lonely planet

France

Steve Fallon
Daniel Robinson
Teresa Fisher
Nicola Williams

LONELY PLANET PUBLICATIONS
Melbourne • Oakland • London • Paris

FRANCE

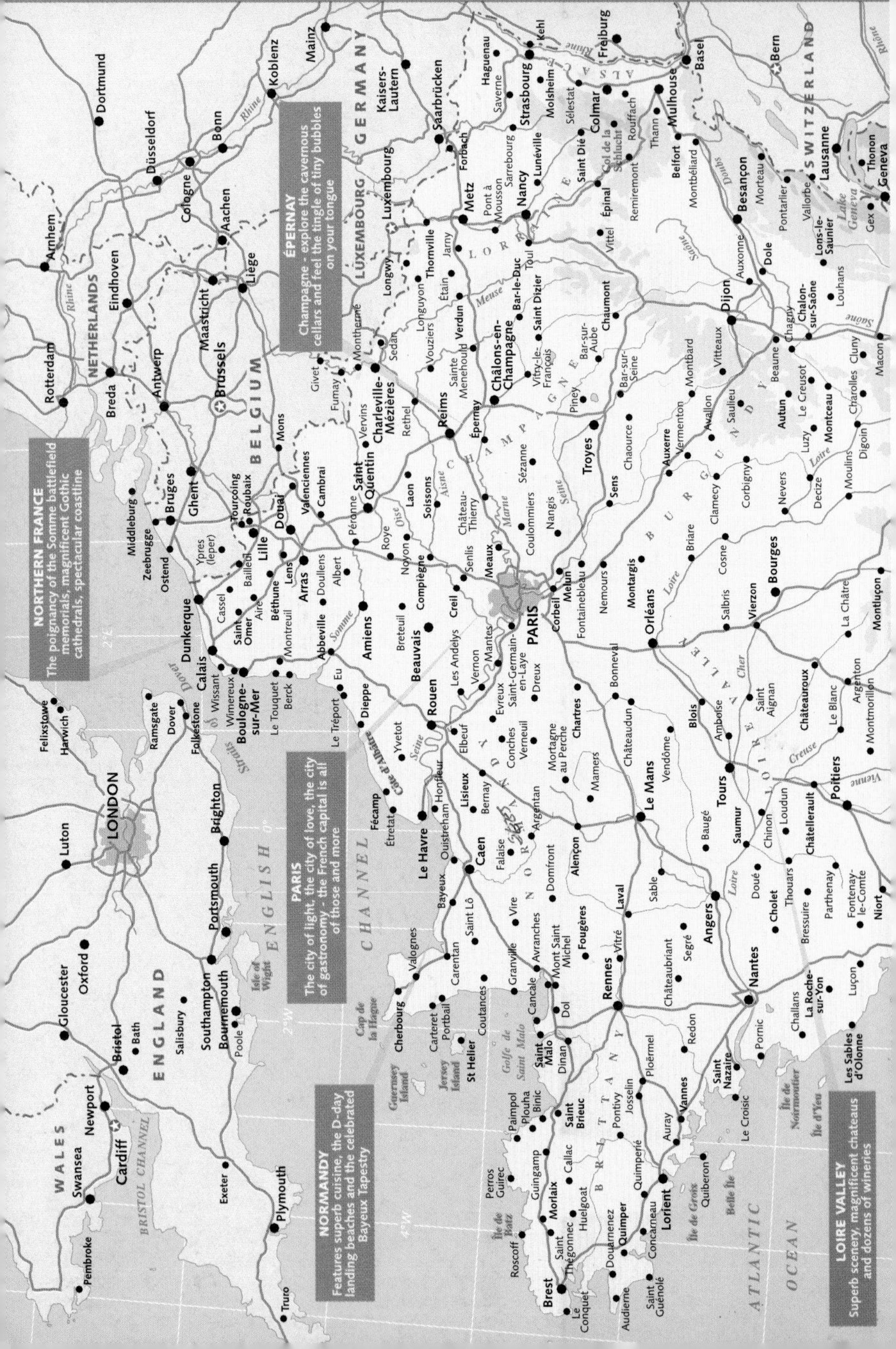
NORTHERN FRANCE
The poignancy of the Somme battlefield memorials, magnificent Gothic cathedrals, spectacular coastline
ÉPERNAY
Champagne - explore the cavernous cellars and feel the tingle of tiny bubbles on your tongue
PARIS
The city of light, the city of love, the city of gastronomy - the French capital is all of those and more
NORMANDY
Features superb cuisine, the D-day landing beaches and the celebrated Bayeux Tapestry
LOIRE VALLEY
Superb scenery, magnificent chateaux and dozens of wineries
ENGLAND
WALES
NETHERLANDS
BELGIUM
LUXEMBOURG
GERMANY
SWITZERLAND
ENGLISH CHANNEL
BRISTOL CHANNEL
ATLANTIC OCEAN
LONDON
PARIS

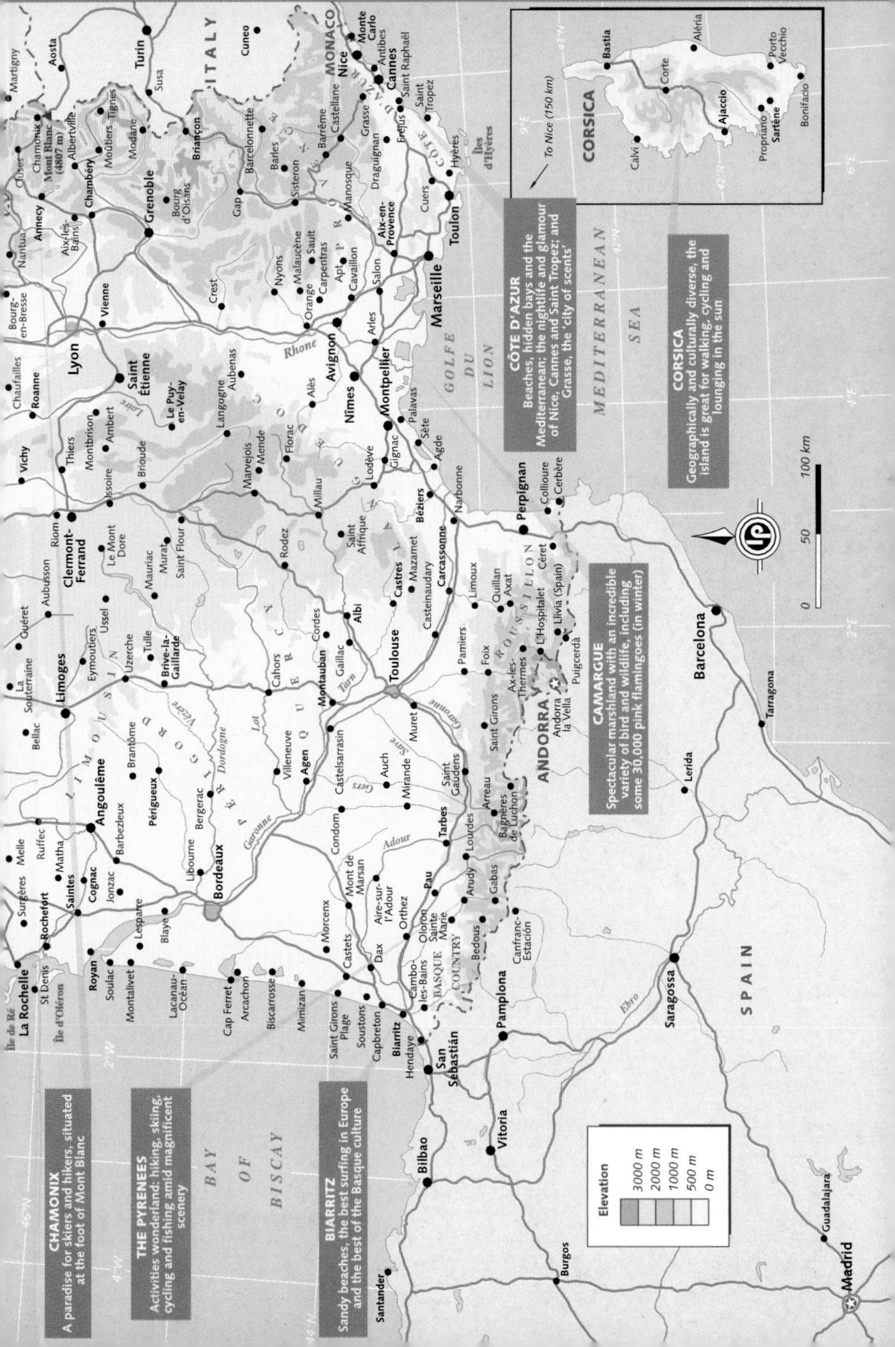
CHAMONIX
A paradise for skiers and hikers, situated at the foot of Mont Blanc
THE PYRENEES
Activities wonderland: hiking, skiing, cycling and fishing amid magnificent scenery
BIARRITZ
Sandy beaches, the best surfing in Europe and the best of the Basque culture
CAMARGUE
Spectacular marshland with an incredible variety of bird and wildlife, including some 30,000 pink flamingoes (in winter)
CÔTE D'AZUR
Beaches, hidden bays and the Mediterranean; the nightlife and glamour of Nice, Cannes and Saint Tropez; and Grasse, the 'city of scents'
CORSICA
Geographically and culturally diverse, the island is great for walking, cycling and lounging in the sun
CORSICA
To Nice (150 km)
Bastia
Calvi
Corte
Aléria
Ajaccio
Propriano
Sartène
Porto Vecchio
Bonifacio
Elevation
3000 m
2000 m
1000 m
500 m
0 m
0
50
100 km
BAY
OF
BISCAY
GOLFE
DU
LION
MEDITERRANEAN
SEA
SPAIN
ITALY
MONACO
ANDORRA
Andorra la Vella
Monte Carlo
Nice
Cannes
Antibes
Saint Raphaël
Saint Tropez
Fréjus
Grasse
Draguignan
Hyères
Îles d'Hyères
Toulon
Cuers
Marseille
Aix-en-Provence
Salon
Arles
Avignon
Nîmes
Montpellier
Palavas
Sète
Agde
Béziers
Narbonne
Perpignan
Collioure
Cerbère
Céret
Carcassonne
Toulouse
Albi
Castres
Mazamet
Rodez
Millau
Lyon
Saint Étienne
Vienne
Grenoble
Chambéry
Annecy
Aix-les-Bains
Chamonix
Mont Blanc (4807 m)
Albertville
Briançon
Gap
Turin
Aosta
Cuneo
Clermont-Ferrand
Vichy
Roanne
Limoges
Angoulême
Périgueux
Bordeaux
Cognac
Saintes
Rochefort
La Rochelle
Île de Ré
Île d'Oléron
Royan
Arcachon
Cap Ferret
Biarritz
Bayonne
Hendaye
San Sebastián
Bilbao
Vitoria
Pamplona
Saragossa
Lerida
Barcelona
Tarragona
Santander
Burgos
Madrid
Guadalajara
Pau
Tarbes
Lourdes
Montauban
Cahors
Agen
Foix
Rhone
Loire
Garonne
Dordogne
Lot
Tarn
Ebro
ROUSSILLON
BASQUE COUNTRY
LIMOUSIN
PÉRIGORD

France
3rd edition – March 1999
First published – April 1994

Published by
Lonely Planet Publications Pty Ltd A.C.N. 005 607 983
192 Burwood Rd, Hawthorn, Victoria 3122, Australia

Lonely Planet Offices
Australia PO Box 617, Hawthorn, Victoria 3122
USA 150 Linden St, Oakland, CA 94607
UK 10a Spring Place, London NW5 3BH
France 1 rue du Dahomey, 75011 Paris

Photographs by
Rachel Black, Simon Bracken, Jean-Bernard Carillet, Bethune Carmichael, CDT Bas-Rhin, Olivier Cirendini, Adrienne Costanzo, Mark Daffey, John Davison, Greg Elms, Steve Fallon, Teresa Fisher, Frances Linzee Gordon, Cristopher Groenhout, Mark Honan, Richard I'Anson, Leanne Logan, James Lyon, Chris Mellor, Richard Nebeský, Daniel Robinson, Brenda Turnnidge, Tony Wheeler, Nicola Williams

Many of the images in this guide are available for licensing from Lonely Planet Images (lpi@lonelyplanet.com.au).

Front cover photograph
Outside the walls of the medieval Cité of Carcassonne
(Guido Alberto Rossi & Jacques Cochin, The Image Bank)

ISBN 0 86442 612 7

Printed by The Bookmaker Pty Ltd
Printed in China

Although the authors and Lonely Planet try to make the information as accurate as possible, we accept no responsibility for any loss, injury or inconvenience sustained by anyone using this book.

Contents – Text

ANDORRA 1043

THE PYRENEES 1063

FRENCH BASQUE COUNTRY 1091

LANGUAGE 1120

GLOSSARY 1129

FOOD GLOSSARY 1132

ACKNOWLEDGMENTS 1136

INDEX 1139

MAP LEGEND back page

METRIC CONVERSION inside back cover

Contents – Maps

FRENCH BASQUE COUNTRY

MAP LEGEND

REGIONAL MAPS

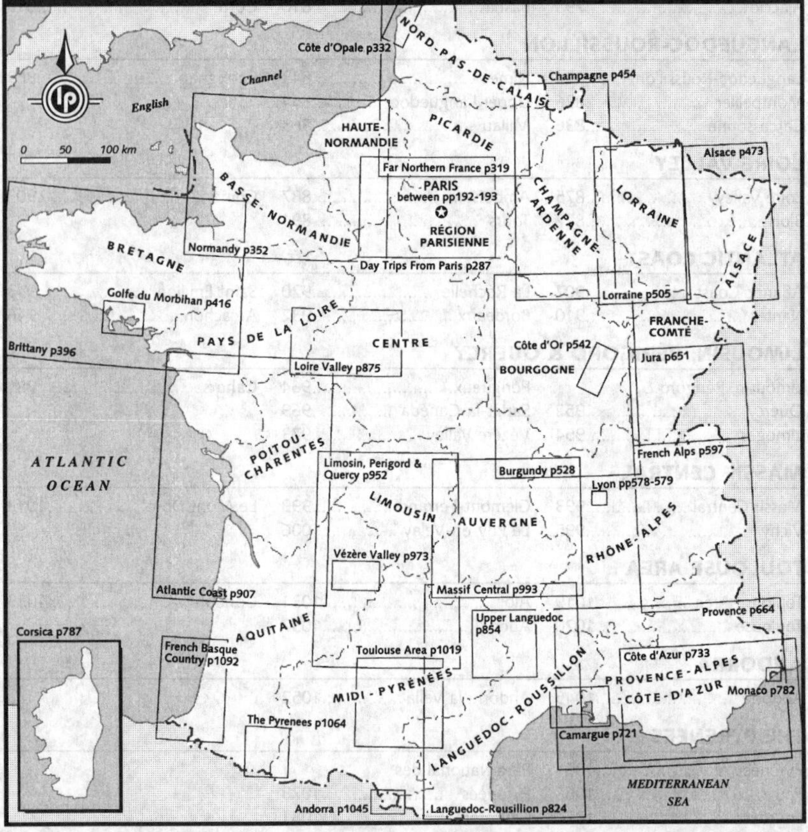
English Channel
0 50 100 km
Côte d'Opale p332
NORD-PAS-DE-CALAIS
Champagne p454
PICARDIE
HAUTE-NORMANDIE
Far Northern France p319
Alsace p473
BASSE-NORMANDIE
PARIS between pp192-193
RÉGION PARISIENNE
CHAMPAGNE-ARDENNE
LORRAINE
ALSACE
BRETAGNE
Normandy p352
Day Trips From Paris p287
Golfe du Morbihan p416
PAYS DE LA LOIRE
Lorraine p505
FRANCHE-COMTÉ
Brittany p396
CENTRE
Côte d'Or p542
Jura p651
Loire Valley p875
BOURGOGNE
ATLANTIC OCEAN
POITOU-CHARENTES
Limosin, Perigord & Quercy p952
French Alps p597
Burgundy p528
Lyon pp578-579
LIMOUSIN
AUVERGNE
RHÔNE-ALPES
Vézère Valley p973
Atlantic Coast p907
Massif Central p993
Provence p664
Upper Languedoc p854
AQUITAINE
Corsica p787
French Basque Country p1092
Toulouse Area p1019
Côte d'Azur p733
MIDI-PYRÉNÉES
LANGUEDOC-ROUSSILLON
PROVENCE-ALPES-CÔTE-D'AZUR
Monaco p782
The Pyrenees p1064
Camargue p721
MEDITERRANEAN SEA
Andorra p1045
Languedoc-Rousillion p824

The Authors

Steve Fallon

Born in Boston, Massachusetts, Steve Fallon can't remember a time when he was not obsessed with travel, other cultures and languages. As a teenager he worked an assortment of jobs to finance trips to Europe and South America, and he graduated from Georgetown University with a Bachelor of Science in modern languages. The following year he taught English at the University of Silesia, near Katowice in Poland. After he had worked for several years for a Gannett newspaper and obtained a master's degree in journalism, his fascination with the 'new' Asia took him to Hong Kong, where he lived and worked for 13 years for a variety of publications and was editor of *Business Traveller* magazine. In 1987, he put journalism on hold when he opened Wanderlust Books, Asia's only travel bookshop. Steve also lived in Budapest for 2½ years, where he wrote Lonely Planet's guides to *Hungary* and *Slovenia* before moving to London in 1994. He has written or contributed to a number of other Lonely Planet titles.

Daniel Robinson

Daniel Robinson was raised in the USA (the San Francisco Bay area and Glen Ellyn, Illinois) and Israel. His first trip, at age 17, was to Cyprus, and since then he has spent several years backpacking around Asia, parts of the Middle East and Europe. His previous work for Lonely Planet includes the Vietnam and Cambodia sections of the 1st edition of *Vietnam, Laos & Cambodia* and, since 1991, all three editions of the *France* guide.

Daniel completed a BA in Near Eastern Studies at Princeton University in 1990 and is currently working on a PhD in Israeli history at Tel Aviv University. He lives in Tel Aviv with his wife, Yael Arami.

Teresa Fisher

Teresa was brought up in Poole, Dorset, on the south coast of England. She gained a BA Honours in Music from Exeter University and, after several years in London working in Sotheby's musical instrument department and teaching business English in-house to companies throughout Europe, she moved to Munich to work as a TEFL teacher and cross-cultural communications consultant to BMW. It was not until 1993 that she became a travel writer and photographer. Since then she has joined the British Guild of Travel Writers and contributes regularly to a variety of newspapers, magazines and guidebooks, both at home and abroad. Although this is her first Lonely Planet book, she is the author of 12 books to date – five of which are on France, making her a confirmed Francophile.

Nicola Williams

Nicola first hit the road as an impoverished student in 1990. After busing and boating it across Indonesia from Jakarta to East Timor and back again, she studied for an MA at London's School of Oriental & African Studies. Following a two year stint as a journalist with the *North Wales Weekly News*, Nicola moved to Latvia to bus it round the Baltics as features editor of the English-language newspaper *The Baltic Observer*. Having travelled the length and breadth of the Baltic region as editor-in-chief of the *In Your Pocket* city guide series, Nicola moved to Lyon in France, where she lives with her husband, Matthias.

Nicola has previously updated Lonely Planet's *Estonia, Latvia & Lithuania*, and written the 1st editions of *Romania & Moldova* and *Provence & the Côte d'Azur*, Lonely Planet's first regional guide to France.

DEDICATIONS FROM THE AUTHORS

Steve Fallon Once again, my share of France is dedicated to Michael Rothschild, a star that will always be in reach, a star that will never fall.

Daniel Robinson I'd like to dedicate my bit of this book to Yael Arami, who became my wife – and began her rabbinical studies at the Jewish Theological Seminary in Jerusalem – as this book was being proofed.

Teresa Fisher I would like to dedicate my share of this book to my parents, Dr and Mrs Ronnie Fisher, whose help and encouragement made this book possible. Also, special thanks to Carl Downing for his patience and support, when I was busy researching rather than helping him build our aeroplane.

This Book

The 1st edition of Lonely Planet's guide to France was the work of Daniel Robinson and Leanne Logan. For the 2nd edition, Daniel teamed up with Steve Fallon, who was the coordinator, and Richard Nebeský. Daniel and Steve teamed up with Nicola Williams and Teresa Fisher for this edition.

Steve coordinated the project once again and also updated the Introduction, Facts about France, Facts for the Visitor, Paris and Day Trips Around Paris chapters. Daniel updated the Getting Around, Getting There & Away, Atlantic Coast, Alsace & Lorraine, Burgundy, Champagne, Far Northern France and Massif Central chapters. Nicola updated the French Alps & the Jura, Lyon, Provence, Côte d'Azur & Monaco, Languedoc-Roussillon and Corsica chapters. And Teresa updated the Normandy, Brittany, Toulouse, Loire Valley, Andorra, Pyrenees, French Basque Country, and Limousin, Périgord & Quercy chapters.

From the Publisher

This book was coerced through the production process at Lonely Planet's Melbourne office by coordinators Darren Elder (editorial) and Lisa Borg (mapping and design). Darren was given generous advice and encouragement throughout the project by Katie Cody and Adrienne Costanzo, and was assisted with editing and proofing by Errol Hunt, Janet Austin, Anne Mulvaney, Arabella Bamber and Martine Lleonart. Jane Hart provided support and guidance to Lisa throughout the project. Lisa was assisted with the mapping by Paul Piaia, Chris Lee Ack, Helen Rowley, Mark Griffiths, Csánad Csutoros, Nicholas Lynagh-Banakoff and Adrian Persoglia. Matt King provided assistance in the book's early stages and with the illustrations. A cast of thousands also assisted throughout: Isabelle Muller and the staff of LP's Paris office, who helped invaluably with the Food & Wine section and various other questions; Emily Cole, who did some last-minute translating; and Rowan McKinnon, who wrote the aside on Jean-Paul Sartre. Tamsin Wilson patiently answered all queries relating to the new book design. Tim Uden provided invaluable assistance during layout; Leonie Mugavin helped with various factual questions throughout; Quentin Frayne edited the language section; the climate charts were drawn by Anthony Phelan; and David Kemp designed the cover. Finally, thanks to the authors, who were a pleasure to work with.

THANKS
Many thanks to the travellers who used the last edition and wrote to us with helpful hints, advice and interesting anecdotes. Your names appear in the back of this book.

Foreword

ABOUT LONELY PLANET GUIDEBOOKS

The story begins with a classic travel adventure: Tony and Maureen Wheeler's 1972 journey across Europe and Asia to Australia. Useful information about the overland trail did not exist at that time, so Tony and Maureen published the first Lonely Planet guidebook to meet a growing need.

From a kitchen table, then from a tiny office in Melbourne (Australia), Lonely Planet has become the largest independent travel publisher in the world, an international company with offices in Melbourne, Oakland (USA), London (UK) and Paris (France).

Today Lonely Planet guidebooks cover the globe. There is an ever-growing list of books and there's information in a variety of forms and media. Some things haven't changed. The main aim is still to help make it possible for adventurous travellers to get out there – to explore and better understand the world.

At Lonely Planet we believe travellers can make a positive contribution to the countries they visit – if they respect their host communities and spend their money wisely. Since 1986 a percentage of the income from each book has been donated to aid projects and human rights campaigns.

Updates Lonely Planet thoroughly updates each guidebook as often as possible. This usually means there are around two years between editions, although for more unusual or more stable destinations the gap can be longer. Check the imprint page (following the colour map at the beginning of the book) for publication dates.

Between editions up-to-date information is available in two free newsletters – the paper *Planet Talk* and email *Comet* (to subscribe, contact any Lonely Planet office) – and on our Web site at www.lonelyplanet.com. The *Upgrades* section of the Web site covers a number of important and volatile destinations and is regularly updated by Lonely Planet authors. *Scoop* covers news and current affairs relevant to travellers. And, lastly, the *Thorn Tree* bulletin board, and *Postcards* section of the site carry unverified, but fascinating, reports from travellers.

Correspondence The process of creating new editions begins with the letters, postcards and emails received from travellers. This correspondence often includes suggestions, criticisms and comments about the current editions. Interesting excerpts are immediately passed on via newsletters and the Web site, and everything goes to our authors to be verified when they're researching on the road. We're keen to get more feedback from organisations or individuals who represent communities visited by travellers.

Lonely Planet gathers information for everyone who's curious about the planet – and especially for those who explore it first-hand. Through guidebooks, phrasebooks, activity guides, maps, literature, newsletters, image library, TV series and web site we act as an information exchange for a worldwide community of travellers.

Research Authors aim to gather sufficient practical information to enable travellers to make informed choices and to make the mechanics of a journey run smoothly. They also research historical and cultural background to help enrich the travel experience and allow travellers to understand and respond appropriately to cultural and environmental issues.

Authors don't stay in every hotel because that would mean spending a couple of months in each medium-sized city and, no, they don't eat at every restaurant because that would mean stretching belts beyond capacity. They do visit hotels and restaurants to check standards and prices, but feedback based on readers' direct experiences can be very helpful.

Many of our authors work undercover, others aren't so secretive. None of them accept freebies in exchange for positive write-ups. And none of our guidebooks contain any advertising.

Production Authors submit their raw manuscripts and maps to offices in Australia, USA, UK or France. Editors and cartographers – all experienced travellers themselves – then begin the process of assembling the pieces. When the book finally hits the shops some things are already out of date, we start getting feedback from readers, and the process begins again....

WARNING & REQUEST

Things change – prices go up, schedules change, good places go bad and bad places go bankrupt – nothing stays the same. So, if you find things better or worse, recently opened or long since closed, please tell us and help make the next edition even more accurate and useful. We genuinely value all the feedback we receive. Julie Young coordinates a well-travelled team that reads and acknowledges every letter, postcard and email and ensures that every morsel of information finds its way to the appropriate authors, editors and cartographers for verification.

Everyone who writes to us will find their name in the next edition of the appropriate guidebook. They will also receive the latest issue of *Planet Talk*, our quarterly printed newsletter, or *Comet*, our monthly email newsletter. Subscriptions to both newsletters are free. The very best contributions will be rewarded with a free guidebook.

Excerpts from your correspondence may appear in new editions of Lonely Planet guidebooks, the Lonely Planet Web site, *Planet Talk* or *Comet*, so please let us know if you *don't* want your letter published or your name acknowledged.

Send all correspondence to the Lonely Planet office closest to you:

Australia: PO Box 617, Hawthorn, Victoria 3122
UK: 10A Spring Place, London NW5 3BH
USA: 150 Linden St, Oakland CA 94607
France: 1 rue du Dahomey, Paris 75011

Or email us at: talk2us@lonelyplanet.com.au

For news, views and updates see our Web site: www.lonelyplanet.com

HOW TO USE A LONELY PLANET GUIDEBOOK

The best way to use a Lonely Planet guidebook is any way you choose. At Lonely Planet we believe the most memorable travel experiences are often those that are unexpected, and the finest discoveries are those you make yourself. Guidebooks are not intended to be used as if they provide a detailed set of infallible instructions!

Contents All Lonely Planet guidebooks follow the same format. The Facts about the Country chapters or sections give background information ranging from history to weather. Facts for the Visitor gives practical information on issues like visas and health. Getting There & Away gives a brief starting point for researching travel to and from the destination. Getting Around gives an overview of the transport options when you arrive.

The peculiar demands of each destination determine how subsequent chapters are broken up, but some things remain constant. We always start with background, then proceed to sights, places to stay, places to eat, entertainment, getting there and away, and getting around information – in that order.

Heading Hierarchy Lonely Planet headings are used in a strict hierarchical structure that can be visualised as a set of Russian dolls. Each heading (and its following text) is encompassed by any preceding heading that is higher on the hierarchical ladder.

Entry Points We do not assume guidebooks will be read from beginning to end, but that people will dip into them. The traditional entry points are the list of contents and the index. In addition, however, there is a complete list of maps and an index map illustrating map coverage.

There's also a colour map that shows highlights. These highlights are dealt with in greater detail in the Facts for the Visitor chapter, along with planning questions and suggested itineraries. Each chapter covering a geographical region begins with a locator map and another list of highlights. Once you find something of interest in a list of highlights, turn to the index.

Maps Maps play a crucial role in Lonely Planet guidebooks and include a huge amount of information. A legend is printed on the back page. We seek to have complete consistency between maps and text, and to have every important place in the text captured on a map. Map key numbers usually start in the top left corner.

Although inclusion in a guidebook usually implies a recommendation we cannot list every good place. Exclusion does not necessarily imply criticism. In fact there are a number of reasons why we might exclude a place – sometimes it is simply inappropriate to encourage an influx of travellers.

Introduction

The largest country in Western Europe, France is also the region's most diverse. It stretches from the rolling plains of the north to the jagged ridges of the Pyrenees, and from the rugged coastline of Brittany to the clear, blue lakes and icy crags of the Alps.

There are mountain peaks and glaciers here, dense forests and vineyards, cliff-lined canyons and endless sandy beaches. And with the country's excellent (and affordable) train network, you can – throughout most of the year – go skiing one day and sunbathing the next. But unless you have a lifetime, you have to make some choices, and this book will help you decide whether you'll go skiing in the Alps or the Pyrenees and swimming in the Atlantic or the Mediterranean.

FRANCE LOCATOR

France's cities and towns are especially alluring. In Paris, celebrated for centuries for its stunning architecture and romantic *joie de vivre*, as well as in other cities, you'll see people strolling along grand boulevards, picnicking in parks and watching the world go by from café terraces. All cities and even many small towns have exceptional museums and galleries devoted to art, regional culture or both. Shopping is generally better in the larger cities, but many villages make products that are consumed and praised throughout the country – a cheese, perhaps, or a particularly fine wine.

Over the centuries, what is now France has received more immigrants than any other country in Europe: from the Celtic Gauls and Romans to arrivals in this century from the nation's former colonies in Indochina and Africa. Elements of the culture, cuisine and the artistic sense of these immigrants have been assimilated into the many streams of French culture and have helped to create the unique and diverse civilisation that is modern France. Today, Vietnamese spring rolls are as French as baguettes, North African raï music as familiar to most people as *chansons françaises*.

Geographically France is on the western edge of Europe, but with the unification of Europe, it is at the crossroads politically: between England and Italy, in the middle of Belgium, Germany and Spain. Of course, this is just how the French have always viewed their nation – at the very centre of things.

Facts about France

HISTORY

Early Inhabitants

France has been inhabited at least since the Middle Palaeolithic period (about 90,000 to 40,000 BC) when Neanderthal people (thought to be early representatives of *Homo sapiens*) hunted animals, made crude flakestone tools and lived in caves. Several of their skeletons have been found in the caves at Le Moustier near Les Eyzies and at Le Bugue (both in modern-day Périgord). Mousterian people, who are associated with Neanderthals, have left the earliest evidence in Western Europe of the use of fire and the practice of burying their dead.

During a dramatic change of climate about 35,000 years ago, the Neanderthal people disappeared. They were followed by Cro-Magnon people, a later variety of *Homo sapiens*. Much taller than their predecessors (over 170cm), these Cro-Magnon people had nimble hands, larger brains, long, narrow skulls and short, wide faces. They were skilful hunters, and with their improved tools and hunting techniques were able to kill reindeer, bison, horses and mammoths.

Prehistoric art began with Cro-Magnon people. They started drawing, painting and sculpting, using a variety of different techniques. Their initial simplistic drawings and engravings of animals gradually became far more detailed and realistic, as at the Lascaux cave in the Vézère Valley of Périgord. They also decorated tools, played music, danced, performed assorted ceremonies (eg magical rituals to enhance fertility) and had fairly complex social patterns.

In the Mesolithic period, which began about 13,000 years ago, hunting and fishing became very efficient and wild grains were harvested. The Neolithic period (about 6000 to 4500 years ago), also known as the New Stone Age, saw the advent of polished stone tools. Warmer weather caused great changes in flora and fauna, ushering in the practice of farming and stock rearing. Cereals were grown, as were peas, beans and lentils. Communities were therefore more settled and villages were built. Pottery decorated with geometric patterns became common, as did woven fabric. This was also the time in which the first megalithic monuments were erected such as the amazing menhirs and dolmens at Carnac in Brittany.

Indo-European tribes from the Aegean region began to use copper tools and weapons in the early 3rd millennium and by about 2500 BC copper was being worked on both sides of the Alps. After the introduction of more durable bronze, forts were built and a military elite developed.

Over the next millennium, iron was introduced in various parts of Europe, but it was a scarce, precious metal and used only for ornaments and small knives. It did not come into common use until the arrival of the Celts.

The Gauls & the Romans

The Celtic Gauls moved into what is now France between 1500 and 500 BC. By about 600 BC, they had established trading links with the Greeks, whose colonies on the Mediterranean coast included Massilia (Marseille). Some 300 years later, members of a Celtic tribe called the Parisii set up a few huts made of wattle and daub on what is now the Île de la Cité in Paris and engaged in fishing and trading.

Centuries of conflict between the Gauls and Romans ended in 52 BC, when Julius Caesar's legions crushed a revolt led by the Gallic chief Vercingétorix and took control of the territory. Christianity was introduced to Roman Gaul early in the 2nd century AD.

France remained under Roman rule until the 5th century, when the Franks (thus the name 'France') and the Alemanii overran the country from the east. These peoples adopted important elements of Gallo-Roman civilisation (including Christianity) and their eventual assimilation resulted in a fusion of Germanic culture with that of the Celts and the Romans.

The Merovingians & the Carolingians

Two Frankish dynasties, the Merovingians and the Carolingians, ruled from the 5th to the 10th century. The Frankish tradition by which the king was succeeded by *all* of his sons led to power struggles and the eventual disintegration of the kingdom into a collection of small feudal states. In 732, Charles Martel defeated the Moors at Poitiers, thus ensuring that France would not fall under Muslim rule as had Spain.

Charles Martel's grandson Charlemagne significantly extended the power and boundaries of the kingdom and was crowned Holy Roman Emperor (Emperor of the West) in 800. But during the 9th century, the Scandinavian Vikings (also known as the Norsemen, ie Normans) began raiding France's western coast. They eventually settled in the lower Seine Valley and formed the duchy of Normandy in the early 10th century.

In addition to uniting all the Christian lands of Western Europe, Charlemagne also inspired a period of great cultural revival.

The Middle Ages

The Capetian dynasty, which would last for the next 800 years, was founded in 987, when the nobles elected Hugh Capet as their king. At that time, the king's domains were quite modest, consisting mostly of land around Paris and Orléans.

In 1066 Norman forces under William the Conqueror, duke of Normandy, occupied England, making Normandy – and, later, Plantagenet-ruled England – a formidable rival of the kingdom of France. A further third of France came under the control of the English crown in 1152, when Eleanor of Aquitaine married Henry of Anjou (later King Henry II of England). The subsequent rivalry between France and England for control of Aquitaine and the vast English territories in France would last for three centuries.

France played a leading role in the Crusades (the First Crusade was preached at Clermont in 1095 by Pope Urban II), and most of France's major cathedrals were erected between the 12th and early 14th centuries. In 1309, the French-born Pope Clement V fled the political turmoil in Rome and moved the Holy See to Avignon, where it remained until 1377, a useful tool of French policy.

The Hundred Years' War By the middle of the 14th century the struggle between the Capetians and England's King Edward III (a member of the Plantagenet family) over the powerful French throne degenerated into the Hundred Years' War, which was fought on and off from 1337 to 1453. The bubonic plague ravaged the country in 1348 and 1349, killing about a third of the population, but the 'Black Death' only briefly interrupted the fighting.

By the early 15th century, things were not going well for the Capetians. French forces were defeated at Agincourt in 1415, and the dukes of Burgundy, allied with the English, occupied Paris five years later. In 1422 John Plantagenet, duke of Bedford, was installed as regent of France for England's King Henry VI, then an infant. Henry was crowned as king of France at Notre Dame less than 10 years later.

In 1429 a 17-year-old peasant girl known to history as Jeanne d'Arc (Joan of Arc) persuaded the French legitimist Charles VII that she had received a divine mission from God to expel the English from France and bring about Charles' coronation. She rallied the French troops and defeated the English near Orléans, and Charles was crowned at Reims. However, Joan of Arc failed in her attempt to capture Paris and in 1430 she was captured by the Burgundians and sold to the English. She was convicted of witchcraft and heresy by a tribunal of French ecclesiastics and burned at the stake two years later at Rouen. Charles VII returned to Paris in 1437, but it was not until 1453 that the English were entirely driven from French territory (with the exception of Calais).

The Renaissance

The culture of the Italian Renaissance (French for 'rebirth') arrived full-swing in France in the early 16th century during the reign of François I partly because of a series of indecisive French military operations in Italy. For the first time, the French aristocracy was exposed to Renaissance ideas of scientific and geographic scholarship and discovery, and the value of secular over religious life.

Writers such as Rabelais, Marot and Ronsard were influential as were the architectural disciples of Michelangelo and Raphael. Evidence of this architectural influence can be seen in François I's chateau at Fontainebleau and the Petit Château at Chantilly.

This new architecture was meant to reflect the splendour of the monarchy, which was fast moving toward absolutism. But all this grandeur and show of strength was not enough to stem the tide of Protestantism that was flowing into France.

The Reformation

By the 1530s the position of the Reformation that was sweeping through Europe had been strengthened in France by the ideas of John Calvin, a Frenchman exiled to Geneva. The Edict of January (1562), which afforded the Protestants certain rights, was met by violent opposition from ultra-Catholic nobles, whose fidelity to their religion was mixed with a desire to strengthen their power base in the provinces.

The Wars of Religion (1562-98) involved three groups: the Huguenots, French Protestants who received help from the English; the Catholic League, led by the House of Guise; and the Catholic monarchy. The fighting severely weakened the position of the king and brought the French state close to disintegration. The most deplorable massacre took place in Paris in 1572, when some 3000 Huguenots who had come to the capital to celebrate the wedding of the Protestant Henri of Navarre (the future Henri IV) were slaughtered in what has become known as the Saint Bartholomew's Day Massacre (23-24 August). In 1588, on the so-called Day of the Barricades, the Catholic League rose up against Henri III and forced him to flee the royal court at the Louvre; he was assassinated the following year.

Henri III was succeeded by Henri IV, starting the Bourbon dynasty. In 1598 Henri IV decreed the Edict of Nantes, which guaranteed the Huguenots many civil and political rights and, most importantly, the freedom of conscience, but this was not universally accepted. Ultra Catholic Paris refused to allow their new Protestant king entry to the city, and a siege of the capital continued for almost five years. Only when Henri IV embraced Catholicism at the cathedral in Saint Denis – *'Paris vaut bien une messe'* (Paris is well worth a Mass), he is reputed to have said upon taking communion there – did the capital submit to him.

Henri IV was succeeded by Louis XIII in 1610, but throughout most of Louis XIII's undistinguished reign he remained under the control of his ruthless chief minister, Cardinal Richelieu. Richelieu is best known for his untiring efforts to establish an all-powerful monarchy in France, opening the door to the absolutism of Louis XIV, and French supremacy in Europe, which would see France fighting Holland, Austria and England almost continuously.

Louis XIV & the Ancien Régime

Le Roi Soleil (the Sun King) ascended the throne as Louis XIV in 1643 at the age of five and ruled until 1715. Throughout his long reign, he sought to project the power of the French monarchy – bolstered by claims of divine right – both at home and abroad. He involved France in a long series of costly wars that gained it territory but terrified its neighbours and nearly bankrupted the treasury.

But Louis XIV, whose widely quoted saying *'L'État c'est moi'* (I am the State) is often taken out of historical context, was able to quash the ambitious, feuding aristocracy and create the first centralised French state, elements of which can still be seen in France today. He did pour huge sums of money into building his extravagant palace at Versailles, 23km south-west of Paris, but by doing so he was able to sidestep the endless intrigues of the capital, by then a city of 600,000 people. And by turning his nobles into courtiers, Louis XIV forced them to compete with each other for royal favour, reducing them to ineffectual sycophancy.

Louis XIV mercilessly persecuted the Protestant minority, which he considered a threat to the unity of the state (and thus his power). In 1685 he revoked the Edict of Nantes, which had guaranteed the Huguenots freedom of conscience.

Louis XIV's successor, his grandson Louis XV (ruled 1715-74), turned out to be an oafish buffoon though his regent, the duke of Orléans, did move the court from Versailles back to Paris; in the Age of the Enlightenment, the French capital had become, in effect, the centre of Europe. It was Louis XV who said *'Après moi, le deluge'* (After me, the flood); in hindsight his words were more than prophetic. He was followed by the incompetent – and later universally despised and powerless – Louis XVI, who ultimately met an early demise.

As the 18th century progressed, new economic and social circumstances rendered the *ancien régime* (old order) dangerously out of step with the needs of the country. The regime was further weakened by the anti-establishment and anticlerical ideas of the Enlightenment, whose leading lights included Voltaire, Rousseau and Montesquieu. But entrenched vested interests, a cumbersome power structure and royal lassitude prevented change from starting until the 1770s, by which time the monarchy's moment had passed.

The Seven Years' War (1756-63), fought by France and Austria against Britain and Prussia, was one of a series of ruinous wars pursued by Louis XV, and it led to the loss of France's flourishing colonies in Canada, the West Indies and India to the English. It was in part to avenge these losses that Louis XVI sided with the colonists in the American War of Independence. But the Seven Years' War cost a fortune and, even more disastrous for the monarchy, it helped to disseminate in France the radical democratic ideas that the American Revolution had thrust on the world stage.

The French Revolution & the First Republic

By the late 1780s, the indecisive Louis XVI and Marie-Antoinette, his overbearing and controlling queen, had managed to alienate virtually every segment of society – from enlightened groups to conservatives. When the king tried to neutralise the power of the more reform-minded delegates at a meeting of the États Généraux (Estates General) at the Jeu de Paume at Versailles in May-June 1789, the urban masses took to the streets and, on 14 July, they raided Invalides for weapons and then stormed the prison at Bastille – the ultimate symbol of the despotism of the ancien régime.

At first, the Revolution was in the hands of relative moderates. France was declared a constitutional monarchy and various reforms were enacted, including the adoption of the

Declaration of the Rights of Man. But as the masses armed themselves against the external threat to the new government posed by Austria, Prussia and the many exiled French nobles, patriotism and nationalism mixed with revolutionary fervour, and then popularised and radicalised the Revolution. It was not long before the moderate republican Girondins lost power to the radical Jacobins, led by Robespierre, Danton and Marat, who abolished the monarchy and declared the First Republic in September 1792 after Louis XVI proved unreliable as a constitutional monarch. The National Assembly was replaced by a 'Revolutionary Convention'.

In January 1793, Louis XVI, who had tried to flee the country with his family but only got as far as Varennes, was convicted of 'conspiring against the liberty of the nation' and guillotined at Place de la Révolution (today's Place de la Concorde) to be followed by his queen in October. In March the Jacobins set up the notorious Committee of Public Safety. This body virtually had dictatorial control over the country during the Reign of Terror (September 1793 to July 1794), which saw religious freedoms revoked, churches desecrated and closed and cathedrals turned into 'Temples of Reason'.

By autumn, following Marat's assassination by Charlotte Corday (a Girondin sympathiser) in July, the Reign of Terror was in full swing, and by the middle of 1794 some 17,000 people in every part of the country had been beheaded. In the end, the Revolution turned on itself, 'devouring its own children' in the words of the Jacobin Saint-Just: Robespierre sent Danton to the guillotine, and later Saint-Just and even Robespierre himself ended their lives with their heads separated from their bodies.

After the Terror, a five man delegation of moderate Republicans led by Paul Barras, who had seen to the arrests of Robespierre and Saint-Just among others, set themselves up as a Directoire (Directory) to rule the Republic. On 13 Vendémiaire in the year VI (ie 5 October 1795; see the boxed text 'Republican Calendar'), a group of Royalist rebels bent on overthrowing the Directory was intercepted in Paris by loyalist forces led by a dashing young Corsican general named Napoleon Bonaparte. His military tactics and skill were immediately recognised and Napoleon was put in command of the army in Italy, where he was particularly successful in the campaign against Austria. His victories soon turned him into an independent political force.

Republican Calendar

During the Revolution, the Convention adopted a new, more 'rational' calendar from which all 'superstitious' associations (eg saints' days) were removed. Year 1 began on 22 September 1792, the day the Republic had been proclaimed. The 12 months – renamed Vendémiaire, Brumaire, Frimaire, Nivôse, Pluviôse, Ventôse, Germinal, Floréal, Prairial, Messidor, Thermidor and Fructidor – were divided into three 10-day weeks called *décades*. Based on the cult of nature, the poetically inspired names of the months were chosen according to the seasons: the autumn months, for instance, were Vendémiaire, derived from *vendange* (grape harvest or vintage), Brumaire (from *brume* (mist or fog), and Frimaire from *frimas* (frost). The last day of each décade was a rest day, and the five or six remaining days of the year were used to celebrate Virtue, Genius, Labour, Opinion and Rewards. These festivals were initially called *sans-culottides* in honour of the *sans-culottes*, the extreme Revolutionaries who wore pantaloons rather than the short breeches favoured by the upper classes. While the Republican calendar worked well in theory, it caused no end of confusion for France in its communication and trade abroad since the months and days kept on changing in relation to those of the Gregorian calendar. Napoleon re-introduced the Gregorian calendar on 1 January 1806.

Napoleon & the First Empire

The post-Revolutionary government was far from stable, and when Napoleon returned to Paris in 1799, he found a chaotic republic in which few had any faith. In November, when it appeared that the Jacobins were again on the ascendancy in the legislature, Napoleon tricked the delegates into leaving Paris for Saint Cloud, to the south-west, 'for their own protection', overthrew the discredited Directory and assumed power himself.

At first, Napoleon took the title of First Consul. In 1802, a referendum declared him 'consul for life' and his birthday became a national holiday. By 1804, when he had himself crowned Emperor of the French by Pope Pius VII at Notre Dame Cathedral in Paris, the scope and nature of Napoleon's ambitions were all too obvious. But to consolidate and legitimise his authority, Napoleon needed more victories on the battlefield. So began a seemingly endless series of wars in which France came to control most of Europe. In 1812, in an attempt to do away with his last major rival on the continent, the tsar, Napoleon invaded Russia. Although his Grande Armée captured Moscow, it was wiped out shortly thereafter by the brutal Russian winter. Prussia and Napoleon's other enemies quickly recovered from their earlier defeats, and less than two years after the fiasco in Russia, the allied armies entered Paris. Napoleon abdicated and left France for the tiny Mediterranean island-kingdom of Elba.

At the Congress of Vienna (1814-15), the Allies restored the House of Bourbon to the French throne, installing Louis XVI's brother as Louis XVIII (the second son of Louis XVI had been declared Louis XVII by monarchist exiles and died in 1795). However, in March 1815, Napoleon escaped from Elba, landed in southern France and gathered a large army as he marched northward towards Paris. His 'Hundred Days' back in power ended, however, when his forces were defeated by the English under the Duke of Wellington at Waterloo in Belgium. They exiled him to the remote South Atlantic island of Saint Helena, where he died in 1821.

Although reactionary in some ways – he re-established slavery in the colonies, for instance – Napoleon instituted a number of important reforms, including a reorganisation of the judicial system, the promulgation

Very much revered in French history, Napoleon Bonaparte instituted reforms that still affect France today.

of a new legal code, the Code Napoléon (or civil code), which forms the basis of the French legal system (and many others in Europe) to this day, and a new education system. More importantly, he preserved the essence of the changes brought about by the Revolution. Napoleon is therefore remembered by the French as a great hero.

The Second Republic

The rule of Louis XVIII (1814-24) was dominated by the struggle among extreme monarchists, who wanted to return to the ancien régime, people who saw the changes wrought by the Revolution as irreversible and the radicals of the working-class neighbourhoods of Paris. Charles X (ruled 1824-30) handled the struggle among them with great ineptitude and was overthrown in the so-called July Revolution of 1830, when a motley group of revolutionaries seized the Hôtel de Ville in Paris. The Colonne de Juillet, in the centre of the Place de la Bastille, honours those killed in the street battles that accompanied the revolution; they are buried in vaults under the column.

Louis-Philippe (ruled 1830-48), an ostensibly constitutional monarch of bourgeois sympathies and tastes, was then chosen by Parliament to head what became known as the July Monarchy. Louis-Philippe was in turn overthrown in the February Revolution of 1848, in whose wake the Second Republic was established.

The Second Empire

In presidential elections held in 1848, Napoleon's almost useless nephew Louis Napoleon Bonaparte was overwhelmingly elected. Legislative deadlock caused Louis Napoleon to lead a coup d'état in 1851, after which he was proclaimed Emperor Napoleon III.

The Second Empire lasted from 1852 until 1870. During this period, France enjoyed significant economic growth and, under Baron Haussmann, Paris was transformed. But as his uncle had done before him, Napoleon III embroiled France in a number of conflicts, including the disastrous Crimean War (1853-56). It was the Prussians, however, who ended the Second Empire. In 1870, Prussian Prime Minister Otto von Bismarck goaded Napoleon III into declaring war on Prussia. Within months the thoroughly unprepared French army had been defeated and the emperor taken prisoner.

When news of the debacle reached the French capital, the Parisian masses took to the streets and demanded that a republic be declared.

The Third Republic & the Belle Époque

The Third Republic began as a provisional government of national defence in September 1870. The Prussians were, at the time, advancing on Paris and would subsequently lay siege to the capital, forcing its starving citizens to bake bread laced with sawdust and consume most of the animals in the zoo. In January 1871 the government negotiated an armistice with the Prussians, who demanded that Assemblée Nationale (National Assembly) elections be held immediately. The republicans, who had called on the nation to continue to resist, lost to the monarchists, who had campaigned on a peace platform.

As expected, the monarchist-controlled assembly ratified the Treaty of Frankfurt (1871). However, when ordinary Parisians heard of its harsh terms – a 5FF billion war indemnity and surrender of the provinces of Alsace and Lorraine – they revolted against the government.

The Communards, as the supporters of the Paris Commune were known, took over the city in March and the French government moved to Versailles. In May, the government launched a week-long offensive, now known as *La Semaine Sanglante* (Bloody Week), on the Commune in which several thousand rebels were killed. A further 20,000 or so Communards, mostly from the working class, were summarily executed. Karl Marx interpreted the Communard insurrection as the first great proletarian uprising against the bourgeoisie, and socialists came to see its victims as martyrs of the class struggle.

Despite this disastrous start, the Third Republic ushered in the glittering *belle époque* (beautiful age), with Art Nouveau architecture, a whole field of artistic 'isms' from impressionism onwards, and advances in science and engineering, including the construction of the first metro line in Paris. Expositions Universelles (World Exhibitions) were held in the capital in 1889 (showcased by the Eiffel Tower, much maligned at the time) and again in 1901 in the purpose-built Petit Palais. The Paris of nightclubs and artistic cafés made its first appearance around this time.

France was obsessed with a desire for revenge after its defeat by Germany in 1871, and jingoistic nationalism, scandals and accusations were the order of the day. But the greatest moral and political crisis of the Third Republic was the infamous Dreyfus Affair, which began in 1894 when Captain Alfred Dreyfus, a Jewish army officer, was accused of betraying military secrets to Germany, court-martialled and sentenced to life imprisonment on Devil's Island, the supposedly inescapable French penal colony off the northern coast of South America. Despite bitter opposition from the army command, right-wing politicians and many Catholic groups, the case was eventually reopened and Dreyfus vindicated. The affair greatly discredited both the army and the Catholic Church. The result was more rigorous civilian control of the military and, in 1905, the legal separation of church and state.

The Entente Cordiale of 1904 ended colonial rivalry between France and Britain in Africa, beginning a period of cooperation that has, more or less, continued to this day.

WWI & the Inter-War Period Central to France's entry into WWI was the desire to regain Alsace and Lorraine, lost to Germany in 1871. Indeed, Raymond Poincaré, president of the Third Republic from 1913 to 1920 and later prime minister, was a native of Lorraine and a firm supporter of war with Germany. However, when the heir to the Austrian throne, Archduke Franz Ferdinand, was assassinated by Serbian nationalists at Sarajevo on 28 June 1914, precipitating what would erupt into a global war, Germany jumped the gun. Within a month, it had declared war on Russia and France.

The defeat of Austria-Hungary and Germany in WWI, which regained Alsace and Lorraine for France, was achieved at an unimaginable human cost. Of the eight million French men who were called to arms, 1.3 million were killed and almost one million crippled. The dead included two of every 10 Frenchmen aged between 20 and 45 years of age. At the Battle of Verdun (1916) alone, the French (led by Général Philippe Pétain) and the Germans each lost about 400,000 men.

Because much of the war – including most of the trench warfare that used thousands of soldiers as cannon fodder to gain a few metres of territory – took place on French territory, large parts of north-eastern France were devastated. Industrial production dropped by 40%, the value of the franc was seriously undermined, and the country faced a devastating financial crisis. The Treaty of Versailles of 1919, which officially ended the war, was heavily influenced by French Prime Minister Georges Clemenceau, the most uncompromising of the Allied leaders, who made sure that its harsh terms included a provision that Germany pay US$33 billion in reparations.

The 1920s and 30s saw France – and Paris in particular – as a centre of the avant-garde, with artists pushing into the new fields of cubism and surrealism, Le Corbusier rewriting the architectural text book, foreign writers like Ernest Hemingway and F Scott Fitzgerald attracted by the city's liberal atmosphere, and nightlife establishing a cutting edge reputation for everything from jazz clubs to striptease.

France's efforts to promote a separatist movement in the Rhineland and its occupation of the Ruhr in 1923 to enforce reparations payments proved disastrous. But it did lead to almost a decade of accommodation and compromise with border guarantees and Germany's admission to the League of Nations. The naming of Adolf Hitler as chancellor in 1933, however, changed all that.

WWII During most of the 1930s, the French, like the British, had done their best to appease Hitler, but two days after Berlin's invasion of Poland in 1939, France joined the British in declaring war on Germany. By June of the following year, France had capitulated. The British expeditionary force sent to help the French barely managed to avoid capture by retreating to Dunkerque and crossing the English Channel in small boats. The very expensive Maginot Line, a supposedly impregnable wall of fortifications along the Franco-German border, had proved useless: the German armoured divisions had simply outflanked it by going through Belgium.

The Germans divided France into a zone under direct German occupation (in the north and along the west coast) and a puppet state based in the spa town of Vichy, which was led by the ageing WWI hero of the Battle of Verdun, Général Pétain. Both Pétain's collaborationist government, whose leaders and supporters assumed that the Nazis were Europe's new masters and had to be accommodated, and French police forces in German-occupied areas were very helpful to the Nazis in rounding up French Jews and others for deportation to Auschwitz and other death camps.

After the capitulation, Général Charles de Gaulle, France's under-secretary of war, fled to London and, in a famous radio broadcast on 18 June 1940, appealed to French patriots to continue resisting the Germans. De Gaulle also set up a French government-in-exile and established the Forces Françaises Libres (Free French Forces), a military force dedicated to continuing the fight against the Germans.

The underground movement known as the Résistance (Resistance), which never included more than perhaps 5% of the population (the other 95% either collaborated or did nothing), engaged in such activities as railway sabotage, collecting intelligence for the Allies, helping Allied airmen who had been shot down and publishing anti-German leaflets.

The liberation of France began with the US, British and Canadian landings in Normandy on D-day (6 June 1944). On 15 August, Allied forces also landed in southern France. After a brief insurrection by the Resistance, Paris was liberated on 25 August by an Allied force spearheaded by Free French units, sent in ahead of the Americans, so the French would have the honour of liberating the capital.

The Fourth Republic

De Gaulle returned to Paris and set up a provisional government, but in January 1946 he resigned as president, miscalculating that such a move would provoke a popular outcry for his return. A few months later, a new constitution was approved by referendum.

The Fourth Republic was a period of unstable coalition cabinets that followed one another with bewildering speed (on average, once every six months) and economic recovery, helped immeasurably by massive US aid. The war to re-assert French colonial control of Indochina ended with the French defeat at Dien Bien Phu in 1954. France also tried to suppress an uprising by Arab nationalists in Algeria, whose population included over one million French settlers.

The Fifth Republic

The Fourth Republic came to an end in 1958, when extreme right-wingers, furious at what they saw as defeatism rather than tough action in dealing with the uprising in Algeria, began conspiring to overthrow the government. De Gaulle was brought back to power to prevent a military coup and possible civil war. He soon drafted a new constitution that gave considerable powers to the president at the expense of the National Assembly.

The Fifth Republic (which continues to this day) was rocked in 1961 by an attempted coup staged in Algiers by a group of right-wing military officers. When it failed, the Organisation de l'Armée Secrète (OAS; a group of French settlers and sympathisers opposed to Algerian independence) turned to terrorism, trying several times to assassinate de Gaulle. The book and film *The Day of the Jackal* portrayed a fictional OAS attempt on de Gaulle's life.

In 1962, de Gaulle negotiated an end to the war in Algeria. Some 750,000 *pieds noirs* (literally, 'black feet' – as Algerian-born French people are known in France) flooded into France. In the meantime, almost all of the other French colonies and protectorates in Africa had demanded and achieved independence. Shrewdly, the French government began a program of economic and military aid to its former colonies in order to bolster France's waning importance internationally and create a bloc of French-speaking nations in the Third World.

However, the loss of the colonies, the surge in immigration and economic difficulties, including a big rise in unemployment, weakened the de Gaulle government. A large demonstration in Paris against the war in Vietnam in March 1968, led by student Daniel Cohn-Bendit ('Danny the Red'), now a European Parliament Member representing the German Green Party, gave impetus to the student movement and protests were staged throughout the spring. A seemingly insignificant incident in May, in which police broke up yet another in a long series of demonstrations by Paris university students, sparked a violent reaction on the streets of the capital; students occupied the Sorbonne, barricades were erected in the Latin Quarter and unrest spread to other universities. Workers joined in the protests and about nine million people participated in a general strike, virtually paralysing the country. It was a period of much creativity and new ideas with slogans appearing everywhere, such as *L'Imagination au Pouvoir* (literally, 'Put Imagination in Power') and *Sous les Pavés, la Plage* ('Under the Cobblestones, the Beach'), a reference to Parisians' favoured material for building barricades and what they could expect to find beneath them.

The alliance between workers and students couldn't last long. While the former wanted a greater share of the consumer market, the latter wanted to destroy it. De Gaulle took advantage of this division and appealed to people's fear of anarchy. Just as the country seemed on the brink of revolution and an overthrow of the Fifth Republic, stability was restored. The government made a number of immediate changes, including the decentralisation of the higher education system, and reforms (eg lowering the voting age to 18, an abortion law, workers self-management) continued through the 1970s.

1969 to the Present In 1969 de Gaulle was succeeded as president by the Gaullist leader Georges Pompidou, who was in turn succeeded by Valéry Giscard d'Estaing in 1974. François Mitterrand, long-time head of the Parti Socialiste (PS; Socialist Party), was elected president in 1981 and, as the business community had feared (the Paris stock market index fell by 30% on news of his victory), immediately set out to nationalise 36 privately owned banks, large industrial groups and various other parts of the economy, increasing the state-owned share of industrial production from 15% to over 30%. During the mid-1980s, however, Mitterrand followed a generally moderate economic policy and in 1988, at the age of 69, was re-elected for a second seven-year term. In the 1986 parliamentary elections, the right-wing opposition led by Jacques Chirac, mayor of Paris from 1977, received a majority in the National Assembly, and for the next two years Mitterrand was forced to work with a prime minister and cabinet from the opposition, an unprecedented arrangement known as *cohabitation*.

In the May 1995 presidential elections Chirac walked away with a comfortable electoral victory. The ailing Mitterrand, who would die in January 1996, had decided not to run again. In his first few months in office, Chirac received high marks for his direct words and actions in matters relating to the European Union (EU) and the war raging in Bosnia. His Cabinet choices, including the selection of 'whiz kid' Foreign Minister Alain Juppé as prime minister, were well received. But Chirac's decision to resume nuclear testing on the Polynesian island of Moruroa and a nearby atoll was met with outrage both in France and abroad.

On the home front, Chirac's moves to restrict welfare payments (a move designed to bring France closer to meeting the criteria of European monetary union) led to the largest protests since 1968. For three weeks in late 1995 Paris was crippled by public sector strikes, leaving the economy battered.

In 1997 Chirac took a big gamble and called an early parliamentary election for June. The move backfired: Chirac remained president but his party, the Rassemblement pour la République (RPR; Rally for the Republic) lost support and a coalition of Socialists, Communists and Greens, led by Lionel Jospin, a former minister of education in the Mitterrand government (who, most notably, promised the French people a shorter working week for the same pay), became prime minister. France had once again entered into a period of cohabitation – with Chirac on the other side this time around.

A year into office, Jospin and his government continued to enjoy the electorate's broad trust and approval, partly due to his political skill and perceived lack of public arrogance (a most unusual trait among French politicians). As president, Chirac retains the power to dissolve Parliament after two years of a government's mandate (ie mid-1999) has elapsed. However, with the fractious right unable to agree on whether or not to opt for economic liberalism and the absence of a uniting leader, this appears unlikely.

GEOGRAPHY

France covers an area of 551,000 sq km and is the largest country in Europe after Russia and Ukraine. It is shaped like a hexagon bordered by either mountains or water except for the north-east frontier. France has been invaded repeatedly across this relatively flat frontier, which abuts Germany, Luxembourg and Belgium.

France's coastline, which is some 3200km long, is remarkably diverse, ranging from the white chalk cliffs of Normandy and the treacherous promontories of Brittany to the fine-sand beaches along the Atlantic. The Mediterranean coast tends to have pebbly and even rocky beaches, though beaches in Languedoc and some in Roussillon are sandy.

France is drained by five major river systems:

The 775km-long Seine, used widely for navigation, passes through Paris on its way from Burgundy to the English Channel.

The Loire, the longest river in the country, stretches for 1020km from the Massif Central to the Atlantic. Its flow is eight times greater in December and January than at the end of summer.

The Rhône, which links Lake Geneva and the Alps with the Mediterranean, is joined by the Saône at Lyon.

The Garonne system, which includes the Tarn, Lot and Dordogne rivers, drains the Pyrenees and the rest of the south-west, emptying into the Atlantic.

The Rhine, which flows into the North Sea, forms the eastern border of Alsace for about 200km. Its tributaries, including the Moselle and Meuse, drain much of the area north and east of Paris.

GEOLOGY

A significant proportion of France is covered by mountains, many of them among the most spectacular in Europe.

The French Alps, which include Mont Blanc (4807m), Europe's highest peak, run along France's eastern border from Lake Geneva (Lac Léman) to the Côte d'Azur. There is permanent snow cover above 2800m. The Jura Range, gentle limestone mountains north of the Alps that peak at just over 1700m, stretches along the Swiss frontier north of Lake Geneva. The Pyrenees run along France's entire 450km border with Spain, from the Atlantic to the Mediterranean. Though the loftiest peak is only 3404m high, the Pyrenees can be almost as rugged as the Alps.

The Alps, the Jura and the Pyrenees, though spectacular, are young ranges in comparison with France's ancient massifs, formed between 225 and 345 million years ago. The most spectacular is the Massif

Central, a huge region in the middle of France whose 91,000 sq km cover one-sixth of the entire country. It is perhaps best known for its chain of extinct volcanoes, such as the Puy de Dôme (1465m).

France's other ancient massifs, worn down over the ages, include the Vosges, a forested upland in the country's north-east corner between Alsace and Lorraine; the Ardennes, most of which lies in Belgium and Germany and whose French part is on the northern edge of Champagne; and the Massif Armoricain, which stretches westward from Normandy and forms the backbone of Brittany and Normandy.

CLIMATE

In general, France has a temperate climate, with mild winters, except in mountainous areas and Alsace.

The Atlantic has a profound impact on the north-west, particularly Brittany, whose weather is characterised by high humidity and lots of rain (200 days a year compared to the national average of 164). The area is also subject to persistent and sometimes violent westerly winds.

France's north-east, especially Alsace, has a continental climate, with fairly hot summers and winters cold enough for snow to stay on the ground for weeks at a time. The wettest months in Alsace are June and July, when storms are common.

Midway between Brittany and Alsace – and affected by the climates of both – is the Paris basin. The region records the nation's lowest annual precipitation (about 575mm), but rainfall patterns are erratic: you're just as likely to be caught in a heavy spring or autumn downpour as in a sudden summer cloudburst. Paris' average yearly temperature is 12°C, but the mercury sometimes drops below zero in January and can climb to the mid-30s or higher in August.

The southern coastal plains are subject to a Mediterranean climate as far inland as the southern Alps, the Massif Central and the eastern Pyrenees. If you like hot summers and mild winters, the south of France is for you: frost is rare, spring and autumn downpours are sudden but brief, and summer is virtually without rain. However, the south is also the region of the mistral, a cold, dry wind that blows down the Rhône Valley for about 100 days a year. Most relentless (and fierce) in spring, it is sometimes blamed for making people ill-tempered or even driving them mad.

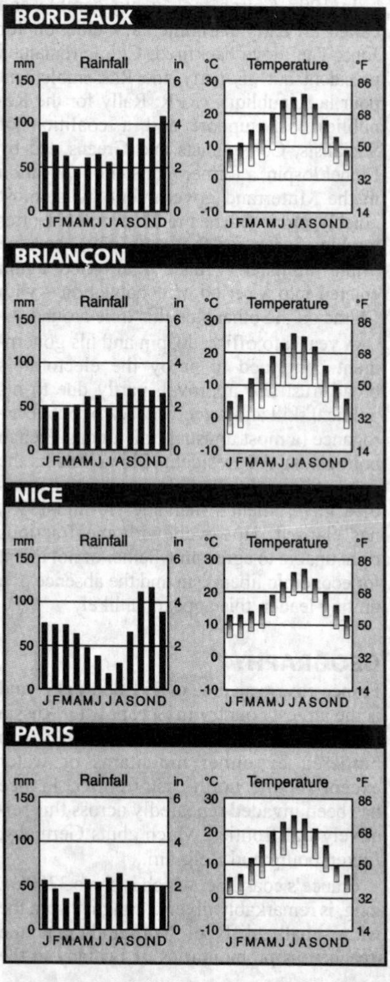

ECOLOGY & ENVIRONMENT

Ecology

France may not have as many nuclear power stations as the USA, but while the US ceased building new ones more than a decade ago, the French program – the most ambitious in the world – is still going strong. Since the late 1980s, the state-owned electric company, Electricité de France (EDF), has produced about three-quarters of the country's electricity using nuclear power. Most of France's nuclear reactors are on main rivers or near the coast. France has also sought to export nuclear technology to various developing countries. Nuclear waste, which is becoming an increasingly important issue, is dumped on the Cotentin Peninsula in Normandy.

EDF also controls France's hydroelectric program. By damming rivers to produce electricity, it has created huge recreational lakes but destroyed the traditional habitats of many animals. High-voltage power lines are a blight on much of the countryside and electrocute at least 1000 birds of prey each year. The EDF has announced that new lines will, as often as possible, run underground.

The French government took a positive step in 1992, when it finally agreed to suspend nuclear testing on the Polynesian island of Moruroa and a nearby atoll. The tests, begun in 1964, were carried out above-ground for a decade before being continued underground. Protesters claimed the tests had disastrous effects on the health of the Moruroa islanders, causing increased rates of birth defects and leukaemia, and disrupted the atoll's food chain. In July 1985 French agents blew up the Greenpeace ship *Rainbow Warrior* in Auckland harbour in an attempt to derail the organisation's campaign against the tests. One person on board was killed. In 1995, however, President Jacques Chirac decided to conduct one last series of tests before supporting a worldwide test ban treaty. This round of tests concluded in January 1996, and France and the UK signed the treaty in April 1998.

Environment

The Office National des Forêts (ONF) manages most of the forests in France, but they are not protected reserves. French ecologists charge that the ONF runs them less to ensure the survival of their ecosystems than to bring in revenue from timber sales.

Summer forest fires are an annual hazard. Great tracts of land are burned each year, often because of careless day-trippers or, as is sometimes the case in the Maures and Esterel ranges in the Côte d'Azur, intentionally set alight in order to get licences to build on the damaged lands. France's northern forests, particularly in the Vosges, have been affected by acid rain.

Wetlands, fantastically productive ecosystems that are essential for the survival of a great number of bird species, reptiles, fish and amphibians, are also shrinking. More than two million hectares – 3% of French territory – are considered important wetlands, but only 4% of this land is protected.

FLORA & FAUNA

France is blessed with a rich variety of flora and fauna. Unfortunately, many fragile species are having a hard time surviving in the face of urbanisation, intensive agriculture, the draining of wetlands, hunting, pollution, the encroachment of industries and the expansion of the tourism infrastructure. Unfortunately, there are precious few established nature reserves so the long-term future of much of the fauna, in particular, appears bleak.

Flora

About 14 million hectares of forest – mostly beech, oak and pine – cover about 20% of France. There are some 4200 species of plants and flowers.

Fauna

All told, France is home to 113 species of mammals (more than any other country in Europe), 363 species of birds, 30 kinds of amphibians, 36 varieties of reptiles and 72 kinds of fish.

Endangered Species

At least three kinds of mammals have disappeared in modern times, and the Pyrenean ibex, Corsican deer, and about 10 species of bats are currently on the endangered list. A quarter of the fish species are also in trouble. Wolves are believed to be extinct, but some reports indicate that there may be a couple of them still roaming the Massif Central. River otters, once abundant, have fallen victim to trappers.

The once common brown bear disappeared from the Alps in the mid-1930s, when about 300 of the animals still lived in the Pyrenees. Today, that number has dwindled to 15. Many birds, including vultures and storks, have all but disappeared from the skies, and Bonnelli's eagle is down to about two dozen pairs from 670 only 20 years ago.

Some animals still live in the wild thanks to a re-introduction program based in certain national and regional parks. Storks are being bred in Alsace, vultures have also been re-introduced in Languedoc, and beavers, once nearly wiped out, are prospering in the Armorique Regional Park in Brittany and in the Rhône Valley. Alpine creatures such as the chamois (a mountain antelope) and the larger bouquetin (a type of ibex) were widely hunted until several national parks were established.

France counts some 1.7 million hunters, many of whom head to the forests and woodlands with their dogs as soon as the five-month season opens at the end of September. To safeguard the passage of migratory birds, long a target of hunters, the Brussels Directive was introduced in 1979 to protect wild birds, their eggs, nests and habitats; it applies to all member states of the EU.

The French government signed the directive but didn't bother to make its provisions part of French law, so birds that can safely fly over other countries may still be shot as they cross France. As a result, environmentalists have in the past rented entire mountain passes on birds' flight paths in order to keep hunters away.

National & Regional Parks

About 0.7% of France's land is within a *parc national* (national park), and another 7% within a *parc naturel régional* (regional park). There are also nearly 100 small *réserves naturelles* (nature reserves) and a few private reserves set up by environmental groups. The proportion of protected land is low relative to France's size.

The national parks, which are uninhabited, are under the direct control of the government and are fully protected by legislation: dogs, vehicles and hunting are banned and camping is restricted. However, the parks themselves are relatively small (all are under 1000 sq km), and the ecosystems they are supposed to protect spill over into what are called 'peripheral zones', populated areas around the parks in which tourism and other economic activities are permitted.

France has six national parks, all of them in the mountains except for the Parc National de Port Cros, an island marine park off the Côte d'Azur. Most national parkland is in the Alps, where the Vanoise, Écrins and Mercantour parks are hugely popular with nature lovers and hikers in summer. The Parc National des Pyrénées runs for 100km along the Spanish border and is a favourite with rock climbers. The wild Parc National des Cévennes, which has a few inhabitants in its central zone, is on the border of the Massif Central and Languedoc.

The country's almost three dozen regional parks and its nature reserves, most of which were established both to improve (or at least maintain) local ecosystems and to encourage economic development and tourism, all support human populations and are locally managed. The regional parks are mainly in areas with diminishing populations that are facing severe economic problems such as the Massif Central and parts of Corsica.

GOVERNMENT & POLITICS

France has had 11 constitutions since 1789. The present one, which was instituted by de Gaulle in 1958, established what is known as the Fifth Republic. It gives considerable power to the President of the Republic. Jacques Chirac took over the presidency from François Mitterrand in May 1995.

The 577 members of the Assemblée Nationale are directly elected in single-member constituencies for five year terms. The 321 members of the rather powerless Sénat (Senate), who serve for nine years, are indirectly elected. The president of France is chosen by direct election for a seven year term. Women were given the right to vote in 1944. The voting age is 18.

Executive power is shared by the president and the Council of Ministers, whose members (including the prime minister) are appointed by the president but are responsible to parliament. The president, who resides in the Palais de l'Élysée (Élysée Palace) in Paris, serves as commander-in-chief of the armed forces and theoretically makes all major policy decisions. In periods of cohabitation, however, when the president and prime minister are not of the same party, the main policy-maker is the prime minister while the president is concerned with foreign affairs only (the office's *domaine reservé*). He or she can also dismiss the prime minister and has the power to dissolve the National Assembly in times of crises and no-confidence.

France is one of the five permanent members of the UN Security Council. It withdrew from NATO's joint military command in 1966 and has maintained an independent arsenal of nuclear weapons since 1960.

Local Administration

France has long been a highly centralised state. Before the Revolution, the country consisted of about two dozen major regions and a variety of smaller ones. Their names (and those of their long-extinct predecessors) are still widely used, but for administrative purposes the country has, since 1790, been divided into units of about 6100 sq km called *départements* (departments). There are 96 departments in metropolitan France – the mainland and Corsica – and another five in overseas territories. Most are named after geographical features, especially rivers, but are commonly known by their two-digit code, which appears as the first two digits of all postcodes in the department and as the last two numbers on number plates of cars registered there.

The national government is represented in each department by a *préfet* (prefect). A department's main town, where the government and the prefect are based, is known as a *préfecture* (prefecture). It is also the seat of an elected *conseil général* (general council). You can tell if a town is a prefecture because the last three digits of the postcode are zeros.

A department is subdivided into a number of *arrondissements* (for a national total of 324), each of whose main town is known as a *sous-préfecture* (subprefecture). The arrondissements are further divided into *cantons* and these are further split into *communes*, the basic administrative unit of local government. Each of France's 36,400 communes is presided over by a *maire* (mayor) based in a *mairie* (town hall). Almost one-third of the communes have populations of less than 200.

Because of their small size, departments are ill-suited for carrying out modern regional coordination. In 1972, the government divided France into 22 regions based roughly on the country's historical divisions. Each of these has an elected council and other organs, but its powers are limited and it plays no direct role in actual administration.

France's five *départements d'outre-mer* (overseas departments) include: the Caribbean islands of Guadeloupe and Martinique; French Guiana (Guyane), a 91,000 sq km territory on the northern coast of South America between Brazil and Suriname; the island of Réunion, which is in the Indian Ocean east of Madagascar; and Saint Pierre et Miquelon in the Atlantic, just off the southern coast of the Canadian province of Newfoundland. The island of Mayotte, one of the Comoros Islands in the Indian Ocean, has quasi-departmental status.

In addition, France has three *territoires d'outre-mer* (overseas territories), all of which are in the South Pacific: French Polynesia, which includes Tahiti and 130 other islands; New Caledonia, which also includes a large tract of the Pacific and several island dependancies; and the Wallis and Futuna islands. France also claims a sizeable chunk of Antarctica. All of these far-flung bits of territory are often referred to collectively as DOM-TOM, the acronym of the *départements d'outre-mer-territoires d'outre-mer*.

ECONOMY

France's economy may not be the powerhouse of Europe – Germany can lay claim to that distinction – but French financial leaders have enough clout to determine the shape of European Monetary Union in 1999. EMU, as it is known, has been the driving force behind much of Europe's financial direction as the millennium nears.

For the traveller the most important consequence will be the disappearance of many of Europe's banknotes and bills in 2003,

REGIONS & DÉPARTEMENTS

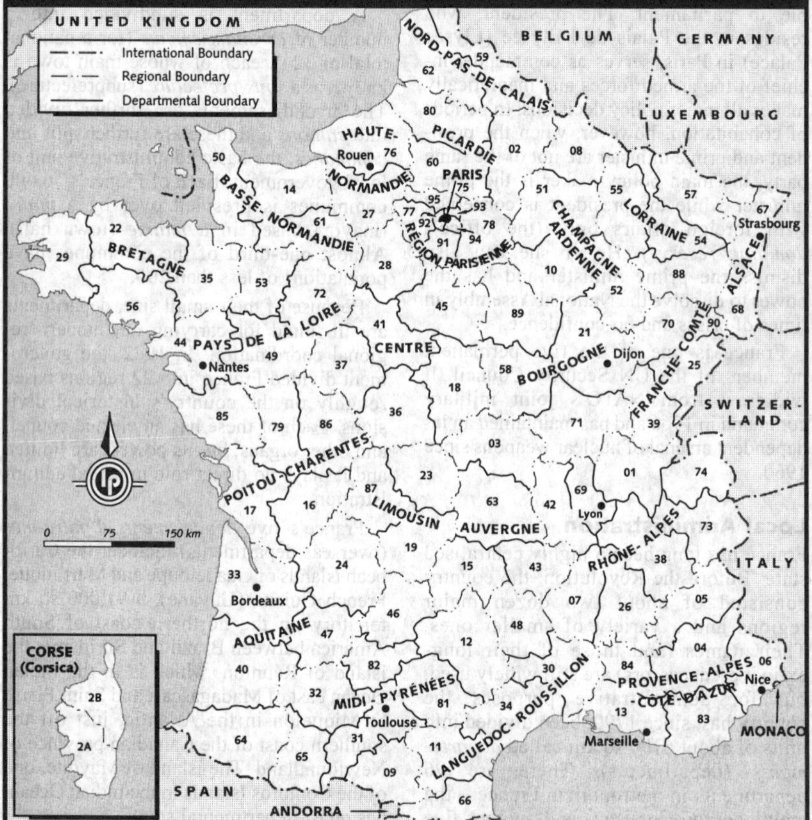

when the euro becomes the standard European Union currency (see the boxed text 'Adieu Franc, Bonjour Euro' in the Facts for the Visitor chapter).

At the heart of financial policy-making will be a central bank. Although France had hoped that its half-hearted attempts at making Paris a regional financial centre would result in the city being selected as the bank's headquarters, the French capital lost out to Frankfurt. However, in May 1998 the French won a victory that surprised many European observers: the central bank's chief would have a much shorter reign than originally envisaged,

REGIONS AND DÉPARTEMENTS

ALSACE
67 Bas-Rhin
68 Haut-Rhin

AQUITAINE
24 Dordogne
33 Gironde
40 Landes
47 Lot-et-Garonne
64 Pyrénées-Atlantiques

AUVERGNE
03 Allier
15 Cantal
43 Haute-Loire
63 Puy-de-Dôme

BASSE-NORMANDIE
14 Calvados
50 Manche
61 Orne

BRETAGNE
22 Côtes d'Armor
29 Finistère
35 Ille-et-Vilaine
56 Morbihan

BOURGOGNE
21 Côte d'Or
58 Nièvre
71 Saône-et-Loire
89 Yonne

CENTRE
18 Cher
28 Eure-et-Loire
36 Indre
37 Indre-et-Loire
41 Loir-et-Cher
45 Loiret

CHAMPAGNE-ARDENNE
08 Ardennes
10 Aube
51 Marne
52 Haute-Marne

CORSE
2A Corse-du-Sud
2B Haute-Corse

FRANCHE-COMTÉ
25 Doubs
39 Jura
70 Haute-Saône
90 Territoire de Belfort

HAUTE-NORMANDIE
27 Eure
76 Seine-Maritime

LANGUEDOC-ROUSSILLON
11 Aude
30 Gard
34 Hérault
48 Lozère
66 Pyrénées-Orientales

LIMOUSIN
19 Corrèze
23 Creuse
87 Haute-Vienne

LORRAINE
54 Meurthe-et-Moselle
55 Meuse
57 Moselle
88 Vosges

MIDI-PYRÉNÉES
09 Ariège
12 Aveyron
31 Haute-Garonne
32 Gers
46 Lot
65 Hautes-Pyrénées
81 Tarn
82 Tarn-et-Garonne

NORD-PAS-DE-CALAIS
59 Nord
62 Pas-de-Calais

PAYS DE LA LOIRE
44 Loire-Atlantique
49 Maine-et-Loire
53 Mayenne
72 Sarthe
85 Vendée

PICARDIE
02 Aisne
60 Oise
80 Somme

POITOU-CHARENTES
16 Charente
17 Charente-Maritime
79 Deux-Sèvres
86 Vienne

PROVENCE-ALPES-CÔTE D'AZUR
04 Alpes-de-Haute-Provence
05 Hautes-Alpes
06 Alpes-Maritimes
13 Bouches-du-Rhône
83 Var
84 Vaucluse

RÉGION PARISIENNE
75 Ville de Paris
77 Seine-et-Marne
78 Yvelines
91 Essonne
92 Hauts-de-Seine
93 Seine-Saint-Denis
94 Val-de-Marne
95 Val-d'Oise

RHÔNE-ALPES
01 Ain
07 Ardèche
26 Drôme
38 Isère
42 Loire
69 Rhône
73 Savoie
74 Haute-Savoie

and its second head would be a French official. The Germans were upset, not so much in losing out to their age-old rivals, but because French financial planners have a reputation for being led by their politicians. The Germans fear that a French central bank chief would be ruled more by the ballot box than by firm economic fundamentals.

Most outsiders are surprised by the degree to which the French state still owns much of France. While French bankers are advising many countries around the world on how to sell off state-owned companies, the French themselves have been slow to privatise their own industry. When the Socialist-dominated government announced in 1998 that France Telecom would be sold to the public in a stock market issue financial markets were relieved. But the sale was contingent on the findings of a special committee that included the trade unions, who were afraid of the negative impact a partial sale would have on jobs.

Pragmatism had something to do with the Socialists going back on their word and opting for privatisation. France continually wrestles with a budget deficit, and in the late 1990s there were fears that the government would overspend to such a degree that France would not be eligible to join the first wave of EMU. Selling off state assets was one way for France to ensure that it met the criteria.

The French economy is growing at about the EU average. This sluggish rise in annual gross domestic product – predicted at just under 3% in 1999 – will keep France's relatively high unemployment at around 12%, a figure that has not budged in years.

France is one of the world's most industrialised nations, with some 40% of the workforce employed in the industrial sector. About 50% of GNP comes from industrial production. However, there is poor coordination between academic research and companies that might turn good ideas into products, and the country has fewer large corporations – an important source of private capital and investment in research and development – than other industrialised nations of similar size.

France can also lay claim to being the largest agricultural producer and exporter in the EU. Its production of wheat, barley, maize (corn) and cheese is particularly significant. The country is to a great extent self-sufficient in food except for certain tropical products, like bananas and coffee. As you savour some delectable morsel of French food, remember that nearly one in 10 workers nationwide is engaged in agricultural production. Despite this, the agricultural sector is the weakest part of the economy, largely because many of the holdings are too small and low-tech for efficient production.

POPULATION & PEOPLE

France has a population of 58.3 million, more than 20% of whom live in the greater metropolitan area of Paris. The number of people living in rural and mountain areas has been declining since the 1950s.

For much of the last two centuries, France has had a considerably lower rate of population growth than its neighbours. On the other hand, over that period the country has accepted more immigrants than any other European nation, including significant numbers of political refugees.

Between 1850 and WWI, the country received 4.3 million immigrants. A further three million immigrants arrived between the world wars, in part because the carnage of WWI had left France with a serious shortage of workers. Most immigrants came from other parts of Europe (especially Italy, Spain, Poland, Russia and Armenia), but the economic boom following WWII, also accompanied by a labour shortage, attracted several million workers – most of them unskilled – along with their families from North Africa and French-speaking sub-Saharan Africa.

During the late 1950s and early 60s, as the French colonial empire collapsed, over one million French settlers returned to metropolitan France from Algeria, other parts of Africa and Indochina. At the same time, millions of non-French immigrants from the same places were welcomed as much needed manpower during France's '30 glorious years' of fast economic growth.

Large-scale immigration was stopped by a 1974 law banning all new foreign workers, but in recent years there has been a racist backlash against the country's non-white immigrant communities, especially Muslims from North Africa, who haven't assimilated into French society and the French economy as quickly as their European predecessors. The extreme-right *Front National* (National Front) party has fanned these racist feelings in a bid to win more votes. In 1993 the French government changed its immigration laws to make it harder for immigrants to get French citizenship or bring their families into the country. In January 1997 the National Assembly approved (by a large margin) new legislation that legitimised the status of some illegal immigrants, but also implemented measures that made it easier to locate and repatriate others.

EDUCATION

France's education system has long been highly centralised, a fact reflected in teachers status as civil servants. Its high standards have produced great intellectuals and almost universal literacy, but equal opportunities are still not available to people of all classes.

Private schools, most of which are Catholic (though Protestant and Jewish schools also exist), educate about 17% of students – and also accounts for almost a quarter of all students planning to attend university. The state pays staff salaries and some of the operating costs at most private schools provided they follow certain curriculum guidelines. Tuition fees are thus very low.

Primary

One-third of all French children begin attending a *crèche* (day nursery), a *jardin d'enfants* (day-care centre) or an *école maternelle* (nursery school) at the age of two. By age three they are joined by virtually all of their peers. Until the age of 10 or 11, all children – rich or poor, gifted or slow – follow pretty much the same curriculum. Primary education became compulsory for all children between the ages of six and 13 in 1882. Education is now obligatory until 16 years of age.

Secondary

Lycée (secondary school) studies are divided into two stages. The first cycle (*collège*), attended by children aged 11 to 15, follows a curriculum of general studies that is more or less the same in all schools. During the second cycle, which is for those aged 15 to 18, pupils can choose between the academic track and the less highly regarded vocational track.

Only students in the academic track can sit for the university entrance exam called the *baccalauréat* (usually shortened to *le bac*). At present, 73% of high school students take the matriculation exam, double the proportion in 1980 and considerably more than in other European countries. There is also a vocational baccalauréat.

Tertiary

Universities Anyone who has passed the bac is entitled to a free place in one of France's 77 universities, an option taken up by about one-third of young people (again, the highest proportion in Western Europe). The catch is that after the first year of study, students must face a gruelling examination that only 30 to 40% of them end up passing (in medicine, one in six). Those who fail must make do with other options, such as attending a two year *collège universitaire*. The drop-out rate is exacerbated by the scarcity of government stipends, received by only one in eight students.

French university degrees are slightly different from their counterparts granted in English-speaking countries. A *licence*, awarded after three years, is similar to a bachelor's degree. It is followed by a *maîtrise*, roughly equivalent to a master's degree, which is in turn followed in some fields by a *diplôme d'études approfondies* (DEA) or a *diplôme d'études supérieures spécialisées* (DESS), taken before completing a PhD. The prestigious *doctorat*, which is necessary to become a full professor, takes many years of highly specialised research. The highest-level teaching qualification is known as an *agrégation*.

In 1793, the Revolutionary government abolished the universities, some of which had been founded in the Middle Ages. They were re-established by Napoleon in 1808. The Sorbonne, founded in the 13th century, was long the country's leading university. Now incorporated into the University of Paris system (part of which occupies the old Sorbonne buildings in the Latin Quarter), it has for centuries helped to draw many of France's most talented and energetic people to Paris, creating a serious provincial brain drain. Today, about one-third of French students study in Paris.

Grandes Écoles Some of France's ablest and most ambitious young people do not attend the overcrowded universities. About 5% of students are enrolled in the country's 140 prestigious *grandes écoles*, institutions offering training in such fields as business management, engineering and the applied sciences. Students do not pay tuition and even receive salaries but they must work as civil servants after graduation – for up to 10 years in some cases. A high percentage of the top positions in the public sector, the traditionally less-prestigious private sector and politics are filled by grandes écoles graduates.

PHILOSOPHY

René Descartes (1586-1650) was the founder of modern philosophy, and the greatest thinker since Aristotle. He was small in stature and poor in health, but he was an intellectual giant who used a rigorous method of wholesale doubt and sought mathematical-like certainty in all things. Descartes' famed phrase '*cogito, ergo sum*' (I think, therefore I am) is the basis of modern philosophical thought, and his method came to be known as Cartesianism.

France produced some other luminary thinkers particularly in the late 19th and early 20th centuries, and these included Henri Louis Bergson, Jean-Paul Sartre (see the boxed text 'Jean-Paul Sartre & Existentialism'), Gabriel Honoré Marcel, Maurice Merleau-Ponty, Michel Foucault, Jacques Derrida (an Algerian) and the French Feminists headed by Simone de Beauvoir. They are collectively known as the French existentialists, although their influences were predominantly German. Their views differed widely, but the theme of human freedom was common to all.

ARTS

Architecture

Prehistoric The earliest monuments made by humans in France were stone megaliths erected during the Neolithic period from about 4000 to 2400 BC. Although these prehistoric monuments are mainly found in Brittany, particularly around Carnac, there are others in northern Languedoc (eg around the town of Mende) and on Corsica (eg Filitosa).

Gallo-Roman The Romans constructed a large number of public works all over the country from the 1st century BC: aqueducts, fortifications, marketplaces, temples, amphitheatres, triumphal arches and bathhouses. They also established regular street grids at many settlements.

Southern France – especially Provence and the coastal plains of Languedoc – is the place to go in search of France's *gallo-romain* legacy. Testimony to the Romans' architectural brilliance includes the Pont du Gard aqueduct between Nîmes and Avignon, the colossal amphitheatres at Nîmes and Arles, the theatre at Orange, the Maison Carrée in Nîmes and the public buildings in Vaison-la-Romaine.

Dark Ages Although quite a few churches were built during the Merovingian and Carolingian periods (5th to 10th century), very little remains of them. However, traces of churches from this period can be seen at Saint Denis (north of Paris) and in Auxerre's Saint Germain Abbey.

Jean-Paul Sartre & Existentialism

The 20th century's most famous French thinker was Jean-Paul Sartre, the quintessential Parisian intellectual who was born in Paris on 21 June 1905 and died there on 15 April 1980. For most people he embodied an obscure idea called existentialism. It's one of the great 'isms' in pop culture, but even philosophers have trouble explaining what existentialism really means.

Sartre was a novelist, a playwright, a critic and a brilliant philosopher. His father was a decorated naval officer, and his mother was the cousin of Albert Schweitzer, the famous Alsatian-German theologian and African missionary doctor. His father died when Sartre was young and he was raised by his grandfather.
He graduated from the Ecole Normale Supérieure in 1929 and in 1938 published his first novel, *La Nausée* (Nausea), which introduced many of the themes of his later philosophical works. He worked as a *lycée* teacher until the outbreak of WWII and spent a year as a prisoner of war. As a result of his war experiences he found a new political commitment and became a key figure in the French Resistance. He announced that he was a communist and became a champion of left-wing political issues. In 1960 he published his last proper philosophical work, *Critique de la raison dialectique* (Critique of Dialectic Reason), where he attempted to reconcile his original existentialist philosophy with Marxism. Ideas of collectivism and solidarity did not sit easily next to Sartre's themes of introspection and subjectivity. He was to renounce communism in later life.

Sartre never used the term existentialism in his early defining works, but it came to represent a body of thought that he, in part, inherited from the German philosopher Edmund Husserl. It was also adopted by a Parisian café clique of writers, dramatists and intellectuals (which included life-long companion Simone de Beauvoir), and even painters and musicians. Jean-Paul's intellectual influences were the German philosophers, in particular Martin Heidegger and Friedrich Nietzche, and he was also influenced by the Dane Søren Kierkegaard. All of these philosophers had existentialist leanings, concerning themselves with the human condition, but they were very different from each other. DE Cooper said that existentialism is a 'tendency rather than a coherent philosophy', and Sartre's existentialism was profoundly original.

Sartre was a Cartesianist; the foundation of his ideas was Descartes' proof of human consciousness, the *cogito* – I think therefore I am. But unlike Descartes and Kierkegaard he was

Continued on next page

Jean-Paul Sartre & Existentialism

also an atheist, and the 'loss of God' was a phrase he used often. In the 1930s he wrote a series of analyses of human self-awareness that culminated in his most important philosophical work *L'Etre et le néant* (Being and Nothingness; 1943). The central idea of this long and difficult book is to distinguish between objective things and human consciousness, and to assert that consciousness is a 'non-thing' (the literal English translation of Sartre's '*néant*' is 'nothingness', but it is too strong). Consciousness is made real by standing back and taking a point of view on things, on 'being'. Since consciousness is not involved in the strictly causal relationship that things have with other things it is free, and freedom makes us human. He claimed that we are 'condemned to be free' – we must choose and act – and must take personal responsibility for our own actions and destinies without deferring to religion, traditional moral structures or society. Even in indecision we choose not to choose, thus freedom is inescapable.

'Existence precedes essence', said Sartre. There is no such thing as human nature – we each become ourselves through our choices and actions, and these comprise who and what we are. We are nothing more than the choices we make. Someone does not tell the truth because they are honest, but defines themselves as honest by telling the truth again and again. Human consciousness is subjective and this is something we cannot overcome, but embracing our subjectivity gives us the power to infinitely redefine and transform ourselves.

For all its lofty language and convoluted philosophical argument, *L'Etre et le néant* is a treatise on a fairly simple way of life that embraces one's own autonomy and seeks to maximise one's choices (or one's awareness of them). Many read Sartre's message as a positive one, but for him this heightened human awareness was characterised by emptiness, boredom and negativity. His language is often dark and brooding: 'It is in anguish that we become conscious of our freedom'. Anguish for Sartre is realisation that many of our actions have profound effects on others, that we are responsible for these and that there is no objective justification for our choices ('I choose for all mankind'). We are 'abandoned' in the world where, with the loss of God, we are left with no external rule or guidance in our choices. We 'despair' because our sphere of influence has limits, and because there are things that we care about over which we have no control. We exercise 'bad faith' when we regard ourselves as not free and not responsible, and 'self-deception' when we claim we have no choice.

Sartre argued, firstly in *Esquisse d'une théorie des émotions* (Sketch for a Theory of the Emotions; 1939), that Freud's notion of the unconscious was flawed and that a human unconscious that motivates a person unknowingly to action could not exist. As a Cartesianist, Sartre held that consciousness must always be aware of itself. The explanation of all thoughts, dreams and feelings should be sought within the consciousness, not outside it. If the mind seeks to repress certain things then it must be aware of which things to repress, and thereby is merely practicing self-deception.

The many literary works, essays, plays and political writings of Sartre were charged with his philosophical ideas, and were often used as vehicles. *No Exit* (*Huis-clos* in French; 1944), his most popular play, is an allegorical and unnerving story about three people who find themselves in a room together with no way out. This work includes Sartre's famous words 'Hell is other people'.

He remained politically active in later life, but his health deteriorated rapidly in his last years. Throughout his life he'd imbibed vast quantities of alcohol, tobacco and amphetamines, and this continued unabated – he ultimately went blind. Jean-Paul Sartre succumbed to lung cancer aged 74. Over 25,000 people attended his funeral procession.

Romanesque A religious revival in the 11th century led to the construction of a large number of *roman* (Romanesque) churches, so-called because their architects adopted many architectural elements (eg vaulting) from Gallo-Roman buildings still standing at the time. Romanesque buildings typically have round arches, heavy walls whose few windows let in very little light, and a lack of ornamentation that borders on the austere.

Many of the most famous Romanesque churches – Saint Sernin basilica in Toulouse, for instance – were built for pilgrims en route to Santiago de Compostela in Spain. Others, like Caen's two famous Romanesque abbeys, were erected by prominent benefactors. Chateaus built during this era tended to be massive, heavily fortified structures that afforded very few luxuries to their inhabitants. The Romanesque style remained popular until the mid-12th century.

Gothic The Gothic style originated in the mid-12th century in northern France, whose great wealth enabled it to attract the finest architects, engineers and artisans. Gothic structures are characterised by ribbed vaults carved with great precision, pointed arches, slender verticals, chapels (often built by rich people or guilds) along the nave and chancel, refined decoration and large stained-glass windows.

The first Gothic building was the basilica in Saint Denis, which combined various late Romanesque elements to create a new kind of structural support in which each arch counteracted and complemented the next. Gothic technology and the width and height it made possible subsequently spread to the rest of Western Europe.

Cathedrals built in the early Gothic style, which lasted until about 1230, were majestic but lacked the lightness and airiness of most later works. Since the stained-glass windows could not support the roof, thick stone buttresses were placed between them. It was soon discovered that reducing the bulk of the buttresses and adding outer piers to carry the thrust created a lighter building without compromising structural integrity.

This discovery gave rise to flying buttresses, which helped lift the Gothic style to its greatest achievements, between 1230 and 1300. During this period, when French architecture dominated the European scene for the first time, Gothic masterpieces such as the seminal cathedral at Chartres and its successors at Reims and Amiens were decorated with ornate tracery (the delicate stone rib-work on stained-glass windows) and huge, colourful rose windows.

Because of the fiascos at Beauvais cathedral, whose 48m vaults collapsed in 1272 and again in 1284, it became clear that Gothic technology had reached its limits. Architects became less interested in sheer size and put more energy into ornamentation.

In the 14th century, the Rayonnant (Radiant) Gothic style – named after the radiating tracery of the rose windows – developed, with interiors becoming even lighter thanks to broader windows and more translucent stained glass. One of the most influential Rayonnant buildings was the Sainte Chapelle in Paris, whose stained glass forms a sheer curtain of glazing.

By the 15th century, decorative extravagance led to Flamboyant Gothic, so named because its wavy stone carving was said to resemble flames. Beautifully lacy examples of Flamboyant architecture include the Clocher Neuf at Chartres, Rouen cathedral's Tour de Beurre, Église Saint Maclou in Rouen, and the spire of Strasbourg cathedral.

Renaissance The Renaissance, which began in Italy in the early 15th century, set out to realise a 'rebirth' of classical Greek and Roman culture. It had its first impact on France at the tail end of the 15th century, when Charles VIII began a series of invasions of Italy.

The French Renaissance is divided into two periods: early Renaissance and Mannerism. During the first period, a variety of classical components and decorative motifs (columns, tunnel vaults, round arches, domes etc) were blended with the rich decoration of Flamboyant Gothic, a synthesis best exemplified by the Château de Chambord in the

Loire Valley. But the transition from late Gothic to Renaissance can be seen most clearly in the Château de Blois, whose Flamboyant section was built only 15 years before its early Renaissance wing.

Mannerism began around 1530, when François I (who had been so deeply impressed by what he'd seen in Italy that he brought Leonardo da Vinci to Amboise in 1516) hired Italian architects and artists – many of them disciples of Michelangelo or Raphael – to design and decorate his new chateau at Fontainebleau.

Over the next couple of decades, French architects who had studied in Italy took over from their Italian colleagues. In 1546 Pierre Lescot designed the richly decorated south-western corner of the Louvre's Cour Carrée. The Petit Château at Chantilly was built about a decade later.

Because French Renaissance architecture was very much the province of the aristocracy and designed by imported artists, the middle classes – resentful French artisans among them – remained loyal to the indigenous Gothic style, and Gothic churches

PARTS OF A CATHEDRAL

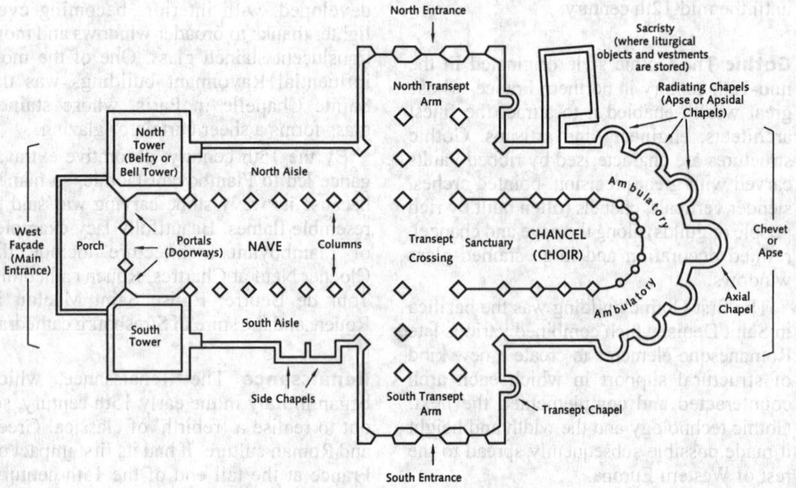

NOTE:
Very few churches incorporate all of the elements shown here, some of which are found only in Gothic cathedrals from certain periods. Romanesque churches have a much simpler layout.

Many French cathedrals are oriented roughly east to west so that the chancel faces more or less east towards Jerusalem. As a result, the main entrance is usually at the base of the west façade and the transept arms extend north and south from the transept crossing as shown here.

continued to be built throughout the 16th century. The Mannerist style lasted until the early 17th century.

Baroque During the baroque period, which lasted from the end of the 16th century to the late 18th century, painting, sculpture and classical architecture were integrated to create structures and interiors of great subtlety, refinement and elegance.

Salomon de Brosse, who designed Paris' Palais du Luxembourg (1615), set the stage for France's two most prominent early baroque architects: François Mansart, designer of the classical wing of the Château de Blois (1635), and his younger rival, Louis Le Vau, the first architect for Louis XIV's palace at Versailles and its predecessor and model, Vaux-le-Vicomte. Baroque elements are particularly in evidence in Versailles' lavish interiors, such as the Galerie des Glaces (Hall of Mirrors). Jules Hardouin-Mansart, Le Vau's successor at Versailles, also designed the Église du Dôme (1670s) at the Invalides in Paris, considered the finest church built in France during the 17th century.

PARTS OF A CATHEDRAL

USEFUL TERMS:

Ambulatory
The ambulatory, a continuation of the aisles of the nave around the chancel, forms a processional path that allows pilgrims relatively easy access to radiating chapels, saints' relics and altars around the chancel and behind the altar.

Clerestory Windows
The clerestory windows, a row of tall windows above the triforium (see below), are often difficult to see because they're so high above the floor.

Cloister
The cloister (*cloître*), a four-sided enclosure surrounded by covered, colonnaded arcades, is often attached to a monastery church or a cathedral. In monasteries, the cloister served as the focal point of the monks' educational and recreational activities.

Narthex
The narthex is an enclosed entrance vestibule just inside the west entrance. It was once reserved for penitents and the unbaptised.

Crypt
The crypt (*crypte*) is a chamber under the church floor, usually at the eastern end, in which saints, martyrs, early church figures and worthy personages are buried. In many Gothic churches, the crypt is often one of the few extant parts of earlier, pre-Gothic structures on the site. A visit to the crypt, usually reached via stairs on one or both sides of the chancel, may involve a small fee.

Rood Screen
A rood screen, also known as a jube (*jubé*), is an often elaborate structure separating the chancel from the nave. Because rood screens made it difficult for worshippers to see religious ceremonies taking place in the chancel, most were removed in the 17th and 18th centuries.

Rose Window
The circular stained-glass windows commonly found in Gothic cathedrals over the west entrance and at the north and south ends of the transept arms are known as rose or wheel windows. The stained-glass panels are usually separated from each other by elaborate stone bar tracery, which people inside the church see in silhouette.

Treasury
A treasury (*trésor*) is a secure room for storing and displaying precious liturgical objects. It may be open shorter hours than the church itself. Visiting often involves a small entry fee.

Triforium
The triforium is an arcaded or colonnaded gallery above the aisle, choir or transept. Most triforia are directly above the columns that separate the aisles from the nave or the ambulatory from the chancel. From the late 13th century, larger clerestory windows often replaced the triforium.

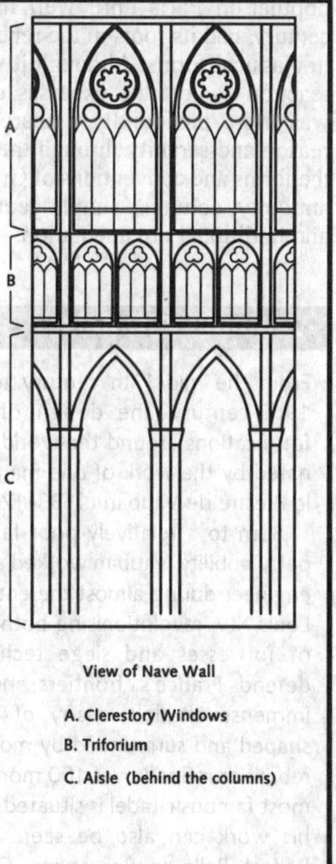

View of Nave Wall

A. Clerestory Windows
B. Triforium
C. Aisle (behind the columns)

Rococo Rococo, a derivation of baroque, was popular during the Enlightenment (1700-80). In France, rococo was confined almost exclusively to the interiors of private residences and had a minimal impact on churches, chateaus and façades, which continued to follow the conventional rules of baroque classicism. Rococo interiors, such as the oval rooms of the Archives Nationales building in Paris, were lighter, smoother and airier than their 17th century predecessors and favoured pastels over vivid colours.

Neoclassicism Neoclassical architecture, which emerged in about 1740 and remained popular in Paris until well into the 19th century, had its roots in the renewed interest in classical forms. Although it was in part a reaction against the excesses of rococo, it was more profoundly a search for order, reason and serenity through the adoption of the forms and conventions of Graeco-Roman antiquity: columns, simple geometric forms and traditional ornamentation.

Vauban's Citadels

From the mid-17th century to the mid-19th century, the design of defensive fortifications around the world was dominated by the work of one man: Sébastien le Prestre de Vauban (1633-1707).

Born to a relatively poor family of the petty nobility, Vauban worked as a military engineer during almost the entire reign of Louis XIV, revolutionising both the design of fortresses and siege techniques. To defend France's frontiers, he built 33 immense citadels, many of them star-shaped and surrounded by moats, and he rebuilt or refined over 100 more. Vauban's most famous citadel is situated at Lille, but his work can also be seen at Antibes, Belfort, Belle Île, Bensançon, Concarneau, Perpignan, Saint Jean Pied de Port, Saint Malo and Verdun.

France's greatest 18th century neoclassical architect was Jacques-Germain Soufflot, who designed the Panthéon in Paris. But neoclassicism really came into its own under Napoleon, who used it extensively for monumental architecture intended to embody the grandeur of imperial France. Well known Paris sights designed (though not necessarily completed) during the First Empire (1804-14) include the Arc de Triomphe, La Madeleine, the façade of the Palais Bourbon, the Arc du Carrousel at the Louvre, the Assemblée Nationale and the Bourse.

Art Nouveau Art Nouveau, which emerged in Europe and the USA in the second half of the 19th century but came to be seen as outdated by around 1910, is characterised by sinuous curves and flowing, asymmetrical forms reminiscent of tendrilous vines, water lilies, the patterns on insect wings and the flowering boughs of trees. It was influenced by the arrival of *objets d'art* from Japan, and its name comes from a Paris gallery that featured works in the new style.

Art Nouveau had a profound impact on all of the applied arts, including interior design, glass work, wrought-iron work, furniture making and graphics. Art Nouveau combined a variety of materials – including iron, brick, glass and ceramics – in ways never seen before. France's major Art Nouveau centres were Nancy and Paris; the latter is still graced by Hector Guimard's noodle-like metro entrances. There are some fine Art Nouveau interiors in the Musée d'Orsay, an Art Nouveau glass roof over the Grand Palais and, on Rue Pavée in the Marais, a synagogue designed by Guimard.

Contemporary Architecture France's most celebrated architect this century, Le Corbusier, was born in Switzerland but settled in Paris in 1917 at the age of 30. A radical modernist, he tried to adapt buildings to their functions in industrialised society without ignoring the human element. At the Cité Radieuse development (1952) in Marseille, for example, he put buildings with related functions in a circular formation and constructed them in standard sizes based on the proportions of the human form. His chapel at Ronchamp (1955), in eastern France, is one of the most important works of modern architecture in France.

France's leaders have long sought to immortalise themselves by erecting huge, public edifices – known as *grands projects* – in Paris. In recent years, the late President Georges Pompidou commissioned the once reviled but now much revered Centre Beaubourg (1977) and his successor, Giscard d'Estaing, was instrumental in transforming a derelict train station into the glorious Musée d'Orsay, which opened in 1986. But François Mitterrand surpassed them both with his monumental commissions.

Since the early 1980s, Paris has seen the construction of such projects as IM Pei's glass pyramid at the Louvre, an architectural *cause célèbre* in the late 1980s; the Opéra-Bastille; the Grande Arche in the skyscraper district of La Défense; the huge science museum and park at La Villette; Parc André Citroën in the western corner of the 15e arrondissement; the new Finance Ministry offices in Bercy; and the controversial new home of the Bibliothèque Nationale (National Library), whose four sun-drenched skyscrapers house the stacks while readers peruse their books underground.

France's first new cathedral in more than a century was inaugurated in 1995 in Evry, a 'new town' 20km south of Paris. Designed by architect Mario Botta and built at a cost of 65FF million, the controversial Cathédrale de la Résurrection is a truncated cylinder of red brick whose sloping roof has two dozen lime trees planted around its rim to symbolise Christ's crown of thorns.

Painting

16th Century & Before Sculpture and stained glass rather than paintings were the main adornments of the medieval Gothic cathedrals of northern France, in part because the many windows left little wall space. The Sienese, French and Spanish artists working at the papal court in Avignon in the 14th century, however, created an influential style of mural painting, examples of which can be seen in the city's Palais des Papes.

In the 15th century, France might have served as a meeting ground for the rich traditions of Italy and Flanders, but the Hundred Years' War got in the way. In the 16th century, the Wars of Religion further hampered the development of French painting. Most French Renaissance painters copied Italian models with little passion or inspiration.

17th Century Voltaire wrote that French painting began with Nicolas Poussin (1594-1665), a baroque painter who frequently set scenes from classical mythology and the Bible in ordered landscapes bathed in golden light. Poussin spent most of his working life in Rome. His main subject was the slanting light of the Roman countryside.

In 1648 Charles le Brun founded the Royal Academy and, as its head, dominated French painting until the arrival of Jean-Antoine Watteau. Watteau's scenes of concerts and picnics are set in gardens with the occasional presence of characters from the Italian commedia dell'arte.

18th Century In the 18th century, Jean-Baptiste Chardin brought the humbler domesticity of the Dutch masters to French art. He was the first painter to regard still life as an essay in composition rather than a show of skill in reproduction.

In 1785 the public reacted with enthusiasm to two large paintings by Jacques Louis David with clear republican messages, *The Oath of the Horatii* and *Brutus Condemning His Son*. David became one of the leaders of the Revolution, and a virtual dictator in matters of art, where he advocated a precise, severe classicism. He was made official state painter by Napoleon and produced such vast pictures as *Le Sacre de Napoléon* (Coronation of Napoleon) in 1804. He is perhaps best remembered for the famous painting of Marat lying dead in his bath.

19th Century Jean Auguste Dominique Ingres, David's most gifted pupil, continued in the neoclassical tradition. The historical pictures to which he devoted most of his life are now generally regarded as inferior to his portraits.

The gripping *Raft of the Medusa* by Théodore Géricault is on the threshold of romanticism; if Géricault had not died young, he would probably have become a leader of the movement along with his friend Eugène Delacroix. The latter searched through the histories and literatures of many countries to find subjects to suit his turbulent, dramatic style. His most famous picture, perhaps, is *La Liberté Conduisant le Peuple* (Freedom Leading the People), which commemorates the July Revolution of 1830.

While the romantics revamped the subject-picture, the members of the Barbizon School effected a parallel transformation of landscape painting. The school derived its name from the village of Barbizon near the forest of Fontainebleau, where Camille Corot and Jean-François Millet, among others, gathered to paint in the open air. Corot is best known for his landscapes, while Millet took many of his subjects from peasant life and had a strong influence on Van Gogh. Reproductions of his *The Angelus* still hang over many mantelpieces in rural France as well as in Catholic grammar schools around the world.

Millet anticipated the realist program of Gustave Courbet, a prominent member of the Paris Commune, whose paintings show the drudgery of manual labour and the difficult lives of the working class.

Édouard Manet used realism to depict the life of the Parisian middle classes, yet he included in his pictures numerous references to the old masters. His *Le Déjeuner sur l'Herbe* and *Olympia* were considered scandalous, largely because they broke with the traditional treatment of their subject matter.

Impressionism, initially a term of derision, was taken from the title of an experimental painting by Claude Monet in 1874, *Impression: Soleil Levant* (Impression: Sunrise). Monet (see the boxed text 'Claude Monet' in the Normandy chapter) was the leading figure of the school, which counted among its members Alfred Sisley, Camille Pissarro, Berthe Morisot and Pierre-Auguste Renoir. The impressionists' main aim was to capture fleeting light effects, and light came to dominate the content of their painting. For instance, Monet painted the same subjects – cathedrals, haystacks, trees, water lilies – many times to show the transient effect of light at different times of day.

Edgar Degas was a fellow traveller of the impressionists, but he preferred his studio to open-air painting. He found his favourite subjects at the racecourse and the ballet. His superb draughtsmanship seized on gestures and movements ignored by earlier artists, and he invented new kinds of composition such as depicting subjects from an oblique angle. Henri de Toulouse-Lautrec was a great admirer of Degas and chose similar subjects: people in the bars, brothels and music halls of Montmartre in Paris. He is best known for his posters and lithographs in which the distortion of the figures is both caricature and decorative.

Paul Cézanne is celebrated for his still lifes and landscapes depicting the south of France, while the name of Paul Gauguin immediately conjures up the South Pacific and his studies of Tahitian women. Both he and Cézanne are usually referred to as postimpressionists, something of a catch-all word for the diverse styles that flowed from impressionism.

In the late 19th century, Gauguin worked for a time in Arles with the Dutch artist Vincent van Gogh, who spent most of his painting life in France. A brilliant and innovative artist, Van Gogh produced haunting self-portraits and landscapes in which colour assumes an expressive and emotive quality. His later technique foreshadowed pointillism, developed by Georges Seurat, who applied paint in small dots or uniform brush strokes of unmixed colour, producing fine mosaics of warm and cool tones.

Henri Rousseau was a contemporary of the postimpressionists, but his 'naive' art was totally unaffected by them. A customs official, he painted on Sundays, and his dreamlike pictures of the Paris suburbs, jungle and desert scenes have had a lasting influence on 20th century art.

Gustave Moreau was a member of the symbolist school. His eerie treatment of mythological subjects can be seen in his old studio south-west of Place Pigalle – now the Musée Gustave Moreau – in Paris.

20th Century French painting in the 20th century has been characterised by a bewildering diversity of styles, two of which are particularly significant: Fauvism and cubism. Fauvism took its name from the slur of a critic who compared the exhibitors at the 1906 autumn salon with *fauves* (wildcats) because of their radical use of intensely bright colours. Among these 'wild' painters were Henri Matisse, André Derain and Maurice de Vlaminck.

Cubism was effectively launched in 1907 by the Spanish prodigy Pablo Picasso with his *Les Demoiselles d'Avignon*. Cubism, as developed by Picasso, Georges Braque and Juan Gris, deconstructed the subject into a system of intersecting planes and presented various aspects of it simultaneously. Collages incorporating bits of cloth, wood, string, newspaper and other things that happened to be lying around were a cubist speciality.

After WWI, the School of Paris was formed by a group of expressionists, mostly foreign-born, such as Amedeo Modigliani from Italy and Russian-born Marc Chagall. The latter's pictures combine fantasy and folklore.

Dada, a literary and artistic movement of revolt, started in Germany and Switzerland during WWI. In France, one of the principal dadaists was Marcel Duchamp, whose Mona Lisa adorned with a moustache and goatee epitomises the spirit of the movement.

The German dadaist Max Ernst moved to Paris in 1922 and was instrumental in starting surrealism, an offshoot of dada that flourished between the wars. Drawing on the theories of Freud, surrealism attempted to reunite the conscious and unconscious realms, to permeate everyday life with fantasies and dreams. The most famous surrealist painter, the Catalan Salvador Dalí, came relatively late to the movement.

WWII ended Paris' role as the world's artistic capital. Many artists left France, and though some returned after the war, the city never regained its old magnetism.

Sculpture

At the end of the 11th century, sculptors began to decorate the portals, capitals, altars and fonts of Romanesque churches, illustrating Bible stories and the lives of the saints for the illiterate. Two centuries later, when the cathedral became the centre of monumental building, sculpture spread from the central portal to the whole façade, whose brightly painted and carved surface offered a symbolic summary of Christian doctrine. In the 14th century, the Dutchman Claus Sluter, working at the court of Burgundy, introduced a vigorous realism with his sculptures for the Chartreuse de Champnol monastery in Dijon.

As well as adorning cathedrals, sculpture was increasingly commissioned for the tombs of the nobility. The royal tombs in the Basilica of St Denis, near Paris, illustrate the progress in naturalism from the 13th to the 15th centuries.

In Renaissance France, Pierre Bontemps decorated the beautiful tomb of François I at Saint Denis, and Jean Goujon created the Fontaine des Innocents near the Forum des Halles in Paris. The baroque style is exemplified by Guillaume Coustou's *Horses of Marly* at the entrance to the Ave des Champs-Élysées.

In the 19th century, memorial statues in public places came to replace sculpted tombs. One of the best artists in the new mode was François Rude, who sculpted the statue of Marshall Ney outside the Closerie des Lilas in Paris and the bas relief on the Arc de Triomphe. Jean-Baptiste Carpeaux began as a romantic sculptor, but *The Dance* on the Opéra-Garnier in Paris and his fountain in the Luxembourg Gardens look back to the warmth and gaiety of the baroque.

At the end of the 19th century, Auguste Rodin overcame the conflict of neoclassicism and romanticism. His sumptuous bronze and marble figures of men and women, often intimately entwined, and often incomplete, did much to revitalise sculpture as an expressive medium. Rodin is regarded by some critics as the finest portraitist in the history of the art. Some of his best known works include *The Kiss*, *The Thinker* and *The Burghers of Calais*. One of Rodin's most gifted pupils was Camille Claudel, whose work can also be seen in the Musée Rodin in Paris.

One of the most important French sculptors of the early 20th century was Aristide Maillol, whose voluptuous female nudes show his attachment to formal analysis, in direct contrast to Rodin's emotive style. Braque and Picasso experimented with sculpture, and in the spirit of Dada, Marcel Duchamp exhibited 'found objects', such as a urinal, which he titled *Fountain* and signed. The Swiss-born sculptor Alberto Giacometti participated in the surrealist movement in Paris during the 1930s. After WWII he produced a disturbing series of emaciated human figures in bronze.

One of the most influential sculptors to emerge after WWII was César Baldaccini (known as César to the world), who was born in Marseille in 1921. He began using iron and scrap metal (most notably crushed car bodies) to create his imaginary insects and animals but later graduated to pliable plastics. Arguably his best known work is the little statue handed to actors at the Césars, the French cinema awards equivalent to Hollywood's Oscars.

Music

When French music comes to mind, most people hear accordions and *chansonniers* (cabaret singers) like Edith Piaf and Jacques Brel. But they're only part of a much larger and more complex picture.

In the 17th and 18th century, French baroque music influenced a great deal of the European musical output. Composers such as François Couperin (1668-1733), especially noted for his harpsichord studies, and Jean Phillipe Rameau (1683-1764), who played a pivotal role in the development of modern harmony, were two major players in this field. French harpsichord music set the precedent for much of the keyboard music that was later to evolve.

France produced a number of musical luminaries in the 19th century. Among these were Hector Berlioz (1803-69), Charles Gounod (1818-93), César Franck (1822-90), Camille Saint-Saëns (1835-1921) and Georges Bizet (1838-75). Nowadays Bizet is chiefly known for his operas *Carmen* and *The Pearl Fishers*, and Gounod for his operas *Faust* and *Romeo and Juliet*.

Berlioz is the greatest figure in the French romantic movement. He was the founder of modern orchestration, and as an orchestrator demanded gargantuan forces; his ideal orchestra included 240 stringed instruments, 30 grand pianos and 30 harps.

Berlioz's operas and symphonies and Franck's organ compositions sparked a musical renaissance in France that would produce such greats as Gabriel Fauré and the impressionists Claude Debussy and Maurice Ravel. Debussy revolutionised classical music with his *Prélude à l'Après-Midi d'un Faune*, creating a light almost Asian musical impressionism, while Ravel's work, including *Boléro*, is often characterised by its sensuousness and tonal colour. Two contemporary composers include Olivier Messiaen, who combined modern, almost mystical music with natural sounds such as birdsong, and his student, the radical Pierre Boulez, who includes computer-generated sound in his compositions.

Jazz hit Paris in the 1920s with a bang and has remained popular, particularly among intellectuals, ever since. France's contribution to the world of jazz has been great: the violinist Stéfane Grappelli and the legendary three-fingered Gypsy guitarist Django Reinhardt from the 1930s, Claude Luter and his Dixieland Band in the 1950s and, more recently, the pianists Martial Solal and Michel Petrucciani.

The most appreciated form of indigenous music is the *chanson française*, with a tradition going back to the troubadours of the Middle Ages. It was an important medium for conveying ideas and information to the illiterate masses, and such enduring greats as *La Marseillaise* and the socialist anthem *L'Internationale*, are rooted in this tradition.

French songs have always favoured lyrics over music and rhythm, which goes some way to explaining the enormous popularity of rap in France.

Eclipsed by the music halls and burlesque of the early 20th century, the chanson tradition was revived from the 1930s by such singers as Piaf (see the boxed text) and Charles Trenet. In the 1950s the cabarets of the Left Bank gave young author-composers the opportunity to break new ground and singers such as Georges Brassens, Léo Ferré, Claude Nougaro, Jacques Brel and Barbara became national stars.

Today's popular music has come a long way since the *yéyé* (imitative rock) of the 1960s sung by Johnny Halliday – watch out

Edith Piaf, the Urchin Sparrow

Like her contemporary Judy Garland in the USA, Edith Piaf (1915-63) was not just a singer but a tragic, stoical figure who the nation took to its heart and never let go.

She was born Edith Giovanna Gassion to a street acrobat and his singer wife, who lived in the poor Belleville district of Paris. Her early childhood was spent with her maternal grandmother, an alcoholic who neglected her, and later her father's parents, who ran a local brothel in Normandy. When she was nine she toured with her father but left home at 15 to sing alone in the streets of Paris. Her first employer, Louis Leplée, called her *la môme piaf* (the urchin sparrow) and introduced her to the cabarets of Pigalle.

When Leplée was murdered in 1935, she faced the streets again. But along came Raymond Asso, an ex-Legionnaire who would become her Pygmalion, forcing her to break with her pimp and hustler friends, putting her in her signature black dress and inspiring her first big hit (*Mon Légionnaire*, 1937). When he succeeded in getting her a contract at one of the most famous Parisian music halls of the time, her career skyrocketed.

This frail women, who sang about street life, drugs, death and whores, seemed to embody all the miseries of the world yet sang in a husky, powerful voice with no self-pity. Her tumultuous love life earned her a reputation as *une dévoreuse d'hommes* (a man-eater), but she launched the careers of several stars, including Yves Montand and Charles Aznavour. Another one of her many lovers was the world middleweight boxing champion Marcel Cerdan; he was killed in a plane crash on his way to join her on her American tour in 1949. True to form, Piaf insisted that the show go on after learning of his death but fainted on stage in the middle of *L'Hymne à l'Amour*, a love song inspired by Cerdan.

After she was involved in a car accident in 1951, Piaf began drinking heavily and became addicted to morphine. Her health declined quickly but she continued to sing around the world (notably at New York's Carnegie Hall in 1956) and record some of her biggest hits, including *Je Ne Regrette Rien* and *Milord*. In 1962, frail and once again penniless, Piaf married a young hairdresser called Théo Sarapo, recorded the duet *À Quoi Ça Sert l'Amour?* (What Use Is Love?) with him and left Paris for southern France, where she died the following year. A crowd of some two million people attended her funeral in Paris, and the grave of the much missed Urchin Sparrow in Père Lachaise Cemetery (20e) is still visited and decorated by thousands of her loyal fans each year.

for rappers MC Solaar, Doc Gynéco and I Am, from Marseille. Evergreen balladeers-folk singers include Francis Cabrel, Julien Clerc, Jean-Jacques Goldman and Jacques Higelin, while the late Serge Gainsbourg remains enormously popular. Some people like the New Age space music of Jean-Michel Jarre; others say his name fits his sound.

But France's main claim to fame over the past decade has been *sono mondial* (world music) – from Algerian *raï* and other North African music (Cheb Khaled, Natache Atlas, Jamel, Cheb Mami, Racid Taha) to Senegalese *mbalax* (Youssou N'Dour), West Indian *zouk* (Kassav, Zouk Machine) and Cuban salsa. Les Négresses Vertes and Mano Negra were two bands in the late 1980s that combined many of these elements – often with brilliant results. Watch for their successors Noir Désir.

Dance

Ballet as we know it today originated in Italy but was brought to France in the late 16th century by Catherine de Médecis. The first Ballet Comique de la Reine (dramatic ballet) in France was performed at an aristocratic wedding at the French court in 1581. It combined music, dance and poetic recitations (usually in praise of the monarchy) and was performed by male courtiers with women of the court forming the corps de ballet. Louis XIV so enjoyed the spectacle that he danced many leading roles himself at Versailles. In 1661 he founded the Académie Royale de Danse (Royal Dance Academy), from which ballet around the world developed.

By the end of the 18th century ballet had developed into a fully fledged art form, and choreographers like Jean-Georges Noverre became more important than the musicians, poets and dancers themselves. In the early 19th century, romantic ballets such as *Giselle* (1841) and *La Sylphide* (1832) were more popular than opera in Paris.

France was at the forefront of classical ballet until the end of the 19th century when the Russian Imperial Ballet was becoming the centre for innovation. This was exacerbated when Marius Petipa, a native of Marseille, left France for Russia. Mixing the French dance tradition with Slavic sensibilities, folklore and music he created such masterpieces as *La Bayadère* (1877) and *Le Lac des Cygnes* (Swan Lake, 1895).

France has lost its pre-eminent position in dance to countries like the USA, Germany and even Japan in this century, though Roland Petit managed to shake French ballet out of its lethargy between 1945 and 1955, creating some innovative ballets such as *Turangalila* with music composed by Olivier Messiaen. Another important figure was Maurice Béjart who shocked the public in 1955 with his *Ballet sur la Symphonie d'un Homme Seul* danced in black, *Le Sacre du Printemps* (1959), and *Le Marteau sans Maître* (1968) with music by Pierre Boulez.

After 1968 many dance centres were created outside Paris mainly at Nancy, La Rochelle and Montpellier, but all have been heavily influenced from the outside by such choreographers as the American Merce Cunningham.

Today French dance seems to be moving in a new, more personal direction with performers like Caroline Marcadé and Maguy Martin and choreographers such as Odile Duboc and Jean-Claude Gallotta.

Literature

Middle Ages The earliest work of French literature is the 11th century *Chanson de Roland* (Song of Roland), an epic poem that recounts the heroic death of Charlemagne's nephew Roland, ambushed on the way back from a campaign against the Muslims in Spain in 778.

Lyric poems of courtly love composed by troubadours dominated medieval French literature, and there was the new genre of the *roman* (literally, 'the romance'), which often drew on Celtic stories such as King Arthur and his court, the search for the Holy Grail, and Tristan and Iseult. The *Roman de la Rose*, a 22,000 line poem written by Guillaume de Lorris and Jean de Meung, was a new departure, manipulating allegorical figures such as Pleasure and Riches, Shame and Fear.

François Villon was condemned to death in 1462 for stabbing a lawyer, but the sentence was commuted to banishment from Paris. As well as a long police record, Villon left a body of poems charged with a highly personal lyricism, among them the *Ballade des Femmes du Temps Jadis* (Ballad of Dead Ladies).

Renaissance The great landmarks of French Renaissance literature are the works of La Pléaide, Rabelais and Montaigne. François Rabelais composed a farcical epic about the adventures of the giant Gargantua and his son Pantagruel. His highly exuberant narrative blends coarse humour with encyclopaedic erudition in a vast panorama that seems to include every kind of person, occupation and jargon found in mid-16th century France.

La Pléaide was a group of poets active in the 1550s and 60s, of whom the best known is Pierre de Ronsard. They are chiefly remembered for their lyric poems. Michel de Montaigne wrote a long series of essays on all sorts of topics that constitutes a fascinating self-portrait.

Classicism The 17th century is known as *le grand siècle* because it is the century of the great French classical writers. In poetry, François de Malherbe brought a new rigour to the treatment of rhythm. Transported by the perfection of Malherbe's verses, Jean de La Fontaine recognised his vocation and went on to write his charming *Fables* in the manner of Aesop.

Molière was an actor who became the most popular comic playwright of his time. Plays such as *Tartuffe* are staples of the classical repertoire, and they are still performed in translation around the world. The tragic playwrights Pierre Corneille and Jean Racine, by contrast, drew their subjects from history and classical mythology. For instance, Racine's *Phèdre*, taken from Euripides, is a story of incest and suicide among the descendants of the Greek gods.

The mood of classical tragedy permeates *La Princesse de Clèves* by Marie de La Fayette, which is widely regarded as the first major French novel.

Enlightenment The literature of the 18th century is dominated by philosophers, among them Voltaire and Jean-Jacques Rousseau. The most durable of Voltaire's works have been his 'philosophical tales', such as *Candide*, which ironically recounts the improbable adventures of a simple soul who is convinced that he is living in the best of all possible worlds despite the many problems that befall him.

Rousseau, a Catholic convert from Protestantism, came from Switzerland and always considered himself a religious exile in France. Voltaire's political writings, in which it is argued that society is fundamentally opposed to nature, were to have a profound and lasting influence on him. Rousseau's sensitivity to landscape and its moods anticipates romanticism, and the insistence on his own singularity in *Les Confessions* makes it the first modern autobiography.

19th Century The 19th century brought Victor Hugo, widely acclaimed for his poetry as well as for his novels *Les Misérables* and *Notre Dame de Paris* (The Hunchback of Notre Dame). By virtue of his enormous output, the breadth of his interests and his technical innovations, Hugo is the key figure of French romanticism. In 1885 some two million people followed his funeral procession.

Other 19th century novelists include Stendhal, author of *Le Rouge et le Noir*, the story of the rise and fall of a poor young man from the provinces who models himself on Napoleon; Honoré de Balzac, whose vast series of novels, known under the general title of *La Comédie Humaine*, approaches a social history of France; Aurore Dupain, better known by nom de plume George Sand, who combined the themes of romantic love and social injustice in her work; and of course Alexandre Dumas the elder, who wrote *Le Comte de Monte Cristo* (The Count of Monte Cristo), *Les Trois Mousquetaires* (The Three Musketeers) and other adventures, as well as several plays and poems.

By the mid-19th century, romanticism was evolving into new movements, both in fiction and poetry. In 1857 two landmarks of French literature appeared: *Madame Bovary* by Gustave Flaubert and *Les Fleurs du Mal* by Charles Baudelaire. Both writers were tried for the supposed immorality of their works. Flaubert won his case, and his novel was distributed without cuts. Less fortunate was Baudelaire (who moonlighted as a translator in Paris – he introduced the works of the American writer Edgar Allan Poe to Europe in translations that have since become French classics), who was obliged to cut several poems from *Les Fleurs du Mal*. He died an early and painful death, practically unknown, but his work influenced all the significant French poetry of the late 19th century and is reflected in much 20th century verse as well.

The aim of Émile Zola, who claimed Flaubert as a precursor of his school of naturalism, was to convert novel writing from an art to a science by the application of experimentation. His theory may seem naive, but his work (especially with regards the *Les Rougon-Macquart* series) was powerful and innovative.

Paul Verlaine and Stéphane Mallarmé created the symbolist movement, which strove to express states of mind rather than simply detail daily reality. Arthur Rimbaud, apart from crowding an extraordinary amount of rugged, exotic travel into his 37 years and having a tempestuous homosexual relationship with Verlaine, produced two enduring pieces of work: *Illuminations* and *Une Saison en Enfer* (A Season in Hell).

20th Century Marcel Proust dominated the early 20th century with his giant seven-volume novel, *A la Recherche du Temps Perdu* (Remembrance of Things Past); it is largely autobiographical and explores in evocative detail the true meaning of past experience recovered from the unconscious by 'involuntary memory'. André Gide found his voice in the celebration of homosexual sensuality and later left-wing politics. *Les Faux-Monnayeurs* (The Counterfeiters) exposes the hypocrisy and self-deception with which people try to avoid sincerity – a common theme with Gide.

Surrealism was a vital force in French literature until WWII. André Breton ruled the group and wrote its three manifestoes, although the first use of the word 'surrealist' is attributed to the writer Guillaume Apollinaire, a fellow traveller. Breton's autobiographical narratives, such as *Nadja*, capture the spirit of the movement: the fascination with dreams, divination and all manifestations of 'the marvellous'. As a poet, Breton was overshadowed by Paul Éluard and Louis Aragon, whose most famous surrealist work was *Le Paysan de Paris*.

Colette enjoyed tweaking the nose of conventionally moral readers with titillating novels that detailed the amorous exploits of such heroines as the schoolgirl Claudine. One of her more interesting works concerned the German occupation of Paris, *Paris de Ma Fenêtre* (Paris from My Window).

After WWII, existentialism, a significant literary movement, developed around Jean-Paul Sartre, Simone de Beauvoir and Albert Camus, who worked and conversed in the cafés of Saint Germain des Prés in Paris. All three stressed the importance of the writer's political engagement. Camus' best work on this theme is *L'Étranger* (The Outsider); he won a Nobel prize for Literature in 1957. De Beauvoir, author of the ground-breaking study *The Second Sex*, had a profound influence on feminist thinking.

In the late 1950s, some younger novelists began to look for new ways of organising the narrative. *Les Fruits d'Or* by Nathalie Sarraute, for example, does away with identifiable characters and has no plot as such. The so-called new novel (*nouveau roman*) refers to the works of Sarraute, Alain Robbe-Grillet, Boris Vian, Julien Gracq and Michel Butor, among others. However, these writers never formed a close-knit group, and their experiments have taken them in divergent directions. Today the nouveau roman is very much out of favour in France. Mention must also be made of *Histoire d'O*, the highly erotic sado-masochistic novel written by Dominique Aury (1907-98) under a pseudonym in 1954. The book sold more copies than any other contemporary French novel outside France.

In 1980 Marguerite Yourcenar, best known for memorable historical novels such as *Mémoires d'Hadrien*, became the first woman to be elected to the French Academy.

Marguerite Duras came to the notice of a larger public when she won the prestigious Prix Goncourt for her novel *L'Amant* (The Lover) in 1984. A prolific writer and film maker, she is also noted for the screenplays of *India Song* and *Hiroshima, Mon Amour*, described by one critic as part nouveau roman, part Mills & Boon.

Philippe Sollers was one of the editors of *Tel Quel*, a highbrow, then left-wing review that was very influential in the 1960s and early 70s. His 60s novels were forbiddingly experimental, but with *Femmes* (Women) he returned to a conventional narrative style.

Another of the editors of *Tel Quel* was Julia Kristeva, best known for theoretical writings on literature and psychoanalysis. Her book *Les Samuraï*, a fictionalised account of the heady days of *Tel Quel*, is an interesting document on the life of the Paris intelligentsia. Roland Barthes and Michel Foucault are other authors and philosophers associated with this period.

More accessible authors who enjoy a wide following include Françoise Sagan, Patrick Modiano, Yann Queffélec, Pascal Quignard and Denis Tillinac. The *roman pólicier* (detective novel) has always been a great favourite with the French and among its greatest exponents has been the Belgian-born Georges Simenon and his novels featuring Inspector Maigret as well as Frédéric Dard (alias San Antonio), Léo Malet and Daniel Pennac, widely read for his witty crime fiction (eg *Au Bonheur des Ogres*, *La Fée Carabine*).

Cinema

Early Days to WWII France's place in the film history books was ensured by those cinematographic pioneers, the Lumière brothers, who invented 'moving pictures' and organised the world's first paying (1FF) public movie screening – a series of two minute reels – in Paris' Grand Café on the Blvd des Capucines on 28 December 1895. They went on to specialise in newsreels and documentaries, leaving Charles Pathé – often called the Napoleon of cinema – to monopolise and rapidly expand France's cinema scene prior to WWI.

The 1920s and 30s were innovative times for film in France, as such avant-garde directors as René Clair, Marcel Carné and the intensely productive Jean Renoir, son of the famous artist, searched for new forms and subjects. Clair created a world of fantasy in his films in which he gave free rein to his penchant for invention. Though Carné's films were visually stunning, he presented a pessimistic world in which violence and poverty dominate. Poetic realism, strong narrative, and a strong sense of social satire mark the work of Jean Renoir.

New Wave After the war, however, ideas and techniques gradually lost innovation, and the big names tended to go somewhat stale. The industry stagnated until the late 1950s, when a large group of new directors burst onto the scene with a new genre, the so-called *nouvelle vague* (new wave).

This group included Jean-Luc Godard, François Truffaut, Claude Chabrol, Eric Rohmer, Jacques Rivette, Louis Malle and Alain Resnais. The one belief that united this disparate group was that a film should be the conception of the film maker rather than the product of a studio or producer, hence giving rise to the term *film d'auteur*.

With small budgets, sometimes self-financed, no extravagant sets or big-name stars, they made films like *Et Dieu Créa la Femme* (And God Created Woman, 1956), which brought sudden stardom to Brigitte Bardot, the little fishing village of Saint

Tropez and the young director Roger Vadim. The film, which examined the amorality of modern youth, received international acclaim.

A ream of films followed, among them Alain Resnais' *Hiroshima, Mon Amour* (1959) and *L'Année Dernière à Marienbad* (Last Year in Marienbad, 1961), which explored the problems of time and memory. François Truffaut's *Les Quatre Cents Coups* (The 400 Blows, 1959) was partly based on his own rebellious adolescence. Jean-Luc Godard made such films as *À Bout de Souffle* (Breathless, 1960), *Alphaville* (1965) and *Pierrot le Fou* (1965), which showed even less concern for sequence and narrative, with frequent jump-cutting and interruptions by pop-art images and actors' comments on the film itself. The new wave continued until the 1970s, by which time it had lost its experimental edge.

Other famous French directors making films at this time included Agnès Varda and Claude Chabrol. Of the non-new wave directors of the 1950s and 60s, one of the most notable was Jacques Tati, who made many comic films based around the charming, bumbling figure of Monsieur Hulot and his struggles to adapt to the modern age.

Contemporary Cinema The most successful directors of the 1980s and 90s have produced original and visually striking films featuring unusual locations, bizarre stories and unique characters. Well regarded directors include Jean-Jacques Beineix, who made *Diva* in 1981 followed five years later by *Betty Blue* (the film's French title was the rather bizarre *37°2 le Matin*), and Luc Besson with *Subway* (1985) and *The Big Blue* (1988). Some of Beineix's work, including *La Lune dans le Caniveau* (The Moon in the Gutter, 1983) with Nastassja Kinski and Gérard Depardieu, has been dismissed as self-indulgent twaddle. Besson's later films have become more commercial, including the action-packed *Nikita* (1990) and *Léon*.

In 1986 Claude Berri came up with *Jean de Florette* followed by *Manon des Sources*, modern versions of writer/film maker Marcel Pagnol's original works, which proved enormously popular both in France and abroad. Léos Carax, in his *Boy Meets Girl* (1983) created a kind of Parisian purgatory of souls lost in the eternal night.

Modern French cinema has a reputation for being intellectual, elitist and, frankly, boring. But French films aren't always so pat and serious. Light social comedies like *Trois Hommes et un Couffin* (Three Men and a Cradle; 1985) and *Romuald et Juliette* (1989) by Coline Serreau and *La Vie Est un Long Fleuve Tranquille* (Life is a Long Quiet River, 1988) by Étienne Chatiliez have been among the biggest hits in France in recent years.

Other well regarded directors today include Bertrand Blier (*Trop Belle pour Toi*), Eric Klapisch (*Un Air de Famille*), Claude Sautet and André Téchiné. Matthieu Kassovitz's award-winning *La Haine* examines the prejudice and violence of the world of the 'Beurs' – young, French-born Algerians. Alain Renais' *On Connaît la Chanson*, based on the life of the late British television playwright Dennis Potter, received international acclaim and six Césars in 1997.

Events & Stars The French film industry's main annual event is the Cannes Film Festival, which, since 1946, has awarded the coveted Palme d'Or and other prizes to French and foreign films. French movie stars, directors, technicians etc are annually honoured with the Césars, created in 1976.

One of the nation's earliest screen heroes was the great comic Fernandel, who was nicknamed 'Horseface' because of his inimitable grin and who starred in the *Don Camillo* series of the 1950s. Maurice Chevalier left for Hollywood in the 1930s, becoming the man who epitomised the dapper Frenchman in musicals such as *The Merry Widow*, *Gigi* and *Can-Can*. Two of France's best loved actors of the 1930s and 40s were Jean Gabin and Arletty. Gabin frequently portrayed strong-willed nonconformists; his most notable role was in Jean Renoir's *La Grande Illusion* (1937). Cast as the downtrodden prostitute in many films, Arletty is best remembered for her role in Carné's *Les Enfants du Paradis* (1945). Stars of the 1950s and 60s included Jean-Paul Belmondo, a kind of impertinent James Bond; the tall, dark and handsome Alain Delon; and the sexy Bardot.

More contemporary is Philippe Noiret, a veteran of over 100 French films whose hang-dog face found international acclaim in 1989 as the Sicilian movie-loving projectionist in *Cinema Paradiso*.

However, it is Gérard Depardieu more than any other French actor who has reached worldwide audiences in the past two decades. Among his most powerful roles were those in François Truffaut's *Le Dernier Métro* (1980), *Jean de Florette* (1986; directed by Claude Berri), *Danton* (1982) by the Polish director Andrzej Wajda, and *Cyrano de Bergerac* (1990), by Jean-Paul Rappeneau). Starring next to Depardieu in *Le Dernier Métro* was the incomparable Catherine Deneuve, generally considered one of France's leading actors. Emmanuelle Béart, Isabelle Huppert, Sandrine Bonnaire, Carole Bouquet, Isabelle Adjani and Oscar-winning Juliette Binoche are among the contemporary female stars of the French cinema.

The 1980s seemed to favour very masculine, almost macho, older actors who had interesting and mysterious pasts like Jean Reno (*Subway*, *The Big Blue*) and Richard Bohringer (*Diva*). In recent years, however, less macho actors like Daniel Auteuil (*Manon des Sources*), Hippolyte Girardot (*Un Monde sans Pitié*) and Fabrice Lucchini (*La Discrète, Beaumarchais*) have gained considerable followings.

Humour

Though it may come as a surprise to some, French people do like to laugh. Such comedians as Bourvil, Fernandel, Bernard Blier, Louis de Funès, Francis Blanche, Jean Poiret and Michel Serrault have enjoyed enormous popularity over the years and their films (eg *La Grande Vadrouille*, *La Vache et le Prisonnier*, *Les Tontons Flingueurs*, *La Cage aux Folles*) have been among the most successful movies made over the past 40 years. Inexplicably, the moronic American comedian Jerry Lewis is immensely popular in France, as is the neurotic film director Woody Allen.

Stand-up comics now considered classics include Fernand Raynaud, whose sketches were based on real characters and situations, and Pierre Dac, who broadcast to the Free French Forces on Radio Londres during WWII.

Among contemporary stars are the pied noirs comics Elie Kakou and Guy Bedos (the latter is left-wing, which, among this generally conservative group, is comical in itself) and the French-Arab comedian Smaïn. Raymond Devos, who builds up extravagant situations, plays with words and pushes logic to a surrealistic extreme also has a large following as does the trio Les Nuls and Patrick Timsi. But one of the biggest phenomenon of the past 20 years was Coluche, who began his career with Gérard Depardieu, Miou-Miou and Josiane Balasko in a small café-théâtre near Beaubourg in Paris. He quickly became famous for his bizarre dress and crude humour, which sometimes bordered on the vulgar. As his humour became more and more political, he was censored and his 'alternative' nightly news on Canal Plus was eventually cancelled. Sadly, he died in a motorcycle accident at the height of his fame in 1986.

Adult comic books (*bandes dessinées*) enjoy a following unimaginable in English-speaking countries with the well known *Astérix* paving the way for more recent publications like *Rubrique à Brac* and the artists Marcel Gotlib and Cabu. The latter's signature character is Le Grand Duduche, a rebellious and lazy student fighting to integrate himself into post-1968 French society and his racist, almost fascist *beau-frére* (brother-in-law). The word *beauf* has passed into the language to describe just such a man. In *Les Bidochon*, Alain Binet caricatures the life of average middle-class citizens who live in council flats, commute to work and go on organised holidays abroad.

One of the few women to have broken into this predominantly male domain is Claire Brétécher, who gently mocks feminist intellectuals in her *Les Mères*, a popular gift for women expecting a baby.

SOCIETY & CONDUCT

Interacting with the French

Some visitors to France conclude that it would be a lovely country if it weren't for the French. As in other countries, however, the more tourists a particular town or area attracts, the less patience the locals tend to have for them.

Making Friends & Avoiding Offence

By following a number of simple guidelines, you can usually win people over and avoid offending anyone.

Here are a few dos:

- The easiest way to improve the quality of your relations with the French is always to say *'Bonjour, monsieur/madame/mademoiselle'* when you walk into a shop, and *'Merci, monsieur ... au revoir'* when you leave. 'Monsieur' means 'sir' and can be used with any male person who isn't a child. 'Madame' is used where 'Mrs' would apply in English, whereas 'mademoiselle' is used when talking to unmarried women. When in doubt, use 'madame'.
- It is customary for people who know each other to exchange kisses (*bises*) as a greeting, though rarely between two men except in the south or if they are related. The usual ritual is one glancing peck on each cheek, but depending on the region (and the personalities involved), some people go for three or even four kisses. People who don't kiss each other will almost always shake hands.
- If invited to someone's home or a party, always bring some sort of gift, such as good wine (not some 10FF *vin de table*). Flowers are another good stand-by, but chrysanthemums are only brought to cemeteries.
- Many French people seem to feel that 'going Dutch' (ie splitting the bill) at restaurants is an uncivilised custom. In general, the person who did the inviting pays for dinner, though close friends and colleagues will sometimes share the cost.

A few don'ts:

- When buying fruit, vegetables or flowers anywhere except at supermarkets, do not touch the produce or blossoms unless invited to do so. Show the shopkeeper what you want and he or she will choose for you.
- In a restaurant, do not summon the waiter by shouting *'garçon'*, which means 'boy'. Saying *'s'il vous plaît'* (please) is the way it's done nowadays.
- When you're being served cheese (eg as the final course for dinner), remember two cardinal rules: never cut off the tip of the pie-shaped soft cheeses (eg Brie, Camembert) and cut cheeses whose middle is the best part (eg blue cheese) in such a way as to take your fair share of the crust.
- Money, particularly income, is a subject that is simply not discussed in France.
- In general, lawns in France are meant to be looked at and praised for their greenness, not sat upon; watch out for *pelouse interdite* (Keep off the Grass!) signs. But this has been changing in recent years, with signs being removed and replaced with *pelouse autorisée*, meaning tourists and locals alike are permitted to sit, eat, play and walk on the grass of certain parks (with some exceptions, such as the Jardin des Tuileries and Jardin du Luxembourg in Paris).

RELIGION

Catholics

Some 80% of French people identify themselves as Catholic but, although most have been baptised, very few ever attend church. *Conversion*, such as that experienced by the poet Paul Claudel (1868-1955) and the novelist Henry de Montherlant (1896-1972), thus actually means 're-conversion' in English. The Catholic Church in France is generally very progressive and ecumenically minded. Cardinal Jean-Marie Lustiger, archbishop of Paris since 1981, was born to Jewish immigrants from Poland in Paris in 1926. He converted to Catholicism at age 14. His mother died in the Nazi extermination camp Auschwitz in 1942.

Protestants

France's Protestants (Huguenots), who were severely persecuted during much of the 16th and 17th centuries, now number about one million. They are concentrated in Alsace, the Jura, the south-eastern part of the Massif Central and along the Atlantic coast.

John Calvin (1509-64), born in Noyon in the far north of France, was educated in Paris, Orléans and Bourges but spent much of his life in Geneva.

Muslims

France has between 4 and 5 million nominally Muslim residents, and they now make up the country's second-largest religious group. The vast majority are immigrants or their offspring who came from North Africa during the 1950s and 60s.

In recent years, France's Muslim community has been the object of racist agitation by right-wing parties and extremist groups. The so-called Muslim scarf affair of 1994, when pupils were expelled from school for wearing scarves (considered 'ostentatious religious signs') brought the matter to the forefront but was more or less resolved two years later when the Constitutional Council ruled that schools may not suspend pupils who wear scarves if no overt religious proselytising is involved. Many North Africans complain of discrimination by the police and employers.

Jews

There has been a Jewish community in France for most of the time since the Roman period. During the Middle Ages, the community suffered persecution and there were a number of mass expulsions. French Jews, the first in Europe to achieve emancipation, were granted full citizenship in 1790-91. Since 1808, the French Jewish community has had an umbrella organisation known as the Consistoire based in Paris.

The country's Jewish community, which now numbers some 650,000 (the largest in Europe), grew substantially during the 1960s as a result of immigration from Algeria, Tunisia and Morocco.

Facts for the Visitor

HIGHLIGHTS

France has a wealth of wonderful places to visit, but some aspects of the country are so outstanding that they deserve special mention. From north to south (roughly), they include:

- Scrutinising the Bayeux Tapestry for 'living scenes' from history – including Halley's Comet
- Visiting Giverny and its gardens in full blossom
- Walking the streets and admiring the architecture of Paris
- Spending the afternoon in Paris' Louvre, Musée d'Orsay, Musée Rodin or Musée Picasso
- Gazing up at the spires and stained glass of Strasbourg's cathedral
- Sampling wines along Alsace's Route du Vin
- Feeling the ocean spray in your face at Pointe du Raz (France's westernmost point) in Brittany
- Cruising to idyllic Île d'Ouessant off Brittany
- Enjoying the folk culture of Brittany's Finistère region
- Viewing Chartres cathedral's stained glass on a bright sunny day
- Visiting the Loire Valley chateaus of Chambord, Chenonceau, Cheverny and/or Azay-le-Rideau
- Dijon's city centre
- Wine tasting in the Côte d'Or region of Burgundy
- Viewing Mont Blanc from the western side of the Chamonix Valley
- Taking the waters in the *belle époque* spa town of Vichy
- Strolling along the avenues and through the squares of central Lyon
- Birdwatching at the Camargue delta
- Walking through the Palais des Papes in Avignon
- Climbing the Pont du Gard Roman aqueduct near Nîmes
- Enjoying an evening performance at Arles' Roman amphitheatre
- Visiting the ochre-red village of Roussillon in Provence
- Walking along Cannes' waterfront at dusk
- Smelling the sweet aromas in Grasse
- Hiking in the Pyrenees
- Watching Corsica's mountains rise up from the sea from the ferry

SUGGESTED ITINERARIES

Depending on the length of your stay, you might want to see and do the following in France:

One week
: Visit Paris – the most beautiful city in the world – and a nearby area, such as the Loire Valley, Champagne, Alsace or Normandy.

Two weeks
: As above, plus one area in the west or south, such as Brittany, the Alps or Provence.

One month
: As above but spending more time in each place and visiting more of the west or south (eg Brittany or the Côte d'Azur).

Two months
: As above, plus hiking in the Pyrenees or Alps; hanging out at one of the beach areas on the Mediterranean or Atlantic coast; spending some time in more remote areas (eg the Basque Country or Corsica).

PLANNING

When to Go

In terms of weather, France is at its best in spring, though winter-like relapses are not unknown and the beach resorts only begin to pick up sometime in May. Autumn is pleasant, too, but the days are fairly short and later on it gets a bit cool for sunbathing, even along the Côte d'Azur. Winter is great for skiing and other snow sports in the Alps, Pyrenees and other mountain areas, but Christmas, New Year's and the February-March school holiday periods create surges in domestic tourism that can make it very difficult or expensive to find accommodation. Paris has various cultural events on offer all winter long.

In July and August, the weather is warm and even hot, especially in the south, and France's beaches, resorts and camping grounds are packed.

Small villages may be almost entirely shut down on Sundays and public holidays. Public transport is likely to be limited or suspended, and food shops – except a morning-only *boulangerie* – may be shut.

Domestic Tourism By law, French wage-earners get five weeks of *congés payés* (paid holiday) each year. Most of them take advantage of their time off between 14 July and 31 August, when the coasts, mountains and other areas upon which France's city dwellers descend like a locust storm suffer from acute shortages of hotel rooms and camp sites.

Meanwhile, in the half-deserted cities of the interior – only partly refilled by foreign tourists – many shops, restaurants, cinemas, cultural institutions and even hotels simply shut down so the proprietors can head out of town along with their customers. A *congé annuel* (annual closure) sign in the window usually means 'come back in September'. Even worse, the people left behind to staff essential services tend to be more irritable and officious than usual.

The February-March school holidays are another period of mass domestic tourism, bringing huge numbers of people (and higher prices) to the Alps, the Pyrenees and Andorra.

School Holiday Periods France's *vacances scolaires* (school holidays), during which millions of families take domestic vacations, generally fall during the following times of year:

Christmas-New Year
: Schools all over the country are closed from 20 December to 4 January.

February-March
: The 'February' holidays last from about 11 February to 11 March; pupils in each of three zones are off for overlapping 15-day periods.

Easter
: The month-long spring break, which begins around Easter, also means pupils have overlapping 15-day holidays.

Summer
: The nationwide summer recess lasts from the tail end of June until very early September.

Weather Forecasts If you understand French (or know someone who does), you can find out the *météo* (weather forecast) by calling the following numbers:

National forecast	☎ 08 36 70 12 34
Regional forecasts	☎ 08 36 68 00 00
Mountain area & snow forecasts	☎ 08 36 68 04 04
Marine forecast	☎ 08 36 68 08 08

For departmental forecasts, dial ☎ 08 36 68 02 plus the two digit departmental number (eg ☎ 08 36 68 02 75 for Paris). Each call costs five télécarte units or 2.23FF per minute. By Minitel, key in 3615 MET or 3617 METPLUS.

What Kind of Trip?

Travelling Companions Travelling alone is not a problem in France; the country is very well developed and generally very safe.

If you decide to travel with others, keep in mind that travel can put relationships to the test like few other experiences can. Many long-term friendships have broken down under the strains of constant negotiations about where to stay and eat, what to see and where to go next. But many friendships have also become closer than ever before. You won't find out until you try it, but make sure you agree on itineraries and routines *beforehand* and try to remain flexible about everything – even in the heat of an August afternoon in Paris.

If travel is a good way of testing established friendships, it's also a great way of making new ones. Hostels and camping grounds are good places to meet fellow travellers, so even if you're travelling alone, you need never be lonely.

Move or Stay? 'If this is Tuesday, it must be Strasbourg.' Though often ridiculed, the mad dash that 'does' an entire country the size of France in a couple of weeks can have its merits. If you've never visited France before, you won't know which areas you'll like, and a quick 'scouting tour' will give an overview of the options. A rail pass that offers unlimited travel within a set period of time can be the best way to do this. For more information, see the Rail Passes sections in the Getting Around chapter.

But if you know where you want to go, have found a place you like or have specific interests like hiking or folk culture, the best advice is to stay put for a while, discover some of the lesser known sights, make a few local friends and settle in. It's also cheaper in the long run.

Maps

Road maps and city maps are available at Maisons de la Presse (large newsagencies found all over France), tourist offices, bookshops and even some newspaper kiosks. Where relevant, advice on maps and where to buy them is given under Orientation in a city or town listing.

Using Map Indexes

Place names that begin with a definite article (eg Le Mont Saint Michel, La Rochelle, L'Île Rousse) may be listed either under Le/La/L' or under the rest of the name in French indexes. Names that start with 'Saint' (abbreviated as St) appear before names that begin with 'Sainte' (Ste), a female saint. Streets named after people are listed either by the last name or, as Michelin seems to prefer, by the first name or title (Général, Maréchal, etc).

When more than one town bears the same name, each one is given a descriptive suffix. For instance, you'll find in various parts of the country Villefranche-sur-Cher (Villefranche on the Cher River), Villefranche-sur-Mer (Villefranche by the Sea) and Villefranche-du-Périgord (Villefranche in Périgord). Unless there's another Villefranche nearby, local people usually drop the suffix.

In Paris, the best place to find a full selection of Institut Géographique National (IGN) maps is at the Espace IGN (☎ 01 43 98 85 00; metro Franklin D Roosevelt) at 107 Rue La Boétie (8e), open Monday to Friday from 9.30 am to 7 pm and on Saturday from 12.30 to 6.30 pm.

Road Maps A variety of *cartes routières* (road maps) are available, but if you're going to be driving a lot, the best road atlas to have in the car is Michelin's *Atlas Routier France*, which covers the whole country in 1:200,000 scale (1cm = 2km). It comes with either spiral or regular binding and costs 119FF.

Driving in and out of Paris can be confusing with a map; without one, it's hopeless. The most useful road map of the greater Paris area is Michelin's 1:100,000 scale *Environs de Paris* (green map No 106).

If you'll be concentrating on just a few regions, it's easier and cheaper to buy Michelin's yellow-jacketed 1:200,000 scale fold-out maps, which come in two sizes: small (about 13FF for each of the 39 sheets), marked with two-digit identification numbers; and large (28FF), identified by three-digit numbers.

The latter cover the country in only 17 sheets but are rather clumsy. IGN covers France with 16 maps in 1:250,000 scale (29FF) and 74 1:100,000 scale maps (29FF), but both are more difficult to drive with than Michelin's maps.

To plot cross-country travel, you have two 1:1,000,000 scale maps to choose from: Michelin's red-series map No 911; and IGN's Map No 901, entitled *France – Routes, Autoroutes* (20FF). Both are updated annually.

Hiking & Cycling Maps Didier et Richard publishes a series of 1:50,000 scale trail maps (about 67FF), perfect for hoofing it or cycling.

IGN covers all of France with about 1100 1:50,000-scale topographical maps and 2200 1:25,000-scale maps. There are two varieties in the 1:25,000 scale: the old kind (46FF), which cover the entire country; and the more recent Top 25 series maps (58FF), which are available for the Mediterranean coast, the Alps, the Pyrenees, the Basque Country and a few other areas. Map No 1748OT (OT is short for *ouest*, ie west) covers an area slightly west of that covered by map No 1748ET (short for *est*, ie east).

IGN's 1:1,000,000 scale grey-jacketed Map No 903 (29FF), entitled *France – Grande Randonnée*, shows all of France's long-distance GR trails. It is useful for strategic planning of a cross-country trek.

IGN No 906 (29FF), known as *France – VTT & Randonnées Cyclos*, indicates dozens of suggested bicycle tours of rural France. Other IGN cycling maps include *90 Circuits Cyclos en Île de France* and various regional *cyclocartes*.

City Maps The *plans* (street maps) distributed free by tourist offices range from the superb to the virtually useless. Michelin's *Guide Rouge* (see Guidebooks later in this chapter) has over 500 city and town maps that show one-way streets and have numbered town entry points that are coordinated with Michelin's yellow-jacketed 1:200,000 scale road maps. Some of them also appear, in a slightly different form, in the company's *Guides Verts* (Green Guides). Michelin publishes excellent 1:10,000-scale maps of Paris and Lyon. Plans-Guides Blay offers orange-jacketed street maps of 125 French cities and towns.

Abbreviations commonly used on city maps include: *R* for *rue* (street); *Bd*, *Boul* or *Bould* for boulevard; *Av* for avenue; *Q* for *quai* (quay); *Cr* for *cours* (avenue); *Pl* for *place* (square); *Pte* for *porte* (gate); *Imp* for *impasse* (dead-end street); *St* for *saint* (masculine) and *Ste* for *sainte* (feminine).

WHAT TO BRING

The cardinal rule in packing is to bring as little as possible. It's better to start off with too little rather than too much, as virtually anything you could possibly need is available locally. Sea mail services have been discontinued in France, so the only way to send packages overseas is by air mail, which can be very expensive, even for low-priority printed matter.

If you'll be doing any walking with your gear, even just from hotels to trains, a backpack is the only way to go. One of the most flexible ways to carry your belongings is in an internal-frame travel pack whose straps can be zipped inside a flap, turning it into something resembling a nylon suitcase. The most useful kind has an exterior pouch that zips off to become a daypack.

If you plan to stay at hostels, pack or buy a towel and a plastic soap container when you arrive. Bedding is always provided or available for hire, though you might want to take along your own sheet bag. You'll sleep easier with a padlock on your storage locker, which are usually provided at hostels.

Other optional items you might need include a torch (flashlight), an adapter plug for electrical appliances (such as a cup or coil immersion heater to make your own tea or instant coffee), a universal bath/sink plug (a plastic film canister sometimes works), sunglasses and a hat, a few clothes pegs and premoistened towelettes or a large cotton handkerchief, which you can soak in fountains and use to cool off while touring cities and towns in the warmer months.

TOURIST OFFICES

Local Tourist Offices

Every city, town, village and hamlet seems to have either an *office de tourisme* (a tourist office run by some unit of local government) or a *syndicat d'initiative* (a tourist office run by an organisation of local merchants). Both are an excellent resource and can almost always provide a local map at the very least. Some will also change foreign currency, especially when banks are closed, though the rate is rarely very good. Many tourist offices will make local hotel reservations, usually for a small fee.

Details on local tourist offices appear under Information at the beginning of each city, town or area listing.

Tourist Offices Abroad

French government tourist offices (usually called Maisons de la France) can provide every imaginable sort of tourist information on Paris as well as the rest of the country, most of it in the form of brochures. They include:

Australia
(☎ 02-9231 5244; fax 9221 8682; frencht@ozemail.com.au)
25 Bligh St, 22nd floor, Sydney, NSW 2000. Open weekdays from 9 am to 5 pm.

Belgium
(☎ 0902 88 025; fax 02-502 0410; maisondelafrance@pophost.eunet.be)
21 Ave de la Toison d'Or, 1050 Brussels. Open weekdays from 10 am to 5 pm.

Canada
(☎ 514-288 4264; fax 845 4868; mfrance@mtl.net)
1981 McGill College Ave, Suite 490, Montreal, Que H3A 2W9. Open weekdays from 9 am to 4 pm.

Germany
Frankfurt:
(☎ 069-758 021; fax 069-745 556; maison_de_la_France@t-online.de)
Westendstrasse 47, D-60325 Frankfurt. Open weekdays from 9 am to 4.30 pm.
Berlin:
(☎ 030-218 2064; fax 214 1238)
Keithstrasse 2-4, D-10787 Berlin. Open weekdays from 10 am to 1 pm and 2 to 5.30 pm (4.30 pm on Friday).

Hong Kong
(☎ 2501 9548; fax 2536 2868)
c/o Air France, Alexandra House, 21st floor, Chater Road, Central. Open weekdays from 9 am to 1 pm and 2 to 6 pm.

Ireland
(☎ 01-703 4046; fax 874 7324)
35 Lower Abbey St, Dublin 1. Open weekdays from 9.30 am to 1.30 pm and 2 to 5 pm.

Italy
(☎ 02-584 861; fax 5848 6222; entf@enter.it)
Via Larga 7, 20122 Milan. Open weekdays from 9.30 am to 5.30 pm.

Netherlands
(☎ 0900 112 2332; fax 020-620 3339; fra_vvv@euronet.nl)
Prinsengracht 670, 1017 KX Amsterdam. Open weekdays from 10 am to 5 pm.

South Africa
(☎ 011-880 8062; fax 880 7722; mdfsa@frenchdoor.co.za)
Oxford Manor, 1st floor, 196 Oxford Road, Illovo 2196. Open weekdays from 9 am to 1 pm and 2 to 4.30 pm.

Spain
(☎ 91-541 8808; fax 541 2412; maisondelafrance@mad.sericom.es)
Alcalá 63, 28014 Madrid. Open weekdays from 9 am to 1.30 pm and 4 to 7 pm (8 am to 3 pm in summer).

Switzerland
Zürich:
(☎ 01-211 3085; fax 212 1644)
Löwenstrasse 59, 8023 Zürich. Open weekdays from 10 am to 1 pm and 2 to 5.30 pm.
Geneva:
(☎ 022-732 8610; fax 731 5873)
2 Rue Thalberg, 1201 Geneva. Open weekdays from 9 am to noon and 1 to 5.45 pm (5 pm on Friday).

UK
(☎ 0891-244 123; fax 0171-493 6594 or, after June 1999, 020-7493 6594; piccadilly@mdlf.demon.co.uk)
178 Piccadilly, London W1V 0AL. Open daily from 10 am to 6 pm (5pm on Saturday, closed Sunday).

USA
New York:
(☎ 212-838 7800; fax 838 7855; info@francetourism.com)
444 Madison Ave, 16th floor, New York, NY 10022-6903. Open weekdays 9 am to 5 pm.
Los Angeles:
(☎ 310-271 6665; fax 276 2835; fgtola@juno.com)
9454 Wiltshire Blvd, Suite 715, Beverly Hills, CA 90212-2967

VISAS & DOCUMENTS

Passport

By law, everyone in France, including tourists, must carry some sort of ID on them at all times. For foreign visitors, this means a passport (if you don't want to carry your passport for security reasons a photocopy should do, although you may be required to report to a police station later to verify your identity) or, for citizens of the EU, a national ID card.

Visas

Tourist There are no entry requirements or restrictions on nationals of the EU, and citizens of Australia, the USA, Canada, New

Zealand and Israel do not need visas to visit France as tourists for up to three months. Except for people from a handful of other European countries, everyone else must have a visa.

Among those who need visas are South Africans. Visa fees depend on the current exchange rate but a transit visa should cost about UK£7, a visa valid for stays of up to 30 days is around UK£18, and a single/ multiple entry visa of up to three months about UK£21.50/25.50. You will need your passport (valid for a period of three months beyond the date of your departure from France), a return ticket, proof of sufficient funds to support yourself, proof of pre-arranged accommodation (possibly), two passport-size photos and the visa fee in cash.

If all the forms are in order, your visa will be issued on the spot. You can also apply for a French visa after arriving in Europe – the fee is the same, but you may not have to produce a return ticket. If you enter France overland, your visa may not be checked at the border, but major problems can arise if you don't have one later on (eg at the airport as you leave the country).

Long-Stay & Student If you'd like to work or study in France or stay for over three months, apply to the French embassy or consulate nearest where you live for the appropriate sort of *long séjour* (long-stay) visa. Unless you live in the EU, it is extremely difficult to get a visa that will allow you to work in France. For any sort of long-stay visa, begin the paperwork in your home country several months before you plan to leave. Applications cannot usually be made in a third country nor can tourist visas be turned into student visas after you arrive in France. People with student visas can apply for permission to work part-time (inquire at your place of study).

Au Pair For details on au pair visas, which must be arranged *before* you leave home (unless you're an EU resident), see Au Pair under Work later in this chapter.

Carte de Séjour If you are issued a long-stay visa valid for six or more months, you'll probably have to apply for a *carte de séjour* (residence permit) within eight days of arrival in France. For details, inquire at your place of study or the local *préfecture* (prefecture), *sous-préfecture* (subprefecture), *hôtel de ville* (city hall), *mairie* (town hall) or *commissariat* (police station).

In Paris, EU passport-holders seeking a carte de séjour should apply to the visa office in the Salle Europe, which is on the ground floor next to *escalier* (stairway) C in the Préfecture de Police, 1 Place Louis Lépine, 4e (metro Cité). It's open weekdays from 8.45 am to 4.30 pm (4 pm on Friday). Foreigners with other passports who are staying in arrondissements 8e, 9e, 11e and 17e to 20e must go to the Hôtel de Police at 19-21 Rue Truffaut, 17e (metro Place Clichy or La Fourche), weekdays between 9 am and 4.30 pm. For those foreigners in other arrondissements, the correct address is the Hôtel de Police at 114-116 Avenue du Maine, 14e (metro Gaîté). Details are available from the Préfecture de Police on ☎ 01 53 71 51 68.

Students of all nationalities must apply for a carte de séjour to the office at 13 Rue Miollis, 15e (metro Cambronne or Ségur), open weekdays from 8.45 am to 4.30 pm (4 pm on Friday).

Visa Extensions Tourist visas *cannot* be extended except in emergencies (eg medical problems). If you're in Paris and have an urgent problem, you should call the Préfecture de Police (☎ 01 53 71 51 68) for guidance.

If you don't need a visa to visit France, you'll almost certainly qualify for another automatic three-month stay if you take the train to Geneva or Brussels, say, and then re-enter France. The fewer recent French entry stamps you have in your passport the easier this is likely to be. If you needed a visa the first time around, one way to extend your stay is to go to a French consulate in a neighbouring country and apply for another one there.

People entering France by rail or road often don't have their passports checked, much less stamped, and even at airports don't be surprised if the official just glances at your passport and hands it back without stamping the date of entry. Fear not: you're in France legally, whether or not you had to apply for a visa before arriving (though at some point, to show your date of entry, you may be asked to produce the plane, train or ferry ticket you arrived with). If you prefer to have your passport stamped (eg you expect to have to prove when you last entered the country), it may take a bit of running around to find the right border official.

Travel Insurance

You should seriously consider taking out travel insurance. This not only covers you for medical expenses and luggage theft or loss but also for cancellation or delays in your travel arrangements. (You could fall seriously ill two days before departure, for example.) Cover depends on your insurance and type of airline ticket, so ask both your insurer and your ticket-issuing agency to explain where you stand. Ticket loss is also covered by travel insurance.

Paying for your airline ticket with a credit card often provides limited travel accident insurance, and you may be able to reclaim the payment if the operator doesn't deliver. In the UK, for instance, institutions issuing credit cards are required by law to reimburse consumers if a company goes into liquidation and the amount in contention is more than UK£100. Ask your credit card company what it's prepared to cover.

Diving Licence & Permits

Many non-European drivers' licences are valid in France, but it's still a good idea to bring along an International Driving Permit, which can make life much simpler, especially when hiring cars and motorbikes. Basically a multilingual translation of the vehicle class and personal details noted on your local driver's licence; an IDP is not valid unless accompanied by your original licence. An IDP can be obtained for a small fee from your local automobile association – bring along a passport photo and a valid licence.

Hostel Card

A Hostelling International (HI) card is necessary only at official *auberges de jeunesse* (youth hostels), but it may get you small discounts at other hostels. If you don't pick one up before leaving home, you can buy one at almost any official French hostel for 70/100FF if you're under/over 26 years of age. One night membership (where available) costs between 10 and 19FF, and a family card is 100FF.

Student, Youth & Teachers' Cards

An International Student Identity Card (ISIC) can pay for itself through half-price admissions, discounted air and ferry tickets, and cheap meals in student cafeterias. Many places stipulate a maximum age, usually 24 or 25. In Paris, ISIC cards are issued by Accueil des Jeunes en France (AJF) and other student travel agencies for 60FF (see Student Travel Agencies under Information in the Paris chapter).

If you're under 26 but not a student, you can apply for a GO25 card issued by the Federation of International Youth Travel Organisations (FIYTO; 60FF), which entitles you to much the same discounts as an ISIC and is also issued by student unions or student travel agencies.

A Carte Jeunes (120FF for one year) is available to anyone under 26 who has been in France for at least six months. It gets you discounts on things like air tickets, car rental, sports events, concerts and movies. In France, details are available from ☎ 08 03 00 12 26; by Minitel key in 3615 CARTE JEUNES. In Paris, qualifying young people can pick one up at AJF and other student travel agencies.

Teachers, professional artists, museum conservators and certain categories of students are admitted to some museums free. Bring along proof of affiliation, eg an International Teacher Identity Card (ITIC; 60FF).

Seniors' Card

Reduced entry prices are charged for people over 60 at most cultural centres, including museums, galleries and public theatres. SNCF issues the Carte Senior (which replaces the Carte Vermeil) to those over 60, which gives reductions of 20 to 50% on train tickets. It costs 140FF for a card valid for purchasing four train tickets or 285FF for a card valid for one year.

Camping Card International

The Camping Card International (CCI; formerly the Camping Carnet) is a camping ground ID that can be used instead of a passport when checking into a camp site and includes third-party insurance (up to Sfr2.5 million) for damage you may cause. As a result, many camping grounds offer a small discount if you sign in with one. CCIs are issued by automobile associations, camping federations and, sometimes, on the spot at camping grounds. In the UK, the AA issues them to its members for UK£4.

Carte Musées et Monuments

The Carte Musées et Monuments (Museums & Monuments Card) can be used to gain quick entry (no queuing) to around 70 venues in Paris and the Île de France, including the Louvre and the Musée d'Orsay. The cost for one/three/five days is 80/160/240FF. There is no reduced rate for students or senior travellers. In France details are available from ☎ 01 44 78 45 81; fax 01 44 78 12 23; www.intermusees.com.

Photocopies

The hassles brought on by losing your passport can be considerably reduced if you have a record of its number and issue date, or even better, photocopies of the relevant data pages. A photocopy of your birth certificate can also be useful.

Also add the serial numbers of your travellers cheques (cross them off as you cash them) and photocopies of your credit cards, airline ticket and other travel documents. Keep all this emergency material separate from your passport, cheques and cash, and leave extra copies with someone you can rely on back home. Add some emergency money, say US$50 in cash, to this separate stash as well. If you do lose your passport, notify the police immediately to get a statement, and contact your nearest consulate.

EMBASSIES & CONSULATES

French Embassies & Consulates

Don't expect France's diplomatic and consular representatives abroad to be helpful or even civil at times, though you do come across the odd exception. Addresses include the following:

Australia
  Embassy:
  (☎ 02-6216 0100; fax 6273 3193)
  6 Perth Ave, Yarralumla, ACT 2600
  Consulate:
  (☎ 03-9820 0944/0921; fax 9820 9363)
  492 St Kilda Rd, Level 4, Melbourne, Vic 3004
  Consulate:
  (☎ 02-9262 5779; fax 9283 1210)
  St Martin's Tower, 20th floor, 31 Market St, Sydney, NSW 2000

Belgium
  Embassy:
  (☎ 02-548 8711; fax 513 6871)
  65 Rue Ducale, 1000 Brussels
  Consulate:
  (☎ 02-229 8500; fax 229 8510)
  12A Place de Louvain, 1000 Brussels

Canada
  Embassy:
  (☎ 613-789 1795; fax 789 0279)
  42 Sussex Drive, Ottawa, Ont K1M 2C9
  Consulate:
  (☎ 514-878 4385; fax 878 3981)
  1 Place Ville Marie, 26th floor, Montreal, Que H3B 4S3
  Consulate:
  (☎ 416-925 8041; fax 925 3076)
  130 Bloor St West, Suite 400, Toronto, Ont M5S 1N5

Germany
  Embassy:
  (☎ 0228-955 6000; fax 955 6055)
  An der Marienkapelle 3, 53179 Bonn
  Consulates:
  (☎ 030-885 90243; fax 885 5295)
  Kurfürstendamm 211, 10719 Berlin
  (☎ 089-419 4110; fax 419 41141)
  Möhlstrasse 5, 81675 Munich

Ireland
(☎ 01-260 1666; fax 283 0178)
36 Ailesbury Rd, Ballsbridge, Dublin 4
Israel
Embassy:
(☎ 03-524 5371; fax 522 6094)
112 Herbert Samuel Drive, 63572 Tel Aviv
Consulate:
(☎ 03-510 1415; fax 510 4370)
Migdalor Building, 11th floor, 1-3 Ben Yehuda St, 63801 Tel Aviv
Italy
Embassy:
(☎ 06-686 011; fax 860 1360)
Piazza Farnese 67, 00186 Rome
Consulate:
(☎ 06-6880 6437; fax 6860 1260)
Via Giulia 251, 00186 Rome
Netherlands
Embassy:
(☎ 070-312 5800; fax 312 5854)
Smidsplein 1, 2514 BT The Hague
Consulate:
(☎ 020-624 8346; fax 626 0841)
Vijzelgracht 2, 1000 HA Amsterdam
New Zealand
(☎ 04-472 0200; fax 472 5887)
1-3 Willeston St, Wellington
South Africa
January-June:
(☎ 021-212 050; fax 261 996)
1009 Main Tower, Cape Town Center, Heerengracht, 8001 Cape Town
July-December:
(☎ 012-435 564; fax 433 481)
807 George Ave, Arcadia, 0132 Pretoria
Spain
Embassy:
(☎ 91-435 5560; fax 435 6655)
Calle de Salustiano Olozaga 9, 28001 Madrid
Consulate:
(☎ 91-319 7188; fax 308 6273)
Calle Marques de la Enseñada 10, 28004 Madrid
Consulate:
(☎ 93-317 8150; fax 412 4282)
Ronda Universitat 22, 08007 Barcelona
Switzerland
Embassy:
(☎ 031-359 2111; fax 352 2191)
Schosshaldenstrasse 46, 3006 Berne
Consulate:
(☎ 022-311 3441; fax 310 8339)
11 Rue Imbert Galloix, 1205 Geneva
Consulate:
(☎ 01-268 8585; fax 268 8500)
Mühlebachstrasse 7, 8008 Zürich
UK
Embassy:
(☎ 0171-201 1000 or, after June 1999, ☎ 020-7201 1000; fax 201 1004 or 7201 1004)
58 Knightsbridge, London SW1X 7JT
Consulate:
(☎ 0171-838 2000 or, after June 1999, ☎ 020-7838 2000; fax 838 2001 or 7838 2001)
21 Cromwell Rd, London SW7 2DQ. The visa section is at 6A Cromwell Place, London SW7 2EW (☎ 0171-838 2051 or, after June 1999, ☎ 020-7838 2051). Dial ☎ 0891-887733 for visa information.
USA
Embassy:
(☎ 202-944 6000; fax 944 6166)
4101 Reservoir Rd NW, Washington, DC 20007
Consulate:
(☎ 212-606 3688; fax 606 3620)
934 Fifth Ave, New York, NY 10021
Consulate:
(☎ 415-397 4330; fax 433 8357)
540 Bush St, San Francisco, CA 94108.
Other consulates are located in Atlanta, Boston, Chicago, Houston, Los Angeles, Miami and New Orleans.

Embassies & Consulates in France

All foreign embassies are in Paris. Canada, the UK and the USA also have consulates in other major cities. The locations of some major embassies are indicated by reference to the colour maps (named Map 1 to 9) that appear in the Paris chapter.

To find an embassy or consulate not listed here, consult the *Yellow Pages* (look under Ambassades et Consulats) in Paris.

Australia
(Map 4; ☎ 01 40 59 33 00; metro Bir Hakeim)
4 Rue Jean Rey, 15e. The consular section, which handles matters concerning Australian nationals, is open Monday to Friday from 9.15 am to noon and 2 to 4.30 pm.
Belgium
(☎ 01 44 09 39 39; metro Charles de Gaulle-Étoile)
9 Rue de Tilsitt, 17e
Canada
Embassy:
(Map 2; ☎ 01 44 43 29 00; metro Alma Marceau or Franklin D Roosevelt)
35 Ave Montaigne, 8e. Canadian citizens in need of consular services should call the

embassy Monday to Friday from 9.30 to 11 am or 2 to 4.30 pm for a weekday appointment.
Consulate:
(☎ 03 88 96 65 02)
Rue du Ried, La Wantzenau, 12km north-east of Strasbourg
Consulate:
(☎ 05 61 99 30 16)
30 Blvd de Strasbourg, Toulouse

Czech Republic
Embassy:
(☎ 01 40 65 13 00; metro Bir Hakeim)
15 Ave Charles Floquet, 7e
Consulate:
(☎ 01 44 32 02 00; metro Saint Germain des Prés)
18 Rue Bonaparte, 6e

Germany
Embassy:
(☎ 01 53 83 45 00; metro Franklin D Roosevelt)
13 Ave Franklin D Roosevelt, 8e
Consulate:
(☎ 01 42 99 78 00; Minitel 3615 ALLEMAGNE; metro Iéna)
34 Ave d'Iéna, 16e
Consulate:
(☎ 03 88 15 03 40)
15 Rue des Francs Bourgeois, 15th floor, Strasbourg

Ireland
(Map 2; ☎ 01 44 17 67 00 or, after hours in an emergency, ☎ 01 44 17 67 67; Minitel 3615 IRLANDE; metro Argentine)
4 Rue Rude, 16e, between Ave de la Grande Armée and Ave Foch. Open Monday to Friday from 9.30 am to noon (or by appointment). The phone is staffed on weekdays from 9.30 am to 1 pm and 2.30 to 5.30 pm.

Israel
(☎ 01 40 76 55 00; metro Franklin D Roosevelt)
3 Rue Rabelais, 8e

Italy
Embassy:
(☎ 01 49 54 03 00; metro Rue du Bac)
51 Rue de Varenne, 7e
Consulate:
(☎ 01 44 30 47 00; metro La Muette)
5 Blvd Émile Augier, 16e
Consulate:
(☎ 04 79 33 20 36)
12 Blvd Lèmenc, Chambery

New Zealand
(Map 2; ☎ 01 45 00 24 11 for 24-hour voice mail and emergencies; metro Victor Hugo)
7ter Rue Léonard de Vinci, 16e, one block south of Ave Foch, across Place du Venezuela from 7 Rue Léonard de Vinci. Open Monday to Friday from 9 am to 1 pm for routine matters and 2 to 5.30 pm for emergencies. In July and August it's also open on Friday from 8.30 am to 2 pm.

South Africa
(☎ 01 53 59 23 23; metro Invalides)
59 Quai d'Orsay, 7e, near the American Church

Spain
(☎ 01 44 43 18 00; metro Alma Marceau)
22 Ave Marceau, 8e

Switzerland
Embassy:
(☎ 01 49 55 67 00; metro Varenne)
142 Rue de Grenelle, 7e
Consulate:
(☎ 03 88 35 00 70)
11 Blvd du Président Edwards, Strasbourg

UK
Consulate:
(Map 2; ☎ 01 44 51 31 00 or, 24 hours a day in an emergency, ☎ 01 42 66 29 79; Minitel 3615 GBRETAGNE; metro Concorde or Saint Augustin)
16 Rue d'Anjou, 8e. Open weekdays (except on bank holidays) from 9.30 am to 12.30 pm and 2.30 to 5 pm.
Consulate:
(☎ 04 72 77 81 70; fax 04 72 77 81 70)
24 Rue Childebert, 4th floor, Lyon
Consulate:
(☎ 04 91 15 72 10; metro Castellane)
24 Ave du Prado, Marseille
Consulate:
(☎ 04 93 82 32 04)
8 Rue Alphonse Kerr, Nice

USA
Consulate:
(Map 2; ☎ 01 43 12 23 for a recorded information service or, 24 hours a day in an emergency, ☎ 01 43 12 49 48; Minitel 3614 ETATS-UNIS; metro Concorde)
2 Rue Saint Florentin, 1er. Except on French and US holidays, the American Services section is open Monday to Friday from 9 am to 3 pm.
Consulate:
(☎ 04 91 54 92 00; fax 04 91 55 09 97)
12 Blvd Paul Peytral, Marseille
Consulate:
(☎ 04 93 88 89 55)
31 Rue Maréchal Joffre, Nice
Consulate:
(☎ 03 88 35 31 04)
15 Ave d'Alsace, Strasbourg

CUSTOMS

The usual allowances apply to *duty-free goods* purchased at airports or on ferries outside the EU (from June 1999): tobacco (200 cigarettes, 50 cigars, or 250g of loose tobacco), alcohol (1L of strong liquor or 2L of less than 22% alcohol by volume; 2L of wine), coffee (500g or 200g of extracts) and perfume (50g of perfume and 0.25L of toilet water).

Do not confuse these with *duty-paid* items (including alcohol and tobacco) bought at normal shops and supermarkets in another EU country and brought into France, where certain goods might be more expensive. Then the allowances are more than generous: 800 cigarettes, 200 cigars, or 1kg of loose tobacco; 10L of spirits (more than 22% alcohol by volume), 20L of fortified wine or aperitif, 90L of wine or 110L of beer.

MONEY

Currency

The national currency is the French franc, abbreviated in this book by the letters 'FF'. One franc is divided into 100 centimes.

Adieu Franc, Bonjour Euro

Don't be surprised if you come across two sets of prices for goods and services in Paris. From 1 January 1999 both the franc and Europe's new currency – the euro – will be legal tender here.

It's all part of the harmonisation of the EU. Along with national borders, venerable currencies like the franc are also being phased out. Not all EU members have agreed to adopt the euro, but the franc, Deutschmark and lira will be among the first of 11 currencies to go the way of the dodo. The euro will end the 650 year reign of the franc, which began in 1360 when King Jean le Bon struck coins to signify that his part of France was *franc des anglois* (free of English domination).

No actual coins or banknotes will be issued until 1 January 2002; until that time, the euro will in effect be 'paperless'. Prices can be quoted in euros, but there won't actually be any euros in circulation. Companies will use the new European currency for their accounting, banks can offer euro accounts and credit card companies can bill in euros. Essentially, the euro can be used any time it is not necessary to hand over hard cash.

This can lead to confusion, and travellers should be forewarned that the scheme is open to abuse. For instance, a restaurant might list prices in both francs and euros. Check your bill carefully – your total might have the amount in francs, but a credit card company may bill you in the euro equivalent.

Things will probably get worse during the first half of 2002. There is a six month period when countries can use both their old currencies and the newly issued euro notes and coins.

The euro will have the same value in all member countries of the EU; the €5 note in France is the same €5 note you will use in Italy. The official exchange rates will be set on 1 January 1999, but unofficial rates are already in use. €1 is nearly equal in value to US$1.

Coins and notes have already been designed. The banknotes come in denominations ranging from €5 to €500. All bills feature a generic 'European' bridge on one side and a vaguely familiar but unidentifiable 'European' arch on the reverse. Each country is permitted to design coins with one side standard for all euro coins and the other bearing a national emblem.

Check out http://europa.eu.int/euro for information on the euro and samples of the banknotes and coins.

French coins come in denominations of 5, 10, 20 and 50 centimes (0.5FF) and 1, 2, 5, 10 and 20FF; the two highest denominations have silvery centres and brass edges. It's a good idea to keep a supply of coins of various denominations for parking meters, laundrettes, tolls etc.

Banknotes are issued in denominations of 20FF (Claude Debussy), 50FF (the Little Prince and his creator, Antoine de Saint Exupéry), 100FF (Paul Cézanne, who now replaces Eugène Delacroix), 200FF (Gustave Eiffel, replacing Montesquieu) and 500FF (Marie and Pierre Curie). Frequently, it can be difficult to get change for a 500FF bill.

Exchange Rates

country	unit		franc
Australia	A$1	=	3.70FF
Canada	C$1	=	4.10FF
EU	€1	=	6.60FF
Germany	DM1	=	3.35FF
Japan	¥100	=	4.30FF
New Zealand	NZ$1	=	3.15FF
Spain	100 pta	=	3.95FF
UK	UK£1	=	9.80FF
USA	US$1	=	6FF

At banks and exchange bureaus, you can tell how good the rate is by checking the spread between the rates for *achat* (buy rates, ie what they'll give you for foreign cash or travellers cheques) and *vente* (sell rates, ie the rate at which they sell foreign currency to people going abroad) – the greater the difference, the further each is from the inter-bank rate (printed daily in newspapers, including the *International Herald Tribune*).

Exchanging Money

Banks and exchange bureaus often give a better rate for travellers cheques than for cash. Major train stations and fancy hotels also have exchange facilities, which usually operate in the evening, on weekends and during holidays, but the rates are usually poor.

Cash In general, cash is not a very good way to carry money. Not only can it be stolen, but in France you don't get an optimal exchange rate. The Banque de France, for instance, usually pays about 2.5% *more* for travellers cheques, more than making up for the 1% commission usually involved in buying travellers cheques.

However, bringing along the equivalent of about US$100 in low-denomination notes will make it easier to change a small sum of money when an inferior rate is on offer or you need just a few francs (eg at the end of your stay).

Because of counterfeiting, it may be difficult to change US$100 notes, and even most Banque de France branches refuse to accept them.

Travellers Cheques Except at exchange bureaus and the Banque de France, you have to pay to cash travellers cheques: at banks, expect a charge of 22 to 30FF per transaction; the post office charges a minimum of 16FF. A percentage fee may apply for large sums. American Express offices do not charge a commission on their own travellers cheques, but holders of other brands must pay 3% on top (minimum charge: 40FF).

The travellers cheques offering the greatest degree of flexibility are those issued by American Express (in US dollars or French francs) and Visa (in French francs) because they can be changed at many post offices.

Keep a record of cheque numbers, where they were purchased and which ones were cashed. Obviously, you should keep all such information separate from the cheques themselves.

Lost or Stolen Travellers Cheques If your American Express travellers cheques are lost or stolen in France, call ☎ 0800 90 86 00, a 24-hour toll-free number. In Paris, the main American Express office (Map 2; ☎ 01 47 77 77 07; metro Auber or Opéra) is at 11 Rue Scribe (9e). Reimbursements are available Monday to Saturday from 9 am to 6.30 or 7 pm (5.30 pm on Saturday). Reimbursements can also be made at the American Express offices in Aix-en-Provence, Bordeaux, Cannes, Disneyland Paris, Le Havre, Lyon, Marseille, Monaco, Nice, Paris, Rouen, Saint Jean de Luz, Strasbourg and in Andorra (see the Money section under the city name in the relevant chapters of the book).

If you lose your Thomas Cook cheques, contact any Thomas Cook bureau – eg in a major train station or at 4 Blvd Saint Michel, 6e (☎ 01 46 34 23 81) – for replacements. The company's customer service bureau can be contacted toll-free by dialling ☎ 0800 90 83 30.

Guaranteed Cheques Eurocheques, available if you have a European bank account, are guaranteed up to a certain limit. When cashing them (eg at post offices), you will be asked to show your Eurocheque card bearing your signature and registration number, and perhaps a passport or ID card. Your Eurocheque card should be kept separately from the cheques. Many hotels and merchants refuse to accept Eurocheques because of the relatively large commissions.

ATMs ATMs are known in French as DABs (*distributeurs automatiques de billets*) or *points d'argent*. ATM cards can give you direct access to your cash reserves back home at a superior exchange rate. Most ATMs will also give you a cash advance through your Visa or MasterCard, functioning as a sort of debit card attached to your bank account. This method of getting an advance usually incurs the lowest fees (see Cash Advances in the following Credit Card section).

Some non-US ATMs won't accept PIN codes with more than four digits – ask your bank how to handle this, and while you're at it find out about withdrawal fees and daily limits. There are plenty of ATMs in France linked to the international Cirrus and Maestro networks. If you normally remember your PIN code as a string of letters, translate it back into numbers, as keyboards may not have letters indicated.

Credit Cards Overall, the cheapest way to take money with you to France is by using a credit or debit card, both to pay for things (in which case the merchant absorbs the commission) and to get cash advances. Visa (Carte Bleue) is the most widely accepted, followed by MasterCard (Access or Eurocard). American Express cards are not very useful except at upmarket establishments, but they do allow you to get cash at certain ATMs and over a dozen American Express offices in France. In general, all three cards can be used to pay for travel by train and in many restaurants.

Exchange rates may vary – to your advantage or disadvantage – between the day you use the card and the date of billing.

It may be impossible to get a lost Visa or MasterCard reissued until you get home (American Express and Diners Club International offer on-the-spot replacement cards); hence, two different credit cards are safer than one. Always keep some spare travellers cheques or cash on hand in the event of such an emergency.

Cash Advances When you get a cash advance against your Visa or MasterCard credit card account, your issuer charges a transaction fee and/or finance charge. With some issuers, the fees can reach as high as US$10 *plus* interest per transaction, so check with your card issuer before leaving home and compare rates. Also, at many banks you also have to pay a commission of 30FF or more. You can avoid paying interest (which accrues from the moment you receive the cash, not from the end of the billing period) by depositing lots of money in your credit card account before you leave home, in effect turning it into a bank account and transforming your credit card into a debit card. The biggest problem with cash advances is that there are all sorts of limits on how much cash you can take out per week or month, regardless of your credit limit.

Cash advances are available at American Express offices to card holders for no charge – except the usual 1% fee to purchase travellers cheques. The usual withdrawal limit is US$500 (US$1000 if you can write a personal cheque) every 21 days for Green Card holders and US$2000 for Gold Card holders.

Some unscrupulous exchange bureaus advertise that they do cash advances, but instead of giving you French francs, they insist that you take your money in US dollars or some other foreign currency, which they make you buy at their disadvantageous 'sell' rate. If you need francs, you then have to change your dollars or pounds back again, and take a second loss on the difference between the buy and sell rates.

Lost or Stolen Cards If your Visa card is lost or stolen, call Carte Bleue at ☎ 01 42 77 11 90 in Paris or ☎ 02 54 42 12 12 in the provinces, 24 hours a day. To get a replacement card you'll have to deal with the issuer.

Report a lost MasterCard, Eurocard or Access to Eurocard France (☎ 01 45 67 53 53) and, if you can, to your credit card issuer back home (for cards from the USA, call ☎ 314-275 6690). In Paris, Eurocard France is at 16 Rue Lecourbe, 15e (metro Sèvres Lecourbe) and is open Monday to Friday from 9.30 am to 5.30 pm.

If your American Express card is lost or stolen, call ☎ 01 47 77 70 00 or ☎ 01 47 77 72 00; both are staffed 24 hours a day. In an emergency, American Express card holders from the USA can call collect on ☎ 202-783 7474 or ☎ 202-677 2442. Replacements can be arranged at any American Express office (see Lost or Stolen Travellers Cheques earlier).

A lost Diners Club card should be reported on ☎ 01 47 62 75 75.

International Transfers Telegraphic transfers are not very expensive but, despite their name, can be quite slow. Be sure to specify the name of the bank and the name and address of the branch where you'd like to pick it up.

It's quicker and easier to have money wired via American Express (US$50 for US$1000). Western Union's Money Transfer system (☎ 01 43 54 46 12) and Thomas Cook's MoneyGram service (☎ 0800 90 83 30) are also popular.

Banque de France Banque de France, France's central bank, offers the best exchange rates in the country. It does not accept Eurocheques or provide credit card cash advances. Most do not accept US$100 notes due to the preponderance of counterfeit ones. Also, due to the high volume of customers and shortage of staff, some branches are limiting their exchange operations to the morning only. Be warned.

Post Offices Many post offices perform exchange transactions for a middling rate. The commission for travellers cheques is 1.2% (minimum 16FF).

Post offices accept banknotes in a variety of currencies as well as travellers cheques issued by American Express (denominated in either US dollars or French francs) or Visa (in French francs only).

Commercial Banks Commercial banks usually charge between 22 and 50FF per foreign currency transaction. The rates offered vary, so it pays to compare.

Commercial banks are generally open either from Monday to Friday or Tuesday to Saturday. Hours are variable but are usually from 8 or 9 am to sometime between 11.30 and 1 pm and 1.30 or 2 to 4.30 or 5 pm. Exchange services may end half an hour before closing time.

Exchange Bureaus In large cities, especially Paris, *bureaux de change* are faster, easier, open longer hours and give better rates than the banks.

Your best bet is to familiarise yourself with the rates offered by various banks (which almost always charge a commission) and compare them with those on offer at exchange bureaus (which are not generally allowed to charge commissions). On relatively small transactions, even exchange places with less-than-optimal rates may leave you with more francs in your pocket.

All major train stations have exchange bureaus – some run by Thomas Cook – but their rates are less than stellar. Changing money at the bureau de change chains like Chequepoint and Exact Change is only slightly less foolish than making your travellers cheques into paper aeroplanes and launching them from the top of Mont Blanc; they offer about 10% less than a fair rate. When using bureaux de change, shop around and beware of the small print – for example, bureaus on the Rue de Rivoli in Paris specialise in offering good rates that only apply if you're changing US$3000 or more. The CCF exchange office at the main tourist office in the capital takes no commission, offers a decent rate and is open daily from 9 am to 7.30 pm.

Costs

If you stay in hostels or showerless, toiletless rooms in budget hotels and have picnics rather than dining out, it is possible to travel around France for about US$35 a day per person (US$45 in Paris). A couple staying in two-star hotels and eating one cheap restaurant meal each day should count on spending at least US$65 a day per person, not including car rental. Lots of moving from place to place, eating in restaurants, drinking wine or treating yourself to France's many little luxuries can increase these figures considerably.

Discounts Museums, cinemas, the SNCF, ferry companies and other institutions offer all sorts of price breaks to people under the age of either 25 or 26; students with ISIC cards (age limits may apply); *le troisième age* (seniors), ie people over 60 or, in some cases, 65. Look for the words *demi-tarif* or *tarif réduit* (half-price tariff or reduced rate) on rate charts and then ask if you qualify.

Those under 18 get an even wider range of discounts, including free entry to Musées Nationaux (museums run by the French government). For information on the Carte Musées et Monuments, which allows entry to around 70 venues in Paris, see that listing under Visas & Documents.

Ways to Save Money There are lots of things you can do to shave francs off your daily expenditures. A few suggestions:

- Travel with someone else – single rooms usually cost only marginally less than doubles. Triples and quads (often with only two beds) are even cheaper per person. Budget hotel rooms often cost less per person than hostel beds.
- You'll get the best exchange rate and save on commissions by changing money at the Banque de France and using a credit card whenever possible (see Changing Money later in this chapter).
- Avoid high-season travel to regions that raise their accommodation prices when demand goes up (eg Corsica and the Côte d'Azur during July and August, the Alps in February).
- If you stay in one place for a while and get to know your way around, your daily costs are likely to come down.
- Avail yourself of France's many free sights: bustling marketplaces, tree-lined avenues, cathedrals, churches, parks, canal towpaths, nature reserves etc.
- Visit museums on days when entry is discounted or even free. In Paris, for instance, the Louvre is more than 40% cheaper after 3 pm and free on the first Sunday of every month.
- When calling home, avoid France's pricey International Direct Dial (IDD) services – use Country Direct services or use your phonecard just long enough to ask to be rung back.
- Bring along a pocketknife and eating utensils so you can have picnics instead of restaurant meals. The cheapest food is sold in supermarkets and at outdoor markets.
- Carry a water bottle wherever you go so you don't have to pay for a pricey cold drink each time you're thirsty (public drinking fountains in France are few and far between).
- In restaurants, order the *menu* (set menu) and ask for tap water rather than soft drinks, mineral water or wine.
- Avoid taking trains for which you have to pay supplements or reservation fees. For information on reduced-rate train tickets, see the Rail Passes and Discount Tickets sections under Train in the Getting Around chapter.
- If you'll be hiring a car, arrange for rental before you leave home. If you'll be staying at least a month, hire a purchase-repurchase car (see Purchase-Repurchase Plans under Car in the Getting Around chapter).
- Buy discount bus/metro passes or carnets of reduced-price tickets rather than single-ride tickets.

Tipping & Bargaining

French law requires that restaurant, café and hotel bills include the service charge (usually 10 to 15%), so a *pourboire* (tip) is neither necessary nor expected in most cases. However, most people leave a few francs in restaurants, unless the service was bad. They rarely tip in cafés and bars when they've just had a coffee or a drink.

In taxis, the usual tip is 2FF no matter what the fare, with the maximum about 5FF. People in France rarely bargain, except at flea markets.

Taxes & Refunds

France's VAT is 20.6% on most goods except food, medicine and books, for which it's 5.5%; it goes as high as 33% on such items as watches, cameras and video cassettes. Prices that include VAT are often marked TTC (*toutes taxes comprises*, ie 'all taxes included').

If you are not a resident of the EU, you can get a refund of most of the VAT (TVA in French) provided that: you're over 15; you'll be spending less than six months in France; you purchase goods (not more than 10 of the same item) worth at least 1200FF (tax included) at a single shop; and the shop offers *vente en détaxe* (duty-free sales).

Present a passport at the time of purchase and ask for a *bordereau de détaxe* (export sales invoice). Some shops may refund 14% of the purchase price rather than the full 17.1% you are entitled to in order to cover the time and expense involved in the refund procedure.

As you leave France or another EU country, have all three pages (two pink and one green) of the bordereau validated by the country's customs officials at the airport or at the border. Customs officials will take the two pink sheets and the stamped self-addressed envelope provided by the store; the green sheet is your receipt. One of the pink sheets will then be sent to the shop where you made your purchase, which will then send you a *virement* (transfer of funds) in the form you have requested, such as by French franc cheque, or directly into your account. Be prepared for a long wait.

Instant Refunds If you're flying out of Orly or Roissy Charles de Gaulle airports certain stores can arrange for you to receive your refund as you're leaving the country. You must make such arrangements at the time of purchase.

When you arrive at the airport you have to do three things:

- Up to three hours before your flight leaves, you need to take your bordereau, passport, air ticket and the things you purchased (don't put them in your checked luggage) to the *douane* (customs) office so they can stamp all three copies of the bordereau (one of which they keep).
- Go to an Aéroports de Paris (ADP) information counter, where they will check the figures and put another stamp on the documents.
- Go to the customs refund window (*douane de détaxe*) or the exchange bureau indicated on your bordereau to pick up your refund.

POST & COMMUNICATIONS

Postal services in France are fast, reliable, bureaucratic and expensive. About three-quarters of domestic letters arrive the day after they've been mailed.

Each of France's 17,000 post offices is marked with a yellow or brown sign reading 'La Poste'; older branches may also be marked with the letters PTT, the abbreviation of *postes, télégraphes, téléphones*. To mail things, go to a postal window marked *toutes opérations*.

Postal Rates

Domestic letters up to 20g cost 3FF. Postcards and letters up to 20g cost 3FF within the EU; 3.80FF to most of the remainder of Europe as well as Africa; 4.40FF to the USA, Canada and the Middle East; and 5.20FF to Australasia. Aerograms cost 5FF to all destinations.

Worldwide express mail delivery, called Chronopost (☎ 01 46 48 10 00; Minitel 3614 CHRONOPOST for information), costs a fortune.

Sea-mail services have been discontinued, so sending packages overseas sometimes costs almost as much as the exorbitant overweight fees charged by airlines, even if you use *économique* (discount) air mail. Packages weighing over 2kg may not be accepted at branch post offices – in Paris, they're handled by the *poste principale* of each arrondissement. Post offices sell smallish boxes in four different sizes for 6.50 to 12.50FF.

Sending Mail

All mail to France *must* include the five digit postcode, which begins with the two digit number of the department. In Paris, virtually all postcodes begin with 750 and end with the two digit arrondissement number, eg 75004 for the 4e arrondissement. The local postcode is listed under the main heading of each city or town in this book.

Mail to France should be addressed as follows:

John SMITH
8, rue de la Poste
75020 Paris
FRANCE

The surname (family name) should be written in capital letters. As you'll notice, the French put a comma after the street number and don't capitalise 'rue', 'av', 'bd' (boulevard) etc as we do in this guide. The notation 'CEDEX' after a city or town name simply means that mail sent to that address is collected at the post office rather than delivered to the door.

Receiving Mail

Poste Restante To have mail sent to you via poste restante (general delivery), available at all French post offices, have it addressed as follows:

SMITH, John
Poste Restante
Recette Principale
76000 Rouen
FRANCE

Since poste restante mail is held alphabetically by last name, it is vital that you follow the French practice of having your *nom de famille* (surname or family name) written first and in capital letters. In case your friends back home forget, always check under the first letter of your *prénom* (first name) as well. There's a 3FF charge for every piece of poste restante mail you pick up weighing less than 20g; for anything between 20 and 100g, the fee is 4FF. It is usually possible to forward (*faire suivre*) mail from one poste restante address to another. When you go to pick up poste restante mail, always have your passport or national ID card handy, otherwise the staff won't hand it over.

Poste restante mail not addressed to a particular branch goes to the city's *recette principale* (main post office) whether or not you include the words Recette Principale in the address. If you want it sent to a specific branch post office mentioned in this book (most of which are generally centrally located and marked on the maps), write the street address mentioned in the text.

In Paris, poste restante mail not addressed to a particular branch is sent to the city's main post office (☎ 01 40 28 20 00; metro Sentier or Les Halles) at 52 Rue du Louvre (1er). See Post & Communications in the Paris chapter for details.

American Express It is also possible to receive mail (but not parcels or envelopes larger than an A4 sheet of paper) in care of American Express.

If you don't have an American Express card or at least one American Express travellers cheque, there's a 5FF charge each time you check to see if you've received something (some offices waive the fee if there's nothing for you). The office will hold mail for 30 days before returning it to the sender. After that, having them forward it to another American Express office costs 15FF for two months.

See Lost or Stolen Travellers Cheques in the Money section of this chapter for a list of cities with American Express offices; addresses are given under Money in the relevant city listings.

Telephone

A quarter of a century ago, France had one of the worst telephone systems in Western Europe. But thanks to massive investment in the late 1970s and early 80s, the country now has one of the most modern and sophisticated telecommunications systems in the world.

International Dialling to France To call the Paris area from outside France, dial your country's international access code, then 33 (France's country code), then omit the 0 at the beginning of the 10-digit local number (ie nine digits, starting with 1). To call anywhere else in France, dial the international access code, then 33, then again ignore the 0 in the 10-digit local number.

International Dialling from France To call someone outside France, dial the international access code (00), the country code, the area code (without the initial zero if there is one) and the local number. International Direct Dial (IDD) calls to almost anywhere in the world can be placed from public telephones. Useful country codes include:

Andorra	☎ 376
Australia	☎ 61
Canada	☎ 1
Hong Kong	☎ 852
Germany	☎ 49
Japan	☎ 81
India	☎ 91
Ireland	☎ 353
Monaco	☎ 377
New Zealand	☎ 64
Singapore	☎ 65
South Africa	☎ 27
UK	☎ 44
USA	☎ 1

If you don't know the country code (*indicatif pays*) and it doesn't appear on the information sheet posted in most telephone cabins, consult a telephone book or dial ☎ 12 (directory inquiries).

To make a reverse-charges (collect) call (*en PCV*, pronounced 'PEY-SEY-VEY') or a person-to-person call (*avec préavis*, pronounced 'ah-VEK preh-ah-VEE'), dial 00, and then dial 33 plus the country code of the place you're calling (for the USA and Canada, dial 11 instead of 1). There won't be a dial tone after you've dialled 00, so don't wait for one. Don't be surprised if you get a recording and have to wait a while. If you're using a public phone, you must insert a télécarte (or, in the case of public coin telephones, 1FF) to place operator-assisted calls through the international operator.

For directory inquiries concerning subscriber numbers outside France, dial 00 then 3312 and finally the relevant country code (again, 11 instead of 1 for the USA and Canada). You often get put on hold for quite a while. In public phones, you can access this service without a télécarte, but from home phones the charge is 7.30FF per inquiry.

Toll-free 1-800 numbers in the USA and Canada cannot be called from overseas except through certain Country Direct services, in which case you bear the cost.

International Rates Daytime calls to other parts of Europe cost from 2.47 to 4.45FF a minute. Reduced tariffs (1.98 to 3.46FF) generally apply on weekdays from 9.30 pm to 8 am, and on weekends and public holidays from 2 pm on Saturday to 8 am on Monday.

Nondiscount calls to continental USA and Canada are 2.97FF a minute on weekdays from 2 to 8 pm. The price then drops to 2.35FF. The rate to Alaska, Hawaii and the Caribbean is a whopping 9.77FF a minute (7.79FF discount rate).

Full-price calls to Australia, Japan, New Zealand, Hong Kong and Singapore are 6.55FF a minute. A discount rate of 5.20FF a minute applies daily from 9.30 pm (Saturday from 2 pm) to 8 am and all day on Sunday and public holidays.

Calls to other parts of Asia, South America and non-Francophone Africa are generally 6.55 to 9.77FF a minute, though to some countries a rate of 5.20 to 7.79FF will apply at certain times.

Country Direct Services Country Direct lets you phone home by billing the long-distance carrier you use at home. The numbers can be dialled from public phones without inserting a phonecard; with some models, you're meant to dial even if there's no dial tone. The numbers listed below will connect you, free of charge, with an operator in your home country, who will verify your method of payment: by credit card, reverse charges etc.

Australia	Telstra	☎ 0800 99 00 61
	Optus	☎ 0800 99 20 61
Canada		☎ 0800 99 00 16
		☎ 0800 99 02 16
Hong Kong		☎ 0800 99 08 52
		☎ 0800 99 28 52
		☎ 0800 99 18 52
Ireland		☎ 0800 99 03 53
New Zealand		☎ 0800 99 00 64
Singapore		☎ 0800 99 00 65
UK	BT	☎ 0800 99 00 44
		☎ 0800 99 02 44
	Mercury	☎ 0800 99 09 44
USA	AT&T	☎ 0800 99 00 11
	MCI	☎ 0800 99 00 19
	Sprint	☎ 0800 99 00 87
	Worldcom	☎ 0800 99 00 13

Domestic Dialling France has five telephone dialling areas. To make calls within any region, just dial the 10-digit number. The same applies for calls between regions and from metropolitan France to French overseas departments and vice versa. The five regional area codes are:

01	the Paris region
02	the north-west
03	the north-east
04	the south-east (including Corsica)
05	the south-west

If you want France Telecom's *service des renseignements* (directory inquiries or assistance), dial ☎ 12. Don't be surprised if the operator does not speak English. The call is free from public phones but costs 3.71FF from private lines.

There is no way to make a domestic reverse-charges call. Instead, ask the person you're calling to ring you back (see Receiving Calls at Public Phones).

Domestic Tariffs Local calls are quite cheap, even at the red tariff (see the following paragraph): one calling unit (0.81FF with a télécarte) lasts for three minutes. For calls over distances of up to 100km, one unit lasts somewhere between 72 seconds (25 to 30km) and 32 seconds (52 to 100km) during red tariff periods. Over distances greater than 100km, one unit lasts just 21 seconds in public phones.

Like so many things in France, colour codes are used to indicate domestic telephone discounts. The regular rate for calls within France, known as the *tarif rouge* (red tariff), applies Monday to Saturday from 8 am to 12.30 pm and Monday to Friday from 1.30 to 6 pm. You pay 30% less than the tarif rouge with the *tarif blanc* (white tariff), which is in force Monday to Saturday from 12.30 to 1.30 pm and Monday to Friday from 6 to 9.30 pm. The rest of the time, you enjoy 50% off with the *tarif bleu* (blue tariff), except between 10.30 pm and 6 am, when the *tarif bleu nuit* (blue night tariff) gives you a 65% discount.

Note: numbers that begin with '08 36' (such as the SNCF's national information number) are always billed at 2.23FF per minute, regardless of the day or the time.

Toll-Free Numbers Two-digit emergency numbers (see Dangers & Annoyances in this chapter), Country Direct numbers and *numéros verts* (toll-free numbers – literally, 'green numbers' – which have 10 digits and begin with 0800), can be dialled from public telephones without inserting a télécarte or coins.

Public Phones Almost all public telephones in France require a télécarte, which can be purchased at post offices, *tabacs* (tobacconists), supermarket check-out counters, SNCF ticket windows, Paris metro stations, and anywhere you see a blue sticker reading *télécarte en vente ici*. Cards worth 50/120 calling units cost 40.60/97.50FF. Make sure your card's plastic wrapper is intact when you buy it.

In small village post offices, you occasionally find old-style phones for which you pay at the counter after you've made your call.

Using a Télécarte To make a domestic or international phone call with a télécarte, follow the instructions on the LCD display.

When a public telephone's display does not read *hors service* (out of order), the word *décrochez* should appear in the LCD window. If the phone has a button displaying two flags linked with an arrow, push it for the explanations in English. If not, when you see the words *introduire carte ou faire numéro libre* (insert the card or dial a toll-free number), insert the card chip-end first with the rectangle of electrical connectors facing upwards. *Patientez SVP* means 'Please wait'.

When the top line of the display tells you your *crédit* or *solde* (how many units you have left), denominated in *unités* (units), the bottom line of the LCD screen will read *numérotez* (dial). As you press the keyboard, the *numéro appelé* (number being called) will appear on the display.

After you dial, you will hear a rapid beeping followed by long beeps (it's ringing) or short beeps (it's busy). When your call is connected, the screen begins counting down your card's value. To redial, push the button inscribed with a telephone receiver icon (not available on all public phones).

If, for any reason, something goes wrong in the dialling process, you'll be asked to *raccrochez SVP* (please hang up). *Crédit épuisé* means that your télécarte has run out of units.

Switching Télécartes Mid-Call It's possible to replace a used-up télécarte with a new one in the middle of a call – an especially useful feature with overseas calls – but only if you follow the instructions exactly. When the screen reads, *crédit = 000 unités – changement de carte*, press the green button, wait for the message *retirez votre carte* and then take out the old télécarte. When you see the words *nouvelle télécarte* (not before!), insert a fresh card.

Coin Phones You occasionally run across phones that take coins (1FF for a local call) rather than télécartes, especially in remote rural areas. Remember that coin phones don't give change.

Most coin phones let you hear the dial tone immediately, but with the very oldest models – the ones with windows down the front and no slot for 2FF pieces – you must deposit your money before you get the tone.

Point Phone Many cafés and restaurants have privately owned, coin-operated telephones – intended primarily for the use of their clients – known as Point Phones. Point Phones require that you deposit 2FF to dial, but you can get half of that back if you make a short call and use two 1FF pieces rather than one 2FF coin. To make another call with your left-over credit (shown on the LCD screen), press the *reprise crédit* button.

You cannot get the international operator or receive calls from a Point Phone, but you can dial emergency numbers (no coins needed) and use Country Direct services (insert the 2FF – you'll get it back at the end). To find a Point Phone, look for blue-on-white window stickers bearing the Point Phone emblem.

Receiving Calls at Public Phones All public phones except Point Phones can receive both domestic and international calls. If you want someone to call you back, just give them France's country code, the area code (where relevant) and the number,

Accessing Email in France

While visiting France, it is eminently possible to access your home email account (and the Web) without making expensive international calls on noisy lines, stopping by pricey hotel business centres or searching out the country's relatively few cybercafés. But doing so takes the right equipment and a fair bit of patience.

Once you've got your laptop and a PC Card modem (be aware that some modems have trouble recognising European dial tones, and others will melt down if accidentally connected to a digital line), the next step is to get roaming Internet access. Your options are:

- Connecting through your service provider back home. Larger companies (eg AOL) have domestic access numbers around the world.
- Tapping into a network of local access numbers coordinated by companies such as Eunet (https://traveller.eu.net), which charge a monthly rate and a small fee for each connection. It may be necessary to configure your email program to present a dialogue box during login.
- Signing up with a French access provider. This can be time-consuming, require payment of a monthly fee of 50 to 150FF *plus* per-hour fees, and involve dealing with technical instructions and customer support people in French.

In any case, you'll need to know your home account's POP user name and the addresses of your SMTP (outgoing mail) and POP (incoming mail) servers.

Getting your modem to talk to the computer you're dialling is where things get tricky – and not only because of configuration problems. French phones use a T-shaped jack virtually unknown outside of France and its former colonies. Modems, on the other hand, generally have wires equipped with the closest thing there is to an international standard, the RJ-11 (modular) plug of the type used in the USA and quite a few other countries. Linking the two requires an adapter, which you can get at Monoprix and Prisunic department stores.

Harder to find is an in-line coupler that turns one RJ-11 socket into two (your best bet is to pick one up before leaving home – in France about the only place they're sold is in BHV stores). Along with an extension phone cord equipped with RJ-11 plugs at both ends and a French adapter, it will let you connect both your modem and a telephone to the same line. This is often crucial, as getting past the hotel's automatic switchboard may require that you use their pulse-dial telephone. To do this you'll have to configure your network-connection program to work in manual dial mode. As soon as you hear the fax-like noise of the access provider, connect your computer and hang up the phone. Don't be surprised if it takes several attempts (perhaps trying different access numbers) to establish a connection.

Unless your server access is local or uses a national access number billed at local rates, be prepared for ruinously high phone bills, especially from hotel rooms, where each France Télécom billing unit – good for just 32 seconds of cross-country connection time at the highest daytime rate – costs around 2FF. The only way to connect a modem to a public phone (or any hard-wired phone, such as those in some hotel rooms) is to use an acoustic coupler, a bulky and slow gadget that costs about US$100.

An Internet site with useful information on connecting your modem to local phone lines while on the road is: www.kropla.com/phones.htm. Companies that sell equipment to enable 'international modem connectivity' include TeleAdapt (www.teleadapt.com) and Road Warrior International (www.warrior.com/cpplus/adapters).

usually written after the words *Ici le* or *No d'appel* on the tariff sheet or on a little sign inside the phone box. When there's an incoming call, the words *décrochez – appel arrivé* will appear in the LCD window.

Minitel Minitel is an extremely useful telephone-connected, computerised information service, though it can be expensive to use and is being given a run for its money by the Internet. The most basic Minitels, equipped with a B&W monitor and a clumsy keyboard, are available for no charge to telephone subscribers. Newer models have colour screens, and many people now access the system with a home computer and a modem.

Minitel numbers consist of four digits (eg 3611, 3614, 3615 etc) and a string of letters. Home users pay a per-minute access charge, but consulting the *annuaire* (directory) is free. Most of the Minitels in post offices are also free for directory inquiries (though some require a 1 or 2FF coin), and many of them let you access pay-as-you-go on-line services.

Fax, Telegraph & Email

Virtually all Parisian post offices can send and receive domestic and international faxes (*télécopies* or *téléfaxes*), telexes and telegrams. It costs about 80FF (20FF within France) to send a one page fax. For information on sending emails from cybercafés, see Internet Resources in the Post & Communications section of the individual cities and towns.

INTERNET RESOURCES

Useful Web sites on France in English include:

French Government Tourism Office
 www.francetourism.com
 (official tourism site with all manner of information on and about travel in France)
Gay & Lesbian
 www.france.qrd.org
 ('queer resources directory' for gay and lesbian travellers)
Guide Web
 www.guideweb.com
 (good site, but only for selected regions)
Maison de la France
 www.maison-de-la-france.fr
Paris Tourist Office
 www.paris-promotion.fr
Real France
 www.realfrance.com
 ('inside' information on arts and crafts, nature, leisure, food, restaurants, wine, museums, sights, events, hotels, guesthouses and chateaux)
Skiing
 www.skifrance.fr
 (ski resorts, services, conditions etc)

Both La Poste and France Telecom have set their sights on the Internet. At the time of going to print, La Poste was setting up Internet access centres at 1000 post offices around France; a chip card costing 90FF would get you three hours access. France Telecom, meanwhile, has been sponsoring 'Internet stations' around France, including ones in Paris (see Internet Resources in the Information section of that chapter), Montpellier and Grenoble. These are not cybercafés but high tech centres where people can surf the Internet, send emails and take free beginners courses on how to use the Internet. Access rates are cheaper than commercial cybercafés: 20/30FF for a half-hour/hour.

Internet devotees can also have their hunger satiated at a number of cybercafés in and around Paris; see Internet Resources in the Information section of that chapter.

BOOKS

Most books are published in different editions by different publishers in different countries. As a result, a book might be a hardcover rarity in one country while it's readily available in paperback in another. Fortunately, bookshops and libraries search by title or author, so your local bookshop or library is best placed to advise you on the availability of the following recommendations.

There are so many excellent books on France that it's hard to choose just a few to recommend, though the list has been shortened considerably by limiting the selection almost exclusively to works available in paperback.

France & the Internet

France's relationship with *l'informatique* (the whole sphere of computer use) in general and the *les autoroutes de l'information* (the information superhighway) in particular has been marked by a certain *technophobie* (technophobia) tinged with Gallic reticence. On the one hand, France is the country that created the world's first on-line service for the masses, France Télécom's popular but primitive and expensive Télétel (Minitel) system. On the other hand, it was President Jacques Chirac who, when told how simple it is to use an *ordinateur* (computer) – 'you just click on the mouse' – replied famously, 'Qu'appelez-vous la souris?' (What is it that you call a mouse?) – this in December of 1996! At the end of the 1990s, though, the Gallocentric view that *le Cyberespace* is an irrelevant Anglophone fad has given way to a national computer and Internet literacy campaign – this despite the selfish, short-term interests of the many powerful French companies who make vast sums of money charging by the minute for Minitel access.

France's linguistic patriots have been waging a rearguard action to save the French language from an invasion of Internet terms from English, the uncontested lingua franca of cyberspace (85 to 90% of Web sites are in English, as opposed to just 2% in French). A lively linguistic debate, with as yet inconclusive results, has ensued. A mouse is either *une souris* or, often tongue in cheek, *un mulot* (field mouse). The Internet remains *l'Internet* (often without the definite article) for now, but the World Wide Web – *le Web* for most people – is also known as *la toile* (spider's web) or, absurdly – in order to avoid that quintessentially un-French letter, the 'W' – the *oueb* or (as in *Le Monde*) the *ouèbe*. A Web surfer is either an *internaute* or a *surfeur*.

To collect your *courier électronique* (email) you'll need to access (*accéder à*) what the locals call *un fournisseur d'accès* (access provider). Before an email address (whose French accents can, in general, safely be ignored), you often see the notation *mél*, short for *message électronique*, which is supposed to look like *tél*, written before phone numbers.

Lonely Planet

Lonely Planet's guide to *Paris* covers the French capital in great depth; *Western Europe* and *Mediterranean Europe* have chapters dealing both with Paris and France as a whole. Lonely Planet also publishes a *French phrasebook*.

Guidebooks

Large travel bookshops carry hundreds of titles on virtually every aspect of visiting France.

History, Art & Architecture Michelin, the huge rubber conglomerate, has been publishing travel guides ever since the earliest days of motorcar touring, when the books were intended to promote sales of its inflatable rubber tyres.

Michelin's *guides verts* (green guides; 59 to 71FF each), which cover all of France in 24 regional volumes – about a dozen of which are currently available in English – are full of historical information, although the editorial approach is very conservative and regional cultures tend to be given short shrift. The green guide to all of France (75FF) has brief entries on the most touristed sights.

The massive *Blue Guide* (£16.99), by Ian Robertson, has reams of detailed information on architecture and history but is a dry read.

Among the French-language guides, useful only if your French is very proficient, the best overall guidebooks are those published by

Guide Bleu (absolutely no relation to its English-language namesake), its blue-jacketed all-France (198FF) and regional guides provide accurate, balanced information on matters historical, cultural and architectural.

It also publishes abridged guides called *Les Petits Bleus,* including one on Paris (50FF).

Paris Lonely Planet's *Paris* is a complete guide to the French capital. Walking guides include: *Paris Step by Step* by Christopher Turner; *Walking Paris* by Gilles Desmons; *Paris Walks* by Alison & Sonia Landes; and *Frommer's Walking Tours Paris* by Lisa Legarde. *The Paris Literary Companion*, by Ian Littlewood, escorts you past the buildings where literary personalities once made their homes. *Paris Pas Cher*, updated annually, lists inexpensive shopping options. Another source of information on penny-wise living in Paris is *Paris aux Meilleurs Prix*.

Hiking & Cycling The Fédération Française de Randonnée Pédestre (FFRP; the French Ramblers' Association; see Hiking under Activities for more information) publishes some 120 topoguides (75 or 99FF), map-equipped booklets on GR, GRP and PR trails. Local organisations also produce topoguides, some of them in the form of a *pochette* (a folder filled with single-sheet itineraries). The information that topoguides provide – in French, of course – includes details on trail conditions, flora, fauna, villages en route, camping grounds, *refuges* etc. In many areas, bookshops and tourist offices stock a selection of titles with local relevance.

The UK publisher Robertson McCarta has translated quite a few topoguides into English. Issued in book form as part of the Footpaths of Europe series, regions covered include Normandy, Brittany, the Loire Valley, the Auvergne, the Dordogne, the Alps, the Pyrenees, Provence and Corsica. They're cheaper and easier to find in the UK than in France.

Wild France (US$16), edited by Douglas Botting and published by the Sierra Club in the USA. Also look out for Lonely Planet's *Walking in France*, due out in May 2000, for an overview of hiking options all over France. A good guide for Alpine hiking is *Walking in the Alps*, by Brian Spencer.

Mountain bike enthusiasts who can read French should look for the books of *Les Guides VTT*, a series of cyclists' topoguides published by Didier et Richard. Robin Neillands' *Cycle Touring in France* (£7.95) is a good companion for independent cyclists, detailing 20 very good cycling tours. *Bicycle Tours of France* (US$10), by Gay & Kathlyn Hendricks, has details on five suggested cycling routes.

Accommodation & Restaurants Many people swear by Michelin's red-jacketed *Guide Rouge* to France (150FF), published each March, which has over 1200 pages of information on 6400 mid and upper-range hotels and 3900 restaurants in every corner of the country. Accompanied by 521 detailed city maps, it is best known for rating France's greatest restaurants with one, two or three stars. Chefs have been known to commit suicide upon losing a star. The icons used instead of text are explained in English at the front of the book. The *Guide Rouge* to Paris is 36FF.

The *Guide Gault Millau France* (175FF), published annually, awards up to four *toques rouges* (red chefs' caps) to restaurants with exceptionally good, creative cuisine; *toques blanches* (white chefs' caps) go to places with superb modern or traditional cuisine. Each establishment is rated on a scale of one to 20. *Gault Millau* is said to be quicker at picking up-and-coming restaurants than the *Guide Rouge*. The symbols used are explained in English and an English edition is also available. The *Food Lover's Guide to France*, by the Paris-based American food reviewer Patricia Wells, is informative and a good read. *Le Guide des Hôtels-Restaurants Logis de France* (95FF) is a complete listing of Logis de France affiliates in France (see Mid-Range Hotels in the Accommodation section in this chapter).

The French-language *Guide du Routard* series is not as highly regarded as it was a few years back, but it's still popular with youngish French people travelling around their own country. The restaurant recommendations generally offer good value, but rock-bottom hotels rarely make an appearance and there are very few maps. Guide du Routard's *Hôtels & Restos de France* (99FF) lists mid-range hotels and restaurants all over the country; their *Restos & Bistrots de Paris* (42FF) deals with the capital.

Vegetarian Food The *Annuaire Vert* (Green Directory; 260FF if bought direct from the publisher, which includes shipping within France), issued annually by Éditions OCEP. (☎ 01 47 00 46 46; metro Saint Amboise), 11 Rue Saint Amboise, 75011 Paris, lists organic and macrobiotic food shops, vegetarian restaurants, *pharmaciens-herboristes* (naturopathic pharmacies) and all sorts of organisations. The listings are broken up by department.

History & Politics

A wide variety of excellent works on French history are available in English.

The Sun King by Nancy Mitford. A classic work on Louis XIV and the country he ruled from Versailles.

Citizens by Simon Schama. A truly monumental work that examines the first few years after the storming of the Bastille in 1789.

A Social History of the French Revolution by Christopher Hibbert. A highly readable social account of the same period.

A History of Modern France by Alfred Cobban. A very readable, three-volume history that covers the period from Louis XIV to 1962.

France – Fin de Siècle by Eugene Weber. A wide-ranging social history portrait of late 19th century France.

Pétain's Crime by Paul Webster. Examines the collaborationist Vichy government that ruled France during WWII.

Is Paris Burning? by Dominique Lapierre and Larry Collins. A dramatic account of the liberation of Paris in 1944.

Paris after the Liberation by Anthony Beevor and Artemis Cooper. A lively account of post-war Paris.

The Age of the Cathedrals by Georges Duby. An authoritative study of the relations between art and society in medieval France.

Cross Channel by Julian Barnes. A witty collection of key moments in shared Anglo-French history – from Joan of Arc to Eurostar.

You might also take a look at any of the books by Alistair Horne, which include *The Fall of Paris* (on the Commune of 1870-71), *The Price of Glory* (on the WWI Battle of Verdun) and *To Lose a Battle* (on the French defeat in 1940).

People, Society & Culture

The following books about France and its people make for fascinating reading and should be easy to find.

The French by Theodore Zeldin (A$19.95, £8.99, US$14). A highly acclaimed and very insightful survey of French passions, peculiarities and perspectives. It's intelligent, informative and humorous.

France Today by John Ardagh (£8.99, US$12). A good introduction to modern-day France, its politics, its people, and their idiosyncrasies.

Cultural Atlas of France by John Ardagh. A superb illustrated synopsis of French culture and history with a short section on each region of the country.

The Identity of France by Fernand Braudel. A very comprehensive (two volumes) look at the country and its people.

Past Imperfect: French Intellectuals, 1944-1956 by Tony Judt. An examination of the lively intellectual life of post-war France.

The Second Sex by Simone de Beauvoir. A systematic examination of women's inferior status. This study helped to inspire the modern feminist movement and is one of the most significant books of the existentialist era.

Feminism in France by Claire Duchen. A work that charts the progress of feminism in France from 1968 to the mid-1980s.

The Food of France by Waverley Root (US$10.95). An absolutely superb – indeed, the definitive – region-by-region introduction to French cuisine, first published in 1958.

French Literature

For suggested reading, see Literature in the Facts about France chapter. Most of the writers mentioned have been translated into English.

Literature & Travelogues by Foreign Writers

France has long attracted writers from all over the world, in part because of its tolerance of those people who deviate from conventional social norms.

A Moveable Feast by Ernest Hemingway. Portrays bohemian life in Paris between the wars.

A Year in Provence and ***Toujours Provence*** by Peter Mayle. Best-selling accounts of life in the Midi that take a witty look at the French through English eyes.

The Autobiography of Alice B Toklas by Gertrude Stein. An autobiographical account of the author's years in Paris, her salon at 27 Rue de Fleurus near the Luxembourg Gardens, and her friendships with Matisse, Picasso, Braque, Hemingway and others.

Tropic of Cancer and ***Tropic of Capricorn*** by Henry Miller. Steamy novels set in Paris, published in France in the 1930s but banned under obscenity laws in the UK and USA until the 1960s.

Down and Out in Paris and London by George Orwell. Orwell's famous account of the time he spent living with tramps in Paris and London in the late 1920s.

Flaubert's Parrot by Julian Barnes. A highly entertaining novel that pays witty homage to the great French writer.

NEWSPAPERS & MAGAZINES

French France's main daily newspapers are *Le Figaro* (right wing; aimed at professionals, business people and the bourgeoisie), *Le Monde* (centre-left; very popular with business people, professionals and intellectuals), *Le Parisien* (centre; middle-class, easy to read if your French is basic), *France Soir* (right; working and middle-class), *Libération* (left; popular with students and intellectuals) and *L'Humanité* (communist; working-class). *L'Équipe* is a daily devoted exclusively to sport.

English In cities and important towns, larger newsagents and those at railway stations usually carry the informative, intelligent *International Herald Tribune* (10FF), published jointly by the *New York Times* and the *Washington Post*. Issued daily (except Sunday), it is edited in Paris and has very good coverage of French news.

Other English-language papers you can find include the *Guardian*; the *Financial Times*; the *Times*; and the colourful *USA Today*. The *European* weekly newspaper is also readily available, as are *Newsweek*, *Time* and the *Economist*.

Paris-based *France USA Contacts* (or *FUSAC*), issued every fortnight, consists of hundreds of ads placed by both companies and individuals. It is distributed free at Paris' English-language bookshops, Anglophone embassies and the American Church (Map 4; ☎ 01 47 05 07 99; metro Pont de l'Alma) at 65 Quai d'Orsay (7e). It can be very helpful if you're looking for au pair work, short-term accommodation etc. To place an ad, contact FUSAC Centre d'Annonces (☎ 01 45 38 56 57; fax 01 45 38 98 94; metro Gaîté or Edgar Quinet) at 3 Rue Larochelle, 14e, weekdays from 10 am to 7 pm.

RADIO & TV

AM & FM Radio

You can pick up a mixture of the BBC World Service and BBC for Europe on 648 kHz AM. The Voice of America (VOA) is on 1197 kHz AM but reception is often poor.

In Paris, you can pick up an hour of Radio France Internationale (RFI) news in English every day at 3 pm on 738 kHz AM. Radio Netherlands often has programming in English on 1512 kHz AM.

France Info broadcasts the news headlines in French every few minutes. It can be picked up on 105.5 MHz FM in Paris.

Short-Wave & Long-Wave Radio

Pocket-size digital short-wave radios, such as those made by Sony and Phillips, make it easy to keep abreast of the world news in English wherever you are.

The BBC World Service can be heard on 6195, 9410, 11955, 12095 (a good daytime frequency) and 15575 kHz. BBC Radio 4 broadcasts on 198 kHz long wave. It carries BBC World Service programming in the wee hours of the morning.

The VOA broadcasts in English at various times of the day on 7170, 9535, 9680, 9760, 9770, 11805, 15135, 15205, 15255, 15410 and 15580 kHz.

Radio Canada International's half-hour English broadcasts, including relays of domestic CBC programs such as the World at Six, regularly come in loud and clear on one or more of these frequencies: 5995, 7235, 11690, 11890, 11935, 13650, 13670, 15150, 15325, 17820 and 17870 kHz.

Although Radio Australia directs most of its broadcasts to the Asia-Pacific region, it can sometimes be picked up in Western Europe. Frequencies to try include 9500, 11660 and 11880 kHz.

RFI can be picked up in English on 6175 kHz at 2 pm and at 6 pm (Central European Time).

Internet

Many local and international radio stations from every corner of the globe now 'broadcast' their program via the Internet, to be picked up by internet surfers using software like RealAudio, which can be easily downloaded. Station Web sites often include write-ups of the latest news and are an excellent source of short-wave schedules. TRS Consultants' Hot Links (www.trsc.com) has dozens of hypertext links relevant to Internet radio.

Stations with Internet relays include the BBC World Service (www.bbc.co.uk/worldservice), Radio Australia (www.abc.net.au/ra), Radio Canada International (www.rcinet.ca), CBC Radio (www.radio.cbc.can), Radio France Internationale (www.rfi.fr) and the Voice of America (www.voa.gov).

TV

Upmarket hotels often offer cable and satellite TV access to CNN, BBC Prime, Sky and other networks. Canal+ (pronounced 'ka-NAHL ploose'), a French subscription TV station available in many mid-range hotels, sometimes shows nondubbed English movies.

A variety of weekend-to-weekend TV listings are sold at all newsstands. Foreign movies that haven't been dubbed and are shown with subtitles are marked 'VO' or 'v.o.' (*version originale*).

VIDEO SYSTEMS

Unlike the rest of Western Europe and Australia, which use PAL (phase alternation line), French TV broadcasts are in SECAM (*système électronique couleur avec mémoire*). North America and Japan use a third incompatible system, NTSC (National Television Systems Committee). Non-SECAM TVs won't work in France. French videotapes can't be played on video recorders and TVs that lack a SECAM capability.

PHOTOGRAPHY & VIDEO

Film & Equipment

Colour-print film produced by Kodak and Fuji is widely available in supermarkets, photo shops and FNAC stores. At FNAC, a 36 exposure roll of Kodacolor costs 37/46FF for 100/400 ASA. One hour developing is widely available.

For slides (*diapositives*), count on paying at least 48/60/70FF for a 36 exposure roll of Ektachrome rated at 100/200/400 ASA; developing costs 28/32FF for 24/36 exposures.

Kodachrome costs 92FF for a 36 exposure roll of 64 ASA, including processing, but it may be a bit difficult to find now that it's no longer developed in France. Processing can take several weeks.

Photography

Photography is rarely forbidden, except in museums and art galleries. Of course, taking snapshots of military installations is not appreciated in any country. When photographing people, it is basic courtesy to ask permission. If you don't know any French, smile while pointing at your camera and they'll get the picture – as you probably will.

Video

Properly used, a video camera can give a fascinating record of your holiday. Unlike still photography, video 'flows' so, for example, you can shoot scenes of the countryside rolling past the train window, to give an overall impression that isn't possible with ordinary photos.

Video cameras these days have very sensitive microphones, and you might be surprised how much sound will be picked up. This can also be a problem if there is a lot of ambient noise – filming by the side of a busy road might seem OK when you do it, but viewing it back home might simply give you a cacophony of traffic noise. One good rule to follow for beginners is to try to film in long takes, and don't move the camera around too much. If your camera has a stabiliser, you can use it to obtain good footage while travelling on various means of transport, even on bumpy roads.

Make sure you keep the batteries charged and have the necessary charger, plugs and transformer for the country you are visiting. In most countries, it is possible to obtain video cartridges easily in large towns and cities, but make sure you buy the correct format. It is usually worth buying at least a few cartridges duty-free to start off your trip.

Finally, remember to follow the same rules regarding people's sensitivities as for still photography – always ask permission first.

Security

Be prepared to have your camera and film run through x-ray machines at airports and the entrances to sensitive public buildings. The gadgets are ostensibly film-safe up to 1000 ASA, and laptops and computer disks appear to pass through without losing data, but there is always some degree of risk.

The police and gendarmes who run x-ray machines often seem to treat a request that they hand-check something as casting doubt on the power and glory of the French Republic. Arguing almost never works, and being polite is only slightly more effective unless you can do it in French. You're most likely to get an affirmative response if you are deferential and your request is moderate: request that they hand-check your film, not your whole camera (which could, after all, conceal a bomb). They are usually amenable to checking computer disks by hand.

TIME

France uses the 24-hour clock, with the hours separated from the minutes by a lower-case letter 'h'. Thus, 15h30 is 3.30 pm, 21h50 is 9.50 pm, 00h30 is 12.30 am etc.

France is one hour ahead of (ie later than) GMT/UTC. During daylight-saving (or summer) time, which runs from the last Sunday in March to the last Sunday in October, France is two hours ahead of GMT/UTC. The UK and France are always one hour apart – when it's 6 pm in London, it's 7 pm in Paris.

New York is generally six hours behind Paris. This may fluctuate a bit depending on exactly when daylight-saving time begins and ends on both sides of the Atlantic.

The time difference to Melbourne and Sydney is complicated because daylight-saving time Down Under takes effect during the northern hemisphere's winter. The Australian east coast is between eight and 10 hours ahead of France.

ELECTRICITY

Voltage & Cycle

France and Monaco run on 220V at 50Hz AC. Andorra has a combination of 220V and 125V, both at 50Hz.

In the USA and Canada, the 120V electric supply is at 60Hz. While the usual travel transformers allow North American appliances to run in France without blowing out, they cannot change the Hz rate, which determines – among other things – the speed of electric motors. As a result, tape recorders not equipped with built-in adapters may function poorly.

There are two types of adapters; mixing them up will destroy either the transformer or your appliance, so be warned.

The 'heavy' kind, usually designed to handle 35 watts or less (see the tag) and often metal-clad, is designed for use with small electric devices such as radios, tape recorders and razors. The other kind, which weighs much less but is rated for up to 1500 watts, is for use only with appliances that contain heating elements, such as hair dryers and irons.

Plugs & Sockets

Old-type wall sockets, often rated at 600 watts, take two round prongs. The new kinds of sockets take fatter prongs and have a protruding earth (ground) prong.

Adapters to make new plugs fit into the old sockets are said to be illegal but are still available at electrical shops. In Paris, adapters and transformers of all sorts are available at the BHV department store (☎ 01 42 74 90 00; metro Hôtel de Ville) at 52-64 Rue de Rivoli (4e).

WEIGHTS & MEASURES

Metric System

France uses the metric system, which was invented by the French Academy of Sciences after the Revolution at the request of the National Assembly and adopted by the French government in 1795. Inspired by the same rationalist spirit in whose name churches were ransacked and turned into 'Temples of Reason', the metric system replaced a confusing welter of traditional units of measure, which lacked all logical basis and made conversion complicated and commerce chaotic.

For a conversion chart, see the inside back cover of this book.

Numbers

For numbers with four or more digits, the French use full stops or spaces where writers in English would use commas: one million therefore appears as 1.000.000 or 1 000 000. For decimals, on the other hand, the French use commas, so 1.75 comes out as 1,75.

LAUNDRY

Doing laundry while on the road in France is a pretty straightforward affair. To find a *laverie libre-service* (an unstaffed, self-service laundrette) near where you're staying, see Laundry under Information at the beginning of each city listing, or ask at your hotel or hostel.

French laundrettes are not cheap. They usually charge 18 to 20FF for a 6 or 7kg machine and 2/5FF for five/12 minutes of drying. Some laundrettes have self-service *nettoyage à sec* (dry cleaning) for about 60FF per 6kg.

In general, you deposit coins into a *monnayeur central* (central control box) – not the machine itself – and push a button that corresponds to the number of the machine you wish to operate. These gadgets are sometimes programmed to deactivate the washing machines an hour or so before closing time.

Except with the most modern systems, you're likely to need all sorts of peculiar coin combinations – change machines are often out of order, so come prepared. Coins, especially 2FF pieces, are handy for the *séchoirs* (dryers) and the *lessive* (laundry powder) dispenser.

You can choose between a number of washing cycles:

blanc – whites
couleur – colours
synthétique – synthetics
laine – woollens
prélavage – prewash cycle
lavage – wash cycle
rinçage – rinse cycle
essorage – spin-dry cycle

TOILETS

Public Toilets

Public toilets, signposted *toilettes* or *w.c.* (pronounced 'VEY SEY' or 'DOO-bluh VEY SEY'), are few and far between, though small towns often have them near the *mairie* (town hall). In Paris, there are a number of superb public toilets from the *belle époque* (eg at Place de la Madeleine), but you're more likely to come upon one of the tan, self-disinfecting toilet pods. Get your change ready: many public toilets cost 2 or 2.50FF.

In the absence of public amenities, you can try ducking into a fast-food outlet or a major department store. Except in the most tourist-filled areas, café owners are usually amenable to your using their toilets provided you ask politely (and with just a hint of urgency): *'Est-ce que je peux utiliser les toilettes, s'il vout plaît?'*. Some toilets are semico-ed: the washbasins and urinals are in a common area through which you pass to get to the closed toilet stalls.

In older cafés and even hotels, the amenities may consist of a *toilette à la turque* (Turkish-style toilet), a squat toilet that people all over Asia prefer to the sit-down type but which some westerners think is primitive and uncomfortable. The high-pressure flushing mechanism will soak your feet if you don't step back before pulling the cord. In some older buildings, the toilets used by ground floor businesses (eg restaurants) are tiny affairs accessed via an interior courtyard. Many hall toilets are in a little room all their own, with the nearest washbasin nowhere to be seen (in hotels, it's more than likely attached to the nearest shower).

In a few cities and towns, you still find flushless, kerbside *urinoirs* (urinals) reeking with generations of urine.

Bidets

In many hotel rooms – even those without toilets or showers – you will find a bidet, a porcelain fixture that looks like a shallow toilet with a pop-up stopper in the base. Originally conceived to improve the personal hygiene of aristocratic women, its primary purpose is for washing the genitals and anal area, though its uses have expanded to include everything from hand-washing laundry to soaking your feet.

HEALTH

France is a healthy place. Your main risks are likely to be sunburn, foot blisters, insect bites and an upset stomach from eating and drinking too much. You might experience mild stomach problems if you're not used to copious amounts of rich cream and olive oil-based sauces, but you'll get used to it after a while.

Predeparture Planning

Immunisations No jabs are required to travel to France, but they may be necessary to visit other European countries if you're coming from an infected area – yellow fever is the most likely requirement. If you are travelling to France with stop-overs in Africa, Latin America or Asia, check with your travel agent or the embassies of the countries you plan to visit as early as you can before you depart.

However, there are a few routine vaccinations that are recommended whether you

Medical Kit Check List

When travelling, consider taking a basic medical kit including the following:

- ☐ **Aspirin** or **paracetamol** (acetaminophen in the US) – for general pain or fever.
- ☐ **Antihistamine** (such as Benadryl) – a decongestant for colds and allergies, to ease the itch from insect bites or stings, and to help prevent motion sickness. Antihistamines may cause sedation and interact with alcohol, so care should be taken when using them; take one you know and have used before, if possible.
- ☐ **Loperamide** (eg Imodium) or Lomotil for diarrhoea; prochlorperazine (eg Stemetil) or metaclopramide (eg Maxalon) is usually very good for nausea and vomiting.
- ☐ **Rehydration mixture** – to treat severe diarrhoea; particularly important when travelling with children.
- ☐ **Antiseptic**, such as povidone-iodine (eg Betadine) – for cuts and grazes.
- ☐ **Calamine lotion** or **aluminium sulphate spray** (eg Stingose) – to ease irritation from bites or stings.
- ☐ **Bandages** and **Band-Aids**.
- ☐ **Scissors, tweezers** and a **thermometer** (note that mercury thermometers are prohibited by airlines).
- ☐ **Cold and flu tablets** and **throat lozenges**. Pseudoephedrine hydrochloride (Sudafed) may be useful if flying with a cold to avoid ear damage.
- ☐ **Insect repellent**, **sunscreen**, a **chap stick** and **water purification tablets**.

are travelling or not, and this Health section assumes that you've had them: polio (usually administered during childhood), tetanus and diphtheria (usually administered during childhood, with a booster shot every 10 years), and sometimes measles. For details, see your doctor.

All vaccinations should be recorded on an International Health Certificate, available from your doctor or government health department. Don't leave this till the last minute, since certain vaccinations have to be spread out over a period of time. For details about getting immunised in Paris, see Vaccinations under Health in the Paris chapter.

Health Insurance Make sure that you have adequate health insurance. See Travel Insurance under documents in the Facts for the Visitor chapter for details.

Other Preparations Ensure that you're healthy before you start travelling. If you are going on a long trip make sure your teeth are OK. If you wear glasses take a spare pair and your prescription.

If you require a particular medication take an adequate supply, as it may not be available locally. Take part of the packaging showing the generic name, rather than the brand, which will make getting replacements easier. It's a good idea to have a legible prescription or letter from your doctor to show that you legally use the medication to avoid any problems.

Medical Treatment in France

Emergency numbers for ambulances, the police and the fire brigade are listed in this chapter under Emergency.

Many major hospitals are indicated on the maps in this book, and their addresses and phone numbers are mentioned in the text. Tourist offices and hotels can put you on to a doctor or dentist, and your embassy or consulate will probably know one who speaks your language. For details on hospitals in Paris, see Medical Services under Information in the Paris chapter.

Public Health System France has an extensive public health care system. Anyone (including foreigners) who is sick, even mildly so, can receive treatment in the *service des urgences* (casualty ward or emergency room) of any public hospital. Hospitals try to have people who speak English in the casualty wards, but this is not done systematically. If necessary, the hospital will call in an interpreter. It's an excellent idea to ask for a copy of the diagnosis – in English, if possible – in case your doctor back home is interested.

Getting treated for illness or injury in a public hospital costs much less in France than in many other western countries, especially the USA: being seen by a doctor (a *consultation*) costs about 150FF (235 to 250FF on Sunday and holidays, 275 to 350FF from 8 pm to 8 am). Seeing a specialist is a bit more expensive. Blood tests and other procedures, each of which has a standard fee, will increase this figure. Full hospitalisation costs from 3000FF a day. Hospitals usually ask that visitors from abroad settle accounts right after receiving treatment (residents of France are sent a bill in the mail).

Dental Care Most major hospitals offer dental services. For details on dental care options in Paris, see Medical Services under Information in the Paris chapter.

Pharmacies French pharmacies are almost always marked by a green cross, the neon components of which are lit when it's open. *Pharmaciens* (pharmacists) can often suggest treatments for minor ailments.

If you are prescribed medication, make sure you understand the dosage, and how often and when you should take it. It's a good idea to ask for a copy of the *ordonnance* (prescription) for your records.

French pharmacies coordinate their days and hours of closure so that a town or district isn't left without a place to buy medication. For details on the nearest *pharmacie de garde* (pharmacy on weekend/night duty), consult the door of any pharmacy, which will have such information posted.

Emergency

The following toll-free numbers can be dialled from any public phone or Point Phone in France without inserting a télécarte or coins:

SAMU medical treatment/ambulance	☎ 15
Police	☎ 17
Fire	☎ 18
Rape crisis hotline	☎ 0800 05 95 95

SOS Help This Paris-based, crisis hotline (☎ 01 47 23 80 80) is staffed daily from 3 to 11 pm. The volunteer staff – all of whom are native English speakers – are there to talk with English-speakers who are having difficulties and to make referrals for specific problems. They're also happy to give out practical information on less urgent matters.

SAMU When you ring ☎ 15 (also ☎ 01 45 67 50 50 in Paris), the 24-hour dispatchers of the Service d'Aide Médicale d'Urgence (Emergency Medical Aid Service) will take down details of your problem (there's usually someone on duty who speaks English) and then send out a private ambulance with a driver (250 to 300FF) or, if necessary, a mobile intensive care unit.

For less serious problems, SAMU can also dispatch a doctor for a house call. If you prefer to be taken to a particular hospital, mention this to the ambulance crew, as the usual procedure is to take you to the nearest one. In emergency cases (ie those requiring intensive care units), billing will be taken care of later. Otherwise, you need to pay in cash at the time you receive assistance.

Highway Emergencies There are *postes d'appel d'urgence* (emergency phones), mounted on bright orange posts, about every 4km along main highways and every 1.5 to 2km on autoroutes.

SOS Voyageurs Many large train stations (eg Marseille) have offices of SOS Voyageurs, an organisation of volunteers (mostly retirees) who try to help travellers having some sort of difficulty. If your pack has been stolen or your ticket lost, or if you just need somewhere to change your baby, they may be able to help. The staff can be sweet and helpful, but they are not very good in a crisis.

Basic Rules

Everyday Health Normal body temperature is 37°C (98.6°F); more than 2°C (4°F) higher indicates a high fever. The normal adult pulse rate is 60 to 100 per minute (children 80 to 100, babies 100 to 140). As a general rule the pulse increases about 20 beats per minute for each 1°C (2°F) rise in fever.

Respiration (breathing) rate is also an indicator of illness. Count the number of breaths per minute: between 12 and 20 is normal for adults and older children (up to 30 for younger children, 40 for babies). People with a high fever or serious respiratory illness breathe more quickly than normal. More than 40 shallow breaths a minute may indicate pneumonia.

Water Tap water all over France is safe to drink. However, unlike Switzerland, the water in most French fountains is not drinkable and – like the taps in some public toilets – may have a sign reading *eau non potable* (undrinkable water).

Always beware of natural sources of water. A burbling Alpine or Pyrenean stream may look crystal clear, but it's inadvisable to drink untreated water unless you're at the source and can see it coming out of the rocks.

It's very easy not to drink enough liquids, especially on hot days or at high altitudes – don't rely on feeling thirsty to indicate when you should drink. Not needing to urinate or very dark-yellow urine is a danger sign. France suffers from a singular lack of drinking fountains, so it's a good idea to carry a water bottle.

Water Purification The simplest way of purifying water is to boil it thoroughly. Vigorously boiling should be satisfactory, but at high altitude water boils at a lower temperature, so germs are less likely to be killed. You'll need to boil it for longer in these environments.

Simple filtering will not remove all dangerous organisms, so if you cannot boil water it should be treated chemically. Chlorine tablets (Puritabs, Steritabs or other brand names) will kill many pathogens, but not some parasites, like amoebic cysts and giardia. Iodine is more effective in purifying water and is available in tablet form (such as Potable Aqua). Follow the directions carefully and remember that too much iodine can be harmful.

Environmental Hazards

Altitude Sickness Lack of oxygen at high altitudes (over 2500m) affects most people to some extent. The affect may be mild or severe and occurs because less oxygen reaches the muscles and the brain at high altitude, requiring the heart and lungs to compensate by working harder. Symptoms of Acute Mountain Sickness (AMS) usually develop during the first 24 hours at altitude but may be delayed up to three weeks. Mild symptoms include headache, lethargy, dizziness, difficulty sleeping and loss of appetite. There is no hard-and-fast rule as to what is too high: AMS has been fatal at 3000m, although 3500 to 4500m is the usual range. Very few treks or ski runs in the Alps and Pyrenees reach heights of 3000m or more, so it's unlikely to be a major concern. Mild altitude problems will generally abate after a day or two, but if symptoms persist or become worse the only treatment is to descend – even 500m can help.

Fungal Infections Fungal infections occur more commonly in hot weather and are usually found on the scalp, between the toes or fingers, in the groin and on the body (ringworm). You get ringworm (which is a fungal infection, not a worm) from infected animals or other people. Moisture encourages these infections.

To prevent fungal infections wear loose, comfortable clothes, avoid artificial fibres, wash frequently and dry carefully. If you do get an infection, wash the infected area at least daily with a disinfectant or medicated soap and water, and rinse and dry well. Apply an antifungal cream or powder like tolnifate (Tinaderm). Try to expose the infected area to air or sunlight as much as possible and wash all towels and underwear in hot water, change them often and let them dry in the sun.

Heat Exhaustion Dehydration and salt deficiency can cause heat exhaustion. Take time to acclimatise to high temperatures, drink sufficient liquids and do not do anything too physically demanding.

Salt deficiency is characterised by fatigue, lethargy, headaches, giddiness and muscle cramps; salt tablets may help, but adding extra salt to your food is better.

Hypothermia Too much cold can be just as dangerous as too much heat. If you are trekking at high altitudes, be prepared.

Hypothermia occurs when the body loses heat faster than it can produce it and the core temperature of the body falls. It is surprisingly easy to progress from very cold to dangerously cold due to a combination of wind, wet clothing, fatigue and hunger, even if the air temperature is above freezing. It is best to dress in layers; silk, wool and some of the new artificial fibres are all good insulating materials. A hat is important, as a lot of heat is lost through the head. A strong, waterproof outer layer and a 'space' blanket for emergencies are essential. Carry basic supplies, including food containing simple sugars to generate heat quickly and fluid to drink.

Symptoms of hypothermia are exhaustion, numb skin (particularly toes and fingers), shivering, slurred speech, irrational or violent behaviour, lethargy, stumbling, dizzy spells, muscle cramps and violent bursts of energy. Irrationality may take the form of sufferers claiming they are warm and trying to take off their clothes.

To treat mild hypothermia, first get the person out of the wind and/or rain, remove their clothing if it's wet and replace it with dry, warm clothing. Give them hot liquids – not alcohol – and some high-kilojoule, easily digestible food. Do not rub victims, instead allow them to slowly warm themselves. This should be enough to treat the early stages of hypothermia. The early recognition and treatment of mild hypothermia is the only way to prevent severe hypothermia, which is a critical condition.

Jet Lag Jet lag is experienced when a person travels by air across more than three time zones (each time zone usually represents a one hour time difference). It occurs because many of the functions of the human body (such as temperature, pulse rate and emptying of the bladder and bowels) are regulated by internal 24-hour cycles. When we travel long distances rapidly, our bodies take time to adjust to the 'new time' of our destination, and we may experience fatigue, disorientation, insomnia, anxiety, impaired concentration and loss of appetite. These effects will usually be gone within three days of arrival, but to minimise the impact of jet lag:

- Rest for a couple of days prior to departure.
- Try to select flight schedules that minimise sleep deprivation; arriving late in the day means you can go to sleep soon after you arrive. For very long flights, try to organise a stopover.
- Avoid excessive eating (which bloats the stomach) and alcohol (which causes dehydration) during the flight. Instead, drink plenty of non-carbonated, non-alcoholic drinks such as fruit juice or water.
- Avoid smoking.
- Make yourself comfortable by wearing loose-fitting clothes and perhaps bringing an eye mask and ear plugs to help you sleep.
- Reset your watch immediately on boarding and try to sleep at the appropriate time for the time zone you are travelling to.

Motion Sickness Eating lightly before and during a trip will reduce the chances of motion sickness. If you are prone to motion sickness try to find a place that minimises movement – near the wing on aircraft, close to midships on boats, near the centre on buses. Fresh air usually helps; reading and cigarette smoke don't. Commercial motion-sickness preparations, which can cause drowsiness, have to be taken before the trip commences. Ginger (available in capsule form) and peppermint (including mint-flavoured sweets) are natural preventatives.

Prickly Heat Prickly heat is an itchy rash caused by excessive perspiration trapped under the skin. It usually strikes people who have just arrived in a hot climate. Keeping cool, bathing often, drying the skin and using a mild talcum or prickly heat powder or resorting to air-conditioning may help.

Sunburn You can get sunburned surprisingly quickly, even through cloud. Use a sunscreen, hat, and barrier cream for your nose and lips. Calamine lotion or Stingose are good for mild sunburn. Protect your eyes with good quality sunglasses, particularly if you will be near water, sand or snow.

Hay Fever Hay fever sufferers should be aware that the pollen count in certain parts of southern France, particularly Provence and Corsica, is especially high in May and June.

Infectious Diseases

Diarrhoea Simple things like a change of water, food or climate can all cause a mild bout of diarrhoea, but a few rushed toilet trips with no other symptoms is not indicative of a major problem.

Dehydration is the main danger with any diarrhoea, particularly in children or the elderly as dehydration can occur quite quickly. Under all circumstances *fluid replacement* (at least equal to the volume being lost) is the most important thing to remember. Weak black tea with a little sugar, soda water, or soft drinks allowed to go flat and diluted 50% with clean water are all good. Keep drinking small amounts often. Stick to a bland diet as you recover.

Hepatitis There are almost 300 million chronic carriers of hepatitis B in the world. It is spread through contact with infected blood, blood products or body fluids, for example through sexual contact, unsterilised needles and blood transfusions, or contact with blood via small breaks in the skin. Other risk situations include having a shave, tattoo, or having your body pierced with contaminated equipment. You should seek medical advice, but there is not much you can do apart from resting, drinking lots of fluids and eating lightly.

HIV & AIDS HIV, the Human Immunodeficiency Virus, develops into AIDS, Acquired Immune Deficiency Syndrome (SIDA in French), which is a fatal disease. HIV is a major problem in many countries. Any exposure to blood, blood products or body fluids may put the individual at risk. The disease is often transmitted through sexual contact or dirty needles – vaccinations, acupuncture, tattooing and body piercing can be potentially as dangerous as intravenous drug use. HIV/AIDS can also be spread through infected blood transfusions; some developing countries cannot afford to screen blood used for transfusions.

If you do need an injection, ask to see the syringe unwrapped in front of you, or take a needle and syringe pack with you.

Fear of HIV infection should never prevent you from seeking treatment for serious medical conditions.

AIDS & HIV Information For information on free and anonymous HIV-testing centres (*centres de dépistage*) in France, ring the SIDA Info Service toll-free, 24 hours a day, on ☎ 0800 84 08 00. Information is also available in the Marais district of Paris at Le Kiosque (☎ 01 44 78 00 00; metro Saint Paul), 36 Rue Geoffroy l'Asnier, 4e, and at another Le Kiosque in the Latin Quarter, 6 Rue Dante, 5e (☎ same; metro Maubert Mutualité). Both are open weekdays from 10 am to 12.30 pm and 1 to 7 pm, and on Saturday from 2 to 7 pm.

The offices of the Paris-based AIDES (☎ 01 44 52 00 00; metro Télégraphe) at 247 Rue de Belleville (19e), an organisation that works for the prevention of AIDS and assists AIDS sufferers, are staffed on weekdays from 2 to 6 pm. FACTS-Line (☎ 01 44 93 16 69) is an English-language help line in Paris for those with HIV or AIDS in operation Monday, Wednesday and Friday from 6 to 10 am.

Sexually Transmitted Diseases Gonorrhoea, herpes and syphilis are among these diseases; sores, blisters or rashes around the genitals, discharges or pain when urinating are common symptoms. In some STDs, such as wart virus or chlamydia, symptoms may be less marked or not observed at all especially in women. Syphilis symptoms eventually disappear completely but the disease continues and can cause severe problems in later years. While abstinence from sexual contact is the only 100% effective prevention, using condoms is also effective. The treatment of gonorrhoea and syphilis is with antibiotics. The different sexually transmitted diseases each require specific antibiotics. There is no cure for herpes or AIDS.

Condoms All pharmacies carry *préservatifs* (condoms), and many have 24 hour automatic condom dispensers outside the door. Some brasseries, discotheques, metro stations and WCs in petrol stations and cafés are also equipped with condom machines. Condoms that conform to French government standards are always marked with the letters NF (*norme française*) in black on a white oval inside a red-and-blue rectangle.

Cuts, Bites & Stings

Rabies is a fatal viral infection found in many countries. Many animals can be infected and it is their saliva that is infectious. Any bite, scratch or even lick from a warm-blooded, furry animal should be cleaned immediately and thoroughly. Scrub with soap and running water, and then apply alcohol or iodine solution. Medical help should be sought promptly to receive a course of injections to prevent the onset of symptoms and death.

Insect Bites & Stings Bee and wasp stings are usually painful rather than dangerous. However, in people who are allergic to them severe breathing difficulties may occur and they may require urgent medical care. Calamine lotion or Stingose spray will give relief, and ice packs will reduce the pain and swelling.

Jellyfish Local advice will help prevent your coming into contact with *méduses* (jellyfish) and their stinging tentacles, often found along the Mediterranean. Dousing the wound in vinegar will de-activate any stingers that have not 'fired'. Calamine lotion, antihistamines and analgesics may reduce the reaction and relieve the pain. The sting of the Portuguese man-of-war, which has a sail-like float and long tentacles, is painful but rarely fatal.

Leeches & Ticks You should check all over your body if you have been walking through a potentially tick-infested area, as ticks can cause skin infections and other more serious diseases. If a tick is found attached, press down around the tick's head with tweezers, grab the head and gently pull upwards. Avoid pulling the rear of the body as this may squeeze the tick's gut contents through the attached mouth parts into the skin, increasing the risk of infection and disease. Smearing chemicals on the tick will not make it let go and is not recommended.

Snakes To minimise your chances of being bitten always wear boots, socks and long trousers when walking through undergrowth where snakes may be present. Don't put your hands into holes or crevices, and be careful when collecting firewood.

Snake bites do not cause instantaneous death and antivenenes are usually available. Immediately wrap the bitten limb tightly, as you would for a sprained ankle, and then attach a splint to immobilise it. Keep the victim still and seek medical help, if possible with the dead snake for identification. Don't attempt to catch the snake if there is a possibility of being bitten again. And the use of tourniquets to stop the poison and sucking it out have now been comprehensively discredited.

Women's Health

Gynaecological Problems Sexually transmitted diseases are a major cause of vaginal problems. Symptoms include a smelly discharge, painful intercourse and sometimes a burning sensation when urinating. Male sexual partners must also be treated. Medical attention should be sought and remember in addition to these diseases HIV or hepatitis B may also be acquired during exposure. Besides abstinence, the best thing is to practise safe sex using condoms.

Antibiotic use, synthetic underwear, sweating and contraceptive pills can lead to fungal vaginal infections in hot climates. Maintaining good personal hygiene, and loose-fitting clothes and cotton underwear will help to prevent these infections.

Fungal infections, characterised by a rash, itch and discharge, can be treated with a vinegar or lemon-juice douche, or with yoghurt. Nystatin, miconazole or clotrimazole pessaries or vaginal cream are the usual treatment.

WOMEN TRAVELLERS

Attitudes Towards Women

Women were given the right to vote in 1945 by De Gaulle's short-lived post-war government, but until 1964 a woman needed her husband's permission to open a bank account or get a passport. It was in such an environment that Simone de Beauvoir wrote *Le Deuxième Sexe* (The Second Sex) in 1949.

Safety Precautions

Women tend to attract more unwanted attention than men, but female travellers need not walk around France in fear: people are rarely assaulted on the street. However, the French seem to have given relatively little thought to sexual harassment (*harcèlement sexuel*), and many men (and some women) still think that to stare suavely at a passing woman is to pay her a flattering compliment.

Physical attack is very unlikely but, of course, it does happen. As in any country, the best way to avoid being assaulted is to be conscious of your surroundings and aware of situations that could be potentially dangerous: deserted streets, lonely beaches, dark corners of large train stations etc. Using the metros until late at night is generally OK, as stations are rarely deserted, but there are a few to avoid. See Dangers & Annoyances in the Paris chapter for details.

France's national rape-crisis hotline (☎ 0800 05 95 95) can be reached toll-free from any telephone without using a phonecard. Staffed by volunteers Monday to Friday from 10 am to 6 pm, it's run by a women's organisation called Viols Femmes Informations, whose Paris office is at 9 Villa d'Este, 13e (metro Porte d'Ivry).

In an emergency, you can always call the police (☎ 17), who will take you to the hospital. In Paris, medical, psychological and legal services are available to people referred by the police at the 24-hour Service Médico-Judiciaire of the Hôtel Dieu (☎ 01 42 34 82 34).

Organisations

France's women's liberation movement flourished along with its counterparts in other western countries in the late 1960s and early 70s but by the mid-80s was pretty moribund. For reasons that have more to do with French society than anything else, few women's groups function as the kind of supportive social institutions that have been formed in the USA, UK and Australia.

The women-only Maison des Femmes (Map 5; ☎ 01 43 43 41 13; metro Reuilly Diderot) at 163 Rue Charenton (12e) is the main meeting place for women of all ages and nationalities. It is staffed on Wednesday from 4 to 7 pm and on Saturday from 3 to 6 pm.

GAY & LESBIAN TRAVELLERS

France is one of Europe's most liberal countries when it comes to homosexuality, in part because of the long French tradition of public tolerance towards groups of people who chose not to live by conventional social codes. In addition to the large gay and lesbian communities in Paris, a thriving gay centre since the late 1970s, there are active communities in Cannes, Lyon, Marseille, Nice, Toulouse and many other provincial cities. France's lesbian scene is much less public than its gay counterpart and is centred mainly around women's cafés and bars.

Gay Pride marches are held in Paris, Marseille, Montpellier, Nantes, Rennes and other cities each year in June. For details, contact Paris' Centre Gai et Lesbien.

For information on AIDS and free, anonymous HIV tests, see HIV & AIDS in the Health section in this chapter.

Organisations

Most of France's major gay organisations are based in Paris and include the following:

Centre Gai et Lesbien (CGL; Map 5; ☎ 01 43 57 21 47; metro Ledru Rollin), 3 Rue Keller, 11e. The bar, library etc are open Monday to Saturday from 2 to 8 pm; Café Positif, open on Sunday from 2 to 7 pm, is mainly for people who are HIV positive.

Écoute Gaie – a hotline (☎ 01 44 93 01 02) for gays and lesbians staffed on weekdays from 6 to 10 pm and on Saturday from 6 to 8 pm.

Act Up Paris (☎ 01 48 06 13 89 for a recording; Minitel 3615 ACTUP; actupp@compuserve.com; www.actupp.org; metro Voltaire), 45 Rue Sedaine, 11e. Meetings are held every Tuesday night at 7.30 pm at the École des Beaux Arts, 14 Rue Bonaparte, 6e (Map 6; metro Saint Germain des Prés).

Association des Médecins Gais (☎ 01 48 05 81 71), BP 433, 75527 Paris CEDEX 11. The Association of Gay Doctors, based in the CGL, deals with health issues of special importance to gays. Staffed on Wednesday from 6 to 8 pm and on Saturday from 2 to 4 pm.

Gay Publications

Among the more serious gay publications are the CGL's monthly called *3 Keller* (15FF) and Act Up's monthly called *Action* (free). *Gay* (35FF) is a monthly national magazine available at newsstands everywhere.

Published weekly, *e.m@le* has interviews, gossip and articles (in French), among the best listings of gay clubs, bars and associations, and personal classifieds.

It is available free at gay venues or for 8FF at newsagents. *VIP*, published monthly, has fewer listings and more articles (20FF; free at gay venues). *Hyzberg*, the 'free gay and lesbian monthly magazine' contains listings and articles on Paris and selected areas in the rest of France – mostly about and for men. The semi-monthly *Homosphere* (free) is essentially just a listing of personal ads. *Le Nouveau HH* (22FF; free at gay venues) has personals and some articles.

Guidebooks include:

Guide Gai Pied A predominantly male, French and English-language annual guide (79FF) to France (about 80 pages on Paris) that is published by Les Éditions du Triangle Rose (☎ 01 43 14 73 00; www.gaipied.fr).

Spartacus International Gay Guide A male-only guide (180FF; US$32.95) to the world with more than 100 pages devoted to France (28 pages on Paris).

Boy's Gay Guide A French & English guide (70FF) to Paris with information of particular interest to gays and lesbians.

Guide Exes An annual guide (60FF) for both gays and lesbians published by Exes.

Lesbian Publications

The monthly national magazine, *Lesbia* (25FF; ☎ 01 43 48 89 54), gives a rundown of what's happening around the country. *Les Nanas*, a freebie appearing every other month, is for women only. *Dyke Guide* is a new bilingual guide (59FF) for lesbians published by AT Productions.

Most of these titles are available from Les Mots à la Bouche (see Bookshops under Information in the Paris chapter).

DISABLED TRAVELLERS

France is not particularly well equipped for *handicapés* (disabled people): kerb ramps are few and far between, older public facilities and budget hotels often lack lifts, cobblestone streets are a nightmare to navigate in a wheelchair, and the Paris metro, most of it built decades ago, is hopeless. But physically challenged people who would like to visit Paris can overcome these problems. Most hotels with two or more stars are equipped with lifts, and Michelin's *Guide Rouge* indicates hotels with lifts and facilities for disabled people. In Paris both the Foyer International d'Accueil de Paris Jean Monnet and the Centre International de Séjour de Paris Kellermann have facilities for disabled travellers (see Hostels & Foyers under Places to Stay in the Paris chapter).

In recent years the SNCF has made efforts to make its trains more accessible to people with physical disabilities. A traveller in a wheelchair (*fauteuil roulant*) can travel in the wheelchair in both TGV and regular trains provided they make a reservation by phone or at a train station at least a few hours before departure. Details are available in SNCF's booklet *Guide du Voyageur à Mobilité Réduite*. You can also contact SNCF Accessibilité on toll-free ☎ 0800 15 47 53.

In some places vehicles outfitted for people in wheelchairs provide transport within the city. Details are available from the Groupement pour l'Insertion des Personnes Handicapées Physiques (☎ 01 41 83 15 15) at 98 Rue de la Porte Jaune, 92210 Saint Cloud.

General publications you might look for include:

Holidays and Travel Abroad: A Guide for Disabled People An annual publication (UK£5) that gives a good overview of facilities available to disabled travellers in Europe. Published in even-numbered years by the Royal Association for Disability & Rehabilitation (☎ 0171-250 3222 or, after June 1999, ☎ 020-7250 3222), 12 City Forum, 250 City Rd, London EC1V 8AF.

Paris & Île de France pour Tous Available from the Paris tourist office (60FF).

Gîtes Accessibles aux Personnes Handicapés A guide (60FF) to *gîtes ruraux* and *chambres d'hôtes* with disabled access. Published by Gîtes de France (see Gîtes Ruraux & B&Bs under Accommodation in this chapter).

Guide du Voyageur à Mobilité Réduite An SNCF pamphlet that details services available to train travellers in wheelchairs. One page is in English.

Access in Paris A complete, 245 page guide to Paris for the disabled is published by Quiller Press (☎ 0171-499 6529 or, after June 1999, ☎ 020-7499 6529), 46 Lillie Rd, SW6 London.

SENIOR TRAVELLERS

Senior citizens are entitled to discounts in France on things like public transport, museum admission fees etc, provided they show proof of their age. In some cases they might need a special pass. See Seniors' Card in the Visas & Documents section for details.

TRAVEL WITH CHILDREN

Successful travel with young children requires planning and effort. Don't try to overdo things; even for adults, packing too much into the time available can cause problems. And make sure the activities include the kids as well – balance that day at the Louvre in Paris with a visit to the city's zoo in the Jardin des Plantes or even Disneyland Paris (see that section in the Day Trips from Paris chapter). Include the kids in the trip planning; if they've helped to work out where you will be going, they will be much more interested when they get there. Lonely Planet's *Travel with Children* is a good source of information.

Most car-rental firms in France have children's safety seats for hire at a nominal cost, but it is essential that you book them in advance. The same goes for highchairs and cots (cribs); they're standard in most restaurants and hotels but numbers are limited. The choice of baby food, infant formulas, soy and cow's milk, disposable nappies (diapers) and the like is as great in French supermarkets as it is back home, but the opening hours may be quite different. Run out of nappies on Saturday afternoon and you're facing a very long and messy weekend.

The weekly entertainment magazine *L'Officiel des Spectacles* advertises babysitting services (*gardes d'enfants*) available in Paris. For a list, see Paris for Children in the Paris chapter.

DANGERS & ANNOYANCES

In general, France is a pretty safe place in which to live and travel. Though property crime – especially theft involving vehicles – is a *major* problem, it is extremely unlikely that you will be physically assaulted while walking down the street.

Theft

By far the biggest crime problem in France for tourists is theft (*vol*). Most thieves are after cash or valuables, but they often end up with passports, address books, personal mementos and other items and their loss is likely to put you in a long-term bad mood. You may also have to rush off to your nearest consulate to sort out the missing documents.

The problems you're most likely to encounter are thefts from – and of – cars, pickpocketing and the snatching of daypacks or women's handbags, particularly in dense crowds (eg at busy train stations, on rush-hour public transport, in fast-food joints and in cinemas). A common ploy is for one person to distract you while another zips through your pockets. The south of France seems to have more crime than the north – the Côte d'Azur and Provence are notorious.

Although there's no need whatsoever to travel in fear, a few simple precautions will minimise your chances of being ripped off.

Before Leaving Home Photocopy your passport, credit cards, driver's licence, plane ticket and other important documents, such as your address book and travellers cheques receipts – leave one copy of each document at home and keep another one with you, separate from the originals. Some people even bring along a photocopy of their birth certificate, which is useful if you have to replace a passport.

Write your name and address on the inside of your suitcase, backpack, daypack, address book, diary etc. If such items are lost or stolen and later recovered, the police will have at least some chance of finding you.

Documents & Money Always keep your money, credit cards, tickets, passport, driver's licence and other important documents in a money belt worn *inside* your trousers or skirt. Never carry them around in a daypack or waist pouches, which are easy for thieves to grab (or slice off) and sprint away with. The same goes for those little pouches that you wear around your neck.

Keep enough money for a day's travel separate from your money belt (eg in your daypack or suitcase). That way, you'll be penniless only if everything gets taken at once.

While theft from hotel rooms is pretty rare, it's a bad idea to leave cash or important documents in your room. Hostels are a fair bit riskier, since so many people are always passing through. If you don't want to carry your documents with you, ask the hotel or hostel's front desk to put them in the *coffre* (safe).

The most valuable things you have with you are exposed film, your address book and your diary: if your camera gets swiped, you can buy a new one, but your photos, address book and diary are irreplaceable. Except when you're travelling by aeroplane, such items are probably safest in your suitcase or main pack rather than in your daypack.

When going swimming, especially along the Côte d'Azur, try to leave valuables in the hotel or hostel safe. And while you're in the water, have members of your party take turns sitting with everyone's packs and clothes.

Watch out for counterfeit US banknotes, especially US$100 bills. And don't be tempted to do anyone a 'favour' by changing US cash for them unless you're sure it's genuine.

Watch out for con artists: if a deal seems too good to be true, it most definitely is. And without being paranoid, be wary of sudden friendships – you never know what your 'new friend' may be after.

While on the Move Be especially careful with your passport and important documents at airports: pickpockets and professional passport thieves know that people are often careless when they first arrive in a foreign country.

When travelling by train, especially if you'll be sleeping, the safest place for small bags is under your seat. Large bags are best off in the overhead rack right above your head, and you may want to fasten them to the rack with the straps or even a small lock. Bags left in the luggage racks at the ends of the carriage are an easy target: as the train is pulling out of a station, a thief can grab your pack and hop off; the authors of this guide have seen it happen. In sleeping compartments, make sure to lock the door at night.

Keep an eagle eye on your bags in train stations, airports, fast-food outlets, cinemas and at the beach. Anything you can do to make your equipment easy to watch and clumsy to carry will make it more difficult to snatch. Some people lock, zip or tie their daypack to their main pack. Affixing tiny locks to the zips will help keep out sticky fingers. When sitting in a cinema or outdoor café, you might also wrap one strap of your daypack around your leg (or the leg of your chair).

If you leave your bags at a left-luggage office or in a luggage locker (where available), treat your claim chit (or locker code) like cash: some audacious daypack thieves have been known to take stolen chits back to the train station and thus claim possession of the rest of their victims' belongings.

While Travelling by Car Parked cars and motorbikes, as well as the contents of vehicles (especially those cars with a rental company stickers or out-of-town, purchase-repurchase (red-coloured) or foreign plates) are favourite targets for thieves. The risk is especially high in the south of France, where theft victims – including one of the authors for this book – abound.

Never, ever leave anything valuable inside your car. Like other Europeans, many French people often carry their removable car radios with them whenever they park their vehicles. In fact, never leave anything at all in a parked car. Even a few old clothes, a handkerchief or an umbrella left lying in the backseat may attract the attention of a passing thief, who won't think twice about breaking a window or smashing a lock to see if there's a camera hidden underneath. Hiding your bags in the trunk is considered very risky; indeed, French people with hatchbacks often remove the plastic panel that covers the boot (trunk) so passing thieves can see that it's empty.

When you arrive in a new city or town, find a hotel and unload your belongings *before* doing any sightseeing that will involve leaving the car unattended. And on your last day in town, ask the hotel manager to store your luggage until after you've done any local touring, shopping or errands.

The threat of car break-ins is most likely to cramp your style when you've decided to leave town A in the morning and explore a few places on your way to town B, where you'll be spending the night. What are you supposed to do with your luggage while taking a day hike or lounging on the beach? If at all possible, design your day so you can check into a hotel *before* the day's sightseeing or leave your luggage in one of the lockers at a train or bus station. One of the authors of this book was consistently allowed to leave his baggage at the reception of various camping grounds; the people staffing these places are usually pretty easygoing and familiar with people on the go. Otherwise, short of parking outside a police station, you're stuck. When you stop for lunch at autoroute rest areas, keep the car in sight.

Racism

The rise in support for the extreme right-wing National Front in recent years reflects the growing racial intolerance in France, particularly against North African Muslims and, to a somewhat lesser extent, blacks from sub-Saharan Africa and France's former colonies and territories in the Caribbean.

In many parts of France, especially in the south (eg Provence and the Côte d'Azur), places of entertainment such as bars and discotheques are, for all intents and purposes, segregated: owners and their ferocious bouncers make it abundantly clear what sort of people are 'invited' to use their nominally private facilities and what sort are not. Such activities are possible in the land of *liberté*, *égalité* and *fraternité* because there is little civil rights enforcement.

Hunters

The hunting season usually runs from the end of September to the end of February. If you see signs reading *chasseurs* or *chasse gardé* strung up or tacked to trees, you might want to think twice about wandering into the area, especially if you're wearing anything that might make you resemble a deer. Unless the area is totally fenced off, it's not illegal to be there, but accidents do happen (50 French hunters die each year after being shot by other hunters).

Natural Dangers

There are strong undertows and currents along the Atlantic coast, particularly in south-western Brittany. If sleeping on a beach, always ensure you are above the high tide mark (especially on the north coast of Brittany).

Thunderstorms in the mountains and hot southern plains can be extremely sudden, violent and dangerous. It's a good idea to check the weather report before you set out on a long hike. If you're heading into the high country of the Alps or Pyrenees ensure you take extra food and water and that you have plenty of warm clothing.

LEGAL MATTERS

Police

Thanks to the Napoleonic Code (on which the French legal system is based), the police can pretty much search anyone they want to at any time – whether or not there is probable cause. They have been known to stop and search chartered coaches for drugs just because they are coming from Amsterdam.

France has two separate police forces. The Police Nationale, under the command of departmental prefects (and, in Paris, the Préfet de Police), includes the Police de l'Air et des Frontières (PAF), the border police. The Gendarmerie Nationale, a paramilitary force under the control of the Ministry of Defence, handles airports, borders etc.

The dreaded Compagnies Républicaines de Sécurité (CRS), riot police heavies, are part of the Police Nationale. You often see hundreds of them, equipped with the latest riot gear, at strikes or demonstrations.

Police with shoulder patches reading 'Police Municipale' are under the control of the local mayor.

If asked a question, cops are likely to be correct and helpful but no more than that (though you may get a salute). If the police stop you for any reason, be polite and remain calm. They have wide powers of search and seizure and, if they take a dislike to you, they may choose to use them. The police can, without any particular reason, decide to examine your passport, visa, carte de séjour etc.

French police are very strict about security, especially at airports. Do not leave baggage unattended: they're serious when they warn that suspicious objects will be summarily blown up.

Drinking & Driving

As elsewhere in the EU, the laws are very tough when it comes to drinking and driving, and for many years the slogan has been: *'Boire ou conduire, il faut choisir'* (To drink or to drive, you have to choose). The acceptable blood-alcohol limit is 0.05%, and drivers exceeding this amount face fines of up to 30,000FF plus up to two years in jail. Licences can also be immediately suspended.

Littering

The fine for littering is about 1000FF.

Drugs

Importing or exporting drugs can lead to a 10 to 30 year jail sentence. The fine for possession of drugs for personal use can be as high as 500,000FF.

Smoking

By nature many French people do not take seriously laws they consider stupid or intrusive; whether others feel the same is another matter. Laws banning smoking in public places do exist, for example, but no one pays much attention to them. In restaurants, diners will often smoke in the nonsmoking sections of restaurants – and the waiter will happily bring them an ashtray.

BUSINESS HOURS

Most museums are closed on either Monday or Tuesday, though in summer some open daily. A few places (eg the Louvre in Paris) stay open until almost 10 pm on one or two nights a week.

Small businesses are open daily, except Sunday and often Monday. Hours are usually 9 or 10 am to 6.30 or 7 pm, with a midday break from noon or 1 pm to 2 or 3 pm.

Supermarkets and hypermarkets are open Monday to Saturday; a few open on Sunday morning in July and August. Small food shops are mostly closed on Sunday morning or afternoon and Monday, so Saturday afternoon may be your last chance to stock up on provisions until Tuesday, unless you come across a supermarket, seven-day grocery or a boulangerie on duty by rotational agreement. Many restaurants in Paris are closed on Sunday.

In some parts of France, local laws require that most business establishments close for at least one day a week. Exceptions include family-run businesses, such as grocery stores and small restaurants, and places large enough to rotate staff so everyone gets to have a day off.

Since you can never tell which day of the week a certain merchant or restaurateur has chosen to take off, this book includes, where possible (summer times can be particularly unpredictable), details on weekly closures.

In July and August, loads of businesses tend to shut down: the owners and employees heading for the hills or the beaches for their annual vacation.

PUBLIC HOLIDAYS & SPECIAL EVENTS

The following *jours fériés* (public holidays) are observed in France:

1 January
Jour de l'An (New Year's Day)

Late March/April
Pâques (Easter Sunday) & *lundi de Pâques* (Easter Monday)

1 May
Fête du Travail (May Day)

8 May
Victoire 1945 – celebrates the Allied victory in Europe that ended WWII

May
L'Ascension (Ascension Thursday) – celebrated on the 40th day after Easter

Mid-May to mid-June
Pentecôte (Pentecost/Whit Sunday) & *lundi de Pentecôte* (Whit Monday) – celebrated on the 7th Sunday after Easter

14 July
Fête Nationale (Bastille Day/National Day)

15 August
L'Assomption (Assumption Day)

1 November
La Toussaint (All Saints' Day)

11 November
Le onze novembre (Remembrance Day) – celebrates the armistice of WWI

25 December
Noël (Christmas)

The following are *not* public holidays in France: Shrove Tuesday (Mardi Gras; the first day of Lent); Maundy (or Holy) Thursday (*jeudi saint*) and Good Friday (*vendredi saint*) just before Easter; and Boxing Day (26 December). Good Friday and Boxing Day, however, are holidays in Alsace.

Most museums and shops (but not cinemas, restaurants or most *boulangeries*) are closed on public holidays. When a holiday falls on a Tuesday or a Thursday, the French have a custom of making a *pont* (bridge) to the nearest weekend by taking off Monday or Friday as well. The doors of banks are a good place to look for announcements of upcoming long weekends.

France's national day, 14 July, commemorates the day in 1789 when defiant Parisians stormed the Bastille prison, thus beginning the French Revolution. Often called Bastille Day by English speakers, it is celebrated with great gusto in most of the country, and in many cities and towns it can seem as if every person and their poodle is out on the streets. In Paris and many provincial towns (eg Carcassonne), Bastille Day ends with a fireworks display.

On May Day, many people – including those marching in the traditional trade union parades – buy *muguets* (lilies of the valley), said to bring good luck, to give to friends. French law allows anyone to sell wild muguet on 1 May without a permit.

Most French cities have at least one major music, dance, theatre, cinema or art festival each year. Some villages hold *foires* (fairs) and *fêtes* (festivals) to honour anything from a local saint to the year's garlic crop. In this book, important annual events are listed under Special Events in many city and town listings; for precise details about dates, which change from year to year, contact the local tourist office. Remember that the largest festivals make it very difficult to find accommodation, so make reservations as far in advance as possible.

ACTIVITIES

France's varied geography and climate make it a superb place for a wide range of outdoor pursuits. Some hostels, eg those run by the Fédération Unie des Auberges de Jeunesse (FUAJ; see Hostels & Foyers in the Accommodation section of this chapter), offer week-long sports *stages* (training courses).

Little of France consists of pristine wilderness. Even the remotest regions are dotted with villages and crisscrossed by roads, power lines, hydroelectric projects etc. Not that there aren't beautiful, unspoiled places, but they're not – as in Australia or North America – a three day walk from the nearest road. On the other hand, to many travellers coming from built-up Britain (which supports roughly the same population) or other parts of continental Europe, parts of France will look almost empty.

Cycling

The French take their cycling very seriously, and whole parts of the country almost grind to a halt during the annual Tour de France (see the boxed text 'Helicopters and Taut Legs on Le Tour' and the Spectator Sports section later in this chapter).

A *vélo tout-terrain* (VTT; mountain bike) is a fantastic tool for exploring the countryside. Some GR and GRP trails (see Hiking later in this chapter) are open to mountain bikes, but take care not to startle hikers. A *piste cyclable* is a bicycle path.

Elsewhere in this chapter, information on topoguides for cyclists can be found under Guidebooks in the Books section, and there's a rundown on hiking/cycling maps in the Maps section.

For information on road rules, cycling organisations, transporting your bicycle and bike rental, see Bicycle in the Getting Around chapter. Details on places that rent bikes appear at the end of each city or town listing under Getting Around.

Skiing

France has more than 400 ski resorts in the Alps, the Jura, the Pyrenees, the Vosges, the Massif Central and even the mountains of Corsica. The ski season generally lasts from December to March or April, though it's shorter at low altitudes and longer high up in the Alps. Snow conditions can vary greatly from year to year. January and February tend to have the best overall conditions, but the slopes can be very crowded during the February-March school holidays. Although prices differ from place to place, *ski de piste* or *ski alpin* (downhill skiing) ends up being quite expensive because of the cost of equipment, lift tickets, accommodation and the customary après-ski drinking sessions. *Ski de fond* (cross-country skiing) is a lot cheaper.

France can claim a fair few superlatives in the world of skiing. The largest ski area in the world is Les Portes du Soleil at Morzine-Avoriaz, north-west of Chamonix. The longest vertical drop (2500m) in France is at Les Arcs, near Bourg Saint Maurice. The highest resort in Europe is Val Thorens (2300m), west of Méribel. Europe's largest skiable glacier, measuring almost 200 hectares, is at Les Deux Alpes in the spectacular Parc National des Écrins. One of the longest unofficial trails (20km) in France is in the Vallée Blanche at Chamonix; the longest official (groomed) one – some 16km – is the black-marked Sarenne Trail at Alpe d'Huez.

The Alps have some of Europe's finest – and priciest – ski facilities. In a few places, you can even ski on glaciers during the summer (for details, see the French Alps & the Jura chapter). The high-altitude downhill ski resorts in the Alps not only satisfy skiers at all levels but also offer good snowboarding and cross-country skiing. Two of the best ski areas are Les Trois Vallées (Three Valleys), which include the resorts of Méribel, Courchevel, Val Thorens and Les Menuires, and L'Espace Killy, with Val d'Isère and Tignes. Almost as good – and cheaper – are the resorts of Les Arcs and Alpe d'Huez. In these resorts the snow is the most plentiful, tends to be more powdery, the runs are long and varied, and off-piste skiing is among the best in the world.

Smaller, low-altitude stations, more suited to beginners and intermediates, include quite a few of the resorts in the Pyrenees (see Andorra, Cauterets and Vallée d'Aspe) and the Massif Central (see Le Mont Dore). They are much cheaper and less glitzy than their classier, more vertically challenging counterparts. In the Alps, low-altitude skiing is popular on the Vercors massif (see Around Grenoble in the French Alps & the Jura chapter).

Cross-country skiing is possible at high-altitude resorts but is usually much better in the valleys (eg on the 200km of trails around Le Grand Bornand and La Clusaz near Annecy). Undoubtedly some of the best trails are in the Jura range, around resorts like Métabief and Les Rousses.

One of the cheapest ways to ski in France is to buy a package deal before leaving home. Ask your travel agent for details.

Many hostels in the Alps offer affordable week-long packages in winter, including room, board, ski passes and sometimes equipment and lessons.

Outside France, French Government Tourist Offices (see Tourist Offices Abroad earlier in this chapter for addresses) can supply you with the annual *France: The Largest Ski Domain in the World*, a brochure with details on more than 50 French ski resorts. It is published by the Association des Mairies des Stations Françaises de Sports d'Hiver et d'Été (☎ 01 47 42 23 32; www .skifrance.fr; metro Havre Caumartin), better known as Ski France, based at 61 Blvd Haussmann, 75008 Paris. The Club Alpin Français office (see Hiking) may also be able to provide information.

During the snow season, the Thursday and Friday editions of the *International Herald Tribune* have a weekend ski report on the back page. By Minitel, information on snow conditions and some 100 ski stations is available on 3615 CORUS.

Hiking

France is crisscrossed by a staggering 120,000km of *sentiers balisés* (marked walking paths), which pass through every imaginable kind of terrain in every region of the country. No permits are needed for hiking, but there are restrictions on where you can camp, especially in national parks.

Probably the best known trails are the *sentiers de grande randonnée*, long-distance footpaths whose alphanumeric names begin with the letters GR and whose track indicators (*jalonnement* or *balisage*) consist of red and white stripes on trees, rocks, walls, posts etc. Some are many hundreds of kilometres long, such as the GR5, which goes from the Netherlands through Belgium, Luxembourg and the spectacular Alpine scenery of eastern France, before ending up in Nice. Others include the GR1, which circumnavigates the Paris metropolitan area; the GR3, which passes through the Loire Valley; the GR4, which meanders through the Massif Central; the popular GR10, which runs along the Pyrenees from the Mediterranean to the Atlantic; and the stunning GR20, which takes you to some of Corsica's highest peaks.

The *grandes randonnées de pays* (GRP) trails, whose markings are yellow and red, usually go in some sort of loop. These 'country walks' are designed for intense exploration of one particular area and usually take from a few days to a week, though some are longer.

Other types of trails include *sentiers de promenade randonnée* (PR), walking paths whose trail markings are yellow; *drailles*, paths used by cattle to get to high-altitude summer pastures; and *chemins de halage*, towpaths built in the days when canal barges were pulled by animals walking along the shore. Shorter day-hike trails are often known as *sentiers de petites randonnées* or *sentiers de pays*; many of them are circular so that you end up where you started.

The Fédération Française de la Randonnée Pédestre (FFRP), the publisher of most major topoguides (see Guidebooks – Hiking & Cycling under Books in this chapter), has an information centre in Paris at 64 Rue de Gergovie, 14e (☎ 01 45 45 31 02; fax 01 43 95 68 07; Minitel 3615 RANDO; metro Pernety), which is open Monday to Saturday from 10 am to 6 pm. There's an FFRP bookshop at 9 Rue Geoffroy Marie, 9e (☎ 01 44 89 93 90; metro Cadet).

Hotel treks are unguided hikes in which a trekking company arranges for accommodation, hearty dinners and transport for your pack so you can hike unencumbered from village to village. Headwater (☎ 0160-648 699), a company based in Cheshire (UK) that arranges such treks, is represented in Australia by Peregrine (☎ 03-9663 8611).

The Club Alpin Français (☎ 01 53 72 88 00; fax 01 42 02 24 18; Minitel 3615 CALPIN; metro Laumière), 24 Ave de Laumière, 75019 Paris, generally provides services (eg courses, group hikes) only to its members, though the *refuges* it maintains are open to everyone. Membership costs 465FF per year (250FF for people aged 18 to 24) and includes various kinds of insurance.

For details on *refuges* and other overnight accommodation for hikers, such as *gîtes d'étape*, see the Accommodation section of this chapter.

Mountaineering & Rock Climbing

If you're interested in *alpinisme* (mountaineering) or *escalade* (rock climbing), you can arrange climbs with professional guides through the Club Alpin Français (see the Hiking section earlier).

Swimming

France has lovely beaches along all of its coasts – the English Channel, the Atlantic and the Mediterranean (including the coast of Corsica) – as well as on lakes such as Lac d'Annecy and Lake Geneva. The fine, sandy beaches along the family-oriented Atlantic coast (eg near La Rochelle) are much less crowded than their rather pebbly counterparts on the Côte d'Azur. Corsica is crowded only during July and August. Beaches along the Channel and in southern Brittany are cooler than those farther south. The public is free to use any beach not marked as private in France.

Topless bathing for women is pretty much the norm in France – if other people are doing it, you can assume it's OK. For information on nude bathing, see Naturism later in this section.

Surfing & Windsurfing

The best surfing in France is on the Atlantic coast around Biarritz, where waves can reach heights of 4m. Windsurfing is popular wherever there's water and a breeze, and renting equipment is often possible on lakes.

Rafting & Canoeing

White-water rafting, canoeing and kayaking are practised on many French rivers, including those that flow down from the Massif Central (eg the Dordogne River) and the Alps. Farther south, the Gorges du Verdon are popular for white-water rafting, while canoe and kayak enthusiasts tend to favour the Gorges du Tarn. The Fédération Française de Canoë-Kayak (FFCK; ☎ 01 45 11 08 50; fax 01 48 86 13 25), 87 Quai de la Marne, 94340 Joinville-le-Pont, can supply information on canoeing and kayaking clubs around the country.

Canal Boating

One of the most relaxing ways to see France is to rent a houseboat for a leisurely cruise along canals and navigable rivers, whose slow-moving and often tree-lined channels pass through some of the most beautiful countryside in Europe. Changes in altitude are taken care of by a system of *écluses* (locks), where you can often hop ashore to meet the lock-keeper, who often sells local cheeses, wine and fruit as a sideline. It is good form to help open the sluice gates. There is no charge to pass through a lock, though some people leave a tip.

Generally, the boats available for hire can accommodate from four to 12 passengers and are outfitted with sleeping berths, a shower, a toilet, sheets, blankets, pillows, a fridge, a hotplate, an oven and kitchen utensils. Anyone over 18 can pilot a river boat without a special licence (though you do need a licence to fish). Before departure, first-time skippers are given instructions on relevant laws and how to operate the boat – learning the ropes takes only about a half-hour. The speed limit is 6km/h on canals and 10km/h on rivers.

Since the canals are usually quite wide (almost 40m in many cases), there's plenty of space to moor your craft (or stop for the night) pretty much wherever you please: near a village, next to an interesting historical site, in the middle of nowhere. Figure on covering about 20 to 25km a day. Personal equipment you might want to bring along includes binoculars, tennis shoes, wet-weather gear and bicycles (the last of which are available from many boat-rental companies).

Rental in France Canal boats can be rented for a weekend (late Friday afternoon to Monday morning), a short week (Monday afternoon to Friday morning), a week (Saturday afternoon to Saturday morning or

Monday afternoon to Monday morning) or a number of weeks. From late June to early September, when demand is very high, the minimum rental period is generally one week.

For a four person craft, the rates for a weekend or short week generally range from 2000FF (mid-October to mid-April) to 4000FF (in summer, if they're not already booked). Weekly rates, generally 3500 to 4000FF in winter, start at 6000FF in July and August. These prices do not include fuel, for which you should figure on paying about 500FF a week, depending on how far you travel.

Although for much of the year rental can be arranged with only a day or two of advance notice, you're better off reserving well in advance, especially if you're not familiar with the exact dates of France's holiday weekends and overlapping school holiday periods. To get a boat in July and August, reservations must be made at least several months ahead.

Many companies require that you pay 30 or 40% of the total at the time you make your reservation and the remainder four weeks before your scheduled holiday. Quite a few companies refuse payment by credit card but do accept personal cheques (even from overseas), bank transfers, bank cheques, Eurocheques and postal money orders. Before sailing away, you have to leave a deposit equal to the boat's insurance excess (deductible), usually somewhere between 2000 and 5000FF.

For details on rental companies, see Canal Boating under Activities in the Paris chapter and in the Burgundy, Languedoc-Roussillon, Brittany, and Limousin, Périgord & Quercy chapters.

For a booklet listing boat rental companies, contact the Syndicat National des Loueurs de Bateaux de Plaisance (☎ 01 44 37 04 00; fax 01 45 77 21 88; metro Javel) at Port de Javel, 75015 Paris.

Rental from Abroad Crown Blue Line offers canal boat rental in Brittany, Alsace, Languedoc and the Camargue area of Provence and along the Canal du Midi in the Toulouse area. In the UK, contact Crown Travel (☎ 01603-630513; fax 664298) at 8 Ber Street, Norwich NR1 3EJ.

Fishing

Fishing in France requires not only the purchase of a licence but familiarity with all sorts of stock conservation rules that differ from region to region and even from river to river. Dates when fishing is permitted are strictly controlled and, during part of the year, may be limited to certain days of the week. There are rules about the types of lures and hooks you can use, the minimum legal size for each species (that, too, can vary from stream to stream) and the number of fish you can catch in the course of a day. Most tackle shops should have details on any local (often department-based) fishing organisations.

Bird Watching

Places of ornithological interest include Le Teich (near Arcachon), Provence's spectacular Camargue delta, and the Parc Naturel Régional des Pyrénées.

Horse Riding

Équitation (horse riding) is popular in many park areas. The opportunities for riding and the variety of trails available is great, from Alpine paths to the trails that run through the Forêt de Fontainebleau. Some GR and GRP trails (see the Hiking section earlier) are open to horses. See the Champagne, Far Northern France, Atlantic Coast, The French Basque Country, The Pyrenees, Provence, Andorra, Languedoc-Roussillon and Burgundy chapters for details or inquire at local tourist offices.

Hang-Gliding & Parapente

Deltaplane (hang-gliding) and *parapente* are all the rage in many parts of France, particularly in the Alps (see the Annecy and Chamonix listings), the Massif Central (see Le Mont Dore), Languedoc (see Millau), Andorra (see Soldeu-El Tarter Ski Area) and the Pyrenees (see Bedous).

Parapente, or parasailing, involves running off the top of a mountain dragging a rectangular parachute behind you until it opens. The chute then fills with air and, acting like an aircraft wing, lifts you up off the ground. If the thermals are good you can stay up for hours, circling the area peacefully.

Newcomers can try out parapente with a *baptême de l'air* (tandem introductory flight) for 250 to 500FF. A five day *stage d'initiation* (beginners course) costs 2000 to 3500FF. See the Pyrenees, Alps, Massif Central and Languedoc-Roussillon chapters for more information.

Gliding

Vol à voile (gliding) is most popular in France's south, where the temperatures are warmer and the thermals better. Causse Méjean (see Florac in the Languedoc-Roussillon chapter) is one of the most popular spots. For the addresses and details of gliding clubs around France, contact the Fédération Française de Vol à Voile (FFVV; ☎ 01 45 44 04 78; fax 01 45 44 71 93; metro Sèvres Babylone) at 29 Rue de Sèvres, 75006 Paris.

Ballooning

For details on *montgolfière* (hot-air balloon) flights, see Hot-Air Ballooning under Activities at the beginning of the Burgundy chapter and under Organised Tours in the Loire Valley chapter.

Spelunking

Speleology, the scientific study of caves, was pioneered by the Frenchman Édouard-André Martel late last century, and France still has some great places for cave exploration. The Club Alpin Français (see Hiking) can supply details about organised activities.

Spas & Thalassotherapy

For over a century, the French have been keen fans of *thermalisme* (water cures), for which visitors with ailments ranging from rheumatism to serious internal disorders flock to hot spring resorts.

Once the domain of the wealthy, spa centres now offer fitness packages intended to appeal to a broad range of people of all ages. Many of the resorts are in the volcanic Massif Central – Vichy is the best known – but there are others along the shore of Lake Geneva and in the Pyrenees (eg Cauterets).

A salty variant of thermalisme is *thalassothérapie* (sea-water therapy). Centres dot the Côte d'Azur, the Atlantic Coast and the Brittany coast.

Naturism

France is one of Europe's most popular venues for *naturisme*. Naturist centres, most of them – not surprisingly – in the sunny south (Languedoc, Roussillon, Provence, the Côte d'Azur, the Gironde region of the Atlantic coast), range from small rural camp sites to large chalet villages with cinemas, tennis courts and shops. Their common denominator is water – virtually all have access to the sea, a lake, a river or, at the very least, a pool. A few are active year-round, but most are open from April to October, and for insurance and security reasons virtually all require that visitors have either a *carte associatif* (membership card) from a naturist club or an International Naturist Federation (INF) *passeport naturiste* (naturist passport). The latter is available at many naturist holiday centres for about 120FF. Nude bathing and sunbathing is also practised all over France on relatively isolated strips of beach.

The Fédération Française du Naturisme (French Naturist Federation; ☎ 01 47 64 32 82; fax 01 47 64 32 63; Minitel 3615 NATURISM; metro Wagram), 65 Rue de Tocqueville, 75017 Paris, has a variety of brochures on *au naturel* clubs and leisure activities, virtually all of them are family-oriented. Their glossy magazine, *Nat-Info* (also known as *Les Nouvelles Vacances*; 30FF), published four times a year, has information on scores of naturist centres and is available from newsstands. Abroad, French Government Tourist Offices can supply you with a copy of *Naturism in France*, which has details on 65 major holiday centres.

COURSES
Language

All manner of French courses, lasting from two weeks to nine months, are held in Paris and a variety of provincial cities and towns. A number of language schools start new courses at the beginning of every month. Many of the organisations detailed below can also arrange homestays or other accommodation.

The Service Culturel (French Cultural Service) has reams of information on studying in France, as do French government tourist offices and consulates. In Paris, you might also contact the Ministry of Tourism-sponsored International Cultural Organisation (ICO; ☎ 01 42 36 47 18; fax 01 40 26 34 45; metro Châtelet) at 55 Rue de Rivoli (1er). The mailing address is 55 Rue de Rivoli, BP 2701, 75027 Paris CEDEX.

Within France, lists of addresses are available from a Centre Régional Information Jeunesse (CRIJ), located in almost two dozen cities nationwide (see Work later in this chapter). The Paris tourist office has a list of programs in Paris.

Among the offices of the French Cultural Service, many of them attached to embassies, are the following:

Australia
(☎ 02-6216 0100; fax 6273 5450)
6 Perth Ave, Yarralumla, ACT 2600

Canada
(☎ 416-925 0025; fax 925 2560)
175 Bloor St East, Suite 606, Toronto, Ont M4W 3R8

Ireland
(☎ 01-676 2197; fax 676 9403)
1 Kildare St, Dublin 2

New Zealand
(☎ 04-494 1320; fax 499 0546)
1-3 Willeston St, PO Box 53, Wellington

Singapore
(☎ 468 4663; fax 466 3296)
5 Gallop Rd, Singapore 258960

South Africa
(☎ 012-435 658)
795 George Ave, Arcadia, 0132 Pretoria

UK
(☎ 0171-838 2055 or, after June 1999, ☎ 020 7838 2055; fax 838 2088 or 7838 2088)
23 Cromwell Rd, London SW7 2EL

USA
(☎ 212-439 1400)
972 Fifth Ave, New York, NY 10021

Paris The many French-language schools in the capital include:

Accord Language School
(Map 7; ☎ 01 42 36 24 95; fax 01 42 21 17 91; accordel@easynet.fr; metro Les Halles)
52 Rue Montmartre, 75002 Paris. A dynamic language school whose classes get high marks from students. Four-week classes on five levels with a maximum of 14 students (and often less) start at the beginning of each month of the year. They cost 1800FF for the *cours semi-intensif* in winter (eight hours a week) and, in summer, 2700FF (15 hours a week over three weeks). The *cours intensif* classes (20 hours a week over four weeks in winter, 25 hours a week over three weeks in summer) cost 3800FF and are held in the morning. The *cours extensif* (three hours a week for three months), which meets at night, costs 1800FF. Another option is the four-week grammar workshop (three hours a week) for 750FF. The school's office is open weekdays from 9 am to 6 pm. If there's space, you can sign up until the first day of class.

Alliance Française
(Map 4; ☎ 01 45 44 38 28; fax 01 45 44 89 42; info@paris.alliancefrancaise.fr; metro Saint Placide)
101 Blvd Raspail, 75006 Paris. This is the Paris headquarters of a venerable institution whose brief is to promote French language and civilisation around the world. Month-long French courses at all levels – but of variable quality, according to readers – begin during the first week of each month; registration takes place during the five business days before the start of each session. If there's space, it's possible to enrol for just two weeks. *Intensif* courses, which meet for four hours a day, cost 3050FF a month; *extensif* courses, which involve two hours of class a day, cost 1525FF a month. The enrolment fee is 250FF. The registration office is open Monday to Friday from 9 am to 5 pm. Bring your passport and a passport-sized photo. Payment, which must be made in advance, can be done with travellers cheques or credit cards. The mailing address of the Alliance Française is 101 Blvd Raspail, 75270 Paris CEDEX 06.

Cours de Langue et Civilisation Françaises de la Sorbonne
(☎ 01 40 46 22 11; fax 01 40 46 32 29)
47 Rue des Écoles, 75005 Paris. The Sorbonne's famous French Civilisation Course, from which one of the authors graduated sometime back in the late Dark Ages, has courses in French language and civilisation for students of all levels. Costs vary, but a four week summer course should cost about 3250FF, while 16 to 20 hours a week of lectures and tutorials is between 6350 and 7400FF per semester. The instructors take a very academic and stilted approach to language teaching; don't expect to learn how to haggle in a market or swear at road hogs even after a year here.

Eurocentre
(☎ 01 40 46 72 00; fax 01 40 46 72 06; par-infi@eurocentres.com; metro Odéon)
13 Passage Dauphiné, 75006 Paris. This is the Paris branch of the Zürich-based, nonprofit Eurocentre chain, which has schools in 10 countries. Two/four week intensive courses with 12 to 15 participants, well reviewed by Lonely Planet readers, cost 3750/7150FF, including – each week – 25 50-minute lessons, three lectures and five to 10 hours in the multimedia learning centre. New courses begin every two, three or four weeks.

Institut Parisien de Langue et de Civilisation Françaises
(Map 4; ☎ 01 40 56 09 53; fax 01 43 06 46 30; institut.parisien@dial.oleane.com)
87 Blvd de Grenelle, 75015 Paris. Four-week courses with a maximum of 12 students per class cost 2440/3600/6040FF for 10/15/25 hours a week; six-week courses cost 3620/5340/8960FF. The office is open on weekdays from 8.30 am to 5 pm.

Langue Onze
(Map 3; ☎ 01 43 38 22 87; fax 01 43 38 36 01; metro Parmentier)
15 Rue Gambey, 11e. This small, independent language school gets good reports. Four/two week intensive courses are 3300/1900FF, evening classes start at 2000FF a trimester and individual lessons are 120FF an hour. Classes have a maximum of nine students.

Provinces There are also several language schools in the provinces, which can also have cheaper accommodation options, including:

Aix-en-Provence

The American University Center
(☎ 04 42 38 42 38; fax 04 42 38 95 66)
409 Ave Jean-Paul Coste. It offers courses of varying length and intensity, which cost 2200FF for 30 hours of instruction and 2500FF for 40 hours spread over two weeks.

Université de Provence
(☎ 04 42 59 22 71)
29 Ave Robert Schumann. Organises cheaper summer courses and can also organise good accommodation.

Amboise

Eurocentre
(☎ 02 47 23 10 60; fax 02 47 30 54 99)
9 Mail Saint Thomas, BP 214, 37402 Amboise CEDEX. A small school in the charming Loire Valley.

Avignon

Centre d'Études Linguistiques d'Avignon
(☎ 04 90 86 04 33; fax 04 90 85 92 01; www.avignon-et-provence.com/cela)
16 Rue Sainte Catherine, 84000 Avignon. Has courses that start at 1500FF a week (from 1800FF in July). B&B accommodation can be arranged at 85FF a night per person.

Besançon

Centre de Linguistique Appliquée
(☎ 03 81 66 52 00; fax 03 81 66 52 25; cla@univ-fcomte.fr)
6 Rue Gabriel Plançon, 25030 Besançon. One of France's largest language schools offering a wide range of French courses at all levels. Four-week summer courses for beginners (100 hours of group tuition) cost 4920FF.

Dijon

Centre International d'Études Françaises
(☎ 03 80 30 50 20; fax 03 80 30 13 08)
36 Rue Chabot Charny, 21000 Dijon

La Rochelle

Eurocentre, Parc de la Francophonie
(☎ 05 46 50 57 33; fax 05 46 44 24 77)
Ave Marillac, 17024 La Rochelle CEDEX 01. Housed in facilities near the Université de La Rochelle's campus, it is a good school and can provide accommodation.

Lyon

Alliance Française
(☎ 04 78 95 24 72; fax 04 78 60 77 28)
11 Rue Pierre Bourdan, 69003 Lyon

Cooking

The major cooking schools in Paris include École Le Cordon Bleu (☎ 01 53 68 22 50; fax 01 48 56 03 96; metro Vaugirard) at 8 Rue Léon Delhomme (15e); École Ritz Escoffier (☎ 01 43 16 30 50; fax 01 43 16 31 50; metro Concorde) at 38 Rue Cambon (1er); and La Toque d'Or (☎ 01 45 44 86 51;

fax 01 45 44 86 81; metro Varenne) at 55 Rue de Varenne (7e). Tuition costs varies widely but count on paying US$200 to US$500 a day.

WORK

Despite France's 12% unemployment rate and laws that forbid people who aren't EU nationals from working in France, working 'in the black' (ie without documents) is still possible. People without documents probably have their best chance of finding work during fruit harvests, at Alpine ski resorts in the ski season and in the Côte d'Azur's tourist industry. Au pair work is also very popular and can be done legally even by non-EU citizens.

The national minimum wage for nonprofessionals (le SMIC, or *salaire minimum interprofessionel de croissance*) is 39.43FF an hour. However, employers willing to hire people in contravention of France's employment laws are also likely to ignore the minimum wage law.

For practical information on employment in France, you might want to pick up *Working in France* by Carol Pineau and Maureen Kelly. Another publication good for summer jobs that is available at bookshops in Paris is *Emploi d'Été en France* (77FF) from Vac-Job.

Residence Permits

To work legally in France you must have a residence permit known as a carte de séjour. Getting one is almost automatic for EU nationals and almost impossible for anyone else except full-time students (see the Visas & Documents section at the start of this chapter).

Non-EU nationals cannot work legally unless they obtain a work permit (*autorisation de travail*) before arriving in France. Obtaining a work permit is no easy matter, because a prospective employer has to convince the authorities that there is no French – and, increasingly these days, no EU – citizen who can do the job being offered to you.

Employment Agencies

The Agence National pour l'Emploi (ANPE), France's national employment service, has offices in the cities and most large towns. It has lists of job openings, but you're not likely to find much temporary or casual work except during the fruit harvests, when certain ANPE offices allow special provisions for people interested in becoming temporary farmworkers. The ANPE has office branches throughout Paris; the one at 20bis Rue Sainte Croix de la Bretonnerie, 4e (☎ 01 42 71 24 68; metro Hôtel de Ville) deals with those people residing in the 1er, 2e and 12e arrondissements for example.

Centres Régionaux Information Jeunesse (CRIJ), which provide all sorts of information for young people on housing, professional training and educational options, also sometimes have noticeboards with work possibilities. The Paris headquarters (☎ 01 44 49 12 00; fax 01 40 65 02 61; metro Champ de Mars-Tour Eiffel) is at 101 Quai Branly (15e). Both these bodies are useless, however, if you don't have a carte de séjour.

Au Pair

Under the au pair system, single young people (aged 18 to about 27) who are studying in France live with a French family and receive lodging, full board and a bit of pocket money in exchange for taking care of the kids, babysitting, doing light housework and perhaps teaching English to the children. Most families prefer young women, but a few positions are also available for young men. Many families want au pairs who are native English speakers, but knowing at least some French may be a prerequisite.

For practical information, pick up *The Au Pair and Nanny's Guide to Working Abroad* by Susan Griffith & Sharon Legg.

Working Conditions Depending on the family and the placement agency, the minimum commitment ranges from two to six months; the maximum initial stay is 12 months, extendable to 18 months. Many families prefer to hire an au pair for the entire school year (from September to late June).

In general, the family provides room and board and gives the au pair 400 to 500FF a week of pocket money in exchange for up to 30 hours of work and two or three evenings of babysitting each week. By law, au pairs must have one full day off a week (usually Sunday). In Paris, some families also provide weekly or monthly metro passes. The family must also pay for French social security (*securité sociale*), which covers about 70% of medical expenses (it's a good idea to get sufficient supplementary insurance).

All this – including pay and maximum working hours – is clearly spelled out in the *accord* (contract), provided by the Direction Départemental du Travail et de l'Emploi (Departmental Office of Work & Employment). It is signed by both the family and the au pair, officially designated as a *stagiaire aide-familiale*.

Paperwork Because the au pair system is seen by the French government as a forum in which people from other cultures can learn about France and improve their language skills, non-EU citizens usually denied working papers can get special long-stay au pair visas. To be eligible, applicants have to arrange to study something (usually a course of French) while in France in an officially recognised framework and must apply for their au pair visa *before* leaving their home country. Applications won't be considered from people already in France.

After you find a suitable family (see Placement Agencies), the family fills out a *engagement d'accueil* (work contract) and mails it to you so you can make a formal application to the French consulate nearest your home. Sign the contract and send it to the consulate along with your passport, two copies of the application form (which the consulate can provide), an application fee, two photos, the results of a medical exam, and proof that you have been admitted to a recognised program of study. Technically, an au pair's visa lets you work only for the family that has hired you.

Residents of the EU can easily arrange for an au pair job and a carte de séjour after arriving in France. Non-EU nationals who decide to try to find an au pair position after entering the country cannot to do so legally and won't be covered by the protections provided for under French law and may be liable to be deported.

Placement Agencies Most agencies charge the au pair 650 (for the short summer period) to 800FF (for the long winter period) and collect an additional 570 to 1270FF from the family. They generally require that applicants know at least a bit of French, enjoy working with children, and have some experience doing so. All ask for letters of reference, either from the parents of children you've taken care of or from teachers or previous employers. Prospective au pairs should ask lots of questions, especially about living conditions and privacy – remember, there are more families looking for au pairs than there are suitable applicants.

If you are not an EU national, you must contact the placement agency from your home country at least three months in advance. Residents of the EU can apply to the agency after arriving in France. In Paris, check the bulletin boards at the American Church and Saint Joseph's Church (see the Cultural Centres listing in the Information section in the Paris chapter) as well as the publication *France USA Contacts* (see Newspapers & Magazines earlier in this chapter) for job ads. The Paris tourist office has a list of au pair placement agencies that include:

Amicale Culturelle Internationale
(☎ 01 47 42 94 21; fax 01 49 24 02 67; metro Havre Caumartin)
27 Rue Godot de Mauroy, 75009 Paris

Accueil Familial des Jeunes Étrangers
(☎ 01 45 49 15 57; fax 01 45 44 60 48; metro Sèvres Babylone)
23 Rue du Cherche Midi, 75006 Paris

Agricultural Work

The French government seems to tolerate undocumented workers helping out with some agricultural work, especially during harvests. To find a field job, ask around in areas where harvesting is taking place – trees with almost-ripe fruit on them are a sure sign that pickers will soon be needed. Many farmers prefer hiring people who know at least a bit of French.

Grape Harvest The *vendange* (grape harvest) is traditionally France's biggest employer of casual labour, requiring some 100,000 extra pairs of hands each year from about mid-September to mid or late October. Increasingly, vendange is being done by machine, though mechanical picking is forbidden in some areas (eg Champagne) and is disdained by the most prestigious chateaus.

The date of the vendange changes from year to year according to the weather and other factors that affect the grapes as they mature. The exact dates are set by the prefecture only a week (or less) before the start of picking, which usually lasts a fortnight. Wages are 39.43FF an hour (minus 20% for taxes). Food is often supplied, but growers offering accommodation (anything from a rough dorm to a room in the house) are getting harder to find.

To find vendange work, one option is to go through ANPE, the national employment agency. If you choose this route, for which you must have a carte de séjour, contact ANPE's Service de Vendange in writing, in French if possible, sometime after June. They'll send you a questionnaire whose answers will help them place you with a vigneron (wine grower). Useful ANPE offices include:

Burgundy
(☎ 03 80 25 07 00; fax 03 80 24 95 84)
6 Blvd Saint Jacques, 21203 Beaune CEDEX. Open weekdays from 8 am to noon and 1.15 to 4.45 pm (3.30 pm on Monday and Friday).

Beaujolais
(☎ 04 74 60 30 03; fax 04 74 09 06 24)
169 Rue Paul Bert, 69665 Villefranche-sur-Saône CEDEX

Bordeaux
(☎ 05 56 50 83 83; fax 05 56 50 52 97)
Ave des 40 Journaux, 33049 Bordeaux CEDEX

Champagne
(☎ 03 26 54 88 29; fax 03 26 54 41 98)
Cour de la Gare, 51331 Épernay CEDEX

Pays de la Loire
(☎ 02 51 88 24 00; fax 02 40 47 70 95)
16 Rue Anatole de Monzie, BP 2129, 44203 Nantes CEDEX 02
(☎ 02 41 58 58 10; fax 02 41 65 68 79)
16 Rue du Docteur Coignard, BP 2132, 49321 Cholet CEDEX

A less bureaucratic option is simply to arrive in the region of your choice right before the harvest and contact local people connected with the wine trade.

Other Harvests Fruits and vegetables are harvested somewhere in France from mid-May straight through to November. Apples are grown nearly all over, with the harvest starting in the south (eg in Languedoc) in September and moving northward to cooler regions (eg Normandy) by October. In the department of Indre, for example, the apple harvest is from mid-September to the end of October. Around Nantes, pears need picking from September to November.

Other important harvesting regions and their crops include Brittany and Normandy for cherries and plums; the Rhône Valley and Provence for strawberries, cherries, apples, peaches, tomatoes and pears; the Languedoc-Roussillon region for apricots and melons; and Périgord for plums and apples and. *Produits maraîchers*, a term you may come across, means market garden crops.

Ski Resorts

The Alps are the most promising of France's ski regions for picking up hospitality work in hotels and restaurants in ski resorts with lots of British holiday-makers. The season runs from about December to April.

If you speak only English, the fashionable resort of Méribel, in the Tarentaise Valley east of Chambéry, may be a good place to start looking, as a large number of British tour companies operate from there.

Côte d'Azur

The season on the Côte d'Azur runs from June to September. Selling goods or services on the beach is one way to make a few francs, though you've got to sell an awful lot of ice cream and wrap a lot of hair with coloured beads to make a living.

A tad more glam is working on a yacht. Cannes and Antibes are the places to start looking and March is the month, as many jobs are filled by mid-April. Yacht owners often take on newcomers for a trial period of day-crewing before hiring them for the full charter season. By late September, long-haul crews are in demand for winter voyages to the West Indies.

Street Performers

If you play an instrument or have some other talent in the performing arts, you could try busking as a street musician, actor, juggler, pavement artist etc.

In Paris, amplifiers, percussion instruments and anything you have to blow are technically forbidden but are widely tolerated by the police so long as they're not too loud or obnoxious. Busking borders on downright legality in front of the Centre Pompidou, around Sacré Cœur and on the metro, where the RATP police are in charge. But wherever you are, the best way to avoid hassles is to talk to other street artists.

ACCOMMODATION

France has accommodation of every sort and for every budget. For details – and, in many cases, help with reservations – contact the nearest tourist office.

In many parts of France, local authorities impose a *taxe de séjour* (tourist tax) on each visitor in their jurisdiction. The prices charged at camping grounds, hotels etc may therefore be as much as 1 to 7FF per person higher than the posted rates.

Reservations

Advance Reservations Advance reservations are a good way to avoid the hassle of searching for a place to stay each time you pull into a new town; they are especially useful if you won't be arriving in the morning. During periods of heavy domestic or foreign tourism (eg around Easter and Christmas-New Year's, during the February-March school holiday and, in some areas, in July and August), having a reservation can mean the difference between finding a room in your price range and moving on.

Tourist Offices Many tourist offices will help people who don't speak French make local hotel reservations, usually for a small fee. In some cases, you pay a deposit that is later deducted from the first night's bill. The staff may also have information on vacancies, but they will usually refuse to make specific recommendations. You cannot take advantage of reservation services by phone – you have to stop by the office.

By Telephone The relative cheapness of international phone calls makes it eminently feasible to call a hotel in France from anywhere in the world to find out if they have space when you'd like to come. Double-check to make sure the hotel proprietor understands the date, day of the week and estimated hour of your arrival, and make sure you know what he or she expects in terms of a deposit or written confirmation. It is not fair to the hotelier to make hotel reservations by telephone and then not show up. If you won't be able to come as planned, call the hotel and inform them as soon as possible.

Deposits Many hotels, particularly budget ones, accept reservations only if they are accompanied by *des arrhes* (pronounced 'dez AR'; a deposit) in French francs. Some places, especially those with two or more stars, don't ask for a deposit if you give them your credit card number or send them confirmation of your plans by letter or fax in clear, simple English. But if you send them a fax, don't expect a response by fax.

Quite a few hotel owners frown upon Eurocheques because of the high exchange commission. If you make a deposit by Eurocheque, don't be surprised if the hotel holds it until you arrive and then returns it in exchange for cash. Most hotels will accept personal or cashiers' cheques only if they're in French francs.

Postal delivery within France usually takes only a couple of days, so deposits can easily be sent by postal money order. After you've made your reservations by phone, go to any post office and purchase a *mandat lettre* (money order) in the proper amount and make it payable to the hotel.

Same-Day Reservations Even during the peak season, most hotels keep a few rooms unreserved, so that at least some of the people who happen by looking for a place can be accommodated. As a result, a hotel that was all booked up when you called three days ago may have space if you ring at 9 or 10 am on the morning of the day you'll be arriving. Except in Paris, you can almost always find a place to stay this way, even in August.

Most places will hold a room only until a set hour, rarely later than 6 or 7 pm (and sometimes earlier). If you are running late, let them know or they're liable to rent out the room to someone else.

Camping

Camping, either in tents or in caravans, is immensely popular in France, and the country has thousands of camping grounds, many of them near streams, rivers, lakes or the ocean. The vast majority of them close for at least a few months in winter, and some are only open in summer. Hostels sometimes let travellers pitch tents in the back garden.

A camping ground's facilities and amenities determine how many stars it has (usually two to four), which, along with location and seasonal demand, influence the prices. Tariffs are generally the same for tents and camping cars, except that the latter are charged an extra fee for electricity. Some places have *forfaits* (fixed price deals) for two or three people. Children up to about age 12 enjoy significant discounts. Few camping grounds are near major sights, so campers without their own wheels may spend a fair bit of money (and time) commuting.

Camping à la ferme (camping on the farm) is coordinated by Gîtes de France (see Gîtes Ruraux & B&Bs), publisher of the annual guide *Camping à la Ferme* (70FF). The sites – of which there are more than 1100 all over the country – are generally accessible only if you have a car or bicycle.

For details on camping grounds not mentioned in the text, inquire at a local tourist office. If you'll be doing lots of car camping, pick up a copy of Michelin's *Camping-Caravanning France* (72FF), which lists 3500 camping grounds.

In July and especially August, when most camping grounds are completely packed, campers who arrive late in the day have a much better chance of getting a spot if they arrive on foot (ie without a vehicle). Camping ground offices are often closed for most of the day – the best times to call for reservations are in the morning (before 10 or 11 am) and in the late afternoon or early evening.

Freelance Camping If you'll be doing overnight backpacking, remember that camping is generally permitted only at designated camp sites. Pitching your tent anywhere else (eg in a road or trailside meadow), known as *camping sauvage* in French, is usually illegal, though it's often tolerated to varying degrees. Except in Corsica, you probably won't have any problems if you're not on private land, have only a small tent, are discreet, stay only one or two nights, take the tent down during the day, do not light a campfire, and are at least 1500m from a camping ground (or, in a national park, at least an hour's walk from a road).

If you camp out on the beach, even where the police tolerate such behaviour (such as in Nice or Saint Tropez), you'll be an easy target for thieves, so be careful where you put your valuables when sleeping. In areas with especially high tidal variations (eg on the northern coast of Brittany and nearby parts of Normandy), sleeping on the beach is not a good idea. If you decide to take the risk ask a local about the high-tide mark.

Rental Accommodation

If you don't speak French or have a local person helping you, it may be very difficult to find a flat for long-term rental. In any case, don't sign any documents without having someone fluent in French legalese take a look at them.

The first hurdle is finding a landlord with a suitable apartment who's willing to entrust it to someone who isn't French. It's not uncommon to be asked on the phone, *'Vous êtes de quelle nationalité?'* ('What nationality are you?'). Most people aren't usually uptight about Australians, Canadians or Americans, but prejudice against North Africans and black Africans is rife and there are few laws to prevent owners from screening prospective tenants. After you've exhausted your personal connections, places to look for apartments to let include the *petites annonces* (classified ads) in local newspapers – *De Particulier à Particulier* (15F) and *La Centrale des Particuliers* (17F), both issued each Thursday – *À Vendre à Louer* (7FF); and, for students, the CROUS office of the nearest university. Estate agents require lots of paperwork and charge commissions of up to one month's rent.

Competition for apartments can be fierce, especially in September and October, when lots of students are searching for places. However, at any time of year, finding an apartment is a matter of making your calls as soon as possible after the information becomes public.

Refuges & Gîtes d'Étape

A *refuge* (mountain hut or shelter; pronounced 'reh-FUUZH') is a very basic dorm room established and operated by national park authorities, the Club Alpin Français or other private organisations along trails in uninhabited mountainous areas that are frequented by hikers and mountain climbers. *Refuges*, some of which are open year-round, are generally marked on hiking and climbing maps.

In general, *refuges* are equipped with bunks (usually wall-to-wall), mattresses and blankets but not sheets, which you have to bring yourself or (sometimes) rent for 15 to 20FF. Overnight charges average between 50 to 70FF a night per person; given how much space you get, *refuges* are more expensive per square metre than most luxury hotels. Meals, prepared by the *gardien* (attendant), are sometimes available. Most *refuges* are equipped with a telephone – often it's a good idea to call ahead and make a reservation.

For details on *refuges*, contact a tourist office near where you'll be hiking or consult the *Guide des Refuges et Gîtes des Alpes*, published by the Grenoble-based Glénat, which covers the Alps; or for the Pyrenees *Hébergement en Montagne*, published by the Saint Girons-based Éditions Randonnées Pyrénéennes. Both should be available in bookshops or Maisons de la Presse.

Gîtes d'étape, which are usually better equipped and more comfortable than *refuges* (some even have showers), are situated in less remote areas, often in villages. They cost around 60 or 70FF per person and are listed in *Gîtes d'Étape et de Séjour* (70FF), published annually by Gîtes de France.

Gîtes Ruraux & B&Bs

Several types of accommodation – often in charming, traditional-style houses with gardens – are available for people who would like to spend time in rural areas and have a vehicle. All are represented by Gîtes de France, an organisation that acts as a liaison between owners and renters.

A *gîte rural* – of which France has some 35,000 – is a holiday cottage (or part of a house) in a village or on a farm. Amenities always include a kitchenette and bathroom facilities.

A gîte rural owned by a *commune* (the smallest unit of local government) is known as a *gîte communal*. In most cases, there is a minimum rental period – often one week, but sometimes only a few days.

A *chambre d'hôte*, basically a B&B (bed and breakfast), is a room in a private house rented to travellers by the night. Breakfast is included. France has about 15,000 chambres d'hôtes.

Each department has a Gîtes de France *antenne* (branch) that publishes a brochure listing the local gîtes. Depending on agreements with individual owners, the branch may be able to handle English-language bookings through its *service de réservation*. Otherwise, you're meant to contact the owner yourself. During holiday periods, it is necessary to reserve rural accommodation in some areas well in advance. Most owners will ask for deposits.

Gîtes de France branches are often affiliated with the *association départementale de tourisme rural* (departmental association for rural tourism) or the department's *maison de l'agriculture* (agriculture office) or *chambre d'agriculture* (chamber of agriculture). Details on how to find or contact the nearest Gîtes de France office are available at any local tourist office, which may also be able to supply a brochure. You can also contact the Fédération Nationale des Gîtes de France (☎ 01 49 70 75 75; fax 01 49 70 80 09; Minitel 3615 GITES DE FRANCE; metro Trinité) at 59 Rue Saint Lazare, 75009 Paris. Office hours on weekdays are 10 am to 6.30 pm, and on Saturday from 10 am to 1 pm and 4 to 6.30 pm. It also publishes *Chambres et Tables d'Hôtes* (95 to 115FF) and *Nouveaux Gîtes Ruraux* (95 to 105FF).

Homestays

Under an arrangement known as *hôtes payants* (literally, 'paying guests') or *hébergement chez l'habitant* (lodging with the owners or occupants of private homes), students, young people and tourists can stay with French families. In general you rent a room and have access (sometimes limited) to the family's kitchen and telephone. Many language schools (see the previous Courses section) can arrange homestays for their students.

For details on each agency's prices and conditions, it's a good idea to call, write or fax at least six weeks in advance, though last-minute arrangements are sometimes possible.

Students and tourists alike should count on paying 3000 to 5200FF a month, 1200 to 1500FF a week, or 130 to 300FF a day for a single room, including breakfast.

Amicale Culturelle Internationale
(☎ 01 47 42 94 21; fax 01 49 24 02 67; metro Havre Caumartin)
27 Rue Godot de Mauroy, 75009 Paris. Arranges stays in French homes in Paris (1500FF a week for B&B, 1800FF for half-board) and elsewhere in France. The minimum stay is two weeks.

France Lodge
(☎ 01 53 20 09 09; fax 01 53 20 01 25; metro Le Peletier)
41 Rue La Fayette, 75009. A nonprofit organisation that arranges accommodation in private homes and apartments. In Paris, prices start at about 130FF a night per person (cheaper by the month). Annual membership costs 85FF, and payment must be made in French francs.

Accueil Familial des Jeunes Étrangers
(☎ 01 45 49 15 57; fax 01 45 44 60 48; metro Sèvres Babylone)
23 Rue du Cherche Midi, 75006 Paris. They'll find you a room with a family for 3000 to 3500FF a month, including breakfast. For stays of less than a month, expect to pay about 140FF a day. There's a subscription fee of 500FF for stays of less than a month. Longer stays incur a 100FF fee per month.

Monasteries

La Procure (☎ 01 45 48 20 25; metro Saint Sulpice), 3 Rue de Mézières, 75006 Paris, publishes *Guide Saint Christophe* (120FF), which has details in French on staying at monasteries all over France. Its office hours are Monday to Saturday from 9.30 am to 7.30 pm.

Hostels & Foyers

Official hostels that belong to one of the three hostel associations in France are known as *auberges de jeunesse* and are so indicated in this book. In university towns, you may also find *foyers* (pronounced 'fwa-YEI'), student dormitories converted for use by travellers during the summer school holidays. In certain cities and towns, young workers are accommodated in dormitories called either *foyers de jeunes travailleurs* or *travailleuses*, and despite the names, most are now co-ed. These places, which often take *passagères* and *passagers* (female and male short-term guests) when they have space, are relatively unknown to most travellers and very frequently have space available when the other kinds of hostels are full. Information on hostels and foyers not mentioned in the text is available from local tourist offices.

In Paris, expect to pay 90 to 120FF a night for a hostel bed, including breakfast. In the provinces, a bunk in the single-sex dorm room generally costs somewhere from 50FF (at an out-of-the-way place with basic facilities) to 70FF, which does not include a sometimes-optional continental breakfast (around 15FF). A few of the better places that aren't official hostels charge more. Most auberges de jeunesse as well as some hostels and foyers have kitchen facilities of one sort or another.

Not all hostels and foyers accept reservations made by telephone, and if they do they will usually only hold a place for a few hours. In July and August, when swarms of summer backpackers descend on France, it's an excellent idea to arrive in town early enough to check in by mid-morning.

Hostel Organisations Most of France's hostels belong to one of three major hostel associations:

Fédération Unie des Auberges de Jeunesse
(FUAJ; ☎ 01 44 89 87 27; fax 01 44 89 87 10; Minitel 3615 FUAJ; www.fuaj.org; metro La Chapelle)
27 Rue Pajol, 75018 Paris

Ligue Française pour les Auberges de la Jeunesse (LFAJ)
(☎ 01 44 16 78 78; fax 01 45 44 57 47; metro Glacière)
67 Rue Vergniaud, 75013 Paris

Union des Centres de Rencontres Internationales de France (UCRIF)
(☎ 01 40 26 57 64; fax 01 40 26 58 20; Minitel 3615 UCRIF; ucrif@aol.com; metro Les Halles or Étienne Marcel)
27 Rue de Turbigo, 75002 Paris

FUAJ and LFAJ affiliates will require Hostelling International or similar cards, available at any hostel for about 100FF (70FF if you're under 26). They also require that you either bring a sleeping sheet or rent one for 13 to 16FF per stay.

Hotels

Most French hotels have between one and four stars; the fanciest places have four stars plus an L (for 'luxury'). A hotel that has no stars (ie that has not been rated) is known as *non-homologué*, sometimes abbreviated as NH. The letters 'NN' after the rating mean the establishment conforms to the *nouvelle norme* (new standards), introduced in 1992. Hotel ratings are based on certain objective criteria (eg the size of the entry hall), not the quality of the service, the décor or cleanliness, so a one-star establishment may be more pleasant than some two or three-star places. Prices often reflect these intangibles far more than they do the number of stars.

Most hotels offer a *petit déjeuner*, which means a continental breakfast consisting of a croissant, French rolls, butter, jam and either coffee or hot chocolate. The charge is usually 20 to 40FF per person, a bit more than you would pay at a café. Some places in heavily touristed areas increase their high-season profits by requiring that guests take breakfast. Even more deplorable from the point of view of budget travellers are hotels that won't rent you a room unless you pay for *demi-pension* (half-board, ie breakfast and either lunch or dinner).

Budget Hotels In general, hotels listed under 'budget' have doubles that cost less than two hostel beds, ie up to 170FF (240FF in Paris), quite a bit less than the budget options available in countries such as the UK or Germany. Most are equipped with a washbasin (and, usually, a bidet) but lack private bath or toilet. Almost all these places also have more expensive rooms equipped with shower, toilet and other amenities.

Most doubles, which generally cost only marginally more than singles, have only one double bed, though some places have rooms with two twin beds (*deux lits séparés*); triples and quads usually have two or three beds. Taking a shower in the hall bathroom is sometimes free but is usually *payant*, which means there's a charge of 10 to 25FF per person. Sometimes you have the option of a bath for the same price as a shower.

Although it's much harder to meet fellow travellers at a hotel than at a hostel, renting a hotel room will free you from cumbersome hostel regulations (eg night-time curfews, daytime room closures and length-of-stay limits) and rambunctious school groups. And while many hostels are well out of the city centre, often making you reliant on public transport, inexpensive hotels can almost always be found near the train station or in the centre of town.

If you're in the market for truly rock-bottom accommodation, you may come across *hôtels de passe*, hotels whose rooms are rented out for use by prostitutes. Certain parts of central Marseille and Paris' Pigalle and Rue Saint Denis areas are known to have such establishments, but so do other cities and towns. Of course, it's not that you can't get a good night's sleep in a hôtel de passe – if the walls are thick enough, that is.

Some cheap hotels have the unpleasant habit of refusing to refund the unused part of your deposit when you decide to switch hotels or leave town earlier than planned. The moral of the story is not to prepay for those nights where there's a chance you won't be staying. In any case, the sooner you tell the manager, the better your chances of being reimbursed.

If you're travelling by car, you'll be able to take advantage of the remarkably cheap hotel chains whose postmodern, pressboard-and-plastic establishments have been springing up on the outskirts of France's cities and towns, usually on a main access route. The best known, Formule 1, charges from 130 to 140FF (according to the season) for a ticky-tacky, shower and toilet-equipped room for up to three people; until 7 pm, there's no penalty to cancel a reservation prepaid by credit card.

Little Surprises The budget hotels listed in the book are often small, family-run affairs that follow their own often idiosyncratic notions of service. Some peculiarities you should be prepared for include:

- You may be asked to *régler* (settle your account) when you check in.
- There may be no lift to your 6th floor room (especially in Paris) and no fire escape either.
- The bed may have a very soft mattress.
- Your bed may have a *traversin* (bolster), a horrible thing shaped like a large hot dog, rather than an *oreiller* (pillow).
- The shower may consist of a curtainless bathtub with nowhere to hang the hand nozzle.
- Some small hotels, especially those attached to bars, may not have any shower facilities at all.

Hôtel Meublé A small hotel that rents out rooms with *cuisinettes* (kitchenettes), generally by the week and often to the same holidaying clients year after year, is known as a *hôtel meublé*. They are very common on the Côte d'Azur, especially in Nice.

Mid-Range Hotels Hotels with double rooms listed under 'middle' in this book come with showers and toilets (unless otherwise noted) and usually have doubles for 170 to about 350FF. Many places listed under 'budget' have rooms that, from the point of view of amenities and price, fall in the mid-range category.

Some 4000 hotels – many of them family-run places in the countryside, by the sea or in the mountains – belong to Logis de France, an organisation whose affiliated establishments meet strict standards of service and amenities. They generally offer very good value. The Fédération Nationale des Logis de France (☎ 01 45 84 70 00; fax 01 44 24 08 74; Minitel 3615 LOGIS DE FRANCE; metro Tolbiac), based at 83 Ave d'Italie, 75013 Paris, issues an annual guide with a detailed map showing how to find each hotel.

FOOD & WINE

FOOD

FRENCH CUISINE

The cuisine of France is remarkably varied, with a great many differences based on the produce and gastronomy of each region. Culinary traditions that have been developed and perfected over the centuries have made French cooking a highly refined art. This is true of even the simplest peasant dishes, which require careful preparation and great attention to detail. However, the secret to success in a French kitchen is not so much elaborate techniques as the use of fresh ingredients that are locally produced and in season. Eating well is still of prime importance to most French people, who spend an amazing amount of time thinking about, talking about and consuming food.

Even if you can't afford to eat in expensive restaurants, you can still enjoy France's epicurean delights by buying food at markets or speciality shops, trying the local delicacies of the particular region you're in, and avoiding the standard fare of tourist menus such as steak-frites, crème caramel and so on.

Regional Specialities

There are all sorts of reasons for the amazing variety of France's regional cuisine. Climatic and geographical factors have been particularly important: the hot south tends to favour olive oil, garlic and tomatoes, while the cooler, pastoral regions farther north emphasise cream and butter. Areas near the coast specialise in mussels, oysters and saltwater fish, while those near lakes and rivers use freshwater fish.

Diverse though it is, French cuisine is typified by certain regions, most notably Normandy, Burgundy, Périgord, Lyon and, to a lesser extent, Provence and Alsace.

Normandy Normandy is famous for the incredible richness and superior quality of its local produce, especially its dairy products. Each Norman cow produces an average of five tonnes of milk annually, which is why the region supplies something like half of France's milk, butter, cream and cheese. Among the cheeses, Camembert (produced in Normandy since the time of William the Conqueror) is supreme, but there are a great many others, including Neufchâtel (or Bondon), Pont l'Évêque and Livarot. Cream and butter go into the creation of the many rich, thick sauces that accompany fish, meat and vegetable dishes in the region.

Charcuteries (delicatessens) abound in Normandy, their windows displaying various terrines, pâtés and tripe. Also common are *galantine*, a cold dish of boned, stuffed, pressed meat (especially pork) that is presented in its own jelly, often with truffles and pistachio nuts. One

Title page photc
Adrienne Costanz

Norman dish that may not be to everyone's taste is *tripes à la mode de Caen*, tripe combined with ox or calf's trotters, cider or Calvados, carrots, leeks, onions and herbs, and slow-cooked in a clay pot.

Rouen is famous for its duck dishes. The ducks are slaughtered by choking in order to retain the blood, which is then used to make the accompanying sauces. A typical dish is *canard à la rouennaise*, but there are countless other duck dishes, and recipes vary from town to town.

Trouville and Honfleur are the places to go for fish and seafood; their markets are crammed with lobsters, crayfish, langoustines, prawns, tiny scallops, plump oysters, delicious small mussels and an endless variety of fish. Specialities include mussel soup, which is made with stock, white wine and cream, and *sole à la normande*.

Apples are another essential of Norman cuisine, and cider is used extensively in cooking, particularly in meat and poultry dishes. Apple *cidre* (cider) is bubbly, lightly alcoholic and refreshing. There are two kinds: *doux* (sweet) and *brut* (dry).

Calvados is to the apple what Cognac is to the grape. This strong apple brandy (whose most celebrated variety comes from the Vallée d'Auge) is sometimes strengthened by adding cider to make *pommeau*, which is drunk as a strong (18% alcohol) apéritif. Calvados is used in the preparation of sauces and also in desserts.

Burgundy Burgundian cuisine is solid, substantial and served in generous portions. The region's best known dish, *bœuf bourguignon*, is beef marinated and cooked in red wine with mushrooms, onions, carrots and bacon bits. Any dish described as *à la bourguignonne* will be prepared with a similar sauce. Quite a few other Burgundian dishes are prepared with cream-based sauces, although *andouillette de Mâcon* (a small raw pork sausage) comes with a mustard sauce.

The region's most famous condiment is mustard, which was introduced to Gaul by the Romans. Burgundy's speciality mustards are made with anything from tarragon to honey and range in taste from delicate to fiery.

Other traditional Burgundian products include gingerbread (which traditionally takes six to eight weeks to prepare), black *escargots* (snails) – those raised on grape leaves are reputed to be the tastiest in France – and blackcurrants. The latter are used to make both jams and *crème de cassis*, a sweet blackcurrant liqueur that is combined with white wine (traditionally Aligoté) to make the apéritif known as kir.

Périgord Regarded as one of the best regional cuisines of France, Périgord is famous for its truffles, foie gras and its poultry. Most prized by chefs is goose, which is turned into pâté de foie gras (goose liver pâte) but also stuffed with chestnuts or plums, roasted, boiled or turned into *confit d'oie* (cooked and stored in its own fat). Goose fat is used a lot in cooking, as is walnut oil. Also popular are ducks and pork, which are also turned into a confit. Regional dishes are usually called *à la périgourdine*, which may (or may not) mean it will come with périgourdine or *périgueux* sauce (a rich brown sauce with foie gras purée and truffles).

Truffles

Périgord is famed for its *truffes* (truffles), edible subterranean fungi that grow on the roots of certain oak and hazelnut trees and can sell for over 2000FF per 100g in exclusive Parisian shops. Specially trained dogs or pigs 'sniff' them out between November and March. The Périgord region's highly prized variety, renowned for its distinctive aroma, is black and rough in texture. Truffles are at their best when eaten fresh – they only keep for a week and lose some of their flavour when preserved. The precious fungus is traditionally added to a variety of sauces and dishes but is also delicious in omelettes and pasta.

The region's cuisine is very diverse and also includes freshwater fish (which can be stuffed with foie gras or cooked with truffles, grilled, marinated or cooked in ashes), crayfish, rabbit and beef. One of the best desserts is chestnut gâteau, but also look out for flans or tarts with plums, quinces, grapes, cherries or pears.

Lyon The city of Lyon, at the crossroads of some of France's richest agricultural regions (Burgundy and its wines, Charolles and its cattle, Dauphiné and its dairy products), enjoys a supply of quality foodstuffs unequalled in France. Indeed, it is considered by most to be the country's *temple de gastronomie*. The most typical dishes are *boudin blanc* (veal sausage) and *quenelles* (light dumplings made of fish or meat, poached and often served in a *sauce Nantua*, a creamy crayfish sauce). Surprisingly, in the very masculine world of French cuisine, Lyon owes most of its reputation to women, the famous *mères lyonnaises*, who have run traditional-style restaurants in that city for generations.

Alsace Most of the dishes on offer in traditional Alsatian restaurants are not found anywhere else in France – except in the brasserie, whose cuisine still reflects that venerable institution's Alsatian origins.

On the savoury side, you're likely to find *baeckeoffe* (baker's oven), a stew made of several kinds of meat (often pork, mutton and beef) and vegetables that have been marinated for two days. It is traditionally prepared at home before being cooked in the oven of a nearby bakery. *Choucroute alsacienne* (or *choucroute garnie*) is sauerkraut served hot with sausage, pork or ham – it is often accompanied by cold, frothy beer or a local wine. *Flammeküche*, a thin layer of pastry topped with cream, onion, bacon and sometimes cheese or mushrooms and cooked in a wood-fired oven, is known in French as *tarte flambée*. A *ziewelküche* (or *tarte à l'oignon)* is an onion tart, while a *tourte* is a raised pie with ham, bacon or ground pork, eggs and leeks. Alsace produces some excellent *charcuterie*, products prepared from what is renowned in these parts as *le seigneur cochon* (the 'noble pig').

The white *asperges* (asparagus) of Alsace are prized throughout France and only available for a couple of weeks in late May.

Alsace's pâtisseries are particularly well stocked with scrumptious pastries, including *kougelhopf* (or *kougloff)*, a mildly sweet sultana and almond cake that is baked in a mould and is easily identified by its ribbed, dome-like shape. *Tarte alsacienne* is a custard tart made with local fruits, which also includes the wonderful Alsatian plums called *quetsches*.

Alsace also has its own kinds of eateries. *Winstub* (VEEN-shtub), warm and wood-panelled, serve wine by the glass or carafe as well as hearty Alsatian pork dishes, many of them prepared, of course, with wine. Places to drink beer were once known as *bierstub* (BEER-shtub), but these days the bierstub exists more in local myth than in day-to-day reality.

Provence Provençal cuisine is prepared with *huile d'olive* (olive oil) and *ail* (garlic). *Tomates* (tomatoes) are another common ingredient, and you can safely assume that any culinary delight described as *à la provençale* will be prepared with garlic-seasoned tomatoes. Other vegetables that frequently appear on local menus are aubergines (eggplant), summer squash or courgettes (zucchini) and *oignons* (onions). Tomatoes, eggplant and squash, stewed together along with green peppers, garlic and various aromatic herbs, produce that perennial Provençal favourite, ratatouille.

Aïoli is a sauce prepared by mixing mayonnaise (made with olive oil) with lots of freshly crushed garlic. It is spread generously on hot or cold vegetables, such as asperges, eggs and especially *morue pochée* (poached codfish).

Provence's most famous soup is *bouillabaisse*, which is made with at least three kinds of fresh fish cooked for 10 minutes or so in broth with onions, tomatoes, saffron and various herbs, including laurel (bay leaves), sage and thyme. It is sometimes prepared with shellfish as well. Bouillabaisse, which is eaten as a main course, is usually served with toast and *rouille*, a spicy sauce that some people mix into the soup but which most spread on the crisp toast. The most renowned bouillabaisse is made in Marseille. A popular starter is *soupe au pistou*, a soup of vegetables, noodles, beans and basil, and a hearty winter meal is *daube de bœuf* (a beef stew cooked in red wine) with *pâtés fraîches* (cold pâté).

Provence is sometimes called 'the garden of France' because of its superb spices, fruits and vegetables. The region is also famous for its locally pressed olive oil, honey and fresh goat cheese. *Truffes* (truffles) are harvested from November to April. Depending on the season, all these delicacies are available fresh at local food markets.

A favourite way to eat *crudités* (raw vegetables) is with *anchoïade* (*anchoýade* in Provençal), a dipping sauce of anchovy paste.

French Basque Country Among the essential ingredients of Basque cooking are the deep-red chillies you'll see hanging out to dry in summer, brightening up houses and adding that extra bite to many of the region's dishes. Equally characteristic is the goose fat that is used to cook almost everything – from eggs to *garbure*, a filling cabbage and bean soup. The pâté de foie gras and the confit d'oie are also excellent. Fish dishes abound on the coast, with tuna and sardines being the speciality of Saint Jean de Luz. A fish stew called *ttoro* may include scampi, hake, eel and monkfish as well as chillies, tomatoes and white wine. Other local delicacies include baby eels, trout and *salmis de palombe*, wood pigeon partially roasted then simmered in a rich sauce of wine and vegetable purée.

The locally cured *jambon de Bayonne* (Bayonne ham) is a salty staple of Basque cuisine, but its cheaper Spanish cousin *jamón serrano* is far more common on *menus*.

Types of Cuisine

There are several different kinds of French cuisine:

Haute cuisine (high cuisine) Originating in the spectacular feasts of French kings, haute cuisine is typified by super-rich, elaborately prepared and beautifully presented multicourse meals.

Cuisine bourgeoise Is French home cooking of the highest quality.

Cuisine des régions Also known as *cuisine campagnarde* (country cuisine), regional cuisine uses the finest ingredients and most refined techniques to prepare traditional rural dishes.

Nouvelle cuisine (new cuisine) This style of cuisine made a big splash at home and abroad in the diet-conscious 1970s and 80s. It features rather small portions served with light sauces. Nouvelle cuisine is prepared and presented in such a way as to emphasise the inherent textures and colours of the ingredients.

Languedoc As in Provence, food in Languedoc is cooked in and laced with liberal amounts of olive oil. France's most famous blue cheese is made at Roquefort, south of Millau. Other regional favourites include Bleu des Causses and Pélardon.

Languedoc's most celebrated dishes are *cassoulet* (a hearty stew of white beans and pork), mutton, confit d'oie and *confit de canard* (preserved duck). The term *à la languedocienne* usually means dishes served with a garlicky garnish of tomatoes, aubergines and *cèpes* (boletus mushrooms).

ETHNIC CUISINES

France has a considerable population of immigrants from its former colonies and protectorates in North and West Africa, Indochina, the Middle East, India, the Caribbean and the South Pacific, as well as refugees from every corner of the globe, so an exceptional variety of reasonably priced ethnic food is available.

North African

One of the most delicious and easy-to-find North African dishes is couscous, steamed semolina garnished with vegetables and a spicy, meat-based sauce just before it is served. It is usually eaten with lamb shish kebab, *merguez* (small, spicy sausages), *méchoui* (barbecued lamb on the bone), chicken or some other meat. The Moroccan, Algerian and Tunisian versions all differ slightly. Another Moroccan favourite, particularly in Paris, is *tajine* (a delicious slow-cooked stew of meat, usually eaten by dipping small pieces of bread into it) with lemons, prunes or confits.

Asian

France's many immigrants from South-East Asia, especially Vietnam and Cambodia, have brought Asian food to every corner of the country. Vietnamese restaurants, many of them run by ethnic Chinese who fled Vietnam, generally offer good value but little authentic food. In the major cities, you can also sample the cuisines of Cambodia, Japan, Korea, Tibet and Thailand.

Kosher

For information on *cacher* (kosher) restaurants in Paris, see the Marais Area, Gare Saint Lazare & Grands Boulevards, and Oberkampf, Ménilmontant & Belleville Areas under Places to Eat in the Paris chapter. Kosher restaurants are also mentioned in the Strasbourg and Marseille sections.

MEALS IN FRANCE

Breakfast

In the Continental tradition, the French start the day with a *petit déjeuner* (breakfast) usually consisting of a croissant and a light bread roll with butter and jam, followed by a *café au lait* (coffee with lots of hot milk), a small black coffee or hot chocolate. Buying rolls or pastries from a pâtisserie is quite a bit cheaper than eating at the hotel or a café.

Lunch & Dinner

For many French people, especially in the provinces, lunch is still the main meal of the day. Restaurants generally serve lunch between noon and 2 or 2.30 pm and dinner from 7 or 7.30 pm to sometime between 9.30 and 10.30 pm. Very few restaurants (except for brasseries, cafés and fast-food places) are open between lunch and dinner.

In many cities and towns, the vast majority of restaurants are closed on Sunday. In cities such as Paris, from where most locals flee for the beaches in August, many restaurateurs lock up and leave town along with their clients.

Traditional Meals

As the pace of French life becomes more hectic, the three-hour midday meal is becoming increasingly rare, at least on weekdays. Dinners, however, are still turned into elaborate affairs whenever time and finances permit. For visitors, the occasional splurge can be the perfect end to a day of sightseeing.

A fully fledged, traditional French meal is an awesome event, often comprising six distinct courses and sometimes more. The meal is always served with wine (red, white or rosé, depending on what you're eating). The fare served at a traditional *déjeuner* (lunch), usually eaten around 1 pm, is largely indistinguishable from that served at *dîner* (dinner), usually begun around 8.30 pm.

The order in which courses are served is as follows:

- an *apéritif* (a predinner drink plus nibblies)
- one or more *entrées* (first course/starters)
- the *plat principal* (main course)
- a *salade* (usually consisting of lettuce and dressing)
- *fromage* (cheese)
- *dessert* (dessert)
- *fruit* (fruit)
- *café* (coffee)
- a *digestif* (an after-dinner drink)

TYPES OF EATERIES

Restaurants & Brasseries

There are lots of restaurants where you can get an excellent French meal for 150 to 200FF – Michelin's *Guide Rouge* is filled with them – but good, inexpensive French restaurants are in short supply. In this book, we have tried to list restaurants that offer what the French call a *bon rapport qualité-prix* (good value for money).

Some of the best French restaurants in the country are attached to hotels, and those on the ground floor of budget hotels often have some of the best deals in town. Almost all are open to nonguests.

Routiers (truckers restaurants), usually found on the outskirts of towns and along major roads, cater to truck drivers and can provide a quick, hearty break from cross-country driving.

Both restaurants and brasseries serve full meals, but with two principal differences:

- Restaurants usually specialise in a particular variety of food (eg regional, traditional, North African, Vietnamese), whereas brasseries – which look very much like cafés – serve more standard fare. This often includes choucroute because the brasserie, which actually means 'brewery', originated in Alsace.
- Restaurants are usually open only for lunch and dinner, whereas brasseries stay open from morning until night and serve meals (or at least something solid) at all times of the day.

Places to eat always have a *carte* (menu) posted outside so you can decide before going in whether the selection and prices are to your liking. It is considered extremely rude to walk out after you have sat down and received your menu.

À la Carte When ordering each dish separately from the menu (ie à la carte), one option is usually the *plat du jour* (dish of the day), some sort of speciality that changes from day to day. Restaurants rarely have minimum charges, so it is possible for people who aren't particularly hungry to order a main dish without the expected three or four accompanying courses. Vegetarians can assemble a meal by ordering one or more side dishes.

Menus Most restaurants offer at least one fixed-price, multicourse meal known in French as a *menu*, *menu à prix fixe* or *menu du jour* (menu of the day). A *menu* (not to be confused with a *carte* – throughout this book we italicise *menu* to distinguish it from the English word 'menu') almost always costs much less than ordering à la carte. In some places, you may also be able to order a *formule*, which usually has fewer choices but allows you to pick two of three courses (eg starter and main course or main course and dessert). In many restaurants, the cheapest lunch *menu* is a much better deal than the equivalent one available at dinner.

When you order a three course *menu*, you usually get to choose an entrée, such as salad, pâté or soup; a main dish (several meat, poultry or fish dishes, including the plat du jour, are generally on offer); and one or more final courses (usually cheese or dessert).

Boissons (drinks), including wine, cost extra unless the menu says *boisson comprise* (drink included), in which case you may get a beer or a glass of mineral water. If the *menu* says *vin compris* (wine included), you'll probably be served a small *pichet* (jug) of wine. The waiter will always ask if you would like coffee to end the meal, but this will almost always cost extra.

Menu prices vary greatly. In routiers, a *menu* can cost as little as 50FF, while at the most elegant establishments (ie those with one or more Michelin stars), they start at several hundred francs. The cheapest *menu* at an average restaurant will cost between 70 and 85FF, and the most expensive *menu* may cost two or three times as much. Many places have a *menu enfant* (children's set menu) available for children under 12.

Restaurant meals are almost always served with bread. If you run out of bread in your basket, don't be afraid to ask the waiter for more (just say, *pourrais je avoir encore du pain, s'il vous plaît*).

Cafés

Cafés are an important focal point for social life in France, and sitting in a café to read, write, talk with friends or just daydream is an integral part of many French people's day-to-day existence. Many people see café-sitting – like shopping at outdoor markets – as a way of keeping in touch with their neighbourhood and maximising their chances of running into friends and acquaintances. Unfortunately, the number of traditional cafés is dropping nationwide – from some 200,000 in 1960 to about 50,000 today.

Only basic food is available in most cafés. Common options include a baguette filled with Camembert or pâté, a *croque-monsieur* or a *croque-madame*.

Three factors determine how much you'll pay in a café: where the café is situated, where you are sitting within the café, and what time of day it is.

A café on a grand boulevard (such as Blvd du Montparnasse or the Champs-Élysées in Paris) will charge considerably more than a place that fronts a quiet side street. Once inside, progressively more expensive tariffs apply at the counter (*comptoir* or *zinc*), in the table area (*salle*) and on the outside terrace (*terrasse*), the best vantage point from which to see and be seen. Some of the cheapest soft drinks may be available only at the bar. The price of drinks goes up at night (usually after 8 pm). It really comes down to this: you are not paying for your espresso or mineral water as much as for the right to occupy an attractive and visible bit of ground. Ordering a cup of coffee (or anything else) earns you the right to sit there for as long as you like. Rarely, if ever, will you feel pressured to order something else.

You usually pay the *addition* (bill) right before you leave, though if your waiter is going off duty you may be asked to pay up at the end of his or her shift.

Vegetarian Eateries

Vegetarians form only a small minority in France and are not very well catered for, as specialised vegetarian restaurants are few and far between. Only the cities are likely to have vegetarian establishments, and these may look more like laid-back cafés than restaurants. Still, their fare is usually better than the omelettes and cheese sandwiches available from ordinary cafés.

Other vegetarian options include *saladeries*, casual restaurants that serve a long list of *salades composées* (mixed salads), though you should carefully scan the menu as many of these also include meat of some sort. Some restaurants have at least one vegetarian dish on the menu, though it may be one of the entrées (starters or first courses). Unfortunately, very few set menus include vegetarian options. For more information on vegetarian options in France, see Vegetarian Food under Guidebooks in the Books section of the Facts for the Visitor chapter.

Salons de Thé

Salons de thé (tearooms) are trendy and somewhat pricey establishments that usually offer quiches, salads, cakes, tarts, pies and pastries in addition to tea and coffee.

Crêperies

Crêperies specialise in crêpes, ultra-thin pancakes cooked on a flat surface and then folded or rolled over a filling. In some parts of France, the word 'crêpe' is used to refer only to sweet crêpes made with *farine de froment* (regular wheat flour), whereas savoury crêpes, often made with *farine de sarrasin* (buckwheat flour) and filled with cheese, mushrooms and the like, are called *galettes*.

Cafeterias

Many cities have cafeteria restaurants offering a good selection of dishes you can see before ordering, a factor that can make life easier if you're travelling with kids. Cafeteria chains include Flunch, Mélodine and Casino.

University Restaurants

All French universities have student restaurants subsidised by the Ministry of Education and operated by the Centre Régional des Œuvres Universitaires et Scolaires, better known as CROUS.

Meal tickets are sold at ticket windows, but since each university seems to have its own policy on feeding students from out-of-town. In Paris, tickets for three-course meals cost 14.10FF for students with ID, 23FF if you have an ISIC card (or Carte Jeune Internationale), and 27.90FF for nonstudent guests. Ticket windows, like the cafeterias themselves, have limited opening hours, and are often closed on weekends and during school holidays (including July and August).

Are You Being Served?

When you enter a shop, as a matter of courtesy, remember to say *'Bonjour, monsieur/madame/mademoiselle'* and when you leave, say *'Merci, monsieur/madame/mademoiselle, au revoir'*.

SHOPPING

France is justly renowned for its extraordinary chefs and restaurants, but one of the country's premier culinary delights is to stock up on delicious fresh breads, pastries, cheese, fruit, vegetables and prepared dishes and sit down for a gourmet *pique-nique*. Note that many food shops are closed on Sunday afternoon and Monday.

French food retailing is arranged so that most people buy a good part of their food from a series of small neighbourhood shops, each with its own speciality. At first, having to go to four shops and stand in four queues to fill the fridge (or assemble a picnic) may seem rather a waste of time, but the whole ritual is an important part of the way many French people live their daily lives.

Since each *commerçant* (shopkeeper) specialises in purveying only one type of food, he or she can almost always provide all sorts of useful tips: which round of Camembert is ripe, which inexpensive wine will complement a certain food, and so on.

As the whole set up is geared to people buying small quantities of fresh food each day, it's perfectly acceptable to purchase only meal-size amounts: a few *tranches* (slices) of meat to make a sandwich, perhaps, or a *petit bout* (small chunk) of sausage. You can also request just enough for one/two people (*pour une/deux personnes*). If you want a bit more, ask for *'encore un petit peu'*, and if you are being given too much, say *'c'est trop'*. Even small villages have a selection of food shops, and remote hamlets are usually served by mobile grocers, butchers and bakers.

Boulangeries

Fresh bread is baked and sold at France's 36,000 *boulangeries*, which supply three-quarters of the country's bread. For more information see the boxed text 'The Staff of Life'.

Pâtisseries

Mouth-watering pastries are available at pâtisseries, which are often attached to boulangeries. Some of the most common pastries include *tarte aux fruits* (fruit tarts), *pain au chocolat* (similar to a croissant but filled with chocolate), *pain aux raisins* (a flat, spiral pastry made with custard and sultanas) and *religieuses* (eclairs with one cream puff perched on top of another to resemble a nun's headdress).

The Staff of Life

Nothing is more French than bread, and it comes in an infinite variety. Don't worry that you will have to buy too much; most *boulangeries* (bakeries) will sell you half a loaf. But you'll probably be able to eat a whole one in any case.

All Parisian boulangeries have 250g baguettes, which are long and thin, and 400g fatter loaves of *pain* (bread), both of which are at their best if eaten within four hours of baking. You can store them for longer in a plastic bag, but the crust becomes soft and chewy; if you leave them out, they'll soon be hard – which is the way many French people like them at breakfast. The *pain* is softer on the inside, has a less crispy crust than the baguette, and is slightly cheaper by weight. If you're not very hungry, ask for a *demi baguette* or *demi pain. Ficelles* are thinner, crustier versions of the baguette – really like very thick breadsticks.

Many boulangeries also have heavier, more expensive breads made with all sorts of grains and cereals, and some of these are so scrumptious they can be eaten plain. You will also find bread flavoured with nuts, raisins or herbs. Other types of bread, which come in a wide range of sizes and shapes, vary from shop to shop, but since they are all on display, making a selection is easy.

Signs you're likely to see in boulangeries include: *pain cuit au feu de bois* (bread baked in a wood-fired oven), *pain de seigle* (rye bread), *pain complet* (wholemeal bread), *pain au son* (bread with bran), *pain de campagne* (country loaf) and *pain au levain* (traditionally made yeast bread that's usually a bit chewy). These heavier breads keep much longer than the baguettes and standard white-flour *pains.*

To facilitate carrying it to your hotel or the park, you can ask for your baguette to be *coupé en deux* (cut in two). If you ask for the bread to be sliced, there's a small charge (usually less than 1FF).

Bread is baked at various times of day, so that fresh bread is readily available as early as 6 am and also in the afternoon. Most boulangeries close for one day a week, but the days are staggered so that a town or neighbourhood is never left without a place to buy bread (except, perhaps, on Sunday afternoon). Places that sell bread but don't bake it on the premises are known as *dépôts de pain.*

You can tell if a croissant has been made with margarine or butter by the shape: margarine croissants have their tips almost touching, while those made with butter have them pointing away from each other.

Confiseries

Chocolate and other sweets made with the finest ingredients can be found at *confiseries*, which are sometimes combined with boulangeries and pâtisseries.

Fromageries

If you buy your cheese in a supermarket, you're likely to end up with unripe and relatively tasteless products unless you know how to select each variety. Here's where a *fromagerie*, also known as a *crémerie*, comes in. The owner, a true expert on matters dairy, can supply you with cheese that is *fait* (ripe) to the exact degree that you request – and will usually let you taste it before you decide what to buy. Just ask *'est-ce que je peux le goûter, s'il vous plaît?'* and they will cut you a little piece from under the rind so as not to damage the cheese's appearance. Most fromageries sell both whole and half-rounds of Camembert, so you don't have to buy more than you're likely to eat in a day or two.

Most cheeses, including Camembert and Emmenthal, will last at least a couple of days without refrigeration, even in summer. Soft and blue cheeses tend to melt, however, especially if you carry them around in your daypack. In cooler weather, you can put them (and other perishables) in a plastic bag and hang it out the window of your hostel or hotel room.

Charcuteries

A charcuterie is a delicatessen offering sliced meats, seafood salads, pâtés, terrines etc. Most supermarkets have a charcuterie counter. If the word *traiteur* (trader) is written on a sign, it means that the establishment sells ready-to-eat takeaway dishes.

Fruit & Vegetables

Fruits and *légumes* are sold by a *marchand de légumes et de fruits* (greengrocer) and at food markets and supermarkets. Most small groceries have only a limited selection. You can buy whatever quantity of produce suits you, even if it's just three carrots and a peach.

The kind of produce on offer varies greatly from region to region and from season to season. Some things are available in only one small region for a limited time of the year. Many *primeurs* (the first fruits and vegetables of the season) come from Provence and Brittany. *Biologique* means grown organically (ie without chemicals).

Meat & Fish

A general butcher is a *boucherie*, but for specialised poultry you have to go to a *marchand de volaille*, where *poulet fermier* (free-range chicken) will cost much more than a regular chicken. A *boucherie chevaline*, easily

CHRIS MELLOR

OLIVIER CIRENDINI

FRANCES LINZEE GORDON

RICHARD NEBESKY

OLIVIER CIRENDINI

OLIVIER CIRENDINI

The food and wine of France is magnificent. Wherever you go in this vast country each region has its speciality, ranging from the mustard of Dijon, wine from Burgundy, Bordeaux or the Loire, cheese and *charcuterie* from … well, all over.

FRANCES LINZEE GORDON

FRANCES LINZEE GORDON

JAMES LYON

OLIVIER CIRENDINI

NICOLA WILLIAMS

BRENDA TURNNIDGE

Eating is a national pastime in France and only the best produce is used to prepare the dishes: Provence, Périgord and Brittany are particularly noted for some fruit and vegetables, dairy products are best from Normandy, and seafood is best from the Atlantic or Mediterranean regions.

identifiable by the gilded horse's head above the entrance, sells horse meat, which some people prefer to beef or mutton, in part because it is less likely to have been produced using artificial hormones and has less fat. Fresh fish and seafood are available from a *poissonnerie*.

Épiceries & Alimentations

A small grocery store with a little bit of everything is known as an *épicerie* (literally, 'spice shop') or an *alimentation générale*. Most épiceries are considerably more expensive than supermarkets, especially in Paris, though some – such as those of the Casino and Comod chains – are more like minimarkets. Some épiceries are open on days when other food shops are closed, and many family-run operations stay open until late at night.

Supermarkets

Both town and city centres usually have at least one department store with a large *supermarché* (supermarket) section in the basement or on the first floor. Stores to look for include Monoprix, Prisunic and Nouvelles Galeries. You may also find one or more small supermarkets of the Casino chain. In Paris, the cheapest edibles are sold at the no-frills supermarkets of Ed l'Épicier. Most larger supermarkets have charcuterie and cheese counters, and many also have in-house boulangeries.

The cheapest place to buy food is a *hypermarché* (hypermarket), such as those of the Auchan, Carrefour, Intermarché, E Leclerc and Rallye chains, where you'll pay up to 40% less for staples than at an épicerie. Unfortunately, they're nearly always on the outskirts of town, often in an area accessible only by car.

Food Markets

In most towns and cities, many of the aforementioned products are available one or more days a week at *marchés en plein air* (open-air markets), also known as *marchés découverts*, and up to six days a week at *marchés couverts* (covered marketplaces), often known as *les halles*. Markets are cheaper than food shops and supermarkets and the merchandise, especially fruit and vegetables, is fresher and of better quality.

In smaller towns and villages, markets have a vital social function. Like cafés, they are an important meeting place, especially for small-scale farmers who have their weekly chat with acquaintances while selling their wares. There is no bargaining, and weighing is often done with hand scales.

A French Cooking Class

Chaud (Warm Goats' Cheese Salad)
Lettuce tossed with a vinaigrette (olive oil, balsamic vinegar, salt and pepper), a few tomatoes and pine nuts. Place the 'crottins de Chavignol' (small goats' milk cheeses), already browned and softened in the oven, on top.

Gratin Dauphinois
Serves 6
Take 1kg of long potatoes, peel and cut into thin rounds. Place in an oven proof dish, which should already be rubbed with a clove of garlic. In a bowl mix 500mL of milk (boiled), one beaten egg, salt, pepper, 100g of grated Gruyére cheese, and a pinch or two of grated nutmeg. Pour mixture over the potatoes. Sprinkle with grated Gruyère. Spread small knobs of butter (50g) over the top. Cover and cook in an oven for 45 minutes at 190-200°C, then uncover and brown for a further 15 minutes.

Pot-au-Feu (Hot Pot)
Add the following to a cast-iron cooking pot: 200g of stewing steak per person (eg ribs, leg, forequarter), a marrowbone, carrots, turnips, leeks, green cabbage (optional), onions pierced with cloves, a bouquet garni (thyme, bay leaves, a stick of celery, parsley), salt and pepper. Add water to cover. Leave to cook for at least 2½ hours (45 minutes in a pressure cooker). Serve the stock separately as a soup/broth before the meat. Eat the marrow on wholemeal bread with cooking salt. The meat and vegetables are eaten with French mustard, gherkins and cooking salt. This dish tastes even better reheated the following day. The recipe can be prepared equally successfully with duck meat.

Escalopes de Veau Flambée (Veal Scallops Flambé)
Flour enough veal scallops for your party and place in a high-sided frying pan with butter and oil; brown and then cook at a medium heat. Remove the veal scallops and keep warm. Place a heaped tablespoon of chopped shallots in the frying pan and cook until golden. Add the veal again and flambé in a young brandy. To flambé, pour the brandy into a stainless steel ladle and light (warm the ladle before adding the brandy, otherwise it may not light). Tip the still flaming liquid onto the meat. Remove the veal once more and arrange on a serving dish. Sprinkle with finely chopped parsley. Add to the frying pan a generous ladleful of fresh cream and a tablespoon of juice from the veal. Reduce and pour over the veal and parsley. Serve with fresh mushrooms cooked in oil.

WINE

Grapes and the art of wine-making were introduced to Gaul by the Romans. In the Middle Ages, important vineyards developed around the monasteries, whose monks needed wine to celebrate the Mass. Large-scale wine production later moved closer to the ports (eg Bordeaux) for export.

In 1863, a kind of aphid known as phylloxera was accidentally brought to Europe from the USA. It ate through the roots of Europe's grapevines, destroying around 10,000 sq km of vineyards in France alone. It looked like European wine production was doomed until phylloxera-resistant root stocks were brought from California and had older varieties grafted onto them.

Wine-making is a complicated chemical process, but ultimately the taste and quality of the wine depends on four key factors: the type(s) of grape used, the climate, the soil, and the art of the wine-maker.

Some viticulturists have honed their skills and techniques to such a degree that their wine is known as a *grand cru* (literally, 'great growth'). If this wine has been produced in a year of optimum climatic conditions it becomes a *millésime* (vintage). Grands crus are aged first in

Wine Quality

Wine production in France is strictly supervised by the government. Under French law, wines are divided into four categories:

***Appellation d'origine contrôlée* (AOC)** These wines have met stringent government regulations governing where, how and under what conditions they are grown, fermented and bottled. They are almost always, at the very least, good and may actually be superb. A bottle of AOC wine can cost from as little as 20FF to many hundreds of francs a bottle, depending on where it's from and which label it bears. The makers of AOC wines are the elite of the French wine industry.

***Vin délimité de qualité supérieure* (VDQS)** These are good wines from a specific place or region – the second rank of French quality control. Prices are similar to AOC wines.

Vin de pays Wines with this label, whose literal meaning is 'country wine', are of reasonable quality and are generally drinkable. They usually sell for between 10 and 15FF a bottle.

Vin de table These table wines are also known as *vins ordinaires* (ordinary wines). You can buy 1L bottles from a supermarket for between 9 and 13FF, but if you buy directly from the producer, you'll pay as little as 5FF a litre (bring your own container). Spending an extra 5 or 10FF can often make a big difference in quality, drinkability and the severity of your hangover.

small oak barrels and then in bottles, sometimes for 20 years or more, before they develop their full taste and aroma. These are the memorable (and pricey) bottles that wine experts talk about with such passion.

There are dozens of wine-producing regions throughout France, but the eight principal regions are Alsace, the Loire Valley, Bordeaux, Burgundy, Champagne, Beaujolais, Languedoc-Roussillon and the Rhône. Wines in France are named after where they're grown rather than the grape varietal, except in Alsace.

In addition to Champagne, which is world renowned for its sparkling wine, two regions produce the most celebrated table wines in France: Bordeaux (Saint Émilion and Pomerol are well known) and Burgundy (eg Côte de Beaune, Côte de Nuits). Vintners can argue interminably about a wine's merits, but it seems that although a Burgundy of the right vintage can be extraordinary, Bordeaux is more reliable.

Wine Regions

Bordeaux Bordeaux wines have always enjoyed a favourable reputation, even from Roman times. Britons (who call the reds 'claret') have hungered for the wines of Bordeaux since the mid-12th century, when King Henry II, who controlled this region of France thanks to his marriage to Eleanor of Aquitaine, tried to gain favour with the citizens of Bordeaux by allowing them, among other concessions, tax-free trade with England. As a result, Bordeaux wine was the cheapest imported wine. This demand has remained ever since. Since those days, Bordeaux's wines have gained a world-wide reputation.

Bordeaux has the perfect climate for producing wine – it is halfway between the North Pole and the equator and its proximity to the Atlantic helps protects it from frosts and excessive heat.

As a result Bordeaux produces more fine wine than any other region in the world. From its 100,000 hectares of vineyards, the region typically produces around one-quarter of France's total *appellation contrôlée* wine, of which 75% is red.

The Bordeaux reds are often described as well-balanced, a quality achieved by blending several grape varieties. The grapes predominantly used are Merlot, Cabernet Sauvignon and Cabernet Franc.

Burgundy This famous wine-growing region is most noted for its great white and red wines. The red wines are produced with Pinot Noir grapes, which although used in other areas produce their best results in Burgundy. The best reds need 10 to 20 years to age and when mature produce a unique mix of aromas. White wine is made from the Chardonnay grape.

The four main wine-growing areas of Burgundy are Chablis, Côte d'Or, Chalonnais and Mâconnais.

Burgundy has produced wines since the days of the Celts (there is some evidence to suggest they introduced wine to the region before the Roman arrival), but developed its reputation in the reign of Charlemagne, when monks first began to produce wine. The Benedictines of Cluny were the first group of monks to gain a significant toehold in the region, but others followed. With cellars to mature the wine, the inclination to keep records and the organisation to make improvements, the monks' influence on wine in Burgundy has meant the region has enjoyed a reputation for great wine ever since.

The vignerons (vine growers) of Burgundy generally only have small vineyards (rarely more than 10 hectares and sometimes only a row or two), partly because the land has always been so valuable but largely because of the Napoleonic Code, which insists every family member receive equal inheritance. Often this sees vignerons produce small quantities of wine (sometimes just one barrel, enough for 25 cases), which merchants then buy and blend, sometimes with spectacular results, but sometimes not.

Beaujolais Unlike their more subtle cousins from Burgundy and Bordeaux, the light but undistinguished reds of Beaujolais age poorly and are therefore drunk young – so young, in fact, that some are considered fit for consumption just a few weeks after the grape harvest. There are 13 different types of Beaujolais in all.

The first day on which the year's new Beaujolais wines – made with Gamay grapes – can officially be sold falls on the third Thursday in November. For many revellers, the chance to sample the year's new *crus* (vintages) provides the perfect excuse for a day and night of partying – and not just in France. Amid the media hype across Europe, bars and cafés hail the new stock's arrival with signs proclaiming '*le Beaujolais nouveau est arrivé!*' (the new Beaujolais has arrived!).

WINE REGIONS

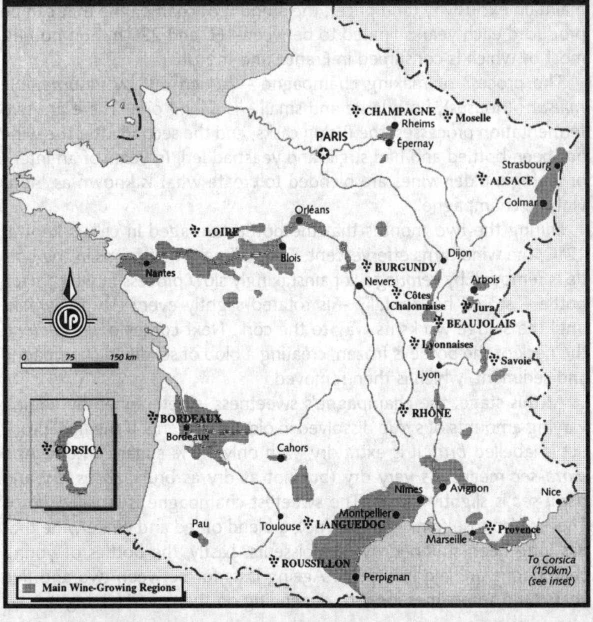

The bright, cherry-red wine, which should be drunk chilled (10°C), has as many detractors (who say it tastes like blackcurrant cordial) as supporters.

The region has 10 appellations: in addition to Nouveau, Chiroubles, Saint Amour and Chénas also tend to age poorly; Régnié is only a new appellation and is still establishing its reputation; Juliénas has some backbone but should still be drunk within two to three years of its vintage; Fleurie is one of the most expensive and is especially renowned for its floral perfume; and Brouilly, Moulin-à-Vent and Morgon all tend to defy the region's reputation and age well.

Champagne Champagne appeared on the French wine scene in the late 17th century thanks to Dom Pierre Pérignon, the innovative cellar master of the Benedictine Abbey at Hautvilliers (near Épernay). He perfected a technique for making sparkling wine of consistent quality (earlier attempts had proved remarkably – even explosively – unpredictable). He proceeded to put his product in strong, English-made bottles (the local bottles couldn't take the enormous pressure) and capped them, thereby sealing in the bubbles, with a new kind of bottle stopper – corks brought from Spain and forced into the mouth of the bottle under high pressure, creating a bulbous, mushroom shape.

Champagne is made using only three varieties of grapes: Chardonnay, Pinot Noir and Pinot Meunier. Each vine is vigorously pruned and trained to produce a small quantity of high quality grapes. Indeed, to maintain exclusivity (and price), the amount of champagne that can be produced each year is limited to between 160 and 220 million bottles, most of which is consumed in France and the UK.

The process of making champagne – carried out by innumerable *maisons* (houses), both large and small – is a long one. There are two fermentation processes, the first in casks, and the second after the wine has been bottled and had sugar and yeast added. In years of an inferior vintage, older wines are blended to create what is known as 'non-vintage champagne'.

During the two months that the bottles are aged in cellars kept at 12°C, the wine turns effervescent. The sediment that forms in the bottle is removed by *remuage*, a painstakingly slow process in which each bottle – stored horizontally – is rotated slightly every day for weeks until the sludge works its way to the cork. Next comes *dégorgement*: the neck of the bottle is frozen, creating a blob of solidified champagne and sediment, which is then removed.

At this stage, the champagne's sweetness is determined by adding varying amounts of syrup dissolved in old champagne. If the final product is labelled *brut*, it is extra dry, with only 1.5% sugar content. And *extra-sec* means it's very dry (but not as dry as brut), *sec* is dry and *demi-sec* is slightly sweet. The sweetest champagne is labelled *doux*. There's also rosé (pink champagne), a blend of red and white wine that has long been snubbed by connoisseurs. Lastly, the bottles of young champagne are laid in a cellar. Ageing lasts for between two and five years (and sometimes longer), depending on the *cuvée* (vintage).

Some of the most famous champagnes are Möet et Chandon, Veuve Cliquot, Mercier, Mumm, Laurent-Perrier, Piper-Heidsieck, Dom Pérignon and Taittinger.

Alsace Alsace has been producing wine since about 300 AD. These days, the region produces almost exclusively white wines – mostly varieties produced nowhere else in France – that are known for their clean, fresh taste and compatibility with the often heavy local cuisine. Some of the fruity Alsatian whites also, unusually, go well with red meat.

Alsace's four most important varietal wines are Riesling, known for its subtlety; the more pungent and highly regarded Gewürztraminer; the robust, high-alcohol Tokay-Pinot Gris; and Muscat d'Alsace, which is not as sweet as that made with Muscat grapes grown farther south. Edelzwicker is light, premium wine made from a blend of different grapes.

Eaux de vie (brandies), are made and flavoured with locally grown fruit and nuts. Of the many varieties, kirsch, a cherry concoction, is the most famous.

Rhône The Rhône River is an important tributary for wine, not only in France but also in Switzerland; however, in wine circles the Rhône always means the area in south-west France.

The French Rhône is divided up into four areas, but the two most important are the northern and southern districts. The different soil, climate, topography and grapes used means there is a dramatic difference in the wines produced by each.

Set on steep hills beside the river, the northern vineyards make red wines exclusively from the Syrah grape, which is a deep ruby-red colour and produces rich wines. The aromatic Viognier grape is the most popular for white wines. The most prestigious wines come from this area, and several rival those of Bordeaux and Burgundy. The south is better known for the quantity of wine it produces. The vineyards are also more spread out and interspersed with fields of lavender and orchards of olives, pears and almonds. The Grenache grape, which ages well when blended, is used in the reds, while the whites use the Ugni Blanc grape.

A Rare Vintage

In 1998 several thousand bottles of 1907 Heidsieck champagne were recovered from the wreck of a Swedish ketch sunk by a German U-boat during WWI. The bottles are expected to fetch US$30,000 each. The bubbly, intended for the tables of tsarist officers in Finland, was preserved by the cold, dark waters of the Baltic Sea and is said by experts to be of exceptional quality.

Languedoc-Roussillon The Languedoc-Roussillon region is the country's most important wine-growing area. Up to 40% of France's wine, mainly cheap, *vin de table* (red table wine), is produced here. About 300,000 hectares of the region is 'under vine', which represents one-third of France's total. And this is in spite of EU led initiatives to reduce Europe's wine surplus by subsidising vignerons to cut down their vines and replant with better quality AOC grapes.

About 10% of the wine produced now is AOC standard. In addition to the well known Fitou label, the area's other AOC wines are Coteaux du Languedoc, Faugères, Corbières and Minervois. The region also produces about 70% of France's *vin de pays* (intermediate category wine), much of which is labelled as Vin de Pays d'Oc. Many vignerons are now also concentrating on producing more and higher quality white wine. A dry rosé, mainly for local consumption, is also produced, as are a muscat and some sparkling wine.

The region's wine producers are also seen as France's most troublesome, often protesting any change that affects their industry, sometimes violently. This is especially true of the appellation laws. Many local vignerons, for instance, prefer to disregard the AOC categories and produce high quality vin de pays instead.

Loire Valley The Loire produces the greatest variety of wines of any region in France: very dry wines to very tart; all manner of colours from the lightest white to the deepest purple; and all types of sparkling wines. A particular speciality of the region is rosé, the most noted of which is Rosé de Anjou.

Many of the Loire wines tend to be underrated by the experts, but obvious exceptions to this are the wines of Pouilly-Fumé, Sancerre, Bourgueil, Chinon and, in particular, Saumur.

Wine at Meals

The French nearly always drink wine with their meals. A fine meal will be accompanied by an equally fine *bouteille* (bottle) of wine – *rouge* (red), *blanc* (white) or rosé – chosen to complement the main course. Unfortunately, wines cost several times more in restaurants than in supermarkets, and the idea of Australian-style BYO (bring your own) is utterly unknown – indeed, the very idea strikes the French as being in unspeakably bad taste.

Ultimately, the taste of any wine is determined by the food with which it is drunk. As a rule, the stronger the food, the stronger the wine. Game will generally be eaten with a full-bodied red wine; beef and lamb with a lighter one; pork, veal and poultry with either a medium white or a light red; fish and shellfish with a dry white; and dessert with a sweet white wine.

Except for champagne, for which the following terms are used a bit differently (see the boxed text 'Champagne, the Sparkling Wine' in the Champagne chapter), brut is very dry, sec is dry, demi-sec is medium sweet, doux is very sweet, and *mousseux* is sparkling.

Wine Tasting

Wine tasting is an art and a tradition. The wine is poured into a small, shallow cup called a *taste-vin*. Tasters use a rich vocabulary to describe wines: wine can be nervous, elegant, fleshy, supple or round and taste of vanilla, strawberry, cherry, cinnamon and even cigars and cedar.

In most wine-growing regions, *caves* (wine cellars) provide an opportunity to purchase wine straight from the vigneron. Quite often, you'll be offered a *dégustation* (tasting), with the wine poured straight from enormous wood barrels or sparkling stainless steel vats (you don't have to spit it out). It's usually free, but you won't be at all popular if you sample several vintages and then leave without buying. Cellars often require that you buy in bulk (*en vrac*) – a 5L minimum is common in some areas.

Study, Swirl, Sniff, Sip, Swallow . . . hic

The art of wine tasting is a complex process and one that takes years to fully appreciate (and usually also requires an extensive vocabulary of adjectives, the more obscure the better), but here's our guide to help you bluff your way through it.

1. Colour Look through the wine towards a source of light. Then tilt the glass slightly and look through it towards a pale background. What you're looking for here is clarity and colour. Clarity is obvious (no good wines have particles floating around in them) but colour is more complex. A deep colour indicates a strong wine. The colour can also reveal the types of grapes used as well as the wine's age (in red wines a blue hue indicates youth, whereas an orange hue indicates age).

2. Smell Swirl the wine around and smell it in one inhalation. The agitation will release the wine's full bouquet. Close your eyes and concentrate: what do you smell? There are 11 main groups of smells associated with wine, ranging from fruits to plants, herbs and spices, and even toasted.

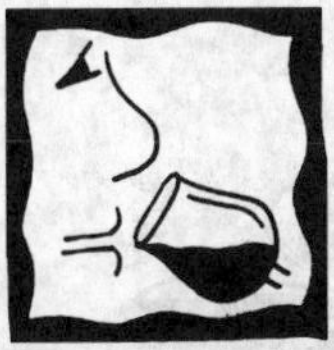

3. Taste Take a sip, swill it around in your mouth and then (here's the tough part) draw in some air to bring out the flavour. Our tastebuds can identify four sensations: bitter, acid, salty and sweet. After doing this swallow the wine. A fine wine should leave an aftertaste.

Wine Bars

Bars à vins, mostly an urban phenomenon, serve a dozen or more selected wines by the glass so you can taste and compare different varieties and vintages. Wines do not keep for very long after the bottle has been opened, but a few years back someone realised that wine in an uncorked bottle can be stabilised by replacing the air inside with a nonoxidising gas.

Wine Shops

Wine is sold by *marchands de vin* (or a *caviste*), such as the shops of the Nicolas chain. Wine shops in close proximity to the vineyards of Burgundy, Bordeaux, Chablis and other wine-growing areas may offer tastings.

The cheapest vintages can cost less than 10FF a bottle – less than a soft drink in a café! – but it's usually worth paying a bit more (at least 20FF) for something more refined. Of course, the better vintages can range in price up to several thousand francs.

DRINKS

Although alcohol consumption has dropped by 20% since the war – the stereotypical Frenchman no longer starts the day by 'killing the worm' (*tuer le ver*) with a shot of red wine (or something stronger) followed by a small, black coffee – the French drink more than any other national group in the world, except the people of Luxembourg. On average, the French consume 11L of pure alcohol a year, compared to 8.3L in the USA and 8.2L in the UK (and with the 18L they drank each year in 1960). Per capita wine consumption fell 30% in the 1980s to 73L a year, this despite recent studies that have shown red wine to be very healthy if drunk regularly and in moderation.

Nonalcoholic Drinks

Water All tap water in France is safe to drink, so there is no need to buy expensive bottled water. Tap water that is not drinkable (eg at most public fountains or in some streams) will usually have a sign reading 'eau non potable'.

If you prefer to have tap water with your meal rather than some pricey soft drink or wine, don't be put off if the waiter scowls: French law mandates that restaurants must serve tap water to clients who so request it. Make sure you ask for *de l'eau* (some water), *une carafe d'eau* (a jug of water), *de l'eau du robinet* (tap water) or, in Paris, raise a smile by asking for *Château Tiberi* (Monsieur Tiberi is the mayor of Paris). Otherwise you'll most likely get *eau de source* (mineral water), which comes *plate* (flat or noncarbonated) or *gazeuse* (fizzy or carbonated).

Mineral waters such as Perrier and Vittel are very fashionable in France, as they are elsewhere. If you're at a café, a *Perrier tranche* is a Perrier with a slice of lemon.

Soft Drinks Soft drinks are expensive in France – in a fashionable café, don't be surprised if you're charged 20FF for a little bottle of Gini or Pschitt. A beer may be cheaper than a Coke. Even in the supermarket, soft drinks are only just cheaper than beer, milk and even some kinds of wine.

One relatively inexpensive café drink is *sirop* (squash, ie fruit syrup), served either *à l'eau* (mixed with water), with *soda* (carbonated water) or Perrier. Basically a strong cordial, popular syrup flavours include *cassis* (blackberry), *grenadine* (pomegranate), *menthe* (mint) and *citron* (lemon). A *citron pressé* is a glass of iced water (either flat or carbonated) with freshly squeezed lemon juice and sugar. A glass of freshly squeezed orange juice is an *orange pressée*. The glass is only half-filled and is accompanied by sugar and water to sweeten and dilute if you choose. *Limonade* is lemon-lime soda (lemonade in the UK). A *panaché* is a shandy (a mixture of limonade and beer). A *diabolo* is limonade with syrup. The French are not particularly fond of drinking very cold things, though this is changing. If you would like your drink with ice cubes, ask for *des glaçons*.

Yoghurt Drinks Yop, made by Yoplait, and Dan'up, produced by Danone, are sweet yoghurt drinks somewhat similar to the sweet *lassi* you get in Indian restaurants. Both are sold in supermarkets.

Coffee A cup of coffee can take various forms, but the most ubiquitous is espresso, made by forcing steam through ground coffee beans. A small, black espresso is called *un café noir*, *un express* or simply *un café*. You can also ask for a *grand* (large) version.

Un café crème is espresso with steamed milk or cream. *Un café au lait* is lots of hot milk with a little coffee served in a large cup or, sometimes, a bowl. A small café crème is a *petit crème*. A *noisette* (literally, 'hazelnut') is an espresso with just a dash of milk.

The French consider American coffee undrinkably weak and dishwatery; they sometimes jokingly call it *jus de chaussettes* (sock juice). They will serve it, or something similar, if you ask for *un café américain* or – because it has been 'lengthened' by adding extra hot water – *un café allongé* or *un café long*. Decaffeinated coffee is *un café décaféiné* or *un déca*.

Tea & Hot Chocolate Other hot drinks that are widely available include *thé* (tea), which is unlikely to be up to the English standard but will be served with milk if you ask for *un peu de lait frais*. Herbal tea, which is widely available, and is very popular as a treatment for minor ailments, is called *tisane* or *infusion*. Popular herbal teas include *menthe* (mint), *camomille* (camomile) and *tilleul* (dried lime flowers).

French *chocolat chaud* (hot chocolate) can be excellent or completely undrinkable.

Alcoholic Drinks

Wine For information on wine, see the Food & Wine section earlier.

Apéritifs Meals are often preceded by an appetite-stirring *apéritif* such as *kir* (white wine sweetened with cassis, ie blackcurrant syrup), *kir royale* (champagne with cassis) and *pineau* (cognac and grape juice). Port is drunk as an apéritif rather than after the meal in France.

Pastis is a 90-proof, anise-flavoured alcoholic drink that, as you mix it with water, turns cloudy. It's strong, refreshing and cheap. Although it's popular all over the country, it's a particular favourite in southern France, where people sip it as an apéritif. Popular brand names are Pernod and Ricard.

Digestifs After-dinner drinks are often ordered along with coffee. France's most famous brandies are Cognac and Armagnac, both of which are made from grapes in regions of those names. The various other sorts of brandies, many of them very strong local products, are known collectively as *eaux de vie* (literally, 'waters of life').

Eaux de vie are a clever way of making use of a bad thing or an over-production of fruit. The grape skins and pulp left over after being pressed for wine are distilled and made into the celebrated Marc de Champagne and Marc de Bourgogne. Calvados is an apple brandy that is made in Normandy; Poire William is a pear-based concoction. Yellow *mirabelle* plums and raspberries are used to make the fiery and highly perfumed *eau de vie de prune* or *eau de vie de framboise*. An invitation to 'une petite prune' or 'une petite framboise' by the head of the house at the end of a meal will mean that you have been truly accepted by a French family.

Produced all over France, most liqueurs are made from grapes, eau de vie, sugar and either fruit or the essences of aromatic herbs. Well known brands include Cointreau, Bénédictine and Chartreuse, all of which are elaborate blends of various ingredients, and orange-spiced Grand Marnier. Sweeter and lighter than the eaux de vie, a liqueur is considered a 'woman's drink' in France. More esoteric is Salers, a bitter concoction made from the roots of the protected wild gentian plant.

Beer Beer, which is served by the demi (about 330mL), is usually either Alsatian (like Kronenbourg, 33 or Pelforth) or imported from Germany or Belgium.

In pubs, beer is cheaper *à la pression* (on draught/tap) than in a *bouteille* (bottle), but prices vary widely depending on what sort of an establishment it is. At a decent but modest sort of place, count on paying 12 to 16FF for a demi of Kronenbourg on tap. Prices often go up two or three francs as the night wears on. Strong Belgian brews such as Trappist beers or cherry-flavoured *kriek* are quite pricey, typically costing about 25FF a bottle.

ENTERTAINMENT

Local tourist offices are generally the best source of information about what's going on in their city or town. In larger towns, the staff will quite frequently be able to give you a free brochure listing the cultural events and entertainment planned for each week, fortnight or month.

Cinema

If you don't want to hear your favourite actor dubbed into French, look in the film listings and on the theatre's billboard for the letters *VO* or *v.o.* (*version originale*) or *v.o.s.t.* (*version originale sous-titrée*), all of which mean that the film retains its original foreign soundtrack but has been given French subtitles. If v.o. is nowhere to be seen, or if you notice the letters *v.f.* (*version française*), it means the film has been dubbed into French. Of course, if the original version of the film was in some language other than English – Chinese, Spanish, Arabic etc – the v.o. version will be too. One of the authors of this book once went to see a film that the ads said was from the UK *and* v.o. only to discover, during the opening scenes, that the soundtrack was in Welsh.

In Paris, the film listings in *Pariscope* and *L'Officiel des Spectacles* (see Listings in the Entertainment section in the Paris chapter) usually also include the original release names of some English-language movies. However, local newspapers, cinema billboards and cinema answering machines generally only use the French titles, which may be completely unrelated (and often also difficult to figure out) to the original English names.

Cinema schedules usually list two times for each film: one for the *séance*, ie when the prescreening ads and trailers begin, and the other, usually 10 to 25 minutes later, for the film itself. No self-respecting French *cinéphile* would dream of missing the ads, which – released from the time limits and content conventions of TV – are generally creative, entertaining and often quite provocative.

Film-going in France does not come cheap – count on paying 40 to 50FF for a first-run film. Most French cinemas offer discounts to students, and people under 18 or over 60 usually get discounts of about 25%, but not on Friday, Saturday and Sunday nights. On Wednesday (and sometimes also on Monday), most cinemas give discounts to everyone.

Discos & Clubs

In French, a discotheque (also called a *boîte*) is any sort of establishment where music (live or recorded) leads to dancing. The music on offer ranges from jazz and raï to Latino and techno, and the crowd may be gay, lesbian, straight or mixed. The sign *'tenue correcte exigée'*, which you may see displayed at various venues, means 'appropriate dress required'. Most discos only begin to hit their stride after midnight (and sometimes much later).

Bouncers These gorillas will eye-ball you suspiciously at the entrance to most clubs and discos. Alas, when it comes to nighttime entertainment, France is the land of the *videur* (bouncer, literally 'emptier'). In some places, the bouncers are big, stupid and paid to indulge their megalomaniacal animalistic tendencies to keep out 'undesirables', which, depending on the place, ranges from unaccompanied men who aren't dressed right to members of certain minority groups (eg North Africans and blacks).

One of the functions of a bouncer is to decide, according to your overall look, if you're suitable for that particular night's entertainment. At some particularly exclusive discotheques, you have to be dressed in a manner appropriate to the night's theme. Although locals can find their night out abruptly reconfigured by a bouncer's snap decision, tourists aren't usually held to such strict standards. All discos, however, are very careful not to admit people who are drunk.

Music

All French cities and many towns put on at least one music festival each year. For details, see Special Events under specific city and town listings or contact the local tourist office. The nationwide Fête de la Musique brings live music to every corner of the country each 21 June.

France's contemporary music scene is dominated by jazz and the sounds of Cuba, Brazil and Africa. Celtic music, such as that featured at the Festival Interceltique, held at Lorient in Brittany in early August, continues to gain popularity. Techno is almost as popular in Paris as it is in Berlin.

The classical music scene is very lively and less Paris-centric than you might think. The dozen or so non-Parisian orchestras include well regarded organisations in Lille, Strasbourg and Toulouse. There are innumerable classical music festivals all over France, especially during the summer; those held in Aix-en-Provence and Orange in July are especially popular. The *chansons* of Edith Piaf, Georges Brassens and Belgian-born Jacques Brel continue to be popular.

Theatre

Long gone is French theatre's post-war golden age, when dramatists and directors such as Anouilh, Beckett, Camus, Genet, Ionesco and Montherlant held audiences spellbound with their innovative works.

These days, the French theatre scene is dominated by the revival of old favourites and the translation of foreign hits, especially in Paris. As it has since the time of Louis XIV, Paris' famous Comédie Française continues to produce French classics, though it has expanded its repertoire in recent years.

One of the highlights of the French theatre year is the Festival d'Avignon and the concurrent Festival Off (fringe festival), held in Avignon from mid-July to mid-August.

SPECTATOR SPORTS

Football and cycling are probably the most popular spectator sports, but the French are also particularly taken with tennis and rugby. Skiing is also quite popular though France hasn't produced any stars since Jean-Claude Killy and Marielle Goitchel in the 1960s. Champion figure skaters Philippe Candeloro and Surya Bonnally have sparked interest in ice skating in the past few years.

For details on upcoming sporting events, consult the sports daily *L'Équipe* (4.90FF) or the *Figaroscope*, published by *Le Figaro*, each Wednesday.

BRENDA TURNIDGE

The French victory in the World Cup triggered a week-long celebration across the whole country.

Football

France's greatest sporting moment came at the 1998 World Cup, which the country hosted and won, beating the reigning champions and tournament favourite, Brazil, in a one-sided final. Reduced to 10 men (as they had been during their semi-final against Croatia) France beat Brazil 3-0 thanks to two goals from Zinedine Zidane and one from Emmanuel Petit. After the match, millions of elated supporters spilled on to the streets of Paris to celebrate.

The early days of France 98 were marred by serious outbreaks of hooligan violence, and rows over ticket allocation. Many football federations claimed their ticket allocations failed to meet demand, while many fans – in particular the Japanese – were promised tickets that never materialised. But as the tournament progressed these problems were overshadowed by some thrilling matches, including the home side's victories over Paraguay, Italy, Croatia and, finally, Brazil.

It was a success the football-mad French had waited a long time for. France's national teams had traditionally been hailed for their flair and imaginative play but had never progressed further than the World Cup semi-finals. It was not until 1984 that France won a major international football trophy – the European Championship, thanks mainly to the brilliant performance of superstar Michel Platini. France also won the 1984 Olympic tournament, again beating Brazil.

At club level, in 1991 Marseille became the first French side to win the European Champions League. Three years later Paris-Saint Germain took the European Cup Winners Cup.

The 1995 Bosman decision – allowing any European club to field as many European players as they wish – has resulted in a great exodus of French players (including Zidane and Petit) to clubs in Italy, Britain, Spain and Germany where they are better paid. This could have a great impact on the future of French club football at both national and European level.

The French team's home matches (friendlies and qualifiers for the 2000 European Championships) are held at the magnificent Stade de France at Saint-Denis, which was built especially for the World Cup. Check the sporting press for details on when and where individual club sides are playing.

Rugby

Rugby league has a strong following in the south and south-west of France with favourite teams being Toulouse, Montauban and Saint Godens. Rugby union is more popular still, as the enduring success of the powerful Paris-Saint Germain club testifies. The French national teams in both codes have always been notoriously difficult to beat at home.

France's home games in the Tournoi des Cinq Nations (Five Nations Tournament) are held in March and April and involve France, England, Scotland, Wales, Ireland and, from the year 2000, Italy. The finals of the Championnat de France de Rugby take place in late May and early June.

Tennis

The French Open, held in Paris's Roland Garros Stadium in late May and early June, is the second of the four Grand Slam tournaments. For more information, see Spectator Sports in the Paris chapter.

Cycling

The Tour de France is the world's most prestigious bicycle race. For three weeks in July, 189 of the world's top cyclists (in 21 teams of nine) take on a 3000km-plus route. The route changes each year, but three things remain constant – the inclusion of the Alps, Pyrenees and, since 1975, the race's finish on the Champs-Élysées in Paris. Frequently the race crosses the border into Switzerland, Spain, Italy and Andorra; in recent years it has even started in England and Ireland! Wherever it goes, the route is blocked off hours before the cyclists stream past.

The race itself is typically divided into 22 daily stages: it starts with a prologue, which is a short time trial used essentially to put a rider (the prologue's winner) in the leader's jersey for the first stage; two other time trials; five or six stages in the mountains;

the rest are usually long flat stages; and, usually, there's at least one rest day. Each stage is timed and the race's overall winner is the rider with the lowest aggregate time – the smallest winning margin was in 1989, when Greg LeMond beat enigmatic Parisian Laurent Fignon by eight seconds after 23 days of racing and 3285km.

There are three special jerseys: the *maillot jaune* (yellow jersey) for race leader, *maillot vert* (green jersey) for points leader, and *maillot à pois rouges* (red polka dot jersey) for the king of the mountains. These jerseys are awarded after every stage in the race and to win one, especially the maillot jaune, even for a day, is certain to make headlines back home for that rider.

France is also the world's number one track cycling nation and has a formidable reputation in the developing sport of mountain biking.

For information on the Paris-Roubaix cycle race and the indoor Grand Prix des Nations competition, see Spectator Sports in the Paris chapter.

The Mondialisation of Le Tour

During the halcyon days of French dominance of the Tour de France in the 1960s, 70s and early 80s, it used to be said that the government could fall, taxes double, trains strike, but there was only one thing the French public cared about in July: who was wearing the *maillot jaune* (yellow (leader's) jersey) in the Tour de France.

With no French winner in the Tour since voracious Breton Bernard Hinault won his fifth Tour crown in 1985, cycling has slipped in the national psyche and football is the nation's number one sporting love – especially so now France is the reigning World Cup champion and since the drugs scandal of 1998. However, the race itself continues in its march towards *mondialisation* (internationalisation).

From its humble beginnings in 1903, when newspaper publisher Henry Desgrange created the race to boost sales of *l'Auto*, Le Tour, as the race is more fondly known, is now the biggest annual sporting event in the world in terms of budget, worldwide TV audiences and spectators, and is only eclipsed in these areas by the World Cup of Football and the Olympic Games (both of which are only held every four years).

The mondialisation of Le Tour was inadvertently started by a core group of English-speaking cyclists in the 1980s (often referred to as the 'Foreign Legion'). These riders were very successful and the subsequent demand for TV coverage has now meant that the race (and the sport of cycling) is well known in the USA, Australia, Ireland and the UK. As a result the traditional European sponsors such as Fiat, Tissot and Crédit Lyonnais are being replaced by US sponsors such as Coca-Cola and Nike.

The Foreign Legion (whose careers are detailed in Rupert Guinness' book of the same name) included the likes of Irishmen Stephen Roche (who won the race in 1987) and Sean Kelly, Brits Graeme Miller and Sean Yates, Australians Phil Anderson and Alan Pieper, and the most successful of them all, America's Greg LeMond, who won the race three times. Although the cyclists of the initial 'regiment' of the Foreign Legion have all retired now, another regiment – including Australia's Stuart O'Grady (the first Australian since Phil Anderson in 1981 and 1982 to wear the maillot jaune) and Robbie McEwen, and Americans Lance Armstrong and Bobby Julich (3rd overall in 1998) – continues to make its mark on Le Tour.

However, it isn't just the English-speaking riders that inspire devotees of Le Tour these days. It's almost impossible to watch the action without appreciating the strength and panache (a highly regarded quality by the French public) of the likes of Marco Pantani, who broke the 32 year drought of wins by Italians in 1998, and French hero Richard Virenque.

Traditional Sports

Pétanque France's most popular traditional games are *pétanque* and the similar, though more formal, *boules* (similar to lawn bowls but played on a hard surface). Unlike lawn bowls, whose white-clad players throw their woods on an immaculate strip of grass, pétanque and boules (which has a 70 page rule book) are usually played by village men in work clothes on a rough gravel or sandy pitch known as a *boulodrome*, scratched out wherever a bit of flat and shady ground can be found. Especially popular in the south, the games are often played in the cool of late afternoon, sometimes with a glass of pastis near to hand. The object is to get your boules (biased metal balls) as close as possible to the 'jack', the small ball thrown at the start. World championships are held for both sports.

Pelote In the Basque Country, the racquet game of *pelote*, the fastest form of which is

Helicopters & Taut Legs on Le Tour

Today it was Pau, gateway to the Pyrenees, but it could be any town lining the route of the Tour de France, in any year, and it would still be the same.

I was just outside the town centre on Rue du 14 Juillet, the main road to the mountains, standing in the gutter, shoulder to shoulder with holidaying Frenchmen and women listening to the race on small radios. Extraordinarily jovial *gendarmes* walked idly up and down the bitumen. And kids and groups of cyclists were everywhere. The talk was loud, the looks wide-eyed and attentive.

It was one of those hot, humid summer's days. A threatening storm had turned the sky a dark slate grey. Everything about the day seemed charged, ready to erupt.

It was the ninth stage of the 1987 Tour. The first significant day for those hoping to win overall honours. The mountains always play a big part in the Tour; they're unforgiving, unrelenting and daunting, so the riders would have been nervous too before the start.

The road was closed to traffic, except official cars: team cars, media cars and the white Fiats of the organisers, all with their lights on full beam and horns trumpeting, were a constant high-speed stream. The first signal of the riders' approach was the helicopters. There were six, hovering and darting across the sky like noisy dragonflies. Seven riders were in the lead group, and they had just turned onto the long straight road that led up to the centre. The crowd surged, strained and stood on tiptoes. The gendarmes, at work now, kept them at bay.

At 100m the crowd could name all the riders: Eric Breukink, the tall Dutchman, was there, and so was Charly Mottet, the perennial French favourite. *'Allez, Charly, allez, allez, allez.' 'Bonne chance, Charly.'* And in a few seconds the brightly coloured jerseys and taut muscled legs of those seven were over the sharp rise and sprinting around Place de Verdun to the finish. But before it could go quiet another group approached. The cheers continued, as did the naming of each of the riders. And then they were gone, up over the rise as well. That's how it went for 50 minutes, the crowd standing an enthusiastic vigil on the side of the road and the riders' taut legs pushing up over the day's final rise to the finish. And all the time the streets thundered with the sounds of car horns, cheering and helicopters.

As it turned out Breukink won the race to the line, but Mottet became the hero of France by earning the maillot jaune. If you're in France in July and have the chance to see Le Tour, do it. It's free. Choose a stage finish, rather than a start, and, if you can, choose a day when the riders finish on a climb. Buy a copy of *L'Équipe* for the daily itineraries during the race or visit the organiser's Web site (www.letour.fr/) if you want to plan ahead.

Darren Elder

called *cesta punta*, is very popular. For details, see the boxed text 'Pelote' in the French Basque Country chapter.

SHOPPING

France is renowned for its luxury goods, particularly *haute couture*, high-quality clothing accessories (eg Hermès scarves), lingerie and perfume. Obviously Paris has the largest selection on offer, but for local crafts and art (eg colourful faïence from Quimper in Brittany, crystal and glassware from Baccarat in southern Lorraine, enamel and porcelain from Limoges in Limousin), it's best to go directly to the source.

This is especially true for wines (eg Bordeaux, Burgundy, Alsace, Champagne) and other alcoholic beverages (eg Izarra from Bayonne in the French Basque Country, Bénédictine from Fécamp in Normandy), cheese (chèvre from Provence, Mont d'Or from the Jura, brocciu from Corsica) and exotic foodstuffs like the delectable black truffles harvested around Vaison-la-Romain in Provence, macaroons from Saint Émilion (see the Atlantic Coast chapter) and candied fruit from Nice on the Côte d'Azur. For information on local shopping options, see Shopping under the individual towns and cities.

Non-EU residents may be able to get a rebate of some of the 20.6% value-added tax (VAT). See Taxes & Refunds under Money in this chapter for details.

Clothing & Shoe Sizes

Clothes and footwear are sized differently in France than in the UK and USA. For the equivalents, see the tables below.

Clothing Sizes

Women's Tops & Dresses			Men's Shirts			Men's Suits		
UK	USA	France	UK	USA	France	UK	USA	France
8	6	36	–	14	36	30	36	38
10	8	38	14½	14½	37	32	37	40
12	10	40	15	15	38	38	38	42-44
14	12	42	15½	15½	39	–	39	44
18	16	46-48	16	16½	41	38	42	48
20	18	50	16½	17	42			
22	20	52						

Shoe Sizes

Women's Shoes			Men's Shoes		
UK	USA	France	UK	USA	France
3	4	35½	5½	6	39
3½	4½	36	6½	7	40
4	5	36½	7	7½	41
4½	5½	37	8	8½	42
5	6	37½	8½	9	43
5½	6½	38	9½	10	44
6	7½	39	10½	11	45

Getting There & Away

AIR

Air France, France's money-losing national carrier, and scores of other airlines link Paris with every part of the globe. Other French airports with direct international air links include Bordeaux, Lyon, Marseille, Metz-Nancy-Lorraine, Mulhouse-Basel (EuroAirport), Nantes, Nice, Strasbourg and Toulouse.

For details on Paris' two main international airports, Orly and Roissy Charles de Gaulle, and the addresses of airline offices in the French capital, see Air under Getting There & Away in the Paris chapter. The various ways to travel between the airports and central Paris are covered under To/From the Airport in that chapter's Getting Around section.

Don't forget to reconfirm your onward or return bookings 72 hours before your flight.

Travel with Children

In general, children under the age of two travel for 10% of the standard fare (or, on some carriers, for free) as long as they don't occupy a seat. They don't get a luggage allowance either. Skycots, baby food, formula, nappies (diapers), etc should be provided by the airline if requested in advance. Children aged between two and 12 can usually occupy a seat for half to two-thirds of the full fare and do get a luggage allowance.

Cheap Air Fares

Return (round-trip) tickets are usually cheaper than two one ways. In some cases, the return fare may actually be less than a one-way ticket. The cheapest tickets often come with cumbersome restrictions: minimum and/or maximum stays, advance reservation requirements, mandatory Saturday overnight, nonrefundability etc.

Round-the-world (RTW) tickets make it possible to combine a visit to the Alps with a trek in the Himalayas and backpacking in the Rockies. If you live in Australasia, they are often no more expensive than an ordinary return fare. Prices start at about UK£900, A$1700 or US$1300. You usually have to book dates for every sector you want to fly, but these can be changed en route. The departure date from your home country usually determines the fare (ie which season you're charged). Validity usually lasts for a year. From New Zealand an RTW ticket with United to Europe (via the USA) and then back with Thai costs about NZ$2500.

Use the fares quoted in this book as a guide only. They are based on the rates advertised by travel agents as we went to press and are likely to have changed somewhat by the time you read this.

Discount Travel Agents Usually only a few travel agents are given access to a particular batch of discounted tickets, so the best way to find cheap tickets is to phone around. Things to check include the total fare, the stopovers allowed (or required), the duration of the journey, the period of validity, cancellation penalties and any other restrictions.

You may discover that those impossibly cheap flights are 'fully booked, but we have another one that costs a bit more ...' Or that the flight is on an airline notorious for its poor safety record and will leave you for 14 hours in the world's least-favourite airport, where you'll be confined to the transit lounge unless you get an expensive visa ... Or the agent may claim that the last two cheap seats until next autumn will be gone in two hours. Don't panic – keep ringing around.

If you are travelling from the USA or South-East Asia, you will sometimes find that the cheapest flights are being advertised by obscure agencies whose names have yet to reach the telephone directory. Many such firms are honest and solvent, but there are a few rogues who will take

Air Travel Glossary

Apex Tickets Apex stands for Advance Purchase Excursion fare. These tickets are usually between 30 and 40% cheaper than the full economy fare, but there are restrictions. You must purchase the ticket at least 21 days in advance (sometimes more), be away for a minimum period (normally 14 days), and return within a maximum period (90 or 180 days). Stopovers are not allowed. Extra charges are payable if you change your dates of travel or destination. Also, the tickets are not fully refundable.

Baggage Allowance This will be written on your ticket; you are usually allowed one 20kg item to go in the hold, plus one item of hand luggage. Some airlines which fly transpacific and transatlantic routes allow for two pieces of luggage (there are pretty generous limits on their dimensions and weight).

Bucket Shops At certain times of the year and/or on certain routes, many airlines fly with empty seats. This isn't profitable and it's more cost-effective for them to fly full, even if that means having to sell a certain number of drastically discounted tickets. They do this by off-loading them onto bucket shops (UK) or consolidators (USA), travel agents who specialise in discounted fares. These tickets are often the cheapest you'll find. Availability varies widely, so you'll not only have to be flexible in your travel plans, you'll also have to be quick off the mark as soon as an advertisement appears in the press.

Bumped Just because you have a confirmed seat doesn't mean you're going to get on the plane – see Overbooking.

Cancellation Penalties If you have to cancel or change a discounted ticket, there are often heavy penalties involved; insurance can sometimes be taken out against these penalties. Some airlines impose penalties on regular tickets as well, particularly against 'no-show' passengers.

Check In Airlines ask you to check in a certain time ahead of the flight departure (usually one to two hours on international flights). If you fail to check in on time and the flight is overbooked, the airline can cancel your booking and give your seat to somebody else.

Confirmation Having a ticket written out with the flight and date you want doesn't mean you have a seat until the agent has checked with the airline that your status is 'OK' or confirmed. Meanwhile you could just be 'on request'.

Courier Fares Businesses often need to send urgent documents or freight securely and quickly. They do it through courier companies. These companies hire people to accompany the package through customs and, in return, offer a bargain ticket. In effect, what the courier companies do is ship their freight as your luggage on the regular commercial flights. This is a legitimate operation – all the freight is completely legal. There are two shortcomings, however: the short turnaround time of the ticket, usually not longer than a month; and the limitation on your luggage allowance. You may be required to surrender all your baggage allowance for the use of the courier company, and be only allowed to take carry-on luggage.

Discounted Tickets There are two types of discounted fares – officially discounted (such as Apex) and unofficially discounted (see Bucket Shops). The latter can save you more than money – you may be able to pay Apex prices without all the requirements. The lowest prices often impose drawbacks, such as flying with unpopular airlines, inconvenient schedules, or unpleasant routes an connections.

Air Travel Glossary

Full Fares Airlines traditionally offer 1st class (coded F), business class (coded J) and economy class (coded Y) tickets. These days there are so many promotional and discounted fares available that few passengers pay full economy fare.

Lost Tickets If you lose your airline ticket an airline will usually treat it like a travellers cheque and, after inquiries, issue you with another one. Legally, however, an airline is entitled to treat it like cash and if you lose it then it's gone forever. Take good care of your tickets.

MCO An MCO, or 'miscellaneous charge order', is a voucher that looks like an airline ticket but carries no destination or date. It can be exchanged through any International Association of Travel Agents (IATA) airline for a ticket on a specific flight. It's a useful alternative to an onward ticket in those countries that demand one, and is more flexible than an ordinary ticket if you're unsure of your route.

No-Shows No-shows are passengers who fail to show up for their flight. Full-fare passengers who fail to turn up are sometimes entitled to travel on a later flight. The rest are penalised.

Overbooking Airlines hate to fly empty seats and since every flight has some passengers who fail to show up, airlines often book more passengers than they have seats. Usually excess passengers make up for the no-shows, but occasionally somebody gets bumped. Guess who it is most likely to be? The passengers who check in late.

Promotional Fares These are officially discounted fares, such as Apex fares, available from travel agencies or direct from the airline.

Reconfirmation At least 72 hours prior to departure time of an onward or return flight, you must contact the airline and 'reconfirm' that you intend to be on the flight. If you don't do this the airline can delete your name from the passenger list and you could lose your seat.

Restrictions Discounted tickets often have various restrictions on them – such as needing to be paid for in advance and incurring a penalty to be altered. Others are restrictions on the minimum and maximum period you must be away.

Round-the-World Tickets RTW tickets give you a limited period (usually a year) in which to circumnavigate the globe. You can go anywhere the carrying airlines go, as long as you don't backtrack. The number of stopovers or total number of separate flights is decided before you set off and they usually cost a bit more than a basic return flight.

Stand-by This is a discounted ticket where you only fly if there is a seat free at the last moment. Stand-by fares are usually available only on domestic routes.

Transferred Tickets Airline tickets cannot be transferred from one person to another. Travellers sometimes try to sell the return half of their ticket, but officials can ask you to prove that you are the person named on the ticket. This is less likely to happen on domestic flights, but on an international flight tickets are compared with passports.

Travel Periods Ticket prices vary with the time of year. There is a low (off-peak) season and a high (peak) season, and often a low-shoulder season and a high-shoulder season as well. Usually the fare depends on your outward flight – if you depart in the high season and return in the low season, you pay the high-season fare.

your money and run – only to reopen elsewhere a month or two later under a new name. If you feel suspicious about a firm, don't give them all the money at once – leave a deposit of 20% or so and pay the balance when you get the ticket. If they insist on cash in advance, go somewhere else or take a very big risk. And once you have the ticket, ring the airline to confirm that you are booked on the flight.

You may decide that it's worthwhile to pay a bit more than the rock-bottom fare in return for the safety of a better known travel agent. Such firms include:

Council Travel
 www.counciltravel.com
 (US-based company)
Nouvelles Frontières
 www.newfrontiers .com
 (French-based)
STA Travel
 www.sta-travel.com
Travel CUTS
 www.travelcuts.com
 (Canadian-based)
USIT
 www.usit.ie
 (Irish-based)
Wasteels
 www.voyages-wasteels.fr
 (French and Belgian based)

Cheap Tickets in France The only way to find the best deal is to shop around – prices and available dates vary greatly, and a clearing house with great prices to Bangkok may not be able to get you the lowest student fare to New York.

Inexpensive flights offered by charter clearing houses can be booked through many regular travel agents – look in agency windows for posters and pamphlets advertising Forum Voyages (☎ 01 53 32 71 72 or ☎ 08 36 68 12 02; Minitel 3615 FV), Go Voyages (☎ 08 36 68 61 00 for a recording at 2.23FF a minute; Minitel 3615 GO VOYAGES), Look Voyages (☎ 01 53 43 13 13 or ☎ 08 36 68 01 20; Minitel 3615 LOOK PROMO, 3615 LOOK INFOR or 3615 SOS CHARTER) and Nouvelle Liberté (Minitel 3615 NLB). Some of the fares advertised in the Paris metro and the free Paris biweekly *France USA Contacts* (*FUSAC*) are sometimes too good to be true.

Nouvelles Frontières (☎ 08 03 33 33 33 at 1.49FF a minute; Minitel 3615 NF), which specialises in long-haul flights and has some cheap routings to Asia through Russia, eastern Europe and the Persian Gulf, has 150 bureaus around the country. Attractive youth fares are available from various student travel agencies (eg AJF, Council Travel, USIT; see Student Travel Agencies in the Paris chapter) and from Voyages Wasteels (☎ 01 43 62 30 00 in Paris; Minitel 3615 WASTEELS), best known for selling BIJ train tickets.

Since London's bucket shops tend to be cheaper than their Parisian counterparts, an option for long-haul flights is to contact Trailfinders (☎ 0171-937 5400 or, after June 1999, ☎ 020-7937 5400) at 194 Kensington High St, London W8 7RG, or STA Travel (☎ 0171-361 6262 or, after June 1999, ☎ 020-7361 6262) at Priory House, 6 Wrights Lane, London W8 6TA.

Aventure du Bout du Monde (☎ 01 43 35 08 95; fax 01 43 22 24 41; www.abm.fr; metro Denfert Rochereau), based in Paris at 7 Rue Gassendi (14e), is an organisation that facilitates the exchange of practical travel information – including advice on cheap flights – between travellers. Membership costs 190FF a year. Its web site has useful information in French on buying aeroplane tickets in France.

Weight Limits

Unless you're flying to/from North America (across the Atlantic or the Pacific), in which case you can usually bring along two suitcases of fairly generous proportions, your checked luggage will be subject to a 20kg weight limit. On most flights (with the exception of certain charters) you won't be charged if you're only three to 5kg over, but beyond that each kilogram will be assessed at 1% of the price of a full-fare 1st class, one-way ticket. This can work out to be very expensive indeed, eg A$58 per kilogram to/from Australia.

The UK

Flights between Paris and London are sometimes available for as little as 500FF return; Air France offers one-way youth fares for 390FF. A straightforward and fully flexible London-Paris ticket with British Airways, British Midland or Air France will cost UK£158/252 one way/return, although a seven day excursion ticket (taking in a Saturday night) should cost somewhere between UK£85 and UK£90. One-way fares as low as UK£49 are available on Air UK.

The Channel Islands

Aurigny Air Services (☎ 01481-822 886 in Alderney; ☎ 02 99 46 70 28 in Dinard) has flights linking Dinard with Guernsey (UK£56 one way) and Jersey (UK£50 one way).

Ireland

USIT Voyages (☎ 01-602 1600 in Dublin, ☎ 01 42 34 56 90 in Paris; by Minitel 3615 USIT) has one-way/return Dublin-Paris flights for young people (25 and under) and students for I£55/99 (I£45/79 for very restrictive tickets to Beauvais airport). Belfast-Paris student fares are I£67/128. In France, non-student return fares to/from Dublin, Shannon, Cork and Galway are in the 900 to 1400FF range.

Continental Europe

Return discount fares from Paris include Athens (1500FF), Berlin (1000FF), Budapest (1900FF), Copenhagen (1500FF), Istanbul (1400FF), Madrid (1500FF), Stockholm (1900FF) and Rome (1150FF). The cheapest fares are available in early spring and late autumn. Air France's youth fares often cost only a bit more than charters.

The USA

The flight options across the North Atlantic, the world's busiest long-haul air corridor, are bewildering. The *New York Times*, *LA Times*, *Chicago Tribune* and *San Francisco Chronicle* all have weekly travel sections in which you'll find any number of travel agents' ads. Council Travel and STA Travel have offices in major cities nationwide.

You should be able to fly from New York to Paris and back for US$400 to US$500 in the low season and US$550 to US$700 in the high season. Equivalent fares from the west coast are US$100 to US$300 higher.

On a stand-by basis, one-way fares can work out to be remarkably cheap. Airhitch (☎ 212-864 2000; www.airhitch.org) specialises in this sort of thing and can get you to/from Europe for US$175/225/255 each way from the east coast/midwest/west coast.

In Paris, one-way discount flights on the Paris-New York route usually cost from 1200 to 1500FF. Return fares of 2000FF are sometimes available, but a more usual fare is 2500FF (3400FF in July and August). Return fares to the west coast are 600 to 1000FF higher.

Courier Flights Another option is a courier flight. A New York-Paris return ticket can be had for as little as US$300 in the low season. You may also be able to fly one way. The drawbacks are that your stay in Europe may be limited to one or two weeks; your luggage is usually restricted to hand luggage; there is unlikely to be more than one courier ticket available for any given flight; and you may have to be a local resident and apply for an interview before they'll take you on.

You can find out more about courier flights from the International Association of Air Travel Couriers (☎ 561-582 8320; fax 561-582 1581; www.courier.org; iaatc@courier.org), As You Like It Travel (☎ 212-679 6949; fax 212-779 9674; www.asulikeit.com) or Now Voyager Travel (☎ 212-431 1616; fax 212-334 5243; www.nowvoyagertravel.com).

Canada

Travel CUTS (☎ 1-888-838 CUTS) has offices in all major cities. You might also scan the budget travel agents' ads in the Toronto *Globe & Mail*, the *Toronto Star* and the *Vancouver Province*.

From Paris, you may find that flights are a bit cheaper to Montreal than to Toronto, with one-way/return fares as low as 1200/2000FF.

Australia

STA Travel and Flight Centres International are major dealers in cheap air fares. Saturday's travel sections in the *Sydney Morning Herald* and the Melbourne *Age* have many ads offering cheap fares to Europe, but don't be surprised if they happen to be 'sold out' when you call: they're usually low-season fares on obscure airlines with conditions attached.

Airlines like Thai, Malaysian, Qantas and Singapore have fares to Paris from about A$1500 (low season) to A$2500 (high season). All have frequent promotional fares so it pays to check daily newspapers. Flights to/from Perth are a couple of hundred dollars cheaper.

From Paris, return trips to Melbourne or Sydney start at about 6200FF (about 1000FF more during the northern summer). Nouvelles Frontières has some of the best fares around.

New Zealand

As in Australia, STA Travel and Flight Centres International are popular travel agents in New Zealand. The cheapest fares to Europe are routed through Asia. Fares (via Bangkok) in the low season start at about NZ$1185 one way and NZ$2049 return. Via the USA, fares in the low season start at NZ$1265/2299 one way/return. A RTW ticket will cost about NZ$2300.

Africa

Nairobi and Johannesburg are probably the best place in Africa to buy tickets to Europe, thanks to the many bucket shops and the lively competition between them. Several West African countries offer cheap charter flights to France. Charter fares from Morocco and Tunisia can be quite cheap if you're lucky enough to find a seat.

From Paris, return charter flights to Tunis cost 1300 to 2000FF; Tangier is 1500 to 2200FF. Return fares start at 2600FF to Dakar, and 3400FF to Abidjan and Mombasa (about 1000FF higher in summer). Nouvelles Frontières has a wide selection of destinations.

Middle East

Paris is well connected with the whole Middle East. Sample cheapie return fares include Amman (2200FF), Bahrain (3500FF), Beirut (2300FF), Cairo (2200FF) and Tel Aviv (1800 to 2300FF; tickets are often cheaper if bought in Israel, eg from the student travel agency ISSTA, ☎ 03-521 4444).

East & South Asia

Singapore and Bangkok are the air fare capitals of the region. Their bucket shops are at least as unreliable as those of other cities, so shop around and ask the advice of other travellers before handing over any money. STA Travel has branches in Hong Kong, Tokyo, Singapore, Bangkok and Kuala Lumpur.

Mumbai and Delhi are the air transport hubs in India, but tickets may be slightly cheaper in Delhi. There are a number of bucket shops around Connaught Place in Delhi, but check with other travellers about their current trustworthiness.

In Paris, sample discount return prices include: Bangkok (3600 to 4900FF, depending on the time of the year), Bombay (3800 to 5000FF), Ho Chi Minh City (4350FF), Hong Kong (3800FF), Jakarta (4300FF), Phnom Penh (4400FF) and Singapore (3800FF). Nouvelles Frontières offers a wide selection of destinations and generally has decent prices.

LAND

Paris, France's main rail and road hub, is linked with every part of Europe. Travel from northern Europe to other parts of France sometimes (though much less frequently than in the past) involves switching train stations in Paris – for details on Paris' six major train stations, see Train under Getting There & Away in the Paris chapter.

For details on rail passes such as Eurail, BIJ tickets and other reduced price rail options, see Rail Passes and Discount Tickets under Train in the Getting Around chapter.

England

The Channel Tunnel, inaugurated in 1994 after massive cost overruns, is the first dry-land link between England and France since the last Ice Age. The three parallel, concrete-lined tunnels – two rail tunnels and one for servicing them – were bored between Folkestone and Calais through a layer of impermeable chalk marl 25 to 45m below the floor of the English Channel. About US$14 billion in private capital was invested in the project, the fourth attempt at tunnelling from England to France (previous efforts were abandoned). The financially struggling consortium that built the tunnel has been awarded a concession to run it for 55 years.

Bus Eurolines (☎ 01582-404511 in Luton, ☎ 01 49 72 51 51 in Paris; Minitel 3615 EUROLINES; www.eurolines.co.uk; euro line@imaginet.fr) has bus services from London's Victoria Coach station to various French cities, including, of course, Paris (UK£31/44 or 280/410FF one way/return, a bit less if you qualify for a discount; 7½ hours) via Dover and Calais. Bookings can be made in London at the Eurolines office (☎ 0171-730 8235 or, after June 1999, ☎ 020-7730 8235), 52 Grosvenor Gardens, London SW1W 0AU; by telephone through the main Eurolines office (☎ 01582-404511) in Luton; or at any office of National Express, whose buses link London and other parts of the UK with the Channel ports.

For details on Eurobus, see Bus under Continental Europe in this chapter.

Eurostar It's an extraordinary experience that may change the way Britain sees the Continent: you're on a sleek, ultra-modern train clickety-clicking through Kent, then it's dark for 20 minutes, and then you're whizzing across Flanders in northern France at 300km/h. The highly civilised Eurostar – the much-heralded passenger train service through the Channel Tunnel – takes only three hours (not including the one hour time change) to get from London to Paris: 70 minutes from London's Waterloo station to Folkestone (via Ashford), 20 minutes to cross the Channel, and 1½ hours from Calais to Paris' Gare du Nord. When the 109km of high-speed Channel Tunnel rail link between London and Folkestone is *finally* completed around 2007, travel on the English side will take a mere 45 minutes. The ride from London to Lille takes two hours. Passport and customs checks are usually done before you board the train.

Eurostar is owned by the French and Belgian state railways and Britain's privatised London & Continental Railways. There are direct services from London and Ashford to Paris and the three other Eurostar stops in France, Calais-Fréthun, Lille and Disneyland Paris. In winter, direct Eurostar Ski Trains link London with the Alps (Bourg Saint Maurice).

Contact Eurostar through the following:

France (in English)	☎ 08 36 35 35 39
Eurostar UK	☎ 0990-186 186
Motor Rail	☎ 0990-848 848
Rail Europe	☎ 0990-300 003
Minitel	3615 SNCF (go to the Eurostar pages)
Internet	www.eurostar.com

The regular 2nd class fare on Eurostar's London-Paris service is UK£120/220 (1140/1950FF) one way/return (UK£179/ 305 or 1700/3400FF in 1st class). If you'll be spending a Saturday night or any three other nights at your destination, you can buy a Leisure (Loisir) ticket, which costs UK£119 (990FF) return. Changes to date and time of travel can be made before each departure, and full refunds are available before the outward trip. The more restrictive Excursion (Sourire) ticket, also available if you spend a Saturday night at your destination, costs just UK£99 (850FF) return. Although changes to date and time of travel can be made before the departure of each train, it is nonrefundable.

The 2nd class Mid Week Travel ticket is the cheapest way to go from London to Paris (UK£79) but carries a lot of restrictions: it must be purchased seven days in advance; it is valid for travel only on Tuesday, Wednesday and Thursday; your trip must include a Saturday night away; and the ticket cannot be changed and is nonrefundable. In France, fully refundable Normal Week-end fares, which cost 750/1290FF one way/return, are valid for 2nd class travel on Friday, Saturday, Sunday and holidays.

Young people aged 25 or under can purchase return tickets for UK£85 (650FF), while people over 60 are charged UK£99 (890FF) return; dates can be changed but reimbursement is limited to 50%. Children under 12 pay 350/550FF one way/return in 2nd class. Special deals (eg a round trip for as little as 590FF return from Paris) are often on offer, so it pays to contact Eurostar for the latest information. As we go to press, tickets are quite a bit more expensive in pounds (ie in the UK) than in francs (ie in France).

In London, Eurostar tickets are available from some travel agents, at many mainline train stations, and from the SNCF-owned Rail Europe at 179 Piccadilly, London W1V 0BA, which also sells other SNCF tickets (refundable only in the UK, not in France). In France, ticketing is handled by SNCF.

Eurotunnel High-speed shuttle trains known as Eurotunnel (formerly Le Shuttle) whisk cars, motorbikes, bicycles and coaches from Folkestone through the Channel Tunnel to Coquelles, 5km southwest of Calais, in air-conditioned and soundproofed comfort. For information and reservations, ask a travel agent or contact Eurotunnel (☎ 0990-353 535 in the UK, staffed until 10 pm on weekdays and 6 pm on weekends; ☎ 03 21 00 61 00 in France; www.eurotunnel.com).

The regular one-way (and same-day return) fare for a passenger car, including all its passengers, ranges from UK£65/645FF (in winter) to UK£110/1095FF (mid-July to early September). Return fares valid for more than five days cost twice as much. The fee for a bicycle, including its rider, is UK£15/150FF return; advance reservations are mandatory.

An excursion (return) fare good for less than five days costs UK£70 to UK£135 (690 to 1290FF) for a passenger car, depending on the season. Incredibly cheap excursion fares good for one to five days are sometimes available.

Eurotunnel runs 24 hours a day, every day of the year, with up to four departures an hour during peak periods (one an hour from midnight to 7 am). If you opt to pay at the toll booth, you can do so with a credit card, Eurocheques and a variety of currencies, but you'll pay full fare: to take advantage of the cheap promotional fares you must order your tickets at least 24 hours before departure.

Vehicles pass through customs and passport control for both countries before driving onto the train, so you should arrive at the terminal at least 25 minutes before departure. During the 35-minute crossing, passengers can sit in their cars, walk around the rail carriage or use the toilets, which the French argued were unnecessary.

Continental Europe

France serves as one of Europe's major transport hubs.

Eurolines Buses Eurolines (☎ 01 49 72 51 51; Minitel 3615 EUROLINES; www.eurolines.co.uk or www.eurolines.fr; euroline@imaginet.fr), an association of companies that together form Europe's largest international bus network, links Paris and other French cities with points all over Western and Central Europe, Scandinavia and Morocco. Buses are slower and less comfortable than trains, but they are cheaper, especially if you qualify for the 10 to 20% discount available to people who are 25 or under or over 60, or take advantage of the discount fares on offer from time to time.

Eurolines' direct buses link Paris and other French cities with destinations including Amsterdam (270FF; 7½ hours), Barcelona (540FF; 15 hours), Berlin (490FF; 14 hours), Budapest (570FF; 23 hours), Madrid (590FF; 17 hours), Prague (440FF; 16 hours), Rome (600FF; 23 hours) and Vilnius (650FF; 36 hours). From late June to early September the company also has buses to Athens (890FF; 55 hours) and Istanbul (560FF; 72 hours). These are non-discounted, one-way adult fares from Paris – return tickets cost quite a bit less than two one ways. In summer, it's not a bad idea to make reservations a few days in advance.

Eurolines-affiliated companies can be found across Europe, including Amsterdam (☎ 020-560 87 87; www.eurolines.nl), Barcelona (☎ 93-490 4000; www.travelcom.es/juliavia), Berlin (☎ 030-86 0960; www.deutsche-touring.com), Brussels (☎ 02-203 0707), Göteborg (☎ 020-987377; www.eurolines.se), Madrid (☎ 91-528 1105), Prague (☎ 02-2421 3420; www.eurolines.cz), Rome (☎ 06-44 23 39 28; www.eurolines.it) and Vienna (☎ 01-712 0435; www.eurolines.at). For details on Eurolines offices in France, see Bus under Getting There & Away in the listings for the relevant cities.

Busabout With Busabout (☎ 0171-950 1661 or, after June 1999, ☎ 020-7950 1661; fax 0171-950 1662 or, after June 1999, 020-7950 1662; busabout.info@virgin.net; www.busabout.com) you buy a ticket valid for two weeks or one, two or three months that lets you get on and off the bus whenever you choose at a wide variety of destinations in Western Europe, Central Europe, Scandinavia and Morocco. The company, based in London at 258 Vauxhall Bridge Road, has a network consisting of interlinked circuits and point-to-point lines whose far-flung destinations – 60 cities and towns in 14 countries during the summer season – include Prague, Budapest, Berlin, Vienna, Rome, Athens, Madrid, Lisbon and Marrakech. In France, Busabout serves Paris, Avignon and Nice (year-round); Albertville (in winter); and Calais, Reims, Dijon, Lyon, Tours and Bordeaux (during the warmer months). From mid-December to late March, its Snow Zone service takes you to snowboarding sites in the Alps.

Tickets, which cost about 20% less than comparable Eurail tickets, are not sold on the bus, but are available through student travel agencies. In winter, for example, a pass good for two months of unlimited travel costs about UK£239 (UK£209 for students). You can start your travels anywhere on the network, but if you want to begin in London there's an additional fee of about UK£15 for the trans-Channel bus. Busabout runs year-round, with service at each pick-up point every two days (daily during the warmer months).

Train Rail services link France with every country in Europe; schedules are available from major train stations in France and abroad. Because of different track gauges and electrification systems, you often have to change trains at the border (eg to Spain). For details on SNCF, including telephone numbers, see Train in the Getting Around chapter.

Most trains to the Iberian Peninsula cross the Franco-Spanish border at Irún (on the Atlantic coast) and Portbou (on the Mediterranean coast), though there are also trains via Puigcerdà (La Tour de Carol). SNCF and the Spanish national railways are planning a high-speed rail link between Narbonne and Barcelona.

Hitching For information on getting to/from other parts of continental Europe with Allostop and Association Pouce, see Hitching in the Getting Around chapter.

East Asia

It *is* possible to get to France by rail from East Asia, though count on spending at least eight days doing it. You can choose from among four different routes to Moscow: the trans-Siberian (9297km from Vladivostok), the trans-Mongolian (7860km from Beijing) and the trans-Manchurian (9001km from Beijing), which all use the same tracks across Siberia but have different routes east of Lake Baikal; and the trans-Kazakhstan, which runs between Moscow and Urumqi in north-western China. Prices vary enormously, depending on where you buy the ticket and what is included – advertised 2nd class fares include US$490 from Vladivostok and US$282 from Beijing. Details are available from the Russian National Tourist Office (www.interknowledge.com/russia/trasib01.htm) and Finnsov (www.finnsov.fi/fs_trsib.html).

SEA

Reservations and tickets for ferry travel to/from England, Ireland, Italy and North Africa are available from most travel agencies in France and the countries served. The prices given below are for standard one-way tickets; return fares generally cost less than two one ways. Children aged four to 14 or 15 travel for half to two-thirds of an adult fare.

Much of the passenger traffic between mainland France and Corsica, Sardinia and North Africa is handled by the Société Nationale Maritime Corse Méditerranée (SNCM).

Food is often expensive on ferries, so it is worth bringing your own. Note that if you're travelling with a vehicle, you are usually denied access to it during the voyage.

England

Fares vary widely according to seasonal demand, and tickets can cost almost three times as much in July and August as in winter. Three or five-day excursion return fares generally cost about the same as regular one-way tickets and are sometimes cheaper. To take advantage of promotional fares you may have to reserve 24 hours or more in advance. Some companies (eg Hoverspeed, Brittany Ferries and Condor) have pricing policies that make it more expensive to buy a ticket in pounds than in francs.

Eurailpasses are *not* valid for ferry travel between England and France, but some discounts are available for students (eg on SeaFrance) and young people (eg on Brittany Ferries), at least for tickets bought in France. Transporting bicycles is often (but not always) free.

Via Far Northern France The shortest Channel crossings are between Kent and the far northern tip of France. In order to compete with the Channel Tunnel, ferry companies have been slashing their fares and improving service. Travellers report that the ferry companies are cracking down on people who buy super-cheap one-day return tickets and then show up at the dock with a backpack big enough for months on the road.

Dover-Calais with Hoverspeed The fastest way to cross the English Channel – the trip typically only takes 35 minutes – is to take one of Hoverspeed's *aéroglisseurs* (hovercraft), which ply the waters between Dover (Douvres) and Calais 10 to 17 times a day. Hovercraft – the first such conveyance crossed the Channel in 1959 – cannot operate in anything more tempestuous than a force-eight gale. The company's SeaCats (giant Australian-designed catamarans), which take 50 minutes to make the crossing, are less subject to the vagaries of the Channel weather because of their design.

For a one-way trip or a return completed within five days, Hoverspeed charges pedestrians UK£25 (150FF). A car with five passengers is charged UK£79 to UK£109 (590 to 890FF) for one-way passage, 10 to 25% more for a five day return, depending on the season. Special promotional fares are often available, including incredibly cheap day trips (50FF for a pedestrian, 250FF for a car) and what may be Europe's cheapest cruise: just UK£5 (9FF) for a trip (available on a stand-by basis only) that takes you across the Channel and back without leaving the terminal on the other side, the idea being that you'll make lots of duty free purchases while on board.

Dover-Calais by Car Ferry SeaFrance Sealink and P&O Stena run a total of about 45 car ferry crossings a day from Dover to Calais (1½ hours). SeaFrance, which has 15 runs a day, charges UK£22 (200 to 220FF) for one-way pedestrian passage (UK£20 for students and seniors). On SeaFrance, cars cost UK£75 to UK£115 (560 to 960FF) one way or for a five day return, and UK£133 to UK£183 (1060 to 1460FF) for a regular return fare; additional passengers pay UK£3 or UK£4 each.

P&O Stena has eight ferries covering this route. They leave and return every hour until 7 am, every 45 minutes after that. They are slightly faster than Sealink and cost a bit more. Return fares start from UK£5 for a day, UK£24 for five days and a flexible return is UK£48. Car tariffs start from

Ferry Companies

Brittany Ferries
Reservations:
France (1.49FF per minute) ☎ 08 03 82 88 28
UK ☎ 0990-360 360
Ireland (Cork) ☎ 021-277 801
Santander ☎ 942-36 06 11
Information:
Saint Malo ☎ 02 99 40 64 41
Minitel: 3615 FERRYPLUS
Internet: www.brittany-ferries.com

Condor Ferries
Offices:
Saint Malo ☎ 02 99 20 03 00
St Helier ☎ 01534-607 080
Weymouth ☎ 01305-761 551
Internet: www.condorferries.co.uk

Émeraude Lines
Reservations:
Carteret ☎ 02 33 52 61 39
Diélette ☎ 02 33 52 61 39
Granville ☎ 02 33 50 16 36
Jersey ☎ 01534-66 566
Paris ☎ 01 47 42 30 61
Saint Malo ☎ 02 99 40 48 40
Minitel: 3615 EMERAUDE LINES
Internet: www.emeraudelines.com

Hoverspeed
Reservations:
France ☎ 08 00 90 17 77
UK ☎ 01304-240 241
Boulogne ☎ 03 21 30 27 26
Calais ☎ 03 21 46 14 14
Dover ☎ 01304-240 774
Folkestone ☎ 01303-715 313
Minitel: 3615 HOVERSPEED
Internet: www.hoverspeed.co.uk

Irish Ferries
Reservations:
UK ☎ 0990-171 717
Cherbourg ☎ 02 33 23 44 44
Dublin ☎ 01-661 0511
Paris ☎ 01 42 66 90 90
Roscoff ☎ 02 98 61 17 17
Rosslare ☎ 053-33 158
Internet: www.irish-ferries.ie

P&O European Ferries
Reservations:
France (1.09FF a minute) ☎ 08 03 01 30 13
UK ☎ 0990-980 555
Dublin ☎ 1 800-409 049
Bilbao ☎ 94 423 4477
Minitel: 3615 POFERRY
Internet: www.poef.com

P&O Stena Line
Reservations:
Calais ☎ 03 21 46 04 40
Dieppe ☎ 02 35 06 39 03
Paris ☎ 01 44 51 00 51
Information:
UK (Dover) ☎ 0990-980 980
Minitel: 3615 POSTENA
Internet: www.postena.com

SeaFrance Sealink
Reservations:
Calais ☎ 03 21 34 55 00
☎ 03 21 46 80 00 (24 hours a day)
Dover ☎ 0990 711 711
Lille ☎ 03 20 06 29 44
Paris ☎ 01 44 94 40 40
Minitel: 3615 SEAFRANCE
Internet: www.seafrance.co.uk

SNCM
Reservations:
France (1.49FF a minute) ☎ 08 36 67 95 00
Ajaccio – town ☎ 04 95 29 66 99
– port ☎ 04 95 29 66 63
Bastia – town ☎ 04 95 54 66 99
– port ☎ 04 95 54 66 60
Porto Torres ☎ 079-51 44 77
Sète ☎ 04 67 46 68 00
Toulon ☎ 04 94 16 66 66
Minitel: 3615 SNCM
Internet: www.sncm.fr

UK£25 for a day, UK£109 for five days and UK£189 for a flexible return. Bicycles are free on both services.

Folkestone-Boulogne Hoverspeed's SeaCats make this 55 minute crossing four times a day year-round. For a one-way trip or a round-trip completed in less than five days, pedestrians pay UK£25 (150FF). A car with five passengers costs from UK£74 to UK£99 (590 to 1130FF). Many of Hoverspeed's Dover-Calais promotions are also available here.

Via Normandy England's south coast has several ferry links with Normandy.

Poole-Cherbourg Brittany Ferries' four-hour crossing (one or two a day, with a few missed days in winter) costs UK£16 to UK£28 (150 to 250FF) one way for foot passengers; in France students get a 10% discount. A car, including the driver, pays UK£70 to UK£130 (630 to 1170FF) one way; car passengers are charged UK£7 (60FF) each. Cheaper five and 10 day excursion fares are available. Bicycles cost 50FF (free from October to March).

Portsmouth-Cherbourg On this run (five hours during the day, 8¼ hours overnight; two or three a day from October to March, four a day the rest of the year), P&O European Ferries charges foot passengers UK£15 to UK£30 (135 to 280FF) one way. A basic overnight cabin with space for two costs UK£24 to UK£32 (230 to 310FF). A car, including the driver, is charged UK£70 to UK£130 (630 to 1250FF) one way; additional car passengers pay UK£7 (65FF) each. Five and 10-day return fares are available. Bicycles cost 50FF (free from October to March).

Portsmouth-Le Havre P&O European Ferries' 5½ hour crossing (eight hours at night; three a day) costs the same as the Portsmouth-Cherbourg service. An overnight cabin with room for four costs UK£30 to UK£46.

Portsmouth-Ouistreham Brittany Ferries' car ferry service to/from Ouistreham runs three times a day year-round and takes six hours. Prices are the same as for the Poole-Cherbourg service.

Via Brittany The services to/from Brittany run much less frequently than those along the Straits of Dover, especially in winter.

Plymouth-Roscoff From mid-March to mid-November, this route (six hours) is served by one to three Brittany Ferries' car ferries a day; the rest of the year there is only one crossing a week. Pedestrians pay UK£17 to UK£27 (150 to 260FF) one way; in France students get a 10% discount. Cars cost UK£74 to UK£126 (670 to 1230FF), including the driver; car passengers pay UK£8 each. Excursion fares are cheaper. Bicycles cost UK£5 (50FF), but are free from October to March.

Portsmouth-Saint Malo Brittany Ferries has Portsmouth-Saint Malo car ferries (eight to 10½ hours) year-round, seven days a week (except some Thursdays, Fridays and/or Saturdays from early November to early March). Regular one-way fares are UK£18 to UK£32 (160 to 290FF) for pedestrians (10% less for students in France) and UK£81 to UK£150 (730 to 1300FF) for a car, including the driver. Car passengers pay UK£7 or UK£9 (80FF). Excursion fares are cheaper. Bicycles cost UK£5 (50FF), but are free from October to March.

Weymouth-Saint Malo From May to mid-October, Condor has one catamaran a day linking Weymouth with Saint Malo (via Guernsey). The 4¼ hour crossing costs UK£25 (250FF) one way for pedestrians; cars (including two passengers) are UK£90 to UK£150 (900 to 1700FF), depending on the season. Bicycles are free.

Via Spain If you'd like to return to England from south-west France (or start your trip there), a couple of ferry services from northern Spain are worth considering. Except in January, P&O European Ferries runs twice-weekly car ferries from Portsmouth to Bilbao (Santurtzi port; 28 to 36 hours), which is only about 150km west of Biarritz. Cars, including the driver, cost UK£150 to UK£275 (1430 to 2630FF); passengers with or without cars pay UK£50 to UK£75 (430 to 780FF) each way, not including a sleeping berth (480 to 670FF for a cabin with two beds). A bicycle costs 70 to 100FF.

From mid-March to mid-November, Brittany Ferries has twice-weekly car ferry services from Plymouth to Santander (24 hours), which is about 240km west of Biarritz. During the winter months, there are two to four monthly sailings. Foot passengers pay UK£51 to UK£88 (390 to 670FF) one way; students get 10% off on the franc fare. The cheapest couchette is UK£18 (160FF). A car, including the driver, costs UK£156 to UK£281 (1240 to 2250FF) each way, depending on the season. A bicycle costs UK£7.50 to UK£10 (free from October to March).

The Channel Islands

From late March to 1 November, Condor's sleek, high-speed catamarans link Saint Malo, Brittany, with the Channel Islands (Îles Anglo-Normandes). For licensing reasons the company is not able to transport vehicles on these routes. One-way/return fares for foot passengers are UK£21/39 (265/435FF) to/from Jersey (70 minutes; two to four times a day) and UK£21/39 (310/525FF) to/from Guernsey (Guernesey in French; 2¾ hours; at least one a day). One day excursion fares on the Saint Malo-Jersey route costs UK£29 (280FF, 198FF for young people aged 15 to 23). From May to mid-September there are passenger services via Jersey to Sark (Sercq). Condor also links Guernsey by car ferry with Poole (April to October) and Weymouth (May to mid-October).

Émeraude Lines' express car ferries from Saint Malo to Jersey (70 minutes) run all year except from early January to early February, with only six sailings a week in winter. Cars pay 725FF one way but only 495 to 695FF for a three day excursion fare; pedestrians are charged 275FF for either a one-way ticket or a one day excursion fare. From late March to 2 November, the company also has services to Guernsey and Sark.

Émeraude Lines' catamarans also link Jersey and/or Guernsey with three small ports on the west coast of Normandy: Granville (mid-April to early October; daily), Carteret (April to mid-October; almost daily) and Diélette (April to early October; six to nine times a month). One-day excursion fares are about 250FF for adults and 195FF for young people aged from 15 to 23; a regular one-way fare is 275 to 310FF.

Ireland

Eurailpass holders pay 50% of the appropriate fare for ferry crossings between Ireland and France on Irish Ferries (make sure you book ahead).

Irish Ferries links Rosslare with Cherbourg (19 hours) and Roscoff (18 hours). There are two or three ferries a week from September to March; sailings are every other day during the rest of the year. Pedestrians pay between I£35 (315FF) and I£70 (650FF) one way; fares for students and people over 60 are I£30 to I£60 (270 to 550FF). A two bed cabin costs I£23 to I£34. The tariff for a car with two passengers ranges from I£99 to I£265 (900 to 2800FF); additional passengers pay up to I£24 (100 to 150FF) each. These prices do not include I£5 per person in Irish taxes. Bicycles are free except in summer, when they cost I£15 to I£20 (140 to 180FF).

From April to early October, Brittany Ferries has weekly car ferries linking Cork (Ringaskiddy) with Roscoff (14 hours). Foot passengers pay from I£30/50 (300/500FF) to I£60/95 (600/950FF) one way/return, depending on the date; a car with two adults costs I£95/155 (960/1550FF) to I£260/410 (2600/4100FF). Bicycles are sometimes free but usually cost an extra I£10 to I£15 (100 to 150FF) one way or I£15 to I£25 (150 to 250FF) return.

Italy

A variety of ferry companies ply the waters between Corsica and Italy. For details, see the introductory Getting There & Away section of the Corsica chapter.

Sardinia From mid-April to September, the SNCM has four to eight car ferries a month from Marseille or Toulon to Porto Torres on the Italian island of Sardinia (Sardaigne in French). The SNCM links the Corsican ports of Ajaccio and Propriano with Porto Torres during approximately the same period but only two to five times a month (eight in May, none out of Porto Torres in July).

For details on ferries from Bonifacio, Corsica, to Santa Teresa, Sardinia, see the Getting There & Away section under Bonifacio in the Corsica chapter.

Tunisia

The SNCM and the Compagnie Tunisienne de Navigation (CTN) operate two weekly car ferries (almost daily services from late June to mid-September) between Marseille and Tunis (about 24 hours). The standard adult fare is 915FF (for an armchair) or 1570FF (in the cheapest cabin). If you're taking along a vehicle (1805/2880FF one way/return), it is important to book ahead, especially in summer. In Tunis, CTN's office (☎ 216-135 33 31) is at 122 Rue de Yougoslavie. In France, ticketing is handled by SNCM.

Morocco

Car ferries run by the Compagnie Marocaine de Navigation (CoMaNav) to/from Tangier (Tanger) dock at the French port of Sète, 29km (20 minutes by train) south-west of Montpellier. The once or twice-weekly crossing takes about 36 hours. A bed in the cheapest cabins costs 1000FF (1360FF from July to September); discounts are available if you're a student, under 26 or in a group of four or more. One way/return, a vehicle costs 1480/2560FF (1970/3150FF in summer). The company's representative in Tangier is CoMaNav-Passages (☎ 09-93 26 49) at 43 Ave Abou El Alaâ El Maâri. In France, ticketing is handled by SNCM, and its Sète office (☎ 04 67 46 68 00) is at 4 Quai d'Alger. In the UK, contact Southern Ferries (☎ 0171-491 4968 or, after June 1999, ☎ 020-7491 4968).

The USA, Canada & Elsewhere

The days of earning your passage on a freighter to Europe have well and truly passed, and long-distance passenger ships disappeared with the advent of cheap air travel, but it's still possible to travel as a passenger on a cargo ship. Such vessels typically take five to 12 passengers and charge about US$100 per person a day. Details are available from Travltips Cruise and Freighter Travel Association (☎ 800-872 8584 in the USA; www.travltips.com), Freighter World Cruises (☎ 800-571 7774 or ☎ 818-449 3106 in the USA), The Cruise People (☎ 0 800 526 313, ☎ 416-444 2410 in Canada; http://members.aol.com/CruiseAZ/home .htm) and the *Freighter Travel Review* (☎ 01206-503798 in the UK; www .ftr-mag.com).

Warning

The information in this chapter is particularly vulnerable to change: prices for international travel are volatile, routes are introduced and cancelled, schedules change, special deals come and go, and rules and visa requirements are amended. Airlines and governments seem to take a perverse pleasure in making price structures and regulations as complicated as possible. You should check directly with the airline or a travel agent to make sure you understand how a fare (and any ticket you may buy) works. In addition, the travel industry is highly competitive and there are many lurks and perks.

The upshot of this is that you should get opinions, quotes and advice from as many airlines and travel agents as possible before you part with your hard-earned cash. The details given in this chapter should be regarded as pointers and are not a substitute for your own careful, up-to-date research.

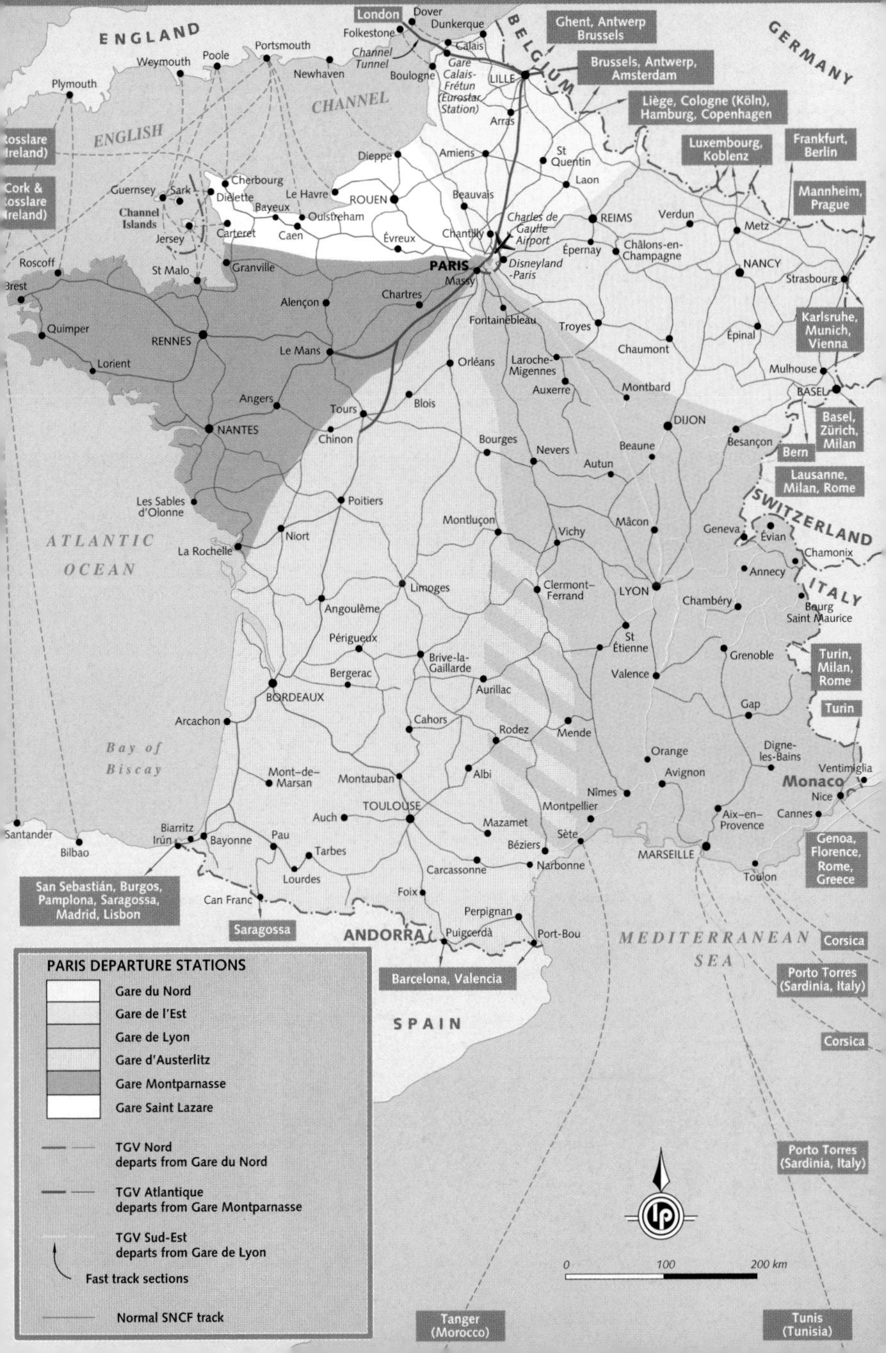
PARIS DEPARTURE STATIONS
Gare du Nord
Gare de l'Est
Gare de Lyon
Gare d'Austerlitz
Gare Montparnasse
Gare Saint Lazare
TGV Nord
departs from Gare du Nord
TGV Atlantique
departs from Gare Montparnasse
TGV Sud-Est
departs from Gare de Lyon
Fast track sections
Normal SNCF track
0
100
200 km
ENGLAND
ENGLISH
CHANNEL
BELGIUM
GERMANY
SWITZERLAND
ITALY
ATLANTIC
OCEAN
Bay of
Biscay
SPAIN
ANDORRA
Monaco
MEDITERRANEAN
SEA
London
Dover
Folkestone
Dunkerque
Calais
Channel
Tunnel
Boulogne
Gare
Calais-
Frétun
(Eurostar
Station)
LILLE
Arras
Portsmouth
Newhaven
Weymouth
Poole
Plymouth
Rosslare
(Ireland)
Cork &
Rosslare
(Ireland)
Ghent, Antwerp
Brussels
Brussels, Antwerp,
Amsterdam
Liège, Cologne (Köln),
Hamburg, Copenhagen
Luxembourg,
Koblenz
Frankfurt,
Berlin
Mannheim,
Prague
Karlsruhe,
Munich,
Vienna
Basel,
Zürich,
Milan
Bern
Lausanne,
Milan, Rome
Turin,
Milan,
Rome
Turin
Genoa,
Florence,
Rome,
Greece
Corsica
Porto Torres
(Sardinia, Italy)
Corsica
Porto Torres
(Sardinia, Italy)
Tanger
(Morocco)
Tunis
(Tunisia)
San Sebastián, Burgos,
Pamplona, Saragossa,
Madrid, Lisbon
Saragossa
Barcelona, Valencia
Dieppe
Amiens
St
Quentin
Laon
Guernsey
Sark
Cherbourg
Diélette
Channel
Islands
Jersey
Carteret
Le Havre
Bayeux
Ouistreham
Caen
ROUEN
Beauvais
Charles de
Gaulle
Airport
Chantilly
Évreux
REIMS
Verdun
Metz
Épernay
Châlons-en-
Champagne
NANCY
Strasbourg
PARIS
Massy
Disneyland
-Paris
Roscoff
Brest
St Malo
Granville
Alençon
Chartres
Quimper
RENNES
Lorient
Le Mans
Fontainebleau
Troyes
Chaumont
Épinal
Mulhouse
BASEL
Orléans
Laroche-
Migennes
Auxerre
Montbard
Angers
Blois
Tours
NANTES
Chinon
DIJON
Besançon
Bourges
Nevers
Beaune
Autun
Poitiers
Les Sables
d'Olonne
Niort
La Rochelle
Montluçon
Vichy
Mâcon
Geneva
Évian
Chamonix
Annecy
Limoges
Clermont-
Ferrand
LYON
Chambéry
Bourg
Saint Maurice
Angoulême
Périgueux
Brive-la-
Gaillarde
St
Étienne
Grenoble
Bergerac
BORDEAUX
Aurillac
Valence
Arcachon
Cahors
Rodez
Mende
Gap
Orange
Digne-
les-Bains
Mont-de-
Marsan
Montauban
Albi
Avignon
Ventimiglia
Nice
TOULOUSE
Nîmes
Montpellier
Cannes
Auch
Mazamet
Aix-en-
Provence
Santander
Biarritz
Irún
Bayonne
Pau
Tarbes
Béziers
Sète
MARSEILLE
Bilbao
Lourdes
Carcassonne
Narbonne
Toulon
Can Franc
Foix
Perpignan
Puigcerdà
Port-Bou

TONY WHEELER

Some of the mechanical fountains of the Centre Pompidou, Paris

NICOLA WILLIAMS

On parade!

CHRIS MELLOR

Le tricolore

RICHARD I'ANSON

Pedestrians chance Paris' traffic in front of the Arc de Triomphe.

CHRIS MELLOR

The city of Chamonix is nestled in a valley surrounded by the Alps.

CDT BAS-RHIN

Woman in folk costume, Alsace

Getting Around

France's domestic transport network, much of it state-owned and subsidised, tends to be monopolistic: the SNCF takes care of virtually all inter-departmental land transport; the SNCM handles most ferry services to Corsica; and short-haul bus companies are either run by the department or grouped so each local company handles a different set of destinations. Eurolines and its privately owned competitors in the long-haul bus field are limited to international routes.

AIR

Carriers with domestic networks include Air France (which now includes Air Inter), Air Liberté (owned by British Airways), AOM, Air Littoral, Corsair (run by the Nouvelles Frontières travel agency), Corse Méditerranée, Flandre Air and Proteus. The government assigns routes and sets prices to avoid 'excessive competition', though the market is slowly being liberalised

Thanks to the TGV, travel between some cities (eg Paris and Lyon) is faster and easier by rail than by air, particularly if you include the time and hassle involved in getting to and from the airports.

Any French travel agent can make bookings for domestic flights and supply details on the complicated fare system. Outside France, Air France representatives sell tickets for many domestic flights. For details on airline addresses, see Airline Offices under Getting There & Away in the Paris chapter.

All Roads Lead to Paris

Certain itineraries around France are inherently faster than others, in large part because of the 'Paris-centric' nature of France's air, rail and road networks. A glance at any map of the country's rail lines and *autoroutes* (motorways/expressways), arranged like the spokes of a wheel with Paris at the hub, will illustrate this perfectly. If two or more widely scattered regions of France especially interest you – Alsace and the French Basque Country, say, or Brittany and Corsica – you can minimise the time you spend getting from one region to the other by taking advantage of domestic air links, super-fast TGV trains, overnight sleeper trains, the 130km/h autoroutes or the SNCF's Train + Auto service (where both you and your car go by rail).

Costs

The cheapest one-way youth/student air fares include the following (adult tickets cost 1½ to four times as much depending on restrictions and when you fly):

Paris-Ajaccio/Bastia	518FF
Paris-Bordeaux	288FF
Paris-Biarritz	338FF
Paris-Nice	338FF
Lyon-Toulouse	288FF
Marseille-Strasbourg	577FF
Lille-Nice	437FF

On most flights, each passenger is allowed one carry-on bag and 23kg of checked luggage. Excess baggage, including bikes and skis, costs just 10FF per kilogram.

Discounts

Children, young people, students, couples, families and seniors – and, on many flights, everyone else – can fly for 50 to 75% less than the full fare.

Air France (☎ 0 802 802 802 at 0.79FF a minute; Minitel 3615 AF; www.airfrance.com) has four regular fare levels, ranging from Tempo 1 (full-fare coach) to Tempo 4 (tickets with all sort of restrictions that require advance booking). The company offers half fares on Tempo 1 and Tempo 2 tickets to people over 60; families, defined as at least one parent or grandparent travelling with one (or more) children aged 24 or under (26 or under in the case of students); and heterosexual couples who are either married or have proof of cohabitation (eg a French government issued *certificat de concubinage*). Gays and lesbians seem to be left out yet again. Even cheaper Tempo Jeunes fares are available to young people 24 and under (26 and under in the case of students).

To/From the Airport

For information on public transport links to French airports, including Orly and Roissy Charles de Gaulle near Paris, see To/From the Airports in the Getting Around section of each city listing.

BUS

Because French transport policy is biased in favour of the state-owned rail system, the country has only extremely limited interregional bus services. However, buses are used quite extensively for short-distance travel within departments, especially in rural areas with relatively few train lines (eg Brittany and Normandy). Over the years, certain uneconomical rail lines have been replaced by SNCF buses – unlike regional buses, these are free for people with rail passes.

TRAIN

France's superb rail network, operated by the state-owned – and heavily subsidised – SNCF (Société Nationale des Chemins de Fer), reaches almost every part of the country. Many towns not on the SNCF train and bus network are linked with nearby railheads by intra-departmental bus lines. SNCF information offices and ticket windows can help you get from any French train station to any other, irrespective of how many *correspondances* (changes/transfers) it takes.

Network

France's most important train lines radiate from Paris like the spokes of a wheel, making rail travel between provincial towns situated on different spokes infrequent and rather slow. In some cases you have to transit through Paris, which sometimes (though these days less and less frequently) requires transferring from one of the capital's six train stations to another. For details, see the colour SNCF Railways map, which shows the parts of France served by each of Paris' stations, and Train under Getting There & Away in the Paris chapter.

Electrified track makes up only 43% of all SNCF track but it carries 80% of the traffic. Many secondary and tertiary lines have infrequent services.

TGV

The pride and joy of the SNCF is the world renowned TGV (*train à grande vitesse*), whose name – pronounced 'TEH-ZHEH-VEH' – means 'high-speed train'. There are now five TGV services:

TGV Sud-Est Links Paris' Gare de Lyon with Lyon and the south-east, including Dijon, Geneva, the Alps, Avignon, Marseille, Nice and Perpignan.

TGV Atlantique Links Paris' Gare Montparnasse with Brittany (Rennes, Quimper, Brest), Nantes, the Loire Valley, La Rochelle, Bordeaux, the French Basque Country and Toulouse.

TGV Nord Links Paris' Gare du Nord with Arras, Lille and Calais.

Eurostar Links Paris' Gare du Nord with Lille, Calais-Fréthun and, via the Channel Tunnel, London Waterloo (three hours), Ashford and other British cities (see To/From England under Land in the Getting There & Away Chapter).

Thalys Links Paris' Gare du Nord with Brussels-Midi (1½ hours), Amsterdam CS (4½ hours) and Cologne's Hauptbahnhof (four hours).

Thanks to a new section of TGV track east and south of Paris, all three domestic TGV lines are now connected to each other, making it possible to go directly from, say, Lyon to Nantes or Bordeaux to Lille – without switching trains (and stations) in Paris. Stops on this link-up include Roissy Charles de Gaulle airport and Disneyland Paris.

TGV Time Trials

In test runs, the TGV Atlantique has reached a top-speed of 515.3km/h, but like the TGV Nord it usually travels at a maximum of 300km/h. The TGV Sud-Est goes up to 280km/h.

The TGV Sud-Est runs on super-fast TGV track only between Paris and Valence, in part because new track costs about US$10 million per kilometre but mostly because of political wrangling and local opposition. The high-speed track is supposed to reach Marseille in late 1999.

A train that is not a TGV is often referred to as a *corail* or *classique*.

Information

Larger train stations generally have both *guichets* (ticket windows) and information/reservation offices; opening hours and phone numbers are listed under Train in the Getting There & Away section of each city or town listing.

If you'll be doing a lot of travel in one region of France, ask at a train station for a *Guide Régional des Transports*, a booklet of SNCF bus and intra-regional rail schedules published by many regional governments. For national coverage, you can purchase an *Indicateur Horaires Ville à Ville* (60FF for a book or a Windows compatible computer diskette), sold in train stations at Relais H newsagents.

Some people swear by the *Thomas Cook European Timetable* (118FF), useful for figuring out which domestic and international routings are feasible so you can use rail passes to their fullest. It is updated monthly and is available from all Thomas Cook exchange bureaus.

Left-Luggage

Most larger SNCF stations have both a *consigne manuelle* (left-luggage office), where you pay 30FF per bag or 35FF per bicycle for 24 hours, and a *consigne automatique*, a 72 hour computerised luggage locker that will issue you with a lock code in exchange for 15, 20 or 30FF, depending on the size. The old mechanical lockers – a dying breed – cost 5 or 20FF per 24 hours. At smaller stations you can usually check your bag with the clerk at the ticket window (30FF). It's a good idea to find out when the left-luggage facilities close; some keep almost banking hours.

As we went to press most luggage lockers were out of service because of the security threat posed by terrorists.

Schedules

SNCF's pocket-size *horaires* (time schedules), available for free at stations, can be a bit complicated to read, especially if you don't know French railway-speak.

At the top of non-TGV schedules there are two rows of boxed numbers: the upper one is the *numéro de train* (train number), while the lower one indicates relevant *notes à consulter* (footnote references). The footnotes, of which there may be dozens, are explained in French at the bottom of the sheet.

Very often a particular train *circule* (runs) only on Sunday or only on certain dates. Alternatively, it may operate *tous les jours* (every day) *sauf* (except) Saturday, Sunday and/or *fêtes* (holidays). Of 20 trains listed on the schedule, only a few may be running on the day you'd like to travel. To be certain that you've understood your options it's a good idea to ask at the information office or, in small stations, at the ticket window.

Classes & Sleepers

Most French trains, including the TGV, have both 1st and 2nd class sections.

Most overnight trains are equipped with couchettes (sleeping berths), for which you must make reservations and pay a fee of 90FF. The 2nd class couchette compartments have six berths, while those in 1st class have four. *Voitures-lits* (sleepers) have one, two or three real beds per compartment and cost from 259 to 907FF per person. On some overnight trains you can guarantee yourself a 2nd class *siège inclinable* (reclining seat) by paying 20FF.

How to Find Rail Information

From 7 am to 10 pm every day, you can get schedule and fare information and make reservations for the SNCF's domestic and international services in a number of languages (2.23FF a minute):

English	☎ 08 36 35 35 39
French	☎ 08 36 35 35 35
German	☎ 08 36 35 35 36
Spanish	☎ 08 36 35 35 37
Italian	☎ 08 36 35 35 38

Using online services, your options include:

Minitel (full schedule details available; credit card purchases possible):
3615 SNCF
3623 SNCF

Internet:

SNCF	www.sncf.fr
Eurostar	www.raileurope.com
Thalys	www.thalys.com
Rail Europe	www.raileurope.com

When you board your train check the destination panel on the exterior of the car – trains are sometimes split up in mid-journey, with several cars sent to a different destination than the rest of the train.

Costs & Reservations

The SNCF's prices are set by a combination of objective factors (eg how many kilometres you'll be travelling) and an analysis of supply and demand. For 2nd class travel, count on paying 50 to 60FF per 100km for cross-country trips and 70 to 100FF per 100km for short hops. (By comparison, autoroute tolls come to about 40FF per 100km, while petrol adds another 40FF.) Regular return (round-trip) passage costs twice as much as one way. Travel in 1st class is 50% more expensive than 2nd class.

Children under four travel free; those aged four through to 11 pay 50% of the adult fare.

Where applicable, Eurailpass holders must pay reservation fees (20FF on all trains, including TGVs) and couchette charges but not supplements.

Reservation Fee The reservation fee (effectively 20FF) is optional *except* under these circumstances:

- If you're travelling by TGV, Eurostar or Thalys.
- If you want a bed or couchette.
- During holiday periods (eg around Easter and 14 July), when it may be necessary to make a reservation several days in advance in order to get a seat on especially popular trains.

Reservations can be made by telephone, Minitel or via the SNCF's Web site (see the boxed text 'How to Find Rail Information'), at any SNCF ticketing office, or using train station ticket machines. Make sure you specify *non-fumeur* (non-smoking) or *fumeur* (smoking).

Before departure time you can change your reservation by telephone. To pick up your new tickets, go to a ticket counter with the reference number you've been given. Reservations can be changed for no charge up to one hour *after* your scheduled departure time, but only if you are actually at your departure station.

Supplements On certain trains to/from Paris, non-TGV passengers travelling during *heures de pointe* (peak periods) have to pay a supplement of up to 60/120FF in 2nd/1st class. Supplements do not generally apply to travel from one provincial station to another but may be levied if you take an international train (eg one coming from Spain) on a domestic segment.

On the small fold-out train schedules, a hatch symbol (#) right below the train number means that supplements have to be paid, at least on certain days of the week. On the platform, departure boards indicate which trains require supplements.

Buying a Ticket

At especially large stations (eg those in Paris), there are separate ticket windows for travel on *international*, *grandes lignes* (long-haul) and *banlieue* (suburban) lines. Tickets bought with cash can be reimbursed for cash (by you or a thief), so keep them in a safe place.

You can almost always use MasterCard, Visa, Diners Club or American Express credit cards to pay for train tickets. At some larger stations, one or two of the ticket windows will exchange enough foreign currency to cover the cost of your train ticket. In the near future it should be possible to purchase tickets online at the SNCF's Web site; payment will be by credit card.

Virtually every SNCF station in the country has at least one easy-to-use on-line ticket machine (*automat point de vente* (APV) or *billeterie automatique*) that accepts credit cards for purchases of at least 15FF. To make the on-screen interface switch to English, touch the Union Jack (UK flag) in the upper right hand corner of the *'bonjour'* screen (if you see a different screen, try touching the screen or pushing the red *annulation* button).

Tickets can be purchased on board the train, but unless the ticket window where you boarded was closed *and* the station didn't have a ticket machine, prohibitive tariffs apply: a flat 130FF for journeys under 75km, 90FF plus the price of a regular ticket for journeys of more than 75km. TGV tickets bought on board cost an extra 100FF, no matter how far you're going.

If you find yourself aboard a train without a ticket it's a good idea to search out the *contrôleur* (ticket inspector or conductor) to inform him/her of your circumstance. By doing this you can probably ensure that the surcharge will be just 40FF (20FF if you're travelling less than 75km).

Some travel agents issue train tickets, but most charge a hefty handling fee, although some student travel places (eg AJF) don't.

Rail Passes for Non-Europeans

These passes do *not* cover reservation fees or couchette charges. However, they do get you discounts on the Eurostar and Thalys. Most of them come in half-price versions for children aged four to 11.

Contrary to popular belief, the rail passes designed for non-Europeans (eg Eurailpass) *can* be purchased at a limited number of places in Europe provided you're not a resident of any European country. However, prices are *much* higher than they would be at home. For instance, a two month Youth Flexipass costs about 30% more than in the USA.

In France, passes are available from the SNCF offices at Orly and Roissy Charles de Gaulle airports; in Paris at Gare du Nord, Gare de Lyon and Gare Saint Lazare; and at the main train stations in Marseille and Nice.

In London, rail passes for residents of Europe, as well as rail passes for overseas visitors, are sold by Rail Europe, a subsidiary of the SNCF, which has offices at 179 Piccadilly, London W1V 0BA (☎ 0990-300 003) and in Victoria Station.

Eurailpass If you are not a resident of Europe and expect to be really clocking up the kilometres in France and other European countries, you might consider buying a Eurailpass. The standard version entitles you to unlimited rail travel over a period of 15 or 21 days or one, two or three months. A Flexipass lets you take trains during any 10 or 15 days you select over a period of two months. The Saverpass and Saver Flexipass, valid for two to five adults travelling together, entitle each member of the group to a 15% discount.

Eurailpasses are not valid in the UK or on cross-Channel ferries. On Irish Ferries routings that link the Irish Republic with France, pass holders pay 50% of the appropriate fare.

Eurailpasses offer reasonable value to people who have not reached their 26th birthday on the first day of travel (people over that age can only get the pricey 1st class versions). One/two months of unlimited travel with the Eurail Youthpass costs US$605/857. The Eurail Youth Flexipass costs US$444/585 for 10/15 days of travel over two months. In any case, a Eurailpass is only worth it if you plan to do a lot of travelling within a short space of time: Eurail itself reckons the pass only starts saving money if you cover more than 2400km.

Europass The Europass, not available to European residents, lets you travel in certain European countries for between five and 15 consecutive or non-consecutive days over a two month period. Regular adult fares, good for 1st class passage within France, Germany, Italy, Spain and Switzerland, range from US$326 for five days to US$746 for 15 days (20% less for two adults travelling together). The Netherlands, Belgium, Luxembourg, Portugal, Austria, Hungary and Greece can be added for a modest surcharge. The Europass Youth, available to people aged 25 and under, ranges in cost from US$216 for five days to US$506 for 15.

France Railpass This flexipass entitles people who are not residents of France to unlimited travel on the SNCF system for three to nine days over the course of a month. In 2nd class, the three-day version costs US$165 (US$132 each for two people travelling together); each additional day of travel costs US$30. Versions involving car rental are also available.

The France Youthpass, available to people aged 25 and under, costs US$150 for four days of travel over two months; additional days (up to a maximum of 10 in total) cost US$25.

Rail Passes for Residents of Europe

The Euro Domino and Inter Rail passes are available to people of all ages and nationalities provided they have been resident in Europe for at least six months. However, you cannot purchase a pass for use in your country of residence. In France, both are sold at most train stations. Holders of these passes get discounts on the Eurostar and Thalys but must pay all SNCF reservation fees and supplements.

Euro Domino France The new Euro Domino flexipass, which comes in various versions for travel within one of the 29 participating countries, gives you three, five or 10 consecutive or non-consecutive days of midnight-to-midnight travel over a period of one month. The pass also gets you 25% off on travel from the place where it was purchased to the border of the country in which you'll be travelling.

Where to Buy Rail Passes

Australia

Thomas Cook	☎ 02-9320 6561

Canada

Rail Europe	☎ 1-800 361 7245

Hong Kong

Thomas Cook	☎ 2853 9712

India

Hans Air Services (New Delhi)	☎ 011-372 2360
Travel Corporation India (Mumbai)	☎ 022-202 1881

Japan

Japan Travel Bureau	☎ 03-3284-7103
Kinetsu	☎ 03-3255-1794

New Zealand

Thomas Cook	☎ 09-379 6800

Singapore

Thomas Cook	☎ 221 0222

UK

Motor Rail	☎ 0990-300 003
Rail Europe	☎ 0990-848 848

USA

Rail Europe	☎ 1-800-438 7245

Outside of Europe, some rail passes are also available from accredited travel agents. Reservations can also be made online (www.raileurope.com).

Euro Domino France – the version good for travel on the SNCF – comes in two versions: the youth version (for people 25 and under) which offers three/five/10 days of 2nd class travel for UK£85/115/185; and the adult version, which costs UK£105/145/220 in 2nd class. Euro Domino France is available from major train stations in most European countries, including France (though not to residents of France).

Inter Rail Pass With the Inter Rail Pass, you can travel in 29 European countries organised into eight zones; France is in Zone E, grouped with the Netherlands, Belgium and Luxembourg. For 22 days of unlimited 2nd class travel in one zone, the cost is 1836FF (1285FF if you're aged 25 and under). One month of 2nd class travel in two/three/eight zones costs 2380/2720/3100FF (1700/1938/2210FF for young people). You also get 50% off on travel from your home country to your zone(s) and between non-adjacent zones.

SNCF Discount Tickets

The fares discussed below are available at all SNCF stations but are not applicable to travel wholly within the Paris Transport Region. There are no residency requirements. Children under four travel free.

Reduced Price Tickets Discounts of 25% on one-way or return travel within France are available at train station ticket windows for certain groups of travellers, subject to availability. Just show the ticket agent proof of eligibility, and you'll get the reduction on the spot. If you're over 12 but have not yet reached your 26th birthday on the date of travel, you are eligible for a Découverte 12/25 fare, which replaces the old BSE tickets. One to four adults travelling with a child aged four to 11 qualify for the Découverte Enfant Plus fare. People over 60 enjoy a fare called Découverte Senior.

In addition, any two people who are travelling together (the old and complex cohabitation requirements have been scrapped) qualify for a Découverte Deux fare, which gives you a 25% reduction in 1st or 2nd class, but only on return travel.

On Thalys trains to Belgium, Holland and Cologne, people aged 12 to 25 get 50% off the full fare; seniors get a 30% discount.

Travel Passes Discounts of 50% (25% if the cheapest seats are sold out) on one-way or return travel within France are available to certain groups of travellers if they purchase a card valid for 12 months. No passport photo is required.

Young people aged 12 to 25 qualify for the Carte 12/25, which costs 270FF. One to four adults travelling with a child aged four to 11 can get the Carte Enfant Plus for 350FF. People over 60 qualify for a Carte Senior, which replaces the Carte Vermeil and costs 285FF.

Découverte Séjour No matter what age you are, you can get a 25% reduction for return travel within France if you meet two conditions: the total distance you'll be travelling is at least 200km, and you'll be spending Saturday night at your destination.

Découverte G30 & G8 These fares, available on over 1000 trains a day serving 470 destinations in France and other countries (ticket windows can supply you with a list, known as the *Guide Découverte G30 et G8*), let anyone of any age save significant sums if they reserve a place on a specific train well in advance, subject to availability. The Découverte G30, which offers a saving of up to 60%, must be purchased 30 days to two months before the date of travel. Discounts of up to 40% are available if you buy a Découverte G8, which must be bought at least eight days before your date of travel. A refund of 70% is available up to four days before departure; after that, it's use it or lose it.

BIJ Tickets These venerable tickets – the acronym stands for Billets Internationals de Jeunesse (International Youth Tickets) – are still available to anyone aged 25 or under and save you 20 to 25% on international

2nd class rail travel (one way or return). A limited number of places are available so the earlier you reserve the better.

To the great inconvenience of young travellers, BIJ tickets are not sold at SNCF ticket windows. Rather, you have to go to a travel agent that issues them, such as Voyages Wasteels (☎ 01 43 62 30 00; Minitel 3615 WASTEELS; www.voyages-wasteels.fr), CIT/Eurotrain or student travel agencies such as AJF, OTU, Council Travel and USIT. There's usually at least one such office in the vicinity of major train stations.

Validating Your Ticket

Before boarding the train you must validate your ticket by time-stamping it in a *composteur*, one of those orange posts situated somewhere between the ticket windows and the tracks. When you insert your ticket (with the printed side up), the machine will take a semicircular bite out of the side and print the time and date on the back.

If you forget to validate your ticket before boarding, find a conductor so he/she can punch it for you (if you wait for your crime to be discovered, you're likely to be fined). Always keep your ticket and reservation card with you until the end of the journey.

Eurail and other rail passes *must* be validated before you begin your first journey to initiate the period of validity. Usually this needs to be done at a train station ticket window.

Breaking Your Journey

A train ticket is good for travel for 24 hours after it's been validated (*composté*), even if it has been punched by the conductor, so there's no problem if you want to break your journey – provided you're not on a line (eg a TGV) that requires a reservation, and you arrive at your final destination before 24 hours is up. So if something out the window looks interesting, you can simply get off at the next station and hop on a later train going in the same direction. Time-stamp your ticket again before you reboard. If you decide to stay for more than 24 hours, it is not possible to get a refund for the unused portion of the ticket.

Reimbursements

Getting a reimbursement for unused, tickets bought in France for domestic or international travel is pretty straightforward. If you have an open ticket (ie one without a reservation) for domestic, Eurostar or Thalys travel, you can get 90% of your money back until the end of the ticket's validity, usually two months from the date of issue (marked on the ticket). For other international tickets, refunds are available up to six months after the date of purchase. Tickets worth 30FF or less cannot be reimbursed.

If you have a ticket for a reserved seat or couchette on a specific train, you can get a 100% refund (or change the reservation for no charge) until the time your train is supposed to depart, or until one hour after the train leaves provided you're actually at the departure station.

Unless your ticket was purchased from a travel agent or outside France (in which case you have to go back to the issuing office), refunds are available from any train station ticket window or a Service Clientèle office in a mainline station. If you paid by credit card your reimbursement will be paid to your account or in the form of a cheque in French francs, sent to you by post.

CAR

Having your own vehicle gives you exceptional freedom. Unfortunately, it can be expensive, and cars are often inconvenient in city centres or anywhere else where parking and traffic are a problem.

Measured relative to the number of kilometres driven, the rate of fatalities on French roads – some 8000 a year – is almost double that of the UK or the USA.

Documents

In France all drivers must carry the following papers with them at all times:

- a national ID card or passport
- a valid driver's permit or licence (*permis de*

conduire); many foreign driving licences can be used in France for up to one year
- car ownership papers, known in France as a *carte grise* (grey card)
- proof of insurance, known in France as a *carte verte* (green card)

If you're caught at a police roadblock without one or more of these documents, you may be subject to a 900FF on the spot fine. Photocopies of all of them should be kept in a safe place. Never leave your car ownership or insurance papers in the vehicle. For information on getting an International Driving Permit, see Documents in the Facts for the Visitor chapter.

A motor vehicle entering a foreign country must display a sticker identifying its country of registration (eg GB for Great Britain, IRL for Ireland, F for France etc).

Equipment

A reflective warning triangle, to be used in the event of breakdown, must be carried in the car. Recommended accessories, which are mandatory in some European countries, are a first-aid kit, a spare bulb kit and a fire extinguisher. In the UK, contact the RAC (☎ 0990-275 600) or the AA (☎ 0990-500 600).

A right-hand drive vehicle brought to France from the UK or Ireland must have deflectors affixed to the headlights to avoid dazzling oncoming traffic. France's famous yellow headlamps are being phased out in favour of the safer white ones.

Road Network

France, along with Belgium, has the densest highway network in Europe. There are four types of intercity roads:

Autoroutes Multilane divided motorways/highways, usually requiring the payment of tolls, whose alphanumeric designations begin with A. Marked by blue symbols showing a divided highway receding into the distance, they often have *aires de repos* (rest areas), some with restaurants and pricey petrol stations.

Routes Nationales Main highways whose names begin with N (or, on older maps and signs, RN). The newer ones are wide, well signposted and lavishly equipped with reflectors.

Routes Departmentales Secondary and tertiary local roads whose names begin with D.

Routes Communales Minor rural roads whose names sometimes begin with C. They are maintained by the smallest unit of local government in rural areas, the commune.

Road Rules

Motoring in Europe (£4.99), published in the UK by the RAC, gives an excellent summary of road regulations in each European country, including parking rules. Motoring organisations in other countries have similar publications.

North American drivers should remember that turning right on a red light is illegal in France.

Speed Limits Unless otherwise posted, a speed limit of 50km/h applies in *all* areas designated as built-up, no matter how rural they may appear. On intercity roads, you must slow to 50km/h the moment you pass a white sign with red borders on which a place name is written in black or blue letters. This limit remains in force until you arrive at the other edge of town, where you'll pass an identical sign with a red diagonal bar across the name.

Outside built-up areas, speed limits are:

- 90km/h (80km/h if it's raining) on undivided N and D highways
- 110km/h (100km/h if it's raining) on dual carriageways (divided highways) or short sections of highway with a divider strip
- 130km/h (110km/h in the rain, 60km/h in icy conditions) on autoroutes

Speed limits are generally not posted unless they deviate from those mentioned above. If you drive at the speed limit, expect to have lots of cars coming to within a few metres of your rear bumper, flashing their lights, and then overtaking at the first opportunity.

Priorité à Droite For overseas tourists, the most confusing – and dangerous – traffic law in France is the notorious 'priority to the right' rule, under which any car entering an intersection (including a T-junction) from a road on your right has right-of-way no matter how small the road it's coming from. To put it another way: if you're turning right from a side road onto a main road, you have priority over vehicles approaching from your left. If you're turning left, though, you have to wait for cars coming from your right. French drivers tend to take full advantage of their rights and will pull boldly into an intersection at which they have priority.

At most larger *ronds-points* (roundabouts or traffic circles) – French road engineers *love* roundabouts – priorité à droite has been suspended so that the cars already in the roundabout have right of way. This circumstance is indicated by signs reading either *'vous n'avez pas la priorité'* (you do not have right of way) or *'cédez le passage'* (give way) or by yield signs displaying a circle made out of three curved arrows.

Priorité à droite is also suspended on *routes à caractère prioritaire* (priority roads), which are marked by a yellow diamond (actually an up-ended square – see illustration) with a black diamond in the middle. Such signs appear every few kilometres and at intersections. Priorité à droite is reinstated if you see the same sign with a diagonal bar through it.

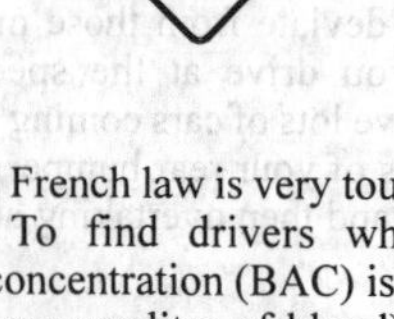

Alcohol French law is very tough on drunk drivers. To find drivers whose blood-alcohol concentration (BAC) is over 0.05% (0.50 grams per litre of blood), the police sometimes conduct random breathalyser tests. Fines range from 500 to 8000FF, and licences can also be suspended.

Fines You seldom see the police pulling anyone over for speeding, which may explain why French drivers seem so fearless as they whiz down the autoroute. In any case, *contraventions* (fines) for serious violations (eg speeding, driving through a red light) range from 1300 to 50,000FF. The police can make tourists pay up immediately.

Road Signs

On information signs indicating how to get to various cities, towns and intersecting highways, an arrow next to the words *toutes directions* (all directions) or *autres directions* (other directions) indicates where to head unless you're going to one of the destinations specifically mentioned elsewhere on the sign.

Sens unique means 'one way'. *Voie unique* means 'one-lane road' (eg at a narrow bridge). *Allumez vos feux* means 'turn on your headlights'. If you come to a *route barrée* (a closed road), you'll usually also find a yellow panel with instructions for a *déviation* (detour). Signs for *poids lourds* (heavyweights) are meant for lorries (trucks), not automobiles. The words *sauf riverains* on a no-entry sign mean 'except residents'.

Road signs with the word *rappel* (remember) written on or under them are telling you something that you were already supposed to know (eg the speed limit).

Motoring Organisations

In Paris, the Automobile Club de l'Île de France (☎ 01 40 55 43 00; metro Argentine) at 14 Ave de la Grande Armée (17e) sells insurance coverage and, if you stop by the office, can supply you with basic maps and suggestions for itineraries. The Automobile Club National no longer exists.

Costs

The convenience of having your own vehicle does not come cheaply, but for two or more people a car may cost less than going by train (this depends in part on what rail discounts you qualify for). In addition, a car will allow you to avail yourself of less expensive camping grounds, hostels and hotels located on city outskirts and in the countryside.

By autoroute, the drive from Paris to Nice, a distance of about 950km (about eight hours of actual driving), costs 380FF for petrol (at 16km per litre) and 349FF for autoroute tolls, for a total of about 729FF. This figure does not include wear and tear, depreciation, repairs, insurance or the risk of damage, theft or accident. By comparison, a regular, one-way, 2nd class train ticket for the six hour Paris-Nice run costs 438FF.

Petrol *Essence* (petrol or gasoline), also known as *carburant* (fuel), is expensive in France, incredibly so if you're used to Australian or North American prices. At the time of writing, unleaded (*sans plomb*) petrol with an IOR octane rating of 98 costs around 6.40FF a litre (US$4 per US gallon). Diesel fuel (*gazole*) is 4.60FF per litre (US$2.90 per US gallon). Filling up (*faire le plein*) is most expensive at the rest stops along the autoroutes and cheapest at small rural petrol stations; the price of a litre of fuel can vary by as much as 20% depending on where you buy it.

Tolls Tolls are charged for travel on almost all autoroutes (except around major cities) and many bridges. On autoroutes, you're essentially paying for the right to drive faster and thus save time. Despite the high speed limits, such travel is also much safer per kilometre driven.

Some autoroutes have toll plazas every few dozen kilometres, while on others a machine issues a little ticket that you hand over at a *péage* (toll booth) when you exit. Count on paying about 40FF per 100km, by credit card if you prefer. From Paris, autoroute destinations with hefty tolls include Paris to Bordeaux (254FF for passenger cars), Calais (105FF), Clermont-Ferrand (175FF), Lyon (154FF), Marseille (267FF), Nantes (170FF) and Strasbourg (182FF).

Parking

In French cities, finding a place to park is likely to be the single greatest hassle you'll face. In city centres, your best bet is usually to ditch the car somewhere and either walk or take public transport.

Gallic Parking Techniques

Most French cars are fairly small, but frequently they're not quite compact enough to fit into the only parking place in the neighbourhood. This is where the French belief that bumpers are meant to be bumped comes in handy: you back up until you tap the car behind, then you drive forward until you touch the car in front, and so on until you work your way to the kerb. Strange as it may sound, some people leave their cars in neutral so that drivers parking nearby can gently push them backwards or forwards in the process of squeezing into a tight spot.

Public parking facilities are marked by signs bearing a white letter 'P' on a blue background.

Parking Meters In most cities and many towns, parking near the city centre requires paying 5 to 10FF an hour and is subject to a time limit, often two hours. This lamentable circumstance is generally indicated either by the word *payant* written on the asphalt or by an upright sign in French.

The French love of gadgetary solutions has led to the installation of sophisticated, kerbside *horodateurs* (parking meters), into which you feed coins (or, in some cities, insert a debit card – these are available at *tabacs*) according to how long you want to park. When you press the correct button (usually the green one – the other ones are for local residents with special permits), the machine spits out a little ticket listing the precise time after which you'll be illegally parked. Take the ticket and place it on the passenger side of the dashboard where it's visible from the pavement.

Most horodateurs are programmed to take into account periods when parking is free, so you can pay the night before for the first hour or two after 9 am (or whatever time metered parking begins).

In many parking garages, the exit gate is unstaffed. You're meant to pay at machines placed at pedestrian entrances – you'll be told how much you owe when you insert the time-stamped magnetic ticket you were issued when you drove in.

Alternate Side Parking Parking on some streets is governed by an arrangement called *stationnement alterné semi-mensuel*, which means you can park on one side of the street from the 1st of the month until the evening of the 15th and on the other side from the 16th until the end of the month.

Dangers & Annoyances

Theft from and of cars is a *major* problem in France, especially in the south. For details, see Theft under Dangers & Annoyances in the Facts for the Visitor chapter.

Repairs If your car is *en panne* (breaks down), you'll have to find a garage that handles your *marque* (make of car). There are Peugeot, Renault and Citroën garages all over the place, but if you have a non-French car you may have trouble finding someone to service it in more remote areas. Michelin's *Guide Rouge* lists garages at the end of each entry.

Accidents If you are involved in a minor accident with no injuries, the easiest way for the drivers to sort things out with their respective insurance companies is to fill out a Constat Aimable d'Accident Automobile (jointly agreed accident report), known in English as a European Accident Statement, which has a standardised way of recording important details about what happened. In rental cars it is usually included in the packet of documents you were given.

If your French is not fluent, find someone who can explain exactly what each word of traffic jargon means. Never sign anything you don't understand – insist on a translation and sign that only if it's acceptable. Make sure you can read the other driver's handwriting. If problems crop up, it's usually not very hard to find a police officer. To alert the police, dial ☎ 17.

Make sure the report includes any information that will help you to prove that the accident was not your fault. For instance, if you were just sitting there and the other person backed into you, mention this under Observations (No 14 on the Constat). Remember, if you *did* cause the accident (or can't prove that you didn't) you may end up paying a hefty excess (deductible), depending on your insurance policy.

Car Rental

Given the cost of getting a car across the English Channel or from mainland France to Corsica, and the expenses involved in driving across France, it may make sense to rent a car after you arrive in the region you'd like to explore. Airport tariffs may be higher than the rates charged in town. *Kilométrage illimité* means that there's no limit on how many kilometres you can drive. Most rental companies require that you be over 21 (or, in some cases, over 23) and have had a driver's licence for at least one year. The packet of documents you are given should include a 24 hour number to call in case of a breakdown or accident.

Rental Companies The Car & Motorbike section under Getting Around in the Paris chapter lists quite a few car-hire companies' offices and reservation numbers. In other city chapters, rental agencies are mentioned under Getting There & Away. Very few places are open on Sunday. It's a good idea to reserve a few days in advance, especially with the less expensive companies.

The multinational rental agencies, such as Hertz, Avis, Budget and Europe's largest, Europcar, are outrageously expensive if you walk into one of their offices and hire a car on the spot – up to 900FF a day for a Twingo (Renault's smallest model) with unlimited kilometres. But if you can plan in advance, their prebooked and prepaid promotional rates can be very reasonable. For instance, weekly rates for Europe, as advertised in the USA, can be as little as US$160, less than a quarter of the rate in France. They may also have fly/drive combinations and other discounts that are worth looking into – ask your travel agent.

For rentals that are not arranged in advance, domestic companies (Rent-a-Car Système, Grand Garage Jean Jaurès) and some of the student travel agencies (eg USIT) have the best rates. The largest French company, ADA Location de Véhicules (☎ 08 36 68 40 02 for 2.23FF a minute; Minitel 3615 ADA), will generally rent a small car (a Ford Ka or an Opel Corsa) for 269/369FF for one day, including 200/400km free (the rate is 1.15FF per kilometre after that) and an excess (deductible) of 3000FF (6000FF if the vehicle is stolen). The rate for a weekend (from 6 pm on Friday to 8 am on Monday) is 549FF, including 800km free. For a full seven days (with 1000/2000km free), you pay 1499/1739FF. The rental fee includes 24-hour breakdown service, provided by Mondial Assistance (☎ 0 800 01 02 97).

Under SNCF's pricey Train + Auto plan, you can reserve an Avis car when you book your train ticket and it will be waiting for you when you arrive at any of over 200 train stations.

Insurance *Assurance* (insurance) for damage or injury you cause to other people is mandatory, but things like collision damage waivers vary greatly from company to company. The policies offered by some small, discount companies may leave you liable for up to 8000FF – when comparing rates, the most important thing to check is the *franchise* (excess/deductible). If you're in an accident where you are at fault, or the car is damaged and the party at fault is unknown (eg someone dents your car while it's parked), or the car is stolen, this is the amount that you are liable for before the collision damage policy kicks in.

Forms of Payment All the major domestic and multinational rental companies accept payment by credit card. Because you'll probably have to leave a deposit for the insurance excess and perhaps the petrol in the tank, many companies *require* that you have a credit card. Some ask you to leave a signed credit card slip without a sum written on it as a deposit. If you don't like this arrangement, ask them to make out two credit card slips: one for the sum of the rental and the other for the sum of the excess. Make sure to have the latter destroyed when you return the car.

Purchase-Repurchase Plans

If you'll be needing a car in Europe for 24 days to six months, by far your cheapest option is to 'purchase' a brand new one from the manufacturer and then, at the end of your trip, 'sell' it back to them. In reality, you only pay for the number of days you use the vehicle, but the tax-free, purchase-repurchase (*achat-rachat*) aspect of the paperwork (none of which is your responsibility) makes this type of leasing much cheaper than renting, especially for longer periods. Eligibility is restricted to people who are not *residents* of the EU (ie citizens of EU countries are eligible provided they live outside the EU).

Everyone we know who's travelled with a purchase-repurchase car has given the Renault and Peugeot programs rave reviews. One minor problem: the red number plates announce to all passing thieves that the car is being driven by a tourist, so be especially careful (see Theft under Dangers & Annoyances in the Facts for the Visitor chapter).

Renault Renault Eurodrive, used with great success by several Lonely Planet authors, lets you drive in 33 countries in Western and Central Europe (not including Hungary and Poland for insurance reasons) as well as North Africa. You just need a credit card, a passport and a driver's licence (not necessarily an international one) valid in the countries in which you'll be driving. The minimum age is 18; there's no maximum age.

Payment for the period for which you would like the car must be made in advance. If you return it early, you can usually get a refund for the unused time (seven days minimum). Extending your contract is also possible but you pay a hefty premium to cover the cost of the added paperwork – call the Paris office (☎ 01 40 40 33 68) at least a week before your original return date.

The car can be picked up and returned in 14 different French cities, in many cases at the airport. It can also be collected or dropped off outside France (eg in Amsterdam, London, Madrid or Rome) but this involves an extra fee.

The Special Export Sales Division of Renault's Paris office (Map 1; metro Porte de Pantin), 186 Ave Jean Jaurès (19e), can arrange a car within one week. However, depending on the exchange rates, it is sometimes cheaper to arrange your Renault purchase-repurchase car outside France, where various discounts may be available. The cheapest rates seem to be those on offer at Renault's Internet site. Telephone and fax numbers of Renault Eurodrive offices in France and abroad are listed in the boxed text 'Renault Eurodrive Offices'; it's best to contact them (or a travel agent) three or four weeks before your trip.

In the USA, the cheapest model available – a 1.2L, three door, five speed Twingo with AM/FM cassette-radio – costs US$480 for the first 17 days and US$16 for each additional day. If arranged through Paris, a Twingo costs 3780FF for the first 17 days and 52FF for each day thereafter. For 1½/three months the price is about US$1168/1664 in the USA and US$986/1250 in France.

These prices include unlimited kilometres, 24 hour towing and breakdown service (☎ 0 800 05 15 15 in France, ☎ 33 1 47 11 13 13 in other countries), and comprehensive insurance with – incredibly – no excess (deductible). Returning a damaged car to Renault is totally hassle-free – as at least that's what one Lonely Planet author discovered. Cars with automatic transmission and diesel engines are also available. If you fall in love with your car (unlikely in the case of the Twingo), you can buy it when your purchase-repurchase agreement comes to an end.

Renault Eurodrive Offices

France	☎ 01 40 40 32 32 fax 01 42 41 83 47 www.eurodrive.com
Australia	☎ 1-800 221 156 ☎ 02-9299 3344 fax 02-9262 4590
Canada	☎ 1-800 361 2411 ☎ 514-461 1149 fax 514-461 0207
New Zealand	☎ 09-525 8800 fax 09-525 8810
USA	☎ 1-800 221 1052 ☎ 212-532 1221 fax 212-725 537

Peugeot The Peugeot Vacation Plan (☎ 1-800 572 9655 in the USA; www.auto-france.com) is very similar to Renault Eurodrive. Details are available from some travel agents.

Buying a Car

The hassle of buying a car and later selling it, the risk of losing your entire investment if something expensive goes wrong, and the cost of registration, insurance, petrol, tolls, taxes and the like make purchasing your own vehicle worthwhile only if you'll be spending a lot of time in Europe. Because of regulations requiring that cars over seven years old pass a regular safety test (*contrôle technique*), dirt-cheap old beaters are a thing of the past. The book value of used cars up to eight years old is listed in *L'Argus* (15FF), available at many newsagents and kiosks.

The seller should provide you with two copies of the *certificat de cession d'un véhicule* (certificate of transfer of a vehicle); the car's carte grise (the vehicle's registration certificate) marked with the words *vendu le* or *cédé le* (sold on) and the date; a contrôle technique form that is up to date; and a *certificat de non-gage* (a certificate from the prefecture attesting that the car has not been pledged as collateral, eg for a loan).

The seller's liability insurance stays in force until midnight of the day you buy the car, but after that it is illegal to drive it until you have a carte verte (a certificate of *garantie au tiers*, ie liability insurance), part of which you display on the right-hand side of the windscreen. In Paris, a reliable insurance agent with decent rates is BUSTA (Map 4; ☎ 01 47 05 05 04; fax 01 45 50 40 94; metro Pont de l'Alma) at 9 Ave Rapp (7e).

Within 15 days of purchase, you must take care of *immatriculation* (vehicle registration) and get a new carte grise. This can be done at the nearest prefecture or, in Paris, the Préfecture de Police on Île de la Cité. Bring along *attestation* (proof) of where you live (eg an official receipt from your hotel or hostel that includes your full name and passport number). All cars are given new license plate numbers when they change hands, so when you get your carte grise you must *immediately* drive to a garage and get them to punch out *plaques d'immatriculation* (number or registration plates).

When you sell your car, cut off the upper right-hand corner of the carte grise, draw a diagonal line across it and write *vendu le* (sold on) plus the date. Take the little green insurance tag out of the sticker on the right-hand side of the windscreen. Make sure to have the buyer sign a *reçu d'achat de véhicule* (receipt for the purchase of a vehicle). When the deal is done, take one copy of the certificat de cession d'un véhicle to the prefecture where the car was registered.

MOTORCYCLE

France is a superb country for motorcycle touring, with winding roads of good quality and lots of stunning scenery. Just make sure your wet-weather gear is up to scratch.

Riders of any type of two-wheel vehicle with a motor must wear a helmet – if you're caught bareheaded, you can be fined and have your bike confiscated until you get one. Bikes of more than 125cc must have their headlights on during the day. No special licence is required to ride a motorbike whose engine is smaller than 50cc, which is why you often find places renting scooters rated at 49.9cc.

Motorcycle Rental

To rent a moped, scooter, motorcycle, etc you usually have to leave a *caution* (deposit) of several thousand francs, which you forfeit – up to the value of the damage – if you're in an accident and it's your fault. Since insurance companies won't cover theft, you'll also lose the deposit if the bike is stolen. Most places accept deposits made by credit card, travellers cheques or Eurocheques.

BICYCLE

France is an eminently cyclable country, thanks in part to its extensive network of secondary and tertiary roads, which carry relatively light traffic. Indeed, many people consider such back roads, a good number of which date from the 19th century or earlier, the ideal vantage point from which to view France's celebrated rural landscapes. One pitfall: they rarely have proper shoulders (verges).

More information of interest to cyclists can be found in the Facts for the Visitor chapter: general information on cycling in France is given under Activities; map options are discussed under Maps; and information on cyclists' topoguides can be found under Hiking & Cycling in the Travel Guides listing of the Books section. The Tour de France appears under Spectator Sports in the Facts for the Visitor chapter.

Road Rules

French law mandates that bicycles must have two functioning brakes, a bell, a red reflector on the back and yellow reflectors on the pedals. After sunset and when visibility is poor, cyclists must turn on a white light in front and a red one in the rear. The name and address of the bike's owner are supposed to appear on a metal plate attached to the front of the bike. When being overtaken by a car or truck, cyclists are required to ride in single file.

Cycling Organisations

In Paris, the Fédération Française de Cyclotourisme (☎ 01 44 16 88 88; fax 01 44 16 88 99; Minitel 3615 FFCT, 3615 VTT or 3615 VELO; metro Corvisart), 8 Rue Jean-Marie Jégo (13e), just north of Rue Bobillot, acts as a liaison among France's 3100 cycling clubs. Run by volunteers, it organises bicycle trips that are open to people visiting France. If you write to them they'll send you a packet of free general information in English, but they cannot answer specific queries. However, if you stop by the Paris office you can usually consult one of the volunteers. The FFCT also sells touring itineraries for one to seven-day excursions, cycling maps and topoguides for cyclists.

In the UK, the Cyclists' Touring Club (☎ 01483-417 217), Cotterell House, 69 Meadrow, Godalming, Surrey GU7 3HS, can supply information to members on cycling conditions in Europe as well as detailed routes, itineraries, cheap cycle and third-party insurance, cycle holidays etc. They also sell maps, topoguides and other publications by mail order. Membership, which includes insurance benefits, costs UK£25 per annum (UK£12.50/16.50 to people aged under 18/over 65, UK£42 for three or more people living at the same address).

European Bike Express (☎ 01642-251 440) facilitates independent cycling holidays by transporting cyclists and their bikes by bus and trailer from the UK to places all over France. Return fares are UK£140 to UK£160 (UK£10 less for members of the Cyclists' Touring Club).

Transporting Your Bicycle

Air It is relatively easy to take your bicycle with you on an aircraft. You can either take it apart and pack everything in a bike bag or box, or simply wheel it to the check-in desk, where it will be treated as a piece of baggage (you may have to supply your own box, available from bike shops). It will probably be necessary to remove the pedals and turn the handlebars sideways so that it takes up less space in the aircraft's hold. Check all this (and weight limits) with the airline well in advance, preferably before you pay for your ticket.

Bus Buses – local or intercity – will almost never take bicycles.

Train Within France, a bicycle can be brought along free of charge as hand luggage on most trains, provided it is enclosed in a *housse* (cover) that measures no more than 1200cm by 90cm. You are responsible for loading and unloading your bicycle from the luggage section of your train car. The SNCF won't accept any responsibility for its condition. You can also *enregistrer* (register) a boxed bicycle as checked baggage to any destination in France and many places in Europe for 135FF plus 15FF for a *emballage* (bike box), but it will probably take three or four days to arrive. Special tariffs apply in Corsica.

Sea Bicycle travel is free on most trans-Channel ferries, though from April to September a fee of UK£5 or 50FF applies on many runs to/from Normandy and Brittany. A cyclist with a bicycle pays UK£15/150FF for return passage on Eurotunnel (through the Channel Tunnel); advance reservations of at least 24 hours are mandatory. Bikes are sometimes free on ferries to/from Ireland but usually cost 100 to 180FF. Taking a bike to Corsica costs 85FF.

Bicycle Rental

Most towns have at least one shop that hires out *vélos tout-terrains* (mountain bikes), popularly known as VTTs (60 to 100FF a day), or cheaper touring bikes. Most places require a 1000 or 2000FF deposit, which you forfeit if the bike is damaged or stolen. In general, deposits can be made in cash, with signed travellers cheques or by credit card (though a passport will often suffice).

For details on rental shops, see the Getting Around or Getting There & Away sections of each city or town listing.

Avoiding Theft

Never leave your bicycle locked up outside overnight if you want to see it or most of its parts again. You can leave your bike in train station left-luggage offices for 35FF a day.

HITCHING

Hitching is never entirely safe in any country in the world, and we don't recommend it. Travellers who decide to hitch should understand that they are taking a small but potentially serious risk. However, many people do choose to hitch, and the advice that follows should help to make their journeys as fast and safe as is possible.

A woman hitching on her own is taking a risk, but two women should be reasonably safe. Two men together may have a harder time getting picked up than a man travelling alone. The best (and safest) combination is probably a man and a woman. In any case, never get in the car with someone you don't trust, even if you have no idea why. Keep your belongings with you on the seat rather than in the boot (trunk).

Dedicated hitchers may wish to invest in the *Hitch-Hikers Manual for Europe* by Simon Calder (Vacation Work; 1993).

Exploring France by Thumb

Hitching is as much a way to meet people as it is a way to get around. If you speak some French (few older people in rural areas know any English), thumbing it affords unmatched opportunities to meet French people from all walks of life. The less like a tourist you look and feel, the better off you'll be.

On the back roads you may not get long-distance rides, but you are more likely to get picked up and to meet people. Drivers will often give you advice on what to see in the immediate vicinity.

Fishing for Rides

Some of our readers report that it is more difficult to hitch in France than almost anywhere else in Europe, while others claim that France is one of the best places in Europe to hitch. And some travellers have had luck getting rides from truck drivers at truck stops, while others find that passenger cars are more likely to pick them up, either on slip or access roads (highway entrances) or at petrol stations. In any case, hitching from city centres is pretty much hopeless: take public transport to the outskirts. It is illegal to hitch on autoroutes, but you can stand near the entrance ramps as long as you don't block traffic. Travelling around the Côte d'Azur is nearly impossible. Remote rural areas are often an excellent bet, but once you get off the busier routes nationales there are few vehicles. If your itinerary includes a ferry crossing, it is worth trying to score a ride before the ferry rather than after, since vehicle tickets sometimes include a number of passengers free of charge. At dusk, give up and think about finding somewhere to stay.

To maximise your chances of being picked up, stand where it's convenient for drivers to stop; look cheerful, presentable and nonthreatening; orient your backpack so it looks as small as possible to oncoming drivers; make eye contact with the people driving by.

It is an excellent idea to hold up a sign with your destination followed by the letters *s.v.p.* (short for *s'il vous plaît*, meaning 'please') written on it. One traveller reports that a destination sign reading *'n'importe où'* (anywhere) works well if you aren't going to any particular place.

Allostop & Association Pouce

Two organisations put people looking for rides in touch with drivers going to the same destination. Allostop Provoya (☎ 01 53 20 42 42 or, from outside Paris, ☎ 01 53 20 42 44; metro Cadet) is based at 8 Rue Rochambeau (9e) in Paris; for opening hours see Hitching under Getting There & Away in the Paris chapter. Association Pouce (☎ /fax 02 99 08 67 02; Minitel 3617 POUCE; www.idonline.net/pouce; allopouce@infonie.fr) is based in Brittany.

Travelling this way offers undeniable environmental advantages, but it requires a fair bit of advance planning (eg contacting either organisation a few days ahead) and is far from free. With Allostop, each passenger pays 22 centimes a kilometre to the driver and is assessed a fee to cover administrative expenses: 30/40/50/60FF for trips under 200/300/400/500km and 70FF for trips over 500km. If you buy an eight trip *abonnement* (membership) for 180FF, which is valid for up to two years, you pay only the charge per-kilometre. Association Pouce, whose interface with the public is in French by answering machine, Minitel and the Internet, has similar per-kilometre fees but no cover charge.

To arrange a trip, contact either organisation (or stop by the Allostop office) and you will be given details on how to contact a driver going your way. Allostop's administrative fee can be paid for by telephone with a credit card.

Possible destinations from Paris include Amsterdam (167FF), Barcelona (294FF), Berlin (301FF), Bordeaux (197FF), Geneva (188FF), Lyon (162FF), Marseille (239FF) and Nice (274FF). These are Allostop's prices and include both what you pay the driver and the administrative fee. Province-to-province transport is also occasionally available.

BOAT

For information on touring France's waterways by boat, see Canal Boating under Activities in the Facts for the Visitor chapter.

LOCAL TRANSPORT

Getting around France's cities is usually pretty straightforward, though taxis are pricey and at times hard to find.

Bus, Tram & Metro

France's cities and larger towns generally have excellent public transport systems, including metros in Paris, Lyon, Marseille, Lille and Toulouse, and ultra-modern trams in such cities as Paris, Nantes, Strasbourg and Grenoble. Details on routes, fares, tourist passes etc are usually available at tourist offices and local bus company information counters; in this book see Getting Around at the end of each city listing.

Taxi

French taxis are rather expensive, especially outside the major cities. All large and medium-sized train stations – and many small ones – have a taxi stand (rank) out front.

Urban Orienteering

When a building is put up in a location where they've run out of consecutive street numbers, a new address is formed by fusing the number of an adjacent building with the notations *bis* (twice), *ter* (thrice) or, rarely, *quater* (four times). Thus, the street numbers 17bis or 89ter are the equivalent of 17A or 89B.

In larger cities, especially Paris, the street doors of many apartment buildings can be opened only if someone has given you the entry code, which is changed periodically. Outside intercoms are more common in provincial cities. In some buildings, the entry code device is de-activated during the day, but to get in (or out) you still have to push a button (usually marked *porte*) to release the catch.

The doors of many French apartments are completely unmarked: not only are the occupants' names nowhere in sight, but there isn't even an apartment number. To know which door to knock on, you'll usually be given cryptic instructions, such as *cinquième étage, premier à gauche* (5th floor, first on the left) or *troisième étage, droite droite* (3rd floor, turn right twice). In France (and in this guidebook), the 1st floor is the floor above the *rez-de-chaussée* (ground floor).

For details on the tariffs and regulations applicable in major cities, see Taxi under Getting Around in the Paris chapter. In small cities and towns, where taxi drivers are unlikely to find another fare anywhere near where they let you off, there are four kinds of tariffs, set by the local prefecture:

Tariff A (about 3.50FF per kilometre) – for return trips taken Monday to Saturday from 7 am to 7 pm
Tariff B (about 5FF per kilometre) – for return travel undertaken from 7 pm to 7 am and all day on Sunday and holidays
Tariff C (about 7FF per kilometre) – for one-way travel undertaken during the day from Monday to Saturday
Tariff D (about 10FF per kilometre) – for one-way travel at night and on Sunday and holidays

Travel under 20km/h (or thereabouts) is calculated by time (75FF an hour) rather than distance. Since the *prise en charge* (flag fall) is about 13.50FF, a one-way, 4km trip taken on a weekday afternoon will cost about 42FF. There may be a surcharge of 5FF to get picked up at a train station or airport and a fee of 6FF per bag.

ORGANISED TOURS

Though independent travel is usually far more rewarding than being led from bus to sight and back again, some areas are difficult to visit unless you have wheels. Where relevant (eg the D-day Beaches in Normandy) your options are mentioned in the Organised Tours sections within the regional chapters.

Paris

Paris (population 2.2 million in the urban area, 10.5 million in the Île de France region) has just about exhausted the superlatives that can reasonably be applied to any city. Notre Dame and the Eiffel Tower – at sunrise, at sunset, at night, in the snow – have been described countless times, as have the Seine and the subtle (and not so subtle) differences between the Left and Right banks. But what writers have been unable to capture is the grandness and even magic of strolling along the broad avenues that lead from impressive public buildings and exceptional museums to parks, gardens and esplanades.

Paris probably has more known landmarks than any city in the world. As a result, first-time visitors often arrive in the French capital with all sorts of expectations: of grand vistas, of intellectuals pontificating at sidewalk cafés, of romance along the Seine, of naughty nightclub revues, of rude people who won't speak English and who rip you off. If you look hard enough, you can probably find all those things. But another approach is to set aside the preconceptions of Paris and to explore the city's avenues and backstreets as if the tip of the Eiffel Tower or the spire of Notre Dame weren't about to pop into view at any moment.

Paris is enchanting almost everywhere, at any time, in every season. And, like a good meal, it excites, it satisfies, the memory lingers. In *A Moveable Feast*, his recollections of Paris in the 1920s, the American author Ernest Hemingway wrote: 'If you are lucky to have lived in Paris as a young man, then wherever you go for the rest of your life, it stays with you, for Paris is a moveable feast.'

Those of us who took Mr Hemingway's advice in our salad days could not agree more. We're still dining out on the feast of memories.

HIGHLIGHTS

- **Louvre** – visit the new Egyptology collection (or any collection that takes your fancy)
- **Musée d'Orsay** – marvel at this beautiful museum's impressionist art
- **Sainte Chapelle** – admire its sublime stained glass on a sunny day
- **Notre Dame** – attend an organ concert
- **Seine River** – enjoy a dinner cruise
- **Views** – take in the views from Eiffel Tower, Tour Montparnasse, La Samaritaine rooftop terrace or Sacré Cœur

What Parisians eat in bistros – *soupe à l'oignon* (onion soup); *pieds de cochon* (pig's trotters); *pot au feu* (stewed beef and vegetables); *moëlle* (beef marrow on bread)

Paris is also popular for ethnic foods – *couscous* and *tajine* from North Africa; Vietnamese *nems* (spring rolls); West Indian *boudin antillais* (blood sausage or black pudding)

ORIENTATION

The city of Paris is relatively small: approximately 9.5km (north to south) by 11km (west to east), not including the Bois de Boulogne and the Bois de Vincennes; its total area is 105 sq km. Within central Paris (which the French call *Intra-Muros* – meaning 'within the walls'), the Rive Droite (Right Bank) is north of the Seine, while the Rive Gauche (Left Bank) is south of the river.

This chapter gives you three ways to find the addresses mentioned: by arrondissement, by map reference and by metro stop.

Arrondissements

Paris is divided into 20 *arrondissements* (districts) that spiral out from the city centre clockwise like a conch shell. Paris addresses always include the arrondissement number, and they're very important: streets with the same names exist in different districts.

In this chapter, arrondissement numbers are listed after the street address using the usual French notation: *1er* for *premier* (1st), *4e* for *quatrième* (4th), 19e for *dix-neuvième* (19th), and so forth (on some signs or commercial maps, you will see the notation 4ème, 19ème etc).

Maps & Map References

The exact location of every museum, hotel, restaurant, exchange bureau etc mentioned in this chapter is indicated on one of the colour maps (between pages 192 and 193). Each address includes the reference number of the relevant map, usually just before the telephone number.

The most useful map of Paris for sale is the 1:10,000 scale *Paris Plan* published by Michelin. It comes in booklet form (No 11 or 14) or by fold-out sheet (No 10 or 12) for 34FF or, under the name *Atlas Paris 15*, in

PARIS ARRONDISSEMENTS

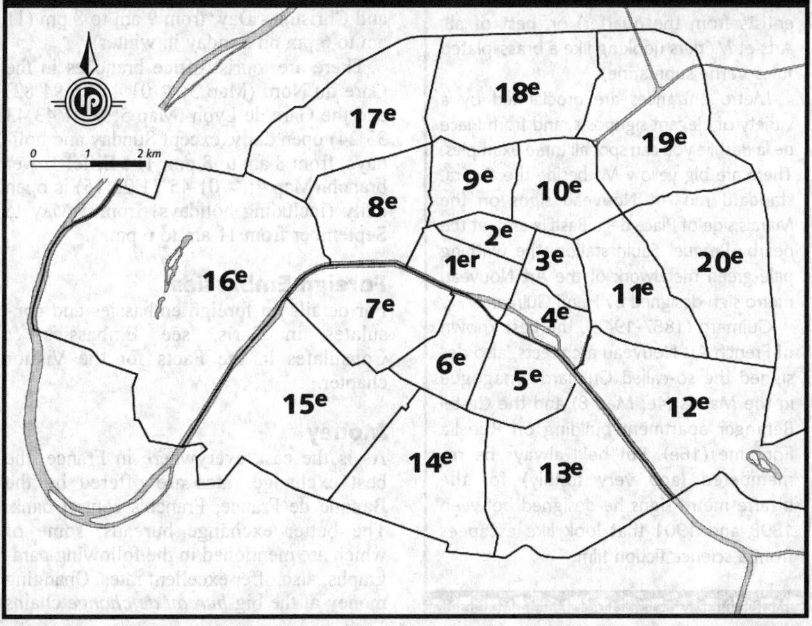

large format (75FF). *Atlas Paris & Banlieues 25* includes the suburbs.

Many Parisians swear by the pocket-size book with hand-drawn maps called *Paris par Arrondissement* (60FF), which has a double-page street plan of each arrondissement. Others find it confusing, though it does list the appropriate metro stop next to streets in the index. A more user-friendly choice is *Paris Practique* (36FF), in a larger format and slimmer.

Art in the Metro

There are more modern subway systems than the Paris metro but few as convenient, reasonably priced or, at the better stations, more elegant. Which is not to say that it can't be very tedious when the metro workers have one of their periodic *grèves* (strikes), or very sleazy at some of the more down and dirty stations late at night ...

Some stations not to be missed are Louvre-Rivoli (a small taste of the nearby Musée du Louvre), Cluny-La Sorbonne (decorated with ceramic replicas of the signatures of intellectuals, artists and scientists from the quarter) or, best of all, Arts et Métiers (looking like a brass-plated Jules Verne submarine).

Metro entrances are proclaimed by a variety of elegant signposts, and from Place de la Bastille you can spot all three examples. There are big yellow Ms beside the Opéra, standard red Art Nouveau signs on the Marais side of Place de la Bastille and, at the nearby Bréguet Sabin station, the writhing pale-green metalwork of the Art Nouveau metro sign designed by Henri Guimard.

Guimard (1867-1942), the best known of French Art Nouveau architects, also designed the so-called Guimard synagogue in the Marais (4e; Map 8) and the Castel Béranger apartment building on Rue La Fontaine (16e). But he'll always be remembered (and very fondly) for the bizarre metro signs he designed between 1898 and 1901 that look like escapees from a science fiction film.

Metro Stations

There is almost always a metro station within 500m of wherever you want to go in Paris, so all offices, museums, hotels, restaurants etc mentioned here have the nearest metro stop written immediately after the telephone number (or, in a few cases, after the street address). Metro stations usually have a *plan du quartier* (map of the neighbourhood) hung on the wall near the exits. It can be an invaluable aid for initial orientation in an unfamiliar area.

INFORMATION

Tourist Offices

Paris' main tourist office (Map 2; ☎ 01 49 52 53 54 or, for information in English, ☎ 01 44 29 12 12; fax 01 49 52 53 00; www.paris-promotion.fr; metro George V) is at 127 Ave des Champs-Élysées (8e). It's open every day of the year, except 1 May and Christmas Day, from 9 am to 8 pm (11 am to 6 pm on Sunday in winter).

There are tourist office branches in the Gare du Nord (Map 3; ☎ 01 45 26 94 82) and the Gare de Lyon (Map 5; ☎ 01 43 43 33 24) open daily, except Sunday and holidays, from 8 am to 8 pm. The Eiffel Tower branch (Map 4; ☎ 01 45 51 22 15) is open daily (including holidays) from 2 May to September from 11 am to 6 pm.

Foreign Embassies

For details on foreign embassies and consulates in Paris, see Embassies & Consulates in the Facts for the Visitor chapter.

Money

As is the case everywhere in France, the best exchange rates are offered by the Banque de France, France's central bank. The better exchange bureaus, some of which are mentioned in the following paragraphs, also offer excellent rates. Changing money at the big *bureau de change* chains like Chequepoint and Exact Change is crazy; they offer about 10% less than a fair rate. Note that not all commercial bank branches handle foreign currency. Also, due to the high volume of customers and shortage of counter staff, some Banque de France branches are limiting their exchange operations, usually to the morning only, and very few accept US$100 notes.

Quite a few Parisian post offices will exchange a variety of foreign banknotes as well as American Express travellers cheques (in US dollars or francs) and Visa travellers cheques (in francs).

Airports The Travelex exchange bureaus at both Orly and Roissy Charles de Gaulle airports are open daily from 6 or 6.30 am until 11 or 11.30 pm.

Train Stations All of Paris' six major train stations have automatic teller machines (ATMs). They also have exchange bureaus, often run by Thomas Cook, which are open seven days a week until at least 7 pm (later in summer), but their rates are less than stellar. Very near each of the stations you'll find a post office (open weekdays from 8 am to 7 pm and on Saturday until noon) with exchange services.

American Express Paris' landmark American Express office (Map 2; ☎ 01 47 77 77 07; metro Auber or Opéra) is at 11 Rue Scribe (9e), facing the west side of Opéra Garnier. Exchange services, cash advances, refunds and poste restante are available Monday to Friday from 8.30 am to 6.30 pm (7 pm in summer), from 9 am to 5.30 pm on Saturday and, for changing money only, on Sunday from 10 am to 5 pm.

Louvre Area The headquarters of the Banque de France (Map 7; ☎ 01 42 92 22 27; metro Palais Royal), 31 Rue Croix des Petits Champs (1er), three blocks north of the Louvre, is open Monday to Friday from 9.30 am to 12.30 pm and 1.30 to 4 pm.

The exchange bureaus along Rue de Rivoli (1er) include the Paris Vision office at No 214 (Map 7; ☎ 01 42 60 30 01; metro Tuileries), open every day of the year from 7 am to 9 pm (to 10 pm in summer). Other places with good rates include Le Change du Louvre (Map 7; ☎ 01 42 97 27 28; metro Palais Royal), on the north side of Le Louvre des Antiquaires at 151 Rue Saint Honoré (1er), open daily from 10 am to 7 pm (in winter, weekdays from 10 am to 4 pm, Saturday from 10.30 am to 4.30 pm), and Le Change de Paris (Map 2; ☎ 01 42 60 30 84; metro Tuileries) at 2 Place Vendôme (1er), open Monday to Saturday from 10 am to 6 or 6.30 pm.

Les Halles Area Best Change (Map 7; ☎ 01 42 21 46 05; metro Louvre-Rivoli) at 21 Rue du Roule (1er), three blocks southwest of Forum des Halles, is open daily from 10 am (11 am on Sunday) to 8 pm.

Bastille Area The Banque de France branch (Map 5; ☎ 01 44 61 15 30; metro Bastille) at 5 Place de la Bastille (4e), directly across from Opéra Bastille, is open weekdays from 9 to 11.45 am and 1.30 to 3.30 pm. Temporary closures due to crowds are not unknown here.

Latin Quarter The Banque Nationale de Paris (Map 6; ☎ 01 43 29 45 50; metro Luxembourg) at 7 Rue Soufflot (5e) exchanges foreign currency and will make Visa and MasterCard cash advances on weekdays from 9 to 5 pm.

6e Arrondissement The Banque de France branch (Map 4; ☎ 01 49 54 27 27; metro Sèvres Babylone) at 48 Blvd Raspail is open weekdays from 8.45 am to 12.15 pm and 2 to 3.30 pm.

Le Change de Paris (Map 6; ☎ 01 43 54 76 55; metro Saint Michel) at 2 Place Saint Michel, has some of the best rates in Paris and is open daily from 10 am to 7 pm. Rates are only marginally lower at the nearby exchange bureau (Map 6; ☎ 01 46 34 70 46) at 1 Rue Hautefeuille (near the southern end of Place Saint Michel), open daily from 9 am to 9 pm.

Champs-Élysées Area The Bureau de Change (Map 2; ☎ 01 42 25 38 14; metro Franklin D Roosevelt) at 25 Ave des Champs-Élysées (8e) has some of the best rates in the city and is an especially good bet on weekends. It is open every day of the year from 9 am to 8 pm.

Near La Madeleine, the Office de Change de Paris (Map 2; ☎ 01 42 66 25 33; metro Madeleine or Concorde) at 13 Rue Royale (8e) is open daily until 6.30 pm (6 pm on Sunday and holidays).

Parc de Monceau Area The Banque de France branch (Map 2; ☎ 01 42 27 78 14; metro Monceau) at 1 Place du Général Catroux (17e), a block north of Parc de Monceau, is open weekdays from 8.45 am to noon and 1.45 to 3.30 pm.

Opéra Garnier Area There's a foreign currency exchange machine that accepts banknotes of eight countries at Barclays Bank (Map 7; metro Opéra), 24bis Ave de l'Opéra (2e).

Montmartre The bureau de change (Map 9; ☎ 01 42 52 67 19; metro Abbesses) at 6 Rue Yvonne Le Tac (18e) usually has excellent rates and is open from 10 am to 6.30 pm (6 pm on weekends); closed Sunday, except from June to September.

There are a couple of banks and another exchange bureau at Place des Abbesses (Map 9), where the post office has a 24 hour banknote exchange machine. The Thomas Cook bureau (Map 9) at Place Blanche, next to the Moulin Rouge, is open daily from 9.30 am to 11.30 pm.

Post & Communications

Post Most post offices in Paris are open Monday to Friday from 8 am to 7 pm and on Saturday from 8 am to noon.

The main post office (Map 7; ☎ 01 40 28 20 00; metro Sentier or Les Halles), 52 Rue du Louvre (1er), five blocks north of the east end of the Louvre, is open 24 hours a day, seven days a week – but only for sending mail, telegrams and domestic faxes, picking up poste restante mail (3FF for up to 20g, 4FF for up to 100g) and making calls with *télécartes* (phonecards). Other services, including currency exchange, are available only during regular post office hours. Be prepared for long queues after 7 pm. Poste restante mail not specifically addressed to a particular branch post office is delivered here.

The post office (Map 2; ☎ 01 42 56 13 71; metro George V) at 71 Ave des Champs-Élysées (8e) has extended hours (weekdays from 8 am to 7.30 pm and Saturday from 10 am to 7 pm), when you can send letters, telegrams and faxes, make télécarte calls and change money.

Each arrondissement has its own five digit postcode, formed by adding 750 or 7500 to the arrondissement number: 75001 for the 1st arrondissement, 75019 for the 19th and so forth. All mail to addresses in France *must* include the postcode. The notation 'CEDEX' after the postcode and Paris simply means that mail sent to that address is collected at the post office rather than delivered to the door.

Telephone For information on how to use French phones, see Telephone under Post & Communications in the Facts for the Visitor chapter. Télécartes are on sale at post offices, *tabacs* (tobacconists), supermarket check-out counters, metro stations, state-owned rail system (SNCF) ticket windows, and anywhere you see a blue sticker reading *télécarte en vente ici*. Cards worth 50/120 units cost 40.60/97.50FF.

Fax, Telegraph & Email Virtually all Paris post offices can send and receive domestic and international faxes, telexes and telegrams. It costs about 80FF (20FF within France) to send a one page fax.

Internet Resources

For several useful Web sites on both Paris and France in general, in English, see the Internet Resources section in the Facts for the Visitor chapter.

At the time of going to print, La Poste was setting up Internet access centres at 1000 post offices around France; a chip card costing 90FF would get you three hours access. France Telecom, meanwhile, has been sponsoring 'Internet stations' around France, including one in Paris called Cyber Espace (☎ 01 40 51 96 16), 35 Rue du Cherche Midi (6e), on the corner of Blvd Raspail. These are not cybercafés as such but high-tech centres where people can surf the Internet, send emails and take free beginners courses on how to use the Internet. Access rates are cheaper than at commercial cybercafés: 20/30FF for a half-hour/hour.

Internet devotees can also have their hunger satiated at a number of cybercafés around Paris. Venues include:

Café Orbital (Map 6; ☎ 01 43 25 76 77; metro Luxembourg) 13 Rue de Médicis (6e). Open daily from 10 am to 10 pm; 55FF per hour, 200/300FF for five/10 hours. Student discounts available.

Web Bar (Map 8; ☎ 01 42 72 66 55; webbar@webbar.fr; metro Filles du Calvaire) 32 Rue de Picardie (3e). Open daily from 11.30 am to 2 am; 40FF per hour or 250FF for 10 hours.

Hi Tech Café (Map 4; ☎ 01 45 38 67 61; metro Montparnasse) 10 Rue de Départ (15e). Open Monday to Saturday from noon to 2 am; 40FF per hour or 320FF for 10 hours.

Travel Agencies

General The following agencies are among the largest in Paris and offer the best services and deals:

Forum Voyages (☎ 01 53 32 71 72 or ☎ 08 36 68 12 02 for information and reservations; Minitel 3615 FV) has 11 branches in Paris proper including one at 11 Ave de l'Opéra (1er; ☎ 01 42 61 20 20; metro Pyramides) and another at 28 Rue Monge (5e; Map 7; ☎ 01 43 25 54 54; metro Cardinal Lemoine). Open weekdays from 9.30 am to 7 pm and on Saturday from 10 am to 6 pm.

Nouvelles Frontières (☎ 08 03 33 33 33; Minitel 3615 NF; www.nouvelles-frontieres.com) has some 13 outlets around the city including at 5 Ave de l'Opéra (1er; Map 7; metro Pyramides), open weekdays from 9 am to 8 pm (7 pm on Saturday), and 66 Blvd Saint Michel (6e; metro Luxembourg), open Monday to Saturday from 9 am to 7 pm.

Student Paris travel agencies that cater to students and young people can supply discount tickets to travellers of all ages. Most issue ISIC student ID cards (60FF) and the Carte Jeunes (120FF), and sell Eurolines tickets.

USIT (Map 6; ☎ 01 42 34 56 90; metro Luxembourg), 6 Rue de Vaugirard (6e). Ireland's student travel outfit is open weekdays from 9.30 am to 6.30 pm and on Saturday from 10 am to 6 pm. For telephone sales, ring ☎ 01 42 44 14 00. For information and reservations by Minitel, dial 3615 USIT. USIT has three other branches including those at 12 Rue Vivienne (2e; Map 7; ☎ 01 42 44 14 00; metro Bourse), open Monday to Friday from 9.30 am to 6 pm (8 pm on Thursday in summer); 85 Blvd Saint Michel (5e; ☎ 01 43 29 69 50; metro Luxembourg), open Monday to Saturday from 10 am to 6 pm; and 31 bis Rue Linné (5e; ☎ 01 44 08 71 20; metro Jussieu), open Monday to Saturday from noon to 7 pm.

Council Travel (Map 7; ☎ 01 44 55 55 44; metro Pyramides), 22 Rue des Pyramides (1er). Holders of plane tickets issued by Council Travel (the US student travel company) and Travel CUTS (its Canadian counterpart) can come here to get lost tickets replaced, make reservations for tickets with open returns and change flight dates (but not routes). Refunds are available from the issuing office only. It is open Monday to Friday from 9.30 am to 6.30 pm and on Saturday from 10 am to 5.30 pm. Council Travel's second bureau (Map 6; ☎ 01 44 41 89 80; metro Odéon) at 1 Place de l'Odéon (6e) is open weekdays from 9.30 am to 6.30 pm and Saturday from 11 am to 3 pm.

Accueil des Jeunes en France (AJF; Map 8; ☎ 01 42 77 87 80; metro Rambuteau), 119 Rue Saint Martin (4e), across the square from the Centre Pompidou. This place does more than find travellers places to stay (see Accommodation Services in the Places to Stay section): it also functions as a travel agency for people of all ages. AJF is open Monday to Friday from 10 am to 6.45 pm and on Saturday to 5.45 pm.

OTU Voyages (Map 6; ☎ 01 44 41 38 50; metro Port Royal), 39 Ave Georges Bernanos (5e). This branch of the French student travel agency is open weekdays from 10 am (11 am from Monday) to 6.45 pm.

Bookshops

Paris has a number of bookshops that cater to Anglophones.

Abbey Bookshop (Map 6; ☎ 01 46 33 16 24; metro Cluny-La Sorbonne), 29 Rue de la Parcheminerie (5e). A mellow place, not far from Place Saint Michel, and known for having free tea and coffee, a supply of Canadian newspapers and a good selection of new and used works of fiction. It is open Monday to Saturday from 10 am to 7 pm; Sunday hours vary according to the owner's whim.

Australian Bookshop (Map 6; ☎ 01 43 29 08 65; metro Saint Michel), 33 Quai des Grands Augustins (6e). Open Tuesday to Sunday from 11 am to 7 pm.

Brentano's (Map 7; ☎ 01 42 61 52 50; metro Opéra), 37 Ave de l'Opéra (2e). Midway between the Louvre and Opéra Garnier, this shop specialises in books from the USA and is open Monday to Saturday from 10 am to 7.30 pm.

La Maison de l'Expatriée (Map 4; ☎ 01 53 59 33 00; metro Assemblée Nationale), 7 Rue de Bourgogne (7e). This bookshop and newsagency due south of the Assemblée Nationale has one of the largest selections of English-language newspapers and magazines in Paris. It's open weekdays from 7 am to 8 pm and on weekends from 9 am to 1 pm and 2 to 7 pm.

Shakespeare & Company (Map 6; ☎ 01 43 26 96 50; metro Saint Michel), 37 Rue de la Bûcherie (5e). Paris' most famous – but very much resting on its laurels – English-language bookshop has a varied and unpredictable collection of new and used books in English, including novels from 10FF. It also has a large selection of books in Russian, German, Spanish and Italian. It is open daily from noon till midnight. This is *not* the original Shakespeare & Company owned by Sylvia Beach and made famous after it published James Joyce's *Ulysses* in 1922. That was at 12 Rue de l'Odéon and was closed by the Germans in 1941.

WH Smith (Map 2; ☎ 01 44 77 88 99; metro Concorde), 248 Rue de Rivoli (1er). One block east of Place de la Concorde, WH Smith is open Monday to Saturday from 9.30 am to 7 pm and on Sunday from 1 to 7 pm.

Village Voice (Map 6; ☎ 01 46 33 36 47; metro Mabillon), 6 Rue Princesse (6e), two blocks south of Église Saint Germain des Prés. A helpful shop with an excellent selection of contemporary North American fiction and European literature in translation. It is open on Monday from 2 to 8 pm and Tuesday to Saturday from 10 am to 8 pm.

Gay Paris' premier gay bookshop is Les Mots à la Bouche (Map 8; ☎ 01 42 78 88 30; metro Hôtel de Ville) at 6 Rue Sainte Croix de la Bretonnerie (4e). Most of the back wall is devoted to English-language books, including lots of novels. It is open Monday to Thursday from 11 am to 11 pm, on Friday and Saturday till midnight and on Sunday from 2 to 8 pm.

Libraries

Bibliothèque Publique d'Information (BPI; Map 8; ☎ 01 44 78 12 33; www.bpi.fr; metro Rambuteau), 11 Rue Brantôme (3e). This huge, noncirculating and free library is usually spread over three floors of the Centre Pompidou but has been relocated to Rue Brantôme until the renovation of the centre is completed (expected to be in late 1999). The 2300 periodicals include quite a few English-language newspapers and magazines from around the world. It is open daily, except Tuesday, from noon (10 am on weekends and public holidays) to 10 pm.

Bibliothèque Nationale de France de François Mitterrand (Map 1; ☎ 01 53 79 53 79; metro Quai de la Gare), 11 Quai Franc Mauriac (13e). This national library contains some 10 million tomes stored on more than 400km of shelves, and can accommodate 3000 readers. It is open to the public (20FF for a day pass, 200FF for an annual pass) Tuesday to Saturday from 10 am to 7 pm and on Sunday from noon to 6 pm.

British Council (Map 4; ☎ 01 49 55 73 23; metro Invalides), 9-11 Rue de Constantine (7e). The council has a lending library that costs 250FF a year to join (200FF with a student card); the reference library charges 30FF per day. It is open weekdays from 11 am to 6 pm (to 7 pm on Wednesday). See Cultural Centres for more information.

American Library in Paris (Map 4; ☎ 01 53 59 12 60; metro Pont de l'Alma or École Militaire), 10 Rue du Général Camou (7e). This is among the largest English-language lending libraries in Europe, with some 90,000 volumes of classic and contemporary fiction, nonfiction and some 450 magazines. Annual membership costs 570FF (460FF for students), 240FF for three months in summer and 70FF a day (library reading privileges only). It is open Tuesday to Saturday from 10 am to 7 pm, with limited hours on Sunday and Monday and in August.

Cultural Centres

British Council The British Council (Map 4; ☎ 01 49 55 73 00; metro Invalides) at 11 Rue de Constantine (7e), whose mission is 'to promote British culture and civilisation', has reference and lending libraries (see Libraries), and also runs language courses through the British Institute. The café in the basement is open weekdays from 9.30 am to 6.45 pm.

American Church The American Church (Map 4; ☎ 01 47 05 07 99; metro Pont de l'Alma), 65 Quai d'Orsay (7e), functions as a community centre for English-speakers and is an excellent source of information on accommodation, jobs etc. Reception is staffed daily from 9 am to 1 pm and 2 to 10.30 pm (7.30 pm on Sunday). The church has three bulletin boards: an informal board downstairs on which people post all sorts of announcements (for no charge), and two identical official bulletin boards – one near reception, the other outside – listing flats, things for sale and jobs, especially work for au pairs, baby-sitters and English-language teachers. The American Church sponsors a variety of classes, workshops, concerts (on Sunday at 6 pm from September to May) and other cultural activities.

Laundry

There are self-service laundrettes around every corner in Paris.

Louvre Area Near the BVJ hostel, the Laverie Libre Service (Map 7; metro Louvre-Rivoli) at 7 Rue Jean-Jacques Rousseau (1er) is open daily from 7.30 am to 10 pm.

Marais The laundrette (Map 8; metro Hôtel de Ville) at 35 Rue Sainte Croix de la Bretonnerie (4e) and the Laverie Libre Service (Map 8; metro Saint Paul) at 25 Rue des Rosiers (4e) are open daily from 7 or 7.30 am to 10 pm. You can start your washing any time until 8.30 pm at the run-down Laverie (Map 8; metro Saint Paul) at 40 Rue du Roi de Sicile (4e).

Bastille Area The laundrette (Map 5; metro Bastille) at 2 Rue de Lappe (11e) is open daily from 7 am to 10 pm.

Latin Quarter Three blocks south-west of the Panthéon, the laundrette (Map 6; metro Luxembourg) at 216 Rue Saint Jacques (5e), near the Hôtel de Médicis, is open from 7 am to 10.30 pm. Just south of the Arènes de Lutèce, the Lavomatique (Map 5; metro Monge) at 63 Rue Monge (5e) is open daily from 6.30 am to 10 pm. Near Place de la Contrescarpe, Le Bateau Lavoir (Map 5; metro Cardinal Lemoine) at 1 Rue Thouin (5e) is open daily from 7 am to 10 pm.

6e Arrondissement The Julice Laverie (Map 6; metro Mabillon) at 56 Rue de Seine (6e) is open daily from 7 am to 10.30 pm. There is a second Julice Laverie (Map 6; metro Saint André des Arts) at 22 Rue des Grands Augustins (6e) which opens daily from 7 am to 9 pm.

Gare de l'Est Area The Lav' Club (Map 3; metro Gare de l'Est) at 55 Blvd de Magenta (10e), near the Franprix supermarket, stays open daily until 10 pm.

Montmartre This area's plentiful laundrettes include two on Rue des Trois Frères (metro Abbesses): the Salon Lavoir Sidec (Map 9) at No 28, open daily from 7 am to 9 pm, and the Lavoir (Map 9) at No 63, open daily from 7 am to 10 pm (both 18e).

West of the Butte de Montmartre (Montmartre Hill), the Laverie Libre Service (Map 9; metro Blanche) at 4 Rue Burq (18e) is open daily from 7.30 am to 10 pm.

Toilets

The tan-coloured, self-cleaning cylindrical toilets you see on Paris pavements are open 24 hours a day and cost 2 or 2.50FF. In general, café owners do not appreciate you using their facilities if you are not a paying customer. If you're desperate try ducking into a fast-food joint, major department store, Forum des Halles or the underground toilets in front of Notre Dame.

Paris for Children

Paris abounds with places that will delight children. Family visits to many areas of the city can be designed around a rest stop or picnic at the following attractions (see the Things to See & Do section for further details):

6e Arrondissement (Map 6): Jardin du Luxembourg
19e Arrondissement (Map 1): Parc de la Villette, Cité des Enfants in the Cité des Sciences et de l'Industrie
Bastille area (4e, 11e and 12e; Map 5): playground at the Port de Plaisance de Paris-Arsenal
Bois de Boulogne (Map 1): Jardin d'Acclimatation
Bois de Vincennes (Map 1): zoo
Champs-Élysées Area (8e; Map 2): Palais de la Découverte
Eiffel Tower Area (7e; Map 4): Champ de Mars
Jardin des Plantes Area (5e; Map 5): Grande Galerie de l'Évolution, zoo, playground
Montmartre (18e; Map 9): playground

The weekly entertainment magazine *L'Officiel des Spectacles* (2FF), which comes out on Wednesday, lists *gardes d'enfants* (babysitting services) available in Paris.

Medical Services

There are some 50 *assistance publique* (public health service) hospitals in Paris. If you need an ambulance, call ☎ 15 or ☎ 01 45 67 50 50. For emergency treatment, call Urgences Médicales on ☎ 01 48 28 40 04 or SOS Médecins on ☎ 01 47 07 77 77. Both offer 24-hour house calls. For information on free and anonymous HIV-testing centres and helplines in Paris, see Health in the Facts for the Visitor chapter.

Some hospitals are:

Hôtel Dieu (Map 6; ☎ 01 42 34 82 34; metro Cité), on the north side of Place du Parvis Notre Dame (4e). After 10 pm use the emergency entrance on Rue de la Cité. The 24 hour emergency room can refer you to the hospital's emergency gynaecological services in cases of sexual assault.

American Hospital (Map 1; ☎ 01 46 41 27 37; fax 01 46 41 27 00; metro Anatole France), 63 Blvd Victor Hugo, offers emergency medical and dental care 24 hours a day.

Hôpital Franco-Britannique (Map 1; ☎ 01 46 39 22 22; metro Anatole France), 3 Rue Barbès, is a less expensive English-speaking option. People from outside the EU are asked to pay up front.

La Pitié-Salpêtrière Hospital (Map 1; metro Chevaleret), on Rue Bruand (13e), is the only dental hospital with extended hours. The after-hours entrance, open from 5.30 pm to 8.30 am, is at 47 Blvd de l'Hôpital (13e; Map 5; metro Gare d'Austerlitz).

Dental Care For emergency dental care contact:

SOS Dentaire (Map 1; ☎ 01 43 37 51 00; metro Port Royal), 87 Blvd de Port Royal (13e), is a private dental office that offers services when most dentists are off duty: Monday to Friday from 8 to 11.40 pm and on weekends and holidays from 9 am to 12.10 pm, 2.20 to 7.10 pm and 8 to 11.40 pm. If you have an urgent problem, call to set up an appointment. A consultation and treatment generally costs 300 to 600FF.

Pharmacies Some pharmacies with extended hours include:

Pharmacie des Champs (Map 2; ☎ 01 45 62 02 41; metro George V), inside the shopping arcade at 84 Ave des Champs-Élysées (8e), is open 24 hours a day year-round.

Pharmacie Européenne de la Place de Clichy (Map 2; ☎ 01 48 74 65 18; metro Place de Clichy), 6 Place de Clichy (17e), is open 24 hours a day year-round.

Pharmacie des Halles (Map 8; ☎ 01 42 72 03 23; metro Châtelet), 10 Blvd de Sébastopol (4e), is open daily from 9 am (noon on Sunday and holidays) to midnight.

Emergency

Emergency telephone numbers include:

Police	☎ 17
Fire brigade	☎ 18
Ambulance (SAMU)	☎ 15
	☎ 01 45 67 50 50
Urgences Médicales (24 hour house calls)	☎ 01 48 28 40 04
SOS Médecin (24 hour house calls)	☎ 01 47 07 77 77

Dangers & Annoyances

Crime In general, Paris is a safe city and occurrences of random street assault are rare. La Ville Lumière (the City of Light), as Paris is called, is generally well lit, and there's no reason not to use the metro until it stops running at around 12.45 am. As you'll notice, women *do* travel alone on the metro late at night in most areas, though not all report feeling 100% comfortable. The Bois de Boulogne and Bois de Vincennes are best avoided after dark.

Nonviolent crime such as pickpocketing and thefts from handbags or packs is a problem wherever there are crowds, especially tourists. Places in which to be especially careful include Montmartre, Pigalle, around Forum des Halles and the Centre Pompidou, on the metro at rush hour and even the Latin Quarter. Be especially wary of children: kids who jostle up against you in the crowd may be diving into your bag with professional aplomb.

Metro stations that are best avoided late at night include: Châtelet-Les Halles, and its seemingly endless corridors; Château Rouge in Montmartre; Gare du Nord; Strasbourg Saint Denis; Réaumur Sébastopol; and Montparnasse Bienvenüe. *Bornes d'alarme* (alarm boxes) are in the centre of each metro/RER platform and in some station corridors.

Lost & Found All objects found anywhere in Paris – except those discovered on trains or in train stations – are eventually brought to the city's Bureau des Objets Trouvés (Lost Property Office; Map 1; ☎ 01 55 76 20 20; metro Convention), 36 Rue des Morillons (15e), run by the Préfecture de Police. Since telephone inquiries are impossible, the only way to find out if a lost item has been located is to go all the way down there and fill in the forms. The office is open from 8.30 am to 5 pm on Monday, Wednesday and Friday, and to 8 pm on Tuesday and Thursday. In July and August, daily closing time is 5 pm.

Items lost in the metro (☎ 01 40 06 75 27 for information) are held by station agents for one day before being sent to the Bureau des Objets Trouvés. Anything found on trains or in train stations is taken to the *objets trouvés* bureau – usually attached to the left-luggage office – of the relevant station. Telephone inquiries (in French) are possible:

Gare d'Austerlitz	☎ 01 53 60 71 98
Gare de l'Est	☎ 01 40 18 88 73
Gare de Lyon	☎ 01 40 19 67 22
Gare Montparnasse	☎ 01 40 48 14 24
Gare du Nord	☎ 01 53 90 20 20
Gare Saint Lazare	☎ 01 53 42 01 44

WALKING TOURS

Paris is a wonderful city to walk around and surprisingly pedestrian-friendly, in part because it's relatively compact. It's also a fairly level city, so apart from toiling up to Montmartre, there's no hill-climbing involved. Traffic can be a problem, though; cars will only stop for you if you absolutely assert your rights on pedestrian crossings. And then there's those damn dogs.

Remembrance of Dogs Past & Present

The Paris municipality spends vast sums of money to keep the city's pavements relatively passable, and the technology it employs is undeniably impressive. But it would seem that repeated campaigns to get people to clean up after their pooches have been less than a howling success. Evidence to this effect takes the form of 'souvenirs' left by recently walked poodles and other breeds, often found smeared along the pavement – by daydreaming strollers, one assumes, or guidebook writers absorbed in jotting something down important. Until that far-off day when Parisians – and their much loved canines – change their ways, the word on the streets remains the same: watch your step.

The sky's the limit on specialised and themed walking tours of Paris, whether self-paced or led by a guide. The entertainment magazine *Pariscope* (3FF) lists different organised walks and tours each week in its 'Guide de Paris: Promenades' section, as does *L'Officiel des Spectacles* (2FF) under 'À Travers Paris: Promenades'.

Paris Walking Tours (☎ 01 48 09 21 49; fax 01 42 43 75 51), 10 Rue Samson in Saint Denis, north of Paris, gets good reports. English-language tours (60FF) of Montmartre leave on Sunday and Thursday at 10.30 am from the Abbesses metro station (Map 9); tours of Marais leave from the Saint Paul metro station (Map 8) on Sunday at 2.30 pm and Wednesday at 10.30 am. A tour called Hemingway's Paris (60FF) takes place every Tuesday at 2 pm, starting from the Cardinal Lemoine metro station (Map 5).

The Bibliothèque Publique d'Information (BPI; Map 8; metro Rambuteau), presently at 11 Rue Brantôme (3e), offers excellent literary tours (100FF; 80FF reduced tariff) that follow the footsteps of such diverse writers as Céline, Rilke, Georges Simenon, Jean Cocteau and Henry Miller. Three-hour tours leave from the BPI on Wednesday and Sunday at 2.30 pm, and an extra tour on Sunday at 10 am. For information and reservations ring ☎ 01 44 78 45 73.

If you want to go it on your own but need some direction (though aimless exploring is half the fun of Paris) consult any of the walking guides listed in the Books section of the Facts for the Visitor chapter.

LOUVRE AREA

The Louvre area (1er) has long been a chic residential area for people of means.

Musée du Louvre

The vast Louvre (Map 7; ☎ 01 40 20 53 17 or, for a recording, ☎ 01 40 20 51 51; metro Palais Royal) was constructed around 1200 as a fortress and rebuilt in the mid-16th century for use as a royal palace. It began its career as a public museum in 1793. The paintings, sculptures and artefacts on display have been assembled by French governments over the past five centuries. Among them are works of art and artisanship from all over Europe and important collections of Assyrian, Etruscan, Greek, Coptic, and Islamic art and antiquities.

The Louvre may be the most actively avoided museum in Paris. Tourists and residents alike, daunted by the richness of the place and its sheer size (the side facing the Seine is almost 750m long), often find the prospect of an afternoon at a smaller museum far more inviting.

Eventually, most people do their duty and come, but many leave overwhelmed, unfulfilled, exhausted and frustrated at having gotten lost on their way to the *Mona Lisa*. Since it takes several serious visits to get anything more than a brief glimpse of the works on offer, your best bet – after checking out a few you really want to see – is to choose a period or section of the museum and pretend that the rest is somewhere across town.

The Louvre was one of the late President François Mitterrand's most ambitious *grands projets*, and the government has invested over US$1 billion in restoring and upgrading its exhibition halls and public spaces.

Unfortunately, in recent years the Louvre has been plagued by thefts – some seven big ones since 1994 – and public access to many of its 500 rooms may be sacrificed to security.

Carte Musées et Monuments

The Museums and Monuments Card is valid for entry to around 70 venues in Paris and the Île de France (see the Day Trips from Paris chapter), including the Louvre and the Musée d'Orsay. The cost for one/three/five days is 80/160/240FF. There is no reduced rate for students or senior travellers. The pass is available from participating venues, tourist offices, FNAC outlets and some metro stations in Paris.

Note that most museums in Paris are free for those under 18 and give a reduced rate for those aged 18 to 25 and over 60. Most museums are closed on Monday or Tuesday.

Orientation The main entrance and ticket windows in the Cour Napoléon (1er) are covered by a 21m-high **glass pyramid** (Map 7) designed by the China-born American architect IM Pei. You can avoid the queues outside the pyramid by entering the Louvre complex via the Carrousel du Louvre shopping area (open daily from 8.30 am to 11 pm), with an entrance at 99 Rue de Rivoli (Map 7), or by following the 'Louvre' exit from the Palais Royal metro stop.

The Louvre is divided into four sections. **Sully** forms the four sides of the Cour Carrée (Square Courtyard) at the eastern end of the building. **Denon** stretches for 500m along the Seine. **Richelieu**, the wing along the Rue de Rivoli, was occupied by the Ministry of Finance until the late 1980s and has some superb new halls. The centrepiece of the underground **Carrousel du Louvre** shopping mall, which stretches from the pyramid to the Arc de Triomphe du Carrousel (see later in the Louvre Area section), is an **inverted glass pyramid**, also by Pei.

The split-level public area under the pyramid is known as **Hall Napoléon**. It has an exhibit on the history of the Louvre, a bookshop, a restaurant, a café and auditoriums for concerts, lectures and films. Maps in English of the complex (*Louvre Plan/Information*) are available at the round information desk. The best publication for a general overview is *Louvre First Visit* (20FF), which leads you past some 50 works of art including the Code of Hammurabi stele, Vermeer's *The Lacemaker,* and the Apollo Gallery with the French crown jewels as well as the *Winged Victory of Samothrace*, *Venus de Milo* and *Mona Lisa*. The more comprehensive *Louvre The Visit* (60FF) illustrates and describes more than 160 works of art. Both publications are available in the museum gift shop.

Hours & Tickets The Louvre is open daily, except Tuesday and certain holidays. From Thursday to Sunday its hours are 9 am to 6 pm. On Monday and Wednesday, hours are 9 am to 9.45 pm, but on Monday only the Richelieu wing or other limited collections are open after 5.30 pm. Ticket sales end 45 minutes before closing time, and the guards begin clearing the halls 30 minutes before that. The Hall Napoléon is open daily, except Tuesday, from 9 am to 9.45 pm.

Entry to the permanent collections (but not temporary exhibitions) costs 45FF (26FF after 3 pm and all day Sunday); the first Sunday of every month is free. There are no discounts for students or senior citizens, but those under 18 get in free. Tickets are valid for the whole day, so you can leave and re-enter as you please. A *billet jumelé* (combination ticket) for the permanent collections and Hall Napoléon costs 60/40FF before/after 3 pm.

Guided Tours English-language guided tours (☎ 01 40 20 52 09) lasting 1½ hours are held three to five times a day (only one on Sunday, at 11.30 am). Tours depart from the Accueil des Groupes area under the glass pyramid. Tickets cost 38FF (22FF for 13 to 18-year-olds; free for children under 13) in addition to the regular entry fee. Groups are limited to 30 people, so it's a good idea to sign up at least 30 minutes before departure time.

Recorded tours (*acoustiguides*) in six languages, available until 4.30 pm, can be rented for 30FF under the pyramid, at the entrance to each wing. The recording lasts 1½ hours.

Église Saint Germain L'Auxerrois

Built between the 13th and 16th centuries in a mixture of Gothic and Renaissance styles, this parish church (Map 7; metro Louvre-Rivoli) stands on a site – facing the eastern side of the Louvre – that has been used for Christian worship since about 500 AD. After being mutilated by 18th century churchmen intent on 'modernisation', and vandals during the Revolution, it was restored by Viollet-le-Duc in the mid-1800s. It is open daily from 8 am to 8 pm.

The square, Romanesque **belfry** that rises from next to the south transept arm contains the bell whose tolling served as a signal to begin the Saint Bartholomew's Day Massacre in August 1572, in which 3000 Protestants were slaughtered according to a plan devised by Catherine de Médicis and approved by her son, the French King Charles IX.

Jardin du Palais Royal

The **Palais Royal** (Map 7; metro Palais Royal), which briefly housed a young Louis XIV in the 1640s, is opposite Place du Palais Royal, north of the Louvre. Construction was begun in the 17th century by Cardinal Richelieu, though most of the present neoclassical complex dates from the latter part of the 18th century. It now contains the Conseil d'État (State Council) and is closed to the public. The colonnaded building facing Place André Malraux is the **Comédie Française** (Map 7), founded in 1680 and the world's oldest national theatre.

Just north of the main part of the palace is the Jardin du Palais Royal, a lovely park surrounded by arcades. Those on the eastern side of the park, **Galerie de Valois**, shelter antiquarian bookshops; on the other side, in **Galerie de Montpensier**, you'll find art galleries, places that make colourful Legion of Honour-style medals (at Nos 3-4 and 7) and others that specialise in toy soldiers (at Nos 30, 34 and 37-38).

The park is open daily from 7 am (7.30 am from October to March) to between 8.30 pm in winter and 11 pm in summer.

Le Louvre des Antiquaires

This impressive building on the eastern side of Place du Palais Royal (Map 7; metro Palais Royal) houses about 250 elegant antique shops. Each is filled with precious objects (*objets d'art*, furniture, clocks, classical antiquities) available to shoppers with oodles of cash. It is open Tuesday to Sunday from 11 am to 7 pm. In July and August it closes on Sunday.

Galerie Véro Dodat

For a quick taste of 19th century Paris, it's hard to beat this shopping arcade (Map 7) between 19 Rue Jean-Jacques Rousseau and 2 Rue du Bouloi, which opened in 1826 and retains its 19th century skylights, ceiling murals and store fronts. The shops here specialise in antiques, *objets d'art*, art books and fashion accessories. There are also a couple of good eateries here too.

Musée des Arts Décoratifs

The Museum of Decorative Arts (Map 7; ☎ 01 44 55 57 50; metro Palais Royal) is on the 3rd floor at 107 Rue de Rivoli (1er) and occupies the western tip of the Louvre's north wing. Displays include furniture, jewellery and *objets d'art* (such as ceramics and glassware) from the Middle Ages and the Renaissance through to the Art Nouveau and Art Deco periods. On the 1st and 2nd floors is the **Musée de la Mode et du Textile** (Museum of Fashion and Textile). The museums are open Tuesday to Friday from 11 am to 6 pm (to 9 pm on Wednesday) and weekends from 10 am to 6 pm. Entrance to both costs 30FF (20FF for those aged 18 to 25).

Place des Pyramides

The brightly gilded, 19th century **statue of Joan of Arc** at Place des Pyramides, next to 192 Rue de Rivoli (Map 7), is a favourite rallying point for royalists and parties of the extreme right.

Arc de Triomphe du Carrousel

Constructed by Napoleon to celebrate his battlefield successes of 1805, this triumphal arch (Map 7) set in the Jardin du Carrousel, at the eastern end of the Jardin des Tuileries, was once crowned by the Horses of Saint Mark's, stolen from Venice by Napoleon but returned after Waterloo. The group of statues on top, added in 1828, celebrates the return of the Bourbons to the French throne after Napoleon's downfall. The sides of the arch are adorned with depictions of Napoleonic victories and eight pink marble columns, atop each of which stands a soldier of the emperor's Grande Armée.

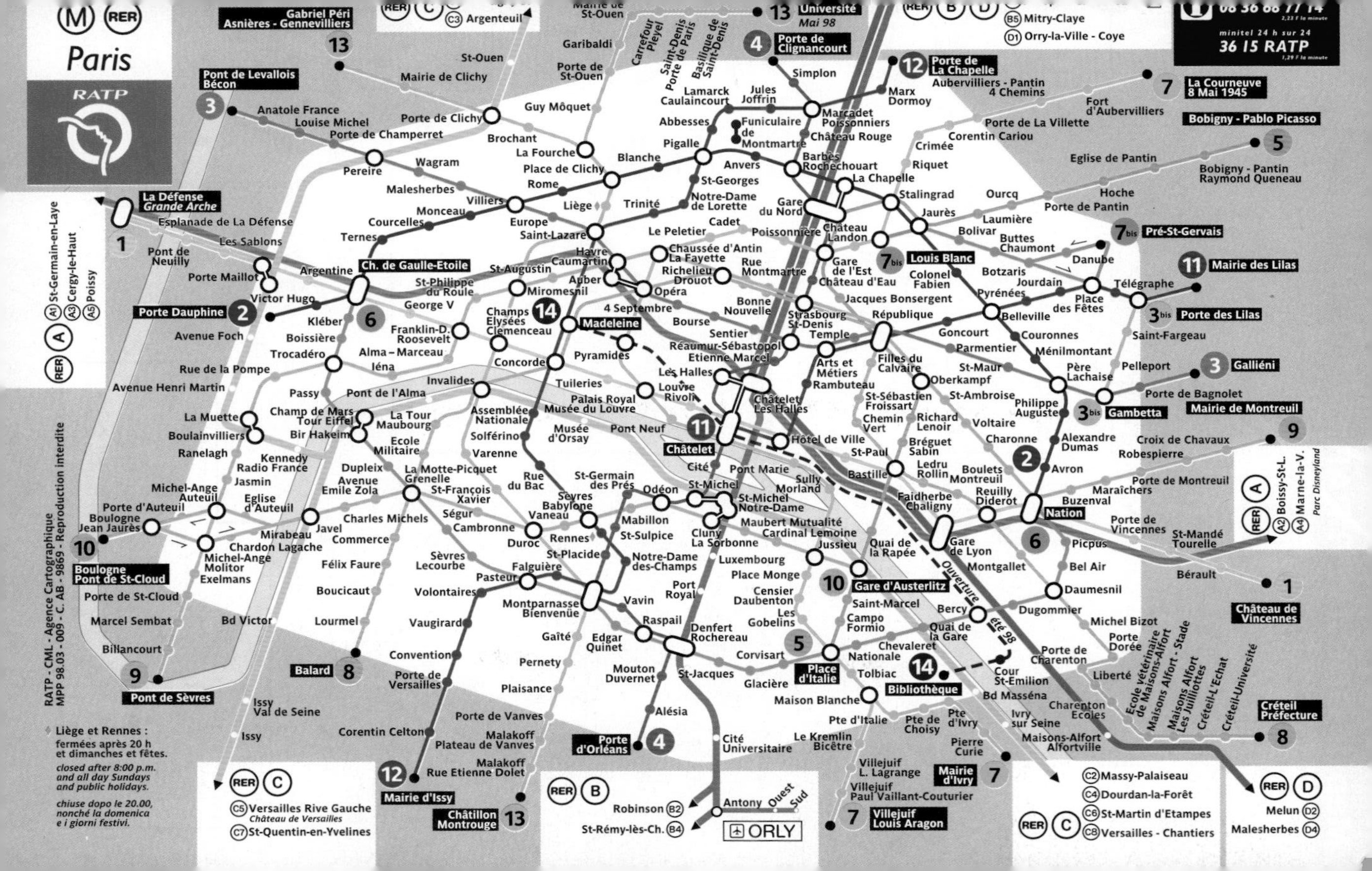

M RER
Paris
RATP
36 15 RATP
minitel 24 h sur 24
La Défense Grande Arche
Pont de Levallois Bécon
Gabriel Péri Asnières - Gennevilliers
Porte de Clignancourt
Université Mai 98
Porte de La Chapelle
La Courneuve 8 Mai 1945
Bobigny - Pablo Picasso
Pré-St-Gervais
Mairie des Lilas
Porte des Lilas
Galliéni
Mairie de Montreuil
Château de Vincennes
Créteil Préfecture
Mairie d'Ivry
Villejuif Louis Aragon
Porte d'Orléans
Châtillon Montrouge
Mairie d'Issy
Balard
Pont de Sèvres
Boulogne Pont de St-Cloud
Porte Dauphine
Ch. de Gaulle-Etoile
Madeleine
Châtelet
Louis Blanc
Gambetta
Nation
Gare d'Austerlitz
Place d'Italie
Bibliothèque
Ouverture été 98
A1 St-Germain-en-Laye
A3 Cergy-le-Haut
A5 Poissy
A2 Boissy-St-L.
A4 Marne-la-V. Parc Disneyland
B5 Mitry-Claye
D1 Orry-la-Ville - Coye
C3 Argenteuil
C5 Versailles Rive Gauche Château de Versailles
C7 St-Quentin-en-Yvelines
B2 Robinson
B4 St-Rémy-lès-Ch.
ORLY
Antony
Ouest
Sud
C2 Massy-Palaiseau
C4 Dourdan-la-Forêt
C6 St-Martin d'Etampes
C8 Versailles - Chantiers
D2 Melun
D4 Malesherbes
Liège et Rennes : fermées après 20 h et dimanches et fêtes.
closed after 8:00 p.m. and all day Sundays and public holidays.
chiuse dopo le 20.00, nonché la domenica e i giorni festivi.
RATP - CML - Agence Cartographique MPP 98.03 - 009 - C. AB - 9869 - Reproduction interdite

Map 1 GREATER PARIS

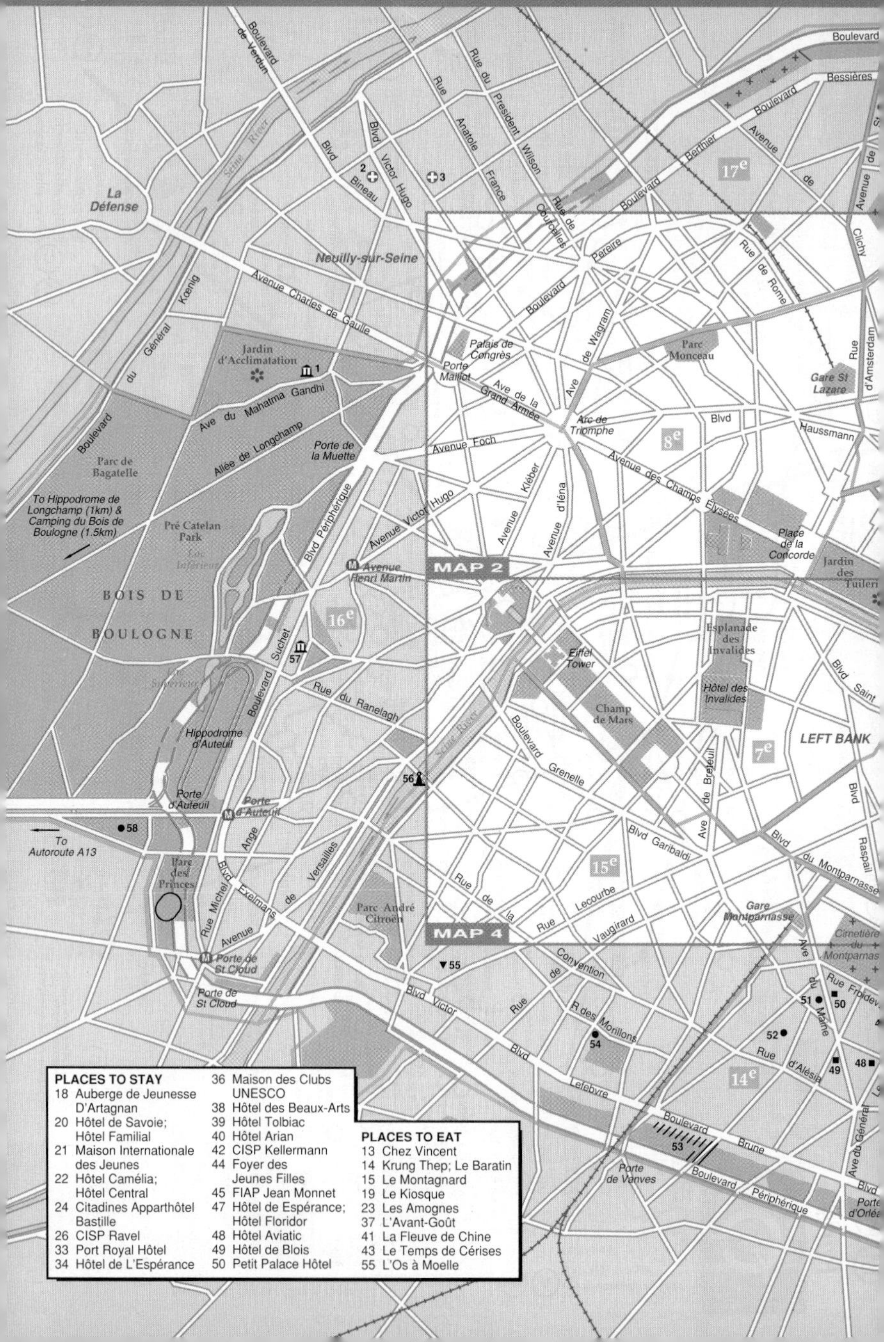

La Défense
Neuilly-sur-Seine
Seine River
Boulevard de Verdun
Blvd Bineau
Blvd Victor Hugo
Rue Anatole France
Rue du President Wilson
Rue de Courcelles
Boulevard Berthier
Boulevard Bessières
Avenue de Clichy
17e
Avenue Charles de Gaulle
Boulevard du Général Kœnig
Jardin d'Acclimatation
Ave du Mahatma Gandhi
Allée de Longchamp
Parc de Bagatelle
To Hippodrome de Longchamp (1km) & Camping du Bois de Boulogne (1.5km)
Pré Catelan Park
Lac Inférieur
BOIS DE BOULOGNE
Lac Supérieur
Porte de la Muette
Blvd Périphérique
Avenue Victor Hugo
Avenue Henri Martin
16e
Boulevard Suchet
Rue du Ranelagh
Hippodrome d'Auteuil
Porte d'Auteuil
To Autoroute A13
Parc des Princes
Rue Michel Ange
Blvd Exelmans
Avenue de Versailles
Porte de St Cloud
Parc André Citroën
Palais de Congrès
Porte Maillot
Ave de la Grand Armée
Boulevard Pereire
Ave de Wagram
Parc Monceau
Rue de Rome
Rue d'Amsterdam
Gare St Lazare
Arc de Triomphe
Avenue Foch
Avenue Kléber
Avenue d'Iéna
Blvd Haussmann
8e
Avenue des Champs Elysées
Place de la Concorde
Jardin des Tuileries
MAP 2
Eiffel Tower
Champ de Mars
Esplanade des Invalides
Hôtel des Invalides
Blvd Saint
LEFT BANK
7e
Blvd Raspail
Boulevard Grenelle
Ave de Breteuil
Blvd Garibaldi
Blvd du Montparnasse
15e
Rue de la Convention
Rue Lecourbe
Rue de Vaugirard
Gare Montparnasse
MAP 4
Cimetière du Montparnasse
Ave du Maine
Rue Froidevaux
Rue d'Alésia
R des Morillons
Blvd Victor
Blvd Lefebvre
14e
Boulevard Brune
Porte de Vanves
Boulevard Périphérique
Ave du Général
Blvd
Porte d'Orléans
1
2
3
48
49
50
51
52
53
54
55
56
57
58
PLACES TO STAY
18 Auberge de Jeunesse D'Artagnan
20 Hôtel de Savoie; Hôtel Familial
21 Maison Internationale des Jeunes
22 Hôtel Camélia; Hôtel Central
24 Citadines Apparthôtel Bastille
26 CISP Ravel
33 Port Royal Hôtel
34 Hôtel de L'Espérance
36 Maison des Clubs UNESCO
38 Hôtel des Beaux-Arts
39 Hôtel Tolbiac
40 Hôtel Arian
42 CISP Kellermann
44 Foyer des Jeunes Filles
45 FIAP Jean Monnet
47 Hôtel de Espérance; Hôtel Floridor
48 Hôtel Aviatic
49 Hôtel de Blois
50 Petit Palace Hôtel
PLACES TO EAT
13 Chez Vincent
14 Krung Thep; Le Baratin
15 Le Montagnard
19 Le Kiosque
23 Les Amognes
37 L'Avant-Goût
41 La Fleuve de Chine
43 Le Temps de Cérises
55 L'Os à Moelle

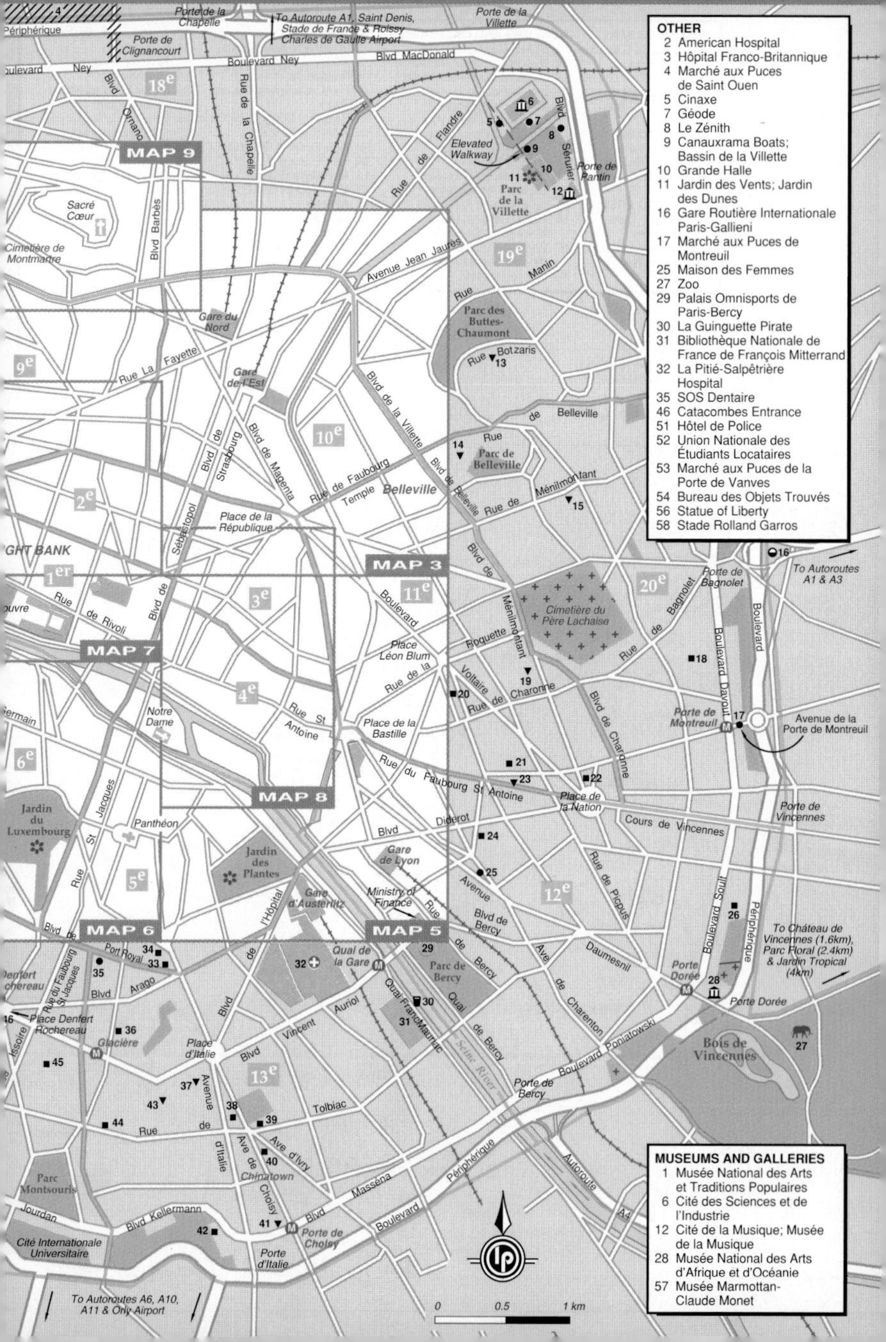
OTHER
2 American Hospital
3 Hôpital Franco-Britannique
4 Marché aux Puces de Saint Ouen
5 Cinaxe
7 Géode
8 Le Zénith
9 Canauxrama Boats; Bassin de la Villette
10 Grande Halle
11 Jardin des Vents; Jardin des Dunes
16 Gare Routière Internationale Paris-Gallieni
17 Marché aux Puces de Montreuil
25 Maison des Femmes
27 Zoo
29 Palais Omnisports de Paris-Bercy
30 La Guinguette Pirate
31 Bibliothèque Nationale de France de François Mitterrand
32 La Pitié-Salpêtrière Hospital
35 SOS Dentaire
46 Catacombes Entrance
51 Hôtel de Police
52 Union Nationale des Étudiants Locataires
53 Marché aux Puces de la Porte de Vanves
54 Bureau des Objets Trouvés
56 Statue of Liberty
58 Stade Rolland Garros
MUSEUMS AND GALLERIES
1 Musée National des Arts et Traditions Populaires
6 Cité des Sciences et de l'Industrie
12 Cité de la Musique; Musée de la Musique
28 Musée National des Arts d'Afrique et d'Océanie
57 Musée Marmottan-Claude Monet
MAP 9
MAP 3
MAP 7
MAP 8
MAP 6
MAP 5
To Autoroute A1, Saint Denis, Stade de France & Roissy Charles de Gaulle Airport
To Autoroutes A1 & A3
To Château de Vincennes (1.6km), Parc Floral (2.4km) & Jardin Tropical (4km)
To Autoroutes A6, A10, A11 & Orly Airport
Porte de la Chapelle
Porte de Clignancourt
Porte de la Villette
Porte de Pantin
Porte de Bagnolet
Porte de Montreuil
Porte de Vincennes
Porte Dorée
Porte de Bercy
Porte de Choisy
Porte d'Italie
Parc de la Villette
Parc des Buttes-Chaumont
Parc de Belleville
Cimetière du Père Lachaise
Cimetière de Montmartre
Sacré Cœur
Gare du Nord
Gare de l'Est
Gare de Lyon
Gare d'Austerlitz
Place de la République
Place Léon Blum
Place de la Bastille
Place de la Nation
Place Denfert Rochereau
Place d'Italie
Notre Dame
Panthéon
Jardin du Luxembourg
Jardin des Plantes
Parc de Bercy
Bois de Vincennes
Parc Montsouris
Cité Internationale Universitaire
Ministry of Finance
Belleville
Chinatown
Seine River
Elevated Walkway
0 0.5 1 km

Map 2 CENTRAL PARIS NORTH-WEST

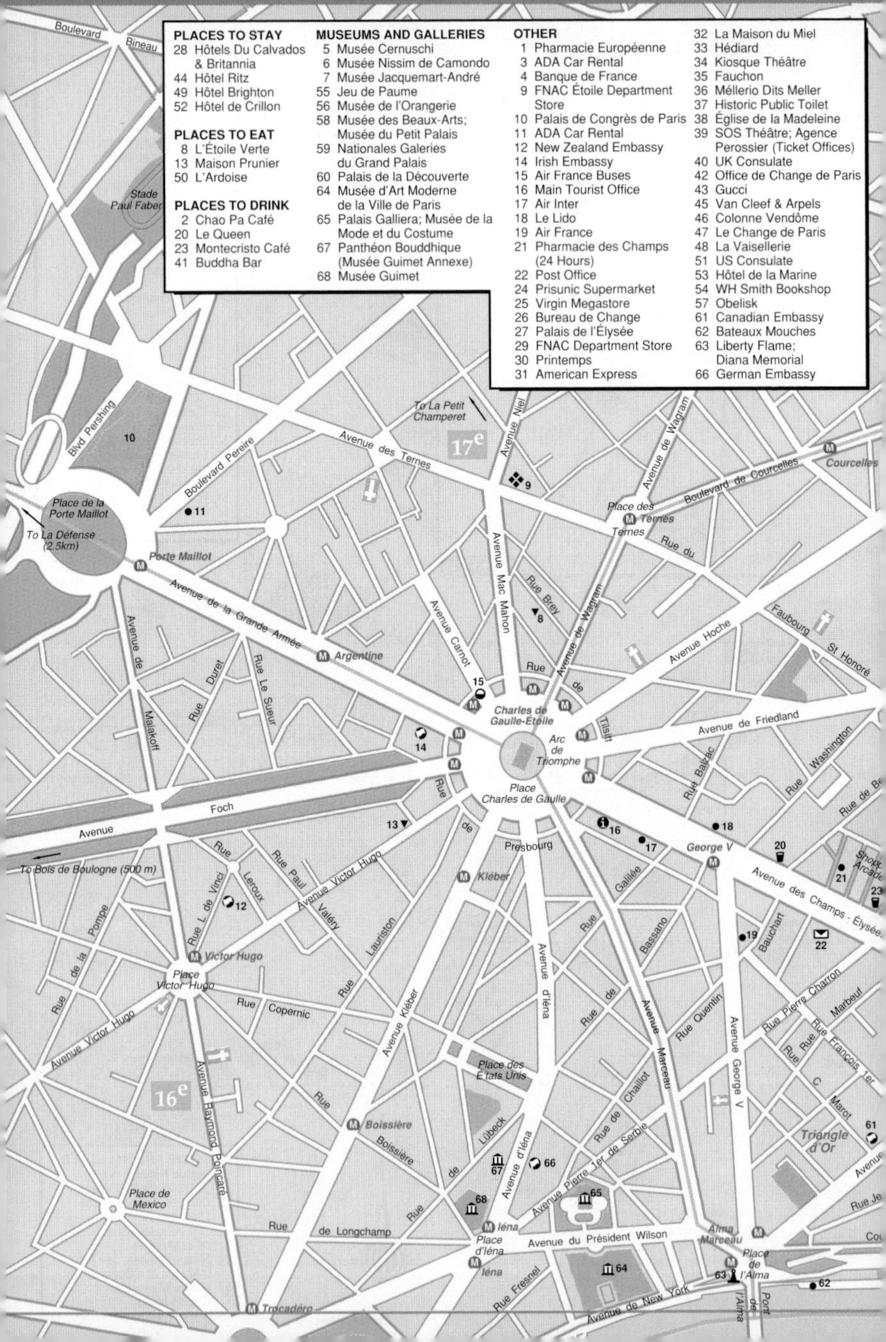
PLACES TO STAY
28 Hôtels Du Calvados & Britannia
44 Hôtel Ritz
49 Hôtel Brighton
52 Hôtel de Crillon
PLACES TO EAT
8 L'Étoile Verte
13 Maison Prunier
50 L'Ardoise
PLACES TO DRINK
2 Chao Pa Café
20 Le Queen
23 Montecristo Café
41 Buddha Bar
MUSEUMS AND GALLERIES
5 Musée Cernuschi
6 Musée Nissim de Camondo
7 Musée Jacquemart-André
55 Jeu de Paume
56 Musée de l'Orangerie
58 Musée des Beaux-Arts; Musée du Petit Palais
59 Nationales Galeries du Grand Palais
60 Palais de la Découverte
64 Musée d'Art Moderne de la Ville de Paris
65 Palais Galliera; Musée de la Mode et du Costume
67 Panthéon Bouddhique (Musée Guimet Annexe)
68 Musée Guimet
OTHER
1 Pharmacie Européenne
3 ADA Car Rental
4 Banque de France
9 FNAC Étoile Department Store
10 Palais de Congrès de Paris
11 ADA Car Rental
12 New Zealand Embassy
14 Irish Embassy
15 Air France Buses
16 Main Tourist Office
17 Air Inter
18 Le Lido
19 Air France
21 Pharmacie des Champs (24 Hours)
22 Post Office
24 Prisunic Supermarket
25 Virgin Megastore
26 Bureau de Change
27 Palais de l'Élysée
29 FNAC Department Store
30 Printemps
31 American Express
32 La Maison du Miel
33 Hédiard
34 Kiosque Théâtre
35 Fauchon
36 Méllerio Dits Meller
37 Historic Public Toilet
38 Église de la Madeleine
39 SOS Théâtre; Agence Perossier (Ticket Offices)
40 UK Consulate
42 Office de Change de Paris
43 Gucci
45 Van Cleef & Arpels
46 Colonne Vendôme
47 Le Change de Paris
48 La Vaisellerie
51 US Consulate
53 Hôtel de la Marine
54 WH Smith Bookshop
57 Obelisk
61 Canadian Embassy
62 Bateaux Mouches
63 Liberty Flame; Diana Memorial
66 German Embassy
Boulevard Bineau
Stade Paul Faber
Blvd Pershing
Boulevard Pereire
Place de la Porte Maillot
To La Défense (2.5km)
Porte Maillot
To La Petit Champeret
17e
Avenue des Ternes
Avenue Niel
Avenue de Wagram
Boulevard de Courcelles
Courcelles
Place des Ternes
Ternes
Rue du Faubourg St Honoré
Avenue Mac Mahon
Rue Brey
Avenue de la Grande Armée
Argentine
Avenue Carnot
Avenue de Malakoff
Rue Duret
Rue Le Sueur
Avenue Hoche
Rue de Tilsitt
Charles de Gaulle-Étoile
Arc de Triomphe
Avenue de Friedland
Rue Balzac
Rue Washington
Place Charles de Gaulle
Avenue Foch
To Bois de Boulogne (500 m)
Rue de Presbourg
Rue Leroux
Rue Paul Valéry
Avenue Victor Hugo
Kléber
George V
Avenue des Champs-Élysées
Rue L de Vinci
Victor Hugo
Place Victor Hugo
Rue de la Pompe
Rue Lauriston
Rue Galilée
Rue Bassano
Rue Bauchart
Rue Copernic
Avenue Kléber
Avenue d'Iéna
Avenue Marceau
Rue Quentin
Avenue George V
Rue Pierre Charron
Rue Marbeuf
Rue François 1er
Rue C Marot
Triangle d'Or
Avenue Raymond Poincaré
16e
Place des États Unis
Rue Boissière
Boissière
Rue de Lübeck
Rue de Chaillot
Rue de Longchamp
Place de Mexico
Avenue Pierre 1er de Serbie
Iéna
Place d'Iéna
Avenue du Président Wilson
Alma Marceau
Place de l'Alma
Rue Fresnel
Avenue de New York
Trocadéro
Pont de l'Alma

Square des Batignolles
Rue Legendre
To Macis et Muscade (50m)
Cimetière de Montmartre
18e
MAP 9
Rue Jouffroy d'Abbans
17e
Boulevard Malesherbes
Rue Legendre
Rue de Rome
0
200
400 m
Avenue de Clichy
Rue Biot
Place de Clichy
Place de Clichy
1
2
Boulevard des Batignolles
Place du Général Catroux
Rome
Avenue de Villiers
4
3
Villiers
Petersbourg
Rue d'Amsterdam
Rue Cardinal Mercier
Monceau
Boulevard de Courcelles
Rue de Constantinople
Rue de Rome
Rue de Clichy
Avenue Vélasquez
5
Rue de Monceau
Liège
MAP 3
Parc de Monceau
6
Rue de
Europe
Place de l'Europe
Rue de
Rue d'Amsterdam
Rue de Madrid
Rue Murillo
Rue de Lisbonne
Rue de Vienne
Londres
9e
Rue Monceau
Avenue de Messine
Boulevard Malesherbes
Gare Saint Lazare
28
Rue de
Rue
Rue de
Saint Lazare
St Lazare
Rue
7
29
Rue de Caumartin
Boulevard Haussmann
Place St Augustin
Rue de la Pépinière
St Augustin
Rue du Havre
Rome
Boulevard Haussmann
Rue la Boétie
30
Auber
Rue de
Miromesnil
Rue de Miromesnil
Havre Caumartin
8e
Faubourg
St Honoré
Rue de l'Arcade
Rue Auber
Auber
Avenue Franklin D Roosevelt
St Philippe du Roule
Rue Tronchet
Rue Vignon
31
Rue La Boétie
Rue du Colisée
32
Rue de Caumartin
Rue Scribe
Boulevard Malesherbes
33
Place de
35
4
25
Avenue Matignon
Rue de Faubourg Saint Honoré
27
34
Avenue de Marigny
Rue d'Anjou
Franklin D Roosevelt
Avenue Gabriel
40
d'Anglas
37
Boulevard des Capucines
Blvd de la Madeleine
39
la Madeleine
38
36
Madeleine
MAP 7
26
Rond-Point des Champs-Élysées
Rue de la Paix
43
Rue Royale
Franklin D Roosevelt
Rue Boissy
41
42
Rue Cambon
44
45
Rue de Marignan
Champs-Élysées Clemenceau
Rue St Honoré
Avenue Montaigne
Avenue des Champs-Élysées
52
51
Place
46
Vendôme
Rue St Florentin
Rue
53
1er
47
Rue Bayard
Grand Palais
59
60
Avenue Franklin D Roosevelt
Ave Winston Churchill
58
Petit Palais
Concorde
54
50
Rue de Castiglione
48
Place de la Concorde
57
55
Rue de Rivoli
Cours la Reine
49
Jardin des Tuileries
Tuileries
Pont Alexandre III
Seine River
56
MAP 4

Map 3 CENTRAL PARIS NORTH-EAST

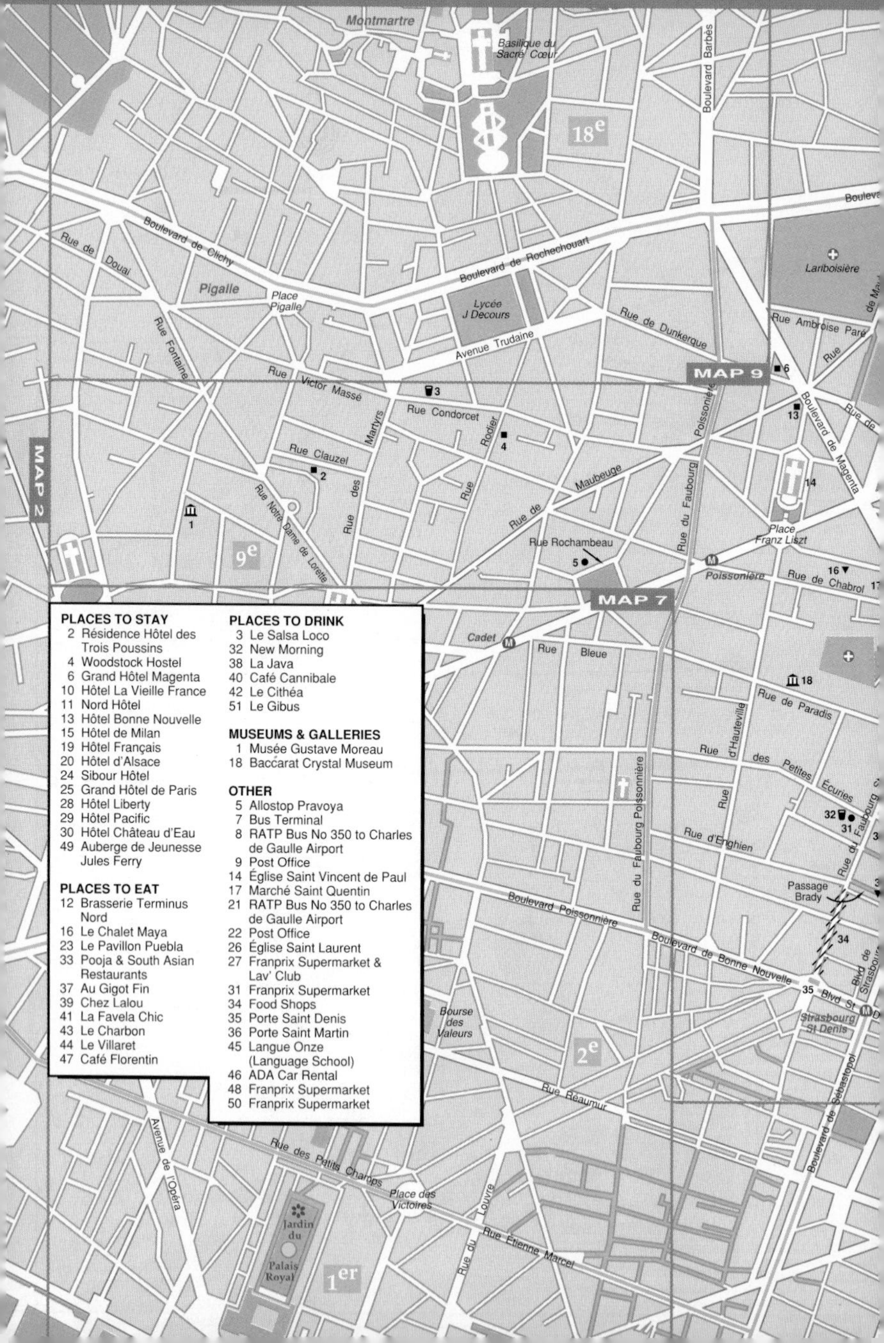
PLACES TO STAY
2 Résidence Hôtel des Trois Poussins
4 Woodstock Hostel
6 Grand Hôtel Magenta
10 Hôtel La Vieille France
11 Nord Hôtel
13 Hôtel Bonne Nouvelle
15 Hôtel de Milan
19 Hôtel Français
20 Hôtel d'Alsace
24 Sibour Hôtel
25 Grand Hôtel de Paris
28 Hôtel Liberty
29 Hôtel Pacific
30 Hôtel Château d'Eau
49 Auberge de Jeunesse Jules Ferry
PLACES TO EAT
12 Brasserie Terminus Nord
16 Le Chalet Maya
23 Le Pavillon Puebla
33 Pooja & South Asian Restaurants
37 Au Gigot Fin
39 Chez Lalou
41 La Favela Chic
43 Le Charbon
44 Le Villaret
47 Café Florentin
PLACES TO DRINK
3 Le Salsa Loco
32 New Morning
38 La Java
40 Café Cannibale
42 Le Cithéa
51 Le Gibus
MUSEUMS & GALLERIES
1 Musée Gustave Moreau
18 Baccarat Crystal Museum
OTHER
5 Allostop Pravoya
7 Bus Terminal
8 RATP Bus No 350 to Charles de Gaulle Airport
9 Post Office
14 Église Saint Vincent de Paul
17 Marché Saint Quentin
21 RATP Bus No 350 to Charles de Gaulle Airport
22 Post Office
26 Église Saint Laurent
27 Franprix Supermarket & Lav' Club
31 Franprix Supermarket
34 Food Shops
35 Porte Saint Denis
36 Porte Saint Martin
45 Langue Onze (Language School)
46 ADA Car Rental
48 Franprix Supermarket
50 Franprix Supermarket
Montmartre
Basilique du Sacré Cœur
18e
Boulevard Barbès
Boulevard de Clichy
Rue de Douai
Boulevard de Rochechouart
Lariboisière
Pigalle
Place Pigalle
Lycée J Decours
Rue de Dunkerque
Rue Ambroise Paré
Rue Fontaine
Avenue Trudaine
MAP 9
Rue Victor Massé
Rue Condorcet
Rue Rodier
Rue des Martyrs
Rue Clauzel
Rue Notre Dame de Lorette
Rue de Maubeuge
Rue du Faubourg Poissonnière
Boulevard de Magenta
MAP 2
9e
Rue Rochambeau
Place Franz Liszt
Poissonière
Rue de Chabrol
MAP 7
Cadet
Rue Bleue
Rue de Paradis
Rue d'Hauteville
Rue des Petites Écuries
Rue d'Enghien
Passage Brady
Boulevard Poissonnière
Boulevard de Bonne Nouvelle
Blvd de Strasbourg
Blvd St
Strasbourg St Denis
Bourse des Valeurs
2e
Rue Réaumur
Boulevard de Sébastopol
Avenue de l'Opéra
Rue des Petits Champs
Place des Victoires
Jardin du Palais Royal
Rue du Louvre
Rue Étienne Marcel
1er

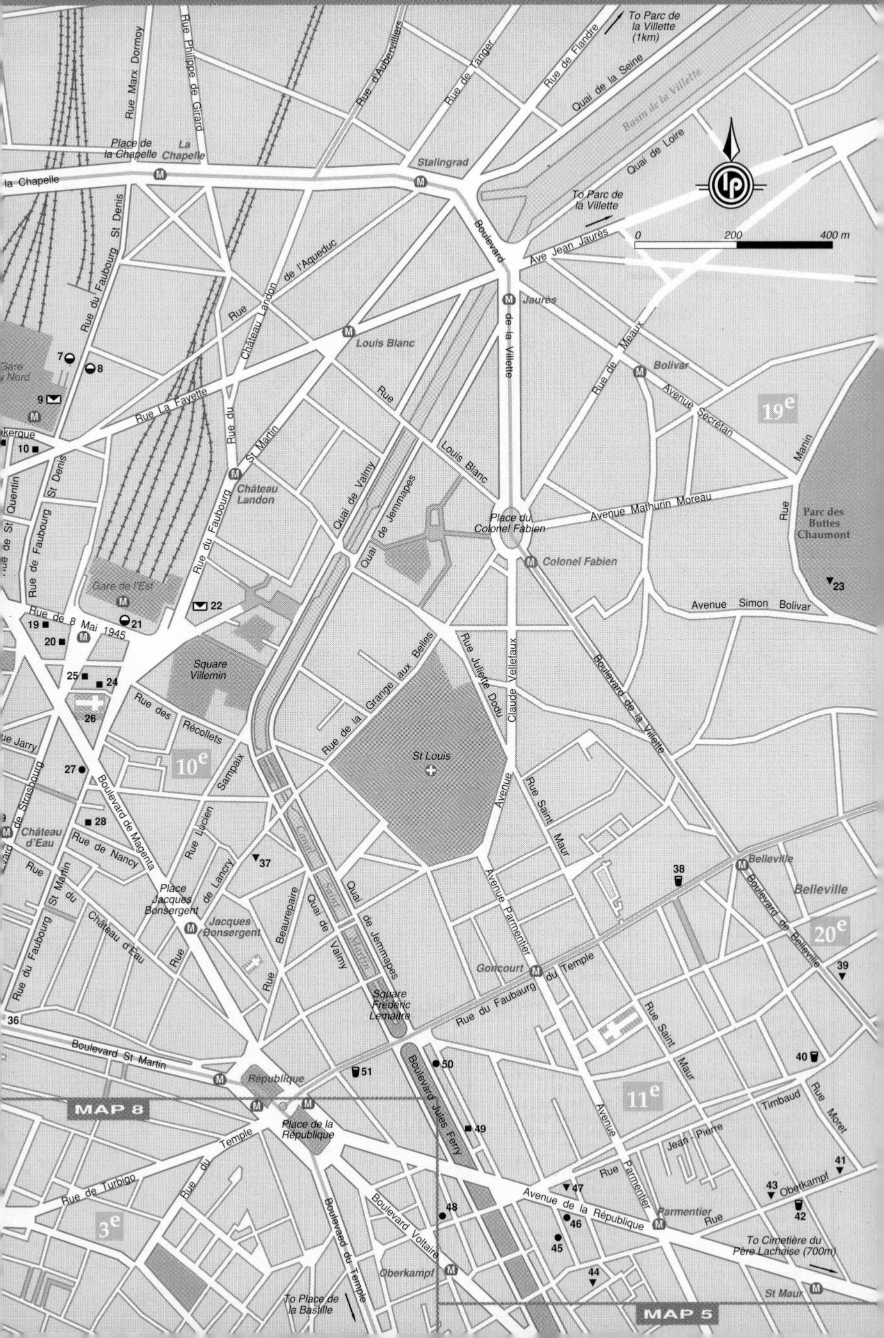
To Parc de la Villette (1km)
Rue de Flandre
Quai de la Seine
Bassin de la Villette
Quai de Loire
To Parc de la Villette
Rue de Tanger
Rue d'Aubervilliers
Rue Marx Dormoy
Rue Philippe de Girard
Place de la Chapelle
La Chapelle
la Chapelle
Stalingrad
Boulevard de la Villette
Ave Jean Jaurès
0
200
400 m
Rue de l'Aqueduc
Rue Château Landon
Rue du Faubourg St Denis
Jaurès
Louis Blanc
Rue Louis Blanc
Rue de Meaux
Bolivar
Avenue Secrétan
19e
Rue Manin
Gare du Nord
Rue La Fayette
Rue du Faubourg St Martin
Château Landon
Quai de Valmy
Quai de Jemmapes
Place du Colonel Fabien
Avenue Mathurin Moreau
Parc des Buttes Chaumont
Colonel Fabien
Rue de St Quentin
Rue de Faubourg St Denis
Gare de l'Est
Avenue Simon Bolivar
Rue du 8 Mai 1945
Square Villemin
Rue de la Grange aux Belles
Rue Juliette Dodu
Claude Vellefaux
Boulevard de la Villette
Rue des Récollets
St Louis
Rue Jarry
10e
Rue Sampaix
Avenue
Rue Saint Maur
Boulevard de Strasbourg
Boulevard de Magenta
Rue Lucien
Canal Saint Martin
Château d'Eau
Rue de Nancy
Rue de Lancry
Belleville
Boulevard de Belleville
Belleville
20e
Place Jacques Bonsergent
Jacques Bonsergent
Rue du Faubourg St Martin
Rue du Château d'Eau
Rue Beaurepaire
Avenue Parmentier
Goncourt
Rue du Faubourg du Temple
Square Frédéric Lemaître
Boulevard St Martin
République
Boulevard Jules Ferry
Rue Saint Maur
Rue Moret
Rue Timbaud
MAP 8
Place de la République
11e
Rue Jean-Pierre Timbaud
Rue du Temple
Rue de Turbigo
Rue du Temple
3e
Boulevard du Temple
Boulevard Voltaire
Avenue de la République
Parmentier
Rue Oberkampf
Oberkampf
To Cimetière du Père Lachaise (700m)
St Maur
To Place de la Bastille
MAP 5

Map 4 CENTRAL PARIS SOUTH-WEST

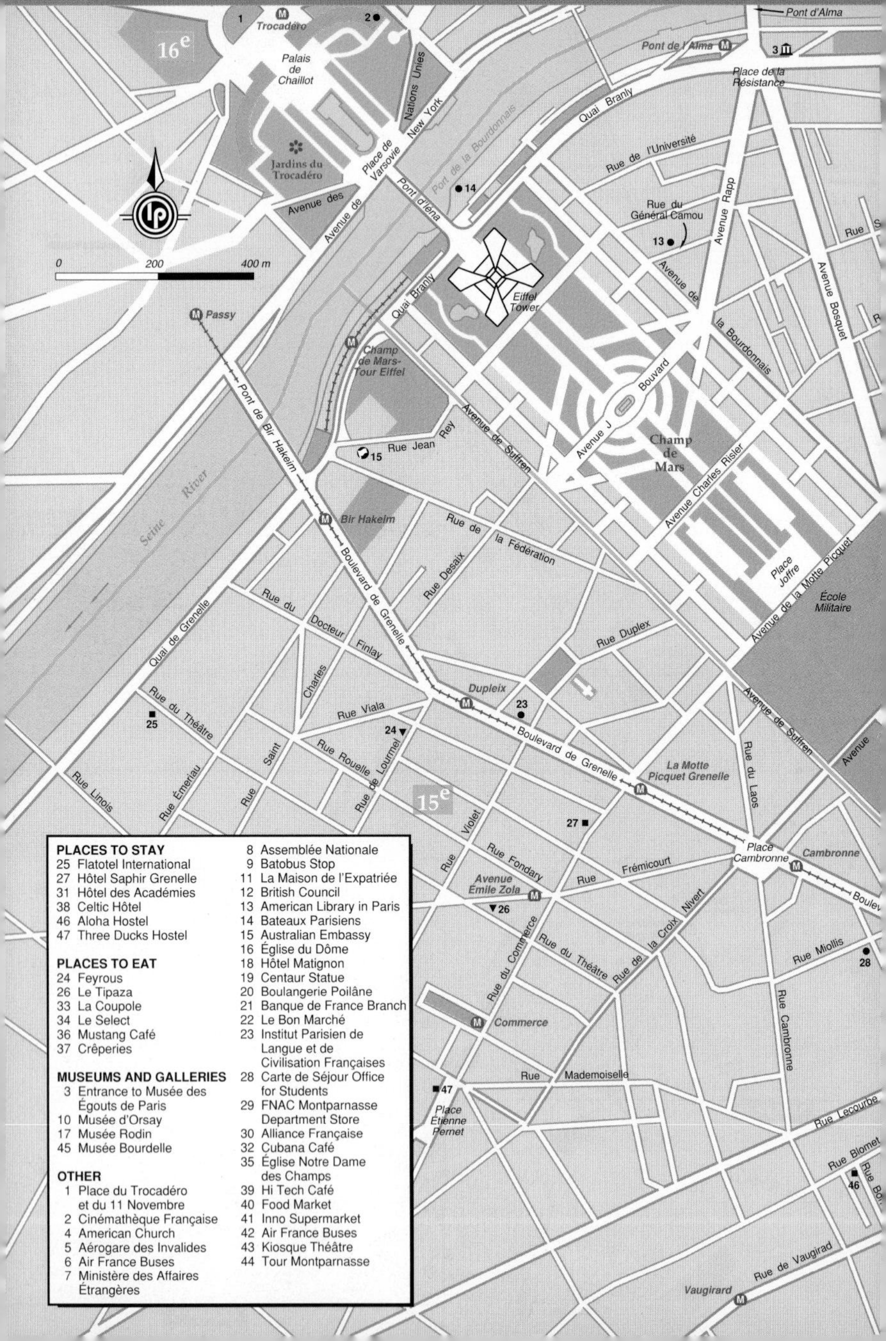

PLACES TO STAY
25 Flatotel International
27 Hôtel Saphir Grenelle
31 Hôtel des Académies
38 Celtic Hôtel
46 Aloha Hostel
47 Three Ducks Hostel

PLACES TO EAT
24 Feyrous
26 Le Tipaza
33 La Coupole
34 Le Select
36 Mustang Café
37 Crêperies

MUSEUMS AND GALLERIES
3 Entrance to Musée des Égouts de Paris
10 Musée d'Orsay
17 Musée Rodin
45 Musée Bourdelle

OTHER
1 Place du Trocadéro et du 11 Novembre
2 Cinémathèque Française
4 American Church
5 Aérogare des Invalides
6 Air France Buses
7 Ministère des Affaires Étrangères
8 Assemblée Nationale
9 Batobus Stop
11 La Maison de l'Expatriée
12 British Council
13 American Library in Paris
14 Bateaux Parisiens
15 Australian Embassy
16 Église du Dôme
18 Hôtel Matignon
19 Centaur Statue
20 Boulangerie Poilâne
21 Banque de France Branch
22 Le Bon Marché
23 Institut Parisien de Langue et de Civilisation Françaises
28 Carte de Séjour Office for Students
29 FNAC Montparnasse Department Store
30 Alliance Française
32 Cubana Café
35 Église Notre Dame des Champs
39 Hi Tech Café
40 Food Market
41 Inno Supermarket
42 Air France Buses
43 Kiosque Théâtre
44 Tour Montparnasse

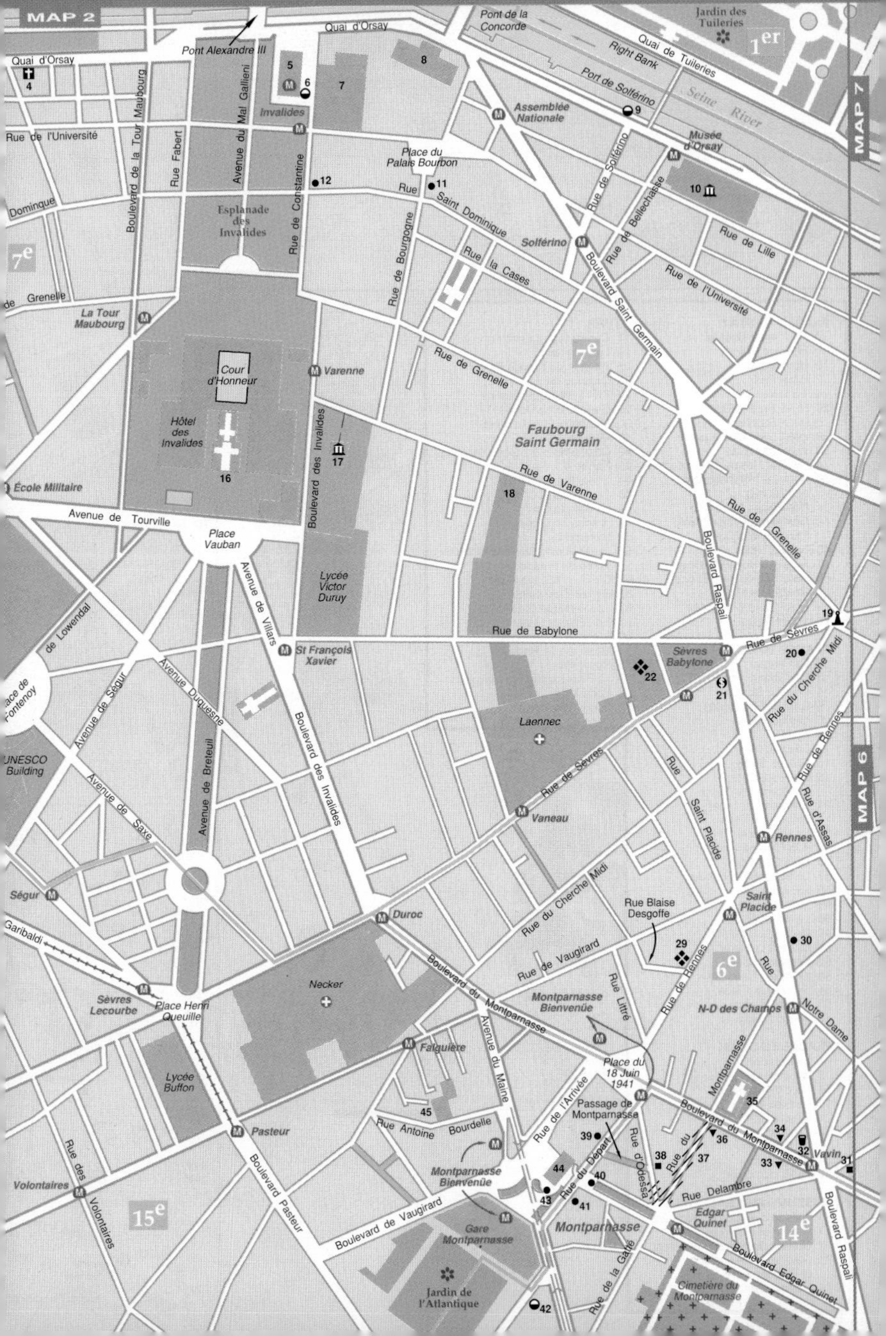
MAP 2
MAP 7
MAP 6
Quai d'Orsay
Pont Alexandre III
Pont de la Concorde
Jardin des Tuileries
1er
Quai de Tuileries
Right Bank
Port de Solférino
Seine River
Invalides
Assemblée Nationale
Musée d'Orsay
Rue de l'Université
Rue Fabert
Avenue du Mal Gallieni
Rue de Constantine
Boulevard de la Tour Maubourg
Place du Palais Bourbon
Rue Saint Dominique
Dominique
Esplanade des Invalides
Solférino
Rue de Solférino
Rue de Bellechasse
Rue de Lille
Rue de Bourgogne
Rue la Cases
Boulevard Saint Germain
Rue de l'Université
7e
Grenelle
La Tour Maubourg
Varenne
Rue de Grenelle
Cour d'Honneur
Hôtel des Invalides
Faubourg Saint Germain
Rue de Varenne
École Militaire
Boulevard des Invalides
Avenue de Tourville
Place Vauban
Rue de Grenelle
Boulevard Raspail
Lycée Victor Duruy
Avenue de Villars
de Lowendal
Rue de Babylone
St François Xavier
Rue de Sèvres
Sèvres Babylone
Rue du Cherche Midi
Place de Fontenoy
Avenue de Ségur
Avenue Duquesne
Laennec
Rue de Rennes
UNESCO Building
Avenue de Breteuil
Rue de Sèvres
Rue Saint Placide
Rue d'Assas
Avenue de Saxe
Vaneau
Rennes
Ségur
Rue du Cherche Midi
Duroc
Saint Placide
Rue Blaise Desgoffe
Garibaldi
Rue de Vaugirard
Boulevard du Montparnasse
6e
Rue de Rennes
Necker
Rue Littré
Sèvres Lecourbe
Place Henri Queuille
Montparnasse Bienvenüe
N-D des Champs
Rue Notre Dame
Falguière
Avenue du Maine
Place du 18 Juin 1941
Montparnasse
Lycée Buffon
Rue de l'Arrivée
Passage de Montparnasse
Boulevard du Montparnasse
Rue Antoine Bourdelle
Pasteur
Rue du Départ
Rue d'Odessa
Rue du
Vavin
Rue des Volontaires
Volontaires
Boulevard Pasteur
Montparnasse Bienvenüe
Rue Delambre
15e
Boulevard de Vaugirard
Edgar Quinet
Montparnasse
Gare Montparnasse
14e
Boulevard Raspail
Boulevard Edgar Quinet
Rue de la Gaîté
Jardin de l'Atlantique
Cimetière du Montparnasse
1 4 5 6 7 8 9 10 11 12 16 17 18 19 20 21 22 29 30 31 32 33 34 35 36 37 38 39 40 41 42 43 44 45

Map 5 CENTRAL PARIS SOUTH-EAST

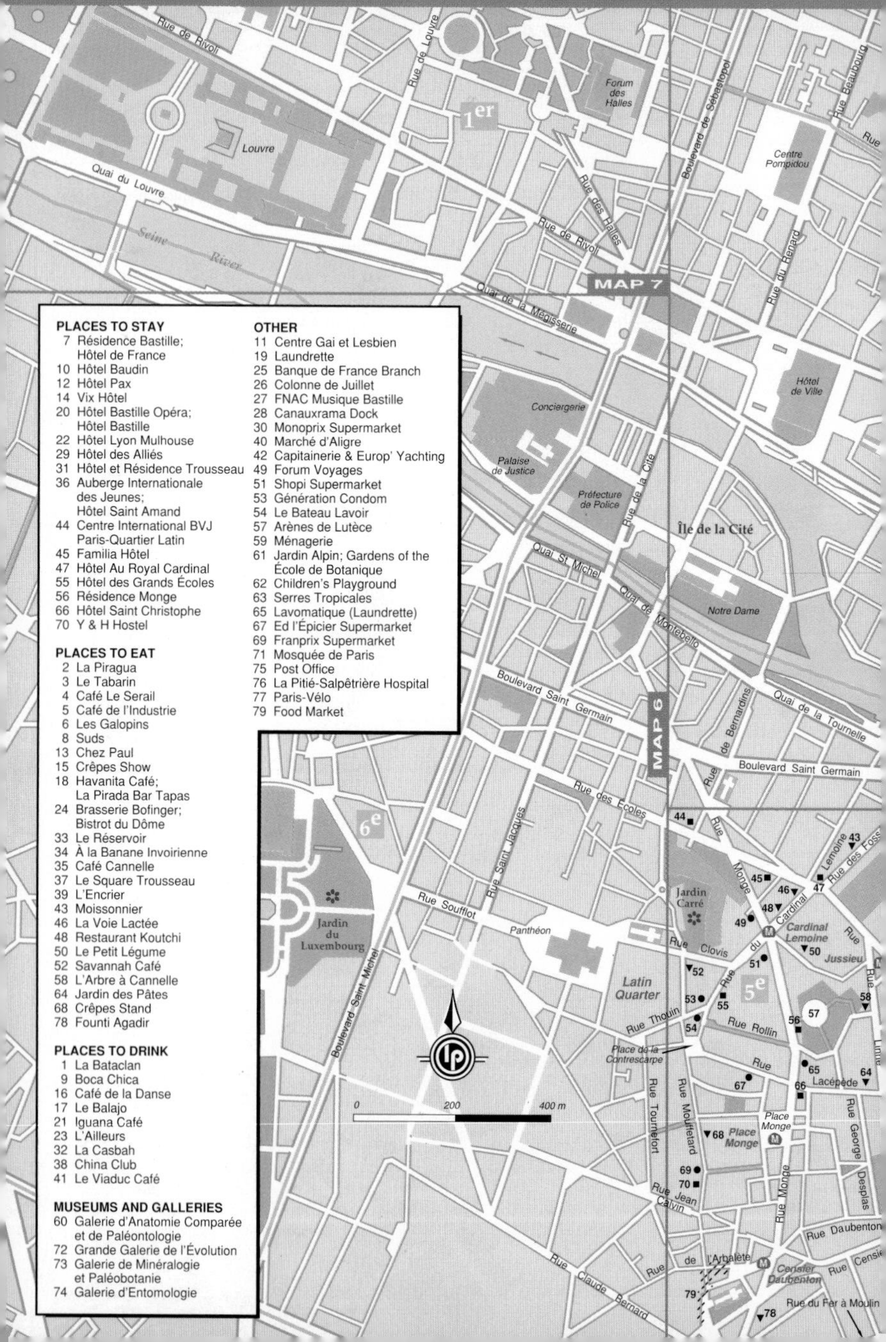

PLACES TO STAY

7 Résidence Bastille; Hôtel de France
10 Hôtel Baudin
12 Hôtel Pax
14 Vix Hôtel
20 Hôtel Bastille Opéra; Hôtel Bastille
22 Hôtel Lyon Mulhouse
29 Hôtel des Alliés
31 Hôtel et Résidence Trousseau
36 Auberge Internationale des Jeunes; Hôtel Saint Amand
44 Centre International BVJ Paris-Quartier Latin
45 Familia Hôtel
47 Hôtel Au Royal Cardinal
55 Hôtel des Grands Écoles
56 Résidence Monge
66 Hôtel Saint Christophe
70 Y & H Hostel

PLACES TO EAT

2 La Piragua
3 Le Tabarin
4 Café Le Serail
5 Café de l'Industrie
6 Les Galopins
8 Suds
13 Chez Paul
15 Crêpes Show
18 Havanita Café; La Pirada Bar Tapas
24 Brasserie Bofinger; Bistrot du Dôme
33 Le Réservoir
34 À la Banane Invoirienne
35 Café Cannelle
37 Le Square Trousseau
39 L'Encrier
43 Moissonnier
46 La Voie Lactée
48 Restaurant Koutchi
50 Le Petit Légume
52 Savannah Café
58 L'Arbre à Cannelle
64 Jardin des Pâtes
68 Crêpes Stand
78 Founti Agadir

PLACES TO DRINK

1 La Bataclan
9 Boca Chica
16 Café de la Danse
17 Le Balajo
21 Iguana Café
23 L'Ailleurs
32 La Casbah
38 China Club
41 Le Viaduc Café

MUSEUMS AND GALLERIES

60 Galerie d'Anatomie Comparée et de Paléontologie
72 Grande Galerie de l'Évolution
73 Galerie de Minéralogie et Paléobotanie
74 Galerie d'Entomologie

OTHER

11 Centre Gai et Lesbien
19 Laundrette
25 Banque de France Branch
26 Colonne de Juillet
27 FNAC Musique Bastille
28 Canauxrama Dock
30 Monoprix Supermarket
40 Marché d'Aligre
42 Capitainerie & Europ' Yachting
49 Forum Voyages
51 Shopi Supermarket
53 Génération Condom
54 Le Bateau Lavoir
57 Arènes de Lutèce
59 Ménagerie
61 Jardin Alpin; Gardens of the École de Botanique
62 Children's Playground
63 Serres Tropicales
65 Lavomatique (Laundrette)
67 Ed l'Épicier Supermarket
69 Franprix Supermarket
71 Mosquée de Paris
75 Post Office
76 La Pitié-Salpêtrière Hospital
77 Paris-Vélo
79 Food Market

CENTRAL PARIS SOUTH-EAST Map 5

Map 6 LATIN QUARTER

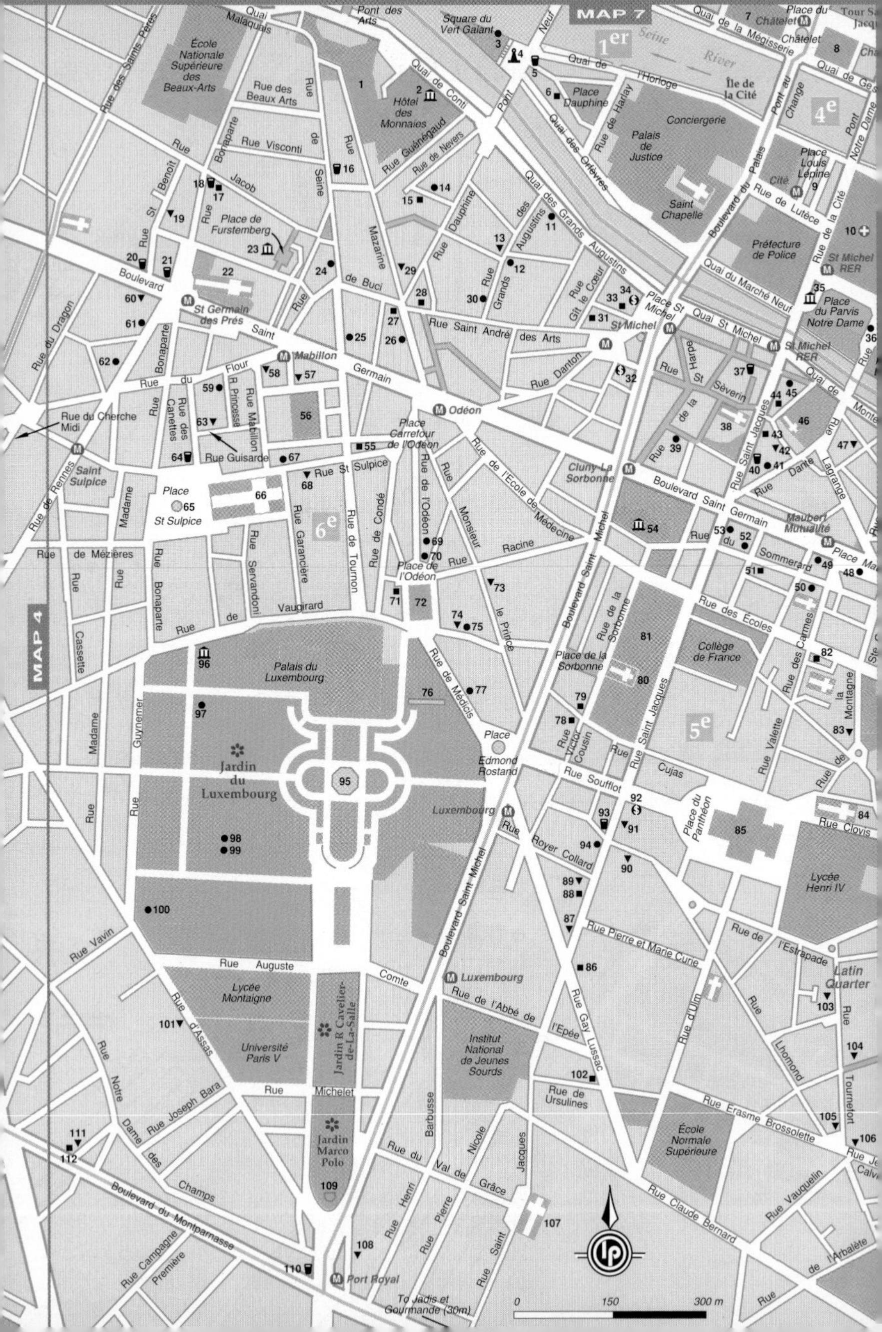

MAP 6 - LATIN QUARTER

PLACES TO STAY
6 Hôtel Henri IV
15 Hôtel de Nesle
17 Hôtel des Deux Continents; Hôtel des Marronniers
27 Hôtel Petit Trianon
28 Hôtel Saint André des Arts
31 Hôtel Saint Michel
33 Delhy's Hôtel
43 Hôtel du Centre
44 Hôtel Esmeralda
51 Hôtel Marignan
55 Hôtel du Globe
71 Hôtel Michelet Odéon
78 Grand Hôtel Saint Michel
79 Hôtel Cluny Sorbonne
82 Hôtel Saint Jacques
86 Hôtel Gay Lussac
88 Hôtel de Médicis & Laundrette
102 Grand Hôtel du Progrès
112 Citadines Apparthôtel Raspail Montparnasse

PLACES TO EAT
13 Rôtisserie d'En Face
19 Le Petit Zinc; All Jazz Club
29 Chez Albert
42 Chez Maï
47 Les Bouchons de François Clerc
57 Le Golfe de Naples
58 Mabillon University Restaurant
60 Brasserie Lipp
63 Le Mâchon d'Henri
68 Lina's
73 Polidor
74 Indonesia
83 L'Étoile de Berger
87 Tao
89 Douce France
90 Tashi Delek
91 Perraudin
101 Assas University Restaurant
103 Castor et Pollux
104 Le Vigneron
105 Chez Léna et Mimille
106 Châtelet University Restaurant
108 Bullier University Restaurant
111 Le Caméléon

PLACES TO DRINK
5 Taverne Henri IV
16 La Palette
18 La Villa Jazz Club
20 Café de Flore
21 Les Deux Magots
37 Le Caveau de la Huchette
40 Le Cloître; Polly Maggoo
56 Coolin; Marché Saint Germain
64 Café de la Mairie
93 Café Oz
110 La Closerie des Lilas

MUSEUMS AND GALLERIES
2 Musée de la Monnaie
23 Musée National Eugène Delacroix
35 Crypte Archéologique
54 Musée National du Moyen Âge
96 Musée du Luxembourg

OTHER
1 Institut de France; Bibliothèque Mazarine
3 Vedettes du Pont Neuf
4 Statue of Henri IV
7 Théâtre Musical de Paris
8 Théâtre de la Ville
9 Flower Market
10 Hôtel Dieu Hospital
11 Australian Bookshop
12 Mariage Frères
14 Théâtre de Nesle
22 Église Saint Germain des Prés
24 Julice Laverie
25 Champion Supermarket
26 Chez Jean-Mi
30 Julice Laverie
32 Exchange Bureau
34 Le Change de Paris
36 Point Zéro
38 Église Saint Séverin
39 Abbey Bookshop
41 Album
45 Shakespeare & Company Bookshop
46 Église Saint Julien le Pauvre
48 Food Market; Food Shops; Fromagerie
49 EOL' Modelisme
50 Au Vieux Campeur Shop
52 Au Vieux Campeur Shop
53 Eurolines Ticket Office
59 Village Voice Bookshop
61 Monoprix Supermarket
62 Kenzo
65 Fontaine des Quatre Évêques
66 Église Saint Sulpice
67 Galerie d'Amon
69 Odimex Paris
70 Council Travel
72 Odéon Théâtre de l'Europe
75 USIT
76 Fontaine des Médicis
77 Café Orbital
80 Chapelle de la Sorbonne
81 Sorbonne (Université de Paris)
84 Église Saint Étienne du Mont
85 Panthéon
92 Banque National de Paris
94 Food Shops
95 Grand Bassin
97 Chess & Card Games
98 Théâtre du Luxembourg
99 Playground
100 Beehives
107 Église Val-de-Grace
108 OTU Voyages
109 Fontaine de l'Observatoire

Map 7 LES HALLES & LOUVRE AREAS

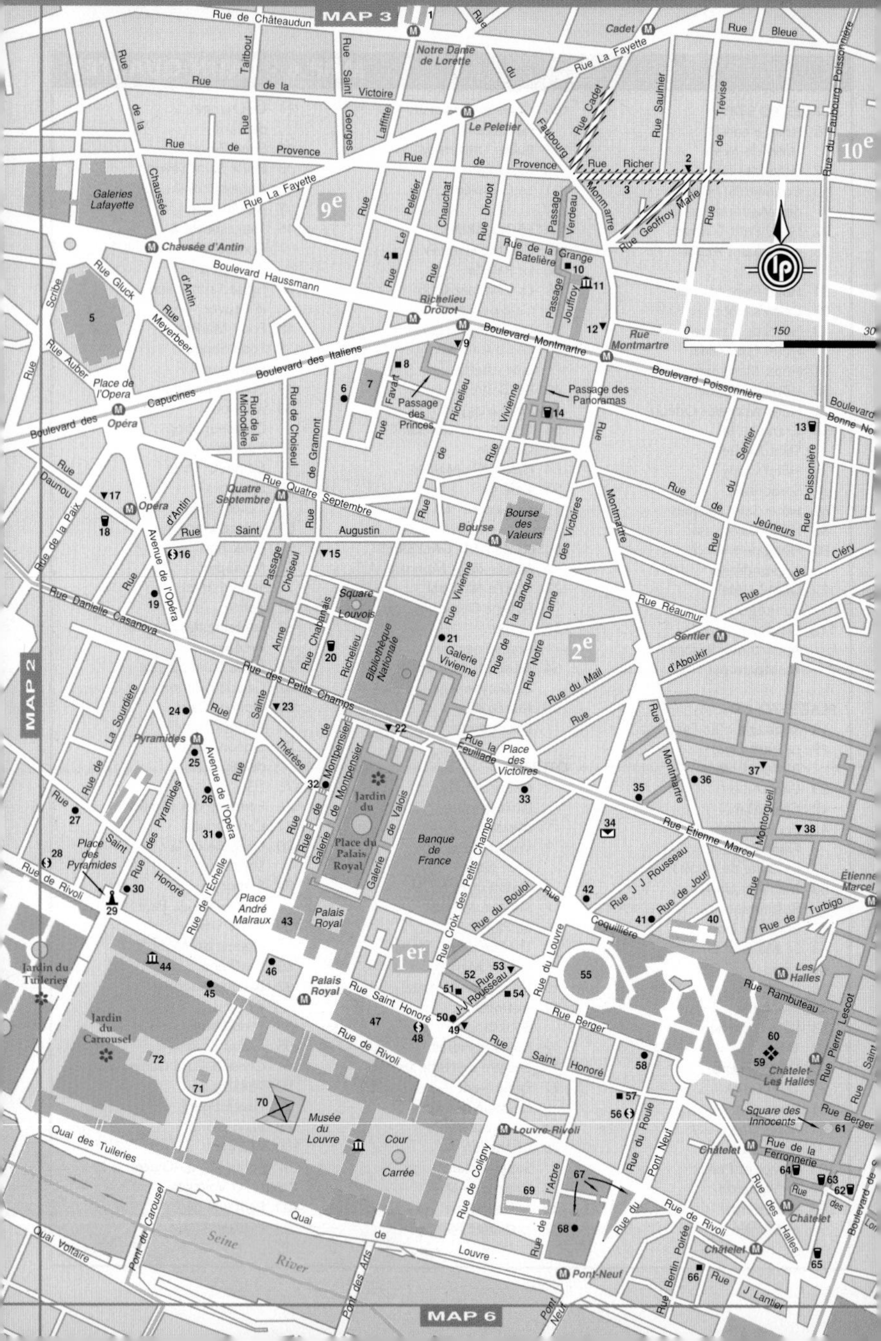
MAP 3
MAP 2
MAP 6
Rue de Châteaudun
Cadet
Rue Bleue
Notre Dame de Lorette
Rue La Fayette
Rue Taitbout
Rue de la Victoire
Rue Saint Georges
Laffitte
Le Peletier
Rue de Provence
Rue Cadet
Rue Saulnier
Rue de Trévise
Rue du Faubourg Poissonnière
10e
Faubourg Montmartre
Rue Richer
Rue Geoffroy Marie
Galeries Lafayette
Rue de la Chaussée
9e
Rue Le Peletier
Chauchat
Rue Drouot
Passage Verdeau
Rue de la Grange Batelière
Passage Jouffroy
Chausée d'Antin
Boulevard Haussmann
Rue Gluck
Scribe
Rue d'Antin
Rue Meyerbeer
Richelieu Drouot
Boulevard Montmartre
Rue Montmartre
Rue Auber
Place de l'Opera
Boulevard des Italiens
Boulevard des Capucines
Opéra
Rue de la Michodière
Rue de Choiseul
Rue de Gramont
Favart
Passage des Princes
Rue de Richelieu
Rue Vivienne
Passage des Panoramas
Boulevard Poissonnière
Boulevard Bonne Nouvelle
Rue du Sentier
Rue Poissonnière
Rue Daunou
Rue de la Paix
Quatre Septembre
Rue Quatre Septembre
Rue Saint Augustin
Avenue de l'Opéra
Rue d'Antin
Passage Choiseul
Bourse
Bourse des Valeurs
Rue des Victoires
Rue de Jeûneurs
Rue de Cléry
Rue Danielle Casanova
Square Louvois
Rue Chabanais
Rue Sainte Anne
Bibliothèque Nationale
Galerie Vivienne
Rue de la Banque
Rue Notre Dame
2e
Rue Réaumur
Sentier
Rue d'Aboukir
Rue du Mail
Rue des Petits Champs
Rue La Sourdière
Pyramides
Rue Thérèse
Rue de Montpensier
Jardin du Place du Palais Royal
Galerie de Valois
Galerie de Montpensier
Rue la Feuillade
Place des Victoires
Banque de France
Rue Montorgueil
Rue Étienne Marcel
Étienne Marcel
Rue des Pyramides
Rue de l'Échelle
Rue Saint Honoré
Place des Pyramides
Rue de Rivoli
Place André Malraux
Palais Royal
Rue Croix des Petits Champs
Rue du Bouloi
Rue J J Rousseau
Rue du Jour
Rue Coquillière
Rue de Turbigo
Jardin du Tuileries
1er
Rue du Louvre
Les Halles
Rue Rambuteau
Rue Pierre Lescot
Palais Royal
Rue Saint Honoré
Rue Berger
Jardin du Carrousel
Musée du Louvre
Cour Carrée
Châtelet-Les Halles
Square des Innocents
Louvre-Rivoli
Rue du Roule
Rue Pont Neuf
Rue de la Ferronnerie
Châtelet
Quai des Tuileries
Rue de Coligny
Rue de l'Arbre
Rue des Halles
Quai du Louvre
Seine River
Quai Voltaire
Pont du Carrousel
Pont des Arts
Pont Neuf
Rue Bertin Poirée
Rue J Lantier
Boulevard de Sébastopol
0 150 300

MAP 7 - LES HALLES & LOUVRE

PLACES TO STAY
4 Hôtel Peletier-Haussmann
8 Citadines Apparthôtel Opera
10 Hôtel Chopin
51 Hôtel de Lille
54 Centre International BVJ Louvre
57 Hôtel Saint Honoré
66 Grand Hôtel de Champagne

PLACES TO EAT
2 Les Ailes; Folies Bergères
3 North African Jewish Restaurants
9 Le Drouot
12 Chartier
15 La Maison Savoureuse
17 Country Life
22 Willi's Wine Bar
23 Higuma
37 Aux Crus de Bourgogne
38 Le Loup Blanc
39 Joe Allen
49 Le Petit Mâchon
53 L'Épi d'Or

PLACES TO DRINK
13 Rex Club
14 Le Croquenote
18 Harry's New York Bar
20 La Champmeslé
62 Au Duc des Lombards
63 Le Baiser Salé; Le Sunset
64 Banana Café
65 Café Oz

MUSEUMS AND GALLERIES
11 Musée Grévin
44 Musée des Arts Décoratifs; Musée de la Mode et du Textile

OTHER
1 Église Notre Dame de Lorette
5 Opéra Garnier
6 Agence des Théâtres
7 Opéra Comique
16 Barclays Bank
19 Brentano's Bookshop
21 USIT
24 Monoprix Supermarket
25 Council Travel
26 Forum Voyages
27 Il Pour l'Homme
28 Paris Vision
29 Joan of Arc Statue
30 Cityrama Bus Tours
31 Nouvelles Frontières
32 Fine Food Shops
33 Kenzo
34 Main Post Office
35 Comme des Garçons
36 Accord Language School
40 Église Saint Eustache
41 Agnès B
42 E Dehillerin
43 Comédie Française
45 Entrance to Carrousel du Louvre
46 Cityrama Ticket Office
47 Le Louvre des Antiquaires
48 Le Change du Louvre
50 Laverie Libre Service (Laundrette)
52 Galérie Véro Dodat
55 Bourse de Commerce
56 Best Change
58 Franprix Supermarket
59 FNAC Forum Department Store
60 Forum des Halles
61 Fontaine des Innocents
67 La Samaritaine
68 La Samaritaine Rooftop Terrace
69 Église Saint Germain L'Auxerrois
70 IM Pei's Glass Pyramid
71 Inverted Glass Pyramid
72 Arc de Triomphe du Carrousel

RICHARD NEBESKÝ

A merry-go-round and the eateries on the rooftop of Les Halles, Paris

Map 8 CENTRE POMPIDOU AREA & MARAIS

MAP 8 - CENTRE POMPIDOU AREA & MARAIS

PLACES TO STAY
36 Hôtel Axial Beaubourg
43 Hôtel Central Marais
59 Hôtel Le Compostelle
61 Hôtel Le Palais des Fès
63 Hôtel Rivoli
64 Hôtel de Nice
67 MIJE Maubuisson
72 MIJE Fourcy
76 Grand Hôtel Malher
77 Hôtel Moderne; Hôtel Pratic
82 Hôtel Sully
83 Hôtel de la Place des Vosges
86 Hôtel de la Herse d'Or
88 Hôtel Castex
90 MIJE Fauconnier
96 Hôtel des Deux Îles
97 Hôtel Saint Louis

PLACES TO EAT
1 Au Bascou
4 404
5 Chinese Restaurants
8 Au Trou Normand
9 Le Clown Bar
11 Chez Omar
13 Mélodine Cafeteria
19 Le Repaire de Cartouche
22 Robert et Louise
23 Aquarius; Le Petit Picard
24 Le Gai Moulin
31 Au P'tit Rémouleur
44 La Truffe; Coffee Shop
48 Chez Rami et Hanna
49 Chez Marianne
52 Caves Saint Gilles
54 Jo Goldenberg
57 Amadéo
62 Minh Chau; Quetzal Bar
65 La Perla
81 Vins des Pyrénées
85 L'Impasse
89 L'Enoteca
94 Les Fous de l'Île
99 Brasserie de l'Île Saint Louis
102 Restaurant A

PLACES TO DRINK
3 Les Bains
6 Le Tango
25 Café Beaubourg
29 Au Vieux Paris
37 Open Café & Laundrette
38 Mixeri Bar
45 Le Petit Fer à Cheval
46 La Chaise au Plafond
47 Amnésia Café
56 Stolly's
60 Le Pick Clops

MUSEUMS AND GALLERIES
16 Centre Pompidou
18 Archives Nationales; Musée de l'Historie de France
20 Musée Picasso
21 Musée de la Serrure
51 Musée Cognacq-Jay
53 Musée Carnavalet
70 Mémorial du Martyr Juif Inconnu
71 Maison Européenne de la Photographie
80 Hôtel de Sully
84 Maison de Victor Hugo
103 Institut du Monde Arabe

OTHER
2 Église St Nicholas des Champs
7 Web Bar
10 Cirque d'Hiver
12 Le Défenseur du Temps
14 Bibliothèque Publique d'Information (BPI)
15 AJF
17 Allô Logement Temporaire
26 Mechanical Fountains
27 Pharmacie des Halles
28 Église Saint Merri
30 Ed l'Épicier Supermarket
32 Noctambus Stops
33 Hôtel de Ville
34 Post Office
35 BHV Department Store
39 Post Office
40 Mariage Frères
41 Point Virgule
42 Les Mots à la Bouche
50 Laverie Libre Service
55 Laverie
58 À l'Olivier
66 Église Saint Gervais-Saint Protais
68 Sic Amor
69 Mélodies Graphiques
73 Supermarché G20
74 Franprix Supermarket
75 Guimard Synagogue
78 Gourmaud
79 Monoprix Supermarket
87 Flo Prestige
91 Hôtel de Sens
92 Église Saint Louis en l'Île
93 Berthillon Ice Cream
95 Le Moule à Gâteau
98 Galerie Alain Carion
100 Mémorial des Martyrs de la Déportation
101 Bateaux Parisiens Dock

CHRISTOPHER GROENHOUT

The view from the Eiffel Tower across the Seine to the Palais de Chaillot and La Défense

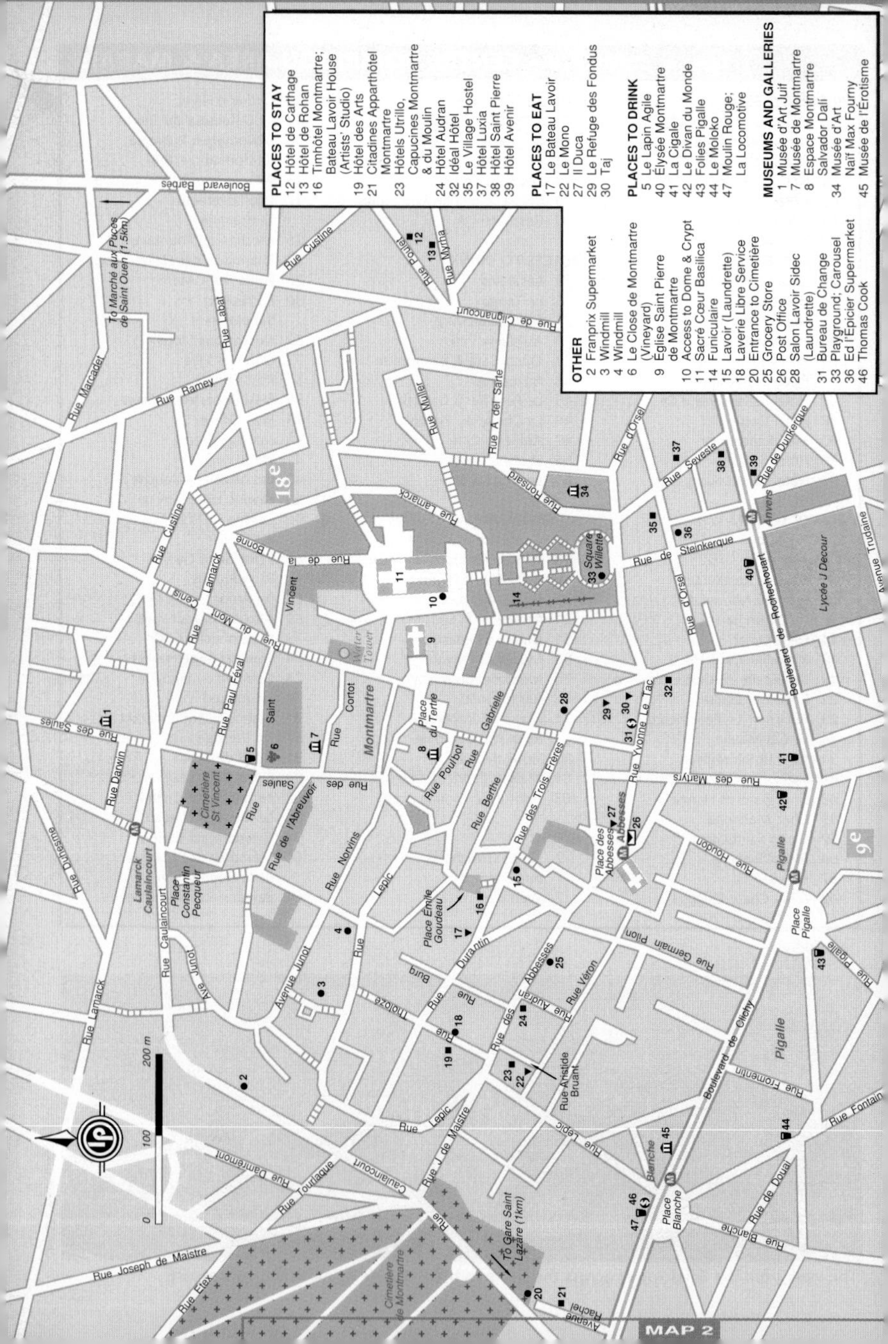
PLACES TO STAY
12 Hôtel de Carthage
13 Hôtel de Rohan
16 Timhôtel Montmartre; Bateau Lavoir House (Artists' Studio)
19 Hôtel des Arts
21 Citadines Apparthôtel Montmartre
23 Hôtels Utrillo, Capucines Montmartre & du Moulin
24 Hôtel Audran
32 Idéal Hôtel
35 Le Village Hostel
37 Hôtel Luxia
38 Hôtel Saint Pierre
39 Hôtel Avenir
PLACES TO EAT
17 Le Bateau Lavoir
22 Le Mono
27 Il Duca
29 Le Refuge des Fondus
30 Taj
PLACES TO DRINK
5 Le Lapin Agile
40 Élysée Montmartre
41 La Cigale
42 Le Divan du Monde
43 Folies Pigalle
44 Le Moloko
47 Moulin Rouge; La Locomotive
MUSEUMS AND GALLERIES
1 Musée d'Art Juif
7 Musée de Montmartre
8 Espace Montmartre Salvador Dalí
34 Musée d'Art Naïf Max Fourny
45 Musée de l'Érotisme
OTHER
2 Franprix Supermarket
3 Windmill
4 Windmill
6 Le Close de Montmartre (Vineyard)
9 Église Saint Pierre de Montmartre
10 Access to Dome & Crypt
11 Sacré Cœur Basilica
14 Funiculaire
15 Lavoir (Laundrette)
18 Laverie Libre Service
20 Entrance to Cimetière
25 Grocery Store
26 Post Office
28 Salon Lavoir Sidec (Laundrette)
31 Bureau de Change
33 Playground; Carousel
36 Ed l'Épicier Supermarket
46 Thomas Cook
To Marché aux Puces de Saint Ouen (1.5km)
To Gare Saint Lazare (1km)
18e
9e
0
100
200 m
Square Willette
Place du Tertre
Place des Abbesses
Place Pigalle
Place Blanche
Place Émile Goudeau
Place Constantin Pecqueur
Cimetière St Vincent
Cimetière de Montmartre
Lycée J Decour
Water Tower
Montmartre
Pigalle
Boulevard Barbès
Boulevard de Rochechouart
Boulevard de Clichy
Rue Custine
Rue Ramey
Rue Marcadet
Rue Lamarck
Rue Caulaincourt
Rue Lepic
Rue des Abbesses
Rue des Trois Frères
Rue Yvonne Le Tac
Rue d'Orsel
Rue de Steinkerque
Rue Ronsard
Rue des Martyrs
Rue de Dunkerque
Rue Norvins
Rue des Saules
Rue Cortot
Rue Poulbot
Rue Berthe
Rue Gabrielle
Rue Durantin
Rue Tholozé
Rue Houdon
Rue Germain Pilon
Rue Véron
Rue Audran
Rue Burq
Rue Junot
Avenue Junot
Rue Darwin
Rue Duhesme
Rue Tourlaque
Rue Damrémont
Rue Joseph de Maistre
Rue J de Maistre
Rue Etex
Avenue Rachel
Rue Blanche
Rue de Douai
Rue Fontaine
Rue Fromentin
Rue Pigalle
Avenue Trudaine
Rue Seveste
Rue Muller
Rue A del Sarte
Rue de Clignancourt
Rue Myrha
Rue Poulet
Rue Labat
Rue du Mont Cenis
Rue de la Bonne
Rue Paul Féval
Rue de l'Abreuvoir
Rue Saint Vincent
Rue Lamarck
Rue Aristide Bruant
Lamarck Caulaincourt
Abbesses
Anvers
Blanche
MAP 2

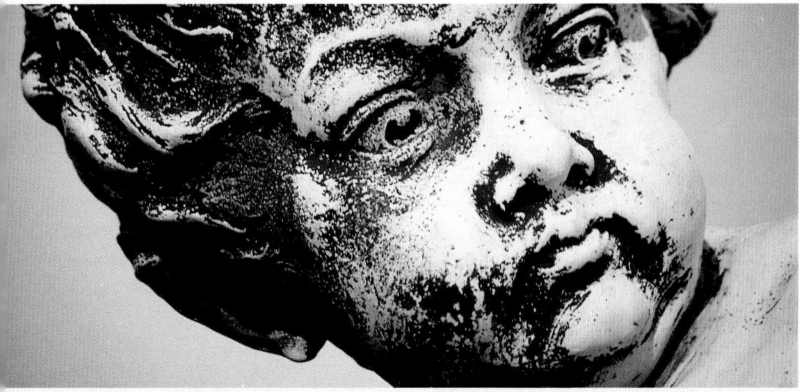

GREG ELMS

Detail of a statue in Paris

BETHUNE CARMICHAEL

A sculpture in the Musée d'Orsay, Paris

RACHEL BLACK

Detail of the ceiling of the Arc de Triomphe

SIMON BRACKEN

Detail from one of Notre Dame's three entrances

RICHARD I'ANSON

The stunning glass pyramid, designed by IM Pei, was added to the Louvre in the late 1980s.

GREG ELMS

Fountain of Saturn, Versailles

SIMON BRACKEN

Statue on the Pont de l'Alma

SIMON BRACKEN

Detail of the Panthéon

The Museums of Paris

The following list contains the names of all museums mentioned in this chapter. For easy reference, they are listed by the English name, followed by the French (the reverse appears in the text).

African & Oceanic Art
Musée National des Arts d'Afrique et d'Océanie (p226; Map 1; ☎ 01 44 74 84 80; metro Porte Dorée), 293 Ave Daumesnil (12e)

Arab World Institute
Institut du Monde Arabe (pp206-7; Map 5; ☎ 01 40 51 38 38; metro Cardinal Lemoine), 1 Rue des Fossés Saint Bernard (5e)

Army
Musée de l'Armée (p213; Map 4; ☎ 01 44 42 37 67; metro Varenne), Hôtel des Invalides, Esplanade des Invalides (7e)

Baccarat Crystal
Musée du Cristal Baccarat (p220; Map 3; ☎ 01 47 70 64 30; metro Château d'Eau), CIAT building, 30bis Rue de Paradis (10e)

Bourdelle
Musée Bourdelle (p211; Map 4; ☎ 01 49 54 73 73; metro Falguière), 18 Rue Antoine Bourdelle (15e)

Buddhist Pantheon
Panthéon Bouddhique (p215; Map 2; ☎ 01 47 23 88 11; metro léna), 19 Ave d'léna (16e)

Carnavalet (History of Paris)
Musée Carnavalet (p199; Map 8; ☎ 01 42 72 21 13; metro Saint Paul or Chemin Vert), 23 Rue de Sévigné (3e)

Cernuschi
Musée Cernuschi (p218; Map 2; ☎ 01 45 63 50 75; metro Villiers), 7 Ave Vélasquez (8e)

Cinema
Musée du Cinéma Henri Langlois (p214; Map 4; ☎ 01 45 53 74 39; metro Trocadéro), Palais de Chaillot, Place du Trocadéro (16e)

City of Music
Cité de la Musique (p224; Map 1; ☎ 01 44 84 44 84; metro Porte de Pantin), Parc de la Villette, 221 Ave Jean Jaurès (19e)

City of Sciences & Industry
Cité des Sciences et de l'Industrie (p223; Map 1; ☎ 01 40 05 12 12 or ☎ 08 36 68 29 30; metro Porte de la Villette), 30 Ave Corentin Cariou (19e)

Cognacq-Jay
Musée Cognacq-Jay (p200; Map 8; ☎ 01 40 27 07 21; metro Saint Paul), 8 Rue Elzévir (3e)

Coins & Medals
Musée de la Monnaie (pp210-11; Map 6; ☎ 01 40 46 55 35 or ☎ 01 34 51 93 53; metro Pont Neuf), 11 Quai de Conti (6e)

Dalí
Espace Montmartre Salvador Dalí (pp221-2; Map 9; ☎ 01 42 64 40 10; metro Abbesses), 9-11 Rue Poulbot (18e)

Decorative Arts
Musée des Arts Décoratifs (p192; Map 7; ☎ 01 44 55 57 50; metro Palais Royal), 107 Rue de Rivoli, 3rd floor (1er)

Eugene Delacroix
Musée National Eugène Delacroix (p210; Map 6; ☎ 01 44 41 86 50; metro Mabillon), 6 Place de Furstemberg

Eroticism
Musée de l'Érotisme (pp222-3; Map 9; ☎ 01 42 58 28 73; metro Blanche), 72 Blvd de Clichy (18e)

Fashion & Clothing
Musée de la Mode et du Costume (p215; Map 2; ☎ 01 47 20 85 23; metro léna), Palais Galliera, 10 Ave Pierre 1er de Serbie (16e)

Fashion & Textile
Musée de la Mode et du Textile (p192; Map 7; ☎ 01 44 55 57 50; metro Palais Royal), 107 Rue de Rivoli (1er)

Fine Arts
Musée des Beaux-Arts de la Ville de Paris (p217; Map 2; ☎ 01 42 65 12 73; metro Champs-Élysées Clemenceau), Petit Palais, Ave Winston Churchill (8e)

French Monuments
Musée des Monuments Français (p214; Map 4; ☎ 01 44 05 39 10; metro Trocadéro), Palais de Chaillot, Place du Trocadéro (16e)

The Museums of Paris

Grand Palais
Nationales Galeries du Grand Palais (p217; Map 2; ☎ 01 44 13 17 17; metro Champs-Élysées Clemenceau), Ave Winston Churchill

Grévin
Musée Grévin (p219; Map 7; ☎ 01 42 46 13 26; metro Rue Montmartre), 10-12 Blvd Montmartre (9e)

Guimet
Musée Guimet (pp214-15; Map 2; ☎ 01 47 23 88 11; metro Iéna), 6 Place d'Iéna (16e)

French History
Musée de l'Histoire de France (p199; Map 8; ☎ 01 40 27 60 96; metro Rambuteau), Hôtel de Soubise, 60 Rue des Francs Bourgeois (3e)

Hôtel de Sully
(p199; Map 8; ☎ 01 42 74 47 75; metro Saint Paul), 62 Rue Saint Antoine (4e)

Victor Hugo
Maison de Victor Hugo (p198; Map 8; ☎ 01 42 72 10 16; metro Saint Paul or Chemin Vert), 6 Place des Vosges (3e)

Jacquemart-André
Musée Jacquemart-André (p218; Map 2; ☎ 01 42 89 04 91; metro Miromesnil), 158 Blvd Haussmann (8e)

Jeu de Paume
Galerie Nationale du Jeu de Paume (p196; Map 2; ☎ 01 47 03 12 50; metro Concorde), Place de la Concorde (1er)

Jewish Art
Musée d'Art Juif (p222; Map 9; ☎ 01 42 57 84 15; metro Lamarck Caulaincourt), 42 Rue des Saules, 3rd floor (18e); soon to move to Hôtel de Saint Aignan, 71 Rue du Temple (3e; metro Rambuteau).

Locks
Musée de la Serrure (p200; Map 8; ☎ 01 42 77 79 62; metro Saint Paul or Chemin Vert), 1 Rue de la Perle (3e)

Louvre
Musée du Louvre (p190; Map 7; ☎ 01 40 20 53 17; metro Palais Royal or Louvre-Rivoli), Cour Napoléon (1er)

Luxembourg
Musée du Luxembourg (p210; Map 6; ☎ 01 42 34 25 94; metro Luxembourg), 19 Rue de Vaugirard (6e)

Mankind
Musée de l'Homme (p214; Map 4; ☎ 01 44 05 72 72; metro Trocadéro), Palais de Chaillot, Place du Trocadéro (16e)

Maritime
Musée de la Marine (p214; Map 4; ☎ 01 53 65 65 69; metro Trocadéro), Palais de Chaillot, Place du Trocadéro (16e)

Middle Ages
Musée National du Moyen Âge (p207; Map 6; ☎ 01 53 73 78 00; metro Cluny-La Sorbonne), Thermes de Cluny, 6 Place Paul Painlevé (5e)

Claude Monet
Musée Marmottan-Claude Monet (p226; Map 1; ☎ 01 42 24 07 02; metro La Muette), 2 Rue Louis Boilly (16e)

Modern Art (City of Paris)
Musée d'Art Moderne de la Ville de Paris (p215; Map 2; ☎ 01 53 67 40 00; metro Iéna or Alma Marceau), Palais de Tokyo, 11 Ave du Président Wilson (16e)

Gustave Moreau Museum
Musée Gustave Moreau (Map 3; ☎ 01 48 74 38 50; metro Trinité), 14 Rue de La Rochefoucauld (9e)

Pompidou Centre (National Museum of Modern Art)
Musée National d'Art Moderne (p197; Maps 5 and 8; ☎ 01 44 78 12 33; metro Châtelet-Les Halles or Rambuteau), Rue Beaubourg (4e)

Montmartre
Musée de Montmartre (p222; Map 9; ☎ 01 46 06 61 11; metro Lamarck Caulaincourt), 12 Rue Cortot (18e)

Nissim de Camondo
Musée Nissim de Camondo (p218; Map 2; ☎ 01 53 89 06 40; metro Monceau or Villiers), 63 Rue de Monceau (8e)

The Museums of Paris

Natural History
Musée National d'Histoire Naturelle (p206; Map 5; ☎ 01 40 79 30 00; metro Censier Daubenton or Gare d'Austerlitz), Jardin des Plantes, 57 Rue Cuvier (5e)

Naive Art
Musée d'Art Naïf Max Fourny (p222; Map 9; ☎ 01 42 58 72 89; metro Anvers), Halle Saint Pierre, 2 Rue Ronsard (18e)

Opera
Musée de l'Opéra (p218; Map 7; ☎ 01 47 42 07 02; metro Opéra), Opéra Garnier, Place de l'Opéra (9e)

Orangerie
Musée de l'Orangerie des Tuileries (p196; Map 2; ☎ 01 42 97 48 16; metro Concorde), Place de la Concorde (1er)

Orsay
Musée d'Orsay (p212; Map 4; ☎ 01 40 49 48 14; metro Musée d'Orsay or Solférino), 1 Rue de Bellechasse (7e)

Palace of Discovery
Palais de la Découverte (p217; Map 2; ☎ 01 40 74 80 00; metro Champs-Élysées Clemenceau or Franklin D Roosevelt), Ave Franklin D Roosevelt (8e)

Petit Palais
Musée du Petit Palais (p217; Map 2; ☎ 01 42 65 12 73; metro Champs-Élysées Clemenceau), Ave Winston Churchill (8e)

Photography
Maison Européenne de la Photographie (p200; Map 8; ☎ 01 44 78 75 00; metro Saint Paul), 5-7 Rue de Fourcy (4e)

Popular Arts & Traditions
Musée National des Arts et Traditions Populaires (p226; Map 1; ☎ 01 44 17 60 00; metro Les Sablons), 6 Ave du M Gandhi (16e)

Sewers
Musée des Égouts de Paris (p213; Map 4; ☎ 01 47 05 10 29; metro Pont de l'Alma), Quai d'Orsay (7e)

Picasso
Musée Picasso (p200; Map 8; ☎ 01 42 71 25 21; metro Saint Paul), 5 Rue de Thorigny (3e)

Rodin
Musée Rodin (pp212-13; Map 4; ☎ 01 47 05 01 34; metro Varenne), 77 Rue de Varenne

Unknown Jewish Martyr
Mémorial du Martyr Juif Inconnu (p200; Map 8; ☎ 01 42 77 44 72; metro Pont Marie or Saint Paul), 17 Rue Geoffroy l'Asnier (4e)

TONY WHEELER

Detail of the Palais de Tokyo façade, Musée d'Art Moderne.

Jardin des Tuileries

The formal Tuileries Gardens (Maps 2 & 7), which begin just west of the Louvre, were laid out in their present form (more or less) in the mid-1600s by André Le Nôtre, who also created the gardens at Versailles and Vaux-le-Vicomte (see the Day Trips from Paris chapter). The Tuileries soon became the most fashionable spot in Paris for parading about in one's finery. The gardens are open daily from 7 am (7.30 am in winter) to between 7.30 and 9 pm, depending on the season.

The Voie Triomphale (also known as the **Grand Axe** or 'Great Axis'), the western continuation of the Tuileries' east-west axis, follows the Champs-Élysées to the Arc de Triomphe and, eventually, to the Grande Arche in the modern skyscraper district of La Défense.

Musée de l'Orangerie des Tuileries

The Orangerie Museum (Map 2; ☎ 01 42 97 48 16; metro Concorde), in the south-west corner of the Jardin des Tuileries at Place de la Concorde (1er), has important impressionist works, including a series of Monet's *Décorations des Nymphéas* (Water Lilies) and paintings by Cézanne, Matisse, Picasso, Renoir and Soutine. It's open daily, except Tuesday, from 9.45 am to 5.15 pm. Entrance costs 30FF (20FF for those aged 18 to 25); everyone pays 18FF on Sunday.

Jeu de Paume

The Galerie Nationale du Jeu de Paume (Map 2; ☎ 01 47 03 12 50; metro Concorde) is housed in a one-time *jeu de paume* (a court for playing real, or royal, tennis) built in 1861 during the reign of Napoleon III in the north-west corner of the Jardin des Tuileries. Once the home of a good part of France's national collection of impressionist works (now housed in the Musée d'Orsay), it reopened in 1992 as a gallery for innovative short-term exhibitions of contemporary art, from the last 20 or 30 years.

It's open Tuesday to Friday from noon to 7 pm (9.30 pm on Tuesday) and on weekends from 10 am to 7 pm. Admission is 38FF (28FF for people aged 13 to 18, students under 26 and people over 60). The Carte Musées is not valid here.

Place Vendôme

Eight-sided Place Vendôme (Map 2) and the arcaded and colonnaded buildings around it were built between 1687 and 1721. In March 1796, Napoleon married Josephine in the building at No 3. The Ministry of Justice has been at Nos 11-13 since 1815.

Today, the buildings around the square house the posh Hôtel Ritz (Map 2) and some of Paris' most fashionable and expensive boutiques, more of which can be found along nearby Rue de Castiglione, Rue Saint Honoré and Rue de la Paix.

The 43.5m-tall column in the centre of the square, **Colonne Vendôme**, consists of a stone core wrapped in a 160m-long bronze spiral made from 1250 Austrian and Russian cannons captured by Napoleon at the Battle of Austerlitz (1805). The bas-reliefs on the spiral depict Napoleon's victories of between 1805 and 1807. The statue on top, placed there in 1873, depicts Napoleon as a Roman emperor.

LES HALLES AREA

The huge pedestrian zone between the Centre Pompidou (1er) and the Forum des Halles is always filled with people, just as it was for the 850-odd years when the area served as Paris' main marketplace.

Forum des Halles

Les Halles, Paris' main wholesale food market, occupied the area just south of Église Saint Eustache from around the early 12th century until 1969, when it was moved out to the suburb of Rungis. In its place, Forum des Halles (Map 7; metro Les Halles or Châtelet-Les Halles) – a huge and aesthetically controversial underground shopping mall – was constructed in the high-tech, glass and chrome style in vogue in the early 1970s. It all looks a bit frayed 30 years on.

Around Forum des Halles

Atop Forum des Halles is a popular **park** where you can picnic, people-watch and sunbathe on the lawn while gazing at the flying buttresses of Église Saint Eustache. During the warmer months, street musicians, fire-eaters and other performers display their talents throughout the area, especially at **Square des Innocents**, whose centre is adorned by a multi-tiered Renaissance fountain, **Fontaine des Innocents** (1549; Map 7). The square and fountain are named after the Cimetière des Innocents, a cemetery on this site from which two million skeletons were disinterred and transferred to the Catacombes (Map 1) in the 14e in the 1780s.

Église Saint Eustache

This majestic church (Map 7; metro Les Halles), one of the most attractive in Paris, is just north of the grassy area on top of Forum des Halles. Constructed between 1532 and 1640, its general design is Gothic. The classical west façade was added in the mid-18th century.

Inside, there's some exceptional Flamboyant Gothic archwork holding up the ceiling of the chancel, though most of the interior ornamentation is Renaissance and classical, as you can see from the cornices and Corinthian columns. The gargantuan, 101 stop, 8000 pipe organ above the west entrance is used for concerts, long a tradition here. The church is open Monday to Saturday from 9 am to 7 pm (8 pm in summer); Sunday from 9 am to 12.30 pm and 2.30 to 7 pm (8 pm in summer).

La Samaritaine Rooftop Terrace

For an amazing 360° panoramic view of central Paris, head to the roof of building No 2 of La Samaritaine department store (Map 7; ☎ 01 40 41 20 20; metro Pont Neuf) on Rue de la Monnaie (1er), just north of Pont Neuf. The 11th floor lookout and its viewpoint indicator are open Monday to Saturday from 9.30 am to 7 pm (10 pm on Thursday).

Centre Pompidou

The Centre Georges Pompidou (Maps 5 & 8; ☎ 01 44 78 12 33; www.cnac-gp.fr; Minitel 3615 BEAUBOURG; metro Rambuteau), also known as the Centre Beaubourg, is dedicated to displaying and promoting modern and contemporary art. Unfortunately, the centre is undergoing massive renovations that will not be completed until late 1999, though temporary exhibition spaces have been set up.

Orientation & Tickets The Tipi (teepee; ☎ 01 44 78 14 63) set up in Place Georges Pompidou (the plaza to the west) has multimedia information on the centre and its activities as well as updates on the works in progress. It is open daily, except Tuesday, from 12.30 pm (2 pm on weekends) to 6 pm. Entry is free.

Many of the 30,000-plus works of the **Musée National d'Art Moderne (MNAM)** here, France's national collection of 20th century art, have been loaned to other museums in France and abroad, but one-person shows (eg Bruce Nauman, Max Ernst, David Hockney) continue at the **Galerie Sud**, on the centre's southern side on Rue Saint Merri. The museum bookshop and gift shop (open to 8 pm) have also been moved here.

On the plaza just north of the Tipi is the **Atelier Brancusi**, the reconstructed studio of Romanian-born sculptor Constantin Brancusi (1876-1957). It contains almost 140 examples of his work as well as drawings, paintings and glass photographic plates. Galeri Sud and the Atelier Brancusi are open daily, except Tuesday, from noon (10 am at the weekend) to 10 pm. Admission to the atelier is 20FF; to both the atelier and Galerie Sud it's 30FF (20FF reduced price).

Around the Centre Pompidou

Place Georges Pompidou This plaza on the west side of the centre and the nearby pedestrianised streets attract buskers, street artists, musicians, jugglers, mime artists and, so Parisians complain, pickpockets and drug dealers. The fanciful **mechanical fountains** (Map 8) of skeletons, dragons, G-clefs and a big pair of ruby-red lips, at Place Igor Stravinsky, on the centre's south side, were created by Jean Tinguely and Niki de Saint-Phalle. They are a delight.

Le Défenseur du Temps (Defender of Time; Map 8), a mechanical clock (1979), whose protagonist does hourly battle from 9 am to 10 pm with the elements (air, water and earth in the form of a phoenix, crab and dragon), is a block north of the Centre Pompidou along Rue Brantôme (3e), in a modern development known as Quartier de l'Horloge. Particularly lively combat takes place at noon and 6 and 10 pm when our hero is attacked by all three 'villains'.

Tour Saint Jacques

The 52m Flamboyant Gothic Tower of Saint James (4e; Maps 6 & 8) is all that remains of the Église Saint Jacques la Boucherie, built by the powerful butchers' guild in 1523. It is not open to the public.

Hôtel de Ville

Paris' city hall (Maps 5 & 8; ☎ 01 42 76 40 40; metro Hôtel de Ville) was rebuilt in the neo-Renaissance style between 1874 and 1882 after having been gutted during the Paris Commune (1871). The ornate façade is decorated with 108 statues of noteworthy Parisians. Free guided tours (☎ 01 42 76 50 49 for reservations) of the interior are held in French on the first Monday of the month at 10.30 am, except on public holidays and during official functions. The visitors entrance is at 29 Rue de Rivoli (4e), where there's a hall used for temporary exhibitions (open Monday to Saturday from 9.30 am to 6 pm).

The Hôtel de Ville faces the majestic **Place de l'Hôtel de Ville**, used since the Middle Ages to stage many of Paris' celebrations, rebellions, book burnings and public executions.

MARAIS

The Marais (literally, 'marsh'; 4e and 3e), the area of the Right Bank directly north of Île Saint Louis, was in fact a swamp until the 13th century when it was converted to agricultural use. In the early 1600s, Henri IV built Place des Vosges, turning the area into Paris' most fashionable residential district and attracting wealthy aristocrats who then erected luxurious but subtle *hôtels particuliers* (private mansions). When the aristocracy moved out of Paris to Versailles and Faubourg Saint Germain (7e) during the late 17th and 18th centuries, the Marais and its townhouses passed into the hands of ordinary Parisians. The 110 hectare area was given a major face-lift in the late 1960s and 70s.

Today, the Marais is one of the few neighbourhoods of Paris most of its pre-Revolutionary architecture; indeed the house at 3 Rue Volta (3e), built in 1292, is thought to be the oldest in the city. In recent years the area has become trendy, but it's still home to a long-established Jewish community and is the centre of Paris' gay life.

Place des Vosges

Place des Vosges (4e; Map 8; metro Bastille or Chemin Vert), inaugurated in 1612 as Place Royale, is a square ensemble of 36 symmetrical houses with ground floor arcades, steep slate roofs and large dormer windows. Only the earliest houses were built of brick: to save time, the rest were given timber frames and faced with plaster, which was later painted to resemble brick.

Today, the arcades around Place des Vosges are occupied by upmarket art galleries, pricey antique shops and elegant places to sip tea.

The much revered author Victor Hugo lived at 6 Place des Vosges (3e) from 1832 to 1848, moving here just after the success of *Notre Dame de Paris* (The Hunchback of Notre Dame). **Maison de Victor Hugo** (Map 8; ☎ 01 42 72 10 16; metro Saint Paul or Chemin Vert) is now a municipal museum, and is open daily, except Monday and holidays, from 10 am to 5.40 pm. The entry fee is 27FF (19FF for students, free for under 18s).

Squares & Courtyards

RICHARD NEBESKÝ

Men playing boules, Les Halles.

Postcard visions of Paris are often constructed around pretty little squares, arrayed with café tables where happy imbibers quaff wine in the spring sunshine. Try the Place du Marché Sainte Catherine (4e; Map 8; metro Saint Paul), in the colourful Marais district, for a perfect example of that sort of square. Place des Vosges (4e; Map 8; metro Bastille) is only a few minutes stroll away if you want a more formal version of the Paris *place*. And while you're in the Marais, search out the intricate courtyards of the Village Saint Paul, just off antique-shop-studded Rue Saint Paul (Map 8; metro Saint Paul), or the two beautifully decorated late Renaissance-style courtyards at the nearby Hôtel de Sully, a lovely 17th century aristocratic mansion at 62 Rue Saint Antoine (4e). On the Left Bank, Place de la Contrescarpe (5e; Map 5; metro Cardinal Lemoine) is a lively and picturesque little roundabout surrounded by cafés, shops and students. Joyce and Ernest were once locals (there's a 'Hemingway lived here from 1922 to 1923' sign just a few steps away at 74 Rue du Cardinal Lemoine). Once upon a time this area was just outside the city walls, and there are large chunks of medieval city walls off Rue du Cardinal Lemoine and Rue Clovis.

Hôtel de Sully

While in the vicinity of Place des Vosges, it's well worth ducking into the Hôtel de Sully (Map 8; metro Saint Paul), a superb, early 17th century aristocratic mansion at 62 Rue Saint Antoine (4e) that is now home to the Caisse Nationale des Monuments Historiques et des Sites (responsible for maintaining many of France's historical monuments). The two beautifully decorated late Renaissance-style courtyards are adorned with bas-reliefs of the seasons and the elements. Photographic exhibitions take place at the Hôtel de Sully (☎ 01 42 74 47 75) from Tuesday to Sunday from 10 am to 10.30 pm.

Musée Carnavalet

Also known as the Musée de l'Histoire de Paris (Map 8; ☎ 01 42 72 21 13; metro Saint Paul or Chemin Vert), 23 Rue de Sévigné (3e), this museum of Parisian history is housed in two hôtels particuliers: the mid-16th century, Renaissance-style Hôtel Carnavalet, once home to the late 17th century writer Madame de Sévigné, and the late 17th century Hôtel Le Peletier de Saint Fargeau. The artefacts on display chart the history of Paris from the Gallo-Roman period to the 20th century. The museum has the country's most important collection of documents, paintings and other objects from the French Revolution. It also has *in situ* Fouquet's Art Nouveau jewellery shop from the Rue Royale and Marcel Proust's cork-lined bedroom from his apartment on Blvd Haussmann.

The museum is open daily (except on Monday and public holidays) from 10 am to 5.40 pm; from 11.50 am for the 19th and 20th century rooms. Entrance costs 27FF (14.50FF reduced price).

Musée Picasso

The Picasso Museum (Map 8; ☎ 01 42 71 25 21; metro Saint Paul or Chemin Vert), 5 Rue de Thorigny (3e), housed in the mid-17th century Hôtel Salé, is one of Paris' best loved art museums. Displays include more than 3500 of Picasso's engravings, paintings, ceramic works, drawings and an unparalleled collection of sculptures. You can also see part of Picasso's personal art collection, which includes works by Braque, Cézanne, Matisse and Degas. The museum is open daily, except Tuesday, from 9.30 am to 6 pm (5.30 pm from October to March); ticket sales end 45 minutes before closing. The entry fee is 30FF (20FF reduced price and on Sunday for everyone).

Musée de la Serrure

The Lock Museum (Map 8; ☎ 01 42 77 79 62; metro Saint Paul or Chemin Vert), 1 Rue de la Perle (3e), also known as the Musée Bricard, showcases a fine collection of locks, keys and door knockers. One lock, made around 1780, traps your hand in the jaws of a bronze lion if you try to use the wrong key. Another, created in the 19th century, shoots anyone who inserts an incorrect key. The museum is open from 10 am to noon and 2 to 5 pm (closed on weekends, holidays, Monday morning and in August). Entrance costs 30FF (15FF for students and seniors, free for under 18s).

Musée Cognacq-Jay

The Musée Cognacq-Jay (Map 8; ☎ 01 40 27 07 21; metro Saint Paul), 8 Rue Elzévir (3e), brings together oil paintings, pastels, sculpture, *objets d'art*, jewellery, porcelain and furniture from the 18th century. It is open from 10 am to 5.40 pm (closed Monday and holidays). Entry costs 17FF (9FF if you're aged 18 to 25; free for those under 18).

Maison Européenne de la Photographie

The Maison Européenne de la Photographie (Map 8; ☎ 01 44 78 75 00; metro Saint Paul or Pont Marie), in an 18th century hôtel particulier at 5-7 Rue de Fourcy (4e), has permanent and temporary exhibits on the history of photography with particular connection to France. The museum is open Wednesday to Sunday from 11 am to 8 pm and entry is 30FF (15FF for those under 26 or over 60 and for everyone on Wednesday after 5 pm).

Archives Nationales

France's National Archives (Map 8; ☎ 01 40 27 60 96; metro Rambuteau) are based in the impressive, early 18th century **Hôtel de Soubise** at 60 Rue des Francs Bourgeois (3e). The complex also contains the **Musée de l'Histoire de France**, where you can view documents dating from the Middle Ages. The ceiling and walls of the early 18th century interior are extravagantly painted and gilded in the rococo style. The museum is open weekdays, except Tuesday, from noon to 5.45 pm and on weekends from 1.45 pm. Entrance costs 15FF (10FF for teachers and people under 25 or over 60).

Jewish Neighbourhood

When renovation of the Marais began in the 1960s the area around **Rue des Rosiers** and **Rue des Écouffes**, known as the Pletzl (Map 8; metro Saint Paul) and long home to a poor but vibrant Jewish community, was pretty run-down. Now expensive and trendy boutiques all coexist with Jewish bookshops and *cacher* (kosher) grocery shops, butcher shops and restaurants. The area is virtually comatose on the Sabbath (Saturday).

The so-called **Guimard synagogue** (1914), 10 Rue Pavée (Map 8), is renowned for its Art Nouveau architecture, which is the work of Hector Guimard, designer of the famous metro entrances (see the boxed text 'Art in the Metro'). The interior is closed to the public.

Mémorial du Martyr Juif Inconnu

The Memorial to the Unknown Jewish Martyr (Map 8; ☎ 01 42 77 44 72; metro

Pont Marie or Saint Paul), 17 Rue Geoffroy l'Asnier (4e), established in 1956, includes a memorial to the victims of the Holocaust, various temporary exhibits and small permanent exhibits on the 1st, 2nd and 3rd floors. It is open daily, except Saturday and on Jewish holidays, from 10 am to 1 pm and 2 to 6 pm (4.30 or 5 pm on Friday). Entry to the crypt and museum is 15FF.

BASTILLE AREA

After years as a run-down immigrant neighbourhood notorious for its high crime rate, the Bastille area, which encompasses mostly the 11e and 12e but also the easternmost part of the 4e, has undergone a fair degree of gentrification, in large part because of the Opéra Bastille, which opened in 1989. The area east of Place de la Bastille retains its lively atmosphere and ethnic flair.

Bastille

The Bastille, built during the 14th century as a fortified royal residence, is the most famous monument in Paris that doesn't exist: the infamous prison – the quintessential symbol of monarchic despotism – was demolished shortly after a mob stormed it on 14 July 1789 and all seven prisoners were freed. The site where it once stood, Place de la Bastille (12e), is now a very busy traffic roundabout.

In the centre of Place de la Bastille is the 52m **Colonne de Juillet** (July Column; Map 5; metro Bastille), whose shaft of greenish bronze is topped by a gilded and winged figure of Liberty. It was erected in 1833 as a memorial to the people killed in the street battles that accompanied the July Revolution of 1830; they are buried in vaults under the column.

Opéra Bastille

Paris' giant 'second' opera house (Map 5; ☎ 01 44 73 13 99 or ☎ 08 36 69 78 68 for inquiries; metro Bastille) at 2-6 Place de la Bastille (12e), designed by the Canadian Carlos Ott, was inaugurated on 14 July 1989, the 200th anniversary of the storming of the Bastille. For details on the 1¼ hour guided tours (50FF for adults, 30FF for children under 16, students and seniors) of the building, which take place on most afternoons, call ☎ 01 40 01 19 70. See the Entertainment section later in this chapter for more detailed information on tickets to performances.

Viaduc des Arts

The arches beneath this railway viaduct along Ave Daumesnil (12e), which went out of service in 1969, have been transformed into a showcase for trendy designers and artisans. The top of the viaduct is a leafy promenade called the **Promenade Plantée** (Map 5) and offers excellent views of the surrounding area. It's open from 8 am (9 am on weekends) to 5.30 pm (9.30 pm from May to August).

ÎLE DE LA CITÉ

The site of the first settlement around the 3rd century BC and later the centre of the Roman town of Lutetia (Lutèce in French), the Île de la Cité (1er and 4e) remained the centre of royal and ecclesiastical power even after the city spread to both banks of the Seine during the Middle Ages. The middle part of the island was demolished and rebuilt during Baron Haussmann's great urban renewal scheme of the late 19th century.

Notre Dame

Notre Dame (Map 8; ☎ 01 42 34 56 10; metro Cité), Paris' cathedral, is one of the most magnificent achievements of Gothic architecture ever built, and certainly to survive in such condition. Built on a site occupied by earlier churches – and, some two millennia ago, a Gallo-Roman temple – it was begun in 1163 and completed around 1345. Viollet-le-Duc carried out extensive renovations in the 19th century. The interior is 130m long, 48m wide and 35m high, and can accommodate over 6000 worshippers. Some 12 million people visit the cathedral each year.

The Hunchback of Notre Dame

The story of the Hunchback of Notre Dame as told by Victor Hugo in his romantic novel *Notre Dame de Paris* – and not the silly Disney cartoon version with the happy ending – goes something like this ...

It's 15th century Paris during the reign of Louis XI. The Gypsy girl Esmeralda is in love with Captain Phoebus, but the evil and jealous archdeacon, Claude Frollo, denounces her as a witch. The hunchbacked bell ringer, Quasimodo, is devoted to Esmeralda and saves her (for a while) when she seeks protection from the mob in the belfry of Notre Dame. We won't give the ending away but suffice it to say that everyone comes to a tragic end – including Captain Phoebus, who gets married.

Was *Notre Dame de Paris*, which has no basis in historical fact except for the setting, just a good story or a commentary on the times? Hugo began the book during the reign of the unpopular and reactionary Charles X, who, with the guidance of his chief minister, had abolished freedom of the press and dissolved parliament. The ascent of Louis-Philippe, a bourgeois king with liberal leanings, in the July Revolution of 1830 took place shortly before the book was published. The novel can thus be seen as a condemnation of absolutism (ie of Charles X) and of a society that allows the likes of people like Frollo and Phoebus to heap scorn and misery on unfortunate characters like Esmeralda and Quasimodo.

But there is more to it than that. Hugo's evocation of the colourful and intense life of the late 15th century is seen by some as a plea for the preservation of Gothic Paris and its decaying architecture. Indeed, the condition of Notre Dame in the early 19th century was so bad that artists, politicians and writers, including Hugo, beseeched Louis-Philippe to rectify it. Hugo was appointed to the new Commission for Monuments and the Arts, where he sat for 10 years. In 1845 the Gothic revivalist architect Viollet-Le-Duc began his renovation of Notre Dame, in which he added the steeple and gargoyles (among other things). The work continued for almost two decades.

If these were the ideals Hugo was advocating in *Notre Dame de Paris*, they were widely held views because the novel was very successful and gained him wider fame than any of his previous work.

SIMON BRACKEN

Notre Dame is known for its sublime balance, although if you look closely you'll see all sorts of minor asymmetrical elements introduced to avoid monotony, in accordance with standard Gothic practice. These include the slightly different shapes of each of the three main entrances. One of the best views of Notre Dame is from **Square Jean XXIII**, the lovely little park behind the cathedral, where you can see the mass of ornate **flying buttresses** that encircle the chancel and support its walls and roof.

Inside, exceptional features include three spectacular **rose windows**, the most renowned of which is the window over the west façade, which is 10m across, and that on the north side of the transept, which has remained virtually unchanged since the 13th century. The 7800 pipe organ was restored between 1990 and 1992.

Notre Dame is open daily from 8 am to 6.45 pm (7.45 pm on weekends). The **trésor** (treasury) at the back of the cathedral, which contains sacred liturgical objects and works of art (entry 15FF, 10FF for students), is open Monday to Saturday from 9.30 am to 6.30 pm. There are free **guided tours** of the cathedral in English on Wednesday and Thursday at noon and on Saturday at 2.30 pm (daily in August).

Distances from Paris throughout France are measured from **Place du Parvis Notre Dame** (Map 6), the square in front of Notre Dame. A bronze star, set in the pavement across the street from the cathedral's main entrance, marks the exact location of *'point zéro des routes de France'*.

North Tower The entrance to Notre Dame's north tower (Map 8; ☎ 01 43 29 50 40) is on Rue du Cloître Notre Dame – to the right and around the corner as you walk out of the main doorway. From the base, a long, spiral climb up 238 steps gets you to the top of the **west façade**, from where you can view many of the cathedral's most frightening gargoyles – not to mention a good part of Paris. Tickets are on sale daily from 9.30 am to 6.45 pm (10 am to 4.45 pm from October to March) and cost 32FF (21FF for those aged 12 to 25, free for children under 12).

Notre Dame's Kestrels

Birdwatchers estimate that about 40 pairs of kestrels (*Falcon tinnunculus*), known as sparrow hawks in the USA and windhovers in the UK, currently nest in Paris, preferring tall old structures like the towers at Notre Dame. Four or five pairs of kestrels regularly breed in cavities high up in the cathedral, and once a year, usually in late June, local ornithologists set up a public kestrel-watching station behind the cathedral, with telescopes and even a camera transmitting close-up pictures of one of the kestrels' nesting sites. The birds form their partnerships in February, eggs are laid in April, the kestrel chicks hatch in May and are ready to depart by early July. In late June, birdwatchers may spot the adult kestrels returning to their young with a tasty mouse or sparrow. Unfortunately, Paris' pigeons – the dirty flying rats that they are – are too large for a kestrel chick to handle!

Crypte Archéologique

Under the square in front of Notre Dame, the Archaeological Crypt (Map 6; ☎ 01 43 29 83 51; metro Cité) displays *in situ* the remains of structures from the Gallo-Roman and later periods. It is open daily from 10 am to 5 pm (6 pm from April to September); ticket sales end 30 minutes before closing. Fees are the same as for the cathedral's north tower. A combination ticket valid for both the crypt and the tower costs 40FF.

Sainte Chapelle

The Sainte Chapelle (Map 6; ☎ 01 53 73 78 51; metro Cité), whose upper chapel is illuminated by a veritable curtain of luminous 13th century **stained glass** (the oldest and finest in Paris), is inside the **Palais de Justice** (Law Courts), on the west side of Blvd du Palais (1er). Consecrated in 1248, Sainte Chapelle was built in only 33 months to house what was believed to be Jesus' crown of thorns, and other relics purchased by King Louis IX (Saint Louis) earlier in the 13th century.

Sainte Chapelle is open daily from 9.30 or 10 am to 5 pm (6.30 pm from April to September); ticket sales end 30 minutes before closing. Entry costs 32FF (21FF for people aged 12 to 25). A ticket valid for both Sainte Chapelle and the nearby Conciergerie costs 50FF. The visitors entrance is directly opposite 7 Blvd du Palais. Be prepared for airport-type security, with x-ray machines, bag searches etc.

Conciergerie

The Conciergerie (Map 6; ☎ 01 53 73 78 50; metro Cité), whose entrance is at 1 Quai de l'Horloge, was a luxurious royal palace when it was built in the 14th century, but it later lost favour with the kings of France and was turned into a prison and torture chamber. During the Reign of Terror (1793-94), the Conciergerie was used to incarcerate alleged enemies of the Revolution before they were brought before the Revolutionary Tribunal, which met next door in the Palais de Justice. Among the 2600 prisoners held here before being sent in tumbrels (a farm cart) to the guillotine were Queen Marie-Antoinette and, as the Revolution began to turn on its own, the Revolutionary radicals Danton, Robespierre and, finally, the judges of the tribunal themselves.

The huge Gothic **Salle des Gens d'Armes** (Cavalrymen's Hall) dates from the 14th century and is a fine example of the Rayonnant Gothic style. It is the largest surviving medieval hall in Europe. **Tour de l'Horloge**, the tower on the corner of Blvd du Palais and Quai de l'Horloge, has held a public clock aloft since 1370. Opening hours and entry fees at the Conciergerie are the same as those at Sainte Chapelle; a combination ticket to both costs 50FF.

Flower Market

The Île de la Cité's famous **marché aux fleurs** (Map 6; metro Cité), Paris' oldest, has been at Place Louis Lépine, the square just north of the Préfecture de Police, since 1808. It is open Monday to Saturday (and when holidays fall on Sunday) from 8 am to about 7 pm.

On Sunday, the marché aux fleurs is transformed into a **marché aux oiseaux** (bird market) open from 9 am to 7 pm.

Mémorial des Martyrs de la Déportation

At the south-eastern tip of the Île de la Cité, behind Notre Dame, is the Deportation Memorial (Map 8), erected in 1962. It's a haunting monument to the 200,000 residents of France – including 76,000 Jews – who were killed in Nazi concentration camps. A single barred 'window' separates the bleak, rough concrete courtyard from the waters of the Seine. The Tomb of the Unknown Deportee is flanked by 200,000 bits of back-lit glass. The memorial is open daily from 10 am to noon and 2 to 5 pm (7 pm from April to September).

Pont Neuf

The now sparkling-white, stone spans of Paris' oldest bridge, Pont Neuf (literally, 'New Bridge'; Map 6), link the western end of the Île de la Cité with both banks of the Seine. Begun in 1578, Pont Neuf was completed in 1607, when the king inaugurated it by crossing the bridge on a white stallion; the occasion is commemorated by an equestrian **statue of Henri IV**. The arches are decorated with humorous and grotesque figures of street dentists, pickpockets, loiterers and the like.

ÎLE SAINT LOUIS

The smaller of the Seine's two islands, the Île Saint Louis (4e; Map 8) is just downstream from the Île de la Cité. It was actually two uninhabited islands – sometimes used for duels – until the early 17th century, when a building contractor and two financiers worked out a deal with

Louis XIII to create one island out of the two and build two stone bridges to the mainland. In exchange they would receive the right to subdivide and sell the newly created real estate. This they did with great success, and between 1613 and 1664 the entire island was covered with fine new houses.

Today, the island's 17th century, grey-stone houses and the small-town shops that line the streets and quays impart a village-like, provincial calm. Rue Saint Louis en l'Île (Map 8) is home to a number of upmarket art galleries. The area around **Pont Saint Louis**, the bridge linking the island with the Île de la Cité, and **Pont Louis-Philippe**, the bridge to the Marais, is one of the most romantic spots in all of Paris.

JARDIN DES PLANTES AREA

This very picturesque area is just east of the Latin Quarter (5e).

Jardin des Plantes

Paris' botanic gardens (Map 5; ☎ 01 40 79 30 00; metro Gare d'Austerlitz or Jussieu), 57 Rue Cuvier (5e), was founded in 1626 as a medicinal herb garden for Louis XIII. The first greenhouse, constructed in 1714, was home to a coffee tree whose offspring helped establish coffee production in South America. The gardens are open daily from 7.30 am until some time between 5.30 pm (in the dead of winter) and 8 pm (in summer).

The **Serres Tropicales** (Tropical Greenhouses; Map 5), also known as the Jardin d'Hiver (Winter Garden), are open on weekdays, except Tuesday, from 1 to 5 pm; weekend hours are 10 am to 5 pm (6 pm from April to September). Admission costs 15FF (10FF for students aged 16 to 25 and people over 60, and 5FF for children). The **Jardin Alpin** (Alpine Garden; Map 5) and the gardens of the **École de Botanique** (Botanical School; Map 5) are both free, and are open on Monday and from Wednesday to Friday from April to September.

Parks & Gardens

Though upwards of 90,000 trees (mostly plane and chestnut) line the streets of Paris, at times the city can feel excessively built-up. You don't have to escape all the way to the Bois de Boulogne (16e; Map 1; metro Porte Dauphine), or the Bois de Vincennes (12e; Map 1; metro Porte Dorée), the city's 'green lungs' to the west and south-east, to get a bit of grass under your feet, though. The Jardin du Luxembourg (6e; Map 6; metro Luxembourg) and Jardin des Tuileries (1er; Map 2; metro Tuileries), while small, formal affairs, can give you the illusion of countryside; and the Parc des Buttes-Chaumont (19e; Map 1; metro Buttes-Chaumont), and the Parc de Monceau (8e; Map 2; metro Monceau), are fully fledged green and open spaces.

In recent years the city government has spent millions of francs transforming vacant lots and derelict industrial land into new parks. Some of the better ones are Parc de la Villette (19e; Map 1; metro Porte de la Villette); Parc de Bercy (12e; Map 1; metro Bercy); Jardin de l'Atlantique, near Gare Montparnasse (15e; Map 4; metro Montparnasse Bienvenüe); and the Promenade Plantée, the 'planted promenade' above the Viaduc des Arts, a disused railway viaduct along Ave Daumesnil (12e; Map 5; metro Gare de Lyon or Daumesnil) that has been transformed into a showcase for trendy designers and artisans.

SIMON BRACKEN

Zoo The northern section of the Jardin des Plantes is taken up by the **Ménagerie** (Map 5; ☎ 01 40 79 37 94; metro Jussieu or Gare d'Austerlitz), a medium-sized zoo founded in 1794. During the Prussian siege of Paris in 1870, most of the animals were eaten by starving Parisians. It is open daily from 9 am to 5 pm (6 pm from April to September, when closing time is 6.30 pm on Sunday and holidays). Entrance costs 30FF (20FF for students aged 16 to 25 and people over 60, and 10FF for children).

Musée National d'Histoire Naturelle

The National Museum of Natural History (☎ 01 40 79 30 00; metro Censier Daubenton or Gare d'Austerlitz), created by a decree of the Convention in 1793, was the site of important scientific research in the 19th century. It is in four buildings along the southern edge of the Jardin des Plantes.

The five level **Grande Galerie de l'Évolution** (Map 5; ☎ 01 40 79 39 39), 36 Rue Geoffroy Saint Hilaire, has some imaginative exhibits on evolution and humankind's effect on the world's ecosystem; the African parade, as Noah would have lined up his cargo for the ark, is quite something. The Salle des Espèces Menacées et des Espèces Disparues, on level 2, displays extremely rare specimens of endangered and extinct species of animals. The Salles de Découverte (Discovery Rooms) house interactive exhibits for kids. They are all open daily, except Tuesday, from 10 am to 6 pm (10 pm on Thursday). Entry costs 40FF (30FF and 10FF reduced prices).

The **Galerie de Minéralogie et Paléobotanie** (Map 5; 30FF, reduced prices 20FF and 10FF), which covers mineralogy and paleobotany (ie fossilised plants), has an amazing exhibit of giant natural crystals and a basement display of precious objects made from minerals. Out the front there's a rose garden. The **Galerie d'Anatomie Comparée et de Paléontologie** (Map 5; 30FF; reduced prices 20FF and 10FF) has displays on comparative anatomy and paleontology. Both are open daily, except Tuesday and holidays, from 10 am to 5 pm (6 pm on weekends). The **Galerie d'Entomologie** (Map 5; 15FF, reduced prices 10FF and 5FF) specialises in the study of insects. It's open Monday and Wednesday to Friday from 1 to 5 pm; weekends from 10 am to 6 pm.

Mosquée de Paris

Paris' central mosque (Map 5; ☎ 01 45 35 97 33; metro Place Monge), whose entrance is at Place du Puits de l'Ermite (next to the square minaret), was built between 1922 and 1926 in an ornate Hispano-Moorish style. Shoes must be removed at the entrance to the prayer hall. Guided tours (15FF, 10FF for children and students) take place daily, except Friday, from 9 am to noon and 2 to 6 pm. Visitors must be modestly and respectfully dressed.

The mosque complex includes a North African-style *salon de thé*, a restaurant (☎ 01 43 31 38 20) with excellent couscous and *tajines* (60 to 110FF) and a **hammam** (bathhouse; ☎ 01 43 31 18 14). The entrances to both the restaurant and hammam are at 39 Rue Geoffroy Saint Hilaire (across from the Grande Galerie de l'Évolution). The hammam (85FF) is open to men on Tuesday and Sunday only; on other days it is reserved for women.

Institut du Monde Arabe

The Arab World Institute (Map 5; ☎ 01 40 51 38 38; metro Cardinal Lemoine or Jussieu), 1 Rue des Fossés Saint Bernard (5e), set up by France and 20 Arab countries to promote cultural contacts between the Arab world and the west, is housed in a highly praised building (1987) that successfully mixes modern and traditional Arab and western elements. The *mushrabiyah* (thousands of very costly aperture-like mechanisms built into the glass walls) were inspired by the traditional latticed wooden windows that let you see out without being seen, and are operated by electric motors regulating the amounts of light and heat that reach the interior of the building.

The 7th floor **museum** displays 9th to 19th century art and crafts from the Muslim world, as well as astrolabes and instruments from other fields of scientific endeavour in which Arab technology once led the world. It is open Tuesday to Sunday from 10 am to 6 pm. Tickets cost 25FF (20FF for students, people under 25 and seniors). Temporary exhibitions (enter from Quai Saint Bernard) involve a separate fee.

Arènes de Lutèce

This heavily reconstructed, 2nd century AD Roman amphitheatre (Map 5; metro Place Monge), discovered in 1869, could once seat around 10,000 people for gladiatorial combats and other events. There are entrances at 49 Rue Monge and opposite 7 Rue de Navarre. Entry is free.

LATIN QUARTER

Known as the Quartier Latin (5e) because all communication between students and professors here took place in Latin until the Revolution, this area has been the centre of Parisian higher education since the Middle Ages. It has become increasingly touristy in recent years, however, and its near monopoly on the city's academic life has waned as students have moved to other campuses, especially since 1968 student protests. The Latin Quarter does have a large population of students and academics affiliated with the Sorbonne (now part of the Université de Paris system), the Collège de France, the École Normale Supérieure (all Map 6) and other institutions of higher learning.

Musée National du Moyen Âge

The Museum of the Middle Ages (Map 6; ☎ 01 53 73 78 00; metro Cluny-La Sorbonne), also known as the Musée de Cluny, is housed in two structures: the frigidarium and other remains of **Gallo-Roman baths** dating from around 200 AD, and the late 15th century **Hôtel de Cluny**, considered the finest example of medieval civil architecture in Paris. The spectacular displays include statuary, illuminated manuscripts, arms, furnishings and objects made of gold, ivory and enamel. A series of late 15th century tapestries from the southern Netherlands known as *La Dame à la Licorne* (Lady and the Unicorn) is hung in a round room on the 1st floor.

The museum, whose entrance is at 6 Place Paul Painlevé (5e), is open from 9.15 am to 5.45 pm (closed Tuesday). The entrance fee is 30FF (20FF for people aged 18 to 25, on Sunday for everyone over 18).

Sorbonne

Paris' most renowned university, the Sorbonne (Map 6) was founded in 1253 by Robert de Sorbon, confessor of King Louis IX, as a college for 16 poor theology students. Closed in 1792 by the Revolutionary government after operating for centuries as France's premier theological centre, it was reopened under Napoleon. Today, the Sorbonne's main complex (bounded by Rue de la Sorbonne, Rue des Écoles, Rue Saint Jacques and Rue Cujas) and other buildings in the vicinity house most of the 13 autonomous universities that were created when the University of Paris was reorganised following the violent student protests of 1968.

Place de la Sorbonne links Blvd Saint Michel with **Chapelle de la Sorbonne** (Map 6), the university's gold-domed church built between 1635 and 1642. The interior is open only when there are special exhibitions on.

Panthéon

The domed landmark now known as the Panthéon (Map 6; ☎ 01 43 54 34 51; metro Luxembourg) was commissioned around 1750 as an abbey church, but because of financial problems wasn't completed until 1789. Two years later, the Constituent Assembly converted it into a secular mausoleum for the *grands hommes de l'époque de la liberté française* (great men of the era of French liberty), removing all Christian symbols and references. After another stint as a church, the Panthéon once again became a secular necropolis. The Panthéon's ornate marble interior is gloomy in the extreme and much of it will be closed – including the colonnaded dome – for a massive renovation.

Permanent residents of the Panthéon's crypt include Voltaire, Louis Braille, Jean-Jacques Rousseau, Victor Hugo, Émile Zola,

Jean Moulin and dual Nobel Prize-winner Marie Curie, who was reburied here (along with her husband, Pierre) in 1995.

The Panthéon is open daily April to September from 9.30 am to 6.30 pm, and October to March from 10 am to 6.15 pm; ticket sales end 45 minutes before closing time. Tickets cost 32FF (21FF for those aged 12 to 25, and free for children under 12).

Église Saint Étienne du Mont

This lovely church (Map 6; metro Cardinal Lemoine) at Place de l'Abbé Basset (behind the Panthéon) was built between 1492 and 1626. The most exceptional feature of the Gothic interior is its graceful **rood screen** (1535) separating the chancel from the nave. Also of interest are the carved **wooden pulpit** (1650), held aloft by a figure of Samson, and the 16th and 17th century **stained glass**. Just inside the entrance, a plaque in the floor marks the spot where a defrocked priest, armed with a knife, murdered an archbishop in 1857.

6E ARRONDISSEMENT

Centuries ago, Église Saint Germain des Prés (Map 6) and its affiliated abbey owned most of the 6e and 7e arrondissements. The neighbourhood around the church began to be built up in the late 1600s, and these days – under the name Saint Germain des Prés – it is celebrated for its 19th century charm. Cafés such as Les Deux Magots and Café de Flore (see Pubs, Bars & Cafés – 6e Arrondissement in the Entertainment section later in this chapter), were favourite hand-outs of post-war Left Bank intellectuals, and are the places where existentialism was born.

Jardin du Luxembourg

When the weather is warm – or even just slightly sunny – Parisians of all ages flock to the formal terraces and chestnut groves of the 25 hectare Luxembourg Gardens (Map 6; metro Luxembourg) to read, write, relax and sunbathe.

Activities for Children The Jardin du Luxembourg offers all of the delights of a Parisian childhood a century ago and is one of the best places in Paris to take kids. The atmosphere of bygone days is enhanced by the kepi-topped Senate guards.

At the Grand Bassin (the octagonal pond; Map 6), **model sailboats** – many old enough to have been sailed by today's grandparents back when they were in grammar school – can be rented on Wednesday, Saturday and Sunday (daily during school holiday periods, including July and August) from 2 pm until some time between 4.30 pm (in winter) and 7 pm (in summer).

About 200m south-west of the pond, at the pint-sized **Théâtre du Luxembourg** (Map 6; ☎ 01 43 26 46 47), visitors are treated to a complete theatre experience in miniature: in a hall filled with child-sized seats, **marionettes** put on shows whose antics can be enjoyed even if you don't understand French. The puppets put on one to five performances (23FF) on Wednesday, Saturday, Sunday and holidays, and daily during school vacation periods, at 2.30, 3.30 and 4.30 pm (3 and 4 pm on weekends).

Next to the Théâtre du Luxembourg, the modern **playground** – one half for kids up to age seven, the other half for children aged seven to 12 – costs 14FF per child (7.50FF for adults). Not far away, the vintage **swings** cost 7FF per child, as does the old-time **carousel**.

One hundred metres north of the theatre, kids weighing up to 35kg can ride Shetland ponies (13FF; carriage rides 10FF) daily unless it's raining, starting at 11 am (2 pm on Monday, Tuesday, Thursday and Saturday).

In the south-west corner of the gardens, you can visit the **ruches** (beehives; Map 6), established here in 1856, where you can take beekeeping courses (☎ 01 45 42 29 08). They are staffed all day on Wednesday and often on Saturday as well. There's a **fruit tree orchard** just south of the beehives.

Activities for Adults In the north-west corner of the Jardin du Luxembourg, just north of the tennis courts, **chess and card games** (Map 6) – often a dozen at a time – are held every afternoon of the year, rain or shine. BYOB (bring your own board).

On the north side of the Théâtre du Luxembourg, there are **basketball** and **volleyball courts** – you could try to join in a game. **Boules courts**, sometimes used by people doing t'ai chi in the morning, are just north of the beehives.

Palais du Luxembourg The Luxembourg Palace (Map 6), at the northern end of the Jardin du Luxembourg along Rue de Vaugirard, was built for Marie de Médicis (queen of France from 1600 to 1610) to assuage her longing for the Pitti Palace in Florence, where she spent her childhood. Just east of the palace is the Italianate **Fontaine des Médicis**, a long, ornate goldfish pond built around 1630. The palace has housed the Senate, the upper house of the French parliament, since 1958. There are tours of the interior (☎ 01 42 34 20 60 for information, ☎ 01 44 61 21 66 for reservations) on the first Sunday of each month at 10 am.

Statues & Sculptures

TONY WHEELER

Modern sculpture outside Église Saint Eustache at the Forum des Halles.

Paris is dotted with outdoor statuary and beautiful fountains, such as the romantic Fontaine des Médicis (Map 6; metro Luxembourg), which combines fountain, pond and statuary in one elegant group in the Jardin du Luxembourg. Like the Tuileries on the Right Bank, these gardens are dotted with sculptures and statuary. The Fontaine de l'Observatoire, at the southern point of the gardens (Map 6; metro Port Royal), is a favourite.

Not far away on foot, but on the other side of the universe in concept, is the very modern *Statue of Centaur* at the junction of Rue du Cherche Midi and Rue du Sèvres (Map 4; metro Saint Sulpice). A much loved modern piece of sculpture is the giant head, looking like it's just rolled away from an equally gigantic guillotine, beside Église Saint Eustache at the Forum des Halles (Map 7; metro Les Halles). Equally striking is Claes Oldenburg's huge *Buried Bicycle*, protruding from the grass in the Parc de la Villette (Map 1; metro Porte de la Villette).

It was the French who gave New York City its *Statue of Liberty*, so it's fitting that they kept a smaller one for Paris. It's right in the middle of the Seine, a short distance downstream from the Eiffel Tower (Map 4; metro Ave du President Kennedy or Maison de Radio France). The *Flame of Liberty*, a replica of the one atop the torch of the State of Liberty in New York placed in Place de l'Alma (Map 2; metro Alma Marceau) by US firms based in Paris in 1989 to honour the bicentennial of the French revolution, has become a memorial to Diana, Princess of Wales. She was killed in a car accident in the underpass below it in August 1997.

Musée du Luxembourg The Luxembourg Museum (Map 6; ☎ 01 42 34 25 94; metro Luxembourg), 19 Rue de Vaugirard (6e), opened at the turn of the century in the *orangerie* of the Palais du Luxembourg and was dedicated to presenting the work of artists still living. It now hosts temporary art exhibitions, often from different regions of France. It is open Tuesday to Sunday from 11 am to 6 pm (to 8 pm on Thursday). Entry is 31FF (21FF reduced price and for everyone on Tuesday).

Église Saint Sulpice

This church (Map 6; metro Saint Sulpice) lined inside with chapels, a block north of the Jardin du Luxembourg at Place Saint Sulpice, was built between 1646 and 1780 on the site of earlier churches dedicated to Saint Sulpicius, a 6th century archbishop of Bourges. The Italianate façade, designed by a Florentine architect, has two rows of superimposed columns and is topped by two towers. The neoclassical décor of the vast interior reflects the influence of the Counter-Reformation.

Place Saint Sulpice is adorned by a very energetic fountain, **Fontaine des Quatre Évêques** (1844; Map 6). Nearby streets are known for their *haute couture* (high fashion) houses (see the Shopping section later in this chapter).

Église Saint Germain des Prés

The Romanesque-style Church of Saint Germanus of the Fields (Map 6; metro Saint Germain des Prés), the oldest (though hardly the most interesting) church in Paris, was built in the 11th century on the site of a 6th century abbey. It has since been altered many times, but the bell tower over the west entrance has changed little since 1000, apart from the addition of the spire in the 19th century.

France's Merovingian kings were buried here during the 6th and 7th centuries, but their tombs disappeared during the Revolution. The interior is disfigured by truly appalling 19th century polychrome paintings and frescoes. The church, often used for concerts, is open daily from 8 am to 7 pm.

Musée National Eugène Delacroix

The Eugène Delacroix Museum (Map 6; ☎ 01 44 41 86 50; metro Mabillon or Saint Germain des Prés), just east of Église Saint Germain des Prés at 6 Place de Furstemberg (6e), was the artist's home and studio at the time of his death in 1863. It is open daily, except Tuesday, from 9.30 am to 5.30 pm (last entry at 4.30 pm). Tickets cost 22FF (15FF reduced price, and for all on Sunday).

Institut de France

The Institut de France was created in 1795 by bringing together five of France's academies of arts and sciences. The most famous of these is the **Académie Française**, founded in 1635, whose 40 members (known as the *Immortels*, ie Immortals) are charged with the Herculean task of safeguarding the purity of the French language. The first female Immortel (Marguerite Yourcenar) was admitted in 1980.

The domed building housing the Institut de France (Map 6; ☎ 01 44 41 44 41; metro Mabillon or Louvre-Rivoli), a masterpiece of French neoclassical architecture from the mid-17th century, is at 23 Quai de Conti, across the Seine from the eastern end of the Louvre.

The only part of the complex that can be visited without joining a tour is the **Bibliothèque Mazarine** (Mazarine Library; Map 6; ☎ 01 44 41 44 06), 25 Quai de Conti, the oldest public library in France (founded in 1643). You can visit the bust-lined, late 17th century reading room or consult the library's collection of 500,000 items on weekdays from 10 am to 6 pm (closed during the first half of August). Entry is free, but you must leave your ID at the office on the left-hand side of the entryway to secure a pass; a second form of ID is needed to gain access to the books.

Musée de la Monnaie

The Museum of Coins and Medals (Map 6; ☎ 01 40 46 55 35 or ☎ 01 34 51 93 53; metro Pont Neuf), 11 Quai de Conti (6e), just across Pont Neuf from Île de la Cité, traces the history of French coinage from antiquity to the present and as well as coins and medals includes presses and other minting equipment. It is open Tuesday to Friday from 11 am to 5.30 pm and from noon to 5.30 pm on weekends. The entry fee is 20FF (15FF for students and people over 60; free for under 16s and, on Sunday, for everyone).

The Hôtel des Monnaies, which houses the museum, became a royal mint during the 18th century and is still used by the Ministry of Finance to produce commemorative medals. Except in August, French-language tours of the mint's workshops are held on Wednesday and Friday at 2.15 pm and cost 20FF.

MONTPARNASSE

After WWI, writers, poets and artists of the avant-garde abandoned Montmartre and crossed the Seine, shifting the centre of artistic ferment to the area around Blvd du Montparnasse (6e, 14e and 15e). Chagall, Modigliani, Léger, Soutine, Miró, Picasso, Kandinsky, Stravinsky, Hemingway, Henry Miller and Cocteau, as well as such political exiles as Lenin and Trotsky, all used to hang out in the cafés and restaurants for which the quarter became famous. Montparnasse remained a creative centre until the mid-1930s.

Although the trendy Latin Quarter crowd considers the area hopelessly nondescript, **Blvd du Montparnasse** (on the southern border of the 6e) and its many fashionable restaurants, cafés and cinemas attract large numbers of people in the evening. Rue d'Odessa and Rue de Montparnasse are known for the *crêperies* founded by Bretons who, after arriving in Paris by train, apparently ventured no farther than the area around Gare Montparnasse.

Tour Montparnasse

The 209m-high Montparnasse Tower (Map 4; ☎ 01 45 38 52 56; metro Montparnasse Bienvenüe), 33 Ave du Maine (15e), built in 1974 of steel and smoked glass, affords spectacular views of the city. The lift to the 56th floor indoor observatory, with shops, an exhibition and a video about Paris, costs 32FF (27FF for those over 60, 24FF for students and those aged 15 to 20, and 17FF for under 14s). If you want to combine the lift trip with a hike up the stairs to the 59th floor open-air terrace, the cost is 42/36/33/26FF. April to September the tower is open daily from 9.30 am to 11.30 pm. The rest of the year its hours are 9.30 am to 10.30 pm (11 pm on Friday, Saturday and holidays). The last ascent is 30 minutes before closing.

Cimetière du Montparnasse

Montparnasse Cemetery (Maps 1 and 4; ☎ 01 44 10 86 50; metro Edgar Quinet or Raspail), accessible from both Blvd Edgar Quinet and Rue Froidevaux (14e), was opened in 1824. It contains the tombs of such illustrious personages as Charles Baudelaire, Guy de Maupassant, Samuel Beckett, François Rude, Frédéric August Bartholdi, Constantin Brancusi, Chaim Soutine, Man Ray, Camille Saint-Saëns, André Citroën, Alfred Dreyfus, Jean Seberg, Simone de Beauvoir and Jean-Paul Sartre. If Père Lachaise has Jim Morrison, the equivalent here is the French singer Serge Gainsbourg (division No 1); fans leave metro tickets with their names inscribed on them in his memory. Maps showing the location of famous tombs are posted near most entrances and are available free from the Conservation office at 3 Blvd Edgar Quinet. The cemetery is open daily from 8 am (8.30 am on Saturday and 9 am on Sunday) to 6 pm (5.30 pm from early November to mid-March).

Musée Bourdelle

The Bourdelle Museum (Map 4; ☎ 01 49 54 73 73; metro Falguière), due north of Gare Montparnasse at 18 Rue Antoine Bourdelle (15e), contains monumental bronzes in the building where sculptor Antoine Bourdelle (1861-1929) lived and worked. The three sculpture gardens are particularly lovely. The museum is open Tuesday to Sunday, except on public holidays, from 11 am to 5.30 pm and entry costs 17.50FF (9FF for students and those over 60).

7E ARRONDISSEMENT

The 7e arrondissement stretches along the Left Bank from Saint Germain des Prés (6e; Map 6) to the Eiffel Tower (Map 4; see the Eiffel Tower Area section later in this chapter) and includes several important museums and sights.

Musée d'Orsay

The Musée d'Orsay (Map 4; ☎ 01 40 49 48 14 or, for a recording, ☎ 01 45 49 11 11; Minitel 3615 ORSAY; metro Musée d'Orsay or Solférino), along the Seine at 1 Rue de Bellechasse (7e), displays France's national collection of paintings, sculptures, *objets d'art* and other works produced between 1848 and 1914, including fruits of the impressionist, postimpressionist and Art Nouveau movements. It is spectacularly housed in a former train station built in 1900 and reinaugurated in its present form in 1986.

Many visitors head straight to the upper level (lit by a skylight) to see the famous **impressionists** (Monet, Renoir, Pissarro, Sisley, Degas, Manet, Van Gogh, Cézanne) and **postimpressionists** (Seurat, Matisse), but there's also a great deal to see on the ground floor, including some early works by Manet, Monet, Renoir and Pissarro. The middle level has some magnificent **Art Nouveau rooms**.

Tickets & Hours The Musée d'Orsay is open daily, except Monday, from 10 am (9 am on Sunday and from mid-June to August) to 6 pm (9.45 pm on Thursday). Ticket sales stop 30 minutes before closing time. Tickets for the permanent exhibits cost 39FF (27FF for those aged 18 to 25 or over 60, and free for under 18s) and are valid all day (ie you can leave and re-enter the museum as you please). There are separate fees for temporary exhibitions.

Guided Tours English-language tours begin at 11 am Tuesday to Saturday and there's an addition one on Thursday at 7 pm; tickets (40FF in addition to the entry fee, no discounts) are sold at the information desk to the left as you enter the building. Audioguides (1½ hour cassette tours), available in six languages, point out 30 major works – many of which had a revolutionary impact on 19th century art – that the uninitiated might easily miss. They can be rented for 30FF (no discounts; ID deposit) on the right just past the ticket windows. The excellent full-colour *Guide to the Musée d'Orsay* (95FF) is available in English.

Faubourg Saint Germain

Faubourg Saint Germain, the area between the Musée d'Orsay and, 1km to the south, Rue de Babylone, was Paris' most fashionable neighbourhood in the 18th century. Some of the most interesting mansions, many of which now serve as embassies or government ministries, are along three east-west oriented streets: Rue de Lille, Rue de Grenelle and Rue de Varenne. The **Hôtel Matignon** (Map 4), since 1958 the official residence of France's prime minister, is at 57 Rue de Varenne (7e).

Assemblée Nationale

The National Assembly, the lower house of the French parliament, meets in the 18th century Palais Bourbon (Map 4; ☎ 01 40 63 60 00; metro Assemblée Nationale) at 33 Quai d'Orsay, right across the Seine from Place de la Concorde (8e). There are free guided tours in French (☎ 01 46 36 41 13) every Saturday at 10 or 11 am and 2 or 3 pm. Admission is on a first-come, first-served basis (each tour has only 30 places), so join the queue early. A national ID card or passport is required.

The Second Empire-style **Ministère des Affaires Étrangères** (Foreign Affairs Ministry; Map 4), built between 1845 and 1855 and popularly referred to as the Quai d'Orsay, is next door at 37 Quai d'Orsay.

Musée Rodin

The Musée Auguste Rodin (Map 4; ☎ 01 47 05 01 34; metro Varenne), 77 Rue de Varenne (7e), often listed by tourists as their favourite Paris museum, is one of the most relaxing spots in the whole city. Rooms on two floors of this private 18th century residence display extraordinarily vital bronze and marble sculptures by Rodin and Camille Claudel, including casts of some of Rodin's most celebrated works: *The Hand of God*, *The Burghers of Calais*, *The Kiss*, *Cathedral* and, of course, that crowd-pleaser *The Thinker*, outside. There's a delightful rear **garden** filled with sculptures and shady trees.

The Musée Rodin is open daily, except Monday, from 9.30 am to 4.45 pm (5.45 pm from April to September). Entrance costs 28FF (18FF if you're 18 to 25 or over 60 and, on Sunday, for everyone; free for under 18s). Just the garden costs 5FF to visit.

Hôtel des Invalides

The Hôtel des Invalides (7e; Map 4; metro Varenne or La Tour Maubourg) was built in the 1670s by Louis XIV to provide housing for 4000 disabled *invalides* (veterans). On 14 July 1789, the Paris mob forced its way into the building and, after fierce fighting, seized 28,000 rifles before heading on to the Bastille. The 500m-long **Esplanade des Invalides** (Map 4; metro Invalides), which stretches from the main building to the Seine, was laid out between 1704 and 1720.

The **Église du Dôme** (Map 4; metro Varenne or La Tour Maubourg), with its sparkling dome, was built between 1677 and 1735 and is considered one of the finest religious edifices erected under Louis XIV. The church's career as a mausoleum for military leaders began in 1800, and in 1861 it received the remains of Napoleon, encased in six concentric coffins. The buildings on either side of the **Cour d'Honneur** (Map 4), the main courtyard, house the **Musée de l'Armée** (☎ 01 44 42 37 67), a huge military museum. The Musée de l'Armée and the very extravagant **Tombeau de Napoléon 1er** (Napoleon's Tomb), inside the church, are open daily from 10 am to 4.45 pm (5.45 pm from April to September). Entrance costs 37FF (27FF for children, students and seniors).

Musée des Égouts de Paris

The Paris Sewers Museum (Map 4; ☎ 01 47 05 10 29; metro Pont de l'Alma) is a working museum whose entrance – a rectangular maintenance hole – is across the street from 93 Quai d'Orsay (7e). Raw sewage with all sorts of vaguely familiar objects floating in it flows beneath your feet as you walk through 480m of odoriferous tunnels, passing artefacts illustrating the development of Paris' waste-water disposal system. The sewers are open Saturday to Wednesday (except, God forbid, when rain threatens to flood the tunnels) from 11 am to 5 pm (6 pm from May to September); the last entry is an hour earlier. Tickets cost 25FF (20FF for children, students and seniors).

EIFFEL TOWER AREA

Paris' most prominent and recognisable landmark, the Eiffel Tower is surrounded by open areas on both banks of the Seine (7e and 16e). Nearby, parts of the Right Bank have several outstanding museums.

SIMON BRACKEN

Today, it's hard to believe that at the time it was built most Parisians hated the Eiffel tower and wanted it torn down.

Eiffel Tower

The Tour Eiffel (Map 4; ☎ 01 44 11 23 23 or ☎ 01 45 50 34 565; metro Champ de Mars-Tour Eiffel or Bir Hakeim) faced massive opposition from Paris' artistic and literary elite when it was built for the 1889 Exposition Universelle (World Fair), held to commemorate the centenary of the Revolution. It was almost torn down in 1909 but was spared for purely practical reasons: it proved an ideal platform for the transmitting antennas needed for the new science of radiotelegraphy. It was the world's tallest structure until Manhattan's Chrysler building was completed in 1930.

The Eiffel Tower, named after its designer, Gustave Eiffel, is 320m high, including the television antenna at the very tip. This figure can vary by as much as 15cm, however, as the tower's 7000 tonnes of iron, held together by 2.5 million rivets, expand in warm weather and contract when it's cold.

When you're done peering upwards through the girders, you can choose to visit any of the three levels open to the public. The lift (west and north pillars), which follows a curved trajectory, costs 20FF for the 1st platform (57m above the ground), 42FF for the 2nd (115m) and 57FF for the 3rd (276m). Children aged four to 12 pay 10/21/27FF respectively; there are no youth or student rates. You can avoid the lift queues by walking up the stairs in the south pillar to the 1st and 2nd platforms (14FF).

The tower is open every day from 9.30 am (9 am from late March to early September) to 11 pm (midnight from early July to early September). The stairs are open from 9 am to 6.30 pm (9 pm in late spring – approximately May and June; 11 pm in July and August).

Champ de Mars

The grassy area south-east of the Eiffel Tower, whose name means 'Field of Mars' (Mars was the Roman god of war), was originally a parade ground for the cadets of the 18th century **École Militaire** (Military Academy; Map 4), the vast, French classical-style building at the south-eastern end of the lawns whose graduates include Napoleon.

When the weather is good, young Parisians flock to the Champ de Mars to skateboard or roller-skate; it's also an excellent place for a picnic. For the young, and young at heart, there are **marionette shows** (☎ 01 48 56 01 44; metro École Militaire) on Wednesday, Saturday, Sunday and public holidays at 3.15 and 4.15 pm (daily during school holidays, including July and August; cost 16FF).

Jardins du Trocadéro

The Trocadéro Gardens (Map 4; metro Trocadéro), whose fountains and statue garden are grandly illuminated at night, are across Pont d'Iéna from the Eiffel Tower in the posh 16e. They are named after the Trocadéro, a Spanish stronghold near Cádiz captured by the French in 1823.

Palais de Chaillot

The two curved, colonnaded wings of the Palais de Chaillot (16e; Map 4; metro Trocadéro), which was built for the World Exhibition of 1937, and the terrace in between them afford an exceptional panorama of the Jardins du Trocadéro, the Seine and the Eiffel Tower.

This vast complex normally houses four museums, but two – the **Musée du Cinéma Henri Langlois** (Henri Langlois Cinema Museum; ☎ 01 45 53 74 39) and the **Musée des Monuments Français** (French Monuments Museum; ☎ 01 44 05 39 10) – will probably be closed until late 1999. The other two, reached from the gap between the two wings, are the **Musée de l'Homme** (Museum of Mankind; ☎ 01 44 05 72 72; 30FF for adults, 20FF reduced price; closed Tuesday), with anthropological and ethnographic exhibits from Africa, Asia, Europe, the Arctic, the Pacific and the Americas; and the **Musée de la Marine** (Maritime Museum; ☎ 01 53 65 65 69; 38FF for adults, 25FF reduced price; closed Tuesday), known for its beautiful model ships.

Musée Guimet

The Guimet Museum (Map 2; ☎ 01 47 23 88 11; metro Iéna), 6 Place d'Iéna (16e), which is about midway between the Eiffel

Tower and the Arc de Triomphe, also called the Musée des Arts Asiatiques (Museum of Asian Arts), usually displays antiquities and works of art from Afghanistan, India, Nepal, Pakistan, Tibet, Cambodia, China, Japan and Korea. However, until massive renovations are completed in 1999, part of the collection will be housed at the **Musée du Panthéon Bouddhique** (Buddhist Pantheon Museum; Map 2; metro Iéna), the Guimet annexe a short distance to the north at 19 Ave d'Iéna (16e), with Chinese and Japanese Buddhist paintings and sculptures brought to Paris in 1876 by Émile Guimet. It is open daily, except Tuesday, from 9.45 am to 5.45 pm. Entrance costs 16FF (12FF reduced price, free for under 18s).

Musée d'Art Moderne de la Ville de Paris

The **Palais de Tokyo**, 11 Ave du Président Wilson (16e), houses the Modern Art Museum of the City of Paris (Map 2; ☎ 01 53 67 40 00; metro Iéna or Alma Marceau). Its collections include representatives of just about every major artistic movement of the 20th century: fauvism, cubism, the School of Paris, surrealism and expressionism. Artists with works on display include Matisse, Picasso, Braque, Soutine, Modigliani, Chagall and Dufy. Part of the museum is being rebuilt as the **Palais du Cinema**.

The museum is open Tuesday to Friday from 10 am to 5.30 pm, and on weekend from 10 am to 6.45 pm. Tickets cost 27FF (19FF reduced price), but more if there's a temporary exhibit.

Musée de la Mode et du Costume

The Fashion and Clothing Museum (Map 2; ☎ 01 47 20 85 23; metro Iéna or Alma Marceau), in the Palais Galliera just opposite the Musée d'Art Moderne de la Ville de Paris (enter from 10 Ave Pierre 1er de Serbie, 16e), contains some 10,000 outfits and accessories from the past three centuries. The lovely building and gardens are in themselves worth a visit. The museum is open Tuesday to Sunday from 10 am to 6.40 pm and costs 45FF (reduced price 32FF).

Place de l'Alma

South-east of the Palais Galliera is Place de l'Alma, an insignificant square that would mostly go unnoticed by most travellers if not for the tragic event that occurred in the underpass running parallel to the Seine shortly after midnight on 31 August 1997: Diana, Princess of Wales, her companion, Dodi Fayed, and their chauffeur, Henri Paul, were killed when the car in which they were travelling struck the 13th concrete pillar in the underpass. (Diana's bodyguard, Trevor Rees-Jones, the only one in the car to be wearing a seat belt at the time of the crash, survived but was badly disfigured and is still suffering from partial amnesia.) The tragedy unleashed a torrent of grief in the UK and around the world unseen since the assassination of US President John F Kennedy in 1963.

Though there was some talk early on about renaming the square Place Diana, the only reminder of the tragedy at present surrounds the bronze **Flame of Liberty** (Map 2; metro Alma Marceau), a replica of the one atop the torch of New York's Statue of Liberty that was placed here by American firms based in Paris in 1987 on the centenary of the *International Herald Tribune* newspaper as a symbol of friendship between France and the USA. It has become something of a **memorial to Diana** and is decorated with flowers and personal notes.

On the first anniversary of Diana's death, the city government, bowing to public sentiment both at home and abroad, announced plans to create its own monument to the late Princess of Wales: a nature garden for children dedicated to Diana at 21 Rue des Blancs Manteaux (4e) in the Marais. The garden was scheduled to open in the spring of 1999.

PLACE DE LA CONCORDE AREA

The cobblestone expanses of Place de la Concorde (8e) are sandwiched between the Jardin des Tuileries and the parks at the eastern end of Ave des Champs-Élysées.

Place de la Concorde

Place de la Concorde was laid out between 1755 and 1775. The 3300-year-old pink granite **obelisk** (Map 2) in the middle was given to France in 1831 by Muhammad Ali, viceroy and pasha of Egypt. Weighing 230 tonnes and towering 23m over the cobblestones, it once stood in the Temple of Ramses at Thebes (modern-day Luxor). The eight female statues adorning the four corners of the square represent France's largest cities.

In 1793, Louis XVI's head was lopped off by a guillotine set up in the north-west corner of the square, near the statue representing the city of Brest. During the next two years, another guillotine – this one near the entrance to the Jardin des Tuileries – was used to behead 1343 more people, including Marie-Antoinette and, six months later, the Revolutionary leader Danton. Shortly thereafter, Robespierre lost his head here, too. The square was given its present name after the Reign of Terror, in the hope that it would be a place of peace and harmony.

The two imposing buildings on the north side of Place de la Concorde are the **Hôtel de la Marine** (Map 2), headquarters of the French navy, and the **Hôtel de Crillon** (Map 2), one of Paris' most exclusive hotels.

Église de la Madeleine

The neoclassical Church of Saint Mary Magdalen (Map 2; metro Madeleine), known as La Madeleine, is 350m north of Place de la Concorde along Rue Royale. Built in the style of a Greek temple, it was consecrated in 1842 after almost a century of design changes and construction delays. It is surrounded by 52 Corinthian columns each standing 20m tall. The marble and gilt interior, topped by three skylighted cupolas, is open Monday to Saturday from 7 am to 7 pm, and on Sunday from 7.30 am to 1 or 1.30 pm and 3.30 to 7 pm. You can hear the massive organ being played at Mass on Saturday at 6 pm and on Sunday at 11 am and 6 pm.

Place de la Madeleine

Paris' cheapest *belle époque* attraction is the **public toilet** (Map 2) on the east side of La Madeleine, which dates from 1905 (2.20FF to sit down, 2FF for the urinals). There has been a **flower market** on the east side of the church since 1832; it's open daily, except Sunday, until 8.30 or 9 pm.

CHAMPS-ÉLYSÉES AREA

Ave des Champs-Élysées (8e; Map 2), whose name means Elysian Fields (Elysium was where happy souls dwelt after death, according to Greek and Roman mythology), links Place de la Concorde (8e) with the Arc de Triomphe. Since the Second Empire (1852-70), the avenue has come to symbolise the style and *joie de vivre* in Paris.

Ave des Champs-Élysées

Popular with the aristocracy of the mid-19th century as a stage on which to parade their wealth, the 2km-long Ave des Champs-Élysées was, after WWII, taken over by airline offices, cinemas, car showrooms and fast-food restaurants. In recent years, however, the municipality's US$48 million investment to regain some of the 72m-wide avenue's former sparkle and prestige has paid off and the Champs-Élysées is a more popular destination than ever. In late July the Champs-Élysées plays host to the final stage of the Tour de France bicycle race; if you want to see this colourful affair find a spot on the barricades before midday.

Rue du Faubourg Saint Honoré

Rue du Faubourg Saint Honoré (8e; the western extension of Rue Saint Honoré), 400m north of the Champs-Élysées, links Rue Royale (metro Concorde) with Place des Ternes (metro Ternes). It is home to some of Paris' most renowned couture houses. Other luxury items available here include jewellery and fine antiques.

The most noteworthy of the avenue's 18th century mansions is the **Palais de l'Élysée** (Map 2), at the intersection of Rue du Faubourg Saint Honoré and Ave de Marigny (8e) and now the official residence of the French president.

Musée du Petit Palais

The Petit Palais (Map 2; ☎ 01 42 65 12 73; metro Champs-Élysées Clemenceau), Ave Winston Churchill (8e), built for the Exposition Universelle of 1900, houses the **Musée des Beaux-Arts de la Ville de Paris**, the Paris municipality's Museum of Fine Arts. It specialises in medieval and Renaissance *objets d'art* (porcelain, clocks etc), tapestries, drawings and 19th century French painting and sculpture. The Petit Palais is open Tuesday to Sunday from 10 am to 5.40 pm (last entry at 5 pm) and to 8 pm on Thursday. Tickets cost 27FF (14.50FF reduced price).

Grand Palais

The Grand Palais (Map 2; ☎ 01 44 13 17 17; metro Champs-Élysées Clemenceau), across Ave Winston Churchill from the Petit Palais (the main entrance faces Ave des Champs-Élysées), houses the **Nationales Galeries du Grand Palais**, which hosts special exhibitions lasting three or four months. Built for the 1900 Exposition Universelle, it has an iron frame and an Art Nouveau-style glass roof. It is open daily, except Tuesday, from 10 am to 8 pm (last entry 7.15 pm), on Wednesday to 10 pm (last entry 9.15 pm).

Palais de la Découverte

The Palace of Discovery (Map 2; ☎ 01 40 74 80 00 or, for a recording, ☎ 01 40 74 81 82; Minitel 3615 DECOUVERTE; metro Champs-Élysées Clemenceau), a fascinating science museum on Ave Franklin D Roosevelt (8e), has interactive exhibits on astronomy, biology and medicine, chemistry, mathematics and computer science, physics and earth sciences. The two **Eureka rooms** have exhibits for young children.

The Palais de la Découverte is open Tuesday to Saturday from 9.30 am to 6 pm, and from 10 am to 7 pm on Sunday and holidays. Entrance costs 27FF (17FF for students and people under 18 or over 60, and free half an hour before closing time). The **planetarium** (☎ 01 40 74 81 73), which has four shows a day in French (usually at 11.30 am and 2, 3.15 and 4.30 pm, plus one on weekends at 5.45 pm), costs an extra 13FF.

Triangle d'Or

Many of Paris' richest residents, finest hotels and most fashionable couture houses can be found in the Triangle d'Or (Golden Triangle), an ultra-exclusive neighbourhood whose corners are at Place de la Concorde, the Arc de Triomphe and Place de l'Alma. Ave Montaigne, home of *haute couture* (see the Shopping section), is a good place from which to start exploring.

Arc de Triomphe

The Arc de Triomphe (Map 2; ☎ 01 43 80 31 31; metro Charles de Gaulle-Étoile) is 2.2km north-west of Place de la Concorde in the middle of Place Charles de Gaulle (or Place de l'Étoile), the world's largest traffic roundabout and the meeting point of 12 avenues. It was commissioned in 1806 by Napoleon to commemorate his imperial victories but remained unfinished when he started losing – first battles and then whole wars. It was finally completed in 1836.

The most famous of the four high-relief panels is to the right as you face the arch from the Ave des Champs-Élysées side. Entitled *Départ des Volontaires de 1792* and also known as *La Marseillaise*, it is the work of François Rude.

Since 1920, the body of an Unknown Soldier from WWI taken from Verdun in Lorraine has lain beneath the arch, his fate and that of countless others is commemorated by a memorial flame that is rekindled each evening around 6.30 pm. France's national remembrance service is held here annually at 11 am on 11 November.

From the viewing platform on top of the arch (284 steps) you can see the 12 avenues – many of them named after Napoleonic victories and illustrious generals – radiating towards every part of Paris. From April to September, the platform can be visited daily, except on major holidays, from 9.30 am to 11 pm; during the rest of the year the hours are 10 am to 10 pm. Tickets cost 35FF (23FF if you're 12 to 25, free for children) and are sold in the underground passageway.

PARC DE MONCEAU AREA

Parc de Monceau

Pass through one of the gates in the elaborate wrought-iron fence around the Parc de Monceau (Map 2; metro Monceau) and you'll find yourself amid immaculately tended lawns, flowerbeds, trees and pseudoclassical statues. The nearby streets are lined with opulent mansions and grand apartment buildings from the mid-19th century. The world's first parachute jump – from a balloon – was made here in 1797. The park is open daily until 8 pm (10 pm from April to October).

Musée Cernuschi

The Cernuschi Museum (Map 2; ☎ 01 45 63 50 75; metro Villiers), 7 Ave Vélasquez (8e), houses a collection of ancient Chinese art (funerary statues, bronzes, ceramics) and works from Japan assembled during the 19th century by the banker Henri Cernuschi. It is open from 10 am to 5.40 pm (closed Monday and holidays). Entry costs 30FF (20FF reduced price).

Musée Nissim de Camondo

The Nissim de Camondo Museum (Map 2; ☎ 01 53 89 06 40; metro Monceau or Villiers), 63 Rue de Monceau (8e), displays 18th century furniture, wood panelling, tapestries, porcelain and other *objets d'art* collected by Count Moïse de Camondo, who established this museum in memory of his son Nissim, who died in WWI. It is open Wednesday to Sunday from 10 am to 5 pm. Tickets cost 27FF (18FF for people under 25 or over 60).

Musée Jacquemart-André

The Jacquemart-André Museum (Map 2; ☎ 01 42 89 04 91; metro Miromesnil), 158 Blvd Haussmann (8e), is housed in an opulent residence built during the mid-19th century. The collection includes furniture, tapestries and enamels, but it is most noted for its paintings by Rembrandt and Van Dyck and the Italian Renaissance works of Bernini, Botticelli, Carpaccio, Donatello, Mantegna, Tintoretto, Titian and Uccello. The museum is open daily from 10 am to 6 pm and entry is 46FF (33FF reduced price), including an audioguide in one of six languages.

OPÉRA GARNIER AREA

Opéra Garnier (9e), Paris' world famous opera house, abuts the Grands Boulevards, broad thoroughfares whose *belle époque* elegance has only partially been compromised by the traffic and pedestrian tumult of modern Paris.

Opéra Garnier

This renowned opera house (Map 7; ☎ 01 40 01 22 63; metro Opéra) at Place de l'Opéra (9e), designed in 1860 by Charles Garnier to showcase the splendour of Napoleon III's France, is one of the most impressive monuments erected during the Second Empire. It contains the **Musée de l'Opéra** (☎ 01 47 42 07 02), which is open daily from 10 am to 5 pm (ticket sales end half an hour before closing time). The entrance fee is 30FF (20FF for children, students and seniors, and free for under 10s) and includes a visit to the opera house unless there's a daytime rehearsal or performance going on. Operas and concerts are staged both here and at the Opéra Bastille (see the Entertainment section for details on both venues).

Blvd Haussmann

Blvd Haussmann (8e and 9e), just north of Opéra Garnier, is the heart of a commercial and banking district and known for its famous department stores, including **Galeries Lafayette** (Map 7) at No 40 and **Printemps** (Map 2) at No 64 (see the Shopping section).

Grands Boulevards

The eight contiguous Grands Boulevards (Maps 2, 3 & 7) – Madeleine, Capucines, Italiens, Montmartre, Poissonière, Bonne Nouvelle, Saint Denis and Saint Martin – stretch from elegant Place de la Madeleine (8e) eastward to the less-than-luxurious Place de la République (3e and 10e), a distance of just under 3km. The Grands Boulevards were laid out in the 1600s on the site of obsolete fortifications and served as a centre of café and theatre life in the 18th and 19th centuries, reaching the height of fashion during the *belle époque*.

Baron Haussmann

Few town planners anywhere in the world have had as great an impact on the city of their birth as Baron Georges-Eugène Haussmann (1809-91) did on Paris. As prefect of the Seine département under Napoleon III for 17 years, Haussmann and his staff of engineers and architects completely rebuilt huge swathes of Paris. He is best known (and most bitterly attacked) for having demolished much of medieval Paris, replacing the chaotic narrow streets – easy to barricade in an uprising – with the handsome, arrow-straight thoroughfares for which the city is celebrated. He also revolutionised Paris' water supply and sewerage systems and laid out many of the city's loveliest parks, including Parc des Buttes-Chaumont (19e), Parc Montsouris (14e), and large areas of the Bois de Boulogne (16e) and Bois de Vincennes (12e).

19th Century Arcades

Stepping into the covered shopping arcades off Blvd Montmartre is the best way to step back into early 19th century Paris. The **Passage des Panoramas** (Map 7; metro Rue Montmartre), 11 Blvd Montmartre (2e), which was opened in 1800 and received Paris' first gas lighting in 1817, was expanded in 1834 with the addition of four other interconnecting passages: Feydeau, Montmartre, Saint Marc and Variétés. The arcades are open daily from 6.30 am to midnight.

On the other side of Blvd Montmartre (9e), between Nos 10 and 12, is **Passage Jouffroy** (Map 7; metro Rue Montmartre), which leads across Rue de la Grange Batelière to **Passage Verdeau**. Both contain shops selling antiques, old postcards, used and antiquarian books, gifts, pet toys, imports from Asia and the like. The arcades are open until 10 pm. A bit to the west at 97 Rue de Richelieu (2e) is the skylighted **Passage des Princes** (Map 7; metro Richelieu Drouot).

Musée Grévin

This waxworks museum (Map 7; ☎ 01 42 46 13 26; metro Rue Montmartre) is most notable for its location: it's inside the Passage Jouffroy at 10-12 Blvd Montmartre (9e). The collection is not up to that of Madame Tussaud's but would you get to see the death masks of French Revolutionary leaders in London? It's open seven days a week from 10 am to 7 pm. The ticket counter closes one hour before closing. Entry is an outrageous 55FF (36FF for children aged from six to 14).

10E ARRONDISSEMENT

The lively working-class area (metro Château d'Eau and Gare de l'Est) around Blvd de Strasbourg and Rue du Faubourg Saint Denis (especially south of Blvd de Magenta) is home to large communities of Indians, Pakistanis, West Indians, Africans, Turks and Kurds. Strolling through **Passage Brady** (Map 3; metro Château d'Eau) is almost like stepping into a back alley in Bombay.

Tranquil Canal Saint Martin links the 10e with Parc de la Villette (19e). Rue de Paradis (10e; metro Château d'Eau) is famed for its crystal, glass and tableware shops.

Porte Saint Denis & Porte Saint Martin

Porte Saint Denis (Map 3; metro Strasbourg Saint Denis), the 24m-high triumphal arch at the intersection of Rue du Faubourg Saint Denis and Blvd Saint Denis, was built in 1672 to commemorate Louis XIV's campaign along the Rhine. On the north side, carvings represent the fall of Maastricht in 1673.

Two blocks east, at the intersection of Rue du Faubourg Saint Martin and Blvd Saint Denis, is another triumphal arch, the 17m-high Porte Saint Martin (Map 3), erected in 1674 to commemorate the capture of Besançon and the Franche-Comté region by Louis XIV's armies.

Baccarat Crystal Museum

The glittering, incredibly pricey Baccarat showroom (Map 3; ☎ 01 47 70 64 30; metro Château d'Eau) at 30bis Rue de Paradis (10e) has an adjoining museum filled with stunning pieces of crystal, many of them custom-made for princes and dictators of desperately poor ex-colonies. It is open weekdays from 9 am to 6 pm, and on Saturday from 10 am to noon and 2 to 5 pm; entry is 15FF.

Canal Saint Martin

The shaded towpaths of the 4.5km-long Saint Martin Canal (Map 3; metro Jaurès, République and others) – speckled with sunlight filtering through the plane trees – are wonderful places for a romantic stroll or bike ride past the nine **locks**, metal bridges and ordinary Parisian neighbourhoods. Parts of the waterway (built in 1806 to link the Seine with the 108km Canal de l'Ourcq) are higher than the surrounding land. For information on barge rides, see the Organised Tours section later in this chapter.

BERCY

Long cut off from the rest of the city by railway tracks and the Seine but now joined with the Left Bank by the new 240FF million Pont Charles de Gaulle, Bercy (12e; Map 5) has some of Paris' most important new buildings. These include the octagonal **Palais Omnisports de Paris-Bercy** (Map 1), Blvd de Bercy, designed to serve as both an indoor sports arena and a concert, ballet and theatre venue, and the giant **Ministry of Finance** (Map 5), also on Blvd de Bercy.

13E ARRONDISSEMENT

The generally nondescript 13e arrondissement begins a few blocks south of the Jardin des Plantes (5e).

Bibliothèque Nationale de France de François Mitterrand

Right across the river from Bercy is the controversial, US$2 billion National Library of France (Map 1; ☎ 01 53 79 59 59; metro Quai de la Gare), 11 Quai Franc Mauriac, conceived by Mitterrand as a 'wonder of the modern world'. No expense was spared to carry out a plan that many said defied logic. While many of the more than 10 million books and historical documents are shelved in the four sun-drenched, 80m-high towers – shaped like half-open books – patrons sit in artificially lit basement halls built around a forest of 126 50-year-old pines, trucked in from Normandy at a cost of US$22,000 each. The towers have since been fitted with a complex shutter system and the basement is prone to flooding from the Seine, but the library has at last been opened to readers (see Libraries in the Information section earlier).

Chinatown

In the triangle bounded by Ave de Choisy, Ave d'Ivry and Blvd Masséna, Paris' high-rise Chinatown (Map 1; metro Tolbiac, Porte d'Ivry or Porte de Choisy) has a distinctly Franco-Chinese ambience, thanks to the scores of east Asian restaurants, shops and travel agencies.

14E ARRONDISSEMENT

The less-than-thrilling 14e is best known for Cimetière du Montparnasse (see the Montparnasse entry earlier in this chapter); **Parc Montsouris** (Map 1; metro Cité Universitaire), a beautiful park across Blvd Jourdan from the lawns and university dorms of the **Cité Internationale Universitaire** (Map 1); and the discount clothing outlets along Rue d'Alésia (Map 1).

Catacombes

In 1785, it was decided to solve the hygiene and aesthetic problems posed by Paris' overflowing cemeteries by exhuming the bones and storing them in the tunnels of three disused quarries. One ossuary created during this period is the Catacombes (Map 1; ☎ 01 43 22 47 63; metro Denfert Rochereau), without a doubt the most macabre place in Paris. After descending 20m from street level, visitors follow 1.6km of underground corridors in which the bones and skulls of millions of Parisians are neatly stacked along the walls. During WWII, these tunnels were used by the Résistance as a headquarters.

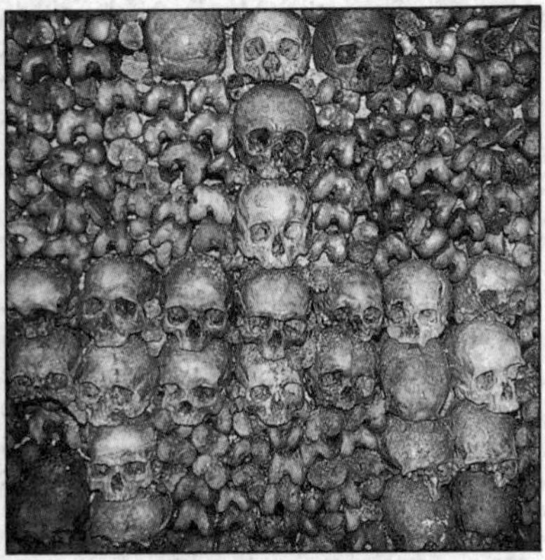

Bones and skulls lining a tunnel in the Catacombes.

The route through the Catacombes begins from the small green building at 1 Place Denfert Rochereau. The site is open Tuesday to Friday from 2 to 4 pm, and on weekends from 9 to 11 am and 2 to 4 pm. Tickets cost 27FF (19FF for students and children). Flash photography is no problem, but tripods are forbidden. It's a good idea to bring along a torch (flashlight).

The exit (metro Mouton Duvernet), where a guard will check your bag for stolen bones, is on Rue Remy Dumoncel, 700m southwest of Place Denfert Rochereau.

MONTMARTRE

During the 19th century the bohemian lifestyle of Montmartre (18e) attracted artists and writers whose presence turned the area into Paris' most important centre of creativity. Although such activity shifted to Montparnasse after WWI, Montmartre retains an upbeat ambience that all the tourists in the world couldn't spoil.

Getting Around

The Régie Autonome des Transports Parisians (RATP) sleek funicular (Map 9) travelling Montmartre's southern slope whisks visitors from Square Willette (metro Anvers) to Sacré Cœur. It runs until 12.40 am and costs one metro/bus ticket each way. Weekly and monthly Carte Orange coupons as well as Paris Visite and Mobilis passes are also valid.

Montmartrobus, run by the RATP, takes a circuitous route all over Montmartre; maps are posted at bus stops.

Basilique du Sacré Cœur

The Basilica of the Sacred Heart (Map 9; ☎ 01 53 41 89 00; metro Lamarck Caulaincourt), perched at the very top of Butte de Montmartre (Montmartre Hill), was built from contributions taken by Parisian Catholics as an act of contrition after the humiliating Franco-Prussian War of 1870-71. Construction began in 1873, but the basilica was not consecrated until 1919.

A 234 step climb up narrow spiral staircases takes you to the **dome** (15FF, 8FF for children and students under 25), which affords one of Paris' most spectacular panoramas; you can see as far away as 30km on a clear day. The chapel lined **crypt** (15FF, 8FF reduced price) is huge but not very interesting.

The basilica is open daily from 7 am to 11 pm. The dome and the crypt, down the stairs to the right as you exit the basilica, are open daily from 9 am to 6 pm (7 pm from April to September).

Place du Tertre

Half a block west of the **Église Saint Pierre de Montmartre** (Map 9), parts of which date from the 12th century (it's the only building left from the great Benedictine abbey of Montmartre, 1147-1680), is Place du Tertre (Map 9; metro Abbesses), once the main square of the village of Montmartre. These days it's filled with cafés, restaurants, portrait artists and tourists and is always animated. Look for the two **windmills** to the west on Rue Lepic.

Espace Montmartre Salvador Dalí

Over 300 works by Salvador Dalí (1904-89), the flamboyant Catalan surrealist sculptor, printmaker, painter and self-promoter, are on display at this museum (Map 9; ☎ 01 42 64 40 10; metro Abbesses) at 9-11 Rue Poulbot (18e), around the corner from Place du Tertre. It is open daily from 10 am to 6 pm, and entry is 35FF (25FF reduced rate).

Musée de Montmartre

The Montmartre Museum (Map 9; ☎ 01 46 06 61 11; metro Lamarck Caulaincourt), 12 Rue Cortot (18e), displays paintings, lithographs and documents mostly relating to the area's rebellious and bohemian/artistic past. It's hard to appreciate what the big deal is (and to justify the admission fee) unless you care about Montmartre's mythology – and can read French. There's a lush little garden out the back. The museum is open Tuesday to Sunday from 11 am to 6 pm. Tickets cost 25FF (20FF for students and seniors).

Musée d'Art Naïf Max Fourny

The Museum of Naive Art, founded in 1986, is housed in Halle Saint Pierre (Map 9; ☎ 01 42 58 72 89; metro Anvers) at 2 Rue Ronsard (18e), across from Square Willette and the base of the funicular. The vivid paintings – gathered from around the world – are immediately appealing, thanks to their whimsical and generally optimistic perspective on life. The museum, whose themed exhibitions change frequently, is open daily from 10 am to 6 pm. Tickets cost a pricey 40FF (30FF for students, seniors and teachers, and 20FF for children). Workshops for children are held on Wednesday and on weekends from 3 to 4 pm.

Musée d'Art Juif

The small Museum of Jewish Art (Map 9; ☎ 01 42 57 84 15; metro Lamarck Caulaincourt), on the 3rd floor of the Jewish community centre at 42 Rue des Saules (18e), has a modest collection of synagogue models, paintings and ritual objects from Eastern Europe and North Africa. It is open Sunday to Thursday from 3 to 6 pm (closed on Jewish holidays and in August). Entrance costs 30FF (20FF for students, 10FF for children). There are plans for the collections to be combined with Jewish artefacts from the Musée National du Moyen Age to create the **Musée d'Art et d'Histoire du Judaïsme**, to be housed in the Hôtel de Saint Aignan at 71 Rue du Temple (3e) in the Marais (metro Rambuteau).

Cimetière de Montmartre

Montmartre Cemetery (Maps 2 & 9; ☎ 01 43 87 64 24; metro Place de Clichy), established in 1798, is the most famous cemetery in Paris after Père Lachaise. It contains the graves of Zola, Alexandre Dumas the younger, Stendhal and Heinrich Heine; Jacques Offenbach and Hector Berlioz; Degas; film director François Truffaut; and Vaslav Nijinsky.

The entrance nearest the Butte de Montmartre is at 20 Ave Rachel, down the stairs from 10 Rue Caulaincourt. From mid-March to early November, the cemetery is open weekdays from 8 am (8.30 am on Saturday, 9 am on Sunday and holidays) to 6 pm (last entry at 5.45 pm). The rest of the year it's open from 8.30 am to 5.30 pm.

Pigalle

Only a few blocks south-west of the tranquil, residential streets of Montmartre is lively, neon-lit Pigalle (9e and 18e; Maps 3 & 9), one of Paris' two main sex districts – the other, near Forum des Halles, is along Rue Saint Denis (1er). But Pigalle is more than simply a sleazy red-light district: though the area around Blvd de Clichy between the Pigalle and Blanche metro stops is lined with erotica shops and striptease parlours and, appropriately enough, the new Musée de l'Érotisme, there are also plenty of trendy nightspots, including La Locomotive disco and the Moulin Rouge (see the Entertainment section).

The **Musée de l'Érotisme** (Museum of Eroticism; Map 9; ☎ 01 42 58 28 73; metro Blanche), 72 Blvd de Clichy (18e), tries to put titillating statuary and sexual aids from days gone by on a loftier plane – with erotic art both antique and new from four continents spread over seven levels – but we all know why we've come here. The museum is open daily from 10 am to 2 am. Entry is 40FF (30FF reduced tariff).

19E ARRONDISSEMENT

The 19e is of interest to visitors mainly because of the Canal Saint Martin (see the 10e Arrondissement entry earlier) and its eastern continuation, Canal de l'Ourcq, and two large parks: Parc de la Villette, next to Paris' largest science museum, and hilly Parc des Buttes-Chaumont.

Parc de la Villette

This whimsical, 30 hectare park (Map 1), which opened in 1993 in the city's far north-eastern corner, stretches for 600m from the Cité des Sciences et de l'Industrie (metro Porte de la Villette) southward to the Cité de la Musique (metro Porte de Pantin) and is split into two sections by Canal de l'Ourcq.

For kids, there's a **merry-go-round** near the Cinaxe, a **playground** between the Géode and the nearest bridge, and two large play areas: the **Jardin des Vents** (Garden of Winds; Map 1) and the adjacent **Jardin des Dunes** (Garden of Dunes). Divided into three areas for children of different ages, the gardens are across Galerie de la Villette (the covered walkway) from the **Grande Halle** (Map 1), a wonderful old slaughterhouse of wrought iron and glass used for concerts, theatre, expositions and conventions.

For information on barge rides to Parc de la Villette from the Port de Plaisance de Paris-Arsenal and Quai Anatole France, near the Musée d'Orsay, see Organised Tours later in this chapter.

Cité des Sciences et de l'Industrie

The enormous City of Sciences and Industry (Map 1; ☎ 01 40 05 12 12 or ☎ 08 36 68 29 30; Minitel 3615 VILLETTE; www.cite-sciences.fr; metro Porte de la Villette), at the northern end of Parc de la Villette at 30 Ave Corentin Cariou (19e), has all sorts of high-tech exhibits.

Musée Explora The huge, rather confusing main museum is open daily, except Monday, from 10 am to 6 pm (7 pm on Sunday). A ticket good for Explora, the planetarium, a 3D film, and the French navy submarine *Argonaute* (commissioned in 1957) costs 50FF (35FF for those aged eight to 25, seniors and teachers, and for everyone on Saturday; free for children) and allows you to enter and exit up to four times during the day. Various combo tickets valid for the Cité des Sciences, the Géode and Cinaxe are available.

A free map-brochure in English and the detailed 80 page *Guide to the Permanent Exhibitions* (20FF) are available from the round information counter at the Cité des Sciences' main entrance.

Cité des Enfants The highlight of the Cité des Sciences is the brilliant Cité des Enfants, whose colourful and imaginative hands-on demonstrations of basic scientific principles are divided into two sections: one for three to five-year-olds, the other for five to 12-year-olds. Younger kids can explore, among other things, the conduct of water (waterproof lab ponchos provided), while older children can build toy houses with industrial robots and stage news broadcasts in a TV studio equipped with real video cameras.

Ninety-minute visits begin four times a day at two-hour intervals from 9.30 or 10.30 am. Each child is charged 25FF and must be accompanied by an adult. During school holiday periods it's a good idea to make reservations two or three days in advance (☎ 08 36 68 29 30 or Minitel 3615 VILLETTE).

Géode

Just south of the Cité des Sciences at 26 Ave Corentin Cariou is the Géode (Map 1; ☎ 01 40 05 12 12), a 36m-high sphere whose mirror-like surface made of thousands of polished, stainless-steel triangles has made it one of the architectural calling cards of modern Paris. Inside, high-resolution, 70mm films – virtual reality, special effects, nature etc – lasting 45 minutes are projected onto a 180° screen that gives viewers a sense of being surrounded by the action. Films begin every hour on the hour from

10 am to 9 pm (closed Monday, except during school holiday periods). Headsets that pick up an English soundtrack are available for no extra charge.

Tickets to the Géode cost 57FF (44FF for under 25s, seniors and teachers; not available on weekends and holidays from 2 to 5 pm). For afternoon shows during school holiday periods and on Tuesday and Thursday from March to June, make advance reservations.

Cinaxe

The Cinaxe (☎ 01 42 09 34 00), a hydraulic cinema with seating for 60 people that moves in synchronisation with the action on the screen, is right across the walkway from the south-western side of the Cité des Sciences. This example of proto-virtual reality technology is open from 11 am to 6 pm (closed Monday) and costs 33FF (29FF for children, students and seniors). Shows begin every 15 minutes.

Cité de la Musique

On the southern edge of Parc de la Villette, the City of Music (Map 1; ☎ 01 44 84 44 84; Minitel 3615 CITEMUSIQUE; www.cite-musique.fr; metro Porte de Pantin), 221 Ave Jean Jaurès (19e), opened in 1995 and is a striking triangular concert hall whose brief is to bring non-elitist music from around the world to Paris' multi-ethnic masses. Some 900 rare musical instruments are on display in its **Musée de la Musique** (Music Museum), which is open Tuesday to Thursday from noon to 6 pm, Friday and Saturday to 7.30 pm and Sunday from 10 am to 6 pm. Entry costs 35FF (25FF for students and seniors, 10FF for those aged six to 18). The **Centre d'Information Musique et Danse** (☎ 01 44 84 46 09; Minitel 3615 MUSIQUE or 3615 DANSE) lets you try out interactive CD-ROMs (many of them in English) connected to music from Tuesday to Saturday from noon to 6 pm (Sunday from 10 am); entry is free.

Parc des Buttes-Chaumont

Encircled by tall apartment blocks, the 25 hectare Buttes-Chaumont Park (Map 1; metro Buttes-Chaumont or Botzaris) is the closest thing in Paris to Manhattan's Central Park. Great for jogging, cycling or tanning, its lush, forested slopes hide grottoes and artificial waterfalls. The romantic **lake** is dominated by a temple-topped **island** linked to the mainland by two bridges. It's open daily from 7 am to 9 pm (11 pm from May to September).

20E ARRONDISSEMENT

Cimetière du Père Lachaise

The most visited necropolis in the world is Père Lachaise Cemetery (Map 1; ☎ 01 43 70 70 33; metro Philippe Auguste, Père Lachaise or Gambetta), founded in 1805, whose 70,000 ornate (and at times ostentatious) tombs of the rich and/or famous form a verdant, open-air sculpture garden. Among the one million people buried here are Chopin, Molière, Apollinaire, Oscar Wilde, Balzac, Proust, Gertrude Stein, Colette, David, Simone Signoret, Pissarro, Seurat, Modigliani, Sarah Bernhardt, Yves Montand, Delacroix, Edith Piaf; Isadora Duncan, and even those immortal 12th century lovers, Abélard and Héloïse. The only tomb most young visitors seem to be interested in is that (in Division 6) of 1960s rock star **Jim Morrison**, who died in an apartment on Rue Beautreillis (4e) in the Marais in 1971.

On 27 May 1871, the last of the Communard insurgents, cornered by the government forces, fought a hopeless, all-night battle among the tombstones. In the morning, the 147 survivors were lined up against the **Mur des Fédérés** (Wall of the Federalists) and shot. They were buried where they fell in a mass grave.

The cemetery, which has five entrances (two of them on Blvd de Ménilmontant), is open weekdays from 8 am to 5.30 pm (Saturday from 8.30 am, Sunday from 9 am). From mid-March to early November the cemetery closes at 6 pm. Maps indicating the location of noteworthy graves are posted around the cemetery and can be obtained free from the Conservation office at 16 Rue du Repos, on the western side of the cemetery. Newsstands and kiosks in the area sell the

The superb Gothic architecture of Notre Dame at dusk

RICHARD I'ANSON

Arc de Triomphe du Carrousel

SIMON BRACKEN

The original gilded station clock of the Musée d'Orsay building

BETHUNE CARMICHAEL

View of a Paris neighbourhood across the Seine

RICHARD I'ANSON

BRENDA TURNNIDGE

SIMON BRACKEN

RACHEL BLACK

Whether it is people watching in a streetside café in Paris or while wandering the streets during the festival in Avignon, France's cities, towns and squares attract a wealth of colourful characters, musicians, buskers and other street performers.

Abélard & Héloïse

He was a brilliant 39-year-old philosopher and logician who had gained something of a reputation for his controversial ideas. She was the beautiful niece of a clergyman at Notre Dame. And like Bogart and Bergman in Casablanca and Romeo and Juliet in Verona – of all damn things – they had to fall in love in medieval Paris.

In 1118, the wandering scholar Pierre Abélard (1079-1142) returned to Paris, having clashed with yet another theologian in the provinces. There he was employed by Canon Fulbert of Notre Dame to tutor his niece Héloïse (1098-1164). One thing led to another and a son, Astrolabe, was born. Abélard did the gentlemanly thing and married his sweetheart secretly, but when Fulbert learned of it he was outraged. The canon had Abélard castrated and sent Héloïse packing to a nunnery. Abélard took monastic vows at the abbey in Saint Denis and continued his studies and controversial writings, falling foul of several clergymen of the day and even being branded a heretic by the pope at one point. Héloïse, meanwhile, was made abbess of a convent.

All the while, however, the star-crossed lovers continued to correspond: he sending tender advice on how to run the convent and she writing passionate, poetic letters to her lost lover. The two were reunited only in death; in 1817 their remains were disinterred and brought to Père Lachaise Cemetery (20e; Map 1), where they lie today beneath a neo-Gothic tombstone.

more detailed *Plan Illustré du Père Lachaise* (Illustrated Map of Père Lachaise) for 10FF. Two-hour tours (☎ 01 40 71 75 23) of the cemetery in French leave every Saturday (and on certain Tuesdays and Sundays as well) from the Conservation office at 2.30 pm. They cost 37FF (26FF reduced rate) and can be general or themed.

Belleville

This buoyant and utterly unpretentious working-class 'village' centred around Blvd de Belleville (Maps 1 & 3; metro Belleville) is home to large numbers of immigrants, especially Muslims and Jews from North Africa and Vietnamese and Chinese from Indochina. In recent years, the area's none-too-solid, late 19th century workers' flats have become a trendy address for avant-garde artists in search of cheap housing and the cachet that comes with slumming it. This is one of the best places in Paris to dine on couscous, with meat either kosher or halal (slaughtered according to either Jewish or Muslim law). See the Oberkampf, Ménilmontant & Belleville Areas entry in the Places to Eat section.

BOIS DE BOULOGNE

The 8.65 sq km Boulogne Woods (16e; Map 1), on the western edge of the city, owes its informal layout to its designer, Baron Haussmann, who took his inspiration from London's Hyde Park rather than the more geometric French models.

The southern reaches of the woods take in **Stade Rolland Garros** (Map 1), home of the French Open tennis tournament, and two horse-racing tracks, the Hippodrome de Longchamp (for flat races) and the Hippodrome d'Auteuil (for steeplechase; Map 1). For details, see Horse Racing in the Spectator Sports section later in this chapter.

Gardens

The enclosed **Parc de Bagatelle** (Map 1), in the north-western corner of the Bois de Boulogne, is renowned for its beautiful gardens, which surround the **Château de Bagatelle**, built in 1775. There are areas dedicated to irises (which bloom in May), roses (June to October) and water lilies (August).

The **Pré Catelan** (Map 1) includes a garden in which you can see plants, flowers and trees mentioned in Shakespeare's plays.

Rowboats & Bicycles Rowboats can be hired at **Lac Inférieur** (Map 1; metro Ave Henri Martin), the largest of the park's lakes and ponds. Paris Cycles (☎ 01 47 47 76 50 for a recorded message or, for bookings, ☎ 01 47 47 22 37) rents bicycles at two locations: on Ave du Mahatma Gandhi (Map 1; metro Les Sablons), across from the Porte Sablons entrance to the Jardin d'Acclimatation amusement park, and near the Pavillon Royal (metro Avenue Foch) at the northern end of Lac Inférieur. Except when it rains, bicycles are available daily mid-April to mid-October from 10 am to sundown and the same hours on Wednesday, Saturday and Sunday only during the rest of the year. The rental cost is 80FF per day.

Musée National des Arts et Traditions Populaires

The National Museum of Popular Arts and Traditions (Map 1; ☎ 01 44 17 60 00; metro Les Sablons), near the Jardin d'Acclimatation at 6 Ave du Mahatma Gandhi (16e), has displays illustrating life in rural France before and during the period of the Industrial Revolution. It is open from 9.45 am to 5.15 pm (closed Tuesday). Tickets cost 25FF (17FF reduced price, available to everyone on Sunday).

Jardin d'Acclimatation

This kids-orientated amusement park (Map 1; ☎ 01 40 67 90 82; metro Les Sablons) on Ave du Mahatma Gandhi is open daily year-round from 10 am to 6 pm. Entrance costs 12FF (6FF reduced price). To the south-west of the park is Bowling de Paris (☎ 01 40 67 94 00), a bowling alley open weekdays from 11 am to 2 am (from 10 am at weekends) where games cost 20 to 32FF per person. The highest tariffs are in force after 8 pm and on weekends.

Musée Marmottan-Claude Monet

Two blocks east of the Bois de Boulogne, between Porte de la Muette and Porte de Passy, the Marmottan-Claude Monet Museum (Map 1; ☎ 01 42 24 07 02; metro La Muette), 2 Rue Louis Boilly (16e), has the world's largest collection of works by the impressionist Monet, as well as paintings by Gauguin and Renoir. It is open Tuesday to Sunday from 10 am to 5.30 pm (last entry 5 pm). Entrance costs 40FF (25FF reduced price).

BOIS DE VINCENNES

Paris' other large English-style park, the 9.3 sq km Bois de Vincennes (12e; Map 1), is in the far south-eastern corner of the city. The **Parc Floral** (Floral Park; metro Château de Vincennes), just south of the Château de Vincennes, is on Route de la Pyramide. The **Jardin Tropical** (Tropical Garden; RER stop Nogent-sur-Marne) is at the park's eastern edge on Ave de la Belle Gabrielle.

Musée National des Arts d'Afrique et d'Océanie

The National Museum of African and Oceanic Art (Map 1; ☎ 01 44 74 84 80; metro Porte Dorée), 293 Ave Daumesnil (12e), is devoted to the art of the south Pacific, North, West and Central Africa. It is open on weekdays, except Tuesday, from 10 am to noon and 1.30 to 5.30 pm (no midday closure during special exhibitions), and on weekends from 12.30 pm (10 am for the aquarium) to 6 pm. The entry fee is 30FF (20FF if you're 18 to 24 or over 60, free for under 18s).

Zoo

The Parc Zoologique de Paris (Map 1; ☎ 01 44 75 20 10; metro Porte Dorée), founded in 1934, is at 53 Ave de Saint Maurice, just east of the Blvd Périphérique (the ring road around Paris). The zoo is open Monday to Saturday from 9 am to 6 pm (5 pm in winter) and on Sunday to 6.30 pm in summer and 5.30 pm in winter; last entry is about 30 minutes before closing.

The entrance fee is 40FF (30FF reduced tariff, 10FF for students).

Château de Vincennes

The Château de Vincennes (☎ 01 48 08 31 20; metro Château de Vincennes), at the northern edge of the Bois de Vincennes, is a bona fide royal chateau complete with massive fortifications and a moat. Louis XIV spent his honeymoon at the mid-17th century **Pavillon du Roi**, the westernmost of the two royal pavilions flanking the **Cour Royale** (Royal Courtyard). The 52m-high **dungeon**, completed in 1369, was used as a prison during the 17th and 18th centuries. It will be closed for repairs until the end of the century.

You can walk around the grounds for free, but the only way to see the Gothic **Chapelle Royale**, built between the 14th and 16th centuries, is to take a guided tour (in French, with an information booklet in English). Tickets cost 32FF (reduced price 21FF) for a long tour, and 25FF (15FF) for a short one. There are five long and five short tours a day from May to September, when the chateau is open from 10 am to 6 pm, and four of each the rest of the year between 10 am and 5 pm.

ACTIVITIES

The entertainment weeklies *Pariscope* and *L'Officiel des Spectacles* (see Listings under Entertainment later in this chapter) have up-to-date information in French on every imaginable sort of activity.

Canal Boating

The Paris area's three rivers (the Seine, Marne and Oise) and its canals (Saint Martin and l'Ourcq) offer a unique vantage point from which to enjoy the delights of Paris. A one or two week rental – less expensive than many hotels if there are four or more of you – can easily be split between quiet canal/river cruises and days spent moored in the city. Within Paris proper, the only places you can stay overnight are Bassin de la Villette (19e; Map 1), and Port de Plaisance de Paris-Arsenal (4e and 12e; Map 5), but it's possible to stop for an hour or two at a number of quays along the Seine.

Europ' Yachting (Map 5; ☎ 01 43 44 66 77; fax 01 43 44 74 18; metro Quai de la Rapée), 11 Blvd de la Bastille (12e), on the ground floor of the Capitainerie of Port de Plaisance de Paris-Arsenal, rents out boats for four to seven people. From mid-March to mid-October you can rent by the week (6000 to 10,000FF). On weekends and holidays year-round, boats are available for 945 to 1900FF a day, depending on the boat and the period. Reservations should be made three weeks ahead, though boats are sometimes available at the last minute. The office is open Monday to Saturday from 10 am to 1 pm and 2.30 to 7 pm.

Sports Facilities

For information (in French) on Paris' sporting activities and facilities (including its three dozen swimming pools), call Allô Sports on ☎ 01 42 76 54 54 or Minitel 3615 PARIS. It is staffed on weekdays from 10.30 am to 5 pm (4.30 pm on Friday).

COURSES

For information on studying French and learning how to cook, see Courses in the Facts for the Visitor chapter.

ORGANISED TOURS

Bus

On Sunday afternoon from mid-April to mid-September, RATP's Balabus follows a 50 minute route from Gare de Lyon to La Défense that passes by many of central Paris' most famous sights. Details are available at metro counters.

Parisbus (☎ 01 42 88 69 15 or ☎ 01 42 88 98 88) runs red, London-style double-decker buses in a 2¼ hour circuit that takes in Notre Dame, the Eiffel Tower and Musée d'Orsay as well as the usual list of Right Bank tourist sights. For 125FF (60FF for children aged four to 13) you can, over a period of two days, get on and off these buses wherever you like; their progress through the city is accompanied by commentary in English and French. Brochures showing the exact locations of Parisbus' stops are available at many hotels.

Cityrama (☎ 01 44 55 61 00) runs two-hour tours of the city daily (150FF), accompanied by taped commentary in a dozen or so languages. The company also has trips to Chartres (270FF), Versailles (195FF) and other places around Paris, and is near the western end of the Louvre at 4 Place des Pyramides (1er; Map 7; metro Tuileries).

Bicycle

Paris-Vélo (Map 5; ☎ 01 43 37 59 22; metro Censier Daubenton) at 2 Rue du Fer à Moulin (5e) runs well reviewed bicycle tours of Paris and its major monuments for between 120 and 180FF. Phone ahead to reserve a place. It's open Monday to Saturday from 10 am to 12.30 pm and 2 to 6 pm (in summer from 10 am to 2 pm and 5 to 7 pm). It also rents bicycles for 90/420FF a day/week (see also Bicycle in the Getting Around section later in this chapter).

Boat

Canal Cruises From March to October, Canauxrama (Map 5; ☎ 01 42 39 15 00) barges travel between Port de Plaisance de Paris-Arsenal (12e) and Parc de la Villette (19e) along the charming Saint Martin and l'Ourcq canals. Departures are at around 9.45 am and 2.30 pm from Parc de la Villette, and 9.45 am and 2.30 pm from Port de Plaisance. The cost is 75FF (60FF for students; 45FF for kids aged six to 12, except on Sunday and holidays when everyone pays 75FF).

Paris Canal Croisières (☎ 01 42 40 96 97) has daily three-hour cruises from late March to mid-November from Quai Anatole France, just north-west of the Musée d'Orsay (Map 4), leaving at 9.30 am and returning from Parc de la Villette at 2.30 pm. There are extra trips at 2.35 pm (from the museum) and 6.15 pm (from the park) from mid-July to August. The cost is 95FF for adults; 70FF for those aged 60 and over, or aged between 12 and 25 (excluding Sunday afternoons and holidays); and 55FF for children aged four to 11.

Seine Shuttle From late April to September, the Bateaux Parisiens Batobus river shuttle (☎ 01 44 11 33 99) docks at the following six stops:

- Eiffel Tower (Port de la Bourdonnais next to the Pont d'Iéna, 7e; Map 4)
- Musée d'Orsay (Port de Solférino; 7e; Map 4)
- Saint Germain des Prés (Quai Malaquais, 6e; Map 6)
- Notre Dame (Quai Montebello, 5e; Map 8)
- Hôtel de Ville (Quai de l'Hôtel de Ville, 4e; Map 8)
- Musée du Louvre (Quai du Louvre, 1er; Map 7)

The boats pass by every 25 minutes from about 10 am to 7 pm (9 pm in July and August) and cost 20FF for the first journey between dockings and 10FF thereafter. Unlimited travel for the whole day costs 60FF (half-price for children under 12); two days is 90/45FF. If you're travelling west the whole trip will cost just 20FF (one stop); in the opposite direction, it's three stops and will cost 40FF.

Seine Cruises From its base just north of the Eiffel Tower (Map 4) at Port de la Bourdonnais (7e; metro Pont de l'Alma), Bateaux Parisiens also runs one hour river circuits (50FF, 25FF for children under 12) and lunch/dinner cruises (300/560FF) year-round. From May to October, boats also depart from the dock (Map 8; ☎ 01 43 26 92 55; metro Maubert Mutualité) opposite Notre Dame, on Quai de Montebello (5e).

Bateaux Mouches (Map 2; ☎ 01 42 25 96 10 or, for an English-language recording, ☎ 01 40 76 99 99; Minitel 3615 MOUCHES; metro Alma Marceau), based on the Right Bank just east of Pont de l'Alma (8e), runs 1000 seat tour boats, the biggest on the Seine. From mid-November to mid-March there are sailings daily at 11 am, 2.30 and 3.15 pm, and on the hour from 4 to 9 pm. Depending on demand, there are additional cruises at 1 and 9.30 pm. The rest of the year boats depart every half-hour from 10 am to 12.30 pm and 1.30 to 11.30 pm. A 1½ hour cruise with commentary costs 40FF (20FF for those under 14). Lunch cruises are 200 to 300FF, dinner cruises are 500 to 650FF.

Vedettes du Pont Neuf (Map 6; ☎ 01 46 33 98 38; metro Pont Neuf), whose home dock is at the far western tip of Île de la Cité (1er), offers one hour boat excursions. Between April and November, boats generally leave every half-hour between 10 am and noon and 1.30 to 7 pm; night cruises depart every half and hour from 9 to 11 pm. From November to March there are about a dozen cruises from Monday to Thursday (when night services stop at 10 or 10.30 pm) and seven on Friday, Saturday and Sunday. A ticket costs 50FF (25FF for children under 12).

SPECIAL EVENTS

Innumerable cultural and sporting events take place in Paris throughout the year; details appear in *Pariscope* and *L'Officiel des Spectacles* (see Listings in the Entertainment section) or are available from the tourist office. The following abbreviated list gives you a taste of what to expect.

31 December/1 January

Ave des Champs-Élysées (8e), Blvd Saint Michel (5e) and Place de la Bastille (11e) are the places to be on New Year's Eve.

La Grande Parade de Montmartre – New Year's Day parade in Montmartre that wends its way from Place Pigalle northward to Place Jules Joffrin (18e; Map 9; metro Pigalle).

Late January/early February

Chinese New Year – dragon parades and other festivities are held in Chinatown, the area of the 13e between Ave d'Ivry and Ave de Choisy (metro Tolbiac) as well as along Rue Au Maire (3e; metro Arts et Métiers), which is south-east of the Conservatoire des Arts et Métiers.

Late February/early March

Salon International de l'Agriculture – a 10 day international agricultural fair with lots to eat, including dishes from all over France. Held at the Parc des Expositions at Porte de Versailles (15e; metro Porte de Versailles).

Early March

Jumping International de Paris – show jumping tournament at the Palais Omnisports de Paris-Bercy (12e; Map 1; metro Bercy).

Late March/mid-April

Banlieues Bleues – jazz festival held in Saint Denis and other Paris suburbs attracts big-name talent.

Mid-April

Marathon International de Paris – the Paris International Marathon starts on the Place de la Concorde (1er) and finishes on the Ave Foch (16e).

Late April/early May

Foire de Paris – huge food and wine fair at the Parc des Expositions at Porte de Versailles (15e; metro Porte de Versailles).

Late May/early June

Internationaux de France de Tennis (French Open Tennis Tournament) – a glitzy tennis tournament held at Stade Roland Garros (Map 1; metro Porte d'Auteuil) at the southern edge of the Bois de Boulogne (16e).

Mid-June in odd-numbered years

Paris Air Show – one of the world's premier exposition of civilian and military air and space technology. Held at Le Bourget airport, in Paris' northern suburbs.

Late June/early July

La Course des Garçons de Café – a Sunday afternoon foot race through central Paris whose participants – hundreds of waiters and waitresses – carry a glass and bottle balanced on a tray. Spilling or breaking anything results in disqualification.

Around 20 June

Gay Pride – a colourful, Saturday afternoon parade through the Marais (4e; Map 8) to celebrate Gay Pride Day. Various bars and clubs sponsor floats.

21 June

Fété de la Musique – a music festival that caters to a great diversity of tastes and features impromptu live performances all over the city.

Early July

La Goutte d'Or en Fête – world music festival (raï, reggae, rap etc) at Place de Léon (18e; metro Barbès Rochechouart).

14 July

Bastille Day – Paris is *the* place to be on France's national day. Late on the night of the 13th, *bals des sapeurs-pompiers* (dances sponsored by Paris fire brigades – considered sex symbols in France) are held at fire stations around the city. At 10 am on the 14th, there's a military and fire brigade parade along Ave des Champs-Élysées, accompanied by a fly-over of fighter aircraft and helicopters. Reviewing stands line Ave des Champs-Élysées, so the only way to get a halfway decent view is to arrive early. Much of the city centre, temporarily pedestrianised, fills with strollers out to celebrate *liberté*, *égalité* and *fraternité* amid the omnipresent riot police.

On the night of the 14th, a huge display of *feux d'artifice* (fireworks) is held at around 11 pm either near the Eiffel Tower or at the Invalides (both Map 4).

3rd or 4th Sunday in July

Tour de France. The last stage of the world's most prestigious cycling event ends with a dash up Ave des Champs-Élysées.

Mid-September to December

Festival d'Automne. Autumn festival of music and theatre held in venues throughout the city.

Early October

Foire Internationale d'Art Contemporain (FIAC). Huge contemporary art fair with some 150 galleries represented at the Espace Eiffel Branly, 29-55 Quai Branly (7e; metro Pont de l'Alma).

24-25 December

Christmas Eve Mass. Midnight Mass is celebrated on Christmas Eve at many Paris churches, including Notre Dame (Map 8; get there by 11 pm to find a place in a pew).

PLACES TO STAY

To determine where any form of accommodation is located, refer to the map whose number (1 to 9) appears before the telephone number.

Accommodation Services

Accueil des Jeunes en France No matter what age you are, the AJF (Map 8; ☎ 01 42 77 87 80; metro Rambuteau), at 119 Rue Saint Martin (4e) across the square from the Centre Pompidou, can *always* find you accommodation, even in summer. It works like this: you come in on the day (or the day before) you need a place to stay and pay the AJF for the accommodation (plus a 10FF fee). The staff then give you a voucher to take to the hostel or hotel. Prices for doubles start at about 250FF and, thanks to AJF discounts, are often less than the price you'd pay if you contacted the hotel yourself. AJF is open Monday to Friday from 10 am to 6.45 pm and on Saturday to 5.45 pm. Be prepared for long queues in summer.

Tourist Offices The main Paris tourist office (Map 2; ☎ 01 49 52 53 54; metro George V), 127 Ave des Champs-Élysées (8e), and its three annexes (in the Gare du Nord and Gare de Lyon and, in summer, at the base of the Eiffel Tower) can find you a place to stay for the night of the day you stop by. It also has a number of brochures on homestays, including one on *pensions de famille*, which are similar to B&Bs.

Camping

Camping du Bois de Boulogne (☎ 01 45 24 30 00; fax 01 42 24 42 95), on Allée du Bord de l'Eau (16e), the only camping ground within the Paris city limits, is along the Seine at the far western edge of the Bois de Boulogne. Two people with a tent are charged 60 to 77FF (89 to 118FF with a vehicle), depending on the season, and reception at this seven hectare site is staffed 24 hours a day. It's very crowded in summer, but there's always space for a small tent (though not necessarily for a car). There are also fully equipped caravans accommodating four people available for between 256 and 461FF, depending on the type and the season. The Porte Maillot metro stop (Map 2), 4.5km to the east, is linked to the camping ground by RATP bus No 244 (which runs from 6 am to 8.30 pm) and, from around Easter to September, by privately operated shuttle bus (11FF).

Homestays

For more information on the arrangement known as *hôtes payants* (literally, 'paying guests') or *hébergement chez l'habitant* (lodging with the occupants of private homes), see Homestays in the Accommodation section of the Facts for the Visitor chapter.

Flats & Apartments

Serviced Serviced flats – like staying in a hotel without all the extras – are an excellent option for those on a budget, particularly those in small groups. There are several locations around Paris.

Citadines Apparthôtels This hotel chain with apartment-style rooms has 10 properties in Paris, including one on the Blvd du Montparnasse (see Hotels – 6e Arrondissement), in Montmartre (see Hotels – Montmartre & Pigalle), near the Opéra Garnier (see Hotels – Gare Saint Lazare & Grands Boulevards) and east of the Gare de Lyon (see Hotels – Bastille Area). Rates are substantially cheaper if you stay longer than seven days in any season.

Flatôtel International (Map 4; ☎ 01 45 75 62 20; fax 01 45 79 73 30; metro Charles Michels), 14 Rue du Théâtre (15e). Studios measuring 35 sq m cost from 680 to 750FF a day and two to five-room apartments from 1200 to 2900FF. All are equipped with kitchen facilities. The minimum stay is one day.

Short-Term Allô Logement Temporaire (Map 8; ☎ 01 42 72 00 06; fax 01 42 72 03 11; metro Hôtel de Ville or Rambuteau), 64 Rue du Temple (3e), is a nonprofit organisation that acts as a liaison between flat owners and foreigners looking for furnished apartments for periods of one week to one year. Small studios of about 20 sq m cost from 1000 to 3000FF a week. October, when university classes resume, is the hardest month in which to find a place, but over summer it's usually possible to find something within a matter of days. Before any deals are signed, the company will arrange for you to talk to the owner by phone, assisted by an interpreter if necessary. There is a 300FF annual membership fee and, in addition to the rent and one month deposit (paid directly to the owner), a charge of 200FF for each month you rent. The office is open Monday to Friday from noon to 8 pm.

Another outfit with short-term furnished apartments available is AES (☎ 01 45 35 02 50 or ☎ 01 45 35 01 01; fax 01 45 35 01 00; asiacenter@aol.com; metro Glacière), 8 Rue des Tanneries (13e).

Long-Term For information about renting a flat for a longer period, see Rental Accommodation in the introductory Facts for the Visitor chapter.

Student The Union Nationale des Étudiants Locataires (National Union of Student Renters; Map 1; ☎ 01 45 41 58 18; Minitel 3615 UNEL; metro Pernety), 2 Rue Pernety (14e), will let anyone with a student card who pays the 120FF annual fee (photo required) consult its lists of available apartments and *chambres de bonne*. The usual rental period is 12 months, though six month or one semester leases do exist. The office is open on weekdays from 10 am to noon and 2 to 6 pm (open afternoons only from about January to April); year-round, Wednesday hours are 10 am to 8 pm.

The Paris tourist office's sheet entitled *Logements pour Étudiants* lists other organisations that can help find accommodation for students who'll be in Paris for at least a semester.

Hostels & Foyers

Paris' hostels and *foyers* (student residence halls) don't come cheaply. Beds under 100FF are few and far between, so two people who don't mind sleeping in the same bed may find basic rooms in budget hotels a less expensive proposition. Groups of three or four willing to share two or three beds will save even more.

Some hostels allow guests to stay only for a maximum of three nights, particularly in summer, though places that have upper age limits (eg 30) tend not to enforce them. Only official *auberges de jeunesse* (youth hostels) require guests to present Hostelling International (HI) cards. Curfews at Paris hostels are generally at 1 or 2 am. Few hostels accept telephone reservations from individuals, but those that do are noted in the text.

Louvre & Les Halles Areas You can't get any more central than the 1er arrondissement between the Louvre and the Forum des Halles.

Centre International BVJ Louvre (Map 7; ☎ 01 53 00 90 90; fax 01 53 00 90 91; metro Louvre-Rivoli), 20 Rue Jean-Jacques Rousseau (1er). This modern, 200 bed BVJ hostel charges 120FF (including breakfast) for a bunk in a single-sex room for two to 10 people. Guests should be aged under 35. Rooms are accessible from 2.30 pm on the day you arrive and all day after that. Kitchen facilities are not available. There is almost always space in the morning, even in summer.

Marais Area The Marais (4e) is one of the liveliest sections of the city centre and its hostels are among the city's finest. The Maison Internationale de la Jeunesse et des Étudiants runs three *hôtels de jeunes* (young people's hostels) in attractively renovated 17th and 18th century residences in the Marais.

Costs and phone number details are the same for all three. A bed in a shower-equipped, single-sex dorm room for four to eight people is 125FF (137FF in a triple, 152FF in a double, 198FF in a single), including breakfast. Rooms are closed from noon to 3 pm; curfew is from 1 to 7 am.

Individuals can make reservations for all three MIJE hostels by calling the switchboard – they'll hold you a bed until 3 pm, and the maximum stay is seven nights. During summer and other busy periods, there may not be space after about mid-morning. There's an annual membership fee of 10FF.

MIJE Fourcy (Map 8; ☎ 01 42 74 23 45; fax 01 40 27 81 64; metro Saint Paul), 6 Rue de Fourcy (4e). This 207 bed place is the largest of the three. There's a cheap restaurant here with a three course *menu* with a drink for 52FF and a *plat du jour* plus drink for 40FF.

MIJE Fauconnier (Map 8; metro Saint Paul or Pont Marie), 11 Rue du Fauconnier. This 118 bed hostel is two blocks south of MIJE Fourcy.

MIJE Maubuisson (Map 8; metro Hôtel de Ville), 12 Rue des Barres. This 114 bed place is half a block south of the *mairie* (town hall) of the 4e.

Latin Quarter The lively, student-filled Latin Quarter, in the western part of the 5e arrondissement, is ideal for young people.

Centre International BVJ Paris-Quartier Latin (Map 5; ☎ 01 43 29 34 80; fax 01 42 33 40 53; metro Maubert Mutualité), 44 Rue des Bernardins (5e). This hostel, which welcomes individual travellers over groups, has the same tariffs and rules as the Centre International BVJ Louvre (see Louvre Area later). Long-term singles/doubles with use of the kitchen are also available for 3900/ 7200FF a month.

Y & H Hostel (Map 5; ☎ 01 45 35 09 53; fax 01 47 07 22 24; young@youngandhappy.fr; metro Place Monge), 80 Rue Mouffetard (5e). This clean, very friendly, English-speaking place – the name is short for 'young & happy' – is in the happening centre of the Latin Quarter and is very popular with a younger crowd. The rooms are closed from 11 am to 5 pm but reception is always open. A bed in a cramped room with washbasin for two to four people costs 97FF, including breakfast; showers are free. The 2 am curfew is strictly enforced. In summer, the best way to get a bed is to stop by at about 9 am.

Bastille Area The relatively untouristed 11e and 12e (the areas north-east, east and south-east of Place de la Bastille) are unpretentious, working-class areas.

Auberge Internationale des Jeunes (Map 5; ☎ 01 47 00 62 00; fax 01 47 00 33 16; aij@aij-paris.com; metro Ledru Rollin), 10 Rue Trousseau (11e). This clean and very friendly hostel, 700m east of Place de la Bastille, attracts a young, international crowd and is very full in summer. Beds in dorms for two to six people cost just 81FF from November to February, 91FF from March to October, including breakfast. Rooms are closed for cleaning between 10 am and 3 pm. You can book in advance, and they'll hold a bed for you if you call from the train station.

Résidence Bastille (Map 5; ☎ 01 43 79 53 86; metro Voltaire), 151 Ave Ledru Rollin (11e). This 150 bed hostel, open year-round, is about 900m north-east of Place de la Bastille. Beds in rooms for two to four people cost 120FF (110FF from November to February), including breakfast, and there are singles for 171FF (160FF in the low season). Reception is open for check-in from 7 am to 12.30 pm and 2 to 10 pm. Curfew is at 1 am – if you'll be coming back later, inform them in advance. Lockers are available between 9 am and 6 pm for 20FF a day.

Maison Internationale des Jeunes pour la Culture et pour la Paix (MIJCP; Map 1; ☎ 01 43 71 99 21; fax 01 43 71 78 58; metro Faidherbe Chaligny), 4 Rue Titon (11e). This MIJCP, 1.3km east of Place de la Bastille, charges 110FF for a bed in a spartan dorm room for up to eight people, including breakfast. Curfew is from 2 to 6 am. The upper age limit of 30 is not strictly enforced. Telephone reservations are accepted –

your chance of finding a bed is greatest if you call or stop by between 8 and 10 am. The maximum stay is theoretically three days, but you can usually stay for a week.

Auberge de Jeunesse Jules Ferry (Map 3; ☎ 01 43 57 55 60; fax 01 40 21 79 92; auberge@micronet.fr; metro République or Oberkampf), 8 Blvd Jules Ferry (11e). This official hostel, a few blocks east of Place de la République, is a bit institutional, but the atmosphere is fairly relaxed and – an added bonus – they don't accept groups. Beds cost 113FF in a four or six person room and 118FF in a double, including breakfast. Rooms are locked from 10.30 am to 2 pm. You must have an HI card to stay here (available for 114FF) or pay an extra 19FF per night. You can send/receive emails and surf the Internet from the computer in the reception area (connection 5FF). There is a Franprix supermarket nearby at 28 Blvd Jules Ferry.

Centre International de Séjour de Paris Ravel (Map 1; ☎ 01 44 75 60 00; metro Porte de Vincennes), 4-6 Ave Maurice Ravel (12e). The 230 bed CISP Ravel, on the south-eastern edge of the city, charges 113FF per bed in a 12 person dormitory, 138FF in a two to five person room, and 181FF in a single, including breakfast. There is no upper age limit. Reception is open from 6.30 am to 1.30 am. Individuals (as opposed to groups, which predominate) can make telephone reservations up to two days ahead. To get there from Porte de Vincennes metro station, walk south on Blvd Soult, turn left onto Rue Jules Lemaître and then go right onto Rue Maurice Ravel.

Chinatown & Montparnasse Areas

The southern 13e, 14e and 15e arrondissements are not particularly exciting places, but neither are they very far from the Left Bank's major sights.

Centre International de Séjour de Paris Kellermann (Map 1; ☎ 01 44 16 37 38; metro Porte d'Italie), 17 Blvd Kellermann (13e). The 350 bed CISP Kellermann has beds in dorm rooms accommodating two to four people for 138FF, and 113FF in those with eight beds. Basic singles are 156FF or 186FF with shower and WC. A double with facilities costs 312FF. Except on Friday and Saturday nights, curfew is at 1.30 am. The maximum stay is five or six nights. Kitchen facilities are not available. Telephone reservations can be made up to 48 hours before you arrive. Facilities for disabled people are available.

Maison des Clubs UNESCO (Map 1; ☎ 01 43 36 00 63; fax 01 45 35 05 96; girardin@fiap.asso.fr; metro Glacière), 43 Rue de la Glacière (13e). This rather institutional place charges 125FF for a bed in a large, unsurprising room for three or four people; singles/doubles are 165/145FF per person. In the multi-bed rooms, priority is given to 18 to 30-year-olds, but older travellers are accepted if there's space. Beds booked by telephone are usually held until 2 pm – if you'll be arriving later, ring them on the day of your arrival.

Foyer des Jeunes Filles (Map 1; ☎ 01 44 16 22 22; fax 01 45 65 46 20; metro Glacière), 234 Rue de Tolbiac (13e). Also known as Foyer Tolbiac, this friendly, Protestant-run dormitory accepts women travellers only, with no minimum or maximum stay and no upper age limit from mid-June to mid-September (or, if there's space, during the rest of the year). A single room costs 120FF (including breakfast, except on Sunday) plus an annual fee of 30FF. There are kitchens on each floor. Reservations can be made by phone or fax, and reception is open 24 hours a day. There's no curfew. The Foyer is about 600m south of the Glacière metro stop so you might want to take bus No 21 or 62 from Châtelet or the Jardin du Luxembourg. Orlybus stops nearby.

Foyer International d'Accueil de Paris Jean Monnet (Map 1; ☎ 01 45 89 89 15; fax 01 45 81 63 91; metro Glacière), 30 Rue Cabanis (14e). FIAP Jean Monnet, a few blocks south-east of Place Denfert Rochereau, has modern, carpeted rooms for eight/four/two people – pretty luxurious by hostel standards – for 131/161/184FF per person (including breakfast); singles are 281FF. Rooms specially outfitted for *handicapés* (disabled people) are available. Curfew is from 2 to 6 am. Telephone reservations are accepted up to 15 days ahead, but priority is given to groups.

Three Ducks Hostel (Map 4; ☎ 01 48 42 04 05; metro Félix Faure or Commerce), 6 Place Étienne Pernet (15e). Named after three ducks who used to live in the courtyard, the friendly, down-to-earth Trois Canards, at the southern end of Rue du Commerce, is a favourite with young backpackers, who apparently can get very noisy at night; we have had a litany of complaints from readers about loud music, drunken parties, tiny kitchens and ice-cold showers. A bunk bed in a very basic room for two to eight people costs 97FF (87FF from November to April), including breakfast. Telephone reservations are accepted on the day of arrival. Kitchen facilities are available. Rooms are closed between 11 am and 5 pm and there's a 2 am curfew.

Aloha Hostel (Map 4; ☎ 01 42 73 03 03; fax 01 42 73 14 14; metro Volontaires), 1 Rue Borromée (15e). Run by the same people (and with the same prices) as the Three Ducks but much more laid-back and quiet, this place is about 1km west of Gare Montparnasse. The rooms, which have two to six beds (some rooms have showers), are closed from 11 am to 5 pm, but reception is always open. Curfew is at 2 am. Kitchen facilities and safe-deposit boxes are available.

Montmartre & Pigalle Both the 9e and 18e arrondissements have fine hostels, one of them brand-new.

Le Village Hostel (Map 9; ☎ 01 42 64 22 02; fax 01 42 64 22 04; village@levillage-hostel.fr; metro Anvers), 20 Rue d'Orsel (18e). This fine new 26 room hostel with beamed ceilings and views of Sacré Cœur has beds in rooms for two to six people for 117FF (97FF from November to March) and doubles/triples/quads for 147/137/127FF per person (137/117/107FF in winter). Singles are 180FF. All rooms have showers and WC. Prices include breakfast, and kitchen facilities are available. There is also a bar and a lovely outside terrace.

Woodstock Hostel (Map 3; ☎ 01 48 78 87 76; fax 01 48 78 01 63; metro Anvers), 48 Rue Rodier (9e). This hostel is just down the hill from rowdy Pigalle in a quiet, residential quarter. A dorm bed in a room for four to six people costs 77FF in the off season and in a double room a bed is 87FF; both tariffs include breakfast. In summer prices rise to 87FF and 97FF respectively. There's a 2 am curfew and rooms are shut from 11.30 am to 5 pm.

20e Arrondissement This official hostel may be away from the centre of the action, but it's just one metro stop from the Paris-Gallieni international bus station.

Auberge de Jeunesse D'Artagnan (Map 1; ☎ 01 40 32 34 56; fax 01 40 32 34 55; 101717.3452@compuserve.com; metro Porte de Bagnolet), 80 Rue Vitruve (20e). The hostel has rooms with two to eight beds, big lockers, laundry facilities, Internet access and even a cinema! It has the same rules and rates as the Auberge de Jeunesse Jules Ferry (see the Bastille Area earlier).

Hotels – Louvre & Les Halles Areas

This area – for the most part the 1er with bits of the western 4e and eastern 8e – may be very central, but don't expect to find tranquillity or many bargains. Both airports are linked to the Châtelet-Les Halles metro/RER station (Map 7) by Roissyrail and Orlyval.

Budget Very few cheapies are left in the 1er.

Hôtel de Lille (Map 7; ☎ 01 42 33 33 42; metro Palais Royal), 8 Rue du Pélican (1er). At this 13 room place clean singles/doubles (200/230FF) come with washbasin, bidet and cheap ceiling tiles. Doubles with shower are 280FF. A token for a 15 minute shower costs an appalling 30FF.

Mid-Range Welcome to the realm of charmless upgrades.

Hôtel Saint Honoré (Map 7; ☎ 01 42 36 20 38; fax 01 42 21 44 08; metro Châtelet), 85 Rue Saint Honoré (1er). This upgraded but cramped one star place offers doubles/quads from 280/450FF; more spacious doubles are 320 to 350FF.

Top End The 1er is the area to come to if you really want to blow the budget.

Grand Hôtel de Champagne (Map 7; ☎ 01 42 36 60 00; fax 01 45 08 43 33; metro Châtelet), 17 Rue Jean Lantier (1er). This very comfortable, three star hotel has 42 rooms costing from 596 to 721FF (in July and August) to 652 to 812FF (in June and from September to November).

Hôtel Brighton (Map 2; ☎ 01 47 03 61 61; fax 01 42 60 41 78; metro Tuileries), 218 Rue de Rivoli (1er). This is a three star, 70 room establishment with lovely singles/doubles/triples starting at 545/580/1025FF and climbing to 915/950/1125FF, depending on the season and the room. The rooms that overlook the Jardin des Tuileries are the most popular; those on the 4th and 5th floors afford views over the trees to the Seine.

Hôtel de Crillon (Map 2; ☎ 01 44 71 15 00; fax 01 44 71 15 02; metro Concorde), 10 Place de la Concorde (8e). The colonnaded, 200 year old Crillon, whose sparkling public areas (including Les Ambassadeurs restaurant, with two Michelin stars) are sumptuously decorated with chandeliers, original sculptures, gilt mouldings, tapestries and inlaid furniture, is the epitome of French luxury. Spacious singles/doubles with pink marble bathrooms start at 2600/3250FF or from 2950/3550 in May-June and September-October. The cheapest suites are 4900FF, larger ones go for 6800 to 8500FF. Breakfast is another 170FF (continental) or 230FF (American).

Hôtel Ritz (Map 2; ☎ 01 43 16 30 30; fax 01 43 16 36 68; metro Opéra), 15 Place Vendôme (1er). As one of the world's most celebrated and expensive hotels, the 142 room, 45 suite Ritz has sparkling rooms starting at 2900/3500FF (3300/3900FF in May-June and September-October). Junior suites begin at 4700FF (5200FF); regular suites start at 6000FF. Facilities include a deluxe health club, a swimming pool and squash courts. The hotel restaurant, L'Espadon, has two Michelin stars, and the renovated Hemingway Bar is supposedly where Papa imbibed.

Hotels – Marais Area

This district is one of the liveliest and trendiest in Paris.

Budget Despite gentrification, the Marais (4e) still has a few cheapies left.

Hôtel Rivoli (Map 8; ☎ 01 42 72 08 41; metro Hôtel de Ville), 44 Rue de Rivoli (4e). This hotel on the corner of Rue des Mauvais Garçons is one of the best deals in town. Basic and somewhat noisy rooms with washbasin start at 160FF. Singles with shower are 180FF; doubles with bath but no toilet are 190 to 220FF, and a double with bath and toilet is 250FF. The hall shower (20FF) is sometimes lukewarm. The front door is locked from 2 to 6.30 am.

Hôtel Le Palais de Fès (Map 8; ☎ 01 42 72 03 68; fax 01 42 60 49 33; metro Hôtel de Ville), 41 Rue du Roi de Sicile (4e). Fairly large, modern doubles cost 200FF with washbasin, 250FF with shower and 280FF with shower and toilet. Singles start at 150FF. Hall showers are 15FF. Reception is in the Moroccan restaurant on the ground floor.

Hôtel Moderne (Map 8; ☎ 01 48 87 97 05; metro Saint Paul), 3 Rue Caron (4e). The less-than-salubrious singles/doubles come with washbasin and start at 130/160FF; doubles with shower are 190FF (220FF with toilet). There's a toilet and shower (15FF) on the stairs halfway between each floor. Telephone reservations are accepted up to a week before your scheduled arrival.

Hôtel Pratic (Map 8; ☎ 01 48 87 80 47; fax 01 48 87 40 04; metro Saint Paul), 9 Rue d'Ormesson (4e). This 23 room hotel has nondescript rooms from 180/245FF (245/290FF with shower). Doubles with bath and toilet are 340FF.

Hôtel Sully (Map 8; ☎ 01 42 78 49 32; metro Bastille), 48 Rue Saint Antoine (4e). You'll find one star doubles for 200FF with washbasin, 250FF with shower, and 270FF with shower and toilet at this hotel, which is only one block south of Place des Vosges. A two bed triple with shower and toilet costs 300FF. The hall shower is free.

Hôtel de la Herse d'Or (Map 8; ☎ 01 48 87 84 09; fax 01 48 87 94 01; metro Bastille), 20 Rue Saint Antoine (4e). This is a friendly place with unsurprising, serviceable singles with washbasin for 160FF and with basin and toilet for 200FF; doubles with toilet and a small shower are 260 to 295FF. Hall showers are 10FF.

Mid-Range There's a good choice of mid-range places in the Marais.

Hôtel de Nice (Map 8; ☎ 01 42 78 55 29; fax 01 42 78 36 07; metro Hôtel de Ville), 42bis Rue de Rivoli (4e). The English-speaking owner of this especially warm, family-run place has 23 comfortable singles/doubles/triples/quads for 380/450/550/650FF. Many rooms have balconies, on which guests have been known to sunbathe in summer.

Hôtel Le Compostelle (Map 8; ☎ 01 42 78 59 99; fax 01 40 29 05 18; metro Hôtel de Ville), 31 Rue du Roi de Sicile (4e). This three star place, whose 26 singles/doubles (from 300/400FF) come with TV, is tasteful but not fancy. Rooms with bath start at 490FF.

Hôtel de la Place des Vosges (Map 8; ☎ 01 42 72 60 46; fax 01 42 72 02 64; metro Bastille), 12 Rue de Birague (4e). Superbly situated right next to Place des Vosges, this 16 room, two star place has rather average singles from 330FF (448FF in summer) and doubles with bathroom from 475 to 664FF. There's a tiny lift from the 1st floor.

Hôtel Castex (Map 8; ☎ 01 42 72 31 52; fax 01 42 72 57 91; metro Bastille), 5 Rue Castex (4e). This cheery, 27 room establishment has been run by the same family since 1919. Quiet, old-fashioned (but immaculate) rooms with shower cost 240/320FF (290 to 360FF with toilet). Triples/quads are 460/530FF. If possible, reserve at least four weeks ahead.

Top End There are top-end hotels in the heart of the Marais as well as in the vicinity of the elegant Place des Vosges.

Hôtel Central Marais (Map 8; ☎ 01 48 87 56 08; fax 01 42 77 06 27; metro Hôtel de Ville), 2 Rue Sainte Croix de la Bretonnerie (4e). This seven room, mostly gay male hotel also welcomes lesbians. Singles/doubles with one bathroom for every two rooms are 400/485FF; suites for two/three people are 595/720FF. After 3 pm reception is around the corner in the bar (33 Rue Vieille du Temple). Reservations should be made four to six weeks ahead – they'll hold a room if you give them a Visa or MasterCard number.

Hôtel Axial Beaubourg (Map 8; ☎ 01 42 72 72 22; fax 01 42 72 03 53; metro Hôtel de Ville), 11 Rue du Temple (4e). The name of this three star place says it all: modern mixed with historic. It's in the heart of the Marais and charges from 450FF for singles and 530FF for doubles.

Grand Hôtel Malher (Map 8; ☎ 01 42 72 60 92; fax 01 42 72 25 37; metro Saint Paul), 5 Rue Malher (4e). The 31 nicely appointed rooms at this family-run, two star establishment start from 475/605FF (580/730FF during high-season periods).

Hotels – Île de la Cité & Île de Saint Louis

The islands in the Seine are an easy walk from central Paris.

Budget Believe it or not, the only hotel on the Île de la Cité (1er) is a cheapie.

Hôtel Henri IV (Map 6; ☎ 01 43 54 44 53; metro Cité or Saint Michel), 25 Place Dauphine (1er). This old-fashioned, very popular hotel is a bit tattered and worn but has 21 adequate rooms: one-bed rooms cost from 116 to 260FF, two beds from 200 to 270FF. Showers in the hall cost 15FF and breakfast is included. The three rooms with their own showers cost 230 to 270FF. Reception is open until 8 pm, but you should make reservations a month in advance. Credit cards are not accepted.

Top End The chichi Île de Saint Louis (4e) remains as pricey as ever.

Hôtel Saint Louis (Map 8; ☎ 01 46 34 04 80; fax 01 46 34 02 13; metro Pont Marie), 75 Rue Saint Louis en l'Île (4e). The 21 doubles (695/895FF with one/two beds) at this three star establishment are appealing but unspectacular, though the public areas are lovely. The basement breakfast room dates from the early 1600s; breakfast costs 49FF.

Hôtel des Deux Îles (Map 8; ☎ 01 43 26 13 35; fax 01 43 29 60 25; metro Pont Marie), 59 Rue Saint Louis en l'Île (4e). This excellent 17 room hotel has singles from 710FF and doubles from 840FF.

Hotels – Latin Quarter

Mid-range hotels in the Latin Quarter are popular with visiting academics so rooms are hardest to find when conferences and seminars are scheduled: usually March to July and in October.

The Luxembourg and Port Royal metro/RER stations are linked to both airports by Roissyrail and Orlyval.

Budget Real cheapies have almost gone the way of the dodo in the Latin Quarter.

Port Royal Hôtel (Map 1; ☎ 01 43 31 70 06; fax 01 43 31 33 67; metro Les Gobelins), 8 Blvd de Port Royal (5e). The clean, quiet and well kept 46 singles/doubles at this older, one star place start at 175/218FF (325FF with shower and toilet). Hall showers are 15FF.

Hôtel de Médicis (Map 6; ☎ 01 43 54 14 66 for reception, ☎ 01 43 29 53 64 for the public phone in the hall; metro Luxembourg), 214 Rue Saint Jacques (5e). This is exactly what a dilapidated Latin Quarter dive for impoverished students should be like. Very basic singles start at 85FF, but don't be surprised if they're occupied; doubles/triples are 160/230FF. Reservations are not accepted.

Hôtel du Centre (Map 6; ☎ 01 43 26 13 07; metro Saint Michel), 5 Rue Saint Jacques (5e). This is a run-down establishment with only basic singles/doubles, which start at 100/150FF; doubles with shower are 180FF, triples 300FF. Hall showers are 20FF. Reservations are not accepted.

Mid-Range There are dozens of two and three-star hotels, including a cluster near the Sorbonne and another group along the lively Rue des Écoles.

Grand Hôtel du Progrès (Map 6; ☎ 01 43 54 53 18; metro Luxembourg), 50 Rue Gay Lussac (5e). Washbasin equipped singles at this older, 36 room hotel start at 150FF; large and old-fashioned doubles with a view and morning sunlight are 240FF (330FF with shower and toilet), including breakfast. Hall showers are free. Credit cards are not accepted. The hotel is closed in August.

Hôtel Gay Lussac (Map 6; ☎ 01 43 54 23 96; fax 01 40 51 79 49; metro Luxembourg), 29 Rue Gay Lussac (5e). This family-run, one star place with a bit of character and a lift has small rooms starting as low as 160FF but averaging 200FF; rooms with toilet cost from 240 to 260FF, and rooms with shower or bath and toilet from 310 to 340FF. Fairly large doubles/three-bed quads with shower, toilet and high ceilings are 360/500FF.

Familia Hôtel (Map 5; ☎ 01 43 54 55 27; fax 01 43 29 61 77; metro Cardinal Lemoine), 11 Rue des Écoles (5e). This is a welcoming, well situated, two star establishment with 30 attractively decorated rooms. Eight have balconies, from which you can catch a glimpse of Notre Dame. Doubles go for 370 to 520FF, triples are 585 to 620FF and quads are 720FF.

Hôtel Saint Jacques (Map 6; ☎ 01 44 07 45 45; fax 01 43 25 65 50; metro Maubert Mutualité), 35 Rue des Écoles (5e). This two star hotel hasn't lost its old-time charm in the slightest. Spacious singles/doubles/triples start at 360/420/560FF; many have ornamented ceilings and balconies.

Hôtel Marignan (Map 6; ☎ 01 43 25 31 03; metro Maubert Mutualité), 13 Rue du Sommerard (5e). This friendly, 30 room place has pleasant, old-fashioned singles/doubles/ triples/quads with washbasin for 190/270/340/410FF, with shower for 330/360/470/520FF; prices include breakfast. About half of the rooms have toilets. Guests also have free use of a fridge, microwave, washing machine and dryer.

Hôtel Cluny Sorbonne (Map 6; ☎ 01 43 54 66 66; fax 01 43 29 68 07; metro Luxembourg), 8 Rue Victor Cousin (5e). The lift in this two star hotel, which has pleasant, well kept singles/doubles/twins for 375/380/400FF, is the size of a telephone booth. If you'll be checking in before 1 pm, you can usually reserve a room by telephone without sending a deposit.

Hôtel Esmeralda (Map 6; ☎ 01 43 54 19 20; fax 01 40 51 00 68; metro Saint Michel), 4 Rue Saint Julien le Pauvre (5e). This 19 room hotel, tucked away in a quiet street with full views of Notre Dame, has been everyone's secret 'find' for years now. As a result you'll need to book well in advance. A simple single with washbasin is 160FF; doubles with shower and toilet are 320FF, with bath and toilet from 450 to 490FF. Triples start at 500FF.

Top End For this category the Latin Quarter generally offers better value than the nearby 6e arrondissement.

Hôtel de L'Espérance (Map 1; ☎ 01 47 07 10 99; fax 01 43 37 56 19; metro Censier Daubenton), 15 Rue Pascal (5e). Just a couple of minutes walk south of lively Rue Mouffetard, this quiet and pleasantly elegant 38 room hotel has singles/doubles with shower and toilet for 360/390FF, or with bath for 390/430FF. Larger rooms with two beds cost 450FF. Triples are 500FF. Breakfast is 35FF.

Hôtel Au Royal Cardinal (Map 5; ☎ 01 43 26 83 64; fax 01 44 07 22 32; metro Cardinal Lemoine), 1 Rue des Écoles (5e). We've heard good things about this very central, 37 room hotel near the Sorbonne. Singles from 300 to 435FF, doubles from 310 to 495FF and triples from 550 to 640FF.

Hôtel Saint Christophe (Map 5; ☎ 01 43 31 81 54; fax 01 43 31 12 54; metro Place Monge), 17 Rue Lacépède (5e). A classy small hotel with 31 well equipped rooms at 500/650FF, although discounts are often available.

Hôtel des Grandes Écoles (Map 5; ☎ 01 43 26 79 23; fax 01 43 25 28 15; metro Cardinal Lemoine), 65 Rue du Cardinal Lemoine (5e). This three star place with 47 rooms just north of Place de la Contrescarpe has one of the loveliest situations in the Latin Quarter, tucked away in a courtyard off a medieval street with its own garden. Singles are 320 to 550FF, doubles 350 to 600FF.

Grand Hôtel Saint Michel (Map 6; ☎ 01 46 33 33 02; fax 01 40 46 96 33; metro Luxembourg), 19 Rue Cujas (5e). This one-time two star hotel has been given an extra *étoile* (star) after a complete renovation and has raised its prices accordingly: singles/doubles (some with balcony) now cost 690/790FF, while triples are 1090FF. The attached salon de thé is quite pleasant.

Résidence Monge (Map 5; ☎ 01 43 26 87 90; fax 01 43 54 47 25), 55 Rue Monge (5e). This clean, well managed hotel with 36 rooms right in the thick of things is an expensive choice if you're alone (singles cost from 380 to 480FF) but a good deal if you've got a companion or two; doubles and triples start at 450FF.

Hotels – 6e Arrondissement

Saint Germain des Prés is a delightful area, but it is quite expensive given the modest comforts offered by most mid-range places.

Mid-Range The mid-range places listed are the least expensive hotels the 6e has to offer.

Hôtel de Nesle (Map 6; ☎ 01 43 54 62 41; metro Odéon or Mabillon), 7 Rue de Nesle (6e). The Nesle is a spirited, often *too* jolly hostelry that's been a favourite with young travellers since it was established in 1971. It remains a good place to meet other travellers. A bed in a simple double is 150FF, if you come alone they'll find you a roommate. Singles with shower are 250FF; doubles with toilet and shower or bath are 400FF. Reservations are not accepted – the only way to get a bed is to stop by in the morning.

Hôtel Saint Michel (Map 6; ☎ 01 43 26 98 70; metro Saint Michel), 17 Rue Gît le Cœur (6e). Comfortable but pretty standard, soundproofed rooms start from 190FF with nothing, from 285FF for rooms with shower but no toilet, and from 325 to 370FF for rooms with shower and toilet. The hall shower costs 12FF.

Delhy's Hôtel (Map 6; ☎ 01 43 26 58 25; fax 01 43 26 51 06; metro Saint Michel), 22 Rue de l'Hirondelle (6e). This 21 room, one star hotel, through the arch from 6 Place Saint Michel, has neat, simple washbasin equipped singles/doubles for as low as 180/290FF; with toilet they're 250/290FF, while a double with shower is 380FF. Hall showers cost 25FF. Breakfast (30FF) is usually obligatory during summer and holiday periods.

Hôtel Petit Trianon (Map 6; ☎ 01 43 54 94 64; metro Odéon), 2 Rue de l'Ancienne Comédie (6e). Plain singles/doubles with washbasin and bidet at this 15 room hotel are 170/260FF; doubles with shower begin at 350FF. Doubles/triples with shower and toilet are 400/450FF. The showers in the hall are free.

Hôtel Saint André des Arts (Map 6; ☎ 01 43 26 96 16; fax 01 43 29 73 34; metro Odéon), 66 Rue Saint André des Arts (6e). Rooms at this 31 room hotel, on a lively, restaurant-lined thoroughfare, start at 360/460/570/620FF for one/two/three/four people, including breakfast.

Hôtel des Académies (Map 4; ☎ 01 43 26 66 44; fax 01 43 26 03 72; metro Vavin), 15 Rue de la Grande Chaumière (6e). This truly charming 21 room hotel has been run by the same friendly family since 1920 and has singles with washbasin for 210FF, and shower equipped doubles for 285FF (325 to 340FF with shower and toilet).

Top End The pricey three-star hotels are around Saint Germain des Prés.

Hôtel Michelet Odéon (Map 6; ☎ 01 46 34 27 80; fax 01 46 34 55 35; metro Odéon), 6 Place de l'Odéon (6e). Only a one minute walk from the Jardin du Luxembourg, this 42 room place has tasteful, generously proportioned singles for 420FF, doubles from 480 to 540FF, triples from 645FF and quads from 700FF. Rooms with bath rather than shower cost 50 to 60FF more.

Hôtel des Deux Continents (Map 6; ☎ 01 43 26 72 46; fax 01 43 25 67 80; metro Saint Germain des Prés), 25 Rue Jacob (6e). This 41 room establishment has spacious singles for 695FF, doubles from 765 to 815FF and triples for 1020FF; breakfast is 45FF.

Hôtel du Globe (Map 6; ☎ 01 43 26 35 50; fax 01 46 33 62 69; metro Odéon), 15 Rue des Quatre Vents (6e). The 15 singles/doubles in this eclectic two star hotel – each with their own theme – cost from 350 to 450FF.

Hôtel des Marronniers (Map 6; ☎ 01 43 25 30 60; fax 01 40 46 83 56; metro Saint Germain des Prés), 21 Rue Jacob (6e). This 37 room place has less-than-huge singles/doubles/triples from 540/735/1060FF and a charming garden out the back.

Citadines Apparthôtel Raspail Montparnasse (Map 6; ☎ 01 43 35 46 35; fax 01 40 47 43 01; metro Vavin), 121 Blvd du Montparnasse (6e). At the southern boundary of the 6e near Gare Montparnasse, the apartment-style rooms here feature kitchen areas. Prices vary during the year from 610 to 670FF for a small 'studette', 710 to 775FF for a two person studio, or 1230 to 1375FF for a two bedroom apartment. Rates are cheaper if you stay longer than seven days.

Hotels – Gare Saint Lazare & Grands Boulevards

The avenues around Blvd Montmartre are a popular nightlife area. Roissybus links Charles de Gaulle airport with Place de l'Opéra.

Budget The better deals are away from Gare Saint Lazare, but there are several places along Rue d'Amsterdam beside the station.

Hôtel Du Calvados (Map 2; ☎ 01 48 74 39 31; fax 01 48 74 33 75; metro Saint Lazare), 20 Rue d'Amsterdam (9e). Singles at this 24 room hotel start at 180FF, while doubles with washbasin and toilet are 220FF (300FF with toilet and shower).

Mid-Range There are quite a few two and three-star hotels along Rue d'Amsterdam, which runs along the eastern side of Gare Saint Lazare.

Hôtel Britannia (Map 2; ☎ 01 42 85 36 36; fax 01 42 85 16 93; metro Saint Lazare), 24 Rue d'Amsterdam (9e). This is a two star, 46 room place with narrow hallways and pleasant, clean doubles with shower/bath for 445/490FF, and triples for 565/610FF that are a bit on the small side.

Hôtel Chopin (Map 7; ☎ 01 47 70 58 10; fax 01 42 47 00 70; metro Rue Montmartre), 46 Passage Jouffroy (9e). This 36 room, two star hotel near 10 Blvd Montmartre is down one of Paris' most delightful 19th century covered shopping arcades. Basic singles start at 355FF; shower equipped singles/doubles/triples cost from 405/450/565FF. After the arcade closes at 10 pm, ring the *sonnette de nuit* (the night doorbell).

Top End There are a few reasonably priced top-end hotels in this area.

Hôtel Peletier-Haussmann (Map 7; ☎ 01 42 46 79 53; fax 01 48 24 12 01; metro Richelieu Drouot), 15 Rue Le Peletier (9e). This friendly 24 room hotel just off Blvd Haussmann has shower equipped singles/doubles/triples/quads at 330/410/475/500FF.

Citadines Apparthôtel Opéra (Map 7; ☎ 01 44 50 23 23; fax 01 44 50 23 50; metro Richelieu Drouot), 18 Rue Favart (2e). Almost opposite the Opéra Comique, this branch of the apartment-style chain has small studios accommodating one person from 675 to 755FF, two-person studios from 755 to 845FF and two-bedroom apartments from 1230 to 1380FF. Rates are lower if you stay more than a week.

Hotels – Gare du Nord Area

This may not be one of the city's most attractive districts, but it's not dangerous, unless you opt to spend the night in the train station. Gare du Nord is linked to Charles de Gaulle airport by Roissyrail and RATP bus No 350 and to Orly airport by Orlyval.

Budget This area of Paris has some pretty good budget deals.

Hôtel de Milan (Map 3; ☎ 01 40 37 88 50; fax 01 46 07 89 48; metro Gare du Nord), 17-19 Rue de Saint Quentin (10e). This friendly, old-fashioned, one star place is equipped with an ancient (and temperamental) lift. Clean, quiet but basic singles and doubles are available from 153 and 186FF. Doubles with toilet and shower are 266 to 346FF, triples cost from 429FF. Hall showers cost 18FF; breakfast is 20FF.

Hôtel Bonne Nouvelle (Map 3; ☎ 01 48 74 99 90; metro Gare du Nord), 125 Blvd de Magenta (10e). The 'Good News' is a modest hotel with simple, clean, shower equipped doubles from 150 to 220FF. Hall toilets are on the landing.

Grand Hôtel Magenta (Map 3; ☎ 01 48 78 03 65; fax 01 48 78 41 64; metro Gare du Nord), 129 Blvd de Magenta (10e). Clean, spacious rooms are available with washbasin and bidet from 130 to 145FF, with shower from 220FF, or with shower and toilet from 260FF. Larger rooms for three to five people are 320 to 450FF. Hall showers are 20FF.

Hôtel La Vieille France (Map 3; ☎ 01 45 26 42 37; fax 01 45 26 99 07; metro Gare du Nord), 151 Rue La Fayette (10e). A 34 room place with spacious, pleasant and soundproofed doubles with washbasin and bidet for 195FF, and with bath or shower and toilet from 265 to 295FF. Triples are 320 to 360FF. Hall showers cost 15FF.

Mid-Range The area around the Gare du Nord has a lot of two-star hotels.

Nord Hôtel (Map 3; ☎ 01 45 26 43 40; fax 01 42 82 90 23), 37 Rue de Saint Quentin (10e). This 46 room hotel, right across from Gare du Nord, has clean, quiet singles for 275 to 330FF or doubles from 330 to 360FF. An extra person costs 95FF. Breakfast is 25FF.

Hotels – Gare de l'Est

This lively, working-class area of Paris has its own attractions even if your train doesn't pull into Gare de l'Est. RATP bus No 350 to/from Charles de Gaulle airport stops right in front of the station.

Budget The 10e has some of Paris' grungiest flophouses, but the few diamonds in the rough offer some real bargains.

Sibour Hôtel (Map 3; ☎ 01 46 07 20 74; fax 01 46 07 37 17; metro Gare de l'Est), 4 Rue Sibour (10e). This friendly, one star place has 45 well kept rooms, including old-fashioned singles/doubles from 175/195FF (285FF with shower, toilet and TV). Hall showers cost 15FF.

Hôtel d'Alsace (Map 3; ☎ 01 40 37 75 41; metro Gare de l'Est), 85 Blvd de Strasbourg (10e). An old, but well maintained, 32 room hostelry with bright, clean singles/doubles/quads with washbasin for 134/187/247FF. Doubles with shower are 227FF. The fireplaces give the rooms a bit of old-time charm. Hall showers cost 10FF. The entrance is on the left-hand side of the passageway.

Hôtel Liberty (Map 3; ☎ 01 42 08 60 58; fax 01 42 40 12 59; metro Château d'Eau), 16 Rue de Nancy, 1st floor (10e). Clean, plain singles/doubles start at 150/160FF (160/185FF with shower, 180/210FF with shower and toilet). A bed for a third person costs 40FF. Hall showers are 10FF.

Hôtel Pacific (Map 3; ☎ 01 47 70 07 91; fax 01 47 70 98 43; metro Château d'Eau), 70 Rue du Château d'Eau (10e). An older one star place, the Pacific has 24 spacious, unpretentious and clean doubles/triples for 130/220FF (250FF with shower). Hall showers are 15FF.

Hôtel Château d'Eau (Map 3; ☎ 01 48 24 67 09; metro Château d'Eau), 61 Rue du Château d'Eau, 1st floor (10e). If you like your linoleum with cigarette burns, this run-down, partly residential hotel is for you. Large, basic singles/doubles cost 120/150FF (220FF with shower). Hall showers are 15FF.

Mid-Range There are quite a few two and three-star places around Gare de l'Est.

Hôtel Français (Map 3; ☎ 01 40 35 94 14; fax 01 40 35 55 40; metro Gare de l'Est), 13 Rue du 8 Mai 1945 (10e). A 71 room place with attractive, almost luxurious, singles/doubles/triples (some with balconies) for 385/430/530FF. Children with parents are free. It costs 30FF to park.

Grand Hôtel de Paris (Map 3; ☎ 01 46 07 40 56; fax 01 42 05 99 18; metro Gare de l'Est), 72 Blvd de Strasbourg (10e). This well run (though extravagantly named) establishment has 49 pleasant, soundproofed singles/doubles/triples/quads (300/350/450/500FF) and a tiny lift. If you stay at least four days in the off season, they may throw in breakfast (30FF) for free.

Hotels – Bastille Area

The area just east of Place de la Bastille (ie around Rue de Lappe) has become one of Paris' trendiest nightlife areas since the construction of the Opéra Bastille. Farther east is an ungentrified, typically Parisian working-class neighbourhood whose hotels cater mainly to French businesspeople of modest means. Place de la Nation (Map 1) is linked to Charles de Gaulle airport by RATP bus No 351.

Budget The 11e has Paris' best selection of respectable, old-time cheapies. The best deals are away from Place de la Bastille.

Hôtel Baudin (Map 5; ☎ 01 47 00 18 91; fax 01 48 07 04 66; metro Ledru Rollin), 113 Ave Ledru Rollin (11e). This once grand, old-fashioned, one star hostelry has 17 mercifully unmodernised singles/doubles from 120/220FF (220/270FF with bath and toilet); triples are 80FF more. Hall showers are free.

Hôtel de France (Map 5; ☎ 01 43 79 53 22; metro Voltaire), 159 Ave Ledru Rollin (11e). At this one star establishment, decent, well maintained singles/doubles/triples with shower go for 150/220/280FF. All the toilets are off the hall.

Hôtel de Savoie (Map 1; ☎ 01 43 72 96 47; metro Voltaire), 27 Rue Richard Lenoir (11e). Nondescript but serviceable singles/doubles start at 120/150FF; showers are free. Rooms with shower are 150/220FF.

Hôtel Familial (Map 1; ☎ 01 43 67 48 24; metro Voltaire), 33 Rue Richard Lenoir (11e). This family run, old-time cheapie with basic, slightly run-down singles/doubles with washbasin start from 100/120FF. Hall showers are 15FF.

Hôtel des Alliés (Map 5; ☎ 01 44 73 01 17; metro Ledru Rollin), 90 Rue du Faubourg Saint Antoine (12e). This uninspiring, 37 room place offers one of the better deals in the Bastille area with singles/doubles/triples/quads ranging from 90/150/195/240FF, to 130/180/210/280FF in the high season. All rooms have a shower (four with bath).

Hôtel Camélia (Map 1; ☎ 01 43 73 67 50; metro Nation), 6 Ave Philippe Auguste (11e). This family-run, one star establishment has 30 pleasant, well kept rooms from 150FF, 210FF with shower, and from 220 to 250FF with shower and toilet. Hall showers cost 20FF. The hotel is closed from late July to late August.

Hôtel Central (Map 1; ☎ 01 43 73 73 53; metro Nation), 16 Ave Philippe Auguste (11e). This quiet and clean place just north of Place de la Nation has singles/doubles/quads with washbasin and bidet for 128/155/260FF. Hall showers cost 20FF (less if you stay for a few days).

Hôtel Saint Amand (Map 5; ☎ 01 47 00 90 55; metro Ledru Rollin), 6 Rue Trousseau (11e). The linoleum floored, washbasin equipped rooms spread over six floors (there's no lift) are nothing fancy, but the prices begin at only 100/120FF (from 170FF with shower). Hall showers are 20FF.

Hôtel Bastille Opéra (Map 5; ☎ 01 43 55 16 06; metro Bastille), 6 Rue de la Roquette (11e). This ageing, 20 room place, just off Place de la Bastille, has basic rooms starting at 130/180FF. Showers are free. Reception, open 24 hours, is on the 1st floor – push the intercom button to get in. Telephone reservations are not accepted, but if you call from the train station they'll hold a room for an hour or two. There are other hotels along the same street.

Vix Hôtel (Map 5; ☎ 01 48 05 12 58; metro Bastille or Ledru Rollin), 19 Rue de Charonne (11e). This place is a bit dreary and not exactly spotless, but it has plenty of basic rooms from 100/120FF; hall showers are 15FF. Doubles with shower cost 150FF. Telephone reservations are not usually accepted.

Mid-Range Two star comfort is less expensive in the 11e than in the inner arrondissements.

Hôtel Bastille (Map 5; ☎ 01 47 00 06 71; fax 01 43 38 54 27; metro Bastille), 24 Rue de la Roquette (11e). The youthful staff at this friendly, two star establishment offer neat, modern singles/doubles/triples for 320/380/430FF, including breakfast. From June to September and around Christmas, a bed in a single-sex shared triple with shower and toilet costs 121FF, including breakfast.

Hôtel Pax (Map 5; ☎ 01 47 00 40 98; fax 01 43 38 57 81; metro Bastille or Ledru Rollin), 12 Rue de Charonne (11e). Large, spotless rooms range from 200 to 250FF (250 to 380FF with toilet and shower).

Hôtel Lyon Mulhouse (Map 5; ☎ 01 47 00 91 50; fax 01 47 00 06 31; metro Bastille), 8 Blvd Beaumarchais (11e). This renovated two star hotel with 40 rooms offers quiet, predictable singles from 330 to 355FF, and doubles with shower and toilet at 480FF; there are also triples (530 to 560FF) and quads (580 to 620FF) available.

Top End If you're looking to stay on in Paris for a spell, the following could be the place for you.

Citadines Apparthôtel Bastille (Map 1; ☎ 01 40 01 15 15; fax 01 40 01 15 20; metro Reuilly Diderot), 14-18 Rue de Chaligny (12e). Just south of the landmark Hôpital Saint Antoine, the apartment-style rooms in this chain hotel feature kitchen areas. Prices vary during the year from 460 to 515FF for a small 'studette' for one person, 545 to 600FF for a two person studio, or 760 to 1035FF for a two bedroom apartment. Staying longer than a week allows cheaper rates.

Hotels – Chinatown Area

Paris' Chinatown is south of Place d'Italie along Ave d'Ivry and Ave de Choisy.

Budget The 13e may not be electrifying, but it has some good deals and there are plenty of good restaurants nearby.

Hôtel Tolbiac (Map 1; ☎ 01 44 24 25 54; fax 01 45 85 43 47; metro Tolbiac), 122 Rue de Tolbiac (13e). Well lit, quiet and spotlessly clean singles/doubles go for 130/155FF with washbasin, 160FF with shower, or 200FF with shower and toilet. Hall showers are free.

Hôtel Arian (Map 1; ☎ 01 45 70 76 00; fax 01 45 70 85 53; metro Tolbiac), 102 Ave de Choisy (13e). This motel-like, one star place has simple singles for 160FF, with shower for 230FF. Doubles and triples with shower and toilet cost from 230 to 290FF.

Hôtel des Beaux-Arts (Map 1; ☎ 01 44 24 22 60; metro Tolbiac), 2 Rue Toussaint Féron (13e). Rooms start at 160/180FF and go up to 210 with shower or up to 290FF with bath and toilet.

Hotels – Montparnasse Area

Though untouristed and less than thrilling, the 14e and the easternmost corner of the 15e do have a number of good deals. Gare Montparnasse is served by Air France buses from both airports. Place Denfert Rochereau is also linked to both airports by Orlybus, Orlyval and Roissyrail.

Budget The budget places in the 14e don't see many foreign tourists.

Celtic Hôtel, (Map 4; ☎ 01 43 20 93 53; fax 01 43 20 66 07; metro Edgar Quinet), 15 Rue d'Odessa (14e). The Celtic is an old-fashioned, one star place that has undergone only partial modernisation. It has bare singles/doubles at 210/240FF, doubles/triples with shower at 280/370FF and with shower and toilet at 300/390FF.

Hôtel de l'Espérance (Map 1; ☎ 01 43 21 63 84; metro Gaîté), 45 Rue de la Gaîté (14e). This is a 14 room place whose doubles (175FF with washbasin, 185 to 195FF with shower) are a bit frayed and dreary. A bed for a third person is 50FF. Hall showers cost 15FF.

Hôtel Aviatic (Map 1; ☎ 01 45 40 59 75; fax 01 45 40 67 48; metro Mouton Duvernet), 10 Rue de Brézin (14e). The clean, basic rooms at this family-run hotel-bar, which come equipped with steel-frame beds and linoleum floors, start at 110/130FF (210 to 230FF with shower and toilet). Hall showers are 10FF.

Hôtel L'Espérance (Map 1; ☎ 01 43 21 41 04; fax 01 43 22 06 02; metro Denfert Rochereau), 1 Rue de Grancey (14e). This 14 room place has basic rooms from 155/190FF (260 to 325FF with shower but no toilet).

Mid-Range Just east of Gare Montparnasse, there are a number of two and three-star places on Rue Vandamme and Rue de la Gaîté; the latter street is dotted with sex shops.

Petit Palace Hôtel (Map 1; ☎ 01 43 22 05 25; fax 01 43 21 79 01; metro Gaîté), 131 Ave du Maine (14e). The same family has run this friendly, ambitiously named, two star place since 1952. It has smallish but spotless doubles/triples for 250/310FF with washbasin and bidet, and 310/400FF with shower and toilet. Hall showers are 20FF.

Hôtel de Blois (Map 1; ☎ 01 45 40 99 48; fax 01 45 40 45 62; metro Mouton Duvernet), 5 Rue des Plantes (14e). This one star establishment offers smallish singles/doubles with washbasin and bidet for 230/280FF. Doubles with shower are 250, and 270FF with shower and toilet. Fully equipped triples are 360FF.

Hôtel Floridor (Map 1; ☎ 01 43 21 35 53; fax 01 43 27 65 81; metro Denfert Rochereau), 28 Place Denfert Rochereau (14e). Shower equipped singles/doubles go for 279/307FF (297/325FF with toilet as well), including breakfast served in your room.

Hotels – 15e Arrondissement

The 15e is conveniently close to the Eiffel Tower and other Left Bank attractions.

Mid-Range There are a number of mid-range hotels along Blvd de Grenelle, particularly around metro La Motte Picquet Grenelle.

Hôtel Saphir Grenelle (Map 4; ☎ 01 45 75 12 23; fax 01 45 75 62 49; metro La Motte Picquet Grenelle), 10 Rue du Commerce (15e). Conveniently close to restaurants and metro lines, this small hotel has modern singles/doubles at 390/460FF. Discount packages are available including a three-night weekend package for 990FF.

Hotels – Montmartre & Pigalle

Montmartre, encompassing the 18e and the northern part of the 9e, is one of the most charming neighbourhoods in Paris.

Budget The flat area around the base of the hill has some surprisingly good deals. The lively, ethnically mixed area east of Sacré Cœur can be a bit rough – some people say it's prudent to avoid the Château Rouge metro stop at night.

Hôtel Saint Pierre (Map 9; ☎ 01 46 06 20 73; metro Anvers), 3 Rue Seveste (18e). This friendly, family run establishment in a renovated older building with 36 simple but serviceable singles/doubles costs from 120/180FF (170/190FF with shower and toilet, 230FF with bath and toilet). With Blvd de Rochechouart so close, though, it can be a bit noisy here.

Hôtel Audran (Map 9; ☎ 01 42 58 79 59; fax 01 42 58 39 11; metro Abbesses), 7 Rue Audran (18e). Basic rooms start at 120/160FF; doubles with shower are 180FF, or 250FF with shower and toilet. Each floor has a toilet; the 1st and 3rd floors have showers (10FF).

Idéal Hôtel (Map 9; ☎ 01 46 06 63 63; fax 01 42 64 97 01; metro Abbesses), 3 Rue des Trois

Frères (18e). This is an older place with 45 simple but adequate rooms costing from 125 to 140FF for singles and 180FF for doubles. Rooms with shower but no toilet are 250FF. If you ring from the station, they'll hold a room for a few hours.

Hôtel de Rohan (Map 9; ☎ 01 46 06 82 74; metro Château Rouge), 90 Rue Myrha (18e). Basic, tidy rooms at this one star establishment go for 110/140FF. Doubles/triples with shower are 170/200FF. Showers in the hall cost 20FF.

Hôtel de Carthage (Map 9; ☎/fax 01 46 06 27 03; metro Château Rouge), 10 Rue Poulet (18e). This 40 room cheapie has basic but serviceable singles costing from 90 to 110FF; doubles are 140 to 160FF. Hall showers cost 15FF. Doubles with shower and toilet cost from 190 to 230FF. Curfew is at 1 am.

Mid-Range The attractive two-star places on Rue Aristide Bruant are generally less full in July and August than in spring and autumn.

Hôtel des Arts (Map 9; ☎ 01 46 06 30 52; fax 01 46 06 10 83; metro Abbesses), 5 Rue Tholozé (18e). This is a friendly, attractive 50 room place with singles/doubles from 340/430FF (460FF with two twin beds). Breakfast costs 30FF.

Timhôtel Montmartre (Map 9; ☎ 01 42 55 74 79; fax 01 42 55 71 01; metro Abbesses), 11 Rue Ravignan and Place Émile Goudeau (18e). This is a good choice if you place more value on location than room size. The 60 neat, modern rooms cost 460/560FF. Some of the rooms on the 4th and 5th floors have stunning views of the city (110FF extra). Buffet breakfast is 49FF.

Hôtel Utrillo (Map 9; ☎ 01 42 58 13 44; fax 01 42 23 93 88; metro Abbesses), 7 Rue Aristide Bruant (18e). The 30 rooms here start at 305/380FF. A double with bath and toilet is 420FF. Buffet breakfast costs 40FF.

Hôtel des Capucines Montmartre (Map 9; ☎ 01 42 52 89 80; fax 01 42 52 29 57; metro Abbesses or Blanche), 5 Rue Aristide Bruant (18e). Singles with TV and minibar cost from 250 to 325FF, doubles from 300 to 350FF and triples from 350 to 420FF. A bed for a third person is 80FF.

Hôtel du Moulin (Map 9; ☎ 01 42 64 33 33; fax 01 46 06 42 66; metro Abbesses or Blanche), 3 Rue Aristide Bruant (18e), is the third of this useful cluster and has 27 rooms with toilet and bath or shower at 250/300FF in winter and 290/380FF in summer.

Hôtel Luxia (Map 9; ☎ 01 46 06 84 24; fax 01 46 06 10 14; metro Anvers), 8 Rue Seveste (18e). This 45 room hotel mainly takes groups, but at least a few rooms are almost always left for independent travellers. Plain, clean singles/doubles/triples with shower, toilet and TV are 280/300/390FF.

Hôtel Avenir (Map 9; ☎ 01 48 78 21 37; fax 01 40 16 92 62; metro Anvers), 39 Blvd Rochechouart (9e). This two star, 42 room place on noisy Blvd Rochechouart has singles/doubles/triples/quads from 240/280/310/400FF. All rooms have a bath or shower and the rates include breakfast.

Top End There are a couple of top-end hotels in the area, one just south of Pigalle and another near the entrance to the Cimetière de Montmartre.

Citadines Apparthôtel Montmartre (Map 9; ☎ 01 53 42 43 44; fax 01 45 22 59 10; metro Blanche), 16 Ave Rachel (18e). Right by the entrance to the Cimetière de Montmartre, and on a quiet street, this branch of the apartment-style hotel chain has small 'studettes' from 480 to 535FF, larger studios for two people from 570 to 630FF, and two-bedroom apartments from 800 to 1065FF. Stays of longer than a week are cheaper.

Résidence Hôtel des Trois Poussins (Map 3; ☎ 01 53 32 81 81; fax 01 53 32 81 82; metro Saint Georges), 15 Rue Clauzel (9e). This two star hotel due south of Place Pigalle has singles/doubles from 350/450FF, but more than half of its 40 rooms are small studios (from 380/450FF) with their own cooking facilities.

Hotels – Airports

Both airports have a wide selection of places, including mid-range Ibis hotels and a rather unusual form of accommodation if you just need to rest.

Hôtel Ibis (☎ 01 49 19 19 19; fax 01 49 19 19 21), next to the Aéroport Charles de Gaulle 1 train station. This large, modern chain hotel with two stars and 556 rooms has doubles and triples for 415FF (320FF at the weekend). The hotel is linked to all three terminals by shuttle bus.

Hôtel Ibis (☎ 01 46 87 33 50; fax 01 46 87 29 92), Orly airport. This 299 room chain hotel is linked to both terminals by the Navette ADP (airport shuttle bus). Doubles cost 395FF.

Cocoon (☎ 01 48 62 06 16; fax 01 48 62 56 97), below departure level (Hall 36) at Aéroport Charles de Gaulle 1. This strange place has 60 'cabins' where you can sleep for up to 16 hours – but no longer than that. The single/double day rates (check in any time between 8 am to 6 pm) are 150/200FF; overnight they're 250/300FF. All cabins have TVs, telephones with fax and, most importantly, alarm clocks.

PLACES TO EAT

Except in touristy areas, most of the city's thousands of restaurants are pretty good value for money – at least by Parisian standards. Intense competition tends to rid the city quickly of places with bad food or prices that are out of line. Still, you can be unlucky. Study the posted *menus* carefully and check to see how full or empty the place is before entering.

Most restaurants (but not brasseries) are closed on Sunday, and very few stay open between 2.30 or 3 and 7 pm.

Louvre & Les Halles Areas

The area between Forum des Halles and the Centre Pompidou (1er and western 4e) is filled with scores of *branché* (plugged-in or trendy) restaurants, but few of them (except the many fast-food joints) are inexpensive. Streets lined with places to eat include Rue des Lombards, the bar and bistro-lined Rue Montorgueil, and the narrow streets north and east of Forum des Halles.

French The 1er and 4e have a diverse selection of French eating establishments.

Au P'tit Rémouleur (Map 8; ☎ 01 48 04 79 24; metro Hôtel de Ville), 2 Rue de la Coutellerie, just west of the Hôtel de Ville (4e). This small, typically French fish restaurant includes bouillabaisse (60FF), mussels and a 65FF *menu* among its specialities. Main dishes cost from 49 to 74FF; *menus* cost 65FF at lunch and 119FF at dinner. It is open Monday to Saturday from noon to 3 pm and 7 to 11 pm.

Willi's Wine Bar (Map 7; ☎ 01 42 61 05 09; metro Bourse), 13 Rue des Petits Champs (1er). This place is a civilised yet convivial wine bar run by two British expats who introduced the wine-bar concept to Paris in the mid-1980s. The lunch *menu* is 148FF, dinner is 189FF. À la carte starters average 60FF, main courses 90FF and desserts 45FF. It is open Monday to Saturday from noon to 11 pm.

L'Épi d'Or (Map 7; ☎ 01 42 36 38 12; metro Châtelet-Les Halles), 25 Rue Jean-Jacques Rousseau (1er). This oh-so-Parisian bistro hard by Les Halles serves classic, well prepared dishes (rabbit terrine, *gigot d'agneau* cooked for seven hours) to a suprisingly well heeled crowd. There's a *menu* for 105FF. It's open daily for lunch and dinner, except on Saturday for lunch and on Sunday.

Aux Crus de Bourgogne (Map 7; ☎ 01 42 33 48 24; metro Châtelet-Les Halles), 3 Rue de Bachaumont (2e). This excellent bistro on a pedestrianised street serves great seafood (fresh lobster with mayonnaise, pike quenelles in Nantua sauce etc) as well as fillet of beef in a morelle sauce. Expect to pay from 180FF per person. It's open weekdays until 10.30 pm.

Le Petit Mâchon (Map 7; ☎ 01 42 60 08 06; metro Palais Royal), 158 Rue Saint Honoré (1er). This new bistro has Lyon-inspired specialities like snails in garlic butter and *andouillette* in mustard sauce. Starters cost from 38 to 70FF, main courses from 72 to 108FF and there's a 98FF *menu*. It's open for lunch and dinner Tuesday to Sunday to 11.30 pm.

Japanese Businesspeople from Japan in search of real Japanese food flock to Rue Sainte Anne and other streets of Paris' 'Japantown', which is just west of the Jardin du Palais Royal. Many of the restaurants are surprisingly good value.

Higuma (Map 7; ☎ 01 47 03 38 59; metro Pyramides), 32bis Rue Sainte Anne (1er). Stepping into this place is like ducking into a corner noodle shop in Shinjuku. To the delight of the almost exclusively Japanese clientele, the high-temperature woks are forever filled with furiously bubbling soups and simmering vegetables. A meal-sized bowl of soup noodles costs from 40 to 48FF. It is open daily from 11.30 am through to 10 pm. *Menus* (63 to 70FF) are not served from 3 to 5 pm.

Other Cuisines This part of Paris is a fast-food lovers' paradise, with a variety of chain outlets close to the Centre Pompidou and Les Halles.

Joe Allen (Map 7; ☎ 01 42 36 70 13; metro Étienne Marcel), 30 Rue Pierre Lescot (1er). A very American bar-restaurant with a great atmosphere and a descent selection of Californian wines, it has two/three course *menus* for 140/170FF. It is open daily from noon to 1.30 am. Sunday brunch is from noon to 4 pm.

Le Loup Blanc (Map 7; ☎ 01 40 13 08 35; metro Étienne Marcel), 42 Rue Tiquetonne (2e). Now we've seen everything – a techno restaurant (though it is hard to see or hear exactly why). This place does do some decent main courses, though, like Thai-style prawns and squid with anise (57 to 85FF). It's open daily from 8 pm to 12.30 am, and brunch is available on Sunday from noon to 5 pm. The area around Rue Tiquetonne is becoming very trendy.

Mélodine Cafeteria (Map 8; ☎ 01 40 29 09 78; metro Rambuteau), 2 Rue Brantôme (4e), across from the north side of the Centre Pompidou. The food at this huge, self-service cafeteria is better than you might expect, and it may satisfy finicky kids. Main dishes cost from only 27 to 40FF, pizzas from 27 to 36FF and salads are available. Food is served daily from 11 am to 10 pm.

La Maison Savoureuse (Map 7; ☎ 01 42 60 03 22; metro Quatre Septembre), 62 Rue Sainte Anne (2e). This cheap and cheerful little place serves excellent value Vietnamese food (lunch *menus* at 36 and 48FF) *à table* or you can take your spring rolls (from 9FF) and vermicelli noodles to Square Louvois, a pretty little park a short distance to the south-east, for a picnic.

Self-Catering There are a number of options along Ave de l'Opéra and Rue de Richelieu, as well as around Forum des Halles, including a ***Monoprix*** at 21 Ave de l'Opéra (2e; Map 7), a ***Franprix*** at 35 Rue Berger (1er; Map 7), open Monday to Saturday from 8.30 am to 8 pm, and a bargain-priced ***Ed l'Épicier*** inside the courtyard at 80 Rue de Rivoli (4e; Map 8), open Monday to Saturday from 9 am to 8 pm. Fine food shops can be found on Rue de Richelieu (1er; Map 7; metro Pyramides), including a ***fromagerie*** at No 38 (closed from 2 to 4 pm, on Sunday and Monday, and in July and August) and ***Evrard***, a *traiteur* (delicatessen or caterer) across the street at No 41 (open Monday to Friday until 7.30 pm, closed in August). The latter has ready-to-eat delicacies.

Marais Area

The Marais (4e and southern 3e), filled with small eateries of every imaginable kind, is one of Paris' premier neighbourhoods for eating out.

French The French places in this area tend to be small and intimate.

Le Petit Picard (Map 8; ☎ 01 42 78 54 03; metro Hôtel de Ville), 42 Rue Sainte Croix de la Bretonnerie (4e). Mainly gay and very popular, this restaurant serves very traditional French cuisine. The *menus* cost 64FF (lunch only) and 84FF, and there's one of Picardie specialities for 129FF. It's closed for lunch on weekends and all day Monday.

Le Gai Moulin (Map 8; ☎ 01 48 87 47 59; metro Rambuteau), 4 Rue Saint Merri (4e). Traditional French cuisine, including a 100FF *menu*, is served daily from 7 pm to midnight at this small, modern place with a mainly (but not exclusively) gay clientele.

Amadéo (Map 8; ☎ 01 48 87 01 02; metro Saint Paul or Hôtel de Ville), 19 Rue François Miron (4e). This restaurant is decidedly gay, although straight diners are very welcome, and it produces delicious and stylish food at a set price of 165FF (85FF at lunch) for almost any starter, main course and dessert on its *carte*. On Tuesday evening, the *menu* is only 100FF and includes a kir. Amadeo is closed on Saturday for lunch and on Sunday.

Vins des Pyrénées (Map 8; ☎ 01 42 72 64 94; metro Bastille), 25 Rue Beautreillis (4e). In a former wine warehouse, this restaurant is a good place to splurge on a French meal, with starters from 35 to 60FF and main courses from around 70 to 110FF. It's open daily for lunch and dinner to 11.30 pm; closed Sunday.

Robert et Louise (Map 8; ☎ 01 42 78 55 89; metro Saint Sébastien Froissart), 64 Rue Vieille du Temple (3e). Delightful, unfussy and inexpensive French food prepared by a husband and wife team including *côte de bœuf* cooked on an open fire. Those who know this place consistently give it rave reviews. Starters cost from 25 to 35FF, main courses from 80 to 90FF, with a plat du jour at 75FF. It's open for lunch and dinner till 10 pm; closed Sunday.

L'Impasse (Map 8; ☎ 01 42 72 08 45; metro Bastille), 4 Impasse Guéménée (4e). This warm restaurant, with its beamed ceiling and stone walls, serves quality dishes 'just like grandma made': fresh cod with lentils, duck leg in wine with fruit, veal with chives. The 135FF fixed *menu* is good value and includes some fabulous desserts (eg *gourmandise au chocolat*). It's open daily for lunch and dinner, except on Sunday and for lunch on Monday and Saturday.

Jewish The kosher and kosher-style restaurants along Rue des Rosiers serve specialities from North Africa, Central Europe and Israel. Many are closed on Friday evening, Saturday and Jewish holidays.

Takeaway falafel and *shwarma* are available all along Rue des Rosiers.

Chez Rami et Hanna (Map 8; ☎ 01 42 78 23 09; metro Saint Paul), 54 Rue des Rosiers (4e). Israeli dishes, including the *assiette royale* (a plate of seven salads; 60FF), are served daily from 11 am to 2 am.

Jo Goldenberg (Map 8; ☎ 01 48 87 20 16; metro Saint Paul), 7 Rue des Rosiers (4e). Founded in 1920, this kosher-style restaurant-deli has become Paris' most famous Jewish eatery. The mixed starters (30FF) and apple strudel (29FF) are excellent, but the plats du jour (80FF) don't measure up to New York deli standards. Still, it's a very convivial, almost festive place for a meal. It's open 364 days a year (closed Yom Kippur) from 8.30 am until midnight or 1 am.

Chez Marianne (Map 8; ☎ 01 42 72 18 86; metro Saint Paul), 2 Rue des Hospitalières Saint Gervais (4e). A kind of Sephardic (Middle Eastern/North African Jewish) alternative to the Jo Goldenberg, with an adjoining delicatessen. Plates with four/five/six different meze (felafel, hummus etc) cost 55/65/75FF. The window at the deli dispenses takeaway felafel sandwiches for 20FF.

Vegetarian The Marais is one of the few neighbourhoods in Paris to actually offer a choice of meatless restaurants.

La Truffe (Map 8; ☎ 01 42 71 08 39; metro Hôtel de Ville), 31 Rue Vieille du Temple (4e). This organic, vegetarian restaurant specialises in dishes made with mushrooms. The *poêlée champignons* (99FF as a starter, 129FF as a main) and vegetable lasagne (69/79FF) are superb. A savoury *tarte* served with vegetables costs from 59 to 89FF. There's a lunchtime *menu* for 59FF. It is open daily from noon to 4 pm and 7 to 11 pm.

Aquarius (Map 8; ☎ 01 48 87 48 71; metro Rambuteau), 54 Rue Sainte Croix de la Bretonnerie (4e). The calming atmosphere of this healthy restaurant makes you think of fresh bean sprouts, which is great if you're in the mood for something as light as that. The two course *menu* (lunch only) costs 62FF; for 92FF you get three courses. It is open Monday to Saturday from noon to 10.30 pm; the plat du jour is available from noon to 2 pm and 7 to 10 pm.

Other Cuisines The Marais has a good selection of ethnic places. If you're looking for authentic Chinese food but can't be bothered going all the way to the 13e, check out any of the small Chinese noodle shops and restaurants along Rue Au Maire (3e; Map 8; metro Arts et Métiers), which is south-east of the Conservatoire des Arts et Métiers.

Au Bascou (Map 8; ☎ 01 42 72 69 25; metro Arts et Métiers), 38 Rue Réaumur (3e). Basque cuisine might sound a little far-fetched but try it, you'll probably like it. Classics include *pipérade basquaise* (a kind of omelette with peppers, garlic, tomatoes and ham), crispy baby squid, milk-fed lamb and Bayonne ham in all its guises. The lunch *menu* is good value at 90FF. At dinner, expect to pay from 180 to 250FF à la carte. Au Bascou is open daily for lunch and dinner, except on Saturday for lunch and on Sunday.

Caves Saint Gilles (Maps 5 & 8; ☎ 01 48 87 22 62; metro Chemin Vert), 4 Rue Saint Gilles (3e). This trendy Spanish wine bar north-east of Place des Vosges is the place for tapas (80FF for a platter) and sangria. The red *banquettes* are always packed, and it's open daily until 2 am.

L'Enoteca (Map 8; ☎ 01 42 78 91 44; metro Pont Marie), 25 Rue Charles V (4e). If you feel like splashing out on an Italian meal in Paris, do it here. Risotto with gorgonzola and pears, tagliatelle with prawns and asparagus, carpaccio with rocket – this is haute cuisine *à l'italienne* and there's an excellent list of Italian wines. The weekday lunch *menu* is good value at 95FF (including wine). À la carte expect to pay between 200 and 250FF.

La Perla (Map 8; ☎ 01 42 77 59 40; metro Saint Paul or Hôtel de Ville), 26 Rue François Miron (4e). A favourite with younger Parisians, this trendy California-style Mexican place is more a bar than a restaurant. Specialities include guacamole (29FF), nachos (30FF) and burritos (from 46FF). Meals are served Monday to Friday from noon to 3 pm and 7 to 11 pm, and on weekends nonstop from noon to 11 pm. Monday to Friday happy hour (cocktails, tequila and mezcal only) is from 6 to 8 pm.

404 (Map 8; ☎ 01 42 74 57 81; metro Arts et Métiers), 69 Rue des Gravilliers (3e). The 404 has some of the best couscous and *tajine* (a meat and vegetable stew cooked in a domed earthenware pot) in Paris (both from 90 to 105FF). It also has excellent grills from 90FF, aniseed bread and *menus* at 59, 79 and 119FF, which are great value. The restaurant, done up like the inside of an old Moroccan home, is owned by the French-Arab comedian Smaïn, so the atmosphere is always upbeat. It's open from Monday to Saturday for lunch and dinner; the *brunch berbère* (Berber brunch; 100FF) is available on Sunday from noon to 5 pm.

Chez Omar (Map 8; ☎ 01 42 72 36 26; metro Arts et Métiers), 47 Rue de Bretagne (3e). Though hardly as refined as the 404, this place – long a favourite of show biz and fashion types – is another excellent choice for couscous (eg couscous royal at 110FF) and tajines. This old converted café is an excellent place for people-watching. It also offers one of the warmest welcomes in Paris. It's open daily for lunch and dinner to 10 pm, except on Sunday for lunch.

Minh Chau (Map 8; ☎ 01 42 71 13 30; metro Hôtel de Ville), 10 Rue de la Verrerie (4e). For only 26 to 32FF you can enjoy tasty main dishes (grilled chicken with lemon grass, roast duck) at this tiny but welcoming Vietnamese place. It is open Monday to Saturday from 11.30 am to 3 pm and 5.30 to 11 pm.

Self-Catering There's a bunch of ***food shops*** on the odd-numbered side of Rue Saint Antoine (4e; Map 8) between the ***Monoprix*** supermarket (open Monday to Saturday from 9 am to 9 pm) at No 71 and the ***Supermarché G20*** at No 117 (open Monday to Saturday from 9 am to 8.30 pm). There's a ***Franprix*** supermarket at No 133 of the same street open Monday to Saturday from 8.30 am to 7.45 pm and on Sunday from 9 am to 12.45 pm.

Gourmaud (Map 8; metro Saint Paul), 91 Rue Saint Antoine (4e). This is one of the few gourmet shops in Paris where you can assemble an entire picnic – everything from herrings, quiches and quenelles to eclairs – in one place. It's open 365 days a year from 9 am to 10 pm.

Flo Prestige (Map 8; ☎ 01 53 01 91 91; metro Bastille) at 10 Rue Saint Antoine (4e), on the corner of Rue des Tournelles. This branch of the famous traiteur, with some 10 outlets around town, has picnic supplies and, more importantly, some of the most delectable pastries and baked goods in Paris. It's open daily from 8 am to 11 pm.

Île Saint Louis

Famed for its ice cream as much as anything else, the Île Saint Louis (4e) is generally an expensive place to eat. It's best suited to those looking for a light snack or the finest ingredients for lunch beside the Seine. Rue Saint Louis en l'Île has several salons de thé, and there are lots of restaurants along this street, but they tend to be either touristy and disappointing or expensive (or both).

Brasserie de l'Île Saint Louis (Map 8; ☎ 01 43 54 02 59; metro Pont Marie), 55 Quai de Bourbon (4e). Founded in 1870, this spectacularly situated brasserie features *choucroute garnie* (sauerkraut with assorted prepared meats) and other Alsatian dishes for under 100FF, but you can enjoy the location by ordering coffee/beer (6/15FF at the bar, 14/20FF at a table or on the terrace). It is open from 11.30 am (6 pm on Thursday) to 1 am (closed Wednesday and in August).

Berthillon (Map 8; ☎ 01 43 54 31 61; metro Pont Marie), 31 Rue Saint Louis en l'Île (4e). This ice-cream parlour is reputed to have Paris' most delicious frozen delicacies. While the fruit flavours are justifiably renowned, the chocolate, coffee, *marrons glacés*, Agenaise (Armagnac and prunes) and *nougat au miel* (honey nougat) are incomparably richer. The takeaway counter is open from 10 am to 8 pm (closed Monday, Tuesday and during school holidays); one/two/three small scoops cost 9/16/20FF. The *salon dégustation* (sit-down area) is open the same days from 1 pm (2 pm on weekends) to 8 pm. Other places on Île Saint Louis also feature Berthillon ice cream but without the long queues.

Les Fous de l'Île (Map 8; ☎ 01 43 25 76 67; metro Pont Marie), 33 Rue des Deux Ponts (4e). An exception to the touristy nature of Île Saint Louis, this friendly and down-to-earth establishment serves meals for between 120 and 150FF per person. It's open Tuesday to

Friday from noon to 11 pm, Saturday from 3 to 11 pm and Sunday from noon to 7 pm.

Self-Catering Île Saint Louis, home to some of Paris' finest and priciest food shops, is a great place to assemble a gourmet picnic. Along Rue Saint Louis en l'Île (4e; Map 8; metro Pont Marie) there are a number of ***fromageries*** and ***groceries*** (usually closed Sunday afternoon and Monday). There are more ***food shops*** on Rue des Deux Ponts.

Le Moule à Gâteau (Map 8; metro Pont Marie), 47 Rue Saint Louis en l'Île (4e). It has some of the most delicious fancy breads in Paris as well as fantastic brownies and chocolate cake (10FF). It is open from 8.30 am to 8 pm (closed Monday).

Latin Quarter

Rue Mouffetard (5e; metro Place Monge) is filled with scores of places to eat. It's especially popular with students, in part because of the unparalleled selection of stands selling baguette sandwiches, *panini* (Italian toasted bread with fillings) and crêpes. Rue Soufflot (metro Luxembourg) is lined with cafés.

Avoid Rue de la Huchette (see the boxed text 'Bacteria Alley') unless you're after *chawarma* (ie shwarma), which is available at several places around No 14.

Bacteria Alley

Paris' largest concentration of tourist restaurants is squeezed into a labyrinth of narrow streets in the 5e arrondissement across the Seine from Notre Dame. The Greek, North African and Middle Eastern restaurants between Rue Saint Jacques, Blvd Saint Germain and Blvd Saint Michel attract mainly foreigners, unaware that some people refer to Rue de la Huchette (Map 6), and nearby streets like Rue Saint Séverin and Rue de la Harpe, as 'bacteria alley'. To add insult to injury, many of the poor souls who eat here are under the impression that that this little maze is the famous Latin Quarter.

Although you'll probably be better off if you avoid the establishments that ripen their meat and seafood in the front window, it's still possible to get a cheap, decent meal in the northern 5e. For details read on for the Latin Quarter's Places to Eat listings.

French The Latin Quarter has a good selection of reasonably priced French places.

Le Vigneron (Map 6; ☎ 01 47 07 29 99; metro Place Monge), 18-20 Rue du Pot de Fer (5e). Just off the lively Rue Mouffetard, the 'Wine Grower' specialises in south-west cuisine (including its award-winning *joue de bœuf*) with *menus* at 108 and 148FF. À la carte prices range from 80 to 110FF for starters, 90 to 120FF for main dishes and from 50 to 65FF for desserts. Wines range from 80 to 150FF, with the average around 110FF. The ambience here is intimate, the service superb.

Chez Léna et Mimille (Map 6; ☎ 01 47 07 72 47; metro Censier Daubenton), 32 Rue Tournefort (5e), a block west of Rue Mouffetard. The three course lunch/dinner *menus* at this elegant French restaurant cost 98/185FF; wines are in the 100 to 165FF range. It closes on Saturday at noon and in winter on Sunday. The terrace overlooks a lovely little park.

Castor et Pollux (Map 6; ☎ 01 43 31 15 00; metro Censier Daubenton), 8 Rue Tournefort (5e). This totally untouristed place is a perfect example of a *restaurant du quartier*, an intimate little place frequented by local residents who appreciate the high quality of the cooking and the amicable welcome. The lunch *menu* is 62FF; there are dinner *menus* at 78 and 120FF. The plat du jour is 48FF.

Perraudin (Map 6; ☎ 01 46 33 15 75; metro Luxembourg), 157 Rue Saint Jacques (5e). If you fancy *bœuf Bourguignon* (59FF), *gigot d'agneau* (leg of lamb; 59FF) or *confit de canard* (59FF), try this reasonably priced traditional French restaurant, which hasn't changed much since the turn of the century. At lunchtime there's a *menu* for 63FF and 250mL of wine is 10FF. It is open from noon to 2.15 pm and 7 to 11.15 pm (closed on Saturday for lunch and on Sunday).

Moissonnier (Map 5; ☎ 01 43 29 87 65; metro Cardinal Lemoine), 28 Rue des Fossés Saint Bernard (5e). Excellent Lyon-inspired cuisine has been served at this elegant restaurant since 1960. There's a *menu* at 150FF; if ordering à la carte, count on a full meal costing about 250FF (starters from 60FF, main courses from

95FF). It is open from noon to 1.30 pm and 7 to 9.30 pm (closed Sunday night and on Monday).

Les Bouchons de François Clerc (Map 6; ☎ 01 43 54 15 34; metro Maubert Mutualité), 12 Rue de l'Hôtel Colbert (5e). Along with excellently prepared dishes like black pudding tart cooked with apples and crispy cod (*menus* at 117 and 219FF), the draws here are very affordable wines (almost wholesale prices) and an excellent cheese selection. It's open daily for lunch and dinner, except on Saturday for lunch and on Sunday.

L'Arbre à Cannelle (Map 5; ☎ 01 43 31 68 31; metro Jussieu), 14 Rue Linné (5e). A bright, upbeat salon de thé known for its brunches (90 to 120FF) and its plats du jour (70FF). It is open daily from noon to 6.30 pm.

Crêpes Stand (Map 5; metro Place Monge), 61 Rue Mouffetard (5e). This sidewalk stand serves some of the best discount crêpes in Paris. Savoury crêpes are only 12 to 25FF; sweet crêpes are 7 to 23FF. It is open daily from 11 am to 12.30 am (2 am on Friday and Saturday nights).

North African & Middle Eastern The Latin Quarter is a good area for couscous and tajines.

Founti Agadir (Map 5; ☎ 01 43 37 85 10; metro Censier Daubenton), 117 Rue Monge (5e). This Moroccan restaurant has some of the best couscous, grills and tajines (70 to 85FF) on the Left Bank. There's a *menu* – with or without couscous – for 84FF. It's open daily, except Monday.

La Voie Lactée (Map 5; ☎ 01 46 34 02 35; metro Cardinal Lemoine), 34 Rue du Cardinal Lemoine (5e). The 'Milky Way' is a Turkish place with modern and traditional Anatolean cuisine, including a buffet of Turkish salads. Starters range from 32 to 55FF, main courses from 52 to 70FF. The 60FF 'lunch' *menu* is available till 9 pm; evening *menus* cost 85, 100 and 120FF. It is open from noon to 3 pm and 7 to 11 pm (closed Sunday). Come Thursday night for some specially prepared dishes.

Koutchi (Map 5; ☎ 01 44 07 20 56; metro Cardinal Lemoine), 40 Rue du Cardinal Lemoine (5e). The décor of this Afghan restaurant is reminiscent of a Central Asian caravanserai. Specialities include Afghan salads (25 to 30FF), meat dishes (65 to 85FF) and desserts (25 to 30FF). The evening *menu* costs 98FF; the lunchtime one is 55FF. It is open from noon to 2.30 pm and 7 to 11 pm (closed on Saturday for lunch and on Sunday).

Asian Asian restaurants of all types abound in the Latin Quarter.

Tashi Delek (Map 6; ☎ 01 43 26 55 55; metro Luxembourg), 4 Rue des Fossés Saint Jacques (5e). The lunch *menu* at this intimate Tibetan restaurant (whose name means 'bonjour' in Tibetan) costs 65FF; the 105FF dinner *menu* includes wine. There are some seven vegetarian choices on the *carte* ranging in price from 36 to 45FF. It is open Monday to Saturday from noon to 2.30 pm and 7 to 10.30 pm.

Chez Maï (Map 6; ☎ 01 43 54 05 33; metro Maubert Mutualité), 65 Rue Galande (5e). This hole-in-the-wall Vietnamese place is open daily from noon to 3 pm and 7 to 11 pm. Main dishes (including excellent shrimp ones) cost only 25 to 30FF; soup is 20FF and salads and omelettes cost from 20FF.

Tao (Map 6; ☎ 01 43 26 75 92; metro Luxembourg), 248 Rue Saint Jacques (5e). Decidedly more upmarket than Chez Maï, this place serves some of the best Vietnamese cuisine in the Latin Quarter; try the warm beef noodle salad or grilled minced prawns. It's not cheap (150 to 200FF per person), but the portions are huge. Open daily, except Sunday, to 10.30 pm.

Restaurant A (Map 8; ☎ 01 46 33 85 54; metro Maubert Mutualité), 5 Rue de Poissy (5e). This place serves standard Chinese favourites (spring rolls, sweet and sour fish, Peking duck) at affordable prices; *menus* are 68 and 88FF at lunch and 108FF at dinner. Check out the artist-owner's sculpted vegetables and ice. Open daily, except on Monday for lunch, until 11 pm.

Vegetarian The choice for vegetarians is not as great in the Latin Quarter as in the Marais, but there are a couple of decent options.

Le Petit Légume (Map 5; ☎ 01 40 46 06 85; metro Cardinal Lemoine), 36 Rue des Boulangers (5e). A good place for a quick vegetarian lunch. Dinner *menus* are 50, 64 and 75FF.

Jardin des Pâtes (Map 5; ☎ 01 43 31 50 71; metro Cardinal Lemoine), 4 Rue Lacépède (5e). OK, not strictly vegetarian but 100% *biologique* (natural), the cosy 'Garden of Pastas' has as many types of the same as you care to name (wholewheat, buckwheat, chestnut etc) from 55 to 80FF. It's open for lunch and dinner to 11 pm, except on Monday for lunch.

Other Cuisines Eclectic is the name of the game at some restaurants in this area.

Savannah Café (Map 5; ☎ 01 43 29 45 77; metro Cardinal Lemoine), 27 Rue Descartes (5e). The food served at this charming little restaurant just north of Place de la Contrescarpe is as eclectic as the carnival-like decorations strewn around the place. Tabouli mixes here with tortellini and *fromage blanc* with baklava – in short, food from 'the south'. *Menus* cost 75FF (at lunch) and 134FF. À la carte entrées are 37 to 60FF, main courses 76 to 84FF and pasta dishes from 72 to 76FF. It's open daily for lunch and dinner till 11.30 pm, except on Sunday and on Monday for lunch.

Self-Catering On Tuesday, Thursday and Saturday from 7 am to 1 pm, Place Maubert (5e; Map 6; metro Maubert Mutualité) is transformed into a lively ***food market***. ***Food shops*** are also found here and along nearby Rue Lagrange.

There's another ***food market*** on Rue Mouffetard, at the bottom end, around Rue de l'Arbalète (5e; Map 5; metro Censier Daubenton). The stalls tend to close on Sunday afternoon and Monday. This is one of Paris' oldest and liveliest market areas, with many interesting shops. There is a ***Franprix*** supermarket at 82 Rue Mouffetard (5e; Map 5; metro Censier Daubenton), open Monday to Saturday from 9 am to 8 pm and on Sunday to 1 pm.

Rue Saint Jacques, just south of Rue Soufflot (5e; Map 6; metro Luxembourg), also has a variety of food shops, and another ***food market*** can be found at Place Monge (5e; Map 5; metro Place Monge), open Wednesday, Friday and Sunday mornings until 1 pm. Nearby at 37 Rue Lacépède (5e; Map 5) is a cheap ***Ed l'Épicier*** supermarket, open Monday to Saturday from 9 am to 7.30 pm. There's a ***Shopi*** supermarket at 34 Rue Monge (5e; Map 5), open Monday to Saturday from 8.30 am to 9 pm.

For sandwiches to take to the Jardin du Luxembourg, try the popular hole-in-the-wall ***Douce France*** at 7 Rue Royer Collard (5e; Map 6; metro Luxembourg), where the lunchtime line of Sorbonne students is testament to the quality of its sandwiches (including vegetarian options; 13.50FF), coffee (3FF) and fruit juices (6FF). It's open weekdays from 11 am to 4 pm.

6e Arrondissement

Rue Saint André des Arts (Map 6; metro Saint Michel or Odéon) is lined with restaurants, including a few down the covered passage between Nos 59 and 61. There are lots of places between Église Saint Sulpice and Église Saint Germain des Prés, especially along Rue des Canettes, Rue Princesse and Rue Guisarde. Place Carrefour de l'Odéon (Map 6; metro Odéon) has a cluster of lively bars, cafés and restaurants.

French Place Saint Germain des Prés is home to three famous cafés: Brasserie Lipp is listed below; Les Deux Magots and Café de Flore are covered under Pubs, Bars & Cafés in the Entertainment section.

Brasserie Lipp (Map 6; ☎ 01 45 48 53 91; metro Saint Germain des Prés), 151 Blvd Saint Germain (6e). Politicians rub shoulders with intellectuals and editors, while tuxedoed waiters serve pricey à la carte dishes (choucroute, 102FF; plats du jour, 120FF) at this old-time, wood panelled café-brasserie. The *menu* costs 196FF (including 250mL of wine). Many people make a big fuss about sitting downstairs rather than upstairs, which is the nonsmoking section and considered nowheresville. Brasserie Lipp is open daily from 8.30 am to 1 am.

Polidor (Map 6; ☎ 01 43 26 95 34; metro Odéon), 41 Rue Monsieur le Prince (6e). A meal at this *crêmerie-restaurant* is like a quick trip back to Victor Hugo's Paris – the restaurant and its décor date from 1845 – but everyone knows about it, and the place has become pretty touristy. Guests are seated together at tables of six, 10 or 16. *Menus* of tasty, family-style French cuisine are available for 55FF (lunch only) and 100FF. Specialities include bœuf Bourguignon (50FF), *blanquette de veau* (veal in white sauce; 68FF) and the most famous *tarte tatin* (caramelised apple pie; 25FF) in Paris. It is open daily from noon to 2.30 pm and 7 pm to 12.30 am (11 pm on Sunday).

Le Mâchon d'Henri (Map 6; ☎ 01 43 29 08 70; metro Saint Sulpice), 8-10 Rue Guisarde (6e). This very Parisian bistro in a street awash with bars serves up Lyon-inspired dishes like lentil salad, various *charcuteries*, *saucisson chaud* (hot Lyon sausage) and *tarte aux pommes* (apple pie). Starters are 35 to 40FF, main courses from 60 to 80FF. It's open daily for lunch and dinner until 11.30 pm.

Le Petit Zinc (Map 6; ☎ 01 42 61 20 60; metro Saint Germain des Prés), 11 Rue Saint Benoît (6e). This wonderful (and expensive – entrées from 52 to 110FF, main courses from 110 to 160FF) place serves regional specialities from the south-west of France in true Art Nouveau splendour. There's a *menu* at 168FF. Try to get a table on the raised level in order to enjoy all the goings-on. It's open daily from noon to 2 am.

Rôtisserie d'En Face (Map 6; ☎ 01 43 26 40 98; metro Odéon), 2 Rue Christine (6e). This *auberge moderne*, a short walk south-east of the Pont Neuf, is a good choice if you're looking for simple, but well prepared French food. The lunch *menu* is 139FF, at dinner there's one at 159FF and another at 210FF. It's open for lunch and dinner to 11 pm, except on Saturday for lunch and on Sunday.

Lina's (Map 6; ☎ 01 43 29 14 14; metro Odéon) at 27 Rue Saint Sulpice (6e). A conveniently situated and comfortable member of a small chain with classy sandwiches in the 21 to 45FF range and soups from 27FF.

Other Cuisines The cuisines of southern Europe and Asia are well represented in the 6e.

Le Golfe de Naples (Map 6; ☎ 01 43 26 98 11; metro Mabillon), 5 Rue de Montfaucon (6e). Italian residents say this restaurant/pizzeria has the best pizza and home-made pasta in Paris, which is not generally celebrated for its Italian food. Pizzas range from 49 to 59FF, and don't forget to try the grilled fresh vegetables (85FF).

Chez Albert (Map 6; ☎ 01 46 33 22 57; metro Odéon), 43 Rue Mazarine (6e). Authentic Portuguese food is not easy to come by in Paris, but this place has it in spades; pork with clams, numerous *bacalha*u (dried cod) dishes and prawns sautéed in lots of garlic. The *menus* are 80 and 135FF, and it's open daily for lunch and dinner (closed on Sunday and on Monday for lunch).

Indonesia (Map 6; ☎ 01 43 25 70 22; metro Luxembourg), 12 Rue de Vaugirard (6e). This 'embassy of Indonesian cooking' run as a non-profit cooperative has all the standards – from an elaborate, multicourse rijsttafel to nasi goreng, *rendang* and *gado-gado*. *Menus* are available at 89, 99 and 129FF. It's open daily for lunch and dinner to 10.30 or 11 pm, except on Sunday for lunch.

Self-Catering With the Jardin du Luxembourg nearby, this is the perfect area for a picnic lunch. Also see the Latin Quarter section earlier for more picnic suggestions.

Poilâne (Map 4; ☎ 01 45 48 42 59; metro Sèvres Babylone), 8 Rue du Cherche Midi (6e). This is the most famous *boulangerie* in Paris. Its delicious sourdough bread, baked in wood-fired ovens every two hours, has a crunchy, slightly burned crust (19FF for a small round loaf). It's open daily, except Sunday, from 7 am to 8.15 pm.

Food shops (metro Mabillon) on Rue de Seine and Rue de Buci (both 6e). This is the largest cluster of shops in the 6e.

Champion (Map 6; metro Mabillon) at 79 Rue de Seine (6e). This supermarket is open Monday to Saturday from 8.40 am to 9 pm.

Chez Jean-Mi (Map 6; metro Odéon), 10 Rue de l'Ancienne Comédie (6e). This boulangerie and restaurant is open 24 hours a day, 365 days a year.

Monoprix (Map 6; metro Saint Germain des Prés) at 52 Rue de Rennes (6e). This store's supermarket, at the back of the basement level, is open Monday to Saturday from 9 am to 9 pm.

Marché Saint Germain (metro Mabillon), Rue Lobineau (6e), just north of the eastern end of Église Saint Germain des Prés (Map 6). This covered market has a huge array of produce and prepared foods.

Champs-Élysées Area

Few places along touristy Ave des Champs-Élysées offer good value, but some of the restaurants in the surrounding areas are very good.

French Generally, you're unlikely to find cheap eats in this area, but there are some exceptions.

L'Étoile Verte (Map 2; ☎ 01 43 80 69 34; metro Charles de Gaulle-Étoile), 13 Rue Brey (17e). When one LP author was a student in Paris, this was the place for a splurge and it still feels like it did way back then. All the old classics remain – the onion soup, the snails, the rabbit – and there are *menus* for 74FF (available weekdays only from 11.30 am till 9 pm), 100FF (with wine) and 145FF (with aperitif, wine and coffee). À la carte entrées start at 39FF, main courses at 59FF.

Maison Prunier (Map 2; ☎ 01 44 17 35 85; fax 01 44 17 90 10; metro Charles de Gaulle-Étoile), 16 Ave Victor Hugo (16e). This venerable fish and seafood restaurant, founded in 1925, is famed for its Art Deco interior. First courses generally cost from 90 to 250FF and mains from 160 to 280FF. It is open from noon to 2.30 pm and 7 to 11 pm (closed on Sunday and on Monday for lunch). Make reservations at least two days ahead.

Fauchon (Map 2; ☎ 01 47 62 60 11; metro Madeleine), 26-30 Place de la Madeleine (8e). Paris' most famous luxury food store (see Food & Wine in the Shopping section) also has five eat-in areas, including a cafeteria, in the basement at No 30, where you can purchase hot drinks, cold dishes, sandwiches and exquisite pastries. It is open Monday to Saturday from 9.40 am to 7 pm. After that and until midnight, the cafeteria turns into a *brasserie*. ***La Trattoria*** (☎ 01 47 42 90 30), an Italian restaurant on the 1st floor at No 26, is open from noon to 3 pm and 7 to 11 pm (closed on Sunday and holidays).

L'Ardoise (Map 2; ☎ 01 42 96 28 18; metro Concorde or Tuileries), 28 Rue du Mont Thabor (1er). The incomparable American food writer Patricia Wells raved about this place, which has no *carte* (*ardoise* means 'blackboard', which is all there is), so who are we to argue? The rabbit and hazelnut terrine, and beef fillet with morels, prepared dexterously by chef Pierre Jay (ex Tour d'Argent), are superb and the 165FF *menu* offers excellent value. It's open daily for lunch and dinner until 11.30 pm, except on Monday and on Tuesday for lunch.

Le Petit Champerret (Map 2; ☎ 01 43 80 01 39; metro Porte de Champerret), 40 Rue Vernier (17e). This little bistro north of Place Charles de Gaulle serves hearty home cooking in an intimate, friendly atmosphere. Try the stuffed rabbit with wild mushrooms or the *tête de veau*. There's a lunch *menu* at 90FF; an à la carte meal will set you back about 180FF. It's open weekdays only.

Self-Catering Place de la Madeleine (8e; Map 2; metro Madeleine) is the luxury food centre of one of the world's food capitals. The delicacies on offer don't come cheap, but even travellers on a modest budget can turn a walk around La Madeleine into a gastronomic odyssey. Most places are open from Monday to Saturday.

Prisunic (Map 2; metro Franklin D Roosevelt) at 62 Ave des Champs-Élysées (8e). This store's supermarket section is buried in the basement. It is open Monday to Saturday from 9 am to midnight.

Gare Saint Lazare & Grands Boulevards

This area, encompassing parts of the 2e and 9e, has a number of fine restaurants. The neon-lit Blvd Montmartre (Map 7; metro Rue Montmartre or Richelieu Drouot) and nearby sections of Rue du Faubourg Montmartre (neither of which are anywhere near the neighbourhood of Montmartre) form one of Paris' most animated café and dining districts.

French This area has among the two cheapest French restaurants in Paris.

Le Drouot (Map 7; ☎ 01 42 96 68 23; metro Richelieu Drouot), 103 Rue de Richelieu, 1st floor (2e). The décor and ambience of this inexpensive restaurant haven't changed since the late 1930s; dining is like a trip back to prewar Paris. A three course traditional French meal with wine should cost less than 100FF: fish and meat main courses from 35 to 60FF, a demi of cider or beer is 13FF. *Menus* cost 55, 62 and 79FF. It is open 365 days a year from 11.45 am to 3 pm and 6.30 to 10 pm. Reservations are not accepted.

Chartier (Map 7; ☎ 01 47 70 86 29; metro Rue Montmartre), 7 Rue du Faubourg Montmartre (9e). A real gem that is justifiably famous for its 330 seat *belle époque* dining room, virtually unaltered since 1896. The prices and fare are similar to those at Le Drouot (the management is the same) and are among the cheapest for a sit-down meal in Paris. It is open every day of the year from 11.30 am to 3 pm and 6 to 10 pm. Reservations are not accepted, so don't be surprised if there's a queue.

North African & Jewish There's a large selection of kosher North African and Jewish restaurants on Rue Richer, Rue Cadet and Rue Geoffroy Marie (all 9e; Map 7) just south of the Cadet metro stop.

Les Ailes (Map 7; ☎ 01 47 70 62 53; metro Cadet), next door to the Folies Bergères at 34 Rue Richer (9e). This kosher Tunisian place has superb couscous with meat or fish starting at 105FF and a good selection of North African salads. It is open daily to the public, except Friday night and Saturday.

Vegetarian Vegetarians are in luck just south-west of Opéra Garnier.

Country Life (Map 7; ☎ 01 42 97 48 51; metro Opéra), 6 Rue Daunou (2e). A food shop-restaurant that serves an all-you-can-eat buffet (65FF) from 11.30 am to 2.30 pm and 6.30 to 10 pm (closed on Friday night, and on Saturday and Sunday).

Gare du Nord & Gare de l'Est Area

This area offers all types of food but most notably Indian and Pakistani, usually elusive cuisines in Paris.

French There's a cluster of brasseries and bistros opposite the façade of Gare du Nord. They're decent options for a final (or first) meal in the City of Lights.

Brasserie Terminus Nord (Map 3; ☎ 01 42 85 05 15; metro Gare du Nord), 23 Rue de Dunkerque (10e). The copper bar, white tablecloths and brass fixtures – reflected brightly in the mirrored walls – look much as they did between the wars. Breakfast (45FF) is available daily from 7 to 11 am; full meals are served from 11 am through to 12.30 am. The 123FF *menu du garçon* is not available from 6 to 10 pm; the late-night (after 10 pm) *faim de nuit menu* costs 121FF.

Au Gigot Fin (Map 3; ☎ 01 42 08 38 81; metro Jacques Bonsergent), 56 Rue de Lancry (10e). This very meaty restaurant serves specialities from Périgord, including cassoulet, duck confit and *gigot d'agneau* in many different ways. It has lovely décor (we liked the wrought-iron circular staircase), but it feels somewhat like a hotel restaurant. There's a lunch *menu* for 85FF and dinner ones at 100 and 175FF. It's open daily for lunch and dinner, except on Saturday for lunch and on Sunday.

Le Chalet Maya (Map 3; ☎ 01 47 70 52 78; metro Poissonière or Gare de l'Est), 5 Rue des Petits Hôtels (10e). A nice little unpretentious restaurant whose food (seafood cassoulet, *tête de veau*) is not about to change the world, but for a 60FF *menu* at lunch and 95FF *menu* at dinner, you shouldn't expect much more. It's open daily for lunch and dinner, except on Sunday and on Monday for lunch.

Other Cuisines The tiny restaurants off Blvd de Strasbourg, many open throughout the afternoon, serve the city's most authentic Indian and Pakistani food.

Passage Brady (Map 3; metro Château d'Eau), running between Blvd de Strasbourg and Rue du Faubourg Saint Denis (10e), this tiny covered arcade could easily be in Bombay or Calcutta. The incredibly cheap (and usually crowded) Indian and Pakistani places are generally open for one of the best lunch deals in Paris (meat curry, rice and a tiny salad from 30FF) and for dinner, with *menus* from 49 to 55FF. They include ***Palais des Rajpout***, ***La Reine du Kashmir***, ***Shalimar***, ***Bhai Bhai***, ***Kashmir Express*** and ***Pooja***, perhaps the best of the lot.

Self-Catering Rue du Faubourg Saint Denis (10e; Map 3; metro Strasbourg Saint Denis), north of Blvd Saint Denis, is one of the cheapest places in Paris to buy food. It has a distinctively Middle Eastern air, and quite a few of the groceries offer Turkish and North African specialities. Many of the food shops, including the fromagerie at No 54, are closed on Sunday afternoon and on Monday.

Marché Saint Quentin (Map 3; metro Gare de l'Est), opposite 92 Blvd de Magenta (10e), at the start of Rue de Chabrol. This huge covered market is open from 8 am to 1 pm and 3.30 to 7.30 pm (closed on Sunday afternoon and on Monday).

Franprix (Map 3; metro Gare de l'Est) at 57 Blvd de Magenta (10e). Open Monday to Saturday from 9 am to 7.30 pm. The Franprix opposite 6 Rue des Petites Écuries (10e; Map 3; metro Château d'Eau) is open the same hours.

Bastille Area

This area, mostly the 11e and 12e but also the westernmost part of the 4e, is chock-a-block with restaurants. Narrow, scruffy Rue de Lappe (11e; Map 5) may not look like much during the day, but it's one of the trendiest café and nightlife streets in Paris, attracting a young, alternative crowd.

French Traditional French food in all price ranges can be found in the Bastille area.

Brasserie Bofinger (Map 5; ☎ 01 42 72 87 82; metro Bastille), 5-7 Rue de la Bastille (4e). This is reputedly the oldest brasserie in Paris (founded in 1864), with Art Deco-style brass, glass and mirrors. Specialities include choucroute (90 to 120FF) and seafood dishes (from 126FF). The 169FF *menu* includes half a bottle of wine. It is open daily from noon to 3 pm and 6.30 pm to 1 am (no afternoon closure on weekends and holidays). Reservations are necessary for dinner, especially on weekends, and for Sunday lunch. Ask for a seat downstairs, under the *coupole* (stained-glass dome) if possible.

Le Bistrot du Dôme (Map 5; ☎ 01 48 04 88 44; metro Bastille), 2 Rue de la Bastille (4e). Opposite Bofinger, this superb restaurant, a distant cousin of the better known Le Dôme Brasserie in Montparnasse, specialises in superbly prepared (and pricey) fish dishes. The blackboard *carte* has starters from 45 to 65FF, main courses from 90 to 130FF.

Le Tabarin (Map 5; ☎ 01 48 07 15 22; metro Bréguet Sabin), 3 Rue du Pasteur-Wagner, corner of Rue Amelot (11e). On the Marais-Bastille border, this friendly café-restaurant manages to combine tradition with a modern approach. Excellent and reasonably priced food like grilled salmon costs from 66 to 96FF. Open daily until midnight.

Café de l'Industrie (Map 5; ☎ 01 47 00 13 53; metro Bréguet Sabin), 16 Rue Saint Sabin (11e). At this very popular restaurant with neo-colonial décor, main courses are in the 50 to 85FF bracket and the desserts – every imaginable kind of tarte – cost from 24 to 34FF. It's open until 1 am every night, except Saturday, and it's wise to book.

Chez Paul (Map 5; ☎ 01 47 00 34 57; metro Ledru Rollin), 13 Rue de Charonne, at the end of Rue de Lappe (11e). This is a convivial and extremely popular bistro with traditional French cuisine. Mains cost 62 to 95FF, so count on paying about 170FF for a meal with wine. It is open daily from noon to 3 pm and 7.30 pm to 12.30 am.

Le Square Trousseau (Map 5; ☎ 01 43 43 06 00; metro Ledru Rollin), 1 Rue Antoine Vollon (12e). This vintage bistro, with its etched glass, zinc bar and polished wood panelling, is comfortable rather than trendy and attracts a jolly and very mixed clientele. The food and standards are of high quality, but we suspect that most people come to enjoy the lovely terrace overlooking a small park. The lunch *menu* is 135FF; à la carte dinner with wine should cost between 180 and 250FF. Diners are received at the bar with a complimentary glass of wine. It's open daily till 11.30 pm.

Les Galopins (Map 5; ☎ 01 47 00 45 35; metro Bastille), 24 Rue des Taillandiers (11e). This little neighbourhood bistro serves simple but high-quality starters and main courses (60 to 80FF) like rabbit with mustard and green salad with foie gras. The reception is warm here; diners are offered a little glass of beer at the bar.

L'Encrier (Map 5; ☎ 01 44 68 08 16; metro Ledru Rollin), 55 Rue Traversière (12e). If you're looking for lunch in the Bastille area, you couldn't do better than at the 'Inkwell', which serves an excellent-value three course *menu* for 58FF. It's open for lunch and dinner from Monday to Friday.

Other Cuisines Cuisines from all over the world are found along Rue de la Roquette and Rue de Lappe, just east of Place de la Bastille, but Tex-Mex (usually rather bland in Paris) is the major attraction.

La Pirada Bar Tapas (Map 5; ☎ 01 47 00 73 61; metro Bastille), 7 Rue de Lappe (11e). This popular place has live music at night. Other nearby Tex-Mex options are ***Café 66*** (named after US Route 66) at No 8 and ***Del Rio Café*** at No 26.

Havanita Café (Map 5; ☎ 01 43 55 96 42; metro Bastille), 11 Rue de Lappe (11e). This bar-restaurant is decorated with posters and murals inspired – like the food and drinks – by Cuba. Not as trendy as it used to be but still worth a look. Draught beers range from 20 to 24FF, cocktails from 40 to 48FF, starters from 34 to 78FF and the excellent main courses from 58 to 160FF. It's open daily from noon to 3 pm and 5 pm to 2 am. Happy hour, when cocktails are 15 to 20FF cheaper, is from 5 to 8 pm.

Suds (Map 5; ☎ 01 43 14 06 36; metro Ledru Rollin), 55 Rue de Charonne (11e). No, not a trendy laundrette but a very branché bar-restaurant with a name that means 'Souths' and jazz in the basement. The cuisine here is anything and everything from the south – from Mexican and Peruvian to Portuguese and North African. Suds packs them in daily for lunch and dinner till 1 am (midnight on Sunday and Monday), but neither the food nor the mainstream music impressed us. Lunch *menus* are available for 59 to 88FF. À la carte starters at dinner range from 29 to 45FF, main courses from 59 to 88FF and desserts from 32 to 39FF; expect to pay about 200FF per person with wine at dinner. The vegetarian plate is 52FF.

Le Kiosque (Map 1; ☎ 01 43 79 74 80; metro Philippe Auguste), 26 Rue de la Folie Régnault (11e). A culinary adventure along the Silk Road, this restaurant serves an amalgamation of Turkish, Indian, Chinese and Lebanese – and it works superbly. The excellent décor (Turkish ceramics, carpets on the walls) sets the tone. Try the mixed meze, the lamb curry Madras-style or the chicken biryani. There's a *menu* at 82FF; ordering à la carte should cost around 160FF per person. It's open weekdays until 2 am.

Café Le Serail (Map 5; ☎ 01 43 38 17 01; metro Bastille), 10 Rue Sedaine (11e). This trendy North African café-restaurant is a lounge lizard's paradise, with deep over-stuffed sofas where you can sit and sip mint tea before or after your meal. There's a lunch *menu* for 100FF; expect to pay about 200FF à la carte at dinner.

Self-Catering There are lots of ***food shops*** and supermarkets along Rue de la Roquette up towards Place Léon Blum (metro Voltaire). There's a ***Monoprix*** at 97 Rue du Faubourg Saint Antoine (11e; Map 5; metro Ledru Rollin), open Monday to Saturday from 9 am to 9 pm.

Oberkampf, Ménilmontant & Belleville Areas

In the northern part of the 11e, east of Place de la République, and into the 20e, Rue Oberkampf and its extension, Rue de Ménilmontant are becoming increasingly popular with diners and denizens of the night. Rue de Belleville is dotted with Chinese, Vietnamese and Turkish places and Blvd de Belleville has loads of kosher couscous restaurants (closed on Saturday).

French French restaurants run the gamut here – from the sublime to the ridiculously cheap.

Au Trou Normand (Map 8; ☎ 01 48 05 80 23; metro Oberkampf), 9 Rue Jean-Pierre Timbaud (11e). Hosted by several grannies, this very French and cosy little restaurant has some of the lowest prices in Paris. Starters range from 10 to 25FF (the vegetable potage is particularly good), main courses from 29 to 39FF, desserts are under 10FF. Diners sit at shared tables covered with plastic tablecloths. It's open daily from noon to 2.30 pm and 7.30 to 11 pm, except on Saturday for lunch and on Sunday.

Le Villaret (Map 3; ☎ 01 43 57 89 76; metro Parmentier), 13 Rue Ternaux (11e). This excellent neighbourhood restaurant, a stone's throw from the Cirque d'Hiver and the great food market on Blvd Richard Lenoir (Map 5; metro Richard Lenoir), has diners coming from across Paris till late to sample such specialities as artichoke and foie gras salad, calf's liver with truffled mashed potatoes, and cod cooked with creamed mussels. Starters cost from 40 to 50FF, main courses from 80 to 135FF and desserts from 40FF. Wines range from 85 to 320FF but average around 150FF. It's open for dinner from Monday to Saturday till 1 am.

Le Repaire de Cartouche (Map 8; ☎ 01 47 00 25 86; metro Saint Sébastien Froissart), 8 Blvd des Filles du Calvaire or 99 Rue Amelot (11e). This old-fashioned place with a distinctly modern approach (rissole of black pudding cooked with figs, cod roasted with leeks) has taken a new direction with the arrival of a young and energetic chef. Starters cost from 35 to 45FF, main courses from 65 to 90FF and desserts from 30 to 40FF. Wines average about 160FF a bottle. It's open daily for lunch and dinner till 11 pm, except on Sunday and on Monday for dinner.

Le Clown Bar (Map 8; ☎ 01 43 55 87 35; metro Filles du Calvaire), 114 Rue Amelot (11e). This wonderful wine bar next to the Cirque d'Hiver is like a museum, with painted ceilings, mosaics on the wall and a lovely zinc bar. The food is simple and unprententious; we loved the rabbit rillettes with onion compote and parmentier (black pudding mixed with mashed potatoes and baked). Starters cost from 30 to 58FF, main courses around 75FF; expect to pay from 150FF per person. It's open daily, except on Sunday from October to April, for lunch and dinner till 11.30 pm.

Le Charbon (Map 3; ☎ 01 43 57 55 13; metro Parmentier), 109 Rue Oberkampf (11e). More of a café than a restaurant, the Charbon serves a Saturday or Sunday brunch (11 am to 5 pm) for 75FF that is just right at a place that's not too chic, not too trendy, not too young and not too conservative. The plat du jour is 68FF. It's open daily from 9 am to 2 am.

Le Baratin (Map 1; ☎ 01 43 49 39 70; metro Pyrénées), 3 Rue Jouye-Rouve (20e). This wine bistro offers some of the best food in the 20e with a choice of two or three starters and the same number of main courses. There's a lunch *menu* for 60FF; à la carte at dinner shouldn't set you back more than 160FF. Thankfully there's no canned music here as seems to be standard in most *bars à vin* in Paris. It's open daily for lunch and dinner, except on Sunday and Monday and on Saturday for lunch.

Other Cuisines The cuisines of southern Europe, North Africa and Asia are well represented here.

Café Florentin (Map 3; ☎ 01 43 55 57 00; metro Parmentier), 40 Rue Jean-Pierre Timbaud (11e). Superb Italian fare can be had here in cosy surroundings. The lunch *menu* is 65FF (including wine); à la carte starters are 21 to 55FF and main courses 58 to 90FF. The two dozen pasta dishes range in price from 56 to 78FF. It's open for lunch and dinner until 11.45 pm, except Saturday lunch and all day Sunday.

Chez Vincent (Map 1; ☎ 01 42 02 22 45; metro Botzaris), 5 Rue du Tunnel (19e). This restaurant on the southern boundary of the Parc des Buttes-Chaumont offers refined (and rather expensive) Italian cuisine in a lively, smoky environment. There's a *menu* at 180FF but ordering à la carte won't leave you with much change from 300FF. It's open for lunch and dinner until 10.30 pm except all day Sunday and at midday on Saturday.

Le Pavillon Puebla (Map 3; ☎ 01 42 08 92 62; metro Buttes-Chaumont), in the Parc des Buttes-Chaumont, near the entrance where Ave Simon Bolivar and Rue Botzaris meet (19e). No, not Mexican but Catalan, this exquisite restaurant in a Second Empire-style pavilion attracts not so much for its wonderful seafood and fish dishes like anchovy tarte, bouillabaisse and cod stuffed with snails, but the wonderful terrace open in summer. *Menus* are 180 and 240FF. For dessert, don't miss the mille-feuille aux fraises (strawberries in layers of flaky pastry). It's open for lunch and dinner Tuesday to Saturday to 10.30 pm.

La Favela Chic (Map 3; ☎ 01 43 57 15 47; metro Ménilmontant), 131 Rue Oberkampf (11e). Very branché Brazilian is the story at this small place with main courses at 50 to 70FF including a massive *feijoada* (65FF). It's open daily from noon to 2 am (from 7 pm on Saturday).

La Piragua (Map 5; ☎ 01 40 21 35 98; metro Saint Ambroise), 6 Rue Rochebrune (11e). Colombian food and good Latino music feature at this small and friendly restaurant. There are *menus* at 96 and 110FF; à la carte starters like *empañadas* and fried plantains start from 22 to 35FF, mains from 59 to 98FF (try the marinated chicken Piragua cooked with smoked bacon and raisins, 60FF). La Piragua is open daily, except Sunday.

Le Montagnard (Map 1; ☎ 01 43 49 42 38; metro Ménilmontant), 132 Blvd Ménilmontant (20e). Don't be fooled by the name – the 'Mountaineer' doesn't serve fondue and *raclette* but couscous and has a 55FF *menu*. There's a decent bar here too.

Chez Lalou (Map 3; ☎ 01 43 58 35 28; metro Couronnes), 78 Blvd de Belleville (20e). The pick of the kosher couscous crop on the Blvd de Belleville, this place has killer couscous from 60 to 80FF, grills from 60FF, *brick à l'oeuf* for 20FF and salads from 25FF. The terrace is a lovely – and lively – place to dine in the warm weather.

Krung Thep (Map 1; ☎ 01 43 66 83 74; metro Pyrénées), 93 Rue Julien Lacroix (20e). Considered by many to be the most authentic Thai restaurant in Paris, the 'Bangkok' is a small place with all our favourites: green curries, *tom yam gung* and fish steamed in banana leaves. Expect to pay about 120FF per person. It's open daily to 11 pm.

Self-Catering There's a ***Franprix*** supermarket at 23 Rue Jean-Pierre Timbaud (11e; Map 3; metro Oberkampf), open Monday to Saturday from 8 am to 8 pm.

Place de la Nation

There are loads of decent restaurants on the roads fanning out from Place de la Nation.

French The French restaurants in this area tend to be real finds.

MARK DAFFEY

Rising steeply out of the Atlantic and with its imposing building and slender spire on the abbey building, Mont Saint Michel is an impressive sight.

FRANCES LINZEE GORDON

A WWII cemetery near Bayeux

FRANCES LINZEE GORDON

Typical rural countryside in Normandy

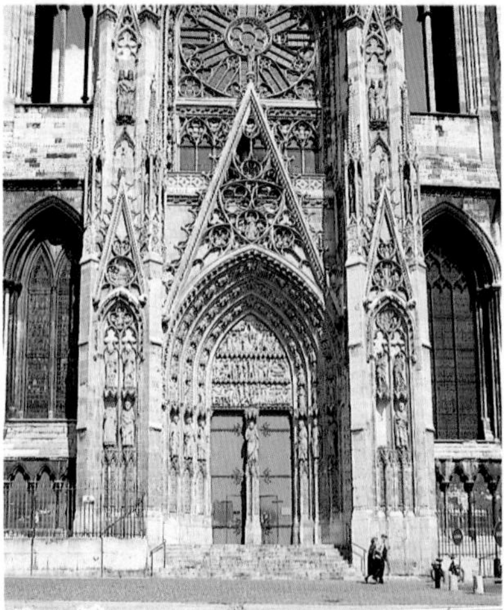
LEANNE LOGAN

Rouen's Cathédrale Notre Dame, Normandy

TERESA FISHER

The white cliffs of the Côte d'Albâtre

Les Amognes (Map 1; ☎ 01 43 72 73 05; metro Faidherbe Chaligny), 243 Rue du Faubourg Saint Antoine (11e). A meal at Les Amognes is a quintessentially French – rather than Parisian – experience: *haute cuisine* at a reasonable 190FF set price, discreet service, an atmosphere that is *correcte*, even a little provincial. Superb dishes include a tarte of marinated sardines, the lightly pan-fried scallops and the stuffed endives. The wines aren't cheap though (from 200FF for a bottle of Burgundy). It's open daily for lunch and dinner until 10.30 pm, except on Sunday and on Monday for lunch.

Other Cuisines Place de la Nation and surrounds has a large number of restaurants serving non-French food.

Le Réservoir (Map 5; ☎ 01 43 56 39 60; metro Ledru Rollin), 16 Rue de la Forge Royale (11e). This warehouse turned Italian-ish restaurant done up in modern kitsch is popular with punters and celebrities headed for the even more kitsch Casbah club (see Entertainment) next door. Count on from 200FF a head. It's open daily till 1 am.

Café Canelle (Map 5; ☎ 01 43 70 48 25; metro Ledru Rollin), 1bis Rue de la Forge Royale (11e). This festive Moroccan restaurant is run by two Algerian brothers who do couscous with a twist; how does it sound flavoured with cinnamon, orange flowers and dates? It's open daily from 7 pm to 2 am.

À La Banane Ivoirienne (Map 5; ☎ 01 43 70 49 90; metro Ledru Rollin), 10 Rue de la Forge Royale (11e). This friendly place serves West African specialities, at dinner only, from Tuesday to Saturday. Entrées start from 20 to 35FF, main courses are in the 60 to 85FF region. There's African music on Thursday from 10 pm.

Chinatown Area

Dozens of East Asian restaurants line the main streets of Paris' Chinatown (13e), including Ave de Choisy, Ave d'Ivry and Rue Baudricourt. The cheapest *menus*, which go for about 50FF, are usually available only at lunch on weekdays.

French It may sound strange, but Chinatown is not all about Asian food. There are also several French restaurants here.

L'Avant-Goût (Map 1; ☎ 01 53 80 24 00; metro Place d'Italie), 26 Rue Bobillot (13e). A prototype of the Parisian 'neo-bistro', this restaurant serves some of the most inventive modern cuisine around (lamb confit with rosemary and polenta) at an affordable 59FF for the lunch *menu* and 135FF for the one at dinner. It's open Tuesday to Saturday for lunch and dinner until 10.30 pm.

Le Temps des Cérises (Map 1; ☎ 01 45 89 69 48; metro Corvisart), 18-20 Rue de la Buttes aux Cailles (13e). The relaxed feeling of this 'anarchistic' restaurant run by a workers' cooperative, the good solid fare (rabbit with mustard, steak *frites*) and especially the low prices keep regulars coming back for more. There are *menus* at 56FF (lunch only) and 118FF; plats du jour are 45FF. Expect to pay about 130FF à la carte. It's open daily, except on Saturday for lunch and on Sunday.

Asian This area has the best Chinese food in Paris.

Le Fleuve de Chine (Map 1; ☎ 01 45 82 06 88; metro Porte de Choisy), 15 Ave de Choisy (13e), or enter through the Tour Bergame housing estate at 130 Blvd Masséna. Take it from the experts, this place has the most authentic Cantonese food in Paris and, as is typical, both the surrounds and the service are as forgettable as the 1997 Hong Kong handover. Main courses range from 40 to 95FF, but settle in at around 40 to 50FF for chicken, prawn and superb claypot dishes. Expect to pay about 110FF per person for a splurge. It's open daily for lunch and dinner.

Montparnasse Area

Since the 1920s, the area around Blvd du Montparnasse (6e and 14e) has been one of the city's premier avenues for enjoying that most Parisian of pastimes: sitting in a café and checking out the passers-by. Many younger Parisians, however, now consider the area passé.

There are several ***crêperies*** at 20 Rue d'Odessa (Map 4) and several more around the corner on Rue du Montparnasse. ***Mustang Café*** (Map 4; ☎ 01 43 35 36 12; metro Montparnasse-Bienvenüe), 84 Blvd du Montparnasse (14e), has passable Tex-Mex (platters and chilli from 45FF; *fajitas* are 98FF) available to 5 am.

French Blvd du Montparnasse, around the Vavin metro stop, is home to a number of legendary places, made famous between the wars by writers (Ernest Hemingway, F Scott Fitzgerald etc) and avant-garde artists (Dalí, Cocteau). Before the Russian Revolution, these cafés attracted exiled revolutionaries such as Lenin and Trotsky.

La Coupole (Map 4; ☎ 01 43 20 14 20; metro Vavin), 102 Blvd du Montparnasse (14e). La Coupole's famous mural-covered columns (decorated by artists including Brancusi and Chagall), dark wood panelling and indirect lighting have hardly changed since the days of Sartre, Soutine, Man Ray and Josephine Baker. Mains at this 450 seat brasserie, which opened in 1927, cost about 100FF, so count on spending about 185FF per person for a meal. A lunchtime express *menu* is 89FF including 250mL of wine; evening *menus* start at 123FF. It is open daily from noon to 2 am. There's dancing on some nights and tea dances on weekends (see Discos & Clubs in the Entertainment section for details).

Le Select (Map 4; ☎ 01 42 22 65 27; metro Vavin), 99 Blvd du Montparnasse (6e). Another Montparnasse legend, the Select's décor has changed very little since 1923. The *menu* costs 90FF, and *tartines* (buttered bread with toppings) made with pain Poilâne start at 30FF. Drinks are served at the tiny, round sidewalk tables, each equipped with Parisian café-style rattan chairs. It is open daily from 7 am to 3 am.

Le Caméléon (Map 6; ☎ 01 43 20 63 43; metro Vavin), 6 Rue de Chevreuse (6e). If you want to eat at a 'nouveau' bistro or brasserie – the distinction isn't that clear even to the French any more – that serves fresh, innovative food in a traditional setting, you couldn't do better than this place. Its lobster ravioli (82FF), among other dishes, is worth dying for. Starters range from 35 to 70FF, main courses from 82 to 135FF, and there's a lunchtime *menu* for 120FF. It also has an excellent wine selection.

Self-Catering There's an ***Inno*** supermarket opposite the Tour Montparnasse (Map 4), open Monday to Saturday from 9 am to 9 pm, and a ***food market*** on Blvd Edgar Quinet (Map 4), open Wednesday and Saturday mornings until 1 pm.

15e Arrondissement

There are quite a few places to eat to the south of Blvd de Grenelle.

French You'll find some lovely French restaurants in quiet neighbourhoods of this area.

L'Os à Moelle (Map 1; ☎ 01 45 57 27 27; metro Lourmel), 3 Rue Vasco de Gama. In the far-flung south-western 15e, the 'Marrow Bone' is well worth the trip, and chef Thierry Faucher (late of the Crillon) offers one of the best and most affordable (145FF at lunch, 190FF at dinner) *dégustation menus* in town. Its four courses could include such delicacies as creamed scallops in the shell with coriander, bass in cumin-flavoured butter and half a quail with endives and chestnuts, plus dessert. Wines are in the 95 to 160FF range and the list is very good. L'Os à Moelle is open for lunch and dinner from Tuesday to Saturday.

North African & Middle Eastern Not surprisingly, these ever popular cuisines can be found throughout the 15e.

Feyrous (Map 4; ☎ 01 45 78 07 02; metro Dupleix), 8 Rue de Lourmel. A bright, busy and outgoing Lebanese traiteur-restaurant with *menus* at 60 and 85FF at lunch and 105FF at dinner. It's open daily from 7 am to 2 am.

Le Tipaza (Map 4; ☎ 01 45 79 22 25; metro Avenue Émile Zola), 150 Ave Émile Zola (15e). This classy Moroccan restaurant has good couscous (65 to 82FF), tajines (76 to 80FF) and other Moroccan specialities with *menus* at 75FF at lunch and 130FF at dinner.

Montmartre & Pigalle

This area encompasses bits of the 9e, 17e and 18e. The restaurants along Rue des Trois Frères (18e; Map 9) are a much better bet than their touristy counterparts at Place du Tertre (Map 9).

French Montmartre's French restaurants, like almost everything else on the Butte, are slightly offbeat.

Le Refuge des Fondus (Map 9; ☎ 01 42 55 22 65; metro Abbesses or Anvers), 17 Rue des Trois Frères (18e). This establishment has been a Montmartre favourite since 1966. For 87FF you get an aperitif, hors d'œuvre, red wine in a baby bottle (or beer or soft drink) and a good quantity of either fondue Savoyarde (cheese) or Bourguignon (meat; minimum order for two). It is open daily from 7 pm to 2 am (last seating at midnight or 12.30 am). It's a good idea to phone ahead (at 5 or 6 pm) for reservations, especially on weekends.

Le Bateau Lavoir (Map 9; ☎ 01 42 54 23 12; metro Abbesses), 8 Rue Garreau (18e). Named after the studio behind it on Place Émile Goudeau where Picasso & Co made art around the turn of the century, this wonderful old-style bistro has good-value *menus* at 98 and 130FF. It's closed on Saturday for lunch and on Monday.

Macis et Muscade (Map 2; ☎ 01 42 26 62 26; metro La Fourche), 110 Rue Legendre (17e). This is another example of an excellent *restaurant du quartier*, and its fine *carte* is changed by chef Thierry Arrouasse every season. The lunch *formule* is 65FF, the dinner *menu* is 120FF. À la carte entrées cost from 30 to 42FF and mains from 50 to 80FF. Wines are in the 120 to 160FF range. It's open daily for lunch and dinner, except on Saturday for lunch and on Sunday.

Other Cuisines French cuisine is not the only option in Montmartre.

Il Duca (Map 9; ☎ 01 46 06 71 98; metro Abbesses), 26 Rue Yvonne le Tac (18e). A neat, tidy and intimate little Italian restaurant with good, straightforward food including a lunchtime *menu* for 69FF and main courses from 70 to 82FF. Home-made pasta dishes are 45 to 75FF.

Le Mono (Map 9; ☎ 01 46 06 99 20; metro Abbesses or Blanche), 40 Rue Véron (18e). The friendly Togolese woman who runs this unpretentious restaurant has been serving great West African cuisine for more than 20 years. Specialities – made with imported ingredients – include *lélé* (flat, steamed cakes of white beans and shrimp and served with tomato sauce; 25FF), *maffé* (beef or chicken served with peanut sauce; 50FF), *gbekui* (a sort of goulash made with spinach, onions, beef, fish and shrimp; 55FF) and *djenkommé* (grilled chicken with semolina noodles). Vegetarian dishes are prepared upon request. It is open from 7 to 11.30 pm (later on Friday and Saturday); closed on Wednesday.

Taj (Map 9; ☎ 01 42 59 88 80), 11 Rue des Trois Frères (18e). This cosy little Indian restaurant has biryanis from 45 to 60FF, curries from 39 to 45FF and *menus* at 59 and 75FF.

Self-Catering Towards Pigalle there are lots of ***groceries***, many of them open until late at night – try the side streets leading off Blvd de Clichy (eg Rue Lepic). Heading south from Blvd de Clichy, Rue des Martyrs (9e; Map 3) is lined with food shops basically all the way to the Notre Dame de Lorette metro stop.

Franprix (Map 9; metro Lamarck Caulaincourt) at 44 Rue Caulaincourt (18e). This supermarket is open Monday to Saturday from 8.30 am to 7.25 pm (7.45 pm on Friday and Saturday). There's an ***Ed l'Épicier*** supermarket (Map 9; metro Anvers) a block south of the bottom of the funicular at 31 Rue d'Orsel (18e), open Monday to Saturday from 9 am to 8 pm.

University Restaurants

Stodgy but rib-sticking cafeteria food is available in copious quantities at Paris' 16 *restaurants universitaires* (student cafeterias), run by the Centre Régional des Œuvres Universitaires et Scolaires (CROUS; ☎ 01 40 51 36 00; Minitel 3615 CROUS). Tickets for three-course meals cost 14.10FF for students with ID, 23FF if you have an ISIC card (or Carte Jeune Internationale) and 27.90FF for nonstudent guests. CROUS restaurants (usually referred to as *restos U*) have variable opening times that change according to school holiday schedules and weekend rotational agreements; check the schedule posted outside any of the following.

Assas (Map 6; ☎ 01 46 33 61 25; metro Port Royal or Notre Dame des Champs), 92 Rue d'Assas, 7th floor (6e), in the Université de Paris' Faculté de Droit et des Sciences Économiques (Law & Economics Faculty). The ticket window is on the 6th floor.

Châtelet (Map 6; ☎ 01 43 31 51 66; metro Censier Daubenton), 10 Rue Jean Calvin (5e), just off Rue Mouffetard.

Bullier (Map 6; ☎ 01 43 54 93 38; metro Port Royal), 39 Ave G Bernanos, 2nd floor (5e), in Centre Jean Sarrailh.

Mabillon (Map 6; ☎ 01 43 25 66 23; metro Mabillon), 3 Rue Mabillon, 3rd floor (6e).

Self-Catering

Buying your own food is one of the best ways to keep travel costs down. For details on how French food shops work, see Self-Catering in the Food section in the Facts for the Visitor chapter. Supermarkets, which are few and far between in central Paris, are much cheaper than *épiceries* (grocery stores), such as those of the Félix Potin chain. Many food shops are closed on Sunday and/or Monday and take a break between 12.30 or 1 pm and 3 or 4 pm.

Paris has an exceptional number of places perfect for picnicking: parks, the courtyards of public buildings, the quays along the Seine and so forth.

Food Markets Paris' neighbourhood food markets offer the freshest and best-quality fruits, vegetables, cheeses, prepared salads etc at the lowest prices in town. The *marchés découverts* (open-air markets) – 60 of which pop up in public squares around the city two or three times a week – are open from 7 am to 1 pm. The dozen or so *marchés couverts* (covered markets) are open from 8 am to some time between 12.30 and 1.30 pm and from 3.30 or 4 to 7.30 pm (closed Sunday afternoon and Monday). To find out when there's a market near your hotel or hostel, ask anyone who lives in the neighbourhood.

ENTERTAINMENT

Listings

It's virtually impossible to sample the richness of Paris' entertainment scene without first perusing *Pariscope* (3FF) or *L'Officiel des Spectacles* (2FF), both of which come out on Wednesday and are available at any newsstand. *Pariscope* includes a five page insert in English courtesy of London's *Time Out* weekly events magazine.

For up-to-date information on clubs and the music scene, pick up a copy of *LYLO* (an acronym for Les Yeux, Les Oreilles – ie The Eyes, The Ears), a free magazine with excellent listings of rock concerts and other live music available at certain cafés, bars and on Minitel at 3615 LYLO. The monthly magazine *Nova* (10FF) is a more mainstream source, but its *Hot Guide* insert of listings is particularly useful. Check out any of the FNAC outlets (see Booking Agencies), especially the one in the Forum des Halles shopping mall, for free flyers and programs.

For less time-sensitive information on the hottest discos, bars and live music venues, the best source is *Le Fêtard en Poche* (Éditions Florent-Massot; 89FF), a 160 page guide to Paris after dark updated annually and available at bookshops and some newsstands.

You can hear recorded English-language information on concerts and other events, prepared by the Paris tourist office, by calling ☎ 01 49 52 53 56 (24 hours), though it's not always as up to date as it could be. Two other excellent sources for what's on are Radio FG on 98.2 MHz FM and Radio Nova on 101.5 MHz FM. For who and what is *caliente* in Latino music, check out Minitel 3615 LATINA.

Booking Agencies

You can buy tickets for many (but not all) cultural events at several ticket outlets, among them FNAC (rhymes with 'snack') outlets and Virgin Megastores. Both accept reservations and ticketing by phone. FNAC will take Visa and MasterCard as will Virgin Megastore, which also accepts American Express and Diners Club. Tickets cannot be returned or exchanged unless a performance is cancelled.

Reservations for a wide variety of theatre and opera productions can be made using Minitel 3615 THEA.

Virgin Megastore (Map 2; ☎ 01 49 53 50 00; metro Franklin D Roosevelt), 52-60 Ave des Champs-Élysées (8e). The *billeterie* (ticket office; ☎ 01 49 53 52 09 for both stores) in the basement, like the rest of this four level emporium, is open daily from 10 am (noon on Sunday) to midnight. Virgin has a second store (☎ 01 49 53 52 90; metro Palais Royal) with a box office next to the inverted glass pyramid in the Carrousel du Louvre shopping mall (Map 7), 99 Rue de Rivoli (1er). It is open daily from 11 am to 8 pm (to 10 pm Wednesday to Saturday).

FNAC (Map 7; ☎ 01 40 41 40 00 or ☎ 08 36 68 04 56 for information; metro Châtelet-Les Halles), 1-7 Rue Pierre Lescot (1er), in the FNAC Forum department store on the 3rd underground level of the Forum des Halles shopping mall, which is open from Monday to Saturday from 10 am to 7.30 pm. The commission is 10 to 20FF a ticket. To purchase tickets by Minitel, key in 3615 FNAC and your credit card number – the tickets will be sent to you by mail. FNAC has several other billeteries (*services des spectacles*) around the city including at the FNAC Montparnasse department store (Map 4; ☎ 01 49 54 30 00; metro Saint Placide) at 136 Rue de Rennes (6e), about 600m north of Gare Montparnasse, open Monday to Saturday from 10 am to 7.30 pm; FNAC Musique Bastille (Map 5; ☎ 01 43 42 04 04; metro Bastille) at 4 Place de la Bastille (12e), open Monday to Saturday from 10 am to 8 pm (10 pm on Wednesday and Friday); and FNAC Étoile department store (Map 2; ☎ 01 44 09 18 00; metro Ternes) at 26-30 Ave des Ternes (17e), open Monday to Saturday from 10 am to 7.30 pm.

Other booking agencies include:

Agence des Théâtres (Map 7; ☎ 01 42 97 46 70; metro Quatre Septembre), 7 Rue de Marivaux (2e).

Agence Perrossier (Map 2; ☎ 01 42 60 58 31; metro Madeleine), 6 Place de la Madeleine (8e). Open Monday to Saturday from 9.15 am to 7 pm.

Cityrama (Map 7; ☎ 01 44 55 60 00; metro Palais Royal), 147 Rue Saint Honoré (1er).

SOS Théâtre (Map 2; ☎ 01 44 77 88 55; metro Madeleine), 6 Place de la Madeleine (8e). Open Monday to Saturday from 10 am to 7 pm.

Discount Tickets

On the day of a performance, the Kiosque Théâtre outlets (no phone) sell theatre tickets for 50% off the usual price (plus a commission of 16FF). The seats on offer are almost always the most desirable (in the orchestra or 1st balcony) and expensive. Tickets to concerts, operas and ballets may also be available.

Both outlets – one across from 15 Place de la Madeleine (8e; Map 2; metro Madeleine) and the other halfway between Gare Montparnasse and the nearby Tour Montparnasse (15e; Map 4; metro Montparnasse Bienvenüe) – are open Tuesday to Saturday from 12.30 to 8 pm and on Sunday from 12.30 to 4 pm.

Cinema

Pariscope and *L'Officiel des Spectacles* list cinematic offerings alphabetically by the French title followed by the English (or German, Italian, Spanish etc). Going to the movies in Paris does not come cheaply: expect to pay 45 to 50FF for a ticket. Students and people under 18 and over 60 usually get discounts of about 25% (except on Friday, Saturday and Sunday nights). On Wednesday (and sometimes Monday), most cinemas give discounts to everyone.

If a movie is labelled 'VO' or 'v.o.' (for *version originale*) it means it will be subtitled rather than dubbed ('v.f.' or *version française*), so Hollywood movies will still be in English.

Cinémathèque Française (☎ 01 45 53 21 86 or, for a recording, ☎ 01 47 04 24 24). This cultural institution (generously supported by the government) almost always leaves its foreign offerings – often seldom-screened classics – in the original, nondubbed version. Screenings take place daily, except Monday, in the far-eastern tip of the Palais de Chaillot on Ave Albert de Mun (16e; Map 4; metro Trocadéro or Iéna). Tickets cost 28FF (17FF reduced price).

Discos & Clubs

A *discothèque* in Paris is just about any sort of place where music leads to dancing. The truly branché crowd considers showing up before 1 am a serious breach of good taste.

The discothèques favoured by the Parisian 'in' crowd change frequently, and many are officially private. Single men may not be admitted, even if their clothes are subculturally appropriate, simply because they're single men. Women, on the other hand, get in for free on some nights. It's always easier to get into the club of your choice during the week, when things may be hopping even more than they are at the weekend. Remember, Parisians tend to go out in groups and don't mingle as much as Anglo-Saxons do.

Paris is great for music, especially techno and there are some mighty fine DJs based here. Latino and Cuban salsa are also huge. Theme nights at clubs are common; for more details consult the sources mentioned under Listings at the start of this section.

Les Bains (Map 8; ☎ 01 48 87 01 80; metro Étienne Marcel), 7 Rue du Bourg l'Abbé (3e). In a renovated old Turkish bath, this club still manages to produce steam heat on particularly hot nights. Les Bains, once renowned for its surly, selective bouncers on the outside and trendy, star-struck revellers inside, has calmed down a bit under new management, but it's still hard to get in at the weekend. Monday is theme night. Mostly techno with a healthy dash of 70s music, it attracts a mixed straight and gay crowd from 11.30 pm to 6.30 am (entry 100FF).

Le Balajo (Map 5; ☎ 01 47 00 07 87; metro Bastille), 9 Rue de Lappe (11e). A mainstay of the Parisian dance-hall scene since 1936. Wednesday night is mambo night; the DJs spin the LPs and CDs (rock, 1970s disco, funk etc) Thursday to Saturday night from 11.30 pm to 5.30 am; dancing begins in earnest at 2 or 3 am. Admission costs 100FF (80FF on Wednesday) and includes one drink. Women can wear pretty much whatever they want, but men should be a bit dressed up. On Sunday (and sometimes Saturday) afternoon from 3 to 7 pm, DJs play old-fashioned *musette* (accordion music) – waltz, tango, cha-cha – for aficionados of *rétro* tea dancing. Entry is 50FF (60FF with a drink).

La Casbah (Map 5; ☎ 01 43 79 69 04; metro Ledru Rollin), 18-20 Rue de la Forge Royale (11e). You might want to brave the gorillas and the big egos of this club just to check out the décor: over-the-top pastel Moorish from floor to ceiling. The music is retro 80s, house and dance and is regaining popularity lost over the past few years. Entry costs 80FF on Thursday, 120FF on Friday and Saturday, including a drink.

Dancing de la Coupole (Map 4; ☎ 01 43 20 14 20; metro Vavin), 102 Blvd du Montparnasse (14e). Tuesday is salsa night at La Coupole (90FF) from 9.30 pm to 3 am, when a 15 member Latin American band attracts a mixed crowd. On Friday and Saturday from 9.30 pm to 4 am there's a retro disco (95FF) and tea dances (40FF) on Saturday from 3 to 7 pm and Sunday from 3 to 9 pm.

Folies Pigalle (Map 9; ☎ 01 48 78 25 56; metro Pigalle), 11 Place Pigalle (9e). A heaving, mixed place that is great for cruising from the balcony above the dance floor. It's open Thursday to Saturday from 11 pm till dawn. Entry costs 100FF.

Le Gibus (Map 3; ☎ 01 47 00 78 88; metro République), 18 Rue du Faubourg du Temple (11e). A former cathedral of rock, this cave-like place now devotes itself to techno (Wednesday and Thursday), trance (Friday) and house (Tuesday, Saturday and Sunday). There are concerts some nights so be sure to inquire. It's open Tuesday to Sunday from 11.30 pm till dawn. Entry is 20 to 70FF, depending on the night.

La Guinguette Pirate (Map 1; ☎ 01 44 24 89 89 or ☎ 01 53 82 02 04; metro Quai de la Gare), 157 Quai de la Gare (13e). This club on a three masted Chinese junk at the foot of the Bibliothèque Nationale de France is as eclectic as it gets: from reggae and ska to Breton rock. There's usually a concert at 10.30 pm (entry 30FF), and the crowd is young (25 to 30) and energetic. Weekend concerts feature French rock groups. It's open daily from about noon (7.30 pm on Monday) to 2 am.

La Java (Map 3; ☎ 01 42 02 20 52; metro Belleville), 105 Rue du Faubourg du Temple (10e). The original dance hall where Piaf got her first break now reverberates to the sound of salsa at the Cuban Jam Sessions held Thursday and Friday (entry 80FF with a drink) from 11 pm to 5 am.

La Locomotive (Map 9; ☎ 01 53 41 88 88; metro Blanche) in Pigalle at 90 Blvd de Clichy (18e). An enormous ever popular disco that's long been one of the favourite dancing venues for teenage out-of-towners. Music at La Loco ranges from techno in the pulsating basement to groove and disco on the 1st floor loft; rock, psychedelic and the like dominate on the huge ground floor. It is open nightly from 11 pm (midnight on Monday) to 6 am (7 am on weekends). Entrance costs 70/55FF with/without a drink on weekdays, and women get in free before 12.30 am. On Friday and Saturday it costs 60FF without a drink before midnight and 100FF with one after that. Men pay 70FF and women get in free on Sunday. Dress rules are mellow: jogging suits and sandals are out but almost everything else is decidedly in. There's a popular gay tea dance here on Sunday from 5 to 11 pm. Entry costs 40/60FF before/after 6 pm.

Le Queen (Map 2; ☎ 01 53 89 08 90; metro George V), 102 Ave des Champs-Élysées (8e). The king (as it were) of gay discos in Paris now reigns even more supreme with special theme parties open to all (eg Respect on Wednesday), if they can get past the hostile bouncers. Queen is open seven days a week from midnight to 6 or 7 am. There's no cover charge, except on Friday and Saturday nights (100FF, including a drink). Dress as outrageously as you can at the weekend.

Rex Club (Map 7; ☎ 01 42 36 83 98; metro Bonne Nouvelle), 5 Rue Poissonière (2e). This huge, popular club is the undisputed hottest (at the moment) for techno and house. It's got both a music DJ and a video one. It's open Tuesday to Saturday from 11 pm till dawn and entry is 60 to 70FF.

Le Tango (Map 8; ☎ 01 42 72 17 78; metro Arts et Métiers), 13 Rue au Maire (3e). An Afro-Caribbean club on the boil Thursday to Saturday night (60FF) and popular with the *frotti/frotta* (rubbing) set, Le Tango is *not* for the shy.

Theatre

Almost all of Paris' theatre productions, including those written in other languages, are performed in French. There are a few English-speaking troupes around, though – look for ads on metro poster boards and in English-language periodicals (eg *France USA Contacts* – see Newspapers & Magazines in the Facts for the Visitor chapter).

Comédie Française (Map 7; ☎ 01 40 15 00 15; metro Palais Royal), 2 Rue de Richelieu (1er), next to the Palais Royal. The world's oldest national theatre, this was founded in 1680 under Louis XIV. Its repertoire is based on the works of such French theatrical luminaries as Corneille, Molière, Racine, Beaumarchais, Marivaux and Musset, though in recent years contemporary and even non-French works have been staged. The box office (☎ 01 44 52 15 15) is open daily from 11 am to 6 pm. Tickets for regular seats cost from 70 to 185FF and can be purchased up to 14 days ahead. Tickets for places near the ceiling (30FF) go on sale one hour before curtain time, which is when – subject to availability – those under 25 and students under 27 can purchase any of the better seats remaining for only 50FF. The discount tickets are available from the window around the corner from the box office and facing Rue de Montpensier.

Odéon Théâtre de l'Europe (Map 6; ☎ 01 44 41 36 36; Minitel 3615 ODEON; metro Odéon), 1 Place Paul Claudel (6e). This huge, ornate theatre, built in the early 1780s, often puts on foreign plays in their original languages (subtitled in French) and hosts theatre troupes from abroad (30 to 170FF). The box office is open daily from 11 am to 7 pm (to 1 pm on Sunday). Tickets can be purchased over the phone with a credit card. People over 60 get a discount on the pricier tickets, while students and people under 26 who purchase a Carte Complice Jeune can get good reserved seats at low prices. Half-price tickets are available to anyone 50 minutes before curtain time. During the first week of a play's run, some rush tickets are available one hour before curtain time for as little as 15 to 25FF.

Point Virgule (Map 8; ☎ 01 42 78 67 03; metro Hôtel de Ville), 7 Rue Sainte Croix de la Bretonnerie (4e). This is café theatre at its best, with stand-up comics, performance artists, musical acts – you name it. There are three shows daily at 8, 9.15 and 10.15 pm. Entry costs 80/130/150FF for one/two/three shows (students 65FF).

Cabaret

Paris' risqué cancan revues – those dazzling, pseudo-bohemian productions featuring hundreds of performers, including female dancers both with and without elaborate costumes – are about as representative of the Paris of the late 1990s as crocodile-wrestling is of Australia or bronco-busting of the USA.

Moulin Rouge (Map 9; ☎ 01 53 09 82 82; metro Blanche), 82 Blvd de Clichy (18e). This legendary cabaret, whose dancers appeared in Toulouse-Lautrec's famous posters, sits under its trademark red windmill (a 1925 copy of the original). The dinner show (at 7 or 8 pm, depending on the season) costs 750FF, including champagne. Tickets cost 350FF (including two drinks) if you stand at the bar; if you prefer to sit down the price jumps to 450 or 510FF, including half a bottle of champagne. Apart from the dinner show, there are performances nightly at 9 or 10 pm and again at 11 pm or midnight, depending on the season.

Folies Bergères (Map 7; ☎ 01 44 79 98 98; metro Cadet), 32 Rue Richer (9e). This place is celebrated for its high-kicking, feather-clad dancers but lately it's been staging musicals such as *Fame* from Tuesday to Sunday at 9 pm with matinees at 3 pm on weekends (100 to 350FF). When the dancers are on show entry costs 130 to 350FF; dinner and the show at 7.30 pm is 510 to 690FF.

Le Lido (Map 2; ☎ 01 40 76 56 10; metro George V), 116bis Ave des Champs-Élysées (8e). The floor show gets top marks for grandiose sets and lavish costumes. Operating since 1946, the nightly shows at 10 pm and midnight cost 540FF for the show with a half-bottle of champagne, 365FF to watch from the bar with two drinks and 770, 880 or 990FF for the show and dinner.

Opera & Classical Music

The Opéra National de Paris now splits its performances between Opéra Garnier, its old home, and Opéra Bastille, which opened in 1989. Both opera houses also stage ballets and concerts put on by the Opéra National's affiliated orchestra, choirs and ballet company. The opera season lasts from mid-September to mid-July.

Paris plays host to dozens of orchestral, organ and chamber music concerts each week.

Opéra Bastille (Map 5; ☎ 01 44 73 13 99 or ☎ 08 36 69 78 68 for inquiries, ☎ 01 44 73 13 00 for reservations, ☎ 01 43 43 96 96 for a recording in French; Minitel 3615 OPERAPARIS; metro Bastille), 2-6 Place de la Bastille (12e). Telephone lines are staffed from 11 am to 6 pm daily, except Sunday and holidays. It's possible to make reservations by phone from abroad – just make sure you pay for the tickets at least one hour before curtain time. Credit cards are accepted only at the box office, which is open Monday to Saturday from 11 am to 6.30 pm. Ticket sales begin 14 days before the date of the performance. According to Parisian opera buffs, however, the only way absolutely to ensure a reservation is by post some two months in advance: 120 Rue de Lyon, 75576 Paris Cedex 12.

Opera tickets cost 145 to 635FF. To have a shot at the cheapest (ie worst) seats in the house (60FF), you have to stop by the ticket office the day tickets go on sale – exactly 14 days before the performance (on a Monday if the performance is on a Sunday). Ballets cost 70 to 280FF (45FF for the cheapest seats), concerts are 85 to 240FF (45FF).

If there are unsold tickets, people under 25 or over 65 and students can get excellent seats for about 100FF only 15 minutes before the curtain goes up. Ask for the *tarif spécial*.

Opéra Garnier (Map 7; same ☎ and Minitel as Opéra Bastille; metro Opéra), Place de l'Opéra (9e). Ticket prices and conditions (including last-minute discounts) are almost the same as at Opéra Bastille. For certain non-opera performances, the cheapest regular tickets, which get you a seat with an obstructed view, cost as little as 20 or 30FF.

Opéra Comique (Map 7; ☎ 01 42 44 45 46 for reservations; metro Richelieu Drouot), 5 Rue Favart (2e). A century-old hall that plays host to classic and less well known works of opera. The season lasts from late October to early July. Tickets, available from FNAC or Virgin, cost 100 to 610FF; 50FF tickets with limited or no visibility are available up to 12 hours before the performance at the box office (opposite 14 Rue Favart), open Monday to Saturday from 11 am to 7 pm. Subject to availability, students and those under 25 or over 65 can get big discounts 15 minutes before curtain time.

Théâtre de la Ville (Map 6; ☎ 01 42 74 22 77; Minitel 3615 THEAVILLE; metro Châtelet), 2 Place du Châtelet (4e). This municipal hall plays host to theatre, dance and all kinds of music, with tickets from 95 to 190FF. Depending on availability, people under 25 and students can buy up to two tickets at a 30 to 50% discount on the day of the performance. Credit cards are accepted at the ticket office, which is open Monday to Saturday from 9 am to 8 pm (6 pm on Monday) and on Sunday an hour before curtain time. There are no performances in July and August.

Théâtre Musical de Paris (Map 6; ☎ 01 42 33 00 00 for information, ☎ 01 40 28 28 40 for reservations; Minitel 3615 CHATELET; metro Châtelet), 2 Rue Édouard Colonne (1er), on the western side of Place du Châtelet. Also called the Théâtre Municipal du Châtelet or just the Théâtre du Châtelet, this hall hosts operas (200 to 750FF for the better seats, 50 to 80FF for seats with limited visibility), ballets (90 to 200FF), concerts (including by the excellent Orchestre de Paris) and theatre performances. Classical music is performed on Sunday at 11.30 am (80FF; free for under 12s) and on Monday, Wednesday and Friday at 12.45 pm (50FF).

The ticket office is open daily from 11 am to 7 pm (8 pm on performance nights); tickets go on sale 14 days before the performance date. Subject to availability, students and people under 25 or over 65 can get seats for all performances, except the operas, for 50FF starting 15 minutes before curtain time. There are no performances in July and August.

Cité de la Musique (Map 1; ☎ 01 44 84 45 45 or, for reservations, ☎ 01 44 84 44 84; Minitel 3615 CITEMUSIQUE; www.cite-musique.fr; metro Porte de Pantin), in the south-eastern tip of Parc de la Villette at 221 Ave Jean Jaurès (19e). The oval, 1200 seat main auditorium, whose blocks of seats can be reconfigured to suit different types of performances, hosts every imaginable type of music and dance, from western classical to North African and Japanese. Tickets, usually available from FNAC and Virgin, cost 75 to 200FF (60 to 170FF reduced rate) for evening concerts. Concerts in the little auditorium on Friday, Saturday and Sunday cost 80/60FF. Sunday afternoon performances, which usually start at 3 pm, cost 80FF. The ticket office, open Tuesday to Saturday from noon to 6 pm and Sunday from 10 am, is opposite the main auditorium next to the Fontaine aux Lions (Lions Fountain).

Church Venues Some of the performances held in Paris' historic churches are free, such as those at Notre Dame Cathedral (Map 8) each Sunday at 5.30 pm (usually 80/60FF for full/reduced tariff on certain other days of the week at 8.30 pm). From April to October, classical concerts are also held in Sainte Chapelle (Map 6; ☎ 01 53 73 78 51) on Île de la Cité (1er); the cheapest seats are about 110FF (80FF for students under 25).

Other noted concert venues with similar admission fees are Église Saint Eustache (1er; Map 7), Église Royale at the Val-de-Grâce (5e; Map 6), Église Saint Sulpice (6e; Map 6), Église Saint Germain des Prés (6e; Map 6), Église de la Madeleine (8e; Map 2) and Église Saint Pierre de Montmartre (18e; Map 9).

Museum Venues Museums featuring concert series include Musée du Louvre (☎ 01 40 20 53 17; Map 7), which holds a series of midday and evening chamber music concerts from September to June, and Musée d'Orsay (☎ 01 40 49 48 14; Map 4).

Rock

There's rock at numerous bars, cafés and clubs around Paris, plus a host of venues regularly put on acts by international performers. It's often easier to see Anglophone acts in Paris than in their home countries. Typically, tickets cost 120 to 220FF. The most popular stadium venues for international acts include Le Zénith (☎ 01 42 08 60 00), at the Cité de la Musique (19e; Map 1), and the Palais Omnisports de Paris-Bercy (12e; Map 1; ☎ 01 44 68 44 68).

Other venues – though not exclusively for rock – include the following:

L'Ailleurs (Map 5; ☎ 01 44 59 82 82; metro Bastille), 13 Rue Jean Beausire (4e). This tiny concert café showcasing local talent (mostly *chansons françaises*) is open seven nights a week. Concerts begin at 9.30 pm (though you should arrive an hour before) and finish at about 11 pm. Entry costs 30, 50 or 80FF depending where you sit. It's open daily from 6.30 pm to 1.30 am.

Le Bataclan (Map 5; ☎ 01 49 23 96 33; metro Saint Ambroise), 50 Blvd Voltaire (11e). A small concert venue with some big acts, Le Bataclan masquerades some weekends as a techno club. It's open from 11.30 pm to 5 am.

La Cigale (Map 9; ☎ 01 49 25 89 99; metro Pigalle), 102 Blvd de Rochechouart (18e). An enormous old music hall that hosts international rock acts and occasionally jazz. There's seating in the balcony and dancing up front. Admission costs from 80 to 120FF.

Café de la Danse (Map 5; ☎ 01 47 00 57 59; metro Bastille), 5 Passage Louis-Philippe (11e). An auditorium with 300 to 500 seats it's located only a few metres from 23 Rue de Lappe. Almost every evening at 8 or 8.30 pm, it plays host to rock concerts, dance performances, musical theatre and poetry readings. Tickets (50 to 150FF) are available from FNAC.

Élysée Montmartre (Map 9; ☎ 01 44 92 45 45; metro Anvers), 72 Blvd de Rochechouart (18e). This huge old music hall is one of the better venues for one-off rock and indy concerts. The Java brings its salsa here every third Saturday of the month (80FF), and the Scream theme party (100FF; drinks 50FF) held on another Saturday each month attracts big-name DJs and a mixed crowd (from supermodels to drag queens). Women shouldn't have any problems getting in any time; single guys might have to wait till late.

Le Divan du Monde (Map 9; ☎ 01 44 92 77 66; metro Pigalle), 75 Rue des Martyrs (18e). One of the best concert venues in town with good visibility and sound; Latino figures at least once a week. It's also a popular club open most nights till dawn.

Jazz

After WWII, Paris was Europe's most important jazz centre and is again very much à la mode; the city's better *boîtes* (clubs) attract top international stars. The Banlieues Bleues (☎ 01 42 43 56 66), a jazz festival held in Saint Denis and other Paris suburbs from late February to early April, attracts big-name talent.

Le Caveau de la Huchette (Map 6; ☎ 01 43 26 65 05; metro Saint Michel), 5 Rue de la Huchette (5e). A medieval *caveau* (cellar) – used as a courtroom and torture chamber during the Revolution – where virtually all the jazz greats have played since 1946. It's touristy – no doubt about that – but the atmosphere can often be more electric than at the more 'serious' jazz clubs. It is open nightly from 9.30 pm to 2 am (4 am on Saturday, Sunday and the night before public holidays); sessions begin at 10.30 pm.

The cover charge is 60FF (55FF for students) during the week, 70FF (no discounts) on Friday, Saturday and the night before holidays. Fruit juice/beer start at 22/26FF. Details on coming attractions are posted on the door; the bands change every week or so.

Le Baiser Salé (Map 7; ☎ 01 42 33 37 71; metro Châtelet), 58 Rue des Lombards (1er). One of three very hip jazz clubs on the same street (see the following two venues) at which a single membership card (150FF a year) gets you significant discounts. The *salle de jazz* on the 1st floor has concerts of Afro jazz, jazz fusion etc nightly from 10 pm to 3 am. The cover charge is 40 to 80FF; it's free on Sunday (when young musicians play) and during jam sessions on Monday night. The bar on the ground floor is open daily from 7 pm to 6 am.

Le Sunset (Map 7; ☎ 01 40 26 46 60; metro Châtelet), 60 Rue des Lombards (1er). Musicians and actors (cinema and theatre) are among the jazz fans who hang out at this trendy club, whose cellar hosts live concerts of funk, Latino, bebop and the like nightly from 10.30 pm to 4 am; most of the big names play Wednesday to Saturday. Entry costs 80FF, including a drink; subsequent liquid refreshment is 28FF a go. At the ground floor bar and restaurant, you can eat until 3 am (closed Sunday); *menus* are 80 and 120FF.

Au Duc des Lombards (Map 7; ☎ 01 42 33 22 88; metro Châtelet), 42 Rue des Lombards (1er). An ultra-cool venue decorated with posters of past jazz greats that attracts a far more relaxed (and less reverent) crowd than other two venues on the street. The ground floor bar vibrates nightly from 8 pm to 4 or 5 am. The cover charge is 50 to 100FF, depending on what's on; drinks are 28FF (juice, beer) to 55FF (cocktails).

La Villa (Map 6; ☎ 01 43 26 60 00; metro Saint Germain des Prés), 29 Rue Jacob (6e). This very cool, high-tech place attracts big-name performers from the USA, the rest of Europe and Japan, with local talent thrown in for good measure between sets. You'll love the odd shaped furniture – stools shaped like teardrops, 'crouching' chairs etc. It's open Monday to Saturday from 10.30 pm to 2 am and entry costs 150FF, including the first drink.

All Jazz Club (Map 6; ☎ 01 42 61 53 53; metro Saint Germain des Prés), 7-11 Rue Saint Benoît (6e). Formerly called Latitudes, this club features a more varied assortment of musicians in stylish club surroundings. The bar is open daily from 6 pm to 2 am; there are sessions every night, except Sunday, at 10 pm (10.30 pm on Friday and Saturday). The price of the first drink (120FF) usually gains entry; some special concerts cost 130 to 150FF.

New Morning (Map 3; ☎ 01 45 23 51 41 for recorded information, ☎ 01 42 31 31 31 for reservations; metro Château d'Eau), 7-9 Rue des Petites Écuries (10e). An informal auditorium that hosts concerts of jazz as well as rock, funk, salsa, Afro-Cuban and Brazilian music three to seven nights a week at 9 pm. The second set ends at about 1 am. Tickets (110 to 140FF), available from FNAC and Virgin, can usually be purchased at the door. There are concerts from time to time on Sunday at 3 pm (30FF).

French Chansons

For details on accordion music at Le Balajo's weekend tea dances, see Discos & Clubs earlier.

Le Croquenote (Map 7; ☎ 01 42 33 60 70; metro Rue Montmartre), 22 Passage des Panoramas (2e). An intimate French restaurant with dinner (170FF) at 8 pm and chansons – in the styles of Brel, Brassens, Léo Ferré and Félix Leclerc – at around 10 pm. It is closed on Sunday and in August. Call ahead to book a table.

Au Vieux Paris (Map 8; ☎ 01 48 87 55 56; metro Hôtel de Ville), 72 Rue de la Verrerie (4e). A real period-piece Parisian bar (closed Sunday and Monday) that hosts sing-alongs of French chansons, accompanied by an accordionist and

Madame Françoise, the feisty proprietress (sheet music provided). The music begins at about 11.45 pm on Thursday, Friday and Saturday nights and carries on till 4 am. The patrons are mostly young Parisians. Come by at around 11 pm to get a seat.

Le Lapin Agile (Map 9; ☎ 01 46 06 85 87; metro Lamarck Caulaincourt), 22 Rue des Saules (18e). A rustic cabaret venue favoured by turn-of-the-century artists and intellectuals. The name derives from *Le Lapin à Gill*, a mural of a rabbit jumping out of a cooking pot by caricaturist André Gill, which can still be seen on the western exterior wall. In 1911 the writer Roland Dorgelès, known for his hatred of modern art, tied a paintbrush to the tail of a donkey and – with the unwitting help of Guillaume Apollinaire, a Lapin Agile regular and a noted exponent of cubism – managed to get the resulting mess into the Salon des Indépendants art show under the title *Sunset over the Adriatic*.

These days, chansons are performed and poetry read nightly, except Monday, from 9 pm to 2 am. Entry costs 130FF (90FF for students, except on Saturday and holidays), including a drink.

Chez Louisette (Map 1; ☎ 01 40 12 10 14; metro Porte de Clignancourt), in the Marché aux Puces de Saint Ouen. This is one of the highlights of a visit to Paris' largest flea market. Market-goers crowd around little tables to eat lunch and hear an old-time *chanteuse* belt out Piaf numbers accompanied by accordion music. It is open from noon to 6 or 7 pm on Saturday, Sunday and Monday. Main dishes are 65 to 135FF. Chez Louisette is inside the maze of Marché Vernaison not far from 130 Ave Michelet, the boulevard on the other side of the highway from the Porte de Clignancourt metro stop (18e).

Pubs, Bars & Cafés

Les Halles Area The area around Forum des Halles is filled with 'in' places for a drink.

Café Beaubourg (Map 8; ☎ 01 48 87 63 96; metro Châtelet-Les Halles), 100 Rue Saint Martin (1er), just opposite the Centre Pompidou. This minimalist café draws an arty crowd, and there's always free entertainment on the large square at the front. Sunday brunch (110FF) on the terrace is excellent. It's open daily from 8 am to 1 am (2 am on Friday and Saturday).

Café Oz (Map 7; ☎ 01 40 39 00 18; metro Châtelet), 18 Rue Saint Denis (1er). An Aussie pub bubbling with the same Down Under (well, let's just call it) enthusiasm as the original across the river on Rue Saint Jacques in the 5e. See the Latin Quarter section for details.

Marais The 4e has quite a few lively places for daytime and after-hours drinks.

Le Petit Fer à Cheval (Map 8; ☎ 01 42 72 47 47; metro Hôtel de Ville or Saint Paul), 30 Rue Vieille du Temple (4e). A slightly offbeat bar-restaurant named after its horseshoe-shaped counter; often filled to overflowing with friendly, mostly straight young regulars. The plat du jour changes each day. The all stainless-steel bathroom is straight out of a Flash Gordon film. This place is open daily from 9 am (11 am on weekends) to 2 am. Food (plat du jour 60FF, sandwiches around 20FF) is available nonstop from noon to about 1.15 am.

La Chaise au Plafond (Map 8; ☎ 01 42 76 03 22; metro Hôtel de Ville), 10 Rue du Trésor (4e). Owned by the same people as Le Petit Fer à Cheval, and with a similar cybertoilet, it's a warm place with tables outside on a pedestrian-only backstreet. It's open daily from 9.30 am to 2 am.

Le Pick Clops (Map 8; ☎ 01 40 29 02 18; metro Hôtel de Ville), 16 Rue Vieille du Temple (4e), at the corner of Rue de Roi du Sicile. This is a straight rock bar in a very gay neighbourhood serving cheap drinks and is a great place to watch the world go by. The brief happy hour is from 8 to 9 pm.

Stolly's (Map 8; ☎ 01 42 76 06 76; metro Hôtel de Ville), 16 Rue de la Cloche Percée (4e). Just off Rue de Rivoli, this Anglophone bar is always overcrowded, particularly during the 5 to 8 pm happy hour. It's open daily. There are chairs on the pavement and a demi/pint of Guinness is 20/35FF. A 1.6L pitcher of cheap *blonde* (house lager) is 50FF.

Mixeri Bar (Map 8; ☎ 01 48 87 55 44; metro Hôtel de Ville), 23 Rue Sainte Croix de la Bretonnerie (4e). The name says it all – straight and gay with eclectic music. It's open daily from 4 pm to 2 am.

Amnésia Café (Map 8; ☎ 01 42 72 16 94; metro Hôtel de Ville), 42 Rue Vieille du Temple (4e). A cosy, warmly lit and very popular place, most of whose clients – but not all – are gay. Beers start at 15FF (19FF after 10 pm), cocktails at

45FF. Breakfast is 70FF, *menus* at brunch (daily from noon to 4 pm) are 90 and 130FF, and the plat du jour is 60FF. It is open daily from 11 am to 2 am.

Île de la Cité The island (1er) is not exactly hopping after dark but there is a good wine bar here.

Taverne Henri IV (Map 6 ; ☎ 01 43 54 27 90; metro Pont Neuf), 13 Place du Pont Neuf (1er). A decent restaurant as well as a serious wine bar, this place attracts lots of people in the legal profession from the nearby Palais de Justice. It's open weekdays from noon to 9 pm, on Saturday to 4 pm.

Latin Quarter The Latin Quarter (5e) has Paris' highest concentration of bars catering to Anglophones.

Café Oz (Map 6; ☎ 01 43 54 30 48; metro Luxembourg), 184 Rue Saint Jacques (5e). A casual, friendly Australian pub with Foster's on tap for 22FF (35FF for a 'schooner' or 400mL), and VB, Coopers, Cascade and Redback as other amber options, plus Australian wines from 22FF a glass. A lunch of pie with salad is 45FF. It is open daily from 4 pm to 2 am (happy hour from opening to 9.30 pm), and the staff are clued in about jobs, apartments etc.

Le Cloître (Map 6; ☎ 01 43 25 19 92; metro Saint Michel), 19 Rue Saint Jacques (5e). An unpretentious, relaxed place where the mellow background music goes down well with the students who congregate here. There's Guinness and other beer on tap, and you can play chess in the back (except after 10 pm on weekends and holidays, when it gets too crowded). It is open daily from 3 pm to 2 am.

Polly Maggoo (Map 6; ☎ 01 46 33 33 64; metro Saint Michel), 11 Rue Saint Jacques (5e). An informal, friendly bar founded in 1967 and still spinning disks from the 60s. The regulars include English-speakers resident in Paris. Chess and backgammon can be played from noon to 8 pm and beer starts at 13FF (18FF after 10 pm). It is open daily from 1 pm to 3 or 4 am.

6e Arrondissement The 6e has some of Paris' most famous cafés and quite a few decent newcomers.

Les Deux Magots (Map 6; ☎ 01 45 48 55 25; metro Saint Germain des Prés), 170 Blvd Saint Germain (6e). There's been a café here since 1881 but the present one – whose name derives from the two *magots* (grotesque figurines) of Chinese dignitaries at the entrance – dates from 1914. It is perhaps best known as the haunt of Sartre, Hemingway and André Breton. On the huge terrace (enclosed in winter), you can sip coffee (22FF), beer on tap (28FF) and its famous home-made hot chocolate (30FF), served in steaming porcelain pitchers by waiters clad in long white aprons. A continental breakfast costs 80FF. Light meals (34 to 48FF) are available. It is open daily from 7.30 am to 1.30 am.

Café de Flore (Map 6; ☎ 01 45 48 55 26; metro Saint Germain des Prés), 172 Blvd Saint Germain (6e). An Art Deco-style café less touristy than the Deux Magots where the red banquettes, mirrors and marble walls haven't changed since the days Sartre, de Beauvoir, Albert Camus and Picasso imbibed the house Pouilly Fumé. The outdoor terrace (glassed-in in winter) is a sought-after place to sip beer (41FF for 400mL), wine (32FF) or coffee (23FF). It is open daily from 7 am to 1.30 am.

La Palette (Map 6; ☎ 01 43 26 68 15; metro Mabillon), 43 Rue de Seine (6e). This turn-of-the-century café, stomping ground of Cézanne and Braque, attracts dealers and shoppers from the local art galleries; it's open Monday to Saturday till 2 am.

Café de la Mairie (Map 6; ☎ 01 43 26 67 82; metro Saint Sulpice), 8 Place Saint Sulpice (6e). A bustling and slightly tacky café on two floors frequented by students, writers and, since the late 1980s, film producers attracted by its tattered Left Bank ambience and tired of the Flore. A beer costs 11FF at the counter, 20FF if you sit down. It is open Monday to Saturday from 7 am to 11 pm or midnight (2 am in the warm months).

Cubana Café (Map 4; ☎ 01 40 46 80 81; metro Vavin), 45 Rue Vavin (6e). The perfect place for a couple of 'starter' drinks before carrying on to the nearby Coupole for a night of salsa and mambo. For those who indulge in cigars, there's a *fumoir* equipped with a bunch of comfy sofas and live Cuban music on Wednesday evenings and on Sunday at 2 pm.

Coolin (Map 6; ☎ 01 44 07 00 92; metro Mabillon), 15 Rue Clément (6e). The only Irish bar we intend including in this section, the Coolin stands out for its location (it's in a renovated covered market) and its odd fusion of Dublin pub and Parisian café. It's open daily from 10 am (noon on Sunday) to 2 am.

Champs-Élysées Area Once considered hopelessly tacky, the Ave des Champs-Élysées (8e) and surrounds have a new lease of life since their costly renovation.

Montecristo Café (Map 2; ☎ 01 45 62 30 86; metro Franklin D Roosevelt), 68 Ave des Champs-Élysées (8e). This bar-restaurant, which bills itself as 'Havana in Paris', brings Latino mainstream and the tourists love it. The music is decent, there's a great bar and the place never closes – it is open 24 hours a day, seven days a week. The first drink costs 100FF on Friday and Saturday. Happy hour is from 3 to 8 pm, and Sunday brunch (90 to 110FF) from 11 am to 5 pm.

Buddha Bar (Map 2; ☎ 01 53 05 90 00; metro Concorde), 8 Rue Boissy d'Anglas (8e). At centre stage in the cavernous cellar of this restaurant-bar frequented by suits, supermodels and hangers-on is an enormous bronze Buddha. Everyone should go at least once for a look, but stick with the drinks (cocktails from 60FF); a Pacific Rim-style meal will cost you upwards of 300FF. The bar is open daily from 6 pm to 2 am.

Grands Boulevards The Grands Boulevards (2e and 9e) are some of the Right Bank's major areas for a night on the town.

Harry's New York Bar (Map 7; ☎ 01 42 61 71 14; metro Opéra), 5 Rue Daunou (2e). Back in the prewar years, when there were several dozen American-style bars in Paris, Harry's was one of the most popular – habitués included F Scott Fitzgerald and Hemingway. The Cuban mahogany interior dates from the mid-19th century and was brought over lock, stock and barrel from Manhattan's Third Ave in 1911. Beer costs 28FF (35FF after 10 pm). Drinks at the basement piano bar – there's live music (usually soft jazz) nightly from 10 pm to 2 or 3 am – cost 40 to 70FF. It is open every day of the year except 24 and 25 December from 10.30 am to 4 am. The copyrighted advertisement for Harry's in the *International Herald Tribune* still reads: 'Tell the Taxi Driver Sank Roo Doe Noo'.

Bastille Area The area just north and east of Place de la Bastille (11e) is enormously popular for dining, drinking and dancing all night long. Rue de Lappe, a dreary narrow lane in the daytime, comes alive at night. The area to the south-east of the square (12e) has a number of excellent after-dark venues.

Iguana Café (Map 5; ☎ 01 40 21 39 99; metro Bastille), 15 Rue de la Roquette (11e). A chic, two level café-pub that attracts exceptionally trendy people in their 20s and early 30s. Cocktails are 42 to 55FF (46 to 59FF after 10 pm); beer on tap is 20 to 28FF (or 24 to 32FF). It is open daily from 9 am to 5 am.

Boca Chica (Map 5; ☎ 01 43 57 93 13; metro Ledru Rollin), 58 Rue de Charonne (11e). An enormous, almost industrial, place close to the bar-restaurant Suds, with three large bars on two floors and a friendly, lively, young crowd. Happy hour is from 4 to 8 pm daily when a 500mL beer is 20FF and all cocktails are half-price. It's open daily till 2 am.

China Club (Map 5; ☎ 01 43 43 82 02; metro Ledru Rollin), 50 Rue de Charenton (12e). If you've got the rich uncle (he's the 'American uncle' in French, surprise, surprise) or aunt in tow, have them take you to this stylish establishment just behind the Opéra Bastille. It's got a huge bar with high ceilings on the ground floor, a fumoir (in case he's into Havanas) open from 7 pm to 2 am (3 am on Friday and Saturday) on the 1st floor, and a jazz club in the cellar open till 3 am – all done up to look like Shanghai circa 1930. Happy hour is from 7 to 9 pm daily when all drinks are 35FF.

Le Viaduc Café (Map 5; ☎ 01 44 74 70 70; metro Gare de Lyon), 43 Ave Daumesnil (12e). The terrace of this very trendy café in one of the glassed-in arches of the Viaduc des Arts is an excellent spot to while away the hours, and the jazz brunch on Sunday is very popular. It's open seven days a week until 4 am.

Oberkampf & Ménilmontant Areas East of Place de la République, Rue Oberkampf (11e) and its extension, Rue de Ménilmontant (20e) are the up-and-coming branché areas of Paris with a number of interesting cafés and bars, like the popular *Le Charbon* (see the Places to Eat section).

Le Cithéa (Map 3; ☎ 01 40 21 70 95; metro Parmentier), 114 Rue Oberkampf (11e). This place has bands playing acid and jungle jazz, Latin, drum and bass, and funk. Wine and beer cost 25FF, cocktails are from 60FF. It is open daily from 8 pm till dawn and it's where most people from the Charbon end up in the wee hours.

Café Cannibale (Map 3; ☎ 01 49 29 95 59; metro Couronnes), 93 Rue Jean-Pierre Timbaud (11e). So laid-back it's almost asleep, this cosy café and bar is a place where you can either linger over a coffee (10FF) or grab a quick beer at the bar (12FF) or *à table* (20FF). The lunch formule is 60FF and brunch *menus*, served from noon to 4 pm, are 75 and 85FF. It's open daily from 8 am to 2 am.

Montparnasse Area The most popular places to while away the hours over a drink or coffee in this area (14e and 6e) are the large café-restaurants like ***La Coupole*** and ***Le Select*** on Blvd du Montparnasse (see the Places to Eat section for details on these places).

La Closerie des Lilas (Map 6; ☎ 01 40 51 34 50; metro Port Royal), 171 Blvd du Montparnasse (6e). Anybody who has read Hemingway knows he did a lot of writing, drinking and eating of oysters here; little brass tags on the tables tell you exactly where he (and other luminaries such as Picasso and Apollinaire) whiled away the hours making art or just gossiping. It's open daily from 11.30 am to 2 am.

Montmartre & Pigalle Areas In between the sleaze there are some interesting bars at the bottom of the Montmartre hill (9e and 18e).

Le Salsa Loco (Map 3; ☎ 01 40 82 91 56; metro Pigalle), 70 Rue Condorcet (9e). Yet another place with a Cuban theme and salsa music, this is where to come in Pigalle when everything else is shutting down. *Mojitos*, rum-based Cuban cocktails, are reasonable at 30FF. It's open daily from 7 pm to 3 am (until 5 am on Saturday).

Le Moloko (Map 9; ☎ 01 48 74 50 26; metro Blanche), 26 Rue Fontaine (9e). An incredibly 'in' *bar de nuit* whose décor is an eclectic mix of the classic (red velvet) and the provocative. There's jukebox dancing (soul, hip-hop) on the ground floor. Entry is free most nights, but not on Saturday, when there are live shows (concerts, striptease etc). It is open daily from 10 pm to 5.30 or 6 am, but things don't pick up until after midnight.

Chao Pa Café (Map 2; ☎ 01 46 06 72 90), 22 Blvd de Clichy (18e). This café-restaurant, transformed from an old-style brasserie into something straight out of Saigon, is open Sunday to Wednesday to 2 am and the rest of the week to 5 am.

Gay Paris

The Marais (4e) – especially those areas around the intersection of Rue Sainte Croix de la Bretonnerie, Rue des Archives and westward to Rue Vieille du Temple – has been Paris' main centre of gay social life since the early 1980s. There are also some decent bars west of Blvd de Sébastopol in the 1er and 2e.

Quetzal Bar (Map 8; ☎ 01 48 87 99 07; metro Hôtel de Ville), 10 Rue de la Verrerie (4e), at the corner of Rue des Mauvais Garçons (literally, 'Street of the Bad Boys'). A neon-lit, modern bar popular with 30-something gay men. A demi on tap is 18FF. It is open daily from 5 to 3 am (4 am on Friday and Saturday). Happy hour is from 5 to 8 pm and 11 pm to midnight.

Open Café (Map 8; ☎ 01 42 72 26 18; metro Hôtel de Ville), 17 Rue des Archives (4e). This is where most people head after work or where they start the evening. It's so packed at those times that the clientele often spills out onto the pavement. It's open from 10 am to 2 am; happy hour is from 6 to 8 pm.

Coffee Shop (Map 8; ☎ 01 42 74 46 29; metro Hôtel de Ville), 3 Rue Sainte Croix de la Bretonnerie (4e). A small, almost exclusively gay café that's open daily from noon to 2 am. Bottled beer, officially served only with the two-course meals (60FF; available all day), costs 17FF. Coffee is 16FF.

Banana Café (Map 7; ☎ 01 42 33 35 31; metro Châtelet-Les Halles), 13 Rue de la Ferronerie (1er). This ever popular cruise bar on two levels has a nice enclosed terrace with stand-up tables and attracts a young crowd. Happy hour (drinks half-price) is between 4.30 and 7.30 pm. It's open daily from 4.15 pm to 6 am.

La Champmeslé (Map 7; ☎ 01 42 96 85 20; metro Pyramides), 4 Rue Chabanais (2e). A relaxed, dimly lit place that plays mellow music for its patrons, about 75% of whom are lesbians (the rest are mostly gay men). The back room is reserved for women only. Works by a different woman artist are displayed each month. Beer or fruit juice cost about 30FF. It is open Monday to Saturday from 5 pm to 2 am, and traditional French chansons are performed live every Thursday from 10 pm.

SPECTATOR SPORTS

For details on upcoming sporting events, consult the sports daily *L'Équipe* (4.90FF) or *Figaroscope*, published by *Le Figaro*, each Wednesday.

Football & Rugby

The Paris-Saint Germain (PSG) football club, one of the best teams in the French first division, often plays at the 50,000 seat Parc des Princes (16e; Map 1; metro Porte de Saint Cloud). Tickets to see PSG in action (usually on Saturday night) are available through FNAC and the Virgin Megastore on Ave des Champs-Élysées (see Booking Agencies in the Entertainment section), as well as at the Parc des Princes box office (☎ 01 49 87 29 29 or ☎ 01 42 88 02 76 for a recording; metro Porte de Saint Cloud) at 24 Rue du Commandant Guilbaud (16e), open weekdays from 9 am to 8 pm and Saturday from 10 am to 5 pm. The Coupe de France finals take place at the Stade de France (SDF) in early May, the Tournoi de Paris in late July.

The Parc des Princes sometimes hosts rugby matches, a sport particularly popular in south-western France, and local rugby champion Le Racing Club de France (☎ 01 45 67 55 86) also play at the SDF. The highlights of the rugby season are the championship finals in early June and the Tournoi des Cinq Nations (Five Nations Tournament), involving France, England, Scotland, Wales and Ireland in March/April.

Tennis

Les Internationaux de France de Tennis (French Open), the second of the four Grand Slam tournaments, is held in late May/early June on red clay at Stade Roland Garros (Map 1; ☎ 01 47 43 48 00; metro Porte d'Auteuil), 2 Ave Gordon Bennett (16e). The capacity of the stadium's main section, Le Central, is about 16,500. Tickets are expensive and hard to come by; bookings must usually be made by March at the latest.

The top indoor tournament is the Open de Tennis de la Ville de Paris (Paris Tennis Open), which usually takes place sometime in late October or early November at the Palais Omnisports de Paris-Bercy (Map 1; ☎ 01 43 46 12 21; metro Bercy), 8-12 Blvd de Bercy (12e).

Cycling

The final stage of the world's most prestigious cycling event, the Tour de France, has, since the 1975, ends with a dash up Ave des Champs-Élysées on the third or fourth Sunday in July some time between noon and 6 pm.

The second biggest 'Parisian' event on the cycling calendar does not even begin in Paris any more. Held on the first Sunday after Easter, the gruelling, one day Paris-Roubaix road race actually begins in Compiègne (see the Day Trips from Paris chapter), 82km north-east of Paris, and continues for 267km over 27 different sections (totalling 50km) of *pavé* (cobblestone) before reaching the *vélodrome* at Roubaix, north-east of Lille.

The biggest indoor cycling event is the Grand Prix des Nations, held in October and pitting the best cyclists from the world's eight best nations against one another on a 250m vélodrome at the Palais Omnisports de Paris-Bercy (Map 1).

Horse Racing

One of the cheapest ways to spend a relaxing afternoon in the company of Parisians of all ages, backgrounds and walks of life is to go to the races. The most accessible of Paris' six racecourses is Hippodrome d'Auteuil (Map 1; ☎ 01 45 27 12 25 or ☎ 01 49 10 20 30; metro Porte d'Auteuil) in the south-east corner of the Bois de Boulogne (16e), which hosts steeplechases from February to early July and from September to early December.

Races are held on Sunday as well as some other days of the week, with half a dozen or so heats scheduled between 2 and 5.30 pm. There's no charge to stand on the *pelouse* (lawn) in the middle of the track; a seat in the *tribune* (stands) costs 25FF (40FF on Sunday and holidays, 50FF during special events). Race schedules are published in almost all national newspapers. If you can read a bit of French, pick up a copy of *Paris Turf* (Minitel 3615 TURF for results), the horse-racing daily available at newsstands for 7FF.

To buy yourself a stake in the proceedings, you can place a bet – the minimum is only 10FF. Information on the horses and their owners, trainers and jockeys is available from the free programs; additional statistics are printed in *Paris Turf*. The odds are displayed on TV screens near the betting windows. You can bet that your horse will come in *gagnant* (1st place), *placé* (1st or 2nd place) or *placé jumelé* (1st, 2nd or 3rd place). If your horse wins, take your ticket to any betting window to collect your windfall.

Show jumping is all the rage in Paris and the Jumping International de Paris held in March at the Palais Omnisports de Paris-Bercy attracts thousands of fans.

SHOPPING

Paris has shopping options to suit all tastes and budgets. Garments, for instance, can be selected at the ultra-chic couture houses along Ave Montaigne or plucked from flea-market tables.

Department Stores

The 'big three' department stores of Paris are Printemps, La Samaritaine and Galeries Lafayette.

Printemps (Map 2; ☎ 01 42 82 57 87 or ☎ 01 42 82 50 00; metro Havre Caumartin), 64 Blvd Haussmann (9e). Printemps has one of the world's largest perfume and cosmetics departments, and is open Monday to Saturday from 9.35 am to 7 pm (to 10 pm on Thursday).

Galeries Lafayette (Map 7; ☎ 01 42 82 36 40; metro Auber or Chaussée d'Antin), 40 Blvd Haussmann (9e). This huge store, in two adjacent buildings linked by a pedestrian bridge, features over 75,000 brand-name items, and has a wide selection of fashion accessories. It is open Monday to Saturday from 9.30 am to 6.45 pm (9 pm on Thursday). There's a fine view from the rooftop restaurant.

La Samaritaine (Map 7; ☎ 01 40 41 20 20; metro Pont Neuf) is in four buildings between Pont Neuf and 142 Rue de Rivoli (1er). An excellent colour-coded brochure in English is available. The arrowhead-shaped building No 1 is devoted solely to toys, stuffed animals and games; building No 4 has a big supermarket in the basement. The main store is in building No 2. It is open Monday to Saturday from 9.30 am to 7 pm (10 pm on Thursday). You can take in the outstanding rooftop view from building No 2 for free.

Le Bon Marché (Map 4; ☎ 01 44 39 80 00; metro Sèvres Babylone), 24 Rue de Sèvres (7e). Paris' first department store, in two adjacent buildings, is less fancy (and expensive) than its upmarket rivals across the river. It's open Monday to Saturday from 9.30 am to 7 pm; the famed grocery department is now a separate store called La Grande Épicerie de Paris at No 26 of the same street. It is open from 8.30 am to 9 pm.

BHV (Bazar de l'Hôtel de Ville; Map 8; ☎ 01 42 74 90 00; metro Hôtel de Ville), 52-64 Rue de Rivoli (4e). BHV is a straightforward department store, apart from its enormous but chaotic hardware/DIY department in the basement with every type of hammer, power tool, nail, plug or hinge you could ask for (which is what you'll have to do since you'll never find it on your own). BHV is open Monday to Saturday from 9.30 am to 7 pm (to 10 pm on Wednesday).

Clothing & Fashion Accessories

New collections are released twice a year – for spring/summer and autumn/winter. There are citywide end-of-season sales from the end of June until some time in August and from late December through January/February.

Triangle d'Or Some of the fanciest clothes in Paris are sold by the *haute couture* houses of the Triangle d'Or (1er and 8e), an ultra-exclusive neighbourhood whose corners are at Place de la Concorde, the Arc de Triomphe and Place de l'Alma (Map 2). Along the even-numbered side of Ave Montaigne (1er; metro Franklin D Roosevelt or Alma Marceau) you'll find Prada at No 10, Inès de la Fressange at No 14, Celine at No 38 and Chanel at No 42. On the odd side you'll pass Valentino at No 17, Nina Ricci at No 39 and Thierry Mugler at No 49. Givenchy (metro Alma Marceau) is nearby at 3 Ave George V (8e); Hermès is at No 42 of the same street.

Rue du Faubourg Saint Honoré & Rue Saint Honoré There is another grouping of couture houses and exclusive clothing and accessories stores just north of Place de la Concorde along Rue du Faubourg Saint Honoré (8e; Map 2; metro Madeleine or Concorde), and its eastern continuation, Rue Saint Honoré (metro Tuileries). Guy Laroche is at 28 Rue du Faubourg Saint Honoré, and Christian Lacroix at No 73.

Place des Victoires Trendy designer boutiques at Place des Victoires (1er and 2e; Map 7; metro Bourse or Sentier) include Kenzo at No 3, Cacharel at No 5, Stephane Kélian at No 6 and Thierry Mugler at No 8. Rue Étienne Marcel, which runs east from Place des Victoires, is the home of Comme des Garçons at No 40 (for men) and No 42 (for women), Yohji Yamamoto at Nos 45 and 47, Chevignon Trading Post at No 49 and Junko Shimada at No 54. The post-modern designs of Jean-Paul Gaultier are on sale a few blocks west of Place des Victoires at 6 Rue Vivienne (2e; metro Bourse). Towards Forum des Halles on Rue du Jour (1er), near Église Saint Eustache, the modern, casual styles of Agnès B (Map 7; metro Les Halles) are available at No 3 (for men) and No 6 (for women).

Marais Rue des Rosiers (4e; Map 8; metro Saint Paul) is attracting a growing number of fashionable clothing shops. Tehen is at No 5bis, L'Éclaireur at No 3, while Lolita Lempicka is not far away at No 2. Under the exclusive arcades of Place des Vosges (4e), Issey Miyake is tucked away at No 3-5. There are other interesting shops along Rue des Francs Bourgeois (3e and 4e), leading out of Place des Vosges. For more everyday clothing, there are lots of shops along Rue de Rivoli, which gets less expensive as you move east from the 1er into the 4e.

6e Arrondissement The largest grouping of chic clothing boutiques in the fashionable 6e – many of them run by younger and more daring designers – is north-west of Place Saint Sulpice (Map 6; metro Saint Sulpice or Saint Germain des Prés). Ultra-chic clothing, footwear and leather goods shops along Rue du Cherche Midi include Il Bisonte at No 17. Along Blvd Saint Germain, Sonia Rykiel has shops at No 175 (for women) and No 194 (for men). Rue de Rennes has Celine at No 58, Kenzo at No 60, and Benneton shops, including one for kids, at Nos 61 and 63. At Place Saint Sulpice, you can pop into Yves Saint Laurent Rive Gauche at No 12 and its Boutique Femme at No 6.

A bit to the south-west, just south of Le Bon Marché, Rue Saint Placide (Map 4; metro Sèvres Babylone) has lots of attractive shops selling clothes and shoes, mainly (but not exclusively) for women.

Reasonably priced clothing and shoe shops are legion along the southern half of Rue de Rennes (Map 4; metro Rennes or Saint Placide).

Rue d'Alésia The part of Rue d'Alésia (14e; Map 1; metro Alésia) between No 54 (just east of Place Victor and Hélène Baschand) and No 149 is lined with places that sell relatively inexpensive brand-name clothes and accessories, including discounted designer seconds with their labels removed (*dégriffés*). Most of the shops are cramped and chaotic, with poorly displayed merchandise and disinterested staff – this is especially true west of Nos 110 and 125. More shops can be found on Ave du Général Leclerc, both north and south of Place Victor and Hélène Baschand.

Jewellery

Around Place Vendôme (1er; Map 2; metro Tuileries), Cartier has shops at Nos 7 and 23, Philippe Patek is at No 10 and Van Cleef & Arpels is at No 22. There are more expensive jewellery shops along nearby Rue de Castiglione (1er) and Rue de la Paix (2e).

Less expensive jewellery is sold at various places around the city. Funky items, many of them imported, can be found in the Marais, including along Rue des Francs Bourgeois (Map 8; 3e and 4e). Costume jewellery is available at the flea markets.

Galerie d'Amon (Map 6; ☎ 01 43 26 96 60; metro Saint Sulpice), 28 Place Saint Sulpice (6e), specialises in modern glass and jewellery. It's open Monday to Saturday from 11 am to 6.45 pm. Sic Amor (Map 8; ☎ 01 42 76 02 37; metro Pont Marie), 20 Rue du Pont Louis-Philippe (4e), sells contemporary jewellery by local designers. Méllerio Dits Meller (Map 2; ☎ 01 42 61 57 53; metro Opéra), 9 Rue de la Paix (2e), has jewellery ranging from the sublime (rings copied from medieval styles) to the ridiculous (traditional swords carried by the Immortals of the Académie Française).

Antiques

For details on Le Louvre des Antiquaires (Map 7), see the Louvre Area in the Things to See & Do section.

In the 6e there are a number of shops selling antique maps and antiquarian books around Rue Bonaparte and Rue Jacob (both Map 6; metro Saint Germain des Prés).

Food & Wine

The food and wine shops of Paris are legendary and well worth seeking out.

Fauchon (Map 2; ☎ 01 47 62 60 11; metro Madeleine), 26-30 Place de la Madeleine (8e). Six departments sell the most incredibly mouthwatering (and expensive) delicacies, such as foie gras for 1000 to 2000FF per kilogram. Fruit – the most perfect you've ever seen – includes exotic items from South-East Asia (mangosteens, rambutans etc). Fauchon is open daily, except on Sunday and holidays, and also has several eat-in options. To place an order from abroad, contact Fauchon's *service export* (☎ 01 47 62 60 11; fax 01 47 42 83 75).

Hédiard (Map 2; metro Madeleine), 21 Place de la Madeleine (8e). This famous luxury food shop consists of two adjacent sections selling prepared dishes, tea, coffee, jams, wine, pastries, fruit and vegetables etc. It is open from 9.30 am to 9 pm (closed on Sunday and certain holidays.

La Maison du Miel (Map 2; ☎ 01 47 42 26 70; metro Madeleine), 24 Rue Vignon (9e), a block north of Fauchon. This store stocks over 40 kinds of honey (17.50 to 42FF for 500g). It is open Monday to Saturday from 9 am to 7 pm.

Mariage Frères (Map 8; ☎ 01 42 72 28 11; metro Hôtel de Ville) at 30-32 Rue du Bourg Tibourg (4e). Paris' premier tea shop, with 450 to 500 varieties from 32 countries; the most expensive is a variety of Japanese *thé vert* (green tea) that costs about 50FF for 100g. It is open daily from 10.30 am to 7.30 pm. The 19th century salon de thé, where in summer you can cool off with tea-flavoured ice cream, is open from noon to 7 pm. A tea lunch here is 140FF. Mariage Frères (founded in 1854) has another shop (Map 6; ☎ 01 40 51 82 50; metro Odéon) at 13 Rue des Grands Augustins (6e). It keeps the same hours.

Jadis et Gourmande (Map 1; ☎ 01 43 26 17 75; metro Port Royal) at 88 Blvd de Port Royal (5e). One of four branches selling chocolate, chocolate and more chocolate in every conceivable shape and size.

À l'Olivier (Map 8; ☎ 01 48 04 86 59; metro Saint Paul), 23 Rue de Rivoli (4e). The place in Paris for oil – from olive to walnut – with a good selection of vineyards and olives too.

Gift & Souvenir Ideas

Paris has a huge number of speciality shops offering gift items.

E Dehillerin (Map 7; ☎ 01 42 36 53 13; metro Les Halles), 18-20 Rue Coquillère (1er). This shop (founded in 1820) carries the most incredible selection of professional-quality cookware – you're sure to find something even the most well equipped kitchen is lacking. It is open Monday to Saturday from 8 am to 6 pm (closed on Monday from 12.30 to 2 pm).

La Vaisellerie (Map 2; ☎ 01 42 60 64 50; metro Tuileries), 332 Rue Saint Honoré (1er). This shop between the Louvre and Place Vendôme specialises in innovative tableware – from decorative butter knives to silver-plated napkin rings.

Mélodies Graphiques (Map 8; ☎ 01 42 74 57 68; metro Pont Marie), 10 Rue du Pont Louis-Philippe (4e). This shop carries all sorts of items made from exquisite Florentine *papier à cuve* (paper hand-decorated with marbled designs). It is open from 11 am (2 pm on Sunday and Monday) to 7 pm. There are several other fine stationery shops along the same street.

Il Pour l'Homme (Map 7; ☎ 01 42 60 43 56; metro Tuileries), 209 Rue Saint Honoré (1er). Housed in an old paint shop with Victorian-era display counters and chests of drawers, 'It for the Man' has everything a man could want or not need – from tie clips and cigar cutters to DIY tools and designer tweezers.

EOL' Modelisme (Map 6; ☎ 01 43 54 01 43; metro Maubert Mutualité), 55 Blvd St Germain (5e) and also at Nos 62 and 70 of the same street. This shop sells expensive toys for big boys and girls, including every sort of model imaginable – from radio-controlled aircraft to huge wooden yachts. The main shop, right by the metro entrance, has an amazing collection of tiny cars and is open weekdays from 8 am to 8 pm.

Album (Map 6; ☎ 01 43 25 85 19; metro Maubert Mutualité), 8 Rue Dante (5e). This shop specialises in *bandes dessinées* (comic books), which have an enormous following in France. Album has everything from *Tintin* to erotic comics and French editions of the latest Japanese *manga*.

Odimex Paris (Map 6; ☎ 01 46 33 98 96; metro Odéon), 17 Rue de l'Odéon (6e). This shop sells teapots: little ones, big ones, sophisticated ones, comic ones and very expensive ones.

Génération Condom (Map 5; ☎ 01 43 54 43 42; metro Cardinal Lemoine), 6 Rue Thouin (5e). Every sort of condom (little ones, big ones, sophisticated ones, comic ones etc) and condom-related item you could ask for. It's open Monday to Saturday from 11 am to 7 pm.

Galerie Alain Carion (Map 8; ☎ 01 43 26 01 16; metro Pont Marie), 92 Rue Saint Louis en l'Île (4e). This shop has a beautiful collection of museum-quality minerals, crystals and fossils from 40 different countries as well as meteorites, some of them in the form of earrings, brooches and pendants. Prices range from 5 to 80,000FF (for a 60kg meteorite). It is open Tuesday to Saturday from 10.30 am to 1 pm and 2 to 7.30 pm.

Flea Markets

Paris' *marchés aux puces* (flea markets), easily accessible by metro, can be great fun if you're in the mood to browse for unexpected treasures among the *brocante* (second-hand goods) and bric-a-brac on display. Some new goods are also available, and a bit of bargaining is expected.

Marché aux Puces de Saint Ouen (Map 1; metro Porte de Clignancourt). This vast flea market, founded in the late 19th century and said to be Europe's largest, is at the northern edge of the 18e. The stalls – of which there are over 2000 – are grouped into nine *marchés* (market areas), each with its own speciality (antiques, cheap clothing etc). It is open Saturday, Sunday and Monday from 7.30 am to 7 pm (later during summer).

If you arrive by metro, walk north along Ave de la Porte de Clignancourt and cross under Blvd Périphérique to the inner suburb of Saint Ouen. The market is centred around Rue des Rosiers and nearby Ave Michelet, Rue Voltaire, Rue Paul Bert and Rue Jean-Henri Fabre. While shopping, watch out for pickpockets.

Marché aux Puces de Montreuil (Map 1; metro Porte de Montreuil). Established in the 19th century, this market is in the south-eastern corner of the 20e on Ave de la Porte de Montreuil, between the metro stop and the ring road. It is known for having good-quality, second-hand clothes and designer seconds. The 500 stalls also sell engravings, jewellery, linen, crockery, old furniture and appliances. It is open on Saturday, Sunday and Monday from 7 am to about 7 pm.

Marché aux Puces de la Porte de Vanves (Map 1; metro Porte de Vanves). This market in the far south-western corner of the 14e arrondissement is known for its fine selection of junk. Ave Georges Lafenestre looks like a giant car-boot sale, with lots of 'curios' that aren't quite old (or classy) enough to qualify as antiques. Ave Marc Sangnier is lined with stalls selling new clothes, shoes, handbags and household items. It is open on Saturday and Sunday from 7 am to 6 pm (7.30 pm in summer).

Marché d'Aligre (Map 5; metro Ledru Rollin). Smaller and more central than the other three, this market in the 12e at Place d'Aligre – 700m south-east of Place de la Bastille – is one of the best places in Paris to rummage through boxes filled with old clothes and one-of-a-kind accessories worn decades ago by Parisians. It is open Tuesday to Sunday until about 1 pm.

GETTING THERE & AWAY

For information on transport options between the city and the airports, see To/From the Airports in the Getting Around section. For information on air links to Paris, see Air in the introductory Getting There & Away chapter.

Air

Orly Airport Aéroport d'Orly, the older and smaller of Paris' two major international airports, is 16km south of central Paris. Air France and some other international carriers (Iberia, TAP Air Portugal etc) use Orly-Ouest (the west terminal), so the traditional division of responsibilities – Orly-Sud (the south terminal) for international flights, Orly-Ouest for domestic services – no longer holds. A driverless overhead rail line linking Orly-Ouest with Orly-Sud – part of the Orlyval system – functions as a free shuttle between the terminals.

For flight and other information call ☎ 01 49 75 15 15 or, via the switchboard, ☎ 01 49 75 52 52. By Minitel, dial 3615 HORAV or 08 36 25 05 05.

Roissy Charles de Gaulle Airport Aéroport Roissy Charles de Gaulle, 27km north of the city centre in the suburb of Roissy, consists of three terminal complexes. Aérogare 2 has six semicircular terminals that face each other in pairs (2A, 2B, 2C, 2D, 2E and 2F); it is used by Air France and Air Inter for international and domestic flights and by certain foreign carriers. Other international carriers use the cylindrical Aérogare 1. Aérogare T9 is used by charter companies. Airport shuttle buses link Aérogare 1 with both train stations and Aérogare 2 (see To/From the Airports in the Getting Around section). Shuttle buses also go to Aérogare T9.

Flight and other information is available in English or French 24 hours a day on ☎ 01 48 62 22 80 or ☎ 08 36 25 05 05. By Minitel, you can get flight information on 3615 HORAV.

Beauvais Airport The city of Beauvais is 56km north-west of Paris and its airport is used by charter flight companies and discount airline Ryanair, for its Paris-Dublin flights.

Airline Offices The following is a list of selected airlines. Airline offices can also be found in the Paris Yellow Pages under *Transports Aériens*.

Air France
: ☎ 0802 802 802 for information and reservations, ☎ 08 36 68 10 48 for recorded information on arrivals and departures; Minitel 3615 or 3616 AF. Offices are generally open Monday to Saturday from 9 am to 6 pm and include one at 40 Ave George V (8e; Map 2; metro George V), just off Ave des Champs-Élysées.

Air Inter
: ☎ 01 45 46 90 00 for information and reservations, ☎ 08 36 68 34 24 for flight information; Minitel 3615 AIRINTER. Offices include one at 119 Ave des Champs-Élysées (8e; Map 2; metro George V).

Air Liberté
: (☎ 01 49 79 09 09 or ☎ 08 03 80 58 05; Minitel 3615 AIR LIBERTE) 3 Rue Pont des Halles, Rungis 94656.

Air Littoral
: (☎ 08 03 83 48 34; metro Vavin) 100 Blvd Montparnasse (14e).

Air UK
: (☎ 01 44 56 18 08; Minitel 3615 AIR UK; metro Madeleine) 2 Rue Chauveau Lagarde (8e).

American Airlines
: (☎ 01 69 32 73 07 or toll-free ☎ 08 01 87 28 72; metro Saint Philippe du Roule) 109 Rue du Faubourg Saint Honoré (8e).

British Airways
: (☎ 08 02 80 29 02; metro Madeleine) 13 Blvd de la Madeleine (1er).

Canadian Airlines International
: (☎ 01 69 32 73 00; metro Miromesnil) 109 Rue du Faubourg Saint Honoré (8e).

Continental
: (☎ 01 42 99 09 09 or toll-free ☎ 08 00 25 31 81; Minitel 3615 CONTINENTAL; metro George V) 92 Ave des Champs-Élysées (8e).

Corsair
: (☎ 01 49 79 49 79) 24 Rue Saarinen, Rungis 94150.

El Al
: (☎ 01 44 55 00 00; metro Madeleine) 35 Blvd des Capucines (2e).

Northwest Airlines
: (☎ 01 42 66 90 00; metro Madeleine) 16 Rue Chauveau Lagarde (8e).

Qantas
: (☎ 01 44 55 52 00; metro Madeleine) 13 Blvd de la Madeleine (1er).

Ryanair
: (☎ 03 44 11 41 41)

SAS
: (☎ 53 43 25 25; Minitel 3615 FLYSAS; metro St Augustin) 18 Blvd Malesherbes (8e).

Singapore Airlines
(☎ 01 45 53 90 90; metro Boissière) 43 Rue Boissière (16e).

South African Airways (SAA)
(☎ 01 49 27 05 50; metro Tuileries) 350 Rue Saint Honoré (1er).

TAT
(☎ 01 49 75 15 15 or ☎ 08 03 80 58 05; Minitel 3615 TAT; metro Opéra) 17 Rue de la Paix (2e).

Thai
(☎ 01 44 20 70 80; metro Franklin D Roosevelt) 23 Ave des Champs-Élysées (8e).

Tower Air
(☎ 01 55 04 80 80; metro Madeleine) 20 Rue Royale (8e).

United
(☎ 01 41 40 30 30; Minitel 3615 UNITED; metro Opéra) 34 Ave de l'Opéra (2e).

Bus

Domestic Because the French government prefers to avoid competition with the state-owned rail system (SNCF) and the heavily regulated domestic airlines, there is no domestic intercity bus service to or from Paris.

International Eurolines runs buses from Paris to cities all over Europe, including London (see Bus under Land in the introductory Getting There & Away chapter). The company's Gare Routière Internationale Paris-Gallieni (international bus terminal; Map 1; ☎ 01 49 72 51 51; metro Gallieni) is on the eastern edge of the 20e arrondissement in the inner suburb of Bagnolet.

The Eurolines ticket office (Map 6; ☎ 01 43 54 11 99; Minitel 3615 EUROLINES; euroline@imaginet.fr; www.eurolines.fr; metro Cluny-La Sorbonne) at 55 Rue Saint Jacques (5e) is open from 9.30 am to 1 pm and 2.30 to 7 pm (6 pm on Monday and Saturday, closed Sunday); from late June to August, there's no midday closure. In summer, it's not a bad idea to make a reservation a few days in advance.

Eurolines tickets are also sold by many student travel agencies (see Travel Agencies – Student under Information at the beginning of this chapter) and Allostop Provoya (see the Hitching entry later in this chapter).

Train

SNCF train information is available for mainline services on ☎ 08 36 35 35 35 (☎ 08 36 35 35 39 in English) and for suburban services on ☎ 01 53 90 20 20 or ☎ 08 36 67 68 69 (recording). By Minitel, key in 3615 SNCF.

Paris has six major train stations, each of which handles passenger traffic to different parts of France and Europe. For more information on the breakup of regional responsibility of trains from each station, see the 'SNCF Railways' map between pages 160 and 161.

Gare d'Austerlitz (Map 5; metro Gare d'Austerlitz), Blvd de l'Hôpital (13e). Responsible for trains to the Loire Valley, Spain and Portugal and non-TGV trains to south-western France (Bordeaux, the Basque Country etc).

Gare de l'Est (Map 3; metro Gare de l'Est), Blvd de Strasbourg (northern end; 10e). Handles traffic to parts of France east of Paris (such as Champagne, Alsace and Lorraine), Luxembourg, parts of Switzerland (Basel, Lucerne, Zürich), southern Germany (Frankfurt, Munich) and points farther east.

Gare de Lyon (Map 5; metro Gare de Lyon), Blvd Diderot (12e). Responsible for both regular and TGV Sud-Est trains to places south-east of Paris, including Dijon, Lyon, Provence, the Côte d'Azur, the Alps, parts of Switzerland (Bern, Geneva, Lausanne), Italy and points beyond.

Gare Montparnasse (Map 4; metro Montparnasse Bienvenüe), intersection of Ave du Maine and Blvd de Vaugirard (15e). Handles trains to Brittany and places between Paris and Brittany (Chartres, Angers, Nantes). It's the Paris terminus of the TGV Atlantique, which serves Tours, Nantes, Bordeaux and other destinations in south-western France.

Gare du Nord (Map 3; metro Gare du Nord), Rue de Dunkerque (10e). Takes care of trains to the northern suburbs of Paris, northern France (Lille, Calais), the UK, Belgium, northern Germany, Scandinavia, Moscow etc. It also handles the TGV Nord, which serves Lille and Calais, and the Eurostar trains to London.

Gare Saint Lazare (Map 2; metro Saint Lazare), intersection of Rue Saint Lazare and Rue d'Amsterdam (8e). Responsible for traffic to Normandy, including Dieppe, Le Havre and Cherbourg.

Fares One-way, 2nd class fares to destinations around France and abroad include:

Destination	Fare (FF)	Duration (hours)
Amsterdam	387	5
Annecy	335	3½
Berlin	879	11
Copenhagen	1133	16
Geneva	370	3½*
Lille	269	1*
Lyon	384	2*
Madrid	631	16
Marseille	367	4¼*
Nantes	345	2*
Nice	438	6 *
Prague	974	16
Rome	644	12
Toulouse	433	5½ *
Strasbourg	210	4

* *by TGV*

Hitching

Getting out of Paris by thumb, by standing near highway entrance ramps or at petrol stations, doesn't usually work very well. Your best bet is probably to take an RER train out to the suburbs and try from there. Remember to exercise care when hitching.

An organisation in Paris that matches travellers and drivers headed for the same destination is Allostop Provoya (Map 3; ☎ 01 53 20 42 42 or ☎ 01 53 20 42 44; metro Cadet), 8 Rue Rochambeau (9e). It is open Monday to Friday from 9 am to 7.30 pm and on Saturday from 9 am to 1 pm and 2 to 6 pm.

GETTING AROUND

Paris' public transit system, most of which is operated by the RATP (Régie Autonome des Transports Parisians), is one of the most efficient in the world. It's also one of the western world's great urban travel bargains. Free metro/RER/bus maps are available at metro station ticket windows.

To/From the Airports

See the map 'To/From the Airports' to get a sense of your options.

Orly Airport All six public transport options linking Orly with the city run daily every 15 minutes or so (less frequently late at night) from some time between 5.30 and 6.30 am to 11 or 11.30 pm. Tickets are sold on board the buses.

Orlyval
: Links the airport with the city centre in 30 minutes, no matter what the traffic situation is like (57FF; 28FF for children aged four to 10). A completely automated shuttle train connects both Orly terminals with the Antony RER station on RER line B in eight minutes; to get to Antony from the city, take line B4 towards Saint-Rémy-les-Chevreuse. Tickets are valid for 1st class passage on the RER and metro travel within the city. Orlyval runs Monday to Saturday from 6 am to 10.30 pm and on Sunday from 7 am to 10.55 pm.

Orlyrail
: Links the airport with RER line C (30FF; 40 minutes to the city centre). An airport shuttle bus, which runs every 15 minutes from just before 6 am to 11.30 pm, takes you to/from the Pont de Rungis-Aéroport d'Orly RER station; to get there from the city, take a C2 train code-named ROMI or MONA towards Pont de Rungis or Massy-Palaiseau. Tickets are valid for onward metro travel.

Orlybus
: An RATP-run bus to/from the Denfert Rochereau metro station, in the heart of the 14e near Place Denfert Rochereau (Map 1; 30FF; 30 minutes; ☎ 01 40 02 32 94). In both directions, it makes several stops in the eastern 14e.

Jetbus
: The cheapest way to get into the city (24FF; 20 minutes; ☎ 01 60 48 00 98). A bus, running every 12 to 15 minutes from about 6 am to about 10 pm, links both terminals with the Villejuif-Louis Aragon metro stop, which is a bit south of the 13e on the city's southern fringe. From there a regular metro ticket will get you into the city.

Air France Bus
: Air France bus No 1 (☎ 01 41 56 89 00) to/from Gare Montparnasse in the 15e (Map 4; metro Montparnasse Bienvenüe) and Aérogare des Invalides in the 7e (Map 4; metro Invalides). The trip costs 40FF (half-price for

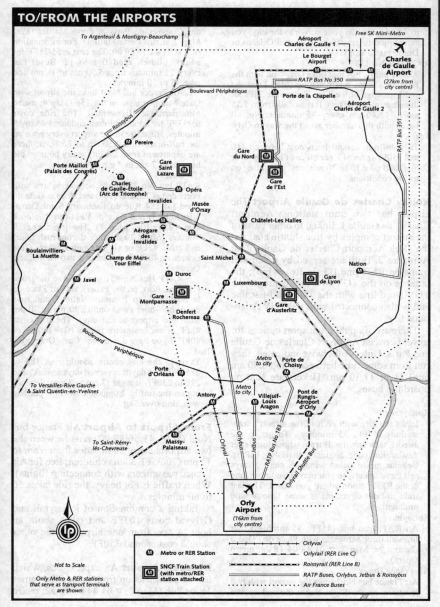

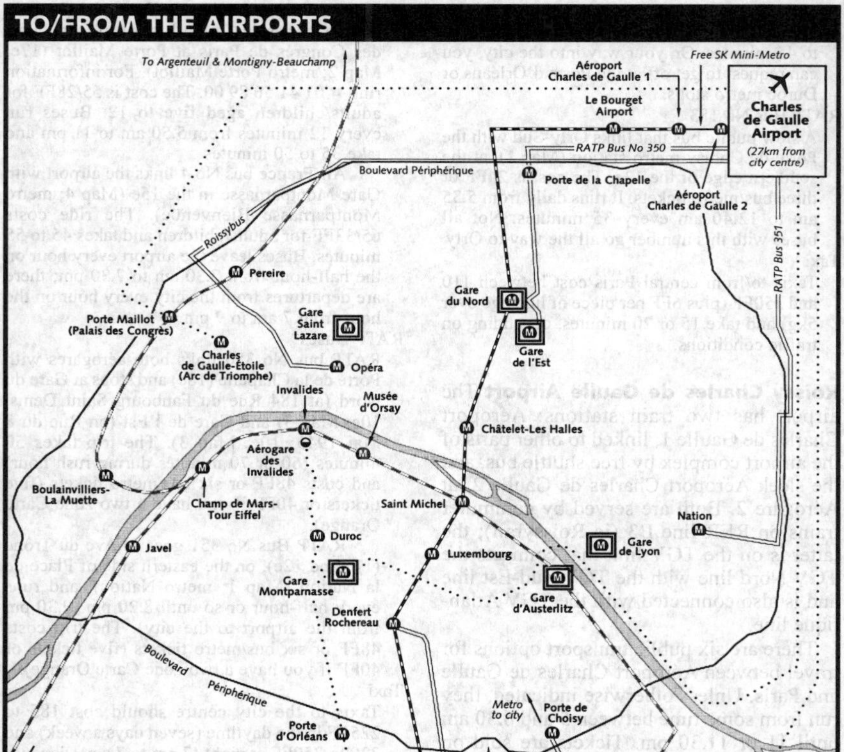
TO/FROM THE AIRPORTS
To Argenteuil & Montigny-Beauchamp
Free SK Mini-Metro
Aéroport Charles de Gaulle 1
Le Bourget Airport
Charles de Gaulle Airport
(27km from city centre)
RATP Bus No 350
Boulevard Périphérique
Porte de la Chapelle
Aéroport Charles de Gaulle 2
Roissybus
RATP Bus 351
Pereire
Gare du Nord
Porte Maillot (Palais des Congrès)
Gare Saint Lazare
Gare de l'Est
Charles de Gaulle-Étoile (Arc de Triomphe)
Opéra
Invalides
Musée d'Orsay
Châtelet-Les Halles
Aérogare des Invalides
Boulainvilliers-La Muette
Champ de Mars-Tour Eiffel
Saint Michel
Nation
Duroc
Gare de Lyon
Javel
Luxembourg
Gare Montparnasse
Gare d'Austerlitz
Denfert Rochereau
Boulevard Périphérique
Metro to city
Porte de Choisy
Porte d'Orléans
To Versailles-Rive Gauche & Saint Quentin-en-Yvelines
Antony
Metro to city
Villejuif-Louis Aragon
Pont de Rungis-Aéroport d'Orly
To Saint-Rémy-lès-Chevreuse
Massy-Palaiseau
Orlyval
Orlybus
Jetbus
RATP Bus No 183
Orlyrail Shuttle Bus
Orly Airport
(16km from city centre)
Not to Scale
Only Metro & RER stations that serve as transport terminals are shown
Metro or RER Station
SNCF Train Station (with metro/RER station attached)
Orlyval
Orlyrail (RER Line C)
Roissyrail (RER Line B)
RATP Buses, Orlybus, Jetbus & Roissybus
Air France Buses

children aged five to 12), runs every 12 minutes from 5.50 am to 11 pm and takes 30 to 45 minutes. On your way into the city, you can request to get off at the Porte d'Orléans or Duroc metro stops.

RATP Bus No 183
A slow public bus that links Orly-Sud with the Porte de Choisy metro station (Map 1), at the southern edge of the 13e. The cost is 24FF or three bus/metro tickets. It runs daily from 5.35 am to 12.40 am every 35 minutes. Not all buses with this number go all the way to Orly.

Taxi
Taxis to/from central Paris cost between 110 and 150FF (plus 6FF per piece of luggage over 5kg) and take 15 or 20 minutes, depending on traffic conditions.

Roissy Charles de Gaulle Airport The airport has two train stations: Aéroport Charles de Gaulle 1, linked to other parts of the airport complex by free shuttle bus, and the sleek Aéroport Charles de Gaulle 2, at Aérogare 2. Both are served by commuter trains on RER line B3 (ie Roissyrail); the latter is on the TGV link that connects the TGV Nord line with the TGV Sud-Est line and is also connected with the TGV Atlantique line.

There are six public transport options for travel between Aéroport Charles de Gaulle and Paris. Unless otherwise indicated, they run from some time between 5 and 6.30 am until 11 or 11.30 pm. Tickets are sold on board the buses.

Roissyrail
Links the city with both of the airport's train stations (47FF; 35 minutes). To get to the airport, take any line B train whose four letter destination code begins with E (eg EIRE). Regular metro ticket windows can't always sell these tickets, so you may have to buy one at the RER station where you board. The last train in both directions is some time around midnight.

Roissybus
An RATP-run bus (45FF; 45 minutes) that links all three aérogares with Place de l'Opéra (2e and 9e; Map 7; ☎ 01 48 04 18 24; metro Opéra).

Air France Buses
Air France bus No 2 links the airport with two locations on the Right Bank: the end of Ave Carnot nearest the Arc de Triomphe (Map 2; metro Charles de Gaulle-Étoile) and the Palais des Congrès de Paris at Porte Maillot (17e; Map 2; metro Porte Maillot). For information ring ☎ 01 41 56 89 00. The cost is 55/28FF for adults/children aged five to 12. Buses run every 12 minutes from 5.50 am to 11 pm and take 35 to 50 minutes.

Air France bus No 4 links the airport with Gare Montparnasse in the 15e (Map 4; metro Montparnasse Bienvenüe). The ride costs 65/33FF for adults/children and takes 45 to 55 minutes. Buses leave the airport every hour on the half-hour from 7.30 am to 7.30 pm; there are departures from the city every hour on the hour from 7 am to 9 pm.

RATP Buses
RATP bus No 350 links both aérogares with Porte de la Chapelle (18e) and stops at Gare du Nord (at 184 Rue du Faubourg Saint Denis, 10e; Map 3) and Gare de l'Est (on Rue du 8 Mai 1945; 10e; Map 3). The trip takes 50 minutes (60 or 70 minutes during rush hour) and costs 48FF or six bus/metro tickets (five tickets or 40FF if you have a two zone Carte Orange).

RATP Bus No 351 goes to Ave du Trône (11e and 12e), on the eastern side of Place de la Nation (Map 1; metro Nation), and runs every half-hour or so until 8.20 pm (9.30 pm from the airport to the city). The trip costs 48FF or six bus/metro tickets (five tickets or 40FF if you have a two zone Carte Orange).

Taxi
Taxis to the city centre should cost 185 to 225FF in the daytime (seven days a week) and 220 to 250FF at night (7 pm to 7 am), depending on the traffic. Luggage costs 6FF per bag weighing over 5kg.

From Airport to Airport Air France bus No 3 (☎ 01 41 56 89 00) runs between the two airports every 20 minutes from 6 am to 11 pm (70/35FF adults/children; free for Air France passengers with connecting flights). When traffic is not heavy, the ride takes 50 to 60 minutes.

Taking a combination of Roissyrail and Orlyval costs 103FF and takes about an hour. A taxi from one airport to the other should cost around 350FF.

Beauvais Airport An express bus, which leaves and picks up from beside the James Joyce Pub (Map 2; ☎ 01 44 09 70 32; metro

Porte Maillot), 71 Blvd Gouvion St-Cyr, open from 7 am to 2 am, departs 2½ hours prior to Ryanair departures and leaves the airport 20 minutes after arrival. Tickets (40FF one way) can be purchased at the Ryanair terminal and the James Joyce.

Metro & RER

Paris' underground network consists of two separate but linked systems: the Métropolitain, known as the *métro*, which has 13 lines and over 300 stations, and the RER, a network of suburban services that pass through the city centre. (A new high-speed line called the Météor and linking the Madeleine stop with the Bibliothèque Nationale de France in the 13e and RER line C will probably have opened by the time you read this.) The term 'metro' is used in this chapter to refer to the Métropolitain as well as any part of the RER system within Paris proper.

For a list of the metro stations you might want to avoid late at night, see the Dangers & Annoyances entry under Information at the start of this chapter.

Information Metro maps are available for free at metro ticket windows. For information on the metro, RER and bus system, call the RATP's 24 hour inquiries number on ☎ 08 36 68 77 14 if you speak French, or ☎ 08 36 68 41 14 for English (2.23FF a minute). By Minitel, key in 3615 RATP.

Information on SNCF's suburban services (including certain RER lines) is available on ☎ 01 53 90 20 20 or ☎ 08 36 67 68 69 (recording). By Minitel, type 3615 SNCF.

Metro Network Each Métropolitain train is known by the name of its end-of-the-line stop, which means that trains on the same line have different names depending on which direction they are travelling in.

Each line is also officially known by a number (1 to 13), but Parisians almost never use these and probably wouldn't understand you if you did.

In the stations, blue on white *direction* signs indicate how to get to the right platform. On metro lines that split into several branches the terminus served by each train is indicated on the cars with back-lit panels.

Black on orange *correspondance* (change or transfer) signs show how to get to connecting trains. In general, the more lines that stop at a station, the longer the *correspondances* will be.

White on blue *sortie* signs indicate the station exits you have to choose from.

The last metro train on each line begins its final run of the night some time between 12.25 and 12.45 am. After about midnight, metro travel is free. The metro starts up again around 5.30 am.

RER Network The RER is faster than the Métropolitain but the stops are more widely spaced. Some parts of the city, such as the Musée d'Orsay and the Eiffel Tower, can be reached far more conveniently by RER than by Métropolitain.

RER lines are known by an alphanumeric combination – the letter (A, B, C or D) refers to the line, the number to the spur it will follow somewhere out in the suburbs. Even-numbered lines head to Paris' southern or eastern suburbs, odd-numbered ones go north or west. All trains whose code begins with the same letter have the same end-of-run stop. Stations served are usually indicated on electronic destination boards above the platform.

The RER 1st class cars, which are in the middle of the trains, can be identified by the yellow stripe across the upper part of the car and the numeral '1'.

Suburban Services The RER and the SNCF's commuter lines serve destinations outside the city, ie in zones 2 to 8. Purchase a special ticket *before* you board the train or you won't be able to get out of the station when you arrive at your destination. You are not allowed to pay the additional fare when you get there.

If you are issued a full-sized SNCF ticket for travel to the suburbs, validate it in one of the orange time-stamp pillars before boarding the train. You may also be given a *contremarque magnétique* (magnetic ticket) to get through any metro/RER-type turnstiles you'll have to cross on the way to/from the platform. If you are travelling on a multi-zone Carte Orange, Paris Visite or Mobilis pass (see the following sections), do *not* punch the magnetic coupon in SNCF's orange time-stamp machines. Some – but not all – RER/SNCF tickets purchased in the suburbs for travel to the city allow you to continue your journey by metro; if in doubt, ask the person selling you the ticket.

For some destinations, tickets can be purchased at any metro ticket window, but for others you'll have to get to an RER station on the line you need in order to buy a ticket. If you're trying to save every franc and have a Carte Orange, Paris Visite or Mobilis, you could get off the train at the last station covered by your coupon and then purchase a separate ticket for the rest of your trip.

Tickets The same 2nd class tickets are valid on buses, trams (eg in the northern suburb of Saint Denis), the Montmartre funicular, the metro and – for travel within the Paris city limits – the RER. They cost 8FF if bought individually and 48FF for a *carnet* of 10. Children under four travel free; children under 10 for half the fare. Tickets are sold at every metro station, though not always at each and every entrance. At some stations, you can pay by credit card if the bill comes to at least 45FF.

One bus/metro ticket lets you travel between any two metro stations for a period of two hours, no matter how many transfers are required. You can also use it on the RER commuter rail system for travel within Paris (that is, within zone 1). However, a single ticket cannot be used to transfer from the metro to a bus, from a bus to the metro or between buses.

Always keep your ticket until you exit from your station.

Weekly & Monthly Tickets The cheapest and easiest way to travel the metro is to get a Carte Orange, a bus/metro/RER pass whose accompanying magnetic coupon comes in weekly and monthly versions. You can get tickets for travel in two to eight urban and suburban zones, but unless you'll be using the suburban commuter lines an awful lot, the basic ticket – valid for zones 1 and 2 – is probably sufficient.

A weekly ticket costs 75FF for zones 1 and 2 and is valid from Monday to Sunday. Even if you'll be in Paris for only three or four days, it may work out cheaper than purchasing a carnet (you'll break even at 16 rides) and it will certainly cost less than buying a daily Mobilis or Paris Visite pass. The monthly Carte Orange ticket (255FF for zones 1 and 2) begins on the first day of each calendar month. Both are on sale in metro and RER stations from 6.30 am to 10 pm and at certain bus terminals.

To get a Carte Orange, bring a photograph (passport size) of yourself to any metro or RER ticket counter (four photos for about 25FF are available from automatic booths in the train stations and certain metro stations). Request a Carte Orange (which is free) and the kind of coupon you'd like. To prevent tickets from being used by more than one person, you must write your surname (*nom*) and given name (*prénom*) on the Carte Orange, and the number of your Carte Orange on each weekly or monthly coupon you buy (next to the words *Carte No*).

Tourist Passes The rather pricey Mobilis and Paris Visite passes allow unlimited travel on the metro, the RER, SNCF's suburban lines, buses, the Noctambus system (see Bus below), trams and the Montmartre funicular railway. They do not require a photo, though you should write your card number on the ticket.

The Mobilis card and its coupon allows unlimited travel for one day in two to eight zones (30 to 110FF). It is on sale at all metro and RER ticket windows as well as SNCF stations in the Paris region, but you would have to make at least six metro trips in a day with a carnet of tickets to break even on this pass.

Paris Visite passes, which allow the holder discounts on entries to certain museums and activities as well as transport, are valid for one/two/three/five consecutive days of travel in either three, five or eight zones. The one to three zone version costs 50/85/120/170FF for one/two/three/five days. Children aged four to 11 pay half-price. They can be purchased at larger metro and RER stations, at SNCF bureaus in Paris and at the airports.

Bus

Regular bus services operate Monday to Saturday from about 7 am to 8.30 pm. Services are drastically reduced on Sunday, holidays and after 8.30 pm. As your bus approaches, signal the driver by waving.

Bus Fares Short bus rides (ie rides in one or two bus zones) cost one bus/metro ticket; longer rides within the city require two tickets. Transfers to other buses or the metro are not allowed on the same ticket. Travel to the suburbs costs two to six tickets, depending on the distance. Special tickets valid only on the bus can be purchased from the driver.

Whatever kind of single-journey ticket you have, you must cancel (*oblitérer*) it in the *composteur* (cancelling machine) next to the driver. If you have a Carte Orange, Mobilis or Paris Visite pass, just flash it at the driver when you board. Do *not* cancel your magnetic *coupon*.

Noctambus After the metro shuts down, the Noctambus network links the area just west of the Hôtel de Ville (4e; Map 8), with lots of places on the Right Bank (served by lines A to H) and a few destinations on the Left Bank (served by lines J and R). Look for the symbol of a little black owl silhouetted against a yellow moon. All 10 lines depart every hour on the half-hour from 1.30 to 5.30 am; line R also leaves at 1, 2, 3, 4 and 5 am.

Noctambus services are free if you have a Carte Orange, Mobilis or Paris Visite pass. Otherwise, a single ride costs three metro tickets (or four if you have to change/transfer to another bus at Châtelet).

Car & Motorcycle

Driving in Paris is nerve-wracking but not impossible, except for the faint-hearted or indecisive. The fastest way to get across Paris is usually on the Périphérique (Map 1), the ring road or beltway that encircles the city.

In many parts of Paris you have to pay 10FF an hour to park your car on the street. Large municipal parking garages usually charge from 12 to 15FF an hour or, for periods of 12 to 24 hours, 80 to 130FF. Parking fines are usually 75 or 200FF and parking attendants dispense them with great abandon, though Parisians appear simply to ignore them.

Rental The easiest (if not cheapest) way to turn a stay in Paris into an uninterrupted series of hassles is to rent a car. If driving the car doesn't destroy your holiday sense of spontaneity, parking the damn thing will. A small car (Peugeot 106) for one day with 400km, plus insurance and taxes, costs about 350FF, but there are better deals from smaller agencies from as low as 199FF a day or 549FF for a three day weekend with 800km.

Most of the larger companies listed below have offices at the airports, and several are also represented at Aérogare des Invalides in the 7e (Map 4; metro Invalides). Higher rates may apply for airport rental, and you may have to return the car there.

To contact the major companies, ring their reservations centres:

Avis	☎ 01 46 10 60 60
Citer/Eurodollar	☎ 01 44 38 61 61
Europcar	☎ 01 30 43 82 82
Hertz	☎ 01 39 38 38 38

For other rental operators check the Yellow Pages under *Location d'automobiles: tourisme et utilitaires*. A number of national and local companies offer relatively reasonable rates. It's a good idea to reserve at least three days ahead, especially for holiday weekends and during summer.

ADA (Map 2; ☎ 01 45 72 36 36 or ☎ 08 36 68 40 02 for general information and reservations; metro Porte Maillot) at 271 Blvd Pereire (17e). ADA has about a dozen other Paris bureaus, including those at 74 Rue de Rome (8e; Map 2; ☎ 01 42 93 65 13; metro Rome); 49 Ave de Versailles (16e; ☎ 01 42 15 06 06; metro Mirabeau); and 34 Ave de la République (11e; Map 3; ☎ 01 48 06 59 74; metro Parmentier).

Rent A Car (Map 5; ☎ 01 43 45 15 15; Minitel 3615 RENTACAR; metro Bercy) at 79 Rue de Bercy (12e). Rent A Car has Seat Marbellas with unlimited kilometres for around 300FF a day and is open Monday to Saturday from 8 am to 8 pm. It has 10 branches in Paris, including one at 84 Ave de Versailles (16e; ☎ 01 42 88 40 04; metro Mirabeau).

OTU Voyages (☎ 01 44 41 38 50 for rental information). The French student travel agency (Map 6) has very good car rental rates through Budget for anyone over 21 who has a student card or is under 26. See Travel Agencies – Student in the Information section at the beginning of this chapter for details on OTU.

Taxi

Parisian taxi drivers have a reputation for arrogance, they're often also hair-raisingly bad drivers and not many of them know where they're going, but, within reason, it's all part of the fun – especially if you end up on the Place Charles de Gaulle (the multi-lane roundabout surrounding the Arc de Triomphe).

The *prise en* charge (flag fall) is 13FF. Within the city, it costs 3.45FF per kilometre for travel undertaken from Monday to Saturday from 7 am to 7 pm (tariff A). At night and on Sunday and holidays (tariff B) it's 5.70FF per kilometre. It costs 130FF an hour to have a taxi wait for you.

There's an extra 8FF charge for taking a fourth passenger, but it is wise to ask permission first, as most drivers are reluctant to take more than three people because of insurance constraints. Each piece of baggage costs 6FF and from certain train stations there's a 5FF supplement. A full list of surcharges is posted on the side window behind the driver. The usual tip is 2FF no matter what the fare, with the maximum about 5FF.

Radio-dispatched taxi companies, on call 24 hours, include:

Alpha Taxis	☎ 01 45 85 85 85
Artaxi	☎ 01 42 41 50 50
G7 Radio	☎ 01 47 39 47 39
Taxis Bleus	☎ 01 49 36 10 10
Taxis-Radio 7000	☎ 01 42 70 00 42

Bicycle

Paris now has almost 100km of bicycle lanes – with another 50km planned by 2000 – that run north-south and east-west through the city; for information ring ☎ 01 40 28 73 73. They're not particularly attractive or safe, but cyclists can be fined about 250FF for failing to use them. The tourist office distributes a free brochure-map produced by the mayor's office called *100km pour Vivre Paris à Vélo*.

There's plenty of space for cyclists in the Bois de Boulogne (16e), the Bois de Vincennes (12e), along Canal Saint Martin (10e) to Parc de la Villette (19e) and then along the south bank of the 108km Canal de l'Ourcq. The quays along the Seine on the Right Bank and the Quai d'Orsay on the Left Bank are closed to motor vehicles on Sunday between 10 am and 5 pm. For information on bicycle tours, see Organised Tours earlier in this chapter.

Bike rental (90 to 150FF a day) is possible in the Bois de Boulogne, at a number of RER/SNCF stations and at the following:

Cycles Peugeot
(☎ 01 45 27 91 39; metro La Muette) 7 Rue Duban (16e)

Cyclic
(☎ 01 43 25 63 67; metro Maubert Mutualité) 19 Rue Monge (5e)

La Maison du Vélo
(☎ 01 42 81 24 72; metro Gare du Nord) 11 Rue Fénelon (10e)

Metro Bike
(☎ 01 43 21 88 38; metro Edgar Quinet) 1 Blvd Edgar Quinet (14e)

Paris à Vélo, C'est Sympa!
(☎ 01 48 87 60 01: metro Bastille) 37 Blvd Bourdon (4e)

Paris Vélo
(☎ 01 43 37 59 22; metro Censier Daubenton) 2 Rue du Fer à Moulin (5e)

Bicycles are not allowed on the metro. You can take your bicycle for free on some RER lines out to the Paris suburbs on weekends and holidays (all day), and on weekdays before 6.30 am, between 9.30 am and 4.30 pm, and after 7.30 pm (ie outside peak travel times). More lenient rules apply to SNCF commuter services. For details, call the SNCF or the RATP or stop by one of their information offices.

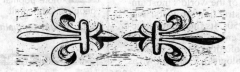

Day Trips from Paris

The 12,000 sq km region surrounding Paris is known as the Île de France (literally, 'Island of France') because of its position between four rivers: the Aube, the Marne, the Oise and the Seine. It was from this relatively small area that, beginning in around 1100, the kingdom of France began to expand.

Today, the region's excellent rail and road links with the French capital and its exceptional sights – the cathedrals of Saint Denis, Chartres, Beauvais and Senlis; the chateaus of Versailles, Fontainebleau and Chantilly; and, of course, Disneyland Paris – make it especially popular with day-trippers. The many woodland areas around the city, which include the forests of Fontainebleau, Chantilly and Compiègne, offer unlimited outdoor activities.

HIGHLIGHTS

- **Versailles** or **Saint Denis Basilica** – relive the glory that was the kingdom of France in the 17th century
- **Disneyland Paris** – become a child again (for a day, at least)
- **Fontainebleu** – go for a walk or ride in this lovely forest
- **Chartres** – learn about the cathedral's awesome stained glass on one of its excellent English-language tours
- **Château de Chantilly** – marvel at the colour and richness of the 15th century *Trés Riches Heures du Duc de Berry* illuminated manuscript

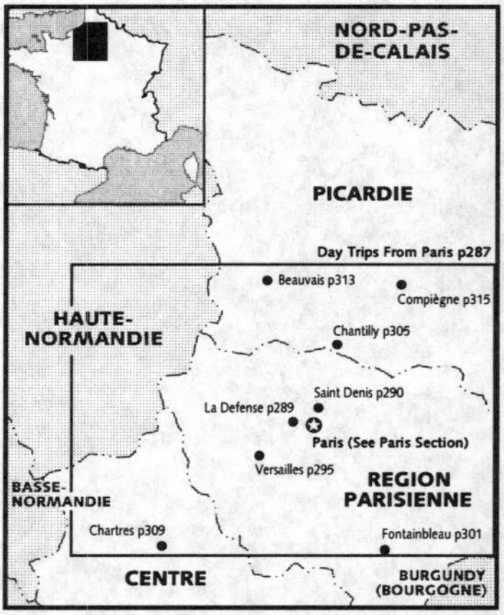

double cheeseburger – at Planet Hollywood in Disneyland Paris, more popular than most French people like to admit

potage Saint-Germain – green pea soup

Information

The Espace du Tourisme Île de France (☎ 01 42 44 10 50), which is in the lower level of the Carrousel du Louvre shopping mall next to IM Pei's inverted glass pyramid (1er), is open daily (except Tuesday) from 10 am to 7 pm. Before you head out, pick up a copy of Michelin's 1:200,000 scale *Île de France* map (No 237) or the 1:100,000 scale *Environs de Paris* one (No 106).

LA DÉFENSE

• pop 30,000 ✉ 92080

La Défense, Paris' skyscraper district, is 3km west of the 17th arrondissement. Set on the sloping west bank of the Seine, its ultramodern architecture and multi-storey office blocks are so radically different from the rest of centuries-old Paris that it's well worth a brief visit.

La Défense, one of the world's most ambitious urban construction projects, was begun in the late 1950s. Its first major structure was the Centre des Nouvelles Industries et Technologies (Centre for New Industries & Technologies), better known as

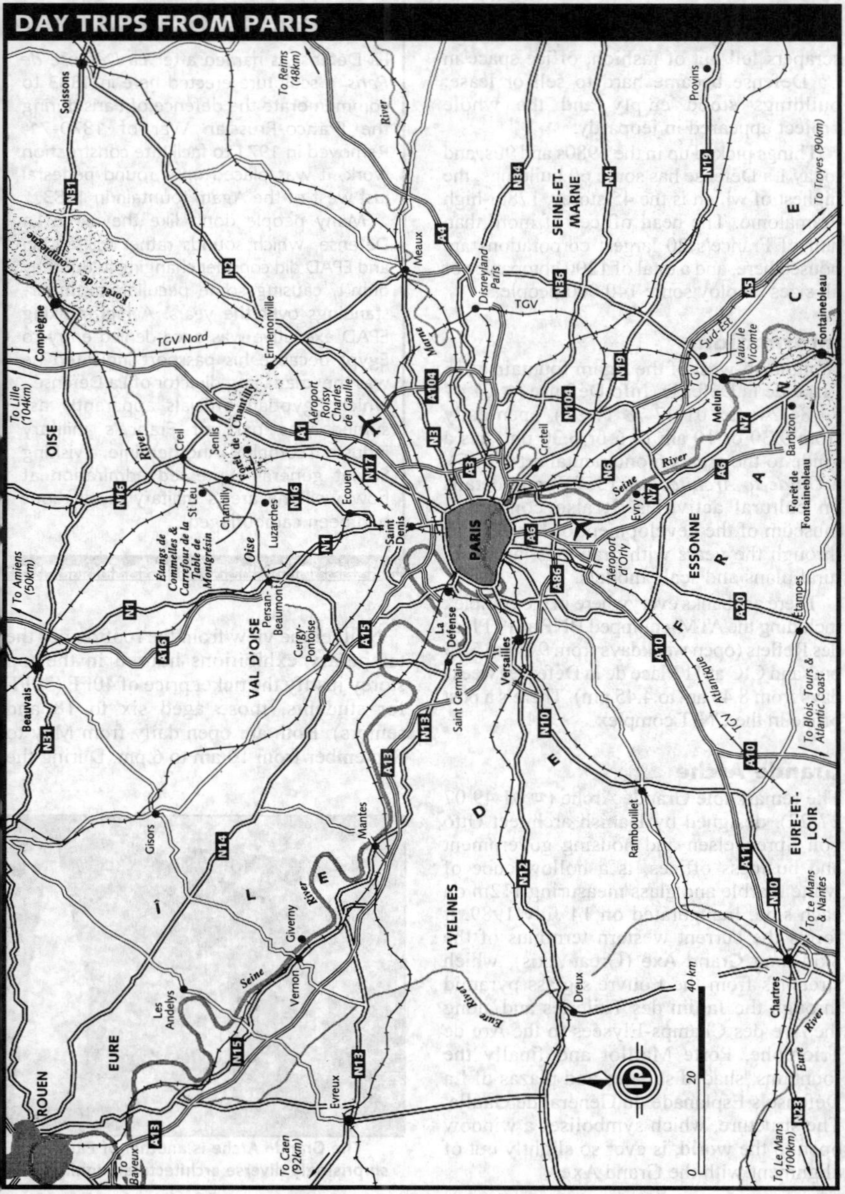

AROUND PARIS

CNIT, inaugurated in 1958 and renovated in 1989. During the mid-1970s, when skyscrapers fell out of fashion, office space in La Défense became hard to sell or lease: buildings stood empty and the whole project appeared in jeopardy.

Things picked up in the 1980s and 90s, and today La Défense has some 60 buildings, the highest of which is the 45 storey, 178m-high Framatome. The head offices of more than half of France's 20 largest corporations are housed here, and a total of 1200 companies of all sizes employ some 140,000 people.

Information

A bit north-west of the Agam fountain at 15 Place de la Défense, Info Défense (☎ 01 47 74 84 24; fax 01 47 78 17 93), open daily from 9.30 or 10 am to 6 or 6.30 pm, has a guide to the area's monumental art (15FF), a *Guide to Architecture* (35FF) and details on cultural activities. It also contains a museum of the development of La Défense through the years with drawings, architectural plans and scale models.

There are banks everywhere in the complex including the ATM-equipped BNP at 19 Place des Reflets (open weekdays from 9 am to 5.15 pm) and CIC at 11 Place de la Défense (weekdays from 8.45 am to 4.45 pm). There's a post office in the CNIT complex.

Grande Arche

The remarkable Grande Arche (☎ 01 49 07 27 27), designed by Danish architect Otto von Spreckelsen and housing government and business offices, is a hollow cube of white marble and glass measuring 112m on each side. Inaugurated on 14 July 1989, it forms the current western terminus of the 8km-long **Grand Axe** (Great Axis), which stretches from the Louvre's glass pyramid through the Jardin des Tuileries and along the Ave des Champs-Élysées to the Arc de Triomphe, Porte Maillot and finally the fountains, shaded squares and plazas of La Défense's Esplanade du Général de Gaulle. The structure, which symbolises a window open to the world, is ever so slightly out of alignment with the Grand Axe.

La Défense de Paris

La Défense is named after *La Défense de Paris*, a sculpture erected here in 1883 to commemorate the defence of Paris during the Franco-Prussian War of 1870-71. Removed in 1971 to facilitate construction work, it was placed on a round pedestal just west of the Agam fountain in 1983.

Many people don't like the name La Défense, which sounds rather militaristic, and EPAD did consider changing it. But they didn't, causing some peculiar misunderstandings over the years. A high-ranking EPAD executive was once denied entry to Egypt because his passport indicated he was the 'managing director of La Défense', which Egyptian officials apparently assumed was part of France's military industrial complex. Another time, a visiting Soviet general expressed admiration at how well the area's military installations had been camouflaged!

Neither the view from the rooftop nor the temporary exhibitions housed in the top storey justify the ticket price of 40FF (30FF for students, those aged six to 18 and seniors). Both are open daily from May to September from 10 am to 6 pm. During the

The Grande Arche is another of Paris' surprisingly diverse architectural highlights.

rest of the year the weekday hours are 11 am to 5 pm, the weekend ones are 10 am to 5 pm.

Parvis & Esplanade

In a largely successful attempt to humanise the district's somewhat harsh mixture of glass, steel and concrete, the Parvis, Place de la Défense and Esplanade du Général de Gaulle, which together form a 1km-long pedestrian precinct, have been turned into a **garden of contemporary art**. The nearly 70 monumental sculptures and murals here – and west of the Grande Arche in the **Quartier du Parc** and **Jardins de l'Arche**, a 2km-long westward extension of the Grand Axe – include colourful and imaginative works by Calder, Miró and Agam.

In the south-east corner of Place de la Défense and opposite the Info Défense office is something much older – a statue honouring the defence of Paris during the Franco-Prussian War of 1870-71 (see the boxed text 'La Défense de Paris').

La Colline de la Défense

This complex, on top of Les Quatre Temps shopping mall, just south of the Grande Arche, houses the huge **Dôme IMAX** (☎ 08 36 67 06 06), a 460 seat, 180° cinema that gives you the feeling of being inside the films on screen. Tickets cost 57FF (44FF for children under 16, students and seniors) and 40FF for the second film. On Saturday a double feature costs 80/70FF. Screenings start every hour from 12.30 to 6.45 pm (8 pm on Saturday).

Of more conventional interest is the **Musée de l'Automobile** (☎ 01 46 92 46 00), whose outstanding collection of vintage motorcars includes lots of very early French models. Many of the signs are in English.

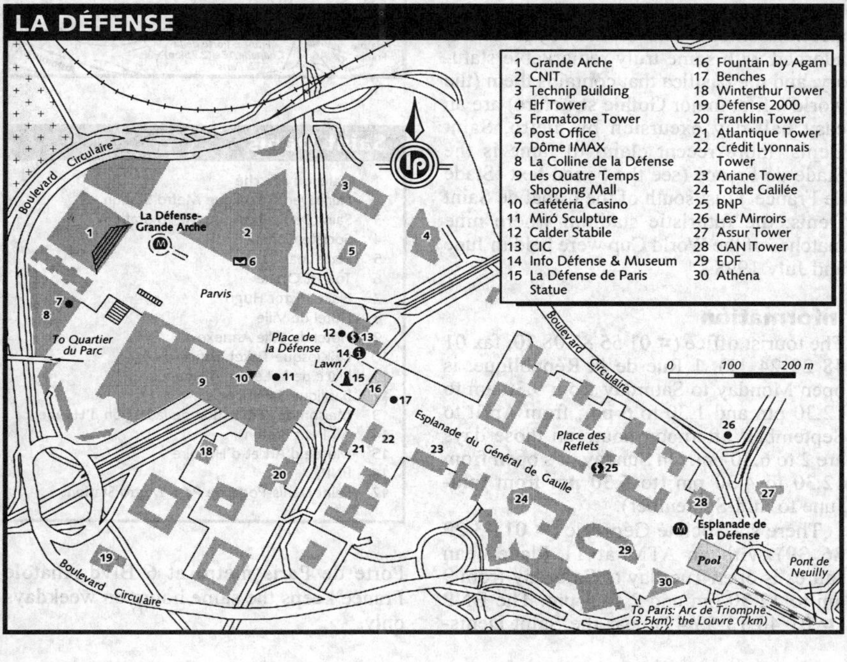

It's open daily from 12.15 to 7.30 pm. Entry is 35FF (20FF reduced price).

Places to Eat

In Les Quatre Temps shopping mall, there are some 30 restaurants, including ***Le Paname Brasserie***, with pizzas from 49 to 65FF and *menus* at 89 and 120FF, and the ***Cafétéria Casino***, which has simple main courses with entrée, dessert or cheese for as little as 29FF.

Getting There & Away

The Grande Arche de la Défense metro station is the western terminus of metro line No 1; the ride from the Louvre takes about 20 minutes. If you take the RER (line A), remember that La Défense is in zone three.

SAINT DENIS

• pop 97,000 ✉ 93200

For 1200 years, Saint Denis was the burial place of the kings of France; today it is an industrial suburb just north of Paris' 18th arrondissement. The ornate royal tombs, adorned with some truly remarkable statuary, and the basilica that contains them (the world's first major Gothic structure) are an easy half-day excursion by metro. Saint Denis' more recent claim to fame is the Stade de France (see the boxed text 'Stade de France') just south of the Canal de Saint Denis, the futuristic stadium where nine matches of the World Cup were held in June and July 1998.

Information

The tourist office (☎ 01 55 87 08 70; fax 01 48 20 24 11), 1 Rue de la République, is open Monday to Saturday from 9.30 am to 12.30 pm and 1.30 to 6 pm; from April to September, afternoon hours on those days are 2 to 6.30 pm. On Sunday, it's open from 12.30 to 4.30 pm (to 6.30 pm from mid-June to mid-September).

There's a Société Générale (☎ 01 43 20 86 39) with an ATM at 11 Place Jean Jaurès is open Tuesday to Saturday from 9 am to 12.30 pm and 2 to 5 pm. The BNP (☎ 01 48 13 53 49) near the Saint Denis-Porte de Paris metro at 6 Blvd Anatole France keeps the same hours on weekdays only.

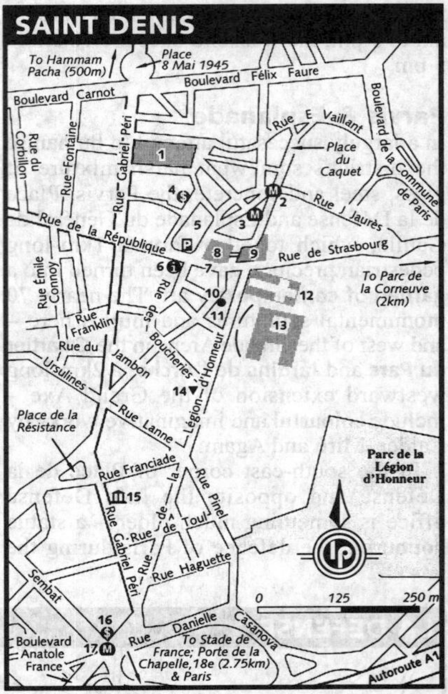

Saint Denis

1. Halle du Marché
2. Saint Denis-Basilique Metro Station
3. Saint Denis-Basilique Metro Station
4. Société Générale
5. Place Jean Jaurès
6. Tourist Office
7. Place Victor Hugo
8. Hôtel de Ville
9. Hôtel de Ville Annexe
10. Le Kiosque Ticket Office
11. Place de la Légion d'Honneur
12. Basilique Saint Denis
13. Maison de l'Éducation de la Légion d'Honneur
14. Au Petit Breton
15. Musée d'Art et d'Histoire
16. BNP
17. Saint Denis-Porte de Paris Metro Station

Stade de France

With a sigh of relief heard round Paris and the nation, the purpose-built 80,000-seat Stade de France (SDF), in the northern suburb of Saint Denis, opened with ample time to spare for France 98, the World Cup of Football. Built at a cost of 2.7FF billion in just two years, this futuristic and very beautiful structure had been from the start the target of much criticism in the French press.

The controversy began early on. In 1991, when France was proposed as host for the 1998 World Cup, the site picked for the new stadium was Melun-Sénart, 35km south-east of Paris. But two years later, after France had been chosen and a certain amount of funding had been earmarked for Melun-Sénart, then-Prime Minister Édouard Balladur abruptly changed the location to Saint Denis, which did in fact have the benefit of being closer to Paris and on a metro line.

The polemics continued as the stadium was being built. Would it be ready on time? What is it going to be called? (A national contest on that point finally arrived at a consensus: the less-than-inspiring 'Stadium of France'). For many even the grass on the pitch wasn't growing fast enough.

On the eve of the World Cup, the next question on everyone's lips was: what the heck is this fantastic stadium going to do for a living afterward? The Paris-Saint Germain (PSG) football club, which usually attracts some 37,000 spectators at the Parc des Princes in the 16e, bowed out as new tenant, citing the high costs of using the SDF. Other more modest clubs, among them the Le Racing Club de France (rugby and athletics) and Red Star (second division football) were also being considered. Meanwhile the SDF will continue to welcome international matches and national finals in football and rugby and 'big event' concerts by foreign and home-grown sensations like the Rolling Stones and Johnny Halliday.

Basilique Saint Denis

The basilica of Saint Denis (☎ 01 48 09 83 54), part of which is currently undergoing renovation, served as the burial place for all but a handful of France's kings from Dagobert I (ruled 629-39) to Louis XVIII (ruled 1814-24). Their tombs and mausoleums constitute one of Europe's most important collections of funerary sculpture.

The present basilica, begun in around 1135 by the irrepressible Abbot Suger, changed the face of western architecture. It was the first major structure to be built in the Gothic style, and it served as a model for many other 12th century French cathedrals, including Chartres. Features illustrating the transition from Romanesque to Gothic can be seen in the **choir** and **ambulatory**, which are adorned with a number of 12th century **stained-glass windows**. The **narthex** (the portico running along the western end of the basilica) also dates from this period. The nave and transept were built a century later.

During the Revolution, the basilica was devastated – the royal tombs were emptied of their human remains, which were then dumped in pits outside the church – but the mausoleums, put into storage in Paris, survived. They were brought back in 1816, and the royal bones were reburied in the crypt a year later. Restoration of the structure was begun under Napoleon, but most of the work was carried out by Viollet-le-Duc from 1858 until his death in 1879.

Tombs The tombs – all of which are now empty – are decorated with life-size figures of the deceased. The ones built before the Renaissance are adorned with *gisants* (recumbent figures). Louis IX (Saint Louis; 1214-70) decided that all his royal predecessors should have elaborate tombs of their own, so though he had little idea what they looked like, he commissioned reclining figures for each of them. Those made after 1285 were carved from death masks and are thus fairly, well, lifelike. The oldest tombs (dating from around 1230) are those of **Clovis I** (died 511) and his son **Childebert I** (died 558), brought to Saint Denis during the early 19th century.

Opening Hours & Entry Fees You can visit the nave for free, but to get to the interesting bits in the transept and chancel there's a charge of 32FF (21FF for those aged 12 to 25, students and seniors; free for those under 12). The basilica is open daily, except on five major holidays, from 10 am (noon on Sunday) to 5 pm (7 pm from April to September). The ticket counters close 30 minutes earlier. Guided tours on CD-ROM headsets lasting 1¼ hours (25FF for one; 35FF for two people sharing) are available at the ticket booth.

Musée d'Art et d'Histoire

Saint Denis' excellent Museum of Art & History (☎ 01 42 43 05 10), 22bis Rue Gabriel Péri, occupies a restored Carmelite convent founded in 1625 and later presided over by Louise de France, the youngest daughter of Louis XV. Displays include reconstructions of the Carmelites' cells, an 18th century apothecary and, in the archaeology section, fascinating items found during excavations around Saint Denis. There's also a section on modern art and, on the 2nd floor, politically charged posters, cartoons, lithographs and paintings from the 1871 Paris Commune. The museum is open daily except Tuesday and holidays; opening hours are 10 am to 5.30 pm (2 to 6.30 pm on Sunday). Entry costs 20FF (10FF for students, teachers and seniors; free for those under 16).

Activities

The immensely popular **Hammam Pacha** (☎ 01 48 29 11 11), a Turkish bathhouse at 147 Rue Gabriel Péri some 500m north of Place 8 Mai 1945, is open to women on Monday, Wednesday and Friday from noon to midnight (10 pm on Wednesday) and on Thursday, Saturday and Sunday from 10 am to midnight. The only mixed day is Tuesday (open 5 pm to midnight). Entry costs 125FF. Men must have a *carte associatif* (membership card) from a naturist club or an International Naturist Federation (INF) *passeport naturiste* (naturist passport). See Naturism under Activities in the Facts for the Visitor chapter for details.

Special Events

From mid-June to mid-July, the Festival de Saint Denis brings mainly classical concerts, opera and dance to the basilica and other venues around town. Tickets (100 to 250FF, reduced rate 50 to 90FF) and information are available from Le Kiosque (☎ 01 48 13 06 07; fax 01 48 13 02 81), 6 Place de la Légion d'Honneur. Many events of the Banlieues Bleues (☎ 01 42 43 56 66; fax 01 42 43 21 90), a jazz festival in the suburbs of Paris in March and April, are held in Saint Denis. Tickets are 100/90FF.

Places to Eat

There are a number of restaurants in the modern shopping area around the Saint Denis-Basilique metro stop and along Rue de la Légion d'Honneur, including ***Au Petit Breton*** (☎ 01 48 20 11 58) at No 18, with a *menu* for 60FF and a *formule* for 55FF. It is open daily, except Saturday night and on Sunday, for lunch and dinner till 9 pm.

On Tuesday, Friday and Sunday from 7 am to 1 pm, there's a large, multi-ethnic ***food market*** – known in particular for its selection of spices – at Place Jean Jaurès, across the street from the tourist office, and in the ***Halle du Marché***, the large covered market to the north-west.

Getting There & Away

Take metro line No 13 to the Saint Denis-Basilique terminus for the basilica and tourist office, or Saint Denis-Porte de Paris for the Museum of Art & History and the Stade de

France. Make sure you don't get on one of the trains going to Asnières-Gennevilliers; the line splits at La Fourche station.

PARC ASTÉRIX

✉ 60128

A home-grown alternative to Disneyland Paris, the Parc Astérix (☎ 03 44 62 31 31 or ☎ 03 44 62 34 04; fax 03 44 62 34 56; Minitel 3615 PARC ASTERIX) is 36km north of Paris, just beyond Roissy Charles de Gaulle airport. Like Disneyland it's divided into a variety of areas – Astérix Village, the Roman City, Ancient Greece and so on, and there are lots of rides, including a particularly hair-raising roller coaster. The park is open daily from early April to mid-October from 10 am to 6 pm. Entry to the park and all the rides is 160FF for adults and 110FF for children under 12.

Getting There & Away

Take RER line train B3 as if you're going to the airport. From the Roissy Charles de Gaulle 1 train station, Courriers Île-de-France buses depart for the park every half-hour from 9.30 am to 1.30 pm. They return from the park every half-hour from 4.30 pm until 30 minutes after the park closes.

DISNEYLAND PARIS

✉ 77777

It took some US$4.4 billion and five years of work to turn the beet fields 50km east of Paris into Disneyland Paris, which opened in 1992 amid much fanfare and controversy. Although Disney stockholders were less than thrilled with the park's performance for the first few years, what was then known as EuroDisney is now in the black, and the many visitors – mostly families with young children – seem to be having a great time. The park is now the single most popular tourist attraction in Europe, having received 12.6 million visitors in 1997.

Information

Disney Information There are information booths scattered around the park, including one in City Hall. In France, information is available (and hotel reservations can be made) on ☎ 01 60 30 60 30 (fax 01 60 30 30 99), in the UK on ☎ 0990 030 303, and in the USA on ☎ 407-WDISNEY. By Minitel, dial 3615 DISNEYLAND. The park also has a Web site (www.disneylandparis.com).

Money The American Express office, hidden away in the wing of the Disneyland Hôtel nearest the train station, has exchange services available daily from 10 am to 6.30 pm (closed on weekends from 1 to 2 pm). The American Express exchange kiosk in Disney Village is open daily from 9.30 am to 10 pm (shorter hours in winter).

Post & Communications In the off season, the Disney Village post office is open from 12.30 to 7 pm. Summer hours are 8.30 am to 10.30 pm (1 to 7.15 pm on Sunday).

Disneyland Paris Theme Park

The theme park, isolated from the outside world by a clever layout and grassy embankments, is divided into five *pays* (lands). **Main Street, USA**, just inside the main entrance, is a spotless avenue reminiscent of Norman Rockwell's idealised small-town America, circa 1900. The adjacent **Frontierland** is a re-creation of the 'rugged, untamed American West'.

Adventureland, intended to evoke the Arabian Nights and the wilds of Africa among other exotic lands, is home to that old favourite, Pirates of the Caribbean, as well as the Indiana Jones roller coaster. **Fantasyland** brings fairy-tale characters such as Sleeping Beauty, Pinocchio and Snow White to life. And in **Discoveryland**, the hitech rides (including the Space Mountain and Big Thunder Mountain) and futuristic movies pay homage to Leonardo da Vinci, HG Wells, George Lucas and – for a bit of local colour – Jules Verne.

Opening Hours & Entry Fees Disneyland Paris is open 365 days a year. From early September to late June, the hours are 10 am to 6 pm (8 pm on Saturdays, some

Sundays and perhaps during school holiday periods). In summer it's open daily from 9 am to 11 pm.

The one-day entry fee, which includes unlimited access to all rides and activities (except the shooting gallery and the video games arcade), costs 200FF (155FF for children aged three to 11) from late March to October. The rest of the year, except during the Christmas holidays, prices drop to 160/130FF. Multiple-day passes are also available.

Places to Stay

Camping & Bungalows The ***Davy Crockett Ranch*** (☎ 01 60 45 69 00), a lovely forested area whose entrance is 7km south-west of the theme park, is open year-round. It costs 400FF to park a caravan or pitch a tent at the 97 camping sites. There are also some 500 bungalows for four to six people costing 400 to 815FF a night, depending on the season. Each has two double beds (plus two bunk beds in the six-person models) and a kitchenette.

Hotels Each of the park's six enormous hotels has its own all-American theme, reflected in the architecture, landscaping, décor, restaurants and entertainment. All the rooms have two double beds (or, in the case of the Hôtel Cheyenne, one double bed and two bunk beds) and can sleep four people.

Rates depend on the dates of stay. Prices are highest during July and August and around Christmas; on Friday and Saturday nights and during holiday periods from April to October; and on Saturday nights from mid-February to March. The least expensive rates are available on most weeknights (ie Sunday to Thursday or, sometimes, Friday) from January to mid-February, from mid-May to June, for most of September, and from November to mid-December.

The cheapest hotel is the 1000 room, New Mexico-style ***Hôtel Santa Fe*** (☎ 01 60 45 78 00), which charges 435 to 780FF for a room. The 14 buildings of the 1000 room ***Hôtel Cheyenne*** (☎ 01 60 45 62 00) – each with its own hokey name – are arranged to resemble a Wild West frontier town. Rooms cost 535 to 925FF.

Places to Eat

There are about 10 American-style restaurants in Disney Village, including ***Planet Hollywood*** (☎ 01 60 43 78 27), which is open daily from 11 or 11.30 am to about midnight.

Getting There & Away

Marne-la-Vallée-Chessy (Disneyland's RER station) is served by RER line A4, which runs every 15 minutes or so. Tickets, available at metro stations, cost 39FF (35FF from the Nation metro stop; 35 to 40 minutes). Trains that go all the way to Marne-la-Vallée-Chessy have four-letter codes beginning with the letter 'Q'. The last train back to Paris leaves Disneyland a few minutes after midnight. A taxi to/from the centre of Paris costs about 350FF (450FF from 7 pm to 8 am and on Sunday and holidays).

VERSAILLES

• pop 95,000 ✉ 78000

Paris' prosperous, leafy and very bourgeois suburb of Versailles is the site of the grandest and most famous chateau in France. It served as the kingdom's political capital and the seat of the royal court for almost the entire period between 1682 and 1789, which was the year Revolutionary mobs massacred the palace guard and dragged Louis XVI and Marie-Antoinette to Paris, where they eventually had their heads lopped off.

Because so many people consider Versailles a must-see destination, the chateau attracts more than three million visitors a year. The best way to avoid the queues is to arrive first thing in the morning; if you're interested in just the Grands Appartements, another good time for you can come is around 3.30 or 4 pm.

Versailles is 23km south-west of Paris.

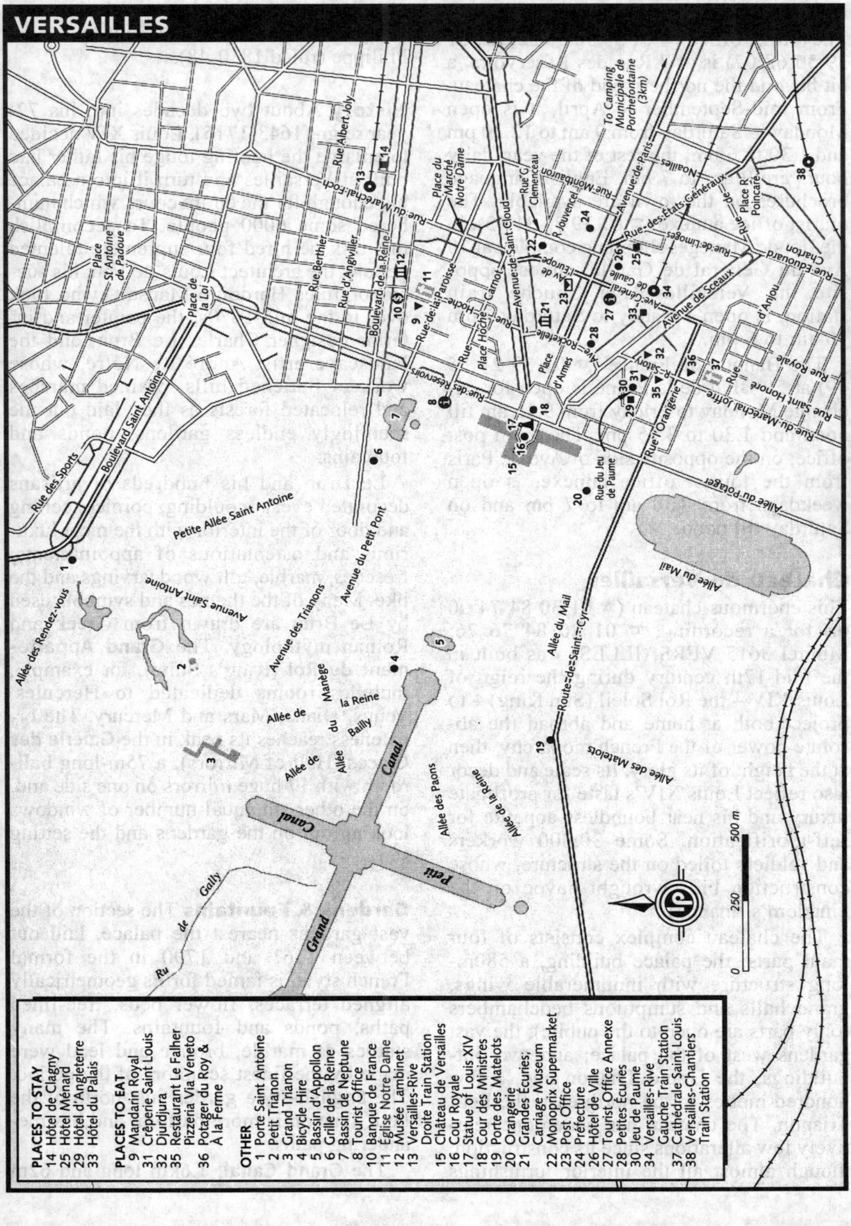
VERSAILLES
PLACES TO STAY
14 Hôtel de Clagny
25 Hôtel Ménard
29 Hôtel d'Angleterre
33 Hôtel du Palais
PLACES TO EAT
9 Mandarin Royal
31 Crêperie Saint Louis
32 Djurdjura
35 Restaurant Le Falher
Pizzeria Via Veneto
36 Potager du Roy &
À la Ferme
OTHER
1 Porte Saint Antoine
2 Petit Trianon
3 Grand Trianon
4 Bicycle Hire
5 Bassin d'Appollon
6 Grille de la Reine
7 Bassin de Neptune
8 Tourist Office
10 Banque de France
11 Église Notre Dame
12 Musée Lambinet
13 Versailles-Rive
Droite Train Station
15 Château de Versailles
16 Cour Royale
17 Statue of Louis XIV
18 Cour des Ministres
19 Porte des Matelots
20 Orangerie
21 Grandes Écuries;
Carriage Museum
22 Monoprix Supermarket
23 Post Office
24 Préfecture
26 Hôtel de Ville
27 Tourist Office Annexe
28 Petites Écuries
30 Jeu de Paume
34 Versailles-Rive
Gauche Train Station
37 Cathédrale Saint Louis
38 Versailles-Chantiers
Train Station
To Camping Municipale de Porchefontaine (3km)
Place du Marché Notre Dame
Place St Antoine de Padoue
Place de la Loi
Place Hoche
Place d'Armes
Place R Poincaré
Boulevard Saint Antoine
Boulevard de la Reine
Rue du Maréchal Foch
Rue Albert Joly
Rue Berthier
Rue d'Angiviller
Rue des Réservoirs
Rue de la Paroisse
Rue Hoche
Rue Carnot
Avenue de Saint Cloud
Avenue de Paris
Avenue de Sceaux
Rue des États Généraux
Rue de l'Orangerie
Rue du Jeu de Paume
Rue Royale
Rue Saint Honoré
Rue du Maréchal Joffre
Allée du Potager
Allée du Mail
Allée des Matelots
Allée de la Reine
Allée des Paons
Allée de Bailly
Allée de Manège
Route de Saint Cyr
Avenue du Petit Pont
Avenue des Trianons
Avenue Saint Antoine
Petite Allée Saint Antoine
Allée des Rendez-vous
Rue des Sports
Grand Canal
Petit Canal
Ru de Gally
0 250 500 m

AROUND PARIS

Information

The tourist office (☎ 01 39 50 36 22; fax 01 39 50 68 07) is at 7 Rue des Réservoirs, a bit beyond the northern end of the chateau. From mid-September to April, it is open Monday to Saturday from 9 am to 12.30 pm and 1.30 to 6 pm; the rest of the year, daily hours are 9 am to 7 pm. English-language brochures on the town are available. The tourist office annexe (☎ 01 39 53 31 63), in the Îlot de Manèges shopping complex at 10 Ave du Général de Gaulle, almost opposite the Versailles-Rive Gauche train station, is open Tuesday to Saturday from 10 am to 6 pm.

The Banque de France (☎ 01 39 24 55 49) at 50 Blvd de la Reine is open for exchange Monday to Friday from 9.15 am till noon and 1.30 to 3.15 pm. The main post office, on the opposite side of Ave de Paris from the tourist office annexe, is open weekdays from 8.30 am to 7 pm and on Saturday till noon.

Château de Versailles

This enormous chateau (☎ 01 30 84 74 00 or, for a recording, ☎ 01 30 84 76 76; Minitel 3615 VERSAILLES) was built in the mid-17th century during the reign of Louis XIV – the Roi Soleil (Sun King) – to project both at home and abroad the absolute power of the French monarchy, then at the height of its glory. Its scale and décor also reflect Louis XIV's taste for profligate luxury and his near boundless appetite for self-glorification. Some 30,000 workers and soldiers toiled on the structure, whose construction bills wrought havoc on the kingdom's finances.

The chateau complex consists of four main parts: the palace building, a 580m-long structure with innumerable wings, grand halls and sumptuous bedchambers (only parts are open to the public); the vast gardens west of the palace; and two outbuildings, the Grand Trianon and, a few hundred metres to the north-east, the Petit Trianon. The chateau has undergone relatively few alterations since its construction, though almost all the interior furnishings disappeared during the Revolution and many of the rooms were rebuilt by Louis-Philippe (ruled 1830-48).

History About two decades into his 72-year reign (1643-1715), Louis XIV decided to enlarge the hunting lodge his father had built at Versailles and turn it into a palace big enough for the entire court, which numbered some 6000 people. To accomplish this task he hired four supremely talented people: the architect Louis Le Vau; his successor Jules Hardouin-Mansart, who took over in the mid-1670s; the painter and interior designer Charles Le Brun; and the landscape artist André Le Nôtre, whose workers flattened hills, drained marshes and relocated forests as they laid out the seemingly endless gardens, ponds and fountains.

Le Brun and his hundreds of artisans decorated every moulding, cornice, ceiling and door of the interior with the most luxurious and ostentatious of appointments: frescoes, marble, gilt woodcarvings and the like. Many of the themes and symbols used by Le Brun are drawn from Greek and Roman mythology. The **Grand Appartement du Roi** (King's Suite), for example, includes rooms dedicated to Hercules, Venus, Diana, Mars and Mercury. The ornateness reaches its peak in the **Galerie des Glaces** (Hall of Mirrors), a 75m-long ballroom with 17 huge mirrors on one side and, on the other, an equal number of windows looking out on the gardens and the setting sun.

Gardens & Fountains The section of the vast gardens nearest the palace, laid out between 1661 and 1700 in the formal French style, is famed for its geometrically aligned terraces, flower beds, tree-lined paths, ponds and fountains. The many statues of marble, bronze and lead were made by the finest sculptors of the period. The **English-style garden** just north of the Petit Trianon is more pastoral and has meandering paths.

The **Grand Canal**, 1.6km long and 62m

wide, is oriented to reflect the setting sun. It is intersected by the 1km **Petit Canal**, creating a cross-shaped body of water with a perimeter of over 5.5km. Louis XIV used to hold boating parties here. From May to mid-October, you too can paddle around the Grand Canal: four-person rowing boats (☎ 01 39 54 22 00) cost 70FF an hour. The dock is at the canal's eastern end. The **Orangerie**, built under the Parterre du Midi (flower bed) on the south side of the palace, is used for the wintertime storage of exotic plants.

The gardens' largest fountains are the 17th century **Bassin de Neptune** (Neptune Fountain), 300m north of the main palace building, whose straight side abuts a small, round pond graced by a winged dragon, and, at the eastern end of the Grand Canal, the **Bassin d'Apollon**, in whose centre Apollo's chariot, pulled by rearing horses, emerges from the water.

On Sunday from early May to early October, the fountains are turned on at 11.15 am for the 20 minute **Grande Perspective** and from 3.30 to 5.30 pm for the longer and more elaborate **Grandes Eaux**. On the days when the fountain shows take place, there is a 25FF fee to get into the gardens.

The Trianons In the middle of the park, about 1.5km north-west of the main building, are Versailles' two smaller palaces, each surrounded by neatly tended flower beds. The pink-colonnaded **Grand Trianon** was built in 1687 for Louis XIV and his family, who used it as a place of escape from the rigid etiquette of court life. Napoleon I had it redone in the Empire style. The much smaller **Petit Trianon**, built in the 1760s, was redecorated in 1867 by the Empress Eugénie, who added Louis XVI-style furnishings similar to the uninspiring pieces that now fill its 1st floor rooms.

A bit farther north is the **Hameau de la Reine** (Queen's Hamlet), a mock rural village of thatch-roofed cottages constructed from 1775 to 1784 for the amusement of Marie-Antoinette.

Opening Hours & Entry Fees The **Grands Appartements** (State Apartments), the main section of the palace that can be visited without a guided tour, include the Galerie des Glaces and the **Appartement de la Reine** (Queen's Suite). Except on Monday and five public holidays, they are open from 9 am to 5.30 pm (6.30 pm from May to September); the ticket windows close 30 minutes earlier. Entry costs 45FF (35FF for people aged 18 to 25 and, after 3.30 pm daily and on Sunday, for everyone; free for under 18s). Tickets are on sale at Entrée A (Entrance A; also known as Porte A), which, as you approach the palace, is off to the right from the equestrian statue of Louis XIV. The queues are worst on Tuesday, when many Paris museums are closed, and on Sunday.

A new exhibit called **Les Grandes Heures du Parlement** (Famous Events of Parliament; ☎ 01 39 67 07 73), which focuses on the history of France's Assemblée Nationale (National Assembly) is in the chateau's south wing. It keeps the same hours as the chateau though the ticket office closes one hour earlier. Entry costs 20FF (15FF for those aged 18 to 25; free for under 18s).

From October to April, the Grand Trianon (25FF; 15FF reduced price; free for under 18s) is open Tuesday to Sunday, 10 am to 12.30 pm and 2 to 5.30 pm (no midday closure on weekends). The rest of the year, hours are 10 am to 6.30 pm. The last entry is 30 minutes before closing time. The Petit Trianon, open the same days and hours, costs 15FF (10FF reduced price; free for under 18s). A combined ticket for both will set you back 30FF (20FF reduced price).

The gardens are open seven days a week (unless it's snowing) from 7 am to nightfall (between 5.30 and 9.30 pm, depending on the season). Entry is free *except* on Sundays from early May to early October, when the fountains are in operation and entry is 25FF.

If you have a Carte Musées et Monuments, you don't have to wait in the queue – go straight to Entrée A2.

Guided Tours One of the best ways to get a sense of the Grands Appartements is to rent the state-of-the-art recorded tour available for 30FF at Entrée A, right behind the ticket booths. The excellent commentary lasts 80 minutes.

The **Appartement de Louis XIV** and the **Appartements du Dauphin et de la Dauphine** can be toured with a 55 minute audioguide, available at Entrée C, for 25FF (17FF for children aged seven to 17). You can begin your visit between 9 am and 3.30 pm (4.15 pm from May to September). This is also a good way to avoid the queues at Entrée A.

Several different guided tours are available in English from 9 am to 3.30 pm (4 pm from May to September). They last one hour, 1½ and two hours and cost 25FF *per hour* (17FF per hour for people aged seven to 17). Tickets are sold at Entrée D; tours begin across the courtyard at Entrée F.

All the tours require that you also purchase a ticket to the Grands Appartements. If you buy it at Entrée C or Entrée D when paying for your tour, you can later avoid the Grands Appartements queue at Entrée A by going straight to Entrée A2.

The Town of Versailles

Like the chateau, the attractive town of Versailles, crisscrossed by wide boulevards, is a creation of Louis XIV. However, most of today's buildings date from the 18th and 19th centuries.

Grandes & Petites Écuries Ave de Paris, Ave de Saint Cloud and Ave de Sceaux, the three wide thoroughfares that fan out eastward from Place d'Armes, are separated by two large, late 17th century stables: the Grandes Écuries (mostly occupied by the army) and the Petites Écuries, which contains an architectural unit and restoration workshops. The **Carriage Museum** in the Grandes Écuries can be visited daily from May to September from 12.30 to 6.30 pm. In April and October the hours on Saturday and Sunday only are 9 am to 12.30 pm and 2 to 5.30 pm. Entry costs 12FF (free for under 18s).

Jeu de Paume The Jeu de Paume, 350m south-east of the chateau on Rue du Jeu de Paume, was built in 1686 and played a pivotal role in the Revolution less than a century later (see the boxed text 'The Tennis Court Oath'). It is open to the public from May to September, when it can be visited Wednesday and Saturday from 2 to 5 pm. Contact the chateau's Bureau d'Action Culturelle (☎ 01 30 84 76 18) for details.

Cathédrale Saint Louis This neoclassical (and slightly baroque) cathedral at 4 Place Saint Louis, a harmonious if austere work by Hardouin-Mansart, was built between 1743 (when Louis XV himself laid the first stone) and 1754. It is known for its 3131-pipe Cliquot organ and is decorated with a number of interesting paintings and

The Tennis Court Oath

In May 1789, in an effort to deal with the huge national debt and to moderate dissent by reforming the tax system, Louis XVI convened at Versailles the États-Généraux (States General), a body made up of over a thousand deputies representing the three estates: the Nobility and the Clergy (most of whom were exempted from paying taxes) and the Third Estate, representing the middle classes. When the Third Estate, whose members constituted a majority of the delegates, was denied entry to the usual meeting place of the États-Généraux, they met separately in the Salle de Jeu de Paume (Royal Tennis Court), where they constituted themselves as the National Assembly on 17 June. Three days later they took the famous Tennis Court Oath, swearing not to dissolve the assembly until Louis XVI had accepted a new constitution. This act of defiance sparked protests of support and, a short while later, open rebellion. Less than a month after the Tennis Court Oath, a Parisian mob would storm the Bastille prison.

stained-glass panels. Its opening hours are from 9 am to noon and 2 to 6 or 7 pm.

Musée Lambinet Housed in a lovely 18th century residence at 54 Blvd de la Reine, the Musée Lambinet (☎ 01 39 50 30 32) displays 18th century furnishings (ceramics, sculpture, paintings, furniture) and objects connected with the history of Versailles (including the Revolutionary period). It is open Tuesday and Friday from 2 to 5 pm, Wednesday and Thursday from 1 to 6 pm, and on Saturday and Sunday from 2 to 6 pm. Entry costs 25FF (15FF reduced tariff).

Église Notre Dame Built by Hardouin-Mansart in 1684, this church at 35 Rue de la Paroisse served as the parish church of the king and his courtiers. It has a fine sculpted pulpit. It is generally open from 8.30 am till noon and 2 to 7.30 pm.

Places to Stay

Camping Municipale de Porchefontaine (☎ 01 39 51 23 61), about 3km south-east of the centre at 31 Rue Berthelot, is 500m from the Versailles-Porchefontaine train station (on RER line C5) and in the Parc Forestier des Nouettes. It charges 50FF per site and 30FF per adult.

The friendly, 17 room ***Hôtel Ménard*** (☎ 01 39 50 47 99), 8 Rue Ménard, has simple, spotless singles with washbasin from 100 to 130FF, doubles for 150 to 170FF. Singles/doubles with shower are 170/190FF.

Across the street from the Versailles-Rive Gauche station on the 2nd floor at 6 Place Lyautay is the ***Hôtel du Palais*** (☎ 01 39 50 39 29; fax 01 39 50 80 41). This well kept hotel has doubles with washbasin for 170FF, and with shower for 220 to 250FF.

Around the corner from the Jeu de Paume at 2bis Rue de Fontenay, the two star, 18 room ***Hôtel d'Angleterre*** (☎ 01 39 51 43 50; fax 01 39 51 45 63) has attractive rooms from 150/250 (300FF with bath).

The ***Hôtel de Clagny*** (☎ 01 39 50 18 09; fax 01 39 50 85 17) is at 6 Impasse de Clagny, half a block from 91 Blvd de la Reine and behind the Versailles-Rive Droite station. Singles with washbasin and toilet at this 21 room, two star place are 200FF. Doubles with shower and toilet are 280FF (300FF with bath and toilet).

Places to Eat

Restaurants The quiet, elegant ***Restaurant Le Falher*** (☎ 01 39 50 57 43), 22 Rue Satory, has French gastronomic *menus* for 115FF (at lunch) and 128, 160FF (with wine) and 180FF. It's closed on Saturday at midday and Sunday.

Traditional French *menus* at the refined ***Potager du Roy*** (☎ 01 39 50 35 34), 1 Rue du Maréchal Joffre, go for 130FF (Tuesday to Saturday at lunch only) and 175FF. It's closed Sunday night and Monday. Two doors away at No 3 of the same street is ***À la Ferme*** (☎ 01 39 53 10 81). This establishment specialises in fish and grilled meats. Two-course formules and *menus* cost 87 to 117FF. It's closed on Monday and on Tuesday for lunch.

The ***Crêperie Saint Louis*** (☎ 01 39 53 40 12) is at 33 Rue du Vieux Versailles, around the corner from 22bis Rue Satory. The Breton specialities at this cosy place include sweet and savoury crêpes (18 to 45FF), and there are *menus* for 55, 65 and 85FF. It is open daily.

The couscous at the friendly ***Djurdjura*** (☎ 01 39 50 47 49), 5 Rue Satory, is prepared in the manner of the Kabyles of eastern Algeria and costs from 49FF; the excellent mixed couscous is 69FF while couscous royal is 85FF. It's open daily till midnight.

There are a dozen other restaurants in the immediate vicinity, including ***Pizzeria Via Veneto*** (☎ 01 39 51 03 89), at 20 Rue Satory, which has pizzas (39 to 50FF) and pasta dishes (43 to 57FF) and is open daily.

The ***Mandarin Royal*** (☎ 01 39 50 48 03), a Chinese restaurant with some Thai and Vietnamese dishes just west of the Église Notre Dame at 5 Rue de Sainte Geneviève, has a lunch *menu* for 49FF and dinner ones for 68, 88 and 118FF. It's open for lunch and dinner daily, except Sunday night and for lunch on Monday.

Self-Catering There's an outdoor ***food market*** at Place du Marché Notre Dame open Tuesday, Friday and Sunday from 8 am to 1 pm; the ***food stalls*** in the covered market are open every morning. The ***Monoprix*** supermarket at 9 Rue Georges Clemenceau, north of the Ave de Paris, is open Monday to Saturday from 8.30 am to 9 pm.

Getting There & Away

Each of Versailles' three train stations is served by RER and/or SNCF trains coming from a different set of Paris stations.

RER line C5 takes you from Paris' Left Bank RER stations to Versailles-Rive Gauche station (14FF), which is only 700m from the chateau. From Paris, catch any train whose four-letter code begins with the letter 'V'. There are 60 trains a day (35 on Sunday); the last train back to Paris leaves just after midnight. Tickets are not sold at regular metro ticket windows.

RER line C7 links Paris' Left Bank with Versailles-Chantiers station (14FF), a 1.3km walk from the chateau. From the city, take any train whose code begins with 'S'. Versailles-Chantiers is also served by 36 SNCF trains a day (20 on Sunday) from Gare Montparnasse (14FF; 14 minutes); all trains on this line continue on to Chartres.

From Paris' Gare Saint Lazare and La Défense, the SNCF has about 70 trains a day to Versailles-Rive Droite (19FF including a metro journey), which is 1.2km from the chateau. The last train to Paris leaves a bit past midnight.

Getting Around

From late February to December, Astel (☎ 01 39 66 97 66) hires out bicycles both at Petite Venise (the eastern end of the Grand Canal) and next to Grille de la Reine. Hours are 10 am to at least 5 pm (later as the days get longer). Fees are a steep 30/20FF per half-hour/hour at Petite Venise and 15/25FF at Grille de la Reine.

FONTAINEBLEAU

• pop 18,000 ✉ 77300

The town of Fontainebleau, 65km south-east of Paris, is renowned for its elegant Renaissance chateau – one of France's largest royal residences – whose splendid furnishings make it particularly worth a visit. It's much less crowded and pressured than Versailles. The town itself has a number of fine restaurants and night spots and is surrounded by the beautiful Forêt de Fontainebleau, a favourite hunting ground of a long line of French kings.

Information

The tourist office (☎ 01 60 74 99 99; fax 01 60 74 80 22; Minitel 3615 FONTAINEBLEAU), 4 Rue Royale, is open May to September from Monday to Saturday from 9.30 am to 6.30 pm and from 10 am to 6 pm on Sunday. During the rest of the year it is open weekdays from 9.30 am to 5.30 pm, on Saturday from 10 am to 6 pm, and on Sunday from 10 am to 12.30 pm and 3 to 5.30 pm. The very helpful staff here can provide information on *chambres d'hôtes* and *gîtes ruraux*. They also rent self-paced audioguide tours of the city in English lasting 1½ hours (30FF).

The Banque de France at 192 Rue Grande is open Monday to Friday from 8.30 to noon and 1.30 to 3.30 pm. The main post office, 2 Rue de la Chancellerie, is open weekdays from 8 am to 7 pm and on Saturday till noon.

Château de Fontainebleau

The enormous, 1900 room Château de Fontainebleau (☎ 01 60 71 50 70), whose list of former tenants reads like a who's who of French royal history, is one of the most beautifully ornamented and furnished chateaus in France. Every centimetre of the wall and ceiling space is richly adorned with wood panelling, gilded carvings, frescoes, tapestries and paintings. The parquet floors are of the finest woods, the fireplaces ornamented with exceptional carvings, and many of the pieces of furniture are Renaissance originals.

FONTAINEBLEAU

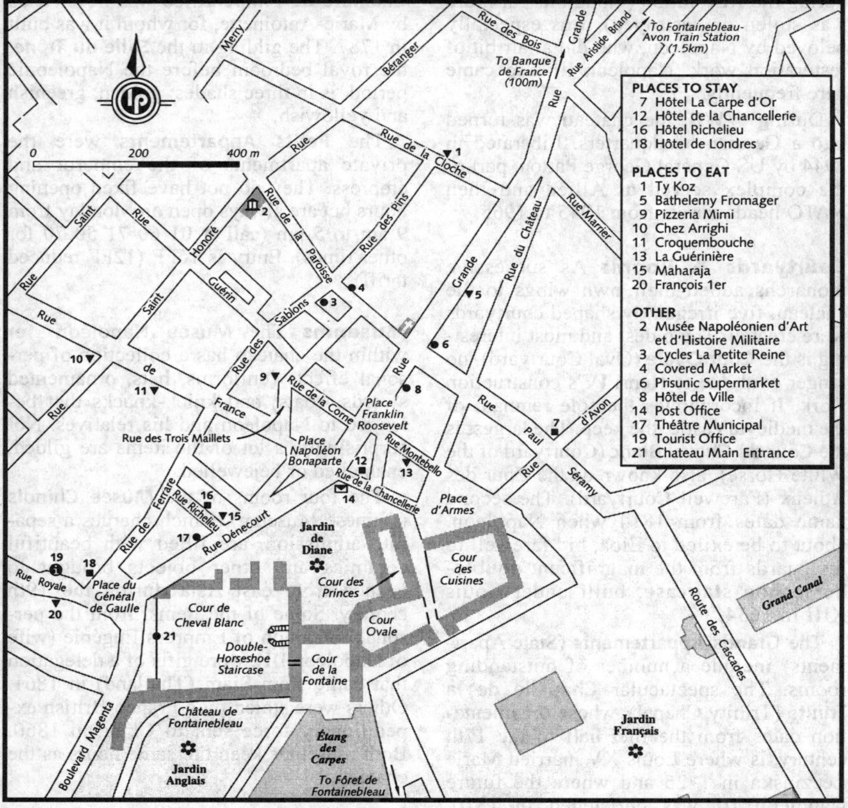

History The first chateau on this site was built sometime in the early 12th century and enlarged by Louis IX in the 13th century. Only a single medieval tower survived the energetic Renaissance-style reconstruction undertaken by François I (ruled 1515-47), whose superb artisans, many of them brought from Italy, blended Italian and French styles to create what is known as the First School of Fontainebleau. During this period, the *Mona Lisa* hung here amidst other fine works of art in the king's collection.

During the latter half of the 16th century, the chateau was further enlarged by Henri II, Catherine de Médicis and Henri IV, whose Flemish and French artists created the Second School of Fontainebleau.

Even Louis XIV got in on the act: it was he who hired Le Nôtre to redesign the gardens. But his most (in)famous act at Fontainebleau was the revocation in 1685 of the Edict of Nantes, which had guaranteed freedom of conscience to France's Protestants since 1598.

Fontainebleau, which was not damaged during the Revolution (though its furniture was stolen or destroyed), was especially beloved by Napoleon, who did a fair bit of restoration work. Napoleon III also came here frequently.

During WWII, the chateau was turned into a German headquarters. Liberated in 1944 by US General George Patton, part of the complex served as Allied and then NATO headquarters from 1945 to 1965.

Courtyards & Rooms As successive monarchs added their own wings to the chateau, five irregularly shaped courtyards were created. The oldest and most interesting is the **Cour Ovale** (Oval Courtyard), no longer oval due to Henri IV's construction work. It incorporates the sole remnant of the medieval castle, the keep. The largest is the **Cour du Cheval Blanc** (Courtyard of the White Horse), also known as the Cour des Adieux (Farewell Courtyard). The second name dates from 1814 when Napoleon, about to be exiled to Elba, bid farewell to his guards from the magnificent **double-horseshoe staircase**, built under Louis XIII in 1634.

The **Grands Appartements** (State Apartments) include a number of outstanding rooms. The spectacular **Chapelle de la Trinité** (Trinity Chapel), whose ornamentation dates from the first half of the 17th century, is where Louis XV married Marie Leczinska in 1725 and where the future Napoleon III was christened in 1810. **Galerie François 1er**, a gem of Renaissance architecture, was decorated from 1533 to 1540 by Il Rosso, a Florentine follower of Michelangelo. In the wood panelling, François I's monogram, a letter 'F', appears repeatedly along with his emblem, a dragon-like salamander.

The **Salle de Bal**, a ballroom 30m long that was also used for receptions and banquets dating from the mid-16th century, is renowned for its mythological frescoes, marquetry floor and Italian-inspired coffered ceiling. The large windows afford views of the Cour Ovale and the gardens. The gilded bed in the 17th and 18th century **Chambre de l'Impératrice** was never used by Marie-Antoinette, for whom it was built in 1787. The gilding in the **Salle du Trône**, the royal bedroom before the Napoleonic period, is in three shades: golden, greenish and yellowish.

The **Petits Appartements** were the private apartments of the emperor and empress. They do not have fixed opening hours but are always open on Monday from 9 am to 5 pm (call ☎ 01 60 71 50 70 for other times). Entry is 16FF (12FF reduced tariff).

Museums The **Musée Napoléon 1er** within the chateau has a collection of personal effects (uniforms, hats, ornamented swords, coats) and knick-knacks that belonged to Napoleon and his relatives. Not surprisingly, a lot of the items are gilded, enamelled or bejewelled.

The four rooms of the **Musée Chinois** (Chinese Museum), which charges a separate admission, are filled with beautiful ceramics and other objects brought to France from east Asia during the 19th century. Some of the items, from the personal collection of Empress Eugénie (wife of Napoleon III), were gifts of a delegation that came from Siam (Thailand) in 1861. Others were stolen by a Franco-British expeditionary force sent to China in 1860. Both museums keep the same hours as the chateau.

Gardens On the north side of the chateau, the **Jardin de Diane**, a formal garden created by Catherine de Médicis, is home to a flock of noisy *paons* (peacocks). The marble fountain in the middle of the garden, decorated with a statue of Diana, goddess of the hunt, and four urinating dogs, dates from 1603.

Le Nôtre's formal, 17th century **Jardin Français** (French Garden), also known as the Grand Parterre, is east of the **Cour de la Fontaine** (Fountain Courtyard) and the **Étang des Carpes** (Carp Pond). The **Grand Canal** was excavated in 1609 and predates the canals at Versailles by over half a century. The informal **Jardin Anglais** (English Garden), laid out in 1812, is west of the pond. The **Forêt de Fontainebleau**, crisscrossed by paths, begins 500m south of the chateau.

Opening Hours & Entry Fees The interior of the chateau (enter from the Cour du Cheval Blanc) is open daily, except Tuesday, from 9.30 am to 12.30 pm and 2 to 5 pm (no midday closure from June to September and until 6 pm in July and August). The last visitors are admitted an hour before closing time. Tickets for the Grands Appartements and the Musée Napoléon, valid for the day, cost 35FF (23FF for people aged 18 to 25 and, on Sunday, for everyone; free for under 18s). The Musée Chinois is an extra 16FF (12FF reduced price). Conducted tours in English of the Grands Appartements depart several times a day from the staircase near the ticket windows.

The gardens (free entry) are open daily from early morning until sundown. In winter, parts of the garden may be closed if personnel are in short supply.

Musée Napoléonien d'Art et d'Histoire Militaire

Fontainebleau's second museum of Napoleoniana (☎ 01 60 74 64 89), housed in a late 19th century mansion at 88 Rue Saint Honoré, has exhibits of military uniforms and weapons. It is open Tuesday to Saturday from 2 to 5 pm. Tickets cost 10FF (free for children under 12).

Forêt de Fontainebleau

This 250 sq km forest, which surrounds the town of Fontainebleau, is one of the loveliest wooded tracts in the Paris region, boasting oaks, beeches, birches and planted pines. The many trails – including parts of the **GR1** and **GR11** – are great for jogging, hiking, cycling and horse riding. The area is covered by IGN's 1:25,000 scale map No 2417OT, entitled *Forêt de Fontainebleau* (57FF). Michelin's green guide entitled *Île de France* (63FF) has several detailed hiking itineraries. The tourist office sells a small topoguide, *Guide des Sentiers de Promenades dans le Massif Forestier de Fontainebleau* (50FF), whose maps and text (in French) cover almost 20 walks in the forest.

Places to Stay

The two star, 25 room ***Hôtel de la Chancellerie*** (☎ 01 64 22 21 70; fax 01 64 22 64 43), 1 Rue de la Chancellerie, has old-fashioned singles/doubles/triples with toilet and shower for 180/250/320FF from November to March and 240/300/380FF the rest of the year. You might also try the 14 room ***Hôtel La Carpe d'Or*** (☎ 01 64 22 28 64), 21bis Rue Paul Séramy (enter from 7 Rue d'Avon), where singles/doubles/triples with washbasin, bidet and toilet cost 162/194/306FF, and 177/224/358FF with toilet and shower.

The 18 room ***Hôtel Richelieu*** (☎ 01 64 22 26 46; fax 01 64 23 40 17), just north of the chateau at 4 Rue Richelieu, has singles with shower from 240 to 270FF, depending on the season, and doubles from 280 to 310FF. If you want to splurge you should choose the 12 room ***Hôtel de Londres*** (☎ 01 64 22 20 21; fax 01 60 72 39 12) opposite the chateau's main entrance on Place du Général de Gaulle. Doubles with everything go for 350 to 450FF in winter and 550 to 650FF in summer.

Places to Eat

Restaurants Two excellent choices on Rue de France are ***Chez Arrighi*** (☎ 01 64 22 29 43) at No 53, whose *menus* cost 95, 125 and 175FF (closed Monday), and ***Croquembouche*** (☎ 01 64 22 01 57) at No 43, where the *menus* go for 88FF (at lunch), 125FF (till 10 pm) and 195FF. The latter is closed all day Wednesday and for lunch on Thursday. The ***François 1er*** (☎ 01 64 22 24 68), 3 Rue Royale, has excellent specialities from Normandy and Brittany (especially seafood) and *menus* at 98, 125 and 150FF. Expect to pay about 230FF per person if ordering à la carte.

AROUND PARIS

La Guérinière (☎ 01 60 72 04 05), 10-12 Rue Montebello, is an excellent choice for quality French cuisine at affordable prices. The lunch formule is 75FF, four-course dinner *menus* are 108 and 160FF, and there's a simple buffet of salads and cold meats available any time for 55FF. It is open for lunch and dinner except on Tuesday and on Wednesday evening.

The ***Maharaja*** (01 64 22 14 64), an Indian restaurant at 15 Rue Dénecourt, has curries (46 to 69FF) and tandoori dishes (29 to 46FF) as well as starters like *pakoras* and *samosas* for 20 to 24FF. There are lunchtime *menus* for 59 and 89FF and one at dinner for 99FF. It's closed on Sunday.

For Breton crêpes and *galettes*, head for ***Ty Koz*** (☎ 01 64 22 00 55) down the little alleyway from 18 Rue de la Cloche. It is open daily for lunch and dinner to 10 pm.

Pizzeria Mimi (☎ 01 64 22 70 77), 17 Rue des Trois Maillets, has pizzas (43 to 56FF), pastas (42 to 58FF) and more elaborate Italian main courses available daily at lunch and dinner.

Self-Catering The ***Prisunic*** at 58 Rue Grande is open Monday to Saturday from 8.45 am to 7.45 pm; the food section is on the 1st floor.

Getting There & Away

Between 22 and 25 daily commuter trains link Paris' Gare de Lyon with Fontainebleau-Avon (47FF; 40 to 60 minutes); in off-peak periods, there's about one train an hour. The last train back to Paris leaves Fontainebleau a bit after 9.45 pm (just after 10.30 pm on Sunday and holidays).

Getting Around

Cycles La Petite Reine (☎ 01 60 74 57 57), 32 Rue des Sablons, rents mountain bikes year-round for 60/80FF per half-day/day (80/100FF on weekends). A 2000FF deposit is required. The shop is open Monday to Saturday from 9 am to 7.30 pm and to 6 pm on Sunday. During the warm months, bikes can be hired at the train station for 80/120FF for a half-day/day. Ring ☎ 01 64 22 36 14 for information.

VAUX-LE-VICOMTE

✉ 77950

This castle and its magnificent gardens (☎ 01 64 14 41 90) 25km north of Fontainebleau were designed and built by Le Brun, Le Vau and Le Nôtre between 1656 and 1661 as a precursor to their more ambitious work at Versailles. Unfortunately, Vaux-le-Vicomte's beauty turned out to be the undoing of its owner Nicolas Fouquet, Louis XIV's minister of finance. It seems that Louis, seething with jealously that he had been upstaged at the chateau's official opening, had Fouquet thrown into prison, where he died in 1680. Today visitors can view the interior of the castle and the formal gardens daily from April to October from 10 am to 6 pm for 56FF (46FF for students, seniors and those aged six to 16). On the second and last Sunday of every month during that period, there are elaborate fountain shows in the gardens from 3 to 6 pm.

Getting There & Away

Vaux-le-Vicomte is not an easy place to reach. The chateau is 7km north-east of Melun, which is served by RER line D2 from Paris (47FF; 45 minutes). To cover the last stretch, however, you'll have to walk or take a taxi from the Melun station (☎ 01 64 52 51 50) for between 100 and 120FF. If you're under your own steam, take the A4 or the A6 from Paris (53km) or the N6 and the N36 from Fontainebleau.

CHANTILLY

• pop 11,300 ✉ 60500

The elegant town of Chantilly, 48km north of Paris, is best known for its heavily restored but imposing chateau, surrounded by gardens, lakes and a vast forest. The chateau is just over 2km east of the train station. The most direct route is to walk through the Forêt de Chantilly along Route de l'Aigle, but you'll get a better sense of the town by taking Ave du Maréchal Joffre and Rue de Paris to Rue du Connétable, Chantilly's main thoroughfare.

AROUND PARIS

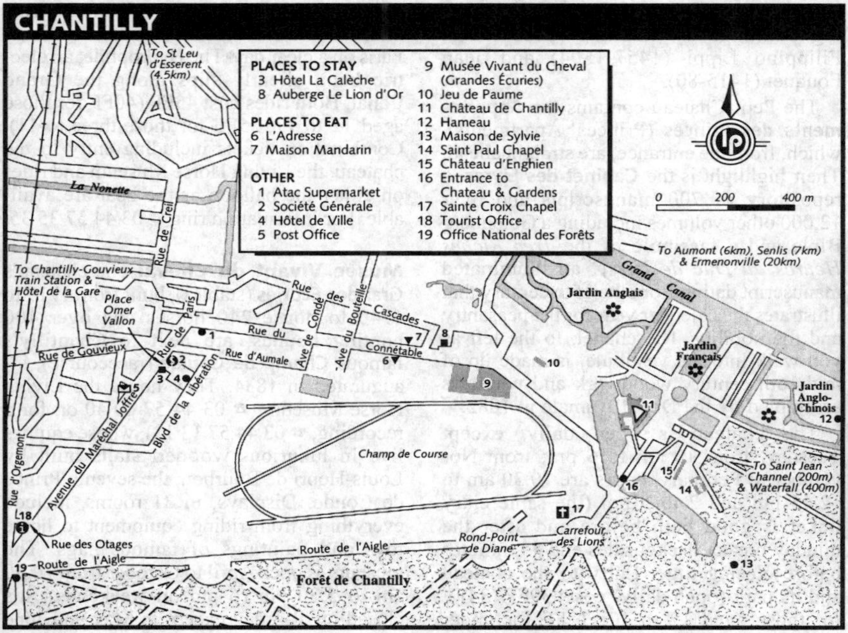

Information

The tourist office (☎ 03 44 57 08 58; fax 03 44 57 74 64), 60 Ave du Maréchal Joffre, is open daily April to September from 9 am to 7 pm. During the rest of the year the Monday to Saturday hours are 9.15 am to 12.45 pm and 2.15 to 6.15 pm.

The Société Générale (☎ 03 44 62 57 00) has a branch at 1 Ave du Maréchal Joffre open Monday to Saturday from 8.30 am till noon and 1.30 to 5.25 pm (4.15 pm on Saturday). There's a post office at 26 Ave du Maréchal Joffre open weekdays from 9 am to 6 pm and on Saturday from 8.30 till noon.

Château de Chantilly

The chateau (☎ 03 44 62 62 62), left in a shambles after the Revolution, is of interest mainly because of its gardens and a number of superb paintings. It consists of two attached buildings entered through the same vestibule. The **Petit Château** was built around 1560 for Anne de Montmorency (1492-1567), who served six French kings as *connétable* (high constable), diplomat and warrior and died in battle against the Protestants. The attached Renaissance-style **Grand Château**, completely demolished during the Revolution, was rebuilt by the Duc d'Aumale in the late 1870s. It served as a French military headquarters during WWI.

The Grand Château, to the right as you enter the vestibule, contains the **Musée Condé**. Its unremarkable 19th century rooms are adorned with furnishings, paintings and sculptures haphazardly arranged according to the whims of the Duc d'Aumale, son of King Louis-Philippe, who donated the chateau to the Institut de France at the end of the 19th century on condition that the exhibits not be reorganised. The most remarkable works are hidden away in a small room called the **Sanctuaire**, including paintings by Raphael (1483-1520), Filippino Lippi (1457-1504) and Jean Fouquet (1415-80).

The Petit Château contains the **Appartements des Princes** (Princes' Apartments), which, from the entrance, are straight ahead. Their highlight is the **Cabinet des Livres**, a repository of 700 manuscripts and over 12,000 other volumes including a Gutenberg Bible and a facsimile of the *Très Riches Heures du Duc de Berry*, an illuminated manuscript dating from the 15th century that illustrates the calendar year for the peasantry and the nobility. The chapel, to the left as you walk into the vestibule, is made up of mid-16th century woodwork and windows assembled by the Duc d'Aumale in 1882.

The chateau is open daily, except Tuesday, from 10 am to 6 pm; from November to February, hours are 10.30 am to 12.45 pm and 2 to 5 pm (the same entry ticket is good both before and after the midday break). Ticket sales end 45 minutes before closing time. Entry to the chateau and its park (open daily) costs 39FF (34FF for those aged 12 to 17; 12FF for under 12s). Entry to the park alone costs 17FF (10FF reduced tariff).

Gardens The chateau's excellent but long-neglected gardens were once among the most spectacular in France. The formal **Jardin Français**, whose flower beds, lakes and Grand Canal were laid out by Le Nôtre in the mid-17th century, is directly north of the main building. To the west, the informal **Jardin Anglais**, was begun in 1817. East of the Jardin Français is the rustic **Jardin Anglo-Chinois** (Anglo-Chinese Garden), created in the 1770s. Its foliage and silted-up waterways surround the **Hameau** (hamlet), a mock rural village whose mill and half-timbered buildings, built in 1774, inspired the Hameau at Versailles.

Activities There are a couple of attractions in the gardens that will keep the kids (and maybe even you) happy. The **Aérophile**, the world's largest hot-air balloon, takes on passengers and soars 150m up into the sky (it's attached to a cable), offering views as far as Paris on a clear day. The **Hydrophile**, an electric boat, silently slips along the Grand Canal. Both rides cost 45FF (40FF for those aged 12 to 17; 25FF for those three to 11). Combination tickets including entry to the chateau, the Living Horse Museum and rides on either the balloon or the boat are available. For information ring ☎ 03 44 57 35 35.

Musée Vivant du Cheval The chateau's **Grandes Écuries** (stables), built from 1719 to 1740 to house 240 horses and over 400 hunting hounds, are next to Chantilly's famous **Champ de Course** (racecourse), inaugurated in 1834. They house the Living Horse Museum (☎ 03 44 57 40 40 or, for a recording, ☎ 03 44 57 13 13), whose equines live in luxurious **wooden stalls** built by Louis-Henri de Bourbon, the seventh Prince de Condé. Displays, in 31 rooms, include everything from riding equipment to horse toys and paintings of famous nags. The museum is open April to October from 10.30 am to 5.30 pm (6 pm on weekends); it's closed on Tuesday except in May and June (open on Tuesday afternoons in July and August). From November to March, the weekday hours are 2 to 5 pm; at the weekend it's open from 10.30 am to 5.30 pm. Entry costs 50FF (40FF for those aged three to 17).

The 30-minute **Présentation Équestre Pédagogique** (Introduction to Dressage Riding), included in the entry price, generally takes place at 11.30 am, 3.30 and 5.15 pm (3.30 pm only from November to March). More elaborate, hour-long demonstrations of dressage riding (80FF, 70FF for children) are held on the first Saturday of the month at 8.30 pm and the first Sunday of the month at 3.15 pm (with an additional one at 4.45 pm from April to October).

Forêt de Chantilly

The Chantilly Forest, once a royal hunting estate, covers 63 sq km. Its tree cover, patchy in places because of poor soil and overgrazing by deer, includes beeches, oaks, chestnuts, limes and pines.

The forest is crisscrossed by a variety of walking and riding trails. In some areas, straight paths laid out centuries ago meet at multi-angled *carrefours* (crossroads). Long-distance trails that pass through the Forêt de Chantilly include the **GR11**, which links the chateau with the town of Senlis (see the following section); the **GR1**, which goes from Luzarches (famed for its 16th century cathedral) to Ermenonville; and the **GR12**, which goes north-eastward from four lakes known as the **Étangs de Commelles** to the Forêt d'Halatte.

The area is covered by IGN's 1:25,000 scale map No 2412OT (57FF), which is entitled *Forêts de Chantilly, d'Halatte and d'Ermenonville*. The *Carte de Découverte des Milieux Naturels et du Patrimoine Bâti* (40FF), a 1:100,000 scale map available at the tourist office, indicates sites of historic and tourist interest (eg churches, chateaus, museums and ruins). *Randonnées autour de Chantilly et Senlis* (24FF), an unbound topoguide available at the tourist office, has details in French on 10 hikes in the vicinity of Chantilly and Senlis.

Places to Stay

The seven room ***Auberge Le Lion d'Or*** (☎ 03 44 57 03 19; fax 03 44 57 92 31), 44 Rue du Connétable, has large and cheery singles with washbasin for 110FF and shower-equipped rooms for two/three people for 180/230FF, or four/five people for 280/330FF. Reception (in the restaurant) is closed on Wednesday. The hotel shuts down from 20 December to 20 January.

Hôtel La Calèche (☎ 03 44 57 02 55), at No 3 of busy Ave du Maréchal Joffre, has rooms for up to three people uniformly priced at 240FF. ***Hôtel de la Gare*** (☎ 03 44 62 56 90; fax 03 44 62 56 99), just opposite the train station on Place de la Gare, is a surprisingly pleasant place with shower-equipped doubles for 290FF.

Places to Eat

The restaurant and crêperie at the ***Auberge Le Lion d'Or***, with *menus* at 114 and 142FF, is highly recommended. Other restaurants on the Rue du Connétable include the bistro-like ***L'Adresse*** (☎ 03 44 57 27 74) at No 49, and the ***Maison Mandarin*** (☎ 03 44 57 00 29), a Chinese restaurant at No 62. L'Adresse has starters from 35 to 48FF, mains for 65 to 90FF, a formule at 95FF and a *menu* for 145FF. It's open for lunch and dinner except Sunday evening and all day Monday from noon to 2 pm and 7 to 10 pm. The Maison Mandarin has starters in the 25 to 35FF range and main courses are 40 to 68FF. It is open for lunch and dinner Tuesday to Sunday.

Midway between the train station and the chateau, the ***Atac*** supermarket at Place Omer Vallon is open Monday to Saturday from 8.30 am to 7.30 pm.

Getting There & Away

Paris' Gare du Nord is linked to Chantilly-Gouvieux train station (☎ 03 44 21 50 50; 41FF; 30 to 45 minutes) by a mixture of RER and SNCF commuter trains, a total of almost 40 a day (26 on Sunday and holidays). In the morning, there are departures from Gare du Nord at least twice an hour; in the evening, there are generally trains back to Paris every hour or so until just before midnight.

The two dozen weekday trains (signposted for a variety of destinations, including Compiègne, Saint Quentin, Amiens and Creil) start at Gare du Nord, where Chantilly-bound trains use both the Grandes Lignes and Banlieue platforms. The bus station is next to the train station.

SENLIS

• pop 15,200 ✉ 60300

Senlis, just 10km north-east of Chantilly through the forest, is an attractive medieval town of winding cobblestone streets, Gallo-Roman ramparts and towers. It was a royal seat from the time of Clovis to Henri IV and contains several fine museums and an important 12th century cathedral. Buses (15FF; 20 minutes) link Senlis with Chantilly about every half-hour.

The Gothic **Cathédrale de Notre Dame**, which is entered through the south portal on Place Notre Dame, was consecrated in 1191. The cathedral is unusually bright, but the stained glass, though original, is unexceptional. The magnificent carved stone **Grand Portal**, on the west side facing the Place du Parvis Notre Dame, has statues and a relief relating to the life of Mary. It was the inspiration for the one at the cathedral in Chartres.

The tourist office (☎ 03 44 53 06 40; fax 03 44 53 29 80) is on the Place du Parvis Notre Dame just opposite (and west) of the cathedral. It is open Wednesday to Monday from 10 am till noon and 2.15 to 6.15 pm.

CHARTRES

• pop 40,000 ✉ 28000

The magnificent 13th century cathedral of Chartres, crowned by two soaring spires – one Gothic, the other Romanesque – rises from the rich farmland 90km south-west of Paris and dominates the medieval town around its base.

The cathedral's varied collection of relics – particularly the Sainte Chemise, a piece of cloth claimed to have been worn by the Virgin Mary when she gave birth to Jesus – attracted many pilgrims during the Middle Ages. Indeed, the town of Chartres has been attracting pilgrims for over 2000 years: Gallic Druids may have had a sanctuary here, and the Romans apparently built themselves a temple dedicated to the Dea Mater (mother goddess), later interpreted by Christian missionaries as prefiguring the Virgin Mary.

Information

The tourist office (☎ 02 37 21 50 00; fax 02 37 21 51 91) is across Place de la Cathédrale from the cathedral's main entrance. From April to September it is open Monday to Saturday from 9 am to 7 pm and on Sunday from 9.30 am to 5.30 pm. During the rest of the year, the Monday to Saturday hours are 10 am to 6 pm and the Sunday ones from 10 am to 1 pm and 2.30 to 4.30 pm. Hotel reservations in the department of Eure-et-Loir cost 10FF (plus a 50FF deposit). The tourist office rents self-guided, one-hour Walkman tours of the old city for 35FF for one person, 40FF for two people sharing (plus a 100FF deposit).

The Banque de France at 32 Rue du Docteur Maunoury is open Monday to Friday from 8.45 am to 12.30 pm and 1.50 to 3.35 pm. The impressive neo-Gothic main post office, Place des Épars, is open Monday to Friday from 8.30 am to 7 pm and on Saturday from 8.30 am to noon.

Cathédrale Notre Dame

Chartres' 130m-long cathedral (☎ 02 37 21 75 02), one of the crowning architectural achievements of western civilisation, was built in the Gothic style during the first quarter of the 13th century to replace a Romanesque cathedral that had been devastated – along with much of the town – by fire on the night of 10 June 1194. Because of effective fundraising among the aristocracy and donations of labour by the common folk, construction took only 25 years, resulting in a high degree of architectural and iconographical unity. It is France's best preserved medieval cathedral, having been spared both post-medieval modifications and the ravages of war and the Revolution (see the boxed text 'Saved by Red Tape').

The cathedral is open daily from 7.30 am (8.30 am on Sunday) to 7.15 pm, except during Mass, weddings and funerals. There are 1½ hour English-language tours conducted by Chartres expert Malcolm Miller (☎ 02 37 28 15 58; fax 02 37 28 33 03) that are held twice daily (noon and 2.45 pm), except on Sunday and holidays, from Easter to sometime in November. The cost is 30FF (20FF for students).

Portals & Towers All three of the cathedral's entrances have superbly ornamented triple portals, but the west entrance, known as the **Portail Royal** (Royal Portal), is the only one that predates the fire. Carved from 1145 to 1155, its superb statues, whose features are elongated in the Romanesque style, represent the glory of Christ. The structure's other main Romanesque feature is the 105m **Clocher Vieux** (Old Bell Tower), also known as the Tour Sud (South Tower), which was begun in the 1140s. It is the tallest Romanesque steeple still standing.

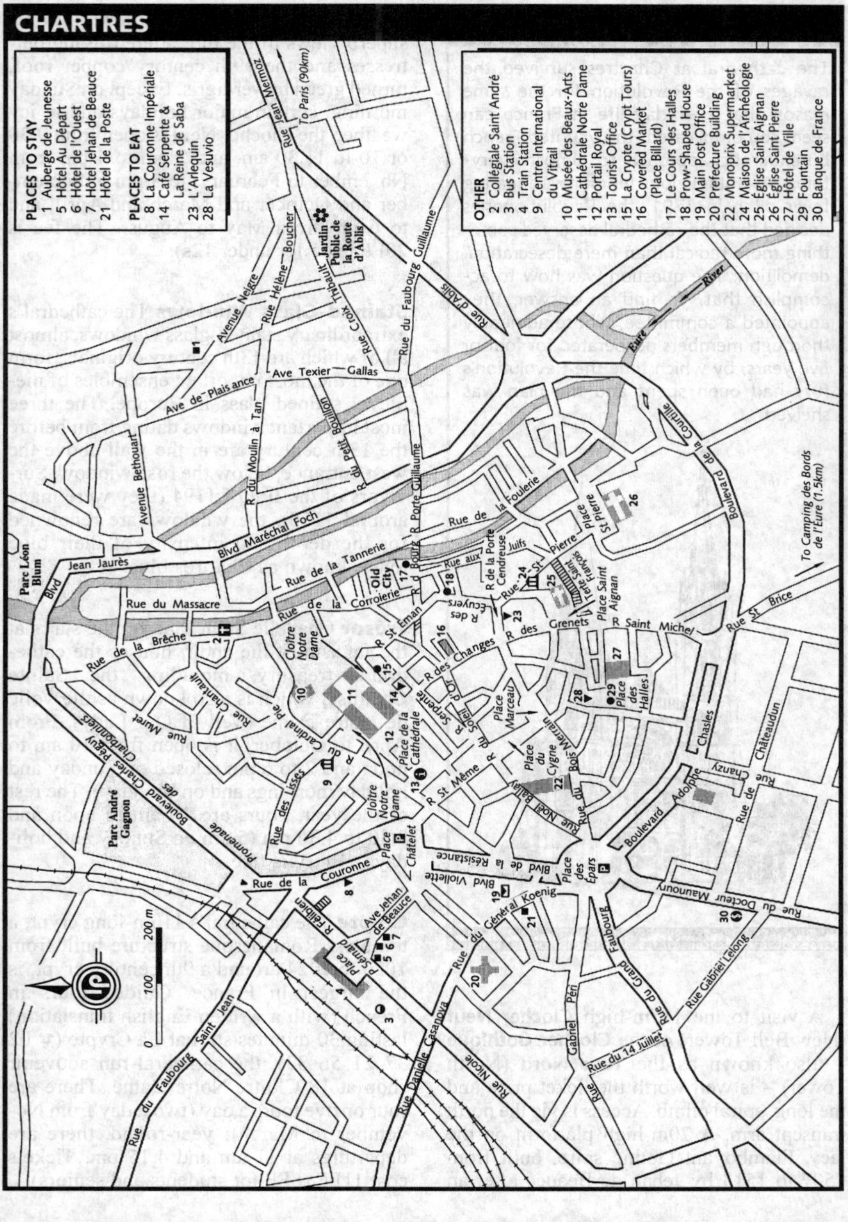

AROUND PARIS

Saved by Red Tape

The cathedral at Chartres survived the ravages of the Revolution for the same reason that everyday life in France can seem so complicated: the vaunted French bureaucratic approach to almost everything. As antireligious fervour was nearing fever pitch in 1791, the Revolutionaries decided that the cathedral deserved something more radical than mere desecration: demolition. The question was how to accomplish that. To find an answer, they appointed a committee, whose admirably thorough members deliberated for four or five years, by which time the Revolution's fury had been spent and the plan was shelved.

A visit to the 115m-high **Clocher Neuf** (New Bell Tower) or the **Clocher Gothique** – also known as the Tour Nord (North Tower) – is well worth the ticket price and the long, spiral climb. Access is via the north transept arm. A 70m-high platform on the lacy, Flamboyant Gothic spire, built from 1507 to 1513 by Jehan de Beauce after an earlier wooden spire burned down, affords superb views of the three-tiered flying buttresses and the 19th century copper roof, turned green by verdigris. Except on Sunday morning, certain major holidays and in icy weather, the Clocher Neuf is open from 9.30 or 10 to 11.30 am, and 2 pm to 4 pm from November to February; to 5 pm in September and October and March and April; and to 6 pm from May to August. The fee is 20FF (free for under 12s).

Stained-Glass Windows The cathedral's extraordinary stained-glass windows, almost all of which are 13th century originals, form one of the most important ensembles of medieval stained glass in Europe. The three most important windows dating from before the 13th century are in the wall above the west entrance, below the rose window. Survivors of the fire of 1194 (they were made around 1150), the windows are renowned for the depth and intensity of their blue tones, known as Chartres blue.

Trésor Chapelle Saint Piat, up the stairs at the far end of the choir, houses the cathedral's treasury, including the Sainte Chemise, which is also known as the Voile de Notre Dame (Veil of Our Lady). From April to October, it is open from 10 am to noon and 2 to 6 pm (closed on Sunday and holiday mornings and on Monday). The rest of the year, hours are 10 am to noon and 2.30 to 4.30 pm (5 pm on Sunday and holidays). Entry is free.

Crypte The cathedral's 110m-long crypt, a tombless Romanesque structure built from 1020 to 1024 around a 9th century crypt, is the largest in France. Guided tours in French (with a written English translation) lasting 30 minutes start at La Crypte (☎ 02 37 21 56 33), the cathedral-run souvenir shop at 18 Cloître Notre Dame. There are four or five tours a day (two a day from November to March); year-round, there are departures at 11 am and 4.15 pm. Tickets cost 11FF (8FF for students and seniors).

Musée des Beaux-Arts

Chartres' Fine Arts Museum (☎ 02 37 36 41 39), 29 Cloître Notre Dame (through the gate next to the cathedral's north portal), is housed in the former **Palais Épiscopal** (Bishop's Palace), most of which was built in the 17th and 18th centuries. Its collections include mid-16th century enamels of the 12 Apostles made by Léonard Limosin for François I, paintings from the 16th to 19th century and wooden sculptures from the Middle Ages. It is open from 10 am to noon and 2 to 5 pm (6 pm from October to May; closed Tuesday and on Sunday morning all year). Entry costs 10FF (5FF for students and people over 60).

Centre International du Vitrail

The International Centre of Stained Glass (☎ 02 37 21 65 72), in a half-timbered former granary at 5 Rue du Cardinal Pie (down the hill from the cathedral's north portal), has three exhibitions a year of contemporary stained glass. It can be visited daily from 9.30 am to 12.30 pm and 1.30 to 6 pm (closed for about two weeks between exhibitions). The entry fee is 20FF (12FF for children, students and seniors).

Old City

Chartres' carefully preserved old city is north-east and east of the cathedral along the narrow western channel of the Eure River, which is spanned by a number of footbridges. From Rue du Cardinal Pie, the stairs known as **Tertre Saint Nicolas** and **Rue Chantault** – the latter is lined with old houses – lead down to the empty shell of the mid-12th century **Collégiale Saint André**, a Romanesque collegiate church closed in 1791 and severely damaged in the early 19th century and 1944.

Rue de la Tannerie, and its continuation **Rue de la Foulerie**, along the river's east bank, are lined with flower gardens, mill-races and the restored remnants of riverside trades: wash houses, tanneries and the like. **Rue aux Juifs** (Street of the Jews) has been extensively renovated. Half a block down the hill there's a riverside promenade and up the hill **Rue des Écuyers** has many houses from around the 16th century, including a prow-shaped, half-timbered structure at No 26 with its upper section supported by beams. **Rue du Bourg** also has some old half-timbered houses.

From Place Saint Pierre, you get a good view of the flying buttresses holding up the 12th and 13th century **Église Saint Pierre**. Once part of a Benedictine monastery founded in the 7th century, it was outside the city walls and was vulnerable to attack; the fortress-like, pre-Romanesque **bell tower** attached to it was used as a refuge by monks and dates from around 1000. The fine, brightly coloured **clerestory windows** in the nave, choir and apse are from the mid-13th and early 14th centuries. It is open daily from 9 am to 5 pm (7 pm in summer).

Église Saint Aignan, Place Saint Aignan, built in the early 16th century, is interesting for its wooden barrel-vault roof (1625) and its painted interior of faded blue and gold floral motifs (circa 1870). The stained glass and the Renaissance Chapelle de Saint Michel date from the 16th century. It's open daily from 8 am to 5 pm (7 pm in summer).

Special Events

For information on the Festival d'Orgue (Organ Festival) in July and August, the Musée des Beaux-Arts' harpsichord festival in May, the Festival de Jazz d'Eure-et-Loir in March, concerts in the cathedral and other cultural events, contact the tourist office.

Places to Stay

Camping About 2.5km south-east of the train station ***Camping des Bords de l'Eure*** (☎ 02 37 28 79 43), 9 Rue de Launay, is open from late April to early September. To get there from the train station or Place des Épars take bus No 8 to the Vignes stop.

Hostel The 70 bed ***Auberge de Jeunesse*** (☎ 02 37 34 27 64; fax 02 37 35 75 85), 23 Ave Neigre, is about 1.5km east of the train station via Blvd Charles Péguy and Blvd Jean Jaurès. A bed in this pleasant and calm

AROUND PARIS

hostel costs about 65FF, including breakfast. Reception is open daily from 2 to 10 pm. Curfew is 10.30 pm in winter and 11.30 pm in summer. To get there from the train station, take bus No 3 to the Rouliers stop.

Hotels The two star, 29 room ***Hôtel de l'Ouest*** (☎ 02 37 21 43 27), 3 Place Pierre Sémard, has somewhat dingy carpeted doubles/triples ranging from 120/170FF (with washbasin and bidet) to 210/260FF (with shower and toilet). The hall shower costs 10FF.

Almost next door is the ***Hôtel Jehan de Beauce*** (☎ 02 37 21 01 41; fax 02 37 21 59 10), on the 1st floor at 19 Ave Jehan de Beauce. This two star, 46 room hotel has clean, decent singles/doubles from 140/160FF (195/225FF with shower and toilet). Triples are also available for 300FF.

You might also try the eight room ***Hôtel Au Départ*** (☎ 02 37 36 80 43), 1 Rue Nicole, where doubles/triples with washbasin and bidet are 110/170FF. Reception (at the bar) is closed on Sunday. The ***Hôtel de la Poste*** (☎ 02 37 21 04 27; fax 02 37 36 42 17), with 57 rooms at 3 Rue du Général Koenig near Place des Épars, has singles with shower for 230FF with shower and toilet (330FF with bath and toilet). Triples/quints cost 370/440FF.

Places to Eat

Restaurants ***L'Arlequin*** (☎ 02 37 34 88 57), 8 Rue de la Porte Cendreuse, features freshly caught fish dishes for 65 to 85FF, with starters for 42 to 70FF and a lunchtime *plat du jour* at 56FF. It's open weekdays for lunch and dinner till 11 pm, and Saturday evening.

The ***Café Serpente*** (☎ 02 37 21 68 81), a brasserie and *salon de thé* at 2 Cloître Notre Dame, serves meals daily from 9 am to 1 am. The plat du jour is 98FF, salads are 35 to 42FF. ***La Reine de Saba*** (☎ 02 37 21 89 16), 8 Cloître Notre Dame, has four lunch *menus* for 59 to 99FF. This casual French restaurant is open daily from 8.30 am to 8 pm (9.30 or 10 pm on weekends and from July to mid-September).

At ***La Vesuvio*** (☎ 02 37 21 56 35), 30 Place des Halles, pizzas (35 to 60FF), salads (42 to 48FF) and light meals are served daily from noon to 3 pm and 7 to 11 pm. ***La Couronne Impériale*** (☎ 02 37 21 87 59), 7-9 Rue de la Couronne, has Chinese and Vietnamese starters for 25 to 42FF, main courses for 38 to 45FF and dim sum for 25FF. *Menus* are available at 58 and 79FF. It's closed on Monday.

Self-Catering There are a number of ***food shops*** around the ***covered market*** on Rue des Changes (open Saturday until about 1 pm). The ***Monoprix*** supermarket at 21 Rue Noël Ballay is open Monday to Saturday from 9 am to 7.30 pm. In the old city, ***Le Cours des Halles***, a grocery at 19 Rue du Bourg, is open daily from 8 am to 7.30 pm (closed on Sunday after 1 pm).

Getting There & Away

There are 36 round trips a day (20 on Sunday) to/from Paris' Gare Montparnasse (71FF one way; 55 to 70 minutes) and Versailles' Chantiers station (59FF; 50 minutes). The last train back to Paris leaves Chartres a bit after 9 pm (7.40 pm on Saturday, sometime after 10 pm on Sunday and holidays).

BEAUVAIS

• pop 55,000 ✉ 60000

The soaring Cathédrale Saint Pierre, whose 48m-high choir has the highest Gothic vaults ever built, and the town's fine museums make Beauvais a great day trip from Paris – or a fine stopover on your way between northern France and the French capital. Beauvais, prefecture of the Oise department, is 81km north of Paris.

Information

The less-than-interested tourist office (☎ 03 44 45 08 18; fax 03 44 45 63 95), 1 Rue Beauregard, on the other side of the Galerie Nationale de la Tapisserie from the cathedral, is open May to October on Monday from 10 am to 1 pm and 2 to 6 pm, Tuesday to Saturday from 9.30 am to 7 pm, and Sunday from 10 am to 5 pm. During the rest of the year it's open Monday to Saturday from 9.30 am to 6.30 pm and on Sunday from 10 am to 1.30 pm.

The Banque de France at 31 Rue du Docteur Gérard, south of the cathedral along Rue Jean Vast, is open for exchange Monday to Friday from 9.15 am till noon and 1.30 to 3.15 pm.

The post office at 1 Rue Gambetta is open weekdays from 8 am to 7 pm and on Saturday till noon.

Cathédrale Saint Pierre

To enthusiasts, Beauvais' unfinished Gothic cathedral (☎ 03 44 48 11 60) is to church architecture what the Venus de Milo is to sculpture: a fantastically beautiful work with certain key extremities missing, in this case the nave; to others it looks like an up-ended dinosaur, frightening in its sheer mass. When the town's Carolingian cathedral was partly destroyed by fire in 1225, a series of ambitious local bishops and noblemen decided that its replacement should

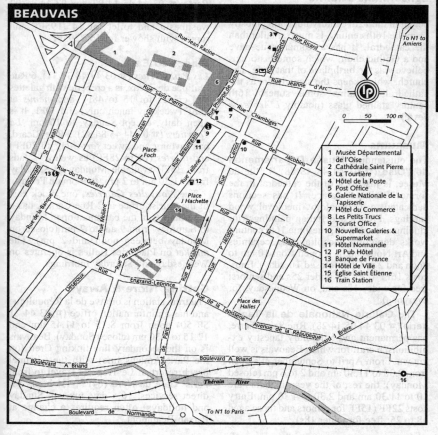

BEAUVAIS

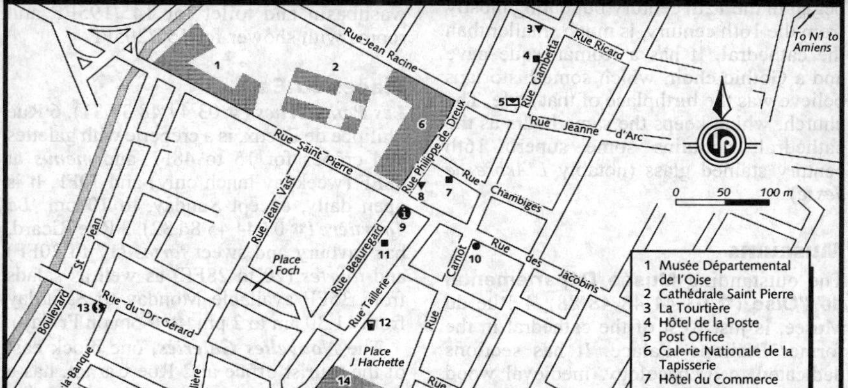

surpass anything ever built. Unfortunately, their soaring and richly adorned creation surpassed not only its rivals but the limits of technology, and in 1272 and again in 1284 the 48m-high vaults collapsed.

The cathedral is open daily from 9 am to 12.15 pm and 2 to 5.30 pm (6.15 pm from May to October). The **astronomical clock** (built 1868) sounds at 10.40 am (Monday to Saturday) and daily at 2.40, 3.40 and 4.40 pm (22FF for adults; 15FF for students; 5FF for children aged four to 14).

Église Saint Étienne

This church on Rue Engrand Leprince, begun in the 12th century but dating mostly from the 16th century, is much smaller than the cathedral. It has a Romanesque nave and a Gothic choir, which some historians believe was the birthplace of that style. The church, which keeps the same hours as the cathedral, contains some superb 16th century stained glass (notably *L'Arbre de Jessé*).

Museums

The outstanding **Musée Départemental de l'Oise** (☎ 03 44 48 48 88), 1 Rue du Musée, is just west of the cathedral in the former Bishops' Palace. It has sections dedicated to archaeology, medieval wood carvings, French and Italian paintings (including a number of gruesome 16th century works depicting decapitations), ceramics and Art Nouveau. It is open from 10 am to noon and 2 to 6 pm (closed Tuesday). Entry costs 16FF (8FF for under 25s and seniors; free for under 18s and, on Wednesday, for everyone).

The **Galerie Nationale de la Tapisserie** (☎ 03 44 05 14 28), Rue Saint Pierre, has permanent and temporary tapestry exhibitions, a craft for which Beauvais is well known. From April to September, it's open from 9.30 to 11.30 am and 2 to 6 pm (closed Monday); the rest of the year, its hours are 10 to 11.30 am and 2.30 to 4.30 pm. Entry costs 22FF (15FF for seniors and those aged 18 to 25; free for under 18s).

Places to Stay

The ***Hôtel Normandie*** (☎ 03 44 45 07 61), 19 Rue Beauregard, a half-block south of the tourist office, has utilitarian doubles from 120FF (140FF with toilet). Reception is closed on Monday.

The cheaper ***Hôtel du Commerce*** (☎ 03 44 48 17 84), 11-13 Rue Chambiges, has basic singles/doubles with washbasin for 100/110FF and ones with shower for 134/144FF. More central is the ***JP Pub Hôtel*** (☎ 03 44 45 07 51; fax 03 44 45 71 25), 15 Place Jeanne Hachette, with rooms with shower from 120/180FF. The ***Hôtel de la Poste*** (☎ 03 44 45 14 97; fax 03 44 45 02 31), 19 Rue Gambetta, has rooms with washbasin and toilet for 145/195FF and rooms with shower for 155/205FF.

Places to Eat

Les Petits Trucs (☎ 03 44 48 31 31), 6 Rue Philippe de Dreux, is a crêperie with galettes and crêpes for 15 to 48FF and *menus* at 58FF (weekday lunch only) and 70FF. It is open daily, except Sunday, to 10 pm. ***La Tourtière*** (☎ 03 44 45 86 32), 3 Rue Ricard, has savoury and sweet *tartes* (17 to 20FF) and *tourtes* (20 to 28FF) as well as salads from 35FF available Monday to Saturday from 11.30 am to 2 pm (to 9 pm on Friday).

The ***Nouvelles Galeries***, one block east of the tourist office at 2 Rue Carnot, has a supermarket in the basement open Monday to Saturday from 9 am to 7 pm (closed on Monday between noon and 2 pm). The ***market*** on Place des Halles is operates on Wednesday and Saturday mornings.

Getting There & Away

The train station is on Ave de la République and has an information office (☎ 03 44 21 50 50) open from 8.15 to 11.45 am and 12.15 to 7.30 pm (closed Sunday). Beauvais is on the secondary line linking Creil (on the Paris-Amiens line) with the Channel beach resort of Le Tréport. Travel to/from Paris' Gare du Nord (64FF; 1½ hours for direct services; 16 a day, nine on Sunday and holidays) often requires a change at Persan-Beaumont.

COMPIÈGNE

• pop 42,000 ✉ 60200

Favoured by the rulers of France as a country retreat since Merovingian times, Compiègne reached the height of its popularity in the mid-19th century under Napoleon III (ruled 1852-70). These days the city, 80km north-east of Paris, is a favourite day trip for Parisians, particularly on Sunday.

On 23 May 1430, Joan of Arc was captured at Compiègne by the Burgundians, who later sold her to their allies, the English. During WWII, thousands of people, including many Jews, were loaded onto trains and sent to Nazi concentration camps from a transit camp in the Compiègne suburb of Royallieu.

Information

The tourist office (☎ 03 44 40 01 00; fax 03 44 40 23 28) is in the 15th century Flamboyant Gothic Hôtel de Ville, on Place de l'Hôtel de Ville opposite the monumental statue of Jeanne d'Arc (complete with its enormous *fleur de lis* banner). It is open Monday to Saturday from 9.15 am to 12.15 pm and 1.45 to 6.30 pm. From mid-April to October it also opens on Sunday from 9.30 am to 12.30 pm and 2.30 to 5 pm.

There's a branch of Société Générale (☎ 03 44 38 57 00) at the corner of Rue Magenta and Rue de l'Étoile, almost opposite the Église Saint Jacques. It is open Tuesday to Saturday from 8.15 am to 12.15 pm and 1.30 to 5.25 pm (4.25 pm on Saturday). The main post office, 7 Rue des Domeliers, is open weekdays from 8 am to 7 pm and on Saturday till noon.

Château de Compiègne

Compiègne's principal draw card is the old royal palace on Place du Général de Gaulle, a favoured hunting ground for generations of French kings and courtiers. Known officially as the Musée National du Château de

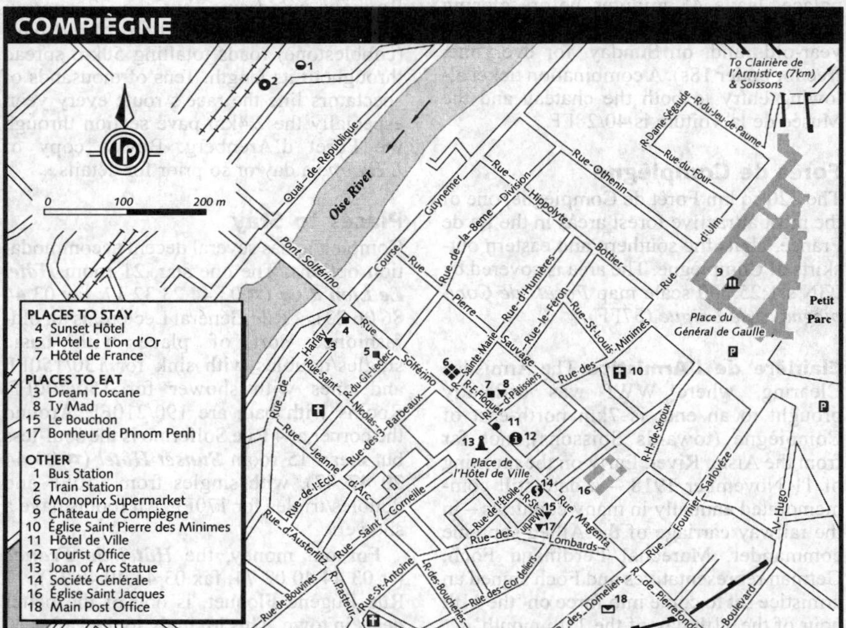

Compiègne (☎ 03 44 38 47 00), it was given its present form between 1752 and 1786 under Louis XV, who commissioned the architect Ange-Jacques Gabriel to rebuild the dilapidated palace left by his great-grandfather, Louis XIV. After the Revolution, the structure – set on the edge of a large forest – was used by Napoleon I, who did some renovation work of his own. Later, it was a special favourite of Napoleon III, who used to throw big hunting parties here.

In addition to the royal apartments, furnished in the styles of the 18th century and the mid-19th century Second Empire and making up the **Musée du Second Empire**, the palace complex houses the **Musée de la Voiture** (☎ 03 44 38 67 00), which displays early motorcars as well as vehicles that predate the age of the internal combustion engine. Except on Tuesday, the chateau is open from 9.15 am to 4.30 pm (6.15 pm from April to September). The last tours (in French), which is the only way to see the palace, leave 45 minutes before closing time. Admission is 35FF (23FF for 18 to 25-year-olds and, on Sunday, for everyone; free for under 18s). A combination ticket allowing entry to both the chateau and the Musée de la Voiture is 40/28FF.

Forêt de Compiègne

The 220 sq km Forêt de Compiègne, one of the most attractive forest areas in the Île de France, abuts the southern and eastern outskirts of Compiègne. The area is covered by IGN's 1:25,000 scale map *Forêts de Compiègne et de Laigue* (57FF).

Clairière de l'Armistice The Armistice Clearing, where WWI was officially brought to an end, is 7km north-east of Compiègne (towards Soissons), not far from the Aisne River. Early on the morning of 11 November 1918 – a date still commemorated annually in many countries – in the railway carriage of the Allied supreme commander, Maréchal Ferdinand Foch, German representatives and Foch signed an armistice set to come into force on 'the 11th hour of the 11th day of the 11th month'.

On 22 June 1940 – shortly after German bombing had destroyed much of Compiègne – in the same railway car, the French were forced to sign the armistice that recognised the German conquest of France. The carriage was later taken for exhibition to Berlin, where it was destroyed by Allied bombing in 1943.

A replica of the original carriage, placed here to commemorate the first signing ceremony (most French guidebooks prefer to forget about the second one) is open daily, except Tuesday, from 9 am to noon or 12.30 pm and 2 to 5.30 pm (6.30 pm from April to mid-October). Admission costs 10FF.

Special Event

Paris-Roubaix, truly one of the world's toughest one-day cycling races, actually starts here in Compiègne, on the first Sunday after Easter. What makes it the 'toughest' for the 170-odd elite cyclists is not so much the 267km of its course to Roubaix *vélodrome*, but the 27 energy-sapping, bone-jarring sections of old *pavé* (cobblestone) roads totalling 50km spread throughout its length. Tens of thousands of spectators line the race's route every year, especially the 2.4km pavé section through the Fôret d'Arenberg. Buy a copy of *L'Équipe* a day or so prior for details.

Places to Stay

Compiègne has several decent accommodation options. The one star, 21 room ***Hôtel Le Lion d'Or*** (☎ 03 44 23 32 17; fax 03 44 86 06 23), 4 Rue Général Leclerc, is an old-fashioned sort of place with basic singles/doubles with sink for 130/150FF and ones with shower for 150/200FF. Rooms with bath are 190/210FF. Around the corner at 4 Rue Solférino is the soul-less but clean 15 room ***Sunset Hôtel*** (☎ 03 44 20 47 47), with singles from 150FF and doubles/triples for 170FF. All rooms have a shower.

For our money, the ***Hôtel de France*** (☎ 03 44 40 02 74; fax 03 44 40 48 37), 17 Rue Eugène Floquet, is one of the better deals in town. This lovingly looked after 20 room hotel has antiques, chintz and dried flowers everywhere and a welcoming, cosy feeling. Simple singles/doubles with washbasin are 110/160FF and 175/250FF with shower. Singles/doubles/triples/quad with bath or shower and toilet are 225/260/400/450FF.

Places to Eat

Restaurants ***Le Bouchon*** (☎ 03 44 40 05 32) is an old-style brasserie in new digs at 5 Rue Saint Martin. Starters and salads are 40 to 70FF, stick-to-the-ribs main courses like *tête de veau*, *bœuf bourguignon*, and *andouilles* range from 48 to 80FF. There's a formule at 69FF.

If you want something lighter to ***Ty Mad*** (☎ 03 44 40 02 64) at 14 Rue des Pâtissiers, which specialises in Breton crêpes and galettes (14 to 39FF). There's a lunch *menu* at 51FF. It is closed on Sunday and Monday.

Rue de Harlay, along the left bank of the Oise River, has a couple of decent restaurants, including the Italian ***Dream Toscane*** (☎ 03 44 23 31 33) at No 5, with pizzas (38 to 52FF) cooked in a wood-burning oven. If you feel like trying Cambodian food (which is sort of like Thai), the friendly, family-run ***Bonheur de Phnom Penh*** (☎ 03 44 40 09 45), 13 Rue des Lombards, has starters for 20 to 30FF, main courses for 32 to 48FF and *menus* at 55FF (lunch) and 80FF. It is open daily, except for lunch on Monday.

Self-Catering There's a ***Monoprix*** at 37 Rue Solférino open Monday to Saturday from 8.30 am to 8 pm. You can also enter from Rue Sainte Marie at the end of Rue Eugène Floquet.

Getting There & Away

Compiègne enjoys frequent rail service from Paris' Gare du Nord (68FF; 1¼ hours). Compiègne's train station is across the Oise River from the town centre.

Getting Around

Bicycles are for rent for the day, week or weekend about 50m to the right as you exit the train station in front of the Brasserie du Nord. Ring ☎ 06 07 54 99 26 for information.

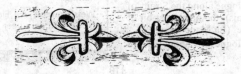

Far Northern France

Many travellers coming from the UK or Belgium first set foot on French soil in the far north, an area made up of the three historical regions at the northern tip of the Hexagon: Flanders (Flandre or Flandres), Artois and Picardy (Picardie). Le Nord de France – densely populated, highly industrialised and with its major heavy industries in decline – is not one of the more fabled corners of France, but if you're up for a short trip from the UK, or inclined to do a little exploring, the region offers lots to do and some excellent dining.

In the Middle Ages, the part of France nearest the Belgian border, together with much of Belgium and a bit of Holland, made up a feudal principality known as Flandres. Even today, many people in the Nord department (along the Belgian border) – especially in the villages – still speak Flemish, which is essentially the same language as Dutch with some differences in vocabulary. Unlike anywhere else in France, the people of the area drink more beer than wine, especially during the carnivals or annual fairs known as *braderies*, when 'giants' (see the boxed text 'The Giants' later in this chapter) come out of hiding to join in the celebrations.

The lively metropolis of Lille, the region's commercial, intellectual and cultural capital, is only two hours from London by Eurostar. Some 50km to the south, the Flemish-style squares in the picturesque city of Arras have no equal anywhere in France. Amiens, not far from a number of sobering battlefield memorials from WWI, is graced by one of France's most magnificent Gothic cathedrals.

Calais' relative prosperity as the premier trans-Channel port has come partly at the expense of its economically depressed rivals, Boulogne-sur-Mer and Dunkerque. The spectacular Côte d'Opale stretches from Calais to Boulogne along the Straits of Dover (Pas de Calais), the narrowest bit of the English Channel (La Manche).

Calais and Boulogne are about 300km north-west of Paris.

HIGHLIGHTS

- **Côte d'Opal** – gaze across at the white cliffs of Dover in England from this spectacular coastline
- **Sangatte** or **Wissant** – lounge in the sun on sandy Channel beaches
- **Lille** – visit the city's superb museums; expore its old town, restaurants and lively nightlife
- **Arras** – stroll among the Flemish-style arcades of the Grand' Place and Place des Héros

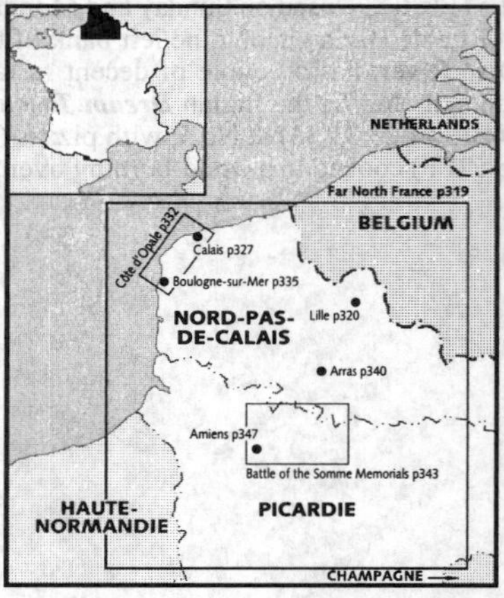

hochepot – a thick Flemish soup made with all sorts of meats and vegetables

freshly cured fish dishes, especially the herrings

Welsh rarebit – a Flemish fondue prepared with dark beer

FAR NORTHERN FRANCE

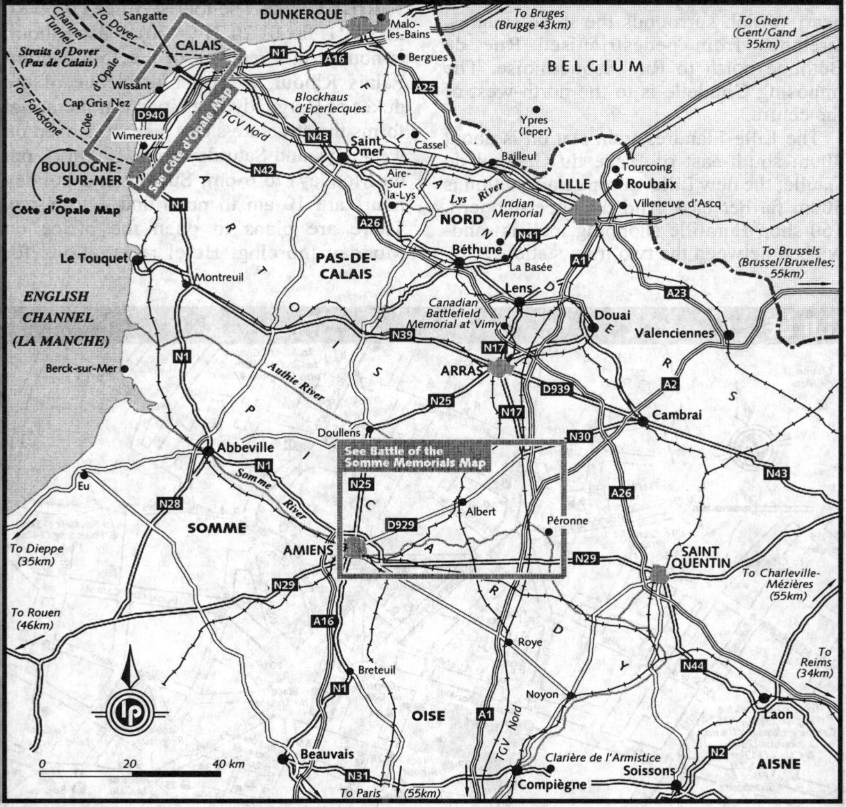

LILLE

• pop 1.1 million

Thanks to the Eurostar and other fast rail links, Lille – France's northern-most metropolis – is an increasingly popular first stop in France for visitors coming from across the Channel and Belgium. Long a major industrial centre – and, a century ago, a symbol of all that was wrong with the Industrial Revolution – today's Lille is a forward-looking place, with two internationally renowned art museums and an attractive old town, graced with ornate Flemish-style buildings, which boasts a lively restaurant and nightlife scene. Also, Charles de Gaulle, one of France's favourite sons, was born in Lille in 1890.

Orientation

Lille is centred around three almost adjacent public squares: Place du Général de Gaulle, also known as the Grand' Place; nearby Place du Théâtre; and Place Rihour, home of the tourist office. Vieux Lille (Old

Town) is north of Place du Général de Gaulle. The city's vibrant commercial heart, which surrounds the three squares, stretches from pedestrianised Rue de Béthune north to Rue Esquermoise. The imposing Citadelle is to the north-west of the centre.

The Lille-Flandres train station is about 400m south-east of Place du Général de Gaulle; the new Lille-Europe train station is 500m farther east. And the super-modern, 160 shop Euralille shopping mall is sandwiched between the two train stations.

Information

Tourist Office The tourist office (☎ 03 20 21 94 21; fax 03 20 21 94 20), Place Rihour, is housed in a remnant of the 15th century Palais Rihour, a former residence of the dukes of Burgundy; the city's war memorial forms the structure's east side. It is open on weekdays and Saturday from 10 am (1 pm on Monday) to 6 pm; Sunday and holiday hours are 10 am to noon and 2 to 5 pm. There are plans to open the office on Monday morning. Hotel reservations for

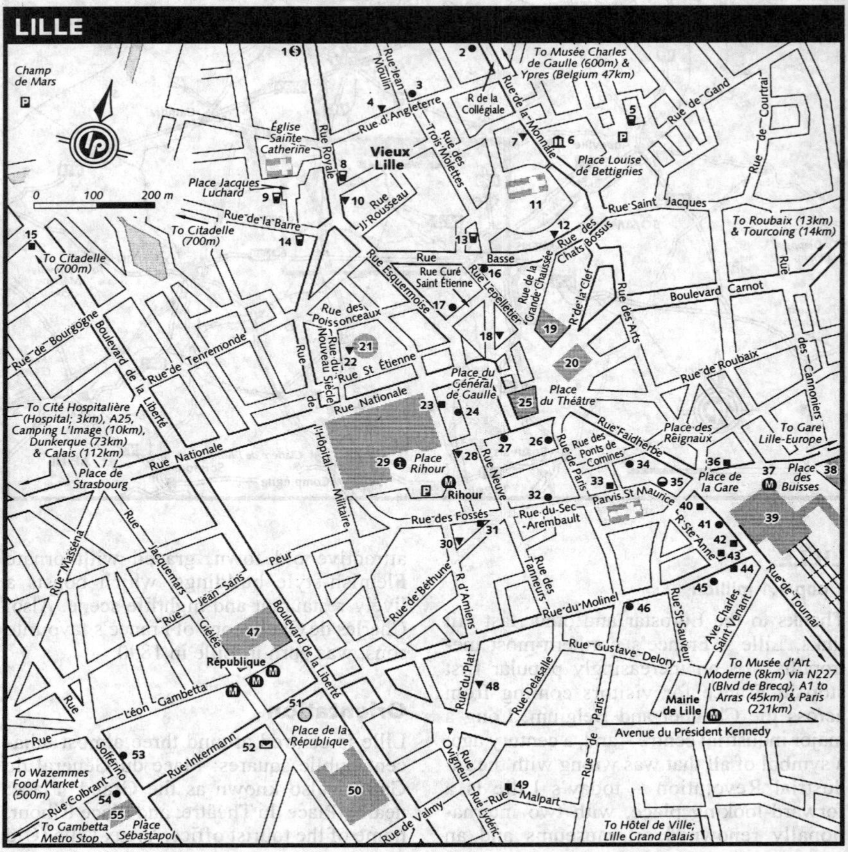

walk-in visitors are free. A brochure of walking tours costs 10FF. Guided walking tours in French (and sometimes also in English) take place in summer.

Money The Banque de France at 75 Rue Royale is open weekdays from 8.30 am to 12.15 pm and 1.15 to 3.45 pm. The tourist office will also change money, but at a mediocre rate.

The Thomas Cook bureau at the Lille-Flandres train station, behind track 8, is open daily from 8 am to 8 pm (10 am to 6 pm on holidays and also, from October to March, on Sunday).

Post The main post office, 8 Place de la République, is open weekdays from 8 am to 7 pm and on Saturday from 8 am to noon. The branch at 1 Blvd Carnot (in the imposing Chambre de Commerce building) closes at 6.30 pm (noon on Saturday). Both do currency exchange.

The city has two postcodes. In central Lille, the postcode of the area east of Blvd de la Liberté is 59800; the area to the west is 59000.

Internet Resources The almost anonymous IRGB Netstation (☎ 03 20 52 94 49), 35 Rue Frédéric Mottez, charges 15/30/50FF for 15/30/60 minutes online. It is open Monday to Saturday from 1 to 9 pm.

Laundry The modern Laverie O'Claire at 57 Rue du Molinel lets you begin your last wash as late as 8 pm and the last dry cycle at 8.30 pm. The Laverie Libre Service at 6 Rue de la Collégiale, a bit north of Vieux Lille, is open daily until 7.30 pm.

Medical Services The Cité Hospitalière (☎ 03 20 44 59 62; metro CHR Oscar Lambret), 3.5km south-west of the city centre, is a large hospital at Place de Verdun. Médecins de Garde de Lille (☎ 03 20 73 57 57) can send a doctor for a house call at night (8 pm to 8 am), on Saturday after 1 pm and on Sunday.

Emergency The Commissariat Central de Police (☎ 03 20 62 47 47; metro Lille Grand Palais), Lille's main police station, is at 6 Blvd du Maréchal Vaillant. It's open 24 hours a day.

LILLE

PLACES TO STAY

- 15 Hôtel Le Globe
- 23 Grand Hôtel Bellevue
- 31 Hôtel de France
- 33 Hôtel Breughel
- 36 Hôtel Flandre-Angleterre
- 40 Hôtel des Voyageurs
- 42 Hôtel Faidherbe
- 43 Hôtel Floréal
- 44 Hôtel Moulin d'Or
- 49 Auberge de Jeunesse

PLACES TO EAT

- 4 African Children
- 7 La Pâte Brisée
- 10 Moroccan Restaurant
- 12 À l'Huîtrière
- 18 La Tarterie de la Voûte
- 22 Le Hochepot
- 28 Brasserie La Chicorée
- 30 Aux Moules
- 48 La Source

OTHER

- 1 Banque de France
- 2 Lavarie Libre Service
- 3 L'Angle Saxo
- 5 Café Oz
- 6 Musée de l'Hospice Comtesse
- 8 L'Illustration Café
- 9 Bar Rocambole
- 11 Cathédrale Notre Dame de la Treille
- 13 Au Lieu d'Elles
- 14 Le Balatum
- 16 Boulangerie
- 17 Fromagerie
- 19 Opéra
- 20 Chambre de Commerce Building; Post Office
- 21 Palais de la Musique
- 24 Furet du Nord Bookshop
- 25 Vieille Bourse
- 26 Le 30
- 27 La Voix du Nord Building
- 29 Tourist Office
- 32 FNAC Billeterie
- 34 Cinéma Metropole
- 35 Eurolines Office
- 37 Gare Lille-Flandres Metro Station; Local-Suburban Bus Terminal
- 38 Euralille Shopping Mall
- 39 Gare de Lille-Flandres
- 41 Europcar Car Rental
- 45 Monoprix Supermarket
- 46 Laverie O'Claire Laundrette
- 47 Préfecture Building
- 50 Palais des Beaux-Arts
- 51 Fountain
- 52 Main Post Office
- 53 Laundrette
- 54 Food Market
- 55 Théâtre Sébastopol

Walking Tour

Place du Général de Gaulle is surrounded by a number of attractive and striking buildings. The ornate, Flemish Renaissance **Vieille Bourse** (Old Stock Exchange), built in 1652, actually consists of 24 separate commercial buildings built around a courtyard. On the south side, the Art Deco home of **La Voix du Nord** (1932), the leading regional daily, has a gilded sculpture of three graces on top. The goddess-topped **column** (1845) in the middle of the fountain commemorates the Austrian siege of Lille in 1792.

Nearby Place du Théâtre is dominated by the neoclassical **Opéra** and the tower-topped neo-Flemish **Chambre de Commerce building**, both built in the early years of the 20th century.

North of Place du Général de Gaulle, **Vieux Lille** (Old Lille), the city's most inviting quarter for wandering, is filled with nicely restored 17th and 18th century houses of brick and stone. The old residences along **Rue de la Monnaie** now house chic shops. Other streets with noteworthy buildings include **Rue de la Grande Chaussée** and **Rue Esquermoise**.

South of the centre at the southern end of Rue de Paris, the **Porte de Paris** is a triumphal arch built between 1685 and 1692 to celebrate the capture of Lille by Louis XIV in 1667. At Place Roger Salengro, the vast, Art Deco-style **Hôtel de Ville**, built from 1924 to 1932, has a slender **beffroi** (belfry). From early April to late September you can climb it on weekdays from 9 to 11 am and 2 to 4 pm, and on Sunday and holidays (but not Saturday) from 9.30 am to noon.

Museums

Lille's truly outstanding **Palais des Beaux-Arts** (Fine Arts Museum; ☎ 03 20 06 78 17; metro République), in a huge, late 19th century building at the southern end of Place de la République, reopened its doors in 1997 after a massive renovation. It has a superb collection of 15th to 20th century paintings and exhibits of archaeology, medieval sculpture and ceramics. Opening hours are noon (from 2 pm on Monday) to 6 pm (8 pm on Friday); closed on Tuesday and bank holidays. Tickets, valid for the whole day, cost 30FF (20FF reduced price).

Hundreds of works of modern art, many from between 1900 and 1940, are on display at the renowned **Musée d'Art Moderne du Nord** (☎ 03 20 19 68 68), 8km east of Lille in the new city of Villeneuve-d'Ascq. Artists represented include Braque, Calder, Léger, Miró, Modigliani and Picasso. It is open daily, except Tuesday, from 10 am to 6 pm. Entry costs 25FF (15FF for students). To get there, take metro line No 1 (towards 4 Cantons) to Pont de Bois; from there take bus No 41 to Parc Urbain-Musée.

The **Musée de l'Hospice Comtesse** (☎ 03 20 49 50 90), 32 Rue de la Monnaie, is housed in a lovely 17th century building that was once a home for the poor; it is named after the Comtesse Jeanne de Flandre, who founded the home in 1236. The wood ceiling of the **Salle des Malades** (Great Hospital Hall) is decorated with Lille tapestries from 1704. Displays include ceramics, faïence wall tiles, 17th and 18th century paintings, furniture and religious art. It is open from 10 am to 12.30 pm and 2 to 6 pm (closed on Tuesday and seven major holidays). Admission costs 15FF (5FF for people aged from 12 to 25).

A few blocks north of Vieux Lille in a now scruffy neighbourhood, the house at 9 Rue Princesse is where Charles de Gaulle was born in 1890. It now houses the **Musée Charles de Gaulle** (☎ 03 20 31 96 03). The building looks much as it did a century ago, which is open from 10 am to noon and 2 to 5 pm (closed Monday, Tuesday and holidays). Entry is 15FF (7FF for those under 12). If the doors are closed ring the bottom bell.

Citadelle

The greatest military architect of the 17th century, Sébastien Le Prestre de Vauban (see the boxed text 'Vauban's Citadels' in the Facts about France chapter), constructed this massive star-shaped fortress, 2.2km in circumference, immediately following the capture of Lille by French forces in

1667. The best preserved of all of Vauban's fortresses, it continues to function as a military base. The outer ramparts, which are open to the public, are surrounded by a large, tree-shaded **park**. On the south-east side there's a **mini-amusement park** and a **children's play area**.

From April to October the tourist office runs two-hour tours (40FF) in French on Sunday afternoon at 3 pm; they begin at Porte Royale, the citadel's main gate.

Special Events

The Fêtes de Lille festival brings street theatre to the city's avenues during the third weekend of June. The Braderie, a vast flea market that fills up almost the whole city centre, is held on the first weekend of September. Based on a different theme each year, the Festival de Lille is a series of concerts and other cultural events that take place over four weeks in September and October. The Festival Mozart, a program of orchestral and opera concerts of works composed mainly by Wolfgang Amadeus, runs from November to early April. Tickets are available from FNAC (see Entertainment). Christmas decorations and the like are on offer at the Marché de Noël (Christmas market), which runs from the end of November to 31 December.

Places to Stay – Budget

Camping *Camping L'Image* (☎ 03 20 35 69 42), 10km north-west of Lille at 140 Rue Brune in the suburb of Houplines, is open year-round. Fees are 18FF for a tent site and 11FF per adult. To get there by car, take the A25 towards Dunkerque and get off at exit No 8 (Chapelle d'Armentières).

Hostel The newly renovated, 170 bed *Auberge de Jeunesse* (☎ 03 20 57 08 94; fax 03 20 63 98 93; aubergedelille@nordnet.fr; metro République or Mairie de Lille), in a former maternity hospital at 12 Rue Malpart, has beds starting at 69FF, including breakfast. Reception is staffed from 8 am to noon and 2 pm to 2 am. It is closed from 20 December to the end of January.

Hotels The two star *Hôtel de France* (☎ 03 20 57 14 78; fax 03 20 57 06 01), 10 Rue de Béthune (the entrance is around the corner on Rue de la Vieille Comédie), has airy singles/doubles with washbasin for 135/190FF (200/255FF with shower and toilet, less on weekends). Hall showers are free. If you arrive by car and would like to unload your luggage, take Rue des Fossés; if the barrier is down push the hotel's button on the barrier's intercom.

The newly gentrified Place de la Gare, next to the Lille-Flandres train station, has quite a few hotels. The *Hôtel des Voyageurs* (☎ 03 20 06 43 14; fax 03 20 74 19 01) at No 10 has simple, clean and fairly large singles/doubles, reached via a vintage lift, starting at 120/150FF (180/220FF with shower and toilet). A hall shower is 10FF. The *Hôtel Faidherbe* (☎ 03 20 06 27 93; fax 03 20 55 95 38) at No 42 has singles/doubles from 130/150FF (210FF with shower and toilet). There's no hall shower.

The quiet, newly redone *Hôtel Floréal* (☎ 03 20 06 36 21; fax 03 20 21 10 76), 21 Rue Sainte Anne, has simple, clean singles/doubles from 120FF (220FF with shower and toilet); there's no hall shower. The one star *Hôtel Moulin d'Or* (☎ 03 20 06 12 67; fax 03 20 06 33 50), 15 Rue du Molinel, also newly refurbished, has very simple, linoleum-floored doubles from 160FF, 195FF with shower, and 215FF with shower and toilet. There are no hall showers. Curfew is midnight.

Near the Citadelle and its park, the 21 room *Hôtel Le Globe* (☎ 03 20 57 29 58) at 1 Blvd Vauban has doubles from 130FF (170FF with shower, 270FF with bath and toilet). There is free parking next to the Citadelle.

Places to Stay – Mid-Range & Top End

The friendly, two-star, 67 room *Hôtel Breughel* (☎ 03 20 06 06 69; fax 03 20 63 25 27), 5 Parvis Saint Maurice, has a range of decent, modern doubles for 170FF (290FF with shower and toilet). The wood and wrought-iron lift is from the 1920s. Enclosed parking is 26FF a night.

Among the two and three star hotels around Place de la Gare you might try the 45 room ***Hôtel Flandre-Angleterre*** (☎ 03 20 06 04 12; fax 03 20 06 37 76) at No 13, which has doubles from 330FF (less on Friday, Saturday and Sunday nights). Two rooms with shower are available for 170FF.

The three-star, Best Western-affiliated ***Grand Hôtel Bellevue*** (☎ 03 20 57 45 64; fax 03 20 40 07 93), 5 Rue Jean Roisin, built in the early part of the century, has very comfortable singles/doubles for 555/595FF.

Places to Eat

Restaurants Lille has an excellent selection of restaurants. Most are closed on Sunday.

Vieux Lille Area The popular, relaxed ***La Pâte Brisée*** (☎ 03 20 74 29 00), 63-65 Rue de la Monnaie, has savoury and sweet *tartes*, salads, meat dishes and the house speciality, gratin, available in one/two/three-course *menus* for 46/69/82FF, including a drink. It is open daily. Tartes (29 to 37FF) and salads are also on offer at the intimate ***La Tarterie de la Voûte*** (☎ 03 20 42 12 16), 4 Rue des Débris Saint Étienne (on the northern side of Place du Général de Gaulle). It is closed on Sunday and on Monday night.

The elegant, brick ***Le Hochepot*** (☎ 03 20 54 17 59), 6 Rue du Nouveau Siècle (in the round Palais de la Musique), serves Flemish dishes such as *coq à la bière* and carbonade (a Flemish beef stew cooked in beer). The *menus* cost 125FF (including drinks) and 140FF (regional dishes). It is closed Saturday for lunch and on Sunday.

À l'Huîtrière (☎ 03 20 55 43 41), at No 3 on the curiously named Rue des Chats Bossus (literally, 'Street of the Hunchback Cats'), has great seafood and traditional French cuisine. Decorated with mosaics dating from 1928, it doubles as a fish shop and gourmet delicatessen. The lunch *menu* is 260FF; mains are about 180FF, à la carte meals cost 300 to 600FF. Reservations are necessary on Friday and Saturday nights. It is open from noon to 2.30 pm and 7 to 9.30 pm (closed on Sunday evening and from late July to late August).

Rue Royale is *the* place for ethnic cuisine; good bets include the ***Moroccan restaurant*** at No 16. African specialities are on offer around the corner at ***African Children*** (☎ 03 20 06 14 54), 44 Rue d'Angleterre, where the *menus* go for 100 to 150FF. Most exotic of all, kangaroo meat and other Down Under specialities are on offer daily, except Sunday, from noon to 3 pm at ***Café Oz*** (see Bars & Pubs under Entertainment).

South of Place de Gaulle There are quite a few restaurants (including a number of pizzerias) in and around the pedestrianised Rue d'Amiens. The brasserie-style ***Aux Moules*** (☎ 03 20 57 12 46), 34 Rue de Béthune, serves Flemish dishes such as Welsh rarebit (fondue prepared with dark beer; 45FF) and, of course, mussels (51FF). It's open daily from noon to midnight.

Brasserie La Chicorée (☎ 03 20 54 81 52), 15 Place Rihour, serves meals (including seafood) all day, every day from 10 am to 4.30 am (until 6 am on Saturday and Sunday mornings). *Menus* start at 68FF. There are other brasseries in the immediate vicinity.

La Source (☎ 03 20 57 53 07), 13 Rue du Plat, is an organic food shop with a vegetarian restaurant out the back. Lunch is served Monday to Saturday from noon to 2 pm; dinner is available on Friday night (7 to 9 pm). The *menus* cost 55 to 75FF. There are a number of ethnic places (Antillean, Spanish, South-East Asian) on the same street; all are closed on Sunday.

Self-Catering The lively ***Wazemmes food market*** (metro Gambetta) at Place Nouvelle Aventure, 1.2km south-west of the centre in the working-class, ethnically diverse Wazemmes quarter, is open nonstop from early morning until 7 pm (closed Monday; most stalls are also closed on Friday). The city's largest ***outdoor market*** takes place nearby on Tuesday, Thursday and Sunday mornings (until 1.30 or 2 pm); Sunday is also flea market day. There's a ***food market*** on Place

FAR NORTHERN FRANCE

Sébastopol (across from 151 Rue Solférino) on Wednesday and Saturday mornings.

The ***Monoprix*** supermarket at 31 Rue du Molinel is open Monday to Saturday from 8.30 am to 8 pm. The vast ***Carrefour*** hypermarket on the top level of the Euralille shopping mall is open until 10 pm (closed Sunday).

In Vieux Lille, the ***fromagerie*** at 3 Rue du Curé Saint Étienne is open Tuesday to Saturday. There's an especially good ***boulangerie*** across the street from 26 Rue Basse (closed Sunday afternoon).

Entertainment

Tickets for cultural events in Lille (and around France and Belgium) are available at the FNAC *billeterie* (ticket agency; ☎ 03 20 15 58 59 for information, ☎ 01 49 87 50 50 in Paris to make reservations), which is across the street from 15 Rue du Sec-Arembault. It is open Monday to Saturday from 10 am to 7.30 pm.

Cinema Nondubbed films are shown daily on the four screens of ***Cinéma Metropole*** (☎ 03 20 15 92 23), 26 Rue des Ponts des Comines.

Classical Music & Jazz The well regarded ***Orchestre National de Lille*** (☎ 03 20 12 82 40) plays in the round Palais de la Musique, which is one block north of Rue Nationale.

Le 30 (☎ 03 20 30 15 54), 30 Rue de Paris, has live jazz nightly (except Sunday) from 10 pm to 4 am. The audience sits on soft, modular couches that make the place look like a 1960s airport VIP lounge. Drinks are 25 to 50FF. There's more live jazz – on Friday and Saturday nights from 10 pm to 2 am – in the cellars of ***L'Angle Saxo*** (☎ 03 20 51 88 89), 36 Rue d'Angleterre. On other nights of the week bands and pianists sometimes make an appearance, also from 10 pm to 2 am. Drinks start at 20FF.

Pubs & Bars ***Café Oz*** (☎ 03 20 55 15 15), 33 Place Louise de Bettignies, the local branch of Paris' famous Australian bar, is very popular with both Lillois and Anglophone students. Foster's on tap costs 15FF for 250mL, but the speciality is cocktails (45FF). It is open daily from 11 am (6 pm on Sunday) to 2 am, becoming a restaurant daily, except Sunday, between noon and 3 pm. There are lots of pubs (and restaurants) nearby, eg on Rue de Gand.

In Vieux Lille, the welcoming, laid-back ***Le Balatum*** (☎ 03 20 57 41 81), 13 Rue de la Barre, is popular; beers start at 13FF. ***L'Illustration Café*** (☎ 03 20 12 00 90), 18 Rue Royale, is a mellow Art Nouveau-style bar with beer from 13FF. Both are open daily until 2 am.

Bar Rocambole, a dark, trendy bar for gay men at 11 Place Jacques Luchard (next to the south side of Église Sainte Catherine), is open Monday to Saturday nights. The small, intimate, women-only ***Au Lieu d'Elles*** (☎ 03 20 51 54 88 or ☎ 03 20 06 61 04), 19 Rue du Cirque (1st floor), is an almost exclusively lesbian *cafette* (mini-café) open on Wednesday evenings (closed in August and perhaps July).

Some of the city's most *branchés* (literally, 'in') and wild pubs and bars are south-west of the centre, along the part of Rue Solférino north of Théâtre Sébastopol.

Getting There & Away

Bus The Eurolines office (☎ 03 20 78 18 88), 23 Parvis Saint Maurice, has direct buses to Brussels (60FF), London (220FF; six hours) and other destinations. It is open from 9 am to 6 or 8 pm (closed on Sunday and, Monday to Wednesday, from noon to 2 pm).

Train Lille has fast, frequent rail links to almost everywhere in France. Its two train stations (☎ 08 36 35 35 35) are linked to each other by metro line No 2 and the tram lines.

Gare Lille-Flandres (metro Gare Lille-Flandres) handles almost all non-TGV (including regional) services and the vast majority of the TGVs to Paris' Gare du Nord (199 to 269FF; one hour; 15 to 26 a day). The information office is open daily from 9 am to 6.45 pm (closed Sunday and holidays).

About 500m to the east, the ultra-modern Gare Lille-Europe (metro Gare Lille-Europe) is used by the Eurostar trains to London (two hours) and the TGVs and Eurostars to Brussels (100FF; 38 minutes; 15 a day); a few of the TGVs to Paris; and all TGVs to destinations not on the TGV-Nord line, including Roissy Charles de Gaulle airport (207 to 267FF), Disneyland-Paris, Lyon (402 to 472FF) and Nice (577 to 677FF; nine hours).

Other options include Paris' Gare du Nord by non-TGV (161FF; 2¼ hours; two a day), Calais (83FF; 1½ hours; seven to 14 a day), Boulogne (104 or 133FF; 2¼ hours; nine a day on weekdays, three on weekends), Arras (52FF; 40 minutes; 11 to 14 a day), Amiens (94FF; 1½ hours; four direct a day), Strasbourg (270FF; 5½ hours; two a day) and Amsterdam (289FF; 3½ to 4¾ hours; 13 a day).

Car There's free, unmetered parking at the Champ de Mars, the huge parking lot between the Citadelle and Vieux Lille; along most of the streets south-west of Rue Solférino; and around the Musée Charles de Gaulle.

Europcar (☎ 03 20 78 18 18) is near the Lille-Flandres train station at 32 Place de la Gare (closed Sunday).

Getting Around

Transpole (☎ 03 20 40 40 40), which has an information window in the Gare Lille-Flandres metro station, runs Lille's two, fully automated metro lines, both of which stop at the Lille-Flandres train station; the two tram lines, both of which serve both train stations; and an extensive network of urban and suburban buses, several of which cross over into Belgium. Tickets, which are sold on the bus but must be purchased (and validated in the orange posts) before boarding the metro or tram, cost 7.80FF. A carnet of 10 (62FF) and a weekly coupon (71FF), good from Monday to Sunday, are available from metro station ticket machines and many *tabacs* (tobacconists). Route maps are available at the tourist office.

CALAIS

• pop 102,000 ✉ 62100

Calais, only 34km from the English town of Dover (Douvres in French), has long been the most popular port for passenger travel between the UK and continental Europe. Its dominance of trans-Channel transport was sealed in 1994 with the opening of the Channel Tunnel, which ducks under La Manche – amid a maze of highways and loading terminals – at Coquelles, 5km south-west of the town centre. More than 20 million people pass through Calais each year as they cross the Straits of Dover, but most continue quickly onward to more alluring destinations: except for a couple of better-than-average museums and Rodin's *The Burghers of Calais*, there's little to see here other than the oversized hypermarkets and the vast Cité de l'Europe shopping mall, designed to attract bargain-hunting British day-trippers. It is, however, a pretty good place for a first or last gourmet meal in France.

The English King Richard I (the Lion-Hearted) helped to launch the town's popularity with trans-Channel travellers in 1190, when he passed through the city on his way to the Third Crusade. The English later so coveted Calais – in part to control its audacious pirates – that King Edward III captured the town in 1346, thus beginning over two centuries of English rule. In mid-1944, the Germans used the Calais area as a base to launch flying bombs against Britain.

Orientation

The flourishing centre of Calais, whose main square is Place d'Armes, is encircled by canals and harbour basins. The Calais-Ville train station is 650m south of Place d'Armes on Blvd Jacquard, the continuation of neon-lit Rue Royale, the main commercial thoroughfare. The centre of the untouristed part of town is 700m farther south along Blvd Jacquard, around Blvd Léon Gambetta and the Place du Théâtre bus hub.

The car ferry terminal is 1.7km north-east of Place d'Armes; the hoverport (for hovercraft and SeaCats) is another 1.5km farther out in the same direction.

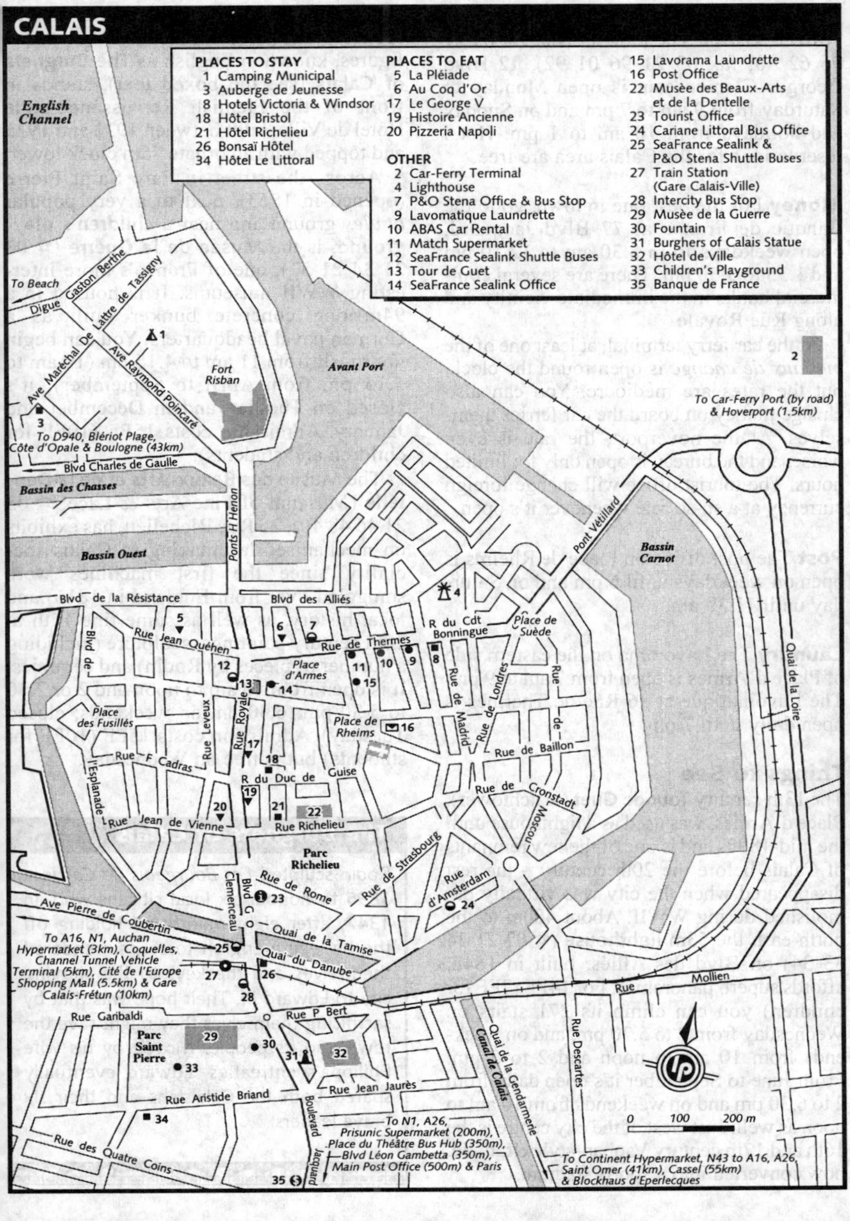
CALAIS
PLACES TO STAY
1 Camping Municipal
3 Auberge de Jeunesse
8 Hotels Victoria & Windsor
18 Hôtel Bristol
21 Hôtel Richelieu
26 Bonsaï Hôtel
34 Hôtel Le Littoral
PLACES TO EAT
5 La Pléiade
6 Au Coq d'Or
17 Le George V
19 Histoire Ancienne
20 Pizzeria Napoli
OTHER
2 Car-Ferry Terminal
4 Lighthouse
7 P&O Stena Office & Bus Stop
9 Lavomatique Laundrette
10 ABAS Car Rental
11 Match Supermarket
12 SeaFrance Sealink Shuttle Buses
13 Tour de Guet
14 SeaFrance Sealink Office
15 Lavorama Laundrette
16 Post Office
22 Musée des Beaux-Arts et de la Dentelle
23 Tourist Office
24 Cariane Littoral Bus Office
25 SeaFrance Sealink & P&O Stena Shuttle Buses
27 Train Station (Gare Calais-Ville)
28 Intercity Bus Stop
29 Musée de la Guerre
30 Fountain
31 Burghers of Calais Statue
32 Hôtel de Ville
33 Children's Playground
35 Banque de France
English Channel
To Beach
Digue Gaston Berthe
Ave Marechal De Lattre de Tassigny
Ave Raymond Poincaré
Fort Risban
Avant Port
To Car-Ferry Port (by road) & Hoverport (1.5km)
To D940, Blériot Plage, Côte d'Opale & Boulogne (43km)
Blvd Charles de Gaulle
Bassin des Chasses
Bassin Ouest
Ponts H Henon
Pont Vétillard
Bassin Carnot
Quai de la Loire
Blvd de la Résistance
Blvd des Alliés
R du Cdt Bonningue
Place de Suède
Rue Jean Quéhen
Rue de Thermes
Place d'Armes
Blvd de l'Esplanade
Place des Fusillés
Rue Leveux
Rue Royale
Place de Rheims
Rue de Madrid
Rue de Londres
Rue de Baillon
Rue F Cadras
R du Duc de Guise
Rue de Cronstadt
Rue Jean de Vienne
Rue Richelieu
Moscou
Parc Richelieu
Rue de Strasbourg
Rue de Rome
Rue d'Amsterdam
Blvd G Clemenceau
Ave Pierre de Coubertin
Quai de la Tamise
Quai du Danube
To A16, N1, Auchan Hypermarket (3km), Coquelles, Channel Tunnel Vehicle Terminal (5km), Cité de l'Europe Shopping Mall (5.5km) & Gare Calais-Frétun (10km)
Rue Mollien
Rue Garibaldi
Rue P Bert
Parc Saint Pierre
Rue Descartes
Quai de la Gendarmerie
Canal de Calais
Rue Jean Jaurès
Rue Aristide Briand
Boulevard Jacquard
Rue des Quatre Coins
0 100 200 m
To N1, A26, Prisunic Supermarket (200m), Place du Théâtre Bus Hub (350m), Blvd Léon Gambetta (350m), Main Post Office (500m) & Paris
To Continent Hypermarket, N43 to A16, A26, Saint Omer (41km), Cassel (55km) & Blockhaus d'Eperlecques

FAR NORTHERN FRANCE

Information

Tourist Office The tourist office (☎ 03 21 96 62 40; fax 03 21 96 01 92), 12 Blvd Georges Clemenceau, is open Monday to Saturday from 9 am to 7 pm and on Sunday and holidays from 10 am to 1 pm. Hotel reservations for the Calais area are free.

Money For the best rate in town, go to the Banque de France at 77 Blvd Jacquard, open weekdays from 8.30 am to 12.10 pm and 1.35 to 3.30 pm. There are several commercial banks in the immediate vicinity and along Rue Royale.

At the car ferry terminal, at least one of the *bureaux de change* is open round the clock, but the rates are mediocre. You can also change money on board the car ferries themselves. At the hoverport, the rate is even worse, and the bureau is open only for limited hours. The tourist office will change foreign currency at a so-so rate whenever it's open.

Post The post office on Place de Rheims is open on weekdays until 6 pm and on Saturday until 11.30 am.

Laundry The Lavorama on the eastern side of Place d'Armes is open from 7 am to 9 pm. The Lavomatique at 36 Rue de Thermes is open daily until 7 pm.

Things to See

The 13th century **Tour de Guet** (watchtower), Place d'Armes, was used as a lighthouse until the mid-1800s and is one of the few remnants of Calais before the 20th century – the rest disappeared when the city was virtually demolished during WWII. About 400m to the north-east, the 53m **lighthouse** (☎ 03 21 34 33 34) on Blvd des Alliés, built in 1848, affords superb panoramas. For 14FF (7FF for children) you can climb its 271 stairs on Wednesday from 2 to 5.30 pm, and on weekends from 10 am to noon and 2 to 5 pm. From June to September it's open daily from 2 to 6.30 pm and on weekends from 10 am to noon as well. Just west of the city centre is the 16th and 17th century Vauban-style **citadelle**, now converted into a sports stadium.

A cast of Auguste Rodin's world-famous bronze statue of six emaciated but proud figures, known in English as **The Burghers of Calais** (see the boxed text), stands in front of the Flemish Renaissance-style Hôtel de Ville, built between 1911 and 1925 and topped with an ornate 75m clock tower.

Across the street in Parc Saint Pierre (opened in 1863), next to a very popular *boules* ground and near a **children's playground**, is the **Musée de la Guerre** (☎ 03 21 34 21 57), one of France's more interesting WWII museums. It is housed in a 94m-long concrete bunker built as a German naval headquarters. You can begin your visit from 11 am to 4.15 pm (10 am to 5.15 pm from April to September); it's closed on Tuesday and in December and January. Admission costs 15FF (10FF for children and students).

The **Musée des Beaux-Arts et de la Dentelle** (Museum of Fine Arts & Lace; ☎ 03 21 46 48 40), 25 Rue Richelieu, has exhibits on mechanised lacemaking (a Calais speciality since the first machines were smuggled over from England in 1816) and local history, as well as some fine 15th to 20th century paintings, sculpture (including a number of pieces by Rodin) and ceramics. It is open from 10 am to noon and 2 or 2.30 to 5.30 pm (6.30 pm on weekends; closed Tuesday). Admission costs 15FF (10FF for students) but is free on Wednesday.

The Burghers of Calais

Rodin sculpted *Les Bourgeois de Calais* in 1895 to honour six local citizens who, in 1347, after eight months of holding off the besieging English forces, surrendered themselves and the keys to the starving city to Edward III. Their hope was that by sacrificing themselves they might save the town and its people. Moved by his wife Philippa's entreaties, Edward eventually spared both the Calaisiens and their six brave leaders.

Calais' sandy, cabin-lined **beach**, from where you can watch huge car ferries sailing off towards the white cliffs of Dover, is a bit under 1km north-west of Place d'Armes. To get there take bus No 3, which continues along the coast westward to 8km-long **Blériot Plage**. It is named after the pioneer French aviator Louis Blériot, who took off from here in 1909 for the first trans-Channel flight.

Places to Stay

Camping The grassy ***Camping Municipal*** (☎ 03 21 97 89 79), just past 16th century Fort Risban on Ave Raymond Poincaré, is open all year. Two people with a tent or camper van are charged 49.80FF. To get there from the train station, take bus No 3 to the Pluviose stop.

Hostel The modern and attractive, 164 bed ***Auberge de Jeunesse*** (☎ 03 21 34 70 20; fax 03 21 96 87 80), also known as the Centre Européen de Séjour, is on Ave Maréchal De Lattre de Tassigny, 200m from the beach. A spot in a two-bed double costs 78FF, including breakfast. Check-in and room access are possible 24 hours a day. To get there from the train station, take bus No 3 to the Pluviose stop.

Hotels Across the park from the train station, the small ***Hôtel Le Littoral*** (☎ 03 21 34 47 28), 71 Rue Aristide Briand, has spacious if spare singles/doubles/quads with washbasin starting at 100/140/180FF; hall showers are 15FF (free if you stay a few days). Reception is closed on Sunday. Plenty of parking is available.

The welcoming ***Hôtel Windsor*** (☎ 03 21 34 59 40; fax 03 21 97 68 59), 2 Rue du Commandant Bonningue, run by an Englishman and his French wife, has decent doubles from 160FF (265FF with shower and toilet). Enclosed parking is available for 30FF. A few doors away at No 8, the two star ***Hôtel Victoria*** (☎ 03 21 34 38 32; fax 03 21 97 12 13) has comfortable singles/doubles from 150/160FF (230/230FF with shower and toilet).

The central and friendly ***Hôtel Bristol*** (☎/fax 03 21 34 53 24), 15 Rue du Duc de Guise, has cosy singles/doubles from 130/160FF (180/220FF with shower and toilet); hall showers are free. Rooms for four and five people are also available.

The family-run ***Hôtel Richelieu*** (☎ 03 21 34 61 60; fax 03 21 85 89 28) is a very quiet, two star place at 17 Rue Richelieu. It has singles/doubles/quads with soft beds and a complete range of amenities for 185/254/314FF.

Right across the street from the train station on Quai du Danube, the prefab, cardboard-walled ***Bonsaï Hôtel*** (☎ 03 21 96 10 10; fax 03 21 96 60 00) has crumbling and utterly characterless rooms for one to three people for 149FF.

Places to Eat

Rue Royale is lined with restaurants and pubs, especially at its northern end.

Restaurants A good bet for a first/last-day splurge in France is the family-run ***La Pléiade*** (☎ 03 21 34 03 70), 32 Rue Jean Quéhen, a truly elegant, mainly seafood restaurant whose *menus* cost 85 and 160FF, not including dessert. Meals are served from noon to 2.30 or 3 pm and 7.30 to 10 pm (closed on Saturday for lunch and on Monday). Another fine French restaurant is ***Le George V*** (☎ 03 21 97 68 00), 36 Rue Royale, where the *menus* range from 95FF (brasserie-style) to 275FF (gastronomique). This place is closed on Saturday for lunch, on Sunday and on holidays in the evening.

Histoire Ancienne (☎ 03 21 34 11 20), a Paris-style bistro at 20 Rue Royale, specialises in meat dishes that are either grilled over a wood fire or cooked in tasty sauces. The *menus* go for 98 to 158FF. It is closed on Monday night and on Sunday. At 31 Place d'Armes, the rustic ***Au Coq d'Or*** (☎ 03 21 34 79 05) serves grilled meat dishes and seafood daily (except Wednesday); the *menus* run from 59 to 245FF.

Pizzeria Napoli (☎ 03 21 34 49 39), 2 Rue Jean de Vienne, serves generous portions of pasta and pizza for 35 to 47FF. It is closed on Monday.

Self-Catering Great places for a picnic include Parc Saint Pierre and Parc Richelieu.

Part of Place d'Armes turns into an outdoor ***food market*** on Wednesday and Saturday mornings. The ***Match*** supermarket on Place d'Armes is open Monday to Saturday from 9.30 am to 12.30 pm and 2.30 to 7.30 pm (no midday break on Saturday; open on Sunday morning in July and August). Near the Banque de France, the ***Prisunic*** supermarket at 17 Blvd Jacquard is open Monday to Saturday from 8.30 am to 7.30 pm, and, from March or April to December, on Sunday from 10 am to 7 pm.

Getting There & Away

For information on the Channel Tunnel and ferry tariffs and schedules, see To/From England under the Land and Sea sections in the introductory Getting There & Away chapter.

Bus Inglard (☎ 03 21 96 49 54) has three buses a day (except Sunday and holidays) from the Calais-Ville train station and Place du Théâtre to Boulogne's Blvd Daunou (27FF; 1¼ hours), via the beautiful Côte d'Opale (the D940) and the many villages en route. Times are posted at the stops. Cariane Littoral (☎ 03 21 34 74 40), 10 Rue d'Amsterdam, has buses from the train station to Saint Omer and express BCD services – intended mainly for students – to Boulogne (38FF) and Dunkerque (40FF).

Train Calais has two train stations: Gare Calais-Ville (also known as Gare Centrale) in the city centre; and Gare Calais-Fréthun, 10km south-west of town in the vicinity of the Channel Tunnel entrance. The train station at the Gare Maritime (ferry terminal) is no longer in operation.

Shop Till You Drop in Calais

The EU has plans – bitterly opposed as we go to press – to end the duty-free discounts available aboard Channel ferries in June 1999. Calais' onshore shops and hypermarkets seem set to continue supplying day-tripping *rosbifs* (Britons) – taking advantage of cheap same-day return fares – with everything except, perhaps, roast beef. Items worth picking up 'on the Continent' include delicious edibles (fresh oysters, foie gras, cheeses, gourmet prepared dishes) and drinks (wine, champagne, beer and spirits) that are hard to find – or much more expensive – in the land of the pound sterling.

The enormous, steel-and-glass **Cité de l'Europe** shopping mall (also known as Cité Europe; ☎ 03 21 46 47 48) is right next to the vehicle loading area for the Channel Tunnel. Its 150 shops include a vast Carrefour hypermarket (open Monday to Saturday from 9 am to 10 pm) and wine shops such as **Victoria Wine** and **Tesco Vin Plus**, where buying in bulk to carry home in the car is easy. Most places in the mall are open from 10 am to 8 pm (9 pm on Friday; closed on Sunday except for the bars, restaurants and cinemas). To get there by car, follow the signs to the 'Tunnel sous La Manche' and then to the Centre Commercial; by public transport, take bus No 7 (8FF) from the Calais-Ville train station.

Calais also has two other hypermarkets, both open Monday to Saturday until about 9 pm. The **Auchan**, 2.5km west of Blvd Jacquard on Ave Roger Salengro (the N1 to Boulogne), is right across the A16 from Cité de l'Europe. It is served by bus No 5. The **Continent**, 2.7km east of Blvd Jacquard on Ave Yervant Toumaniantz, can be reached by bus No 4.

In town, the main shopping area is along Rue Jacquard, Blvd Léon Gambetta and Blvd La Fayette – the latter two thoroughfares intersect Rue Jacquard 700m south of the train station. Warehouses in the industrial estates near the city centre are home to such wine retailers as **Eastenders** and **The Wine and Beer Company**.

At Gare Calais-Ville (☎ 08 36 35 35 35) the information office is open from 9 am to 6.30 pm (5.30 pm on Saturday, closed Sunday). Calais-Ville has direct, non-TGV trains to Paris' Gare du Nord (178FF; 3½ hours; three to six a day), Boulogne (41FF; 35 minutes; 10 to 16 a day), Amiens (115FF; two hours; six to eight a day), Arras (99FF; two hours; four to eight a day) and Lille-Flandres (83FF; 1½ hours; seven to 14 a day). The last train from Calais-Ville to Amiens and Paris is at 6 pm (7 pm on Sunday).

Calais-Fréthun is used by all but one of the TGVs linking Calais with Paris' Gare du Nord (204 to 274FF; 1½ hours; two a day) as well as the Eurostar to London (1¾ hours; one a day). The last Eurostar to Paris departs at 8.20 pm. Around the time that trains arrive or depart, Calais-Fréthun is linked to the Calais-Ville station by Opale Bus No 7 (10FF).

Car To get to the Channel Tunnel's vehicle loading area at Coquelles, follow the road signs on the A16 to the 'Tunnel Sous La Manche' (tunnel under the Channel).

Car rental firms in Calais include ABAS (☎ 03 21 34 67 67), 14 Rue de Thermes, which charges 219/521FF for a day/weekend (including 100km a day). It's closed on Sunday. Eurorent, Hertz, Avis, Budget and Europcar have agencies at Place d'Armes. These same companies, as well as National-Citer, also have bureaus at the car ferry terminal, though they're not always staffed. The rental companies' desks at the hoverport are staffed only when an arriving passenger has made advance reservations.

Boat P&O Stena and SeaFrance Sealink car ferries to and from Dover dock at the very busy, seven-berth car ferry terminal (also known as the Terminal Est), situated a little over 1km north-east of Place d'Armes.

In town, P&O Stena's office (☎ 03 21 46 04 40) at 41 Place d'Armes is open on weekdays from 8.30 am to 6 pm and on Saturday until noon. Also nearby at 2 Place d'Armes is SeaFrance Sealink's office (☎ 03 21 34 55 00), open from 9.30 am to 12.30 pm and 1.30 to 6 pm (5.30 pm on Friday, closed on Saturday afternoon and on Sunday). Both companies' ferry terminal bureaus (☎ 03 21 46 10 10 for P&O Stena, ☎ 03 21 46 80 00 for SeaFrance Sealink) are open 24 hours a day.

SeaCats and hovercraft to/from Dover, operated by Hoverspeed (☎ 0 800 90 17 77 or ☎ 03 21 46 14 14), use the hoverport, which is 3km north-east of the town centre. The hovercraft run up onto the tarmac a few hundred metres from the water's edge; the SeaCats dock nearby.

Getting Around

Bus To get to the car ferry terminal, take one of the free shuttles run by SeaFrance Sealink and P&O Stena – they stop at the Calais-Ville train station and near each company's office at Place d'Armes. Times, coordinated with the arrival and departure of boats, are posted. Hoverspeed's buses to the hoverport (4FF) leave the train station about 45 minutes before each departure.

Local buses, run by Opale Bus (☎ 03 21 00 75 75), operate from a hub at Place du Théâtre, which is 700m south of the train station near the intersection of Blvd Jacquard and Blvd Gambetta. Almost all the lines also stop at the Calais-Ville train station.

Taxi To order a cab, call Eurotaxi (☎ 03 21 97 35 35) or TRL (☎ 03 21 97 13 14). A taxi from the train station to the hoverport costs about 40FF (50FF at night).

AROUND CALAIS

The hilltop village of **Cassel** (population 2200), 29km south of Dunkerque, affords panoramic views of the verdant Flanders plain. It served as Maréchal Ferdinand Foch's headquarters from 1914 to 1915 and, in 1940, was the site of very intensiver rear-guard resistance by British troops defending Dunkerque during the evacuation.

Excellent lunches (and, on Saturday, dinner) are on offer at the friendly, two room ***Hôtel Le Foch*** (☎ 03 28 42 47 73) at 41 Grand' Place.

The quiet town of **Saint Omer** (population 15,000) is known for its **basilica**, the only large Gothic church in the region. The 20 room ***Hôtel Les Frangins*** (☎ 03 21 38 12 47; fax 03 21 98 72 78), 33 Place Victor Hugo, has doubles for 330FF.

The 22m-high **Blockhaus d'Eperlecques** (☎ 03 21 88 44 22), off the D600 between Dunkerque and Saint Omer, was built by the Nazis in 1943 as a V2 rocket assembly and launching site. The construction was carried out by 3000 forced labourers, many of whom were killed in the 25 Allied air raids that eventually prevented the site from becoming operational. It is now a memorial. On weekends in March and daily in April, May, October and November, it can be visited from 2.15 to 6 pm (5 pm in November). From June to September it is open daily until 7 pm.

CÔTE D'OPALE

The 40km of cliffs, sand dunes and beaches between Calais and Boulogne, known as the Opal Coast, are a stunningly beautiful introduction to France, despite the fact that the area is frequently buffeted by gale-force winds. The coastal peaks are dotted with the remains of Nazi Germany's Atlantic Wall, a chain of fortifications and gun emplacements built to prevent an Allied invasion.

Part of the **Parc Naturel Régional Nord-Pas-de-Calais**, the Côte d'Opale area is crisscrossed by hiking paths, including the GR Littoral trail that follows the coast; some routes are also suitable for mountain biking and horse riding (for details, pick up a copy of the free, French-language booklet *Randonnées en Côte d'Opale* at a tourist office).

If you arrive in Calais by car, the Côte d'Opale's main highway, the D940, offers some spectacular vistas. All the sights and villages mentioned below are served by the Calais-Boulogne bus line operated by Inglard (☎ 03 21 96 49 54). See Getting There & Away under Calais for details about schedules and fares.

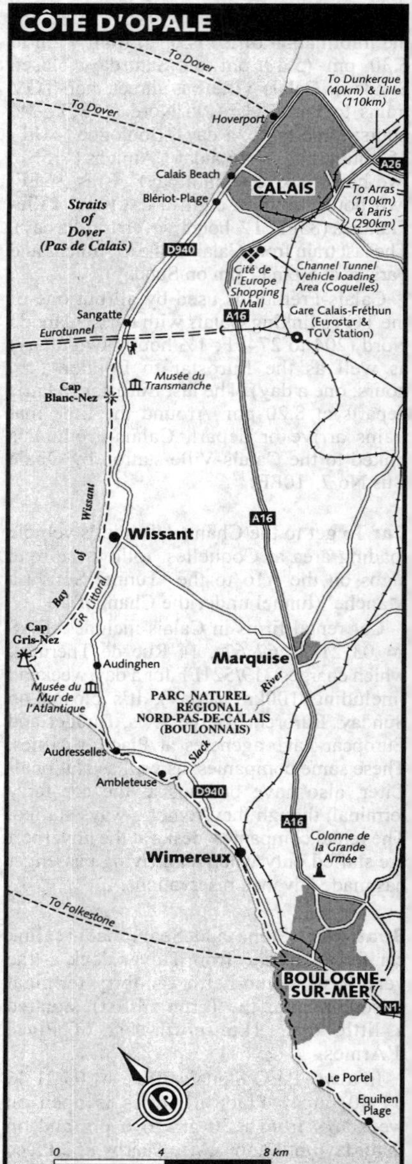

Sangatte

The village of Sangatte, 8km west of Calais, sits right on top of where the Channel Tunnel slips under the Straits of Dover. It is known for its long, dune-lined beach.

Cap Blanc-Nez

The windswept, 134m-high Cap Blanc-Nez affords truly spectacular views of the Bay of Wissant, Cap Gris-Nez, the port of Calais, the verdant Flemish countryside and the cliffs of Kent. The road leading up to the grey **obelisk** honouring the WWI Dover Patrol passes by scrubland dotted with German fortifications and Allied bomb craters.

Atop the bomb-pocked hill across the highway, at the base of the antenna, is the **Musée du Transmanche** (☎ 03 21 85 57 42), whose exhibits relate the history of the many attempts – some serious, others hare-brained – to cross the Channel by balloon, biplane, bridge, tunnel and the like. From April to September it's open daily, except Monday (daily in July and August), from 10 am to 6 pm (tickets sold until 5.15 pm). Admission costs 20FF (15FF for under 18s and students).

Wissant

The cute, upmarket seaside resort of Wissant is midway between Cap Blanc-Nez and Cap Gris-Nez on a vast, fine-sand beach. In 55 BC, Julius Caesar launched his invasion of Britain from here.

Places to Stay Each town along the Côte d'Opale has at least one camping ground – Wissant's municipal ***Camping de la Source*** (☎ 03 21 35 92 46), open from mid-March to November, is only 200m from the beach.

The ***Hôtel Le Vivier*** (☎ 03 21 35 93 61; fax 03 21 82 10 99), on Place de l'Église, has doubles from 270 to 380FF, including breakfast.

Audinghen

The inland village of Audinghen, 3km south-east of Cap Gris-Nez, was rebuilt after being completely destroyed in 1944.

Place to Stay Audinghen has one of the Côte d'Opale's cheapest hotels, the five room ***Hôtel Chez Monique*** (☎ 03 21 87 30 09), 98 Grand' Place, across the highway from the striking, post-war church. Doubles cost 120FF with washbasin and 160FF with shower. Hall showers are not available.

Cap Gris-Nez

Topped by a lighthouse and a radar station intended to keep the 500 ships that pass by here each day from crashing into each other, the 45m-high cliffs of Cap Gris-Nez – the name 'Grey Nose' is actually a corruption of the archaic English 'craig ness', which means 'rocky promontory' – are only 28km from the English coast. The area is a favourite stopping-off point for millions of migrating birds.

About 500m from the roundabout at the turn-off to Cap Gris-Nez is the **Musée du Mur de l'Atlantique** (Atlantic Wall Museum; ☎ 03 21 32 97 33), a WWII museum housed in an artillery emplacement whose 380mm gun could lob 800kg shells all the way to England. From mid-February to October it is open daily from 9 am to 12.30 pm and 1.30 to 6 pm. Admission costs 30FF (12FF for children aged eight to 14).

Ambleteuse

The village of Ambleteuse, on the northern side of the mouth of the Slack River, is blessed by a lovely **beach** once defended from attack by 17th century **Fort Mahon**. A bit south of town is a protected area of grass-covered dunes known as **Dunes de la Slack** (the Slack is a small river).

The large and well organised **Musée 39-45** (☎ 03 21 87 33 01) in Ambleteuse is open daily from April to mid-October from 9.30 am to 7 pm. The rest of the year – except December and January, when it's closed – it's open on weekends and holidays from 10 am to 6 pm. Tickets cost 30FF (20FF for children aged seven to 14), including a film in English.

FAR NORTHERN FRANCE

BOULOGNE-SUR-MER

• pop 44,000 ✉ 62200

Boulogne is by far the most interesting of France's Channel ports. Most of the city is an uninspiring mass of post-war reconstruction, but the attractive Ville Haute (Upper City), perched high above the rest of town, is surrounded by a 13th century wall and endowed with a surprising museum. The city is also home to one of France's premier aquariums. In recent years most trans-Channel vehicle and passenger traffic has moved up the coast to Calais.

Orientation

Central Boulogne consists of three distinct areas: the walled, hilltop Ville Haute, about 1km east of the tourist office along the Grande Rue; the Basse Ville (Lower City), sandwiched between the Ville Haute and the Liane River; and the port area, across the Liane River from the Basse Ville. The commercial district stretches from the tourist office to the Ville Haute and includes the Grande Rue, Rue Faidherbe, Rue Victor Hugo, Rue Adolphe Thiers and Rue de la Lampe. The main train station, Gare Boulogne-Ville, is 1200m south-east of the tourist office along Blvd Daunou.

Information

Tourist Office The tourist office (☎ 03 21 31 68 38; fax 03 21 33 81 09) is on Quai de la Poste and is open Monday to Saturday from 8.45 am to 12.30 pm and 1.30 to 6.15 pm; Sunday hours are 9.30 am to 12.30 pm and 2 to 5.30 pm. In July and August its daily hours are 9 am to 7 pm. Local hotel reservations are free, as is a brochure (in French) on nearby hiking, cycling and equestrian trails.

Money The best rates are available at the Banque de France at 1 Place Angleterre, open weekdays from 8.30 am to noon and 1.15 to 3.30 pm. Several commercial banks have bureaus on or near Rue Victor Hugo. Thomas Cook has exchange bureaus aboard the SeaCats.

Post The main post office, next to the bus hub at Place de France, is open on weekdays from 8 am to 7 pm and on Saturday from 8.30 am to 12.30 pm. Currency exchange is available.

Laundry The Lavomatique at 235 Rue Nationale is open daily from 5.30 am to 9.30 pm. Le Lavoir Boulonnais is at the north-east end of Rue Saint Louis.

Ville Haute

The Upper City is an island of centuries-old buildings and cobblestone streets perched high above the bustle of the Basse Ville. You can walk completely around the Ville Haute atop the rectangular, tree-shaded **ramparts**, a distance of just under 1.5km.

The square, medieval **belfry** of the 18th century Hôtel de Ville (☎ 03 21 87 80 80), open from 8 am to 6 pm (closed Saturday afternoon and Sunday), affords spectacular views of the city; access (free) is from Place Godefroy de Bouillon, named after a local lord crowned King of Jerusalem during the First Crusade. Among the impressive buildings around the square is the neoclassical **Hôtel Desandrouin**, built in the 1780s and later used by Napoleon.

The dominant feature of the Ville Haute is **Basilique Notre Dame** (☎ 03 21 99 75 98), built from 1827 to 1866, whose towering, colonnaded dome (of Italian inspiration) is visible all over town. The interior can be visited, via the side entrance on Rue de Lille, Monday to Saturday from 8 am to noon and 2 to 7 pm. Sunday hours are from 8.30 am to 12.30 pm and 2.30 to 6 pm (7 pm in July and August). The uninteresting, partly Romanesque **crypt** and **treasury** (10/5FF for adults/children) is open from 2 pm (2.30 pm on Sunday) to 5 pm (closed Monday).

Everything from Egyptian and Greek antiquities (including a mummy) to 19th century Inuit masks from Alaska and ceremonial weapons from the South Pacific is on view in the castle-like, moat-encircled **Château-Musée** (☎ 03 21 10 02 20), built by the counts of Boulogne beginning in the

FAR NORTHERN FRANCE

BOULOGNE-SUR-MER

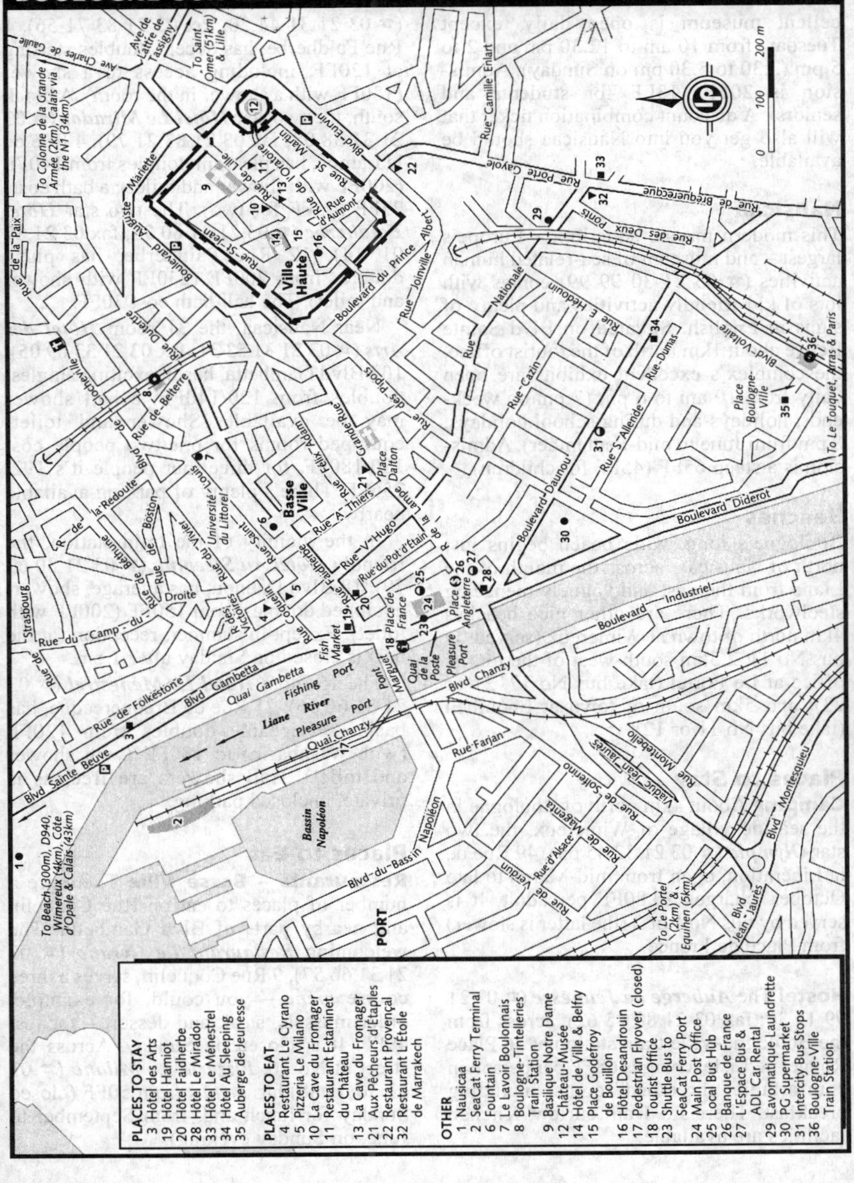
PLACES TO STAY
3 Hôtel des Arts
19 Hôtel Hamiot
20 Hôtel Faidherbe
28 Hôtel Le Mirador
33 Hôtel Le Ménestrel
34 Hôtel Au Sleeping
35 Auberge de Jeunesse
PLACES TO EAT
4 Restaurant Le Cyrano
5 Pizzeria Le Milano
10 La Cave du Fromager
11 Restaurant Estaminet du Château
13 La Cave du Fromager
21 Aux Pêcheurs d'Étaples
22 Restaurant Provençal
32 Restaurant L'Étoile de Marrakech
OTHER
1 Nausicaä
2 SeaCat Ferry Terminal
6 Fountain
7 Le Lavoir Boulonnais
8 Boulogne-Tintelleries Train Station
9 Basilique Notre Dame
12 Château-Musée
14 Hôtel de Ville & Belfry
15 Place Godefroy de Bouillon
16 Hôtel Desandrouin
17 Pedestrian Flyover (closed)
18 Tourist Office
23 Shuttle Bus to SeaCat Ferry Port
24 Main Post Office
25 Local Bus Hub
26 Banque de France
27 L'Espace Bus & ADL Car Rental
29 Lavomatique Laundrette
30 PG Supermarket
31 Intercity Bus Stops
36 Boulogne-Ville Train Station
To Colonne de la Grande Armée (2km), Calais via the N1 (34km)
To Saint Omer (51km) & Lille
To Le Touquet, Arras & Paris
To Le Portel (2km) & Equihen (5km)
To Beach (300m), Wimereux (4km), D940, Côte d'Opale & Calais (43km)
Ville Haute
Basse Ville
PORT
Liane River
Bassin Napoléon
Fishing Port
Pleasure Port
Fish Market
Boulevard du Prince Albert
Boulevard Diderot
Boulevard Industriel
Boulevard Daunou
Blvd Gambetta
Quai Gambetta
Quai Chanzy
Blvd Chanzy
Blvd Sainte Beuve
Blvd-du-Bassin Napoléon
Blvd Montesquieu
Blvd Jean Jaurès
Viaduc Jean Jaurès
Place Dalton
Place de France
Place Angleterre
Place Boulogne-Ville
Quai de la Poste
Grande Rue
Rue Faidherbe
Rue V Hugo
Rue A Thiers
Rue de Lille
Rue St Martin
Rue St Jean
Rue de Brequerecque
Rue des Deux Ponts
Rue Porte Gayole
Rue Nationale
Rue Joinville
Rue Cazin
Rue S Allende
Rue Farjan
Rue de Solferino
Rue de Magenta
Rue d'Alsace
Rue de Verdun
Rue Montebello
Blvd Voltaire
Rue de Folkestone
Rue du Camp de Droite
Rue de la Paix
Ave Charles de Gaulle
Ave de Lattre de Tassigny
0 100 200 m

13th century. Situated at the north-east end of Rue de l'Oratoire, this eclectic but excellent museum is open daily, except Tuesday, from 10 am to 12.30 pm and 2 to 5 pm (2.30 to 5.30 pm on Sunday). Admission is 20FF (13FF for students and seniors). A discount combination ticket that will also get you into Nausicaa should be available.

Nausicaa

This modern marine aquarium – Europe's largest – and museum of sea-related human activities (☎ 03 21 30 99 99) comes with lots of kid-friendly activities and plenty of signs in English. Situated on Blvd Sainte Beuve about 1km north of the tourist office, the complex's excellent exhibits are open daily from 10 am to 6 pm (7 pm on weekends, holidays and during school holidays; 8 pm from June to mid-September). Admission is a steep 65FF (45FF for children).

Beaches

Boulogne's long, wide beach begins just north of Nausicaa, across the mouth of the Liane from the vast and vaguely menacing steelworks. There are other nice beaches 4km north of town at Wimereux (served by bus No 1); 2.5km south-west of the tourist office at Le Portel (take bus No 17, 21 or 23); and 5km south of town at Enquihen (take bus No 11 or 12).

Places to Stay

Camping About 4km north of Boulogne in the seaside village of Wimereux, the two star ***Olympic*** (☎ 03 21 32 45 63), 49 Rue de la Libération, open from mid-March to late October, charges 20.80FF per adult. It is served by bus No 1 or 2 (the latter is slower) from Place de France.

Hostel The ***Auberge de Jeunesse*** (☎ 03 21 99 15 30; fax 03 21 80 45 62), across from the Boulogne-Ville train station at 56 Place Rouget de Lisle, charges 68FF per person in comfortable, three-bed rooms, including breakfast. There's a 1 am curfew. Kitchen facilities are available.

Hotels There are a number of very average places near the river. The ***Hôtel Hamiot*** (☎ 03 21 31 44 20; fax 03 21 83 71 56), 1 Rue Faidherbe, has decent doubles starting at 120FF, including access to a shower (180FF with a shower in the room). A block south, the two star ***Hôtel Le Mirador*** (☎ 03 21 31 38 08; fax 03 21 83 21 79), 4 Rue de la Lampe, has pleasant doubles from 140FF (200FF with shower and toilet); a bath costs 25FF (45FF for two). The two star ***Hôtel Faidherbe*** (☎ 03 21 31 60 93; fax 03 21 87 01 14), 12 Rue Faidherbe, has plush doubles from 200FF (250FF with shower and toilet). The hall bath cost 30FF.

Near Nausicaa, the 31 room ***Hôtel des Arts*** (☎ 03 21 31 53 31; fax 03 21 33 69 05), 102 Blvd Gambetta, has unexciting singles/doubles from 120/140FF; a hall shower may be available. Shower and toilet-equipped rooms for one/two people cost 150/180FF, for three/four people it's 192/256FF. There's plenty of parking available nearby.

In the vicinity of the train station, the friendly ***Hôtel Au Sleeping*** (☎ 03 21 80 62 79), 18 Blvd Daunou, has average, shower-equipped doubles from 150FF (200FF with toilet). Except in summer, reception (at the bar) is closed on Sunday after 1 pm.

The 15 room ***Hôtel Le Ménestrel*** (☎ 03 21 31 60 16), 21 Rue de Bréquerecque, has basic, serviceable doubles from 120FF (with washbasin) to 180FF (with shower and toilet). Hall showers are free, as is private, enclosed parking.

Places to Eat

Restaurants – Basse Ville There are a number of places to eat on Rue Coquelin and nearby parts of Blvd Gambetta. The welcoming ***Restaurant Le Cyrano*** (☎ 03 21 31 66 57), 9 Rue Coquelin, serves a three course *menu* – you could, for example, order mussels, steak and dessert – for just 49FF. It is closed on Sunday. Across the street at No 16, ***Pizzeria Le Milano*** (☎ 03 21 30 01 88) has *menus* from 50FF (closed Sunday for lunch and, from September to June, on Sunday evening).

Walk past the fresh fish on ice at the entrance to ***Aux Pêcheurs d'Étaples*** (☎ 03 21 30 29 29), 31 Grande Rue, and you get to the restaurant, a fine place for a seafood splurge. The 95 and 130FF *menus* are available from noon to 2 pm and 7 to 10 pm (closed Sunday evening).

Have a hankering for a steaming portion of couscous before heading to England? A good choice is ***Restaurant L'Étoile de Marrakech*** (☎ 03 21 31 38 42) at 228 Rue Nationale (closed Wednesday).

Restaurants – Ville Haute The restaurants along pedestrianised Rue de Lille include ***La Cave du Fromager*** (☎ 03 21 80 49 69) at No 30, a cheese restaurant with specialities such as raclette, Welsh rarebit, gratin and fondue Savoyarde. *Menus* are available from 79.50FF (closed Tuesday). ***Restaurant Estaminet du Château*** (☎ 03 21 91 49 66), 2 Rue du Château (across from the entrance to the basilica), is closed on Wednesday night and Thursday; fish and meat *menus* cost from 69 to 168FF.

Just outside the ramparts, ***Restaurant Provençal*** (☎ 03 21 80 49 03), 107 Rue Porte Gayole, serves tasty Moroccan couscous (from 60FF) amid slightly exaggerated Oriental décor.

Self-Catering In the Basse Ville, there's a ***food market*** at Place Dalton on Wednesday and Saturday mornings. The ***PG*** supermarket in the Centre Commercial La Liane at 53 Blvd Daunou is open Monday to Saturday from 8 am to 8 pm. There are a number of ***food shops*** along Rue de la Lampe.

In the Ville Haute there are several ***food shops*** on Rue de Lille, including a ***La Cave du Fromager***, a fromagerie at No 23, open from 9 am to 7 pm (closed on Sunday after 4 pm and on Tuesday).

Getting There & Away

Bus Buses to the Côte d'Opale and Calais stop across the street from 75 Blvd Daunou. For details see Getting There & Away under Calais.

Dumont (☎ 03 21 31 77 48) has four or five buses a day (except Sunday and holidays) from Blvd Daunou that go southward to the beach resorts of Le Touquet (40 minutes) and Berck-sur-Mer (1¼ hours).

Train Boulogne has two train stations: Gare Boulogne-Ville (also known as the Gare Centrale) on Blvd Voltaire, and the smaller, poorly served Gare Boulogne-Tintelleries on Rue de Belterre. The Gare Maritime (ferry terminal) train station is no longer used.

The information office at Boulogne-Ville (☎ 08 36 35 35 35) is open Monday to Saturday from 9.15 am to noon and 2 to 6.45 pm. You can get to Paris' Gare du Nord by regular train (160FF; 2¾ hours; seven a day), TGV (221 to 271FF; only one direct on weekdays) and, from Calais-Fréthun (linked to Calais by SNCF bus), by Eurostar (204FF; 1½ hours; four a day). The Eurostar can also get you to London. Other destinations include Lille-Flandres (104FF; 2¼ hours; nine a day on weekdays, three on weekends), Amiens (91FF; 1¼ hours; five to eight a day), Arras (94FF; two hours; seven on weekdays, three or four on weekends) and Calais (41FF; 40 minutes; 10 to 17 a day).

Car ADL (☎ 03 21 80 97 34), 26 Rue de la Lampe, may be a bit less expensive than Euroto (☎ 03 21 30 32 23), which is at 96 Rue Nationale.

Boat Regular ferry services between Boulogne and the English coast began shortly after 43 AD, when Roman Emperor Claudius launched his conquest of England from here. These days, Calais' dominance of cross-Channel traffic has brought hard times to Boulogne, though the town is still linked to Folkestone (only 45km away) by Hoverspeed's SeaCats (☎ 03 21 30 27 26 at the ferry terminal). For details on tariffs and schedules, see To/From England under Sea in the introductory Getting There & Away chapter.

Getting Around

Bus The local bus company, TCRB, has an information office, known as L'Espace Bus (☎ 03 21 83 51 51), at 14 Rue de la Lampe. Virtually all the lines stop at the main bus hub on Place de France, which is across the street from the tourist office. A single ride costs 6FF.

Shuttle buses coordinated with ferry sailings link the pleasure port side of the main post office with the SeaCat port, a distance of about 600m.

Taxi To order a taxi, ring ☎ 03 21 91 25 00. Count on paying 35FF (45FF at night) to get from the ferry terminal to the Boulogne-Ville train station.

DUNKERQUE

• pop 190,000 ✉ 59140

Dunkerque had the great misfortune of being flattened shortly before one of the most uninspired periods in the whole of western architecture. Some day, this industrial port city may be hailed as having a unique and exceptionally harmonious ensemble of superb, 1950s-style brick low-rise buildings, but until the world develops a taste for the architecture of post-war reconstruction, the town is unlikely to inspire many tourists to reach for their cameras. In recent years, matters have been made worse by the economic crisis that has ravaged the industrial heartland of northern France, leaving shuttered hotels and empty shops in its wake. Unless you're planning to spend some time on the beach or participate in the colourful, pre-Lent carnival festivities, there's little reason to spend the night here.

Under Louis XIV, Dunkerque – whose name means 'church of the dunes' in Flemish – served as a base for French privateers, including the infamous Jean Bart (1650-1702), whose daring attacks on English and Dutch ships have ensured his status as a local hero. Indeed, the city centre's main square, suitably adorned with a dashing statue, bears his name.

These days, Dunkerque is no longer linked to England by ferry.

FAR NORTHERN FRANCE

The Evacuation of Dunkerque

In May and June of 1940, Dunkerque earned a place in the history books when British Expeditionary Force and French and Belgian units found themselves almost completely surrounded by Hitler's armies, which had advanced into far northern France. In an effort to salvage what it could, Churchill's government ordered British units to make their way to Dunkerque, where naval vessels and hundreds of fishing boats and pleasure craft, many manned by civilian volunteers, braved intense German artillery and air attacks to ferry 340,000 men to the safety of England. Conducted in the difficult first year of WWII, this unplanned and chaotic evacuation – dubbed Operation Dynamo – failed to save any of the units' heavy equipment but was seen as an important demonstration of Britain's resourcefulness and determination.

Orientation & Information

The train station is 600m south-west of Dunkerque's main square, Place Jean Bart. The beach and its waterfront esplanade, Digue de Mer, are 2km north-east of the centre – via Ave des Bains – in the suburb of Malo-les-Bains, whose main square is Place Turenne.

The helpful tourist office (☎ 03 28 26 27 28; fax 03 28 63 38 40), in the base of the medieval former belfry on Rue de l'Amiral Ronarc'h, is open from 9 am to 12.30 pm and 1.30 to 6.30 pm (no midday closure on Saturday); Sunday hours are 10 am to noon and 3 to 5 pm. Hotel reservations in the Flandres region are free.

Things to See & Do

The **Musée Portuaire** (Harbour Museum; ☎ 03 28 63 33 39), 9 Quai de la Citadelle, housed in a yellow brick structure built in 1869 as a warehouse for imported tobacco, has lots of splendid ship models and exhibits on the history of Dunkerque as a port. It is open daily, except Tuesday, from 10 am to 12.45 pm and 1.30 to 6 pm (no lunchtime closure in July and August). Entry costs 25FF (20FF for under 18s and students).

The one-hour **boat tours** (☎ 03 28 58 85 12 for reservations) that depart from Place du Minck from April to September (40FF) afford views of the huge port and some of France's most important steelworks and petroleum works.

Dunkerque's wide, promenade-lined beach, **Plage des Alliés**, is about 2km north-east of the city centre at **Malo-les-Bains**, an inexpensive, faded turn-of-the century seaside resort. The tourist office has a map-brochure on walking trails in the **Dewulf and Marchand dunes**, 5km north-east of Malo-les-Bains near Bray-Dunes. To get there, take bus No 2 or 2AM.

Organised Tours

Tours of some of far northern France's industrial plants, both large and small, take place from about 20 July to 20 September. For details contact the tourist offices in Lille, Calais, Boulogne or Dunkerque, or the Chambre Régionale de Commerce et d'Industrie (☎ 03 20 63 79 62; fax 03 20 10 02 00; crcinpdc@nordnet.fr).

Special Events

Dunkerque's carnival, held at the beginning of Lent, evolved into its present form thanks to the town's cod fishermen, for whom it served as a final fling before setting out for months of work in the cold waters off Iceland. The most colourful celebrations take place on the Sundays before and after Mardi Gras – on the first Sunday, costumed locals gather at the Hôtel de Ville, where the mayor and other dignitaries, assembled on the balcony, pelt the crowd with herrings.

Places to Stay

At the train station, one of the best budget bets is the ***Hôtel Au Chemin de Fer*** (☎ 03 28 63 16 98), 24 Rue du Chemin de Fer, whose simple but bright, shower-equipped singles/doubles cost 110/130FF. Across from the tourist office, the two star ***Hôtel du Tigre*** (☎/fax 03 28 66 75 17), 8 Rue Clemenceau, has singles/doubles from 90/130FF (180/230FF with shower and toilet).

ARRAS

• pop 40,000 ✉ 62000

Arras (the final 's' is pronounced), former capital of Artois, is renowned for its harmonious, picturesque ensemble of 17th and 18th century Flemish-style buildings in the town centre. The rest of the city, seriously damaged during both world wars, is nothing to write home about.

Orientation

Arras is centred around the Grand' Place and almost-adjoining Place des Héros (the Petite Place), where you'll find the Hôtel de Ville. The train station is 600m south-east of Place des Héros at the south-eastern end of Rue Gambetta, Arras' main commercial thoroughfare. The commercial centre is around Rue Ronville, in the pedestrianised area south-east of Place des Héros.

Information

Tourist Office The tourist office (☎ 03 21 51 26 95; fax 03 21 71 07 34), inside the Hôtel de Ville at Place des Héros, is open Monday to Saturday from 9 am to noon and 2 to 6 pm, and on Sunday and holidays from 10 am to 12.30 pm and 3 to 6.30 pm. From late April to early October its hours are 9 am (10 am on Sunday and holidays) to 6.30 pm, with a break from 1 to 2.30 pm on Sunday and holidays.

Money The Banque de France at 1 Rue Ernestale changes money Tuesday to Saturday from 9 am to noon. There are lots of commercial banks along Rue Gambetta and its continuation, Rue Ernestale.

Post The post office on Rue Gambetta is open on weekdays from 8 am to 6.30 pm and on Saturday until noon. Currency exchange is possible.

Laundry The Super-Lav at 17 Place d'Ipswich is open daily from 7 am to 8 pm.

ARRAS

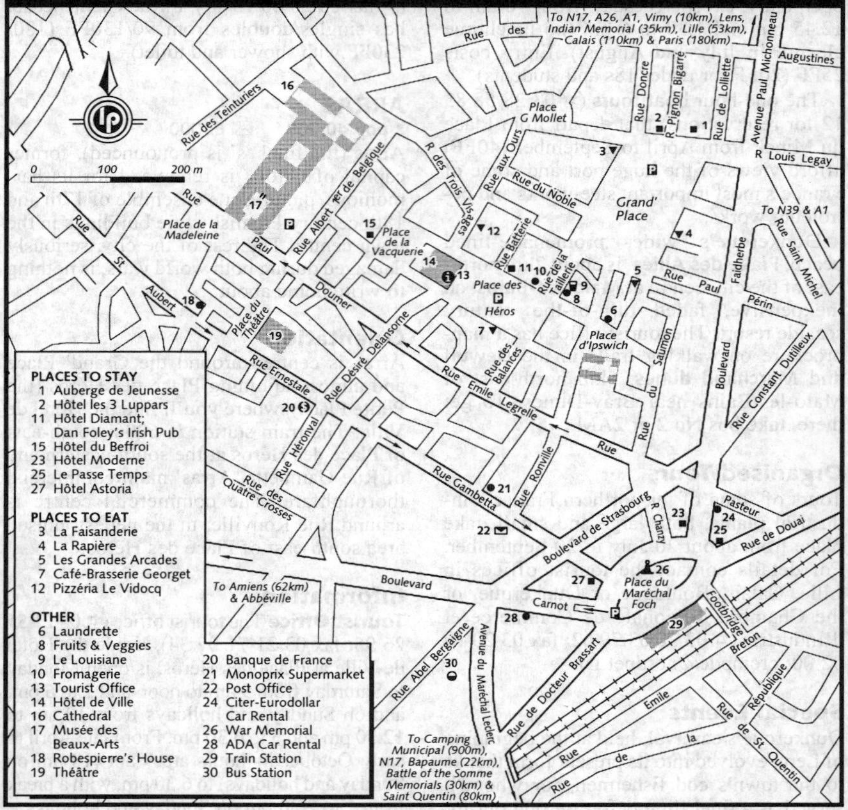

Walking Tour

The city centre's two 11th century market squares, **Place des Héros** and **Grand' Place**, surrounded by some 155 Flemish baroque houses from the 17th and 18th centuries, are the pride of Arras. Although they vary in details (eg the rounded gables are of different sizes), the brick and stone structures have a basic symmetry, and their 345 sandstone columns form a common arcade. The area was heavily damaged in WWII and restoration of the houses was completed only relatively recently.

The Flemish Gothic **Hôtel de Ville** at Place des Héros dates from the 16th century but was completely rebuilt after WWI. Two giants (see the boxed text 'The Giants'), Colas and Jacqueline, are on display in the lobby.

From the basement you can hop on a lift to the top of the 75m **belfry** (14FF/10FF for adults/students), open daily until 6 pm. You can also take a 40 minute guided tour with English translation (20FF/10FF for children/students) of the slimy but fascinating **souterrains** (tunnels) – also known as *boves* (cellars) – under Place des Héros, which were turned into British command posts, hospitals, barracks etc during WWI (at the time, the front lines were only 1500m east of the city centre). Tours generally begin daily at 11 am, 3 and 4.30 pm. A ticket to both and the **Historama**, a slide show covering the city's past, costs 35FF (20FF reduced price).

The **Musée des Beaux-Arts** (Fine Arts Museum; ☎ 03 21 71 26 43), 22 Rue Paul Doumer, is housed in the central section of the neoclassical former Benedictine abbey of Saint Vaast (or Vedast). Displays include the original, 16th century copper lion from the Hôtel de Ville belfry, Gallo-Roman artefacts, medieval sculpture (including a skeletal, recumbent figure from 1446 whose stomach cavity is being devoured by worms), tapestries and paintings. It's open daily, except Tuesday, from 10 am to noon and 2 to 6 pm (5 pm from October to March); Sunday hours are 10 am to noon and 3 to 6 pm. Admission is 20FF (10FF for children, students and seniors; free on the first Wednesday of the month).

The imposing façade of the neoclassical, cruciform **cathedral** (built between 1773 and 1833), just north of the abbey, is decorated with two rows of huge Corinthian columns. Theoretically, the interior can be visited daily from 2.15 to 5 or 6.30 pm.

Just before the Revolution (from 1787-89, to be exact), the Arras-born lawyer and Jacobin radical **Robespierre** lived in the bourgeois, 18th century house (built 1730) at 9 Rue Maximilien Robespierre. It has recently been restored.

The Giants

In far northern France, as in a number of other parts of Western Europe, *géants* (giants) – huge wickerwork body-masks up to 8.5m tall and animated by a person inside – emerge to run about, dance and add to the general merrymaking of local carnivals and feast days. Each has a name and a personality, usually based either on characters from legends or on personages from local history. The giants marry each other and have children, creating, over the years, complicated family relationships. When they get old and tatty they die, providing an occasion for all the locals to turn out for the 'cremation'.

The giants have been a tradition in this region (though nowhere else in France) since the 16th century; nearly 200 of the creatures now 'live' in towns in far northern France, including Dunkerque, Douai, Bailleul, Aire-sur-la-Lys and Cassel. Your best chance to see them is at pre-Lenten carnivals, during Easter (eg Easter Monday) and at summer festivals – dates and places appear in the annual brochure *L'Année des Géants – Fêtes et Sorties*, available at tourist offices.

Places to Stay

Camping The *Camping Municipal* (☎ 03 21 71 55 06), open from April to September, is at 138 Rue du Temple, a 10 minute walk south of the train station along Ave du Maréchal Leclerc. Adults pay 14FF each; there are charges of 8.50FF for a tent and 8FF for a car.

Hostel The central, 54 bed *Auberge de Jeunesse* (☎ 03 21 22 70 02; fax 03 21 07 46 15), 59 Grand' Place, charges 46FF for a bed. Reception is open from 7.30 am to noon and 5 to 11 pm. It is closed in December and January. Curfew is 11 pm. Rooms must be vacated by 10 am.

Hotels Near the train station, the 16 room *Le Passe Temps* (☎ 03 21 71 58 38), 1 Place du Maréchal Foch, has plain but spacious singles/doubles from 130/150FF (210FF with bath and toilet). The two-star, 30 room *Hôtel Astoria* (☎ 03 21 71 08 14; fax 03 21 71 60 95), 10 Place du Maréchal Foch, has singles/doubles in a contemporary style from 220/240FF.

At the Grand' Place, the charming, 42 room *Hôtel des 3 Luppars* (☎ 03 21 07 41 41; fax 03 21 24 24 80) at No 47 occupies the only non-Flemish-style building on the Grand' Place – it's Gothic and dates from 1467, and these days is outfitted with a sauna.

Very comfortable singles/doubles/triples start at 190/260/340FF. The 12-room, two star ***Hôtel Diamant*** (☎ 03 21 71 23 23; fax 03 21 71 84 13), 5 Place des Héros, has unexciting doubles with shower and toilet from 230FF.

The very central, 17 room ***Hôtel du Beffroi*** (☎ 03 21 23 13 78; fax 03 21 23 03 08), 28 Place de la Vacquerie, has recently renovated singles/doubles from 150/170FF (230FF with shower and toilet).

Places to Eat

Restaurants At the Grand' Place, ***La Rapière*** (☎ 03 21 55 09 92) at No 44, which specialises in traditional French and regional cuisine, has *menus* starting at 82FF (closed Sunday night). For a splurge, you might try ***La Faisanderie*** (☎ 03 21 48 20 76), a French restaurant at No 45 with *menus* for 200 and 300FF. It is open from noon to 2 pm and 7.30 to 9.30 pm (closed Sunday night and Monday). The brasserie-style ***Les Grandes Arcades*** (☎ 03 21 23 30 89) at No 10 has *menus* from 84FF and plats du jour for 65FF (open from October to April, closed on Sunday night).

From Monday to Saturday for lunch, the unpretentious ***Café-Brasserie Georget*** (☎ 03 21 71 13 07), 42 Place des Héros, offers a simple, home-made *plat du jour* for 40FF. The popular ***Pizzéria Le Vidocq*** (☎ 03 21 23 79 50), 24 Rue des Trois Visages, has pasta dishes and pizzas (37 to 64FF) baked in a wood-fired oven. It's open from noon to 2 pm and 7 to 10 pm (closed Saturday for lunch and on Sunday).

Near the train station, a number of restaurants can be found along the edges of Place du Maréchal Foch.

Self-Catering ***Food markets*** are held on Wednesday and Saturday mornings (until 1 pm) around the Hôtel de Ville and at the Grand' Place. The boulangerie-equipped ***Monoprix*** supermarket at 30 Rue Gambetta is open Monday to Saturday from 8.30 am to 8 pm.

There's a ***fromagerie*** at 37 Place des Héros (closed from 1 to 2.30 pm and on Sunday and Monday). ***Fruit and vegetables*** are available across the street at 18 Rue de la Taillerie (closed Monday morning and on Sunday).

Entertainment

There are a number of cafés and pubs along the northern side of Place des Héros and along Rue de la Taillerie, the short street linking the two main squares. ***Dan Foley's Irish Pub*** (☎ 03 21 71 46 08), 7 Place des Héros, is open daily until 1 am. There is live music on Thursday, Friday and Saturday nights starting at 10 pm. ***Le Louisiane*** (☎ 03 21 23 18 00), 12 Rue de la Taillerie, which often has live music (especially piano and jazz), is open daily until 1 or 2 am.

Getting There & Away

Bus The information office at the modern bus station (☎ 03 21 51 34 64), on Rue Abel Bergaigne, is open all day until 7 pm (until noon on Saturday; closed Sunday). During school holiday periods, hours are 8 am to noon and 4 to 6.30 pm (closed on Saturday afternoon and on Sunday).

Train The information desk at the train station (☎ 08 36 35 35 35) is open from 8 am to 7 pm (6 pm on Saturday, closed Sunday and holidays).

Arras, on the main Lille-Paris line and other secondary lines, has direct trains to destinations including Paris' Gare du Nord (131FF by non-TGV, 154 to 206FF by TGV; 50 to 90 minutes; six to 13 a day), Albert (39FF; 25 minutes; six to eight a day), Amiens (58FF; 45 minutes; four to six a day), Boulogne (94FF; two hours; seven on weekdays, three or four on weekends), Calais (99FF; two hours; four to eight a day) and Lille-Flandres (52FF; 40 minutes; 11 to 14 a day).

Car ADA (☎ 03 21 24 04 33) is at 60 Blvd Carnot, just west of the train station (closed Sunday). Citer-Eurodollar (☎ 03 21 71 49 14) is at 14 Blvd Faidherbe (closed Saturday afternoon and on Sunday).

Taxi Allo Taxi (☎ 03 21 58 18 17), available 24 hours, can take you around town as well as to nearby battlefield sites.

BATTLE OF THE SOMME MEMORIALS

The WWI Allied offensive known as the First Battle of the Somme, waged in the villages and woodlands north-east of Amiens, was designed to relieve pressure on the beleaguered French troops at Verdun (for more information see the Alsace & Lorraine chapter). On 1 July 1916, British, Commonwealth and French troops 'went over the top' in a massive assault along a 34km front. But German positions proved virtually unbreachable, and on the first day of the battle an astounding 20,000 British troops were killed and another 40,000 were wounded. The majority of the casualties were infantrymen mowed down by German machine guns.

By the time the offensive was called off in mid-November, casualties on all sides had reached 1.2 million. The British had advanced 12km, the French only 8km. The Battle of the Somme has since become a metaphor for the meaningless slaughter of war, and its killing fields have become a site of pilgrimage.

Commonwealth Cemeteries & Memorials

Over 750,000 soldiers from Canada, Australia, New Zealand, South Africa, the Indian subcontinent, the West Indies and other parts of the British Empire died on the Western Front, two-thirds of them in France. By Commonwealth tradition, they were buried where they fell, in over 1000 military cemeteries and 2000 civilian cemeteries. Today, hundreds of neatly tended Commonwealth plots dot the landscape along a wide line running roughly from Albert and Cambrai north via Arras and Béthune to Armentières and Ypres (Ieper) in Belgium. Many of the Commonwealth headstones bear personal inscriptions composed by family members. Some 26 memorials (20 of them in France) bear the names of over 300,000 Commonwealth soldiers whose bodies were never recovered or identified. The French, Americans and Germans reburied their dead in large war cemeteries after the war.

Except where noted, all the monuments listed here are always open. Larger Commonwealth cemeteries usually have a plaque

BATTLE OF THE SOMME MEMORIALS

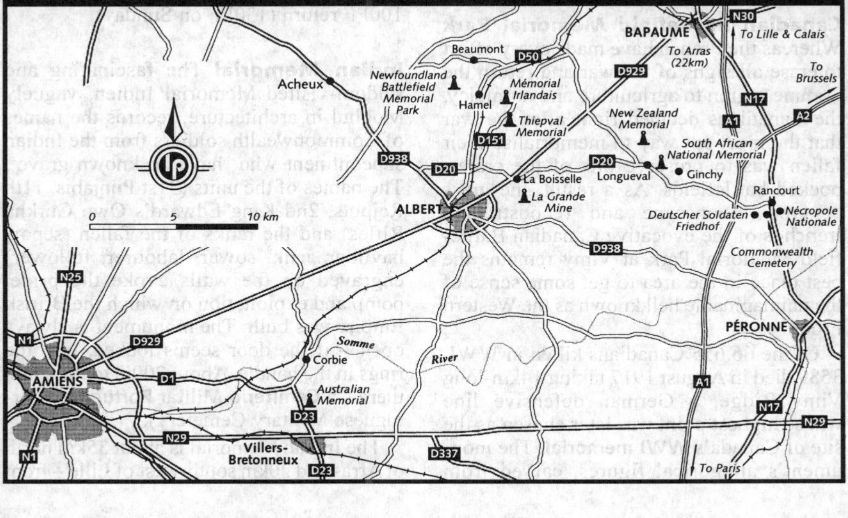

(often inside a little marble pavilion) with historical information in English. Touring the area is only really feasible by car or bicycle.

Maps & Brochures All of the memorials and cemeteries mentioned here (and hundreds of others) are indicated on Michelin's 1:200,000 scale maps. For more complete information, pick up a copy of Michelin's yellow maps Nos 51 and/or 52 overprinted by the Commonwealth War Graves Commission (☎ 03 21 21 77 00 in Beaurains) with all the Commonwealth cemeteries in the region. These are available for 25FF from some tourist offices (eg Arras). The brochure *The Somme – Remembrance Tour of the Great War* (5FF) is also on offer at area tourist offices.

To visit WWI sites farther north, in the departments of Nord and Pas-de-Calais, you might want to pick up *Along the Track of the First World War* (35FF), available at tourist offices (eg in Lille). It provides driving instructions for a car tour.

North of Arras

The area north of Arras has a couple of noteworthy memorials and numerous military cemeteries.

Canadian Battlefield Memorial Park

Whereas the French have made every effort to erase all signs of the war and return the Somme region to agriculture and normalcy, the Canadians decided right after the war that the most apt way to memorialise their fallen was to preserve bits of the crater-pocked battlefields. As a result, the grass covered moonscape and reconstructed **trenches** of the evocative Canadian Battlefield Memorial Park at Vimy remains the best place in the area to get some sense of the unimaginable hell known as the Western Front.

Of the 66,655 Canadians killed in WWI, 3589 died in August 1917 taking 14km-long Vimy Ridge, a German defensive line whose highest point was later chosen as the site of Canada's **WWI memorial**. The monument's allegorical figures, carved from huge blocks of limestone, include a cloaked, downcast female figure representing a young Canada mourning her fallen. The base is inscribed with the names of 11,285 Canadian troops who went missing in action. The 1 sq km park also includes two **Canadian cemeteries** and, at the vehicle entrance to the main memorial, a monument (in French and Arabic) to the **Moroccan Division**.

The information booths at the memorial's parking lot (☎ 03 21 48 79 03) and the trenches (☎ 03 21 48 98 97), usually staffed by Canadian students from April to mid-November and by security guards the rest of the year, have informative brochures (and, when the students are around, free guided tours). The trenches can be visited until sundown, and the memorial is open even later, until the illumination is turned off.

The Canadian Memorial is 10km north of Arras – take the N17 and follow the signs. From Arras, eight trains a day (one on Sunday and holidays) go to the town of Vimy (14FF), 6km east of the memorial. You can also take bus No 20 from Arras (12FF; 20 minutes; seven a day except on Sunday) – ask the driver to let you off at the Vimy Ridge turn-off, 3km from the memorial. A taxi from Arras should cost about 100FF return (130FF on Sunday).

Indian Memorial The fascinating and seldom-visited Mémorial Indien, vaguely Moghul in architecture, records the names of Commonwealth soldiers from the Indian subcontinent who 'have no known grave'. The names of the units (31st Punjabis, 11th Rajputs, 2nd King Edward's Own Gurkha Rifles) and the ranks of the fallen (sepoy, havildar, naik, sowar, labourer, follower) engraved on the walls evoke the pride, pomp and exploitation on which the British Empire was built. The monument is always open – if the door seems locked, turn the rings in the handle. About 200m to the south there's a **Cemiterio Militar Português** (Portuguese Military Cemetery).

The Indian Memorial is about 35km north of Arras and 20km south-west of Lille – from

La Bassée, take the poorly signposted, northbound D947 (marked as the N347 on some signs) to its intersection with the D171.

Around Albert

Some of the bloodiest fighting of WWI took place around the town of Albert, which is on the Amiens-Arras train line. The farmland north and east of the town is dotted with dozens of Commonwealth cemeteries.

Albert's tourist office (☎ 03 22 75 16 42) is at 9 Rue Gambetta, across the street from **Église Notre-Dame de Brebières**, whose 70m tower is topped by a gilded dome and statue of the Virgin Mary. Bicycles (50 or 60FF per day) can be rented year-round from Brasselet Père et Fils (☎ 03 22 75 05 11), 10 Rue Hippolyte Devaux, open from 9 am to noon and 2 to 7 pm (closed on Sunday and Monday).

Australian National War Memorial Situated on a hill from which Australian and British troops repulsed a German assault on 24 April 1918, Australia's National War Memorial at Villers-Bretonneux is a 32m tower on which the names of 10,982 soldiers who went missing in action are engraved. It was dedicated in 1938; only two years later, its stone walls were scarred by German guns as French forces entrenched here briefly slowed Hitler's invading armies. During WWI, 313,000 Aussies (out of a total population of 4.5 million) volunteered for military service; of the 60,000 men who never returned, 46,000 met their deaths on the Western Front.

In the **Commonwealth military cemetery** between the road and the monument there are Australian and Canadian sections. Many of the headstones are marked simply 'A Soldier of the Great War/Known Unto God' from 'An Australian Regiment'.

The Australian memorial is 16km southwest of Albert and 15km east of Amiens – from the latter take the N29 or D1, then the D23. The Villers-Bretonneux train station, linked to Amiens (18FF; 12 minutes; five to seven a day), is 3km south of the memorial.

Newfoundland Battlefield Memorial Park The evocative Parc Terre-Neuvien, site of an infantry assault on German trenches in which the volunteer Royal Newfoundland Regiment was nearly wiped out on 1 July 1916, preserves part of the Western Front as it looked at fighting's end. The zigzag trench system (which still fills with mud in winter) is clearly visible, as are the countless shell craters and the remains of barbed wire barriers. You can get a view of the whole battlefield from the base of the **caribou statue** – in 1918, hundreds of square kilometres of northern France looked like this. Opened in 1925, the memorial sits on land 'purchased with funds subscribed by the government and women of Newfoundland' (as a sign explains).

The park is 8km north of Albert along the D50.

Thiepval Memorial Dedicated to 'the Missing of the Somme', this memorial was built in the early 1930s on the site of a German stronghold that was stormed on 1 July 1916 with unimaginable casualties. The columns of the arches are inscribed with the names of 73,367 British and South African soldiers whose remains were never found. When two or more soldiers have the same surname and first initial, their serial numbers are indicated. Locals still dig up shrapnel from the nearby fields.

In the **Thiepval Anglo-French cemetery** behind the memorial, most of the gravestones are marked either *'Inconnu'* or 'A Soldier of the Great War/Known Unto God'.

Thiepval is about 8km north-east of Albert along the D929, the D20 and finally the D151. These roads pass a number of Commonwealth cemeteries.

Mémorial Irlandais Built on a German frontline position assaulted by the 36th (Ulster) Division on 1 July 1916, the **Tour d'Ulster** (Ulster Tower), dedicated in 1921 and something of a Unionist pilgrimage site, is a replica of Helen's Tower near Bangor, County Down in Northern Ireland, where the unit had done its training. The **memorial room** inside the tower and the gardens are especially well tended. A black obelisk known as the **Orange Memorial to Fallen Brethren** stands near the entrance.

The Mémorial Irlandais is about 1km north of Thiepval.

La Grande Mine Officially known as the Lochnagar Crater Memorial, this enormous crater – one of many made by tunnelling under enemy (in this case German) trenches and planting vast quantities of explosives – looks like a meteor hit it. It was made at 7.30 am on 1 July 1916. The nearby grassy area is pocked with smaller craters.

To get there from Albert, take the D929 north-eastward for about 3km to its intersection with the D20 (at La Boisselle). Then turn south-eastward for 500m along the C9 (also known as Route de la Grande Mine).

South African National Memorial The Mémorial Sud-Africain, founded in 1920, is in the middle of shell-pocked **Delville Wood**, which was almost captured by a South African brigade in the third week of July 1916. The avenues through the trees are named after streets in London and Edinburgh. The star-shaped **museum** (☎ 03 22 85 02 17), opened in 1986, can be visited from 10 am to 3.45 pm (5.45 pm from April to mid-October); it's closed on Monday, holidays and in December and January. There's a **Commonwealth cemetery** across the street.

To get to Delville Wood, which is about 15km east of Albert between the villages of Longueval and Ginchy, take the D20.

The **New Zealand Memorial** is 1.5km due north of Longueval.

Rancourt This village, 20km east of Albert, is the site of three military cemeteries. The French **Nécropole Nationale** (National Necropolis), on the N17 just south of the edge of town, has 54,665 graves marked with double rows of cement crosses and, for Muslims, Jews and *libre-penseurs* (freethinkers), tablet-shaped markers. The **chapel**, built with private donations, is lined with memorial plaques marked *mort pour la patrie* (meaning 'died for the homeland'); some include heroic descriptions of battlefield valour. There's a small **Commonwealth cemetery** across the street.

The **Deutscher Soldaten Friedhof** (Cimetière Militaire Allemand, ie German Military Cemetery), 500m due west of the French cemetery (near the intersection of the N17 and the N20), contains the remains of 11,422 German soldiers, many of whom are buried in the mass graves at the top of the slope.

Péronne About 25km south-east of Albert in the town of Péronne is the innovative and informative **Historial de la Grande Guerre** (☎ 03 22 83 14 18), which examines the origins and consequences of WWI from the perspective of France, Germany and Great Britain and their respective soldiers and civilians. It is open daily, except Monday, from 10 am to 5.30 pm (6 pm from May to September, when it's open seven days a week). It is closed from 19 December to 16 January. Entry costs 39FF (20FF for under 18s, students, teachers and ex-servicemen or veterans).

AMIENS

• pop 132,000 ✉ 80000

Amiens, the friendly if austere former capital of Picardy, is home to one of France's most magnificent cathedrals. The city's 23,000 students give the city a young, lively feel. Seriously damaged during both world wars, it is a good base for visits to the Battle of the Somme memorials.

Orientation

The centre of the partly pedestrianised commercial district is two blocks west of the cathedral around grassy Place Gambetta. The main shopping street is Rue des Vergeaux. The train station, about 1km east of Place Gambetta, faces a 26 storey concrete apartment tower known as Tour Perret.

AMIENS

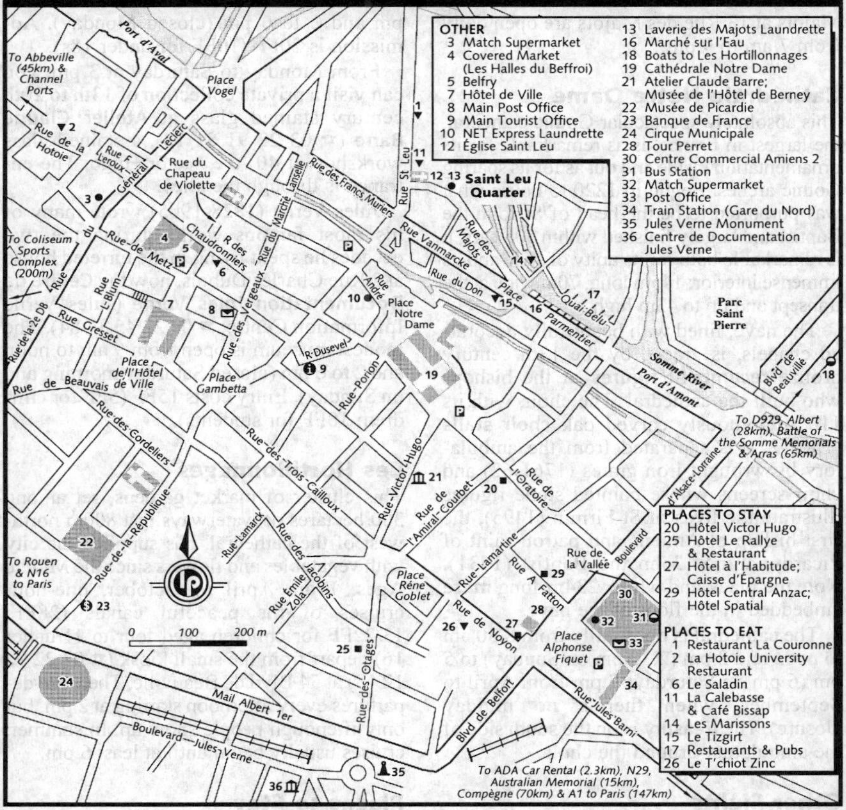

Information

Tourist Office The main tourist office (☎ 03 22 71 60 50; fax 03 22 71 60 51; www.amiens.com), 6bis Rue Dusvel, is open Monday to Saturday from 9 am to 6.30 pm; Sunday hours are 2 to 5 pm (6.30 pm from Easter to October). Hotel reservations cost 20FF. Brochures on the Somme war monuments are available.

Money The Banque de France on Rue de la République is open weekdays from 9 am to noon and 1.45 to 3.30 pm but may do exchange operations only in the morning. There are several commercial banks around Place René Goblet and a Caisse d'Épargne across Place Alphonse Fiquet from the train station; many are open from Tuesday to Saturday.

Post The main post office, 7 Rue des Vergeaux, and the branch post office at 35 Place Alphonse Fiquet (next to the train station) are open weekdays from 8 am to 7 pm and on Saturday until noon. The former will exchange foreign currency.

Laundry NET Express at 10 Rue André (facing the cathedral) and Laverie des Majots at 13 Rue des Majots are open daily from 7 am to 9 pm.

Cathédrale Notre Dame

This absolutely spectacular Gothic cathedral, the largest in France, is as remarkable for its ornamentation inside and out as for its soaring Gothic arches. Begun in 1220 to house what was purported to be the head of St John the Baptist and largely finished within 50 years, it is remarkable both for its unity of style and its immense interior: 145m long, 70m wide at the transept and up to 43m high.

The nave, lined with beautifully decorated chapels, is graced by the 13th century bronze **recumbent figures** of the bishops who built the cathedral. The choir, with its 110 sumptuously carved oak **choir stalls** (1508-22), is separated from the ambulatory by wrought-iron grates (1761-62) and choir screens whose painted stone figures illustrate the lives of St Firmin (1495), the first bishop of Amiens and patron saint of Picardy, and St John the Baptist (1531). Note the black and white, 234m-long **maze** embedded in the floor of the nave.

The cathedral is open daily from 8.30 am to noon and 2 pm (2.30 pm on Sunday) to 5 pm (6 pm on Saturday; 7 pm from April to September, when there's no midday closure). The **treasury** is on the south side of the ambulatory around the choir.

Other Sights

The medieval **Saint Leu Quarter**, north of the cathedral, is the best place in town for a riverside stroll. Overenthusiastic post-war renovations have left parts of the area a bit too picturesque, but the many neon-lit, riverside restaurants and pubs make it lively at night. At **Place Gambetta**, the throbbing heart of the city's commercial district, two glass-covered shafts expose remains of the Gallo-Roman city of Samarobriva.

The **Musée de Picardie** (☎ 03 22 97 14 00), housed in a gorgeous Second Empire building at 48 Rue de la République, has displays of archaeology, medieval art, 18th century French paintings and Revolutionary era ceramics. It is open from 10 am to 12.30 pm and 2 to 6 pm (closed Monday). Admission is 20FF (10FF for under 18s).

From Monday to Saturday at 3 pm, you can visit a private collection of 13th to 20th century stained glass at **Atelier Claude Barre** (☎ 03 22 91 81 18), a stained-glass workshop at 40 Ave Victor Hugo. The entrance is through the alley.

Jules Verne (1828-1905) wrote many of his most famous works during the two decades he spent living in the turreted house at 2 Rue Charles Dubois, now the **Centre de Documentation Jules Verne** (Jules Verne Information Centre; ☎ 03 22 45 37 84). The modest museum is open from 9 am to noon and 2 to 6 pm (closed Saturday morning and on Sunday). Entry costs 15FF (5FF for children; 10FF for students).

Les Hortillonnages

This cluster of market gardens, set among 300 hectares of waterways just 800m northwest of the cathedral, has supplied the city with vegetables and flowers since the Middle Ages. From April to October, one-hour cruises of the peaceful canals (28FF; 13/22FF for children aged four to 11/under 16) depart from the small kiosk (☎ 03 22 92 12 18) at 54 Blvd de Beauvillé. There are departures every afternoon starting at 2 pm, but only if enough people show up. In summer, cruises usually begin until at least 6 pm.

Places to Stay

The lovely and very central ***Hôtel Victor Hugo*** (☎ 03 22 91 57 91; fax 03 22 92 74 02), 2 Rue de l'Oratoire, has modern, stylish doubles from 135FF (200FF with shower and toilet). Reception is open 24 hours a day.

The two star ***Hôtel Central Anzac*** (☎ 03 22 91 34 08; fax 03 22 91 36 02), 17 Rue Alexandre Fatton, was started decades ago by an Australian ex-serviceman. It has clean and comfortable (if small) singles/doubles from 150/175FF (215/240FF with shower and toilet). The two star ***Hôtel Spatial*** (☎ 03 22 91 53 23; fax 03 22 92 27 87), next door at No 15, has recently renovated, modern singles/doubles from 150/170FF (225/250FF with shower and toilet). Free, enclosed parking is available. The ***Hôtel à l'Habitude*** (☎ 03 22 91 69 78; fax 03 22 91 84 48), 7 Place Alphonse Fiquet, has doubles with shower and toilet for 195 to 230FF.

The ***Hôtel Le Rallye*** (☎ 03 22 91 76 03; fax 03 22 91 16 77), 24 Rue des Otages, built in the 1920s, has slightly tatty doubles from 120FF (180FF with shower and toilet).

Places to Eat

Restaurants *Les Marissons* (☎ 03 22 92 96 66), a very elegant restaurant housed in a 14th century boatwright's workshop on Pont de la Dodane, has *menus* of Picardy cuisine for 110 to 255FF (closed Saturday for lunch and on Sunday). French and regional cuisine are on offer at the attractive ***Restaurant La Couronne*** (☎ 03 22 91 88 57), 64 Rue Saint Leu. The *menus* cost 92 and 135FF. It is closed on Saturday and on Sunday night.

The restaurant attached to the ***Hôtel Le Rallye*** (see Places to Stay) has *menus* for 60 to 170FF (closed Saturday evening and on Sunday). ***Le T'chiot Zinc*** (☎ 03 22 91 43 79), a small, inviting bistro at 18 Rue de Noyon, has Picardy-style *menus* for 68 to 139FF (closed Monday for lunch and on Sunday).

Cold and warm salads (49 to 83FF) are the speciality of ***Le Saladin*** (☎ 03 22 92 05 15), an upbeat place at 4 Rue des Chaudronniers (closed Sunday).

Algerian Berber-style couscous (60 to 135FF) is on offer at ***Le Tizgirt*** (☎ 03 22 91 42 55), a colourful place at 60 Rue Vanmarcke (closed Saturday for lunch, Monday night and on Sunday). ***La Calabesse*** (☎ 03 22 91 28 00), 48 Rue Saint Leu, serves Afro-Antillean dishes (closed Saturday for lunch and on Sunday).

During the school year, ***La Hotoie*** (☎ 03 22 91 30 35), a large university cafeteria at 4 Rue de la Hotoie, is open weekdays from 11.35 am to 11.15 pm and 6.35 to 8 pm.

Self-Catering Fruits and vegetables grown in the hortillonnages are on offer at the ***marché sur l'eau*** (floating market), now held on dry land at Place Parmentier on Saturday morning.

The modern ***covered market*** that occupies the eastern bit of Les Halles du Beffroi, a shopping mall on Rue de Metz, is open Tuesday to Saturday from 8 am to 7 pm (12.30 pm on Saturday). Outside, there's also a ***food market*** on Wednesday and Saturday from 9 am to 6 pm.

The ***Match*** supermarket deep inside the Amiens 2 Centre Commercial, next to the train station, is open Monday to Saturday from 8 am to 8 pm. The ***Match*** supermarket at 29 Rue du Général Leclerc is open daily, except Sunday afternoon and Monday morning.

Entertainment

Café Bissap (☎ 03 22 92 36 41), 50 Rue Saint Leu, open Monday to Saturday from 4 pm to 3 am, is a mellow bar with African décor and a world music ambience.

Getting There & Away

Bus The bus station (☎ 03 22 92 27 03), next to the train station in the basement of the Centre Commercial, has daily buses to Beauvais (44 or 68FF; 1¼ hours; 10 on weekdays, two on weekends), Albert (23FF; 35 to 60 minutes; four a day except Sunday, the first at about noon) and Arras (46.50FF; two hours; two a day except Sunday). The information office is staffed from Monday to Saturday from 6 am to 1 pm and 1 to 7 pm.

Train Gare du Nord (☎ 03 36 35 35 35), Place Alphonse Fiquet, the city's main train station, is on the Paris-Calais line. The information office is open from 8.45 am to 6.20 pm (closed Sunday and holidays).

Destinations served include Paris' Gare du Nord (96FF; 1¼ to two hours; 10 to 14 a day), Lille (94FF; 1½ hours; four direct a day), Arras (58FF; 45 minutes; four to six a day) via Albert (34FF; 25 minutes; 13 on weekdays, five to eight on weekends), Villers-Bretonneux (18FF; 12 minutes; five to seven a day), Calais (115FF; two hours;

six to eight a day) via Boulogne (91FF; 1¼ hours; five to eight a day) and Rouen (90FF; 1½ to two hours; three or four a day). SNCF buses, timed with the TGVs, link Amiens with the Haute Picardie TGV station (41FF).

Car ADA car rental (☎ 03 22 46 49 49) is 2.5km south-east of the train station at 387 Chaussée Jules Ferry (closed Sunday). By car, take Rue Jules Barni; by bus, take line No 1 or 16.

Getting Around

Car Free, unmetered parking is available along the streets that are on the other side of Rue Jules Barni from the train station.

Normandy

Often compared with the countryside of southern England, Normandy (Normandie) is the land of the *bocage*, farmland subdivided by hedges and trees. The hedgerows (*haies*) made fighting difficult in WWII, and for the past half century there has been a trend to cut them down.

In many areas, however, they still break the landscape up into a patchwork of enclosed fields. Winding through these hedgerows are sunken lanes, whose grassy sides are covered with yellow primroses and gorse. At various points, the lanes are deep enough to hide the half-timbered houses.

Set among this peaceful, pastoral landscape are Normandy's cities and towns. Rouen is well endowed with medieval architecture, including a spectacular cathedral; Caen boasts some fine Norman Romanesque abbeys; Bayeux, home to the 11th century Bayeux Tapestry, is only a dozen kilometres from the D-day landing beaches. Between Rouen and Paris is Giverny, the home and garden of Claude Monet. In Normandy's south-western corner, on the border with Brittany, is the celebrated island abbey of Mont Saint Michel. Normandy's most important port cities are Cherbourg and Le Havre.

Along the Côte d'Albâtre (Alabaster Coast), the area south-west of Dieppe, dramatic chalk cliffs rise above the pebble beaches. Farther west, the coastline is padded by sand.

Because it is only a couple of hours by train from Paris, much of Normandy's coast is lined with seaside resorts, including those at Fécamp, Honfleur, and the fashionable twin towns of Deauville and Trouville. During the second half of the 19th century, the Norman coast attracted a number of impressionist painters.

The Battle of Normandy (1944) left its mark on the region. It is most evident in cities like Le Havre and Caen, where postwar architecture predominates.

HIGHLIGHTS

- **Mont Saint Michel** – explore this fascinating island's myriad network of narrow streets
- **Bayeux** – marvel at the magnificent Bayeux Tapestry
- **Giverny** – visit the Musée Claude Monet, Monet's famous house and diverse gardens
- **D-day landing beaches** – pay homage to those who fell during Operation Overlord in WWII

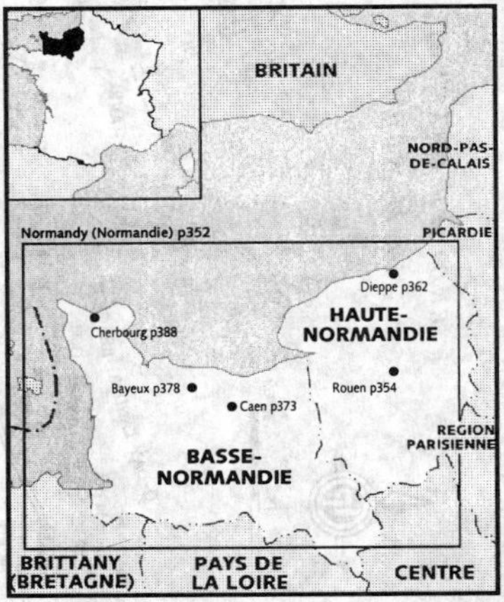

moules frites – mussels with chips, Normandy's best are in picturesque Honfleur

dairy products – Normandy is renowned for its rich milk, butter, cheeses and cream

apple drinks – *cidre* (cider) and Vallée d'Auge apple brandy

NORMANDY (NORMANDIE)

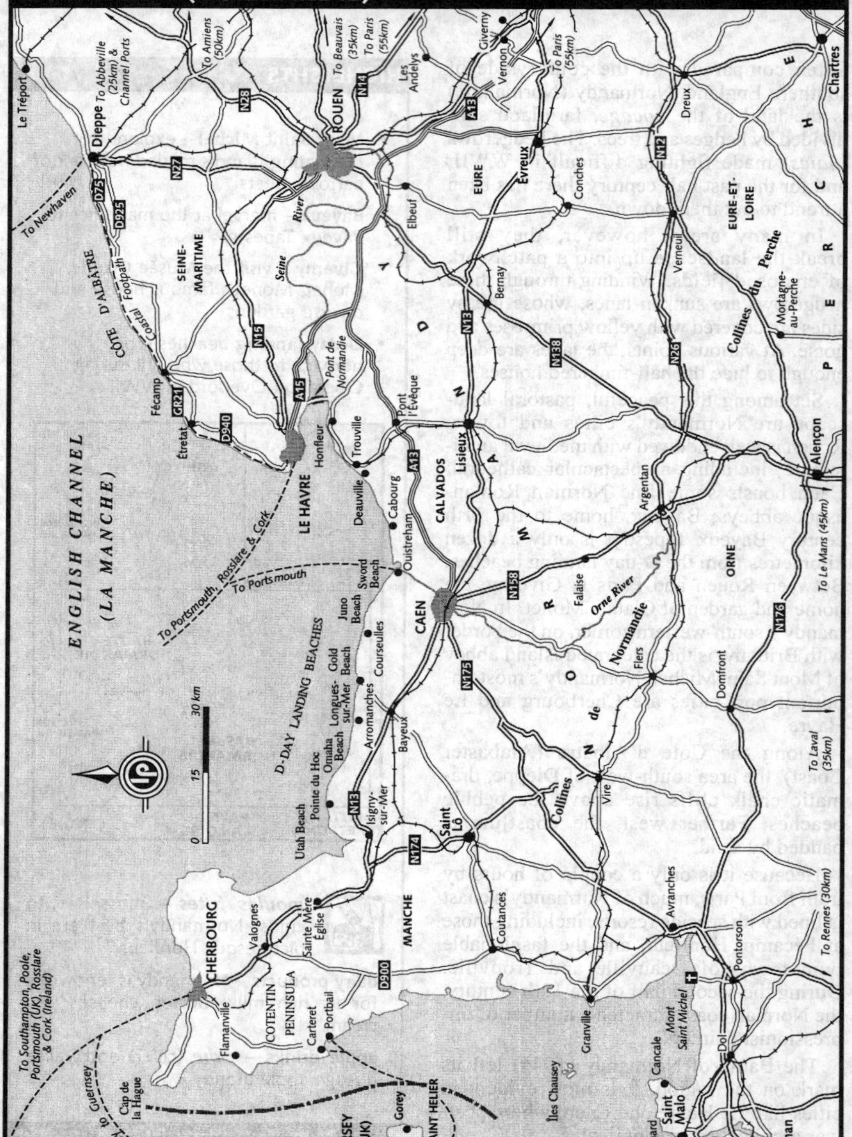

NORMANDY

History

Normandy's evolution as a historical entity began with the invasions by the Vikings in the 9th century. Originally made up of bands of plundering pirates, many of these raiding groups from Scandinavia established settlements in the area and adopted Christianity. In 911 the French king Charles the Simple and the Viking chief Hrölfr agreed to make the Rouen region home to these Norsemen (or Normans), who gave their name to the region.

In 1066 the duke of Normandy crossed the English Channel with 6000 soldiers. His forces crushed the English in the Battle of Hastings, and the duke – who became known to history as William the Conqueror – was crowned king of England. The Channel Islands (Îles Anglo-Normandes), just off the Norman coast, came under English rule in the same year and remain British crown dependencies to this day. During the 11th and 12th centuries, many abbeys and churches were built in Normandy and England in the Romanesque style.

During the Hundred Years' War (1337-1453), the duchy switched back and forth between French and English rule. England dominated Normandy (except for Mont Saint Michel) for about 30 years until France gained permanent control in 1450. In the 16th century Normandy, a Protestant stronghold, was the scene of much fighting between Catholics and Huguenots.

In 1942, a force of 6000, mostly Canadian, troops participated in a disastrous landing near Dieppe. On 6 June 1944 – better known as D-day – 45,000 Allied troops landed on beaches near Bayeux. The Battle of Normandy followed, and after several months and 100,000 deaths, German resistance was finally broken.

Geography

The English Channel (La Manche) and north-eastern Brittany form the western border of Normandy, and the Paris basin and Picardy form its eastern border. The region's two divisions – Haute Normandie (Upper Normandy) and Basse Normandie (Lower Normandy) – are separated by the Seine River, which flows from Paris through Rouen before emptying into the Channel near Le Havre at the Baie de la Seine.

The Cotentin Peninsula, with Cherbourg at its northern tip, divides the Baie de la Seine from the Golfe de Saint Malo, which is famed for its extraordinary tides. The Channel Islands lie to the west of the peninsula.

Getting There & Away

Ferries to and from England dock at Cherbourg, Dieppe, Le Havre and Ouistreham, north-east of Caen. Ireland is connected by ferry with Cherbourg. The Channel Islands are mostly accessible from the Breton port of Saint Malo, but in the warm season from Cherbourg, Carteret, Granville and Portbail as well. For details on ferry schedules and fares, see the Sea section of the introductory Getting There & Away chapter.

Normandy is easily accessible by train from Paris.

Getting Around

All major cities and towns in Normandy are adequately connected by rail, but the buses between smaller towns and villages are somewhat infrequent as they mostly serve school routes. Hitching is no problem on major roads, but off the main tracks it can be slow going. Visitors who would like to explore Normandy's rural areas might consider renting a car. See Getting There & Away under D-day Beaches, Caen and Rouen for information on rental companies.

Rouen & Côte d'Albâtre

ROUEN

• pop 105,000 ✉ 76000

The city of Rouen, for centuries the farthest point downriver where you could cross the Seine by bridge, is known for its many spires and church towers. The old city has around 2000 half-timbered houses, quite a few of which have rough-hewn

ROUEN

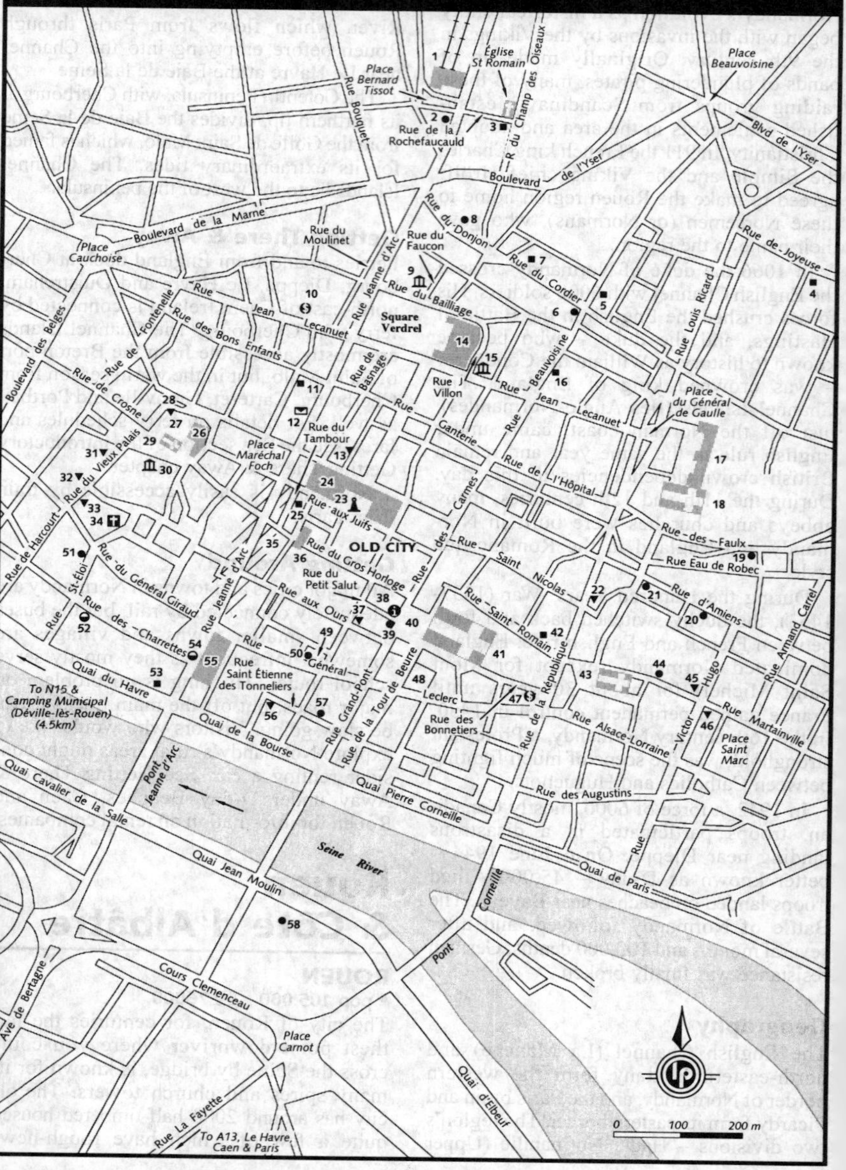
Place Bernard Tissot
Rue Bouquet
Église St Romain
R. du Champ des Oiseaux
Place Beauvoisine
Rue de la Rochefaucauld
Blvd de l'Yser
Boulevard de l'Yser
Boulevard de la Marne
Rue du Moulinet
Rue du Donjon
Rue du Faucon
Place Cauchoise
Rue de Joyeuse
Rue Jeanne d'Arc
Rue du Cordier
Rue du Bailliage
Rue Jean Lecanuet
Square Verdrel
Rue Louis Ricard
Rue de Fontenelle
Rue des Bons Enfants
Boulevard des Belges
Rue de Crosne
Rue de Basnage
Rue Beauvoisine
Rue Villon
Rue Jean Lecanuet
Place du Général de Gaulle
Rue du Tambour
Rue Ganterie
Place Maréchal Foch
Rue du Vieux Palais
Rue des Carmes
Rue de l'Hôpital
Rue aux Juifs
Rue des Faulx
Rue de Harcourt
Rue Eau de Robec
OLD CITY
Rue du Gros Horloge
Rue Saint Nicolas
Rue du Petit Salut
Rue St-Eloi
Rue du Général Giraud
Rue Jeanne d'Arc
Rue aux Ours
Rue d'Amiens
Rue des Charrettes
Rue Saint Romain
Rue Armand Carrel
Rue Général Leclerc
Quai du Havre
Rue Saint Étienne des Tonneliers
To N15 & Camping Municipal (Déville-lès-Rouen) (4.5km)
Rue Grand-Pont
Rue de la Tour de Beurre
Rue de la République
Rue des Bonnetiers
Rue Victor Hugo
Rue Martainville
Quai de la Bourse
Rue Alsace-Lorraine
Place Saint Marc
Pont Jeanne d'Arc
Quai Cavalier de la Salle
Quai Pierre Corneille
Rue des Augustins
Seine River
Quai Jean Moulin
Rue Corneille
Quai de Paris
Pont Corneille
Ave de Bertagne
Cours Clemenceau
Place Carnot
Quai d'Elbeuf
Rue La Fayette
To A13, Le Havre, Caen & Paris
0
100
200 m
1
2
3
4
5
6
7
8
9
10
11
12
13
14
15
16
17
18
19
20
21
22
23
24
25
26
27
28
29
30
31
32
33
34
35
36
37
38
39
40
41
42
43
44
45
46
47
48
49
50
51
52
53
54
55
56
57
58

NORMANDY

beams, posts and diagonals leaning this way and that. Rouen also has a renowned Gothic cathedral and a number of excellent museums. The city was occupied by the English during the Hundred Years' War, and it was at this time that the young French heroine Joan of Arc (Jeanne d'Arc) was tried for heresy and burned at the stake in Rouen.

Rouen can be visited on an overnight or even a day trip from Paris. It is an excellent base for visiting Monet's home in Giverny.

Orientation

The train station (Gare Rouen-Rive Droite) is at the northern end of Rue Jeanne d'Arc, the main thoroughfare running south to the Seine. The old city is centred around Rue du Gros Horloge between the Place du Vieux Marché and the cathedral.

Information

Tourist Office The tourist office (☎ 02 32 08 32 40; fax 02 32 08 32 44) is in a lovely, early 16th century building at 25 Place de la Cathédrale, opposite the western façade of the Cathédrale Notre Dame. It is open Monday to Saturday from 9 am to 6.30 pm and on Sunday from 10 am to 1 pm. From May to September, opening hours are Monday to Saturday from 9 am to 7 pm, and on Sunday from 9.30 am to 12.30 pm and 2.30 to 6 pm. The staff can make hotel reservations in the area for 15FF.

The tourist office conducts two-hour guided tours of the city daily at 10.30 am and 3 pm during July and August, and at weekends during the rest of the year (33FF for adults; 25FF for children).

Money The Banque de France at 32 Rue Jean Lecanuet is open weekdays from 8.45 am to 12.15 pm and 1.30 to 3.30 pm. The Bureau de Change near the cathedral at 7-9 Rue des Bonnetiers has decent exchange rates and does not take a commission. It is open daily, except Sunday, from 10 am to 7 pm. Half a dozen banks line Rue Jeanne d'Arc between the Théâtre des Arts and Place Maréchal Foch, in front of the Palais de Justice.

American Express (☎ 02 32 08 19 20) is at 1-3 Place Jacques Le Lieur. It is open on weekdays from 8.45 am to noon and 1.30 to

ROUEN

PLACES TO STAY

- 3 Hôtel de la Rochefaucauld
- 4 Hostellerie du Vieux Logis
- 5 Hôtel Sphinx
- 7 Hôtel Normandya
- 11 Hôtel des Flandres
- 16 Hôtel Napoléon
- 25 Hôtel Le Palais
- 42 Hôtel de la Cathédrale
- 53 Hôtel Viking

PLACES TO EAT

- 13 Pascaline
- 22 Alimentation Générale
- 28 Les Maraichers
- 31 Kyoto
- 32 Chez Pépé
- 33 La Galetteria
- 37 Gourmand'grain
- 45 Kim Ngoc
- 46 Chez Zaza
- 56 La Vieille Auberge

OTHER

- 1 Gare Rouen-Rive Droite
- 2 Voyages Wasteels (Travel Agency)
- 6 Laundrette
- 8 La Tour Jeanne d'Arc
- 9 Musée de la Céramique
- 10 Banque de France
- 12 Main Post Office
- 14 Musée des Beaux-Arts
- 15 Musée Le Secq des Tournelles
- 17 Hôtel de Ville
- 18 Église Saint Ouen
- 19 ABC Bookshop
- 20 Laundrette
- 21 Laundrette
- 23 Palais de Justice Courtyard; Monument Juif
- 24 Palais de Justice
- 26 Covered Food Market
- 27 Place du Vieux Marché
- 29 Église Jeanne d'Arc
- 30 Musée Jeanne d'Arc
- 34 Église St Éloi
- 35 Banks
- 36 Gros Horloge
- 38 Tourist Office
- 39 American Express
- 40 Place de la Cathédrale
- 41 Cathédrale Notre Dame
- 43 Église Saint Maclou
- 44 Aître Saint Maclou
- 47 Bureau de Change
- 48 Place de la Calende
- 49 Place Jacques Le Lieur
- 50 American Express
- 51 Rouen Cycles
- 52 Bus Station
- 54 Espace Métrobus
- 55 Théâtre des Arts
- 57 Cinéma Le Melville
- 58 Prefecture

6 pm. There's a second American Express office (☎ 02 35 89 48 60) at 25 Place de la Cathédrale. It's open Monday to Saturday from 9 am to 1 pm and 2 to 7 pm, and Sunday 9.30 am to 12.30 pm and 2.30 to 6 pm.

Post The main post office, where you can also change foreign currency, is at 45 Rue Jeanne d'Arc and opens weekdays from 8 am to 7 pm and Saturday to noon.

Travel Agencies Voyages Wasteels (☎ 02 35 71 92 56), 70m south of the train station at 111bis Rue Jeanne d'Arc, sells discount air tickets. It's open Monday to Friday from 9 am to noon and 2 to 7 pm, and to 6 pm on Saturday.

Bookshops For English-language books, the ABC Bookshop (☎ 02 35 71 08 67) at 11 Rue des Faulx near the Église Saint Ouen is open from Tuesday to Saturday between 10 am and 6 pm.

Laundry North of the centre, there's a laundrette at 73 Rue Beauvoisine open from 8 am to 8.30 pm daily. The laundrette diagonally opposite 44 Rue d'Amiens is open every day from 7 am to 9 pm, as is the one next to 53 Rue d'Amiens.

Old City

Rouen's old city suffered enormous damage during WWII, but has since been painstakingly restored. The main street is **Rue du Gros Horloge**, which runs from the cathedral to **Place du Vieux Marché**, where 19-year-old Joan of Arc was executed for heresy in 1431. The striking **Église Jeanne d'Arc** marking the site was completed in 1979; you'll learn more about her life from its stained-glass windows than at the tacky **Musée Jeanne d'Arc**, across the square at No 33. The church is open daily, except Friday and Sunday mornings, from 10 am to 12.30 pm and 2 to 6 pm. Entry to the museum costs 24/12FF for adults/students.

The pedestrianised Rue du Gros Horloge is spanned by an early 16th century gatehouse holding aloft the **Gros Horloge**, a large medieval clock with only one hand. Visits to the late 14th century belfry of the Gros Horloge have been suspended until the year 2000 because of a major renovation project.

The incredibly ornate **Palais de Justice** (Law Courts), which was left a shell at the end of WWII, has been restored to its early 16th century Gothic glory, though the 19th century western façade facing Place Maréchal Foch still shows extensive bullet and shell damage. In recent years, during construction of the city's underground (subway) system, important archaeological discoveries were made, including a 3rd century Gallo-Roman settlement.

The courtyard of the Palais de Justice, which you can enter through a gate on Rue aux Juifs, is worth a look for its spires, gargoyles and statuary. Under the courtyard is the **Monument Juif**, a stone building used as a synagogue by Rouen's Jewish community in the early 12th century. Hour-long guided visits (in French) to the site take place on Saturday at 2.30 pm. Entrance is 35FF (25FF for students).

Cathédrale Notre Dame

Rouen's cathedral, which was the subject of a series of paintings by the impressionist artist Claude Monet, is considered a masterpiece of French Gothic architecture. Erected between 1201 and 1514, it suffered severe damage during WWII and has been undergoing restoration and cleaning for decades. The Romanesque **crypt** was part of a cathedral completed in 1062 and destroyed by fire in 1200. Note also the Flamboyant Gothic **Tour de Beurre**, with its apt yellow stonework, paid for out of the alms donated by members of the congregation who wanted to eat butter during Lent. There are several guided visits (10FF) a day to the crypt, ambulatory and **Chapel of the Virgin** during Easter, July and August, but only at weekends the rest of the year. The cathedral is open Monday to Saturday from 8 am to 7 pm on Sunday to 6 pm. Access is restricted on Sunday mornings, when several Masses are held.

Musée Le Secq des Tournelles

This fascinating museum (☎ 02 35 71 28 40) devoted to the blacksmith's craft displays some 12,000 locks, keys, scissors, tongs and other wrought-iron utensils made between the 3rd and 19th centuries. Located in a desanctified 16th century church at 2 Rue Jacques Villon (opposite 27 Rue Jean Lecanuet), it is open daily, except Tuesday, from 10 am to 1 pm and 2 to 6 pm. Entry is 13FF (9FF for students).

Other Museums

The **Musée des Beaux-Arts** (Fine Arts Museum; ☎ 02 35 71 28 40), facing Square Verdrel at 26bis Rue Jean Lecanuet, features paintings from the 15th to the 20th centuries on two floors. Adults/students pay 20/13FF admission.

The **Musée de la Céramique** (☎ 02 35 07 31 74), whose speciality is 16th to 19th century faïence (decorated earthenware), most notably that produced in Rouen, is north of the square and up a flight of steps at 1 Rue du Faucon. The building it occupies, with a fine courtyard, dates from 1657. Ticket prices are 13/9FF for adults/students.

Both museums keep the same hours as the Musée Le Secq des Tournelles.

Église Saint Maclou

Although this Flamboyant Gothic church (entrance next to 56 Rue de la République) was built between 1437 and 1521, much of the decoration dates from the Renaissance. It is open daily from 10 am to noon and 2 to 6 pm (3 to 5.30 pm on Sunday).

Aître Saint Maclou

This curious ensemble of half-timbered buildings, built between 1526 and 1533, is decorated with macabre carvings of skulls, crossbones, grave-diggers' tools and hourglasses reminding visitors of their mortality. The courtyard was used as a burial ground for victims of the plague as late as 1781 and is now the municipal École des Beaux-Arts. It can be visited for free daily from 8 am to 8 pm; enter at 186 Rue Martainville, behind the Église Saint Maclou.

Église Saint Ouen

Église Saint Ouen, a 14th century abbey church, is an especially refined example of the High Gothic style. The entrance is through a lovely garden along Rue des Faulx. It is open from 10 am to 12.30 pm and 2 to 4.30 pm, and to 6.30 pm in summer (closed Tuesday).

La Tour Jeanne d'Arc

This tower (☎ 02 35 98 16 21), in Rue du Donjon south of the train station, is the only one left of the eight that once ringed a huge chateau built by Philippe Auguste in the early 13th century. Joan of Arc was imprisoned here before her execution. The tower and its two exhibition rooms are open daily (except Tuesday) from 10 am to noon and 2 to 5 pm, and to 5.30 pm in summer. Entrance is 10FF (free for students).

Places to Stay

Rouen has heaps of very cheap hotels. Most are north of the city centre, but there are also a few good options in the old city.

Camping The *Camping Municipal* (☎ 02 35 74 07 59), in Déville-lès-Rouen, is 5km north-west of the train station on Rue Jules Ferry. From the Théâtre des Arts or the bus station, take bus No 2 (last bus at 11 pm) and get off at the *mairie* of Déville-lès-Rouen. Two people with a tent are charged 56FF. It is open year-round.

Hostel Rouen's Auberge de Jeunesse has recently closed but there are plans for a new one to open soon. Contact the tourist office for the latest update.

Gîtes d'Étape The tourist office has information on these in the Rouen area.

Hotels – North of the Centre Just a stone's throw from the train station, the welcoming ***Hôtel de la Rochefaucauld*** (☎ 02 35 71 86 58), opposite the Saint Romain church, offers simple singles/doubles for one or two people from 120/150FF, including breakfast. Showers cost 15FF. The spotless ***Hôtel Normandya*** (☎ 02 35 71 46 15), a pleasant, family-run place at 32 Rue du Cordier, is on a quiet street 300m south-east of the train station. Singles (some with shower) are 110 to 140FF, doubles are 10 to 20FF more and a hall shower is 10FF.

The ***Hôtel Sphinx*** (☎ 02 35 71 35 86), 130 Rue Beauvoisine, is a cosy, friendly place with some timbered rooms. Doubles range from 90 to 100FF; an additional bed is 60FF. Showers cost 10FF. The small, comfortable ***Hôtel Napoléon*** (☎ 02 35 71 43 59), farther down the same street at No 58, has rooms with washbasin for 90/100FF. Hall showers are included in the price of the room.

The very French ***Hostellerie du Vieux Logis*** (☎ 02 35 71 55 30), 5 Rue de Joyeuse, almost a kilometre east of the train station, has a relaxed and pleasantly frayed air with a delightful little garden out the back. Singles/doubles start at 100FF and two-bed triples cost 150FF. You can shower for free.

Hotels – City Centre The ***Hôtel des Flandres*** (☎ 02 35 71 56 88), 5 Rue des Bons Enfants, has doubles for 125FF with washbasin and bidet, 140FF with shower, and 160FF with shower and toilet. The ***Hôtel Le Palais*** (☎ 02 35 71 41 40), between the Palais de Justice and the Gros Horloge at 12 Rue du Tambour, has singles/doubles for 120FF with shower. The somewhat pricier ***Hôtel Viking*** (☎ 02 35 70 34 95), near the bus station at 21 Quai du Havre, has singles/doubles with shower overlooking the river for 270/285FF.

If you're feeling really flush, the two star ***Hôtel de la Cathédrale*** (☎ 02 35 71 57 95; fax 02 35 70 15 54) sits in the shadow of Rouen's Gothic wonder in a 17th century house at 12 Rue Saint Romain. Rooms run from 270 to 415FF, with all the comforts you'd expect. Ask for a room looking onto the inner courtyard.

Places to Eat

Restaurants The ***Paris-Maraîchers*** (☎ 02 35 71 57 73), 37 Place du Vieux Marché, is definitely the pick of the Vieux Marché's many restaurants, with its lively pavement terrace and varied *menus* from 69FF. For hybrid Japanese/Korean/Chinese food, try ***Kyoto*** (☎ 02 35 07 76 77)), which is open for lunch and dinner daily (except Sunday and Monday lunch) at 35 Rue du Vieux Palais.

Chez Pépé (☎ 02 35 15 01 50), 19 Rue du Vieux Palais, is a pizzeria that is open daily from 11.30 am to 2 pm and 7 to 11.30 pm. ***Gourmand'grain*** (☎ 02 35 98 15 74), 3 Rue du Petit Salut, is a lunchtime vegetarian café with good salads and health-food *menus* for 45 and 69FF.

Near the Église Saint Maclou at 85 Rue Martainville, ***Chez Zaza*** (☎ 02 35 71 33 57) specialises in couscous (from 45FF) and is open daily for lunch and dinner. ***Kim Ngoc*** (☎ 02 35 98 76 33), nearby at No 166, is one of Rouen's many Vietnamese restaurants and has *menus* for 69 and 90FF. It's open daily, except Monday, for lunch and dinner. The ground floor restaurant at the ***Hostellerie du Vieux Logis*** is reminiscent of the 1920s, with a massive candelabra of melting wax, and an ageing *patron* softly padding between the tables. A multicourse *menu* costs 65FF.

For something a bit more stylish, you won't do better than ***Pascaline*** (☎ 02 35 89 67 44), an old-time bistro at 5 Rue de la Poterne with a player piano and some wonderful duck dishes. It is open daily for lunch and dinner with two and three-course *menus* for 59 and 97FF. The intimate ***La Vieille Auberge*** (☎ 02 35 70 56 65), 37 Rue Saint Étienne des Tonneliers, has an enticing 89FF *menu* including such local specialities as *canard* (duck) *flambé au Calvados*. It's closed on Monday.

Self-Catering Dairy products, fish and fresh produce are on sale daily, except Monday, from 6 am to 1.30 pm at the ***covered market*** at Place du Vieux Marché. But if you're in Rouen on a Thursday, Friday, Saturday or Sunday, head for the much more lively food and clothing ***market*** on Place Saint Marc, east of Église Saint Maclou.

The ***Alimentation Générale*** at 78 Rue de la République is open daily from 8 am to

10.30 pm. There are more food shops on Rue Alsace-Lorraine.

Entertainment

Cinema *Cinéma Le Melville* (☎ 02 35 98 79 79), 12 Rue Saint Étienne des Tonneliers, very occasionally has nondubbed English-language films, though French and dubbed films predominate. Tickets are 40/32FF for adults/students. The tourist office can provide you with monthly listings.

Classical Music From May or June to September, concerts are frequently held in Rouen's cathedral and churches. Inquire at the tourist office for details.

The ***Théâtre des Arts*** (☎ 02 35 71 41 36), on Place des Arts, is home to the Opéra de Normandie.

Getting There & Away

Bus The grim brick bus station (☎ 02 35 52 92 00), 25 Rue des Charrettes, near the Théâtre des Arts, has hardly changed since the 1960s. The information office, on the bottom level next to the bus ramps, is open weekdays from 8 am to 6.30 pm and on Saturday from 8 to 11.30 am.

Four companies, represented by SATAR, serve Dieppe (66FF; two hours; three a day) and towns along the coast west of Dieppe, including Fécamp (80FF; one a day) and Le Havre (84FF; three hours; five a day). Destinations around Rouen include Elbeuf (via Les Essarts, the motorcar racetrack; 23FF), Évreux (62FF; six a day), Jumièges (28FF) and Louviers (39FF). The buses to Dieppe and Le Havre are much slower than the train and are more expensive.

Train The Art Nouveau Gare Rouen-Rive Droite (☎ 08 36 35 35 35), built between 1912 and 1928, sits at the northern end of Rue Jeanne d'Arc on Place Bernard Tissot. The information office is open Monday to Saturday from 8.30 am to 7.45 pm. Luggage lockers are available from 5.15 or 6 am to 11 pm.

Rouen is only 70 minutes by express train from Paris' Gare Saint Lazare (102FF). There are two dozen trains a day in each direction, the latest at about 10 pm (towards Rouen) and 9 pm (towards Paris). There are also trains to Amiens (90FF; 1½ hours; four a day), Caen (113FF; two hours; four a day), Dieppe (54FF; 45 minutes; 10 a day), Le Havre (71FF; one hour; 16 a day) and, by TGV, to Lyon (321FF).

Car For car rental, you might try one of the following companies:

ADA
(☎ 02 35 72 25 88) 34 Ave Jean Rondeaux
Avis
(☎ 02 35 53 17 20) train station bureau
Hertz
main office (☎ 02 35 98 16 57), 38 Quai Gaston; train station bureau (☎ 02 35 70 70 71), 130 rue Jeanne d'Arc

Getting Around

Bus & Metro TCAR operates Rouen's extensive local bus network as well as its metro line. The latter runs under Rue Jeanne d'Arc and links the train station with the Théâtre des Arts before crossing the Seine and branching off into the southern suburbs. The metro runs between 5 am (6 am on Sunday) and 11.30 pm daily.

TCAR (also known as Métrobus) has an information office (☎ 02 35 52 52 52) at the modern Espace Métrobus, opposite the Théâtre des Arts on Rue Jeanne d'Arc. It is open Monday to Saturday from 7 am to 7 pm. Tickets, valid for an hour (and unlimited kilometres), cost 8FF if bought individually or 59FF for a magnetic card good for 10 rides. A Carte Découverte, valid for unlimited travel for one/two/three days, is available at the tourist office for 20/30/40FF.

Taxi To order a taxi 24 hours a day ring Radio Taxi (☎ 02 35 88 50 50).

Bicycle Rouen Cycles (☎ 02 35 71 34 30), 45 Rue Saint Éloi, rents mountain bikes for 120FF a day with a deposit of 2000FF. It's open Tuesday to Saturday from 8.30 am to 12.15 pm and 2 to 7.15 pm.

GIVERNY

• pop 548 ✉ 27620

Situated between Paris and Rouen and an ideal day trip from either, this small village contains the Musée Claude Monet, the home and flower-filled garden from 1883 to 1926 of one of France's leading impressionist painters. Here Monet painted some of his most famous series of works, including *Décorations des Nymphéas* (Water Lilies).

First opened to the public in 1980, the museum attracts almost 400,000 visitors a year, many of whom also come to view the fine impressionist collection of the Musée Américain.

Musée Claude Monet

Monet's home (☎ 02 32 51 28 21) is open daily, except Monday, from April to October from 10 am to 6 pm. Admission to the house and gardens costs 35/25/20FF for adults/students/children.

Seasons have an enormous effect on the gardens at Giverny. From early to late spring, daffodils, tulips, rhododendrons, wisteria and irises appear, followed by poppies and lilies. By June, nasturtiums, roses and sweet peas are in flower. Around September, there are dahlias, sunflowers and hollyhocks.

The hectare of land that Monet owned has become two distinct areas, cut by the

Claude Monet

One of the most important figures in modern art, Claude Monet, born in Paris in 1840, was the undisputed leader of the impressionists. He grew up near Le Havre, where in his late teens he started painting nature in the open air, a practice that was to affect his work throughout the rest of his career.

By the time he was 17, Monet was studying in Paris at the Académie Suisse with such artists as Pissarro. Influenced by the intensity of the light and colours of Algeria, where he spent some time during his military service, Monet concentrated on painting landscapes, developing an individual style that aimed to capture on canvas the immediate impression of the scene before him, rather than precise detail.

During the Franco-Prussian War of 1870-71, Monet travelled to London, where he discovered the works of Turner and Constable. Consequently, painting from his houseboat on the Seine at Argenteuil, he focused on the effects of air and light, and in particular on the latter's effect on the water's surface. He also began using the undisguised, broken brush strokes that best characterise the impressionist style.

It was in the late 1870s that Monet first began painting pictures in series, in order to study the effects of the changing conditions of light and the atmosphere. The best known of these include the Rouen cathedral series, which were painted in the 1890s. In 1883, four years after the death of his first wife, Camille, he moved to Giverny with Alice Hoschedé, her five children from a previous marriage, and his two sons. Here he set about creating an environment where he could study and paint the subtle effects and changes of colour that varying tones of sunlight had on nature.

Alice died in 1911, followed three years later by Monet's eldest son, Jean. Soon after, the portly, bearded artist built a new studio and started painting the *Nymphéas* (Water Lilies) series. The huge dimensions of some of these works, together with the fact that the pond's surface takes up the entire canvas, meant the abandonment of composition in the traditional sense and the virtual disintegration of form. Monet completed the series just before his death in 1926.

Chemin du Roy, a small railway line that, unfortunately, was converted into what is now the busy D5 road.

The northern part is the **Clos Normand**, where Monet's famous pastel pink and green house and the Water Lily studio stand. These days the studio is the entrance hall, adorned with precise reproductions of his works and ringing with cash register bells from busy souvenir stands. Outside are the symmetrically laid-out gardens.

From the Clos Normand's far corner, a tunnel leads under the D5 to the **Jardin d'Eau** (Water Garden). Having bought this piece of land in 1895 after his reputation had been established, Monet dug a pool (fed by the Epte, a tributary of the nearby Seine), planted water lilies and constructed the Japanese bridge, which has since been rebuilt. Draped with purple wisteria, the bridge blends into the asymmetrical foreground and background, creating the intimate atmosphere for which the 'Painter of Light' was famous.

Musée Américain

The American Impressionist Museum (☎ 02 32 51 94 65) contains the works of many of the American impressionist painters who flocked to France in the late 19th and early 20th centuries. It lies 100m down the road from Musée Claude Monet at 99 Rue Claude Monet, and it has the same opening hours as the Musée Claude Monet. Entry costs 35FF (20FF for students, 15FF for children aged seven to 12).

Getting There & Away

Giverny is 76km north-west of Paris and 66km south-east of Rouen. The nearest town is Vernon (☎ 08 36 35 35 35 for train information), nearly 7km to the north-west on the Paris-Rouen train line.

From Paris' Gare Saint Lazare (65FF; 50 minutes), there are two trains before noon to Vernon. For the return trip there's roughly one train an hour between 5 and 9 pm. From Rouen (56FF; 40 minutes), four trains leave before noon; to get back, there's about one train every hour between 5 and 10 pm.

Once in Vernon it's still a hike to Giverny. Buses (☎ 02 35 71 32 99) meet most trains and cost 14FF, but bikes are a good alternative and can be hired from the train station for 55FF a day. A hefty 1000FF deposit is required. The other options are to walk or hitch.

DIEPPE

• pop 36,000 ✉ 76200

Dieppe is an ancient seaside town and long a favourite among British weekend visitors. It's not the prettiest place in Normandy, but its location – set between two limestone cliffs – and its medieval castle are dramatic. Dieppe also has the attractive, gritty appeal of an old-fashioned port.

Dieppe has not really been affected by the opening of the Channel Tunnel. Most visitors consider it a destination or are headed for other points west in Normandy or Brittany. It remains, however, the closest Channel port to Paris (171km). Newhaven, to which Dieppe is linked by ferry, is the Channel port nearest to London (120km).

History

Privateers based in Dieppe pillaged Southampton in 1338 and blockaded Lisbon two centuries later. The first European settlers in Canada included many Dieppois. The town was one of France's most important ports during the 16th century, when ships regularly sailed from Dieppe to West Africa and Brazil.

Orientation

The town centre is largely surrounded by water. Blvd de Verdun runs along the lawns – a favourite spot for kite-flyers – that border the beach. Most of the Grande Rue and Rue de la Barre has been turned into a pedestrian mall. Quai Duquesne and its continuation Quai Henri IV follow the west and north sides of the port area. Ferries dock at the terminal on the north-east side of the port, just under 2km on foot from the tourist office but almost 5km by the circuitous highway access road into town.

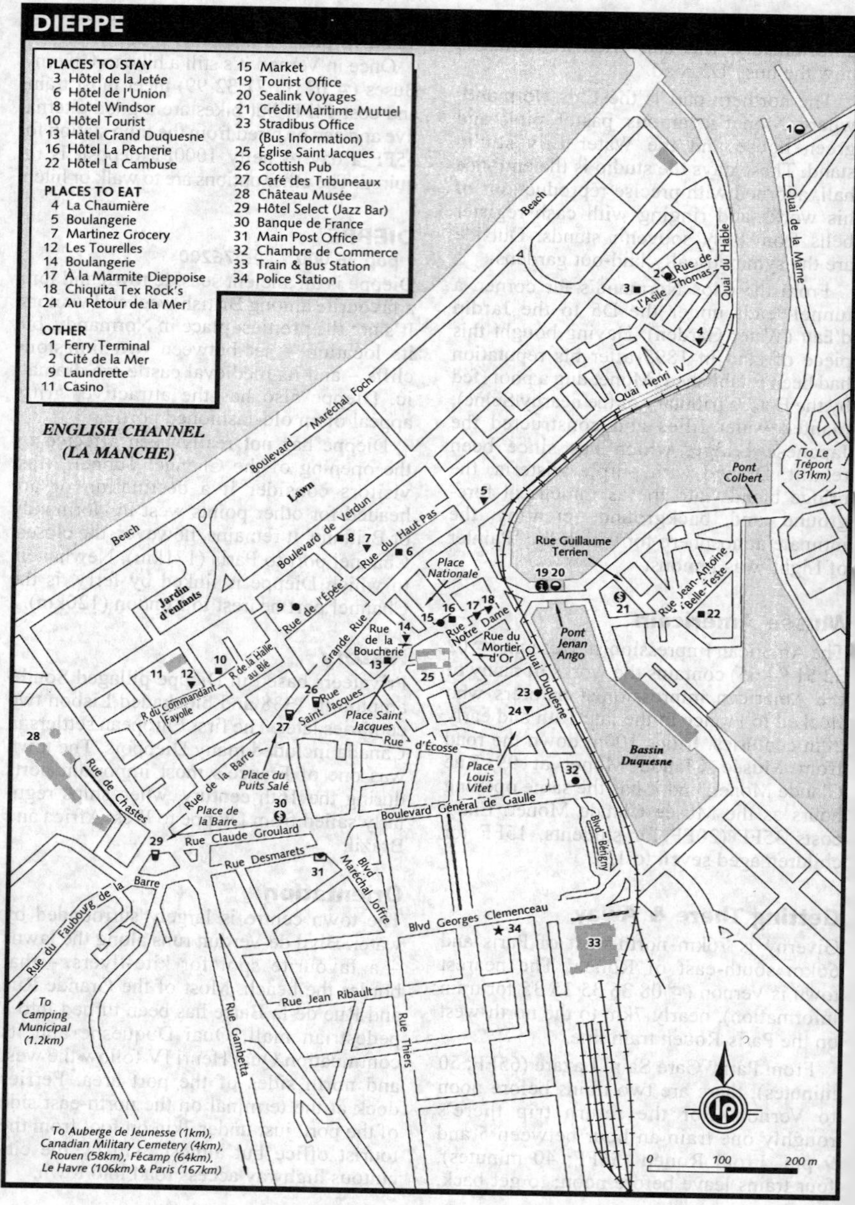
DIEPPE
PLACES TO STAY
3 Hôtel de la Jetée
6 Hôtel de l'Union
8 Hotel Windsor
10 Hôtel Tourist
13 Hàtel Grand Duquesne
16 Hôtel La Pêcherie
22 Hôtel La Cambuse
PLACES TO EAT
4 La Chaumière
5 Boulangerie
7 Martinez Grocery
12 Les Tourelles
14 Boulangerie
17 À la Marmite Dieppoise
18 Chiquita Tex Rock's
24 Au Retour de la Mer
OTHER
1 Ferry Terminal
2 Cité de la Mer
9 Laundrette
11 Casino
15 Market
19 Tourist Office
20 Sealink Voyages
21 Crédit Maritime Mutuel
23 Stradibus Office
(Bus Information)
25 Église Saint Jacques
26 Scottish Pub
27 Café des Tribuneaux
28 Château Musée
29 Hôtel Select (Jazz Bar)
30 Banque de France
31 Main Post Office
32 Chambre de Commerce
33 Train & Bus Station
34 Police Station
ENGLISH CHANNEL
(LA MANCHE)
Beach
Lawn
Jardin d'enfants
Boulevard Maréchal Foch
Boulevard de Verdun
Rue du Haut Pas
Rue de l'Epée
Grande Rue
Rue de la Boucherie
Place Nationale
Rue Notre Dame
Rue du Mortier d'Or
R de la Halle au Blé
R du Commandant Fayolle
Rue Saint Jacques
Place Saint Jacques
Rue d'Écosse
Place du Puits Salé
Rue de la Barre
Place de la Barre
Rue de Chastes
Place Louis Vitet
Boulevard Général de Gaulle
Rue Claude Groulard
Rue Desmarets
Blvd Maréchal Joffre
Blvd Bérigny
Blvd Georges Clemenceau
Rue du Faubourg de la Barre
Rue Jean Ribault
Rue Gambetta
Rue Thiers
Quai Duquesne
Pont Jenan Ango
Rue Guillaume Terrien
Rue Jean-Antoine Belle-Teste
Bassin Duquesne
Quai Henri IV
Rue de l'Asile Thomas
Quai du Hable
Quai de la Marne
Pont Colbert
To Le Tréport (31km)
To Camping Municipal (1.2km)
To Auberge de Jeunesse (1km), Canadian Military Cemetery (4km), Rouen (58km), Fécamp (64km), Le Havre (106km) & Paris (167km)
0
100
200 m

Information

Tourist Office The tourist office (☎ 02 35 84 11 77; fax 02 35 06 27 66) is situated on Pont Jehan Ango, on the west side of the port area. From May to September, it's open Monday to Saturday from 9 am to 1 pm and 2 to 7 pm (8 pm in July and August), and on Sunday from 10 am to 1 pm and 3 to 6 pm. The rest of the year, it's open Monday to Saturday from 9 am to noon and 2 to 6 pm. Hotel reservations in the Dieppe area cost 20FF.

City tours are held in English every Friday at 2.30 pm in July and August for 25FF.

Money All banks in Dieppe are closed on Monday except the Crédit Maritime Mutuel, a short distance east of the tourist office at 3 Rue Guillaume Terrien, which is open Monday to Friday from 8.30 am to noon and 1.30 to 5.30 pm, and the Banque de France at 4 Rue Claude Groulard, which is open weekdays from 8.45 to 11.45 am and 1.30 to 3.45 pm.

Several other banks are found around Place Nationale, including a Banque Populaire at No 15, open from 10 am to noon and 2 to 5 pm Tuesday to Saturday. There are also limited exchange facilities at the train station.

Post The main post office, 2 Blvd Maréchal Joffre, is open on weekdays from 8.30 am to 6 pm and on Saturday until noon.

Laundry The laundrette, two doors down from the tattoo parlour at 44 Rue de l'Épée, is open daily from 7 am to 9 pm.

Things to See & Do

Though the white cliffs on either side of Dieppe have been compared to those at Dover, the **beach** is gravelly and at times very windy. The vast **lawns** between Blvd de Verdun and the beach were laid out in the 1860s by that seashore-loving imperial duo, Napoleon III and his wife, Eugénie. **Église Saint Jacques**, a Norman Gothic church at Place Saint Jacques, has been reconstructed several times since the early 13th century.

The **Château-Musée** (☎ 02 35 84 19 76), in the castle perched on the cliff to the west of the city centre on Rue de Chastes, displays model ships and ivory carvings made in Dieppe from tusks brought from West Africa, a trade that began in the early 16th century. It's open from 10 am to noon and 2 to 5 pm (closed Tuesday). From June to September, it's open daily until 6 pm. Admission is 13/7.50FF for adults/children.

If you want to learn more about what Dieppe takes from – and gives back to – the sea around it, visit the **Cité de la Mer** (☎ 02 35 06 93 20) at 37 Rue de l'Asile Thomas. Aquariums and exhibits devoted to fishing, shipbuilding, cliffs and even pebbles crowd some 1650 sq m of floor space. It is open from 10 am to noon and 2 to 6 pm from September to April, and from 10 am to 7 pm from May to August. Admission is 28FF for adults and 16FF for children up to 16 years old.

The **Canadian Military Cemetery** is 4km towards Rouen. To get there, take Ave des Canadiens (the continuation of Rue Gambetta) southward and follow the signs.

The **GR21 hiking trail** follows the Côte d'Albâtre (see the following Côte d'Albâtre section) south-westward from Dieppe all the way to Le Havre. A map (35FF) is available at the tourist office. For easy walks in the surrounding areas ranging from one to three hours, pick up a copy of *Chemins Pédestres* for 15FF.

Places to Stay

It may be difficult finding a place to stay in July and August. Some hotels raise their prices during this period.

Places to Stay – Budget

Camping Open year-round, the two star ***Camping Municipal du Pré Saint Nicolas*** (☎ 02 35 84 11 39) is on Route de Pourville about 2km west of the train station. Two people with a tent are charged 33FF. From Monday to Saturday bus Nos 1 and 3 run out there from the train station six times a day until about 5 pm. Otherwise, head along Rue du Faubourg de la Barre, turn right into Chemin du Prêche and follow it to the camping ground.

Hostel The ***Auberge de Jeunesse*** (☎ 02 35 84 85 73; fax 02 35 84 89 62), 48 Rue Louis Fromager, about 1.5km south-west of the train station, is open from mid-February to mid-November. A bed costs 46FF a night, breakfast 18FF and sheets are 16FF. There's a kitchen and laundry, and you can pitch a tent on the grounds for about 25FF a night. From the train station, walk straight up Blvd Bérigny to the Chambre de Commerce from where you take bus No 2 (direction: Val Druel) to the Château Michel stop. The last bus departs at 8 pm.

Hotels The ***Hôtel Tourist*** (☎ 02 35 06 10 10), 16 Rue de la Halle au Blé, one block back from the beach behind the Casino, has plain but adequate singles/doubles with shower for 140/240FF and one double without shower for 160FF.

Hôtel La Pêcherie (☎ 02 35 82 04 62), in the heart of the old city at 3 Rue du Mortier d'Or, is a little hotel with simple doubles from 210FF, and doubles with shower from 220FF. Nearby, the recently refurbished ***Hôtel Grand Duquesne*** (☎ 02 35 84 10 18), 15 Place Saint Jacques, has rooms without showers for 175/195FF. The showers are free.

A number of popular small hotels along Rue du Haut Pas and its continuation, Rue de l'Épée, include the ***Hôtel de l'Union*** (☎ 02 35 84 35 52) at 47-49 Rue du Haut Pas. Basic singles/doubles with hall showers cost 110/150FF.

Places to Stay – Mid-Range

The ***Hôtel de la Jetée*** (☎ 02 35 84 89 98), 5 Rue de l'Asile Thomas, has pleasant singles and doubles from 145FF with wash-basin and 210FF with shower.

The ***Hôtel La Cambuse*** (☎ 02 35 84 19 46), 42 Rue Jean-Antoine Belle-Teste, has clean, renovated doubles with shower for 150 or 280FF. An extra bed is 38FF.

The two star ***Hôtel Windsor*** (☎ 02 35 84 15 23; fax 02 35 84 74 52), on the seafront (though a long way from the water across those lawns) at 18 Blvd de Verdun, has small, garishly decorated doubles with wash-basin from 210FF and with full amenities from 340FF. If you don't mind facing the city side, you'll pay only 190FF.

Places to Eat

There are quite a few tourist restaurants – some serving chips and pies to homesick Britons – along Quai Henri IV (often written Quai Henry IV). The peninsula across Pont Jehan Ango from Quai Duquesne contains several cafés.

Restaurants One of the cheapest and least touristy restaurants in town is at the ***Hôtel de l'Union***. Its 55FF *menu* is available daily, except Wednesday, and in summer it's also available for dinner.

At No 31 Place Louis Vitet, ***Au Retour de la Mer*** (☎ 02 35 84 04 81) has a standard *menu* for 65FF. Two blocks up at 1 Arcades de la Poissonnerie, ***Chiquita Tex Rock's*** (☎ 02 35 84 17 54) serves American-style hamburgers and Tex-Mex dishes with *menus* from 80FF – perhaps not every-body's cup of tequila in a town noted for seafood ...

Just behind the Casino at 43 Rue du Commandant Fayolle, ***Les Tourelles*** (☎ 02 35 84 15 88) serves good-value *menus* from 59FF and generous paellas from 85F (which must be ordered 24 hours in advance). The friendly ***La Chaumière*** (☎ 02 35 40 18 54), on the waterfront at 1 Quai du Hâble, has an excellent 68FF seafood *menu*, but if you really want to taste Dieppe's *fruits de la mer* at their best, head for ***À la Marmite Dieppoise*** (☎ 02 35 84 24 26) at 8 Rue Saint Jean in the old city. *Menus* are from 85 to 145FF, and the restaurant is closed Sunday evening and all day Monday.

Self-Catering The ***food market*** between Place Saint Jacques and Place Nationale is open on Tuesday and Thursday mornings and all day Saturday.

The ***boulangerie*** at 15 Quai Henri IV is open daily from 7 am to 7.30 pm (closed Monday). There are other bakeries along the Grande Rue, Rue Saint Jacques and at 14 Rue de la Boucherie (closed Wednes-day). You'll find ***grocery stores*** on Rue de la Barre, Rue de l'Épée and Rue du Haut Pas. The ***Martinez grocery*** at 44 Rue du Haut Pas is open from 7.30 am to 8.30 pm (closed Monday).

Entertainment

Dieppe has loads of pubs and bars full of interesting characters, but don't be surprised if you have to buzz to be let in. It's not a particularly rough town, but sailors (and many travellers from across the Channel) tend to overindulge from time to time. The ***Scottish Pub***, 12 Rue Saint Jacques, is a good place to start a crawl, and the friendly bar staff will point you in the right direction. ***Café des Tribunaux*** is in an early 18th century building on Place du Puits Salé. Farther west on Place de la Barre, the ***Hôtel Select*** (☎ 02 35 84 14 66), another British-owned establishment, features live jazz most Friday nights in the bar.

Getting There & Away

Bus The bus station (☎ 02 35 84 21 97), in the same cavernous building as the train station, south of the city centre on Blvd Georges Clemenceau, is open from 8 am to noon and 2 to 6 pm daily, except Saturday and Sunday afternoon, and when there are no buses. There are services to Fécamp (72FF; two a day, two or three a day in July and August), Le Tréport (39FF; four a day) and Rouen (69FF; two hours; three a day).

Train The information office at the train station (☎ 08 36 35 35 35) is open daily, except Sunday, from 9.40 am to 12.30 pm and from 2 to 6 pm.

The paucity of direct trains to Paris' Gare Saint Lazare (144FF; 2¼ hours) is offset by frequent services to Rouen (54FF), which is 45 to 60 minutes from Dieppe and 70 minutes from Gare Saint Lazare. The last train from Dieppe to Paris (via Rouen) leaves just after 6.30 pm Monday to Saturday; on Sunday, there is a service to Paris (via Rouen) at 8.09 pm.

Boat The first ferry service from Dieppe to England (Brighton, to be exact) began in 1790. These days, Stena Sealink (☎ 02 35 06 39 03) runs car ferries between Dieppe and Newhaven. The ferry terminal for pedestrians and cars is on the north-east side of the port area at the end of Quai de la Marne. Tickets and information are also available from Sealink Voyages (☎ 08 36 68 88 89). For details on prices and schedules, see the Sea section in the introductory Getting There & Away chapter.

Getting Around

Bus The local bus network, Stradibus, runs 11 lines, which vary considerably in frequency. Some run on Sunday, others don't; some run until 6 pm, others until 8 pm. All buses stop at either the train station or the nearby Chambre de Commerce, on Quai Duquesne. Stradibus' information office (☎ 02 32 14 03 03), 56 Quai Duquesne, near the fire station, has timetables and is open weekdays from 8 am till noon and 1.30 to 6.30 pm. A single ticket costs 6.20FF, a 10 ticket carnet 41FF.

A free bus timed to meet incoming and outgoing ferries shuttles foot passengers between the terminal and the tourist office.

Taxi Taxis can be ordered by calling ☎ 02 35 84 20 05. The fare from the ferry pier to the city centre is about 30FF.

CÔTE D'ALBÂTRE

Stretching 100km from Dieppe south to Étretat, the tall, white cliffs and stony beaches of the Côte d'Albâtre (Alabaster Coast) are reminiscent of the coast of southern England. Small villages and a few resorts nestle in the dry valleys leading down from the Pays de Caux, a chalky inland plateau.

Without a car, the Côte d'Albâtre is rather inaccessible. However, hikers can follow the coastal GR21 from Dieppe to Le Havre. If you are driving, take the coastal road, which starts as the D75 west of Dieppe, and not the inland D925. The Côte d'Albâtre's two main centres are Fécamp and Étretat, both of which are at the southern end.

Fécamp

• pop 21,000 ✉ 76400

Fécamp was little more than a fishing village until the 6th century, when a few drops of Christ's blood miraculously found their way here and it became a pilgrimage centre. An order of Benedictine monks soon established a monastery, and the 'medicinal elixir' concocted there in the early 16th century helped keep Fécamp on the map. The recipe, lost during the Revolution, was rediscovered in the 19th century and the after-dinner liqueur was produced commercially. Today, Bénédictine is one of the most popular and widely marketed digestives in the world.

Information The tourist office (☎ 02 35 28 51 01; fax 02 35 27 07 77) is south of the Palais Bénédictine at 113 Rue Alexandre Le Grand. It is open daily from 10 am to 12.15 pm and 1.45 to 6 pm (and continually from 10 am to 6 pm in July and August).

Palais Bénédictine The Bénédictine Distillery (☎ 02 35 10 26 10) is at 110 Rue Alexandre Le Grand in an ornate building (1900) mixing Flamboyant Gothic and eclectic styles, inspired by the 15th century Hôtel de Cluny in Paris. It is geared up to tell you everything about the history and making of its aromatic liqueur – except the exact recipe. Tours start in the Art Museum, which houses the private collection of founder Alexandre Le Grand, and continues through a hall where hundreds of bottles of bootlegged Bénédictine are proudly displayed. In the fragrant Plant & Spice Room, you can smell a handful of some of the ingredients used to make the potent drink. Saffron, myrrh and cinnamon (along with two dozen other herbs and spices) are blended in copper vats in the nearby distillery. The tour ends in the attractive Modern Art Gallery, which has changing exhibits.

Opening hours for the Palais vary. From mid-March to mid-May and early September to mid-November, it's open from 10 am to noon and 2 to 5.30 pm; from mid-May to early September the hours are 9.30 am to 6 pm. From mid-November to mid-March there are only two visits a day – at 10.30 am and 3.30 pm. Admission is 27/20/13.50FF for adults/students/children and includes a free shot of Bénédictine at the end – before you exit via the gift shop.

Getting There & Away Fécamp is accessible by bus from Dieppe, Le Havre and Rouen, and by train from Le Havre. See those sections for more information.

Getting Around Mountain bikes and 10-speeds (80FF a day) are available for rent from Location Vélo-VTT (☎ 02 35 28 45 09), north-east of the tourist office and Palais Bénédictine at 2 Ave Gambetta.

Étretat

• pop 1600 ✉ 76280

The small village of Étretat, which is 20km south-west of Fécamp, has long been renowned for its two cliffs: the Falaise d'Amont and the Falaise d'Aval. Featuring the most unusual rock formations in the area, you'll see them long before you arrive, plastered on all the region's tourist brochures and postcards, and appearing somewhat deceivingly to be one rock.

Beyond the Falaise d'Aval to the south-west of the village is the simply stunning Manneporte rock arch and the 70m-high Aiguille (Needle), which pierces the surface of the water behind the arch. From the western end of Étretat's stony beach, a steep path leads to the top of the cliff, which affords a fine view of the rocks. On the Falaise d'Amont opposite, a memorial marks the spot where two aviators were last seen before their attempt to cross the Atlantic in 1927. Do not try to explore the base of the cliffs outside low tide.

Information The tourist office (☎ 02 35 27 05 21), in the centre of the village on Place Maurice Guillard, has lists of accommodation available in the area and sensibly posts them on the door for inspection outside its opening hours. It's open daily from 10 am till noon and 2 to 6 pm. It also has a map of the cliff trails.

Getting There & Away The easiest way to reach Étretat is by bus from Le Havre, 28km to the south. For information, see that section.

LE HAVRE

• pop 196,000 ✉ 76600

Le Havre, France's second most important port, is also a bustling gateway for ferries to Britain and Ireland. Unfortunately, there's not much more you can say in favour of this coastal city at the mouth of the Seine. All but obliterated by WWII bombing raids that killed 5000 citizens, Le Havre was rebuilt around its historical remains by Auguste Perret, one of the leading modern architects of the time, who also designed the city's 100m-high 'Stalinist baroque' Église Saint Joseph, which is, unfortunately, visible from all points. The result is a regimented grid of wide, straight central streets – there are more roads per inhabitant here than anywhere else in France – lined with row upon row of three storey, reinforced-concrete buildings. West of the city, the area north of the Seine is lined with shipyards, chemical plants and other industries.

Orientation

With such a rigid layout of streets, Le Havre is easy to navigate. The main square is the enormous Place de l'Hôtel de Ville with its lovely gardens, fountains and equally huge town hall on the north side. Ave Foch runs westward to the sea and the Port de Plaisance recreational area; Blvd de Strasbourg goes eastward to the train and bus stations. Rue de Paris cuts southward past the Espace Oscar Niemeyer, a square named after the Brazilian who designed two cultural centre buildings (which have been compared to a truncated cooling tower and a toilet bowl).

Rue de Paris ends at the Quai de Southampton and the Bassin de la Manche, from where ferries to Britain set sail out of the Terminal de la Citadelle, south-east of the central square. Within easy walking distance of the terminal and Place de l'Hôtel de Ville is the Quartier Saint François, Le Havre's 'old city' where there are several good restaurants.

Information

Tourist Office The tourist office (☎ 02 32 74 04 04; fax 02 35 42 38 39) is on the ground floor of the Hôtel de Ville, entered on the northern side. It's open Monday to Saturday from 8.45 am to 6 pm and on Sunday from 10 am to 1 pm. From May to September it's open daily from 8.45 am to 7 pm, except Sunday when it is open from 10 am to 12.30 pm and 2.30 to 6 pm.

Money The Société Générale opposite the main post office at 2 Place Léon Meyer is open Monday to Friday from 8 am to 5 pm. There are lots more banks on Blvd de Strasbourg. An exchange bureau opposite the old Irish Ferries terminal at 41 Blvd Kennedy is open Monday to Saturday from 8 am to 12.30 pm and 1.30 to 7 pm; in July and August hours are 8 am to 7.30 pm.

American Express (☎ 02 32 74 75 76) is at 57 Quai Georges V, which is south of Blvd de Strasbourg and runs parallel to it. It is open weekdays from 8.45 till noon and 1.30 to 6 pm.

Post Le Havre's main post office, 62 Rue Jules Siegfried, is open weekdays from 8 am to 7 pm and on Saturday till noon. There's also a post office at the southern end of Rue de Paris, opposite the old Irish Ferries terminal.

Laundry The laundrette at 23 Rue Jean de la Fontaine is open daily from 7 am to 9 pm.

Musée des Beaux-Arts

There's only one thing really worth seeing in Le Havre and that's the Fine Arts Museum (☎ 02 35 42 33 97), on Blvd Kennedy about 200m west of the old Irish Ferries terminal. Noted for its excellent collection of impressionist paintings, including some by Monet, it also has a good selection of works by Raoul Dufy, a native of Le Havre, and Eugène Boudin, an early impressionist who spent part of his youth here. The museum is closed for renovations until March 1999. Check with the tourist office for opening hours and prices.

Places to Stay

Though there is no surfeit of cheap places in Le Havre, some budget accommodation can be found.

Places to Stay – Budget & Mid-Range

Camping The closest camping ground to the centre is ***Camping de la Forêt de Montgeon*** (☎ 02 35 46 52 39), nearly 3km north of town in a 250 hectare forest. It's open from April to September and charges 52FF for one or two people with a tent. From the station, take bus No 11 and alight after it has gone through the 700m-long Jenner Tunnel. Then walk north through the park for another 1.5km.

Hotels A line of nondescript hotels faces the train station. However, hidden down an alley opposite the station (to the right of the Hertz office) is the ***Hôtel d'Yport*** (☎ 02 35 25 21 08; fax 02 35 24 06 34) at 27 Cours de la République. It's a friendly place with a range of rooms including basic singles/doubles/triples from 141/167/213FF. A hall shower costs a whopping 25FF extra. Rooms with a shower start at 171/182/243FF. The hotel has a private garage (30FF).

Also close to the station is the ***Grand Hôtel Parisien*** (☎ 02 35 25 23 83; fax 02 35 25 05 06), on the corner of Blvd de Strasbourg at 1 Cours de la République. Clean and pleasant, it has singles/doubles from 210/240FF with shower and TV.

Near the old Irish Ferries terminal, there are a couple of decent places. The ***Hôtel Le Monaco*** (☎ 02 35 42 21 01), 16 Rue de Paris (turn right as you leave the ferry building and take the first left), has shipshape rooms from 140/165FF. Nearby at 11 Quai de Southampton, the tiny ***Le Ferry Boat*** (☎ 02 35 42 29 55) has seven rooms from 145FF, but it's often full. Hall showers are free.

Places to Stay – Top End

The shocking-pink ***Hôtel Le Mercure*** (☎ 02 35 19 50 50; fax 02 35 19 50 99) is on Chaussée d'Angoulême, across from the Bassin du Commerce and next to the World Trade Centre building. It's one of the top hotels in town and charges from 545FF.

Near the opposite end of the Bassin du Commerce is the ***Hôtel Le Bordeaux*** (☎ 02 35 22 69 44; fax 02 35 42 09 27), 147 Rue Louis Brindeau. Rooms cost 385/470FF with discounted rates at weekends.

Places to Eat

The area around the train station has several decently priced restaurants, including ***Flunch*** (☎ 02 35 46 59 82), a cheap, cheerful self-service restaurant attached to Auchan hypermarket in the Mont Gaillard shopping centre (clearly signed from the station). Another budget option is the restaurant at the ***YMCA*** (☎ 02 35 19 87 87), 153 Blvd de Strasbourg, about 400m west of the train station. (Accommodation at the YMCA is for long-term guests only.)

The Quartier Saint François is the best place to eat, with almost 50 restaurants to choose from. Crêperies and couscous restaurants are in abundance. For the former, try ***Au Petit Breton*** (☎ 02 35 21 44 14), 11 Rue Dauphine. Couscous starts at 60FF.

The restaurant at the ***Hôtel Le Monaco*** has excellent seafood *menus* from 130FF.

Getting There & Away

Bus The bus station (☎ 02 35 26 67 23) lies just south of the train station on Blvd de Strasbourg. Caen-based Bus Verts du Calvados (☎ 02 31 44 77 44) and Rouen's CNA (☎ 02 35 52 92 00) run regional services from here to Caen, Honfleur, Rouen and other destinations. Auto-Cars Gris (☎ 02 35 27 04 25) has 10 buses a day to Fécamp (44FF; 1½ hours) via Étretat, but that frequency is halved on Sunday. The bus information office is open weekdays from 8 am to noon and 2 to 6 pm.

Train Le Havre's train station (☎ 08 36 35 35 35) is about 1km east of the city centre on Cours de la République. The information office is open daily from 5.15 am (7.15 am on Sunday) to 8 pm. The main rail destinations are Rouen (91FF; one hour; 15 a day) and Paris' Gare Saint Lazare (147FF; 2¼ hours; 10 a day). A secondary line goes north to Fécamp (43FF; 1¼ hours; five a day), but you must be sure to change at Bréauté-Beuzeville.

Boat P&O European Ferries (☎ 02 35 19 78 78), which links Le Havre with Portsmouth, uses the new Terminal de la Citadelle on Ave Lucien Corbeaux just over a kilometre south-west of the train station. The information desk is open daily from 9 am to 7 pm. A special bus (7.50FF) takes passengers from the terminal to the tourist office and the train station 15 minutes after the arrival of each ferry.

For information on schedules and prices see the Sea section in the Getting There & Away chapter.

Getting Around

Bus Bus Océane runs 14 lines in and around Le Havre as well as a small funicular linking Place Thiers with Rue Félix Faure near the hilltop Fort de Tournville. Bus Océane's information office (☎ 02 35 43 46 00), in a kiosk east of the tourist office on Place de l'Hôtel de Ville, is open Monday to Saturday from 7 am to 7 pm. A single ticket is 8FF, a carnet of 10 is 53FF, and a Ticket Ville, valid for a day, is 18FF. The three-minute funicular ride costs 2FF up and 1FF down.

Taxi To order a taxi, ring ☎ 02 35 25 81 81 or ☎ 02 35 25 81 00.

Calvados

The department of Calvados stretches from Honfleur in the east to Isigny-sur-Mer in the west. It is famed for its rich pastures and farm products: butter, cheese, cider and an apple-flavoured brandy called Calvados. The D-day beaches extend along almost the entire coast of Calvados.

HONFLEUR

• pop 8300 ✉ 14600

The picturesque seaside town of Honfleur sits opposite Le Havre at the mouth of the Seine. Because it's only about 200km north-west of Paris – closer to the capital than almost any other point on the coast – multitudes of Parisian day-trippers flock to the town. There are no beaches in Honfleur, but there are some fine stretches of sand not far away. Just 15km south-west are the up-market coastal resorts of Deauville and Trouville.

In the 19th century, Honfleur attracted a steady stream of artists, among them many impressionists. The town escaped damage during WWII and retains much of its traditional architecture. Because of extensive siltation, centuries-old wooden houses that once lined the seafront quay now lie several hundred metres inland. The graceful, 2km-long Pont de Normandie over the Seine, linking Honfleur with Le Havre for the first time, opened to great fanfare in January 1995.

History

Honfleur's seafaring tradition dates back over a millennium. After the Norman invasion of England in 1066, goods bound for the conquered territory were shipped across the Channel from Honfleur.

In 1608, Samuel de Champlain set sail from here on his way to found Quebec City. In 1681, Cavelier de la Salle started out from Honfleur to explore what is now the USA. He reached the mouth of the Mississippi and named the area Louisiana in honour of King Louis XIV, ruler of France at the time. During the 17th and 18th centuries, Honfleur achieved a certain degree of prosperity through trade with the West Indies, the Azores and the colonies on the west coast of Africa.

Orientation

Honfleur is centred around the Vieux Bassin, the old harbour. To the east is the heart of the old city, known as the Enclos because it was once enclosed by fortifications. To the north is the Avant Port (Outer Harbour), where the fishing fleet is based. Quai Sainte Catherine fronts the Vieux Bassin on the west, while Rue de la République runs southward from it. The Plateau de Grâce, with Chapelle Notre Dame de Grâce on top, is west of town.

Information

Tourist Office The tourist office (☎ 02 31 89 23 30; fax 02 31 89 31 82) is in the Enclos at Place Arthur Boudin, a couple of blocks south-east of the Vieux Bassin. Between Easter and September it is open Monday to Saturday from 9.30 am to 12.30 pm and 2 to 6 pm. The rest of the year, it closes at 5.30 pm. From Easter to October the office is open on Sunday from 10 am to 1 pm.

From July to September the tourist office has two-hour guided tours of Honfleur on Saturday at 3 pm. The cost is 32/28FF for adults/children.

Post The main post office is south-west of the centre on Rue de la République, just past Place Albert Sorel.

Église Sainte Catherine

This wooden church, whose stone predecessor was destroyed during the Hundred Years' War, was built by the people of Honfleur during the second half of the 15th and the early 16th centuries. It is thought that they chose wood, which could be worked by local shipwrights, in an effort to save money in order to strengthen the fortifications of the Enclos. The structure that the town's ship's carpenters created, which was intended to be temporary, has a vaulted roof that looks like an overturned ship's hull. The church is also remarkable for its twin naves. Église Sainte Catherine is open to visitors daily from 9 am to noon and 2 to 6 pm except during services.

Clocher Sainte Catherine

The church's freestanding wooden bell tower, Clocher Sainte Catherine (☎ 02 31 89 54 00), was constructed during the second half of the 15th century. It was built apart from the church for both structural reasons (so the church roof would not be subject to the bells' weight and vibrations) and for reasons of safety (a high tower was more likely to be hit by lightning). The former bell-ringer's residence at the base of the tower houses a small museum of liturgical objects, but the huge, rough-hewn beams are of more interest.

From mid-March to September the bell tower is open from 10 am to noon and from 2 to 6 pm (closed Tuesday). The rest of the year, it's open weekdays, except Tuesday, from 2.30 to 5 pm and on weekends from 10 am to noon and 2.30 to 5 pm. Tickets, which cost 30FF (25FF for students), also get you into the Musée Eugène Boudin. Tickets are 10FF for Clocher Sainte Catherine only.

Musée Eugène Boudin

Named in honour of the early impressionist painter born here in 1824, this museum (☎ 02 31 89 54 00), on Rue de l'Homme de Bois at Place Erik Satie, has an excellent collection of impressionist paintings from Normandy, including works by Boudin, Dubourg, Dufy and Monet. It has the same opening hours as the Clocher Sainte Catherine.

Harbours

The **Vieux Bassin**, from where ships bound for the New World once set sail, now shelters mainly pleasure boats. The nearby quays and streets, especially **Quai Sainte Catherine**, are lined with tall, narrow houses – many faced with bluish-grey slate shingles – dating from the 16th to 18th centuries. The **Lieutenance**, once the residence of the town's royal governor, is at the mouth of the old harbour.

The **Avant Port**, on the other side of the Lieutenance, is home to Honfleur's 50 or so fishing vessels. Farther north, dikes line both sides of the entrance to the port.

Either harbour makes a pleasant route for a walk to the seashore. One-hour **boat tours** of the Vieux Bassin and the port area are available on the *Calypso* for 20FF. Ask at the tourist office where to board.

Musée de la Marine

Honfleur's small Maritime Museum (☎ 02 31 89 14 12) is on the eastern side of the Vieux Bassin in the deconsecrated Église Saint Étienne, which was begun in 1369 and enlarged during the English occupation of Honfleur (1415-50). Displays include assorted model ships, ship's carpenters' tools and engravings.

From April to late September, it's open daily, except Monday, from 10 am to noon and 2 to 6 pm. At other times, the museum is open weekdays from 2 to 6 pm, and weekends from 10 am to noon and 2 to 6 pm; closed from mid-November to mid-February. Entrance to both the Musée de la Marine and the Musée d'Ethnographie et d'Art Populaire Normand is 25/15FF for adults/students.

Musée d'Ethnographie et d'Art Populaire Normand

Next to the Musée de la Marine on Rue de la Prison, the Museum of Ethnography & Norman Folk Art (☎ 02 31 89 14 12) occupies a couple of houses and a former prison dating from the 16th and 17th centuries. It contains 12 furnished rooms of the sort you would have found in the shops and wealthy homes of Honfleur between the 16th and 19th centuries.

It can be visited only if you join one of the guided tours (in French), which leave about once an hour. Opening hours and entry fees are the same as those at the Musée de la Marine.

Greniers à Sel

The two huge salt stores (☎ 02 31 89 02 30) on Rue de la Ville, down the block from the tourist office, were built in the late 17th century of stone and oak in order to store the salt needed by the fishing fleet to cure its catch of herring and cod. For most of the year, the only way to see the Greniers à Sel is to take a guided tour (inquire at the tourist office). During July and August the stores host art exhibitions and concerts.

Chapelle Notre Dame de Grâce

This chapel, built between 1600 and 1613, is at the top of the Plateau de Grâce, a wooded, 100m-high hill about 1km west of the Vieux Bassin. There's a great view of the town and port.

Beach

The beach nearest Honfleur is a bit under 1km west of the Vieux Bassin, but it is not very attractive – its ambiance spoiled by the views of oil refineries in the distance. There are better beaches to the west in the direction of Trouville.

Places to Stay

Honfleur is not a cheap place to spend the night, but it is an easy day trip from Le Havre.

Camping *Camping du Phare* (☎ 02 31 89 10 26), about 500m north-west of the Vieux Bassin along Blvd Charles V, is open from April to September. To reach it from the centre of town, follow Rue Haute. It costs 25FF per person and 35FF for a tent site and car.

Hotels The ***Bar de la Salle des Fêtes*** (☎ 02 31 89 19 69), 8 Place Albert Sorel, 400m south-west of the Vieux Bassin along Rue de la République, charges 160FF (including breakfast) for each of its four double rooms. The ***Auberge de la Claire*** (☎ 02 31 89 05 95; fax 02 31 89 11 37), 77 Cours Albert Manuel, 700m south-west, has apartments from 400FF.

More centrally located, the ***Hôtel Le Hamelin*** (☎ 02 31 89 16 25), near the Église Sainte Catherine at 16 Place Hamelin, has doubles with shower from 180FF. Near the tourist office, the ***Hôtel des Cascades*** (☎ 02 31 89 05 83; fax 02 31 89 32 13), 17 Place Thiers, has rooms from 200FF.

The ***Hôtel Le Moderne*** (☎ 02 31 89 44 11), 20 Quai Lepaulmier, has very simple singles/doubles for 125/195FF as well as doubles with shower for 300FF.

Places to Eat

Restaurants Places to dine are abundant (especially along Quai Sainte Catherine) but they don't come cheaply: *menus* start at about 85FF. The ***Hôtel Le Moderne*** is one of the less expensive places, with *menus* from 70FF. Otherwise you'll just have to splurge along with everyone else. One highly recommended spot is the cosy ***La Tortue*** (☎ 02 31 89 04 93), near the Musée Eugène Boudin at 36 Rue de l'Homme de Bois, whose succulent seafood *menus* start at 99FF.

Self-Catering The Saturday ***market*** at Place Sainte Catherine runs from 8 am to 1 pm. There's a ***Champion*** supermarket just west of Rue de la République, near Place Albert Sorel. It's open Monday to Friday from 8.30 am to 12.30 pm and 2.30 to 7.30 pm, and 8.30 am to 7.30 pm on Saturday. The large ***Marché U***, on Ave de Canteloup, is open Tuesday to Saturday from 9 am to 12.30 pm and 3 to 7.30 pm, and on Sunday and Monday mornings.

Shopping

There are quite a few art galleries and crafts shops along the streets east and north of Église Sainte Catherine. On Saturday mornings, local artisans sell their work at Place Arthur Boudin and along Rue de la Ville.

Getting There & Away

Bus The bus station (☎ 02 31 89 28 41) is south-east of the Vieux Bassin on Rue des Vases. The information kiosk is open from 9 am to 12.15 pm and 2.30 to 5.30 pm on weekdays and on Saturday morning.

Bus Verts (☎ 02 31 44 77 44 in Caen) has services via Deauville (20.80FF; 30 minutes; line No 20) to Caen (67FF or 86FF by express bus). In the other direction, the same line goes northward to Le Havre (41.60FF; 30 minutes; five a day) via the Pont de Normandie. Line No 50 goes to Lisieux (one hour). Bus Verts offers a 12% discount for people under 26 on Wednesday, Saturday afternoon and Sunday.

CAEN

• pop 115,000 ✉ 14000

Caen, the capital of Basse Normandie, was one of the many Norman cities to suffer heavily in WWII. Bombed on D-day, the city burned for over a week before being liberated by the Canadians – only to be then shelled by the Germans. Three-quarters of the city was flattened, the only vestiges of the past to survive being the ramparts around the chateau and the two great abbeys, all built by William the Conqueror when he founded the city in the 11th century. Much of the medieval city was built from 'Caen stone', a creamy local limestone exported for centuries over the channel to England.

Linked to the sea by a canal running parallel to the Orne River, Caen has seen rapid expansion in recent years and these days is a bustling university city. It is also the gateway for Ouistreham, a minor passenger port for ferries to England.

Orientation

Caen's modern heart is made up of a few pedestrianised shopping streets and some busy boulevards. The largest, Ave du 6 Juin, links the centre, which is based around the southern end of the chateau, with the canal and train station to the south-east. What's left of the old city is centred around Rue du Vaugueux, a short distance south-east of the chateau.

Information

Tourist Office The modern tourist office (☎ 02 31 27 14 14; fax 02 31 27 14 13), on Place Saint Pierre, is open Monday to Saturday from 10 am to 1 pm and 2 to 6 pm. On Sunday the hours are 10 am to 1 pm. In July and August it is open Monday to Saturday from 10 am to 7 pm, and on Sunday from 10 am to 1 pm and 2 to 5 pm. Hotel reservations within the city cost 10FF. The office sells various maps including one to the D-day beaches (39FF).

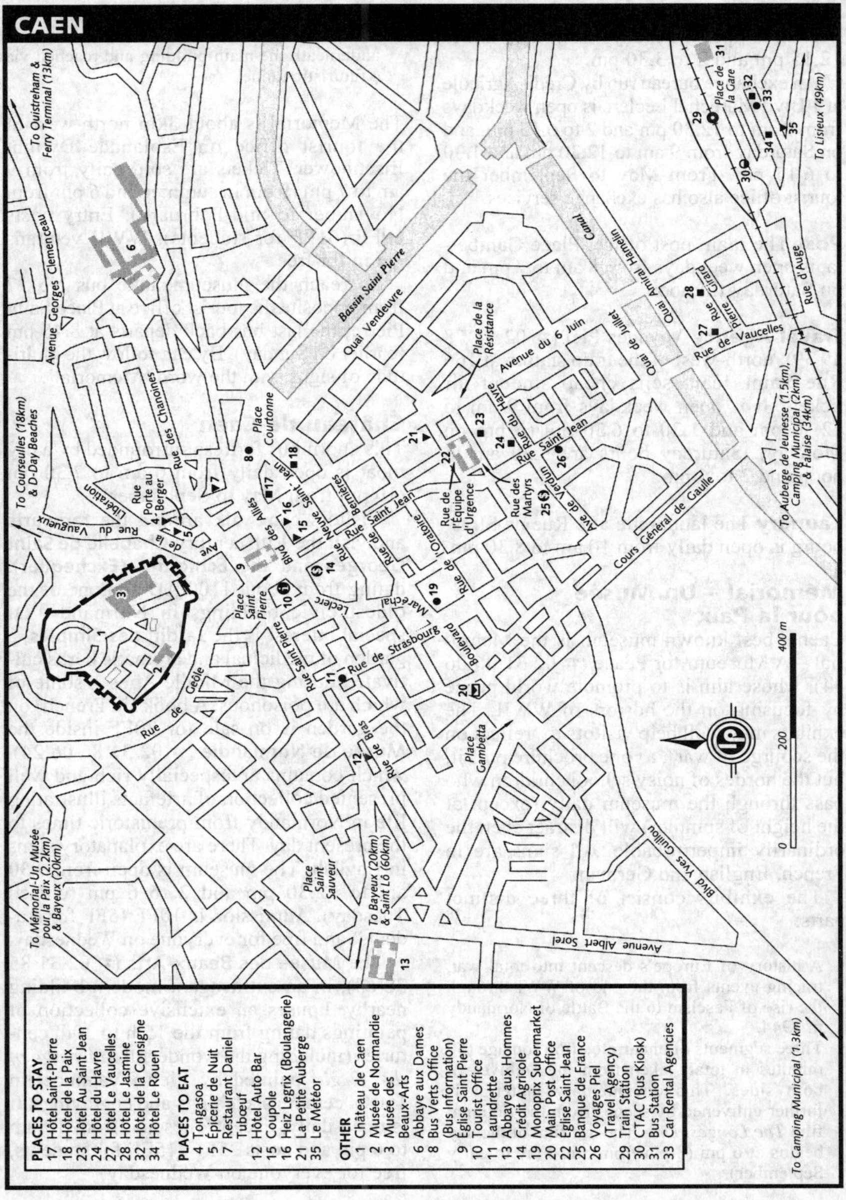
CAEN
To Ouistreham & Ferry Terminal (13km)
To Courseulles (18km) & D-Day Beaches
To Mémorial-Un Musée pour la Paix (2.2km) & Bayeux (20km)
To Bayeux (20km) & Saint Lô (60km)
To Auberge de Jeunesse (1.5km), Camping Municipal (2km) & Falaise (34km)
To Camping Municipal (1.3km)
To Lisieux (49km)
Avenue Georges Clemenceau
Bassin Saint Pierre
Quai Vendeuvre
Rue des Chanoines
Place Courtonne
Rue du Vaugueux
Ave de la Libération
Rue Porte au Berger
Place Saint Pierre
Blvd des Alliés
Rue Neuve Saint Jean
Rue Saint Pierre
Rue de Geôle
Rue de Strasbourg
Blvd Maréchal Leclerc
Rue Bernières
Rue de Saint Jean
Rue de l'Oratoire
Rue de l'Équipe d'Urgence
Place de la Résistance
Avenue du 6 Juin
Quai de Juillet
Quai Amiral Hamelin
Canal
Rue du Havre
Rue des Martyrs
Rue Saint Jean
Ave de Verdun
Cours Général de Gaulle
Boulevard
Place Gambetta
Rue de Bras
Place Saint Sauveur
Blvd Yves Guillou
Avenue Albert Sorel
Place de la Gare
Rue de Vaucelles
Rue Pierre Girard
Rue d'Auge
0 200 400 m
PLACES TO STAY
17 Hôtel Saint-Pierre
18 Hôtel de la Paix
23 Hôtel Au Saint Jean
24 Hôtel du Havre
27 Hôtel Le Vaucelles
28 Hôtel Le Jasmine
32 Hôtel de la Consigne
34 Hôtel Le Rouen
PLACES TO EAT
4 Tongasoa
5 Épicerie de Nuit
7 Restaurant Daniel Tubœuf
12 Hôtel Auto Bar
15 Coupole
16 Heiz Legrix (Boulangerie)
21 La Petite Auberge
35 Le Météor
OTHER
1 Château de Caen
2 Musée de Normandie
3 Musée des Beaux-Arts
6 Abbaye aux Dames
8 Bus Verts Office (Bus Information)
9 Église Saint Pierre
10 Tourist Office
11 Laundrette
13 Abbaye aux Hommes
14 Crédit Agricole
19 Monoprix Supermarket
20 Main Post Office
22 Église Saint Jean
25 Banque de France
26 Voyages Piel (Travel Agency)
29 Train Station
30 CTAC (Bus Kiosk)
31 Bus Station
33 Car Rental Agencies

Money The Banque de France at 14 Ave de Verdun is open weekdays from 8.45 am to 12.15 pm and 2 to 3.30 pm.

An exchange bureau run by Crédit Agricole at 1 Blvd Maréchal Leclerc is open weekdays from 9 am to 12.30 pm and 2 to 6.15 pm, and on Saturday from 9 am to 12.30 pm and 1.30 to 6.15 pm. From May to September the tourist office also has exchange services.

Post The main post office, Place Gambetta, is open weekdays from 8 am to 7 pm and on Saturday till noon.

Travel Agency Voyages Piel (☎ 02 31 78 39 39), north-west of the train station at 166 Rue Saint Jean, sells cheap student air tickets. It is open weekdays from 9 am to 12.30 pm and 1.30 to 6.30 pm (6 pm on Monday). Saturday hours are 9.30 am to noon and 2 to 6 pm.

Laundry The laundrette at 8 Rue de Strasbourg is open daily from 10 am to 8.30 pm.

Mémorial – Un Musée pour la Paix

Caen's best known museum is the Memorial – A Museum for Peace (☎ 02 31 06 06 44), whose aim is to promote world peace by focusing on the horrors of WWII. The exhibits may well help visitors to 'reflect on the scourge of war', as one brochure puts it, but the hordes of noisy school children who pass through the museum daily (except at the height of summer) will distract even the ordinarily imperturbable. All signs are in French, English and German.

The exhibits consist of three distinct parts:

- A history of Europe's descent into total war, tracing events from the end of WWI through the rise of Fascism to the Battle of Normandy in 1944.
- Three segments of unnarrated film footage (50 minutes in total) taken from the archives of both sides. This documentary material is further enlivened by scenes from the fictional film *The Longest Day*. The last film of the day begins at 6 pm (8 pm from mid-May to early September).
- An exhibit on Nobel Peace Prize laureates, housed in a former German command post underneath the main building and reached via a futuristic tunnel.

The Mémorial is about 3km north-west of the tourist office on Esplanade Dwight Eisenhower. Tickets are sold daily from 9 am to 7 pm (9 pm in summer and 6 pm from November to mid-February). Entry costs 69FF (61FF for students). WWII veterans get in for free.

To reach the museum, take bus No 17 from opposite the tourist office at Place Saint Pierre; the last bus back departs at 8.45 pm (earlier on Sunday). By car, follow the multitude of signs with the word 'Mémorial'.

Château de Caen

This enormous fortress surrounded by a dry moat is open daily from 6 am to 7.30 pm (10 pm from May to September).

Visitors can walk around the **ramparts** and visit the 12th century **Chapelle de Saint Georges** and the **Échiquier (Exchequer)**, dating from about 1100 AD and one of the oldest civic buildings in Normandy. Of special interest is the **Jardin des Simples**, a garden of medicinal and aromatic herbs cultivated during the Middle Ages – some of which are poisonous. A book (in French) on the garden is on sale for 30FF inside the **Musée de Normandie** (☎ 02 31 86 06 24), which contains an especially rich and well presented collection of artefacts illustrating life in Normandy from prehistoric times to the present day. There are explanatory signs in English. The museum is open from 9.30 am to 12.30 pm and 2 to 6 pm (closed Tuesday). Admission is 10FF (5FF for students) and free for everyone on Wednesday.

The **Musée des Beaux-Arts** (☎ 02 31 85 28 63), in an extravagant modern building nearby, houses an extensive collection of paintings dating from the 15th to 20th centuries (including the wonderful *Marriage of the Virgin* painted by Pietro Vannucci in 1504), ceramics, etchings and engravings. It is open daily, except Tuesday, from 10 am to 6 pm and costs 25FF (15FF for students, free for everyone on Wednesday).

Abbeys

Caen's two Romanesque abbeys were built on opposite sides of town by William the Conqueror and his wife, Matilda of Flanders, after the distant cousins had been absolved by the Roman Catholic church for marrying. The **Abbaye aux Hommes** (Abbey for Men; ☎ 02 31 30 42 81), with its multiturreted Église Saint Étienne, is at the end of Rue Saint Pierre and once contained William's mortal remains. It was here that many townsfolk sheltered during the bombing raids of 1944. Today it is home to the Hôtel de Ville and can be visited by guided tour daily at 9.30 and 11 am and 2.30 and 4 pm. Entrance costs 10FF. Entry to the church is free, which is open daily from 8.15 am to noon and 2 to 7.30 pm.

The starker **Abbaye aux Dames** (Abbey for Women; ☎ 02 31 06 98 98), at the eastern end of Rue des Chanoines, incorporates the Église de la Trinité; look for Matilda's tomb behind the main altar. Access to the abbey, which houses regional government offices, is by guided tour daily at 2.30 and 4 pm. Entry is free.

Places to Stay – Budget

Camping On the bank of the Orne River, the ***Camping Municipal*** (☎ 02 31 73 60 92), on Route de Louvigny, 2.5km south-west of the train station, is open from late April to September. It charges 18FF per person and 10FF for a tent site. To reach the camping ground, take bus No 13 to the Camping stop (last bus at 8 pm).

Near the coast at Ouistreham, ***Camping des Pommiers*** (☎ 02 31 97 12 66), on Rue de la Haie Breton, is open all year, except from mid-December to mid-February. Prices are 19FF per person and the same for a tent site.

Hostel The ***Auberge de Jeunesse*** (☎ 02 31 52 19 96; fax 02 31 84 29 49), 68 Rue Eustache Restout, charges 62FF (plus 10FF for breakfast) but is only open from June to September. It's 2km south-west of the train station – take bus No 5 or 17 (the last one is at 9 pm) to the Cimetière de Vaucelles stop.

Hotels The ***Hôtel de la Paix*** (☎ 02 31 86 18 99), 14 Rue Neuve Saint Jean, has plain, medium-sized singles/doubles starting at 129/139FF. The ***Hôtel du Havre*** (☎ 02 31 86 19 80), 11 Rue du Havre, has average rooms of more than average size from 150FF with washbasin or toilet, and 210/230FF with shower. The ***Hôtel Au Saint Jean*** (☎ 02 31 86 23 35; fax 02 31 86 74 15), 20 Rue des Martyrs, has nicely done singles or doubles for 140FF (with shower) or 190FF (with full bathroom). You'll rest easy here knowing that the belfry of the church next door is empty. There's free enclosed parking.

Near the train station, ***Hôtel Le Vaucelles*** (☎ 02 31 82 23 14), 13 Rue de Vaucelles, has rooms starting at 115FF (140FF with shower and TV). Hall showers are free. ***Hôtel Le Jasmine*** (☎ 02 31 52 00 11), where rooms with shower cost 100/120FF, is nearby at 39 Rue Pierre Girard. The hard-to-miss yellow and green ***Hôtel de la Consigne*** (☎ 02 31 82 23 59), 48-50 Place de la Gare, has doubles from 140FF.

Places to Stay – Mid-Range

Two-star hotels vary considerably in price and quality, with doubles from a low of 100FF to a high of 350FF. A couple of cheaper ones in this bracket face the train station at Place de la Gare.

The ***Hôtel Le Rouen*** (☎ 02 31 34 06 03), 8 Place de la Gare, has decent rooms with washbasin from 115FF and ones with shower from 180FF. In the city centre, ***Hôtel Saint-Pierre*** (☎ 02 31 86 28 20; fax 02 31 85 17 21), 40 Blvd des Alliés, has comfortable but basic rooms from 120/130FF.

Places to Eat

Restaurants The pedestrianised quarter around Rue du Vaugueux to the south-east of the chateau is one of Caen's most popular dining areas. Lots of little, mid-priced restaurants compete here for the custom of tourists and locals alike and serve a vast range of cuisines: North African, Chinese and even Malagasy at ***Tongasoa*** (☎ 02 31 43 87 15), 7 Rue du Vaugueux. The diverse range of main courses start at 55FF. Tongasoa is closed on Sunday for lunch.

Coupole (☎ 02 31 86 37 75), south of the chateau at 6 Blvd des Alliés, has a good-value *menu* for 63FF, salads from 38FF and a selection of local dishes including *tripes à la mode de Caen*. Another central option is ***Hôtel Auto Bar*** (☎ 02 31 86 12 48), 40 Rue de Bras, a local hang-out (closed Saturday evening and Sunday) with a string of *menus*, the cheapest costing 58FF for a three course meal including a glass of wine.

La Petite Auberge (☎ 02 31 86 43 30), 17 Rue de l'Équipe d'Urgence, is a homely little place with *menus* of home-cooked food from 68FF and *plats du jour* from 55FF. Down near the train station at 55 Rue d'Auge is ***Le Météor*** (☎ 02 31 82 31 35). This tiny haunt charges only 48FF for a three course *menu*, including a glass of wine.

For a splurge that won't break the bank, try the tasteful ***Restaurant Daniel Tubœuf*** (☎ 02 31 43 64 48), 8 Rue Buquet. The chef's inventive dishes (and the wonderful 'original contemporary décor') have earned the restaurant one Michelin star. *Menus* for dinner are priced at 110/140/150/220FF. Daniel Tubœuf is closed Sunday, Monday and most of August.

Self-Catering In the city centre, the ***Monoprix*** at 45 Blvd Maréchal Leclerc has a downstairs supermarket that's open Monday to Saturday from 8.30 am to 8.30 pm. Late-night purchases can be made at ***Épicerie de Nuit***, 23 Rue Porte au Berger, open nightly (except Monday) from 8 pm to 2 am. Exquisite *gâteaux* and dozens of types of bread are available at ***Heiz Legrix***, 8 Blvd des Alliés, open daily from 7 am to 7.30 pm, except Monday.

For ***food markets*** head to Place Saint Sauveur on Friday, Blvd Leroy (behind the train station) on Saturday and Place Courtonne on Sunday.

Entertainment

Summer nightlife centres on the brasseries along the Bassin Saint Pierre (marked on some maps as the Port de Plaisance).

Getting There & Away

Bus The modern bus station (☎ 02 31 44 77 44) is next to the train station at Place de la Gare, about 1.5km south-east of the tourist office. Bus Verts serves the entire Calvados department, including Bayeux (36FF; 50 minutes), the eastern D-day beaches, Honfleur (67FF via Cabourg and Deauville, or 86FF by express bus), the ferry port at Ouistreham (21FF; 35 minutes), Falaise, Lisieux and Vire. It also runs two buses a day to Le Havre (1½ hours). The office is open weekdays from 7.30 am (6.30 am on Monday) to 7 pm (7.30 pm on Friday) and on Saturday from 8.30 am to 7 pm.

Most buses stop both at the bus station and in the centre of town at Place Courtonne, where there's a Bus Verts information kiosk. During the summer school holidays (July and August, more or less), the Ligne Côte du Nacre goes to Bayeux (one hour and 20 minutes) twice a day via Ouistreham and the eastern D-day beaches. A line (No 44) to Bayeux takes in the Mémorial, Arromanches, Pointe du Hoc and the American Military Cemetery.

If you arrive in Caen by bus, your ticket is valid on CTAC city buses for one hour. If you purchase your intercity ticket in advance, your ride *to* the bus station to catch your bus is free.

Train The train station's information office (☎ 08 36 35 35 35) and the ticket windows are open daily from 6.30 am to 8 pm.

Caen is on the Paris-Cherbourg line. There are connections to Paris' Gare Saint Lazare (152FF; 2½ hours; 13 a day); Bayeux (31FF; 20 minutes); Cherbourg (97FF; 1½ hours; four a day); Pontorson (119FF; six a day), which is near Mont Saint Michel; Rennes (163FF; three hours; two a day); Rouen (113FF; two hours; 10 a day); and Tours (170FF; 3¾ hours, five a day) via Le Mans.

Car Rental agencies on Place de la Gare include Hertz (☎ 02 31 84 64 50) at No 34, Europcar (☎ 02 31 84 61 61) at No 36 and Avis (☎ 02 31 84 73 80) at No 44. Avis has a bargain-basement rate of 401FF per day plus a per kilometre charge of 1.20FF.

Boat Brittany Ferries (☎ 02 31 36 36 36) sails from Ouistreham, 14km north-east of Caen, to Portsmouth in England. For more information, see the Sea section in the introductory Getting There & Away chapter.

Getting Around

Bus CTAC city bus No 7 and the more direct No 15 run between the train station, where the company has an information kiosk, to the tourist office (stop: Saint Pierre). A single ride costs 5.90FF, and a carnet of 10 is 50.50FF. Services generally end between 6 and 8 pm.

Taxi To order a local taxi, ring ☎ 02 31 26 62 00 or ☎ 02 31 52 17 89.

BAYEUX

• pop 15,000 ✉ 14400

Bayeux is celebrated for two trans-Channel invasions: the conquest of England by the Normans under William the Conqueror in 1066 (an event chronicled in the celebrated Bayeux Tapestry) and the Allied D-day landings of 6 June 1944, which launched the liberation of Nazi-occupied France. Bayeux was the first town in France to be freed and, remarkably, survived virtually unscathed.

Bayeux is a very attractive – though fairly touristy – town with several excellent museums. It also serves as a base for visits to the D-day beaches.

Orientation

The Cathédrale Notre Dame, the major landmark in the centre of Bayeux and visible throughout the town, is 1km north-west of the train station. The Aure River, with several attractive little mills along its banks, flows northward on the eastern side of the centre.

Information

A *billet jumelé* (multipass ticket), valid for four of the five museums listed in this section (excluding the Musée Mémorial) and available at each, costs 38FF (22FF for students).

Tourist Office The tourist office (☎ 02 31 51 28 28; fax 02 31 51 28 29) is at Pont Saint Jean, just off the northern end of Rue Larcher. It is open Monday to Saturday from 9 am to noon and 2 to 6 pm. During July and August, it opens on Sunday from 9.30 am to noon and 2.30 to 6 pm.

Money Banks are open Tuesday to Saturday from 8.30 am to noon and 2 to 5 pm. A Société Générale is at 26 Rue Saint Malo, and a Caisse d'Épargne at No 59 on the same street. The tourist office will change money when the banks are closed (public holidays and Monday).

Post The main post office, opposite the Hôtel de Ville at 14 Rue Larcher, is open weekdays from 8 am to 6.30 pm and on Saturday until noon. It has exchange facilities.

Bookshop The Maison de la Presse (☎ 02 31 92 05 36) at 53 Rue Saint Martin has various maps of the D-day beaches from about 30FF. It is open Monday to Saturday from 8.15 am to 12.30 pm and 2 to 7 pm.

Laundry There's a laundrette at 13 Rue du Maréchal Foch open daily from 8 am to 8 pm.

Bayeux Tapestry

The world-famous Bayeux Tapestry – actually a 70m-long strip of coarse embroidered linen – was commissioned by Bishop Odo of Bayeux, half-brother to William the Conqueror, sometime between the Norman invasion of England in 1066 and 1082. The tapestry, which was probably made in England, recounts the dramatic story of the Norman invasion and the events that led up to it – from the Norman perspective. The story is told in 58 panels, with action-packed scenes following each other in quick succession. The events are accompanied by written commentary in dog Latin. The scenes are filled with depictions of 11th century Norman and Saxon dress, food, tools, cooking utensils and weapons. The Saxons are depicted with moustaches and the backs of the Norman soldiers' heads are shaved. Halley's Comet, which passed through our part of the solar system in 1066, also makes an appearance.

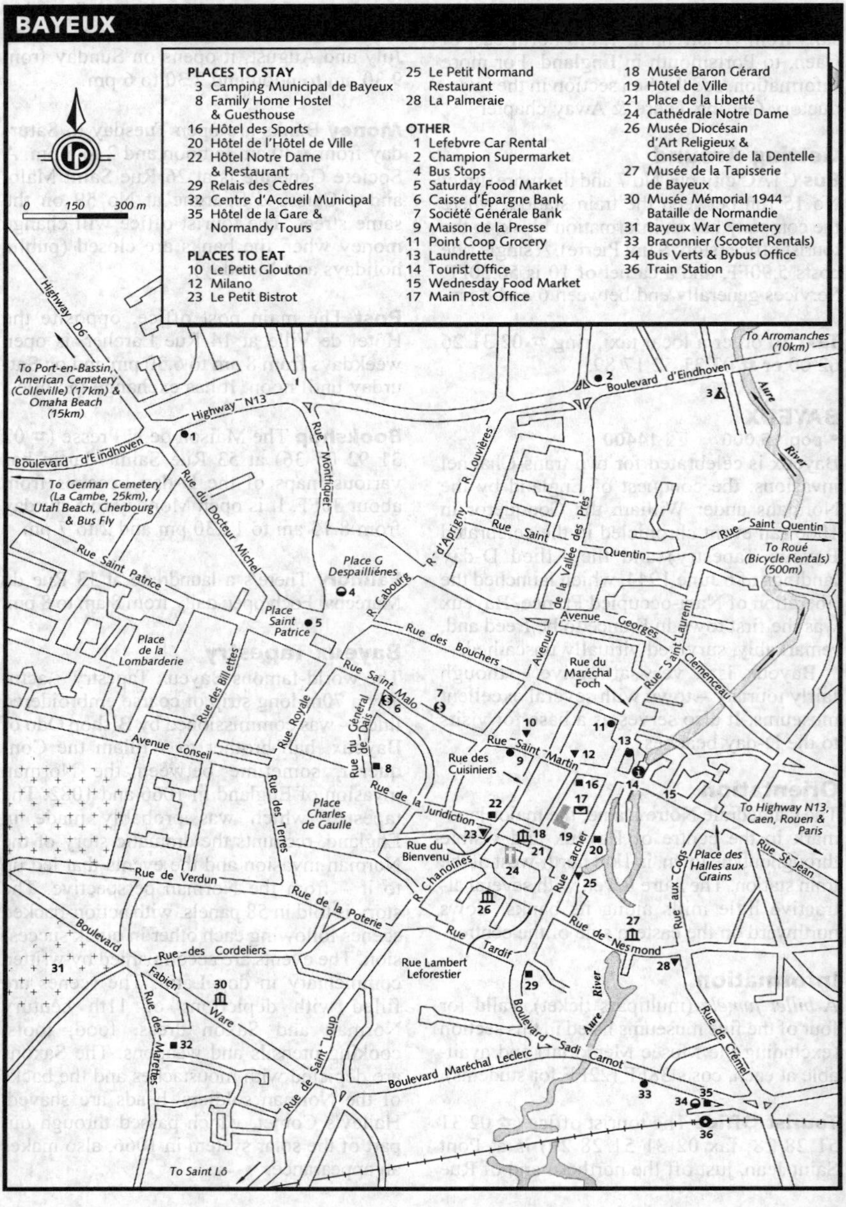
BAYEUX
PLACES TO STAY
3 Camping Municipal de Bayeux
8 Family Home Hostel & Guesthouse
16 Hôtel des Sports
20 Hôtel de l'Hôtel de Ville
22 Hôtel Notre Dame & Restaurant
29 Relais des Cèdres
32 Centre d'Accueil Municipal
35 Hôtel de la Gare & Normandy Tours
PLACES TO EAT
10 Le Petit Glouton
12 Milano
23 Le Petit Bistrot
25 Le Petit Normand Restaurant
28 La Palmeraie
OTHER
1 Lefebvre Car Rental
2 Champion Supermarket
4 Bus Stops
5 Saturday Food Market
6 Caisse d'Épargne Bank
7 Société Générale Bank
9 Maison de la Presse
11 Point Coop Grocery
13 Laundrette
14 Tourist Office
15 Wednesday Food Market
17 Main Post Office
18 Musée Baron Gérard
19 Hôtel de Ville
21 Place de la Liberté
24 Cathédrale Notre Dame
26 Musée Diocésain d'Art Religieux & Conservatoire de la Dentelle
27 Musée de la Tapisserie de Bayeux
30 Musée Mémorial 1944 Bataille de Normandie
31 Bayeux War Cemetery
33 Braconnier (Scooter Rentals)
34 Bus Verts & Bybus Office
36 Train Station
0 150 300 m
To Arromanches (10km)
To Port-en-Bassin, American Cemetery (Colleville) (17km) & Omaha Beach (15km)
To German Cemetery (La Cambe, 25km), Utah Beach, Cherbourg & Bus Fly
To Roué (Bicycle Rentals) (500m)
To Highway N13, Caen, Rouen & Paris
To Saint Lô
Highway D6
Highway N13
Boulevard d'Eindhoven
Rue Montfiquet
Rue du Docteur Michel
Rue Saint Patrice
Place G Despailliénes
Place Saint Patrice
Place de la Lombarderie
Rue des Billettes
Rue Royale
Rue Saint Malo
Rue du Général de Dais
Avenue Conseil
Rue des Terres
Place Charles de Gaulle
Rue de Verdun
Rue de la Poterie
Rue des Cordeliers
Boulevard Fabien Ware
Rue des Marettes
Rue de Saint Loup
Boulevard Maréchal Leclerc
Boulevard Sadi Carnot
R Cabourg
R d'Aprigny
R Louvières
Rue Saint Quentin
Avenue de la Vallée des Prés
Avenue Georges Clemenceau
Rue Saint Laurent
Rue des Bouchers
Rue du Maréchal Foch
Rue Saint Martin
Rue des Cuisiniers
Rue de la Juridiction
Rue du Bienvenu
R Chanoines
Rue Tardif
Rue Lambert Leforestier
Rue Larcher
Rue de Nesmond
Rue aux Cogs
Place des Halles aux Grains
Rue St Jean
Rue de Crémel
Aure River

The tapestry is housed in the **Musée de la Tapisserie de Bayeux** (☎ 02 31 51 25 50), part of the Centre Guillaume le Conquérant on Rue de Nesmond. It is open daily from 9 or 9.30 am to 12.30 pm and 2 to 6 pm. From May to mid-September, the museum does not close at midday and stays open to 7 pm. Entry is 38FF (22FF for students). The excellent taped commentary (which is available in six languages for 5FF) makes viewing the upstairs exhibits somewhat unnecessary. A 14 minute film is screened between eight and 13 times a day in English on the 2nd floor in the Salle Odon. The last showing is at 5.15 pm (5.45 pm from May to mid-September).

Cathédrale Notre Dame

Most of Bayeux's spectacular cathedral, a fine example of Norman Gothic architecture, dates from the 13th century, though the crypt, the arches of the nave and the lower portions of the towers on either side of the main entrance are late 11th century Romanesque. The central tower was added in the 15th century; the copper dome dates from the 1860s. The cathedral is open daily from 8.30 am to 6 pm. In July and August the hours are 8 am to 7 pm.

Musée Diocésain d'Art Religieux

The Diocesan Museum of Religious Art (☎ 02 31 92 14 21), an Aladdin's cave of vestments and liturgical objects, is just south of the cathedral at 6 Rue Lambert Leforestier. It is open daily from 10 am to 12.30 pm and 2 to 6 pm (9 am to 7 pm from July to September). The entry fee is 38FF (22FF for students), which allows you entry to the Conservatoire de la Dentelle in the same building.

Conservatoire de la Dentelle

The fascinating Lace Conservatory (☎ 02 31 92 73 80) is dedicated to the preservation of traditional Norman lacemaking techniques. This is claimed to be the only place where you can watch some of France's most celebrated lacemakers, who are creating the intricate designs using dozens of bobbins and hundreds of pins.

Lace is meant to be looked through, and its quality is judged by the contrast between areas with different knot densities. In the mid-19th century, the Bayeux region had some 60,000 lacemakers. Sections of lace were made by 'subcontractors' in the countryside and assembled into seamless pieces in Bayeux's great manufactory, Lefébère. Much of the production was destined for the South American market.

The Conservatoire also gives lacemaking classes and sells lacemaking materials (pins, bobbins, thread etc). Small lace objects, the product of something like 50 hours work, are on sale for around 750FF. The museum is open the same hours as the Musée Diocésain d'Art Religieux. The admission charge for the Diocesan Museum also allows you into the conservatory (except during exhibitions).

Musée Baron Gérard

This pleasant museum (☎ 02 31 92 14 21), next to the cathedral at Place de la Liberté, specialises in local porcelain, lace and 15th to 19th century paintings (Italian, Flemish, impressionist). Out front there is a huge plane tree known as the Arbre de la Liberté, which, like many such 'Freedom Trees', was planted in the years after the Revolution. It is one of only nine left in France. The museum is open daily from 10 am to 12.30 pm and 2 to 6 pm (9 am to 7 pm from June to mid-September). The entry fee is 38FF (22FF for students).

Musée Mémorial 1944 Bataille de Normandie

Bayeux's huge war museum (☎ 02 31 92 93 41), Blvd Fabien Ware, rather haphazardly displays thousands of photos, uniforms, weapons, newspaper clippings and life-like scenes associated with D-day and the Battle of Normandy. It is open daily from 10 am to 12.30 pm and 2 to 6 pm. From May to mid-September, the opening hours are from 9.30 am to 6.30 pm. Entry costs 31FF (15FF for students). A 30 minute film in English is screened two to five times a day (always at 10.45 am and 5 pm).

William Conquers England

From an unpromising beginning, William the Conqueror (1027-87) became one of the most powerful men of the early Middle Ages and ruler of two kingdoms. The son of Robert I of Normandy and his concubine Arlette (during his lifetime, he was commonly referred to as 'William the Bastard'), William ascended the throne of Normandy at the age of five. In spite of several attempts by rivals – including members of his own family – to kill him and his advisers, William took over the running of Normandy at age 15. For a period of about five years, from when he was about 20, he set about regaining his lost territory and feudal rights, quashing several rebellions along the way. He then began to think of expanding Norman influence.

In England, King Ethelred II (William's relative) had apparently promised William that upon his death, the throne would pass to the young Norman ruler. And when the most powerful Saxon lord in England, Harold Godwinson of Wessex, was shipwrecked on the Norman coast, he was obliged to swear to William that the English crown would pass to Normandy.

In January 1066 Ethelred died without an heir. The great nobles of England (and very likely the majority of the Saxon people) supported Harold's claim to the throne, and he was crowned on 5 January. He immediately faced several pretenders to his throne, William being the most obvious one. But while William was preparing to send an invasion fleet across the Channel, a rival army consisting of an alliance between Harold's estranged brother Tostig and Harold Hardrada of Norway landed in the north of England. Harold marched north and engaged them in battle at Stamford Bridge, near York, on 25 September. He was victorious, and both Harold Hardrada and Tostig were killed.

Meanwhile, William had crossed the Channel unopposed with an army of about 6000 men, including a large cavalry force. They landed at Pevensey before marching to Hastings. Making remarkably quick time southward from York, Harold faced William with about 7000 men from a strong defensive position on 13 October. William put his army into an offensive position, and the battle began the next day.

Although William's archers scored many hits among the densely packed and ill-trained Saxon peasants, the latter's ferocious defence terminated a charge by the Norman cavalry and drove them back in disarray. For a while, William faced the real possibility of losing the battle. However, summoning all the knowledge and tactical ability he had gained in numerous campaigns against his rivals in Normandy, he used the cavalry's rout to draw the Saxon infantry out from their defensive positions, whereupon the Norman infantry turned and caused heavy casualties on the undisciplined Saxon troops. The battle started to turn against Harold – his two other brothers were slain, and he himself was killed (by an arrow through the eye, according to the Bayeux Tapestry) late in the afternoon. The embattled Saxons fought on until sunset and then fled, leaving the Normans effectively in charge of England. William immediately marched to London, ruthlessly quelled the opposition, and was crowned king of England on Christmas Day.

William thus became king of two realms and entrenched England's feudal system of government under the control of Norman nobles. Ongoing unrest among the Saxon peasantry soured his opinion of the country, however, and he spent most of the rest of his life after 1072 in Normandy, only going to England when compelled to do so. He left most of the governance of the country to the bishops.

In Normandy, William continued to expand his influence by military campaigns or by strategic marriages; in 1077, he took control of the Maine region, but then fought Philip I of France over several towns on their mutual border. In 1087 he was injured during an attack on Mantes. He died at Rouen a few weeks later and was buried at Caen.

Bayeux War Cemetery

This peaceful cemetery, on Blvd Fabien Ware a few hundred metres west of the war museum, is the largest of the 18 Commonwealth military cemeteries in Normandy. It contains 4868 graves of soldiers from the UK and 10 other countries. Many of the 466 Germans buried here were never identified, and the headstones are simply marked 'Ein Deutscher Soldat' (A German Soldier). There is an explanatory plaque in the small chapel to the right as you enter the grounds. The structure across Blvd Fabien Ware commemorates the 1807 Commonwealth soldiers missing in action.

Places to Stay

Camping ***Camping Municipal de Bayeux*** (☎ 02 31 92 08 43) is about 2km north of the town centre, just south of Blvd d'Eindhoven. It's open from mid-March to mid-November and you can check in from 8 to 9 am and 5 to 7 pm (7 am to 9 pm in July and August). A tent site costs 8.40FF, adults pay 16.20FF each and children under seven pay 8.40FF.

A limited number of tents can be pitched in the back garden of the ***Family Home*** hostel (see the following section) for about 30FF per person, including breakfast.

Hostels The ***Family Home*** (☎ 02 31 92 15 22; fax 02 31 92 55 72) hostel and guesthouse, in three old buildings at 39 Rue du Général de Dais, is an excellent place to meet other travellers. A bed in a dorm room costs 100FF (90FF if you've got a Hostelling International card), including breakfast. Singles are 160FF. The hostel is open all day, but curfew is (theoretically) at 11 pm; just ask for a key to the main door. Multicourse French dinners cost 65FF, including wine. Vegetarian dishes are available on request or you can cook for yourself. There are also facilities for washing clothes.

The efficient ***Centre d'Accueil Municipal*** (☎ 02 31 92 08 19) is housed in a large, modern building at 21 Rue des Marettes, 1km south-west of the cathedral. Antiseptic but comfortable singles (which is all that's available) are a great deal at 92FF, including breakfast. Reservations by telephone are usually accepted.

Chambres d'Hôtes The tourist office has a list of chambres d'hôtes in the Bayeux area. The cheapest cost about 150FF for two people, with breakfast.

Hotels The old but well maintained ***Hôtel de la Gare*** (☎ 02 31 92 10 70; fax 02 31 51 95 99), 26 Place de la Gare, opposite the train station, has singles/doubles from 85/140FF. Two-bed triples/quads are 160FF and showers are free. There are no late trains so it's usually pretty quiet at night.

The ***Hôtel de l'Hôtel de Ville*** (☎ 02 31 92 30 08), in the centre of town at 31ter Rue Larcher, has large, quiet singles/doubles for 130/150FF including free use of showers. An extra bed is 50FF. Telephone reservations are not accepted. A few hundred metres north at 19 Rue Saint Martin, the ***Hôtel des Sports*** (☎ 02 31 92 28 53) is a cut above, with tastefully appointed rooms (most with shower or free use of those in the hall) starting at 160/200FF.

The ***Relais des Cèdres*** (☎ 02 31 21 98 07), somewhat fussily done up in 'French country' style, is in an old mansion at 1 Blvd Sadi Carnot. Doubles cost 150FF with washbasin and toilet, 220FF with shower, and 250FF with shower or bath and toilet. Showers are free.

If you can afford something more luxurious, you might try ***Hôtel Notre Dame*** (☎ 02 31 92 87 24; fax 02 31 92 67 11), 44 Rue des Cuisiniers, a one star place opposite the western façade of the cathedral. Doubles are 250 to 260FF with shower or bath, but they have half a dozen cheaper rooms without shower for 160FF. Hall showers cost 20FF.

Places to Eat

Restaurants *Le Petit Normand* (☎ 02 31 22 88 66), 35 Rue Larcher, specialises in traditional Norman food prepared with apple cider and is popular with English tourists. Simple fixed-price *menus* start at 58FF; more expensive *menus* are available at 95 and 125FF.

The restaurant is open for lunch and dinner daily, except Wednesday and Sunday nights. It opens daily in July and August.

For couscous (from 55FF), try ***La Palmeraie*** (☎ 02 31 92 72 08) near the Bayeux Tapestry Museum at 62-64 Rue de Nesmond. It's open for lunch and dinner every day except Monday. ***Milano*** (☎ 02 31 92 15 10), 18 Rue Saint Martin, serves very good pizza. It's open Monday to Saturday for lunch and dinner (daily from June to August) from 11.30 am to 10 pm.

The food at the ***Hôtel Notre Dame*** restaurant is Norman at its finest; count on 60FF for a lunch *menu* and 90FF per person minimum at dinner. It is closed for Sunday lunch and all day Monday from November to March. Just south at 2 Rue du Bienvenu, ***Le Petit Bistrot*** (☎ 02 31 51 85 40) is a charming little eatery with excellent fish and duck *menus* from 98FF. It closes on Sunday and Monday.

Self-Catering There are lots of takeaway and food shops along or near Rue Saint Martin and Rue Saint Jean, including ***Le Petit Glouton*** at 42 Rue Saint Martin and the ***Point Coop grocery*** at 25 Rue du Maréchal Foch. The latter is open Tuesday to Saturday from 8.30 am to 12.15 pm and 2.30 to 7.15 pm, and on Sunday from 9 am to noon. Rue Saint Jean is the site of an open-air ***food market*** on Wednesday morning, as is Place Saint Patrice on Saturday morning. *Teurgoule*, a sweet, cinnamon-flavoured rice pudding typical of the Bayeux region, is available.

The ***Champion*** supermarket across the road from the Camping Municipal is open Monday to Saturday from 9 am to 8 pm.

Getting There & Away

Bus Bus Verts (☎ 02 31 92 02 92, 02 31 44 77 44 in Caen) offers rather infrequent service from the train station and Place G Despallières to Caen, the D-day beaches (see Getting There & Away in the following section), Vire and elsewhere in the Calvados department.

The schedules are arranged for the convenience of school children coming into Bayeux for school in the morning and going home in the afternoon. The Bus Verts office, across the parking lot from the train station, is open weekdays from 10 am to noon and 3 to 6 pm. It is closed during most of July. There are timetables posted in the train station and at Place G Despallières.

Train The train station (☎ 02 31 92 80 50), Place de la Gare, is open daily from about 7 am to 8.45 pm (9 pm Sunday). Trains from here serve Paris' Gare Saint Lazare (184FF) via Caen (31FF; 20 minutes; 15 a day) as well as Cherbourg (78FF; one hour; 10 a day). There's a service to Quimper (267FF) via Rennes.

Getting Around

Bus The local bus line, Bybus (☎ 02 31 92 02 92), which shares an office with Bus Verts, has four routes traversing Bayeux, all of which end up at Place G Despallières. From the train station, take bus No 3.

Taxi Taxis can be ordered 24 hours a day by calling ☎ 02 31 92 92 40 or ☎ 02 31 92 04 10.

D-DAY BEACHES

The D-day landings, codenamed 'Operation Overlord', were the largest military operation in history. Early on the morning of 6 June 1944, swarms of landing craft – part of a flotilla of almost 7000 boats – hit the beaches, and tens of thousands of soldiers from the USA, UK, Canada and elsewhere began pouring onto French soil.

Most of the 135,000 Allied troops stormed ashore along 80km of beach north of Bayeux codenamed (from west to east) Utah and Omaha (in the US sector) and Gold, Juno and Sword (in the British and Canadian ones). The landings on D-day – called Jour J in French – were followed by the Battle of Normandy, which would lead to the liberation of Europe from Nazi occupation. In the 76 days of fighting, the Allies suffered 210,000 casualties, including 37,000 troops killed. German casualties are believed to be around 200,000; and another 200,000 German soldiers were taken prisoner. Caen's Memorial museum provides

NORMANDY

the best introduction to the history of what took place here and also attempts to explain the rationale behind each event. Once on the coast, travellers can take a well marked circuit that links the battle sites, close to where holiday-makers sunbathe.

Fat Norman cows with udders the size of beach balls use the bombed-out bunkers to shield themselves from the wind. Many of the villages near the D-day beaches have small museums with war memorabilia on display collected by local people after the fighting.

Information

Maps of the D-day beaches are available at *tabacs* (tobacconists), newsagents and bookshops in Bayeux and elsewhere. The best one is called *D-day 6.6.44 Jour J* and sells for about 40FF. Note that the area is also known as the Côte du Nacre (Mother-of-Pearl Coast).

Arromanches

To make it possible to unload the quantities of cargo necessary, the Allies established two prefabricated ports codenamed **Mulberry Harbours**.

The harbour established at Omaha Beach was completely destroyed by a ferocious gale just two weeks after D-day, but one of them, Port Winston, can still be viewed at Arromanches, a seaside town 10km north-east of Bayeux.

The harbour consists of 146 massive cement caissons towed from England and sunk to form a semicircular breakwater in which floating bridge spans were moored. In the three months after D-day, 2.5 million men, four million tonnes of equipment and 500,000 vehicles were unloaded there. At low tide you can walk out to many of the caissons. The best view of Port Winston is from the hill, east of town, topped with a statue of the Virgin Mary.

The well regarded **Musée du Débarquement** (Invasion Museum; ☎ 02 31 22 34 31), on Place de 6 Juin right in the centre of Arromanches by the sea, explains the logistics and importance of Port Winston and makes a good first stop before visiting the beaches. Museum hours are 9 am to 6 pm in April, 9 am to 7 pm from May to September, 9.30 am to 5 pm from October to December and from February to March. It's closed on Monday and throughout January. Entrance is 35FF (20FF for students). The last guided tour (in French, with a written text in English) leaves 45 minutes before closing time. An unimpressive seven minute diorama/slide show in English is held throughout the day.

Longues-sur-Mer

The massive 152mm German guns on the coast near Longues-sur-Mer, 6km west of Arromanches, were designed to hit targets some 20km away, which in June 1944 included both Gold Beach (to the east) and Omaha Beach (to the west). Half a century later, the mammoth artillery pieces are still sitting in their colossal concrete emplacements. (In wartime they were covered with camouflage nets and tufts of grass.)

Parts of an American film about D-day, *The Longest Day* (1962), were filmed both here and at Pointe du Hoc. On clear days, Bayeux's cathedral, 8km away, is visible to the south.

Omaha & Juno Beaches

The most brutal fighting on D-day took place 15km north-west of Bayeux along 7km of coastline known as Omaha Beach, which had to be abandoned in storms two weeks later.

As you stand on the gently sloping sand, try to imagine how the US soldiers must have felt running inland towards the German positions on the nearby ridge.

A memorial marks the site of the first US military cemetery on French soil, where soldiers killed on the beach were buried. Their remains were later reinterred at the American Military Cemetery at Colleville-sur-Mer or in the USA.

These days, Omaha Beach is lined with holiday cottages and is popular with swimmers and sunbathers. Little evidence of the war remains apart from a single concrete boat used to carry tanks ashore and, 1km farther west, the bunkers and munitions sites of a German fortified point (look for the tall obelisk on the hill).

The Battle of Normandy

In early 1944 an Allied invasion of continental Europe seemed inevitable. Hitler's folly on the Russian front and the Luftwaffe's inability to control the skies had left Germany vulnerable.

Normandy was to be the spearhead into Europe. Codenamed Operation Overlord, the invasion entailed an assault by three paratroop divisions and five seaborne divisions, along with 1000 planes, 300 gliders and countless ships and boats. The total invasion force was 45,000, and 15 divisions were to follow once successful beachheads had been established.

Allied intelligence confused the Germans about the landing site. The narrow Channel crossing to Calais seemed more likely, although Hitler and Field Marshal Rommel both felt that Normandy would be the choice. As a result, fortifications were much stronger around Calais than in Normandy.

Because of the tides and unpredictable weather patterns, Allied planners had only a few days available each month to launch the invasion. On 4 June, the date chosen, very bad weather set in, delaying the operation. The weather had only improved slightly the next day, but General Dwight D Eisenhower, Allied commander-in-chief, gave the go-ahead: 6 June would be D-day.

D-day, 6 June 1944

In the very early hours of 6 June the first troops were on the ground. British commandos captured key bridges and destroyed German communications, while the paratroops weren't far behind them. Although the paratroops' tactical victories were few, they caused enormous confusion in German ranks. More importantly, because of their relatively small numbers, at first, the German high command didn't believe that the real invasion had begun.

Sword, Juno & Gold Beaches These beaches, stretching for about 35km from Ouistreham to Arromanches, were attacked by the British 2nd Army, which included sizable detachments of Canadians and smaller groups of Commonwealth, Free French and Polish forces.

At Sword Beach, initial German resistance was quickly overcome, and the beach was secured after about two hours. Infantry pushed inland from Ouistreham to link up with paratroops around Ranville, but soon suffered heavy casualties as their supporting armour fell behind, trapped in a huge traffic jam on the narrow coastal roads. Nevertheless, they were within 5km of Caen by 4 pm, but a heavy German armoured counterattack forced them to dig in. Thus, in spite of the Allies' successes, Caen, one of the prime D-day objectives, was not taken on the first day as planned.

At Juno Beach, Canadian brigades cleared the beach in 15 minutes and headed inland. Mines took a heavy toll on the infantry, but by noon they were south and east of Creuilly. Late in the afternoon, the German armoured divisions that had halted the British from Sword were deflected towards the coast and held Douvres, thus threatening to drive a wedge between the Sword and Juno forces. However, the threat of encirclement caused them to withdraw by the next day.

At Gold Beach, the attack by the British forces was at first chaotic; the initial ferocious bombardment of German positions by air and sea hadn't silenced enough of the defenders' big guns. By 9 am, though, Allied armoured divisions were on the beach and several brigades pushed inland. By afternoon, they had joined up with the Juno forces and were only 3km from Bayeux.

On all three beaches, odd-looking 'Funnies' – specially designed armoured amphibious vehicles designed to clear minefields, breach walls and wire entanglements and provide support and protection for infantry – proved their worth. Their construction and successful deployment was due to the ingenuity and foresight of British Major-General Hobart.

Omaha & Utah Beaches For some reason, US General Omar Bradley decided that his US 1st Army didn't need the Funnies – a mistake that was to cost his men dearly at Omaha. It was compounded by the loss of 27 tanks that been launched from landing craft too far out from the beach. Thus, the US 5th Corps had to land on a well defended beach with virtually

The Battle of Normandy

no armoured cover at all. The landing itself was close to a shambles; troops had to struggle though deep water to the beach, where they collected in exhausted little groups, facing devastating fire from enemy positions and with little prospect of support. Eventually, a precarious toehold was gained; the Germans, lacking reserves, were forced to fall back a short distance. Nevertheless, 1000 Allied soldiers were killed at Omaha on D-day, out of a total of 2500.

At Utah, US forces faced little resistance, and got off the beach after two hours. By noon, the beach had been cleared with the loss of only 12 men. Pockets of troops held large tracts of territory to the west of the landing site, and the town of Sainte Mère Église was captured.

The Beginning of the End

Four days later, the Allies held a coastal strip about 100km long and 10km deep. British Field Marshal Montgomery's plan successfully drew the weight of German armour towards Caen, where fierce fighting continued for more than a month and reduced the city to rubble, thus leaving the US army farther west to consolidate and push northward up the Cotentin Peninsula.

The port of Cherbourg was a major prize; after a series of fierce battles, it fell to the Allies on 29 June. However, its valuable facilities were blown up by the Germans, so it remained out of service until autumn. To overcome likely logistical problems, the Allies had devised the remarkable 'Mulberry Harbours'. These were enormous floating harbours that were towed from England, and set up off the Norman coast. They were indispensable in allowing large amounts of supplies to be taken quickly off ships and onto the roads leading to the front. A big storm from 19 to 22 June, however, destroyed the harbour stationed at Omaha Beach and damaged the Gold Beach installation.

The fierce Battle of the Hedgerows was fought mainly by the Americans up and down the Cotentin Peninsula. The land of the *bocage*, divided into countless fields bordered by walled roads and hedgerows, made ideal territory for defending. Nevertheless, once the Allies broke out from the beachheads their superior numbers meant the end was nigh for the Germans in Normandy.

By the end of July, US army units had smashed through to the border of Brittany. By mid-August, two German armies had been surrounded and destroyed near Falaise and Argentan, and on 20 August, US forces crossed the Seine at several points about 40km north and south of Paris.

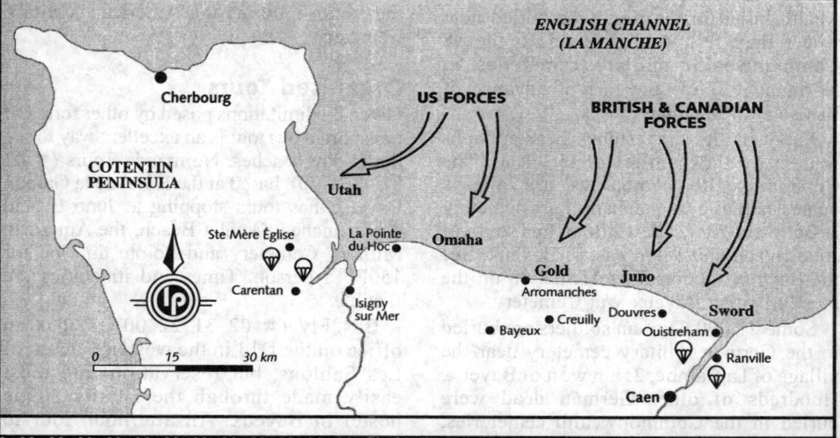

Dune-lined Juno Beach, 12km east of Arromanches, was stormed by Canadian troops on D-day. A Cross of Lorraine marks the spot where General Charles de Gaulle came ashore shortly after the landings.

Military Cemeteries

The bodies of the American soldiers who lost their lives during the pivotal Battle of Normandy were either sent back to the USA (if their families so requested) or buried in the **American Military Cemetery** (☎ 02 31 51 62 00) at Colleville-sur-Mer, 17km north-west of Bayeux. The cemetery contains the graves of 9386 American soldiers and a memorial to 1557 others whose remains were never found.

The huge, immaculately tended expanse of lawn, with white crosses and Stars of David and set on a hill overlooking Omaha Beach, testifies to the extent of the killings that took place around here in 1944. There's a large colonnaded memorial, a reflecting pond and chapel for silent meditation. The cemetery is open from 8 am to 5 pm (9 am to 6 pm from about mid-April to mid-October). From Bayeux, it can be reached by Bus Verts' line No 70, but service is infrequent. Bus No 44 from Caen will also drop you off here.

By tradition, soldiers from the Commonwealth killed in the war were buried near where they fell. And as a result, the 18 **Commonwealth military cemeteries** in Normandy follow the line of advance of British and Canadian troops.

Many of the gravestones bear epitaphs written by the families of the dead. The Commonwealth cemeteries are always open. There is a Canadian military cemetery at **Bény-sur-Mer**, a few kilometres south of Juno Beach and 18km east of Bayeux. See the Bayeux section for information on the mostly British Bayeux War Cemetery.

Some 21,000 German soldiers are buried in the German military cemetery near the village of **La Cambe**, 25km west of Bayeux. Hundreds of other German dead were buried in the Commonwealth cemeteries, including the one in Bayeux.

Pointe du Hoc Ranger Memorial

At 7.10 am on 6 June 1944, 225 US Army Rangers scaled the 30m cliffs at Pointe du Hoc, where the Germans had emplaced a battery of huge artillery guns.

The guns, as it turned out, had been transferred elsewhere, but the Americans captured the gun emplacements (the two huge circular cement structures) and the German command post (next to the two flag poles), and then fought off German counterattacks for two days. By the time they were relieved on 8 June, 81 of the rangers had been killed and 58 more had been wounded.

Today, the site, which France turned over in perpetuity to the US government in 1979, looks much as it did half a century ago.

The ground is still pockmarked with 3m bomb craters. Visitors can walk among and inside the German fortifications, but they are warned not to dig: there may still be mines and explosive materials below the surface. In the German command post, you can see where the wooden ceilings were charred by American flame-throwers. As you face the sea, Utah Beach, which runs roughly perpendicular to the cliffs here, is 14km to the left. Pointe du Hoc, which is 12km west of the American cemetery, is always open. The command post is open the same hours as the American Military Cemetery.

Organised Tours

Given the limitations posed by other forms of transport, a bus tour is an excellent way to see the D-day beaches. Normandy Tours (☎ 02 31 92 10 70), based at the Hôtel de la Gare in Bayeux, has tours stopping at Juno Beach, Arromanches, Omaha Beach, the American Military Cemetery and Pointe du Hoc for 150FF a person. Times and itineraries are flexible.

Bus Fly (☎ 02 31 22 00 08) has an office on the D13 in the western suburb of Les Sablons, but reservations are most easily made through the Family Home hostel in Bayeux. An afternoon tour to major D-day sites costs 160FF (140FF for students), including museum entry fees, and they'll collect you from your hotel or the tourist office in Bayeux.

Getting There & Away

Bus Bus No 70 run by Bus Verts (☎ 02 31 92 02 92 in Bayeux, 02 31 44 77 44 in Caen) goes westward to the American Military Cemetery at Colleville-sur-Mer and Omaha Beach, and on to Pointe du Hoc and the town of Grandcamp-Maisy. Bus No 74 (No 75 during summer) serves Arromanches, Gold and Juno beaches, and Courseulles. During July and August only, the Côte du Nacre line goes to Caen via Arromanches, Gold, Juno and Sword beaches, and Ouistreham; and Circuit 44 links Bayeux and Caen via Pointe du Hoc, the American Military Cemetery, Arromanches and the Mémorial museum.

Car For three or more people, renting a car can be cheaper than a tour. Lefebvre Car Rental (☎ 02 31 92 05 96), on Blvd d'Eindhoven (at the Esso petrol station) in Bayeux, charges 320FF per day with 200km free (more than enough for a circuit to the beaches along coastal route D514) and 640FF for two days with 400km free. The excess (deductible) is 2000FF. The office is open every day from 8 am to 8 pm.

Bicycle Ten-speeds are available from the Family Home hostel in Bayeux for 60FF a day (plus 100FF deposit). Cycles 14 (☎ 02 31 92 27 75), on Blvd Winston Churchill, rents mountain bikes for 70FF a day (340FF a week), but you have to leave a deposit of 1500FF. Cycles 14 is open daily, except Sunday, from 9 am to 12.15 pm and 2 to 7 pm.

Manche

The department of Manche, surrounded on three sides by the English Channel (La Manche), includes the entire Cotentin Peninsula. Its 320km of coastline stretches from Utah Beach north-westward to the port city of Cherbourg and then south to the magnificent Mont Saint Michel. The fertile inland areas, crisscrossed with hedgerows, produce an abundance of cattle, dairy products and apples.

The Cotentin Peninsula's north-west corner is especially lovely, with unspoiled stretches of rocky coastline sheltering tranquil bays and villages. Due west lie the Channel Islands of Jersey (25km from the coast) and Guernsey (45km), accessible by ferry from Saint Malo in Brittany and, in season, from the Norman towns of Carteret, Portbail and Granville.

Sadly, over the past two decades, the Manche region has become known as 'Europe's nuclear dump'. On the peninsula's western tip at Cap de la Hague is France's first uranium waste treatment plant, which is well hidden until you reach its heavily fortified perimeter. Farther south at Flamanville is a sprawling power plant, and at the Cherbourg shipyards the latest nuclear submarines are built.

Getting Around

Trains run to and from Cherbourg, but local buses are few and far between in the Manche region.

CHERBOURG

• pop 28,000 ✉ 50100

At the very tip of the Cotentin Peninsula sits Cherbourg, the largest but hardly the most appealing town in this part of Normandy. A port city and naval base, it's too busy with transatlantic cargo ships and passenger ferries crossing to England and Ireland to think about much else. Don't expect to find any of the romance portrayed in Jacques Demy's 1964 classic film *Les Parapluies de Cherbourg* (The Umbrellas of Cherbourg) here.

Orientation

The Bassin du Commerce, a wide central waterway, separates the 'living' half of Cherbourg to the west from the deserted streets of the Basin de Commerce to the east. The attractive Avant Port (Outer Harbour) lies to the north.

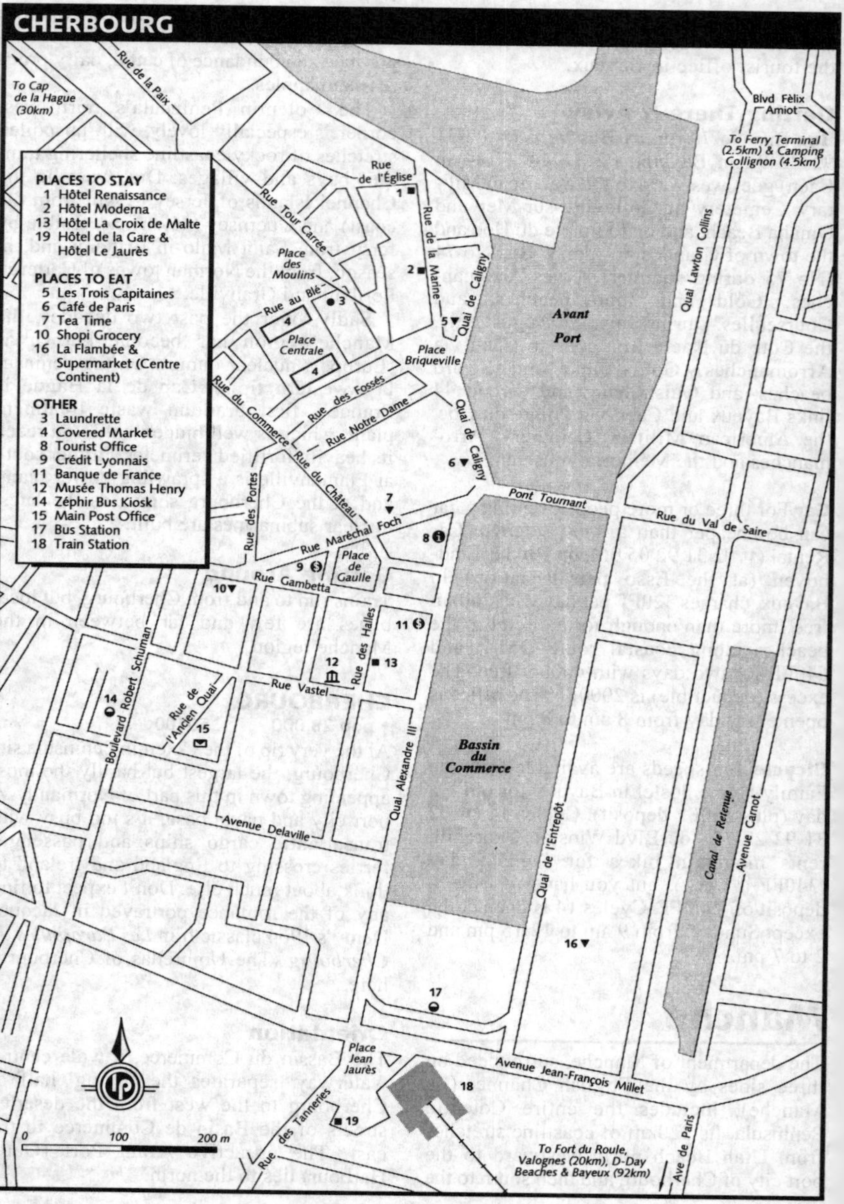
CHERBOURG
PLACES TO STAY
1 Hôtel Renaissance
2 Hôtel Moderna
13 Hôtel La Croix de Malte
19 Hôtel de la Gare & Hôtel Le Jaurès
PLACES TO EAT
5 Les Trois Capitaines
6 Café de Paris
7 Tea Time
10 Shopi Grocery
16 La Flambée & Supermarket (Centre Continent)
OTHER
3 Laundrette
4 Covered Market
8 Tourist Office
9 Crédit Lyonnais
11 Banque de France
12 Musée Thomas Henry
14 Zéphir Bus Kiosk
15 Main Post Office
17 Bus Station
18 Train Station
To Cap de la Hague (30km)
Rue de la Paix
Blvd Fèlix Amiot
To Ferry Terminal (2.5km) & Camping Collignon (4.5km)
Rue de l'Église
Rue Tour Carrée
Rue de la Marine
Place des Moulins
Rue au Blé
Place Centrale
Quai de Caligny
Avant Port
Quai Lawton Collins
Place Briqueville
Rue des Fossés
Rue Notre Dame
Rue du Commerce
Rue du Château
Rue des Portes
Pont Tournant
Rue du Val de Saire
Rue Maréchal Foch
Place de Gaulle
Rue Gambetta
Rue des Halles
Rue Vastel
Boulevard Robert Schuman
Rue de l'Ancien Quai
Quai Alexandre III
Bassin du Commerce
Quai de l'Entrepôt
Canal de Retenue
Avenue Carnot
Avenue Delaville
Place Jean Jaurès
Avenue Jean-François Millet
Rue des Tanneries
Ave de Paris
To Fort du Roule, Valognes (20km), D-Day Beaches & Bayeux (92km)
0 100 200 m

Information

Tourist Office The tourist office (☎ 02 33 93 52 02; fax 02 33 53 66 97), 2 Quai Alexandre III, is open weekdays from 9 am to noon and 2 to 6 pm, and on Saturday morning. From June to September it's open Monday to Saturday from 9 am to noon and 2 to 6 pm. The annexe (☎ 02 33 44 39 92) at the ferry terminal is open daily from 7 to 9 am and 2 to 3 pm. The tourist office can make hotel reservations for 10FF.

Money The Banque de France at 22 Quai Alexandre III is open weekdays from 9 am to noon and 1.30 to 3.30 pm.

Crédit Lyonnais at 16 Rue Maréchal Foch is open weekdays from 8.30 am to noon and 1.30 to 5.15 pm. Foreign currency can also be exchanged at the post office. Whenever a ferry arrives, the exchange desk at the ferry terminal opens, but the rates are lower than those of the banks.

Post The main post office, 1 Rue de l'Ancien Quai, is open weekdays from 8 am to 7 pm and on Saturday until noon.

Laundry The laundrette at 62 Rue au Blé is open daily from 7 am to 10 pm.

Breakwater

Even from the Avant Port, the breakwater (*jetée*) is hard to see. A good vantage point is **Fort du Roule**, which watches over the city from the south-east. A road weaves up from Ave Étienne Lecarpentier, which runs off Ave de Paris, a short distance south-east of the train station.

Musée Thomas Henry

This museum (☎ 02 33 23 02 23), upstairs in the cultural centre on Rue Vastel, has 200 works by French, Flemish, Italian and other artists, but the 30 paintings by Jean-François Millet alone make it worth the visit. The museum is open daily, except Monday, from 9 am (10 am Sunday) to noon and 2 to 6 pm. Entry costs 15FF (7FF for students).

Nuclear Tours

Those who think they might like to glow in the dark can take guided 'technical' tours of the Cogema uranium waste **reprocessing plant** (☎ 02 33 02 64 00) at La Hague or the **Flamanville nuclear power plant** (☎ 02 33 04 12 99). Each tour lasts about three hours, and you must present your passport or national ID card. The facility at Cap de la Hague is open daily from 10 am to 6 pm between April and September, and on weekends only during the rest of the year. The Flamanville station's opening hours are Monday to Saturday from 9 am till noon and 2 to 6.30 pm.

Hiking

The tourist office organises hikes of 12km or more in the surrounding countryside some Saturdays from April to October, and every Saturday in July and August.

Places to Stay

Camping The nearest camping ground is *Camping Collignon* (☎ 02 33 20 16 88) in Tourlaville, on the coast about 5km north-east of town. It is open from June to September. Adults pay 18FF each and a tent site is 29FF. Bus No 5 makes two runs a day Monday to Saturday from the train station and there are frequent shuttles (*navettes*) in summer. There's a large indoor swimming pool near the camp site.

Camping du Fort (☎ 02 33 22 27 60) is a further 5km to the east at Bretteville-en-Saire. The site is open all year and charges 6.30/3.75/3.75FF per person/tent site/car. To get there, take one of the two daily buses (No 1) to Bretteville.

Hostel The ***Auberge de Jeunesse***, Rue de l'Abbaye, was expected to open as we went to press. Contact the tourist office for more information.

Hotels Quai de Caligny has plenty of mid-range options. There are cheaper places in the backstreets north of the tourist office.

The ***Hôtel Moderna*** (☎ 02 33 43 05 30; fax 02 33 43 97 37), one block back from the harbour at 28 Rue de la Marine, has decent, basic rooms from 140FF (190FF with shower). At the end of Rue de la Marine, the ***Hôtel Renaissance*** (☎ 02 33 43 23 90; fax 02 33 43 96 10), 4 Rue de l'Église, has comfortable rooms (ask for one with views of the port) starting at 140/160FF or with shower for 160/180FF.

Hôtel La Croix de Malte (☎ 02 33 43 19 16; fax 02 33 43 65 66), near the sumptuous Théâtre de Cherbourg (1882) at 5 Rue des Halles, has well equipped doubles from 170FF.

Facing the train station at 10 Place Jean Jaurès, the ***Hôtel de la Gare*** (☎ 02 33 43 06 81; fax 02 33 43 12 20) has adequate rooms from 105/125FF. A couple of doors along at No 4, the ***Hôtel Le Jaurès*** (☎ 02 33 43 06 35) has basic rooms for 120/130FF and ones with shower for 150/170FF. The hotel is closed on Sunday. The brasserie below can get pretty lively.

Places to Eat

Restaurants Quai de Caligny is lined with restaurants, but the view of the fishing boats bobbing up and down tends to drive up the prices. Two of the best seafood restaurants, with *menus* from around 110FF, are ***Café de Paris*** (☎ 02 33 43 12 36) at No 40, and ***Les Trois Capitaines*** (☎ 02 33 20 11 66) at No 16. In the streets to the north-west – Rue Tour Carrée and Rue de la Paix – and around Place Centrale you'll find a wider choice of both cuisine and price.

Just round the corner from the tourist office at 39 Rue Maréchal Foch is a place called ***Tea Time*** (☎ 02 33 94 46 47), which has salads from 39/50FF as well as grilled dishes. If you can forgo the atmosphere, ***La Flambée***, on the 1st floor of the Centre Continent at Quai de l'Entrepôt, across Ave Jean-François Millet from the train station, has a reasonable 54FF three course *menu*.

Self-Catering ***Market*** days are Tuesday and, especially, Thursday until about 5 pm at Place de Gaulle and Place Centrale. The latter, which is covered, also operates on Saturday morning. There's a flower marke on Place de Gaulle on Saturday morning.

Opposite the train station in the Centr Continent at Quai de l'Entrepôt, is a hug ***supermarket*** open Monday to Saturda from 8.30 am to 9.30 pm (10 pm Sunday) The little ***Shopi grocery store*** at 57 Ru Gambetta is open Monday to Saturday fron 8.30 am to 12.30 pm and 2.30 to 7.30 pm.

Getting There & Away

Bus Buses operate from the Autogare (☎ 0. 33 44 32 22) on Ave Jean-François Mille across the road to the north of the trai station. The information desk is open week days from 8.45 am to noon and 2 or 2.30 t 6.30 pm. The main regional bus line tha operates from here is STN (☎ 02 33 88 5 00 in Tourlaville), which has services to th camping ground in Bretteville-en-Sair (12.80FF).

Train Cherbourg's little train station (☎ 02 3. 44 18 74) is at the southern end of the Bassi du Commerce, about 600m from the touris office. The information desk is open dail from 9.30 am to 8 pm (6 pm on Saturday).

Destinations served include Paris' Gar Saint Lazare (232FF; 3½ hours; seven day) via Caen (97FF; 1½ hours), Pontorso (128FF; 2½ hours; two a day) and Renne (171FF; 3½ hours; two a day).

Boat The three companies with services t either England or Ireland have bureaus i the reception hall of the ferry terminal (*gar maritime*), which is 3km north-east of th train station just off Blvd Maritime. Th companies generally make sure their desk are open two hours before departure and fo 30 minutes after the arrival of each ferry The hall is open from 5.30 am to 11.30 pm

Brittany Ferries (☎ 02 33 43 43 68) oper ates to Poole in England; Irish Ferries (☎ 0. 35 19 24 00) sails to Rosslare, Ireland; an P&O European Ferries (☎ 02 33 88 65 70 handles the link to Portsmouth as well a freight ferries to Rosslare, which sometime take the occasional passenger although ther is no reservation system. For details on price and schedules see the Sea section of the introductory Getting There & Away chapter.

Local buses run between the ferry terminal and the tourist office between three and 10 times a day, depending on the season. The fare is 5FF.

Getting Around

Bus City buses are run by Zéphir (☎ 02 33 22 40 58). The information kiosk at 40 Blvd Robert Schuman is open weekdays from 9 to 11.45 am and 1.30 to 6.30 pm (closed Monday morning), and on Saturday from 9.30 am to noon and 2 to 6 pm. Buses leave from either outside the kiosk or at various points around Place Jean Jaurès, in front of the train station. Single tickets cost 5.80FF, and a carnet of 10 is 50FF.

Taxi Taxis can be called on ☎ 02 33 53 36 38. The trip between the train station and ferry terminal costs about 35FF.

MONT SAINT MICHEL

• **pop 120** ✉ **51016**

It is difficult not to be impressed with your first sighting of Mont Saint Michel. Covering the summit is the massive abbey, a soaring ensemble of buildings in a hotchpotch of architectural styles. The abbey (80m above the sea) is topped by a slender spire at the tip of which is a gilded copper statue of Michael the Archangel slaying a dragon. Around the base are the ancient ramparts and a jumble of buildings that house the 120 people who still live here. At night the whole structure is brilliantly illuminated.

Mont Saint Michel's fame is derived equally from the bay's extraordinary tides. Depending on the orbits of the moon and, to a lesser extent, the sun, the difference in the level of the sea between low and high tides can reach 15m. At low tide, the Mont looks out on bare sand stretching many kilometres into the distance. At high tide – only about six hours later – this huge expanse of tideland is under water (though the Mont and its causeway are completely surrounded by the sea only at the highest of tides, which occur at seasonal equinoxes).

History

According to Celtic mythology, Mont Saint Michel was one of the sea tombs to which the souls of the dead were sent. In 708 AD the saint appeared to Bishop Aubert of Avranches and told him to build a devotional chapel at the top of the summit. In 966, Richard I, duke of Normandy, gave Mont Saint Michel to the Benedictines, who turned it into an important centre of learning and, in the 11th century, into something of an ecclesiastical fortress, with a military garrison at the disposal of the abbot and the king.

In the early 15th century, during the Hundred Years' War, the English blockaded and besieged Mont Saint Michel three times. But the fortified abbey withstood these assaults; it was the only place in western and northern France not to fall into English hands. After the Revolution, Mont Saint Michel was turned into a prison. In 1966 the abbey was symbolically returned to the Benedictines as part of the celebrations marking its millennium.

Orientation

There is only one opening in the ramparts, Porte de l'Avancée, immediately to the left as you walk down the causeway. The Mont's single street – Grande Rue – is lined with restaurants, a few hotels, souvenir shops and entrances to some rather tacky exhibits in the crypts below. There are several large carparks (15FF) near the Mont.

Pontorson, the nearest town to Mont Saint Michel, is 9km south and the base for most travellers. Route D976 from Mont Saint Michel runs right into Pontorson's main thoroughfare, Rue du Couësnon.

Information

Tourist Offices The tourist office (☎ 02 33 60 14 30; fax 02 33 60 06 75) is up the stairs to the left as you enter Porte de l'Avancée. It is open Monday to Saturday from 9 am to noon and 2 to 5.45 pm. From Easter to September, daily hours are from 9.30 am to noon and 1 to 6.30 pm. In July and August it's open daily from 9 am to 7 pm.

If you are interested in what the tide will be doing during your visit, look for the *horaire des marées* posted outside. In July and August – when up to 9000 people a day visit and the gates are sometimes closed to stop the flow – children under eight can be left with a *gardien* (baby-sitter) near the abbey church. A detailed map of the Mont is available at the tourist office for 16FF.

The friendly staff at Pontorson's tourist office (☎ 02 33 60 20 65), in the Place de l'Église just west of the Place de l'Hôtel de Ville, are on duty Tuesday to Friday from 9.30 am to noon and 2.30 to 5 pm (to 7.30 pm daily from mid-June to mid-September).

Money There are several places to change money at Mont Saint Michel, but for a better rate go to the CIN bank at 98 Rue du Couësnon in Pontorson. It's open Tuesday to Saturday from 8.30 am to 12.15 pm and from 1.45 to 5.45 pm (4.50 pm on Saturday). There are more banks on Rue du Couësnon and Place de l'Hôtel de Ville.

Post The Pontorson post office (☎ 02 33 60 01 66) is on the eastern side of the Place de l'Hôtel de Ville. It is open weekdays from 8.30 to noon and from 2 to 5.30 pm, and on Saturday morning.

Books *The Mont Saint Michel*, a booklet written by Lucien Bély and published by Éditions Ouest-France, is a surprisingly readable history of the abbey and its inhabitants. Souvenir shops along the Grande Rue sell it for 50FF.

Walking Tour

When the tide is out, it's possible to walk all the way around Mont Saint Michel, a distance of about 1km. Straying too far from the Mont could be risky: you might get stuck in wet sand – from which Norman soldiers are depicted being rescued in one scene of the Bayeux Tapestry.

Abbaye du Mont Saint Michel

The Mont's major attraction is the renowned abbey (☎ 02 33 89 80 00), open daily from 9.30 am to 4.30 pm (5.30 pm during public holidays). From May to September the hours are 9 am to 5.30 pm. To reach it, walk to the top of the Grande Rue and then climb the stairway. From mid-May to September (except Sunday) there are self-paced night-time illuminated visits (60FF; 35FF for those under 25) of Mont Saint Michel complete with music starting at 9 or 10 pm and lasting for three hours.

Most rooms can be visited without a guide but it's worthwhile taking the guided tour included in the ticket price (36FF for adults, 22FF for students and those aged 18 to 25, 10FF for children). One-hour tours in English depart three to eight times a day (the last leaves about half an hour before closing).

The **Église Abbatiale** (Abbey Church) was built at the rocky tip of the mountain cone. To be more precise, the transept rests on solid rock while the nave, choir and transept arms are supported by the massive rooms below. The church is famous for its mixture of architectural styles: the nave and south transept (11th and 12th centuries) are Norman Romanesque, while the choir (late 15th century) is Flamboyant Gothic. Mass is said here daily year-round at 12.15 pm.

The buildings on the north side of the Mont are known as **La Merveille** (literally, 'the wonder' or 'marvel'). The famous **cloître** (cloister) is an ambulatory surrounded by a double row of delicately carved arches resting on granite pillars. The early 13th century **réfectoire** (dining hall) is illuminated by a wall of recessed windows – a remarkable arrangement given that the sheer drop precluded the use of flying buttresses – which diffuses the light beautifully. The Gothic **Salle des Hôtes** (Guest Hall), which dates from 1213, has two giant fireplaces. Watch out for the **promenoire** (ambulatory), with one of the oldest ribbed vaulted ceilings in Europe, and **La Chapelle de Notre de Dame sous Terre** (Underground Chapel of Our Lady), one of the earliest rooms built in the abbey and rediscovered in 1903.

The stones originally used to build the abbey were brought to the Mont by boat and then pulled up the hillside using ropes. What looks like a treadmill for gargantuan gerbils was in fact powered in the 19th century by half a dozen prisoners who, by turning the wheel, hoisted the supply sledge up the side of the abbey. The French government is currently spending over US$86 million in restoring the Mont to its former glory, so don't be disappointed if you find it covered in scaffolding.

Museums

The Grande Rue at times resembles a fair, with touts trying to talk you into visiting the 20 minute **Archéoscope** (☎ 02 33 60 14 36) multimedia show or the **Musée Grévin** (☎ 02 33 60 14 09), a wax museum with a mishmash of pseudo-historical exhibits. The **Musée Maritime** (☎ 02 33 60 14 09) is a bit more serious with explanations about the bay. A combined ticket for the three venues costs 75FF for adults, 60FF for students and 45FF for children; individually they're 45/30FF. The museums are open daily from 9 am to 6 pm.

Église Notre Dame de Pontorson

Though it wouldn't think of trying to compete with its dramatic sister to the north, the 12th century Church of Our Lady in Pontorson is a good example of the Norman Romanesque style of architecture. To the left of the main altar is a 15th century relief of Christ's Passion, which was mutilated during the Religious Wars and again during the Revolution.

Places to Stay

Camping ***Camping du Mont Saint Michel*** (☎ 02 33 60 09 33) is on the shop-lined D976 to Pontorson, only 2km from the Mont. This grassy camping ground is open from mid-February to mid-November, and charges 22FF per person and 20FF for a tent and car. It also has bungalows with shower and toilet for two people for 220FF. There are several other camping grounds – one called ***Camping sous les Pommiers*** (☎ 02 33 60 11 36) – a couple of kilometres farther south towards Pontorson. It is open from April to mid-October and charges 40FF for two people, car and tent, then 12.70FF for every extra person.

In Pontorson the ***Camping Municipal*** (☎ 02 33 68 11 59), to the west of the train station near the Centre Duguesclin (see the following), is open from April to September. Charges are 12.70FF for adults, 5.30FF for children, 12.70FF for a tent or caravan site and 6.30FF to park a car.

Hostel ***Centre Duguesclin*** (☎ 02 33 60 18 65), in Pontorson, operates as a 10 room hostel from Easter to mid-September. A bed in a dormitory room accommodating four to six people costs 41FF a night, but you must bring your own sheets. There are kitchen facilities on the ground floor. The hostel is closed from 10 am to 6 pm, but there is no curfew. The hostel is about 1km west of the train station on Blvd du Général Patton, which lies near the Couësnon River north of Rue du Couësnon. The hostel is on the left side in an old three storey stone building opposite No 26.

Gîtes d'Étape The tourist office at Pontorson can arrange private accommodation or farm stays from 150 to 200FF per double, including breakfast.

Hotels Mont Saint Michel has about 15 hotels, but almost all are rated with two or more stars and are expensive. ***Hôtel de la Mère Poulard*** (☎ 02 33 60 14 01; fax 02 33 48 52 31), the first hotel on the left as you walk up the Grande Rue, has doubles with shower from 250FF.

Your best bet is to stay in Pontorson. Across Place de la Gare from the train station are a couple of cheap hotels. The ***Hôtel de l'Arrivée*** (☎ 02 33 60 01 57), 14 Rue du Docteur Tizon, has doubles for 87FF with washbasin, 110FF with washbasin and toilet, and 155FF with shower. Triples/quads with washbasin or toilet are 160/180FF and from 200FF with shower. Hall showers are 15FF. The ***Hôtel Le Rénové*** (☎ 02 33 60 00 21), nearby at 4 Rue de Rennes, has simple doubles for 150FF (with washbasin) and 180FF (with shower). Triples or quads cost 250FF. Hall showers are free.

The ***Hôtel La Tour de Brette*** (☎ 02 33 60 10 69), 8 Rue du Couësnon, is an excellent deal. Rooms – all with shower and TV – are 149FF (220FF in summer).

At the top end, the ***Hôtel Montgomery*** (☎ 02 33 60 00 09), in a lovely 16th century townhouse at 13 Rue du Couësnon, has rooms with shower from 240FF.

Places to Eat

Restaurants The tourist restaurants around the base of the Mont have lovely views, but they aren't bargains; *menus* start at about 90FF.

In Pontorson, ***La Squadra*** (☎ 02 33 68 31 17), 102 Rue Couësnon, has decent pizza from 36FF, salads from 16FF and pasta. It's open daily, except Monday, for lunch and dinner. For crêpes and savoury galettes (about 20FF), try ***La Crêperie du Couësnon*** (☎ 02 33 60 16 67) at 21 Rue du Couësnon. The restaurant at the ***Hôtel La Tour de Brette*** has *menus* for 56, 70 and 94FF.

For something a little more formal, try the dining room of the ***Hôtel de Bretagne*** (☎ 02 33 60 10 55), 59 Rue du Couësnon, with excellent food (*menus* from 80FF) and service. The restaurant at the ***Hôtel Montgomery*** is the poshest in town. Expect to pay at least 128FF for a three course meal.

Self-Catering The ***supermarket*** nearest the Mont is next to the Camping du Mont Saint Michel on the D976. It is open daily (except Sunday) from mid-February to October from 8 am to 8 pm (10 pm in July and August). In Pontorson, the ***8 à 8*** at 5 Rue du Couësnon is open Monday to Saturday from 8.30 am to 12.30 pm and 3 to 7.15 pm, and Sunday from 9 am to 12.30 pm.

Getting There & Away

Bus Bus No 15 run by STN (☎ 02 33 58 03 07 in Avranches) goes from Pontorson train station to Mont Saint Michel. There are nine buses a day in July and August (six on weekends) and three or four during the rest of the year. Most buses connect with trains to/from Paris, Rennes and Caen.

For information on bus transport to/from Saint Malo, 54km to the west, or Rennes, see Getting There & Away in those sections. The Pontorson office of the Courriers Bretons bus company (☎ 02 33 60 11 43; in Saint Malo ☎ 02 99 56 79 09) is 50m west of the train station at 2 Rue du Docteur Bailleul. It is open weekdays from 10.30 to noon and 5.45 to 7 pm. Courriers Bretons buses on their way *to* Mont Saint Michel from Saint Malo do *not* pick up passengers in Pontorson but will pick up in the opposite direction.

Train There are trains to the tiny Pontorson station (☎ 08 36 35 35 35) from Caen (120FF; 2¼ hours; one a day) via Folligny; Rennes (65FF; 50 minutes; two a day) via Dol; and Cherbourg (145FF; 2½ hours; two a day). Train schedules are posted at the station. From Paris, take the train to Caen (from Gare Saint Lazare), to Rennes (from Gare Montparnasse) or travel directly to Pontorson via Folligny (from Gare Montparnasse; 247FF). The train station, which has a left-luggage office (30FF) and lockers (3FF), is open weekdays from 8.30 to noon and 1.30 to 7.30 pm, Saturday from 8.30 to noon and 2 to 6.15 pm, and Sunday from 2.30 to 9.30 pm.

Getting Around

Bikes can be rented at the train station (55FF per day plus 1000FF deposit), and from E Videloup (☎ 02 33 60 11 40) at 1bis Rue du Couësnon, which charges 35FF per day for city bicycles and 70FF for mountain bikes. E Videloup is open Monday afternoon to Saturday from 8.30 am to 12.30 pm and from 2 to 7 pm.

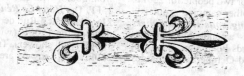

Brittany

Brittany (Bretagne in French, Breizh in Breton) commands the rugged western tip of France. Centuries of independence followed by relative isolation from the rest of the country have forged a distinctive Breton culture, language and way of life.

Many people say that there are two Brittanys: the 1100km-long coast, known as Armor (meaning 'Land of the Sea'), and the secretive interior, Argoat (meaning 'Land of the Woods'). The coastline, swept by the rough Atlantic Ocean and the somewhat calmer waters of the English Channel, is dotted with lighthouses and is characterised by rocky coves that shelter tiny port villages and tidal inlets. Unfortunately, much of the coastline is lined with holiday houses. The offshore islands, some of which are protected areas for sea birds, can get quite overcrowded by tourists during summer.

Inland, paths lead to ruined castles, legendary forests and farms built in pink, grey and black local stone. However, the sea is never more than 60km away from even the remotest parts of the interior. Though many of the villages are picturesque and easily accessible, Argoat remains relatively unfrequented by tourists. On the whole, they tend to stick to the main cities like Quimper and Saint Malo and to towns like Vannes or Dinan, all proud of their rich historical and architectural heritage. The mysterious megaliths which dot the land, especially around Carnac, are even older.

HIGHLIGHTS

- **Quimper** – take in the Festival de Cornouaille (late July)
- **Île d'Ouessant** – explore this or one of Brittany's other rugged islands
- **Carnac** – marvel at the extraordinary standing stones
- **Forêt de Paimpont** – trace the legends of King Arthur and Merlin the magician

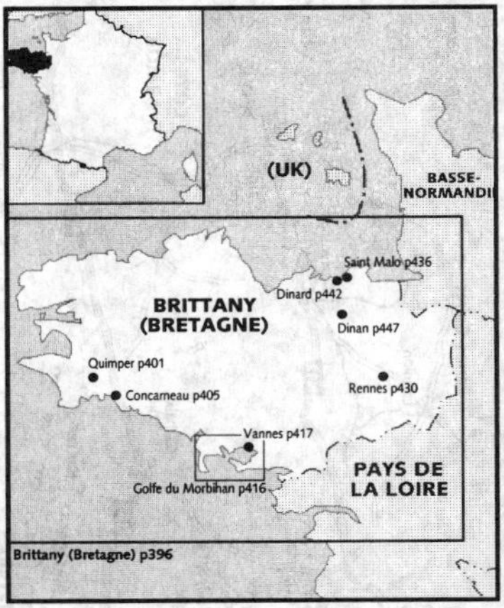

homard a l'Américaine – chunks of lobster sautéed with shallots, tomatoes and onions, flavoured with white wine and cognac

seafood – Belon oysters, clams, lobster and *coquilles Saint-Jacques* (scallops)

crêpes – especially good are seafood crêpes, savoury *galettes* and the sweet dessert crêpes

History

Brittany was first inhabited by Neolithic tribes, whose menhirs and dolmens are still scattered throughout the region (see the boxed text 'The Megaliths of Carnac'). Around the 6th century BC, they were joined by the region's first wave of Celts. Julius Caesar conquered the region in 56 BC, and it remained in Roman hands until the 5th century AD.

Following the departure of the Romans, a second wave of Celts – driven from what is now Britain and Ireland by the Anglo-Saxon

BRITTANY (BRETAGNE)

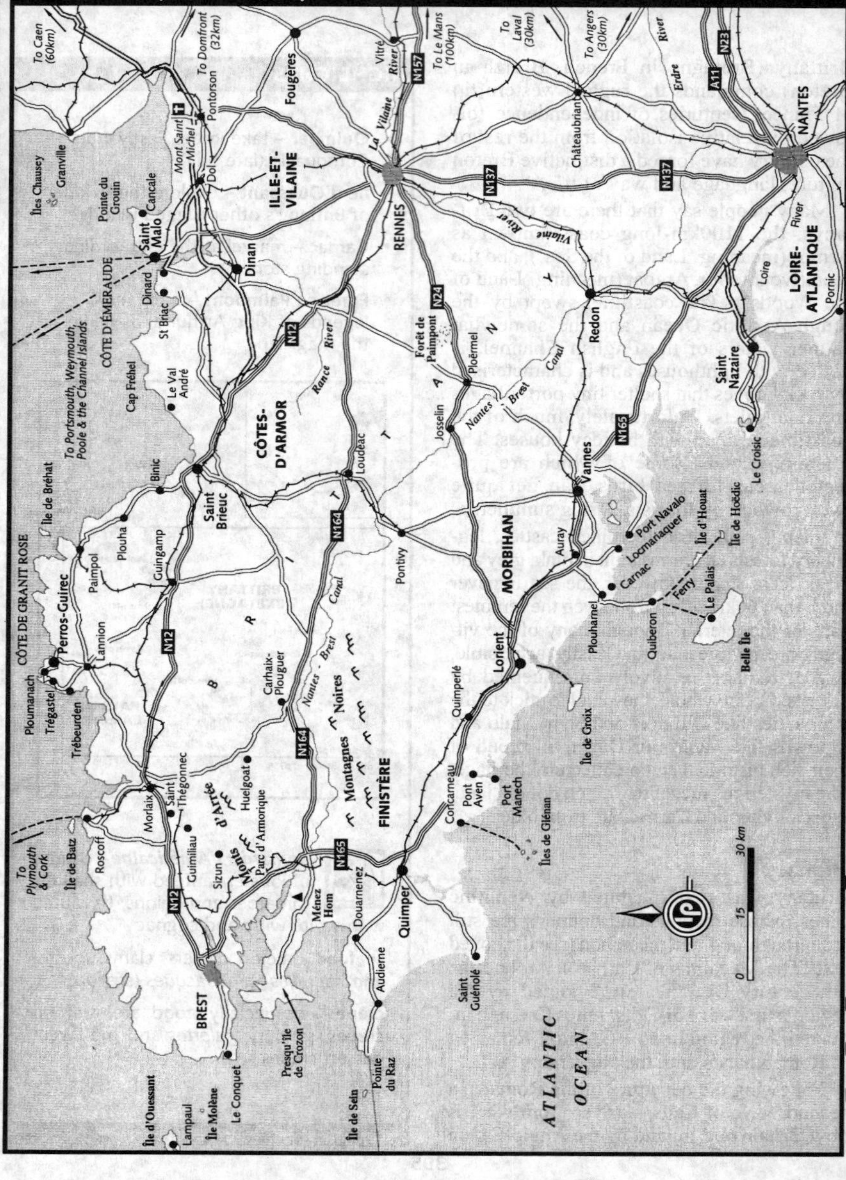

invasions – crossed the Channel and settled in Brittany. In the 5th and 6th centuries, the region was gradually Christianised by Celtic missionaries, after whom many Breton towns (eg Saint Malo and Saint Brieuc) are named.

In the 9th century, Brittany's national hero, Nominoë, revolted against French rule, taking control of both Rennes and Nantes. Shortly thereafter, his successors managed to repulse the Normans (Vikings). Because of its location, the duchy of Brittany was contested by the kings of both France and England throughout the Middle Ages. After a series of royal weddings, the region became part of France in 1532.

Over the centuries, Brittany has retained a separate regional identity and has become far less assimilated into the French mainstream than most areas of the country. Recently, there has been a drive for cultural and linguistic renewal, and stronger ties have been established with the Celtic cultures of Ireland, Wales, Scotland, Cornwall and Galicia in Spain.

To this day, some Bretons have not abandoned the hope that their region will one day regain its independence. In the late 1960s and 70s, Breton separatists carried out numerous violent actions in support of an independent Breton state, culminating in a bomb attack on the palace at Versailles in 1978. However, although many locals still put 'Breizh' stickers on their cars, violent separatist agitation appears to be a thing of the past.

King Arthur

While Breton culture abounds in legends, the most famous is the story of King Arthur, linked to both Brittany and, via Cornwall, England since the Middle Ages. In Brittany many sites are tied to Arthur, Lancelot, Merlin, the fairies Vivian and Morgan le Fay and others.

The Île Grande and Île d'Aval, close to Perros-Guirec, are both said to be the island of Avalon where Morgan le Fay (the sister of Arthur according to Chrétien de Troyes' version of the tale) lived and where Arthur was buried. Hidden in the last stronghold of the old inland forest, the Forêt d'Huelgoat is the place where Arthur should have found the Holy Grail. The Forêt de Paimpont (or Brocéliande) south-west of Rennes contains Merlin's spring of eternal youth and was home to his mistress, Vivian, the mysterious Lady of the Lake. Vannes was the capital of the kingdom ruled by Ban, the father of Lancelot, while Nantes appears in many versions of the myth as the court of King Arthur himself.

Geography

Although Brittany occupies a good part of the ancient Massif Armoricain, 300 million years of erosion have turned most of the region into an expanse of low-lying plains and gentle uplands. The only exceptions are the north-western Monts d'Arrée and the south-central Montagnes Noires.

White, sandy beaches and pleasant inlets leading to picturesque small ports are commonplace along a great deal of the coast. Spectacular rocky cliffs can be found in many areas, particularly at the end of the westernmost peninsulas and on the Île d'Ouessant. Deep tidal inlets or gorges, called *abers*, are common on the northern coast.

For administrative purposes, Brittany is divided into four departments. Finistère occupies the far western quarter of the peninsula. The central section is divided between the Côtes d'Armor (to the north) and Morbihan (to the south). In the east and north-east, next to Normandy, is the mainly inland department of Ille-et-Vilaine, which includes the regional capital, Rennes.

Climate

Brittany's coast is washed by the Gulf Stream, a warm ocean current flowing from the Gulf of Mexico towards north-western Europe. As a result, the region enjoys a very mild climate. Brittany does record France's highest annual precipitation, but it rarely rains for many days, even during the wettest months (from January to May).

Society & Conduct

Breton customs – like the Breton language – are most evident in Basse Bretagne (Lower Brittany), the western half of the peninsula, and particularly in Cornouaille, the south-western tip. Haute Bretagne (Upper Brittany), the eastern half of the peninsula (which includes Saint Malo), has retained little of its traditional way of life.

Traditional costumes, including various versions of the tall lace headdresses of the women, can sometimes still be seen at *fest-noz* (night-time dance and music festivals) and *pardons* (colourful religious celebrations). The region's two most important cultural festivals are Quimper's Festival de Cornouaille in late July and the Festival Interceltique, which takes place in Lorient in early August.

Religious Art

The stone *calvaires* (calvaries) at Lampaul-Guimiliau, Saint Thégonnec and Sizun, with their sculpted stories of saints and other figures, speak eloquently of the strong Celtic influence which is evident in Breton religious art. Brittany has a long list of saints unrecognised by Rome.

Also typically Breton is the *enclos paroissial* (enclosed parish), which consists of a walled enclosure containing a church, an ossuary and a calvary. Good examples can be found at Lampaul-Guimiliau, Saint Thégonnec and Plougastel-Daoulas.

Language

The indigenous language of Brittany is Breton (Breiz), a Celtic language related to Cornish and Welsh and, more distantly, to Irish and Scottish Gaelic. Breton can sometimes still be heard in western Brittany (especially in Cornouaille), where as many as 600,000 people have some degree of fluency. However, the number of Breton-speaking households is diminishing.

After the Revolution, the new government made a concerted effort to suppress the Breton language and replace it with French. Even 20 years ago, if school children spoke Breton in the classroom they were punished. Things have changed, however, and about 20 privately subsidised schools now teach in Breton, several at the secondary level.

The Breton Flag & Emblems

The flag of Brittany consists of nine horizontal black and white stripes, representing each of the nine ancient *évêchés* (bishoprics) of Upper and Lower Brittany. In the top left-hand corner of the flag is a field of stylised ermines, stoats with black and white fur that symbolise the duchy of Brittany. You'll see ermines on many city and town flags and seals in the region.

A symbol also often encountered is the triskelion (from the Greek *triskelês* – 'three-legged'), a decorative motif consisting of three curved branches, arms or legs radiating from a centre. It was first used by the Celts around 450 BC and remains an important symbol in Celtic countries, evoking images of the sun or the eternal wheel of life and death.

A few helpful Breton expressions are:

Breton	French	English
demad, demat	bonjour	hello
d'ur wech all	à une autre fois	see you again
kenavo	au revoir	goodbye
trugarez	merci	thank you
yehed mad, yec'hed mat	à votre santé	cheers

The following are some Breton words you may come across, especially in place names. Note that the spelling may vary.

aber	embouchure	mouth
ar	le, la	the
aven	rivière, fleuve	river
bae	baie	bay
bed	monde	world
bihan	petit	little
deiz	jour	day
dol	table	table
douar	terre	earth
dour	eau	water
du	noir	black
enez	île	island
fao, faou	hêtre	beech tree
fest-noz	fête de nuit	night festival
gall	français	French
gwenn	blanc	white
hir	long	long
...ig, ic	-ette	diminutive suffix = little
iliz	église	church
izel	bas	low
kember, kemper	confluent	confluence
ker	cher	dear
koad, goat	forêt	forest
koan	dîner	dinner
kromm, crom	courbé	curved
men/mein	pierre	stone
menez	montagne	mountain
mor	mer	sea
nant	vallée	valley
pen	tête, bout	head, end
plou, plo, ple... (used only as a prefix in place names)	paroisse	parish
poull	mare	pond
pred	déjeuner	lunch
raz	détroit	strait
roz, ros	tertre	hillock, mound
ster, stêr, steir	rivière, fleuve	river
stif, stivell	source	spring
tann	chêne	oak tree
telenn	harpe	Celtic harp
ti, ty	maison	house
trev, tre, treo	trêve	parish division
trez	sable	sand
uhel	haut	high

Activities

Sailing and windsurfing are very popular in Brittany. Scuba diving around the rocky archipelagos is among the best in France.

A slow but interesting way to cross the region is by canal boat along the canals and waterways from Brest or Dinan to Nantes. See Canal Boats under Activities in the Facts for the Visitor chapter for details. For information on canal boats, moorings and locks contact the Service de la Navigation (☎ 02 99 59 20 60 in Rennes; ☎ 02 97 64 85 20 in Lorient).

Getting There & Away

Ferries of various sorts link Saint Malo with the Channel Islands, the English ports of Weymouth and Portsmouth and Cork in Ireland. From Roscoff, there are ferries to Plymouth (England) and Cork (Ireland). For more information, see England and Ireland under Sea in the Getting There & Away chapter as well as the Getting There & Away listings under Saint Malo and Roscoff.

Getting Around

All of Brittany's major towns and cities are linked by rail but the tracks basically follow the coast, and there are no services to or across the interior. This is where the bus network takes over. It is extensive but services are often infrequent.

The lack of convenient, intercity public transport and the appeal of exploring out-of-the-way destinations make renting a car or motorbike worth considering. Brittany – especially Cornouaille – is an excellent area for cycling, and bike-rental places are never hard to find.

Finistère

Brittany's westernmost region, Finistère (Land's End) is also the most Breton in character. It is known for its numerous calvaries and *pardons*, especially in Cornouaille, the area of southern Finistère whose name commemorates the early Celts who sailed from Cornwall and other parts of Britain to settle here. This is where you're most likely to hear people speaking Breton. The area's major city, Quimper, stages an annual summer festival celebrating Celtic culture.

Brest, Finistère's other main city, is at the far western tip of the peninsula. Along the southern coast there are numerous fishing ports, including the engaging town of Concarneau.

Finistère is surrounded by the sea, which pounds the rocky cliffs and deep inlets making up much of the rugged coastline. The sea breeze sweeps as far inland as the Monts d'Arrée, the eastern frontier of the Parc Naturel Régional d'Armorique. Islands off the coast like Ouessant, Molène and Sein are buffeted by very strong currents. Some 350 lighthouses, beacons, buoys and radar installations make the area's busy and treacherous sea routes more navigable.

QUIMPER

• pop 60,000 ✉ 29000

At the confluence of the Odet and Steïr rivers, Quimper (Kemper in Breton) has successfully preserved its Breton architecture and atmosphere and is considered by many to be the cultural and artistic capital of the region. Some even refer to Quimper (pronounced 'kam-PAIR') as the 'soul of Brittany'.

Orientation

The old city, much of it for pedestrians only, is to the west and north-west of the cathedral. The train and bus stations are just under 1km east of the old city. Mont Frugy overlooks the centre from the south bank of the Odet River.

Information

Tourist Office The tourist office (☎ 02 98 53 04 05; fax 02 98 53 31 33) at Place de la Résistance is open Monday to Saturday from 9 am to 12.30 pm and 1.30 to 6.30 pm. In July and August, it is open from 9 am to 7 pm. From May to mid-September, the office is also open on Sunday from 10 am to 1 pm and 3 to 7 pm. A tour of the city in English leaves the tourist office at 2 pm every Tuesday in July and August.

Money The Banque de France is 150m from the train station at 29 Ave de la Gare. It is open weekdays from 8.45 am to noon and 1.30 to 3.30 pm. The Crédit Lyonnais in Place Saint Corentin is open Tuesday to Saturday from 8 am to noon and 1.50 to 5 pm. In the centre, the Banque de Bretagne at 18 Quai de l'Odet keeps similar hours.

Crédit Agricole at 10 Rue René Madec is open Monday to Saturday from 8.45 am to 12.15 pm and 1.45 to 5.30 pm (4 pm on Saturday).

Post The main post office at 37 Blvd Amiral de Kerguélen is open weekdays from 8 am to 6.30 pm and on Saturday until noon.

Travel Agency Bretagne Voyages (☎ 02 98 95 61 24), 20 Rue du Parc, sells air and boat tickets. It is open Monday to Saturday from 9 am to noon and 1.30 to 6.30 pm (5.30 pm on Saturday).

Laundry The Lav' Seul laundrette at 9 Rue de Locronan, two blocks north of Église Saint Mathieu, is open daily from 7 am to 9 pm. The Laverie de la Gare, west of the bus station parking lot at 2 Rue Jacques Cartier, keeps the same hours.

Walking Tour

Strolling along the quays that flank both banks of the Odet is a fine way to get a feel for the city. The old city is known for its centuries-old houses, which are especially in evidence on **Rue Kéréon** and around **Place au Beurre**. To climb 72m-high **Mont Frugy**, which offers great views of the city, follow the switchback **Promenade du Mont Frugy**, which starts just east of the tourist office.

QUIMPER

PLACES TO STAY
- 3 Hôtel Le Celtic
- 22 Hôtel La Tour d'Auvergne
- 27 Hôtel Dupleix
- 40 Hotels
- 41 Hôtel de l'Ouest

PLACES TO EAT
- 19 La Folle Blanche
- 20 Trattoria Mario
- 28 Rue Ste Catherine Crêperies
- 35 Crêperie du Frugy
- 42 Le Lotus d'Or

OTHER
- 1 Torch VTT (Bicycle Rental)
- 2 Laundrette
- 4 Blue Note
- 5 Euzen Traiteur
- 6 Musée des Beaux-Arts; Hôtel de Ville
- 7 Église Saint Mathieu
- 8 Crédit Agricole Bank
- 9 Monoprix Supermarket
- 10 Covered Market
- 11 Bretagne Voyages (Travel Agency)
- 12 Crédit Lyonnais
- 13 Ar Bed Keltiek; François le Villec Shops
- 14 Place Saint Corentin
- 15 Cathédrale Saint Corentin
- 16 Café/Coffeeshop
- 17 Cathedral Garden
- 18 Musée Départemental Breton
- 21 Main Post Office
- 23 Lennez (Bicycle Rental)
- 24 Laundrette
- 25 Theatre
- 26 Police Station
- 29 Préfecture
- 30 QUB Office (Bus Information)
- 31 Banque de Bretagne
- 32 Place de la Résistance
- 33 Tourist Office
- 34 Promenade du Mont Frugy
- 36 Unico Grocery
- 37 Banque de France
- 38 Bus Station
- 39 Train Station
- 43 Musée de la Faïence
- 44 Faïenceries HB Henriot

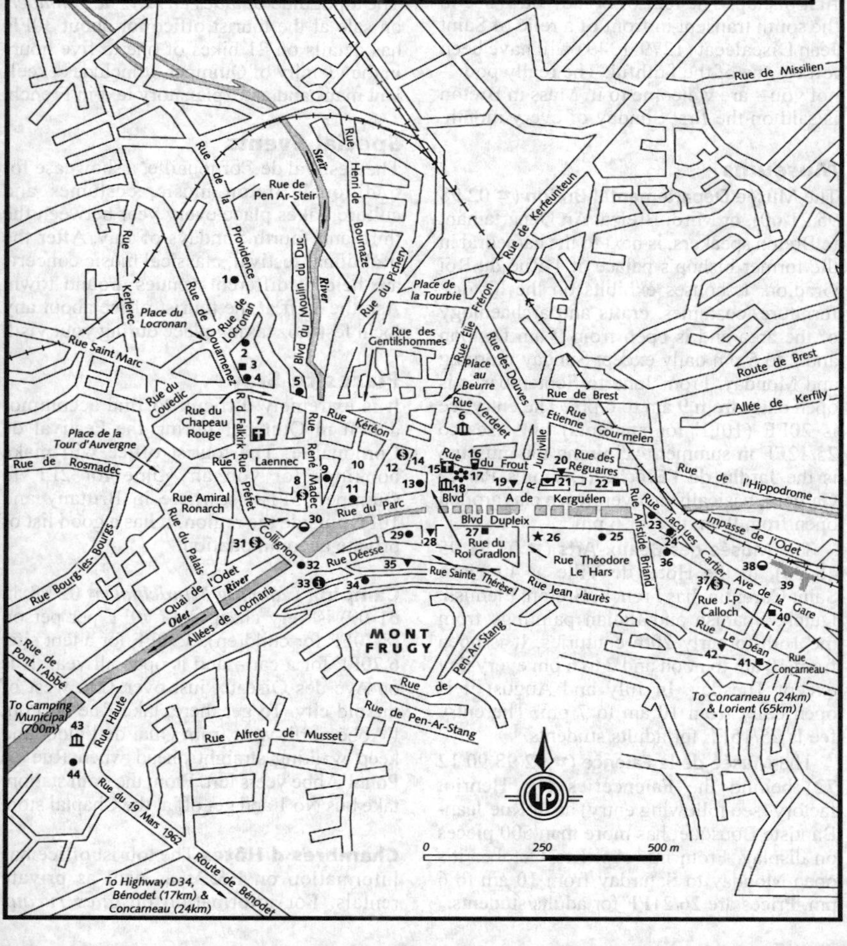

Cathédrale Saint Corentin

Built between 1239 and 1515 (with spires added in the 1850s), Quimper's newly cleaned cathedral incorporates many Breton elements, including – on the western façade between the spires – an equestrian statue of King Gradlon, the city's mythical 5th century founder. The early 15th century nave is out of line with the choir, built two centuries earlier. The cathedral's patron saint is Saint Corentin, who was Quimper's first bishop. The loaf of bread you'll see in the south transept in front of a relic of Saint Jean Discalcéat (1279-1349) will have been left by one of the faithful. The really poor – not you – are welcome to it. Mass in Breton is said on the first Sunday of every month.

Museums

The **Musée Départemental Breton** (☎ 02 98 95 21 60), or Mirdi Breizat An Departamant to Breton speakers, is next to the cathedral in the former bishop's palace at 1 Rue du Roi Gradlon. It houses exhibits on the history, furniture, costumes, crafts and archaeology of the area and is open from 9 am to noon and 2 to 5 pm daily except Sunday morning and Monday. From June to September it is open daily from 9 am to 6 pm. The entry fee is 20FF (10FF for students) but rises to 25/12FF in summer. Adjoining the museum is the **Jardin de l'Évêché** (Bishop's Palace Garden), basically an overgrown playground open from 9 am to 5 or 6 pm.

The **Musée des Beaux-Arts** (☎ 02 98 95 45 20), in the Hôtel de Ville at 40 Place Saint Corentin, has French, Breton, Flemish, Dutch, Spanish and Italian paintings from the 16th to early 20th centuries. It is open from 10 am to noon and 2 to 6 pm every day except Tuesday. In July and August it is open daily from 10 am to 7 pm. The entry fee is 25/15FF for adults/students.

The **Musée de la Faïence** (☎ 02 98 90 12 72) behind the Faïenceries HB Henriot factory (see following entry) at 14 Rue Jean-Baptiste Bousquet has more than 500 pieces on display. From mid-April to October it's open Monday to Saturday from 10 am to 6 pm. Prices are 26/21FF for adults/students.

Faïencerie Tour

Faïenceries HB Henriot (☎ 02 98 90 09 36) has been turning out colourful Quimper faïence (glazed earthenware) since 1690. There are organised tours of the factory, which is on Rue Haute south-west of the cathedral, on weekdays from 9 to 11.15 am and 2 to 4.15 pm (5.15 pm in July and August). The cost is 20FF.

Hiking

The topoguide *Balades en Pays de Quimper*, on sale at the tourist office for about 30FF, has details on 21 hikes of one to five hours in the vicinity of Quimper. It includes excellent maps and an explanatory text in French.

Special Events

The Festival de Cornouaille, a showcase for traditional Breton music, costumes and culture, takes place every year between the third and fourth Sundays of July. After the traditional festival, classical music concerts are held at different venues around town. Ask the staff at the tourist office about any local fest-noz taking place during your visit.

Places to Stay

It is extremely difficult to find accommodation in Quimper during the Festival de Cornouaille. The tourist office will make bookings for you any time for 2FF in Quimper, 5FF elsewhere in Brittany and 10FF outside the region. It has a good list of private accommodation.

Camping *Camping Municipal* (☎ 02 98 55 61 09) is very cheap – 17.70FF per person (8.70FF for children), 3.90FF for a tent site, 6.70FF for a car – and is open all year. It is on Ave des Oiseaux just over 1km west of the old city. To get there, take Rue de Pont l'Abbé north-west from Quai de l'Odet and keep walking straight ahead when Rue de Pont l'Abbé veers left. From the train station, take bus No 1 and get off at the Chaptal stop.

Chambres d'Hôtes The tourist office has information on B&Bs as well as private rentals. For information on *gîtes ruraux* (farm B&Bs), contact the ***Chambre d'Agriculture*** (☎ 02 98 52 48 00) on Allée Sully.

Hotels The spotless ***Hôtel de l'Ouest*** (☎ 02 98 90 28 35), up Rue Jean-Pierre Calloch from the train station at 63 Rue Le Déan, has large, pleasant singles from 100FF, doubles from 150FF and triples/quads from 220/250FF. Singles/doubles with shower are 180/190FF. Hall showers are 15FF.

There are several hotels opposite the train station. ***Hôtel Pascal*** (☎ 02 98 90 00 81; fax 02 98 53 21 81) at 17 Ave de la Gare provides a few doubles for 120FF, but most of the singles/doubles have showers and cost from 155/180FF.

The ***Hôtel Derby*** (☎ 02 98 52 06 91; fax 02 98 53 39 04) at 13 Ave de la Gare has good-sized rooms with shower, toilet and TV from 150/200FF. You could also try the ***Hôtel Café Nantaïs*** (☎ 02 98 90 07 84) at 23 Ave de la Gare, which has rooms (with washbasin and bidet) at 118FF.

Closer to the action at 13 Rue de Douarnenez (100m north of Église Saint Mathieu), the rather noisy ***Hôtel Le Celtic*** (☎ 02 98 55 59 35) has doubles without/with shower for 125/165FF. Doubles with bath and toilet are 215FF.

More upmarket is the modern ***Hôtel Dupleix*** (☎ 02 98 90 53 35; fax 02 98 52 05 31), east of the Préfecture building at 34 Blvd Dupleix, with doubles from 410FF. The charming ***Hôtel La Tour d'Auvergne*** (☎ 02 98 95 08 70; fax 02 98 95 17 31), in a quiet area at 13 Rue des Réguaires, has doubles with washbasin and toilet from 295FF.

Places to Eat

Restaurants Crêpes and savoury galettes – Breton specialities – are your best bets for a cheap and filling meal. Along Rue Sainte Catherine, directly across the river from the cathedral, there are crêperies at No 9, No 11 and No 15. ***Crêperie du Frugy*** (☎ 02 98 90 32 49) at No 9 Rue Sainte Thérèse is open for lunch and dinner daily except Sunday lunchtime and Monday. Crêpes range in price from 7 to 32FF.

You'll find several decent restaurants on Rue Le Déan not far from the train station. These include a Vietnamese place called ***Le Lotus d'Or*** (☎ 02 98 53 02 54), which is at No 53.

There is a strip of ***ethnic restaurants*** – from Chinese and Indian to Italian – on Ave de la Libération, the continuation of Ave de la Gare running east of the train station.

Trattoria Mario (☎ 02 98 95 42 15), behind the post office at 35 Rue des Réguaires, specialises in pizza and is open from Tuesday to Sunday from 11 am to 2 pm and 7 to 11.30 pm.

If you want to splurge, try ***La Folle Blanche*** (☎ 02 98 95 76 76), an attractive restaurant at 39 Blvd Amiral de Kerguélen that looks onto part of the Jardin l'Évêché. It specialises in Lyonnais cuisine (*menus* from 80FF) and is open for lunch and dinner every day but Sunday.

Self-Catering ***Euzen Traiteur***, a delicatessen at 10 Rue du Chapeau Rouge, has excellent meats, prepared dishes and especially tasty gnocchi. It is open from 8 am to 7.30 pm daily except Sunday. The ***Monoprix*** supermarket on Quai du Port au Vin (near the covered market) is open daily, except Sunday, from 9 am to 7 pm.

Near the train station, the ***Unico*** grocery at 39 Ave de la Gare is open daily from 8 am (7.30 am on Saturday, 8.30 am on Sunday) to 8 pm.

Entertainment

From late June to the first week in September, traditional Breton music is performed every Thursday evening at 9 pm in the Jardin de l'Évêché. The entrance fee is about 25FF.

The ***Blue Note*** (☎ 02 98 53 47 47), a bar next to the Hôtel Le Celtic at 7 Rue de Douarnenez, features jazz and blues some nights. Rue du Frout near the cathedral has a couple of small pubs that attract a Breton-speaking clientele. The ***Café/Coffee Shop*** at No 26 is a popular gay venue open nightly from 5 pm to 1 am.

Shopping

Ar Bed Keltiek (Celtic World; ☎ 02 98 95 42 82) at 2 Rue du Roi Gradlon has a wide selection of Celtic books, music, pottery and jewellery. The store is open Tuesday to Saturday from 9 am to 1 pm and 2 to 7 pm. During July and August it is open every day from 8 am to 8 pm.

For faïence and textiles decorated with traditionally inspired Breton designs, go to the excellent shop of François Le Villec (☎ 02 98 95 31 54) at 4 Rue du Roi Gradlon. It is open Monday to Saturday from 9.30 am to 12.30 pm and 2 to 7 pm (daily with no midday break in summer). The shop just behind the Faïenceries HB Henriot factory at Place Bérardier has a large selection of Quimper-ware plates, cups, bowls etc. It is open Monday to Saturday from 9.30 am to 6 pm.

Getting There & Away

Bus The bus station is in the modern building to the right (west) as you exit the train station on Ave de la Gare; schedules are posted inside. The office (☎ 02 98 90 88 89) serves half a dozen bus companies, including SCETA (☎ 02 98 93 06 98 in Carhaix-Plouguer), Castric (☎ 02 98 56 33 03 in Combrit) and Le Cœur (☎ 02 98 54 40 15 in Pouldreuzic, 15km west of Quimper). It is open from 7.15 am to 12.30 pm and 1 to 7.15 pm on weekdays (to 5 pm on Saturday) and from 5 to 7.30 pm on Sunday. There is reduced service on Sunday and during the off season.

Another bus company, CAT (☎ 02 98 90 68 40), has buses to Brest (84FF), Pointe du Raz (France's westernmost point; 47FF), Roscoff (118FF) and other destinations.

Caoudal (☎ 02 98 56 96 72 in La Forêt Fouësnant, near Concarneau) has a service to Concarneau (24.50FF) and Quimperlé (47FF).

For information on SNCF buses to Douarnenez, Camaret (which is at the tip of the Presqu'île de Crozon), Concarneau and Quiberon, inquire at the train station.

Train The train station (☎ 02 98 98 31 26 or ☎ 08 36 35 35 35) is next to the bus station on Ave de la Gare. The information counters are open daily from 8 am to 7.15 pm except Friday and Sunday (8 am to 7 pm in July and August). TGV trains can be picked up in Rennes, Lorient and Nantes. A one-way ticket to Paris' Gare Montparnasse costs 368FF. The trip between Paris and Quimper takes about four hours. Destinations within Brittany include Brest (83FF; 1½ hours; six to eight a day), Vannes (92FF; 1½ hours; seven a day) and Saint Malo (206FF; three hours; four a day) via Rennes. The station has luggage lockers (15 to 30FF).

Car ADA (☎ 02 98 52 25 25) has an office near the train station at 2 Ave de la Gare. Europcar (☎ 02 98 90 00 68) is nearby at 12 Rue de Concarneau.

Getting Around

Bus QUB, which runs the seven local bus lines, has an information office (☎ 02 98 95 26 27) opposite the tourist office at 2 Quai de l'Odet. It's open weekdays from 8 am to 12.15 pm and 1.30 to 6.30 pm and on Saturday from 9 am to noon and 2 to 6 pm. Tickets are 6FF each or 45FF for a carnet of 10. Buses stop running around 7 pm and do not operate on Sunday except for bus No 8. To reach the old city from the station, take bus No 1 or 6.

Taxi Taxis can be reached on ☎ 02 98 90 21 21 or ☎ 02 98 90 16 45.

Bicycle Torch VTT (☎ 02 98 53 84 41) at 58 Rue de la Providence rents mountain bikes for 65/90FF a half-day/day (70/45FF from October to April). The shop, which is open from 9.30 am to 12.30 pm and 2 to 7 pm daily except Sunday and Monday morning, is a good source of information on cycling routes. Cycles Lennez (☎ 02 98 90 14 81), just west of the train station at 13 Rue Aristide Briand, has regular bikes for 69/95/125FF for one/two/three days and mountain bikes for 95/145FF for one/two days.

CONCARNEAU

• pop 18,500 ✉ 29900

Concarneau (Konk-Kerne in Breton), France's third most important trawler port, is 24km south-east of Quimper. Much of the tuna brought ashore here is caught in the Indian Ocean or off the coast of Africa; you'll see handbills announcing the size of the incoming fleet's catch all around town. Concarneau is slightly scruffy and at the same time a bit touristy, but it's refreshingly unpretentious and is near several decent beaches.

Orientation

Concarneau curls around the protected harbour that houses the Port de Plaisance and the busy fisheries area of Port de Pêche. Quai d'Aiguillon, the site where the tourist office is located, runs north-south along the harbour, turning into Quai Peneroff as it passes the Ville Close, the walled town. Quai Peneroff continues southward to the Port de Plaisance, with its multitude of pleasure boats, and Quai de la Croix.

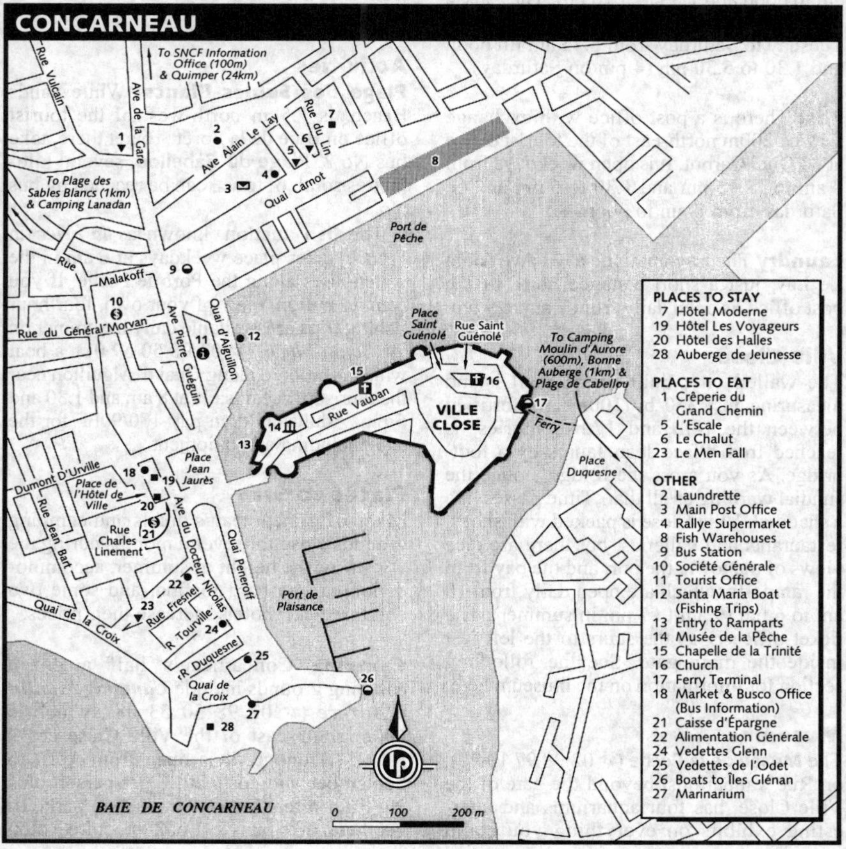

Information

Tourist Office The tourist office (☎ 02 98 97 01 44; fax 02 98 50 88 81), on Quai d'Aiguillon, is 200m north of the main (western) gate to the Ville Close. It is open Monday to Saturday from 9 am to 12.30 pm and from 1.45 to 7 pm. From May to June, it's open Sunday from 9.30 am to 12.30 pm, and in July and August it's open daily from 9 am to 8 pm.

Money The Société Générale at 10 Rue du Général Morvan, half a block west of the tourist office, is open weekdays from 8.10 am to noon and 1.35 to 5.10 pm. The Caisse d'Épargne on Rue Charles Linement opens Tuesday to Saturday from 8.45 am till noon and 1.30 to 5.30 pm (4 pm on Saturday).

Post There is a post office with exchange service 200m north-east of the tourist office at 14 Quai Carnot. It is open weekdays from 8 am to 12.15 pm and 1.30 to 6 pm and on Saturday from 8 am to noon.

Laundry The Lavomatique at 21 Ave Alain Le Lay, just a short distance north of the post office, is open daily from 7 am to 9 pm.

Ville Close

The walled city, built on a small island measuring just 350 by 100m and fortified between the 14th and 17th centuries, is reached from Place Jean Jaurès by a foot-bridge. As you cross the bridge, notice the sundial warning us all that 'Time passes like a shadow'. Ville Close is packed with shops, restaurants and galleries, but there are nice views of the town, the port and the bay from the **ramparts**, which are open daily from 10 am to 6 pm (9 am to 7 pm in summer). The ticket office is up the stairs to the left just inside the main gate. See the following section for information on the museum here.

Museums

The **Musée de la Pêche** (☎ 02 98 97 10 20), on Rue Vauban just beyond the gate of the Ville Close, has four aquariums and interesting exhibits on everything you could possibly want to know about fish and the fishing industry in Concarneau over the centuries. It's open daily from 10 am to noon and 2 to 6 pm (9.30 am to 7 pm in July and August). Prices are 30/20FF for adults/those under 16. A few steps farther along at No 36 is an interesting little church called **Chapelle de la Trinité**, which now houses a theatre.

The more serious **Marinarium** (☎ 02 98 97 06 59) next to the hostel at Quai de la Croix has aquariums as well as exhibits dealing with oceanography and marine biology. It is open Easter to September daily from 2 to 6.30 pm. Prices are 20/12FF for adults/children.

Activities

Plage des Sables Blancs 'White Sands Beach' is 1.5km north-west of the tourist office on Baie de la Forêt. To get there, take bus No 2. **Plage du Cabellou**, several kilometres south of town, can be reached by bus No 1.

The **fish auction**, known as *la criée* in French, takes place weekdays at 6 am in the warehouses along the Port de Pêche. If you want to pull in a few of your own, four-hour **fishing trips** are available daily in summer on the *Santa Maria* (☎ 02 98 50 69 01), a boat which is moored along Quai d'Aiguillon near the tourist office. It sails at 8 am and 1.30 and 6 pm. Adults/children pay 180/90FF for the trip, including all equipment.

Places to Stay

Many of Concarneau's hotels and camping grounds close for several months during the winter. At the height of summer, accommodation can be hard to find, and some two and three-star hotels increase their prices.

Camping Concarneau's half a dozen camping grounds include ***Camping Moulin d'Aurore*** (☎ 02 98 50 53 08), which is 600m south-east of the Ville Close at 49 Rue de Tregunc. It is open from April to September and costs 20FF per person plus 19FF for a tent site and a place to park. To get there, take bus No 1 or 2 (stop: Le Rouz) or the little ferry from Ville Close to Place Duquesne and walk south along Rue Mauduit Duplessis.

Camping Lanadan (☎ 02 98 97 17 78), about 100m north of the Plage des Sables Blancs on Route de la Forêt, is open from mid-June to mid-September. It is served by bus No 2 (stop: Poulgazec). The charges per person/tent/car are 13/16/8FF.

Hostel The ***Auberge de Jeunesse*** (☎ 02 98 97 03 47; fax 02 98 50 87 57) is right on the water at Quai de la Croix, next to the Marinarium. To get there from the tourist office, walk south to the end of Quai Peneroff and turn right. A bed is 46FF, and breakfast is 19FF. Reception is open from 9 am to noon and 6 to 8 pm, but you can leave your bags in the dining room, which is open all day.

Hotels The ***Hôtel Les Voyageurs*** (☎ 02 98 97 08 06), 9 Place Jean Jaurès, has slightly overpriced doubles for 175FF with washbasin and bidet and 200FF with shower. Hall showers are free. If you can afford a bit more, ***Hôtel des Halles*** (☎ 02 98 97 11 41; fax 02 98 50 58 54), just around the corner on Place de l'Hôtel de Ville, charges 220FF for a double with shower and TV and 290FF with shower, TV and toilet. Or try the ***Hôtel Modern*** (☎ 02 98 97 03 36; fax 02 98 97 89 06), 5 Rue du Lin, a quiet backstreet. It has rooms with washbasin for 200FF and with shower from 280FF. Use of the private garage costs 40FF.

About 1km out of town, the friendly ***Bonne Auberge*** is perfectly situated on the beach at Le Cabellou and surrounded by gardens. Singles/doubles start at 120/150FF with washbasin and at 200/240FF with shower.

Places to Eat

Restaurants *Le Men Fall* (☎ 02 98 50 80 80), down narrow Rue Fresnel from Quai de la Croix, has good pizzas and pasta and is open daily to 11 pm (closed Monday and Sunday for lunch except in summer). There are lots more restaurants along Ave du Docteur Nicolas.

A number of eateries north of the fishing port offer good value for money. ***L'Escale*** (☎ 02 98 97 03 31) at 19 Quai Carnot is particularly popular with local Concarnois – a hearty lunch or dinner *menu* (available daily except Saturday night and all day Sunday) costs just 51FF. Next door at No 20, the similar ***Le Chalut*** (☎ 02 98 97 02 12) has a 50FF *menu* (closed Friday and Saturday nights).

For excellent home-style crêpes, try the unpretentious little crêperie called ***Crêperie du Grand Chemin*** (☎ 02 98 97 36 57) at 17 Ave de la Gare. Your basic *crêpe au beurre* (buttered crêpe) costs only 7FF – and there's a big discount if you order them by the pair. More extravagant varieties are 15 to 23FF.

Self-Catering The stalls in the ***covered market*** on Place Jean Jaurès sell all the basics and are open daily until 1 pm. The big market day is Friday.

The ***Rallye*** supermarket on Quai Carnot next to the post office is open Monday to Saturday from 8.45 am to 7.30 pm. During most of July and August it's also open on Sunday from 9.30 am to 12.30 pm. The ***Alimentation Générale*** at 8 Ave du Docteur Nicolas is open Monday to Saturday from 7.30 am to 9.30 pm (8 pm on Saturday) and on Sunday from 7.30 am to 1 pm and 6 to 8.30 pm.

Getting There & Away

Bus The bus station is in the parking lot north of the tourist office. Caoudal (☎ 02 98 56 96 72 in La Forêt Fouësnant) runs up to four buses a day (three on Sunday) between Quimper and Quimperlé via Concarneau, Pont Aven and La Forêt Fouësnant. The trip from Quimper to Concarneau costs 24.50FF.

SCETA (☎ 02 98 93 06 98 in Carhaix-Plouguer) links Concarneau with Rosporden (20FF) 10km to the north-east six times a day Monday to Saturday and once a day on Sunday. Autocars Castilla-Le Naour (☎ 02 98 06 82 18 in Nevez) sends buses eastward along the coast to Port Manech (16FF) five times a day except Sunday and holidays. The tourist office has bus details and timetables.

Train Trains no longer stop at the old station north-west of the centre, but the SNCF office (☎ 08 36 35 35 35) there can provide train information nationwide.

Getting Around

Bus Concarneau's three bus lines run by Busco operate between 7.20 am and 7.20 pm daily except Sunday. All of them stop at the bus terminal next to the tourist office and tickets are 5FF (45FF for a 10 ticket carnet). For information, consult the Busco office (☎ 02 98 60 53 76) in the covered market on Place Jean Jaurès. It's open from 10 am to noon and 2 to 5 pm on weekdays except Tuesday.

Taxi You can book taxis in Concarneau on ☎ 02 98 97 10 93 or ☎ 02 98 97 06 06.

Boat A small passenger ferry links the Ville Close with Place Duquesne on Concarneau's eastern shore year-round. From mid-June through August, the ferry departs when it's full between 7.30 am and 10 pm. In the off season, they start an hour later, take a lunch break and finish at 6.20 pm (7.20 pm on Saturday and Sunday). One-way tickets cost 3FF (or 20FF for 10 tickets).

AROUND CONCARNEAU

From April to September, three companies offer excursions to **Îles de Glénan**, a group of nine little islands about 20km south of Concarneau with an 18th century fort, sailing and scuba-diving schools, an interesting bird sanctuary, as well as a couple of houses.

Vedettes Glenn (☎ 02 98 97 10 31), 17 Ave du Docteur Nicolas, and Vedette Taxi (☎ 02 98 97 25 25), based in Quimper, charge 100FF return (50FF for children). A return trip with Vedettes de l'Odet (☎ 02 98 50 72 12 in Concarneau, 02 98 57 00 58 in Bénodet) costs 120/60FF for adult/children. Vedettes de l'Odet and Vedettes Glenn also offer four-hour excursions up the **Odet River** (110/55FF) from Bénodet, near the river mouth.

BREST

• pop 154,000 ✉ 29200

Sheltered by a wide natural harbour known as the Rade, rainy Brest is one of France's most important naval ports. Flattened by continual air attacks during WWII, it was rebuilt as a modern, not particularly attractive, city. The medieval port area and its narrow streets, where Jean Genet set his homoerotic novel *Querelle* (and Fassbinder his film), are long gone. You'll still see the starched white uniforms of the French navy everywhere, though, as well as sailors from other countries lurching and staggering about on shore leave.

Orientation

The centre of Brest lies north of the Rade and the Port de Commerce; to the west are the Arsenal Maritime and the Penfeld River. From Place de la Liberté, the main square, Rue de Siam runs south-west and Rue de Jean Jaurès north-east. Both are lined with restaurants, cafés and bars. The Château de Brest lies to the south-west.

Information

Tourist Office The tourist office (☎ 02 98 44 24 96; fax 02 98 44 53 73) is south of Place de la Liberté at 8 Ave Georges Clemenceau, next to the modern Quartz cultural and convention centre. It's open Monday to Saturday from 10 am to 12.30 pm and 2 to 6 pm. In July and August, the hours are 10 am to 6 pm from Monday to Saturday and 10 am to noon and 2 to 6 pm on Sunday.

If you're interested in doing some walking or hiking in the area, pick up a copy of *30 Circuits Pédestres autour de Brest* (50FF) from the tourist office.

Money The Banque de France, south-west of the tourist office at 39 Rue du Château, is open weekdays from 8.45 am to 12.15 pm and 1.30 to 3.30 pm. Crédit Mutuel de Bretagne at 2 Place de la Liberté is open Tuesday to Saturday from 8.30 am to noon and 1.30 to 6 pm (4 pm on Saturday). There are lots more banks along Rue de Siam.

Post The main post office, which has exchange services, is south-west of Place de la Liberté at Place Général Leclerc. It is open weekdays from 8 am to 7 pm and on Saturday from 8 am to noon.

Laundry The laundrette at 8 Place de la Liberté is open daily from 7 am to 8.30 pm.

Océanopolis

The ultramodern Océanopolis (☎ 02 98 34 40 40) at the Port de Plaisance, about 3km east of the city centre, has lovely aquariums with algae forests, seals, crabs, anemones, sea urchins and Brest's famed scallops. There are also interesting exhibitions on all aspects of sea life from ocean currents to algae, and even a section on cooking with seaweed. From mid-June to September, when prices are 50/30FF for adults/those under 18, it's open daily from 9.30 am to 6 pm (the rest of the year it's open Monday from 2 to 5 pm, Tuesday to Friday from 9.30 am to 5 pm and weekends to 6 pm). Océanopolis can be reached on bus No 7 from in front of the Quartz centre.

Musée de la Marine

The Maritime Museum (☎ 02 98 22 12 39) is housed in the fortified Château de Brest, which dates from the 13th century and is one of the few buildings in the city to survive the 'rain', as the poet Jacques Prévert described the bombing of WWII. The rather feeble exhibits examine the city's maritime tradition, but the views of the Rade and the naval port from the thick walls are striking. Just don't stray too far: most of the chateau is military property and off-limits to civilians. The Musée de la Marine is open daily except Tuesday from 9.15 am to noon and 2 to 6 pm. Prices are 29/19FF for adults/children.

Tour Tanguy

The paintings, photographs and dioramas in this round 14th century tower (☎ 02 98 00 88 60), which is across the Penfeld River on Place Pierre Péron, trace the history of Brest from earliest times with emphasis on how the city looked on the eve of WWII. Among the more interesting events documented is the visit of three Siamese ambassadors in 1686 who were on their way to the court of Louis XIV with gifts of gold, silver and lacquer. Rue de Siam was renamed to commemorate the occasion. Tour Tanguy is open on Wednesday, Thursday and weekends from 2 until 5 or 6 pm from October to May, and daily from 10 am till noon and 2 to 7 pm in June and September. In July and August, daily hours are 10 am to noon and 2 to 7 pm. Admission is free.

Places to Stay

Hostel The ***Auberge de Jeunesse*** (☎ 02 98 41 90 41; fax 02 98 41 82 66) is on Rue de Kerbriant near Océanopolis and a stone's throw from the artificial beach at Moulin Blanc. It charges 68FF (breakfast included) per person and is open all year. To get there, take bus No 7 from the train station and get off at Port de Plaisance, the last stop.

Hotels Most of Brest's hotels offer weekend packages, with discounts of between 20 and 30% for Friday, Saturday or Sunday night stays.

The ***Hôtel Vauban*** (☎ 02 98 46 06 88; fax 02 98 44 87 54), a fairly grand place south-east of the tourist office at 17 Ave Georges Clemenceau, has simple doubles for 130FF and ones with shower, toilet and TV from 220FF. Overall, it's an excellent deal.

The ***Hôtel Abalis*** (☎ 02 98 44 21 86; fax 02 98 43 68 32), two blocks south at 7 Ave Georges Clemenceau, charges 195/220FF for a single/double with shower and TV.

Places to Eat

Alsatian may not be your cuisine of choice in Brittany, but ***La Taverne Saint Martin*** (☎ 02 98 80 48 17) at 92 Rue Jean Jaurès has generous *menus* starting at 62FF, six beers (including Belgian cherry-flavoured *kriek*) on tap and is open seven days a week till midnight.

The ***Brasserie Le Palais*** at the Hôtel Vauban has a 50FF *menu* and plats du jour for 40FF.

Ma Petite Folie (☎ 02 98 42 44 42), an old lobster boat beached at Moulin Blanc near the hostel, has very affordable fish *menus*.

The *Monoprix* supermarket at 49 Rue de Siam has a large grocery section in the basement. It's open Monday to Saturday from 8.30 am to 7.30 pm.

Getting There & Away

Bus Brest's bus station (☎ 02 98 44 46 73), south-east of the tourist office on Place du 19ème Régiment d'Infanterie, serves a number of independent lines. The information office is open weekdays from 7 am to 12.30 pm and 1 to 7 pm, on Saturday from 8 am to 1.15 pm and 3.45 to 6.30 pm and on Sunday from 4 to 7 pm.

CAT (☎ 02 98 44 32 19) has up to seven buses a day to Quimper (80FF; 1¼ hours). Les Cars de St Mathieu (☎ 02 98 89 12 02 in Le Conquet) links Brest with Le Conquet (24.50FF; 45 minutes; up to six a day except Sunday) while Kreisker (☎ 02 98 69 00 93 in St Pol de Léon) goes to Roscoff (54FF; 1½ hours) up to four times a day.

Train The information office at the train station (☎ 02 98 31 51 67 or ☎ 08 36 35 35 35), which is just east of the bus station, is open daily from 8.45 am to 8 pm (7 pm on Saturday and Sunday). Trains from here run south-east to Quimper (81FF; 80 minutes) or north-east to Morlaix (54FF; 40 minutes), from where there are connections to Roscoff (30FF; 20 minutes). TGV trains to Paris' Gare Montparnasse (352FF) take just over four hours.

Car ADA (☎ 02 98 44 44 88) has an office next to the Hôtel Abalis at 9 Ave Georges Clemenceau. Avis (☎ 02 98 44 63 02) is at 20bis Rue de Siam.

Boat Ferries to the Île d'Ouessant leave from the Port de Commerce east of the chateau. See Getting There & Away in the Île d'Ouessant section for details.

Getting Around

Bus The local bus network is run by Bibus, which has an information kiosk (☎ 02 98 80 30 30) on Place de la Liberté. It is open Monday to Saturday from 8 am to 12.15 pm and 1.15 to 7 pm (8.30 am to 12.15 pm and 1.15 to 6 pm on Saturday). Single tickets cost 6FF, and a carnet of 10 is 50FF. There are also day passes available for 18FF.

Taxi You can order a taxi in Brest by ringing ☎ 02 98 80 43 43.

Bicycle Torch VTT (☎ 02 98 41 93 71) at 87 Rue de Paris, a branch of the shop in Quimper, rents mountain bikes for 90FF a day and 65FF for half a day (70 and 45FF respectively from October to May). They can help you with routes and itineraries.

ÎLE D'OUESSANT

• pop 1060 ✉ 29242

Île d'Ouessant (in Breton, Enez Eusa, meaning 'Island of Terror'; Ushant in English), a wild but hauntingly beautiful island 20km from the mainland, epitomises the ruggedness of the Breton coast. About 7km long and 4km wide, it serves as a beacon for more than 50,000 ships entering the Channel each year.

Traditionally, the sea played a pivotal role in the everyday life of the islanders, providing them with both a livelihood and the resources they needed. Boys would go to sea at the age of 11. The interiors of the houses, partitioned by little more than wooden panels, resembled the insides of a boat and were decorated with furniture made from driftwood. Outside, the houses were painted in symbolic colours: blue and white for the Virgin Mary, green and white for hope.

While the island's isolation from the rest of Brittany is to an extent over, some traditions and customs remain. Old women still make lace crosses in memory of the husbands who never returned from the sea; the little black Ushant sheep are free to roam about; and *ragoût de mouton* (lamb baked for five hours under a layer of roots and herbs) retains its popularity.

Orientation & Information

The only village of any size is Lampaul, 3km from where the ferries dock. It has a handful of hotels and shops.

In the heart of Lampaul on Place de l'Église is the tiny tourist office (☎ 02 98 48 85 83; fax 02 98 48 87 09), open Monday to Saturday from 10.30 am to noon and 2 to 5 pm, and 10 am to 12.30 pm on Sunday. It sells brochures (10FF) with maps outlining four walks of between 10 and 17km in length; the text is in French.

Lighthouses

About 7km separate Ouessant's western and eastern extremities, each boldly marked by a powerful lighthouse. Standing tall before the setting sun is the striped **Phare de Créac'h**, the world's most powerful lighthouse. Just north of the ferry dock is the **Phare du Stiff**.

The entire island is ideal for (very windy) walks. A 45km path follows the craggy, rocky coastline, passing some very grand scenery.

Museums

Heading west from Lampaul, the **Écomusée d'Ouessant** (☎ 02 98 48 86 37), also known as the Maison du Niou, has simple but moving displays on local life arranged in two colourful houses furnished in the traditional style. From October to April it's open from 10 am to noon and 2 to 4 pm (6.30 pm in April and May; closed Monday year-round). From June to September it's open daily from 10.30 am to 6.30 pm. Prices are 25/15FF for adults/children.

Musée des Phares et des Balises (☎ 02 98 48 80 70), a lighthouse and beacon museum positioned under the Phare de Créac'h, tells the intriguing story of these vital installations. A 30 minute walk west of Lampaul, the museum is open daily, except Monday, between October and March from 2 to 4 pm, and in April from 2 to 6.30 pm. From May to September it is open daily from 10.30 am to 6.30 pm. Prices are 25/15FF for adults/children.

Places to Stay & Eat

The ***Camping Municipal*** (☎ 02 98 48 84 65) in Lampaul looks more like a football field than a camping ground. It's open from March to November and costs 14/14FF per person/tent site.

Although Lampaul has four hotels, only the ***Hôtel L'Océan*** (☎ 02 98 48 80 03) is open all year. It has bay-view rooms and a lively bar underneath. Singles/doubles with shower are 305/550FF for demi-pension including breakfast and dinner. In the warmer months, a cheaper option is the ***Duchesse Anne*** (☎ 02 98 48 80 25) which offers rooms from 130/170FF.

The hotels, notably the Duchesse Anne, have decent restaurants specialising in lamb and stingray. There is a small ***supermarket*** in Lampaul.

Getting There & Away

Air If time (but not money) is a concern, Finist'air (☎ 02 98 84 64 87) will fly you from the Aéroport International de Brest-Guipavas, about 9km north-east of Brest, to Ouessant in 20 minutes. The company schedules two return flights a day throughout the year. The one-way fare is 340FF (170FF for children between two and 12 years old).

Boat Year-round ferries to Ouessant are run by Penn Ar Bed (meaning 'End of the World'; ☎ 02 98 80 24 68), which sails either from Brest's Port de Commerce or from Le Conquet, 24km west of Brest. The voyage from Brest takes 2½ hours, while from Le Conquet it's 1½ hours. Almost all boats call at tiny Île Molène en route.

From April to September there are between three and five boats a day, with the first sailing at 8 or 8.30 am. In July and August, daily boats leave from Brest at 8.30 am and from Le Conquet at 8.45, 9.45 and 11 am and at 5.30 pm. Returning from Ouessant, there are boats bound for Le Conquet at 9.45 am and 4.30, 5 and 7 pm – only the 5 pm boat continues to Brest. In winter (October to March), there is a daily boat leaving from Brest at 8.30 am and from

Le Conquet at 9.45 am. From Ouessant, boats leave for Le Conquet and Brest at 4.30 pm.

A return adult ticket costs 180/152FF from Brest/Le Conquet; children up to 16 years pay 108/90FF.

Finist'mer (☎ 02 98 89 16 61 in Le Conquet) runs faster boats up to eight times a day between Le Conquet and Ouessant from May to September. The crossing takes 45 minutes and costs 145/75FF for adults/children.

Getting Around

Bus A shuttle bus covers the 3km from the ferry terminal to Lampaul (10FF).

Bicycle Cycling around Ouessant is popular but the strong headwinds can make the going difficult. OuessanCycles (☎ 02 98 48 83 44), which has a kiosk at the ferry terminal on the island's eastern side, rents bicycles/mountain bikes for 60/80FF a day, as does Locacycles (☎ 02 98 48 80 44), also at the ferry terminal.

PARC NATUREL RÉGIONAL D'ARMORIQUE

Of France's almost three dozen regional parks, the 1100 sq km Armorique Regional Park (Park An Arvorig in Breton) is among the most diverse. Taking in the Monts d'Arrée and the unspoiled forests around Huelgoat, it stretches westward for some 70km along the Presqu'île de Crozon (Crozon Peninsula) and includes the reserves of Île d'Ouessant and the Molène archipelago.

For more information, contact the park's head office (☎ 02 98 21 90 69) at Ménez-Meur near Hanvec, 50km north of Quimper on the D18.

Huelgoat

• pop 1740 ✉ 29690

The small town of Huelgoat (An Uhelgoat in Breton) is an excellent base for exploring what's left of the forested Argoat. On the edge of the town is the unspoiled Forêt d'Huelgoat – where King Arthur's treasure is said to be buried – with its unusual rock formations, caves, menhirs and abandoned silver and lead mines, which were being exploited as early as the 15th century.

To the east and north-east, are the Forêt de Saint Ambroise and the Forêt de Fréau. All are connected by a good network of hiking trails.

Orientation & Information Huelgoat lies to the east of a small wishbone-shaped lake, which empties into the Argent River. The tourist office (☎ 02 98 99 72 32; fax 02 98 99 75 72) is in the *mairie* (town hall) on Rue des Cendres, which runs off tiny Place Aristide Briand. It is open from Tuesday to Saturday from 2 to 6 pm. From June to August, it's open Monday to Saturday from 10 am to noon and 2 to 6 pm.

The Crédit Agricole at 16 Rue des Cendres is open Tuesday to Saturday from 9 am to noon and 1.30 to 5.30 pm. The post office, due south of the square at 22 Rue des Cieux, is open from 9 am to noon and 2 to 5 pm on weekdays and on Saturday morning.

Things to See & Do The **Moulin du Chaos** (☎ 02 98 99 77 83), on the Argent River about 1km east of town, takes its name from the steady erosion of the forest's granite base. It contains exhibits on the archaeology, geology, flora and fauna of the Argoat. It is open daily (except Monday) in July and August from 1.30 to 6.30 pm.

Most of the **hiking trails** fan out from the end of Rue du Lac. There are large signposts directing you, but be sure to bring a map. The tourist office sells a number of excellent guides and maps to the area.

Places to Stay The ***Camping Municipal du Lac*** (☎ 02 98 99 78 80), 500m west of the centre on Rue du Général de Gaulle, is open from April to mid-September and charges 15.50/17.50FF per person/tent site and access to the swimming pool. The tourist office has information on ***chambres d'hôtes*** (from 150FF) and ***gîtes ruraux*** in the surrounding areas.

Huelgoat's most central hotel is ***Hôtel de l'Armorique*** (☎ 02 98 99 71 24) at 1 Place Aristide Briand. It is currently closed, but the tourist office staff are hopeful that it will reopen again soon. In the meantime, the ***Hôtel du Lac*** (☎ 02 98 99 71 14) at 9 Rue du Général de Gaulle is a good bet. It charges 230/250FF for singles/doubles, all with shower, toilet and TV.

Places to Eat There are several restaurants on Place Aristide Briand, including the ***Crêperie des Myrtilles*** with crêpes from 8 to 32FF. The restaurant at the ***Hôtel du Lac*** is a popular place for a pizza (from 40FF) or salad (from 28FF). ***La Chouette Bleue*** (☎ 02 98 99 78 19) at 1 Rue du Lac has crêpes and quiches for 30 to 39FF and main courses for 35 to 69FF.

Getting There & Away SCETA buses (☎ 02 98 93 06 98 in Carhaix-Plouguer) link Huelgoat with Morlaix to the north (24km) and Carhaix-Plouguer to the south-east (17km). There are up to four buses a day to Morlaix (48FF; one hour) but only one on Sunday (at 5.05 pm). Count on three to Carhaix-Plouguer (20FF; 30 minutes) from Monday to Saturday and one on Sunday (at 7.15 pm). Buses stop in front of the Chapelle de Notre Dame at Place Aristide Briand.

ROSCOFF

• pop 3700 ✉ 29680

Protected from the furious seas by the little offshore island of Batz, the town of Roscoff (Rosko in Breton), whose 16th century granite houses surround a small bay, is the southernmost – and arguably the most attractive – Channel port for entering France by ferry from Britain or Ireland.

Nearby areas of the Channel are home to a wide variety of algae, some of which are used in *thalassothérapie*, a health treatment using sea water. Roscoff's hinterland is known for its *primeurs* (early fruits and vegetables), such as cauliflower, onions, tomatoes, new potatoes and artichokes, which flourish here. Before the advent of large vehicular ferries, Roscoff farmers, known as 'Johnnies', would load up boats with the small pink onions grown locally, sail to England and deliver them to markets by bicycle.

Orientation

Roscoff is arrayed around the fishing and pleasure craft port, which is sheltered by several cement piers. Place de la République lies to the west of Quai d'Auxerre, where there are several restaurants. The town's focal point, though, is Rue Amiral Réveillère leading north-westward to Place Lacaze-Duthiers and Église Notre Dame de Kroaz-Batz.

Information

Tourist Office The tourist office (☎ 02 98 61 12 13; fax 02 98 69 75 75) is housed in a fine old stone building just north of Place de la République at 46 Rue Gambetta. It is open Monday to Saturday from 9 am to noon and 2 to 6 pm (though in winter it may open an hour later and close an hour earlier). In July and August it's open Monday to Saturday from 9 am to 12.30 pm and 1.30 to 7 pm and on Sunday from 10.30 am to 12.30 pm.

Money The Crédit Mutuel de Bretagne 200m north-west of the tourist office at 10 Rue Louis Pasteur is open Monday to Saturday from 8.30 am to 12.15 pm and 1.30 to 5 pm (4.30 pm on Saturday). The Caisse d'Épargne, near the tourist office at 9 Rue Gambetta, is open Tuesday to Saturday from 8.45 am to noon and 1.30 to 5.30 pm (4 pm on Saturday). There's a 24 hour banknote exchange and ATM in the ferry terminal.

Post The post office at 19 Rue Gambetta is open weekdays from 9 am to noon and 2 to 5 pm and on Saturday morning.

Laundry The Ferry Laverie at 23 Rue Jules Ferry south of the tourist office is open from 8 am to 8 pm daily.

Things to See & Do

Roscoff is not overly endowed with historical sites, but the Flamboyant Gothic **Église Notre Dame de Kroaz-Batz** and its 16th century Renaissance belfry are worth a look.

The Station Biologique de Roscoff (☎ 02 98 29 23 23), which is at Place Georges Teissier a short distance north-west of the church, contains both an **aquarium** and **marine museum**. It is open June to August from 10 am to noon and 1 to 6 pm (7 pm in summer) and afternoons only in April, May, September and October. It closes in winter. Prices are 26/22FF for adults/students.

Next to the tourist office, the desanctified **Chapelle de Sainte Anne**, which was turned into a Temple of Reason during the Revolution, houses the **Maison des Johnnies** (☎ 02 98 61 12 13). This museum is devoted to the onion growers and sellers, who are much revered and awarded almost hero status in these parts.

The Centre Nautique on Quai d'Auxerre (☎ 02 98 69 72 79) rents **sailboards** and **catamarans** for 150 and 350FF for three hours.

If you're interested in thalassotherapy, you can take the cure at Roc Kroum (☎ 02 98 29 20 00) on the Anse inlet west of the centre on Ave Victor Hugo. Roc Kroum also has a large pool (40FF) as well as a jacuzzi and sauna (50FF each), where you can while away the hours. It is open from 12.45 to 2.30 pm and 5.30 to 8.30 pm (1.30 to 2.30 pm on Thursday). On Sunday the hours are 9.30 am to noon and 3 to 6 pm.

Places to Stay

Camping *Camping de Kérestat* (☎ 02 98 69 71 92), 2.5km south of Roscoff, charges 24/12FF per adult/child and 40/14FF for a tent site/car. It is open all year. *Camping Municipal de Perharidy* (☎ 02 98 69 70 86), which is situated about 6km south-west of the centre on the south-western side of the Anse inlet and open May to September, is much cheaper. Adults/children pay 8/6FF or 13/8FF, depending on the season, while a tent site/parking place is 8/5FF or 11/6FF. Showers are free. Bungalows sleeping four are also available for between 800 and 1500FF a week. Both camp sites are very close to sandy beaches, but neither is served by public transport.

Hotels Hotels are relatively expensive in Roscoff, and most raise their prices in July and August. Be advised that many shut down in winter – usually from November to March.

One of the better deals in town can be had at the two star ***Hôtel Les Arcades*** (☎ 02 98 69 70 45; fax 02 98 61 12 34), 15 Rue Amiral Réveillère, with simple but modern singles/doubles from 170/195FF and ones with shower from 260/275FF. Hall showers are free. Les Arcades closes in winter.

The ***Hôtel Le Centre*** (☎ 02 98 61 24 25; fax 02 98 61 15 43), 5 Rue Gambetta, near the tourist office, has simple doubles without/with showers for 200/280FF and charming old photos of Johnnies in the bar. Doubles with shower at the ***Hôtel Les Alizés*** (☎ 02 98 69 72 22; fax 02 98 61 11 40), on Quai d'Auxerre, are 160 or 260FF, depending on the season.

Places to Eat

There are pizzerias and crêperies everywhere, but seafood reigns in Roscoff, France's premier crabbing port. Many restaurants close in winter.

L'Écume du Jour (☎ 02 98 61 22 83), overlooking the port and the Île de Batz at Quai d'Auxerre, is a good choice for fish. It closes on Wednesday. Nearby on the same quay, ***Les Korrigans*** (☎ 02 98 61 22 15) serves all manner of crêpes and galettes and has seafood *menus* for 71 and 93FF.

Chez Gaston (☎ 02 98 69 75 65) on Rue Joseph Barra south-east of the port is an intimate little restaurant, but seafood *menus* are cheaper (and the views better) at the ***Hôtel Les Arcades restaurant*** (see Places to Stay) which faces the sea.

Getting There & Away

Bus & Train The combined bus and train station (☎ 02 98 69 70 20 or ☎ 08 36 35 35 35) is on Rue Ropartz Morvan about 500m from the tourist office. To get to the tourist office, turn right into Rue Vloche as you leave the station, then right onto Rue Brizeux. Follow it until it curves around to the left into Rue Jules Ferry, which leads to Place de la République, Rue Gambetta and the tourist office. The ticket office at the station is open Monday to Saturday from 6.30 am to 12.50 pm and 1.45 to 7 pm (8.30 am to noon and 2 to 5.30 pm on Sunday), daily in summer from 6.30 am to 7.30 pm.

There are trains or buses to Morlaix (30FF; one hour), from where you can make connections west to Brest (70FF; 1½ hours), south to Quimper (107FF; 1¾ hours) and Huelgoat (34FF; one hour; four daily), and east to Lannion (120FF; three hours; five daily) and Saint Brieuc (98FF; 1¾ hours; five daily).

Boat Brittany Ferries (☎ 02 98 29 28 28) sails to Plymouth in England and Cork in Ireland. Boats leave from the Gare Maritime de Bloscon, which is open daily from 9 am to midnight. It's about 2km east of the tourist office; to get to town, head straight up the hill as you leave the ferry terminal, turn right and then take the first left into Rue de Plymouth. This leads down to Quai d'Auxerre.

Getting Around

Desbordes (☎ 02 98 69 72 44), near the train station at 13 Rue Brizeux, rents bikes.

AROUND ROSCOFF

Île de Batz

• pop 750 ✉ 29253

Just 2km offshore and visible from the port, the four sq km Île de Batz (Enez Vaz in Breton) is a charming island with some good beaches, a lovely garden (Jardins Georges Delaselle; open daily in summer; 20FF) and lots of seaweed. The ***Auberge de Jeunesse*** (☎ 02 98 61 77 69) on the island is open from April to October and charges 65FF per person including breakfast.

Getting There & Away Boats to Île de Batz take 15 minutes and are run by CFTM Vedettes (☎ 02 98 61 78 87). At high tide, they leave from the pier running eastward into the old port. When the tide is out, you must cross the long, narrow footbridge to the north of the port. Return tickets cost 32/16FF for adults/children. In July and August boats sail every 15 minutes between 8 am and 8 pm; during the rest of the year, services are less frequent, with about eight sailings a day.

Morbihan Coast

Morbihan, the department which covers Brittany's south-central section, stretches from Redon in the east to Lorient near the Finistère border. Naturally enough, it is the coast – particularly around the regional capital, Vannes – that attracts most visitors. The Golfe du Morbihan (Morbihan Gulf), enclosed by arms of land which leave only a narrow outlet to the Atlantic, is virtually an inland sea (*mor bihan* means 'little sea' in Breton). About 40 of its islands are inhabited. Oysters are cultivated around the gulf, which is also a bird sanctuary of international importance.

West of the gulf, the Presqu'île de Quiberon, a narrow, claw-shaped peninsula, makes it about halfway to Belle Île, an island separated from the town of Quiberon by 12km of open sea.

The whole Morbihan region is a showcase of the architectural achievements of the Neolithic period. At nearly every crossroads, you'll see signs pointing to megalithic sites, of which the ones at Carnac are the most famous.

VANNES

• pop 48,000 ✉ 56000

Gateway to the islands of the Golfe du Morbihan, Vannes (Gwened in Breton) is a lovely town – small enough to feel intimate, close enough to the sea to taste the salt air and old enough to have an interesting history. The medieval heart of town, full of students from the Vannes branch of the Université de Rennes, is almost as lively as it was centuries ago.

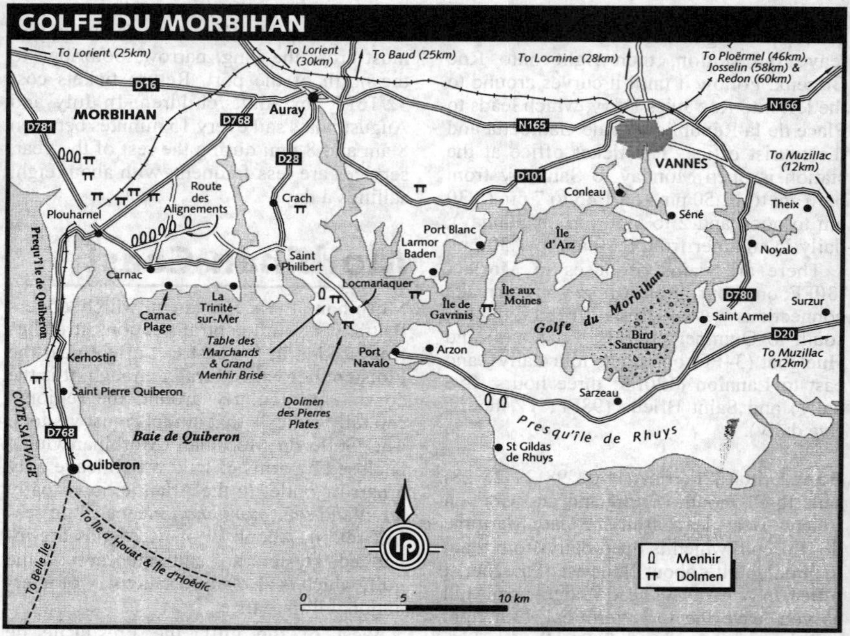

GOLFE DU MORBIHAN

History

In pre-Roman times Vannes was the capital of the Veneti, a Gallic tribe of intrepid sailors who fortified their town with a sturdy wall (a long section of which remains) and built a formidable fleet of sailing ships. The Veneti were conquered by Julius Caesar after a Roman fleet defeated them in a battle off Brittany's south-eastern coast in the 1st century BC. Under the 9th century Breton hero Nominoë, the town became the centre of Breton unity. In 1532 the union of the duchy of Brittany with France – achieved through a series of royal marriages – was proclaimed in Vannes.

Orientation

Except for the salty sea breeze, you'd hardly know Vannes was on the coast. Its small, yacht-filled port sits at the end of a canal-like waterway 1.5km from the gulf's entrance. The Île de Conleau, about 3.5km south of the town, is now connected to the mainland by a causeway and is sometimes called Presqu'île de Conleau (Conleau Peninsula). The centre of the old city is Place des Lices. Cafés ring the semicircular Place Gambetta at the northern end of the port.

The train station is about 1.5km north-east of the tourist office on Place de la Gare.

Information

Tourist Office The tourist office (☎ 02 97 47 24 34; fax 02 97 47 29 49), in a lovely 17th century half-timbered house at 1 Rue Thiers, is open Monday to Saturday from 9 am to noon and 2 to 6 pm. In the peak season (roughly June to September) it opens without a break from 9 am to 7 pm and on Sunday from 10 am to 1 pm and 3 to 7 pm. It can exchange foreign currency but only in July and August.

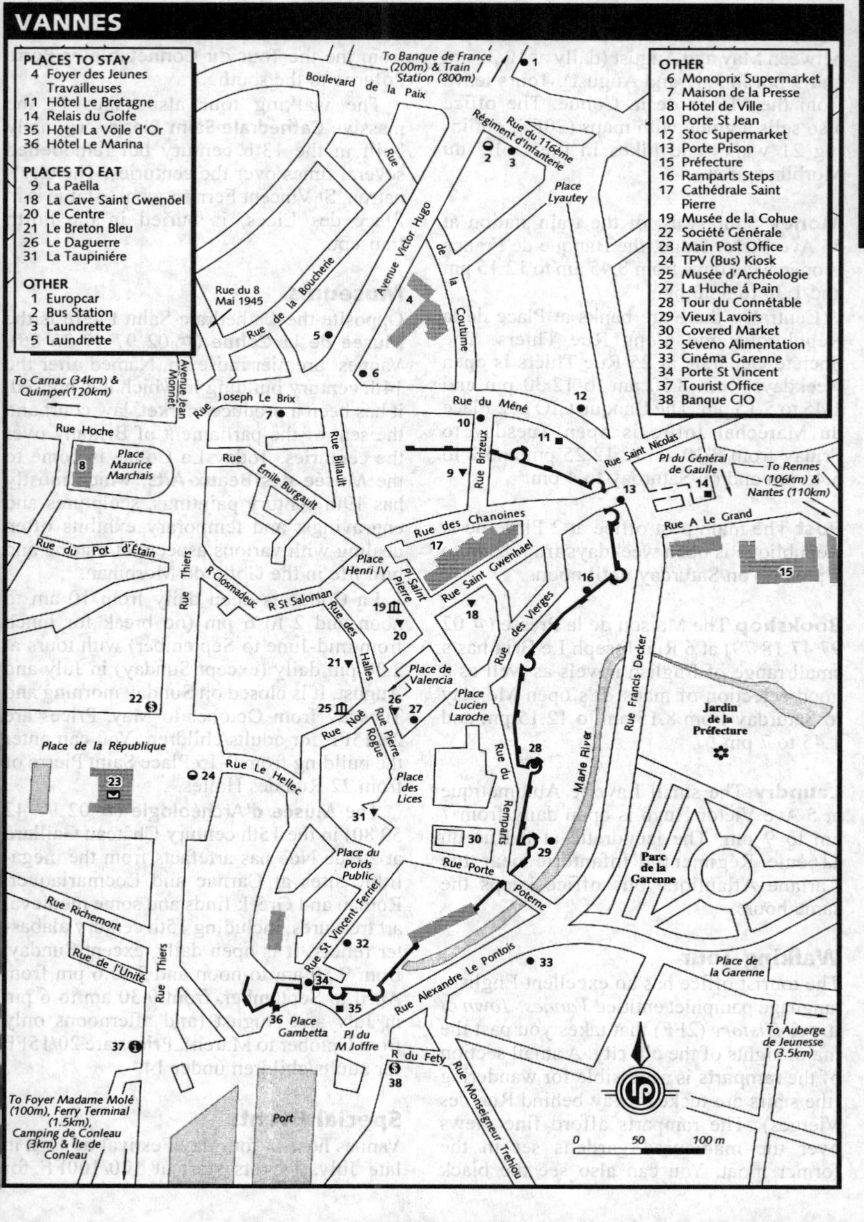
VANNES
PLACES TO STAY
4 Foyer des Jeunes Travailleuses
11 Hôtel Le Bretagne
14 Relais du Golfe
35 Hôtel La Voile d'Or
36 Hôtel La Marina
PLACES TO EAT
9 La Paëlla
18 La Cave Saint Gwenoël
20 Le Centre
21 Le Breton Bleu
26 Le Daguerre
31 La Taupiniére
OTHER
1 Europcar
2 Bus Station
3 Laundrette
5 Laundrette
OTHER
6 Monoprix Supermarket
7 Maison de la Presse
8 Hôtel de Ville
10 Porte St Jean
12 Stoc Supermarket
13 Porte Prison
15 Préfecture
16 Ramparts Steps
17 Cathédrale Saint Pierre
19 Musée de la Cohue
22 Société Générale
23 Main Post Office
24 TPV (Bus) Kiosk
25 Musée d'Archéologie
27 La Huche á Pain
28 Tour du Connétable
29 Vieux Lavoirs
30 Covered Market
32 Séveno Alimentation
33 Cinéma Garenne
34 Porte St Vincent
37 Tourist Office
38 Banque CIO
To Banque de France (200m) & Train Station (800m)
Boulevard de la Paix
Rue du 116ème Régiment d'Infanterie
Place Lyautey
Avenue Victor Hugo
Rue de la Coutume
Rue de la Boucherie
Rue du 8 Mai 1945
Avenue Jean Monnet
To Carnac (34km) & Quimper(120km)
Rue Joseph Le Brix
Rue du Méné
Rue Hoche
Place Maurice Marchais
Rue Émile Burgault
Rue Billault
Rue Brizeux
Rue Saint Nicolas
Pl du Général de Gaulle
To Rennes (106km) & Nantes (110km)
Rue A Le Grand
Rue du Pot d'Étain
Rue des Chanoines
Place Henri IV
Pl Saint Pierre
Rue Saint Gwenhael
Rue Thiers
R Closmadeuc
R St Saloman
Rue des Halles
Rue des Vierges
Place de Valencia
Place Lucien Laroche
Rue Francis Decker
Marle River
Jardin de la Préfecture
Rue Noë
Rue Pierre Rogue
Place de la République
Rue Le Hellec
Place des Lices
Rue du Rempart
Place du Poids Public
Rue Porte Poterne
Parc de la Garenne
Rue Richemont
Rue de l'Unité
Rue St Vincent Ferrier
Rue Alexandre Le Pontois
Place de la Garenne
Place Gambetta
Pl du M Joffre
R du Fety
Rue Monseigneur Trehiou
To Auberge de Jeunesse (3.5km)
To Foyer Madame Molé (100m), Ferry Terminal (1.5km), Camping de Conleau (3km) & Île de Conleau
Port
0 50 100 m

The tourist office conducts tours of the city on Wednesday and Saturday at 3 pm between May and August (daily at 10.30 am and 3 pm in July and August). Tours leave from the Musée de la Cohue. The office also sells a guide with maps (20FF) outlining 21 walks and hikes in the Golfe du Morbihan area.

Money South-west of the train station at 55 Ave Victor Hugo, the Banque de France is open weekdays from 8.45 am to 12.15 pm and 1.30 to 3.30 pm.

Centrally, there are banks at Place de la République and along Rue Thiers. The Société Générale at 25 Rue Thiers is open weekdays from 8.30 am to 12.30 pm and 1.45 to 5.15 pm. The Banque CIO at 2 Place du Maréchal Joffre is open Tuesday to Friday from 8.30 am to 12.25 pm and 2 to 5.45 pm and on Saturday to 4 pm.

Post The main post office at 2 Place de la République is open weekdays from 8 am to 7 pm and on Saturday until noon.

Bookshop The Maison de la Presse (☎ 02 97 47 18 79) at 6 Rue Joseph Le Brix has a small range of English novels as well as a good selection of maps. It's open Monday to Saturday from 8.15 am to 12.15 pm and 1.45 to 7 pm.

Laundry The small Laverie Automatique at 5 Ave Victor Hugo is open daily from 7 am to 9 pm. The laundrette at 8 Rue du 116ème Régiment d'Infanterie near the Cariane Atlantique bus office keeps the same hours.

Walking Tour

The tourist office has an excellent English-language pamphlet entitled *Vannes: Town of Art & History* (2FF) that takes you past the major sights of the **old city**. A small section of the **ramparts** is accessible for wandering (the stairs are tucked away behind Rue des Vierges). The ramparts afford fine views over the manicured gardens set in the former moat. You can also see the black tops of the **Vieux Lavoirs** (old laundry houses), though better views are afforded from the the **Tour du Connétable** or **Porte Poterne** to the south.

The walking tour also takes in the massive **Cathédrale Saint Pierre**, originally built in the 13th century but remodelled several times over the centuries. The city's patron, St Vincent Ferrier, whose statue is in Place des Lices, is buried in the north transept.

Museums

Opposite the Cathédrale Saint Pierre is the **Musée de la Cohue** (☎ 02 97 47 35 86), Vannes' premier museum. Named after the 14th century building in which it is housed, it has been a produce market, law court and the seat of the parliament of Brittany over the centuries. Today La Cohue is home to the **Musée des Beaux-Arts**, which mostly has 19th century paintings, sculptures and engravings, and temporary exhibits often dealing with various aspects of marine and bird life in the Golfe du Morbihan.

La Cohue is open daily from 10 am to noon and 2 to 6 pm (no break for lunch from mid-June to September) with tours at 2.30 pm daily (except Sunday) in July and August. It is closed on Sunday morning and Tuesday from October to May. Prices are 25/15FF for adults/children. You can enter the building from 9-15 Place Saint Pierre or from 22 Rue des Halles.

The **Musée d'Archéologie** (☎ 02 97 42 59 80) in the 15th century Château Gaillard at 2 Rue Noë has artefacts from the megalithic sites at Carnac and Locmariaquer, Roman and Greek finds and some medieval art treasures, including 15th century alabaster reliefs. It is open daily, except Sunday, from 9.30 am to noon and 2 to 6 pm from April to September, from 9.30 am to 6 pm in July and August (and afternoons only from October to March). Prices are 20/15FF for adults/children under 14.

Special Events

Vannes hosts a four day Festival de Jazz in late July. Tickets start at 120/100FF for adults/students. Classical music concerts called Les Nuits Musicales du Golfe take place from mid-July to early August.

Places to Stay

Camping About 3km south of the tourist office, the three star ***Camping de Conleau*** (☎ 02 97 63 13 88) on Ave du Maréchal Juin has views over the calm waters of the gulf. It's open from April to September and charges 68FF for one person with a tent and car. An extra person is 25FF. Bus No 2 (last one at 7.40 pm) from Place de la République stops at the gate.

Hostels The ***Auberge de Jeunesse*** (☎ 02 97 66 94 25; fax 02 97 66 94 15) on Route de Moustérian in Séné, 4km south-east of Vannes, is open year-round and costs 70FF with breakfast and sheets. To reach it, take bus No 4 from Place de la République and get off at Le Stade stop.

Foyer des Jeunes Travailleuses (☎ 02 97 54 33 13) at 14 Ave Victor Hugo is open to all. It has single rooms with washbasin for 90FF (75FF for people under 26), breakfast for 13FF, and sheets for 28FF.

There's also the ***Foyer Madame Molé*** (☎ 02 97 47 29 60) at 10 Place Théodore Decker, along the port a couple of blocks south of the tourist office, which offers studios with bathroom and kitchen for 500FF per week (including bed linen).

Hotels – Train Station Area Facing the station, ***Le Richemont*** (☎ 02 97 47 12 95; fax 02 97 54 92 79) at 26 Place de la Gare has decent, basic rooms from 150FF (200FF with shower). The friendly ***Hôtel Anne de Bretagne*** (☎ 02 97 54 22 19; fax 02 97 42 69 10) at 42 Rue Olivier de Clisson – go right as you exit the station then take the first left – has singles/doubles with washbasin for 170/200FF or with TV and shower for 240/290FF.

Hotels – Old City Place Gambetta overlooking the port has two of the best choices in town. The ***Hôtel Le Marina*** (☎ 02 97 47 22 81; fax 02 97 47 00 34) at No 4 has relaxing, modern rooms which receive the morning sun and have views over the marina and the crowded cafés below. Prices start at 180FF. If you prefer your sun after lunch, the ***Hôtel La Voile d'Or*** (☎ 02 97 42 71 81; fax 02 97 42 42 95) opposite at No 1 has doubles with washbasin for 160FF and ones with shower for 220FF.

Just outside the old city walls, the very clean and tidy ***Hôtel Le Bretagne*** (☎ 02 97 47 20 21; fax 02 97 47 90 78) at 36 Rue du Méné has one simple single for 110FF and singles/doubles with shower from 160/180FF. A block away, the ***Relais du Golfe*** (☎ 02 97 47 14 74; fax 02 97 42 52 28) on Place du Général de Gaulle has rooms from 150FF with washbasin and from 180FF with shower.

Places to Eat

Restaurants Hidden under a medieval turret on Place des Lices, the popular ***La Taupinière*** (☎ 02 97 42 57 82) at No 9 offers crêpes from 28 to 40FF. It is closed on Wednesday.

The warm atmosphere and the crêpes of ***La Cave Saint Gwenöel*** (☎ 02 97 47 47 94) at 23 Rue Saint Gwenhael come highly recommended. It is closed on Monday and Sunday.

The very popular ***La Paëlla***, in an ancient townhouse at 7 Rue Brizeux, serves plates of its namesake (from 44FF) and jugs of sangria (from 30FF). It's closed Sunday and Monday. ***Le Centre*** (☎ 02 97 54 25 14), at 7 Place Saint Pierre opposite the cathedral, has a standard, three course *menu* from 56FF. ***Le Daguerre*** (☎ 02 97 47 21 94), upstairs at 8 Rue Pierre Rogue and facing Place de Valencia, has salads, grills and good-value *menus* from 59FF (closed Sunday). The Breton *menus* (from 78FF) at ***Le Breton Bleu***, 13 Rue des Halles, go beyond crêpes and galettes.

Self-Catering On Wednesday and Saturday mornings, a ***produce market*** takes over Place du Poids Public and the surrounding area. Fresh meat is sold in the ***covered market*** round the corner.

The ***Monoprix*** supermarket at 1 Place Joseph Le Brix has a *boulangerie* as well as an upstairs grocery section. It is open Monday to Saturday from 8.35 am to 8.30 pm. The new ***Stoc*** supermarket at 19 Rue du Méné is open Monday to Saturday from 8.30 am to 8 pm.

Near the 18th century gate, Porte Saint Vincent, ***Séveno Alimentation*** at 12 Rue Saint Vincent Ferrier is open Monday to Saturday from 8.30 am to 12.30 pm and 3 to 7.30 pm and on Sunday from 10 am to noon. ***La Huche à Pains*** (☎ 02 97 47 23 76) at 23 Place des Lices is a popular *pâtisserie* for such Breton pastries as *kouign amman*.

Entertainment

A few nondubbed films are shown at the ***Cinéma Garenne*** (five screens) at 12bis Rue Alexandre Le Pontois.

Getting There & Away

Bus Regional buses are run by two companies – CTM and Cariane Atlantique. CTM buses (☎ 02 97 01 22 10) cover destinations in Morbihan including Port Navalo (35FF), Pontivy (48FF) and Ploërmel (47FF). They leave from the parking lot opposite the train station.

The Cariane Atlantique office (☎ 02 97 47 29 64), at 4 Rue du 116ème Régiment d'Infanterie at the intersection of Ave Victor Hugo and Blvd de la Paix, is open weekdays from 8 am to noon and 2 to 6 pm and on Saturday from 8.30 am to noon and 2.30 to 5 pm. Line Nos 23 and 24 go via Auray to Carnac (38FF; 1¼ hours; four a day) and on to Plouharnel (43FF) and Quiberon (52FF; 1¾ hours). Line No 20 serves Nantes (93.50FF), while No 16 goes to Rennes (92.50FF) via Josselin (35FF) and Ploërmel (43FF).

Train Vannes' train station (☎ 02 97 26 72 16 or ☎ 08 36 35 35 35) is on Place de la Gare north-east of town. The information office is open daily from 9 am to 6.50 pm.

There are trains via Rennes (107FF; 1½ hours) to Paris' Gare Montparnasse (317FF; 3½ hours; three a day), Auray (21FF; 12 minutes), Quimper (102FF; 1¼ hours; seven a day) and Nantes (101FF; 1¼ hours; six a day). For details on trains to Quiberon via Plouharnel near Carnac, see Getting There & Away in the Quiberon section.

Car To contact ADA, call ☎ 02 97 42 59 10. Europcar (☎ 02 97 42 43 43) at 48 Ave Victor Hugo is open Monday to Saturday from 8 am to noon and 2 to 7 pm (6 pm on Saturday).

Getting Around

Bus The city bus company TPV has an information kiosk (☎ 02 97 01 22 23) at the main bus hub on Place de la République. It's open weekdays from 8.30 am to 12.30 pm and 1.30 to 6.30 pm. A single ticket costs 6.40FF (47FF for a carnet of 10).

The seven main lines run Monday to Saturday from 6.15 am to 8.15 pm. There is very limited service on Sunday. Bus Nos 3 and 4 link the train station with Place de la République.

Taxi To order a taxi, ring ☎ 02 97 54 34 34.

Bicycle Bikes can be hired from the train station luggage office for about 44FF a day (slightly more in July and August) plus a 500FF deposit. The office is open daily from 8 to 11.50 am and 2 to 6.30 pm.

AROUND VANNES

Golfe du Morbihan Islands

There are about 40 inhabited islands in the Golfe du Morbihan, 36 of them privately owned by artists, actors and the like.

The two largest islands, **Île d'Arz** and **Île aux Moines**, are home to several small villages. Though there's little on them apart from palm groves and beaches, they're popular day trips from Vannes.

Between Easter and October, two boats a day (at 10 and 11.30 am) run by Navix (☎ 02 97 46 60 00) and stopping at both islands leave from the ferry terminal opposite the Parc du Golfe at the end of Ave Maréchal de Lattre de Tassigny in Vannes. The return fare is 150/100FF for adults/

children under 14. Boats calling at just one island sail at 11.30 am and 2.15 and 5 pm and cost 100/77FF. La Compagnie des Îles (☎ 02 97 46 18 19) charges roughly the same prices and also has five or six cruises a day in the high season.

Navix also runs boats to Belle Île south of Quiberon (see Belle Île later in this chapter). The return fare for adults/children is 150/90FF. Out of season, the noticeboard in the tourist office can tell you when the next boat excursion around the gulf will be leaving.

Both islands are also accessible by regular ferries year-round. To Île d'Arz, boats run by Le Didroux (☎ 02 97 66 92 06) leave from Île de Conleau between 10 and 13 times a day. To Île aux Moines, boats owned by Société Izenah (☎ 02 97 26 31 45) sail from Port Blanc, 13km south-west of Vannes, about every half an hour between 7 am and 10 pm in summer (8 pm at other times). The fare to Île aux Moines is 20/10FF for adults/children up to 10.

CARNAC

• pop 4200 ✉ 56340

Carnac (Garnag in Breton) sits on the doorstep of some of the world's foremost megalithic sites. Located about 32km west of Vannes, the town is made up of the attractive old village, Carnac Ville, and a more modern seaside resort, Carnac Plage, with a 2km-long sandy beach (Grande Plage) on the sheltered Baie de Quiberon.

Orientation

Carnac Ville and Carnac Plage are 500m apart. They're joined by Ave de Salines and Ave de l'Atlantique, which head south to the beachfront Blvd de la Plage.

Information

Tourist Office The very efficient main tourist office (☎ 02 97 52 13 52; fax 02 97 52 86 10) is in Carnac Plage at 74 Ave des Druides, two blocks north of the beach. It's open Monday to Saturday from 9 am to noon and 2 to 6 pm. In July and August it's open from 9 am to 7 pm and on Sunday from 3 to 6.30 pm.

The tourist office annexe (same telephone number) in Carnac Ville is behind the church on the central Place de l'Église. From April to November it's open Monday to Saturday from 9.30 am to 12.30 pm and 2 to 6 pm. In July and August the hours are 9.30 am to 12.30 pm and 2.30 to 7 pm and on Sunday from 10 am to 1 pm. The annexe sells a number of books and guides on the megalithic sites.

Money There are several banks on Rue Saint Cornély, west of Place de l'Église, including Crédit Mutuel de Bretagne at No 27. Société Générale's ATM at the main tourist office in Carnac Plage accepts Visa and other cards.

Post The main post office, with exchange services, is opposite 27 Rue de la Poste, which runs southward from Place de l'Église. It is open from 9 am to noon and 2 to 5 pm on weekdays and on Saturday morning.

Megaliths

Carnac's megalithic sites start north of Carnac Ville and stretch for 13km north and east as far as the village of Locmariaquer. To see inside many of the dolmens, you'll need a torch (flashlight).

In Carnac, **Tumulus Saint Michel**, 200m north-east of Place de l'Église at the end of Rue du Tumulus, dates back to at least 5000 BC and is topped with a 16th century cross and the **Chapelle Saint Michel**.

The closest and largest line of menhirs is the **Alignements du Ménec**, 1km north of Carnac Ville; to get there from Place de l'Église, head straight up Rue de Courdiec, which is a block north-west of the church. The area is fenced off to protect the 1100 menhirs that were being damaged by people trampling around and on them. But they're easily seen from the road or the roof of the nearby Archéoscope. Don't expect Stonehenge, though; most of them are no more than 1m high.

The Megaliths of Carnac

Megalithic culture arose during the Neolithic period between 4500 and 2000 BC, created by people whose lives were based on agriculture and herding – a radical change from the hunting and gathering of the earlier Palaeolithic era.

The most enduring monuments left by this culture include: *menhirs*, stones between 1m and 20m high, weighing between two and 200 tonnes and planted upright in the ground (in Breton, *men* means stone and *hir* means long); *dolmens* (*dol* meaning table), stone burial chambers, standing on their own or accessed by a narrow passage, often engraved with symmetrical designs; and *tumuli*, earth mounds which covered the dolmens. The most spectacularly decorated dolmens and the largest tumuli are on Gavrinis, an island in the Golfe du Morbihan.

While menhirs and dolmens are found in other parts of France and the rest of Europe, their concentration around Carnac has made this region famous. There's a wealth of sites, from solitary menhirs protruding from a field to the most impressive feature, the *alignements*, which are parallel lines of menhirs running for several kilometres and capped by a *cromlech*, a semicircle of stones.

The meaning of menhirs – unlike that of dolmens – has not been deciphered, though theories abound. Solitary rocks have been interpreted as being everything from phallic symbols to signposts indicating that a burial ground is nearby. It has been suggested that the alignments have astronomical and religious significance, though the mystery remains unsolved.

From here, Route de Kerlescan heads east for about 1.5km to the very impressive **Alignements de Kermario** (1029 menhirs in 10 lines), which is also a protected site but with a specially built viewing platform. Another 500m farther is the **Alignements de Kerlescan**, a much smaller grouping (555 menhirs in 13 lines), but the only one where you're free to wander around.

Between the two alignments is the **Géant de Manio**, a huge dolmen that apparently points the way to the **Quadrilatère**, an unusual group of menhirs arranged in a square. South of the Géant is the small **Tumulus de Kercado** in the grounds of a chateau with the same name. It dates from 3800 BC and was the burial ground of a Neolithic chieftain. During the Revolution it was used as a hiding place by Breton royalists.

Near Locmariaquer, the big monuments are the **Table des Marchands**, a 30m-long dolmen, and the **Grand Menhir Brisé**, the region's largest menhir, which once stood 20m high but is now lying broken on its side. These two are off the D781 just before the village. The site is open in April and May from 10 am to 1 pm and 2 to 6 pm. From June to September the hours are 10 am to 7 pm and in October from 10 am to 1 pm and 2 to 5 pm. Tours costing 25/6FF for adults/children are available. For detailed information contact the tourist office in Locmariaquer (Place de la Mairie; ☎ 02 97 57 33 05).

Just south of Locmariaquer by the sea is the **Dolmen des Pierres Plates**, a 24m-long chamber whose rocky walls are decorated with impressive, multishaped engravings.

Unfortunately, no buses run to Locmariaquer from Carnac (there's a very infrequent service from Auray in the late morning and late afternoon), but it's cyclable and not an impossible hitch along the D781.

Musée de Préhistoire

This Museum of Prehistory (☎ 02 97 52 22 04) at 10 Place de la Chapelle in Carnac Ville, a block north-east of Place de l'Église, is an excellent introduction to the megalithic sites. It chronicles life in and around Carnac from the Palaeolithic and Neolithic eras to the Middle Ages. A free English-language booklet will guide you adequately through the two floors.

The museum is open daily except Tuesday from 10 am to noon and 2 to 5 pm. In June and September it's open daily from 10 am to noon and 2 to 6 pm; the daily hours in July and August are 10 am to 6 pm (closed during lunch hours on weekends). Prices are 30/15FF for adults/students and children and 25/15FF from October to March.

Archéoscope

Sitting partially hidden opposite the Alignements du Ménec on Route des Alignements is the Archéoscope (☎ 02 97 52 07 49). The 25 minute show uses light, sound and special movement effects to take you back to Neolithic times.

From mid-February to mid-November, it's open daily from 10 am to noon and 1.30 to 5.30 pm. From May to October only, there are two English-language shows a day at 10.30 am and 2.30 pm and in July and August there is a third at 6 pm. Prices are 45/30/25FF for adults/students/children. A viewing stand on top of the building gives a good view of the menhirs.

Places to Stay

Camping There's a cluster of camping grounds about 2km north of Carnac Ville – head straight up Rue de Courdiec past the menhirs until you see the signs. The three star ***Les Pins*** (☎ 02 97 52 18 90) is open from April to mid-November and charges 20/13FF for adults/children under seven plus 40FF for a tent site and parking. Prices are dearer in July and August.

In Carnac Plage, the three star ***Camping Nicolas*** (☎ 02 97 52 95 42), on Blvd de Légenèse, west of the tourist office one block from the sea, is open from April to October. In addition to the usual facilities it also has a laundry. Adults/children pay 22/14FF. A tent site and car are 32FF.

Hotels Hotels are no bargain in Carnac Ville. About the cheapest is the lovely little ***Chez Nous*** (☎ 02 97 52 07 28) at 5 Place de la Chapelle, where a double with shower costs 210FF (230FF in summer). ***Auberge Le Râtelier*** (☎ 02 97 52 05 04; fax 02 97 52 76 11) at 4 Chemin du Douet, a quiet street one block south-west of Place de l'Église, has rustic charm, low ceilings and timber furnishings. Rooms with shower start at 230FF (250FF in summer).

In Carnac Plage, the ***Hôtel Hoty*** (☎ 02 97 52 11 12; fax 02 97 52 80 03) at 15 Ave de Kermario, two blocks east of the tourist office, is open all year round. Rooms start at 160FF. Another cheapie is ***La Frégate*** (☎ 02 97 52 97 90) at 14 Allée des Alignements (next to the tourist office). It is open from April to September. For a room with a view, try ***Hôtel Bord de Mer*** (☎ 02 97 52 10 84; fax 02 97 52 87 63) on the beach at 13 Blvd de la Plage. It is open from Easter to October with singles/doubles with shower starting from 295/350FF.

Places to Eat

Restaurants In Carnac Ville, ***Auberge Le Râtelier*** (see Places to Stay) has gourmet *menus*, served in a dining room illuminated by stained-glass windows, for 95/138/170FF (closed in February). ***La Caliorne*** (☎ 02 97 52 92 05) at 8 Rue de Colary has snacks and standard *menus* from 52FF while, just south of Place de l'Église, ***Chez Yannick*** (☎ 02 97 52 08 67) at 8 Rue du Tumulus is a lush garden crêperie serving galettes priced from 16FF.

In summer, Ave des Druides and the small streets around the tourist office in Carnac Plage are packed with crêperies, pizzerias and restaurants. ***La Frégate*** (see Places to Stay) is very popular, with a lunch *menu* (including wine) for 65FF and dinner ones from 75FF.

Self-Catering On Wednesday and Sunday there's a ***produce market*** just off Place de l'Église in Carnac Ville.

There are several supermarkets along Route de Plouharnel as you enter Carnac Ville. The ***Intermarché*** is open Monday to

Saturday from 8.30 am to 12.30 pm and 3 to 7 pm. In summer, it's open Monday to Saturday from 8.30 am to 8 pm and on Sunday from 9.30 am to 12.30 pm.

In Carnac Plage, the ***Super U*** supermarket at 188 Ave des Druides, about 1km east of the tourist office, is open Monday to Saturday from 9 am to 12.30 pm and 3 to 7 pm (there's no midday closure on Saturday or in July and August). In summer it's also open Sunday morning. The ***Marché U*** next to the tourist office at 68 Ave des Druides is open from 8.30 am to 1 pm and 3 to 8 pm in July and August only.

Getting There & Away

Bus Cariane Atlantique buses (☎ 02 97 47 29 64 in Vannes) between Vannes (38FF) and Quiberon (21FF) stop in Carnac Ville just outside the *gendarmerie* (police station) on Rue Saint Cornély, leading into Place de l'Église. In Carnac Plage the stop is in front of the tourist office. There are also daily buses to Auray (22FF), Plouharnel (10FF) and Lorient (38FF).

Train The nearest train station is in Plouharnel, 4km north-west of Carnac Ville. Plouharnel is on the Auray-Quiberon line which runs in summer only (see Getting There & Away under Quiberon for details). Otherwise you'll have to make your way by bus to/from Auray, 12km to the north-east. SNCF has an office on the 1st floor of the main tourist office in Carnac Plage. It is open daily from mid-June to August from 9 am to 12.30 pm and 2 to 5 pm. During the rest of the year, it opens on Saturday only.

Getting Around

In summer, bikes can be hired in Carnac Ville from Lorcy (☎ 02 97 52 09 73) at 6 Rue de Courdiec. In Carnac Plage, a few blocks from the tourist office, you can rent three-speeds for 37FF a day (27FF a half-day) at Le Randonneur (☎ 02 97 52 02 55), 20 Ave des Druides, and three-speeds and mountain bikes at Cycl'Up (☎ 02 97 52 91 76) at No 40 of the same street. Three or five-speeds at the latter are 37FF a day (27FF a half-day) and 155FF a week. Cycl'Up is open daily from 9 am to 7 pm from April to September. Cycling on the beach is *interdit* (prohibited).

QUIBERON

• pop 4600 ✉ 56170

At the end of a narrow, 14km-long peninsula south-west of Carnac lies Quiberon (Kiberen in Breton), a popular seaside town surrounded by sandy beaches and a wild coastline swept by enormous seas. It's also the port for ferries to Belle Île.

Orientation

One main road, the D768, leads into Quiberon; at the end of it is the train station. From here Rue de Verdun winds down to a sheltered bay (Port Maria), which is lined by the town's main beach, the Grande Plage.

Information

Tourist Office The tourist office (☎ 02 97 50 07 84; fax 02 97 30 58 22) is between the train station and the Grande Plage at 14 Rue de Verdun. It is open Monday to Saturday from 9 am to 12.30 pm and 2 to 6.30 pm. In July and August it's open from 9 am to 8 pm and on Sunday from 10 am to noon and 5 to 8 pm.

Money The Banque CIO just north of the tourist office on Rue de Verdun is open weekdays from 8.30 am to 12.20 pm and 1.30 to 5 pm. The Caisse d'Épargne south of the tourist office at Place Hoche and Rue de Verdun is also open on Saturday from 8.45 am to noon and 1.30 to 4 pm.

Post The main post office is north-west of the tourist office on Place Duchesse Anne. It is open from 9 am to noon and 2 to 6 pm on weekdays and on Saturday morning.

Beaches

The wide, sandy beach is *the* attraction in and around Quiberon. The Grande Plage attracts families while bathing spots towards the peninsula's tip are larger and less crowded. The peninsula's rocky western side is known as the Côte Sauvage (Wild Coast). It's great for a windy cycle but too rough for swimming. The spooky, Gothic-style mansion perched on the rocks is the privately owned Château de Turpault.

Places to Stay

Many hotels and other forms of accommodation in Quiberon close between November and March or April.

Camping All of the peninsula's 14 camping grounds are very close to the shore, mostly on the east and south-east coasts. The closest public site is ***Camping Municipal du Rohu*** (☎ 02 97 30 95 25) in Le Petit Rohu, about 4km north-east of the centre. It charges 45FF (including tent, two people and car) or 48FF for a site by the sea and is open from April to September.

The much closer – and more expensive – privately run ***Camping du Conguel*** (☎ 02 97 50 19 11; fax 02 97 30 46 66) at Blvd de la Teignouse is south-east of the centre. It is open from April to October and costs 20/14.50FF per adult/child and 79.50FF for a tent site. The Conguel's prices double in July and August.

Hostel Quiberon's ***Auberge de Jeunesse*** (☎ 02 97 50 15 54; fax 02 97 36 90 83) is in a quiet part of town south-east of the train station at 45 Rue du Roch Priol. Open from May to September, it charges 49FF for a dorm bed, 19FF for breakfast and 17FF for sheets. A bed in a tent for two in the back garden costs 39FF and you can pitch your own tent for 33FF. The hostel is closed from 10 am to 6 pm.

Hotels About the cheapest place in town is the ***Hôtel Bon Accueil*** (☎ 02 97 50 07 92), 6 Quai de l'Houat, along the waterfront to the west. It provides rooms with washbasin/shower from 160/190FF. Moving eastward and more upmarket, the ***Hôtel L'Océan*** (☎ 02 97 50 07 58; fax 02 97 50 27 81) at 7 Quai de l'Océan has rooms with washbasin/shower from 160/240FF in the low season and 170/250FF in summer.

Facing the pier from where boats sail to Belle Île, the ***Hôtel Albatros*** (☎ 02 97 50 15 05; fax 02 97 50 27 61) at 19 Rue de Port Maria has rooms with shower starting at 265FF. Prices rise dramatically in summer.

The ***Hôtel L'Idéal*** (☎ 02 97 50 12 72; fax 02 97 50 39 99), at 43 Rue de Port Haliguen several blocks south-east of the train station, has singles/doubles from 200/250FF.

Places to Eat

Restaurants Like its hotels, Quiberon's restaurants tend to be expensive. Crêperies, pizzerias and snack stands line Quai de Belle Île and Rue de Port Maria, while the restaurants in the ***Hôtel Bon Accueil*** and ***Hôtel Albatros*** (see Places to Stay) have reasonably priced *menus*. ***Le Vietnam*** (☎ 02 97 30 44 25) at 15 Place Hoche serves Chinese as well as Vietnamese food.

Self-Catering The ***Stoc*** supermarket on Rue de Verdun south of the tourist office is open Monday to Saturday from 8.45 am to 12.30 pm and 3 to 7.15 pm. Sunday hours are 9 am to noon.

Getting There & Away

Bus Cariane Atlantique buses (☎ 02 97 47 29 64 in Vannes) connect Quiberon with Carnac (21FF), Auray (35FF) and Vannes (52FF; 1¾ hours). Buses stop at the train station and Place Hoche near the tourist office and beach.

Train Trains run to/from Quiberon only in July and August. The little station (☎ 02 97 50 07 07 or ☎ 08 36 35 35 35) is on Rue de la Gare, the northern extension of Rue de Verdun.

The nearest major train station is at Auray (☎ 02 97 24 44 69 or ☎ 08 36 35 35 35), 23km north-east on the Lorient-Paris rail line. Quiberon-Auray trains all stop at Plouharnel, the closest station to Carnac. In summer, a normal SNCF train to Auray from Quiberon takes 40 minutes and costs 27FF. There's also the much slower Tire-Buchon (Corkscrew) train, which costs a flat 12FF between any two stations.

Boat For information about getting to Belle Île and the smaller islands of Houat and Hoëdic, see Getting There & Away in the following Belle Île section.

Getting Around

Taxi To order a taxi in Quiberon, ring ☎ 02 97 50 11 11.

Bicycle Cycles Loisirs (☎ 02 97 50 10 69) at 3 Rue Victor Golvan north-west of the tourist office has five-speeds/mountain bikes for 41/78FF a day and 175/329FF a week. Scooters cost 140/217FF a half-day/day.

BELLE ÎLE

• **pop 4300** ✉ **56360**

Belle Île, about 15km south of Quiberon, is what its name says it is: a beautiful island. Vauban built one of his citadels here, but it is far less impressive than the island's natural rock formations.

About 20km long and 9km wide, Belle Île is bounded by relatively calm waters to the east and by the crashing force of the Atlantic to the west. The population swells to 35,000 in summer. Fortunately, the island is large enough to accommodate that many visitors without feeling crowded.

Information

Tourist Office The tourist office (☎ 02 97 31 81 93; fax 02 97 31 56 17) is in Le Palais, the main village, on Quai Bonnelle to the left as you get off the ferry. From July to mid-September it's open Monday to Saturday from 9 am to 7.30 pm. During the rest of the year it's open from 9.30 am to 6.30 pm. It's open on Sunday morning all year from 9 or 10 am to noon or 1 pm.

Things to See & Do

Le Palais is a cosy port dominated by the citadel which Vauban strengthened in 1682 after centuries of Anglo-French disputes over control of the area. The citadel now houses the **Musée Historique** (☎ 02 97 31 84 17), which examines Belle Île's past.

Belle Île's wild southern side has spectacular rock formations, a few small, natural ports and a number of caves. The most famous, **Grotte de l'Apothicairerie** (Cave of the Apothecary's Shop), is an awesome cavern into which the waves roll from two sides.

A pedestrians-only track follows the island's entire coastline. If you're travelling by bike, ask at the tourist office for its brochure of *sentiers côtiers* (coastal paths), which shows the best cycling routes.

Places to Stay

Camping There are 11 camping grounds dotted around Belle Île; most are two-star places open only from April or May to September or October. The municipal ***Les Glacis*** site (☎ 02 97 31 41 76) in Le Palais at the base of the citadel is the closest to the port. It charges 15/10FF for adults/children and 10FF for a tent site and is open from April to September.

Hostel & Gîtes d'Étape The ***Auberge de Jeunesse*** (☎ 02 97 31 81 33; fax 02 97 31 58 38) in Le Palais is open all year except October and charges 51FF a night (70FF with breakfast). For hikers, there are a couple of ***gîtes d'étape*** on the island – one along the coast at Port Gouen about 1km south of Le Palais (☎ 02 97 31 55 88; 45FF) and another in Locmaria (☎ 02 97 31 70 48). The latter charges 36FF for a dorm bed and 136FF for a room with three beds.

Hotels & B&Bs The hotels on Belle Île are pricey. The cheapest is the ***Hôtel La Frégate*** (☎ 02 97 31 54 16) open from April to October, facing the dock in Le Palais at Quai de l'Acadie, with rooms from 220FF. The local ***chambres chez l'habitant*** (B&Bs) are better – ask at the tourist office for a list. Prices average about 250FF for a double room with breakfast.

Places to Eat

On Belle Île seafood is king. For a sumptuous repast, try the highly recommended ***La Saline*** (☎ 02 97 31 84 70) on Route du Phare heading out of Le Palais.

Getting There & Away

Ferries from Quiberon to Belle Île and the smaller islands of Houat and Hoëdic are run by CMN (☎ 02 97 50 06 90 in Quiberon) and leave from the terminal at the western end of Port Maria. On Belle Île, ferries dock at the terminal in Le Palais (☎ 02 97 31 80 01). The trip to Belle Île takes 45 minutes. Ferries run all year with up to six sailings a day, though in summer and on weekends there are many more (as many as 13).

Return fares are 85/58FF for adults/children under 12. Transporting a bike back and forth costs 40FF; cars cost from 404 to 728FF depending on their size. Passenger prices are the same to the car-free islands of Houat and Hoëdic, but services to these islands are much less frequent (sometimes only one a day in the low season). The return trip between Houat and Hoëdic costs 42.50/31FF for adults/children.

You can also reach Belle Île from Vannes by boat in summer. Navix (☎ 02 97 46 60 00) charges 150FF for an adult return and 90FF for children under 14.

Getting Around

In Le Palais, Les Cars Verts (☎ 02 97 31 81 88) on Quai de Lysère rents 2CV Citroën *décapotables* (convertibles) for 355FF a day.

There's a handful of bicycle and scooter rental places near Le Palais' port.

LORIENT

• pop 59,000 ✉ 56100

In the 17th century the Compagnie des Indes (the French East India Company) founded the Port de l'Orient; the name was later abbreviated to Lorient. Ever since, it has been one of the most important ports in France. In WWII, it held U-boat pens; during fierce fighting in 1945, the city was almost entirely destroyed.

Lorient (An Oriant in Breton) contains little of specific interest to travellers, but its tidy streets, upbeat atmosphere and large student community make it well worth a visit.

Fans of Celtic culture will enjoy the Festival Interceltique, which takes the city by storm every summer, and Lorient's variety of accommodation makes it a useful base for exploring the nearby areas of Morbihan and Finistère.

Orientation

Lorient is set on a large natural harbour and the Scorff River. The centre of town is about 1km south of the train and bus stations near the narrow Port de Plaisance. You can reach it by walking down Cours de Chazelles and its continuation, Rue Maréchal Foch.

Information

Tourist Office The helpful tourist office (☎ 02 97 21 07 84; fax 02 97 21 99 44) is on the Quai de Rohan on the southern side of the Port de Plaisance. In July and August it's open on weekdays from 9 am to 7 pm, the same hours (with a two hour lunch break from noon) on Saturday, and from 10 am to noon and 2 to 5 pm on Sunday. The rest of the year it is open weekdays from 9 am to 12.30 pm and 1.30 to 6 pm and on Saturday from 9 am to noon and 2 to 6 pm.

Money There are several banks along Cours de Chazelles, including the Société Générale at No 24. It is open weekdays from 8.45 am to 12.25 pm and 2.25 to 5.45 pm. On Saturday the hours are 8.15 am to 12.15 pm and 1.30 to 4.30 pm.

Post The main post office is in the centre of town at 9 Quai des Indes. It is open weekdays from 8 am to 7 pm and on Saturday morning till noon.

Laundry The Cleanfil laundrette at 2 Rue George Gaigneux, just off Rue Maréchal Foch, is open daily from 8 am to 9 pm.

Musée de la Compagnie des Indes

This fascinating museum (☎ 02 97 82 19 13), located in a 17th century citadel in the Port Louis area south-east of Lorient's centre, traces the history of the French East India Company and its lucrative trade with India, China, Africa and the New World from

1660 to the end of the 18th century. It is open daily except Tuesday from 10 am to 7 pm (1.30 to 6 pm only from October to March). Prices are 29/19FF for adults/students.

To reach Port Louis and the museum most comfortably, take the 10 minute ferry from the Embarcadère de la Rade (☎ 02 97 33 40 55) at the end of Quai des Indes and opposite the tourist office. From Monday to Saturday, ferries run every half-hour between 6.45 am and 8.15 pm. There are seven ferries on Sunday between 10.30 am and 6.30 pm. The one-way fare is 6.70FF, and taking a bike along costs an extra 6.30FF.

Special Events

For 10 days in early August, Lorient is given over to a celebration of Celtic culture, especially music, literature and dance, called the Festival Interceltique. People from the Celtic countries or regions (*broiou keltiek* in Breton) – Ireland, Scotland, Wales, Cornwall, Isle of Man and certain parts of north-western Spain – join the Bretons to pay homage to their common heritage.

Places to Stay

Hostel The ***Auberge de Jeunesse*** (☎ 02 97 37 11 65; fax 02 97 87 95 49) is 3km out of town at 41 Rue Victor Schoelcher. Dorm beds cost 68FF, with breakfast included. The hostel is closed from 22 December to the end of January. To get there from the station take bus C and get off at the Auberge de Jeunesse stop.

Hotels Lorient has a large number of hotels in all price ranges so, except during the Festival Interceltique, it shouldn't be difficult to find a place to stay.

The one star ***Hôtel d'Arvor*** (☎ 02 97 21 07 55) at 104 Rue Lazare Carnot is a small, friendly place about 600m south-west of Quai de Rohan. Rooms, some of which have antique furnishings, cost from 130FF (with washbasin) to 150FF (with shower and toilet). From the train station, take bus D (direction: Nouvelle Ville) and get off at the Carnot stop.

Moving upmarket, the two star ***Hôtel Victor Hugo*** (☎ 02 97 21 16 24; fax 02 97 84 95 13) is well situated at 36 Rue Lazare Carnot, close to the port. Comfortable rooms with shower and TV cost 230FF. There are a few doubles with just washbasin for 160FF.

The top-end but rather characterless ***Hôtel Mercure*** (☎ 02 97 21 35 73; fax 02 97 64 48 62) is at 31 Place Jules Ferry. Rooms with TV, shower and toilet cost 325/375FF for singles/doubles but are cheaper on weekends, except in summer.

Places to Eat

Restaurants The Hôtel d'Arvor has a very good restaurant, with *menus* for 85 and 120FF, and is open daily except Sunday. *Menus* at the Hôtel Victor Hugo start at 85FF. See Places to Stay for details.

The ***Royal Couscous*** (☎ 02 97 64 45 78) at 65 Rue Lazare Carnot serves North African specialities, including tajines (from 60FF), daily until midnight.

The intimate ***Le Saint Louis*** (☎ 02 97 21 50 45) at 48 Rue Jules Le Grand has two good *menus* for 62 and 98FF (closed Tuesday night and Wednesday), but an even better bet is the ***Bistrot du Yachtman*** (☎ 02 97 21 31 91) north of the tourist office at 14 Rue Poissonière. *Menus* start at 79FF.

Self-Catering ***Le Garde Manger***, a small grocery at 79 Rue Lazare Carnot, is open daily, except Sunday, from 8.30 am to 1 pm and 4 to 9 pm.

Getting There & Away

Bus Some 20 different bus companies serving the Morbihan department operate out of the bus station (☎ 02 97 21 28 29) next to the train station. Destinations, among many others, include Josselin (60FF) and Carnac (35FF).

Train Lorient's enormous train and bus station complex, known as the Gare d'Échanges, is at 7 Cours de Chazelles. The train information office (☎ 02 97 85 41 41) is open daily from 9 am to 7.30 pm. Lorient is served by TGVs from Paris' Gare Montparnasse (342FF; 3½ hours). Other trains go to Brest (135FF; 2¼ hours), Quimper (63FF; 45 minutes), Vannes (60FF; 35 minutes), Rennes (139FF; 1½ hours) and places in between.

Boat Car ferries run by CMN (☎ 02 97 64 77 64) depart frequently in summer for Île de Groix, an 8km-long island with some fine beaches and accommodation south-west of Lorient. They leave from the Embarcadère Île de Groix, about 150m south-east of the tourist office on Blvd Adolphe Pierre. The return fare is 85/58FF for adults/children up to 12 and students up to 25 years of age. Transporting a bicycle costs 38FF return, but you can just as easily rent a bicycle/mountain bike/scooter there from Loca Loisirs (Quai de Port Tudy; ☎ 02 97 86 80 03) for 49/71/260FF a day.

In July and August you can also reach Belle Île on Tuesday, Thursday and Friday (see the previous section) from Lorient, but passages must be booked well in advance, and you cannot transport a car from here.

Getting Around

Bus Lorient's Vitaville city buses are run by CTRL, which has an information office (☎ 02 97 21 28 29) in the Gare d'Échanges. It is open Monday to Saturday from 7 am to 7 pm. Most of the 11 lines (designated by letters, not numbers) meet at the train station and run between about 7 am and 8 pm daily except Sunday, when services are greatly reduced. Tickets cost 6.70FF each or 55FF for a carnet of 10. A daily pass is 20FF. One Passe Partout for 115FF gets you three days bus travel as well as ferry trips to Île de Groix, Port Louis and/or museum entries and an entrance to the Citadelle Port Louis.

Bus D links the train station with the Quai de Rohan and the tourist office.

Taxi Taxis in Lorient can be reached on ☎ 02 97 21 29 29.

Eastern & Central Brittany

Eastern Brittany, encompassing the inland portion of the department of Ille-et-Vilaine, is less popular with tourists than any other part of the region and, frankly, that's not surprising. The area has retained almost nothing of its traditional way of life and has little in common with the rest of Brittany. Rennes, the capital of Ille-et-Vilaine and of Brittany as a whole, feels less Breton than any other city in the region. Rennes is, however, a very useful transport centre.

Parts of central Brittany, split between the departments of Côtes d'Armor (to the north) and Morbihan (to the south), are no more Breton than Rennes. But the Forêt de Paimpont (or Brocéliande), where King Arthur and his court once held sway (see the boxed text 'King Arthur'), is a wonderful place to explore. To the south-west is Josselin, a picturesque little town with an important chateau dating from the 14th century.

RENNES

• pop 203,000 ✉ 35000

Rennes, a university centre, has sat at an important crossroads since Roman times. Capital of Brittany since its incorporation into France in the 16th century, the city developed at the junction of the highways linking the northern and western ports of Saint Malo and Brest with the former capital, Nantes (see the Atlantic Coast chapter), and the inland city of Le Mans.

Orientation

The city centre is divided into northern and southern sectors by La Vilaine, a river channelled into a cement-lined canal which disappears underground just before the central square, Place de la République. The northern area, which includes the pedestrianised old city, is the most appealing. To the south, Rennes is garishly modern, with enormous shopping complexes like the Centre Colombier.

RENNES

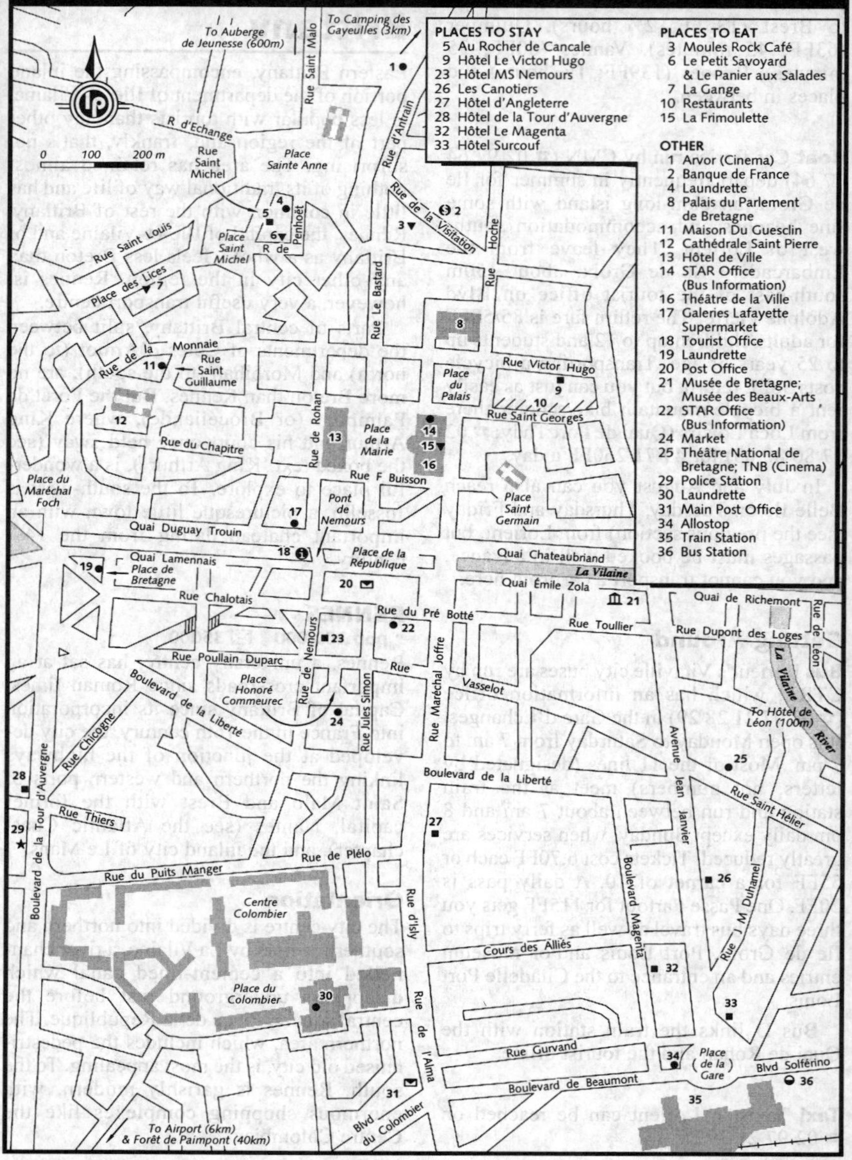
PLACES TO STAY
5 Au Rocher de Cancale
9 Hôtel Le Victor Hugo
23 Hôtel MS Nemours
26 Les Canotiers
27 Hôtel d'Angleterre
28 Hôtel de la Tour d'Auvergne
32 Hôtel Le Magenta
33 Hôtel Surcouf
PLACES TO EAT
3 Moules Rock Café
6 Le Petit Savoyard & Le Panier aux Salades
7 La Gange
10 Restaurants
15 La Frimoulette
OTHER
1 Arvor (Cinema)
2 Banque de France
4 Laundrette
8 Palais du Parlement de Bretagne
11 Maison Du Gueslin
12 Cathédrale Saint Pierre
13 Hôtel de Ville
14 STAR Office (Bus Information)
16 Théâtre de la Ville
17 Galeries Lafayette Supermarket
18 Tourist Office
19 Laundrette
20 Post Office
21 Musée de Bretagne; Musée des Beaux-Arts
22 STAR Office (Bus Information)
24 Market
25 Théâtre National de Bretagne; TNB (Cinema)
29 Police Station
30 Laundrette
31 Main Post Office
34 Allostop
35 Train Station
36 Bus Station
0 100 200 m
To Auberge de Jeunesse (600m)
To Camping des Gayeulles (3km)
Rue Saint Malo
R d'Echange
Rue Saint Michel
Place Sainte Anne
Rue d'Antrain
Rue de la Visitation
Rue Hoche
Place Saint Michel
R de Penhoët
Rue Saint Louis
Place des Lices
Rue Le Bastard
Rue de la Monnaie
Rue Saint Guillaume
Rue Victor Hugo
Place du Palais
Rue Saint Georges
Rue de Rohan
Place de la Mairie
Rue du Chapitre
Rue F Buisson
Place du Maréchal Foch
Pont de Nemours
Place Saint Germain
Quai Duguay Trouin
Quai Lamennais
Place de la République
Place de Bretagne
Quai Chateaubriand
La Vilaine
Quai Émile Zola
Rue Chalotais
Rue du Pré Botté
Rue Toullier
Quai de Richemont
Rue Dupont des Loges
Rue de Léon
La Vilaine River
Rue de Nemours
Rue Poullain Duparc
Rue Vasselot
Place Honoré Commeurec
Boulevard de la Liberté
Rue Jules Simon
Rue Maréchal Joffre
To Hôtel de Léon (100m)
Rue Chicogne
Boulevard de la Tour d'Auvergne
Avenue Jean Janvier
Rue Saint Hélier
Rue Thiers
Rue de Pléło
Boulevard Magenta
Rue du Puits Manger
Rue J M Duhamel
Centre Colombier
Rue d'Isly
Cours des Alliés
Place du Colombier
Rue de l'Alma
Rue Gurvand
Place de la Gare
Blvd Solférino
Boulevard de Beaumont
Blvd du Colombier
To Airport (6km) & Forêt de Paimpont (40km)

Information

Tourist Office The main tourist office (☎ 02 99 79 01 98; fax 02 99 79 31 38) is on Pont de Nemours at Place de la République. It is open Tuesday to Saturday from 9 am to 6 pm and Monday from 1 to 6 pm. The tourist office annexe (☎ 02 99 53 23 23) at the train station is open weekdays from 8 am to 7 pm and weekends from 10 am to 1 pm and 3 to 6 pm.

Money The Banque de France at 25 Rue de la Visitation is open weekdays from 8.45 am to noon and 1.30 to 3.30 pm. Inside the train station, the Crédit Agricole is open Tuesday to Friday from 9.30 am to 1 pm and 2.15 to 6.45 pm. On Saturday the hours are 9 am to 1 pm and 2 to 4 pm.

Post The main post office at 27 Blvd du Colombier is open weekdays from 8 am to 7 pm and on Saturday from 8 am to noon. There's another post office at Place de la République, which keeps the same hours. Both have currency-exchange services.

Laundry The laundrette at 23 Rue de Penhoët is open daily from 7 am to 8 pm. Near the train station, the more upmarket Cleanfil on Place du Colombier in the Centre Colombier is open Monday to Saturday from 7.30 am to 9 pm. Close to the tourist office, the laundrette at 3 Place de Bretagne is open daily from 7 am to 10 pm.

Old City

Much of medieval Rennes was gutted by *le grand incendie*, the great fire of 1720 started by a drunken carpenter who accidentally set a pile of shavings alight. It engulfed 900 homes in an eight day conflagration. The half-timbered houses that survived now make up the old city, Rennes' most picturesque quarter. It is bordered by Place Sainte Anne, Place des Lices and the streets north-west of the tourist office.

Among the prettiest streets are **Rue Saint Michel** and **Rue Saint Georges**. The latter intersects the enormous Place de la Mairie and Place du Palais, site of the 17th century **Palais du Parlement de Bretagne**, the former seat of the rebellious Breton parliament and more recently the Palais de Justice. In February 1994 the building was largely destroyed by fire caused by the maritime flares fired by angry fishermen during a protest over income rates. It is now being restored at a cost of 350FF million. On **Rue Saint Guillaume**, the superbly carved but crumbling **Maison Du Guesclin** at No 3 was named after a 14th century Breton warrior. Nearby is the outwardly reserved 17th century **Cathédrale Saint Pierre**, whose golden neoclassical interior comes as a warm surprise. It is open daily from 9 am to noon and 2 to 7 pm.

Museums

Jointly housed in the city's old university at 20 Quai Émile Zola are the **Musée de Bretagne** (☎ 02 99 28 55 84) and the **Musée des Beaux-Arts** (☎ 02 99 28 55 85). The former offers an insightful introduction to Brittany's history and culture from the Gallo-Roman period to just before WWI.

Upstairs, the Fine Arts Museum is unexceptional apart from the room devoted to Picasso. The two museums are open daily, except Tuesday, from 10 am to noon and 2 to 6 pm. The prices for each are 15/7.50FF for adults/students and children. A ticket valid for both museums costs 20/10FF.

Special Events

Rennes is at its most lively in the first week of July during the Tombées de la Nuit, when the old city is filled with music, theatre and people in medieval costume.

Places to Stay

Camping Rennes' only camping ground is the municipal ***Camping des Gayeulles*** (☎ 02 99 36 91 22) on Rue du Professeur Maurice Audin in the Parc des Bois, about 4.5km north-east of the station. It is open from April to September and charges 13/15/5FF per person/tent site/car. To get there from Place de la Mairie, take bus No 3 to the Gayeulles stop.

Hostel The ***Auberge de Jeunesse*** (☎ 02 99 33 22 33; fax 02 99 59 06 21) is at 10-12 Canal Saint Martin, 2.5km north-west of the train station. A bed in a room for three costs 80FF, including breakfast. A single/double is 130/180FF. The hostel is served by buses from the train station or Place de la Mairie (last one at about 8 pm). Take bus No 20 on weekdays and bus No 18 on weekends; get off at the Coétlogon stop, and walk straight down Rue de Saint Malo.

Hotels – Train Station Area The semi-circular Place de la Gare and the streets leading north to the city centre are brimming with hotels. The ***Hôtel Surcouf*** (☎ 02 99 30 59 79; fax 02 99 31 72 71) at 13 Place de la Gare has basic rooms from 209FF (from 229FF with shower). ***Hôtel d'Angleterre*** (☎ 02 99 79 38 61; fax 02 99 79 43 85) at 19 Rue du Maréchal-Joffre is well placed between the river and the station with rooms from 150FF (197FF with shower).

Hôtel Le Magenta (☎ 02 99 30 85 37; fax 02 99 31 21 31) at 35 Blvd Magenta has ordinary rooms from 130FF (190FF with shower), and triples from 250FF. The hall shower costs 20FF. Rooms at ***Les Canotiers*** (☎ 02 99 31 69 11; fax 02 99 31 40 11) at 35 Ave Jean Janvier are 195FF with shower.

Hotels – Old City The old city is filled with character but not hotels. ***Au Rocher de Cancale*** (☎ 02 99 79 20 83), which is in a half-timbered house at 10 Rue Saint Michel, has rooms from 220FF. It's closed on weekends and, given the nearby student bars, could be very noisy.

Hotels – Elsewhere East of the old city, ***Hôtel Le Victor Hugo*** (☎ 02 99 38 85 33; fax 02 99 36 54 95) at 14 Rue Victor Hugo has a good location but ordinary singles/doubles with washbasin for 135/175FF and with shower from 230FF. South of the tourist office, the shipshape ***Hôtel MS Nemours*** (☎ 02 99 78 26 26; fax 02 99 78 25 40) at No 5 on the bus-only Rue de Nemours has particularly neat singles/doubles with shower and TV from 240/285FF.

South-west of the tourist office, at 20 Blvd de la Tour d'Auvergne, the warm ***Hôtel de la Tour d'Auvergne*** (☎ 02 99 30 84 16) has basic rooms for 135FF and ones with shower for 165FF. Hall showers are 15FF.

On the other side of town three blocks south-east of the museums, ***Hôtel de Léon*** (☎ 02 99 30 55 28) at 15 Rue de Léon is a quirky, art-bedecked place with simple but large singles/doubles for 125/155FF and ones with shower for 175/180FF. Hall showers are 18FF. This is a very quiet part of town.

Places to Eat

Despite such a large student population, Rennes has few cheap restaurants. Lovely Rue Saint Georges is *the* street for indulging in crêpes, pizza and ethnic food from Indian to Brazilian.

Restaurants In the old city, ***Le Petit Savoyard*** (☎ 02 99 78 21 29) at 13 Rue de Penhoët has a lunch-only *menu* for 56FF. ***Le Panier aux Salades*** (☎ 02 99 79 20 97), next door at No 15, has salads from 36FF. The ***Moules Rock Café***, featuring bivalves and Elvis at 34 Rue de la Visitation, has all-you-can-eat mussel platters.

In the small alleyway behind the Théâtre de la Ville on Place de la Mairie, ***La Frimoulette*** (☎ 02 99 79 44 63) has mussels with chips for 43FF and *menus* for 55 and 71FF. It is open till midnight, but closed Sunday and Monday evening. At 34 Place des Lices, Indian restaurant ***Le Gange*** (☎ 02 99 30 18 37) serves *menus* from 85FF and a wide variety of vegetarian dishes.

Self-Catering There's a large covered ***market hall*** on Place Honoré Commeurec. Stalls are open Monday to Saturday from 7 am to 6.30 pm, though some vendors take a couple of hours off for lunch. A ***market*** is held at Place des Lices on Saturday morning.

The ***Galeries Lafayette*** on Quai Duguay Trouin has a grocery section open Monday to Saturday from 9 am to 8 pm. If you'd like fresh bread on Sunday, the ***boulangerie*** in the old city on Rue Saint Michel is open from 7 am to 1 pm and 2 to 8 pm. There's another Sunday ***boulangerie*** at the train station on Blvd Magenta; it's open from 7 am to 1.30 pm and 3 to 8.30 pm.

Entertainment

Cinema Two cinemas screen nondubbed films: ***Arvor*** (☎ 02 99 38 72 40) at 29 Rue d'Antrain and ***TNB*** (☎ 02 99 30 88 88) at the Théâtre National de Bretagne at 1 Rue Saint Hélier. Ask at the tourist office for *Ciné Spectacles*, a free weekly guide that lists their programs, or call ☎ 08 36 68 00 39 for a recorded listing.

Getting There & Away

Air Rennes' Saint Jacques airport (☎ 02 99 29 60 00) is about 6km south-west of town.

Bus Several lines operate from the bus station on Blvd Solférino east of the train station, including: Cariane Atlantique, which offers service to Nantes (95FF; two hours), Vannes (85FF; 2½ hours) and Josselin (58FF); TAE, which goes to Dinan (48FF; 1¼ hours) and Dinard (62FF; 1¾ hours); Courriers Bretons, which has buses to Pontorson (55FF; one hour) and Mont Saint Michel (60FF; 1¼ hours); and TIV, which serves Fougères (48FF; one hour) and Paimpont.

Train The modern train station (☎ 02 99 29 11 63 or ☎ 08 36 35 35 35) on Place de la Gare is equipped with banks, shops and a large train information office, which is open Monday to Saturday from 8 am to 7.30 pm (from 10 am on Sunday).

Some of the major destinations served include Paris' Gare Montparnasse by TGV (263FF; two hours; hourly trains until 8 pm), Saint Malo (67FF; one hour; seven a day), Vannes (107FF; one hour; 10 a day), Nantes (112FF; two hours; six a day), Brest (159FF; 2½ hours) and Quimper (181FF; 2½ hours).

Car ADA can be contacted on ☎ 02 99 38 59 88. Europcar (☎ 02 99 51 60 61) has a bureau at the train station.

Hitching Allostop (☎ 02 99 30 93 93), which matches up hitchers and drivers for a fee, is at 37 Blvd de Beaumont, opposite the station. It is open weekdays from 9 am to 7 pm, Saturday from 10 am to 1 pm and 2 to 5 pm. There is a flat fee depending on the distance of the journey and a per kilometre charge of 0.20FF.

Getting Around

To/From the Airport Saint Jacques airport is connected to the city by bus No 57, which stops at Place de la République.

Bus Local buses are run by STAR (☎ 02 99 79 37 37), whose information kiosk at 12 Rue du Pré Botté is open Monday to Saturday from 7 am to 7 pm. It has another office at Place de la Mairie, which keeps the same hours. Single tickets cost 6.50FF and a carnet of 10 is 47FF. Most buses leave from or pass by one of two major hubs – Place de la République and Place de la Mairie. Some also leave from the train station. To reach Place de la République from the station, take bus No 1, 17 or 20.

Taxi Taxis (☎ 02 99 30 79 79) line up outside the train station.

AROUND RENNES

Forêt de Paimpont

The Paimpont Forest is about 40km south-west of Rennes. It was here that the young Arthur supposedly received the sword Excalibur from the fairy Vivian, the very mysterious Lady of the Lake and later Merlin's mistress. Visitors still come here in search of the spring of eternal youth, where the magician first met his lover.

The best base for exploring the Forêt de Paimpont is the village of **Paimpont**, whose tourist office (☎ 02 99 07 84 23) is next to the 12th century **Église Abbatiale** (Abbey Church). The tourist office is open April to September daily, except Tuesday, from 10 am till noon and 2 to 5 pm. It has a free annotated walking/cycling map of the forest (62km of trails) or you can buy the more complete *Tour de Brocéliande* topoguide covering 162km of trails. On Thursday and Saturday in July and August, there are guided tours of the lower forest (10 am; 15FF) and upper forest (2 pm; 25FF). A guided tour for the whole day costs 35FF.

Places to Stay & Eat The small ***Camping Municipal de Paimpont*** (☎ 02 99 07 89 16) near the lake is open from mid-April to September and charges 14/12/4FF per person/tent site/car. Two *gîtes d'étape* just outside the village – ***Les Forges*** (☎ 02 99 06 81 59) and ***Trudeau*** (☎ 02 99 07 81 40) – charge 50/46FF per person respectively. Trudeau also offers hotel accommodation, with a double including breakfast costing 210FF. If you must have your comfort, the central ***Relais de Brocéliande*** (☎ 02 99 07 81 07; fax 02 99 07 80 60) is for you. It has rooms with shower from 220FF (180FF without shower) and excellent *menus* from 70FF. For crêpes and galettes, try the ***Crêperie du Porche*** (☎ 04 91 07 81 88).

Getting There & Around Paimpont is accessible by TIV bus (☎ 02 99 30 87 80) from Rennes (one hour; up to seven a day from Monday to Saturday). Once there you can rent bikes for about 50FF a day from Trudeau (see Places to Stay & Eat) or mountain bikes (90FF a day) from Le Brécilien (☎ 02 99 07 81 13), a bar next to the tourist office.

Josselin

• pop 2400 ✉ 56120

The picturesque if somewhat touristy town of Josselin was the seat of a dynastic line of counts for several centuries in the Middle Ages. They built the large chateau, which hosted many of the dukes of Brittany during their wanderings through the duchy. The best time to visit Josselin is Bastille Day (14 July), when the entire town dresses up for the Festival Médiéval.

Orientation Josselin lies on the Oust River, 43km north-east of Vannes and 78km south-west of Rennes. The centre of the village is Place Notre Dame, a beautiful square of 16th century half-timbered houses. The shop-lined Rue Olivier de Clisson runs north from the square.

Information The tourist office (☎ 02 97 22 36 43; fax 02 97 22 20 44) on Place de la Congrégation is open daily from 10 am to noon and 2 to 6 pm from April to October. From November to March it is closed Monday morning and Saturday afternoon.

There's a Caisse d'Épargne at 14 Rue Olivier de Clisson open Tuesday to Saturday from 9 am to 12.15 pm and 1.30 to 5.30 pm (4 pm on Saturday). The main post office is a few doors down at No 10. It is open from 8 am till noon and 2 to 5 pm on weekdays, and on Saturday morning.

Things to See The **Basilique Notre Dame du Roncier**, parts of which date back to the 12th century, is on Place Notre Dame. It contains some superb 15th and 16th century stained glass on the south wall. In the chapel on the north-east side of the choir is the tomb of Olivier de Clisson, high constable (*connétable*) of France who fortified the chateau during the Hundred Years' War in the late 14th century.

The **Château de Josselin** (☎ 02 97 22 36 45), south-west of the tourist office down Rue du Château, was built in the 12th century and retains four of its original round towers. The chateau's rooms, most of which were restored in the 19th century, are open for inspection daily in July and August from 10 am to 6 pm and in June and September from 2 to 6 pm. In April, May and October you can visit only in the afternoon on Wednesday, Saturday and Sunday. Prices are 29/18FF for adults/students and children to 14 years.

Places to Stay & Eat The ***Camping du Bas de la Lande*** (☎ 02 97 22 22 20; fax 02 97 73 93 85), about 2km south-west of the centre and open-year round, charges 12/12/10FF per person/tent site/car. There's no hostel in Josselin, but the village-run ***gîte d'étape*** (☎ 02 97 22 21 69) south-east of the chateau by the Oust River has dormitory beds for 43FF and stays open all year.

The ***Hôtel de France*** (☎ 02 97 22 23 06; fax 02 97 22 35 78) at 6 Place Notre Dame has rooms with shower from 230FF (270FF in summer).

The less attractive ***Hôtel Le Pélican*** (☎ 02 97 22 22 05), west of the tourist office at 87 Rue Glatinier, charges 168/185FF for singles/doubles.

Menus at the ***Hôtel de France*** start at 78FF. For something lighter, try the crêpes (from 15FF) and salads (from 22FF) at the ***Crêperie de Clisson*** at 2 Rue Olivier de Clisson.

Getting There & Away Between two and four Cariane Atlantique buses (☎ 02 97 47 29 64 in Vannes) a day link Josselin with Rennes (58FF; two hours) and Vannes (42FF; 45 minutes). They stop at Place de la Résistance, which is at the northern end of Rue Olivier de Clisson. Buses to/from Rennes also call at Ploërmel (15FF; 20 minutes), 13km south-east, which has the closest train station to Josselin. On Friday and Sunday, Breton Sud Autocars (☎ 02 97 39 02 45 in Baud) runs a bus at 8 or 9 pm to Lorient (58FF; 1½ hours).

North Coast

The central part of Brittany's north coast belongs to the Côtes d'Armor department, which stretches from Perros-Guirec, near the north-east corner of Finistère, to Saint Briac, which is just west of the upmarket beach resort of Dinard. Dinard, ever popular Saint Malo, the oyster-producing town of Cancale and other points along the Baie du Mont Saint Michel are in the department of Ille-et-Vilaine.

The rugged stretch of coast between Le Val André in the west and Pointe du Grouin in the east is known as the Côte d'Émeraude (Emerald Coast). The area, which includes Dinard, Saint Malo and the Rance Estuary, is famous for its numerous peninsulas and promontories, many of which have spectacular sea views.

The best way to explore the Côte d'Émeraude is to walk part of the GR34 trail, which runs along the entire coast of both departments. The largest offshore islands are Île de Bréhat, 8km north of the port town of Paimpol, and Les Sept Îles, 18km west of Perros-Guirec. The medieval town of Dinan, which is about 20km from the coast, is on the Rance River south of Saint Malo.

SAINT MALO

• pop 48,000 ✉ 35400

The Channel port of Saint Malo is one of the most popular tourist destinations in Brittany – and with good reason. Situated at the mouth of the Rance River, it is famed for its walled city and nearby beaches. The Saint Malo area has some of the highest tidal variations in the world.

Saint Malo is an excellent base from which to explore the Côte d'Émeraude between Pointe du Grouin and Le Val André.

History

Saint Malo was one of France's most important ports during the 17th and 18th centuries, serving as a base for both merchant ships and government-sanctioned pirates, known more politely as privateers. Although fortification of the city was begun in the 12th century, the most imposing military architecture dates from the 17th and 18th centuries, when the English – the favourite targets of Malouin privateers – posed a constant threat.

Orientation

Saint Malo consists of the resort towns of Saint Servan, Saint Malo, Paramé and Rothéneuf. Saint Malo's old city, signposted as Intra-Muros (meaning 'within the walls') and also known as the Ville Close, is connected to Paramé by the Sillon Isthmus.

Information

Tourist Office Saint Malo's tourist office (☎ 02 99 56 64 48; fax 02 99 40 93 13) is just outside the old city on Esplanade Saint Vincent. It is open Monday to Saturday from 9 am to noon and 2 to 6 pm. From April to June and in September, it stays open to 7 pm and keeps Sunday hours from 10 am to noon

SAINT MALO

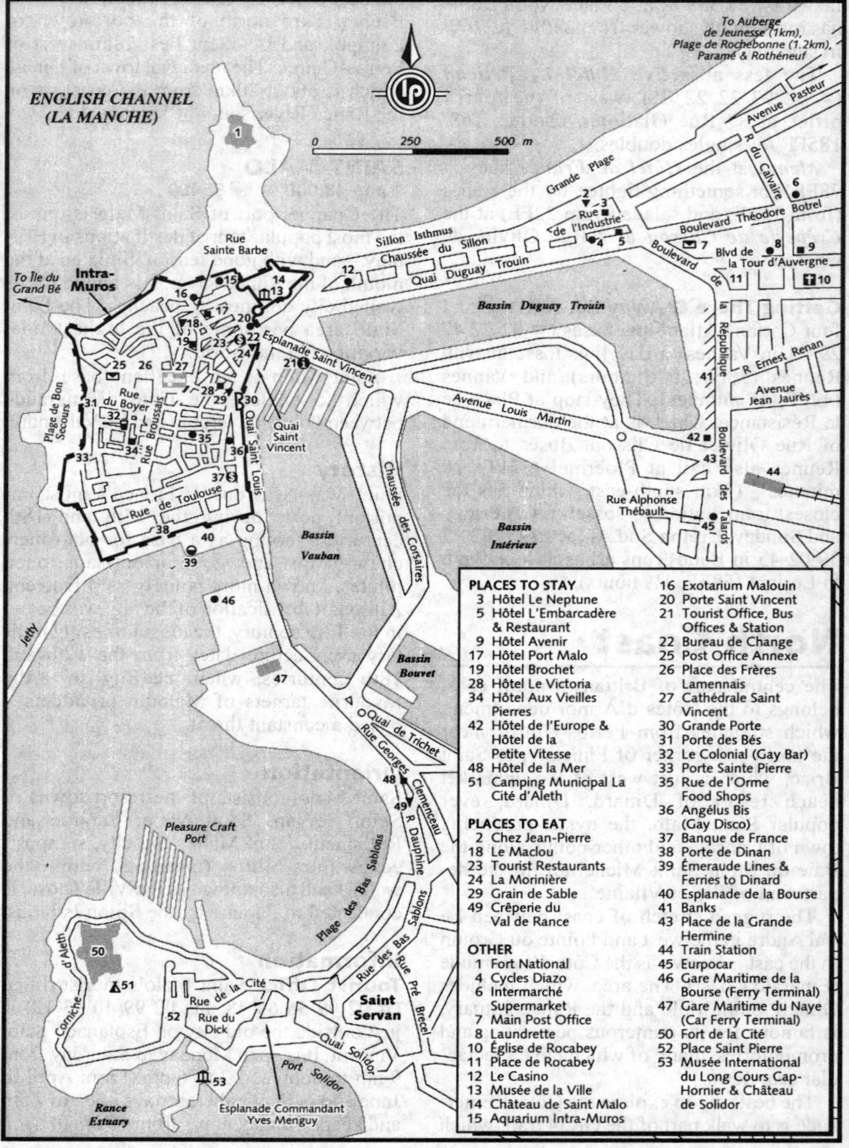

To Auberge de Jeunesse (1km), Plage de Rochebonne (1.2km), Paramé & Rothéneuf
ENGLISH CHANNEL (LA MANCHE)
0 250 500 m
Avenue Pasteur
R du Calvaire
Grande Plage
Rue de l'Industrie
Boulevard Théodore Botrel
Sillon Isthmus
Chaussée du Sillon
Quai Duguay Trouin
Boulevard de la République
Blvd de la Tour d'Auvergne
Rue Sainte Barbe
To Île du Grand Bé
Intra-Muros
Bassin Duguay Trouin
Esplanade Saint Vincent
R. Ernest Renan
Avenue Jean Jaurès
Avenue Louis Martin
Plage de Bon Secours
Rue du Boyer
Rue Broussais
Quai Saint Vincent
Quai Saint Louis
Boulevard des Talards
Rue de Toulouse
Rue Alphonse Thébault
Bassin Vauban
Chaussée des Corsaires
Bassin Intérieur
Jetty
Bassin Bouvet
Quai de Trichet
Rue Georges Clemenceau
R Dauphine
Pleasure Craft Port
Plage des Bas Sablons
Rue des Bas Sablons
Rue Pré Brecel
Corniche d'Aleth
Rue de la Cité
Rue du Dick
Saint Servan
Quai Solidor
Port Solidor
Rance Estuary
Esplanade Commandant Yves Menguy
PLACES TO STAY
3 Hôtel Le Neptune
5 Hôtel L'Embarcadère & Restaurant
9 Hôtel Avenir
17 Hôtel Port Malo
19 Hôtel Brochet
28 Hôtel Le Victoria
34 Hôtel Aux Vieilles Pierres
42 Hôtel de l'Europe & Hôtel de la Petite Vitesse
48 Hôtel de la Mer
51 Camping Municipal La Cité d'Aleth
PLACES TO EAT
2 Chez Jean-Pierre
18 Le Maclou
23 Tourist Restaurants
24 La Morinière
29 Grain de Sable
49 Crêperie du Val de Rance
OTHER
1 Fort National
4 Cycles Diazo
6 Intermarché Supermarket
7 Main Post Office
8 Laundrette
10 Église de Rocabey
11 Place de Rocabey
12 Le Casino
13 Musée de la Ville
14 Château de Saint Malo
15 Aquarium Intra-Muros
16 Exotarium Malouin
20 Porte Saint Vincent
21 Tourist Office, Bus Offices & Station
22 Bureau de Change
25 Post Office Annexe
26 Place des Frères Lamennais
27 Cathédrale Saint Vincent
30 Grande Porte
31 Porte des Bés
32 Le Colonial (Gay Bar)
33 Porte Sainte Pierre
35 Rue de l'Orme Food Shops
36 Angélus Bis (Gay Disco)
37 Banque de France
38 Porte de Dinan
39 Émeraude Lines & Ferries to Dinard
40 Esplanade de la Bourse
41 Banks
43 Place de la Grande Hermine
44 Train Station
45 Europcar
46 Gare Maritime de la Bourse (Ferry Terminal)
47 Gare Maritime du Naye (Car Ferry Terminal)
50 Fort de la Cité
52 Place Saint Pierre
53 Musée International du Long Cours Cap-Hornier & Château de Solidor

and 2 to 6 pm. In July and August, it's open Monday to Saturday from 8.30 am to 8 pm and on Sunday from 10 am to 7 pm.

Money There are half a dozen banks near the train station, along Blvd de la République and at Place de Rocabey. All are open on weekdays and keep about the same hours: 8.30 am to noon and 1.30 to 4.30 pm.

In the old city, Banque de France at 7 Rue d'Asfeld is open weekdays from 8.45 am to noon and 1.30 to 3.30 pm. The Caisse d'Épargne at 14 Rue de Dinan (three blocks up from Porte de Dinan) is open weekdays from 8.45 am to noon and 1.30 to 5.30 pm (5 pm on Friday). The Bureau de Change at 2 Rue Saint Vincent gives a horrible rate, but it's open daily from mid-March to mid-November from 10 am to 7 pm (9 am to 10 pm from June to September).

Post Saint Malo's main post office is near Place de Rocabey at 1 Blvd de la Tour d'Auvergne. It is open weekdays from 8 am to 7 pm and on Saturday till noon. More convenient is the branch in the old city at 4 Place des Frères Lamennais. It opens weekdays from 8.30 am to 12.30 pm and 1.30 to 6.30 pm. On Saturday it closes at noon. Both offices offer exchange services.

Laundry The laundrette at 25 Blvd de la Tour d'Auvergne, north-east of Place de Rocabey, is open daily from 7 am to 9 pm.

Old City

During the fighting of August 1944, which drove the Germans from Saint Malo, 80% of the old city was destroyed. After the war, the principal historical monuments were faithfully reconstructed, but the rest of the area was rebuilt in the style of the 17th and 18th centuries. **Cathédrale Saint Vincent**, begun in the 11th century, is noted for its medieval stained-glass windows. The striking modern altar in bronze reveals a Celtic influence.

The **ramparts**, which were built at various times through the centuries, survived the war and are largely original. They afford superb views in all directions: the freight port, the interior of the old city and the Channel. There is free access to the **ramparts walk** at Porte de Dinan, the Grande Porte, Porte Saint Vincent and elsewhere. The remains of the 17th century **Fort National** (☎ 02 99 46 91 25), built by Vauban and used for many years as a prison, are just beyond the northern stretch. They can be visited from Easter to late October.

Museums The **Musée de la Ville** (☎ 02 99 40 71 57), in the Château de Saint Malo at Porte Saint Vincent, deals with the history of the city and the Pays Malouin (the area around Saint Malo). It opens daily from 10 am to noon and 2 to 6 pm (closed on Monday in winter). Prices are 26/13FF for adults/students. For 40/20FF, you can visit the Musée International du Long Cours Cap-Hornier in Saint Servan too.

The **Aquarium Intra-Muros** (☎ 02 99 40 91 86), which has about 100 tanks, is built into the walls of the old city around the corner, next to Place Vauban. It is open daily from 10 am to 7 pm (10 pm in July and August). Prices for adults/students are 30/20FF. The **Grand Aquarium Saint Malo** (☎ 02 99 21 19 02) is Europe's first circular aquarium. From mid-June to September it's open from 9 am to 9 pm and costs 50/44FF for adults/students. The rest of the year it is open from 9.30 am to 6 pm and costs 44/30FF. To get there take bus No 5 from the train station and hop off at La Madeleine stop.

Île du Grand Bé

You can reach the Île du Grand Bé, where the 18th century writer Chateaubriand is buried, on foot at low tide via the Porte des Bés and the nearby old city gates. Be warned though: when the tide comes in (and it comes in fast), the causeway remains impassable for about six hours.

Saint Servan

Saint Servan's fortress, **Fort de la Cité**, was built in the mid-18th century and served as a German base for several years during WWII. The German pillboxes of thick steel flanking the fortress walls were heavily scarred by Allied shells in August 1944.

The interesting **Musée International du Long Cours Cap-Hornier** (☎ 02 99 40 71 58) is housed in the 14th century Château de Solidor on Esplanade Menguy. The museum has nautical instruments, ship models and other exhibits related to the sailors who sailed around Cape Horn between the early 17th and early 20th centuries. There is a great view from the top of the tower. The museum is open from 10 am to noon and 2 to 6 pm daily (closed Monday from October to April). Prices are 20/10FF for adults/students or 40/20FF if you want to visit the Musée de la Ville in the old city as well.

Beaches

Just outside the old city walls to the west is **Plage de Bon Secours** with a protected tidal pool for bathing. Saint Servan's **Plage des Bas Sablons** has a cement wall that keeps the sea from receding all the way to the yacht harbour at low tide. The **Grande Plage**, which stretches north-eastward from the Sillon Isthmus, is spiked with tree trunks that act as breakers. **Plage de Rochebonne** is 1km or so to the north-east. The walk from the Grande Plage to the Plage des Bas Sablons via the ramparts of the Intra-Muros is especially enjoyable at sunset.

Walking & Cycling

From Saint Malo or the Château de Solidor in Saint Servan, you can walk (or cycle) via the Barrage de la Rance to Dinard, a distance of about 12km.

Organised Tours

Bus For information on bus tours of the Saint Malo area (including Mont Saint Michel), see Bus under the Getting There & Away section.

Boat From April or May to September, Émeraude Lines (☎ 02 99 40 48 40) runs small ferries from its dock just outside the old city's Porte de Dinan to the Îles Chausey (60/125FF one way/return; 90 minutes each way), the Île Cézembre (50FF return; 20 minutes each way) and Dinan (90/120FF one way/return; 2½ hours each way). For details on its ferry service to Dinard, see Getting There & Away in the Dinard section.

Places to Stay

Camping The *Camping Municipal La Cité d'Aleth* (☎ 02 99 81 60 91), at the western tip of Saint Servan next to Fort de la Cité, has an exceptional view in all directions. This place stays open all year and always has room for another small tent. It costs 85FF for a tent site for three people with a car. People pay 18.50FF each, and a tent site and a place to park is 26FF. In summer, take bus No 1. During the rest of the year, your best bet is bus No 6.

Hostel The *Auberge de Jeunesse* (☎ 02 99 40 29 80; fax 02 99 40 29 02) is at 37 Ave du Père Umbricht in Paramé, just under 2km north-east of the train station. A bed in a room for four or six people is 64FF (69FF from June to August), while doubles cost 77FF (82FF in summer) per person and singles with washbasin are 70FF (all including breakfast). From the train station, take bus No 5.

Hotels – Place de Rocabey The small *Hôtel Avenir* (☎ 02 99 56 13 33) at 31 Blvd de la Tour d'Auvergne has rooms for 120FF (150FF with shower). Hall showers cost 15FF. Close to the Grande Plage, ***Hôtel Le Neptune*** (☎ 02 99 56 82 15) is an older, family-run place at 21 Rue de l'Industrie. Adequate doubles with washbasin cost from 120FF. Doubles with shower and toilet cost 190FF. Hall showers are 15FF.

The ***Hôtel L'Embarcadère*** (☎ 02 99 40 39 58) at 53 Quai Duguay Trouin is on the Sillon Isthmus a few hundred metres west of Place de Rocabey. Ordinary doubles with one bed start at 120FF, while a twin is 160FF. Showers cost 10FF. Parking is easy in the Place de Rocabey area.

Hotels – Train Station Area The ***Hôtel de l'Europe*** (☎ 02 99 56 13 42) is at 44 Blvd de la République, across the roundabout from the train station. Modern, nondescript doubles start at 160FF (170FF from mid-April to August). Rooms with a shower and without/with a toilet are 190/200FF (230/260FF from May to August). There are no hall showers. Like other places in this area, the hotel is somewhat noisy. The ***Hôtel de la Petite Vitesse*** (☎ 02 99 56 01 93), next door at No 42, has good-sized but noisy doubles from 160FF (190FF with shower) and two-bed quads from 290FF. Hall showers are 25FF. Telephone reservations are not accepted in summer.

Hotels – Old City The friendly, family-run ***Hôtel Aux Vieilles Pierres*** (☎ 02 99 56 46 80) is in a quiet part of the old city at 4 Rue des Lauriers (or 9 Rue Thévenard). Rooms start at 130FF (160FF with shower); hall showers are free. The ***Hôtel Le Victoria*** (☎ 02 99 56 34 01; fax 02 99 40 32 78) is more in the thick of things at 4 Rue des Orbettes. It has doubles from 150FF (185FF with shower), 167FF in summer. Hall showers are free.

The ***Hôtel Port Malo*** (☎ 02 99 20 52 99; fax 02 99 40 29 53) is a medium-sized place 150m from Porte Saint Vincent at 15 Rue Sainte Barbe. Singles/doubles with shower and toilet are 145/175FF (175/220FF in July and August). The ***Hôtel Brochet*** (☎ 02 99 56 30 00), due south at 1 Rue de la Corne de Cerf, is excellent value for its category. Its singles/doubles (accessible by lift) with shower and TV start at 200/235FF (more in summer), depending on the room size.

Hotel – Saint Servan The ***Hôtel de la Mer*** (☎ 02 99 81 61 05) at 3 Rue Dauphine is right next to Plage des Bas Sablons and about 1km from the old city. Singles/doubles start at 145/165FF (165/190FF in summer). If you call after arriving in Saint Malo, they'll hold a room for an hour or so. To get there, take bus No 2 or 3 and get off at Rue Georges Clemenceau.

Places to Eat

Restaurants The old city has lots of ***tourist restaurants***, crêperies and pizzerias in the area between Porte Saint Vincent, the cathedral and the Grande Porte. There are several crêperies just inside Porte de Dinan. More tourist restaurants line the streets nearest the Plage de Bon Secours.

As good as any place for seafood is ***La Morinière*** (☎ 02 99 40 85 77) at 9 Rue Jacques Cartier with *menus* at 70 and 90FF (closed Wednesday). Or try the more intimate ***Grain de Sable*** (☎ 02 99 56 68 72), on the same street at No 2, which serves an excellent fish soup. For takeaway sandwiches available until 1 am daily (closed from 2.30 to 5.30 pm), head for ***Le Maclou*** (☎ 02 99 56 50 41) at 22 Rue Sainte Barbe.

Chez Jean-Pierre (☎ 02 99 40 40 48), popular for pizza and pasta (from 50FF), has an enviable location across from the Grande Plage at 60 Chaussée du Sillon. It's open seven days a week. The restaurant at the ***Hôtel L'Embarcadère*** (see Places to Stay), which is very popular with dock workers, has excellent-value *menus* for 49 and 65FF.

Near Plage des Bas Sablons in Saint Servan, ***Crêperie du Val de Rance*** (☎ 02 99 81 64 68) at 11 Rue Dauphine serves Breton-style crêpes and galettes (8 to 35FF) all day. Order a bottle of dry Val de Rance cider and drink it – as they all do here – from a teacup.

Self-Catering In the old city, you'll find a number of ***food shops*** along Rue de l'Orme, including an excellent cheese shop (closed Sunday and Monday) at No 9, a fruit and vegetable shop (closed Sunday) at No 8 and two boulangeries. An ***Intermarché*** supermarket is on Blvd Théodore Botrel. It's open from Monday to Saturday from 9 am to 7.15 pm. In July and August, it's also open on Sunday morning.

Entertainment

During July and August, classical music concerts are held in Cathédrale Saint Vincent and elsewhere in the city. Ask the tourist office for details.

For nightlife, try ***Le Casino*** (☎ 02 99 40 64 00) with its bars, brasserie, pizzeria, slot machines and disco just outside the Intra-Muros on Quai Duguay Trouin.

Getting There & Away

Bus The bus station, from which several companies operate, is at Esplanade Saint Vincent beside the tourist office. Many of the buses departing from here also stop at the train station.

Courriers Bretons (☎ 02 99 56 79 09) has regular services to Cancale (some via Pointe du Grouin; 20.50FF), Fougères (48FF; Monday to Saturday only), Pontorson (45FF; one hour) and Mont Saint Michel (50FF; 1¼ hours). The daily bus to Mont Saint Michel leaves at 11.10 am and returns around 5.30 pm. During July and August, there are five return trips a day. Courriers Bretons' office is open weekdays from 8.30 am to 12.15 pm and 2 to 6.15 pm and Saturday morning (all day in summer).

TIV (☎ 02 99 40 82 67), with identical opening hours, has buses to Cancale (20FF), Dinan (33.50FF), Dinard (19FF) and Rennes (54.50FF).

Pansart Voyages (☎ 02 99 40 85 96), whose office is open Monday to Saturday (daily in July and August), offers various excursions. All-day tours to Mont Saint Michel (115/55/104FF for adults/children/students) operate about two times a week from April to October, three times in July and August.

Train The train station (☎ 02 99 56 04 40 or ☎ 08 36 35 35 35) is 1.5km east of the old city along Ave Louis Martin. The information counters are open weekdays from 5.30 am to 8 pm (Saturday from 6 am, Sunday from 7.30 am). There is direct service to Paris' Gare Montparnasse (290FF; 4¼ hours) in July and August only. During the rest of the year, you have to change trains at Rennes (67FF; one hour), but the trip takes as little as three hours. More locally, there are services to Dinan (44FF; one hour; six a day) and to Lannion (155FF; four hours; six a day). You can also get to Quimper (206FF).

Car To contact ADA, call ☎ 02 99 56 06 15. Avis (☎ 02 99 40 18 54) and Budget (☎ 02 99 40 15 10) have desks at the Gare Maritime du Naye. Europcar (☎ 02 99 56 75 17) is near the train station at 16 Blvd des Talards.

Boat Ferries link Saint Malo with the Channel Islands (Îles Anglo-Normandes), Weymouth and Portsmouth. Services are significantly reduced in winter. For information on schedules and tariffs, see the Sea section in the Getting There & Away chapter.

Hydrofoils, catamarans and the like depart from the Gare Maritime de la Bourse; car ferries leave from the Gare Maritime du Naye. Both are south of the walled city.

Condor (☎ 02 99 20 03 00) has catamaran and jetfoil services to Jersey (275FF one day excursion) and Guernsey (315FF) from mid-March to mid-November and up to mid-September to Sark and Alderney (525FF for a three day excursion). Condor's service to Weymouth (250FF one way; 5½ hours) operates daily from late April to October.

Émeraude Lines (☎ 02 99 40 48 40) has ferries to Jersey, Guernsey and Sark. Service is most regular between late March and mid-November. Car ferries to Jersey run all year except in January and to Guernsey from April to October only.

Between mid-March and mid-December, Brittany Ferries (☎ 02 99 40 64 41) has boats to Portsmouth once or twice a day leaving from the Gare Maritime du Naye. One-way passenger fares are 180 to 260FF and, for a car, 580 to 1370FF including driver. In winter, ferries sail four to five times a week.

Getting Around

Bus Saint Malo Bus has seven lines, but line No 1 runs in summer only. Tickets cost 7FF and can be used as transfers for one hour after they're time-stamped; a carnet of 10 costs 49FF and there's a one day pass for 20FF. In summer, Saint Malo Bus tickets are also valid on Courriers Bretons buses for travel within Saint Malo. Buses usually operate until about 7.30 pm, but in summer certain lines keep running until about midnight.

The company's information office at Esplanade Saint Vincent (☎ 02 99 56 06 06) is open from 8.30 or 9 am to noon and 2 to 6.15 or 6.30 pm daily in summer and from 2.15 to 6 pm from September to June.

Esplanade Saint Vincent is linked with the train station by bus Nos 1, 2, 3 and 4.

Taxi Taxis can be ordered on ☎ 02 99 81 30 30.

Boat Shuttles to Dinard (see the Dinard section for details) depart from just outside the old city's Porte de Dinan.

Bicycle Cycles Diazo (☎ 02 99 40 31 63) at 47 Quai Duguay Trouin is open Monday to Saturday from 9 am to noon and 2 to 6 pm. Three-speeds cost 55FF and mountain bikes 85FF a day.

DINARD

• pop 10,000 ✉ 35800

While Saint Malo's old city and beaches are oriented towards middle-class families, Dinard attracts a well heeled clientele (especially from the UK), who have been coming here since the mid-19th century. Indeed, Dinard has the feel of a turn-of-the-century beach resort, especially in summer, with its striped bathing tents, beachside carnival rides and spike-roofed *belle époque* mansions perched above the water. The air is cool and fragrant thanks to the many pine and cedar trees scattered around the town.

Staying in Dinard can be a bit hard on the budget, but since the town is just across the Rance Estuary from Saint Malo (12km by road), you can easily come over by bus or boat for the day.

Orientation

Plage de l'Écluse (also called Grande Plage), which is right down the hill from the tourist office, runs along the northern edge of town between Pointe du Moulinet and Pointe de la Malouine. To get there from the Embarcadère (the pier where boats from Saint Malo dock) climb the stairs and walk 200m north-west along Rue Georges Clemenceau. Place de Newquay, with a couple of budget hotels, is 1km south-west of the tourist office.

Information

Tourist Office The tourist office (☎ 02 99 46 94 12; fax 02 99 88 21 07) is in a round, colonnaded building at 2 Blvd Féart. It is open Monday to Saturday from 9 am to noon and 2 to 6 pm (to 7.30 pm with no midday break in July and August).

Money There are a number of banks on Rue Levavasseur and a Caisse d'Épargne at 30 Blvd Féart, opposite the police station and open weekdays from 8.45 am to 12.15 pm and 1.45 to 5.30 pm (4 pm on Saturday).

Post The main post office is just south of Ave Édouard VII at Place Rochaid. It is open weekdays from 8 am till noon and 1.30 to 6.30 pm and on Saturday morning.

St Bartholomew Church

This Anglican church (☎ 02 99 46 77 00), built from contributions in 1871, is at 3 Rue Faber, 50m up the hill from 25 Ave George V. The church and its library are open every day from 10 am to 6 pm.

Musée du Site Balnéaire

The town's only real museum (☎ 02 99 46 81 05), at 12 Rue des Français Libres, focuses on the history of the area and, in particular, Dinard's development as a seaside resort. But it's really more interesting as a building than a museum. The Villa Eugénie was built in 1868 for the wife of Napoleon III who – alas – never got to stay here. It is open from April to October from 10 am to noon and 2 to 6 pm. Prices are 16/10FF for adults/students.

Aquarium

The unspectacular aquarium (☎ 02 99 46 13 90) of the Muséum National d'Histoire Naturelle is at 17 Ave George V. It's open daily mid-May to mid-September from 10.30 am to 12.30 pm and 3.30 pm (2.30 pm on Sunday) to 7.30 pm. Prices are 10/5FF for adults/students up to the age of 25.

DINARD

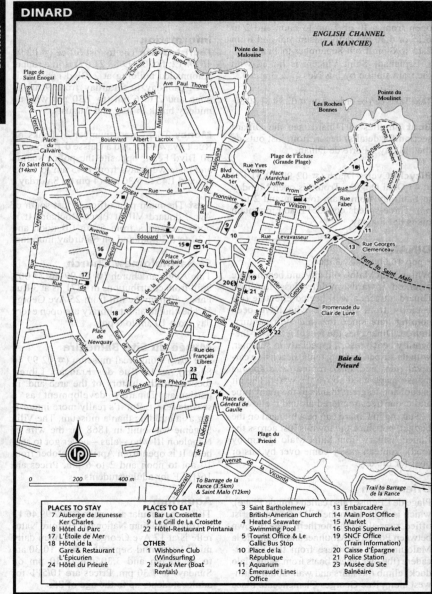

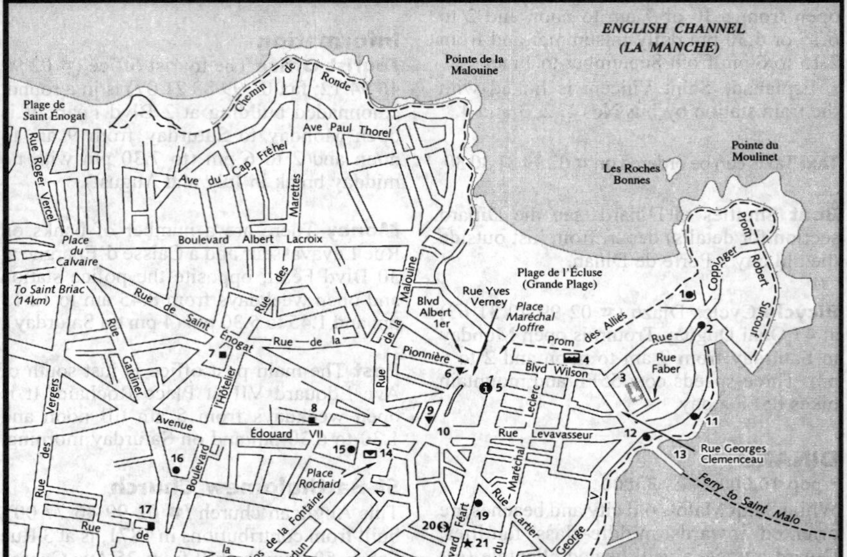

PLACES TO STAY
- 7 Auberge de Jeunesse Ker Charles
- 8 Hôtel du Parc
- 17 L'Étoile de Mer
- 18 Hôtel de la Gare & Restaurant L'Épicurien
- 24 Hôtel du Prieuré

PLACES TO EAT
- 6 Bar La Croisette
- 9 Le Grill de La Croisette
- 22 Hôtel-Restaurant Printania

OTHER
- 1 Wishbone Club (Windsurfing)
- 2 Kayak Mer (Boat Rentals)
- 3 Saint Bartholemew British-American Church
- 4 Heated Seawater Swimming Pool
- 5 Tourist Office & Le Gallic Bus Stop
- 10 Place de la République
- 11 Aquarium
- 12 Émeraude Lines Office
- 13 Embarcadère
- 14 Main Post Office
- 15 Market
- 16 Shopi Supermarket
- 19 SNCF Office (Train Information)
- 20 Caisse d'Épargne
- 21 Police Station
- 23 Musée du Site Balnéaire

Barrage de la Rance

If you drive or walk (12km) between Saint Malo and Dinard along the D168, you'll pass the Usine Marémotrice de la Rance (Rance Tidal Power Station; ☎ 02 99 16 37 00), a hydroelectric dam across the estuary of the Rance River that uses Saint Malo's extraordinarily high tides to generate nearly 10% of the electricity consumed in Brittany. The 750m-long dam, built between 1963 and 1967, has 24 turbines that are turned on an incoming tide by sea water flowing into the estuary and on an outgoing tide by water draining into the sea. Near the lock on the Dinard side is a small, subterranean visitors centre that is open daily from 8.30 am to 8 pm. It has an interesting film in English on how the power station works. Entrance is free.

Activities

Swimming Wide, sandy **Plage de l'Écluse** is surrounded by fashionable hotels, a casino and changing cubicles. Picasso used the beach as the setting for several of his tableaux in the 1920s, and you'll see reproductions of them planted in the sand. Next to the beach is the **Piscine Olympique** (☎ 02 99 46 22 77), an Olympic-sized swimming pool filled with heated sea water. It's open daily from 10 am to 12.30 pm and 3 to 7.30 pm (Sunday to 6.30 pm), and prices are 12/10FF for adults/students on weekdays and 24/15FF on weekends and holidays. **Plage du Prieuré**, 1km to the south along Blvd Féart, isn't as smart as Plage de l'Écluse but is less crowded. **Plage de Saint Énogat** is 1km west of Plage de l'Écluse on the other side of Pointe de la Malouine.

Windsurfing The Wishbone Club (☎ 02 99 88 15 20), next to the swimming pool on Plage de l'Écluse, offers windsurfing instruction for 150FF per hour and also hires out boards. Depending on the type, they cost from 70 to 110FF per hour (180 to 250FF for a half-day). Wishbone operates every day from 9 am to 10 pm in July and August, and on weekends only during the rest of the year. It also rents catamarans and kayaks for 180/60FF per hour.

Kayaking Kayak Mer (☎ 02 99 46 90 46) near Plage de l'Écluse at 10 Ave George V rents kayaks (120FF a half-day) and gives instruction in July and August.

Walking & Hiking Beautiful seaside trails extend along the coast in both directions from Dinard. The tourist office sells a topoguide (5FF) with maps and information in French on five coastal trails entitled *Sentiers du Littoral du Canton de Dinard*.

Dinard's famous **Promenade du Clair de Lune** (Moonlight Promenade) runs along the Baie du Prieuré, south-west from the Embarcadère to Place du Général de Gaulle. What may be the town's most attractive walk links the Promenade du Clair de Lune with Plage de l'Écluse via the rocky coast of **Pointe du Moulinet**, from where Saint Malo's old city can be seen across the water. This trail continues westward along the coast, passing Plage de Saint Énogat en route to Saint Briac, some 14km away. Bikes are not allowed. Ask the tourist office for details of the sound-and-light show on the Promenade du Clair de Lune from mid-June to mid-September.

Special Events

A festival of British film is held in Dinard in early October – thus the statue of director Alfred Hitchcock, two seagulls perched on his shoulders, standing near the entrance to Plage de l'Écluse.

Places to Stay

Hostel The small but attractive ***Auberge de Jeunesse Ker Charles*** (☎ 02 99 46 40 02) at 8 Blvd l'Hôtelier (about 600m west of the tourist office) is open all year. A bed costs 80FF including breakfast.

Hotels A number of relatively inexpensive hotels can be found around Place de Newquay. The ordinary ***Hôtel de la Gare*** (☎ 02 99 46 10 84) at 28 Rue de la Corbinais has doubles with washbasin and bidet from

120FF. Reception is inside the ground floor restaurant. The friendly ***L'Étoile de Mer*** (☎ 02 99 46 11 19) at 52 Rue de la Gare has rooms with shower starting from 220FF.

The ***Hôtel du Parc*** (☎ 02 99 46 11 39; fax 02 99 88 10 58), a bit closer to the centre of town at 20 Ave Édouard VII, is a medium-sized hotel with half a dozen cheap rooms starting at 140FF for one or two people, 160FF with shower and 230FF with shower and TV.

If you can afford a little more, ***Hôtel du Prieuré*** (☎ 02 99 46 13 74; fax 02 99 46 81 90) is a lovely little place overlooking the beach and Saint Malo at 1 Place du Général de Gaulle. Singles and doubles with shower are 260FF.

Places to Eat

Restaurants There are plenty of places around the tourist office that sell crêpes and the like. ***L'Épicurien*** at the Hôtel de la Gare (see Places to Stay) is a family-style restaurant with a good-value lunch *menu* for 45FF which includes a choice from the salad bar.

Bar La Croisette (☎ 02 99 46 43 32), a few steps west of the tourist office at 4 Rue Yves Verney, has a good, four course *menu* available for 59FF. It is closed on Monday evening and Tuesday, except during holidays. It has a branch a few steps away at 4 Place de la République.

Hôtel-Restaurant Printania (☎ 02 99 46 13 07) at 5 Ave George V on the seafront near the Port de Plaisance is not cheap (*menus* start at 90FF) but worth it for the view from the sunny terrace which looks out towards Saint Malo.

Self-Catering The ***Shopi*** supermarket north of Place de Newquay at 45 Rue Gardiner is open from 8.30 am to 12.30 pm and 2.30 to 7.30 pm Monday to Saturday and on Sunday morning from 9.30 am to 12.30 pm. There's a large ***covered market*** west of the post office on Place Rochaid.

Getting There & Away

Bus TIV buses (☎ 02 99 40 82 67 in Saint Malo) leave Esplanade Saint Vincent in Saint Malo and pick up passengers at the train station there before continuing on via the Barrage de la Rance to Dinard and the tourist office (stop: Le Gallic). The buses run slightly less often than once an hour until about 6 pm (to Saint Malo) and 7 pm (to Dinard). The one-way fare is 19FF.

Train Trains no longer stop in Dinard, but SNCF has an information office (☎ 02 99 29 10 35 or ☎ 08 36 35 35 35) at 31bis Blvd Féart. It is open Tuesday to Saturday from 10 am till noon and 2 to 6.30 pm.

Boat From April to late September, the Bus de Mer (Sea Bus) run by Émeraude Lines (☎ 02 99 40 48 40 in Saint Malo, ☎ 02 99 46 10 45 in Dinard) links Saint Malo's Porte de Dinan with Dinard's Embarcadère at 27 Ave George V. The trip costs 20/30FF one way/return (12/20FF for children under 12) and takes 10 minutes. Transporting a bicycle costs 15FF one way. There are eight to 16 runs a day between 9.30 or 10 am and sometime around 6 or 7 pm. In July and August, there are three or four evening sailings.

Getting Around

You can order a taxi on ☎ 02 99 46 88 80 or ☎ 02 99 88 15 15.

POINTE DU GROUIN DOMAINE NATUREL DÉPARTEMENTAL

This nature reserve is on the beautiful and very wild coast between Saint Malo and Cancale. An effort is being made to protect and revitalise the vegetation here. Île des Landes, just off the coast, is home to a large number of giant black cormorants. Some 90cm long and with a wingspan of 170cm, the cormorants are among the largest sea birds in Europe. The tourist office in Cancale has a basic map of the area and French-language brochures that describe the local flora and fauna.

Getting There & Away

Via the GR34 coastal trail (also called the Chemin des Douaniers in this area), Pointe du Grouin is 7km from Cancale and 18km from Saint Malo. Count on about five hours of walking from Saint Malo. By road (the D201), it's 4km from Cancale and 18km from Saint Malo.

There is bus service from Saint Malo and Cancale during the summer school holidays (roughly July and August). Daily during the rest of the year, at least one of nine Courriers Bretons buses (☎ 02 99 56 79 09 in Saint Malo) on the Saint Malo-Cancale run (21FF) stops at the reserve.

CANCALE

• pop 5000 ✉ 35260

Cancale, a relaxed fishing port 14km east of Saint Malo, is famed for its offshore *parcs à huîtres* (oyster beds). The town even has a museum dedicated to oyster farming and shellfish, the **Ferme Marine** (☎ 02 99 89 69 99), which is on the Corniche de l'Aurore south-west of the port. It is open daily from mid-February to October and prices are 38/30/18FF for adults/students/children.

Orientation

Port de la Houle occupies one side of a small bay. Cancale's fleet of small fishing boats moors just off the sandy bathing beach to the north-east within sight of the oyster beds. The town overlooks Port de la Houle from the north. Its centre is Place de l'Église.

Information

Tourist Office The tourist office (☎ 02 99 89 63 72) is south-west of Place de l'Église at 44 Rue du Port. It is open Monday to Saturday from 10 am to 12.30 pm and 2 to 7 pm. Sunday hours are 10 am to 1 pm. In summer it's open daily from 9 am to 6 pm.

From June to August there's a tourist office annexe at Port de la Houle, which is open daily from 11 am to 1 pm and 4.30 to 8.30 pm.

Money There are several banks around Place de l'Église, including the Banque Populaire, which is open weekdays.

Post The main post office is north-west of the tourist office on Ave du Général de Gaulle. It is open weekdays from 8 am to noon and 2.30 to 5.30 pm. The hours on Saturday are 9 am to noon.

Places to Stay

Camping The ***Camping Municipal Le Grouin*** (☎ 02 99 89 63 79) is 6km north of Cancale near Pointe du Grouin and a fine beach. It's open from early March to mid-September. There are several other private camp sites in the area.

Hotels The ***Hôtel La Cotriade*** (☎ 02 99 89 61 78), 23 Quai Gambetta, has doubles with washbasin/shower from 150/190FF. It is closed from mid-November to March. Just a short distance to the west and a block inland from the water, the ***Hôtel de l'Arrivée*** (☎ 02 99 89 80 46), situated at 28 Rue Victor Hugo, has doubles/triples for 150/200FF. It is open all year.

Up Rue du Port at No 39, the small ***Hôtel de la Mairie*** (☎ 02 99 89 60 10) has doubles from 180FF.

Places to Eat

Most of the restaurants at Port de la Houle specialise, appropriately enough, in oysters, which cost a minimum 62FF a dozen. ***Le Pêcheur*** (☎ 02 99 89 61 58), at the southern end of Rue du Port at 1 Place de la Chapelle, is a good choice. It has *menus* from 75FF.

If, however, you prefer your oysters cheaper and direct from the source, walk 100m east in the direction of Pointe des Crolles and its lighthouse. Along the quay are several kiosks selling a dozen different types of oyster (numbered according to size and quality) and costing only 16 to 30FF a dozen.

In town, the ***Comod*** supermarket at Place de l'Église is open Monday to Saturday from 8.30 am to 12.30 pm and 2.45 to 7 pm. From mid-June to mid-September, it is open Monday to Saturday from 8.30 am to 1 pm and 2.30 to 7.30 pm, and on Sunday from 9 am to 12.30 pm.

Getting There & Away

Cancale has two bus stops, one behind the church on Place Lucidas and another a few hundred metres down the hill at Port de la

Houle next to the pungent Halle des Poissons (fish market). Courriers Bretons (☎ 02 99 56 79 09 in Saint Malo) and TIV (☎ 02 99 40 82 67 in Saint Malo) have year-round services to/from Saint Malo (21FF).

Getting Around

Loca'cycles (☎ 02 99 89 62 97), in the Bazar Parisien next to the tourist office at 42 Rue du Port, rents bicycles/mountain bikes for a flat 65/80FF fee plus an hourly supplement (35/40FF for the first hour, 10/9FF for subsequent ones). Thus an eight hour rental would be a costly 170/183FF. Loca'cycles is open from 8.30 am to 12.15 pm and 2.30 to 7 pm Monday to Saturday. In July and August there is no midday break.

DINAN

• pop 12,000 ✉ 22100

Perched above the Rance River Valley about 34km south-west of Saint Malo and 22km south of Dinard, the medieval town of Dinan has been attracting visitors for centuries. It was once completely surrounded by ramparts and more than a dozen stone towers and a good portion of the walls are still standing today, as are some beautiful 15th century half-timbered houses. The town's historic air is most palpable at the end of September during the Fête des Remparts, when Dinannais dressed in medieval garb are joined by some 40,000 visitors for a rollicking, two day festival in the tiny old city.

Orientation

Nearly everything of interest – except the picturesque port area on the Rance River to the north-east – is within the tight confines of the old city, which is centred around Place des Cordeliers and Place des Merciers. Place Duclos is the centre of the modern town.

Information

Tourist Office The tourist office (☎ 02 96 39 75 40; fax 02 96 39 01 64) at 6 Rue de l'Horloge is open Monday to Saturday from 8.30 am to 12.30 pm and 2 to 5.45 pm. From mid-June to September, it's open from 9 am to 7 pm and on Sunday from 10 am to 12.30 pm and 3 to 5.30 pm. The tourist office sells an excellent map and guide to Dinan for 15FF.

Money The Banque de France on Rue Thiers is open on weekdays from 8.45 am to noon and 1.30 to 3.45 pm.

Post The main post office at 7 Place Duclos is open on weekdays from 8.30 am to 6.30 pm, and on Saturday until noon.

Old City

Wandering the cobbled streets of the old city is Dinan's main attraction. Two streets not to miss – particularly if you're heading down to the port – are **Rue du Jerzual** and its continuation, the steep **Rue du Petit Fort**. They both have an endless number of galleries, expensive shops and some restaurants. The latter ends with a neck-craning view of the Viaduct de Dinan over the Rance.

Back up in the old city, the most attractive half-timbered houses hang over the central **Place des Merciers**. A few paces south, the **Tour de l'Horloge**, a clock tower whose tinny chimes rattle over the rooftops every quarter of an hour, rises from Rue de l'Horloge. Between April and September, you can climb up to its tiny balcony (14/8FF for adults/those under 18). **Église Saint Malo**, opposite 33 Grande Rue, dates from the late 15th century.

The pride of Dinan is the **Basilique Saint Sauveur**, which is on the square of the same name west of the park-like **Jardin Anglais** (English Garden). Its construction started in the 12th century. Inside you'll find a crypt containing the heart of Bertrand du Guesclin, a 14th century knight most noted for his hatred of the English, his fierce (and successful) battles to expel them from France and his rather ugly countenance.

East of the basilica, there's an excellent view over the Rance valley from **Tour Sainte Cathérine** and **Tour Cardinal**.

Musée du Château

Housed in the keep of the ruins of the 14th century castle on Rue du Château, the Musée du Château (☎ 02 96 39 45 20) relates the history of Dinan and includes a collection of polychrome carved wooden statues from the 16th century. The museum's hours vary depending on the season. From June to mid-October, it's open daily from 10 am to 6.30 pm; from mid-March to May and mid-October to mid-November it's open from 10 to 11.15 am and 2 to 5.15 pm (closed Tuesday); and from February to mid-March and mid-November to December it's open daily, except Tuesday, from 1.30 to 5.30 pm. Prices are 25FF for adults and 10FF for children and students.

Organised Tours

From April to September, Émeraude Lines (☎ 02 96 39 18 04) runs boats from Quai de la Rance at the riverside port (below the town and to the north of the viaduct) to Dinard and Saint Malo (2½ hours one way). There's usually only a single boat a day,

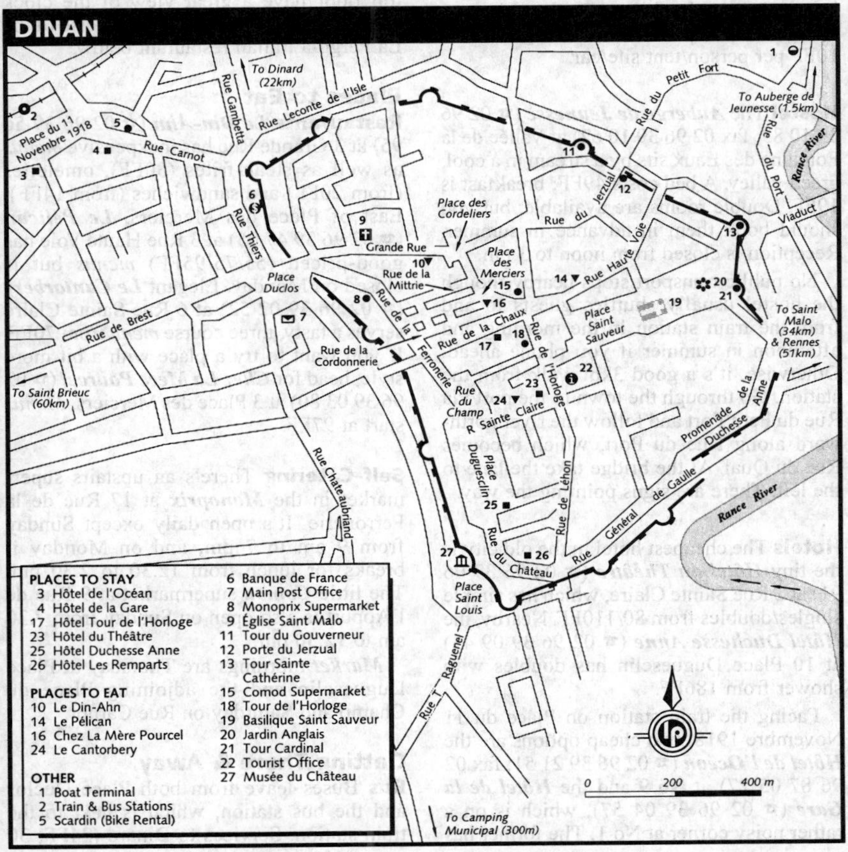

with the departure time dependent on the tide. The boat can leave Dinan any time in the morning or afternoon and doesn't make the return trip until the next day. When you get to Dinard or Saint Malo, you can easily return to Dinan by bus (or, from Saint Malo, by train too). For adults/children, tickets cost 90/55FF one way and 120/70FF return.

Places to Stay

Camping The nearest camping ground is the two star ***Camping Municipal*** (☎ 02 96 39 11 96) at 103 Rue Chateaubriand, which is just 2km south of Place Duclos. It's open from June to September and charges 13/13/10FF per person/tent site/car.

Hostel The ***Auberge de Jeunesse*** (☎ 02 96 39 10 83; fax 02 96 39 10 62) at Vallée de la Fontaine des Eaux sits by a stream in a cool, green valley. A bed costs 49FF; breakfast is 19FF. Double rooms are available, but you should book them in advance in summer. Reception is closed from noon to 3 pm.

No public transport stops nearby though the hostel usually shuttles guests to and from the train station in the morning and afternoon in summer if you phone ahead. Otherwise, it's a good 3km walk from the station. Go through the town to the port via Rue du Petit Fort and follow the river northward along Rue du Port, which becomes Rue du Quai. At the bridge take the lane to the left. There are signs pointing the way.

Hotels The cheapest hotel in the old city is the tiny ***Hôtel du Théâtre*** (☎ 02 96 39 06 91) at 2 Rue Sainte Claire, which has simple singles/doubles from 80/110FF. Nearby, the ***Hôtel Duchesse Anne*** (☎ 02 96 39 09 43) at 10 Place Duguesclin has doubles with shower from 186FF.

Facing the train station on Place du 11 Novembre 1918, two cheap options are the ***Hôtel de l'Océan*** (☎ 02 96 39 21 51; fax 02 96 87 05 27) at No 9 and the ***Hôtel de la Gare*** (☎ 02 96 39 04 57), which is on a rather noisy corner at No 1. The former has singles/doubles for 130/155FF, and the latter for 135/165FF.

Around from the chateau, the ***Hôtel Les Remparts*** (☎ 02 96 39 10 16; fax 02 96 85 33 69) at 6 Rue du Château has rooms with washbasin for 165FF and with shower for 265FF. It's on a busy road but most of the rooms are in the back. There's private parking (25FF) available.

The ***Hôtel Tour de l'Horloge*** (☎ 02 96 39 96 92; fax 02 96 85 06 99) is in a charming 18th century house at 5 Rue de la Chaux. It's on a cobbled, pedestrianised lane and has large rooms from 295FF. Those on the top floor have a great view of the clock tower and are unaffected by the noise of the La Pergola Italian restaurant below.

Places to Eat

Restaurants ***Le Din-Ahn*** (☎ 02 96 39 56 95) at 3 Grande Rue has inexpensive *menus* as well as steak-frites (30FF), omelettes (from 20FF) and sandwiches (from 14FF). East of Place des Merciers, ***Le Pélican*** (☎ 02 96 39 47 05) at 3 Rue Haute Voie has good-priced (55/75/95FF) *menus* but is closed on Monday. Elegant ***Le Cantorbery*** (☎ 02 96 39 02 52) at 6 Rue Sainte Claire serves a tasty, three course *menu* from 70FF. If you want to try a place with a bit more style, head for ***Chez La Mère Pourcel*** (☎ 02 96 39 03 80) at 3 Place des Merciers. *Menus* start at 97FF.

Self-Catering There's an upstairs supermarket in the ***Monoprix*** at 17 Rue de la Ferronerie. It's open daily except Sunday from 9 am to 7 pm, and on Monday it breaks for lunch from 12.30 to 2.30 pm. The little ***Comod*** supermarket at 9 Rue de l'Apport is also open on Sunday from 7.30 am to 12.30 pm.

Market mornings are Thursday at Place Duguesclin and the adjoining Place du Champ and Saturday on Rue Carnot.

Getting There & Away

Bus Buses leave from both Place Duclos and the bus station, which is next to the train station. Services to Dinard (24FF; 30

FRANCES LINZEE GORDON

Musée d'Unterlinden, Colmar

DANIEL ROBINSON

Place de la Carrière in Nancy, Lorraine

FRANCES LINZEE GORDON

Château de Chaumont, Loire Valley

FRANCES LINZEE GORDON

Cathédrale Notre Dame in Strasbourg, Lorraine

RICHARD NEBESKÝ

RICHARD NEBESKÝ

CHRIS MELLOR

RICHARD NEBESKÝ

RICHARD NEBESKÝ

The French Alps is a winter wonderland for those intent on a little adventure, whether it is skiing, parapente or just soaking up the sights, sounds and atmosphere of a typical Alpine village.

minutes) and Saint Malo (32FF; 40 minutes) are run by CAT (☎ 02 96 39 21 05), which has an office at the station and is open daily except Sunday from 8 am to noon and 2 to 6 pm. Buses to Rennes (46FF; 1¼ hours) are run by TAE.

Train The train station (☎ 02 96 39 22 39 or ☎ 08 36 35 35 35) is on Place du 11 Novembre 1918, about 1km north-west of the tourist office. Trains to Paris' Gare Montparnasse (302FF; 3¼ hours; up to seven a day) go via Rennes (71FF; one hour). More locally, there are services to Saint Malo (46FF; one hour; six a day).

Getting Around

Taxi You can call a taxi in Dinan on ☎ 02 96 39 06 00 or ☎ 02 96 39 10 60.

Bicycle Scardin (☎ 02 96 39 21 94), which is just up the road from the train station at 30 Rue Carnot, rents city bikes for 50/300FF a day/week.

PAIMPOL

• pop 7800 ✉ 22500

Paimpol (Pempoull in Breton) is a small fishing port on the Côte du Goëlo, the border region between the 'real' Brittany and the rest of the region. Until early this century, many of the fishermen who set sail from here would fish in the waters off Iceland for seven months at a stretch. Many never returned, the victims of storms and disease and now the subjects of folk tales and *chants de marins* (sea ditties).

Paimpol is the closest port to the Île de Bréhat (Enez Vriad in Breton), a tiny island 8km north of town whose local population of 450 is virtually overwhelmed by sun-worshipping tourists in summer.

Orientation

The centre of Paimpol is Place du Martray. A short distance to the east and north-east are the two *bassins* of the Port de Plaisance and the Baie de Paimpol. Place de la République lies between the train station and the port.

The 'Real' Brittany

Le Goëlo is the region marking the northern end of an imaginary line running from north to south that separates 'Breton Brittany' to the west from what the local people call 'Gallic Brittany' to the east. The demarcation line makes its way from Plouha (between Paimpol and Binic) south to Vannes in Morbihan. Someone from Paimpol, then, is a 'real' Breton, whereas a neighbour from Binic, a mere 25km south-east, is a 'Gallo-Breton' (in Breton, *gal* means 'abroad'). Gallic Brittany (also known as Upper Brittany, or Haute Bretagne) is predominantly French-speaking, while in Breton Brittany (Bretagne Basse, or Lower Brittany) many people still speak the regional tongue, heard these days mainly in Finistère.

Information

Tourist Office The tourist office (☎ 02 96 20 83 16) in Place de la République west of Place du Martray is open Tuesday to Saturday from 10 am to 12.30 pm and 2.30 to 6 pm. In July and August it's open Monday to Saturday from 9 am to 7.30 pm and Sunday from 10 am to 1.30 pm.

Money The Banque de Bretagne on Place du Martray is open Tuesday to Saturday from 8.30 am to 12.15 pm and 1.30 to 5.15 pm.

Post The main post office, which has exchange services, is north-east of the train station on Ave du Général de Gaulle. It is open weekdays from 9 am to noon and 1 to 5.30 pm. Saturday hours are 8 am to noon.

Laundry The laundrette at 23 Rue 18 Juin north of the train station is open daily from 8 am to 10 pm.

Places to Stay

The quiet, two star ***Camping Municipal de Cruckin*** (☎ 02 96 20 78 47) on Rue de

Cruckin is on the beautiful Baie de Kérity, 2km south-east of town off the road to Plouha. It is open from Easter to September and costs 7.50/6.50/5FF per person/tent site/car. For 25FF, you can also camp on the grounds of the ***Auberge de Jeunesse*** (☎ 02 96 20 83 60; fax 02 96 20 96 46) at the Château de Kerraoul, 1.5km north-west of the centre. A dorm bed with breakfast at the hostel costs 63FF, and it stays open all year.

There are a few inexpensive hotels fronting the port. The ***Hôtel Le Goëlo*** (☎ 02 96 20 82 74; fax 02 96 20 58 93) on Quai Duguay Trouin has simple singles/doubles for 130/170FF and rooms with shower from 200FF. ***Hôtel Le Berthelot*** (☎ 02 96 20 88 66) at 1 Rue du Port is slightly pricier with singles/doubles for 150/170FF and rooms with bath from 220FF.

Places to Eat

The few restaurants on the port are fairly touristy and expensive. Instead, try the ***Crêperie-Restaurant Morel*** (☎ 02 96 20 86 34) at 11 Place du Martray.

There's an ***Intermarché*** supermarket on Ave du Général de Gaulle, just west of the train station. It's open weekdays from 8.30 am to 12.15 pm and 2.30 to 7.15 pm. On Saturday there is no midday break.

A ***market*** is held on Tuesday morning at Place Gambetta, south-west of Place du Martray. There are ***oyster vendors*** selling freshly shucked bivalves at Quai Duguay Trouin on weekends.

Getting There & Away

Bus & Train Buses to and from Saint Brieuc run by CAT (☎ 02 96 33 36 60 in Saint Brieuc) cost 39.50FF and take 1½ hours. They leave from and arrive at Paimpol's train station (☎ 02 96 20 81 22) on Ave du Général de Gaulle. From there it's a few minutes walk to the tourist office. Head north up Rue du 18 Juin, turn left into Rue de l'Église, take the first right and then turn left on Rue Sylvain Bertho. The tourist office is at the end.

The closest significant rail junction to Paimpol is Guingamp, which you can reach by bus (36FF; 40 minutes; seven a day), from where there are frequent trains west to Brest (108FF) and east to Dinan (92FF).

Boat Ferries to Île de Bréhat, run by Vedettes de Bréhat (☎ 02 96 20 03 47), leave from the port at Pointe de l'Arcouest, 6km north of town. The trip takes 10 minutes and costs 40/34FF return for adults/children under 11. Taking a bicycle along costs 50FF return, but no bikes are allowed on board when the boat is full. There are hourly sailings in summer between 8.30 am and 8 pm and five or six sailings a day in winter.

Getting Around

Bus CAT buses leave four times a day in winter (six or seven times in summer) from Paimpol's train station (11.50FF one way) to Pointe de l'Arcouest to connect with the Île de Bréhat ferries.

Bicycle Bikes can be hired for 70FF a day from Cycles du Vieux Clocher (☎ 02 96 20 83 58) at Place de Verdun. It is due south of the tourist office near the Vieux Tour (Old Tower).

PERROS-GUIREC & LANNION

One of the oldest resorts along the Côte de Granit Rose (Pink Granite Coast), Perros-Guirec (Perroz Gireg in Breton; population 8000) sits at the top end of Brittany's northernmost peninsula. It's a rather exclusive resort town, flanked by two harbours – the sheltered new marina to the south-east and the old fishing port of Ploumanach about 2km to the north-west. Between the two harbours winds a coastline of rose-coloured granite, sculpted and smoothed by the elements into some pretty strange shapes. These are interrupted by a few small beaches and coves where sea otters still feel at home.

While Perros can be pricey for overnight halts, the town of Lannion (Lannuon in Breton; population 17,000), 12km inland and the nearest town served by train, has a decent hostel.

Orientation

Perros has two distinct parts: the main upper town on the hill and the marina area at its base. They're about 1km apart if you make your way up along the small roads, or double that distance if you follow the coastal Blvd de la Mer and Blvd Clemenceau around Pointe du Château, the peninsula that extends eastward from town.

Information

Tourist Office The tourist office (☎ 02 96 23 21 15; fax 02 96 23 04 72) is in the upper town at 21 Place de l'Hôtel de Ville. It is open Monday to Saturday from 9 am to 12.30 pm and 2 to 6.30 pm. In summer, the hours are 9 am to 7.30 pm and on Sunday from 10 am to 12.30 pm and 4 to 6.30 pm.

Money The Crédit Maritime Mutuel at 20 Place de l'Hôtel de Ville has exchange services, as does the Société Général at 4 Rue de la Poste.

Post The main post office is east of the tourist office on Rue de la Poste. It is open from 9 am to noon and 2 to 5.30 pm on weekdays and on Saturday morning.

Swimming

There are several beaches close to Perros. The main one is **Plage de Trestraou**, to the north about 1km from the tourist office. The others, attractive **Plage de Trestrignel** and **Plage du Château** on either side of Pointe du Château, are much smaller and more isolated.

Walking & Hiking

For a fantastic walk along the coast, you can follow the GR34 from Plage de Trestraou along the pink rocks to the Port de Ploumanach. It's about 5km each way.

Places to Stay

Camping Four camping grounds are dotted around the area. The four star ***Camping Le Ranolien*** (☎ 02 96 91 43 58) has the best location: it's close to the sea, between the rocks just off the road to Ploumanach. It is open from February to mid-November and charges 75FF for two people with a tent (130FF in the high season).

Hostels There are two year-round youth hostels outside of Perros. Inland at Lannion (12km), ***Les Korrigans*** (☎ 02 96 37 91 28; fax 02 96 37 02 06) at 6 Rue du 73 Territorial is a two minute walk from the train station. It charges 52FF a night plus 22FF for breakfast. Reception is open Monday to Saturday from 9 am to 9 pm and on Sunday from 10 am to noon and 6 to 9 pm.

The other hostel, ***Le Toëno*** (☎ 02 96 23 52 22; fax 02 96 15 44 34), is on the coast, 10km west of Perros near the town of Trébeurden on Route de la Corniche. It charges 45FF for a bed and 20FF for breakfast. To get there take CAT bus No 15 from the train station in Lannion or from Perros' mairie.

Hotels In Perros' upper town, the ***Hôtel Les Violettes*** (☎ 02 96 23 21 33), a Victorian-style house south-west of the tourist office at 19 Rue du Calvaire, has rooms with washbasin/shower starting at 155/215FF. The ***Hôtel de la Mairie*** (☎ 02 96 23 22 41; fax 02 96 23 33 04) at 28 Place de l'Hôtel de Ville has doubles with washbasin for 160FF and ones with shower and toilet for 220FF.

Opposite the train station in Lannion, the ***Hôtel de Bretagne*** (☎ 02 96 37 00 33), situated at 32 Ave du Général de Gaulle, has rooms with shower starting from 260FF.

Places to Eat

The Perros hotels listed here have decent *menus* from 54FF (at the Hôtel Les Violettes) to 68FF.

Self-caterers will find a ***Comod*** supermarket just south-west of the tourist office on Blvd Aristide Briand. It's open Monday to Saturday from 8.30 am to 12.30 pm and 3 to 7.30 pm. In summer, it's also open on Sunday morning.

Getting There & Away

Buses operated by CAT (☎ 02 96 37 02 40) shuttle between Lannion's train station and

Perros (15FF), where they stop at both the marina and Place de l'Hôtel de Ville.

From the Lannion train station (☎ 02 96 37 04 59), there are rail connections via Plouaret Trégor eastward to Guingamp and on to Saint Brieuc; and westward via Morlaix to Roscoff (61.50FF; three hours) and Brest (80FF; 2½ hours; six a day).

Getting Around

Bus CAT bus No 15 runs from Lannion's train station to Perros, before continuing on north-west to Ploumanach and then on to Trébeurden and Trégastel. There are up to nine buses daily on weekdays, a few less on Saturday and none on Sunday.

Taxi Taxis can be reached in Lannion by ringing ☎ 02 96 48 09 50.

Bicycle In Perros at 41 Blvd Aristide Briand, rental bikes are available from Perros Deux Roues (☎ 02 96 91 03 33) for 60FF per day.

Champagne

Champagne, known in Roman times as Campania (literally, 'Land of Plains'), is a largely agricultural region famed around the world for the sparkling wines that have been made here since the days of Dom Pérignon. According to French law, only bubbly from very limited parts of the region – grown, aged and bottled according to the strictest standards – can be labelled as champagne.

The production of the celebrated wine takes place mainly in two departments: Marne, whose metropolis is the 'Coronation City' of Reims; and the less prestigious Aube, whose prefecture is the ancient, picturesque city of Troyes. The town of Épernay, a bit south of Reims, is the de facto capital of champagne (the drink) and is the best place to head for *dégustation* (tasting). The Route Touristique du Champagne (Champagne Tourist Route) wends its way through the region's vineyards.

Activities

Champagne Air Show (☎ 03 26 82 59 60; fax 03 26 82 48 62), based at 15bis Place Saint Niçaise in Reims, runs hot-air balloon flights all over the Champagne region.

HIGHLIGHTS

- **Reims** or **Épernay** – inhale the potent odours of maturing champagne and mould on a cellar tour
- **Route Touristique du Champagne** – explore the region's vineyards on this scenic drive
- **Verzy** – consider the contortions of the dwarf-mutant beech trees
- **Troyes** – admire the woodwork tools and modern art in the city's museums

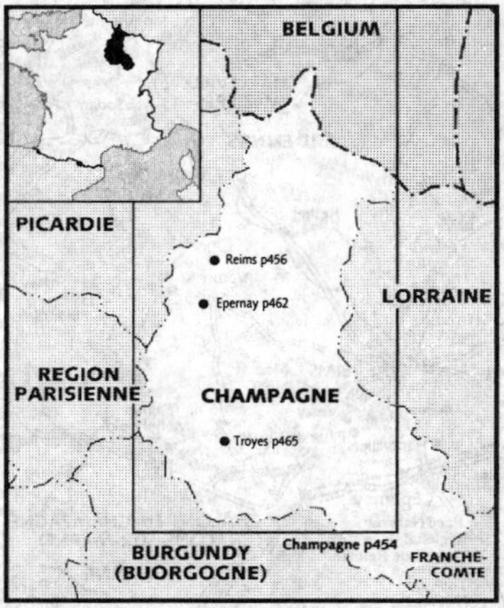

champagne – savour the moment as the tiny bubbles tingle on your tongue and you nibble on *biscuits de Reims* (a type of macaroon)

REIMS

• pop 206,000 ✉ 51100 alt 85m

After Clovis I, founder of the Frankish kingdom, was baptised here in 496 AD, Reims (rhymes with the French pronunciation of *prince*; often anglicised as Rheims) became the traditional site of French coronations. From 816 to 1825, 34 sovereigns, among them 25 kings – including Charles VII, crowned here on 17 July 1429 with Joan of Arc at his side – began their reigns as Christian rulers in the city's famed cathedral. In 1996, the city marked the 1500th anniversary of Clovis' conversion.

Some 85% of Reims' houses were destroyed by German artillery shells during WWI. On 7 May 1945, Germany's unconditional surrender was signed here, effectively bringing an end to WWII in Europe. Meticulously reconstructed after the world wars, modern-day Reims is a neat and orderly city,

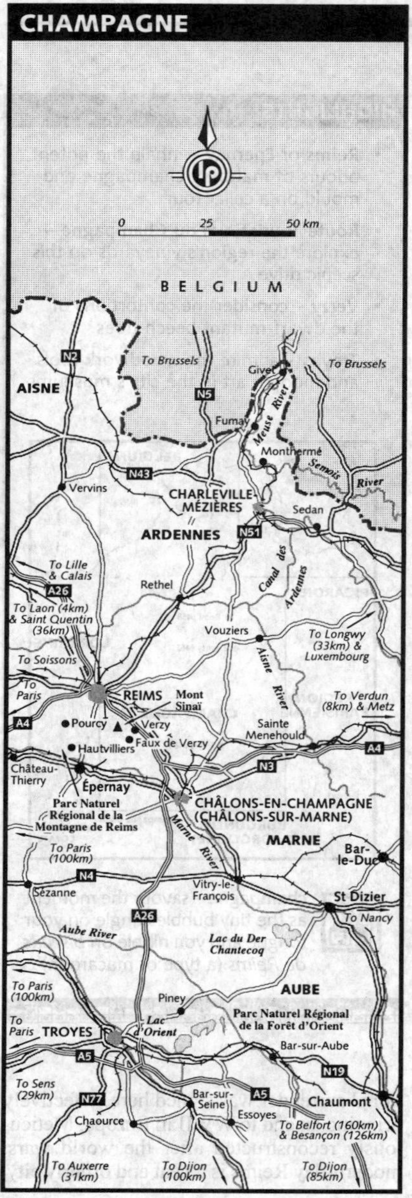

with wide avenues and neatly tended parks. With Épernay, it is the most important centre of champagne production.

Orientation

The main streets of Reims' commercial centre, the area north-west of the cathedral, are Rue Carnot, Rue de Vesle, Rue Condorcet and Rue de Talleyrand. The train station is about 1km north-west of the cathedral, across Square Colbert from the pedestrianised Place Drouet d'Erlon, a major nightlife area. Virtually every street in the city centre is one way.

Information

Tourist Office The tourist office (☎ 03 26 77 45 25; fax 03 26 77 45 27) is across the street from the cathedral at 2 Rue Guillaume de Machault. From Easter to September it is open from 9 or 9.30 am to 7.30 pm (6.30 or 7 pm on Sunday and holidays); the rest of the year it closes at 6.30 pm (5.30 pm on Sunday and holidays). In July and August closing time is 8 pm (7 pm on Sunday). Local hotel reservations are free. A three hour Walkman tour of the area around the cathedral costs 50FF. Subject to availability, you can pick up brochures on the region of Champagne and the free weekly *Les Rendez-Vous Rémois*, which lists concerts, films and other cultural events.

Money The Banque de France on Rue Docteur Jacquin opposite the building marked 'Galeries Rémoises' is open weekdays from 8.45 am to 12.20 pm and 1.40 to 3.45 pm.

There's a cluster of commercial banks on Rue Carnot, one block north of the cathedral. Several more can be found at the southern end of Place Drouet d'Erlon. The tourist office changes money on Saturday, Sunday and holidays.

Post The main post office is at Place du Boulingrin. It's open weekdays from 8 am to 7 pm and Saturday from 8 am to noon. The branch at 2 Rue Cérès, through the arches on the east side of Place Royale, is open weekdays from 8.30 am to 6 pm and Saturday from 8 am to noon. Both exchange foreign currency.

Laundry The Lav-o-Clair at 59 Rue Chanzy is open daily from 7 am to 9.30 pm. The Laverie Automatique at 129 Rue de Vesle is open daily from 7 am to 9 pm.

Public Squares

The huge pedestrianised square that has runway lights down the middle and places to eat and drink along the sides is the **Place Drouet d'Erlon**. Its flower-filled fountain is topped with a gilded, winged female figure that looks like she's playing horseshoes with a garland. At Rue Condorcet, the 12th to 14th century **Église Saint Jacques** has some pretty awful post-war stained glass. About 1km to the north-east, the **Porte de Mars**, a Roman triumphal arch from the 3rd century AD, is in a small park at **Place de la République**.

In the town centre, the 18th century **Place Royale**, graced by a statue of Louis XV and still crisscrossed by the old tram tracks, is surrounded by impressive neoclassical arcades. At **Place du Forum**, excavations have uncovered the **Cryptoportique**, a 3rd century gallery of the Roman forum whose interior can be visited from mid-June to mid-September; hours are 2 to 5 pm (closed Monday).

Cathédrale Notre Dame

Reims' world-famous Gothic cathedral, which was begun in 1211 (on a site occupied by churches since the 5th century) and largely completed 100 years later, was for centuries the traditional site of French coronations. Badly damaged by artillery and fire during WWI, it was restored, in large part with funds donated by John D Rockefeller; reconsecration took place in 1938, just in time for the next war.

The long (138m) and relatively narrow structure is noted for its lightness, elegance and harmony, but can hardly be called sublime and, frankly, is more interesting for its history than for its heavily restored architectural features. The finest stained glass is the west façade's 12 petalled **great rose window** and its smaller neighbour downstairs. There's a window by Chagall in the axial chapel (directly behind the high altar) and, two chapels to the left, a statue of Joan of Arc. Along the north aisle, near the Flamboyant Gothic organ case (15th and 18th centuries), is a 15th century **astronomical clock**, restored after WWI. The interior of the west façade is decorated with 120 statues in niches, some of them badly damaged.

The cathedral, which is at the north-east end of Rue Libergier, is open daily from 7.30 am to 7.30 pm, except during services.

Palais du Tau

The Tau Palace (☎ 03 26 47 81 79), a former archbishop's residence constructed in 1690 and rebuilt in the decades after WWII, was once the residence of princes about to be crowned king. Now a museum housing exceptional tapestries, statues and ritual objects from the cathedral, it is open daily from 9.30 am to 12.30 pm and 2 to 6 pm (6.30 pm in July and August, when there's no midday closure). From mid-November to mid-March it's open from 10.30 am to noon and 2 to 5 pm (6 pm on weekends). Admission is 32FF (21FF for young people aged 12 to 25 and teachers with ID). The entrance is inside the cathedral, to the right of the high altar.

Basilique Saint Rémi

Named after Remigius, the bishop who baptised Clovis and 3000 Frankish warriors in the 5th century, this former Benedictine abbey church is worn but stunning. Its 121m-long interior, restored after the damage of WWI, is still a pilgrimage site. The Romanesque nave and transept are mainly from the mid-11th century; the choir (1162-90) is in the early Gothic style, with a large triforium gallery and tiny clerestory windows. The 12th century-style chandelier has 96 candles, one for each year of the life of Saint Rémi, whose tomb (in the choir) is marked by a mausoleum from the mid-17th century.

To get to the basilica, which is about 1.5km south-east of the tourist office at

Place Saint Rémi, take bus No A from the train station or bus A, F or I from the Théâtre bus hub; get off at the Saint Rémi or Saint Timothée stops. The entrance is on Rue Saint Julien, through the southern portal.

Musée Saint Rémi

The Saint Rémi Museum (☎ 03 26 85 23 36), 53 Rue Simon, 100m from the basilica's west façade, is housed in buildings constructed for the abbey between the 12th and 18th centuries. Displays include archaeological items, tapestries and 16th to 19th century weapons. It is open daily from 2 to 6.30 pm (7 pm on weekends). Admission costs 10FF.

Musée de la Reddition

Nazi Germany capitulated on 7 May 1945 in US General Dwight D Eisenhower's war room, now a museum (☎ 03 26 47 84 19) known as the Salle de Reddition (Surrender Room). The original battle maps are still affixed to the walls. Located inside a school at 12 Rue Franklin Roosevelt, it is open

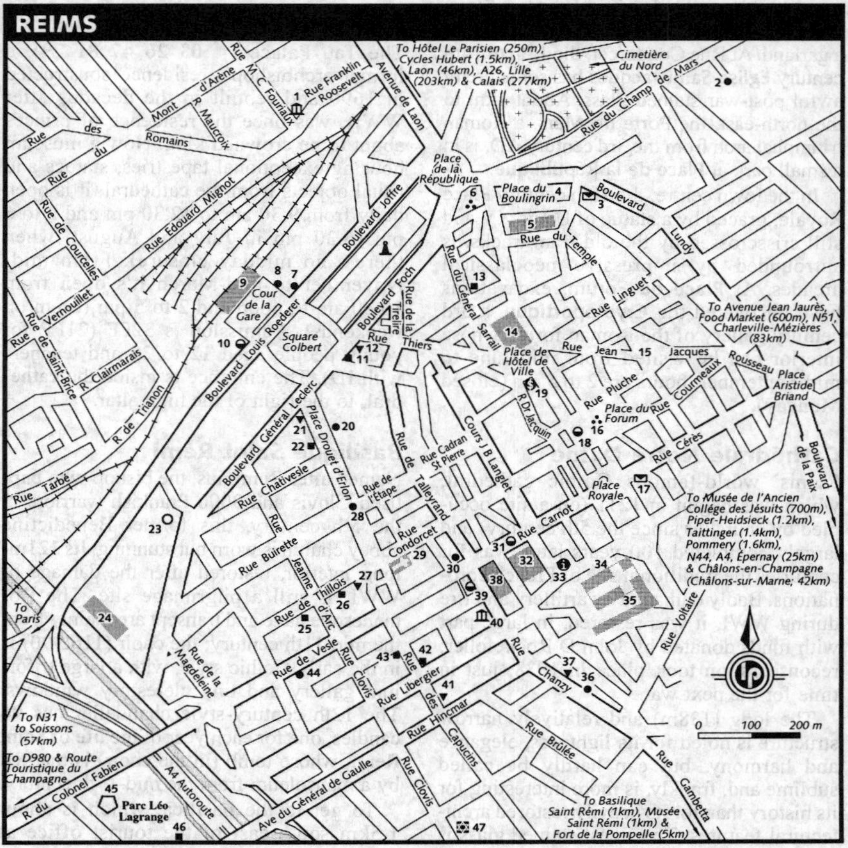

April to November from 10 am to noon and 2 to 6 pm (closed Tuesday). Admission costs 10FF (free for students).

Fort de la Pompelle

This WWI fortress, about 5km south-east of Reims on the N44 (towards Châlons-en-Champagne, which is also widely known as Châlons-sur-Marne), now houses a military museum (☎ 03 26 49 11 85; 20FF). It's opening hours are 10 am to 5 pm (7 pm from April to October, closed for two weeks around New Year).

Champagne Cellars

The musty *caves* (cellars) and dusty bottles of about a dozen Reims-area champagne houses can be visited on guided tours that include explanations of how champagne is made. The tourist office has a brochure with details. Places that charge fees generally don't require advance reservations.

Mumm One of the largest producers in Reims, with an output of six to seven million bottles a year, Mumm's cellar (☎ 03 26 49 59 70) is at 34 Rue du Champ de Mars. It offers 45-minute guided cellar tours (20FF, free for children under 16) that include, at the end, a glass of bubbly. Tours, often in English, are held daily from November to March from 9 to 11 am and 2 to 5 pm (closed on weekend mornings). To get there, take bus K from near the Théâtre bus hub to the Justice stop.

Taittinger Taittinger (☎ 03 26 85 84 33), 9 Place Saint Niçaise, is located 1.5km south-east of the cathedral. Tours (20FF, free for under 12s), which last an hour, include a video and a visit to the 13th century cellars, followed by a tasting session. The tours run on weekdays from 9.30 am to noon and 2 to 4.30 pm; from March to November tours also take place on weekends and holidays from 9 to 11 am and 2 to 5 pm. Phone for details about tours in English. To get there from the train station or the Théâtre bus hub, take bus A to the Saint Timothée stop.

Pommery This champagne house (☎ 03 26 61 62 56) is headquartered on a hilltop at 5 Place du Général Gouraud, 1.8km south-east of the cathedral. From April to October, 45-minute tours (including four or five a day in English – call for details), which end with a tasting, depart daily from 10.20 am

REIMS

PLACES TO STAY

- 11 Hôtel L'Univers & Restaurant Au Congrès
- 13 Hôtel Alsace
- 22 Grand Hôtel du Nord
- 25 Hôtel Au Bon Accueil
- 26 Hôtel Thillois
- 42 Hôtel de la Cathédral
- 43 Le Bon Moine Hotel & Restaurant
- 46 Centre International de Séjour

PLACES TO EAT

- 12 Le Foch
- 21 Le Continental
- 27 Il Colosseo
- 37 Le Bouchon Champenois
- 41 Le Chamois & Cactus Café

OTHER

- 1 Musée de la Reddition
- 2 Mumm Cellar
- 3 Main Post Office
- 4 Food Market
- 5 Old Covered Market
- 6 Porte de Mars
- 7 Rent-a-Car Système
- 8 ADA & National Citer Car Rental
- 9 Train Station
- 10 Intercity Bus Stops
- 14 Hôtel de Ville
- 15 Place Léon Bourgeois
- 16 Cryptoportique
- 17 Post Office
- 18 Intercity Bus Stops
- 19 Banque de France
- 20 Cinéma Gaumont
- 23 Cirque
- 24 Centre des Congrès (Convention Centre)
- 28 Fountain
- 29 Église Saint Jacques
- 30 Monoprix Supermarket
- 31 Théâtre Bus Hub
- 32 Palais de Justice
- 33 Tourist Office
- 34 Cathédrale Notre Dame
- 35 Palais du Tau
- 36 Lav-o-Clair Laundrette
- 38 Grand Théâtre
- 39 La Boutique TUR
- 40 Musée des Beaux-Arts
- 44 Laverie Automatique
- 45 Comédie de Reims
- 47 Synagogue

to 5.20 pm. The rest of the year tours take place only on weekdays from 10 am to noon and 2 to 4 pm. The charge is 40FF (20FF for students; free for children 13 and under). In the winter it's a good idea to make reservations a day ahead (or, for an afternoon visit, in the morning). Bus A will take you to the Saint Timothée stop, from where you can either take bus R to the Gouraud stop or walk about 600m.

Piper-Heidsieck Champagne meets Disneyland at Piper-Heidsieck (☎ 03 26 84 43 44), 51 Blvd Henry Vasnier, which is 1.2km south-east of the cathedral. For 35FF (15FF for children aged seven to 16), you get a 20 minute tour with automated commentary (in English) and a dégustation. There are departures daily from 9 to 11.45 am and 2 to 5.15 pm. To get there by bus, follow the same directions as to Pommery but get off bus R at the Henry Vasnier stop (or walk from the line A Saint Timothée stop).

CHAMPAGNE

Special Events

Sometime in early June, the four day Les Sacres du Folklore, one of northern France's most celebrated and colourful folk festivals, takes place concurrently with Les Fêtes Johanniques, a medieval celebration that re-enacts Joan of Arc's arrival in Reims. From the end of June through August, Les Flâneries Musicales d'Été brings mostly free concerts to historic venues all over town.

Places to Stay – Budget

Reims' hotels, at their fullest in July and August, offer good value for money.

Hostel The ***Centre International de Séjour*** (CIS; ☎ 03 26 40 52 60; fax 03 26 47 35 70) is on Allée Polonceau in Parc Léo Lagrange, a bit over 1km west of the cathedral (just over the canal). This place has beds for 69FF in a double or triple, and 89FF in a single; breakfast is 10FF. Reception is open until 8 pm. To get there take bus B, K or N to the Colin stop or bus H to the Pont De Gaulle stop.

Hotels The friendly ***Hôtel Alsace*** (☎ 03 26 47 44 08; fax 03 26 47 44 52), 6 Rue du Général Sarrail, has large and pleasant doubles/triples from 130/160FF (180/ 220FF with shower and toilet). Hall showers are free if you stay for several days. From December to March, reception is closed on Sunday until 6 pm.

The 29 room ***Hôtel Au Bon Accueil*** (☎ 03 26 88 55 74), 31 Rue de Thillois, lives up to its name, offering clean, decent singles/doubles with washbasin for 80/100FF; singles/doubles/triples with shower cost 120/15/170FF (170/170/200FF with toilet too). Hall showers are 10FF. The quiet, 19 room ***Hôtel Thillois*** (☎ 03 26 40 65 65), 17 Rue de Thillois, provides pretty average singles/doubles from 120/140FF (150/170FF with shower and toilet). There are no hall showers; toilets are on the landing. Reception is generally closed on Sunday.

About 900m north-east of the train station at 3 Rue Périn (next to 73 Ave de Laon), the quiet ***Hôtel Le Parisien*** (☎ 03 26 47 32 89; fax 03 26 86 81 39) has clean, very serviceable doubles with washbasin for 110 to 150FF; doubles with shower are 180FF. Hall showers cost 20FF. From the station, walk to Place de la République and then north along Ave de Laon, or take bus A or C to the Saint Thomas stop. Free street parking is available.

Places to Stay – Mid-Range

On lively Place Drouet d'Erlon, the charming, old-time ***Grand Hôtel du Nord*** (☎ 03 26 47 39 03; fax 03 26 40 92 26), a two star, 50 room establishment at No 75, has spacious, tasteful doubles – some with great views – for 250FF. Directly opposite the train station at 41 Blvd Foch, the 40 room, three star ***Hôtel L'Univers*** (☎ 03 26 88 68 08; fax 03 26 40 95 61) has spacious and up-to-date singles/doubles from about 320/360FF.

The quiet, family-run, two star ***Hôtel de la Cathédrale*** (☎ 03 26 47 28 46; fax 03 26

88 65 81), 250m west of the cathedral at 20 Rue Libergier (a great location), has 17 tidy, tasteful rooms from 265/400FF for two/four people. The two star, 10 room ***Le Bon Moine*** (☎ 03 26 47 33 64; fax 03 26 40 43 87), 14 Rue des Capucins, has singles/doubles from 200/220FF. Reception may be closed on Sunday – call ahead if you'll be arriving then.

Places to Eat

Restaurants – French One of the best lunch deals around is on offer at the ***Hôtel Alsace*** (see Places to Stay), whose generous, four course, bistro-style lunch *menu*, available Monday to Saturday for just 58FF, attracts a crowd of friendly regulars.

Le Bouchon Champenois (☎ 03 26 88 50 35), 45 Rue Chanzy, specialises in the cuisine of Champagne, which is often prepared with sauces based on champagne or ratafia (an almond-flavoured aperitif). The *menus* start at 69FF. It is closed on Sunday and Monday evenings. ***Le Bon Moine*** (☎ 03 26 47 33 64), a brasserie-restaurant at 14 Rue des Capucins, specialises in traditional French fare, including steak tartare (56FF) and home-made *andouillette* (tripe sausage; 52FF). The *menus* cost 59, 80 and 100FF. It's closed on Sunday.

Le Foch (☎ 03 26 47 48 22), 37 Blvd Foch, whose speciality is fish, has *menus* for 165 to 220FF. It's open from noon to 2.30 pm and 7.15 to 9.30 pm (closed on Sunday night and Monday). A few buildings away, ***Au Congrès***, a formal French restaurant attached to the Hôtel L'Univers (see Places to Stay), has *menus* for 80 to 168FF (open daily). ***Le Continental*** (☎ 03 26 47 01 47), 95 Place Drouet d'Erlon, has French and regional *menus* for 97 to 198FF. It's open daily, with dinner service until 11.30 pm.

Le Chamois (☎ 03 26 88 69 75), 45 Rue des Capucins, serves large salads and Savoyard specialities, including *pierre à feu* (meat you cook yourself on a hot volcanic rock; 73FF) and fondue (66FF). The *menus* cost 45 and 59FF (lunch only) and 75FF (not available on Friday night, Saturday or Sunday). It's closed on Wednesday and for lunch on Sunday.

Restaurants – Other ***Il Colosseo*** (☎ 03 26 47 68 50), 9 Rue de Thillois, reached through an ornate, dilapidated former theatre façade, has pizzas and pastas for 38 to 74FF. It is open from 11.30 am to 2.30 pm and 6.30 to 11.30 pm (closed Sunday and Monday).

There are several East Asian restaurants on Rue de Thillois (near the Hôtel Au Bon Accueil) and the parallel Rue de Vesle (near the laundrette).

Self-Catering ***Food markets*** take over parts of Place du Boulingrin on Wednesday and Saturday mornings (until 2 pm) and Ave Jean Jaurès (east of Place Aristide Briand) on Sunday morning (until 1 pm). The ***Monoprix*** supermarket at 1 Rue de Talleyrand has a good *boulangerie*, and is open Monday to Saturday from 8.30 am to 9 pm.

Entertainment

Cinéma Gaumont (☎ 03 26 47 32 02), 72 Place Drouet d'Erlon, screens nondubbed films every Tuesday.

Brasseries and cafés with terraces line Place Drouet d'Erlon, the focal point of Reims' nightlife. To the south the ***Cactus Café*** (☎ 03 26 88 16 99), 47 Rue des Capucins, is a mellow Tex-Mex bar with Mexican beers (from 20FF) and 20 kinds of tequila. Popular with students, it's open from 11 am (4 pm on Saturday) to 12.30 am (1.30 am on Friday and Saturday nights; closed Sunday).

Getting There & Away

Bus TransChampagne (STDM; ☎ 03 26 65 17 07; staffed on weekdays from 8.30 am to 5.30 pm) has four buses a day (two or three on weekend afternoons) to Troyes (1½ hours by autoroute for 112FF or two hours by highway for 108FF). In Reims, buses served by a circular local line known as La Citadine stop at Place du Forum (hours posted) and next to the train station.

Train Reims is on the secondary Paris-Longwy line. The train station information office (☎ 08 36 35 35 35) is open from 8.30 am to 7 pm (9 am to 6 pm on Saturday; closed Sunday and holidays).

Destinations served by direct trains include Paris' Gare de l'Est (118FF; 1½ hours; seven to 11 a day), Épernay (33FF; 20 to 40 minutes; 10 to 19 a day) and Dijon (187FF; 3½ hours; five a day). There are also services to Nancy (152FF; three hours; three or four a day), Metz (154FF), Verdun (100FF), Lyon, Nice (12½ hours overnight) and Strasbourg (221FF). The best way to reach Troyes is by bus.

Car ADA (☎ 03 26 50 08 40) and National Citer (03 26 40 43 38) are both at the train station parking lot; the cheaper Rent-a-Car Système (☎ 03 26 47 27 77) is around the corner. All three are closed from noon to 2 pm and on Sunday.

Getting Around

Bus The local bus company's information office, La Boutique TUR (☎ 03 26 88 25 38), is at 6 Rue Chanzy, right at the Théâtre bus hub (ie the streets in front of or on either side of the Grand Théâtre), which is served by almost all TUR lines. A single ticket, available from drivers, costs 5FF; a carnet of 10, sold at La Boutique TUR and *tabacs* (tobacconists), is 34FF. The boutique is open from 7 am to 8 pm (7 pm on Saturday; closed on Sunday and holidays).

The train station is linked to the Théâtre bus hub (and thus the tourist office) by buses A, C, F, K and T. Most lines begin their last runs at about 8.45 pm. The five night lines (A, B, C, G and H) make their last pass by the Théâtre bus hub at about 11.45 pm.

Taxi For a taxi, call ☎ 03 26 47 05 05 or ☎ 03 26 02 15 02.

Bicycle Bike of various types can be rented from Cycles Hubert (☎ 03 26 09 16 93), 82 Rue de Neufchâtel, which is about 1.5km due north of Place de la République (by bus take line C towards Orgeval).

ROUTE TOURISTIQUE DU CHAMPAGNE

The signposted tertiary roads that make up the Champagne Tourist Route – 600km in all – meander through the region's three most important wine-growing areas: the **Montagne de Reims**, between Reims and Épernay; the **Côte des Blancs**, south of Épernay towards Sézanne; and the **Vallée de la Marne**, west of Épernay towards Château Thierry. **Hautvilliers**, where Dom Pérignon created champagne three centuries ago, is about 6km north of Épernay.

The Route Touristique weaves its way among the neatly tended vines that cover the slopes between very average-looking villages where small *producteurs* (champagne producers) welcome travellers in search of bubbly; brown (or black) and white signs point the way to each winery. Beautiful panoramas abound. Tourist offices can supply you with the colour-coded brochure *La Route Touristique du Champagne – Visites de Caves*, available in English, which includes maps and the addresses and opening hours of many *viticulteurs* (wine growers).

For details on the Route Touristique's Côtes des Bar section east of Troyes, see the Around Troyes section at the end of this chapter.

Parc Naturel Régional de la Montagne de Reims

The section of the Route Touristique nearest Reims skirts the Montagne de Reims Regional Park, endowed with lush forests and a botanical curiosity, the mutant beech trees known as **Faux de Verzy** (see the boxed text 'Dwarf-Mutant Beech Trees'). To get there from the village of Verzy, follow the signs up the D34; the first trees can be seen about 1km from 'Les Faux' parking lot. Across the D34, a short trail leads through the forest to the *point de vue* (panoramic viewpoint) atop 288m-high **Mont Sinaï**.

Dwarf-Mutant Beech Trees

No-one knows why the forests near the village of Verzy are home to 800-odd bizarrely malformed beech trees, but their presence has been documented since at least the 6th century. Scientists have determined that the phenomenon is genetic, but that hardly explains why so many of these so-called *faux* are to be found in the same small area (similar mutants sometimes grow elsewhere in ones and twos) or why the vertically challenged beeches have as neighbours two dwarf-mutant oaks. One thing is certain though: the faux, whose gnarled and contorted branches droop towards the ground to form an umbrella-shaped dome, suffer in the competition for light with their non-mutant companions and need to be protected.

Some of the mutant trees, which grow slowly and live a very long time, are fertile and can reproduce sexually, but to help nature along and ensure the survival of these botanical curiosities, experts from the University of Reims carry out in vitro fertilisation of the trees. City-dwelling faux, transplanted from Verzy, can often be seen around France in public parks.

Nothing much happens at the Maison du Parc (visitors centre; ☎ 03 26 59 44 44) in the village of Pourcy (next to Marfaux), but it can supply brochures on the park, including a few in English, and details on sporting options, local events and *gîtes*. It is open on weekdays from 8.30 am to noon and 1.30 to 6 pm (5.30 pm on Friday) and, from Easter to October, on weekends and holidays from 2.30 to 6.30 pm.

Hiking & Cycling An excellent brochure entitled *Balades Champenoises* is available at area tourist offices, and comes with fold-out maps of the many hiking trails around Reims and Épernay (including the GR14, which pass through and around the Parc Naturel Régional de la Montagne de Reims). It also has details on horse riding, accommodation and bike rental. Topoguides for the area are also available.

Épernay-based Argos VTT (☎ 03 26 51 95 36) publishes colour-coded maps of several marked cycling trails in and around the regional park. They are available for 2FF each at tourist offices (eg in Épernay). Cycl'o Vert (☎ 03 26 97 97 77), based at 34 Rue Carnot in Verzy, rents out bikes – call them in advance to make arrangements.

ÉPERNAY

• pop 28,000 ✉ 51200 alt 75m

Épernay, an ordinary-looking (but prosperous) provincial town 25km south of Reims, is home to some of the world's most famous champagne houses. Underneath the streets, in some 100km of subterranean cellars, tens of millions of bottles of champagne, just waiting to be popped open for some sparkling celebration, are being aged. In 1950, one such cellar – owned by the irrepressible Mercier – hosted a car rally without the loss of a single bottle. The town, set amid the gentle vineyard-covered slopes of the Marne River valley, is the best place in Champagne to tour cellars and sample fizzy wine. It can easily be visited as a day trip from Reims.

Orientation

The mansion-lined Ave de Champagne, where many of Épernay's champagne houses are based, stretches eastward from the town's commercial heart, whose liveliest streets are Rue Général Leclerc and Rue Saint Thibault. The most attractive part of town is, surprisingly, around the train station, where you'll find generous green spaces (including a handsome formal garden around the Hôtel de Ville). The area south of Place de la République is given over to parking lots.

Information

Tourist Office The helpful and well equipped tourist office (☎ 03 26 53 33 00; fax 03 26 51 95 22), 7 Ave de Champagne, can supply you with details on cellar visits

CHAMPAGNE

as well as hiking and cycling information. It is open Monday to Saturday from 9.30 am to 12.30 pm and 1.30 to 5.30 pm (7 pm from Easter to mid-October, when it's also open on Sunday and holidays from 11 am to 4 pm). Hotel reservations cost 20FF.

Money The Banque de France at Place de la République is open weekdays from 8.45 am to noon and 1.45 to 4 pm.

Post The main post office, on Place Hugues Plomb, is open weekdays from 8 am to 7 pm and on Saturday until noon. Foreign currency can also be exchanged here.

Laundry The Lavoclair at 40 Rue du Docteur Rousseau is open until 6 pm in winter, later during the rest of the year. The laundrette at 18 Ave Jean Jaurès is supposed to be open daily until 8 pm.

Champagne Houses

Épernay's champagne houses cannot be accused of ever cowering behind excessive modesty or aristocratic understatement. When

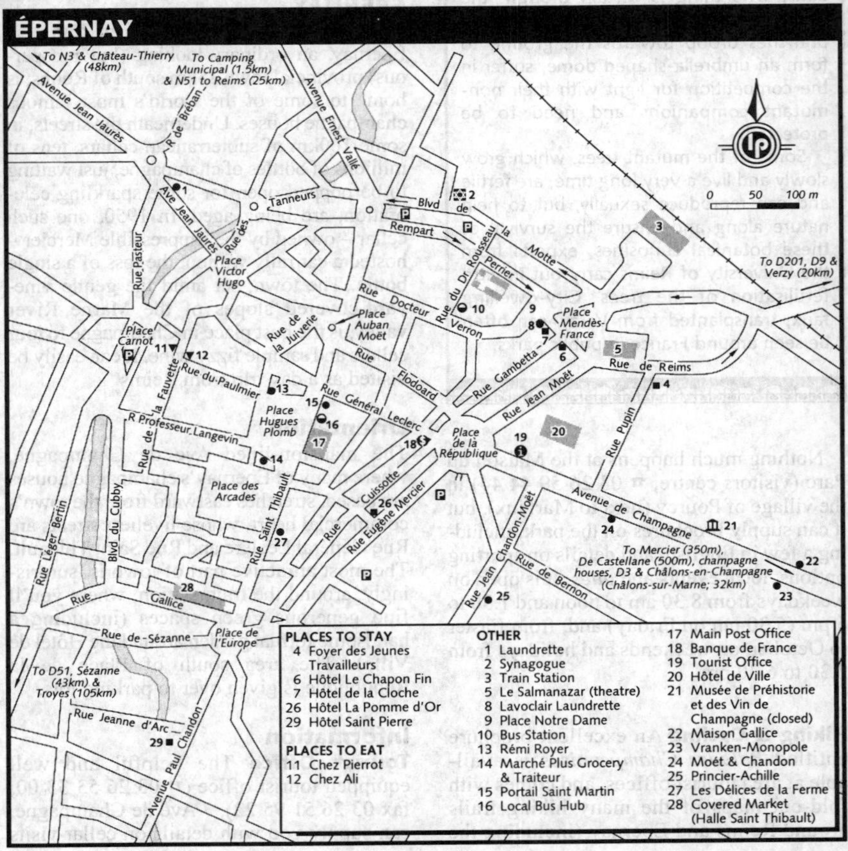

it comes to PR for brand-name bubbly, dignified razzle-dazzle is the name of the game. Many of the well touristed maisons on or near Ave de Champagne offer interesting, informative tours, followed by a visit to the factory outlet bubbly shop. Reservations are not necessary for those listed below.

Moët & Chandon This prestigious house (☎ 03 26 51 20 00), 18 Ave de Champagne, offers 45 to 60-minute tours (35FF, 20FF for children aged 12 to 16) that are among the region's most interesting and informative. Tours (in English), which include a short film and end with a tasting session, depart every 15 or 20 minutes from 9.30 to 11.30 am and 2 to 4.30 pm (closed on weekends from sometime in November through to Easter). For an extra fee it may be possible to sample and compare two or three different champagnes.

De Castellane Just down the hill from 64 Ave de Champagne is De Castellane (☎ 03 26 51 19 19) at 57 Rue de Verdun. The 45-minute cellar tours (20FF, 15FF for children aged five to 15), held in English pretty much whenever Anglophone visitors arrive, include a visit to an informative museum whose exhibits of old machinery illustrate all the stages in making and bottling champagne. At the end there's a dégustation. From Easter to October tours are held from 10 to 11.15 am and 2 to 5.15 pm; to see the production lines in action, come on a weekday. The 60m-high tower, reached via 237 steps, affords panoramic views.

Mercier The most popular brand in France, Mercier (☎ 03 26 51 22 22), based at 68-70 Ave de Champagne, has thrived on unabashed self-promotion since it was founded in 1847 by Eugène Mercier, a trailblazer in the field of eye-catching publicity stunts and the virtual creator of the cellar tour. Everything here is flashy, including the 160,000L barrel that took two decades to build and the lift that transports you 30m underground to a laser-guided train that – yes, there's a glitch in the glitz – gets confused by camera flashes and has been known to veer into the bottles that line its route.

Entertaining tours (25FF on weekdays, 30FF on weekends; 10FF for children aged 12 to 16), which end with a tasting, are held daily from 9.30 to 11.30 am and 2 to 4.30 pm (5.30 pm on Sunday and holidays); from December to February it's closed on Tuesday and Wednesday. From April to November there are tours in English about once an hour; the rest of the year phone ahead for times.

Places to Stay

Épernay has a handful of cheap hotels but, overall, Reims offers better deals.

Camping The *Camping Municipal* (☎ 03 26 55 32 14), on Allée de Cumières near the Marne River, 2km north-west of the train station. It is open from April to mid-September. Fees are 16FF per adult and 19FF for a tent site plus parking.

Hostels The *Foyer de Jeunes Travailleurs* (FJT; ☎ 03 26 51 62 51; fax 03 26 54 13 60), 2 Rue Pupin, also known as the Centre International de Séjour, has beds for travellers for 70FF in two to six-person rooms. Reception is open daily (except Sunday) from 2 to 8 pm. It's a good idea to reserve in advance by phone.

Hotels The best deal in town is the *Hôtel Saint Pierre* (☎ 03 26 54 40 80), 1 Rue Jeanne d'Arc, which occupies an elegant, early 20th century mansion on the southern edge of town. Charming singles/doubles start at 113/125FF; shower and toilet-equipped doubles are 180FF. Reception is closed on Sunday from 2 to 7 pm. Private parking is available.

Across the shady square from the train station, the *Hôtel Le Chapon Fin* (☎ 03 26 55 40 03; fax 03 26 54 94 17), 2 Place Mendès-France, has medium-sized doubles with shower for 170FF. The two star, 19 room *Hôtel de la Cloche* (☎ 03 26 55 24 05; fax 03 26 51 88 05), 5 Place Mendès-France, has nondescript doubles with shower and toilet from 170FF. Reception is closed daily from 3 to 5.30 pm.

The two star, 26 room ***Hôtel La Pomme d'Or*** (☎ 03 26 55 59 44; fax 03 26 55 10 88), 12 Rue Eugène Mercier, has uninspiring but serviceable singles/doubles/triples from 180/200/265FF.

Places to Eat

Restaurants The restaurant of the ***Hôtel de la Cloche*** (see Places to Stay) offers *menus* of traditional French cuisine for 69 to 230FF (open daily, except Sunday evening in winter). The rustic restaurant attached to the ***Hôtel Le Chapon Fin*** (see Places to Stay) has French and Champenois *menus* from 56 to 160FF. It's open daily from noon to 2.30 pm and 7 to 11 pm.

Chez Pierrot (☎ 03 26 55 16 93), an elegant restaurant at 16 Rue de la Fauvette, serves French bourgeois-style cuisine, including a *menu* for 120FF (closed Sunday).

Couscous (60 to 90FF) is on offer at ***Chez Ali*** (☎ 03 26 51 80 82), 27 Rue de la Fauvette (closed Monday for lunch).

Self-Catering On Wednesday and Saturday mornings there's a ***covered market*** on the corner of Rue Saint Thibault and Rue Gallice. On Sunday mornings a small ***open-air market*** pops up on Place Auban Moët.

At 13 Place Hugues Plomb, ***Marché Plus*** grocery is open from 7 am to 9 pm (7 am to 1 pm on Sunday). Next door at No 9, the ***traiteur*** sells scrumptious prepared dishes (closed from 12.45 to 3 pm and on Sunday afternoon and Wednesday). ***Les Délices de la Ferme***, a fromagerie nearby at 19 Rue Saint Thibault, is open Tuesday to Saturday (closed from 12.30 to 3 pm).

Getting There & Away

The train station information office (☎ 08 36 35 35 35), Place Mendès-France, is open from 9 am to noon and 2 to 6 pm (closed Sunday and holidays). Destinations served by direct trains include Paris' Gare de l'Est (105FF; 1¼ hours; seven to 11 a day), Reims (33FF; 20 to 40 minutes; 10 to 19 a day), Metz (142FF) and Nancy (141FF; two hours; three a day). You can also get to Strasbourg (direct or via Nancy; 213FF) and Verdun (via Châlons-en-Champagne; 106FF).

Getting Around

Rémi Royer (☎ 03 26 55 29 61), 10 Place Hugues Plomb, is open from 9 am to noon and 2 to 7 pm (closed Sunday and Monday). It has mountain bikes for 70/120FF per half-day/day.

TROYES

• pop 122,000 ✉ 10000 alt 113m

Troyes – like Reims, one of the historic capitals of Champagne – is a pleasant enough city, with lots of medieval and Renaissance houses, a number of interesting churches and some worthwhile museums. Effective town planning has, in recent years, added several well conceived features, including pedestrian malls and a modern covered food market.

Troyes does not have any champagne cellars; however, if shopping is on your mind, of recent times it has become known for its scores of clothing factory outlet stores.

Orientation

Although Troyes hardly benefits from the champagne trade, the medieval city centre – bounded by Blvd Gambetta, Blvd Victor Hugo, Blvd du 14 Juillet and the Seine – is, ironically, shaped like a champagne cork (*bouchon*). The main commercial street is Rue Émile Zola.

The train station and the tourist office are at the cork's westernmost extremity, about 500m west of the old town. Most of the city's sights and activities are in the square part of the cork 'below' (ie south-west of) the bulbous cap. However, the cathedral and the Musée d'Art Moderne are in the 'cap', in a district known as Quartier de la Cité. The old town is centred around the 17th century Hôtel de Ville and nearby Église Saint Jean.

CHAMPAGNE

TROYES

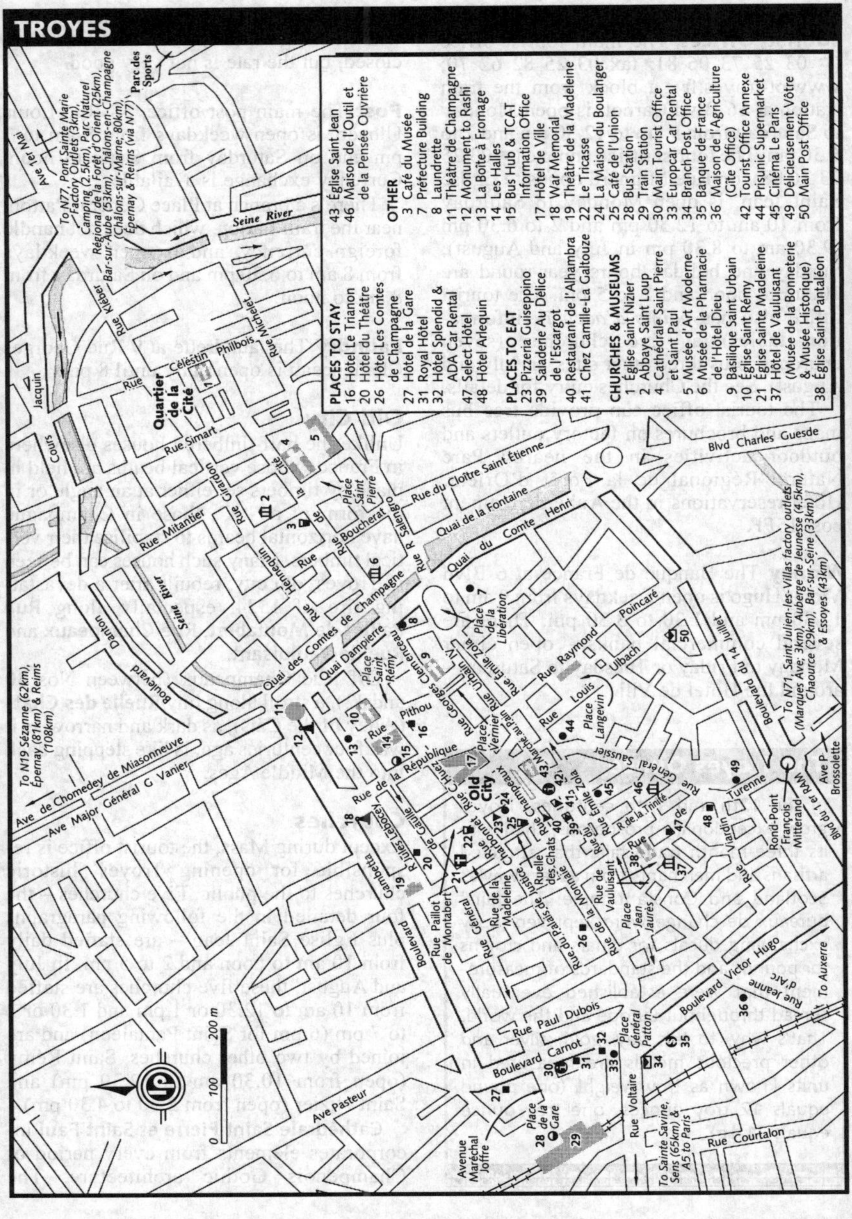
PLACES TO STAY
16 Hôtel Le Trianon
20 Hôtel du Théâtre
26 Hôtel Les Comtes de Champagne
27 Hôtel de la Gare
31 Royal Hôtel
32 Hôtel Splendid & ADA Car Rental
47 Select Hôtel
48 Hôtel Arlequin
PLACES TO EAT
23 Pizzeria Guiseppino
39 Saladerie Au Délice de l'Escargot
40 Restaurant de l'Alhambra
41 Chez Camille-La Galtouze
CHURCHES & MUSEUMS
1 Église Saint Nizier
2 Abbaye Saint Loup
4 Cathédrale Saint Pierre et Saint Paul
5 Musée d'Art Moderne
6 Musée de la Pharmacie de l'Hôtel Dieu
9 Basilique Saint Urbain
10 Église Saint Rémy
21 Église Sainte Madeleine
37 Hôtel de Vauluisant (Musée de la Bonneterie & Musée Historique)
38 Église Saint Pantaléon
43 Église Saint Jean
46 Maison de l'Outil et de la Pensée Ouvrière
OTHER
3 Café du Musée
7 Préfecture Building
8 Laundrette
11 Théâtre de Champagne
12 Monument to Rashi
13 La Boîte à Fromage
14 Les Halles
15 Bus Hub & TCAT Information Office
17 Hôtel de Ville
18 War Memorial
19 Théâtre de la Madeleine
22 Le Tricasse
24 La Maison du Boulanger
25 Café de l'Union
28 Bus Station
29 Train Station
30 Main Tourist Office
33 Europcar Car Rental
34 Branch Post Office
35 Banque de France
36 Maison de l'Agriculture (Gîte Office)
42 Tourist Office Annexe
44 Prisunic Supermarket
45 Cinéma Le Paris
49 Délicieusement Vôtre
50 Main Post Office

Information

Tourist Offices The main tourist office (☎ 03 25 73 06 81; fax 03 25 82 62 70; www.ot-troyes.fr), a block from the train station at 16 Blvd Carnot, is open Monday to Saturday from 9 am to 12.30 pm and 2 to 6.30 pm. The tourist office annexe (☎ 03 25 73 36 88), on Rue Mignard opposite Église Saint Jean, is open Monday to Saturday from 10 am to 12.30 pm and 2 to 6.30 pm (9.30 am to 8.30 pm in July and August); Sunday and holiday hours year-round are 10 am to noon and 2 to 5 pm. The tourist office also has *points d'accueil* (information tables) at five churches (seven churches, plus three other sites, in July and August). See the Churches entry for details.

The tourist office can provide free bus maps and brochures on factory outlets and outdoor activities in the nearby Parc Naturel Régional de la Forêt d'Orient. Hotel reservations in the Aube department cost 15FF.

Money The Banque de France at 6 Blvd Victor Hugo is open weekdays from 9 am to 12.30 pm and 1.30 to 3.30 pm. There are several commercial banks – open either Monday to Friday or Tuesday to Saturday – around the Hôtel de Ville.

The Troyes Ounce

In the 12th and 13th centuries, Troyes grew exceptionally prosperous, thanks to its three-month trade fairs that attracted artisans and merchants from as far away as Scotland and Constantinople. The fairs' bureaux de change were kept very busy exchanging ducats for dinars and crowns for pounds and the standards of measurement that were established eventually spread throughout Europe and the world. That's why, to this day, gold, silver and other precious metals are measured in units known as troy weight (one pound equals 12 troy ounces, one troy ounce equals 31.1g).

The tourist office's Rue Mignard annexe will exchange money when the banks are closed, but the rate is not very good.

Post The main post office, 38 Rue Louis Ulbach, is open weekdays from 8 am to 7 pm and on Saturday from 8 am to noon. Currency exchange is available.

There's a branch at Place Général Patton, near the train station, which does not handle foreign currency, and is open weekdays from 8 am to 6.30 pm and on Saturday from 8 am to noon.

Laundry The laundrette at 9 Rue Georges Clemenceau is open daily until 8 pm.

Old City

Unlike the half-timbered houses elsewhere in France, whose vertical beams are held in place by timbers set either at an angle or in the form of an 'X', those in Champagne have horizontal beams to stabilise their vertical timbers. Many such houses can be seen in Troyes' old city, rebuilt after a devastating fire of 1524, especially along **Rue Paillot de Montabert**, **Rue Champeaux** and **Rue de Vauluisant**.

Off Rue Champeaux (between Nos 30 and 32), a stroll along tiny **Ruelle des Chats** (Alley of the Cats), as dark and narrow as it was four centuries ago, is like stepping back into the Middle Ages.

Churches

Except during Mass, the tourist office is responsible for opening Troyes' historic churches to the public. Five churches – the four detailed in the following paragraphs plus Église Saint Jean – are staffed daily from 10 am to noon and 2 to 5 pm. In July and August, these five churches are staffed from 10 am to 12.30 or 1 pm and 1.30 or 2 to 7 pm (6 pm for Saint Pantaléon) and are joined by two other churches, Saint Rémy (open from 10.30 am to 12.30 pm) and Saint Nizier (open from 2.30 to 4.30 pm).

Cathédrale Saint Pierre et Saint Paul incorporates elements from every period of Champenois Gothic architecture. The

Flamboyant Gothic **west façade**, for instance, is from the mid-16th century, whereas the chancel and transepts are over 250 years older. The interior is illuminated by a spectacular series of about 180 **stained-glass windows** dating from the 13th to 17th centuries. There's also a tiny **treasury**.

Église Sainte Madeleine, Troyes' oldest (and most interesting) church, is on the corner of Rue Général de Gaulle and Rue de la Madeleine. The early Gothic nave and transept date from the mid-12th century; the choir and tower weren't built until the Renaissance. The main attraction is the splendid Flamboyant Gothic **rood screen**, which dates from the early 1500s. The statue of a deadly serious **Sainte Marthe** (St Martha), around the pillar from the wooden pulpit in the nave, is considered a masterpiece of the 15th century Troyes School. There's colourful, Renaissance stained glass in the apse.

Rashi

During the 11th and 12th centuries, a small Jewish community was established in Troyes under the protection of the counts of Champagne. Its most illustrious member was Rabbi Shlomo Yitzhaki (1040-1105), who is better known by his acronym, Rashi (Rachi in French). His commentaries on the Bible and the Talmud are still vastly important to Jews and have had an impact on Christian Bible interpretation; they combine literal and nonliteral methods of interpretation, and make extensive use of allegory, symbolism and parable. In 1475 his Bible commentary became the first book to be printed in Hebrew. Rashi's habit of explaining difficult words and passages in the vernacular (written in Hebrew characters) has made his writings an important source for scholars of Old French. In Troyes there's a striking monument to Rashi across from 5 Rue Louis Mony (next to the Théâtre de Champagne).

Troyes' other old churches include the Renaissance-style **Église Saint Pantaléon**, on Rue de Turenne, which was built from 1508 to 1672 on the one-time site of a synagogue. The interior is decorated with dozens of 16th century statues, most of them carved locally. The Gothic **Basilique Saint Urbain**, at Place Vernier, was begun in 1262 by Pope Urban IV, who was born in Troyes and whose father's shoemaking shop once stood on this spot. The west porch was added in the late 19th century. While the choir is being reinforced, the fine 13th century stained-glass windows will remain in storage. The church's best known statue is that of **La Vierge au Raisin**, a graceful, early 15th century stone carving of the Virgin in the choir.

Museums

A combined ticket (*billet groupé*) valid for entry to the four municipal museums – the Hôtel de Vauluisant, the Musée d'Art Moderne, the Musée de la Pharmacie de l'Hôtel Dieu and the Abbaye Saint Loup – costs 60FF (10FF if you're under 18). All are free on Wednesday and closed on Tuesday and some holidays.

Maison de l'Outil et de la Pensée Ouvrière The Museum of Tools & Crafts (☎ 03 25 73 28 26), 7 Rue de la Trinité, has thousands of lovingly displayed hand tools – many from the 1700s – worn down over many years by workers' hands and the materials they were shaping. Established by a national craftsmen's association, it is housed in the beautifully restored 16th century Renaissance-style Hôtel de Mauroy. It is open daily from 9 am (10 am on weekends and holidays) to 1 pm and 2 to 6.30 pm (6 pm on weekends and holidays); admission is 30FF (20FF for students and seniors).

Musée d'Art Moderne Housed in the former bishop's palace (16th, 17th and 19th centuries) at Place Saint Pierre (next to the cathedral), the Museum of Modern Art (☎ 03 25 76 21 68) has an amazing collection dating from 1850 to 1950, including works by Modigliani, Derain, Matisse, Picasso, Cézanne and Soutine. There are also some delightful works by local artist Maurice Marinot and exhibits of African and South Pacific art. It is open from 11 am to 6 pm (closed Tuesday and holidays). Entry costs 30FF (5FF for people aged under 18 and students).

Musée de la Pharmacie de l'Hôtel Dieu The one-time hospital (☎ 03 25 80 98 97) on Quai des Comtes de Champagne, founded in the 12th century, houses a fully outfitted, wood-panelled **pharmacy** that looks just as it did in the early 1700s. It is open from 10 am to noon and 2 to 6 pm (closed Tuesday and holidays). Entrance costs 20FF (5FF for people under 18 and students).

Hôtel de Vauluisant In the 16th century Renaissance-style Hôtel de Vauluisant, 4 Rue de Vauluisant (just behind Église Saint Pantaléon), the **Musée de la Bonneterie** (Hosiery & Knitwear Museum; ☎ 03 25 42 33 33) traces the knitwear industry's rise to fame and fortune with displays of old night-caps, slippers and knitting machines. In the same building, the **Musée Historique de Troyes et de la Champagne** has exhibits on the history of Troyes as well as displays of religious statuary, paintings (especially from the 16th century) and coins. Both are open from 10 am to noon and 2 to 6 pm (closed Tuesday and holidays). Admission is 30FF (5FF for those aged under 18 and students).

Special Events

La Ville en Musique brings music of all sorts (classical, jazz etc) to Troyes from late June to late August. The Semaine Chantante, a week of choral concerts (especially by children's choirs), takes place in even-numbered years in the middle of July. The Nuits de Champagne is a colourful festival of all sorts of music (rock, jazz, French chansons etc) held each year, usually in late October. For further information and tickets contact the tourist office or call ☎ 03 25 43 55 00.

Places to Stay – Budget

The *gîtes office* (☎ 03 25 73 00 11; fax 03 25 73 94 85) in the Maison d'Agriculture, Rue Jeanne d'Arc, can supply you with information on rural accommodation. It is open weekdays from 9 am to noon and 2 to 5 pm (4 pm on Friday).

Camping The three star *Camping Municipal* (☎ 03 25 81 02 64) is about 3.5km north-east of the train station at 7 Rue Roger Salengro in Pont Sainte Marie. It is open from about April to 15 October and charges 29FF for a tent site and parking plus 25FF per adult. There's a supermarket nearby. To get there, take bus No 1 (last one at about 8.30 pm) to the Stade de l'Aube stop.

You can also camp at the Auberge de Jeunesse (see Hostels) for 27FF per person.

Hostels The 100 bed *Auberge de Jeunesse* (☎ 03 25 82 00 65; fax 03 25 72 93 78), at 2 Rue Jules Ferry in the Troyes suburb of Rosières, is about 5.5km south of the train station. A bed costs 46FF; breakfast is 19FF. Reception is open daily from 8 am to 10 pm. To get there take bus No 8.

Hotels – City Centre The superbly situated, eight room *Hôtel Le Trianon* (☎ 03 25 73 18 52), 2 Rue Pithou (across from Les Halles), has doubles with washbasin from 130FF; shower-equipped rooms for two/four people are 220/250FF. Reception is closed after 9 pm and on Sunday after noon or 1 pm.

The pleasant, 28 room *Hôtel Les Comtes de Champagne* (☎ 03 25 73 11 70; fax 03 25 73 06 02), 56 Rue de la Monnaie, has doubles starting at 120FF (150FF with toilet); singles/doubles with shower and toilet are 175/190FF. The rooms away from the street are quietest. Hall showers are free. Enclosed parking is 25FF. The friendly *Hôtel du Théâtre* (☎ 03 25 73 18 47; fax 03 25 73 85 73), 35 Rue Jules Lebocey, has singles/doubles with shower for 150/170FF. Reception is closed on Sunday after 4 pm.

The *Select Hôtel* (☎/fax 03 25 73 36 16), a slightly run-down place at 1 Rue de

Vauluisant, has very basic but serviceable washbasin-equipped singles/doubles/quads with linoleum floors and tacky wallpaper from 80/110/185FF. Half-pension costs 50FF extra per person. Hall showers are free. On Sunday, reception is closed until 6 pm, so call ahead if you'll be arriving on Sunday afternoon.

Hotels – Train Station Area The uninspiring, two star ***Hôtel de la Gare*** (☎ 03 25 78 22 84; fax 03 25 74 16 26), 8 Blvd Carnot, has quiet, modern singles/doubles with shower and toilet from 185/265FF. There's plenty of street parking out front. The ***Hôtel Splendid*** (☎ 03 25 73 08 52; fax 03 25 73 41 04), 44 Blvd Carnot, has decent singles/doubles from 140/155FF (215/230FF with shower and toilet).

Places to Stay – Mid-Range

The two star ***Hôtel Arlequin*** (☎ 03 25 83 12 70; fax 03 25 83 12 99), 50 Rue de Turenne, is one of the best deals in town. Its charming, newly renovated singles/doubles/triples with antique furnishings and high ceilings – each different – start at 200/250/300FF.

The three star ***Royal Hôtel*** (☎ 03 25 73 19 99; fax 03 25 73 47 85), 22 Blvd Carnot, run by a friendly and welcoming couple, has large, soundproofed and delightfully tasteful singles/doubles for 231/350FF, triples for 400FF.

Places to Eat

Restaurants – French ***Chez Camille-La Galtouze*** (☎ 03 25 73 22 75), 82 Rue Urbain IV, has gastronomic French *menus* for 58, 79 and 98FF (open daily). ***Saladerie Au Délice de l'Escargot*** (☎ 03 25 73 02 27), on the same street at No 90, has 30 kinds of salads, fondues and fried meat dishes (closed all day Sunday and Monday evening). The *menus* cost 65 and 95FF. ***Le Théâtre***, a brasserie-restaurant affiliated with the hotel of the same name (see Places to Stay – Budget), has decent *menus* from 68FF (closed on Sunday night).

The elegant ***Restaurant du Royal Hôtel*** (see Places to Stay – Mid-Range) serves traditional French cuisine from noon to 2 pm and 7.30 to 9.30 pm (closed Saturday and Monday for lunch and on Sunday night). The *menus* cost 119 and 165FF.

Restaurants – Other The informal and chummy ***Pizzeria Guiseppino*** (☎ 03 25 73 92 44), at No 26 on narrow, medieval Rue Paillot de Montabert, serves pasta and ultra-thin, crispy pizzas for 35 to 48FF. It is open from noon to 2 pm and 7.30 to 11 pm (until midnight on Friday and Saturday; closed Monday for lunch and on Sunday).

Restaurant de l'Alhambra (☎ 03 25 73 18 41), 31 Rue Champeaux, open daily from noon to 3 pm and 7 pm till midnight, serves Algerian couscous (60 to 80FF) amid Moorish-style décor. The same pedestrianised street is home to a number of other eateries. Several ethnic restaurants can be found along Rue de la Cité between the cathedral and the Musée de la Pharmacie.

Self-Catering Ideal picnicking spots include the park along Blvd Carnot (near the train station) and flowery Place de la Libération.

Les Halles, a lively 19th century marketplace near the intersection of Rue Général de Gaulle and Rue de la République, is open until 7 pm (closed from 12.45 to 3.30 pm and on Sunday). Nearby parts of Rue Général de Gaulle have lots of food stores, including ***La Boîte à Fromage***, a cheese shop at No 18 that stays open until 7.30 pm (closed from 12.30 to 3 pm and on Sunday afternoon, Monday and holidays) and several Asian groceries (at Nos 14, 30 and 56).

The ***Prisunic*** supermarket at 71 Rue Émile Zola is open Monday to Saturday from 8.30 am to 8 pm.

Délicieusement Vôtre at 63 Rue de Turenne sells cheese and jams and, at lunchtime, hot dishes. It is open from 9.30 am to 2 pm and 4 to at least 7.30 pm (closed on Sunday afternoon).

Entertainment

Except in summer, ***Cinéma Le Paris*** (☎ 03 25 73 18 53), 107 Rue Émile Zola, screens a nondubbed film each Tuesday.

The relaxed ***Café du Musée*** (☎ 03 25 80 58 64), 59 Rue de la Cité, popular with students, is open from 9 am to 3 am (closed on Sunday). Beers start at 12FF. ***Café de l'Union*** (☎ 03 25 40 35 67), a bar and brasserie at 34 Rue Champeaux, has 1930s-style décor, including red banquettes. Its hours are 11 am to 3 am (closed Sunday). ***Le Tricasse*** (☎ 03 25 73 14 80), a pub with a billiard table at 16 Rue Paillot de Montabert, is popular with students and expats. Beers on tap start at 15FF; Guinness is 17FF. It is open from 11 am (3 pm on Saturday) to 3 am; closed Sunday.

Shopping

Troyes is known for its scores of *magasins d'usine* (factory outlets), whose discounted (and perhaps delabelled) brand-name sportswear, shoes, baby clothes, underwear etc attract bargain-hunting French people by the coach load. They are situated in two main zones:

- Saint Julien-les-Villas – about 3km south of the city centre on Blvd de Dijon (the N71 to Dijon). Some 100 shops occupy the six buildings of Marques Avenue (☎ 03 25 82 39 19), centred around 114 Blvd de Dijon. Hours are 10 am (9.30 am on Saturday) to 7 pm (closed Monday morning and Sunday). By bus, take line No 2 towards Bréviandes.
- Pont Sainte Marie – about 3km north-east of the city centre along Rue Marc Verdier, which links Ave Jean Jaurès (the N77 to Châlons-sur-Marne) with Ave Jules Guesde (the D960 to Nancy). McArthur Glen (☎ 03 25 70 47 10) is a strip mall with 60 shops; hours are 10 am (9.30 am on Saturday) to 7 pm (closed on Monday morning and on Sunday). By bus take line No 1 towards Pont Sainte Marie.

Knitwear Capital of France

Troyes first began to produce *bonneterie* (hosiery) in the early 16th century. Later, especially after mechanical looms based on English designs were introduced in the mid-18th century, production expanded to include stockings, socks and various headwear. Hosiery's hold over life in Troyes continued to grow until even the poor children living in the local charity hospital had to earn their keep by working the looms. Before long, the town had become the knitwear capital of France, a title it has retained to this day.

Getting There & Away

Bus Coach services fill some of the gaping holes left by Troyes' rather pathetic rail services. The bus station office (☎ 03 25 71 28 42), run by Courriers de l'Aube, is in a corner of the train station building. It is open weekdays from 8.30 am to 12.30 pm and 3.30 to 6.30 pm (longer hours in July and August). Bus schedules are posted outside on the sign next to the oval toilet pod; some are also available at the tourist office.

TransChampagne (STDM; ☎ 03 26 65 17 07; staffed on weekdays from 8.30 am to 5.30 pm) has four buses a day (two or three on weekend afternoons) to Reims (1½ hours by autoroute for 112FF or two hours by highway for 108FF). Les Courriers de l'Aube (☎ 03 25 71 28 40) has lines to Sens (78FF; three a day on weekdays, one on Saturday) and Châtillon-sur-Seine (70FF; 1¾ hours; three or four times a day, except on Sunday), from where there's a bus at noon to Dijon. Les Rapides de Bourgogne (☎ 03 86 46 90 90) runs two or three SNCF buses a day to Laroche-Migennes (60FF; one to 1¾ hours; four/one a day on weekdays/weekends), a stop on the Paris-Dijon rail line. From Monday to Thursday the company has a 4 pm service to Auxerre in Burgundy (about 2¼ hours).

Train Troyes is on the rather isolated Paris-Basel line. The train station information office (☎ 08 36 35 35 35) is open from 8.30 am to noon and 2 to 7 pm (closed Sunday and holidays). Major destinations include Paris' Gare de l'Est (115FF; 1½ to two hours; nine or 10 a day) and Basel (Bâle in French; 207FF; about 3½ hours; three to five a day). To get to Dijon (142FF; at least three hours; three to six a day) and Lyon

(231FF), you have to change trains. The best way to travel to northern Champagne (including Reims) and to Burgundy is by bus.

Car ADA (☎ 03 25 73 41 68) is at 36 Blvd Carnot; Europcar (☎ 03 25 73 27 66) is around the corner at 2 Rue Voltaire.

Getting Around

Bus The main bus hub of the TCAT system (☎ 03 25 70 49 00), known as Halle, is on Rue de la République near Les Halles. The eight regular lines run every 10 or 20 minutes (30 to 60 minutes on Sunday) until 7.30 or 8 pm; schedules are posted at each stop. Magnetic tickets valid for one/three rides are available from drivers for 7/17FF.

Taxi To order a taxi, call ☎ 03 25 78 30 30.

AROUND TROYES

Parc de la Forêt d'Orient

The Parc Naturel Régional de la Forêt d'Orient, 700 sq km of forest, fields, villages and water, is about 25km east of Troyes. In the warm season, you can swim, sail, windsurf, kayak, water-ski, jet ski etc on the three large lakes. The Maison du Parc (park headquarters; ☎ 03 25 43 81 90), in Piney, is open on weekdays from 9 am to noon and 2 to 6 pm; weekends and holiday hours are 9.30 am to 12.30 pm and 2.30 pm to sometime between 5.30 pm (in winter) and 6.30 pm (in the warm months).

Les Courriers de l'Aube (☎ 03 25 71 28 42) has buses from Troyes' train station to Piney (30 minutes; at least two a day) and other villages in the park. From late June to late August, the company's buses link Troyes with the **Lac d'Orient**, a large lake that offers lots of water sports.

Route Touristique du Champagne

Although the Aube department, of which Troyes is the capital, is a major producer of champagne (about 20 million bottles a year), it gets none of the recognition accorded the Marne department and the big maisons around Reims and Épernay. Much of the acrimony dates to 1909, when the Aube growers were excluded from the growing area for Champagne's Appellation d'Origine Contrôlée (AOC). Two years later, they were also forbidden to sell their grapes to producers up north, resulting in months of strikes and chaos; eventually, the army was called in. It was another 16 years before the Aube wine growers could again display the prestigious (and lucrative) AOC tag on their labels, but by then the northern producers had come to dominate the market.

Today, champagne production in the Troyes area takes place on a modest scale. However, Aube does have its own section of the Route Touristique du Champagne, the **Côtes des Bar**, which passes through Bar-sur-Seine (about 33km south-east of Troyes) and Bar-sur-Aube (about 35km north-east of Bar-sur-Seine). Private cellars en route are open to visitors. Tourist offices can provide you with an excellent English-language brochure on the route.

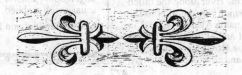

Alsace & Lorraine

Though often spoken as if they were one, Alsace and Lorraine, neighbouring regions in France's north-eastern corner, are linked by little more than an accident of history. Alsace and part of Lorraine were annexed by Germany in 1871, and in the decades before WWI they became a focal point of French nationalism.

Alsace

The charming and beautiful region of Alsace, long a meeting place of Europe's Latin and Germanic cultures, is nestled between the Vosges Mountains and the Rhine River – along which the long disputed Franco-German border seems also to have found its final resting place. Popularly known as a land of storks' nests and colourful, half-timbered houses sprouting geraniums, Alsace also offers a wide variety of outdoor activities – including hiking, mountain biking and skiing – in and around its gentle, forested mountains. Throughout France, the people of Alsace have a reputation for being hard-working, well organised and tax-paying.

Alsace, which occupies an area 190km long and no more than 50km wide, is made up of just two departments: Bas-Rhin (Lower Rhine), the area around the dynamic regional capital, Strasbourg; and Haut-Rhin (Upper Rhine), which covers the region's more southerly reaches, including the department's picturesque capital, Colmar. Germany is just across the busy, barge-laden Rhine, whose western bank is in Alsace as far south as the Swiss city of Basel.

Because the Rhine used to flood periodically, Alsace's major towns were built a few kilometres west of the river along the much smaller Ill River, which runs parallel to the Rhine. Indeed, the name Alsace – *Illsass* in Alsatian – means 'Land of the Ill'. Alsace's Route du Vin (Wine Route), which begins west of Strasbourg and continues southward

HIGHLIGHTS

- **Strasbourg** – gaze up at the spires and stained glass of the city's Gothic cathedral
- **Munster** or **Hunawihr** – watch the storks clacking their beaks
- **Colmar** – marvel at the Issenheim Altarpiece
- **Grand Ballon** or **Ballon d'Alsace** – take in the panorama of the Black Forest and the Alps
- **Nancy** – visit the curvaceous Art Nouveau furniture at the Musée de l'École de Nancy

baeckeoffe (baker's oven) – a stew of several meats and vegetables

kugelhopf – sultana and almond cake, usually with a ribbed, dome-like shape

Gewürztraminer and Reisling wines

to Colmar and beyond, snakes through the vineyards and picture-postcard villages along the eastern foothills of the Vosges.

History

During the Reformation, Protestantism made significant inroads in Alsace, particularly in Strasbourg, and to this day about one-fifth of Alsatians are Protestants. French influence in Alsace began at the end of the 1500s during the Wars of Religion (1562-98) and increased during the Thirty Years' War (1618-48), when Alsatian cities, caught between opposing Catholic and Protestant factions, turned to France for assistance. Most of the region was attached to France in 1648 under the Treaty of Westphalia.

By the time of the French Revolution, after more than a century of enjoying considerable autonomy, the Alsatians felt far more connected to France than to Germany. Indeed, the upper classes had already begun to adopt the French language. But more than two centuries of French rule did little to dampen 19th century Germany's enthusiasm for a foothold on the west bank of the southern Rhine. The Franco-Prussian War of 1870-71, a supremely humiliating episode in French history, ended with the Treaty of Frankfurt (1871), by which an embittered France was forced to cede Alsace and the northern part of the present-day region of Lorraine to Germany.

Following Germany's defeat in WWI, Alsace and Lorraine were returned to France, but the French government's program to re-assimilate the area (eg by replacing church schools with state-run ones and banning German-language newspapers) gave rise to a strong movement for home rule.

Germany's second annexation of Alsace and Lorraine in 1940 (and indeed the occupation of all of France) was supposed to have been made impossible by the state-of-the-art Maginot Line (see the boxed text 'The Maginot Line'). Immediately after Nazi Germany took over the area, about half a million people fled to occupied France. This time, the Germanisation campaign was

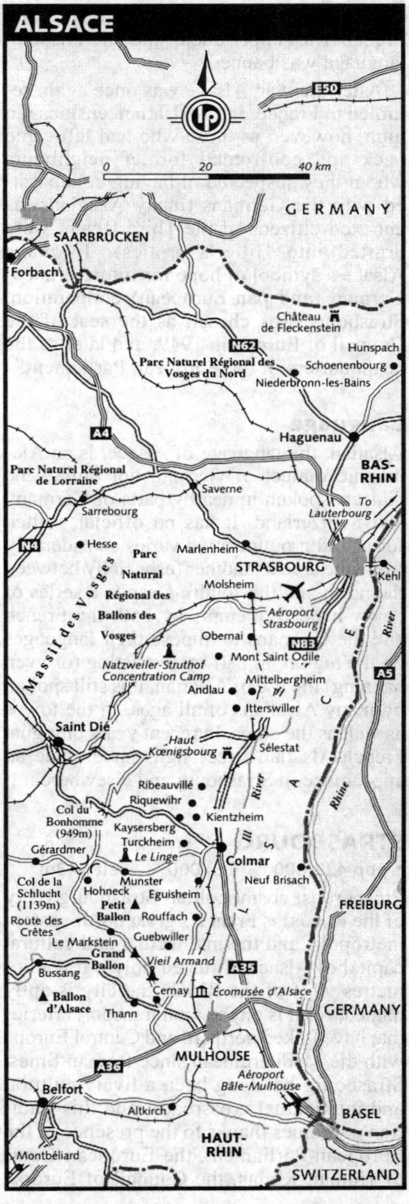

particularly harsh: anyone caught speaking French was imprisoned, and the Alsatian language was banned.

After the war, Alsace was once again returned to France. Intra-Alsatian tensions ran high, however, as those who had left came back and confronted former neighbours whom they suspected of having collaborated with the Germans (many Alsatians, as annexed citizens of the Third Reich, were drafted into Hitler's armies). To make Alsace a symbol of hope for future Franco-German (and pan-European) cooperation, Strasbourg was chosen as the seat of the Council of Europe in 1949, and later as the headquarters of the European Parliament.

Language

Alsatian, the language of Alsace, is an Alemannic dialect of German not unlike the dialects spoken in nearby parts of Germany and Switzerland. It has no official written form, and pronunciation varies considerably from one area to another (especially between the north and the south). Despite a series of heavy-handed attempts by both the French and the Germans to impose their languages on the region, in part by restricting (or even banning) the use of Alsatian, it is still spoken by many Alsatians of all ages, in the towns as well as the cities. In recent years bilingual French-Alsatian street signs have made an appearance in Strasbourg and elsewhere.

STRASBOURG

• pop 423,000 ✉ 67000 alt 143m

Prosperous, cosmopolitan Strasbourg (City of the Roads) is France's great north-eastern metropolis and the intellectual and cultural capital of Alsace. Situated only a few kilometres west of the Rhine, the city is aptly named, for it is on the vital transport arteries that have linked northern and Central Europe with the Mediterranean since Roman times. Strasbourg has long been a lively cultural and intellectual crossroads, and this tradition continues thanks to the presence of the European Parliament, the European Court of Human Rights, the Council of Europe, and an international student population of some 55,000.

Towering above the restaurants, *winstubs* (traditional Alsatian eateries) and pubs of the lively old city – a wonderful area to explore on foot – is the cathedral, a medieval marvel in pink sandstone. Nearby you'll find one of the finest ensembles of museums in France.

Accommodation is extremely difficult to find during European Parliament sessions – see Places to Stay for details.

History

Before it was attached to France in 1681, Strasbourg was effectively ruled for several centuries by a guild of citizens whose tenure accorded the city a certain democratic character. A university was founded in 1566 and several leaders of the Reformation took up residence here. Johann Gutenberg worked in Strasbourg from about 1434 to 1444, perfecting his printing press and the moveable metal type that made it so revolutionary. Three centuries later, the German poet, playwright, novelist and philosopher Johann Wolfgang von Goethe (1749-1832) studied law here.

The religious struggles that followed the Reformation hit Strasbourg with particular ferocity. To this day, several pairs of churches – one Catholic, the other Protestant – bear the same name (eg Église Saint Pierre-le-Jeune). In one case, Église Saint Pierre-le-Vieux, the same structure houses two churches, with separate entrances for the Protestant and Catholic faithful.

Orientation

The city centre is about 3.5km west of Pont de l'Europe, the bridge that links the French bank of the Rhine River with the German city of Kehl.

Strasbourg's train station is 400m west of the Grande Île (Big Island), the core of ancient and modern-day Strasbourg. Almost half of the Grande Île, which is surrounded by the Ill River and its branch, the Fossé du Faux Rempart, is now pedestrianised.

The Grande Île's main squares are Place

Kléber, Place Broglie, Place Gutenberg and Place du Château. They are linked by a number of relatively narrow traffic arteries, including east-west Rue du Vieux Marché aux Vins (and its eastward continuation) and the pedestrianised Grand' Rue; and the north-south Rue des Francs Bourgeois (down whose middle runs the tram line) and Rue des Grandes Arcades. Most of Strasbourg's museums are clustered around the cathedral, whose spire is visible from all over town. The quaint Petite France area in the Grande Île's south-western corner is subdivided by canals.

Palais de l'Europe, seat of the European Parliament, is about 2km north-east of the cathedral.

Information

Tourist Offices The main tourist office (☎ 03 88 52 28 28; fax 03 88 52 28 29; otsr@strasbourg.com; www.strasbourg.com) is just north of the cathedral at 17 Place de la Cathédrale, next to the ornate, 16th century Maison Kammerzell. It is open daily from 9 am to 6 pm (7 pm from June to September). Just outside the train station's arrival hall there's a tourist office annexe (☎ 03 88 32 51 49) in the subterranean Galerie de l'En-Verre, which is underneath Place de la Gare. It is open from 8.30 am to 12.30 pm and 1.45 to 6 pm (closed on Sunday from November to Easter). From June to early October its daily hours are 9 am to 7 pm.

At any of the three bureaus you can make same-day reservations (10FF) for tourist office-affiliated hotels anywhere in Alsace. Carnets of bus/tram tickets are available, as are free route maps. A map of cycling paths in and around Strasbourg costs 15FF; a free booklet entitled *Carte des Parcours Cyclables en Bas-Rhin* covers cycling routes around the department. *Strasbourg Actualités*, a French-language monthly listing concerts, expositions etc is also available free of charge. The 'Strasbourg Pass' (58FF), valid for three days, gets you a boat tour, one museum entry, a second museum entry for half-price, a 50% discount on a guided tour of the city, a free climb to the top of the cathedral's west façade, and – in the warm months – tickets to an organ concert in the cathedral.

For information on the Alsace region and the Route du Vin, you might also stop by the Agence de Développement Touristique en Bas-Rhin (☎ 03 88 15 45 80; www.tourisme-alsace.com), south of Place Broglie at 9 Rue du Dôme. It is open weekdays from 9.30 am till noon and 2 to 6 pm.

Money The Banque de France at 3 Place Broglie is open weekdays from 9 am to 12.30 pm and 1.30 to 3.30 pm. The first performance of the French national anthem, *La Marseillaise* (see the boxed text 'La Marseillaise'), was held on this spot in 1792. The American Express office (☎ 03 88 21 96 59), 19 Rue des Francs Bourgeois, is open on weekdays from 8.45 am to noon and 1.30 to 6 pm.

La Marseillaise

Though you'd never know it from the name, France's stirring national anthem, *La Marseillaise*, was written in Strasbourg. In April 1792, at the beginning of the war with Austria, the mayor of Strasbourg – in whose city a garrison was getting ready for battle – suggested that the Revolutionary army have a catchy and patriotic tune to sing while marching off to spread the blessings of liberty throughout the rest of Europe. He approached Claude Rouget de Lisle, a young army engineer with a minor reputation as a composer, who after a furious all-night effort came up with a marching song entitled *Chant de Guerre de l'Armée du Rhin* (War Song of the Rhine Army). It was first performed in the mayor's house (on the site of the present-day Banque de France building) by the mayor himself. The soul-stirring tune and its bloody lyrics became popular immediately, and by August it was on the lips of volunteer troops from Marseille as they marched northward to defend the Revolution.

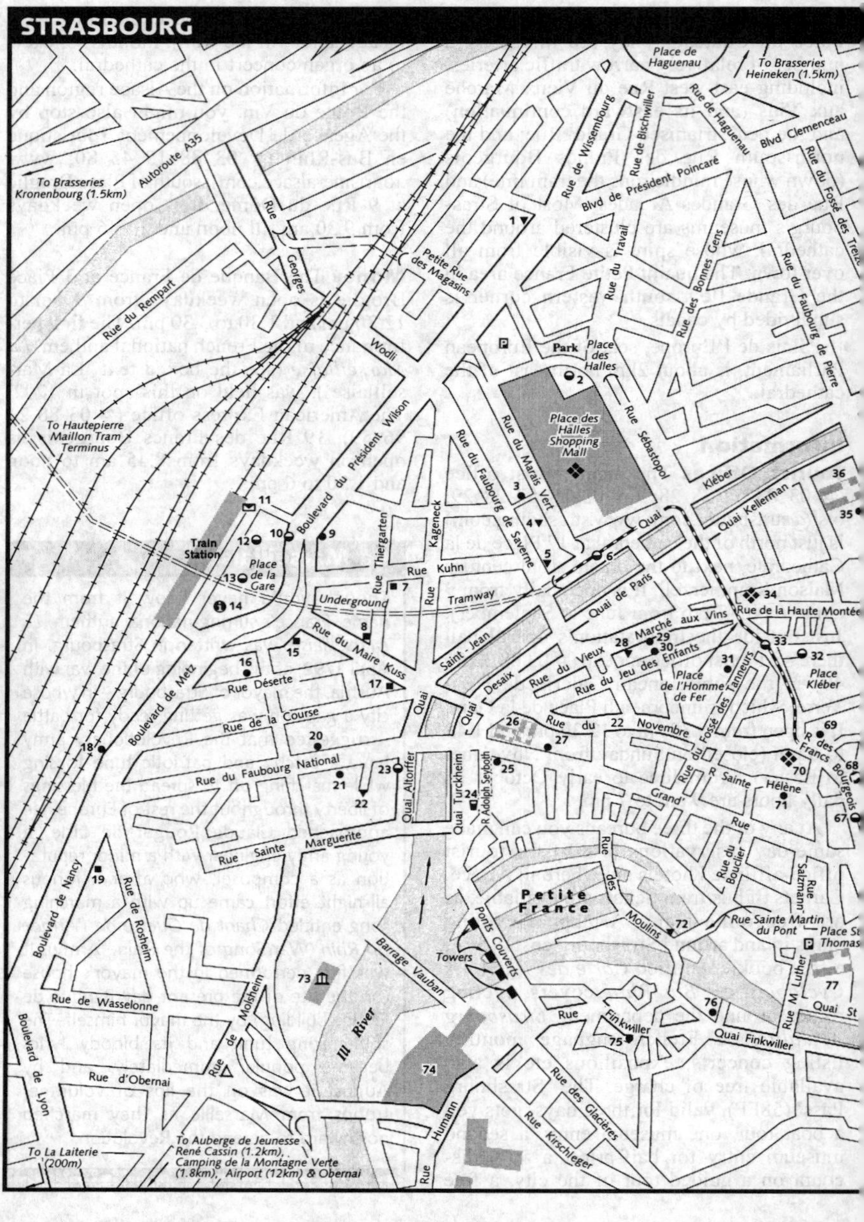
STRASBOURG
Place de Haguenau
To Brasseries Heineken (1.5km)
To Brasseries Kronenbourg (1.5km)
Autoroute A35
Rue de Wissembourg
Rue de Bischwiller
Rue de Haguenau
Blvd Clemenceau
Rue du Fossé des Treize
Blvd de Président Poincaré
Rue du Travail
Rue des Bonnes Gens
Rue du Faubourg de Pierre
Rue Georges
Petite Rue des Magasins
Rue du Rempart
Wodli
Park
Place des Halles
Place des Halles Shopping Mall
Rue Sébastopol
Rue du Marais Vert
Rue du Faubourg de Saverne
To Hautepierre Maillon Tram Terminus
Boulevard du Président Wilson
Train Station
Place de la Gare
Rue Thiergarten
Kageneck
Rue Kuhn
Rue
Tramway
Underground
Quai Kellerman
Kléber
Quai
Quai de Paris
Rue de la Haute Montée
Rue du Maire Kuss
Saint - Jean
Marché aux Vins
Rue du Vieux
Rue du Jeu des Enfants
Place de l'Homme de Fer
Rue du Fossé des Tanneurs
Place Kléber
Rue Déserte
Boulevard de Metz
Rue de la Course
Quai
Quai Desaix
Rue du 22 Novembre
R des Francs Bourgeois
Rue du Faubourg National
Quai Altorffer
Quai Turckheim
R Adolph Seyboth
R Sainte Hélène
Grand' Rue
Rue Sainte Marguerite
Rue des Moulins
Rue du Bouclier
Rue Salzmann
Petite France
Ponts Couverts
Towers
Rue Sainte Martin du Pont
Place St Thomas
Boulevard de Nancy
Rue de Rosheim
Barrage Vauban
Rue M Luther
Ill River
Rue de Molsheim
Rue de Wasselonne
Rue Finkwiller
Quai Finkwiller
Quai St
Boulevard de Lyon
Rue d'Obernai
Rue Humann
Rue des Glacières
Rue Kirschleger
To La Laiterie (200m)
To Auberge de Jeunesse René Cassin (1.2km), Camping de la Montagne Verte (1.8km), Airport (12km) & Obernai
1
2
3
4
5
6
7
8
9
10
11
12
13
14
15
16
17
18
19
20
21
22
23
24
25
26
27
28
29
30
31
32
33
34
35
36
67
68
69
70
71
72
73
74
75
76
77

ALSACE

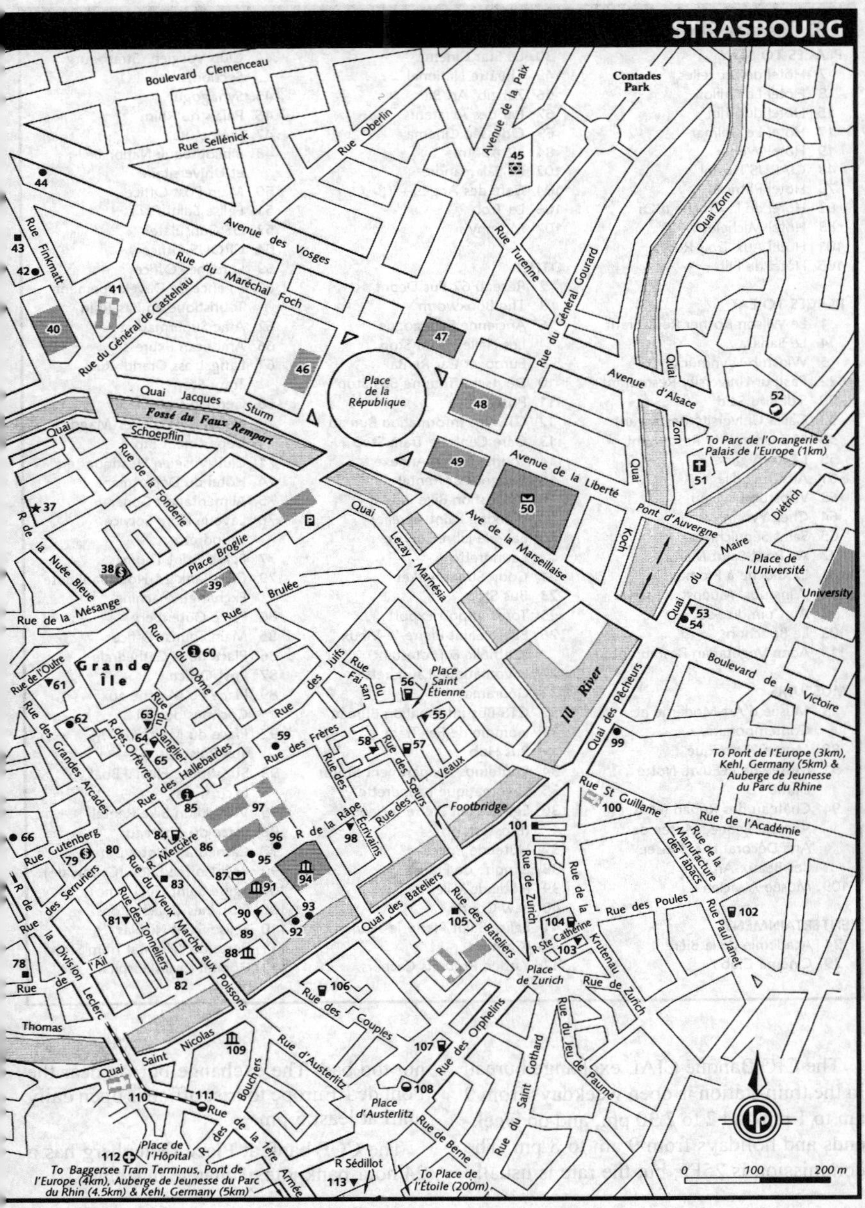
STRASBOURG
Boulevard Clemenceau
Rue Sellénick
Rue Finkmatt
Avenue des Vosges
Rue du Maréchal Foch
Rue du Général de Castelnau
Rue Oberlin
Avenue de la Paix
Contades Park
Rue Turenne
Rue du Général Gourard
Quai Zorn
Avenue d'Alsace
Quai Zorn
Place de la République
Quai Jacques Sturm
Fossé du Faux Rempart
Quai Schoepflin
Rue de la Fonderie
R de la Nuée Bleue
Place Broglie
Rue Brulée
Rue de la Mésange
Avenue de la Liberté
Quai Koch
Ave de la Marseillaise
Quai Lezay - Marnésia
Pont d'Auvergne
To Parc de l'Orangerie & Palais de l'Europe (1km)
Dietrich
Rue du Maire
Place de l'Université
University
Quai des Pêcheurs
Boulevard de la Victoire
Ill River
Grande Île
Rue de l'Outre
Rue du Dôme
Rue des Juifs
Rue du Fai san
Place Saint Étienne
Rue des Frères
Rue du Sanglier
R des Orfèvres
Rue des Hallebardes
Rue des Grandes Arcades
Rue des Sœurs
Rue des Veaux
Rue des Écrivains
R de la Râpe
Footbridge
To Pont de l'Europe (3km), Kehl, Germany (5km) & Auberge de Jeunesse du Parc du Rhine
Rue St Guillame
Rue de l'Académie
Rue de la Manufacture des Tabacs
Rue Gutenberg
R Mercière
Rue des Serruriers
Rue du Vieux Marché aux Poissons
Rue des Tonneliers
R de la Division Leclerc
Rue de l'Ail
Rue Thomas
Quai des Bateliers
Rue des Bateliers
Rue de Zurich
Rue de la Krutenau
R Ste Catherine
Place de Zurich
Rue des Poules
Rue Paul Janet
Rue de Zurich
Quai Saint Nicolas
Rue des Couples
Rue d'Austerlitz
Rue des Orphelins
Rue du Saint Gothard
Rue du Jeu de Paume
Place d'Austerlitz
Rue de Berne
R Sédillot
Rue des Bouchers
Rue de la 1ère Armée
Place de l'Hôpital
To Baggersee Tram Terminus, Pont de l'Europe (4km), Auberge de Jeunesse du Parc du Rhin (4.5km) & Kehl, Germany (5km)
To Place de l'Étoile (200m)
0 100 200 m
37 38 39 40 41 42 43 44 45 46 47 48 49 50 51 52 53 54 55 56 57 58 59 60 61 62 63 64 65 66 78 79 80 81 82 83 84 85 86 87 88 89 90 91 92 93 94 95 96 97 98 99 100 101 102 103 104 105 106 107 108 109 110 111 112 113

STRASBOURG

PLACES TO STAY
- 7 Hôtel de Bruxelles
- 8 Hôtel Le Grillon
- 15 Hôtel du Rhin
- 17 Hôtel Le Colmar
- 19 Hôtel Weber
- 43 CIARUS Hostel
- 78 Hôtel Patricia
- 82 Hôtel de la Cruche d'Or
- 83 Hôtel Michelet
- 101 Hôtel Aux Trois Roses
- 105 Hôtel de l'Ill

PLACES TO EAT
- 1 Le Wilson Kosher Restaurant
- 4 Le Sahara
- 5 Winstub Wynmuck
- 22 Pasteur University Restaurant
- 28 Sidi Bou Saïd
- 53 Gallia University Restaurant
- 55 FEC University Restaurant
- 58 La Korrygane
- 61 Au Crocodile
- 63 Winstub Le Clou
- 64 Chez Yvonne
- 65 Saint Sépulchre
- 72 Au Pont Saint Martin
- 81 La Cloche à Fromage
- 90 Winstubs' Muensterstuewel
- 98 Au Coin du Feu
- 103 Le Bouchon
- 113 Adan Vegetarian Restaurant

MUSEUMS
- 73 Musée d'Art Moderne et Contemporain
- 88 Musée Historique
- 91 Musée de l'Œuvre Notre Dame
- 94 Château des Rohan (Musée Archéologique, Musée des Arts Décoratifs & Musée des Beaux-Arts)
- 109 Musée Alsacien

ENTERTAINMENT
- 24 Académie de la Bière
- 29 Cinéma Club
- 30 Le Star Cinema
- 49 Théâtre National
- 56 Zanzib' Art Bar
- 57 Bar des Aviateurs
- 69 Odyssée Cinema
- 84 12 Apôtres
- 102 La Salamandre
- 104 Café des Anges
- 106 Le Trou
- 107 Murphy's

OTHER
- 2 Réseau 67 Bus Depot
- 3 The Bookworm
- 6 Ancienne Synagogue Les Halles Tram Stop
- 9 Europcar Car Rental
- 10 Deutsche Touring Bus Stop
- 11 Post Office
- 12 CTS Bus Information Bureau
- 13 Gare Centrale Tram Stop
- 14 Tourist Office Annexe
- 16 Budget Car Rental
- 18 Vélocation Bike Rental (Parking Saint Aurélie)
- 20 Laverie Libre Service Laundrette
- 21 Coop Supermarket
- 23 Bus Stop
- 25 Toros Import Export
- 26 Église Saint Pierre-le-Vieux (Catholic & Protestant)
- 27 Lavomatique Laundrette
- 31 Géorama
- 32 CTS Bus Information Bureau
- 33 Homme de Fer Tram; Bus Hub
- 34 Printemps (Department Store)
- 35 Lavomatique Laundrette
- 36 Église Saint Pierre-le-Jeune (Prostestant)
- 37 Hôtel de Police
- 38 Banque de France
- 39 Hôtel de Ville
- 40 Law Courts
- 41 Église Saint Pierre-le-Jeune (Catholic)
- 42 Yarden Produits Cachers
- 44 Club Vosgien (Strasbourg Section)
- 45 Synagogue
- 46 Palais du Rhin
- 47 Préfecture
- 48 Bibliothèque Nationale et Universitaire
- 50 Main Post Office
- 51 Église Saint Paul
- 52 US Consulate
- 54 CROUS Office
- 59 Eurolines Office
- 60 Agence de Développement Touristique en Bas-Rhin
- 62 Atac Supermarket
- 66 American Express
- 67 Langstross Grand' Rue Tram Stop
- 68 German Consulate
- 70 Nouvelles Galeries-Magmod Department Store
- 71 Club Vosgien Headquarters
- 74 Hôtel du Department
- 75 Alimentation Générale
- 76 Laverie Libre Service Laundrette
- 77 Église Saint Thomas
- 79 CCF Bank 24-Hour Banknote Exchange Machine
- 80 Place Gutenberg
- 85 Main Tourist Office
- 86 Place de la Cathédrale
- 87 Post Office
- 89 Place du Marché aux Cochons de Lait
- 92 Place du Marché aux Poissons
- 93 Strasbourg Fluvial Boat Excursions
- 95 Vélocation Bike Rental
- 96 Place du Château
- 97 Cathédrale Notre Dame
- 99 Best Coffee Shop (Cybercafé)
- 100 Église Saint Guillaume
- 108 Eurolines Coach Stops
- 110 Église Saint Nicolas
- 111 Porte de l'Hôpital Tram Stop
- 112 Hôpital Civil (Hospital)

The CIC Banque CIAL exchange bureau in the train station is open weekdays from 9 am to 1 pm and 2 to 7.30 pm, and on weekends and holidays from 9 am to 8 pm. The commission is 25FF, but the rate is usually not too bad. The exchange bureau near the Pont de l'Europe tourist office is open daily until at least 5 pm.

The CCF bank at Place Gutenberg has a 24 hour banknote exchange machine.

ALSACE

Post The main post office, 5 Ave de la Marseillaise, is open weekdays from 8 am to 7 pm and on Saturday until noon. The branch post office in the train station building is open the same hours. The branch at Place de la Cathédrale is open on weekdays until 6.30 pm and on Saturday until noon. All three have exchange services.

Internet Resources The Best Coffee Shop (mobile ☎ 06 80 46 43 15), 10 Quai des Pêcheurs, charges 35FF an hour to use its three or four terminals. For 180FF you get unlimited use for a month and an email account. Opening hours are 11 am (2 pm on Saturday) to 1 am; it's closed on Sunday.

Bookshops The Bookworm (☎ 03 88 32 26 99; bookwormfr@aol.com), an English-language bookshop at 3 Rue de Pâques, has a wide selection of new and used books, videos and audio cassettes, including Lonely Planet guides in English. It is open from 10 am (1.30 pm on Monday) to 6.30 pm (6 pm on Saturday); closed Sunday.

Géorama (☎ 03 88 75 01 95), 20-22 Rue du Fossé des Tanneurs, has an excellent selection of local and national maps. It is open from 9.30 am (2 pm on Monday) to 7 pm; closed Sunday. The headquarters of the 34,000 member Club Vosgien hiking organisation (☎ 03 88 32 57 96; fax 03 88 22 04 72), 16 Rue Sainte Hélène, also carries hiking maps and topoguides. It is open Monday to Saturday from 8.30 or 9 am to noon and 2 to 6 pm.

Strassbuch, put out each year by local students and often available for no charge in bookshops, has details on virtually every sort of establishment, including places to eat and shop.

Laundry On the Grande Île, the Lavomatique at 29 Grand' Rue is open daily from 8 am to 8 pm, while the Lavomatique at 8 Rue de la Nuée Bleue is open from 7 am to 9 pm. Near the train station, the Laverie Libre Service at 38 Rue du Faubourg National is open daily from 7 am to 9 pm. In Petite France, the Laverie Libre Service at 2 Quai Finkwiller overlooks the river, affording the finest view from a laundrette you'll fine anywhere in France. It is open daily from 8 am to 9 pm.

Medical Services The Hôpital Civil (☎ 03 88 11 67 68; tram stop Porte de l'Hôpital), 1 Place de l'Hôpital, accepts patients 24 hours a day.

Emergency The Police Nationale's Hôtel de Police (☎ 03 88 15 37 37), 11 Rue de la Nuée Bleue, is staffed 24 hours a day.

Walking Tour

With its bustling public squares, busy pedestrianised areas and upmarket shopping streets, the Grande Île is a great place for aimless ambling. The narrow streets of the **old city**, particularly around the cathedral, are especially enchanting at night. There are watery views from the paths along the **Ill River** and the canal known as the **Fossé du Faux Rempart** – the grassy quays along the latter are a wonderful venue for a picnic or just a rest in the shade.

Crisscrossed by narrow lanes, canals and locks, **Petite France**, in the south-west corner of the Grande Île, is the stuff of fairy tales. The half-timbered houses, meticulously maintained and sprouting veritable thickets of geraniums, and the riverside parks attract multitudes of tourists, but the area still manages to retain its Alsatian atmosphere and charm, especially in the early morning or late evening.

The Terrasse Panoramique (free) atop **Barrage Vauban**, a dam built to prevent river-borne attacks on the city, affords panoramas of the Ill River. Four square, 13th century fortified towers and the quaint, half-timbered houses of Petite France stand to one side, while the ultramodern Musée d'Art Moderne and the Hôtel du Département can be seen to the other. The terrace is open daily from 9 am to 7 or 8 pm.

The city's parks (see Parc de l'Orangerie) provide a welcome respite from the traffic and congestion of the Grande Île.

ALSACE

Cathédrale Notre Dame

Strasbourg's lacy, almost fragile-looking Gothic cathedral was begun in 1176 to replace a cathedral that had burned down three decades earlier. The west façade – which can be viewed to best advantage from Rue Mercière – was completed in 1284, but the 142m spire, the tallest of its time, was not in place until 1439; its southern companion was never built. After the Reformation and a long period of bitter struggle, the cathedral came under Protestant control, and was not returned to the Catholic Church until Louis XIV took over the city in 1681. During the Revolution, hundreds of the cathedral's statues were smashed, but fortunately a plan to get rid of the spire was never carried out. The structure was damaged by Prussian artillery in 1870 and by Allied bombing in 1944.

The cathedral (☎ 03 88 32 75 78) can be visited daily, except during Mass, from 7 to 11.40 am and 12.35 to 7 pm. The 12th to 14th century **stained-glass windows**, especially the rose window over the west portal, shine like jewels on bright days. The colourful **organ case** on the north side dates from the 14th century, while the 30m-high Gothic and Renaissance contraption just inside the south entrance is the **horloge astronomique** (astronomical clock), a late 16th century clock (the mechanism dates from 1842) that strikes 'noon' every day at precisely 12.30 pm. There is a 5FF charge to see the carved wooden figures whirl through their paces, which is why only the cathedral's south entrance is open between 11.40 am and the end of the show.

The 66m-high platform above the façade (from which the **tower** and its Gothic openwork **spire** soar another 76m) affords a stork's-eye view of Strasbourg. If you don't mind climbing up a 330 step spiral staircase, it can be visited daily from 9 am to 4.30 pm (November to February), 5.30 pm (March and October), 6.30 pm (April to June and September) or 7 pm (July and August, when opening time is 8.30 am). The entrance (☎ 03 88 43 60 40) is at the base of the bell tower that was never built. Tickets cost 20FF (10FF for students).

From May to early October, 35-minute concerts of organ music accompanied by various instruments are held several times a week at 9 pm. Tickets (34FF) are sold at the cathedral's south entrance from 7 pm.

Museums

Except for the Musée de l'Œuvre Notre-Dame and the new Musée d'Art Moderne et Contemporain, which close on Monday, all of the city's museums are open daily (except Tuesday). Except for Musée d'Art Moderne, opening hours are 10 am to noon and 1.30 to 6 pm (10 am to 5 pm on Sunday). Most museums charge 20FF (10FF for students up to age 25 and seniors); entrance is free if you're under 15 or disabled. From November to March all the museums are free on Sunday if you get there before noon. Unless otherwise noted the telephone number for Strasbourg's museums is ☎ 03 88 52 50 00.

The **Musée de l'Œuvre Notre-Dame**, housed in a group of 14th and 16th century buildings at 3 Place du Château, is Strasbourg's single most outstanding museum. It houses a magnificent collection of Romanesque, Gothic and Renaissance sculpture in both stone and wood, including a number of the cathedral's original statues, brought here for preservation and display. The *Tête du Christ* (Head of Christ), part of a stained-glass window from the mid-11th century – the oldest work of its kind in France – is in Room II. The celebrated figures of a downcast and blindfolded *Synagoga* (representing Judaism) and a victorious *Église* (the Church), which date from around 1230 and once flanked the south entrance to the cathedral (now replaced by copies), are in Room VI.

The **Château des Rohan**, 2 Place du Château, also known as the Palais Rohan, was built between 1732 and 1742 as a residence for the city's princely bishops, including Cardinal Louis de Rohan. Today, the chateau houses three museums and a gallery, each with a separate 20FF entrance

CHRIS MELLOR
The spectacular scenery of the Alps is perfect for hiking.

RICHARD NEBESKY
Argentière in the Savoy region of the Alps

FRANCES LINZEE GORDON
The canals of Annecy's old city

RICHARD NEBESKY
La Clusaz is one of the Alps' oldest skiing resorts.

STEVE FALLON

The red stone village of Roussillon in Provence is especially popular with painters.

NICOLA WILLIAMS

The Vaucluse boasts spectacular countryside, which is often brightened in spring by poppies.

fee. The whole place can be visited for 40FF (20FF for students and seniors).

In the basement, the reasonably intertesting **Musée Archéologique** covers the period from the Palaeolithic period to 800 AD. On the ground floor is the **Musée des Arts Décoratifs**, which includes a series of lavish rooms that illustrate the lifestyle of the rich and powerful during the 18th century. Louis XV and Marie-Antoinette once slept here (in 1744 and 1770 respectively). There are also rooms dedicated to 18th century faïence from Strasbourg and Haguenau and oversized clocks, including their inner workings. On the 1st floor, the **Musée des Beaux-Arts** has a rather staid collection of French, Spanish, Italian, Dutch and Flemish masters from the 14th to the 19th century. The small **Galerie Robert Heitz** hosts temporary exhibits.

The very impressive new **Musée d'Art Moderne et Contemporain** (☎ 03 88 23 31 31), at Place Sainte Marguerite, has a fine collection of paintings and sculpture from the impressionists to the present, including works by Monet, Manet, Chagall, Klimt and lots of other big names. It is open daily, except Monday, from 11 am to 7 pm (10 pm on Thursday). Entry costs 30FF (20FF reduced price).

The **Musée Alsacien** (☎ 03 88 35 55 36), 23 Quai Saint Nicolas, housed in three 16th and 17th century houses, affords a fascinating glimpse into Alsatian life over the centuries. Displays in the two dozen rooms include kitchen equipment (stoves, ceramics, biscuit cutters), colourful furniture, children's toys and even a tiny, 18th century synagogue.

The **Musée Historique** (☎ 03 88 32 25 63), in a late 16th century abattoir at 3 Place de la Grande Boucherie, traces the history of Strasbourg, but is closed for renovation until at least 2000.

Palais de l'Europe

Palais de l'Europe (☎ 03 88 17 20 07), home of the European Parliament since it was built in 1977, is 2km north-east of the cathedral. The interior can be visited on one-hour tours weekdays at 2.30 pm (in French) and at 4.30 pm (in either English and German) except when parliamentary sessions are being held. Call a day in advance to make reservations and find out when English tours are to be conducted. Visits, which are more frequent in July and August, begin at the Centre de la Presse on Allée Spach. To get there by bus, take No 23, 30 or 72.

Parc de l'Orangerie

The shaded paths, flowerbeds, children's playgrounds and swan-dotted lake of Parc de l'Orangerie are favourites with local families, especially on sunny Sunday afternoons. From April to mid-October you can rent **rowing boats** (☎ 03 88 61 07 89) on Lac de l'Orangerie for about 25FF per half-hour. The **bowling alley** (☎ 03 88 61 36 24), which also has billiard tables, is open daily until at least midnight.

Parc de l'Orangerie is across Ave de l'Europe from Palais de l'Europe. To get there by bus, take No 23, 30 or 72 to the Palais de l'Europe stop or No 15 to the Quartier des Quinze stop.

Hiking

The Strasbourg section of the Club Vosgien (☎ 03 88 35 30 76), a regional hiking organisation founded in 1872, sponsors group hikes and ski trips in the Vosges and other parts of Alsace in which visitors are welcome to participate. Reservations for the excursions, which are usually held on Sunday and either Wednesday or Thursday, should be made a few days ahead at the Strasbourg section office at 71 Ave des Vosges. It is staffed weekdays from 4 to 6.30 pm and on Saturday from 10 am to noon. The price is usually 65FF, plus 25FF for insurance for nonmembers. Bus trips leave from in front of the Palais du Rhin at Place de la République. Trip schedules are posted outside the Club Vosgien's regional headquarters (see Bookshops under Information), which can provide you with hiking information as well as maps.

Organised Tours

City From May to October the tourist office runs 1½-hour guided tours of the city, some of them in English, several times a week at 2.30 pm. In July and August tours take place daily at 10.30 am and 8.30 pm. The fee is 38FF (19FF for children and students).

Boat Boat excursions (40/20FF for adults/students; 1¼ hours) run by Strasbourg Fluvial (☎ 03 88 84 13 13 or ☎ 03 88 32 75 25) leave from the *embarcadère* (dock) behind the Château des Rohan.

Brewery Tours Two of Strasbourg's largest *brasseries* (breweries) offer guided tours of their production facilities.

Brasseries Heineken (☎ 03 88 19 59 53) is 2.5km north of the Grande Île at 4 Rue Saint Charles (near the corner of Route de Bischwiller) in Strasbourg's inner suburb of Schiltigheim. There are free, 1½-hour tours in French, German or English (depending on group bookings) at various times on weekdays. Reservations are mandatory. To get there, take bus No 4 (northbound) from Place de l'Homme de Fer and get off at the Schiltigheim Mairie stop.

Brasseries Kronenbourg (☎ 03 88 27 41 59) is 2.5km north-west of the Grande Île at 68 Route d'Oberhausbergen. Free tours in French, German and English are conducted at 9 and 10 am and 2 and 3 pm (and from June to August from 11 am and 4 pm) on weekdays (and Saturday from early May to September), except on holidays. Call ahead to reserve a place. To get to the brewery, take the tram to the Saint Florent stop. Bus No 7 from the Homme de Fer hub also goes there (get off at the Jacob stop).

Special Events

Strasbourg's summer season is enlivened by a variety of cultural events, including the Festival de Musique de Strasbourg (☎ 03 88 32 42 38), which takes place from early June to early July. Musica (☎ 03 88 21 02 02), a festival of contemporary music, is held from mid-September to early October.

One of Alsace's biggest fairs is the Marché de Noël (Christmas Market), held at Place Broglie, Place de la Cathédrale and Place de la Gare from early December until New Year's Eve (until 24 December at Place Broglie).

Places to Stay

Many of the city's hotel rooms are reserved up to a year in advance from Monday to Thursday during the one week each month (except August) when the European Parliament is in session. It is *extremely* difficult to find last-minute accommodation during these periods, so unless you'll be staying in one of the hostels, which are usually relatively unaffected, it's a good idea to ring the tourist office (or check its Web site) to find out the session dates. If you find yourself without a place to stay, the tourist office can tell you, by phone or in person, if there have been any last-minute hotel cancellations for that evening (but not for subsequent nights).

Places to Stay – Budget

Camping The grassy municipal ***Camping de la Montagne Verte*** (☎ 03 88 30 25 46), 2 Rue Robert Forrer, open year-round, charges 26FF to park and pitch a tent; each adult is charged 20FF. To get there by bus, follow the instructions for the Auberge de Jeunesse René Cassin (see Hostels), which itself has room at the back to pitch about 60 tents. The charge, including breakfast, is 42FF per person.

Hostels The city's newest and most central hostel is the stylish, modern ***Centre International d'Accueil et de Rencontre Unioniste de Strasbourg*** (CIARUS; ☎ 03 88 15 27 88; fax 03 88 15 27 89), a 285 bed, Protestant-run hostel at 7 Rue Finkmatt. People of all ages and faiths are welcome, and no hostelling card is necessary. Per-person tariffs (including breakfast) range from 86FF in a room with six or eight beds to 118FF in a double, usually containing a bunk bed. Singles are 185FF. Rooms are single-sex and equipped with shower and toilet. CIARUS also has rooms and facilities for the disabled.

Curfew is at 1 am. This place is so attractive that at least a few European MPs choose to stay here. From the train station, take bus No 10 or 20 (northbound) and get off at the Place de Pierre stop.

The ***Auberge de Jeunesse René Cassin*** (☎ 03 88 30 26 46; fax 03 88 30 35 16) is at 9 Rue de l'Auberge de Jeunesse, about 2km south-west of the station. A bed costs 69FF in a room for four to six people and 99/149FF in a double/single, including breakfast. Reception is open daily from 7 am to 12.30 pm, 1.30 to 7.30 pm and 8.30 to 11.30 pm. A HI card is mandatory. To get there from the train station, walk to Quai Altorffer and take bus No 3 or 23, which run every 10 to 15 minutes (less frequently on weekends) from 6 am to 11.30 pm, to the Auberge de Jeunesse stop.

About 6km east of the train station near Pont de l'Europe, the ***Auberge de Jeunesse du Parc du Rhin*** (☎ 03 88 45 54 20; fax 03 88 45 54 21), on Rue des Cavaliers, charges 98/138/184FF per person (including breakfast) in a quad/double/single; prices are 86/118/155FF in July and August and from mid-November to December. It is closed during the first half of November. The hostel is linked to the city centre, including Quai Altorffer, by bus Nos 2 and 21. From the Parc du Rhin stop walk south for about 800m.

Hotels – Train Station Area The 15 room ***Hôtel Le Colmar*** (☎ 03 88 32 16 89; fax 03 88 21 97 17), 1 Rue du Maire Kuss (1st floor), isn't stylish, but it's cheap and convenient. Clean, serviceable singles/doubles/triples start at 135/155/200FF; doubles with shower and toilet are 200FF. Hall showers cost 15FF. Reception may be closed on Sunday from 2 to 5.30 pm.

The ***Hôtel Weber*** (☎ 03 88 32 36 47; fax 03 88 32 19 08; ficelles@wanadoo.fr), 22 Blvd de Nancy, is hardly in the most attractive part of town, but it's convenient if you arrive by train. Clean, quiet doubles start at 130FF; doubles/triples with shower and toilet are 220/310FF. Hall showers are 12FF. If you have a car, unmetered parking is available if you drive south on Blvd de Nancy to Rue de Kœnigshoffen and turn right under the railroad tracks.

Hotels – Grande Île A good bet is the ***Hôtel Patricia*** (☎ 03 88 32 14 60; fax 03 88 32 19 08; ficelles@wanadoo.fr), 1a Rue du Puits, a quiet backstreet near Rue des Serruriers. Its generally dark, rustic interior (the 16th century building was once a convent) fits in well with the local ambience. Ordinary doubles with washbasin cost 170FF; doubles with shower and toilet are 220FF. The hall shower costs 12FF. Reception is open from 8 am to 8 pm.

The very central, 16 room ***Hôtel Michelet*** (☎ 03 88 32 47 38) is a small, family-run establishment at 48 Rue du Vieux Marché aux Poissons, a busy street whose name means 'Street of the Old Fish Market'. Simple singles/doubles start at 140/165FF (201/250FF with shower and toilet). Hall showers are free.

Places to Stay – Mid-Range & Top End

The city is fairly well supplied with tourist-class hotels.

Train Station Area Place de la Gare and nearby Rue du Maire Kuss are lined with two and three star hotels. Among the best bets is the ***Hôtel du Rhin*** (☎ 03 88 32 35 00; fax 03 88 23 51 92), 7-8 Place de la Gare, which has top-storey doubles – there's a lift – starting at 200FF. Doubles with shower and toilet are 360FF.

The cheery, informal ***Hôtel Le Grillon*** (☎ 03 88 32 71 88; fax 03 88 32 22 01), a 35 room, two star place at 2 Rue Thiergarten, has singles/doubles from 170/220FF (with washbasin) to 230/270FF (with shower and toilet). Extra beds (up to a total of five people) are 70FF each. Hall showers are free.

The older, two star ***Hôtel de Bruxelles*** (☎ 03 88 32 45 31; fax 03 88 32 06 22), 13 Rue Kuhn (the entrance is around the corner), has clean and fairly large doubles with washbasin for 145FF. Rooms with shower and toilet are 250/320/350FF for doubles/triples/quads. Some of the rooms can be a bit noisy, especially those facing the street.

Cathedral Area The small, two star ***Hôtel de la Cruche d'Or*** (☎ 03 88 32 11 23; fax 03 88 21 94 78) is at No 6 on the quiet Rue des Tonneliers, a bit south-west of the cathedral. Singles/doubles with shower and toilet start at 170/290FF. An extra bed is 60FF.

On the right (south) bank of the Ill River, the 27 room, two star ***Hôtel de l'Ill*** (☎ 03 88 36 20 01; fax 03 88 35 30 03), 8 Rue des Bateliers, has rooms with shower for 180/240FF, and with shower and toilet for 245/280FF. The two star ***Hôtel Aux Trois Roses*** (☎ 03 88 36 56 95; fax 03 88 35 06 14), 7 Rue de Zurich, has comfortable but rather small rooms with minibar for 290/395FF. The largest doubles, which cost 470FF, can take a third bed for 70FF extra. Two rooms are outfitted for disabled guests. There's no charge to use the hotel's private sauna. A few free parking places are available behind the hotel.

ALSACE

Places to Eat

The city's largest concentration of places to eat and drink is along the narrow streets east and north of the cathedral, especially on and around Rue des Frères.

Restaurants – Winstubs & Alsatian The narrow streets north of the cathedral offer three excellent, intimate places specialising in authentic Alsatian cuisine. ***Saint Sépulchre*** (☎ 03 88 32 39 97), 15 Rue des Orfèvres, a block north of the cathedral, is exalted by some locals as the city's last authentic winstub. Here you'll find solid traditional everyday dishes such as *jambonneau* (knuckle of ham) and *jambon en croûte* (ham wrapped in a crust); 75FF each. This place is open from 11 am to 2 pm and 4 to 10 pm (closed Sunday and Monday).

Winstub Le Clou (☎ 03 88 32 11 67), 3 Rue du Chaudron (a tiny alley north of the cathedral), is another warm, authentic Alsatian eatery; diners are seated together at long tables. Specialities include baeckeoffe (97FF) and *wädele braisé au pinot noir* (ham knuckles in wine; 86FF). About 15 kinds of wine are on offer starting at 23FF per 250mL. Meals are served from 11.45 am to 2.15 pm and 5.30 pm to 12.30 am (closed Wednesday for lunch and on Sunday and holidays). Another favourite is the upmarket ***Chez Yvonne*** (☎ 03 88 32 84 15), 10 Rue du Sanglier, frequented by Jacques Chirac and other politicos. Traditional Alsatian baeckeoffe is available for 90FF. Opening hours are noon to 2 pm and 6 pm to midnight (closed Monday for lunch and on Sunday).

The area just south of the cathedral has several rather touristy winstubs, including ***Winstubs'Muensterstuewel*** (☎ 03 88 32 17 63) at 8 Place du Marché aux Cochons de Lait (closed Sunday and Monday).

North-west of the Grande Île, the homey ***Winstub Wynmuck*** (☎ 03 88 32 40 86), 2 Rue du Faubourg de Saverne, caters primarily to Strasbourgeois. Specialities include huge portions of baeckeoffe (88FF), *choucroute* (78FF) and *fleichkechele* (mixed grilled meats; 60FF) with green salad. Alsatian wines start at 18FF for 250mL. This place is open from 11.30 am to 2 pm and 6 to 11 pm (closed on Sunday).

Petite France's many tourist-oriented restaurants include ***Au Pont Saint Martin*** (☎ 03 88 32 45 13), 15 Rue des Moulins, which is not a winstub but specialises in Alsatian dishes such as choucroute (70FF) and baeckeoffe (88FF). Vegetarians can select the *fricassée de champignons* (mushroom fricassee; 48FF) and one or two other dishes. The lunch *menu* costs 60FF. Meals are served every day from noon to 2.30 pm and 6.30 to 11 pm. Regional specialities can also be sampled at ***Au Coin du Feu*** (☎ 03 88 35 44 85), 10 Rue de la Râpe, which has decent *menus* for 50FF (two courses, including wine; lunch only) and 108FF (three courses). This place is closed Tuesday for lunch and on Monday.

Restaurants – French The lively ***Le Bouchon*** (☎ 03 88 37 32 40), 6 Rue Sainte Catherine, offers Lyonnaise specialities at reasonable prices – starters begin at 28FF and main courses at 68FF. It's open Monday to Saturday from 7 pm to 2 am (11.30 pm on Monday). The proprietor is a *chansonnière* of local repute and performs most nights at about 11 pm.

For Breton crêpes in a relaxed environment, try ***La Korrygane*** (☎ 03 88 37 07 34), 12 Place du Marché Gayot, off Rue des Frères; open daily. Crêpes and *galettes* (cakes) range from 17 to 49FF. The same courtyard is home to several other eateries.

What is claimed to be the world's largest cheese platter is prepared at ***La Cloche à Fromage*** (☎ 03 88 23 13 19), one of several restaurants around 27 Rue des Tonneliers. Cheese plates start at 93FF, *fondue Savoyarde* is 109FF and there are three-course *menus* for 129FF (closed on Sunday for lunch).

For all-out indulgence, *the* place to go is ***Au Crocodile*** (☎ 03 88 32 13 02), 10 Rue de l'Outre, which boasts three Michelin stars and often plays host to visiting heads of state. The four course *menu* costs 295/430FF for lunch/dinner (395/720FF with wine). Au Crocodile is closed on Sunday (except certain holidays) and Monday and during the last three weeks of July.

Restaurants – North African The ***Le Sahara*** (☎ 03 88 22 64 50), 3 Rue du Marais Vert, serves up copious portions of *tajine* (65FF) and couscous (42 to 95FF). *Menus* are available for 53 and 75FF. It is open daily from 11.30 am to 2 pm and 6.30 to 11.30 pm. On the Grande Île, ***Sidi Bou Saïd*** (☎ 03 88 32 35 88), 22 Rue du Vieux Marché aux Vins, has couscous for 55 to 70FF.

Restaurant – Vegetarian The *Adan* (☎ 03 88 35 70 84), a popular, vegetarian self-service restaurant at 6 Rue Sédillot, serves lunch from 11.45 am to 2 pm (closed on Sunday). *Menus* start at 59FF.

Restaurants – Kosher Strasbourg has a number of places that cater to the city's large Jewish population. ***Le Wilson*** (☎ 03 88 52 06 66), 25 Blvd du Président Wilson, is a large kosher meat restaurant that also functions as a takeaway, a dairy pizzeria (dinner only) and a patisserie. *Menus* start at 85FF; plats du jour are 60FF. Le Wilson is open daily for lunch and dinner except on Friday night and Saturday (open on Saturday night in winter).

Student Restaurants Unfortunately for travellers, to get the full student discount at Strasbourg's university restaurants you need to buy a *carte à puce*, a rechargeable and reimbursable magnetic debit card that costs 200FF (including a 50FF deposit). It is on sale at the CROUS office (☎ 03 88 21 28 00) at 1 Quai du Maire Diétrich, which is open weekdays from 9 am to 1 pm, and at lunchtime at the Pasteur restaurant. Otherwise, you can buy one-time tickets for *hôtes* (guests) for 28FF, double the regular student price, at lunchtime at the CROUS restaurants.

Student restaurants with good reputations include ***FEC*** (☎ 03 88 35 36 20), in the courtyard at 17 Place Saint Étienne, and ***Gallia*** (☎ 03 88 35 22 32), next to the CROUS office at 1 Place de l'Université. Both are open weekdays (and one weekend a month) from 11 am to 1.30 pm and 6 to 8 pm. ***Pasteur***, 7 Rue du Faubourg National, is open on weekdays and some weekends from 11.30 am to 1.30 pm and 6.30 to 7.45 pm. In the check-out line of the cafeteria (as opposed to the restaurant) you can pay in cash.

Self-Catering Near Place Kléber, ***Le Marché*** supermarket on the 3rd floor of the Nouvelles Galeries-Magmod department store, 34 Rue du 22 Novembre, is open Monday to Saturday from 9 am to 7 pm. Also near Place Kléber, the ***Atac*** supermarket at 47 Rue des Grandes Arcades is open Monday to Saturday from 8.30 am to 8 pm. ***Toros Import Export*** at 8 Grand' Rue is open seven day a week from 8 am to 8 pm.

In the Petite France area, the ***Alimentation Générale*** at 12 Rue Finkwiller is open Monday to Saturday from 7 am to 7 pm. There are several other food shops nearby.

Yarden Produits Cachers, 3 Rue Finkmatt, is a well stocked kosher grocery that is open from 9.30 am to 12.30 pm (1 pm on Sunday) and 3 to 7.30 pm (until sometime between 4 and 5 pm on Friday, when there may not be a midday closure). It is closed all day Saturday as well as on Sunday afternoon.

Near the train station, the ***Coop*** supermarket at 19 Rue du Faubourg National is open weekdays from 8 am to 12.30 pm and 3 to 7 pm, and on Saturday from 8 am to 6 pm.

Strasbourg's 19 weekly outdoor markets include an all-day ***food market*** at Place Broglie on Wednesday and Friday. On Saturday from 7 am to 1 pm, farmers come to town to sell their own produce at the ***farmers' market*** in Place du Marché aux Poissons (near the cathedral).

Entertainment

Cinemas Nondubbed films are on offer at ***Odyssée*** (☎ 03 88 75 11 52), an art cinema at 3 Rue des Francs Bourgeois that bills itself as an *espace cinématographique culturel européen*; the five screen ***Cinéma Club*** (☎ 03 88 32 01 48), 32 Rue du Vieux Marché aux Vins; and the five screen ***Le Star*** (☎ 03 88 22 33 95), which is one street away at 27 Rue du Jeu des Enfants.

Discos & Clubs Strasbourg's most vibrant venue for live music is ***La Laiterie*** (☎ 03 88 23 72 37) at 11-13 Rue du Hohwald, about 1km south-west of the train station. Live groups – including some of international repute (Pat Matheney was in town while this chapter was being researched) – play pop, jazz, blues, rap, reggae, French chansons etc almost every night of the week. In general, a back-up group begins playing at 8.30 pm, while the main attraction of the evening takes the stage at 10 pm. Tickets usually cost from 50 to 130FF and are available either at the door (telephone bookings are not accepted) or, for a slight surcharge, at a FNAC ticket outlet. More popular groups are often sold out. To get to La Laiterie by bus, take line No 2, 3 or 23 to the Boulevard de Lyon stop.

From Wednesday to Saturday ***La Salamandre*** (☎ 03 88 25 79 42), 3 Rue Paul Janet, a dance club popular with students, has either live bands (salsa, house, 70s etc – but no techno) or themed DJ nights from 9 pm to 3 am. From October to April it also has a *bal musette* (dancing to French accordion music) on Sunday from 5 to 10 pm. Tickets for the themed evenings cost about 30FF; concerts range from 60 to 80FF.

The mellow, informal ***Café des Anges*** (☎ 03 88 37 12 67), 5 Rue Sainte Catherine, has dancing to jazz, soul, R&B, funk and acid in the cellar, while on the ground floor the bods move to salsa and assorted other Latin music. This place is open from 9 pm to 4 am (closed on Sunday and Monday except on holidays), but things only really get going around 11 pm. There's no entry fee; drinks start at 15 or 20FF.

Pubs & Bars Pubs and bars that specialise in beer include the modern, well lit ***12 Apôtres*** (☎ 03 88 32 08 24), 7 Rue Mercière, a stone's throw from the cathedral. A favourite of locals, it has 14 beers on tap (prices start at 22FF for 400mL) and is open daily from 4 pm (noon on Saturday and in summer) to midnight (1 am on Saturday night).

At the friendly ***Académie de la Bière*** (☎ 03 88 32 61 08), 17 Rue Adolphe Seyboth, you can sit amid rough-hewn wooden beams – or, if you prefer, in the cellar below – and choose from among 70 beers; prices start at 12FF (17FF after 9 pm). *Tartes flambées*, little pizzas and quiches are available all day long. This place, popular with students, is open daily from 9 am to 4 am. Irish music has been known to be heard here. ***Le Trou*** (☎ 03 88 36 91 04), in a vaulted brick cellar at 5 Rue des Couples, has about 50 kinds of beer. Prices for a draught demi (330mL) start at 15FF (10FF from 8 to 9 pm); bottles are in the 20 to 50FF range. Le Trou, which also serves munchies and sandwiches, is open daily from 8 pm (6 pm on Sunday) to 4 am.

The friendly, laid-back ***Zanzib' Art Bar*** (☎ 03 88 37 91 81), 1 Place Saint Étienne, is open daily from 11 am until as late as 4 am.

Beers start at 10FF (15FF after 9 pm). ***Bar des Aviateurs*** (☎ 03 88 36 52 69), 12 Rue des Sœurs, whose poster and photo-covered walls and long wooden counter give the place a 1940s sort of feel, is open every day from 8 pm to 4 am. Beers start at 18FF. The clients often start dancing at around 2 am.

On the south bank of the Ill River there are several pubs along Rue des Orphelins, including ***Murphy's*** (☎ 03 88 36 52 29) at No 11, which is open daily until 1.30 am.

Getting There & Away

Air Strasbourg airport (☎ 03 88 64 67 67) is 12km south-west of the city centre (towards Molsheim) near the village of Entzheim.

Bus Réseau 67 (☎ 03 88 23 43 23), the department's network of commuter and school bus lines and companies (it's named after the first two digits of Bas-Rhin's postal code), serves towns and villages north, west and south of Strasbourg, but not the Route du Vin except for Molsheim and Obernai; the latter (40 to 60 minutes; eight times a day except Sunday, with the last bus back at 5.25 pm) is on the Otrott line. Other destinations that may be of interest include Haguenau and Saverne. Sunday and holiday services are limited or nonexistent. Réseau 67's Strasbourg depot is a parking lot just north of the Place des Halles shopping mall; the office is open Monday to Saturday from 6 am to 7 pm.

Eurolines (☎ 03 88 22 73 74) has an office at 5 Rue des Frères (closed on Saturday afternoon and Sunday), but its coaches arrive and depart from Place d'Austerlitz.

Strasbourg city bus No 21 links Place Gutenberg with the Stadthalle in Kehl, the German town just across the Rhine. The German company Deutsche Touring (☎ 07851-72082 in Kehl) has twice-daily buses from Place de la Gare northward to the German cities of Tübingen (35DM) and Reutlingen.

Train The train station building, constructed in 1883, is open 24 hours a day; the information windows (☎ 08 36 35 35 35) are staffed daily from 5 am to 9 pm. The left-luggage office (☎ 03 88 75 41 63) is open daily from 8 am to 8 pm.

Route du Vin towns with frequent SNCF bus or train services include Molsheim (20FF; 20 minutes; 20 on weekdays, five to seven on weekends and holidays), Obernai (28FF; 30 minutes; 10 on weekdays, four to six on weekends and holidays) and Sélestat (one hour; 10 on weekdays, four to six on weekends and holidays).

Strasbourg has direct trains to Paris' Gare de l'Est (210FF, except for some early evening trains that require supplements; four hours; 10 to 12 a day), Colmar (58FF; 30 to 50 minutes; 18 to 28 a day), Metz (112FF; 1¼ hours; nine a day), Mulhouse (one hour; 16 to 24 a day), Nancy (108FF; 1¼ hours; 10 to 13 a day), Lille (270FF; five hours; two a day) and Lyon (253FF; five hours; five or six a day). There are also connections, some via Lyon, to Nice (463FF; 11 hours; three a day).

Internationally, there are regular trains to Basel (Bâle; 102FF; 1½ hours; nine to 15 a day), Amsterdam (417FF via Brussels; eight hours; three a day), Frankfurt (215FF; three hours; six a day), Prague (590FF via Stuttgart; nightly; 14 hours) and Budapest (880FF; nightly; 14 hours).

Car Near the train station, Europcar (☎ 03 88 22 18 00), 16 Place de la Gare, is open Monday to Saturday from 8 am to noon and 2 to 7 pm (5 pm on Saturday, closed Sunday). Budget (☎ 03 88 52 87 52), 14 Rue Déserte, is open from 8 am to noon and 2 to 6 pm (closed Saturday afternoon and Sunday).

Getting Around

To/From the Airport To get to Strasbourg's international airport in Entzheim, take tram line A to the Baggersee terminus and then hop on a CTS *navette* (shuttle; ☎ 03 88 77 70 70), which run every 15 minutes. It costs 25FF and takes 12 minutes to get to the airport. Lufthansa and a company called Check Line (☎ 03 89 49 06 21) have buses to Frankfurt airport; Swissair has buses to Basel's airport.

Bus & Tram Strasbourg's excellent public transport network, run by CTS (☎ 03 88 77 70 70), combines highly civilised trams and good geographical coverage with frequent service. The futuristic, three car bubble that you see sliding almost silently down the middle of the street is the city's one and only tram line, ambitiously named Ligne A.

Single bus/tram tickets, sold by bus drivers and the ticket machines at tram stops, cost 7FF. A Multipass good for five/10 trips costs 31/62FF and is available from the tourist office, CTS information bureaus (eg at 31 Place Kléber and in the Galerie de l'En-Verre below Place de la Gare), some post offices, some *tabacs* (tobacconists) and tram stop ticket machines. The tourist office, CTS bureaus and ticket dispensers also sell the Tourpass (20FF), which is valid for 24 hours of travel from the moment you time-stamp it. The weekly Hebdopass (64FF) is good from Monday to Sunday.

The bus hubs are Place de l'Homme de Fer, a block north-west of Place Kléber, marked by a huge doughnut-shaped shelter of glass and steel; and Place Gutenberg. Quite a few buses can also be caught at Place Broglie. Buses from the city centre run until about 11.30 pm.

Taxi France Taxi (☎ 03 88 22 19 19) and Taxi Treize (☎ 03 88 36 13 13) operate round the clock.

Bicycle & Electric Car Strasbourg has an extensive *réseau cyclable* (network of cycling paths); maps are available at the tourist office for 15FF.

The city government has set up a wonderful system called Vélocation (☎ 03 88 52 01 01) whereby you can rent bicycles from three spots around town: Parking Saint Aurélie, a block south of the train station at 1 Blvd de Metz; in the parking lot between the cathedral and the Musée de l'Œuvre Notre-Dame; and at Place de l'Étoile, 500m due south of Place d'Austerlitz. Bicycles cost a mere 20/30FF a half-day/day; a tandem is 40FF. The Vélocation sites are open daily from 9 am to 7 pm; the Saint Aurélie site's hours are a bit longer. A map/guide with cycling itineraries costs 15FF.

The Saint Aurélie garage also hires out electric cars, which run for about 50km on a single charge and cost 100FF a half-day. You must present your passport/national identity card and leave a deposit of 1000FF.

ROUTE DU VIN D'ALSACE

Meandering for some 120km along the eastern foothills of the Vosges, the Alsace Wine Route wends its way through villages brightened by colourful half-timbered houses, surrounded by vine-clad slopes and guarded by ruined hilltop castles. Combine these vistas with numerous roadside *caves* (wine cellars), where you can sample Alsace's crisp white wines (Riesling and Gewürztraminer in particular), and you have one of the region's busiest tourist tracks. Local tourist offices can supply you with an English-language map-brochure, *The Alsace Wine Route*, which details the Route du Vin's course and gives a bit of information on each town or village it passes.

The Route du Vin stretches from Marlenheim, about 20km west of Strasbourg, southward to Thann, about 35km south-west of Colmar. En route are some of Alsace's most colourful villages, many extensively rebuilt after being flattened in WWII. Though often twee and touristy, the area is still a working centre of wine production, its economy based on the 130 sq km of vines and the 'liquid gold' that they produce.

Some of the slightly less touristy places include (from north to south) Mittelbergheim, Andlau, Itterswiller, Turckheim and Eguisheim. Also worth visiting are the very popular Ribeauvillé, Riquewihr, Kintzheim, Kaysersberg and the chateau at Haut Kœnigsbourg, all of which can easily be seen on a day trip from Colmar. Just try not to go on a holiday weekend or during the summer school holidays, when the route is positively overrun with French and German visitors.

The villages mentioned below – listed from north to south – all have plenty of hotels, camping grounds and restaurants, but very few of them cater to the budget-conscious. If money is tight your best bet is to ask any tourist office for its list of *chambres d'hôtes* (B&Bs), which cost as little as 130/160FF for a single/double.

Organised Tours

For the carless, Tourisme Fleury (☎ 06 07 26 68 15) at 40 Rue de Wattwiller in Strasbourg, offers tours that take in as many as nine villages in an eight hour day (9 am to 5 pm). Travelling in a nine passenger minibus costs up to 390FF per person, but the price drops as the number of participants increases.

Getting There & Away

The Route du Vin, which is not just one road but a composite of several (the D422, D35, D1bis etc), can be easily travelled by car or bicycle. It is very well signposted along its entire course, but drivers might want to pick up a copy of Blay's colour-coded map, *Alsace Touristique* (40FF at tourist offices). Parking can be a nightmare in the high season, especially in Ribeauvillé and Riquewihr.

Getting to and around the Route du Vin by public transport can be a bit tricky but is eminently possible, and most of the towns mentioned below are served by train and/or bus – for details see Getting There & Away under Colmar and Strasbourg. The Colmar tourist office has comprehensive information on regional bus schedules and can suggest ways to take full advantage of your options.

Molsheim

Less than 30km south-west of Strasbourg, this ancient town is one of the largest on the Route du Vin and is a popular day trip from the Alsatian capital. Among its attractions are the medieval fortifications, including the tall **Porte des Forgerons** (Blacksmiths' Gate), the 16th century **Metzig** (Town Hall) and an enormous late Gothic church built in pink sandstone in 1615 and known as the **Église des Jésuites**.

The tourist office (☎ 03 88 38 11 61; fax 03 88 49 80 40), 19 Place de l'Hôtel de Ville, near the Metzig, has a list of available rooms.

Obernai

This picturesque town, 8km south of Molsheim, was once the residence of the Dukes of Alsace. These days it is home to many buildings of historic interest, including a **belfry** from the 13th and 16th centuries and the **Halle aux Blés** (Corn Exchange; 1554) on Place du Marché. The cool, flower-bedecked courtyards (eg Cour Fastinger off Rue Général Gouraud) are fun to explore.

The tourist office (☎ 03 88 95 64 13; fax 03 88 49 90 84) is opposite the belfry on Place du Beffroi. A good place for a meal, with Alsatian *menus* from 75FF, is the ***Restaurant La Halle aux Blés*** (☎ 03 88 95 56 09) on the ground floor of its namesake.

Mittelbergheim & Andlau

Some 10km south-west of Obernai and 2km apart, these two villages are – refreshingly – not as geared up for tourism as their flashier siblings to the north and south. Mittelbergheim is a hilly village awash in vines with no real centre and tiny streets lined with Renaissance houses. Private accommodation is reasonably easy to come by ('chambres/zimmer frei' signs are in windows all over town).

Andlau, on lower ground but surrounded by hills, has plenty of *caves* for wine-tasting (the labels to try here are Kastelberg, Mœnchberg and Wiebelsberg). Among Andlau's sights are the dilapidated **Haut Andlau** and **Spesbourg castles**, accessible on foot in about three hours, and a Romanesque **abbey church** with an eerie, 11th century crypt. The tourist office (☎ 03 88 08 22 57; fax 03 88 08 42 22), which is open on most afternoons, is at 5 Rue du Général de Gaulle.

Haut Kœnigsbourg

Built on a forested promontory high above the town of Saint Hippolyte, the imposing, red-sandstone **Château du Haut Kœnigsbourg** (☎ 03 88 82 50 60) was reconstructed early this century by Germany's Kaiser Wilhelm II (ruled 1888-1918) on the site of a 12th century fortress. Hours change according to the season, but the chateau can be visited daily from 9 or 9.30 am to noon and 1 pm to sometime between 4 pm (in the dead of winter) to 5.30 or 6 pm (from June to September). Admission costs 40FF (25FF for students and children).

Ribeauvillé

Some 19km north-west of Colmar, Ribeauvillé is arguably the most touristed of all the villages on the Route du Vin. It's easy to see why: the little village, nestled in a valley and brimming with 18th century overhanging houses and narrow alleys, is picture perfect. Don't miss the 13th and 14th century **Tour des Bouchers** (Butchers' Tower), Place de la Mairie, or the **Pfifferhaus** at 99 Grand' Rue, which once housed the town's marching minstrels. The ruins of three 12th and 13th century **castles** west and north-west of Ribeauvillé can be reached on foot in three hours. One of them – **Château du Haut Ribeaupierre** – is visible from the village centre.

The tourist office (☎ 03 89 73 62 22; fax 03 89 73 23 62) is at No 1 on the pedestrianised Grand' Rue. It can supply you with a brochure, *Le Pays de Ribeauvillée et Riquewihr*, which should be available in English and has a useful map.

Riquewihr

This partially walled village is every bit as popular with visitors as Ribeauvillé, 5km to the north, but somehow, despite all the crowds, it feels just a tad more authentic. The 16th century **ramparts** are great for exploring, as are the inner courtyards. Other sights include the **Dolder Tour Beffroi**, a 13th century gate with a bell tower, and the **Château de Riquewihr**, built in 1539 and now housing the less-than-riveting **Musée d'Histoire des PTT d'Alsace** (Alsace Postal Museum; ☎ 03 89 47 93 80). Instead, head for the **Tour des Voleurs** (Thieves' Tower), a former dungeon containing some extremely efficient-looking implements of torture. The tower is open from Easter to 1 November; hours are 9.15 am to noon and 1.30 to 6 pm. Admission costs 10FF.

The tourist office (☎ 03 89 49 08 40; fax 03 89 49 08 49), 2 Rue de la Armée, can supply you with a map indicating everything of interest.

Kaysersberg

This touristy, picture-perfect town, 10km north-west of Colmar along the N415, is known for its **fortified bridge** over the Weiss River and its 12th to 15th century red-sandstone **church**, which has a Renaissance **fountain** on one side and the ornate, Renaissance **Hôtel de Ville**, built in 1605, on the other. The house where the musicologist, medical doctor and 1952 Nobel Peace Prize winner **Albert Schweitzer** (1875-1965) was born is now a cultural centre (there's a museum dedicated to the good doctor in the Vallée de Munster town of Gunsbach). The remains of the **chateau**, on a hillside a few hundred metres north of the centre, are surrounded by trimmed and trained grape vines. Footpaths lead in all directions; possible destinations include Riquewihr (1½ hours), Labaroche (2½ hours) and Ribeauvillé (three hours).

The tourist office (☎ 03 89 78 22 78; fax 03 89 78 27 44; OT.kaysersberg@rmcnet.fr) is at No 39 on the main street, officially called Rue du Général de Gaulle.

The only inexpensive eatery is the ***kebab place***, 68 Rue du Général de Gaulle.

Eguisheim

• pop 1500 ✉ 68420 alt 210m

Just 5km south-west of Colmar, the village of Eguisheim, surrounded by vineyards, has a circular town centre in whose middle sits the **Château d'Eguisheim**, founded in the 8th century, where Pope Leo IX was born in 1002. Bisected by the Grand' Rue, the village centre is known for its gabled, geranium-adorned houses, two **Renaissance-style fountains** and, on a hill above the town, three square **dungeons** (fortified towers) made of red sandstone. The latter are linked to the town by a variety of walking trails that also go to neighbouring villages. During the warm months the town fills with wine-seeking tourists drawn by some three dozen small wineries. The most famous *grands crus* (vintages) are Eichberg and Pfersigberg, whose vineyards are north-west of town.

The tourist office (☎ 03 89 23 40 33) is on the Grand' Rue.

Eguisheim has a number of two star hotels. The ***Auberge des Comtes*** (☎ 03 89 41 16 99; fax 03 89 24 97 10), 1 Place Charles de Gaulle, on the western edge of the town centre, has comfortable doubles/triples for 320/420FF (290/360FF in the off season).

NATZWEILER-STRUTHOF CONCENTRATION CAMP

The only Nazi concentration camp on French soil, Natzweiler-Struthof (☎ 03 88 97 04 49) was established about 30km west of Obernai in May 1941. The site was chosen because of the nearby quarries, in which many of the inmates were worked to death as slave labourers. In all, some 25,000 of the camp's prisoners, most of them Jews from around Europe and French Résistance fighters (including many women), died or were executed here. In April 1944, as the Allies approached Alsace, the surviving inmates were sent to Dachau.

The camp provided Reich University in Strasbourg with inmates for use in often lethal pseudo-medical experiments involving combat gases and infectious diseases such as hepatitis. In April 1943 about 100 Jewish prisoners, specially brought from Auschwitz, were gassed at Natzweiler-Struthof to supply the anatomical institute of the university with skeletons for its anthropological and racial skeleton collection.

Today visitors can see the remains of the barracks, prison cells and crematorium as well as a museum, a cemetery and a memorial. From March to 24 December, Struthof can be visited daily from 10 to 11.30 am and 2 to 4.30 pm (10 am to 5 pm in July and August). Entry costs 8FF. To get there by car, take the D426, D214 and D130 from Obernai.

COLMAR

• pop 65,000 ✉ 68000 alt 194m

The centre of the colourful, harmonious town of Colmar, capital of Haut-Rhin, is a maze of cobbled pedestrian malls and restored, Alsatian-style buildings from the late Middle Ages and the Renaissance. Many of the half-timbered houses are painted in bold tones of blue, orange, red or green. The Musée d'Unterlinden is world renowned for the spectacular Issenheim Altarpiece.

Colmar is at its liveliest during 10 days in the first half of August, when the town throws its annual Foire des Vins (see Special Events). Many villages along the Route du Vin, which can easily be explored by car, bus or bike using Colmar as a base, have similar celebrations that continue to the end of summer.

Orientation

Avenue de la République links the charmless area around the train station and bus terminal with the Musée d'Unterlinden and the nearby tourist office, a distance of about 1km. The old city, much of it pedestrianised, is south-east of the Musée d'Unterlinden. The Petite Venise quarter runs along the Lauch River, at the southern edge of the old city.

Information

Tourist Office The efficient tourist office (☎ 03 89 20 68 92; fax 03 89 41 34 13; www.tourisme.fr/COLMAR), across the street from the Musée d'Unterlinden at 4 Rue des Unterlinden, is open Monday to Saturday from 9 am to noon and 2 to 6 pm (no midday closure from April to October; open until 7 pm in July and August). Sunday hours are 10 am to 2 pm. The staff will make reservations for both hotels and rental cars for no charge, but only if you stop by. In the warm months you might want to pick up a *Calendrier des Manifestations* (Calendar of Events), which lists things going on in and around Colmar. See Hiking & Cycling under both Colmar and the Massif des Vosges for details on brochures you might want to also pick up.

Money The Banque de France at 46 Ave de la République is open on weekdays from 8.45 am to 12.10 pm and 1.50 to 3.30 pm. The tourist office will change money, but the rate is not very good. There are 24-hour banknote exchange machines at the Crédit Commercial de France opposite the Monoprix on Rue des Clefs, and at the Sogenal bank at 17 Rue des Têtes.

Post The main post office, 36 Ave de la République, is open weekdays from 8 am to 6.30 pm and Saturday from 8.30 am to noon. Exchange services are available.

Laundry The Point Laverie at 1 Rue Ruest is open daily.

Medical Services Hôpital Pasteur (☎ 03 89 80 40 00, 24 hours a day), 700m west of the train station at 39 Ave de la Liberté, has a 24 hour casualty ward. It is served by bus Nos 1, 3, A and C.

ALSACE

Old City

The medieval streets of the old city, including **Rue des Clefs**, the **Grand' Rue** and **Rue des Marchands**, are lined with dozens of half-timbered houses. **Maison Pfister**, which is opposite 36 Rue des Marchands, was built in 1537 and is remarkable for its exterior decoration, including delicately painted panels, an elaborate oriel window and a carved wooden balcony. The house next door at 9 Rue des Marchands, which dates from 1419, has a wooden sculpture of a sombre-looking *marchand* (merchant) on the corner. The **Maison des Têtes** (House of the Heads), 19 Rue des Têtes, built in 1609, has a fantastic façade crowded with 106 grimacing stone faces and animal heads.

Colmar has a number of small **quartiers** (quarters, or neighbourhoods) – not much more than single streets in a few cases – which preserve some of the ambience that existed back when each was home to a specific guild. At the south-eastern end of Rue des Marchands, near the **Quartier des Tanneurs** (Tanners' District), is the **Ancienne Douane** (or Koïfhus in Alsatian; Old Customs House), built in 1480. Now used for temporary exhibitions and concerts, it is the town's most interesting example of late medieval civil architecture.

Rue des Tanneurs, with its tall houses and rooftop verandas for drying hides, intersects **Quai de la Poissonnerie**, the former fishers' quarter, which runs along the Lauch River. The river provides the delightful **Petite Venise** (Little Venice) area – also known as Quartier de la Krutenau – with its rather fanciful appellation, best appreciated from the **Rue de Turenne bridge**.

On Friday and Saturday and during holiday periods, Colmar's historic sites are all lit up at night by special computer-controlled spotlights of different colours and varying intensities. Blue, representing air, is used for roofs; green, symbolising life-giving water, illuminates rivers and their banks; amber, the colour of earth, often shines on tree branches; and the warmth of the hearth is represented by white, often used to illuminate the half-timbered houses.

Musée d'Unterlinden

The most renowned work in the Unterlinden Museum (☎ 03 89 20 15 50) is the **Issenheim Altarpiece** (Rétable d'Issenheim), which has been acclaimed as one of the most dramatic and moving works of art ever created. The museum also displays several other medieval altarpieces, an Alsatian wine cellar (including a 17th century press), armour and weapons from the 15th and 16th centuries, pewterware, Strasbourg faïence and memorabilia from the Revolutionary period.

From November to March the Musée d'Unterlinden is open daily, except Tuesday, from 9 am to noon and 2 to 5 pm. During the rest of the year it's open daily from 9 am to 6 pm. Ticket sales end half an hour before closing time. Admission costs 32FF (27FF for seniors, 22FF for children and students under 26).

Other Museums

Dedicated to the life and work of the Colmar native who created New York's *Statue of Liberty*, the **Musée Bartholdi** (☎ 03 89 41 90 60), 30 Rue des Marchands, displays some of the work and personal memorabilia of Frédéric Auguste Bartholdi (1834-1904) in the house where he was born. It is open daily, except Tuesday, from 10 am to noon and 2 to 6 pm. Admission is 20FF (15FF for students).

The **Musée du Jouet** (☎ 03 89 41 93 10), 40 Rue Vauban, has an impressive collection of wind-up antique toys and trains. It is open from 10 am to noon and 2 to 6 pm (closed Tuesday). Admission costs 25FF (10FF for children and students).

Churches

The 13th and 14th century **Collégiale Saint Martin** is an unusually intimate Gothic basilica, Place de la Cathédrale. Commonly referred to as a cathedral (though Colmar is not a bishopric), this structure of yellow and pink sandstone is known for its sombre ambulatory around a hexagonal choir and, outside, its peculiar, Mongol-style copper spire (1572). The Collégiale is open daily from 8 am to 7 pm except during Masses.

Église des Dominicains, in Place des Dominicains, a desanctified Gothic church once used as a corn market, is known for its 14th and 15th century stained glass and the celebrated triptych *La Vierge au Buisson de Roses* (1473; The Virgin in the Rose Bush), painted by Martin Schongauer. This masterpiece, of a doe-eyed Mary holding the Infant Jesus, made world headlines when it was stolen for 18 months in 1972. The interior is open daily from 10 am to 1 pm and 3 to 6 pm (closed from January to late March). Entrance costs 8FF (6FF for students under 30).

At the northern end of the Grand' Rue, **Église Protestante Saint Mathieu** was, until 1937, both a Catholic and Protestant church. Once administered by the Franciscans, it contains a rare medieval *jubé* (rood screen) separating the chancel from the nave. The interior can be visited daily, except on Sunday morning from mid-June to mid-October and for most of the period between Easter and May; hours are 10 am to noon and 3 to 5 pm.

Hiking & Cycling

The tourist office can supply a variety of maps and topoguides. *Proposals of Walking Tours in the Region of Colmar* (10FF) provides basic outlines of 11 day hikes in the Colmar area and the Vosges. You can plan your own route using the network of 14 *sentiers viticoles* (signposted vineyard trails), which take walkers through small villages and colourful, fragrant vineyards. The tourist office also sells IGN-Club Vosgien maps (56FF) and several topoguides for cyclists.

Organised Tours

On Saturday and Sunday from April to October, the tourist office has – one after the other – tours of the Musée d'Unterlinden (52FF) and the old city (25FF); the first begins at 10.15 am. A combined ticket for both tours, each of which lasts 1¼ hours, costs 60FF. On Saturday evening a bit after nightfall (and, from late November to early January, three or four times a week), the tourist office has 1½ hour guided tours (25FF) of Colmar's historic sites, which are lit up by spotlights.

Special Events

Alsatian vintners display their wine for tasting and sale at the Foire Régionale des Vins d'Alsace (Regional Wine Fair of Alsace), which attracts large numbers of visitors to Colmar for 10 days during the first half of August. The fair is also a good place to sample local food specialities.

From July to mid-September, Colmar plays host to a number of music festivals, including the classical Festival International de Colmar, held during the first half of July. Jazz en Ville, Jazz au Champ is a jazz festival that takes place in early September. Details are available from the tourist office.

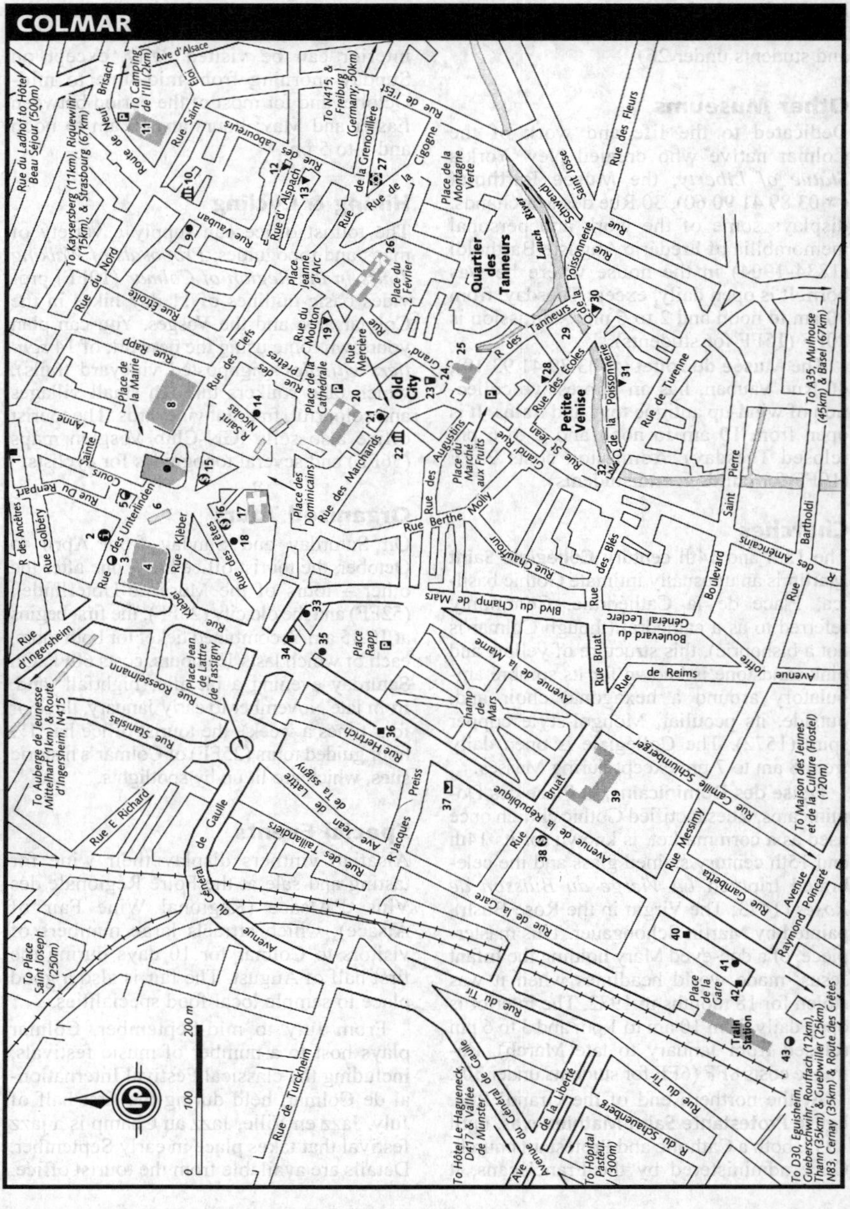
COLMAR
Old City
Petite Venise
Quartier des Tanneurs
Place de la Cathédrale
Place Jeanne d'Arc
Place des Dominicains
Place du Marché aux Fruits
Place Rapp
Champ de Mars
Place de la Gare
Place de la Montagne Verte
Place du 2 Février
Place Jean de Lattre de Tassigny
Place de la Mairie
Train Station
Lauch River
Rue des Clefs
Rue Vauban
Rue Rapp
Rue Kléber
Rue des Marchands
Rue Mercière
Rue des Augustins
Rue Berthe Molly
Rue des Tanneurs
Rue de Turenne
Rue des Écoles
Rue Saint Jean
Grand Rue
Rue des Têtes
Rue Stanislas
Rue Roesselmann
Rue Golbéry
Rue d'Ingersheim
Rue du Nord
Rue Étroite
Rue Saint Eloi
Route de Neuf Brisach
Ave d'Alsace
Rue des Laboureurs
Rue de la Grenouillère
Rue de la Cigogne
Rue de l'Est
Rue d'Alspach
Rue du Mouton
Rue des Prêtres
Rue des Fleurs
Rue Saint Josse
Rue Schwendi
Rue de la Poissonnerie
Rue de la République
Rue Bruat
Rue des Blés
Rue Chauffour
Rue de Reims
Rue Messimy
Rue Gambetta
Rue Camille Schlumberger
Rue de la Gare
Rue du Tir
Rue du Schauenberg
Rue de la Liberté
Rue E Richard
Rue Henner
Rue des Taillandiers
Rue de Turckheim
Rue du Rempart
Rue des Ancêtres
Rue Sainte Anne
Cours Sainte Anne
Rue des Unterlinden
Rue Saint Nicolas
R Jacques Preiss
Ave Jean de Lattre de Tassigny
Avenue du Général de Gaulle
Avenue de la Marne
Avenue Raymond Poincaré
Avenue Joffre
Boulevard du Général Leclerc
Blvd du Champ de Mars
Boulevard Saint Pierre
Rue des Américains
Rue Bartholdi
To Kaysersberg (11km), Riquewihr (15km), & Strasbourg (67km)
Rue du Ladhof to Hôtel Beau Séjour (500m)
To Camping de l'Ill (2km)
To N415, & Freiburg (Germany; 50km)
To A35, Mulhouse (45km) & Basel (67km)
To Maison des Jeunes et de la Culture (Hostel) (120m)
To D30, Eguisheim, Gueberschwihr, Rouffach (12km), Thann (35km) & Guebwiller (25km) N83, Cernay (35km) & Route des Crêtes
To Hôpital Pasteur (300m)
To Hôtel Le Hagueneck, D417 & Vallée de Munster
To Place Saint Joseph (250m)
To Auberge de Jeunesse Mittelhart (1km) & Route d'Ingersheim, N415
200 m
100
0

COLMAR

PLACES TO STAY
1 Hôtel Primo 99
34 Hôtel Kempf
36 Hôtel Rhin et Danube
40 Hôtel La Chaumière
42 Hôtel Terminus-Bristol

PLACES TO EAT
12 Le Petit Bouchon
13 Les Gourmets d'Asie
19 Djerba La Douce
28 La Maison Rouge
30 Aux Trois Poissons
31 Le Petit Gourmand

OTHER
2 Tourist Office
3 Unterlinden/Point Central Bus Hub
4 Musée d'Unterlinden
5 TRACE Bus Information Office
6 Quai de la Sinn
7 Monoprix Supermarket
8 Hôtel de Ville
9 Point Laverie Laundrette
10 Musée du Jouet
11 Atac Supermarket
14 Fromagerie Saint Nicolas
15 Crédit Commercial de France
16 Sogenal Bank
17 Église des Dominicains
18 Maison des Têtes; Restaurant Maison des Têtes
20 Collégiale Saint Martin
21 Maison Pfister
22 Musée Bartholdi
23 Murphy's Irish Pub
24 Ancienne Douane
25 Place de l'Ancienne Douane (Koïfhúsplätz)
26 Église Protestante Saint Mathieu
27 Synagogue
29 Old Covered Market
32 Panorama
33 Cycles Geiswiller
35 Europcar Car Rental
37 Main Post Office
38 Banque de France
39 Prefecture
41 Grand Garage Jean Jaurès Car Rental
43 Bus Terminal

Places to Stay

During parts of the spring and summer, especially around Easter and from mid-July to mid-August, most hotel rooms are booked up in advance. The period of the Wine Fair (early August) is especially busy.

Camping The three star *Camping de l'Ill* (☎ 03 89 41 15 94), on Route de Neuf Brisach in Horbourg-Wihr, is just over 3km east of Colmar. It is open from February to November and charges 19FF for a tent or caravan plus 17FF per adult. To get there take bus No 1 from the train station or the Unterlinden/Point Central hub to the Plage de l'Ill stop.

Hostels The friendly *Maison des Jeunes et de la Culture* (MJC; ☎ 03 89 41 26 87; fax 03 89 23 20 16), a bit south of the train station at 17 Rue Camille Schlumberger, is more flexible than the youth hostel. Also known as the Centre International de Séjour (CIS), it charges 46FF for a bed, not including breakfast (20FF), in rooms for two or more people. Reception is open Monday to Saturday from 7.30 am to noon and 2 to 10 pm, and on Sunday from 8 am to noon. Call ahead if you'll be arriving on Sunday afternoon.

The *Auberge de Jeunesse Mittelhart* (☎ 03 89 80 57 39; fax 03 89 80 76 16), 2 Rue Pasteur, charges 66FF per person, including breakfast. Reception is open from 7 to 10 am and 5 pm to midnight; curfew is at midnight (11 pm in winter). From the train station, the hostel is just over 2km north along the railway tracks and then west on Route d'Ingersheim. From the train station or Unterlinden/Point Central, take bus No 4 and get off at the Pont Rouge stop.

Hotels In the centre of town, the friendly *Hôtel Kempf* (☎ 03 89 41 21 72; fax 03 89 23 06 94), 1 Ave de la République (a rather busy street corner), has simple, relatively spacious singles/doubles with washbasin and bidet for 140/160FF. Rooms with shower and toilet are 225FF. Unmetered parking is available along Ave de la Marne.

Near the train station, the cosy *Hôtel La Chaumière* (☎ 03 89 41 08 99), 74 Ave de la République, has simple and rather small rooms with washbasin and bidet from 150 to 180FF. Rooms with shower and toilet are 220/240FF. Hall showers are free. Reception is closed on Sunday from 1 to 5 pm.

The ***Hôtel Rhin et Danube*** (☎ 03 89 41 31 44; fax 03 89 24 54 37), a two star place at 26 Ave de la République, is about midway between the train station and the Musée d'Unterlinden. It has old-fashioned, shower-equipped doubles with high ceilings for 170FF; doubles with shower and toilet are 240 to 260FF, depending on the season. Adding up to two extra beds costs 50FF each. The three star ***Hôtel Terminus-Bristol*** (☎ 03 89 23 59 59; fax 03 89 23 92 26), founded in 1925, is opposite the train station at 7 Place de la Gare. From December to March, doubles with shower start at 295FF; prices begin at 400FF the rest of the year.

A short walk north-east of the centre, the venerable ***Hôtel Beau Séjour*** (☎ 03 89 41 37 16; fax 03 89 41 43 07), 25 Rue du Ladhof, which has been around since 1913, has rooms with all the amenities from 250/280FF. The blush-pink (but fading) ***Hôtel Primo 99*** (☎ 03 89 24 22 24; fax 03 89 24 55 96), 5 Rue des Ancêtres, has rooms with washbasin for up to three people for 159FF. Rooms with shower and toilet for one/two/three/four people cost 269/329/349/399FF. Hall showers are free. There's a huge public parking lot across the street.

About 700m west of the train station, the ***Hôtel Le Hagueneck*** (☎ 03 89 80 68 98; fax 03 89 79 55 29), 83 Ave du Général de Gaulle, compensates for its distance from the town centre with rooms with shower and toilet from 160/230FF.

Places to Eat

Restaurants – Alsatian & French In terms of both cuisine and décor, one of Colmar's most enjoyable splurges can be had at ***Le Petit Bouchon*** (☎ 03 89 23 45 57), 11 Rue d'Alspach. Set in an old Alsatian house, this place has Alsatian *menus* from 92FF and a Lyonnaise *menu* (the chef is from Lyon) for 89FF. It is closed on Wednesday and, in winter, on Sunday night.

La Maison Rouge (☎ 03 89 23 53 22), 9 Rue des Écoles, specialises in Alsatian cuisine, including spit-roasted ham (57FF); the two course Alsatian *menu* costs 85FF. It is open from noon to 2 pm and 6.30 to 9.30 or 10 pm (closed on Sunday evening and on Wednesday).

The tiny, intimate ***Le Petit Gourmand*** (☎ 03 89 41 09 32), 9 Quai de la Poissonnerie, has outside seating along the Lauch River in the warm months. Alsatian *menus* cost 95 and 145FF. It is open daily, except Monday night and Tuesday; dinner is served until 9.30 pm. ***Aux Trois Poissons*** (☎ 03 89 41 25 21), an elegant fish restaurant appropriately situated at 15 Quai de la Poissonnerie, has *menus* from 130 to 225FF (closed on Tuesday evening and on Wednesday).

The unpretentious French restaurant of the ***Hôtel Kempf*** has tasty steak main courses starting at 75FF (closed Wednesday).

The very classy ***Restaurant La Maison des Têtes*** (☎ 03 89 24 43 43), in the spectacular Maison des Têtes at 19 Rue des Têtes, has gourmet *menus* from 165FF and a superb wine list. It is closed Sunday evening and on Monday.

Restaurants – Other For traditional Vietnamese (rather than Chinese-Vietnamese) food, try ***Les Gourmets d'Asie*** (☎ 03 89 41 75 10), 20b Rue d'Alspach, which has exceptionally elegant service. The cheapest *menus*, not available on Saturday night, cost 65 and 75FF; the *plat du jour* is 39FF. It is closed on Monday.

Djerba La Douce (☎ 03 89 24 17 12), 10 Rue du Mouton, has Tunisian couscous for 48 to 95FF. It is closed on Monday, except from May to early September.

Self-Catering The ***Monoprix*** supermarket directly across the square from the entrance to the Musée d'Unterlinden has an in-house *boulangerie*. It is open Monday to Saturday from 8.30 am to 8.30 pm (7.30 pm on Saturday). Just north-east of the old city on Route de Neuf Brisach, the large ***Atac*** supermarket is open Monday to Saturday from 8.30 am to 7.30 pm. Plenty of parking is available.

The old covered market on Rue des Écoles plays host to a ***food market*** on Thursday morning (until 1 pm).

In the old city, ***Fromagerie Saint Nicolas*** (☎ 03 89 24 90 45), 18 Rue Saint Nicolas, sells only the finest traditionally made cheeses, yoghurts, honey and jams from 9 am to 12.30 pm and 2 to 7 pm (closed on Monday morning and on Sunday). It serves an excellent cheese sandwich for 20FF.

Entertainment

Murphy's Irish Pub (☎ 03 89 29 06 66), 48 Grand' Rue, is open daily from 11 am to 1.30 am. A pint of Murphy's stout or Irish red on tap costs 30FF.

Getting There & Away

Bus The bus terminal – little more than a parking lot – is to the right as you exit the train station. Several companies have buses to nearby villages; most follow either the Route du Vin or major highways. Hours are posted. Note that service is severely reduced on Sunday and holidays. The tourist office can supply bus schedules (ask for the free annual pamphlet *Dernières Nouvelles d'Alsace* (*DNA*) or the free monthly booklet *Actualités Colmar*) and advice on how to best take advantage of your bus options.

Route du Vin Public bus may not be the most efficient way to explore Alsace's Wine Route (see the Route du Vin section), but it is an option.

From Monday to Saturday, Riquewihr (25 minutes) and Ribeauvillé (50 minutes) are served by five or six daily buses run by Pauli. The first leaves Colmar at about 8 am; the last run back is a bit after 5 pm. Martinken also links Colmar with Ribeauvillé (30 minutes; six a day, except Sunday). On school days Martinken has two buses to Hunawihr (35 minutes), but only one very inconvenient one coming back, at 7 am.

Kienzheim (11FF) and Kaysersberg (12FF; 30 minutes) are served by 19 buses a day (one on Sunday) operated by STAHV.

Regular service to points south of Colmar, including Eguisheim (10 minutes), Gueberschwihr (20 minutes), Rouffach (30 minutes) and Guebwiller (one hour), is shared by Kunegel and Sodag. Eguisheim (25 minutes) can also be reached by Pauli buses three times a day, except Sunday.

The Vosges Colmar's train station is linked with the Vallée de Munster towns of Gunsbach (35 minutes) and Munster (40 minutes) six times a day, including Sunday, by STAHV and SALTA. Twice a day, the companies' buses continue on to Col de la Schlucht (1¼ hours), Gérardmer (1½ hours), Remiremont and the Lorraine town of Épinal (three hours).

On weekdays, Sodag has five buses a day to Cernay, starting point of the Route des Crêtes.

Germany Kunegel (☎ 03 89 24 65 65) and SüdbadenBus (SBG; ☎ 0761-36172 in Freiburg) have eight buses a day (three on weekends) from Colmar's train station to one of two locations in the German university city of Freiburg – either the bus station or Hans Bunte Nord (37FF/10DM; 70 minutes).

Train The train station's information office (☎ 08 36 35 35 35) is open from 9 am to 7 pm (6 pm on Saturday, closed Sunday). There are services to Strasbourg (58FF; 30 to 50 minutes; 18 to 28 a day), Mulhouse (42FF; 20 minutes; 20 a day) and Besançon (129FF; two hours; eight a day), as well as to Lyon (232FF; 4½ hours; five direct a day) and Basel (63FF; 50 minutes; nine to 14 a day). To get to Paris' Gare de l'Est you have to change trains – via Strasbourg it takes six hours and costs 239FF.

Route du Vin & The Vosges To get to Obernai (44FF; 1½ hours) and Molsheim (49FF; 70 minutes) you have to change trains at Sélestat (25FF; 15 minutes).

Six or seven autorails a day (four on Sunday and holidays) link Colmar with the Vallée de Munster towns of Gunsbach (25 minutes), Munster (21FF; 30 minutes) and Metzeral (45 minutes). The last train back begins its run at about 6.45 pm.

Car The cheapest rental agency in town is Grand Garage Jean Jaurès (☎ 03 89 41 30 26; fax 03 89 41 77 29), 80 Ave de la République (closed Sunday). Europcar (☎ 03 89 24 11 80), 9 Ave de la République (Place Rapp), is open Monday to Saturday from 8 am to noon and 2 to 6 pm.

Getting Around

To/From the Airport EuroAir'Bus (☎ 03 89 90 25 11) links Bâle-Mulhouse airport (EuroAirport) with Colmar's train station (50 minutes; five a day).

Bus Colmar's local buses are operated by TRACE (☎ 03 89 20 80 80), which has an office around the corner from the tourist office in Galerie du Rempart. All 10 lines – which run from Monday to Saturday until sometime between 6 and 8 pm – stop at the Unterlinden/Point Central hub, which is next to the tourist office, and most also stop at the train station. Service is drastically reduced on Sunday.

A single ride costs 5.50FF, and a carnet of 10 tickets is 41FF. A Billet Pass is good for between one day (15FF) and seven days (40FF) – just time-stamp it the first time your use it and then show it to the driver each time you board.

Taxi You can order a taxi 24 hours a day by calling Radios Taxis (☎ 03 89 80 71 71) or Taxi Gare (☎ 03 89 41 40 19).

Bicycle Cycles Geiswiller (☎ 03 89 41 30 59), 4-6 Blvd du Champ de Mars, has bicycles for 60/100FF per half-day/day. It is open from 8.30 am to noon and 2 to 6.30 pm (closed on Sunday and Monday). Cycles Meyer (☎ 03 89 79 12 47), 6 Rue du Pont Rouge, across Route d'Ingersheim from Auberge de Jeunesse Mittelhart, rents bicycles for 70FF a day (closed Sunday and Monday).

MASSIF DES VOSGES

The delightful and sublimely beautiful Parc Naturel Régional des Ballons des Vosges, founded in 1989, covers about 3000 sq km in the southern part of the Vosges range. Roughly speaking, it is bounded by Sélestat and Cernay in Alsace, Belfort in Franche-Comté and Remiremont and Saint Dié in Lorraine.

Hiking & Cycling

In the warm months, the gentle, rounded mountains, deep forests, glacial lakes, rolling pastureland and tiny villages are a hikers paradise, with an astounding 7000km of marked trails, including a variety of GR trails and their variants (the GR5, GR7, GR53 etc). Trail maps published jointly by the IGN and the Club Vosgien generally cost about 56FF at tourist offices and larger newsagents. The Colmar tourist office can supply you with *Proposals of Walking Tours in the Region of Colmar* (10FF), which outlines a number of day hikes in the Vosges.

For details on group hikes sponsored by the Club Vosgien, see Hiking in the Strasbourg section.

Cyclists also have hundreds of kilometres of idyllic trails – and several topoguides (available at the Colmar tourist office) – to choose from.

Skiing

The Massif des Vosges has 1000km of cross-country trails (the use charge is 22 to 40FF a day) and 36 modest skiing areas with 170 ski lifts, mostly tow lines. Lift tickets cost from 65 to 95FF a day, depending on the date. Information on snow conditions is available on ☎ 03 89 41 34 76 (in Colmar) or, from Friday to Sunday, on ☎ 03 29 25 47 02 (in La Bresse); by Minitel dial 3615 METEO or 3615 VOTEL.

Getting There & Away

For details on bus and train services to Cernay, the Vallée de Munster and Col de la Schlucht, see the Bus and Train entries under Getting There & Away in the Colmar section.

Vallée de Munster

This lush, verdant river valley, its pastureland dotted with tiny villages, its upper slopes thickly forested, is one of the loveliest in the Vosges range. It is crisscrossed by over 500km of marked hiking trails, including the

ALSACE

GR5, the GR531 and the GR532, and 300km of mountain bike tracks. In winter, the area grooms close to 100km of cross-country ski trails, and nearby slopes are home to six small downhill ski stations. The D417 links up with the Route des Crêtes at Col de la Schlucht.

The best hiking map for the valley is the IGN-Club Vosgien map entitled *Colmar, Munster, Gérardmer, Saint-Dié* (55FF). The area is also covered by four IGN Top 25 maps.

Munster The town of Munster (population 4700; the name means 'monastery'), famed for its eponymous cheese, grew up around Abbaye Saint Grégoire, a Benedictine abbey founded in 660 AD by monks from Ireland. At Place du Marché, across from the neo-Romanesque **Protestant church** (built between 1867 and 1873), the roof and chimneys of the **Maison du Prélat** (former prelate's quarters) are the year-round home of a half-dozen pairs of **storks**. Munster is an excellent base for exploring the Vallée de Munster and is the best place in the area to pick up information and provisions.

The stork reintroduction centre in Hunawihr (see the boxed text 'Storks') has an **Enclos Cigognes** (stork enclosure), home to about a dozen frisky young birds, 250m behind the Renaissance **Hôtel de Ville** (built in 1550). This is a great place to observe the majestic birds up close, whose food consists mainly of fish and day-old male chicks (sorry cuddly-chick lovers, but storks are carnivores).

Information The tourist office (☎ 03 89 77 31 80; fax 03 89 77 07 17) is at 1 Rue du Couvent, which is either through the arch of the Maison du Prélat or behind the *bibliothèque* (library), depending on which direction you come from. Opening hours

Storks

Cigognes (white storks), long a feature of Alsatian folklore, are one of the region's most beloved symbols. Believed to bring luck (as well as babies), they spend the winter in Africa and then migrate to Europe for the warmer months, feeding from marshes (their favourite delicacies include small rodents, moles, lizards, all sorts of insects and, to a lesser extent, frogs) and building their nests of twigs and sticks on church steeples, rooftops and tall trees. Beginning in about 1960, however, the draining of the marshes along the Rhine, hunting in Africa, chemical poisons and – most lethal of all – high-tension lines reduced stork numbers catastrophically. By the early 1980s there were only three pairs left in all of Alsace.

When cold weather arrives, instinct tells young storks – at the age of just a few months – to fly south for a two or three year, 12,000km trek to sub-Saharan Africa, from which they return to Alsace ready to breed – if they return at all. Research has shown that 90% die en route because of electrocution, hunting, exhaustion and dehydration. In subsequent years, the adult storks – 1m long, with a 2m wingspan and weighing 3.5kg – make only a short trek south for the winter, returning to Alsace to breed after a few months in Africa.

In the 1980s, research and breeding centres were set up with the goal of establishing a permanent, year-round Alsatian stork population. The young birds spend the first three years of their lives in captivity, which causes them to lose their migratory instinct and thus avoid the rigours and dangers of migration. The program has been a huge success, and today Alsace – the western extremity of the storks' range – is home to some 700 of these majestic birds. The **Centre de Réintroduction des Cigognes** (☎ 03 89 73 72 62) is in Hunawihr, just south of Ribeauvillé, and can be visited from April to 11 November. Its hours are 10 am to noon and from 2 pm to sometime between 5 and 7 pm. Entry costs 30FF (20FF for children). Storks can also be seen in the town of Munster (see The Vosges section) and along the Route du Vin.

ALSACE

are 9.30 am to 12.30 pm and 2 to 6 pm (7 pm in July and August, 4 pm on off-season Saturdays). It is closed on Sunday, except from May to September and during school holiday periods, when its hours are 10 am to noon or 12.30 pm.

Information on the Parc Régional is also available from the Maison du Parc (☎ 03 89 73 90 20; fax 03 89 77 90 30), which is in the same building as the tourist office but around the other side. It is open on weekdays from 10 am to noon and 2 to 6 pm.

Munster's postcode is 68140.

Places to Stay & Eat The family-run, 13 room ***Hôtel des Vosges*** (☎ 03 89 77 31 41; fax 03 89 77 59 86), 58 Grand' Rue (the main commercial street), has spacious, simply furnished doubles from 180FF (260FF with shower and toilet). Hall showers are 10FF. Reception is closed on Sunday afternoon and Monday except during school holiday periods.

A ***food market*** is held at Place du Marché on Saturday mornings. There are ***Super U*** and ***Match*** supermarkets east of the town centre (towards Colmar).

Getting Around In the town centre, bicycles can be rented from La Godille Sport (☎ 03 89 77 08 77), 8 Grand' Rue and, nearby, Cycles Stey (☎ 03 89 77 35 45). The tourist office has details on other rental agencies.

Soultzbach-les-Bains This untouristed hamlet, whose houses and market gardens straddle a creek called the Kresbach River, is 5km east of Munster in a lovely valley surrounded by forested hillsides; several trails lead north, east and west to nearby hills and villages. During the latter half of the 19th century Soultzbach's now shuttered spa, built over the *source* (natural spring) that gave the village its name, was very popular with curists.

Soultzbach's only hotel, the 10 room, one star ***Hôtel Saint Christophe*** (☎ 03 89 71 13 09; fax 03 89 71 06 84), 4 Rue de l'Église (the D43), has singles/doubles from 120/145FF; doubles/triples with shower and toilet are 210/245FF.

Soultzbach-les-Bains' postcode is 68230.

Hohrodberg The hillside hamlet of Hohrodberg (760m), 7km north of Munster, affords gorgeous views of the valley. It is home to the ***Hôtel Roess*** (☎ 03 89 77 36 00; 03 89 77 01 95), 16 Route du Linge (the D5bis-I), a two star hotel that has been run by the same family for five generations. Singles/doubles/triples start at 160/240/350FF (240/310/440FF with shower and toilet), but half-pension (250 to 300FF per person, including the room) is obligatory from Easter to September. In the restaurant, the *menus* cost 106 to 187FF.

Hohrodberg's postcode is 68140.

Le Linge The German fortifications at Le Linge (986m), carved into the sandstone hilltop, were the object of a French offensive launched in July of 1915. Some 10,000 French troops and 7000 Germans died in the assaults and subsequent static trench warfare, in which soldiers of the opposing sides fought hand-to-hand from trenches only metres apart. The battle site, which has one of the best preserved WWI trench networks in France (it's kept in good repair by volunteers), is still surrounded by rusted tangles of the original barbed wire, areas that have yet to be cleared of live munitions, and the hidden remains of never-exhumed human corpses. The forested memorial site, on the D11-VI, affords gorgeous views of tree-covered hills and pastoral hamlets – these contrast jarringly with the trenches and rifle slits. The small **museum** is open from 15 April to 1 November.

About 500m south-east of Le Linge, at the intersection of the D11-VI and the D5bis-I, is a **Deutscher Soldatenfriedhof 1914-18** (WWI German military cemetery), whose long, even rows of black, metal crosses are interspersed with stone Stars of David.

Route des Crêtes

The Route of the Crests, part of it built during WWI to supply French frontline troops, takes you to (or near) the Vosges' highest *ballons* (bald, rounded mountain peaks) and road passes, as well as to several WWI sites. Mountaintop lookouts afford spectacular views of the Alsace plain, the Schwartzwald (Black Forest) across the Rhine in Germany, the Jura and – on clear days – the Alps.

Beginning in Cernay, the Route des Crêtes continues north-east and then north along the D431, D430, D61 and D148 to the Col du Bonhomme (949m). During the winter months and early spring it is often impassable due to snow. The sites mentioned below are listed from south to north.

Vieil Armand Site of the bloodiest WWI fighting in Alsace, Hartmannswillerkopf – renamed Vieil Armand by the French troops – saw the deaths of some 30,000 French and German soldiers as the strategic hilltop fortress changed hands several times. Today, a crypt containing the remains of 12,000 unidentified soldiers forms the **Monument National**, topped by a bronze altar. Beyond the French **military cemetery**, a path leads up the forested hill to the actual site of the fortress (956m), marked by a 22m-high white cross. The remains of trenches and fortifications, most of them German, can be seen nearby.

Grand Ballon The dramatic, windblown summit of the 1424m-high Grand Ballon, the highest point in the Vosges, is marked by a radar ball, a weather station and a monument to the Diables Bleus, French special infantry troops known as the Blue Devils. A short trail links all three to the highway. If the unsurpassed panorama doesn't blow you away, the howling wind just might. On foot, the Grand Ballon is two hours from Murback, 2½ hours from Vieil Armand and 3½ hours from Guebwiller.

At the top of the road pass (1325m), you'll find the chalet-style ***Grand Hôtel Ballon*** (☎ 03 89 48 77 99), run by the Club Vosgien.

Le Markstein The tiny, low-budget ski station of Le Markstein (1240m; ☎ 03 89 82 74 98 at the tourist office, ☎ 03 89 82 14 46 at the ski lift) consists of a number of scattered hotels, sandwich bars and ski lifts. The D430 to Guebwiller is kept open year-round.

The ***Hôtel Wolf*** (☎ 03 89 82 64 36; fax 03 89 38 72 06) is a 20 room, two star place with doubles from 175FF (with washbasin) to 315FF (with shower and toilet). The rooms are simple and unadorned, as befits a mountain retreat. It is open year-round, except from 10 November to 10 December.

Le Markstein's postcode is 68610.

Hohneck The bald, 1362m-high summit of Hohneck (literally, 'high place'), marked by a single, slope-roofed wooden lodge, affords panoramic views in every direction. Via the GR5, it is one hour from Col de la Schlucht and 4¼ hours from Le Markstein. Hohneck may be snowbound into April. Nearby ski areas include Col de la Schlucht (☎ 03 29 63 11 38 for the ski lift) and La Bresse-Hohneck (☎ 03 29 25 41 71 for the ski lift).

A couple of kilometres south of Hohneck in the one-horse hamlet of Breitzousen is the ***Ferme-Auberge Deybach*** (☎ 03 29 63 22 92; fax 03 29 63 03 21), accessible in winter only on skis, which offers accommodation in dorm rooms for 180FF per person, including half-pension (restaurant closed on Monday). The whole place shuts down in December.

Hohneck's postcode is 88400.

Col de la Schlucht This 1139m-high mountain pass is 36km west of Colmar on the D417 and 29km north-west of the Grand Ballon. It is home to a small ski station and a modern church. Trails lead in various directions; walking north along the GR5 will take you to three lakes with colours for names: **Lac Vert**, **Lac Noir** and **Lac Blanc**.

Ballon d'Alsace

The 1250m-high Ballon d'Alsace, 20km south-west of the Grand Ballon as the crow flies (by road, take the D465 from Saint Maurice), is the meeting point of four departments (Haut-Rhin, Territoire-de-Belfort, Haute-Saône and Vosges) and three regions

(Alsace, Franche-Comté and Lorraine). Between 1871 and WWI, the border between France and Germany passed by here, attracting French tourists eager to catch a glimpse of France's 'lost province' of Alsace. During WWI the mountaintop was heavily fortified, but the trenches, whose shallow remains can still be seen, were never used in battle.

The Ballon d'Alsace is a good base for day hikes. The GR5 passes by here, as do other walking trails; possible destinations include a number of lakes (eg the **Lac des Perches**). In winter, the area has snow-shoeing, cross-country skiing (☎ 03 29 25 20 38) and, on the ballon's northern slopes, downhill runs served by the Jumenterie lift (☎ 03 29 25 39 00). For information on parapente lessons and introductory flights, contact Centre École Pent'Air (☎ 03 84 23 20 40).

The 18 room, two star ***Grand Hôtel du Sommet*** (☎ 03 84 29 30 60; fax 03 84 23 95 60), open year-round, has doubles/triples/quads with shower and toilet for 200/260/300FF. It also has a restaurant – the plat du jour costs 50FF, the *menu* is 80FF. In July and August the hotel serves as a *point d'information*, providing visitors with hiking information.

Bussang The riverside town of Bussang (population 1800), north of the Ballon d'Alsace near the very beginning of the Moselle River, is another good base for hikers, cyclists and skiers of both the downhill and cross-country variety. The area is covered by IGN maps *3619 Ouest* and *3620 Ouest*.

The two star ***Hôtel Le Tremplin*** (☎ 03 29 61 50 30; fax 03 29 61 50 89), on the N66 (the main road through town), has doubles for 150FF (with washbasin) and 250FF (with shower and toilet); quads with all the amenities are 340FF. The hotel's ***restaurant***, whose traditional French *menus* range from 75 to 190FF, is closed on Sunday night and Monday except during school holiday periods. Provisions can be picked up at a number of ***food shops***.

SNCF buses link Bussang with Remiremont (one hour; five a day), from where there are trains to Nancy (1½ hours; five to eight a day).

Mountain bikes can be rented from Bar Apollo XVIII (☎ 03 29 61 50 78), 43 Route de Santé.

Bussang's postcode is 88540.

The Continental Divide

The Massif des Vosges serves as a *ligne de partage des eaux* (continental divide). A raindrop or snowflake that falls on the range's eastern slopes will flow to the Rhine and eventually make its way to the North Sea. A drop of rain that lands on the western slopes of the Vosges – perhaps only a few metres from its Rhine-bound counterpart – will eventually end up in the Rhône before joining with the warm waters of the Mediterranean.

MULHOUSE

• pop 110,000 ✉ 68100 alt 240m

The industrial city of Mulhouse (pronounced 'Moo-LOOZE'), 43km south of Colmar, has little of the quaint Alsatian charm that typifies its northern neighbours. In fact, in recent years it has made the news mainly because of ethnic tensions and urban violence. However, the city's dozen museums, several of them world class, are well worth a stop even if you're not a sworn fan of the various types of industrial technology that they highlight.

Information

The tourist office (☎ 03 89 35 48 48; fax 03 89 45 66 16; www.ot-ville-mulhouse.fr) is 200m north of the train station at 9 Ave du Maréchal Foch. It is open Monday to Saturday from 9 am to 7 pm (5 pm on Saturday, 6 or 7 pm on Saturday from June to September). In July and August it's also open on Sunday from 10 am to 1 pm. The office distributes two excellent pamphlets (in English) for self-guided walking tours of the city.

Museums

The **Musée Français du Chemin de Fer** (☎ 03 89 42 25 67), 2 Rue Alfred de Glehn, displays locomotives, carriages and switching equipment of all types and periods. It shares its space – a disused railway station – with the **Musée du Sapeur-Pompier** (Firefighters' Museum), which has a collection of fire engines and helmets reminiscent of a Gilbert and Sullivan opera. Both are open daily from 9 am to 5 pm (6 pm from April to September); entry to both costs 45FF (20FF for students and children). To get there by car, take the A36 and get off at the Mulhouse Ouest exit and follow the signs. By bus, take the hourly line No 17 from the train station.

The **Musée National de l'Automobile** (☎ 03 89 33 23 23), 192 Ave de Colmar, displays some 500 rare and historic motorcars made since 1878 by 98 different companies – especially Bugatti, whose factory was in nearby Molsheim – and collected by the textile magnate Schlumpf brothers. Opening hours are 10 am to 6 pm (closed on Tuesday). The entrance fee is as upmarket as the cars on display: 57FF (27FF for students and children). To get there from the A36 take exit Mulhouse Centre and follow the signs. By bus, take the hourly line No 17 from the train station.

The **Musée de l'Impression sur Étoffes** (Museum of Textile Printing; ☎ 03 89 46 83 00), across from the train station at 3 Rue Jean-Jacques Henner, has a collection (assembled since 1833) of some three million printed fabric samples from all over the world. The museum, which recently underwent extensive renovation, is open daily from 9 or 10 am to 6 pm. Tickets cost 32FF (16FF for students).

The delightful **Musée du Papier Peint** (☎ 03 89 64 24 56), in the 18th century Commanderie at 28 Rue Zuber in Rixheim, a couple of kilometres south-east of Mulhouse on the D66, is without doubt the most complete Wallpaper Museum in the world. Some 130,000 different wallpapers and painted panels from as far back as the 18th century, and the machines used to make them, are on display. The museum is open daily from 9 or 10 am to noon and 2 to 6 pm (closed on Tuesday from October to May). From June to September printing demonstrations are held on Tuesday, Thursday and Saturday at 3.30 pm. Admission costs 30FF (20FF for students and children). To get there by car, take the A36 towards Basel (Bâle) and get off at Rixheim. By bus, take No 10 from Tour de l'Europe.

Getting There & Away

The information office (☎ 08 36 35 35 35) at the train station, which is south of the centre at 10 Ave du Général Leclerc, is open weekdays from 8.30 am to 7 pm (5.30 pm on Saturday). There are frequent services to Colmar (42FF; 20 minutes; 20 a day), Strasbourg (81FF; one hour; 16 to 24 a day), Besançon (104FF; 1¾ hours) and Paris' Gare de l'Est.

Buses, which leave from the terminus next to the station, serve towns and villages north, west and south of Mulhouse, including Colmar (30FF; 1½ hours; five a day, except Sunday).

ÉCOMUSÉE D'ALSACE

The largest open-air museum in France, the Écomusée d'Alsace (☎ 03 89 74 44 54) at Ungersheim, about 17km north-west of Mulhouse off the A35 to Colmar, is a reconstructed Alsatian village modelled on the still plentiful real thing. Some 70 derelict houses and other buildings were taken from their original sites and reassembled here to create a 'living museum' in which traditional artisans and craftspeople do their thing for the wide-eyed crowds. Frankly, it's all a bit corny. The Écomusée, which hosts special events year-round, is open daily from 9 or 9.30 am (10.30 am from November to February) to sometime between 4.30 pm (November to February) and 7 pm (July and August). Admission costs 76FF for an adult, 63FF for students and 46FF for children (52, 44 and 34FF respectively from November to March).

Lorraine

Lorraine is probably associated more with quiche and De Gaulle's double-barred cross (*croix de Lorraine*) than with the early medieval kingdom of Lotharingia from which its name derives. It is one of France's chief industrial regions, so though a third of the land is forested (eg along the Vosges range) it has little of the picturesque quaintness of Alsace. Population centres tend to be sturdy towns once based on now declining heavy industries such as coal, iron and salt mining, and steel production – this is particularly true near the border with Luxembourg and Germany. Agriculture also plays an important role in the economy, especially in the central Lorraine plateau and areas farther south. Lorraine is fed by the Meurthe, Moselle and Meuse rivers.

Historically, Lorraine has had two capitals. Nancy, among France's most refined and attractive cities, is famed for its Art Nouveau architecture. Metz, 54km to the south, is an attractive, dynamic city known for the stunning stained glass of its cathedral. To the west, the town of Verdun, site of wholesale slaughter between 1916 and 1917, bears silent testimony to the destruction and insanity of WWI.

For information on the Parc Naturel Régional des Ballons des Vosges, part of which covers far south-eastern Lorraine, see the Massif des Vosges section earlier.

History

Lorraine was the birthplace of Jeanne d'Arc (1412-31), who became France's national heroine during the Hundred Years' War by stirring the French royalist army to resist the English and their allies. Lorraine became part of France in 1766 upon the death of Stanislaw I, the former king of Poland and father-in-law of Louis XV, who had been given Lorraine in 1738 by the treaties that ended the War of the Polish Succession (1733-38).

During the 17th century, Lorraine was fortified by the construction of a number of massive fortresses designed by the foremost military architect of the period, Vauban (see the boxed text 'Vauban's Citadels' in the Facts about France chapter). Along with the Verdun battlefields and the Maginot Line, these fortifications are a major draw for those interested in military history.

NANCY

• pop 329,000 ✉ 54000 alt 206m

Delightful Nancy has an air of refinement found nowhere else in Lorraine. With a stunning, gilded central square, sumptuous cream-coloured buildings and shop windows filled with fine chocolates and fragile works of glass, the former capital of the Dukes of Lorraine seems as opulent today as it did during the 16th to 18th centuries, when much of the city centre was built.

Nancy thrives on a combination of innovation and sophistication. The Musée de l'École de Nancy, the city's premier museum, houses many of the dream-like, sinuous works of the Art Nouveau movement that flourished here (as the Nancy School) thanks to the rebellious spirit of local artists, including Émile Gallé. Further examples of their work can be found throughout the city: look for the stained-glass windows and elaborate grillwork that grace the entrances to many banks, shops and private homes.

Orientation

In the heart of Nancy is the beautifully proportioned, 18th century Place Stanislas and the adjoining Place de la Carrière. These grand public spaces connect the narrow, twisting streets of the 11th century Vieille Ville (Old Town), centred around the Grande Rue, with the rigid right angles of the 16th century Ville Neuve (New Town) to the south, whose main thoroughfares are Rue Saint Dizier, Rue Saint Jean and Rue Saint Georges. The train station, at the bottom of busy Rue Stanislas, is 800m south-west of Place Stanislas.

Nancy's sights and hotels are scattered around both the new and old towns. Most sights (except the Musée de l'École de Nancy) are within easy walking distance of Place Stanislas.

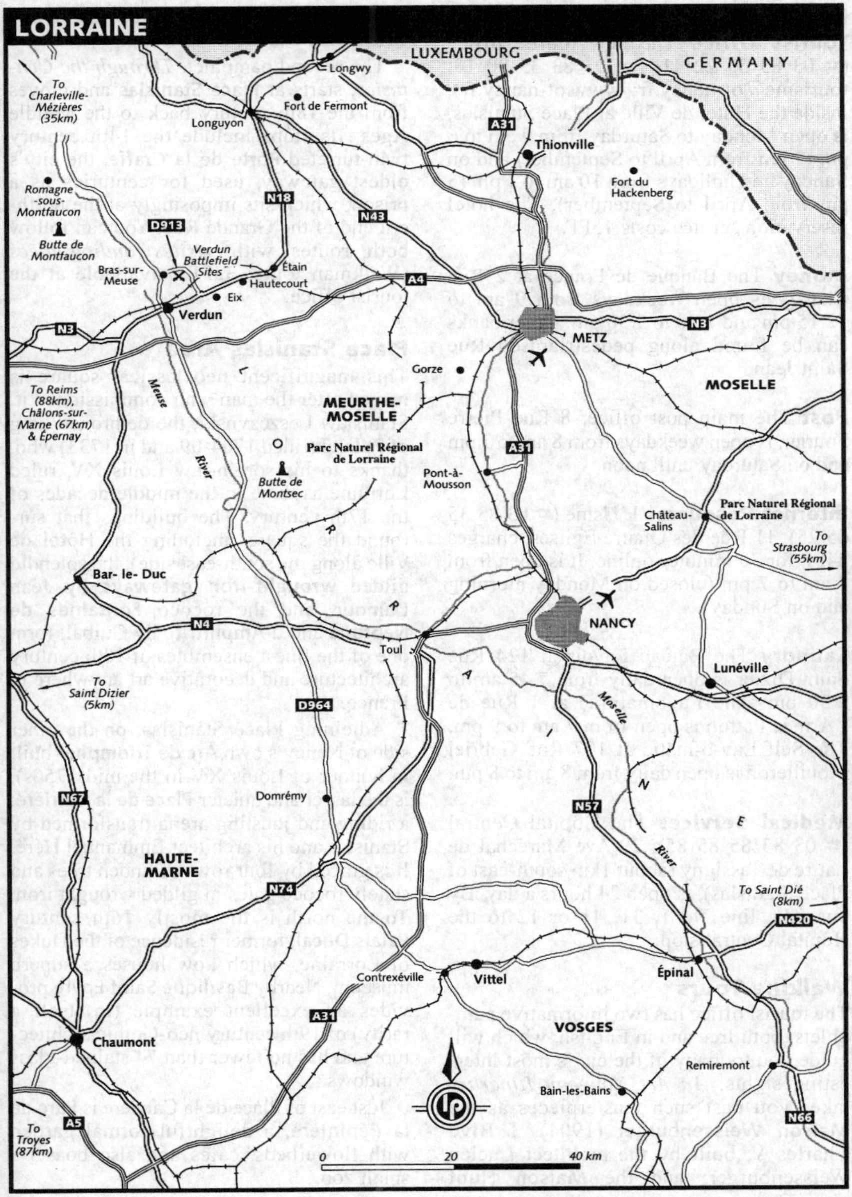
LORRAINE
LUXEMBOURG
GERMANY
Longwy
To Charleville-Mézières (35km)
Fort de Fermont
Longuyon
Thionville
Fort du Hackenberg
A31
N18
N43
D913
Romagne-sous-Montfaucon
Butte de Montfaucon
Verdun Battlefield Sites
Bras-sur-Meuse
Étain
Hautecourt
Eix
A4
Verdun
N3
METZ
MOSELLE
To Reims (88km), Châlons-sur-Marne (67km) & Épernay
Gorze
MEURTHE-MOSELLE
Parc Naturel Régional de Lorraine
Butte de Montsec
Meuse River
Pont-à-Mousson
Château-Salins
To Strasbourg (55km)
Bar-le-Duc
N4
Toul
NANCY
Lunéville
To Saint Dizier (5km)
D964
Moselle River
L O R R A I N E
N57
N67
Domrémy
HAUTE-MARNE
N74
To Saint Dié (8km)
N420
Contrexéville
Vittel
Épinal
A31
VOSGES
Chaumont
Remiremont
Bain-les-Bains
A5
To Troyes (87km)
N66
0
20
40 km

Information

Tourist Office The new tourist office (☎ 03 83 35 22 41; fax 03 83 35 90 10; tourisme@ot-nancy.fr; www.ot-nancy.fr), inside the Hôtel de Ville at Place Stanislas, is open Monday to Saturday from 9 am to 6 pm (7 pm from April to September) and on Sunday and holidays from 10 am to 1 pm (5 pm from April to September). The hotel reservation service costs 15FF.

Money The Banque de France at 2 Rue Chanzy is open weekdays from 9 am to 12.15 pm and 1.30 to 3.30 pm. Other banks can be found along pedestrianised Rue Saint Jean.

Post The main post office, 8 Rue Pierre Fourier, is open weekdays from 8 am to 7 pm and on Saturday until noon.

Internet Resources L'Usine (☎ 03 83 35 65 25), 11 Rue des Quatre Églises, charges 24FF for 30 minutes online. It is open from 7 am to 7 pm (closed on Monday morning and on Sunday).

Laundry The Bateau Lavoir at 124 Rue Saint Dizier is open daily from 7.45 am to 9.30 pm. The Lavomatique at 1 Rue de l'Armée Patton is open from 7 am to 9 pm. The Self Lav-o-matic at 107 Rue Gabriel Mouilleron is open daily from 8 am to 8 pm.

Medical Services The Hôpital Central (☎ 03 83 85 85 85), 29 Ave Maréchal de Lattre de Tassigny (about 1km south-east of Place Stanislas), is open 24 hours a day. By bus take line No 1, 31, 41 or 12 to the Hôpital Central stop.

Walking Tours

The tourist office has two informative pamphlets, both free and in English, which will guide you to many of the city's most interesting sights. *An Art Nouveau Itinerary* takes you past such masterpieces as the **Maison Weissenburger** (1904), 1 Blvd Charles V, built by the architect Lucien Weissenburger; and the **Maison Huot** (1903), actually two houses at Nos 92 and 92bis Quai Claude de Lorrain.

The second pamphlet, *Through the Centuries*, starts at **Place Stanislas** and moves from the 18th century back to the Middle Ages. Its stops include the 14th century twin-turreted **Porte de la Craffe**, the city's oldest gateway, used for centuries as a prison, which sits imposingly at the northern end of the Grande Rue. You can follow both routes with *visites audioguidées* (Walkman tours; 35FF), available at the tourist office.

Place Stanislas Area

This magnificent neoclassical square is named after the man who commissioned it, Stanislaw Leszczynski, the dethroned king of Poland (ruled 1704-09 and in 1733) who, thanks to his son-in-law Louis XV, ruled Lorraine as duke in the middle decades of the 17th century. The buildings that surround the square (including the **Hôtel de Ville** along the south-east side), the splendid gilded **wrought-iron gateways** by Jean Lamour, and the rococo **Fontaines de Neptune** and **d'Amphitrite** by Guibal, form one of the finest ensembles of 18th century architecture and decorative art anywhere in France.

Adjoining Place Stanislas, on the other side of Nancy's own **Arc de Triomphe** (built in honour of Louis XV in the mid-1750s), is the larger and quieter **Place de la Carrière**, a riding and jousting arena transformed by Stanislas and his architect Emmanuel Héré. It is graced by four rows of linden trees and stately rococo gates in gilded wrought iron. To the north is the mostly 16th century **Palais Ducal**, former residence of the Dukes of Lorraine, which now houses a superb museum. Nearby **Basilique Saint Epvre** provides an excellent example (in itself a rarity) of 19th century neo-Gothic architecture and has no fewer than 74 stained-glass windows.

Just east of Place de la Carrière is **Parc de la Pépinière**, a delightful formal garden with flowerbeds, cafés and also boasts a small zoo.

Museums

Musée de l'École de Nancy Housed in a 19th century villa about 2km south-west of the city centre, the outstanding School of Nancy Museum (☎ 03 83 40 14 86), 36-38 Rue du Sergent Blandan, brings together a heady collection of colourful, curvaceous pieces produced by the turn-of-the-century Art Nouveau movement (see Architecture under Arts in the Facts about France chapter). Don't miss the enormous dining room (the walls, floor, ceiling and furniture are all made of mahogany), the bedstead of ash and crystal called *Aube et Crépuscule* (Dawn and Dusk), and the decadent ceramic bathtub around the back of it. The garden, with its bizarre glass-topped Chapel of Rest, is also worth a look.

The museum is open daily, except Tuesday, from 10.30 am (2 pm on Monday) to 6 pm. Entry costs 20FF (15FF for students and children over 10). By bus, take No 5 or 25 to the Nancy Thermal stop or No 6, 16 or 46 to the Painlevé stop and walk south for 200m.

Musée Historique Lorrain The mostly 16th century **Palais Ducal** (Ducal Palace) houses two sections of the excellent Lorraine Historical Museum (☎ 03 83 32 18 74). The part dedicated to fine arts and history at 64 Grande Rue traces the region's history from Gallo-Roman times to the 19th century. It has rich collections of medieval statuary, engravings and faïence, as well as Judaica from before and after the Revolution. At 66 Grande Rue is the Arts et Traditions Populaires (Regional Art and Folklore) section, housed in the 15th century **Couvent des Cordeliers**, a former Franciscan monastery. The late 15th century Gothic **Église des Cordeliers** and the adjacent **Chapelle Ducale** (Ducal Chapel; 1607), modelled on the Medici Chapel in Florence, served as the burial place of the Dukes of Lorraine.

From May to late September both are open daily, except Tuesday, from 10 am to 6 pm; during the rest of the year its hours are 10 am to noon and 2 to 5 pm (6 pm on Sunday and holidays). Each museum costs 20FF (15FF for students, 10FF for children). A combination ticket may be available.

Musée des Beaux-Arts The Fine Arts Museum (☎ 03 83 85 30 72), 3 Place Stanislas, is housed in an 18th century mansion that is arguably more interesting than the exhibition of French and Italian Renaissance, baroque, rococo and contemporary works inside. Fans of delicate glassware will enjoy the gallery of Daum crystal, with more than 200 pieces on display. This museum is being renovated and is set to reopen in 1999.

Places to Stay

Camping The leafy ***Camping de Brabois*** (☎ 03 83 27 18 28; fax 03 83 91 83 45) is on Ave Paul Muller, on a hill about 5km south-west of the centre. It is open from April to mid-October and costs about 15FF for a spot, 15FF per adult and 6FF to park. By bus, take No 26 or 46 to the Camping stop (see Hostel for more details).

Hostel The ***Auberge de Jeunesse Remicourt*** (☎ 03 83 27 73 67; fax 03 83 41 41 35), in a fantastic old chateau surrounded by a peaceful park, is 4km south of the centre at 149 Rue de Vandœuvre in Villers-lès-Nancy. A bed costs 75FF (95FF in a shower-equipped double), including breakfast. Meals are available from 30FF. Check-in is possible only from 5.30 to 10 pm, but you can drop off your bags all day long. By bus take the No 26 from near the train station (Rue Raymond Poincaré) or the Point Central to the Saint Fiacre stop, or – less conveniently – the No 46 to the Albert 1er stop.

Hotels – Old & New Towns The (formerly Grand) ***Hôtel de la Poste*** (☎ 03 83 32 11 52; fax 03 83 37 58 74), 56 Place Monseigneur Ruch, next to the sombre cathedral, was once a classy establishment. These days its large, if simple, singles/doubles start at 145/165FF with shower (165/185FF with toilet as well).

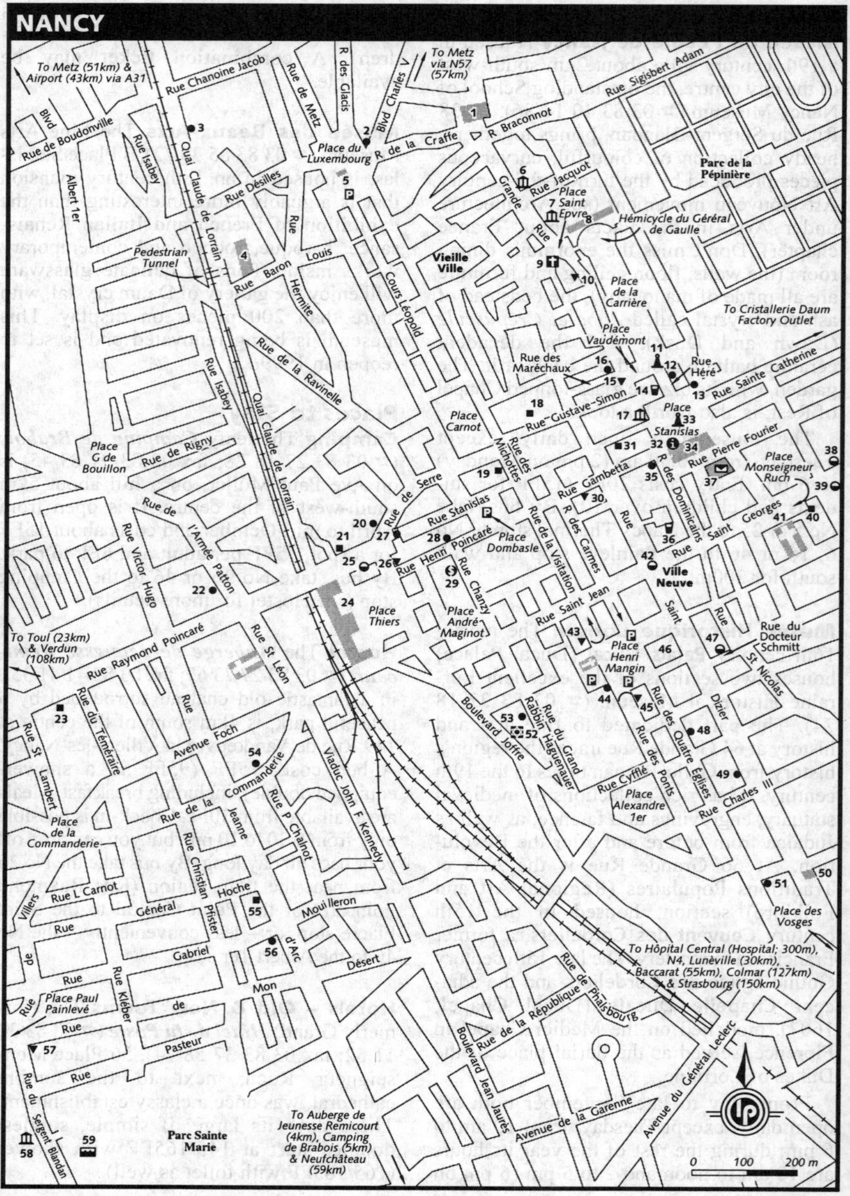
NANCY
To Metz (51km) & Airport (43km) via A31
To Metz via N57 (57km)
Rue Chanoine Jacob
R des Glacis
Rue de Metz
Blvd Charles V
Rue Sigisbert Adam
Blvd
Rue de Boudonville
Rue Isabey
Albert 1er
Quai Claude de Lorrain
Place du Luxembourg
R de la Craffe
R Braconnot
Parc de la Pépinière
Rue Désilles
Rue Jacquot
Grande
Place Saint Epvre
Hémicycle du Géréral de Gaulle
Pedestrian Tunnel
Rue Baron Louis
Hermite
Rue
Cours Léopold
Vieille Ville
Place de la Carrière
To Cristallerie Daum Factory Outlet
Rue de la Ravinelle
Place Vaudémont
Rue des Maréchaux
Rue Héré
Rue Sainte Catherine
Rue Isabey
Quai Claude de Lorrain
Rue-Gustave-Simon
Place Carnot
Place Stanislas
Place G de Bouillon
Rue de Rigny
Rue des Michottes
Rue Pierre Fourier
Place Monseigneur Ruch
Rue Gambetta
R des Dominicains
Rue de
Rue de Serre
Rue Stanislas
Rue Saint Georges
R des Carmes
Rue de la Visitation
l'Armée Patton
Rue Victor Hugo
Rue Henri Poincaré
Place Dombasle
Rue Chanzy
Ville Neuve
Place Thiers
Place André Maginot
Rue Saint Jean
Saint
Rue
To Toul (23km) & Verdun (108km)
Rue Raymond Poincaré
Rue St Léon
Rue du Docteur Schmitt
Place Henri Mangin
St Nicolas
Rue du Téméraire
Rue St Lambert
Rue
Avenue Foch
Boulevard Joffre
Rue du Grand Rabbin Haguenauer
Rue des Quatre Eglises
Rue des Ponts
Dizier
Rue Cyfflé
Rue de la Commanderie
Jeanne
Rue P Chalnot
Viaduc John F Kennedy
Place Alexandre 1er
Rue Charles III
Place de la Commanderie
Rue Christian Pfister
Rue L Carnot
Villers
Général
Hoche
Mouilleron
Place des Vosges
Rue
Gabriel
d'Arc
Désert
To Hôpital Central (Hospital; 300m), N4, Lunèville (30km), Baccarat (55km), Colmar (127km) & Strasbourg (150km)
Rue de Phalsbourg
Mon
de
Rue
Rue Kléber
Place Paul Painlevé
Rue de la République
Boulevard Jean Jaurès
Rue
Pasteur
Rue
Avenue du Général Leclerc
Avenue de la Garenne
Rue du Sergent Blandan
Parc Sainte Marie
To Auberge de Jeunesse Remicourt (4km), Camping de Brabois (5km) & Neufchâteau (59km)
0
100
200 m
1
2
3
4
5
6
7
8
9
10
11
12
13
14
15
16
17
18
19
20
21
22
23
24
25
26
27
28
29
30
31
32
33
34
35
36
37
38
39
40
41
42
43
44
45
46
47
48
49
50
51
52
53
54
55
56
57
58
59

LORRAINE

NANCY

PLACES TO STAY

- 18 Hôtel Le Grenier à Sel
- 19 Hôtel de l'Académie; Blue Note Piano Bar
- 21 Hôtel Piroux; Hôtel de Flore
- 23 Hôtel Poincaré
- 31 Hôtel des Portes d'Or
- 40 Hôtel de la Poste
- 55 Hôtel de la Croix de Bourgogne

PLACES TO EAT

- 10 Chez Bagot-Le Chardon Bleu
- 15 Le Petit Gastrolâtre
- 26 Brasserie Excelsior
- 30 Restaurant Capucin Gourmand
- 43 La Cigogne
- 45 La Bocca
- 57 Café Au Bon Coin

MUSEUMS

- 6 Musée Historique Lorrain (Arts et Traditions Populaires); Église des Cordeliers
- 7 Palais Ducal; Musée Historique Lorrain (Fine Arts)
- 17 Musée des Beaux-Arts
- 58 Musée de l'École de Nancy

OTHER

- 1 Porte de la Craffe
- 2 Maison Weissenburger
- 3 Maison Huot
- 4 Théâtre de la Manufacture
- 5 Mémorial Désilles
- 8 Palais du Gouvernement
- 9 Basilique Saint Epvre
- 11 Arc de Triomphe
- 12 Daum Crystal Shop
- 13 Wrought-Iron Gateway
- 14 L'Arquebuse
- 16 Aux Croustillants (Boulangerie)
- 20 Europcar Car Rental
- 22 Lavomatique Laundrette
- 24 Train Station
- 25 Bus to Auberge de Jeunesse & Navettes Aérolor (Airport Bus)
- 27 Porte Stanislas
- 28 Chambre de Commerce Building
- 29 Banque de France
- 32 Tourist Office
- 33 Statue of Stanislaw Leszczynski
- 34 Hôtel de Ville
- 35 Baccarat Crystal Shop; Espace 54
- 36 Caveau des Dom's
- 37 Main Post Office
- 38 Les Rapides de Lorraine Bus Office
- 39 Intercity Bus Terminal
- 41 Cathedral
- 42 Point Central Bus Hub
- 44 Casino Supermarket
- 46 Covered Market
- 47 CGFTE Bus Information Office
- 48 L'Usine Cybercafé
- 49 Bateau Lavoir Laundrette
- 50 Porte Saint Nicolas
- 51 Michenon Bike Rentals
- 52 Synagogue
- 53 Match Supermarket
- 54 Caméo Cinema
- 56 Self Lav-o-matic Laundrette
- 59 Piscine Louison Bobet

The welcoming and slightly off-beat, 28 room ***Hôtel de l'Académie*** (☎ 03 83 35 52 31; fax 03 83 32 55 78), 7bis Rue des Michottes, offers excellent value: rooms with shower start at 100/150FF (from 165FF with toilet, too). Some rooms can take an extra bed for 30FF. Around the corner, the ***Hôtel Le Grenier à Sel*** (☎ 03 83 32 31 98; fax 03 83 35 32 88), 28 Rue Gustave Simon, which has been around since 1875, has rustic rooms with low, beamed roofs. Basic rooms with bath start at 160/180FF. Reception is closed on Sunday after 4 pm and all day Monday; if you'll be arriving on Monday call ahead.

At 21 Rue Stanislas, the two star ***Hôtel des Portes d'Or*** (☎ 03 83 35 42 34) has rooms from 250/280FF.

Hotels – Train Station Area The ***Hôtel Piroux*** (☎ 03 83 32 01 10; fax 03 83 35 44 92), 12 Rue Raymond Poincaré, has shower-equipped doubles starting at 160FF (200FF with bath, toilet and TV). On Saturday and Sunday reception is closed from noon to 7 pm. Four blocks west, the two star ***Hôtel Poincaré*** (☎ 03 83 40 25 99; fax 03 83 27 22 43), 81 Rue Raymond Poincaré, has decent singles from 110FF. Singles/doubles cost 150/160FF with toilet and 190/200FF with shower, too. Private parking costs 20FF extra. You might also try the 13 room, two star ***Hôtel de Flore*** (☎ 03 83 37 63 28), 8 Rue Raymond Poincaré, where rooms start at 150/200FF.

The spotless, friendly ***Hôtel de la Croix de Bourgogne*** (☎ 03 83 40 01 86), 68bis Rue Jeanne d'Arc, 1km from the train station, has cheery doubles from 120FF (160FF with shower); hall showers are 10FF extra. To get there, take bus No 7, 8, 17 or 44 to the Croix de Bourgogne stop. There's plenty of parking available around the corner.

Places to Eat

Nancy's many restaurants are to be found in several clusters in and around the city centre. Place Vaudémont is filled with cafés in summer.

Restaurants – Old Town In Nancy for some two decades, ***Le Petit Gastrolâtre*** (☎ 03 83 35 51 94), 1 Place Vaudémont, has been a favourite place for Lorraine-style dishes. Its *menus* run from 95 to 195FF. This place is closed on Monday for lunch and on Sunday. Around the corner, Rue des Maréchaux is lined with about a dozen restaurants of all sorts.

Chez Bagot-Le Chardon Bleu (☎ 03 83 37 42 43), in a delightful 18th century house at 45 Grande Rue, has excellent and innovative French *menus* for 128 to 190FF (and 78FF for lunch, except on Sunday). Specialities include fish. It is closed on Sunday night and on Monday.

Restaurants – New Town For a seafood splurge amid Art Nouveau and Art Deco elegance, try ***Brasserie Excelsior*** (☎ 03 83 35 24 57), opposite the train station at 50 Rue Henri Poincaré. The *menus* at this Parisian-style brasserie, which dates back to 1910, start at 109FF (after 10 pm), 112FF (for lunch) and 155FF (for dinner). It is open daily from 7.30 am to 12.30 am; full meals are served from 11.45 am to 3 pm and 7 pm to 12.30 am. ***Restaurant Capucin Gourmand*** (☎ 03 83 35 26 98), 31 Rue Gambetta, has classic French cuisine with a modern twist, served in a grand, turn-of-the-century dining room. The *menu* costs 180FF (closed on Sunday and Monday).

Near Place Henri Mangin, ***La Bocca*** (☎ 03 83 32 74 47), 33 Rue des Ponts, has pasta (from 44FF) and lets you compose your own pizzas (46FF) from its selection of 34 toppings. It is open daily, except Sunday, from noon to 2.30 pm and 7 to 11 pm (midnight on Saturday). There are several other restaurants nearby.

La Cigogne (☎ 03 83 32 11 13), a small brasserie-restaurant-café at 4bis Rue des Ponts, has three-course meat or fish *menus* from 62.50FF (closed Sunday).

Just north of the Musée de l'École de Nancy, the ***Café au Bon Coin*** (☎ 03 83 40 04 01), 33 Rue de Villers, has *menus* from 71 to 135FF. It is closed on Sunday.

Self-Catering The ***covered market*** at Place Henri Mangin is open Tuesday to Saturday from about 6 am to 6 pm. There's a ***Casino*** supermarket on the other side of Place Henri Mangin. The ***Match*** supermarket on Rue du Grand Rabbin Haguenauer is open Monday to Saturday from 7 am to midnight.

Aux Croustillants, a boulangerie near Place Stanislas at 10 Rue des Maréchaux, is open 24 hours a day, except from 10 pm on Sunday to 5.30 am on Tuesday.

Entertainment

Much of Nancy's nightlife is centred around Rue Saint Jean and nearby streets in the new town.

Cinema There's a good selection of non-dubbed films at ***Caméo*** (☎ 03 83 40 35 68), 16 Rue de la Commanderie.

Discos, Clubs & Bars The ***Blue Note Piano Bar*** (☎ 03 83 30 31 18), 3 Rue des Michottes, open nightly from 9.30 pm to 4 am (5 am on weekends), has live concerts on Thursday night and a disco on Friday and Saturday nights (60FF, including a drink). The rest of the week, the four vaulted cellar rooms function as a bar. ***Caveau des Dom's*** (or Dominicains; ☎ 03 83 35 04 00), in the courtyard at 21bis Rue Saint Dizier, is another favourite.

L'Arquebuse, 13 Rue Héré, is a very stylish and mellow bar with comfortable armchairs and modern, nautical styling. It is open from 6.30 pm to 4 am (5 am on weekends). It's closed on Sunday and Monday.

Shopping

If you can't make it to Baccarat (see the Around Nancy section), you can admire

LORRAINE

and buy famous (and expensive) crystal right near Place Stanislas. Cristallerie Daum has an outlet (☎ 03 83 32 21 65) at 22 Rue Héré. The Baccarat shop (☎ 03 83 30 55 11) is at 2 Rue des Dominicains. Espace 54 (☎ 03 83 32 34 00), next door at 3 Rue Gambetta, specialises in stunning glass by contemporary French artists. All three are closed on Monday morning and on Sunday.

Daum's factory outlet (☎ 03 83 32 14 55), 17 Rue des Cristalleries, which leads off Rue Henri Bazin, the continuation of Rue Sainte Catherine, sells discontinued designs and seconds (closed Sunday).

Getting There & Away

Air The Metz-Nancy-Lorraine airport (☎ 03 87 56 70 00) is 43km north-east of Nancy off the A31.

Bus Les Rapides de Lorraine (☎ 03 83 32 80 00) has an office at 89 Rue Saint Georges. It is open from 7.45 am to noon and 2 to 6.15 pm (noon on Saturday, closed Sunday). The intercity bus terminal is across the street. Destinations served include Épinal (57FF; two hours; five a day, except Sunday), Contrexéville (70FF), Vittel (70FF; two hours), Lunéville (33FF) and Verdun (91 or 95FF; 2¾ hours; six a day, one on Sunday and holidays).

Train The information office (☎ 08 36 35 35 35) of the train station, on Place Thiers, is open daily from 9 am to 7.30 pm (6.30 pm on Saturday). Destinations with direct services include Paris' Gare de l'Est (203FF; three hours; 10 to 12 a day), Épernay (141FF; two hours; three a day), Épinal (61FF; one hour; 10 to 17 a day), Metz (50FF; 40 minutes to one hour; 21 to 32 a day), Remiremont (1¼ hours; six to eight a day) and Strasbourg (108FF; 1¼ hours; 10 to 12 a day).

Car Europcar (☎ 03 83 37 57 24) is near the train station at 18 Rue de Serre (closed Sunday).

Getting Around

To/From the Airport Navettes Aérolor (☎ 03 83 65 15 15 or ☎ 03 87 34 60 00 in Metz; Minitel 3615 HORAVLOR) links Nancy's train station (the Hôtel Mercure tower) with Metz-Nancy-Lorraine airport (40FF; 40 minutes; seven times a day on weekdays).

Bus The local bus company CGFTE (☎ 03 83 35 54 54) has an office at 3 Rue du Docteur Schmitt; it's open Monday to Saturday from 7.30 am to 7 pm. Almost all the lines stop at or near the intersection of Rue Saint Georges and Rue Saint Dizier, known as the Point Central. A single ticket costs 7FF (10FF after 9.20 pm on night buses); a magnetic ticket good for 10/20 rides is 50/90FF. The weekly Pass Stanislas costs 67FF.

Taxi To order a taxi, call ☎ 03 83 37 65 37.

Bicycle Bikes can be rented from Michenon (☎ 03 83 17 59 59), 91 Rue des Quatre Églises, which is open Tuesday to Saturday from 9 am to noon and 2 to 7 pm.

AROUND NANCY

Baccarat

For centuries Nancy and southern Lorraine have produced some of the world's finest crystal and glassware. The most famous *cristallerie* of all is at Baccarat, 55km to the south-east of Nancy. The Baccarat workshops are not open to the public, but at the **Musée de Baccarat** (☎ 03 83 76 61 37), housed in a 19th century chateau, you can admire some 1100 pieces, including a 2m-high crystal candelabra and carafes created for Tsar Nicholas II of Russia. In one room you can watch artisans at work, but if you suddenly have an urge to sing, try not to reach high C. From April to October the museum is open daily from 9.30 am to 12.30 pm and 2 to 6.30 pm; the rest of the year its hours are 10 am to noon and 2 to 6 pm. Admission is 15FF. Baccarat is linked to Nancy by train (50FF; 45 minutes; six to 10 a day).

METZ

• pop 193,000 ✉ 57000 alt 173m

Metz, present-day capital of Lorraine, is a dignified, cosmopolitan city with stately public spaces, riverside parks and a large university. Many of the most impressive buildings date from the period when Metz was part of the German Empire. The magnificent Gothic cathedral, with its stunning stained glass, is the major attraction.

In the Middle Ages, Metz was a prosperous and autonomous city within the Holy Roman Empire. Although predominantly Protestant after the Reformation, a siege by forces loyal to the Holy Roman Empire in 1552 was successfully resisted with the help of the Catholic king of France, Henry II. The city was ceded to France in 1648 by the Treaty of Westphalia. When Metz was annexed by Germany in 1871, a quarter of the population fled to French territory.

Orientation

The cathedral, situated on a hill above the Moselle River, is a bit over 1km due north of the train station. The most important public spaces in the city centre are the 18th century Place d'Armes, next to the cathedral; Place de la Comédie, on a small island north-west of the cathedral; Place Saint Jacques, in the heart of the pedestrianised commercial district – this area's main thoroughfare is Rue Serpenoise, once a Roman highway; Place de la République, on the south-west side of the city's commercial centre; and the adjacent Esplanade, which overlooks a lovely riverside park and one of the channels of the Moselle River. The main university campus is 600m west of the cathedral on the Île de Saulcy.

Information

Tourist Offices The highly professional tourist office (☎ 03 87 55 53 76; fax 03 87 36 59 43) is across Place d'Armes from the cathedral. It's open Monday to Saturday from 9 am to 7 pm (9 pm in July and August); Sunday hours are 10 am to 1 pm and 3 pm (2 pm in July and August) to 5 pm. Hotel reservations cost 10FF.

The tourist office offers 1½-hour visites audioguidées of the city in a variety of languages (45FF). In summer, guided tours of the city in French (45FF) leave the tourist office daily, except Sunday, at 3 pm.

Money The Banque de France at 12 Ave Robert Schuman is open weekdays from 8.30 am to 12.30 pm and 1.30 to 3.30 pm. Opposite the train station, the Banque Populaire de Lorraine at 3 Rue François de Curel is open weekdays from 8.30 am to 6 pm. There are several banks at Place Saint Louis. The tourist office also has an exchange service.

Post The imposing main post office is at 9 Rue Gambetta and is open weekdays from 8 am to 7 pm and on Saturday until noon. Foreign exchange services are available.

Internet Resources Net Café (☎ 03 87 76 30 64), in the courtyard at 11 Place de la Cathédrale, is open Monday to Saturday from 1 to 6 pm. A half-hour online costs 35FF.

Laundry The Lavomatique laundrettes at 4 Rue des Allemands, 11 Rue de la Fontaine and 22 Rue du Pont des Morts are open daily from 7 am to 8 pm.

Medical Services Notre Dame de Bonsecours CHR (☎ 03 87 55 31 31), a huge hospital at 1 Place Philippe de Vigneulles, is open 24 hours a day.

Emergency The Police Nationale's Hôtel de Police (☎ 03 87 37 91 19) at 6 Rue Belle Isle is staffed 24 hours a day.

Cathédrale Saint Étienne

The spectacular, Gothic-style Cathedral of Saint Stephen (☎ 03 87 75 54 61) is famed for its veritable curtains of stained glass, some of the finest in France. The three decks of windows, remarkable for their richness and diversity, date from the 13th to 20th centuries. The superb **Flamboyant Gothic windows** by Thiébault de Lixheim (1504), on the **main wall** of the left-hand transept arm, provide a remarkable stylistic contrast with Valentin Brousch's magnificent Renaissance windows on the main wall of the right-hand transept arm, created a mere two decades later. The most celebrated recent panes are by Jacques Villon (1957; next to the information kiosk) and Marc Chagall (1960-63; in the left-hand transept arm opposite the statue of the Virgin and in the choir above the entrance to the **trésor**, ie treasury).

Built of yellow-tan limestone between 1220 and 1522 on the site of earlier churches (including a 6th century cathedral and Saint Étienne's 5th century oratory), the cathedral has a 42m-high nave – one of the highest in France – and soaring flying buttresses. The structure was created by fusing a pre-existing 13th century church, Notre Dame-la-Ronde, with Pierre Perrat's late 14th century nave. The neo-Gothic main portal was added between 1894 and 1903 and includes a figure of the prophet Daniel (on the far right). Because the statue bore a remarkable resemblance to the German Kaiser Wilhelm II, it was a source of jokes until its moustache was 'shaved off' in 1940.

The cathedral is open daily from 7 am to noon and 2 to 6 pm (6.30 pm from June to September, when there's usually no midday closure). It costs 12FF to see the treasury and 15th century **crypt** (below the altar, on the right-hand side), from whose ceiling hangs the Graoully ('GRAU-lee' or 'GRAU-yee'), a legendary monster carried in processions from at least the 12th century; both are open from 9.30 am to noon and 2 to 5.30 pm (from June to September its afternoon hours are 1 to 6.30 pm). The cathedral is worth two or three visits. Try to come on a bright day.

Place de la Comédie

This lovely neoclassical square, bounded by one of the channels of the Moselle River, is home to the city's **Théâtre** (1738-53), the oldest theatre building in France that's still in use. During the Revolution, when the *place* was known as Place de l'Égalité, a guillotine emplaced here lopped off the heads of 63 'enemies of the people'.

On the square's south-west side stands the **Temple Neuf** (Protestant Church), a Rhenish-style neo-Romanesque structure built by the Germans in 1903.

Musée d'Art et d'Histoire

The excellent Art & History Museum (☎ 03 87 75 10 18), 2 Rue du Haut Poirier, has an outstanding collection of Gallo-Roman antiquities, early medieval religious art and stonework, and paintings from various periods. It is housed in a maze-like series of 60 rooms that were originally part of a 15th century granary and a 17th century convent.

The museum, worth at least two or three hours, is open daily from 10 am to noon and 2 to 6 pm. Admission costs 30FF (10FF for students). It is free for children under 12 and, on Wednesday and Sunday mornings, for everyone.

Place Saint Louis

This attractive square is surrounded by medieval arcades and merchants' houses dating from the Renaissance.

The Esplanade

The Esplanade's formal flowerbeds and its statue (1859) of a gallant-looking Marshall Ney, sword dangling at his side, are flanked by imposing public buildings, including the **Arsenal**, built under Napoleon III in 1863 and turned into a concert hall in 1989, and the late 18th century **Palais de Justice**, built in a sober neoclassical style.

Just south of the Esplanade is **Église Saint Pierre-aux-Nonains**, originally built between 380 and 400 AD as part of a Gallo-Roman spa complex. The parts of the walls that have horizontal stripes of red bricks are Roman originals. Later additions to the structure show Roman, barbarian, Coptic, Byzantine, Syrian and Germanic architectural influences. From the 6th to 16th centuries the structure served as the abbey church of a women's monastery. From April to September the church can be visited daily, except Monday, from 2 to 6.30 pm; the rest of the year it's open the same hours on Saturday and Sunday.

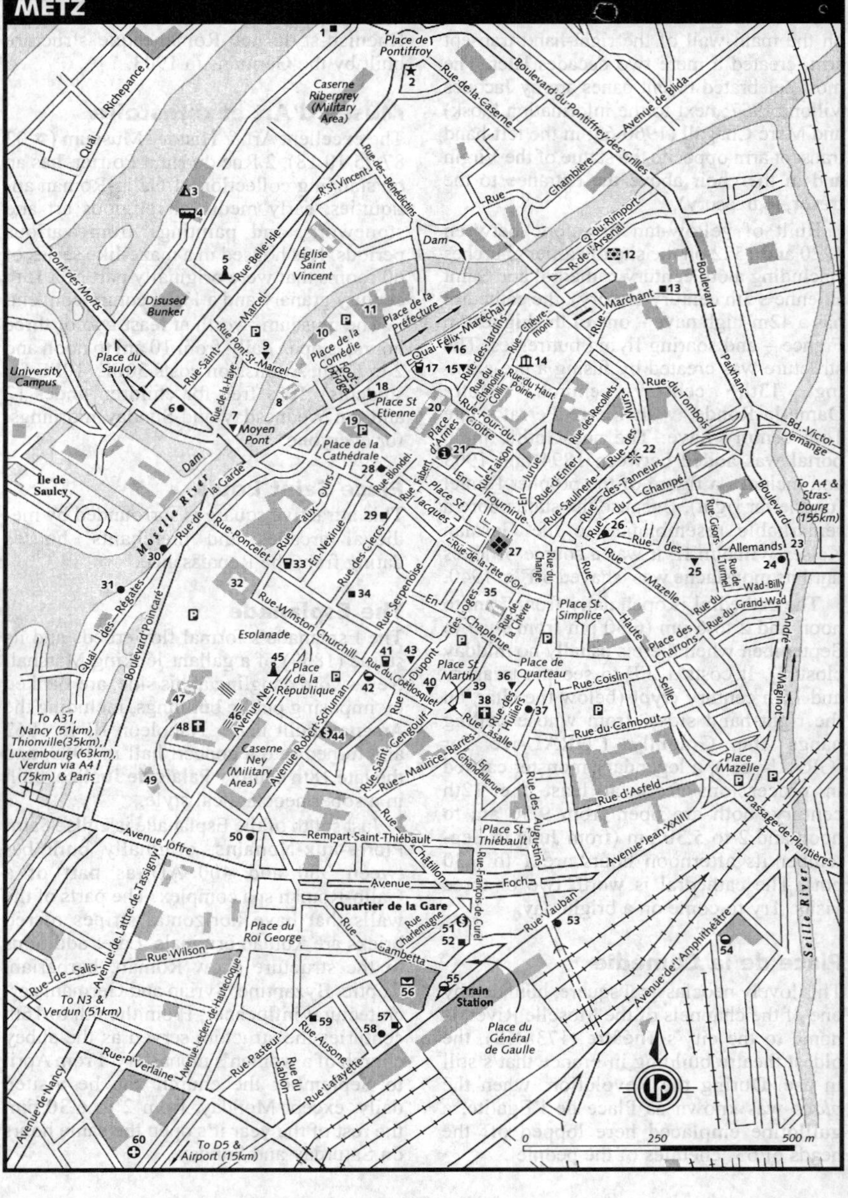
METZ
Place de Pontiffroy
Caserne Riberprey (Military Area)
Rue de la Caserne
Boulevard du Pontiffrey des Grilles
Avenue de Blida
Quai Richepance
R. St Vincent
Rue des Bénédictins
Rue Chambière
Q. du Rimport
R. de l'Arsenal
Rue Belle Isle
Pont des Morts
Église Saint Vincent
Dam
Disused Bunker
Rue Marcel
Rue Pont-St-Marcel
Place de la Préfecture
Place de la Comédie
Quai Félix Maréchal
Rue Chèvremont
Rue Marchant
Boulevard Paixhans
University Campus
Place du Saulcy
Rue Saint-Marcel
Rue de la Haye
Foot Bridge
Place St Etienne
Rue des Jardins
Rue du Chanoine Collin
Rue du Haut Poirier
Rue des Récollets
Rue des Murs
Rue du Tombois
Bd. Victor Demange
Moyen Pont
Place de la Cathédrale
Place d'Armes
Rue Four du Cloître
Rue Taison
En Jurue
Rue d'Enfer
Île de Saulcy
Moselle River
Rue de la Garde
Rue Blondel
Rue Fabert
Place St Jacques
En Fournirue
Rue Saulnerie
Rue des Tanneurs
Rue du Champé
Rue Gisors
Boulevard
To A4 & Strasbourg (155km)
Rue aux Ours
Rue Poncelet
En Nexirue
Rue des Clercs
Rue de la Tête d'Or
Rue du Change
Rue des Allemands
Rue de Turmel
Rue Mazelle
Rue du Wad-Billy
Rue du Grand-Wad
Quai des Régates
Boulevard Poincaré
Esplanade
Rue Winston Churchill
Rue Serpenoise
En Chaplerue
Rue des Loges
Rue de la Chèvre
Place St Simplice
Rue Haute Seille
Place des Charrons
Avenue André Maginot
Place de la République
Avenue Ney
Avenue Robert Schuman
Rue du Coëtlosquet
Rue Dupont des Loges
Place St Martin
Place de Quarteau
Rue Coislin
Rue des Huilliers
Rue Lasalle
Rue du Gambout
To A31, Nancy (51km), Thionville (35km), Luxembourg (63km), Verdun via A4 (75km) & Paris
Caserne Ney (Military Area)
Rue Saint-Gengoulf
Rue Maurice Barrès
Chandellerue
Rue des Augustins
Place Mazelle
Rue d'Asfeld
Passage de Plantières
Avenue Joffre
Rempart Saint-Thiébault
Rue Châtillon
Place St Thiébault
Rue François de Curel
Avenue Jean XXIII
Avenue Foch
Rue Vauban
Quartier de la Gare
Rue Charlemagne
Place du Roi George
Rue Wilson
Rue Gambetta
Avenue de Lattre de Tassigny
Rue de Salis
Avenue Leclerc de Hauteclocque
To N3 & Verdun (51km)
Train Station
Avenue de l'Amphithéâtre
Seille River
Place du Général de Gaulle
Rue P. Verlaine
Rue Pasteur
Rue Ausone
Rue du Sablon
Rue Lafayette
Avenue de Nancy
To D5 & Airport (15km)
0
250
500 m

LORRAINE

METZ

PLACES TO STAY
- 1 Auberge de Jeunesse Metz-Plage
- 3 Metz-Plage Camping
- 13 Auberge de Jeunesse Carrefour
- 18 Hôtel de la Cathédrale
- 29 Grand Hôtel de Metz
- 34 Hôtel Lafayette
- 39 Hôtel Chez Françoise
- 52 Hôtel Métropole
- 57 Hôtel Moderne
- 59 Cécil Hôtel

PLACES TO EAT
- 7 Restaurant Mairie
- 9 Restaurant du Pont Saint Marcel
- 15 Taj Mahal
- 16 À La Ville de Lyon
- 25 Tâm Traiteur
- 36 L'Étoile du Maroc
- 40 Au Pied de Vigne
- 43 Pizzerias

OTHER
- 2 Hôtel de Police
- 4 Swimming Pool
- 5 Bell Tower
- 6 Laundrette
- 8 Temple Neuf
- 10 Théâtre
- 11 Préfecture Building
- 12 Synagogue
- 14 Musée d'Art et d'Histoire
- 17 Irish Pub
- 19 Covered Market
- 20 Cathédrale Saint Étienne
- 21 Tourist Office
- 22 Panorama
- 23 Porte des Allemands
- 24 Peugeot Cycles
- 26 Laundrette
- 27 Suma Supermarket; Centre Saint Jacques Shopping Mall
- 28 Net Café
- 30 Paddleboat Rental
- 31 Pleasure Boat Dock
- 32 Palais de Justice
- 33 Le Privilège
- 35 Notre Dame
- 37 Laundrette
- 38 St Martin
- 41 Le Tiffany
- 42 TCRM Bus Information Office
- 44 Banque de France
- 45 Statue of Marshall Ney
- 46 Arsenal Cultural Centre
- 47 Église Saint Pierre-aux-Nonains
- 48 Ancienne Chapelle des Templiers
- 49 Palais du Gouverneur
- 50 Porte Serpenoise
- 51 Banque Populaire de Lorraine
- 53 Water Tower
- 54 Bus Station
- 55 Aérolor Airport Shuttle
- 56 Main Post Office
- 58 Eurorent Car Rental
- 60 Notre Dame de Bonsecours

West and north-west of the Esplanade, on both sides of Blvd Poincaré, is a lovely **riverside park**, graced with statues, ponds, swans, ducks and a fountain. **Paddleboats** can be rented in the warm months.

Quartier de la Gare

The solid, bourgeois buildings and broad avenues of the handsome quarter north-west of the train station, including Rue Gambetta and Ave Foch, were constructed around the turn of the century when the city was part of the German Empire. The public and commercial buildings are in either the round-arched, neo-Romanesque style or the Flemish neo-Renaissance style, both popular in Wilhelm II's Second Reich. Intended to Germanise the city by emphasising Metz's post-1871 status as an inalienable part of the German Empire, they were built using dark-hued sandstone, granite and basalt rather than the yellow-tan Jaumont limestone characteristic of French-built neoclassical structures.

The huge, grey-sandstone **train station**, completed in 1908 and decorated with sculptures whose common theme is German imperial might, was designed with military needs in mind: 300m long, it can load or unload 20,000 troops and their equipment in 24 hours. Wilhelm II himself had lodgings in the building's south-western section. The massive **main post office**, built in 1911 of red Vosges sandstone, is as solid and heavy as the cathedral is light and lacy.

Porte des Allemands

First erected around 1230 when a wall to surround this part of the city was constructed, the crenellated 'Gate of the Germans' owes its name to a medieval hospital, run by the brothers of Notre Dame-des-Allemands, which was situated nearby. Of the eight city gates that existed at the end of the 15th century, this is the only one that remains. Situated on the Seille River, it was severely damaged during the liberation of the city by Allied forces in November 1944.

Places to Stay

Several of the city's two-star places have a few cheap rooms on offer.

Camping The shady *Metz-Plage Camping* (☎ 03 87 32 05 58) is on the bank of the Moselle about 500m north-west of the centre. Open from early May to September, it charges 40FF for a caravan site, 15FF for a tent site and 15FF per adult. It is served by bus Nos 2, 5, 9, 25, 27, 29 and U.

Hostels The ***Auberge de Jeunesse Metz-Plage*** (☎ 03 87 30 44 02; fax 03 87 33 19 80), on the river just off Place du Pontiffroy, charges 49FF for a bed and 19FF for a self-service breakfast. Reception is open from 7 to 10 am and 5 to 10 pm; there's no curfew. Kitchen facilities are available, and the hostel loans out bicycles for free. From the train station take bus No 3 or 11 to the Pontiffroy stop.

The ***Auberge de Jeunesse Carrefour*** (☎ 03 87 75 07 26; fax 03 87 36 71 44), 6 Rue Marchant, charges 80.40FF for a single and 69FF for a bed in a room for three, four or eight. Prices include breakfast. Rooms are accessible all day long. From the train station take bus No 11 to the Rimport stop.

Hotels – Train Station Area The attractive train station area has some excellent deals. Many of the hotels offer 24 hour, underground parking for just 20FF.

Your best bet is probably the comfortable, 80 room, two star ***Hôtel Métropole*** (☎ 03 87 66 26 22; fax 03 87 66 29 91), in an attractive neoclassical building at 5 Place du Général de Gaulle. It has clean, modern singles with washbasin for 125FF; doubles with shower and toilet start at 185FF. Another place offering good value is the slightly more expensive, two star ***Cécil Hôtel*** (☎ 03 87 66 66 13; fax 03 87 56 96 02), 14 Rue Pasteur. The 43 room, two star ***Hôtel Moderne*** (☎ 03 87 66 57 33; fax 03 87 55 98 59), in a beautiful building at 1 Rue Lafayette, charges 120FF for a basic single; singles/doubles with shower and toilet start at 165/205FF.

Halfway between the station and the cathedral is Metz's cheapest hotel, the nine room ***Hôtel Chez Françoise*** (☎ 03 87 75 29 79), 8 Rue des Parmentiers, where doubles with washbasin cost 120FF. Hall showers are free. Reception is closed on Sunday. Many of the rooms are let by the week (650FF) or month (2200FF), so it's often full.

Hotels – City Centre On pedestrianised Rue des Clercs, the ***Hôtel Lafayette*** (☎ 03 87 75 21 09) at No 24 has simple doubles with old-fashioned touches for 145FF (180FF with shower and toilet); quads start at 210FF. A hall shower is 20FF. Nearby, the recently renovated, two star ***Grand Hôtel de Metz*** (☎ 03 87 36 16 33; fax 03 87 74 17 04), 3 Rue des Clercs, has singles/doubles/triples from 295/335/375FF. Parking in the hotel garage costs 40FF.

The very attractive ***Hôtel de la Cathédrale*** (☎ 03 87 75 00 02; fax 03 87 75 40 75), 25 Place de Chambre, just west of the cathedral in a 17th century townhouse, has charming – even romantic – singles/doubles for 360/380FF; a suite is 500FF.

Places to Eat

Place Saint Jacques is given over almost entirely to cafés in the warmer months.

Restaurants – French An excellent option for local dishes is ***Restaurant du Pont Saint Marcel*** (☎ 03 87 30 12 29), 1 Rue du Pont Saint Marcel, where everything is typical of Lorraine, from the succulent dishes to the billowy cotton shirts and black trousers worn by the waiters. This is the place to try such Moselle wines as Müller Thurgau or Pinot Gris Auxerrois. The *menus* cost 98 and 168FF. It is open daily.

Traditional French gastronomic fare is on offer at ***Au Pied de Vigne*** (☎ 03 87 21 01 07), 34 Rue du Coëtlosquet (open daily for lunch and dinner). The *menus* cost 80 to 195FF.

For a splurge, an excellent bet is the elegant, formal ***À la Ville de Lyon*** (☎ 03 87 36 07 01), next to 13 Rue des Piques (the building has been a restaurant since 1847), whose selection of traditional French dishes varies with what's available fresh in the marketplace. The *menus* cost 110, 185 and 300FF. It is closed on Sunday evening and on Monday. ***Restaurant Maire*** (☎ 03 87 32 43 12), next to the Moyen Pont at 1 Rue du Pont des Morts, specialises in French gastronomic cuisine. The *menus* cost 150FF (available on weekdays for lunch and dinner), 270 and 380FF. It is open daily from noon to 2.30 pm and 7.30 to 10 pm.

Restaurants – Other A block east of Place de la République, Rue Dupont des Loges is home to a number of ***pizzerias***. Behind the cathedral, there are several ethnic restaurants along Rue des Jardins, including ***Taj Mahal*** (☎ 03 87 74 33 23) at No 16, where the lunch *menu* costs 45FF and vegetarian mains also are about 45FF.

L'Étoile du Maroc (☎ 03 87 76 33 66), 5 Rue des Huiliers, has couscous and tajines for 60 to 90FF. It is open daily from noon to 3 pm and 7 to 11 pm.

Self-Catering There's a ***Suma*** supermarket on the lowest level of the modern Centre Saint Jacques shopping mall, which is accessible from the south-eastern edge of Place Saint Jacques (Rue de Ladoucette). It is open Monday to Saturday from 8.30 am to 7.30 pm.

The ***covered market*** at Place de la Cathédrale was begun in the late 18th century but wasn't completed until 1830 (the Revolution delayed things a bit). It is open daily, except Sunday and Monday, from 7 am to 5 pm. On Saturday morning, there's a large, outdoor ***food market*** at either Place Saint Jacques (October to April) or Place d'Armes (May to September).

Inexpensive but tasty Vietnamese takeaway dishes, offered in generous portions, are available at Tâm Traiteur (☎ 03 87 74 96 93), open until 8 pm (closed Sunday).

Entertainment

The ***Arsenal cultural centre*** (☎ 03 87 39 92 00), Metz's main concert hall, is right next to the Esplanade.

The pulsating, gyrating bodies and modernistic décor would have knocked the socks off the people who built the vaulted cellar that houses ***Le Tiffany*** (☎ 03 87 75 23 32), a discotheque at 24 Rue du Coëtlosquet, which is open from 11 pm to 5 am (closed on Tuesday night). Entry costs 50FF (60FF on Friday and Saturday nights). Sports shoes are forbidden.

Le Privilège (☎ 03 87 36 29 29), a friendly gay bar and techno-metal disco at 20 Rue aux Ours, is open nightly, except Monday, from 10 pm to 5 am.

Just down the hill from the cathedral, ***Irish Pub*** (☎ 03 87 37 01 38), 3 Place de Chambre, is open daily until 2 am (1 am on Sunday night).

Getting There & Away

Air Metz-Nancy-Lorraine airport (☎ 03 87 56 70 00) is 16km south of the city centre off the A31.

Bus Two regional bus companies operate from the bus station on Ave de l'Amphithéâtre, which is on the other side of the tracks from the train station. Hours are posted at the bus stops. Some lines also stop at the train station.

Les Rapides de Lorraine (☎ 03 87 63 65 65) links Metz with Veckring (near the Maginot Line fortress of Hackenberg; 24.70FF; about two hours; via Thionville) and Verdun (69.10FF; 1¾ hours; seven a day, except Sunday). Les Courriers Mosellans (☎ 03 87 34 60 12), which handles Eurolines ticketing, has buses to Gorze (29.60FF; 50 minutes) on weekdays and Saturday at 11.15 am and 6.15 pm, but there's no way to get back the same day. Both companies' offices are open on weekdays until at least 5 pm (4 pm on Friday) and are closed from noon to 2 pm.

Train Metz is on two main rail lines, Paris-Frankfurt and Brussels-Basel. The train station's information office (☎ 08 36 35 35 35) is open weekdays from 9 am to 7.30 pm, on Saturday until 6 pm. Direct trains link Metz with Paris' Gare de l'Est (204FF or, on a few Friday and Sunday trains, 254FF; 2¾ hours; six to eight a day), Nancy (50FF; 35 minutes; at least hourly), Verdun (71FF; 1¼ hours; three on weekdays, one on weekends), Strasbourg (112FF; 1½ hours; seven to 11 a day), Colmar (148FF; two hours; four direct a day) and Frankfurt (272FF; 3¼ hours; four a day).

Car Eurorent (☎ 03 87 66 36 31), 5 Rue Lafayette, is open Monday to Saturday.

Getting Around

To/From the Airport Aérolor shuttles (☎ 03 83 65 15 15 or ☎ 03 87 34 60 00 in Nancy) link Metz's train station with Metz-Nancy-Lorraine airport (40FF; 30 minutes) six times a day on weekdays.

Bus TCRM (☎ 03 87 76 31 11), the local bus company, has an information and ticket office at 1 Ave Robert Schuman (Place de la République; closed Sunday). Most lines operate daily from 6 am to about 8 pm, though bus No 11 has runs nightly at about 10 and 11 pm and midnight.

Taxi You can order a taxi 24 hours a day by ringing ☎ 03 87 56 91 92.

Bicycle Ten-speeds/mountain bikes can be hired for 50/80FF a day from Peugeot Cycles (☎ 03 87 74 13 14), 71 Rue des Allemands. It is open from 8 am to noon and 2 to 7 pm daily (closed Monday morning and on Sunday).

LORRAINE

AROUND METZ

Parc Naturel Régional de Lorraine

The Lorraine Regional Park, created in 1974, is split into two sections: the larger part is situated south-west of Metz and west and north-west of Nancy, while the smaller part is south-east of Metz and north-east of Nancy. Both areas, covering a total area of 2000 sq km, are forested and dotted with lakes that attract fishers and families on holiday. They also contain some of Lorraine's most picturesque villages, including **Gorze** (population 1380), the site of a Benedictine abbey founded in the 8th century. Gorze is 18km south-west of Metz and can be reached from Metz by bus (see Bus under Getting There & Away in the Metz section) or bike.

The park headquarters (☎ 03 83 81 12 77) is in Pont-à-Mousson, which is 32km south of Metz and 31km north of Nancy and linked to both cities by the A31. You can pick up brochures and buy topoguides and the like on weekdays from 9 am to noon and 2 to 5 pm.

Fort du Hackenberg

The Metz area was heavily fortified by the Germans before WWI and, as part of the Maginot Line, by the French between the wars. The largest single Maginot Line bastion in the area was the 1000 man Hackenberg fort (☎ 03 82 82 30 08), whose 10km of galleries were designed to be self-sufficient for three months and, in battle, to fire four tonnes of shells a minute. Situated 15km east of Thionville and 30km north-east of Metz near the village of Veckring, it can be visited from April to October on Saturday, Sunday and holidays at 2 pm (3 pm in July and August). An electric trolley takes visitors along 4km of the fortress' underground tunnels, past such subterranean installations as a kitchen, a hospital, a generating plant and ammunition stores. For information on buses from Metz to Veckring, see Bus under Getting There & Away in the Metz section.

VERDUN

• pop 20,700 ✉ 55100 alt 198m

The horrific events that took place in and around Verdun between February 1916 and August 1917 – *l'enfer de Verdun* (the hell of Verdun) – have turned the town's name into a byword for wartime slaughter. During the last two years of WWI, over 800,000 soldiers – some 400,000 French and almost as many Germans, along with thousands of Americans who arrived in 1918 – lost their lives here.

After the annexation of Alsace and part of Lorraine by Germany in 1871, Verdun became a frontline outpost. Over the next four decades, it was turned into the most important – and most heavily fortified – element in France's eastern defensive line. During WWI, Verdun itself was never taken by the Germans, but the evacuated town was almost totally destroyed by artillery bombardments. In the hills to the north and east of Verdun, where most of the fighting took place, the brutal combat, carried out with artillery, flame-throwers and poison gas, completely wiped nine villages off the map.

These days, Verdun is an economically depressed and profoundly provincial backwater that attracts an inordinate number of short-term tourists, a circumstance that may go some way to explaining some locals' suspicious and less-than-welcoming attitude to foreign visitors. It is also still something of a garrison town – the French army has a boot camp near town – and one often sees groups of fresh recruits shouting military chants along the main streets.

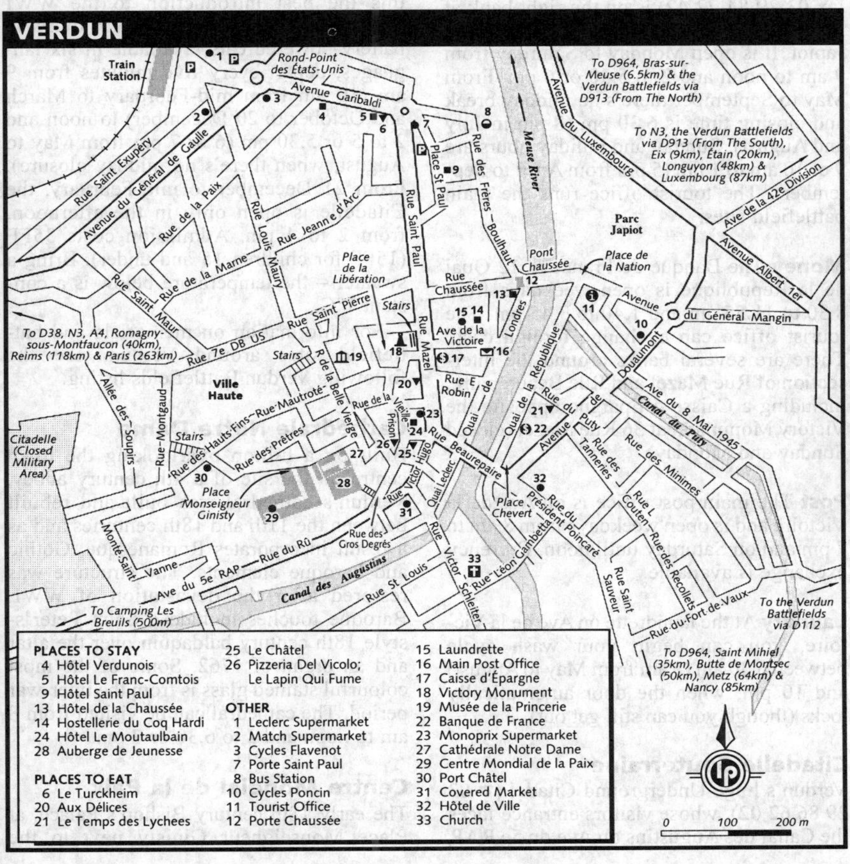

LORRAINE

Orientation

Central Verdun straddles the Meuse River and its two canals, but the livelier part of town, the Ville Haute (Upper Town), is on the river's left (western) bank, which rises to the cathedral. The train station is 700m north-west of the cathedral. Verdun's wide streets, such as Rue Mazel, the main drag, and its continuation Rue Saint Paul, were laid out in the years following WWI.

Information

Tourist Office Verdun's helpful but poorly managed tourist office (☎ 03 29 86 14 18; fax 03 29 84 22 42) is on the right bank at Place de la Nation, south of the large Parc Japiot. It is open Monday to Saturday from 9 am to noon and 2 to 5.30 or 6 pm. From May to September there's no midday break and closing time is 6.30 pm (8 pm in July and August). Sunday and holiday hours are 9 or 10 am to 1 pm (5 pm from April to September). The tourist office runs the main battlefield sites.

Money The Banque de France at 12 Quai de la République is open weekdays from 8.30 to 11.55 am and 1.40 to 3.45 pm. The tourist office can exchange foreign cash. There are several banks around the intersection of Rue Mazel and Rue Beaurepaire, including a Caisse d'Épargne opposite the Victory Monument at 36 Rue Mazel (closed Sunday and Monday).

Post The main post office is on Ave de la Victoire and is open weekdays from 8 am to 7 pm and on Saturday until noon. Currency exchange is available.

Laundry At the laundrette on Ave de la Victoire, you can begin your wash cycle between 6.30 am (5 am from May to August) and 10 pm, when the door automatically locks (though you can still get out).

Citadelle Souterraine

Verdun's huge Underground Citadel (☎ 03 29 86 62 02), whose visitors entrance faces the Canal des Augustins on Ave du 5e RAP, was designed by Vauban in the 17th century and completed in 1838. In 1916, its 7km of underground galleries were turned into an impregnable command centre in which 10,000 men lived, many while waiting to be dispatched to the front. Its subterranean facilities included a bakery, a hospital and a petrol supply station, all serviced by a narrow-gauge rail system. These days, the above-ground parts of the Citadelle are still used by the French army and are off-limits.

About 10% of the galleries have been converted into an imaginative, audiovisual re-enactment of Verdun in 1916, making this the best introduction to the WWI history of the area. Half-hour tours in battery-powered cars, available in six languages, depart every five minutes from 9 am (10 am from mid-February to March and October to 20 December) to noon and 2 to 5 or 5.30 pm (6 or 7 pm from May to August, when there's no midday closure). From 21 December to mid-February, the Citadelle is open only in the afternoon, from 2 to 4 pm. Admission costs 35FF (15FF for children 15 and under). Bring a sweater – the temperature below is a constant 7°C.

For information on memorials and battlefield sites around Verdun, see the following Verdun Battlefields listing.

Cathédrale Notre Dame

Built on a hilltop overlooking the town centre on the site of a 4th century abbey, Verdun's cathedral was built and rebuilt between the 11th and 18th centuries and as a result incorporates Romanesque, Gothic and baroque elements. The structure was restored after the devastation of WWI. Baroque touches include a Saint Peter's-style 18th century baldaquin over the altar and an organ of 1762. Some of the most colourful stained glass is from the inter-war period. The cathedral can be visited from 8 am to noon and 2 to 6.30 or 7 pm.

Centre Mondial de la Paix

The early 18th century Bishop's Palace, at Place Monseigneur Ginisty next to the

The Unknown Soldier

On 10 November 1920, one day short of two years after the end of WWI, in a chamber deep inside Verdun's Citadelle Souterraine, an infantryman named Auguste Thin solemnly walked up to eight coffins draped with the tricolour, each containing an unidentified corpse exhumed from a different Verdun battlefield. He had been chosen to select the set of anonymous remains to be interred in France's Tomb of the Unknown Soldier, and his role in the ceremony was to place the white, red and blue bouquet handed to him by War Veterans' Minister – later Minister of War – André Maginot on top of one of the coffins. Thin added up the digits of his unit number – the 132nd Infantry Regiment – and placed the flowers on the sixth coffin, which was then transported to Paris for reburial under the Arc de Triomphe. There it remains to this day, a memorial to all the men who died for France (*morts pour la France*) during WWI.

cathedral, now houses the World Centre for Peace (☎ 03 29 86 55 00), whose innovative audiovisual museum, part of which you visit with an infrared headset, has imaginative and moving exhibits on the themes of peace and human rights in light of the horrific carnage of WWI. English documentation is available. It can be visited from 10 am to 1 pm and 2 to 6 pm (closed on Tuesday, except from June to mid-September, when there's no midday closure). Entry costs 35FF (20FF if you're aged 12 to 18).

Musée de la Princerie

Verdun's municipal museum (☎ 03 29 86 10 62), housed in a 16th century townhouse at 16 Rue de la Belle Vierge, displays Romanesque and Gothic sculptures, medieval bits and bobs, ceramics and Lorraine-style furnishings. It's open daily, except Tuesday, from April to October from 9.30 am to noon and 2 to 6 pm. Admission is 10FF.

Victory Monument

Overlooking Rue Mazel is the colossal, almost Fascist-looking **Monument à la Victoire**, which honours those who died in the Battle of Verdun. Portraying a warrior and flanked by two cannons, it was built from 1920 to 1929.

City Gates

On the west bank of the Meuse, the imposing **Porte Chaussée** was built in the 14th century as part of the city walls; it later served as a prison. **Porte Châtel**, which dates from the 13th century, is two blocks west of the cathedral on Rue Mautroté. Across from the bus station, **Porte Saint Paul**, rebuilt between 1919 and 1929, is adorned with a bronze by Rodin, given to the city by the Netherlands.

Dragées Braquier

Verdun doesn't have a *dragée* queen, but it does have tours (10FF) of the Braquier factory (☎ 03 29 84 30 00), 50 Rue du Fort de Vaux, where you can see dragées (pronounced 'dra-ZHAY' – not to be confused with *draguer* ('dra-GAY'), which means to flirt or chat up), ie sugared almonds – a Verdun speciality – being made. Reservations and ticketing are handled by the tourist office.

Places to Stay

Camping The three star, swimming pool-equipped ***Camping Les Breuils*** (☎ 03 29 86 15 31), open from April to mid-October, is on Allée des Breuils about 500m west of the Citadelle Souterraine. Charges are 21FF per adult and 15/18FF for a tent/caravan. To get there take bus No 3 to the Cité Verte École stop.

Hostel The new 69 bed ***Auberge de Jeunesse*** (☎ 03 29 86 28 28; fax 03 29 86 28 82), situated behind the cathedral, is affiliated with the Centre Mondial de la Paix. Reception is staffed from 8 am to noon (10 am on weekends) and 5 to 11 pm. A modern bunk

LORRAINE

of generous proportions costs 68FF, including breakfast. Rooms are accessible all day long, but the curfew is 11 pm. It may be closed in January.

Hotels Near the train station, the ***Hôtel Le Franc-Comtois*** (☎ 03 29 86 05 46), 9 Ave Garibaldi, has singles/doubles with shower and toilet for 150/170FF; the rooms out back are quietest. Basic but comfortable singles with washbasin start at just 110FF. There are no hall showers. It's easy to park in this area. The ***Hôtel Verdunois*** (☎ 03 29 86 17 45), 13 Ave Garibaldi, has basic rooms from 120/140FF (20FF more with shower), but may soon change proprietors. There's private parking out back.

Near the bus station, the ***Hôtel Saint Paul*** (☎/fax 03 29 86 02 16), 12 Place Saint Paul, has dull but well lit rooms from 160FF (230FF with shower and toilet).

In the centre of town, the 17 room ***Hôtel de la Porte Chaussée*** (☎ 03 29 86 00 78), next to Porte Chaussée at 67 Quai de Londres, has plain but spacious doubles from 150FF (180FF with shower). Hall showers are 15FF. The attractive, two star ***Hôtel Le Montaulbain*** (☎ 03 29 86 00 47; fax 03 29 84 75 70), 4 Rue de la Vieille Prison, has spacious, cheerful rooms with shower and toilet for one/two/three people for 170/190/230FF. Free parking is available nearby. The pretentious, three star ***Hostellerie du Coq Hardi*** (☎ 03 29 86 36 36; fax 03 29 86 09 21), 8 Ave de la Victoire, has spacious but tacky singles/doubles from 300/450FF.

LORRAINE

Places to Eat

There are brasseries and bars along the strollable riverside Quai de Londres and nearby streets.

Restaurants *Le Turckheim* (☎ 03 29 83 91 40), a congenial French restaurant at 7 Ave Garibaldi, has *menus* from 57FF, including a four course *menu surprise* (100FF) that changes according to what's available in the market. From November to March it is closed on Sunday.

Le Châtel (☎ 03 29 86 20 14), directly opposite 14 Rue des Gros Degrés, is a real *restaurant du quartier* (neighbourhood restaurant), with simple decoration and good, reasonably priced food. It has three-course *menus* starting at 60FF (86FF on the weekend), a Lorraine-style *menu* for 98FF, as well as two-course *formules* for 47 and 70FF. It is closed on Saturday for lunch and on Sunday.

Aux Délices, 19 Rue Mazel, has a small sit-down area and a superb choice of quiches with onions, Roquefort and even *escargots* (snails), as well as Lorraine chocolates. It is open from 7.15 am to 7.15 pm (closed Monday).

Pizzeria Del Vicolo (☎ 03 29 86 43 14), 33 Rue des Gros Degrés, has decent pizzas for 30 to 60FF. It is closed on Monday for lunch and on Sunday. ***Le Temps des Lychees*** (☎ 03 29 86 26 26), 8 Rue du Puty, has Chinese, Vietnamese and Thai dishes. *Menus* start at 55FF for weekday lunches, 90FF the rest of the time. It is open daily.

Self-Catering On Friday from 7 am to 12.30 pm there's a ***food market*** in and around the old covered market on Rue Victor Hugo.

The ***Monoprix*** supermarket at the southern end of Rue Mazel is open Monday to Saturday from 9 am to noon and 2 to 7 pm. Next to the train station, the ***Match*** supermarket on Ave du Général de Gaulle is open Monday to Saturday from 9 am to 12.15 pm and 2.15 to 7.30 pm (no midday closure on Saturday). On the other side of the station, the cavernous ***Leclerc*** hypermarket is open from 9 am to 8 pm (8.30 pm on Friday, closed on Sunday).

Entertainment

Le Lapin Qui Fume (☎ 03 29 86 15 84), 31 Rue des Gros Degrés, is a friendly bar that's a favourite with neighbourhood regulars. (The name Le Lapin Qui Fume, which dates from early in the century, means 'the rabbit who smokes'.) It is open from 10 am (3 or 4 pm on Sunday) to 2 am (closed Monday). Beers start at 10FF.

Getting There & Away

Bus At the bus station, Les Rapides de la Meuse (☎ 03 29 86 02 71) has an information desk that is open from 5.30 am to 8 pm (closed on Saturday after 12.30 pm and Sunday). Destinations served include Metz (69.10FF; 1¾ hours; seven a day, except Sunday) and Nancy (91 or 95FF; 2¾ hours; six a day, one on Sunday and holidays).

Train The little train station (☎ 08 36 35 35 35) at the western end of Ave Garibaldi, built in 1868 by the Eiffel Company, served as a hospital from 1914 to 1916. It is from here that the Unknown Soldier made his final journey in 1920 (see the boxed text 'The Unknown Soldier').

Verdun is on a tertiary rail line so service is poor. Destinations include Paris' Gare de l'Est (177FF; 3¼ hours; two to four a day), Metz (71FF; 1¼ hours; three on weekdays, one on weekends), Nancy (88FF; 1½ to 2¼ hours; one to three a day), Reims (100FF) and Strasbourg (161FF; via Metz).

Getting Around

Taxi To order a local taxi, ring ☎ 03 29 86 05 46 or ☎ 03 29 86 05 22.

Bicycle Cycles Flavenot (☎ 03 29 86 12 43), Rond Point des États-Unis, the local Cannondale dealer, rents mountain bikes for 100FF a day and can supply information on local group rides. It's open from 9 am to noon and 2 to 7 pm (closed on Monday morning and on Sunday). Cycles Poncin (☎ 03 29 84 14 12), 25 Ave de Douaumont, rents mountain bikes for 60/150/300FF for a day/weekend/week. It is open Tuesday to Saturday from 9 am to noon and 2 to 6.45 pm.

VERDUN BATTLEFIELDS

The outbreak of WWI in August 1914 was followed, on the Western Front, by a long period of trench warfare in which neither side made any significant gains. To break the stalemate, the Germans decided to change tactics, attacking a target so vital for both military and symbolic reasons that the French would throw every man they had into its defence. These troops would then be slaughtered, 'bleeding France white' and causing the French people to lose their will to resist. Germany, so the German general staff believed, would then win the war. The target selected for this bloody plan was the heavily fortified city of Verdun.

The Battle of Verdun began on the morning of 21 February 1916. After the heaviest shelling of the war to that date (something like two million shells in 10 hours), German forces went on the attack and advanced with little opposition for four days, capturing, among other unprepared French positions, the Fort de Douaumont. Thus began a 300 day battle fought by hundreds of thousands of cold, wet, miserable and ill-fed men, sheltering in their muddy trenches and foxholes amid a moonscape of craters.

French forces were regrouped and rallied by General Philippe Pétain (later the leader of the collaborationist Vichy government during WWII), who slowed the German advance by launching several French counterattacks. He also oversaw the massive resupply of Verdun via the **Voie Sacrée** (Sacred Way), the 75km road from Bar-le-Duc, which was maintained by territorial troops from Senegal and over which 35,000 vehicles (including lorries, Paris buses and private cars) – one every 15 seconds, day and night – carried 90,000 *poilus* (French WWI soldiers) and thousands of tonnes of war material every week. During March and April, the ridges and hills north and north-west of Verdun – including what came to be known as *Le Mort Homme* (Dead Man's Hill) – were taken and retaken by both sides with incredible casualties. The Fort de Vaux fell to the Germans on 7 June.

By July, German advance units were only 5km from Verdun at the Fort de Souville, but their offensive had ground to a halt. From October 1916 to October 1917 French forces recaptured most of the territory they had lost at the beginning of the battle, but the Germans were not pushed back beyond the positions they had held in February 1916 until American troops and French forces launched a coordinated offensive in September 1918.

The Maginot Line

The famed Maginot Line, named after André Maginot (1877-1932), French minister of war from 1929 to 1931, was one of the most spectacular blunders of WWII. This elaborate, mostly subterranean defence network, built between 1930 and 1940, was the pride of pre-war France. It included everything France's finest military architects thought would be needed to defend the nation in a 'modern war' of poisonous gas, tanks and aeroplanes: reinforced concrete blockhouses, infantry bunkers (some housing 600 soldiers), subterranean lines of supply and communication, minefields, antitank canals, floodable basins and even artillery emplacements that popped out of the ground to fire and then disappeared. The only things visible above ground were firing posts and lookout towers. The line stretched along the Franco-German frontier from the Swiss border all the way round to Belgium where, for political and budgetary reasons, it stopped.

The Maginot Line even had a slogan: '*Ils ne passeront pas*' (They won't get through). 'They' – the Germans – never did break the barrier. Rather than attack the Maginot Line straight on, Hitler's armoured divisions simply circled around through Belgium and invaded France across its unprotected northern frontier. They then attacked the Maginot Line from the rear. Against all the odds – and with most of northern France already in German hands – some of the fortifications held out for a few weeks. When resistance became hopeless, thousands of French troops managed to escape to Switzerland, where the Swiss promptly interned them (they weren't freed until the following year).

Parts of the Maginot Line are open to visitors, but without your own wheels they're a bit hard to get to. In Lorraine, visitors can tour Fort du Hackenberg and Fort de Fermont. In Alsace, it's possible to visit Schoenenbourg (☎ 03 88 73 44 43), which is about 45km north of Strasbourg near the village of Betschdorf. From March to October, it is open on the first Sunday of the month and on certain holidays from 9 am to 4 pm. From July to the first week in September it can be visited daily from 2 to 4 pm (9 am to 4 pm on Sunday and holidays). Entry costs 25FF.

LORRAINE

Information

Most of the battle sites detailed below are managed by the Verdun tourist office, which can supply historical and practical information on the battlefields.

The area and its trails are covered in detail by the IGN Top 25 map No 3112 ET (*Forêts de Verdun et du Mort-Homme*), which sells for 58FF.

Organised Tours

From May to mid-September the Verdun tourist office runs guided minibus tours of the five main battlefield sites. The tours, which begin at 2 pm and last until about 6 pm, cost 145FF for adults, including entry fees where applicable.

Getting Around

All the battle sites, which are very well signposted (follow the signs to the 'Champ de Bataille 14-18'), are about 10km north-east of Verdun in a forested area served by the D913 and D112. By car, you can easily visit the area on a day trip from the attractive city of Metz. You could also take a taxi from Verdun.

Les Rapides de la Meuse (☎ 03 29 86 02 71) can get you from Verdun to both ends of the D913, the highway along which most of the monuments are situated. Buses on their way to Metz stop at the intersection of the N3 and the D913 (8FF; eight a day), while buses to Sedan stop at Bras-sur-Meuse (12.20FF; 10 minutes; four a day, except Sunday).

Mémorial de Verdun

The village of Fleury, wiped off the face of the earth in the course of being captured and recaptured 16 times, is now the site of the Verdun Memorial (☎ 03 29 84 35 34), also known as the Musée Mémorial de Fleury. The informative and interesting exhibits tell the story of the Battle of Verdun using evocative photos, documents, weapons and other objects from the battle. One wall panel shows post-war French government documents, complete with grotesque photographs, classifying various types of war wounds and their associated entitlements. Downstairs is a re-creation of the Verdun battlefield the way it looked on the day the guns finally fell silent. Some of the signs are in English.

The museum is open daily from 9 am to 6 pm (5 or 5.30 pm from November to February). Entrance costs 20FF (10FF for children aged 11 to 16) and includes a film on the Battle of Verdun, available in English.

Fleury

The Mémorial de Verdun actually sits atop Fleury's former train station – the town centre was a few hundred metres down the road. Today, a memorial chapel known as **Notre Dame de l'Europe** (Our Lady of Europe) marks the grassy, crater-pocked site, surrounded by low ruins and signs indicating the layout of the village.

Mémorial Ossuaire

The 137m-long Memorial Ossuary (☎ 03 29 84 54 81), inaugurated in 1932 and also known as the Ossuaire de Douaumont, is France's most important WWI memorial. It houses the remains of about 130,000 unidentified French and German soldiers, collected from the battlefields after the war and interred in mass tombs identified by the sector of the battlefield from which the remains were exhumed. The site is open from 9 am to noon and from 2 pm to sometime between 5 pm (in November) and 6.30 pm (from May to early September). There's no midday closure from early April to early September. Entry is free.

Downstairs, you can view a truly excellent, 20 minute audiovisual presentation on the battle and its participants. An excellent translation, provided by infrared headset, is included in the entry fee of 16FF (10FF for children). It is screened every 30 minutes. Climbing to the top of the 46m-high, projectile-shaped **bell tower** costs 6FF (4FF for children).

Nécropole Nationale

Outside the Mémorial Ossuaire, the 15,000 cement crosses (and a few non-Christian markers) of the French military cemetery extend down the hill from a black stone plaque signed in 1984 by the late French President François Mitterrand and West German Chancellor Helmut Kohl and engraved with the words: 'We have forgiven, we have understood, we have become friends'.

Nearby, tablets inscribed in Hebrew with the Ten Commandments form the **Mémorial Israélite** (Jewish Memorial).

Fort de Douaumont

About 2km north-east of the ossuary on the highest of the area's hills stands Douaumont (☎ 03 29 84 41 91 or ☎ 03 29 84 18 85), the strongest of the 39 forts and bastions built along a 45km front to protect Verdun. Because the French high command disregarded warnings of an impending German offensive, Douaumont had only a skeleton crew when the Battle of Verdun began. By the fourth day it had been easily captured by a small contingent of Germans. Despite the loss of 679 German soldiers in a munitions depot explosion inside the fort in May 1916, Douaumont was not recaptured until October of that year, when colonial troops from Morocco retook it.

The 3km network of cold, dripping galleries inside Douaumont, built between 1885 and 1912, can be visited daily from 10.30 am to 1 pm and 2 to 4.30 or 5 pm (6.30 pm from April to September). From 21 December to mid-February its hours are 11 am to 4 pm. Entry costs 15FF (8FF for children aged eight to 16). The exterior of the fortress can be visited all the time.

Tranchée des Baïonnettes

On 12 June 1916, two companies of the 137th Infantry Regiment of the French army were sheltering in their *tranchées* (trenches), *baïonnettes* (bayonets) fixed, waiting for a ferocious artillery bombardment to end. It never did – the incoming shells covered their positions with mud and debris, burying them alive. They weren't found for three years, when several hundred bayonet tips sticking through the ground were spotted. A heavy cement memorial, built with contributions from the USA, now marks the site. A line of plain wooden crosses stands atop the trench, whose victims were left where they died, their bayonets still poking through the soil. The site is always open.

The tree-filled valley across the D913 is known as the **Ravin de la Mort** (Ravine of Death).

Fort de Vaux

On 1 June 1916 German troops managed to enter the tunnel system of the Vaux Fortress (☎ 03 29 88 32 88 or ☎ 03 29 84 18 85), attacking the French defenders from inside their own ramparts. After six days and seven nights of brutal, metre-by-metre combat along the narrow passageways – the most effective weapons were grenades, flame throwers and poison gas – the steadfast French defenders, dying of thirst (licking drops of moisture off the walls had become their only source of water), were forced to surrender. The fort was recaptured by the French five months later.

The interior of Vaux, built between 1881 and 1912 and encased in 2.5m of concrete, is smaller, more reconstructed and less dreary – and thus less interesting – than Douaumont. It can be visited from 9 or 9.30 am to noon and 1 to 4.30 or 5 pm (6 or 6.30 pm from April to mid-September, when there's no midday closure). Tickets cost 15FF (8FF for children aged eight to 16). The outer ramparts and the roof of the fort are open all the time.

Military Cemeteries

The French military cemetery nearest the town of Verdun is the **Nécropole Nationale Verdun-Faubourg Pavé**, which is about 1.5km north-east of the centre along Ave du 30e Corps. The **Deutscher Soldatenfriedhof 1914-18** (German military cemetery) at Hautecourt, 15km north-east of Verdun along the N3, has rows of simple, black metal crosses and grey stone Stars of David. Each cross marks the final resting place of four soldiers, many of them unidentified.

American Memorials

The largest US military cemetery in Europe is at **Romagne-sous-Montfaucon**, 37km north-west of Verdun along the D38 and D123. About 10km south-east, a 58m-high column atop the 336m-high **Butte de Montfaucon**, just east of Montfaucon-d'Argonne, commemorates the Meuse-Argonne offence of 1918 by the US 1st Army.

South-east of Verdun another US monument sits in a forest on the 375m-high **Butte de Montsec**.

FORT DE FERMONT

One of the larger underground fortresses of the Maginot Line (see the boxed text 'The Maginot Line'), Fermont (☎ 03 82 39 35 34) is about 56km north of Verdun. Around 30m deep, it withstood three days of heavy bombardment when the Germans attacked on 21 June 1940, but surrendered a few days later. It was retaken by the French in September 1944. These days, you can take a 2½ hour tour (30FF, 20FF for children aged six to 12), in English if there's demand, during which a small electric trolley transports you from one subterranean army block to another. From June to August tours begin daily at 2 and 3.30 pm; in April, May and September there are tours at the same times on Saturday, Sunday and holidays.

Fermont is about 6km north-east of Longuyon. Longuyon's tourist office (☎ 03 82 39 21 21) is at Place Allende.

Burgundy

The dukedom of Burgundy (Bourgogne), situated on the great trade route between the Mediterranean and northern Europe, waxed wealthier and more powerful than the Kingdom of France during the 14th and 15th centuries. It was also larger, and at its height counted Holland, Flanders, Luxembourg and much of what is now Belgium and northern France (Picardy, Artois) among its noncontiguous territories. Some of the finest musicians, artists and architects from these lands were brought to the Burgundian capital, Dijon, where their artistic legacy still graces the city. Six centuries ago, it seemed that France might one day find itself absorbed into Burgundy (it was the Burgundians who took Joan of Arc prisoner before selling her to the English), but in the end Burgundy became part of France, in 1477.

These days, Burgundy's four departments (Yonne, Côte d'Or, Saône-et-Loire and Nièvre) are renowned for their superb wines, excellent gastronomy and rich architectural heritage. Buildings of note include a large number of medieval and Renaissance-era homes, churches (many topped by the region's distinctive, multihued tile roofs) and monasteries. Most of the latter belonged to either the ascetic, Cîteaux-based Cistercian order or its bitter rivals at the time, the powerful and wealthy Benedictines, directed from Cluny.

Activities

See the Parc Naturel Régional du Morvan section of this chapter for information on outdoor activities.

The department of Côte d'Or (of which Dijon and Beaune are a part) has many hundreds of kilometres of hiking trails, including parts of the GR2, GR7 and GR76; a number of these trails take you through some of France's most beautiful wine-growing areas. *La Côte d'Or – Hiking Tours* is a free brochure that has details on hiking itineraries, trail maps and accommodation options (*gîtes*, camping grounds etc).

HIGHLIGHTS

- **Dijon** – wander among the city's medieval and Renaissance churches and townhouses
- **Beaune** – visit the spectacular Hôtel-Dieu des Hospices de Beaune
- **Autun** – admire the Roman gates and other ancient sites in and around the town
- **Noyers-sur-Serein** – ramble around this tiny walled village
- **Canals** – cruise peacefully along one of Burgundy's many waterways in a canal boat

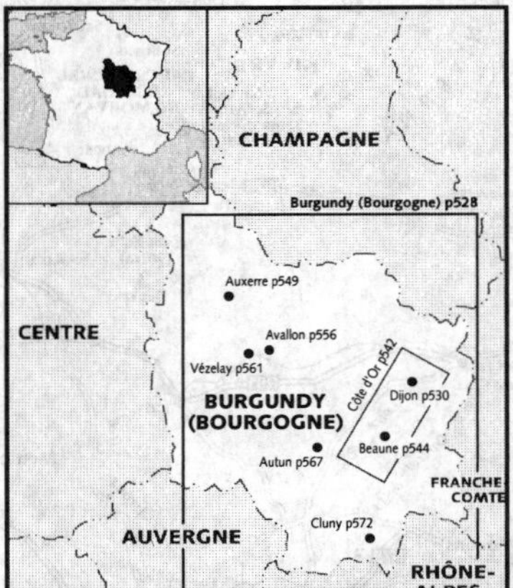

bœuf à la bourguignon – beef cooked in red wine with mushrooms, onions and bacon

Burgundy red and white wines

Dijon mustard – which ranges from sweet to super-spicy

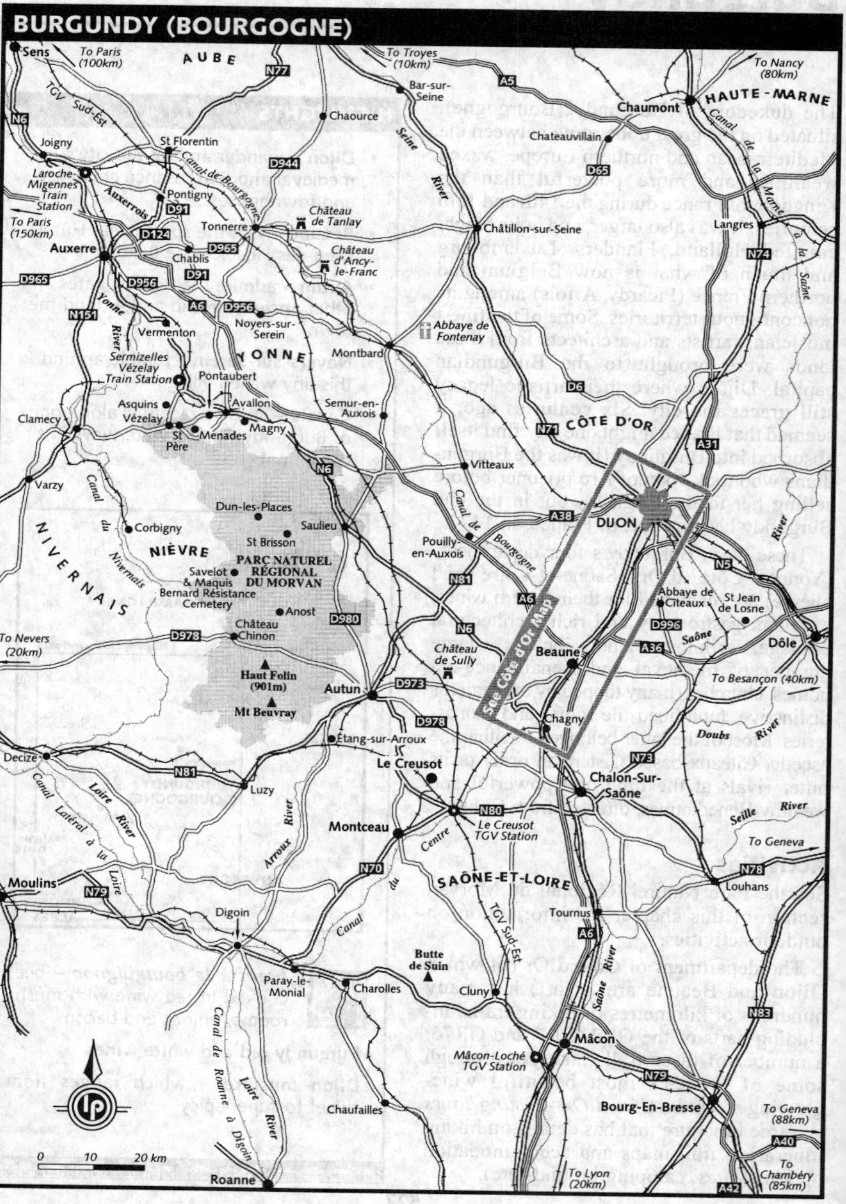
BURGUNDY (BOURGOGNE)
Sens
To Paris (100km)
AUBE
To Troyes (10km)
To Nancy (80km)
TGV Sud-Est
Bar-sur-Seine
Chaource
St Florentin
Joigny
Laroche-Migennes Train Station
Canal de Bourgogne
Auxerrois
Pontigny
To Paris (150km)
Château de Tanlay
Tonnerre
Auxerre
Chablis
Château d'Ancy-le-Franc
Yonne River
Vermenton
Noyers-sur-Serein
Sermizelles Vézelay Train Station
YONNE
Pontaubert
Asquins
Vézelay
Avallon
Clamecy
St Père
Menades
Magny
Varzy
Canal du Nivernais
Dun-les-Places
Corbigny
Saulieu
St Brisson
NIÈVRE
PARC NATUREL RÉGIONAL DU MORVAN
Savelot & Maquis Bernard Résistance Cemetery
NIVERNAIS
Anost
Château Chinon
To Nevers (20km)
Haut Folin (901m)
Mt Beuvray
Autun
Étang-sur-Arroux
Le Creusot
Decize
Luzy
Canal Latéral à la Loire
Loire River
Arroux River
Le Creusot TGV Station
Montceau
Canal du Centre
Moulins
Digoin
Paray-le-Monial
Charolles
Canal de Roanne à Digoin
Loire River
Chaufailles
Roanne
0 10 20 km
Chaumont
HAUTE-MARNE
Chateauvillain
Canal de la Marne à la Saône
Seine River
Châtillon-sur-Seine
Langres
Abbaye de Fontenay
Montbard
Semur-en-Auxois
CÔTE D'OR
Vitteaux
Canal de Bourgogne
Pouilly-en-Auxois
DIJON
Saône River
Abbaye de Citeaux
St Jean de Losne
Dôle
Saône
Château de Sully
Beaune
See Côte d'Or Map
To Besançon (40km)
Chagny
Doubs River
Chalon-Sur-Saône
Seille River
To Geneva
SAÔNE-ET-LOIRE
Louhans
TGV Sud-Est
Tournus
Saône River
Butte de Suin
Cluny
Mâcon
Mâcon-Loché TGV Station
Bourg-En-Bresse
To Geneva (88km)
To Lyon (20km)
To Chambéry (85km)
N77 A5 N6 D944 D65 D91 D124 D965 D91 D956 A6 D956 N151 N74 D6 N71 A31 A38 N6 N5 N81 A6 D996 A36 D980 N6 D978 D973 D978 N73 N81 N80 N79 N70 N78 A6 N83 N79 A40 A42

Hot-Air Ballooning A number of companies offer *montgolfière* (hot-air balloon) rides over Burgundy for about 1250FF per person. Many travel agents in France can make bookings.

Air Adventures (☎ 03 80 90 74 23; fax 03 80 90 72 86), based 43km west of Dijon in Pouilly-en-Auxois, has flights year-round, weather permitting, with discounts for groups of five or more.

Air Escargot (☎ 03 85 87 12 30; fax 03 85 87 08 84) is based 16km south of Beaune in Remigny. Children under 12 get 50% off.

Boating For general information on houseboat holidays, see Canal Boats under Activities in the Facts for the Visitor chapter.

Burgundy's 1200km of navigable waterways includes the rivers Yonne, Saône and Seille and a network of canals excavated between the 17th and 19th centuries to link three of France's most important rivers: the Saône, the Loire and the Rhône. Navigational charts and guidebooks for the area are published by Éditions Cartographiques Maritimes and Vagnon and are available either where you pick up your boat or at well stocked bookshops.

Between mid-October and mid-March, quite a few canals (or sections of them) are emptied of water to facilitate upkeep. Known as *chômages*, these closures can last from several weeks to a couple of months. The rivers, of course, are almost always open for navigation. The locks are open daily except on major holidays.

The Comité Régional de Tourisme de Bourgogne (☎ 03 80 50 90 00; fax 03 80 30 59 45; crt.bourgogne@hol.fr; www.bourgogne-tourisme.com), whose mailing address is BP 1602, 21035 Dijon CEDEX, publishes an excellent annual brochure entitled *Boating Holidays in Burgundy*. It is available at many tourist offices.

Boat Rental Reliable, experienced rental companies based in Burgundy include:

Bateaux de Bourgogne (☎ 03 86 72 92 10; fax 03 86 72 92 14), 1-2 Quai de la République, 89000 Auxerre. This grouping of 15 rental companies has over 200 boats. From late April to late October, the office – one floor above Auxerre's tourist office – is open from 9 am to noon and 2 to 6 pm (6.30 pm in summer, 5.30 pm on Friday; closed on Sunday and, from late October to late April, on Saturday).

Aquarelle (☎ 03 86 46 96 77; fax 03 86 52 55 31), Quai Saint Martin, Port de Plaisance, 89000 Auxerre. The company's 10 Dutch-built Linssen boats are available from April to October. The office, right across the river from the tourist office, is open daily from 9 am to noon and 2 to 7 pm (6 pm from November to March, when it's closed on weekends). Credit cards are accepted, as are French franc travellers cheques and Eurocheques.

France Afloat (Burgundy Cruisers; ☎ 03 86 81 54 55; fax 03 86 81 67 87; UK ☎/fax 0171-704 0700 or, after June 1999, ☎/fax 020-7704 0700; france.afloat@wanadoo.fr), 1 Quai du Port, 89270 Vermenton. This company, based 23km south-east of Auxerre, acts as an agent for about a dozen rental companies.

Locaboat Plaisance (☎ 03 86 91 72 72; fax 03 86 62 42 41; locaboat@locaboat.com; www.locaboat.com), Port au Bois, BP 150, 89303 Joigny CEDEX. This company has boats leaving from a variety of places, including Dijon, Joigny (27km north-west of Auxerre) and Corre (110km north-east of Dijon).

Work

For information on picking grapes, see Work in the Facts for the Visitor chapter.

DIJON

• pop 230,000 ✉ 21000 alt 245m

The prosperous city of Dijon, capital of the dukes of Burgundy from the early 11th century until the late 1400s, reached the height of its brilliance during the 14th and 15th centuries under Philippe le Hardi (Philip the Bold), Jean sans Peur (John the Fearless) and Philippe le Bon (Philip the Good). During their reigns, the Burgundian court was among Europe's most illustrious, and Dijon was turned into one of the great centres of western art.

Modern Dijon, mustard capital of the universe, is one of the most appealing of France's provincial cities, with an inviting city centre graced by elegant medieval and Renaissance buildings. Despite its long and venerable history, the city has a distinctly

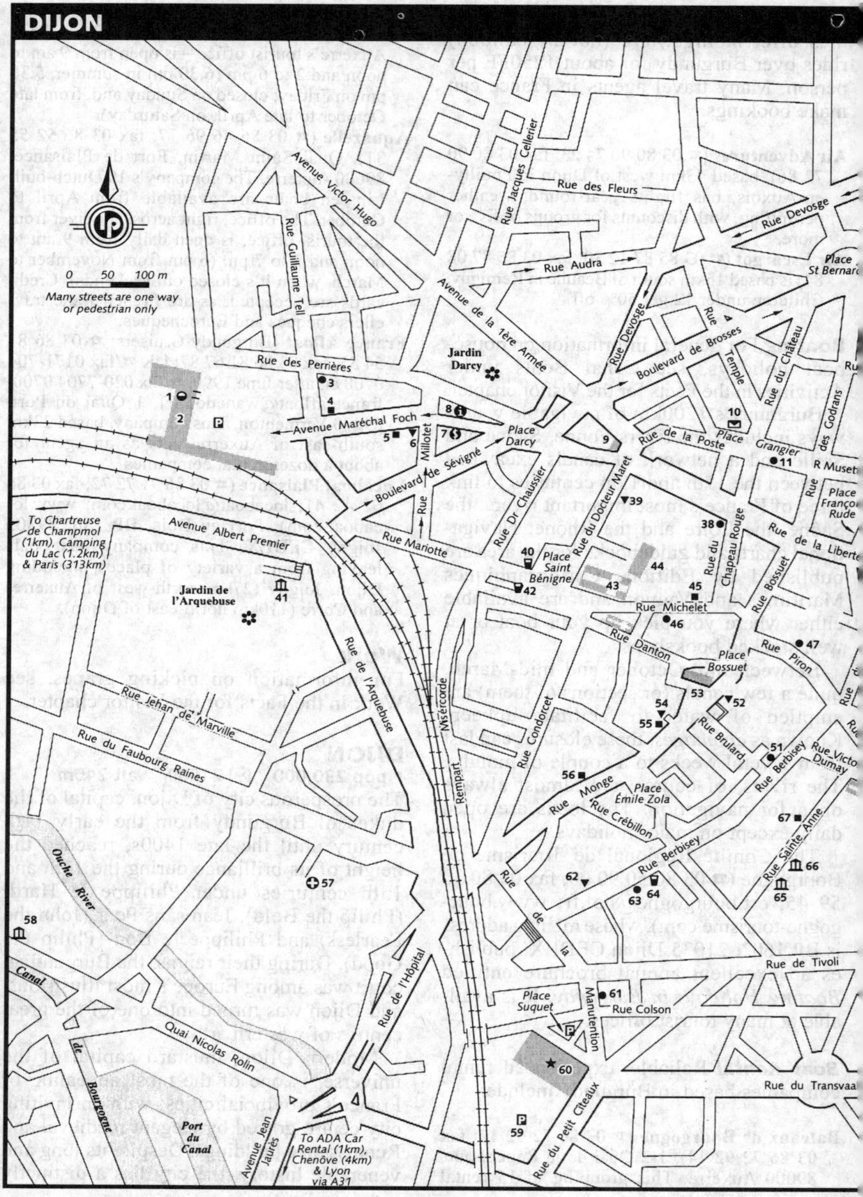
DIJON
0 50 100 m
Many streets are one way or pedestrian only
Avenue Victor Hugo
Rue Guillaume Tell
Rue Jacques Cellerier
Rue des Fleurs
Rue Devosge
Place St Bernard
Rue Audra
Avenue de la 1ère Armée
Rue Devosge
Rue Temple
Rue du Château
Boulevard de Brosses
Rue des Godrans
Rue des Perrières
Jardin Darcy
Avenue Maréchal Foch
Millotet
Place Darcy
Rue de la Poste
Place Grangier
R Musette
Boulevard de Sévigné
Rue Dr Chaussier
Rue du Docteur Maret
Place François Rude
To Chartreuse de Champmol (1km), Camping du Lac (1.2km) & Paris (313km)
Avenue Albert Premier
Rue Mariotte
Rue du Chapeau Rouge
Rue Bossuet
Rue de la Liberté
Place Saint Bénigne
Jardin de l'Arquebuse
Rue Michelet
Rue Danton
Rue Piron
Place Bossuet
Rue de l'Arquebuse
Rue Jehan de Marville
Miséricorde
Rue Condorcet
Rue Brulard
Rue Berbisey
Rue Victor Dumay
Rue du Faubourg Raines
Rempart
Rue Monge
Place Émile Zola
Rue Crébillon
Rue Sainte Anne
Ouche River
Rue Berbisey
Rue de la Manutention
Rue de l'Hôpital
Canal
Rue de Tivoli
Place Suquet
Rue Colson
Quai Nicolas Rolin
de Bourgogne
Rue du Transvaal
Rue du Petit Cîteaux
Port du Canal
Avenue Jean Jaurès
To ADA Car Rental (1km), Chenôve (4km) & Lyon via A31
1 2 3 4 5 6 7 8 9 10 11 38 39 40 41 42 43 44 45 46 47 51 52 53 54 55 56 57 58 59 60 61 62 63 64 65 66 67

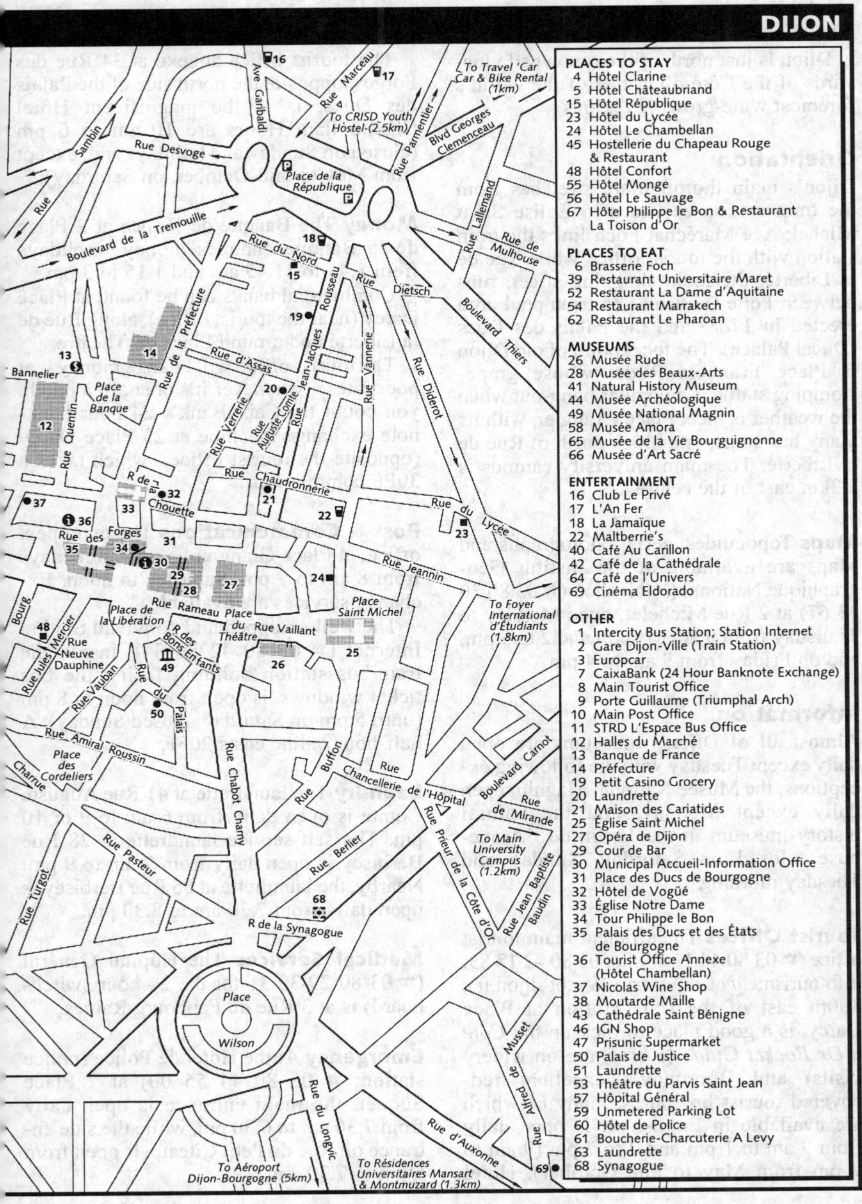
DIJON
PLACES TO STAY
4 Hôtel Clarine
5 Hôtel Châteaubriand
15 Hôtel République
23 Hôtel du Lycée
24 Hôtel Le Chambellan
45 Hostellerie du Chapeau Rouge & Restaurant
48 Hôtel Confort
55 Hôtel Monge
56 Hôtel Le Sauvage
67 Hôtel Philippe le Bon & Restaurant La Toison d'Or
PLACES TO EAT
6 Brasserie Foch
39 Restaurant Universitaire Maret
52 Restaurant La Dame d'Aquitaine
54 Restaurant Marrakech
62 Restaurant Le Pharoan
MUSEUMS
26 Musée Rude
28 Musée des Beaux-Arts
41 Natural History Museum
44 Musée Archéologique
49 Musée National Magnin
58 Musée Amora
65 Musée de la Vie Bourguignonne
66 Musée d'Art Sacré
ENTERTAINMENT
16 Club Le Privé
17 L'An Fer
18 La Jamaïque
22 Maltberrie's
40 Café Au Carillon
42 Café de la Cathédrale
64 Café de l'Univers
69 Cinéma Eldorado
OTHER
1 Intercity Bus Station; Station Internet
2 Gare Dijon-Ville (Train Station)
3 Europcar
7 CaixaBank (24 Hour Banknote Exchange)
8 Main Tourist Office
9 Porte Guillaume (Triumphal Arch)
10 Main Post Office
11 STRD L'Espace Bus Office
12 Halles du Marché
13 Banque de France
14 Préfecture
19 Petit Casino Grocery
20 Laundrette
21 Maison des Cariatides
25 Église Saint Michel
27 Opéra de Dijon
29 Cour de Bar
30 Municipal Accueil-Information Office
31 Place des Ducs de Bourgogne
32 Hôtel de Vogüé
33 Église Notre Dame
34 Tour Philippe le Bon
35 Palais des Ducs et des États de Bourgogne
36 Tourist Office Annexe (Hôtel Chambellan)
37 Nicolas Wine Shop
38 Moutarde Maille
43 Cathédrale Saint Bénigne
46 IGN Shop
47 Prisunic Supermarket
50 Palais de Justice
51 Laundrette
53 Théâtre du Parvis Saint Jean
57 Hôpital Général
59 Unmetered Parking Lot
60 Hôtel de Police
61 Boucherie-Charcuterie A Levy
63 Laundrette
68 Synagogue
To Travel 'Car Car & Bike Rental (1km)
To CRISD Youth Hostel (2.5km)
To Foyer International d'Étudiants (1.8km)
To Main University Campus (1.2km)
To Aéroport Dijon-Bourgogne (5km)
To Résidences Universitaires Mansart & Montmuzard (1.3km)

youthful air, thanks to the presence of some 30,000 university and other students.

Dijon is just north of the renowned vineyards of the Côte d'Or, one of the world's foremost wine-growing regions.

Orientation

Dijon's main thoroughfare stretches from the train station eastward to Église Saint Michel: Ave Maréchal Foch links the train station with the tourist office while Rue de la Liberté, the main shopping street, runs between Porte Guillaume (a triumphal arch erected in 1788) and the Palais des Ducs (Ducal Palace). The focal point of old Dijon is Place François Rude, whose grape-stomping statue is a popular hang-out when the weather is nice. Place Grangier, with its many bus stops, is a block north of Rue de la Liberté. The main university campus is 2.3km east of the centre.

Maps Topoguides, aerial photographs and Maps are available at the Institut Géographique National (IGN) shop (☎ 03 80 30 33 67) at 2 Rue Michelet, open Monday to Thursday from 9 am to noon and 2 to 5 pm, and on Friday from 9 am to 4 pm.

Information

Almost all of Dijon's museums are open daily except Tuesday with the following exceptions: the Musée National Magnin, open daily except Monday, and the natural history museum in the Jardin de l'Arquebuse, closed on Saturday, Sunday and Tuesday mornings.

Tourist Offices The efficient main tourist office (☎ 03 80 44 11 44; fax 03 80 42 18 83; infotourisme@ot-dijon.fr; www.ot-dijon.fr), 300m east of the train station at Place Darcy, is a good place to pick up the *Côte d'Or Pocket Guide* (a brochure on winery visits) and Burgundy's excellent red-covered tourist brochures, many of which are available in English. It is open daily from 9 am to 1 pm and 2 to 7 pm (9 am to 9 pm from May to mid-October). Hotel reservations within the region cost 15FF plus a deposit of 10%.

The tourist office annexe at 34 Rue des Forges, opposite the north side of the Palais des Ducs, is in the magnificent Hôtel Chambellan. Hours are 10 am to 6 pm (closed on Sunday and holidays and, except from May to mid-October, on Saturday).

Money The Banque de France at 2 Place de la Banque changes money weekdays from 8.45 to 11.45 am and 1.15 to 3 pm.

Commercial banks can be found at Place Darcy (near the tourist office), along Rue de la Liberté and around Place du Théâtre.

The tourist office will change money – at poor rates – whenever it's open. In a pinch, you could try CaixaBank's 24 hour banknote exchange machine at 23 Place Darcy (opposite the tourist office), which takes a 30FF commission.

Post & Communications The main post office, at Place Grangier, is open weekdays from 8 am to 7 pm, Saturday to noon. Exchange services are available.

The well equipped and convivial Station Internet (☎ 03 80 42 89 84), inside the train/bus station building facing the bus ticket windows, is open from noon to 8 pm (until 5 pm on Saturday; closed Sunday). A half-hour online costs 20FF.

Laundry The laundrette at 41 Rue Auguste Comte is open daily from 6 am to 9 or 10 pm. The self-service laundrette at 28 Rue Berbisey is open daily from 7 am to 9 pm. Nearby, the laundrette at 55 Rue Berbisey is open daily from 7.30 am to 8.30 pm.

Medical Services The Hôpital Général (☎ 03 80 29 30 31 for the 24 hour switchboard) is at 3 Rue du Faubourg Raines.

Emergency At the Hôtel de Police (police station; ☎ 03 80 44 55 00) at 2 Place Suquet, the main entrance is open daily from 7.30 am to 6.30 pm, while the side entrance on Rue du Petit Cîteaux is open from 6 pm to 7.30 am.

Palais des Ducs

Palais des Ducs et des États de Bourgogne (Palace of the Dukes and States General of Burgundy) was once the palace of the powerful dukes of Burgundy. Its classical appearance is the result of 17th and 18th century remodelling and additions carried out at the behest of the States General of Burgundy, which used to meet here every three years from 1688.

The front of the palace looks out across the Cour d'Honneur to the semicircular **Place de la Libération**, a gracious, arcaded public square laid out by Jules Hardouin Mansart (one of the architects of Versailles) in 1686. Inside the middle section of the building you'll find the entrance to the 46m-high, 15th century **Tour Philippe le Bon** (Tower of Philip the Good), which affords great views of the city. At the time of going to press it was closed to the public as part of a national campaign to prevent terrorist attacks, but it can usually be climbed. From Easter to the third Sunday in November, accompanied visits begin every 45 minutes or so from 9 am to noon and 1.45 to 5.30 pm; the rest of the year, it's open on Wednesday afternoons, and weekends from 9 to 11 am and 1.30 to 3.30 pm. Tickets are available from the municipal Accueil-Information office (☎ 03 80 74 52 71) in the Cour d'Honneur.

Most of the western part of the palace is occupied by Dijon's Hôtel de Ville (City Hall). The Salle des États is closed to the public, but you can at least see (through glass doors) the **Escalier Gabriel**, a monumental marble staircase (1733-38) off the passageway through the south side of the Cour de Flore (the complex's western courtyard). The room at the top of the stairs is sometimes used for art and photography exhibitions.

The newest part of the building, the east wing, completed in 1852, houses the Musée des Beaux-Arts (see the following entry). The entrance to the museum is on the **Cour de Bar**, whose name derives from the oldest part of the complex, the **Tour de Bar**, a squat, four storey tower built by Philip the Bold in the 1360s. Across the courtyard, the vaulted **Cuisines Ducales** (Ducal Kitchens; closed daily from about 11.45 am to 1.45 pm and on Tuesday), probably constructed around 1445, are a fine example of Gothic civic architecture. The six mammoth open hearths could each spit-roast an entire steer.

Musée des Beaux-Arts

Dijon's outstanding Musée des Beaux-Arts (Fine Arts Museum; ☎ 03 80 74 52 70) in the Palais des Ducs is one of the richest and most renowned in France. The magnificent **Salle des Gardes** (Guards' Room), rebuilt after a fire in 1502, houses the extraordinary 14th and 15th century Flamboyant Gothic sepulchres of two of the first Valois dukes of Burgundy: Philip the Bold (1342-1404), and John the Fearless (1371-1419) and his wife Margaret of Bavaria. The tombs and a couple of amazing gilded altarpieces, created around 1400, were originally installed in the Chartreuse de Champmol.

The museum is open from 10 am to 6 pm (closed Tuesday); the modern and contemporary art section is closed from noon to 1.30 pm. Admission is 22FF (10FF for people over 65, students 25 and under and those under 18). Summertime special expositions cost a bit more.

Museum Passes

The Carte d'Accès aux Musées gets you into all six of Dijon's major museums for just 30FF (15FF for those under 18 or over 65 and for students 25 and under). Sold at each of the museums, its coupons are valid for a year.

La Clé de la Ville combination ticket (45FF) not only gets you all the benefits of the Carte d'Accès aux Musées, but is also good for one of the tourist office's guided or Walkman tours (see the Organised Tours section).

Église Notre Dame

One block north of the Palais des Ducs is Église Notre Dame, built in the Burgundian Gothic style between 1220 and 1240. The three tiers of the extraordinary façade are decorated with dozens of false gargoyles (false because they aren't there to throw rainwater clear of the building) separated by two rows of tall, thin columns. The present gargoyles are late 19th century replacements of the originals.

On top of the façade to the right is the 14th century **Horloge à Jacquemart** (Jacquemart Clock), which was brought to Dijon from Kortrijk (Courtrai) in Flanders in 1382 by Philip the Bold, who had come across it while putting down a rebellion. Hours are sounded by the figures of a man (Jacquemart, who's been there since the late 14th century) and a woman (his wife, added in 1610), who strike the bell with axe-like hammers. The half and quarter hours are struck by their children, Jacquelinet and Jacquelinette, who were added in 1714 and 1881 respectively.

Thanks to the tower, the graceful interior of the church has a particularly high transept crossing. Some of the stained glass dates from the 13th century. The Gobelins tapestry of birds and animals in the south transept arm dates from 1946 and commemorates Dijon's liberation from German occupation on 11 September 1944. In the nearby chapel is an 11th century **Black Madonna**.

Medieval & Renaissance Houses

Some of the finest of Dijon's many medieval and Renaissance *hôtels particuliers* (aristocratic townhouses) are north of the Palais des Ducs on **Rue Verrerie** and **Rue des Forges** (eg Nos 38, 40 and 50), Dijon's main street until the 18th century.

The splendid Flamboyant Gothic **Hôtel Chambellan** (built in 1490) at 34 Rue des Forges is now home to a branch of the tourist office. At the top of the spiral stone staircase, there's a remarkable bit of vaulting – a male figure holding a basket supports the roof.

Rue de la Chouette, where there are more old residences, runs along the north side of Église Notre Dame. It is named for the small, stone *chouette* (owl) – said to grant happiness and wisdom to passers-by who stroke it – carved into the corner of one of the chapels on the north side of the church. The **Hôtel de Vogüé** at 8 Rue de la Chouette, erected around 1614, is known for its ornate Renaissance style courtyard. Now occupied by municipal offices, the courtyard is reached via an arched entrance (open daily) built in the early 18th century.

A couple of blocks farther east at 28 Rue Chaudronnerie, the **Maison des Cariatides** (House of the Caryatids), built in the early 17th century by a rich family of copper merchants, has a façade decorated with stone caryatids (figures used as supporting columns) and faces.

Église Saint Michel

Construction of Église Saint Michel was begun in the 15th century in the Flamboyant Gothic style. By the 16th century, when it came time to build the west façade, architectural tastes had changed and the church was given an impressive, richly ornamented Renaissance façade, considered among the most beautiful in France. The two cupola-topped towers date from 1667.

Musée Rude

The small Rude Museum (☎ 03 80 66 87 95), housed in a desanctified church on Rue Vaillant (opposite the west façade of Église Saint Michel), is not what you might think it is about. It has quite a few works (and copies of works) by the Dijon-born sculptor François Rude (1784-1855), creator of the *Marseillaise* panel on the Arc de Triomphe in Paris. From June to September, it's open from 10 am to noon and 2 to 5.45 pm (closed Tuesday). Admission is free.

Musée National Magnin

Some 2000 assorted works of art, assembled around the turn of the century by the sister and brother team of Jeanne and Maurice Magnin, are on display in the magnificent Magnin family ancestral home (☎ 03 80 67 11 10), a mid-17th century residence at 4 Rue des Bons Enfants. It is open from 10 am to noon and 2 to 6 pm (closed Monday). The entrance fee is 18FF (12FF reduced price).

Palais de Justice

The law courts, which are one block southeast of Place de la Libération on Rue du Palais, were built in the 16th and 17th centuries as the Palais du Parlement du Bourgogne (Palace of the Burgundian Parliament). Although modified in the 19th century, the structure retains its Renaissance-style façade from 1572. The wooden door is a copy; the original is in the Musée des Beaux-Arts.

Inside, the **Chambre Dorée**, which dates from 1522, retains much of its original decoration; it can be visited on weekdays provided the court is not in session. When the court is in session, it may be possible to sit in on a trial.

Cathédrale Saint Bénigne

Situated on top of what may be the tomb of St Benignus (who by tradition is believed to have brought Christianity to Burgundy in the 2nd century), Dijon's Burgundian Gothic cathedral was built as an abbey church between 1280 and the early 1300s. Many of the great figures of Burgundy's history are buried inside. From April to October, the enormous **organ** (1743) is used for concerts, some of them free. The large **crypt** (7FF) – all that remains of a Romanesque abbey church constructed between 1001 and 1026 – is usually open daily from 8.45 am to 7 pm (until 6 pm in winter).

Musée Archéologique

The Musée Archéologique (Archaeological Museum; ☎ 03 80 30 88 54), next to the cathedral at 5 Rue du Docteur Maret, displays a number of extremely rare Celtic (Gallic and Gallo-Roman) artefacts made of wood, stone and metal, including jewellery from 950 BC, votive figures from the 1st century AD and a bronze representation of the goddess Sequana standing on a boat, also from the 1st century. The Romanesque chamber on the lowest level, once part of a Benedictine abbey, dates from the early 11th century. Upstairs, the vaulted early Gothic hall, at one time the abbey's dormitory, was built in the 12th and 13th centuries. Hours are 9 am to noon and 2 to 6 pm (June to September from 10 am to 8 pm); closed on Tuesday and some holidays. Entry costs 14FF (free for children, students and teachers and, on Sunday and holidays, for everyone). A free English brochure with details on the most important artefacts is available at the ticket window.

Musée d'Art Sacré

This museum (☎ 03 80 44 12 69) at 15 Rue Sainte Anne, housed in the copper domed rotunda and chapels of a neoclassical church completed in 1709, displays ecclesiastical objects from the 12th to 19th centuries. It's worth visiting just to see the building – check out the cloud-enveloped putti over the gabled entrance and the radiant sun emblems of the Sun King, Louis XIV, during whose reign it was built. It's open from 9 am to noon and 2 to 6 pm (closed Tuesday). Admission is 10FF (5FF reduced price).

Musée de la Vie Bourguignonne

Almost next door at 17 Rue Sainte Anne is the city's folklore museum (☎ 03 80 44 12 69), whose period rooms – installed in a 17th century Cistercian convent – illustrate how the rural people of Burgundy lived in centuries past. All the signs are in French, but it should be possible to borrow a brochure in English. Opening hours are the same as at the Musée d'Art Sacré. Admission is 14FF (7FF for students and people over 65; free for people under 18).

Jardin de l'Arquebuse

The centrepiece of Dijon's delightful botanic gardens, across Ave Albert Premier from the train station, is a formal garden whose hundreds of plants – some of them aquatic – are labelled in botanical Latin. Ducks dive for weed and swans paddle around proudly in the pond and stream, while along the park's southern edge children frolic in the two **playgrounds** and locals match their skills and wits in games of boules.

The **Muséum** (☎ 03 80 76 82 76) in the north-eastern corner features natural history and is open from 9 am to noon and 2 to 6 pm (closed on Saturday, Sunday and on Tuesday mornings). Admission is 14FF for adults (7FF for students). The park itself is open from 7.30 am until sometime between 5 pm (in the middle of winter) and 8 pm (in summer).

Synagogue

Dijon's domed and turreted main synagogue, on Rue de la Synagogue, was built in Romano-Byzantine style in 1879.

Chartreuse de Champmol

This one-time *chartreuse* (charterhouse, ie Carthusian monastery), founded in 1383 by Philip the Bold as a burial place for himself and his Valois successors, was almost completely destroyed during the Revolution. The famous **Puits de Moïse** (Well of Moses), a hexagonal grouping of six Old Testament figures created between 1395 and 1405 by Dutch sculptor Claus Sluter, is presently closed for long-term restoration, but you can still visit Sluter's **Portail de la Chapelle** (Chapel Doorway). Although the site, 1.2km west of the train station at 1 Blvd Chanoine Kir, is now occupied by a psychiatric hospital, the chapel (☎ 03 80 42 48 48 for the gatehouse) is open to the public all day every day. To get there, follow the directions to Camping du Lac (see Places to Stay).

Organised Tours

The tourist office's two hour Visite Audioguidée (audioguided city tour; 39FF) is very informative, providing you with a Walkman, a cassette tape in English, French, German or Italian and a map.

In July and August daily at 10 pm, the tourist office runs bilingual French and English tours of Dijon's floodlit monuments. The cost is 35FF (60FF for a couple; 25FF for students and seniors; free for kids under 12). The many other walking tours on offer are mostly in French.

Tours of the **Musée Amora** (Mustard Museum), 48 Quai Nicolas Rolin, are held on Wednesday and Saturday at 3 pm (daily at 3 pm in summer, beginning mid-June). Tickets (15FF; free for children under 12) are available at the tourist office.

The tourist office also has information and tickets for tours into the countryside. Its Circuits des Châteaux bus tours, which take you to the region's chateaux, churches and abbeys, are held almost every Sunday from July to September; destinations change each week. The cost is 220/260FF for a half-day/day, not including a meal. The tourist office also handles ticketing for minibus tours (in French and English) run by Wine & Voyages (☎ 03 80 62 72 63; winevoyages@bourgogne.net), including Circuits en Vignoble (250 to 290FF), two or three-hour tours of the Côte de Nuits vineyards (held daily in both the morning and afternoon from March or April to November); and visits to the Cistercian abbey of **Cîteaux** (280FF), where the monks earn a living making cheese and honey. The company can also provide details about two-hour boat excursions on the Canal de Bourgogne (60FF).

Special Events

Dance and music troupes come from around the world participate in the Folkloriades Internationales et Fêtes de la Vigne, a week-long folklore festival held each year in late August or early September. The Foire Internationale et Gastronomique, held at the Parc des Expositions from 30 October to 11 November, gives visitors the chance to sample cuisines from Burgundy and around the world. From May to July, Dijon hosts a wide variety of cultural events (theatre, jazz, classical music etc).

Places to Stay – Budget

Many of Dijon's smaller hotels are closed on Sunday from noon to 5 pm.

Camping The two-star *Camping du Lac* (☎ 03 80 43 54 72) at 3 Blvd Chanoine Kir is 1.4km west of the train station behind the psychiatric hospital. It is open from April to mid-October. Charges are 16FF per adult, 12FF for a tent and 8FF for a car. If you arrive on foot, there's almost always room for a small tent. To get there from the train station, take bus No 12 (towards Fontaine d'Ouche) and get off at the Hôpital des Chartreux stop; services stop at around 8 pm.

Hostels The ***Foyer International d'Étudiants*** (☎ 03 80 71 70 00), a student dorm 2.5km east of the centre at 6 Rue Maréchal Leclerc, accepts travellers year-round if there's space, though rooms (75FF for a single) are most likely to be available from April to early October. To get there, catch bus No 4 (towards Saint Apollinaire) along Ave Victor Hugo or Rue de la Liberté and get off at the Vélodrome stop. At night take line A to Billardon.

The ***Centre de Rencontres Internationales et de Séjour de Dijon*** (CRISD; ☎ 03 80 72 95 20; fax 03 80 70 00 61), Dijon's large (265 bed) and institutional hostel, is 2.5km north-east of the centre at 1 Blvd Champollion. A bed in a newly renovated dorm room for up to six people costs 71FF, including breakfast. A room equipped with shower and toilet, with space for one to three people, costs 144FF, not including breakfast. Guests without a student or hostelling card pay 8FF extra for the first four nights. Amenities include washing machines and, next door, a municipal swimming pool (6FF). Check-in is available 24 hours a day. To get there, take bus No 5 (towards Épirey) from Place Grangier. At night take line A to the Épirey Centre Commercial stop.

From May to September (and during the rest of the year if there's space), travellers can stay on the main university campus at the ***Résidence Universitaire Mansart*** (☎ 03 80 68 27 68), a university dorm 2.2km south-east of the centre at 94 Rue Mansart (also spelt 'Mansard'). The *secrétariat* (reception), in a building fronted with green glass, is open weekdays from 10 am to noon and 1.15 to 4.45 pm. When it's closed, a sign on the door will direct you to the concierge or, after 9 pm, the night staff. New guests can register any time of the day or night. If you have student ID, the charge is 66.80FF per person; otherwise, it's 84.70FF. To get there, take bus No 9 (towards Campus) at either the train station or along Rue de la Liberté and get off at the Mansart stop. At night, take line C to Mansart.

You might also try the ***Résidence Universitaire Montmuzard*** (☎ 03 80 39 68 01; fax 03 80 39 68 20), which is a 10 minute walk north at 8 Ave Alain Savary behind the Faculté de Droit (Law Faculty). The secretariat, in Pavillon Bossuet, is open weekdays from 9 am to noon and 1.30 to 4.30 pm. Prices and conditions are the same as at Mansart, as is the 24 hour presence of a concierge or night staff. To get there, take bus No 9 or line C to the RU Montmuzard stop.

Hotels – Train Station Area The ***Hôtel Châteaubriand*** (☎ 03 80 41 42 18; fax 03 80 59 16 28) at 3 Ave Maréchal Foch (1st floor) has doubles for 165 to 182FF (206 to 251FF with shower and toilet). The rooms, some with two twin beds, are not exactly cheery, but they do exude a certain old-fashioned charm. The hall showers are free.

Hotels – City Centre The friendly and accommodating, 23 room ***Hôtel Monge*** (☎ 03 80 30 55 41; fax 03 80 30 30 15) at 20 Rue Monge has singles/doubles/quads starting at 125/135/260FF; rooms with shower, toilet and TV cost 200/210/340FF. Some of the mattresses are very soft. Hall showers cost 15FF. Students with ID get a 5% discount (10% if you stay four or more days). It may be possible to park in the tiny courtyard.

The very central, 14-room ***Hôtel Confort*** (☎ 03 80 30 37 47; fax 03 80 30 03 43) is at 12 Rue Jules Mercier, an alley off Rue de la Liberté. Decent, plain singles/doubles with shower start at 155/165FF (175/195FF with toilet as well); an extra bed costs 50FF. Reception is closed on Sunday from noon to 5 pm and nightly after about 10 pm. To get there by car, drive slowly along the pedestrianised Rue du Bourg to Rue Neuve Dauphine. By bus from the train station (Blvd de Sévigné), take No 9 or 12 and get off at the Liberation stop.

The two star, 23 room ***Hôtel Le Chambellan*** (☎ 03 80 67 12 67; fax 03 80 38 00 39), half a block north of Église Saint Michel at 92 Rue Vannerie, has antique-style doubles from 120FF; shower-equipped rooms are 170FF (220FF with toilet). Breakfast (35FF) can be taken in the 17th century courtyard. The hotel is linked to the train station by bus No 12; get off at the Théâtre Vaillant stop.

Hotels – East of the City Centre The 16 room ***Hôtel du Lycée*** (☎ 03 80 67 12 35; fax 03 80 63 84 69) at 28 Rue du Lycée has ordinary rooms with new mattresses from 120FF (150FF with shower, 175FF with toilet as well). For 240FF you get a room with shower and toilet for up to five people. Hall showers are free. Reception is closed on Sunday from noon to 5 pm and nightly after 10 pm. Free parking is available on Rue Diderot north of Rue du Lycée. From the train station, take bus No 12 (towards Quetigny) from Blvd de Sévigné and get off at the Théâtre Vaillant stop.

Hotels – Suburbs There's a cluster of cheap, postmodern motor hotels – including ***Formule 1*** (☎ 03 80 52 08 52), ***Fimotel*** (☎ 03 80 51 70 70) and ***One Star Plus*** (☎ 03 80 52 15 11) – 4km south of Dijon in Chenôve, on Rue de Longvic near the E Leclerc hypermarket. If you're driving from the city centre, follow the signs to Lyon via the A31. The area is linked to the train station by bus No 7.

Places to Stay – Mid-Range

The two star, 21 room ***Hôtel Le Sauvage*** (☎ 03 80 41 31 21; fax 03 80 42 06 07) at 64 Rue Monge, also signposted as the Hostellerie du Sauvage, occupies a *relais de poste* (relay posthouse), parts of which date from the 15th century. The decent, quiet rooms around the grapevine-shaded courtyard are decorated with old-fashioned furniture; prices for singles/doubles start at 210/230FF.

The quiet, 22 room ***Hôtel République*** (☎ 03 80 73 36 76; fax 03 80 72 46 04), 3 Rue du Nord, has ordinary but fairly large doubles/triples/quints with shower and toilet for 195/240/400FF. Reception closes at 11 pm (from about December to May, at 6 pm on Sunday). To get there from the train station (Blvd de Sévigné), take bus No 6 (towards La Fleuriée) or No 7 (towards Roosevelt) and get off at the République Rousseau stop.

Near the train station, the two and three-star hotels along Ave Maréchal Foch include the 45 room, lift-equipped ***Hôtel Clarine*** (☎ 03 80 43 53 78; fax 03 80 42 84 17) at No 22, whose huge, comfortable one or two-bed doubles go for 290FF; an extra bed costs 50FF. Reception is open 24 hours a day.

Places to Stay – Top End

The 30 room ***Hôtel Philippe le Bon*** (☎ 03 80 30 73 52; fax 03 80 30 95 51), a three star place at 18 Rue Sainte Anne, has fairly luxurious, contemporary singles/doubles with cable TV from 370/450FF. Private parking is available at no extra cost. The four star, 30 room ***Hostellerie du Chapeau Rouge*** (☎ 03 80 30 28 10; fax 03 80 30 33 89) at 5 Rue Michelet has been at this site since 1847. Most of the elegant, air-con rooms cost between 600 and 790FF, though there are a few small rooms for 350FF. Private parking is available for 20FF.

Places to Eat

Dijon's restaurants are of a particularly high standard, especially relative to the prices. There are lots of small café-restaurants, including quite a few ethnic places, a few blocks south-west of the Palais des Ducs on and around Rue Berbisey, Place Émile Zola and Rue Monge.

Restaurants – French The ***La Toison d'Or*** (☎ 03 80 30 73 52), 18 Rue Sainte Anne, serves up Burgundian and French cuisine in a rustic medieval setting. If ordered à la carte, the main dishes cost 90 to 170FF; *menus* are available for 160FF (including wine; weekday lunches only),

205 and 250FF. It's open daily from noon to 2 pm and 7 to 9.15 pm.

La Dame d'Aquitaine (☎ 03 80 30 45 65), 23 Place Bossuet, purveys Burgundian and south-western French cuisine under the soaring arches of a 13th century crypt. The *menus*, served to the accompaniment of classical music, cost 138FF (including wine; lunch only) to 245FF. It's open daily from noon to 1.30 pm and 7 to 11 pm.

The super-elegant restaurant of the ***Hostellerie du Chapeau Rouge*** (see Places to Stay) has *menus* from 150FF (including a glass of wine) to 390FF. It's open daily from noon to 1.45 pm and 7.30 to 9.45 pm.

Restaurants – Other The ***Restaurant Marrakech*** (☎ 03 80 30 82 69), 20 Rue Monge, offers copious portions of excellent tajines and couscous for 60 to 95FF. It's open from noon to 2.30 pm and 7 to 11 pm (midnight on Friday and Saturday; closed Monday for lunch). ***Le Pharaon*** (☎ 03 80 30 11 36), one of France's few Egyptian restaurants (Lebanese fare is also on offer), is at 116 Rue Berbisey. *Menus* cost 58FF (weekday lunch only), 70FF (vegetarian), 75, 90 and 110FF. Hours are noon to 1.30 pm and 7 to 11 pm (closed Sunday for lunch and Monday).

Brasseries & Cafés The inexpensive brasseries, cafés and sandwich shops along Ave Maréchal Foch include ***Brasserie Foch*** (☎ 03 80 41 27 93) at No 1bis, where the plat du jour (39FF) and *menus* (57 and 78FF) are served from 11.30 am to 10 pm (closed Sunday).

University Restaurant The ***Restaurant Universitaire Maret*** (☎ 03 80 40 40 34), at 3 Rue du Docteur Maret, is open on weekdays and one weekend a month from 11.40 am to 2 pm and 6.40 to 8 pm (closed in July and August). Tickets (14.10FF for students) are on sale on the ground floor at lunchtime (until 1.15 pm) and during Monday dinner.

Self-Catering Parks perfect for picnics include Jardin de l'Arquebuse; the fountain-adorned Jardin Darcy; Place des Ducs de Bourgogne (just north of the Musée des Beaux-Arts); and Place Saint Michel (next to Église Saint Michel).

On Tuesday, Friday and Saturday mornings (until 1 pm), the ***Halles du Marché***, a 19th century covered market 150m north of Rue de la Liberté, and the whole pedestrian zone around it, fill with street stalls offering edibles and flea market goods (the latter are also on sale Saturday afternoon). Food shops along nearby Rue François Rude include the ***Nicolas*** wine shop at No 6 (closed all day Sunday and Monday morning) and several ***boulangeries***. Two blocks south of Rue de la Liberté, the upstairs supermarket of the ***Prisunic*** at 11-13 Rue Piron is open Monday to Saturday from 8.30 am to 8 pm.

North of the Palais des Ducs, there's a cluster of ***boulangeries*** and ***food shops*** along Rue Jean-Jacques Rousseau, including a ***Petit Casino*** grocery at No 16 (open from 8 am to 12.45 pm and 3.15 to 7.45 pm, closed Sunday afternoon and Monday morning).

Kosher grocery items are available at ***Boucherie-Charcuterie A Levy*** at 25 Rue de la Manutention, open from 8 am to 12.30 pm and 2 to 7.30 pm (until sometime between 3 and 7 pm on Friday; closed Saturday).

Entertainment

Dijon's club and bar scene is centred around Place de la République, especially along its northern side. There are a number of convivial cafés on and around Rue Berbisey.

For details (in French) on Dijon's lively cultural scene, pick up a copy of *Dijon Nuit et Jour*, published every three months (except in summer) by the municipality, or the monthly *Dijon Culture*. Both are available for no charge at the tourist office and some hotels.

Cinema Non-dubbed films flicker nightly on the three screens of ***Cinéma Eldorado*** (☎ 03 80 66 51 89 for the office, ☎ 03 80 66 12 34 for a recording in French, ☎ 08 38 68 01 74 for an interactive answering machine), an art cinema at 21 Rue Alfred de Musset. It's closed from mid-July to mid-August.

Discos & Clubs The *Club Le Privé* (☎ 03 80 73 39 57), 20 Ave Garibaldi, has flashing lights, pulsating speakers and banquettes with leopard-skin upholstery; music on the two dance floors ranges from rock and retro to tango and reggae. It is open nightly from 10 am to 4 am (5 am on Friday and Saturday nights), but things tend to be slow until midnight. Entrance costs 50FF, including a drink (30FF with a non-alcoholic beverage from Sunday to Thursday). Ages here range from 18 to 84.

L'An-Fer (☎ 03 80 71 32 44 daytime, ☎ 03 80 70 03 69 at night), 8 Rue Marceau, achieved fame for pioneering techno music, now presented on Friday and Saturday nights by DJs of international repute. Especially popular with students, it becomes mainly gay every Sunday night. Hours are 11 pm to 4 am (5 am on Friday and Saturday nights; closed Monday). Entry costs 50FF (60FF on Friday), including a drink.

Pubs & Bars Two hopping, informal cafés across from the west façade of the cathedral attract lots of lively young locals: *Café Au Carillon* (☎ 03 80 30 63 71) at 2 Rue Mariotte; and, across the street at 4 Place Saint Bénigne, *Café de la Cathédrale* (☎ 03 80 30 42 10). Both are open Monday to Saturday from 6.30 am to 1 or 2 am; the latter is also open on Sunday until 8 or 9 pm. Both charge 12FF for a demi of beer.

The only gay-oriented bar in the city centre is *Café de l'Univers* (☎ 03 80 30 98 29), 47 Rue Berbisey, whose hetero ground floor and terrace are open daily from 10 am to 2 am. The mainly gay and lesbian cellar, which has a small dance floor, is open from 9 pm to 2 am. Beers start at 15FF.

At 14 Place de la République, *La Jamaïque* (☎ 03 80 73 52 19) – also known as La Rhumerie – is a large bar whose décor and music are inspired by the Caribbean. Beers start at 15FF; rum-based cocktails are 20 to 70FF. Hours are 3 pm to 4 am (closed Sunday). On Tuesday to Saturday nights, there's live music (jazz, rock, flamenco, Brazilian etc) from about 10.30 pm to 2.30 or 3 am.

Maltberrie's (☎ 03 80 67 51 14), an Irish-style pub at 70 Rue Vannerie, has concerts and jam sessions of traditional Celtic music, pop and rock several times a week. It is open daily from 11 am (5 pm during school holiday periods) to 2 am. Guinness on tap is 17FF.

Shopping

Moutarde Maille (☎ 03 80 30 41 02) at 32 Rue de la Liberté, the factory shop of the company that makes Grey Poupon and other mustards, sells nothing but fancy mustard (from 12FF), vinegar and faïence mustard pots (135 to 1700FF). It's open from 9 am to noon and 2.15 to 7 pm (closed Sunday, and in January and February on Monday).

Getting There & Away

Air Dijon-Bourgogne airport (☎ 03 80 67 67 67) is 6km south-east of the city centre.

Bus The intercity bus station (☎ 03 80 42 11 00) is in the same building as the train station. The Transco information counter is open weekdays from 7.30 am to 6.30 pm and on Saturday until 12.30 pm; the *chef de gare* (station master), in an office facing the departure platforms, will gladly answer questions on weekdays from 6.30 to 7 pm, on Saturday from 4.30 to 7 pm, and on Sunday from 11 am to 12.30 pm and 5 to 7.30 pm.

There's good bus service to destinations all over the department of Côte d'Or; hours are posted on the platforms. Transco bus No 44 to Beaune (38.40FF; one hour) stops at lots of wine-making villages along the way; see the Beaune section for details. There's one bus a day to Autun (78.60FF; 2¼ hours); departure from Dijon is at 12.15 pm (11.10 am on Sunday and holidays). Three buses a day (one on Sunday, at 11.30 am) go to Avallon (92.60FF; two hours). To get to Troyes, change buses at Châtillon-sur-Seine.

Train The Dijon-Ville train station (☎ 08 36 35 35 35) was built to replace a structure destroyed in 1944. The information office is open from 9 am to 7 pm (6 pm on Saturday; closed Sunday and holidays).

Getting to/from Paris' Gare de Lyon by TGV (217 to 267FF; a dozen a day) takes only 1¾ hours; non-TGV trains (187FF; five to eight a day), also to/from Gare de Lyon, take 2¾ to 3½ hours. The services to Lyon's Gare de la Part-Dieu and/or Gare de Perrache cost 131FF (141FF by TGV) and run 13 to 17 times a day. Non-TGV trains also serve Nice (368FF; four direct a day; eight hours) and Strasbourg (199FF; one direct on most days; four hours). For details on train services to Beaune (37FF), Autun (94FF via Étang), Auxerre (122FF), Avallon (90FF via Montbard) and Vézelay, see each town's section in this chapter.

Car Travel 'Car (☎ 03 80 72 31 00), which has cars for as little as 190FF a day with 100km free and a 5000FF excess (deductible), is 1.3km east of Place de la République at 2 Ave Raymond Poincaré. It is served by bus Nos 5 and 6; get off at the Hugues III stop. ADA (☎ 03 80 51 90 90) is 2km south of the train station at 109 Ave Jean Jaurès; by bus, take No 16 to Bourroches Jaurès. Europcar (☎ 03 80 43 28 44) is half a block from the train station at 47 Rue Guillaume Tell. All three are closed on Sunday.

Getting Around

To/From the Airport From the train station or Rue de la Liberté, take local bus No 1 (towards Longvic) and get off at the Longvic Mairie stop, from where it's a 10 minute walk to the airport.

Bus Dijon's extensive urban bus network is run by STRD (☎ 03 80 30 60 90). Tickets, valid for any combination of transfers for one hour after time-stamping, cost 5.20FF and can be bought on the bus; a Carte 12 Trajets, good for a dozen rides, costs 42.50FF (not valid after 8.30 pm). A Forfait Journée ticket, valid all day, costs 16FF. STRD's L'Espace Bus (information and ticket office) at Place Grangier is open Monday to Saturday from 6.30 am to 7.15 pm.

Bus lines are known by their number and the name of the terminus station. In the city centre, seven different buses stop along Rue de la Liberté, and five more have stops around Place Grangier. Standard STRD lines operate from 6 am (1 pm on Sunday and holidays) to 8 or 8.30 pm. Every night from 8.30 pm to 12.15 am, the six lines of the Réseau du Soir (A, B, C, D, E and F) link the city centre with outlying areas every 30 minutes or so. On Sunday and holiday mornings from 9.30 am to about 12.45 pm, four P'tiBus minibus lines (D1 to D4) link the train station with certain outlying districts.

Car There's unmetered parking in the lot just south of the Hôtel de Police at Place Suquet.

Taxi To order a taxi 24 hours a day, call ☎ 03 80 41 41 12.

Bicycle All year-round, Travel 'Car (see Car under Getting There & Away) rents bikes for 100FF per 24 hours.

CÔTE D'OR

Burgundy's finest vintages come from the vine-covered Côte d'Or (Golden Hillside), the narrow, eastern slopes of the limestone, flint and clay escarpment running south from Dijon for about 60km. The northern section, the **Côte de Nuits**, stretches from the village of Fixin south to Corgoloin and produces reds known for their full-bodied, robust character. The southern section, the **Côte de Beaune**, lies between Aloxe-Corton and Santenay and produces both great reds and great whites.

The reds are made from Pinot Noir grapes, while for the whites both Pinot Blanc and Chardonnay are used. After the phylloxera beetle devastated the region's vines in the late 19th century, the vineyards were replanted by grafting traditional varieties onto phylloxera-resistant rootstock imported from the USA.

Some of the Côte d'Or's outstanding winemaking villages are: Marsannay-la-Côte, Fixin, Brochon, Gevrey-Chambertin, Nuits Saint Georges, Vougeot, Vosne-Romanée, Pernand Vergelesses, Aloxe-Corton and Savigny-lès-Beaune, all north of Beaune; and, south of Beaune: Pommard, Volnay, Saint

Romain, Puligny-Montrachet, Meursault, Auxey-Duresses, Rochepot and Santenay.

Detailed information on the region's vintages is available in *The Wines of Burgundy* (9th edition; 75FF) by Sylvain Pitiot & Jean-Charles Servant, published by Presses Universitaires de France and available at the Beaune tourist office.

Wine-Tasting

The villages of the Côte d'Or offer innumerable opportunities to sample excellent wines and purchase them where (or very near) they've been grown and aged. Just look for signs reading *dégustation* (tasting), *domaine* (wine-making estate), château, *cave* (wine cellar), *caveau* (a small cellar) or just plain *vins*. Another key vocabulary item is *gratuit* (free). Places that offer more than a few wines for sampling almost always charge a fee. Many wineries will ship wines home for you.

Villages in the Beaune area with cellars that offer tastings include:

Aloxe-Corton

Château Corton-André (☎ 03 80 26 44 25). Open daily year-round from 10 am to 12.30 pm and 2 to 6 pm.

Clos des Langres (☎ 03 80 62 98 73). Open year-round from 9 am to noon and 2 to 6 pm (closed on Sunday).

Savigny-lès-Beaune

Metairie de Villamont (☎ 03 80 21 52 13). Open mid-March to late November from 10 am to 6.30 pm (closed Tuesday).

Pommard

Château de Pommard (☎ 03 80 22 12 59 or ☎ 03 80 22 07 99), 3km south of Beaune. A 25 minute guided tour of the early 18th century chateau, including a glass of wine, costs 25FF (free for children under 16). From April to late November, tours begin daily from 9 am to 5.30 or 5.45 pm. There's a cluster of small cellars and wine merchants a few hundred metres to the south in the village.

Meursault

Domaine Bernard et Philippe Delagrange (☎ 03 80 21 22 72), 10 Rue du 11 Novembre. The 15th century cellars here can be visited daily from 9.30 am to 7 pm (6 pm in winter).

Château de Meursault (☎ 03 80 26 22 75). For 50FF you can taste seven wines in the cellars. Open daily from 9.30 am to noon and 2.30 to 6 or 6.30 pm (5.30 pm in winter).

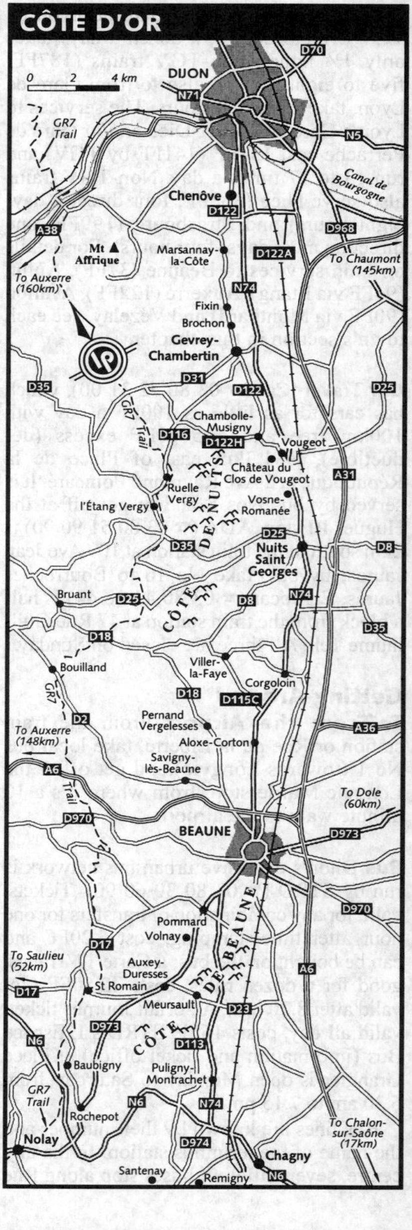

Hiking & Cycling

The GR7 and its variant, the GR76, run along the Côte d'Or from a bit west of Dijon to the hills west of Beaune, from where they continue southward. Much of the route follows tertiary roads that wend their way up and down the slopes west of the N74.

To get from Dijon to Beaune by bike – the ride takes three or four hours at an easy pace (it's a bit over 40km) – you might want to follow the quiet D122 through the vineyards until Nuits Saint Georges, and then take the D8 and D115C. To avoid riding both ways, you can take your bike on the train for the return trip, but this is possible only on certain runs – contact the SNCF for details.

Car Tour

The **Route du Chancelier Rolin** takes car-equipped visitors through the beautiful countryside of southern Burgundy to sites related to the life of the illustrious Chancellor Nicolas Rolin (1376-1461). It links Beaune (where Rolin and his wife founded the Hôtel-Dieu) with Autun (where you can visit his former residence, now a museum). A brochure in English is available at tourist offices.

Places to Stay

If you'd prefer to stay in one of the Côte d'Or villages rather than in Dijon or Beaune, a brochure listing the area's camp sites, gîtes, B&Bs and hotels is available from tourist offices, many of which can also help with reservations.

Getting Around

Unless you hire a hot-air balloon (see the Activities section at the beginning of this chapter), the best way to see the Côte d'Or is by car, though travelling by bus and/or train is also possible. Free brochures with suggested motoring itineraries are available from tourist offices. Bus services to and around the Côte d'Or are covered under Getting There & Away in the Beaune and Dijon sections of this chapter.

BEAUNE

• pop 21,000   ✉ 21200   alt 220m

Beaune (pronounced roughly like 'bone'), about 44km south of Dijon, is the unofficial capital of the Côte d'Or. The town's primary vocation is the production, ageing and sale of fine wines, which makes it one of the best places in France for wine-tasting. The most famous historical site in Beaune is the magnificent Hôtel-Dieu, France's most fascinating medieval charity hospital.

Beaune makes an excellent day trip from Dijon. The best time to visit is in spring; the town is pretty dead in the colder months, especially from December to February.

Orientation

The old city, shaped rather like a drop of water and partly enclosed by ramparts and a stream, is encircled by a one-way boulevard with seven names. The tourist office, which is 1km west of the train station, is a short walk from the Hôtel-Dieu, the basilica, a number of wine cellars and the pedestrian mall (Rue Monge and Rue Carnot).

Information

Tourist Office Beaune's tourist office (☎ 03 80 26 21 30; fax 03 80 26 21 39; otbeaune@hol.fr) is on Rue de l'Hôtel-Dieu opposite the entrance to the Hôtel-Dieu. It is open daily from 9 am to sometime between 6 pm (in winter) and 8 pm (Monday to Saturday from mid-June to late September). Staff can supply you with a free map and lists of cellars in both Beaune and its environs that offer wine-tasting.

Money The Banque de France at 26 Place Monge is open weekdays from 8.45 am to noon and 1.45 to 3.30 pm.

Some of Beaune's commercial banks are open Monday to Friday, while others are open Tuesday to Saturday. Several banks with exchange services can be found near the Banque de France. The tourist office will change money on Saturday afternoon, Sunday (usually until 5 pm) and holidays (until at least 5 pm).

Post The post office at 7 Blvd Saint Jacques is open weekdays from 8 am to 7 pm and on Saturday from 8 am to noon. Currency exchange is available.

Bookshop Athenæum de la Vigne et du Vin (☎ 03 80 25 08 31), 7 Rue de l'Hôtel-Dieu (next to the tourist office), carries IGN maps and thousands of titles on *œnologie* (the art and science of wine-making), some in English, as well as books on the Burgundy region and its cuisine. It is open daily from 10 am to 7 pm (8 pm from May to August).

Laundry The Blanc-Matic laundrettes at 24 Rue du Faubourg Saint Nicolas and 28 Rue du Faubourg Madeleine (through the arch) are open daily from 7 am to 7 pm.

Hôtel-Dieu

The celebrated Hôtel-Dieu des Hospices de Beaune (☎ 03 80 24 45 00), a charity hospital founded in 1443 by Nicolas Rolin (chancellor to Philip the Good) and his wife Guigone de Salins, is one of France's architectural highlights. The Flemish-Burgundian Gothic-style structure, topped by a multicoloured roof of

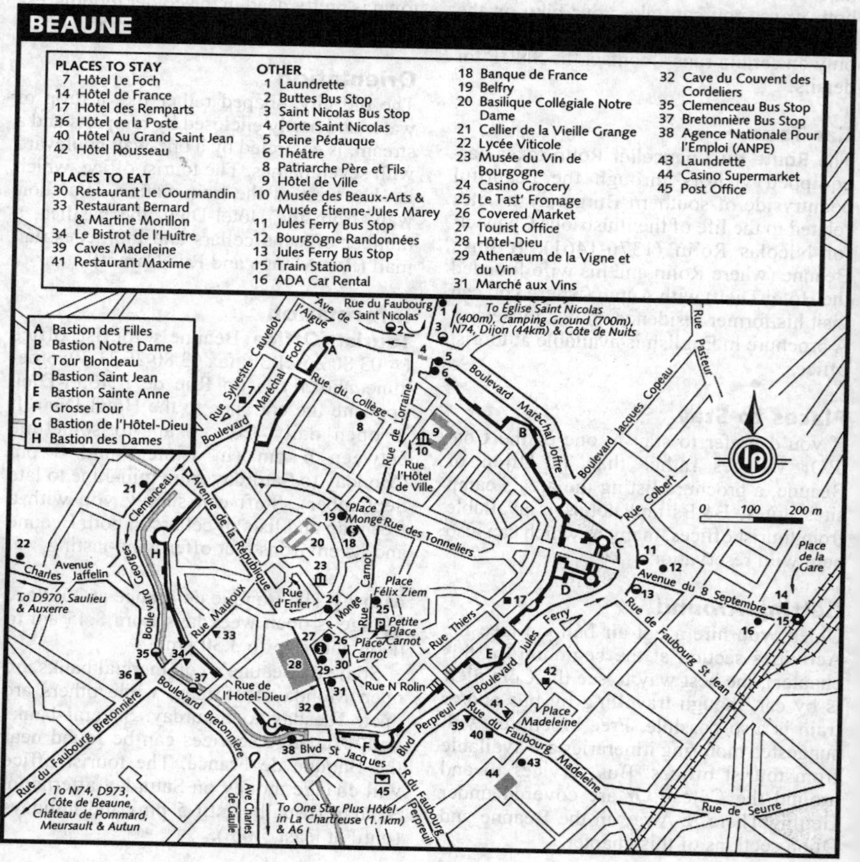

geometrically arranged glazed tiles, incorporates halls, wards, a pharmacy, a kitchen and various exhibits (eg medical utensils) that provide a fascinating look at late medieval life.

The hospital's valuable endowment – 58 hectares of prime vineyards bequeathed by Rolin – produces wine that is still auctioned each year, on the third Sunday in November, to raise money for medical care and research.

The darkened room off the hall lined with several outstanding tapestries contains the brilliant *Polyptych of the Last Judgement*, a multipanelled masterpiece commissioned by Rolin in 1443 from the Flemish artist Roger van der Weyden. At the bottom of this very literal interpretation of the Last Judgement, naked dead people climb out of their graves: those on the left are welcomed into heaven (a golden cathedral), while on the right the terror-stricken damned are dragged into the fires of hell.

The Hôtel-Dieu is open daily from 9 to 11.30 am and 2 to 5.30 pm; from a week before Easter to mid-November, it's open from 9 am to 6.30 pm. Admission is 32FF (25FF for students and children aged 10 to 14). There's an excellent English-language brochure available at the ticket window.

Basilique Collégiale Notre Dame

Construction of this collegiate church, once affiliated with the Benedictine monastery at Cluny, was begun in 1120. The ambulatory, nave and apsidal chapels are all Burgundian-style Romanesque; the rest is Gothic (13th to 15th centuries). The five wool and silk panels of the *Tapisseries de la Vie de la Vierge Marie* (Tapestries of the Life of the Virgin Mary) in the choir date from the late 15th century. There's access to the cloister via the door of the south transept arm.

The basilica is open daily from about 8.30 am to 6.45 pm. It is surrounded by a neighbourhood of quaint, narrow streets.

Ramparts

The thick stone walls of the fortifications around the old city, surrounded by a wild, overgrown area given over in part to cultivating cherries and vegetables, shelter privately owned wine cellars. The ramparts can easily be circumnavigated on foot.

Museums

Housed in a one-time palace of the dukes of Burgundy (built between the 14th and 18th centuries) on Rue d'Enfer, the **Musée du Vin de Bourgogne** (Museum of the Wines of Burgundy; ☎ 03 80 22 08 19) has exhibits on how vines are tended, grapes picked and wines aged, barrelled and bottled. It is open from 9.30 am to 6 pm (closed on Tuesday from December to March). A booklet with a room-by-room tour is available at the ticket counter.

Across the street from 9 Rue de l'Hôtel de Ville, the south wing of the 17th century Hôtel de Ville (formerly an Ursuline convent) contains two museums (☎ 03 80 24 56 98 for both): the **Musée des Beaux-Arts**, which features Gallo-Roman stone carvings and assorted paintings from the 15th to 19th centuries, including works by Beaune native Félix Ziem (1821-1911); and the **Musée Étienne-Jules Marey**, which is dedicated to the work of one of the pioneers of *chronophotographie* (the art of recording an action sequence by making a series of still photographs), a precursor of motion-picture photography. From April to October, both museums are open daily from 2 to 6 pm.

A ticket valid for all three museums costs 25FF (15FF for children over 12, students and people aged over 60).

Wine-Tasting

Under Beaune's buildings, streets and ramparts, millions of dusty bottles of wine are, at this very moment, being aged to perfection in cool, dark, cobweb-lined cellars. A number of places present an excellent opportunity to sample and compare different Burgundy wines.

Marché aux Vins (☎ 03 80 25 08 20), on Rue Nicolas Rolin 30m south of the tourist office. For 50FF, you get a *taste-vin* (a flat metal cup whose convex and concave surfaces help you admire the wine's colour) with which you can sample 18 wines (mainly reds) in the candle-lit, barrel-lined Église des Cordeliers (a desanctified church built from the 13th to 15th centuries) and the cellars beneath it. The best reds are near the exit. By special request visitors can sample older vintages and wine from the Hospices de Beaune endowment. It is possible to begin visits daily from 9.30 am to noon (11.30 am in winter) and 2 to 6 pm (5.30 pm in winter).

Cave du Couvent des Cordeliers (☎ 03 80 24 53 79), 6 Rue de l'Hôtel-Dieu. In this 13th century cellar of a one-time convent, *sommeliers* (wine waiters) provide advice to visitors as they sample, self-service style, two whites and four reds. Entry costs just 20FF. It is open daily from 9.30 am to 6.30 pm (9.30 am to noon and 2 to 6 pm from December to March).

Reine Pédauque (☎ 03 80 22 23 11), on Rue de Lorraine next to Porte Saint Nicolas. At this family-run winery, 30FF gets you a 30 to 45 minute guided tour of the cellars (available in English mainly from April to October) and the opportunity to taste one white, two reds and Belen, an apéritif. Given the thick cobwebs on the ceiling of the slimy 18th century *cave* (filled with crud-encrusted bottles) you wouldn't want to be in here if gravity reversed itself. Visits are held daily from 9 to 11 am and 2 to 5 pm; the cellars close one hour later.

Patriarche Père et Fils (☎ 03 80 24 53 01), 6 Rue du Collège. One of the largest *caves* in Burgundy, Patriarche is a lot like Paris' Catacombs except that the cellars are lined with dusty wine bottles instead of human bones. A self-guided tour with taped English commentary and the opportunity to taste 13 wines costs 40FF (10FF less if you return the taste-vin; free for accompanied under 18s who won't be sipping anything). It's open daily from 9.30 to 11.30 am and 2 to 5.30 pm.

Lycée Viticole (☎ 03 80 26 35 81), 16 Ave Charles Jaffelin, is one of 14 French secondary schools that train young people to plant and grow vines and ferment, age and bottle wine. From 8 am to noon and 2 to 5.30 pm (closed on Saturday afternoon and Sunday), you can taste and purchase the excellent, relatively inexpensive wines made by the students as part of their studies; proceeds are reinvested in the school. Cellar visits are also possible.

BURGUNDY

Organised Tours

Daily in July and August, on weekends in May, June and September and on certain weekends in October and November, the tourist office runs English-language tours of the town (38FF for an individual, 60FF for a couple, 90FF for a family) at noon. From early April to mid-November, an English-language sound and light show takes place nightly in the Hôtel-Dieu courtyard.

The tourist office handles ticketing for hot-air balloon rides, two-hour minibus tours of the Côte (180FF) and wine-tasting courses.

Special Events

From about the end of June to the beginning of August, the Festival International de Musique Baroque brings concerts and operas to Beaune on Friday, Saturday and Sunday evenings at 9 pm. On the third Sunday in November, the Hospices de Beaune auctions the premium wines from its vineyards in the covered market.

Places to Stay

Beaune's hotels are often full in September and October, when people come for the grape harvest and to enjoy the autumn weather.

Camping The four star ***camping ground*** (☎ 03 80 22 03 91) at 10 Rue Auguste Dubois, open from mid-March to October, charges 59FF for two adults with a tent and a car. To get there from the town centre, go north on Rue du Faubourg Saint Nicolas for 1km and turn left at Église Saint Nicolas.

About 7km south of Beaune in Meursault, ***Camping de la Grappe d'Or*** (☎ 03 80 21 22 48), surrounded by vineyards, is open from April to October. Two adults with a tent and car pay 67.50FF (84.50FF in July and August).

Hotels – Budget The ***Hôtel Rousseau*** (☎ 03 80 22 13 59), 11 Place Madeleine, run by a friendly older woman, has large, old-fashioned singles/doubles from 135/180FF; a room with toilet accommodating five is 380FF. All prices include breakfast. Some of the rooms have showers or toilets; the hall shower costs 20FF. Reception is sometimes closed for a couple of hours.

The nine room ***Hôtel Le Foch*** (☎ 03 80 24 05 65; fax 03 80 24 75 59), 24 Blvd Maréchal Foch, has plain, slightly idiosyncratic doubles from 175FF (200FF with shower, 230FF with toilet as well). Hall showers are free. Use of the garage costs 30FF. Reception is closed on Sunday from 1 to 4 pm.

The impersonal, 38 room ***One Star Plus*** (☎ 03 80 22 53 17; fax 03 80 24 10 14), 8 rue André-Marie Ampère, charges 149FF a night for a smallish double with pressboard walls, shower and toilet. It is one of half a dozen cheap chain hotels around Rue Burgalat in La Chartreuse, an area a bit over 1km south of the old city near the Beaune exit of the A6 (the Paris-Lyon autoroute).

Hotels – Mid-Range The quiet, two star, 22 room ***Hôtel de France*** (☎ 03 80 24 10 34; fax 03 80 24 96 78), opposite the train station at 35 Ave du 8 Septembre, has large, spotless one/two-bed doubles with shower and toilet for 260/310FF; quads are 460FF. The impersonal, 106 room ***Hôtel Au Grand Saint Jean*** (☎ 03 80 24 12 22; fax 03 80 24 15 43), a two star place at 18 Rue du Faubourg Madeleine, has garish hallways but decent doubles/quads from 228/285FF. There are several other two and three-star hotels nearby at Place Madeleine.

Hotels – Top End The ***Hôtel des Remparts*** (☎ 03 80 24 94 94; fax 03 80 24 97 08; hotel.des.remparts@wanadoo.fr; www.webstore.fr/hotel-remparts), a three star place in a 17th century mansion at 48 Rue Thiers, has huge doubles, some with beam ceilings, for 290 to 470FF, and quads from 520FF; prices are 10% lower from December to mid-March. Enclosed parking costs 45FF for 24 hours. The luxurious, four star ***Hôtel de la Poste*** (☎ 03 80 22 08 11; fax 03 80 24 19 71), 5 Blvd Georges Clemenceau, has doubles starting at 650FF.

Places to Eat

Restaurants ***Restaurant Maxime*** (☎ 03 80 22 17 82), 3 Place Madeleine, offers reasonably priced Burgundian cuisine in a rustic yet elegant dining room. *Menus* cost 78, 96 and 148FF; à la carte, *bœuf bourguignon* is 65FF. It's open from noon to 2 pm and 7 to 10 pm (closed Monday and during February). There are a number of other restaurants nearby.

The intimate ***Restaurant Le Gourmandin*** (☎ 03 80 24 07 88), 8 Place Carnot, whose French and regional specialities include bœuf bourguignon (68FF), is open from noon to 2 pm and 7 to 10.30 pm (closed on Wednesday for lunch and on Tuesday). The *menus* cost 89 to 175FF. There are a number of cafés and restaurants – many with warm-weather terraces – nearby, especially around Place Carnot, Petite Place Carnot and Place Félix Ziem.

Caves Madeleine (☎ 03 80 22 93 30), a cosy wine bar at 8 Rue du Faubourg Madeleine, serves at least a dozen wines by the glass (from 13.30FF) and family-style Burgundian *menus* for 69 and 89FF. It is open Monday to Saturday, and on Sundays that are also holidays.

Le Bistrot de l'Huître (☎ 03 80 24 71 28), 45 Rue Maufoux, serves fresh oysters from both Brittany and the Île d'Oléron; half a dozen of the luscious bivalves cost 41 to 76FF, depending on size and provenance. This place, which also offers escargots, salads, patés and wine by the glass, is generally open daily.

The elegant ***Restaurant Bernard & Martine Morillon*** (☎ 03 80 24 12 06), 31 Rue Maufoux, bearer of one Michelin star, has traditional French *menus* for 180, 330, 400 and 480FF. À la carte main dishes (eg fish) cost from 190 to 360FF (closed Tuesday for lunch and Monday).

Self-Catering The covered market and nearby Place Carnot play host to a ***food market*** every Saturday until about 1 pm. On Wednesday morning, the covered market hosts a smaller ***marché gourmand*** (gourmet market).

The ***Casino*** grocery at 14 Rue Monge is open daily from 7.30 am to 7.30 pm (closed from 12.30 to 3 pm and on Sunday and Tuesday afternoons); in July and August there's no midday closure and it's open daily except Sunday afternoon. There are several ***food shops*** along the pedestrianised Rue Carnot, including ***Le Tast' Fromage***, a fromagerie at the intersection of Rue Carnot and Rue Monge (closed Sunday and Monday from late November to Easter; open daily except Sunday afternoon the rest of the year).

The ***Casino*** supermarket at 28 Rue du Faubourg Madeleine is open Monday to Saturday from 8.30 am to 7.30 pm.

Shopping

Wine is sold *en vrac* (in bulk) for as little as 6.10FF a litre, not including the container, at a number of places, including Cellier de la Vieille Grange (☎ 03 80 22 40 06) at 27 Blvd Georges Clemenceau (closed Sunday afternoon). The minimum sale is supposed to be 5L but flexibility is often practised.

Getting There & Away

Bus Transco bus No 44, which runs nine or so times a day (seven times a day during the summer school holidays; twice on Sunday and holidays), passes a number of wine-growing villages (eg Vougeot, Nuits Saint Georges, Aloxe-Corton) on the way from Dijon to Beaune (38.40FF; one hour) and vice versa. On weekdays and Saturday during the school year, buses leave Dijon at 6.35, 7.45 and 11.05 am and 12.15, 2.30, 5.05, 5.50 and 6.20 pm (and, except on Saturday, at 7.15 pm). Buses leave Beaune at about 6.25, 6.40, 7.40 and 8.28 am and 12.45 pm (except Saturday), 1.05, 1.25, 5.05, 6 and 6.25 pm. Sunday departures from Beaune are at 12.35 and 6.25 pm.

Certain buses on the No 44 run also serve villages south of Beaune, including Pommard, Volnay, Meursault and Rochepot, though during the summer school holidays this section is covered by only three buses a day. Bus No 44 goes once a day to Autun, departing Beaune at about 1.10 pm (12.05 pm on Sunday and holidays).

In Beaune, Transco buses stop at several places around the boulevards that encircle the old city, using different stops for different lines and directions (see the Beaune map). Buses coming from Dijon stop at Jules Ferry, Buttes and then Clemenceau; buses to Dijon pick up passengers at Bretonnière, Jules Ferry and Saint Nicolas.

Train Beaune's train station (☎ 08 36 35 35 35), whose ticket windows are open daily until 8.30 pm, is served by local trains on the Dijon-Lyon line. The service to Dijon (37FF; 14 to 20 a day) takes 20 to 25 minutes; the last train from Beaune to Dijon leaves at about 11.15 pm (a bit later on Sunday night). It is possible to bring along a bicycle only on certain runs – check with the SNCF for details.

Trains to/from Lyon (112FF; 1½ to 2¼ hours; six or seven a day) sometimes stop at both of Lyon's train stations. Beaune is linked to Paris' Gare de Lyon (233 to 283FF) by one or two direct TGVs a day. To get to Autun (71FF), change at Étang-sur-Arroux.

Car ADA car rental (☎ 03 80 22 72 90) has an office at 26 Ave du 8 Septembre.

Getting Around

Taxi To order a taxi, ring ☎ 06 09 42 36 80.

Bicycle The tourist office has a brochure with details on bike circuits of 10 to 45km.From April to mid-November, Bourgogne Randonées (☎ 03 80 22 06 03) at 7 Ave du 8 Septembre rents all-terrain bikes for 100FF a day, including printed information on route options. It is open seven days a week until 7 pm.

AUXERRE

• pop 38,800 ✉ 89000 alt 130m

Auxerre (pronounced 'oh-SAIR') grew up around its attractive old city, whose slopes – graced by belfries, spires and steep-roofed, half-timbered houses – overlook the still waters of the Yonne River. Its narrow streets are easily explored on foot. Noteworthy sights include the cathedral and a 9th century Carolingian crypt.

Auxerre, famed for its first-rate football teams, is a good base for visiting northern Burgundy, including the Chablis area. The city's pleasure-boat port makes this an excellent place to rent a canal boat (see Activities at the beginning of this chapter).

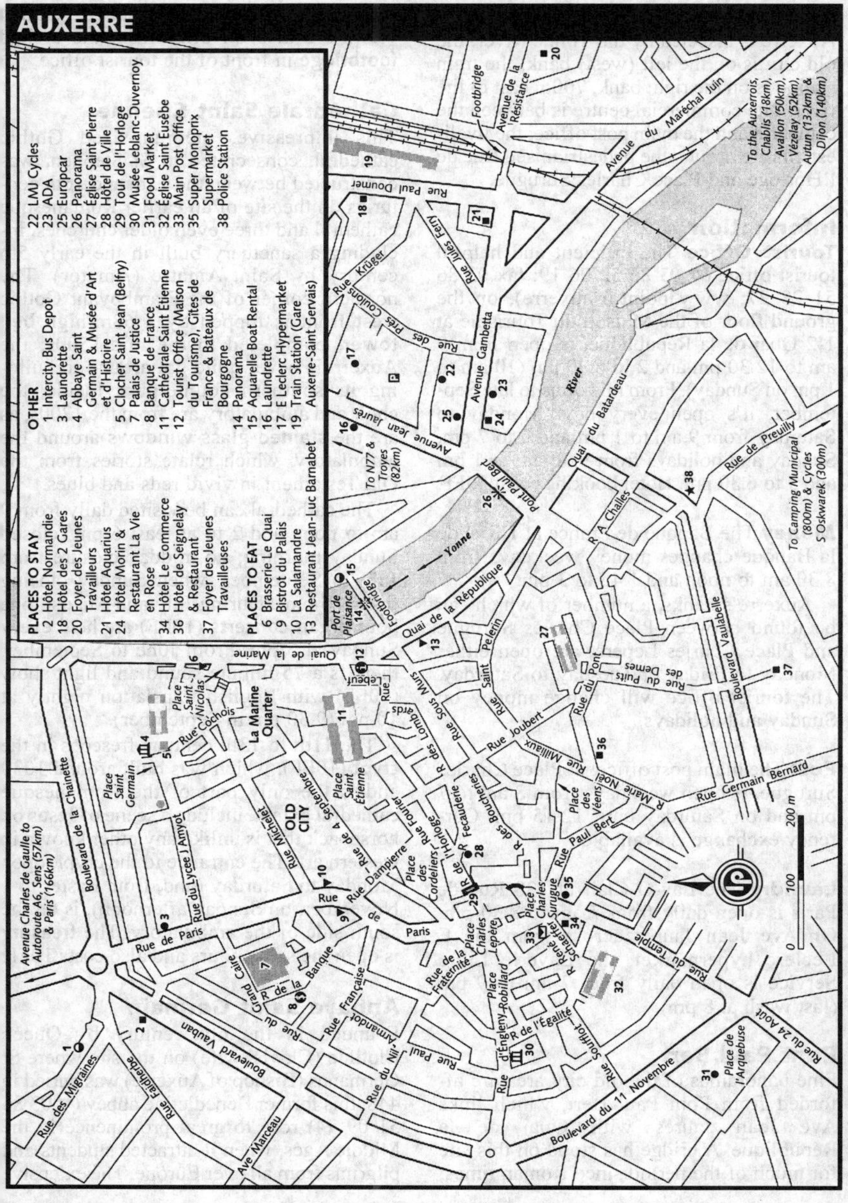
AUXERRE
PLACES TO STAY
2 Hôtel Normandie
18 Hôtel des 2 Gares
20 Foyer des Jeunes Travailleurs
21 Hôtel Aquarius
24 Hôtel Morin & Restaurant La Vie en Rose
34 Hôtel Le Commerce
36 Hôtel de Seignelay & Restaurant
37 Foyer des Jeunes Travailleuses
PLACES TO EAT
6 Brasserie Le Quai
9 Bistrot du Palais
10 La Salamandre
13 Restaurant Jean-Luc Barnabet
OTHER
1 Intercity Bus Depot
3 Laundrette
4 Abbaye Saint Germain & Musée d'Art et d'Histoire
5 Clocher Saint Jean (Belfry)
7 Palais de Justice
8 Banque de France
11 Cathédrale Saint Étienne
12 Tourist Office (Maison du Tourisme), Gîtes de France & Bateaux de Bourgogne
14 Panorama
15 Aquarelle Boat Rental
16 Laundrette
17 E Leclerc Hypermarket
19 Train Station (Gare Auxerre-Saint Gervais)
22 LMJ Cycles
23 ADA
25 Europcar
26 Panorama
27 Eglise Saint Pierre
28 Hôtel de Ville
29 Tour de l'Horloge
30 Musée Leblanc-Duvernoy
31 Food Market
32 Eglise Saint Eusèbe
33 Main Post Office
35 Super Monoprix Supermarket
38 Police Station
Avenue Charles de Gaulle to Autoroute A6, Sens (57km) & Paris (166km)
To N77 & Troyes (82km)
To the Auxerrois, Chablis (18km), Avallon (50km), Vézelay (52km), Autun (132km) & Dijon (140km)
To Camping Municipal (800m) & Cycles S Oskwarek (300m)
Yonne
River
La Marine Quarter
OLD CITY
Port de Plaisance
Footbridge
Place Saint Germain
Place Saint Nicolas
Place Saint Étienne
Place des Cordeliers
Place Charles Lepère
Place Charles Surugue
Place Robillard
Place des Véens
Place de l'Arquebuse
Boulevard de la Chainette
Boulevard Vaulabelle
Boulevard Vauban
Boulevard du 11 Novembre
Quai de la République
Quai de la Marine
Quai du Batardeau
Pont Paul Bert
Avenue Jean Jaurès
Avenue Gambetta
Avenue du Maréchal Juin
Avenue de la Résistance
Rue Paul Doumer
Rue de Paris
Rue du Temple
Rue Germain Bernard
Rue de Preuilly
Rue du 24 Août
Rue Joubert
Rue Dampierre
Rue Fécauderie
Rue de l'Horloge
Rue Française
Rue des Migraines
Ave Marceau
0 100 200 m

Orientation

Auxerre is bisected by the Yonne River: the old city is on the left (west) bank; the train station is on the right bank, 700m east of the river. The commercial centre is between the cathedral and the main post office; the liveliest bits are around the pedestrianised Rue de l'Horloge and Place Charles Surugue.

Information

Tourist Office The efficient and helpful tourist office (☎ 03 86 52 06 19; fax 03 86 51 23 27; www.ipoint.fr/auxerre), on the ground floor of the Maison du Tourisme at 1-2 Quai de la République, is open from 9 am to 12.30 pm and 2 to 6.30 pm (10 am to 1 pm on Sunday). From mid-June to late September, it's open every day: Monday to Saturday from 9 am to 1 pm and 2 to 7 pm, Sunday and holidays from 9.30 am to 1 pm and 3 to 6.30 pm. Hotel bookings cost 15FF.

Money The Banque de France at 1 Rue de la Banque changes money weekdays from 8.30 am to noon and 1.45 to 3 pm.

Auxerre's banks, a number of which can be found between Place Charles Surugue and Place Charles Lepère, are open either Monday to Friday or Tuesday to Saturday. The tourist office will change money on Sunday and holidays.

Post The main post office, at Place Charles Surugue, is open weekdays from 8 am to 7 pm and on Saturday until 12.15 pm. Currency exchange is available.

Laundry The Lav-O-Clair at 138 Rue de Paris is open daily from 7 am to 8.30 pm. On Ave Jean Jaurès across from the E Leclerc hypermarket, the Laverie Libre Service is open daily from 7 am to 9 pm (last wash at 8 pm).

BURGUNDY

Pont Paul Bert

Fine panoramas of the old city area are afforded from Pont Paul Bert, which links Ave Jean Jaurès with Quai de la République. A bridge has stood on this site for much of the period since Roman times; the present structure dates from 1857. Great views are also on offer from the arched **footbridge** in front of the tourist office.

Cathédrale Saint Étienne

This impressive, medium-sized Gothic cathedral, consecrated to St Stephen, was constructed between the 13th and 16th centuries on the site of an earlier Romanesque cathedral and three even older churches, including a sanctuary built in the early 5th century by Saint Amatre (Amator). The northern corner of the Flamboyant Gothic west front is topped by a 68m-high **bell tower**, completed in the mid-1500s; the Auxerrois never quite got around to building its southern counterpart. Inside, the choir and ambulatory are from the 1200s, as are the **stained-glass windows** around the ambulatory, which relate stories from the Old Testament in vivid reds and blues.

The cathedral can be visited daily from 9 am to noon and 2 to at least 6 pm (closed Sunday morning; no midday closure from July to September, when Sunday closing time is 5 pm). During July and August, one hour **organ concerts** (10FF) are held every Sunday at 5 pm. From June to September, there is a 75 minute sound and light show (30FF) with English translation nightly at 10 pm (9.30 pm in September).

The 11th to 13th century frescoes in the **crypt** (10FF), which was built around 1030 and is the only part of the Romanesque cathedral extant, include a scene of Jesus on horseback that is unlike any other known in western art. The entrance to the crypt, open Monday to Saturday (and, from Easter to 1 November, on Sunday afternoon), is on the south side of the ambulatory. The **treasury** is open the same hours and also costs 10FF.

Abbaye Saint Germain

Founded in the 6th century by Queen Clotilde (Clovis' wife) on the site where St Germanus (Bishop of Auxerre) was buried in 448, this former Benedictine abbey (☎ 03 86 51 09 74) rose to great prominence in the Middle Ages, when it attracted students and pilgrims from all over Europe. The extensive

Carolingian crypts are decorated with exceptional frescoes from 858 that are among the oldest in France. The 51m-high **belfry** ended up being detached from the mostly Gothic **abbey church** (13th and 15th centuries) when several bays at the west end of the nave were razed in 1811.

The monastery buildings around the cloister, which date from the 14th to 17th centuries, house Auxerre's **Musée d'Art et d'Histoire**, where you can see prehistoric stone implements and Gallo-Roman antiquities. Other sections are devoted to paintings, sculpture and contemporary art.

The abbey is open from 10 am to noon and 2 to 6 pm (closed Tuesday and some holidays); from June to September, hours are 10 am to 6.30 pm. The crypts must be visited with a guide – tours (in French, with printed information in English) begin every hour (every half-hour in summer); the last one leaves at 5 pm (5.30 pm in summer). Admission costs 20FF but is free for students, those under 16 and, on Wednesday, for everyone; the same ticket is valid for the Musée Leblanc-Duvernoy.

Tour de l'Horloge

The spire-topped clock tower over Rue de l'Horloge, built in 1483 as part of the city's fortifications, stands on the site of the city's main gate during Gallo-Roman times. Its spire was destroyed by fire in 1825 and rebuilt in 1891. On the 17th century clock face, the hand with a sun on one end indicates the time of day. The other hand, decorated with an orb, shows what day of the lunar month it is, making a complete rotation every 29½ days.

Musée Leblanc-Duvernoy

This museum (☎ 03 86 51 09 74), housed in an 18th century mansion at 9bis Rue d'Églény, displays early 18th century tapestries from Beauvais (four of which have Chinese motifs), faïence from Burgundy and elsewhere, paintings and other fine arts. It is open from 2 to 6 pm (closed Tuesday and some holidays). Admission costs 12FF, but it's free for students and, on Wednesday, for everyone. A ticket also valid for the Abbaye Saint Germain costs 20FF.

Special Events

From 21 to 28 June, Jazz à Auxerre brings to town about a dozen jazz concerts, most of them free. Piano à Auxerre is a week-long festival of piano recitals held each year in late September.

Places to Stay – Budget

Camping The shaded, grassy ***Camping Municipal*** (☎ 03 86 52 11 15) at 8 Route de Vaux (across the street from the football stadium) is 1.5km south of the train station. It is open April to September and charges 14FF per adult and 12FF for a tent site. By bus, take line A from the old city (Place Robillard or Blvd du 11 Novembre) to the Stades Arbre Sec stop.

Hostels Two co-ed dormitories for young working people offer travellers basic singles for 77FF, including breakfast; doubles (available only at Ave de la Résistance) are 132FF. Rooms are open all day, and there's no curfew. The cafeteria-equipped, 135 room ***Foyer des Jeunes Travailleuses*** (☎ 03 86 52 45 38) is slightly south of the old city at 16 Blvd Vaulabelle; to get there from the train station, take bus line B or D to the Vaulabelle stop. The 150 room ***Foyer des Jeunes Travailleurs*** (☎ 03 86 46 95 11) is behind the train station at 16 Ave de la Résistance; to get there, follow the signs to the 'Maison du Quartier Rive Droite'.

Gîtes Reservations for ***gîtes ruraux*** can be made at the Gîtes de France booking office (☎ 03 86 72 92 15; fax 03 86 72 92 09), on the 1st floor of the tourist office building (closed Sunday and, from November to Easter, on Saturday). Credit cards are accepted.

Hotels The 12 room ***Hôtel des 2 Gares*** (☎ 03 86 46 90 06), opposite the train station at 10 Rue Paul Doumer, has basic doubles with shower and toilet for 130FF. Reception (at the bar) is closed on Sunday.

Near the river, the seven room ***Hôtel Morin*** (☎ 03 86 46 90 26; fax 03 86 46 73 57) at 4 Ave Gambetta can provide adequate singles/doubles/triples/quads with shower and toilet for 139/159/199/239FF. Reception is open daily until 11 pm.

Places to Stay – Mid-Range

Part of the pleasant ***Hôtel de Seignelay*** (☎ 03 86 52 03 48; fax 03 86 52 32 39) at 2 Rue du Pont, centred around a quiet courtyard, dates from the 17th century. Quite spacious doubles/quads cost 280/320FF; the handful of rooms with washbasins go for 140/170FF. Parking in the locked garage is 25FF. The 19 room ***Hôtel Le Commerce*** (☎ 03 86 52 03 16; fax 03 86 52 42 37) at 5 Rue René Schaeffer (a very central location) provides very attractive doubles/triples for 230/290FF; rooms for five are 360FF. The private garage costs 35FF. Reception is closed on Sunday after 3 pm.

The two star, 47 room ***Hôtel Normandie*** (☎ 03 86 52 57 80; fax 03 86 51 54 33), a gem of a hotel on the northern edge of the old city at 41 Blvd Vauban, offers excellent value, with elegant doubles starting at 290FF. Room service, a billiard table, bar and sauna (30FF) are all available 24 hours a day. The private garage costs 26FF.

The two star, 13 room ***Hôtel Aquarius*** (☎ 03 86 46 95 02; fax 03 86 51 29 80), 33 Ave Gambetta, has small, soundproofed singles/doubles/triples for 190/220/280FF. Reception is closed daily from 3 to 5 pm and on Sunday after 3 pm.

Places to Eat

Restaurants – French The ***Restaurant de Seignelay*** in the Hôtel de Seignelay serves classic French and Burgundian cuisine in a rustic dining room that has been much upgraded since it served as a stable in the 17th century. The four *menus* cost between 59 and 135FF. Hours are noon to 1.30 pm and 7 to 9 pm (closed Monday). The unpretentious, old-time ***Bistrot du Palais*** (☎ 03 86 51 47 02) at 69 Rue de Paris serves Lyon-style meat mains for 55FF; starters and desserts cost 25FF. Hours are noon to 2 or 2.30 pm and 7.15 to 11 or 11.30 pm (closed Sunday and Monday). There are several other small restaurants along the same street.

Brasserie Le Quai (☎ 03 86 51 66 67) is a restaurant/bar at 4 Place Saint Nicolas, a picturesque public square in La Marine, once Auxerre's commercial quarter. The plat du jour (60 to 70FF, depending on the day) and the *menus* – which cost between 59FF (lunch only; not available on weekends or holidays) and 190FF (50FF for children) – are served daily from noon to 2.30 pm and 7 to 10 pm (11 pm in summer, when you can dine outside). Drinks are served from 9 am to 1 am.

La Salamandre (☎ 03 86 52 87 87) at 84 Rue de Paris, a refined restaurant that specialises in fish (85 to 185FF) and seafood, has *menus* for 108FF (not available in the evening on weekends or holidays), 178, 258 and 298FF. It's closed Saturday for lunch and on Sunday.

At the geranium-bedecked ***Restaurant Jean-Luc Barnabet*** (☎ 03 86 51 68 88), 14 Quai de la République, a row of windows enables you to watch the chefs preparing the innovative versions of traditional French dishes that have earned this place one Michelin star. *Menus* are available for 295FF (380FF with wine, 95FF for children) from 12.30 to 2.30 pm and 8 to 9.30 pm (closed on Sunday evening and Monday). Reservations are recommended for dinner on Friday and Saturday and lunch on Sunday.

Restaurants – Other The inexpensive ***La Vie en Rose*** (☎ 03 86 46 90 26) at 4 Ave Gambetta offers pizzas (39 to 55FF) and *menus* that include a hors d'œuvre buffet for 59, 79 and 149FF. It's open daily from 11.30 am to 2 pm and 7 to 11 pm.

Self-Catering The ***food market*** a few blocks south-west of the old city at Place de l'Arquebuse springs to life on Tuesday and Friday mornings. In the old city Place Charles Surugue has a ***food market*** on Wednesday mornings. The ***Super Monoprix*** supermarket on Place Charles Surugue is open from 8.30 am to 8 pm (7.30 pm on Saturday). It's closed on Sunday.

Near the train station, the ***E Leclerc*** hypermarket, between Rue des Prés Coulons and Ave Jean Jaurès, is open from Monday to Saturday from 9 am to 7.30 pm (8 pm on Friday).

Getting There & Away

Bus The intercity bus depot on Rue des Migraines is linked to the old city and the train station by local bus line B. Some intercity lines also stop at the train station and/or Place de l'Arquebuse. Schedules can be picked up on weekdays (until 5.30 pm) and Saturday morning at the Accueil office (☎ 03 86 72 43 00) in the Hôtel de Ville at Place de l'Hôtel de Ville.

Les Rapides de Bourgogne (☎ 03 86 94 95 00) has buses to Chablis (26FF; 40 minutes; two a day on weekdays), Pontigny (one a day except Sunday) and Tonnerre (41.50FF; 70 minutes; two a day on weekdays). From Monday to Thursday, there's a direct bus to Troyes (2¼ hours) at 8.40 am.

Train The Auxerre-Saint Gervais train station (☎ 08 36 35 35 35) on Rue Paul Doumer has 10 to 14 daily connections to Laroche-Migennes (20 minutes), a rail junction on the main line linking Paris' Gare de Lyon (120FF; about two hours; six to nine a day) with Tonnerre (52FF), Montbard (near Fontenay; 82FF) and Dijon (122FF; 2¼ hours; three to five a day). The SNCF has buses from Laroche-Migennes to Troyes (60FF; one to 1¾ hours; four/one a day on weekdays/ weekends).

Except to Sermizelles-Vézelay (40FF; 50 minutes; three to five a day) and Avallon (49FF; one hour; three to five a day), services south-eastward towards the Étang-sur-Arroux junction – eg to Saulieu and Autun (102FF; at least 2¾ hours) – are very slow and require a change at Avallon.

Car ADA (☎ 03 86 46 01 02) is at 6bis Ave Gambetta. Europcar (☎ 03 86 46 99 08), nearby at 9 Ave Gambetta, is closed on Sunday and holidays.

Getting Around

Bus The five main local bus lines (A, B, C, D and E), operated by Le Bus (☎ 03 86 46 90 90), run once or twice an hour until about 7 pm. Lines B, D and E link the train station with the city centre.

Taxi To order a taxi, ring ☎ 03 86 52 51 52.

Bicycle The tourist office can supply details on cycling routes and may itself hire out bikes for 60FF a day. LMJ Cycles (☎ 03 86 46 30 60) at 4 Rue du Sparre rents out bikes for 50/90FF per half-day/day (closed Sunday). South-east of the old city at 22 Rue de Preuilly (100m past the rail overpass), Cycles S Oskwarek (☎ 03 86 52 71 19) charges 100/150/300FF per day/ weekend/week (closed Sunday).

EAST OF AUXERRE

Between the Yonne River and the Canal de Bourgogne lie the Auxerrois and the Tonnerrois, rural areas whose rolling hills are dotted with farmhouses and hay bales and carpeted with forests, fields, pastures and – especially around Chablis – meticulously tended vineyards. The area has lots of quiet back roads (eg the D124) and hiking trails that can be cycled; brochures are available at tourist offices.

Chablis

• pop 2600 ✉ 89800 alt 135m

The well-to-do but sleepy town of Chablis, 19km east of Auxerre, has made its fortune growing, ageing and marketing the delicate, dry white wines that bear its name. Made from Chardonnay grapes grown on the area's sunny, well drained limestone marl slopes, Chablis is divided into four Appelations d'Origine Contrôlées (AOC): Petit Chablis, Chablis, Premier Cru and, most prestigious of all, Grand Cru.

From December to February many wine cellars close down, but you can still drop in on nearby domaines. The rest of the year, the town is very quiet from about noon to 3 pm; most of the shops are closed on Monday.

A Knight in Shining Petticoats

Speculation about the cross-dressing habits of the French secret agent Charles Chevalier d'Éon de Beaumont (1728-1810), born 15km east of Chablis in Tonnerre, has been rife for centuries, especially in sex-obsessed England, where he spent a good part of his life wearing the latest in women's fashion and spying for Louis XV. The locals, at least, have no doubt about the brave chevalier's suitability as a role model for contemporary youth: they've named the local secondary school after him.

Orientation & Information In the centre of Chablis (ie west of the main square, Place Charles de Gaulle), the D965 is known as Rue Auxerroise.

The tourist office (☎ 03 86 42 80 80), 1 Rue de Chichée (follow the signs), is open from 10 am to 12.30 pm and 1.30 to 6.30 pm (closed on Sunday, except from May to September).

The banks around Place Charles de Gaulle are open Tuesday to Saturday.

Walking Tour The 13th century **Église Saint Martin**, founded in the 9th century by monks fleeing the Norman attacks on Tours, is one block north of Place Charles de Gaulle. Two blocks south of here – follow Rue Porte Noël – you'll come upon the two round bastions of **Porte Noël**. Around the corner, at 12 Rue des Juifs, is the shell of a centuries-old **synagogue**.

Across the courtyard from the tourist office, **Petit Pontigny** was once used by the Cistercian monks of Pontigny as a fermentation cellar (visits are by appointment only).

Wine-Tasting Chablis can be sampled at quite a few wine shops along Rue Auxerroise. La Chablisienne (☎ 03 86 42 89 89), a co-operative cellar owned by 300 small producers, is about 1km south of town on Blvd Pasteur (the D91 towards Noyers). Dégustation (25FF) is possible daily, year-round.

Places to Stay The ***Hôtel de l'Étoile*** (☎ 03 86 42 10 50; fax 03 86 42 81 21) at 4 Rue des Moulins (across from the Casino grocery on Place Charles de Gaulle) has doubles for 230FF (210FF with toilet but without shower). From November to March reception is closed on Sunday night and Monday. The three star ***Hostellerie des Clos*** (☎ 03 86 42 10 63; fax 03 86 42 17 11) at Place Général Gras has doubles from 298FF. In the off season, it is closed all day Wednesday and on Thursday until 3 pm or so.

Places to Eat The ***Au Vrai Chablis*** (☎ 03 86 42 11 43), Place Charles de Gaulle, has inexpensive *menus* (closed Tuesday evening, Wednesday and in January). There are other restaurants nearby. The restaurant of the ***Hostellerie des Clos*** (see Places to Stay), bearer of one Michelin star, has *menus* for 178, 298 and 394FF. In the off season, it is closed on Wednesday and on Thursday for lunch.

On Sunday morning, there's an ***outdoor market*** at Place Charles de Gaulle. Except for the ***Casino*** grocery (open from 7 am to 12.30 pm and 3.30 to 7.30 or 8 pm; closed on Sunday), the ***food shops*** around Place Charles de Gaulle are all closed on Monday. The ***Casino*** grocery on Place Général Gras, around the corner from the tourist office, is closed from 12.30 to 3 pm and on Wednesday and Sunday afternoons.

Getting There & Away From Monday to Friday, Les Rapides de Bourgogne (☎ 03 86 94 95 00) operates two Auxerre-Chablis-Tonnerre return trips a day. Buses depart from Auxerre (26FF; 40 minutes) at 11.15 am (12.15 pm on Wednesday) and at 5.40 pm; there are departures from Chablis at 7.10 am and 2.30 pm.

Pontigny

• pop 825 ✉ 89230 alt 113m

The quiet town of Pontigny, on the Serein River 25km north-east of Auxerre, is best known for its superbly preserved **Abbatiale** (abbey church; ☎ 03 86 47 54 99), whose harmonious, 108m-long sanctuary, lined with 23 chapels, was built in the mid-12th century in the Gothic style. The simplicity of its lines and the lack of ornamentation (except for the choir screen and stalls, added in the 17th and 18th centuries) reflect the Cistercian order's rigorous austerity. Monks from the abbey were the first to perfect the production of Chablis wine. The abbey, surrounded by farmland, can be visited daily.

Places to Stay & Eat Almost every village around here has a camping ground.

The six room ***Hôtel Saint Vincent*** (☎ 03 86 47 42 61), opposite the town hall at 40 Rue Paul Desjardins (the N77), has doubles with washbasin for 130 to 150FF. Hall showers are free. Except from May to October, reception is closed on Sunday. The hotel shuts down in February and for a fortnight around 1 October.

The ***Proximarché*** grocery at 43 Rue Paul Desjardins is closed on Sunday afternoon.

Getting There & Away Les Rapides de Bourgogne (☎ 03 86 94 95 00) has two runs a day (except Sunday) between Auxerre and Pontigny.

Noyers-sur-Serein

• pop 850 ✉ 89310

In the centre of this tiny, medieval village (pronounced 'nwa-YER'), reached via fortified stone gates, narrow streets wind past 15th and 16th century stone and half-timbered houses. Lines carved into the façade of the 18th century **Hôtel de Ville**, right next to the ancient stone arcade of the library building, mark the level at which historic floods crested.

The **Musée de Noyers** (☎ 03 86 82 89 09), not far from the 15th century church on Rue de l'Église, displays 100 or so works of naive art. Except in January, it is open from 2.30 to 6.30 pm on weekends and holidays and, except on Thursday, during school vacations; from June to September, daily opening hours are 11 am to 6.30 pm. Admission is 20FF (15FF for students; 10FF for children and seniors).

Just outside the rectangular, clock-adorned south gate, Chemin des Fossés leads eastward to the Serein and a **riverside walk** around Noyers' 13th century walls.

Places to Stay & Eat The friendly, 10 room ***Hôtel de la Vieille Tour*** (☎ 03 86 82 87 69; fax 03 86 82 66 04), at Place du Grenier à Sel, is the perfect place for a truly relaxing break. It is open from Easter to sometime in early November (and for part of the winter – call for details). Doubles start at 180FF (250FF with shower and toilet). The best time to phone is between 8 and 10 am and after 5 pm.

At least one of the two ***groceries*** just inside the village's south gate is open daily except Sunday afternoon.

Getting There & Away When school is in session, Les Rapides de Bourgogne (☎ 03 86 34 00 00) has one bus a day on weekdays to/from Avallon (30FF; one hour).

ABBAYE DE FONTENAY

The Abbey of Fontenay (☎ 03 80 92 15 00), founded in 1118 and restored to its medieval glory over the past century, offers a glimpse of how the Cistercians used to live. Visits begin daily from 9 am to noon and 2 to 6 pm (5 pm from late September to late March). Entry costs 45FF (22FF for children and students). A taxi ride from the Montbard train station (on the line linking Paris' Gare de Lyon with Dijon), 6km to the west, should cost about 50FF one way.

The English Connection

Three archbishops of Canterbury played a role in the medieval history of Pontigny's abbey: Thomas à Becket spent the first three years of his exile here (1164-66); Stephen Langton, a refugee from political turmoil in England, lived here for six years (1207-13); and Edmund Rich, who fell ill and died at Soissy in 1240 while on his way to the Vatican, was brought here for burial.

AVALLON

• pop 9500 ✉ 89200 alt 250m

The once-strategic walled town of Avallon is set on a picturesque hilltop overlooking the Cousin River. The urban charms of the old city's medieval and Renaissance buildings are only a few hundred metres from the wooded slopes along the river and two of its tributaries. The town, very quiet from November to Easter, is at its liveliest during the popular Saturday morning market along Rue Mathé.

Avallon is a good base for visits to the northern section of the Parc Naturel Régional du Morvan, including Vézelay.

Orientation

The train station is 900m north of Place Vauban, which along with the contiguous Promenade des Terreaux, Place des Odebert and Rue Mathé, forms Avallon's main square. The walled old city, which begins just south of Place Vauban, is built on a roughly triangular, granite hilltop with

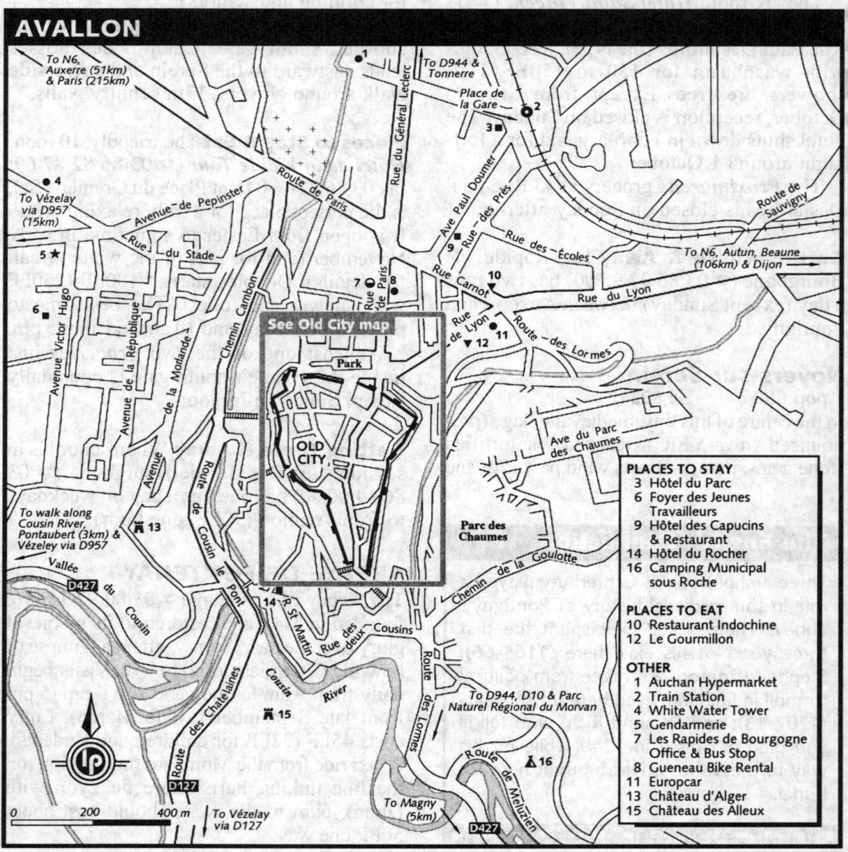

BURGUNDY

ravines to the east and west. The old city's main commercial thoroughfare is Grande Rue Aristide Briand.

Information

Tourist Office The mediocre tourist office (☎ 03 86 34 14 19; fax 03 86 34 28 29), in a 15th century house at 4 Rue Bocquillot, is open Monday to Saturday (daily from Easter to September) from 9.30 am to 12.30 pm and 2 to 6.30 pm; in July and August hours are 9.30 am to 7.30 pm. A free brochure in English gives details on a self-guided tour of the old city. Maps and topoguides on the Morvan region are also available.

Money Avallon's banks, several of which can be found on Place Vauban and along nearby Rue de Lyon, are open Tuesday to Saturday.

Post The post office at 9 Place des Odebert is open on weekdays from 8 am to noon and 1.30 to 6 pm and on Saturday until noon. Currency exchange is possible.

Bookshop Topoguides and maps of the Morvan are available at the Maison de la Presse at 19 Place Vauban (closed in the afternoon on Sundays and holidays and, except in summer, on Sunday morning).

Walking Tour

Construction of Avallon's fortifications, which tower over the lush, terraced slopes of two tiny tributaries of the Cousin River, was begun in the 9th century following devastating attacks on the town by Muslim armies from Moorish Spain (731) and the Normans (843). A walk around the walls, with their many 15th to 18th century towers and bastions, is a fine way to get a sense of the town's geography.

Intra-muros (literally, 'within the walls'), the main street – Grande Rue Aristide Briand and its continuation, Rue Bocquillot – passes by the city's most interesting sights, including **Tour de l'Horloge**, built in the mid-15th century. Medieval and Renaissance houses grace many side streets.

Soon after **Église Saint Lazare** was completed at the start of the 12th century, the huge numbers of pilgrims drawn here by a piece of the skull of St Lazarus (believed to provide protection from leprosy) rendered the structure inadequate, so in the mid-12th century the nave was made larger (though somewhat crooked) by moving the façade 20m to the west.

The church's two **portals** (a third was crushed when the north belfry collapsed in 1633) are magnificently decorated in the Burgundian Romanesque style. A sanctuary dedicated to St Mary was erected on this site in the 4th century; its crypt is under the choir.

Temporary expositions are held next door in **Église Saint Pierre** from about April to September and across the street in the 18th century **Grenier à Sel** (salt store) during July and August.

The **Musée de l'Avallonnais** (☎ 03 86 34 03 19) at Place de la Collégiale (behind the tourist office), founded in 1862, has a little bit of everything: minerals, fossils, armaments, popular religious art and paintings, including 58 expressionist sketches by Georges Rouault (1871-1958). From May to October it's open daily, except Tuesday, from 10 am to noon and 2 to 6 pm. Admission is 20FF (15FF for students; free for under 16s).

About 100 costumes from the 18th to 20th centuries are displayed in period tableaux at the **Musée du Costume** (☎ 03 86 34 19 95) at 6 Rue Belgrand. From Easter until 1 November, it is open daily from 10.30 am to 12.30 pm and 1.30 to 5.30 pm (a bit later in summer). The entrance fee of 25FF (15FF for students) includes an optional 45 minute guided tour (in French).

Hiking & Cycling

A lovely route for a walk or bike ride in the verdant **Vallée du Cousin** is the shaded, one-lane D427, which follows the gentle rapids of the Cousin River as it flows through dense forests and lush meadows. From the Hôtel du Rocher (see the main Avallon map), you can head either west towards Pontaubert (cross under the viaduct; 3km) and the D957 to Vézelay, or east towards Magny.

The tourist office has free but rudimentary hiking maps of the Vallée du Cousin and for an 8km, two hour tour of the old city walls and nearby bits of the countryside – ask for *Avallon Découverte*.

Places to Stay – Budget

Camping Set in the middle of a forest on the banks of the shallow Cousin River, the grassy and very attractive ***Camping Municipal sous Roche*** (☎/fax 03 86 34 10 39) 2km south-east of the old city (3km south of the train station) is open mid-March to mid-October. Charges are 18FF per adult, 13FF for a tent site and 13FF for parking.

Hostel The 150 room ***Foyer des Jeunes Travailleurs*** (☎ 03 86 34 01 88) at 10 Ave Victor Hugo, in an area of 1970s apartment blocks 2km south-west of the train station, accepts travellers whenever there's space, which is almost always (though call first). A dorm bed is 60FF; singles/doubles cost 78/120FF (73/110FF for the second and subsequent nights). Meals are available for 50FF; breakfast for 16 or 19FF. Reception is staffed 24 hours a day.

Hotels The 10 room ***Hôtel du Parc*** (☎ 03 86 34 17 00; fax 03 86 34 28 48), across the street from the train station, has ordinary but serviceable singles/doubles with washbasin for 115/130FF (no hall showers available). Doubles with shower start at 149FF. Reception is closed on Sunday.

The 14 room ***Hôtel du Rocher*** (☎ 03 86 34 19 03) at 11 Rue des Îles Labaume, in the Vallée du Cousin about 2.5km south-west of the train station (from Place des Odebert, take Rue de la Fontaine Neuve), is the best deal in town. Plain, old-fashioned, wood-panelled doubles/two-bed quads are just 100/150FF. One or two 2FF coins get you a shower. Reception is closed on Monday

AVALLON – OLD CITY

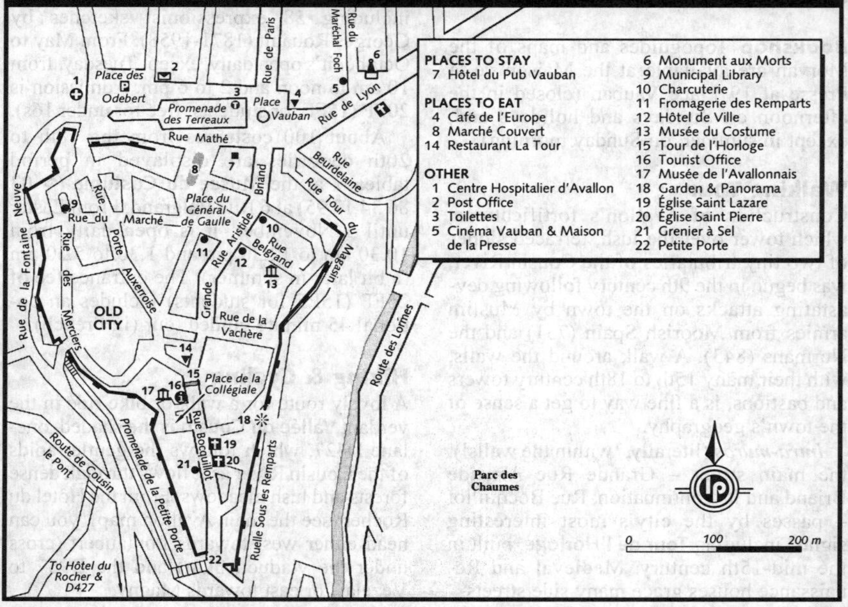

unless it's a holiday. The hotel closes from mid or late December to mid or late January.

Places to Stay – Mid-Range

The pleasant, eight room ***Hôtel des Capucins*** (☎ 03 86 34 06 52; fax 03 86 34 58 47) at 6 Ave Paul Doumer has modern, quiet doubles for 290FF. The owners prefer that guests take their dinner at the hotel's elegant restaurant. Reception is closed on Wednesday and, except from July to September, on Tuesday night. Free private parking is available. The five room ***Hôtel du Pub Vauban*** (☎ 03 86 34 02 20) at 3 Rue Mathé has nondescript but comfortable doubles with shower, toilet and TV for 220 to 260FF.

Places to Eat

Restaurants French and Burgundian dishes, including fish, are on offer at ***Le Gourmillon*** (☎ 03 86 31 62 01) at 8 Rue de Lyon, whose *menus* go for 79FF (not available on Sunday and holidays), 98, 132 and 156FF. Except from about May to September, it is closed on Sunday night and Monday. The rustically elegant restaurant attached to the ***Hôtel des Capucins*** (see Places to Stay) has French gastronomic and Burgundian *menus* for 85FF (weekday lunches only), 100, 137, 190 and 260FF. It is closed on Wednesday and, except from July to September, on Tuesday night; hours are noon to 2 pm and 7 to 9 pm.

Restaurant La Tour (☎ 03 86 34 24 84), next to the Tour de l'Horloge at 84 Grande Rue Aristide Briand, has pizzas (34 to 50FF), pasta (45 to 48FF) and sweet crêpes (17 to 30FF). It is open from 11.30 am to 2.30 pm and 7 to 10.30 pm (11 pm on Friday and Saturday). Except in July and August, it's closed on Sunday for lunch and on Monday. ***Restaurant Indochine*** (☎ 03 86 34 51 24) at 4 Rue Carnot serves Chinese and Vietnamese food daily, except for lunch on both Monday and Wednesday. The weekday lunch *menu* costs 58FF.

Self-Catering Good places for a picnic include the garden behind Église Saint Lazare, and on Promenade de la Petite Porte just outside the southern end of the old city.

On Saturday morning until 12.30 pm or so, the ***marché couvert*** (covered market) on Rue Mathé and nearby Place du Général de Gaulle fill with food stalls. Among the ***food shops*** at and near Place du Général de Gaulle is the ***charcuterie*** at 17 Grande Rue Aristide Briand, which has superb prepared dishes (closed Sunday afternoon and Monday). ***Fromagerie des Remparts*** at 3 Place du Général de Gaulle, open Tuesday to Saturday, also sells Burgundian specialities. Both are open from 8 or 9 am to 12.30 pm and 2.30 or 3 to 7 pm.

The vast ***Auchan*** hypermarket/mall on Rue du Général Leclerc is open Monday to Saturday from 8.30 am to 9 pm.

Entertainment

Except in July and August, ***Cinéma Vauban*** (☎ 03 86 34 22 87) at 1 Rue Maréchal Foch screens a nondubbed film each Wednesday at about 8 pm.

Getting There & Away

For information on getting to Vézelay, see the Vézelay section of this chapter.

Bus Transco bus No 49 (☎ 03 80 42 11 00 in Dijon), which connects Avallon's train station with Dijon (92.60FF; two hours; three a day, once on Sunday), is faster and cheaper than the train. Schedules may be available at the tourist office.

Les Rapides de Bourgogne (☎ 03 86 34 00 00), 39 Rue de Paris, is open from 8 am to noon (11.30 am on Saturday) and 3 to 6 pm (closed Saturday afternoon and Sunday). It has services to Noyers-sur-Serein (30FF; one hour; once a day on weekdays). Most buses stop at the company's office and the train station.

Train Three to five trains a day link Avallon's train station (☎ 03 86 34 01 01 or ☎ 08 36 35 35 35) with Auxerre (49FF; one hour) and Laroche-Migennes (61FF; 1½ hours), from where there are non-TGV connections to Paris' Gare de Lyon (148FF from

Avallon; three hours) and Dijon (90FF from Avallon; three or more hours). Les Rapides de Bourgogne operates two SNCF buses a day to Montbard (46FF), which is on the mainly-TGV line that connects Paris' Gare de Lyon (about 200 to 250FF by TGV from Avallon) with Dijon. There are infrequent trains/buses to Saulieu (41FF; one hour; four a day) and Autun (70FF; 1¾ hours; two a day, one on Sunday and holidays).

Car Europcar (☎ 03 86 34 39 36) is at 28 Rue de Lyon (closed weekends).

Getting Around

Gueneau (☎ 03 86 34 28 11) at 26 Rue de Paris rents mountain bikes for 40/80FF for a half-day/day. It is open from 8 am to noon and 2 to 7 pm (closed Sunday).

VÉZELAY

• pop 570 ✉ 89450 alt 285m

Despite the hordes of tourists who descend on Vézelay during the warm season, this tiny, fortified village is one of France's architectural gems. It is surrounded by some of the most beautiful countryside in Burgundy, a patchwork of vineyards, sunflower fields, hay and grazing sheep. Vézelay lies just within the Parc Naturel Régional du Morvan.

History

Vézelay's Benedictine monastery was established in the 9th century after an earlier monastery, at what is now the neighbouring village of Saint Père, had been ravaged by the Normans (Vikings). Thanks to the relics of St Mary Magdalene, to which great miracles were attributed, Vézelay became an important pilgrimage site in the 11th and 12th centuries; it also served as the starting point for one of the four pilgrimage routes to Saint Jacques de Compostelle (Santiago de Compostela) in Spain. In recent decades the Franciscans and the Fraternité Monastique de Jérusalem have brought monastic life (and pilgrims) back to the town.

Vézelay reached the height of its renown and power in the 12th century. St Bernard, leader of the Cistercian order, preached the Second Crusade here in the presence of King Louis VII (1146), and King Philip Augustus of France and King Richard the Lion-Heart of England met up here before setting out on the Third Crusade (1190). King Louis IX visited the town several times in the 13th century.

Orientation

Place du Champ-de-Foire (essentially a parking lot) is linked to the basilica at the top of the hill by touristy Rue Saint Étienne and its continuation, Rue Saint Pierre. The village's half-dozen streets are lined with picturesque old houses.

Information

The tourist office (☎ 03 86 33 23 69; fax 03 86 33 34 00), at the top of Rue Saint Pierre, is open from 10 am to 1 pm and 2 to 6 pm (closed on Thursday except from mid-June to October).

The post office on Rue Saint Étienne, which has an automatic teller machine around the side (through the square arch), is open on weekdays from 9 am to noon and 2 to 5 pm, and on Saturday from 8.45 to 11.45 am. It also has an exchange service, and the tourist office also changes money.

Basilique Sainte Madeleine

Vézelay's basilica (☎ 03 86 33 26 73 for the secretariat), founded in the 880s, was completely rebuilt between the 11th and 13th centuries. Later trashed by the Huguenots (1569), desecrated during the Revolution and, to top off the human ravages, repeatedly struck by lightning, it was, by the mid-1800s, on the point of collapse. In 1840, the restoration architect Viollet-le-Duc undertook the daunting task of rescuing the structure. His work, which included reconstructing significant parts of the building (eg the west façade and its doorways), helped Vézelay – previously a ghost town – spring back to life.

Basilique Sainte Madeleine houses what, during the Middle Ages, were believed to be the relics of St Mary Magdalene. During the 11th and 12th centuries, when this was an abbey church affiliated with Cluny, huge numbers of pilgrims came to Vézelay to celebrate her feast day, 22 July, a tradition that has been revived in recent years. In 1120, during the annual pilgrimage, the nave caught fire and over a thousand pilgrims perished.

On the 12th century **tympanum**, located between the mid-12th century narthex (the portico along the west end of the basilica) and the nave, superb Burgundian-style Romanesque carvings show Jesus seated on a throne in the almond-shaped panel in the middle, radiating his holy spirit to the Apostles. His hands are outstretched to welcome all the known peoples of the earth, including Arabs, Armenians, Jews, Byzantines, Cappadocians (Turks) and Ethiopians, represented by the figures on the eight panels above the Apostles. The fantastic figures on the lintels, representing pagan peoples marching towards Jesus and the True Faith, are endowed with all sorts of bizarre features such as grotesquely large ears or the heads of dogs. On the recessed arch enclos-

VÉZELAY

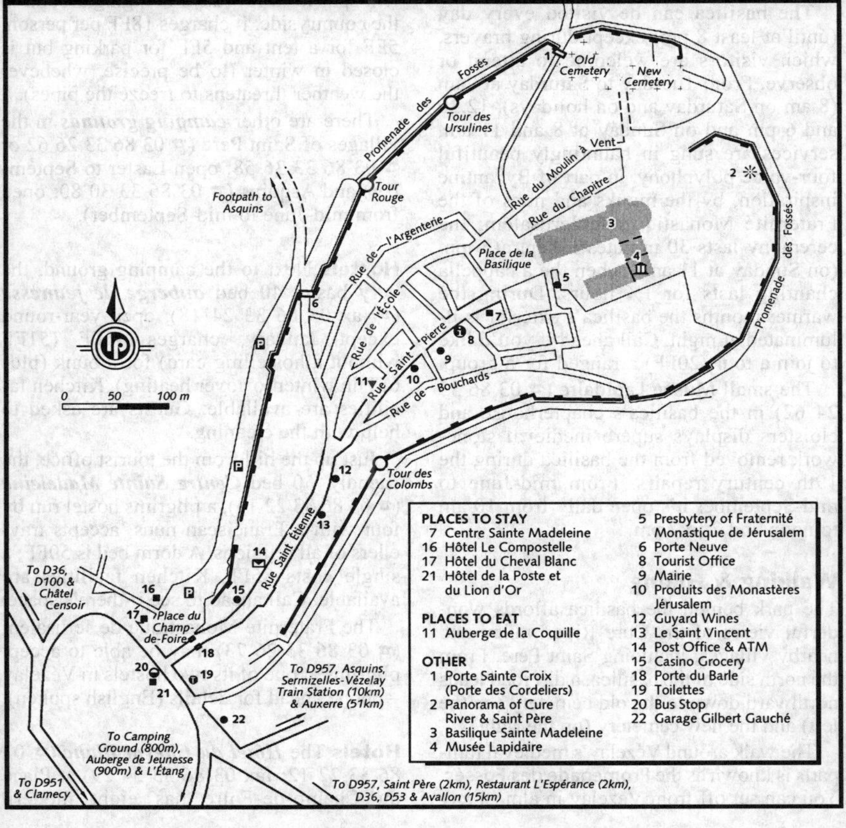

ing the whole scene, the signs of the zodiac alternate with medallions depicting the labours of each month.

The basilica's interior is a study in comparative architecture. The Romanesque **nave**, rebuilt using stone of various shades in the decade and a half following the great fire of 1120, is endowed with round arches and very small windows, features typical of the Romanesque style. The transept and choir (1185) have ogival arches and much larger windows, two of the hallmarks of Gothic architecture. The two rows of columns in the nave are topped by **sculpted capitals**. There's a mid-12th century **crypt** under the transept crossing.

The basilica can be visited every day (until at least 8 pm) except during prayers, which visitors are welcome to attend or observe. From Tuesday to Saturday at 7am (8 am on Saturday and on holidays), 12.30 and 6 pm and on Sunday at 8 and 11 am, services are sung in hauntingly beautiful four-voice polyphony, in part of Byzantine inspiration, by the monks and nuns of the Fraternité Monastique de Jérusalem; the ceremony lasts 30 minutes except at 6 pm (on Sunday at 11 am), when the a cappella chanting lasts for 1¼ hours. During the warmer months the basilica's exterior is illuminated at night. Call ahead if you'd like to join a tour (20FF) arranged for a group.

The small **Musée Lapidaire** (☎ 03 86 33 24 62) in the basilica's chapterhouse and cloisters displays superb medieval stonework removed from the basilica during the 19th century repairs. From mid-June to mid-September it's open daily from 10 am to noon and 2 to 7 pm.

Walking & Hiking

The park behind the basilica affords wonderful views of the Cure River valley and nearby villages, including Saint Père. From the north side of the basilica, a dirt road leads northward down to the old cemetery (on the left) and the new cemetery (on the right).

The walk around Vézelay's medieval ramparts is known as the **Promenade des Fossés**. You can set off from Vézelay in almost any direction and find yourself, almost instantly, far from the madding crowd – and in the midst of the gorgeous countryside of the Morvan. A footpath links the Promenade des Fossés with the village of Asquins, from where trails lead to the Cure River.

The tourist office sells brochures on mountain bike and walking trails around Vézelay.

Places to Stay

Camping The ***camping ground*** (☎/fax 03 86 33 24 18), on a grassy hillside 900m south-west of Place du Champ-de-Foire along the road towards L'Étang, is an excellent spot for a few days lounging around in the countryside. It charges 18FF per person, 5FF for a tent and 5FF for parking but is closed in winter (to be precise, whenever the weather threatens to freeze the pipes).

There are other ***camping grounds*** in the villages of Saint Père (☎ 03 86 33 26 62 or ☎ 03 86 33 36 58; open Easter to September) and Asquins (☎ 03 86 33 30 80; open from mid-June to mid-September).

Hostels Next to the camping ground, the very basic, 40 bed ***auberge de jeunesse*** (☎/fax 03 86 33 24 18), open year-round except January, charges 45FF (51FF without a hostelling card) for a bunk (plus 6FF in winter to cover heating). Kitchen facilities are available. Guests are asked to help with the cleaning.

Just up the hill from the tourist office, the friendly, 50 bed ***Centre Sainte Madeleine*** (☎ 03 86 33 22 14), a pilgrims hostel run by four with-it Franciscan nuns, accepts travellers of all religions. A dorm bed is 50FF; a single costs 85FF. Kitchen facilities are available. Call ahead to see if there's space.

The Fraternité Monastique de Jérusalem (☎ 03 86 33 26 73) may be able to accept pilgrims at one of its two hostels in Vézelay – phone ahead for details (English spoken).

Hotels The ***Hôtel du Cheval Blanc*** (☎ 03 86 33 22 12; fax 03 86 33 34 29) at Place du Champ-de-Foire has eight modern rooms for 190 to 300FF. It is closed from late November to mid-February.

The two star, 18 room ***Hôtel Le Compostelle*** (☎ 03 86 33 28 63; fax 03 86 33 34 34) at 1 Place du Champ-de-Foire has modern, spotless doubles and triples from 270 and 370FF, quads from 400FF; the pricier rooms have a more inspiring view. This place is closed for a few weeks in January. The three star ***Hôtel de la Poste et du Lion d'Or*** (☎ 03 86 33 21 23; fax 03 86 32 30 92), also on Place du Champ-de-Foire and open from late March to early November, has attractive doubles for 320 to 600FF.

The luxury hotel attached to ***Restaurant L'Espérance*** (see Places to Eat) in Saint Père has rooms for 600 to 2500FF. Reserve two weeks ahead (a month ahead for Saturday nights).

Places to Eat

Restaurants The restaurants along Rue Saint Pierre include ***Auberge de la Coquille*** (☎ 03 86 33 35 57) at No 81, which serves traditional French cuisine as well as crêpes; *menus* cost 45 to 109FF. It is open daily from mid-February to 11 November and, the rest of the year, on weekends and during school holidays. Most of the hotels around Place du Champ-de-Foire have restaurants.

Restaurant L'Espérance (☎ 03 86 33 39 10; fax 03 86 33 26 15) in Saint Père-sous-Vézelay, 3km towards Avallon from Vézelay along the D957, is one of only about 20 restaurants in France that have been awarded three stars by Michelin. French gastronomic *menus* range from 490 to 860FF. Dinner reservations should be made at least a week in advance (a month in advance for Saturday). It is closed on Tuesday and on Wednesday for lunch.

Self-Catering The *Casino* grocery on Rue Saint Étienne is open until 7 pm (closed from 12.30 to 4 pm and in the afternoon on Monday, Wednesday and Sunday). In summer it's open daily, without a midday break, until 8 or 8.30 pm.

Shopping

Vézelay's wines (mainly whites), produced only since the mid-1970s, can be sampled and purchased at Guyard (☎ 03 86 33 33 29) at 32 Rue Saint Étienne, whose panoramic back patio looks out on the winery's grape vines. The wine is not only aged but also pressed in the 11th century cellars under the shop, which can be visited.

Burgundy-made jams, *pains d'épices* (spice breads), mustards, vinegar, terrines etc are sold at Le Saint Vincent (☎ 03 86 33 27 79), 28 Rue Saint Étienne (open daily from a week before Easter until 11 November). Food items made by monks are sold at Produits des Monastères Jérusalem (☎ 03 86 33 37 43) at 78 Rue Saint Pierre (closed on Monday except in July and August).

There are several art galleries along Rue Saint Pierre. A number of potters have studios in Vézelay, Saint Père and nearby villages – look for signs reading '*potier*'.

Getting There & Away

Vézelay is 15km from Avallon (19km if you take the gorgeous D427 to Pontaubert) and 51km from Auxerre. All parking in Vézelay is metered.

Bus & Train From June to late September, one SNCF bus a day, on the run from Montbard, links Avallon's train station with Vézelay (22FF; 20 minutes); departures are at 5.20 pm from Avallon and 9.45 am (10.50 am on weekends) from Vézelay (the stop is in front of the Hôtel de la Poste et du Lion d'Or). For details, contact the SNCF in Avallon (☎ 03 86 34 01 01).

The Sermizelles-Vézelay train station (☎ 03 86 33 41 78; 15FF from Avallon), about 10km north of Vézelay, is on the rail line linking Laroche-Migennes (on the Paris-Dijon line) with Auxerre and Avallon (three to five trains a day). On weekdays (except holidays), buses run by Cars de la Madeleine (☎ 03 86 33 35 95) link Vézelay with the train station, departing from Sermizelles-Vézelay at 10 am and from Vézelay at 9.30 am. In July and August, there's a second round trip at around 3 pm.

Taxi To order a taxi (eg for travel to/from the Sermizelles-Vézelay train station), call ☎ 03 86 32 31 88 or ☎ 03 86 33 24 45.

Getting Around

Garage Gilbert Gauché (☎ 03 86 33 30 17), at the entrance to Vézelay's old city, rents mountain bikes for 120FF a day (60 to 80FF a half-day). Hours are 8 am (9.30 am on Sunday) to 12.30 pm and 2.15 to 8 or 8.30 pm (7 or 7.30 pm on Sunday); closed on Monday except in July and August. In winter call ahead.

If riding to/from Avallon, it's a good idea to avoid the heavy traffic on the D957. The less direct (and somewhat hilly) D53 and the D36 (via Island and Menades) are much quieter and more scenic.

PARC NATUREL RÉGIONAL DU MORVAN

The 1750 sq km Parc Naturel Régional du Morvan (Morvan Regional Park), a sparsely populated granite plateau bounded by Vézelay, Avallon, Saulieu, Autun and Château Chinon, includes 700 sq km of dense woodland, 13 sq km of lakes and lots of rolling farmland subdivided by hedgerows, stone walls and stands of trees: beech, hornbeam, oak and, at higher elevations, conifers. Many of the area's 30,000 residents earn a living from such traditional pursuits as farming, ranching, logging and even growing Christmas trees, though the time when the impoverished Morvan (the name, of Celtic origin, means 'Black Mountain') supplied wet nurses to rich Parisians and took in the capital's orphans has long passed.

Maps & Topoguides

Useful maps with English keys include the *Carte de Randonnées Morvan* (53FF), a 1:50,000 scale map in IGN's Culture & Environment series which is absolutely perfect for hiking, cycling and horse riding; and IGN No 306 (*Parc Naturel Régional du Morvan*), a 1:100,000 scale map that indicates trails (the GR13, the Tour du Morvan, local walking paths), gîtes d'étape, B&Bs and sites of interest to tourists. Over a dozen 1:25,000 scale IGN Série Bleue maps (46FF) are also available.

French-language topoguides include *Tour du Morvan – Les Grands Lacs* (No 032; 72FF) in the GR Pays series, and *Traversée du Morvan* (No 111; 80FF), which covers the GR13.

For cycling, you can't beat *Le Morvan en Vélo Tout Terrain* (40FF), a packet of colour-coded map sheets detailing 1400km of marked itineraries.

Activities

The Parc du Morvan offers hiking, mountain biking, canoeing (on the Chalaux, Cousin, Cure and Yonne rivers), rafting, horse riding, fishing and, on the lakes, water sports.

Saulieu

• pop 2900 ✉ 21210 alt 535m

The village of Saulieu is not only an excellent base for a visit to the Morvan region, it's also a renowned gastronomic centre. Once an overnight stop on the Paris-Lyon coach road, the town learned centuries ago to cater to visitors with high culinary expectations.

Orientation The N6 is known as Rue d'Argentine as it passes through town. From the Auberge du Relais at 8 Rue d'Argentine, the tourist office is 100m north, the basilica is 200m up the hill (south-west) and the train station is 400m down the hill (north-east).

Information The well equipped Maison du Tourisme (☎ 03 80 64 00 21; fax 03 80 64 21 96) at 24 Rue d'Argentine can supply you with all relevant information on the Parc du Morvan and can help with reservations for gîtes d'étape, B&Bs etc. It is open Tuesday to Saturday from 9.30 am to noon and 2 to 6 pm and, from Easter to October, on Sunday and holidays from 10 am to noon. In July and August, hours are 9.30 am to 7 pm (10 am to noon and 2 to 5 pm on Sunday).

Things to See The Burgundian Romanesque **Basilique Saint Andoche**, 200m west of the N6, is known for its 60 vividly sculpted capitals illustrating Biblical stories, fauna and flora. Next door, the well conceived **Musée François Pompon** (☎ 03 80 64 19 51) at 3 Rue du Docteur Roclore displays Gallo-Roman steles, medieval statuary and sleek sculptures by the noted animal sculptor François Pompon (1855-1933). It is open daily, except Tuesday, from 10 am to 12.30 pm and 2 to 5.30 pm (5 pm on Sunday and holidays; 6 pm from April to September). Admission is 20FF (15FF for under 16s).

Places to Stay The 16 room ***Hôtel de la Tour d'Auxois*** (☎/fax 03 80 64 13 30), on Rue d'Argentine across from No 8, has doubles from 140FF (170FF with shower).

Places to Eat Most of Saulieu's restaurants are open seven days a week.

The ***Auberge du Relais*** (☎ 03 80 64 13 16) at 8 Rue d'Argentine serves gastronomic and Burgundian *menus* for 60FF (children only), 100, 128 and 158FF. It is open daily from noon to 2.30 pm and 7 to about 9.30 pm (10 pm in summer). The restaurant of ***Hôtel de la Tour d'Auxois*** (see Places to Stay) has French and Burgundian *menus* for 65 to 190FF.

Restaurant Bernard Loiseau-La Côte d'Or (☎ 03 80 90 53 53; fax 03 80 64 08 92; loiseau@relaischateaux.fr; www.integra.fr/relaischateaux/loiseau) at 2 Rue d'Argentine, proud bearer of three Michelin stars, offers *menus* of fine country cuisine for 490FF (weekday lunches only), 650FF (except Saturday night) and 920FF (for the *menu dégustation*). It is open daily from noon to 2.30 pm and 7 to 10 pm. Reservations are necessary on holidays, for Sunday lunch and for dinner on Friday and Saturday.

There's an ***Atac*** supermarket 300m down Rue Jean Bertin (the D26) from Restaurant Bernard Loiseau-La Côte d'Or. It is open from Monday to Saturday from 8.45 am to 12.15 pm and 2.45 to 7 pm.

Getting There & Away SNCF buses link Saulieu's train station with the Montbard train station (on the Paris-Dijon line; 50 minutes) three times a day (twice a day on Sunday and holidays). Another SNCF line, served mostly by buses, links Saulieu with Autun (43FF; one hour) and Avallon (41FF; one hour) four times a day. Hours are posted inside the terminal building.

Saint Brisson

The Parc Régional's *maison du parc* (headquarters and visitors centre; ☎ 03 86 78 79 00; fax 03 86 78 74 22), 14km west of Saulieu in Saint Brisson, is surrounded by rolling hills, forests and small lakes. Topoguides, maps and a wide range of hiking brochures are available year-round, either in the building marked *administration* (open weekdays from 8.45 am to 12.15 pm and 1.30 to 5.30 pm; 5 pm on Friday) or, from Easter to 11 November, nearby at the Point d'Information, which is open daily from 10.15 am to 6 pm). Half a dozen trails pass by here.

The **Musée de la Résistance en Morvan** (☎ 03 86 78 72 99), which chronicles the heroism that made the Morvan a Résistance stronghold during WWII, is open from early June to mid-September from 10 am to noon and 2 to 6 pm (closed on Friday). Admission is 25FF (5FF for children). The **Herbularium**, a garden of 160 local plant species (many of them with medicinal properties), is open year-round.

Château Chinon

This rather ordinary village, best known for having had François Mitterand as its mayor from 1959 to 1981, makes a good base for exploring the Morvan.

Orientation Hôtel Le Vieux Morvan is 200m up the hill from the fountain roundabout on the D978; the tourist office is 200m farther up the slope. The two museums are 300m up the main street from the tourist office.

Information The tourist office (☎/fax 03 86 85 06 58), in the Maison du Morvan at 2 Place Saint Christophe, has a good supply of brochures, maps and topoguides. When school is in session it's open in the afternoon, except on Wednesday and Sunday; during the rest of the year, it's open daily, except on Sunday afternoon.

Things to See The **Musée du Septennat** (☎ 03 86 85 19 23) at 6 Rue du Château displays all sorts of official gifts presented to Mitterand during his two *septennats* (seven-year terms as President of France). It's open from Easter to December (closed on Tuesday except in July and August). Admission is 26FF (13FF for children and students). A ticket also valid for the **Musée du Costume** (☎ 03 86 85 18 55) next door costs 40FF (20FF reduced price).

You can get a 360° view of Château Chinon and its environs from the summit of the hill that overlooks the town's steep rooftops from the north. To get there, go up the residents-only road opposite the Musée du Septennat for 250m – just follow the signs to the *table d'orientation* (viewpoint indicator).

Places to Stay Mitterand used to keep a room at the two star ***Hôtel Le Vieux Morvan*** (☎ 03 86 85 05 01; fax 03 86 85 02 78) at 8 Place Gudin, where doubles start at 260FF. It is closed from 20 December to late January. The ***Hôtel Lion d'Or*** (☎ 03 86 85 13 56) has two entrances: one is through the arch from the fountain roundabout, the other is at 10 Rue des Fossés, on the other side of the fat, round tower from the roundabout. Doubles start at 150FF (200FF with shower and toilet). Reception is closed on Sunday after 5 pm and on Monday.

Places to Eat The restaurant in the ***Hôtel Le Vieux Morvan*** (see Places to Stay), open daily, has *menus* for 65FF (for children), 95FF (not available on Saturday night, Sunday or holidays), 120, 150 and 200FF.

The ***Casino*** grocery at 32 Blvd de la République, on the other side of the small fountain from the Hôtel Le Vieux Morvan, is open until 7.30 pm (closed from 12.30 to 3 pm, on Sunday afternoon and, except in July and August, on Wednesday afternoon). The ***Maximarché*** supermarket, 200m towards Autun from the fountain roundabout, is open Monday to Saturday.

Getting There & Away RSL (☎ 03 85 52 30 02) has a daily bus (except Sunday) from Autun to Château Chinon (35.50FF; one hour) via Roussillon-en-Morvan and Arleuf.

Maquis Bernard Résistance Cemetery

Seven RAF airmen – the crew of a bomber shot down near here in 1944 – and 21 *résistants* are buried in this neatly tended *cimetière Franco-Anglais* (Franco-English cemetery), deep in a dense forest in which a battalion of British paratroops operated jointly with Free French forces. The nearby **drop zone** is marked with bilingual signs.

The cemetery, near the tiny hamlet of Savelot, is about 8km south-west of Montsauche-les-Settons (along the D977) and 5.6km east of Oroux-en-Morvan (along the D12). From the D977bis, go 2.8km along the one-lane dirt road to Savelot.

AUTUN

• pop 17,900 ✉ 71400 alt 326m

Autun, a tidy, attractive town 85km south-west of Dijon, is set on a low rise nestled between tree-covered hills (to the south-east) and farmland (to the north). Today, it is a quiet subprefecture, but in the early centuries AD it was one of the most important cities in Roman Gaul. Then known as Augustodunum (in honour of the Roman Emperor Augustus, who founded the city around 10 BC), its 6km of ramparts were topped by 54 towers and pierced by four gates. The city also had all the usual infrastructure typical of a Roman metropolis: two theatres, an amphitheatre, a system of aqueducts, a circus etc. Autun was repeatedly sacked by Barbarian tribes beginning in 269 AD, but its fortunes revived in the Middle Ages, when an impressive cathedral was erected. Many of the buildings in the city centre date from the 17th and 18th centuries.

Autun is a good base for exploring the southern part of the Parc Naturel Régional du Morvan.

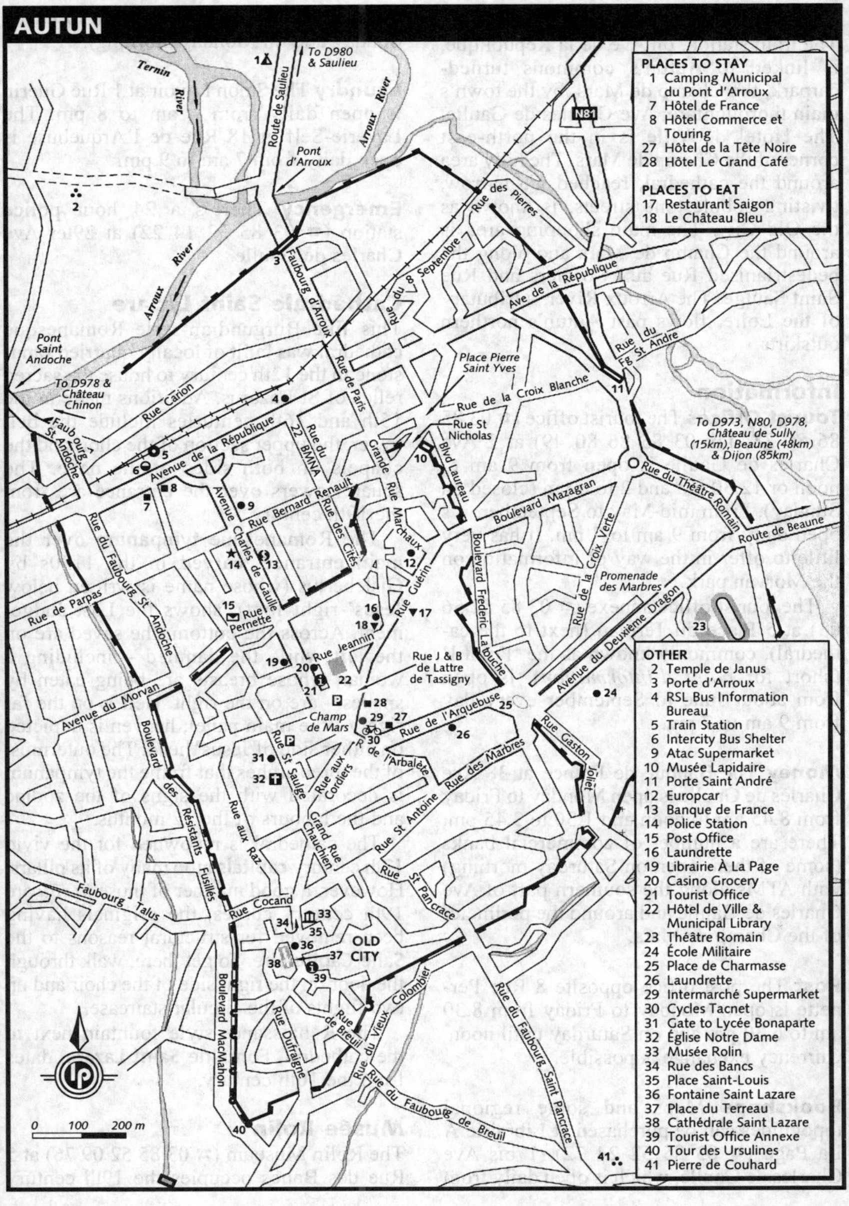
AUTUN
PLACES TO STAY
1 Camping Municipal du Pont d'Arroux
7 Hôtel de France
8 Hôtel Commerce et Touring
27 Hôtel de la Tête Noire
28 Hôtel Le Grand Café
PLACES TO EAT
17 Restaurant Saigon
18 Le Château Bleu
OTHER
2 Temple de Janus
3 Porte d'Arroux
4 RSL Bus Information Bureau
5 Train Station
6 Intercity Bus Shelter
9 Atac Supermarket
10 Musée Lapidaire
11 Porte Saint André
12 Europcar
13 Banque de France
14 Police Station
15 Post Office
16 Laundrette
19 Librairie À La Page
20 Casino Grocery
21 Tourist Office
22 Hôtel de Ville & Municipal Library
23 Théâtre Romain
24 École Militaire
25 Place de Charmasse
26 Laundrette
29 Intermarché Supermarket
30 Cycles Tacnet
31 Gate to Lycée Bonaparte
32 Église Notre Dame
33 Musée Rolin
34 Rue des Bancs
35 Place Saint-Louis
36 Fontaine Saint Lazare
37 Place du Terreau
38 Cathédrale Saint Lazare
39 Tourist Office Annexe
40 Tour des Ursulines
41 Pierre de Couhard
To D980 & Saulieu
To D978 & Château Chinon
To D973, N80, D978, Château de Sully (15km), Beaune (48km) & Dijon (85km)
N81
Ternin River
Arroux River
Pont d'Arroux
Pont Saint Andoche
Place Pierre Saint Yves
Champ de Mars
Promenade des Marbres
OLD CITY
Route de Saulieu
Faubourg d'Arroux
Rue du 8 Septembre
Rue des Pierres
Ave de la République
Rue du Fg St Andre
Rue de la Croix Blanche
Rue St Nicholas
Blvd Laureau
Rue du Théâtre Romain
Route de Beaune
Boulevard Mazagran
Boulevard Frederic Latouche
Rue de la Croix Verte
Avenue du Deuxième Dragon
Rue Carion
Rue de Paris
Avenue de la République
Faubourg St Andoche
Rue du 22 BMNA
Avenue Charles de Gaulle
Rue Bernard Renault
Rue des Cités
Grande Rue Marchaux
Rue Guérin
Rue du Faubourg St Andoche
Rue de Parpas
Rue Pernette
Rue Jeannin
Rue J & B de Lattre de Tassigny
Avenue du Morvan
Boulevard des Résistants Fusillés
Rue aux Raz
Rue St Saulge
Rue aux Cordiers
Grand Rue Chauchien
Rue de l'Arquebuse
Rue de l'Arbalète
Rue des Marbres
Rue St Antoine
Rue Gaston Joliet
Rue St Pancrace
Rue Cocand
Faubourg Talus
Boulevard MacMahon
Rue Dufraigne
Rue de Breuil
Rue du Vieux Colombier
Rue du Faubourg de Breuil
Rue du Faubourg Saint Pancrace
0 100 200 m

BURGUNDY

Orientation

The train station, on Ave de la République, is linked to Autun's commons turned-carpark, the Champ de Mars, by the town's main thoroughfare, Ave Charles de Gaulle. The Hôtel de Ville is in the north-east corner of the Champ de Mars. The hilly area around the cathedral, reached via narrow, twisting cobblestone streets, is known as the Old City. The main shopping area is around the Champ de Mars and along the pedestrianised Rue aux Cordiers and Rue Saint Saulge. The Arroux River, a tributary of the Loire, flows past Autun's northern outskirts.

Information

Tourist Offices The tourist office (☎ 03 85 86 80 38; fax 03 85 86 80 49) at 2 Ave Charles de Gaulle is open from 9 am to noon or 12.30 pm and 2 to 6 pm (closed on Sunday). From mid-May to September, it's open daily from 9 am to 7 pm. It has very little to offer in the way of information on the Morvan park.

The tourist office annexe (☎ 03 85 52 56 03) at 5 Place du Terreau (next to the cathedral), commonly known as the 'Point I' (short for *point d'information*), is open from about June to September every day from 9 am to 7 pm.

Money The Banque de France at 38 Ave Charles de Gaulle is open Monday to Friday from 8.45 am to noon and 1.30 to 3.45 pm. There are a number of commercial banks (some of them open on Saturday morning) with ATMs along the southern part of Ave Charles de Gaulle and around the perimeter of the Champ de Mars.

Post The post office opposite 8 Rue Pernette is open Monday to Friday from 8.30 am to 6.30 pm and on Saturday until noon. Currency exchange is possible.

Bookshops Maps and some regional topoguides can be purchased at Librairie À La Page (☎ 03 85 52 24 72), 17bis Ave Charles de Gaulle, which is open daily from 9 am to noon and 2 to 7 pm (closed on Sunday and on Monday morning).

Laundry The Salon Lavoir at 1 Rue Guérin is open daily from 6 am to 8 pm. The Laverie-Self at 18 Rue de l'Arquebuse is open daily from 7 am to 9 pm.

Emergency There's a 24 hour police station (☎ 03 85 52 14 22) at 29ter Ave Charles de Gaulle.

Cathédrale Saint Lazare

This fine Burgundian-style Romanesque cathedral was built of locally quarried sandstone in the 12th century to house the sacred relics of St Lazarus. Additions made in the 15th and 16th centuries include the bell tower, the upper section of the choir and the chapels on both sides of the nave. The square towers over the entrance are from the 19th century.

The Romanesque **tympanum** over the main entrance, carved in the 1130s by Gislebertus (whose name is written below Jesus' right foot), shows the Last Judgement. Across the bottom, the saved are on the left while the damned – including a woman whose breasts are being eaten by snakes – are on the right. Hell is on the far right of the main panel; heaven is depicted on either side of Jesus' head. The outermost of the three arches that frame the tympanum is decorated with the signs of the zodiac and the labours of the 12 months.

The cathedral is renowned for the vivid 12th century **capitals** atop many of its pillars. However, a good number of those *in situ* are 19th century copies, the originals having been removed for structural reasons to the **Salle Capitulaire**. To get there, walk through the door on the right side of the choir and up two flights of the circular staircase.

The Renaissance-style fountain next to the cathedral, **Fontaine Saint Lazare**, dates from the 16th century.

Musée Rolin

The Rolin Museum (☎ 03 85 52 09 76) at 5 Rue des Bancs occupies the 19th century

Hôtel Lacomme and, across the courtyard, the 15th century Hôtel Rolin, once the home of Nicolas Rolin, chancellor to the duke of Burgundy and founder of Beaune's Hôtel-Dieu. Displays include Gallo-Roman artefacts of local provenance, 12th century Romanesque sculptures and a well known collection of 15th and 16th century French and Flemish works, many of them created in Autun. It is open from 9.30 or 10 am to noon and 2 pm to sometime between 4 pm (in winter) and 6 pm (April to September); closed on Tuesday and, from 12 November to March, on Monday. Admission is 20FF (10FF for students).

Musée Lapidaire

The Lapidary Museum (☎ 03 85 52 35 71) at 10 Rue Saint Nicolas, whose Gallo-Roman statuary is displayed in a delightful flower garden, is open in July and August (closed Tuesday; entry is free).

Roman Gates

Built during the reign of Constantine, **Porte d'Arroux**, one of Augustodunum's four gates, is particularly well preserved. Constructed without mortar, it has four arches (two large ones for vehicular traffic and two smaller ones for pedestrians) that are still used for their original purposes. From the river side of the gate, you can see, above the arches, fluted pilasters topped with delicate Corinthian capitals. The two pyramid-shaped hills visible to the north of town are mine tailings.

The **Porte Saint André** dating from the 1st century is similar in design to Porte d'Arroux.

Théâtre Romain

Autun's Roman Theatre, designed to hold some 16,000 people, was once the largest theatre in Roman Gaul. It was severely damaged in the Middle Ages (much of its stone was hauled off for new buildings), but 19th century restorations make it possible to imagine how the theatre must have looked when filled with cheering spectators. Today, it is used for concerts.

From the top of the theatre, you can see on the forested hillside to the south-west the **Pierre de Couhard** (Rock of Couhard), the 27m-high remains of a Gallo-Roman pyramid that was probably either a tomb or a cenotaph.

Temple de Janus

Long associated (incorrectly) with the Roman god Janus, this massive 24m high square tower, only two of whose walls are extant, seems to have been built in the 1st century AD for worship according to the Celtic tradition of the Gauls. The interior was once painted in vermilion. The temple, open all the time, is in the middle of farmland 800m north of the train station – to get there, you can either take the path along the north bank of the Arroux River from Pont d'Arroux or head north from Pont Saint Andoche.

Short Walks

For a stroll along the exterior of the tower-topped and crenellated city walls, parts of which date from Roman times but most of whose upper sections are late medieval, walk from Ave du Morvan (three blocks west of Ave Charles de Gaulle) south to the 12th century **Tour des Ursulines** (the statue-topped tower at the city's southern tip); then turn north-eastward.

From the walled city's southern edge, you can take Rue du Faubourg Saint Pancrace into the countryside and out to the Pierre de Couhard.

Organised Tours

From July to mid-September every day at 3 pm, the tourist office runs two-hour walking tours (30FF) of the Old City and the cathedral (in French and, if the guide is able, in English). A different itinerary is followed each day. In July and August, the tourist office also organises four-hour bicycle tours (70FF, including bike rental) on Tuesday, Thursday and Saturday.

Special Events

The Musique en Morvan festival, which brings concerts (especially choral ones) to

Autun and other places in the Morvan area, is held for 10 days during the latter half of July.

Autun's Gallo-Roman past is re-enacted by 300 local residents on three weekends (Friday and Saturday nights) in August, in a night-time spectacle known as Il Était une Fois Augustodunum (Once Upon a Time in Augustodunum). Tickets cost 70FF (40FF for children aged six to 12). Information on both events is available from the tourist office.

Places to Stay

Autun has a fair number of inexpensive accommodation options.

Camping ***Camping Municipal du Pont d'Arroux*** (☎ 03 85 52 10 82) on Route de Saulieu, which occupies a shady and beautiful (though densely packed) spot on the Ternin River, is open from a week before Easter to October. Fees are 13.50FF per adult, 13FF for a tent site and 8.50FF for parking; there may be a surcharge in July and August.

Hotels Opposite the train station, the tidy, two star, 20 room ***Hôtel Commerce et Touring*** (☎ 03 85 52 17 90; fax 03 85 52 37 63) at 20 Ave de la République has unsurprising doubles from 145FF (185FF with shower). Doubles/triples with shower and toilet are 195/230FF. Free enclosed parking is available. This establishment is closed in December. The 26 room ***Hôtel de France*** (☎ 03 85 52 14 00; ☎ 03 85 86 14 52) at 18 Ave de la République has pleasant, soundproofed doubles with shower and toilet from 220FF; doubles with washbasin and bidet start at 130FF.

The attractive, 27 room ***Hôtel de la Tête Noire*** (☎ 03 85 86 59 99; fax 03 85 86 33 90), a two star, lift-equipped place at 3 Rue de l'Arquebuse, has comfortable, newly renovated rooms with shower and toilet for 260 to 285FF. You might also try the nine room ***Hôtel Le Grand Café*** (☎ 03 85 52 27 66), on the Champ de Mars at 19 Rue J & B de Lattre de Tassigny. Doubles with shower cost 170FF (235FF with bath and toilet). Reception (at the bar) is closed on Sunday and holidays.

Places to Eat

Restaurants For Burgundian and creative French cuisine, ***Le Château Bleu*** (☎ 03 85 86 27 30) at 3 Rue Jeannin, open daily except Monday evening and Tuesday, is an excellent choice. The *menus* cost 85FF (not available on Saturday night, Sunday or holidays), 130, 175, 195 and 245FF. Bookings are a good idea for Sunday lunch and on holidays. For details on the ***Hôtel de la Tête Noire***, where traditional French *menus* cost 79 to 160FF, and the ***Hôtel Commerce et Touring***, whose Burgundian and French *menus* cost 62, 85 and 140FF, see Places to Stay.

Restaurant Saigon (☎ 03 85 86 37 95) at 12 Rue Guérin serves authentic Vietnamese cuisine daily, except on Monday for lunch. The *menus* cost 60FF (weekday lunches only), 100 and 130FF.

Self-Catering The street level of the Hôtel de Ville building and the surrounding square is brought to life by a ***food market*** on Wednesday and Friday mornings (until noon or 12.30 pm).

The bakery-equipped ***Intermarché*** supermarket at 21 Rue J & B de Lattre de Tassigny is open Monday to Saturday from 8.30 am to 7.30 pm (closed from 12.30 to 2.30 pm on Monday and Tuesday). North of the Champ de Mars, there are a number of ***food shops*** along Rue Guérin and the perpendicular Grande Rue Marchaux.

On Ave Charles de Gaulle, you'll find a ***Casino*** grocery at No 6 (open Tuesday to Sunday) and an ***Atac*** supermarket opposite No 35 (open Monday to Saturday), both open until 7 pm but closed for lunch.

Getting There & Away

Bus RSL (☎ 03 85 52 30 02) has a limited bus service linking the bus shelter (hours posted) next to Autun's train station with Le Creusot TGV station (63FF) and, west of Autun in the Parc Naturel Régional du

Morvan, Château Chinon (35.50FF; one hour; one per day, except on Sunday) via Roussillon-en-Morvan and Arleuf. The bus to La Petite Verrière, Cussy-en-Morvan and Anost, also in the Morvan park, runs three times a day (once a day on Saturday, none on Sunday) when school is in session (three times a week the rest of the time). RSL's information bureau at 13 Ave de la République is open weekdays from 8 am to noon and 2 to 6 pm (5 pm on Friday). Bus schedules are usually available at the tourist office.

Transco (☎ 03 80 42 11 00 in Dijon) has one return trip a day to and from Dijon (78.60FF; 2¼ hours) via Beaune and the Côte d'Or wine-making villages; buses depart from Autun's train station seven days a week at 5.10 pm.

Train Autun's train station (☎ 08 36 35 35 35) on Ave de la République is on a slow, tertiary SNCF line that requires a change of train/bus to get almost anywhere except Saulieu (43FF; one hour; four a day) and Avallon (70FF; 1¾ hours; two a day, one on Sunday and holidays). Even getting to Auxerre (102FF; 2¾ hours) and Sermizelles-Vézelay (78FF) usually requires that you change at Avallon.

The fastest way to get to/from Lyon (130FF; 1¾ hours; five or six a day) and Paris' Gare de Lyon (235 to 333FF; 2½ hours; five to seven a day) involves switching at Le Creusot from a TGV train to an RSL bus (63FF in addition to the train fare); bus times are coordinated with train schedules but not every single TGV is met by a bus, especially on weekends. To Paris' Gare de Lyon, it's much cheaper to take a non-TGV (213FF) via Étang or Nevers. The best way to get to Dijon (94FF; three or four convenient connections a day) and Beaune (71FF) is to change at Étang-sur-Arroux (18 minutes; six to eight a day, four on Sunday).

Car Europcar (☎ 03 85 52 13 31) is at 3 Grande Rue Marchaux (closed Sunday and holidays).

Getting Around

Cycles Tacnet (☎ 03 85 86 37 83) at 1 Rue de l'Arquebuse, open from 9 am to noon and 2 to 7 pm (closed on Monday morning and Sunday), has mountain bikes for 60/110FF per half-day/day or 200/500FF per weekend/week.

AROUND AUTUN

The **Château de Sully** (☎ 03 85 82 01 08), a 16th century Renaissance-style chateau whose northern façade was rebuilt in the 18th century, was the birthplace of Marshal MacMahon (1808-93), President of France from 1873 to 1879. From Easter to 1 November, the huge gardens (15FF) can be visited daily from 8 or 9 am to 6 or 7 pm; from June to September the interior – now home to the 4th duke of Magenta and his family – is open to the public every day from 2 to 6 pm (35FF, including the gardens).

Wine is produced on the estate and can be purchased from the concierge.

The chateau is 15km east of Autun on the outskirts of the quiet village of Sully. It makes a good cycling destination, if you're feeling inergetic, or it's a lovely drive: from Autun, take the D973 eastward (towards Beaune) and then the D326 north-east.

The very impressive Château de Sully also has excellent gardens.

BURGUNDY

CLUNY

• pop 4400 ✉ 71250 alt 248m

The remains of Cluny's great abbey (Christendom's largest church until St Peter's Basilica in the Vatican was constructed in the 16th century) are fragmentary and scattered, barely discernible among the streets and buildings of the stone-built, modern-day town, which has the same number of residents as it did 900 years ago. But with a bit of imagination, it's possible to picture how things must have looked in the 12th century, when Cluny's Benedictine abbey, renowned for its wealth and power – and answerable only to the Pope – held sway over 1100 Cluniac priories and monasteries stretching from Poland to Portugal.

Orientation

Cluny's tourist-oriented main drag is known (from south-east to north-west) as Place du Commerce, Rue Filaterie, Rue Lamartine and Rue Mercière. The SNCF bus stop is on Rue Porte de Paris, north of the main drag when it's called Place du Commerce.

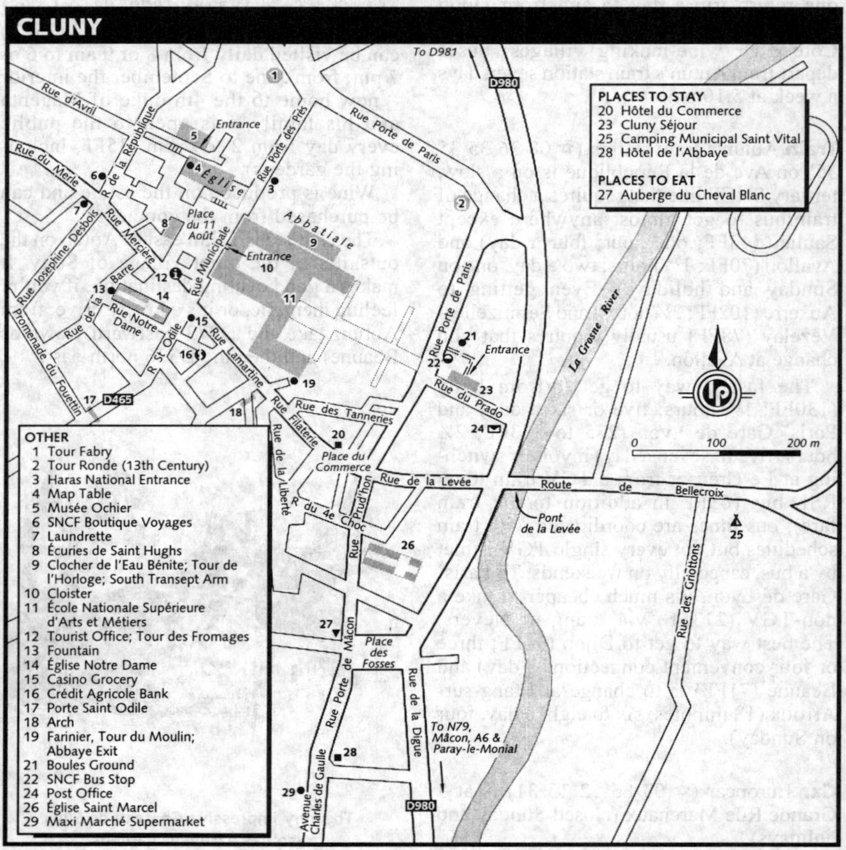

Information

Tourist Office The tourist office (☎ 03 85 59 05 34; fax 03 85 59 06 95; cluny@wanadoo.fr) at 6 Rue Mercière, which distributes several excellent English brochures, is open Monday to Saturday from 10 am to 12.30 pm and 2.30 to 6 pm (until 7 pm from April to October, when it's open the same hours on Sunday); there's no midday closure in July, August and September.

Money Cluny's banks, including the Crédit Agricole opposite 28 Rue Lamartine, are open Tuesday to Saturday. From April to October, the tourist office will change money on Sunday, Monday and holidays.

Post The post office, on the corner of Rue du Prado and the D980, is open weekdays from 8 am to noon and 2 to 6 pm and on Saturday until noon. It offers currency exchange.

Laundry The Laverie Automatique at 1 Rue du Merle is open daily from 8.30 am to 8 pm (last wash at 7.30 pm).

Église Abbatiale

Cluny's vast abbey church (☎ 03 85 59 12 79), founded in 910 and built between 1088 and 1130, once stretched from the narthex – now marked by a **map table** (in front of the Musée Ochier) – all the way to the line of tall trees on the other side of the octagonal 62m-high **Clocher de l'Eau Bénite** (Tower of the Holy Water) and its smaller neighbour, the square **Tour de l'Horloge**, a distance of 187m. The church was shut during the Revolution and the structure sold in 1798 to entrepreneurs who, over the following 25 years, demolished it stone by stone for reuse as building materials.

A visit to the abbey begins at the **Musée Ochier** (☎ 03 85 59 23 97), housed in the 15th century abbot's palace, whose displays include a fascinating model of the Cluny complex at the height of its power, superb Romanesque carvings from the abbey and a high tech video presentation.

The entrance to the mid-18th century **cloister**, presently occupied by one of the campuses of the École Nationale Supérieure d'Arts et Métiers (an institute for training mechanical and industrial engineers), is through a small door in the restored 13th century façade on the eastern side of Place du 11 Août. A grey wall chart in the entry hall shows, to scale, the outlines of Europe's most important medieval churches; other diagrams provide fascinating information on the sprawling Cluniac order. Inside the school complex – remember to follow the '*sens de la visite*' signs – you can visit the remains of the once great edifice: the **south arm of the transept**, several chapels and the chestnut-roofed 13th century **farinier** (*granary*).

Tickets for the whole ensemble (32FF for adults, 21FF for people aged 12 to 25) are sold at the Musée Ochier daily (except some holidays) from 9 or 9.30 am to noon and 2 to 6 pm (7 pm in July and August; no midday closure from July to September). From October to March, hours are 10 am to noon and 2 to 4 or 5 pm. Semi-officially you can wander around the École Nationale Supérieure grounds at midday and for an hour or so after closing time as long as you enter during opening hours, exiting via the grated students' entrance (next to the visitor's entrance) if necessary. An explanatory sheet in English is available at the cloister entrance. In July and August, free 90-minute guided tours in English take place twice a day.

Other Sights

A spectacular panorama of Cluny's many Romanesque houses – built when the abbey, humming with activity, brought prosperity to the town – can be admired from the top of **Tour des Fromages** (Tower of Cheeses), a solid tower right next to the tourist office. So named because it was once used to ripen and sell cheeses, its steep staircases are accessible whenever the tourist office is open. Admission is 6FF (4FF for children and students).

The **Haras National** (National Stud Farm) at 2 Rue Porte des Prés, founded by Napoleon I in 1806, is a laid-back place: visitors are welcome to wander through the five spacious stables, built in the 1800s, and admire some of France's finest stallions (thoroughbreds, ponies and draught horses). It's open daily from 9 am to 7 pm.

Cluny has two other churches of note: the late Romanesque **Église Saint Marcel** on Rue Prud'hon, topped by an octagonal three storey belfry; and the late 13th century **Église Notre Dame**, across the street from the tourist office.

Each summer, the **Écuries de Saint Hughs**, across the square from the École Nationale Supérieure, houses a temporary exhibition.

Places to Stay

The grassy ***Camping Municipal Saint Vital*** (☎ 03 85 59 08 34), open from Easter to early October, is a bit east of town on Rue des Griottons.

Cluny Séjour (☎ 03 85 59 08 83; fax 03 85 59 26 27) on Rue du Prado, a 71 bed hostel run by the municipality, charges 114FF for a single and 76FF per bed in functional rooms for two to four people, including breakfast (but not towels). Reception is open from 5.30 to 9 pm (5 to 10 pm from about Easter to September); during the day it's deserted, so if you've got luggage you might try leaving it at the tourist office or in a café (after ordering at least a coffee). The hostel is closed for three weeks around New Year.

The central, 17 room ***Hôtel du Commerce*** (☎ 03 85 59 03 09) at 8 Place du Commerce has singles/doubles from 110/140FF (230FF with shower and toilet). Hall showers are free. Reception is closed from noon to 3 pm. The two star, 16 room ***Hôtel de l'Abbaye*** (☎ 03 85 59 11 14; fax 03 85 59 09 76), opposite 17 Ave Charles de Gaulle, has small rooms from 150FF; rooms with shower and toilet for one to five people cost 260 to 380FF. Reception is closed on Sunday after 4 pm and on Monday until 5 or 6 pm.

Places to Eat

The ***Auberge du Cheval Blanc*** (☎ 03 85 59 01 13) at 1 Rue Porte de Mâcon has good-value French *menus* for 80 to 200FF (closed December to February and on Friday night and Saturday). The restaurant attached to ***Hôtel de l'Abbaye*** (see Places to Stay) has *menus* starting at 79FF (89FF for dinner and on Sunday and holidays). It is closed on Sunday night and Monday. There are several touristy eateries along Cluny's main drag.

Cluny's ***food shops*** – virtually all closed on Monday – are spread out along Place du Commerce, Rue Lamartine and Rue Mercière. The ***Casino*** grocery at 29 Rue Lamartine is open from 8 am to 12.30 pm (noon on Sunday) and 3 to 7.30 pm (closed on Sunday afternoon and, except in July and August, on Monday). The small ***Maxi Marché*** supermarket on Ave Charles de Gaulle is also closed on Sunday afternoon and Monday.

Getting There & Away

Bus & Train Cluny's toilet-equipped bus stop on Rue Porte de Paris is served by the SNCF coach line that links Chalon-sur-Saône's train station (46FF; 85 minutes; three or four a day) with Mâcon's train station (25FF; 45 minutes; five or six a day) and the nearby Mâcon-Loché TGV station. The SNCF's Boutique Voyages (☎ 03 85 59 07 72) at 9 Rue de la République, which functions as a regular SNCF information and ticket office, is open from 9 am to noon (12.30 pm on Saturday) and 1.30 to 5.30 pm (closed Saturday afternoon, Sunday, Monday and holidays).

Getting Around

Bicycle From about Easter to early October, Association Le Pont (☎ 03 85 59 08 34, or ☎ 03 85 59 03 97 in winter), based at Camping Municipal Saint Vital (see Places to Stay), rents bikes for 10/40/60FF an hour/day/weekend; tandems cost only marginally more (closed Tuesday and Thursday mornings and on Sunday).

PARAY-LE-MONIAL

The 11th and 12th century Burgundian Romanesque **basilica** in the pious, flower-filled town of Paray-le-Monial, 40km west of Cluny, is very similar in design to Cluny's lost abbey church. Built as part of a Cluniac abbey, it is much smaller than its erstwhile mother-house but is remarkably well preserved.

Information

The tourist office (☎ 03 85 81 10 92; fax 03 85 81 36 61) is next to the basilica (closed on Sunday and Monday from November to Easter).

Places to Stay

The two star ***Grand Hôtel de la Basilique*** (☎ 03 85 81 11 13) at 18 Rue de la Visitation, run by the same family since 1904, is open from late March to October. Singles/doubles with shower and toilet start at 190/220FF. Near the train station, the ***Hôtel du Nord*** (☎ 03 85 81 05 12) at 1 Ave de la Gare, open year-round, has doubles from 145FF (175FF with shower and toilet). Except in July and August, reception is usually closed on Saturday.

Getting There & Away

Paray-le-Monial, on the secondary train line between Moulins and Montchanin, has limited direct services to Dijon (97FF) and Vichy (107FF).

Lyon

The grand city of Lyon (Lyons in English; population 415,000) has spent the last 500 years as a commercial, industrial and banking powerhouse. Despite its reputation for being somewhat staid and even austere, modern-day Lyon – the focal point of a prosperous urban area of almost two million people, the second largest conurbation in France – is endowed with outstanding museums, a dynamic cultural life, an important university, classy shopping and lively pedestrian malls. Since 1989 the international police agency Interpol has had its headquarters here.

More importantly, Lyon is renowned for its cuisine: it is one of France's great gastronomic capitals, with pleasures to sample for those on the tightest – or loosest – of budgets!

History

Lyon, founded in 43 BC as the Roman military colony of Lugdunum, served as the capital of the Roman territories known as the Three Gauls under Augustus. Christianity was introduced in the 2nd century AD, when the city was at the height of its Roman glory.

Lyon's extraordinary prosperity began in the 16th century, when banks were established and great commercial fairs – begun in the early 15th century – were held, giving an impetus to trade. Moveable type arrived in 1473, a mere two decades after its invention, and within 50 years Lyon was one of Europe's foremost publishing centres, with several hundred resident printers.

Silk weaving had been introduced to Lyon in the 15th century, but it was not until the mid-18th century that the city became Europe's silk-weaving capital.

The city's famous *traboules* (see the boxed text 'Traboules') proved extremely useful to the Resistance during WWII. On 2 September 1944, the retreating Germans blew up all but two of Lyon's 28 road, rail and pedestrian bridges.

Lyon has been an important centre of scientific research since the 18th century and

HIGHLIGHTS

- ***Traboules*** – discover Lyon's underworld of passageways, courtyards and alleyways
- **Maison des Canuts** – see how 16th century silk weavers worked
- **Fourvière** – scale this hill for a superb panoramic view of Lyon
- **Parc de la Tête d'Or** – grab a picnic and laze away the day
- **Vieux Lyon** – shop until you drop and then drink (coffee, of course) until you pop

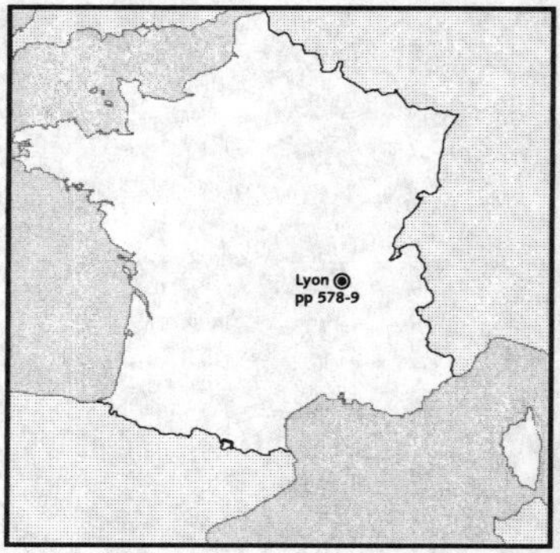

grillades de bœuf à la moelle (grilled beef with marrow) or ***poularde demi-deuil*** (chicken with truffles) – particularly famous Lyonnais dishes, among others

Beaujolais red wine

bouchon – eat out at a traditional Lyonnais restaurant

has produced such eminent scientists as the physicist André-Marie Ampère (1775-1836), after whom the basic unit of electric current was named, and the Lumière brothers, Auguste (1862-1954) and Louis (1864-1948), photographic pioneers and creators of the world's first motion picture in 1895.

Orientation

Lyon's bustling city centre is on the Presqu'île, a 500 to 800m-wide peninsula bounded by the mighty Rhône and smaller Saône rivers. The line of impressive public squares running down the middle of the peninsula includes (from north to south): Place de la Croix Rousse, in the hilltop neighbourhood of Croix Rousse; Place Louis Pradel, just north of the Opéra; Place des Terreaux, bounded by the Hôtel de Ville and the Musée des Beaux-Arts; Place de la République, attached to the pedestrian Rue de la République; Place des Jacobins, just west of Place de la République; vast Place Bellecour; Place Ampère, on pedestrianised Rue Victor Hugo; and Place Carnot, just north of Gare de Perrache, one of Lyon's two mainline train stations. North of Place Bellecour is the quaint Mercière-St Antoine district, the old commercial quarter dominated by the 14th century Église St Nizier. South of Place des Jacobins stretch Rue des Archers, Rue Gasparin and Rue Émile Zola – *the* streets for designer clothes and fashion accessories.

On the west bank of the Saône, Vieux Lyon (Old Lyons) is sandwiched between the river and the hilltop area of Fourvière.

The districts east of the Rhône are known as Lyon-Rive Gauche (Lyons-Left Bank). Gare de la Part-Dieu, the city's other mainline train station, is 1.5km east of the Rhône in La Part-Dieu, a modernistic commercial centre constructed on the sight of a former army barracks and dominated by the pencil-shaped Crédit Lyonnais building – a reddish cylindrical tower topped with a pyramid.

Arrondissements Lyon proper is divided into nine arrondissements. The area of the Presqu'île south of Rue Neuve forms the 2nd arrondissement; the area north of Rue Neuve is in the 1st arrondissement. Vieux Lyon and Fourvière are in the 5th arrondissement, and Croix Rousse in the 4th. The left (east) bank of the Rhône is covered by the 6th, 3rd and 7th arrondissements.

The arrondissement number (1er for the 1st arrondissement, 2e for the 2nd arrondissement etc) of each place mentioned in the text is written in parentheses after the address. When places mentioned are within 600m of a metro station, the stop is listed.

Maps & Guides The best street plan of Lyon is Michelin's 1:10,000 scale map (No 30, or No 31 with a street index). Otherwise, the tourist office gives away free city maps that include short historical explanations (in English) on the reverse side.

Le Petit Paumé is a fabulous French-language city guide to Lyon written by local university students. Unfortunately, it is only distributed (for free) for one day in October, meaning most visitors never get to see it.

The Butcher of Lyon

Klaus Barbie (1913-91) – better known as 'the butcher of Lyon' – served as Lyon's Gestapo commander from 1942 to 1944. He was responsible for ordering the deaths of some 4000 people (including Resistance leader Jean Moulin) and deporting 7500 others to Nazi death camps.

After the war, Barbie worked for US counter-intelligence (1947-51), then settled in Bolivia with his family under the name Klaus Altmann. In 1952 and again in 1954, he was sentenced to death in absentia by a Lyon court but it was not until 1987, following his extradition from Bolivia in 1983, that he was tried in person for crimes against humanity. Barbie was sentenced to life imprisonment but died of leukaemia in prison three years later.

The life and times of Klaus Barbie was the subject of the 4½ hour-long epic film *Hôtel Terminus*, which was awarded the International Critics' Prize at Cannes in 1988.

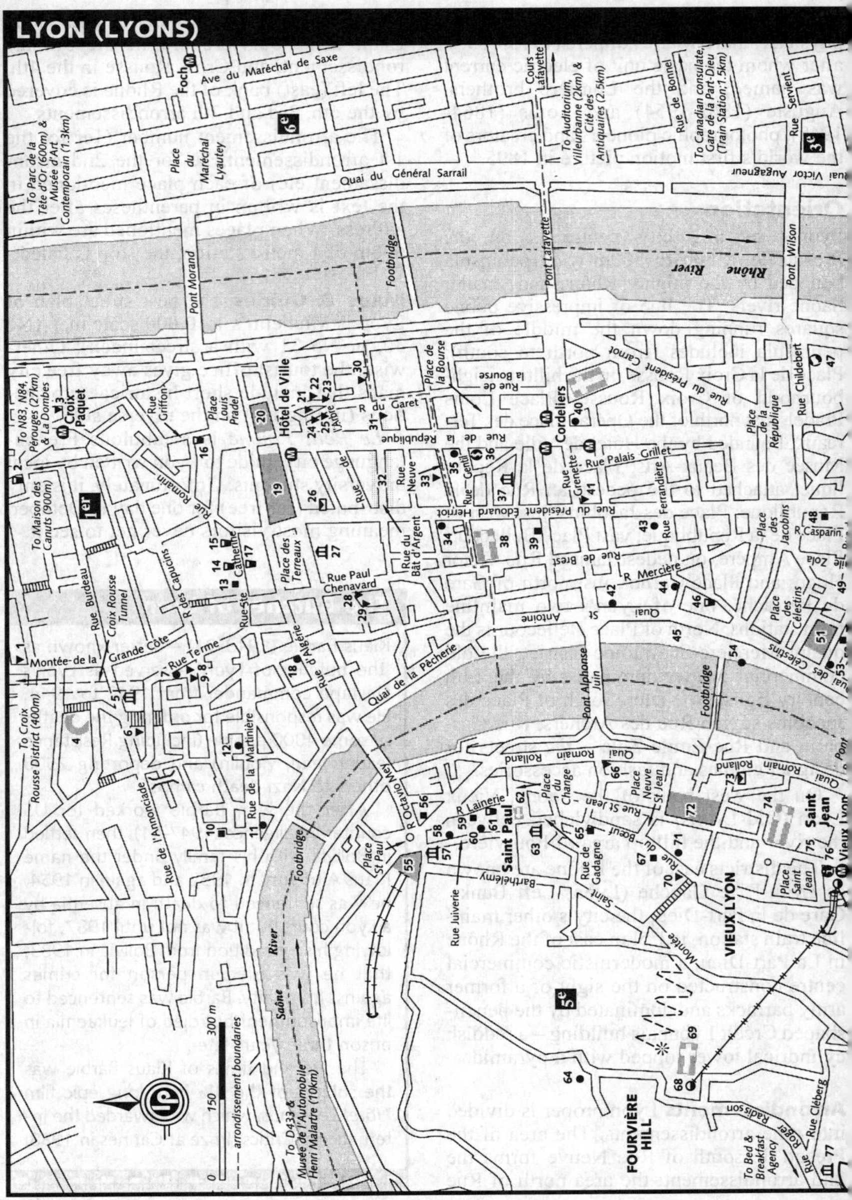
LYON (LYONS)
Foch
Ave du Maréchal de Saxe
6e
Place du Maréchal Lyautey
Quai du Général Sarrail
To Parc de la Tête d'Or (600m) & Musée d'Art Contemporain (1.3km)
Cours Lafayette
To Auditorium, Villeurbanne (2km) & Cité des Antiquaires (2.5km)
Rue de Bonnel
To Canadian consulate, Gare de la Part-Dieu (Train Station; 1.5km)
Rue Servient
3e
Quai Victor Augagneur
Pont Wilson
Rhône River
Pont Lafayette
Footbridge
Pont Morand
Place de la Bourse
Rue de la Bourse
Rue du Président Carnot
Cordeliers
Rue Childebert
Place de la République
Rue de la République
Rue Palais Grillet
Rue Grenette
Rue du Président Edouard Herriot
Rue Ferrandière
Place des Jacobins
R Casparin
Rue de Brest
R. Mercière
Quai St Antoine
Zola
Place des Célestins
Quai des Célestins
Rue Gentil
Rue Neuve
R du Garet
l'Arbre
Hôtel de Ville
Place Louis Pradel
Croix Paquet
To N83, N84, Pérouges (27km) & La Dombes
To Maison des Canuts (900m)
1er
Rue Griffon
Rue Romarin
Rue Ste Catherine
Place des Terreaux
Rue Paul Chenavard
Rue du Bât d'Argent
R des Capucins
Croix Rousse Tunnel
Rue Burdeau
Montée de la Grande Côte
Rue Terme
To Croix Rousse District (400m)
Rue d'Algérie
Quai de la Pêcherie
Rue de la Martinière
Rue de l'Annonciade
R Octavio Mey
Pont Alphonse Juin
Footbridge
Quai Romain Rolland
Place du Change
Place Neuve St Jean
Rue St Jean
R Lainerie
Saint Paul
Rue du Boeuf
Rue de Gadagne
Saint Barthélemy
Rue Juiverie
Place St Paul
Montée
Saint Jean
Place Saint Jean
Vieux Lyon
VIEUX LYON
5e
Rue Roger Radisson
Rue Cléberg
FOURVIÈRE HILL
To Bed & Breakfast Agency
Footbridge
Saône River
To D433 & Musée de l'Automobile Henri Malartre (10km)
arrondissement boundaries
0 150 300 m
Rue

LYON (LYONS)

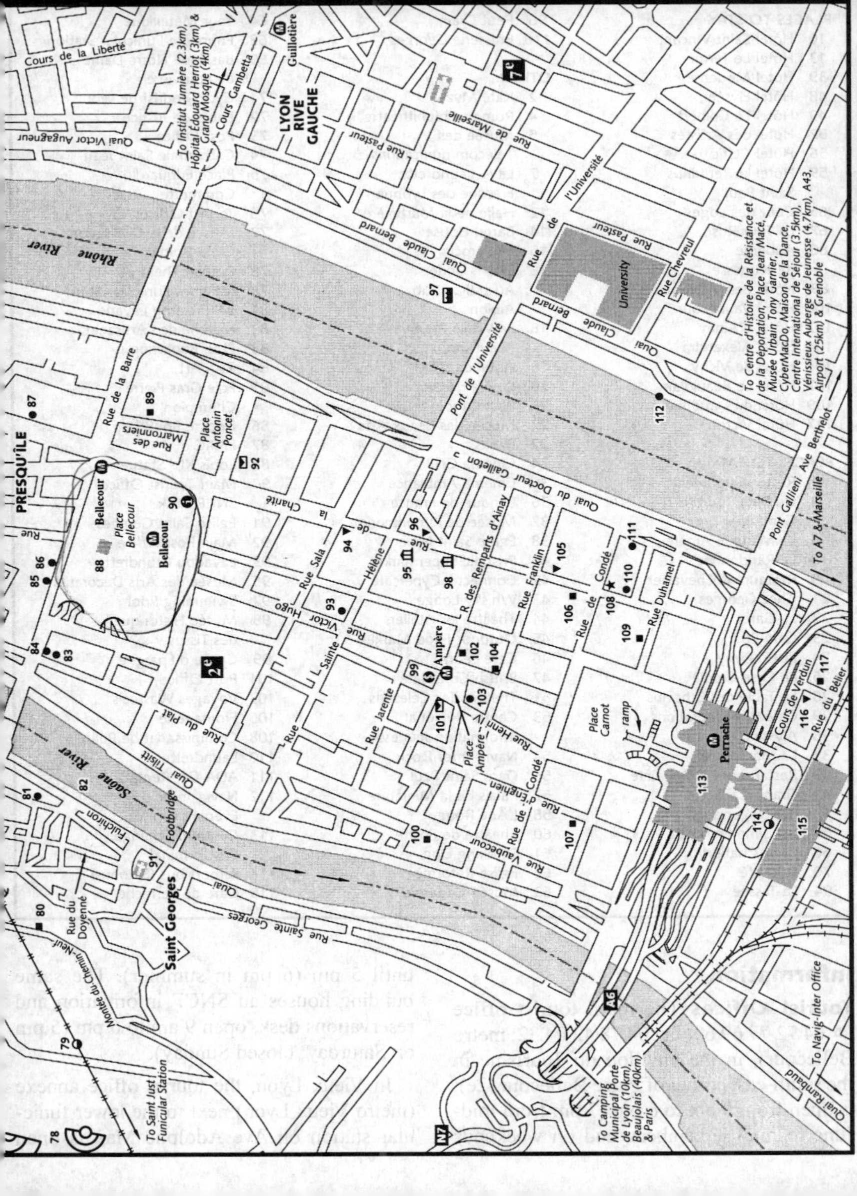
Cours de la Liberté
Quai Victor Augagneur
Cours Gambetta
Guillotière
To Institut Lumière (2.3km), Hôpital Édouard Herriot (3km) & Grand Mosque (4km)
LYON RIVE GAUCHE
Rue de Marseille
Rue Pasteur
Rue de l'Université
Quai Claude Bernard
University
Rue Chevreul
Rhône River
Pont de l'Université
PRESQU'ILE
Rue de la Barre
Rue des Marronniers
Place Antonin Poncet
Bellecour
Place Bellecour
Rue de la Charité
Rue Sala
Rue Sainte Hélène
Rue Victor Hugo
Rue Jarente
R. des Remparts d'Ainay
Rue Franklin
Rue de Condé
Quai du Docteur Gailleton
Rue Duhamel
Pont Gallieni
Ave Berthelot
To A7 & Marseille
Place Carnot
ramp
Perrache
Cours de Verdun
Rue du Bélier
Place Ampère
Ampère
Rue Henri IV
Rue d'Enghien
Rue Vaubecour
Rue du Plat
Quai Tilsitt
Saône River
Footbridge
Quai Fulchiron
Rue du Doyenné
Saint Georges
Quai Saint Georges
Rue Sainte Georges
Montée du Chemin-Neuf
To Saint Just Funicular Station
To Camping Municipal Porte de Lyon (10km), Beaujolais (40km) & Paris
A6
N7
To Navig-Inter Office
Quai Rambaud
To Centre d'Histoire de la Résistance et de la Déportation, Place Jean Macé, Musée Urbain Tony Garnier, CyberMacDo, Maison de la Dance, Centre International de Séjour (3.5km), Vénissieux Auberge de Jeunesse (4.7km), A43, Airport (25km) & Grenoble

LYON (LYONS)

PLACES TO STAY
10 Hôtel Saint Vincent
13 Hôtel Le Terme
39 Hôtel Moderne
48 Hôtel Élysée
49 Hôtel Le Colbert
52 Hotel des Artistes
56 Hôtel Celtic
59 Hôtel Le Terminus Saint Paul
65 Cour des Loges
67 La Tour Rose
80 Auberge de Jeunesse
89 Hôtel des Marronniers
100 Hôtel Vaubecour
102 Hôtel d'Ainay
104 Hôtel Alexandra
106 Hôtel de Vichy
107 Hôtel Le Beaujolais
109 Hôtel du Dauphiné
117 Hôtel Victoria

PLACES TO EAT
1 Resto Vegetarien
3 Un Petit Tour de Camargue
6 La Mangue Amère
8 La Randonnée
9 Restaurant Chevallier
21 Chez Georges
22 Le Garet
23 Café 203
24 Bistro Pizay
25 La Case Créole
28 La Table des Échevins
29 Café des Fédérations
30 Alyssaar
31 La Mamounia
33 Restaurant La Meunière
41 Grand Café des Negociants
50 Brasserie Francotte
66 Chez Chabert
70 Sol Café
94 La Tassée
96 Petit Grain
116 Brasserie Georges

OTHER
2 Kafé Myzik
4 Roman Amphitheatre
5 Musée des Télécommunications
7 Lav+ Laundrette
11 Fresque des Lyonnais
12 Halle de la Martinière
14 Barrel House
15 Shamrock
16 Down Under Australian Pub
17 Albion
18 La Vieille Reserve (wine shop)
19 Hôtel de Ville
20 Opéra de Lyon
26 Post Office
27 Musée des Beaux-Arts
32 Banks
34 Cinéma CNP
35 Cinéma Ambiance
36 Banque de France
37 Musée de l'Imprimerie
38 Église Saint Nizier
40 Prisunic Supermarket
42 Connectik Cybercafé
43 Whisky Lodge
44 Théâtre les Ateliers
45 Outdoor Food Market
46 Café Léon
47 British Consulate
51 Théâtre des Célestins
53 Centre Régional Information Jeunesse
54 Navig-Inter Dock
55 Gare Saint Paul
57 Palais de la Miniature
58 L'Âne Rouge
60 Théâtre de Poche
61 Smoking Dog
62 Église Réformée
63 Musée Gadagne
64 Tour Métallique
68 Fourvière Funicular Station
69 Basilique Notre Dame de Fourvière
71 Cyclo-Tourist de Lyon
72 Palais de Justice
73 Post Office
74 Cathédrale Saint Jean
75 Place Édouard Commette
76 Tourist Office
77 Musée de la Civilisation Gallo-Romain
78 Roman Theatres
79 Minimes Funicular Stop
81 J-P Pressing Lavarie
82 Marché de l'Artisanat
83 Eton Bookshop
84 Rich Art
85 Foie Gras Pierre Champion
86 Decitre Bookshop
87 FNAC
88 Louis XIV Statue
90 Main Tourist Office; SNCF Desk
91 Église Saint Georges
92 Main Post Office
93 Lavadou Laundrette
95 Musée des Arts Décoratifs
97 Swimming Pool
98 Musée Historique des Tissus
99 Caisse d'Épargne
101 Post Office
103 Voyages Wasteels
105 Fromagerie
108 Commissariat de Police
110 Laundrette
111 ADA Car Rental
112 Navig-Inter Evening Cruises
113 Centre d'Échange; Bus Terminal
114 Airport bus (Satobus)
115 Gare de Perrache

Information

Tourist Offices The main tourist office (☎ 04 72 77 69 69; fax 04 78 42 04 32; metro Bellecour), in the Pavillon du Tourisme in the south-east corner of Place Bellecour (2e), is open from 9 am to 6 pm (7 pm from mid-June to mid-September), and on weekends until 5 pm (6 pm in summer). The same building houses an SNCF information and reservations desk, open 9 am to 6 pm (5 pm on Saturday; closed Sunday).

In Vieux Lyon, the tourist office annexe (metro Vieux Lyon) next to the lower funicular station on Ave Adolphe Max is open from 9 am to 1 pm and 2 to 6 pm (Saturday from 9 am to 5 pm). From mid-June to mid-September its hours are 10.30 am to 7.30 pm.

Money The Banque de France (metro Cordeliers) at 14 Rue de la République (2e) is open from 8.45 am to 12.15 pm and 1.30 to 3.30 pm (closed on weekends). The American Express office (☎ 04 72 77 74 50; metro Bellecour), 6 Rue Childebert (2e), is open from 9 am to 12.30 pm and 2 to 6 pm (closed on weekends). From May to September it's open on Saturday morning.

Plenty of commercial banks can be found along Rue Victor Hugo (north of Place Ampère) and, just south of Place des Terreaux, along Rue du Bât d'Argent and nearby sections of Rue de la République. There are Thomas Cook exchange offices at both mainline train stations.

Post & Communications The main post office (metro Bellecour), 10 Place Antonin Poncet (2e), is open from 8 am to 7 pm (Saturday until noon; closed Sunday). The branch post office (metro Hôtel de Ville) at 3 Rue du Président Édouard Herriot (1er) is open the same hours but also breaks for lunch on Wednesday between 12.45 and 1.45 pm. Both change foreign currency. At 8 Place Ampère (2e), the branch post office (metro Ampère) is open from 8.30 am to 6.30 pm (Saturday from 8 am to noon; closed Sunday). In Vieux Lyon, the post office close to the Palais de Justice on Quai Romain Rolland is open from 8.15 am to 6.45 pm (Saturday from 9 am to noon; closed Sunday).

Internet Resources Download and upload at the Connectik Café (☎ 04 72 77 98 85; info@connectik.fr; www.connectik.fr; metro Cordeliers), 19 Quai Saint Antoine (2e). One/five hours online costs 75/250FF. If you want a shake while you surf, head to France's first CyberMacDo (☎ 04 72 76 27 27) on the corner of Ave Tony Garnier and Rue de Gerland (7e). Internet access costs 35/60FF for half an hour/one hour and the place is open from 7.30 am to 10.30 pm.

Travel Agencies The very active Centre Régional Information Jeunesse (☎ 04 72 77 00 66; fax 04 72 77 04 39; metro Bellecour), 9 Quai des Célestins (2e), is open from 10 am (noon on Monday) to 6 pm (5 pm on Saturday; closed Sunday). Voyages Wasteels (☎ 04 78 37 80 17; metro Perrache) has an office on the upper level of the Centre d'Échange, next to Gare de Perrache, and at 5 Place Ampère (☎ 04 78 42 65 37; metro Ampère; 2e). Rue Gentil (metro Hôtel de Ville; 2e) is lined with specialist travel agencies.

Bookshops The Eton English-language bookshop (☎ 04 78 92 92 36; metro Bellecour), 1 Rue du Plat (2e), is open from 10 am to 12.30 pm and 1.45 or 2 to 7 pm (closed all day Sunday and Monday morning). Decitre (☎ 04 72 40 54 54), 6 Place Bellecour, has a good English-language section too and stocks a huge array of maps.

Library The huge Bibliothèque Municipale (Municipal Library; ☎ 04 78 62 85 20; metro Part-Dieu), 30 Blvd Vivier Merle (3e), opposite Part-Dieu train station, is open from 10 am to 7 pm (6 pm on Saturday; closed Sunday and Monday). English-language newspapers, books and periodicals are available for your perusal here too.

Laundry The Lav+ (metro Hôtel de Ville), Rue Terme, is open from 6 am to 9 pm. Three

Passes

An all-day pass (*carte d'entrées groupes*) to Lyon's four municipal museums (Beaux-Arts, Tissus, Gadagne and Imprimerie and Centre de la Résistance et de la Déportation) as well as the suburban Musée de l'Automobile, is available at the museums concerned for 30/15FF for adults/students and seniors. The tourist office has a 90FF Clé de la Ville (Key to the City) valid for three days, which includes entry to six museums plus a bus or walking city tour.

blocks south of Place Bellecour, the Lavadou (metro Ampère), 19 Rue Sainte Hélène (2e), is open from 7.30 am to 8.30 pm. The laundrette (metro Perrache) at 51 Rue de la Charité (2e) is open from 6 am to 10 pm. The hours at Vieux Lyon's J-P Pressing Laverie (metro Vieux Lyon), 11 Monseigneur Lavarenne (5e), are 8 am to 9 pm.

Medical Services Hôpital Édouard Herriot (☎ 04 72 11 73 11; metro Grange Blanche), 5 Place d'Arsonval (3e), 4km south-east of Place Bellecour, has a 24 hour emergency room.

Emergency The Commissariat de Police (☎ 04 78 42 26 56; metro Perrache or Ampère), 47 Rue de la Charité (2e), is responsible for the 2nd arrondissement.

Vieux Lyon

Old Lyon, whose narrow cobble streets are lined with a picture-postcard ensemble of over 300 meticulously restored **medieval and Renaissance houses** (15th to 17th century), lies at the base of Fourvière hill. It comprises three districts: Saint Paul at the northern end, Saint Jean in the middle and Saint Georges in the south. The area underwent urban renewal two decades ago and has since become a trendy and quaint area in which to live, eat and shop for art.

Many of the most interesting old buildings are on Rue du Bœuf, Rue Juiverie, Rue Saint Jean and Rue des Trois Maries. Fronting Vieux Lyon on Quai Romain Rolland is the 19th century, 24 column **Palais de Justice**.

Cathédrale Saint Jean Built between 1180 and 1480, this mainly Romanesque cathedral has a Flamboyant Gothic façade – damaged by the Huguenots and again during the Revolution – whose portals are decorated with 368 square, stone medallions from the early 14th century. The 14th century **astronomical clock** in the north transept chimes daily at noon, 2, 3 and 4 pm. The cathedral is open from 7.30 am to noon and 2 to 7.30 pm (5 pm on weekends and holidays).

Musée Gadagne This museum (☎ 04 78 42 03 61; metro Vieux Lyon), housed in a 16th century mansion formerly owned by two rich Florentine bankers at 12 Rue de Gadagne (5e), has two sections: the **Musée de la Marionette** (Puppet Museum) and the **Musée Historique**. The former was founded by Laurent Mourguet (1769-1844), creator of the Punch and Judy-type puppet Guignol, one of the symbols of Lyon. Both are open from 10.45 am to 6 pm (8.30 pm on Friday; closed Tuesday). Admission is 25/15FF for adults/students.

Traboules

There's more to Lyon that meets the eye. Beneath the city façade of chic shopping malls and crowded cafes, there is a maze of *traboules* (secret passages) – 50km long with 315 passages linking 230 streets – which winds its way through apartment blocks, under streets and into courtyards.

Some of Vieux Lyon's traboules date from Roman times. Many of the 140 traboules that snake their way up the *pentes* (slopes) to the Croix Rousse plateau were constructed by *canuts* (silk weavers) in the 19th century to facilitate the transport of silk in inclement weather. Resistance fighters found them equally handy during WWII.

Genuine traboules (derived from the Latin *trans ambulare* meaning 'to pass through') cut from one street to another, often wending their way up fabulous spiral staircases en route. Traboules that fan out into a courtyard or lead into a cul de sac are not traboules, but rather *miraboules*.

Lyon's most celebrated traboules link 26 Rue Saint Jean in Vieux Lyon to 1 Rue du Bœuf, and 12 Quai Romain Rolland to 2 Place du Governement. In Croix Rousse, you can step into the city's underworld at 9 Place Colbert, crossing the Cours des Voraces renowned for its monumental staircase that zigzags up seven floors, and emerging at 29 Rue Imbert Colomès.

Palais de la Miniature The doll-sized domestic scenes and tiny, handmade objects on display at this museum (☎ 04 72 00 24 77; metro Vieux Lyon), 2 Rue Juiverie (5e), will delight the young *and* young-at-heart. It is open from 10 am to noon and 2 to 6 pm. Entry costs 25/20FF for adults/children and students.

Fourvière

Two millennia ago, the Romans built the city of Lugdunum on the slopes of Fourvière. Today, Lyon's 'hill of prayer' (topped by a basilica and the **Tour Métallique**, a grey, Eiffel Tower-like structure erected in 1893 and now used as a TV transmitter) affords spectacular views of Lyon and its two rivers. There are several footpaths up the slope. The easiest way to the top is to take the funicular from Place Saint Jean in Vieux Lyon (metro Vieux Lyon). The Fourvière line, whose upper terminus is right behind the basilica, operates daily until 10 pm; trains run every five or 10 minutes. Use bus/metro tickets or buy a funicular return ticket for 12.50FF.

Basilique Notre Dame de Fourvière Like Sacré Cœur in Paris, this ungainly basilica served by the Fourvière funicular station and completed in 1896, was built by subscription to fulfil a vow taken by local Catholics during the disastrous Franco-Prussian War of 1870-71. The august *Blue Guide France* declares it 'hideous ... in a depraved taste which should be seen to be believed', and indeed, its ornamentation is a superb example of the exaggerated enthusiasm for embellishment that dominated French ecclesiastical architecture during the late 19th century. If overwrought marble and gilded mosaics are not your cup of tea, the **panoramic view** from the nearby terrace still merits a visit. The basilica is open from 6 am to 7 pm.

Musée de la Civilisation Gallo-Romaine Among the extraordinary artefacts – almost all found in the Rhône Valley – on display at the truly exceptional Museum of Gallo-Roman Civilisation (☎ 04 72 38 81 90; Fourvière funicular station), 17 Rue Cléberg (5e), are the remains of a four-wheeled vehicle from around 700 BC, several sumptuous mosaics and lots of Latin inscriptions, including the text of a speech made by Lyon-born Roman Emperor Claudius in 48 AD. It is open from 9.30 am to noon and 2 to 6 pm (closed Monday and Tuesday). Admission is 20/10FF for adults/students.

The two rebuilt **Roman theatres** next to the museum are open from 9 am to dusk. Concerts are occasionally held here.

Presqu'île

The face of Lyon – both past and present – peers out of the **Fresque des Lyonnais**, a fantastic example of trompe l'oeil, at the intersection of Rue de la Martinière and Quai de la Pêcherie on the banks of the Saône. Some 30 personalities are featured on the seven-storey building, including chef Paul Bocuse, loom inventor Joseph-Marie Jacquard (1752-1834), Renaissance poet Maurice Scève (1599-1560) and 16th century explorer Giovanni da Verrazzano, a Florentine shipmaster navigator from Lyon who discovered what is now New York in 1524 (he left it untouched, enabling the Dutch to settle it a century later). The yellow-haired 'little prince' painted on the wall is a tribute to his creator, author Antoine de Saint-Exupéry, who was born in Lyon in 1900.

Heading east, you then come to **Place des Terreaux** (metro Hôtel de Ville), the centrepiece of which is a 19th century fountain incorporating 21 tonnes of lead and sculpted by Frédéric-Auguste Bartholdi, also responsible for New York's Statue of Liberty. The four horses pulling the chariot symbolise rivers galloping seaward. Fronting the square is the **Hôtel de Ville**, built in 1655 but given its present façade in 1702. The remaining fountains spread over the remaining area of the square were designed by Burden.

To the south, there are upmarket shops along and around **Rue de la République**, known for its 19th century buildings; its southern half is a pedestrian mall. Two blocks west of here is the **Mercière-Saint Antoine quarter**, a web of narrow streets bearing the names of Lyon's traditional traders.

Pedestrianised **Rue Victor Hugo** runs southward from **Place Bellecour** (metro Bellecour), one of the largest public squares in Europe. Laid out in the 17th century, it has an equestrian statue of Louis XIV in the middle. Adjacent areas were razed during the Reign of Terror (1793-94) by Revolutionary radicals furious at the city's resistance to the Convention. Thousands of Lyonnais were executed before Robespierre's downfall spared the city from even greater devastation. The area was rebuilt in the early 19th century.

Musée des Beaux-Arts The 90 rooms of Lyon's Museum of Fine Arts (☎ 04 72 10 17 40; metro Hôtel de Ville), 20 Place des Terreaux (1er), house a truly outstanding collection of sculptures and paintings from every period of European art. It is open from 10.30 am to 6 pm (closed Monday and Tuesday). Admission is 25F/15F for adults/students. The museum gardens are open from 7.30 am to 7 pm (until 6 pm in winter; from 9 am on weekends).

Musée Historique des Tissus & Musée des Arts Décoratifs The Lyonnais are especially proud of their Textile History Museum (☎ 04 78 37 15 05; metro Ampère), housed in a luxurious, 18th century former private residence at 34 Rue de la Charité (2e). Its collections include extraordinary Lyonnais silks, French and Asian textiles (tapestries, lace) and carpets. A couple of doors down at 30 Rue de la Charité is the Museum of Decorative Arts (☎ 04 78 37 15 05; metro Ampère). Here, three storeys of rooms are filled with mainly 18th century furniture, tapestries, wallpaper, ceramics, silver and so forth. Both museums are open from 10 am to 5.30 pm; the Musée des Arts Décoratifs closes between noon and 2 pm. A ticket valid for both costs 28/15FF for adults/students.

Musée de l'Imprimerie The Museum of Printing (☎ 04 78 37 65 98; metro Cordeliers), 37 Rue de la Poulaillerie (2e), focuses on the history of a technology that had firmly established itself in Lyon by the 1480s. Among the exhibits housed in what served as the city hall until 1652 are some of the first books ever printed, including a page of a Gutenberg Bible (1450s) and several incunabula (books printed before the year 1500). Don't miss the fantastic Renaissance courtyard. Museum hours are 9.30 am to noon and 2 to 6 pm (closed Monday and Tuesday; no midday closure on Friday except during school holiday periods). Admission is 25/15FF for adults/students.

Croix Rousse

The hilltop neighbourhood of Croix Rousse (literally 'russet cross'), just north of Lyon centre, is known for its bustling outdoor markets and street entertainers. In summer, films are screened under the trees on Place Colbert, halfway up the *pentes* (slopes) that lead up to the Croix Rousse plateau. By day, old men gather here to play *boules lyonnaises* (Lyonnais bowls) and chess.

In 1805, following the introduction of the mechanical Jacquard weaving loom, it was in Croix Rousse, Lyon's traditional working-class district, that Lyonnais silk weavers (*canuts*) built new workshops equipped with extraordinarily high, beamed ceilings to accommodate the new 3.9m-tall loom. During the bitter 1830-31 canut uprisings, prompted by bad pay and dire working conditions, hundreds of people were killed.

The history and tradition of Croix Rousse's canuts is celebrated on the **Fresque des Canuts**, painted trompe l'oeil-style on the building face on the corner of Blvd des Canuts and Rue Denfert-Rochereau.

Maison des Canuts Set up by the guild of canuts, this museum (☎ 04 78 28 62 04; metro Croix Rousse), 10-12 Rue d'Ivry (4e), traces the history of Lyon's silk weaving industry and often has weavers on hand to demonstrate the art of operating a traditional loom. It is open weekdays from

8.30 am to noon and 2 to 6.30 pm, and Saturday from 9 am to noon and 2 to 6 pm. Entry costs 15/10FF for adults/students.

Musée des Télécommunications France Télécom has turned an old telephone exchange at 12bis Rue Burdeau (1er), half a block down the hill from the Roman amphitheatre, into a telecommunications museum (☎ 04 78 39 88 89; metro Hôtel de Ville) whose antique equipment is almost all in working order. It's open from 8 am to noon and 2 to 5 pm (closed on weekends). Ring the *musée* button on the intercom to enter.

Opposite the museum are the excavations of the Roman **Amphithéâtre des Trois Gaulles** (19 AD; metro Hôtel de Ville), Rue L Sportisse (1er), where early Christian martyrs were killed in 177 AD.

Left Bank

Centre d'Histoire de la Résistance et de la Déportation The WWII headquarters of Lyon's notorious Gestapo chief, Klaus Barbie, right across the Rhône from Gare de Perrache at 14 Ave Berthelot (7e), has been transformed into an evocative, multimedia museum (☎ 04 78 72 23 11; metro Perrache or Jean Macé) that commemorates both Nazi atrocities (including torture and executions planned or carried out in this very building) and the heroism of French Resistance fighters. The centre is open from 9 am to 5.30 pm (last entry at 5 pm; closed Monday and Tuesday). Admission is 25/10FF for adults/students and seniors.

Musée d'Art Contemporain The Museum of Contemporary Art (☎ 04 72 69 17 17; stella@lyon.asi.fr), which specialises in works created after 1960, is housed in the Cité Internationale overlooking Parc de la Tête d'Or at 81 Quai Charles de Gaulle (not far from the Interpol headquarters). Take bus No 47 from Gare de la Part-Dieu or bus No 71 from Gare de Perrache or the quays along the east side of the Presqu'île. The museum is only open when there are exhibitions on (ask at the tourist office for further details).

Mosqué de Lyon Badr Eddine Lyon's dazzling Grand Mosque (☎ 04 78 76 00 23; metro Laënnec), 5km east of the Presqu'île at 146 Blvd Pinel (8e), is a striking, all white structure that fuses traditional North African architecture and calligraphy with late 20th century western aesthetics. A religious focal point for Lyon's 130,000-strong Muslim community, it is open to modestly dressed visitors (10FF) from 9 am to noon and 4 to 5 pm (closed Friday). The prayer room on the ground floor can hold 1500 worshippers; the balconies are for women only. Shoes should be left in the *vestiaire chaussures* (shoe storage area).

Institut Lumière Lyon is the birthplace of cinema, the glorious beginnings of which are unravelled in the Institut Lumière, moved into the family home of Antoine Lumière who, together with his sons Auguste and Louis, set the whole ball rolling. On 19 March 1885 they shot the first reels of the pioneering motion picture *La Sortie des Usines Lumières* (*The Exit of the Lumières' Workshops*). The exhibition in the Institute includes a model of the vast workshop that once stood opposite the family house. The remaining part still standing is currently being restored to house a cinema that was due to open as we went to press. In July and August films are screened outside (see Cinema in the Entertainment section).

The Institut Lumière (☎ 04 78 78 18 95; metro Monplaisir Lumière), 25 Rue du Premier Film (8e), 3km south-east of Place Bellecour along Cours Gambetta, is open from 2 to 7 pm (closed Monday). Admission is 25/20FF for adults/students.

Musée Urbain Tony Garnier This unusual open-air museum – the only one of its kind in France – pays homage to Lyonnais architect Tony Garnier (1869-1948) who, in the 1930s, designed and built the low-cost council housing estate in which this urban museum is housed. A tour of the 50 seven-storey apartment blocks – home to some 5000 people – reveals 24 fantastic wall murals illustrating different aspects of Garnier's 'ideal city'. Each mural, painted on the side of the one of the apartment blocks, is 220 sq metres and took one month to paint. The last six murals feature 'ideal cities' painted by Egyptian, Indian, African, Mexican, Russian and American artists.

As the Musée Urbain Tony Garnier is, in fact, a rejuvenated housing estate, you can stroll its streets any time. For information contact the Atelier Tony Garnier (☎ 04 78 75 16 15), 4 Rue des Serpollières (8e). It runs guided tours (25FF) on Saturday at 2 and 4 pm and also sells a 15FF information booklet (in English or French) that is well worth picking up. You can also visit an apartment on the estate (10FF), furnished as it was in the 1930s with the help of the residents who contributed most of the items. The Atelier Tony Garnier is open from 2 to 6 pm (closed Sunday and Monday).

Bus No 53 from Gare de Perrache stops outside the museum.

Parc de la Tête d'Or This 105 hectare English-style park (☎ 04 78 89 53 52; metro Masséna), laid out in the 1860s, is graced by a lake, botanical garden, zoo and renowned **roseraie** (rose garden). In fine weather, you can rent boats and play miniature golf here. Take bus No 71 from the Rhône-side quay of the Presqu'île and across the river by the Churchill Bridge, or No 41 or 47 from Gare de la Part-Dieu.

The park is open from 6 am to 9 pm (11 pm from April to September). The open-air section of the **Jardin Botanique** (☎ 04 72 82 35 00), in the park's south-eastern corner, can be visited from 9 to 11.30 am and 1.30 to 5 pm; the greenhouses, including one with carnivorous plants, are open slightly shorter hours. From March to October, the **Jardin Alpin** (Alpine Garden) is open daily from 8 to 11.30 am only.

Also in the park, **Guignol puppet shows** (☎ 04 78 93 71 75) are held at Place de l'Observatoire throughout the year (weather permitting). Tickets cost 15FF for adults and 12FF for children.

Organised Tours

The tourist office has a mind-boggling choice of thematic city tours (50/25FF adults/students) on offer. Alternatively you can hire a set of headphones to guide yourself round the city, or hop on a bus (☎ 04 78 98 56 00) for a two hour tour.

Navig-Inter (☎ 04 78 42 96 81; fax 04 78 42 11 09), 13bis Quai Rambaud, conducts river excursions (42FF for adults, 30FF for children; one to 1½ hours) from the dock opposite 3 Quai des Célestins (metro Bellecour or Vieux Lyon; 2e). Its evening cruise (54/42FF; one hour), departing on Saturday at 9.30 pm from mid-July to mid-August, is particularly pleasant, as are its year-round dinner cruises (210/140FF; 2¾ hours), which depart from the Left Bank, next to 23 Quai Claude Bernard (7e). Advance bookings are essential.

Special Events

All summer long, the streets of Vieux Lyon ring with the sound of buskers, street entertainers and various musical festivals. In mid-September it plays host to the two-day Vieux Lyon Tupiniers (Old Lyon Pottery Festival), and in December it celebrates the Festival de Musique du Vieux Lyon (☎ 04 78 42 39 04 for information). On 8 December, the city is lit up with the Fête des Lumières (Festival of Lights), marking the Feast of the Immaculate Conception. Around 8 pm, a procession of people carrying candles wends its way from Place Saint Jean in Vieux Lyon to Basilique Notre Dame de Fourvière. The faithful not in the procession place candles in the windows of their homes.

From mid-September in even-numbered years, there is the month-long dance festival, Biennale de la Danse, and in odd-numbered years during the same period, the Biennale d'Art Contemporain (Contemporary Art Biennial).

Places to Stay – Budget

Camping The *Camping Municipal Porte de Lyon* (☎ 04 78 35 64 55) is some 10km north-west of Lyon in Dardilly. Open all year, this attractive and well equipped camping ground charges 66FF for two people with a tent and vehicle. Bus No 19 (towards Ecully-Dardilly) from the Hôtel de Ville metro station stops right out front. By car, take the A6 towards Paris.

Hostels A new 180 bed ***Auberge de Jeunesse*** (☎ 04 78 15 05 50; fax 04 78 15 05 51), 40-45 Montée du Chemin Neuf, Vieux Lyon, has recently opened. A dorm bed here costs 69FF per person, including breakfast. Sheets cost 17FF. The ***Vénissieux Auberge de Jeunesse*** (☎ 04 78 76 39 23; fax 04 78 77 51 11), 5.5 km south-east of Gare de Perrache at 51 Rue Roger Salengro in Vénissieux. A dorm bed for the night here costs 48FF and the hostel is open from 7.30 to 12.30 am. From the Presqu'île, take bus No 35 from next to the main post office (metro Bellecour) to the Georges Lévy stop. From Gare de la Part-Dieu, take bus No 36 (towards Minguettes) and get off at the Viviani-Joliot-Curie stop. From Gare de Perrache, take bus No 53, which stops 500m north of the hostel at the États-Unis-Viviani stop.

The ***Centre International de Séjour*** (☎ 04 78 76 14 22), 46 Rue du Commandant Pégoud (8e), is 4km south-east of Gare de Perrache and just behind 101 Blvd des États-Unis. A bed in a quad/double/single costs 82/104/130FF (78/93/123FF on weekends) per person, including breakfast. The centre is served by the same buses as the Vénissieux Auberge de Jeunesse; get off at the États-Unis-Beauvisage stop (the Viviani stop if you're on the No 35).

Gîtes Lyon's numerous chambres d'hôtes are listed in the *Guide Hébergements – Le Rhône*, distributed free at the tourist office.

Gîtes de France (☎ 04 72 77 17 50; fax 04 78 38 21 15; metro Perrache), 1 Rue Général Plessier (2e), arranges B&B-type accommodation in family homes on and around town. B&B accommodation booked through the ***Bed & Breakfast*** (☎ 04 72 57 99 22; fax 04 72 57 92 51), 4 Rue Joliot (5e), costs 120 to 170FF per person a night.

Hotels – Presqu'île Presqu'île's cheap hotels are pretty scattered. The friendly ***Hôtel Vaubecour*** (☎ 04 78 37 44 91; fax 04 78 42 90 17; metro Ampère), on the 2nd floor at 28 Rue Vaubecour (2e), is a spotless place a few blocks west of the Rue Victor Hugo pedestrian mall. Basic singles/doubles start at 110/140FF, triples/quads with washbasin and bidet at 199FF. Hall showers are 15FF. There's free parking south of Rue Fanklin.

One block north of Place des Terreaux, ***Hôtel Le Terme*** (☎ 04 78 28 30 45; fax 04 78 27 38 29; metro Hôtel de Ville), on the 1st floor at 7 Rue Sainte Catherine (1er), has simply furnished singles/doubles/triples with washbasin and bidet for 130/180/200FF. Doubles with shower are 250FF.

The ***Hôtel des Marronniers*** (☎ 04 78 37 04 82; metro Bellecour), on the 2nd floor at 5 Rue des Marronniers (2e), has serviceable washbasin and bidet-equipped rooms starting at 125/150/180/200FF for one/two/three/four people.

Hôtel d'Ainay (☎ 04 78 42 43 42; metro Ampère), 14 Rue des Remparts d'Ainay (2e), just off Place Ampère, has singles/doubles from 139/175FF (20/218FF with shower, 223/235FF with shower and toilet). Hall showers are 15FF.

Nearby is the ***Hôtel Alexandra*** (☎ 04 78 37 75 79; fax 04 72 40 94 34; metro Perrache), 49 Rue Victor Hugo (2e), with rooms for one or two people with shower/bath for 190/249FF.

The ***Hôtel de Vichy*** (☎ 04 78 37 42 58; metro Perrache), 60bis Rue de la Charité (2e), has rock-bottom rooms for 135/145FF for one/two people.

Hôtel Le Beaujolais (☎ 04 78 37 39 15; metro Perrache), 22 Rue d'Enghien (2e), is an unfriendly, last-resort sort of place in the seedy area west of Place Carnot. Frighteningly basic rooms for one or two people with/without shower are 170/140FF.

The ***Hôtel Victoria*** (☎ 04 78 37 57 61; fax 04 78 42 91 07; metro Perrache), 3 Rue Delandine (2e), is a two star, lift-equipped place with singles/doubles from 103/127FF.

Hotels – Vieux Lyon The ***Hôtel Celtic*** (☎ 04 78 28 01 12; fax 04 78 28 01 34; metro Vieux Lyon), 10 Rue François Vernay (5e), smells a bit like a swimming pool but at least it's clean. Singles/doubles with shared shower cost 130/160FF. A private shower is 30FF extra. Spitting distance away is the ***Hôtel Le Terminus Saint Paul*** (☎ 04 78 28 13 29; fax 04 72 00 97 27; metro Vieux Lyon), 6 Rue Lainerie (5e). Doubles with shower cost from 170FF (from 260FF with bath).

Hotels – Croix Rousse The friendly and very local ***Hôtel Croix Rousse*** (☎ 04 78 28 29 85; fax 04 78 27 00 26; metro Croix Rousse), 157 Blvd de la Croix Rousse (4e), has spotlessly clean doubles with shower and toilet for 220FF. Round the corner at 1 Rue Victor Fort (4e) is the cheaper ***Hôtel de la Poste*** (☎ 04 78 28 62 67; metro Croix Rousse), where bargain-basement rooms for one or two people start at 100FF.

Places to Stay – Mid-Range

Presqu'île Cheaper two-star places in Lyon's commercial centre include the 20 room ***Hôtel Le Colbert*** (☎ 04 72 56 08 98; fax 04 72 56 08 65; metro Bellecour), on the 1st floor at 4 Rue des Archers (2e). It has bright but antiseptic doubles for 285FF.

Hôtel Saint Vincent (☎ 04 78 27 22 56; fax 04 78 30 92 87; 1er), 9 Rue Pareille, is just across the Saône from the northern end of Vieux Lyon. Saint Vincent has singles/doubles/triples with shower and toilet for 210/250/270FF.

Singles/doubles at the classy hostelry-style ***Hôtel Élysée***, (☎ 04 78 42 03 15; fax 04 78 37 76 49; metro Bellecour), 92 Rue du Président Édouard Herriot (2e), start at 280/350FF.

The very red, three star ***Hotel des Artistes*** (☎ 04 78 42 04 88; fax 04 78 42 93 76; metro Cordeliers), overlooking the Théâtre des Célestins at 8 Rue Gaspard André (2e), has comfortable singles/doubles with shower for 350/390FF.

Five blocks south of Place des Terreaux is the ***Hôtel Moderne*** (☎ 04 78 42 21 83; fax 04 72 41 04 40; metro Cordeliers), 13 Rue Dubois (1er), which has basic singles/doubles for 200/240FF and rooms with shower for 290/315FF.

Near Gare de Perrache Hotels next to Perrache train station include the two star ***Hôtel du Dauphiné*** (☎ 04 78 37 24 19; fax 04 78 92 81 52; metro Perrache), 3 Rue Duhamel (2e). Small, functional singles with shower start at 180FF; tacky doubles/quads with shower and toilet are 250/280FF.

There are several other two and three-star hotels situated in the immediate vicinity.

Places to Stay – Top End

Lyon has plenty of upmarket hotels geared more to a corporate bank account than a backpacker's wallet. Truly, madly, deeply worthy of the cash is the lavish ***Cour des Loges*** (☎ 04 78 42 75 75; fax 04 72 40 93 61; metro Vieux Lyon), housed in a Renaissance mansion wrapped around a traboule on Rue du Bœuf (5e). Modern, split-level duplex suites with sunken baths and avant-garde paintings adorning the walls start at around 1000FF.

Equally historic is ***La Tour Rose*** (☎ 04 78 37 25 90; fax 04 78 42 26 02; metro Vieux Lyon), 22 Rue du Bœuf (5e). Lushly furnished suites are a celebration of Lyon's past silk tradition while the hotel restaurant is housed in a former chapel topped with a glass and steel roof. Expect to pay at least 950/1400FF for the privilege.

Places to Eat

Lyonnaiseries (Lyon specialities) are not for the faint hearted. Meaty dishes worth sinking your teeth into include *boudin blanc* (veal sausage), *quenelles* (lighter-than-light flour, egg and cream dumplings), *quenelles de brochet* (pike quenelles, usually served in a creamy crayfish sauce Nantua), and *andouillette* (sausages made from pigs' intestines). Yum.

Bouchons

In the world of Lyonnais gastronomy, a *bouchon* is a small, friendly, unpretentious restaurant that serves traditional Lyonnais cuisine. In most of France, however, the strict definition of the word conjures up the more prosaic meanings of 'bottle stopper', 'cork' or 'traffic jam'.

When ordering wine in a bouchon, always ask for wine in a *pot*, a 460mL glass bottle with a solid 3cm-thick glass bottom and sometimes adorned with an elastic band round its neck to prevent wine drips when pouring. Contrary to what your mother taught you as a child, you might well be required to keep your knife and fork for the duration of the meal; wiping your eating gadgets clean with a piece of bread between courses is allowed.

In keeping with tradition, many bouchons are closed in July and August.

Bouchons The ***Café des Fédérations*** (☎ 04 78 28 26 00; metro Hôtel de Ville), 8 Rue Major Martin (1er), is one of Lyon's most splendid bouchons (see the boxed text 'Bouchons'). And it's always packed, despite the entertaining apron-clad patron offering evening diners no choice beyond one 145FF *menu* comprising a plate of cold meats and Croix Rousse caviar (lentils dressed in a creamy sauce) as well as a main dish (usually tripe) and cheese or dessert. Reservations here are essential. It's closed on weekends.

Another place always full is ***Le Garet*** (☎ 04 78 28 16 94; metro Hôtel de Ville), 7 Rue du Garet (1er). This is a warm and convivial bouchon where old friends have been meeting for years. The *plat du jour* costs 56FF and *menus* range from 86FF (lunch only) to 115FF. It is also closed on weekends.

Chez Georges (☎ 04 78 28 30 46; metro Hôtel de Ville), 8 Rue du Garet (1er), is a homely bouchon with house specialities such as tripe and *cervelle d'agneau* (lamb's brains). It is open weekdays from noon to 2 pm and 7.30 to 10 pm.

Typical Lyonnais specialities are laid out for all to see at the friendly and unpretentious ***Restaurant La Meunière*** (☎ 04 78 28 62 91; metro Cordeliers), 11 Rue Neuve (1er). Cold dishes are displayed in a large banquet-style table that dominates this elegant bouchon. *Menus* start at 95FF and it is open from 12.15 to 1.45 pm and 8 to 9.45 pm (closed Sunday and Monday). Reservations are recommended.

Another place always packed is the ***Bistro Pizay*** (☎ 04 78 28 37 26; metro Hôtel de Ville), 4 Rue Verdi (1er). A terrace around the back is opened in summer and they serve unusual *lasagne de foie gras aux pommes* (duck liver pâté lasagne with apples). *Menus* are 72 or 98FF and it is open until 11.30 pm (closed all day Monday and Tuesday lunchtime).

Less frequented by tourists is ***Chez Chabert*** (☎ 04 78 42 99 65), 14 Quai Romain Rolland in Vieux Lyon. Liver lovers will adore the succulent foie (liver) here. Beware of the potent liquor served free of charge with coffee and topped up constantly! It has *menus* for 110 and 180FF and is open from 7.30 pm.

Brasseries Famed among European brasseries and featured in most French school textbooks is the very large ***Brasserie Georges*** (☎ 04 72 56 54 54; metro Perrache), 30 Cours de Verdun (2e), where over 500 people dine amid the splendour of ornate 1920s ceiling murals, floor tiles and upholstered red banquettes. The brasserie, which actually dates from 1836, set world records in 1986 and again in 1996 for dishing up the largest dish of *choucroute* (sauerkraut) weighing a grotesque 1.5 tonnes and, 10 years on, for producing the biggest baked Alaska (34m-long). The numerous choucroutes and baked Alaska dishes for which the brasserie is famed today are thankfully a tad smaller in size. It's open from 7 am to 12.15 am, and has live music on Saturday nights.

The ***Brasserie Francotte*** (☎ 04 78 37 38 64; metro Cordeliers), overlooking the Théâtre des Célestins at 8 Place des Célestins (2e), is popular with the theatre crowd as well as early risers in search of breakfast (35FF). It's open from 8 am to midnight and sporadically hosts live jazz bands. Equally refined is the large ***Grand Café des Negociants*** (☎ 04 78 42 50 05; metro Cordeliers), 2 Place Francisque Regaud (2e). The walls are lined with mirrors and the service, by charming waiters, is impeccable. It serves lovely light fish dishes among other things and is open until midnight.

Other Lyonnais Restaurants Cheap and cheerful and favoured for its elephant-sized portions is ***La Randonnée*** (☎ 04 78 27 86 81; metro Hôtel de Ville), 4 Rue Terme (1er). It has a vegetarian plate for 30FF, a *rapide buffet* comprising omelettes, pasta and the like for 25FF, and evening *menus* from 49FF. It's closed Sunday lunchtime and all day Monday.

Not the type of place you'd be feel comfortable strolling in with jeans is the ***Restaurant Chevallier*** (☎ 04 78 28 19 83; metro Hôtel de Ville), 40 Rue de Sergent Blandan (1er). Fine French cuisine is served here with lunchtime/evening *menus* starting at 90/105FF. It is open until 9.45 pm (closed Saturday lunchtime).

Harking back in history is the nearby ***La Table des Échevins*** (☎ 04 78 39 98 33; metro Hôtel de Ville), 12 Rue Major Martin (1er), which specialises in medieval Lyonnais cuisine such as *agneau au persil* (lamb with parsley). There are 78, 98 and 138FF evening *menus*, a 55FF lunch *menu* and a 36FF plat du jour.

Heading up the pentes to Croix Rousse along Rue d'Austerlitz, you come to the fun ***Petit Gadin*** (☎ 04 78 39 72 85; metro Croix Paquet) at No 17 (4e). It has good-value lunchtime/evening *menus* for 65/115FF, serves the best *tiramisu* in the whole of Lyon and has extremely funky 3D glass-topped tables. Close by, Rue Royale (metro Croix Paquet) is lined with fun places to eat. The rustic decor at the ***Un Petit Tour de Camargue*** (☎ 04 78 39 32 33) at No 74 (4e) is particularly charming.

La Tassée, (☎ 04 72 77 79 00; metro Bellecour; 2e), 20 Rue de la Charité, is said by some to be one of the best places in town for local culinary specialities and superb Beaujolais. Either way, it's pricey and closed Sunday.

About 12km north of the city France's most famous chef presides over his three Michelin star restaurant ***Paul Bocuse*** (☎ 04 72 42 90 90; fax 04 72 27 85 87), at 50 Quai de la Plage, Collonges-au-Mont-d'Or. Larger-than-life portraits of France's gastronomic 'emperor' and king of nouvelle cuisine adorn the outside walls of the restaurant, while inside you can treat yourself to a whole host of 'Bocuse wonders' including truffle soup or chicken baked and served inside a sealed pig's bladder. There are *menus* for 510, 610, 710 and 740FF (410FF for weekday lunches) and reservations are mandatory. Take bus No 184 from Gare de Perrache; a taxi from the centre of Lyon costs around 130FF.

Ethnic Cuisines For an oriental snack standing up, stroll the length of Rue Sainte Marie des Terreaux and Rue Sainte Catherine (metro Hôtel de Ville), both of which are lined with Chinese, Turkish etc quick-eating joints.

On the way to Croix Rousse is the small and cosy African ***La Mangue Amère*** (☎ 04 78 39 15 42; metro Croix Paquet), 7 Montée de l'Ampithéâtre (1er). *Menus* cost 75 or 105FF and its *mousse d'avocat* (avocado mousse) simply melts in your mouth. The 'Bitter Mango' is open until 11 pm (closed Monday).

Always packed is ***La Case Créole*** (☎ 04 78 29 41 70; metro Hôtel de Ville), a young and trendy Creole place at 4 Rue Verdi (1er). *Menus* start at 68FF and it is open until 11 pm (closed all day Tuesday and Wednesday lunchtime). ***La Mamounia*** (☎ 04 78 28 68 44; metro Hôtel de Ville), close by at 20 Rue du Bât d'Argent (1er), is a Moroccan place. All entrées/main dishes cost 28/99FF.

The Syrian ***Alyssaar*** (☎ 04 78 29 57 66; metro Hôtel de Ville), 29 Rue du Bât d'Argent, specialises in the cuisine of Aleppo, 'the gastronomic capital of the Middle East' as far as the Syrian-born owner is concerned. The *assiette du khalife* (seven varieties of hors d'œuvres) costs 76FF and *menus* go for 78, 87 and 105FF. It is open from 7.30 pm to midnight (closed Sunday).

Cafés Outside cafés spill across every square and empty patch of street in Vieux Lyon on sunny days. Fountain-flooded Place des Terreaux is likewise one big outside café in summer.

Particularly tasteful is the ***Sol Café*** (☎ 04 72 77 66 69; metro Vieux Lyon), 28 Rue du Bœuf (5e), which is permanently adorned with fresh sunflowers and serves light tapas-style snacks. It's open from noon to midnight (closed Sunday and Monday).

Across the Saône and on the Presqu'île is the artsy ***Café 203*** (☎ 04 78 28 66 65; metro Hôtel de Ville), 9 Rue Garet (1er), popular with the opera crowd for its good-value 65FF *menu* that includes a glass of wine.

Handy for a quick nibble after a museum tour is the small but busy Vietnamese ***Petit Grain*** (☎ 04 72 41 77 85; metro Ampère), close to the Textile History Museum at 19 Rue de la Charité (2e) in the Presqu'île. The 'Little Grain' is open from 10 am to 8 pm and has healthy salads, spicy meats and the like for 40FF.

The full flavour of 1960s flower power is still alive and well at Croix Rousse's much loved ***Resto Végétarien***, a bohemian vegetarian place on one of the pentes leading up to the Croix Rousse plateau at 59 Montée de la Grande Côte (1er). Seating is around flower-filled communal tables or on floor cushions. It is the only place in town to practise a *prix libre* policy, meaning that there are no fixed prices: you simply pay what you think your meal is worth (Scrooges not welcome). It is open from 4 to 7.30 pm (closed Sunday).

Self-Catering Lush fruit, vegetables, olives, cheese and an abundance of fresh bread in all shapes and sizes are sold at the colourful ***outdoor food markets***, held each morning, except Monday, on Blvd de la Croix Rousse (metro Croix Rousse; 4e) and on Quai Saint Antoine (metro Bellecour; 2e).

In the northern Presqu'île, the covered ***Halle de la Martinière*** (metro Hôtel de Ville), 24 Rue de la Martinière (1er), is open from 6.30 am to 12.30 pm and 4 to 7.30 pm (closed Sunday afternoon and Monday). There is a giant ***Carrefour*** supermarket (metro Part-Dieu) in the Part Dieu Centre (closed Sunday).

Seeking a bit of a taste-bud tickle? Head for the expensive and exclusive ***La Vieille Réserve*** for wine (metro Hôtel de Ville), on the corner of Rue d'Algerie and Place Tobie Robatel (1er); ***Foie Gras Pierre Champion*** for duck liver pâté (metro Bellecour), 4 Place Bellecour (2e); ***Rich Art*** for designer chocolate (metro Bellecour), 1 Rue du Plat (2e); ***Fromagerie*** for cheese (metro Perrache or Ampère), 39 Rue de la Charité (2e); or the ***Whisky Lodge*** for 118 types of whisky (metro Bellecour), 7 Rue Ferrandière (2e).

Entertainment

The tourist office has full details on Lyon's rich and varied cultural and entertainment scene. It also distributes the free fortnightly *Le Petit Bulletin*, which lists what's on where, as does the weekly *Lyon Poche* (7FF at newsagents). Tickets for many events are sold at FNAC (☎ 04 72 40 49 49; metro Bellcour), 85 Rue de la République (2e).

Cinemas Lyon has no less than 15 cinemas. Tickets cost around 45FF. For English-language film screenings try the ***Cinéma Ambiance*** (☎ 04 78 28 07 52; metro Cordeliers), 12 Rue de la République (2e), or ***Cinéma CNP*** (☎ 04 78 27 26 25; metro Hôtel de Ville or Cordeliers), 40 Rue du Président Édouard Herriot (1er).

On warm summer evenings films are shown under the stars on the square in front of the ***Institut Lumière*** (☎ 04 78 78 18 95;

metro Monplaisir Lumière), 25 Rue du Premier Film (8e), and under the trees on Place Colbert (metro Croix Paquet; 1er).

Opera, Theatre & Classical Music From October to June, Lyon's neoclassical ***opera house*** (☎ 04 72 00 45 45; metro Hôtel de Ville; 1er), Place de la Comédie, which was built in 1832 and completely remodelled in 1993, stages opera, ballet, classical concerts and recitals. Opera tickets cost 90 to 380FF. The box office is open from 11 am to 7 pm (closed Sunday). The ***Auditorium*** (☎ 04 78 95 95 95; metro Garibaldi), 149 Rue Garibaldi (1er), is a popular venue for classical concerts.

The box office at the ***Théâtre des Célestins*** (☎ 04 72 77 40 00; metro Cordeliers), Place des Célestins (2e), dating from 1877, is open from 11 am to 6 pm (closed Sunday). ***Théâtre les Ateliers*** (☎ 04 78 37 46 30; metro Cordeliers) is at 5 Rue du Petit David (2e).

Café-theatres include the comic ***L'Âne Rouge*** (☎ 04 78 39 37 55; metro Vieux Lyon), 11 rue Juiverie (5e), and the ***Café des Arts*** (☎ 04 72 41 89 90; metro Vieux Lyon), 4 Rue Saint Georges (5e).

Dance Contemporary dance, cabarets and occasional rock concerts take place at the ***Maison de la Dance*** (☎ 04 72 78 18 00; metro Grange Blanche), 8 Ave Jean Mermoz (8e).

Pubs & Clubs Top drinking holes include the Irish ***Shamrock*** (metro Hôtel de Ville), 15 Rue Sainte Catherine (1er); the ***Barrel House***, next door at No 13; and the ***Albion***, immediately opposite at No 12. All three are open until 3 am on weekends. For more of a down-under touch try the ***Down Under Australian Pub*** (metro Hôtel de Ville), 12 Rue du Griffon (1er). ***Café Léon*** (metro Cordeliers), 8 Rue de la Monnaie (2e), is a busy but pricey, late-night tapas bar. In Vieux Lyon, head for the smoky ***Smoking Dog***, 16 Rue Lainerie (5e), open until 1 am.

Kafé Myzik (☎ 04 72 07 04 26; metro Croix Paquet) is a hole-in-the-wall bar-cum-club at 20 Montée St Sébastien (1er) that often hosts live bands. Admission costs a token 1FF. The very local ***Whisky Ping Pong*** (metro Croix Rousse), 4ter Rue Belfort (4e), is also packed thanks to its house specialities – *cassoulet* (a hearty stew), whisky and backgammon. This one is open until 3 am (closed Sunday and Monday).

Shopping

On Sunday morning from 7 am to 1 pm, in Vieux Lyon (metro Vieux Lyon; 5e), head for the Marché de l'Artisanat (Artists' Market) along Quai Fulchiron, which has items produced by local crafters and artists (jewellery, pottery etc). On Place Bellecour, a postage stamp and telephone card market is held each Sunday from 8.30 am to 12.30 pm (metro Place Bellecour; 2e). Books – old and new – can be browsed through and bought at the outdoor book market along Quai de la Pêcherie (metro Hôtel de Ville; 1er) on Saturday and Sunday from 10 am to 6 pm.

La Cité des Antiquaires (☎ 04 72 44 91 98), 117 Blvd Stalingrad (6e), in the Villeurbanne suburb is the third largest antique market in Europe. It is open Thursday, Saturday and Sunday from 9.30 am to 12.30 pm and 2.30 to 7 pm. Also in Villeurbanne, there is a giant flea market at 1 Rue du Canal, which is a lot of fun and open on Thursday and Saturday from 8 am to noon and Sunday from 6 am to 1 pm.

Getting There & Away

Air Lyon-Satolas airport (☎ 04 72 22 76 91 for information, ☎ 04 72 22 72 21 for the switchboard) is 25km east of the city.

Bus Most of the intercity buses to destinations north, east and south of Lyon (eg Annecy, Chambéry, Grenoble, Pérouges, Valence, Saint Étienne) depart from the bus terminal under the Centre d'Échange, next to Gare de Perrache. Timetables and other information are available from the information office of Lyon's mass transit authority, TCL (☎ 04 78 71 70 00; www.tcl.fr). Tickets are sold by the driver. Buses to places west of Lyon (information ☎ 04 78 43 40 74) leave from outside the Gorge de Loup metro station.

The Eurolines office (☎ 04 72 41 09 09; metro Perrache), on the bus station level of the Centre d'Échange (follow the 'Lignes Internationales' signs), is open from 9 am to 6.30 pm (closed Sunday).

Train Lyon has two mainline train stations (☎ 08 36 35 35 35 for both): Gare de Perrache, on the Presqu'île; and Gare de la Part-Dieu, about 1.5km east of the Rhône in an area of modern office blocks. Only a handful of local trains use Gare Saint Paul in Vieux Lyon.

In general, trains that begin or end their runs in Lyon (including most short-haul lines) use Perrache, while trains passing through the city (including most trains to southern France and the TGVs to Roissy Charles de Gaulle airport and Lille) stop at Part-Dieu. Some trains – such as the TGVs to/from Paris and most runs to the Alps and Geneva – stop at both stations.

TGV travel to and from Paris's Gare de Lyon (two hours; hourly) costs 232 to 304FF. On some days, there's also a non-TGV train overnight (250FF; five hours). Lyon has direct rail links to *all* parts of France and Europe. Destinations accessible by direct TGV include Roissy Charles de Gaulle airport (325 to 405FF; 2¼ hours), Disneyland Paris, Lille-Europe (402 to 509FF; three hours) and Nantes (350FF; five hours). Following the completion of the new high-speed railroad southbound (see TGV in the Getting Around chapter), Lyon will have direct TGV links to Avignon, Marseille and Monpellier.

Gare de Perrache The complex that includes Gare de Perrache (metro Perrache) consists of two main buildings: the Centre d'Échange, whose lower levels serve as a bus terminal and metro station, and the train station itself, southward across the pedestrian bridge.

The SNCF information office (☎ 04 72 40 10 65) on the station's lower level is open from 9 am to 7 pm (6.30 pm on Saturday; closed Sunday and holidays). At least one ticket counter is staffed 24 hours a day. SOS Voyageurs (☎ 04 78 37 03 31), the travellers aid organisation, has an office (open weekdays until 8 pm) on the station's upper level. From 4.30 am to 1 am, you can take a shower (about 15FF), it's down the half flight of stairs near the Thomas Cook bureau.

Gare de la Part-Dieu The information office of the Part-Dieu train station (metro Part-Dieu; ☎ 08 36 35 35 35), on the courtyard reached via the Vivier Merle exit, is open from 9 am to 7.30 pm (6.30 pm on Saturday; closed Sunday). The Service Clientèle office, which handles reimbursements, is in the same building, open from 10 am to 12.30 pm and 1.45 to 6.15 pm (closed on weekends).

There are luggage lockers under one of the stairways up to platforms G and H. The Part-Dieu branch of SOS Voyageurs (☎ 04 72 34 12 16), at the foot of the stairs up to platforms I and J, is open from 8 am to 8 pm. Showers (15.20FF) under the stairs to platforms A and B are closed between 12.45 and 4.45 am.

Car ADA (☎ 04 78 37 93 93; metro Perrache) has an office at 42 Quai du Docteur Gailleton (2e). At Gare de Perrache, Europcar (☎ 04 78 95 94 94; metro Perrache) has an office on the upper level of the Centre d'Échange. All the major car rental companies have an office at Gare de la Part-Dieu, on the courtyard accessed by the Porte Villette exit.

Getting Around

To/From the Airport Buses (known as Satobus) from the city to Lyon-Satolas airport cost 46/34.50FF for adults/students and take 45 minutes from Gare de Perrache (the stop is between the train station and the Centre d'Échange near the taxis) and 35 minutes from Gare de la Part-Dieu (the stop is across the plaza from the Vivier Merle exit). Buses run every 20 minutes (every 30 minutes on Saturday afternoons, Sunday and holidays) from 5 am to 9 pm (later if there are incoming flights). Lyon-Satolas is also served by buses from Annecy (by reservation), Chambéry, Geneva, Grenoble, Valence and Vienne.

Avoid taking a taxi between the town centre and the airport. Theoretically the 15 minute trip into town costs no more than 220FF. In reality it's at least 300FF.

Metro & Bus Lyon's metro system is run by TCL. The four fast, quiet metro lines are known as A, B, C and D; the last is fully automated (ie driverless). The two funicular railway lines that link Vieux Lyon with Fourvière and Saint Just are known by their initial F and SJ. The metro runs from 5 am to midnight. Tickets must be time-stamped before proceed to the platforms, which incidentally, have no turnstiles.

Tickets Tickets, which cost 8FF singly and 68FF for a carnet of 10, are valid for one-way travel on buses, trolley buses, the metro and the funiculars. They can be used for an hour after being time-stamped for the first time. Up to three transfers are allowed but return trips are not.

The Ticket Liberté (24FF), good for a day of unlimited travel, can be bought on or before the day you use it at some metro ticket machines, on buses and at TCL information offices.

TCL Offices Near Gare de la Part-Dieu, TCL's information and sales bureau (☎ 04 78 71 70 00; metro Part-Dieu), 19 Blvd Vivier Merle (3e), is open weekdays from 7 am to 6.30 pm and Saturday from 9 am to 5 pm. At Gare de Perrache, there's a TCL office on the middle level of the Centre d'Échange, it's open until 7 pm (5 pm on Saturday; closed Sunday). There are other TCL offices in or next to the Bellecour, Vieux Lyon, Croix Rousse and Gorge de Loup metro stations and at 43 Rue de la République (2e; metro Cordeliers).

Taxi To order a taxi, call Taxis Lyonnais (☎ 04 78 26 81 81) or Allô Taxi (☎ 04 78 28 23 23). There is a taxi stand (☎ 04 78 28 08 79) close to Place Terreaux (metro Hôtel de Ville) at the north end of Rue du Président Édouard Herriot.

Bicycle Cycling aficionados are invited to participate in the group rides of Cyclo-Tourist de Lyon (☎ 04 78 42 44 08; metro Vieux Lyon), a cycling club at 19 Rue du Bœuf (5e) in Vieux Lyon. The office is open on Tuesday, Thursday and Friday from 3 to 7 pm. While you're here, pick up a copy of the useful *40 Randonnées ou Pedestres VTT dans le Rhone* (70FF) detailing 40 hiking and cycling routes in the region.

AROUND LYON

Couvent Sainte Marie de la Tourette

The modernistic convent, 30km east of Lyon in La Tourette, is the next best thing after the chapel at Ronchamp (see the French Alps & Jura chapter) for dedicated fans of the architect Le Corbusier (1887-1965), renowned for his stark, concrete building and innovative furniture designs which won him acclaim around the world as one of the 20th century's architectural gods.

Admission to the Couvent Sainte Marie (☎ 04 74 26 79 70; fax 04 74 26 79 99) costs 25/15FF for adults/students. Guided tours are available between 15 June and 15 September daily at 10 and 11 am, and 2, 3, 4, 5 and 6 pm (no tour at 11 am on Sunday). In winter there are hourly afternoon tours on weekends.

La Tourette is 1.5km from L'Arbresle. By car follow the westbound N7 out of Lyon. From Lyon's Gare Saint Paul (metro Vieux Lyon; 5e) there are regular trains to L'Arbresle (25FF; 45 minutes; every 15 to 30 minutes).

Pérouges & La Dombes

The heavily restored medieval village of Pérouges (population 850), perched on a hill 27km north-east of Lyon, is linked to Lyon by bus. Day-trippers flock here year-round to stroll its cobbled streets and munch on *galettes de Perouges* (sweet, light tarts served warm and crusted with sugar) and cider, the traditional Pérougien feast.

Immediately to the south-west is La Dombes, a marshy area whose hundreds of shallow lakes, created over the past six centuries by local farmers, are used primarily as fish ponds for a while and then drained so crops can be grown on the fertile lake bed.

The area, bisected by the N83, attracts lots of wildlife, especially waterfowl. Our feathered friends – including many species from other continents – can be observed at the **Parc des Oiseaux** (bird park; ☎ 04 74 98 05 54) just outside Villars-les-Dombes.

Beaujolais

The hilly Beaujolais region, just north of Villefranche-sur-Saône (and only 40km north of Lyon) is a land of rivers (all tributaries of the Saône), granite peaks (the highest is the 1012m-Mont Saint Rigaud), pastures, small farms and forests. Touring by mountain bike is popular in these parts; 15 routes (230km) for two-wheelers are detailed in the Topoguide entitled *Le Beaujolais à VTT*.

The region is most famous, however, for its wines (see the boxed text 'Beaujolais Wines'), boasting some 150 sq km of terraced vineyards occupying a narrow, 60km-long strip along the right bank of the Saône. Beaujolais' other gastronomic wonders include its fine virgin oils – including pecan nut oil, almond oil and pine kernel oil – available at the Huilerie Beaujolaise (☎ 04 74 69 28 06), 29 Rue des Echarmeaux in Beaujeu; the annual Chestnut Fair (☎ 04 74 64 85 14) held on the last Sunday of October in Thel; and the Pear Fair (☎ 04 78 47 62 43), hosted by Chasselay village on the third Sunday in October.

French Alps & the Jura

'Lances des glaciers fiers, rois blancs' (Lances of proud glaciers, white kings)

Arthur Rimbaud

The French Alps, where fertile, green valleys meet soaring peaks topped with craggy, snowbound summits, form one of the most awesome mountain ranges in the world. In summer, visitors take advantage of hundreds of kilometres of magnificent hiking trails and engage in all sorts of warm-weather sporting activities. In winter, the area's fine ski resorts attract downhill and cross-country enthusiasts from around the globe.

The first half of this chapter covers mountainous areas where you can hike and ski, including the mountains and valleys around Mont Blanc. During the warm months, Annecy, Thonon-les-Bains and Chambéry offer the best of the French Alps' lowland delights: swimming, hiking, parapente (paragliding) and the like. Grenoble, capital of the historical region of Dauphiné, provides big-city amenities and hiking opportunities, while nearby there are less expensive low-altitude ski stations. North of Lake Geneva, Besançon and the Jura towns of Métabief Mont d'Or and Les Rousses offer a taste of the refreshingly untouched Franche-Comté region.

HIGHLIGHTS

- **Chamonix** – marvel at Mont Blanc from the world's highest cable car
- **Bonneval-sur-Arc** – stroll around its cobbled streets
- **Baume-les-Messieurs** – explore the caves and waterfalls
- **Ronchamp** – visit Le Corbusier's chapel

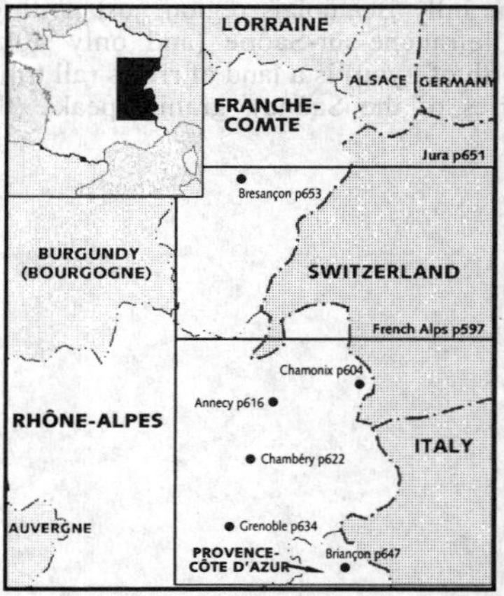

regional cheese specialities – fondue, *raclette, tartiflette* and *gratin Dauphinois*

Chartreuse liqueur – made by the monks in Voiron

Geography

The Alps – whose name is derived from the Ligurian word for pasture – have served as a barrier between Europe's peoples and nations since ancient times. Formed some 44 million years ago, the peaks and valleys have been sculpted by erosion and, especially over the past 1.6 million years, massive glaciers. Both these factors have endowed the Alpine river valleys with mild climates and rich soils, making them very suitable for human settlement.

The Alps stretch for 370km from Lake Geneva (Lac Léman) in the north, almost to Provence in the south. France's border with Italy follows the Alps' highest ridges and peaks.

The Alps' two major historic regions are Savoy and Dauphiné. Savoy covers the northern portion of the Alps and culminates in Europe's highest mountain, Mont Blanc (4808m), with the town of Chamonix at its base. To the west, Annecy acts as the gateway to much of Savoy, while farther south sits the region's historic capital, Chambéry. Dauphiné, which is south of Savoy and stretches eastward all the way to Briançon and the Italian border, is home to Grenoble, the capital of the Alps.

North of Lake Geneva, the Jura Mountains form an arc that extends northward along the Doubs River towards Alsace.

Climate

The Alps are characterised by extreme climatic diversity. As you would expect, the southern slopes are warmer than areas with northern exposure.

There's enough snow most years from December to April for skiing even at lower-altitude stations. In spring (late spring and summer at higher elevations), carpets of flowers bloom next to and within the magnificent forests. Throughout the year, weather conditions can change rapidly.

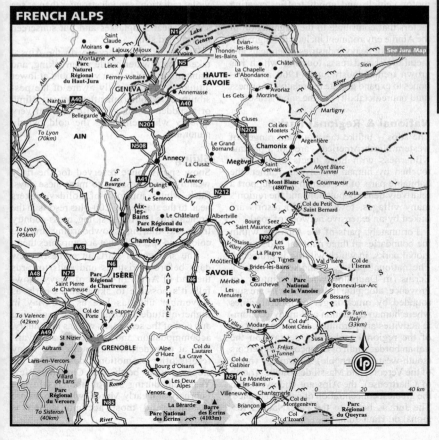

FRENCH ALPS

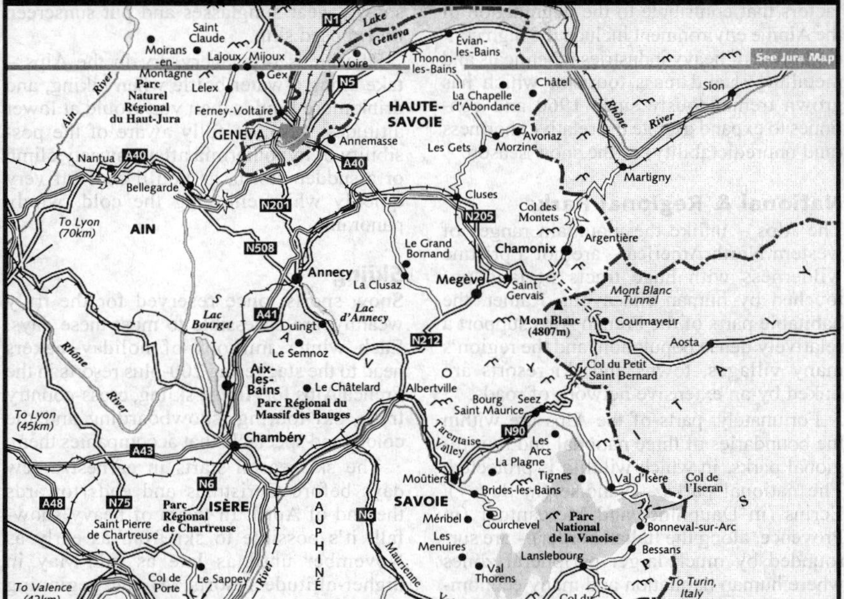

For weather information, call the *météo* (weather bureau information) on ☎ 08 36 68 00 00 for the regional report or ☎ 08 36 68 04 04 for the snow and mountain report. For the departmental report, dial ☎ 08 36 68 02 followed by the two-digit departmental number (see the Regions & Départments map in the Facts about France chapter). Year-round, daily weather bulletins are pinned outside the tourist office in ski resorts.

Ecology & Environment

The Alps' dense road network handles a significant proportion of Western Europe's motor vehicle and goods traffic, creating enormous air-pollution problems. Other factors that contribute to the degradation of the Alpine environment include the high concentration of heavy industries (chemicals and metallurgy) and mass tourism, which has grown tremendously since 1960 and continues to expand despite the relative shortness (and unpredictability) of the snow season.

National & Regional Parks

The Alps – unlike the mountain ranges of western North America – are not a pristine wilderness with huge tracts of land untouched by human endeavour. Rather, the habitable parts of the French Alps support a relatively dense population, and the region's many villages, towns and ski resorts are linked by an extensive network of roads.

Fortunately, parts of the Alps are within the boundaries of three national and four regional parks, in which wildlife is protected. The national parks – Vanoise (in Savoy), Écrins (in Dauphiné) and Mercantour (in Provence, along the Italian border) – are surrounded by much larger peripheral zones where human habitation and many economic activities are permitted. With the addition of the regional parks of Queyras (on the Italian border south of Briançon), the Vercors (south-west of Grenoble), Chartreuse (north of the Vercors) and Massif des Bauges (north of Chartreuse), the Alps are endowed with the greatest concentration of parks in France. The Jura is home to the Parc Naturel Régional du Haut-Jura.

Dangers & Annoyances

Despite precautions such as expensive anti-avalanche fences and tunnels, avalanches pose a very real danger in snowbound areas. Each year many people die as a result of these disasters, and whole valleys can be cut off for days. All avalanche warning signs should be strictly obeyed, whether they are along roads or on ski slopes. They are there for a reason.

On glaciers, be careful of crevasses. A fall or accident in an isolated area can be fatal so never ski, hike or climb alone.

At high altitudes, where the sun's ultraviolet radiation is much stronger than at sea level (and is intensified by reflection off the snow), wear sunglasses and put sunscreen on exposed skin.

The air is often very dry in the Alps – take along a water bottle when hiking, and drink more liquids than you would at lower altitudes. Also, be fully aware of the possibility of hypothermia after a sweaty climb or a sudden storm, as you'll cool off very quickly while enjoying the cold, windy panorama.

Skiing

Snow sports, once reserved for the truly wealthy, are accessible to most these days. Each winter millions of holiday-makers head to the staggering 200-plus resorts in the French Alps for Alpine skiing, cross-country treks, ski touring, snowboarding and the colour and spectacle that accompanies them.

The ski season starts in earnest a few days before Christmas and ends towards the end of April. In years of heavy snowfall, it's possible to ski from as early as November until as late as mid-May in higher-altitude resorts. At the beginning and end of the season, as well as in January, accommodation and lift tickets are available at considerable discounts, and many resorts offer promotional deals. Give the slopes a wide berth over Christmas-New Year, and during school holidays in late February and early March, when prices are sky-high and most accommodation is booked out.

FRENCH ALPS

Summer skiing on high-altitude glaciers is usually possible in July and August in some areas. Most resorts typically have a combination of both cross-country and Alpine (downhill) runs. Some also have snowparks for snowboarders.

Ski Information Every ski station and nearby town has a tourist office providing exhaustive information on skiing, indoor and outdoor activities, and public transport. The local accommodation service (which makes reservations for hotels, chalets etc), ski school and Bureau des Guides are often in the same building. All resorts have post offices, banks, bakeries and supermarkets.

SkiFrance (☎ 01 47 42 23 32; fax 01 47 66 15 94; skifrance@laposte.fr; www.skifrance.fr), 61 Blvd Haussmann, F-75008 Paris, and the Fédération Française de Ski (☎ 04 50 51 40 34; fax 04 50 51 75 90; ski@ffs.fr; www.ffs.fr), 50 Rue des Marguisats, BP 2451, F-74011 Annecy, can both provide information on all French ski resorts.

Alpine Skiing Downhill runs range in length from a few hundred metres to 20km and are colour-coded to indicate the level of difficulty: green (for beginners), blue (for intermediate skiers), red (for advanced skiers) and black (for experts). Summer skiing on glaciers tends to be on short green or blue runs.

Off-Piste Skiing Off-piste skiing, known in French as *hors piste* (skiing outside groomed trails on fresh or powder snow), is popular. However, off-piste skiers should always exercise extreme caution as these areas usually do not have any warning signs. Take a guide with you.

Cross-Country Skiing Known in French as *ski de fond*, cross-country skiing is most popular in the Jura. Cross-country stations are more relaxed and casual than the higher downhill ski resorts, with prices reflecting the lower altitudes, smaller snowfalls and shorter ski season.

Cross-country ski trails are designated as easy or difficult. Resorts charge fees for the upkeep of the trails. Cross-country ski passes cost between 35/140 and 80/320FF per day/week.

Snowboarding Snowboards (*snowboard* or *le surf* in French) and boots can be hired from ski rental shops, while the École de Ski Français (ESF; see Ski Schools) offers group or private snowboarding lessons that cost approximately the same as skiing lessons. Chamonix, Chamrousse, Les Arcs, Les Deux Alpes, La Plagne, Méribel and Espace Killy all have large snowparks equipped with half-pipes, quarters, gaps, tables and other tricky delights.

Ski Equipment Skis, boots and poles can be hired on a daily or weekly basis from ski shops in every resort. Alpine equipment starts at 100/300FF per day/week depending on the resort and the type of skis you hire. Cross-country equipment ranges from 40/200FF to 75/380FF per day/week, and snowboards and boots from around 100/ 750FF to 760/1200FF. You can hire monoskis and telemark skis in most resorts too.

Take a note of the serial number marked on your skis. If you lose them, you have to pay for a replacement pair (take out insurance to cover this cost – see Insurance following). Most ski shops have a locker room where you can leave your skis free of charge overnight.

Always equip yourself with sunglasses, gloves, a *plan des pistes* (free from tourist offices), warm and water-resistant clothing, and sunscreen.

Lifts & Ski Passes A daunting range of contraptions (*remontées mecaniques*) cover the slopes to whisk skiers uphill. Lifts include *téléskis* (drag lifts), *télésièges* (chair lifts), *télécabines* (gondolas), *téléphériques* (cable cars) and *funiculaires* (funicular railways).

Daily, weekly, monthly or seasonal *forfaits* (ski passes) are the best way to use the above. Passes give access to a group of lifts, the lifts in one sector of the resort or the station's entire skiable domain, plus that of neighbouring resorts (including across the border into Switzerland or Italy in some resorts).

Passes are cheaper for children and seniors. Many resorts offer a cheaper package deal covering a six day ski pass and six half-day group lessons. Others offer packages incorporating a six day ski pass and accommodation or ski school.

Ski Schools France's leading ski school, the École de Ski Français has branches in most stations and generally offers private or group tuition at better rates than the smaller, independent ski schools that are in some resorts.

A six day course (three hours of group tuition a day) costs between 400 and 900FF depending on the resort. Private one-hour lessons (for up to four people) cost between 180 and 200FF. All resorts offer lessons for children; some have snow gardens for toddlers aged from three to five (those at Les Deux Alpes, Les Arcs and Val d'Isère are reputedly the best).

Ski Touring Experienced off-piste skiers can ski tour – skiing and climbing some of the less accessible peaks, ridges and glaciers outside resort areas. Tours require mountaineering and ice-climbing skills, are for one or several days, and include accommodation in mountain *refuges*. Seven-day tours start at 4000FF. Experienced guides – essential for these tours – can be contacted in most resorts at the Bureau des Guides or ESF.

Package Deals Package deals are the cheapest way to ski. Most resorts offer excellent-value discount packages (mainly during quiet periods) that typically include a week's accommodation (in a hotel, studio or apartment), a ski pass, and sometimes ski equipment hire and lessons.

The FUAJ (see Accommodation in the Facts for the Visitor chapter) has 17 hostels in the French Alps and offers good-value package deals in winter, starting from 1150/2440FF in the low/high season for six days' hostel accommodation, meals, ski pass and equipment hire. Full details are

Skiing in the Alps

Resort	Trademarks	Alpine Runs
Chamonix-Mont Blanc	High in altitude and attitude. Young, trendy and full of fun	162km
Portes du Soleil	Exclusive resort attracting a more sedate crowd.	650km
Saint Gervais & Megève	Pricey, chic and full of Alpine charm.	300km
La Clusaz	A cheaper spot. Popular locally.	132km
Le Grand Bornand	A day trip from Annecy.	65km
Trois Vallées	Méribel: heavy traffic and heaving bars and clubs.	600km
La Plagne	The family choice. Olympic bobsleigh run.	210km
Les Arcs	Top skiing and snowboarding. Car-free but little charm.	200km
Val d'Isère	Unrivalled alpine skiing. Dizzying nightlife.	300km
Les Deux Alpes	Snowboarders' delight. Summer skiing and lively bar scene.	200km
Alpe d'Huez	Snowboarding park, longest black run, summer skiing.	220km
Le Grand Serre Chevalier	Strung-out resort with door-to-door skiing.	250km
Métabief Mont d'Or	Low altitude village. Snow not guaranteed.	42km
Les Rousses	Popular with French and Swiss day-trippers.	40km
Chartreuse	A series of small, quiet villages.	30km

listed in *Destination Montagne*, published annually by the FUAJ.

Insurance Most package deals include insurance. If you don't have a package deal, take out Carré Neige insurance when you buy your ski pass. It covers mountain rescue costs, breakage or theft of skis etc and costs 14FF per day.

Some resorts offer discounts on lift tickets and lessons if you have a Carte Neige – an annual insurance plan sold at all resorts costing 225/130FF for Alpine/cross-country skiers.

Warm-Weather Activities

Fantastic hiking trails wend their way up and around the mountains near Mont Blanc and crisscross the national parks; the GR5 traverses the entire Alps. Rafting, canoeing and mountain biking are also popular, as are the more gentle pastimes of horse riding and ice-skating. Warm-weather activities such as these can be enjoyed at most larger ski resorts.

A particularly popular Alpine activity is parapente (paragliding), the sport of floating down from somewhere high suspended from a wing-shaped, steerable parachute that allows you (if you're lucky and skilled) to catch updraughts and fly around for quite a while. The ESF in most resorts offers courses: a *baptême de l'air* (initiation flight) costs from 350 to 500FF. A five day *stage d'initiation* (beginners' course) costs from 2000 to 3250FF. A second five-day course, which prepares you to pursue the sport on your own, costs the same.

Parachutisme (skydiving) will cost you a lot more: 900FF for a day of instruction and a *saut d'initiation* (first jump) from 1200m (or 1900FF from a heart-destroying 3500m).

Places to Stay & Eat

Most resorts have a central reservation service that books accommodation in hotels, studios, apartments and chalets. Prices vary drastically between the low and high seasons. Hotels generally offer full or half-board. Most apartments and studios

Skiing in the Alps

Cross-Country Runs	Skiing Expertise Required	Ski Lifts	Ski Pass (6 days)
42km	Intermediate, advanced, off-piste	64	930/1080FF
40km	All abilities, off-piste	220	928FF
84km	Beginners, intermediate	81	871/1080FF
70km	Beginners, intermediate	56	750FF
56km	Beginners, intermediate	39	640FF
90km	All abilities	200	1080FF
90km	Beginners, intermediate	110	1005FF
45km	All abilities, off-piste	77	995FF
24km	Intermediate, advanced, off-piste	102	1005FF
20km	Intermediate, advanced	63	908FF
50km	All abilities	86	1000FF
45km	All abilities, off-piste	72	900FF
120km	Predominantly cross-country	33	525FF
220km	Predominantly cross-country	40	601FF
80km	Beginners, cross-country	19	520FF

have a self-catering kitchenette – the cheapest option for budget travellers. Gîtes de France (see Gîtes Ruraux & B&Bs in the Facts for the Visitor chapter) publishes the annual *Gîtes de Neige* guide.

The Club Alpin Français (CAF) has numerous mountain *refuges* in the Alps. Full details are available from the CAF offices listed in this chapter. Advance reservations are required for most *refuges*.

Restaurants in ski resorts tend to offer poor-quality cuisine at rip-off prices. On the slopes, you'll ski past plenty of restaurants with prices to reflect the altitude.

Getting There & Away

The Alps' closest international airports are Genève-Cointrin airport near Geneva, Switzerland, and Lyon-Satolas airport, just outside Lyon. On a clear day and with the right flight path, the view through the plane window is the best introduction to the Alps you can get. In winter there are direct bus connections from both airports to numerous ski resorts with Geneva's Aeroski bus (☎ 022-798 20 00) and Lyon's Satobus-Alpes (☎ 04 72 35 94 96; mail@satobus-alps.com; www.satobus-alps.com).

The Eurostar speeds its way through the Channel Tunnel from London-Waterloo to Moûtiers (8¾ hours) and Bourg Saint Maurice (9½ hours) on Saturday during the ski season. Train services within France to many parts of the Alps are excellent. Full details are published in the SNCF's *La Neige en Direct* brochure.

To get to some ski resorts by car you may need snow chains after heavy snowfalls. In the high season, traffic on the *cols* (high mountain passes) leading to the resorts can be hellish. The Mont Blanc and Fréjus road tunnels connect the French Alps with Italy, as do a number of major cols: Petit Saint Bernard (2188m), near Bourg Saint Maurice; Mont Cénis (2083m), in the Haute Maurienne Valley; and Montgenèvre (1850m), near Briançon. Certain mountain passes, such as the Col du Galibier (2558m) and the Col de l'Iseran (2770m), are usually closed between November and June, depending on snowfall. Road signs indicate if passes are blocked well in advance.

Savoy

Bordered by Switzerland and Italy, Savoy (Savoie – pronounced 'sav-WA') rises from the southern shores of Lake Geneva and keeps rising until it reaches the massive Mont Blanc, which dominates the town of Chamonix. Farther south, long U-shaped valleys are obvious relics of ancient glaciers that created lakes such as Lac d'Annecy as well as France's largest natural lake, Lac Bourget, near Aix-les-Bains.

Savoy is divided into two departments, Haute-Savoie and Savoie, and the people of the whole region are known as Savoyards. Despite centuries of French cultural influence, they have managed to keep their identity, and often speak their own dialect, which reveals Provençal influences. In the remote valleys, such as in the Haute Maurienne, rural life goes on as it has for centuries, and the people continue to struggle with the harsh climate and the ever present threat of avalanches.

History

Savoy was long ruled by the House of Savoy, which was founded by Humbert I (or the Whitehanded, as he was known) in the mid-11th century. During the Middle Ages, the dukes of Savoy extended their territory eastward to other areas of the western Alps, including the Piedmont region of what is now Italy.

In the 16th century the dukes of Savoy began to shift their interest from Savoy to their Italian territories; in 1563 they moved their capital from Chambéry to Turin. However, they continued to rule Savoy and managed to resist repeated French attempts to take over the mostly French-speaking region. Savoy was annexed by France in 1792 but was returned 23 years later.

In 1720, Victor Amadeus II, duke of Savoy, became king of Sardinia, and over the next century important territories in northern Italy, including Genoa, came under

Savoyard control. In the mid-19th century, the House of Savoy worked to bring about the unification of Italy under Piedmontese leadership, a goal they achieved in 1861 with the formation of the Kingdom of Italy under King Victor Emmanuel II of the House of Savoy. However, in exchange for Napoleon III's acceptance of the new arrangement and the international agreements that led up to it, Savoy – along with the area around Nice – was ceded to France.

CHAMONIX

• pop 97,000 ✉ 74400 alt 1037m

The town of Chamonix (pronounced 'shah-mo-NEE') sits in a valley surrounded by the most spectacular scenery in the French Alps. The area, a leading mountaineering centre, is almost Himalayan: tongues of deeply crevassed glaciers point toward the valley from the icy spikes and needles of Mont Blanc, which soars 3.8km above the valley floor. Chamonix has been a summer resort since the late 18th century and a winter one from 1903. Since 1965, when the 11.6km-long Mont Blanc tunnel – the world's highest rock-covered tunnel (2480m) – opened, Chamonix has been linked by road to Courmayeur in Italy.

Unlike many other resorts in the Alps, the town's nine ski areas are not connected by a lift system but only by a bus network, making it awkward to change from one area to the next during the day. The mountain range to the east of the valley, the Aiguilles de Chamonix, is characterised by many glaciers and includes the mind-boggling mass of Mont Blanc (4808m). The almost glacier-free Aiguilles Rouges range, whose highest peak is Le Brévent (2525m), runs along the western side of the valley. Argentière, a fine base for hikers and advanced skiers, is a quiet valley village 9km north-east of Chamonix and 9km from the Swiss border.

Information

Tourist Office Chamonix's tourist office (☎ 04 50 53 00 24; fax 04 50 53 58 90; info@chamonix.com; www.chamonix.com), 85 Place du Triangle de l'Amitié, is open from 8.30 am to 12.30 pm and 2 to 7 pm (closed Sunday). It has useful brochures on ski lift hours and costs, *refuges* and camping grounds, and the town's many recreational activities. Ski passes are also sold here. Upstairs, the Centrale de Réservation (☎ 04 50 53 23 33; fax 04 50 53 58 90; reservation@chamonix.com) takes accommodation bookings. In Argentière the tourist office (☎ 04 50 54 02 14; fax 04 50 54 06 39) is at 24 Route du Village.

The CAF (☎ 04 50 53 16 03; fax 04 50 53 27 52), 136 Ave Michel Croz, is usually open from 3 to 7 pm (3 to 6.15 pm on Thursday and from 9 am to noon on Saturday); closed Wednesday and Sunday.

Maison de la Montagne The Maison de la Montagne is near the tourist office at 109 Place de l'Église. On the ground floor is the Compagnie des Guides (☎ 04 50 53 00 88; fax 04 50 53 48 04; chamonix.guides@mont-blanc.com), where mountain guides can be hired year-round. In winter it is open from 8 am to noon and 3 to 7 pm, and during July and August from 6 am to 5 pm. The cost for a guide is from 1220FF per day for up to four people. The 1st floor is home to the ESF (☎ 04 50 53 22 57; fax 04 50 53 65 30), open from 8.15 am to 7 pm in winter.

On the 2nd floor, the Office de Haute Montagne (☎ 04 50 53 22 08), which serves walkers, hikers and mountain climbers, has maps and information on trails, hiking conditions, the weather and *refuges* (they can help non-French speakers make reservations). It is open from 9 am to 12.30 pm and 2.30 to 6.30 pm (closed Sunday).

Money Between the tourist and post offices there are several places to change money. Le Change at 21 Place Balmat offers a decent rate and is usually open from 9 am to 1 pm and 3 to 7 pm (8 am to 8 pm from July to early September and December to April). Outside is a 24 hour exchange machine that accepts banknotes of 15 different currencies. The Banque Laydernier opposite the post office does not charge commission for exchanging French franc travellers cheques.

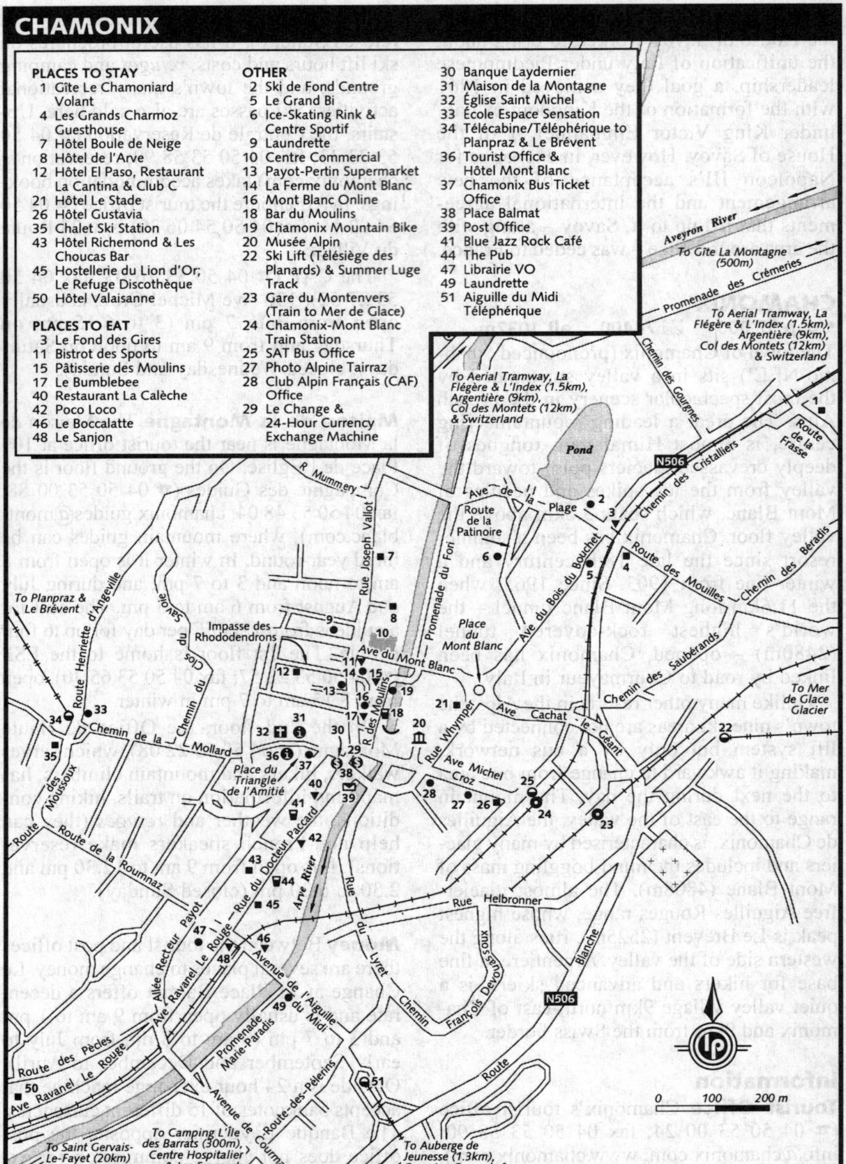
CHAMONIX
PLACES TO STAY
1 Gîte Le Chamoniard Volant
4 Les Grands Charmoz Guesthouse
7 Hôtel Boule de Neige
8 Hôtel de l'Arve
12 Hôtel El Paso, Restaurant La Cantina & Club C
21 Hôtel Le Stade
26 Hôtel Gustavia
35 Chalet Ski Station
43 Hôtel Richemond & Les Choucas Bar
45 Hostellerie du Lion d'Or; Le Refuge Discothèque
50 Hôtel Valaisanne
PLACES TO EAT
3 Le Fond des Gires
11 Bistrot des Sports
15 Pâtisserie des Moulins
17 Le Bumblebee
40 Restaurant La Calèche
42 Poco Loco
46 Le Boccalatte
48 Le Sanjon
OTHER
2 Ski de Fond Centre
5 Le Grand Bi
6 Ice-Skating Rink & Centre Sportif
9 Laundrette
10 Centre Commercial
13 Payot-Pertin Supermarket
14 La Ferme du Mont Blanc
16 Mont Blanc Online
18 Bar du Moulins
19 Chamonix Mountain Bike
20 Musée Alpin
22 Ski Lift (Télésiège des Planards) & Summer Luge Track
23 Gare du Montenvers (Train to Mer de Glace)
24 Chamonix-Mont Blanc Train Station
25 SAT Bus Office
27 Photo Alpine Tairraz
28 Club Alpin Français (CAF) Office
29 Le Change & 24-Hour Currency Exchange Machine
30 Banque Laydernier
31 Maison de la Montagne
32 Église Saint Michel
33 École Espace Sensation
34 Télécabine/Téléphérique to Planpraz & Le Brévent
36 Tourist Office & Hôtel Mont Blanc
37 Chamonix Bus Ticket Office
38 Place Balmat
39 Post Office
41 Blue Jazz Rock Café
44 The Pub
47 Librairie VO
49 Laundrette
51 Aiguille du Midi Téléphérique
Aveyron River
To Gîte La Montagne (500m)
Promenade des Crêmeries
To Aerial Tramway, La Flégère & L'Index (1.5km), Argentière (9km), Col des Montets (12km) & Switzerland
Chemin des Gourgnes
Pond
N506
Route de la Frasse
Chemin des Cristalliers
Ave de la Plage
Route de la Patinoire
R Mummery
Promenade du Fori
Rue Joseph Vallot
Route des Mouilles
Chemin des Béradis
Ave du Bois du Bouchet
To Planpraz & Le Brévent
Route Henriette d'Angeville
Clos du Savoie
Impasse des Rhododendrons
Place du Mont Blanc
Ave du Mont Blanc
Chemin des Saubérands
Chemin du Mollard
Chemin de la Mollard
R. des Moulins
Rue Whymper
Ave Cachat le Géant
To Mer de Glace Glacier
Place du Triangle de l'Amitié
Ave Michel Croz
Route des Moussoux
Route de la Rouмnaz
Rue du Docteur Paccard
Arve River
Rue du Lyret
Rue Helbronner
Allée Recteur Payot
Ave Ravanel Le Rouge
Avenue de l'Aiguille du Midi
Chemin François Devouassoux
Blanche
Promenade Marie-Paradis
Route des Pècles
Ave Ravanel Le Rouge
Avenue de Courmayeur
Route-des-Pèlerins
Route
To Saint Gervais-Le-Fayet (20km)
To Camping L'Île des Barrats (300m), Centre Hospitalier & Les Faurands
To Auberge de Jeunesse (1.3km), Camping Grounds & Mont Blanc Tunnel
0
100
200 m

Post & Communications The post office on Place Balmat is open weekdays from 8 am to noon and 2 to 6 pm, and on Saturday until noon. During July and August, weekday hours are 8 am to 7 pm.

Log into the Internet and send emails from Mont Blanc Online (☎ 04 50 53 23 19; fax 04 50 53 87 21; chamonix@montblanconline.fr), 85 Rue des Moulins. It costs 30/55FF for 30 minutes/one hour online and the centre is open from 9 am to 7 pm (closed Sunday).

Bookshop English books are sold at Librairie VO, 20 Ave Ravanel Le Rouge. It's open from 9 am to noon and 2 to 7.30 pm (closed Sunday).

Laundry The Lav' Matic, 223 Rue Joseph Vallot (on the ground floor of a building called The Mummery), charges 30FF per load, one of the highest rates in the Alps. It's open from 8 am to 8 pm. The more modern laundrette at 174 Ave de l'Aiguille du Midi is open from 9 am to 8 pm. There is a third laundrette inside the Centre Commercial, 35 Ave du Mont Blanc.

Medical Services The Centre Hospitalier (☎ 04 50 53 84 00) is at Route des Pélerins in Les Favrands.

Aiguille du Midi

The Aiguille (pronounced 'ay-GWEE') du Midi, a lone spire of rock looming across glaciers, snowfields and rocky crags, 8km from the summit of Mont Blanc, is unique in its accessibility to people interested in scaling sheer cliffs. The views in all directions are truly breathtaking and should not be missed (there is a lift for those not into climbing).

The téléphérique (☎ 04 50 53 30 80) from Chamonix to the Aiguille du Midi (3842m) is the highest cable car in Europe. From the Aiguille du Midi, between April and September, you can make the 5km transglacial ride (30 minutes) in the Panoramic Mont Blanc cable car to **Pointe Helbronner** (3466m) on the Italian border, where there's some summer skiing. The Italian ski resort of Courmayeur is accessible from here too. The views alone from the cable car are worth the trip.

Return tickets from Chamonix to the Aiguille du Midi cost 194FF; it's an extra 96FF return to Pointe Helbronner. One-way tickets are only 20% less than a return. A ride to the téléphérique's halfway point, Plan de l'Aiguille (2308m) – an excellent place to start hikes in summer – costs 64/82FF one way/return.

The téléphérique, which you can board at the station south of town at the end of Ave de l'Aiguille du Midi, runs year-round from 8 am (6 am between 5 July and 24 August). The last ride up is at 3.45 pm (4.45 in summer). It takes 40 minutes to get to Italy. Be prepared for long queues – the earlier in the morning you get there, the better. You can make advance reservations 24 hours a day by calling ☎ 04 50 53 40 00.

Le Brévent

Le Brévent (2525m), the highest peak on the western side of the valley, is known for its great views of Mont Blanc and the rest of the eastern side of the valley. It can be reached by a combination of the télécabine and téléphérique (☎ 04 50 53 13 18), which costs 55/80FF one way/return. To reach it from the tourist office, walk west on Chemin de la Mollard. Service begins at 8 am (9 am in winter); the last trips up/down are at 5/5.45 pm in summer and an hour or so earlier in winter. Quite a few hiking trails (including various routes back to the valley) can be picked up either at Le Brévent or at the télécabine's midway station, Planpraz (1999m; 46/55FF one way/return).

Mer de Glace

The heavily crevassed Mer de Glace (Sea of Ice), the second largest glacier in the Alps, is 14km long, 1800m wide and up to 400m deep. It moves 45m a year at the edges and up to 90m a year in the middle. It has become a popular tourist attraction thanks to a cogwheel rail line built between 1897 and 1908. In the 17th century, the Mer de

Glace – like other glaciers in the area – reached the bottom of the valley, destroying houses and burying cultivated land.

The **Grotte de la Mer de Glace**, an ice cave that lets you get a look at the glacier from the inside for 14FF, is open from the end of May to the end of September. The interior temperature is -2° to -5°C. Since 1946, the cave has been carved anew each spring – the work is begun in February and takes just over three months. Look down the slope for last year's cave to see how far the glacier has moved.

With new avalanche-proofing over parts of the railway tracks, the train – which leaves from Gare du Montenvers (☎ 04 50 53 12 54) in Chamonix and takes you to Montenvers (1913m) – runs year-round. The last train up departs at 5.30 or 6 pm (earlier after mid-September) and comes down a half-hour later. The 20 minute trip costs 56/67FF one way/return. From Montenvers, a téléphérique (15FF return) takes tourists to the cave. A combined ticket valid for the train, téléphérique, and admission to the cave itself costs 105/66FF for adults/children.

The Mer de Glace can also be reached on foot via the Grand Balcon Nord trail from Plan de l'Aiguille. The uphill trail from Chamonix (two hours) begins near the summer luge track. Traversing the glacier and its many crevasses is dangerous without proper equipment and a guide.

Réserve des Aiguilles Rouges

This nature reserve (3300 hectares), 12km north of Chamonix at Col des Montets, is known for its particularly beautiful and diverse Alpine vegetation. The visitors centre (☎ 04 50 54 02 24) is open between June and September from 9.30 am to 12.30 pm and 1.30 to 7 pm (6.30 pm in June and September). Nearby is a 2km botanical trail lined with scores of Alpine plants. Transport to the Col des Montets is infrequent (see Bus under Getting Around for details).

Musée Alpin

The Musée Alpin (☎ 04 50 53 25 93), just off Ave Michel Croz in Chamonix, displays artefacts, lithographs and photos illustrating the history of mountain climbing and other Alpine sports. From June to mid-October, it's open from 2 to 7 pm; between Christmas and Easter its hours are 3 to 7 pm. It's closed during the rest of the year. Entrance costs about 20FF.

Skiing

Of Chamonix's nine skiing areas, the best areas for beginners are Le Tour, Les Planards, Le Brévent and La Flégère. The latter two are connected by téléphérique. Les Chosalets and Les Grands Montets, accessible from Argentière, offer intermediate and advanced skiers the most challenging skiing. Les Grands Montets also has a snowpark equipped with a half-pipe for snowboarders.

The region also has a number of marked but ungroomed trails suitable for advanced skiers in search of some off-piste thrills. The famous off-piste 20km-long Vallée Blanche descent, which leads from the top of the Aiguille du Midi over the Mer de Glace and through the forests back to Chamonix, should *only* be tackled with a guide. It takes four to five hours to complete and a guide costs 1220FF for up to four people. Contact the ESF or Compagnie des Guides for full details.

Ski Passes The tourist office sells a variety of ski passes, the most popular being the Cham' Ski pass, which is valid for all the lifts in the valley and entitles pass holders to one day's skiing in Courmayeur in Italy and free bus transport in the Chamonix region. Family and beginners' passes are available too.

The more expensive Ski Pass Mont Blanc covers the Megève-Saint Gervais ski area as well as the Chamonix Valley.

Ski Touring Ski touring is superb in spring around Mont Blanc but is not restricted to that area; it is possible to go for a week or longer and ski to Switzerland or Italy, staying in *refuges* or tents along the way. A four day trip with an experienced local

FRENCH ALPS

guide costs 2650FF per person. During winter, it is against the law to make overnight trips in the Chamonix-Mont Blanc area without the permission of the Compagnie des Guides, due to the danger of avalanches and crevasses.

The king of ski tours is the classic six day Haute Route between Chamonix and Zermatt in Switzerland. The trail is skiable from March until early May and costs 4250FF per person. It should only be attempted with an experienced local guide. Skiers should be at an advanced to expert level in off-piste skiing and have a high level of fitness, as the trail is quite physically demanding.

Heli-skiing is also possible. Contact Chamonix Mont Blanc Helicopters (☎ 04 50 54 13 82), SAF Chamonix Helicopters (☎ 04 50 54 07 86), or the Compagnie des Guides for details. A 10 minute panoramic helicopter flight costs 350FF per person.

In summer, there is limited (and expensive) skiing from Pointe Helbronner (see Aiguille du Midi) on the Italian frontier. The runs, which are down a glacier, are only about 800m long and are served by four téléskis.

Warm-Weather Activities

Hiking In late spring and summer (more or less from mid-June to October), the Chamonix area has 310km of hiking trails, some of the most spectacular anywhere in the Alps. The more rewarding trails are at higher elevations, which can be reached in minutes by cable car. The téléphériques shut down in the late afternoon, but in June and July there is enough light to hike until 9 pm or even later.

The combined map and guide, *Carte des Sentiers du Mont Blanc* (Mountain Trail Map; 75FF), is ideal for straightforward day hikes. The most useful map of the area is the 1:25,000 scale IGN map entitled *Chamonix-Massif du Mont Blanc* (No 3630OT; 58FF). Both are sold at Photo Alpine Tairraz (☎ 04 50 53 14 23), 162 Ave Michel Croz. *The Most Beautiful Hikes for Everyone* (Editions Aio; 25FF) maps out easy day hikes in the Mont Blanc region.

The fairly flat **Grand Balcon Sud** trail along the Aiguilles Rouges (western) side of the valley stays up around 2000m and affords great views of Mont Blanc and nearby glaciers. On foot, it can be reached from behind Le Brévent's télécabine station. If you want to avoid a lot of uphill walking, take either the Planpraz (46FF) or La Flégère (43FF) lifts.

From Plan de l'Aiguille (64FF), the **Grand Balcon Nord** takes you to the Mer de Glace, from where you can hike or take the cogwheel train down to Chamonix. There are a number of other trails from Plan de l'Aiguille.

There are trails to **Lac Blanc** (2350m), a turquoise lake (despite its name) surrounded by mountains, from either the top of the Les Praz-l'Index cable car (61FF) or La Flégère (43FF), the line's midway transfer point.

From the southern end of the Réserve des Aiguilles Rouges' botanical walk at Col de Montets (1461m), 12km north of Chamonix, a trail on the east side of the road leads up to l'Aiguillette des Posettes (2201m). Count on it taking 2½ hours up and 1½ hours down.

Canyoning The Compagnie des Guides organises canyoning expeditions from April to October. A half-day/day initiation course costs 350/750FF.

Summer Luge The summer luge track (☎ 04 50 53 08 97), near the télésiège des Planards, is open in June on weekends from 1.30 to 6 pm. During July and August its opening hours are 10 am to 7.30 pm. If there is no snow the luge is also open in May. It costs 32FF a ride.

Cycling Many of the trails around the bottom of the valley (eg the Petit Balcon Sud) are perfect for mountain biking. See Getting Around for information on bike rental.

In season, Chamonix's Club de Cyclotourisme has a group ride every Sunday. It begins some time between 7 and 8 am at Le Grand Bi ski rental shop, 240 Ave du Bois du Bouchet.

FRENCH ALPS

The Compagnie des Guides (see the Information section) can arrange one-day mountain bike tours for 1700/130FF for adults/children. It also offers three, four or five day tours of the Mont Blanc region costing 1140FF for three days plus 300FF for each additional day.

Horse-Drawn Carriage Rides A 25 minute tour of the city in a horse-drawn carriage costs an outrageous 300FF. Carriages usually await tourists year-round on Ave Michel Croz.

Parapente The sky above Chamonix is often dotted with colourful paragliders floating slowly down from the snowy heights. Initiation flights, with an instructor, from Planpraz (2000m) cost 500FF (1400FF from the Aiguille du Midi and 3600FF from Mont Blanc). A five day course costs 2960FF. For details, contact Parapente Azur (☎ 04 50 53 50 14; pazur@club-internet.fr), 128 Rue des Moulins, or Chamonix Parapente (☎ 04 50 55 99 22), 16 Cours du Bartavel. École Espace Sensation (☎ 04 50 55 99 49), another parapente school, is at 8 Route Henriette d'Angeville.

Ice-Skating The indoor ice-skating rink, in the Centre Sportif (☎ 04 50 53 12 36), Ave de la Plage, is open from 10 am to noon and 3 to 6 pm (Wednesday from 9 to 11 pm). Admission is 23/18FF for adults/children; *location patins* (skate rental) is 16FF.

The Centre Sportif's Club des Sports (☎ 04 50 53 11 57) has information on other activities available in the valley.

Places to Stay

During July, August and the ski season, hotels are heavily booked. Many prefer guests who take full or half-board. Book all accommodation in advance through the Centrale de Réservation (see Information earlier). *Les Carnets de l'Hébergement*, published annually by the tourist office, contains a very comprehensive list of the region's camp sites, *refuges*, *gîtes d'étape*, *chambres d'hôtes*, apartment rental agencies and hotels. Expect to pay at least 1000/1800FF a week for a two person studio in the low/high season.

Places to Stay – Budget

Camping There are some 13 camp sites in the Chamonix region. In general, camping costs 25FF per person and 12 to 26FF for a tent site. Because of the altitude, it's often chilly at night.

L'Île des Barrats (☎ 04 50 53 51 44), near the base of the Aiguille du Midi téléphérique, is open from mid-April to mid-October. The three star ***Les Deux Glaciers*** (☎ 04 50 53 15 84), on Route des Tissières in Les Bossons, 3km south of Chamonix, is open year-round (except from mid-November to mid-December). To get there, take the train to Les Bossons or the Chamonix Bus (see Getting Around) to the Tremplin-le-Mont stop.

In Argentière, ***Glacier d'Argentière*** (☎ 04 50 54 17 36; fax 04 50 54 03 73), 58 Chemin des Moilettes, open from May to September, is 700m towards Switzerland from the Argentière train station. Campers pay 23FF each and 20FF for a tent site.

Hostels The ***Auberge de Jeunesse*** (☎ 04 50 53 14 52; fax 04 50 55 92 34; chamonix@wanadoo.fr) is 2km south-west of Chamonix at 127 Montée Jacques Balmat in Les Pélerins. By bus, take the Chamonix-Les Houches line and get off at the Pélerins École stop. In winter, only weekly packages are available, including bed, food, ski pass and ski hire for six days from 1150/2790FF in the low/high season. In summer a bed in a room of four or six costs 74FF, including breakfast. There's no kitchen and meals cost 50FF. You can't check in until after 5 pm. The hostel is closed from October to mid-December.

In summer, ***El Paso*** (see Places to Stay) offers a bed in a dorm for 70FF a night.

Refuges Most ***mountain refuges***, which cost 90 to 100FF a night, are accessible to hikers, though a few can be reached only by mountain climbers. Breakfast and dinner, prepared by the warden, are often available for an extra fee. Call ahead to reserve a place. For information on *refuges*, contact the CAF (see Tourist Office under Information). When the office is closed, pick up a list detailing CAF *refuges* and access routes from outside the office.

There are two easier to reach *refuges*: one at Plan de l'Aiguille (2308m; ☎ 04 50 53 55 60), which is the intermediate stop on the Aiguille du Midi téléphérique, and another at La Flégère (1877m; ☎ 04 50 53 06 13), the midway station on the Les Praz-l'Index cable car.

Gîtes d'Étape The ***Chalet Ski Station*** (☎ 04 50 53 20 25), near the Planpraz and Le Brévent télécabine station at 6 Route des Moussoux, has beds costing 60FF a night. Sheets are 15FF and showers cost 5FF. It's closed from mid-May to late June and mid-September to mid-December.

The semi-rustic ***Gîte Le Chamoniard Volant*** (☎ 04 50 53 14 09; fax 04 50 53 23 25) is on the north-eastern outskirts of town at 45 Route de la Frasse. A bunk in a cramped, functional room for four, six or eight people costs 66FF and sheets are 20FF. Breakfast is 27FF and dinner costs 66FF. The nearest bus stop is La Frasse.

Gîte La Montagne (☎ 04 50 53 11 60), by far the most attractive of Chamonix's three gîtes, is on a beautiful, forested site at 789 Promenade des Crémeries, 1.5km north of the train station (if arriving by bus, get off at La Frasse stop). A bunk in a jam-packed room costs 65FF (including use of the kitchen). This place is closed from 11 November to 20 December.

Argentière has several very well-regarded gîtes. The relaxed and exceptionally friendly ***Le Belvédère*** (☎/fax 04 50 54 02 59) is 250m down the hill from Argentière train station and near the Argentière Sud bus stop at 501 Route du Plagnolet. A bed here in summer/winter costs 60/68FF a night. The ***Gîte du Moulin*** (☎/fax 04 50 54 05 37) is 1km north of Argentière at 32 Chemin du Moulin. The closest train station is Montroc, about 200m away. A dorm bed costs 60FF. Bring your own sheets. The Gîte de Moulin is closed from the end of September to 20 December.

Hotels ***Les Grands Charmoz Guesthouse*** (☎ 04 50 53 45 57), 468 Chemin des Cristalliers, 600m north of Chamonix train station, has doubles for 184FF.

The ***Hôtel Valaisanne*** (☎ 04 50 53 17 98) is a small, family-owned place at 454 Ave Ravanel Le Rouge, 900m south-west of Chamonix town centre. It has doubles for 165/266FF in the low/high season. At the ***Hostellerie du Lion d'Or*** (☎ 04 50 53 15 09), 255 Rue du Docteur Paccard, singles/doubles start at 150/220FF. Reception is in the ground floor restaurant or the bar next door.

The lively ***Hôtel El Paso*** (☎ 04 50 53 64 20; fax 04 50 53 64 22), 37 Impasse des Rhododendrons, is great value. Doubles with shared bath in the low/high season cost 166/224FF, triples are 236/306FF and quads are 288/358FF. In summer a bed in a dorm costs 70FF.

Places to Stay – Mid-Range & Top End

Hôtel Le Stade (☎ 04 50 53 05 44), 83 Rue Whymper (the entrance is around the back on the 1st floor), has simple but pleasant singles/doubles/triples from 149/245/345FF.

Off a quiet lane farther north, the pleasant, local-style ***Hôtel de l'Arve*** (☎ 04 50 53 02 31; fax 04 50 53 56 92), 60 Impasse des Anémones, has singles/doubles/triples from 213/270/549FF in the high season. In the low season rooms cost from 169/21/430FF.

The little ***Hôtel Boule de Neige*** (☎ 04 50 53 04 48), 362 Rue Joseph Vallot, has a lively bar and singles/doubles/triples from 160/205/285FF with shared bathroom. The enormous ***Hôtel Richemond*** (☎ 04 50 53 08 85; fax 04 50 55 91 69), 228 Rue du Docteur Paccard, has rooms for one/two people from 274/414FF.

The three-star, chalet-style ***Hôtel Gustavia*** (☎ 04 50 53 00 31; fax 04 50 55 86 39), 272 Ave Michel Croz, has attractive double rooms for 440/720FF in the low/high season. The four star ***Hôtel Mont Blanc*** (☎ 04 50 53 05 64; fax 04 50 55 89 44), just south of the tourist office at 62 Allée Majestic, has luxurious doubles with half-board for 530/837FF per person in the low/high season.

Places to Eat

Locals scorn Chamonix's mind-blowing array of restaurants. Instead, many trek to ***Chalet de Miage*** (1559m), accessible only by foot and renowned for serving the best fondue this side of Mont Blanc. A three-hour hiking trail is marked from the top of the Bellevue téléphérique in Les Houches, 10km south of Chamonix. Alternatively, contact Allibert (☎ 04 50 53 88 00), 156 Ave de l'Aiguille du Midi, for a 4WD expedition out there.

Restaurants Always packed is ***Le Boccalatte*** (☎ 04 50 53 52 14), 59 Ave de l'Aiguille du Midi, which has a happy hour between 5 and 7 pm and serves hearty portions of fondue, *tarte flambée*, and the like. Advance bookings are recommended. ***Restaurant La Calèche*** (☎ 04 50 55 94 68), 18 Rue du Docteur Paccard, dishes out fondue and folklore shows to undiscriminating tourists. Evening *menus* start at 99FF.

Popular locally is the ***Bistro des Sports*** (☎ 04 50 53 00 46), 182 Rue Joseph Vallot, which has *menus* from 69FF. A favourite with people staying at the nearby gîtes is the self-service ***Le Fond des Gires*** (☎ 04 50 55 85 76), 350 Ave du Bois du Bouchet.

There are lots of restaurants offering pizza, fondue etc, in the streets leading off from Place Balmat. Nearby at 47 Rue du Docteur Paccard, ***Poco Loco*** (☎ 04 50 53 43 03) has pizzas from 33 to 45FF and *menus* from 50FF. It also serves great hot sandwiches (from 23FF), sweet crêpes (from 8FF), and burgers to eat in or take away. ***Le Bumblebee***, 67 Rue Moulins, specialises in good old British food.

For Mexican food, try ***La Cantina*** (☎ 04 50 53 64 20) at the small Hôtel El Paso, 37 Impasse des Rhododendrons, which is run by an Australian. ***Le Sanjon*** (☎ 04 50 53 56 44), 5 Ave Ravanel le Rouge, is a picturesque wooden chalet restaurant serving *raclette* (a block of melted cheese, usually eaten with potatoes and cold meats) and fondue (69F). A favourite is *pierrade* – three different meats that you prepare yourself on a small grill, including six sauces (98FF).

Snacks and the greatest cakes, pastries and hot chocolate in town are served at the ***Pâtisserie des Moulins*** (☎ 04 50 53 58 95), 95 Rue des Moulins. It also offers a lunchtime *menu* for 50FF.

Self-Catering The ***Payot-Pertin*** supermarket, 117 Rue Joseph Vallot, is open from 8.15 am to 7.30 pm (8.15 am to 12.45 pm on Sunday in winter). ***Le Refuge Payot***, opposite the supermarket at 166 Rue Joseph Vallot, and ***Le Ferme du Mont Blanc***, 202 Rue Joseph Vallot, both stock an excellent range of cheeses, meats and other local products.

Entertainment

Nightlife is plentiful and good. A popular après-ski place is the café-bar of the ***Hôtel Gustavia*** (see Places to Stay), which has a happy hour until 7 pm most evenings. ***Club C***, beneath La Cantina (see Places to Eat) at the Hôtel El Paso, hosts occasional bands. Next to the Hôtel Richemond on Rue du Docteur Paccard is ***Les Choucas*** bar which plays loud music and shows snowboard and ski videos to a packed crowd. ***The Pub***, opposite, is another good bet, as is the ***Bar du Moulins***, 80 Rue Moulins.

Most nightclubs have cover charges, although ***Le Refuge***, 275 Rue du Docteur Paccard, does not. The ***Blue Jazz Rock Café***, 32 Rue du Docteur Paccard, is free from Sunday to Wednesday but charges 70FF entry on other nights.

Getting There & Away

Bus The bus station is in the train station building. The office of SAT Autocar (☎ 04 50 53 01 15) has opening hours posted on the door, but in general it's open weekdays from 8.45 to 11.30 am and 1.45 to 6 pm, and on weekends from 6.45 to 7.05 am, 8.45 to 11.05 am and 1.45 to 5.35 pm. Buses also run to Annecy (95.30FF), Grenoble (157FF),

Geneva bus station (165FF; 1½ to two hours) and Geneva airport (188FF; two to 2¼ hours). Destinations in Italy include Courmayeur (53FF; 40 minutes) and Turin (138FF; three hours).

Tickets to Lyon-Satolas airport (340FF; 3¼ hours) are sold at the Chamonix Bus ticket office outside the tourist office on Place du Triangle de l'Amitié. There are two buses a day on weekdays and three a day on weekends.

Train The narrow-gauge train line from Saint Gervais-le-Fayet (23km west of Chamonix) to Martigny, Switzerland (42km north of Chamonix), stops at 11 towns in the valley, including Argentière. There are nine to 12 return trips a day. To enter Switzerland, you have to switch trains at the border (at Châtelard or Vallorcine) because the track gauge changes. From Saint Gervais-le-Fayet, there are trains to all parts of France.

The Chamonix-Mont Blanc train station (☎ 04 50 53 00 44) is in the middle of town at the end of Ave Michel Croz. Ticket counters are staffed from 6 am to 8 pm. The left luggage counter is open from 6.45 am to 8.45 pm (20FF for the first piece of luggage; 10FF for each additional piece).

Major destinations include Paris' Gare de Lyon (374FF; six to seven hours; five a day), Lyon (184FF; four to 4½ hours; four to five a day), Geneva (93FF; two to 2½ hours via Saint Gervais, longer via Martigny), and Annecy (121FF; 2½ hours). There's an overnight train to Paris every day year-round.

Getting Around

Bus Bus transport in the valley is handled by Chamonix Bus (☎ 04 50 53 05 55), Place du Triangle de l'Amitié. In winter it's open from 8 am to 7 pm. The rest of the year its hours are 8 am to noon and 2 to 6.30 pm (7 pm from June to August).

Bus stops are marked by black-on-yellow roadside signs. From mid-December to mid-May, there are 13 lines to all the ski lifts in the area. During the rest of the year, there are only two lines, both of which leave from Place de l'Église (which adjoins Place du Triangle de l'Amitié) and pass by the Chamonix Sud stop. One line goes south to Les Houches via either Les Moussoux (nine a day) or Les Pélerins (eight a day). The other goes north via Argentière to Col des Montets. Buses do not run after 7 pm (6 or 6.30 pm in June and September). In winter, buses are free for holders of ski passes; all others pay 7.50FF for one sector, 15FF for a second sector.

Buses to the Réserve des Aiguilles Rouges go via Les Nants to Col des Montets.

Taxi There's a taxi stand (☎ 04 50 53 13 94) outside the train station.

Bicycle Between April and October, Le Grand Bi (☎ 04 50 53 14 16), 240 Ave du Bois du Bouchet, has three and 10-speeds bicycles for 65FF a day, and mountain bikes for 100FF. It's open from 8.30 am to noon and 2 to 7 pm (closed Sunday).

Chamonix Mountain Bike (☎ 04 50 53 54 76), 138 Rue des Moulins, is open from 9 am to noon and 2 to 7 pm (no midday break during summer and winter holidays). The tariff is 50/95FF for two hours/day.

MEGÈVE & SAINT GERVAIS

Megève (population 4700; 1113m), 36km south-west of Chamonix, and neighbouring Saint Gervais (population 5000; 810m), sit below Mont Blanc and are connected by a common network of ski lifts. These tiny ski villages are among the oldest in the Alps: Megève was developed as a resort in the 1920s for a French baroness following her disillusionment with Switzerland's crowded St Moritz. Today it remains an expensive, trendy resort with a charming old square from which old narrow medieval-style streets and lanes fan out. On the eastern outskirts of the village are chapels and oratories that trace the Stations of the Cross in baroque, rococo and Tuscan-style wood carvings.

Summer hiking trails in the Mont d'Arbois, Bettex and Mont Joly areas are accessible from both villages. Mountain biking is equally popular; some of the best terrain is found along marked trails between Val d'Arly, Mont Blanc and Beaufortain.

Information

Tourist Offices Megève's tourist office (☎ 04 50 21 27 28; fax 04 50 93 03 09; megeve@laposte.fr), Rue de Monseigneur Conseil, is open in season from 9 am to 12.30 pm and 2 (4 pm on Sunday) to 7 pm. The accommodation service (☎ 04 50 21 29 52; fax 04 50 91 85 67) is based here too. Megève's ESF (☎ 04 50 21 00 97) and the Bureau des Guides (☎ 04 50 21 55 11) are inside the Maison de la Montagne, 76 Rue Ambroise Martin.

In Saint Gervais the tourist office (☎ 04 50 47 76 08; fax 04 50 47 75 69), 115 Ave Mont Paccard, is open from 9 am to 1 pm and from 2 to 7.30 pm (9 am to noon and 2 to 6 pm in the low season). It also has an accommodation service (☎ 04 50 93 53 63). The ESF (☎ 04 50 47 76 21) is on Promenade du Mont Blanc and the Bureau des Guides (☎ 04 50 47 76 55) is at Place du Mont Blanc.

Places to Stay

Both tourist offices stock lists of all types of accommodation available. Bookings for CAF *refuges* in Saint Gervais and Megève can be made through the CAF office in Chamonix (see Information in the Chamonix section) or through the Refuge du Val-Monjoie (☎ 04 50 47 76 70; fax 04 50 47 76 71), 73 Ave de Miage, Saint Gervais.

Studios for two people start at 1500/2000FF per week in the low/high season. In Megève the family-run ***La Marmotte*** (☎ 04 50 21 24 49), Route du Jaillet, has smallish wood-lined singles/doubles from 190/250FF, including breakfast. The three star ***Hôtel Au Coeur de Megève*** (☎ 04 50 21 25 30; fax 04 50 91 91 27), Rue Charles Feige, has rooms from 460FF.

In Saint Gervais, the one star ***Hôtel Les Capucines*** (☎ 04 50 47 75 87), 138 Rue du Mont Blanc, has older rooms with washbasin for 140/210FF for a single/double and with shower for 175/260FF, including breakfast. A notch up is the ***Hôtel Maison Blanche*** (☎ 04 50 47 75 81; fax 04 50 93 68 36), a two star hotel (in a lane behind the tourist office) with rooms for two people from 180FF.

Getting There & Away

There's a SAT bus and SNCF office (☎ 04 50 47 73 88) opposite the tourist office in Saint Gervais, and in Megève (☎ 04 50 21 23 42) a couple of blocks south-west of the tourist office.

Many trains to/from Paris via Annecy stop at Sallanches (13km from Megève) and Saint Gervais-le-Fayet (16km from Megève and 2km from Saint Gervais). All trains terminate in Saint Gervais-le-Fayet.

There are four buses a day between Saint Gervais, Megève and Chamonix (48.40FF; 55 minutes). Seven buses a day link Megève and Saint Gervais with the Saint Gervais-le-Fayet and Sallanches train stations. There are also four buses a day in winter to/from Geneva airport (190FF; 1½ hours).

From Saint Gervais-le-Fayet and Saint Gervais, the Mont Blanc tramway (☎ 04 50 47 51 83) rattles its way up to Bellevue (1800m), offering staggering mountain views en route. A return ticket costs 88/126FF in the low/high season.

LES PORTES DU SOLEIL

The dozen villages linked by lifts along the French/Swiss border in the northern Chablais area – dubbed the Portes du Soleil (Gates of the Sun) – is the largest ski area linked by lifts in France. Some 650km of slopes and cross-country trails crisscross the region. You can buy a ski pass covering some or all of them.

Morzine (population 3000; 1000m) in Haute Savoie is the largest village, retaining something (but not a lot) of its traditional Alpine village atmosphere. Accommodation can be booked through the central accommodation service (☎ 04 50 79 11 57; fax 04 50 79 03 48) inside the tourist office (☎ 04 50 74 72 72; fax 04 50 79 03 48). A bed in the ***Auberge de Jeunesse*** (☎ 04 50 79 14 86) costs 65FF in summer. The hostel is open from Christmas to Easter and mid-June to early September.

Avoriaz (1800m), a few kilometres up the valley from Morzine, is among the most expensive of the French ski resorts. Built in the 1960s, it is made up almost entirely of high-rise apartment blocks that, surprisingly, blend into their surroundings because each one is covered with wooden shingles. Apart from two four-star hotels and the ***Club Méditerranée*** (☎ 04 50 74 28 70), all other accommodation is in studios or apartments, which can be booked through the tourist office (☎ 04 50 74 02 11; fax 04 50 74 24 29; avoriaz@wanadoo.fr). Avoriaz is a car-free resort and transport is by horse and sleigh in winter. There's a special course for mountain bikes (with jumps and other obstacles) where those inclined can practise. It's free but only open in summer.

If you're arriving by road via Cluses, **Les Gets** (population 1300; 1172m) is the first village of the Portes du Soleil. Quieter than Morzine and cheaper than Avoriaz, it has plenty of accommodation. Contact the tourist office (☎ 04 50 75 80 80; fax 04 50 79 76 90) or the accommodation booking office (☎ 04 50 75 80 51; fax 04 50 75 85 13). The busy ***Auberge de Jeunesse*** (☎ 04 50 79 14 86) is open from late December to mid-April and July to mid-September.

The other villages on the French side of the border are quieter, cheaper and have more of a village atmosphere. They include **Châtel** (1200m; tourist office ☎ 04 50 73 22 44, fax 04 50 73 22 87, ch@tel.icor.fr; accommodation service ☎ 04 50 81 30 34; fax 04 50 81 30 34) and **La Chapelle d'Abondance** (1000m; tourist office ☎ 04 50 73 02 90; fax 04 50 73 56 04), 28km to the north-east.

Getting There & Away

Free ski shuttle buses take skiers from Morzine to the lifts of Télécabine Super Morzine, Télécabine du Pléney and Téléphérique Avoriaz.

During the ski season, Morzine is linked by bus to Lyon-Satolas (390FF) and Geneva airport (185FF). The latter, 50km north of Morzine, is the closest.

From Morzine there are frequent daily SAT buses (☎ 04 50 79 15 69) to Les Gets and Avoriaz. There are also buses from Morzine to its closest train stations: Thonon (34km to the north) and Cluses (31km to the south).

THONON-LES-BAINS

• pop 30,000 ✉ 74202 alt 370m

Thonon-les-Bains is the main town on the French side of Lake Geneva. The Chablais peaks are behind the city and just across the water is the Swiss city of Lausanne. Geneva is 33km south-east of Thonon.

A residence of the dukes of Savoy in the Middle Ages, today Thonon makes for a peaceful overnight stop in summer, with serene lake cruises to keep you occupied during the day. Avoid it in winter, though: it's dead.

Orientation

The centre of town, built up above the lake, is between Place de l'Hôtel de Ville and the train station, just south of the main square, Place des Arts. Ave du Général Leclerc is the main road down to the lake and the boat docks at Port des Rives. From the port, Quai de Ripaille follows the lake around to the duke's chateau.

Information

Tourist Offices The tourist office (☎ 04 50 71 55 55; fax 04 50 26 68 33; thonon@thononlesbains.com; www.thononlesbains.com), Place du Marché, is open from 8.30 am to noon and 2 to 6.30 pm (closed Sunday). In July and August there's no midday break, and it's open on Sunday from 10 am to noon. To get there from the train station, head straight up Ave de la Gare to Blvd du Canal. Turn right and follow it past the next big intersection into Ave Jules Ferry. The first street to the left leads onto Place du Marché. Between June and September the lakeside tourist office annexe (☎ 04 50 26 19 94) at Port des Rives is open from 10 am to 7 pm. Boat tickets for Lake Geneva cruises are also sold here (see the Getting There & Away section).

FRENCH ALPS

The Bureau Information Jeunesse (☎ 04 50 26 22 23; fax 04 50 81 74 45), 67 Grande Rue, is only open weekdays from 1.30 to 6.30 pm.

Places to Stay & Eat

Given its lakeside location, Thonon's accommodation is expensive. Cheaper options include ***Camping de Saint Disdille*** (☎ 04 50 26 13 59), 3km north-east of town near Port Ripaille, which charges 80FF for up to three people with a tent or caravan. The site is open between May and September. Take bus No 4 from the train station to the Saint Disdille bus stop.

The ***Centre International de Séjour*** (☎ 04 50 71 77 80; fax 04 50 26 68 57), 1.5km south-west of town off the N5 to Geneva at La Grangette, has beds in single or twin rooms for 120FF. Take bus A from the train station to La Grangette.

The central ***Hôtel de la Renovation*** (☎ 04 50 71 11 27), 4 Place du Château, has singles/doubles from 205/241FF. The ***Hôtel Terminus*** (☎ 04 50 26 52 52; fax 04 50 26 00 92), opposite the train station on Place de la Gare, has rooms for 159/189FF.

The two star ***Hôtel l'Union*** (☎ 04 50 73 81 02), 17km south of Thonon in Lullin, has delightful doubles for 220FF plus a cosy restaurant serving traditional cuisine.

Getting There & Away

Bus The SAT bus company (☎ 04 50 71 00 88), 11 Ave Jules Ferry, has regular lines to Évian and into the Chablais Mountains, including to Morzine.

Train The train station (☎ 08 36 35 35 35) is a block south-west of Place des Arts on Place de la Gare. Trains go south-west to Geneva (39FF) and Bellegarde (57FF; 1¼ hours), where you can pick up the TGV connection to Paris' Gare de Lyon. Most days there are six trains a day to Évian (11FF; 10 minutes).

Boat The Swiss CGN company (☎ 04 50 71 14 71 in summer only or ☎ 021-617 06 66; fax 021-617 04 65 in Lausanne) serves the main cities and towns around the lake, hopping from one port to another. In Thonon, boats leave from Port des Rives (☎ 04 50 71 44 00), stopping in Yvoire before continuing via several Swiss villages to Geneva. Boats heading in the other direction go to Évian then across to Lausanne or east to Montreux. One-day passes for unlimited travel (and sundeck basking) are available.

Getting Around

Local buses are run by BUT (☎ 04 50 26 50 74) and depart from Place des Arts. Bus No 8 (July and August only) goes to Port des Rives. A funicular links Place du Château, near the Hôtel de Ville, with Port des Rives for 7FF; daily from 8 am to noon and 1.30 to 6.30 pm.

Lake Geneva

Crescent-shaped Lake Geneva (372m) – known as Lac Léman in French – is Europe's largest Alpine lake. It's almost an inland sea, complete with cities (Geneva and Lausanne are the largest), fishing ports and stony beaches. Measuring 72km in length, it is an average 8km wide (13km at its maximum) and 80m deep (310m at its deepest).

Forming a natural border between Switzerland and France, the lake is fed and drained mainly by the Rhône River. It has very clear and unpolluted waters, despite the many activities that take place upon and around it. Its appearance changes constantly: the surrounding mountains may disappear in fog or clouds and sudden winds can make the surface swell up as if on a sea.

The north side (the *adret*), which lies along the so-called Swiss Riviera and is bordered by vineyards, offers visitors an almost Mediterranean climate and a great view of the Alps. From the south shore (the *avers*), the horizon is limited to the almost-straight line of the Jura range.

AROUND THONON-LES-BAINS

At the northern tip of a blunt peninsula 16km west of Thonon is **Yvoire**, a medieval stone village with a small port, pebbled coves and a multitude of geraniums. In the other direction, is **Évian-les-Bains**, a more luxurious and exclusive version of Thonon (9km east), whose spring waters are famed worldwide. Known as the 'Pearl of Lake Geneva', it was in this town that the Accord d'Évian recognising Algerian independence was signed in 1962. It is possible to visit the Évian water bottling factory; ask at the tourist office (☎ 04 50 75 04 26; fax 04 50 75 61 08), Place d'Allinges, for details or go to the factory's public relations office (☎ 04 50 26 80 80) at 22 Ave des Sources.

ANNECY

• pop 50,000 ✉ 74000 alt 448m

Annecy, the rather chic but friendly capital of the Haute-Savoie department, is the perfect place to spend a relaxing holiday – discounting the bumper to bumper traffic that can be a touch troublesome in July and August. Visitors in a sedentary mood can sit along the lakefront and feed the swans or mosey around the geranium-lined canals of the old city in full view of the Alps.

The town – at the most northern tip of the blue-green, 15km-long Lac d'Annecy – is an excellent base for water sports, as well as hiking, gliding, cycling and rollerblading.

Orientation

The train and bus stations are 500m northwest of the Vieille Ville (Old City), which is centred around the Thiou River (split into Canal du Thiou to the south and Canal du Vassé to the north). The modern town centre is between the main post office and the Centre Bonlieu, where the tourist office is.

The lakefront town of Annecy-le-Vieux is 1.5km east of Annecy.

Information

Tourist Office The tourist office (☎ 04 50 45 00 33; fax 04 50 51 87 20; ancytour@cyberaccess.fr; www.lac-annecy.com), inside the Centre Bonlieu shopping centre at 1 Rue Jean Jaurès, is open from 9 am to noon and 1.45 to 6.30 pm (closed Sunday). There's no midday closure during July and August and it's open on Sunday between 9 am and noon and 1.45 to 6 pm from mid-May to mid-October.

The Bureau Information Jeunesse (☎ 04 50 33 87 40) and Annecy Sport Information (☎ 04 50 33 88 31), also in the Centre Bonlieu, are open Monday from 3 to 7 pm, Tuesday to Friday from 2.30 to 7 pm, and Saturday from 10 am to noon.

Money The Banque de France at 9bis Ave de Chambéry is open weekdays from 8.45 am to noon and 1.45 to 3.45 pm. There's a 24 hour currency exchange machine in the Crédit Lyonnais, Centre Bonlieu, which accepts 15 different currencies.

Post & Communications The main post office, 4bis Rue des Glières, is open weekdays from 8 am to 7 pm (Saturday until noon).

The Syndrome Cybercafé (☎ 04 50 45 39 75; fax 04 50 45 85 65; infos@syndrome.com; www.syndrome.com), 3bis Ave de Chevêne, is open from 9 am to midnight (closed Monday and Tuesday). One hour online access costs 40FF.

Walking Tour

Walking around and taking in the lake, flowers and quaint buildings is the essence of a visit to Annecy. Just east of the old city, behind the Hôtel de Ville, are the flowery **Jardins de l'Europe**, shaded by giant redwoods from California. The grassy expanse of the **Champ de Mars**, across the Canal du Vassé from the redwoods, is a popular park.

A fine stroll can be had by walking from the Jardins de l'Europe along Quai de Bayreuth and Quai de la Tournette to the Base Nautique des Marquisats (see Water Sports) and beyond. Another fine promenade begins at the Champ de Mars and goes eastward around the lake towards Annecy-le-Vieux.

Annecy abounds in interesting architecture. Beyond the Vieille Ville explore Rue Royale (there's an Art Nouveau building at No 15) and Rue des Glières (Art Deco building at No 3).

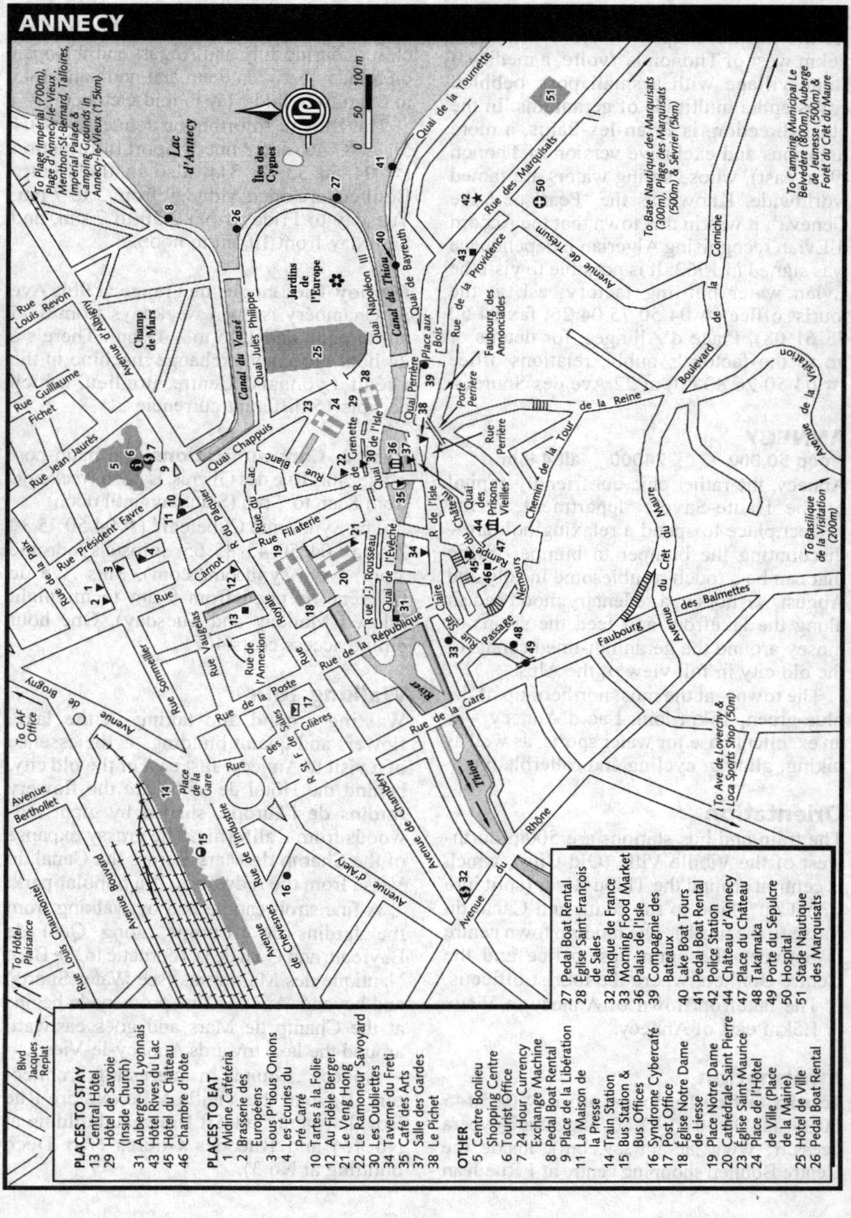
ANNECY
Lac d'Annecy
Îles des Cygnes
Jardins de l'Europe
Champ de Mars
Canal du Vassé
Canal du Thiou
River Thiou
0 50 100 m
To Plage Impérial (700m), Plage d'Annecy-le-Vieux, Menthon-St-Bernard, Talloires, Impérial Palace & Camping Grounds in Annecy-le-Vieux (1.5km)
To Base Nautique des Marquisats (300m), Plage des Marquisats (500m) & Sévrier (5km)
To Camping Municipal Le Belvédère (800m), Auberge de Jeunesse (500m) & Forêt du Crêt du Maure
To Basilique de la Visitation (200m)
To Ave de Loverchy & Loca Sports Shop (50m)
To CAF Office
To Hôtel Plaisance
PLACES TO STAY
13 Central Hôtel
29 Hôtel de Savoie (Inside Church)
31 Auberge du Lyonnais
43 Hôtel Rives du Lac
45 Hôtel du Château
46 Chambre d'hôte
PLACES TO EAT
1 Midine Cafétéria
2 Brasserie des Européens
3 Lous P'tious Onions
4 Les Écuries du Pré Carré
10 Tartes à la Folie
12 Au Fidèle Berger
21 Le Veng Hong
22 Le Ramoneur Savoyard
30 Les Oubliettes
34 Taverne du Freti
35 Café des Arts
37 Salle des Gardes
38 Le Pichet
OTHER
5 Centre Bonlieu Shopping Centre
6 Tourist Office
7 24 Hour Currency Exchange Machine
8 Pedal Boat Rental
9 Place de la Libération
11 La Maison de la Presse
14 Train Station
15 Bus Station & Bus Offices
16 Syndrome Cybercafé
17 Post Office
18 Église Notre Dame de Liesse
19 Place Notre Dame
20 Cathédrale Saint Pierre
23 Église Saint Maurice
24 Place de l'Hôtel de Ville (Place de la Mairie)
25 Hôtel de Ville
26 Pedal Boat Rental
27 Pedal Boat Rental
28 Église Saint François de Sales
32 Banque de France
33 Morning Food Market
36 Palais de l'Isle
39 Compagnie des Bateaux
40 Lake Boat Tours
41 Pedal Boat Rental
42 Police Station
44 Château d'Annecy
47 Place du Château
48 Takamaka
49 Porte du Sépulcre
50 Hospital
51 Stade Nautique des Marquisats

Vieille Ville

The Vieille Ville, an area of narrow streets on either side of the Canal du Thiou, retains much of its 17th century appearance despite efforts to make it quaint for tourists. On the island in the middle, the **Palais de l'Isle** (☎ 04 50 33 87 31), a former prison, houses a display of the city's and region's history and culture. It's open daily, except Tuesday, from 10 am to noon and 2 to 6 pm (daily from June to September from 10 am to 6 pm). Entrance is 20/5FF for adults/students.

From mid-June to September there are guided tours in English (32FF) of the Vieille Ville. The tourist office has details.

Château d'Annecy

The **Musée Château** (☎ 04 50 33 87 30), housed in the 13th to 16th century chateau overlooking the town, has a permanent collection that includes examples of local artisanship and miscellaneous objects about the region's natural history. It also puts on innovative temporary exhibitions. It's open from 10 am to noon and 2 to 6 pm (closed on Tuesday in winter). Admission is 30/10FF for adults/students, but is free on Wednesday to all (except during school holidays). The climb up to the chateau is worth it just for the view.

Carillon Concert

From mid-June to mid-September, a carillon concert is held at the **Basilique de la Visitation** (☎ 04 50 66 17 37) every Saturday. At 4 pm, immediately preceding the concert, there is a guided visit (20FF) of the 37-bell chromatic carillon and various displays on carillon playing. The basilica is south of (ie straight up the hill from) the old city at the top of Ave de la Visitation.

Sunbathing & Swimming

In the warm months there are all sorts of grassy areas along the lakefront in which to hang-out, have a picnic, sunbathe and swim. There is a free beach, **Plage d'Annecy-le-Vieux**, 1km east of the Champ de Mars. Slightly closer to town is **Plage Impérial**, which costs 18FF and is equipped with changing rooms and other amenities.

Perhaps Annecy's most pleasant stretch of lawn-lined swimming beach is the free **Plage des Marquisats**, 1km south of the old city along Rue des Marquisats. The beaches are officially open from June to September.

The **Stade Nautique des Marquisats** (☎ 04 50 45 39 18), 29 Rue des Marquisats, has three outdoor swimming pools and plenty of lawn. From 1 May to 1 September, the complex is open from 9 am (10 am on Sunday and holidays) to 7 pm (7.30 pm from July to early September). The entrance fee is 19FF for those 18 or over (15FF for under 18s).

Hiking & Climbing

The **Forêt du Crêt du Maure**, south of Annecy, has many walking trails but is hardly a pristine wilderness. There are better hiking areas in and around two nature reserves: **Bout du Lac** (20km from Annecy on the southern tip of the lake) and the **Roc de Chère** (10km from town on the east coast of the lake). Both can be reached by Voyages Crolard buses (see Getting There & Away).

Maps and topoguides can be purchased at La Maison de la Presse, 13 Rue Vaugelas, and the tourist office. One of the better hiking maps is *Sentiers Forestiers Crêt du Maure: Sainte Catherine-Annecy-Sévrier* (20FF). The 1:25,000 scale Top 25 IGN map entitled *Lac d'Annecy* (No 3431OT; 57FF) is another goodie for serious hikers.

The CAF (☎ 04 50 09 82 09 or ☎ 04 50 27 29 45) has an office at 77 Rue du Mont Blanc, about 1.5km north-east of the train station. Takamaka (see Water Sports) arranges guided hikes and climbs.

Cycling & Rollerblading

There's a *piste cyclable* (bicycle path), suitable for rollerbladers as well, along the west coast of the lake. It starts 1.5km south of Annecy (on Rue des Marquisats) and goes all the way to Duingt, 12km farther south. See Getting Around for information on bicycle and rollerblade rental.

Water Sports

The Base Nautique des Marquisats, 31 Rue des Marquisats, is a centre for aquatic activities. One-person kayaks and canoes for two can be rented from the Canoë-Kayak Club d'Annecy (☎ 04 50 45 03 98). Between June and September, the office is open from 9 am to noon and 1 to 5 pm.

Between June and mid-September, the Société des Régates à Voile d'Annecy (SRVA; ☎ 04 50 45 48 39; fax 04 50 45 64 64) next door rents all sorts of sailing boats (Laser X4s, catamarans etc) and *planches à voile* (sailboards). The office is open weekdays from 9 am to noon and 2 to 5 pm. From late March to late October, pedal boats and small boats with outboard motors can be hired along the quays of the Canal du Thiou and Canal du Vassé.

Takamaka (☎ 04 50 45 00 33; fax 04 50 51 87 20), 17 Faubourg Sainte-Claire, arranges rafting, kayaking and canyoning expeditions.

Parapente

Col de la Forclaz, the huge ridge overlooking Lake Annecy from the east, is a perfect spot to paraglide. For details on courses (2700FF for five days) and initiation flights (390 to 450FF), contact Takamaka (see Water Sports). The Club École de Parapente (☎ 04 50 57 92 95) is at 12 Rue Louis Bach.

Boat Excursions

Compagnie des Bateaux (☎ 04 50 51 08 40), 2 Place aux Bois, has one-hour boat tours of the lake in summer costing 59/45FF for adults/children. Boats leave from the south bank of the Canal du Thiou on Quai Bayreuth. Tickets have to be bought one hour before departure from the blue wooden huts on the lakeside or direct from the Compagnie des Bateaux office. In summer there are also boat trips across the lake to Menthon-Saint-Bernard and Talloires (see Around Annecy).

Places to Stay – Budget

Camping The ***Camping Municipal Le Belvédère*** (☎ 04 50 45 48 30; fax 04 50 45 55 56) is 2.5km south of the train station in the Forêt du Crêt du Maure. It costs about 45/65FF for one/two people to pitch a tent. To get there, turn off Rue des Marquisats onto Ave de Trésum, take the first left and follow Blvd de la Corniche. From mid-June to early September take bus No 91 (Ligne des Vacances, meaning 'Holiday Line') from the train station.

There are several other camping grounds near the lake in Annecy-le-Vieux.

Hostel The ***Auberge de Jeunesse*** (☎ 04 50 45 33 19; fax 04 50 52 77 52) is 1km south of town at 4 Route du Semnoz in the Forêt du Semnoz. A bed costs 68FF, including breakfast. Sheets are 17FF. From mid-June to early September only, bus No 91 (the Ligne des Vacances) runs from the train station and the Hôtel de Ville to the hostel between 9 am and 7 pm. The rest of the year, take bus No 1 to the Marquisats stop.

Chambre d'Hôte The regional Gîtes de France accommodation office (☎ 04 50 23 92 74; fax 04 79 86 71 32) overlooks the lake at 17 Ave d'Albigny.

There is a ***chambre d'hôte*** (☎ 04 50 23 34 43) overlooking the lake next to the Impérial Palace at 2 Ave de la Mavéria. Doubles with shower/bath cost 200/270FF and breakfast is 30FF. Also brilliantly located is another ***chambre d'hôte*** in a private home (☎ 04 50 45 72 28), next to the Hôtel du Château on Rampe du Château.

Hotels Cheap hotels are hard to find from mid-July to mid-August. Book in advance.

The small ***Hôtel Rives du Lac*** (☎ 04 50 51 32 85; fax 04 50 45 77 40), superbly located near the Vieille Ville and the lake at 6 Rue des Marquisats, has one or two-bed rooms with shower for 136FF. Breakfast costs an extra 24FF.

The ***Hôtel Plaisance*** (☎ 04 50 57 30 42), 17 Rue de Narvik, has simple but neat singles/doubles from 130/140FF. Triples cost from 235FF. Rooms with shower for one or two people are 180FF. The spacious hall shower is 11FF and breakfast costs an extra 25FF.

One of the cheapest places close to the Vieille Ville is the ***Central Hôtel*** (☎ 04 50 45 05 37) in a quiet courtyard at 6bis Rue Royale. Doubles start at 160FF. Triples/ quads cost 220/230FF.

In the heart of the old city, the ***Auberge du Lyonnais*** (☎ 04 50 51 26 10; fax 04 50 51 05 04), 14 Quai de l'Évêché, occupies an idyllic setting next to the canal. Singles/doubles with toilet are 160/200FF. Rooms with shower and toilet are 240/290FF. It only has 10 rooms so be quick.

Places to Stay – Mid-Range & Top End

For a serene view over Annecy's lantern-lit lanes it's hard to beat the ***Hôtel du Château*** (☎ 04 50 45 27 66; fax 04 50 52 75 26), 16 Rampe du Château, just below one of the towers of its namesake. Cosy singles/ doubles start at 230/270FF with shower and toilet. There's a large terrace and plenty of private parking.

One of the most oddly placed hotels in Savoy – if not all of France – is the ***Hôtel de Savoie*** (☎ 04 50 45 15 45; fax 04 50 45 11 99; hotel.savoie@dotcom.fr), 1 Place de Saint François, with its entrance on the left side of a (still functioning) church ... spooky. Simple rooms with washbasin cost from 150/220FF.

Top of the range is the fantastic ***Impérial Palace*** (☎ 04 50 09 30 00; fax 04 50 09 33 33), which sits like a big white ship in a turn-of-the century casino on the lakeside at 13 Ave d'Albigny. Doubles start at 800FF.

Places to Eat

Restaurants In the Vieille Ville, the streets on both sides of the Canal du Thiou are lined with touristy restaurants, most of which are remarkably similar to each other.

Les Oubliettes (☎ 04 50 45 39 78), 10 Quai de l'Isle, has pizzas from 38 to 55FF and a wide choice of other main courses. Just across the canal, ***Le Pichet*** (☎ 04 50 45 32 41), 13 Rue Perrière, has a big terrace and three-course *menus* for 62 and 74FF. A Vietnamese-Chinese place called ***Le Veng Hong*** (☎ 04 50 45 35 43), 4 Rue Jean-Jacques Rousseau, has a 59FF lunchtime *menu* and a takeaway service. It's open from 10.30 am to 12.30 pm and 4 to 11 pm.

Exquisite sweet and savoury tarts can be had at the ***Tartes à la Folie***, 7-9 Rue Vaugelas. There is a 38FF lunchtime *menu*, comprising a savoury tart, salad and soft drink. Don't miss out on the scrumptiously sweet rhubarb and nut tarts. Nearby, in a small courtyard off the same street at 10 Rue Vaugelas, is the excellent ***Les Écuries du Pré Carré***. The *plat du jour* is 50FF; there are *menus* from 79 to 120FF and the service is top-class.

Another place popular with the local crowd is the ***Brasserie des Européens***, 23 Rue Sommeiller, which specialises in *moules* (mussels) starting from 90FF. They also have steak tartare for 84FF and a fresh seafood takeaway counter.

The popular ***Le Ramoneur Savoyard*** (☎ 04 50 51 99 99), 7 Rue de Grenette, has reasonably priced regional dishes, with *menus* from 71 to 155FF. The rather touristy ***Salle des Gardes*** (☎ 04 50 51 52 00), Quai des Vieilles Prisons, facing the old prison, has Savoyard specialities, such as fondue and *tartiflette* (sliced potatoes and reblochon cheese baked in the oven). As does the ***Taverne du Freti*** (☎ 04 50 51 29 52), 12 Rue Sainte Claire. Its authentic raclette is worth every centime at 68FF per person. Book a table in advance.

In the town centre, there are good pizzas (from 33FF), large salads (30 to 40FF) and a children's menu (35FF) at ***Lous P'tious Onions*** (☎ 04 50 51 34 41), in the Grand Passage at 36 Rue Sommeiller. *Menus* start at 60FF. There are also a number of inexpensive places to eat along Rue du Pâquier.

Cafés Rue Perrière and Rue de l'Isle have several cheap, hole-in-the-wall ***sandwich shops***. Cheap and cheerful dishes are served at ***Midine Cafétéria***, a speedy buffet-style eatery at 23 Rue Sommeiller. Tartiflette and salad is 36FF, mussels are 40FF, and there is a children's *menu* for 25FF. It's open daily from 11 am to 9.30 pm (weekends until 10 pm).

Heavenly hot chocolate is served at ***Au Fidèle Berger***, a traditional tea room and chocolate shop on the corner of Rue Royale and Rue Carnot. The ***Café des Arts***, 4 Passage de l'Isle, is a small, dimly lit and intimate café, popular for its bohemian touch and live bands, which play on weekends. It's open from 9 to 1 am.

Self-Catering In the Vieille Ville, there's a popular ***food market*** held along Rue Sainte Claire on Sunday, Tuesday and Friday from 6 am to 12.30 pm.

Getting There & Away

Bus The bus station, Gare Routière Sud, is next to the train station on Rue de l'Industrie. Voyages Crolard (☎ 04 50 45 08 12), open from 6.15 am to 12.30 pm and 1.15 to 7.30 pm (closed Sunday), has regular services to various points around Lake Annecy, including Menthon, Talloires and Roc de Chère on the eastern shore, Sévrier on the western shore, and Bout du Lac on the southern tip. Other services include to/from the ski stations east of Annecy, including La Clusaz (50 minutes), Le Grand Bornand (one hour), Albertville (1¼ hours) and Chamonix. Services on shorter runs cease around 7 pm (earlier on Sunday and holidays).

Autocars Frossard (☎ 04 50 45 73 90), open from 7.45 am to 12.30 pm and 1.45 to 7 pm (closed Sunday), sells tickets to Annemasse, Chambéry (45FF; 50 minutes; seven a day), Évian, Geneva (49.60FF; 1¼ hours; six a day), Grenoble, Nice and Thonon.

Autocars Francony (☎ 04 50 45 02 43) has buses to destinations including Chamonix, Chambéry and Megève (55FF). Most do not run on Sunday or holidays. Its office is open weekdays from 7.15 to 11 am and 2.15 to 6.15 pm.

Train The train station (☎ 04 50 66 50 50) is on Place de la Gare. The information counters are open from 9 am to noon and 2 to 7 pm. The ticket windows are open weekdays from 6.10 am to 7.20 pm, and 9.10 am to 8 pm on weekends.

There are frequent trains to Paris' Gare de Lyon (360FF by TGV; 3¾ hours), Nice (340FF via Lyon, 353FF via Aix-les-Bains; eight to nine hours, faster with a change of train), Lyon (110FF; two hours), Chamonix (104FF; 2½ to three hours), Aix-les-Bains (39FF; 30 to 45 minutes) and Chambéry (48FF; one hour).

The night train to Paris (eight hours), often full on Friday and Saturday, leaves at 10.30 or 11.20 pm. Couchettes cost 90FF extra.

Getting Around

Bus The municipal bus company SIBRA (☎ 04 50 51 72 72) has an information bureau (☎ 04 50 51 70 33) inside the Centre Bonlieu. It's open from 9 am to 7 pm (closed Sunday).

Buses run Monday to Saturday from 6 am to 8 pm. On Sunday, 20 seat minibuses – identified by letters rather than numbers – provide a limited service. Bus No 91 (the Ligne des Vacances), which serves the hostel, runs only from mid-June to early September. Bus tickets cost 7FF; a carnet for eight rides is 37.50FF. Weekly coupons cost 50FF.

Taxi For taxis based at the bus station call ☎ 04 50 45 05 67.

Bicycle & Rollerblades Bikes can be rented from Loca Sports (☎ 04 50 45 44 33), south-west of the Vieille Ville at 37 Ave de Loverchy. Sévrier Sport Location (☎ 04 50 52 42 68), 65 Place de la Mairie, rents tandems, mountain bikes and rollerblades.

AROUND ANNECY

When the sun shines, the charming villages of **Sévrier**, 5km south of Annecy on Lake Annecy's western shore, and **Menthon-Saint-Bernard**, 7km south on its eastern shore, are well worth a day trip. **Talloires**, just a few kilometres south of Menthon, is Annecy's most exclusive lakeside spot. Romantic, luxurious and delightful if you can afford it, is the four star ***Auberge du Père Bise*** (☎ 04 50 60 71 10; fax 04 50 60 73 05; bise@silicone.fr), which overlooks Talloires' picturesque little harbour on Route du Port. The former Haitian dictator Jean Claude Duvalier (better known as Baby Doc) stayed in the 18th century Abbaye hotel for three weeks following his overthrow and subsequent exile in 1986.

Skiing is the Annéciens' main weekend activity in winter. Just 18km south of the city is the predominantly cross-country resort of **Le Semnoz** (1700m), which also has a couple of tame downhill slopes for beginners. Farther afield are the larger village resorts of **La Clusaz** (1100m), 32km east of Annecy, and **Le Grand Bornand** (1000m), 34km north-east of Annecy. There is an ***Auberge de Jeunesse*** (☎ 04 50 02 41 73; fax 04 50 02 65 85; fuaj.la.clusaz@wanadoo.fr) 3km up the valley from La Clusaz at Route du Col de Croix Fry, Le Marcoret. Daily buses to and from Annecy serve all three resorts.

CHAMBÉRY

• pop 54,000 ✉ 73000 alt 270m

Charming Chambéry, which lies in a wide valley between Annecy and Grenoble, has long served as one of the principal gateways between France and Italy. Occupying the entrance to the valleys that lead to the main Alpine passes, the town was the capital of Savoy from the 13th century until 1563. Its charming old quarter, crammed with unexplored courtyards and narrow cobbled streets, was built around the castle of one of the dukes of Savoy.

Orientation

Busy dual carriageways along a narrow canal separate the town's compact old section and the northern sprawl, which starts near the train station at the northern end of Rue Sommeiller. Place des Éléphants – the old city's focal point – is at the north-east end of Rue de Boigne.

Information

Tourist Offices The tourist office (☎ 04 79 33 42 47; fax 04 79 85 71 39; ot.chambery@wanadoo.fr; www.chambery.com) in the Maison du Tourisme, 24 Blvd de la Colonne, is open from 9 am to noon and 1.30 to 6 pm (closed Sunday). Between mid-June and mid-September it's open from 9 am to 12.30 pm and 1.30 to 6.30 pm (Sunday from 10 am to 12.30 pm).

It sells a myriad of useful maps and guides of the surrounding areas, including *Promenades autour de Chambéry* (50FF), which details 16 city walks. In July and August the tourist office arranges city walking tours (25 to 30FF) daily at 4 pm, with an additional one at 9 pm from 15 July. It also organises fun theme tours that take in everything from Chambéry's meandering alleyways to its colourful trompe l'oeil wall paintings.

The 2nd and 3rd floors of the same building are home to the Agence Touristique Départementale de Savoie (☎ 04 79 85 12 45; fax 04 79 85 54 68), where you can get information on the Savoy region. It is open weekdays from 9 am to noon and 2 to 6 pm. On the 4th floor is the Gîtes de France office (☎ 04 79 85 01 09; fax 04 79 85 71 32), open the same hours.

Savoie Information Jeunesse (☎ 04 79 62 66 87), 79 Place de la Gare, has information on hostels, sports, transport and housing. It is open weekdays from 9 am to 12.30 pm and 1.30 to 6 pm (9 am to 5 pm on Tuesday and Friday).

National Park Office The Parc National de la Vanoise headquarters (☎ 04 79 62 30 54; fax 04 79 96 37 18), 135 Rue du Docteur Julliand, is open weekdays from 9 am to noon. Travellers can stop by in the afternoon if they telephone ahead.

Hiking & Touring Information The Bureau des Guides et Accompagnateurs de Montagne (☎ 04 79 62 62 48 or ☎ 04 79 85 05 29) has an information desk inside the tourist office, open in July and August from 5.30 to 6.30 pm. It arranges canyoning, rock and ice climbing, skiing and caving expeditions, as well as hikes in the region. Alternatively, contact the CAF (☎ 04 79 33 05 52), just south of the cathedral at 70 Rue Criox d'Or, open from 5.30 to 7.30 pm (Saturday from 10 am to noon; closed Sunday and Monday).

Les Cyclotouristes Chambériens (☎ 04 79 96 18 27 or ☎ 04 79 85 90 57), 400m north-east of the Fontaine des Éléphants at 7 Chemin des Martinettes, arranges bicycle tours in the region. The members meet at their clubhouse between March and October on Tuesday at 8.15 pm.

The tourist office sells the invaluable guidebooks *Cyclotourisme VTT* and *Escalade via Ferrata Canyoning*, each of which lists some 70-plus cycling and climbing routes in the Savoy region. It stocks hiking maps of the Chartreuse and Vanoise parks too, as does La Piste Verte, 172 Rue Croix d'Or, and La Maison de la Presse, 139 Place Saint Léger.

Money The Crédit Lyonnais next to the tourist office at 26 Blvd de la Colonne is open daily, except Sunday, from 8.15 am to 12.55 pm and 1.30 to 5.15 pm (3.45 pm on Saturday). The Banque de Savoie at 6 Blvd du Théâtre is open weekdays from 8.10 am to noon and 1.35 to 5.20 pm (Saturday until 4.20 pm; closed Sunday).

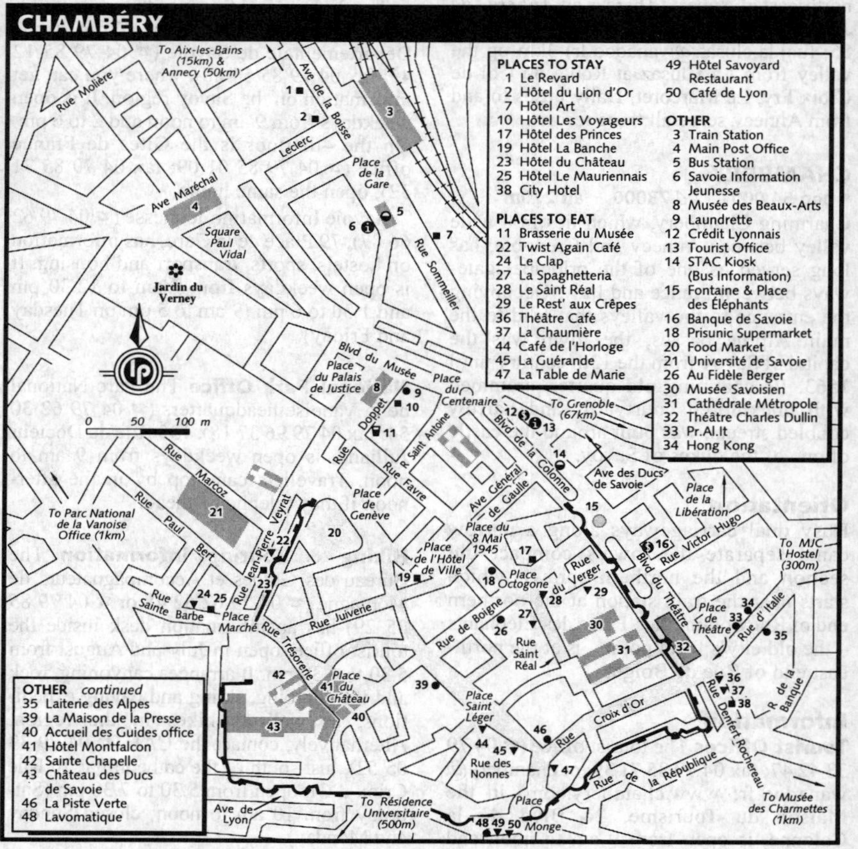

Post The main post office, on Square Paul Vidal, is open weekdays from 8 am to 7 pm and on Saturday until noon.

Laundry The laundrette at 1 Rue Doppet is open from 7.30 am to 8 pm. The Lavomatique at 37 Place Monge is open from 7 am to 10 pm.

Château des Ducs de Savoie

The chateau around which the town was built is an opulent 14th century castle on Place du Château. It houses the region's Conseil Général (County Council). The grounds are open from 7.30 am to 7 pm, but the chateau itself can only be visited on a guided one hour tour (25FF) organised by the tourist office. In July and August tours take place daily at 10.30 am, 2.30, 3.30, 4.30 and 5.30 pm. In April, May, June, September and October there is one tour daily at 2.30 pm. Tours start – and they should be booked in advance – at the tourist office. Between January and March, tours (Saturday and Sunday at 2.30 pm in January and March; daily in February) start outside the Accueil des Guides office (☎ 04 79 85 93 73), beneath the 18th century Hôtel Montfalcon, 6 Place du Château. The office is open from 1.30 to 5.30 pm (closed Wednesday and on weekends).

Tours take in the adjoining **Sainte Chapelle**, built in the 15th century to house what later became known as the Shroud of Turin (the sacred cloth believed to have been used to wrap the crucified Christ before burial). The *suaire* (shroud) was taken to Turin in 1860, when Savoy became part of France. You can visit the 70-bell **Grand Carillon** in Sainte Chapelle – Europe's largest bell chamber – on a guided tour (30FF) on Saturday at 11 am and 6 pm between May and September and at 4 pm from October to April.

Fontaine des Éléphants

Splendidly dominating Place des Éléphants at the intersection of Blvd de la Colonne and Rue de Boigne, this fountain, which could be the model for an Indian postage stamp with its four great elephants, was sculpted in 1838 in honour of Général de Boigne (1751-1830), a local who made a fortune in the East Indies. When he returned home, he bestowed some of his wealth on the town and was honoured posthumously with this monument. The arcaded street that leads from the fountain to the Château des Ducs and bears his name was one of his most important local projects.

Museums

Chambéry's three museums each cost 20/10FF for adults/students. A block south of the elephant fountain and just north of the 15th and 16th century Cathédrale Métropole is the **Musée Savoisien** (☎ 04 79 33 44 48), just off Blvd du Théâtre on Square de Lannoy de Bissy. Occupying a 13th century Franciscan monastery, it exhibits local archaeological finds, including a gallery of 13th century wall paintings that had been hidden by a false roof inside a local mansion. Exhibits of traditional Savoyard mountain life are displayed on the 2nd floor. The museum is open from 10 am to noon and 2 to 6 pm (closed Tuesday). The **Musée des Beaux-Arts** (☎ 04 79 33 75 03), Place du Palais de Justice, houses a rich collection of 14th to 18th century Italian works. It's open the same hours as the Musée Savoisien.

The **Musée des Charmettes** (☎ 04 79 33 39 44), 1.5km south-east of the town, occupies the country house of philosopher and writer Jean-Jacques Rousseau, who lived here in bliss from 1736 to 1742 with his lover, Baronne Louise Éléonore de Warens. From April to September it's open from 10 am to noon and 2 to 6 pm (closed Tuesday). The rest of the year it closes at 4.30 pm. In July and August *only*, a special bus leaves from the tourist office at 2.30 pm on Monday, Thursday, Friday and Saturday. It returns at 4 pm. A bus ticket costs 6.50FF and admission to the museum is 20FF.

Musical evenings are also held here on Wednesday and Friday in summer. Book in advance at the tourist office.

FRENCH ALPS

Places to Stay

Camping There are several camping grounds outside Chambéry, all open from May to September.

The closest is the two star ***Camping Le Nivolet*** (☎ 04 79 85 47 79) in Bassens, 3km north-east of the centre. The fees are 15/15/8FF per person/tent/car. To get there take bus C. Heading north from Chambéry, you might try the three star ***L'Île aux Cygnes*** (☎ 04 79 25 01 76) at Le Bourget du Lac. Take bus H from the Éléphants stop or the train station to the terminus, from where it's a 400m walk.

To the south-east at Challes-les-Eaux, the two star ***Le Mont Saint Michel*** (☎ 04 79 72 84 45), Chemin Saint Vincent, charges 15/12/8FF for a caravan/tent/car. It costs 15/8FF for adults/children. Take bus G from the train station or the Éléphants stop to the Centre Challes stop, from where it's a 15 minute walk.

Hostel In Chambéry there are several *foyers* that take people under 25 – the tourist office has details. The ***Maison des Jeunes et de la Culture*** (MJC; ☎ 04 79 85 05 84), 311 Faubourg Montmélian, is open year-round and charges 75FF per person. There's a shower in the hallway.

The nearest ***Auberge de Jeunesse*** is in Aix-les-Bains (see Around Chambéry).

Hotels In the old city, the ***Hôtel La Banche*** (☎ 04 79 33 15 62), 10 Place de l'Hôtel de Ville, is quiet, with average singles/doubles/triples from 130/180/240FF. Rooms with shower start at 220FF. A short distance to the east, the upmarket ***Hôtel des Princes*** (☎ 04 79 33 45 36; fax 04 79 70 31 47), in one of the arcaded buildings at 4 Rue de Boigne, has singles/doubles with all the mod-cons for 300/350FF. Breakfast is a hefty 50FF.

South-east of the centre, the ***City Hotel*** (☎ 04 79 85 76 79; fax 04 79 85 86 11), 9 Rue Denfert Rochereau, has rooms with washbasin for 170/190FF, and rooms with shower for 195/260FF. Private parking costs 30FF.

Just outside the old city to the west, the ***Hôtel Le Mauriennais*** (☎ 04 79 69 42 78; fax 04 79 69 46 86), 2 Rue Sainte Barbe, offers a chateau view and no-frills singles/doubles/triples from 110/120/170FF. The ***Hôtel du Château*** (☎ 04 79 69 48 78), with its own bar-cum-tattoo parlour at 37 Rue Jean-Pierre Veyrat, has singles/doubles/triples/quads with washbasin for 90/130/170/290FF. Both hotels are on or near a busy road.

Behind the Musée des Beaux-Arts, the ***Hôtel Les Voyageurs*** (☎ 04 79 33 57 00), 3 Rue Doppet, is one of the best deals in town with large, clean rooms with washbasin for 130FF and triples/quads with washbasin for 180/240FF. Rooms with shower cost 150FF. Double rooms with twin beds cost 30FF more. Reception is at the bar below.

Directly opposite the train station, ***Hôtel du Lion d'Or*** (☎ 04 79 69 04 96; fax 04 79 96 93 20), 13 Ave de la Boisse, provides decent singles/doubles with toilet from 140/165FF and with shower from 200/225FF. Breakfast is 30FF, and there's a busy brasserie adjoining the hotel. ***Le Revard*** (☎ 04 79 62 04 64; fax 04 79 96 37 6), close by at 41 Ave de la Boisse, has basic singles/doubles from 150/195FF. The modern ***Hôtel Art*** (☎ 04 79 62 37 26; fax 04 79 62 49 98), directly opposite the bus station at 154 Rue Sommeiller, has beautifully furnished singles/doubles with bath and TV from 230/275FF. Breakfast costs 35FF.

Places to Eat

Restaurants The best restaurant in Chambéry is ***Le Saint Réal*** (☎ 04 79 70 09 33), 10 Rue Saint Réal. *Menus* range from four-course ones for 180FF (220FF with wine and coffee) to six and seven-course *séduction* and *passion menus* for 350 and 460FF. It's closed on Sunday.

Le Rest' aux Crêpes (☎ 04 79 75 00 07), in a side street near the Fontaine des Éléphants at 35 Rue du Verger, specialises in Breton crêpes and *galettes* – hardly Alpine treats. However, the 48FF lunch-only *menu* is good value and includes a glass of kir. It is closed on Sunday and at lunch on Monday.

For Italian-inspired cuisine, try ***La Spaghetteria*** (☎ 04 79 33 27 62), 43 Rue Saint Réal, which boasts 19 pizza and 21 pasta variations, as well as good-value *menus* for 70 and 102FF and a 40FF children's *menu*. Dishes at ***Le Clap*** (☎ 04 79 96 27 08), 4 Rue Sainte Barbe, are poetically named after famous films.

If you want to sample local Savoyard specialities, try the restaurant at the ***Hôtel Savoyard*** (☎ 04 79 33 36 55), 35 Place Monge. Its tartiflette and *gratin de crozets* (Savoyard pasta with cheese) are out of this world. *Menus* start at 78FF; the four-course *menu Savoyard* for 125FF is excellent value. It also has a children's *menu* for 45FF. Have a glass or two of Mondeuse (45FF a half-bottle), Savoy's almost berry-like red wine.

Another good choice for local cuisine in a rustic atmosphere is ***La Chaumière*** (☎ 04 79 33 16 26), 14-16 Rue Denfert Rochereau. It has *menus* for 75, 120 and 150FF. House specialities include *foie gras de canard* and *fondue Savoyarde*. ***La Table de Marie*** (☎ 04 79 85 99 76), 193 Croix d'Or, serves Savoyarde dishes daily until 11 pm. *Menus* start at 85FF.

University Restaurant If you don't mind the 15 minute hike out of town, there's a ***university restaurant*** in the Résidence Universitaire on Rue du Chaney, south-west of the centre. Tickets cost 15FF.

Cafés The ***Brasserie du Musée***, opposite the Musée des Beaux-Arts at 4 Rue Doppet, is a favourite student haunt (though the television with MTV blaring nonstop gets a bit much). The ***Twist Again Café***, 31 Rue Jean-Pierre Veyrat, is a modern place with a little terrace backing onto the marketplace. The ***Théâtre Café***, opposite the Théâtre Charles Dullin on Place du Théâtre, has a popular terrace, which is lively until very late on summer nights. You've got to see the ***bar-cum-tattoo parlour*** at the Hôtel du Château (see Places to Stay) to believe it.

The ***Café de Lyon***, on Place Monge, is always packed. It has a lunch *menu* for 57FF and the café-bar is open from 8 to 1.30 am. Hot spots in summer include ***La Guérande***, 7 Place Saint Léger, and ***Café de l'Horloge***, 11 Place Saint Léger. Both have large outside terraces.

Self-Catering On Saturday morning a ***food market*** is held on Place de Genève. The ***Prisunic*** supermarket at Place du 8 Mai 1945 is open from 8.15 am to 7.30 pm (closed Sunday). The ***Laiterie des Alpes***, 88 Rue d'Italie, stocks a good range of local cheeses and dairy products. Italian products are sold at ***Pr.Al.It***, 67 Rue d'Italie, while ***Hong Kong*** is the place to go for Vietnamese-Chinese supplies.

Au Fidèle Berger, a *chocolatier* founded in 1838 at 15 Rue de Boigne, has some of the best chocolates this side of Brussels.

Getting There & Away

Bus The ticket office at Chambéry bus station (☎ 04 79 69 11 88), south of the train station on Place de la Gare, is open from 6.15 am to 7.15 pm. From here there are buses to Aix-les-Bains (15.50FF; 35 minutes; five a day), Annecy (46.50FF; 50 minutes; seven a day), Grenoble (49FF; 1½ hours; 10 a day) and Voiron (55FF; 1¼ hours; six a day). There is one daily bus to Geneva and Nice, and six a day to Lyon-Satolas airport (130FF; one hour).

Train Chambéry's train station (☎ 08 36 35 35 35) is 400m north-west of the tourist office at the end of Rue Sommeiller on Place de la Gare. The information office is open weekdays from 8.30 am to 12.30 pm and 1.30 to 6.30 pm, Saturday from 8.30 am to 5.50 pm.

There are major rail connections to Paris' Gare de Lyon (334FF by TGV via Lyon; 3¼ hours; six a day), Lyon (82FF; 1¼ hours; 10 a day), Annecy (48FF; one hour; 10 a day) and Grenoble (53FF; one hour; 14 a day).

There are also trains up the Maurienne Valley to Modane (78FF; 1¾ hours; five a day), which continue on to Turin, Rome and Naples in Italy.

Getting Around

Bus The main hub for local buses run by STAC (☎ 04 79 69 61 12) is along Blvd de la Colonne near the Fontaine des Éléphants, where the company has an information kiosk (☎ 04 79 70 26 27), open from 7.15 am to 12.45 pm and from 1 to 7.15 pm (Saturday from 7.20 to 12.20 pm and 2.20 to 5.40 pm; closed Sunday). Many buses also stop at the train station. In general, they run Monday to Saturday until about 8 pm. Single tickets cost 6.50FF and a carnet of 10 is 36.60FF.

AROUND CHAMBÉRY

Chambéry is wedged neatly between two regional parks – the **Parc Naturel Régional de Chartreuse** in the south-west (see Around Grenoble) and the **Parc Naturel Régional du Massif des Bauges**, to the north-east. Covering an area of 80,000 hectares, the Massif des Bauges offers unlimited hiking opportunities. The nature reserve in the north of the park is home to more than 600 chamois and mouflon. The park headquarters (☎ 04 79 54 86 40) is in Le Châtelard.

From the thermal spa of **Aix-les-Bains**, 11km north-west of Chambéry, you can tour **Lac Bourget** – France's largest natural lake – by boat. Contact Bateaux d'Aix-les-Bains (☎ 04 79 88 92 09) at the Grand Port or Aix-les-Bains tourist office (☎ 04 79 35 05 92; fax 04 79 88 88 01), next to the port on Ave du Grand Rue. Aix-les-Bains' ***Auberge de Jeunesse*** (☎ 04 79 88 32 88; fax 04 79 61 14 05; fuaj.montagne@wanadoo), Promenade du Sierroz, overlooks the lake.

Albertville, 39km from Chambéry on the eastern park boundary, played host to the 1992 Winter Olympics. The Olympic highs and lows are colourfully told at the Maison des Jeux Olympiques (☎ 04 79 37 75 71), 11 Rue Pargoud.

MÉRIBEL

✉ 73500 alt 1450m

Méribel lies at the heart of one of the largest skiable areas in the world – the Trois Vallées (Three Valleys). The wealthy purpose-built ski station – 42km south-east of Albertville and 88km from Annecy and Chambéry – was established in 1938 by Scotsman Colonel Peter Lindsay and today remains one of France's most 'British' resorts. Despite the circus of British pubs and grocery stores that have cropped up in recent years to appease its predominantly British clientele, Méribel has retained in part an Alpine village atmosphere thanks to a decision made in the mid-1940s to employ only traditional Savoyard architectural styles.

Méribel is the most central of four resorts tucked in the Trois Vallées. Over the next ridge to the east of the town lies the cheaper **Brides-les-Bains** (580m) and the large, concrete resort of **Courchevel**, spread on the slopes at 1550, 1650 and 1850m. To the south, the Belleville Valley is home to **Saint Martin de Belleville** (1400m), **Les Menuires** (1815m) and **Val Thorens** (2300m), which is Europe's highest ski resort. These main villages – with eight other smaller hamlets spread out around them – are all connected by lifts and marked runs.

Information

Tourist Office Méribel's central Maison du Tourisme houses the tourist office (☎ 04 79 08 60 01; fax 04 79 00 59 61; meribel@laposte.fr; www.les3vallees.com), the accommodation service (☎ 04 79 00 50 00; fax 04 79 00 31 19; www.meribel.net), the ESF (☎ 04 79 08 60 31; fax 04 79 08 60 80) and a transport information counter. The Maison du Tourisme is open from 9 am to 7 pm.

Skiing & Snowboarding

Skiing is between 1300 and 3200m. One of the best skiing resorts in France, the vast area can satisfy skiers all levels. Above Val Thorens, there is summer skiing on the Glacier de Péclet.

Méribel Valley alone has 73 Alpine ski runs (150km), 47 ski lifts, two snowboarding parks, a slalom stadium, and two Olympic downhill runs built for the 1992 Games. Many of these start or pass through Mottaret, a transit point 300m above the town, from where the valley's highest lift

(2910m) climbs Mont Vallon. Cheaper ski passes that only cover Méribel Valley (ideal for beginners) are available. For more competent skiers, there is the Trois Vallées pass, which allows use of all area lifts. Passes valid for more than six days also allow one day of skiing at Espace Killy, La Plagne, Les Arcs, Peisey Vallandry, Pralognan la Vanoise or Les Saisies.

The ESF (see Tourist Office) offers Alpine and cross-country skiing lessons as well as slalom racing and snowboarding courses. Off-piste skiing and ski tours are also available, one of the most popular routes being to La Meije (3983m). Contact the ESF or the Bureau des Guides (☎/fax 04 79 00 30 38) in the Parc Olympique at La Chaudanne.

Summer Activities

The *Guide des Sentiers*, costing 30FF at the tourist office, details 20 marked hiking trails in Méribel Valley. Particularly enticing is the botanical trail marked around Lake Tueda in the Réserve Naturelle de Tueda (Tueda Nature Reserve).

The Bureau des Guides organises rock climbing, hiking and mountain biking expeditions. Contact Chardon Loisirs (☎ 04 79 24 08 84) for white-water rafting courses.

Places to Stay

Of the seven hotels built for the 1992 Olympics, all but two have three or four stars – one-star hotels became almost extinct in Méribel long ago. Accommodation prices are pretty high, but studio and apartment prices are bearable (from 1459FF per week for two in the low season). A cheaper alternative is to base yourself in Les Menuires (accommodation office ☎ 04 79 00 79 79; fax 04 79 00 60 92) or in Brides-les-Bains (tourist office ☎ 04 79 55 20 64; fax 04 79 55 28 91), just 10km east and connected by lifts to Méribel.

If you're intent on staying in Méribel, the ***Hôtel du Moulin*** (☎ 04 79 00 52 23; fax 04 79 00 58 84) has doubles from 440FF a night, including breakfast. ***Hôtel Le Doron*** (☎ 04 79 08 60 02; fax 04 79 00 59 95; hotel_doron@msn.com), in the heart of the village near the tourist office, has doubles for 650FF, also including breakfast. Up the slope from the village, the ***Hôtel Neige et Soleil*** (☎ 04 79 08 62 39; fax 04 79 08 66 98) has rooms on a demi-pension basis from 480/620FF in the low/high season.

Getting There & Away

Vehicle access to Méribel has been made easier thanks to the four-lane A43, built for the Olympics. It links Chambéry (88km north-west) with the nearest town, Moûtiers, 18km north of Méribel.

Geneva and Lyon-Satolas airports are connected to Méribel by shuttle bus services. There's an SNCF information bureau (☎ 04 79 00 53 28) at the tourist office. The closest train station is in Moûtiers (☎ 08 36 35 35 35), from where there are connections to Paris (319FF; five hours) and Chambéry (64FF; 1¼ hours).

Regional buses are operated by Transavoie (☎ 04 79 24 21 58) and run between Méribel and Moûtiers (61FF; four a day on weekdays, more on weekends).

Getting Around

Bus Méribel provides a free shuttle bus service. Buses to Courchevel cost 50FF and a taxi about 250FF.

LA PLAGNE

✉ 73210 alt 1250m

La Plagne is the next resort along the Tarentaise Valley from Méribel in the direction of Bourg Saint Maurice and south of the N90. It is one of those drab apartment-block ski resorts not uncommon in the French Alps, comprising 10 villages crowned by La Plagne 1800. Plagne Centre is the resort's main centre of activity.

The luge and bobsled events of the 1992 Winter Olympics were held at La Plagne 1800, and the daredevil course is open to the public. A 1½ minute ride in a bob-raft (a driverless, four-person bobsleigh) costs 175FF per person, and a 50 second-twirl in a taxi-bob (a competition bobsled complete with driver and braker that holds two terrified passengers) is 460FF per person.

Bookings can be made at the tourist office (see Places to Stay) or at the ESF (☎ 04 79 09 04 40). The run is open to tourists on Tuesday and Sunday from mid-December to mid-March.

Snowboarding is also big in La Plagne – it has a snowboard park. In the valleys around La Plagne there are 80km of cross-country trails, with the most challenging being in the Champagny-en-Vanoise area. In July and August Alpine skiers can ski on the Bellecôte Glacier.

Places to Stay The vast majority of accommodation is in self-contained studios and apartments, starts at 1300FF per week in the low season for two people. The tourist office (☎ 04 79 09 79 79; fax 04 79 09 70 10; ot.laplagne@wanadoo.fr) in Plagne Centre can help with accommodation bookings. Otherwise there are only a handful of upmarket hotels.

Getting There & Away The SNCF booking office and the Autocars Bernard ticket office are in the building adjacent to the tourist office in Plagne Centre. There are four buses a day (more on weekends) to Aime, where the nearest train station is (45FF; 40 minutes). A taxi to Aime costs about 250FF.

BOURG SAINT MAURICE & LES ARCS

• pop 6000 ✉ 73700 alt 810m

Lying deep in the Tarentaise Valley, Bourg Saint Maurice is an old market town surrounded by mountains. Known locally as Bourg, it sits at the gateway to some of Savoy's best known ski resorts, including Les Arcs (1600 to 2000m), which is straight up the hill from Bourg. The modern Arc-en-Ciel funicular zips skiers up to Arc Pierre Blanche (1600m) – the lower village in Les Arcs – in seven minutes (14km by road), making it feasible to stay in Bourg where accommodation is slightly cheaper.

Bourg Saint Maurice is one of the Alps' leading transport hubs: TGVs direct from Paris and the Eurostar, direct from London, both stop here.

Orientation & Information

Les Arcs is split between three stations – Arc Pierre Blanche (1600m), Arc 1800 (1800m) in Charvet, and Arc 2000 (2000m) embracing Villards and Charmettoger. All three are purpose-built and not very pretty.

Tourist Offices Bourg's tourist office (☎ 04 79 07 04 92; fax 04 79 07 24 90; wlesarcs@lesarcs.com; www.lesarcs.com), opposite the train station on Place de la Gare, is open from 8 am to noon and 2 to 7 pm, Friday and Saturday from 8 am to 7.30 pm, Sunday from 8 to noon and 2 to 7 pm. It can be contacted for information on all types of summer and winter activities, not only in Bourg and Les Arcs, but also in Val d'Isère and Tignes. Year-round, it arranges baroque art guided tours, local art and craft tours, Beaufort cheese tours, as well as city tours of Bourg's historic quarter.

There are smaller tourist offices in Arc Pierre Blanche (☎/fax 04 79 07 70 70) in the Galerie Commerciale; in Arc 1800 (☎ 04 79 07 61 11; fax 04 79 07 45 96) in La Pagode building; and in Arc 2000 (☎ 04 79 07 13 78; fax 04 79 07 14 09) on Place Haute. For ski information, contact the Société des Montagnes de l'Arc (☎ 04 79 41 55 18) at Arc 1800.

Activities

Despite its ugly façade, Les Arcs offers solid door-to-door skiing and snowboarding at all levels. The snowboard park at Arc 1800 has a half-pipe, there are flood-lit runs for night skiing, and off-piste areas are patrolled.

The Arc-en-Ciel funicular (☎ 04 79 07 29 03) from Bourg Saint Maurice to Arc 1600 costs 32/58FF one way/return if you do not have a ski pass. In winter it's open from 8.30 am to 4.30 pm (until 6 pm on weekends), and from 8.30 am to 7.30 pm in July and August. A two day ski pass allows you one day of skiing in Tignes and Val d'Isère. A three day pass gives skiers one day of access to La Thuile in Italy.

The ESF has branches in all three stations. In Arc Pierre Blanche the ESF (☎ 04 79 07 43 90) is in the same building as the tourist office. The In Extremis snowboarding school (☎ 04 79 07 21 72) is also here.

The Bureau des Guides (☎ 04 79 07 71 19) in Arc 2000 organises ice climbing in winter and rock climbing, canyoning and parapente in summer. It also arranges thematic hikes such as exploring Arc 2000's frozen lakes in winter and visiting shepherds in Beaufort in summer.

Places to Stay

All types of accommodation can be booked through the Centrale de Réservation (☎ 04 79 07 68 00; fax 04 79 07 68 99).

The ***Verdache*** hostel (☎ 04 79 41 01 93; fax 04 79 41 03 36; fuaj.seez.les.arcs@wanadoo.fr), 4km east of Bourg in Seez, is open from 20 December to mid-September. In winter you must buy a package: six days accommodation, food (including packed lunches), ski pass and ski hire for 2070/2650FF in the low/high season. To get there, take the Val d'Isère bus (see Getting There & Away for details).

Affordable hotels in Bourg include the ***Hostellerie du Petit Saint Bernard*** (☎ 04 79 07 04 32; fax 04 79 07 32 80), Ave du Stade, which charges 210FF per person for B&B; and ***Le Concorde*** (☎ 04 79 07 08 90), Ave Maréchal Leclerc, which has single/double rooms on a half-board basis for 360/300FF per person a night. ***La Vallée de l'Arc*** (☎ 04 79 07 04 12), 49 Grande Rue, charges 200/280FF a night for single/double rooms.

Accommodation is plentiful in all three stations in Les Arcs. The cheapest hotel is the affordable ***Hôtel Béguin*** (☎ 04 79 07 02 92; fax 04 79 07 72 61) in Arc Pierre Blanche. Singles/doubles with shower and toilet cost 210/240FF a night.

Getting There & Away

Bus Regional buses, operated by Autocars Martin (☎ 04 79 07 04 49), leave from next to Bourg's train station. There are two buses a day (13 on weekends) to Les Arcs 1600 and 1800 (50FF) and 2000 (60FF), seven to Seez (24FF), and four to Val d'Isère and Tignes-le-Lac (64FF). Return tickets are not available and you should book your ticket back to Bourg Saint Maurice a couple of days in advance during the high season and on weekends. Buses to Geneva cost 280FF one way.

Satobus-Alpes (☎ 04 72 35 94 96) runs direct buses to Lyon-Satolas airport (about 2¾ hours).

Train There is an SNCF office (☎ 04 79 07 04 46) in Arc 1800. Major train connections from Bourg's modern train station (☎ 08 36 35 35 35), Place de la Gare, include Paris' Gare de Lyon (from 329FF on TGV via Aix-les-Bains; 5½ hours), Chambéry (81FF; two hours; seven a day) and Lyon (174FF; three hours; five a day, some via Chambéry).

There's a direct night train to Paris, and a direct Eurostar train to and from London (828/1656FF single/return; 9½ hours) every Saturday between 20 December and 25 April.

Getting Around

Free shuttle buses run between all three Les Arcs stations from 7.45 am to 7.35 pm.

VAL D'ISÈRE

• pop 1700 ✉ 73150 alt 1850m

It's hip to be seen in Val d'Isère, a trendy resort in the upper reaches of the Tarentaise Valley, 31km south-east of Bourg Saint Maurice, and close to the Italian border. Together with **Tignes** (2100m), Val d'Isère and four other small villages combine to form **Espace Killy**.

Val d'Isère – a forming hunting ground for the dukes of Savoy – has grown from a village since 1932, when skiing was introduced to the region, but a settlement in the valley goes back thousands of years. The oldest building still standing is the 11th century church, with the rest of the village being a mixture of traditional Savoyard stone homes, chalet-type hotels and apartment blocks.

Tignes, a modern resort with unspectacular apartment blocks and hotels that make the valley look like a moonscape, is home to the Alps' leading freestyle ski school.

If this does not appeal, other options are two small Alpine villages, **Les Boisses** and **Les Brévières**, off the main road to Tignes, below Lac du Chevril. Both are traditional villages with no apartment blocks and few hotels. They are quiet at the best of times and almost deserted outside peak season.

Information

Tourist Offices The Val d'Isère tourist office (☎ 04 79 06 06 60; fax 04 79 06 04 56; info@val-disere.com; www.val-disere.com), Place Jacques Mouflier, is open from 8.30 am to 7.30 pm. The Bureau des Guides has a desk inside the tourist office and the accommodation service (☎ 04 79 06 18 90; fax 04 79 06 11 88) is above.

Tignes has two tourist offices – one in Tignes-le-Lac (☎ 04 79 40 04 40; fax 04 79 40 03 15; tignes@laposte.fr) and another in Val Claret (☎ 04 79 40 03 13). The Tignes-le-Lac office is open in winter from 8.30 am to 7 pm (Saturday from 8 am to 8 pm). In summer it's open from 9 am to noon and 2 to 7 pm. There is an SNCF booking desk nearby. The accommodation service (☎ 04 79 06 56 71) is in the same area.

Winter Activities

Espace Killy offers some of the best skiing in the country – between 1550 and 3450m. Ski touring is also excellent in Espace Killy, especially in the Parc National de la Vanoise. The snowboarders Snowspace Park in La Deille has a half-pipe, tables, gaps, quarters and hips. In July and August you can ski on the glacier.

Val d'Isère has no less than four ski schools and seven independent instructors. The ESF (☎ 04 79 06 02 34; fax 04 79 41 15 80) is housed in a large building off Place Jacques Mouflier. Hors Limites (☎ 04 79 41 97 02; lionel@hors-limites.com) specialises in snowboarding. A six day Espace Killy ski pass also entitles skiers to one day of skiing in La Plagne, Les Arcs or Les Trois Vallées.

Heli-skiing, ice diving, ice climbing, showshoeing and sledge and husky-drawn sledge rides are also available. The tourist offices have details.

Summer Activities

One of the more popular hikes is from Val d'Isère to Tignes along the Gorges de la Daille or the high road along Vallon de la Tovière. Other possibilities are to Col de l'Iseran or Glacier des Sources d'Isère, but many other routes in the Parc National de la Vanoise are possible. The valleys and gentle hiking trails also offer many possibilities for mountain biking and fishing.

The Bureau des Guides organises, among other things, visits to a local farm where you can see cheese being made, and Alpine bird-watching treks. Safaris Vanoise (☎ 04 79 06 00 03; fax 04 79 06 10 28) organises animal photography and filming expeditions. The ESF runs parapente lessons in summer.

Places to Stay

Advance bookings, imperative throughout the ski season, can be made through the accommodation service (see Tourist Office). Two-person studios and apartments start at 1300/2900FF a week in the low/high season.

One of the more affordable hotels is ***Relais du Ski*** (☎ 04 79 06 02 06; fax 04 79 41 10 64), south-east of the tourist office, where basic double rooms cost 260/290FF in the low/high season. The two star ***Hôtel l'Avancher*** (☎ 04 79 06 02 00; fax 04 79 41 16 07), Route Fornet, east of the tourist office, has double rooms from 386/465FF in low/high season with half-board. Another mid-range place is the ***Hôtel Kandahar*** (☎ 04 79 06 02 39; fax 04 79 41 15 54), on the main street about 100m north-west of the tourist office, with decent doubles for 310/630FF in low/high season.

Getting There & Away

Autocars Martin (☎ 04 79 06 00 42) runs four buses a day to Val d'Isère and Tignes (65FF) from Bourg Saint Maurice, the nearest train station. It's essential to book your seat back to Bourg Saint Maurice. The office is open weekdays from 9 am to noon and 2 to 7.30 pm, Saturday from 7 am to 1 pm and 1.45 to

FRENCH ALPS

9 pm, Sunday from 7.30 am to noon and 2 to 7.30 pm. There is an SNCF counter here too, open from 9 am to noon and 3 to 7 pm.

Satobus-Alpes (☎ 04 72 35 94 96) runs four buses a day (three on Sunday) from Val d'Isère to Lyon-Satolas airport via Bourg Saint Maurice. A single ticket costs 250FF. There are also buses to Geneva airport (285FF; five hours; three a day and eight on weekends).

Getting Around

In both Val d'Isère and Tignes there are complimentary buses around each centre. The *train rouge* (red train) – a network of 23 shuttle buses – connects Val d'Isère and Tignes to neighbouring villages including Les Boisses and the Grand Motte funicular. Timetables are posted at the bus stops.

PARC NATIONAL DE LA VANOISE

A wild mix of high mountains, steep valleys and glaciers, the Parc National de la Vanoise became France's first national park in 1963. It covers 530 sq km – basically the eastern part of the massif between the Tarentaise Valley to the north and the Maurienne Valley to the south. It's a hiker's heaven, with nearly 500km of marked trails (including the GR5 and GR55) and 42 *refuges* dotted around the rugged terrain. The scenery is spectacular – snowcapped peaks mirrored in icy lakes are just the start. Marmots and chamois, as well as France's largest colony of Alpine ibex (*bouquetin*), graze free and undisturbed among the larch trees, and over them all reigns the eagle.

Though you can get to the park on foot from many of the famous ski resorts, including Méribel and Tignes, the easiest route to the park is through the somewhat forgotten and isolated Haute Maurienne Valley, the part of the Maurienne Valley above the town of Modane. From here, a chain of rough-hewn, shaggy stone villages stretches up to the hamlet of Bonneval-sur-Arc, behind which rises the Col de l'Iseran (2770m). Bonneval-sur-Arc (1800m) and Lanslebourg (1400m), 19km farther southwest, make good bases from which to explore the park.

Orientation & Information

The Parc National de la Vanoise administration office (☎ 04 79 62 30 54; fax 04 79 96 37 18; Minitel 3615 VANOISE) in Chambéry has information on the park and a list of *refuges*, which cost 68FF per night. To book one in June, July or August call ☎ 04 79 08 71 49. The park newspaper, *Estive*, published seasonally and freely distributed in tourist offices, contains a full listing of all *refuges* complete with direct contact numbers.

Park information is also available at the tourist office (☎ 04 79 05 95 95; fax 04 79 05 86 87) in Bonneval-sur-Arc and the Maison du Val Cénis (☎ 04 79 05 23 66; fax 04 79 05 82 17) in Lanslebourg. A good map of the region is the 1:50,000 scale IGN map *Parc de la Vanoise* (No 11).

Baroque Chapels & Museum

One of the particular curiosities of the Haute Maurienne Valley are the many local chapels, whose humble exteriors hide rich interiors of superb baroque religious art; some also have murals from the 15th century. Much of the decoration was done by artists from Turin, one of the centres of baroque art, who came to the valley by crossing over the Col du Mont Cénis.

Unfortunately, in recent years most of the chapels have had to be locked to prevent theft and vandalism. If you inquire at the Maison du Parc or the Espace Baroque they'll be able to arrange a key for you. Ask for the free brochure entitled *Chemins du Baroque*, which lists all the churches on offer. Up the valley from Lanslebourg, **Lanslevillard** (2km) and **Bessans** (12km) have chapels with exceptional painted walls, ceilings, statues and ornamentation.

The **Espace Baroque** (☎ 04 79 05 90 42), a museum housed in an old church in Lanslebourg, is a good place to become acquainted with the valley's baroque tradition. Its contemporary displays are exceptionally good. From late June to mid-September the museum is open from 3 to 7 pm (and from 10 am to noon as well on Tuesday, Wednesday and Saturday; closed Sunday). Entry is 25/15FF for adults/children.

Skiing

Lanslebourg and Bonneval-sur-Arc are popular cross-country skiing resorts. Both offer limited Alpine skiing as well. The ESF (☎ 04 79 05 95 70) is inside the Bonneval-sur-Arc tourist office.

In summer it's possible to ski on the Grand Pissaillas glacier at Col de l'Iseran, 23km north-east of Lanslebourg. The best skiing is between March and early May.

Hiking

Hikers have a fine network of small trails to choose from – the Maison du Val Cénis has a *randonnées* booklet, which details, with maps, a dozen half-day or day treks. The Bureau des Guides (☎ 04 79 05 95 70 or ☎ 04 79 05 96 33) inside the Bonneval-sur-Arc tourist office and Guide de Haute-Montagne (☎ 04 79 05 94 74) both organise guided hikes and climbs.

The trail from Lanslebourg up to the Turra Fort (2500m), from where there are great views over the Lac du Mont Cénis, generally takes about three hours. To really take in the region, you can follow all or part of Le Grand Tour de Haute Maurienne – a hike of five days or more around the upper reaches of the valley. There are 15 *refuges* or gîtes d'étape en route.

The GR5 and GR55 pass through the park and there are also paths linked to the Écrins National Park to the south and the Grand Paradiso National Park in Italy. Tracks are usually passable from June to the end of October.

The old quarter (vieux village) of Bonneval-sur-Arc is *the* place for less-energetic strollers seeking nothing more than a gentle amble. The village's stone cottages and narrow, car-free lanes have been beautifully preserved, earning it the title of one of France's prettiest villages. No visit is complete without a trip to the village *fromagerie*.

The tourist office sells the walking guide *Bonneval-sur-Arc – Promenades et Randonnées* for 5FF.

Places to Stay

In Lanslebourg, ***Camping Les Balmasses*** (☎ 04 79 05 82 83) is open from June to September. The ***Auberge de Jeunesse Hameau des Champs*** (☎ 04 79 05 90 96; fax 04 79 05 82 52) is in the hamlet of Les Champs, which is on the east side of Lanslevillard. It's open from mid-December to September (closed in May) and costs 45FF per night. A shower costs 4.50FF. The CAF has a ***refuge*** (☎ 04 79 05 95 07) next to the tourist office in Bonneval-sur-Arc.

There are five hotels in Lanslebourg. The warm and welcoming two star ***Hôtel La Vieille Poste*** (☎ 04 79 05 93 47; fax 04 79 05 86 85), on the main road through town, has doubles with shower from 250FF. It is closed for a fortnight in April and again from November to Christmas. In Bonneval-sur-Arc the ***Hôtel du Glacier des Evettes*** (☎ 04 79 05 94 06; fax 04 79 05 85 00) has doubles with shower/bath for 280/300FF. Bonneval also has plenty of delightful old stone cottages for rent. The tourist office has details.

Getting There & Away

The trains serving the valley leave from Chambéry and run as far as the Modane train station (☎ 08 36 35 35 35), 23km south-west of Lanslebourg.

From Modane, Transavoie buses (☎ 04 79 05 01 32) go to Lanslebourg (one hour). Once a day (in the evening) they continue to Bessans and Bonneval-sur-arc. In winter a shuttle bus runs four times a day between Lanslebourg and Bonneval-sur-Arc.

Dauphiné

Dauphiné, which encompasses the territories south and south-west of Savoy, stretches from the Rhône River in the west to the Italian border in the east. It includes the city of Grenoble and, a little farther east, the mountainous Écrins National Park. The gentler terrain of the western part of

Dauphiné is typified by the Vercors Regional Park, much loved by cross-country skiers. In the east, the town of Briançon stands guard like a sentinel near the Italian frontier.

History

The area now known as Dauphiné was inhabited by the Celts and then the Romans. By the 11th century it was under the rule of Guigues I, the count of Albon, whose great-grandson Guigues IV (ruled 1133-42) was the first local count to bear the name of 'dauphin'. By the end of the 13th century, the name 'dauphin' had been transformed into a title and the fiefs held by the region's ruling house, La Tour du Pin, were known collectively as Dauphiné. The rulers of Dauphiné continued to expand their territories, which gave them control of all the passes through the southern Alps.

In 1339 Humbert II established a university at Grenoble. A decade later, however, lacking both money and a successor, he sold Dauphiné to the French king, Charles V, who started the tradition whereby the eldest son of the king of France (ie the crown prince) ruled Dauphiné and bore the title 'dauphin'. The region was annexed to France by Charles VII in 1457.

GRENOBLE

• pop 155,000 ✉ 38000 alt 213m

Grenoble, site of the 1968 Winter Olympics, is the intellectual and economic capital of the French Alps. It's also the centre of the Dauphiné region, spectacularly sitting in a broad valley surrounded by mountains – the Chartreuse to the north, the Vercors to the south-west and Alpine peaks stretching east to Italy.

Grenoble gained a reputation for progress in the 1960s, when the Socialist Hubert Dubedout served as mayor. People from all over France flocked here, attracted by social, artistic and technological innovations, and eventually came to outnumber the native Grenoblois. The large university serves a student body of 36,000 and has a thriving foreign student exchange program. Grenoble also has important facilities for nuclear and microelectronic research and is home to many large foreign companies.

The city hosts a jazz festival in March, a rock festival in April, and a European theatre festival in June and July. Given Grenoble is the capital of Dauphiné, this is *the* place to sample the popular French dish, *gratin Dauphinois*. *Noix de Grenoble* (a sweet walnut candy) and *gâteau aux noix* (walnut cake) are the local specialities for those with a sweet tooth.

Orientation

Grenoble can be a particularly difficult city to negotiate, especially from behind the wheel, and street parking is virtually nonexistent. The old city is centred around Place Grenette and Place Notre Dame, both of which are about 1km east of the train and bus stations. The main university campus is a couple of kilometres east of the old centre on the south side of the Isère River.

Information

Tourist Office The ground floor of the Maison du Tourisme, 14 Rue de la République, houses the tourist office (☎ 04 76 42 41 41; fax 04 76 51 28 69), an SNCF counter, a kiosk for tickets to all forms of entertainment, an office of the local bus company (TAG), and the Bureau des Guides (☎/fax 04 76 03 28 63). The first three are open from 9 am to 12.30 pm and 1.30 to 6 pm (closed Sunday). From June to mid-September, the tourist office is open on Sunday from 10 am to noon. The TAG counter is open from 8.30 am to 6.30 pm (Saturday from 9 am to 6 pm; closed Sunday). The Bureau des Guides is open on Thursday between 2 and 6 pm (telephone or fax at other times).

The Maison du Tourisme is served by both tram lines (see Getting Around).

Hiking Information Info-Montagne (☎ 04 76 42 45 90; fax 04 76 15 3 91), on the first floor of the Maison du Tourisme, is the place to go for first-hand information from dedicated outdoor enthusiasts on hiking, climbing, mountain biking and every other imaginable mountain activity *except* skiing.

GRENOBLE

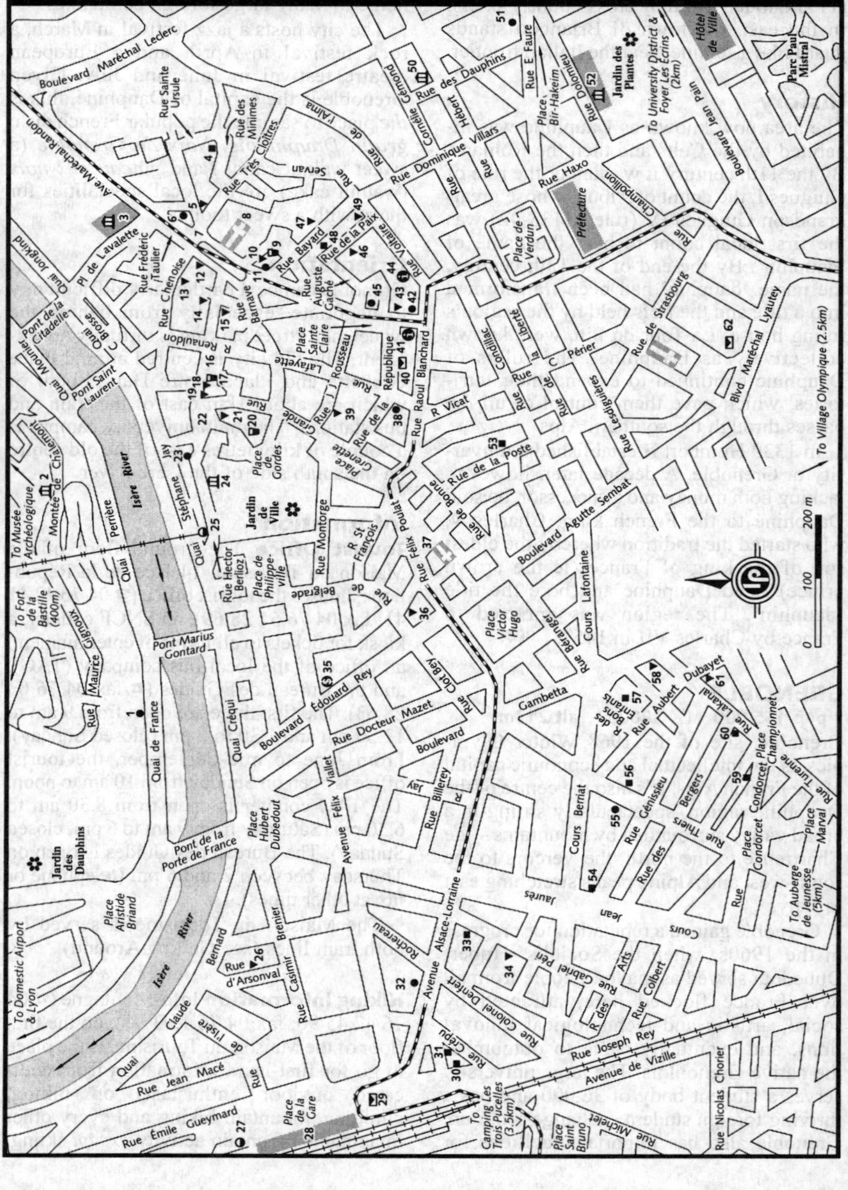
Boulevard Maréchal Leclerc
Rue Sainte Ursule
Ave Maréchal Randon
Quai Jongkind
Pl de Lavalette
Rue Frédéric Taulier
Rue Chenoise
Rue des Minimes
Rue Très Cloîtres
Rue Servan
Rue de l'Alma
Rue Bayard
Rue de la Paix
Rue Voltaire
Rue Auguste Gaché
Rue Barnave
Rue Renauldon
Quai Brosse
Pont de la Citadelle
Quai Mounier
Montée de Chalemont
Pont Saint Laurent
Place Sainte Claire
Rue Lafayette
Rue J J Rousseau
Grande Rue
Rue de la République
Rue Raoul Blanchard
Place Grenette
Place de Gordes
Jardin de Ville
Rue Stéphane Jay
Quai Perrière
Isère River
To Musée Archéologique
To Fort de la Bastille (400m)
Rue Hector Berlioz
Place de Philippeville
Rue Montorge
R St François
Rue de Belgrade
Rue Félix Poulat
Pont Marius Gontard
Rue Maurice Gignoux
Quai de France
Quai Créqui
Boulevard Édouard Rey
Rue Docteur Mazet
Rue Clot Bey
Boulevard Gambetta
Rue Billerey
Rue Jay
Place Hubert Dubedout
Avenue Félix Viallet
Jardin des Dauphins
Place Aristide Briand
Pont de la Porte de France
Isère River
Rue Bernard
Rue Brenier
Rue Casimir
Rue d'Arsonval
Rue Claude
Quai de l'Isère
Rue Jean Macé
Rue Émile Gueymard
Place de la Gare
Rue Rocherau
Avenue Alsace-Lorraine
Rue Crépu
To Domestic Airport & Lyon
To Camping Les Trois Pucelles (3.5km)
Rue Corneille
Rue Gémond
Rue des Dauphins
Rue Hébert
Rue Dominique Villars
Rue E Faure
Place Bir-Hakeim
Rue Dolomieu
Jardin des Plantes
To University District & Foyer Les Ecrins (2km)
Boulevard Jean Pain
Hôtel de Ville
Parc Paul Mistral
Rue Haxo
Rue Champollion
Préfecture
Place de Verdun
Rue Condillac
Rue la Liberté
Rue de Strasbourg
Rue C Périer
Blvd Maréchal Lyautey
R Vicat
Rue Lesdiguières
Rue de la Poste
Rue de Bonne
Boulevard Agutte Sembat
Place Victor Hugo
Rue Béranger
Cours Lafontaine
To Village Olympique (2.5km)
Rue Gambetta
Rue des Bons Enfants
Rue Aubert Dubayet
Rue Lakanal
Place Championnet
Rue Turenne
Cours Berriat
Rue Génissieu
Rue des Bergers
Rue Thiers
Place Condorcet
Place Marval
Rue Condorcet
Cours Jean Jaurès
To Auberge de Jeunesse (5km)
Rue Gabriel Péri
Rue des Arts
Rue Colbert
Rue Colonel Denfert
Rue Joseph Rey
Avenue de Vizille
Rue Nicolas Chorier
Place Saint Bruno
Rue Michelet
0 100 200 m

It sells hiking maps and has detailed info on gîtes d'étape and *refuges*. The office is open from 9 am to noon and 2 to 6 pm (from 10 am on Saturday; closed Sunday).

The CAF (☎ 04 76 42 49 92), 1 Rue Hauquelin, provides information on its *refuges* and organises hiking, mountain-bike and skiing trips. It is open Tuesday from 2.30 pm to 7.30 pm, Thursday to 8.30 pm, and Friday to 8 pm. Other friendly hiking clubs include Mountain Wilderness (☎ 04 76 84 54 42; fax 04 76 84 54 44), Maison de la Nature et de l'Environment, 5 Place Bir-Hakeim; and Grenoble Amitié Nature (☎ 04 76 51 32 36), 5 Passage du Palais de Justice.

Skiing Information The tourist office has comprehensive information, including accommodation lists, for all of Grenoble's surrounding ski resorts (see Around Grenoble). The Grenoble Université Club (☎ 04 76 57 47 72), near the train station at 25 Rue Casimir Brenier, offers inexpensive skiing for students and nonstudents of all ages. There's a 295FF membership fee that includes insurance. The FUAJ ski club, based in the Auberge de Jeunesse (see Hostels under Places to Stay) also offers cheap skiing deals. Its office is open from 10 am to 6 pm in season.

Money The Banque de France, on the corner of Blvd Édouard Rey and Ave Félix Viallet, is open weekdays from 8.45 am to 12.15 pm and 1.30 to 3.30 pm.

Post & Communications The main post office, inconveniently located at 7 Blvd Maréchal Lyautey, is open weekdays from 8 am to 6.45 pm (Saturday until noon). More central is the post office next to the tourist office, open daily, except Sunday and Monday, from 8 am to 6.30 pm. The branch across the tram tracks from the train station is open weekdays from 9.45 am until noon and 1.30 to 5 pm (9.45 to 11.45 am and 1.45 to 5 pm on Tuesday, 9.30 am to noon on Saturday).

GRENOBLE

PLACES TO STAY
- 4 Foyer de l'Étudiante (Summer Hostel)
- 30 Hôtel Alizé
- 31 Hôtel Lux
- 33 Hôtel Royal
- 48 Hôtel du Moucherotte
- 53 Hôtel de la Poste
- 54 Hôtel des Doges
- 56 Hôtel Victoria
- 57 Hôtel Beau Soleil
- 59 Hôtel Condorcet
- 60 Hôtel Lakanal

PLACES TO EAT
- 5 La Galerie Rome
- 10 Le Valgo
- 12 Le Tonneau de Diogène
- 13 L'Amphitryon
- 14 Chorus Café
- 15 Restaurant des Montagnes
- 18 Encore +
- 19 Café Tamara
- 21 Café de la Table Ronde
- 26 Restaurant Universitaire
- 34 Tchou Tchoura
- 36 Les Archers
- 39 La Mère Ticket
- 43 La Forêt Noire
- 46 Ciao a Te
- 47 Le Mal Assis
- 49 La Panse
- 58 Subway
- 61 Chouette! Un Tonneau!

OTHER
- 1 Mountain Bike Grenoble
- 2 Musée Dauphinois
- 3 Musée de Grenoble
- 6 Le New Age Cyber Café
- 7 Place Notre Dame
- 8 Notre Dame Cathedral; Bishop's Palace
- 9 Barberousse
- 11 Cybernet
- 16 Place aux Herbes
- 17 Le Couche Tard
- 20 Le Saxo Pub
- 22 Place Saint André
- 23 Théâtre de Grenoble
- 24 La Musée Stendhal
- 25 Téléphérique to Fort de la Bastille
- 27 Bus Station
- 28 Train Station
- 29 Post Office; TAG Office; Gare Europole Tram Station
- 32 Voyages Wasteels
- 35 Banque de France
- 37 Église Saint Louis
- 38 Prisunic Supermarket
- 40 Post Office
- 41 Maison du Tourisme
- 42 Laundrette
- 44 Centre Information Jeunesse
- 45 Les Halles; Place Sainte Claire Market
- 50 Musée de la Résistance
- 51 Maison de la Nature et de l'Environment
- 52 Musée d'Histoire Naturelle
- 55 Laundrette
- 62 Main Post Office

Internet Resources Surf the Internet and send emails at Cybernet (☎ 04 76 51 73 18; fax 04 76 03 20 33; services@neptune.fr; www.neptune.fr/CyberNetCafe), 3 Rue Bayard. A 30 minute/one hour connection costs 30/47FF. It is open from noon to 2 pm and 10 pm to 1 am. Le New Age Cyber Café (☎ 04 76 51 94 43), opposite the Musée de Grenoble at 1 Rue Frédéric Taulier, charges the same rates and is open from 9.30 am to 9 pm.

Travel Agencies Voyages Wasteels (☎ 04 76 47 34 54; fax 04 76 85 31 78), 50 Ave Alsace Lorraine, sells air tickets. It's open weekdays from 9 am to noon and 2 to 7 pm (until 6 pm on Saturday; closed Sunday).

Laundry The Lavomatique opposite Hotel Victoria, 14 Rue Thiers, is open from 7 am to 10 pm. The no-name laundrette opposite the Maison du Tourisme is open from 7 am to 9.30 pm.

Museum Pass Museum buffs planning to visit all of Grenoble's museums should consider a *Pass' Musées*. It costs 50FF, is valid for a year, and entitles you admission to 16 museums in and around Grenoble. The pass is sold at the Musée Dauphinois.

Fort de la Bastille

Fort de la Bastille, built in the 16th century (and expanded in the 19th) to control the approaches to the city, sits on the north side of the Isère River, 263m above the old city. It affords spectacular views, including Mont Blanc on clear days. Three viewpoint indicators – one just west of the téléphérique station, the other two on the roof of the building just east of it – explain what you're looking at. A sign near the disused Mont Jalla chair lift (300m beyond the arch next to the bathrooms) indicates the hiking trails that pass by here.

To get to the fort, a téléphérique (☎ 04 76 44 33 65) leaves from Quai Stéphane Jay between the Marius Gontard and Saint Laurent bridges. One-way/return tickets cost 22/33FF (17/26FF for students). From November to March the téléphérique runs from 10.30 am to 6.30 pm (from 11 am on Monday). The rest of the year the last trip up is at 11.30 pm and the last trip down is at 11.45 pm – except on Sunday (9 am to 7.15 pm) and Monday (11 am to 7.15 pm) from April to June and September and October. A variety of trails and a road lead up the hillside to the fort.

Musée Dauphinois

Occupying a beautiful 17th century convent, this museum (☎ 04 76 85 19 01; musee-dauphinois@cg38.alpes-net.fr) at 30 Rue Maurice Gignoux sits near the bottom of the hill topped by Fort de la Bastille. From the city centre, it is most easily reached by the Pont Saint Laurent footbridge. The museum has good displays on the crafts and history of the Dauphiné region, with a particular focus on the mountain people's traditional way of life. It's open from 10 am to 7 pm (closed Tuesday), and until 6 pm between November and April. Admission is 20/10FF for adults/students.

East of the museum, also in the historic Saint Laurent quarter of town, is the excellent **Musée Archéologique** (☎ 04 76 44 78 68), housed in a church dating from the 12th century. It's open from 9 am to noon and 2 to 6 pm (closed Tuesday).

Musée de Grenoble

Also called the Musée des Beaux-Arts (Fine Arts Museum), the Grenoble Museum (☎ 04 76 63 44 44), 5 Place de Lavalette, is known for its outstanding collection of paintings and sculpture. Exhibits include an enormous work by the Flemish artist Pierre-Paul Rubens as well as a renowned modern collection that features pieces by Chagall, Léger, Matisse, Modigliani, Monet, Picasso, Sisley and many others.

The museum is open daily, except on Monday and Tuesday, from 11 am to 7 pm (until 10 pm on Wednesday). Admission is 25/15FF for adults/students. There are 1½-hour guided tours (25FF) daily at 3 pm (at 12.15 pm on Monday).

Cathédrale Notre Dame et Ancien Évêché

The double Notre Dame and Saint Hugues Cathedral on Place Notre Dame and the adjoining 14th century Bishop's Palace have recently had complete face-lifts and now contain three museums (expected to open in early 1999): the **crypte archéologique**, with its Roman-era walls and baptistery dating from the 4th to 10th century; the **Musée d'Art Sacré**, containing liturgical and other religious objects; and the **Centre Jean Achard**, with exhibits of art from the Dauphiné region.

Musée de la Résistance et de la Déportation de l'Isère

This museum (☎ 04 76 42 38 53) at 14 Rue Hébert examines the deportation of Jews and others from Grenoble to Nazi concentration and labour camps during WWII and the role of the Vercors region in the Resistance. Captions are in French, English and German. It is open from 9 am to noon and 2 to 6 pm (closed Tuesday). Admission is 20/10FF for adults/students.

Musée Stendhal

Stendhal, author of *Le Rouge et le Noir*, was born in Grenoble in 1783. The tourist office distributes a free brochure called *Route Historique – Stendhal*, which traces the life and works of the French writer from his birthplace and home where he lived for 18 years through to outlying villages that inspired him. The Musée Stendhal (☎ 04 76 54 44 14), overlooking the Jardin de Ville at 1 Rue Hector Berlioz, is open from 10 am to noon and 2 to 6 pm (afternoons only in winter; closed Sunday).

Musée d'Histoire Naturelle

Various Alpine flora and fauna typical to the French Alps as well as a 'carnival of insects' and an aquarium is housed in the natural history museum (☎ 04 76 44 05 35), 1 Rue Dolomieu, overlooking the Jardin des Plantes. There is a botanic garden in its grounds. The complex is open daily, except Tuesday, from 9.30 am to noon and 1.30 to 5.30 pm (Sunday afternoon only from 2 to 6 pm). Admission costs 15FF for adults and 10FF for students.

Hiking

A number of beautiful trails can be picked up in Grenoble or very nearby (eg from Fort de la Bastille). The northern part of Parc Naturel Régional du Vercors (☎ 04 76 95 15 99; fax 04 76 95 97 12 in Villard de Lans for information) is just west of the city.

Places to Stay

Camping *Camping Les Trois Pucelles* (☎ 04 76 96 45 73), open all year, is at 58 Rue des Allobroges (one block west of the Drac River) in Grenoble's western suburb of Seyssins. From the train station, take the tram towards Fontaine and get off at the Maisonnat stop. Then take bus No 51 (the last one goes at around 9 pm) to Mas des Îles and walk east on Rue du Dauphiné. A place to camp and park costs 30/43FF for one/two people.

Hostels The ***Auberge de Jeunesse*** (☎ 04 76 09 33 52; fax 04 76 09 38 09; grenoble .echirolles@wanadoo.fr), 10 Ave du Grésivaudan, is 5km south of the train station in the Echirolles district. It charges 67FF per person including breakfast; reception is open from 7.30 am to 11 pm. To get there from Cours Jean Jaurès, take bus No 8 (direction Pont de Claix; last one is at about 9 pm) to the Quinzaine stop (look for the Casino supermarket).

At 4 Rue Sainte Ursule, the friendly and central ***Foyer de l'Étudiante*** (☎ 04 76 42 00 84) accepts travellers of both sexes from the end of June to the end of September. Singles/doubles cost 90/130FF a day and, for those who want to stay put, 400/ 600FF a week.

Hotels – Train Station Area The ***Hôtel Alizé*** (☎ 04 76 43 12 91; fax 04 76 47 62 79), 1 Rue Amiral Courbet, has modern singles/doubles with washbasin for 126/ 150FF and doubles with shower for 182FF. The ***Hôtel Lux*** (☎ 04 76 46 41 89; fax 04 76 46 51 61), nearby at 6 Rue Crépu, a quiet back street south of the station, is tidy and friendly. Basic rooms are 147/165FF, and rooms with shower start at 188FF.

The good-value ***Hôtel Royal*** (☎ 04 76 46 18 92; fax 04 76 87 15 37), 2 Rue Gabriel Péri, has doubles/triples with shower and toilet for 215/235FF.

Hotels – Place Condorcet Area There are lots of inexpensive hotels in this vicinity. One of the best is the ***Hôtel Lakanal*** (☎ 04 76 46 03 42), 1km south-east of the station off Place Championnet at 26 Rue des Bergers. It attracts a young and friendly crowd and has simple singles/doubles with toilet for just 100/120FF. Rooms with shower and toilet cost 140/180FF. Hall showers are 15FF and breakfast is 20FF.

A block away, the ***Hôtel Condorcet*** (☎ 04 76 46 20 64), 8 Rue Condorcet, has rooms with washbasin for 110/152FF and with bath for 175FF. The noisy ***Hôtel des Doges*** (☎ 04 76 46 13 19; fax 04 76 47 67 95), 29 Cours Jean Jaurès, has basic rooms from 100/120FF and doubles with shower from 160FF. Hall showers cost 15FF and breakfast is 25FF.

The quiet, comfortable ***Hôtel Victoria*** (☎ 04 76 46 06 36), in a courtyard at 17 Rue Thiers, has rooms with shower and TV for 170/190FF and with toilet as well for 195/215FF. The hotel is closed in August.

The relaxed ***Hôtel Beau Soleil*** (☎ 04 76 46 29 40), 9 Rue des Bons Enfants, has rooms from 130/140FF (155/170FF with shower). Hall showers/breakfast are 16/22FF.

Hotels – City Centre The ***Hôtel du Moucherotte*** (☎ 04 76 54 61 40; fax 04 76 44 62 52), 1 Rue Auguste Gaché, is a dark, rather old-fashioned place with huge, clean rooms. Singles/doubles with shower start at 145/194FF, triples/quads cost 218/256FF. Breakfast is 30FF extra.

The pleasant and friendly, family-run ***Hôtel de la Poste*** (☎ 04 76 46 67 25), 25 Rue de la Poste, has basic rooms for 100/160FF; showers are free and a traditional English breakfast is 30FF.

Places to Eat

Grenoble has a fine array of funky restaurants and bistros serving traditional as well as foreign cuisine. North African places are scattered along and around Rue Renauldon and Rue Chenoise; while Place Condorcet and Rue de la Poste are the hot spots for Chinese fare. There are 20 or more pizza joints on Quai Perrière, bang next door to each other.

Restaurants For good food at reasonable prices, try ***Le Tonneau de Diogène*** (☎ 04 76 42 38 40), 6 Place Notre Dame, which attracts a young, lively crowd. The plat du jour is 55FF, salads cost from 15 to 38FF. It's open from 8.30 am to 1 am. The owner's other restaurant, ***Chouette! Un Tonneau!*** (☎ 04 76 46 92 36), a few blocks east of Place Condorcet at 5 Rue Aubert Dubayet, is open from 11.30 am to 10.30 pm (closed Sunday and Monday).

Le Mal Assis (literally 'badly seated'; ☎ 04 76 54 75 93), 9 Rue Bayard, is a cosy upmarket restaurant serving delicious and authentic *cuisine bourgeoise*. Its menu is 128FF and reservations are recommended. It's open until 11 pm (closed Sunday and Monday). ***Le Valgo*** (☎ 04 76 51 38 85), close by at 2 Rue Saint Hugues, has *menus* for 65 and 98FF. *Pieds paquets* (lamb tripe) is its house speciality.

La Mère Ticket, Rue Jean-Jacques Rousseau, serves astonishingly delicious *poulet aux écrevisses* (chicken with crayfish) on its 85FF *menu*. This tiny, homely restaurant is open until 11 pm.

La Panse (☎ 04 76 54 09 54), 7 Rue de la Paix, offers an 85FF lunch *menu* and a 100FF day and night *menu* that are especially good value. It is open from noon to 1.30 pm and 7.15 to 10 pm (closed Sunday).

For local fondue and tartiflette look no farther than the ***Restaurant des Montagnes*** (☎ 04 76 15 20 72), 5 Rue Brocherie. Salads start at 34FF, and there are 13 types of fondue (42FF per person). It is open from 7 am to midnight.

Les Archers (☎ 04 76 46 27 76), 2 Rue Docteur Bailly, is a brasserie-style restaurant with great outside seating in summer.

The plat du jour is 57FF, *huîtres* (oysters) are 106FF a dozen, and it is open from 10 am to 10 pm.

Taking a more modern approach is ***La Galerie Rome*** (☎ 04 76 42 82 01), housed inside a smart art gallery on the corner of Rue du Vieux Temple and Rue Très Cloîtres. It is open from 10 am to 10 pm (closed Sunday and Monday). *Menus* cost 58 and 90FF.

Encore + (☎ 04 76 00 07 77), 3 Rue du Palais, has a bar built from washing machines, has laundry strung from the ceiling, and ironing boards doubling as 'tables for two'. It specialises in moules (mussels), starting at 52FF. Jazz bands play here on Sunday from 9.30 pm.

Ciao a Te (☎ 04 76 42 54 41), 2 Rue de la Paix, is a trendy Italian place, serving great pasta *menus* from 58FF. It is open from 7.45 pm (closed Sunday). The ultra-modern ***L'Amphitryon*** (☎ 04 76 51 38 07), 9 Rue Chenoise, is the place for couscous – and the funkiest entrance in town. ***Tchou Tchoura*** (☎ 04 76 47 35 95), 16 Rue Gabriel Péri, is a Bulgarian restaurant.

University Restaurant The ***Restaurant Universitaire*** at 5 Rue d'Arsonval is open weekdays between mid-September and mid-June from 11.20 am to 1.15 pm and 6.20 to 7.50 pm. Tickets (about 15/30FF for students/nonstudents) are sold at lunchtime only.

Cafés The best breakfast option in town is the trendy ***Subway*** (☎ 04 76 87 31 67), a five minute walk from the train station on the corner of Rue Lakanal and Blvd Gambetta. Hot sandwiches are 20FF, and it has a lunch of sausage, chips (French fries) and drink for 15FF. It's open from 7 to 1 am (Sunday from 5 pm).

Great for afternoon tea is ***La Forêt Noire***, opposite the Maison du Tourisme at the south end of Place Sainte Claire. This delightful *salon de thé* (tea salon) serves a good range of salads, creamy cakes and a *menu minceur* (slimmers menu) for 48FF.

The ***Café Tamara***, 1 Rue du Palais, is a chic place for a cup of coffee. Graffiti covers the walls of the fun, jukebox playing ***Chorus Café*** opposite Restaurant des Montagnes on Rue Brocherie.

Dating from 1739 and an old haunt of Stendhal and Rousseau is the historic ***Café de la Table Ronde*** (☎ 04 76 44 51 41), 7 Place Saint André. The lunch menu costs 75FF. It closes at midnight.

Self-Catering Near the tourist office, the lovely old ***Les Halles*** covered market is open from 6 am to 1 pm (closed Monday). There's a ***food market*** on Place Sainte Claire daily, except Tuesday.

The ***Prisunic*** supermarket, on the corner of Rue de la République and Rue Lafayette, has a basement grocery section and an in-house *boulangerie*. It's open from 8.30 am to 7.30 pm (closed Sunday).

FRENCH ALPS

Entertainment

Le Journal de Saison, issued monthly by the tourist office, lists cultural events. Most cultural events take place at the ***Théâtre de Grenoble*** (☎ 04 76 44 03 44), 4 Rue Hector Berlioz.

Night-time hip bars include ***Barberousse*** (☎ 04 76 57 14 53), a small dimly lit bar at 8 Rue Hache which has 33 sorts of aromatic rum fermenting in giant glass flasks behind the bar. Down a shot of cherry, apple, papaya or other fruit-flavoured liquor for 12FF. The bar is open from 5 pm to 1 am.

Le Couche Tard (☎ 04 76 44 18 79), 7 Rue du Palais, open from 4 pm to 1 am, and ***Le Saxo Pub*** (☎ 04 76 51 06 01), 7 Rue d'Agier, open from 6 pm to 2 am, are Grenoble's most popular, late-night drinking spots.

Getting There & Away

Air Grenoble-Saint Geoirs airport (☎ 04 76 65 48 48), 45km north of Grenoble, is for domestic flights only. International flights operate to/from Lyon-Satolas airport (☎ 04 72 22 72 21), 95km north-west of the city off the A43 to Lyon.

Bus The bus station (☎ 04 76 87 90 31) is next to the train station on Rue Émile Gueymard. Numerous bus companies operate services from here. VFD (☎ 04 76 47 77 77), runs buses to Geneva (143FF; 2½ hours), Nice (293FF; five hours; via Castellane, near the Gorges du Verdon) and most Alpine destinations including Annecy (93FF; 1¾ hours), Bourg d'Oisans (65FF; 50 minutes), Les Deux Alpes (102FF; 1¾ hours), Chamonix (152FF; three hours), and the ski stations on the Vercors range.

Intercars (☎ 04 76 46 19 77; fax 04 76 47 96 34) handles long-haul destinations such as Budapest (580FF), Madrid (540FF), Lisbon (830FF), London (550FF), Prague (520FF) and Venice (260FF). It operates buses departing from Annecy, Chamonix and Lyon too. Its office is open from 9 am to noon and 2 to 6 pm (until noon on Saturday; closed Sunday).

Train The huge, modern train station (☎ 08 36 35 35 35), Rue Émile Gueymard, is next to the Gare Europole tram stop, which is served by both tram lines (see Getting Around). The information office is open from 9 am to noon and 2 to 5.30 pm. The station and at least one ticket window are open from 4 am to 2 am.

Destinations served include Paris' Gare de Lyon (from 348FF; 3½ hours by TGV), Chambéry (53FF; one hour; 14 a day), and Lyon (93FF; 1½ hours; five a day). Change in Lyon for trains to Nice and Monaco. There are three trains a day to Turin (201FF) and Milan (240FF) in Italy; and two trains a day to Geneva (115FF; two hours). For Rome and Naples, change in Chambéry.

Getting Around

To/From the Airport The bus to Lyon-Satolas airport (130/195FF single/return; 65 minutes), operated by Valencin-based Cars Faure (☎ 04 78 96 11 44), stops at the bus station. Buses to the Grenoble-Saint Geoirs airport depart from the bus station (65/98FF single/return; 45 minutes).

Bus & Tram The local mass transit company, TAG, has two ultramodern tram lines – called A and B. Both stop at the tourist office and the train station. Bus and tram tickets cost 7.50FF and are available from ticket machines at tram stops or from bus drivers. They must be time-stamped in the little blue machines located at each tram stop before boarding. Tickets are valid for transfers – but not return trips – within one hour of being time-stamped.

A carnet of 10 tickets costs 53FF. Daily/weekly passes – Visitag and Avantag – are available for 23/70FF at the TAG information desk (☎ 04 76 20 66 66) at the tourist office, or from the TAG office next to the post office outside the train station.

Most of the buses on the 20 different lines cease functioning rather early, sometime between 6 and 9 pm. Trams run daily from 5 am (6.15 am on Sunday) to midnight.

Taxi Radio-dispatched taxis can be ordered by calling ☎ 04 76 54 42 54.

Bicycle Mountain Bike Grenoble (☎ 04 76 47 58 76), 6 Quai de France, has mountain bikes for 55/90FF for a half-day/day, and 160FF for two days (70FF for each subsequent day). A 2000FF deposit is required. The shop also stocks an excellent range of maps, VTT and hiking guides, and is open from 10 am to noon and 2 to 7 pm (closed Sunday and Monday).

The tourist office (see Information) also rents out bicycles costing 10/25/40FF for one hour/half-day/day. For an extra 5FF, a guide will take you on a two hour theme tour of Grenoble. Choose between the city's fountains and gardens, the old town, or – bearing in mind that cement was invented in Grenoble – its cement and concrete architecture (poetically described in the tour brochure as 'grey gold').

AROUND GRENOBLE

Grenoble's surrounding low-altitude regions attract a relaxed crowd in search of cheap winter skiing or summer hiking rather than the hard-core experts and flashy fluoro crowds drawn to the more expensive, higher-altitude resorts farther north.

Stations better known for their good cross-country skiing include Lans-en-Vercors and

TERESA FISHER

Villefranche-sur-Mer harbour, Côte d'Azur

JON DAVISON

The tiered village of Gordes, Provence

ADRIENNE COSTANZO

The Pont du Gard, an exceptional Roman aqueduct near Nîmes, Provence

JEAN-BERNARD CARILLET

Snorkelling in the crystal clear waters surrounding Îles de Lavezzi near Bonifacio, Corsica

TONY WHEELER

The landscape of red, orange and grey granite cliffs, spikes and outcrops of Les Calanche, Corsica

Villard de Lans, south-west of Grenoble in the Vercors range; and Col de Porte and Le Sappey, north of Grenoble in the Chartreuse range. Chamrousse, the nearest resort to Grenoble in the Belledonne range to the east, was built for the 1968 Winter Olympics. Skiers keen to take to the slopes in summer have to head farther east (see Les Deux Alpes and Alpe d'Huez sections).

Chartreuse, a potent liqueur, is made by Carthusian monks in Voiron, about 26km north of Grenoble.

Chamrousse

City dwellers flock to Chamrousse (1400m), 30km east of Grenoble, in winter. The family resort, popular for its wide and gentle slopes, has a snowpark too and attracts more snowboarders than the average resort. The snowboarding World Cup and the French freestyle ski championships are held here each year in March.

The tourist office (☎ 04 76 89 92 65; fax 04 76 89 98 06), in the centre of the resort, has full accommodation lists. The FUAJ ski club in Grenoble (see Skiing Information in the Grenoble section) arranges six-day skiing trips to Chamrousse from 2100FF, including ski pass, ski hire and full-board hostel accommodation at the ***Auberge de Jeunesse*** (☎ 04 76 89 91 31; fax 04 76 89 96 66; chamrousse@wanadoo.fr) in Chamrousse. The CAF also has a *refuge* here: contact the ***Chalet du CAF*** (☎ 04 76 87 03 73; fax 04 76 85 26 77) in Chamrousse.

There are four VFD buses a day from Grenoble to Chamrousse (1¼ hours).

Parc Naturel Régional de Chartreuse

The Chartreuse massif, dubbed the 'emerald of the Alps' by 19th century French novelist Stendhal, lies north and north-west of Grenoble. Covering a protected area of 63,000 hectares, the park is most popular for the cheap, easy downhill skiing and more challenging cross-country skiing offered at its neighbouring resorts of **Le Sappey-Col de Porte** (1000m), **Saint Pierre de Chartreuse** (900m) and **Saint Hugues** (900m).

Voiron, which straddles the park's western boundary, is home to the **Chartreuse distillery**. The liqueur – 55% proof and pea-green in colour – has been made by the Pères Chartreux (Carthusian fathers) in Chartreuse since 1737. Between 1903 and 1918 the monks were expelled from France so they opened a Chartreuse distillery in Tarragone, Spain, instead to continue making what they claimed was purely a medicinal drink.

Free guided tours of the distillery (☎ 04 76 05 81 77) and the 164m-long *caves* (wine cellars), dating from 1860 and said to be the largest liquor vaults in the world, are available year-round from 8.30 to 11 am and 2 to 6.30 pm (until 5.30 pm on weekdays in winter). Tours end with a *dégustation* (tasting) session, in which you can sample the different types of Chartreuse liqueur. Beware of the Élixir Végétal, which is a mind-blowing 71% proof! The distillery is located at 10 Blvd Edgar Kofler, which is only a five minute walk from Voiron bus and train station.

The history of the Carthusian Order, founded in Chartreuse by Saint Bruno in 1084, is vividly portrayed in the **Musée de la Grande Chartreuse** (☎ 04 76 88 60 45) in La Correrie, some 15km east of Voiron en route to Saint Pierre de Chartreuse. Because the monks take a vow of silence and solitude, it is impossible to visit the Grande Chartreuse monastery, 2km west of here. The museum is open between May and September from 9.30 am to noon and 2 to 6.30 pm, and in April and October from 10 am to noon and 2 to 6 pm. Admission for adults/children is 15/8FF.

The central tourist office of the Parc Naturel Régional de Chartreuse is in Saint Pierre de Chartreuse (☎ 04 76 88 62 08; fax 04 76 88 75 10; chartreuse@wanadoo.fr), Place de la Mairie. Its branch office in Le Sappey (☎ 04 76 88 84 05; fax 04 76 88 87 16) is in the village *mairie*. Both offices, plus their Grenoble counterpart, distribute comprehensive lists of available accommodation. Expect to pay from 1500/2000FF in the low/high season for a four person apartment.

Getting There & Away Transport is a problem unless you have a car, as there are only two buses a day between Grenoble and Le Sappey (23.50FF; 40 minutes). On weekends there is one bus between Grenoble and Saint Pierre de Chartreuse.

There are some 10 buses a day from Grenoble to Voiron (VFD; ☎ 04 76 05 03 47; 15FF; 50 minutes). La Correrie is only accessible with private transport.

Parc Naturel Régional du Vercors

The Parc Naturel Régional du Vercors (175,000 hectares), immediately south-west of Grenoble, is a large cross-country skiing, caving and hiking area. During WWII it became a stronghold of the Resistance movement and was dubbed the 'fortresse de la Résistance'.

Lans-en-Vercors (population 1450; 1020m), 25km south-west of Grenoble, is the leading ski village on the Vercors plateau. There's none of the adrenalin of high-Alpine descents here, nor is there a bustling nightlife. Families abound and, outside school holidays, the hotels often have *non complet* (vacancy) signs up. From Lans-en-Vercors, hourly shuttle buses run to the Stade de Neige (Snow Stadium), an area of moderate, wooded slopes crowned by Le Grand Cheval (1807m), about 4km east.

The equally sedate village of **Villard de Lans** (population 3350; 1050m), 9km up the valley from Lans-en-Vercors, is linked by ski lifts and roads to the neighbouring resort of **Corrençon-en-Vercors** (1111m).

Information The park headquarters (☎ 04 76 94 38 26; fax 04 76 94 38 39; info@pnr vercors.fr; www.pnr-vercors.fr) is inside the Maison du Parc at Chemin des Fusillés in Lans-en-Vercors. The tourist offices in Lans- en-Vercors (☎ 04 76 95 42 62; fax 04 76 95 49 70; www.ot-lans-en-vercors.fr), Place de l'Église, and in Villard de Lans (☎ 04 76 95 10 38; fax 04 76 95 98 39; villard.correncon@wanadoo.fr), Place Mure Ravaud, can both provide extensive information on activities in the park. The free brochure entitled *Welcome to Vercors* lists numerous walks in the park as well as driving and caving tours; *Site National Historique de la Résistance en Vercors* traces the footsteps of the Resistance movement in the region.

Places to Stay The tourist offices in both villages can help with accommodation bookings. In Lans-en-Vercors, ***Vercors Immobilier Montagne*** (☎ 04 76 95 41 64; fax 04 76 95 48 33), Place du Village, arranges accommodation in chalets for two to 11 people. In the high season expect to pay from 2300 to 3390FF for a four person studio.

There are numerous gîtes d'étape in the region, the most central being ***Chalet de la Piste de Luge*** (☎ 04 76 94 10 66; fax 04 76 94 11 55), on the eastern edge of Villard de Lans, which costs 60FF per person. A bed for the night costs 50FF at the ***Refuge Garde les Hauts Plateaux*** (☎ 04 76 95 83 51) in Corrençon-en-Vercors.

Getting There & Away From Lans-en-Vercors, VFD (☎ 04 76 95 11 24) runs four buses a day (fewer on weekends) to and from Grenoble (32.50FF; 50 minutes), Villard de Lans (10FF; 20 minutes) and Corrençon (15FF; 35 minutes).

Shuttle buses (11FF) run every half-hour between Lans-en-Vercors and Villard de Lans.

PARC NATIONAL DES ÉCRINS

The spectacular Parc National des Écrins was created in 1973 and is France's second largest national park, taking in nearly everything between the towns of Bourg d'Oisans, Briançon and Gap. The park's 917 sq km of fully protected land are surrounded by 1770 sq km of peripheral areas, most of which are largely unspoiled thanks to their relative inaccessibility. The area is enclosed by steep narrow valleys, sculpted by the Romanche, Durance and Drac rivers and their erstwhile glaciers. The overhanging cliffs look like battle-scarred layered cakes.

Bourg d'Oisans (population 3000; 720m), 50km south-east of Grenoble in the Romanche Valley, and Briançon, another

67km in the same direction, make great bases for exploring the park.

Geography

The park includes the Massif des Écrins, whose summit is Barre des Écrins (4103m), and is surrounded by other equally majestic peaks, such as La Meije (3983m) and Pelvoux (3954m). During the last ice age glaciers from this area reached points as far away as Lyon.

Flora & Fauna

The meeting of Atlantic, Continental and Mediterranean climatic influences has created conditions ideal for a wide variety of vegetation, ranging from fir trees in the north to fields of lavender in the south. One-third of France's flora – some 2000 species – grows in the park, which is known for its reindeer moss and desert plants. Animals inhabiting the park include hares, marmots, foxes, chamois and golden eagles. Ibex were reintroduced in the late 1970s.

Information

Several Maisons du Parc, open all year, provide detailed information. The park headquarters (☎ 04 92 40 20 10; fax 04 92 52 38 34) is at the Domaine de la Charance, F-05000 Gap. There's a large park office in Briançon (☎ 04 92 21 42 55).

In Bourg d'Oisans, the Maison du Parc (☎ 04 76 80 00 51), Rue Gambetta, is open in summer from 9 am to noon and 3 to 7 pm. It sells detailed guides (in French), topoguides and hiking maps, including the invaluable IGN 1:25,000 *Les Deux Alpes-Le Parc National des Écrins* (No 3336ET) and *Bourg d'Oisans-Alpe d'Huez* (No 3335ET). The Bureau des Guides, housed in a wooden hut in front of the grounds of the Maison du Parc, is another good information source (see Other Activities).

The town's tourist office (☎ 04 76 80 03 25; fax 04 76 80 10 38), on the main road just before the Romanche River at Quai Girard, is well stocked with park information too. It's open from 9 am to noon and 2 to 6 pm (closed Sunday).

Musée des Minéraux et de la Faune des Alpes

This museum (☎ 04 76 80 27 54), off Rue du Docteur Daday behind the church in Bourg d'Oisans, is an introduction to what you can (or once could) see in the park. It houses displays of current or vanishing Alpine fauna and rare minerals. It's open daily from 2 to 6 pm (11 am to 7 pm in July and August); closed from 15 November to 15 December. Admission is 25FF for adults (10FF for children).

Hiking

There are plenty of zigzagging paths used for centuries by shepherds and smugglers from points all along the Romanche Valley. From Bourg d'Oisans there is a path to Villard Notre Dame (1525m; two hours). From Venosc, a tiny mountain village in the Vénéon Valley, 12km south-east of Bourg d'Oisans, there's a trail to the popular ski resort of Les Deux Alpes (1660m; 1½ hours). The national park French-only publication *Dix Itinéraires* is a good companion for 10 different treks and climbs of up to seven hours. *Venosc/Vallée de Vénéon* (10FF) is another good publication. The Bourg d'Oisans tourist office sells six different hiking maps (in English and French) entitled *Oisans au Bout des Pieds* (Oisans under Your Feet).

From the Venosc tourist office (☎ 04 76 80 06 82; fax 04 76 80 18 95) you can also take a télécabine up the sheer mountainside to Les Deux Alpes (six minutes), home to one of France's most fantastic glaciers, which shelters an ice cave (see Les Deux Alpes).

Experienced hikers can take the GR54, also known as the Tour de l'Oisans (215km), which follows the contours of the land at altitudes ranging between 700 and 2800m. It's a difficult 10 to 20 day trek. Places to stock up on provisions can be five days apart and avalanches are possible.

There's a hiking guide office (☎ 04 76 79 54 83) in the tiny village of La Bérarde, 31km south-east of Bourg d'Oisans at the end of the Vénéon Valley (at the base of Barre des Écrins). It is open in summer only. The CAF (☎ 04 76 79 53 83) has an office here too.

Other Activities

The Bureau des Guides (☎ 04 76 80 11 27) in front of the Maison du Parc in Bourg d'Oisans organises rafting (140FF for a half-day), rock climbing (120FF for 2½ hours), parapente (650FF for a half-day), hot dogging (150FF for two or three people in an inflatable canoe) and other summer activities in the park. The Air Écrins Club de Parapente de l'Oisans (☎/fax 04 76 11 00 35), 23 Rue Général de Gaulle, Bourg d'Oisans, runs canoeing, kayaking and parapente schools.

At Saint Christophe, near Venosc, Vénéon Eaux Vives (☎ 04 76 80 23 99) organises similar activities. It also hires out mountain bikes for 90FF a day.

Places to Stay & Eat

Within the park's central zone there are about 32 ***refuges***, most of them run by the CAF. The charge is 62FF a night (31/20FF for CAF members/under 18s).

A handful of ***gîtes d'étape*** are on the outskirts of the park, many open year-round. Expect to pay about 65FF a night. For a full listing, ask at the Bourg d'Oisans tourist office for the free brochure entitled *Guide des Hèbergements*.

There are plenty of camping grounds in Bourg d'Oisans, including a cluster just down from the tourist office, on the road to Alpe d'Huez. The four star ***La Cascade*** (☎ 04 76 80 02 42; fax 04 76 80 22 63) is open from mid-December to September. It charges 120FF for two people. Most of the cheaper grounds are only open from June to September.

In Bourg d'Oisans, the ***Maison des Jeunes Le Paradis*** (☎ 04 76 80 01 76), 50 Rue Thiers, charges 65FF for a dorm bed in rooms for 12 people and can also arrange mountain biking, kayaking, canoeing etc. It is closed in May and October.

The town also has about 10 hotels, the cheaper ones being around the bus station on Rue de la Gare. Simple doubles start from 140FF at ***Le Moulin des Fruites Bleues*** (☎ 04 76 80 00 26), 150FF at ***Hôtel Le Rocher*** (☎ 04 76 80 01 53; fax 04 76 79 11 94), and from 200FF at ***Hôtel de l'Oberland Français*** (☎ 04 76 80 24 24).

More upmarket is the cosy ***Hôtel Beau Rivage*** (☎ 04 76 80 03 19; fax 04 76 80 00 77), on Rue des Maquis de l'Oisans, the road running behind the tourist office. Doubles with washbasin cost from 185FF, and from 255FF with TV, shower and toilet. ***Hôtel Le Réghaia*** (☎ 04 76 80 03 37), Ave Aristide Briand, has rooms with washbasin/shower for 160/195FF. It's closed between 5 May and 5 June and in November. These two hotels also have excellent ***restaurants***.

There are plenty of small ***supermarkets*** and grocery stores in Bourg d'Oisans to stock up on supplies.

Getting There & Away

VFD buses (☎ 04 76 80 00 90 in Bourg d'Oisans) serve the Romanche Valley and Briançon. They operate from the bus station on Ave de la Gare, the main road into Bourg d'Oisans.

From Grenoble, VFD bus No 300 goes to Bourg d'Oisans (65FF; 80 minutes) eight times a day, while the No 303 and the No 302 from Grenoble stop in Bourg d'Oisans on their way to Les Deux Alpes (46FF; 40 minutes) and Alpe d'Huez (45FF; 45 minutes) respectively. From Briançon, VFD's bus No 306 stops in Bourg d'Oisans (71FF; 1¾ hours; two a day).

From Bourg d'Oisans to Venosc, La Bérarde and most other smaller places in the valley you'll have to rely on your thumb, except in July and August when a *navette* (shuttle bus) makes a loop between Bourg d'Oisans and La Bérarde via Venosc once a day.

LES DEUX ALPES

✉ 38860 alt 1600m

Les Deux Alpes, 28km south-east of Bourg d'Oisans, has the largest summer skiing area in Europe. From mid-June to early September, you can ski on the Glacier du Mont de Lans (3200 to 3425m), which, year-round, offers good panoramic views of Mont Blanc (east), Massif Central (west) and Mont Ventoux (south).

Les Deux Alpes is a popular winter skiing resort too, as well as one of the top spots in France for snowboarding. The never ending stream of traffic clogging up the entire length of Les Deux Alpes' 1.5km-long main street (D213) belies its lowly beginnings as a mountain pasture for the flocks of Mont de Lans and Venosc, villages neighbouring the resort to the north and south respectively.

Information

Tourist Office Everything in town revolves around the Maison des Deux Alpes on Place des Deux Alpes. It houses the tourist office (☎ 04 76 79 22 00; fax 04 76 79 01 38), the accommodation service (see Places to Stay), the ESF (see Skiing & Snowboarding), and the Bureau des Guides (☎ 04 76 80 52 72; fax 04 76 79 58 42). The Bureau des Guides (☎ 06 11 32 71 88) inside the Maison de la Montagne, Ave de la Muzelle, arranges ice climbing on frozen waterfalls, rock climbing, hiking, rafting and mountain bike expeditions with experienced guides.

Skiing & Snowboarding

The main skiing domain lies below La Meije (3983m), one of the highest peaks in the Parc National des Écrins. There's some 200km of marked pistes, 20km of cross-country trails, and in the snowpark (2600m), a 600m-long axe pipe, 110m-long half-pipe and numerous jumps for snowboarders (all to the blare of pop music).

The ESF (☎ 04 76 79 21 21; fax 04 76 79 22 07) and the more expensive École de Ski International St Christophe (☎ 04 76 79 04 21; fax 04 76 79 29 14), close to Place des Deux Alpes on Ave de la Muzelle, both run ski and snowboarding schools.

SAF Delta Invasion (☎ 04 76 80 65 49; fax 04 76 80 42 29) organises heli-skiing from Les Deux Alpes to Alpe d'Huez, costing 350FF per person.

Grotte de Glace

A 6m-tall dinosaur, Alpine flowers and shepherds are just some of the fantastic ice sculptures exhibited inside the *grotte de glace* (ice cave) cut inside the Glacier du Mont de Lans at Dôme de Puy Salié (3421m). The cave is open year-round from 9.30 am to 4.30 pm. Admission is 20/15/10FF for adults/students/children.

Nonskiers can access the glacier too. Take the Jandri Express télécabine to 3200m (change of télécabine at 2600m), from where you can take the underground Dôme Express funicular to 3400m. A return ticket costs 105FF.

Museums

For a glimpse at traditional Alpine life the way it was before mass tourism swallowed it, visit the **Maison de la Montagne** (☎ 04 76 79 53 15), at the west end of the main street, Ave de la Muzelle. Traditional 19th century dwellings as well as the history of wool farming are displayed in the village museum in Mont de Lans, **Le Chasal Lento** (☎ 04 76 80 23 97). In Venosc, a permanent arts and crafts exhibition is held in the tourist office (☎ 04 76 80 06 82; fax 04 76 80 18 95).

The museums are open in summer from 10 am to noon and 3 to 7 pm, and in winter from 2 to 6 pm. Admission to both is 20FF. A free shuttle bus to Mont de Lans departs daily from outside the Maison de la Montagne at 2 pm and returns to Les Deux Alpes at 4 pm. You can also take a télésiège. To get to Venosc, take a télécabine from the east end of Les Deux Alpes. A return ticket for either is 38FF.

Warm-Weather Activities

Numerous hikes are listed in the free brochure *Le Guide des Randonnées Pédestres au Départ des Deux Alpes?* available at the tourist office.

Parapente ESF (☎ 06 97 72 26 60), inside the Maison des Deux Alpes, offers five-day paragliding courses in summer for 2300FF. A morning/afternoon session is 300/350FF. Its office is open from 6 to 7.30 pm.

Aspiring parachutists should contact SAF Delta Invasion (see Skiing & Snowboarding earlier). To bungee jump from a télécabine contact the tourist office.

Places to Stay

The *Auberge de Jeunesse* (☎ 04 76 79 22 80; fax 04 76 79 26 15; fuaj.les.deux.alpes@wanadoo.fr) is in the heart of town at Les Brûleurs de Loups. A dorm bed in rooms for up to six people costs 49FF per person in summer. In winter only weekly packages are available, including seven days accommodation, food and a ski lift pass. Prices start at 2180/2680FF in the low/high season.

The accommodation service (☎ 04 76 79 24 38; fax 04 76 79 01 38; www.les2alpes.com) inside the Maison des Deux Alpes takes bookings for all types of accommodation. Two-person studios and apartments can be found from 1150/2600FF a week in the low/high season. All hotel reservations should be made well in advance.

Getting There & Away

VFD runs buses to Les Deux Alpes from Grenoble (102FF; 1¾ hours; six a day), 77km north-west. In Les Deux Alpes, reserve tickets in advance from the VFD office (☎ 04 76 80 51 22) on Place de Mont de Lans or Rue de l'Irarde. Buses stop at Bourg d'Oisans (40 minutes) en route. There are also services to Briançon, Alpe d'Huez, Lyon-Satolas and Geneva airports.

ALPE D'HUEZ

✉ 38750 alt 1860m

The ski resort of Alpe d'Huez sits just above Bourg d'Oisans, 13km away by a steep, twisting road (*La Montée de l'Alpe d'Huez*) best known as one of the 'classic' gruelling ascents often included in the Tour de France cycle race.

Alpe d'Huez has excellent winter runs for skiers and snowboarders of all abilities. At 16km, La Sarenne is the longest black run in the French Alps. Experienced skiers can also ski here in July and part of August on glaciers (ranging from 2530m to 3330m). The panoramic view from Pic du Lac Blanc (3330m), the highest point accessible year-round from the village by the Tronçon télécabines, is particularly impressive and well worth the effort.

Information

The tourist office (☎ 04 76 11 44 44; fax 04 76 80 69 54; www.skifrance.fr/~alped'huez), accommodation centre, and ESF (☎ 04 76 80 31 69; fax 04 76 80 49 33) are inside the Maison de l'Alpe, Place Joseph Paganon. The Bureau des Guides (☎ 04 76 80 42 55) and the Taburle École du Snowboard Français (☎ 04 76 80 95 82) are both off Place du Cognet at the Rond Point des Pistes, the northernmost point of the village.

Places to Stay

The accommodation centre (☎ 04 76 11 44 44; fax 04 76 80 69 54) takes bookings for all types of accommodation. Expect to pay 1278/1745FF in the low/high season for a small, self-contained studio for two. An FUAJ *Auberge de Jeunesse* will open in Alpe d'Huez in 1999.

One of the least expensive hotels in town is *Le Chamois* (☎ 04 76 80 31 19), Ave des Jeux, where rooms start at around 170/200FF in the low/high season. The friendly, helpful *Hôtel Alp Azur* (☎ 04 76 80 34 02), Place Jean Molin, has doubles from 270/440FF.

Getting There & Away

There are some seven VFD buses a day from Grenoble via Bourg d'Oisans to Alpe d'Huez (☎ 04 76 80 31 61; 130FF; 2¾ hours). On Wednesday there is a shuttle bus between Les Deux Alpes and Alpe d'Huez (51FF; one hour).

BRIANÇON

• pop 11,000 ✉ 05100 alt 1026m

Briançon is a town of mixed delights. Sitting on a rocky outcrop at the meeting of five valleys, it is one of the highest cities in Europe and boasts 300 days of sunshine a year. Long a frontier post, its beautiful fortified old city guards the road to the Col de Montgenèvre (1850m), a Roman mountain pass leading to Italy, 20km north-east.

In the late 17th century, the famous military architect Vauban was called in to make the town impregnable after it was razed during a regional war. Since then the population has expanded and the town has crept down the slopes to encompass the Durance Valley. The modern lower town, which has a lift station (Briançon-Serre-Chevalier 1200) to the neighbouring ski resort of Le Grand Serre Chevalier, is nothing short of ugly.

Briançon is sandwiched between the awesome terrain of the Parc National des Écrins to the west and the Parc Naturel Régional du Queyras to the south, making it an excellent base to partake in all sorts of outdoor activities.

Orientation

The town is split into two sections. The upper Vieille Ville, with its quaint pedestrianised streets, sits high above its counterpart, the new Ville Basse (Lower Town). The train station is to the south in the suburb of Sainte Catherine. The upper and lower towns are connected by Ave de la République. Entry to the Vieille Ville is either from the Place du Champ de Mars (on the old city's northern side) or, if you're walking up the hill from the lower town, through the Porte d'Embrun.

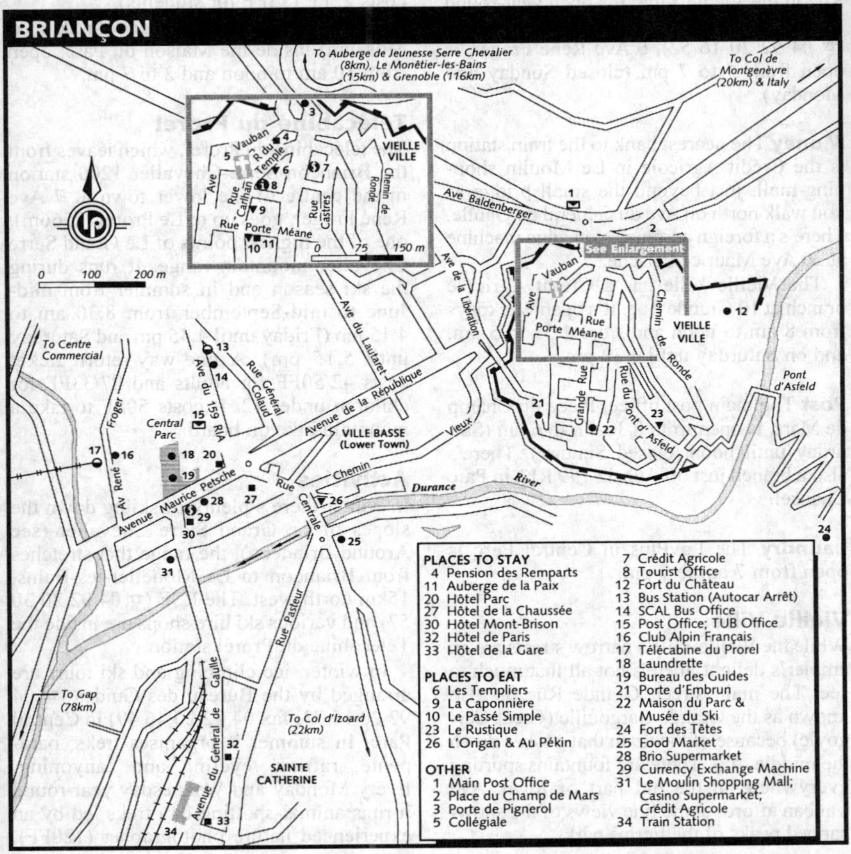

Information

Tourist Offices The tourist office (☎ 04 92 21 08 50; fax 04 92 20 56 45), in the Vieille Ville at 1 Place du Temple, is open Monday to Saturday from 8.30 am to noon and 1.30 to 6 pm. From mid-June to September it is also open on Sunday from 9 am to noon and 1.30 to 5 pm. City tours are organised by the Service du Patrimoine (☎ 04 92 20 29 49; fax 04 92 21 38 45), which is located beneath the Porte de Pignerol.

For information on the Parc National des Écrins, go to the Maison du Parc (☎ 04 92 20 29 29), which is at the south end of Grande Rue in the Vieille Ville. It's open year-round from 10 am to noon and 2 to 7 pm. The CAF (☎ 04 92 20 16 52), 6 Ave René Froger, is open from 4 to 7 pm (closed Sunday and Monday).

Money The nearest bank to the train station is the Crédit Agricole in Le Moulin shopping mall, just beyond the small bridge as you walk north on Ave du Général de Gaulle. There's a foreign currency exchange machine at 20 Ave Maurice Petsche.

The Vieille Ville has a Crédit Agricole branch at 10 Grande Rue. It's open weekdays from 8 am to noon and from 1.55 to 5 pm, and on Saturday until 4.30 pm.

Post The main post office, Place du Champ de Mars, is open from 8.30 am to 6 pm (Saturday until noon; closed Sunday). There's also a branch just off Ave du 159 RIA in Parc Chancel.

Laundry The LavPlus in Central Parc is open from 7 am to 7 pm.

Vieille Ville

While the Vieille Ville's narrow streets are an ambler's delight, there's not all that much to see. The main street, Grande Rue, is also known as the Grande Gargouille (Great Gargoyle) because of the drain that gushes down the middle of it. There are fountains spurting everywhere in the old part of town. Ave Vauban affords some fine views of the snow-capped peaks of the Écrins park.

The **Collégiale** – or the Church of Our Lady & St Nicholas – was built by Vauban in the early 18th century and is characteristically heavy and fortified, its twin towers dominating the Vieille Ville skyline. The baroque paintings and gilt chapels around a circular choir are worth a look. The church is open daily.

The 18th century **Fort du Château** (Castle Fort) sits imposingly above the Vieille Ville. You can visit it daily in July and August and on Wednesday and Saturday in September, but only on a guided tour organised by the tourist office. The tour costs 22FF (15FF for students).

There is an excellent **Musée du Ski** (Ski Museum) inside the Maison du Parc, open from 10 am to noon and 2 to 7 pm.

Télécabine du Prorel

The télécabine du Prorel, which leaves from the Briançon-Serre-Chevalier 1200 station in the centre of the lower town at 7 Ave René Froger, goes up to Le Prorel (2566m), one of the highest points of Le Grand Serre Chevalier mountain range. It runs during the ski season and in summer from mid-June to mid-September from 8.30 am to 4.15 pm (Friday until 4.45 pm and Saturday until 5.15 pm). A one-way/return ticket costs 42/50FF for adults and 27/33FF for children under 12. It costs 50FF to take a mountain bike on board.

Activities

In winter there's plenty of skiing down the slopes of Le Grand Serre Chevalier (see Around Briançon), the range that stretches from Briançon to Le Monêtier-les-Bains, 15km north-west. The ESF (☎ 04 92 20 30 57) and various ski hire shops are inside the Télécabine du Prorel station.

In winter, ice climbing and ski tours are arranged by the Bureau des Guides (☎ 04 92 20 15 73; fax 04 92 20 46 49) in Central Parc. In summer it organises treks, parapente, rafting, cycling and canyoning. Every Monday and Wednesday year-round it runs animal-spotting day treks led by an experienced nature photographer (120FF).

The office is open from 5 to 7 pm, and in July and August from 9 am to 7 pm.

The Maison du Parc sells the useful *Promenades* booklets (35FF), which detail numerous walks and hikes in the Briançon, Oisans and Vanoise region. It's only open between June and August.

Places to Stay

Hostel The nearest hostel is ***Auberge de Jeunesse Serre Chevalier*** (☎ 04 92 24 74 54; fax 04 92 24 83 39; fuaj.serre.chevalier@wanadoo.fr), about 8km north-west at Serre Chevalier-le-Bez near Villeneuve-la-Salle. It charges 45FF a night and 18FF for breakfast. In winter, when it's a popular skiing base, only seven-day packages are available for 2155/2880FF in the low/high season including board, meals, a ski pass and equipment rental. To get to the hostel from the train station or the Place du Champ de Mars, take the Rignon bus (every two hours; last one at 6.45 pm) in the direction of Le Monêtier-les-Bains to Villeneuve-la-Salle, from where it's a 500m walk.

Hotels The hotels in the Vieille Ville are the best in town but a bit away from any action Briançon has to offer. One of the cheapest is the ***Pension des Remparts*** (☎ 04 92 21 08 73) at 14 Ave Vauban. The rooms at the front bask in the afternoon sun and have a good view of the mountains. Prices range from 150 to 259FF, and parking is available. The ***Auberge de la Paix*** (☎ 04 92 21 37 43; fax 04 92 20 44 45), 3 Rue Porte Méane, has comfortable single/double/triple rooms with modern furnishings from 170/185/255FF. Rooms with shower and toilet cost 240/255/315FF.

In the lower town, the ***Hôtel de la Chaussée*** (☎ 04 92 21 10 37; fax 04 92 20 03 94), 4 Rue Centrale, has upmarket doubles with shower from 250FF. The ***Hôtel Mont-Brison*** (☎ 04 92 21 14 55), Ave du Général de Gaulle, has doubles without/with shower for 190/200FF.

Other inexpensive options in the lower town and Sainte Catherine include the ***Hôtel de la Gare*** (☎ 04 92 21 00 49), opposite the train station on Ave Général de Gaulle, which has singles/doubles with washbasin from 110/130FF. At No 41 on the same street, the ***Hôtel de Paris*** (☎ 04 92 20 15 30; fax 04 92 20 30 82) has singles with washbasin/shower for 175/220FF. Doubles with washbasin/shower cost 190/235FF. Prices rise by 30FF in the high season.

The central ***Hôtel Parc*** (☎ 04 92 20 37 47; fax 04 92 20 53 74), on the corner of Ave Maurice Petsche and Ave du 159 RIA, has singles/doubles/triples/quads with all the mod cons from 390/440/525/600FF.

Places to Eat

Restaurants As with hotels, the higher up the hill you are, the more you pay to eat. Nightlife revolves around the few bars along Rue Centrale.

The ***Pension des Remparts*** (see Places to Stay) has some of the least expensive *menus* around – 59FF for three courses or 69FF for four. Good Savoyard fondues for 75FF per person simmer at ***Les Templiers*** (☎ 04 92 20 29 04), 20 Place du Temple.

For a pricier fondue and a variety of other local dishes, try the cavernous ***Le Rustique*** (☎ 04 92 21 00 10), a steep climb up a hill at 36 Rue du Pont d'Asfeld. It is open until 11 pm, has a nonsmoking room, and specialises in trout. Don't miss out on its delicious apple tart with foie gras or quail roasted in honey.

La Caponnière (☎ 04 92 20 36 77), in the Vieille Ville at 12 Rue Commandant Carlhan, has *menus* oozing with local delicacies for 78, 89, 98 or 115FF. ***Le Passé Simple***, adjoining the Auberge de la Paix at 3 Rue Porte Méane, is another traditional place recommended locally.

In the lower town, the ***Hôtel de la Gare*** (see Places to Stay) has a 58FF *menu* that includes a 250mL carafe of wine and a coffee. At 25 Rue Centrale, ***l'Origan*** (☎ 04 92 20 10 09) has 16 varieties of pizzas starting at 32FF, as well as 32 different varieties of sweet and savoury crêpes. Upstairs in the same building, ***Au Pékin*** (☎ 04 92 21 24 22) has *menus* from 68FF and is open from 11 am to 2 pm and 6 to 11 pm. The duck with five-spice powder is acceptable but portions are small, and if the owner offers you a glass of sake at the end of your meal, expect to pay for it.

Self-Catering On Wednesday there's a ***food market*** in the carpark next to the fire station just off Rue Centrale. Numerous quaint ***food shops*** line Grande Rue in the Vieille Ville. On Ave Maurice Petsche the ***Brio*** supermarket is open from 8.30 am to 12.30 pm and 2.15 to 7.30 pm (no break on Saturday; closed Sunday). There is a huge ***Casino*** supermarket in Le Moulin shopping mall.

Getting There & Away

Bus The so-called bus station – a simple bus stop marked Autocar Arrêt – is at the intersection of Ave du 159 RIA and Rue Général Colaud. SCAL (☎ 04 92 21 12 00) has an office next door at 14 Ave du 159 RIA that is open weekdays from 8.30 am to 12.30 pm and 4.30 to 6 pm. It runs a daily bus to Gap (51FF; two hours), Digne (101FF; 3¼ hours; except Sunday), Marseille (157FF; 5¾ hours), Aix-en-Provence (141FF; five hours), and Oulx (51FF; 1½ hours) in Italy. VFD buses (☎ 04 76 47 77 77 in Grenoble) travel via Bourg d'Oisans (71FF; 1¾ hours) to Grenoble (140FF; 2¼ hours; two a day).

Train Briançon's station (☎ 04 92 51 50 50, 04 92 25 66 00), at the end of the line from Gap, is at the southern end of Ave du Général de Gaulle, about 1.5km from the Vieille Ville. The ticket windows are open from 5.30 am to 11.15 pm (until 10 pm on Saturday). Luggage lockers are accessible from 5.30 am to 8.15 pm.

To Paris' Gare de Lyon (400FF; 10½ hours) there's a direct overnight train leaving at 8.05 pm. Two quicker daytime services (seven hours) go via Grenoble or Valence, where they connect with the TGV (430FF). Other major destinations include Gap (67FF; 1¼ hours; five a day), Grenoble (142FF; 4½ hours; four a day) and Marseille (185FF; four hours; three a day).

Getting Around

Bus Two local bus lines run by TUB – the No 1 and the D – both go from the train station to Place du Champ de Mars, Monday to Saturday from 6.40 am to 6.40 pm and from 9 am to noon on Sunday. A single ticket costs 6FF and a carnet of 10 is 41FF. The TUB office (☎ 04 92 20 34 91) is on Place de Suze in Parc Chancel, north of Central Parc.

Bicycle Hire two wheels from Intersport (☎ 04 92 21 10 00) in the Centre Commercial on Ave du Dauphiné, or from its branch beneath the Télécabine du Prorel on Ave René Froger. The Mountain Cycles shop (☎ 04 92 20 23 49), opposite the bus station on Ave du 159 RIA, is only open in summer.

Taxi To summon a taxi in Briançon, ring ☎ 04 92 21 14 42.

AROUND BRIANÇON

Le Grand Serre Chevalier

Le Grand Serre Chevalier is the name given to a large ski area that rises above the Serre Chevalier Valley in the Hautes Alpes region. There are 13 villages that spread out along the valley floor from the town of Briançon to the village of Le Monêtier-les-Bains, 14.5km to the north-west. The skiing is below the peaks and down the slopes of Serre Chevalier to the valley floor, but the lift system only reaches Briançon and the three villages of Chantemerle, Villeneuve-la-Salle and Le Monêtier-les-Bains.

Chantemerle (1350m) and Villeneuve-la-Salle (1400m) are the two central resorts with all the facilities and better nightlife. Le Monêtier-les-Bains (1500m) retains a quieter atmosphere while Briançon has the cheapest accommodation.

Le Grand Serre Chevalier's main tourist office is in Briançon, but there are small offices in Chantemerle (☎ 04 92 98 97), Villeneuve-La Salle les Alpes (☎ 04 92 24 98 98), and Le Monêtier-les-Bains (☎ 04 92 24 98 99). Accommodation can be booked in advance through the central reservation office (☎ 04 92 24 98 90; fax 04 92 24 98 84). Ski touring for a day or overnight in the Parc National des Écrins is particularly rewarding. The Bureau des Guides in Briançon (see Activities in the Briançon section) and the Maison de la Montagne (☎ 04 92 24 75 90) in Villeneuve-la-Salle offer various winter ski tours and summer mountaineering trips.

Getting Around There are up to 10 buses a day from Briançon (22FF; 20 minutes) to Villeneuve-la-Salle. In winter, lifts operate and free shuttle buses ply the route between Le Monêtier-les-Bains and Briançon.

The Jura

The Jura Mountains, a range of dark, wooded hills and undulating plateaus, stretch for 360km along the Franco-Swiss border from the Rhine to the Rhône (ie from near Basel to just north of Geneva). Part of the historic Franche-Comté region, the French Jura is one of the least explored regions in France and hence a fine retreat for people in search of tranquillity away from the tourist crowd. Franche-Comté's capital is Besançon. Le Corbusier's chapel near Ronchamp (see Belfort & Around) has long been a place of pilgrimage for architecture buffs worldwide, while the little-known Saugeais Republic close to the Swiss border (see Around Métabief Mont D'Or) is a must for anyone seeking a glimpse at the region's rich ethnographical treasures.

The Jura – whose name comes from a Gaulish word meaning 'forest' – is also France's premier cross-country skiing area. The range is dotted with ski stations from north of Pontarlier all the way south to Bellegarde. Métabief Mont d'Or, north of the Parc Naturel Régional du Haut-Jura, is one of the better known stations, as popular for its superb hiking and nature trails as for its gentle slopes.

Although not as well known as other wine-growing regions in France, the Jura produces several fine appellations. Because of the altitude the vintners use rarer, sturdier grape varieties, and as a result the area produces some very unique wines.

JURA

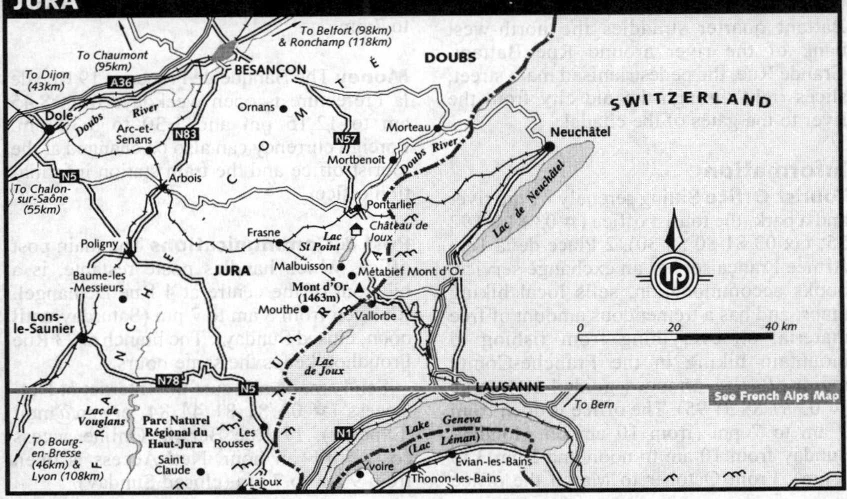

BESANÇON

• pop 114,000 ✉ 25000 alt 250m

Besançon, capital of the Franche-Comté region, is surrounded by hills on the northern reaches of the Jura range. First settled in Gallo-Roman times, it later became an important stop on the early trade routes between Italy, the Alps and the Rhine. Since the 18th century, it has been a noted clock-making centre. Victor Hugo, author of *Les Misérables*, and the film-pioneering Lumière brothers, were born within a stone's throw of each other on Place Victor Hugo in Besançon's old town.

Besançon, noted for its vast parks, clean streets and few tourists, is considered one of the 'greenest' and most liveable cities in France. It has one of the country's largest foreign student populations and the old town's cobble streets hum with fun bars and bistros. Besançon's charming Battant quarter, originally settled by wine-makers, is the most historic area of town.

Orientation

Besançon's old city is neatly encased by the horseshoe-shaped curve of the Doubs River called the Boucle du Doubs. The tourist office and train station are both just outside this loop to the north-west and north. The Battant quarter straddles the north-west bank of the river around Rue Battant. Grande Rue, the pedestrianised main street, slices right through the old city from the river to the gates of the citadel.

Information

Tourist Office Sitting serenely by the river and a park, the tourist office (☎ 03 81 80 92 55; fax 03 81 80 58 30), 2 Place de la 1ère Armée Française, has an exchange service, books accommodation, sells local hiking maps, and has a tremendous amount of free material on everything from fishing to mountain biking in the Franche-Comté region. It also arranges guided city tours (☎ 03 81 88 31 95). The office is open from 9 am to 7 pm (from 10 am on Monday; Sunday from 10 am to noon and from 3 to 5 pm). From October to March the office shuts at 6 pm and is only open on Sunday between mid-September and mid-June from 10 am to noon.

Those wanting to complete their free brochure collection should head for the Comité Régional de Tourisme (☎ 03 81 25 08 08; fax 03 81 83 35 82), 28 Rue de la République, which has dozens of useful ones for travellers. It's open weekdays from 8.30 am to 12.30 pm and 2 to 6 pm (5 pm on Friday).

Centre Régional Information Jeunesse This youth information centre (☎ 03 81 21 16 16; fax 03 81 82 83 17,crijfc@fc-net.fr), 27 Rue de la République, has a travel/accommodation noticeboard, gives away free city maps, and is home to the Autostop office that arranges shared and *payant* (paying) rides in France and abroad. The centre is open Monday and Saturday from 1 to 8 pm, Tuesday to Friday from 10 am to noon and 1.30 to 6 pm.

Club Alpin Français The Besançon branch of the CAF national hiking club (☎ 03 81 81 02 77), 14 Rue Luc Breton, has information on hiking, skiing and mountain biking, and sells useful topoguides and maps. It is open Tuesday to Friday from 5 to 7 pm.

Money The Banque de France at 19 Rue de la Préfecture is open weekdays from 8.45 am to 12.15 pm and 1.30 to 3.30 pm. Foreign currency can also be changed at the tourist office and the train station information office.

Post & Communications The main post office, which handles poste restante, is a hike out of the centre at 4 Rue Demangel. It's open from 8 am to 7 pm (Saturday until noon; closed Sunday). The branch at 23 Rue Proudhon keeps the same hours.

Send emails and surf the Internet at Net' Access (☎ 03 81 81 44 84, erwan@mail.fc-net.fr), 17 Rue Bersot. Online access costs 50FF an hour. Net' Access is open from 9 am to 7 pm (closed Sunday).

Laundry The Blanc-Matic laundrette at 54 Rue Bersot is open from 7 am to 8 pm. Another branch at 14 Rue de la Madeleine is open from 6.30 am and 8.30 pm.

Musée des Beaux-Arts et d'Archéologie

Thought to be France's oldest museum, the Musée des Beaux-Arts (☎ 03 81 82 39 92 or ☎ 03 81 81 44 47), 1 Place de la Révolution, houses an impressive collection of paintings, including primitive and Renaissance works. Franche-Comté's long history of clock-making is also displayed here. The museum is open daily, except Tuesday, from 9.30 am to noon and 2 to 6 pm. Admission is 30/21FF for adults/students (free to all on Sunday).

Citadelle

Built by Vauban for Louis XIV between 1688 and 1711, Besançon's citadel (☎ 03 81 65 07 50) sits at the top of Rue des Fusillés de la Résistance. It is a steep 15 minute walk from the **Porte Noire** (Black Gate), one of the few remains of Besançon's

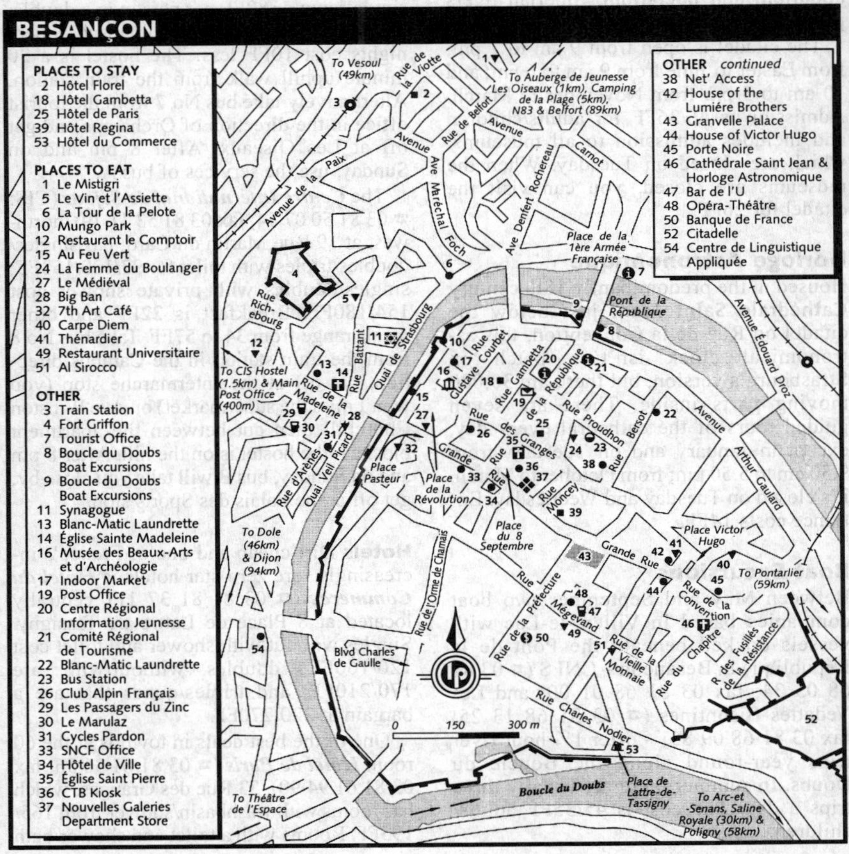

Roman days and dating from the 2nd century AD. Get a sense of the strength of this well preserved citadel by walking along the ramparts.

Within the 15 to 20m-thick walls there are three museums focusing on local culture: the **Musée Comtois**, the **Musée d'Histoire Naturelle** (Natural History Museum) and the **Musée de la Résistance et de la Déportation**, which examines the rise of Nazism and fascism and the French Resistance movement. Less sobering are the colourful collections of insects, fish and nocturnal rodents exhibited in the **insectarium**, **aquarium** and **noctarium**. Siberian tigers prowl in the **parc zoologique**.

The citadel is open from 9 am to 7 pm; from Easter to June from 9 am to 6 pm; and 10 am to 5 pm from November to March. Admission is 46/36FF for adults/children and includes admission to all museums, which are closed on Tuesday. When the museums are closed, you can visit the citadel for 26FF.

Horloge Astronomique

Housed in the predominantly 18th century **Cathédrale Saint Jean**, just below the citadel on Rue de la Convention, this astronomical clock isn't a patch on Strasbourg's version, but there are 30,000 moving parts inside. There are seven guided tours of the cathedral every day, except in January and on Tuesday, from 9.50 am to 5.50 pm; from October to March, it's closed on Tuesday and Wednesday. Entrance costs 14FF.

Boat Excursions

Between May and September two boat companies based in Villers-le-Lac with vessels docked beneath the Pont de la République in Besançon – CNFS (☎ 03 81 68 05 34; fax 03 81 68 01 00) and Les Vedettes Bisontines (☎ 03 81 68 13 25; fax 03 81 68 09 85) – offer 1¼-hour river trips year-round along the Boucle du Doubs. In summer there are usually three trips a day. The cost is 45/35FF adults/children.

Places to Stay

Camping The closest camping ground is the four star ***Camping de la Plage*** (☎ 03 81 88 04 26), Route de Belfort, Chalezeule, 5km north-east of town on the N83. It's open from May to September and costs 11.50/7.50/18/9.50FF per adult/child/tent/car. TGB (☎ 03 81 83 37 38) runs very infrequent buses out to here, usually only one or two a day, in the late afternoon.

Hostels The ***Auberge de Jeunesse Les Oiseaux*** (☎ 03 81 88 43 11; fax 03 81 80 77 97), 48 Rue des Cras, charges 90FF for a single room or 80FF per person in a double, including breakfast and bedding; subsequent nights cost 10FF less. The hostel is a 20 minute uphill walk from the train station. Alternatively take bus No 7 from the tourist office in the direction of Orchamps and get off at Les Oiseaux. After 8 pm and on Sunday, use the services of bus A.

The ***Centre International de Séjour*** (CIS; ☎ 03 81 50 07 54; fax 03 81 53 11 79), north-west at 19 Rue Martin du Gard, has singles/doubles/triples with toilet for 97/120/153FF; singles/doubles with private shower cost 154/180FF. Breakfast is 22FF and other meals range from 34 to 57FF. Take bus No 8 from the train station in the Campus direction, get off at the Intermarché stop (you won't miss the supermarket) on Ave Winston Churchill then cut between the apartment blocks – the hostel is on the hill. After 8 pm and on Sunday, bus B will take you close by; get off at the Palais des Sports stop.

Hotels Dirt-cheap and one of France's increasingly rare zero-star hotels is ***Hôtel du Commerce*** (☎ 03 81 81 37 11), centrally located at 8 Place de Lattre de Tassigny. Singles without/with shower and toilet cost 120/160FF; doubles without/with are 170/210FF; and triples/quads that are a bargain at 220/270FF.

One of the best deals in town is at the 60 room ***Hôtel de Paris*** (☎ 03 81 81 36 56; fax 03 81 61 94 90), 33 Rue des Granges, which has rooms with washbasin/shower from 165/195FF. Rooms with a toilet and shower/bath start at 230/250FF and breakfast costs 38FF. The enormous wooden staircase and garden at the back are quite a delight.

Another excellent choice but too far from the action is ***Hôtel Florel*** (☎ 03 81 80 41 08; fax 03 81 50 44 40), north of the old city and the river at 6 Rue de la Viotte. It has singles/doubles with shower for 190/215FF or with bath for 195/225FF. Breakfast is 29FF extra.

The ***Hôtel Gambetta*** (☎ 03 81 82 02 33; fax 03 81 82 31 16), 13 Rue Gambetta, is unspectacular. Singles with a washbasin are 135FF, doubles with shower are 200FF, and singles/doubles/triples with bath are 225/255/285FF. Breakfast is an extra 30FF.

Down a quiet alley in the heart of the old city, the two star ***Hôtel Regina*** (☎ 03 81 81 50 22; fax 03 81 81 60 20), 91 Grande Rue, offers cosy, floral singles/doubles/triples with shower, toilet and TV for 198/235/265FF. There's parking for a total of three cars in the lane.

Places to Eat

Restaurants Popular for its large tasty portions of local cuisine at favourable prices, ***Le Mistigri***, is a five minute walk from the train station at 1a Rue Général Roland. Its *menu* and its house speciality, *jambon de montagne* (mountain ham), both cost 65FF. It's open from 10 am to 2 pm and from 5 to 10 pm (closed Monday).

Equally cheap and cheerful is ***Au Feu Vert*** (☎ 03 81 82 17 20), 11 Place de la Révolution. It's a simple place with *menus* from 59FF and seven types of couscous from 55FF. It's open from noon to 2 am.

Among Besançon's more stylish options is ***Le Médiéval*** (☎ 03 81 81 12 89), 13 Grande Rue. Waiting staff serve delicious *hypocras* (mulled wine) in goblets and don medieval garb on weekends. Reserve in advance if you want to be sure of a table. It is open from 6 pm to 1 am (closed Sunday).

Equally popular with tourists is ***La Tour de la Pelote*** (☎ 03 81 82 14 58), which is housed inside a 16th century stone tower at 41 Quai de Strasbourg. *Menus* start at 134FF. It's open from noon to 2 pm and from 5 pm to 12.30 am (closed Monday).

Housed above the Caves Marcellin (Marcellin wine cellars) is ***Le Vin et l'Assiette*** (☎ 03 81 81 48 18), 97 Rue Battant. This intimate bistro and wine bar has a *menu* for 95FF and is open from noon to 2 pm and from 5 to 11 pm (closed Sunday and Monday).

Also favoured among the local 'in' crowd is the small but chic ***Restaurant le Comptoir*** (☎ 03 81 83 59 09), 12 Rue Richebourg, which is open from 9 am to 3 pm and from 7 pm to 2 am. Le Comptoir is just one of a handful of charming places to eat along this narrow, old-world street in the Battant quarter of town.

Thénardier (☎ 03 81 82 06 18), 11 Rue Victor Hugo, is great for lunch. *Menus* start at 55FF and service is speedy. If the first floor is full, ask to sit in the cosy cellar. Thénardier is open from 10 am to 2 pm and from 5 to 11 pm.

Mungo Park (☎ 03 81 81 28 01), 11 Rue Jean Petit, which is named after a Scottish explorer, is *the* place for a splurge. *Menus* start at 230FF with the ultimate gourmand menu satisfying the appetite for 490FF. The lunchtime *menu* without/with wine is 195/235FF. The restaurant is open from noon to 3.30 pm and from 5.30 to 9.30 pm (closed Sunday and Monday).

Rue Bersot overflows with ***pizzerias***. The best pizza in town, however, is served at ***Al Sirocco*** (☎ 03 81 82 24 05), 1 Rue Chifflet, which also has a takeaway service. Its 24 varieties of pizza start at 44FF. It's open from noon to 2 pm and from 7.30 to 11 pm (closed on Sunday and on Monday for lunch). For late-night snacks, try ***Big Ban***, 13 Quai Veil Picard, which slaps out hot dogs, steaks and salads from 11.30 am to 1 am (2 am on weekends).

University Restaurant Almost broke? A cheap but tasteless meal (about 15FF for three courses) is available at the ***Restaurant Universitaire***, 36 Rue Mégevand, which is open from 7.30 to 10.30 am and 2.30 to 5 pm.

Cafés ***Carpe Diem***, (☎ 03 81 83 11 18), 2 Place Jean Gigoux, could well *save* the day for lost bohemians in search of a hang-out. This small and simple café-restaurant serves a good range of salads starting at 12FF; the plat du jour is 45FF. Newspapers are free for customers to peruse. It is open from 7 to 2 am.

Delicious homemade breads, sweet and savoury tarts, and healthy breakfasts are served with finesse at ***La Femme du Boulanger*** (☎ 03 81 82 86 93), 6 Rue Morand, which specialises in local artisan produce. The plat du jour is 58FF; don't miss its scrumptious apple bread. The 'Baker's Wife' is open from 7.30 am to 7.30 pm.

Flashy but favoured for its outside summer seating is the ***7th Art Café*** (☎ 03 81 81 90 54), overlooking the river on Quai Vauban and open until 2 am on weekends.

Self-Catering Fresh fish, meat, vegetables and dairy products are sold at the large ***indoor market*** on the corner of Rue Paris and Rue Goudimel. The nearby ***outdoor market*** on Place de la Révolution sells mainly fruit and vegetables.

The ***Nouvelles Galeries***, entered from 69 Grande Rue or opposite the Hôtel de Paris on Rue des Granges, has a grocery section in the basement. It's open from 9 am to 7 pm (closed Sunday).

Entertainment

The Orchestre de Besançon (☎ 03 81 61 51 01) performs at the ***Opéra-Théâtre*** (☎ 03 81 83 03 33), 2 Rue Mégevand. The ***Théâtre de l'Espace*** (☎ 03 81 83 50 50), south-west of the centre at Place de l'Europe, is the venue for colourful hip-hop operas, contemporary dance and theatre, alternative films, puppet shows and cabarets.

Besançon's hip brigade can be found by night at ***Les Passagers du Zinc*** (☎ 03 81 81 54 70), a funky bar and club at 5 Rue de Vignier that hosts tapas nights, live bands, a host of eclectic 'worst record' competitions and other kitsch delights. Step through the bonnet of an old Citröen DS to reach the cellar. It's open from 5 pm to 1 am (2 am on weekends; closed Monday). Small, packed, and equally fun is ***Le Marulaz*** jazz bar (☎ 03 81 01 40 30), 2 Place Marulaz, open from 11 am to 1 am.

The student ***Bar de l'U*** (☎ 03 81 81 68 17), 5 Rue Mairet, hosts an international students evening on Tuesday, a debating forum on Wednesday and live bands on Friday. It's open from 8 am to 1 am.

Getting There & Away

Bus Buses operated by Monts Jura (☎ 03 81 21 22 00) depart from the bus station (☎ 03 81 83 06 11), 9 Rue Proudhon, open weekdays from 8 am to 6.30 pm, and Saturday from 8 am to 1 pm and 2.30 to 5.30 pm. There are daily connections to Morteau (52FF), Ornans (25FF) and Pontarlier (49FF).

Train The train station (☎ 08 36 35 35 35) is 800m up the hill from the city centre at the north-western end of Ave Maréchal Foch. The information office is open from 9.30 am to 12.15 pm and 1.15 to 6.30 pm. Train tickets can be bought in advance at the SNCF office, 44 Grande Rue. It's open from 10 am to 6 pm (closed Sunday).

Major connections include Paris' Gare de Lyon (from 280FF; 2½ hours; five a day), Dijon (72FF; one hour; 20 a day), Lyon (141FF; 2½ hours; five a day), Belfort (77FF; 1¼ hours; four a day), and Arc-et-Senans (33FF; 35 minutes; four a day). To get to Frasne (near Métabief), change trains in Mouchard or Dole (68FF; two hours).

Getting Around

Bus Local buses are run by CTB (☎ 03 81 48 12 12), which has a ticket/information kiosk on Place du 8 Septembre, open Monday to Saturday from 9 am to 12.30 pm and 1 to 7 pm. A single ticket/carnet of 10 costs 6/50FF. Bus Nos 8 and 24 link the train station with the centre.

Taxi To order a taxi, call ☎ 03 81 88 80 80.

Bicycle If you have strong leg muscles, why not tackle Besançon's hilly terrain with a mountain bike hired from Cycles Pardon

(☎ 03 81 81 08 79), 31 Rue d'Arènes. It costs 60/100/180FF for a half-day/day/weekend (plus 3000FF deposit). The shop is open from 9 am to noon and from 2 to 7 pm (closed on Sunday and Monday).

AROUND BESANÇON

Saline Royal

Envisaged by its late 18th century designer, Claude-Nicolas Ledoux, as the 'ideal city', the Saline Royale (Royal Salt Works; ☎ 03 81 54 45 45; fax 03 81 54 45 46) at Arc-et-Senans, 30km south-west of town off the N83 to Chalezeule, is a showpiece of early Industrial Age town planning. Although his dream was never realised, Ledoux's semi-circular saltworks is listed as a UNESCO World Heritage List sight and is a must for anyone interested in town planning.

Opening hours and prices vary depending on the month, but it's usually open from 9 or 10 am to noon and 2 to 5 or 6 pm. In July and August, the hours are 9 am to 7 pm. Admission is 38/30/15FF for adults/students/children under 16.

The family-run ***Hotel Relais*** (☎ 03 81 57 40 60; fax 03 81 57 46 17), in the centre of Arc-et-Senans village, has 10 cosy double rooms costing 180FF. Its lunchtime *menu* at 55FF is excellent value. Campers can pitch their tents at ***Camping des Bords de Loue*** (☎ 03 81 57 42 20, 03 81 57 43 21), a 1.5km-hike signposted off the main road (open from May to October). There are four trains a day from Besançon (33FF; 35 minutes) to Arc-et-Senans.

Ornans

• pop 4015 ✉ 25290

Ornans, 25km south-west of Besançon, is Franche-Comté's 'Little Venice'. The River Loue cuts through the heart of the old town, above which towers the **Château d'Ornans**. The birthplace of Gustave Courbet (1819-77), an 18th century house on the banks of Loue, today houses a museum dedicated to the realist painter. Exhibits include works by Courbet. The **Musée Courbet** (☎ 03 81 62 23 30) is open from 10 am to noon and 2 to 6 pm (closed on Tuesday in winter). Admission is 40/20FF in summer/winter.

Ornan's surrounding **Vallée de la Loue** (Loue Valley) is a popular spot for mountain biking, canoeing and kayaking. Contact the Syratu sports club (☎ 03 81 57 10 82; fax 03 81 57 18 49), 2 Route de Montgesoye. Ornans tourist office (☎/fax 03 81 61 21 50), 7 Rue Pierre Vernier, distributes the excellent free brochure *VTT et Cyclotourisme en Franche-Comté*.

There are eight buses a day (25FF; 45 minutes) from Besançon to Ornans.

Route Pasteur & Route du Vin

Louis Pasteur (1822-95) was born in **Dole**, 20km north-west of Arc-et-Senans along the D472. His childhood home, La Maison Natale de Pasteur (☎ 03 84 72 20 61), overlooking the Canal des Tanneurs in the old town, houses a museum dedicated to the man who invented both pasteurisation and the first rabies vaccine. The Pasteur family later moved to **Arbois**, 35km east of Dole. Pasteur's former laboratory and workshops in Arbois inside Pasteur's house (☎ 03 84 66 11 72), 83 Rue de Courcelles, are open between May and September from 9.45 am to 5.15 pm. Admission is 30FF.

No visit to Arbois, the wine capital of Jura, is complete without sampling a glass of local *vin jaune*. The history of wine-making and of this nutty 'yellow wine', which is matured for six years in oak casks, is recounted in the **Musée de la Vigne et du Vin** (☎ 03 84 66 26 14; percee@jura.vins.com) inside Arbois's medieval Château Pécauld. The museum is open between February and September daily, except Tuesday, from 10 am to noon and 2 to 6 pm (no lunch-break in July and August). The tourist office (☎ 03 84 37 47 37; fax 03 84 66 25 50; www.arbois.com), Rue de l'Hôtel de Ville, arranges guided tours and accommodation. To get to Arbois from Besançon (45km) take a train to Mouchard, 8km north of Arbois.

For the ultimate *dégustation* experience, head 3km south along the Route du Vin to **Pupillin**, a beautifully quaint, yellow-brick village (population 220) brimming with wealth from its wine production. Some 10 different *caves* are open to visitors who can taste (and buy) Arbois-Pupillin wines. Pupillin is not served by public transport; hire a bicycle in Arbois from Rock Sports (☎ 03 84 66 07 90), 62 Grande Rue.

Poligny & Baume-les-Messieurs

Poligny, 10km south of Arbois, lies at the heart of France's lucrative Comté cheese-making industry, the history of which is displayed in the town's **Maison du Comté** (☎ 03 84 7 23 51), Ave de la Résistance. Some 40 million tonnes of Comté cheese are produced each year, much of which is made by *fruitières* (cheese dairies) in the Franche-Comté region. Museum staff run five daily guided tours in summer between 10 am and 4.30 pm (admission 15FF); from October to June the museum is open from 9 to 11 am and 2 to 5 pm (free admission). Poligny tourist office (☎ 03 84 37 24 21; fax 03 84 37 22 37), Rue Victor Hugo, has a list of local fromageries that visitors can tour.

Traditional Jurassien life is still firmly intact in **Baume-les-Messieurs** (population 200), an extraordinarily pretty village sunk between three valleys 20km south of Poligny. Its Benedictine abbey (☎ 03 84 44 61 41), established by Irish monk St Columban at the end of the 14th century, is open from mid-June to mid-September between 10 am and 6 pm. Admission is 20FF. Equally spectacular is the **Grottes de Baume** (Baume Caves), accessible by road from the foot of the 10m-tall **Cascade de Baume** (Baume Waterfall). Guided tours of the 30 million-year-old caves (☎ 03 84 44 61 58) are available between April and September from 9 am to 6 pm.

Immediately east of Baume-les-Messieurs is the Jura's **Région des Lacs** (Lakes District).

Places to Stay & Eat The ***Le Grand Jardin*** (☎ 03 84 44 68 37), opposite Baume-les-Messieurs abbey, has quaint double rooms for 200FF. Book rooms well in advance in summer. ***Le Comptois*** (☎/fax 03 84 25 71 21), some 5km east in Doucier, has singles/doubles with shower for 170/295FF. Rooms with shared bathroom are 140/220FF. Don't miss out on its restaurant's delicious Jurassien fondue, served between March and November to appease tourists hungry for a dip into the region's best known winter speciality (the French only eat fondue in winter). Le Comptois also organises gastronomic tours of the region.

BELFORT & AROUND

Belfort (population 50,125), just across the border from Germany and Switzerland, is as Alsatian as it is Jurassien. Historically part of Alsace, it became part of the Franche-Comté region in 1921. Today, the city is best known as the manufacturer of the TGV train.

The **Musée d'Art et d'Histoire** (☎ 03 84 54 25 51), inside the **Vauban citadel**, is open from 10 am to 7 pm (closed on Tuesday between October and April). Open-air concerts are held on Wednesday in summer. At the foot of the citadel stands **Le Lion de Belfort**, created by sculptor Frédéric-Auguste Bartholdi, who also designed the Statue of Liberty in New York. The 11m-tall lion commemorates Belfort's resistance to the Prussians in 1870-71, following which all of Alsace – except Belfort – was annexed by Germany.

In July, Belfort hosts **Les Eurockéennes** (☎ 03 84 57 01 92; fax 03 84 28 15 12), a three day open-air rock festival that, in the past, has attracted the likes of David Bowie, Garbage, and the Red Hot Chilli Peppers. A one/three day ticket costs 180/440FF and includes use of the festival camp site that overlooks Malsaucy lake.

In Sochaux, near Montbéliard 12km south of Belfort, car enthusiasts can visit the **Musée Peugeot** (☎ 03 81 94 48 21). Guided tours of the car factory are available Monday to Thursday at 8.30 am and 4 pm. The modernist **Église Audicourt** (Audicourt Church), 2km south-east, is a must for architecture buffs. The **Massif du Ballon d'Alsace** (1247m), 20km north of Belfort in the southern part of the Vosges Mountains, provides ample opportunity for winter skiing, and summer hiking, mountain biking, kayaking, and hot-air ballooning.

Ronchamp

La Chapelle de Notre-Dame du Haut (the Chapel of our Lady of the Height; ☎ 03 81 20 65 13), on a hill overlooking the old mining town of Ronchamp (population 3000), 20km west of Belfort, is considered one of the 20th century's architectural masterpieces – making it a pilgrimage site for thousands of architects every year. The white chapel, unique for its surreal, sculpture-like form, was designed between 1950 and 1955 by France's most celebrated architect, Le Corbusier. Its sweeping, concrete roof is said to have been inspired by a hermit crab shell.

The chapel (☎ 03 84 20 65 13) is open from 9 am to 7 pm (to 4 pm between November and March). Admission is 10FF. In summer, Sunday service takes place at 11 am. Over 3000 pilgrims gather here each year on 8 September. A 15 minute hiking trail leads uphill from the centre of Ronchamp to the chapel.

Ronchamp tourist office (☎ 03 84 63 50 82), 14 Place du 14 Juillet, is open between June and October on Monday, Friday and Saturday from 9 am to noon and 2 to 6 pm (5 pm on Saturday).

Places to Stay & Eat

Belfort tourist office (☎ 03 84 55 90 90; fax 03 84 55 90 99), 2 Rue Clémenceau, has the free *Accommodation and Restaurant* brochure containing a city map and a comprehensive list of hotels and camp sites in and around Belfort.

In Belfort, a bed at the ***Auberge de Jeunesse*** (☎ 03 84 21 39 16), 6 Rue de Madrid, is 70FF a night.

In Ronchamp, ***Hôtel à la Pomme d'Or*** (☎ 03 84 20 62 12; fax 03 84 63 59 45), at the foot of the hill leading up to the chapel, has doubles from 210FF. More idyllic is ***Hôtel Carrer*** (☎ 03 84 20 62 32; fax 03 84 63 57 08), 2km north of Ronchamp in Le Rhien. Singles/doubles start at 170/280FF.

Don't leave Belfort without biting into a local Belfore, a scrumptious almond-flavoured pastry filled with raspberries and topped with hazel nuts.

Getting There & Away

Major connections from Belfort train station include Paris' Gare de Lyon via Besançon (278FF; five hours; three a day), Besançon (77FF; 1¼ hours; four a day) and Montbéliard (20FF; 15 minutes; 20 a day).

From Belfort there are one or two trains a day to/from Ronchamp (25FF; 25 minutes). On weekdays there are also two buses a day to/from Ronchamp (25FF; 35 minutes).

MÉTABIEF MONT D'OR

• pop 500 ✉ 25370 alt 1000m

Métabief Mont d'Or, 18km south of Pontarlier on the main road to Lausanne in the central part of the Jura range, is the region's leading cross-country ski resort. Year-round, lifts take you almost to the top of Mont d'Or (1463m), the area's highest peak, from where a fantastic 180° panorama stretches over the foggy Swiss plain to Lake Geneva and from the Matterhorn to Mont Blanc.

Métabief is famed for its unique *vacherin Mont d'Or* cheese.

Orientation & Information

The resort comprises six traditional villages. The main lift station for downhill skiers is in Métabief. There are smaller lifts in Les Hôpitaux Neufs, 2km north-east.

In Métabief, the tourist office (☎ 03 81 49 16 79) and École du Ski Français (ESF; ☎ 03 81 49 04 21) are inside the Centre d'Accueil, 6 Place du Xavier. Both are open from 9 am to noon and 2 to 5 pm. The tourist office (☎ 03 81 49 13 81; fax 03 81 49 09 27), 1 Place de la Mairie, Les Hôpitaux Neufs, is open until 6 pm.

Fromagerie du Mont d'Or

Comté, *morbier* and vacherin Mont d'Or cheese have been made by the Sancey-Richard family in Métabief since 1953. The Fromagerie du Mont d'Or (☎ 03 81 49 02 36; fax 03 81 49 25 07), Rue Moulin, which produces over 200 tonnes of cheese a year, is open year-round to visitors. Guided tours include a visit to the dairy's salting rooms, where the vacherin Mont d'Or cheeses are washed daily with salt water, and the maturing cellars where the hefty 45kg-rounds of Comté cheese are turned by hand twice weekly for up to 12 months.

The fromagerie is open from 9 am to noon and 3 to 6.30 pm (closed Sunday afternoon). Arrive here with the milk lorry before 10.30 am if you want to see cheese being made. Admission is free.

Places to Stay & Eat

Both tourist offices have comprehensive lists of hotels and apartments to rent.

In Métabief, the family-run ***Hôtel Étoile des Neiges*** (☎ 03 81 49 11 21; fax 03 81 49 26 91), Rue du Village, has singles/doubles for 185/235FF. Half-board costs 240/270FF. Strictly local dishes such as raclette, fondue Comtoise, *Mont d'Or chaud* and *la saucisse Jésus de Morteau* are served in its excellent restaurant, also open to nonguests. Tickle your tastebuds first though with a hearty shot of *anis de Pontarlier* (a liquorice-flavoured aperitif), the Jura's answer to Provençal *pastis*.

Getting There & Away

The closest train station is at Frasne (☎ 08 36 35 35 35), 25km north-west on the rail line between Dijon, Arc-et-Senans and Vallorbe (9km east in Switzerland). From Frasne, there are six buses a day that pass through both Métabief and Les Hôpitaux Neufs (21FF; 50 minutes). You can reach both Métabief Ville (21FF) and the ski station (21FF) from Besançon, 78km to the north-west, in about two hours.

Hot Box, Christmas Ice & Jesus

It's hot, it's soft and it's packed in a box. Vacherin Mont d'Or is the only French cheese to be eaten with a spoon – hot (or cold for that matter). Made between 15 August and 15 March with unpasteurised milk (*lait cru*) from red cows grazing above an altitude of 800m, it derives its unique nutty taste from the spruce bark in which it's wrapped.

Louis XV adored it. In the 18th century it was called fat cheese, wood cheese or box cheese. Today, vacherin Mont d'Or is named after the mountain village from which it originates. Connoisseurs top the soft-crusted cheese with chopped onions, garlic and white wine, then wrap it in aluminium foil and cook it in the oven for 45 minutes to create a *boîte chaude* (hot box).

Just 11 factories in the Jura are licensed to produce vacherin Mont d'Or, which ironically, has sold like hot cakes since 1987 when 10 people in Switzerland died from listeriosis after consuming the Swiss version of Mont d'Or, made just a few kilometres across the border. Old-fashioned cheese buffs are quite frank about the Swiss scandal's popularisation of their own centuries-old cheese. They believe the bacterial tragedy, which claimed 34 lives in total between 1983 and 1987, only happened because the Swiss copycats pasteurised their milk.

Mouthe, 15km south of Métabief Mont d'Or, is the mother of *liqueur de sapin* (fir tree liqueur). *Glace de sapin* (fir tree ice-cream) also comes from this village, known as the North Pole of France due to its seasonal sub-zero temperatures (record low -38°). Sampling either is rather like ingesting a Christmas tree.

Then there's Jesus. *Jésus* – a fat little version of regular *saucisse de Morteau* (Morteau sausage) – is the village of Morteau's gastronomic delight. Jesus is easily identifiable by the wooden peg on its back end, attached after being smoked with pine-wood sawdust in a traditional *tuyé* (mountain hut) above 600m. Morteau residents claim their sausage is bigger, better and fatter than any other French sausage. They host a sausage festival (☎ 03 81 50 69 43) each year in August.

AROUND MÉTABIEF MONT D'OR

Winter skiers keen for a break from the slopes should head a few kilometres south to the **l'Odyssée Blanche – Parc du Chien Polaire** (White Odyssey Polar Dog Park; ☎ 03 81 69 20 20; fax 03 81 69 13 02) in Chaux Neuve. Try your hand at 'mushing' – that is exploring the region by dog-drawn sledge, or simply tour the kennels and coo over the Siberian huskies and Alaskan malamutes instead. White Odyssey is open between 20 December and 31 March from 10 am to 5 pm. A half-day/day expedition costs 450/900FF,

The **Château de Joux** (☎ 03 81 69 47 95), 10km north of Métabief on the Route de Pontarlier, guards the entrance from Switzerland into north and central France. It sits atop Mont Larmont (922m), overlooking a dramatic *cluse* (transverse valley) that cuts through the mountain to form a passage just wide enough for the road to snake between. Part of *Les Misérables* (1995) was filmed here. During the First Empire, the castle was a state prison. Today it houses France's most impressive arms museum. The chateau is open in summer from 9 am to 6 pm, and between October and February from 10 to 11.15 am and 2 to 3.30 pm. Admission is 32/27/16FF for adults/students. The music and theatre festival, **Festival des Nuits de Joux**, takes place here in mid-July.

Montbenoît (population 230), 20km farther north, is the capital of the tiny **Saugeais Republic**. The folkloric republic, declared in 1947, has its own flag, national anthem, postage stamp, and a 92-year-old president, Gabrielle Pourchet, who is featured on the Saugeais banknote. In summer a Sauget customs officer greets tourists as they enter the town.

PARC NATUREL RÉGIONAL DU HAUT-JURA

The Haut-Jura regional park covers an area of 75,672 hectares, stretching from Chapelle-des-Bois in the north and almost to the western tip of Lake Geneva in the south. Each year in February, its abundant lakes, mountains and low-lying valleys play host to the Transjurassienne, the world's second longest cross-country skiing race (see the boxed text 'Grande Traversée du Jura'). Exploring this region is difficult without private transport.

Saint Claude, the largest town in the park (population 12,704), is best known for its illustrious wooden pipe-making and diamond cutting tradition, the history of which unfolds in the local pipe and diamond museum. The CAF (☎ 03 84 45 58 62; fax 03 84 60 36 88),

Grande Traversée du Jura

The Grande Traversée du Jura (GTJ) – the Grand Jura Crossing – is a 210km cross-country skiing track from Villers-le-Lac (north of Pontarlier) to Hauteville-Lompnes (south-west of Bellegarde). The path peaks at 1500m near the town of Mouthe (south of Métabief) and follows one of the coldest valleys in France. After the first 20km the route briefly crosses into Switzerland, but most of the time it runs close to the border on the French side. Well maintained and very popular, the crossing takes 10 full days of skiing to cover – a feat for the ultrafit and dedicated.

Part of the GTJ – the 76km from Lamoura to Mouthe – is traversed each year during the world's second largest cross-country skiing competition, the Transjurassienne. Held in late February, the challenge is taken up by more than 4000 skiers, who charge off in an incredible blaze of colour.

For information on the GTJ and accommodation possibilities along the route, contact Relais de Randonnée Étapes Jura (☎ 03 84 41 20 34), F-39310 Lajoux; or GTJ-Espace Nordique Jurassien (☎ 03 84 52 58 10; fax 03 84 52 35 56), Rue Baronne-Delort, F-39300 Champagnole. The best map of the area is the IGN 1:50,000 scale map entitled *Ski de Fond – Massif du Jura*.

8 Blvd de la République, provides information on its *refuges* in the Jura. Dubbed the French capital of wooden toys, **Moirans-en-Montagne**, 14km west, is an apt home for the playful **Musée du Jouet** (Toy Museum).

Les Rousses (population 2850; 1100m), on the north-east edge of the park, is the main centre for winter sports, hiking and mountain biking. Three of its four small, gently-sloped downhill ski areas – Les Jouvencelles, Le Noirmont and La Serra – are in France; the fourth – La Dole – is in Switzerland. Extensive cross-country trails take skiers as far north as Métabief Mont d'Or as well as eastwards across the border. The tourist office (☎ 03 84 60 02 55), SNCF bureau (☎ 03 84 60 01 90), and the Club des Sports (☎ 03 84 60 35 14), are inside the Maison du Tourisme, next to the bus station on Route Blanche.

The Jura's most staggering view can be savoured from the **Col de la Faucille**, 20km south of Les Rousses. As the N5 twists and turns its way down the Jura Mountains past the small ski resort of **Mijoux**, the panoramic view of Lake Geneva embraced by the French Alps and Mont Blanc beyond is startling. By sunset, it is a sight never forgotten – easily rivalling Paris in the romantic spot stakes. Take a télécabine from Mijoux or gaze in the warmth from the terrace bar of the classy ***La Mainaz*** hotel-restaurant (☎ 04 50 41 31 10; fax 04 50 41 31 77) on the Cole de la Faucille. Half-board starts at 405FF per person.

Continuing a farther 25km south-east you arrive at the French-Swiss border, passing through **Ferney-Voltaire**, 5km north of Geneva en route. Following his banishment from Switzerland in 1759, Voltaire lived in Ferney until his return to Paris and death in 1778. Guided tours of his estate – chateau, chapel and 17 acre park – are available in July and August on Saturday at 3, 4 and 5 pm. Past visitors include Auden, Blake and Flaubert, all of whom wrote about the philosopher's home in exile.

Provence

For the vast majority of the year, Provence is bathed in the most glorious southern sunshine, with a warmth and intensity of light unknown in other parts of France. Along the coast, the Mediterranean reflects and refracts the sun's rays, making for sharp, distinct colours. Inland, the hues are more subtle: the red tile roofs and blue skies are softened by an infinite variety of greens and by the looming presence of limestone hills, often wrapped in a gentle haze.

Many Provençal cities and towns date from at least Roman times and offer a wonderful array of cultural treasures, ranging from Roman theatres (still used for music and other festivals) and medieval fortifications to outstanding art museums. The region's population centres boast generous public spaces – just as they did under Augustus – and the locals spend a good part of their lives outdoors, sipping *pastis* (a liquorice-flavoured aperitif) in cafés or playing *pétanque*, a type of bowls using heavy metal balls, under the shade of the region's plane trees.

History

Provence was settled over the centuries by the Ligurians, the Celts and the Greeks, but it was only after its conquest by Julius Caesar in the mid-1st century BC and its integration into the Roman Empire that the region really began to flourish. Many exceptionally well preserved Roman theatres, aqueducts, baths and other ancient buildings can still be seen in towns such as Arles, Orange and Vaison-la-Romaine. After the collapse of the empire in the late 5th century, Provence suffered invasions by the Visigoths, Burgundians and the Ostrogoths. The Arabs – who for some time held the Iberian Peninsula and parts of France – were defeated in the 8th century.

During the 14th century, the Catholic Church – under a series of French-born popes – moved its headquarters from feud-riven Rome to Avignon, thus beginning the most

HIGHLIGHTS

- **Avignon** – tour the Palais des Papes
- **Gordes** or **Les Baux de Provence** – stroll the streets of these remarkable *villages perchés* (perched villages)
- **Activities** – climb Mont Ventoux or go white-water rafting along the Gorges du Verdon
- **Arles** – follow in the footsteps of Van Gogh, see sketches by Picasso in the Musée Réattu and watch a bullfight in the Roman amphitheatre
- **Digne-les-Bains** – travel by narrow-gauge train to Nice

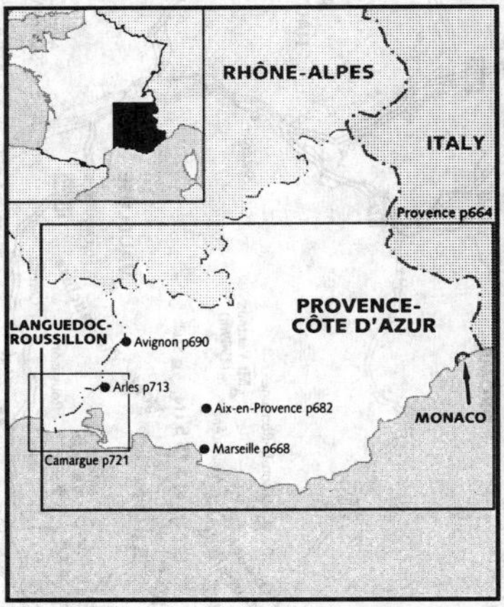

Carpentras market – for local specialities like fruits, vegetables, olives and lavender marmalade

bouillabaisse – a seafood stew with onions, white wine, tomatoes, flavoured with fennel and saffron

pastis and Châteauneuf-du-Pape wine

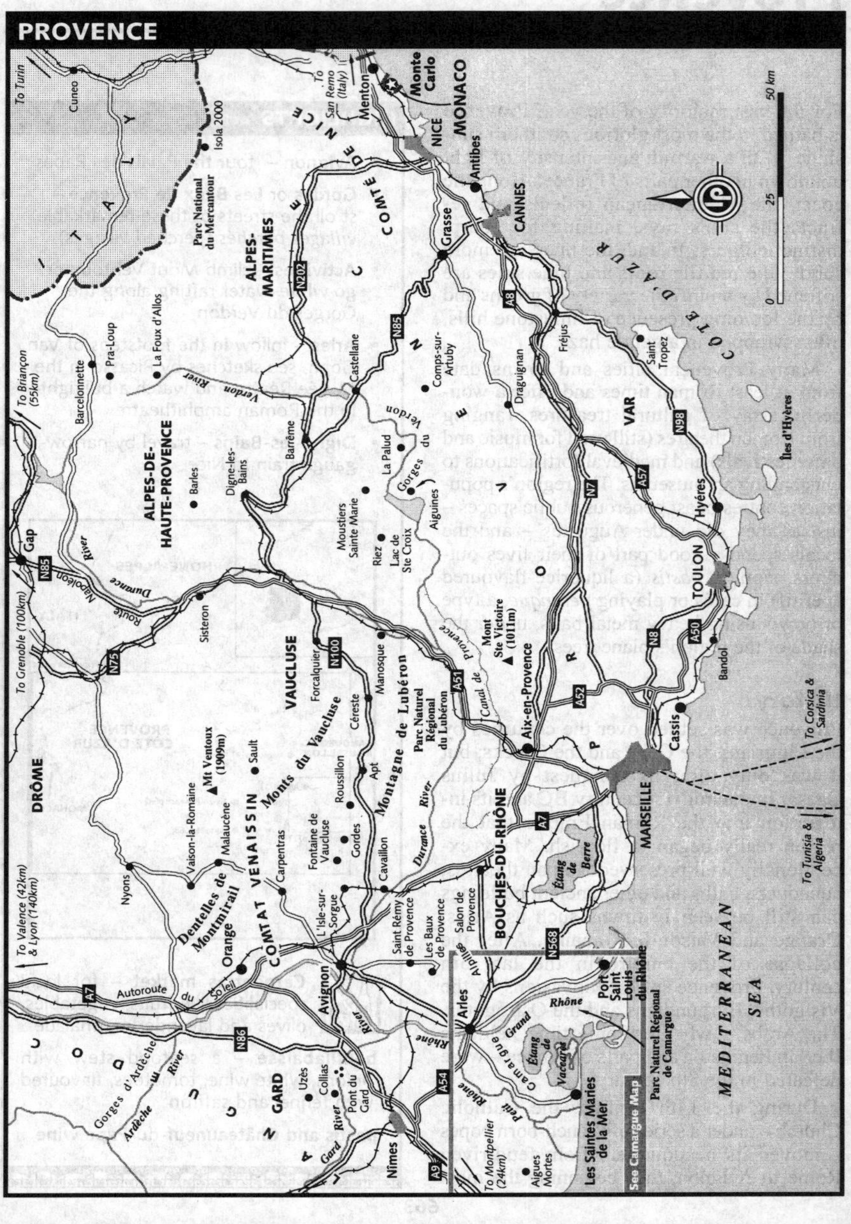
PROVENCE
ITALY
To Turin
Cuneo
Isola 2000
Parc National du Mercantour
To San Remo (Italy)
Menton
Monte Carlo
MONACO
NICE
Antibes
CANNES
Grasse
COMTÉ DE NICE
ALPES-MARITIMES
N202
N85
Castellane
La Foux d'Allos
Pra-Loup
Barcelonnette
To Briançon (55km)
Verdon River
Comps-sur-Artuby
Draguignan
Fréjus
Saint Tropez
CÔTE D'AZUR
A8
VAR
N98
Îles d'Hyères
Hyères
A57
N7
TOULON
A50
N8
Bandol
To Corsica & Sardinia
Cassis
MARSEILLE
A52
A51
Aix-en-Provence
Mont Ste Victoire (1011m)
Canal de Provence
PROVENCE
ALPES-DE-HAUTE-PROVENCE
Barles
Digne-les-Bains
Barrême
La Palud
Gorges du Verdon
Aiguines
Moustiers Sainte Marie
Riez
Lac de Ste Croix
Gap
N85
Route Napoléon
Durance River
Sisteron
N75
To Grenoble (100km)
DRÔME
VAUCLUSE
Forcalquier
N100
Manosque
Céreste
Parc Naturel Régional du Lubéron
Montagne de Lubéron
Mt Ventoux (1909m)
Sault
Monts du Vaucluse
Roussillon
Apt
Gordes
Fontaine de Vaucluse
Cavaillon
Durance River
COMTAT VENAISSIN
Carpentras
Malaucène
Vaison-la-Romaine
Nyons
Dentelles de Montmirail
Orange
To Valence (42km) & Lyon (140km)
A7
Autoroute du Soleil
L'Isle-sur-Sorgue
Saint Rémy de Provence
Les Baux de Provence
Salon de Provence
BOUCHES-DU-RHÔNE
Étang de Berre
N568
Alpilles
Avignon
Rhône River
N86
Gorges d'Ardèche
Ardèche River
GARD
Uzès
Collias
Pont du Gard
Gard River
Nîmes
A9
A54
Arles
Grand Rhône
Petit Rhône
Camargue
Étang de Vaccarès
Port Saint Louis du Rhône
Parc Naturel Régional de Camargue
Les Saintes Maries de la Mer
Aigues Mortes
To Montpellier (24km)
See Camargue Map
MEDITERRANEAN SEA
To Tunisia & Algeria
LANGUEDOC
0 25 50 km

PROVENCE

resplendent period in that city's history. Provence became part of France in 1481, but Avignon and Comtat Venaissin, with its seat at Carpentras, remained under papal control until the Revolution.

Geography

Provence stretches along both sides of the Rhône River from just north of Orange down to the Mediterranean, and along France's southern coast from the Camargue salt marshes in the west to Marseille in the east. Beyond Marseille is the Côte d'Azur, which, though historically part of Provence, appears in a separate chapter in this book. (Monaco also appears in the Côte d'Azur chapter.)

South of Arles, the Camargue marshlands – actually the delta of the Rhône River – are within a triangle formed by the Grand Rhône to the east and the Petit Rhône to the west.

East of the Rhône are most of the region's mountains and hills: the Baronnies; 1909m Mont Ventoux; the Vaucluse plateau (Vaucluse hills); the rugged Lubéron range; and the little Alpilles. Farther east is Europe's most spectacular canyon, the Gorges du Verdon.

Climate

Provence's weather is bright, sunny and dry for much of the year. Indeed, the region's extraordinary light served as an important inspiration for such painters as Van Gogh, Cézanne and Picasso. But the cold, dry winds of the mistral gain surprising fury with little warning as they blow southward down the narrow Rhône Valley, and can turn a fine spring day into a bone-chilling wintry one.

The mistral tends to blow continuously for several days and can reach speeds of more than 100km/h, damaging crops, whipping up forest fires and generally driving everybody around the bend. It is caused by the coincidence of a high-pressure area over central France and a low-pressure area over the Mediterranean, and is most common in winter and spring.

The Perfume of Provence

If there's any one aroma associated with Provence, it's lavender (*lavande*). Lavender fields – once seen, never forgotten – include those at the Abbaye de Sénanque (near Gordes), the Musée de la Lavande (Lavender Museum; ☎ 04 90 76 91 23; in Coustellet) and those which carpet the arid Sault region, east of Mont Ventoux on the Vaucluse plateau.

The sweet purple flower is harvested between 15 July and 15 August. Lavender farms, distilleries and ornamental gardens open to visitors are listed in the English-language brochure *Les Routes de la Lavande* (free from tourist offices).

The Maison de l'Environment et de la Chasse (☎ 04 90 64 13 96), Ave de l'Oratoire, Sault, organises lavender tours, which take in the lavender farms where the crop is grown and the essense extracted.

Language

The various dialects of Provençal – whose grammar is more closely related to Catalan and Spanish than French – are still spoken every day by hundreds of thousands of people across southern France, especially by older residents of rural areas.

From the 12th to 14th century, Provençal was the literary language of France and northern Spain, and was used as far afield as Italy. During that period, it was the principal language of the medieval troubadours, poets – often courtiers and nobles – whose melodies and elegant poems were motivated by the ideal of courtly love.

A movement for the revival of Provençal literature, culture and identity began in the mid-19th century. Its most prominent member was the poet Frédéric Mistral (1830-1914), recipient of the Nobel prize for literature in 1904. In recent years, the language has again enjoyed something of a revival, and in many areas signs are written in Provençal and French.

Getting There & Away

For information on ferry services from Marseille to Sardinia and Tunisia, see Sea in the introductory Getting There & Away chapter. For details on ferries from Marseille to Corsica, see Getting There & Away in the Corsica chapter.

Marseille Region

MARSEILLE

• pop 800,000

The cosmopolitan port of Marseille (Marseilles in English; Marsihès in Provençal) is France's second city and its third largest metropolitan area, with some 1.23 million inhabitants. The city is not in the least bit quaintified for the benefit of tourists, its urban geography and atmosphere – utterly atypical of Provence, by the way – being a function of the diversity of its inhabitants, the majority of whom are immigrants (or their children or grandchildren) from Greece, Italy, Armenia, Spain, North Africa (Muslims, Jews, *pieds noirs*), West Africa and Indochina.

Marseille is notorious for organised crime and racial tensions. The extreme right polls about 25% city-wide and a member of the extremist National Front won the mayoralty in the aerospace-industry centre of Marignane, north-west of Marseille, in the 1995 municipal elections. The National Front secured a stronger footing in the Marseille region in February 1997 when Catherine Mégret, the wife of a National Front theorist, unseated the Socialist mayor in Vitrolles, a Marseille suburb.

Regardless of the city's dubious political leaning, visitors who enjoy exploring on foot will be rewarded with more sights, sounds, smells and big-city commotion than almost anywhere else in the country. There really is no other city quite like it in France; you'll either love it or hate it.

PROVENCE

History

Around 600 BC, a trading post known as Massilia was founded at what is now Marseille's old port by Greek mariners from Phocaea, a city in Asia Minor. In the 1st century BC, the city backed Pompey the Great rather than Julius Caesar, whose forces captured Massilia in 49 BC and exacted commercial revenge by confiscating the fleet and directing Roman trade elsewhere. Massilia retained its status as a free port and was, for a while, the last western centre of Greek learning, but the city soon declined and became little more than a collection of ruins. It was revived in the early 10th century by the counts of Provence.

Marseille was pillaged by the Aragonese in 1423, but the greatest calamity in its history took place in 1720, when the plague (carried by a merchant vessel from Syria) killed around 50,000 of the city's 90,000 inhabitants.

Marseille – like the rest of Provence – became part of France in the 1480s, but the city soon acquired a reputation for rebelling against the central government. The local population enthusiastically embraced the Revolution, and in 1792 some 500 volunteers were sent to defend Paris. As the troops made their way northward, they took to singing a catchy new march composed a few months earlier in Strasbourg. The song, which was soon dubbed *La Marseillaise*, subsequently became France's national anthem (see the boxed text 'La Marseillaise' in the Alsace chapter).

In the 19th century, Marseille grew prosperous from colonial trade. Commerce with North Africa grew rapidly after the French occupation of Algeria in 1830, and maritime opportunities expanded further when the Suez Canal opened in 1869. During WWII, Marseille was bombed by the Germans and Italians in 1940, and by the Allies in 1943-44.

Today, Marseille is renowned as France's most important seaport and the second largest port in Europe after Rotterdam. Following the completion of the new TGV Méditerranée rail line (see the Getting Around chapter at the front of this book), Marseille will be linked by high-speed train to Avignon, Lyon and Paris.

Orientation

The city's main thoroughfare, the wide boulevard called La Canebière, stretches eastward from the Vieux Port (old port). The train station is north of La Canebière at the northern end of Blvd d'Athènes. Just a few blocks south of La Canebière is bohemian Cours Julien, a large pedestrianised square dominated by a water garden, fountains and palm trees, and lined with some of Marseille's hippest cafés, restaurants and theatres. Not *all* the wild graffiti covering the buildings is considered street art. The city's commercial heart is around Rue Paradis, which gets more fashionable as you move south. The new ferry terminal is west of Place de la Joliette, a few minutes walk from the Nouvelle Cathédrale.

Marseille is divided into 16 arrondissements, however, most travellers will only be concerned with three or four. Places mentioned in the text have the arrondissement (1er, 2e etc) listed in parentheses after the street address.

Information

Tourist Offices The tourist office (☎ 04 91 13 89 00; fax 04 91 13 89 20; www.marseilles.com, www.visitprovence.com; metro Vieux Port), 4 La Canebière (1er), is open from 9 am to 7 pm (Sunday from 10 am to 5 pm). From mid-June to mid-September, it is open daily until 8 pm. Staff can make hotel reservations.

The tourist office annexe (☎ 04 91 50 59 18; metro Gare Saint Charles), to the left through the main train station entrance, is open from 10 am to 1 pm and 1.30 to 6 pm (closed on weekends); during July and August, it's open from 9 am to 7 pm (closed on Sunday).

Money The Banque de France on Place Estrangin Pastré (metro Estrangin Préfecture; 6e), a block west of Place de la Préfecture, is open from 8.45 am to 12.30 pm and 1.30 to 3.30 pm (closed on weekends).

There are a number of banks and exchange bureaus near the old port on La Canebière (metro Vieux Port). American Express (☎ 04 91 13 71 21; metro Vieux Port or Noailles), 39 La Canebière (1er), is open from 8 am to 6 pm (Saturday from 8 am to noon and 2 to 5 pm; closed on Sunday).

Post & Communications The main post office (metro Colbert), 1 Place de l'Hôtel des Postes (1er), is open from 8 am to 7 pm (Saturday till noon; closed on Sunday). Exchange services are available.

Near the train station, the crowded branch post office (☎ 04 91 50 89 25; metro Gare Saint Charles), 11 Rue Honnorat (3e) – which does not change money – is open from 8.30 am to 6.30 pm (Saturday until noon; closed on Sunday).

Marseille's postcodes are '130' plus the arrondissement number – postcode 13001 for addresses in the 1st arrondissement (1er) etc.

The Internet Café (☎ 04 91 42 09 37; cafe@icr.internetcafe.fr; metro Estrangin Préfecture), 25 Rue de Village (6e), charges 30/50FF for 30 minutes/one hour access. It's open from 10 am to 8 pm (until 4.30 pm on Friday and from 2.30 pm on Sunday). Definitely more 'in' is Le Rezo Cybercafé (☎ 04 91 42 70 02; rezo@wanadoo.fr; metro Notre Dame du Mont-Cours Julien), 68 Cours Julien (6e). It charges the same rates and is open from 10 am to 8 pm (midnight on Friday and Saturday).

Bookshops The northern end of Rue Paradis (1er) is lined with bookshops, including the Librairie Feuri Lamy (☎ 04 91 33 57 91; metro Vieux Port) at No 21, which has a very good selection of English-language novels. It is open from 9 am to 12.30 pm and 1.45 to 6.45 pm (closed on Sunday).

For the best range of maps, travel books and Lonely Planet guides in the whole of Provence, look no farther than the Librairie de la Bourse (☎ 04 91 33 63 06), 8 Rue Paradis (1er). Lonely Planet guides are also sold by FNAC (☎ 04 91 39 94 00), on the top floor of the Centre Bourse shopping mall (metro Vieux Port), off Cours Belsunce (1er).

MARSEILLE (MARSEILLES)

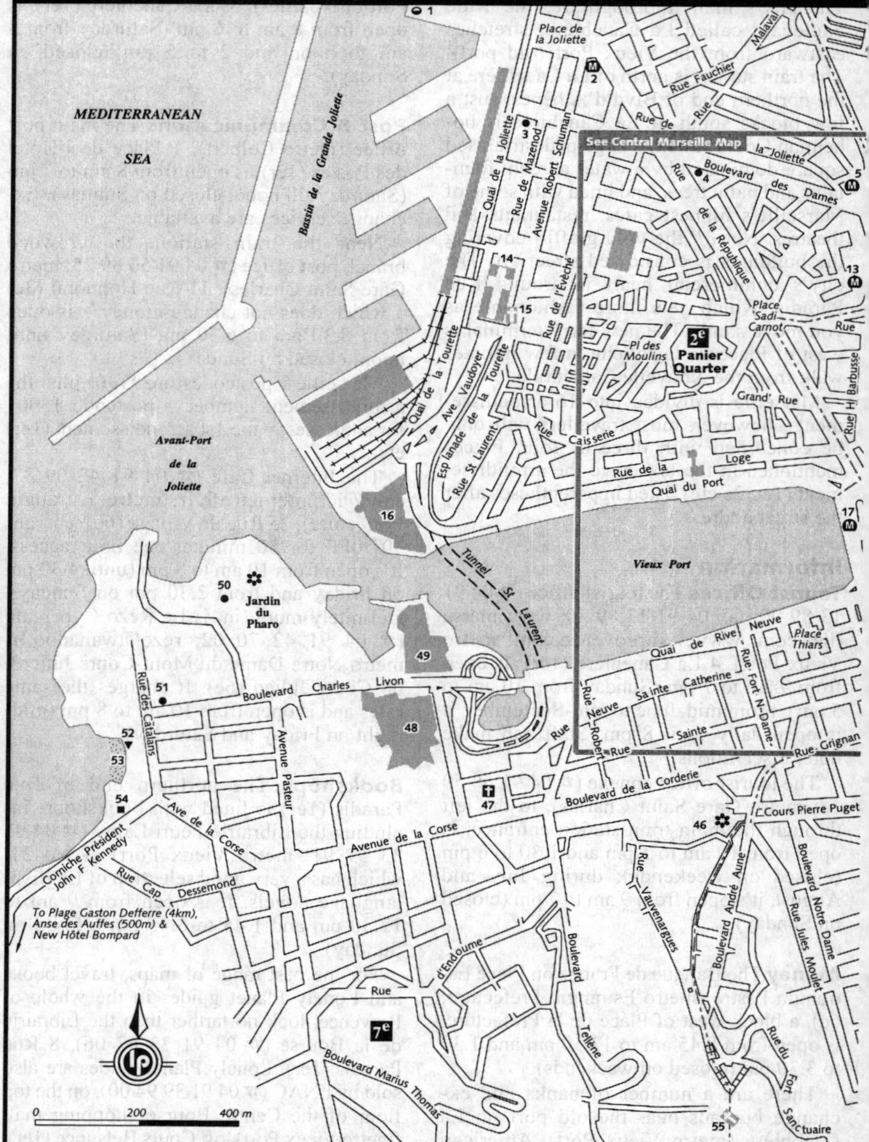

MEDITERRANEAN
SEA
Bassin de la Grande Joliette
Avant-Port de la Joliette
Place de la Joliette
Rue Fauchier
Malaval
Rue de
Rue
See Central Marseille Map
la Joliette
Boulevard des Dames
Rue de la République
Quai de la Joliette
Rue de Mazenod
Avenue Robert Schuman
Rue de l'Evêché
Place Sadi Carnot
Rue
Rue H Barbusse
Pl des Moulins
2e
Panier Quarter
Grand Rue
Quai de la Tourette
Ave Vaudoyer
Esplanade de la Tourette
Rue St Laurent
Rue Caisserie
Rue de la Loge
Quai du Port
Vieux Port
Tunnel St Laurent
Jardin du Pharo
Quai de Rive Neuve
Place Thiars
Rue Neuve Sainte Catherine
Rue Fort N-Dame
Rue Sainte
Rue Robert
Rue
Rue Grignan
Boulevard Charles Livon
Rue des Catalans
Avenue Pasteur
Boulevard de la Corderie
Cours Pierre Puget
Ave de la Corse
Avenue de la Corse
Corniche Président John F Kennedy
Rue Cap Dessemond
Rue Vauvenargues
Boulevard André Aune
Boulevard Notre Dame
Rue Jules Moulet
Rue du Fort Sanctuaire
d'Endoume
Boulevard Tellène
Rue
7e
Boulevard Marius Thomas
To Plage Gaston Defferre (4km), Anse des Auffes (500m) & New Hôtel Bompard
0
200
400 m
1
2
3
4
5
13
14
15
16
17
46
47
48
49
50
51
52
53
54
55

MARSEILLE (MARSEILLES)

PLACES TO STAY
10 Hôtel Ibis Saint Charles
12 Hôtel Gambetta
19 Cheap Hotels
20 Hôtel Sphinx
23 Hôtel de Nice
25 Hôtel Ozea; Hôtel Pied-à-Terre
34 Hôtel Manon
35 Hôtel Massilla
36 Grand Hôtel Le Préfecture
37 Le Président
38 Hôtel Salvator
54 Hôtel le Richelieu
56 Hôtel Béarn

PLACES TO EAT
26 Restaurant Antillais
27 Rétro Julien; Eden Café Rock
28 Le Caucase
29 Le Resto Provençal
32 Le Sud du Haut
52 Pizzeria des Catalans

METRO STATIONS
2 Metro Joliette
5 Metro Jules Guesde
9 Metro Gare Saint Charles & Gare Saint Charles
11 Metro Canebière-Réformés
13 Metro Colbert
17 Metro Vieux Port-Hétel de Ville
18 Metro Noailles
33 Metro Notre Dame du Mont-Cours Julien
43 Metro Estrangin Préfecture
58 Metro Castellane

ENTERTAINMENT
21 Drag Queen Café
22 New Can-Can Disco
31 La Maison Hantée

OTHER
1 Passenger Ferry Terminal
3 SNCM Ferries Office
4 Algérie Ferries
6 Bus Station
7 Taxi Stand
8 Post Office
14 Nouvelle Cathédrale
15 Ancienne Cathédrale de la Major
16 Fort Saint Jean
24 Square Léon Blum
30 Le Rezo Cybercafé
39 Préfecture de Police
40 Préfecture
41 US Consulate
42 Place Estrangin Pastré
44 Banque de France
45 Fruit & Vegetable Morning Market
46 Jardin Pierre Puget
47 Abbaye Saint Victor
48 Fort d'Entrecasteaux & Fort St Nicholas
49 Bas Fort Saint Nicolas
50 Palais du Pharo
51 Laundrette
53 Plage des Catalans
55 Basilique Notre Dame de la Garde
57 Internet Café

Laundry The Laverie Self-Service (metro Vieux Port), 5 Rue Justice Breteuil (1er), is open from 6.30 am to 8 pm. The laundrette at 15 Allées Léon Gambetta (metro Vieux Port; 1er), near Place des Capucins, is open from 8 am to 9 pm. Bizarrely, there is a laundrette inside the Total petrol station (metro Vieux Port) at 104 Blvd Charles Livon (7e).

Medical Services Hôpital de la Timone (☎ 04 91 38 60 00; metro La Timone) is at 264 Rue Saint Pierre (5e).

Emergency The Préfecture de Police (☎ 04 91 39 80 00; metro Estrangin Préfecture), Place de la Préfecture (1er), is open 24 hours.

Dangers & Annoyances Despite its fearsome reputation for crime, Marseille is no more dangerous than other French cities. As elsewhere, street crime (bag-snatching, pickpocketing) is best avoided by keeping your wits about you and your valuables hard to get at. *Never* leave anything you value in a parked car.

At night, avoid walking alone in the Belsunce area, a poor, immigrant neighbourhood south-west of the train station bounded by La Canebière, Cours Belsunce and Rue d'Aix, Rue Bernard du Bois and Blvd d'Athènes.

PROVENCE

Walking Tours

Old Port Area Marseille grew up around the old port (metro Vieux Port), where ships have docked for at least 26 centuries. The main commercial docks were transferred to the Joliette area on the coast north of here in the 1840s, but the old port is still active as a harbour for fishing craft, pleasure yachts and ferries to the Château d'If.

The harbour entrance is guarded by **Bas Fort Saint Nicolas** (on the south side) and, across the water, **Fort Saint Jean**, founded in the 13th century by the Knights Hospitaller of St John of Jerusalem.

In 1943, the neighbourhood on the north side of the Quai du Port – at the time a seedy area with a strong Résistance presence – was systematically dynamited by the Germans. It was rebuilt after the war. There are two museums near the 17th century **Hôtel de Ville**: the Musée des Docks Romains and the Musée du Vieux Marseille. The **Panier Quarter**, most of whose residents are North African immigrants, is a bit farther north. The Centre de la Vieille Charité and its museums sit at the top of the hill.

On the south side of the old port, the large and lively **Place Thiars** and **Cours Honoré d'Estienne d'Orves** pedestrian zone (metro Vieux Port; 1er), with its late-night restaurants and cafés, stretches southward from Quai de Rive Neuve.

To get from one side of the harbour entrance to the other, you could walk through the **Tunnel Saint Laurent** – which surfaces in front of the cathedral (near Fort Saint Jean) and, on the south side, just east of Fort Saint Nicolas – but the heavy traffic, narrow pavement and noxious fumes will probably keep you above ground.

The liveliest part of Marseille – always crowded with people of all ages and ethnic groups – is situated around the intersection of La Canebière and Cours Belsunce (metro Vieux Port or Noailles). The area just north of La Canebière and east of Cours Belsunce, which is known as **Belsunce** (metro Noailles), is a poor immigrant neighbourhood currently undergoing rehabilitation.

The fashionable **6th arrondissement** is worth a stroll, especially the area between La Canebière and the **Prefecture building** (metro Estrangin Préfecture). Rue Saint Ferréol, half a block east of the Musée Cantini, is a pedestrian shopping street.

Along the Coast Another fine place for a stroll is along **Corniche Président John F Kennedy** (7e), which follows the coast for 4.5km. It begins 200m west of the **Jardin du Pharo**, a park with breathtaking views of the old and new ports, and home to the **Palais du Pharo**, built by Napoleon III at 58 Blvd Charles Livon. The road then continues southward past the small but busy **Plage des Catalans** – which resembles a scene from *Baywatch* with its bronzed,

CENTRAL MARSEILLE

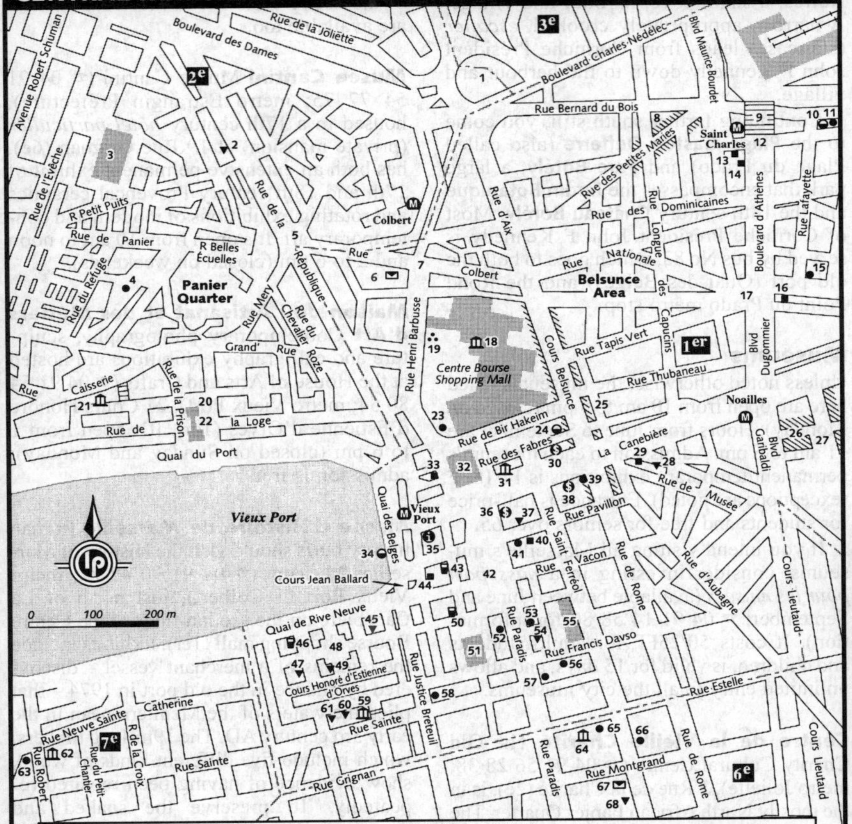

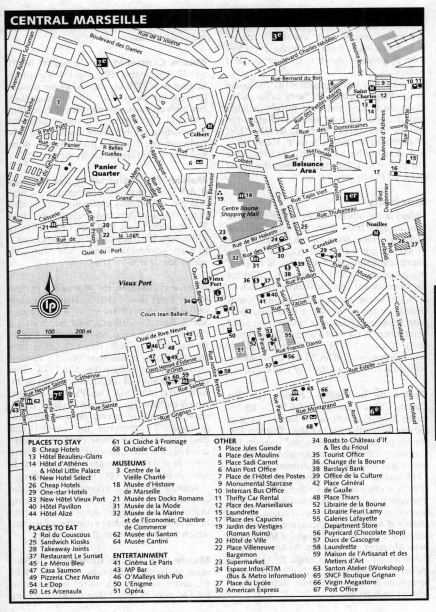

PLACES TO STAY
- 8 Cheap Hotels
- 13 Hôtel Beaulieu-Glaris
- 14 Hôtel d'Athénes & Hôtel Little Palace
- 16 New Hotel Select
- 26 Cheap Hotels
- 29 One-star Hotels
- 33 New Hôtel Vieux Port
- 40 Hôtel Pavillon
- 44 Hôtel Alizé

PLACES TO EAT
- 2 Roi du Couscous
- 25 Sandwich Kiosks
- 28 Takeaway Joints
- 37 Restaurant Le Sunset
- 45 Le Mérou Bleu
- 47 Casa Saumon
- 49 Pizzeria Chez Mario
- 54 Le Dop
- 60 Les Arcenaulx
- 61 La Cloche à Fromage
- 68 Outside Cafés

MUSEUMS
- 3 Centre de la Vieille Charité
- 18 Musée d'Histoire de Marseille
- 21 Musée des Docks Romains
- 31 Musée de la Mode
- 32 Musée de la Marine et de l'Economie; Chambre de Commerce
- 62 Musée du Santon
- 64 Musée Cantini

ENTERTAINMENT
- 41 Cinéma Le Paris
- 43 MP Bar
- 46 O'Malleys Irish Pub
- 50 L'Enigme
- 51 Opéra

OTHER
- 1 Place Jules Guesde
- 4 Place des Moulins
- 5 Place Sadi Carnot
- 6 Main Post Office
- 7 Place de l'Hôtel des Postes
- 9 Monumental Staircase
- 10 Intercars Bus Office
- 11 Thrifty Car Rental
- 12 Place des Marseillaises
- 15 Laundrette
- 17 Place des Capucins
- 19 Jardin des Vestiges (Roman Ruins)
- 20 Hôtel de Ville
- 22 Place Villeneuve Bargemon
- 23 Supermarket
- 24 Espace Infos-RTM (Bus & Metro Information)
- 27 Place du Lycée
- 30 American Express
- 34 Boats to Château d'If & Îles du Frioul
- 35 Tourist Office
- 36 Change de la Bourse
- 38 Barclays Bank
- 39 Office de la Culture
- 42 Place Général de Gaulle
- 48 Place Thiars
- 52 Librairie de la Bourse
- 53 Librairie Feuri Lamy
- 55 Galeries Lafayette Department Store
- 56 Puyricard (Chocolate Shop)
- 57 Ducs de Gascogne
- 58 Laundrette
- 59 Maison de l'Artisanat et des Metiers d'Art
- 63 Santon Atelier (Workshop)
- 65 SNCF Boutique Grignan
- 66 Virgin Megastore
- 67 Post Office

bikini-clad volleyball players – to **Anse des Auffes**, a small cove, harbour and village. A narrow, appropriately crooked, *escalier* (staircase) leads from Corniche Président John F Kennedy down to the harbour and village.

Continuing farther south still, you come to the **Plage Gaston Defferre** (also called Plage du Prado) and **Parc Borély**, a large park that encompasses the **Jardin Botanique** and the 18th century **Château Borély**. Most of Corniche Président John F Kennedy is served by bus No 83, which goes to both the old port (Quai des Belges) and the Rond Point du Prado metro stop.

Museums

Unless noted otherwise, the museums listed here are open from 10 am to 5 pm (closed on Monday). Hours from June to September are 11 am to 6 pm. Admission to each museum's permanent/temporary exhibitions is 12/18FF (exceptions are noted). Entrance is half-price for students and free for seniors over 65.

If you intend visiting all Marseille's museums, consider investing in a *passeport pour les musées* (available between June and September; ☎ 04 91 14 58 80 for information). It costs 50/25FF for adults/students and children, is valid for 15 days, and allows unlimited entry to all the city museums.

Centre de la Vieille Charité The Old Charity Cultural Centre (☎ 04 91 56 28 38; metro Joliette), 2 Rue de la Charité (2e), is in the mostly North African Panier Quarter. The superb permanent exhibits and imaginative temporary exhibitions are housed in a workhouse and hospice built between 1671 and 1745, and restored after serving as a barracks (1905), a rest home for soldiers (WWI) and low-cost housing for people who lost their homes in WWII. It is also home to the **Musée d'Archéologie** (Museum of Archaeology; ☎ 04 91 14 58 80) and the **Musée des Arts Africains, Océaniens & Amérindiens** (Museum of African, Oceanic & American Indian Art; ☎ 04 91 14 58 38). The centre is open from 9 am to noon and 1.30 to 4.45 pm (closed on weekends).

A combined entrance ticket covering all of the above costs 30FF; individual tickets are available too.

Musée Cantini Musée Cantini (☎ 04 91 54 77 75; metro Estrangin Préfecture), housed in a 17th century *hôtel particulier* (private mansion) at 19 Rue Grignan (6e), has both an extensive permanent exhibit of 17th and 18th century Provençal ceramics and rotating exhibitions of modern and contemporary art. It's open from 10 am to noon and 2 to 6 pm (closed on weekends).

Maison de l'Artisanat et des Métiers d'Art Contemporary photography, sculpture and calligraphy exhibitions are hosted at the House of Arts and Crafts (☎ 04 91 54 80 54; metro Vieux Port), 21 Cours Honoré d'Estienne d'Orves (1er). It's open from 1 to 6 pm (closed on Sunday and Monday); admission is free.

Musée d'Histoire de Marseille Roman history buffs should visit the History of Marseilles Museum (☎ 04 91 90 42 22; metro Vieux Port or Colbert), just north of La Canebière on the ground floor of the Centre Bourse shopping mall (1er). Exhibits include the remains of a merchant vessel – discovered by chance in the old port in 1974 – that plied the waters of the Mediterranean in the early 3rd century AD. The 19m-long timbers, which include five different kinds of wood, show evidence of having been repaired repeatedly. To preserve the soaked and decaying wood, the whole thing was freeze-dried right where it now sits – hidden behind glass in a dimly lit room. The museum is open from noon to 7 pm (closed Tuesday).

Roman buildings, uncovered during the construction of the Centre Bourse shopping centre, can be seen just outside the museum in the **Jardin des Vestiges** (Garden of Ruins), which fronts Rue Henri Barbusse (1er).

Musée des Docks Romains The Museum of Roman Warehouses (☎ 04 91 91 24 62; metro Vieux Port), on the north side of the old port in ugly Place de Vivaux (2e),

TONY WHEELER

NICOLA WILLIAMS

OLIVIER CIRENDINI

OLIVIER CIRENDINI

The mountainous and culturally diverse island of Corsica has many attractions. In addition to its obvious French and Italian influences in the cuisine, architecture and language, it also boasts superb hiking, diving and other activities, quaint fishing villages like Centuri Port ... and plenty of goats.

OLIVIER CIRENDINI

In the Ville Haute (Upper City) area of Bonifacio, Corsica, the views can be spectacular.

displays *in situ* part of the 1st century Roman structures discovered in 1947 during post-war reconstruction. The huge jars on display could store 800 to 2000L of wine or oil.

Musée de la Mode Glitz and glamour is the name of the game at the Fashion Museum (☎ 04 91 56 59 57; metro Vieux Port), 11 La Canebière (1er). Housed in Marseille's superb Espace Mode Méditerranée (Mediterranean Fashion Space), the museum looks at French fashion trends over the past 30 years and displays over 2000 different items of clothing and accessories. Contemporary art and photography exhibitions are held in the reception area. The museum is open from 2 to 6 pm (closed on weekends).

Musée du Santon The private collection of 18th and 19th century *santons* (fingernail-size nativity figures that are typical of Provence) collected by santon-maker Marcel Carbonnel is housed in Marseille's Santon Museum (☎ 04 91 54 26 58; metro Vieux Port), 47 Rue Neuve Sainte Catherine (7e). The museum is open from 9.30 am to 12.30 pm and 2 to 6.30 pm (closed on Monday). Admission is free, as is entrance to the adjoining *ateliers* (workshops) where you can watch the minuscule 2.5 to 15cm-tall figures being crafted. Guided tours (in French only) are usually conducted on Tuesday and Thursday at 2.30 pm. The workshops are open from 8.30 am to 1 pm and 2 to 5.30 pm (closed Friday afternoon and on weekends).

Continuing 100m farther up the hill from the museum, you come to the imposing Romanesque **Abbaye Saint Victor** (☎ 04 91 05 84 48; metro Vieux Port), built in the 12th century on the site of a 4th century martyr's tomb. Marseille's annual sacred music festival is held here.

Palais de Longchamp Colonnaded Longchamp Palace (metro Longchamp-Cinq Avenues), constructed in the 1860s, is at the eastern end of Blvd Longchamp on Blvd Philippon (4e). It was designed in part to disguise a *château d'eau* (water tower) built at the terminus of an aqueduct from the Durance River. The two wings house Marseille's oldest museum, the **Musée des Beaux-Arts** (☎ 04 91 14 59 30; 10FF), which specialises in 15th to 19th century paintings, as well as the **Musée d'Histoire Naturelle** (☎ 04 91 62 30 78).

Musée César A new museum is being built to house the collection of sculptor César Baldaccini, born in Marseille in 1921. Among other things, he designed the little statue handed to actors and actresses at the Césars, the French cinema awards. The museum will be on Place du Mazeau; ask the tourist office for details.

Basilique Notre Dame de la Garde

Not to be missed, particularly if you like great panoramas or overwrought 19th century architecture, is a hike up to the Basilique Notre Dame de la Garde (☎ 04 91 13 40 80), an enormous Romano-Byzantine basilica 1km south of the old port. It stands on a hilltop (162m) – the highest point in the city – and provides staggering views of sprawling Marseille.

The domed basilica, ornamented with all manner of coloured marble, intricate mosaics, murals and gilded objects, was erected between 1853 and 1864. The bell tower is topped by a 9.7m-tall gilded statue of the Virgin Mary on a 12m-high pedestal. The great bell inside is 2.5m tall and weighs a hefty 8324kg (the clapper alone is 387kg). Bullet marks from Marseille's Battle of Liberation (15-25 August 1944) scar the cathedral's northern façade.

The basilica and its crypt are open daily from 7 am to 7 pm in winter and 7 am to 8 pm in summer (7 am to 10 pm from mid-June to mid-August). Admission is free; dress conservatively. Bus No 60 links the old port (from Cours Jean Ballard) with the basilica. Count on 30 minutes each way by foot.

Nouvelle Cathédrale

Marseille's Romano-Byzantine cathedral (also called Basilique de Sainte Marie Majeure; ☎ 04 91 90 53 57; metro Joliette), just off Quai de la Tourette (2e), is topped with cupolas, towers and turrets of all shapes and sizes. The structure, built from 1852 to 1893 – a period not known for decorative or architectural understatement – is enormous: 140m long and 60m high. It dwarfs the nearby **Ancienne Cathédrale de la Major** (also called the Vieille Major), a mid-11th century Provençal Romanesque structure that stands on the site of what was once a temple to the goddess Diana. It can only be visited by appointment (☎ 04 91 90 53 57). The Nouvelle Cathédrale is open from 9 am to noon and 2.30 to 5.30 pm (closed on Monday).

Château d'If

Château d'If (☎ 04 91 59 02 30), the 16th century fortress-turned-prison made infamous by Alexandre Dumas' classic work of fiction, *Le Comte de Monte Cristo* (The Count of Monte Cristo), is on a three hectare island 3.5km west of the entrance to the old port. Among the people incarcerated here were all sorts of political prisoners, hundreds of Protestants (many of whom perished in the dungeons), the Revolutionary hero Mirabeau, the rebels of 1848 and the Communards of 1871.

The chateau can be visited between October and March from 9.15 am to 5.15 pm (closed on Monday) and between April and September daily from 9 am to 7 pm. Admission is 22FF.

Boats run by GACM (☎ 04 91 55 50 09; fax 04 91 55 60 23; metro Vieux Port), 1 Quai des Belges (1er), to the Château d'If leave from outside the GACM office in the old port. Hourly boats run between 9 am and noon and 2 and 5 pm (20 minutes; 50FF return). There are sailings at 6.45 am and 6.30 pm too.

Îles du Frioul

The islands of Ratonneau and Pomègues, each of which is about 2.5km long, are a few hundred metres west of the Château d'If. They were linked by a dike in the 1820s. From the 17th to 19th centuries the islands were used as a place of quarantine for people suspected of carrying plague or cholera. Today, the rather barren islands (total area about 200 hectares) shelter sea birds, rare plants and bathers, and are dotted with fortifications (used by German troops during WWII), the ruins of the old quarantine hospital, **Hôpital Caroline**, and Fort Ratonneau.

Boats to the Château d'If also serve the Îles du Frioul (50FF return; 80FF if you want to stop at Château d'If too).

Beaches

Marseille's main beach, 1km-long **Plage Gaston Defferre** (also called Plage du Prado), is about 5km south of the city centre. Take bus No 19, 72 or 83 from the Rond Point du Prado metro stop or bus No 83 (No 583 at night) from the old port (Quai des Belges) and get off at either La Plage or Plage David stops. On foot, follow Corniche Président John F Kennedy, which runs along the coast, past the short **Plage des Catalans**.

Markets

Marseille is home to a colourful array of markets, the most 'aromatic' being the daily fresh fish market, held from 8 am to 1 pm on Quai des Belges (metro Vieux Port; 1er).

Cours Julien (Metro Notre Dame du Mont-Cours Julien; 1er) hosts a variety of morning markets. Shop here for fresh flowers on Wednesday and Saturday, fruit and vegetables on Friday, antique books every second Saturday and stamps or antique books on Sunday. Stalls laden with everything from second-hand clothing to pots and pans fill nearby Place Jean Jaurès (Metro Notre Dame du Mont-Cours Julien; 6e) on Saturday from 8 am to 1 pm.

Organised Tours

The tourist office offers various guided tours, including a walking tour of the city (40FF) departing from outside the tourist office on Sunday at 2 or 2.30 pm.

In summer, GACM (☎ 04 91 55 50 09) runs boat trips from the old port to Cassis and back (120FF), which pass by the stunning Calanques, dramatic formations of coastal rock that attract unusual wildlife.

Places to Stay

Marseille has some of France's cheapest hotels – as cheap as 50FF a night, in fact! The bad news is that many are filthy dives in dodgy areas whose main business is renting out rooms by the hour. Some don't even have any showers. Those we mention here appeared, to us at least, to be relatively clean and reputable.

Places to Stay – Budget

Camping Tents usually can be set up on the grounds of the ***Auberge de Jeunesse Château de Bois Luzy*** (see Hostels) for 26FF per person.

Hostels The ***Auberge de Jeunesse de Bonneveine*** (☎ 04 91 73 21 81; fax 04 91 73 97 23), Impasse du Docteur Bonfils (8e), is about 4.5km south of the centre and charges 72FF, including breakfast. It is open year-round (closed January). Take bus No 44 from the Rond Point du Prado metro stop and get off at the Place Bonnefons stop. Alternatively, take bus No 19 from the Castellane metro stop or No 47 from the Sainte Marguerite Dromel metro stop.

Auberge de Jeunesse Château de Bois Luzy (☎/fax 04 91 49 06 18), Allées des Primevères (12e), is 4.5km east of the centre in the Montolivet neighbourhood. A bed costs 44FF; breakfast is 17FF. A hostelling card is mandatory. Take bus No 6 from near the Réformés metro stop or bus No 8 from La Canebière.

Hotels – Train Station Area The hotels around the train station are convenient if you arrive by train, but you'll find better value elsewhere. There's a cluster of small, extremely cheap hotels of less than stellar reputation along Rue des Petites Maries (1er).

The two star ***Hôtel d'Athènes*** (Central Marseille map; ☎ 04 91 90 12 93; metro Gare Saint Charles), 37-39 Blvd d'Athènes (1er), is at the foot of the grand staircase leading from the train station into town. Average but well kept singles and doubles with shower and toilet cost 190 to 270FF. Rooms in its adjoining one star annexe called the ***Hôtel Little Palace*** cost 120/140/220FF for singles/doubles/triples.

The one star ***Hôtel Beaulieu-Glaris*** (Central Marseille map; ☎ 04 91 90 70 59; fax 04 91 56 14 04; metro Gare Saint Charles), 1-3 Place des Marseillaises (1er), is down the grand staircase from the train station. It has poorly maintained singles with washbasin from 126FF and similar doubles from 180FF. Hall showers are 15FF. Rooms overlooking the street are noisy.

Hotels – North of La Canebière Except for the New Hôtel Vieux Port (see below), all the hotels listed in this section appear on the Marseille map.

Overlooking the bustling old port, the ***New Hôtel Vieux Port*** (☎ 04 91 90 51 42; fax 04 91 90 76 24; info@new-hotel.com), 3bis Rue Reine Elisabeth (1er), is a large renovated complex with modern singles/doubles for 380/420FF. On weekends and from 7 July to 1 September, the rate for all rooms drops to 335FF, making it good value. Rooms at the ***New Hotel Select*** (☎ 04 91 50 65 50; fax 04 91 50 45 56; metro Réformés), run by the same company at 4 Allées Léon Gambetta (1er), are marginally cheaper (275FF on weekends and in July/August).

Hôtel Gambetta (☎ 04 91 62 07 88; fax 04 91 64 81 54; metro Réformés), 49 Allées Léon Gambetta (1er), has singles without shower for 95FF and singles/doubles with shower from 130/160FF. Hall showers cost 15FF.

Hôtel Ozea (☎ 04 91 47 91 84; metro Réformés), 12 Rue Barbaroux (1er), is across Square Léon Blum from the eastern end of Allées Léon Gambetta. It welcomes new guests 24 hours a day (at night just ring the bell to wake up the night clerk). Clean, old-fashioned doubles without/with shower are 120/150FF. There are no hall showers.

There are well kept singles and doubles at the ***Hôtel Pied-à-Terre*** (☎ 04 91 92 00 95;

metro Réformés), 18 Rue Barbaroux (1er), costing 120/150FF without/with shower. There are no hall showers. Reception is open until 1 am.

Hotels – South of La Canebière There are many rock-bottom, very sleazy hotels along Rue Sénac de Meilhan, Rue Mazagran and Rue du Théâtre Français, and around Place du Lycée (all near metro Réformés Canebière; 1er). Slightly to the west, Rue des Feuillants (metro Noailles) has a number of one-star hotels.

A cut above its neighbours, the ***Hôtel Sphinx*** (Marseille map; ☎ 04 91 48 70 59; metro Réformés Canebière), 16 Rue Sénac de Meilhan (1er), has well kept rooms with toilet for one or two people for 70 to 120FF, and with shower for 130 to 160FF. Hall showers are 17FF.

The ***Hôtel de Nice*** (Marseille map; ☎ 04 91 48 73 07; metro Réformés Canebière), 11 Rue Sénac de Meilhan (1er), is a small step up from other hotels in this area too. Unfortunately, the ladies in the house next door welcome more customers throughout the day than a lemonade stand in the Sahara. Doubles without/with shower are 100/120FF; hall showers cost 20FF per person.

Equally good value is the ***Hôtel Pavillon*** (Central Marseille map; ☎ 04 91 33 76 90; metro Vieux Port), 27 Rue Pavillon (1er). Rooms with shower/bath start at 139/149FF and rock-bottom singles with no perks cost from 99FF.

Hotels – Prefecture Area All the hotels in this section are on the Marseille map.

Blvd Louis Salvator (6e), located in a decent neighbourhood, has a number of clean and renovated two-star hotels touting bright rooms with modern décor. At No 9 is the ***Grand Hôtel Le Préfecture*** (☎ 04 91 54 31 60; fax 04 91 54 24 95; metro Estrangin Préfecture), which has perfectly respectable rooms with shower, toilet and TV for 180FF and ones with a bath for 210FF. ***Le Président*** (☎ 04 91 48 67 29; fax 04 91 94 24 44; metro Estrangin Préfecture) at No 12 has rooms with shower, toilet and TV for 190FF and ones with a bath for 240FF.

Continuing up the hill you come to the one star ***Hôtel Massilla*** (☎ 04 91 54 79 28; metro Estrangin Préfecture), 25 Blvd Louis Salvator, which has doubles with shower and toilet for 160FF, doubles with shower only for 140FF and shower-equipped singles for 120FF. Guests have to punch in a secret code to enter this security-conscious hotel. Almost opposite at No 36 is the more upmarket ***Hôtel Manon*** (☎ 04 91 48 67 01; fax 04 91 47 23 04; metro Estrangin Préfecture), which has bright singles/doubles with all the mod-cons from 170/230FF.

Half a block east of the Préfecture building, the ***Hôtel Salvator*** (☎ 04 91 48 78 25; metro Estrangin Préfecture), 6 Blvd Louis Salvator, has doubles with high ceilings and almost antique furniture for 120FF with shower.

Hôtel Béarn (☎ 04 91 37 75 83; metro Estrangin Préfecture), 63 Rue Sylvabelle (6e), is quiet with colourfully decorated singles/doubles for 100/120FF with shower and from 180/210FF with shower and toilet. Guests can watch TV in the common room. Reception closes at 11 pm or midnight.

Places to Stay – Mid-Range & Top End

Hôtel Alizé (Central Marseille map; ☎ 04 91 33 66 97; fax 04 91 54 80 06; metro Vieux Port), 35 Quai des Belges (1er), is an elegant old pile overlooking the old port. It has pleasant singles/doubles with air-con and soundproof windows from 275/300FF.

Built into the rocks and offering fantastic sea and beach views is the idyllic, two star ***Hôtel Le Richelieu*** (Marseille map; ☎ 04 91 31 01 92), next to the Plage des Catalans at 52 Corniche Président John F Kennedy (7e). Rooms for one or two people cost 190FF with shower, 185 to 215FF with shower and toilet, and 220 to 240FF for a room with TV too. Rooms facing the street can also be quite noisy.

The ***New Hôtel Bompard*** (☎ 04 91 52 10 93; fax 04 91 31 02 14), 1 Rue des Flots Bleues, just off Corniche Président John F

Kennedy (7e), sports three stars thanks to its elegant sea views, swimming pool and extensive grounds. Singles/doubles with all the gadgets cost 400/440FF on weekdays (390/430FF on weekends and in July and August).

Places to Eat

Marseille's restaurants offer an incredible variety of cuisines but no trip to Marseille is complete without sampling bouillabaisse. Unless noted otherwise, the places listed below are on the Central Marseille map.

Restaurants – French Fish is the predominant dish in Marseille, be it soup, *huîtres* (oysters), *moules* (mussels) or other shellfish, all of which are plentiful in this port city. The length of Quai de Rive Neuve (1er) is plastered with outside cafés and touristy restaurants touting bouillabaisse on its menu boards; those along Quai du Port on the northern side of the old port are pricier. To the south, the pedestrian streets around Place Thiars are packed with terrace cafés and restaurants in the warmer months.

The upmarket ***Casa Saumon*** (☎ 04 91 54 22 89; metro Vieux Port), 22 Rue de la Paix (1er), serves salmon in a rustic but refined atmosphere. It's open from noon to 2.30 pm and 7.30 to 10.30 pm (closed on Sunday).

Le Mérou Bleu (☎ 04 91 54 23 25; metro Vieux Port), 32-36 Rue Saint Saëns (1er), is a popular restaurant with a lovely terrace. It has bouillabaisse (from 89 to 135FF), other seafood dishes (72 to 125FF), first courses (38 to 78FF), pasta etc.

Pizzeria Chez Mario (☎ 04 91 54 48 54; metro Vieux Port), 8 Rue Euthymènes (1er), is more than just a plain old pizzeria. Chez Mario has fish and grilled meats (85 to 110FF) and pasta (from 50FF) too. It's open from noon to 2.30 pm and 7.30 to 11.30 pm.

La Cloche à Fromage (metro Vieux Port), 27 Cours Honoré d'Estienne d'Orves (1er), has cheese, cheese and more cheese – 70 types in fact. Various *plateaux* (trays) are available from 93FF and there is a lunchtime *menu* for 59FF. Close by is the delightful restaurant-cum-*salon de thé* (tea room) inside the unusual ***Les Arcenaulx***, a beautifully restored complex wrapped around Cours des Arcenaulx at 27 Cours Honoré d'Estienne d'Orves (1er). Advance bookings are recommended.

There is a colourful choice of French eateries on Cours Julien (Marseille map; metro Notre Dame du Mont-Cours Julien; 6e). Particularly tasty places include ***Le Resto Provençal*** (☎ 04 91 48 85 12) at No 64, which has one of the most idyllic outside terraces in the city. It has a *menu* offering (predominantly fishy) regional fare for 110FF, a *plat du jour* for 43FF and a good-value lunchtime *menu* for 65FF. ***Le Sud du Haut*** (☎ 04 91 92 66 64) at No 80 is painted bright blue and yellow on the outside and furnished with an eclectic collection of obscure items inside. Strictly Provençal dishes are served here too.

Restaurants – North African & Asian Given its number of North African immigrants, it's not surprising that couscous reigns supreme in certain parts of Marseille. ***Roi du Couscous*** (☎ 04 91 91 45 46; metro Colbert or Joliette), 63 Rue de la République (2e), is just a short distance north of the Panier Quarter. This 'King of Couscous' dishes up the steamed semolina with meats and vegetables for 35 to 60FF, while a three course lunchtime *menu* is just 50FF, including 0.25L of wine. The King holds court from noon to 2.30 or 3 pm and 7 to 10.30 pm (closed on Monday).

For Vietnamese and Chinese fare, one of the many restaurants on, or just off, Rue de la République (metro Vieux Port) are worth a visit.

Restaurants – Other Ethnic Cours Julien (Marseille map; metro Notre Dame du Mont-Cours Julien; 6e), Marseille's trendy, more bohemian bit of town, is lined with fun and funky restaurants offering a tantalising variety of ethnic cuisines: Indian, Antillean, Pakistani, Thai, Armenian, Lebanese, Tunisian, Italian and so on.

Noteworthy options include the upstairs Caribbean ***Restaurant Antillais*** (☎ 04 91 48 71 89) at No 10. It is run by a congenial couple from the West Indies who offer a 100FF *menu* (including a *pichet* of house wine), plus a colourful range of starters (from 20FF) and main dishes (from 40FF).

The Armenian restaurant ***Le Caucase*** (☎ 04 91 48 36 30), 62 Cours Julien, serves all sorts of unpronounceable (to non-Hayaren speakers, that is) dishes that are as tasty as they are unrecognisable. The *menu* is 88FF. Le Caucase is only open in the evening.

Restaurants – Kosher The ***Restaurant Le Sunset*** (☎ 04 91 33 27 77; metro Vieux Port), 24 Rue Pavillon (1er), has kosher Israeli food and a midday 59FF *menu*. It is open from noon to 2 pm (closed Saturday).

Restaurants – By the Beach Famed for its exquisite – and expensive – bouillabaisse is ***Chez Fonfon*** (☎ 04 91 52 14 38), idyllically set overlooking the harbour of Anse des Auffes, 140 Vallon des Auffes (7e). Fish dishes are the house speciality, with *bouillabaisse du pêcheur* costing 250FF per person and langoustine 100FF per 100g. Bookings are advised.

Not quite so pricey but equally packed is the ***Pizzeria Chez Jeannot*** (☎ 04 91 5 11 28), 129 Vallon des Auffes (7e), which despite its name serves a good range of fresh salads, pastas, oysters and shellfish dishes as well as plain old pizza. Its rooftop restaurant is a great boat-watching spot.

Farther down the coast, ***Pizzeria des Catalans*** (☎ 04 91 52 37 82) has a terrace overlooking the courts of the volleyball club on Plages des Catalans. ***Bistrot Plage & Restaurant de la Corniche*** (☎ 04 91 31 80 32), midway between Marseille's Vieux Port and the main Plage Gaston Defferre at 60 Corniche Président John F Kennedy, has a wonderful terrace which juts out into the sea offering unbeatable views of the coast and the Château d'If. It has a tasty 110FF *menu*.

Cafés Cafés crowd Quai de Rive Neuve and Cours Honoré d'Estienne d'Orves (1er), a large, long, open square two blocks south of the quay. There is another cluster overlooking Place de la Préfecture, at the south end of Rue Saint Ferréol (1er).

The ***salon de thé*** inside the Virgin Megastore (☎ 04 91 55 55 00; metro Place Estrangin Préfecture), 75 Rue Saint Ferréol (1er), is open from 10 am to 8 pm (until midnight on Saturday; closed on Sunday). Equally modern and chic is ***Le Dop***, a small, clean and very green café specialising in pasta on Rue Dumarsais (just off Rue Paradis). Salads cost from 35 to 42FF.

Dressed to kill? Then head for the elitist ***Café de la Mode*** (Fashion Café; ☎ 04 91 91 21 36; metro Vieux Port) inside the Musée de la Mode, 11 La Canebière (1er), open from noon to 7 pm (closed on Monday).

Cours Julien has a colourful cluster of great cafés at its northern end, including the bright yellow ***Rétro Julien,*** serving crêpes at No 22, and ***Eden Café Rock*** (☎ 04 91 92 03 02) next door, whose walls are splashed with wild graffiti-style paintings.

Self-Catering Fresh fruit and vegetables are sold at the ***Marché des Capucins*** (metro Noailles), one block north of La Canebière on Place des Capucins (1er); and the ***fruit and vegetable market*** (metro Estrangin Préfecture), Cours Pierre Puget (6e). Both are closed on Sunday.

For a mouthwatering selection of foie gras (goose liver pâté), Provençal wines and other culinary delights, shop at ***Ducs de Gascogne*** (☎ 04 91 33 87 28), 39 Rue Paradis. ***Puyricard*** (☎ 04 91 55 67 49), 25 Rue Francis Davso, a *chocolatier*, is more suited to those with a sweet tooth.

A rich array of coffee, tea and chocolate is sold at the ***Maison Debout*** (☎ 04 91 33 00 12; metro Estrangin Préfecture), a traditional and very quaint shop at 46 Rue Francis Davso (1er).

Entertainment

Cultural event listings appear in the monthly *Vox Mag* and weekly *Taktik* and *Sortir*, all distributed for free at the tourist office, cinemas and the ticket offices mentioned below. Comprehensive listings also

PROVENCE

appear in the weekly *L'Officiel des Loisirs* (2FF at newspaper kiosks).

Tickets for most cultural events are sold at *billetteries* (ticket counters; ☎ 04 91 39 94 00; metro Vieux Port) in FNAC (☎ 04 91 39 94 00) on the top floor of the Centre Bourse shopping mall; the Virgin Megastore (☎ 04 91 55 55 00; metro Place Estrangin Préfecture), 75 Rue Saint Ferréol (1er); Arcenaulx (☎ 04 91 59 80 37; metro Vieux Port), 25 Cours Honoré d'Estienne d'Orves (1er); and the Office de la Culture (☎ 04 91 33 33 79), 42 La Canebière (1er).

Clubs & Bars For a good selection of rock, reggae, country and other live music, try ***La Maison Hantée*** (☎ 04 91 92 09 40), 10 Rue Vian (6e), a very hip street between Cours Julien and Rue des Trois Rois; or ***La Machine à Coudre*** (☎ 04 91 55 62 65), 6 Rue Jean Roque (1er).

Il Caffé, 63 Cours Julien, open until 10 pm (closed on Sunday), is a pleasant watering hole. Marseille's Irish pub, ***O'Malleys*** (metro Vieux Port), overlooks the old port on the corner of Rue de la Paix and Quai de Rive Neuve (metro Vieux Port). Popular gay bars include ***Énigme*** (☎ 04 91 33 79 20; metro Vieux Port), 22 Rue Beauvau (1er), and the ***MP Bar*** (☎ 04 91 33 64 79) at No 10 on the same street. Camper than a row of tents and full of fun is the lively ***Drag Queen Café*** (☎ 04 91 94 21 41; metro Noailles), 2 Rue Sénac de Meilhan (1er), which hosts live bands and is open until 5.30 am at weekends. Opposite is the equally hectic ***New Can-Can Disco*** (☎ 04 91 48 59 76; metro Réformés Canebière) at No 3, open until 6 am.

Getting There & Away

Air The Marseille-Provence airport (☎ 04 42 14 14 14), also known as the Marseille-Marignane aiport, is 28km north-west of the city in Marignane.

Bus The bus station (*gare des autocars*; ☎ 04 91 08 16 40; metro Gare Saint Charles), Place Victor Hugo (3e), is 150m to the right as you exit the train station. The information counter (☎ 04 91 08 16 40) is open from 7 am to 6 pm (Sunday from 9 am to noon and 2 to 6 pm). It doubles as a left-luggage office (10FF per bag a day). Tickets are sold either at company ticket counters (closed most of the time) or on the bus. Scrappy handwritten schedules are stuck up on a noticeboard outside the bus station building.

There are buses to Aix-en-Provence (26FF; 35 minutes via the autoroute/one hour via the N8), Avignon (91FF; 35 minutes; seven a day), Cannes (120FF; two hours), Carpentras (74FF), Cassis (23FF), Cavaillon (54FF), Digne-les-Bains (80FF; 2½ hours; four a day), Nice (133FF; 2¾ hours), Nice airport, Orange, Salon-de-Provence and other destinations. There is an infrequent service to Castellane (see Getting There & Away in the Gorges du Verdon section).

Eurolines (☎ 04 91 50 57 55; fax 04 91 08 32 21) has buses to Spain, Belgium, the Netherlands, Italy, Morocco, the UK and other countries. Its counter in the bus station is open from 8 am to noon and 2 to 6 pm (7.30 am to noon and 1 to 5 pm on Saturday; closed on Sunday).

Intercars (☎ 04 91 50 08 66; metro Gare Saint Charles), down the staircase from the train station at 14 Place des Marseillaises (1er), has buses to the UK, Spain, Portugal, Morocco, Poland and Slovakia. The office is open from 9 am to noon and 2 to 6 pm (until noon only Saturday; closed on Sunday).

Train Marseille's passenger train station, served by both metro lines, is called Gare Saint Charles (☎ 08 36 35 35 35 or ☎ 04 91 50 00 00; metro Gare Saint Charles). The information and ticket reservation office, one level below the tracks next to the metro entrance, is open from 9 am to 8 pm (closed on Sunday). The luggage lockers are accessible between 8 am and 10 pm (15/20/30FF for a small/medium/large locker).

In town, train tickets can be bought in advance at the SNCF Boutique Grignan, 17 Rue Grignan (1er), which is open from 9 am to 4.30 pm (closed on weekends).

All the trains to Paris' Gare de Lyon (367 to 447FF) are TGVs (4¼ hours; 10 a day) except one daytime run (7¾ hours) and at least two overnight sleepers. There are direct trains to Aix-en-Provence (38FF; 40 minutes; at least 18 a day), Arles (79FF; 40 minutes), Avignon (100FF; one hour), Barcelona via Montpellier (275FF; 8½ hours), Bayonne (376FF; 9½ hours; two a day), Bordeaux (355FF; six hours; five a day), Colmar (369FF; nine hours), Geneva (268FF; 6½ hours), Lourdes (307FF; seven hours; two a day), Lyon (223FF; 3¼ hours; 13 to 15 a day), Montpellier (122FF; 1¾ hours), Nantes (455FF; 12 hours; at least two a day), Nice (145FF; 1½ to two hours; over two dozen a day), Nîmes (114FF; 1¼ hours; 12 a day), Orange (107FF; 1½ hours; 10 a day), Pau (338FF; 6½ hours; two a day), Strasbourg (386FF; nine to 12 hours; two or more a day), Toulouse (235FF; four hours; nine a day) and many other destinations. There's even a night train to Calais (500FF; 12 hours), Lille and Brussels.

The volunteer retirees in the SOS Voyageurs office (☎ 04 91 62 12 80), across the corridor from the police post, help problem-plagued passengers.

Car Rental agencies offering the better rates include Thrifty (☎ 04 91 05 92 18; metro Gare Saint Charles), 8 Blvd Voltaire (1er), and Europcar (☎ 04 91 99 40 90; metro Gare Saint Charles), next to the train station at 7 Blvd Maurice Bourdet (1er).

Boat Marseille's new passenger ferry terminal (*gare maritime*; ☎ 04 91 56 38 63; fax 04 91 56 38 70; metro Joliette) is 250m west of Place de la Joliette (2e).

The Société Nationale Maritime Corse Méditerranée (SNCM; ☎ 08 36 67 95 00; fax 04 91 56 35 86; www.sncm.fr) links Marseille with Corsica (see Getting There & Away in the Corsica chapter), Sardinia and Tunisia. It serves the ports of Algiers, Annaba, Bejaia, Oran and Skikda in Algeria, though services are prone to disruption/cancellation because of the political troubles there. SNCM's office (metro Joliette), 61 Blvd des Dames (2e), is open from 8 am to 6 pm (Saturday from 8.30 am to noon and 2 to 5.30 pm; closed on Sunday).

Algérie Ferries (☎ 04 91 90 64 70; metro Joliette), 29 Blvd des Dames (2e), is open from 8.15 to 11.45 am and 1 to 4.45 pm (closed on weekends). Ticketing and reservations for the Tunisian and Moroccan ferry companies, Compagnie Tunisienne de Navigation (CTN) and Compagnie Marocaine de Navigation (COMANAV; departures from 4 Quai d'Alger in Sète; ☎ 04 67 46 68 00), are handled by SNCM.

For more information on ferry services to/from North Africa and Sardinia, see the Sea section in the introductory Getting There & Away chapter.

Getting Around

To/From the Airport Navette shuttle buses operated by TRPA (☎ 04 91 50 59 34 in Marseille; ☎ 04 42 14 31 27 at the airport) link Marseille-Provence airport (45FF; one hour) with Marseille train station. Buses to the airport leave from outside the train station's main entrance every 20 minutes between 5.30 am and 9.50 pm; buses from the airport depart between 6.30 am and 10.50 pm.

Bus & Metro Marseille has two fast, well maintained metro lines (Métro 1 and Métro 2), a tram line and an extensive bus network.

The metro, which began operation in 1977, trams and most buses run from about 5 am to 9 pm. From 9.25 pm to 12.30 am, metro and tram routes are covered every 15 minutes by buses M1 and M2 and Tramway 68; stops are marked with fluorescent green signs reading *métro en bus* (metro by bus). Most of the 11 Fluobus night buses (☎ 04 91 91 92 10 for information) begin their runs in front of the Espace Infos-RTM office (metro Vieux Port), 6 Rue des Fabres (1er), which distributes route maps.

Bus/metro tickets (9FF) can be used on any combination of metro, bus and tram for one hour after they've been time-stamped (no return trips). A carnet of six costs 42FF; a day pass is 25FF. Tram stops have modern blue ticket *composteurs* (cancelling machines)

PROVENCE

that should be used to time-stamp your ticket before you board.

For information on Marseille's public transport system, drop into Espace Infos-RTM (☎ 04 91 91 92 10). It is open from 8.30 am to 6 pm (9 am to 5.30 pm on Saturday). Tickets can be purchased here from as early as 6.10 am until 7.50 pm.

Taxi There's a taxi stand to the right as you exit the train station through the main entrance. Marseille Taxi (☎ 04 91 02 20 20) and Taxis France (☎ 04 91 49 91 00) dispatch taxis 24 hours a day.

AIX-EN-PROVENCE

• pop 124,000 ✉ 13100

Aix-en-Provence, which most people just call Aix (pronounced like the letter 'x'), is one of France's most graceful – and popular – cities, prompting one reader to slam it as '... a waste because it is too touristy' and another to say '... the nearest thing to traffic hell'. Either way, its harmonious fusion of majestic public squares, shaded avenues and mossy fountains, many of which have gurgled since the 18th century, cannot be disputed. Some 200 elegant hôtels particuliers date from the 17th and 18th centuries, many exhibiting the unmistakable influence of Italian baroque, and coloured that distinctive Provençal yellow.

The city is enlivened by the University of Aix-Marseille, whose forerunner was established in 1409. It counts a student body of about 30,000, many of whom are foreigners undertaking intensive French-language courses.

History

Aix was founded as a military camp under the name of Aquae Sextiae (Waters of Sextius) in 123 BC on the site of thermal springs, which are still flowing to this day. Fortunately for stuck-up Aix, the settlement became known as Aix – not Sex.

The town was established after Roman forces under the proconsul Sextius Calvinus had destroyed the Ligurian Celtic stronghold of Entremont, 3km to the north, and enslaved its inhabitants. In the 12th century, the counts of Provence made Aix their capital.

The city reached its zenith as a centre of art and learning under the enlightened King René (1409-80), a brilliant polyglot who brought painters to his court from around Europe (especially Flanders) and instituted administrative reforms for the benefit of his subjects.

Orientation

Cours Mirabeau, Aix's main boulevard, stretches from La Rotonde, a roundabout with a huge fountain (dry at the time of research) and also called Place du Général de Gaulle, eastward to Place Forbin. The oldest part of the city, Vieil Aix, is north of Cours Mirabeau; most of the streets, alleys and public squares in this part of town are closed to traffic. South of Cours Mirabeau is the Quartier Mazarin, whose regular street grid was laid out in the 17th century. The entire city centre is ringed by a series of one-way boulevards.

Aix's chic shops (designer clothes, hats, accessories etc) are clustered along pedestrian Rue Marius Reinaud, which winds it way behind the Palais de Justice on Place de Verdun.

Information

Tourist Office Aix's highly efficient – and very busy – tourist office (☎ 04 42 16 11 61; fax 04 42 16 11 62; aixtour@aix.pacwan.mn-soft.fr; www.aix-en-provence.com/aixofftour), 2 Place du Général de Gaulle, is open from 8.30 am to 8 pm (10 pm in July and August; Sunday year-round from 10 am to 1 pm and 2 to 6 pm). Hotel bookings cost 5FF, which is set against the cost of the room.

Money Near the graceful Place des Quatre Dauphins, the Banque de France, 18 Rue du Quatre Septembre, is open from 9.15 am to 12.15 pm and 1.30 to 3 pm (closed on weekends).

Commercial banks mass along Cours Mirabeau and Cours Sextius which runs north-south to the west of La Rotonde.

AIX-EN-PROVENCE

PLACES TO STAY
18 Hôtel du Globe
26 Hôtel des Arts-Le Sully
40 Hôtel du Casino
42 Hôtel de France
46 Grand Hôtel Nègre Coste
57 Hôtel Saint Christophe
64 Hôtel Cardinale
65 Hôtel Cardinale (Annexe)
69 Hôtel des Quatre Dauphins
70 Grand Hôtel Roi René

PLACES TO EAT
13 L'Arbre à Pain
20 Restaurant Nem d'Asie
21 La Fontaine
22 Le Platanos
24 University Restaurant
36 Les Bacchanales
37 L'Éclipse
41 Mondial Café
47 Les Deux Garçons
49 Gu et Fils
59 Yôji

OTHER
1 Spar Supermarket
2 ADA Car Rental
3 Cathédrale Saint Sauveur
4 Musée des Tapisseries
5 Place des Martyrs de la Résistance
6 Université d'Aix-Marseilles III (Foreign student language department)
7 Musée du Vieil Aix
8 Galerie du Festival
9 Libre Service de l'Hôtel de Ville
10 La Boulangerie traditionnelle
11 Laundrette
12 Loc 2 Roues Bike Rental
14 Hub Lot Cybercafé
15 Place de l'Hôtel de Ville
16 Hôtel de Ville
17 Cave du Felibrige (Wine shop)
19 Laundrette
23 Église de la Madeleine
25 Laundrette
27 Studio Keaton Cinema
28 Théâtre
29 Rich Art (Chocolate shop)
30 Place des Prêcheurs
31 Palais de Justice
32 Place Saint Honoré
33 Place d'Albertas
34 Change Nazareth
35 Fromagerie des Augustins
38 Council Travel
39 Laundrette
43 Change L'Agence
44 Espace 13 Art Contemporain
45 Monoprix Supermarket
48 Boulangerie
50 Bechard Fabrique de Calissons (Sweet Shop)
51 Banque Nationale de Paris
52 La Rotonde
53 Post Office
54 Bus Station
55 Car Go Car Rental
56 Citer Car Rental
58 Tourist Office
60 Le Cézanne
61 Cinéma Mazarin
62 Musée Paul Arbaud
63 Banque de France
66 Église Saint Jean de Malte
67 Musée Granet
68 Paradox Librairie Internationale
71 Pétanque Course
72 Parc Jourdan; Boulodrome Municipal
73 Train Station

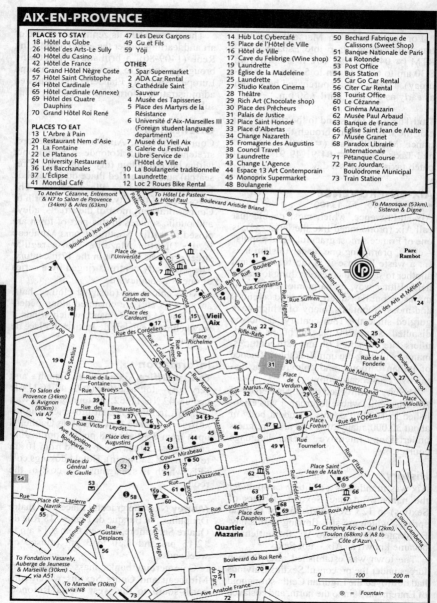

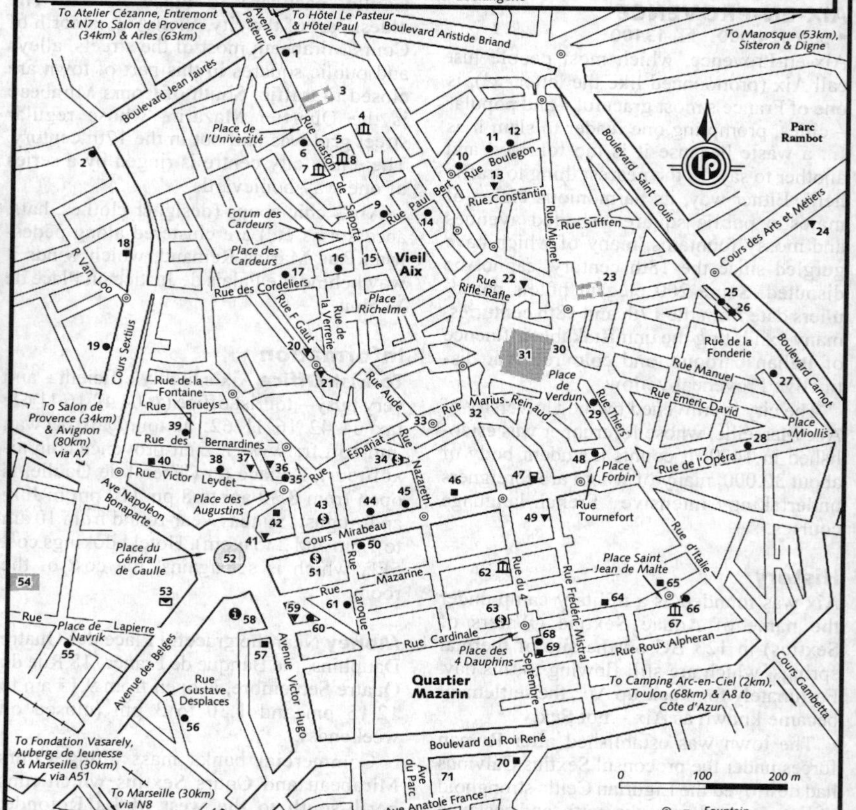

Local American Express agent, Change L'Agence (☎ 04 42 26 84 77), is at 15 Cours Mirabeau. The Change Nazareth (☎ 04 42 38 28 28) exchange bureau, 7 Rue Nazareth, is open from 9 am to 7 pm (5 pm on Sunday) in July and August.

Post & Communications The post office, on the corner of Ave des Belges and Rue Lapierre, is open from 8.30 am to 7 pm (Saturday until noon; closed on Sunday).

The hourly rate at Aix's lone cybercafé, the Hub Lot Cybercafé (☎ 04 42 21 37 31; hub1@mail.vif.fr), 15-27 Rue Paul Bert, is 50FF.

Bookshop The Paradox Librairie Internationale (☎ 04 42 26 47 99), 15 Rue du Quatre Septembre, sells English-language novels and guidebooks, including Lonely Planet guides. It buys/sells second-hand books too, and is open from 9 am to 12.30 pm and 2 to 6.30 pm (closed on Sunday).

Laundry Laundrettes abound – at 3 Rue de la Fontaine, 34 Cours Sextius, 3 Rue de la Fonderie, 15 Rue Jacques de la Roque, 6 Rue Félibre Gaut and 60 Rue Boulegon. All are open from 7 or 8 am to 8 pm.

Walking Tour

Aix's social scene centres on shaded **Cours Mirabeau**, a wide avenue laid out during the latter half of the 1600s and named after the heroic revolutionary Comte de Mirabeau. Trendy cafés spill out onto the pavements on the sunny northern side of the street, which is crowned by a leafy rooftop of plane trees. The shady southern side shelters a string of elegant Renaissance hôtels particuliers, the **Hôtel d'Espargnet** (1647) at No 38 being among the most impressive (today it houses the university's economics department). The Marquis of Entrecasteau murdered his wife in their family home, the **Hôtel d'Isoard de Vauvenarges** (1710), at No 10.

The large, cast-iron fountain at the western end of Cours Mirabeau, **Fontaine de la Rotonde**, dates from 1860. At the avenue's eastern end, the fountain at Place Forbin is decorated with a 19th century statue of King René holding a bunch of Muscat grapes, a varietal he is credited with introducing to the region. The moss-covered **Fontaine d'Eau Thermale** at the intersection of Cours Mirabeau and Rue du Quatre Septembre spouts water at a temperature of 34°C.

Other streets and squares lined with hôtels particuliers include **Rue Mazarine**, one block south of Cours Mirabeau; **Place des Quatre Dauphins**, two blocks farther south, whose fountain dates from 1667; the eastern continuation of Cours Mirabeau, **Rue de l'Opéra** (at Nos 18, 24 and 26); and the pretty, fountain-clad **Place d'Albertas** just west of Place St Honoré, where live music is sometimes performed on balmy summer evenings. Sunday strollers should not miss a jaunt to **Place de l'Hôtel de Ville**, where the city brass band entertains the crowds most Sunday mornings.

South of Aix's historic centre is the pleasing **Parc Jourdan**, a spacious green park dominated by Aix's largest fountain and home to the town's **Boulodrome Municipal**, where old men gather beneath the shade of the trees to play pétanque on sunny days. Pétanque is also the name of the game on the tree-studded court opposite the park entrance on Ave du Parc. Spectators are welcome.

Museums

The tourist office sells a Passeport Musées for 60FF that gets you into the Atelier Cézanne, the Musée Granet, the Musée des Tapisseries, the Musée d'Histoire Naturelle and the Pavillon de Vendôme.

Aix's finest is the **Musée Granet** (☎ 04 42 38 14 70), Place Saint Jean de Malte, housed in a 17th century priory of the Knights of Malta. Exhibits include Celtic statues from Entremont as well as Roman artefacts, while the museum's collection of paintings boasts 16th to 19th century Italian, Dutch and French works as well as some of Aix-born Cézanne's lesser known paintings and watercolours. The museum is open from 10 am to noon and 2 to 6 pm daily except Tuesday. Admission is 10FF for adults (free for students under 25).

An unexceptional collection of artefacts and documents pertaining to the city's history is housed in the **Musée du Vieil Aix** (☎ 04 42 21 43 55), 17 Rue Gaston de Saporta. It's open from 10 am to noon and 2 to 5 pm (closed on Monday; open from 2.30 to 6 pm between April and October). Admission is 15/10FF for adults/students. The **Musée des Tapisseries** (Tapestry Museum; ☎ 04 42 23 09 91), in the Ancien Archevêché (Former Archbishop's Palace), 28 Place des Martyrs de la Résistance, reopened in May 1998 after months of renovation. It is open from 10 am to noon and 2 to 5.45 pm (closed on Sunday); admission is 15FF. The **Musée Paul Arbaud** (☎ 04 42 38 38 95), 2a Rue du Quatre Septembre, displays books, manuscripts and a collection of Provençal faïence; it is open from 2 to 5 pm (closed on Sunday).

Art lovers should not miss the **Petit Musée Cézanne** (☎ 04 42 23 42 53; fax 04 42 21 60 30) inside the Galerie du Festival straddling Rue de Littera at 24 Rue Gaston de Saporta. Next door at No 22 is the chic **Galerie Mosca** (☎ 04 42 21 07 51), which hosts interesting and unusual art exhibitions. The **Espace 13 Art Contemporain** (☎ 04 42 93 03 67), 21bis Cours Mirabeau, also has exhibitions and is open from 10.30 am to 6 pm (closed on Sunday and Monday).

PROVENCE

Cathédrale Saint Sauveur

Aix's cathedral incorporates the architectural features of every major period from the 5th to 18th centuries. The main Gothic structure, built between 1285 and 1350, includes the Romanesque nave of a 12th century church as part of its south aisle; the chapels were added in the 14th and 15th centuries, and there is a 5th century sarcophagus in the apse. The cathedral is open from 8 am to noon and 2 to 6 pm. Mass is held here at 8 am (Saturday at 6.30 pm, Sunday at 9 and 10.30 am and 7 pm). Gregorian chants are often sung here at 4.30 pm on Sunday – an experience not to be missed.

The 15th century *Triptyque du Buisson Ardent* (Triptych of the Burning Bush) in the nave is by Nicolas Froment; it is usually only opened for groups. Near it is a triptych panel illustrating Christ's passion. The tapestries encircling the choir date from the 18th century and the fabulous gilt organ is baroque. There's a *son et lumière* (sound and light) show at 9.30 pm most nights in summer.

Cézanne Trail

Paul Cézanne (1839-1906), Aix's most celebrated son (at least after his death), did much of his painting in and around the city. If you're interested in the minutiae of his day-to-day life – where he ate, drank, played and worked – just follow the **Circuit de Cézanne**, marked by round bronze markers in the pavement that begin at the tourist office. The markers are coordinated with a trilingual guide called *In the Footsteps of Paul Cézanne*, available free from the tourist office.

Cézanne's last studio, now opened to the public as the **Atelier Paul Cézanne** (☎ 04 42 21 06 53), is atop a hill about 1.5km north of the tourist office at 9 Ave Paul Cézanne. It has been left exactly as it was when he died and though none of his works hang here, his tools do. It's open from 10 am to noon and 2 to 5 pm (2.30 to 6 pm from June to September) daily except Tuesday. Entrance is 16/10FF for adults/students. Take bus No 1 to the Cézanne stop.

Markets

Aix is the premier market town in Provence. A mass of fruit and vegetable stands are set up each morning on **Place Richelme**, just as they have been for centuries. Depending on the season, you can buy olives, goat's cheese, garlic, lavender, honey, peaches, melons and a whole host of other sun-kissed products. Another *marché d'alimentation* (grocery market) is set up on **Place des Prêcheurs** on Tuesday, Thursday and Saturday mornings.

A **flower market** is set up on Place des Prêcheurs on Sunday mornings, and on Tuesday, Thursday and Saturday mornings on Place de l'Hôtel de Ville. There's a **flea market** (*marché aux puces*) on Place de Verdun.

Language Courses

In summer Aix teems with young Americans attempting to twist their tongues round those fiddly French r's and the like. See Courses in the Facts for the Visitor chapter for details on language courses at the American University Center in Aix.

Organised Tours

Between April and October, the tourist office runs a packed schedule of guided bus tours around the region in English and in French. Ask for the free brochure entitled *Excursions en Provence* at the tourist office or study the noticeboard outside.

Special Events

Aix has a sumptuous cultural calendar. The most sought-after tickets are for the week-long Festival Provençal d'Aix et du Pays d'Aix, which brings the most refined classical music, opera and ballet each July to such city venues as the Cathédrale Saint Sauveur and the old Théâtre Municipal, 17 Rue de l'Opéra. Fortunately, practitioners of more casual musical expression – buskers – bring the festival spirit to Cours Mirabeau.

Other festivals include the two day Festival du Tambourin (Tambourine Festival) in mid-April, the Aix Jazz Festival in early July and the Fête Mistralienne marking the birthday of Provençal hero Frédéric Mistral on 13 September. For detailed information contact the Comité Officiel des Fêtes (☎ 04 42 63 06 75) or the tourist office.

Places to Stay

Despite being a student town, Aix is not cheap. In July and August, when hotel prices rise precipitously, it may be possible to stay in the university dorms – the tourist office has details or you can call the student accommodation outfit CROUS (☎ 04 42 26 47 00), Ave Jules Ferry, in the Cité des Gazelles.

The tourist office has comprehensive details on *chambres d'hôtes* and *gîtes ruraux* in and around Aix; it also has a list (updated weekly) of all types of accommodation – including farmhouses – to rent on a long-term basis.

Places to Stay – Budget

Camping The *Camping Arc-en-Ciel* (☎ 04 42 26 14 28), open from April to September, is at Pont des Trois Sautets, 2km south-east of town on the Route de Nice. It costs 90FF for a person with tent site. Take bus No 3 to Les Trois Sautets stop.

Hostel The ***Auberge de Jeunesse du Jas de Bouffan*** (☎ 04 42 20 15 99; fax 04 42 59 36 12), 3 Ave Marcel Pagnol, is almost 2km west of the centre. Bed and breakfast is 68FF and sheets cost 11FF a night. Rooms are locked between 10 am and 5 pm. Take bus No 12 from La Rotonde to the Vasarely stop.

Hotels On the city centre's eastern fringe, the laid-back and friendly ***Hôtel des Arts-Le Sully*** (☎ 04 42 38 11 77; fax 04 42 26 77 31), 69 Blvd Carnot (second entrance at 5 Rue de la Fonderie), is strategically situated a touch away from the milling crowds. It has decent singles/doubles with shower and toilet for 149/175FF and TV-equipped doubles for 195FF.

Just north of Blvd Jean Jaurès, the ***Hôtel Paul*** (☎ 04 42 23 23 89; fax 04 42 63 17 80), 10 Ave Pasteur, has rooms for one or two with shower and toilet for 197FF. The hotel is a 10 minute walk from the tourist office; alternatively take minibus No 2 from La Rotonde or the bus station.

Places to Stay – Mid-Range

One of the best and most central places in this range is the cosy ***Hôtel du Casino*** (☎ 04 42 26 06 88; fax 04 42 27 76 58), north-west of La Rotonde at 38 Rue Victor Leydet. It has one smallish single with shower for 200FF; the other rooms are doubles with toilet/shower and toilet for 260/380FF. All prices include breakfast, and the management is exceedingly friendly.

The ***Hôtel Cardinale*** (☎ 04 42 38 32 30; fax 04 42 26 39 05), 24 Rue Cardinale, is a charming place in a charming street and has large rooms with shower, toilet and a mix of modern and period furniture. Year-round prices are 220 to 300FF for a single, 260 to 320FF for a double and 350 to 420FF for a small self-catering suite in its annexe at 12 Rue Cardinale. The similar ***Hôtel de France*** (☎ 04 42 27 90 15; fax 04 42 26 11 47), 63 Rue Espariat, has serviceable singles/doubles with washbasin from 190/210FF and with shower for 300/350FF.

Just out of the pedestrianised area, the ***Hôtel du Globe*** (☎ 04 42 26 03 58; fax 04 42 26 13 68), 74 Cours Sextius, has pleasant singles with toilet from 170FF and doubles/triples with shower and toilet from 260/320FF. Garage parking costs 45FF a night. Farther north, the two star ***Hôtel Le Pasteur*** (☎ 04 42 21 11 76), 14 Ave Pasteur, has singles/doubles with washbasin and shower for 250/350FF.

Places to Stay – Top End

Aix is well endowed with three and four-star hotels, though many are on the outskirts of town. Those close to the centre include the charming and highly recommended ***Hôtel des Quatre Dauphins*** (☎ 04 42 38 16 39; fax 04 42 38 60 19), 54 Rue Roux Alpheran, which charges 290/330/490FF for singles/doubles/triples with period furnishings and shower. The ***Hôtel Saint Christophe*** (☎ 04 42 26 01 24; fax 04 42 38 53 17), sporting a pleasant breakfast terrace at 2 Ave Victor Hugo, has singles/doubles with shower for 350/390FF.

The three star ***Grand Hôtel Nègre Coste*** (☎ 04 42 27 74 22; fax 04 42 26 80 93), 33 Cours Mirabeau, has rooms overlooking what many consider to be France's most beautiful main street for around 350/700FF. Garage parking is available.

Places to Eat

Aix has lots of lovely places to dine, but the prices do little to moderate the town's upmarket gastronomic image. Fortunately, ethnic cuisines are both plentiful and of high quality. Aix's cheapest dining street is Rue Van Loo, which is lined with tiny restaurants offering Italian, Chinese, Thai and other Asian cuisines.

Aix's pastry speciality is the *calisson*, a sweet biscuit made with almond paste comprising 40% almonds and 60% fruit syrup.

Restaurants The area around Rue de la Verrerie and Rue Félibre Gaut offers various options, though Vietnamese-Chinese eateries predominate. The ***Restaurant Nem d'Asie*** (☎ 04 42 26 53 06), 22 Rue Félibre Gaut, is one of the least expensive places, with lunchtime *menus* starting at 45FF. Numerous cafés, brasseries and restaurants can be found nearby in the heart of the city on Place des Cardeurs and Place de l'Hôtel de Ville.

La Fontaine (☎ 04 42 27 53 35) is named after the pretty little fountain that plays on its outside terrace at 5 Rue Fontaine d'Argent. Strictly Provençal cuisine is cooked up here, as is the case at the upmarket ***Les Bacchanales*** (☎ 04 42 27 21 06), 10 Rue de la Couronne, which offers a delectable *menu gourmand* for 295FF and a cheaper, less rich *menu* for adults/children for 145/75FF.

For Greek food, ***Le Platanos*** (☎ 04 42 21 33 19), 13 Rue Rifle-Rafle, offers a 55FF *menu* for lunch and an 85FF *menu* for dinner. ***Yôji*** (☎ 04 42 38 84 48), 7 Ave Victor Hugo, is an upmarket Japanese place that offers succulent *menus* for 119 to 198FF in the evening and from 75FF at lunchtime.

L'Arbre à Pain (☎ 04 42 96 99 95), 12 Rue Constantin, is a vegetarian place which prides itself on its low calorie, full flavoured dishes. Its home-made ice cream, which comes in such flavours as melon, violet and lavender, is particularly enticing.

If you're on the Peter Mayle trail, head straight for ***Gu et Fils*** (☎ 04 42 26 75 12), 3 Rue Frédéric Mistral, or rather 'Chez Gu' as the author of *A Year in Provence* described the place before launching into verbal raptures about the patron's moustache and culinary skills. It serves purely Provençal dishes.

University Restaurant If it's a very cheap meal you're after, there's a ***restaurant universitaire*** (☎ 04 42 38 03 68) at 10 Cours des Arts et Métiers. You may have to buy a ticket from a student for about 15FF. It is generally open from 11.15 am to 1.15 pm and 6.30 to 7.30 pm.

Cafés No visit to Aix is complete without a quick pose behind your shades at Aix's most renowned café, ***Les Deux Garçons*** (☎ 04 42 26 00 51), on the sunny side of Cours Mirabeau at No 53. Dating from 1792, this pricey café-cum-brasserie (a former intellectual hang-out) is just one of many people-watching spots along Cours Mirabeau.

Not quite so conspicuous are the plentiful open-air cafés which sprawl across squares such as Place des Cardeurs, Forum des Cardeurs, Place de Verdun and Place de l'Hôtel de Ville. The ***Mondial Café***, overlooking La Rotunde at the western end of Cours Mirabeau, specialises in shellfish dishes and super-sized salads (from 48FF).

Self-Catering The next best thing to bread from the ***market*** is the fresh and often warm loaves sold at ***La Boulangerie Traditionnelle***, 4 Rue Boulegon. It is also one of the few *boulangeries* to bake on Sunday, along with the one on Rue Tournefort that never closes.

A splendid array of local wines are sold at the ***Cave du Felibrige***, 18 Rue des Cordeliers. For fresh, soft, hard, high or creamy cheeses of all shapes, sizes and smells head for the ***Fromagerie des Augustins***, Rue Espariat.

And what sweeter way to end that sunny summer picnic than with a couple of calissons from ***Bechard Fabrique de Calissons***, a classy *pâtisserie* and *confiseur* at 12 Cours Mirabeau. Aix's traditional almond confections weigh in here at 17FF per 100g (50FF per 100g including ornate packaging). Designer chocolates are sold at ***Rich Art***, 6 Rue Thiers, open from 9.30 am to 12.30 pm and 3 to 7 pm.

The ***Monoprix*** supermarket on Cours Mirabeau has groceries in the basement, open from 8.30 am to 8 pm (closed Sunday). For late-night supplies, try ***Libre Service de l'Hôtel de Ville***, 4 Rue Paul Bert, open until 11 pm, or ***Spar***, 4 Rue Jacques de la Roque.

Entertainment

Pick up a free copy of the monthly *Le Mois à Aix* at the tourist office to find out what's on where and when.

Cinema The people of Aix are particularly fond of what the French call *le septième art* (the seventh art), and two cinemas are dedicated solely to screening nondubbed films: ***Cinéma Mazarin*** (☎ 04 42 26 99 85), 6 Rue Laroque, and the small ***Studio Keaton*** (☎ 04 42 26 86 11), 45 Rue Manuel. The massive 12 theatre ***Le Cézanne*** (☎ 04 36 68 04 06), 3 Rue Marcel Guillaume, has both dubbed and nondubbed films.

Getting There & Away

Bus The small but busy and very run-down bus station located at the western end of Rue Lapierre is served by numerous companies. The information office (☎ 04 42 27 17 91) is open from 7.30 am to 6.30 pm (closed on Sunday). In July and August it's also open on Sunday from 9 am to 5.30 pm.

There are buses to Marseille (26FF; 35 minutes via the autoroute/one hour via the N8; every five to 10 minutes), Arles (65FF; 1¾ hours; two a day); Avignon via the autoroute (85FF; one hour; six a day) or via the national road (70FF; 1½ hours; four a day) and Toulon (82FF; one hour; four a day).

Sumian buses serve Apt, Castellane and the Gorges du Verdon via La Palud (see the Gorges du Verdon section for details).

Train Aix's tiny train station, at the southern end of Ave Victor Hugo, is open from 5.45 am to 10 pm. The information office (☎ 08 36 35 35 35) is open daily from 9 am to 7 pm. Luggage lockers (15 to 20FF) are accessible between 5 am and 10 pm. There are frequent services to Briançon (190FF; 3½ hours), Gap (151FF; two hours) and, of course, Marseille (37FF; 35 minutes; at least 18 a day), from where there are connections to just about everywhere.

Car Rental agencies include Citer (☎ 04 42 93 10 14), 32 Rue Gustave Desplaces; ADA (☎ 04 42 96 20 14), 114 Cours Sextius; and the cheaper Car Go (☎ 04 42 27 92 34), 5 Rue Lapierre, and Le Système (☎ 04 42 38 58 29), 35 Rue de la Molle.

PROVENCE

Getting Around

Bus The city's 14 bus and three minibus lines are operated by Aix en Bus (☎ 04 42 26 37 28), whose information desk inside the tourist office is open from 10 am to 6 pm (Saturday from 10 am to 12.30 pm; closed on Sunday).

La Rotonde is the main bus hub. Most services run until 8 pm. A single/carnet of 10 bus tickets costs 7/41FF. Minibus No 1 links the train and bus stations with La Rotonde and Cours Mirabeau. Minibus 2 starts at the bus station and then follows much the same route.

Taxi Taxis can usually be found outside the bus station. To order one, call Taxi Radio Aixois (☎ 04 42 27 71 11) or Taxi Mirabeau (☎ 04 42 21 61 61).

Bicycle Loc 2 Roues (☎ 04 42 21 37 40), 62 Rue Boulegon, rents city bicycles for 80FF a day (deposit 1000FF). Mountain bikes cost 60/100FF for a half-day/day (plus 1500FF deposit). The shop is open from 9 am to noon and 2 to 5 pm (3 to 7 pm in summer; closed on Sunday). Cycles Naddeo (☎ 04 42 21 06 93), 54 Ave de Lattre de Tassigny, also rents bikes.

The Vaucluse

The Vaucluse is Provence at its most picturesque. Many of the area's towns date from Roman times and still boast impressive Gallo-Roman structures. The villages, which spring to life on market days, are surrounded by some of France's most attractive countryside, brightened by the rich hues of wild herbs, lavender and vines. The Vaucluse is watched over by Mont Ventoux, at 1909m Provence's highest peak.

Geography

The Vaucluse is shaped like a fan, with Avignon, the region's capital, at the hinge. Orange, famed for its Roman theatre, and the smaller Roman town of Vaison-la-Romaine are north of Avignon and west of Mont Ventoux. Carpentras, near the centre of the Vaucluse, also dates from Roman times but is better known for its ancient Jewish community. Just to the south is Fontaine de Vaucluse, to the east of which are Gordes and Roussillon, enticing Provençal villages overlooking a fertile valley. Farther east still is Apt, one of the best bases for exploring the Lubéron range to the south.

Getting Around

If you don't have access to a car, it is possible to get from town to town by local bus, but the frequency and pace of services are very much in keeping with the relaxed tempo of Provençal life.

AVIGNON

• pop 87,000 ✉ 84000

Avignon will enter the next millennium as the European Capital of Culture. It acquired its ramparts and its reputation as a city of art and culture during the 14th century, when Pope Clement V and his court fled political turmoil in Rome and established themselves near Avignon. From 1309 to 1377, the Holy See was based in the city under seven French-born popes, and huge sums of money were invested in building and decorating the papal palace and other important church edifices. Under the popes' tolerant rule, the city became a place of asylum for Jews and political dissidents.

Opponents of the move to Avignon – many of them Italians, like the celebrated poet Petrarch, who lived in Fontaine de Vaucluse at the time – called Avignon 'the second Babylonian captivity' and charged that the city had become a den of criminals and brothel-goers, and was unfit for papal habitation. Pope Gregory XI left Avignon in 1376, but his death two years later led to the Great Schism (1378-1417), during which rival popes – up to three at one time, each with his own College of Cardinals – resided at Rome and Avignon and spent most of their energies denouncing and excommunicating one another. They also expended great efforts on gaining control of church revenues, among whose sources was the sale of indulgences.

Even after the schism was settled and a pope – Martin V – acceptable to all factions established himself in Rome, Avignon remained under papal rule and continued to serve as an important cultural centre. The city and the nearby Comtat Venaissin (now the department of Vaucluse) were ruled by papal legates until 1791, when they were annexed to France.

Today, Avignon continues its traditional role as a patron of the arts, most notably through its annual performing arts festival. Avignon's other attractions include its Pont d'Avignon (Avignon bridge), a bustling (and also very touristy) walled city and a number of interesting museums, including several across the Rhône River in the town of Villeneuve-lès-Avignon.

Orientation

The main avenue within the walled city (*intra-muros*) runs northward from the train station to Place de l'Horloge; it's called Cours Jean Jaurès south of the tourist office and Rue de la République north of it.

Place de l'Horloge is 300m south of Place du Palais, which abuts the Palais des Papes. The city gate nearest the train station is Porte de la République, while the city gate next to Pont Édouard Daladier, which leads to Villeneuve-lès-Avignon, is Porte de l'Oulle. The rehabilitated Quartier des Teinturiers (old dyers' quarter), centred around Rue des Teinturiers, south-east of Place Pie, is Avignon's bohemian – and increasingly trendy – part of town.

Villeneuve-lès-Avignon (occasionally it's written Villeneuve-lez-Avignon), the suburb on the right (north-west) bank of the Rhône, is reached by crossing the two branches of the river and Île de la Barthelasse, the island that divides them. Villeneuve-lès-Avignon's main street is Rue de la République.

Information

Tourist Offices The tourist office (☎ 04 90 82 65 11; fax 04 90 82 95 03; information@ot-avignon.fr; www.ot-avignon.fr), 41 Cours Jean Jaurès, is 300m north of the train station. It's open from 9 am to 1 pm and 2 to 6 pm (5 pm on Saturday; closed on Sunday). In July and August it is open weekdays from 10 am to 7 pm. From mid-April to mid-August it keeps Sunday hours as well, from 10 am to 5 pm.

Between 1 April and 31 October, two-hour city tours (in English and French; 50/30FF for adults/children) depart from the tourist office on Tuesday and Thursday at 10 am.

At the Pont Saint Bénézet, Le Châtelet tourist office annexe (☎ 04 90 85 60 16), which doubles as a ticket office for the bridge and museum, is open from 9 am to 1 pm and 2 to 7 pm (closed on Monday).

In Villeneuve-lès-Avignon, the tourist office (☎ 04 90 25 61 33; fax 04 90 25 91 55), 1 Place Charles David (also called Place du Marché; foot access from the carpark), is open from 8.45 am to 12.30 pm and 2 to 6 pm (until 6.30 pm in July and August; closed on Sunday year-round). In July and August it runs two-hour tours around the old city on Tuesday and Friday at 4 pm (25FF; in French only).

Money The Banque de France, at the northern end of Place de l'Horloge, is open from 8.35 am to 12.05 pm and 1.35 to 3.35 pm (closed on weekends).

There are 24-hour currency exchange machines at the Lyonnais de Banque, 13 Rue de la République, and at the Caixa Bank, 67 Rue Joseph Vernet (opposite the Musée Requien).

The Change Chaix Conseil (☎ 04 90 27 27 89), 43 Cours Jean Jaurès, is open April to October from 10 am to 1 pm and 3 to 7 pm. In July and August the hours are 8.30 am to 8.30 pm.

Post & Communications The main post office, on Cours Président Kennedy, is open from 8 am to 7 pm (Saturday until noon; closed on Sunday). Currency exchange stops at 5 pm on weekdays and 11 am on Saturday. The branch on the corner of Rue Carnot and Rue Général Leclerc is open from 8.30 am to noon and 1.30 to 6.30 pm (Saturday until noon; closed on Sunday).

Cyberdrome (☎ 04 90 16 05 15; fax 04

AVIGNON

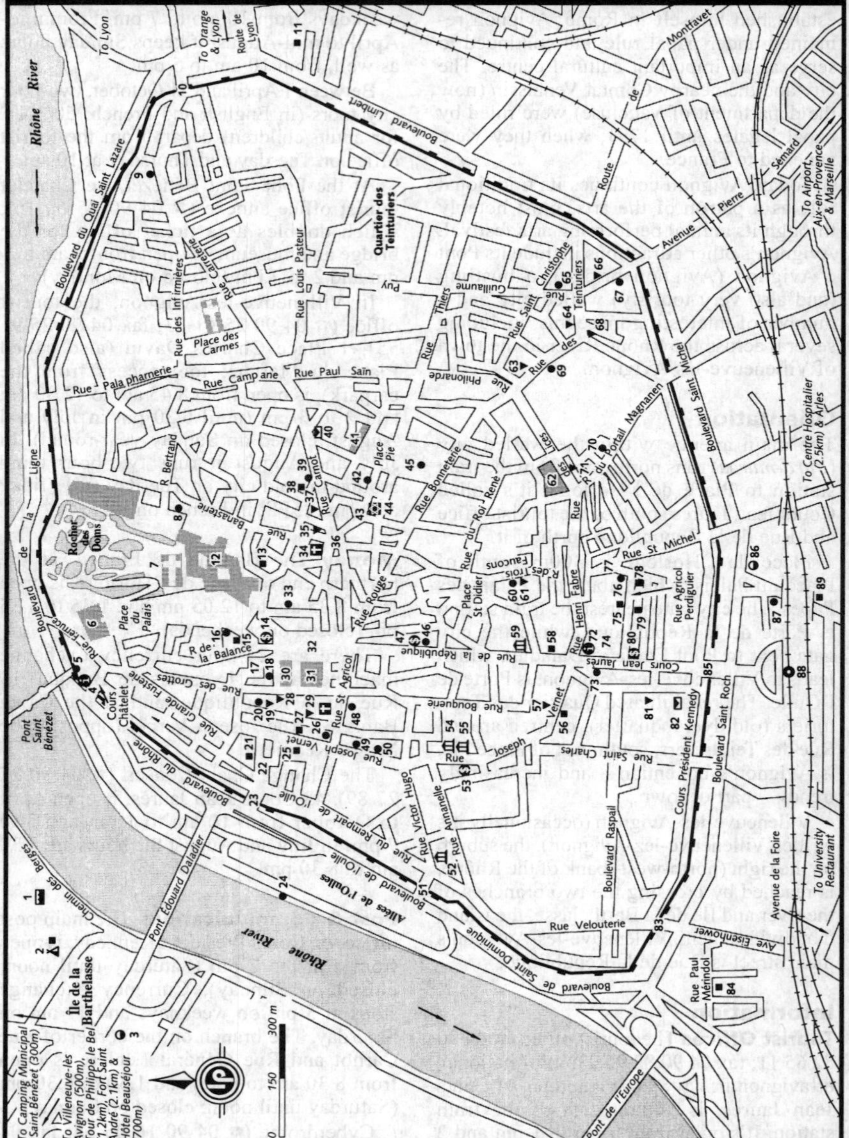
To Lyon
To Orange & Lyon
Route de Lyon
Rhône River
Boulevard du Quai Saint Lazare
Boulevard Limbert
Route de Montfavet
Quartier des Teinturiers
Rue des Infirmières
Rue Carreterie
Rue Louis Pasteur
Place des Carmes
Rue Guillaume Puy
Rue Thiers
Rue Saint Christophe
Rue des Teinturiers
Avenue Pierre Sémard
To Airport, Aix-en-Provence & Marseille
Rue Palapharnerie
Rue Campane
Rue Paul Saïn
Rue Philonarde
Boulevard de la Ligne
R Bertrand
Rue Banasterie
Rue Carnot
Place Pie
Rue Bonneterie
Rue des Lices
Rue du Portail Magnanen
Boulevard Saint Michel
To Centre Hospitalier (2.5km) & Arles
Rocher des Doms
Place du Palais
R de la Balance
Rue du Roi René
Rue des Trois Faucons
Rue St Michel
Place St Didier
Rue Henri Fabre
Rue Agricol Perdiguier
Rue Ferruce
Pont Saint Bénézet
Cours Châtelet
Rue Grande Fusterie
Rue des Grottes
Rue Rouge
Rue St Agricol
Rue de la République
Cours Jean Jaurès
Rue Bouquerie
Rue Vernet
Rue Joseph Vernet
Rue Saint Charles
Cours Président Kennedy
Boulevard Saint Roch
Boulevard du Rhône
Rue de l'Oulle
Rue Victor Hugo
Rue Annanelle
Boulevard Raspail
Avenue de la Foire
Pont Edouard Daladier
Rue du Rempart de l'Oulle
Boulevard de l'Oulle
Allées de l'Oulles
Rue Velouterie
Ave Eisenhower
To University Restaurant
Chemin des Berges
Rhône River
Boulevard Saint Dominique
Boulevard de Saint Dominique
Rue Paul Mérindol
Île de la Barthelasse
To Camping Municipal Saint Bénézet (300m)
To Villeneuve-lès-Avignon (500m), Tour de Philippe le Bel (1.2km), Fort Saint André (2.1km) & Hôtel Beauséjour (700m)
Pont de l'Europe
0 150 300 m

90 16 05 14; cyberdrome@cyberdrome.fr) charges 25FF for 30 minutes online access and is open from 7 am to 1 am.

France's only cyber restaurant, Le Site (☎ 04 90 27 12 00; lesite@web-office.fr), 25 Rue Carnot, charges 25FF for 30 minutes of surfing and has *menus* for 79FF. It is open from noon to midnight (Saturday from 4 pm; closed on Sunday). From Rue Carnot, walk under the arch between the Red Zone Bar and the Piano Bar.

Bookshops The Maison de la Presse (☎ 04 90 86 57 42), opposite the tourist office at 34 Cours Jean Jaurès, has a good selection of maps and French-language regional guides. Alternatively, try the Shakespeare (☎ 04 90 27 38 50), 155 Rue Carreterie, an English bookshop and tea room open from 9.30 am to 12.30 pm and 2 to 6.30 pm (closed on Sunday and Monday).

Laundry The Lavmatic, 27 Rue du Portail Magnanen, is open from 7 am to 7.30 pm. Laverie La Fontaine, 66 Place des Corps Saints, is open from 7 am to 8 pm.

Medical Services The Centre Hospitalier (☎ 04 90 80 12 90), 2.5km south of the train station on Rue Raoul Follereau, is at the southern terminus of bus line Nos 1 and 3 (marked on bus maps as 'Hôpital Sud').

AVIGNON

PLACES TO STAY

- 2 Camping Bagatelle & Auberge Bagatelle
- 11 Avignon Squash Club (Hostel)
- 13 Hôtel de la Mirande
- 15 Hôtel du Palais des Papes
- 21 Hôtel L'Europe
- 25 Hôtel Mignon
- 27 Hôtel Le Provençal
- 38 Hôtel Médiéval
- 56 Hôtel Innova
- 58 Hôtel Central
- 75 Hôtel du Parc
- 78 Hôtel Colbert
- 79 Hôtel Splendid
- 84 Hôtel Saint Roch
- 89 Hôtel Monclar

PLACES TO EAT

- 19 Simple Simon Tea Lunch
- 28 Natural Café & La Fourchette
- 29 Le Brantes
- 35 Le Belgocargo
- 37 Restaurant Song Long
- 57 La Cuisine de Reine
- 61 Le Caveau du Théâtre & Les Caulisses
- 63 Le Bistro Russe
- 64 Sindabad
- 66 Restaurant Au 19éme
- 68 Woolloomooloo
- 71 Le Petit Comptoir
- 81 Restaurant Le Saint Louis

MUSEUMS

- 6 Musée du Petit Palais
- 52 Musée Louis Vouland
- 54 Musée Calvet
- 55 Musée Requien
- 59 Musée Lapidaire

OTHER

- 1 Swimming Pool
- 3 La Barthelasse Bus Stop
- 4 Le Châtelet Tourist Office; Musée en Images
- 5 Tour de Châtelet & Entrance to Pont Saint Bénézet
- 7 Cathédrale Notre Dame des Doms
- 8 La Manutention (Cinéma Utopia)
- 9 Shakespeare (Bookshop)
- 10 Porte Saint Lazare
- 12 Palais des Papes
- 14 Banque de France
- 16 Conservatoire de Musique
- 17 Place Campana
- 18 Maison des Pays de Vaucluse
- 20 Le Val d'Arômes (Luxury Food Shop)
- 22 Place Crillon
- 23 Porte de l'Oulle
- 24 Mireio Embarcadère (Boat Excursions)
- 26 Casino Grocery
- 30 Opéra d'Avignon
- 31 Hôtel de Ville
- 32 Place de l'Horloge
- 33 Bureau du Festival
- 34 Église Saint Pierre
- 36 Place Carnot
- 39 Le Site (Cybercafé)
- 40 Post Office
- 41 Palais de Justice
- 42 TCRA Bus Information Kiosk
- 43 Place Jérusalem
- 44 Synagogue
- 45 Les Halles
- 46 FNAC
- 47 Lyonnais de Banque
- 48 Boulangerie Pâtisserie
- 49 Puyricard (Chocolate Shop)
- 50 Université d'Avignon
- 51 Porte Sainte Dominique
- 53 Caixa Bank
- 60 Maison des Vins
- 62 École des Beaux-Arts
- 65 Cyberdrome (Cybercafé)
- 67 Cycles Peugeot
- 69 Chapelle des Pénitents Gris
- 70 Laundrette
- 72 Tourist Office
- 73 Maison de la Presse
- 74 Square Agricol Perdiguier
- 76 Laundrette
- 77 Place des Corps Saints
- 80 Change Chaix Conseil
- 82 Main Post Office; Bus No 10 (to Villeneuve-lès-Avignon)
- 83 Porte Saint Roch
- 85 Porte de la République; Local Bus Information Office
- 86 Bus Station
- 87 Car Rental Agencies
- 88 Train Station

Pont Saint Bénézet (Le Pont d'Avignon)

St Bénézet's Bridge (☎ 04 90 85 60 16) was built between 1177 and 1185 to link Avignon with the settlement across the Rhône that later became Villeneuve-lès-Avignon. By tradition, the construction of the bridge is said to have begun when Bénézet (Benedict the Bridge Builder), a pious young lad from Savoy, was told in three visions to get the Rhône spanned at any cost. Yes, this is also the **Pont d'Avignon** mentioned in the French nursery rhyme. In actual fact, people did not dance *sur le pont d'Avignon* (on the bridge of Avignon) but *sous* (under) it in between the arches.

The 900m-long wooden structure was repaired and rebuilt several times before all but four of its 22 spans – over both channels of the Rhône and the island in the middle, Île de la Barthelasse – were washed away once and for all in the mid-1600s. To celebrate the dawn of the new millennium and to honour Avignon's crowning as the European Capital of Culture in 2000, the lost 18 arches will be rebuilt – enabling visitors to walk across to Île de la Barthelasse. Incredibly, the authorities plan to pull down the entire reconstructed structure in 2001.

Entry to the bridge via Cours Châtelet – on, under, dancing, whatever – is 15/7FF for adults/students and seniors. It's open from 9 am to 1 pm and 2 to 5 pm (closed on Monday). Between April and September it is open from 9 am to 6.30 pm. Many people find a distant view of the bridge from the Rocher des Doms or Pont Édouard Daladier much more interesting. And they are, of course, free.

The **Musée en Images** (☎ 04 90 82 56 96), which is on Cours Châtelet, traces the history of Avignon and the bridge in a very tacky multimedia *spectacle* (show). The museum is open daily, except Monday and throughout January, from 9 am to 7 pm (5 pm from October to March). Entry costs 26FF for adults and 21FF for students and seniors.

Walled City

Avignon's most interesting bits are within the roughly oval walled city, which is surrounded by almost 4.5km of ramparts built between 1359 and 1370. The ramparts were restored during the 19th century, but the original moats were not, leaving the crenellated fortifications looking purposeless and certainly less imposing than they once did. Even in the 14th century this defence system was hardly state-of-the-art: the towers were left open on the side facing the city, and machicolations (openings in the parapets for dropping things like boiling oil or for shooting arrows at attackers) are lacking in many sections.

Palais des Papes The huge Gothic Palace of the Popes (☎ 04 90 27 50 74; rmg@palais-des-papes.com; www.palais-des-papes.com), Place du Palais, was built during the 14th century as a fortified palace for the pontifical court. It is mainly of interest because of the dramatic events that took place here, since the undecorated stone halls, though impressive, are nearly empty except for occasional art exhibits. The best view of the Palais des Papes complex is from across the river in Villeneuve-lès-Avignon. The fabulous Cours d'Honneur – the palace's main courtyard – has played host to the Avignon theatre festival since 1947.

The Palais des Papes is open from 9.30 am to 5.45 pm (9 am to 7 pm from April to November; until 8 pm from 4 August to 30 September). Visiting the palace's interior costs 40/32FF for adults/students and seniors (including hire of a very user-friendly audioguide in English). One-hour guided tours are available in English from April to October, usually at 11.30 am and 2.30 and 4.45 pm. Occasionally, special exhibits may raise the entrance fees by 9FF or more.

Musée du Petit Palais This museum (☎ 04 90 86 44 58), which served as a bishop's and archbishop's palace during the 14th and 15th centuries, is at the far northern end of Place du Palais. It houses an outstanding collection of 13th to 16th century

Italian religious paintings. It is open from 9.30 am to noon and 2 to 6 pm (closed Tuesday). In July and August daily hours are 10 am to 6 pm. Tickets cost 30/15FF for adults/students and seniors.

Cathédrale Notre Dame des Doms This unexciting Romanesque cathedral, on the north side of the Palais des Papes, was built in the mid-12th century but repeatedly redecorated. Like all of Avignon's other churches, the cathedral was sacked during the Revolution.

Rocher des Doms Just up the hill from the cathedral is the Rocher des Doms, a delightful bluff-top park that affords great views of the Rhône, Pont Saint Bénézet, Villeneuve-lès-Avignon, the Alpilles etc. A semicircular viewpoint indicator tells you what you're looking at.

Conservatoire de Musique Avignon's Conservatory of Music, across Place du Palais from the Palais des Papes, occupies the former Hôtel des Monnaies, which was built in 1619 to house a papal legation led by Cardinal Scipione Borghese. His enormous coat of arms decorates the ornate, baroque façade.

Musée Calvet The Musée Calvet (☎ 04 90 86 33 84), 65 Rue Joseph Vernet, housed in the elegant Hôtel de Villeneuve-Martignan (1741-54), has a large archaeological collection of artefacts from prehistory to Roman times and paintings from the 16th to 20th centuries. Admission is 30/15FF for adults/students and seniors. It is open from 10 am to 1 pm and 2 to 6 pm (closed Tuesday; 10 am to 7 pm from June to September).

Musée Requien This museum (☎ 04 90 82 43 51), next door to the Musée Calvet at 67 Rue Joseph Vernet, houses the city's natural history museum. It's open from 9 am to noon and 2 to 6 pm (closed on Sunday and Monday). Admission is free.

Musée Lapidaire The Statuary Museum (☎ 04 90 85 75 38), 27 Rue de la République, housed in the baroque, 17th century former chapel of a Jesuit college, is an annexe of the Musée Calvet. Displays include stone carvings from the Gallo-Roman, Romanesque and Gothic periods. It is open from 10 am to noon and 2 to 6 pm (closed Tuesday). Entrance is 10FF.

Musée Louis Vouland This small but interesting museum (☎ 04 90 86 03 79), 17 Rue Victor Hugo, displays a fine collection of 17th and 18th century decorative arts, including faïence and some superb French furniture. It is open from 2 to 6 pm (closed on Sunday and Monday). From June to September, it's also open from 10 am to noon. Admission is 20/10FF for adults/students and seniors.

Synagogue The synagogue (☎ 04 90 85 21 24), 2 Place Jérusalem, was first built in 1221. A 13th century oven used to bake unleavened bread for Passover can still be seen, but the rest of the present round and domed neoclassical structure dates from 1846. It can be visited from 10 am to noon and 3 to 5 pm (closed Friday afternoon and on weekends). Visitors should be modestly dressed, and men need to cover their heads.

Wine-Tasting The Maison des Vins, run by the Comité Interprofessionnel des Vins d'AOC Côtes du Rhône (☎ 04 90 27 24 00), is in the Hôtel du Marquis de Rochegude, 6 Rue des Trois Faucons. Head here for information on where to taste Côte du Rhône wines, including the Avignon popes' favourite tipple, Châteauneuf-du-Pape, which happens to boast the highest alcoholic content of all French wines (up to 15%).

Villeneuve-lès-Avignon

Villeneuve-lès-Avignon (population 11,500; postcode 30400), which is across the Rhône from Avignon (and in a different department), was founded in the late 13th century. It became known as the City of Cardinals because many primates affiliated with the papal court built large residences (known as *livrées*) in the town, despite the fact that it was in territory ruled by the French crown and not the pope.

The Passeport pour l'Art (45FF) gets you into the Chartreuse du Val de Bénédiction, Fort Saint André, Musée Pierre de Luxembourg, the Collégiale Notre Dame, Cloître and Tour de Philippe le Bel. The last three are all open from 10 am to 12.30 pm and 3 to 7 pm (10 am to noon and 2 to 5.30 pm from April to September; closed on Monday and in February).

Chartreuse du Val de Bénédiction The Val de Bénédiction Charterhouse (☎ 04 90 25 05 46 or ☎ 04 90 15 24 24), 60 Rue de la République, was founded in 1356 by Pope Innocent VI and, with its 40 cells and three cloisters, was once the largest and most important Carthusian monastery in France. Today it is home to the Centre National des Écritures du Spectacle (National Centre of Playwrights), which offers an inspiring shelter to aspiring playwrights resident in the old monks' quarters.

The largest cloister, **Cloître Saint Jean**, gives you an idea of the architecture and layout of the charterhouse. In the 14th century church, the very delicately carved **mausoleum of Pope Innocent VI** (died 1362) is an extraordinary example of Gothic artisanship. It was removed during the Revolution and only returned in 1963.

The centre is open from 9.30 am to 5.30 pm (9 am to 6.30 pm from April to September). Entrance is 32/21FF for adults/students and seniors.

Musée Pierre de Luxembourg This museum (☎ 04 90 27 49 66), inside the Hôtel Pierre at 3 Rue de la République, has a fine collection of religious art taken from the Chartreuse during the Revolution, including paintings from the 15th to 17th centuries. The museum's most exceptional objects include

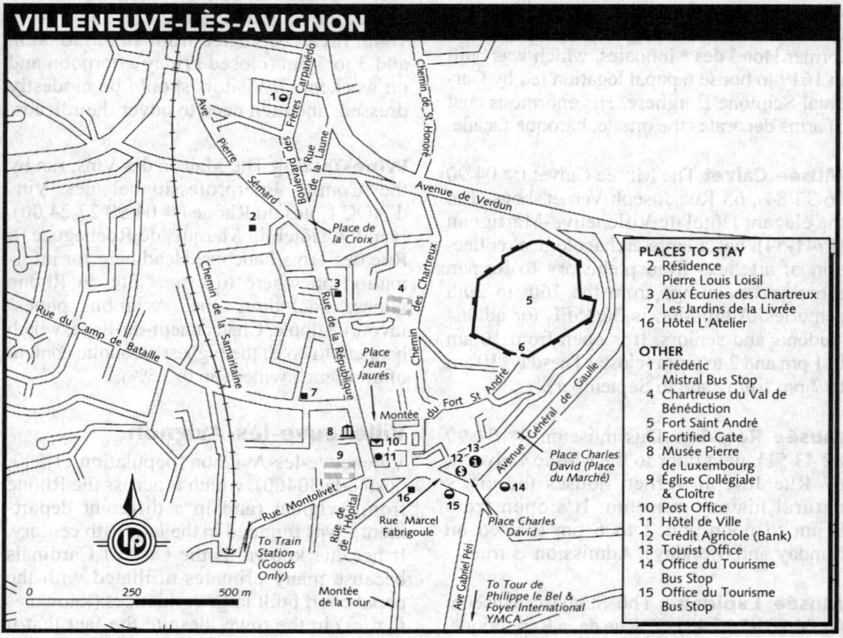

the *Vierge en Ivoire* (Ivory Virgin), a superb 14th century icon carved from an elephant's tusk; the nearby 15th century *Vierge Double Face*, a marble Virgin whose two faces point in opposite directions; and *Couronnement de la Vierge* (Coronation of the Virgin), painted by Enguerrand Quarton in 1453, which is displayed on the 1st floor. Entrance is 20/12FF and includes a visit to the cloister of the Collégiale Notre Dame et Cloître around the corner.

Collégiale Notre Dame et Cloître This former collegiate (and now parish) church on Rue Montolivet, just off Rue de la République, was established in 1333. To visit the rather empty, late 14th century **cloître**, part of which has been privately owned since church property was sold off during the Revolution, ring the bell of the sacristy, which is to the left of the 18th century altar. A visit to the cloister costs 7/5FF; if you have a ticket to the Musée Pierre de Luxembourg, you enter for free.

Tour de Philippe le Bel This 32m-high defensive tower (☎ 04 90 27 49 68) was built in the 14th century at what was, at the time, the western end of Pont Saint Bénézet. The platform on top, reached after a dizzying climb up a 172 step spiral staircase, affords a magnificent panorama of Avignon's walled city, the river and the surrounding countryside. Entrance is 10/6FF.

Fort Saint André This 14th century fortress (☎ 04 90 25 45 35), built on Mont Andaon by the king of France to keep an eye on events across the river in the papal domains, also affords lovely views. The **fortified gate** is a fine example of medieval military architecture. Admission is 25/15FF for adults/students and seniors. Opening hours are from 10 am to noon and 2 to 5 pm (10 am to 12.30 pm and 2 to 6 pm from April to September).

Boat Excursions

Les Grands Bateaux de Provence (☎ 04 90 85 62 25; fax 04 90 85 61 14), based at the Mireio Embarcadère on Allées de l'Oulle, opposite the Porte de l'Oulle, runs excursions from Avignon down the Rhône to Arles, vineyard towns and even the Camargue (four to seven hours; 160 to 345FF including a meal).

Bateau Bus (same ☎ and address) makes less ambitious trips seven times a day in July and August to Villeneuve-lès-Avignon (near the Tour de Philippe le Bel) and back (1½ hours; 35/18FF for adults/children).

Organised Tours

Autocars Lieutard (☎ 04 90 86 36 75; fax 04 90 85 57 07; cars.lieutard@wanadoo.fr), based at the bus station, offers a variety of thematic bus tours between April and October, including to Nîmes and the Pont du Gard (4½ hours; 100FF), Vaison-la-Romaine and Orange (4½ hours; 100FF), the Lubéron (4½ hours; 100FF) and to the wine cellars at Châteauneuf-du-Pape (three hours; 100FF).

Special Events

The world-famous Festival d'Avignon, founded in the late 1940s, is held every year from early July to early August. It attracts many hundreds of performance artists (actors, dancers, musicians etc) who put on some 300 *spectacles* of all sorts each day in every imaginable venue. There are, in fact, two simultaneous events: the prestigious, expensive and government-subsidised official festival, and the fringe one called Festival Off. Tickets for official festival performances in the Palais des Papes' Cours d'Honneur cost 130 to 190FF. A Carte Public Adhérent (65FF) gets you a 30% discount on all Festival Off performances.

Information on the official festival can be obtained by contacting the Bureau du Festival (☎ 04 90 27 66 50 or ☎ 04 90 14 14 26; fax 04 90 27 66 83; www.festival-avignon.com), 8bis Rue de Mons, F-84000 Avignon. Tickets can be reserved from mid-June onwards.

Places to Stay

During the festival, it's practically impossible to find a hotel room unless you've reserved months in advance. The tourist office has information on special dormitory accommodation. Hotel rooms are readily available in August however, when places in the rest of the Vaucluse department are at a premium. Hotel and gîtes reservations anywhere in Vaucluse can be made through the Maison des Pays de Vaucluse (☎ 04 90 82 05 81; fax 04 90 86 54 77), Place Campana.

Places to Stay – Budget

Camping The ***Camping Bagatelle*** (☎ 04 90 85 78 45), open year-round, is an attractive, shaded camping ground just north of Pont Édouard Daladier, 850m from the walled city on Île de la Barthelasse. Charges are 17.80FF per adult, 8.50FF to pitch a tent and 6.50FF for parking. Reception is open from 8 am to 9 pm, but you can arrive any time. Take bus No 10 from in front of the main post office to the La Barthelasse stop.

Camping Municipal Saint Bénézet (☎ 04 90 82 63 50), Île de la Barthelasse, is a bit farther north on Chemin de la Barthelasse. It is open from March to October, and costs 60/80FF in the low/high season for two people plus a caravan/tent site and parking.

Hostels – Avignon The 210-bed ***Auberge Bagatelle*** (☎ 04 90 85 78 45; fax 04 90 27 16 23) is part of a large, park-like area on Île de la Barthelasse that includes Camping Bagatelle. A bed in a room costs 59FF.

From April to September a bunk in a converted squash court at the ***Avignon Squash Club*** (☎ 04 90 85 27 78), 32 Blvd Limbert, costs 58FF. Reception is open from 9 am to 10 pm (closed on Sunday from September to June; open from 8 to 11 am and 5 to 11 pm in July and August). Take bus No 7 from the train station to the Université stop.

Hostels – Villeneuve-lès-Avignon The well managed ***Résidence Pierre Louis Loisil*** (☎ 04 90 25 07 92; fax 04 90 25 88 03), Ave Pierre Sémard, accepts groups but welcomes individual travellers if there's room. Telephone reservations are accepted. A bed in a three or four person room costs 68FF. There are facilities for the disabled. Take bus No 10 from Avignon train station to the Frédéric Mistral stop.

A bed in a basic room for two to four people at the ***Foyer International YMCA*** (☎ 04 90 25 46 20; fax 04 90 25 30 64), 7bis Chemin de la Justice, costs 96FF, including breakfast. Take bus No 10 to the Pont d'Avignon stop.

Hotels – Within the Walls The ***Hôtel du Parc*** (☎ 04 90 82 71 55), 18 Rue Agricol Perdiguier, has singles/doubles without shower for 140/160FF and 180/195FF with shower. Hall showers are 5FF.

The friendly ***Hôtel Splendid*** (☎ 04 90 86 14 46; fax 04 90 85 38 55), 17 Rue Agricol Perdiguier, has singles/doubles with shower for 130/200FF and rooms with shower and toilet for 170/280FF. The hotel rents bikes too (see the Getting Around section).

The third in the trio, the ***Hôtel Colbert*** (☎ 04 90 86 20 20; fax 04 90 85 97 00), 7 Rue Agricol Perdiguier, smells of disinfectant but has well priced singles with shower for 150FF and doubles/triples with shower and toilet for 250/300FF.

The always busy ***Hôtel Innova*** (☎ 04 90 82 54 10; fax 04 90 82 52 39), 100 Rue Joseph Vernet, has bright, comfortable and soundproofed doubles without/with shower for 140/150FF; rooms for two/three/four people with shower and toilet cost 200/240/260FF. Hall showers are free and breakfast is 25FF. Nearby, at 31-33 Rue de la République, is the less than friendly ***Hôtel Central*** (☎ 04 90 86 07 81; fax 04 90 27 99 54), which has uninspiring doubles from 160FF.

The one star ***Hôtel Mignon*** (☎ 04 90 82 17 30; fax 04 90 85 78 46), 12 Rue Joseph Vernet, has spotless, well kept and soundproofed singles/doubles with shower for 150/185FF and doubles with shower and toilet for 220FF. Take bus No 10 from in front of the main post office to the Porte de l'Oulle stop.

Hotels – Outside the Walls The noisy, family-run ***Hôtel Monclar*** (☎ 04 90 86 20 14; fax 04 90 85 94 94), 13 Ave Monclar, is in an 18th century building just across the tracks from the train station. Eminently serviceable doubles start at 165FF with sink and bidet. The hotel has its own parking lot (20FF) and a pretty little back garden.

In Villeneuve-lès-Avignon, the ***Hôtel Beauséjour*** (☎ 04 90 25 20 56), 61 Ave Gabriel Péri, has bargain-basement rooms for one or two people without/with shower for 130/160FF.

Places to Stay – Mid-Range

The two star ***Hôtel Le Provençal*** (☎ 04 90 85 25 24; fax 04 90 82 75 81), 13 Rue Joseph Vernet, has singles/doubles with toilet for 180FF and rooms with shower, toilet and TV for 237FF. Take bus No 10 from in front of the main post office to the Porte de l'Oulle stop.

The very charming, old-world ***Hôtel du Palais des Papes*** (☎ 04 90 86 04 13 or ☎ 04 90 82 47 31; fax 04 90 27 91 17), 1 Rue Gérard Philippe, has doubles with shower, TV and toilet for 280 to 480FF; the pricier rooms sport a view of the Palais des Papes. Triples start at 520FF and dogs cost an extra 50FF.

The splendid two star ***Hôtel Médiéval*** (☎ 04 90 86 11 06; fax 04 90 82 08 64), 15 Rue Petite Saunerie, housed in a restored 17th century house down a quiet street not far from the Palais des Papes, has singles/doubles with all the trimmings from 195/240FF. It also has studios to rent on a weekly, monthly or long-term basis.

Outside the walls, the ***Hôtel Saint Roch*** (☎ 04 90 82 18 63; fax 04 90 82 78 30), 9 Rue Paul Mérindol, has airy doubles with shower, toilet and TV for 250FF; triples and quads are 330FF.

In Villeneuve-lès-Avignon, the beautifully situated ***Hôtel L'Atelier*** (☎ 04 90 25 01 84) has charming doubles with toilet from 250FF and with bath and toilet for 360FF. Equally idyllic is the small and select ***Les Jardins de la Livrée*** (☎ 04 90 26 05 05), 4bis Rue du Camp de Bataille. It has a small stone terrace, swimming pool, Provençal kitchen and quiet rooms for 250 to 370FF. Book in advance. The Gîte de France ***Aux Écuries des Chartreux*** (☎/fax 04 90 25 79 93), next to the entrance to the Chartreuse monastery at 66 Rue de la République, has studios to let for one to four people from 260FF a night.

Places to Stay – Top End

'A place of pilgrimage for men and women of taste' is how the French newspaper *Le Figaro* summed up the ***Hôtel de la Mirande*** (☎ 04 90 85 93 93; fax 04 90 86 26 85), Avignon's most exclusive hotel, housed in a former 14th century cardinal's palace behind the Palais des Papes at 4 Place de la Mirande. Exquisitely furnished rooms start at 1700FF (1850FF from April to October). The hotel has its own cooking school.

The four star ***Hôtel L'Europe*** (☎ 04 90 14 76 76), 12 Place Crillon, is cheap in comparison – rooms cost 630 to 2500FF (dogs an extra 50FF), breakfast is 89FF and *menus* in its restaurant are 210, 285 and 400FF. On Sunday it serves a good-value 160FF brunch from 11.30 am.

Places to Eat

From Easter until mid-November, half of Place de l'Horloge is taken over by tourist restaurants and cafés. *Menus* start at about 75FF. Many restaurants open just for the festival; most have special festival *menus*.

Restaurants – Around Place de l'Horloge For hearty and healthy fodder in a rustic setting (tree trunks for benches etc) look no farther than the atmospheric ***Natural Café*** (☎ 04 90 85 90 82), behind the opera house at 17 Rue Racine (closed on Sunday and Monday). Adjoining it is the more conventional ***La Fourchette*** (☎ 04 90 85 20 93), a Michelin-recommended place with *menus* for 150FF. 'The Fork' is closed on weekends.

Nearby, the ***Simple Simon Tea Lunch*** (☎ 04 90 86 62 70), 26 Rue Petite Fusterie, is an endearing, *très anglais* place for an afternoon cuppa (20 to 23FF) with cake, pie, scones or cheesecake (27FF). Light meals (40 to 52FF) are available all afternoon. Simple Simon is closed on Sunday and in August. ***Le Brantes*** (☎ 04 90 86 35 14), No 22 on the same street, is a large pizza and grill that has excellent-value *menus* from 69FF. Pizzas/pasta dishes cost 42/33FF upwards and there is a kids' *menu* for 35FF. Don't miss the great flower-filled courtyard at the rear.

South of the square on Rue des Trois Faucons is ***Le Caveau du Théâtre*** (☎ 04 90 82 60 91). It has a lunchtime *formule* comprising a *tarte salée* (savoury tart) and dessert for 65FF and evening *menus* for 110FF. You can also taste wine here, also possible at the less formal ***Les Caulisses*** next door. Both are open from noon to 2 pm and 7.30 to 10.30 pm.

Heading east from Place de l'Horloge, you come to Rue Carnot, home to a handful of Vietnamese and Chinese places. ***Restaurant Song Long*** (☎ 04 90 86 35 00) at No 1 offers a wide variety of excellent Vietnamese dishes, including 16 *plats végétariens* (vegetarian soups, salads, starters and main dishes). Lunch/dinner *menus* start at 55/78FF. Song Long is open daily.

Le Belgocargo (☎ 04 90 85 72 99), a Belgian place tucked behind Église Saint Pierre at 7 Rue Armand de Pontmartin, serves mussels 16 different ways for 49 to 68FF and *waterzooi de volaille* (a creamy Belgian stew of chicken, leeks and herbs) for 58FF. Swill it down with a glass of cherry-flavoured kriek beer, served on tap.

Restaurants – Quartier des Teinturiers & Area Rue des Teinturiers is one of Avignon's most fun streets by both day and night. Pleasant bohemian-style restaurants and bistros include the small ***Sindabad*** (☎ 04 90 14 69 45), 53 Rue des Teinturiers, which offers good Tunisian, Asian and Provençal home cooking. It has a 50FF plat du jour and is open from noon and from 6 pm (closed on Sunday).

At No 13 is ***Le Bistro Russe*** (☎ 04 90 85 64 35), a Russian bistro specialising in vodka-inspired treats. Lunchtime/evening *menus* start at 60/80FF (closed on Monday).

The highlight is ***Woolloomooloo*** (☎ 04 90 85 28 44), next to the old paper mill at No 16. Each week the jumble of eclectic antique and contemporary furnishings is rearranged to create a 'new look' for this eccentric restaurant. *Menus* are around 60FF and there are vegetarian and Antillean dishes too. Woolloomooloo is open from noon and from 7.30 pm (closed on Sunday and Monday).

On the western fringe of this old dyers' quarter is ***Le Petit Comptoir*** (☎ 04 90 86 10 94), opposite the crumbling arched façade of the *très belle* École des Beaux-Arts at 52 Rue des Lices. This tiny, eight-table place offers diners the choice of a main course and dessert or entrée for 40FF, or all three for 70FF. The pork kebab marinated in lemon and ginger is particularly tasty.

For a more classical approach, try the very refined ***Restaurant Au 19éme*** (☎ 04 90 27 16 00), 75 Rue Guillaume Puy, housed in the 19th century townhouse where absinthe beverage inventor Jules Pernod once lived. It hosts live jazz on Saturday evening, harp recitals on Friday evening, and has lunchtime/evening *menus* from 89/120FF (closed Saturday lunchtime and Monday evening).

Restaurants – Top End ***La Cuisine de Reine*** (☎ 04 90 85 99 04), opposite the Hôtel Innova inside Le Cloître des Arts, is an elegant restaurant and salon de thé wrapped around an 18th century courtyard. *Menus* start at 110FF and include a surprise *pique-nique à la maison* comprising smoked meats, olives and crusty bread. Calorie-killer cakes and pastries are served in its heavenly art café (closed on Sunday and Monday).

Equally worth the cash are the gastronomic feasts served at the ***Restaurant Le Saint Louis*** (☎ 04 90 27 55 55), overlooking a fabulous 16th century cloister courtyard dominated by a huge moss-covered fountain at 20 Rue du Portail Boquier. Lunch/dinner *menus* start at 99/140FF.

University Restaurant The ***restaurant universitaire*** of the Faculté de Droit (Law Faculty), south-west of the train station on Ave du Blanchissage, is open from October to June except during university holidays. Meals are served from 11.30 am to 1.30 pm and 6.30 to 7.30 pm (closed Saturday evening and Sunday). People with student cards can buy tickets (about 15 or 30FF) at the CROUS office (☎ 04 90 82 42 18), 29 Blvd Limbert, open Monday, Tuesday, Wednesday and Friday from 10.30 am to 12.30 pm.

Self-Catering Les Halles on Place Pie has a ***food market*** open from 7 am to 1 pm (closed on Monday). The complex is open from 6 am to 1.30 pm. Luxury local foods in jars, tins and bottles are sold at the upmarket ***Le Val d'Arômes***, 28 Rue Petite Fusterie. ***Puyricard***, 33 Rue Joseph Vernet, is the place for designer chocolate.

Near Place de l'Horloge, the ***Boulangerie Pâtisserie***, 17 Rue Saint Agricol, is open from 7.45 am to 7.30 pm (closed on Sunday). The ***Casino*** grocery, 22 Rue Saint Agricol, is open from 8 am to 12.45 pm and 3 to 7.30 pm (closed on Sunday).

Entertainment

For information on the Festival d'Avignon and Festival Off, see Special Events earlier in this section. Tickets for many cultural events and performances are sold at the tourist office. Events listings are included in the free *César* weekly magazine and in the tourist office's fortnightly newsletter, *Rendez-vous d'Avignon*. Tickets for most events are sold at FNAC (☎ 04 90 14 35 35), 19 Rue de la République, open from 10 am to 7 pm (closed on Sunday).

Concerts From October to June, the ***Opéra d'Avignon*** (☎ 04 90 82 23 44), housed in an imposing structure built in 1847, Place de l'Horloge, stages operas, operettas, plays, symphonic concerts, chamber music concerts and ballet. The box office is open from 11 am to 6 pm (closed on Sunday).

Cinemas The ***Cinéma Utopia*** (☎ 04 90 82 65 36), 4 Rue des Escaliers Sainte Anne, La Manutention complex (follow the 'Promenade des Papes' signs east from Place du Palais), is a student entertainment/cultural centre with a jazz club, café and four cinemas screening nondubbed films (30FF). Its program is featured in the free weekly *Utopia*.

Getting There & Away

Air Avignon-Caumont airport (☎ 04 90 81 51 51) is 8km south-east of Avignon.

Bus The bus station (*halte routière*; ☎ 04 90 82 07 35) is in the basement of the building down the ramp to the right as you exit the train station on Blvd Saint Roch. The information window is open from 8 am to noon and 1.30 to 6 pm (Saturday until noon; closed on Sunday). You can leave luggage here (10FF). Tickets are sold on the buses, which are run by about 20 different companies.

Places you can get to by bus include Aix-en-Provence (86FF for the one hour trip via the highway, 79FF for the 1½ hour trip along secondary roads; four to six a day), Apt (41FF; 1¼ hours; three or four a day), Arles (37.50FF; 1½ hours; four or five direct a day), Carpentras (20FF; 45 minutes; about 15 a day), Cavaillon (19FF; 35 minutes), Fontaine de Vaucluse (25FF; one hour; two or three a day), Marseille (89FF; 35 minutes by direct bus; seven a day), Montelimar (65FF; two hours), Nice (165FF; one a day), Nîmes (40FF; 1¼ hours; five a day), Orange (28.50FF; 40 minutes; about 20 a day), Pertuis (44.50FF; two hours), Pont du Gard (32FF; 45 minutes), Uzès (45FF; one hour; five a day) and Vaison-la-Romaine (36FF; 1¼ hours; three a day and two on Sunday). Most lines operate on Sunday at reduced frequency.

Long-haul bus companies Linebus (☎ 04 90 85 30 48) and Eurolines (☎ 04 90 85 27 60) have offices at the far end of the bus platforms.

Train The train station (☎ 08 36 35 35 35) is across Blvd Saint Roch from Porte de la République. The information counters are open from 9 am to 6.15 pm (closed on Sunday). The left-luggage room, to the right as you exit the station, is open from 8 am to noon and 2 to 5.30 pm (20FF). Villeneuve-lès-Avignon's small SNCF station only handles goods trains but it sells tickets for passenger trains departing from Avignon.

There are frequent trains to Arles (35FF; 20 minutes; 14 to 18 a day), Marseille (89FF;

one hour), Nice (201FF; 2½ hours), Nîmes (45FF; 30 minutes; 15 a day), Orange (29FF; 20 minutes; 17 a day) and, by TGV, Paris' Gare de Lyon (356 to 418FF; 3¼ hours).

Car Most car rental agencies are signposted from the train station. Europcar (☎ 04 90 85 01 40) is in the Ibis building. Budget (☎ 04 90 27 34 95) is down the ramp to the right as you exit the station, and Hertz (☎ 04 90 82 37 67) is at 4 Blvd Saint Michel.

Getting Around

Bus Local TCRA bus tickets cost 6.50FF each if bought from the driver; a carnet of five tickets (good for 10 rides) costs 48FF at TCRA offices. Buses run from 7 am to about 7.40 pm (8 am to 6 pm and less frequently on Sunday). The two most important bus transfer points are the Poste stop at the main post office and Place Pie.

Carnets and free bus maps (*plan du réseau*) are available at the Point d'Accueil-Vente (☎ 04 90 82 68 19) in the tower wall (La Tourelle) of the old city at Porte de la République across from the train station, and from the Espace Bus kiosk (☎ 04 90 85 44 93), Place Pie. Both are open from 8.15 am to noon and 1.45 to 6.30 pm (Saturday from 8.45 am to noon).

Villeneuve-lès-Avignon is linked with Avignon by bus No 10, which stops in front of Avignon's main post office and on the western side of the walled city near Porte de l'Oulle. Unless you want to take the grand tour of the Avignon suburb of Les Angles, take a bus marked 'Villeneuve puis Les Angles' (rather than 'Les Angles puis Villeneuve'). For the major sights, get off at the Office du Tourisme or the Frédéric Mistral stops in Villeneuve. Bus No 10 runs two or three times an hour from 7.07 am to 8.15 pm. On Sunday and holidays, there are five Villeneuve-puis-Les Angles buses a day; the last return bus is at 5.49 pm.

Taxi Pick up a taxi outside the train station or call the Place Pie taxi stand (☎ 04 90 82 20 20), open 24 hours.

Bicycle Cycles Peugeot (☎ 04 90 86 32 49), 80 Rue Guillaume Puy, has three-speeds and 10-speeds for 60/130/240FF for one day/three days/a week (plus 1000FF deposit). It is open from 8 am to noon and 2 to 7 pm (closed on Sunday).

The Hôtel Splendid (☎ 04 90 23 96 08), 17 Rue Agricol Perdiguier, has mountain bikes to rent for 100/180/650FF a day/weekend/week (plus 2500FF deposit).

AROUND AVIGNON

Twenty-five kilometres south of Avignon, past the small town of **Saint Rémy de Provence** (population 9340), vividly immortalised on canvas by Van Gogh during his stay in an asylum in 1889-90, is **Les Baux de Provence** (population 468). This fortified village, named after the 245m-high *baou* (rocky spur) on which it is perched, pulls in some 2.5 million tourists a year (putting it on a par with Mont Saint Michel in Normandy as one of France's biggest tourist attractions outside of Paris). The most pleasant time to visit the Château des Baux (☎ 04 90 54 55 56; open from 7 am to 7.30 pm, until 8.30 pm in July and August), a former feudal home of Monaco's Grimaldi royal family, is early evening after the caterpillar of tourist coaches has evacuated the village for the day. The tourist office (☎ 04 90 54 34 39; fax 04 90 54 51 51) has information on Les Baux's few accommodation options.

ORANGE

• **pop 27,000** ✉ **84100**

Through a 16th century marriage with the German House of Nassau, the House of Orange (the princely dynasty that had ruled Orange since the 12th century) became active in the history of the Netherlands and later, through William III (William of Orange), also in England. Orange (Arenja in Provençal), which had earlier been a stronghold of the Reformation, was ceded to France in 1713 by the Treaty of Utrecht, but to this day many members of the royal house of the Netherlands are known as the princes and princesses of Orange-Nassau.

Since 1995, Orange – along with Toulon on the Côte d'Azur and Marignane, north-west of Marseille – has been in the hands of a National Front mayor. In February 1997, the Marseille suburb of Vitrolles became the fourth hot spot in France to be controlled by the extreme-right party that for years has been accused of racism and anti-Semitism.

Orientation

The train station is just over 1km east of Place de la République, the city centre, along Ave Frédéric Mistral and Rue de la République. Rue Saint Martin links Place de la République and nearby Place Clemenceau with the tourist office, which is 250m to the west. The Théâtre Antique, Orange's magnificent Roman theatre, is two blocks south of Place de la République. The tiny Meyne River lies north of the city centre.

From the train station, bus No 2 from Rue Jean Reboul (first left after exiting the station) goes to the Théâtre Antique or République stop.

Information

Tourist Office The tourist office (☎ 04 90 34 70 88; fax 04 90 34 99 62; officetourisme@infonie.fr; www.provence-orange.com), 5 Cours Aristide Briand, is open from 9 am to 6 pm (closed on Sunday; 9 am to 7 pm and 10 am to 6 pm on Sunday from April to September).

Money The Banque de France at 5 Rue Frédéric Mistral is open weekdays from 8.30 am to noon and 1.30 to 3.30 pm.

Post & Communications The post office, opposite the bus station on Blvd Édouard Daladier, is open from 8.30 am to 6.30 pm (Saturday from 8 am to noon; closed on Sunday).

The Cyber Station (☎ 04 90 34 27 27; cybersta@club-internet.fr), just north of the tourist office at 2 Cours Aristide Briand, charges 1/25/45FF for one/30/60 minutes online access. It's open from 7.30 am to 7 pm (Friday until 11 pm; Saturday from 11 am to 11 pm; closed on Sunday).

Laundry The laundrette at 5 Rue Saint Florent is open from 7 am to 8 pm.

Théâtre Antique

Orange's magnificent Roman theatre (☎ 04 90 51 17 60), designed to seat about 10,000 spectators, was probably built during the time of Augustus Caesar (ruled 27 BC to 14 AD). Its **stage wall** (*mur de scène*), the only such Roman structure still standing in its entirety (minus a few mosaics and the roof), is 103m wide and almost 37m high. Its plain exterior can be viewed from adjacent Place des Frères Mounets to the north.

For a panoramic view of the Roman masterpiece, follow Montée Philbert de Chalons or Montée Lambert to the top of **Colline Saint Eutrope** (Saint Eutrope Hill; 97m), where a circular viewing table explains what's what. En route you pass the ruins of a 12th century **chateau**, the former residence of the princes of Orange. Those not into walking can always hop aboard the 54 seat *Orangeois* **tourist train** that departs every 30 minutes or so from outside the Théâtre Antique. The city tour (25FF) lasts one hour and takes in all the major sights as well as scaling the Colline Saint Eutrope.

From April to early October, the theatre is open daily from 9 am to 6.30 pm (9 am to noon and 1.30 to 5 pm during the rest of the year). Tickets costing 30/25FF for adults/students also get you into the unexciting **Musée Municipal** (☎ 04 90 51 18 24; fax 04 90 34 55 89), housed in the 17th century Hôtel Van Cuyl opposite on Rue Madeleine Roch. This museum is known for its Roman cadasters, or land survey registers (yawn). From April to October it's open from 9.30 am to 7 pm (9 am to noon and 1.30 to 5.30 pm during the rest of the year).

Arc de Triomphe

Orange's Roman triumphal arch, one of the most remarkable of its kind in France, is at the northern end of plane tree-lined Ave de l'Arc de Triomphe about 450m from the

PROVENCE

centre of town. Probably built around 20 BC, it is 19m in height and width, and 8m thick. The exceptional friezes commemorate Julius Caesar's victories over the Gauls in 49 BC, triumphs of which the Romans wished to remind every traveller approaching the city. The arch has been restored several times since 1825.

Overlooking the eastern side of the arch is the local **pétanque** court where old men gather under the shade of the trees on sunny days to play Provençal *boules* (bowls). Fancy a go? Kit yourself up with balls from Pêche Chasse Bourgeois, 20 Cours Aristide Briand.

Special Events

In June and August, the Théâtre Antique comes alive with all-night concerts, cinema screenings and various musical events during Les Nuits du Théâtre Antique. During the last fortnight in July, it plays host to Les Chorégies d'Orange (www.choregies.asso.fr), a series of weekend operas, classical concerts and choral performances. Seats (50 to 900FF) for this prestigious festival have to be reserved months beforehand; it is possible to catch a free glimpse of the action from the lookout atop Colline Saint Eutrope. Orange also plays host to a week-long jazz festival in June.

Tickets for events held in the Théâtre Antique can be reserved at the Location Théâtre Antique (☎ 04 90 34 24 24 or ☎ 04 90 34 15 52; fax 04 90 11 00 85), 14 Place Silvain, which is open from 9 am to noon and 2 to 5 pm (closed on weekends). To buy tickets for other cultural events (including those held at the modern Palais des Princes, Cours Pourtoules), go next door to the Service Culturel (☎ 04 90 51 57 57; fax 04 90 51 60 51), open from 8.30 am to 5.30 pm (closed on weekends).

Places to Stay

Camping The three star ***Camping Le Jonquier*** (☎ 04 90 34 19 83; fax 04 90 34 86 54), near the Arc de Triomphe on Rue Alexis Carrel, is open from mid-March to the end of October. It charges 28FF per person and 30FF for a tent. Take bus No 1 from the République stop (on Ave Frédéric Mistral, 600m from the train station) to the Arc de Triomphe. From there, walk 100m back, turn right onto Rue des Phocéens and right again onto Rue des Étudiants. The camping ground is across the football field.

Hotels The cheapest joint in town is the ***Bar Hôtel*** (☎ 04 90 34 13 31), 22 Rue Caristie, which has basic rooms for one or two people with shower for 136FF or with shower and toilet for 146FF. The reception is the bar downstairs.

Also cheap is the ***Hôtel de la Gare***, next to the train station on Ave Frédéric Mistral, where rooms start at 160FF.

Close to the bus station, the ***Hôtel Saint Jean*** (☎ 04 90 51 15 16; fax 04 90 11 05 45), 7 Cours Pourtoules, has singles/doubles with washbasin and toilet from 180/260FF. A block north of the Théâtre Antique, the extremely welcoming ***Hôtel Arcotel*** (☎ 04 90 34 09 23; fax 04 90 51 61 12), 8 Place aux Herbes, has singles/doubles/triples/quads from 110/150/160/300FF. Around the corner, the atmospheric ***Hôtel Saint Florent*** (☎ 04 90 34 18 53; fax 04 90 51 17 25), 4 Rue du Mazeau, has great rooms with giant murals painted on the walls and fantastic *belle époque* antique wooden beds adorned with crushed and studded velvet. Rooms cost 160/200FF with shower.

Places to Eat

East of Place Clemenceau, there are a number of moderately priced restaurants on Rue du Pont Neuf; the food at ***Le Bambou*** (☎ 04 90 51 65 19) at No 17 is said to be particularly tasty.

La Sangria (☎ 04 90 34 31 96), 3 Place de la République, has *menus* for 50FF (lunch only), 68 and 100FF. Close by, ***Chez Daniel*** (☎ 04 90 34 63 48), on the corner of Rue Second Weber and Rue Boissy, dishes out oysters,mussels and other shellfish by the dozen. Daniel also offers inspirational fish platters costing 120 to 180FF, to eat in or take away.

For a taste of India, head to the Indian ***New Kasmir*** (☎ 04 90 34 90 09), just west of the

Théâtre Antique on Rue de Tourre, which has spicy *menus* for 79 and 95FF. Highly recommended for its local fare is ***Le Yaca*** (☎ 04 90 34 70 03), close by at 24 Place Silvain. It has a regional *menu* for 65FF. Don't miss the *soupe au pistou* at ***Le Povençal*** (☎ 04 90 34 01 89), 27 Rue de la République.

For a real treat, head for ***Le Garden*** (☎ 04 90 34 64 47), a block west of Place Clemenceau at 6 Place de Langes. The restaurant is furnished in 1930s style and specialises in truffles. Its *brouillade aux truffes* with salad (180FF) is a veritable feast of pricey (and local) black fungi.

Thursday is market day in Orange.

Getting There & Away

Bus The bus station (☎ 04 90 34 15 59 or ☎ 04 90 34 13 39) is south-east of the centre of the city on Cours Pourtoules. Buses from here go to Avignon, Carpentras, Marseille and Vaison-la-Romaine.

Train Orange's tiny train station (☎ 04 90 11 88 64), at the eastern end of Ave Frédéric Mistral, is 1.5km east of the tourist office.

Trains go in two directions: northward to Lyon (134FF; 2¼ hours; 13 a day) and Paris' Gare de Lyon (365FF; 3¼ hours), and southward to Avignon (29FF; 15 minutes; 17 a day), Marseille (127FF; 1½ hours; 10 a day) and beyond.

Getting Around

MTS (☎/fax 04 90 34 94 92), 571 Blvd Édouard Daladier, rents mountain bikes/tandems for 120/350FF a day or 200/600FF a weekend. The shop is open from 8 am to noon and 3 to 8 pm (closed on weekends).

VAISON-LA-ROMAINE

• pop 5900 ✉ 84110

Vaison-la-Romaine, 23 and 47km north-east of Orange and Avignon respectively, is endowed with extensive Roman ruins, a picturesque medieval old city and plenty of tourists.

In the 2nd century BC, the Romans conquered an important Celtic city on this site and renamed it Vasio Vocontiorum. The Roman city flourished, in part because it was granted considerable autonomy, but around the 6th century the Great Migrations forced the population to move to the hill across the river, which was easier to defend. The counts of Toulouse built a castle on top of the hill in the 12th century. The resettlement of the original site began in the 17th century.

The Roman remains discovered at Vaison include villas decorated with mosaics, colonnaded streets, public baths, a theatre and an aqueduct; the latter brought water down from Mont Ventoux. The two week Choralies, a choral festival held each year in August in the Roman theatre, is said to be the largest of its kind in Europe.

Vaison, like Malaucène and Carpentras, 10 and 27km to the south, is a good base for exploring the Mont Ventoux region.

Orientation

Vaison is bisected by the ever flooding Ouvèze River. The Roman city centre, on top of which the modern city centre has been built, is on the river's right (north) bank; the medieval Haute Ville is on the left (south) bank. In the modern city, pedestrianised Grand' Rue heads north-westward from the Pont Romain bridge, changing its name near the Roman ruins to Ave du Général de Gaulle.

To get from the bus station to the tourist office, turn left as you leave the station then left into Rue Colonel Parazols, which leads past the Fouilles de Puymin excavations along Rue Burrhus to the tourist office.

Information

Tourist Office The tourist office (☎ 04 90 36 02 11; fax 04 90 28 76 04), inside the Maison du Tourisme et des Vins, is just off Ave du Général de Gaulle on Place du Chanoine Sautel. It's open from 9 am to noon and 2 to 5.45 pm. Sunday hours from Easter to September are 9 am to 1 pm. In July and August daily hours are 9 am to 6.45 pm.

Post & Communications The post office, which has an exchange service, is diagonally opposite Place du 11 Novembre. It is open from 8.30 am to noon and 2 to 5 pm (until noon Saturday; closed on Sunday).

Gallo-Roman Ruins

The Gallo-Roman ruins that have been unearthed in Vaison can be visited at two sites: **Fouilles de Puymin**, the excavations on the east side of Ave du Général de Gaulle, and **Fouilles de la Villasse**, which are to the west of the same road.

Fouilles de Puymin, whose entrance is opposite the tourist office, is the more interesting of the pair. It includes houses, mosaics and a theatre (designed to accommodate some 6000 people) built around 20 AD under the reign of Tiberius. The **Musée Archéologique** displays some of the artefacts found. Its collection of statues includes the silver bust of a 3rd century patrician and likenesses of Hadrian and his wife Sabina. At Fouilles de la Villasse, you can visit the mosaic and fresco-decorated house in which the silver bust was discovered.

Both sites are open November to February from 10 am to noon and 2 to 4.30 pm (closed Tuesday). From March to October, daily hours are 9 or 9.30 am to 12.30 pm and 2 to 6 or 7 pm. Admission to both sites is 40/22/14FF for adults/students/children. From April to October, there are guided tours (10FF) in English; check the schedule at the tourist office.

Medieval Quarter

Across the much repaired **Pont Romain**, on the south bank of the Ouvèze, lies the **Haute Ville**, which dates from the 13th and 14th centuries. Narrow, cobblestone alleyways lead up the hill past restored houses. At the summit, which affords a nice view, is an imposing 12th century **chateau**, modernised in the 15th century only to be later abandoned.

Places to Stay

The tourist office has comprehensive accommodation lists, including details on chambres d'hôtes and self-catering places in the surrounding region.

Camping The *Camping du Théâtre Romain* (☎ 04 90 28 78 66), Chemin de Brusquet, is opposite the Théâtre Antique in the northern section of the Fouilles de Puymin. It is open from mid-March to October and charges 65/80FF for two people with a tent or caravan in the low/high season. The larger *Camping Carpe Diem* (☎ 04 90 36 02 02), south-east of the centre on Route de Saint Marcellin, is open from mid-March to November. Both sites have swimming pools.

Hostels The quiet but expensive *Centre à Cœur Joie* (☎ 04 90 36 00 78; fax 04 90 36 09 89), 500m south-east of town along the river at the end of Ave César Geoffray, has views of Mont Ventoux. Singles/doubles/triples with breakfast cost 220/280/ 345FF.

Hotels Hotels are few and far between. The 24 room *Hôtel Le Burrhus* (☎ 04 90 36 00 11; fax 04 90 36 39 05), 2 Place Montfort, and the eight room *Hôtel des Lis* (same ☎/fax), 20 Cours Henri Fabre, practically next door and owned by the same people, charge from 240 and 350FF respectively for a double with shower and toilet. Both close from mid-November to 20 December and on Sunday in January and February.

Shopping

Wine (Gigondas, Châteauneuf-du-Pape and Villages des Côtes du Rhône), honey and *nougat au miel* (honey nougat) are all local specialities but nothing can compare with the delectable black truffles harvested around Vaison-la-Romain. Sure they don't come cheap (90FF for 12.5g), but just a few shavings of the costly black fungus will turn the most prosaic plate of pasta into a bite-sized helping of heaven itself.

Local wines and *produits du terroir* (local food products) can be tasted and bought at the Maison des Vins, in the basement of the Maison du Tourisme et des Vins.

Getting There & Away

The bus station, where Lieutard buses (☎ 04 90 36 09 90 in Vaison; ☎ 04 90 86 36 75 in

Avignon) has an office, is east of the modern town on Ave des Choralies. There are limited services from Vaison to Orange (45 minutes), Avignon (1¼ hours) and Carpentras (45 minutes). The office is open from 9 am to noon and 2 to 7 pm.

MONT VENTOUX

The narrow ridge running east to west known as Mont Ventoux is the most prominent geographical feature in northern Provence, thanks to its height (1909m) and its isolation. The radar and antenna-studded summit, accessible by road, affords spectacular views of Provence, the southern Alps and – when it's especially clear – even the Pyrenees.

Mont Ventoux marks the boundary between the fauna and flora of northern France and that of southern France. Some species – including the snake eagle, numerous spiders and a variety of butterflies – are found only here. The mountain's forests were felled 400 years ago to build ships, but since 1860 some areas have been reforested with a variety of species, including the majestic cedar of Lebanon. The mix of deciduous trees makes the mountain especially colourful in autumn.

Since the summit is considerably cooler than the surrounding plains – there can be a difference of up to 20°C – and receives twice as much precipitation, bring warm clothes and rain gear at any time of the year. Areas above 1300m are usually snow-covered from December to April.

Mont Ventoux is regularly included in the route of the Tour de France, and it was here that British cyclist Tommy Simpson collapsed and died during the 1967 event. There is a memorial to him.

Just west of Mont Ventoux rise the sharp pinnacles of the limestone **Dentelles de Montmirail**; the surrounding area makes great hiking terrain. Near the eastern end of the Mont Ventoux massif is the village of **Sault** (800m), surrounded in summer by a patchwork of purple lavender. **Malaucène**, 10km south of Vaison-la-Romaine and the former summer residence of the Avignon popes, is where most people begin their forays into the surrounds of Mont Ventoux, which is 21km to the east. Come winter, **Mont Serein** (1445m), 16km east of Malaucène and 5km from Mont Ventoux's summit on the D974, is transformed into a bustling ski station.

Information

Tourist Offices The Malaucène tourist office (☎/fax 04 90 65 22 59), Place de la Mairie, is open from 10 am (9 am in summer) to noon and 3.30 pm (3 pm in summer) to 5.30 pm (closed on Sunday). Its efficient counterpart on Ave de la Promenade in Sault (☎ 04 90 64 01 21) is open daily from 1 April to 30 September from 9 am to noon and 2 to 7 pm. There is an information chalet on Mont Serein (☎ 04 90 63 42 02).

Maps Didier-Richard's 1:50,000 scale map No 27, entitled *Massif du Ventoux*, includes Mont Ventoux, the Monts du Vaucluse and the Dentelles de Montmirail. It is available at some of the area's larger tourist offices, and many bookshops and newsagents. More detailed is IGN's Série Bleue 1:25,000 *Mont Ventoux* (No 3140ET; 57FF).

Hiking

The GR4, running from the Ardèche River to the west, crosses the Dentelles de Montmirail before climbing up the northern face of Mont Ventoux. It then joins the GR9, and both trails follow the bare, white ridge before parting ways, with the GR4 winding eastward to the Gorges du Verdon. The GR9, which takes you to most of the area's ranges (including the Monts du Vaucluse and Lubéron range), is arguably the most spectacular trail in Provence.

Getting There & Around

If you've got a car, the summit of Mont Ventoux can be reached from Sault via the D164 or – in summer – from Malaucène or Saint Estève via the switchback D974, built in the 1930s. This mountain road is often snow-blocked until as late as April. For information on bus services in the area, see Getting There & Away under Carpentras.

PROVENCE

The EgoBike Shop (☎ 04 90 65 22 15 or ☎ 04 90 60 90 08) in Malaucène rents mountain bikes.

CARPENTRAS

• pop 25,000 ✉ 84200

The drowsy, agricultural town of Carpentras was an important trading centre in Greek times and later a Gallo-Roman city before becoming the capital of the papal territory of the Comtat Venaissin in 1320. It flourished in the 14th century, when it was visited frequently by Pope Clement V (who preferred it to Avignon) and numerous cardinals. During the same period, Jews expelled from territory controlled by the French crown (especially in Languedoc and Provence) sought refuge in the Comtat Venaissin, where they could live – subject to certain restrictions – under the protection of the pope. Today, Carpentras' 14th century synagogue is the oldest such structure in France still in use. In March 1997, skinheads apologised in court for desecrating tombs in the Jewish cemetery several years previous.

Carpentras is equidistant (25km) from Avignon to the south-west and Orange to the north-west. The town is small, easy to navigate on foot, and best known for its bustling Friday markets. It hosts the eclectic Estivales de Carpentras, a two week music, dance and theatre festival, in July.

PROVENCE

Orientation

In the 19th century, the city's fortifications and walls were replaced by a ring of boulevards: Ave Jean Jaurès, Blvd Alfred Rogier, Blvd du Nord, Blvd Maréchal Leclerc, Blvd Gambetta and Blvd Albin Durand. The partly pedestrianised old city lies inside.

If you arrive by bus, walk north-east to Place Aristide Briand, a major traffic intersection at the southernmost point on the almost heart-shaped ring of boulevards. Ave Jean Jaurès leads to the tourist office, while pedestrians-only Rue de la République, which heads due north, takes you straight to the cathedral and the 17th century Palais de Justice (Law Courts). The Hôtel de Ville is a few blocks north-east of the cathedral.

Information

Tourist Office The tourist office (☎ 04 90 63 00 78 or ☎ 04 90 63 57 88; fax 04 90 60 41 02), 170 Ave Jean Jaurès, sells a good range of regional maps and guides, and organises guided city tours (25/10FF for adults/children). Ask for the free English-language brochure *The Discover Carpentras Tour* if you prefer a do-it-yourself job.

The office is open from 9 am to 12.30 pm and 2 to 6.30 pm (6 pm on Saturday; closed on Sunday). Hours in July and August are 9 am to 7 pm (Sunday from 9.30 am to 12.30 pm). Staff exchange foreign currency when the banks are closed.

Money The Banque de France at 161 Blvd Albin Durand is open from 9 am to noon and 1.30 to 3.30 pm (closed on weekends). Commercial banks are on central Place Aristide Briand and Blvd Albin Durand.

Post & Communications The post office, 65 Rue d'Inguimbert, is open from 8.30 am to 7 pm (Saturday until noon only).

Laundry The laundrette, 118 Rue Porte de Monteux (the road linking Place du Général de Gaulle and Blvd Albin Durand), is open from 7 am to 8 pm.

Synagogue

Carpentras' wonderful synagogue was founded on this site in 1367, rebuilt in 1741-43 and restored in 1929 and 1954. For centuries, it served as the focal point of the town's 1000-strong Jewish community. The sanctuary on the 1st floor is decorated with wood panelling and liturgical objects from the 18th century. Down below, there's an oven that was used until 1904 to bake matzo (*pain azyme* in French), the unleavened bread eaten at Passover.

The synagogue, opposite the Hôtel de Ville on Place Juiverie, can be identified by a stone plaque, positioned high on the wall, which is inscribed with Hebrew letters. About 100 Jewish families live in Carpentras today. It can be visited from 10 am to noon and 3 to 5 pm (4 pm on Friday; closed on weekends). The tourist office sells the informative English booklet *The Road to Jewish Heritage in the South of France* (15FF).

Cathedral

Carpentras' one-time cathedral, now officially known as Église Saint Siffrein, was built in the Méridional (southern French) Gothic style between 1405 and 1519. The doorway, whose design is classical and badly in need of renovation, was added in the 17th century. The bell tower is modern. The **Trésor d'Art Sacré** (Treasury of Religious Art) displays various liturgical objects and reliquaries from the 14th to 19th centuries, including the **Saint Mors**, the Holy Bridle bit supposedly made by St Helen for her son Constantine from a nail taken from the True Cross. The cathedral is open from 10 am to noon and 2 to 4 pm (until 6 pm in summer; closed Tuesday year-round).

Arc de Triomphe

Hidden in a corner just off Rue d'Inguimbert – next to the cathedral and behind the Palais de Justice – this triumphal arch (or what's left of it) is the town's only Roman relic. Built under Augustus in the 1st century AD, it has regrettably become little more than a convenient public urinal. One of the carvings on the east side depicts two Barbarian captives (note the beards and chains), their faces all but worn away by time and weather.

Museums

Carpentras' museums are open from 10 am to noon and 2 to 4 pm (until 6 pm in summer; closed Tuesday year-round). The **Musée Comtadin**, which displays artefacts related to local history and folklore, and the **Musée Duplessis**, whose paintings are from the personal collection of Monseigneur d'Inguimbert, are both on the western side of the old city at 234 Blvd Albin Durand. The same 18th century building houses the **Bibliothèque Inguimbertine**, a large library with numerous rare books, incunabula and manuscripts.

The **Musée Sobirats**, one block west of the cathedral at 112 Rue du Collège, is an 18th century private residence decorated and crammed with furniture, faïence and *objets d'art* in the Louis XV and Louis XVI styles.

The hospital in the 18th century **Hôtel Dieu**, Place Aristide Briand, has an old-time pharmacy, complete with pharmaceutical ceramics. It's open to the public (8FF) on Monday, Wednesday and Thursday from 9 to 11.30 am. The hospital's chapel is also of interest, but you must make arrangements with the tourist office to visit it.

Markets

Friday is market day in Carpentras, to our mind one of the most colourful in Provence. Place Aristide Briand and Rue de la République have the usual knock-off jeans, generic T-shirts and junk, but Rue d'Inguimbert and most of Ave Jean Jaurès are laden with tables covered with nougat, strong local cheeses, orange and lavender marmalade, cauldrons of paella, buckets of olives and fresh fruit (especially the wonderful local melons). From November to the beginning of March, truffles are sold on Place Aristide Briand every Friday from 8 to 10 am. Carpentras' biggest fair is held on the Fête de Saint Siffrein (Feast of St Siffrein) on 27 November. In July and August, there's a wine market in front of the tourist office.

Swimming

Art Deco fans who enjoy taking the plunge should head for the **Piscine Couverte Renovée 1930** (☎ 04 90 60 92 03), Rue du Mont de Piété, a lovely covered swimming pool built by the Caisse d'Épargne almost seven decades ago and now fully restored to its geometric glory. The water temperature is 20°C. In general it's open between 3 and 5.15 pm and 6 to 8 pm. Admission is 12.50/8.80FF for adults/children and seniors.

Places to Stay

Camping Outside town on the Route de Saint Didier is ***Camping Lou Comtadou en Provence*** (☎ 04 90 67 03 16), Ave Pierre de

PROVENCE

Coubertin, open from Easter to October. It charges 22FF per person and 29FF for a tent or car. ***Camping Le Brégoux*** (☎ 04 90 62 62 50), Chemin du Vas at Aubignan, 8km to the north-west, is open from March to October.

Hotels Arguably the best place in town to stay for travellers watching their wallets is the one star ***Hôtel du Théâtre*** (☎ 04 90 63 02 90), a very friendly establishment overlooking Place Aristide Briand at 7 Blvd Albin Durand. Large, quiet (the windows are double-glazed) rooms for one or two start at 145FF; triples are 250FF.

At the northern end of town, the eight room ***Hôtel La Lavande*** (☎ 04 90 63 13 49), 282 Blvd Alfred Rogier, has doubles without/with shower for 145/175FF. From the tourist office, follow Blvd Jean Jaurès north-eastward into Blvd Alfred Rogier; the hotel is on the left just past the intersection of Rue Porte de Mazan.

Le Fiacre (☎ 04 90 63 03 15; fax 04 90 60 49 73), a short distance north of the tourist office at 153 Rue Vigne, has single/double rooms from 240/290FF.

Places to Eat

Regional fare rules at ***Le Marijo*** (☎ 04 90 60 42 65), 73 Rue Raspail, which serves up superb three and four-course locally inspired *menus* from around 80FF. For the cheese course, order the *chèvre* (goat's cheese) marinated for 15 days in herbs and olive oil and sprinkled with *marc*, a local eau de vie. This place is closed on Sunday.

Equally palatable are the truffles served in season (January to March) at ***Le Vert Galant*** (☎ 04 90 67 15 50), 12 Rue de Clapiès. Expect to pay at least 100FF a head, plus a lot more if you intend sampling the precious bits of black fungi. Le Vert Galant, honoured with one Michelin star, is closed during the last three weeks of August.

L'Oriental (☎ 04 90 63 19 57), 26 Rue de la Monnaie, specialises in Moroccan couscous from 69FF. ***El Mexicano*** (☎ 04 90 67 21 80), just north of the bus station at 34 Ave Georges Clemenceau, is a hybrid of an American-style steakhouse and a Tex-Mex joint, with beef fondue, every conceivable cut of steak, tacos and chilli and the more exotic bison and *autruche* (ostrich).

Getting There & Away

The train station is served by goods trains only, so buses operated by Cars Comtadins and Cars Arnaud provide Carpentras' only intercity public transport. The bus station, Place Terradou, is 150m south-west of Place Aristide Briand. Schedules are available from the Cars Comtadins office (☎ 04 90 67 20 25) across the square at 38 Ave Wilson. It is open from 8 am to noon and 2 to 6 pm (closed on weekends). The tourist office can also help.

There are hourly services to Avignon (45 minutes) and less frequent runs to Orange (40 minutes), Cavaillon (45 minutes) and L'Isle-sur-Sorgue (20 minutes), 7km west of Fontaine de Vaucluse. Even less frequent are buses (weekdays only) to Vaison-la-Romaine (45 minutes) via Malaucène, Bédoin (40 minutes) at the south-western foot of Mont Ventoux, and Sault (1½ hours) on the south-eastern side of Mont Ventoux.

FONTAINE DE VAUCLUSE

• pop 600 ⊠ 84800

The mighty spring for which Fontaine de Vaucluse (Vau-Cluso La Font in Provençal) is named is actually the spot where the Sorgue River ends its subterranean course and gushes to the surface. At the end of winter and in early spring, up to 200 cubic metres of water per second spill forth magnificently from the base of the cliff, forming one of the world's most powerful springs. During drier periods, the much reduced flow simply seeps through the rocks at various points downstream from the cliff, and the spring itself becomes little more than a still, very deep pond. Following numerous unsuccessful human and robotical attempts to reach the bottom, an unmanned submarine touched base – 315m-deep in 1985.

Some 1.5 million visitors descend upon pretty Fontaine de Vaucluse each year to stroll its streets and throw pebbles into its deep, deep pond.

Information

The tourist office (☎ 04 90 20 32 22; fax 04 90 20 21 37; officetourisme.vaucluse@wanadoo.fr) is on pedestrianised Chemin de la Fontaine, south-east of central Place de la Colonne on the way to the spring. It is open from 10 am to 6 pm (closed on Sunday).

Museums

For its size, the attractive village of Fontaine de Vaucluse has an inordinate number of small museums, dealing with such diverse subjects as the Résistance movement (**Musée d'Histoire 1939-1945**; ☎ 04 90 20 24 00; adjoining the tourist office; 20FF), speleology, and even justice and punishment (**Musée Historique de la Justice et des Châtiments**; ☎ 04 90 20 24 58; Chemin de la Fontaine; 20FF).

The **Moulin à Papier** on the river banks opposite the tourist office is an impressive reconstruction of a paper mill, built on the site of Fontaine de Vaucluse's old mill, whose wheel turned and whose pinewood mallets steadily beat away from 1522 until 1968. It's open from 9 am to 12.30 pm and 2 to 6 pm (Sunday from 10.30 am). Hours in July and August are 9 am to 7 pm; admission is free. Beautiful flower-encrusted paper, made as it was in the 16th century, is sold in the adjoining boutique and art gallery.

The Italian Renaissance poet Petrarch (Pétrarque in French) lived in Fontaine de Vaucluse from 1337 to 1353, immortalising his true love, Laura, wife of Hugues de Sade, in verse. The **Musée Pétrarque** (☎ 04 90 20 37 20; 10FF) on the left bank of the Sorgue is devoted to his work, sojourn and broken heart.

Places to Stay

Camping Municipal Les Prés (☎ 04 90 20 32 38) is west of the village centre near the large public carpark and the Sorgue on Route du Cavaillon. The ***Auberge de Jeunesse*** (☎ 04 90 20 31 65; fax 04 90 20 26 20), Chemin de la Vignasse, is south of the Fontaine de Vaucluse in the direction of Lagnes (walk uphill from the bus stop).

The tourist office has a list of chambres d'hôtes in the village. Fontaine de Vaucluse has three hotels, the most affordable being the 12 room ***Hôtel Les Sources*** (☎ 04 90 20 31 84), Route de Cavaillon. Doubles cost 170FF.

Getting There & Away

Fontaine de Vaucluse is 21km south-east of Carpentras and some 7km east of L'Isle-sur-Sorgue, the nearest 'real' town. From Avignon, Voyages Arnaud runs a bus (25FF; one hour; two or three a day) with a stop at Fontaine de Vaucluse, from where it's a short walk to the spring. There are Arnaud buses from Carpentras to L'Isle-sur-Sorgue (20 minutes).

GORDES

• pop 2000 ✉ 84220

On the white, rocky southern face of the Vaucluse plateau, the tiered village of Gordes forms an amphitheatre overlooking the Sorgue and Calavon rivers. The top of the village is crowned by a sturdy **chateau** built between the 11th and 16th centuries. In summer, this once typical Provençal village is frighteningly overrun with tourists, but it's still worth a wander around if you've got the wheels to get you there.

Information

The tourist office (☎ 04 90 72 02 75; fax 04 90 72 04 39), in the chateau's Salle des Gardes (Guards' Hall), Place du Château, is open from 9 am to noon and 2 to 6 pm.

Getting There & Away

Gordes is some 18km east of Fontaine de Vaucluse and about 20km west of Apt. The closest town is Cavaillon, 16km to the south-west, which is served by train (☎ 04 90 71 04 40 for information) and bus (☎ 04 90 78 32 39) from many cities and towns in Provence. Buses run by Les Express de la Durance (☎ 04 90 71 03 00 in Cavaillon) link Gordes with Cavaillon twice a day except Sunday.

AROUND GORDES

The main reason people come to Gordes is to visit the walled **Village des Bories** (☎ 04 90 72 03 48), 4km south-west of Gordes, just off the D2 heading for Cavaillon.

Bories are one or two-storey beehive-shaped huts constructed without mortar using thin wedges of limestone. They were first built in the area in the Bronze Age and were continuously lived in, renovated and even built anew until as late as the 18th century. It is not known what purpose they first served, but over the centuries they have been used as shelters, workshops, wine cellars and storage sheds. The 'village' contains about 20 such structures, restored to their appearance of about 150 years ago. Some people say the bories remind them of Ireland's *clochán*. The site is open to visitors daily from 9 am to 7.30 pm. Admission is 30/22FF for adults/under 17s.

Some 4km north-west of Gordes and off the D177 is the Cistercian **Abbaye de Sénanque** (Sénanque Abbey; ☎ 04 90 72 05 72) which, in summer, is framed by fields of lilac lavender. The abbey, founded in 1148 and today inhabited by just five monks, is open from 10 am to noon and 2 to 6 pm (2 to 5 pm only between November and March). Sunday hours year-round are 2 to 6 pm (morning Mass at 9 am). Admission is 25/20FF for adults/students.

ROUSSILLON

• pop 1200 ✉ 84220

Roussillon lies in the valley between the Vaucluse plateau and the Lubéron range. Some two millennia ago, the Romans used its distinctive ochre earth for producing pottery glazes. These days the whole village – even the gravestones in the cemetery – is built of the reddish local stone, making it a popular place for painters eager to try out the range of their palettes. The red and orange hues are especially striking given the yellow-white bareness of the surrounding area and the green conifers sprinkled around town.

Information

The tourist office (☎/fax 04 90 05 60 25), in the centre of Roussillon on Place de la Poste, is open from 10 am to noon and 2 to 6.30 pm (closed on Sunday in winter). It changes money from 10 to 11.30 am and 2 to 6 pm. A complete list of hotels, chambres d'hôtes and restaurants in and around Roussillon is pinned up outside the office.

Sentier des Ocres

The 1km-long Ochre Trail begins about 100m north of Roussillon's centre and will lead you through fairy-tale groves of chestnuts, maritime pines and scrub to the bizarre and beautiful ochre formations created by erosion and fierce winds over the centuries. It can be steep at times, but there are lead ropes to hold onto. Don't wear white; you'll return smudged from head to toe in rust-coloured dust.

Getting There & Away

Roussillon, 9km east of Gordes in the direction of Apt (11km east again), is inaccessible by public transport. The GR6 hiking trail passes through here.

APT & THE LUBÉRON

The Lubéron hills stretch from Cavaillon in the west to Manosque in the east, and from Apt southward to the Durance River. The area is named after the main range, a compact massif with a gentle, 1100m-high summit. Its oak-covered northern face is steep and uneven, while its southern face is drier and more Mediterranean in both climate and flora. Much of the Lubéron is within the boundaries of the Parc Naturel Régional du Lubéron. The area has some great hiking trails and is an excellent place for bicycling.

The Lubéron area is dotted with bories (see Around Gordes). The town of Apt (population 11,500), is a very good base for exploring the Lubéron, is largely unexceptional except for its grapes, cherries and *fleurions*, candied or crystallised fruits, which are sold everywhere. It celebrates its Fête de la Cerise (Cherry Festival) each year in May.

Information

Tourist Office As you enter Apt from Cavaillon, the tourist office (☎ 04 90 74 03 18; fax 04 90 04 64 30; tourisme.apt@avignon.pacwan.net) is just over the bridge at 20 Ave Philippe de Girard. It's open from

9 am to noon and 2 to 6 pm (closed on Sunday). In July and August it is open until 7 pm and on Sunday from 9 am to noon. Ask for the leaflet entitled *Apt Cœur du Lubéron – à Découvrir* which details, in English as well as French, two one-hour city tours, signposted around town with colour-coded markers.

The tourist office sells regional maps such as the IGN map of the Vaucluse and Didier-Richard's 1:50,000 Lubéron-Mont Sainte Victoire.

Park Office Information on the Parc Naturel Régional du Lubéron, including details on the park's two dozen *gîtes d'étape*, is available in Apt from the Maison du Parc (☎ 04 90 04 42 00; fax 04 90 04 81 15), 60 Place Jean Jaurès. The centre has plenty of information on hiking and cycling in the park, and sells an excellent range of guides including the recommended topoguide *Le Parc Naturel Régional du Lubéron à Pied* (75FF), which details 24 hikes including the GR9, GR92 and GR97 trails.

The park office is open from 8.30 am to noon and 1.30 to 7 pm (closed on Sunday; open until 6 pm from October to March and closed Saturday afternoon).

Lubéron by Bike

Vélo Loisir en Lubéron (☎ 04 92 79 05 82), BP 14, F-04280 Céreste, assists cyclists wanting to explore the Lubéron by pedal-power. It provides accommodation, bicycle rental and technical support to cyclists following the Lubéron by the cycle route that stretches for 100km across the Parc Naturel Régional du Lubéron.

White markers signpost the eastbound route from Cavaillon, through Ménerbes, Lacoste and Bonnieux (Peter Mayle country) to Apt and farther on eastward to Forcalquier. Orange-ochre signs mark the westbound route. Colourful information boards provide details on accommodation, places to eat and sights in and around the 19 villages cyclists pass en route.

Parc Naturel Régional du Lubéron

The Lubéron Regional Park's 1200 sq km encompass numerous villages, desolate forests (some of them recently scarred by fire), unexpected gorges and abandoned farmhouses, well on the way to falling into ruin – or perhaps restoration by fans of Peter Mayle, whose purchase and renovation of a house just outside the pretty village of **Ménerbes** in the late 1980s formed the basis of his witty, best-selling books *A Year in Provence* and *Toujours Provence*.

Places to Stay

Camping The ***Camping Municipal Les Cèdres*** (☎ 04 90 74 14 61), by the river just out of town on Route de Rustrel, is open from mid-February to mid-November. It charges 10.70FF per person and 7.70FF for a tent or car. ***Camping Le Lubéron*** (☎ 04 90 04 85 40; fax 04 90 74 12 19), south-east of Apt on Route de Saignon, is open from April to September.

Hostel The ***Auberge de Jeunesse*** (☎ 04 90 74 39 34), 6km south-east of Apt in the village of Saignon, offers bed and breakfast for 75FF. The hostel is closed from mid-January to mid-February. To get there without a car, use your feet or thumb.

Hotels In Apt, the welcoming ***Hôtel du Palais*** (☎ 04 90 04 89 32), Place Gabriel Péri (behind Place de la Bouquerie), provides fairly basic doubles with washbasin for 160FF, with shower for 180FF and with shower and toilet for 200FF; triples with shower are 210FF, with bath and toilet 260FF. *Menus* in its popular streetside restaurant start at 89FF.

The ***Hôtel L'Aptois*** (☎ 04 90 74 02 02; fax 04 90 74 64 79), 289 Cours Lauze de Perret, has doubles from 170/320FF with washbasin/shower and toilet. It is closed from about mid-February to mid-March.

Part of the Logis de France chain is the cosy ***Auberge du Lubéron*** (☎ 04 90 74 12 50;

fax 04 90 04 79 49), on the opposite side of the river at 8 Place Faubourg du Ballet. Comfortable singles/doubles in the low season are 250/290FF, rising to 290/420FF in July and August.

Getting There & Away

Buses to Aix-en-Provence (45FF; 1½ hours; two a day) leave from the bus station (☎ 04 90 74 20 21) east of the centre at 250 Ave de la Libération. The trip to Avignon (41FF; three or four a day) takes 1¼ hours. There is also a service to/from Digne-les-Bains (62FF; two hours; two a day), Cavaillon (26.50FF; 40 minutes; two a day), Manosque (one hour; twice daily) and Marseille (55FF; 2½ hours; two a day). The station is open daily from 8 am to noon and 2.30 to 4.45 pm.

Getting Around

Hire a mountain bike from Cycles Agnel (☎ 04 90 74 17 16), along the river east of Place de la Bouquerie at 86 Quai Général Leclerc, or Cycles Ricaud (☎ 04 90 74 16 43), 44 Quai Général Leclerc. Rates are 80/400FF a day/week.

Arles & the Camargue

ARLES

• pop 52,000 ✉ 13200

The attractive city of Arles sits on the northern tip of the Camargue alluvial plain on the Grand Rhône River, just south of where the Petit Rhône splits off from it. Avignon is 36km to the north-east, while Nîmes (see the Languedoc-Roussillon chapter) is 31km to the north-west.

Arles began its ascent to prosperity and political importance in 49 BC, when the victorious Julius Caesar – to whom the city had given its support – captured and plundered Marseille, which had backed Caesar's rival, the general and statesman Pompey the Great. Arles soon replaced Marseille as the region's major port and became the sort of Roman provincial centre that, within a century and a half, needed a 20,000 seat amphitheatre and a 12,000 seat theatre to entertain its citizens. These days, the two structures are still used to stage cultural events and bullfights.

Arles' most famous resident was Vincent Van Gogh (1853-90), who settled in the town for a year in 1888 and immortalised on canvas many of the city's most picturesque streets and surrounding rural areas.

Bullfighting

In *mise à mort* bullfighting (*corrida*), which is popular in Spain, Latin America and parts of southern France, a bull bred to be aggressive is killed in a colourful and bloody ceremony involving picadors, toreadors, matadors and horses. But not all bullfighting ends with a dead animal. In a *course Camarguaise* (Camargue-style bullfight), white-clad *razeteurs* try to remove ribbons tied to the bull's horns with hooks held between their fingers.

In Arles, the bullfighting season begins around Easter with a bullfighting festival known as the Feria (or Féria) and runs until September. The Feria incorporates both the course Camarguaise and corrida, and is held in the Arènes.

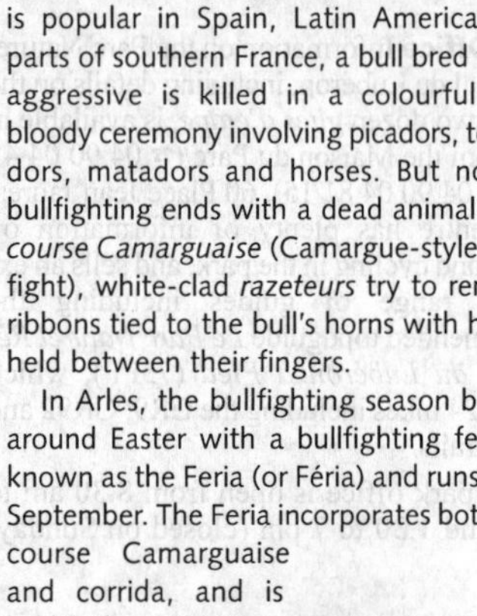

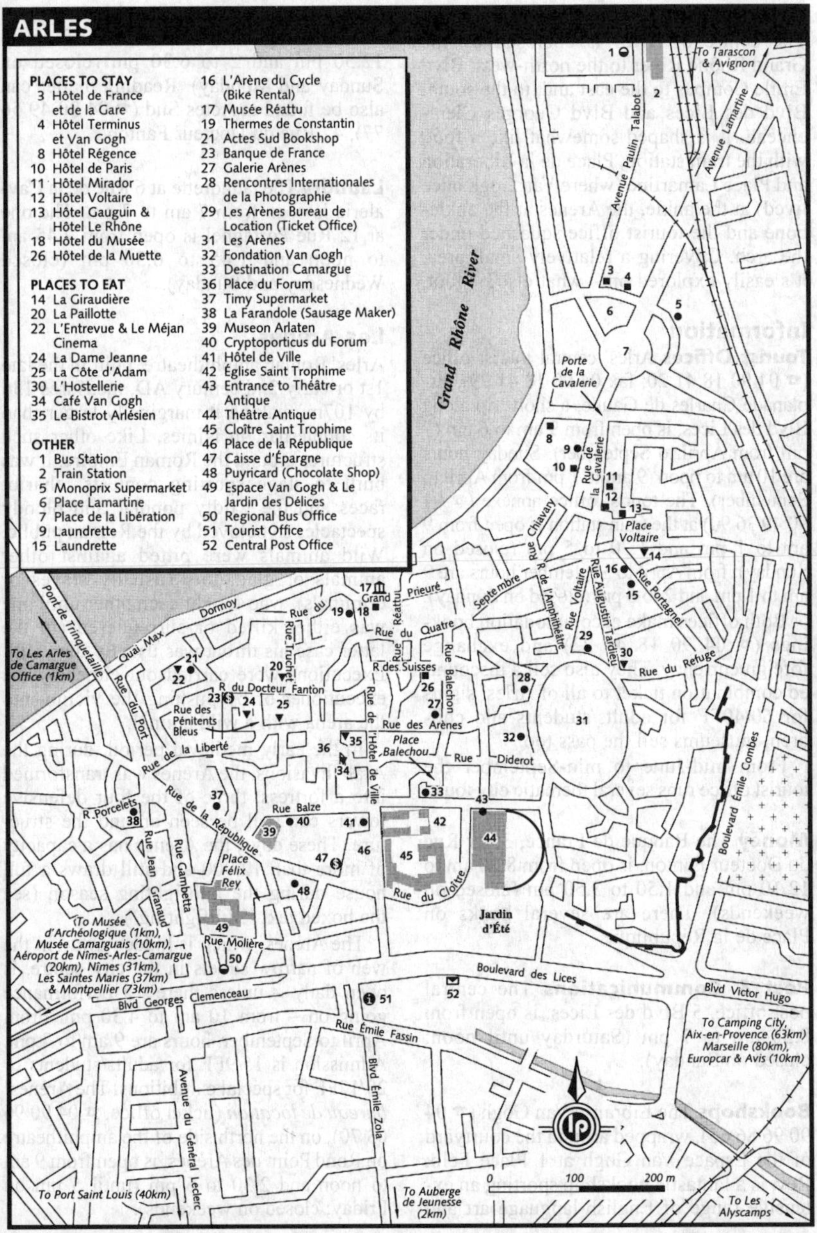
ARLES
PLACES TO STAY
3 Hôtel de France et de la Gare
4 Hôtel Terminus et Van Gogh
8 Hôtel Régence
10 Hôtel de Paris
11 Hôtel Mirador
12 Hôtel Voltaire
13 Hôtel Gauguin & Hôtel Le Rhône
18 Hôtel du Musée
26 Hôtel de la Muette
PLACES TO EAT
14 La Giraudière
20 La Paillotte
22 L'Entrevue & Le Méjan Cinema
24 La Dame Jeanne
25 La Côte d'Adam
30 L'Hostellerie
34 Café Van Gogh
35 Le Bistrot Arlésien
OTHER
1 Bus Station
2 Train Station
5 Monoprix Supermarket
6 Place Lamartine
7 Place de la Libération
9 Laundrette
15 Laundrette
16 L'Arène du Cycle (Bike Rental)
17 Musée Réattu
19 Thermes de Constantin
21 Actes Sud Bookshop
23 Banque de France
27 Galerie Arènes
28 Rencontres Internationales de la Photographie
29 Les Arènes Bureau de Location (Ticket Office)
31 Les Arènes
32 Fondation Van Gogh
33 Destination Camargue
36 Place du Forum
37 Timy Supermarket
38 La Farandole (Sausage Maker)
39 Museon Arlaten
40 Cryptoporticus du Forum
41 Hôtel de Ville
42 Église Saint Trophime
43 Entrance to Théâtre Antique
44 Théâtre Antique
45 Cloître Saint Trophime
46 Place de la République
47 Caisse d'Épargne
48 Puyricard (Chocolate Shop)
49 Espace Van Gogh & Le Jardin des Délices
50 Regional Bus Office
51 Tourist Office
52 Central Post Office
To Tarascon & Avignon
Avenue Paulin Talabot
Avenue Lamartine
Grand Rhône River
Porte de la Cavalerie
Rue de la Cavalerie
Rue Chiavary
Place Voltaire
Rue Portagnel
Rue Voltaire
Rue Augustin Tardieu
R. de l'Amphithéâtre
Rue du Refuge
Septembre
Rue du Quatre
Rue Balechon
R. des Suisses
Rue des Arènes
Place Balechou
Rue Diderot
Rue de l'Hôtel de Ville
Rue Réattu
Prieuré
Grand
Rue du
Rue Truchet
Pont de Trinquetaille
To Les Arles de Camargue Office (1km)
Quai Max Dormoy
Rue du Port
R. du Docteur Fanton
Rue des Pénitents Bleus
Rue de la Liberté
Rue de la République
R. Porcelets
Rue Balze
Rue Jean Granaud
Rue Gambetta
Place Félix Rey
Rue du Cloître
Jardin d'Été
Boulevard Émile Combes
Boulevard des Lices
Blvd Victor Hugo
Rue Molière
(To Musée d'Archéologique (1km), Musée Camarguais (10km), Aéroport de Nîmes-Arles-Camargue (20km), Nîmes (31km), Les Saintes Maries (37km) & Montpellier (73km)
Blvd Georges Clemenceau
Rue Émile Fassin
Blvd Émile Zola
Avenue du Général Leclerc
To Camping City, Aix-en-Provence (63km) Marseille (80km), Europcar & Avis (10km)
0 100 200 m
To Port Saint Louis (40km)
To Auberge de Jeunesse (2km)
To Les Alyscamps

Orientation

The centre of Arles is enclosed by the Grand Rhône River to the north-west, Blvd Émile Combes to the east and, to the south, Blvd des Lices and Blvd Georges Clemenceau. It is shaped somewhat like a foot, with the train station, Place de la Libération and Place Lamartine (where Van Gogh once lived) at the ankle, the Arènes at the ankle-bone and the tourist office squashed under the arch. Covering a relatively small area, it's easily explored on – what else? – foot.

Information

Tourist Offices Arles' central tourist office (☎ 04 90 18 41 20; fax 04 90 18 41 29), Esplanade Charles de Gaulle, a short trip along Blvd des Lices, is open from 9 am to 6 pm (7 pm from April to September). Sunday hours are 10 am to noon (9 am to 1 pm from April to September). The tourist office annexe (☎ 04 90 49 36 90) at the train station is open from 9 am to 1 pm and 1.30 to 5 pm (closed on Sunday); from April to September hours are 9 am to 1 pm and 2 to 6 pm (closed on Sunday).

Both offices make accommodation bookings (☎ 04 90 18 41 22) and exchange foreign currency. They also sell a discounted combination ticket to all of Arles' sights for 60/40FF for adults/students and children; museums sell the pass too.

From mid-June to mid-September the tourist office runs several thematic city tours.

Money The Banque de France, 35ter Rue du Docteur Fanton, is open from 8.30 am to 12.10 pm and 1.50 to 3.50 pm (closed on weekends). There are several banks on Place de la République.

Post & Communications The central post office, 5 Blvd des Lices, is open from 8.30 am to 7 pm (Saturday until noon; closed on Sunday).

Bookshops The Librairie Van Gogh (☎ 04 90 96 86 65), wrapped around the courtyard of the Espace Van Gogh at 1 Place Félix Rey, is a fantastic bookshop sporting an extensive range of English-language art and history books, as well as books and guides about the region. It's open from 10 am to 12.30 pm and 2 to 6.30 pm (closed on Sunday and Monday). Reading matter can also be found at Actes Sud (☎ 04 90 49 56 77), 47 Rue du Docteur Fanton.

Laundry The laundrette at 6 Rue de la Cavalerie is open from 7 am to 7 pm. The one at 12 Rue Portagnel is open from 7.45 am to noon and 1.45 to 6.30 pm (closed Wednesday and Sunday).

Les Arènes

Arles' Roman amphitheatre, built in the late 1st or early 2nd century AD, measures 136 by 107m, making it marginally larger than its counterpart in Nîmes. Like other such structures around the Roman Empire, it was built to stage sporting contests, chariot races and the wildly popular and bloody spectacles so beloved by the Roman public. Wild animals were pitted against other animals or gladiators (usually slaves or criminals), who fought each other until one was either killed or surrendered (in the latter case his throat was usually then slit). Executions were carried out either by the executioner or by pushing the victim into the arena with a wild animal.

In the early medieval period, during the Arab invasions, the Arènes was transformed into a fortress; three of the four defensive towers can still be seen around the structure. These days, the Arènes has a capacity of more than 12,000 and still draws a full house during the bullfighting season (see the boxed text 'Bullfighting').

The Arènes, which is hidden away in the web of narrow streets in the city centre, is open daily – unless there's a performance going on – from 10 am to 4.30 pm. From April to September, hours are 9 am to 7 pm. Admission is 15/9FF for adults/students or 20/12FF for special exhibitions. The Arènes' *bureau de location* (ticket office; ☎ 04 90 96 03 70), on the north side of the amphitheatre on Rond Point des Arènes, is open from 9 am to noon and 2.30 to 6 pm (until 5 pm on Friday; closed on weekends).

Théâtre Antique

The Roman theatre (☎ 04 90 96 93 30), which dates from the end of the 1st century BC, was used for many hundreds of years as a convenient source of construction materials, so little of the original structure – measuring 102m in diameter – remains except for two imposing columns. Entered through the Jardin d'Été (Summer Garden) on Blvd des Lices, it hosts open-air dance, film and music festivals in summer. The Théâtre Antique has the same opening hours as the Arènes and charges the same admission.

Église Saint Trophime

This austere Provençal Romanesque-style church was once a cathedral, as Arles was an archbishopric from the 4th century until 1790. It stands on the site of several earlier churches, and was built in the late 11th and 12th centuries – perhaps using stone cut from the Théâtre Antique. The church is named after St Trophimus, a late 2nd or early 3rd century bishop of Arles.

Across the courtyard is the serene **Cloître Saint Trophime** (☎ 04 90 49 36 36), surrounded by superbly sculptured columns. The two Romanesque galleries date from the 1100s, while the two Gothic galleries are from the 14th century. The cloister is open the same hours as the Arènes and charges 20/14FF admission for adults/students.

Les Alyscamps

This large necropolis (☎ 04 90 49 36 36), 1km south-east of the Arènes, was founded by the Romans and taken over by Christians in the 4th century. Because of the reputed presence among the dead of Christian martyrs said to work miracles, Les Alyscamps became a very popular last resting place.

The necropolis was treated very badly during and after the Renaissance, and today the area is but a shadow of its former glorious self. Some of the original marble sarcophagi are preserved in the Musée d'Archéologique d'Arles. Both Van Gogh and Gauguin painted Les Alyscamps with great vividness. Les Alyscamps is open the same hours as the Arènes; admission is 15/9FF for adults/students.

Other Roman Sites

The partly preserved **Thermes de Constantin**, near the river on Rue du Grand Prieuré, were built in the 4th century. The Roman baths are due to reopen following extensive renovations, and hours should be 10 am to noon and 2 to 4.30 pm (9 am to noon and 2 to 7 pm from April to September). Admission is 15/9FF for adults/students.

The **Cryptoporticus du Forum** are underground storerooms, most of which were carved out in the 1st century BC. To gain access you need to go through a 17th century Jesuit chapel on Rue Balze, they keep the same hours as the Arènes and cost 12/7FF for adults/students.

Museums

The **Musée d'Archéologique d'Arles** (also called the Musée de l'Arles Antique; ☎ 04 90 18 88 88 or ☎ 04 90 18 88 89), in a strikingly modern building, brings together the rich collections of the former Musée d'Art Païen (Museum of Pagan Art) and Musée d'Art Chrétien (Museum of Christian Art). Exhibits include Roman statues, artefacts, marble sarcophagi and a renowned assortment of early Christian sarcophagi from the 4th century. The archaeology museum is 1.5km south-west of the tourist office at Ave de la 1ère Division Française Libre on the Presqu'île du Cirque Romain. It is open from 10 am to 6 pm (closed Tuesday); hours from April to September are 9 am to 8 pm. Admission is 35/25FF for adults/ students.

The **Museon Arlaten** (☎ 04 90 96 08 23), Rue de la République, founded by the Nobel prize-winning poet Frédéric Mistral (see Language at the beginning of this chapter), is dedicated to preserving and displaying everyday objects related to traditional Provençal life: furniture, crafts, costumes, ceramics, wigs, a model of the Tarasque (a people-eating amphibious monster of Provençal legend) etc. It occupies a 16th century townhouse constructed around Roman ruins, and is open from 9 am to noon and 2 to 5 pm (6 pm in April, May and September, 6.30 pm in June and 7 pm in July and August). The museum is closed on Monday between October and June. Admission is 20/15FF for adults/students.

The **Musée Réattu** (☎ 04 90 96 37 68), housed in a former 15th century priory at 10 Rue du Grand Prieuré, exhibits works by some of the world's finest photographers, modern and contemporary works of art, and paintings by 18th and 19th century Provençal artists. The museum also has 57 Picasso drawings, sketched by the eccentric artist between December 1970 and November 1971. His more conventional portrait of his mother Maria, painted in Côte d'Antibes in 1923, is particularly fine. The museum is open daily from 10.30 am to noon and 2 to 5.30 pm (9 am to noon and 2 to 7 pm from April to September). Admission costs 15/ 9FF for adults/students or 20/12FF when there are special exhibits.

Van Gogh Trail

The **Fondation Vincent Van Gogh** (☎ 04 90 49 94 04 or ☎ 04 90 93 08 08; fax 04 90 49 55 49; www.tourismeplus.com/fond-vangogh-arles), inside the Palais de Luppé at 24bis Rond Point des Arènes, markets itself as a 'tribute to Van Gogh through international artists'. It displays a wealth of paintings by other artists inspired by Arles' most famous resident. The centre is open from 9.30 am to noon and 2 to 5.40 pm (10 am to 7 pm between April and October). Admission is 30/20FF for adults/students.

The gallery **La Rose des Vents** (☎ 04 90 93 25 96), 18 Rue Diderot, displays various Van Gogh reproductions as well as copies of letters written by the artist to his brother Theo. It's open from 10.30 am to 12.30 pm and 3 to 7 pm (closed on Sunday morning and Monday).

Various art exhibitions take place at the **Espace Van Gogh** (☎ 04 90 49 39 39; fax 04 90 43 80 85), housed in the old Hôtel Dieu

Vincent Van Gogh

When Vincent Van Gogh (1853-90) arrived in Provence in 1888, the quality of the light and colours were a great revelation to him. He spent an intensely productive year at Arles, during which he painted all sorts of local scenes, among them the Pont de Langlois, a little bridge that has been rebuilt 3km south of Arles (from town, take bus No 1 to the Pont Van Gogh terminus). His famous painting of the bridge entitled *The Bridge at Arles* is on display in the Netherlands at the Kröller-Müller National Museum in Otterlo. Some of Van Gogh's other best known canvases – *Sunflowers*, *Van Gogh's Chair* and *Café at Night* – were all painted in Arles.

In 1888, Van Gogh's friend and fellow artist Gauguin came to stay with him for several months. But their different temperaments and approaches to art soon led to a quarrel, after which Van Gogh – overcome with despair – chopped off part of his left ear. In May 1889, because of recurrent bouts of madness, he voluntarily entered an asylum in Saint Rémy de Provence (25km north-east of Arles over the Alpilles). He stayed there for a year, during which time he continued to be amazingly productive. In 1890, while staying in Auvers-sur-Oise (just north of Paris), Van Gogh – lonely to the point of desperation and afraid his madness was incurable – shot and killed himself.

There are few tangible remains of Vincent Van Gogh's stay in Arles. All traces of his rented yellow house and the nearby café on Place Lamartine – both of which appear in his paintings – were wiped out during WWII. Despite this being his most prolific period – he produced some 200 canvases in the space of a year – not a single piece of Van Gogh's work remains in Arles today.

and former hospital on Place Félix Rey where Van Gogh spent some time.

Organised Tours

Tours of the Camargue by jeep are organised by many companies, including Provence Camargue Tours (☎ 04 90 49 85 58), 1 Rue Émile Fassin; Havas Voyages (☎ 04 90 96 13 25), 4 Blvd des Lices; and Destination Camargue (☎ 04 90 96 94 44; fax 04 90 49 84 31), 29 Rue Balechou. The latter organises half-day trips (180/100FF for adults/children), departing daily from Arles at 3 pm in summer. Reservations can also be made at La Boutique Provençal (☎ 04 90 49 84 31), 8 Rond Point des Arènes. For more information see the Camargue section.

Special Events

Arles has a full calendar of summertime cultural events. In early July, Les Rencontres Internationales de la Photographie (International Photography Festival) and its exhibits attract photographers and aficionados from around the world. The two week Fêtes d'Arles, which usually kicks off at the end of June, brings dance, theatre, music and poetry readings to the city. For more information contact the Festiv'Arles office (☎ 04 90 96 47 00 or ☎ 04 90 96 81 18; fax 04 90 96 81 17), 35 Place de la République. Other fascinating events include the Festival Mosaïque Gitane in mid-July, which celebrates Gypsy culture, and the week-long Fête des Prémices du Riz in mid-August marking the start of the rice harvest.

Places to Stay

Except during festivals, bullfights and July and August, Arles has plenty of reasonably priced accommodation. There are lots of gîtes ruraux (☎ 04 90 59 49 40 for reservations) in the surrounding countryside, especially the Camargue. Ask the tourist office for the list.

Places to Stay – Budget

Camping The nearest camping ground to Arles is the two star ***Camping City*** (☎ 04 90 93 08 86; fax 04 90 93 91 07), 67 Route de Crau, 1km south-east of the city centre on the road to Marseille. It's open from March to October and charges 21/15FF per adult/child plus 22FF for a tent and car. Take bus No 2 to the Hermite stop.

Camargue Cowboys

Gardians are Camargue cowboys who herd the region's cattle and, during the bullfighting season, bulls. The Fête des Gardians, held in Arles on the first weekend of May, honours these mounted herdsmen who, clad in leather hats, chequered shirts and cowboy boots, usher the horned beasts through town on horseback to the Arènes. Traditionally, gardians live in *cabanes de gardians*, tiny whitewashed cottages crowned with a thatched roof and sealed with a strip of mortar.

Hostel The 100 bed ***Auberge de Jeunesse*** (☎ 04 90 96 18 25; fax 04 90 96 31 26), 2km from the centre at 20 Ave Maréchal Foch, charges 75FF including breakfast. It is closed during the first half of February. Take bus No 3 or 8 from Blvd Georges Clemenceau (No 8 from Place Lamartine) to the Fournier stop.

Hotels Close to the train station, the ***Hôtel de France et de la Gare*** (☎ 04 90 96 01 24; fax 04 90 96 90 87), 1-3 Place Lamartine, has rooms for one or two people with shower and toilet for 185FF. Next door at No 5, the renovated ***Hôtel Terminus et Van Gogh*** (☎/fax 04 90 96 12 32) has similar rooms with washbasin, for one or two people, for 140FF. Doubles/triples/quads with shower are 180/270/320FF.

Heading into town you come to a couple more cheapies. The ***Hôtel Régence***, 5 Rue Marius Jouveau, overlooks the Rhône and has uninspiring singles/doubles from 140/175FF. The nearby ***Hôtel de Paris***, above a cheap café at 10 Rue de la Cavalerie, has equally cheap rooms for 160FF.

The ***Hôtel Voltaire*** (☎ 04 90 96 13 58), 1 Place Voltaire, has serviceable rooms, some overlooking the pretty square, from 120/ 140FF with washbasin/shower.

The old-fashioned and cluttered ***Hôtel Le Rhône*** (☎ 04 90 96 43 70), 11 Place Voltaire, has rooms with washbasin from 130FF, rooms with shower from 170FF, and rooms with shower and toilet from 210FF.

Places to Stay – Mid-Range

The renovated, two star ***Hôtel Gauguin*** (☎ 04 90 96 14 35; fax 04 90 18 98 87), 5 Place Voltaire, has doubles equipped with alarm clocks and showers for 180FF (with toilet too for 210FF). Nearby, rooms for one or two people at the 15 room ***Hôtel Mirador*** (☎ 04 90 96 28 05; fax 04 90 96 59 89), 3 Rue Voltaire, cost 230/255FF with toilet and shower/bath. Cheaper rooms with no toilet – just shower – are 190FF.

The appealing, 20 room ***Hôtel du Musée*** (☎ 04 90 93 88 88; fax 04 90 49 98 15), 11 Rue du Grand Prieuré, occupies a fine 12th to 13th century building and is spacious and has a rear terrace garden. Doubles with shower/bath and toilet start at 220/ 320FF.

The family-run, two star ***Hôtel de la Muette*** (☎ 04 90 96 15 39; fax 04 90 49 73 16) at 15 Rue des Suisses is part of the Logis de France chain and has appropriately prettily furnished rooms with toilet and shower/bath from 220/300FF. Rooms with shower only (no toilet) cost 210FF.

PROVENCE

Places to Eat

Blvd Georges Clemenceau and Blvd des Lices are lined with plane trees and brasseries with terraces. The latter are fine for a meal if you don't mind dining à la traffic fumes.

Restaurants Place du Forum, an intimate square shaded by eight large plane trees, turns into one big dining table at lunch and dinner. Most of the restaurants here are mid-range, though ***Le Bistrot Arlésien*** on the corner of Rue des Arènes has salads for 20 to 60FF and reasonably priced plats du jour for 55 to 60FF. ***La Côte d'Adam*** (☎ 04 90 49 62 29), a cosy and popular place nearby at 12 Rue de la Liberté, is slightly cheaper than its counterparts on the square.

The unpretentious ***La Dame Jeanne*** (☎ 04 90 96 37 09), to the west at 4 Rue des Pénitents Bleus, offers a three course *menu* for 72FF and a four course one for 98FF.

The calm and cool ***L'Entrevue*** (☎ 04 90 93 37 28), down by the riverfront in a cinema and bookshop complex at 23 Quai Max Dormoy, doesn't in fact offer a view of the water but is a stylish, laid-back place serving Asian and Caribbean-inspired cuisine, including a fantastic couscous royal (98FF) and wonderfully refreshing mint and pine kernel tea.

The ***L'Hostellerie*** (☎ 04 90 96 13 05), 62 Rue du Refuge, has a terrace with an excellent view towards the amphitheatre. It offers a good selection of salads (18 to 52FF) and a *menu* for 75FF. It is closed on Tuesday. Decked out with wooden blue shutters, ***La Giraudière*** (☎ 04 90 93 27 52), 53-55 Rue Condorcet, is an attractive place overlooking Place Voltaire. It also has a tempting regional *menu* for 79FF.

La Paillotte (☎ 04 90 96 33 15), 26 Rue du Docteur Fanton, is very popular with locals and dishes up great *aïoli Provençal* for 78FF, and an excellent *petite bouillabaisse* for 108FF.

Cafés Arles' most idyllic café is ***Le Jardin Délices*** at the Espace Van Gogh, overlooking ornamental gardens inspired by Van Gogh's painting *The Hospital Garden at Arles*. A variety of salads and light meals are served here, costing between 40 and 50FF for a set formule.

Also paying homage to Vincent's Arles roots is the very yellow ***Café Van Gogh***, Place du Forum, reminiscent of the yellow house on Place Lamartine that Van Gogh chose as the subject for his canvas *Café at Night*. The Café Van Gogh, which is a busy bar by night, has *menus* for 75 and 99FF.

Self-Catering The ***Timy*** supermarket, 19 Rue de la République, is open from 8.30 am to 12.15 pm and 3.30 to 7.30 pm. ***Monoprix***, Place Lamartine, is open from 8.30 am to 7.25 pm. Both are closed on Sunday.

On Wednesday, ***market stalls*** sprawl the length of Blvd Émile Combes along the outside of the city walls. The food section is at the northern end. On Saturday morning, the market moves to Blvd des Lices and Blvd Georges Clemenceau.

Locally made *saucisson d'Arles* (Arles sausage) is sold at sausage-makers ***La Farandole***, 11 Rue des Porcelets. The sweet-toothed can purchase exquisite Provençal chocolates from the ***Puyricard*** chocolatier, Rue de la République.

Getting There & Away

Air Nîmes-Arles-Camargue airport (also called Garons airport; ☎ 04 66 70 49 49) is 20km north-west of the city on the A54.

Bus The bus station, at the end of Ave Paulin Talabot, is about 1km north of the Arènes. The information office (☎ 04 90 49 38 01) is open from 9 am to 4 pm (Saturday until noon; closed on Sunday and Monday). Most intercity buses stop here. Some also stop at 24 Blvd Georges Clemenceau, where the regional bus company Les Cars de Camargue (☎ 04 90 96 94 78) has an office; it also has an office at 4 Rue Jean Mathieu Artaud. It runs services to Nîmes (33FF; 50 minutes; six a day) and Marseille (82FF; 2½ hours; two a day) via Aix-en-Provence (65FF; 1¾ hours).

Les Cars de Camargue buses also link Arles with various parts of the Camargue, including Les Saintes Maries de la Mer (36.50FF; one hour; two a day in winter and six to nine a day in summer), Port Saint Louis (36FF; 65 minutes; six a day) and many places en route such as Mas du Pont de Rousty, Pioch Badet and Pont de Gau. If you'll be staying in the Camargue for a few days, it might be worth purchasing a Passe Camargue (140FF), which gives you three days of unlimited travel on the two main bus routes.

Ceyte Tourisme Méditerranée (CTM; ☎ 04 90 93 74 90), 21 Chemin du Temple, has regular bus services to Marseille, Aix-en-Provence and Avignon (37.50FF; five a day).

Train Arles train station (☎ 08 36 35 35 35) is opposite the bus station. The information office is open from 8 am to noon and 2 to 6 pm (closed on Sunday). Major rail destinations include Nîmes (61FF; 30 minutes), Montpellier (93FF; one hour), Marseille (79FF; 40 minutes) and Avignon (35FF; 20 minutes).

Eurolines (☎ 04 90 96 94 78), the long-haul bus company, sells tickets at 24 Blvd Georges Clemenceau.

Car Leading car rental companies with offices in Arles include ADA (☎ 04 90 96 92 69), 4 Rue Camille Pelleton; Avis (☎ 04 90 96 82 42), Ave Paulin Talabot; and Europcar (☎ 04 90 93 23 24) and Hertz (☎ 04 90 96 75 23), both on Blvd Victor Hugo.

Getting Around

To/From the Airport CTM (☎ 04 90 93 74 90) runs bus regular services to Nîmes-Arles-Camargue airport from Blvd Georges Clemenceau.

Bus Local buses are run by STAR (☎ 04 90 96 87 47). The information office at 16 Blvd Georges Clemenceau, west of the tourist office, is open from 8.30 am to 12.30 pm and 1.30 pm (2 pm in summer) to 6 pm (closed on weekends). This is the main bus hub, though most buses also stop at Place Lamartine, a short walk south of the train station. In general, STAR buses run from 7 am to 7 pm (5 pm on Sunday). A single ticket costs 5FF; a 10 ticket carnet is 42FF. In addition to its 11 bus lines, STAR runs minibuses called Starlets that circle most of the old city every half-hour from 7.15 am to 7.40 pm (not on Sunday). Best of all, they're free.

Taxi To order a taxi, ring ☎ 04 90 49 69 59.

Bicycle Various types of bikes can be hired from Peugeot (☎ 04 90 96 03 77), 15 Rue du Pont, or L'Arène du Cycle/Dall'Oppio (☎ 04 90 96 46 83), 10 Rue Portagnel.

CAMARGUE

The sparsely populated, 780 sq km delta of the Rhône River known as the Camargue (La Camargo in Provençal) is famed for its desolate beauty and the incredibly varied bird life that its wetlands support. Over 400 species of land and water birds inhabit the region, including storks, bee-eaters and some 160 other migratory species. Most impressive of all are the huge flocks of pink flamingoes (*flamants roses*) that come here to nest during the spring and summer; many set up house near the Étang de Vaccarès (a large lake) and Étang du Fangassier. In 1997 some 30,000 flamingoes wintered in the Camargue, with some 15,000 to 20,000 couples hatching and raising their offspring in the spring of 1998.

The Camargue has been formed over the ages by sediment deposited by the Rhône (*Rose* in Provençal) River as it flows into the Mediterranean. In the southern Camargue, the areas between the sea-wall embankments (*digues à la mer*) that line water channels are taken up by shallow salt marshes, inland lakes and lagoons whose brackish waters positively shimmer in the Provençal sun. The northern part of the delta consists of dry land, and in the years following WWII huge tracts were desalinated as part of a costly drainage and irrigation program designed to make the area suitable for large-scale agriculture, especially the cultivation of rice. Rice production has dropped sharply since the 1960s, but it is still a very important part of the Camarguais economy.

At some places along the coast, the delta has continued to grow, leaving one-time seaside towns many kilometres inland from the Mediterranean. Elsewhere, sea currents and storms have, in recent centuries, swept away land that had been around long enough for people to build on. The course of the Rhône has changed repeatedly over the millennia, but the Grand Rhône (which carries 90% of the river's flow) and the Petit Rhône have followed their present channels for about 500 years.

Most of the Camargue wetlands are within the Parc Naturel Régional de Camargue, which was set up in 1970 (some areas had been declared protected in 1927) to preserve the area's fragile ecosystems by maintaining a balance between ecological considerations and the region's economic mainstays of agriculture, salt production, hunting, grazing and tourism.

In certain areas, the Camargue's famous herds of cream-coloured horses can still be seen, along with the black *bious* (bulls) that are raised for bullfighting and roam free under the watchful eyes of a mounted *gardian* (see the boxed text 'Camargue Cowboys'). But you're much more likely to see bulls grazing in fenced-in fields and horses that are saddled and tethered, waiting in rows under the blazing sun for tourists willing to pay for a ride.

At least one traditional Camargue phenomenon is alive and well: the area's savage mosquitoes are flourishing, feeding on the blood of hapless passers-by just as they have for countless eons. Pack *plenty* of insect repellent – then pack more.

Orientation

Shaped like a croissant with the Étang de Vaccarès in the centre, the 850 sq km Parc Naturel Régional de Camargue is enclosed by the Petit Rhône and Grand Rhône rivers. The Étang de Vaccarès and nearby peninsulas and islands form the Réserve Nationale de Camargue, a 135 sq km nature reserve.

Rice is cultivated in the northern sections of the delta. There are enormous salt evaporation pools around Salin de Giraud on the Camargue's south-eastern tip.

The Camargue's two most important centres are the seaside resort of Les Saintes Maries de la Mer and the tiny walled town of Aigues Mortes to the north-west.

Information

Tourist Offices Les Saintes Maries de la Mer's tourist office (☎ 04 90 97 82 55; fax 04 90 97 71 15; saintes-maries@enprovence.com; www.saintes-maries-camargue.enprovence.com), 5 Ave Van Gogh, is open from 9 am to 6 pm (until 7 pm from Easter to September, and 8 pm in July and August).

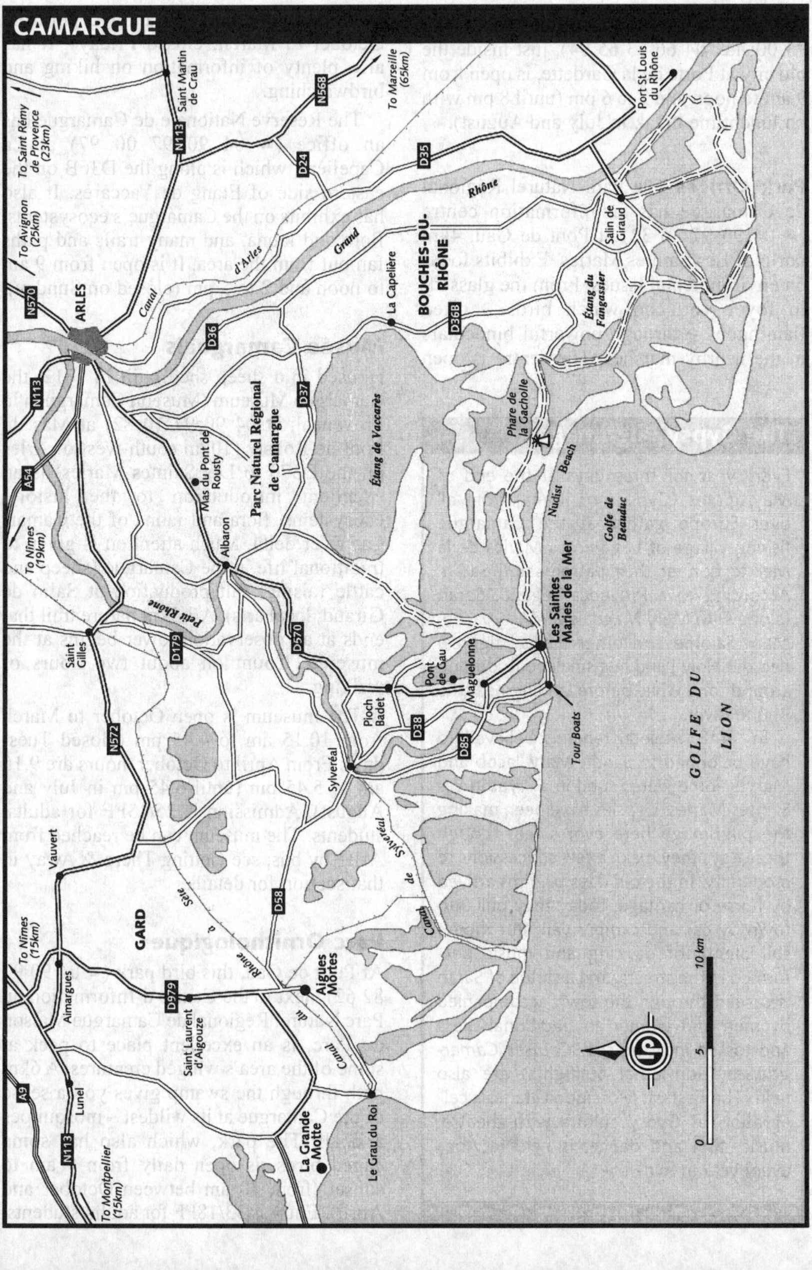
CAMARGUE
ARLES
To Avignon (25km)
To Saint Rémy de Provence (23km)
Saint Martin de Crau
To Marseille (65km)
N570
N113
N568
D24
D35
D36
D36B
D37
D570
D179
D38
D85
D58
D979
N572
A54
A9
Canal d'Arles
Grand Rhône
Petit Rhône
La Capelière
BOUCHES-DU-RHÔNE
Salin de Giraud
Port St Louis du Rhône
Étang du Fangassier
Phare de la Gacholle
Nudist Beach
Golfe de Beauduc
Parc Naturel Régional de Camargue
Étang de Vaccarès
Mas du Pont de Rousty
Albaron
To Nîmes (19km)
Saint Gilles
Les Saintes Maries de la Mer
Pont de Gau
Maguelonne
Pioch Badet
Tour Boats
Sylveréal
Canal de Sylveréal
Vauvert
GARD
Rhône à Sète
To Nîmes (15km)
Aimargues
Saint Laurent d'Aigouze
Aigues Mortes
Canal du Rhône
Lunel
La Grande Motte
Le Grau du Roi
To Montpellier (15km)
GOLFE DU LION
0
5
10 km

PROVENCE

Aigues Mortes' tourist office (☎ 04 66 53 73 00; fax 04 66 53 65 94), just inside the old city at Porte de la Gardette, is open from 9 am to noon and 2 to 6 pm (until 8 pm with no lunchtime break in July and August).

Park Offices The Parc Naturel Régional de Camargue has an information centre (☎ 04 90 97 86 32) at Pont de Gau, 4km north of Les Saintes Maries. Exhibits focus on environmental issues. From the glassed-in foyer you can watch birds – often flamingoes – through powerful binoculars in the nearby marshes. The centre is open from 9 am to 6 pm (9.30 am to 5 pm from October to March; closed Friday). It has also plenty of information on hiking and birdwatching.

The Réserve Nationale de Camargue has an office (☎ 04 90 97 00 97) at La Capelière, which is along the D36B on the eastern side of Étang de Vaccarès. It also has exhibits on the Camargue's ecosystems, flora and fauna, and many trails and paths fan out from the area. It is open from 9 am to noon and 2 to 5 pm (closed on Sunday).

The Gypsy Pilgrimage

Every year for three days at the end of May, *gitans* (Gypsies or Roma) from all over Europe gather at the Camargue fishing village of Les Saintes Maries de la Mer to honour their patron saint, Sarah. According to a Provençal legend, Sarah (along with Mary Magdalene, Mary Jacob, Mary Salome and other Biblical figures) fled the Holy Land in a small boat, drifting around for a while before landing near the Rhône River.

In 1448, skeletal remains believed to have belonged to Sarah, Mary Jacob and Mary Salome were found in a crypt in Les Saintes Maries. Gypsies have been making the pilgrimage here ever since, though these days they make a few concessions to modernity. In the old days pilgrims arrived by horse or carriage; today they pull into town by car and camper van. But there's still plenty of dancing and music performed in the streets, and a statue of Sarah is carried through the town accompanied by men and women in traditional dress and tossed into the sea. *Courses Camarguaises* (non-lethal bullfights) are also held. The Festival Mosaïque Gitane, a celebration of Gypsy culture with theatre, music, film and dance, is held in Arles every year in mid-July.

Musée Camarguais

Housed in a sheep shed built in 1812, the Camargue Museum (Museon Camarguen in Provençal; ☎ 04 90 97 10 82) at Mas du Pont de Rousty (10km south-west of Arles on the D570 to Les Saintes Maries) is an excellent introduction to the history, ecosystems, flora and fauna of the Camargue river delta. Much attention is given to traditional life in the Camargue (sheep and cattle raising, salt production at Salin de Giraud, local arts). A 3.5km nature trail that ends at an observation tower begins at the museum. Count on about two hours of walking.

The museum is open October to March from 10.15 am to 4.45 pm (closed Tuesday). From April to October, hours are 9.15 am to 5.45 pm (until 6.45 pm in July and August). Admission is 25/13FF for adults/students. The museum can be reached from Arles by bus; see Getting There & Away in that section for details.

Parc Ornithologique

At Pont de Gau, this bird park (☎ 04 90 97 82 62), next to the Centre d'Information du Parc Naturel Régional de Camargue Maison du Parc, is an excellent place to peek at some of the area's winged creatures. A 6km path through the swamp gives you a sense of the Camargue at its wildest – mosquitoes and all. The park, which also has some caged birds, is open daily from 9 am to sunset (from 10 am between October and April). Entry is 33/18FF for adults/students.

Aigues Mortes

On the western edge of the Camargue, 28km north-west of Les Saintes Maries, is the curiously named walled town of Aigues Mortes (which could be translated as 'Dead Waters'). Aigues Mortes (population 5000) was established on marshy flat land in the mid-13th century by Louis IX (Saint Louis) so the French crown would have a Mediterranean port under its direct control. (At the time, the area's other ports were controlled by various rival powers, including the counts of Provence.) In 1248, Louis IX's ships – all 1500 of them – gathered here before setting sail to the Holy Land for the Sixth Crusade.

Aigues Mortes' sturdy, rectangular ramparts, the tops of which afford great views over the marshlands, can be easily circumambulated from Tour de Constance. Inside the walls, there's a fair bit of tourist hype though the restored Église Notre Dame des Sablons is worth a look.

Les Saintes Maries de la Mer

• pop 2200 ✉ 13732

This coastal resort is known for its nearby beaches and fortified Romanesque church (12th to 15th centuries), a pilgrimage site for centuries.

Les Saintes Maries is most animated during the annual Gypsy pilgrimage (see the boxed text 'The Gypsy Pilgrimage') on 24-25 May. There is a **Musée des Gitanes** (Gypsy Museum; ☎ 04 90 97 52 85), also known as the 'Panorama du Voyage', next to the Auberge de Jeunesse in Pioch Badet.

Tickets for **bullfights** held in Les Saintes Maries' Arènes on Ave Van Gogh are sold at the ticket office, tucked into its outer walls, between 3 and 7 pm (closed on Sunday). Reservations can also be made by phoning ☎ 04 90 97 10 60.

Beaches

The coast near Les Saintes Maries is lined with around 30km of uninterrupted fine-sand beaches. The area around **Phare de la Gacholle**, the lighthouse 11km east of town, is frequented by *naturalistes* (nudists).

Hiking

There are numerous walking paths and trails in the Parc Naturel Régional and the Réserve Nationale, on the embankments and along the coast. Both park offices sell detailed hiking maps of the area, including the 1:25,000 IGN Série Bleue maps Nos 2944E and 2944O.

Boat Excursions

Several companies with offices in Les Saintes Maries have boat excursions of the Camargue, including Camargue Bateau de Promenade (☎ 04 90 97 84 72), 5 Rue des Launes, and Quatre Maries (☎ 04 90 97 70 10), 36 Ave Théodore Aubanel. Both depart from the Port Gardian in the centre of Les Saintes Maries.

Le Tiki III (☎ 04 90 97 81 68 or ☎ 04 90 97 81 22) is a beat-up old paddleboat that plies the delta's shallow waters and charges 60FF for a 1½ hour tour. Le Tiki is docked at the mouth of the Petit Rhône 1.5km west of Les Saintes Maries.

Other Activities

There are numerous horse farms offering *promenade à cheval* (horse riding) along the D570 (Route d'Arles) leading into Les Saintes Maries. Expect to pay about 75/350FF an hour/day. For detailed info on equestrian activities in the Camargue contact the Association Camarguaise de Tourisme Équestre (☎ 04 90 97 86 32; fax 04 90 97 70 82), Centre de Gines, Pont de Gau.

In Les Saintes Maries, Camprolan (☎ 04 90 97 96 82), 17 Place des Gitans, organises all types of activities including three-hour fishing expeditions for 195FF.

Kayak Vert Camargue (☎ 06 09 56 06 47 or ☎ 04 90 97 88 89; fax 04 90 97 88 91; www.canoe.france.com), Mas des Baumelles, 8km north of Les Saintes Maries off the D38, arranges canoeing and kayaking on the Petit Rhône.

Organised Tours

La Maison du Guide (☎ 04 66 73 52 30; fax 04 66 88 71 25), F-30600 Montcalm, between Aigues-Mortes and Les Saintes Maries on the D58, organises a variety of guided tours on foot, by boat and by bike.

Many companies in Arles organise tours of the Camargue by jeep (see Organised Tours in the Arles section). In Les Saintes Maries, Camargue-Safaris Photo-Loisirs (☎ 04 90 97 86 93 or ☎ 04 09 97 84 12), opposite the Arènes at 22 Ave Van Gogh, organises tours on horseback, by helicopter and by jeep (250FF for a 3½ hour trip).

Places to Stay

Camping The ***Camping La Brise*** (☎ 04 90 97 84 67; fax 04 90 97 72 01), Ave Marcle Carrière, is north-east of the centre of Les Saintes Maries. ***Camping Le Clos du Rhône*** (☎ 04 90 97 85 99; fax 04 90 97 78 85) is on the Route d'Aigues Mortes. Both sites have swimming pools. Expect to pay about 75FF a night at either.

Hostel There's an ***Auberge de Jeunesse*** (☎ 04 90 97 51 72; fax 04 90 97 54 88) in the hamlet of Pioch Badet, 8km north of Les Saintes Maries on the D570 to Arles. Bed and breakfast costs 65FF. Reception is open from 7.30 to 10.30 am and 5 to 11 pm (5 pm to midnight in July and August). Les Cars de Camargue buses from Arles to Les Saintes Maries (36.50FF; one hour; six to nine a day) drop you at the door (see Bus under Getting There & Away in the Arles section for details).

Farmhouses Numerous old *mas* (farmhouses) surround Les Saintes Maries; many have rooms to let. Particularly good value is the ***Mas de la Grenouillère*** (☎ 04 90 97 90 22; fax 04 90 97 70 94), 1.5km down a dirt track signposted 1km north of Les Saintes Maries off the D570. The small but comfortable rooms have a terrace overlooking open fields full of frogs which sing guests to sleep each night. Doubles/triples/quads start at 260/380/460FF. La Grenouillère (literally, 'the frog farm') has a swimming pool and stables, and organises horse riding.

Even more idyllic – if you can afford it the splurge – is the nearby ***Étrier Camarguais*** (☎ 04 90 97 81 14; fax 04 90 97 88 11), a farmhouse-hotel built from 'a dream, flowers and the sun' 500m before La Grenouillère along the same dirt track. Doubles cost 400/540FF in the low/high season. The reception of the 'Camargue Stirrup' is in a traditional *cabane de gardian* (see the boxed text 'Camargue Cowboys').

Hotels Heaps of hotels – mostly three or four stars and at least 300FF a night – line the D570, the main road from Arles into Les Saintes Maries. Hotels in town are equally dear. The cheapest rooms can be had at ***Les Vagues*** (☎/fax 04 90 97 84 40), on the road that runs along the port west of the tourist office at 12 Ave Théodore Aubanel, or ***Le Delta*** (☎ 04 90 97 81 12; fax 04 90 97 72 85) on the right as you enter Les Saintes Maries from the north at 1 Place Mireille. Doubles at Les Vagues start at 190FF. Le Delta has shower-equipped singles/doubles/triples/quads for 185/205/245/275FF.

The cheapest place to stay in Aigues Mortes' historical centre is ***Hôtel Carrière*** (☎ 04 66 53 73 07; fax 04 66 53 84 75), 18 Rue Pasteur, with rooms from 200FF. A cut above it is ***Hôtel Saint Louis*** (☎ 04 66 53 72 68; fax 04 66 53 75 92), 10 Rue Amiral Courbet, with rooms from 280 to 490FF. The Saint Louis closes from January to mid-March. Both hotels have good restaurants with *menus* from 79 and 98FF respectively.

If you want to be closer to the birds, the ***Hostellerie du Pont de Gau*** (☎ 04 90 97 81 53; fax 04 90 97 98 54) is for you. A Logis de France hotel with an excellent restaurant (*menus* from 95FF), it's next to the Parc Ornithologique on the D570 and has doubles for 255FF. It is closed from January to mid-February.

Getting There & Away

For details about bus connections to/from Arles (via Pont de Gau and Mas du Pont de Rousty) and the three day Passe Camargue ticket, see Bus under Getting There & Away in the Arles section. In the high season, there are two buses a day from Les Saintes Maries to Nîmes (1¼ hours) via Aigues Mortes.

Getting Around

As long as you can put up with the insects and stiff sea breezes, bicycles are a fine way to explore the Camargue, which is, of course, very flat. East of Les Saintes Maries, areas along the seafront and farther inland are reserved for hikers and cyclists. For a list of cycling routes (in English) go to Le Vélo Saintois (☎/fax 04 90 97 74 56), 19 Ave de la République, which hires out mountain bikes for 80/200FF a day/three days. It also has tandems and delivers bikes to your hotel door.

The Pioch Badet hostel and Le Vélociste (☎ 04 90 97 83 26), Place des Remparts, both rent bikes too. The latter offers bike, horse and canoe packages.

North-Eastern Provence

DIGNE-LES-BAINS

• pop 16,000 ✉ 04000

Provence hits the Alps, and the land of snow and melted cheese meets the land of sun and olives, around Digne-les-Bains, which is 106km north-east of Aix-en-Provence and 152km north-west of Nice. This laid-back town is named after its thermal springs, visited annually by 11,000 people in search of a water cure for rheumatism, respiratory ailments and other medical conditions. The area is also known for its production of lavender, which is harvested in August and honoured in Digne with the five day festival, Corso de la Lavande, starting on the first weekend of the month, and with Les Journées Lavande throughout the region in mid-August. In summer, you'll smell the little purple flower everywhere. In spring, flowering poppies sprinkle the green fields with buttons of bright red.

Digne itself is unremarkable, though it was the home of a very remarkable woman, Alexandra David-Neel, an adventurer whose travels to Tibet brought her wide acclaim. The shale around Digne is rich in fossils.

The Route Napoléon (now the N85 in these parts), which Bonaparte followed in 1815 on his way to Paris after his escape from Elba, passes through Digne and Castellane, the gateway to the Gorges du Verdon.

Orientation

Digne is built on the eastern bank of the shallow Bléone River. The major roads into town converge at the Point Rond du 11 Novembre 1918, a roundabout 400m north-east of the train station. The main street is plane tree-lined Blvd Gassendi, which heads north-eastward from the Point Rond and passes the large Place du Général de Gaulle, the town's main public square.

Information

Tourist Offices The tourist office (☎ 04 92 31 42 73; fax 04 92 32 27 24) inside the Maison du Tourisme, 11 Point Rond du 11 Novembre 1918, is open from 8.45 am to noon and 2 to 6 pm (closed on Sunday). From May to October hours are 8.45 am to 12.30 pm and 2 to 7 pm (Sunday from 10.30 am to noon and 3 to 7 pm). The office has information on a variety of guided tours in the region.

The Relais Départemental des Gîtes de France (☎ 04 92 31 52 39; fax 04 92 32 32 63), also in the Maison du Tourisme, books accommodation at gîtes in the area. It is open from 8 am to noon and 2 to 6 pm (5 pm on Friday; closed on weekends). Bookings are only made between 9 and 11 am and 1 to 4 pm.

In the same building, the Bureau de Jeunesse (☎ 04 92 36 10 31; fax 04 92 36 10 37) is open from 2 to 6 pm (closed on weekends).

Money The Banque de France, 16 Blvd Soustre, is open from 8.45 am to noon and 1.45 to 3.45 pm (closed on weekends).

Post & Communications Digne's main post office, east of the tourist office at 4 Rue André Honnorat, is open from 8 am to 7 pm (Saturday until noon; closed on Sunday).

Laundry The laundrette in the old city, 4 Place du Marché, is open from 8 am to 7 pm (closed on Sunday). The one at 99 Blvd Gassendi is open daily from 9 am to 7 pm.

Fondation Alexandra David-Neel

Paris-born writer and philosopher Alexandra David-Neel, who spent her last years in Digne, is known for the incognito voyage she made early in the 1900s to Tibet. Her memory – and her interest in Tibet – are kept enthusiastically alive by the Fondation Alexandra David-Neel (☎ 04 92 31 32 38), which occupies her erstwhile residence at 27 Ave Maréchal Juin, as well as by the Journées Tibétaines, an annual celebration of Tibetan culture held at the end of August. Fondation Alexandra David-Neel is just over 1km from town on the road to Nice. From October to June, free tours (with headphones for English speakers) start at 10.30 am and 2 and 4 pm; from July to September, tours begin at 10.30 am and 2, 3.30 and 5 pm. To get there take TUD bus No 3 to the Stade Rolland stop.

Museums

The small **Musée de Digne** (☎ 04 92 31 45 29), 64 Blvd Gassendi, which is closed for renovation until 1999, has displays of art, archaeology and mineralogy. It is usually open from 1.30 to 5.30 pm (closed on Monday). In July and August hours are 10.30 am to noon and 1.30 to 6.30 pm.

In the old city, the **Musée d'Art Religieux** (☎ 04 92 32 35 37), Place des Récollets, south-east of the cathedral in the Chapelle des Pénitents, displays liturgical objects and religious art. It is open from July to October from 10 am to 6 pm. To visit at other times telephone in advance (☎ 04 92 36 75 00).

PROVENCE

Réserve Naturelle Géologique

Digne is in the middle of the Réserve Naturelle Géologique, whose spectacular fossil deposits include the footprints of prehistoric birds as well as ammonites, spiral shells that look something like a ram's horn. You'll need a detailed regional map or a topoguide to the Digne and Sisteron areas (sold at the tourist office) and your own transport (or a patient thumb) to get to the 18 sites, most of which are around **Barles** (24km north of Digne) and **Barrême** (28km south-east of Digne). There's an impressive limestone slab with some 500 ammonites 3km north of Digne on the road to Barles (and 1km north of the Centre de Géologie).

The Réserve Naturelle's headquarters, the **Centre de Géologie** (☎ 04 92 36 70 70; fax 04 92 36 70 71) at Saint Benoît, is 2km north of town off the road to Barles. Its exhibits on matters mineral and geological are open from 9 am to noon and 2 to 5.30 pm (4.30 pm on Friday; closed on weekends from November to March). Entry to the centre is 25/18/15FF for adults/students/children. Take TUD bus No 2, get off over the bridge at the Champourcin stop, then take the road to the left. Cars aren't allowed up, so it's a 15 minute walk along the rocky overhang above the river. Wear flat shoes.

Thermal Spa

You can take to the waters from February to early December at the Établissement Thermal (☎ 04 92 32 32 92) 2km east of Digne's centre. The cost of a good soak is 35FF but you may require a doctor's certificate. Voyeurs rather than *curistes* can join the weekly free tour on Thursday at 2 pm from March to August.

Places to Stay

In July and August you may be required to take half-pension at many of Digne's hotels.

Camping The ***Camping du Bourg*** (☎ 04 92 31 04 87), nearly 2km north-east of Digne on Route de Barcelonnette, is open from April to October and costs 63FF for two people with a car and tent or caravan (58FF if you're taking a cure). Take bus No 2 towards Barcelonnette and get off at the Notre Dame du Bourg stop. From there it's a 600m walk.

Camping des Eaux Chaudes (☎ 04 92 32 31 04), Route des Thermes, near the Établissement Thermal about 1.5km from Digne, is open from April to November and charges 73FF for two people with a car and tent or caravan (65FF for curistes).

Gites d'Étape Hikers can avail themselves of the ***Gîte du Château des Sièyes*** (☎ 04 92 31 20 30), Ave Georges Pompidou, nearly

2km north-west of the town centre off the road to Sisteron. It costs 55FF per person for a dormitory bed. Take bus No 1 headed for Sisteron, and get off at the Pompidou stop.

The peaceful ***Centre de Géologie*** (☎ 04 92 36 70 70) at Saint Benoît has beds in rooms for one, two and four people for 60FF per head.

Hotels The ***Hôtel Petit Saint Jean*** (☎ 04 92 31 30 04; fax 04 92 36 05 80), overlooking the central Place du Général de Gaulle at 14 Cours des Arès, has good-value singles/doubles with washbasin and bidet for 120/140FF, ones with toilet for 130/150FF and ones with shower and toilet for 160/190FF. Triples with toilet cost 190FF. *Menus* in its terrace restaurant start at 67FF.

In the old city, the little ***Hôtel L'Origan*** (☎ 04 92 31 62 13), 6 Rue Pied de Ville, has an upmarket restaurant (*menus* for 70, 98, 125 and 170FF) but affordable singles with washbasin from 90FF and doubles with shower from 140FF.

The two star ***Hôtel Central*** (☎ 04 92 31 31 91; fax 04 92 31 49 78), 26 Blvd Gassendi, has doubles from 150 to 315FF. Also with two stars, the ***Hôtel Le Coin Fleuri*** (☎ 04 92 31 04 51), 9 Blvd Victor Hugo, has functional doubles with washbasin/shower from 170/250FF and a great garden to relax in.

For something a bit more upmarket there's ***Hostellerie de L'Aiglon*** (☎ 04 92 31 02 70; fax 04 92 32 45 83), 1 Rue de Provence, whose entrance attached to the Chapelle Saint Esprit leads to calm, pastel rooms starting at 240FF. It costs 15FF to park in the private garage. Its restaurant, La Chapelle, serves good regional fare.

Places to Eat

Restaurants One of the cheapest places in town for lunch is the ***Restaurant-Cafétéria Le Victor Hugo*** (☎ 04 92 31 57 23), 8-10 Blvd Victor Hugo, with plats du jour from around 35FF. ***Le Point Chaud*** (☎ 04 92 31 30 71), 95 Blvd Gassendi, is a dark, cheap and local haunt.

Away from the terraces on Place du Général de Gaulle, ***La Braisière*** (☎ 04 92 31 59 63), 19 Place de l'Évêché, has a good lunch *menu* for 68FF, a dinner *menu* for 90FF and a fine view over the town. It does excellent *tartiflette* (85FF) and *raclette* (95FF). It is closed on Tuesday night and Wednesday in the off season.

Self-Catering A ***food market*** takes over Place du Général de Gaulle on Wednesday and Saturday mornings. Luxury local products are sold at ***Saveurs et Couleurs***, 7 Blvd Gassendi. The ***Casino*** supermarket, 42 Blvd Gassendi, is open from 7.30 am to 12.30 pm and 3.30 to 7.30 pm (closed on Sunday except from July to September).

Getting There & Away

Bus The bus station (☎ 04 92 31 50 00) is behind the tourist office on Place du Tampinet. Some 11 regional companies operate buses to Nice (144FF; 2¼ hours; at 1.15 pm) via Castellane (near the Gorges du Verdon; 62FF; 1¼ hours; one daily) as well as Marseille (76FF; 2½ hours; four a day) and Apt (60FF; two hours; two a day). The bus station is open from 8.40 am to 12.30 pm and 2.30 to 6.30 pm (closed on Sunday).

Train The train station (☎ 04 92 31 00 67) is a 10 minute walk westward from the tourist office on Ave Pierre Sémard. The ticket windows are open from 8.15 am to 12.30 pm and 1 to 8 pm (Saturday from 8.15 am to 12.30 pm and 1.45 to 4.45 pm). There are four trains a day to Marseille (135FF; 2¼ hours) and three to Briançon (151FF) via Saint Auban.

The two-car diesel trains operated by the government-owned Chemins de Fer de la Provence (☎ 04 92 31 01 58 in Digne; ☎ 04 93 82 10 72 in Nice) run along a scenic and winding narrow-gauge line to Nice's Gare du Sud (☎ 04 93 82 10 17) via Saint Martin du Var, 26km south-east of Nice. The entire trip takes about 3¼ hours and costs 106FF one way. There are four runs in each direction a day.

GORGES DU VERDON

The gorgeous 25km-long Gorges du Verdon (also known as the Grand Canyon du Verdon), the largest canyon in Europe, slice through the limestone plateau midway between Avignon and Nice. They begin at Rougon (near the confluence of the Verdon and Jabron rivers) and continue westward until the river flows into Lac de Sainte Croix. The village of Castellane (population 1349) is east of Rougon and is the main gateway for the gorges.

Carved by the greenish waters of the Verdon River, the gorges are 250 to 700m deep. The bottom is 8 to 90m wide, while the rims are 200 to 1500m apart.

Information

Tourist Offices The best source of information for the Gorges du Verdon is the Castellane tourist office (☎ 04 92 83 61 14; fax 04 92 83 76 89), Rue Nationale, or its counterpart in Moustiers Sainte Marie (☎ 04 92 74 67 84; fax 04 92 74 60 65; www.ville-moustiers-sainte-marie.fr). The Castellane office is open from 9 am to 1 pm and 2 to 7 pm (closed on Sunday afternoon). Moustiers is open from 10 am to noon and 2 to 7 pm.

There's a small tourist office in the centre of La Palud-sur-Verdon (☎/fax 04 92 77 32 02 or ☎ 04 92 77 38 02), and a Syndicat d'Initiative (☎/fax 04 94 85 68 40) in Trigance.

The Canyon

The bottom of the gorges can be visited only on foot or by raft, but motorists and cyclists can enjoy spectacular (if dizzying) views from two cliff-side roads.

La Route des Crêtes (the D952 and D23) follows the northern rim and passes the **Point Sublime** viewpoint at the canyon's entrance, from where the GR4 trail leads to the bottom of the gorge.

Another stunning view is offered by **La Corniche Sublime** (the D19 to the D71), which goes along the southern rim and takes you to such landmarks as the **Balcons de la Mescla** (Mescla Terraces) and **Pont de l'Artuby** (Artuby Bridge), the highest bridge in Europe.

A complete circuit of the Gorges du Verdon via Moustiers Sainte Marie involves about 140km of driving; the tourist office in Castellane has the good English-language brochure *Driving Tours* with 11 itineraries. The only real village en route is **La Palud-sur-Verdon** (930m), 2km north-east of the northern bank of the gorges. In summer, heavy traffic often slows travel to a crawl.

The bottom of the canyon, first explored in its entirety in 1905, presents hikers and white-water rafters with an overwhelming series of cliffs and narrows. You can walk most of it along the often difficult GR4, which is covered by Didier-Richard's 1:50,000 scale map No 19, *Haute Provence-Verdon* (70FF). It is also included in the excellent English-language book, *Canyon du Verdon – The Most Beautiful Hikes* (25FF at Castellane or Moustiers tourist offices), which lists 28 hikes in the gorges. The full GR4 takes two days, though short descents into the canyon are possible from a number of points. Bring along a torch (flashlight) and drinking water. Camping rough on gravel beaches along the way is illegal, but people do it.

The water level of the river in the upper part of the canyon can rise suddenly if the EDF (France's electricity company) opens the hydroelectric dams upstream, making it difficult if not impossible to ford the river. Before setting out, call ☎ 04 92 83 62 68 to find out the level of the Verdon and ☎ 08 36 68 02 04 for the local weather report.

Activities

Castellane's tourist office has a complete list of companies offering rafting, canyoning, horse riding, mountaineering, biking and other outdoor pursuits. Aboard Rafting (☎/fax 04 92 83 76 11), 8 Place Marcel Sauvaire, runs white-water rafting trips (180 to 440FF) as well as canyoning (200 to 350FF), hot-dogging (200FF), windsurfing, paragliding and mountain biking. It is open from April to September.

PROVENCE

Places to Stay & Eat

Camping *Camping de Bourbon* (☎ 04 92 77 38 17), just east of La Palud, charges about 14FF per person and 6FF for a tent. It is open from May to September. Near Castellane, the river is lined with some 15 seasonal camping grounds that tend to be crowded and pricey. The *Domaine de Charteuil Provence* (☎ 04 92 83 79 39), just south of Castellane and open from June to mid-October, charges 58/71FF for two people with a car and tent in the low/high season.

Hostels The *Auberge de Jeunesse Le Trait d'Union* (☎ 04 92 77 38 72; fax 04 92 77 30 48), 500m south of La Palud at the beginning of La Route des Crêtes (here called Route de la Maline), is open from April to October. Bed and breakfast costs 66FF. If you don't have a HI card or equivalent, you can buy a 'foreigners' welcome stamp' for 19FF (six make up a HI card). Sheets cost 17FF.

The *Gîte d'Étape de Fontaine Basse* (☎ 04 94 85 68 36 or ☎ 04 94 85 68 60; fax 04 94 85 68 50), 16km south-east of Castellane in Trigance, charges 100FF for bed and breakfast; sheets are 10FF. In Castellane, a bed at *L'Oustaou* gîte d'étape (☎ 04 92 83 77 27), Chemin des Listes, is 60FF a night.

Hotels If you're not looking for something expensive, Castellane is the place for you. Numerous hotels line the central square, Place Marcel Sauvaire, and adjoining Place de l'Église. For particularly good value there's the *Grand Hôtel du Levant* (☎ 04 92 83 60 05; fax 04 92 83 72 14), an impressive pile on Place Marcel Sauvaire, which has singles/doubles with shower and toilet for 150/180FF.

Shower-equipped doubles with toilet at the *Hôtel La Forge* (☎ 04 92 83 62 61), Place de l'Église, start at 200FF, while the *Hostellerie du Roc* (04 92 83 62 65) next door has doubles/triples from 225/300FF.

On Rue de la République, which leads off Place Marcel Sauvaire, *Hôtel du Verdon* (☎ 04 92 83 62 02; fax 04 92 83 73 80) has doubles with washbasin/shower for 160/180FF. On the same street, *Ma Petite Auberge* (☎ 04 92 83 62 06; fax 04 92 83 68 49) has doubles with shower for 190FF and ones with toilet too for 240FF.

A 10 minute walk from town there's the excellent-value *Stadi Hôtel* (☎ 04 92 83 76 47 or ☎ 04 94 70 34 67; fax 04 94 84 63 36), on the N85 out of Castellane (direction Digne-les-Bains). It has a swimming pool, shows English-language films every evening and has doubles for 220FF. A week's stay in a two to four person studio is 2700FF.

About 10km south-east of the canyon in Comps-sur-Artuby, the *Grand Hôtel Bain* (☎ 04 94 76 90 06; fax 04 94 76 92 24) has rooms for 250 to 370FF. The hotel has been run by the same family for eight generations (since 1737).

If you are looking for something expensive head for the three star *Château de Trigance* (☎ 04 94 76 91 18; fax 04 94 85 68 99), 16km south-east of Castellane in the hilltop village of Trigance. Rooms in the restored 10th century castle start at 600FF.

Getting There & Away

Public transport to, from and around the Gorges du Verdon is limited. Autocars Sumian (☎ 04 42 67 60 34 in Jouques) runs buses from Marseille to Castellane via Aix-en-Provence (109FF), La Palud and Moustiers. VFD (☎ 04 76 47 77 77 in Grenoble; ☎ 04 93 85 24 56 in Nice) runs a daily bus from Grenoble to Nice via Digne and Grasse, stopping in Castellane en route. The tourist offices have schedules.

Getting Around

Bus In July and August, Navettes Autocar (☎ 04 92 83 40 27) runs shuttle buses around the gorges daily except Sunday, linking Castellane with the Point Sublime, La Palud, La Maline etc. Ask at the tourist office in Castellane for schedules and fares.

Bicycle The Stadi Hôtel (see Places to Stay) rents mountain bikes for 50/75FF a half/full day. L'Arc-en-Ciel (☎ 04 92 77 37 40), a restaurant and gîte near central Place de l'Église in La Palud, rents bikes too.

PRA-LOUP

The ski resort of Pra-Loup (1600m), 8.5km south-west of Barcelonnette and 70km south-east of Gap, is connected by a lift system across the Vallon des Agneliers with another ski resort called La Foux d'Allos. The upper part of the Pra-Loup has been built up with many apartment blocks, while the lower part (Les Molanès or Pra-Loup 1500) has chalet-style accommodation.

There is a large variety of runs for all levels of skiers and snowboarders, but the majority are for intermediates and advanced. Cross-country skiing is limited around Pra-Loup and is better in the Ubaye Valley. Saint Paul-sur-Ubaye, in a valley below and to the north-east of Pra-Loup, has 25km of cross-country runs at 1400 to 1500m and Larche has 30km of runs at 1700 to 2000m.

Pra-Loup's 53 lifts are between 1600 and 2600m, with 160km of runs and a vertical drop of almost 1000m.

Information

The tourist office (☎ 04 92 84 10 04; fax 04 92 84 02 93), École de Ski Français (ESF; 04 92 84 11 05) and post office, where you can change money too, are all inside the Maison de Pra-Loup.

Places to Stay

Studios and apartments are the best option and cost from 1090FF per week for two during the low season. At the bottom end of the hotel range is ***Auberge de Pra-Loup*** (☎ 04 92 84 10 05) in the eastern part of the village, which has doubles from 150FF. The mid-range ***Hôtel Manon*** (☎ 04 92 84 17 82; fax 04 92 84 15 08) in the western part of the village has decent rooms from 280FF. ***Hôtel Les Airelles*** (☎ 04 92 84 13 24; fax 04 92 84 64 09) in the centre of the village is at the top end with rooms from 350/500FF in the low/high season.

Getting There & Away

The nearest train station is Gap, from where there are a couple of buses a day to Pra-Loup (48FF; 1½ hours) via Barcelonnette.

LA FOUX D'ALLOS

La Foux d'Allos (1800m) is connected by a lift system to Pra-Loup. By road, Pra-Loup is 23.5km to the north, but there is no public transport available between the two resorts. The tourist office (☎ 04 92 83 80 70; fax 04 92 83 86 27) is in the Maison de la Foux, on the main square.

Places to Stay

The ***Auberge de Jeunesse*** (☎ 04 92 83 81 08; fax 04 92 83 83 70) is in the upper part of the village near the major lift stations. In summer, a bed in a room for two, four, six or eight people costs around 80FF. In winter, only weekly packages are available.

Apartments are the main type of accommodation here and studios for two start at 1300FF per week during the low season and 2800FF in the high season. One of the few hotels at La Foux is the ***Hôtel Le Toukal*** (☎ 04 92 83 82 76) on the main square, which has rooms from 180/330FF, depending on the season. Fine rooms at the three star ***Hôtel Le Sestrière*** (☎ 04 92 83 81 70; fax 04 92 83 11 62) near the main square cost between 300 and 400FF.

Getting There & Away

Buses link the village of La Foux d'Allos, which is 9km south-east of the resort, with Digne-les-Bains and Avignon.

It is possible to get to La Foux d'Allos from Nice by train departing from Nice's Gare des Chemins de Fer de Provence (☎ 04 93 88 34 72), 4bis Rue Alfred-Binet. Take a train to La Vœsubie-Plan-du-Var. The rest of the trip is by bus, with a change required at Thorame.

Another option is to take an Autocars Girieud bus (☎ 04 92 83 40 27) from Nice and Digne, changing buses in Thorame.

ISOLA 2000

Isola 2000 (2000m), the only major ski resort in the Alpes-Maritimes department, is 93km north of Nice. One of France's many purpose-built ski resorts, it's full of unsightly apartment blocks. The skiing can be good, but the snow tends to be a bit heavy due to its proximity to the Mediterranean. It is also known for the unusually high number of sunny days, and a couple of accommodation agencies actually give snow-and-sun guarantees, with accommodation vouchers given for another time if the sun doesn't shine for three consecutive days.

Isola 2000 has runs for skiers and snowboarders of all levels, but the majority of slopes are for intermediate skiers, with a limited number for beginners and experts. There is some good off-piste and tree skiing below Mount Mené. Skiing is between 1800 and 2610m, with 120km of runs covered by 25 chair lifts and a vertical drop of about 800m. There are only 15km of cross-country ski trails around the resort. The ski school can organise ski touring in the Parc National du Mercantour.

An annual Snow Carnival is held here in the first week of March.

Information

The tourist office (☎ 04 93 23 15 15; fax 04 93 23 14 25), banks, post office, ESF (☎ 04 93 23 11 78), rental shops, restaurants, bars, supermarket, food shops, cinema, apartments and hotels are all in the Galerie Marchande high-rise complex.

Places to Stay

Isola 2000 is not cheap. The Isola Location (☎ 04 93 23 14 07; fax 04 93 23 15 62) and Les Adrets (☎ 04 93 23 20 00; fax 04 93 23 20 03) rental agencies rent out apartments and two-person studios. The two star ***Hôtel Druos*** (☎ 04 93 23 12 20; fax 04 93 23 12 38) has ageing rooms with bath, toilet and TV from 300 to 820FF depending on the season. Sitting above the village, and more appealing, the chalet-style ***Hôtel Diva*** (☎ 04 93 23 17 71; fax 04 93 23 12 14) has similarly priced rooms.

The village of Isola, 17km down the valley to the west on the D2205, has a handful of cheaper hotels. The ***Hôtel de France*** (☎ 04 93 02 17 04) has rooms from 215FF per person, including half-pension.

Getting There & Away

There are four buses a day to/from Nice, year-round (87FF; 2¼ hours).

Côte d'Azur & Monaco

The Côte d'Azur, also known as the French Riviera, stretches along France's Mediterranean coast from Toulon to the Italian border. Technically part of Provence, it also includes most of the departments of Alpes-Maritimes and Var. Many of the towns along the coast – Nice, Monaco, Antibes, Cannes, Saint Tropez – are well known as the playgrounds of the rich, famous and tanned, and publicised in films and in the tabloids and glossy magazines. The reality is rather less glamorous, but the Côte d'Azur still has a great deal to attract visitors: sun, 40km of beach, sea water as warm as 25°C, all sorts of cultural activities and – sometimes – even a sprinkle of glitter.

The capital of the Côte d'Azur is Nice, whose plentiful hotels and excellent rail links make it a good base for exploring the region. As you follow the coast westward, you come to the attractive town of Antibes, the wealthy resort of Cannes and, just west of the stunning red mountain known as the Massif de l'Estérel, the twin towns of Saint Raphaël and Fréjus. Inland, the hills overlooking the coast are dotted with towns and villages such as Grasse (renowned for its perfumes), Vence, Saint Paul de Vence and Bormes-les-Mimosas.

The forested Massif des Maures stretches from Saint Raphaël to Hyères. West of the fashionable port town of Saint Tropez you'll find the region's most unspoiled coastline, where capes and cliffs alternate with streams and beaches, many of the latter sheltered from the open sea by the Îles d'Hyères – three large islands (and a couple of tiny ones) some 10km offshore. Ugly Toulon, best known for its role as a naval base, is at the western edge of the Côte d'Azur.

East of Nice, the foothills of the Alps plummet precipitously into the Mediterranean. Three roads, known as *corniches*, take you eastward from Nice past a number of villages overlooking the sea to Menton and the Italian border. The tiny Principality

HIGHLIGHTS

- **Nice** – admire the colours and form of Matisse's work in the Musée Matisse
- **Grasse** – learn what it takes to be a *nez* (nose) at the *parfumeries*
- **Cannes** – go for a stroll along Blvd de la Croisette or lay on the beach
- **Monaco** – see how royalty lives in the Palais du Prince and risk all in Monte Carlo's casino
- **Îles de Lérins** or **Îles d'Hyères** – explore these fascinating islands

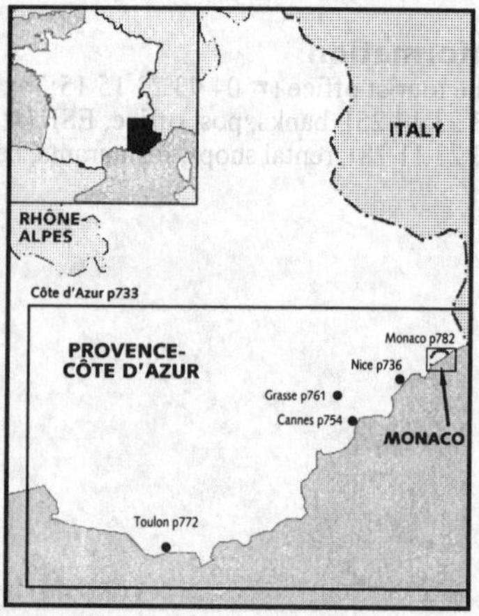

specialities of Nice – *socca* (a croquette covered in chickpea flour and olive oil batter fried on a griddle), *salade Niçoise*, and *pissaladière* (pastry shell with onions, anchovies and *pissala*, and olives)

tarte Tropézienne – a particularly sweet confection from Saint Tropez of Monaco, with its centre at Monte Carlo, is roughly midway between Nice and Menton.

This chapter begins in Nice and follows the coast westward to Toulon. It then covers the stretch of the Côte d'Azur between Nice and the Italian border, including Monaco.

History

Occupied by the Ligurians from the 1st millennium BC, the eastern part of France's Mediterranean coast was colonised around 600 BC by Greeks from Asia Minor, who settled in Massilia (modern-day Marseille). The colony soon expanded to other points along the coast, including what are now Hyères, Saint Tropez, Antibes and Nice. Called in to help Massilia against the threat of invasion by Celto-Ligurians from Entremont in 125 BC, the Romans defeated the Celts and Ligurians and created the Provincia Romana – the area between the Alps, the sea and the Rhône River – from which the name Provence is derived.

In 1388 Nice and its hinterland, also known as the County of Nice, were incorporated into the lands of the House of Savoy. The rest of Provence became part of the French kingdom in 1482; the centralist policies of the French kings saw the region's autonomy greatly reduced. In 1860, after an agreement between Napoleon III and the House of Savoy helped drive the Austrians from northern Italy, France took possession of Savoy and the area around Nice.

In the 19th century, wealthy French, English, American and Russian tourists discovered the Côte d'Azur. Primarily a winter resort, the area attracted an increasing number of affluent visitors thanks to its beauty and temperate climate. The intensity and clarity of the region's colours and light appealed to many painters – particularly the impressionists – including Cézanne, Van Gogh, Matisse and Picasso. Writers and other celebrities were also attracted to the region and contributed to its fame. Little fishing ports became exclusive resorts, and in no time the most beautiful spots were occupied by private villas that looked more like castles. With improved rail and road access and the advent of paid holidays for all French workers in 1936, even more tourists flocked to the region, leading to its development as a summer resort.

CÔTE D'AZUR

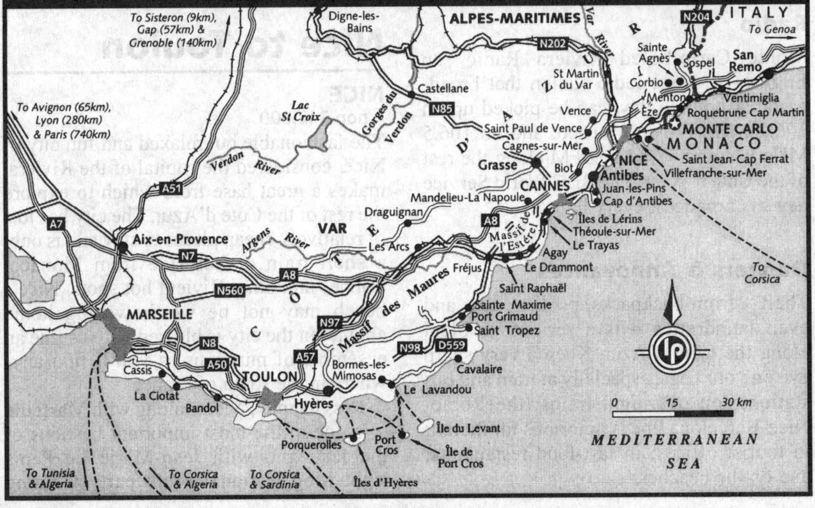

CÔTE D

Passport to the Riviera

Museums in Nice are free every first Sunday of the month. Beyond that, you have to pay to view Matisse's *Blue Nude*, Warhol's *Dollar Sign* or Christo's wrapped shopping trolley (unless you're seven years old or less that is, in which case museums are free anyway).

The Carte Musées Côte d'Azur entitles cardholders to free admission to some 60 Côte d'Azur museums, including Nice's Musée Matisse, Musée Marc Chagall and Musée d'Art Moderne et d'Art Contemporain; Biot's Musée Fernand Léger; Antibes' Musée Picasso; Menton's Musée Jean Cocteau; and most other museums listed in this chapter.

The card is valid for three or seven consecutive days and is sold for 70 or 140FF respectively from participating museums, tourist offices and FNAC stores.

If you intend straying no farther than the museums in Nice, you can purchase a seven day Passe Musée from the Promenade des Anglais tourist office in Nice. It allows one visit to each of Nice's museums.

Radio

Monte Carlo-based Riviera Radio, an English-language radio station that broadcasts 24 hours a day, can be picked up on 106.3 MHz FM in Monaco, and on 106.5 MHz FM and 98.8 MHz FM along the rest of the Côte d'Azur. The BBC World Service news is broadcast every hour.

Dangers & Annoyances

Theft – from backpacks, pockets, cars and even laundrettes – is a serious problem along the Côte d'Azur. Keep a very sharp eye on your bags, especially at train and bus stations; on overnight trains (the Rome-Nice-Barcelona line is notorious for thefts); in tourist offices; in fast-food restaurants; and on the beaches.

Getting There & Away

For information on ferry services from Nice and Toulon to Corsica, see the Getting There & Away section in the Corsica chapter.

Getting Around

SNCF trains shuttle back and forth along the coast between Saint Raphaël and the Italian border, making Nice (Nizza in Italian) a great base for exploring the eastern half of the Côte d'Azur. The area between Saint Raphaël – where the train line veers inland – and Toulon can be reached by bus.

If you're planning to drive along the coast in summer, be prepared for some mighty slow going. It can sometimes take hours to move just a few kilometres, no doubt the reason why the well heeled have taken to reaching their seaside properties by helicopter.

Except for the traffic-plagued high season, the Côte d'Azur is easily accessible by car. The fastest way to get around is by the boring A8 autoroute which, travelling west to east, starts near Aix-en-Provence, approaches the coast at Fréjus, skirts the Estérel range and runs more or less parallel to the coast from Cannes all the way to the Italian border at Ventimiglia (Vintimille in French).

Nice to Toulon

NICE

• pop 342,000

The fashionable but relaxed and fun city of Nice, considered the capital of the Riviera, makes a great base from which to explore the rest of the Côte d'Azur. The city has lots of relatively cheap places to stay and is only a short train or bus ride from Monaco, Cannes and other Riviera hot spots. Nice's beach may not be worth writing home about, but the city is blessed with as fine an ensemble of museums as you'll find anywhere in the south of France.

Less happily, Nice – along with Marseille – is one of the most important bastions of the far right, with Jean-Marie Le Pen's right-wing National Front party winning about 25% of the city-wide vote in most elections. Racist comments are not uncommon here. In part, the city's inter-ethnic tensions are a result of the great gap between rich and poor; beggars are as common as owners of flashy sports cars.

Nice's former mayor, the corrupt right-wing Jacques Médecin (son of another former mayor, Jean Médecin), escaped to Uruguay before being convicted (*in absentia*) in 1992 of misuse of public funds. He was extradited two years later and imprisoned in Grenoble.

Plans are afoot to grace Nice with a tramway in the next century.

History

Nice was founded around 350 BC by the Greek seafarers who had settled Marseille. They named the colony Nikaia, apparently to commemorate a victory (*nike* in Greek) over a nearby town. In 154 BC the Greeks were followed by the Romans, who settled farther uphill around what is now Cimiez, site of a number of Roman ruins.

By the 10th century, Nice was ruled by the counts of Provence. In 1388 the town refused to recognise the new count of Provence, Louis of Anjou, and turned instead to Amadeus VII of the House of Savoy. In the 18th and 19th centuries Nice was temporarily occupied several times by the French, but did not definitively become part of France until 1860, when Napoleon III struck a deal with the House of Savoy. The agreement (known as the Treaty of Turin) was ratified by a vote.

During the Victorian period Nice became popular with the English aristocracy, who came to enjoy the city's mild winter climate. European royalty soon followed.

Orientation

Ave Jean Médecin runs south from near the train station to Place Masséna. The modern city centre, the area north and west of Place Masséna, includes the upmarket pedestrianised streets of Rue de France and Rue Masséna. The Station Centrale and intercity bus station are three blocks east of Place Masséna.

The famous Promenade des Anglais follows the gently curved beachfront from the city centre to the airport, 6km to the west. Vieux Nice (Old Nice) is delineated by Blvd Jean Jaurès, Quai des États-Unis and – to the east – the hill known as Le Château. Place Garibaldi is at the north-eastern tip of Vieux Nice.

The wealthy residential neighbourhood of Cimiez, home to several outstanding museums, is just north of the city centre.

Information

Tourist Offices The most convenient tourist office (☎ 04 93 87 07 07; fax 04 93 16 85 16; otc@nice.coteazur.org; www.nice.coteazur.org) is next to the train station on Ave Thiers. It's open from 8 am to 7 pm (8 pm from July to September). Another (less crowded) office (☎ 04 92 14 48 00; fax 04 92 14 49 03) at 5 Promenade des Anglais is open from 8 am to 6 pm (closed Sunday; 8 pm from May to September).

Near the airport is the Nice Ferber branch office (☎ 04 93 83 32 64; fax 04 93 72 08 27), Promenade des Anglais (towards town from the airport terminal). Inside the airport is an info desk (☎ 04 93 21 44 11; fax 04 93 21 44 50) at Terminal 1.

The Centre Information Jeunesse (☎ 04 93 80 93 93), 19 Rue Gioffredo, is open from 8.45 am to 6.45 pm (closed on weekends).

National Park Office The headquarters of the Parc National du Mercantour (☎ 04 93 16 78 88; fax 04 93 88 79 05), 23 Rue d'Italie, is open weekdays from 9 am to 6 pm. It stocks numerous guides including the free *Les Guides Randoxygène* series which details 25 canyoning routes, 40 mountain biking (VTT) trails and hiking trails in the park (see Around Menton for more details).

Money The Banque de France at 14 Ave Félix Faure is open from 8.45 am to 12.15 pm and 1.30 to 3.30 pm (closed on weekends).

American Express (☎ 04 93 16 53 53), 11 Promenade des Anglais, is open from 9 am to noon and 2 to 6 pm (closed on weekends). From May to September it's open

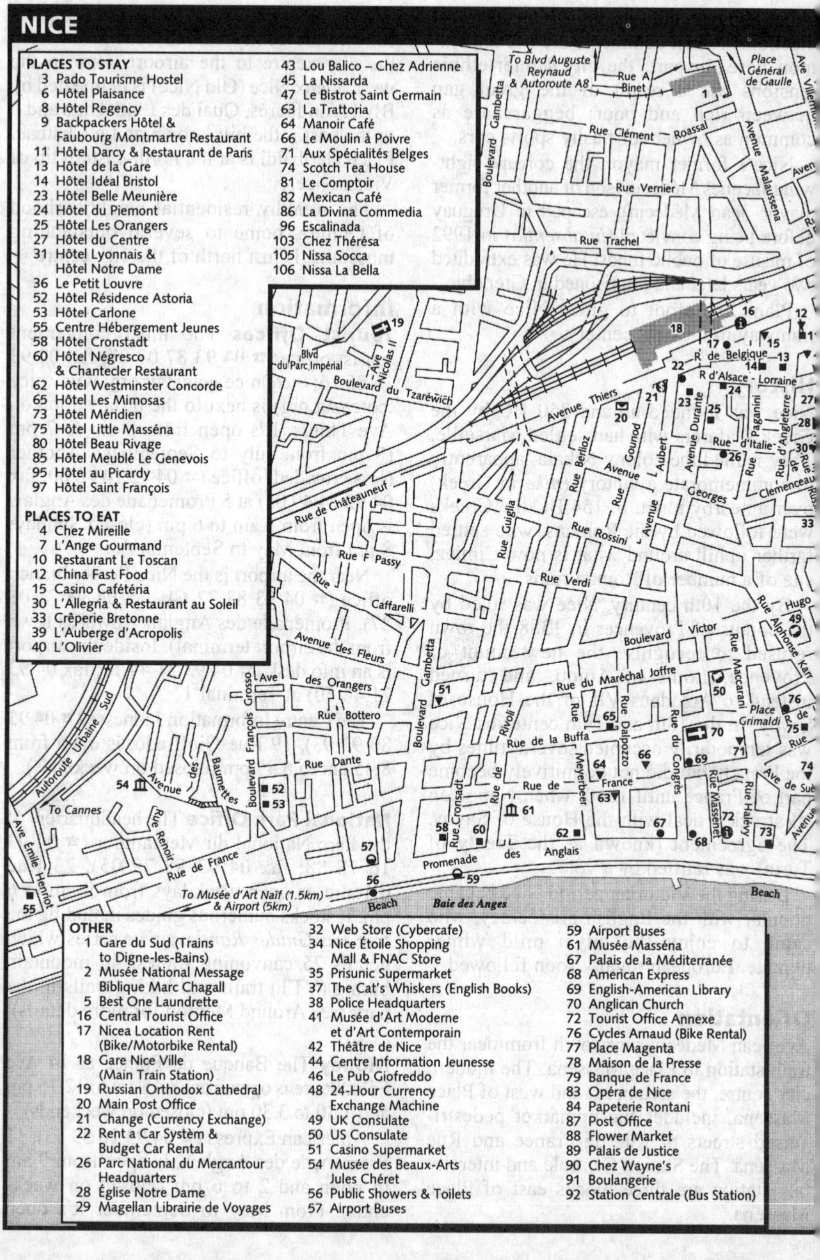
NICE
PLACES TO STAY
3 Pado Tourisme Hostel
6 Hôtel Plaisance
8 Hôtel Regency
9 Backpackers Hôtel & Faubourg Montmartre Restaurant
11 Hôtel Darcy & Restaurant de Paris
13 Hôtel de la Gare
14 Hôtel Idéal Bristol
23 Hôtel Belle Meunière
24 Hôtel du Piemont
25 Hôtel Les Orangers
27 Hôtel du Centre
31 Hôtel Lyonnais & Hôtel Notre Dame
36 Le Petit Louvre
52 Hôtel Résidence Astoria
53 Hôtel Carlone
55 Centre Hébergement Jeunes
58 Hôtel Cronstadt
60 Hôtel Négresco & Chantecler Restaurant
62 Hôtel Westminster Concorde
65 Hôtel Les Mimosas
73 Hôtel Méridien
75 Hôtel Little Masséna
80 Hôtel Beau Rivage
85 Hôtel Meublé Le Genevois
95 Hôtel au Picardy
97 Hôtel Saint François
PLACES TO EAT
4 Chez Mireille
7 L'Ange Gourmand
10 Restaurant Le Toscan
12 China Fast Food
15 Casino Cafétéria
30 L'Allegria & Restaurant au Soleil
33 Crêperie Bretonne
39 L'Auberge d'Acropolis
40 L'Olivier
43 Lou Balico – Chez Adrienne
45 La Nissarda
47 Le Bistrot Saint Germain
63 La Trattoria
64 Manoir Café
66 Le Moulin à Poivre
71 Aux Spécialités Belges
74 Scotch Tea House
81 Le Comptoir
82 Mexican Café
86 La Divina Commedia
96 Escalinada
103 Chez Thérésa
105 Nissa Socca
106 Nissa La Bella
OTHER
1 Gare du Sud (Trains to Digne-les-Bains)
2 Musée National Message Biblique Marc Chagall
5 Best One Laundrette
16 Central Tourist Office
17 Nicea Location Rent (Bike/Motorbike Rental)
18 Gare Nice Ville (Main Train Station)
19 Russian Orthodox Cathedral
20 Main Post Office
21 Change (Currency Exchange)
22 Rent a Car Systèm & Budget Car Rental
26 Parc National du Mercantour Headquarters
28 Église Notre Dame
29 Magellan Librairie de Voyages
32 Web Store (Cybercafe)
34 Nice Étoile Shopping Mall & FNAC Store
35 Prisunic Supermarket
37 The Cat's Whiskers (English Books)
38 Police Headquarters
41 Musée d'Art Moderne et d'Art Contemporain
42 Théâtre de Nice
44 Centre Information Jeunesse
46 Le Pub Giofreddo
48 24-Hour Currency Exchange Machine
49 UK Consulate
50 US Consulate
51 Casino Supermarket
54 Musée des Beaux-Arts Jules Chéret
56 Public Showers & Toilets
57 Airport Buses
59 Airport Buses
61 Musée Masséna
67 Palais de la Méditerranée
68 American Express
69 English-American Library
70 Anglican Church
72 Tourist Office Annexe
76 Cycles Arnaud (Bike Rental)
77 Place Magenta
78 Maison de la Presse
79 Banque de France
83 Opéra de Nice
84 Papeterie Rontani
87 Post Office
88 Flower Market
89 Palais de Justice
90 Chez Wayne's
91 Boulangerie
92 Station Centrale (Bus Station)
To Blvd Auguste Reynaud & Autoroute A8
Rue A Binet
Place Général de Gaulle
Rue Clément Roassal
Avenue Malaussena
Boulevard Gambetta
Rue Vernier
Rue Trachel
Blvd du Parc Impérial
Ave Nicolas II
Boulevard du Tzaréwich
Avenue Thiers
R de Belgique
R d'Alsace - Lorraine
Avenue Durante
Rue Paganini
Rue d'Italie
Rue d'Angleterre
Rue Berlioz
Rue Gounod
Rue Aubert
Avenue Georges Clemenceau
Rue de Châteauneuf
Rue Rossini
Rue Guiglia
Rue F Passy
Rue Verdi
Rue Caffarelli
Boulevard Victor Hugo
Rue Alphonse Karr
Avenue des Fleurs
Ave des Orangers
Rue Bottero
Rue Dante
Boulevard François Grosso
Rue du Maréchal Joffre
Rue Maccarani
Place Grimaldi
Rue de la Buffa
Rue de Rivoli
Rue Dalpozzo
Rue du Congrès
Rue Meyerbeer
Rue de France
Rue Massenet
Rue Halévy
Rue Cronstadt
Autoroute Urbaine Sud
Avenue des Baumettes
To Cannes
Rue Renoir
Ave Émile Henriot
Promenade des Anglais
To Musée d'Art Naïf (1.5km) & Airport (5km)
Beach
Baie des Anges

CÔTE D'AZUR

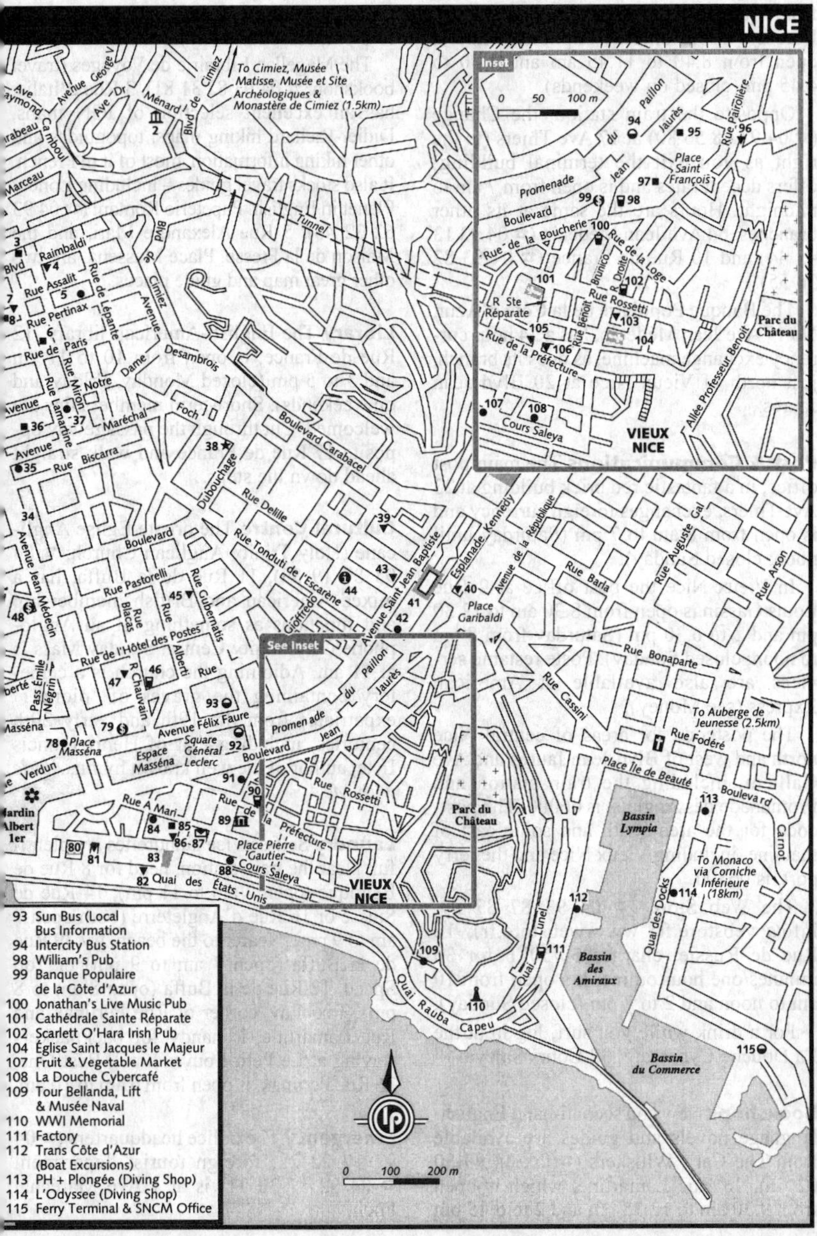
NICE
To Cimiez, Musée Matisse, Musée et Site Archéologiques & Monastère de Cimiez (1.5km)
Avenue George V
Ave Raymond
Ave Dr Ménard
Blvd de Cimiez
Cambou
Marceau
Tunnel
Blvd Raimbaldi
Rue Assalit
Rue Pertinax
Rue de Paris
Rue de Lépante
Rue Miron
Rue Lamartine
Avenue Notre Dame
Desambrois
Avenue Maréchal Foch
Boulevard Carabacel
Rue Biscarra
Dubouchage
Rue Delille
Boulevard
Rue Tonduti de l'Escarène
Avenue Jean Médecin
Rue Pastorelli
Rue Blacas
Rue Gubernatis
Rue de l'Hôtel des Postes
Rue Alberti
R Chauvain
Pass Émile Négrin
Avenue Félix Faure
Place Masséna
Espace Masséna
Square Général Leclerc
Boulevard
Verdun
Jardin Albert 1er
Rue A Mari
Quai des États-Unis
Place Pierre Gautier
Cours Saleya
Rue de la Préfecture
Rue Rossetti
Promenade du Paillon
Jean Jaurès
Gioffredo
Avenue Saint Jean Baptiste
Esplanade Kennedy
Avenue de la République
Place Garibaldi
Rue Barla
Rue Auguste Gal
Rue Arson
Rue Bonaparte
Rue Cassini
To Auberge de Jeunesse (2.5km)
Rue Fodéré
Place Île de Beauté
Boulevard Carnot
Bassin Lympia
To Monaco via Corniche Inférieure (18km)
Quai des Docks
Quai Lunel
Bassin des Amiraux
Bassin du Commerce
Quai Rauba Capeu
Parc du Château
VIEUX NICE
See Inset
Inset
0 50 100 m
Place Saint François
Rue Pairolière
Promenade du Paillon
Boulevard Jean Jaurès
Rue de la Boucherie
Rue de la Loge
Brunico
R Droite
Rue Rossetti
R Ste Réparate
Rue Benoît Bunico
Rue de la Préfecture
Allée Professeur Benoit
Cours Saleya
0 100 200 m
93 Sun Bus (Local Bus Information
94 Intercity Bus Station
98 William's Pub
99 Banque Populaire de la Côte d'Azur
100 Jonathan's Live Music Pub
101 Cathédrale Sainte Réparate
102 Scarlett O'Hara Irish Pub
104 Église Saint Jacques le Majeur
107 Fruit & Vegetable Market
108 La Douche Cybercafé
109 Tour Bellanda, Lift & Musée Naval
110 WWI Memorial
111 Factory
112 Trans Côte d'Azur (Boat Excursions)
113 PH + Plongée (Diving Shop)
114 L'Odyssee (Diving Shop)
115 Ferry Terminal & SNCM Office

from 9 am to 9 pm (Saturday until 1 pm). Barclays Bank on Rue Alphonse Karr is open from 8.40 to 11.45 am and 1.30 to 4.45 pm (closed on weekends).

Opposite the train station, the Change (☎ 04 93 88 56 80) at 17 Ave Thiers (to the right as you exit the terminal building) offers decent rates and is open from 7 am to midnight. Hours are the same at its other branches: 64 Ave Jean Médecin (☎ 04 93 13 45 44) and 10 Rue de France (☎ 04 93 82 16 55).

The Banque Populaire de la Côte d'Azur, No 17 Ave Jean Médecin, has a 24 hour currency exchange machine, as does its branch, just north of Vieux Nice at 20 Blvd Jean Jaurès.

Post & Communications The main post office, in a fantastic red brick building at 23 Ave Thiers, exchanges foreign currency and is open from 8 am to 7 pm (Saturday until noon; closed Sunday).

In Vieux Nice the post office at 2 Rue Louis Gassin is open from 8.30 am to 12.30 pm and 2 to 6.30 pm (Saturday from 8 am to noon; closed Sunday). Poste restante services are also available at American Express (see Money).

The postcode for areas of central Nice north and west of Blvd Jean Jaurès and Ave Galliéni, including the train station and Promenade des Anglais, is 06000. The postcode for the area south and south-east of that line, including Vieux Nice and the ferry port, is 06300.

The Web Store (☎ 04 93 87 87 99; info@webstore.fr; www.webstore.fr), 12 Rue de Russie, charges 30/50FF for 30 minutes/one hour online. It's open from 10 am to noon and 2 to 7 pm (closed Sunday).

For a drink while you surf, log in at the La Douche Cybercafé, 32 Cours Saleya.

Bookshops New and second-hand English-language novels and guides are available from The Cat's Whiskers (☎/fax 04 93 80 02 66), 26 Rue Lamartine, which is open from 9.30 am to 12.15 pm and 2 to 6.45 pm (Saturday from 9.30 am to 12.15 pm and 3 to 6 pm; closed Sunday).

The Magellan Librairie de Voyages (travel bookshop; ☎ 04 93 82 31 81), 3 Rue d'Italie, has an excellent selection of IGN maps, Didier-Richard hiking maps, topoguides and other hiking information, most of it in French. It also stocks travel guides – including Lonely Planet in English. Papeterie Rontani (☎ 04 93 62 32 43), 5 Rue Alexandre Mari, and the Maison de la Presse, Place Masséna, are two other great map and guide places.

Library The English-American library, 12 Rue de France, is open from 10 to 11 am and 3 to 5 pm (closed Monday, Friday and on weekends). Short-term memberships are welcomed. Cut through the passageway opposite 17 Rue de France and walk straight ahead down the steps.

Cultural Centre The ornate Église Anglicane (Holy Trinity Anglican Church; ☎ 04 93 87 19 83), 11 Rue de la Buffa, has a mixed American and British membership and functions as something of an Anglophone Community Centre. Sunday Mass is at 11 am. Adjoining the church is a cemetery containing the graves of 'pioneer' expatriates from the 19th and early 20th centuries, including that of Henri Francis Lyte, author of the well known hymn, *Abide with Me*.

Laundry Self-service laundrettes are plentiful. Near the train station, head for 8 Rue de Belgique (open 7 am to 11 pm), 14 Rue de Suisse or 16 Rue d'Angleterre (both open 7 am to 9 pm). Nearer to the beach, try 39 Rue de la Buffa (open 7 am to 9 pm) or Top Speed, 12 Rue de la Buffa (open 8 am to 8 pm). Taxi Lav, corner of Rue Pertinax and Rue Lamartine, is handy for backpackers staying at Le Petit Louvre hotel. Best One, 26 Rue Pertinax, is open from 6 am to 10 pm.

Emergency The police headquarters (☎ 04 92 17 22 22; foreign tourist department ☎ 04 92 17 20 31) is at 1 Ave Maréchal Foch.

Promenade des Anglais

The palm-lined 'English Promenade', established by Nice's English colony in 1822 as a seaside walking path, provides a fine stage for a stroll along the beach and the Baie des Anges (Bay of Angels). Don't miss the façade of the Art Deco **Palais de la Méditerranée**, crumbling in all its magnificence at 13-17 Promenade des Anglais; former mayor Jacques Médecin was responsible for gutting it in the 1980s.

Other pleasant places for a walk include **Quai des États-Unis**, the promenade leading east to Vieux Nice that honours US President Wilson's decision in 1917 for the USA to join WWI (a colossal memorial commemorating the 4000 people from Nice who died during the war is carved in the rock at the east end of the quay); the **Jardin Albert 1er**, laid out in the late 19th century; **Espace Masséna**, a public square enlivened by fountains; **Place Masséna**, whose early 19th century, neoclassical arcaded buildings are painted in various shades of ochre and red; **Ave Jean Médecin**, Nice's main commercial street; and **Cimiez**, the most exclusive quarter in Nice.

Vieux Nice

This area of narrow, winding streets between Quai des États-Unis and the Musée d'Art Moderne et d'Art Contemporain has looked pretty much the same since the 1700s. Arcade-lined **Place Garibaldi**, built during the latter half of the 18th century, is named after Giuseppe Garibaldi (1807-82), one of the great heroes of Italian unification, who was born in Nice and is also buried in the cemetery in the Parc du Château).

Interesting churches in Vieux Nice include the baroque **Cathédrale Sainte Réparate** at Place Rossetti, built around 1650; the blue-grey and yellow **Église Saint Jacques Le Majeur** at Place du Gésu (close to Rue Rossetti), whose baroque ornamentation dates from the mid-17th century; as well as the mid-18th century **Chapelle de la Miséricorde**, next to Place Pierre Gautier.

Rue Benoît Bunico, which runs perpendicular to Rue Rossetti, served as Nice's Jewish ghetto after a 1430 law restricted where Jews could live. Gates at each end were locked at sunset.

Absolutely Fabulous

Belle époque Nice was absolutely fabulous: the wedding cake mansions, palaces and pastel-painted concrete gâteaux that sprang up in abundance at this time were not just fabulous, they were absolutely fantastical.

Cimiez remains the pearl of this lavish, turn-of-the-century legacy; the Haussmann-style **Conservatoire de Music**, 8 Blvd de Cimiez, dates from 1902. Continuing north along Blvd de Cimiez to No 46 is **L'Alhambra** (1901), an opulent private mansion set on a small, palm tree-studded mound and surrounded by a high wall. No wall can hide the Moorish minarets that top the sparkling white building. The **Villa Raphaeli-Surany** (1900), opposite at No 35, is adorned with intricate mosaic reliefs. The boulevard's crowning jewel is the **Hôtel Excelsior Régina Palace**, 71 Ave Régina, at the north end of Blvd de Cimiez. It was built in 1896 to welcome Queen Victoria to Nice (a statue of her stands in front) and was later home to Henri Matisse.

The pink wedding cake atop Mont Boron you see from the Nice ferry port is the **Château des Anglais**, built in 1859 by English engineer Colonel Robert Smith, inspired by structures he'd restored in India, for a Scotsman, who was renowned at the time as being the only foreigner to live in Nice year-round.

Parc du Château

At the eastern end of Quai des États-Unis, atop a 92m-high hill, is this shady public park, where local families come to stroll, admire the panoramic views of Nice and the sparkling Baie des Anges, or visit the artificial waterfall. It's a great place to escape the heat on a summer afternoon (open 7 am to 8 pm).

The chateau after which the hill and park are named was established in the 12th century but was razed by Louis XIV in 1706. In the one remaining tower, the 16th century **Tour Bellanda**, above the eastern end of Quai des États-Unis, is the **Musée Naval** (☎ 04 93 80 47 61). It is open from 10 am to noon and 2 to 5 pm (7 pm in summer; closed Monday and Tuesday). The cemetery where Garibaldi (see Vieux Nice) is buried covers the north-west of the park.

To get to the top of the chateau, take the *ascenseur* (lift; 3.50/5FF single/return, 1.80/3.60FF for children) from under the Tour Bellanda. It operates from 9 am to 5.50 pm (7.50 pm in summer). Alternatively, walk up Montée Lesage or up the steps at the east end of Rue Rossetti.

Musée d'Art Moderne et d'Art Contemporain

The Museum of Modern & Contemporary Art (☎ 04 93 62 61 62) – Nice's pride and joy in the architectural stakes – specialises in French and American avant-garde works from the 1960s to the present. Glass walkways connect the four marble-coated towers, on top of which is a must-see rooftop garden and gallery featuring pieces by Nice-born Yves Klein (1928-62). Other highlights include Andy Warhol's *Campbell's Soup Can* (1965), a shopping trolley (cart) wrapped by Christo, and a pea-green Model T Ford compressed into a 1.6m-high block by Marseille-born French sculptor César.

The museum, at Ave Saint Jean Baptiste, is open from 10 am to 6 pm (closed Tuesday). Admission is 25/15FF for adults/students. Art films and cult movies are screened most Thursdays at 3 and 8.30 pm in the auditorium. Take bus No 17 from the train station to the Station Centrale, from where the museum is a three minute walk north-east.

Musée National Message Biblique Marc Chagall

The Marc Chagall Biblical Message Museum (☎ 04 93 53 87 20), whose main exhibit is in five small rooms, is across the street from 4 Ave Docteur Ménard, close to Blvd de Cimiez. Don't miss the mosaic of the rose window at Metz Cathedral viewed through a plate-glass window across a small pond. The museum is open from 10 am to 5 pm (6 pm from July to October; closed Tuesday year-round). Admission is 30/20FF for adults/students. Take bus No 15 from Place Masséna to the stop in front of the museum or walk.

Musée Masséna

The Masséna Museum (☎ 04 93 88 11 34), also known as the Musée d'Art et d'Histoire, is in the Palais Masséna, 65 Rue de France. The eclectic collection of paintings, furniture, icons, ceramics and religious art, housed in an Italian-style villa dating from 1898, can be viewed between 10 am and noon and 2 and 6 pm (closed Monday). Entry is 25/15FF for adults/students.

The palm tree-studded gardens behind the museum are equipped with the same blue chairs as the Promenade des Anglais, making for a shady hideaway from the posing crowds on the packed promenade. The gardens close at 7 pm in summer.

Musée des Beaux-Arts Jules Chéret

The Jules Chéret Fine Arts Museum (☎ 04 93 44 50 72), 33 Ave des Baumettes, is housed in a fantastic, yellow and ochre-coloured late 19th century villa – the former residence of a Ukrainian princess – just off Rue de France. The six-column terrace around the back that overlooks the small, pretty public garden, is worth a glance too.

Opening hours/admission fees are the same as at the Musée Masséna. The one hour guided tour on Wednesday at 3 pm (in French only) costs an extra 20FF. Bus No 38 from the Station Centrale stops outside.

Musée Matisse

The Matisse Museum (☎ 04 93 81 08 08), 164 Ave des Arènes de Cimiez, which houses a fine collection of works by Henri Matisse, is 2.5km north-east of the train station in the bourgeois district of Cimiez. The museum's permanent collection is displayed in a red-ochre, 17th century Genoese mansion overlooking an olive grove and the **Parc des Arènes**. Temporary exhibitions are hosted in the futuristic basement building that leads through to the stucco-decorated villa. Well known pieces in the permanent collection include Matisse's blue paper cutouts of *Blue Nude IV* and *Woman with Amphora*.

The Many Phases of Matisse

One of the most famous French artists of this century, Henri Matisse (1869-1954) was renowned for his passion for pure colour. As a leader of the Fauvists (who came to prominence in 1905), his paintings epitomised their radical use of violent colour, heavy outlines and simplified forms. Although Fauvism was a short-lived movement, Matisse continued to employ the method of setting striking complementary colours against one another throughout his career.

Compared to other important painters, Matisse was a latecomer, only developing an interest in painting when he was 20. By the time he was 22 he had given up his law career in his home region, Picardy, and moved to Paris.

Matisse studied art for many years under the symbolist painter Gustave Moreau. While visiting Brittany, he met Australian artist John Russell, who introduced him to the works of Van Gogh, Monet and other impressionists, prompting (so it is believed) Matisse's change from a rather sombre palette to brighter colours. He also spent time in Corsica, whose clear and rich Mediterranean light was to have a lasting influence on his work. By the early 1900s he was well known in Paris among followers of modern art and his paintings were being exhibited, but he was still struggling financially. It wasn't until the first Fauvist exhibition in 1905, which followed a summer of innovative painting in the fishing village of Colliourе in Roussillon, that his financial situation improved. By 1913 he had paintings on display in London and New York.

Matisse spent the winters from 1916 onwards in Nice, often staying in the Hôtel Beau Rivage, Promenade des Anglais. In the 1920s he moved his home to the Côte d'Azur but still spent much time travelling – to Étretat in Normandy and abroad to Italy and Tahiti. During these years he painted prolifically but was less radical; his work's characteristic sensuality and optimism, however, were always present. The 1930s saw him rent an apartment overlooking Place Charles Félix in Nice. His work was marked by a return to more experimental techniques and a renewed search for simplicity, in which the subject matter was reduced to essential elements only.

In 1948 he began working on a set of stained-glass windows for the Chapelle du Rosaire in Vence, run by Dominican nuns. He ended up designing not only the windows but nearly the entire chapel – a project that took several years. During his mainly bedridden final years Matisse rented two apartments in the Hôtel Excelsior Régina Palace in Nice's upmarket Cimiez region. It was here that he turned his hand to *découpage*, the art of creating pictures from brightly coloured paper cutouts. The brilliantly blue *Blue Nude IV* and *Woman with Amphora* were among the results. Matisse died in Cimiez, aged 85, in 1954. His grave in Cimiez cemetery aptly faces out to sea.

Matisse is buried in the cemetery of the **Monastère de Cimiez** (Cimiez Monastery; ☎ 04 93 81 00 04), which today houses a small museum run by – and unravelling the history of – the monastery's Franciscan monks. The artist's grave is signposted *sépulture Henri Matisse* from the cemetery's main entrance (next to the monastery church on Ave Bellanda). A flight of stairs leads from the east end of the olive grove to Ave Bellanda.

The museum is open from 10 am to 5 pm (from 10 am to 6 pm April to September; closed Tuesday year-round). Admission is 25/15FF for adults/students. Guided tours (in French) take place on Wednesday at 3 pm; you can arrange tours in English (☎ 04 93 26 31 77 or ☎ 04 93 46 49 14). Take bus No 15, 17, 20, 22 or 25 from the Station Centrale to the Arènes stop.

Musée et Site Archéologiques

Behind the Musée Matisse, on the east side of the Parc des Arènes, lie the ruins of the Roman city of Cemenelum – the focus of the Archaeology Museum (☎ 04 93 81 59 57), 160 Ave des Arènes de Cimiez. The public baths and the amphitheatre – the venue for outdoor concerts during the Nice Jazz Festival – can both be visited.

Opening hours and admission fees for the Musée et Site Archéologiques are the same as the Musée Matisse. To get here from the latter, turn left out of the main park entrance on Ave des Arènes de Cimiez, walk 100m, then turn left again onto Ave Monte Croce, where the main entrance to the archaeological site is located.

Musée International d'Art Naïf Anatole Jakovsky

The Anatole Jakovsky International Naive Art Museum (☎ 04 93 71 78 33), with a collection of naive art from all over the world, is less than 2km west of the city centre on Ave du Val Marie. Take bus No 10, 12 or 24 from the Station Centrale to the Fabron stop, then walk or take bus No 34 to the Musée Art Naïf stop. The museum is open from 10 am to noon and 2 to 5 pm (6 pm from May to September; closed Tuesday year-round). Admission is 25/15FF for adults/students.

Cathédrale Orthodoxe Russe Saint Nicolas

The multicoloured Russian Orthodox Cathedral of Saint Nicolas (☎ 04 93 96 88 02), crowned by six onion domes, was built between 1902 and 1912 in early 17th century style and is an easy 15 minute walk from the train station. Step inside and you're transported to Imperial Russia. The cathedral, on Ave Nicolas II opposite 17 Blvd du Tzaréwich, is open from 9 or 9.30 am to noon and 2.30 to 5.30 pm (closed Sunday morning). Entrance is 12/10FF. Shorts, miniskirts and sleeveless shirts are forbidden.

Activities

If you don't like the feel of sand between your toes, Nice's **beach** is for you: it's covered with smooth round pebbles. Sections of beach open to the public without charge alternate with 15 *plages concédées* (private beaches), which you have to pay for by renting a chair (around 60FF a day) or mattress (around 55FF).

Along the beach you can hire catamarans, paddleboats (80 to 90FF an hour) or sailboards and jet skis (300FF for a half-hour), take a parachute ride from the back of a speed boat (220FF for 15 minutes) and go water-skiing (100 to 130FF for 10 minutes) or paragliding (200FF for 10 minutes). There are public indoor showers (15FF) and toilets (2FF) opposite 50 Promenade des Anglais.

PH+ Plongée (☎ 04 93 26 09 03), 3 Quai des Deux Emmanuel, and L'Odyssee (☎ 04 93 89 42 44), 14 Quai des Docks, both offer **diving courses**, organise diving expeditions and rent equipment. An introductory dive costs around 160FF; equipment is extra.

Trans Côte d'Azur (☎ 04 92 00 42 30), Quai Lunel, organises **glass-bottomed boat trips** around the Baie des Anges (60/40FF for adults/children), to the Îles de Lérins (see the Cannes section later in the chapter), Saint Tropez and Monaco. The ticket office is open from 8 am to 7 pm (Saturday until 11.45 pm; closed Sunday).

For detailed **hiking** and **mountain-biking** trails in the region, go to the headquarters of the Parc National du Mercantour (see Information) or the Club Alpin Français (☎ 04 93 62 59 99), 14 Ave Mirabeau.

Rollerblading The Promenade des Anglais is *the* place to rollerblade. City Sport, inside the Nice Étoile shopping centre, Ave Jean Médecin, rents rollerblades (and protective kneepads for those not too proud to don something so un-chic) for 30/50/80FF per half-day/day/two days. Super Sports (☎ 04 93 62 28 92), 9 Rue Saint François de Paule, and the Roller Station (☎ 04 93 26 63 35), 10 Rue Cassini, also rent rollerblades.

The latest trends in rollerblade fashions are sold at the 4 Wheels Skate Shop, 4 Place SP Garibaldi.

Special Events

The colourful Carnaval de Nice, held every spring around Mardi Gras (Shrove Tuesday), fills the streets with floats and musicians. The week-long Nice Jazz Festival sets the town jiving in July; the main venue (fabulous!) is the olive grove behind the Musée Matisse in the Cimiez district.

Places to Stay

Nice has a surfeit of reasonably priced places to stay. During the Easter university holidays, lots of American students descend on Nice for a transatlantic 'College Week', making cheap accommodation hard to find after 10 or 11 am. Nice is also crowded with budget travellers during July and August. Inexpensive places fill up by late morning.

Hôtels meublés (literally, 'furnished hotels') are rooms with cooking facilities in 'hotels' (often just private flats) where little or no service is provided.

In summer, many young people sleep on the beach. This is theoretically illegal and public beaches are supposed to be closed between midnight and 6 am, but the Nice (and nice) police usually look the other way. However, watch out for thieves.

The information desk at the bus station (see the Getting There & Away section) has information on Logis de France hotels and other rural properties in the region.

Places to Stay – Budget

Hostels Touting a great tree-studded garden decked out with tables and chairs for guests to lounge on is the busy ***Hôtel Belle Meunière***, 21 Ave Durante, which has dorm beds for 76FF (96FF with shower and 101FF with shower and toilet), including breakfast.

Equally popular is the rambling ***Hôtel Les Orangers*** (☎/fax 04 93 87 51 41), almost opposite in a turn-of-the-century townhouse at 10bis Ave Durante. A bed in a snug four, five or six-bed room with shower and fantastic, huge windows costs 85FF. The cheerful owner speaks excellent English after dealing with Anglophone backpackers for the past 17 years. Nearby, the ***Hôtel Darcy***, 28 Rue d'Angleterre (see Hotels – Train Station Area), has dorm beds for 92FF.

Heading into town along Ave Jean Médecin, you come to the popular 20 bed ***Backpackers Hôtel*** (☎ 04 93 80 30 72) at 32 Rue Pertinax. A dorm bed is 70FF a night, there's no curfew or daytime closure and Patrick, who runs the place, is said to be an absolute darling (and great at directing party-mad backpackers to the hot spot of the moment). The hotel is above the Faubourg Montmartre restaurant.

The ***Pado Tourisme*** hostel (☎ 04 93 80 98 00), 26 Blvd Raimbaldi, charges 60FF for a bed in a mixed dorm. Reception is open from 8 am to noon and 6 to 9 pm; there is a daytime closure between noon and 6 pm.

Nice's ***Auberge de Jeunesse*** (☎ 04 93 89 23 64; fax 04 92 04 03 10), Route Forestière de Mont Alban, is 5km east of the train station. Bed and breakfast is 66FF. Curfew is at midnight and rooms are locked from 10 am to 5 pm. Take bus No 14 (last one at 8.20 pm) from the Station Centrale bus terminal on Square Général Leclerc, which is linked to the train station by bus Nos 15 and 17, and get off at the L'Auberge stop.

The *Centre Hébergement Jeunes* (☎ 04 93 86 28 75; fax 04 93 44 93 22), 31 Rue Louis de Coppet (in the Espace Magnan building), is open from mid-June to mid-September. A bed in a six-person room costs only 50FF. Rooms are locked from 10 am to 6 pm, there's a midnight curfew, and bags must be stored in the luggage room during the day.

Hotels – Train Station Area The quickest way to get to all these hotels is to walk straight down the steps opposite the train station onto Ave Durante. The first place you hit is the clean, warm and welcoming *Hôtel Belle Meunière* (☎ 04 93 88 66 15), 21 Ave Durante, always packed with backpackers. As well as dorms, it has large doubles/triples with high ceilings, some with century-old décor, from 182/243FF (with shower and toilet). There's private parking in the front courtyard. This hotel is closed in December and January.

The highly recommended *Hôtel Les Orangers* (see Hostels) has great doubles and triples with shower and a balcony overlooking palm-tree gardens, for 210FF. Rooms are gloriously sunlit thanks to their great century-old windows and come with fridge (and hotplate on request).

Hard cash and nothing else is accepted at the dreary *Hôtel Idéal Bristol* (☎ 04 93 88 60 72), 22 Rue Paganini, which has basic doubles from 145FF (180FF with shower and toilet). Rooms for four people with shower and toilet are 425FF. It also has a 5th floor terrace where guests can sunbathe and picnic. More dubiously, the Bristol has 130FF rooms to rent during the day for 'passengers waiting for a train'.

The *Hôtel Darcy* (☎ 04 93 88 67 06), 28 Rue d'Angleterre, has singles/doubles/ triples for 125/150/195FF (210/255/300FF with shower and toilet). At 38 Rue d'Angleterre is the new, clean and attractive *Hôtel de la Gare* (☎/fax 04 93 88 75 07), which has modern singles with washbasin/ shower and toilet for 115/175FF. Doubles/ triples/quads cost 155/240/320FF.

The *Hôtel Regency* (☎ 04 93 62 17 44; fax 04 93 92 23 26), 2 Rue Saint Siagre (2nd floor), has large split-level studios with shower, toilet, kitchenette and fridge for two/three people for 220/270FF. Ring the bell to enter.

Rue d'Alsace-Lorraine is dotted with more upmarket two-star hotels: one of the cheapest is the *Hôtel du Piemont* (☎ 04 93 88 25 15) at No 19, which has bargain singles/doubles/ triples with washbasin from 110/130/190FF. Singles/doubles with shower start at 130/ 160FF, while rooms with shower and toilet cost from 180/200FF. Triples/ quads are 225/300FF. It rents rooms on a long-term basis too.

Hotels – City Centre The reception of the friendly *Hôtel Little Masséna* (☎ 04 93 87 72 34), 22 Rue Masséna, is on the 5th floor (open until 8 pm). Doubles with washbasin/ shower/toilet and shower are 140/180/ 220FF. Rooms come with a hot plate and fridge.

The relaxed, family-style *Hôtel Les Mimosas* (☎ 04 93 88 05 59) is two blocks north-east of the Musée Masséna at 26 Rue de la Buffa (2nd floor). Utilitarian rooms of a good size for one/two people cost 120/190FF. Showers cost 10FF.

Midway between the sea and the station is the colourful *Le Petit Louvre* (☎ 04 93 80 15 54; fax 04 93 62 45 08), 10 Rue Emma Tiranty, run by a humorous musician and his wife for 17 years. A faceless Mona Lisa greets guests as they enter, and corridors are adorned with an eclectic bunch of paintings. Singles/doubles with shower, washbasin, fridge and hotplate are 171/205FF; rooms with shower and toilet are 191/230FF; and triples cost 249FF. Breakfast comprises cereal and fruit as well as the usual baguette, croissant and coffee and costs 25FF.

On a side street off Ave Jean Médecin is the one star *Hôtel Lyonnais* (☎ 04 93 88 70 74; fax 04 93 16 25 56), 20 Rue de Russie, which has unrenovated singles/doubles with washbasin for 110/140FF. Nightly rates increase by about 30FF in the high season. Triples/quads start at 210/240FF. It's not the brightest of places but busy in summer nonetheless.

Hotels – Vieux Nice The ***Hôtel Saint François*** (☎ 04 93 85 88 69; fax 04 93 85 10 67), 3 Rue Saint François, has singles/doubles/triples for 130/168/237FF. Showers cost 15FF. Reception is open until 10 pm.

The ***Hôtel au Picardy*** (☎ 04 93 85 75 51), 10 Blvd Jean Jaurès, has single/ double rooms from 120/140FF; there are also pricier rooms that include toilet and shower. Hall showers are 10FF.

The ***Hôtel Meublé Le Genevois*** (☎ 04 93 85 00 58), 11 Rue Alexandre Mari (3rd floor), has 1950s-style singles/doubles with kitchenette from 130/180FF. Huge studios with shower and toilet are 180 to 240FF for two people. If no-one answers the *sonnerie* (bell), push the little red button.

Places to Stay – Mid-Range

Near the train station there are lots of two-star hotels along Rue d'Angleterre, Rue d'Alsace-Lorraine, Rue de Suisse, Rue de Russie and Ave Durante.

In the centre, the ***Hôtel Plaisance*** (☎ 04 93 85 11 90; fax 04 93 80 88 92), 20 Rue de Paris, is a pleasing old two star place with air-conditioned doubles from 320FF.

Named after its location near the Église Notre Dame is the very clean and modern ***Hôtel Notre Dame*** (☎ 04 93 88 70 44; fax 04 93 82 20 38), 22 Rue de Russie, which has spacious doubles/triples with private shower and toilet for 240/300FF. Its 17 rooms fill quickly so get there early. Another good-value place, little publicised, is the modest, 28 room ***Hôtel du Centre*** (☎ 04 93 88 83 85; fax 04 93 82 29 80), 2 Rue de Suisse, which has rooms with shared/private shower for 144/174FF. After 11.30 pm guests need a door code to enter.

A stone's throw from the sea and from the Musée des Beaux-Arts is the good-value ***Hôtel Carlone*** (☎/fax 04 93 44 71 61), 2 Blvd François Grosso. Light and airy rooms for one or two with washbasin/shower and toilet start at 170/250FF and it has triples/ quads from 340/400FF. The ***Hôtel Résidence Astoria*** (☎ 04 95 15 25 45), next door, has rooms with bathroom, fridge, hotplate etc to let on a nightly/weekly/monthly or longer basis. Rates depend on the season, starting from 190/1000/2800FF in the low season and peaking at 250/1650FF per night/week (no monthly rentals) in August. The Astoria also has a pretty garden.

Fabulously like home and equally close to the sea is the welcoming ***Hôtel Cronstadt*** (☎ 04 93 82 00 30), 3 Rue Cronstadt. Exceptionally quiet and graceful rooms cost 270/310/400/580FF for singles/doubles/triples/rooms for four or five people. Prices include breakfast.

Places to Stay – Top End

The pink-domed, green-shuttered, four star ***Hôtel Négresco*** (☎ 04 93 16 64 00 or ☎ 04 93 88 00 58; fax 04 93 88 35 68; negresco@nicematin.fr), 37 Promenade des Anglais, built in the *belle époque* style (see the boxed text 'Absolutely Fabulous'), is Nice's fanciest hotel. It dates from the early 1900s and is protected as an historic monument. Rooms with a sea/sea and garden view start at 1300/1750FF from January to April and 1700/2150FF from May to September. And a continental/American-style breakfast is only another 130/190FF. The Négresco's restaurant is also considered the best in town (see Places to Eat).

The stylish four star ***Hôtel Méridien*** (☎ 04 93 82 25 25; fax 04 93 16 08 90), 1 Promenade des Anglais, is known for its very comfortable rooms and rooftop pool. Rooms cost 1450 to 3300FF. For a touch of class for less cash, try the ***Hôtel Westminster Concorde*** (☎ 04 93 88 29 44; fax 04 93 82 45 35), 27 Promenade des Anglais. Rooms start at 750FF.

Matisse stayed at the ***Hôtel Beau Rivage*** (☎ 04 93 80 80 70; fax 04 93 80 55 77; info@new-hotel.com), 24 Rue Saint François de Paule, when he was in town in 1916. Before that, in 1891, Russian playwright Anton Chekhov (1860-1904) graced the place with his presence. Sea views from the hotel, which today touts four stars, remain superb. The cheapest rooms cost 650/850FF in the low/high season.

Places to Eat

Restaurants – Train Station Area The ***Restaurant Le Toscan*** (☎ 04 93 88 40 54), 1 Rue de Belgique, is a family-run Italian place offering large portions of tripe or home-made pasta from noon to 2 pm and 6.45 to 10 pm (closed Sunday).

Corsican chants and energetic guitar duets are some of the Île de Beauté delights performed every Thursday, Friday and Saturday evening at the Corsican ***L'Allegria*** (☎ 04 93 87 42 00) at 7 Rue d'Italie. Next door is the unpretentious and very friendly ***Restaurant au Soleil***, which offers good local cuisine at unbeatable prices, including an all-day omelette breakfast for 33FF. Another inexpensive favourite is the bustling ***Restaurant de Paris*** (☎ 04 93 88 99 88), 28 Rue d'Angleterre, adjoining the Hôtel Darcy, which has a bargain 38FF *menu*.

Adorned with fat contented cherubs on its outside walls is the atmospheric ***L'Ange Gourmand***, 47 Rue Lamartine. Its *carte*, which changes daily and is handwritten, includes an 85FF *menu*. Close by, on the corner of Blvd Raimbaldi and Rue Miron is the handsome ***Chez Mireille*** (☎ 04 93 85 27 23), which specialises in paella, paella and more paella. It is closed Monday, Tuesday, in June and early July.

Bursting with hungry backpackers is the cheap and cheerful ***Le Faubourg Montmartre*** (☎ 04 93 62 55 03), 32 Rue Pertinax. The house speciality is bouillabaisse (120FF for two) and there's a 68FF *menu*. It's opens for lunch at noon and for dinner from 5.30 pm.

Asian There are over a dozen Vietnamese and Chinese restaurants on Rue Paganini, Rue d'Italie and Rue d'Alsace-Lorraine. Don't expect miracles – except maybe at ***China Fast Food***, a spanking-clean fast-food place on the corner of Ave Thiers and Ave Jean Médecin. Choose from beautifully presented meat dishes for 27 to 38FF and rice variations for 14 to 20FF. It's open from 9 am to midnight.

Restaurants – City Centre The Rue Masséna pedestrian mall and nearby streets and squares, including Rue de France and Place Magenta, are crammed with touristy outdoor cafés and restaurants, although most don't offer particularly good value.

One worth sampling is ***La Trattoria***, whose terrace restaurant fills the entire southern stretch of Rue Dalpozzo. It specialises in pizza *au feu de bois* (cooked with a wood fire). Nearby is the small and homely ***Le Moulin à Poivre***, a couple of doors west of the Manoir Café on Rue de France. The 'Pepper Mill' has a *plat du jour* for 50FF, a 120FF *menu* and plenty of home-made pasta dishes.

Near the port, ***L'Olivier*** (☎ 04 93 26 89 09), 2 Place Garibaldi, is a small, simple and very local place. A meal guaranteed to fill you up costs around 100FF; it is closed Wednesday evening, Sunday and in August.

La Nissarda (☎ 04 93 85 26 29), 17 Rue Gubernatis, serves specialities of Nice and Normandy. The *menus* are reasonably priced at 60FF (lunch only), 78, 98 and 138FF (closed on Sunday and in August). Nearby, ***Le Bistrot Saint Germain*** (☎ 04 93 13 45 12; closed Sunday), 9 Rue Chauvain, brings a touch of Paris to Nice, with walls decorated with photos of Parisian scenes.

Graceful and very local is ***Le Comptoir*** (☎ 04 93 92 08 80), 20 Rue Saint François de Paule, close to the seashore. The restaurant, which has an adjoining nightclub, is decked out in Art Deco style and has a terrace too. Pasta/fish dishes start at 52/90FF.

For a mind-blowing traditional French meal in a luxurious setting, try the Michelin two star ***Chantecler*** (☎ 04 93 88 39 51) inside the Hôtel Négresco. Impeccable service and tantalising cuisine add up to a hefty 500FF-per-head (at least) bill.

Restaurants – Vieux Nice Many of the narrow streets of Vieux Nice are lined with restaurants, cafés, pizzerias and so on that draw locals and visitors alike. There are dozens of cafés and restaurants on Cours Saleya, Place Rossetti and Place Pierre

Gautier, many of which buzz until well past midnight (later during the summer).

A perennial favourite with locals is ***Nissa Socca*** (☎ 04 93 80 18 35), 5 Rue Sainte Réparate, which specialises in delicious Niçois dishes such as *socca* (a thin layer of chickpea flour and olive oil batter fried on a griddle), *salade Niçoise*, *farcis* (stuffed vegetables) and *ratatouille*. Nissa Socca is open daily (closed in January and June). If you don't want to stand in line (inevitable), try ***Nissa La Bella*** (☎ 04 93 62 10 20), opposite, which serves similar (but not as good) dishes. ***Chez Thérésa*** (☎ 04 93 85 00 04) has home-made socca served from a little hole in the wall at 28 Rue Droite from 8 am to 1 pm (closed Monday).

A short distance north of Vieux Nice ***Lou Balico – Chez Adrienne*** (☎ 04 93 85 93 71), 20 Ave Saint Jean Baptiste, serves excellent Niçois specialities, as well as bouillabaisse (250FF), really a Marseille speciality. Mains range from 80 to 125FF, and it's open daily. Nearby is the equally local ***L'Auberge d'Acropolis***, 9 Rue Penchienatti, which has a regional plat du jour for 45FF, a wholesome lunch *menu* for 60FF and evening ones for 95 and 120FF.

Small, select and decked out with colourful furnishings is ***La Divina Commedia*** (☎ 04 93 80 71 84), 7 Rue de la Terrasse. Its plat du jour costs 62FF and it serves a 48FF lunchtime *menu*.

The house speciality at the enchanting (smiling staff, candlelit terrace etc) ***Escalinada*** (☎ 04 93 62 11 71), 22 Rue Pairolière, is *testicules de mouton panés* (sheeps' testicles in batter).

Cafés For home-made cakes and hearty tarts like grandma bakes, look no farther than the cosy ***Scotch Tea House*** (☎ 04 93 87 75 62), tucked between designer clothing shops at 4 Ave de Suède. It's open from 9 am to 7 pm and is *the* place to go for good old-fashioned afternoon tea.

Cool, chic and always packed is the refined ***Manoir Café*** (☎ 04 93 16 36 16), 32 Rue de France. Jazz bands play here on Wednesday evenings. Reserve a table in advance if you want to dine here.

Aux Spécialités Belges, 3 Rue Maccarani, is a small *salon de thé* (tea room) that serves delicious cakes, pastries and other treats.

Sweet crêpes, savoury galettes, punchy ciders and a great range of ice creams are beautifully presented at the busy ***Crêperie Bretonne*** (☎ 04 93 16 02 98), 3 Rue de Russie (closed on Monday).

Guess what type of cuisine the dynamic ***Mexican Café***, 14 Rue Saint François de Paule, specialises in? Wild salsa nights are hosted here on weekends.

Cafeterias Dirt-cheap places near the train station include the ***Flunch Cafétéria*** (☎ 04 93 88 41 35), to the left as you exit the station building; open from 11 am to 10 pm.

The ***Cafétéria Casino*** (☎ 04 93 82 44 44), 7 Ave Thiers, serves breakfast (10 to 17FF) from 8 to 11 am and other meals until 9.30 pm. Its good-value 29FF *formule* comprises its plat du jour plus an entrée, cheese or dessert.

Self-Catering There's a ***fruit & vegetable market*** in front of the prefecture, Cours Saleya, from 6 am to 5.30 pm (closed Sunday afternoon and on Monday), and a fresh fish market every morning on Place Saint François. The ***boulangerie*** without a name at the south end of Rue du Marché is the best place for cheap sandwiches, pizza slices, traditional *michettes* (savoury bread stuffed with cheese, olives, anchovies and onions) and other local breads. Otherwise take a mouthwatering stroll along Rue Pairolière, which is lined with fromageries, boulangeries and fruit shops.

The ***Ducs de Gascogne***, 4 Rue de France, sells foie gras, fine wines and other pricey culinary delights. ***La Ferme Fromagerie***, 3 Rue Maccarani, sells fantastic cheeses.

For a mind-boggling array of different breads, head for ***Le Capitole*** (☎ 04 93 44 67 77), 78 Rue de France. Just around the corner on the south end of Blvd Gambetta is the ***Intermarché*** supermarket, open from 8.45 am to 8 pm (closed Sunday).

The ***Prisunic*** supermarket opposite 33 Ave Jean Médecin is open from 8.30 am to 8.30 pm (closed Sunday); the branch at Place Garibaldi closes at 8 pm. The ***Casino*** supermarket at 27 Blvd Gambetta, on the west side of the city, has the same hours.

Entertainment

The tourist office has detailed information on Nice's abundant cultural activities, many of which are listed in its free monthly brochure, *Le Mois à Nice*. More useful is the weekly *L'Officiel des Loisirs Côte d'Azur* (2FF) available from newsstands on Wednesday. Tickets to events of all sorts can be purchased at FNAC (☎ 04 92 17 77 77), 24 Ave Jean Médecin (inside the Nice Étoile shopping mall).

Cinema Nice has two cinemas offering nondubbed films, many of them in English: the ***Cinéma Nouveau Mercury*** (☎ 04 93 55 32 31 for a recorded message in French), 16 Place Garibaldi, and the ***Cinéma Rialto*** (☎ 04 93 88 08 41), 4 Rue de Rivoli.

Art films (usually in French or with French subtitles) are screened in the auditorium inside the Musée d'Art Moderne et d'Art Contemporain.

Classical Music Operas and orchestral concerts are held at the ornate ***Opéra de Nice*** (☎ 04 92 17 40 40), built in 1885 and undergoing a three year face-lift, at 4-6 Rue Saint François de Paule (around the corner from Quai des États-Unis). The box office is open from 10 am to 6 pm (closed Sunday). The best tickets for operas/concerts and ballets cost 50/20FF; the opera house is closed between mid-June and September.

Theatre The superbly modern ***Théâtre de Nice*** (☎ 04 93 80 52 60), whose entrance on Promenade des Arts faces the Musée d'Art Moderne et d'Art Contemporain, is one block west of Place Garibaldi. The two halls host a wide variety of first-rate theatre performances and concerts. Ticket prices range from 60 to 170FF. The information desk is open from 1 to 7 pm (closed Sunday and Monday) and one hour before each performance.

Pubs & Bars Bars and terraced cafés – perfect for quaffing beers and sipping pastis – abound in Nice. For a taste of some excellent Belgian brew or one of 70-plus types of beer, try ***Le Pub Gioffredo***, corner of Rue Chauvain and Rue Gioffredo. For a pint of Guinness head straight for the ***Scarlett O'Hara Irish Pub***, corner of Rue Rossetti and Rue Droite in Vieux Nice.

Nice boasts a rash of pubs run by Anglophones, with happy hours and live music. Best known is ***Chez Wayne's*** (☎ 04 93 13 46 99; www.waynes.fr), 15 Rue de la Préfecture, which hosts a bilingual quiz on Tuesday, a ladies' night on Wednesday, karaoke on Sunday, and live bands on Friday and Saturday. Wayne's is open from 3 pm to midnight (later on weekends). Happy hour is until 9 pm.

Another hot spot is ***Jonathan's Live Music Pub*** (☎ 04 93 62 57 62), also a *bar à musique*, 1 Rue de la Loge. Live bands (country, boogie-woogie, Irish folk etc) play every night in summer. ***William's Pub*** (☎ 04 93 85 84 66), 4 Rue Centrale, has live music from around 9 pm (not Sunday); the pub is open from 6 pm to 2.30 am. There's pool, darts and chess in the basement. Still bored? Head for the ***Thor Pub*** (☎ 04 93 62 49 90), 32 Cours Saleya.

The ***Hole-in-the-Wall*** (☎ 04 93 80 40 16), 3 Rue de l'Abbaye, is both a restaurant and a venue for live music; open from 8 pm to midnight (closed Monday).

Gay Venues Gay clubs close to the centre include ***Blue Boy*** (☎ 04 93 44 68 24), 9 Rue Spinetta, just off Blvd François Grosso (open 11 pm to 6 am), and the equally popular ***Factory*** (☎ 04 93 56 12 26), east of Le Château at 26 Quai Lunel. It's hard to believe the local headquarters of the National Front was until very recently at the same address.

Shopping

Cours Saleya hosts a wonderful flower market Tuesday to Saturday from 6 am to 5.30 pm and on Sunday morning. There are a number of vendors selling *fruits glacés* (glazed or candied fruits), a speciality of the region. The figs, tangerine slices and pears have to be tasted to be believed. The best-value place for wine-tasting and buying is the traditional wine cellar, and a good one is the Cave de la Buffa (☎ 04 93 88 10 26), 49 Rue de la Buffa. Olive oil is sold in excess at the quaint Moulin à Huile d'Olive Alziari shop, 14 Rue Saint François de Paule.

Designer names abound above the beautiful fashion boutiques languishing along Rue Paradis, Rue de Suède, Rue Alphonse Karr and Rue du Maréchal Joffre. Shop for unusual handmade art, crafts and jewellery at the *marché nocturne* (night market), held from 6.30 pm to midnight on Cours Saleya between July and September.

Close to the train station, Sports Évasion (☎ 04 93 16 88 44), 16 Ave Thiers, is a top-rate hiking and climbing shop that sells all the gear, including maps, compasses etc.

Getting There & Away

Air Nice's international airport, Aéroport International Nice-Côte d'Azur (☎ 04 93 21 30 30), is 6km west of the city centre.

Bus Lines operated by some two dozen bus companies stop at the intercity bus station (☎ 04 93 85 61 81), 5 Blvd Jean Jaurès. The busy information counter (☎ 04 93 85 03 90) is open from 8 am to 6.30 pm (closed Sunday).

There are slow but frequent services daily until about 7.30 pm to Antibes (25FF; 1¼ hours), Cannes (32FF; 1½ hours), Grasse (37FF; 1¼ hours), Menton (24FF return; 1¼ hours), Monaco (17FF return; 45 minutes) and Saint Raphaël (50FF; two hours). Hourly buses run to Vence (21FF; 50 minutes). To Castellane, the gateway to the Gorges du Verdon, there's one bus a day at 7.30 am (97FF; 1½ hours). Buses run to the ski resort of Isola 2000 (87FF; 2¼ hours) four times a day.

For long-haul travel, Intercars (☎ 04 93 80 08 70), at the bus station, takes you to various European destinations; it sells Eurolines tickets for buses to London, Brussels and Amsterdam.

Train Nice's main train station, Gare Nice Ville (or Gare Thiers), Ave Thiers, is 1200m north of the beach. The information office is open from 8 am to 6.30 pm (closed Sunday).

There are fast, frequent services (up to 40 trains a day in each direction) to towns along the coast between Saint Raphaël and Ventimiglia across the Italian border, including Antibes (17FF; 25 minutes), Cannes (32FF; 40 minutes), Menton (28FF; 35 minutes), Monaco (40FF; 20 minutes) and Saint Raphaël (57FF; 45 minutes).

The two or three TGVs that link Nice with Paris' Gare de Lyon (530FF; seven hours) are infrequent, so you may find it more convenient to go via Marseille.

The luggage lockers (15 to 30FF depending on bag size), are open from 6.30 am to 11 pm. You can also store bags at the left-luggage office (☎ 04 93 86 57 49; 30FF a bag); open from 7 am to 10 pm. Reimbursements for train tickets are available in the office (☎ 04 93 82 62 11) near the left-luggage window, open from 9 am to noon and 1 to 4 pm (closed on weekends). Lost luggage and other problems are handled by SOS Voyageurs (☎ 04 93 82 62 11), open from 9 am to noon and 3 to 6 pm (closed on weekends).

The ever-popular two-car diesel trains operated by Les Chemins de Fer de la Provence (☎ 04 93 88 34 72 in Nice; ☎ 04 92 31 01 58 in Digne-les-Bains) make the scenic trip four times daily from Nice's Gare du Sud (☎ 04 93 82 10 17), 4bis Rue Alfred Binet, to Digne-les-Bains (109FF; 3¼ hours).

Boat The fastest and least expensive SNCM ferries from mainland France to Corsica depart from Nice (see Getting There & Away at the start of the Corsica chapter).

The SNCM office (☎ 04 93 13 66 66), ferry terminal, Quai du Commerce, issues tickets (otherwise try a travel agency in town). It is open from 8 am to 7 pm (until 11.45 am on Saturday; open two hours before a scheduled departure on Sunday). From Ave Jean Médecin take bus No 1 or 2 to the Port stop.

Getting Around

To/From the Airport Sunbus route No 23 (8FF), which runs every 20 or 30 minutes from about 6 am to 8 pm, can be picked up at the train station or on Blvd Gambetta, Rue de France or Rue de la Californie. From the intercity bus station or Promenade des Anglais (near the Hôtel Négresco), you can also take the yellow ANT bus (21FF; ☎ 04 93 56 35 40), which bears a symbol of an aeroplane pointing upward (every 20 minutes; 30 minutes on Sunday). Buses also make the run from the train station.

A taxi from the airport to the centre of Nice will cost between 85 and 125FF, depending on the time of day and whether you're at Terminal 1 or 2.

Bus Local buses, run by Sunbus, cost 8/68FF for a single/10 rides. After you time-stamp your ticket, it's valid for one hour and can be used for one transfer. The Nice by Bus pass, valid for one/five/seven days costs 22/85/110FF and includes a return trip to the airport. Passes are sold at the Sunbus information office (☎ 04 93 16 52 10), 10 Ave Félix Faure, which is open from 7.15 am to 7 pm (Saturday until 6 pm; closed Sunday). Bus information and route maps are available here too.

The Station Centrale, Sunbus' main hub, takes up three sides of Square Général Leclerc, which is between Ave Félix Faure and Blvd Jean Jaurès (near Vieux Nice and the intercity bus station). The Sunbus kiosk at Station Centrale is open from 6.15 am to 7.30 pm.

Bus No 12 links the train station with Promenade des Anglais and the beach. To get from the train station to Vieux Nice and the intercity bus station, take bus No 2, 5 or 17. At night, four Noctambuses run north, east and west from Place Masséna.

Car & Motorcycle Rent a Car Système (☎ 04 93 88 69 69; fax 04 93 88 43 36; www.rentacar.fr), in the same building as Budget car rental opposite the train station at 38 Ave Aubert (corner of Ave Thiers), offers the best rates. Around the corner, JML (☎ 04 93 16 07 00; fax 04 93 16 07 48), 36 Ave Aubert, is another cheapie. Budget (☎ 04 97 03 35 03) has an office in town at 1bis Ave Gustave V.

Nicea Location Rent (☎ 04 93 82 42 71; fax 04 93 87 76 36), 9 Ave Thiers, rents mopeds from 250FF a day (extra for petrol and a helmet), 50cc scooters for 390FF a day, and 125cc motorcycles for 465FF a day. The office is open from 9 am to 6 pm (closed Sunday).

The Motor Vespa Center (☎ 04 93 85 34 04), 1 Rue Alfred Mortier, does not rent bikes but sells spare parts, flashy gear and accessories.

Taxi There are taxi stands right outside the train station and on Ave Félix Faure near Place Masséna; otherwise order a taxi (☎ 04 93 13 78 78).

Bicycle Cycles Arnaud (☎ 04 93 87 88 55), 4 Place Grimaldi, has mountain bikes for 100/180FF a day/weekend; a deposit of 2000FF is also required. The shop is open from 9 am to noon and 2 to 4 pm (closed Monday morning and Sunday). Nicea Location Rent (see Car & Motorcycle) rents mountain bikes for 80FF a day.

AROUND NICE

Vence

• pop 15,300 ✉ 06140 alt 325m

More serene than its coastal counterparts, Vence is a beautiful but very touristy little inland town 21km north-west of Nice. Though the area is rather built-up with holiday homes and villas, the medieval centre is perfect for a stroll past the town's art galleries. Porte du Peyra, the main gate of the 13th century wall that encircles the old city, leads to pretty little Place du Peyra with its fountain. The Romanesque cathedral in the centre of the old city was originally built in the 11th century but was extensively reworked in the 17th and 18th centuries.

Some 800m north of Vence on the Route de Saint Jeannet is the **Chapelle du Rosaire** (☎ 04 93 58 03 26), whose interior was designed and decorated by Matisse. It is only open on Tuesday and Thursday from 10 to 11.30 am and 2.30 to 5.30 pm, and during holidays and on Wednesday, Friday and Saturday from 2.30 to 5.30 pm.

Vence tourist office (☎ 04 93 58 06 38; fax 04 93 58 91 81) is at Place du Grand Jardin.

Saint Paul de Vence

• pop 2900 ✉ 06570 alt 180m

This picturesque and *very* touristy hilltop village 4km south of Vence is home to a great many artists and writers. It is most famous for the nearby **Fondation Maeght** (☎ 04 93 32 81 63), one of France's foremost centres for contemporary art. Set on a hill in the beautiful Provençal countryside amid gardens embellished with sculptures and fountains, the gallery was opened in 1964. Along with an exceptional permanent collection of 20th century works featuring such artists as Braque, Bonnard, Matisse and Miró, it also organises important exhibitions, concerts and other performances. It is open from 10 am to 12.30 pm and 2.30 to 6 pm (10 am to 7 pm from July to September). Entry costs 40/30FF for adults/students.

The tourist office (☎ 04 93 32 86 95; fax 04 93 32 60 27) is on Rue Grande.

ANTIBES AREA

Cagnes-sur-Mer

• pop 41,000 ✉ 06804

Cagnes-sur-Mer is made up of Le Haut de Cagnes, the old hill town; Le Cros de Cagnes, the former fishing village by the beach; and Cagnes Ville, a fast-growing modern quarter. The old city with its ramparts is dominated by the 14th century **Château Grimaldi** (☎ 04 93 20 85 57), Place Grimaldi, which houses a museum of contemporary Mediterranean art and stages an annual international art festival. Near Cagnes Ville is the **Musée Renoir** (☎ 04 93 20 61 07), Chemin des Collettes, the home and studio of Renoir from 1907 to 1919. It has retained its original décor and has several of the artist's works on display; the villa is set within a magnificent olive grove.

Both museums are open from 10 am to noon and 2 to 6 pm (closed Tuesday year-round; open between May and September from 10.30 am to 12.30 pm and 1.30 to 6 pm). Admission to each costs 20/10FF for adults/children.

The tourist office (☎ 04 93 20 61 64; fax 04 93 20 52 63), 6 Blvd Maréchal Juin, Cagnes Ville, is just off the A8.

Biot

• pop 5500 ✉ 06410 alt 80m

This charming *village perché* (perched village) was once an important pottery manufacturing centre specialising in large earthenware oil and wine containers. Metal containers brought an end to this industry, but Biot is still active in the production of handicrafts. The village streets are a pleasant place for a stroll, but you will have to get there early to beat the hordes. The attractive **Place des Arcades** dates from the 13th and 14th centuries. At the foot of the village is a **glass factory** where you can watch glass-blowers at work. The tourist office (☎ 04 93 65 05 85) is at Place de la Chapelle. Biot can be reached by bus from Antibes.

Musée National Fernand Léger This museum (☎ 04 92 91 50 30), Chemin du Val de Pôme, dedicated to the artist Fernand Léger (1881-1955) contains 360 of his works, including paintings, mosaics, ceramics and stained-glass windows. A huge, colourful mosaic decorates the museum's façade. It is open from 10 am to 12.30 pm and 2 to 5.30 pm (closed Tuesday year-round; open from 11 am to 6 pm between July and October). Admission is 28/18FF.

Antibes

• pop 71,000 ✉ 06600

Directly across the Baie des Anges from Nice, Antibes has as many attractions as its larger neighbour but is not as crowded. It has beautiful sandy beaches, 16th century ramparts that run right along the shore, an attractive pleasure-boat harbour (Port Vauban) and an old city with narrow, winding streets and flower-bedecked houses.

The city was first settled around the 4th century BC by Greeks from Marseille, who named it Antipolis. It was later taken over by the Romans and then by the Grimaldi family, who ruled it from 1384 to 1608. Because of its position on the border of France and Savoy, it was fortified in the 17th and 18th centuries, but these fortifications were torn down in 1894 to give the city room to expand. Antibes has appealed to many artists over the years, most notably Picasso, Max Ernst and Nicolas de Staël.

Orientation Greater Antibes is made up of three parts: the commercial centre around Place Général de Gaulle; Viel Antibes (Old Antibes) south of Port Vauban; and, to the south-west, the contiguous community of Juan-les-Pins. The principal streets in the centre are Blvd Albert 1er and Rue de la République, which leads westward to the tree-lined Place Nationale. The narrow Promenade Amiral de Grasse hugs the waterfront east of the old city. The train station is north of Place Général de Gaulle at the end of Ave Robert Soleau, close to Port Vauban.

Information Staff at the tourist office (☎ 04 92 90 53 00; fax 04 92 90 53 01), 11 Place Général de Gaulle, distribute a good free map of the city as well as lots of other useful information. The office is open from 9 am to 12.30 pm and 2 to 7 pm (Saturday until noon and 6 pm; closed Sunday). Hours in July and August are 9 am to 8 pm (Sunday from 10 am to 1 pm).

The main post office in Antibes, east of the tourist office on Place des Martyrs de la Résistance, is open from 8 am to 7 pm (Saturday until noon; closed Sunday).

Things to See & Do In the attractive old city on Rue Saint Esprit, Antibes' **cathedral** (known as the Church of the Immaculate Conception) has an ochre-coloured neo-classical façade and a tall Romanesque bell tower.

Steps lead up to the **Château Grimaldi**, which is set on a spectacular site overlooking the sea and the cathedral. It served as Picasso's workshop during part of 1946. Now the **Musée Picasso** (☎ 04 92 90 54 20), it contains an excellent collection of paintings, lithographs, drawings and ceramics as well as interesting displays about the artist's life. The sculpture-lined terrace overlooks the sea.

The museum, which also has a collection of contemporary art, is open from 10 am to noon and 2 to 6 pm (no midday break from mid-June to mid-September; closed Monday year-round). Admission is 20/10FF for adults/students.

The **Musée Archéologique** (☎ 04 92 90 54 35) in Bastion Saint André, south-west of the Château Grimaldi on Promenade Amiral de Grasse, has displays devoted to Antibes' history as a Greek city. It is open daily, except Monday, from 10 am to noon and 2 to 6 pm. Entry is 10/5FF for adults/students.

Places to Stay Accommodation in Antibes is fairly expensive. If you're on a tight budget, the best choice is the ***Relais International de la Jeunesse*** (☎ 04 93 61 34 40; open from mid-March to mid-November), which is idyllically set on Blvd de la Garoupe on the Cap d'Antibes, south of the centre. A bed costs 70FF, including breakfast; sheets are an extra 10FF. From Antibes' bus station, take bus No 2A (direction Eden Roc) to L'Antiquité stop.

The ***Hôtel Caméo*** (☎ 04 93 34 24 17), 62 Rue de la République, just off Place Nationale, has rooms with shower from 280FF. Nearby, the small and welcoming, one star ***Auberge Provençale*** (☎ 04 93 34 13 24; fax 04 93 34 89 88), 61 Place Nationale, charges 240/250FF for a single/double with all *conforts* (mod-cons).

Getting There & Away The bus station (☎ 04 93 34 37 60) is just off Rue de la République, a short distance south-east of Place Général de Gaulle. The information office is open from 8 am (9 am on Saturday) to noon and 2 to 6 pm (closed Sunday).

Buses serve Nice, Valbonne, Cannes, Cagnes-sur-Mer and Biot. There are buses to Square du Lys in Juan-les-Pins (8FF) every 20 minutes (40 minutes on Sunday).

There are frequent trains to/from Nice (17FF; 25 minutes) and Cannes (17FF; 15 minutes).

Juan-les-Pins

✉ 06160

Juan-les-Pins, contiguous to Antibes, is known for both its beautiful 2km-long sandy beach, backed by pine trees, and its outrageous nightlife – a legacy of the 1920s when Americans swung into town with their jazz music and oh-so-brief swimsuits. Party town it might be, but it's an expensive place to sleep; stay in Antibes and commute by bus, train or on foot. The tourist office (☎ 04 92 90 53 05), 51 Blvd Guillaumont, keeps the same hours as the one in Antibes.

A jazz festival – Jazz à Juan – is held here each year in the second half of July, attracting musicians and music-lovers from around the world.

Between April and September, six daily ferries go to Îles de Lérins (see the Cannes section) from the Embarcadère Courbet (☎ 04 93 68 98 98) in Juan-les-Pins.

Cap d'Antibes

Luxurious villas and the Hôtel du Cap, Côte d'Azur's top hotel, are well hidden behind a thick screen of plants and trees on this select peninsula, south-east of Juan-les-Pins. The **Jardin Thuret** (☎ 04 93 67 88 00), 41 Blvd du Cap, was established in 1856 and is home to a wide variety of exotic plants. Opening hours are 8.30 am to 5.30 pm (closed on weekends).

The lovely gardens at the **Villa Eilenroc** (☎ 04 93 67 74 33), right on the tip of Cap d'Antibes, are open on Wednesday from 1.30 to 5 pm (9 am to 5 pm in summer).

CANNES

• pop 69,363 ✉ 06400

It's the money of the affluent, spent with fashionable nonchalance, that keeps Cannes' many expensive hotels, fancy restaurants and exorbitant boutiques in business and its yachts as big as ocean liners afloat. But the harbour, the bay, the hill called Le Suquet, the beachside promenade, the beaches and the people sunning themselves provide more than enough natural beauty to make at least a day trip here well worth the effort.

Cannes is famous for its cultural activities and many festivals, the most renowned being the 10 day International Film Festival in mid-May, which sees the city's population treble overnight. Cannes has just one museum and, since its speciality is ethnography, the only art you're likely to come across is in the many rather pretty galleries scattered around town. Cannes' town motto may be 'Life is a festival', but the main tourist season only runs from May to October.

From Cannes, the Route Napoléon winds northward passing through Grasse, Castellane and Digne-les-Bains on its way to Gap and beyond. It is named after Napoleon I, who, after escaping from Elba in March 1815, passed by here as he headed for Paris, gathering an army en route for his triumphal return to the capital on 20 May.

Orientation

Don't expect to be struck down by glitz and glamour the minute you step foot in Cannes: seedy sex shops and peep shows abound around the train station on Rue Jean Jaurès. Things get better along Rue d'Antibes, the main shopping street a couple of blocks south of here. Several blocks farther south still is the huge Palais des Festivals et des Congrès, just east of the Vieux Port (Old Port).

Cannes' most famous promenade, the magnificent, hotel-lined Blvd de la Croisette, begins at the Palais des Festivals and continues eastward along the Baie de Cannes to Pointe de la Croisette. Place Bernard Cornut Gentille, where the bus station is located, is on the north-west corner of the Vieux Port. The hill west of the port is called Le Suquet.

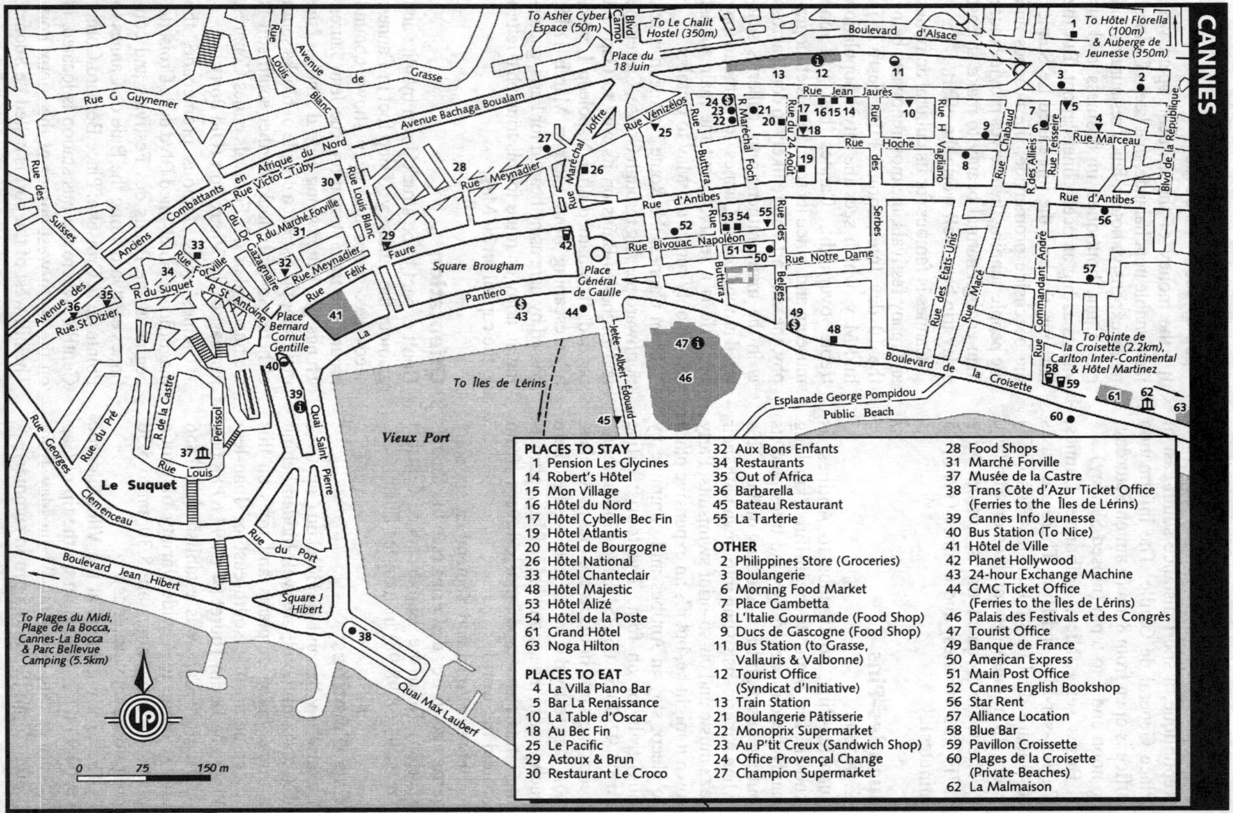
CANNES
PLACES TO STAY
1 Pension Les Glycines
14 Robert's Hôtel
15 Mon Village
16 Hôtel du Nord
17 Hôtel Cybelle Bec Fin
19 Hôtel Atlantis
20 Hôtel de Bourgogne
26 Hôtel National
33 Hôtel Chanteclair
48 Hôtel Majestic
53 Hôtel Alizé
54 Hôtel de la Poste
61 Grand Hôtel
63 Noga Hilton
PLACES TO EAT
4 La Villa Piano Bar
5 Bar La Renaissance
10 La Table d'Oscar
18 Au Bec Fin
25 Le Pacific
29 Astoux & Brun
30 Restaurant Le Croco
32 Aux Bons Enfants
34 Restaurants
35 Out of Africa
36 Barbarella
45 Bateau Restaurant
55 La Tarterie
OTHER
2 Philippines Store (Groceries)
3 Boulangerie
6 Morning Food Market
7 Place Gambetta
8 L'Italie Gourmande (Food Shop)
9 Ducs de Gascogne (Food Shop)
11 Bus Station (to Grasse, Vallauris & Valbonne)
12 Tourist Office (Syndicat d'Initiative)
13 Train Station
21 Boulangerie Pâtisserie
22 Monoprix Supermarket
23 Au P'tit Creux (Sandwich Shop)
24 Office Provençal Change
27 Champion Supermarket
28 Food Shops
31 Marché Forville
37 Musée de la Castre
38 Trans Côte d'Azur Ticket Office (Ferries to the Îles de Lérins)
39 Cannes Info Jeunesse
40 Bus Station (To Nice)
41 Hôtel de Ville
42 Planet Hollywood
43 24-hour Exchange Machine
44 CMC Ticket Office (Ferries to the Îles de Lérins)
46 Palais des Festivals et des Congrès
47 Tourist Office
49 Banque de France
50 American Express
51 Main Post Office
52 Cannes English Bookshop
56 Star Rent
57 Alliance Location
58 Blue Bar
59 Pavillon Croissette
60 Plages de la Croisette (Private Beaches)
62 La Malmaison
To Asher Cyber Espace (50m)
To Le Chalit Hostel (350m)
To Hôtel Florella (100m) & Auberge de Jeunesse (350m)
To Pointe de la Croisette (2.2km), Carlton Inter-Continental & Hôtel Martinez
To Îles de Lérins
To Plages du Midi, Plage de la Bocca, Cannes-La Bocca & Parc Bellevue Camping (5.5km)
Vieux Port
Le Suquet
Public Beach
0 75 150 m

Information

Tourist Offices The tourist office (☎ 04 93 39 24 53, ☎ 04 93 39 01 01; fax 04 92 99 84 23; www.cannes-on-line.com) on the ground floor of the Palais des Festivals is open from 9 am to 6.30 pm (closed Sunday). Daily hours in July and August are 9 am to 7.30 pm.

The tourist office annexe (☎ 04 93 99 19 77), 1st floor of the train station, is open from 9 am to 7 pm (Saturday until 1 pm; closed Sunday). The office is signposted 'Syndicat d'Initiative'; exit the train station, turn left and walk up the flight of stairs.

The Cannes Info Jeunesse office (☎ 04 93 06 31 31; fax 04 93 06 31 59), 5 Quai Saint Pierre, is open from 9 am to noon and 2 to 6 pm (closed on weekends).

Money The Banque de France at 8 Blvd de la Croisette is open from 8.30 am to noon and 1.30 to 3.30 pm. There are banks along Rue d'Antibes and on Rue Buttura.

American Express (☎ 04 93 38 15 87), 8 Rue des Belges, is open from 9 am to noon and 2 to 6 pm (Saturday until noon; closed Sunday). Office Provençal Change (☎ 04 93 39 34 37) is inside the Maison de la Chance, corner of Rue Maréchal Foch and Rue Jean Jaurès. There is a 24 hour currency exchange machine behind the port building on La Pantiero.

Post & Communications The main post office, 22 Rue Bivouac Napoléon, is open from 8 am to 7 pm (Saturday until noon; closed Sunday). It offers foreign currency exchange.

Asher Cyber Espace (☎ 04 92 99 03 01; asher@riviera.net), 44 Blvd Carnot, is open from 9 am to 7 pm (Friday and Sunday from 9 am to noon; closed Saturday).

Bookshop English-language novels are available at the Cannes English Bookshop (☎ 04 93 99 40 08), 11 Rue Bivouac Napoléon, open from 9.30 am to 1 pm and 2 to 7 pm (closed Sunday).

Musée de la Castre

The Musée de la Castre (☎ 04 93 38 55 26), housed in the chateau atop Le Suquet, has a diverse collection of Mediterranean and Middle Eastern antiquities as well as objects of ethnographic interest from all over the world. It is open from 10 am to noon and 2 to 5 pm (closed Tuesday). From April to June afternoon hours are 2 to 6 pm; in July and August, they're 3 to 7 pm. Admission is 10FF (free for students and children).

Walking

Since people-watching is the main reason to come to Cannes, and people are best watched while strolling, and strolling is one of the few activities in Cannes that doesn't cost anything, taking a leisurely walk is highly recommended.

The best places to walk are not far from the water. The pine and palm-shaded walkway along **Blvd de la Croisette** is probably the classiest promenade on the whole Riviera; **La Malmaison** (1863), tucked between the awesome Grand Hôtel and the flashy Noga Hilton at No 47, hosts various art exhibitions (10FF; open from 10.30 am to 12.30 pm and 4 to 8 pm; closed Tuesday). Some of the biggest yachts you'll ever see are likely to be bobbing gently in the **Vieux Port**, which was once Cannes' inner fishing harbour. The nearby streets are particularly pleasant on a summer's night, when the many cafés and restaurants – overflowing with laughing patrons in the latest fashions – light up the area with coloured neon signs.

Just west of the Vieux Port, **Le Suquet** hill affords quite spectacular views of Cannes, especially in the late afternoon and on clear nights.

Beaches

Unlike Nice, Cannes is endowed with a beach of the sandy variety, most of which is sectioned off for guests of the fancy hotels lining Blvd de la Croisette. Here, sun worshippers lap up the beachside equivalent of room service (65FF for a less-than-generous tomato salad delivered to your deck chair; strips of carpet leading to the water's edge etc). This arrangement leaves only a relatively small strip of sand near the Palais des Festivals for the bathing pleasure of picnicking hoi polloi.

However, free public beaches, **Plages du Midi** and **Plages de la Bocca**, stretch for several kilometres westward from the Vieux Port along Blvd Jean Hibert and Blvd du Midi.

Places to Stay

Hotel prices in Cannes fluctuate wildly according to seasonal demand. Tariffs can be up to 50% higher in July and August – when you're lucky to find a room at any price – than they are in winter. Don't even consider staying in Cannes during the film festival in May unless you have booked months in advance (a year in advance at the budget places). Most upmarket places only accept 12-day bookings during this period.

The closest glimpse you're likely to get of where the rich and famous relax is in the windows of John Taylor (☎ 04 93 38 00 66), 55 Blvd de la Croisette, where snaps of absolutely fabulous properties handled by Christie's auction house are displayed.

Places to Stay – Budget

Camping Camping in Cannes is not cheap. ***Parc Bellevue*** (☎ 04 93 47 28 97; fax 04 93 48 66 25), 67 Ave Maurice Chevalier, Cannes-La Bocca, about 5.5km west of the centre of town, is open from April to October. It charges 102FF for two people with a tent and car. Bus No 9 from the bus station on Place Bernard Cornut Gentille stops about 400m away.

Hostels Cannes' modern ***Auberge de Jeunesse*** (☎/fax 04 93 99 26 79), 35 Ave de Vallauris, is about 400m north-east of the train station. A bed in a four to six-person dorm is 80FF, including one free breakfast (4FF). If you don't have an HI card (available for 70/100FF for those under/over 26) you can buy a 10FF card for one night. Each of the three floors has a kitchen, and there's a laundry room. Reception is open from 8 am to 12.30 pm and 2.30 to 10.30 pm (3

Starring at Cannes

The Festival International du Film is a closed shop: unless you're John Travolta, Brigitte Bardot or simply damn rich, beautiful and worth a tabloid splash, you have absolutely no chance of scoring a ticket to the legendary Cannes film festival.

The 10 day festival revolves around the 60,000 sq m Palais des Festivals, likened to an Egyptian tomb by Liza Minnelli and called 'the bunker' by the local population. Around its stark concrete base, it is adorned with the hand imprints and autographs of celebrities – Timothy Dalton, Brooke Shields, Bardot, David Lynch, Johnny Halliday and the like. The largest of the Film Palace's 12 theatres seats 2300 people.

At the centre of the competition is the prestigious Palme d'Or, awarded by the jury and its president to the winning film – generally not a box office hit. Notable exceptions include Coppola's *Apocolypse Now* (1979), *Sex, Lies & Video Tape* (1989), David Lynch's *Wild at Heart* (1990) and Tarentino's *Pulp Fiction* (1994).

An equally integral part of the annual festival is the Marché du Film (Film Market) where an estimated US$200 million worth of business takes place.

Around 7000 'names' – trailed by 3000 journalists – attend the star-studded spectacle. Most stay at the Carlton, Majestic or Noga Hilton hotels. They eat at Roger Vergé's ***Le Moulin de Mougins*** (☎ 04 93 75 78 24), a converted 16th century mill 8km north of Cannes. The festival's annual US$2000-a-head Cinema Against AIDS charity dinner is often held here. In 1997 Hollywood star Sharon Stone auctioned off her belly-button ring over dinner.

The Festival International du Film was created in 1939 to counter Mussolini's fascist propaganda film festival in Venice. It was not until 1946, however, after WWII, that the first festival starred at Cannes.

to 10 pm on weekends). Curfew is at midnight (1 am on weekends).

The very pleasant private hostel, ***Le Chalit*** (☎ 04 93 99 22 11; fax 04 93 39 00 28), 27 Ave du Maréchal Galliéni, is 300m north-west of the station. It charges 80FF for a bed in rooms for four to eight people. Sheets are extra. There are two kitchens. Le Chalit is open year-round and there is no curfew, but you must leave a deposit to get a key.

Hotels Cannes has a handful of handy hotels for budget travellers that won't break the bank. Directly opposite the train station is the uninspiring, but cheap, ***Hôtel du Nord*** (☎ 04 93 38 48 79; fax 04 92 99 28 20), 6 Rue Jean Jaurès. Basic one star singles/doubles with washbasin are 140/180FF. On the same street at No 10, there are 110FF rooms in the small makeshift hotel above the ***Mon Village*** bar (☎ 04 93 38 57 70).

Close by, ***Hôtel Cybelle Bec Fin*** (☎ 04 93 38 31 33; fax 04 93 38 43 47), 14 Rue du 24 Août, has single/double rooms with washbasin for 120/150FF, doubles with shower for 170FF, and doubles with shower and toilet from 200FF.

Heading towards the Auberge de Jeunesse, you pass the excellent-value but little known ***Hôtel Florella*** (☎ 04 93 38 48 11), 55 Blvd République. Rooms just like home for one/two people with washbasin cost 140/170FF; doubles with shower and TV are 190FF.

The friendly 17 room ***Hôtel Chanteclair*** (☎/fax 04 93 39 68 88), 12 Rue Forville, has simple singles/doubles for 130/150FF (mid-October to mid-April) and 160/190FF (peak periods). Two-wheeled conveyances can be parked in the courtyard.

The ***Hôtel National*** (☎ 04 93 39 91 92; fax 04 92 98 44 06), 8 Rue Maréchal Joffre, has singles/doubles from 150/220FF. Doubles/triples with shower and toilet are 250/350FF.

The large ***Hôtel Atlantis*** (☎ 04 93 39 18 72; fax 04 93 68 37 65), 4 Rue du 24 Août, may have a two star rating, but its cheapest singles/doubles with TV cost only 145/180FF during the low season. The price jumps to 340/395FF during festival periods and in July and August. The ***Hôtel de Bourgogne*** (☎ 04 93 38 36 73; fax 04 92 99 28 41), 13 Rue du 24 Août, has singles/doubles with washbasin for 150/180FF, and doubles with shower/shower and toilet for 220/250FF.

The ***Pension Les Glycines*** (☎ 04 93 38 41 28), 32 Blvd d'Alsace, in an old villa east of the train station, has basic singles/doubles from 130/150FF (150/200FF in summer). A huge room for three or four people costs 190/200FF in winter/summer.

Places to Stay – Mid-Range

Opposite the main post office, the rule-happy ***Hôtel de la Poste*** (☎ 04 93 39 22 58; fax 04 93 39 52 58), 31 Rue Bivouac Napoléon, has singles/doubles with shower for 220/240FF (280/340FF in summer). Next door at No 29, the ***Hôtel Alizé*** (☎ 04 93 39 62 17; fax 04 93 39 64 32) has singles/doubles with all the mod-cons for 300/350FF.

Opposite the train station, ***Robert's Hôtel*** (☎ 04 93 38 06 07), 16 Rue Jean Jaurès, has singles/doubles with shower and toilet from 240/300FF.

Places to Stay – Top End

During the film festival, Cannes' horribly expensive hotels buzz with the frantic comings-and-goings of journalists, paparazzi and stars. Fortunately for their fans – who can only dream of staying in such a place during Cannes' most precious days of May – all of the top-end hotels are along Blvd de la Croisette. The best known ones include the ***Carlton Inter-Continental*** (☎ 04 93 06 40 06; fax 04 93 06 40 25; cannes@interconti.com) at No 58; the Art Deco ***Hôtel Martinez*** (☎ 04 92 98 73 00; fax 04 93 39 67 82; martinez@concorde-hotels.com) at No 73; the ***Grand Hôtel*** (☎ 04 93 38 15 45; fax 04 93 68 97 45) at No 45; and the ***Noga Hilton*** (☎ 04 92 99 70 00; fax 04 92 99 70 11) at No 50. Guests pay at least 2000FF for a double.

Places to Eat

Restaurants There are a few inexpensive restaurants around Rue du Marché Forville and lots of little, though not necessarily cheap, restaurants along Rue Saint Antoine and Rue du Suquet. Up in Le Suquet, try the beautifully furnished, African-inspired ***Out of Africa*** (☎ 04 93 68 98 06), 6-8 Rue Saint Dizier, or the less tame ***Barbarella*** (☎ 04 92 99 17 33), a couple of doors down the hill at 12-14 Rue Saint Dizier.

Near the train station, ***La Table d'Oscar*** (☎ 04 93 38 42 46), 26 Rue Jean Jaurès, has daily specialities – *aïoli garni* (boiled fish with garlic mayonnaise), rabbit, farcis for 50 to 75FF, and a 98FF *menu* in summer. It is closed on Sunday night and on Monday. Nearby, ***Au Bec Fin*** (☎ 04 93 38 35 86), 12 Rue du 24 Août, is often filled with regulars. You can choose from two excellent plats du jour for 45 to 60FF or a 79, 85 or 99FF *menu*. Try the *daube de bœuf* (beef stew) *à la Provençale*. This place is closed Saturday evening and Sunday.

Close by is the atmospheric ***La Villa Piano Bar*** (☎ 04 93 38 79 73), 7 Rue Marceau, housed in a fine 19th century villa. Main dishes start at around 100FF, and it has live music most evenings. The terrace, tucked beneath rambling plants in the shade of deep ochre walls, is particularly enchanting. La Villa is open from 8 pm to 2.30 am.

For fish, dine at ***Astoux & Brun*** (☎ 04 93 39 21 87), 21 Rue Félix Faure. Every type and size of oyster is available by the dozen here, as well as elaborate fish platters, mussels stuffed with garlic and parsley, scallops etc. In summer, chefs draw the crowds by preparing the shellfish on the pavement outside. It's open from 10 am to 1 am. For dinner afloat, try the ***Bateau Restaurant*** (☎ 04 93 68 98 88), moored on the Jetée Albert Édouard.

In the centre of town, ***Le Pacific*** (☎ 04 93 39 46 71), 14 Rue Vénizélos, is a favourite with local Cannois – its generous, three course 60FF *menu* is the major draw card. It is closed Friday evening and on Saturday.

Another good choice is the popular ***Aux Bons Enfants***, 80 Rue Meynadier. It offers regional dishes like aïoli garni and *mesclun* (a rather bitter salad of dandelion greens and other roughage) in a convivial atmosphere. It has a 94FF *menu* and is open for lunch and dinner weekdays and for lunch on Saturday (only open Saturday evenings in June and July). There are several other small restaurants at this end of Rue Meynadier.

One of the cheapest restaurants in Cannes is ***Restaurant Le Croco*** (☎ 04 93 68 60 55), 11 Rue Louis Blanc, just south of Blvd Victor Tuby. Pizzas, grilled meat and fish and shish kebabs are the main items on the *carte*. The plat du jour is 49FF and *menus* are 59FF (lunch) and 89FF.

Cafés Cafés, coffee houses and salons de thé abound in upmarket Cannes: one very down-to-earth place worth a bite (or at least a pastis before dining) is the small and cosy ***Bar La Renaissance***, overlooking the bustling Place Gambetta market from the corner of Rue Teisseire and Rue Marceau. Black and white photos of yesterday's stars and glamour queens line the walls – a pleasant contrast to the simple wooden tables and chairs.

La Tarterie (☎ 04 93 39 67 43), 33 Rue Bivouac Napoléon, has a range of salads from 30FF, but it's the house specialities – sweet/savoury tarts costing no more than 15/35FF a slice – that bring in the crowds.

Self-Catering The ***food market***, Place Gambetta, is held every morning (closed Monday in winter). The ***Marché Forville***, a fruit and vegetable market on Rue du Marché Forville, two blocks north of Place Bernard Cornut Gentille, is open every morning except Monday (when a flea market takes pride of place).

Square Brougham, next to the Vieux Port, is a great place for a picnic; buy filled baguettes and other lunchtime snacks from the ***Boulangerie-Pâtisserie*** at 12 Rue Maréchal Foch or from ***Au P'tit Creux***, which is opposite.

Food shops in the vicinity include a ***boulangerie*** (closed Tuesday), 9 Rue Jean Jaurès; the ***Philippines Store*** a few doors farther east on Rue Jean Jaurès (open from 9 am to 8 pm); the very upmarket ***Ducs de Gascogne***, 41 Rue Hoche; and ***L'Italie***

Gourmande, 32 Rue Hoche (it has great home-made pasta!).

Large supermarkets include ***Monoprix*** at 9 Rue Maréchal Foch (second entrance on the corner of Rue Jean Jaurès and Rue Buttura), and ***Champion*** at 6 Rue Meynadier.

Entertainment

Ask the tourist office for a copy of the monthly *Le Mois à Cannes*, which lists what's on and where. Nondubbed films are screened from time to time at the cinemas along Rue Félix Faure and its continuation, Rue d'Antibes.

Hot spots guaranteed to draw a crowd (and various stars when they roll into town) include the ***Blue Bar***, opposite Christian Dior on the corner of Blvd de la Croissette and Rue Commandant André; the ***Pavillon Croisette***, 42 Blvd de la Croisette, which has oyster platters for 135FF; ***Planet Hollywood*** (☎ 04 93 06 78 27), 1 Allée de la Liberté, where superwaif Kate Moss and actor Johnny Depp were caught eating burgers after doing a runner from some official function during the 1998 film festival; and ***Le Bar des Célébrités***, Carlton Inter-Continental, named after the people sufficiently rich to afford its 2000FF bottles of champagne. Drag queens hang out in and around the gay ***Zanzi Bar*** (☎ 04 93 39 30 75), 85 Rue Félix Faure.

Getting There & Away

Bus Buses to Nice (30FF; 1½ hours; every 20 minutes), Nice airport (70FF for the 40 minute trip via the autoroute, 47FF for the 1½ hour trip via the regular road; hourly from 8 am to 7 pm) and other destinations leave from Place Bernard Cornut Gentille, next to the Hôtel de Ville in Cannes centre. Most are operated by Rapides Côte d'Azur. The information office (☎ 04 93 39 11 39) is open from 7 am to 7 pm (closed Sunday).

Buses to Grasse (line No 600; 45 minutes), Vallauris (line No 640), Valbonne (line No 630) and elsewhere depart from the bus station to the left as you exit the train station.

Train The information desk at the train station (☎ 04 93 99 50 50 or ☎ 08 36 35 35 35), Rue Jean Jaurès, is open from 8.30 am to 6 pm (7 pm from mid-July to September).

Destinations within easy reach include Saint Raphaël (31FF; 25 minutes; two an hour), from where you can get buses to Saint Tropez and Toulon. Other destinations include Nice (32FF; 40 minutes) and Marseille (150FF; two hours).

Getting Around

Helicopter Héli-Inter (☎ 04 93 21 46 46; fax 04 93 21 46 47) can whirl high-fliers from Nice airport to the Palm Beach helipad on La Pointe de la Croisette in Cannes in a mere six minutes. The one-way fare is around 400FF.

Bus Bus Azur serves Cannes and destinations up to 7km from town. Its office (☎ 04 93 39 18 71), Place Bernard Cornut Gentille (same building as Rapides Côte d'Azur), is open from 7 am to 7 pm. Single/10 tickets cost 7.50/49FF. A weekly Carte Palm'Hebdo/monthly Carte Croisette is 54/190FF. Bus No 8 runs along the coast from Place Bernard Cornut Gentille to the port and Palm Beach Casino on La Pointe de la Croisette.

Car & Motorcycle Star Rent (☎ 04 93 38 13 48), 92 Rue d'Antibes, and Excellence (☎ 04 93 94 67 67; sales@excellence.fr) rent out cars fit for a star (Ferraris for 13,900FF a day etc). If you prefer something a little more economical, try Thrifty (☎ 04 93 94 61 00), 16 Rue du 14 Juillet, which has simple Fiat Cinquecento from 250FF a day.

Parking can be a nightmare in Cannes; city carparks charge at least 10FF an hour. Tell your chauffeur there are usually free spaces north of the old city across Ave des Anciens Combattants en Afrique du Nord.

Alliance Location (☎ 04 93 38 62 62; alliance.location@wanadoo.fr), 19 Rue des Frères, rents motorcycles (from 260FF a day) and scooters (160/200FF for one/two people) as well as mobile phones (70FF plus calls). The shop is open from 9 am to 7 pm.

Taxi Call ☎ 04 93 38 91 91 or ☎ 04 93 49 59 20 to order a taxi.

Bicycle Alliance Location (see Car & Motorcycle) rents mountain bikes for 80FF a day. Thrifty (☎ 04 93 94 61 00), 16 Rue du 14 Juillet, rents bikes too.

AROUND CANNES

Îles de Lérins

The eucalyptus and pine-covered **Île Sainte Marguerite**, where the enigmatic Man in the Iron Mask – immortalised by Alexandre Dumas in his novel *Le Vicomte de Bragelonne* (The Viscount of Bragelonne) and in the more recent 1998 Hollywood release *The Man in the Iron Mask* – was held during the late 17th century, lies 1km from the mainland.

The island, home to 20 families and measuring only 3.25km by 1km, is encircled and crisscrossed by trails and paths. The **Musée de la Mer** in the Fort Royal has interesting exhibits dealing with the fort's history and various ships that have been wrecked off the island's coast. The door to the left as you enter leads to the old state prisons, built under Louis XIV and the home in 1685 to Huguenots imprisoned for their refusal to renounce their Protestant faith. The inventor of the steam boat, Claude François Dorothée, is said to have come up with the idea while in prison here in 1773. The museum and cells are open from 10.30 am to 12.15 pm and 2 to 5.40 pm (closed Tuesday); it closes at 5.30 pm between April and June; at 6.30 pm from July to September. Admission is 10FF.

The smaller, forested **Île Saint Honorat**, which is just 1.5km long and 400m wide, was once the site of a renowned and powerful monastery founded in the 5th century. Today it is home to Cistercian monks who own the island but welcome people to visit their monastery and seven small chapels dotted around the island.

Neither island has a fantastic beach; in some places, sunbathers lie on mounds of dried seaweed. Camping, cycling and smoking (theoretically – people still light up) are forbidden on both islands. There are no hotels, *gîtes* or camp sites.

The Compagnie Maritime Cannoise (CMC; ☎ 04 93 38 66 33; fax 04 93 38 66 44) runs ferries to Île Saint Honorat (45FF return; 20 minutes) and Île Sainte Marguerite (40FF return; 15 minutes); both islands can be visited for 60FF. The ticket office (☎ 04 92 98 71 36), at the Vieux Port across Jetée Albert Édouard from the Palais des Festivals, is open from 8.30 am to 12.30 pm and 1.30 to 6.30 pm (open later in July and August).

Trans Côte d'Azur (☎ 04 92 98 71 30; fax 04 93 38 69 02) charges the same price for trips to/from both islands. Its office is opposite the Hôtel Sofitel on Quai Max Luberf. It also runs boats to Saint Tropez (120FF return), Monaco (120FF), Île de Port Cros (250FF), Île de Porquerolles (250FF) and San Remo (220FF) in Italy.

For part of the year there are boats to the Îles de Lérins from Juan-les-Pins. See Juan-les-Pins under Antibes Area for more information.

GRASSE

• pop 42,000 ✉ 06130 alt 333m

If it weren't for the scents wafting through Grasse – just 17km north of Cannes and the Mediterranean – your olfactories might detect a sea breeze. But for centuries, Grasse, with its distinct red and orange tile roofs rising up the slopes of the pre-Alps, has been one of France's most important centres of perfume production, along with Paris and Montpellier.

These days there are five master perfumers – or *nez* (noses), as they're called – in the world. Combining their natural gift with seven years of study, they are able to identify, from no more than a whiff, about 6000 scents. Somewhere between 200 and 500 of these fragrances are used to make just one perfume. Compelling reading associated with Grasse is *Perfume*, a novel by Patrick Süskind about the fantastic life and amazing nose of Jean-Baptiste Grenouille.

Grasse and the surrounding region also produce some of France's most highly prized flowers, including lavender (which you'll see growing profusely in the countryside), jasmine, centifolia roses, mimosa, orange blossom and violets.

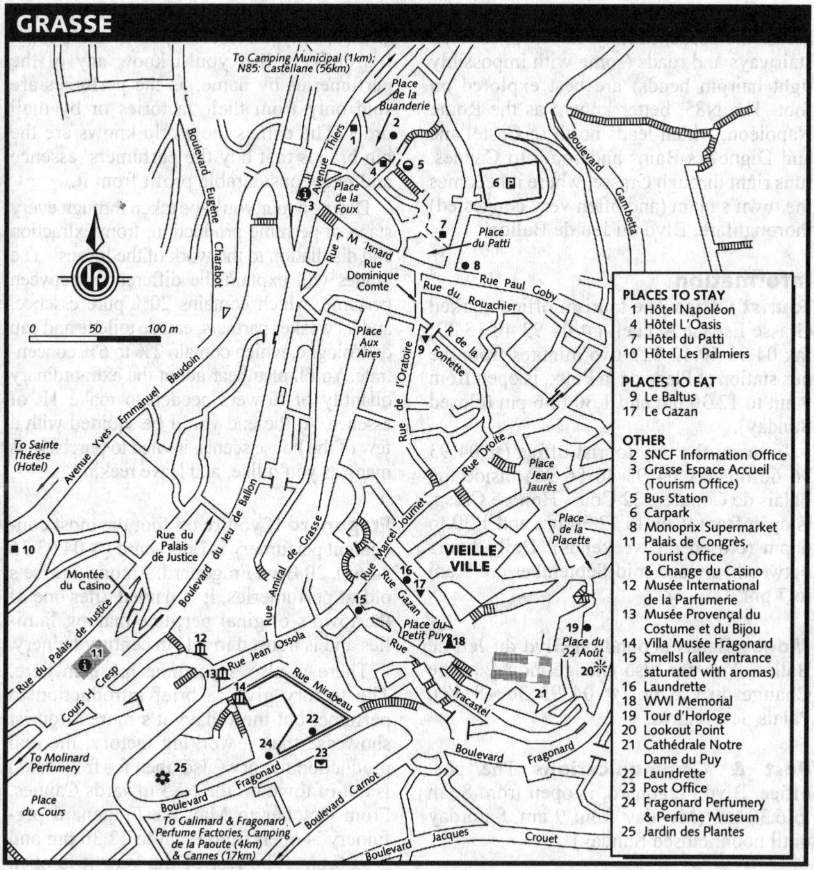

History

Founded by the Romans, Grasse became a small republic by the early Middle Ages, exporting tanned skins and oil (from which it may have earned its name – *gras* or *matière grasse* means 'fat' in French). It was taken over by the counts of Provence in 1226 and became part of France in the 16th century. Already a strong trading centre, Grasse grew even richer with the advent of perfumed gloves in the 1500s. Once established, the glove-makers split from the tanners, setting up a separate industry that eventually led to the creation of perfumeries. These in turn flourished in the 18th century, when perfume became fashionable, and members of high society never went anywhere without leaving a distinct aroma in their wake. Of course, it was a fashion necessity, not accessory; people seldom – if ever – took a bath in the 18th century.

Orientation

While the town of Grasse and its suburbs sprawl over a wide area of hill and valley, the old city is a small area, densely packed into the hillside like so many of the towns across the border in Italy. Its steep, cobbled stairways and roads (some with impossibly tight hairpin bends) are best explored on foot. The N85, better known as the Route Napoléon, which leads north to Castellane and Digne-les-Bains and south to Cannes, runs right through Grasse, where it becomes the town's main (and often very congested) thoroughfare, Blvd du Jeu de Ballon.

Information

Tourist Office The tourism office marked Grasse Espace Accueil (☎ 04 93 40 13 13; fax 04 93 40 12 82), two minutes from the bus station at Place de la Foux, is open from 9 am to 12.30 pm and 1.30 to 6 pm (closed Sunday).

In town, the tiny tourist office (☎ 04 93 36 66 66; fax 04 93 36 86 36) inside the Palais de Congrès, 22 Cours Honoré Cresp, is open from 9 am to 12.30 pm and 1.30 to 6 pm (closed on weekends). Daily hours between July and mid-September are 9 am to 7 pm.

Money Banks abound on Blvd du Jeu de Ballon. You can also change money at the Change du Casino (☎ 04 93 36 48 48), Palais de Congrès.

Post & Communications The post office, Blvd Fragonard, is open from 8 am to 6.30 pm (Monday from 9 am, Saturday until noon; closed Sunday).

Laundry The laundrette at 1bis Rue Gazan is open from 6 am to 9 pm. Hours at the laundrette at 10 Blvd Fragonard, opposite the post office, are 7 am to 9 pm.

Perfumeries

Follow your nose along Rue Jean Ossola to the archway at the beginning of Rue Tracastel, where several perfumeries have been conjuring up new scents for many years. The air around the alley entrance is saturated with aromas. Seasoned (as it were) travellers will be reminded of visits to Delhi, Cairo or Istanbul.

While more than 40 perfumeries exist in Grasse, only three are open to the public. It's unlikely that you'll know any of the perfumeries by name, as the perfumes are sold only from their factories or by mail order. The names the world knows are the big brands that buy the perfumers' essence and reap considerable profit from it.

During a tour you'll be taken through every stage of perfume production, from extraction and distillation to the work of the 'noses'. The guides will explain the differences between perfume, which contains 20% pure essence, and its weaker partners, eau de toilette and eau de Cologne, which contain 2% to 6% concentrate. You'll also hear about the extraordinary quantity of flowers needed to make 1L of essence. At the end you'll be squirted with a few of the house scents, invited to purchase as many as you'd like, and leave reeking.

Fragonard If you're on foot the most convenient perfumery is Fragonard (☎ 04 93 36 44 65), 20 Blvd Fragonard. Among Grasse's oldest perfumeries, it is named after one of the town's original perfume-making families and is housed in a 17th century tannery.

There is also a perfume museum here. The factory gives a brief introduction to perfume, but these days it's more a tourist showcase than a working factory; the real production factory (also open for free visits) is out of town on the N85 towards Cannes. From October to May the Fragonard perfumery is open from 9 am to 12.30 pm and 2 to 6 pm. The rest of the year it is open daily from 9 am to 6.30 pm.

Galimard The second perfumery, Galimard (☎ 04 93 09 20 00; fax 04 93 70 36 22), 73 Route de Cannes, is not far from Fragonard's factory, about 3km out of town. Unless you have wheels it's not a feasible option. The factory is open from 9 am to noon and 2 to 5.30 pm (9 am to 6 pm in summer).

Close by is the Galimard Studio des Fragrances (same ☎/fax), Route de Pégomas, where you can create your own unique fragrance under the guidance of a professional nez (two hours; 200FF).

Molinard Housed in a turreted, Provençal-style villa surrounded by immaculate lawns and a blaze of flowers, Molinard (☎ 04 93 36 01 62; fax 04 93 36 03 91), 60 Blvd Victor Hugo, is a much ritzier affair than Fragonard. Molinard also offers 'create your own perfume' sessions (1¼ hours; 200FF) as well as a seminar about the history of perfume (one hour; 150FF), after which participants walk away with a Molinard diploma. The perfumerie is open from 9 am to 12.30 pm and 2 to 6 pm (closed Sunday); from July to September daily hours are 9 am to 6.30 pm.

Museums

Villa Musée Fragonard Named after the artist Jean-Honoré Fragonard, who was born in Grasse in 1732, this villa (☎ 04 93 40 32 64), 23 Blvd Fragonard, now a museum, is where the artist lived for a year in 1790. The artist's paintings, famous for their licentious scenes, are on display in the museum. It is open from 10 am to noon and 2 to 5 pm (closed Monday and Tuesday). From June to September it's open daily from 10 am to 1 pm and 2 to 7 pm. Admission is free.

Musée Provençal du Costume et du Bijou Visiting Grasse's colourful costume and jewellery museum comes as a breath of fresh air after touring the town's perfumeries. The museum (☎ 04 93 36 44 65), 2 Rue Jean Ossola, is housed inside the stately Hôtel de Clapiers Cabris, the private mansion of the sister of revolutionary Mirabeau – the Marquise de Cabris – who lived in Grasse from 1769. It is open from 10 am to 1 pm and 2 to 6 pm. Admission is free.

Musée International de la Parfumerie Opened in 1989, the International Perfume Museum (☎ 04 93 36 80 20), 8 Blvd Fragonard, examines every detail of perfume production – from extraction techniques to sales and publicity – and traces its 400 years of history in Grasse. One of the most appealing sections of the museum is the rooftop conservatory, where lavender, mint, thyme and jasmine are grown in a heady mix of aromatic scents. It is open from 10 am to noon and 2 to 5 pm (closed Monday and Tuesday). Daily hours from June to September are 10 am to 7 pm. Admission is 25/12.50FF for adults/students.

Cathédrale Notre Dame du Puy

Although rather uninteresting in itself, the former cathedral, built in Provençal Romanesque style in the 12th and 13th centuries and reworked in the 18th century, contains a painting by Fragonard entitled *Washing of the Feet* and several early paintings by Rubens, including *The Crown of Thorns* and *Christ Crucified*. The cathedral is open from 9.30 am (8.30 am on Saturday) to 11.30 am and 2.30 to 6 pm (3 to 7 pm on Saturday).

Special Events

Grasse's two main events – related to flowers and scents *naturellement* – are Exporose in May and La Jasminade, held during the first weekend in August.

Places to Stay

Camping The two star ***Camping Municipal*** (☎ 04 93 36 28 69), Blvd Alice de Rothschild (continuation of Ave Thiers), is 1km northeast of the bus station. It charges 57FF for one person with tent and car. It is closed in January. Bus No 8, marked 'Piscine', leaves from the bus station and stops at the front of the camping ground. Another site is ***Camping de la Paoute*** (☎ 04 93 09 11 42), 160 Route de Cannes, 4km south of Grasse.

Hotels The cheapest option in town is the ***Hôtel Napoléon*** (☎ 04 93 36 05 87), 6 Ave Thiers. Singles/doubles/triples/quads with washbasin start at 130/160/200/350FF. The hotel is closed from the end of December to the end of January. Opposite is the small, rather run-down ***Hôtel L'Oasis*** (☎ 04 93 36 02 72), Place de la Buanderie, which has rooms with washbasin for 170/180FF and singles/doubles/triples with shower for 190/225/270FF.

If you have a car or don't mind an uphill amble, the two star ***Sainte Thérèse*** (☎ 04 93 36 10 29), 39 Ave Yves Emmanuel Baudoin, just over 1km from the tourist office, is a good choice. From the hotel you get a panoramic view of the valley and the dusty, orange-roofed town. Singles/doubles start at 180/200FF; private parking is available. The hotel is closed from October to mid-November. Another option on the same road is ***Hôtel Les Palmiers*** (☎ 04 93 36 07 24) at No 17. Prices in winter/summer start at 160/240FF.

For something more upmarket, try the modern, rather unattractive ***Hôtel du Patti*** (☎ 04 93 36 01 00; fax 04 93 36 36 40), Place du Patti, in the heart of the old city. It has pleasant singles/doubles/triples with private bath and toilet from 330/420/520FF. Parking is available.

Places to Eat

Very charming is the very small Provençal ***Le Baltus*** (☎ 04 93 36 32 90), in the heart of the old town at 15 Rue de la Fontette. It has a *menu* for 90FF, a plat du jour for 60FF, bouillabaisse for 280FF per person and, upon special request, *langouste* (crayfish) for 450FF per person. Le Baltus is open from 12.15 to 2 pm and from 7.30 to 9.30 pm (closed the first two weeks of July). Close by, ***Le Gazan*** (☎ 04 93 36 22 88), Rue Gazan, offers good-value 65FF lunchtime *menus*.

Getting There & Away

Bus The ticket office at the bus station (☎ 04 93 36 08 43), Place de la Buanderie, closes at 5.15 pm. Several companies operate from here. Rapides Côte d'Azur (☎ 04 92 96 88 88) has buses to Nice (37FF; 1¼ hours) via Cannes (19.50FF; 45 minutes) every half-hour (hourly on Sunday). VFD has a morning bus to Grenoble (six hours), which stops in Castellane (near the Gorges du Verdon) and Digne-les-Bains, and from Grenoble continues on to Chambéry, Annecy and Geneva.

Train The train line does not reach Grasse but SNCF has an information office (☎ 04 93 36 06 13) at the bus station, open from 8.30 am to 5.30 pm (closed Sunday).

MASSIF DE L'ESTÉREL

The most stunning natural feature of the entire Côte d'Azur (apart from the azure-blue sea) is the lump of red porphyry rock known as the Massif de l'Estérel. Covered by pine, oak and eucalyptus trees until devastating fires in 1985 and 1986 and now beginning to return to life, this range lies between Saint Raphaël and Mandelieu-La Napoule, which is inland from Cannes.

A drive or walk along the Corniche de l'Estérel (also known as the Corniche d'Or and the N98) – the coastal road that runs along the base of the range – is not to be missed as the views are spectacular. Along the way you'll find many small summer resorts and inlets where you can swim. Some of the places worth visiting include **Le Dramont**, where the 36th US Division landed on 15 August 1944; **Agay**, a sheltered bay with an excellent beach; the resorts of **Le Trayas** and **Théoule-sur-Mer**; and **Mandelieu-La Napoule**, a pleasant resort with a large pleasure-boat harbour near a fabulously restored 14th century castle. In summer, when the Corniche de l'Estérel gets very crowded, choose the inland N7, which runs through the hills and feels like a whole different world.

There are all sorts of walks you can go on in the Massif de l'Estérel, but for the more difficult trails you will need to come equipped with a good map, such as IGN's *Série Bleue* (1:25,000) No 3544ET. Many of the walks, such as those up to the Pic de l'Ours (496m) and the Pic du Cap Roux (452m), are signposted.

Places to Stay

There are camping grounds at various places along the coast, including Le Dramont, Agay, Anthéor, Le Trayas and Mandelieu-La Napoule.

The ***Auberge de Jeunesse*** (☎ 04 93 75 40 23; fax 04 93 75 43 45), Le Trayas, midway between Cannes and Fréjus (about 20km from each), is on a beautiful site overlooking the sea. The hostel at 9 Ave de la Véronèse is 1.5km up the hill from the Auberge Blanche bus stop. The hostel is closed from 10 am to 5 pm and in January. Bed and breakfast is 66FF. You must have an HI card. Telephone reservations are not accepted. You can camp for 44FF (including breakfast).

FRÉJUS & SAINT RAPHAËL

Fréjus (population 41,000), first settled by Massiliots (the Greeks who founded Marseille) and colonised by Julius Caesar around 49 BC as Forum Julii, is known for its Roman ruins. Once an important port, the town was sacked by various invaders, including the Saracens in the 10th century. Much of the town's commercial activity ceased after its harbour silted up in the 16th century.

At the foot of the Massif de l'Estérel is Saint Raphaël (population 26,500), a beachside resort town a couple of kilometres south-east of Fréjus. This was one of the main landing bases of US and French troops in August 1944.

Orientation

Although Saint Raphaël is 2km south-east of Fréjus, the suburbs of the two have now become so intertwined that they seem almost to form a single town. Fréjus comprises the hillside Fréjus Ville, about 3km from the seafront, and Fréjus Plage, on the Gulf of Fréjus. The Roman remains are almost all in Fréjus Ville.

Information

Tourist Offices The Fréjus tourist office (☎ 04 94 17 19 19; fax 04 91 51 00 26), 325 Rue Jean Jaurès, is open from 9 am to noon and 2 to 6.30 pm (Sunday from 10 am to noon and 2.30 to 5.30 pm). Staff make hotel reservations and distribute a good map of Fréjus locating its archaeological treasures. From June to mid-September the tourist office kiosk (☎ 04 94 51 48 42) by the beach (opposite 11 Blvd de la Libération) is open from 10 am to noon and 2.30 to 5.30 pm.

Saint Raphaël's tourist office (☎ 04 94 19 52 52; fax 04 94 83 85 40), Rue Waldeck Rousseau, across the street from the train station, is open from 8.15 am to noon and 1.30 to 6 pm (closed Sunday). Hours in July and August are 9 am to 8 pm (Sunday from 8.30 am to noon).

Money The Banque National de Paris (BNP) is just west of the Fréjus Ville tourist office on Rue Jean Jaurès and is open from 8.30 am to noon and 1.45 to 5 pm (closed on weekends).

Post & Communications In Fréjus (postcode 83600), the post office on Ave Aristide Briand is open from 8.30 am to 7 pm (Saturday until noon; closed Sunday). There's another on Blvd de la Libération opposite the tourist office.

In Saint Raphaël (postcode 83700), the post office is east of the tourist office on Ave Victor Hugo.

Roman Ruins

West of Fréjus' old city on Rue Henri Vadon (past the Porte des Gaules) is the mostly rebuilt 1st and 2nd century **Arènes** (amphitheatre; ☎ 04 94 17 19 19). It once sat an audience of 10,000 and is today used for rock concerts and bullfights. It is open from 9 or 9.30 am to noon and 2 to 6 or 6.30 pm (closed Tuesday). At the south-eastern end of Rue des Moulins, is the **Porte d'Orée**, the only arcade of the thermal baths still standing. North of the old town on Rue du Théâtre Romain are the remains of a **Roman theatre**, open from 9 or 9.30 am to 5 or 6.30 pm (closed Tuesday).

Le Groupe Épiscopal

In the centre of town on Place Formigé, on the site of a Roman temple, is an episcopal ensemble, comprising an 11th and 12th century **cathédrale** (☎ 04 94 51 26 30), one of the first Gothic buildings in the region, though it retains certain Roman features. The carved-wood doors at the main entrance were added during the Renaissance.

To the left of the cathedral is the octagonal 5th century **baptistère** (baptistry), with a Roman column on each of its eight corners. Stairs from the narthex lead up to the stunning 12th and 13th century **cloister**, whose features include some of the columns of the Roman temple and painted wooden ceilings from the 14th and 15th centuries. It looks onto a beautiful courtyard with a well tended garden and a well.

In the cathedral's cloister is the Musée Archéologique (Archaeological Museum), which has a marble statue of Hermes, a head of Jupiter, and a magnificent 3rd century mosaic depicting a leopard. The museum is open from 9 am to noon and 2 to 5 pm (closed Tuesday); from April to October, daily hours are 9 am to 7 pm. Admission, which includes entry to the baptistry and cloister, is 20/15FF for adults/students.

Beaches

Fréjus Plage, lined with buildings from the 1950s, and Saint Raphaël have excellent sandy beaches.

Saint Raphaël is a leading **diving** centre, thanks in part to the **WWII shipwrecks** off the coast. Most diving clubs in town organise dives to the wrecks, which range from a 42m-long US minesweeper to a landing craft destroyed by a rocket in 1944 during the Allied landings. Plongée 83 (☎ 04 94 95 27 18), 29 Ave de la Gare, and CIP Saint Raphaël Odyssée (☎ 04 94 83 66 65), Vieux Port, organise night and day dives, courses for beginners etc.

Les Bateaux de Saint Raphaël (☎ 04 94 95 17 46; fax 04 94 82 71 45), Gare Maritime, organises daily **boat excursions** in summer from Saint Raphaël to the Îles de Lérins (160FF return), and the Fréjus and Saint Tropez gulfs (60FF return). It also runs daily boats to Saint Tropez and Port Grimaud (see Getting There & Away in the Saint Tropez section).

Places to Stay

Accommodation in Fréjus and Saint Raphaël is not cheap.

Camping Fréjus has more than a dozen camping grounds, one of the best being the four star ***Holiday Green*** (☎ 04 94 19 88 30; fax 04 94 40 78 59), on the road to Bagnols, open from April to mid-October. It's 6km from the beach but has its own large pool. Nightly rates are 38/24FF per adult/child and 42/60FF per tent in the low/high season.

Closest to the beach is the ***Parc de Camping de Saint Aygulf Plage*** (☎ 04 94 17 62 49), 270 Ave Salvarelli, in Saint Aygulf, south of Fréjus. This huge camp site – with space for 1600-plus tents – is open from April to October.

Hostels The ***Auberge de Jeunesse Fréjus-Saint Raphaël*** (☎ 04 94 53 18 75; fax 04 94 53 25 86), Chemin du Counillier, near Fréjus Ville, is set in a seven hectare park. Dorm beds cost 66FF, including breakfast. You can camp here for 30FF a night. If you arrive by train get off at Saint Raphaël, take bus No 7 and walk up the hill. In July and August bus No 6 goes directly to the hostel. From Fréjus' train station or from Place Paul Vernet bus No 3 is the best option.

The very comfortable ***Centre International du Manoir*** (☎ 04 94 95 20 58; fax 04 94 83 85 06), Chemin de l'Escale, is 5km south-east of Saint Raphaël in Boulouris. Prices start at 110/119FF for a dorm bed/bed in a double or triple room with shower and toilet in the low season and 115/145FF in summer.

Hotels In Fréjus, the 11 room, no star ***Hôtel Bellevue*** (☎ 04 94 51 39 04; fax 04 94 51 35 20), Place Paul Vernet, has basic singles/doubles from 149/170FF (doubles with shower for 280FF). The two star ***Auberge du Vieux Four*** (☎ 04 94 51 56 38), 49 Rue Grisolle, has well kept singles/doubles with shower and toilet for 200/250FF – and a good restaurant too. Next door at No 35, the two star ***Hôtel Le Flore*** (☎ 04 94 51 38 35; fax 04 94 52 28 20) has rooms from 180FF.

At Fréjus Plage, the 27 room ***Hôtel L'Oasis*** (☎ 04 94 51 50 44), set amid pine trees at Impasse Jean-Baptiste Charcot, has comfortable rooms with TV for 350FF. It is closed from November to mid-February. Also at Fréjus Plage is the ***Hôtel Sable et Soleil*** (☎ 04 94 51 08 70; fax 04 94 53 49 12), facing an ugly carpark at 158 Ave Paul Arène, where singles/doubles cost 280/350FF. The 'Sand and Sun' has facilities for disabled people too.

Getting There & Away

Bus No 5, run by Forum Cars (☎ 04 94 95 16 71 in Fréjus), links Fréjus' train station and Place Paul Vernet with Saint Raphaël.

Both Fréjus and Saint Raphaël are on the train line from Nice to Marseille. For information, call ☎ 08 36 35 35 35. There's an especially frequent service from Nice to Gare de Saint Raphaël-Valescure, south-east of the centre. The information office here is open from 9.15 am to 1 pm and 2.30 to 6 pm.

SAINT TROPEZ

• pop 5700 ✉ 83990

In 1956 Saint Tropez was the setting for the film *Et Dieu Créa la Femme* (And God Created Woman) starring Brigitte Bardot. Its stunning success brought about Saint Tropez's rise to stardom – or destruction, depending on your point of view. But one thing is clear: the peaceful little fishing village of Saint Tropez, somewhat isolated from the rest of the Côte d'Azur at the end of its own peninsula, suddenly became the favourite of the jet set. Ever since, Saint Tropez has lived on its sexy image.

Attempts to keep Saint Tropez small and exclusive have created at least one tangible result: you'll probably have to wait in huge traffic queues to drive into town. Yachts, way out of proportion to the size of the old harbour and irritatingly blocking the view, chased away the simple fishing boats a long time ago. And while painters and their easels jostle each other for space along the harbour quay, in summer there's little of the intimate village air that artists such as the pointillist Paul Signac found so alluring. Still, sitting in a café on Place des Lices in late May, watching the locals engage in a game of *pétanque* in the shade of the age-old plane trees, you could be in any little Provençal village.

Once seen, never forgotten, is the fantastic food, flower and clothing market-cum-antique fair that fills Place des Lices on Tuesday and Saturday morning. Equally memorable is the spectacle of stupidly rich people dining aboard their floating palaces within spitting distance of the crowds gathered on the prom to gawk at them eating dinner.

Locally, Saint Tropez is – rather aptly – known as Saint Trop (literally, 'Saint Too Much').

Orientation

Saint Tropez lies at the southern end of the narrow Bay of Saint Tropez, opposite the Massif des Maures. The old city, with its narrow streets, is packed between Quai Jean Jaurès, the main quay of the Vieux Port; Place des Lices, a lovely shady rectangular 'square' a few blocks inland; and what's left of the 16th century citadel overlooking the town from the north-east.

Information

Tourist Offices The tourist office (☎ 04 94 97 45 21; fax 04 94 97 82 66; tourisme@nova.fr; www.nova.fr/saint-tropez), Quai Jean Jaurès, is open from 9.30 am to 1 pm and 3.30 to 8.30 pm. Hours are shorter in winter. It organises guided city tours in French and English (20/10FF for adults/children).

Money At the port, the Crédit Lyonnais, 21 Quai Suffren, is open from 8 am to noon and 1.30 to 4.45 pm (closed on weekends). It has a 24 hour exchange machine. The Thomas Cook branch (☎ 04 94 97 88 00), 10 Rue Allard, one street from the port, is open from 9 am to 4.30 pm (8.30 am to 9.30 pm from June to September).

Post & Communications The post office, Place Celli, one block from the port, is open from 9 am to noon and 2 to 5 pm (Saturday until noon; closed Sunday). There is an exchange service.

Laundry C'est Wash, 19 Ave du Général Leclerc, a block from the tourist office, is open from 8 am to 11 pm.

Musée de l'Annonciade

The Musée de l'Annonciade (☎ 04 94 97 04 01), in a disused chapel on Place Grammont, Vieux Port, contains an impressive collection of modern art, including works by Matisse, Bonnard, Dufy, Derain and Rouault. Signac, who set up his home and studio in Saint Tropez, is well represented. The museum is open from 10 am to noon and 2 to 6 pm (closed Tuesday). Between June and September its hours are 10 am to noon and 3 to 7 pm (closed in November). Admission is 30/15FF for adults/students.

Musée Naval

If you're really bored with watching the antics of the rich and (maybe not so) famous, visit the Naval Museum (☎ 04 94 97 59 43) in the dungeon of the citadel at the end of Montée de la Citadelle. It is open from 10 am to 5 or 6 pm (closed Tuesday). Apart from displays concerning the town's maritime history, it also has information about the Allied landings that took place here in August 1944. The best photographs of Saint Tropez can be taken from the citadel grounds. Admission is 25/15FF.

La Maison des Papillons

We can't imagine how animal-rights activist Bardot feels about the House of Butterflies (☎ 04 94 97 63 45), 9 Rue Étienne Berny, with some 4500 of the colourful winged creatures pinned to the wall. It is open from 10 am to noon and 3 to 6 or 7 pm (closed Tuesday from April to September).

Beaches

About 4km south-east of the town is the start of a magnificent sandy beach, Plage de Tahiti, and its continuation, Plage de Pampelonne. It runs for about 9km between Cap du Pinet and the rocky Cap Camarat. To get there on foot, head out of town along Ave de la Résistance (south of Place des Lices) to Route de la Belle Isnarde and then Route de Tahiti. Otherwise, the bus to Ramatuelle, a village south of Saint Tropez, stops at various points along a road that runs about 1km inland from the beach.

The coastline east of Toulon, from Le Lavandou to the Saint Tropez peninsula (including spots around the peninsula), is well endowed with *naturiste* (nudist) beaches. It's also legal in some other places, mostly in secluded spots or along sheltered streams farther inland.

On the south side of Cap Camarat is a secluded nudist beach, **Plage de l'Escalet**. Several streams around here also attract bathers in the buff. To get there you can take the bus to Ramatuelle, but you'll have to walk or, if lucky, hitch the 4km south-east to the beach. Closer to Saint Tropez is **La Moutte**, a naturiste beach 4.5km east of town – take Route des Salins, which runs between two of the houses owned by BB (as Bardot is known in France).

Walks

The Sentier Littoral (coastal path) goes all the way from Saint Tropez south to the beach of Cavalaire along some 35km of splendid rocky outcrops and hidden bays. In parts the setting is reminiscent of the tropics minus the coconut palms. If the distance is too great, you can walk as far as Ramatuelle and return on the bus.

If you can read French, invest in the pocket-sized *Promenez-vous à Pied – Le Golfe de Saint Tropez* (45FF), which details 26 hikes around Saint Tropez; buy a copy from the Maison de la Presse on Quai Jean Jaurès.

Places to Stay – Budget & Mid-Range

Surprise, surprise! There's not a cheap hotel to be found in Saint Tropez. To the south-east along Plage de Pampelonne there are plenty of multi-star camping grounds.

Saint Tropez's cheapest hotel is the dingy ***Hôtel La Méditerranée*** (☎ 04 94 97 00 44; fax 04 94 97 47 83), 21 Blvd Louis Blanc. Doubles start at 200FF. One rung up the price ladder is the ***Hôtel Les Chimères*** (☎ 04 94 97 02 90), near Port du Pilon, at the south-western end of Ave du Général Leclerc. Singles/doubles with shower and breakfast cost 328/358FF.

Well worth the cash is the calm and quiet ***Le Baron*** (☎ 04 94 97 06 57), 23 Rue de l'Aïoli. Rooms – all with TV and private bath – overlook the citadel and cost between 350 and 450FF.

Places to Stay – Top End

Saint Tropez's top-end hotels are open from around Easter to mid-October.

The town's most choice offering – and among the Côte d'Azur's most sumptuous – is the four star ***Hôtel Byblos*** (☎ 04 94 97 00 04; fax 04 94 56 68 01), Ave Paul Signac, near the citadel. Outside, it's painted in muted colours of the rainbow, from terracotta through to lavender-blue. Inside, luxurious rooms warranting no complaints cost 1500 to 3070FF, depending on the season. Its in-house restaurant, ***Les Arcades***, is equally worthy of a postcard home.

Places to Eat

Restaurants Quai Jean Jaurès is lined with restaurants, most with *menus* from 100 or 150FF and with a strategic view of the silverware and crystal of those dining on the decks of their yachts.

Extremely tasteful and not too expensive is the informal ***Café Sud*** (☎ 04 94 97 71 72), tucked down a narrow street off Places des Lices at 12 Rue Étienne Berny. It has a *menu* for 140FF and tables are outside in a star-topped courtyard. Close by, the ***Bistrot des Lices*** (☎ 04 94 97 29 00), 3 Places des Lices, serves traditional Provençal cuisine, including wonderful *ratatouille*.

Le Petit Charron (☎ 04 94 97 73 78), 5 Rue Charrons, is another delicious bet. For locals, the top place to eat is the ***Auberge des Maures*** (☎ 04 94 97 01 50), 15km north of Saint Tropez in the village of La Mole.

Cafés Former haunts of BB and her glam friends and foes include ***Le Café*** (☎ 04 94 97 02 25), Place des Lices, which is Saint Tropez's most historic café. Formally called the Café des Arts, it is not to be confused with the place of the same name on the corner of Place des Lices and Ave du Mai Foch. Another good people-watching spot, also with a large terrace, is ***Sénéquier***, Quai Suffren, by the old harbour. ***Le Gorille***, on the same quay, is open 24 hours and is a perfect place for breakfast after dancing the night away.

Self-Catering The ***Prisunic*** supermarket at 9 Ave du Général Leclerc is open from 8 am to 8 pm (closed Sunday). The Place des Lices ***market*** is held on Tuesday and Saturday mornings; the one on Place aux Herbes behind Quai Jean Jaurès is open daily until about noon.

Micka, 36 Rue Clemenceau, sells traditional *tartes Tropéziennes*, a sweet and creamy confection you shouldn't leave Saint Tropez without trying.

Shopping

Saint Tropez is loaded with expensive designer boutiques, gourmet food shops and galleries overflowing with bad art. La BB has a gift shop in Place Croix de Fer to support her animal-welfare charity. Some of the postcards on sale portray her sitting among her furry friends, looking like the Virgin Mary as she calls the faithful to prayer.

Traditional leather sandals are sold at Sandales Tropéziennes (☎ 04 94 97 19 55), 16 Rue Georges Clemenceau.

Getting There & Away

Bus Saint Tropez bus station, Ave Général de Gaulle, is on the south-western edge of town on the one main road out of town. The information office (☎ 04 94 54 62 36) is open from 8 am to noon and 2 to 6 pm (until noon Saturday; closed Sunday). Buses to Ramatuelle (five a day), a village in the middle of the peninsula, leave from the bus station and run parallel to the coast about 1km inland. Sodetrav (☎ 04 94 12 55 12 in Hyères) has eight daily buses to/from Saint Raphaël-Valescure train station to Saint Tropez bus station, via Fréjus (48FF; 1¼ hours). Buses from Saint Tropez to Toulon (95FF; 2¼ hours) go inland before joining the coast at Cavalaire; they also stop at Le Lavandou and Hyères.

Boat In July and August, MMG (☎ 04 94 95 17 46 in Sainte Maxime) operates a shuttle boat service from Saint Tropez to Sainte Maxime (32FF; 30 minutes; 26 daily) and Port Grimaud (26FF; 20 minutes; 11 daily). Between April and July, Les Bateaux de

Saint Raphaël (☎ 04 94 95 17 46; fax 04 94 83 88 55 in Saint Raphaël) runs two boats daily from Saint Tropez to Saint Raphaël (50FF; 50 minutes).

Getting Around

MAS (☎/fax 04 94 97 00 60), 3-5 Rue Joseph Quaranta, rents mountain bikes (80FF per day, plus 2000FF deposit) and scooters (190 to 290FF, plus 2500FF deposit).

There are several hire places along Ave du Général Leclerc. To order a taxi in Saint Tropez, ring ☎ 04 94 97 05 27. To order a taxi boat call Taxi de Mer (☎ 06 09 53 15 47), 5 Quartier Neuf.

SAINT TROPEZ TO TOULON

Massif des Maures

Stretching from Hyères to Fréjus, this arc-shaped massif is covered with pine, chestnut and cork oak trees. The vegetation makes it appear almost black and gives rise to its name, which comes from the Provençal word *mauro* (dark pine wood).

The Massif des Maures offers superb walking and cycling opportunities. There are four roads you can take through the hills, the northernmost being a ridge road, the 85km-long **Route des Crêtes**, which runs close to La Sauvette (779m), the massif's highest peak. It continues east through the village of **La Garde Freinet**, a perfect getaway from the summer hordes. Within the massif are a number of places worth visiting. If you like chestnuts, the place to go is **Collobrières**, a small town renowned for its chestnut purée and *marrons glacés* (chestnuts cooked in syrup and glazed). About 12km east of Collobrières are the ruins of a 12th to 13th century monastery, **La Chartreuse de la Verne**. North-east of the monastery is the village of **Grimaud**, notable for its castle ruins, small Roman church, windmill and pretty streets.

The tourist office in Saint Tropez distributes a map/guide called *Tours in the Golfe of St Tropez – Pays des Maures*, which describes four driving, cycling or walking itineraries.

Bormes-les-Mimosas

• pop 5000 ✉ 83230

Within the Massif des Maures is the 12th century village of Bormes-les-Mimosas, famous for its great diversity of flora. This beautiful village has attracted lots of artists and craftspeople, many of whom you will see at work as you wander through the tiny streets. With stretches of fine sand and numerous inlets, the seafront offers lots of water sports. Various festivals are held here throughout the year – if you're around in September, don't miss the Fête des Vendanges (Grape Harvest Festival). The tourist office (☎ 04 94 71 15 17; fax 04 94 64 79 57) is on Place Gambetta.

Le Lavandou

• pop 5200 ✉ 83980

Once a fishing village, Le Lavandou, is about 5km south-east of Bormes-les-Mimosas, has become a very popular destination, thanks mainly to its 12km-long sandy beach. Although the town itself may not have much to offer, it is a good base for exploring the nearby Massif des Maures, especially if you are interested in doing some cycling. The resort is also close to the three idyllic Îles d'Hyères, which you can reach easily by boat.

Le Lavandou's tourist office (☎ 04 94 71 00 61; fax 04 94 64 73 79) is on Quai Gabriel Péri.

Corniche des Maures

This 26km-long coastal road (part of the D559) stretches from Le Lavandou north-east to La Croix-Valmer. All along here you can enjoy breathtaking views. There are also lots of great beaches for swimming, sunbathing or windsurfing. Among the towns that the road passes through are Cavalière, Pramousquier and Le Rayol.

Îles d'Hyères

The oldest and largest naturiste colony in the region is on Île du Levant, the easternmost of the three Hyères Islands. Indeed, half of this 8km-long island is reserved for naturists.

Vedettes Îles d'Or (☎ 04 94 71 01 02), which has an office at the ferry terminal in

Le Lavandou, operates boats to Île du Levant and Port Cros (both cost 120/75FF return for adults/children; 35 minutes). There are at least four boats a day in the warmer months (hourly in summer) but only four a week in winter. To Porquerolles there is a boat three times a week (daily in July and August); the return fare is 130/95FF. Boats also sail from Hyères (one hour) in the high season.

Parc National de Port Cros Created in 1963 to protect at least one small part of the Côte d'Azur from overdevelopment, Port Cros is France's smallest national park, encompassing just 700 hectares of land – essentially the island of Port Cros – as well as an 1800 hectare zone of water around it. The middle island of the Îles d'Hyères, Port Cros is a marine reserve but is also known for its rich variety of insects and butterflies. Keeping the water around it clean (compared with the rest of the coast) is one of the reserve's big problems.

The park's head office (☎ 04 94 12 82 30) is on the mainland at 50 Rue St Claire in Hyères. The island can be visited all year, but hikers must stick to the marked paths. Fishing, camping and fires are not allowed.

Getting There & Away Boats to the Îles d'Hyères leave from various towns along the coast, including Le Lavandou and Hyères. Boats from Toulon run only from Easter to September (see Boats under Getting There & Away in the Toulon section).

TOULON

• pop 168,000 ✉ 83000

Toulon is France's most important naval port, serving as a base for the French navy's Mediterranean fleet. As a result of heavy bombing in WWII, the city's run-down centre looks very grim when compared to Nice, Cannes or even Marseille.

Initially a Roman colony, Toulon only became part of France in 1481; the city grew in importance after Henri IV founded an arsenal here. In the 17th century the port was enlarged by Vauban. The young Napoleon Bonaparte first made a name for himself in 1793 during a siege in which the English, who had taken over Toulon, were expelled.

As in any large port, there's a lively quarter with heaps of bars where locals and sailors seem to spill out of every door. Women travelling on their own should avoid some of the old city streets at night, particularly around Rue Chevalier Paul and the western end of Rue Pierre Sémard.

All in all, it's a city like no other on the Côte d'Azur, though it's unclear why anyone would want to spend much time here when pulsating Marseille, fine beaches and the tranquil Îles d'Hyères are so close. And with Toulon holding the dubious distinction of having elected a mayor from the extreme right National Front in 1995, you have every good reason to avoid this unfortunate city.

Orientation

Toulon is built around the *rade*, a sheltered bay lined with quays. To the west is the naval base and to the east the ferry terminal, from where boats set sail for Corsica. The city is at its liveliest along Quai de la Sinse and Quai Stalingrad, from where ferries depart for the Îles d'Hyères, and in the old city. North-west of the old city is the train station.

Separating the old city from the northern section is a multilane, multinamed thoroughfare (known as Ave du Maréchal Leclerc and Blvd de Strasbourg as it runs through the centre), which teems with traffic. It continues west to Marseille and east to the French Riviera. Immediately north-west of here, off Rue Chalucet, is a pleasant city park. Toulon's central square is the enormous Place de la Liberté.

Information

Tourist Offices The main tourist office (☎ 04 94 18 53 00; fax 04 94 18 53 09), Place Raimu, is open from 9 am to 6 pm (Sunday from 10 am to noon).

The Maison de l'Étudiant (☎ 04 94 93 14 21), Rue de la Glacière, is also a handy information source.

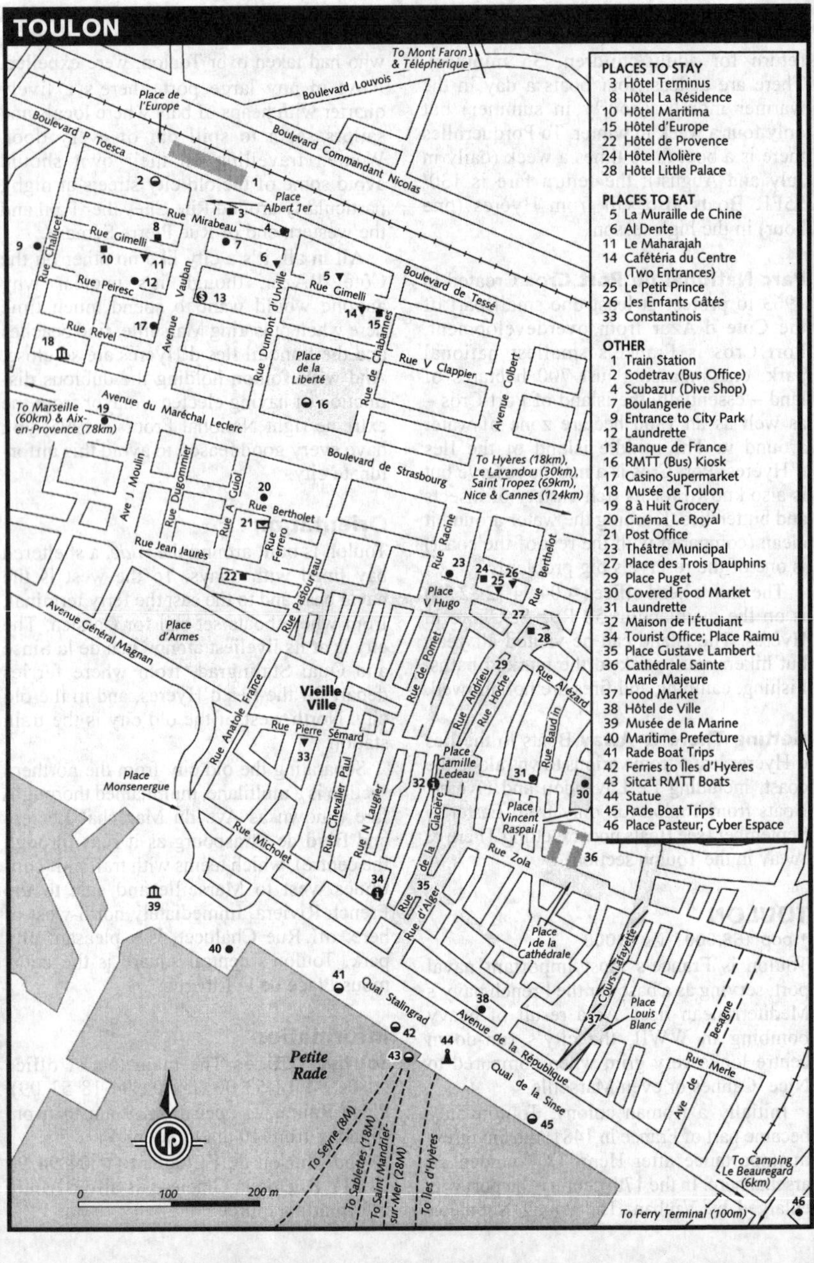
TOULON
PLACES TO STAY
3 Hôtel Terminus
8 Hôtel La Résidence
10 Hôtel Maritima
15 Hôtel d'Europe
22 Hôtel de Provence
24 Hôtel Molière
28 Hôtel Little Palace
PLACES TO EAT
5 La Muraille de Chine
6 Al Dente
11 Le Maharajah
14 Cafétéria du Centre (Two Entrances)
25 Le Petit Prince
26 Les Enfants Gâtés
33 Constantinois
OTHER
1 Train Station
2 Sodetrav (Bus Office)
4 Scubazur (Dive Shop)
7 Boulangerie
9 Entrance to City Park
12 Laundrette
13 Banque de France
16 RMTT (Bus) Kiosk
17 Casino Supermarket
18 Musée de Toulon
19 8 à Huit Grocery
20 Cinéma Le Royal
21 Post Office
23 Théâtre Municipal
27 Place des Trois Dauphins
29 Place Puget
30 Covered Food Market
31 Laundrette
32 Maison de l'Étudiant
34 Tourist Office; Place Raimu
35 Place Gustave Lambert
36 Cathédrale Sainte Marie Majeure
37 Food Market
38 Hôtel de Ville
39 Musée de la Marine
40 Maritime Prefecture
41 Rade Boat Trips
42 Ferries to Îles d'Hyères
43 Sitcat RMTT Boats
44 Statue
45 Rade Boat Trips
46 Place Pasteur; Cyber Espace
To Mont Faron & Téléphérique
Boulevard Louvois
Place de l'Europe
Boulevard P Toesca
Boulevard Commandant Nicolas
Place Albert 1er
Rue Mirabeau
Rue Gimelli
Rue Chalucet
Rue Peiresc
Avenue Vauban
Rue Revel
Rue Dumont d'Urville
Boulevard de Tessé
Rue de Chabannes
Rue V Clappier
Avenue Colbert
Place de la Liberté
To Marseille (60km) & Aix-en-Provence (78km)
Avenue du Maréchal Leclerc
Boulevard de Strasbourg
To Hyères (18km), Le Lavandou (30km), Saint Tropez (69km), Nice & Cannes (124km)
Ave J Moulin
Rue Dugommier
Rue A Guiol
Rue Bertholet
Rue Ferrero
Rue Jean Jaurès
Rue Racine
Rue Berthelot
Rue Pastoureau
Place V Hugo
Avenue Général Magnan
Place d'Armes
Rue de Pomet
Rue Andrieu
Rue Hoche
Rue Alézard
Rue Baudin
Vieille Ville
Rue Anatole France
Rue Pierre Sémard
Place Camille Ledeau
Place Monsenergue
Rue Chevalier Paul
Rue N Laugier
Rue de la Glacière
Place Vincent Raspail
Rue Zola
Rue Micholet
Rue d'Alger
Place de la Cathédrale
Cours Lafayette
Place Louis Blanc
Besagne
Quai Stalingrad
Avenue de la République
Quai de la Sinse
Rue Merle
Ave de
Petite Rade
To Seyne (8M)
To Sablettes (18M)
To Saint Mandrier-sur-Mer (28M)
To Îles d'Hyères
To Camping Le Beauregard (6km)
To Ferry Terminal (100m)
0
100
200 m

CÔTE D'AZUR

Money The Banque de France on Ave Vauban is open from 8.30 am to noon and 1.30 to 5.30 pm (closed on weekends). Commercial banks line Blvd de Strasbourg.

Post & Communications The post office on Rue Bertholet (second entrance on Rue Ferrero) is open from 8 am to 7 pm (Tuesday until 6 pm, Saturday until noon; closed Sunday).

For an Internet connection, contact Cyber Espace (☎ 04 94 41 06 05), 10 Place Pasteur. It is open from 10 am to 8 pm.

Laundry There are several laundrettes in the old city, including one at 25 Rue Baudin (open from 7 am to 9 pm); another is at 16 Rue Peiresc (open from 7 am to 8.30 pm; Sunday until 8 pm).

Musée de Toulon

The Toulon Museum (☎ 04 94 93 15 54), 113 Ave du Maréchal Leclerc, houses an unexceptional **art museum** and a rather moth-eaten **natural history museum** in a Renaissance-style building. The museum is open from 9.30 am to noon and 2 to 6 pm (Sunday from 1 to 6 pm only). Admission is free.

Musée de la Marine

The Naval Museum (☎ 04 94 02 02 01), in the lovely old arsenal building on Place Monsenergue, is open from 9.30 am to noon and 2 to 6 pm (closed Tuesday). In July and August its daily hours are 9.30 am to noon and 3 to 7 pm. Admission is 29/19FF for adults/students and children.

Mont Faron

Overlooking the old city from the north is Mont Faron (580m), from which you can see Toulon's port in its true magnificence. Near the hill's summit is the **Tour Beaumont Mémorial du Débarquement**, which commemorates the Allied landings that took place along the coast here in August 1944. The steep road up to the summit is also consistently used for the Tour de Méditerranée (February) and Paris-Nice (March) professional cycling races.

A *téléphérique* (cableway; ☎ 04 94 92 68 25) climbs the mountain from Ave de Vence. It runs from 9 am to noon and 2 to 5.30 pm (closed Monday) and costs 37/25FF return for adults/children. Take bus No 40 from Place de la Liberté.

Boat Excursions

Excursions around the rade, with a commentary (in French only) on the events that took place here during WWII, leave from Quai Stalingrad or its continuation, Quai de la Sinse. Trips cost an average of 45FF for one hour. Les Batelier de la Rade (☎ 04 94 46 24 65), Quai de la Sinse, also does three-hour tours of the Îles d'Hyères (120FF). Between June and September, SNRTM (☎ 04 94 93 07 56) runs several trips, some with a meal on board, to Cannes and Saint Tropez.

Sitcat boats (☎ 04 94 46 35 46) run by RMTT, the local transport company, link Quai Stalingrad with the towns on the peninsula across the harbour, including La Seyne (line 8M), Saint Mandrier-sur-Mer (line 28M) and Sablettes (line 18M). The 20 minute ride costs the same as a bus ticket: 8FF (10FF if you buy your ticket aboard). The ticket office is open from 8.45 am to 12.10 pm and 1.30 to 6.15 pm. Boats run from around 6 am to 8 pm.

Scubazur (☎ 04 94 92 19 29; fax 04 94 92 24 13), 26 Rue Mirabeau, is a first-class diving shop that has plenty of information on all the **diving clubs and schools** along the Côte d'Azur.

Places to Stay

Camping The closest camping ground to Toulon, ***Le Beauregard*** (☎ 04 94 20 56 35), is on the coast some 6km east in Quartier Sainte Marguerite. It costs 22.50/11FF per adult/child and 19.50FF for a tent. Take bus No 7 from the train station to the La Terre Promise stop.

Hotels There are plenty of cheap options in the old city, though some – particularly those at the western end of Rue Jean Jaurès – are said to double as brothels.

Immediately opposite the train station is the cheap and unsmiling ***Hôtel Terminus*** (☎ 04 94 89 23 54), 7 Blvd de Tessé, which has singles/doubles from 115/185FF. It flogs 59FF *menus* in its adjoining restaurant. Another one, conveniently close to the bus and train stations, is ***Hôtel La Résidence*** (☎ 04 94 92 92 81), 18 Rue Gimelli. The rooms are not as impressive as the lobby, with its enormous gilt mirror and balding Oriental carpets, but they're a bargain. Simple singles/doubles are 120/130FF and those with shower are 190FF. Showers costs 15FF – and the *patron* guards the key as if it opened the very gates of heaven itself. It's easy to park around here.

Heading into town, the ***Hôtel Maritima*** (☎ 04 94 92 39 33), 9 Rue Gimelli, has equally simple single/double rooms for 125/140FF. Rooms with a shower are 180FF and ones with a toilet too are 220FF. The pleasant ***Hôtel Little Palace*** (☎ 04 94 92 26 62; fax 04 94 89 13 77), 6 Rue Berthollet, has simple rooms from 80/125FF and from 150FF with shower. Beside the opera house, the one star ***Hôtel Molière*** (☎ 04 94 92 78 35; fax 04 94 62 85 82), 12 Rue Molière, has doubles from 110FF.

At 53 Rue Jean Jaurès, ***Hôtel de Provence*** (☎ 04 94 93 19 00) is welcoming but often full. Basic rooms start at around 115/125FF, or 150/190FF with shower.

East of the train station is the ***Hôtel d'Europe*** (☎ 04 94 92 37 44; fax 04 94 62 37 50), 7 Rue de Chabannes, which has rooms for one or two people for 198, 230, 250 and 310FF. Photos of each room category accompany the price list displayed in reception. Some rooms have little balconies.

Places to Eat

Pricey restaurants, terraces and bars with occasional live music are abundant along the quays; *menus* start at 100FF and a tiny bouillabaisse or aïoli garni will set you back 80 to 100FF. Another lively area is Place Victor Hugo and neighbouring Place Puget. Cheaper fare can be found in the old city's more dilapidated streets around Rue Chevalier Paul. Plenty of prostitutes ply their trade in this area, pursued by some very unsavoury-looking men.

Restaurants In Rue Pierre Sémard you can have a hearty meal in the humble Algerian restaurant ***Constantinois***. It's mainly frequented by local men, but friendly outsiders – particularly in these tense times in Toulon – are more than welcome. A generous serving of couscous with salad costs as little as 30FF and the coffee is black, thick and sweet.

Another very popular and modern place is ***Les Enfants Gâtés*** (☎ 04 94 09 14 67), 7 Rue Corneille. The 'Spoiled Children' is run by a young crowd and is one of the most pleasant places in town to dine without breaking the bank. The plat du jour is 60FF. Close by is the equally charming ***Le Petit Prince***, 10 Rue de l'Humilité, named after Antoine de Saint-Exupéry's book for children.

There are some decent restaurants on Rue Gimelli near the train station: ***La Muraille de Chine*** (☎ 04 94 92 04 21) at No 32 has Chinese *menus* for 58 and 85FF. It's closed on Sunday. Nearby at No 30 is ***Al Dente*** (☎ 04 94 93 02 50), a cool and elegant Italian place serving eight types of homemade pasta (40FF) and salads for 38 to 46FF. The lunch/evening *menu* is 59/100FF. Al Dente is open for lunch (except Sunday) and dinner to 10.30 or 11 pm. ***Le Maharajah*** (☎ 04 94 91 93 46), an Indian eatery at 15 Rue Gimelli, has lunch/dinner *menus* for 59/129FF and *thalis* (trays with an assortment of dishes) for 145FF. It is closed on Monday.

Cafétéria du Centre (☎ 04 94 92 68 57), 27-29 Rue Gimelli and 4-8 Rue de Chabannes, has cheap three-course *menus* for around 30FF. It is open from 11 am to 2.30 pm and 6.30 to 10 pm (closed Sunday).

Self-Catering The southern half of Cours Lafayette is one long open-air ***food market*** held, in typical Provençal style, under the plane trees. There's a covered ***food market*** on Place Vincent Raspail. Both are open daily except Monday.

Near the train station, the ***boulangerie*** at 21 Rue Mirabeau serves sandwiches, pizza and quiche. It is open daily from 5 am to 7 pm. Close by there is a small ***Casino*** supermarket at 7 Ave Vauban, and ***8 à Huit*** grocery on Ave du Maréchal Leclerc.

Getting There & Away

Bus Intercity buses leave from the bus terminal on Place de l'Europe, to the right as you exit the train station. Information and bus tickets for the several companies that serve the region are available from Sodetrav (☎ 04 94 28 93 40), 4 Blvd Pierre Toesca (opposite the terminal), open from 6.15 am to 7 pm (6.20 to 9.20 am, 11.15 am to 12.30 pm and 2 to 6.25 pm on weekends).

The buses to Hyères (35FF; 40 minutes; seven a day) continue eastward along the coast, stopping at Le Lavandou (58FF; 1¼ hours) and other towns, before arriving in Saint Tropez (92FF; 2¼ hours). Francelignes Comett (☎ 04 91 61 83 00 in Marseille) has buses to Aix-en-Provence (84/134FF one way/return; 1¼ hours). There are four daily (two on Sunday in July and August). Phocéens Cars (☎ 04 93 85 66 61 in Nice) goes to Nice (132FF; 2½ hours) via Hyères and Cannes (120FF; two hours) twice daily (except Sunday).

Train The train station (☎ 08 36 35 35 35) is at Place Albert 1er, near Blvd Pierre Toesca. The information office is open from 8 am to 7 pm (closed Sunday). There are frequent connections to cities along the coast, including Marseille (55FF; 40 minutes), Saint Raphaël (94FF; 50 minutes; hourly) and Nice (129FF; 1½ hours; hourly). Trains to Paris' Gare de Lyon (464FF; 5¾ hours) go via Marseille.

Boat Ferries to Corsica and Sardinia are run by the SNCM (☎ 04 94 16 66 66), which has an office at 49 Ave de l'Infanterie de Marine (opposite the ferry terminal). It is open from 8.30 am to noon (11.30 am on Saturday) and 2 to 5.45 pm (closed Sunday). For more information, see the introductory Getting There & Away section of the Corsica chapter.

Car ferries to Porto Torres in Sardinia operate four to six times a month from mid-April to September. For more information, refer to the Sea section in the introductory Getting There & Away chapter.

Boats from Toulon to the Îles d'Hyères only run from Easter to September and are operated by several companies, such as Trans Med 2000 (☎ 04 94 92 55 88). All depart from Quai Stalingrad. The trip to Porquerolles (100FF return) takes one hour. It's another 40 minutes to Port Cros, from where it's a 20 minute hop to Île du Levant (160FF return to tour all three islands).

Getting Around

Bus Local buses are run by RMTT (☎ 04 94 03 87 03), which has an information kiosk at the main local bus hub on Place de la Liberté. It is open from 7.30 am to noon and 1.30 to 6.30 pm (closed on weekends). Single/10 tickets cost 8/56FF. Buses generally run until around 7.30 or 8.30 pm. Sunday service is limited.

Bus Nos 7 and 13 link the train station with Quai Stalingrad.

Nice to Menton

THE CORNICHES

Nice and Menton (and the 30km of towns in between) are linked by three corniches (coastal roads), each one higher up the hill than the last. If you're in a hurry and don't mind missing the scenery, you can drive a bit farther inland and take the A8.

Corniche Inférieure

The Corniche Inférieure (also known as the Basse Corniche or Lower Corniche; the N98) sticks pretty close to the villa-lined waterfront and the nearby train line, passing (as it goes from Nice eastward to Menton) through Villefranche-sur-Mer, Saint Jean-Cap Ferrat, Beaulieu-sur-Mer, Èze-sur-Mer, Cap d'Ail (where there's a seaside hostel; ☎ 04 93 78 18 58) and Monaco.

Villefranche-sur-Mer Set in one of the Côte d'Azur's most charming harbours, this little port (population 8000) overlooks the Cap Ferrat peninsula. It has a well preserved 14th century old city with a 16th century citadel and a church dating from 100 years later. Steps break up the tiny streets that weave through the old city, the most interesting of which is Rue Obscure. Keep a lookout for occasional glimpses of the sea as you wander through the streets that lead down to the fishing port. Villefranche was a particular favourite of Jean Cocteau, who painted the frescoes (1957) in the 17th century **Chapelle Saint Pierre**.

Saint Jean-Cap Ferrat Once a fishing village, the seaside resort of Saint Jean-Cap Ferrat (population 2250) lies on the spectacular wooded peninsula of Cap Ferrat, which conceals a bounty of millionaires' villas. On the narrow isthmus of Cap Ferrat is the **Musée de Béatrice Ephrussi de Rothschild** (☎ 04 93 01 33 09), housed in the Villa Île de France, which was built in the style of the great houses of Tuscany for the Baroness de Rothschild in 1912. It abounds with antique furniture, paintings, tapestries and porcelain and is surrounded by beautiful gardens. From mid-February to October it is open from 10 am to 6 pm (7 pm in July and August); during the rest of the year its hours are 2 to 6 pm (10 am to 6 pm on weekends). Admission is 46/35FF for adults/students and includes entry to the gardens and the collections on the *rez-de-chaussée* (ground floor). It costs an extra 15FF to view those on the 1st floor.

Moyenne Corniche

The Moyenne Corniche – the middle coastal road (the N7) – clings to the hillside, affording great views if you can find somewhere to pull over. It takes you from Nice past the Col de Villefranche, Èze and Beausoleil, the French town up the hill from Monte Carlo.

Èze Perched on a rocky peak at an altitude of 427m is the picturesque village of Èze (population 2450), once occupied by Ligurians and Phoenicians. Below is its coastal counterpart, Èze-sur-Mer. Make your way to the exotic garden for fabulous views up and down the coast. The German philosopher Friedrich Nietzsche (1844-1900) spent some time here, during which time he started to write *Thus Spoke Zarathustra*. The path that links Èze-sur-Mer and Èze is named after him.

Grande Corniche

The Grande Corniche – whose panoramas are by far the most spectacular – leaves Nice as the D2564. It passes the **Col d'Èze**, where there's a great view; **La Turbie**, which is on a promontory directly above Monaco and offers a stunning night-time vista of the principality; and **Le Vistaëro**.

Roquebrune Dominating this appealing hilltop village (population 12,300), which lies just between Monaco and Menton, is a medieval dungeon that is complete with a re-created manor house. Roquebrune's tortuous little streets, which lead up to the castle, are lined with shops selling handicrafts and souvenirs and are overrun with tourists in the high season. Carved out of the rock is the impressive Rue Moncollet, with arcaded passages and stairways.

For more information, contact the tourist office (☎ 04 93 35 62 87; fax 04 93 28 57 00), 20 Ave Paul Doumer, in nearby **Cap Martin**, an exclusive suburb of Menton known for its sumptuous villas and famous past residents (Winston Churchill and the architect Le Corbusier among them).

MENTON

• pop 29,000 ✉ 06500

Menton, reputed to be the warmest spot on the Côte d'Azur (especially during winter), is only a few kilometres from the Italian border. In part because of the weather, Menton is popular with older holidaymakers, whose way of life and preferences have made the town's after-dark a tad tranquil compared to other spots along the coast. Guy de Maupassant, Robert Louis Stevenson, Gustave Flaubert and Katherine

Mansfield all found solace in Menton. Today, the town draws Italians from across the border, retaining a magnetic charm free of the airs and pretensions found in other areas of the Côte d'Azur.

Menton is famed for its cultivation of lemons. Giant, larger-than-life sculptures made from lemons, lemons and more lemons take over the town for two weeks during Menton's fabulous Fête des Citrons (Lemon Festival) in February. The festival kicks off on Mardi Gras.

Orientation

Promenade du Soleil runs south-west to north-east along the beach; the train line runs approximately parallel about 500m inland. Ave Édouard VII links the train station with the beach; Ave Boyer, where the tourist office is, is 350m to the east. From the station, walk along Ave de la Gare and take the second right off what appears to be a two way divided promenade. The tourist office is about halfway down Ave Boyer.

The Vieille Ville is on and around the hill at the north-eastern end of Promenade du Soleil. The Vieux Port lies just beyond it.

Information

Tourist Office The tourist office (☎ 04 93 57 57 00; fax 04 93 57 51 00), inside the Palais de l'Europe at 8 Ave Boyer, is open from 8.30 am to 12.30 pm and 1.30 to 6 pm (Saturday from 9 am to noon and 2 to 6 pm; closed Sunday).

Thematic organised tours (Menton and the *belle époque*, artists, gardens etc) are arranged by the Maison du Patrimoine (☎ 04 92 10 33 66; fax 04 93 28 46 85), 5 Rue Ciapetta; it has a more central information office (☎ 04 92 10 97 10) at 24 Rue St Michel. Tours cost 30FF per person.

Money There are plenty of banks along Rue Partouneaux. Barclays Bank (☎ 04 93 28 60 00) at 39 Ave Félix Faure is open from 8.30 am to noon and 1.50 to 4.30 pm (closed on weekends). It has an automatic exchange machine outside. Another 24 hour currency machine is outside the Crédit Lyonnais that is two doors down from the tourist office on Ave Boyer.

Post & Communications The post office, Cours George V, is open from 8 am to 6.30 pm (6 pm on Thursday, until noon on Saturday; closed Sunday).

Bookshop A fine range of guides, travel books and foreign-language newspapers are available at the Maison de la Presse at 25 Ave Félix Faure.

Église Saint Michel

The early 17th century Church of Saint Michael, the grandest baroque church in this part of France, sits perched in the centre of the Vieille Ville, which has many narrow, winding passageways. The church is usually open from 10 am to noon and 3 to 6 pm (closed Saturday morning). The ornate interior is Italian in inspiration.

Cemeteries

Farther up the hill via the Montée du Souvenir is the cypress-shaded **Cimetière du Vieux Château** (☎ 04 93 35 87 21), open from 7 am to 6 pm (8 pm from May to September). The graves of English, Americans, Irish, New Zealanders and other foreigners who died here during the 19th century can be seen in the cemetery's south-west corner. The view alone is worth the climb.

If you continue north along the steep Chemin du Trabuquet you'll soon reach the **Cimetière du Trabuquet**, a much larger, multilevel and landscaped cemetery with stunning panoramic views over Menton and the sea and into Italy.

Musée Jean Cocteau

The Jean Cocteau Museum (☎ 04 93 57 72 30), Quai Napoléon III, south-west of the Vieux Port, displays work by Jean Cocteau (1889-1963) – poet, dramatist and film director – in a seafront bastion dating from 1636. Cocteau's work includes drawings, tapestries, ceramics and mosaics such as the pebble designs that decorate the fort's outside walls.

The museum is open from 10 am to noon and 2 to 6 pm (closed Tuesday). Admission is free. Don't miss Cocteau's frescoes in the **Salle des Mariages** (Marriage Hall; ☎ 04 92 10 50 00) in the Hôtel de Ville, Place Ardoïno, open from 8.30 am to 12.30 pm and 1.30 to 5 pm (closed on weekends). Admission is 5FF.

Palais Carnolès

This former summer residence of Monaco's royal family houses Menton's **Musée des Beaux-Arts** (☎ 04 93 35 49 71), 3 Ave de la Madone, at the far western end of Promenade du Soleil. Works dating from the 13th to 19th centuries are displayed here, but one room is also devoted to contemporary art. The palace's surrounding **Jardin de Sculptures** (Sculpture Garden), set amid a lemon and orange grove, makes for a delightful afternoon stroll. Carnolès Palace is open from 10 am to noon and 2 to 6 pm (closed Tuesday).

Beach

The beach along Promenade du Soleil is public but, like its counterpart in Nice, it's covered with smooth little rocks. There are more beaches directly north of the Vieux Port, including Plages des Sablettes with sand and clean water, and east of Port de Garavan, the main pleasure-boat harbour.

The Centre Nautique (☎ 04 93 35 49 70; fax 04 93 35 77 05), Promenade de la Mer, rents laser boats/catamarans/kayaks for 100/120/50FF an hour. The **sailing school** also runs two-hour courses and arranges water-skiing (120FF).

The Compagnie de Navigation et de Tourisme de Menton (☎ 04 93 35 51 72), Vieux Port, organises boat trips to Monaco (60FF) and the Italian Riviera (90FF).

Places to Stay

Camping The two star ***Camping Saint Michel*** (☎ 04 93 35 81 23), Route des Ciappes de Castellar, open from April to mid-October, is 1km north-east of the train station up Plateau Saint Michel. It costs 16/16/17FF per person/tent/car. The two star ***Camping Fleur de Mai*** (☎ 04 93 57 22 36), 67 Route de Gorbio, just 2km north-west of the train station, is open from late March or early April to September.

Hostel The ***Auberge de Jeunesse*** (☎ 04 93 35 93 14; fax 04 93 35 93 07), Plateau Saint Michel, is a short distance from Camping Saint Michel. Bed and breakfast is 66FF. It's closed from 10 am to 5 pm; curfew is at midnight. The walk from the train station is quite a hike uphill, and there are lots of steps.

Hotels Just next door to the train station, the ***Hôtel Le Chouchou*** (☎/fax 04 93 57 69 87) on Place de la Gare has basic singles/doubles above the bar for 180/250FF. Opposite on the same square, the ***Hôtel Le Terminus*** (☎ 04 93 35 77 00) has a few rooms starting at 140/160FF. Hall showers are free. Reception is closed after 11 am on Saturday and after 5 pm on Sunday, but you can always find someone to help you in the bar-restaurant areas during opening times. The ***Hôtel de Belgique*** (☎ 04 93 35 72 66), 1 Ave de la Gare, has rooms from 145/195FF; rooms with a private shower start at 260FF. The hotel is closed in November.

Heading to the sea, ***Hôtel Claridges*** (☎ 04 93 35 72 53), corner of Ave de la Gare and Ave de Verdun, has comfortable rooms starting at 160/220FF. The ***Hôtel Le Globe*** (☎ 04 92 10 59 70; fax 04 92 10 59 71), 21 Ave de Verdun, opposite the tourist office, is part of the Logis de France chain; rooms are around 350FF.

In town, the ***Hôtel des Arcades*** (☎ 04 93 35 70 62; fax 04 93 35 35 97), under the arches at 41 Ave Félix Faure, is one of Menton's most picturesque options. Rooms with washbasin cost 180/220FF in the low season, rising to 260FF in the high season. The best sea views are to be found at ***Le Grand Bleu*** (☎ 04 93 57 46 33), 1684 Promenade du Soleil. Rooms are 250/350FF in summer.

Places to Eat

Restaurants There are places to eat galore – at any time of day – along Ave Félix Faure and its pedestrianised continuation, Rue Saint Michel. Place Clemenceau and Place aux Herbes in the Vieille Ville are equally popular. There are more pricey restaurants with terraces fanned by cool breezes along Promenade du Soleil.

Notable places include ***Le Chaudron*** (☎ 04 93 35 90 25), 28 Rue Saint Michel, which has filling salads from 38 to 63FF and *menus* for 89 and 115FF; and ***L'Ulïvo*** (☎ 04 93 35 45 65), Place du Cap, which is run by an Italian family and specialises in mussel dishes. Some 10 different types – all for 45FF – are on offer. Pasta dishes start at 42FF and giant salads kick off at 25FF.

Slightly cheaper places, including pizzerias, line Quai de Monléon in the Vieille Ville. Along pedestrianised Rue Saint Michel delicious takeaway crêpes or *gauffres* (waffles) are available for between 10 and 25FF, depending on the topping.

Self-Catering In the Vieille Ville, the ***Marché Municipal*** (also known as Les Halles) on Quai de Monléon sells all kinds of food. It's open from 5 am to 1 pm (closed Monday morning).

The ***Marché U*** supermarket at 38 Rue Partouneaux is open from 8.30 am to 7.15 pm (Saturday until 7 pm; closed Sunday). The ***Comtesse du Barry*** shop, next door, serves luxury foie gras products. Sweet treats, chocolate chessboards and a game of draughts made from almond-flavoured calissons from Aix-en-Provence are sold at ***Bosio-Lalone*** (☎ 04 93 35 70 95), a *chocolaterie-pâtisserie* at No 19 on the same street. Wonderful lemon curd and the like are sold at ***L'Arche des Confitures***, 2 Rue du Vieux Collège.

Getting There & Away

Bus The bus station (☎ 04 93 28 43 27) is next to 12 Promenade Maréchal Leclerc, the northern continuation of Ave Boyer. The information office (☎ 04 93 35 93 60 or ☎ 04 93 28 43 27 for international services) is open from 8 am to noon and 2 to 6 pm (closed Saturday afternoon and on Sunday).

There are buses to Monaco (12FF return; 30 minutes), Nice (28FF return; 1¼ hours), Sainte Agnès (44FF return; 45 minutes), Sospel (50FF return; 45 minutes) and, just across the border in Italy, Ventimiglia (Vintimille in French; 12FF; 30 minutes). There are also buses to the Nice-Côte d'Azur airport (95FF; 1½ hours) via Monaco run by Bus RCA (☎ 04 93 21 30 83).

Train The information office (☎ 08 36 35 35 35) at the train station is open from 8.45 am to noon and 2 to 6 pm (Saturday from 8.30 am to noon and 2 to 6 pm; closed Sunday). Trains to Ventimiglia cost 12FF and take 10 minutes. For more information on rail services along the Côte d'Azur see Trains under Getting There & Away in the Nice section.

Getting Around

ADA (☎ 04 92 10 20 25), 7 Cours George V, rents scooters for 189/359FF a day/weekend.

AROUND MENTON

There are many interesting places to visit near Menton, including the Vallée de la Roya (Roya Valley), the Vallée des Merveilles (Valley of Wonders) and the Parc National du Mercantour (see Information in the Nice section). Nearby villages worth visiting include Gorbio and Sainte Agnès (9km and 10km to the north-west respectively), and Castellar and Sospel (7km and 19km north of Menton). There are good walking and hiking areas near each of these places as well as some great views over the Riviera.

The **Vallée de la Roya** once served as a hunting ground for King Victor Emmanuel II of Italy and only became part of France in 1947. In this valley is the pretty village of **Breuil-sur-Roya**. Overlooking the valley is the fortified village of **Saorge**, set in a natural amphitheatre and remarkable for its maze of narrow, stepped streets and its 15th to 17th century houses. A good map for walks in the area, particularly in the Parc National du Mercantour, is the Didier & Richard No 9. IGN's Série Bleue maps Nos 3741OT (*Vallée de la Vesubie, Parc National du Mercantour*) and 3841OT (*Vallée de la Roya, Vallée des Merveilles*) cover the areas in a scale of 1:25,000.

The Gorges de Bergue in the Vallée de la Roya lead to **Saint Dalmas de Tende**, a good base for excursions to the **Vallée des Merveilles**, which is famous for its thousands of Bronze Age rock engravings of human figures and bulls. They are thought to have been done by a Ligurian cult. The best time to visit the valley is between July and September, as the engravings are often covered with snow during the rest of the year. You will need a guide to help you find them. Take sturdy walking shoes and warm, waterproof gear. Jeeps and guides can be hired at Saint Dalmas de Tende. There is also a tourist office (☎ 04 93 04 73 71), Ave du 16 Septembre 1947, Tende, where you can get more information.

Monaco

• pop 30,000 ✉ 98000

The tiny Principality of Monaco, which has been under the rule of the Grimaldi family for most of the period since 1297, is a sovereign state whose territory, surrounded by France, covers only 1.95 sq km. It has been ruled since 1949 by Prince Rainier III (born in 1923), whose sweeping constitutional powers make him much more then a mere figurehead. For decades, the family has been featured on the front pages of the tabloids, though since the death in 1982 of the beloved Princess Grace (remembered from her Hollywood days as the actress Grace Kelly), the media has concentrated on the not-so-successful love lives of the couple's two daughters, Caroline and Stephanie.

Glamorous Monte Carlo is famed for its casino and its role, since 1911, as host to the annual Formula One Grand Prix in May, which sees drivers from around the world tear round a track that winds its way through the town and around the port.

The citizens of Monaco (known as Monégasques), of whom there are only about 5000 out of a total population of 30,000, pay no taxes. They have their own flag (red and white), own national holiday (19 November), own country telephone code (377) and own traditional dialect (Monégasque, which is broadly speaking a mixture of French and Italian). The official language is French although many street signs, particularly in Monaco Ville, are in French and Monégasque. The official religion is Roman Catholic. There are no border formalities upon entering Monaco. The principality was admitted to the UN as a full member in 1993.

By law, it is forbidden to walk around town bare chested, barefooted or bikini-clad.

Orientation

Monaco consists of five principal areas: Monaco Ville (also known as the old city and the Rocher de Monaco), a 60m-high outcrop of rock 800m long on the south side of the Port de Monaco where the Palais du Prince (Prince's Palace) is; Monte Carlo, famous for its casino and annual Formula One Grand Prix, which is north of the port; La Condamine, the flat area south-west of the port; Fontvieille, the industrial area south of Monaco Ville; and Larvotto, the beach area east of Monte Carlo. The French town of Beausoleil is just three streets up the hill from Monte Carlo.

Information

Tourist Offices The Office National de Tourisme (☎ 92 16 61 66; fax 92 16 60 00; mgto@monaco1.org; www.monaco.mc), 2a Blvd des Moulins, is across the public gardens from the casino. It's open from 9 am to 7 pm (Sunday from 10 am to noon). From mid-June to mid-September there are several tourist office kiosks open around the principality, including one at the train station, another next to the Jardin Exotique, one on Blvd Albert 1er, one on Quai des États-Unis (the street that runs along the north side of the port), and another north of the palace between Place du Canton and Place d'Armes.

Money Monaco uses the French franc. Both French and Monégasque franc coins are in circulation, but the latter are difficult to find and not widely accepted outside the principality. The entire Monégasque collection of currency dating from 1640 can be seen in the Musée des Timbres et des Monnaies (Stamp

& Money Museum; ☎ 93 15 41 50; fax 93 15 41 45), 11 Terrasses de Fontvieille.

In Monte Carlo there are numerous banks in the vicinity of the casino. In La Condamine, try Blvd Albert 1er. American Express (☎ 93 25 74 45), 35 Blvd Princesse Charlotte, is open from 9 am to noon and 2 to 6 pm (Saturday until noon; closed Sunday).

Post & Communications Monégasque stamps are valid only within Monaco. Postal rates are the same as those in France. Monaco's public telephones accept Monégasque or French *télécartes*.

Telephone numbers in Monaco only have eight digits. Calls between Monaco and the rest of France are treated as international calls. Dial 00 followed by Monaco's country code (377) when calling Monaco from the rest of France or abroad. To call France from Monaco, dial 00 and France's country code (33). This applies even if you are only making a call from the east side of Blvd de France (in Monaco) to its west side (in France)!

The main post office is in Monte Carlo at 1 Ave Henri Dunant inside the Palais de la Scala. It is open from 8 am to 7 pm (Saturday until noon; closed Sunday), but it does not exchange foreign currency. There are post offices in each of the other four principal areas, including those at Place de la Visitation (near the Musée Océanographique) in Monaco Ville; and across the road from the train station (look for the sign to the Hôtel Terminus) in La Condamine (open from 8 am to 7 pm, Saturday until noon; closed Sunday).

There is a cybercorner inside Stars 'n' Bars (☎ 93 50 95 95; info@starsnbars.com; www.isp-riviera.com/starsnbars), 6 Quai Antoine 1er, open from 11 am to midnight (40FF for 30 minutes online).

Bookshop Scruples (☎ 93 50 43 52), 9 Rue Princesse Caroline, is an English-language bookshop open from 9.30 am to noon and 2.30 to 7 pm (6.30 pm on Saturday; closed Sunday).

Laundry In Beausoleil, on the border between Monaco and France, there is a laundrette at 1 Rue Jean Jaurès. Closer to the centre, there's a laundrette at 1 Escalier de la Riviéra. Both are open daily from 7 am to 9 pm.

Musée Océanographique

If you're planning to see just one aquarium on your whole trip, the world-renowned Musée Océanographique de Monaco (☎ 93 15 36 00) should be it. It has 90 tanks, and upstairs there are all sorts of exhibits on ocean exploration. The museum, on Ave Saint Martin in Monaco Ville, is open from 9 am to 7 pm (8 pm in July and August). The stiff entrance fee is 60/30FF for adults/students. Bus Nos 1 and 2 are the alternatives to a relatively long walk up the hill.

The train stop for the slightly tacky *Azur Express* tourist train (☎ 92 05 64 38; azurtrain@imcn.mc) is opposite the museum entrance. The 35 minute city tour costs 35FF. Tackier still is the underground **Monte Carlo Story** (☎ 93 25 32 33), reached by an escalator opposite the Musée Océanographique. The 45 minute soap opera-style film, screened in seven languages, recalls the history of the Grimaldi dynasty. A cassette recording of the Monégasque national anthem (20FF) is sold at the ticket booth. Reclining gracefully beside both museums is the coastal **Jardin Saint Martin**, open from 7 am to 6 pm (until 8 pm from April to September).

Palais du Prince

The changing of the guard takes place daily outside the Palace of the Prince (☎ 93 25 18 31), at the southern end of Rue des Remparts in Monaco Ville, at precisely 11.55 am. The guards, who carry out their duties of state in spiffy dress uniform (white in summer, black in winter), are apparently resigned to the comic-opera nature of their duties.

From June to October only, you can visit the palace's **state apartments**, open from 9.30 am to 6.20 pm. Half-hour guided visits in English begin every 15 or 20 minutes. Admission is 30/15FF for adults/children. A combined ticket for entry to the **Musée des Souvenirs Napoléoniens** – a display of Napoleon's personal effects in the south wing of the palace – is 40/20FF.

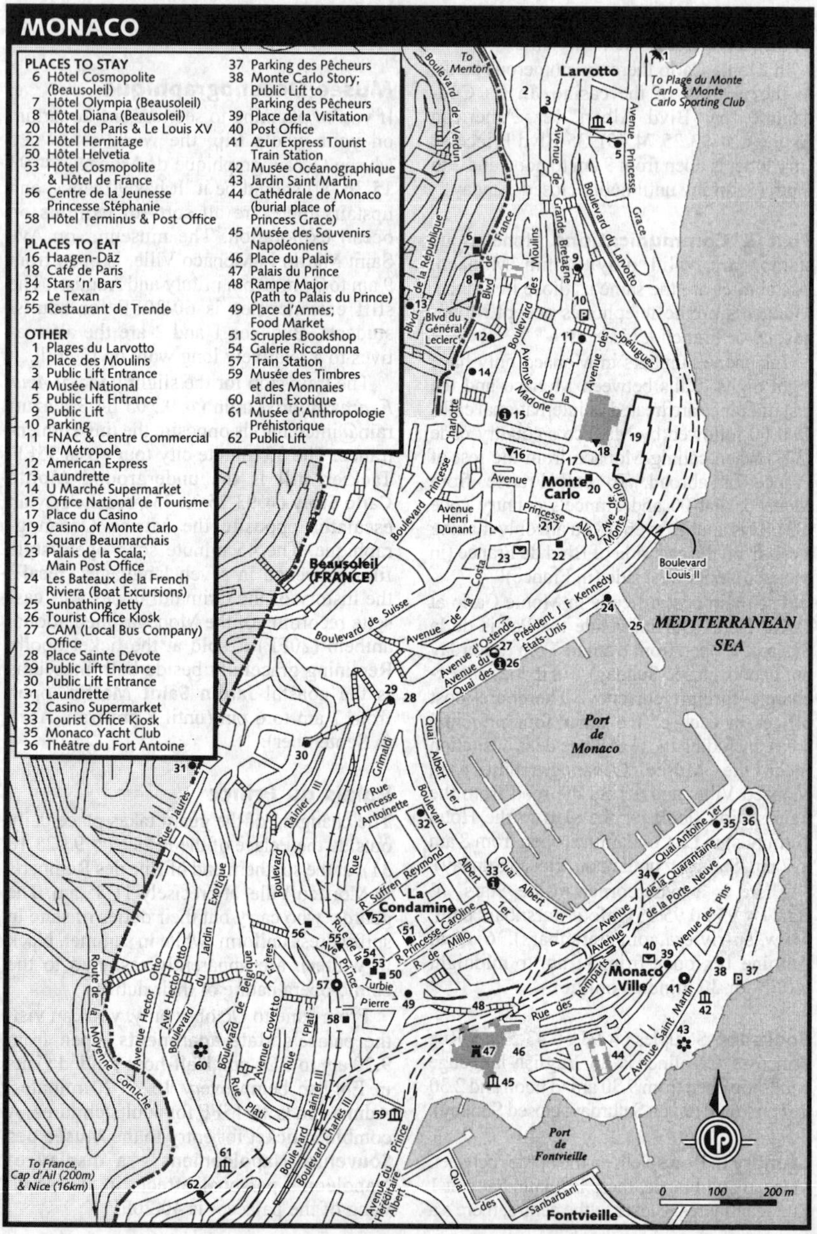
MONACO
PLACES TO STAY
6 Hôtel Cosmopolite (Beausoleil)
7 Hôtel Olympia (Beausoleil)
8 Hôtel Diana (Beausoleil)
20 Hôtel de Paris & Le Louis XV
22 Hôtel Hermitage
50 Hôtel Helvetia
53 Hôtel Cosmopolite & Hôtel de France
56 Centre de la Jeunesse Princesse Stéphanie
58 Hôtel Terminus & Post Office
PLACES TO EAT
16 Haagen-Däz
18 Café de Paris
34 Stars 'n' Bars
52 Le Texan
55 Restaurant de Trende
OTHER
1 Plages du Larvotto
2 Place des Moulins
3 Public Lift Entrance
4 Musée National
5 Public Lift Entrance
9 Public Lift
10 Parking
11 FNAC & Centre Commercial le Métropole
12 American Express
13 Laundrette
14 U Marché Supermarket
15 Office National de Tourisme
17 Place du Casino
19 Casino of Monte Carlo
21 Square Beaumarchais
23 Palais de la Scala; Main Post Office
24 Les Bateaux de la French Riviera (Boat Excursions)
25 Sunbathing Jetty
26 Tourist Office Kiosk
27 CAM (Local Bus Company) Office
28 Place Sainte Dévote
29 Public Lift Entrance
30 Public Lift Entrance
31 Laundrette
32 Casino Supermarket
33 Tourist Office Kiosk
35 Monaco Yacht Club
36 Théatre du Fort Antoine
37 Parking des Pêcheurs
38 Monte Carlo Story; Public Lift to Parking des Pêcheurs
39 Place de la Visitation
40 Post Office
41 Azur Express Tourist Train Station
42 Musée Océanographique
43 Jardin Saint Martin
44 Cathédrale de Monaco (burial place of Princess Grace)
45 Musée des Souvenirs Napoléoniens
46 Place du Palais
47 Palais du Prince
48 Rampe Major (Path to Palais du Prince)
49 Place d'Armes; Food Market
51 Scruples Bookshop
54 Galerie Riccadonna
57 Train Station
59 Musée des Timbres et des Monnaies
60 Jardin Exotique
61 Musée d'Anthropologie Préhistorique
62 Public Lift
To Menton
Larvotto
To Plage du Monte Carlo & Monte Carlo Sporting Club
Boulevard de Verdun
Avenue de Grande Bretagne
Avenue Princesse Grace
Boulevard du Larvotto
Boulevard de France
Boulevard des Moulins
Avenue des Spélugues
Avenue de la Madone
Blvd de la République
Blvd du Général Leclerc
Boulevard Princesse Charlotte
Avenue Henri Dunant
Monte Carlo
Princesse Alice
Ave de Monte Carlo
Boulevard Louis II
Beausoleil (FRANCE)
Boulevard de Suisse
Avenue de la Costa
Avenue d'Ostende
Avenue du Président J F Kennedy
Quai des États-Unis
MEDITERRANEAN SEA
Port de Monaco
Quai Albert 1er
Boulevard Albert 1er
Rue Grimaldi
Rue Princesse Antoinette
Boulevard Rainier III
R Suffren Reymond
La Condamine
R Princesse Caroline
R de Millo
Rue de la Turbie
Ave Prince Pierre
Quai Antoine 1er
Avenue de la Quarantaine
Avenue de la Porte Neuve
Avenue des Pins
Monaco Ville
Rue des Remparts
Avenue Saint Martin
Rue Jaurès
Boulevard du Jardin Exotique
Avenue Hector Otto
Ave Hector Otto
Route de la Moyenne Corniche
Boulevard de Belgique
Avenue Crovetto Frères
Rue Plati
Boulevard Rainier III
Boulevard Charles III
Avenue du Prince Héréditaire Albert
Port de Fontvieille
Quai des Sanbarbani
Fontvieille
To France, Cap d'Ail (200m) & Nice (16km)
0 100 200 m

MONACO

Cathédrale de Monaco

The unspectacular Romanesque-Byzantine cathedral (1875), 4 Rue Colonel, has one draw: the grave of former Hollywood film star Grace Kelly (1929-82), which lies on the west side of the cathedral choir. Her modest tombstone, inscribed with the Latin words *Gratia Patricia Principis Rainerii III*, is heavily adorned with flowers. Tourists usually do a quick march around the cathedral in order to see her grave. Grace Patricia Kelly wed Prince Rainier III in 1956 and died in a car crash in 1982. The remains of other members of the royal family, buried in the church crypt since 1885, today rest behind Princess Grace's grave.

Between September and June, Sunday Mass at 10 am is sung by Monaco's boys choir, Les Petits Chanteurs de Monaco.

Jardin Exotique

The steep slopes of the wonderful Jardin Exotique (☎ 93 15 29 80; jardin-exotique@monte-carlo.mc), 62 Blvd du Jardin Exotique, are home to some 7000 varieties of cacti and succulents from all over the world. The spectacular view alone is worth at least half the entrance fee of 37FF (18FF for students), which also gets you into the **Musée d'Anthropologie Préhistorique** and includes a half-hour guided visit to the **Grottes de l'Observatoire**, a network of stalactite and stalagmite caves 279 steps down the hillside.

The Jardin Exotique is open from mid-September to mid-May from 9 am until 6 pm (or dusk) and until 7 pm the rest of the year. From the tourist office, take bus No 2 to the Jardin Exotique terminus.

Casino

The drama of watching people risk their money in Monte Carlo's spectacularly ornate casino (☎ 92 96 21 21), built between 1878 and 1910, makes visiting the gaming rooms almost worth the stiff entry fees: 50/120FF for a day/week pass into the Salon Ordinaire, which has French roulette and *trente et quarante*; and 100FF for the Salons Privés, which offer baccarat, blackjack, craps, American roulette etc. You must be aged at least 21 to enter (everybody is required to show some form of ID). Short shorts (but not short skirts) are forbidden in the Salon Ordinaire. For the Salons Privés, men must wear a tie and jacket. Gambling accounts for 4.3% of Monaco's GDP (it used to account for most of the government's budget).

Musée National

Housed in a villa built by Charles Garnier, the Musée National (☎ 93 30 91 26), 17 Ave Princesse Grace, contains a fascinating collection of 18th and 19th century dolls and mechanical toys. The museum is open from 10 am to 12.15 pm and 2.30 to 6.30 pm (no midday closure from Easter to September) and costs 26/15FF for adults/students.

Boat Excursions

You can explore the waters off Monaco in a glass-bottomed boat (55 minutes; 70/50FF for adults/students) with Les Bateaux de la French Riviera (☎ 92 16 15 12), Quai des États-Unis. Boats depart at 11 am, 2.30 and 4 pm.

The nearest **beaches**, Plages du Larvotto and Plage de Monte Carlo, are a couple of kilometres east of Monte Carlo. In town, sun worshippers lie their oiled bodies out to bake on giant concrete slabs on the eastern side of the jetty, at the north end of Quai des États-Unis.

Places to Stay

Cheap accommodation is almost nonexistent in Monaco. Mid-range rooms are equally scarce and often full. Indeed, over three-quarters of Monaco's hotel rooms are classified as 'four star deluxe'. Fortunately, Nice is not too far away.

Places to Stay – Budget & Mid-Range

Hostel The *Centre de la Jeunesse Princesse Stéphanie* (☎ 93 50 83 20; fax 93 25 29 82), 24 Ave Prince Pierre, is 120m up the hill from the train station. Only travellers aged between 16 and 31 can stay here – for 70FF per person, including breakfast, shower and sheets. Stays are usually limited to three nights during the summer. Beds are given out each morning on a first-come first-served basis; numbered tickets are distributed from 9 am (or even earlier) near the front gate. Registration begins at 11 am.

Hotels In La Condamine, the clean and pleasant ***Hôtel Cosmopolite*** (☎ 93 30 16 95), 4 Rue de la Turbie, has decent singles/doubles with shower for 288/322FF and doubles without shower for 240FF. The ***Hôtel de France*** (☎ 93 30 24 64), 6 Rue de la Turbie, has rooms with shower, toilet and TV starting at 350/460FF, including breakfast.

Hôtel Terminus (☎ 92 05 63 00; fax 92 05 20 10), Ave Prince Pierre, and ***Hôtel Helvetia*** (☎ 93 30 21 71; fax 92 16 70 51), 1bis Rue Grimaldi, are two cheapies (by Monaco standards) by the train station. Rooms at each are around 350 to 450FF.

In French Beausoleil, there are three hotels virtually in a row on Blvd du Général Leclerc, three streets up from the casino and close to the Beausoleil market. When calling these hotels from Monaco (eg from the train station), dial ☎ 00 33, then the 10 digit number (dropping the first 0).

At No 17, the ***Hôtel Diana*** (☎ 04 93 78 47 58; fax 04 93 41 88 94) has rooms for one or two with shower/bath for 280/380FF. At No 19, the ***Hôtel Cosmopolite*** (☎ 04 93 78 36 00), unrelated to the hotel of the same name in La Condamine, has rooms with shower and TV for 195FF (270/290FF with toilet for one/two people). Between them at No 17bis is the ***Hôtel Olympia*** (☎ 04 93 78 12 70), which has rooms with shower, TV and toilet for 265/300FF.

The even-numbered side of Blvd du Général Leclerc is in Monaco and is called Blvd de France. The nearest bus stop is named Crémaillère and is served by bus Nos 2 and 4. For those confused by this number system (and, seriously, who wouldn't be), the Beausoleil side (ie Blvd du Général Leclerc) begins with a pavement tiled with smiling faces of the *beau soleil* (beautiful sun).

Places to Stay – Top End

World-famous places include the ***Hôtel de Paris*** (☎ 92 16 30 00; fax 92 16 38 50; hp@sbm.mc), Place du Casino, where writer Colette spent the last years of her life; and the four star ***Hôtel Hermitage*** (☎ 92 16 40 00; fax 93 16 38 52; hh@sbm.mc) in Square Beaumarchais. Prices reflect the luxurious, *belle époque* ambience of both hotels; expect to pay a minimum of 2100FF for a double.

Places to Eat

In Monte Carlo, the place to people-watch is from the sprawling terrace of the ***Café de Paris*** (☎ 92 16 20 20), Place du Casino.

Restaurants There are a few cheap restaurants in La Condamine along Rue de la Turbie. Farther down the hill overlooking the port and yacht club is the flashy ***Stars 'n' Bars*** (☎ 93 50 95 95), 6 Quai Antoine 1er, open from noon to 3 am (closed Monday). Billed as a blues bar and restaurant, it is more like a huge country and western saloon. Here you can eat main dishes of American-sized portions and excellent salads (60 to 70FF), listen to live music and watch the staff strut their stuff in starred-and-striped leather shorts and boots. There's live music on Thursday, Friday and Saturday nights in the upstairs night club until 3 am; the restaurant closes at midnight. The same Texan businessman runs ***Le Texan*** (☎ 93 30 34 54), 4 Rue Suffren Reymond.

Very traditional and cosy is the small ***Restaurant de Trende*** (☎ 93 30 37 72), 19 Rue de la Turbie. The décor is totally 1930s and the food absolutely Provençal.

On a totally different plain is ***Le Louis XV*** (☎ 92 16 30 01), sporting three Michelin stars and in the Hôtel de Paris (see Places to Stay); some say it's the best restaurant on the Riviera. It offers high-quality dishes (with prices to match) prepared by French chef Alain Ducasse. *Menus* start at 780FF; an à la carte meal will cost around 1000FF.

Self-Catering ***Haagen-Däz*** has a great little ice cream outlet in the pavilion in the public gardens in front of the casino.

In La Condamine, there's a ***food market*** at Place d'Armes and a ***Casino*** supermarket on Blvd Albert 1er, which is open from 8.45 am to 12.30 pm and 2.45 to 7.30 pm (no break on Friday; Saturday; closed Sunday). Summer hours are 8.30 am to 8 pm (closed Sunday).

Entertainment

Tickets for most cultural events are sold at FNAC (☎ 93 10 81 81), Centre Commercial le Métropole, 17 Ave Spélugues.

Cinema In summer, films are screened at the open-air ***Cinéma d'Été*** (☎ 93 25 86 80) in the Monte Carlo Sporting Club, Ave Princesse Grace, Larvotto. Nondubbed films with French subtitles are shown daily at 9.30 pm (50 to 90FF).

Theatre A charming spot to while away a summer evening is the 18th century fortress ***Théâtre du Fort Antoine*** (☎ 93 50 80 00; fax 93 50 66 94), Ave de la Quarantaine, which is now used as an outside theatre. In July and August plays are staged here on Monday at 9.30 pm (50 to 70FF).

Shopping

The 155 page, pocket-size *Monaco Shopping* guide, published annually and distributed for free by the tourist office, is indispensable to serious shoppers. The Galerie Riccadonna (☎ 93 50 84 46; fax 92 16 06 78), 7 Rue Grimaldi, sells seriously funky designer furniture for very serious amounts of money.

Getting There & Away

Bus There is no bus station in Monaco. Intercity buses leave from various stops around the city.

Train Trains to/from Monaco are run by the French SNCF. The information desk at Monaco train station, Ave Prince Pierre, is open from 9.30 am to noon and 2.30 to 6.30 pm. The automatic luggage lockers (20FF for 72 hours) are accessible round the clock.

Taking the train along the coast is highly recommended – the sea and the mountains provide a truly magnificent sight. There are frequent trains eastward to Menton (12FF; 10 minutes) and the first town across the border in Italy, Ventimiglia (Vintimille in French; 19FF; 25 minutes). For trains to Nice and connections to other towns, see Getting There & Away in the Nice section.

Car If you are driving out of Monaco, either eastward towards Italy or westward to Nice, and you want to go via the A8, you first have to join the Moyenne Corniche (middle coastal road, numbered N7). For Italy, look for signs indicating Gênes (Genoa; Genova in Italian). Blvd du Jardin Exotique leads to the N7 in the direction of Nice.

Getting Around

Bus Monaco's urban bus system has six lines. Line No 2 links Monaco Ville with Monte Carlo and then loops back to the Jardin Exotique. Line No 4 links the train station with the tourist office, the casino and the Larvotto district. A ticket costs 8.50FF. Much better value are the four/eight-ride magnetic cards on sale from bus drivers and vending machines at all stops for 19/30FF, or the one day tourist pass (21FF). Buses run until 7 or 9 pm.

The local bus company, Compagnie des Autobus de Monaco (CAM; ☎ 93 50 62 41), 3 Ave du Président John F Kennedy is open from 8.30 am to noon and 2 to 6 pm (Friday until 5 pm; closed on weekends).

Lifts Some 15 public lifts (*ascenseurs publics*) run up and down the hillside, all marked on the free brochure distributed by the tourist office entitled *Monaco: Getting There & Getting About*. Most operate 24 hours, others run between 6 am and midnight or 1 am only.

Taxi To order a taxi, call ☎ 93 15 01 01.

Helicopter Heli-Air Monaco (☎ 92 05 00 50) will twirl you anywhere along the coast your heart desires – for a not-so-small fee of course.

Bicycle Hire two wheels from the Auto-Moto Garage (☎ 93 50 10 80), 7 Rue de Milo.

Corsica

Corsica (Corse in French) is the most mountainous and geographically diverse of the Mediterranean islands, earning it the perfectly justified title of *l'île de beauté* (the island of beauty). Although it covers only 8720 sq km, Corsica in many ways resembles a miniature continent, with 1000km of coastline lapped by azure seas, soaring granite mountains that stay snowcapped until July, a huge national park (Parc Naturel Régional de Corse), flatland marshes (along the east coast), an uninhabited desert (Désert des Agriates) in the north-west and a 'continental divide' running down the middle of the island. Much of the land is covered with *maquis*, a typically Corsican form of vegetation whose low, dense shrubs provide many of the spices used in Corsican cooking. During WWII, the fighters of the French Résistance became known as 'maquis' because the movement was very active in Corsica.

History

From the 11th to the 13th century, Corsica was ruled by the Italian city-state of Pisa, which sent Tuscan architects and stonemasons to build numerous Romanesque churches on the island. Pisa's supremacy was contested – and in 1284 ended – by its commercial rival, Genoa, whose authority was in turn challenged by Aragon. In the mid-15th century the Genoese handed over the governing of Corsica – beset at the time by near anarchy, in part because of Muslim raids on coastal areas – to the Office de Saint Georges, a powerful financial organisation with its own army. To prevent seaborne raids from North Africa, the office built a massive early-warning and defence system that included hilltop watchtowers along the coast (many of which can be seen to this day) and several citadels.

On a number of occasions, Corsican discontent with foreign rule led to open revolt. In 1755, after 25 years of intermittent warfare

HIGHLIGHTS

- **Ajaccio to Calvi** – roll down the windows, tune the radio and head up the scenic west coast road
- **Pointe de la Parata** – watch the sunset and the Îles Sanguinaires turn iridescent red
- **Calvi** – stroll the old town's narrow streets
- **Porticcio** – relax on this fine-sand beach and soak up the rays
- **Les Calanche** – challenge yourself on one of the four walking trails through this spectacular mountain landscape

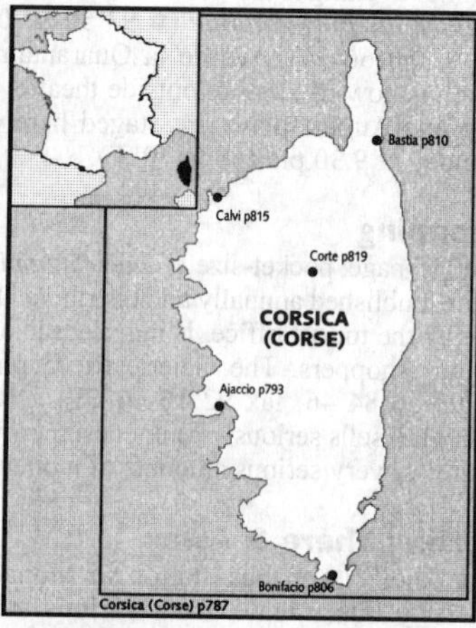

figatelli, coppa, lonzo – Corsican *charcuterie* (prepared meats)

brocciu frais – a soft, white, ewe's-milk cheese

delice à la châtaigne (chestnut cake) and pastries and bread made with chestnut flour

CORSICA (CORSE)

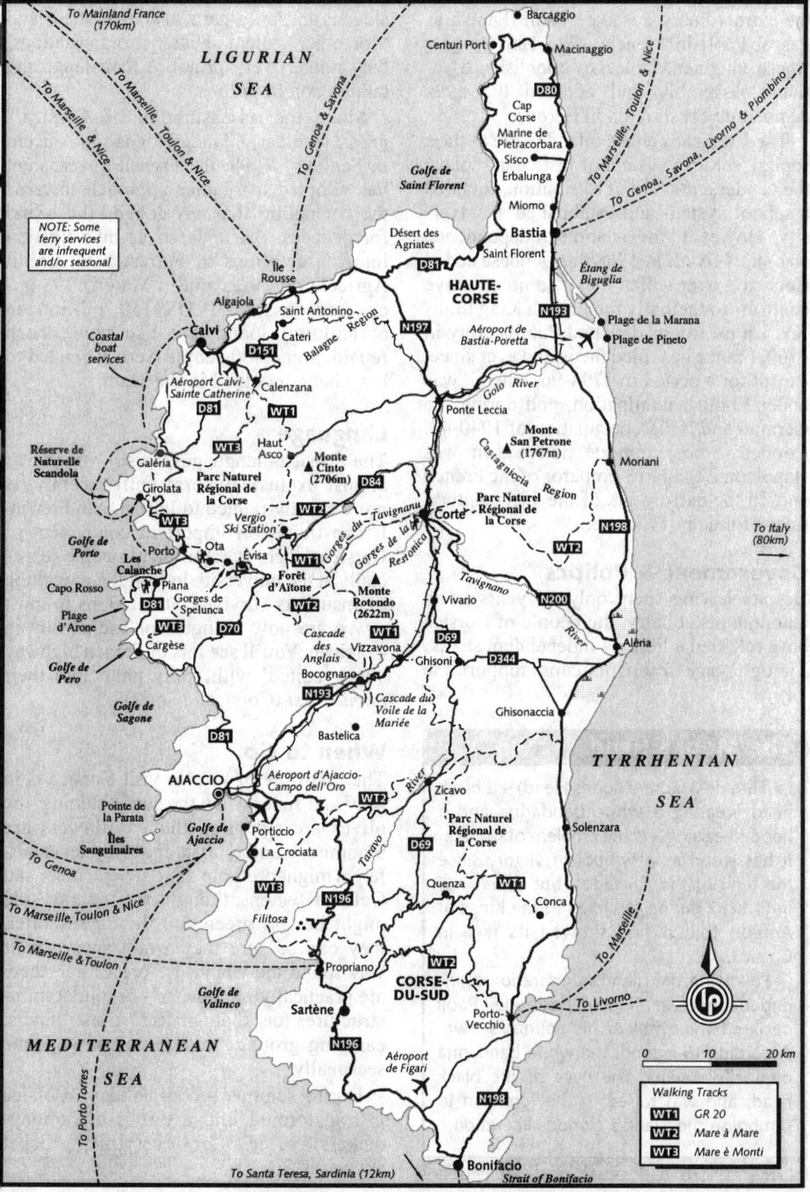

against the Genoese, the Corsicans declared their island independent. They were led by the extraordinary Pasquale Paoli (known as Pascal Paoli in French; 1725-1807), under whose enlightened rule they established a National Assembly and adopted the most democratic constitution in Europe.

The Corsicans chose inland Corte as their capital, set up a system of justice to replace the vendetta method of retribution, founded a school system and established a university. However, the island's independence was short-lived: in 1768 the Genoese ceded Corsica – over which they had no effective control – to their ally the French King Louis XV, whose troops defeated Paoli's army in 1769. France has ruled the island ever since, except for a period in 1794-96, when it was under English domination, and during the German and Italian occupation of 1940-43. Corsica's most famous native son was Napoleon Bonaparte, emperor of the French and, in the early years of the 19th century, ruler of much of Europe.

Government & Politics

Despite having spent only 14 years as an autonomous country, the people of Corsica have retained a fiercely independent streak. Though very few Corsicans support the Front de Libération Nationale de la Corse (FLNC) – whose initials and nationalist slogans are spray-painted all over the island – or other violent separatist organisations, they remain very proud of their language, culture and traditions.

Since the assassination of Corsica's *préfet* (prefect) Claude Erignac in Ajaccio in February 1998, the French government has adopted a tougher approach towards the corruption that has dogged the island for decades. An undercover investigation into the activities of French bank Crédit Agricole on the island in March 1998 uncovered losses of US$150 million in agricultural loans that had never been repaid. Some 400 people were estimated to have been involved in the scam.

The Moor's Head

La Tête de Maure (Moor's Head) – a black head wearing a white bandanna and a hooped earring – is the emblem of Corsica. It has stood as a symbol of victory since the time of the Crusades, but it was not until 1297 during the reign of the Kings of Aragon that it first showed its face in Corsica.

Following the island's declaration of independence in 1755, Pasquale Paoli declared the emblem his country's own. According to legend, the white bandanna originally covered the eyes of the black head, and was raised to the forehead to symbolise the island's glorious liberation.

Language

The Corsican language (Corsu), which was almost exclusively oral until recently, is more closely related to Italian than French. It constitutes an important component of Corsican identity, and many people (especially at the university in Corte) are working to ensure its survival. Street signs in most towns are now bilingual or exclusively in Corsican. You'll see lots of French highway signs 'edited' with spray paint into their *nomi Corsi* (Corsican names).

When to Go

The best time of year to visit Corsica is in May and June, when the sun is shining, the olives are ripening, the wildflowers are blooming – and tourists few. Hay fever sufferers might prefer to visit in September and October when, though the countryside might be less green and the days shorter, they can be sure they won't sneeze their way round the island. Before Easter, there are practically no tourists – or tourist infrastructure for that matter; most hotels, camping grounds and restaurants operate seasonally.

During summer school holidays, Corsica is transformed into a circus of holidaymakers. Prices for everything rocket skywards.

Corsican Polyphony

Corsican band Les Nouvelles Polyphonies Corses won the heart of a nation – and not just Corsicans – with its magnetic polyphonic performance at the opening ceremony of the 1992 Winter Olympics in Albertville, mainland France.

Bewitching in their simplicity, *polyphonies* (Corsican chants) are traditionally sung by a choir of voices *a capella* (without musical accompaniment). *Paghjellas* are sung by three male voices – a tenor, baritone and bass – and mark the passage of life: the *O Culomba* paghjella celebrates women's beauty and its power over men; *A Mio Ghjallinuccia Nera* features a farmer who, eager to travel the world, asks one of his black hens to lend him her wings.

Equally compelling are the sacred chants sung in village churches in the mountainous Castagniccia region east of Corte. In Pigna, south of Île Rousse, polyphonic evenings are held in summer in the Casa Musicale (☎ 04 95 61 77 31). Calvi hosts the five-day Rencontres Polyphoniques festival each year in mid-September.

The recordings of the Sartène Male Voice Choir and contemporary bands I Muvrini, Canta U Populu Corsu and Les Nouvelles Polyphonies Corses are widely available on CD. In Corsica, tune into Radio Corse-Frequenza Mora (100.5 MHz FM in Ajaccio, 101.7 MHz FM in Bastia, 97.7 MHz FM in Corte and 91.7 MHz FM in Calvi).

Dangers & Annoyances

When Corsica makes the headlines, it's often because nationalist militants seeking Corsican independence (usually affiliated with one of the quarrelling factions of the largest separatist organisation, the FLNC) have engaged in some act of violence, such as bombing a public building, robbing a bank, blowing up a vacant holiday villa or murdering the préfet. But the violence, which in 1997 included 290 bombings and 22 murders (some inter-factional), is *not* targeted at tourists, and there is no reason for visitors to fear for their safety.

Activities

Hiking Corsica's superb hiking trails – most of which take in the 330,000 hectare Parc Naturel Régional de la Corse – include the legendary **GR20**, also known as Frà Li Monti (literally, 'between the mountains'), which stretches over 160km from Calenzana (10km south-east of Calvi) to Conca (20km north of Porto Vecchio). Since it follows the island's continental divide, much of the route is above 2000m and hence passable only from mid-June to October. Walking the entire length of the trail takes at least two weeks.

Three Mare à Mare (meaning 'sea to sea') trails cross the island from west to east. In the south, the **Mare à Mare Sud** trail, open year-round, allows you to walk from Propriano to Porto Vecchio in about five days. In the centre of the island, the seven day **Mare à Mare Centre** links La Crociata (about 25km south of Ajaccio) with Ghisonaccia; it is open from about May to November. The **Mare à Mare Nord**, which connects Cargèse (via Évisa) with Moriani (40km south of Bastia), takes seven to 12 days (depending on your route) and is passable only from about May to November. On the north-west coast, the **Mare è Monti** (sea and mountains) trail from Cargèse to Calenzana (via Évisa, Ota, Girolata and Galéria) takes about 10 days. It is open all year but is at its best in spring and autumn.

Some 600km of trails, including the GR20, are covered in *Walks in Corsica* (120FF), an invaluable topoguide published in London by Robertson McCarta. In Ajaccio, the Maison d'Informations Randonées of the Parc Naturel Régional de la Corse sells a host of hiking guides (French only) for the region. It also distributes a series of free brochures entitled *Balades en Corse – Sentiers de Pays* which map out shorter hikes (taking from one to eight hours) in the region; many conveniently start from Corsica's remote mountain train stations.

Organised Tours Objectif Nature (☎/fax 04 95 32 54 34), 3 Rue Notre Dame de Lourdes, Bastia, arranges guided cycling, hiking, horse riding and fishing trips to the island's interior (eg along parts of the GR20) as well as sea kayaking and diving.

In Ajaccio, contact the Maison d'Informations Randonées of the Parc Naturel Régional de la Corse (see Information in the Ajaccio section) or Muntagne Corse (☎ 04 95 20 53 14) at 2 Ave de la Grande Armée.

Places to Stay

Camping Most of Corsica's many camping grounds are open only from June to September. *Camping sauvage* (literally 'wild camping', ie camping outside recognised camping grounds) is prohibited, in part because of the danger of fires (especially in the maquis). In remote areas hikers can bivouac in *refuge* grounds for 20FF a night.

Refuges & Gîtes d'Étape The Maison d'Informations Randonées of the Parc Naturel Régional de la Corse provides hikers with lists of mountain *refuges* and *gîtes d'étape* along the GR20 and other hiking trails (see Hiking in the previous Activities section). A night's accommodation in a park *refuge* is 50FF. Nightly rates in a gîte d'étape are 40 to 80FF; most offer half-board too (145 to 185FF a night).

Gîtes Depending on how far away the beach is, *gîtes ruraux* (country cottages, also called *meublés ruraux*) with shower and toilet for two or more people can be rented for 1000 to 2200FF a week; prices double or triple between June and September when most places are booked up months in advance. In Ajaccio, Relais des Gîtes Ruraux (☎ 04 95 51 72 82; fax 04 95 51 72 89), 1 Rue du Général Fiorella, provides information on available cottages.

Hotels Corsica's budget hotel rooms are more expensive than their mainland counterparts; virtually nothing is available for less than 140FF. Outside of Bastia, Ajaccio and Corte, the vast majority of hotels close between November and Easter.

Corse-Corsica Hotels-Restaurants published by the Logis de France (info@logis-de-france.fr; www.logis-de-france.fr) lists comfortable hotels in Corsica. Book through the Association des Logis de France office in Bastia (☎ 04 95 54 44 30), BP 210, F-20293, or in Porto Vecchio (☎ 04 95 70 05 93; fax 04 95 70 47 82), 12 Rue Jean Jaurès, F-20137.

Getting There & Away

Visitors are charged a 'regional tax' of 30FF upon arrival *and* departure. It is not included in the prices quoted below but will usually be included in your quoted air or ferry fare.

Air Corsica's four main airports are at Ajaccio, Bastia, Figari (near Bonifacio) and Calvi. Return airfares to Corsica from Nice/Marseille/Paris cost 700/800/1200FF. People under 25 or over 60 may qualify for a 600/700/800FF return fare.

Boat Details on ferry services are available from many French travel agents. During the summer – especially from mid-July to early September – reservations for vehicles and couchettes (sleeping berths) on *all* routes must be made well in advance.

In addition to the basic fares listed below, each port levies an additional tax on visitors and vehicles, ranging from 24 to 44FF for a passenger and 35 to 64FF for a vehicle, depending on which port you are coming from and arriving at.

To/From Mainland France Almost all ferry services between the French mainland (Nice, Marseille and Toulon) and Corsica (Ajaccio, Bastia, Calvi, Île Rousse, Porto Vecchio and Propriano) are handled by the state-owned Société Nationale Maritime Corse-Méditerranée (SNCM; ☎ 08 36 67 95 00 in Marseille; ☎ 04 93 13 66 99 in Nice; www.sncm.fr).

Schedules and fares are comprehensively listed in the SNCM pocket timetable, freely distributed at tourist offices, some hotels and SNCM offices. In the height of summer there are up to eight ferries a day; in winter there are as few as eight a week and fares are substantially cheaper.

For one-way passage in a *fauteuil* (which means 'armchair' but in most cases is a rather hard, straight-backed chair in a small cabin), individuals pay 210FF (240FF from late June to early September) to and from Nice, and 256FF (292FF in summer) to and from Marseille or Toulon. Daytime crossings take about 6½ hours. For overnight trips, the cheapest couchette/most comfortable cabin costs an additional 66/288FF.

For people under 25 and seniors, one-way passage costs 184/210FF in winter/summer for all sailings to/from Nice and 224/256FF to/from Marseille and Toulon. Children under 12 pay 50% less than the adult fare.

Transporting a small car costs between 214FF and 612FF depending on the season. Motorcycles under/over 100cc cost 136/149 to 437FF; bicycles cost 91FF and dogs in a kennel/vehicle cost 173/92FF.

Corsica Ferries and SNCM also run a 70km/h express NGV (Navire à Grande Vitesse) service from Nice to Calvi (2¾ hours) and Bastia (3½ hours). Fares on these zippy NGVs, which carry 500 passengers and 148 vehicles, are similar to those charged for passage on the regular ferries.

To/From Italy Corsica Ferries (☎ 04 95 32 95 95 in Bastia; ☎ 019-216 0041 in Savona; ☎ 0586-88 13 80 in Livorno; www.corsicaferries.com) has year-round car ferry services to Bastia from Savona (Savone in French), 32km west of Genoa (Gênes in French, Genova in Italian), and Livorno (Livourne in French, Leghorn in English). Except for overnight runs, the crossing takes four to five hours (1½ hours on the NGV Bastia-Livorno service). From mid-May to mid-September the company also runs ferries from Savona to Île Rousse. Depending on which route you take and when you travel, individuals pay 124 to 180FF (no student or senior discounts). Small cars cost between 250 and 630FF each way; bicycles are free. Cabins for up to three people start at 250FF.

From mid-April to October, Moby Lines (☎ 04 95 34 84 94 or ☎ 04 95 34 84 90 in Bastia; ☎ 0586-82 68 23 or ☎ 0586-82 68 25 in Livorno) links Bastia with the Italian ports of Genoa (seven to eight hours) and Livorno (four hours). From July to early September, Moby Lines' car ferries also link Bastia with Piombino (3½ hours). Depending on when you travel, the one-way fare is 110 to 195FF for passengers and 270 to 460FF for a small car. Cabins with two couchettes start at 105FF.

Between April and September, Corsica Marittima (☎ 04 95 54 66 66 in Bastia; ☎ 010-589 595 in Genoa; ☎ 0586-21 05 07 in Livorno; www.Corsica-Marittima.com) runs express NGV ferries from Bastia to Genoa (3¼ hours) and Livorno (1¾ hours).

For information on ferries from Sardinia to Bonifacio, see Getting There & Away in the Bonifacio section.

Getting Around

Bus Bus transport around the island is slow, infrequent, relatively expensive and handled by a network of independent companies. On longer routes, most of which are operated by Eurocorse, there are only one or two and at most four runs a day. Except during July and August, only a handful of intercity buses operate on Sunday and holidays.

Train This is the most interesting, fun and comfortable way to tour the island – despite Corsica's metre-gauge single-track rail system being a good century behind the TGV. The two and four-car trains screech and crawl their way through the stunning mountain scenery of the interior, stopping at tiny rural stations and, when necessary, for sheep, goats and cows. Sometimes the wind blows sand onto the beachside tracks near Calvi and the conductor has to hop out and shovel these mini-dunes off the rails. At higher elevations, special snowploughs keep the tracks passable in winter. Passengers frequently include Foreign Legionnaires in starched uniforms and white kepis on their way to or from the Foreign Legion base near Calvi.

The 232km network, which runs seven days a week, consists of two lines that meet to exchange passengers at Ponte Leccia. Between September and July, the Ajaccio-Corte-Bastia line is served by four trains a day (two on Sunday and holidays). Services are slightly reduced in winter and increased in August. Two daily trains year-round (coordinated with the Ajaccio-Corte-Bastia service) link Bastia with Ponte Leccia, Île Rousse and Calvi. Printed schedules are available at train stations, tourist offices and some hotels.

Single fares include Ajaccio-Bastia (121FF; 3¼ to four hours), Ajaccio-Calvi (140FF; 3½ to 4½ hours), Ajaccio-Corte (64FF; two hours), Bastia-Calvi (92FF; three hours), Bastia-Corte (56FF; 1¾ hours) and Calvi-Corte (76FF; 2½ hours). Children under 12 are entitled to half-price tickets; those under four travel for free.

For further information contact Chemins de Fer de la Corse (CFC) in Bastia (☎ 04 95 32 80 57 or ☎ 04 95 32 80 61).

Transporting a bicycle costs a flat 73FF no matter how far you're going. The surcharge for bulky hand luggage (6FF) is rarely applied. Leaving luggage at train station ticket windows costs 20FF for 24 hours.

Rail Passes Most rail passes are not valid on the CFC system, though holders of Inter-Rail passes get 50% off.

If you are making a return journey of less than 200km within 48 hours, you are eligible for a *billet touristique* (tourist ticket) which is 25% cheaper than a regular return ticket. These tickets are not available in July, August or the first half of September.

Year-round, the CFC sells its own rail pass – La Carte Zoom – which is well worth buying if you intend making more than a couple of train journeys within Corsica. The Carte Zoom costs 290FF (no reductions for students or seniors) and is valid for seven days, entitling you to unlimited travel on the entire CFC rail network for that period.

Car & Motorcycle Travelling by road is a convenient but stressful way to explore Corsica. Most of the roads are spectacular but narrow and harrowing: the hairpin curves are not preceded by any sort of warning, and guard rails – if there are any at all – are usually little more than low stone walls. Shoulders are narrow or nonexistent and bridges are often single-lane. Count on averaging 50km/h.

It is not uncommon for local motorcyclists (and especially those on scooters) to cruise round town or along country roads without helmets – and with a frightening number of children piled aboard.

The most beautiful roads in Corsica include the D84 from Porto to the Vergio ski station via Évisa and the Forêt d'Aïtone, and the D69 from the N193 (near Vivario) via the forests of the Parc Régional to Ghisoni (linked to the east coast by the D344) and Sartène. The fastest road on the island is the N198, which runs along the flat east coast from Bastia to Bonifacio. A good road map (such as Michelin's yellow-jacketed 1:200,000 map No 90) is indispensable.

Details on car rental are listed in the Getting There & Away sections under Ajaccio, Bonifacio, Bastia and Calvi.

Ajaccio to Porto

Corsica's wildest, most spectacularly scenic coast runs from Ajaccio northward to Calvi. The entries in this section are listed from south to north.

AJACCIO

• pop 60,000 ✉ 20000

The port city of Ajaccio, birthplace of Napoleon Bonaparte (1769-1821), is a great place to begin a visit to Corsica. This pastel-shaded Mediterranean town is a fine place for strolling, but spending some time here can also be educational: Ajaccio's several museums and many statues dedicated to Bonaparte (who, local people will neglect to mention, never came back to visit after becoming emperor) speak volumes, not about Napoleon himself, but about how the people of his native town prefer to think of him.

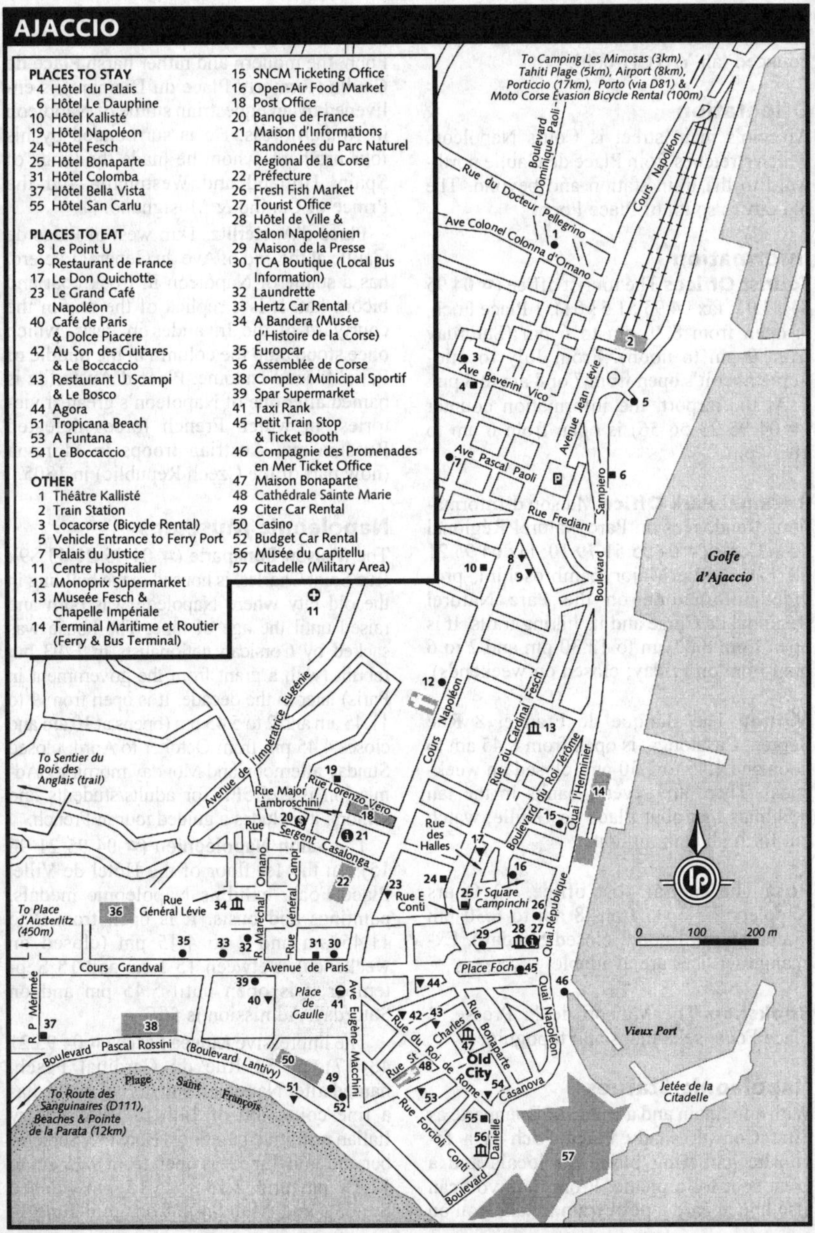
AJACCIO
PLACES TO STAY
4 Hôtel du Palais
6 Hôtel Le Dauphine
10 Hôtel Kallisté
19 Hôtel Napoléon
24 Hôtel Fesch
25 Hôtel Bonaparte
31 Hôtel Colomba
37 Hôtel Bella Vista
55 Hôtel San Carlu
PLACES TO EAT
8 Le Point U
9 Restaurant de France
17 Le Don Quichotte
23 Le Grand Café Napoléon
40 Café de Paris & Dolce Piacere
42 Au Son des Guitares & Le Boccaccio
43 Restaurant U Scampi & Le Bosco
44 Agora
51 Tropicana Beach
53 A Funtana
54 Le Boccaccio
OTHER
1 Théâtre Kallisté
2 Train Station
3 Locacorse (Bicycle Rental)
5 Vehicle Entrance to Ferry Port
7 Palais du Justice
11 Centre Hospitalier
12 Monoprix Supermarket
13 Museée Fesch & Chapelle Impériale
14 Terminal Maritime et Routier (Ferry & Bus Terminal)
15 SNCM Ticketing Office
16 Open-Air Food Market
18 Post Office
20 Banque de France
21 Maison d'Informations Randonées du Parc Naturel Régional de la Corse
22 Préfecture
26 Fresh Fish Market
27 Tourist Office
28 Hôtel de Ville & Salon Napoléonien
29 Maison de la Presse
30 TCA Boutique (Local Bus Information)
32 Laundrette
33 Hertz Car Rental
34 A Bandera (Musée d'Histoire de la Corse)
35 Europcar
36 Assemblée de Corse
38 Complex Municipal Sportif
39 Spar Supermarket
41 Taxi Rank
45 Petit Train Stop & Ticket Booth
46 Compagnie des Promenades en Mer Ticket Office
47 Maison Bonaparte
48 Cathédrale Sainte Marie
49 Citer Car Rental
50 Casino
52 Budget Car Rental
56 Musée du Capitellu
57 Citadelle (Military Area)
To Camping Les Mimosas (3km), Tahiti Plage (5km), Airport (8km), Porticcio (17km), Porto (via D81) & Moto Corse Évasion Bicycle Rental (100m)
Boulevard Dominique Paoli
Cours Napoléon
Rue du Docteur Pellegrino
Ave Colonel Colonna d'Ornano
Ave Beverini Vico
Avenue Jean Lévie
Ave Pascal Paoli
Rue Frediani
Boulevard Sampiero
Golfe d'Ajaccio
Avenue de l'Impératrice Eugénie
To Sentier du Bois des Anglais (trail)
Rue Major Lambroschini
Rue Lorenzo Vero
Rue Sergent Casalonga
Rue du Cardinal Fesch
Boulevard du Roi Jérôme
Quai l'Herminier
Rue des Halles
Rue E Conti
Square Campinchi
Quai République
To Place d'Austerlitz (450m)
Rue Général Lévie
R Maréchal Ornano
Rue Général Campi
Cours Grandval
Avenue de Paris
Place Foch
Quai Napoléon
R P Mérimée
Place de Gaulle
Ave Eugène Macchini
Rue St Charles
Rue du Roi de Rome
Rue Bonaparte
Old City
Vieux Port
Jetée de la Citadelle
Boulevard Pascal Rossini (Boulevard Lantivy)
Plage Saint François
To Route des Sanguinaires (D111), Beaches & Pointe de la Parata (12km)
Rue Forcioli Conti
Boulevard Danielle Casanova
0 100 200 m

Ajaccio is pronounced 'ah-ZHAK-syo'; the city's Corsican name, Aiacciu, is pronounced 'ah-YATCH-ooh'.

Orientation

Ajaccio's main street is Cours Napoléon, which stretches from Place de Gaulle northward to the train station and beyond. The old city is south of Place Foch.

Information

Tourist Offices The tourist office (☎ 04 95 51 53 03; fax 04 95 51 53 01), 1 Place Foch, is open from 8.30 am to 6 pm (Saturday from 9 am to noon). From July to mid-September it's open from 7 or 8 am to 8 pm.

At the airport, the information counter (☎ 04 95 23 56 56) is open from 6 am to 10.30 pm.

Regional Park Office Maison d'Informations Randonées du Parc Naturel Régional de la Corse (☎ 04 95 51 79 10; fax 04 95 21 88 17), 2 Rue Major Lambroschini, provides information on the Parc Naturel Régional de Corse and its hiking trails. It is open from 8.30 am to 12.30 pm and 2 to 6 pm (5 pm on Friday; closed on weekends).

Money The Banque de France, 8 Rue Sergent Casalonga, is open from 8.45 am to noon and 1.45 to 3.30 pm (closed on weekends). There are several banks in the tan buildings that abut Place de Gaulle; watch out for high commissions.

Post The central post office, 13 Cours Napoléon, is open from 8 am to 6.30 pm (Saturday until noon; closed Sunday). Exchange services are available.

Bookshop The Maison de la Presse, 2 Place Foch, sells maps and topoguides.

Napoleonic Statues

With a fountain and a statue of Bonaparte as First Consul, shady **Place Foch** is a favourite gathering place for locals and a great spot for a picnic. From here you can also hop aboard a **petit train** to take you on a 45 minute city tour (35/15FF for adults/children). Just up the hill from Place Foch, the modern and rather harsh **Place de Gaulle** (formerly Place du Diamant) is enlivened by an equestrian statue of Napoleon in Roman dress. He is surrounded by his four brothers, whom he made the kings of Spain, Holland and Westphalia and the Prince of Canino & Musignano.

Place d'Austerlitz, 1km west of Place de Gaulle at the end of Ave du Général Leclerc, has a statue of Napoleon in frock coat and bicorn hat. It is a replica of the one in the courtyard of the Invalides in Paris, which once stood atop the column in the middle of Paris' Place Vendôme. Place d'Austerlitz is named after one of Napoleon's greatest victories, in which French forces defeated Russian and Austrian troops in Moravia (now part of the Czech Republic) in 1805.

Napoleonic Museums

The **Maison Bonaparte** (☎ 04 95 21 43 89), Rue Saint Charles, is housed in the building in the old city where Napoleon was born and raised until the age of nine. The house was sacked by Corsican nationalists in 1793 but rebuilt (with a grant from the government in Paris) later in the decade. It is open from 9 to 11.45 am and 2 to 5.45 pm (opens at 10 am and closes 4.45 pm from October to April; closed Sunday afternoon and Monday morning). Admission is 22/15FF for adults/students and seniors; it includes a guided tour in French.

The **Salon Napoléonien** (☎ 04 95 21 90 15), on the 1st floor of the Hôtel de Ville, Place Foch, exhibits Napoleonic medals, paintings and busts. It is open from 9 to 11.45 am and 2 to 4.45 pm (closed on weekends). Between 15 June and 15 September it is open until 5.45 pm and on Saturday. Admission is 5FF.

The impressive **Musée Fesch** (☎ 04 95 21 48 17), 50-52 Rue du Cardinal Fesch, named after Napoleon's maternal uncle, has a fine collection of 14th to 19th century Italian primitive paintings. Between September and mid-June it is open from 9.15 am to 12.15 pm and 2.15 to 5.15 pm (closed Sunday and Monday); from mid-June to mid-September it's open from 10 am to 5.30 pm (Friday night from 9.30 pm to midnight; closed Tuesday). Entry costs 25/15FF for adults/students. There is a separate fee of 10/5FF for the Renaissance **Chapelle Impériale**, built in the 1850s as a sepulchre for members of the Bonaparte family. Napoleon himself is buried in the Invalides in Paris.

A Bandera (☎ 04 95 51 07 34), 1 Rue Général Lévie, also known as the Musée d'Histoire de la Corse, has exhibits on the island's military history. Entrance costs 20/10FF for adults/students. It is open from 9 am to noon and 2 to 6 pm (closed Sunday). The island's history is also recounted in the **Musée du Capitellu** (☎ 04 95 21 50 57), 18 Blvd Danielle Casanova. Admission is 25/10FF for adults/children and opening hours are 10 am to noon and 2 to 6 pm (closed Sunday afternoon). In July and August the museum is open from 9 to 11 pm too.

Napoleonic Cathedral

Ajaccio's Venetian Renaissance-style **Cathédrale Sainte Marie**, built during the latter half of the 16th century, is in the old city on the corner of Rue Forcioli Conti and Rue Saint Charles. It contains Napoleon's marble baptismal font, to the right of the entrance, and the painting *Vierge au Sacré-Cœur* by Eugène Delacroix (1798-1863), on the wall of the chapel in the back corner of the left-hand wall. It is open from 7 to 11.30 am and 3 to 6.30 pm (6 pm in winter; closed Sunday afternoon year-round).

Pointe de la Parata

Pointe de la Parata, a wild, black-granite promontory 12km west of the city on Route des Sanguinaires (D111), is famed for its sunsets, which can be contemplated from the base of a crenellated, early 17th century Genoese watchtower. To get there, take bus No 5, which runs six to eight times a day in winter and every 20 minutes in July and August. On foot, follow the Sentier du Bois des Anglais, which begins 1.5km west of Place de Gaulle on Ave Nicolas Piétri. En route you pass the baroque-style Chapelle des Grecs (Greeks' Chapel) dating from 1731, the eerie Cimetière Marin, which appears like a miniature town behind its high walls, and the former mansion of Ajaccio-born singer Tino Rossi (1907-83) who recorded over 1000 songs and 24 films during his lifetime.

The **Îles Sanguinaires**, a group of small islands visible offshore, turn a deep red as the sun sets – hence the name Bloody Islands. Nothing but a huge squawking colony of seagulls inhabits these islands. From mid-April to October, they can be visited on two-hour boat excursions that set sail from the Compagnie des Promenades en Mer ticket office (☎ 04 95 51 31 31 or ☎ 04 95 23 23 38; fax 04 95 23 23 27) on the quayside opposite Place Foch (the Vieux Port), usually at 5.30 pm. Cost is 100/50FF for adults/children (120/60FF in July and August).

The same company also runs boat trips to the UNESCO-protected **Réserve Naturelle Scandola** (see Boat Excursions in the Porto section for details). A boat sets sail from Ajaccio's old port at 9 am and returns at 6 pm (220/110FF for adults/children).

Beaches

Ajaccio's beaches are nothing special. Plage de Ricanto, popularly known as **Tahiti Plage**, is about 5km east of town on the way to the airport; it is served by bus No 1. The small, segmented beaches between Ajaccio and Pointe de la Parata (Ariane, Neptune, Palm Beach and Marinella) are served by bus No 5. The ritzy resort town of **Porticcio**, 17km south of Ajaccio across the bay, has a great – if somewhat crowded – beach. Between mid-April and October, there are two boats a day from Ajaccio, departing from Ajaccio's quayside opposite Place Foch at 2.30 and 6 pm (30 minutes; 30/50FF single/return).

Special Events

The biggest day of the year on Ajaccio's calendar is 15 August – both Assumption Day and Napoleon's birthday. The traditional religious procession is accompanied by fireworks and other events.

Places to Stay – Budget

Camping The *Camping Les Mimosas* (☎ 04 95 20 99 85; fax 04 95 10 01 77), open from April to mid-October, is about 3km north of the centre of town on Route d'Alata. It costs 28/11/11FF per adult/tent site/car. Prices drop by 10% out of season. Take bus No 4 from Place de Gaulle or Cours Napoléon to the roundabout (*rond point*) at the western end of Cours Jean Nicoli and walk up Route d'Alata for 1km.

Hotels The nine room *Hôtel Colomba* (☎ 04 95 21 12 66), 8 Ave de Paris, has clean, pleasant singles/doubles from 140/200FF; doubles with shower are 180FF. Reservations (by phone or post) must be in French.

The one star, nine room *Hôtel du Palais* (☎ 04 95 23 36 42; fax 04 95 23 06 96), 5 Ave Beverini Vico, is grotty. It has shower-equipped rooms for one/two/three people starting at 150/190/250FF.

Places to Stay – Mid-Range

The friendly and efficiently run *Hôtel Kallisté* (☎ 04 95 51 34 45; fax 04 95 21 79 00), 51 Cours Napoléon, has spotless and charming singles/doubles/triples/quads with shower and toilet for 200/250/325/400FF in low season (220/275/365/455FF in June, July and September; 300/340/450/560FF in August). Some rooms have air-conditioning and a minibar. Breakfast (35FF) is served in your room. The hotel also lets out self-catering studios.

Also well located on Rue Cardinal Fesch is the colourful three star *Hôtel Fesch* (☎ 04 95 51 62 62; fax 04 95 21 83 36) at No 7. Good value singles/doubles with shower start at 240/280FF.

The two star *Hôtel Bella Vista* (☎ 04 95 51 71 00; fax 04 95 21 81 88) overlooks the bay at the intersection of Blvd Pascal Rossini and Rue Prosper Merimée, and has stunning views of the palm tree-studded beach and the sea. Simple but tasteful singles/doubles/triples with shower and toilet start at 210/220/280FF. It has some 'economy' rooms for one or two people for 200FF.

The two star *Hôtel Bonaparte* (☎ 04 95 21 44 19), 1-2 Rue Étienne Conti, has ordinary singles/doubles/triples/quads with shower and toilet for 260/300/360/390FF.

For great views of the bay (and the heavy traffic along the quay), look no farther than the simple but friendly *Hôtel Le Dauphine* (☎ 04 95 21 12 94; fax 04 95 21 88 69), close to the ferry port at 11 Blvd Sampiero. Singles/doubles/triples start at 230/260/320FF in low season, rising to 250/290/390FF in July and August.

Places to Stay – Top End

The calm *Hôtel San Carlu* (☎ 04 95 21 13 84; fax 04 95 21 09 99), overlooking the citadel in a quiet and graceful part of town at 8 Blvd Danielle Casanova, has spacious singles/doubles with all the perks from 345/388FF.

The modern *Hôtel Napoléon* (☎ 04 95 51 54 00; fax 04 95 21 80 40), 4 Rue Lorenzo Vero, has three star singles/doubles warranting no complaints for 320/370FF.

Places to Eat

Restaurants Ajaccio's restaurants are mostly seasonal and mediocre. Cafés can be found along Blvd du Roi Jérôme, Quai Napoléon and the north side of Place de Gaulle; *Café de Paris* and the neighbouring *Dolce Piacere*, on the east side of Place de Gaulle, both have giant terraces offering good square and sea views.

In the old city Rue Saint Charles and Rue Conventionnel Chiappe are lined with eating places. The popular *Restaurant U Scampi* (☎ 04 95 21 38 09), 11 Rue Conventionnel Chiappe, serves fish and other Corsican specialities (including octopus stew) on a fine, flower-filled terrace. Lunch and dinner *menus* start at 85FF. It is open year-round (closed Friday night and Saturday lunchtime). *Le Bosco* (☎ 04 95 21 25 06) next door shares the same terrace as the Scampi and seems to offer pretty much the same sort of *menus*, including a 195FF shellfish platter.

At 19 Rue de Roi de Rome on, ***Le Boccaccio*** (☎ 04 95 21 16 77) serves high-quality Italian cuisine with spaghetti costing 61 to 88FF and mains (meat and fish) 55 to 94FF. Le Boccaccio is open from noon to 2 pm and 7 to 10 pm (closed Monday in winter).

For a splurge in the old city, consider ***A Funtana*** (☎ 04 95 21 78 04), 7 Rue Notre Dame, with a regional *menu* for 120FF and fish dishes for 90 to 180FF. Hours are noon to 2 pm and 8 to 11 pm (closed Sunday, Monday lunchtime and in June).

Just off Place Foch on Rue Emmanuel Arène is the arty ***Agora*** (☎ 04 95 21 08 29), a modern place with crêpes, couscous and light snacks that adjoins a small book and music boutique. Despite a sign advertising otherwise, this place does *not* double as an Internet café. ***Le Don Quichotte*** (☎ 04 95 21 27 30) on Rue des Halles has pizzas from 40 to 50FF and *menus* from 73FF.

For an unsurpassable sea view, try ***Tropicana Beach*** (☎ 04 95 51 12 98) on Blvd Pascal Rossini, which, despite its tacky name, is home to an elegant indoor restaurant as well as a fantastic terrace built on stilts above the lapping waves. *Menus* start at 75FF; ice cream and light snacks are served on the verandah.

Le Grand Café Napoléon (☎ 04 95 21 42 54), opposite the prefecture at 10 Cours Napoléon, is considered the queen of Cours Napoléon's terrace cafés.

Self-Catering On Square Campinchi, an ***open-air food market*** operates until 1 pm (closed Monday except between June and September). There is a ***fresh fish market*** every morning in the tan-painted building behind the food market, on the corner of Place Foch and Quai l'Herminier.

Near Place de Gaulle, the ***Spar*** supermarket, opposite 4 Cours Grandval, is open from 8.30 am to 12.30 pm and 3 to 7.30 pm (closed Sunday). Along Cours Napoléon, the ***Monoprix*** supermarket, opposite No 40, is open from 8.30 am to 7.15 pm (closed Sunday).

Entertainment

Music, dance and dramas are hosted at Ajaccio's municipal ***Théâtre Kallisté*** (☎ 04 95 22 78 54), 6 Rue Colonel Colonna d'Ornano. For traditional music, try ***Au Son des Guitares*** (☎ 04 95 51 15 47), 7 Rue du Roi de Rome, which hosts local guitar bands every evening from 10 pm onwards.

The resort of Porticcio, 17km west of Ajaccio, attracts a wealthy, somewhat snobby clientele whose preferences have made the village a lively night spot. The Porticcio tourist office (☎ 04 95 25 07 02; fax 04 95 25 06 21) is near the beach. In summer it is sometimes possible to get from Ajaccio's Vieux Port to Porticcio by water taxi.

Getting There & Away

Air Ajaccio-Campo dell'Oro airport (☎ 04 95 23 56 56) is 8km east of the city.

Bus The Terminal Maritime et Routier on Quai l'Herminier houses Ajaccio's bus station. About a dozen companies have services from here, daily except Sunday and holidays, to Bastia (105FF; two a day), Bonifacio (105FF; two or three a day), Calvi (125FF; with a change at Ponte Leccia), Corte (60FF; two a day), Porto and Ota (70FF; 2½ hours; two a day), Sartène (64FF; two or three a day) and many small villages.

The bus station's information counter (☎ 04 95 51 55 45), which can provide schedules, is staffed daily from 7 am to 7 or 8 pm. Eurocorse (☎ 04 95 21 06 30 or ☎ 04 95 51 05 08), responsible for most of the long-distance lines, keeps its kiosk open from 8.30 am to 4 pm (closed Sunday).

Train The train station (☎ 04 95 23 11 03), Blvd Sampiero (Place de la Gare), is staffed daily from 6.15 or 7.30 am to 6.30 pm (8 pm from late May to late September).

Car About a dozen car-rental companies have airport bureaus that are open whenever there are incoming flights. The tourist office has a complete list.

The Hôtel Kallisté (see Places to Stay – Mid-Range) rents cars, offering rates that undercut all the major car-rental companies. A three-door vehicle costs 300/1560FF for a day/week, including unlimited mileage. Prices rise in July and August.

Leading car rental companies in town include Hertz (☎ 04 95 21 70 94; fax 04 95 21 72 50), 8 Cours Grandval; Europcar (☎ 04 95 21 05 49; fax 04 95 51 39 38), 16 Cours Grandval; and Budget (☎ 04 95 21 17 18; fax 04 95 21 00 07), 1 Blvd Lantivy.

Boat The ferry terminal is in the Terminal Maritime et Routier on Quai l'Herminier. SNCM's ticketing office (☎ 04 95 29 66 99), across the street at 3 Quai l'Herminier, is open from 8 to 11.45 am and 2 to 6 pm (closed Saturday afternoon and Sunday). When there's an evening ferry, the SNCM bureau in the ferry terminal sells tickets for pedestrian passengers two or three hours before departure time; tickets for vehicles are available at the port's vehicle entrance.

From mid-April to October, Compagnie des Promenades en Mer (☎ 04 95 51 31 31 or ☎ 04 95 23 23 38; fax 04 95 23 23 27) runs boats from Ajaccio's Vieux Port to Bonifacio (240/120FF return for adults/children).

Getting Around

To/From the Airport TCA bus No 1 (or, late at night, the No 6) links the airport with Ajaccio train and bus stations; tickets cost 20FF. The downside is there's only one bus an hour (departing on the hour from the airport, and on the half-hour from town). Buses run between 6.30 am and 10.30 pm, depending on flight schedules.

A taxi from the airport to the centre of Ajaccio costs around 120FF (140FF at night), including the 10FF airport surcharge.

Bus Local bus maps and timetables can be picked up at the TCA Boutique (☎ 04 95 51 43 23), 2 Ave de Paris, open from 8 am to noon and 2.30 to 6 pm (closed Sunday). A single bus ticket/carnet of 10 costs 7.50/58FF.

Taxi There's a taxi rank (☎ 04 95 21 00 87) on the east side of Place de Gaulle or you can call Radio Taxis Ajacciens on ☎ 04 95 25 09 13.

Bicycle The Hôtel Kallisté (see Places to Stay – Mid-Range) rents mountain bikes/scooters for 80/195FF a day and 470/1210FF for a week. Prices drop between October and April.

About 500m north of the train station on Montée Saint Jean, Moto Corse Évasion (☎ 04 95 20 52 05; fax 04 95 22 48 11) has mountain bikes to rent for 50/85FF a half-day/day.

CARGÈSE

• pop 900 ✉ 20130

Perched on a steep promontory between the Golfe de Sagone (south) and Golfe de Pero (north), Cargèse – founded just over two centuries ago by Greek settlers – retains the appearance and ambience of a Greek village.

In 1676, about 600 Greeks from Itilo in the southern Peloponnese fled their Ottoman-controlled homeland and were given refuge on Corsica by the Republic of Genoa. Loyal to the Genoese and relatively prosperous, the Greek settlers soon became objects of hostility for their Corsican neighbours. After suffering repeated attacks elsewhere on the island, the descendants of the original settlers founded Cargèse, also known as Cargèse-la-Grecque because of its Greek foundation, in 1774. Each year on Easter Monday and 15 August, a colourful religious procession led by Cargèse's Greek Catholic congregation wends its way through the village.

Orientation

The D81, Cargèse's main street, is known as both Ave de la République (towards Ajaccio from the post office) and Rue Colonel Fieschi (towards Porto from the post office). The square stone object 250m up Rue Colonel Fieschi from the post office is an old *lavoir*, traditionally used for washing clothes.

Information

The tourist office (☎ 04 95 26 41 31) on Rue du Docteur Dragacci is open year-round from 4 to 6 pm (closed on weekends). Between June and September, daily hours are 9 am to noon and 4 to 7 pm.

Churches

Cargèse is well known for its two Catholic churches – one eastern (Greek) rite, the other western (Latin) – which face each other across a patchwork of neatly tended hillside vegetable plots. Both afford fine views of the town and of the turquoise Golfe de Sagone.

The 19th century **Latin-rite church** has a square white bell tower on the side of the structure, while the **Greek church** has stone buttresses and a polygonal bell tower on top of the building. The interior of the Greek church – constructed from 1852 to 1870 by the faithful, who worked on Sunday after attending Divine Liturgy – is adorned with a number of icons brought from Greece in the 1670s by the original settlers. Services are held in Greek using prayer books that include both a transliteration of the Greek text and a French translation.

Beaches

The Genoese towers atop Pointe d'Omigna (accessible by a footpath) and Pointe de Cargèse overlook **Plage de Pero**, a long, wide stretch of sand about 1km north of the town centre. Take the road leading down the hill from the lavoir on Rue Colonel Fieschi.

Other beaches include **Plage de Ménasina** (2.5km south of town), **Plage de Stagnoli** (7.5km south) and **Plage de Chiuni** (6km north).

Places to Stay & Eat

The one star ***Hôtel Helios*** (☎ 04 95 26 40 03; fax 04 95 26 47 19), open from mid-March to mid-October, is 2km south of Cargèse on the Ajaccio-Cargèse road. Rooms for two with shower start at 220FF.

The ***Motel Punta e Mare*** (☎ 04 95 26 44 33; fax 04 95 26 49 54) on Route de Paomia has pleasant doubles with shower and toilet from 180 to 250FF. Just down Rue Colonel Fieschi, the ***Hôtel de France*** (☎ 04 95 26 41 07), open from April to October only, has doubles with shower and toilet for 160FF. In July and August, only half-board (230FF per person) is available.

About 100m towards Porto from the laundry stone on Place Saint Jean, the ***Hôtel Le Continental*** (☎ 04 95 26 42 24) has doubles/triples – some with a view of the Golfe de Pero – for 180/240FF. Next door is the elegant ***Hôtel Le Saint Jean*** (☎ 04 95 26 46 68; fax 04 95 26 43 93) which has doubles, also with a sea view from 250FF. Its restaurant has a good value 88FF regional *menu* featuring *figatelli* (a rich liver sausage).

Getting There & Away

Two daily buses from Ota (37km north-east) via Porto (32km north) to Ajaccio (50km south) stop in front of the post office.

PIANA

• pop 500 ✉ 20115 alt 438m

The hillside village of Piana affords breathtaking views of the Golfe de Porto and the soaring mountains of the interior. It is a good base for hikes to nearby Les Calanche, and has somehow managed to remain admirably untouched by the hordes of summer tourists it attracts. The eve of Good Friday is marked by La Granitola, a traditional festival during which hooded penitents, bearing crosses and dressed in white gowns and blue capes, parade through the village to Piana's Église Saint Marie.

The village's *syndicat d'initiative* (tourist office; ☎ 04 95 27 80 28) has hiking information and distributes the free leaflet *Piana Randonnées*. Nearby beaches include the **Anse de Ficajola**, right below Piana and reached by an extremely narrow 4km road (signposted 'Marine de Figajola'), and **Plage d'Arone**, 11km south-west of town via the scenic D824. From the D824, a trail leads westward to the tower-topped **Capo Rosso**. From the D81, opposite the Hôtel Le Scandola at the south end of Piana, a mountain road leads up to the **Belvédère de Saliccio** from where there are staggering views of the village and Les Calanche.

Places to Stay & Eat

The one star, 17 room ***Hôtel Continental*** (☎ 04 95 27 82 02), 100m up the hill from the church, has spacious doubles with washbasin and bidet for 180 to 250FF (270FF with shower or bath and toilet). It is open from April to September. On the D81 towards Cargèse, the two star ***Hôtel Le Scandola*** (☎ 04 95 27 80 07; fax 04 95 27 83 88) has doubles/triples with balconies for around 250/300FF. It is open from April to mid-October.

Below the D81 on the other side of the village, the grand old 30 room ***Hôtel des Roches Rouges*** (☎ 04 95 27 81 81; fax 04 95 27 81 76) dating from 1912 is one of Corsica's most romantic places to stay. Spacious and renovated double rooms with a view of Les Calanche, Piana village and the Anse de Ficajola and with shower, toilet and balcony cost 320FF (340FF for half-board). The ground-floor restaurant, which serves a wonderful 150FF regional *menu*, is a historic monument. The 'Red Rocks' is open from April to mid-November.

Getting There & Away

Buses between Porto and Ajaccio stop near the church and the post office.

LES CALANCHE

The most stunning natural sight in Corsica is Les Calanche (Les Calanques de Piana in French), a spectacular mountain landscape of red, orange and grey granite cliffs, spikes and outcrops. Created by the rock's uneven response to the forces of erosion, these amazing formations, some of which resemble animals, buildings and the like, have been made even more intricate by *taffoni*, spherical cavities carved out of the rock face by the dissolving action of water. Less rocky areas support pine and chestnut forests, whose dark green foliage contrasts dramatically with the coloured granite.

The multicoloured spires of Les Calanche tower 300m above the deep blue waters of the sea below. When it's clear, the D81 and various hiking paths afford breathtaking views.

Calanche is the plural of the Corsican word *calanca* and is pronounced 'kah-LAHNK', the same as its French equivalent, *calanques*.

Hiking

Piana's syndicat d'initiative (see the previous section) has information on hiking in the region. About 8km south-west of Porto on the D81 is **Le Chalet des Roches Bleues**, a modern wood and granite souvenir shop that serves as a useful landmark. Four trails begin in the immediate vicinity:

La Corniche A steep, forested 40 minute walk which leads up to a fantastic view of Les Calanche. It begins on the inland side of the bridge situated 50m down the hill (towards Porto) from the chalet. Trail markings are yellow.

Chemin du Château Fort A one hour trail to a solid block of rock that looks like a fortress and affords stunning views of the Golfe de Porto. It begins 700m down the hill (towards Porto) from the chalet; the trailhead is on the seaward side of the D81 to the right of the rock that looks like a *tête de chien* (dog's head). Trail markings are blue.

Chemin des Muletiers The steep, one hour Mule-Drivers' Trail begins 400m up the hill (towards Piana) from the chalet on the inland side of the D81; the trailhead is 15m down the hill from the roadside sanctuary dedicated to the Virgin Mary. Trail markings are blue.

La Châtaigneraie A three hour circuit through chestnut groves that begins 25m up the hill and across the road from the chalet.

Getting There & Away

Buses from Ajaccio to Porto will drop you off at the chalet.

PORTO

• pop 460 ✉ 20150

The pleasant (if somewhat purpose-built and touristy) seaside village of Porto (Portu in Corsican), nestled among huge outcrops of red granite and renowned for its sunsets, is an excellent base for exploring some of Corsica's most beautiful sights, including Les Calanche, Girolata and the Gorges de Spelunca.

Information

The tourist office (☎ 04 95 26 10 55; fax 04 95 26 14 25), built into the wall separating the marina's upper and lower parking lots, has lots of hiking information, some of it free and in English. It is open year-round from 9.30 am to noon and 2.30 to 6.30 pm (closed on weekends). July and August hours are 9 am to 8 pm (closed Sunday).

The Parc Naturel Régional de Corse has an office inside the Maison de Porto (☎ 04 95 26 15 14), just around the corner from the tourist office.

Things to See & Do

The overdeveloped **marina** is surrounded by hotels and places to eat. A short trail leads to a **Genoese tower** (10FF), open between April and October from 10 am to 6 pm. From the marina, the estuary of the Porto River is behind the line of buildings to the left as you face the sea. On the far side of the river, reached by a footbridge, there's a modest **beach** of grey gravel and sand, a small harbour and one of Corsica's best known **eucalyptus groves**.

Boat Excursions

From mid-April to October, the Compagnie des Promenades en Mer (☎ 04 95 26 15 16) has excursions (by regular or glass-bottomed boat; 170FF) to the fishing village of **Girolata**. The boats sail by the **Réserve Naturelle de Scandola** (Scandola Nature Reserve), home to numerous rare birds and listed as a UNESCO World Heritage List site by for its unique seagull and fishing eagles populations. It may be possible to catch another boat from Girolata to Calvi – see Boat Excursions in the Calvi section. From Porto there are also excursions to Les Calanche (80FF). Ask at the tourist office for booking information.

Motorboats and zodiacs can be rented along the Porto River estuary near the footbridge. On the beach, Porto Locations (☎ 04 95 26 10 13) rents out pedal boats for 40/60FF per half-hour/hour. Canyoning enthusiasts should contact Corsica Treck (☎ 04 95 26 14 49; fax 04 95 26 12 49) based at Camping Les Oliviers.

Places to Stay

Camping The pricey ***Camping Les Oliviers*** (☎ 04 95 26 14 49; fax 04 95 26 12 49) is a few hundred metres down the D81, next to the bridge over the Porto River, on an olive-treed hillside. It is open from April to early November.

The friendly ***Funtana al' Ora*** (☎ 04 95 26 11 65 or ☎ 04 95 26 15 48; fax 04 95 26 15 48), 2km east of Porto on the road to Évisa, charges 28FF per person and 11FF for a tent or car. It is open from May to November.

Hotels On the left-hand side of the marina (as you face the sea), the one star, 10 room ***Hôtel du Golfe*** (☎ 04 95 26 13 33) provides shower-equipped doubles without/with toilet for 160/180FF and triples for 250FF. Prices rise by 20FF per person in July and August.

Also at the marina, the two star ***Hôtel Monte Rosso*** (☎ 04 95 26 11 50; fax 04 95 26 12 30), in the third building from the Genoese tower, has decent doubles with bath and toilet for 240FF (300FF in July and August). It is open from April to mid-October. ***Hôtel Le Riviera*** (☎ 04 95 26 13 61; fax 04 95 26 10 15) next door has doubles/triples with shower and toilet from 160/200FF.

On the east edge of town towards Ota, the ***Hôtel Le Maquis*** (☎ 04 95 26 12 19; fax 04 95 26 12 77) has singles/doubles from 130/180FF. Rooms for two in the less attractive ***Hôtel Colombo*** (☎ 04 95 26 10 14) next door start at 160FF. Both are open May to September.

Getting There & Around

Bus Autocars SAIB (☎ 04 95 22 41 99) has two buses a day linking Porto and nearby Ota with Ajaccio (2½ hours). From mid-May to mid-October the company also runs a return bus from Porto to Calvi (three hours).

Car & Motorcycle From May to late September, two and four wheels can be hired from Porto Locations (☎/fax 04 95 26 10 13), across the street from the supermarket down the hill from the pharmacy. Daily rates for a scooter are 300FF.

Bicycle Porto Locations (see Boat Excursions) rents mountain bikes for 42FF a day.

OTA

• pop 200 ✉ 20150 alt 310m

Ota, a tiny village of stone houses perched above the Porto River, is 5km inland from Porto. It is blessed with some of the best budget accommodation on the island and is not far from the trail climbing up to the celebrated Gorges de Spelunca.

Hiking

The **Pont de Pianella**, an especially graceful Genoese bridge, is just under 2km east of Ota along the D124. About 300m away, the two single-lane Ponts d'Ota span the Onca and Aïtone rivers, which meet here to form the Porto River.

The trail (once a mule track) up the **Gorges de Spelunca** to Évisa (three hours) via the **Pont de Zaglia** (another Genoese bridge) begins on the left bank of the Aïtone (ie on the far side of the farther of the two Ponts d'Ota if you're coming from Ota). The trail markings are orange. If you'd like to walk one way and ride the other, Gîte d'Étape Chez Félix (see Places to Stay & Eat) can supply a taxi for 200FF one way.

The Mare è Monti trail from Cargèse to Calenzana passes through Ota.

Places to Stay & Eat

The ***Gîte d'Étape Chez Marie*** (☎ 04 95 26 11 37) is open year-round and charges 60FF for a bed in a spanking-clean and very modern dormitory room and 120FF for a double. There is a large, pleasant communal kitchen too. Reception is in ***Bar-Restaurant Chez Marie***.

Gîte d'Étape Chez Félix (☎ 04 95 26 12 92) has beds in four and six-person rooms for 50FF. Doubles/triples with shower and toilet cost 200/240FF. Kitchen facilities are available. The reception is in the ***Restaurant Chez Félix*** on Place de la Fontaine.

Both restaurants offer wholesome Corsican home cooking aimed primarily at a backpacking budget.

Getting There & Away

Place de la Fontaine in Ota, 5km east of Porto's pharmacy via the D124, is linked to both Porto and Ajaccio by a bus in the morning and a minibus in the afternoon (no service on Sunday and holidays except July to mid-September).

ÉVISA

• pop 250 ✉ 20126 alt 830m

Surrounded by chestnut groves (*les châtaigneraies*), the peaceful highland village of Évisa – between the Gorges de Spelunca and the majestic Forêt d'Aïtone – is something of a hill station, with fresh, crisp mountain air and a wealth of worthy walking trails.

Chestnut Bread & Beer

The Corsicans have been planting and tending *châtaigniers* (chestnut trees) since the 16th century at least, when the island's Genoese rulers started requisitioning Corsica's grain crop for use back home. The tree became known as *l'arbre à pain* (the bread tree) because of the many uses the Corsicans found for chestnut flour (*farine de châtaigne*). These days the flour is primarily used to make pastries.

The meat of pigs raised on chestnuts is famous for its flavour. Other chestnutty delights worth a nibble include *falculelli* (pressed and frittered Corsican *brocciu* cheese served on a chestnut leaf), *beignets au brocciu à la farine de châtaigne* (brocciu cheese frittered in chestnut flour), *delice à la châtaigne* (Corsican chestnut cake) and, last but not least, *bière à la châtaigne* (chestnut beer).

Forêt d'Aïtone

The Aïtone Forest (800 to 2057m), which surrounds the upper reaches of the Aïtone River, has some of Corsica's most impressive stands of laricio pines, perfectly straight trees rising up to 60m tall and two centuries old. This forest once provided beams and masts for Genoese ships. The forest begins a few kilometres east of Évisa and stretches to the 1477m-high **Col de Vergio** (Bocca di Verghju).

The **Cascades d'Aïtone** (Aïtone Falls) are 4km north-east of Évisa via the D84 and a half-kilometre footpath.

Places to Stay

Hostel The *gîte d'étape* (☎ 04 95 26 21 88), open from early April to October, charges 60FF for a bed. From the post office, follow the concrete path down the stairs to the road, turn left, and walk 100m to the white building with brown shutters.

Hotels Pleasant doubles with bath/shower go for 200/180FF at the aptly named ***La Châtaigneraie*** (Chestnut Grove; ☎ 04 95 26 24 47), on the western edge of the village. In the village centre, the ***Hôtel Restaurant du Centre*** (☎ 04 95 26 20 92) has doubles with shower and toilet for 200FF.

The two star ***Hôtel L'Aïtone*** (☎ 04 95 26 20 04; fax 04 95 26 24 18), closed in mid-November and mid-January, is on the upper outskirts of town. Rustic shower-equipped rooms without/with toilet cost between 180/220FF and 200/320FF, depending on the season. Don't miss out on a swim in the pool while you're here; the hotel restaurant offers a fantastic panorama stretching as far as the Golfe de Porto.

Getting There & Away

The D84, which links Porto with Évisa, Vergio and Corte, is one of the most spectacular roads in Corsica – and one of the most frightening to drive.

There are two buses a day from Évisa to Ajaccio. A taxi (☎ 04 95 26 20 22) to Ota costs around 200FF.

South of Ajaccio

FILITOSA

Corsica's most important prehistoric site, Filitosa (☎ 04 95 74 00 91) is about 25km north-west of Propriano; take the N196 and then follow the D57 for 9km. Inhabited from 5850 BC until the Roman period, its fortifications, buildings, megaliths and statue-menhirs – armed with swords and daggers – have been the subject of intense study since their accidental discovery in 1946. The hilltop site, shaded by olive trees (some up to 1000 years old), and the small **museum** are open daily from 8 am until sunset. Admission is 25FF.

The syndicat d'initiative (☎ 04 95 74 07 64), on your right as you approach the site, has hiking information. Hours are 1 to 5 pm.

SARTÈNE

• pop 3500 ✉ 20100

The sombre and introverted hillside town of Sartène (Sartè in Corsican), built mostly of grey stone, has long been suspicious of outsiders, and for good reason. In 1583, pirates from Algiers raided the town and carried 400 local people off into slavery in North Africa; such raids did not end until the 18th century. The town was long notorious for its banditry and bloody vendettas, and in the early 19th century a violent struggle between rival landowners deteriorated into house-to-house fighting, forcing most of the population to flee. Today's Sartène, whose unofficial slogan is 'the most Corsican of Corsica's towns' is a fascinating place to spend half a day.

Orientation & Information

From Place de la Libération, Sartène's main square, Cours Sœur Amélie leads south up the hill, while Cours Général de Gaulle heads north down the hill. The old Santa Anna quarter is north of Place de la Libération.

The tourist office (☎ 04 95 77 15 40), 6 Rue Borgo, is 30m up the hill from Place de la Libération. It's open weekdays from 9 am to noon and 3 to 6 pm. In July and August it is open until 7 pm (closed Sunday); from October to April it is open mornings only.

Procession du Catenacciu

On the eve of Good Friday, the people of Sartène perform an ancient ritual known as the Procession du Catenacciu. In a colourful re-enactment of the Passion, the Catenacciu (literally, 'the chained one'), an anonymous, barefoot penitent covered from head to foot in a red robe and cowl, carries a huge cross through the town while dragging a heavy chain shackled to the ankle. The Catenacciu is followed by a procession of other penitents, members of the clergy and local notables. As the chain clatters by on the cobblestones, local people look on in great (if rather humourless) excitement. Needless to say, everyone is curious to find out the identity of the penitent, who is selected by the parish priest from among applicants seeking to expiate a grave sin.

Things to See

Near the WWI **memorial** in the middle of Place de la Libération is the granite **Église Sainte Marie**. Inside, on the wall to the left of the entrance, hang the 32kg oak cross and 14kg chain that are carried and dragged by the red-robed penitent in the annual Procession du Catenacciu (see the boxed text 'Procession du Catenacciu'). The baroque marble altar was crafted in Italy in the 17th century. The arch through the middle of the **Hôtel de Ville** (formerly the Palace of the Genoese Governors), on the north side of the square, leads to the **Santa Anna quarter**, a residential neighbourhood of austere, grey-granite houses and sombre, almost medieval alleyways and staircases.

The **Musée de la Préhistoire Corse** (Museum of Corsican Prehistory; ☎ 04 95 77 01 09), housed in a three storey stone building built as a prison in the 1840s, is open from 10 am to noon and 2 to 5 pm (6 pm from mid-June to mid-September; closed on weekends). Admission is 10/5FF for adults/children and students.

Places to Stay

Camping U Farrandu (☎ 04 95 73 41 69), open year-round, is in a quiet, shaded gully a few kilometres towards Ajaccio. Adults pay 40FF.

The only hotel in central Sartène is the two star ***Hôtel Les Roches*** (☎ 04 95 77 07 61; fax 04 95 77 19 93), off Ave Jean Jaurès just below the Santa Anna quarter. From April to October, singles/doubles with shower and toilet cost 240/260FF; a valley view costs a little more. Nightly rates rise in July and August.

A very pleasant alternative is the two star, 31 room ***Hôtel La Villa Piana*** (☎ 04 95 77 07 04; fax 04 95 73 45 65), part of the Logis de France chain on the N196 about 1.5km towards Ajaccio and Propiano. The cheapest doubles with shower and toilet cost 220FF, although those with a private terrace balcony and valley view for 330FF are worth the splurge. Guests have free use of the luxury swimming pool on the hillside above the hotel. Villa Piana is open from April to mid-October.

Also pool-equipped is the next door ***Hôtel Rossi*** (☎ 04 95 77 01 80; fax 04 95 77 09 58), which has doubles with shower from 230/265FF in the low/high season.

Places to Eat

Restaurants Sartène's top eating spot is the small and simple ***Aux Gourmets*** (☎ 04 95 77 16 08), 10 Cours Sœur Amélie. It not only serves delicious Corsican specialities such as courgettes stuffed with *brocciu frais* (a soft white ewe's milk cheese unique to Corsica, made between October and June), but it is also excellent value, with *menus* from 78FF upward.

La Chaumière (☎ 04 95 77 07 13), another Corsican restaurant at 39 Rue Médecin-Capitaine Louis Bénédetti (up the hill from the tourist office), has a *menu* for 90FF. Several other Corsican restaurants can be found in the Santa Anna quarter. Café-filled Place de la Libération is the perfect place in summer to munch a light snack and watch the world go by.

The top place in town to dine for that ultimate (and pricey) treat is the ***Auberge***

Santa Barbara (☎ 04 95 77 09 06), opposite La Villa Piana on the Route de Propriano.

Self-Catering Wines from the Sartène area, sold straight from 300L barrels (bring your own container), are available from ***La Cave Sartenaise***, an old-time wine shop on the ground floor of the Hôtel de Ville. ***Épicerie Bruschini***, 12 Cours Général de Gaulle, is an old-fashioned grocery.

Getting There & Away

Sartène, on the bus line linking Ajaccio (86km) with Bonifacio (53km), is served by at least two buses in each direction; Sunday buses only run in July and August.

Buses operated by Eurocorse stop at the Ollandini travel agency (☎ 04 95 77 18 41), Cours Gabriel Péri (near the bottom of Cours Sœur Amélie). Buses run by Ricci (☎ 04 95 51 08 19) stop at Bar Le Cyrnos (☎ 04 95 77 11 22), 14 Cours Général de Gaulle.

BONIFACIO

• pop 2700 ✉ 20169

The Citadelle of Bonifacio (Bunifaziu in Corsican) sits 70m above the turquoise waters of the Mediterranean atop a long, narrow and eminently defensible promontory sometimes referred to as 'Corsica's Gibraltar'.

On all sides, white limestone cliffs sculpted by the wind and the waves – topped in places with precariously perched, multistorey apartment houses – drop almost vertically to the sea. The north side of the promontory looks out on Bonifacio Sound (Goulet de Bonifacio), a 1.5km-long fjord only 100 to 150m wide, while the citadel's southern ramparts afford views of the coast of Sardinia (Sardaigne in French), 12km to the south across the Strait of Bonifacio (Bouches de Bonifacio). Not surprisingly, the city is overflowing with tourists and the shops that cater to them.

Given the geographical details supplied by Homer about Ulysses' encounter with the cannibalistic Laestrygonians, it is possible that this episode of the *Odyssey* was set in Bonifacio Sound.

Orientation

Bonifacio consists of two main areas: the marina, in the south-eastern corner of Bonifacio Sound, and the Citadelle – also known as the Vieille Ville (old city) or the Ville Haute (upper city) – which occupies the middle section of the 250m-wide promontory.

The Citadelle, linked to the marina by Ave Charles de Gaulle, has three gates: Porte de Gênes, open only to pedestrians; Porte de France, a one-way exit for cars (with a nearby pedestrian exit); and the entrance-only road under Fort Saint Nicolas that ends up at the Foreign Legion monument.

The ferry port is below the Citadelle on the southern side of Bonifacio Sound.

Information

Tourist Office In the Citadelle, the tourist office (☎ 04 95 73 11 88; fax 04 95 73 14 97; www.planetepc.fr/bonifacio), across the street from the Foreign Legion monument on Place de l'Europe, is open from 9 am to 12.30 pm and 1.30 to 5.30 pm (closed on weekends). In May and June it's open from 9 or 10 am to noon and 2 to 6 pm (until 4 pm on Saturday; closed Sunday). In July and August it's open from 9 am to 8 pm.

Money The Société Générale, outside the Citadelle at 38 Rue Saint Érasme, has poor rates and a 25FF commission (closed on weekends). In summer, there are several exchange bureaus along the marina.

Post In the Citadelle, the post office at Place Carrega is open from 9 am to noon and 2 to 5 pm (Saturday until noon; closed Sunday). From July to mid-September, weekday hours are 8.30 am to 6 pm.

Citadelle

Bonifacio Sound is linked to the Citadelle via two sets of stairs. One – known as Montée Rastello and, farther up, Montée Saint Roch – links Rue Saint Érasme with Porte de Gênes. The other one connects the ferry port with the Porte de France.

The old city has something of a medieval ambience, in part because of the cramped

BONIFACIO

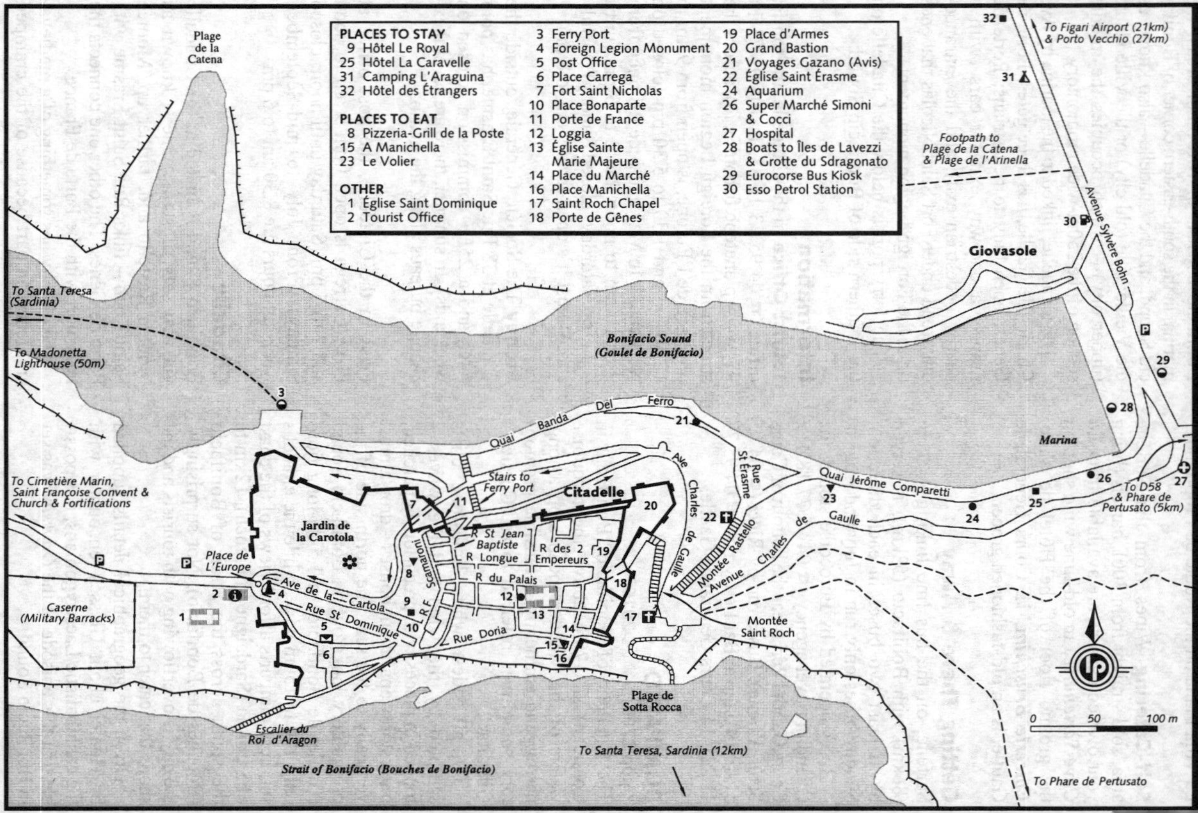
PLACES TO STAY
9 Hôtel Le Royal
25 Hôtel La Caravelle
31 Camping L'Araguina
32 Hôtel des Étrangers
PLACES TO EAT
8 Pizzeria-Grill de la Poste
15 A Manichella
23 Le Volier
OTHER
1 Église Saint Dominique
2 Tourist Office
3 Ferry Port
4 Foreign Legion Monument
5 Post Office
6 Place Carrega
7 Fort Saint Nicholas
10 Place Bonaparte
11 Porte de France
12 Loggia
13 Église Sainte Marie Majeure
14 Place du Marché
16 Place Manichella
17 Saint Roch Chapel
18 Porte de Gênes
19 Place d'Armes
20 Grand Bastion
21 Voyages Gazano (Avis)
22 Église Saint Érasme
24 Aquarium
26 Super Marché Simoni & Cocci
27 Hospital
28 Boats to Îles de Lavezzi & Grotte du Sdragonato
29 Eurocorse Bus Kiosk
30 Esso Petrol Station
Plage de la Catena
To Santa Teresa (Sardinia)
To Madonetta Lighthouse (50m)
Bonifacio Sound (Goulet de Bonifacio)
To Figari Airport (21km) & Porto Vecchio (27km)
Footpath to Plage de la Catena & Plage de l'Arinella
Avenue Sylvère Bohn
Giovasole
Marina
Quai Banda Del Ferro
Stairs to Ferry Port
Citadelle
To Cimetière Marin, Saint Françoise Convent & Church & Fortifications
Jardin de la Carotola
Place de L'Europe
Ave de la Cartola
Rue St Dominique
Caserne (Military Barracks)
R St Jean Baptiste
R des 2 Empereurs
R Longue
R du Palais
Scamaroni
R F
Rue Doria
Ave Charles de Gaulle
Rue St Érasme
Montée Rastello
Avenue Charles de Gaulle
Quai Jérôme Comparetti
Montée Saint Roch
To D58 & Phare de Pertusato (5km)
Plage de Sotta Rocca
Escalier du Roi d'Aragon
To Santa Teresa, Sardinia (12km)
Strait of Bonifacio (Bouches de Bonifacio)
To Phare de Pertusato
0
50
100 m

alleyways, which are lined with tall, narrow stone houses. The flying buttresses overhead carry rainwater to cisterns. **Rue des Deux Empereurs** is aptly named because Charles V and Napoleon once slept in the houses at Nos 4 and 7 respectively. Charles V spent three days in Bonifacio on his way to Algiers in 1541, while Lieutenant Colonel Bonaparte was based here for several months in early 1793 while planning an expedition to Sardinia.

Église Sainte Marie Majeure, a Romanesque structure built in the 14th century but significantly modified later, is known for its square campanile and its **loggia** (roofed porch), under which is a large communal **cistern**, a vital asset in time of siege. The cistern is now used as a conference hall. The marble altar inside dates from the early 17th century.

The impressive **Porte de Gênes**, reached by a drawbridge dating from 1598, was the only entrance to the Citadelle until the Porte de France was built in 1854. A visit to the **Grand Bastion**, above the Porte de Gênes, costs 10FF; it's open from April to mid-October. There are great sea views from nearby **Place du Marché** and **Place Manichella**. The two holes in the ground topped by twin glass pyramids in the centre of Place Manichella were used during the 13th century to store grain, salted meats and other food supplies to feed the town's inhabitants in case of siege.

From the south-western corner of the Citadelle, the **Escalier du Roi d'Aragon** (Staircase of the King of Aragon), whose 187 steps were built, according to legend, by Aragonese troops during the siege of 1420, leads down the cliff. Unless it's windy or stormy, the staircase (10FF) can be visited from June to September.

The road up to the Citadelle enters the old city next to the **Monument de la Légion Étrangère** (Foreign Legion Monument), which originally stood in the Algerian village of Saida but was relocated to Bonifacio in 1963 when Algeria achieved independence and part of the Foreign Legion was transferred from Algeria to Bonifacio.

West of the Citadelle

The rather desolate and derelict plateau at the western end of the promontory is worth a wander, if only for the view. The round towers are all that remain of Bonifacio's erstwhile windmills. The simple **Église Saint Dominique**, built by the Dominicans between 1270 and 1343, is one of the only Gothic churches on Corsica. Farther west you pass the **caserne** (barracks), which served as a Foreign Legion base from 1963 until the 1980s. Today the barracks are only occupied by security guards (ie no military personnel). At the far-western tip of the plateau, just before the concrete fortifications, a neighbourhood of family crypts in a hotchpotch of architectural styles.

Bread of the Dead & Other Treats

Bonifacio's pastry speciality is *paides morts*, a nut and raisin bread which delightfully translates as 'bread of the dead'. Other sweet Corsican delights include *fougazi* (big, flat, sugar-covered, aniseed-flavoured biscuits), *canistrelli* (sugar-crusted biscuits, often flavoured with lemon, almonds or even white wine), *canistrone* (cheese tarts) and *moustachole* (bread with big sugar crystals on top).

In the Citadelle, all these breads are baked at ***Boulangerie-Pâtisserie Faby***, 4 Rue Saint Jean Baptiste, open daily from 8 am to 12.30 pm and 4 to 7 pm (8 pm in July and August, when there's no midday closure). At the marina, try ***Boulangerie-Pâtisserie Michel Sorba***, 1-3 Rue Saint Érasme, which is open from 8 am to 12.30 pm and 4.30 to 7 pm (closed Sunday afternoon and Monday); in July and August, it's open daily from 6 am to 8 pm.

Beaches

To get to **Plage de Sotta Rocca**, a small bit of rocky coast below the south-east corner of the Citadelle, walk down the steps that lead down the hill from the hairpin curve on Ave Charles de Gaulle.

There are several sandy coves on the north side of Bonifacio Sound, including **Plage de la Catena** and **Plage de l'Arinella**. By foot follow the trail that begins on Ave Sylvère Bohn a bit up the hill from the Esso petrol station.

Walks

The **Phare de Pertusato**, a lighthouse several kilometres south-east of the Citadelle on Capo Pertusato (Cape Pertusato), can be reached on foot along the 45 minute clifftop path that begins at the hairpin curve on Ave Charles de Gaulle. By car, take the first right as you head east out of town on the D58.

Boat Excursions

From June to September, marina-based Vedettes Christina (☎ 04 95 73 13 15) and a bunch of other companies run trips to the **Îles de Lavezzi**, an island nature reserve where you can swim and picnic etc; tickets cost around 100FF (be sure to bargain!). The company also offers one-hour excursions to the **Grotte du Sdragonato**, whose roof is pierced by a hole that is said to resemble a backwards silhouette of Corsica.

Places to Stay

Camping Shaded by olive trees, ***Camping L'Araguina*** (☎ 04 95 73 02 96) is 400m north of the marina on Ave Sylvère Bohn and open from mid-March to October. It charges 31/34FF per person in the low/high season, plus 11FF for a tent and 11FF to park a car.

Hotels The 32 room ***Hôtel des Étrangers*** (☎ 04 95 73 01 09; fax 04 95 73 16 97), Ave Sylvère Bohn, 500m north of the marina, is open from early April to October. Doubles with shower and toilet cost 220FF (280 to 390FF from July to September).

In the Citadelle, the two star ***Hôtel Le Royal*** (☎ 04 95 73 00 51; fax 04 95 73 04 68), Rue Fred Scamaroni, has singles/doubles for 190/250FF from October to April; prices double in July and August. At the marina, the three star ***Hôtel La Caravelle*** (☎ 04 95 73 00 03; fax 04 95 73 00 41), 35 Quai Jérôme Comparetti, has doubles for 450 to 750FF (including breakfast). It is open from April to mid-October.

Places to Eat

Restaurants In the Citadelle, the ***Pizzeria-Grill de la Poste*** (☎ 04 95 73 13 31), 5 Rue Fred Scamaroni, has Corsican dishes as well as pizza and pasta (45 to 50FF).

There are lots of touristy restaurants along the south side of the marina: the waterside ***Le Volier*** (☎ 04 95 73 07 06), Quai Jérôme Comparetti, has a tempting 'island of beauty' *menu* for 110FF, a sea fish *menu* for 190FF and a good value 'Citadelle' 65FF *menu*.

In the Citadelle, ***A Manichella*** (☎ 04 95 73 12 75), Place du Marché, is a pleasant snack bar offering light lunches and fine panoramic sea views.

Self-Catering At the marina, the ***Super Marché Simoni***, 93 Quai Jérôme Comparetti, is open from 8 am to 12.30 pm and 3.30 to 7.30 pm (closed Sunday afternoon). The ***Cocci*** supermarket next door has a fresh bakery counter.

Local products, including a mouthwatering range of *saucisses Corse* (Corsican sausages), can be found in abundance at *L'Aliméa*, Quai Jérôme Comparetti.

Getting There & Away

Air Bonifacio's international airport, Aéroport de Figari (☎ 04 95 71 10 10), is 21km north of town.

Bus Eurocorse (☎ 04 95 70 13 83 in Porto Vecchio) has buses to Ajaccio via Sartène. To get to Bastia, change buses at Porto Vecchio which is served by two daily buses (four in summer). All buses leave from the parking lot next to the Eurocorse kiosk (open in summer only).

Car Voyages Gazano (☎ 04 95 73 01 28), 13 Quai Banda Del Ferro, is an agent for Avis. Hertz (☎ 04 95 73 06 41) has an office on the same quay.

Boat Up until the 1960s, the only way to get your car across the Strait of Bonifacio to Sardinia was to have it winched aboard a fishing boat. Thankfully, things are much simpler these days. Saremar (☎ 04 95 73 00 96 in Bonifacio; ☎ 0789-754 156 in Santa Teresa) and Moby Lines (☎ 04 95 73 00 29 in Bonifacio; ☎ 0789-751 449 in Santa Teresa) both offer a daily car ferry service year-round from Bonifacio's ferry port to Santa Teresa (50 minutes; two to seven a day). Both lines charge adults 58 to 70FF depending on the date, including a 30FF regional tax. Small cars cost 140 to 194FF.

Bastia Area

BASTIA

• pop 37,800 ✉ 20200

Bustling Bastia is Corsica's main centre of business and commerce, and has an Italian atmosphere found nowhere else on the island. It was the seat of the Genoese governors of Corsica from the 15th century, when construction of the *bastiglia* (fortress), from which the city's name comes, was begun. You can easily spend a day wandering around, the Vieux Port being Bastia's definite highlight; but most visitors move on pretty quickly.

If you have a car, Bastia is a convenient base for exploring Cap Corse, the 40km-long peninsula north of Bastia.

Orientation

The focal point of the modern city centre is 300m-long Place Saint Nicolas. Bastia's principal thoroughfares are the east-west oriented Ave Maréchal Sebastiani, which links the ferry terminal with the train station, and the north-south oriented Blvd Paoli, a fashionable shopping street one block west of Place Saint Nicolas.

South of Place Saint Nicolas are the town's three older neighbourhoods: Terra Vecchia (which is centred around Place de l'Hôtel de Ville, also known as Place du Marché), the Vieux Port (old port) and the Citadelle.

Information

Tourist Office The tourist office (☎ 04 95 55 96 85; fax 04 95 55 96 00), Place Saint Nicolas, is open from 8 am to noon and 2 to 6 pm (closed on Sunday afternoon). In July and August it's open daily from 8 am to 8 pm.

Money The Banque de France, 2bis Cours Henri Pierangeli, is open from 8.45 am to 12.10 pm and 1.55 to 3.30 pm (closed on weekends). Commercial banks are dotted along the west side of Place Saint Nicolas, along Rue César Campinchi and Rue du Conventionnel Salicetti.

Post The post office on Ave Maréchal Sebastiani is open weekdays from 8 am to 7 pm (Saturday until noon). Exchange services are available.

Bookshop Hiking maps and topoguides are available at Librairie Jean-Patrice Marzocchi (☎ 04 95 34 02 95), 2 Rue du Conventionnel Salicetti, open from 9.30 am to noon and 2.30 to 7 pm (closed all day Sunday and Monday morning).

Laundry Le Lavoir du Port, in the parking lot at the northern end of Rue du Commandant Luce de Casabianca, is open daily from 7 am to 9 pm.

Walking Tour

Lined with palm and plane trees, **Place Saint Nicolas** is an esplanade almost as long as three football pitches, laid out in the late 19th century. There's usually at least one game of *boules* (bowls) being played in the spaces between the war memorial, the bandstand, the statue of Napoleon (dressed as a Roman emperor) and the trees. The west side of the square is lined with shops and cafés.

Just south of Place Saint Nicolas is **Terra Vecchia**, a neighbourhood of old houses (some 18th century), towering tenements and narrow streets. It is centred around the shady

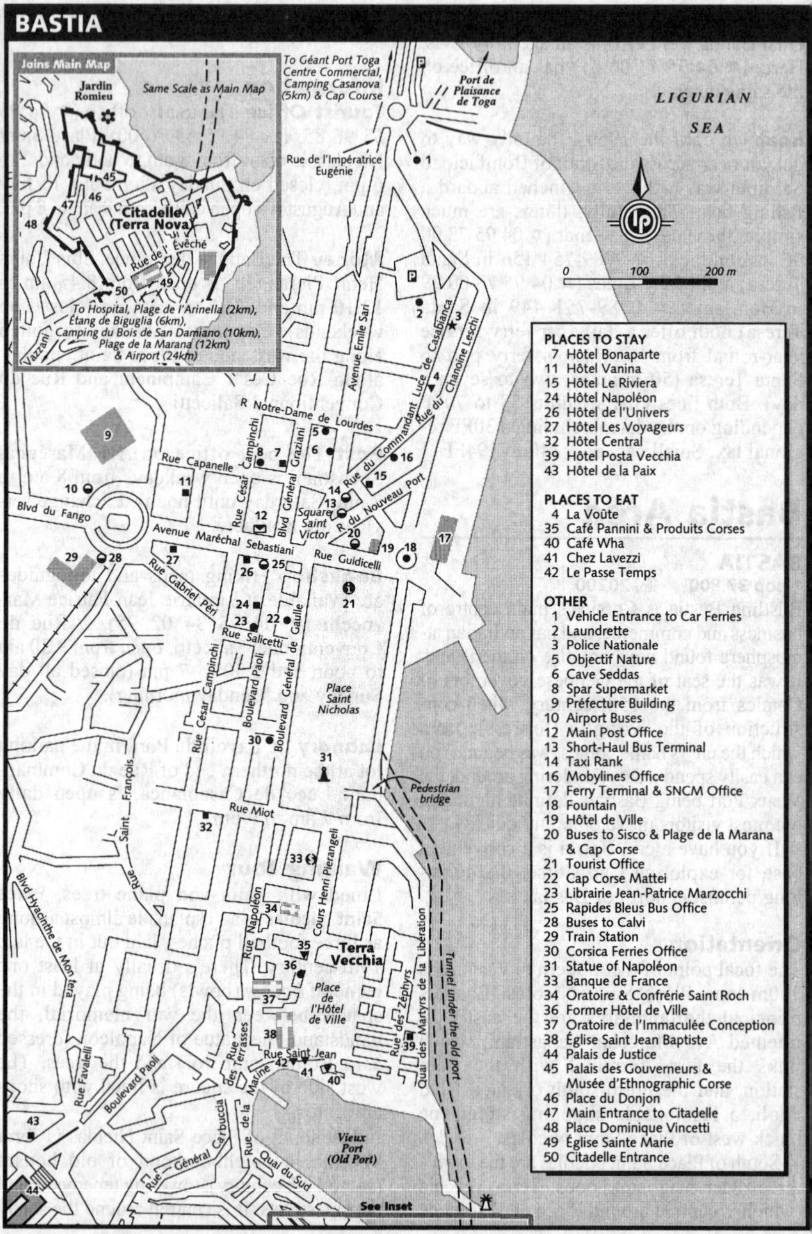
BASTIA
Joins Main Map
Same Scale as Main Map
Jardin Romieu
Citadelle (Terra Nova)
Rue de l'Évêché
To Hospital, Plage de l'Arinella (2km), Étang de Biguglia (6km), Camping du Bois de San Damiano (10km), Plage de la Marana (12km) & Airport (24km)
Vazzani
To Géant Port Toga Centre Commercial, Camping Casanova (5km) & Cap Course
Port de Plaisance de Toga
LIGURIAN SEA
0
100
200 m
Rue de l'Impératrice Eugénie
Avenue Emile Sari
Rue du Commandant Luce de Casabianca
Rue du Chanoine Leschi
R Notre-Dame de Lourdes
Rue Capanelle
Rue César Campinchi
Blvd Général Graziani
Rue du Nouveau Port
Square Saint Victor
Blvd du Fango
Avenue Maréchal Sebastiani
Rue Guidicelli
Rue Gabriel Péri
Rue Salicetti
Boulevard Paoli
Boulevard Général de Gaulle
Place Saint Nicholas
Rue Saint François
Rue Miot
Pedestrian bridge
Blvd Hyacinthe de Montera
Rue Napoléon
Cours Henri Pierangeli
Terra Vecchia
Place de l'Hôtel de Ville
Rue des Zéphyrs
Quai des Martyrs de la Libération
Tunnel under the old port
Rue Saint Jean
Rue des Terrasses
Rue de la Marine
Rue Favalelli
Rue Général Carbuccia
Quai du Sud
Vieux Port (Old Port)
See Inset
PLACES TO STAY
7 Hôtel Bonaparte
11 Hôtel Vanina
15 Hôtel Le Riviera
24 Hôtel Napoléon
26 Hôtel de l'Univers
27 Hôtel Les Voyageurs
32 Hôtel Central
39 Hôtel Posta Vecchia
43 Hôtel de la Paix
PLACES TO EAT
4 La Voûte
35 Café Pannini & Produits Corses
40 Café Wha
41 Chez Lavezzi
42 Le Passe Temps
OTHER
1 Vehicle Entrance to Car Ferries
2 Laundrette
3 Police Nationale
5 Objectif Nature
6 Cave Seddas
8 Spar Supermarket
9 Préfecture Building
10 Airport Buses
12 Main Post Office
13 Short-Haul Bus Terminal
14 Taxi Rank
16 Mobylines Office
17 Ferry Terminal & SNCM Office
18 Fountain
19 Hôtel de Ville
20 Buses to Sisco & Plage de la Marana & Cap Corse
21 Tourist Office
22 Cap Corse Mattei
23 Librairie Jean-Patrice Marzocchi
25 Rapides Bleus Bus Office
28 Buses to Calvi
29 Train Station
30 Corsica Ferries Office
31 Statue of Napoléon
33 Banque de France
34 Oratoire & Confrérie Saint Roch
36 Former Hôtel de Ville
37 Oratoire de l'Immaculée Conception
38 Église Saint Jean Baptiste
44 Palais de Justice
45 Palais des Gouverneurs & Musée d'Ethnographic Corse
46 Place du Donjon
47 Main Entrance to Citadelle
48 Place Dominique Vincetti
49 Église Sainte Marie
50 Citadelle Entrance

Place de l'Hôtel de Ville, now an open-air marketplace and parking lot. Nearby, opposite 3 Rue Napoléon, is the **Oratoire de l'Immaculée Conception** (Oratory of the Immaculate Conception), construction of which began in the late 16th century; its rich baroque interior decoration is from the 18th century.

On the southern side of Place de l'Hôtel de Ville is the back of **Église Saint Jean Baptiste** (closed after noon on Sunday and holidays), whose classical façade, graced by two towers, overlooks the picturesque, horseshoe-shaped **Vieux Port**. Built in the mid-17th century and redecorated in the 18th century, this church has become Bastia's most recognisable architectural symbol.

The entrance to the Vieux Port is guarded by two beacons. **Jetée du Dragon**, the jetty that leads to the southern (red) beacon, affords great views of the harbour, where pleasure craft mingle with the local fleet of bright blue and white wooden boats.

Farther south still is the **Citadelle**, also known as Terra Nova, built by the Genoese between the 15th and 17th centuries. It can be reached by climbing the stairs through **Jardin Romieu**, the hillside park on the south side of the Vieux Port.

Inside the double gates of the Citadelle, at Place du Donjon, is the mustard-yellow **Palais des Gouverneurs** (Governors' Palace). It houses a rather dusty and dull anthropology museum, called the **Musée d'Ethnographic Corse** (☎ 04 95 31 09 12), and an old **Genoese prison**. It is open from 9 or 10 am to noon and 2 to 6 pm (5 pm on off-season weekends, 7 pm from May to September); there is no midday closure from April to October. Entry costs 15FF (including the prison).

Up the stairs from the courtyard of the Palais des Gouverneurs, the ramparts have been turned into a garden with panoramic views of Bastia and the sea. The **conning tower** you pass on the museum terrace is from the WWII submarine *Casabianca*, which helped Corsica keep contact with Free French forces based in Algeria from 1942 to 1943.

Église Sainte Marie, whose entrance is through the side of the building facing Rue de l'Évêché, was begun in 1495 and served as a cathedral from 1570 to 1801. Its interior ornamentation is in the baroque style. The alleyways around the church can be explored on foot.

Activities

Objectif Nature (☎/fax 04 95 32 54 34), 3 Rue Notre Dame de Lourdes, organises a host of outdoor activities including kayaking expeditions (250FF a day), day and night sea fishing trips (from 350FF per person for groups of six or more), hiking, mountaineering, horse riding (350FF a day including lunch) and diving (180FF for a first-time dive). Its office is open from 9 am to 6 pm (closed Sunday).

Places to Stay

Most of Bastia's hotels are open year-round. The tourist office can provide a comprehensive list of all available accommodation.

Places to Stay – Budget

Camping *Camping Casanova* (☎ 04 95 33 91 42), open mid-May to mid-October, is about 5km north of Bastia in Miomo. Fees are 12/10/24FF for a tent site/parking/per adult. Take the bus to Sisco from opposite the tourist office.

Camping du Bois de San Damiano (☎ 04 95 33 68 02), open April to October, is about 10km south of Bastia. Charges for an adult/tent site/parking are 30/12/12FF. Take the airport bus to get here.

Hotels The one star ***Hôtel Le Riviera*** (☎ 04 95 31 07 16; fax 04 95 34 17 39), 1bis Rue du Nouveau Port, has doubles with shower and toilet for 200/250FF in the low/high season. The family-run and not very friendly ***Hôtel Central*** (☎ 04 95 31 71 12; fax 04 95 31 82 40), 3 Rue Miot, has renovated singles/doubles with shower and toilet from 230/250FF. Singles/doubles/triples with shower and shared toilet start at 220/240/280FF.

One of the most convenient (if insalubrious) hotels in Bastia is the 34 room ***Hôtel*** *de l'Univers* (☎ 04 95 31 03 38), 3 Ave Maréchal Sébastiani. Less-than-spotless singles/doubles/triples cost 150/180/220FF (190/210/250FF with shower, 230/270/310FF with shower and toilet). Decidedly more upmarket is the nearby ***Hôtel Les Voyageurs*** (☎ 04 95 34 90 80; fax 04 95 34 00 65) at No 9 on the same street. Doubles with shower and toilet here start at 250FF. Rooms at the ***Hôtel Vanina*** (☎ 04 95 31 50 25), 1 Rue Carnot (2nd floor), are also good value.

Places to Stay – Mid-Range

The very central ***Hôtel Napoléon*** (☎ 04 95 31 60 30; fax 04 95 31 77 83), 43 Blvd Paoli, has small but comfortable doubles equipped with all the amenities for around 300 to 450FF. Prices rise precipitously from early July to early September. From April to October, the two star, 23 room ***Hôtel Bonaparte*** (☎ 04 95 34 07 10; fax 04 95 32 35 62), 45 Blvd Général Graziani, has doubles with shower and toilet for 250 to 400FF, including breakfast.

Up the hill from the Vieux Port, the two star ***Hôtel de la Paix*** (☎ 04 95 31 06 71; fax 04 95 33 16 95), 1 Blvd Hyacinthe de Montera, has fairly spacious doubles/triples for 350/400FF from late June to mid-September. Prices are marginally lower off season.

Overlooking the sea on Quai des Martyrs de la Libération is the ***Hôtel Posta Vecchia*** (☎ 04 95 32 32 38; fax 04 95 46 07 37), which has excellent value singles/doubles with shower and toilet for 200/240FF. Rates rise 40FF in July and August.

Places to Eat

Restaurants & Cafés Cafés and brasseries line the western side of Place Saint Nicolas. Many more restaurants and cafés can be found along the north side of the Vieux Port, on Quai des Martyrs de la Libération and on Place de l'Hôtel de Ville in Terra Vecchia, where the ***Café Pannini*** on the north-eastern corner of the square is popular for its jumbo sandwiches.

In the new town, ***La Voûte*** (☎ 04 95 32 47 11), 6bis Rue du Commandant Luce de Casabianca, is the most inspiring option, offering some French cuisine but mainly pizzas under brick vaults and on a terrace overlooking the port. Mains cost 65 to 99FF and the *menu* is 125FF.

Thankfully, the Vieux Port area is crammed with small, cosy restaurants which ooze charm. Many boast fabulous port views too, such as the pricey but delicious ***Chez Lavezzi*** (☎ 04 95 31 05 73), 8 Rue Saint Jean, which serves exquisitely presented dishes on its pink waterfront terrace. Expect to pay at least 150FF a head.

Le Passe Temps (☎ 04 95 31 72 13) is another recommended place on the old port's north side. It has *menus* for 130, 150 and 195FF.

For a cheap and cheerful approach, head straight for the fun-loving ***Café Wha*** (☎ 04 95 34 25 79), which also has a terrace facing the water. It serves a range of fast-food Mexican dishes and is always packed.

Self-Catering A bustling ***food market*** is held at Place de l'Hôtel de Ville in Terra Vecchio every morning except Monday. For Corsican wines, look no farther than the richly stocked ***Cave Seddas***, 3 Ave Emile Sari. The local liqueur, Cap Corse, is sold at the atmospheric ***Cap Corse Mattei***, 15 Blvd de Gaulle, which hosts a permanent exhibition on the Corsican aperitif. For honey and chestnut flour try ***Produits Corses***, Place de l'Hôtel de Ville.

There is a large ***Spar*** supermarket, on the corner of Rue César Campinchi and Rue Capanelle. Across from the vehicle entrance to the ferry port, the huge Géant Port Toga Centre Commercial houses a ***Casino*** supermarket.

Getting There & Away

Air The Bastia-Poretta airport (☎ 04 95 54 54 54) is 24km south of the city.

Bus Rapides Bleus (☎ 04 95 31 03 79), 1 Ave Maréchal Sebastiani, has buses to Porto Vecchio and Bonifacio (via Porto Vecchio), and handles tickets for the Eurocorse service to Corte and Ajaccio. The afternoon bus to Calvi run by Les Beaux Voyages

(☎ 04 95 65 02 10) leaves from outside the train station.

Rue du Nouveau Port, north of the tourist office, has been turned into a bus terminal for short-haul buses serving villages south and west of Bastia. Buses to Cap Corse (eg Sisco) leave from Ave Pietri, across the street from the tourist office.

Train The train station (☎ 04 95 32 80 61), Ave Maréchal Sebastiani, is open from 6.30 am to 8 pm; Sunday hours are 7 am to noon and 2 to 7 pm.

Car There are a handful of rental agencies at the airport.

Boat The ferry terminal is at the eastern end of Ave Pietri; the left-luggage office, open from 8 to 11.30 am and 2 to 7 pm, charges 10FF a bag. The port's vehicle entrance is 600m to the north.

The SNCM office (☎ 04 95 54 66 81) inside the main terminal is open from 8 to 11.45 am and 2 to 5.45 pm (Saturday until noon; closed Sunday). Tickets are sold two hours before departure in the Corsica Marittima ticket section of the terminal building.

Moby Lines (☎ 04 95 34 84 94 or ☎ 04 95 34 84 90), 4 Rue du Commandant Luce de Casabianca, is open from 8 am to noon and 2 to 6 pm (until noon Saturday; closed Sunday). The company's bureau in the ferry terminal is open two hours before each sailing.

Corsica Ferries (☎ 04 95 32 95 95), 7 Blvd Général de Gaulle, is open from 8.30 am to noon and 2 to 6.30 pm (closed on Sunday and, except in summer, on Saturday afternoon); there's no midday closure from mid-June to mid-September.

Getting Around

To/From the Airport Municipal buses to the airport (48FF; around 10 a day) depart from the Préfecture building, across the roundabout from the train station. The tourist office has schedules. A taxi to the airport will cost 120 to 180FF.

Bicycle Objectif Nature (see Activities) rents mountain bikes for 100FF a day (80FF per person for groups of four or more). Weekend rental costs 150FF. It is open year-round from 9 am to noon and 2 to 5 pm (closed Sunday).

CAP CORSE

The long, narrow peninsula at Corsica's northern tip stretches about 40km northwards from Bastia. Cap Corse's 15km-wide strip of valleys and mountains (up to 1300m high) affords spectacular views of the sea, particularly along the steep and rocky west coast. Once intensively cultivated, the maquis has now reclaimed areas where grapevines, olive trees and fruit orchards once flourished. Cap Corse can be visited as a car or bus excursion from Bastia; the tourist office has details.

On the east coast, there are sandy beaches at **Marine de Pietracorbara**, about 10km north of **Erbalunga**; and slightly north of **Macinaggio**, a small fishing village near the northern tip of Cap Corse. The west coast has many sandy coves.

ÉTANG DE BIGUGLIA

This 12km-long lagoon, a favourite waterfowl nesting site, is connected to the sea by a narrow neck of water 4km south of Bastia. Two beaches, **Plage de la Marana** and **Plage de Pineto**, are along the 500m-wide peninsula that separates the lagoon from the sea. Plage de la Marana is served by SAB bus No 8, whose main Bastia stop is on the north side of Ave Pietri.

CASTAGNICCIA REGION

La Castagniccia, the mountainous area east of Ponte Leccia and Corte, is known for its chestnut tree forests. In the 18th century, it was the cradle of the Corsican nationalist rebellion against Genoese rule. The nationalist leader Pasquale Paoli was born here in the village of Morosaglia in 1725.

Once the richest area of the island thanks to the chestnut crop and products made from chestnut wood, the hills and mountains – which in the 17th century supported 100 people per sq km – are now dotted with abandoned hamlets.

CORSICA

The North Coast

CALVI

• pop 4800 ✉ 20260

The prosperous citadel town of Calvi sits atop a promontory at the western end of a beach-lined, half-moon-shaped bay. Seaside sunbathers can either admire the iridescent turquoise waters of the Golfe de Calvi or, if they turn around, ponder Monte Cinto (2706m) and its soaring neighbours only 20km inland, snowcapped during all but the hottest months.

In 1794, a British expeditionary fleet assisting Pasquale Paoli's Corsican nationalist forces, who had fallen out with the island's post-Revolutionary government, besieged and bombarded Calvi. In the course of the battle, one Captain Horatio Nelson was wounded by rock splinters and lost the use of his right eye.

Calvi hosts a week-long jazz festival in mid-June.

Orientation

The Citadelle – also known as the Haute Ville (upper city) – is on a rocky promontory north-east of the Basse Ville (lower city). Blvd Wilson, which is the major thoroughfare in the commercial centre, is up the hill from Quai Landry and the marina (*port de plaisance*).

Information

Tourist Offices The tourist office (☎ 04 95 65 16 67; fax 04 95 65 14 09), near the marina on the upper floor of the Capitainerie (harbour master's office), is open from 9 am to noon and 2 to 6 pm (Saturday from 9 am to noon and 2.30 to 6 pm). The syndicat d'initiative kiosk next to the train station is permanently closed.

From mid-June to mid-September, the tourist office has an annexe inside the gate to the Citadelle (closed Saturday afternoon and Sunday).

Money The Crédit Lyonnais, Blvd Wilson, is open until 4.30 pm (closed on weekends). There are several banks and exchange places (mostly seasonal) along Blvd Wilson and Quai Landry.

Post The post office, where Blvd Wilson meets Ave de la République, is open from 8.30 am to 5 pm (Saturday until noon; closed Sunday). Exchange services are available.

Bookshop Topoguides and hiking maps are sold at Hall de la Presse (☎ 04 95 65 05 14), 13 Blvd Wilson.

Citadelle

Set atop an 80m-high granite promontory surrounded by massive Genoese fortifications, the Citadelle affords great views. The town's renowned loyalty to Genoa is recalled by the motto *Civitas Calvi Semper Fidelis* (the city of Calvi, forever faithful), accorded to the town by the Republic of Genoa in 1562 and carved over the gate to the Citadelle.

The imposing **Palais des Gouverneurs** (Governors' Palace) on Place d'Armes was built in the 13th century and enlarged in the mid-16th century. It now serves – under the name Caserne Sampiero – as a barracks and mess hall for officers of the Foreign Legion.

Up the street from Caserne Sampiero is **Église Saint Jean Baptiste**, built in the 13th century and rebuilt in 1570; the main altar dates from the 17th century. The women of the local elite used to sit in the screened boxes, whose grilles served to shelter them from the inquisitive (or lustful) gaze of the rabble. To the right of the altar is *Christ des Miracles*, an ebony statue of Jesus that was paraded around town in 1553 shortly before the besieging Turkish forces fell back. Credited with saving Calvi from the Saracens, the statue has since been the object of great veneration.

In the northern part of the Citadelle, a marble plaque marks the site of the house where, according to local tradition, the Genoese navigator Christopher Columbus was born. The stone boat jutting out of the western citadel wall behind the war memorial on Place Christophe Colomb is also in honour of the great explorer.

Notre Dame de la Serra

This 19th century chapel, whose hilltop perch affords spectacular views of the area, is about 6km south-west of town. To get there, walk up Route de Santore.

Beaches

Calvi's 4km-long beach begins at the marina and stretches east around the Golfe de Calvi. See the following Getting There & Away section for details on Tramways de la Balagne and travelling along the coast.

Boat Excursions

From April to October, Croisières Colombo Line (☎ 04 95 65 32 10; fax 04 95 65 03 40) offers six-hour, glass-bottomed boat excursions (260FF) from Calvi's marina to the seaside hamlets of Galéria and Girolata via the Réserve de Naturelle Scandola. For information on onward travel to Girolata from Porto, see Boat Excursions in the Porto section. The Croisières Colombo Line ticket and reservation office is on Quai Landry.

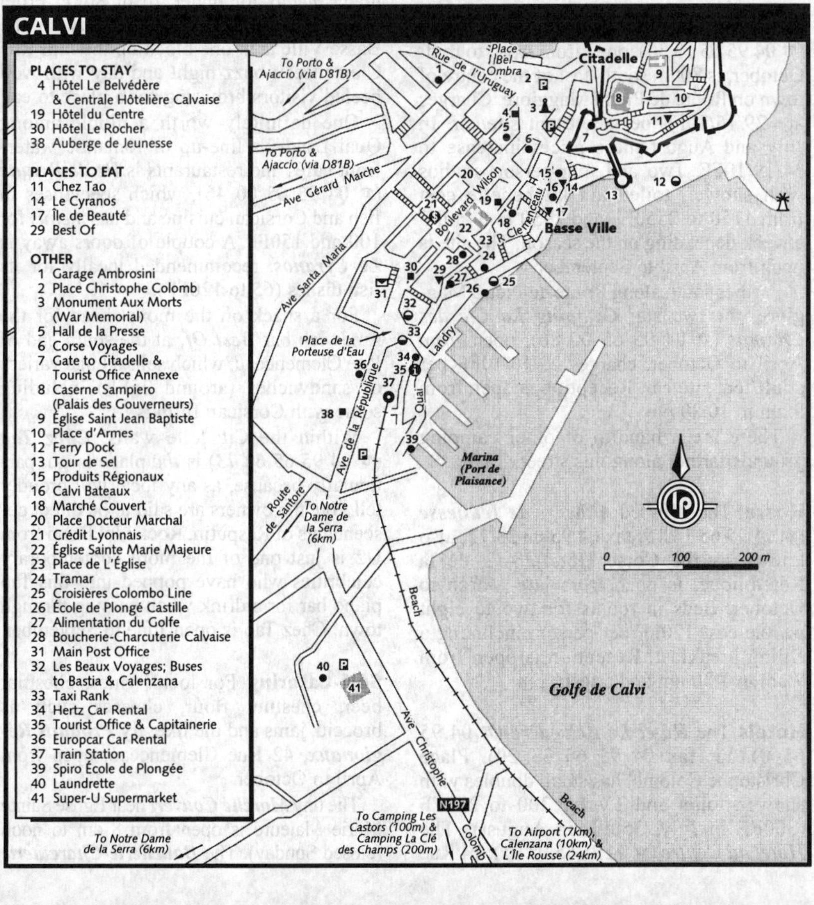

Other Activities

There are a number of scuba diving schools on Quai Landry. Contact the Spiro École de Plongée (☎ 04 95 65 42 22; fax 04 95 65 42 23) or Calvi Bateaux (☎ 04 95 65 02 91), which rents out scuba equipment and can refill diving tanks.

Places to Stay

The Centrale Hôtelière Calvaise (☎ 05 65 22 87; fax 04 95 65 33 20; am.ceccaldi@wanadoo.fr), beneath the Hôtel Le Belvédère on Place Christophe Colomb, takes bookings for all accommodation.

Camping Three star ***Camping Les Castors*** (☎ 04 95 65 13 30), open from April to mid-October, is 800m south-east of the centre of town on Route de Pietra Maggiore. Charges are 29/15/10FF per adult/tent site/car. In July and August these prices increase to 34/19/10FF. Two and four-person studios with shower, toilet and kitchenette cost from 1150 to 2550FF and 1950 to 3750FF a week depending on the season. The site is open from April to September.

Farther south along Route de Pietra Maggiore, the two star ***Camping La Clé des Champs*** (☎ 04 95 65 00 86), open from April to October, charges 23/10/10FF per adult/tent site/car. Reception is open from 9 am to 10.30 pm.

There are a handful of other camping grounds farther along this street.

Hostel The 130-bed ***Auberge de Jeunesse*** (☎ 04 95 65 14 15; fax 04 95 65 33 72; also known as the Corse Hôtel), Ave de la République, is open from late March to October. Beds in rooms for two to eight people cost 120FF per person, including a filling breakfast. Reception is open from 7 am to 1.30 pm and 5 to 10 pm.

Hotels The ***Hôtel Le Belvédère*** (☎ 04 95 65 01 25; fax 04 95 65 33 20), Place Christophe Colomb, has small doubles with shower, toilet and TV for 200 to 250FF (300FF in July, 350FF in August). The ***Hôtel du Centre*** (☎ 04 95 65 02 01), 14 Rue Alsace-Lorraine, is open from June to mid-October and charges similar rates.

Hôtel Le Rocher (☎ 04 95 65 20 04; fax 04 95 65 29 26), across Blvd Wilson from the post office, provides mini-apartments with kitchenettes, fridges, air-con etc for two/four people ranging from 355/550FF to 740/980FF, depending on the season. From November to early April, when reception is unstaffed, ring ☎ 04 95 65 11 35 a day or two ahead.

Places to Eat

Restaurants Calvi's restaurants generally offer excellent quality, but you won't find many *menus* for under 70 or 80FF. From May to September, Quai Landry in the Basse Ville and, one block up the hill, Rue Clemenceau buzz night and day with well heeled visitors browsing for a place to eat.

One definitely worth a nibble among Quai Landry's line-up of romantic waterfront cafés and restaurants is ***Île de Beauté*** (☎ 04 95 65 00 46), which specialises in fish and Corsican cuisine and has *menus* for 100 and 150FF. A couple of doors away is ***Le Cyranos***, recommended locally for its fish dishes (65 to 120FF).

For a snack on the move, head for the sandwich bar ***Best Of***, at the south end of Rue Clemenceau, which sells a huge variety of sandwiches (around 25FF) including some with Corsican fillings.

Within the Citadelle walls, ***Chez Tao*** (☎ 04 95 65 60 73) is *the* place to go, particularly because, as any local will proudly tell you, the owners are said to be direct descendants of Rasputin. Rock idol Bono from U2 is just one of the more contemporary celebrities who have popped into this fun piano bar for a drink when passing through town. Chez Tao is open June to September.

Self-Catering For local wines, chestnut beer, chestnut flour, cheeses such as brocciu, jams and the like, try ***Produits Régionaux***, 42 Rue Clemenceau, open from April to October.

The tiny ***Marché Couvert*** near Église Sainte Marie Majeure is open from 8 am to noon (closed Sunday). The ***Boucherie-Charcuterie***

Calvaise, 5 Rue Clemenceau, sells prepared dishes, local cheeses and wines (open from April to October).

South of the train station along Ave Christophe Colomb, there is the large ***Super-U*** supermarket. Alternatively, try ***Alimentation du Golfe*** at the south end of Rue Clemenceau.

Getting There & Away

Air Calvi-Sainte Catherine airport (☎ 04 95 65 88 88) is 7km south-east of Calvi.

Bus The tourist office has bus information and can supply photocopied time schedules. Buses to Bastia and Calenzana (only in summer) are run by Les Beaux Voyages (☎ 04 95 65 15 02), Place de la Porteuse d'Eau. From mid-May to mid-October, Autocars SAIB (☎ 04 95 26 13 70) has a bus down the island's spectacular north-west coast from Calvi's Monument aux Morts (war memorial) to Galéria (1¼ hours) and Porto (three hours).

Train Calvi's train station (☎ 04 95 65 00 61), just off Ave de la République, is open until 7.30 pm.

From mid-April to mid-October, the one-car diesel *navettes* (shuttle trains) of CFC's Le Tramway de la Balagne make 19 stops along the coast between Calvi and Île Rousse (22km, 45 minutes). The line is divided into three sectors – you need one ticket (available on board for 10FF) for each sector. Carnets of six tickets are sold at stations.

Car Rental companies with offices at the airport include Citer (☎ 04 95 65 16 06) and Budget (☎ 04 95 65 88 34). Europcar (☎ 04 95 65 10 35) has an office on Ave de la République.

Boat The ferry dock is below the south side of the Citadelle; schedules are posted at the tourist office. From Calvi there are express NGV ferries to Nice (2½ hours).

Ferry tickets can only be bought at the port two hours before departure. At all other times, SNCM tickets are handled by Tramar (☎ 04 95 65 01 38), Quai Landry, open from 8.25 am to noon and 1 to 5.30 pm (Saturday until noon; closed Sunday). Les Beaux Voyages (☎ 04 95 65 15 02), Place de la Porteuse d'Eau, is an agent for Corsica Ferries (closed Sunday and, except from May to October, on Saturday too).

For information on getting from Calvi to Porto by sea, see Boat Excursions in the Calvi and Porto sections.

Getting Around

To/From the Airport There is no bus service from Calvi to the airport. Taxis (☎ 04 95 65 03 10), 24 hours a day from Place de la Porteuse d'Eau, cost 70FF (100FF after 7 pm and on Sunday).

Bicycle Garage Ambrosini (☎ 04 95 65 02 13), just off Rue de l'Uruguay, rents mountain bikes for 100/250/600FF for one/three/seven days, plus a 1500FF deposit. It is open from 8 am to noon and 2 to 6 pm (closed Sunday).

AROUND CALVI

The Balagne Region

La Balagne is an area of low hills between the Monte Cinto massif and the sea. Its coastline stretches from Galéria north-east all the way to the **Désert des Agriates**, the desert area that begins 18km east of Île Rousse. The coast between Calvi and Île Rousse is dotted with a string of fine-sand beaches (eg at **Algajola**), many of them served by Le Tramway de la Balagne (see Getting There & Away under Calvi).

Inland, La Balagne, known as the 'Garden of Corsica', is renowned for the fertility of its soil, whose bounty once made the region among Corsica's wealthiest. Traditional products include olive oil, wine, cheese and fruit. The area has a number of 11th and 12th century Pisan churches. The main inland town, **Calenzana**, is 10km south-east of Calvi, to which it is linked by bus during the summer. Calenzana is the northern terminus of the GR20 and Mare è Monti trails.

From Calenzana, the D151 to Île Rousse is a particularly picturesque drive. After the village of **Cateri**, bear right along the D413 for 2.5km to the beautiful, crumbling village of **Saint Antonino**, dramatically perched on a hilltop and offering stunning views of the region.

ÎLE ROUSSE

• pop 2300 ✉ 20220

The uninspiring port and beach resort of Île Rousse, 24km north-east of Calvi, was founded by the Corsican nationalist leader Pasquale Paoli in 1758 to compete with fiercely pro-Genoese Calvi. Known as Isola Rossa in Corsican, its name is derived from the red granite of Île de la Pietra, a rocky island (now connected to the mainland) whose Genoese watchtower presides over an active passenger and freight port.

Orientation & Information

The ferry port is on a peninsula about 500m north of the train station, which is 400m north-west of Place Paoli, the main square. The old city is between Place Paoli and the train station.

The tourist office (☎ 04 95 60 04 35 or ☎ 04 95 60 24 74) on the south side of Place Paoli operates from April to October. It is open from 9 am to noon and 2.30 or 3 to 6 or 7.30 pm (open on Saturday from May, daily in July and August).

Things to See

The beachfront **Promenade Marinella** runs along the coast between the train tracks and the sand. There's more sandy coastline east of town past the rocks, near the pricey **Musée Océanographique** (aquarium; ☎ 04 95 60 27 81). The area of narrow streets north of Place Paoli is known as the **Vieille Ville** (old city).

On **Île de la Pietra**, the reddish island-turned-peninsula where the ferry port is located, there's a **Genoese tower** and, at the far end, a **lighthouse**, from which there are views of nearby islets.

Places to Stay

The ***Hôtel Le Grillon*** (☎ 04 95 60 00 49; fax 04 95 60 43 69), 10 Ave Paul Doumer, has decent singles/doubles/triples with shower and toilet for 170/190/220FF.

The 20 room, two star ***Hôtel L'Isola Rossa*** (☎ 04 95 60 01 32; fax 04 95 60 33 02) is just one of a handful of overpriced hotels lining Promenade du Port, the street running towards the port from the train station. L'Isola Rossa has doubles for 280 to 300FF in May, with prices rising to around 500FF for the same rooms in July and August.

Getting There & Away

Bus Buses on the Calvi-Bastia run stop in front of Café de la Paix, 3 Ave Piccioni (just south of Place Paoli).

Train The train station (☎ 04 95 60 00 50) is midway between Place Paoli and the ferry port. Île Rousse makes an easy day trip from Calvi.

Boat Agence Tramar (☎ 04 95 60 09 56), 200m south-east of Place Paoli on Ave Joseph Calizi, handles SNCM, Corsica Ferries and Moby Lines ticketing. It is open from 8.30 am to noon and 2 to 5.30 pm (closed Saturday afternoon and Sunday).

Getting Around

From March to October, Sport Action Passion (☎ 04 95 60 15 76), 150m south of Place Paoli on Ave Paul Doumer, rents mountain bikes for 100FF a day.

Corte Area

CORTE

• pop 5700 ✉ 20250 alt 400m

When Pasquale Paoli led Corsica to independence in 1755, one of his first acts was to make this fortified town at the geographical centre of the island the country's capital. To this day, Corte (Corti in Corsican) remains a potent symbol of Corsican independence.

Paoli, whose world-view was steeped in the ideas of the Enlightenment, founded a national university here in 1765, but it was closed four years later when the short-lived Corsican republic was taken over by France. The Università di Corsica Pasquale Paoli was reopened in 1981 and now has about 3000 students; it is they who make Corte the island's youngest, liveliest and least touristy town.

Ringed with mountains snow-kissed until as late as early June, Corte is an excellent base for hiking; some of the island's highest peaks are a bit west of town. To the east lies the Castagniccia region (see that section).

Orientation

Corte's main street is the shop-lined Cours Paoli. At its southern end is Place Paoli, from where the narrow streets of the Ville Haute (upper city) wend their way west up to the Citadelle.

The train station, Ave Jean Nicoli, is 1km south-east (down the hill) from Cours Paoli.

Information

Tourist Office The tourist office (☎ 04 95 46 26 70), 15 Quartier des Quatre Fontaines,

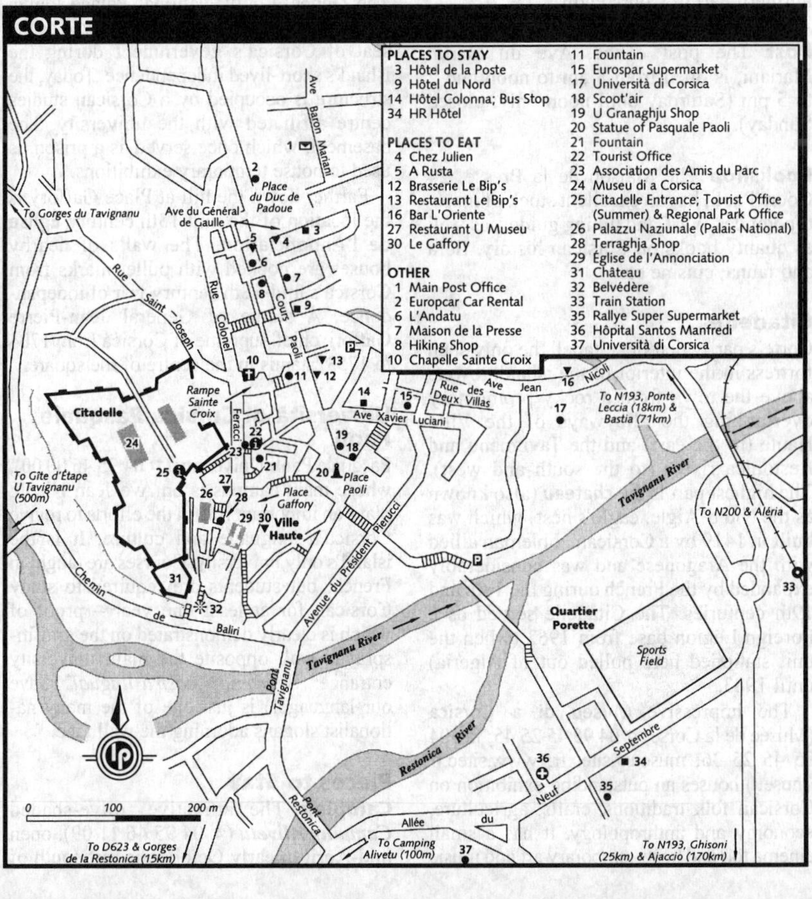

CORTE

is open from 9 am to noon and 2 to 5 pm (closed on weekends). In July and August it is open from 9 am to 8 pm.

Regional Park Office From 15 June to September, the Parc Naturel Régional de Corse has an information office (☎ 04 95 46 27 44) just inside the Citadelle gate, open summer only. The Association des Amis du Parc – Service Haute Montagne (Friends of the Park Association; ☎ 04 95 46 25 26), 15 Rue du C Feracci, is also only open in summer.

Money There are several banks along the northern part of Cours Paoli.

Post The post office, Ave du Baron Mariani, is open from 8 am to noon and 2 to 5 pm (Saturday until noon only; closed Sunday).

Bookshop The Maison de la Presse, 24 Cours Paoli, has an excellent stock of maps, topoguides, VTT and hiking guides, as well as quality books on Corsican history, flora and fauna, cuisine etc.

Citadelle

Corte's partly derelict citadel, the only such fortress in the interior of the island, towers above the town from a rocky promontory overlooking the alleyways of the Ville Haute (to the east) and the Tavignanu and Restonica rivers (to the south and west). The highest part is the **chateau** (also known as the Nid d'Aigle, eagle's nest) which was built in 1419 by a Corsican nobleman allied with the Aragonese and was considerably expanded by the French during the 18th and 19th centuries. The Citadelle served as a Foreign Legion base from 1962 (when the unit stationed here pulled out of Algeria) until 1983.

The impressive **Museu di a Corsica** (Musée de la Corse; ☎ 04 95 45 25 45; fax 04 95 45 25 36; museu@sitec.fr; www.sitec.fr/museu) houses an outstanding exhibition on Corsican folk traditions, crafts, agriculture, economy and anthropology. It has a small cinema too and hosts temporary art and music exhibitions on the ground floor. Captions are in French and Corsican. The museum is open from 10 am to 8 pm in July and August (between April and June until 6 pm, closed on Monday); between September and March until 5 pm (closed Sunday and Monday). Admission (20/15FF for adults/ students) includes a visit to the chateau too, accessed from a side door inside the museum.

Outside the ramparts, a staircase leads from just below the **belvédère** (viewing platform) down to the river.

Palazzu Naziunale

The Genoese-built National Palace, down the hill from the Citadelle gate, served as the seat of Corsica's government during the island's short-lived independence. Today, the structure is occupied by a Corsican studies centre affiliated with the university. The basement, which once served as a prison, is used to house temporary exhibitions.

Farther down the hill at Place Gaffory is the location of the mid-15th century **Église de l'Annonciation**. The walls of nearby houses are pocked with bullet marks from Corsica's mid-18th century war of independence. A statue of Général Jean-Pierre Gaffori, chief-supreme of Corsica from 1704 to 1753, stands in the centre of the square.

Università di Corsica Pasquale Paoli

Pasquale Paoli University (☎ 04 95 45 00 00), whose main campus is on Ave Jean Nicoli, plays an important role in the efforts to revive Corsica's language and culture. It is the island's only university. Courses are taught in French, but students are required to study Corsican for at least one year – proof of which is clearly demonstrated on the graffiti-sprayed wall opposite the main university entrance: '*Salvemu a nostra lingua!*' (Save our language!) is just one of the many nationalist slogans adorning the wall face.

Places to Stay

Camping The attractive, olive-shaded *Camping Alivetu* (☎ 04 95 46 11 09), open mid-April to early October, is just south of

Pont Restonica on Allée du Neuf Septembre. It charges 30/15/15FF per adult/tent site/car. You can camp under the trees at ***Gîte d'Étape U Tavignanu*** (see Hostels) for 10FF per tent plus 20FF per person.

Hostels The 16 bed ***Gîte d'Étape U Tavignanu*** (☎ 04 95 46 16 85) is quiet – except for birds and rushing water. It's open all year and charges 80FF for bed and breakfast. From Pont Tavignanu, walk west along Chemin de Baliri and follow the signs. The gîte is about 500m over the small bridge and 250m from the end of the narrow road.

For details on staying in the university dorms during July and August, contact the CROUS secrétariat (☎ 04 95 45 21 00), Résidence Pasquale Paoli, on the university's main campus.

Hotels The 135 room ***HR Hôtel*** (☎ 04 95 45 11 11; fax 04 95 61 02 85), 6 Allée du Neuf Septembre, has clean, utilitarian rooms for one/two people for 135/145FF (180/195FF with shower and toilet and triples for 290FF). The gloomier ***Hôtel Colonna*** (☎ 04 95 46 26 21 or ☎ 04 95 46 01 09), 3 Ave Xavier Luciani, also known as the Hôtel Cyrnos, has doubles with shower and toilet for 180 to 250FF. Reception is usually at the bar.

From mid-May to mid-October, the one star, 12 room ***Hôtel de la Poste*** (☎ 04 95 46 01 37), 2 Place du Duc de Padoue (Corte's most elegant avenue), has spacious, simply furnished, doubles/triples with shower for 170/220FF or 230/250FF with toilet. Some rooms don't have much of a window. The family-run, 11 room ***Hôtel du Nord*** (☎ 04 95 46 00 68), 22 Cours Paoli, accepts travellers from June to September. Rooms with shower for two/three/four people cost 190/280/310FF.

Places to Eat

Restaurants Corsican cuisine is on offer at ***A Rusta*** (☎ 04 95 46 28 56), 19 Cours Paoli, whose *menu* is 75FF and mains are 45 to 65FF; and opposite at ***Chez Julien*** (☎ 04 95 46 02 90), 24 Cours Paoli, which serves a good value 68FF *menu* in a rustic decor.

Local fare is also served at ***Restaurant Le Bip's*** (☎ 04 95 46 06 26), a cellar restaurant at 14 Cours Paoli at the bottom of the flight of stairs 20m down the hill from ***Brasserie Le Bip's*** (☎ 04 95 46 04 48). The restaurant's 80FF *menu* changes daily; fish dishes are 50 to 120FF. Heading uphill to the citadel, there is the ***Restaurant U Museu***, which has a great range of local fare including yummy chestnut cake and *fiadone* (Corsican cake), and ***Le Gaffory*** (☎ 04 95 61 05 58), Place Gaffory, which has 60FF lunchtime *menus*.

There are a number of student-oriented sandwich and pizza takeaways on Place Paoli and along Cours Paoli. ***Bar L'Oriente*** (☎ 04 95 61 11 17), opposite the university on Ave Jean Nicoli, is a popular student hang-out; its terrace café is particularly pleasant.

The ***restaurant universitaire*** on the main campus of the Università di Corsica on Ave Jean Nicoli, in Résidence Pasquale Paoli, is open from October to June from 11.30 am to 1.30 pm and 6.30 to 9 pm (closed on weekends). Meal tickets are sold from 11 am to 1 pm.

Self-Catering Corte's top ***boulangerie*** is inside the main train station building – and does a roaring trade as a result! The tantalising cellar-shop ***L'Andatu***, Cours Paoli, sells local wines, honey, cold meats and brocciu (Corsican cheese).

There is a ***Eurospar*** supermarket at 7 Ave Xavier Luciani and a ***Rallye Super*** supermarket at Allée du Neuf Septembre (opposite the hospital).

Shopping

Corsican products, including pottery and things to eat and drink, are available at U Granaghju, 2 Cours Paoli. Pottery and crafts shops are situated between the Citadelle and Place Paoli, including Terraghja on Place Gaffory.

There is a well stocked hiking and sports shop, close to L'Andatu, on Cours Paioli.

Getting There & Away

Bus Corte is on Eurocorse's Bastia-Ajaccio route, served by two buses a day in each direction (no Sunday service). The stop is in front of the Hôtel Colonna, 3 Ave Xavier Luciani; a schedule is posted.

Train The train station (☎ 04 95 46 00 97) is staffed from 8 am to noon and 2 to 6.30 pm (closed on Sunday after 11 am from early September to late June).

Car Europcar (☎ 04 95 46 02 79) is at 28bis Cours Paoli.

Getting Around

From March to November, Scoot'air (☎ 04 95 46 01 85), 1 Place Paoli, whose sign reads Telefunken – Thomson, rents mountain bikes and scooters. It is open from 8.30 am to noon and 2 to 7 pm (closed on Sunday from October to April).

AROUND CORTE

South-west of Corte, the clear, greenish-blue waters of the Restonica River flow past pine and chestnut groves as they tumble down **Gorges de la Restonica**, a deep valley whose grey-white granite walls are studded with bushes and trees. Some of the area's choicest trails begin about 16km south-west of Corte at the **Bergeries de Grotelle** (1375m), which can be reached by car via the narrow D623. Trails from here lead to a number of glacial lakes, including **Lac de Mello (Melu)** (1711m), a one hour walk from the Bergeries (sheepfolds), and **Lac de Capitello (Capitellu)** (1930m), 40 minutes beyond Lac de Mello near the GR20. Both are ice-covered half the year.

West of Corte, there are some arduous hiking trails in and around the **Tavignanu River Valley**, including one to **Lac Nino (Ninu)** (1743m; 9½ hours walk from Corte). About 20km south of Corte lies the fine 1526 hectare **Forêt de Vizzavona** (Vizzavona Forest; 800 to 1650m), cut through with 43km of forest trails. The magnificent **Cascade des Anglais**, accessible on foot from Vizzavona village, and the equally fantastic **Cascade du Voile de la Mariée**, farther south-west near Bocognano, are both worth the hike.

In Vizzavona, the wonderful old-world ***Hôtel du Monte d'Oro*** (☎ 04 95 47 21 06; fax 01 95 47 22 05; monte.oro@sitec.fr), dating from 1880, has been run by the same family since 1906 and panders to all budgets. Doubles boasting original early furnishings start at 280FF; overnighting in a gîte is 75FF; and a bed in a forest *refuge* (bedding not provided) is 60FF.

Languedoc-Roussillon

The region of Languedoc-Roussillon, formed in the 1960s from two historic provinces, comprises the five departments of Lozère, Gard, Hérault, Pyrénées-Orientales and Aude. Languedoc-Roussillon, whose capital is the vibrant city of Montpellier, stretches in an arc along the coast from Provence to the Pyrenees; in the north it borders the Massif Central. The region has everything a traveller could want: mountains, sea, great cities and towns, and a lot of history.

HIGHLIGHTS

- **Nîmes** – attend a bullfight at the Roman amphitheatre
- **Gorges de la Jonte** – spot vultures looping and swooping high above
- **Pont du Gard** – swim under the bridge
- **Montpellier** – explore the historic backstreets and go shopping
- **Cévennes** – try Robert Louis Stevenson's donkey trek
- **Canal du Midi** – take a slow boat down the canal

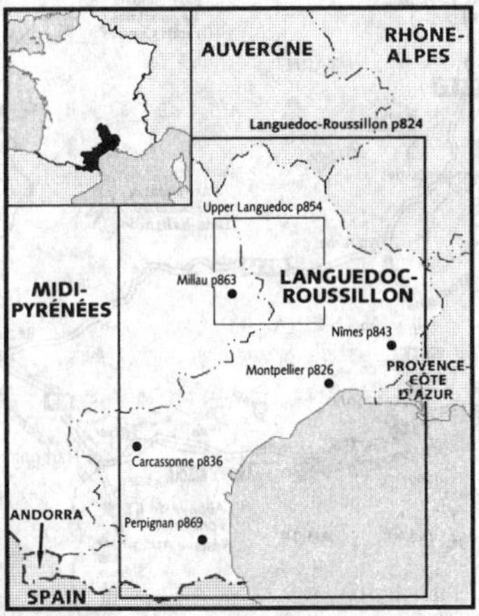

cheese – Roquefort (France's king of cheeses), Bleu des Causses and Pélardon

cassoulet – a hearty stew of white beans prepared with pork, mutton, confit d'oie and/or confit de canard

vins de table (red table wines)

Languedoc

Languedoc takes its name from the *langue d'oc*, a language closely related to today's Catalan but quite distinct from the *langue d'oïl*, the forerunner of modern French spoken north of the Loire. (The words *oc* and *oïl* meant 'yes'.) When France's new regional boundaries were mapped out, Languedoc's traditional centre, Toulouse to the south-west, was excluded from Languedoc-Roussillon.

History

Languedoc was settled as early as 450,000 BC. Phoenicians, Greeks, Romans, Visigoths and Moors all passed through the region before it came under Frankish control in about the 8th century. For the most part, the Franks were happy to leave affairs in the hands of local rulers, and around the 12th century Occitania (today's Languedoc) reached its zenith. At the time, Occitan was the language of the troubadours and the cultured speech of southern France. Eventually, however, the Albigensian Crusade, launched to suppress the 'heresy' of Catharism in 1208, led to Languedoc's complete annexation by the French kingdom. The treaty of Villers-Cotterêts (1539), which made the langue d'oïl the realm's official language, sounded the death knell for Occitan, though a revival spearheaded by the poet Frédéric Mistral in the 19th century breathed new life into the

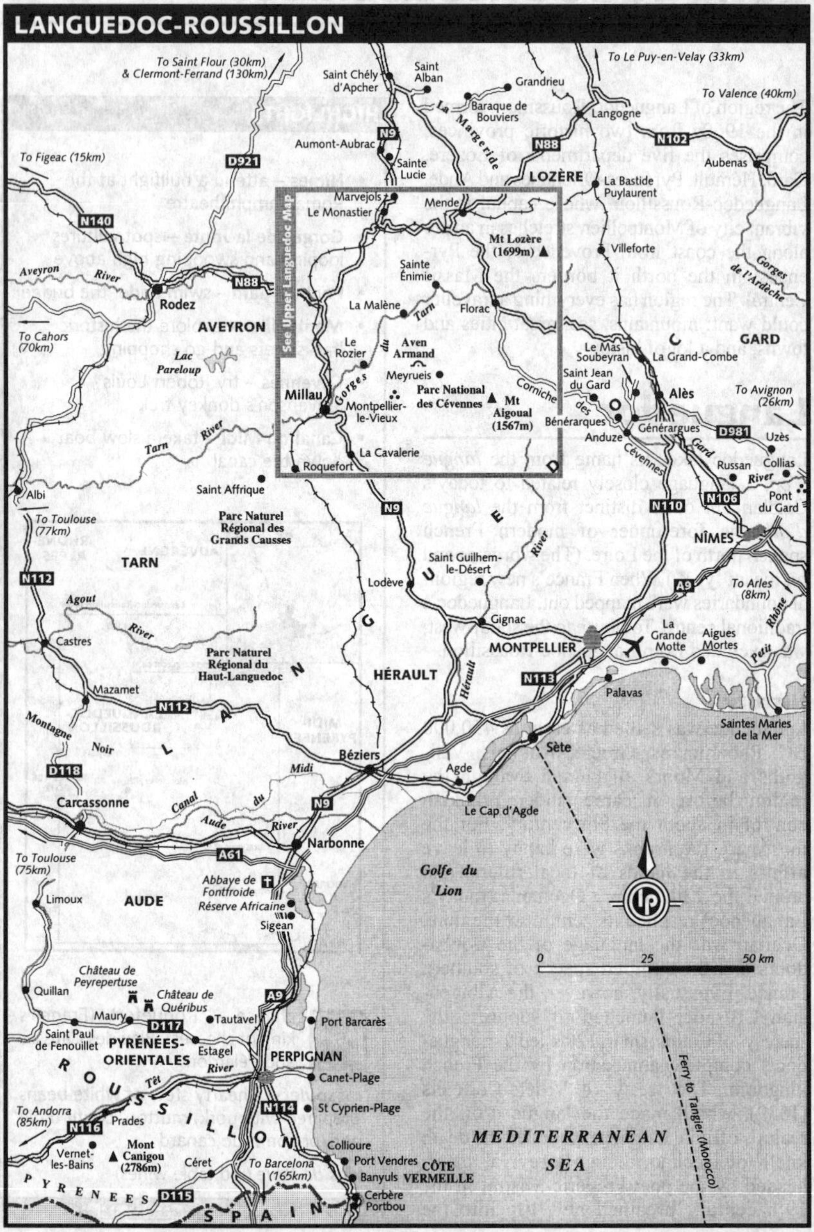

LANGUEDOC-ROUSSILLON
To Saint Flour (30km) & Clermont-Ferrand (130km)
Saint Chély d'Apcher
Saint Alban
Grandrieu
To Le Puy-en-Velay (33km)
Baraque de Bouviers
La Margeride
Langogne
To Valence (40km)
N9
N88
N102
Aumont-Aubrac
Sainte Lucie
D921
To Figeac (15km)
LOZÈRE
La Bastide Puylaurent
Aubenas
Marvejols
Le Monastier
Mende
See Upper Languedoc Map
N140
Mt Lozère (1699m)
Villeforte
Gorges de l'Ardèche
Aveyron River
N88
Sainte Énimie
Rodez
La Malène
Tarn
Florac
AVEYRON
To Cahors (70km)
Le Rozier
du
Aven Armand
Le Mas Soubeyran
La Grand-Combe
GARD
Lac Pareloup
Meyrueis
Saint Jean du Gard
Parc National des Cévennes
Millau
Gorges
Montpellier-le-Vieux
Mt Aigoual (1567m)
Corniche des Cévennes
Alès
To Avignon (26km)
Bénérarques
Générargues
Anduze
D981
Uzès
Tarn River
La Cavalerie
Roquefort
Russan
Collias
Gard River
Pont du Gard
Albi
Saint Affrique
N106
N110
N9
To Toulouse (77km)
Parc Naturel Régional des Grands Causses
NÎMES
TARN
Saint Guilhem-le-Désert
River
N112
Lodève
A9
To Arles (8km)
Agout River
Gignac
Rhône
Castres
La Grande Motte
Aigues Mortes
MONTPELLIER
Parc Naturel Régional du Haut-Languedoc
HÉRAULT
Hérault
Petit
N113
Palavas
Mazamet
N112
Montagne Noir
Saintes Maries de la Mer
Sète
Béziers
D118
Midi
Agde
Carcassonne
Canal du
N9
Le Cap d'Agde
Aude River
Narbonne
To Toulouse (75km)
A61
Golfe du Lion
Abbaye de Fontfroide
Réserve Africaine
Limoux
AUDE
Sigean
0
25
50 km
Château de Peyrepertuse
Quillan
Château de Quéribus
A9
Maury
D117
Tautavel
Port Barcarès
Saint Paul de Fenouillet
PYRÉNÉES-ORIENTALES
Estagel
PERPIGNAN
River
Têt
Canet-Plage
Ferry to Tangier (Morocco)
To Andorra (85km)
N116
Prades
N114
St Cyprien-Plage
Mont Canigou (2786m)
Vernet-les-Bains
Céret
To Barcelona (165km)
Collioure
Port Vendres
CÔTE VERMEILLE
Banyuls
MEDITERRANEAN SEA
PYRENEES
D115
Cerbère
Portbou
SPAIN
L A N G U E D O C
R O U S S I L L O N

language now called Provençal. You'll see a fair few street signs in Provençal, even in Montpellier.

Geography

Languedoc has two distinct areas: the plains of Lower Languedoc (Bas Languedoc), and the rugged, mountainous terrain of Upper Languedoc (Haut Languedoc) to the north. From the plains rise the region's towns and cities, including Montpellier, a leading university centre. Bordering Provence to the east is the sun-baked old Roman town of Nîmes. Follow the coast south-westward and you come to the attractive port of Sète. Just inland lie the cities of Béziers and Narbonne. Farther inland, the walled city of Carcassonne hovers over the hot plain like a medieval mirage.

The coastline of Lower Languedoc is broken by a string of lagoons (*étang* in French, literally 'ponds') that are separated from the sea by sandy beaches. A number of ugly modern resorts have been built, the most well known being the futuristic La Grand Motte, near Montpellier. The coast has some *naturiste* (nudist) resorts including Le Cap d'Agde, France's largest.

Away from the coast, the scene is dominated by ruined castles crowning rocky outcrops, and the countless vineyards that make Languedoc the prime wine-producing area of France. Rising above this plain is Upper Languedoc.

Upper Languedoc is quite distinct from the sun-soaked lowlands or the Auvergne region of the Massif Central. It has a sense of isolation that is appealing to visitors in search of the great outdoors. It includes Lozère, France's most sparsely populated region, which takes in the Parc National des Cévennes, a wild, mountainous area long the refuge of hermits and exiles.

To the west of here are the Grands Causses, bare limestone plateaus fascinating in their isolation, which rise above deep canyons like the Gorges du Tarn. The small towns of Mende, Florac, Alès and Millau are like little oases sprinkled through this wilderness.

Getting There & Away

Ferries sail from the port of Sète to Tangier in Morocco. For details, see Getting There & Away under Montpellier in this chapter, and Sea in the Getting There & Away chapter at the start of this book.

Getting Around

Travel between cities by rail or bus is no problem. Getting to remote hilltop castles will pose a challenge for those without their own wheels, as will travelling around most of Upper Languedoc (eg Lozère, the Grands Causses and the Cévennes).

MONTPELLIER

• pop 211,000 ✉ 34000

The 17th century philosopher John Locke may have had one glass of Minervois too many when he wrote: 'I find it much better to go twise (*sic*) to Montpellier than once to the other world'. Paradise it ain't, but Montpellier continues to attract visitors with its reputation for innovation and vitality.

Not so very long ago, Languedoc's largest city simply slumbered in the Midi sun. Things began changing in the 1960s, however, when many *pieds noirs* (Algerian-born French) left North Africa and settled here, swelling the population. Later a dynamic left-wing local government came to power, promoting the pedestrianisation of the old city, designing an unusual central housing project and attracting high-tech industries. The result is one of France's fastest-growing cities whose focus is to slash traffic pollution by building a high-tech tramway through the city centre (to be completed by 2001).

Nearly a quarter of the city's population is made up of students, and the university is celebrated for its science, law, literature and especially medical faculties; Europe's first medical school was founded here early in the 12th century. Though there is little that would qualify as a 'must see', the old city remains charming – with its stone arches, fine *hôtels particuliers* (private mansions) and decaying splendour. The beach is 12km away.

Montpellier hosts a two week international dance festival in June.

MONTPELLIER

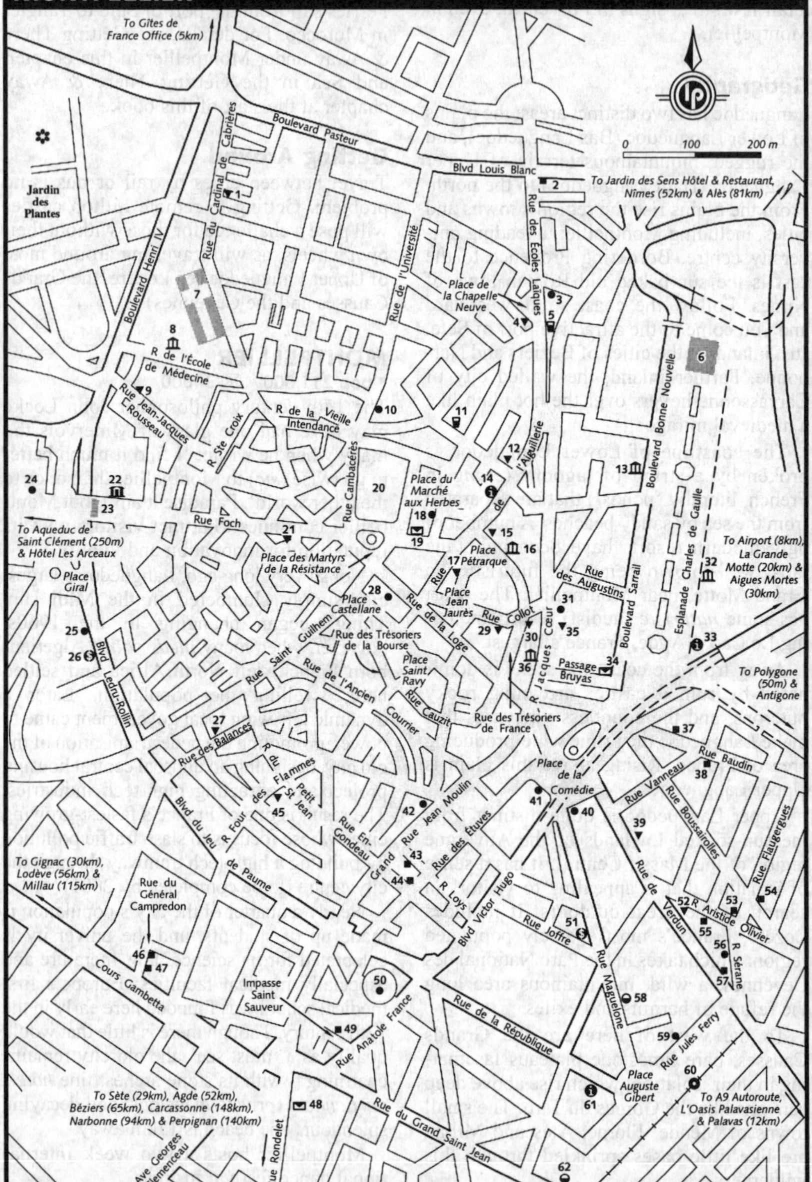
To Gîtes de France Office (5km)
0
100
200 m
Boulevard Pasteur
Rue du Cardinal de Cabrières
Blvd Louis Blanc
To Jardin des Sens Hôtel & Restaurant, Nîmes (52km) & Alès (81km)
Jardin des Plantes
Boulevard Henri IV
Rue de l'Université
Rue des Écoles Laïques
Place de la Chapelle Neuve
R de l'École de Médecine
Rue Jean-Jacques Rousseau
R Ste Croix
R de la Vieille Intendance
Rue de l'Aiguillerie
Boulevard Bonne Nouvelle
Place du Marché aux Herbes
Rue Cambacérès
Rue Foch
To Aqueduc de Saint Clément (250m) & Hôtel Les Arceaux
Place des Martyrs de la Résistance
Place Pétrarque
Rue des Augustins
Boulevard Sarrail
Esplanade Charles de Gaulle
To Airport (8km), La Grande Motte (20km) & Aigues Mortes (30km)
Place Giral
Place Jean Jaurès
Place Castellane
Rue Saint Guilhem
Rue de la Loge
Rue Collot
Rue des Trésoriers de la Bourse
Place Saint Ravy
Rue Jacques Cœur
Passage Bruyas
To Polygone (50m) & Antigone
Blvd Ledru-Rollin
Rue de l'Ancien Courrier
Rue Cauzit
Rue des Trésoriers de France
Rue des Balances
R du Four des Flammes
Petit St Jean
Place de la Comédie
Rue Baudin
Rue Vanneau
Rue Boussairolles
Rue Flaugergues
Blvd du Jeu de Paume
Rue En-Gondeau
Grand Rue Jean Moulin
Rue des Étuves
To Gignac (30km), Lodève (56km) & Millau (115km)
Rue du Général Campredon
R Loys
Blvd Victor Hugo
Rue Joffre
Rue de Verdun
R Aristide Olivier
R Sérane
Cours Gambetta
Impasse Saint Sauveur
Rue Anatole France
Rue de la République
Rue Maguelone
Rue Jules Ferry
Place Auguste Gibert
To Sète (29km), Agde (52km), Béziers (65km), Carcassonne (148km), Narbonne (94km) & Perpignan (140km)
To A9 Autoroute, L'Oasis Palavasienne & Palavas (12km)
Rue du Grand Saint Jean
Rue Rondelet
Ave Georges Clemenceau

Orientation

Surrounded by wide boulevards, the heart of Montpellier is the teardrop-shaped Centre Historique. The centre of this is Place de la Comédie, an enormous pedestrianised square.

North-east of the square is Esplanade Charles de Gaulle, a pleasant tree-lined promenade. To the east is Le Polygone, a modern shopping complex, and Antigone, a housing project with grand colonnaded façades designed for middle-income tenants.

West of Place de la Comédie is the city's oldest quarter, a web of pedestrianised lanes weaving between Rue de la Loge and Grand Rue Jean Moulin. Just north-west of here is the university's medical faculty, next to the twin-turreted Cathédrale Saint Pierre. Outside the main boulevards to the south are the bus and train stations; a huge palm tree greets travellers as they exit the latter.

Information

Tourist Offices Montpellier's main tourist office (☎ 04 67 60 60 60; fax 04 67 60 60 61) is behind the Pavillon de l'Hôtel de Ville at the south end of Esplanade Charles de Gaulle. Staff take accommodation bookings and exchange currency. It's open from 9 am to 1 pm and 2 to 6 pm (Saturday from 10 am, Sunday from 10 am to 1 pm and 2 to 5 pm). Between 15 June and 15 September, Sunday afternoon hours are 3 to 6 pm.

There is a small tourist office (☎ 04 67 92 90 03) on the ground floor of the train station (open weekdays from May to September from 9 am to 1 pm and 3 to 7 pm); other offices are at 78 Ave du Pirée (☎ 04 67 22 06 16; open year-round) on the road to the airport (east), and at the Rond Point Près d'Arènes (☎ 04 67 22 08 80; open summer only) at the southern entrance to the A9 autoroute.

All these offices have reams of information on the Hérault department; alternatively try the Comité Régional du Tourisme (☎ 04 67 22 81 00; fax 04 67 58 06 10; contact.crtlr@cnusc.fr; www.cr-languedocroussillon.fr/tourisme), 20 Rue de la République.

For information on neighbouring Lozère, go to the Maison de la Lozère (☎ 04 67 66 36 10; fax 04 67 60 33 22), 27 Rue de

MONTPELLIER

PLACES TO STAY
- 2 Auberge de Jeunesse
- 37 Hôtel de la Comédie
- 38 Hôtel des Touristes
- 43 Hôtel Majestic
- 44 Hôtel des Étuves
- 46 Hôtel Cosmos
- 47 Hôtel Abysse
- 49 Hôtel du Littoral
- 53 Hôtel le Paris
- 54 Hôtel Mistral
- 55 Hôtel Édouard VII
- 57 Hôtel Colisée Verdun

PLACES TO EAT
- 1 L'Épicurien
- 4 Le Vieil Écu
- 9 Le Petit Jardin
- 12 L'Heure Bleue
- 15 La Diligence
- 17 Salmon Shop
- 21 Le Menestrel
- 27 Dimension 4 Cybercafé
- 29 Restaurant Cerdan
- 30 Simple Simon
- 35 Tripti Kulai
- 39 Factory Café
- 45 Crêperie Les Blés Noirs
- 52 Restaurant Verdi

OTHER
- 3 Laundrette
- 5 Volt Face
- 6 Le Corum
- 7 Cathédrale Saint Pierre
- 8 Musée Atger; Musée d'Anatomie; Medical Faculty
- 10 Bookshop
- 11 Martin's
- 13 Musée Fabre
- 14 Maison de la Lozère
- 16 Musée du Vieux Montpellier; Musée Fougau; Hôtel de Varennes
- 18 St@tion Internet
- 19 Post Office
- 20 Prefecture
- 22 Palais de Justice
- 23 Arc de Triomphe
- 24 Promenade du Peyrou
- 25 Caisse d'Épargne
- 26 Banque de France
- 28 Halles Castellane Market
- 31 Les Cinq Continents
- 32 Pavillon du Musée Fabre
- 33 Main Tourist Office
- 34 Post Office
- 36 Musée Languedocien
- 40 Monoprix Supermarket
- 41 Opéra-Comédie
- 42 Hôtel Saint Côme
- 48 Main Post Office
- 50 Halles Laissac Market
- 51 BNP
- 56 Laundrette
- 58 SMTU Bus Office
- 59 Europcar
- 60 Train Station
- 61 Comité Régional du Tourisme
- 62 Bus Station; Vill' à Vélo

l'Aiguillerie. It takes bookings for rural accommodation in Lozère and is open from 9 am to 12.30 pm and 1.30 to 6 pm (closed Sunday and Monday).

Money The Banque de France, 6 Blvd Ledru-Rollin, is open from 8.30 am to noon and 1.30 to 3 pm (closed on weekends). The Caisse d'Épargne is next door at No 2.

Not far from the train station, the Banque Nationale de Paris at 8 Rue Maguelone is open weekdays from 8.30 am to 4.30 pm. Crédit Lyonnais is at 20 Blvd Victor Hugo.

Post & Communications The main post office, 13 Place Rondelet, is open from 8 am to 7 pm (Saturday until noon; closed Sunday). The branch close to the tourist office at 1 Passage Bruyas is open from 10 am to 6 pm (from noon on Monday; closed Sunday). The city centre branch, Place des Martyrs de la Résistance, is open from 10 am to noon and 1 to 5 pm (Saturday from 9 am to noon; closed Sunday).

You can surf the Internet and send emails from France Telecom's St@tion Internet (fax 04 67 60 62 26; contact@station-internet.com; www.station-internet.com), behind the city centre post office at 6-8 Place du Marché aux Herbes. Half an hour/one hour online costs 20/30FF. St@tion Internet is open from 10 am to 8 pm (Monday from 2 pm; closed Sunday).

Those who seek nourishment while surfing should go to the Dimension 4 Cybercafé (☎ 04 67 60 57 57), 11 Rue des Balances.

Bookshops Rue de l'Université is lined with specialist bookshops, including the English-Language Bookshop (☎ 04 67 66 09 08) at No 4, which has novels and travel guides. It's open from 9.30 am to 1 pm and 2.30 to 7 pm (closed Sunday).

Les Cinq Continents, 20 Rue Jacques Cœur, is a specialist travel bookshop, selling Lonely Planet guides and other English-language books and maps.

Laundry Near the Auberge de Jeunesse, the laundrette at 8 Rue des Écoles Laïques is open daily from 7.30 am to 9 pm. The one at 11 Rue Sérane is open from 7.30 am to 10 pm.

Hôtels Particuliers

During the 17th and 18th centuries, Montpellier's wealthier merchants built tastefully designed private mansions with large inner courtyards. Two of the most interesting are the **Hôtel de Varennes** on Place Pétrarque, a harmonious blend of Romanesque and Gothic styles, and the **Hôtel Saint Côme** on Grand Rue Jean Moulin. The latter, the city's first anatomy theatre for medical students, now houses the Chambre de Commerce and has a superb stained-glass window visible from the courtyard. The Musée Languedocien is housed in the 17th century **Hôtel des Trésoriers de France**, at 7 Rue Jacques Cœur.

Museums

The city's cultural showpiece is the **Musée Fabre** (☎ 04 67 14 83 00), 39 Blvd Bonne Nouvelle. Founded in 1825, it is home to one of France's richest collections of French, Italian, Flemish and Dutch works from the 16th century onward. A small room is devoted to the 19th century realist painter Gustave Courbet; the top floor has more contemporary works. In summer the museum hosts temporary exhibitions in the **Pavillon du Musée Fabre** (☎ 04 67 66 13 46), Esplanade Charles de Gaulle. The museum itself is open from 9 am to 5.30 pm (weekends from 9.30 am to 5 pm; closed Monday). Admission is 20/10FF for adults/students.

The **Musée Languedocien** (☎ 04 67 52 93 03), 7 Rue Jacques Cœur, focuses on the region's archaeological finds as well as *objets d'art* from the 17th to 19th centuries. Hours are 2 to 5 pm (6 pm in July and August; closed Sunday). Admission is 20/10FF.

There are four other museums (admission is free). Two are upstairs in the Hôtel de Varennes on Place Pétrarque: **Musée du Vieux Montpellier** (☎ 04 67 66 02 94), a storehouse of the city's memorabilia from the Middle Ages to the Revolution, is open from 9.30 am to noon and 1.30 to 5 pm (closed Sunday and Monday). Continue upstairs for **Musée Fougau**, which deals with traditional Occitan life. It's only open Wednesday and Thursday from 3 to 6 pm.

The other pair of museums is in the medical faculty, 2 Rue de l'École de Médecine (closed during university holidays). **Musée Atger** (☎ 04 67 66 27 77), housing a striking collection of French, Italian and Flemish drawings, is open Monday, Wednesday and Friday from 1.30 to 4.30 pm. **Musée d'Anatomie** (☎ 04 67 60 73 71), worth a visit if you're into looking at body parts in jars, is open from 2.30 to 5 pm (closed on weekends).

Promenade du Peyrou

Overlooking the city at the western end of Rue Foch, this large, tree-lined square is a peaceful spot to spend a lazy afternoon. Designed in the 17th and 18th centuries, it is dominated by the **Arc de Triomphe** (1692) at one end, and the **Château d'Eau** – a hexagonal water tower – at the other. Stretching away from the latter is the 18th century **Aqueduc de Saint Clément**, under which there's a bustling flea market on Saturday and *pétanque* (bowling) games most afternoons. To the north off Blvd Henri IV is the **Jardin des Plantes**, France's oldest botanic garden, founded by Henry IV in 1593. Opposite the garden is the **Cathédrale Saint Pierre**, with a strange, oversized 15th century porch.

Beaches

The closest beach is at **Palavas-les-Flots**, 12km south of the city and is backed by a nasty concrete skyline. It's easy to reach by local bus (No 17 or 28).

About 20km south-east of Montpellier is **La Grande Motte**, a resort famous for its futuristic, wacky architecture. Aigues Mortes, on the western edge of the Camargue (see the Provence chapter), is another 11km to the north-east. For bus details, see Getting There & Away later in this section.

Organised Tours

For the energetic, there are bicycle city tours (see Bicycle under Getting Around). For those who prefer ambling, the tourist office on Esplanade Charles de Gaulle offers two-hour walking tours of the city, leaving from outside the tourist office on Wednesday and Saturday at 3 pm. Tours cost 39/25FF for adults/students; phone ☎ 04 67 60 60 60 for details. If you want to do it alone ask one of the tourist offices for a copy of *Pedestrians: Welcome to Montpellier*, an excellent brochure and map detailing five easy walks in the old city.

Places to Stay – Budget

Camping The closest camping grounds are around the suburb of Lattes, some 4km south of the city centre. Among the nine camping grounds there is ***L'Oasis Palavasienne*** (☎ 04 67 15 11 61; fax 04 67 15 10 62), Route de Palavas. It is open from April to September and charges 88FF for two people with a tent or caravan. Take bus No 17 from Montpellier bus station to the Lattes stop.

Hostel The ***Auberge de Jeunesse*** (☎ 04 67 60 32 22; fax 04 67 60 32 30), 2 Impasse de la Petite Corraterie on the corner of Rue des Écoles Laïques, is ideally located within the old city. The grandiose mosaic entrance contrasts with the basic dorms but who can complain when a bed costs just 65FF a night. Reception closes at midnight and a hostelling card (available here) is mandatory. Take bus No 2, 4, 5 or 6 from the station to the Ursulines stop. Le Rabelais night buses stop here too.

Gîtes You can book B&B accommodation through the regional ***Gîtes de France*** office (☎ 04 67 67 71 62 or ☎ 04 67 67 71 66; fax 04 67 67 71 77), north-west of the centre inside the Maison du Tourisme, 1977 Ave des Moulins.

Hotels A two minute walk from the train station is the two star ***Hôtel Colisée Verdun*** (☎ 04 67 58 42 63; fax 04 67 58 98 27), 33 Rue de Verdun, which has singles/doubles with toilet and bidet from 145/155FF. Doubles/triples with shower start at 210/300FF.

Popular for its low prices is the weathered and chaotically run ***Hôtel des Touristes***

LANGUEDOC

(☎ 04 67 58 42 37; fax 04 67 92 61 37), 10 Rue Baudin, which has good-sized rooms, all with showers. Singles/doubles/triples start at 120/150/220FF. Close by, ***Hôtel le Paris*** (☎ 04 67 58 37 11; fax 04 67 92 79 72), 15 Rue Aristide Olivier, is an unpretentious two star joint which lists prices both in French francs and euros. Basic but bright singles/doubles cost 120/160FF. Rooms with a shower are 200/270FF.

North-west of the train station, ***Hôtel des Étuves*** (☎ 04 67 60 78 19), 24 Rue des Étuves, is on a pedestrianised street in the old city. Inside, the place creeps up like a vine around a spiral staircase. Singles with toilet start at 95FF, and there are singles/doubles with toilet and shower from 105/150FF. Close by, the clean and cheerful, no star ***Hôtel Majestic*** (☎ 04 67 66 26 85), 4 Rue du Cheval Blanc, has rooms with toilet for 110/130FF.

Near the Halles Laissac market, ***Hôtel du Littoral*** (☎ 04 67 92 28 10; fax 04 67 58 93 41), 3 Impasse Saint Sauveur (off Rue Anatole France), is relatively peaceful, although it's down a grim alley. Large, basic rooms start at 120/155FF; rooms with shower cost from 170/175FF. Hall showers are 15FF.

Three blocks away, ***Hôtel Abysse*** (☎ 04 67 92 39 05) at 13 Rue du Général Campredon has basic but pleasant singles from 99FF or singles/doubles with shower from 129/149FF. Just a few doors down at No 7, ***Hôtel Cosmos*** (☎ 04 67 92 43 97) affords a warmer welcome. Singles/doubles/triples with shower cost from 150 to 250FF. Street parking – a rarity in Montpellier – is available nearby.

Places to Stay – Mid-Range & Top End

Hôtel Mistral (☎ 04 67 58 45 25; fax 04 67 58 23 95), named after the southern wind, is at 25 Rue Boussairolles and is rather a grand place with basic singles without shower for 147FF and singles/doubles with shower from 200/225FF. Given that there's no hall shower, it's worth investing in the latter option.

Another two star place is ***Hôtel Édouard VII*** (☎ 04 67 58 42 13; fax 04 67 58 93 66), 10 Rue Aristide Olivier. It's more modern in tone and has shower-equipped rooms from 190FF.

Closer to the action is ***Hôtel de la Comédie*** (☎ 04 67 58 43 64; fax 04 67 58 58 43), 1bis Rue Baudin. Rooms with shower are 175/255FF.

Next to the Aqueduc de Saint Clément, ***Hôtel Les Arceaux*** (☎ 04 67 92 03 03; fax 04 67 92 05 09), 33 Blvd des Arceaux, has rooms from 235/315FF.

Feeling decadent? Head for the height of luxury at the much-acclaimed ***Jardin des Sens*** (☎ 04 67 79 63 38; fax 04 67 72 13 05), beautifully located in the old city at 11 Ave Saint Lazare. Its 11 rooms range in price from 650 to 2000FF, while breakfast in the 'Garden of Senses' costs a staggering 85FF.

Places to Eat

Restaurants Eating places abound in every nook and cranny of Montpellier's crammed old quarter. Through the stone arch at 20 Rue Jacques Cœur is ***Tripti Kulai*** (☎ 04 67 66 30 51), a popular vegetarian place with salads from 49FF and a *menu* for 69FF. It's open from noon to 9.30 pm (closed Sunday). The brasserie-style ***Restaurant Cerdan*** (☎ 04 67 60 86 96), 8 Rue Collot, has five different *menus* of mostly local fare ranging from 71 to 190FF. It is open until 11.30 pm (closed Sunday).

The back patio of ***La Diligence*** (☎ 04 67 66 12 21), 2 Place Pétrarque, is spanned by one of the Hôtel de Varennes' Gothic-style galleries. An 86/145FF *menu* is served at lunch/dinner. Close by at 27 Rue de l'Aiguillerie is ***Maison de la Lozère***, home to a truly superb restaurant with a vaulted Gothic-style décor. Its regional 159FF *menu* includes tripe, cold meats and cheeses.

West at Place des Martyrs de la Résistance is the quaint ***Le Menestrel*** (☎ 04 67 60 62 51), a 13th century vaulted place at 2 Impasse Périer. Lunch/evening *menus* start at 78/90FF.

Close to the train station, there are a couple of Chinese places on Rue Sérane. For delicious Italian fare, try the cosy

Restaurant Verdi (☎ 04 67 58 68 55), next to the Hôtel Édouard VII on Rue Aristide Olivier. *Menus* start at 75FF and it's open from noon to 3 pm and 7 pm to midnight (closed Sunday).

At the top end of Rue de l'Aiguillerie is Place de la Chapelle Neuve, a shady square lined with little restaurants including ***Le Vieil Écu*** (☎ 04 67 66 39 44) at No 1, which specialises in regional fare and has a three course *menu* for 99FF. Just north of the cathedral at 24 Rue du Cardinal de Cabrières, ***L'Épicurien*** (☎ 04 67 66 09 43) is a popular, hole-in-the-wall restaurant with local specialities. If you prefer greener surrounds, try the lovely ***Le Petit Jardin*** (☎ 04 67 60 78 78), 20 Rue Jean-Jacques Rousseau, which overlooks a fairy-tale little garden. Lunch and dinner *menus* are 80/110FF.

Still feeling decadent? Head back to ***Jardin des Sens*** (see Places to Stay) and dine at the restaurant here run by French twin chefs Jacques and Laurent Pourcel. Sadly, our budget could not stretch to testing the 350 to 530FF *menus*, but they must be tasty: Michelin crowns this place with three stars. Reservations are required.

Cafés All summer long, Place de la Comédie is strewn with cafés where you can grab a quick bite and watch street entertainers perform. Smaller, more intimate squares – equally chair-filled – include Place Jean Jaurès, and the lovely Place Saint Ravy, just south of Place Castellane and off Rue Cauzit.

L'Heure Bleue (☎ 04 67 66 41 65), just round the corner from the Maison de la Lozère on Rue de la Carbonnerie, is a beautifully decorated tea salon where you can sip Earl Grey amid a backdrop of classical music. As well as lunch, the 'Blue Hour' serves a 35FF breakfast and is open from 10 am to 7 pm (closed Sunday).

Simple Simon (☎ 04 67 66 03 43), 1 Rue des Trésoriers de France, is an English tearoom serving cheese scones, cheese and onion pies, 18 types of tea and other British delights. It is open from 10.30 am to 7 pm (closed Sunday).

For fishy treats, head for the welcoming ***Salmon Shop***, 5 Rue de la Petite Lodge, which has a salmon-based *plat du jour* for 55FF, smoked salmon sandwiches for 29FF and salmon salads for 36FF.

The ***Crêperie Les Blés Noirs*** (☎ 04 67 60 43 03), just off Rue du Petit Saint Jean at 5 Rue Four des Flammes, is a cosy spot with *sarrasin* (buckwheat) crêpes from 20 to 51FF and seafood or vegetarian salads from 32 to 43FF. The ***Factory Café*** at the north end of Rue de Verdun has a terrace in the shade.

Self-Catering ***Food markets*** operating daily until about noon include one on Place Jean Jaurès, the adjoining ***Halles Castellane***, and another in the car park-like ***Halles Laissac*** on Place Laissac. ***Le Polygone*** shopping complex is bursting with shops – *boulangeries*, *fromageries* etc – that are generally open until 6 or 7 pm (closed Sunday). ***Monoprix***, Place de la Comédie, has a ground floor grocery section open from 8.30 am to 8 pm (closed Sunday).

Luxury local food products – cheeses, honey with almonds, sweet chestnuts, truffles and the like – are sold at the ***Maison de la Lozère*** (see Tourist Offices under Information earlier in this section), and at ***Pinto***, 14 Rue d'Argenterie.

Entertainment

Montpellier has a bursting cultural calendar. To find out what's on where, pick up the free weekly *Agenda* guide at the tourist office.

Tickets for performances held at Montpellier's numerous theatres are sold at the ***Opéra-Comédie*** box office (☎ 04 67 60 05 45), Place de la Comédie. Contemporary opera, theatre and classical concerts are also hosted by the very modern ***Le Corum*** (☎ 04 67 61 67 61; corum@corum-montpellier.fr), at the north end of Esplanade Charles de Gaulle.

For a drink, a handful of local haunts flank Rue En-Gondeau, off Rue Grand Jean Moulin. Gay bars include ***Martin's*** (☎ 04 67 60 37 15), 5 Rue de Girone, and ***Volt Face*** (☎ 04 67 52 86 89), 4 Rue des Écoles Laïques.

Getting There & Away

Air Montpellier's airport (☎ 04 67 20 85 00), off Route de Carnon, is 8km south-east of the city.

Bus The bus station (☎ 04 67 92 01 43), Place du Bicentenaire, is to the left as you exit the train station.

Courriers du Midi (☎ 04 67 06 03 67) operates an hourly bus to La Grande Motte (22FF; 40 minutes); a few of these buses continue on to Aigues Mortes (33.50FF; 1½ hours; six a day) and, in summer, Les Saintes Maries de la Mer in the Camargue (63FF; two hours). Autocars du Languedoc (☎ 04 67 92 60 35) has buses to Gignac (40 minutes) and points farther inland as well as to the beaches at Palavas and La Grande Motte.

Eurolines (☎ 04 67 58 57 59; fax 04 67 58 86 33), open from 9 am to noon and 2 to 6 pm (closed Sunday), runs buses to most European destinations including Barcelona (295FF; five hours), London (590FF; 17 hours) and Amsterdam (580FF; 21 hours). Linebus (☎ 04 67 58 53 16), open from 9 am to noon and 2 to 9 pm (closed Sunday), operates buses to Spain.

Train The two storey train station (☎ 08 36 35 35 35), Place Auguste Gibert, is 500m south of Place de la Comédie. The information office is open from 8 am to 8 pm (closed Sunday), while the station's upper level and the ticket windows are open from 5 am to 10 pm. On the ground floor there's a left-luggage room (10 to 30FF a day depending on luggage size), open from 8 am to noon and 2 to 5.30 pm. The station itself is open from 5.15 am to 10.30 pm.

Major connections from Montpellier include Paris' Gare de Lyon (312FF via TGV; four to five hours; about 10 a day), Carcassonne (120FF; 1½ hours; 16 a day), Millau (134FF; three hours; six a day) and Perpignan (120FF; two hours; 16 a day) via Narbonne. Locally, there are connections to Nîmes (66FF; 30 minutes; 20 a day), Sète (35FF; 20 minutes), Agde (66FF; 30 minutes), Béziers (79FF; 45 minutes) and Narbonne (88FF; one hour).

Car All the major car-rental companies have offices at the airport. In town, try Europcar (☎ 04 67 06 89 00) in front of the train station at 6 Rue Jules Ferry or Budget (☎ 04 67 92 69 00) and Avis (☎ 04 67 92 92 00), both of which have offices inside the train station.

Boat Compagnie Marocaine de Navigation (COMNAV) runs ferries to the Moroccan port of Tangier from the port of Sète, 26km (20 minutes by train) south-west of Montpellier. Tickets, schedules and information are available from SNCM (☎ 04 67 46 68 00; fax 04 67 74 93 05) at 4 Quai d'Alger in Sète.

A ferry departs every four days year-round from Sète at 7 am, arriving in Tangier 36 hours later. The return boat, which also leaves every four days, departs from Tangier at 6 pm. Single/return fares start at 1360/2180FF, and student fares start at 950/1900FF. Single tariffs for cars/motorcycles start at around 1970/900FF, but discounts are available if you're a student, under 26 or in a group of at least four people.

Getting Around

To/From the Airport The regional bus company Courriers du Midi runs a Navette shuttle bus (☎ 04 67 06 03 78) between the airport and the bus station (20FF; 15 minutes).

Bus City buses are run by SMTU (☎ 04 67 22 87 87), whose office at 27 Rue Maguelone is open from 7 am to 7 pm (closed Sunday). Regular buses run daily until about 8.30 pm, though the Petibus electric minibuses that circulate through the restricted old city can be caught until 7.30 pm from Monday to Saturday. At night, a service called Le Rabelais takes over. It makes a loop around the old city from the train station, and the last bus departs at 12.30 am. Individual bus tickets cost 7FF. A pass that entites you to unlimited transport for one day, including the Le Rabelais service, is 20FF and a 10 ticket carnet is 53FF.

towers, an interesting façade and a huge 14th century rose window.

The Biterrois are keen on rugby. Bullfighting is also very popular, and opponents of that activity would be wise to stay away during the four day *féria* (bullfighting festival) in early August.

Buses run by Courriers du Midi (☎ 04 67 28 23 85) and other companies leave from the north and south sides of the enormous Place Jean Jaurès for Agde, Castres, Colombiers, Montpellier, Narbonne and Valras. The train station (☎ 08 36 35 35 35) is south of the centre on Blvd de Verdun.

NARBONNE

• pop 47,086 ✉ 11100

Once a coastal port but now 13km inland as a result of siltation, Narbonne is a quiet provincial town with a long history. As the capital of Gallia Narbonensis, it was one of the main centres of Roman rule in Gaul. With the collapse of Rome, it became the capital of the Visigoth kingdom before passing to the Moors and then the Franks. It was incorporated into France in 1507.

The town is dominated by the massive **Cathédrale Saint Just**. Construction of the cathedral was halted in the early 14th century, but its unfinished Gothic choir is still one of the highest in France. The cathedral **treasury** contains a beautiful Flemish tapestry of the Creation; the lovely **cloister** dates from the 15th and 16th centuries. You can climb the 105 steps to the top of the **Tour du Nord** (North Tower).

Adjoining the cathedral to the south and facing Place de l'Hôtel de Ville, the fortified **Palais des Archevêques** (Archbishops' Palace) comprises a number of buildings, including the **Donjon Gilles Aycelin**, a large, square tower dating from the 13th century, and Viollet-le-Duc's 19th century **Hôtel de Ville**, which houses the **Musée d'Art et d'Histoire** and **Musée Archéologique** (☎ 04 68 90 30 54).

Out of town, just north of Sigean (15km south of Narbonne) on the western shores of the Étang de Bages et de Sigean, is the **Réserve Africaine de Sigean** (☎ 04 68 48 20 20; fax 04 68 48 80 85), where lions, tigers and other 'safari' specimens live in semi-liberty. For more information contact the Narbonne tourist office (☎ 04 68 65 15 60; fax 04 68 65 59 12) on Place Roger Salengro.

CARCASSONNE

• pop 43,500 ✉ 11000

From afar, Carcassonne looks like a fairy-tale medieval city come back to life. Bathed in the late-afternoon sun and highlighted by dark clouds, the Cité (as the old walled city is known) is truly breathtaking.

Once inside the fortified walls, however, Carcassonne is far from magical. Luring some 200,000 visitors in July and August alone, it is nothing short of a tourist hell in summer. American actor/director Kevin Costner might well have deemed it the perfect location for *Robin Hood, Prince of Thieves* in 1991, but for history buffs in search of genuine old fortifications, Carcassonne's 'medieval' Cité, which actually only dates from the 19th century, is very disappointing.

The Cité's defences are the culmination of many centuries of fortifications built on this spot by the Gauls, Romans, Visigoths, Moors and Franks. In the 13th century, they served as one of the major strongholds of the Cathars (see the boxed text 'The Cathars'). By the 18th century the Cité was 'little more than a slum', however, and it was only thanks to the zeal of Viollet-le-Duc that a decree in 1850 calling for the remaining fortifications to be demolished was not put into effect. Restoration work on the ancient ramparts, keeps, barbicans and towers was completed in 1910.

Carcassonne is not just the Cité, however. The lower town (known as the Ville Basse), an ugly stepsister to camp Cinderella up on the hill, was established in the mid-13th century after the city's inhabitants tried (and failed) to recapture the Cité, which Simon de Montfort had seized during the Albigensian Crusade. They were eventually permitted to return on the condition they rebuild their city on the lowlands on the left bank of the Aude River.

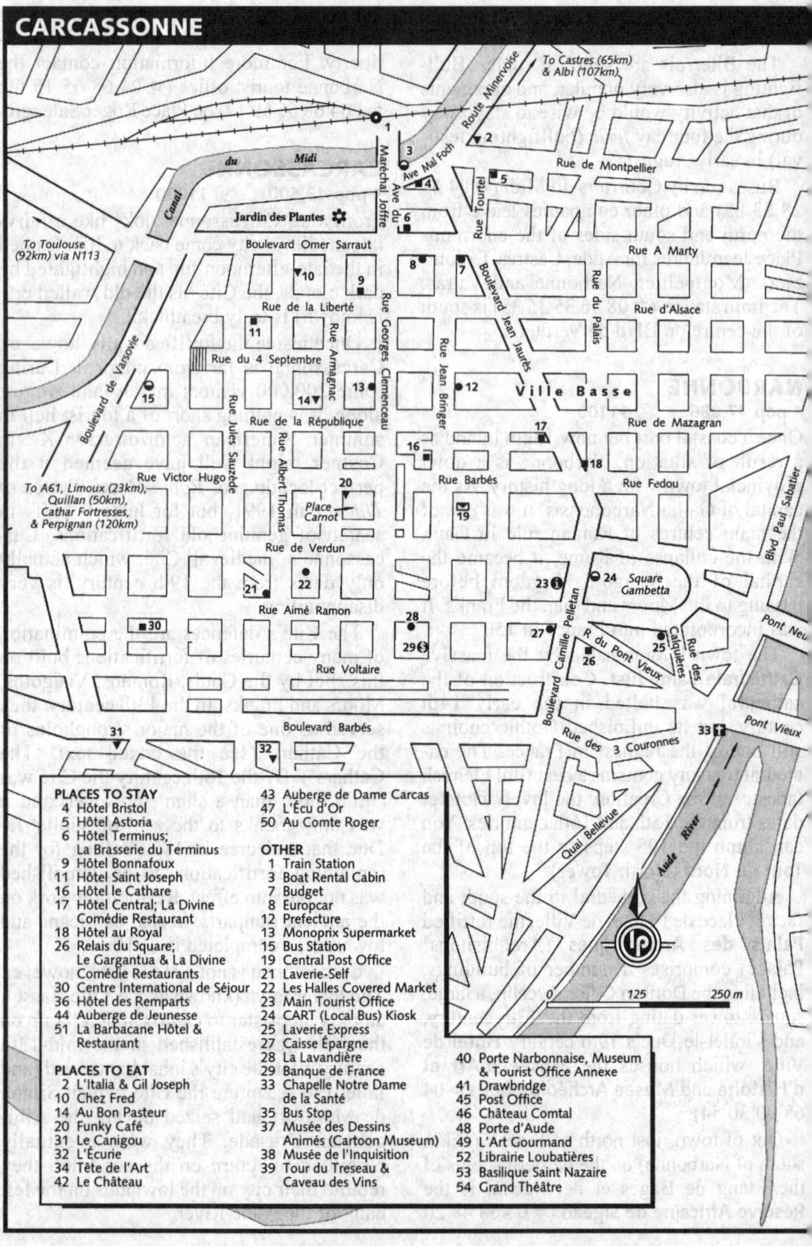

CARCASSONNE
To Castres (65km) & Albi (107km)
Route Minervoise
Canal du Midi
Ave du Maréchal Joffre
Ave Mal Foch
Rue de Montpellier
Rue Tourtel
Jardin des Plantes
To Toulouse (92km) via N113
Boulevard Omer Sarrault
Rue A Marty
Boulevard Jean Jaurès
Rue du Palais
Rue d'Alsace
Rue de la Liberté
Rue Armagnac
Rue Georges Clemenceau
Rue Jean Bringer
Rue du 4 Septembre
Boulevard de Varsovie
Ville Basse
Rue de Mazagran
Rue de la République
Rue Jules Sauzède
Rue Albert Thomas
Rue Victor Hugo
Rue Barbés
Rue Fedou
Blvd Paul Sabatier
To A61, Limoux (23km), Quillan (50km), Cathar Fortresses, & Perpignan (120km)
Place Carnot
Rue de Verdun
Square Gambetta
Rue Aimé Ramon
Boulevard Camille Pelletan
R du Pont Vieux
Rue des Calquières
Pont Neuf
Rue Voltaire
Boulevard Barbés
Rue des 3 Couronnes
Pont Vieux
Quai Bellevue
Aude River
0
125
250 m
PLACES TO STAY
4 Hôtel Bristol
5 Hôtel Astoria
6 Hôtel Terminus; La Brasserie du Terminus
9 Hôtel Bonnafoux
11 Hôtel Saint Joseph
16 Hôtel le Cathare
17 Hôtel Central; La Divine Comédie Restaurant
18 Hôtel au Royal
26 Relais du Square; Le Gargantua & La Divine Comédie Restaurants
30 Centre International de Séjour
36 Hôtel des Remparts
44 Auberge de Jeunesse
51 La Barbacane Hôtel & Restaurant
PLACES TO EAT
2 L'Italia & Gil Joseph
10 Chez Fred
14 Au Bon Pasteur
20 Funky Café
31 Le Canigou
32 L'Écurie
34 Tête de l'Art
42 Le Château
43 Auberge de Dame Carcas
47 L'Écu d'Or
50 Au Comte Roger
OTHER
1 Train Station
3 Boat Rental Cabin
7 Budget
8 Europcar
12 Prefecture
13 Monoprix Supermarket
15 Bus Station
19 Central Post Office
21 Laverie-Self
22 Les Halles Covered Market
23 Main Tourist Office
24 CART (Local Bus) Kiosk
25 Laverie Express
27 Caisse Épargne
28 La Lavandière
29 Banque de France
33 Chapelle Notre Dame de la Santé
35 Bus Stop
37 Musée des Dessins Animés (Cartoon Museum)
38 Musée de l'Inquisition
39 Tour du Treseau & Caveau des Vins
40 Porte Narbonnaise, Museum & Tourist Office Annexe
41 Drawbridge
45 Post Office
46 Château Comtal
48 Porte d'Aude
49 L'Art Gourmand
52 Librairie Loubatières
53 Basilique Saint Nazaire
54 Grand Théâtre

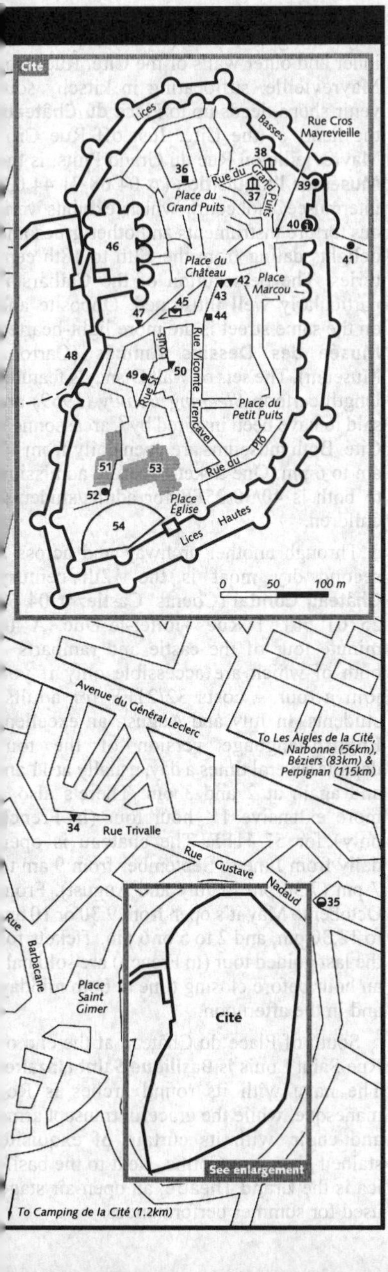

Orientation

The Aude River separates the Ville Basse – a perfect grid of one-way streets enclosed by boulevards – from the Cité, which is on a hill 500m to the south-east. The train station is on the northern edge of the Ville Basse, just over the Canal du Midi from the northern end of the pedestrianised Rue Georges Clemenceau.

The main gate to the Cité is called Porte Narbonnaise, from which Rue Cros Mayrevieille leads up to Place du Château and the Château Comtal. Basilique Saint Nazaire is about 150m to the south.

Information

Tourist Offices The main tourist office (☎ 04 68 10 24 30; fax 04 68 10 24 38; www.tourisme.fr/carcassonne) is in the Ville Basse at 15 Blvd Camille Pelletan opposite Square Gambetta, about halfway between the train station and the Cité. It's open from 9 am to noon and 1.45 to 6.30 pm (closed Sunday). The staff exchange money on weekends. There's a 5FF charge for hotel reservations.

In the Cité, there's a small tourist office (☎ 04 68 10 24 36; fax 04 68 10 24 37) in the Tour Narbonnaise, open from 9 am to 1 pm and 2 to 6 pm.

Money The Banque de France, 5 Rue Jean Bringer, is open from 8.30 am to 12.30 pm and 1.50 to 3.50 pm (closed on weekends). Other major banks are centred on Place Carnot in the Ville Basse.

Post The central post office, 40 Rue Jean Bringer, is open from 8 am to 7 pm (until noon on Saturday; closed Sunday). In the Cité, the branch opposite 17 Rue Porte d'Aude is open from 9 am to noon and 1.50 to 5 pm on weekdays, Saturday from 8.45 to 11.45 am (closed Sunday). Both exchange foreign currency.

Bookshop The Librairie Loubatières adjoining the Hôtel Barbacane on Place Église sells an excellent range of maps and guides, as well as quality art and history books on the region. It is open from 9 am to 6 pm (closed Sunday in winter).

Laundry La Lavandière, 37 Rue Aimé Ramon, is open from 8.30 am to 9.30 pm. The Laverie-Self, 63 Rue Aimé Ramon, is open from 9 am to 9 pm. The Laverie Express, 5 Square Gambetta, is open from 7 am to 7 pm.

Cité

While streets in the Ville Basse and the towpaths along the Canal du Midi are pleasant enough for wandering, the Cité – illuminated at night – is Carcassonne's only major sight. It is enclosed by two walls – the inner one 1.3km long, the outer 1.7km – that constitute one of the largest city fortifications in Europe. The ramparts are broken up by 52 stone towers.

Only the lower sections of the Cité's walls are original. The rest – including the anachronistic roofs shaped like witches' hats (the originals were flatter and weren't covered with slate) – were added by Viollet-le-Duc in the 19th century.

To get to the Cité's main entrance from the train station or Square Gambetta, take bus No 4, which runs every 30 minutes. On foot, the walk from the station takes 35 to 40 minutes – from Square Gambetta, the nicest route is along Rue du Pont Vieux, over the humped old bridge, along Rue Trivalle and Rue Gustave Nadaud to the main entrance. There's a smaller entrance for those on foot at Porte d'Aude. People with cars/caravans can park them at the main entrance for 20/30FF.

Once across the drawbridge (*pont-levis*) over the dry moat, you're immediately faced with a massive bastion, the **Porte Narbonnaise**. There's a tacky and rather dull **art museum** above the tourist office annexe; entry is free. Continuing past the tourist office you come to the **Tour du Treseau**, home to the Cité's **Caveau des Vins** (☎ 04 68 25 29 38). Inside this 13th century tower, which has been transformed into a wine cellar, you can taste and buy Languedoc wines. Dégustation for individual travellers is only possible in summer. The cellar is open year-round from 8 am to 9 pm.

You can also wander around the walkways and grassy *lices* (fields) between th inner and outer walls of the Cité. Rue Cro Mayrevieille, suffocating in kitschy souvenir shops, leads up to **Place du Château** the heart of the Cité. Just off Rue Cro Mayrevieille on Rue du Grand Puits, is th **Musée de l'Inquisition** (☎ 04 68 71 44 03 intermusee@aol.com), which exhibits various torture instruments and other gruesom delights dating from the 13th to 18th centuries. The persecution of the Cathars i particularly well illustrated. Opposite an on the same street is the more light-hearte **Musée des Dessins Animés** (Cartoo Museum). The sets of Walt Disney's feature length cartoon *Sleeping Beauty* (1959) ar said to have been inspired by Carcassonne' Cité. Both museums are open daily from 1 am to 6 pm. One ticket covering admissio to both is 40/30/25FF for adults/students children.

Through another archway and across second dry moat is the 12th centur **Château Comtal** (Counts' Castle; ☎ 04 6 25 01 66), 1 Rue Viollet-le-Duc. A 4 minute tour of the castle and ramparts both of which are accessible only if yo join a tour – costs 32/21FF for adults students. In July and August, an excellen English-language version of the tou departs several times a day, usually at 11 an and again at 2 and 3 pm. There's also more extensive 1½ hour tour (in Frencl only) for 57/41FF. The chateau is ope daily from June to September from 9 am t 7 pm (7.30 pm in July and August). Fron October to May it's open from 9.30 or 10 an to 12.30 pm, and 2 to 5 or 6 pm. Tickets fo the last guided tour (in French) are sold hal an hour before closing time at both midda and in the afternoon.

South of Place du Château at the end o Rue Saint Louis is **Basilique Saint Nazaire** The nave with its round arches is Romanesque, while the graceful transept arm and choir, with its curtain of exquisit stained glass, are Gothic. Next to the basilica is the **Grand Théâtre**, an open-air stag used for summer performances.

Falconry

The medieval art of falconry is demonstrated at **Les Aigles de la Cité** (☎ 04 68 47 88 89; fax 04 68 47 87 05), 800m south of the Cité walls on the Colline de Pech Mary. *Faucons* (falcons), *aigles* (eagles) and *vautours* (vultures) are just some of the birds of prey that can be seen here. Les Aigles is open from 2 pm (11 am in July and August) and a 45 minute demonstration is held at 3 pm.

Special Events

On 14 July at 10.30 pm, the Cité is illuminated with a mass of fireworks to celebrate Bastille Day. Known as Embrasement de la Cité, it's quite a spectacle.

Between June and September during the Festivales d'Orgue de la Cité (☎ 04 68 47 26 97 for information), classical music concerts are held on Sunday at 5 pm in the Basilique Saint Nazaire. Performances are preceded by a 30 minute carillon concert. Throughout July, the Festival de Carcassonne (☎ 04 68 77 71 26) brings music, opera, dance and theatre to the city. Tickets start at 140FF and should be booked in advance.

The first three weeks of August grace the Cité with a barrage of medieval music concerts, tournaments and theatre performances. October brings forth the Fête des Vendanges, primarily a drinking festival hosted by the Caveau des Vins to celebrate the region's grape harvest.

Places to Stay

Camping The ***Camping de la Cité*** (☎ 04 68 25 11 77), on Route de Saint Hilaire about 3.5km south of the main tourist office, charges around 65/90FF for two people with a tent or caravan depending on the season. It's open between March and early October. Take bus No 5 (hourly until 6.40 pm) from Square Gambetta to the Route de Cazilhac stop.

Hostels In the heart of the Cité on Rue Vicomte Trencavel, the very pleasant 120 bed ***Auberge de Jeunesse*** (☎ 04 68 25 23 16; fax 04 68 71 14 84) has dorm beds for 70FF, including breakfast. Sheets are 14FF. There is a snack bar offering light meals and a wonderful outside terrace where occasional theatre performances are held in summer. The hostel is open from 7 am to 11.30 pm. Annual closure is from 10 December to the end of January. Take bus No 4 (last one at 6.50 pm) from the train station to La Cité stop.

A bed at the ***Centre International de Séjour*** (☎ 04 68 25 86 68; fax 04 68 25 48 96), 91 Rue Aimé Ramon in the Ville Basse, costs 68FF a night including breakfast.

Gîtes For B&B accommodation in the city and more rural accommodation contact the ***Gîtes de France*** office (☎ 04 68 11 40 70; fax 04 68 11 40 72), 78 Rue Barbacane, west of the Cité.

Hotels – Train Station Area Just a five minute walk from the train station is the warm and highly recommended ***Hôtel Astoria*** (☎ 04 68 25 31 38; fax 04 68 71 34 14) at 18 Rue Tourtel. It has a lovely reception area and immaculate, renovated rooms – basic singles/doubles with basin and bidet cost 110/130FF. A hall shower is 10FF and parking next to the Astoria's annexe on Rue de Montpellier is free.

Hôtel Bonnafoux (☎ 04 68 25 01 45), 40 Rue de la Liberté, has basic rooms from 100/120FF or with shower for 140/146FF. A hall shower is 15FF. Rooms are sparsely furnished.

A statue of the saint guards the entrance to the ***Hôtel Saint Joseph*** (☎ 04 68 25 10 94; fax 04 68 71 36 28), 81 Rue de la Liberté, which has doubles with/without shower from 120/130FF.

Facing the station, the huge three star ***Hôtel Bristol*** (☎ 04 68 25 07 24; fax 04 68 25 71 89), 7 Ave Maréchal Foch, has singles/doubles with shower and toilet for 175/250FF. It is part of the reliable Logis de France chain. Adjoining it at 2 Ave du Maréchal Joffre is the equally giant ***Hôtel Terminus*** (☎ 04 68 25 25 00) which has rooms with shower for 260/293FF and with bath for 290/340FF.

Hotels – Ville Basse There are several places within a two or three block radius of the main tourist office. The ***Relais du Square*** (☎ 04 68 72 31 72; fax 04 68 25 01 08), 51 Rue du Pont Vieux, is amiable, with a good selection of large rooms – a double costs 140FF, a double with shower is 170FF, and two-bed triples are 230FF. ***Hôtel le Cathare*** (☎ 04 68 25 65 92), 53 Rue Jean Bringer, has smaller, ordinary doubles with/without shower from 170/115FF. In the off season, it offers singles/doubles with shower for 140/165FF including breakfast.

On Blvd Jean Jaurès, the two star ***Hôtel Central*** (☎ 04 68 25 03 84; fax 04 68 72 46 41) at No 27 has sparsely furnished, adequate doubles with shower and TV from 180FF. Opposite at No 22, ***Hôtel au Royal*** (☎ 04 68 25 19 12; fax 04 68 47 33 01) has rooms with shower, TV and toilet from 220FF. Both hotels face a busy street; ask for a room at the back.

Hotels – Cité Rooms start at around 250FF in the vicinity of the Cité. Inside the walls, ***Hôtel des Remparts*** (☎ 04 68 71 27 72; fax 04 68 72 73 26), 3-5 Place du Grand Puits, has a lovely stone façade that hides quite garish modern rooms (from 300/330FF for singles/doubles).

For the ultimate splurge check into ***La Barbacane Hôtel*** (☎ 04 68 25 03 34; fax 04 68 71 50 15), Place Église. Rooms fit for royalty start at 1000FF.

Places to Eat

Restaurants – Ville Basse Highly favoured locally is the small and cosy ***Au Bon Pasteur*** (☎ 04 68 25 46 58), 29 Rue Armagnac. Pluses include an apron-clad chef who has been greeting guests as they enter for the past 20 or so years, nine different seafood dishes, yummy *cassoulet* and foie gras, and *menus* from 72FF. It is open at lunchtime from noon and in the evening from 7.30 pm.

Equally popular is ***Chez Fred***, close to the train station at the north end of Rue Albert Thomas. It has rustic décor and a great outside terrace where traditional live bands play some evenings. The good-value lunchtime *menu* is 98FF including coffee and a glass of wine; evening *menus* start at 105FF. Fred opens at noon. Other handy little numbers close to the station include ***L'Italia*** (☎ 04 68 47 08 64), a pizzeria at 32 Route Minervoise; ***Gil Joseph*** (☎ 04 68 47 85 23), next door on the same street; and ***La Brasserie du Terminus*** (☎ 94 68 71 50 40), 2 Ave du Maréchal Joffre.

Possibly the cheapest *menu* in town can be found at the ***Relais du Square*** (see Places to Stay). It has two restaurants: the more upmarket, street-front ***Le Gargantua***, with *menus* from 78FF, and the unpretentious, nameless diner out the back, which has a bargain 54FF *menu du jour*. ***La Divine Comédie***, a pizzeria at the ***Hôtel Central*** (see Places to Stay), has a very pleasant outside terrace.

If you want to escape from other tourists, dine at ***Le Canigou*** (☎ 04 68 25 22 01), 97 Blvd Barbés, or ***L'Écurie*** (☎ 04 68 72 04 04), 1 Rue d'Alembert. Both serve hearty local cuisine at heart-warming prices.

Restaurants – Cité Thankfully Carcassonne's Cité chefs have not let their standards drop despite the onslaught of undiscerning tourists that bombard their establishments. ***Le Château*** (☎ 04 68 25 05 16), 4 Place du Château, is an upscale place with *menus* from 88FF. Next door is the more casual ***Auberge de Dame Carcas*** (☎ 04 68 71 23 23).

Close by at 7 Rue Porte d'Aude ***L'Écu d'Or*** (☎ 04 68 25 49 03) serves various cassoulet dishes and touts a kids' *menu* (60FF) as well as adult-sized ones (from 120FF). Favoured more for its delightful terrace enclosed in a pretty courtyard away from the milling crowds is the ***Au Comte Roger*** (☎ 04 68 25 31 78), 14 Rue Saint Louis.

Graced with a single Michelin star is the chic ***Barbacane*** (see Places to Stay), housed in a neo-Gothic edifice overlooking the Basilique Saint Nazaire on Place Église. Specialities include *lotte en rôti* (roasted monkfish) and *rable de lapin farci de blettes* saddle of rabbit stuffed with Swiss chard). Book in advance – and expect to pay at least 300FF a head.

Cafés The cafés overlooking Place Carnot spill out onto the fountain-clad square in summer. The café on the corner of Place Carnot and Rue Victor Hugo is a particularly funky place favoured for its outside seating and mind-boggling choice of coffee.

In the Cité, Place Marcou is one big outside café when the sun shines. At the foot of the Cité walls is ***Tête de l'Art*** (☎ 04 68 47 36 36), 37bis Rue Trivalle. Live bands play here some nights and its house specialities are 'pork dishes and good humour'. It's open from 8 am to 2 am.

Self-Catering Fresh flowers, fruit and vegetables are sold in abundance at the morning ***open-air market*** held on Place Carnot on Tuesday, Thursday and Saturday. For fresh fish and meat head for the covered ***Les Halles*** market on Rue de Verdun (open daily except Sunday).

The ***Monoprix*** supermarket on Rue Georges Clemenceau is open from 8.30 am to 7 pm (closed Sunday). Chocolate fiends should head straight for the irresistible ***L'Art Gourmand***, 13 Rue Saint Louis, selling a creative range of calorie-laced goodies. Its ice cream is pretty hot too.

Getting There & Away

Bus The bus station (☎ 04 68 25 12 74) is next to 20bis Blvd de Varsovie up the steps at the western end of Rue du 4 Septembre, about 500m south-west of the train station. Regional buses are run by Trans Aude, which has services to Narbonne (41FF; 1½ hours) and Toulouse (56FF; 2½ hours).

Eurolines, whose buses mainly serve Spain and Portugal, drops off and picks up passengers at the bus station.

Train The train station (☎ 08 36 35 35 35) is at the end of Rue Georges Clemenceau, 1km north of the main tourist office and 2km from the Cité. The information office is open from 9 am until noon and 1.30 to 6.20 pm (closed Sunday). The luggage room is open between 5.30 am and 11 pm.

Carcassonne is on the important rail line linking Toulouse (92FF; 50 minutes; 15 trains a day) with Béziers (89FF; 50 minutes; seven a day), Narbonne (74FF; 30 minutes; 14 a day), Sète (96FF; two hours via Narbonne) and Montpellier (120FF; 1½ hours; 16 a day via Narbonne). There are two direct trains a day south to Perpignan (110FF; 1½ hours); alternatively, change at Narbonne.

Getting Around

Bus Local buses are run by CART (☎ 04 68 47 82 22), which has an information kiosk on Square Gambetta, the central bus hub. Bus No 4 runs every half-hour between the train station, Square Gambetta and Rue Gustave Nadaud near the Cité's Porte Narbonnaise. Single tickets/carnet of 10 cost 5.30/46FF. Buses run until about 7 pm, there's no service on Sunday and some schedules are curtailed in July and August.

Car Europcar (☎ 04 68 25 05 09), 7 Blvd Omer Sarraut; Hertz (☎ 04 68 25 41 26), 33 Blvd Omer Sarraut; and Budget (☎ 04 68 72 31 31), 72bis Alée d'Iéna, are all a two minute walk from the train station.

Taxi Taxis loiter outside the train station. Alternatively, order one on ☎ 04 68 71 50 50.

Boat Motorboats and houseboats can be hired under the bridge linking the train station with the Ville Basse. For information call Nautic (☎ 04 68 71 88 95; fax 04 67 94 05 41), Ave Maréchal Foch in Carcassonne, or Nicols (☎ 04 68 32 47 24; fax 04 68 32 47 28), 36 Quai Valière in Narbonne. Both arrange boats departing from Carcassonne.

Bicycle You cannot rent two wheels in Carcassonne but L'Olive Bleue (☎ 04 68 24 03 03; fax 04 68 24 02 89), 12 Ave Malbec in Montlaur some 20km south-east, rents mountain bikes and delivers them to your doorstep in Carcassonne. Rental costs 80/160/350FF for a day/weekend/one week.

LANGUEDOC

AROUND CARCASSONNE

Cathar Fortresses

Some of the most inaccessible fortresses in which the Cathars sought refuge were built along the boundary between the French and Aragonese spheres of influence a century or more before the Albigensian Crusade. The two most famous fortresses, Peyrepertuse and Quéribus, are about halfway between Carcassonne and Perpignan along the D14. Both are open between Easter and September from 9 or 10 am to 6 or 8 pm.

The tourist offices in Carcassonne has two English-language brochures, indispensable for any trip to the Cathar Land). *In the Footsteps of the Cathars* provides historical detail on 20-plus fortresses and includes a regional map with them all marked on. *Les Sentiers du Pays Cathare* (Cathar Land Paths) lists 12 different hikes in the region from 11 to 26km long. For further information contact the Centre for Cathar Studies (CEC; ☎ 04 68 47 24 66), Maison des Mémoires, 53 Rue de Verdun, F-11000 Carcassonne.

The fortresses are impossible to reach without your own wheels. From Carcassonne, the only way to get to the castles by public transport is to take a bus to Quillan (48FF; 1 hour 20 minutes; three a day) and then a Perpignan bound bus (two a day) to the village of Maury, on the D117. From here it's a 7km uphill walk to Quéribus and a farther 8km to Peyrepertuse.

From the village of Saint Paul de Fenouillet, 8km west of Maury on the D117, the GR36 hiking trail also leads to Peyrepertuse (about 10km). The Quillan-Perpignan bus stops in Saint Paul as well. Up-to-date bus schedules and information on hiking routes to the fortresses are available from Quillan tourist office (☎ 04 68 20 07 78).

NÎMES

• pop 133,000 ✉ 30000

Nîmes, a little bit Provençal (Avignon is only 47km to the north-east) but with a soul as Languedocien as cassoulet, is graced by

The Canal du Midi

This beautiful canal, which affords great views over the sun-baked Languedoc plain, runs from the Bassin de Thau between Agde and Sète on the Mediterranean coast to Toulouse, where it connects with another canal leading west to the Atlantic Ocean at Bordeaux. Built in the late 17th century by 15,000 labourers under the tutelage of Paul Riquet (1604-80) of Béziers, this 240km-long waterway was designed to enable cargo vessels to sail from the Atlantic to the Mediterranean without having to go all the way around Spain.

The Canal du Midi passes many villages and cities as it follows the curve of the Montagne Noire foothills via aqueducts and more than 100 *écluses* (locks), sometimes as many as nine in a row (as is the case near Béziers). Along its entire length it is flanked by plane trees that provide shade and control evaporation. Although its importance to trade has greatly diminished, barges still ply the waters of the canal and its connecting waterways.

In summer they are joined by canal boats hired by tourists, and queues often develop at the locks. Crown Blue Line (☎ 04 68 94 52 72; fax 04 68 94 52 73; boathols@crown-blueline.com; www.crown-blueline.com), Le Grand Bassin BP 21, F-11401 Castelnaudary, arranges one week boat holidays on the Canal du Midi, ranging in length from 130km (26 hours navigation time and 44 locks) to 177km (36 hours navigation time and 98 locks). See Boat in the Getting Around chapter at the beginning of this book for more details.

Before setting sail pick up a copy of the excellent brochures entitled *Canal du Midi et de la Robine – Tourisme Fluvial* and *Autour du Canal du Midi et de la Robine*. Both are available in English also from Carcassonne's tourist offices.

ome of the best preserved Roman public uildings in Europe. Most famous are the rènes, an amphitheatre reminiscent of the Colosseum in Rome, and a 1st century emple known as the Maison Carrée. ounded by Augustus, the Roman Colonia emausensis reached its zenith during the nd century AD, receiving its water supply rom a Roman aqueduct system that includ-d the Pont du Gard, an awesome arched ridge 23km north-east of town. The acking of the city by the Vandals in the arly 5th century began a downward spiral from which it has never recovered. Mind you, lazy and laid-back Nîmes does get more than 300 days of sunshine every year.

Nîmes becomes more Spanish than French during its férias. The surrounding countryside is composed of vineyards and *garrigue*, Languedoc moors whose herbal vegetation gives off a powerful fragrance in spring and early summer. Nîmes is a good base from which to explore the nearby limestone hills, the picturesque village of Uzès and the Pont du Gard.

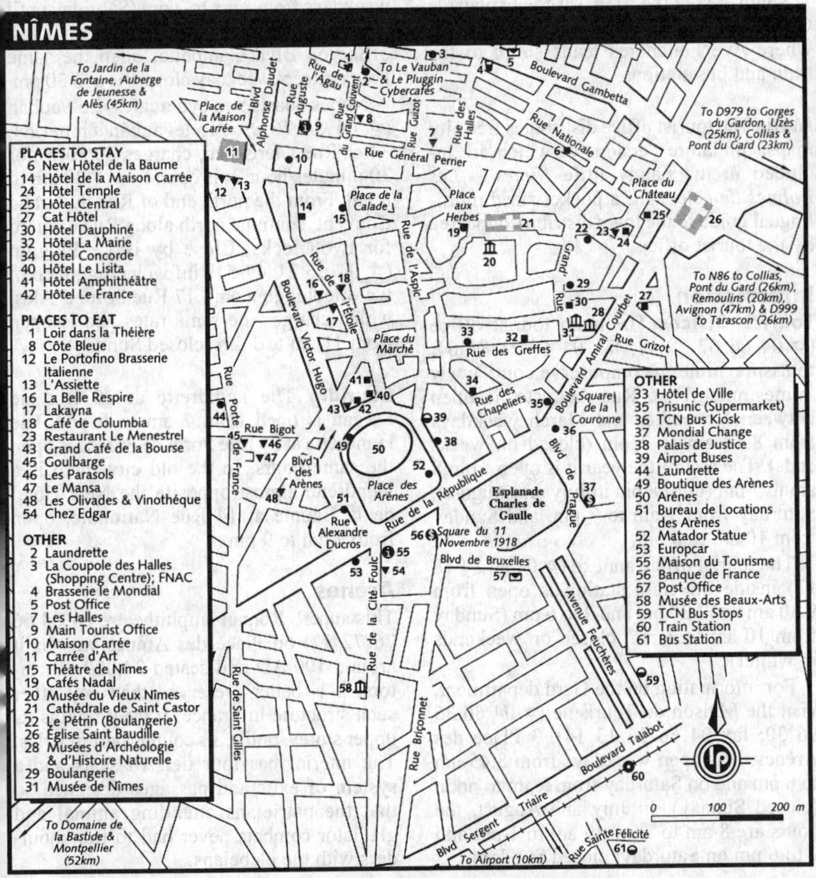

Orientation

Almost everything, including traffic, revolves around the Arènes. Just north of the amphitheatre, the fan-shaped, largely pedestrianised old city is bounded by Blvd Victor Hugo, Blvd Amiral Courbet and Blvd Gambetta. The main squares are Place de la Maison Carrée, Place du Marché and Place aux Herbes, just north of which lies the carefully preserved Îlot Littré, the old dyer's quarter where Nîmes *serge* (better known as denim; see the boxed text 'Denim de Nîmes') was made in the 18th century.

South-east of the Arènes is the Esplanade Charles de Gaulle, a large open square from where Ave Feuchères leads south to the train and bus stations.

Maps The tourist office distributes free city maps, miniature versions of which are included in the handy little *Nîmes – Les Palmes de l'Accueil*, a pocket-sized multilingual guide to the town distributed for free by the tourist office.

Information

Tourist Offices The main tourist office (☎ 04 66 67 29 11; fax 04 66 21 81 04; tourisme_nimes@compuserve.com; www.nimes.mnet.fr), 6 Rue Auguste, is open between November and March weekdays from 8.30 am to 7 pm (closed on weekends). The rest of the year it is open from 8 am to 7 pm (until 8 pm in July and August), Saturday from 9 am to 7 pm, and Sunday from 10 am to 6 pm.

The tourist office annexe (☎ 04 66 84 18 13) inside the train station is open from 9.30 am to 12.30 pm and 2 to 6 pm (Sunday from 10 am to 3 pm; closed on weekends in winter).

For information on the Gard department, visit the Maison du Tourisme (☎ 04 66 36 96 30; fax 04 66 36 13 14), 3 Place des Arènes. It is open weekdays from 8.45 am to 6 pm and on Saturday from 9 am to noon (closed Sunday). In July and August, the hours are 8 am to 7 pm (9 am to 1 pm and 2 to 6 pm on Saturday; closed Sunday).

Money Across from Place des Arènes, the Banque de France on Square du 11 Novembre 1918 is open from 8.30 am to 12.15 pm and 1.45 to 3.30 pm (closed on weekends). Blvd Victor Hugo and Blvd Amiral Courbet are lined with banks.

Mondial Change (☎ 04 66 21 93 94), 5 Blvd de Prague, has decent rates and even better opening hours: 9 am to 7 pm seven days a week year-round.

Post & Communications The central post office, on the north-west corner of Ave Feuchères at 1 Blvd de Bruxelles, is open weekdays from 8 am to 7 pm (Saturday until noon; closed Sunday). There's a branch post office on Blvd Gambetta, open the same hours, except weekday closure is at 6.30 pm.

Nîmes boasts two cybercafés. Le Vauban (☎ 04 66 76 09 71; levauban@mnet.fr), 34ter Rue Clérisseau, charges 30/50FF for 30 minutes/hour. It is open from 8.30 am to 8 pm. From the north end of Rue du Grand Couvent, continue north along Rue Menard for two blocks. Close by is Le Pluggin (☎ 04 66 21 49 51; info@lepluggin.com; www.lepluggin.com), 17 Rue Porte d'Alés, which charges the same rates and is open from 11 am to 1 am (closed Sunday).

Laundry The laundrette at 20 Rue de l'Agau is open from 7 am to 9 pm. The laundrette at 26 Rue Porte de France is open the same hours. In the old city there is a laundrette almost opposite the New Hôtel de la Baume at 14 Rue Nationale, open from 7 am to 9 pm.

Arènes

This superb Roman amphitheatre (☎ 04 66 76 72 77) on Place des Arènes was built around 100 AD and seated 24,000 spectators; it is better preserved than any other such structure in France. It even retains its upper storey, unlike its counterpart in Arles. The interior has four tiers of seats and a system of exits and passages designed so that the patricians attending animal and gladiator combats never had to rub shoulders with the plebeians.

Throughout the year the Arènes, which is covered by a high-tech removable roof from October to April, is used for theatre performances, music concerts and bullfights. Unless there's something on, it's open from 9 am to 12.30 pm and 2 to 6 pm (9 am to 6.30 pm in summer). Admission costs 26FF for adults and 20FF for students and children. Tickets, available until 30 minutes before it closes, are sold at the Boutique des Arènes (☎ 04 66 67 29 11), tucked into the amphitheatre's northern walls.

Maison Carrée

The rectangular, Greek-style temple known as the Maison Carrée (Square House; ☎ 04 66 36 26 76), Place de la Maison Carrée, is one of the most remarkably preserved Roman temples in the world. Built around 5 AD to honour Augustus' two nephews, it survived the centuries as a meeting hall (during the Middle Ages), a private residence, a stable (in the 17th century), a church and, after the Revolution, an archive.

The Maison Carrée, entered through six symmetrical Corinthian columns, sits at the southern end of Rue Auguste. It is open from 9 am to noon or 12.30 pm and from 2.30 to 7 pm (until 6 pm in winter). Admission is free.

The striking glass and steel building to the west across the square was completed in 1993 and is the modern **Carrée d'Art** (Square of Art; ☎ 04 66 76 35 77), containing the municipal library and Musée d'Art Contemporain (see Museums). It is the work of British architect Sir Norman Foster, who designed the seminal Hongkong & Shanghai Bank building in Hong Kong and Stansted airport north-east of London. It perfectly reflects the Maison Carrée and is everything modern architecture should be: innovative, complementary and beautiful.

Jardin de la Fontaine

The Fountain Garden, home to Nîmes' other important Roman monuments, is laid out around the Source de la Fontaine (the site of a spring, temple and baths in Roman times). It retains its rather elegant air, with statue-adorned paths running around deep, slimy-green waterways. The **Temple de Diane** is to the left through the main entrance.

A 10 minute walk through the gardens takes you to the crumbling shell of the **Tour Magne** (☎ 04 66 67 65 56), the largest of the many towers that once ran along the city's 7km-long Roman ramparts. Admission to the tower, which affords a fine view of the countryside around Nîmes, is 12FF for adults, and 10FF for students and children. A combination ticket allowing entry to the Arènes as well costs 32/26FF. The tower is open from 9 am to 7 pm (until 5 pm in winter).

The garden is almost 1km north-west of the amphitheatre. Bus No 2 from Ave Feuchères or the Esplanade Charles de Gaulle stops near the main entrance at the intersection of Ave Jean Jaurès and Quai de la Fontaine, the city's most interesting thoroughfare. The grounds close at around sunset.

Denim de Nîmes

During the 18th century, Nîmes' sizeable Protestant middle class – banned from government posts and various ways of earning a living – turned its energies to trade and manufacturing. Among the products made in Protestant-owned factories was a twilled fabric known as *serge*. This soft but durable fabric became very popular among workers and, stained blue, was the uniform of the fishermen of Genoa.

When Levi Strauss (1829-1902), a Bavarian-Jewish immigrant to the USA, began producing trousers in California during and after the gold rush of 1849, he soon realised that miners needed garments that would last. After trying tent canvas, he began importing the *serge de Nîmes*, now better known as denim.

LANGUEDOC

Museums

Nîmes' half-dozen museums are open daily from 11 am to 6 pm (closed Monday) and charge 26/20FF for adults/students. Museum buffs should buy a three day pass (60/30FF) from the tourist office, entitling you to entry to most sights in Nîmes.

The **Musée du Vieux Nîmes** (☎ 04 66 36 00 64), housed in the 17th century episcopal palace south of the rather unimpressive **Cathédrale de Saint Castor** on Place aux Herbes, is the city's most unappealing museum. Though themes change annually, the emphasis is always on some aspect of Nîmes' history. Equally fusty is the **Musée de Nîmes** (☎ 04 66 67 39 14), 19 Grande Rue.

The **Musée d'Archéologie** (☎ 04 66 67 25 57), 13 Blvd Amiral Courbet, brings together columns, mosaics, sculptures and personal effects from the Roman and pre-Roman periods that have been unearthed around Nîmes. In the same building, the **Musée d'Histoire Naturelle** has a musty collection of stuffed animals and rows of bulls' horns.

The **Musée des Beaux-Arts** (☎ 04 66 67 38 21), on Rue de la Cité Foulc between Nos 20 and 22, has an unsurprising collection of Flemish, Italian and French works as well as a Roman mosaic.

The ultramodern **Musée d'Art Contemporain** (☎ 04 66 76 35 70) in the Carrée d'Art on Place de la Maison Carrée has rotating exhibits of modern art. It's worth a visit just to see the insides of this striking building and the view of the Roman temple across the square. It opens at 10 am and charges 28/20FF admission for adults/students.

Organised Tours

The tourist office (see Information earlier in this section) offers various two-hour city tours (in French only) at 10 am and 2.30 pm on Tuesday, Thursday and Saturday in summer (10 am on Saturday in winter). Tours cost 25/20FF for adults/students and children. A 40 minute tour of the city by taxi (see Getting Around later) seating four people is 140FF.

The Centre Ornithologique du Gard (☎/fax 04 66 26 82 77), Centre André Malroux, Ave de Lattre de Tassigny, organises day trips for birdwatchers in and around Nîmes.

Special Events

In March Nîmes hosts the week-long Printemps du Jazz festival. July and August bring forth an abundance of dances, theatre, rock, pop and jazz events. A yearly calendar of events is available at the tourist office, or pick up a copy of the annual *Guide Culturel Nîmes*.

Férias & Bullfights The three férias – the three day Féria Primavera (Spring Festival) in February, the five day Féria de Pentecôte (Pentecost Festival) in June, and the three day Féria des Vendanges to mark the start of the grape harvest on the third weekend in September – revolve around a series of *corridas* (bullfights), one or two of which are held each day. Tickets to a corrida cost between 100 and 500FF; reservations generally have to be made months in advance through the Bureau de Locations des Arènes (☎ 04 66 67 28 02), on the south-west side of the Arènes at 1 Rue Alexandre Ducros. The bureau is open from 10 am to 12.30 pm and from 3 to 6.30 pm (without a break during férias). It accepts telephone bookings.

Bullfights without victims are known as *courses Camarguaises* or *courses à la cocarde* in which tokens or acorns are plucked from between the bull's horns. They are held on the weekend before a féria and at other times during the bullfighting season. Tickets cost between 50 and 100FF. The best bulls are rewarded with a couple of bars from the opera *Carmen* as they leave the arena.

Places to Stay – Budget

Camping The ***Domaine de la Bastide*** (☎ 04 66 38 09 21) on Route de Générac is about 4km south of town on the D13 heading towards Générac. Two people with a tent pay about 60FF and the site is open all year. From the station, take bus No 1 in the direction of Caremeau. At the Jean Jaurès stop, change to bus D and get off at La Bastide stop. For information on camping near the Pont du Gard, see Pont du Gard in the Around Nîmes section.

Hostel The ***Auberge de Jeunesse*** (☎ 04 66 23 25 04; fax 04 66 23 84 27) is on Chemin de la Cigale, out of the town centre and 3.5km north-west of the train station. A bed costs 47FF. Sheets are an extra 17FF and breakfast an extra 19FF. From the train station, take bus No 2 in the direction of Alès or Villeverte and get off at the Stade stop. The hostel also rents out mountain bikes (see Getting Around later in this section).

Gîtes The ***Gîtes de France*** office (☎ 04 66 27 94 94; fax 04 66 27 94 95) inside the Maison du Tourisme on Place des Arènes arranges all types of rural accommodation as well as B&B in Nîmes.

Hotels Surprisingly, Nîmes has plenty of cheap, decent hotels, many of which are conveniently situated in the old city.

For supposedly excellent views of the Arènes (if the wooden shutters covering the windows open that is), ***Hôtel Le France*** (☎ 04 66 67 23 05; fax 04 66 67 76 93), 4 Blvd des Arènes, has an assortment of dreary rooms and a pricing policy not unlike that used by the Romans at the amphitheatre: the higher up you go, the cheaper the room gets. Singles on the 4th floor (no lift) with washbasin start at 120FF, 3rd floor rooms with shower at 140FF, and triples with bath at 250FF. Between September and Easter the hotel reception is closed between 3 and 6.30 pm. Next door at No 2, ***Le Lisita*** (☎ 04 66 67 66 20; fax 04 66 76 22 30) is a bit cheaper, with shower-equipped singles/doubles from 100/180FF.

Hôtel Concorde (☎ 04 66 67 91 03), 3 Rue des Chapeliers, has small but adequate rooms from 110/115FF. Those with shower are 135/140FF.

The friendly ***Hôtel de la Maison Carrée*** (☎ 04 66 67 32 89; fax 04 66 76 22 57), 14 Rue de la Maison Carrée, has slightly poky rooms, most with shower, toilet and TV. Some have terraces. Prices for singles with washbasin start at around 115FF; singles/doubles with shower are 125/180FF, triples/quads are 270/330FF.

Doubles with washbasin/shower start at 115/150FF at the two star ***Hôtel La Mairie*** (☎ 04 66 67 65 91), 11 Rue des Greffes. Triples/quads with shower are 220/240FF.

Just south and west of the Église Saint Baudille there are several bargain-basement hotels: the spartan ***Hôtel Temple*** (☎ 04 66 67 54 61; fax 04 66 36 04 36), 1 Rue Charles Dabut, has singles/doubles/ quads with shower for 160/200/300FF. Equally sterile is the ***Cat Hôtel*** (☎ 04 66 67 22 88; fax 04 66 21 57 51), 22 Blvd Amiral Courbet, which has unrefined singles with toilet for 135FF and doubles with shower for 159FF. Breakfast is cheap at 22FF. By far the cheapest of the bunch is ***Hôtel Dauphiné***, 12 Grand Rue, where old men permanently cluster around a table in the reception hall playing cards. Rock-bottom rooms with no mod-cons cost 110/120FF for one/two people.

Places to Stay – Mid-Range

Just up from its Roman namesake, the 17 room ***Hôtel Amphithéâtre*** (☎ 04 66 67 28 51; fax 04 66 67 07 79), 4 Rue des Arènes, is one of the city's loveliest options. Rooms are fitted out with an eclectic array of furnishings; most have shower and toilet. Singles/doubles/triples start at 170/170/290FF.

Equally atmospheric is the colourful ***Hôtel Central*** (☎ 04 66 67 27 75; fax 04 66 21 77 79), 2 Place du Château. This place, complete with creaky floorboards and bunches of wild flowers painted on each of the guestroom doors, oozes charm. Singles/doubles/triples with private bath and TV are 210/230/250FF.

Places to Stay – Top End

Most of Nîmes' starred hotels belong to a chain and are scattered around the city's periphery. A touch more individual in both setting and décor is the multi star ***New Hôtel de la Baume*** (☎ 04 66 76 28 42; fax 04 66 76 28 45; info@new-hotel.com), 21 Rue Nationale, just north of the old city's winding streets. Singles/doubles equipped with everything your heart could desire (including air-con) start at 360/400FF.

Places to Eat

Nîmes' gastronomy is as Provençal as it is Languedocienne. *Aïoli*, *rouille* and other spicy southern delights (see the Provence chapter) are as abundant in this city as cassoulet. Don't miss out on sampling the Costières de Nîmes wines, which come from the pebbly vineyards to the south, while in town. If you're a teetotaller, your mineral water couldn't come fresher: Perrier, the famous fizzy French mineral water, gushes out and is bottled at Vergèze, 13km to south-west.

Restaurants Just west of Place des Arènes is the packed ***Les Olivades*** (☎ 04 66 21 71 78), 18 Rue Jean Reboul, which specialises in local wines. It has *menus* for 85 and 120FF and a popular lunchtime one for 65FF.

Across Rue de la République at 3 Rue de la Cité Foulc, ***Chez Edgar*** has excellent regional *menus* from 86FF, an express *menu* for 60FF and one for kids costing 36FF.

Le Portofino Brasserie Italienne (☎ 04 66 36 16 14), 3 Rue Corneille, and ***L'Assiette*** (☎ 04 66 21 03 03), next door, both offer startling views of the Carrée d'Art. The Portofino serves great home-made pasta dishes; the *carbonara* topped with a raw egg (45FF) is particularly tasty. It also offers breakfast/lunchtime *menus* for 19/55FF. The more upmarket 'Plate' serves local cuisine, has a lunchtime *menu* for 60FF, and is open from 9 am to 8 pm. Both have summer terraces that spill onto the pedestrianised street.

Tucked down a small street close to Église Saint Baudille is the very local ***Restaurant Le Menestrel*** (☎ 04 66 67 54 45), 6 Rue le Bavarois Nîmois. The Minstrel conjures up *menus* for 60, 75 and 110FF (closed all day Sunday and Monday lunchtime).

Delightfully small and charming is the very blue ***Côte Bleue*** on the corner of Rue Littré and Rue du Grand Couvent in the heart of the Îlot Littré quarter. The 'Blue Coast' serves strictly local dishes, both inside and outside on its quaint straw-covered terrace.

Rue de l'Étoile has several mid-range restaurants: at No 12, ***La Belle Respire*** (☎ 04 66 21 27 21) has designer décor and bad service. Main dishes range from 75 to 87FF and include regional specialities such as *pistou* (vegetable soup with garlic and basil; 43FF), *toro à la gardianne* (a rich stew of beef, herbs and red wine; 75FF) and various Roquefort concoctions. It is closed on Wednesday and at lunch on Thursday. ***Lakayna*** (☎ 04 66 21 10 96), an attractive North African cellar restaurant at No 18 of the same street, has couscous and *tajines* prepared in the manner of the Kabyles of eastern Algeria from about 70FF. An overly generous couscous royal – just one of 13 variations – is 130FF.

Rue Porte de France offers a good selection of international cuisines too. ***Goulbarge*** (☎ 04 66 67 37 53) at No 15 is an Indian place, while ***Le Mansa*** (☎ 04 66 21 09 18), nearby at No 17bis, offers African cuisine in a kaleidoscopic interior. Around the corner ***Les Parasols*** (☎ 04 66 21 74 99), 11 Rue Bigot, has Sicilian specialities, tonnes of pizza and spaghetti dishes, and *menus* for 85 and 115FF. Rue des Greffes is home to a couple of Chinese and Vietnamese places.

Cafés Place aux Herbes is one communal outside café in summer. Equally bustling, beneath the huge palm tree that sprawls in its centre, is Place du Marché. Young bohemians snub both; they hang out around the columns and cafés of the Maison Carrée.

The minuscule ***Loir dans la Théière*** (☎ 04 66 67 23 07), 29 Rue du Grand Couvent, an alternative *salon de thé* (tea salon) decorated in bold primary colours, serves a mouth-watering array of sweet and savoury crêpes. The 'Dormouse in the Teapot' is open from 11 am to 11 pm (closed Sunday).

Café de Columbia, on the corner of Rue de l'Étoile and Rue Maubet, is a cheap and cheerful Columbian joint touting a 47FF *menu* that includes a glass of wine.

Great for breakfast or a quick coffee on the outside terrace or inside is the ***Grand Café de la Bourse*** (☎ 04 66 67 21 91), opposite the Arènes ticket booth at 2 Blvd des Arènes. It is open from 8 am.

Self-Catering Nîmes plays host to colourful ***markets*** in the old city on Thursday in July and August. ***Les Halles***, the large, modern covered food market between Rue Guizot and Rue des Halles, is open daily until midday. There is a ***Prisunic*** supermarket at the south end of Blvd Amiral Courbet.

For bread shaped like a bull's head look no farther than the ***boulangerie*** on Grand Rue, open from 6.30 am to 1 pm and 2.30 to 8 pm (closed Sunday). Traditional breads of all shapes, sizes and grains are also sold at ***Le Pétrin***, Rue de la Curaterie, open from 7 am to noon and 3 to 7 pm (closed Sunday).

Local herbs, oils and spices are sold at the quaint ***Cafés Nadal***, overlooking Place aux Herbes at 4 Rue Marchands. An unbeatable choice of local wines is sold by knowledgeable staff at the ***Vinothéque*** adjoining Les Olivades (see Places to Eat). The wine shop is open from 9.30 am to 12.30 pm and from 3 to 8 pm (closed Sunday and Monday).

Entertainment

The bimonthly *Nîmescope* is a free entertainment listing. Pick up a copy at the tourist office. Year-round, music concerts, theatre performances and movie screenings are held in the Arènes – less frequently in summer, however.

The ***Théâtre de Nîmes*** (☎ 04 66 36 02 04), Place de la Calade, is the focal point of the city's cultural life, with theatre, music and opera performances scheduled throughout the year. Tickets are available from the theatre box office (☎ 04 66 36 65 10) between 12.30 and 6.30 pm, or from FNAC (☎ 04 66 36 33 33) in La Coupole des Halles shopping centre (entrance at 22 Blvd Gambetta). The latter is open from 9.30 am to 7 pm (until 7.30 pm on Saturday; closed Sunday). Both sell tickets for jazz performances hosted at the ***Odéon***, 7 Rue Pierre Sernard, too.

Live local rock can be heard some nights at ***Brasserie Le Mondial***, 34 Blvd Gambetta.

Getting There & Away

Air Nîmes' airport (☎ 04 66 70 49 49) is 10km south-east of the city on the A54 to Arles. It only serves domestic flights to/from Paris.

Bus Nîmes' bus station is just behind the train station on Rue Sainte Félicité. The information booths for regional operators such as STD Gard (☎ 04 66 84 96 86), Cariane (☎ 04 66 38 13 98), Les Rapides de Camargue (☎ 04 66 29 52 57), and Les Cars de Camargue (☎ 04 90 96 36 25 in Arles) are at one end of the terminal, while long-haul operators like Eurolines and Intercars are at the other. The general bus information counter (☎ 04 66 29 52 00) is open from 8 am to noon and 2 to 6 pm (closed on weekends).

Destinations served include Pont du Gard (32FF; 35 minutes; five a day), Collias (on the Gard River; 35FF; one hour; two daily), Uzès (32FF; 40 minutes; eight a day) and Alès (39.50FF; four daily). There are also buses to/from Avignon (41FF; 1¼ hours; five a day) and Arles (31FF; one hour; five a day). STD Gard organises day excursions to Nice, Menton and other coastal destinations in summer.

Spain, Portugal, Morocco and many other European destinations are served by Eurolines (☎ 04 66 29 49 02; fax 04 66 29 18 82), open from 9 am to 8.15 pm (closed Sunday); and Line Buses (☎ 04 66 29 50 52 or ☎ 04 66 29 50 87), open from 9.30 am to noon and 4.15 to 8.15 pm (closed Sunday). There are weekly services from Nîmes to Barcelona (295FF; 6½ hours), London (550FF; 16 hours), Valencia (390FF; 12 hours) and Prague (520FF; 19 hours).

Train The train station (☎ 08 36 35 35 35) is at the south-eastern end of Ave Feuchères. The information office is open daily, except Sunday, from 8 am to 6.30 pm, while the left-luggage room is open from 8 am to 8 pm.

Major destinations include Paris' Gare de Lyon by TGV (328FF; five hours), Alès (46FF; 40 minutes; 12 a day), Arles (61FF; 30 minutes; nine a day), Avignon (65FF; 30 minutes; 15 a day), Marseille (114FF; 1¼ hours; 12 a day) and Montpellier (66FF; 30 minutes; 20 a day). Two SNCF buses and a couple of trains a day head for Aigues Mortes (39FF; one hour) in the Camargue.

Car To contact ADA, call ☎ 04 67 58 34 35. Avis has an office inside the train station building. Europcar (☎ 04 66 21 31 35) is close by at 1bis Rue de la République.

Getting Around

To/From the Airport Airport buses (☎ 04 66 67 94 77) depart from the bus station four times daily to coincide with flights. En route, the bus (28FF; 30 minutes) stops at Blvd des Arènes, Blvd de Prague near the Esplanade Charles de Gaulle, and Blvd Gambetta.

Bus Local buses are run by TCN (☎ 04 66 38 15 40), whose ticket and information kiosk is in the north-east corner of Esplanade Charles de Gaulle, the main bus hub, opposite the Prisunic supermarket. Many buses stop on Ave Feuchères and Blvd Talabot (to the right as you exit the train station). A single ticket/carnet of 10 costs 6/43FF.

Taxi Taxis hover around Esplanade Charles de Gaulle. To order one by phone, call ☎ 04 66 29 40 11. TRAN taxis (☎ 04 66 29 40 11) offers guided city tours by taxi.

Bicycle The Auberge de Jeunesse (see Places to Stay) rents out mountain bikes for 50FF a day, plus a 100FF deposit.

Alternatively head for MC Cycles (☎ 04 66 04 02 54), 116 Blvd Sergent Triaire. Rental costs 100/150FF a day/weekend, plus deposit.

AROUND NÎMES

Pont du Gard

The exceptionally well preserved, three tiered Roman aqueduct known as the Pont du Gard was once part of a 50km-long system of canals built around 19 BC by Agrippa, Augustus' powerful deputy and son-in-law, to bring water from near Uzès to Nîmes. The 35 small arches of the 275m-long upper tier, which is 49m above the Gard River, contain a watercourse 1.2 by 1.75m that was designed to carry 20,000 cubic metres of water a day. The Romans built the aqueduct with stone from the nearby Vers quarry. The largest boulders weigh over five tonnes.

From carparks either side of the river, you can walk along the road bridge, built in 1743 alongside the top of the aqueduct's lower tier on the Gard's upstream side. Once extensive renovation works (280 cubic metres of stone are being replaced) are completed in 2000, visitors will be able to amble along the aqueduct's middle (and maybe) top tier too. The best view of the Pont du Gard is from the hill on the northern side (left bank) about 200m from the aqueduct (signposted 'Panorama'). On hot days you can swim in the river. The Pont du Gard is frequented by two million people a year (averaging a horrendous 5000-plus visitors a day).

Information The Maison de Tourisme (☎ 04 66 37 00 02), near the aqueduct on the southern side (right bank), is only open from June to September from 9 am to 7 pm. Otherwise the closest one (☎ 04 66 37 22 34; fax 04 66 37 22 02) is another 4km south-east in Remoulins.

Renovations will include a massive tourist centre on the site of the present carpark on the north side of the river. A new carpark will be built farther away, but still within walking distance of the aqueduct.

Places to Stay There are a couple of camp sites near the Pont du Gard including the two star ***Camping International*** (☎ 04 66 22 81 81), 2km from the bridge's northern side on Chemin Barque Vieille. The rate is around 65FF for two people with a tent. It's open from mid-March to mid-October. On the southern side (right bank), ***Camping Municipal La Sousta***, a five minute walk from the bridge on Ave du Pont du Gard, charges 64FF for two people with a tent. Each additional person costs 16FF.

Near the carpark on the northern side, ***Le Vieux Moulin*** (☎ 04 66 37 14 35; fax 04 66 37 26 48), an attractive inn with some truly splendid views of the Pont du Gard, has rooms for one or two people with washbasin and bidet for 205FF, with shower and toilet for 310FF, and with bath and toilet for 460FF. It is open from mid-March to early November.

Getting There & Away The Pont du Gard is 23km north-east of Nîmes, 26km west of Avignon and 12km south-east of Uzès. Buses from Avignon, Nîmes and Uzès stop 1km north of the bridge. The extensive carparks on the north/south side of the river cost 22/17FF.

Gard River

The beautiful and wild Gard River descends from the Cévennes Mountains. It's known for its unpredictability, and torrential rains can raise the water level by 2 to 5m in almost no time. During long dry spells, though, the Gard sometimes virtually disappears.

The Gard flows through the hills in a long gorge from **Russan** to the village of **Collias**. About 6km downstream it passes under the Pont du Gard.

Boating In Collias, Kayak Vert Gardon (☎ 04 66 22 84 83 or ☎ 04 66 22 80 76; fax 04 66 22 88 78) and Canoë Le Tourbillon (☎ 04 66 22 85 54), both based under the town's single bridge, offer excursions by kayak and canoe. You can paddle down to the Pont du Gard (175/100FF for a canoe/kayak for two) with a group in half a day or arrange to be dropped off 22km upstream at Russan, from where there's a great descent back. The latter is a full day trip and is usually available between March and May only. Canoes/kayaks rent for 50/35FF an hour and 145/90FF a day.

Mountain Biking Canoë Le Tourbillon rents mountain bikes for 80/110FF a half-day/day.

Hiking The GR6 follows the river from Collias to the Pont du Gard.

Getting There & Away Bus No 168 from Nîmes' bus station stops in Collias (33.50FF; one hour). There are just two daily.

Uzès

• pop 7700 ✉ 30700

Uzès is a laid-back 'backgammon-in-the-streets' little town set among the hills 25km north of Nîmes. It proved the perfect film set for *Cyrano de Bergerac* (1990) starring Gérard Depardieu and, with its Renaissance façades, impressive Duché (Ducal Palace), narrow streets and ancient towers, remains a charming place to wander around.

Orientation & Information The Château Ducal is a short distance north-east of Place aux Herbes. West of this shady square on Ave de la Libération are the post office (exchange services available) and, just opposite, the bus station (☎ 04 66 29 52 00) and adjacent tourist office (☎ 04 66 22 68 88; fax 04 66 22 95 19). The latter is open from 9 am to noon and 1.30 to 6 pm (closed on weekends).

Duché Also known as the Château Ducal (☎ 04 66 22 18 96), this medieval fortress which was built almost continuously from the 11th to 18th centuries, has been turned into something of a fun fair, with a wax museum and in the Salle du Fantôme (Ghost Room), laser-generated spooks. There are still enough period furniture, tapestries and paintings to satisfy the culture vulture though. The Duché, visitable only by guided tour, is open July to September from 10 am to 6.30 pm; the rest of the year the hours are 10 am to noon and 2 to 6 pm. Admission is 48/35FF for adults/students.

Close by at the end of Impasse Port Royal, off Rue Port Royal, is the beautifully landscaped **Jardin Médiéval** (Medieval Garden; ☎ 04 66 03 10 72). It is open in June and September from 3 to 7 pm (closed on weekends), and in July and August mornings as well from 10 am to 12.30 pm (only afternoons on weekends). Admission costs 10FF.

Special Events Uzès is big on festivals and fairs – one of the more animated is the Foire à l'Ail (Garlic Fair), held on 24 June. On Saturday mornings from November to March, there's a truffle market in Place aux Herbes, and on the third Sunday in January there is a full-blown Truffle Fair. Uzès is also celebrated for its International Festival of Ancient Music held in various places throughout town in the second half of July.

Places to Stay & Eat Uzès is a pleasant day trip from either Nîmes or Avignon. If you decide to stay the night, there is a handful of hotels in town and the tourist office has a complete list of *chambres d'hôtes*. The least expensive hotel is the ***Hostellerie Provençale*** (☎ 04 66 22 11 06), south-east of the tourist office at 1 Rue Grande Bourgade, which has singles/doubles from 180/200FF and a good restaurant with a 76FF *menu*. Outside, cafés sprawl the length of Blvd Gambetta in summer.

Getting There & Away Half of the buses linking Uzès with Nîmes stop near the Pont du Gard, as do buses to/from Avignon. There are three buses a day to Alès on the Cévennes border.

ALÈS & AROUND

Alès en Cévennes (population 41,000), the second largest town in the Gard department, is an industrial centre on the Gard river some 44km north-west of Nîmes and 70km north-east of Montpellier. Coal mining has long been the town's focus, making it a pretty miserable place to visit. But there is light at the end of the tunnel: you can pick up the bus to Florac from here while just a few kilometres south is a bamboo farm, and a museum dedicated to the persecution of Protestants in the 17th and 18th centuries.

Alès' tourist office (☎ 04 66 52 32 15; fax 04 66 52 57 09), on the bank of the Gard at Place Gabriel Péri, is open in summer from 9 am to noon and 1.30 to 6.30 pm. Hours are shorter in winter.

La Bambouseraie de Prafrance

If any place in France should get an award for self-promotion, it's the huge Bamboo Grove and Nursery (☎ 04 66 61 70 47) in Générargues, 12km south-west of Alès on the road to the Corniche des Cévennes. Founded in 1850 by a spice merchant, the Bambouseraie contains 150 bamboo species (red, golden, giant etc) as well as aquatic gardens and an Asian village. Come in early winter and you might experience an evocative and very rare sight: bamboo with a light dusting of snow.

The Bambouseraie is open between March and October from 9.30 am to 7 pm; in November and December from 10 am to 6 pm (closed Monday and Tuesday and in January and February). Admission is 32/18FF for adults/children.

Musée du Désert

Those interested in the clandestine way of life of the Camisards (see the boxed text 'The Camisard Revolt') should visit the interesting Musée du Désert (☎ 04 66 85 02 72), in the charming hamlet of Le Mas Soubeyran which is 5km north of the Bambouseraie. It's open from 9.30 am to noon and 2.30 to 6 pm (no break in July and August). Admission is 20/12FF for adults/students and children.

To reach Le Mas Soubeyran from the Bambouseraie, head west along the D50 and then turn right onto the D509 after Luziers village.

Places to Stay

The Alès tourist office stocks accommodation lists for the region. ***Camping Les Châtaigniers*** (☎ 04 66 52 53 57), Chemin des Sports, is 1.5km south-east of the tourist office. Between June and August, the ***Foyer Mixte de Jeunes Travailleurs*** (☎ 04 66 86 19 80), 2 Ave Jean-Baptiste Dumas, 1km north-west of the train station, accepts travellers. A bed for the night is 80FF.

Highly recommended, as much for its fine restaurant as for its pleasant rooms, is ***Hôtel Le Riche*** (☎ 04 66 86 00 33; fax 04 66 30 02 63) opposite the train station at 42 Place Pierre Sémard. Modern singles/doubles start at 170/250FF.

Getting There & Away

Bus From Alès' bus station (☎ 04 66 30 24 86), on Place Pierre Sémard, there is one daily bus heading into the Cévennes to Florac (58.50FF; 1½ hours), and three to Uzès (37FF; one hour). To get to the Bambouseraie take the lone daily bus to Saint Jean du Gard (29.50FF; one hour) and get off at Anduze, 2km south-west of the Bambouseraie; you'll have to hitch from there.

Train Destinations south from Alès' train station (next to the bus station), include Nîmes (46FF; 40 minutes; 12 a day) and Montpellier (78FF; one hour; two or three a day).

From April to October from Saint Jean du Gard, the little Cévennes steam train (*train à vapeur*; ☎ 04 66 85 13 17), takes 40 minutes to chug to the Bambouseraie via Anduze. Schedules vary according to the season, but count on four return trips a day in July and August, on weekends only in early April and October, daily except Monday from mid-April to June and on Tuesday, Thursday, Saturday and Sunday in September. One-way/return fares are 45/55FF for adults and 33/38FF for children under 12. Bikes and dogs cost 20FF one way or return.

PARC NATIONAL DES CÉVENNES

The diverse Parc National des Cévennes (378 to 1699m) is home to isolated hamlets and a wide variety of flora and fauna – much of the latter, including red deer, beavers and vultures, has been reintroduced over the last two decades.

The park comprises four main areas: Mont Lozère, much of the Causse Méjean, the Cévennes valleys (Vallées Cévenoles) and Mont Aigoual. Though not within the park, the town of Florac, where you'll find the Maison du Parc information centre, is arguably the best base for exploration. However, Alès and Anduze to the south-east also serve as gateways to the park.

History

The 910 sq km park was created in 1970 to bring ecological stability to a region that, because of religious and later economic upheavals, has long had a destabilising human presence. Population influxes, which saw the destruction of the forests for logging and pastures, were followed by mass desertions as people gave up the fight against the inhospitable climate and terrain.

Since the mid-19th century emigration has resulted in the abandonment of many hamlets and farms, which were bought up in the 1960s by wealthy Parisians and foreigners. The newcomers brought money but also new threats to the environment; tourism has therefore been heavily controlled. It's illegal to build new houses in the central zone of the park, for example, and hotels are few and far between except in towns along the

The Camisard Revolt

Early in the 18th century, the Cévennes region was the setting of what some historians describe as the first guerilla war in modern history, fought by Protestants against Louis XIV's army.

The revocation of the Edict of Nantes in 1685 took away the rights that the Huguenots had enjoyed since 1598. Many French Protestants emigrated, while others fled into the wilderness of the Cévennes, from where a local leader named Roland (1680-1704) led the resistance against the French army sent to crush them in 1702. Poorly equipped but with great motivation and an intimate knowledge of the countryside, the outlaws held out for two years. They fought in their shirts – *camiso* in langue d'oc, thus their popular name, Camisards. The royal army slowly gained the upper hand, and on the king's orders the local population was either massacred or forced to flee from the region. Roland was killed and most of the villages were methodically destroyed.

Each year, on the first Sunday of September, thousands of French Protestants meet at Roland's birthplace in Le Mas Soubeyran, a sleepy hamlet near the village of Mialet between Saint Jean du Gard and Anduze along the Corniche des Cévennes. The house where he was born is now the Musée du Désert in which the persecution of Protestantism in the Cévennes between 1685 and the reintroduction of religious freedom with Louis XVI's Edict of Tolerance in 1787 is detailed. The museum shares the same name as that by which this entire period was known: *le Désert* (the desert).

periphery. However, *gîtes ruraux* (country cottages with accommodation), are certainly increasing in number.

Mont Lozère

This 1699m-high lump of granite in the north of the park is shrouded in cloud and ice in winter and covered with heather and blueberries, peat bogs and flowing streams in summer. The headquarters of the **Écomusée du Mont Lozère** (☎ 04 66 45 80 73) in the Maison du Mont Lozère in Pont de Montvert, 2km north-east of Florac, has full details on the region. The museum (admission 20/15FF for adults/students) and the Maison du Mont Lozère are open between 15 April and 30 September from 10.30 am to 12.30 pm and 2.30 to 6.30 pm.

Cévennes Valleys

Sweet chestnut trees (*châtaigniers*), first planted back in the Middle Ages, carpet the valleys of the Cévennes, the park's central region of inaccessible ravines and jagged ridges, along one of which runs the breathtaking Corniche des Cévennes (see Getting

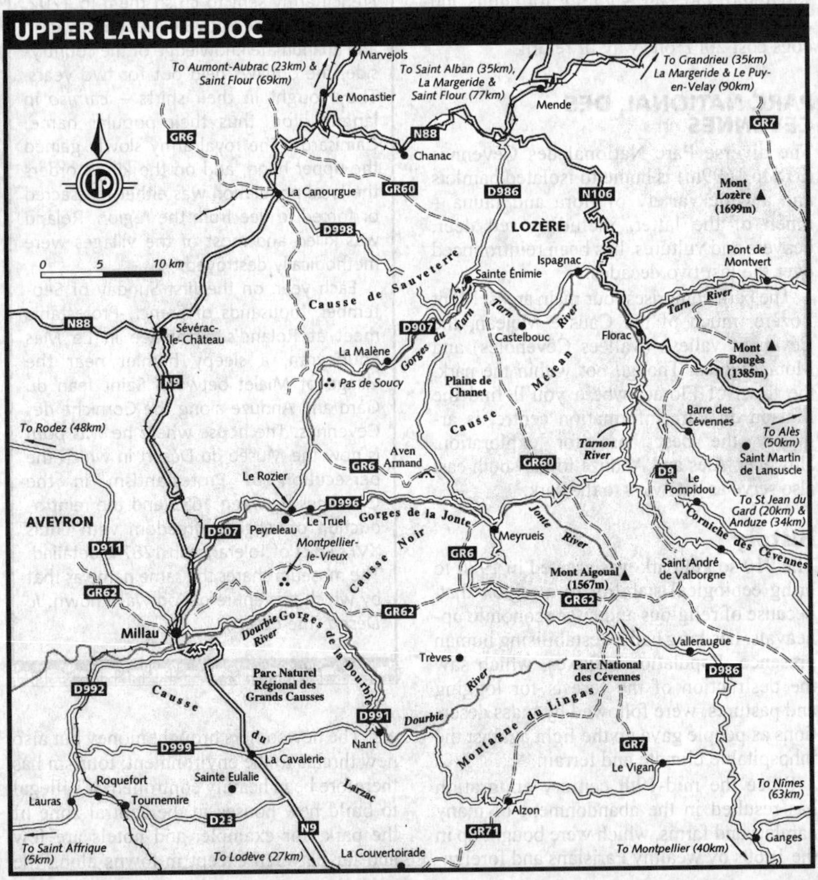

There & Away later in this section for details). Chestnuts, a staple of the mountain people's diet, were once eaten raw, roasted or dried after the meat had been separated from the burr by walking over them in shoes fitted with long serrated spikes. These days they are the preferred meal of the valleys' *sangliers* (wild boars) though they are still used in the preparation of certain sauces and desserts.

Mont Aigoual

Only 70km from the coast, Mont Aigoual (1567m) and the neighbouring Montagne du Lingas region are known more for searing winds and heavy snowfall than Mediterranean climes. Cross-country skiing is popular, as is summer tourism. The area is thick with beech trees thanks to a successful reforestation program begun in 1875 to counteract years of uncontrolled logging.

The meteorological station on Mont Aigoual (☎ 04 67 82 60 01) offers a stunning 360° view over the Cévennes.

Activities

There's cross-country skiing (100km of marked trails) on Mont Aigoual in winter, and donkey treks are immensely popular in the area in warmer months (see Activities in the Florac section). There are 600km of donkey and horse-riding trails and 200km marked out for VTT enthusiasts. An equally well developed network of footpaths attracts hikers year-round. The park authorities have added 22 paths to the six GR trails crossing the area, which include the Vosges-Pyrenees track (GR7) and the Aigoual (GR66), Cévennes (GR67) and Mont Lozère (GR68) circuits. Maps and booklets are available at the Maison du Parc in Florac, where you can also pick up a free *gîtes d'étape* brochure listing some 100 places to spend the night. Ask about the Festival Nature held between June and October when various outdoor activities, lectures and field trips are conducted.

Getting There & Away

If you don't have your own transport, the region is practically as impenetrable as it was centuries ago. A limited bus service runs between Florac and Alès (see Getting There & Away in those sections for details). By car, the most spectacular route between the two towns is the Corniche des Cévennes, a ridge road that winds along the mountain crests of the Cévennes for 56km from Saint Jean du Gard to Florac. The route numbers are D260 and D9.

FLORAC

• pop 2100 ✉ 48400 alt 542m

Florac, 68km north-west of Alès and 38km south-east of Mende, is a pleasant little town and a great base for exploring the Parc National des Cévennes. At the northern end of the wild Corniche des Cévennes, Florac is draped along the Tarnon River, one of the tributaries of the Tarn, while the fortress-like cliffs of the Causse Méjean loom 1000m overhead.

Orientation

The town has one main road, Ave Jean Monestier, which runs parallel to the Tarnon. Most of the medieval streets run off it to the west. The central squares are tiny Place de la Mairie and the tree-lined Esplanade Marceau Farelle.

Information

Tourist Office The tourist office (☎ 04 66 45 01 14; fax 04 66 45 25 80), Ave Jean Monestier, has varied opening hours: between July and September it's open from 8.30 am to 12.30 pm and 2 to 7.30 pm (Sunday from 9 am to noon); from October to June it's open from 9 am to noon and 2 to 5 pm (closed Sunday).

Maison du Parc National des Cévennes

Located in the restored 17th century Château de Florac on Place du Palais, the Maison du Parc (☎ 04 66 49 53 01; fax 04 66 49 53 02; pnc@bsi.fr) has a surfeit of information, maps, wildlife books and guides on the park. Most of the detailed guides are in French, but the *Parc National des Cévennes* guidebook (70FF) is available in English.

The best map overall for the park is the 1:100,000 *Parc National des Cévennes* in

IGN's Culture & Environment series (46FF), but six Série Bleue IGN maps (54FF) cover the area on a 1:25,000 scale: 2641ET, 2641OT, 2640OT, 2739OT, 2740ET and 2741ET. The Maison du Parc is open daily in July and August from 9 am to 7 pm; the rest of the year it's open from 8 am to noon and 2 to 6 pm (closed on weekends).

Money Exchange money at the Caisse d'Épargne at 50 Ave Jean Monestier or the Banque Populaire at 70 Ave Jean Monestier, which is open from 8.30 to noon and 1.30 to 5 pm (closed Sunday and Monday).

Post The post office, 92 Ave Jean Monestier, is open from 9 am to noon and 2 to 5 pm (closed Saturday afternoon and all day Sunday).

Activities

The tourist office has details on all sorts of outdoor activities, including caving, canyon descents, kayaking and canoeing. For hiking details, contact the Maison du Parc (see also Activities in the earlier Parc National des Cévennes section).

Glider Flights Gliders take off from the Florac aerodrome (☎ 04 66 45 15 46; fax 04 66 45 67 89) on the Plaine de Chanet in the centre of the Causse Méjean, about 17km south-west of Florac. A flight costs 270FF an hour for two people or 450 to 700FF for three for a plane flight over the Gorges du Tarn. The airstrip is open between mid-April and September from 9 am to 7 pm.

Donkey Treks Follow the lead of Robert Louis Stevenson (see the boxed text 'Making an Ass of It') and hire a donkey, either from Gentiane (☎ 04 66 41 04 16; fax 04 66 41 03 23 in Pont de Montvert) or Tramontane (☎ 04 66 45 92 44) in Saint Martin de Lansuscle. It costs 250/450/600/1050FF for one/two/three/six days. These places can book accommodation at hotels or gîtes for you, but if you require a guide it's 600 to 800FF a day extra. Though both companies are located outside Florac they do transport the beasties to Florac for you for a small fee (5FF/km).

The Association Sur le Chemin de RL Stevenson (☎/fax 04 66 45 86 31) in Pont de Montvert has route maps with chambres d'hôtes, camp sites and restaurants marked on. The Maison du Parc sells the topoguide *Le Chemin de Stevenson* (90FF) which follows the GR70. An English version is available.

Cycling Bikes can be hired from Cévennes Évasion (☎/fax 04 66 45 18 31), 5 Place Boyer, at the northern end of Esplanade

Making an Ass of Himself

It was the fantastically wild, untamed Cévennes that Scottish writer Robert Louis Stevenson bizarrely chose to cross with a *âne* (donkey) in October 1878.

'I was looked upon with contempt, like a man who should project a journey to the moon, but yet with a respectful interest, like one setting forth for the inclement Pole', Stevenson wrote in *Travels with a Donkey in the Cévennes*, published the following year.

Accompanied by the mouse-coloured Modestine purchased at the market for 65FF and a glass of brandy, Stevenson took 12 days to travel the 220km on foot (Modestine, carried his gear) from Le Monastier to St Jean du Gard. Afterwards, he sold his ass – and wept.

The Stevenson trail, first retraced and marked with the cross of St Andrew by a Scottish woman in 1978, today follows the GR70, crossing Mont du Goulet (1497m) and Mont Lozère (1699m) en route. Donkeys, which can be hired in Florac, carry between 30 to 50kg and cover 10 to 25km a day.

Marceau Farelle in the centre of Florac. Rental rates are 70/110FF for a half-day/day. It's open from 9 am to 12.30 pm and from 2 to 5.30 pm (closed Sunday).

Climbing & Caving Cévennes Évasion (see Cycling) can arrange potholing and rock climbing expeditions for groups of seven to nine people. It charges 210FF per person for a day's potholing, including equipment hire, and 130FF for a half-day's climbing. It also arranges weekend trips. The Sporting Club Florac (☎ 04 66 45 00 71; fax 04 66 45 07 39), Rue Célestin Freinet, offers similar deals.

Places to Stay

Camping The two municipal camping grounds are 1.5km from the town centre in opposite directions. Both charge 14/7FF for adults/children and 24FF for a car plus a tent. ***Le Pont du Tarn*** (☎ 04 66 45 18 26; fax 04 66 45 26 43), off the N106 as it heads north towards Mende, is open from 1 April to 15 October. To the south, ***La Tière*** (☎ 04 66 45 00 53) on the D907 is open from 15 June to 1 September.

Gîtes d'Étape There are a couple of private gîtes d'étape in Florac, including ***L'Ancien Presbytère*** (☎ 04 66 45 24 54), 18 Rue du Pêcher. The town-run, central ***gîte*** (☎ 04 66 45 14 93), 1 Rue du Four, is open all year. A bed at either costs 50FF. In Pont de Montvert there is the ***Gîte le Ron du Chastel*** (☎/fax 04 66 45 84 93), Rue de la Jalerie.

Hotels The frayed ***Hôtel Central et de la Poste*** (☎ 04 66 45 00 01; fax 04 66 45 14 04), 4 Ave Maurice Tour, near Place du Souvenir, has rooms with shower from 170FF. It's closed in January and February.

Hôtel Les Gorges du Tarn (☎ 04 66 45 00 63; fax 04 66 45 10 56), 48 Rue du Pêcher, has adequate rooms with washbasin from 180FF and doubles with shower for 250FF. It is open from Easter to November.

Much better value is the two star ***Grand Hôtel du Parc*** (☎ 04 66 45 03 05; fax 04 66 45 11 81), 47 Ave Jean Monestier. This place has spacious rooms, a pool, delightful gardens and is a wonderful spot to recharge your batteries. Doubles/triples with shower start at 240/290FF. It is open from mid-March to November.

The modern ***Hôtel Le Pont Neuf*** (☎ 04 66 45 01 67), Quartier Pont Neuf, is open year-round. The cheapest rooms start at 260FF, all with bath and toilet.

Places to Eat

You can eat at most of the hotels in Florac. ***La Source du Pêcher*** (☎ 04 66 45 03 01), near the town hall at 1 Rue du Rémuret, has a wonderful location on the little Pêcher River.

For a treat, head for ***Chapeau Rouge*** (☎ 04 66 45 23 40), 4 Rue Théophile Roussel. The 'Red Hat' may be little more than a shed, but the food is excellent, with regional *menus* for 70, 90 and 140FF and a good wine selection. Don't miss one of the desserts made with chestnuts.

Local edibles – liqueurs, jams, Pélardon cheese, chestnuts in all their guises – are sold at the Maison du Pays Cévenol, 3 Rue du Pêcher.

Getting There & Away

There's no train station and buses are sporadic (they do not run at all on Sunday). There's a daily bus to Alès (58.50FF; 1½ hours) and in July and August there's a bus to Mende. Buses leave from the Salle des Fêtes parking lot on the western side of Ave Jean Monestier.

MENDE

• pop 12,000 ✉ 48000 alt 731m

Mende, a quiet little place straddling the Lot River, is the capital of Lozère, France's least populous department. If you are travelling under your own steam, it makes a good base for exploring the northern part of Upper Languedoc, the Lot Valley and the Gorges du Tarn.

Orientation & Information

Mende's oval-shaped centre is enclosed by a one-way ring road. The tourist office (☎/fax 04 66 65 02 69) is two blocks south-west of central Place Urbain V and its landmark cathedral. Most of the year it's open from 9 am to noon and 2 to 6 pm (until noon on Saturday; closed Sunday). In July and August it's open until 8 pm (no lunchtime break).

Things to See & Do

You can wander through Mende in a matter of minutes, but if you have time on your hands, the tourist office has a brochure with a walking tour in English that points out every nook and cranny of historical interest. The most outstanding feature of the town is clearly the 14th century, twin-towered **Cathédrale Notre Dame** on Place Urbain V; ask the tourist office for its descriptive plan of the cathedral. If you arrive from the north, the cathedral is set off strikingly against the high mountains. The highest of the two towers, the **Clocher de l'Évêque** (84m), offers a fine view of the town and Lot Valley.

For an aerial view, take to the skies with members of the Aéroclub de la Lozère (☎ 04 66 65 39 50) from the Mende-Brenouz aerodrome.

Places to Stay

Camping The two star ***Camping Le Tivoli*** (☎ 04 66 65 00 38), 2km west of town on the N88 to Florac, charges about 60FF for two people with a tent and is open all year.

Gîtes The ***Gîtes de France*** regional office (☎ 04 66 65 60 00; fax 04 66 49 27 96) is at 16 Blvd Henri Bourrillon.

Hotels The cheapest accommodation option is ***Hôtel du Gévaudan*** (☎ 04 66 65 14 74), 2 Rue d'Aigues Passes, four blocks north of the tourist office. Small, nondescript singles/doubles cost 120/130FF with washbasin and 160/170FF with shower.

Centrally located on Place Urbain V (entrance on tiny Rue de l'Ormeau), ***Hôtel du Palais*** (☎ 04 66 49 01 59) has lovely views of the cathedral and rooms with washbasin or shower for 150/190FF.

Opposite the bus station on the busy ring road, the two star ***Hôtel du Commerce*** (☎ 04 66 65 13 73), 2 Blvd Henri Bourrillon, is a labyrinthine place. Modern rooms with shower and toilet go from 200/240FF.

Hôtel de France (☎ 04 66 65 00 04; fax 04 66 49 30 47), part of the Logis de France chain, at 9 Blvd Lucien Arnault, has pleasing rooms with shower for 240/280FF.

Places to Eat

Munching options are limited. ***Le Mazel*** (☎ 04 66 65 05 33), 25 Rue Collège, with *menus* for 79 and 140FF, is the best bet for local cuisine. Otherwise, try the nearby ***Bodega Casa del Sol*** (☎ 04 66 49 20 00), 13 Rue Basse, which serves numerous tapas dishes for 10FF each. For a swift half, nip into the packed ***Irish Pub*** on Place de la République.

Local foodies don't dine out in town. They follow their stomachs 57km east to the ***Balme*** hotel and restaurant (☎ 04 66 46 80 14; fax 04 66 46 85 26) in Villefort or 42km north-west to Aumont-Aubrac, where the ***Prouhèze*** (☎ 04 66 42 80 07; fax 04 66 42 87 78) cooks up various gastronomic feasts and is honoured with one star by Michelin.

Getting There & Away

Bus Buses leave from the bus station on Place du Foirail, 100m south-east of the tourist office, or from the train station. One bus a day goes to Rodez (three hours), Marvejols (50 minutes) and Le Puy-en-Velay (two hours). There's an evening bus to Florac via Ispagnac in July and August only.

Train The train station (☎ 04 66 49 00 39 or ☎ 08 36 35 35 35) is 1km north of the town centre across the Lot River.

There are infrequent trains in two directions. The principal line goes east to La Bastide Saint Laurent (44FF; one hour), which is on the main north-south line between Clermont-Ferrand in the Massif Central (150FF; four hours) and Nîmes (113FF; three hours). The other line heads west to Le Monastier (31FF; 35 minutes), from where there are connections to Marvejols (35FF; 40 minutes), Rodez (84FF; three hours with two changes) and Montpellier (139FF; 3½ hours).

Getting Around

Bicycle You can rent a bicycle from Espace Bike (☎/fax 04 66 65 01 81), opposite the bus station at 1 Blvd du Soubeyran. It's open from 9 am to noon and 2 to 6 pm (closed Sunday and Monday). Rental costs 70/350FF per day/week.

AROUND MENDE

Wolf Reserve

Wolves (*loups*) used to roam freely through the forests in Lozère, but today they're seen only in the Parc du Gévaudan (☎ 04 66 32 09 22 or ☎ 04 66 32 42 97) at Sainte Lucie, 7km north of Marvejols (30km west of Mende and accessible by train). The reserve was set up with help from the Brigitte Bardot Foundation by a local man with a love for wolves. Mongolian, Canadian, Siberian and Polish wolves live here in semi-liberty, although it's still sad to see these animals surrounded by wire and disturbed by noisy school groups. Admission is 33/19FF for adults/children and the park is open daily from 10 am to 4.30 pm (6 pm from June to September). For details on getting to Marvejols, see the Getting There & Away entry under Mende. There's no public transport from Marvejols to the park.

La Margeride

One of the most isolated areas of Lozère, La Margeride is a granite range running north-south from the Massif Central towards Mende. This high plateau is covered with pine forests and patches of sunburned moss. Dotted with occasional old stone villages and without a major town as its base, it's ideal hiking and cross-country cycling terrain. In winter you can ski. The region is also home to a European bison reserve, set up to ensure the survival of this endangered species.

A good base for exploring La Margeride is **Baraque de Bouviers** (1418m), on the D5 about halfway between the two nearest towns worth mentioning, Saint Alban and Grandrieu. *Bouviers* is the name of the local herders who bring their flocks to the high country in summer. Around one of their old shelters has grown a small centre (☎ 04 66 47 41 54) open all year to those engaging in outdoor pursuits. It's an excellent base for hiking (the GR4 and GR43 pass by here to the north and west), mountain biking, rock climbing and cross-country skiing. All the necessary equipment can be hired here and you can stay in its *gîte d'étape* for 60FF a night.

Bison Reserve Above the village of Sainte Eulalie en Margeride, 8km north-west of Baraque de Bouviers, is the Réserve de Bisons d'Europe (☎ 04 66 31 40 40; fax 04 66 31 40 34). It was set up in 1992 with 25 European bison brought over from Bialowieza Forest in Poland.

Within the 200 hectare reserve the bison roam freely. From the Maison du Bison at the reserve's entrance, horse-drawn carriages take visitors on a tour. A protected walking path also allows you a glimpse of these mighty animals. Entry to the reserve costs 20/15FF for adults/children if you go on foot and 60/30FF if you take a carriage. The reserve is open from 10 am to noon and 2 to 5 pm (10 am to 7 pm from mid-June to mid-September).

Getting There & Away The 40km from Mende to Baraque de Bouviers can be hitched if you're patient and have a good map – IGN's 2637E and 2638E (scale 1:25,000) in the Série Bleue are the most detailed.

GORGES DU TARN

From the village of Ispagnac situated between Mende and Florac, the spectacular Gorges du Tarn wind south-west for about 50km, ending just north of Millau. En route are two villages, the medieval Sainte Énimie (a good base for canoeing and hiking along the gorges), and 13km downstream the equally attractive La Malène.

The gorge, which is 400 to 600m deep, marks the boundary between the Causse de Sauveterre to the north and the Causse Méjean to the south. From these plateaus, the gorge looks like a white, limestone abyss. The green waters deep down below are dotted here and there with colourful canoes and kayaks. In summer, the riverside road (the D907bis) is often jammed with cars, buses and caravans.

Information

Sainte Énimie's tourist office (☎ 04 66 48 53 44; fax 04 66 48 52 28), in the little Hôtel de Ville north of the bridge, is open between May and mid-September from 9.30 am to noon and 1.30 to 5 pm (7 pm in July and August). The rest of the year it is open from 9.30 am until noon and 1.15 to 4.30 pm (closed on weekends). It stocks an extensive range of maps and hiking guides, including the excellent IGN map entitled *Gorges du Tarn* (No 2640OT; 58FF).

The post office next door to the tourist office exchanges money. It is open weekdays from 9 am to noon and 2 to 5 pm and on Saturday morning (closed Sunday).

Sainte Énimie

• pop 500 ✉ 48210 alt 470m

Beautiful Sainte Énimie is named after a Merovingian princess who founded a monastery here in the 6th century after she bathed in a local spring and recovered from leprosy. Like an avalanche of grey-brown stone, this village blends perfectly into the steep slope behind it. Long isolated, Sainte Énimie is now a popular destination for day-trippers from Millau, Mende and Florac and one of the starting points for descending the Tarn by canoe or kayak.

The little Romanesque **Église de Sainte Énimie** in the centre of the village dates from the 12th century. Just behind it on Place du Presbytère, the tiny **Écomusée Le Vieux Logis** (☎ 04 66 48 53 44) has one vaulted room in a reconstructed old house full of antique local furniture, lamps, tableware and costumes.

Boating

Riding the Tarn River is possible only in summer when the river is (usually) low and the descent a lazy trip over mostly calm water. You can get as far as the impassable Pas de Soucy, which is a barrier of boulders about 9km downriver from La Malène.

A handful of companies, including Canoë Paradan (☎ 04 66 48 56 90 or ☎ 04 66 48 53 58) and L'Évasion Nature (☎ 04 66 48 55 57) in Sainte Énimie, and Le Moulin de la Malène (☎ 04 66 48 51 14 or ☎ 04 66 48 55 17) in La Malène, organise canoe and kayak descents. Their prices are roughly the same. From Sainte Énimie to La Malène (13km; 3½ hours) it costs 200FF for a two person canoe or 100FF for a one person kayak. To the Pas de Soucy (23km; 6½ hours) from Sainte Énimie, it's 260/130FF for a canoe/kayak. Other routes include from Sainte Énimie to Castelbouc (7km; two hours) and then on from Castelbouc to Le Pas de Savoy (30km; two days).

Le Moulin de la Malène sells the useful guide, *Découvertes en Canoë-Kayak – Gorges du Tarn* (40FF). The Sainte Énimie tourist office has information on rafting and hot dogging on the Tarn.

Hiking & Mountain Biking

These are the other ideal ways to see the gorge. The GR60 winds down from the Causse de Sauveterre to Sainte Énimie, crosses the bridge, and then continues southward up to the Causse Méjean in the direction of Mont Aigoual.

La Périgouse (see Horse Riding later) rents mountain bikes for 70/100FF a half-day/day. The Sainte Énimie tourist office sells the useful *Vallée et Gorges du Tarn – Balades à Pied et à VTT* (98FF) guide, which details various hiking and cycling routes in the region.

Horse Riding

The Centre Équestre La Périgouse (☎ 04 66 48 53 71; fax 04 66 48 81 20) in Sainte Énimie has horses for hire for 75FF an hour or 180/250FF per half-day/day.

Places to Stay

The camping grounds along the riverside road are expensive, but ***Camping Les Gorges du Tarn*** (☎ 04 66 48 50 51), about 800m above the village on the road to Florac, costs only 30FF for two people with a tent. It's open from Easter to October.

The tourist office in Sainte Énimie takes bookings for B&B accommodation in the region's local homes and gîtes d'étape. Many houses in La Malène have chambre d'hôte signs hanging outside. Hotels in Sainte Énimie and La Malène are pricey and usually full. Try ***Hôtel Le Central*** (☎ 04 66 48 50 23) facing the Tarn on Rue Basse or ***Hôtel du Commerce*** (☎/fax 04 66 48 50 01) across the little bridge. The Central has singles/doubles for 140/200FF; the Commerce for 130/250FF. Both are closed in winter.

A fabulous place to stay if you have the cash is at the 15th century ***Château de la Caze*** (☎ 04 66 48 51 01; fax 04 66 48 55 75), just 2km north of La Malène on the banks of the Tarn. Luxury rooms start at 600FF and the hotel/restaurant is open from 15 March to 15 November.

Getting There & Away

Public transport along the Gorges du Tarn is virtually nonexistent. The only regularly scheduled bus links Sainte Énimie with Millau, and that's only in July and August. There are other buses from Millau in summer, however; see Organised Tours in the Millau section for more information.

PARC NATUREL RÉGIONAL DES GRANDS CAUSSES

Lying to the west of the Cévennes, the Parc Naturel Régional des Grands Causses (315,640 hectares) embraces an area of harsh limestone plateaus on the southern rim of the Massif Central. Scorched in summer and windswept in winter, their stony surfaces hold little moisture – the water filters through the limestone to form an underground world of caves ideal for speleologists and adventurers.

Over the millennia, the Tarn, Jonte and Dourbie rivers have cut deep gorges through the 5000 sq km plateau, creating four distinct plateaus: Sauveterre, Méjean, Noir and Larzac. Each is different in its delicate geological forms. One may look like a dark lunar surface and another like a Scottish moor covered with the thinnest layer of grass, while the next is gentler and more fertile. But all of them are eerie, and empty except for the occasional shepherd wandering with his flock.

The town of Millau in the centre of the park is a good base for exploring this wild region. The southern part of the park, home to France's 'king of cheeses', is known as Le Pays du Roquefort (the Land of Roquefort). The Gorges de la Jonte, home to swooping birds of prey and rivalling the neighbouring Gorges du Tarn in beauty, skim the park's eastern boundary.

Causse de Sauveterre

The northernmost causse is a gentle, hilly plateau dotted with a few isolated farms. Compact and curiously built, these farms resemble fortified villages. Every possible patch of fertile earth is cultivated, creating irregular, intricately patterned wheat fields.

Causse Méjean

The Causse Méjean, the highest of the causses at an average altitude of around 1000m, is also the most barren and isolated. Occasional fertile depressions dot the poor pastures, and streams disappear into the limestone through sinkholes, funnels and fissures.

Underground, this combination of water and limestone has created some spectacular scenery. One of the most famous caves is **Aven Armand** (for information phone ☎ 04 66 45 61 31; fax 04 66 45 67 38) on the plateau's south-west side. Lying about 75m below the surface, the cavern stretches some 200m and encompasses a subterranean forest of stalagmites and stalactites. Discovered in 1897 by Louis Armand, a colleague of the father of speleology, Édouard-André Martel, it's 19km south of Sainte Énimie and 29km north-east of Millau. The one hour guided visit costs 43/20FF for adults/children. A combination ticket which also includes admission to the Chaos de Montpellier-le-Vieux (see the Causse Noir section) costs 50/25FF. The cave is open from mid-March to early November. For details on getting to Aven Armand, see the Organised Tours and Getting There & Away entries in the Millau section.

The GR60 hiking trail cuts through the Causse Méjean to the east, and there are a lot of gîtes d'étape along the way where you can spend the night for between 35 and 40FF. For cycling on the Causse Méjean, see Activities in the Florac section.

Causse Noir

Rising immediately east of Millau, this 'black' causse is encircled by gorges. It's best known for **Montpellier-le-Vieux** (☎ 05 65 60 66 30 in Peyreleau for information), an area of jagged rocks called *chaos* 18km north-east of Millau overlooking the Gorges de la Dourbie. Created by water erosion over the limestone plateau, the result is 120 hectares of formations with fanciful names such as the Sphinx and the Elephant. Three trails, lasting from one to three hours, cover the site, as does a tourist train.

Officially Montpellier-le-Vieux is open between mid-March and early November from 9 am to 7 pm. Admission is 27/10FF for adults/children and the little train costs 15/10FF return. In the months when it's closed, there's nothing to stop you from freely wandering in. For details on buses and organised tours to the Causse Noir, see the Millau section.

Causse du Larzac

The Causse du Larzac (800 to 1000m) is the largest of the four causses. An endless sweep of distant horizons and rocky steppes broken by medieval villages, it is known as the 'French Desert'. To the west is the Roquefort region; Millau is to the north.

This area is known in particular for its old, fortified villages such as **Sainte Eulalie**, long the capital of the Larzac region and **La Couvertoirade**. They were built by the Knights Templar, a religious military order that distinguished itself during the Crusades of the 12th century. For information on how to reach these villages, see Organised Tours in the Millau section.

Gorges de la Jonte

The dramatic Gorges de la Jonte cut eastward from Le Rozier to Meyrueis, along the north-western slopes of the Aigoual massif. Midway between the two villages, just west of Le Truel on the D996, is the **Belvédère des Vautours** (Vulture Viewing Point) from where you can watch vultures circling and nesting on the surrounding cliffs and learn about their fate. Vultures had all but disappeared from the Causses skies by the 1950s, but in recent years a colony of 20 has been reintroduced into the gorges.

The vulture centre (☎ 05 65 62 69 69; fax 05 65 62 69 67) also houses an exhibition devoted to these majestic birds of prey. In conjunction with Fonds d'Intervention pour Les Rapaces (Emergency Fund for Birds of Prey; ☎ 05 65 62 61 40; fax 05 65 62 63 66), F-12720 Peyreleau, the vulture centre organises half-day treks to the surrounding gorges to watch the vultures (60/30FF for adults/children). The centre is open from 10 am to 6 pm (7 pm in summer). Admission costs 33/19FF for adults/children aged from 6 to 14.

MILLAU

• pop 22,500 ✉ 12100 alt 372m

Actually just over the border in the Midi-Pyrénées department of Aveyron but tied with Languedoc historically and culturally, Millau (pronounced 'mee-YOH') sits between the Causse Noir and Causse du Larzac at the confluence of the Tarn and Dourbie rivers. It is a prosperous town enjoying the benefits of being the main centre for the Parc Naturel Régional des Grand Causses.

Convenient places for take-offs and good thermals have turned Millau into a thriving hang-gliding and parapente centre.

Information

Tourist Office In an attractive garden with fountains at 1 Ave Alfred Merle, the tourist office (☎ 05 65 60 02 42; fax 05 65 61 36 08) is open September to March from 9 am to 12.30 pm and 2 to 6.30 pm (closed Saturday afternoon and all day Sunday). From April to June it's open from 9 am to noon and 2 to 6 pm (closed Sunday), and in July and August daily from 9 am to 12.30 pm and 2 to 7 pm. Ask for a copy of *Millau – Guide Circuits*, a pamphlet with six excellent day trips by car ranging from 130 to 175km.

Park Office For information about the Parc Naturel Régional des Grands Causses go to the park office (☎ 05 65 61 35 50; fax 05 65 61 34 80) at 71 Blvd de l'Ayrolle.

Money The Banque de France at the east of the train station on Place Bion Marlavagne is open from 8.45 am to 12.15 pm and 1.30 to 4.30 pm. There are more banks on Ave Jean Jaurès and Ave de la République.

Post & Communications The main post office, 12 Ave Alfred Merle, is open weekdays from 8.30 am to 7 pm and until noon on Saturday.

You can surf the Internet and send emails from Virus Jeux Video (☎ 05 65 61 07 01), 21 Rue Droite. Access costs 30/50FF for half-hour/hour. It's open Tuesday to Saturday from 9.30 am to noon and 2.30 to 7.30 pm.

Le Beffroi

This 42m-tall belfry on Rue Droite, with a square base from the 12th century and a 17th century octagonal tower, is the centrepiece of the old city. It affords excellent

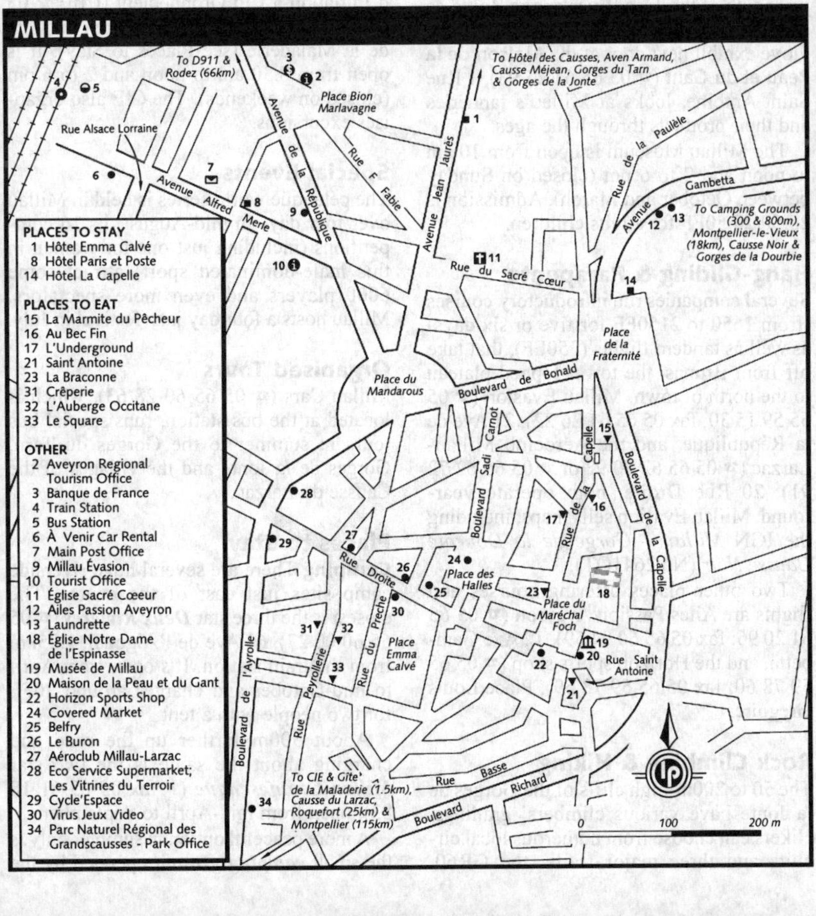

views and can be climbed (15/5FF for adults/children). It is open from 3 to 7 pm (closed Sunday from September to June).

Musée de Millau

The Millau Museum (☎ 05 65 59 01 08) in the Hôtel de Pégayrolles on Place du Maréchal Foch has a rich collection of fossils, including mammoth molars and a dinosaur skeleton dug up from the Causse du Larzac. In the cellar is a huge array of plates and vases excavated at the **Site Archéologique La Graufesenque**, the former site of Gallo-Roman pottery workshops just south of the Tarn River on the Route de Montpellier. The museum's leather and glove exhibit next door at the **Maison de la Peau et du Gant** (☎ 05 65 61 25 93), 1 Rue Saint Antoine, looks at Millau's tanneries and their products through the ages.

The Millau Museum is open from 10 am to noon and 2 to 6 pm (closed on Sunday between October and March). Admission is 25.50/20.50FF for adults/children.

Hang-Gliding & Parapente

Several companies run introductory courses (from 1650 to 2150FF for five or six days) as well as tandem flights (350FF), that take off from Brunas, the tower-topped plateau to the north of town. Millau Évasion (☎ 05 65 59 15 30; fax 05 65 61 26 22), 21 Ave de la République, and the Aéroclub Millau-Larzac (☎ 05 65 62 70 92 or ☎ 05 65 62 72 91), 20 Rue Droite, both operate year-round. Millau Évasion sells maps, including the IGN *Millau – Gorge de la Dourbie Causse Noir* (No 2641OT).

Two other places offering courses and flights are Ailes Passion Aveyron (☎ 05 65 61 20 96; fax 05 65 60 04 59), 12 Ave Gambetta, and the Horizon sports shop (☎ 05 65 59 78 60; fax 05 65 59 78 59), Place Louis Gregoire.

Rock Climbing & Hiking

The 50 to 200m-high cliffs of the Gorges de la Jonte have various climbers' gradings. Hikers can choose from numerous local circuits and three major trails: the GR60, which traverses the Gorges du Tarn at Sainte Énimie and crosses the Causse Méjean; the GR62, which leaves the Cévennes, crosses the Causse Noir and passes Montpellier-le-Vieux before winding down to Millau and heading west to Lac Pareloup; and the GR71 and its spurs, which concentrate on the Causse du Larzac and the Templar villages there.

Millau's tourist office sells maps and guides of the region, including *Randonnées Pédestres: Millau-Gorges du Tarn-Grands Causses* (40FF). For more detailed maps and hiking information, head for the Centre d'Initiation à l'Environnement (CIE; ☎ 05 65 61 06 57), which operates from the Gîte de la Maladerie (see Places to Stay). It is open from 8.30 am to noon and 2 to 6 pm (closed on weekends). The CIE also organises excursions.

Special Events

The pétanque world series is held in Millau over four days in mid-August; its 16 competitions (including just one for women in this male-dominated sport) attract some 6000 players and even more spectators. Millau hosts a four day jazz festival in July.

Organised Tours

Millau Cars (☎ 05 65 60 28 63), which is located at the bus station, runs special bus tours in summer to the Gorges du Tarn, Gorges de la Jonte and the villages of the Causse du Larzac.

Places to Stay

Camping There are several huge riverside camp sites just east of the centre. The closest is the three star ***Deux Rivières*** (☎ 05 65 60 00 27), 61 Ave de l'Aigoual, 1.25km from the train station. It's open from April to mid-October and charges around 70FF for two people with a tent.

About 500m farther up the road and charging about the same is the two star ***Millau Graufesenque*** (☎/fax 05 65 61 18 83), open from mid-April to September.

A more peaceful option in summer only is the small ***camping ground*** operated by the

Gîte de la Maladerie (see Gîte d'Étape). It's basic, fairly isolated and charges about 15FF per person a night.

Gîte d'Étape In a calm setting but hard to get to, the ***Gîte de la Maladerie*** (☎ 05 65 61 06 57; fax 05 65 60 26 02), Chemin de la Graufesenque, charges 55FF a night for a dorm bed. Kitchen facilities are available, and it is open year-round. The gîte is about 2.5km from the train station. To get there cross Pont Lerouge and follow the river to the left.

Hotels Many hotels are closed between October and Easter. One that isn't is ***Hôtel Paris et Poste*** (☎ 05 65 60 00 52), close to the train station at 10 Ave Alfred Merle. Rooms with toilet/shower are 140/200FF.

Also open year-round is the stylish ***Hôtel Emma Calvé*** (☎ 05 65 60 13 49), 28 Ave Jean Jaurès. Its rooms, all with bath and toilet, start at 205FF.

Central but quiet, ***Hôtel La Capelle*** (☎ 05 65 60 14 72), in part of a reconditioned old leather factory just beyond the trees at 7 Place de la Fraternité, is one of the best options in town. The rooms are fine, and the large terrace out the front is perfect for breakfast with a view of the start of the Causse Noir. Fairly basic doubles start at 145FF (200/215FF with shower/shower and toilet). Private parking is free. This place is closed in winter, as is ***Hôtel des Causses*** (☎ 05 65 60 03 19; fax 05 65 60 86 90), 56 Ave Jean Jaurès, a two star Logis de France hotel with pleasant, shower-equipped rooms from 220FF.

Places to Eat

Restaurants ***La Braconne*** (☎ 05 65 60 30 93), 7 Place du Maréchal Foch, has excellent regional *menus* and is famed for its grilled trotters. It has a good selection of Faugères wines and fine outside seating overlooking an attractive square. It's closed Sunday night and Monday.

Just off Place du Maréchal Foch and slightly hidden by an archway is the hole-in-the-wall ***Saint Antoine***, which has a four course *menu* for 60FF.

L'Underground (☎ 05 65 60 09 86), 13 Rue de la Capelle, is one of Millau's most fun hideouts, offering a cheap plat du jour for 25FF. It's open daily from 11 am to 11 pm. Farther up the street at 14 Rue de la Capelle is the welcoming ***La Marmite du Pêcheur*** (☎ 05 65 61 20 44). The 'Fisherman's Pot' has hearty regional *menus* for 60, 91 and 138FF. Don't miss its delicious *salade au Roquefort et noix* (Roquefort and nut salad). ***Au Bec Fin*** (☎ 05 65 60 13 20) at No 20 of the same street also serves regional dishes with *menus* from 60 to 155FF.

Various Roquefort concoctions are also dished up at ***L'Auberge Occitane*** (☎ 05 65 60 45 54), a cosy place at 15 Rue Peyrollerie. Its *médaillon de bœuf au Roquefort* is definitely worth sinking your teeth into. The *menu* is 110FF. Directly opposite at No 10 is a ***crêperie*** serving 23 types of sweet, savoury and flambée crêpes. It's open from 11 am to 8 pm.

Close by at 10 Rue Saint Martin is ***Le Square*** (☎ 05 65 61 26 00), which has *menus* for 92 and 148FF.

Self-Catering The ***market*** mornings are Wednesday and Friday on Place du Maréchal Foch and in the covered market on Place des Halles. The ***Eco Service*** supermarket, 15 Blvd de l'Ayrolle, is open from 8.30 am to 12.30 pm and 2.30 to 7.30 pm (closed Sunday). ***Les Vitrines du Terroir***, next door at No 17, and ***Le Buron*** on the corner of Rue Droite and Rue du Beffroi are two fromageries selling local specialities including Roquefort and Perail du Larzc cheeses.

Getting There & Away

Bus The bus station (☎ 05 65 60 28 63) is in front of the train station at the end of Ave Alfred Merle, about 500m north-west of the centre. Its office is open from 8.15 am to noon and 3.30 to 6.30 pm (Saturday from 8.45 to 11.45 am; closed Sunday). Regularly scheduled buses go to Montpellier (85FF; 2¼ hours; five a day), Rodez (52FF; 1¾ hours; four a day) and Albi (80FF; two a day).

Regional services are very limited in summer. Generally there's only one bus a day to Le Rozier (30FF; 30 minutes), the closest stop (10km north) to Montpellier-le-Vieux. The closest bus stop to Aven Armand is at Meyrueis (45FF; 1¼ hours), some 12km away. To Sainte Énimie (60FF; 1¾ hours) on the Gorges du Tarn there's one regular daily bus in July and August.

To Roquefort (25FF) you have to take the Toulouse bus (two daily, except Sunday, at 7 am and 12.45 pm) and get off at Lauras, from where it's a 4km but pleasant walk uphill.

Train Connections from Millau's train station (☎ 05 65 60 11 65) include Paris' Gare de Lyon (339FF; 9½ hours; three a day), Béziers (88FF; two hours; six a day), Clermont-Ferrand (168FF; 4½ hours), Montpellier (134FF; three hours) and Toulouse (149FF; 3½ hours). Via Rodez (61FF; 1¼ hours), there are trains to Albi (111FF; 2½ hours on the direct morning train). The train station (☎ 05 65 60 34 02) closest to Roquefort is at Tournemire (26FF; 30 minutes; seven a day), a tiny village 3km east of town from where you have to hitch or walk.

Car À Venir (☎ 05 65 61 20 77), 7 Rue Alfred Merle, is an agent for Budget. Try to call a couple of days in advance as the cars have to be brought over from Rodez. Europcar (☎ 05 65 59 19 19) is at 3 Place Frédéric Bompaire.

Getting Around

Bicycle Mountain bikes and normal bikes can be hired at Cycle Espace (☎ 05 65 61 14 29), 21 Blvd de l'Ayrolle, for around 90/130/390FF a day/weekend/week. It is open from 9 am to 12.15 pm and 2 to 7.15 pm (closed Sunday and Monday).

La Barbotte cycles (☎ 05 65 62 66 26) in Le Rozier (from where you could cycle to Montpellier-le-Vieux) rents bikes for about the same price.

AROUND MILLAU

Roquefort

About 25km south-west of Millau, in the heart of the Parc Naturel Régional des Grands Causses is the village of Roquefort-sur-Soulzon (population 780) where *lait de brebis* (ewe's milk) is turned into France's most famous blue cheese. Clinging to a hillside, its steep, narrow streets – permeated with a cheesy smell – are crammed with tourists making their way to the cool natural caves where a dozen different producers ripen some 22,000 tonnes of Roquefort cheese a year.

If you want to see how the cheeses are made, La Société (☎ 05 65 59 93 30 or ☎ 05 65 58 58 58), Rue de la Cave, has one hour guided tours (15FF) that include a sound and light show in the caves and a dégustation session. La Société, established in 1842, is the largest Roquefort producer, churning out 80% of the world's supply. It is open daily from 9.30 to 11.30 am and 2 to 5 pm (9.30 am to 6 pm in July and August). Tours of the equally pungent *caves* of Le Papillon (☎ 05 65 58 50 08), Rue de la Fontaine, dating from 1906 and open from 9.30 to 11.30 am and 1.30 to 4.30 pm, are free.

After enduring a dégustation session of 10 different Roqueforts at Le Moderne (see Places to Stay & Eat below), this author's palate reeled in ecstasy over the buttery Roquefort made by Le Vieux Berger (☎ 05 65 59 91 48), the smallest of the Roquefort producers.

It is also possible to visit the dairy farms in the region, from which some 130 million litres of ewe's milk are collected a year. For information contact the tourist office (☎ 05 65 59 93 19; fax 05 65 58 91 44; www.roquefort.com), Ave Lauras, which is open Monday to Wednesday from 10 am to 5 pm, and Thursday and Friday from 9 am to noon and 2 to 5 pm. In July and August its hours are 9 am to 6 pm.

Places to Stay & Eat There are no hotels in Roquefort. The closest is ***Le Combalou*** (☎ 05 65 59 91 70; fax 05 65 59 98 18),

2.5km west of the village towards Saint Affrique. Truckers rather than tourists tend to stop here. Doubles cost 180FF.

Better value and more aesthetically pleasing is ***Le Moderne*** (☎ 05 65 49 20 44; fax 05 65 49 36 55), directly opposite the train station at 54 Ave Alphonse-Pezet in Saint Affrique, 5.5km from Roquefort. Comfortable singles/doubles in the main hotel building are 200/250FF while more basic rooms in its ***Annexe Les Tilleuls***, immediately opposite, are 90/120FF. All guests can eat in Le Moderne's fantastic restaurant. Its Roquefort-based *menus* starting at 100FF – and allowing you to taste 10 different Roquefort cheeses – should not be missed. The hotel also arranges Évasion Gourmande (literally, 'greedy escape') weekends in Le Pays du Roquefort during which you eat your way around the region. Yum!

Equally fine but less refined are the hearty portions of local fodder dished out at ***Hôtel de la Gare*** (☎ 05 65 59 91 06; fax 05 65 58 91 94) in Tournemire, 3km east of Roquefort. *Menus* start at 75FF, rooms at 160FF for two.

Getting There & Away Roquefort is hard to get to without a car. For information regarding trains, buses and organised tours, see the Millau section earlier.

Roussillon

Roussillon, sometimes known as French Catalonia, lies at the eastern end of the Pyrenees on the doorstep of Spain. The main city is Perpignan, capital of the department of Pyrénées-Orientales.

Roussillon was long a part of Catalonia (the autonomous region in the north-east of modern-day Spain), and it has kept many symbols of Catalan unity. The *sardane*, a dance expressing both peace and revolt, is still performed during festivals, and the Catalan language (Occitan), closely related to Provençal, is widely spoken.

History

Roussillon was inhabited in prehistoric times, and one of the oldest skulls in Europe was found in a cave near Perpignan. After a series of invasions by the same groups who passed through Languedoc, Roussillon came under the control of Catalonia-Aragon in 1172. In the 13th and 14th centuries, Perpignan was the capital of the kingdom of Majorca but, apart from a brief period of French rule in the 15th century, Roussillon spent much of the late Middle Ages under Aragonese rule.

In 1640, the Catalans revolted against the Castilian kings in Madrid, who had engulfed Aragon. After a two year siege, Perpignan was relieved with the help of the French King Louis XIII and his ruthless

The King of Cheeses

The mouldy blue-green veins running through Roquefort are, in fact, the seeds of microscopic mushrooms, picked in the caves at Roquefort then cultivated on leavened bread.

During the cheese's ripening process – which takes place in the same natural caves cut in the mountainside – delicate draughts of air called *fleurines* cut through the cave like a sieve, encouraging the blue *penicillium roqueforti* to eat its way through the white cheese curds. The word 'fleurine' is derived from the langue d'oc word *flarina*, meaning 'to blow'.

At around 100FF a kilogram, Roquefort ranks as one of France's priciest and most noble cheeses. In 1407 Charles VI granted exclusive Roquefort cheese-making rights to the villagers of Roquefort. In the 17th century, the Sovereign Court of the Parliament of Toulouse imposed severe penalties against fraudulent cheese makers trading under the Roquefort name.

chief minister, Cardinal Richelieu. This led in 1659 to the Treaty of the Pyrenees, which defined the border between Spain and France once and for all. The northern section of Catalonia, Roussillon, was handed over to the French, much to the indignation of the locals.

Geography

The southern end of the plain of Lower Languedoc is dominated by Perpignan, to the west of which rises Mont Canigou (2786m), a peak sacred to the Catalan people. All around is a mosaic of vineyards, olive and fig groves and vegetable fields. The flat coastline ends abruptly with the rocky foothills of the Pyrenees at the Côte Vermeille, an area of deep red rocks and soil which inspired the most renowned Fauvist artists.

PERPIGNAN

• pop 110,000 ✉ 66000

More Catalan than French, Perpignan (Perpinyà in Catalan) was the capital of the kingdom of Majorca from 1278 to 1344, which stretched from here to Montpellier and included the Balearic Islands. Perpignan developed into an important commercial centre in the following centuries, and it is still the second largest Catalan city after Barcelona.

Today Perpignan is not the most attractive city in southern France, though it's certainly not the 'villainous ugly town' that the traveller Henry Swinburne said it was in 1775. Situated at the foothills of the Pyrenees and with the Côte Vermeille not far to the south-east, Perpignan makes a great base for day trips into the mountains or along the coast.

Orientation

Perpignan lies south of the Têt River, but it is the crystal-clear Basse River running through the city centre and banked either side with immaculate gardens that you're more likely to encounter. The heart of the old city, encircled by boulevards and partly pedestrianised, lies at Place de la Loge and Place de Verdun.

Information

Tourist Office The tourist office (☎ 04 68 66 30 30; fax 04 68 66 30 26; contact-office@smi-telecom.fr; www.little-france.com/perpignan) is in the Palais des Congrès, Place Armand Lanoux, on the north-eastern edge of Promenade des Platanes. It is open from 8.30 am to noon and 2 to 6.30 pm (closed Sunday). From June to September it's open from 9 am to 7 pm (Sunday from 9 am to noon and 2 to 5 pm).

Copious amounts of information about Roussillon can be picked up at the Comité Départemental du Tourisme (CDT; ☎ 04 68 34 29 94; fax 04 68 34 71 01), 7 Quai de Lattre de Tassigny.

The Catalan Cultural Centre (☎ 04 68 34 11 70), opposite the police station at 42 Ave de Grande Bretagne, promotes Catalan language and culture.

Money The Banque de France, 3 Place Jean Payra, is open from 8.45 am to noon and 1.30 to 3.30 pm (closed on weekends). There are several banks to the north-east on Blvd Clemenceau. Most ATMs dispense Spanish pesetas as well as French francs.

Post The main post office, Rue du Docteur Zamenhof, is open from 8 am (9 am on Wednesday) to 7 pm (Saturday until noon).

Laundry The laundrette at 23 Rue du Maréchal Foch is open from 7 am to 8 pm. The one on Place Jean Payra is open from 9 am to 7 pm (closed Sunday).

Place de la Loge

Place de la Loge has a few lovely old stone structures, including **La Loge de Mer**, a 14th century building rebuilt during the Renaissance that once housed the exchange and maritime tribunal and is now home to a fast-food joint. Next door, the **Hôtel de Ville**, in typical Roussillon style, has a pebbled façade of river stones.

Casa Païral

This museum of Roussillon and Catalan folklore (☎ 04 68 35 42 05) is in the 14th

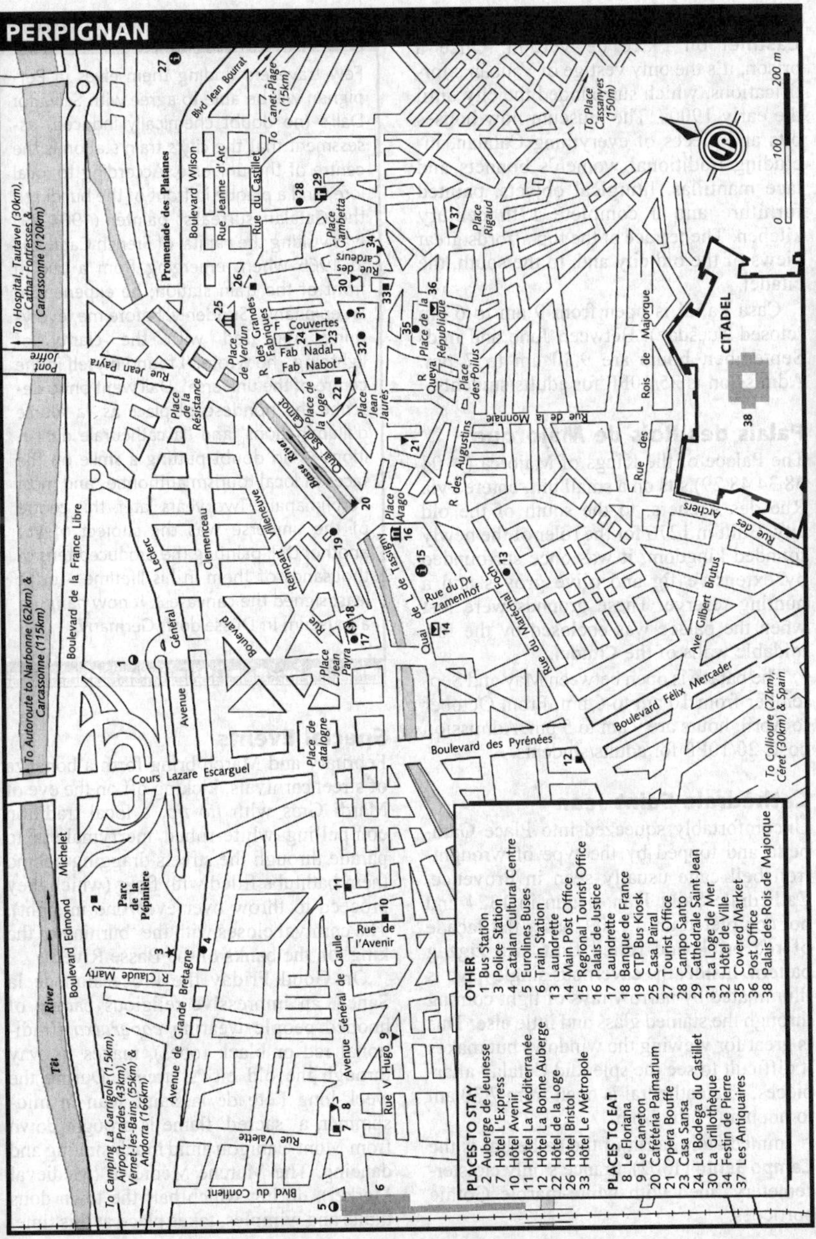
PERPIGNAN
PLACES TO STAY
2 Auberge de Jeunesse
7 Hôtel L'Express
10 Hôtel Avenir
11 Hôtel La Méditerranée
12 Hôtel La Bonne Auberge
17 Hôtel de la Loge
22 Hôtel Bristol
33 Hôtel Le Métropole
PLACES TO EAT
8 Le Floriana
9 Le Caneton
20 Cafétéria Palmarium
21 Opéra Bouffe
23 Casa Sansa
24 La Bodega du Castillet
30 La Grillothèque
34 Festin de Pierre
37 Les Antiquaires
OTHER
1 Bus Station
3 Police Station
4 Catalan Cultural Centre
5 Eurolines Buses
6 Train Station
13 Laundrette
14 Main Post Office
15 Regional Tourist Office
16 Palais de Justice
17 Laundrette
18 Banque de France
19 CTP Bus Kiosk
25 Casa Païral
27 Tourist Office
28 Campo Santo
29 Cathédrale Saint Jean
31 La Loge de Mer
32 Hôtel de Ville
35 Covered Market
36 Post Office
38 Palais des Rois de Majorque
To Hospital, Tautavel (30km), Cathar Fortresses & Carcassonne (120km)
To Autoroute to Narbonne (62km) & Carcassonne (115km)
To Camping La Garrigole (1.5km), Airport, Prades (43km), Vernet-les-Bains (55km) & Andorra (166km)
To Canet-Plage (15km)
To Place Cassanyes (150m)
To Collioure (27km), Céret (30km) & Spain
Têt River
Basse River
CITADEL
Promenade des Platanes
Parc de la Pépinière
Boulevard Wilson
Boulevard de la France Libre
Boulevard Edmond Michelet
Avenue de Grande Bretagne
Avenue Général de Gaulle
Avenue Général Leclerc
Boulevard Clemenceau
Cours Lazare Escarguel
Boulevard des Pyrénées
Boulevard Félix Mercader
Rue Jean Payra
Place de la Résistance
Place de Verdun
Place de la Loge
Place Gambetta
Place Jean Jaurès
Place Arago
Place de Catalogne
Place Rigaud
Place des Poilus
Rue du Maréchal Foch
Rue de la Monnaie
Rue des Archers
Quai Sadi Carnot
0 100 200 m

century red-brick town gate known as **Le Castillet** on Place de Verdun. Once a prison, it's the only vestige of Vauban's fortifications, which surrounded the city until the early 1900s. The museum now houses bits and pieces of everything Catalan, including traditional women's bonnets and lace mantillas, liturgical objects, painted furniture and a complete 17th century kitchen. The terrace at the top affords great views of the old city and, to the south, the citadel.

Casa Païral is open from 9 am to 6 pm (closed Tuesday). Between June and mid-September, hours are 9.30 am to 7 pm. Admission is 25/10FF for adults/students.

Palais des Rois de Majorque

The Palace of the Kings of Majorca (☎ 04 68 34 48 29) sits on a small hill, entered via Rue des Archers, to the south of the old city. Built in 1276 for the ruler of the newly founded kingdom, it was once surrounded by extensive fig and olive groves and a hunting reserve. These grounds were lost when the palace was enclosed by the formidable walls of the **Citadel**.

The palace is open between May and September from 10 am to 6 pm. From October to April, hours are 9 am to 5 pm. Admission costs 20/10FF for adults/students.

Cathédrale Saint Jean

Uncomfortably squeezed into Place Gambetta and topped by the type of wrought-iron bell cage usually seen in Provence, Cathédrale Saint Jean, begun in 1324 and not completed until 1509, has a flat façade of red brick and rolled flint in a zigzag pattern. Inside, the cavernous single nave is illuminated by narrow rays of light coming through the stained glass and little else. This is great for viewing the windows but makes it difficult to see the splendid Catalan altarpieces. The cathedral is open from 7.30 am to noon and 3 to 7 pm.

Immediately north of the cathedral is the **Campo Santo** (1302), France's only cloister-cemetery lined with white-marble Gothic porticoes.

Dalí's Train of Thought

Few travellers finding themselves in Perpignan will be able to agree with Salvador Dalí's (no doubt chemically induced) assessment that the city's train station is the centre of the universe. According to local lore (and a plaque in front of the building), the Catalan surrealist painter (1904-89) was visiting the capital of French Catalonia in 1965 when, emerging from a taxi in front of the train station, he experienced an epiphany. 'Suddenly, before me, everything appeared with the clarity of lightning,' he wrote. 'I found myself in the centre of the universe'. Dalí went on to describe this nondescript place as 'la source d'illuminations' and 'la cathédrale d'intuitions' – no doubt putting a smile on the faces of local tourism authorities and most Perpignanais. Two years later, this centre of the universe was the subject of yet another Dalí painting (he produced tens of thousands of them in his lifetime – or at least signed the canvases). It now hangs in a museum in Düsseldorf, Germany.

Special Events

February and March bring forth a bonanza of street carnivals, kicking off on the eve of Mardi Gras with *tio tio*, a local tradition compelling white-robed merrymakers to parade through the streets dragging behind them bathtubs filled with flour (which they proceed to throw over everyone in sight). The carnival closes with the 'burning of the king' on the banks of the Basse River.

On Good Friday the Procession de la Sanch, an impressive religious parade of hooded people wearing *caperutxa* (traditional red or black robes), makes its way through the old city's streets. During the week-long Fête de la Saint Jean in mid-summer, a 'sacred' flame is brought down from Mont Canigou amid much singing and dancing. The Marché Médiéval (Medieval Market), during which half the town dons tights and wimples, takes place at this time.

Perpignan hosts a two week jazz festival in mid-October and, on the third Thursday in October, a wine festival during which a barrel of the year's new wine is carried through the streets to the Cathédrale Saint Jean to be blessed.

Places to Stay

Camping ***La Garrigole*** (☎ 04 68 54 66 10), 2 Rue Maurice Lévy, 1.5km west of the train station, charges 60FF for two people with a tent and is open year-round except December. Take bus No 2 from the station or Place Arago in the town centre and get off at the Garrigole stop.

Hostel Behind the police station in the Parc de la Pépinière on Ave de Grande Bretagne, the ***Auberge de Jeunesse*** (☎ 04 68 34 63 32; fax 04 68 51 16 02) is a villa-like place at the end of Rue Claude Marty. Beds in dorms or four-person rooms cost 68FF, including breakfast. The hostel is closed between 10 am and 4 pm and from 20 December to 20 January.

Gîtes For B&B and accommodation in rural surrounds contact ***Gîtes de France*** (☎ 04 68 55 60 95; fax 04 68 55 60 94), 30 Rue Pierre Bretonneau.

Hotels – Train Station Area There's a string of hotels along Ave du Général de Gaulle. ***Hôtel L'Express*** (☎ 04 68 34 89 96) at No 3 has small but functional rooms for one or two people without/with shower for 94/114FF. Triples with shower cost 184FF. About 400m farther along from the station, the friendly ***La Méditerranée*** (☎ 04 68 34 87 48) at No 62bis has nicer but still basic singles/doubles (a few with private terrace) from 120/150FF. Use of the hall shower costs 15FF. Rooms with shower start at 170/200FF, triples at 240FF.

The clean, one star ***Hôtel Avenir*** (☎ 04 68 34 20 30; fax 04 68 34 15 63), 11 Rue de l'Avenir, has basic rooms for 90/120FF, rooms for one or two people with shower for 145FF, and triples without/with shower for 170/190FF.

Hotels – City Centre Close to Casa Païral, ***Hôtel Bristol*** (☎ 04 68 34 32 68), 5 Rue des Grandes Fabriques, is a cavernous place with rooms for one or two people with shower for 190FF. The unfriendly ***Hôtel Le Métropole*** (☎ 04 68 34 43 34), 3 Rue des Cardeurs, is about the cheapest option in the city centre. It has an attractive foyer, but the rooms are not nearly as appealing. Still, they're good value at 135FF for one or two people with shower. Two-bed triples cost 175FF.

For a splurge, ***Hôtel de la Loge*** (☎ 04 68 34 41 02; fax 04 68 34 25 13), 1 Rue des Fabriques d'En Nabot, overlooking the Hôtel de Ville, has rustic singles/doubles with everything you need from 205/260FF.

Places to Eat

Restaurants In the city centre, ***Casa Sansa*** (☎ 04 68 34 21 84), 2 Rue des Fabriques Nadal, is a very popular Catalan restaurant-cum-art gallery. Main dishes range from 38 to 89FF; parillade de poisson is 120FF. Casa Sansa is closed all day Sunday and Monday lunchtime. ***La Bodega du Castillet*** (☎ 04 68 34 88 98) is in the narrow Rue des Fabriques Couvertes one street east. The ambience – unmistakably Catalan – is enhanced by the aroma of grilled *calamares* (caramelised desserts) which occasionally wafts through the place. Tapas start at 28FF a serving.

An excellent choice for regional specialities like *esqueixade de bacallà* and *boles de picolat* is ***Opéra Bouffe*** (☎ 04 68 34 83 83), Impasse de la Division, south-west of Place Jean Jaurès. *Menus* range from 67 to 125FF, and it is closed on Sunday. Other goodies for regional fare include ***Festin de Pierre*** (☎ 04 68 51 28 74), 7 Rue Théâtre, and ***Les Antiquaires*** close by at Place Desprès. *Menus* start at around 125FF.

For substantial fare, ***La Grillothèque*** (☎ 04 68 34 06 99), 7 Rue des Cardeurs, has a 68FF *menu* and salads from 42FF. ***Cafétéria Palmarium*** (☎ 04 68 34 51 31), Place Arago, is a large self-service place open daily until 9.30 pm.

A block from the train station along Ave du Général de Gaulle are the good-value ***Le***

Floriana (☎ 04 68 34 60 40) at No 11 which has a *menu* for 60FF and salads from 42FF, and ***Le Caneton***, 12 Rue Victor Hugo, which must be one of the cheapest smallest restaurants in France. Little more than a room in a private house, it is very simple but the three course 30FF *menu* will fill you up.

Self-Catering ***Food markets*** are held every morning on Place des Poilus, as well as in the covered market hall on Place de la République from 7 am to 1 pm and 4 to 7.30 pm (closed Monday).

Getting There & Away

Air Perpignan's airport (☎ 04 68 52 60 70; fax 04 68 52 31 03), Ave Maurice Bellonte, is 5km north-west of the town centre.

Bus The bus station (☎ 04 68 35 67 51) is on Ave Général Leclerc. Bus companies based there include Les Courriers Catalans (☎ 04 68 55 68 00).

Bus No 35 goes to Céret (34FF; 40 minutes; 14 a day) and No 44 to Collioure (31FF; 45 minutes; seven a day), Port Vendres and Banyuls. No 20 goes to Vernet-les-Bains (53FF; 1½ hours; six a day), though with some services you have to change to a connecting bus in Villefranche. Bus No 10 goes to Estagel (25FF; 25 minutes), Maury (37FF; 34 minutes) and Quillan (67FF; 1½ hours). To get to Andorra, change buses at La Tour de Carol; see Getting There & Away in the Andorra chapter.

Buses run by Eurolines (☎ 04 68 34 11 46) leave from outside the office to the left as you exit the train station.

Train Perpignan's small train station (☎ 08 36 35 35 35), the centre of the universe according to Salvador Dalí (see the earlier boxed text 'Dalí's Train of Thought'), is the last major stop before entering Spain at Cerbère/Portbou. It's at the end of Ave Général de Gaulle, about 2km from the tourist office (take bus No 3 to the Palais des Congrès stop). The information office is open daily from 5.45 am to 9.45 pm.

Major destinations include Paris (443FF; 12 to 15 hours; several daily), Montpellier (120FF; two hours; 16 a day), Carcassonne (110FF; 1½ hours; two a day), Narbonne (68FF; 45 minutes) and Barcelona (101FF; 4½ hours; 10 a day). Closer to home are Collioure (28FF; 25 minutes; hourly), Prades (39FF; 45 minutes; seven a day) and Cerbère (43FF; 45 minutes).

The closest you can get to Andorra by train is La Tour de Carol (117FF; 3½ hours; six a day) via Villefranche. For information on transport from there to Andorra la Vella, see Getting There & Away in the Andorra chapter.

Car ADA (☎ 04 68 35 69 80) has an office at 31 Blvd Félix Mercader. Eurorent (☎ 04 68 56 96 96) is at 2 Blvd des Pyrénées.

Getting Around

Bus Local buses are run by CTP, which has an information kiosk (☎ 04 68 61 01 13) on Place Arago open from 8 am to noon and 1.45 to 6.15 pm (from 9 am on Saturday; closed Sunday). Buses leave from several hubs: the train station, Place Arago or along Promenade des Platanes. CTP's 15 lines run until between 7 and 8 pm daily except Sunday when services are curtailed drastically. Single tickets cost 7FF and a 10 ticket carnet is 55FF. Bus Nos 2 and 3 link the train station with Place Arago and the Palais des Congrès (tourist office).

AROUND PERPIGNAN

Coastal Beaches

East of Perpignan is the southernmost stretch of the monotonous Languedoc-Roussillon coast. The nearest beach is **Canet-Plage**, 15km away, connected by bus No 1 daily from Place de Catalogne, Place Arago and the tourist office. Tickets cost 13FF or 55FF for a carnet of six. Nudists are tolerated south of Torreilles (itself just north of Canet) and at Saint Cyprien-Plage to the south.

From late June to mid-July and late August to early September, Bus Interplages (☎ 04 68 35 67 51) links the coast from Canet-Plage to Port Vendres with two buses a day (at 10 am and 2.30 pm) from Monday to Saturday. From mid-July to the end of August they go daily from Canet-Plage as far as Cerbère at 9.30 am and 2 and 4.30 pm.

Côte Vermeille

Near the Spanish border is the Côte Vermeille (Vermilion Coast), which starts where the Pyrenees foothills reach the sea. Set against a backdrop of vineyards, this coastline is riddled with small, rocky bays and little ports that once engaged in sardine and anchovy fishing but now have economies based on tourism.

One such port is the very picturesque **Collioure** (population 2700), whose small harbour is filled with fishing boats (though the coast is more dramatic farther south and ports like Port Vendres and Banyuls are far less touristy). Known to the Phoenicians and once Perpignan's port, Collioure found fame early this century when it inspired the Fauvist art of Henri Matisse and André Dérain. The port's castle, **Château Royal** (☎ 04 68 82 06 43) was the summer residence of the kings of Majorca and is now a museum. The tourist office (☎ 04 68 82 15 47), opposite the castle at Place 18 Juin on the waterfront, can provide all the details.

For information on getting to Collioure, see Bus in the Perpignan Getting There & Away section. Bus Interplages buses stop here in summer.

Tautavel

Some 30km north-west of Perpignan, the village of Tautavel is home to what is thought to be Europe's oldest known human skull. Estimated at 450,000 years old, it can be viewed in the **Musée de la Préhistoire** (☎ 04 68 29 07 76), along with all the other prehistoric items found in the Arago Cave, which is a few kilometres north of town. The museum is open from 10 am to 12.30 pm and 2 to 6 pm (no lunch break in April, June and September), and 9 am to 9 pm in July and August. Entry is 20/10FF for adults/children. There's a tourist office (☎ 04 68 29 12 08) in the town hall.

To get there, take bus No 10 towards Quillan and get off at the crossroads 2km after the village of Estagel (25FF; 30 minutes; five a day). From here, it's a 6km walk.

Vernet-les-Bains

A thermal town long beloved by elderly Britons, Vernet-les-Bains (population 1500; altitude 650m) is the best base for climbing **Mont Canigou** (2786m), the easternmost peak in the Pyrenees. Three tracks wind up from Vernet. The wealthy and/or lazy can take a jeep (about 150FF; ☎ 04 68 05 51 14 or ☎ 04 68 05 54 39 for information) from Vernet to Les Cortalets (2175m) and walk the rest of the way (three hours return). See Organised Tours in the Perpignan section for more information. The tourist office (☎ 04 68 05 55 35; fax 04 68 05 60 33) is on Rue Jules Ferry.

Vernet is accessible from Perpignan, 55km to the east, by bus No 20 (53FF; 1½ hours; six a day) though you may have to change at Villefranche.

Loire Valley

From the 15th to the 18th century, the Loire Valley served as the playground of kings, princes, dukes and nobles, who expended family fortunes and the wealth of the nation to turn it into a vast neighbourhood of lavish (and not-so-lavish) chateaus. Today, the region is a favourite destination of tourists seeking architectural testimony to the glories of the Middle Ages and the Renaissance.

The earliest chateaus in the Loire Valley were medieval *châteaux forts* (fortresses), some constructed hastily in the 9th century as a defence against the marauding Vikings (Norsemen). These structures were built on high ground and from the 11th century – when stone came into wide use – were often outfitted with massive walls topped with battlements, fortified keeps, loopholes (arrow slits) and moats spanned by drawbridges.

As the threat of invasion diminished – and the cannon, introduced in the mid-15th century, rendered castles almost useless for defence – the architecture of new chateaus (and the new wings added to older ones) began to reflect a different set of priorities, including aesthetics and comfort. Under the influence of the Renaissance, whose many innovations were introduced to France from Italy at the end of the 15th century, the defensive structures so prominent in the early chateaus developed into whimsical, decorative features, prominent at Azay-le-Rideau, Chambord and Chenonceau. Instead of being built on isolated hilltops, the Renaissance chateaus were placed near a body of water or in a valley and proportioned to harmonise with their surroundings. By contrast, most chateaus from the 17th and 18th centuries are grand country houses, built in the neoclassical style and set amidst formal gardens.

Activities

There are a couple of interesting ways to take in the views of the Loire Valley.

HIGHLIGHTS

- **Castles** – visit the magnificent castles of Villandry, Cheverny and Chenonceau
- **Loire River** – go hot-air ballooning along the Loire
- **Blois** – discover the tricks of the trade at the new Museum of Magic

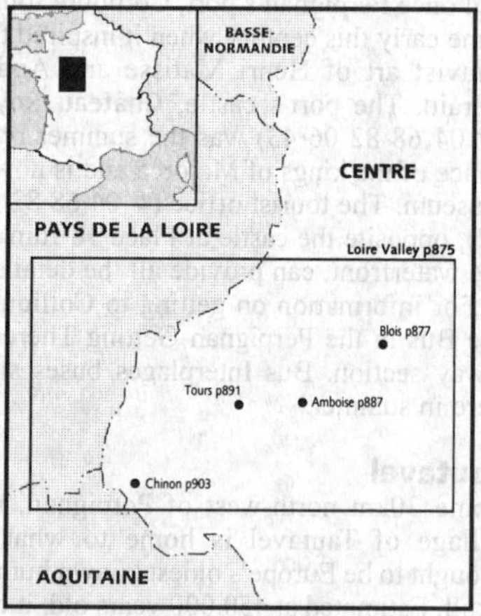

Loire wines – the appellations of Muscadet, Sancerre, Chinon or Bourgueil in particular

cheeses – Saint-Paulin and Feuille de Dreux

Hot-Air Ballooning France Montgolfière (☎ 02 54 71 75 40; fax 02 54 71 75 78), run by a group of English, Welsh and Americans and based in Monthou-sur-Cher (about 30km south of Blois), runs hot-air balloon flights (weather permitting) year-round from almost anywhere in the Loire Valley.

A one to 1½ hour flight, including a round of champagne at the end, costs 1400FF per person (800FF for kids under 12), or 950FF for a stand-by flight; a group of six to eight pays 1200FF per adult. Flights generally take place just after dawn or a couple of hours before sunset, when the wind conditions are the most stable. Make reservations several days ahead for weekday flights, four weeks ahead for weekend (especially Saturday night) flights.

Helicopter Tours For information on helicopter tours, available from mid-June to September, call the heliport (☎ 02 54 90 41 41), 2km north-east of Blois near Pont Charles de Gaulle. A flight of 10/45/55/70 minutes, designed to let you admire the chateaus from the air, costs 250/900/1100/1400FF (minimum four passengers).

Getting There & Away

The Loire Valley is only an hour or two by train from Paris' Gare d'Austerlitz (for regular trains) and Gare Montparnasse (for TGVs). If you're in Paris, the area can easily be visited as a short excursion or as a stopover on the way to Brittany, the Atlantic coast, French Basque country or Bordeaux.

Getting Around

For three or four people, car rental may be cheaper than the bus, train or a tour, especially if you can take advantage of reduced weekend rates. For rental information, see Car under Getting There & Away in the Blois, Tours and Chinon sections.

Bicycle Cycling through the beautiful (and very flat) countryside is an excellent way to get around, though you will really clock up the kilometres if you schedule more than one chateau per outing. The highways that run right along the river are to be avoided – not only do they get heavy traffic, but they are often built atop dikes, the steep sides of which leave little room for verges (shoulders). A 1:200,000 scale Michelin road map or a 1:50,000 scale IGN map is indispensable to find your way around the rural back roads.

Bike rental information appears under Getting Around in the Amboise, Tours and Chinon sections. On certain trains (but not buses), you can take along a bicycle free of

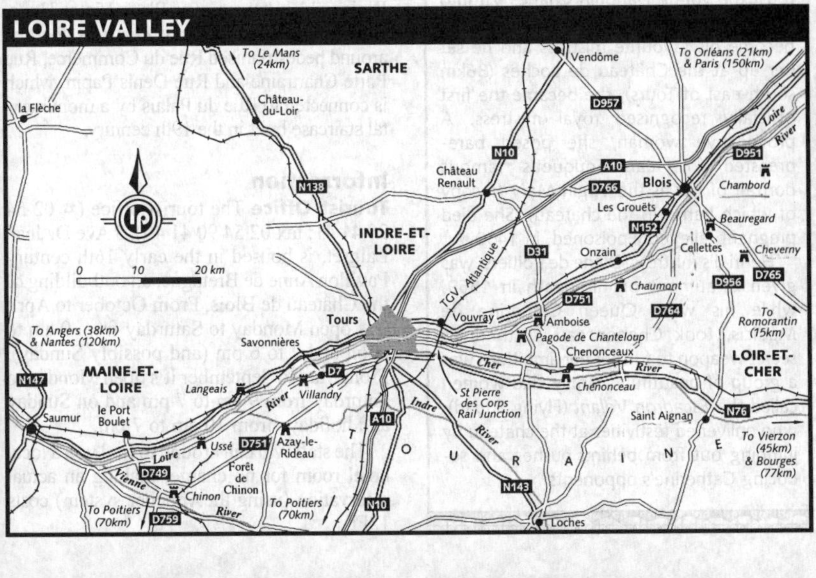

charge, allowing you to cycle either to or from your destinations. Further details are available from SNCF information offices.

BLOIS

• pop 49,000   ✉ 41000   alt 100m

The medieval town of Blois (pronounced 'Blwah') was once the seat of the powerful counts of Blois, from whom France's Capetian kings were descended. From the 15th to the 17th century, the town was a major centre of court intrigue, and during the 16th century it served as something of a second capital of France. A number of truly dramatic events – involving some of the most important personages in French history such as the kings Louis XII, François I and Henri III – took place inside the city's outstanding attraction, the Château de Blois.

The old city, seriously damaged by German attacks in 1940, retains its steep, twisting medieval streets. Blois is quiet at night, but if you're not exhausted after a day of touring you could check out the bowling alley (see Entertainment).

Several of the most rewarding chateaus in the Loire Valley, including Chambord and Cheverny, are situated within a 20km radius of Blois. See the sections Blois Area Chateaus, Amboise and Tours Area Chateaus for further details.

Ladies of the Loire

It's not just the men of the Loire who have made an impact on the world, but countless women – whether peasant, mistress, seductress or queen – have also left an indelible mark on history.

Without the beautiful and wealthy Eleanor of Aquitaine, the Hundred Years' War between England and France would never have taken place. Initially married to King Louis VII of France, in 1152 she married Henry of Anjou who became Henry II of England, bringing to the throne her dowry – one-third of France.

In 1429, Joan of Arc rode into Chinon to roust the young Dauphin Charles VII into regaining his throne. Agnès Sorel was to become his favourite mistress and he set her up at the Château de Loches (36km south-east of Tours), she became the first officially recognised royal mistress. A provocative woman, she posed bare-breasted for Jean Fouquet's famous portrait of her as the Virgin Mary (a copy of which hangs in the chateau). She died pregnant, allegedly poisoned, in 1450.

Henri II's mistress, Diane de Poitiers, was given Chaumont on his death in 1559, while his wife, Queen Catherine de Médicis, took Chenonceau. Catherine's secret weapon to further her ambitions was a group of beautiful, scantily clad women called the *Escadron Volant* (Flying Squad), who enlivened festivities at the chateau by jumping out from behind bushes and seducing Catherine's opponents.

Orientation

Blois, on the north bank of the River Loire, is a compact town – almost everything is within 10 minutes walk of the train station. The old city is the area south and east of the Château de Blois, which towers over Place Victor Hugo. Blois' modern commercial centre is focused around pedestrianised Rue du Commerce, Rue Porte Chartraine and Rue Denis Papin, which is connected to Rue du Palais by a monumental staircase built in the 19th century.

Information

Tourist Office The tourist office (☎ 02 54 90 41 41; fax 02 54 90 41 49), 3 Ave Dr Jean Laigret, is housed in the early 16th century Pavillon Anne de Bretagne, an outbuilding of the Château de Blois. From October to April it is open Monday to Saturday from 9 am to noon and 2 to 6 pm (and possibly Sunday). From May to September it's open Monday to Saturday from 9 am to 7 pm and on Sunday and holidays from 10 am to 7 pm.

The staff will call around to find you a local hotel room for no charge; making an actual reservation (using the voucher system) costs 12FF.

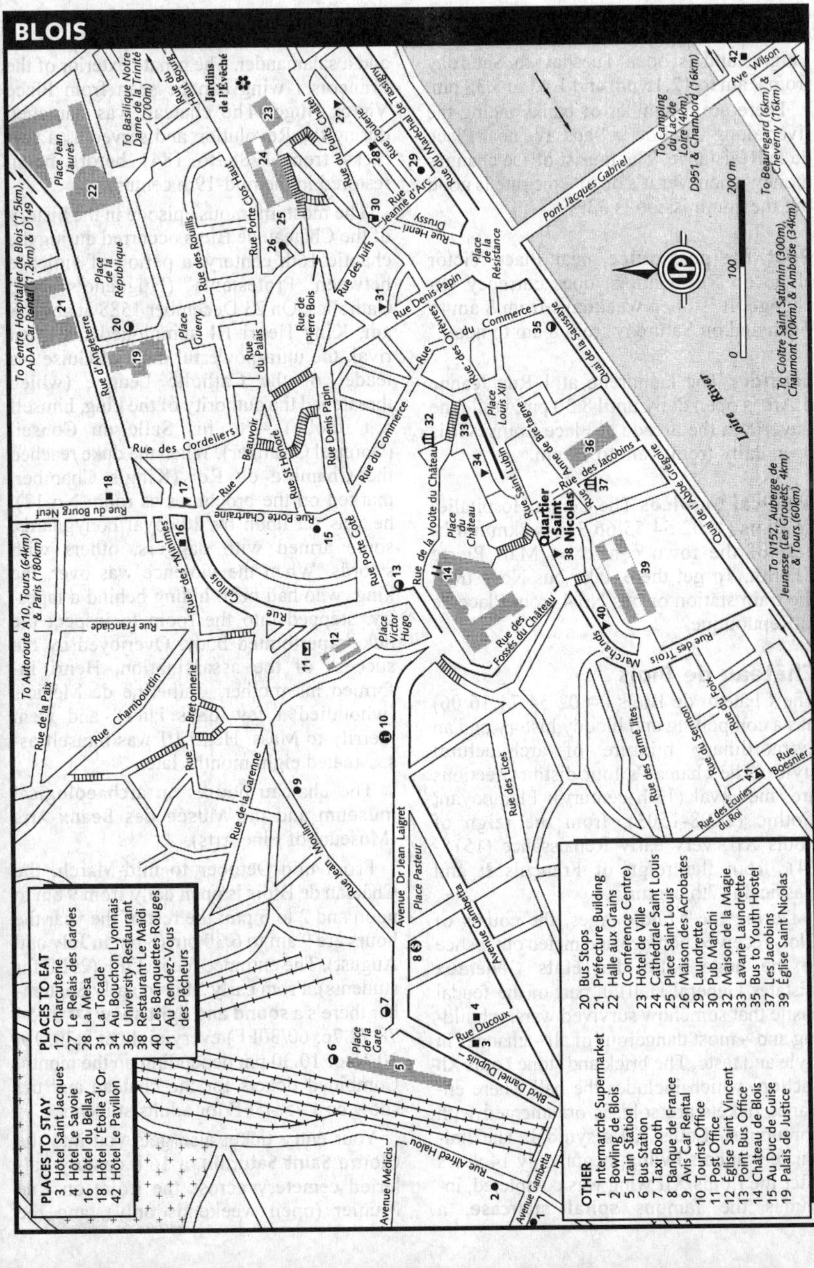
BLOIS
PLACES TO STAY
3 Hôtel Saint Jacques
4 Hôtel Le Savoie
16 Hôtel du Bellay
18 Hôtel L'Étoile d'Or
42 Hôtel Le Pavillon
PLACES TO EAT
17 Charcuterie
27 Le Relais des Gardes
28 La Mesa
31 La Tocade
34 Au Bouchon Lyonnais
36 University Restaurant
38 Restaurant Le Maïdi
40 Les Banquettes Rouges
41 Au Rendez-Vous des Pêcheurs
OTHER
1 Intermarché Supermarket
2 Bowling de Blois
5 Train Station
6 Bus Station
7 Taxi Booth
8 Banque de France
9 Avis Car Rental
10 Tourist Office
11 Post Office
12 Église Saint Vincent
13 Point Bus Office
14 Château de Blois
15 Au Duc de Guise
19 Palais de Justice
20 Bus Stops
21 Préfecture Building
22 Halle aux Grains (Conference Centre)
23 Hôtel de Ville
24 Cathédrale Saint Louis
25 Place Saint Louis
26 Maison des Acrobates
29 Laundrette
30 Pub Mancini
32 Maison de la Magie
33 Lavarie Laundrette
35 Bus to Youth Hostel
37 Les Jacobins
39 Église Saint Nicolas
To Autoroute A10, Tours (64km) & Paris (180km)
To Centre Hospitalier de Blois (1.5km), ADA Car Rental (1.2km) & D149
To Basilique Notre Dame de la Trinité (700m)
To Camping du Lac de Loire (4km), D951 & Chambord (16km)
To Beauregard (6km) & Cheverny (16km)
To Cloître Saint Saturnin (300m), Chaumont (20km) & Amboise (34km)
To N152, Auberge de Jeunesse (Les Grouëts; 4km) & Tours (60km)
Loire River
Pont Jacques Gabriel
Quartier Saint Nicolas
Jardins de l'Évêché
Place Jean Jaurès
Place de la République
Place Victor Hugo
Place du Château
Place Louis XII
Place de la Résistance
Place de la Gare
Place Pasteur
Rue Denis Papin
Rue du Commerce
Avenue Gambetta
Avenue Dr Jean Laigret
Avenue Médicis
Quai de la Saussaye
Quai de l'Abbé Grégoire
0 100 200 m

Money The Banque de France is down the road from the train station at 4 Ave Jean Laigret and is open Tuesday to Saturday from 9 am to 12.15 pm and 1.45 to 3.30 pm.

There are a number of banks facing the river along Quai de la Saussaye near Place de la Résistance. The tourist office changes money whenever it's open – the rate is good but the commission is 33FF.

Post The post office, near Place Victor Hugo on Rue Gallois, does currency exchange. It is open weekdays from 8 am to 7 pm and on Saturday from 8 am to noon.

Laundry The laundrette at 1 Rue Jeanne d'Arc is open daily until 8.30 pm, while the Laverie in the arcade at Place Louis XII is open daily from 7 am to 10 pm.

Medical Services The Centre Hospitalier de Blois (☎ 02 54 55 66 33) is 2km northeast of the town centre on Mail Pierre Charlot. To get there, take bus No 1 from the train station or bus No 4 from Place de la République.

Château de Blois

The Château de Blois (☎ 02 54 74 16 06) has a compelling and bloody history and an extraordinary mixture of architectural styles. The chateau's four distinct sections are: medieval (13th century); Flamboyant Gothic (1498-1503), from the reign of Louis XII; very early Renaissance (1515-24), from the reign of François I; and classical (17th century).

During the Middle Ages, the counts of Blois received homage and meted out justice in the huge **Salle des États Généraux** (Estates General Hall), a part of the feudal castle that somehow survived wars, rebuilding and – most dangerous of all – changes in style and taste. The brick and stone **Louis XII section**, which includes the hall where entrance tickets are sold, is ornamented with porcupines, Louis XII's symbol. The Italianate **François I wing**, begun only 14 years after the Louis XII wing was completed, includes the famous **spiral staircase**, a magnificent structure decorated with repetitions of François I's insignia, a capital 'F' and a salamander. The ornate exterior of the François I wing can be seen from Place Victor Hugo. The chateau was damaged during the Revolution and served as a barracks from 1788 to 1841 before being restored in the mid-19th century.

The most infamous episode in the history of the Château de Blois occurred during the chaotic 16th century, a period of violence between Protestants (Huguenots) and Catholics. On 23 December 1588 at about 8 am, King Henri III summoned his great rival, the ultra-powerful duke of Guise – a leader of the Catholic League (which threatened the authority of the king, himself a Catholic) – to his Salle du Conseil (Counsel Chamber). When the duke reached the Chambre du Roi (King's Chamber, marked on the brochures as room No 12), he was set upon by 20 royal bodyguards, some armed with daggers, others with swords. When the violence was over, the king, who had been hiding behind a tapestry, stepped into the room to inspect the duke's perforated body. Overjoyed by the success of the assassination, Henri informed his mother, Catherine de Médicis (who died a few days later), and went merrily to Mass. Henri III was himself assassinated eight months later.

The chateau houses an **archaeological museum** and the **Musée des Beaux-Arts** (Museum of Fine Arts).

From mid-October to mid-March, the Château de Blois is open daily from 9 am to noon and 2 to 5 pm; the rest of the year the hours are 9 am to 6.30 pm (8 pm in July and August). The entrance fee is 35FF (25FF for students). From early May to early September there's a **sound and light show** (☎ 02 54 78 72 76; 60/30FF) every night at 9.30, 10, 10.15 or 10.30 pm depending on the month. Combined tickets for the chateau and the show cost 75/45FF for adults/students.

Your entry ticket also gets you into the **Cloître Saint Saturnin**, a 16th century galleried cemetery across the Loire on Rue Munier (open weekends only), and the

museum of religious art, housed in **Les Jacobins**, a 15th and 16th century Dominican convent across from 15 Rue Anne de Bretagne. Entry to the **Musée d'Histoire Naturelle** (National History Museum), which is also housed in Les Jacobins, costs an extra 15FF. Both museums here open daily (except Monday) from 2 to 6 pm.

Maison de la Magie

The National Centre for the Art of Magic (☎ 02 54 55 26 26), also known as the Maison Robert-Houdin, is situated across the square from the chateau at 1 Place du Château. It has magic shows, interactive exhibits and displays of clocks and other objects invented by the Blois-born magician Jean-Eugène Robert-Houdin (1805-71), after whom the great Houdini named himself. It is open from June to September from 10 am to 1 pm and 2 to 6 pm (10 am to 6 pm in July and August), and from October to November from 10 am to 12.30 pm and 2 to 5.30 pm. Tickets cost 43/37/30FF for adults/students/children.

Old City

Around the old city, the large brown explanatory signs indicating tourist sights are both informative and in English. Part of the area has been turned into a pedestrian mall, where many of the buildings have attractive white façades, red brick chimneys and roofs of bluish slate.

Cathédrale Saint Louis was rebuilt in a late Gothic style after the devastating hurricane of 1678. The crypt dates from the 10th century. The cathedral *may* be closed between noon and 3 pm and after 6 pm.

The **Hôtel de Ville** is right behind the cathedral. Note the **sundial**, across the courtyard in a corner of the Ecclesiastical Tribunal building. There's a great view of Blois and both banks of the Loire from the lovely **Jardins de l'Évêché** (Gardens of the Bishop's Palace), directly behind the cathedral.

The 15th century **Maison des Acrobates** (House of the Acrobats), 3 Place Saint Louis, across the square from the west façade of the cathedral, is so-named because its timbers are decorated with characters taken from medieval farces, including acrobats and jugglers. It was one of the few medieval houses in Blois to survive the bombings of WWII.

Places to Stay

Camping The two star ***Camping du Lac de Loire*** (☎ 02 54 78 82 05), open from April to mid-October, is about 4km from the centre of Blois, south of the river on the Route de Chambord in Vineuil. Two people with a tent are charged 49FF. There is no bus service from town except in July and August (phone the camp site or the tourist office for details).

Hostel The ***Auberge de Jeunesse*** (☎ 02 54 78 27 21), at 18 Rue de l'Hôtel Pasquier in the village of Les Grouëts, is 4.5km southwest of the train station. It is open from March to mid-November, but call before arriving – it's often full. Beds in the two large, single-sex dorm rooms cost 60FF; the optional breakfast is 19FF. Kitchen facilities are available. Rooms are locked from 10 am to 6 pm, but it's often possible to drop off your bags during the day.

To get to the hostel from Blois, take local TUB bus No 4, which runs until a bit after 7 pm, from Place de la République (linked to the train station by TUB bus Nos 1, 2, 3 and 6) or – if you prefer to avoid a long detour – from 13 Quai de la Saussaye, along the river. If hitching, head south-westward along the northern quay of the Loire, which becomes the N152. At Les Grouëts, walk along Rue Basse des Grouëts to house No 32 and turn onto Rue de l'Hôtel Pasquier; follow it under the tracks and then up the hill for a few hundred metres.

Hotels Near the train station, your best bet is the comfortable, one star ***Hôtel Saint Jacques*** (☎ 02 54 78 04 15; fax 02 54 78 33 05) at 7 Rue Ducoux, whose staff go out of their way to be friendly. Small, ordinary doubles with washbasin and bidet start at 125FF (115FF in the warm months). Doubles/quads with shower, toilet and TV are 190 to 215/225FF. A bath or shower is 15/25FF for one/two people. Across the street at 6 Rue Ducoux, the family-run, two star ***Hôtel Le Savoie*** (☎ 02 54 74 32 21; fax 02 54 74 29 58) has neat, well kept singles/doubles with shower, toilet and TV from 230/280FF.

North of the old city, the 12 room ***Hôtel du Bellay*** (☎ 02 54 78 23 62; fax 02 54 78 52 04), 12 Rue des Minimes, has a few very pleasant doubles for 135 to 160FF; hall showers are free. Double rooms with bath and toilet are 185FF (a bit less from October to March). The ***Hôtel L'Étoile d'Or*** (☎ 02 54 78 46 93), 7 Rue du Bourg Neuf, has ordinary doubles from 150FF (220FF with shower and toilet). Showers are free. Reception (in the Tex-Mex bar) is closed on Sunday.

Across the river from the old city at 2 Ave Wilson, the ***Hôtel Le Pavillon*** (☎ 02 54 74 23 27) has ordinary doubles with washbasin and high ceilings for 120 to 150FF; hall showers cost 15FF (free if you stay more than one night, depending on the season). Doubles/quads with shower and toilet are 150/260FF.

LOIRE VALLEY

Places to Eat

Most of Blois' restaurants and other eateries are closed on Sunday for lunch.

Restaurants – French There's a cluster of popular restaurants along Rue Foulerie, including ***Le Relais des Gardes*** (☎ 02 54 74 36 56) at No 52, a stone, stucco and wood-beamed place that specialises in crêpes (12 to 38FF), *gallettes* (29 to 48FF) and cider. It's closed at midday Sunday and on Monday. A 65FF *menu* is available.

La Tocade (☎ 02 54 78 07 78), 23 Rue Denis Papin, offers inexpensive French food daily except Sunday night and on Monday (daily from June to August). Hours are 11.30 am to 2.30 pm and 6.30 to 10 pm (11 pm in the summer). Main courses cost from 42FF and *menus* are good value at 63, 90 and 135FF. There are a number of café-brasseries at Place de la Résistance.

The cosy ***Les Banquettes Rouges*** (☎ 02 54 78 74 92), 16 Rue des Trois Marchands, serves traditional French cuisine from noon to 2 pm and 7 to 11 pm (closed for lunch on the weekend). *Menus* are 99FF (lunch on weekdays), 105 and 145FF.

Crowds of people out for a splurge make ***Au Bouchon Lyonnais*** (☎ 02 54 74 12 87), 25 Rue des Violettes (above Rue Saint Lubin), a busy place. Main dishes of traditional French and Lyon-style cuisine cost 78 to 128FF; *menus* are 115 and 165FF. Open Tuesday to Saturday from noon to 2 pm and 7 to 10 pm; also open on Sunday night in July and August.

Au Rendez-Vous des Pêcheurs (☎ 02 54 74 67 48), 27 Rue du Foix, specialises in fish (88 to 120FF) brought fresh each morning from the Loire and the sea. The *menu* costs 145FF. Hours are noon to 2 pm and 7.30 to 10 pm (closed all day Sunday and Monday at midday).

Restaurants – Other ***La Mesa*** (☎ 02 54 78 70 70), a very popular Franco-Italian joint, is at 11 Rue Vauvert, up the alleyway from 44 Rue Foulerie. *Menus* are 75 and 130FF; a good selection of salads is also on offer. The large courtyard is perfect for dining alfresco. It's open Monday to Saturday (daily from July to September) from noon to 2 pm and 7 to 11 pm.

Restaurant Le Maïdi (☎ 02 54 74 38 58), in the old city at 42 Rue Saint Lubin, has Moroccan *menus* of couscous, *tajines* and *brochettes* from 65FF. Hours are noon to 2 pm and 6.30 to 10 pm (midnight in summer); closed on Thursday (open on Thursday evening in July and August and holiday weekends). On Rue Foulerie, there's another popular ***Moroccan place*** at No 46 and an ***Indian restaurant*** at No 54.

University Restaurant CROUS has a university restaurant in the former covered market on Rue des Jacobins.

Self-Catering Across the tracks from the train station on Ave Gambetta, the giant, boulangerie-equipped ***Intermarché*** supermarket is open Monday to Saturday until 7.15 pm (closed from 12.30 to 3 pm except on Friday).

In the old city, there's a ***food market*** along Rue Anne de Bretagne on Tuesday, Thursday and Saturday until 1 pm. ***Au Duc de Guise***, a *fromagerie* and wine shop at 10 Rue Porte Chartraine, is open Tuesday to Saturday from 7.30 am to 7.30 pm. The ***charcuterie*** at 57 Rue du Bourg Neuf has a fine selection of prepared dishes (closed from 12.45 to 3.30 pm, on Sunday afternoon and on Monday).

Entertainment

The pedestrian zone in the old city (around Rue du Commerce) is almost dead after nightfall, but things are a bit livelier east of Rue Denis Papin and around Place Louis XII. ***Pub Mancini*** (☎ 02 54 78 04 36), 1 Rue du Puits Châtel, open daily from 3 pm to 5 am, occasionally has live music on weekends from mid-June to August; things get going at about 9 pm on Friday and 6 pm on Saturday.

One of the town's few nightspots is a bowling alley, ***Bowling de Blois*** (☎ 02 54 42 42 27), which is right across the tracks from the train station at 6 Rue Alfred Halou. Games cost 25 to 31FF per person (nights and weekends are the most expensive); shoe rental is 9FF. Billiards costs 10FF a game. It's open daily from 3 pm to 2 am.

Shopping

The **Marché Régional de la Brocante** (Regional Flea Market) is held on the second Sunday of each month along the river at the foot of Rue Jeanne d'Arc.

Getting There & Away

For information on transport to and from nearby chateaus, see Organised Tours and/or Getting There & Away under Blois Area Chateaus and Amboise. Further details appear under each chateau listing.

Train The train station (☎ 08 36 35 35 35) is at the western terminus of Ave Dr Jean Laigret. The information office is open from 9 am to 6.30 pm (closed Sunday and holidays).

Service from Blois to Paris' Gare d'Austerlitz (122FF; at least 11 a day, some with a change of trains at Orléans) takes about 1½ hours. Bordeaux (from 240FF; nine a day) is four hours by direct train but only 3¼ hours if you switch to a TGV at Saint Pierre des Corps, near Tours. To get to La Rochelle (200FF) you have to change at either Saint Pierre des Corps or Poitiers (120FF; nine a day) unless you take the one daily direct service. There are frequent trains to Tours (51FF; 40 minutes; 11 to 17 a day). Nantes (170FF; two to three hours) can be reached via Tours or Saint Pierre des Corps.

Car ADA (☎ 02 54 74 02 47) is 3km northeast of the train station at 108 Ave du Maréchal Maunoury (the D149). It is open Monday to Saturday from 8 am to noon and 2 to 6.30 pm. To get there, take bus No 1 from the train station or bus No 4 from Place de la République to the Cornillettes stop.

Avis (☎ 02 54 74 48 15), 6 Rue Jean Moulin, is open Monday to Saturday from 8 am to noon and 2 to 7 pm.

Getting Around

Bus Buses within Blois, run by TUB, operate from Monday to Saturday until 8 or 8.30 pm. On Sunday and holidays, service is greatly reduced. All buses except the No 4 stop at the train station. Route maps are posted in most bus shelters. Tickets cost 6FF (41FF for a carnet of 10). For information, inquire at the Point Bus office (☎ 02 54 78 15 66) at 2 Place Victor Hugo. The office is open from 8 am (9 am on Saturday) to 12.10 pm and 1.30 to 6 pm (4.30 pm on Saturday); closed on Sunday and on Monday morning. In July and August its hours are 8.30 am to noon and 1.30 to 5.30 pm (closed Saturday afternoon, Sunday and on Monday morning).

Taxi To order a taxi, contact the taxi booth (☎ 02 54 78 07 65) in front of the train station.

BLOIS AREA CHATEAUS

The Blois area is graced with some of the finest chateaus in the Loire Valley, including the spectacular and stunning Chambord, the magnificently furnished Cheverny, romantic Chaumont (also accessible from Tours), and the modest but more personal Beauregard. The town of Amboise is also easily accessible from Blois.

The Blois tourist office has information on *spectacles* (sound and light shows etc) held at many of the chateaus during the summer.

Organised Tours

From about 10 June to 10 September, TLC (☎ 02 54 58 55 61), the Blois area's public bus company, operates two chateau excursions. The circuit to Chambord and Cheverny, which runs twice a day, costs 65FF (50FF for students and those over 60) and picks up passengers both at the Blois train station and at TLC's Point Bus information office at 2 Place Victor Hugo. The bus to Chaumont, Chenonceau and Amboise (four times a week) costs 110FF (90FF reduced price); if requested, it stops at the hostel in Les Grouëts. Prices do not include admission fees, but tour participants are eligible for reduced tariffs.

Getting There & Away

Additional transport details are listed under Getting There & Away at the end of each chateau listing. All times quoted are approximate and should be verified before you make plans.

Bus The departmental TLC bus system is set up to transport school kids into Blois in the morning and to get them home in the afternoon. As a result, afternoon service *to* Blois is limited on some lines. There is reduced service during the summer school holidays and on Sunday and holidays.

Your best source of bus information is the Point Bus office at 2 Place Victor Hugo in Blois, see Getting Around in the Blois section for contact details and opening hours.

TLC buses to destinations in the vicinity of Blois leave from Place Victor Hugo (in front of the Point Bus office) and the bus station – little more than a patch of parking lot with schedules posted – next to Blois' train station.

Train About three-quarters of the trains on the line from Blois to Tours stop at Amboise (33FF; 20 minutes). See Getting There & Away under Tours Area Chateaus for details on getting to places a bit farther afield.

Taxi At the taxi booth (☎ 02 54 78 07 65) in front of the Blois train station, it is possible to hire a taxi or a minibus, with space for eight passengers. A return trip (including a one hour stop at each destination) costs 240FF to Cheverny, 260FF to Chambord and 425FF to Chenonceau; Sunday and holiday rates are 340, 365 and 640FF respectively. Various chateau combinations are possible.

Château de Chambord

The construction of the Château de Chambord (☎ 02 54 50 50 02) was begun in 1519 by King François I, who reigned from 1515 to 1547. It is the largest and most spectacular chateau in the entire Loire Valley. Its Renaissance architecture and decoration, grafted onto a feudal ground plan, may have been inspired by Leonardo da Vinci, who lived in Amboise (34km south-west of here) at the invitation of François I from 1516 until his death three years later. If you're going to see more than one chateau, leave the 440 room Chambord for last or the others may seem unbelievably small by comparison.

François I's emblems – the royal monogram (a letter 'F') and salamanders of a particularly fierce disposition – adorn many parts of the building. Though forced by liquidity problems to leave his two sons unransomed in Spain and to help himself to both the wealth of his churches and his subjects' silver, the king kept 1800 construction workers and artisans busy for 15 years. At one point, he even suggested that the Loire be rerouted so it would pass by Chambord. Eventually a smaller river, the Cosson, was diverted instead. François I died before the building was completed, a task left to his

The chateau at Chambord is the Loire Valley's largest and most spectacular.

royal successors and frequent visitors to the castle – Henri II and Louis XIV. Molière premiered two of his most famous plays at Chambord to audiences that included Louis XIV.

The chateau's famed **double-helix staircase**, attributed by some to Leonardo himself, consists of two spiral staircases that wind around the same central axis but never meet. The rich ornamentation is in the style of the early French Renaissance. It's easy to imagine mistresses and lovers chasing each other up and down the staircases.

The royal court used to assemble on the Italianate **rooftop terrace**, reached via the double-helix staircase, to watch military exercises, tournaments and the hounds and hunters returning from a day of stalking deer. As you stand on the terrace (once described as resembling an overcrowded chessboard), you're surrounded by the towers, cupolas, domes, chimneys, dormers, mosaic slate roofs and lightning rods that form the chateau's imposing skyline.

Tickets to the chateau are on sale daily from 9.30 am to 4.45 pm (October to March) or 5.45 pm (April to June and September) or 6.30 pm (July and August). Guests already in the chateau can stay there for three-quarters of an hour after ticket sales end. The entrance fee is 40FF (25FF if you're aged 12 to 25 on production of a student card). Guide books in half a dozen languages are available for 30FF but are unnecessary, as the chateau is blessed with excellent explanatory signs in French, English, German, Spanish and Italian.

Information Tourist information is available at the entrance to the chateau and at the Centre d'Information Touristique (☎ 02 54 20 34 86), Place Saint Michel (the parking lot surrounded by tourist shops), open daily from early April to September from 9.30 or 10 am to 6 or 7 pm with a break usually between 12.30 and 1.30 pm.

Domaine de Chambord The chateau is in the middle of the Domaine de Chambord, a 54 sq km hunting preserve reserved solely for the use of the president of France. The public is allowed to stroll around just 12 sq km on the western side of the property, which is surrounded by a 33km-long wall, the longest such barrier in France. Trail maps and bicycles are available at the Centre d'Information Touristique.

Entertainment From May to September the **Spectacle d'Art Équestre** (equestrian show; ☎ 02 54 20 31 01) is held at the *écuries* (stables) near the chateau. Performances begin daily at 11.45 am. A second show is held at 4 pm on weekends and holidays and daily in July and August. The cost is 45FF (30FF for children under 13).

There's a sound and light show in French every night from mid-April to mid-October.

Getting There & Away Chambord is 16km east of Blois and 20km north-east of Cheverny.

During the school year, TLC line No 2 averages three daily round trips from Blois to Chambord (18.50FF each way). From Monday to Saturday the first bus out to Chambord departs from Blois just past noon. The last bus back to Blois leaves Chambord at 6.40 pm (5.10 pm on weekends and holidays). During July and August, your *only* bus option is TLC's tourist bus (see Bus under Organised Tours earlier in the Blois Area Chateaus section).

Getting Around Bicycles (great for exploring the grounds) are available from the Centre d'Information Touristique for 25FF an hour, 35FF for two hours and 80FF a day.

Between April and September bicycles can also be rented at the Château de Chambord.

The countryside around Chambard, with its many quiet country back roads, is perfect for cycling. Blois and Cheverny are each 17km from Chambard. A round trip embracing all three towns is 46km – quite a bit for one day if you're not an active cyclist.

Château de Cheverny

The Château de Cheverny (☎ 02 54 79 96 29), the region's most magnificently furnished chateau, was built between 1625 and 1634. After entering the building through its finely proportioned neoclassical façade, visitors are treated to room after sumptuous room outfitted with the finest of period appointments: furniture, paintings, canopied beds, tapestries (eg the amazing *Abduction of Helen* in the Salle d'Armes, the former armoury), chimney pieces, parquet floors, painted ceilings and walls covered with embossed Córdoba leather. The most richly furnished rooms are the **Chambre du Roi** (in which no king ever slept because no king ever stayed at Cheverny) and the **Grand Salon** (Great Drawing Room). Don't miss the three dozen panels illustrating the story of *Don Quixote* in the 1st floor dining room.

As was the custom among the nobility of centuries past, Viscount Arnaud de Sigalas, whose family has owned Cheverny since it was built, maintains an active interest in hunting with hounds. His 80 dogs, each a cross between English fox terriers and French Poitevins, are quite beautiful no matter what you think of using them to kill deer. The **soupe des chiens** (feeding of the dogs) takes place at the kennels (a small cement enclosure not far from the entrance to the grounds) at 5 pm daily, except Sunday and holidays (from mid-September to March it's open daily except for Tuesday, weekends and holidays). Next to the kennels is the **trophy room**, a macabre chamber whose walls, pillars and ceiling are covered with the antlers of almost 2000 stags hunted since the 1850s.

Cheverny is open every day of the year from 9.15 or 9.30 am to noon and 2.15 to 5 pm (November to February), 5.30 pm (October and March), 6 pm (the last half of September) or 6.30 pm (April and May). From June to mid-September the chateau stays open from 9.15 am to 6.45 pm. The entry fee is 33FF (25FF for students, 17FF for children aged seven to 14). Visitors are given a useful information sheet in one of nine languages. The park around the chateau is closed to visitors.

Entertainment During July and August the chateau plays host to a **spectacle historique** (historical re-enactment).

Getting There & Away Cheverny is 16km south-east of Blois and 20km south-west of Chambord.

TLC bus No 4 from Blois to Romorantin stops at Cheverny (13.80FF one way). Buses leave Blois year-round Monday to Saturday at 6.45 am and 12.15 pm. Coming back to Blois, the last bus leaves Cheverny at 6.50 pm (Monday to Friday), 8.15 pm (Sunday and holidays) or 12.50 pm (Saturday).

Château de Chaumont

The Château de Chaumont (☎ 02 54 51 26 26), set on a bluff overlooking the Loire, looks as much like a feudal castle as any chateau in the area. Its most famous feature is the luxurious **écuries**, where it's not difficult to imagine a team of horses being hitched to the ornate coach of a duke or prince. Present your entrance ticket from the main building to get in.

In 1560, Catherine de Médicis (France's powerful queen mother) took revenge on Diane de Poitiers, the mistress of her late husband, King Henry II, by forcing her to accept Chaumont in exchange for her much more favoured residence, the Château de Chenonceau (see Tours Area Chateaux). During the years after America won independence, Benjamin Franklin, at the time US ambassador to France, was a frequent guest at Chaumont.

Tickets to this state owned chateau are on sale daily from 9.30 am to 6 pm (10 am to 4.30 pm from October to mid-March); the chateau itself closes half an hour later. The entrance fee is 31FF (21FF if you're aged 12 to 25). Some of the rooms have explanatory plaques in English. The **park** surrounding the chateau, with its many cedars, is free and is open daily from 9 am until nightfall.

Wine Tasting From Easter to September there is free wine tasting in the small building 50m up Rue du Village Neuf (from the bottom of the path up to the chateau). A dozen wine producers from the Touraine area take turns displaying and selling their products, especially premium AOC wines. Its opening hours depend on the preferences of each vineyard's representative.

Festival International des Parcs et Jardins From mid-June to mid-October the chateau gardens play host to the International Festival of Parks and Gardens (☎ 02 54 20 99 22), the highlight of which is 30 themed gardens laid out by landscape gardeners from around the world. Entry costs 45/35/20FF for adults/students/children aged 8 to 12. It is open daily from 9 am to nightfall.

Getting There & Away The Château de Chaumont is 20km south-west of Blois and 20km north-east of Amboise in the village of Chaumont-sur-Loire, which is on the south bank of the Loire. The path leading up to the park and chateau begins at the intersection of Rue du Village Neuf and the D751, known in town as Rue Maréchal Leclerc.

You can also take a local train on the Orléans-Tours line and get off at Onzain (18FF from Blois; eight or more a day; 10 minutes), which is a 2km walk across the river from the chateau.

If you're coming by bicycle you're best off taking the quiet back roads on the south bank of the river.

Château de Beauregard

Beauregard (☎ 02 54 70 40 05) is the closest chateau to Blois, just 6km south of town. It is relatively modest in size and a bit scruffy on the outside, but this somehow adds to its charm. Built in the early 16th century as a hunting lodge for François I and enlarged 100 years later, it is set in the middle of a large park. The count and countess who own the place still live in one wing, which is why only five rooms are open to the public.

Beauregard's most famous feature is the **Galerie des Portraits** on the 1st floor, featuring 327 portraits of 'who was who' in France from the 14th to the 17th century. The very unusual floor is covered with 17th century Dutch tiles.

From April to September, Beauregard is open daily from 9.30 am to noon and 2 to 6.30 pm; there is no closure at midday during July and August. During the rest of the year (except from early January to mid-February, when it's closed), the chateau is open from 9.30 am to noon and 2 to 5 pm (closed Wednesday). Tariffs are 40FF (30FF for students under 25 and children) for combined entry into the chateau and the gardens. A free information handout in a number of languages is available at reception.

Getting There & Away The Château de Beauregard makes a good destination for a short bike ride from Blois. It can also be visited on the way to Cheverny. There is road access to the chateau from both the D765 (the Blois-Cheverny road) and the D956 (turn left at the village of Cellettes).

TLC bus No 5 from Blois towards Saint Aignan stops at the village of Cellettes (8.30FF), 1km south-west of the chateau, on Wednesday, Friday and Saturday; the first Blois-Cellettes bus leaves at noon. Unfortunately, there's no afternoon bus back except the Châteauroux-Blois line operated by Transports Boutet (☎ 02 54 34 43 95), which passes through Cellettes around 6.30 pm from Monday to Saturday and – except during August – at about 6 pm on Sunday.

AMBOISE

• pop 11,000 ✉ 37400 alt 112m

The picturesque town of Amboise, nestling under its fortified chateau on the south bank of the Loire, reached its peak during the decades around 1500, when the luxury-loving King Charles VIII enlarged it and King François I held raucous parties there. These days, the town makes the most of its association with Leonardo da Vinci, who lived out his last years here under the patronage of François I.

Amboise makes an easy day trip from Blois or Tours. It is 34km downstream (south-west) of Blois, 23km upstream (east) of Tours, and only 10km north-west of the Château de Chenonceau (see Tours Area Chateaus).

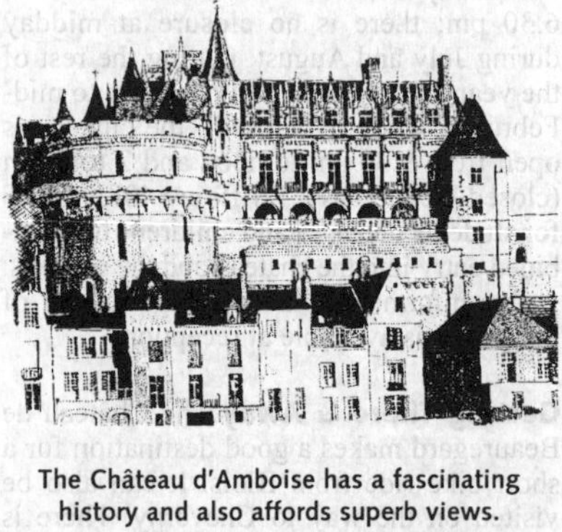

The Château d'Amboise has a fascinating history and also affords superb views.

Orientation

The train station across the river from the centre of town (follow the signs to 'Centre Ville'), is about 800m from the chateau. Le Clos Lucé, once home to Leonardo da Vinci, is 500m south-east of the chateau entrance along Rue Victor Hugo. Amboise's main commercial (and tourist) street is Rue Nationale, which runs roughly parallel to the river.

Information

Tourist Office The tourist office (Accueil d'Amboise; ☎ 02 47 57 09 28; fax 02 47 57 14 35), in a little round pavilion along the river opposite 7 Quai Général de Gaulle, has a free English-language brochure for walking around Amboise. Local hotel reservations cost 2FF per phone call. Ask here for hiking and cycling maps of the Amboise area, including the strenuous 65km *Circuit des Trois Châteaux – Amboise, Chenonceaux et Chaumont* and a free pamphlet entitled *Tourisme à Bicyclette*, which lists nearby *vélotels* and *vélocamps* (bicycle-friendly hotels and camp sites).

From Monday to Saturday its hours are 9 am to 12.30 pm and 2 pm to 6.30 pm; from mid-June to August its hours are 9 am to 8.30 pm. It is also open on Sunday morning (10 am to noon) from Easter to October, and on Sunday afternoon (4 to 7 pm) from mid-June to August.

Money There are a number of banks, open Tuesday to Saturday, on Rue Nationale. Opposite the chateau entrance, the Banque Populaire at 14 Place Général Leclerc is open Monday to Friday. The exchange bureau in the tourist office is open daily from April to October until 6.30 pm (later in summer).

Post The post office at 20 Quai Général de Gaulle is open on weekdays from 8.30 am to noon and 1.30 to 6 pm (no midday closure from early May to September), and on Saturday until noon. Exchange services are available.

Maps Maps of all sorts are sold at the Maison de la Presse at 24 Rue Nationale (closed Sunday afternoon).

River View

Amboise is protected from the river by a dike, whose flower-covered heights are a fine place for a riverside promenade. Some of the best views of town are from the bridge.

Château d'Amboise

The rocky outcrop topped by the Château d'Amboise (☎ 02 47 57 00 98) has been fortified ever since Roman times. King Charles VIII (1470-98), who was born and brought up here, began work to enlarge the chateau in 1492 after a visit to Italy, where he was deeply impressed by that country's artistic creativity and luxurious lifestyle. He died only six years later after hitting his head on a low lintel while on his way to a tennis game in the moat.

King François I also grew up here – as did his sister, the reform-minded French Renaissance author Margaret of Angoulême, also known as Margaret of Navarre. François I lived in the chateau for the first few years of his reign, a lively period marked by balls, masquerade parties, tournaments and festivities of all sorts.

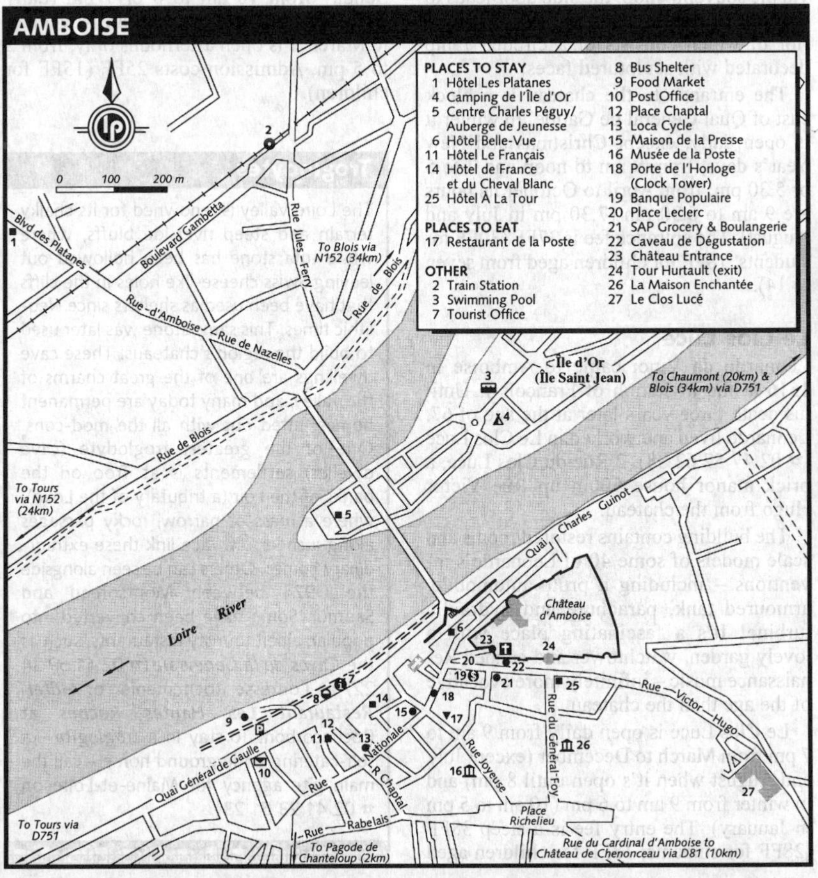

Today, only a few of the 15th and 16th century structures have survived. These include the Flamboyant Gothic **Chapelle Saint Hubert** and, inside the main building, the **Salle des États** (Estates Hall), where a group of Protestant conspirators were tried before being hanged from the balcony in 1560. From 1848 to 1852, Abdelkader, the military and political leader of the Algerian resistance to French colonialism, was imprisoned here.

The chateau's **ramparts** afford a panoramic view of the town and the Loire Valley. The best way to exit the chateau is via the souvenir shop: the side door leads to the **Tour Hurtault** (begun in 1495), the interior of which consists of a circular ramp decorated with sculptured faces.

The entrance to the chateau is a block east of Quai Général de Gaulle. In winter it is open daily, except Christmas and New Year's days, from 9 am to noon and 2 to 5 or 5.30 pm; from April to October its hours are 9 am to 6.30 pm (7.30 pm in July and August). The entrance fee is 37FF (30FF for students, 18FF for children aged from seven to 14).

Le Clos Lucé

Leonardo da Vinci came to Amboise in 1516 at the invitation of François I. Until his death three years later at the age of 67, Leonardo lived and worked in Le Clos Lucé (☎ 02 47 57 62 88), 2 Rue du Clos Lucé, a brick manor house 500m up Rue Victor Hugo from the chateau.

The building contains restored rooms and scale models of some 40 of Leonardo's inventions – including a proto-automobile, armoured tank, parachute and hydraulic turbine! It's a fascinating place with a lovely garden, watchtower and canned Renaissance music – infinitely more evocative of the age than the chateau.

Le Clos Lucé is open daily from 9 am to 7 pm from March to December (except July and August when it's open until 8 pm) and in winter from 9 am to 6 pm (10 am to 5 pm in January). The entry fee is a steep 38FF (28FF for students, 18FF for children aged six to 15). A free brochure in English is available at the turnstile.

The road to Le Clos Lucé passes **troglodytic dwellings**, caves in the limestone hillside in which local people still live (with all the mod-cons and a mortgage, of course).

La Maison Enchantée

This privately run museum (☎ 02 47 23 24 50) at 7 Rue du Général Foy displays over 300 *automates* (automaton dolls), cleverly and comically arranged in miniature scenes. In summer it is open Tuesday to Sunday from 10 am to 6 or 7 pm (daily from May to September); from November to March it is open afternoons only, from 2 to 5 pm. Admission costs 25FF (15FF for children).

Troglodytes

The Loire Valley is renowned for its chalky terrain and steep riverside bluffs, where white tufa stone has been hollowed out leaving Swiss cheese-like holes in the cliffs that have been used as shelters since Neolithic times. This same stone was later used to build the region's chateaus. These cave dwellings are one of the great charms of the valley, and many today are permanent homes, fitted out with all the mod-cons. One of the greatest troglodyte (cave dweller) settlements is at Troo on the banks of the Loir (a tributary of the Loire), where a mass of narrow, rocky passages along a sheer cliff face link these extraordinary homes. Others can be seen alongside the D974 between Montsoreau and Saumur. Some have been converted into popular, albeit touristy restaurants, such as the ***Caves de la Genevraie*** (☎ 02 41 59 34 22) at Louresse-Rochemenier or ***Hôtel-Restaurant Les Hautes Roches*** at Rochecorbon. To stay in a ***troglogîte*** – a self-catering underground home – call the main gîte agency for Maine-et-Loire on ☎ 02 41 23 51 23.

LOIRE VALLEY

Musée de la Poste

The municipal postal museum (☎ 02 47 56 00 11), 6 Rue Joyeuse, housed in the 16th century Hôtel Joyeuse, built by Italian architects, has an interesting collection of stagecoach and ship models, mail carriers' uniforms, lithographs and the like. It's open daily (except Monday) from 9.30 or 10 am to noon and 2 to 5.30 pm (6.30 pm from April to September). Tickets cost 20FF (10FF for children and students).

Wine Tasting

The Caveau de Dégustation (☎ 02 47 57 23 69), opposite 14 Rue Victor Hugo, run by local *viticulteurs* (winegrowers), is open daily from early May to late September from 10 am to 7 pm. The tasting is free but you have to pay 1FF to use the toilets next door.

Places to Stay – Budget

Camping The huge 400 site, two star municipal ***Camping de l'Île d'Or*** (☎ 02 47 57 23 37), attractively situated on the Île d'Or (the island in the middle of the Loire, also known as Île Saint Jean), is open from April to mid-October. There's a charge of 15.60FF for a tent (23.60FF if you've got a car) and 12.50FF per adult. The swimming pool next door costs 12.50FF.

Hostel The ***Centre Charles Péguy-Auberge de Jeunesse*** (☎ 02 47 57 06 36; fax 02 47 23 15 80) is also on the Île d'Or. Beds cost 50FF; breakfast is 15FF. Reception is open weekdays from 3 to 9 pm, 6 to 8 pm on weekends – if you arrive when it's closed, try using the intercom.

Hotels The older ***Hôtel de France et du Cheval Blanc*** (☎ 02 47 57 02 44; fax 02 47 57 69 54), 6-7 Quai Général de Gaulle, is nothing fancy, but large doubles cost only 150FF (195FF with shower, TV and toilet). There is no hall shower. It's closed from mid-November to mid-March.

The 18 room ***Hôtel Les Platanes*** (☎ 02 47 57 08 60), about 600m west of the train station at 7 Blvd des Platanes, provides some plain but spacious doubles from 150FF; doubles/triples/quads with shower and toilet start at 180/220/260FF. Hall showers are free.

The unfriendly ***Hôtel À La Tour*** (☎ 02 47 57 25 04), 32 Rue Victor Hugo, has eight singles/doubles/triples with washbasin and bidet for 120/175/230FF; showers are free. Reception (at the bar) is closed on Thursday except during July and August.

Places to Stay – Mid-Range

The 14 room, two star ***Hôtel Le Français*** (☎ 02 47 57 11 38; fax 02 47 57 71 42), 1 Place Chaptal (or 6 Rue Voltaire), has comfortable, sound-proofed doubles with shower and toilet from 230FF (250FF with a view of the Loire). It also has a couple of shower-equipped rooms without toilet for 190FF.

There are a number of hotels at the south end of the bridge over the Loire, including the three star ***Hôtel Belle-Vue*** (☎ 02 47 57 02 26; fax 02 47 30 51 23) at 12 Quai Charles Guinot, where singles/doubles start at 280/340FF. It is closed from early November to mid-March.

Places to Eat

Restaurants There are lots of touristy ***fast-food outlets*** along Rue Victor Hugo (below the chateau), Rue Nationale and Quai Général de Gaulle. The informal ***Restaurant de la Poste*** (☎ 02 47 23 16 16), 5 Rue d'Orange, has *menus* of traditional French food for 78 to 165FF. It's closed on Tuesday, except from mid-June to September.

Self-Catering There are a number of ***food shops*** along Rue Nationale. Near the chateau entrance on Rue Victor Hugo, you'll find an ***SAP grocery*** at No 2 (closed from 12.30 to 3 pm and on Sunday) and a ***boulangerie*** at No 10 (closed on Monday, except in summer).

On Friday and Sunday mornings a ***food market*** is held right along the river, on the other side of the dike from the town.

Getting There & Away

Bus Buses to and from Amboise stop at the bus shelter across the parking lot from the tourist office, a far more convenient place to begin a visit than the train station on the other side of the river, even though the buses are much slower. The hours are usually posted.

CAT's line No 10 links the town with Tours' bus terminal (25.30FF one way, 45.50FF return; 30 to 50 minutes); it runs eight times a day from Monday to Saturday, six times a day during the summer school holidays.

From Monday to Saturday, one or two daily round trips link Amboise with the Château de Chenonceau (11.30FF one way, 20.70FF return). Buses leave Amboise at 10.45 am (and, during July and August, at 2.45 pm); buses back to Amboise depart from Chenonceau at 12.30 pm (and, during July and August, at around 4.45 pm).

Train The train station (☎ 08 36 35 35 35), on Blvd Gambetta across the river from the centre of town, is served by five or six daily trains from Paris' Gare d'Austerlitz (214FF; two hours).

About three-quarters of the trains on the Blois-Tours line (11 to 17 a day) stop at Amboise. Fares are 33FF to Blois (20 minutes) and 28FF to Tours (20 minutes). The last train to Tours departs at 9.30 pm (an hour later on Sunday and holidays); the last train to Blois is at 9 pm (6.40 pm on Saturday, 10.40 pm on Sunday and holidays).

Getting Around

Taxi Taxis wait at the train station when trains arrive. To order one by phone, ring ☎ 02 47 57 30 39.

Bicycle Loca Cycles (☎ 02 47 57 00 28), on the south bank of the river at 2bis Rue Jean Jacques Rousseau, rent mountain bikes for 90FF a day. The shop is open daily from 9 am to 12.30 pm and 2 to 7 pm.

AROUND AMBOISE

Pagode de Chanteloup

This seven storey Chinese-style pagoda, 44m high, is one of the more pleasing follies left over from the 18th century, and a delightful picnic venue. Built between 1775 and 1778, it combines contemporary French architectural fashions with elements from China, a subject of great fascination at the time. From the top of the pagoda, visitors are rewarded with an impressive view of the Loire Valley. Also visible are the overgrown outlines of the once splendid pools, gardens and forest paths that surrounded the estate's 18th century chateau, torn down in 1823.

From May to September the Pagode de Chanteloup (☎ 02 47 57 20 97) is open every day from 10 am to 6 pm (7 pm in June, 8 pm in July and August). The rest of the year – except from 11 November to mid-February, when it's closed – its hours are 10 am to noon and 2 to 5 pm. Admission costs 30FF (24FF for students, 20FF for children aged seven to 15).

Getting There & Away The pagoda is about 2.5km south of Amboise. Go south on Rue Bretonneau and follow the signs to 'La Pagode'.

TOURS

• pop 270,000 ✉ 37000 alt 108m

Whereas Blois remains essentially medieval in layout and small-townish in atmosphere, lively Tours has the cosmopolitan and bourgeois air of a miniature Paris, with wide 18th century avenues, formal public gardens, café-lined boulevards and a major university. There are also a number of worthwhile museums. Tours is the only town in the Loire Valley with much nightlife, and the restaurants are among the best in the region. It is also said that the French spoken in Tours is the purest in all of France.

Tours makes an excellent base for forays out to nearby chateaus, especially if you're looking for inexpensive accommodation. See Tours Area Chateaus, Blois Area Chateaus and Amboise for details.

History

Tours, founded under the Romans, has twice served as France's capital, albeit briefly. In 1870, during the Franco-Prussian War, the provisional government of national defence fled Paris – Interior Minister Gambetta got

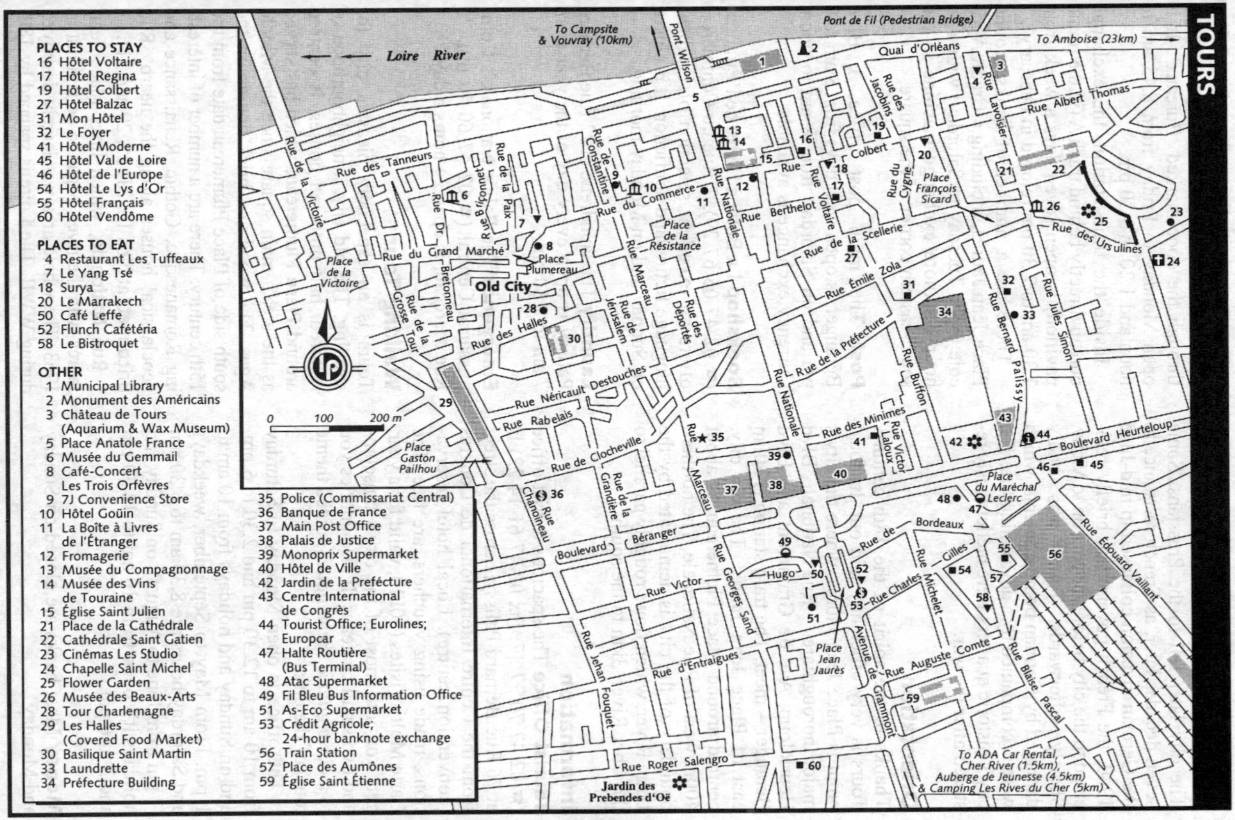
TOURS
PLACES TO STAY
16 Hôtel Voltaire
17 Hôtel Regina
19 Hôtel Colbert
27 Hôtel Balzac
31 Mon Hôtel
32 Le Foyer
41 Hôtel Moderne
45 Hôtel Val de Loire
46 Hôtel de l'Europe
54 Hôtel Le Lys d'Or
55 Hôtel Français
60 Hôtel Vendôme
PLACES TO EAT
4 Restaurant Les Tuffeaux
7 Le Yang Tsé
18 Surya
20 Le Marrakech
50 Café Leffe
52 Flunch Cafétéria
58 Le Bistroquet
OTHER
1 Municipal Library
2 Monument des Américains
3 Château de Tours (Aquarium & Wax Museum)
5 Place Anatole France
6 Musée du Gemmail
8 Café-Concert Les Trois Orfèvres
9 7J Convenience Store
10 Hôtel Goüin
11 La Boîte à Livres de l'Étranger
12 Fromagerie
13 Musée du Compagnonnage
14 Musée des Vins de Touraine
15 Église Saint Julien
21 Place de la Cathédrale
22 Cathédrale Saint Gatien
23 Cinémas Les Studio
24 Chapelle Saint Michel
25 Flower Garden
26 Musée des Beaux-Arts
28 Tour Charlemagne
29 Les Halles (Covered Food Market)
30 Basilique Saint Martin
33 Laundrette
34 Préfecture Building
35 Police (Commissariat Central)
36 Banque de France
37 Main Post Office
38 Palais de Justice
39 Monoprix Supermarket
40 Hôtel de Ville
42 Jardin de la Préfécture
43 Centre International de Congrès
44 Tourist Office; Eurolines; Europcar
47 Halte Routière (Bus Terminal)
48 Atac Supermarket
49 Fil Bleu Bus Information Office
51 As-Eco Supermarket
53 Crédit Agricole; 24-hour banknote exchange
56 Train Station
57 Place des Aumônes
59 Église Saint Étienne
To Campsite & Vouvray (10km)
Pont de Fil (Pedestrian Bridge)
To Amboise (23km)
To ADA Car Rental, Cher River (1.5km), Auberge de Jeunesse (4.5km) & Camping Les Rives du Cher (5km)
0 100 200 m

LOIRE VALLEY

out of the besieged city by balloon – and established itself at Tours for several months. The city later fell to the Prussians. Some seven decades later, as French resistance to the German invasion collapsed in mid-June 1940, the French government briefly relocated to the city before moving on to Vichy. Shortly afterwards Tours was badly damaged by German bombardments, which were accompanied by a devastating fire. The city's historic quarters were meticulously restored after the war.

Orientation

Thanks to the spirit of the 18th century, Tours is very efficiently laid out. Its focal point is Place Jean Jaurès, where the city's major thoroughfares – Rue Nationale, Blvd Heurteloup, Ave de Grammont and Blvd Béranger – meet. The train station is 300m east of Place Jean Jaurès. The old city, centred around Place Plumereau, is about 400m west of Rue Nationale. The northern boundary of the city is demarcated by the Loire River, which flows roughly parallel to the Cher River, 3km to the south.

Information

Tourist Office The spacious tourist office (☎ 02 47 70 37 37; fax 02 47 61 14 22) is at 76 Rue Bernard Palissy, across the street from the Centre International de Congrès (convention centre). Local hotel reservations, made using vouchers, are free. The Carte Multi-Visites (50FF), valid for a year, gets you into most of the city's museums and two small chateaus. It also entitles you to a *visite guidée thématique* (guided theme tour) of the city.

The office is open Monday to Saturday from 10 am to 12.30 pm and 2.30 to 5 pm, and on Sunday and holidays from 10 am to 1 pm. From May to September, weekdays and Saturday hours are 8.30 am to 6.30 pm (7 pm from June to August); on Sunday and holidays it's open from 10 am to 12.30 pm and 3 to 6 pm.

Money Most banks are closed on Sunday and Monday.

The Banque de France branch at 2 Rue Chanoineau has its exchange service through the door marked 'Bureaux'. It is open Monday to Friday from 8.45 am to noon and 1.20 to 3.30 pm.

Inside the train station, the exchange bureau directly behind track A (in the round pavilion) is open seven days a week from 7.30 am to 7.30 pm (closed in February).

There are a number of banks around Place Jean Jaurès, including a Crédit Agricole (open Tuesday to Saturday) with a 24 hour banknote exchange machine in the south-eastern corner of the square.

Post The main post office, 1 Blvd Béranger, is open weekdays from 8 am to 7 pm and on Saturday from 8 am to noon. Currency exchange is available.

Bookshop La Boîte à Livres de l'Étranger (☎ 02 47 05 67 29), 2 Rue du Commerce, offers an excellent selection of English-language fiction and nonfiction. It is closed on Sunday and on Monday morning.

Laundry The laundrette at 22 Rue Bernard Palissy is open every day of the year from 7 am to 8.30 pm.

Emergency The Police Nationale's Commissariat Central (☎ 02 47 60 70 69), 70 Rue Marceau, is open 24 hours a day.

Walking Tour

Tours is an especially pleasant city for strolling. The **old city**, a neighbourhood of restored, half-timbered houses, is centred around **Place Plumereau**, which has served as the area's main square since the Middle Ages. The wood and brick houses on the south side of Place Plumereau date from the 15th century. There are a number of interesting Romanesque, Gothic, Renaissance and neoclassical houses along the nearby **Rue Briçonnet** (at Nos 16, 21, 25, 29 and 31).

Rue Nationale, which links Place Jean Jaurès with the river, began to be laid out in 1763. The whole area was largely destroyed during WWII. The Loire is spanned by 18th century Pont Wilson, which was rebuilt after it collapsed in 1978. Also of interest is the area around the Musée des Beaux-Arts, which includes a lovely park and the Cathédrale Saint Gatien.

Musée des Beaux-Arts

The Fine Arts Museum (☎ 02 47 05 68 73), which is housed in the 17th and 18th century Palais de l'Ancien Archevêché (Former Archbishop's Palace) at 18 Place François Sicard, has an excellent collection of paintings, furniture and *objets d'art* from the 14th to the 20th century. It is especially proud of two 15th century altar paintings by Mantegna that were taken from Italy by Napoleon.

The museum is open from 9 am to 12.45 pm and 2 to 6 pm (closed Tuesday and most major holidays). Entrance costs 30FF (15FF for students and people over 65). The magnificent **cedar of Lebanon** in the courtyard was planted during Napoleon's reign. There's a charming **flower garden** behind it.

Cathédrale Saint Gatien

Various parts of Tours' Gothic-style cathedral represent the 13th century (the choir), the 14th century (the transept), the 14th and 15th centuries (the nave) and the 15th and 16th centuries (the west façade). The domed tops of the two 70m-high **towers** (closed to the public) date from the Renaissance. There's a fine view of the **flying buttresses** from behind.

The interior, which is open from 9 am to 7 pm (and occasionally closed from noon to 2 or 3 pm), is renowned for its **stained-glass windows**, many of which date from the 13th to 15th century. Volunteers at the tourist office table often give free guided tours on a daily basis (except Sunday), but only some of them speak English. Brochures in English are available for 1FF from a self-service table.

The Renaissance **cloître** (cloister) can be visited with a guide (15FF) daily, except Sunday morning, from 9 am to noon and 2 until 5 pm (6 pm from April to September). You can get a glimpse of the cloister – including the **spiral staircase**, the extra buttresses for the north transept and the partly brick remains of the city's **Roman walls** – through the wrought-iron fence to the right as you exit through the west façade.

Musée du Compagnonnage

Tours' unique Guild Museum (☎ 02 47 61 07 93), overlooking the courtyard of **Abbaye Saint Julien** at 8 Rue Nationale, displays the crafts produced by the French chapter of the freemasons – skilful crafts still practised today, from stone sculpting to horseshoeing. The three associations of artisans that founded it have existed since at least the 16th century. The museum is open daily (except Tuesday) from 9 am to noon (12.30 pm from mid-June to mid-September) and 2 to 6 pm. Tickets cost 25FF (15FF for students and over 65s, free for children under 12).

Musée des Vins de Touraine

The Touraine Wine Museum (☎ 02 47 61 07 93), 16 Rue Nationale, occupies the vaulted, 13th century wine cellars of Saint Julien Abbey, whose former abbey church, the Gothic **Église Saint Julien**, is next door. The museum does not give out wine samples, but it does have a roomful of displays on the significance of wine and the traditions associated with it. It is open daily (except Tuesday) from 9 am to noon and 2 to 6 pm. Entry costs 15FF (10FF for students and people over 65).

Musée du Gemmail

This museum (☎ 02 47 61 01 19) at 7 Rue du Mûrier specialises in *gemmail* (pronounced 'zheh-MAI'), an artistic medium that consists of superimposed pieces of coloured glass embedded in a colourless enamel and lit from behind. Gemmail was conceived in 1935, perfected in 1950 and popular in the 50s and 60s. The museum is open Tuesday to Sunday from April to mid-November; hours are 10 am to noon and 2 to 6.30 pm. Tickets cost 30FF (20/10FF for students/children).

Hôtel Goüin

The **Touraine Archaeological Museum** (☎ 02 47 66 22 32), 25 Rue du Commerce, is housed in the Hôtel Goüin, a splendid Renaissance residence built around 1510 for a wealthy merchant. Its Italian-style façade (all that was left after the conflagration of June 1940) is worth seeing even if the eclectic assemblage of prehistoric, Gallo-Roman, medieval, Renaissance and 18th century artefacts doesn't interest you.

The museum is open daily from 10 am to 12.30 pm and 2 to 6.30 pm (5.30 pm from January to mid-March and during October and November, when it's closed on Friday). During July and August, daily hours are 10 am to 7 pm. The entrance fee is 20FF (12FF for children and students, 15FF for people over 60).

Basilique Saint Martin Area

Fans of late 19th century ecclesiastical architecture may want to drop by this extravagant, pseudo-Byzantine church on Rue Descartes, erected between 1886 and 1924. It's open from 8 am to 7 pm, although in winter it may be closed from noon to 2 pm. **Tour Charlemagne**, one of the few remains of a 12th century basilica that was torn down to make way for Rue des Halles in 1802, is across the street from the northern end of the basilica.

Aquarium & Wax Museum

The unimpressive buildings of the **Château de Tours**, 25 Quai d'Orléans, across the street from the Pont de Fil pedestrian suspension bridge, house the nicely done **Aquarium Tropical** (☎ 02 47 64 29 52). Entry costs 30FF (22FF for students and over 60s, 18FF for children under 12). It is open daily from April to mid-November from 9.30 am to noon and 2 to 6 pm (July and August 9.30 am to 7 pm), and afternoons only for the rest of the year. It is closed Sunday morning.

The **Historial de Touraine** (☎ 02 47 61 02 95), a wax museum in the same building, is open daily.

Organised Tours

From mid-April to mid-September the tourist office runs two-hour walking tours of the city about five days a week at 10 am. The cost is 30FF (25FF for children); narration is in French and, if requested, in English. From June to September there are thematic guided tours, also on foot, a couple of times a week.

For details on visiting nearby chateaus by bus or minibus, see Organised Tours in the Tours Area Chateaus section.

Places to Stay – Budget

Camping The closest camp site is the three star ***Camping Les Rives du Cher*** (☎ 02 47 27 27 60) at 61 Rue de Rochpinard in St Avertin, 5km south of Tours. It is open from April to mid-October and charges 14/14/8/8FF per tent/person/child/ car. To get there from Place Jean Jaurès, take bus No 5 straight to the St Avertin's bus terminal, then follow the signs.

About 10km north-east of Tours in Vouvray (see Around Tours), the riverside ***Camping du Bec de Cisse*** (☎ 02 47 52 68 81) is across the N152 and 200m down the hill from the Office du Tourisme. Open from late May to September, it charges 23FF for a tent site (less if you don't have a car) and 16FF per adult.

Hostels *Le Foyer* (☎ 02 47 60 51 51), 16 Rue Bernard Palissy, 400m north of the train station, is a dormitory for workers of both sexes aged 16 to 25. If they have space (availability is best from June to August), they accept travellers of all ages for 65FF a person (70FF in a single). Breakfast is 9FF. Check-in is possible on weekdays from 9 am to 6 pm and on Saturday from 8.30 to 11 am.

Tours' ***Auberge de Jeunesse*** (☎ 02 47 25 14 45) is 5km south of the train station (and 2km south of the Cher River) at Ave d'Arsonval in Parc de Grandmont. A bed in a room of four or six costs 47FF; breakfast is 19FF. Until 8.30 or 8.45 pm, you can take bus No 1 or No 6 from Place Jean Jaurès; between 9.20 pm and about midnight, take Bleu de Nuit line N1 (southbound).

Hotels – Train Station Area The two star ***Hôtel Val de Loire*** (☎ 02 47 05 37 86), 33 Blvd Heurteloup, looks almost like it did when it was a turn-of-the-century bourgeois home, with hardwood floors, high ceilings and some of the gas lighting still in place. Singles/doubles/triples are available at 100/150/200FF (130/180/230FF with shower, 170/220/280FF with bath and toilet). Hall showers cost 15FF.

Hôtel Le Lys d'Or (☎ 02 47 05 33 45; fax 02 47 64 19 00), just round the corner from the station at 21-23 Rue de la Vendée, has quiet, comfortable singles/doubles starting from 120FF, or 185FF with shower and toilet. Ask for a room overlooking the garden. ***Hôtel Français*** (☎ 02 47 05 59 12), 11 Rue de Nantes, provides a cold welcome to match their linoleum-floored doubles/triples/quads from 120/150/170FF (190/220/250FF with shower). Hall showers cost 10FF. Reception is closed on Sunday afternoon, and they don't accept telephone reservations.

Mon Hôtel (☎ 02 47 05 67 53), 500m north of the train station at 40 Rue de la Préfecture, can provide singles/doubles with an oversized bed starting at 100/115FF (170/200FF with shower and toilet). Showers are 15FF. The reception area is lacklustre, but the rooms are modern.

An excellent choice a bit farther from the station is the ***Hôtel Vendôme*** (☎ 02 47 64 33 54) at 24 Rue Roger Salengro. This cheerful place, run by a friendly couple, has simple but decent singles/doubles starting at 120/130FF (150/175 with shower and toilet). A triple with shower is 200FF. Hall showers are free. Free parking is available out front.

Hotels – Near the River There are two excellent bets not far from the Loire. The ***Hôtel Voltaire*** (☎ 02 47 05 77 51), 13 Rue Voltaire, has basic but pleasant doubles from 100FF (130FF with shower). Shower and toilet-equipped rooms for two/three people cost 150/180FF. Down the block at 2 Rue Pimbert, the ***Hôtel Regina*** (☎ 02 47 05 25 36; fax 02 47 66 08 72) has neat, well maintained singles/doubles from 110/120FF (135/150FF with shower and toilet). Hall showers cost 15FF. Both of these places are open all year except for one or two weeks around Christmas and New Year's.

Places to Stay – Mid-Range

Train Station Area To the right as you exit the train station, the two star ***Hôtel de l'Europe*** (☎ 02 47 05 42 07; fax 02 47 20 13 89), 12 Place du Maréchal Leclerc, has high ceilings and strip-carpeted hallways that give it an early 20th century ambience. The huge rooms, equipped with old-fashioned furnishings, cost around 250/300/350FF for a single/double/triple with shower and toilet. An extra bed is 40FF.

The warm, family-run ***Hôtel Moderne*** (☎ 02 47 05 32 81; fax 02 47 05 71 50), 1-3 Rue Victor Laloux, has decent doubles with high ceilings from 245FF; similar rooms without toilet are 194FF.

Near the River The two star ***Hôtel Colbert*** (☎ 02 47 66 61 56; fax 02 47 66 01 55), 78 Rue Colbert, has rooms that range in size from large to enormous. Singles/doubles including shower, toilet and TV start at 230/270FF; an additional bed is 70FF. Slightly farther from the river, the centrally placed ***Hôtel Balzac*** (☎ 02 47 05 40 87), 47 Rue de la Scellerie, has 18 comfortable rooms (most with shower and toilet) from 220FF.

Places to Eat

In the old city, Place Plumereau and nearby streets such as Rue du Grand Marché have quite a few restaurants, pizza places, cafés, crêperies and boulangeries. There's another cluster of food shops and restaurants along semi-pedestrianised Rue Colbert.

Restaurants – French For café-restaurants, you can't beat Place Jean Jaurès and nearby bits of Ave de Grammont, with countless popular eateries, notably ***Flunch Cafétéria*** (☎ 02 47 64 56 70) at 14 Place Jean Jaurès (open daily from 10 am to 2.30 pm and from 6 to 10 pm). ***Café Leffe*** (☎ 02 47 61 48 54), 15 Place Jean Jaurès, named after a Belgian beer called Abbaye de Leffe, is open daily from 7 am to 2 am; brasserie meals are served from noon to 3 pm and 7 to 11.30 pm. *Moules marinières* (mussels cooked with white wine and onions) and chips cost 49FF.

Near the train station at 17 Rue Blaise Pascal, the simple but attractive ***Le Bistroquet*** (☎ 02 47 05 12 76) has *menus* of solid French food for 50FF (dinner only), 58 and 62 (lunch only). Their speciality is paella. Open weekdays from noon to 1.30 pm and 7 to 9.15 pm.

Restaurant Les Tuffeaux (☎ 02 47 47 19 89), 19-21 Rue Lavoisier, specialises in very innovative *cuisine gastronomique* made with lots of fresh local products. *Menus* cost 110 to 200FF. It's open from noon to 1.30 pm and 7.30 to 9.30 pm (closed all day Sunday and Monday at midday). Bookings are a good idea for dinner, especially on Saturday.

Restaurants – Other The cluster of restaurants along Rue Colbert includes ***Le Marrakèch*** (☎ 02 47 66 64 65) at No 111, whose Moroccan couscous and tajines costs from 63 to 75FF. Open daily, except Tuesday.

Surya (☎ 02 47 64 34 04), 65 Rue Colbert, has a selection of North Indian dishes including curries, tandoori items and all sorts of rice biryani. It is open from noon to 2.30 pm and 7 to 11 pm (closed for lunch on Monday). The weekday lunch *menu* costs 59FF.

The hole-in-the-wall ***Le Yang Tsé*** (☎ 02 47 61 47 59), 83bis Rue du Commerce, has Chinese mains for 30 to 35FF, including rice. Open daily from noon to 11 pm (closed for lunch on Monday from December to February).

Self-Catering Pleasant places for a picnic include Place François Sicard (near the Musée des Beaux-Arts), the garden of the Musée des Beaux-Arts (behind the cedar tree) and the Jardin de la Préfecture.

Les Halles, Tours' large covered market, is 500m west of Rue Nationale at Place Gaston Pailhou. It is open Monday to Saturday until 7 pm and on Sunday until 1 pm.

In front of the train station, the ***Atac*** supermarket at 5 Place du Maréchal Leclerc is open Monday to Saturday from 8.30 am to 8 pm and on Sunday from 9.30 am to 12.30 pm. At No 19bis (inside the L'Orangerie shopping mall) Place Jean Jaurès, the boulangerie-equipped ***As-Eco*** supermarket has a mouth-watering selection of prepared salads. It is open Monday to Saturday from 7.30 am to 8 pm and on Sunday from 9 am to 12.30 pm. The ***Monoprix*** supermarket at 77 Rue Nationale is open from 7 am to 7 pm (closed Sunday).

In the old city, the ***7J*** convenience store at 14 Rue de Constantine, is open every day from 8 am to midnight.

East of Rue Nationale, there are lots of food shops along Rue Colbert, including a ***fromagerie*** at No 11 (closed from 12.30 to 3 pm, on Sunday and on Monday morning).

Entertainment

Nondubbed films are screened at ***Cinémas Les Studio*** (☎ 02 47 20 27 00 or, for a recorded message, ☎ 02 47 05 22 80), the entrance of which is opposite 17 Rue des Ursulines. Tickets cost 41FF for non-members (39FF on Wednesday).

Café nightlife is centred around Place Plumereau. Nearby, several cosy pubs line Rue des Orfèvres. The ***Café-Concert Les Trois Orfèvres*** (☎ 02 47 64 02 73), 6 Rue des Orfèvres (off Rue du Commerce), has live music (rhythm and blues, blues, rock, soul, jazz etc) from Tuesday or Wednesday to Saturday starting at 9 or 10 pm. Entry usually costs 35 to 50FF; students often get a reduction. A *demi* (330mL) of draught beer costs 20FF.

Getting There & Away

Many of the chateaus in the vicinity of Tours can be reached by train or bus. For details, see Organised Tours and/or Getting There & Away under Blois Area Chateaus, Amboise, Tours Area Chateaus and Chinon. Further details appear under each chateau listing.

Bus Eurolines' ticket office (☎ 02 47 66 45 56), next to the tourist office at 74 Rue Bernard Palissy, is open weekdays from 9 am

LOIRE VALLEY

FRANCES LINZEE GORDON

The sumptuous interior of the neoclassical Château de Cheverny is the finest in the Loire Valley.

RICHARD NEBESKY

The Pas de la Casa ski resort, near the French border, is one of Andorra's most popular.

TERESA FISHER

The Château des Comtes de Foix stands like a sentinel over the town of Foix, Pyrenees.

TERESA FISHER

Bayonne, French Basque country

TERESA FISHER

Vieux Pont, Saint Jean Pied de Port

TERESA FISHER

Saint Jean de Luz's colourful history includes whaling and piracy, but today it is known for fishing.

to noon and from 1.30 to 6.30 pm (2 to 6 pm on Monday), and Saturday from 9 am to noon and 1.30 to 5.30 pm.

Train The train station (☎ 08 36 35 35 35) is off Blvd Heurteloup at Place du Maréchal Leclerc. The information office is open from 8.30 am to 6.30 pm (closed Sunday and holidays). Tours is linked to Saint Pierre des Corps by shuttle trains synchronised to meet mainline trains.

To get from Paris to Tours by rail you can either take a TGV from Gare Montparnasse (201FF; 70 minutes; 10 to 15 a day), which often requires a change of trains at Saint Pierre des Corps, or you can take a direct non-TGV train from Gare d'Austerlitz (153FF; two to 2½ hours; five to eight a day). There are TGV and non-TGV services to Bordeaux (about 217FF; 2½ hours by TGV) and Poitiers (90FF; about one hour; a dozen a day), frequent non-TGVs to Nantes (147FF; 1¾ hours), and infrequent services to La Rochelle (170FF; three hours).

Car ADA (☎ 02 47 64 94 94) is a bit south of the centre of town at 49 Blvd Thiers, 250m west of the huge Hôtel Altéa at Place Thiers (the intersection of Ave de Grammont and Blvd Thiers). It's open Monday to Saturday from 8 am to noon and 2 to 6.30 pm. By bus, take No 3 or 6 from the train station or bus No 1, 2, 3, 5 or 9 (southbound) from Place Jean Jaurès; get off at the Thiers stop.

Europcar (☎ 02 47 64 47 76), next to the tourist office at 76 Blvd Bernard Palissy, is open from 8 am to noon and 2 to 6.30 pm (6 pm on Saturday; closed Sunday and holidays).

Getting Around

Bus The bus network serving Tours and its suburbs is known as Fil Bleu. Almost all the lines stop around the periphery of Place Jean Jaurès. Two Bleu de Nuit lines – N1 and N2 – operate every 55 minutes from about 9.30 pm until a bit past midnight. Tickets, which cost 6.50FF if bought singly, are valid for one hour after being time-stamped. A carnet of five/10 tickets costs 32/59FF from *tabacs* (tobacconists).

Fil Bleu has an information office (☎ 02 47 66 70 70) at 5bis Rue de la Dolve, 50m west of Place Jean Jaurès. It is open daily, except Sunday, from 7.30 am until 7 pm (9 am to 5.30 pm on Saturday).

Taxi Call Taxi Radio (☎ 02 47 20 30 40) to order a taxi 24 hours a day.

Bicycle From May to September, Amster' Cycles (☎ 02 47 61 22 23) has a rental point 30m to the right of the main entrance of the train station. To rent an 18-speed/tandem for 24 hours, the price is 80/160FF (cheaper for longer periods). They will also lend you maps.

AROUND TOURS

Vouvray

• **pop 2900** ✉ **37210** **alt 115m**

The village of Vouvray, 10km east of Tours, is not an overly attractive place, but its redeaming feature is the fact that it is home to about 40 *caves* (cellars). To find them, look for signs reading '*dégustation*' or '*cave*' or drop by one of the tourist offices for a list. Most can be visited year-round (except, in some cases, on Sunday and holidays).

Information Two municipal tourist offices can give you information on wine-tasting options: the Office du Tourisme (☎ 02 47 52 68 73), on the corner of the N152 and the D46 (Ave Brulé), and Syndicat d'Initiative (☎ 02 47 52 70 48), at the intersection of Rue de la République and Rue Gambetta. Both are open daily, except Sunday and holiday afternoons, from June to September. The rest of the year the Syndicat d'Initiative is open on Tuesday morning, Friday and Saturday.

Places to Eat On Tuesday and Friday morning, there's a ***food market*** on Ave André Maginot, which is near the ***Atac*** supermarket (closed Sunday) at 12 Rue Rabelais.

Getting There & Away Vouvray is on the north bank of the Loire along the N152.

Semitrat's bus No 61 links Tours' Place Jean Jaurès with Vouvray (20 minutes; a dozen a day from Monday to Saturday, three on Sunday afternoon). The last bus back to Tours leaves at around 7.30 pm (6.30 pm on Sunday).

TOURS AREA CHATEAUS

Tours, with its many cheap hotels and decent train and bus links, makes a good base for visits to some of the most interesting of the Loire chateaus, including Chenonceau, Villandry, Azay-le-Rideau, Langeais, Amboise (see the Amboise section) and Chaumont (see Blois Area Chateaus). If you're using the train to get to the chateaus, Tours is your best railhead.

The tourist office in Tours can provide details of sound and light shows, medieval re-enactments, and other spectacles performed at the chateaus during the summer.

Organised Tours

Getting out to the chateaus by public transport is a slow and fairly pricey proposition, so even veteran backpackers may want to consider an organised tour.

Several companies offer very interesting English-language tours of the major Loire Valley chateaus, with different itineraries available each day of the week. Prices often include entrance fees or entitle you to discounts (such fees are a major expense if you go on your own). Reservations can be made at the Tours tourist office; pick-up is usually nearby. If you can get five to seven people together, you can design your own minibus itinerary.

Acco-Dispo (☎ 02 47 57 67 13; fax 02 47 23 15 73) has minibus excursions year-round, except January. Half-day/day tours cost 130/170FF, not including entry fees.

Touraine Évasion (☎ 02 47 63 25 64; fax 02 47 44 31 10) runs half-day/day trips by eight-person minibus for 95/170FF, not including entry fees, from early April to mid-November.

Services Touristiques de Touraine (☎ 02 47 05 46 09) has full-sized coaches that run from April to October. Half-day tours of two chateaus cost 185 to 200FF; all-day tours are about 290FF, including entry fees. STT's office is inside the Tours train station opposite the *Buffet de la Gare*.

Getting There & Away

Transport details are listed under Getting There & Away at the end of each chateau listing. All times quoted are approximate and should be verified before you make plans.

Bus Except on Sunday and holidays, buses to destinations all over the department of Indre-et-Loire leave from the Halte Routière (bus terminal) in front of the Tours train station. Schedules are posted. The information desk (☎ 02 47 05 30 49) is open Monday to Saturday from 7.30 am to noon and 2 to 6.30 pm. Tickets are sold on board.

From Tours, you can make an all-day circuit by public bus to Chenonceau and Amboise (70.90FF) by taking CAT bus No 10 for the hour-long ride to Chenonceau (38FF) at 10 am; catching the bus from Chenonceau to Amboise (11.30FF; 35 minutes) at 12.30 pm (during July and August, there's another bus at 4.40 pm); and then returning to Tours either by bus (at 5.20 or 6 pm; 24.10FF) or train (see Getting There & Away under Amboise). Double-check these times and schedules before setting out.

Train Many of the chateaus of the Loire Valley can be reached from Tours by train or SNCF bus. These include Amboise (28FF), Azay-le-Rideau (28FF), Blois (51FF), Chenonceau (34FF), Chinon (46FF), Langeais (27FF) and Saumur (57FF) and, somewhat less conveniently, Villandry (18FF to Savonnières). Up-to-date travel options are detailed in *Les Châteaux de la Loire en Train*, an SNCF pamphlet issued each year in late May and available at train stations. The *Guide Régional TER*, also available at many train stations, has a more complete schedule.

Château de Chenonceau

With its stylised (rather than defensive) moat, drawbridge, towers and turrets, the 16th century Château de Chenonceau (☎ 02 47 23 90 07) is everything you imagine a fairy-tale castle to be. The chateau's exterior and its gardens are outstanding but the interior, filled with period furniture, tourists, paintings, tourists, tapestries, tourists and more tourists, is of only moderate interest.

The nicest thing about Chenonceau, which straddles the Cher River, is its landscaping and forests and the vistas they afford of the castle's exterior. One of the series of most remarkable women who created Chenonceau, Diane de Poitiers, mistress of King Henri II, planted the garden to the left (east) as you approach the chateau down the avenue of plane trees. After the death of Henri II in 1559, she was forced to give up her beloved Chenonceau by the vengeful Catherine de Médicis, Henri II's widow, who then applied her own formidable energies to the chateau and, among other works, laid out the garden to the right (west) as you approach the castle. Diane's is prettier.

In the 18th century, Madame Dupin, the chateau's owner at the time, brought Jean-Jacques Rousseau to Chenonceau as a tutor for her son. During the Revolution, the affection with which the peasantry regarded Mme Dupin saved the chateau from the violent fate of many of its neighbours.

The 60m-long **Galerie** over the Cher River, built by Catherine de Médicis, was converted into a hospital during WWI.

The fairy-tale castle of Château de Chenonceau has superb gardens.

Between 1940 and 1942, the demarcation line between Vichy-ruled France and the German-occupied zone ran down the middle of the Cher: the castle itself was under direct German occupation, but the Galerie's southern entrance was in the area controlled by Marshal Pétain. For many people trying to escape to the Vichy zone, this room served as a crossing point.

Two other 'must sees' are Catherine's lovely little library on the ground floor, with the oldest original ceiling (1521) in the chateau, and the bedroom where Louise de Lorraine lived out her final days after the assassination of her husband, Henri III, in 1589. Macabre illustrations of bones, skulls, shovels and teardrops adorn the dark walls.

Chenonceau is open all year from 9 am until sometime between 4.30 pm (mid-November to January) and 7 pm (mid-March to mid-September). The entrance fee is 45FF (30FF for children and students). During July and August you can paddle around the moat and the Cher River in four-person rowboats for 10FF per half-hour.

Getting There & Away The Château de Chenonceau, in the town of Chenonceaux (the town has an 'x' at the end), is 34km east of Tours, 10km south-east of Amboise and 40km south-west of Blois.

Milk-run local trains (*omnibus*) on the Tours-Vierzon line stop at Chisseaux (33FF), 2km east of Chenonceaux. There may also be two or three trains a day from Tours to Chenonceaux station, which is only 500m from the chateau.

Year-round from Monday to Saturday, CAT bus No 10 leaves Tours for Chenonceaux (39.40FF one way, 69.90FF return) at 10 am; a bus back to Tours departs at 4.45 pm. For details on bus links to Amboise, see Getting There & Away in the Amboise section.

Château de Villandry

The Château de Villandry (☎ 02 47 50 02 09) has some of the most spectacular formal gardens anywhere in France. The **Jardin d'Ornement** (Ornamental Garden) is made up of intricate, geometrically pruned hedges and flowerbeds loaded with abstract, romantic symbolism (explained in the free English-language brochure you can pick up at the entrance).

Between the chateau and the nearby village church, the **potager** (kitchen garden) is a cross between the vegetable plots in which medieval monks grew their food and the formal gardens so beloved in 16th century France. Vegetables of various hues as well as pear trees, roses and other flowers are used to form nine squares, each one different from the next. Between the potager and the church there's a plot of **herbs** and **medicinal plants**.

All told, Villandry's gardens occupy five hectares and include over 1150 lime trees, hundreds of grape trellises, and some 52km of landscaped plant rows. Villandry is at its most colourful from May to mid-June and from August to October, but is well worth a visit at other times of the year as well.

The chateau itself was completed in 1536, making it the last of the major Renaissance chateaus to be built in this area. The interior, whose sparsely furnished, 18th century rooms and hallways are adorned with mediocre paintings, can easily be skipped, though the 13th century Moorish **mosque ceiling** from Spain is of moderate interest. The view from the tower – from which the intricate gardens can be seen in their entirety, as can the parallel Loire and Cher rivers – is only slightly better than the magnificent one that can be had for no extra cost from the terraced hill east of the chateau.

Villandry's gardens are open every day of the year from 8.30 or 9 am to nightfall (8 pm in July and August). The chateau itself – which, unlike the gardens, is closed from 11 November to mid-February – can be visited until sometime between 5.30 and 6.30 pm. Entry to the gardens costs 32FF (25FF for children and students aged 18 to 25); it's an additional 13FF to see the chateau interior.

Getting There & Away The Château de Villandry is in the village of Villandry, which is 17km south-west of Tours, 31km north-east of Chinon and 11km north-east of Azay-le-Rideau. By road, the shortest route from Tours is the D7, but cyclists will find less traffic on the D88 (which runs along the south bank of the Loire) and the D288 (which links the D88 with Savonnières). If heading south-westward from Villandry towards Langeais, the best bike route is the D16, which has no verges (shoulders) but has light traffic.

The only public transport from Tours to Villandry is the train to Savonnières (18FF; 10 to 20 minutes; two or three a day), which is about 4km east of Villandry. The first train from Tours is at about 12.20 pm (noon on Sunday and holidays); unfortunately, the last train back to Tours is early at 1.30 pm (5.30 pm on Saturday). It may be possible to bring your bicycle along with you.

Château d'Azay-le-Rideau

Azay-le-Rideau (☎ 02 47 45 42 04), built on an island in the Indre River and surrounded by a quiet pool and park, is one of the most harmonious and elegant of the Loire chateaus. It is adorned with stylised fortifications and turrets intended both as decoration and to indicate the rank of the owners. Only seven rooms are open to the public, and their contents are disappointing (apart from a few 16th century Flemish tapestries).

The bloodiest incident in the chateau's history – a subject of invariable fascination for modern-day chateau-goers – occurred in 1418. During a visit to Azay, then a fortified castle, the crown prince (later King Charles VII) was insulted by the Burgundian guard. Enraged, he had the town burned and executed some 350 soldiers and officers. The present chateau was begun exactly a century later by Giles Berthelot, one of François I's less-than-selfless financiers. When the prospect of being audited and hanged drew near, Berthelot fled abroad and never completed the structure. The finishing touches weren't put on until the 19th century.

From April to October the chateau is open daily from 9.30 am to 6 pm (until 7 pm in July and August). The rest of the year its hours are 9.30 am to 12.30 pm and 2 to

5.30 pm. The park stays open half an hour later. Tickets cost 32FF (21FF if you're aged 12 to 25). You can either walk around on your own, guided by the sketchy and confusing brochure, or join a guided tour in French at no extra cost.

Getting There & Away Azay-le-Rideau, in the town of the same name, is 26km south-west of Tours. It is on the SNCF's Tours-Chinon line (two or three a day, one on Sunday); from Tours, the 35 minute trip by either train or bus costs 28FF; the station is 2.5km from the chateau. The last train/bus to Tours leaves Azay at about 6 pm (8 pm on Sunday).

Langeais

• pop 4000 ✉ 37130 alt 102m

The main attraction in the flowery little town of Langeais is the massive Château de Langeais at Place Pierre de Brosse.

Information The town's tourist office (☎ 02 47 96 58 22; fax 02 47 96 83 41), near the chateau in Place du 14 Juillet, has information on places to stay and eat, wine cellars and walks. From Easter to mid-October it's open Monday to Saturday from 9.15 am to 12.45 pm and 2.30 to 6 pm (7pm from late June to mid-September), and on Sunday from 10 am to 12.30 pm (also open in the afternoon in summer months). Off-season hours are 3 to 6 pm (closed Sunday).

Château de Langeais Built in the late 1460s to cut the most likely invasion route from Brittany, the Château de Langeais (☎ 02 47 96 72 60) presents two faces to the world. From the town you see a 15th century fortified castle – its nearly windowless, machicolated ramparts (ie walls from which missiles and boiling liquids could be dropped on attackers) rise forbiddingly from the drawbridge. The sections facing the courtyard, however, are outfitted with the large windows, dormers and decorative stonework characteristic of later chateaus designed for more refined living. The **ruined dungeon** across the garden from the courtyard dates from around 944 and is the oldest such structure in France.

Langeais has the Loire Valley chateaus' most interesting interior after that of Cheverny. The unmodernised configuration of the rooms and the **period furnishings** (chests, beds, stools, tables, chairs etc) give you a pretty good idea of what the place looked like during the 15th and 16th centuries (ie before and during the early Renaissance period). The walls are decorated with fine but somewhat faded Flemish and Aubusson **tapestries**, many of which are in the mille-fleurs (thousand flowers) style.

In one room, wax figures re-enact the marriage of King Charles VIII and Duchess Anne of Brittany, which took place here on 6 December 1491 and which brought about the final union of France and Brittany. The event also put an end to the chateau's strategic importance.

The Château de Langeais, which is owned by the Institut de France, is open every day of the year (except Christmas Day) from 9 am to noon and 2 to 5 pm. From April to September its hours are 9 am to 6.30 pm (9 pm from mid-July to August). Entrance costs 40FF (35FF for people over 60, students and children). The guided tours are in French, but there are explanatory signs in English and several other languages.

Places to Eat There are a number of ***restaurants*** and ***food shops*** along the streets around the walls of the chateau.

Getting There & Away Langeais is 24km south-west of Tours and 14km west of Villandry.

The Langeais train station (☎ 02 47 96 82 19), 400m from the Château de Langeais, is on the Tours-Savonnières-Saumur line. The trip from Tours (27FF; three to six a day) takes 20 to 30 minutes. The last train back to Tours is at 6.40 pm (5.30 pm on Saturday, 7.15 or 8.20 pm on Sunday and holidays). Tickets cost 13FF to Savonnières (4km from Villandry) and 37FF to Saumur.

CHINON

• pop 8627 ✉ 37500

Chinon's massive, 400m-long castle looms over the town's medieval quarter, a fine place for a stroll when the tourists aren't too thick (as it were). The uneven, cobblestone streets are lined with ancient houses, some built of decaying tufa stone, others half-timbered and brick. The contrast between the triangular, black slate roofs and the whitish-tan tufa gives the town its distinctive appearance.

Villandry, Azay-le-Rideau and Langeais can easily be visited from Chinon if you have your own transport.

Orientation

Rue Haute Saint Maurice, the main street in the medieval quarter, becomes Rue Voltaire as you move east. The train station is 1km east of the town's commercial hub, Place Général de Gaulle, also known as Place de l'Hôtel de Ville and Place de la Fontaine.

Information

Tourist Office The tourist office (☎ 02 47 93 17 85; fax 02 47 93 93 05), 12 Rue Voltaire, is open Monday to Saturday from 9 am to 12.15 pm and 2 to 6.30 pm (from mid-June to mid-September its hours are 9 am to 7 pm). From November to February, afternoon hours are 1.30 to 5pm.

Money The Banque CIO at 13 Place Général de Gaulle is open Monday to Friday from 8.30 am to 12.30 pm and 1.40 to 5.30 pm (5.05 pm on Friday).

Post The post office on Quai Jeanne d'Arc is open on weekdays from 8 am to noon and 1.30 to 5.45 pm, and on Saturday until noon.

Laundry The GTI Laverie Libre-Service at 40 Quai Charles VII is open daily from 7 am to 9 pm.

Château de Chinon

Perched atop a rocky spur high above the Vienne River, this huge, mostly ruined medieval fortress (☎ 02 47 93 13 45) consists of three parts separated by waterless moats: little remains of the 12th century **Fort Saint Georges**, which protected the chateau's vulnerable eastern flank; the **Château du Milieu** (the Middle Castle); and, at the western tip, the **Château du Coudray**. From the ramparts there are great views in all directions. The chateau is illuminated at night during the summer months.

After crossing the moat (once spanned by a drawbridge) and entering the Château du Milieu, you pass under the **Tour de l'Horloge** (Clock Tower). The four rooms inside are dedicated to the career of Joan of Arc, who picked out Charles VII from among a crowd of courtiers in 1429 in the castle's **Salle du Trône** (Throne Room), of which little more than the giant fireplace remains. Other parts of the almost undecorated **Grand Logis Royal** (Royal Apartments), built during the 12th, 14th and 15th centuries, are in slightly better condition and house a number of exhibits.

The Château du Coudray has several cylindrical and polygonal dungeons from the 12th and 13th centuries.

The chateau, which is owned by the department of Indre-et-Loire, is open daily from 9 am to 6 pm (7 pm in July and August). From November to mid-March its hours are 9 am to noon and 2 to 5 pm. Entry costs 27FF (18FF for people over 60, 16FF for children and students). Free guided tours in English are held seven times a day all year long.

To get to the chateau from town, walk up the hill to Rue du Puits des Bancs and turn left. By car, Route de Tours (the continuation of the D751 from Tours) takes you to the back of the chateau, where parking is available.

Musée Animé du Vin

This rather kitsch museum (☎ 02 47 93 25 63) at 12 Rue Voltaire (20m up the hill from the tourist office) has life-sized mechanical figures that demonstrate how wine and wine barrels are made, accompanied by piped commentary in English. It is open daily from April to September from 10.30 am to 12.30 pm and from 2 to 7.30 pm. Entry costs 23FF, including a sample of local wine and *confiture de vin* (sweet wine sauce).

LOIRE VALLEY

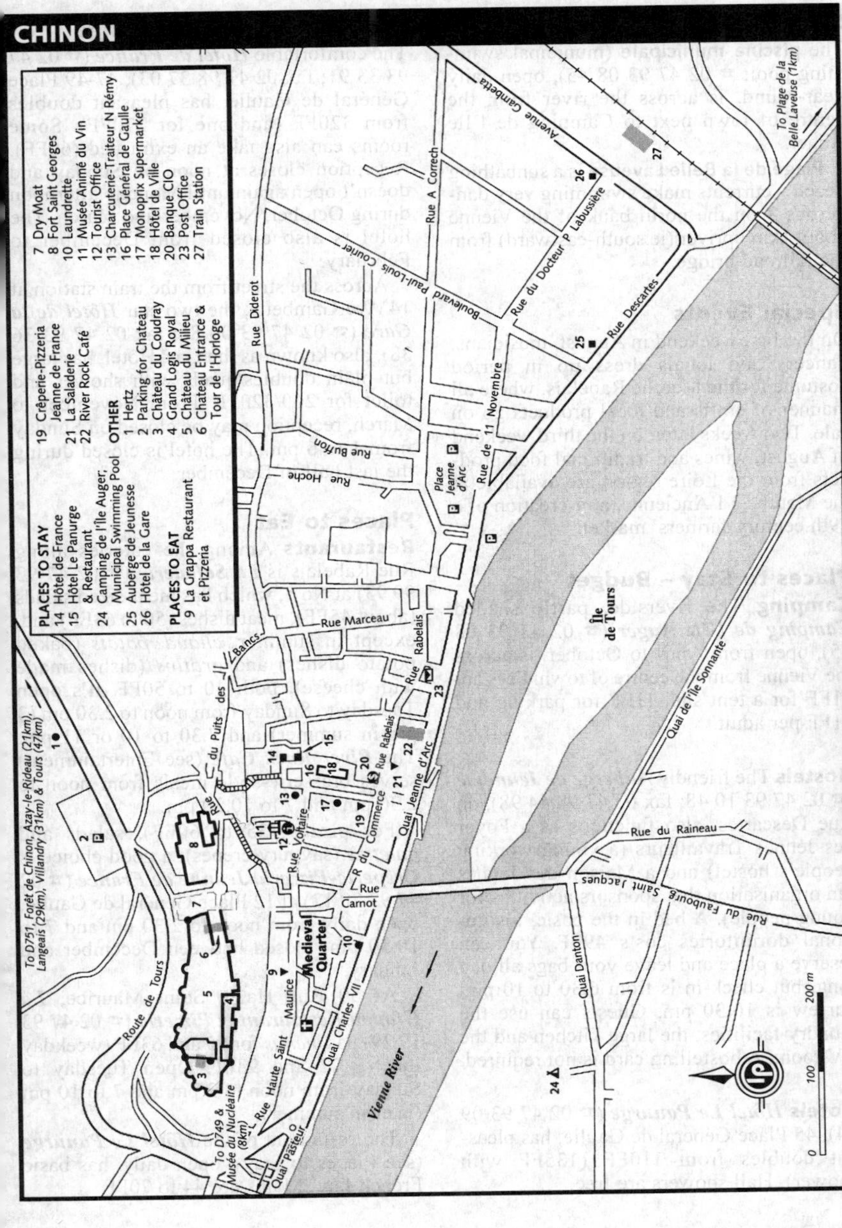
CHINON
PLACES TO STAY
14 Hôtel de France
15 Hôtel Le Panurge & Restaurant
24 Camping de l'Île Auger, Municipal Swimming Pool
25 Auberge de Jeunesse
26 Hôtel de la Gare
PLACES TO EAT
9 La Grappa Restaurant et Pizzeria
19 Crêperie-Pizzeria Jeanne de France
21 La Saladerie
22 River Rock Café
OTHER
1 Hertz
2 Parking for Chateau
3 Château du Coudray
4 Grand Logis Royal
5 Château du Milieu
6 Chateau Entrance & Tour de l'Horloge
7 Dry Moat
8 Fort Saint Georges
10 Laundrette
11 Musée Animé du Vin
12 Tourist Office
13 Charcuterie-Traiteur N Rémy
16 Place Général de Gaulle
17 Monoprix Supermarket
18 Hôtel de Ville
20 Banque CIO
23 Post Office
27 Train Station
Avenue Gambetta
To Plage de la Belle Laveuse (1km)
Rue A Correch
Rue du Docteur P Labussière
Boulevard Paul-Louis Courier
Rue Descartes
Rue Diderot
Rue Buffon
Rue Hoche
Place Jeanne d'Arc
Rue de 11 Novembre
Île de Tours
Rue Marceau
Rue du Puits des Bancs
Rue Rabelais
Quai Jeanne d'Arc
Rue du Commerce
Rue Voltaire
Rue Carnot
Medieval Quarter
Rue Haute Saint Maurice
Quai Charles VII
Vienne River
Quai Pasteur
Route de Tours
Quai de l'Île Sonnante
Rue du Raineau
Rue du Faubourg Saint Jacques
Quai Danton
To D751, Forêt de Chinon, Azay-le-Rideau (21km), Langeais (29km), Villandry (31km) & Tours (47km)
To D749 & Musée du Nucléaire (8km)
0 100 200 m

Swimming

The **piscine municipale** (municipal swimming pool; ☎ 02 47 93 08 45), open daily year-round, is across the river from the centre of town next to Camping de l'Île Auger.

Plage de la Belle Laveuse is a sunbathing beach – currents make swimming very dangerous – on the north bank of the Vienne about 1km upriver (ie south-eastward) from the railroad bridge.

Special Events

On the first weekend in August, musicians, dancers and locals dress up in period costume for the Marché Rabelais, where all manner of crafts and local products go on sale. Two weeks later, on the third weekend of August, wines and traditional food products from the Loire region are available at the Marché à l'Ancienne, a re-creation of a 19th century farmers' market.

Places to Stay – Budget

Camping The riverside, partly shaded ***Camping de l'Île Auger*** (☎ 02 47 93 08 35), open from April to October, is across the Vienne from the centre of town. Fees are 11FF for a tent site, 11FF for parking and 11FF per adult.

Hostels The friendly ***Auberge de Jeunesse*** (☎ 02 47 93 10 48; fax 02 47 98 44 98), on Rue Descartes, also functions as a Foyer des Jeunes Travailleurs (a young working people's hostel) and a Maison des Jeunes (an organisation that sponsors activities for young people). A bed in the basic, institutional dormitories costs 49FF. You can reserve a place and leave your bags all day long, but check-in is from 6.30 to 10 pm; curfew is 10.30 pm. Guests can use the laundry facilities, the large kitchen and the TV room. A hostelling card is not required.

Hotels ***Hôtel Le Panurge*** (☎ 02 47 93 09 84), 45 Place Général de Gaulle, has pleasant doubles from 110FF (135FF with shower). Hall showers are free.

LOIRE VALLEY

Places to Stay – Mid-Range

The comfortable ***Hôtel de France*** (☎ 02 47 93 33 91; fax 02 47 98 37 03), 47-49 Place Général de Gaulle, has pleasant doubles from 320FF (and one for 270FF). Some rooms can also take an extra bed (60FF). Reception closes at noon on Sunday and doesn't open again until Monday afternoon during October, November and March. The hotel is also closed from December to February.

Across the street from the train station at 14 Ave Gambetta, the two star ***Hôtel de la Gare*** (☎ 02 47 93 00 86; fax 02 47 93 36 38), also known as the Gar' Hôtel, has large but plain doubles/quads with shower and toilet for 260/320FF. From November to March, reception may be closed on Sunday from 1 to 6 pm. The hotel is closed during the last half of December.

Places to Eat

Restaurants Among the eateries along Rue Rabelais is ***La Saladerie*** (☎ 02 47 93 99 93) at No 5, which has meal-sized salads (about 45FF), meat dishes (50 to 63FF) and, except in summer, *chaud' patats* (baked potato dishes) and *gratins* (dishes made with cheese), both 40 to 50FF. It's open Tuesday to Sunday from noon to 2.30 pm (3 pm in summer) and 7.30 to 10 or 11 pm. The ***River Rock Café*** (see Entertainment) serves brasserie-style meals from noon to 2.30 pm and 7 to 10.30 pm.

For pizzas (35 to 60FF), salads and *galettes* (savoury crepes), a good choice is ***Crêperie-Pizzeria Jeanne de France*** (☎ 02 47 93 20 12) at 12 Place Général de Gaulle, open daily from noon to 2.30 pm and 7 to 10.30 pm; closed between December and January.

At 50 Rue Haute Saint Maurice, ***La Grappa Restaurant et Pizzeria*** (☎ 02 47 93 19 29) has *menus* for 55 and 63FF (weekday lunch), 72 and 98FF. Open Tuesday to Sunday from noon to 2 pm and 7 to 10 pm (later in summer).

The restaurant of the ***Hôtel Le Panurge*** (see Places to Stay), open daily, has basic French fare. Mains are 44 to 70FF.

Self-Catering The *Monoprix* at 22 Place Général de Gaulle is open Monday to Saturday from 9 am to 12.30 pm and 2.15 to 7.15 pm (no midday closure in summer).

At the northern end of Place Général de Gaulle, there's an ***outdoor market*** on Thursday, Saturday and Sunday mornings until 1 pm. Nearby, ***Charcuterie-Traiteur N Rémy*** on Rue Voltaire has delicious prepared foods (closed Sunday afternoon and Monday). Place Jeanne d'Arc plays host to a ***food market*** on Thursday morning.

Entertainment

The most popular bar in town is the English-style ***River Rock Café*** (☎ 02 47 93 94 94) at 58 Quai Jeanne d'Arc, open Tuesday to Sunday from 11 am to 1 am. Beer starts at 11FF.

Getting There & Away

Chinon is 46km south-west of Tours, 21km south-west of Azay-le-Rideau and 80km north of Poitiers.

Train The train station (☎ 02 47 93 11 04), 1km east of the medieval quarter, is linked by a tertiary line with Tours (46FF; one hour; six to eight a day, four on Saturday, two on Sunday and holidays) and Azay-le-Rideau (25FF). The last transport to Tours is an *autorail* (railcar) at 5.30 pm (7.40 pm on Sunday and holidays).

Car Hertz (☎ 02 47 93 04 65) has an office just beyond the castel on the Route du Tours.

Getting Around

Taxi To order a taxi, ring ☎ 02 47 93 04 86.

Bicycle You might still be able to rent 10-speeds for 30/50FF a half-day/day at the Auberge de Jeunesse (see Places to Stay). Alternatively, rent one at the train station (☎ 02 47 93 08 08) for 40/60FF a half-day/day.

AROUND CHINON

Forêt de Chinon

The Chinon Forest, a wooded area that's great for walking and cycling, begins a few kilometres north-east of town and stretches along the D751 all the way to Azay-le-Rideau.

Route du Vin de Chinon

There are vineyards north, south and east of Chinon, on both banks of the Vienne; they stretch from Beaumont-en-Véron east to Crouzilles and south to Ligré. The tourist office has a brochure on the 'Route du Vin de Chinon' and details on places that sell wine.

Museé du Nucléaire

The Centrale Nucléaire d'Avoine (☎ 02 47 98 77 77), where France's first commercial reactor, erected between 1957 and 1963, has been turned into a museum. The station, 8km north-west of Chinon on the D749, also has two other decommissioned units and four active, pressurised water reactors rated at 900 megawatts.

To arrange a free visit you'll need to call the station a few days ahead (a day ahead in July and August); bring along some form of ID. On weekdays from May to September there are four tours a day; tours are less frequent the rest of the year. The working reactors can only be visited on weekdays.

Getting There & Away The train station at Port Boulet, 2km away on the north bank of the Indre River, is on the Tours-Langeais-Saumur line.

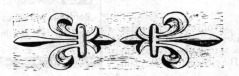

Atlantic Coast

The pristine beaches, sand dunes, pine forests and salt marshes of France's unpretentious Atlantic coast stretch from the English Channel all the way to the Spanish frontier. The region's major attractions include the commodious city of Nantes, near the mouth of the Loire River; Poitiers, famed for its superb Romanesque churches; the ancient and picturesque port of La Rochelle, once an important Huguenot stronghold; the beach fringed Île de Ré; the brandy town of Cognac; Bordeaux, capital of one of the world's most renowned wine-growing regions; and the coastal resort of Arcachon, which boasts an enormous sand dune.

The northern part of the Atlantic seaboard is covered in the Brittany chapter; details on the far south are in the French Basque Country chapter.

NANTES

• pop 496,000 ✉ 44000

Nantes, France's seventh largest city, is the most important commercial and industrial centre in west-central France. A lively place with a mild Atlantic climate and an unbelievable number of cafés and restaurants, it also has fine museums, carefully tended parks and gardens and an ultra-modern tram system.

The Edict of Nantes, a landmark royal charter guaranteeing civil rights and freedom of conscience and worship to France's Protestants, was signed here by Henri IV in 1598. During the Reign of Terror, the guillotine was deemed too slow by the local representative of the Committee of Public Safety. Instead, suspected counter-Revolutionaries were stripped, tied together in pairs and loaded onto barges that were then sunk in the middle of the Loire River.

Orientation

Nantes, historically part of Brittany but today in the Pays de la Loire administrative region, is on the north bank of the Loire River 56km from the Atlantic. The city centre's two main

HIGHLIGHTS

- **Nantes** – stroll by the neoclassical buildings and through the exquisite Jardin des Plantes
- **La Rochelle** – take in the atmosphere around picturesque Vieux Port at different times of the day and night
- **Île de Ré** – lounge around on the fine-sand beaches
- **Poitiers** – try deciphering the medieval carvings on the façade of Église Notre Dame la Grande
- **Bordeaux** – delve into its superb museums and lively nightlife

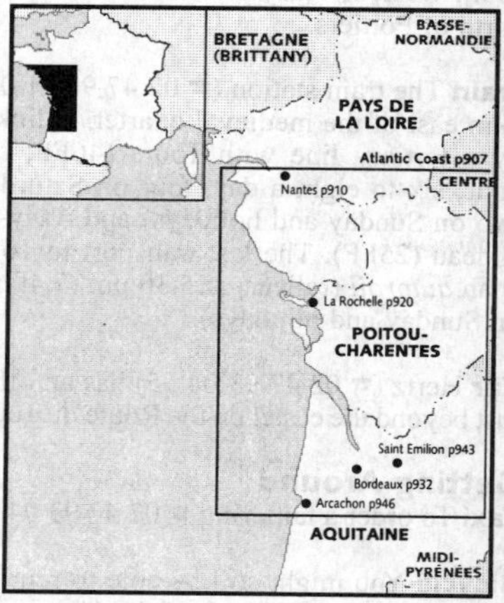

mouclade Rochelaise – mussels in a cream and curry sauce, a speciality of La Rochelle

Bordeaux red wines and Cognac

oysters from Bassin d'Arcachon or the Île de Ré

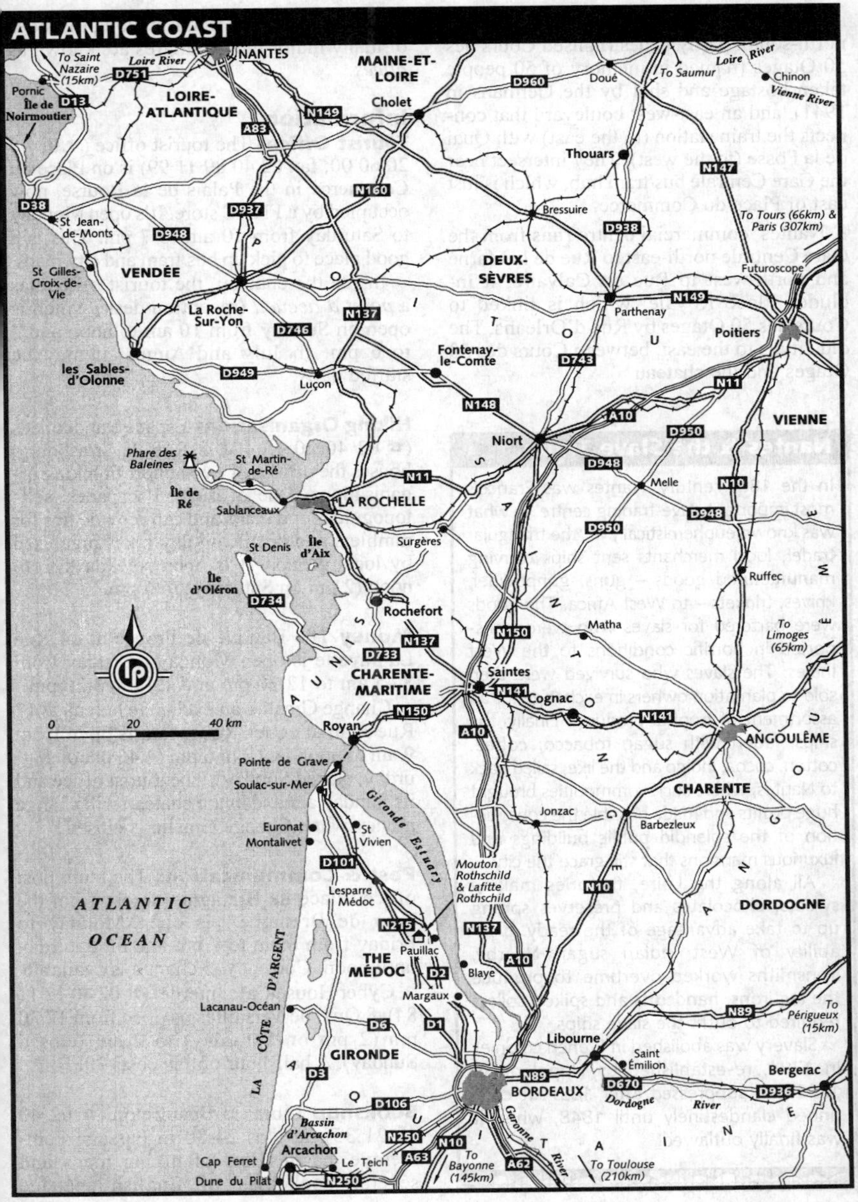
ATLANTIC COAST
NANTES
To Saint Nazaire (15km)
Loire River
D751
Pornic
Île de Noirmoutier
D13
LOIRE-ATLANTIQUE
MAINE-ET-LOIRE
Cholet
N149
A83
D960
Doué
To Saumur
Loire River
Chinon
Vienne River
Thouars
N147
N160
D38
D937
St Jean-de-Monts
D948
Bressuire
D938
To Tours (66km) & Paris (307km)
St Gilles-Croix-de-Vie
VENDÉE
DEUX-SÈVRES
Futuroscope
La Roche-Sur-Yon
N137
N149
Parthenay
Poitiers
D746
les Sables-d'Olonne
D949
Luçon
Fontenay-le-Comte
D743
N11
N148
A10
VIENNE
Niort
D950
Phare des Baleines
St Martin-de-Ré
D948
Melle
N11
Île de Ré
Sablanceaux
LA ROCHELLE
N10
D948
D950
Surgères
Île d'Aix
St Denis
Ruffec
Île d'Oléron
D734
Rochefort
Matha
To Limoges (65km)
N150
N137
D733
CHARENTE-MARITIME
Saintes
N141
Cognac
0
20
40 km
N150
Royan
N141
A10
ANGOULÊME
Pointe de Grave
Soulac-sur-Mer
CHARENTE
Euronat
Montalivet
St Vivien
Gironde Estuary
Jonzac
Barbezieux
D101
Mouton Rothschild & Lafitte Rothschild
Lesparre Médoc
N10
DORDOGNE
ATLANTIC OCEAN
N215
Pauillac
N137
THE MÉDOC
D2
Blaye
A10
Margaux
Lacanau-Océan
CÔTE D'ARGENT
D6
D1
N89
To Périgueux (15km)
GIRONDE
Libourne
Saint Émilion
Bergerac
D3
N89
D670
D936
BORDEAUX
Dordogne
River
D106
Bassin d'Arcachon
Garonne River
N250
N10
Arcachon
A63
To Bayonne (145km)
A62
To Toulouse (210km)
Cap Ferret
Le Teich
Dune du Pilat
N250
LA
POITOU
SAINTONGE
AUNIS
AQUITAINE
ANGOUMOIS
LIMOUSIN

arteries, both served by tram lines, are the north-south, partly pedestrianised Cours des 50 Otages (named in memory of 50 people taken hostage and shot by the Germans in 1941), and an east-west boulevard that connects the train station (to the east) with Quai de la Fosse (to the west). They intersect near the Gare Centrale bus/tram hub, which is just east of Place du Commerce.

Nantes' commercial centre runs from the Gare Centrale north-east to Rue de la Marne and north-west to Rue du Calvaire; it includes Place Royale, which is linked to Cours des 50 Otages by Rue d'Orléans. The old city is to the east, between Cours des 50 Otages and the chateau.

Nantes & the Slave Trade

In the 18th century, Nantes was France's most important slave-trading centre. In what was known euphemistically as 'the triangular trade', local merchants sent ships carrying manufactured goods – guns, gunpowder, knives, trinkets – to West Africa. The goods were bartered for slaves who were transported in horrific conditions to the West Indies. The slaves who survived were then sold to plantation owners in exchange for an assortment of tropical products. Finally, the ships, laden with sugar, tobacco, coffee, cotton, cocoa, indigo and the like, sailed back to Nantes, where such commodities brought huge profits and made possible the construction of the splendid public buildings and luxurious mansions that still grace the city.

All along the Loire, factories making sweets, chocolates and preserves sprang up to take advantage of the ready availability of West Indian sugar. Nearby, ironsmiths worked overtime to produce the leg irons, handcuffs and spiked collars required to outfit the slave ships.

Slavery was abolished in French colonies in 1794, re-established by Napoleon in 1802 and suppressed after 1827. It continued clandestinely until 1848, when it was finally outlawed.

The small streets that run along the sides of many major thoroughfares are known as *allées*.

Information

Tourist Offices The tourist office (☎ 02 40 20 60 00; fax 02 40 89 11 99) is on Place du Commerce in the Palais de la Bourse, now occupied by a FNAC store. It's open Monday to Saturday from 10 am to 7 pm. This is a good place to pick up bus/tram and city maps.

Inside the chateau, the tourist office has a *point d'accueil* (reception desk) which is open on Sunday from 10 am to noon and 2 to 6 pm. In July and August it may be staffed daily.

Hiking Organisations Espace Randonnées (☎ 02 40 20 15 10), 2 Rue de Strasbourg, houses the offices of two nonprofit hiking organisations. One of them, Escapades, sells topoguides and maps and can provide tips for ramblers and details on day hikes organised by local groups. It is open weekdays from noon (2 pm on Saturday) to 6 pm.

Money The Banque de France at 14 Rue La Fayette is open Monday to Friday from 8.45 am to 12.30 pm and 1.45 to 3.30 pm.

Change Graslin, an exchange bureau at 17 Rue Jean-Jacques Rousseau, is open from 9 am to noon and 2 to 6 pm (4.45 pm on Saturday; closed Sunday). The tourist office and its Sunday annexe in the chateau will change money when Change Graslin is closed.

Post & Communications The main post office, Place de Bretagne (across from the Tour de Bretagne), is open Monday to Friday from 8 am to 7 pm and on Saturday until noon. Currency exchange is available.

Cyber House Café Internet (☎ 02 40 12 11 84), 8 Quai de Versailles, is open from 12.30 pm (2 pm on Saturday) to 2 am (closed Sunday). A half-hour online costs 30FF.

Bookshop Librairie Beaufreton (☎ 02 40 48 21 35), at Nos 24-30 in Passage Pommeraye, carries lots of hiking maps and several bookcases of English-language novels. It's open from 10 am to 7 pm (closed Monday morning, Sunday and, in July and August, on Monday afternoon).

Laundry The laundrettes at 8 Allée des Tanneurs (along Cours des 50 Otages) and 3 Allée Duguay Trouin (along Cours Franklin Roosevelt) are open daily from 7 am to 8.30 pm. The full-service Laverie du Bouffay at 3 Rue du Bouffay is open Monday to Saturday from 8.45 am to 7 pm. It costs about the same as a self-service place.

Medical Services The 24 hour Service d'Urgence (emergency room; ☎ 02 40 08 38 95) of the vast CHR de Nantes is along the river on Quai Moncousu.

Emergency The Police Nationale's Hôtel de Police (☎ 02 40 37 21 21; tram stop Motte Rouge) at Place Waldeck Rousseau (1km north-east of the Monument des 50 Otages) is staffed 24 hours a day; look for the sign reading *Entrée du Public*.

Château des Ducs de Bretagne

The impressive Chateau of the Dukes of Brittany (☎ 02 40 41 56 56), surrounded by a moat, was built by François II, duke of Brittany, beginning in 1466. From the outside it looks like your standard medieval castle, with high walls and crenellated towers, but the parts facing the inner courtyard are in the style of a Renaissance pleasure palace. Entry to the courtyard is free, as is walking along part of the ramparts. Sections of the complex will be under renovation until 2008. The building opposite the entrance arch usually houses temporary exhibitions.

Cathédrale Saint Pierre et Saint Paul

This Flamboyant Gothic cathedral at Place Saint Pierre was built over a period of four and a half centuries. The west façade and the towers are from the latter half of the 15th century; the nave is from the 16th century; and the transept and choir were begun in the mid-17th century. The pristine interior was completely restored after a devastating fire in 1972.

The **tomb of François II** (ruled 1458-88), duke of Brittany, and his second wife, Marguerite de Foix, is considered a masterpiece of Renaissance art. The statue facing the nave, which represents **Prudence**, has a female body and face on one side and a bearded male face on the other. Entry to the 11th century **crypt** was not allowed at the time of writing. The cathedral is open from 8.45 am to nightfall or 7 pm, whichever comes first.

Jardin des Plantes

Nantes' Jardin des Plantes, across Blvd de Stalingrad from the train station, is one of the most exquisite botanic gardens in France. Founded in the early 19th century, it has lawns like putting greens, beautiful flower beds, duck ponds, fountains and even a few California redwoods (sequoias). There are **hothouses** and a **children's playground** at the northern end.

Île Feydeau

The channels of the Loire that once surrounded Feydeau Island (the neighbourhood south of the Gare Centrale) were filled in after WWII, but the area's 18th century mansions, built by rich merchants from the ill-gotten profits of the slave trade, are still standing. Some of them are adorned with stone carvings of the heads of African slaves.

Passage Pommeray, a delightful shopping arcade opened in 1843 and hardly changed since, is two blocks north-west of Île Feydeau.

Museums

The renowned **Musée des Beaux-Arts** (Fine Arts Museum; ☎ 02 40 41 65 65), 10 Rue Georges Clemenceau, constructed in the 1890s, displays mainly paintings, including three works by Georges de La Tour. It is open from 10 am (11 am on Sunday) to 6 pm (9 pm on Friday); closed Tuesday and holidays. Some of the exhibits are closed from 11.45 am to 2 pm. Entry costs 20FF (10FF for children, students and people over 65) except on Sunday, when it's free.

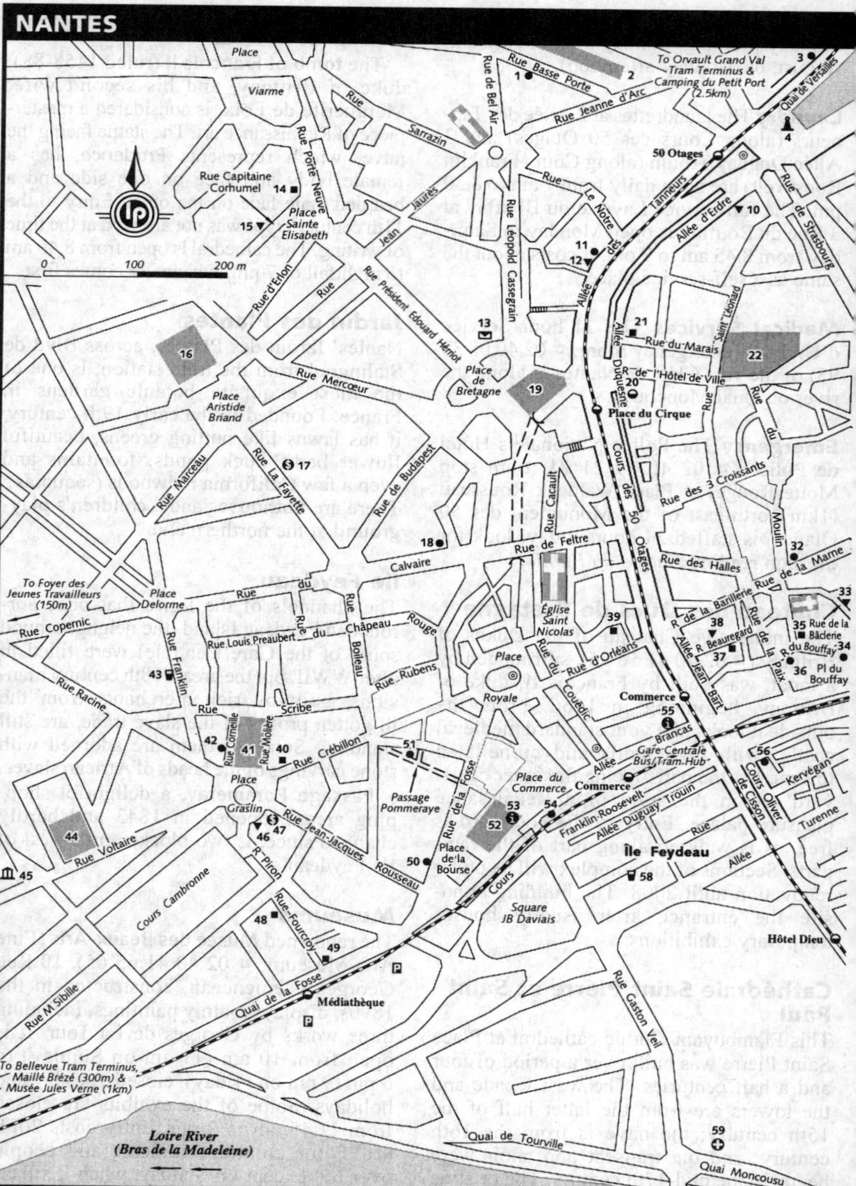
NANTES
Place Viarme
Rue Sarrazin
Rue Porte Neuve
Rue Capitaine Corhumel
Place Sainte Elisabeth
Rue de Bel Air
Rue Basse Porte
Rue Jeanne d'Arc
To Orvault Grand Val Tram Terminus & Camping du Petit Port (2.5km)
Quai de Versailles
50 Otages
Rue Jean Jaurès
Rue Léopold Cassegrain
Rue Le Nôtre
Allée des Tanneurs
Allée d'Erdre
Rue de Strasbourg
Rue Saint Léonard
0
100
200 m
Rue d'Erlon
Rue Président Edouard Herriot
Rue du Marais
R de l'Hôtel de Ville
Allée Duquesne
Place de Bretagne
Place du Cirque
Rue Mercœur
Place Aristide Briand
Rue Marceau
Rue La Fayette
Rue de Budapest
Rue Cacault
Cours des 50 Otages
Rue des 3 Croissants
Rue du Moulin
Rue de Feltre
Rue des Halles
Rue de la Marne
Rue du Calvaire
To Foyer des Jeunes Travailleurs (150m)
Place Delorme
Rue Copernic
Rue Franklin
Rue du Chapeau Rouge
Rue Louis Preaubert
Rue Boileau
Église Saint Nicolas
R de la Barillerie
R Beauregard
Allée Jean Bart
Rue de la Paix
Rue de la Bâclerie
R du Bouffay
Pl du Bouffay
Rue Racine
Rue Rubens
Rue Scribe
Rue Corneille
Rue Molière
Place Royale
Rue d'Orléans
Rue du Couëdic
Commerce
Rue Crébillon
Passage Pommeraye
Place Graslin
Rue de la Fosse
Allée Brancas
Gare Centrale Bus/Tram Hub
Place du Commerce
Cours Olivier de Clisson
Rue Kervégan
Rue Voltaire
Rue Jean-Jacques Rousseau
R Piron
Place de la Bourse
Cours Franklin-Roosevelt
Allée Duguay Trouin
Rue Turenne
Île Feydeau
Allée
Cours Cambronne
Rue Fourcroy
Square JB Daviais
Hôtel Dieu
Rue M Sibille
Quai de la Fosse
Médiathèque
Rue Gaston Veil
To Bellevue Tram Terminus, Maillé Brézé (300m) & Musée Jules Verne (1km)
Quai de Tourville
Quai Moncousu
Loire River (Bras de la Madeleine)

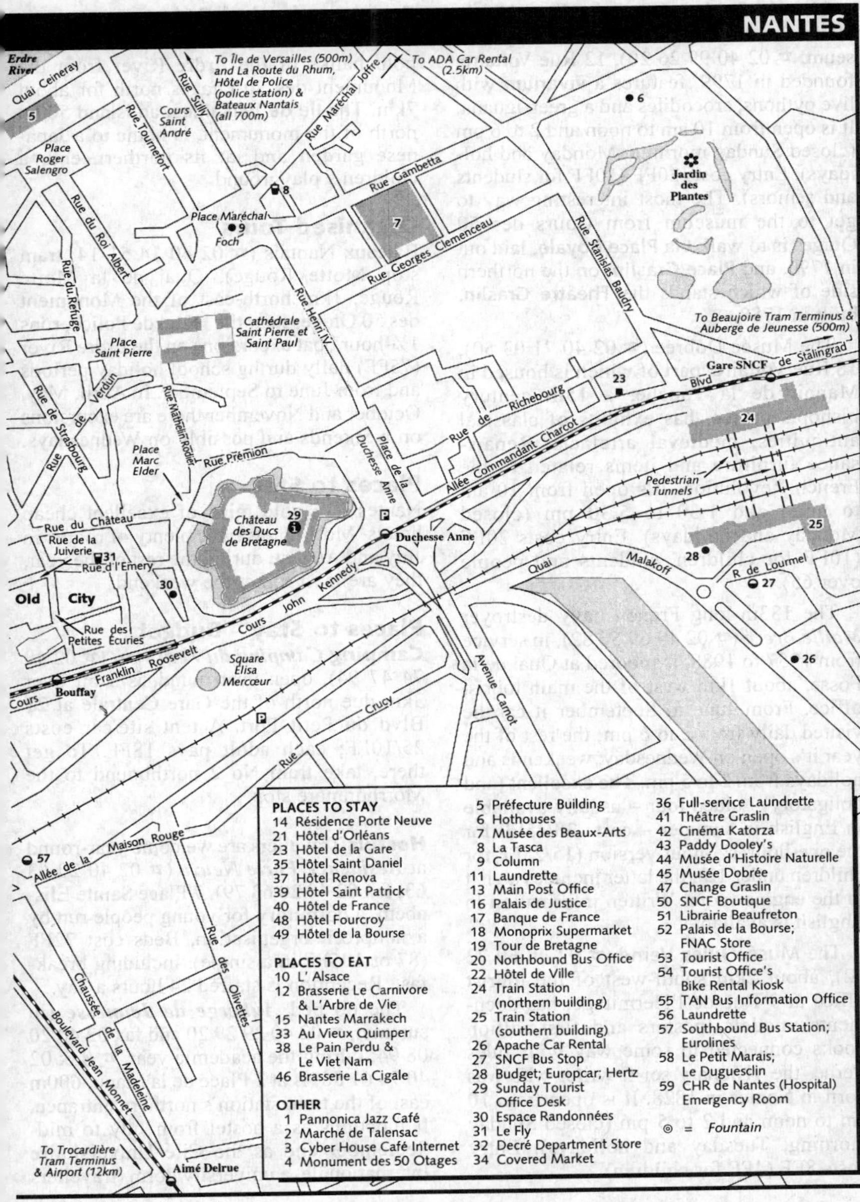
NANTES
Erdre River
Quai Ceineray
To Île de Versailles (500m) and La Route du Rhum, Hôtel de Police (police station) & Bateaux Nantais (all 700m)
To ADA Car Rental (2.5km)
Rue Sully
Rue Maréchal Joffre
Cours Saint André
Place Roger Salengro
Rue Tournefort
Rue Gambetta
Jardin des Plantes
Place Maréchal Foch
Rue du Roi Albert
Rue Georges Clemenceau
Rue Stanislas Baudry
Rue du Refuge
Rue Henri IV
Cathédrale Saint Pierre et Saint Paul
Place Saint Pierre
To Beaujoire Tram Terminus & Auberge de Jeunesse (500m)
Gare SNCF
Blvd de Stalingrad
Rue de Verdun
Rue de Strasbourg
Rue Mathelin Rodier
Rue de Richebourg
Allée Commandant Charcot
Place Marc Elder
Rue Prémion
Duchesse Anne
Place de la Duchesse Anne
Pedestrian Tunnels
Rue du Château
Château des Ducs de Bretagne
Rue de la Juiverie
Rue d'l'Emery
Quai Malakoff
R de Lourmel
Old City
Cours John Kennedy
Rue des Petites Écuries
Square Élisa Mercœur
Cours Franklin Roosevelt
Bouffay
Rue Crucy
Avenue Carnot
Allée de la Maison Rouge
Rue des Olivettes
Chaussée de la Madeleine
Boulevard Jean Monnet
To Trocardière Tram Terminus & Airport (12km)
Aimé Delrue
PLACES TO STAY
14 Résidence Porte Neuve
21 Hôtel d'Orléans
23 Hôtel de la Gare
35 Hôtel Saint Daniel
37 Hôtel Renova
39 Hôtel Saint Patrick
40 Hôtel de France
48 Hôtel Fourcroy
49 Hôtel de la Bourse
PLACES TO EAT
10 L' Alsace
12 Brasserie Le Carnivore & L'Arbre de Vie
15 Nantes Marrakech
33 Au Vieux Quimper
38 Le Pain Perdu & Le Viet Nam
46 Brasserie La Cigale
OTHER
1 Pannonica Jazz Café
2 Marché de Talensac
3 Cyber House Café Internet
4 Monument des 50 Otages
5 Préfecture Building
6 Hothouses
7 Musée des Beaux-Arts
8 La Tasca
9 Column
11 Laundrette
13 Main Post Office
16 Palais de Justice
17 Banque de France
18 Monoprix Supermarket
19 Tour de Bretagne
20 Northbound Bus Office
22 Hôtel de Ville
24 Train Station (northern building)
25 Train Station (southern building)
26 Apache Car Rental
27 SNCF Bus Stop
28 Budget; Europcar; Hertz
29 Sunday Tourist Office Desk
30 Espace Randonnées
31 Le Fly
32 Decré Department Store
34 Covered Market
36 Full-service Laundrette
41 Théâtre Graslin
42 Cinéma Katorza
43 Paddy Dooley's
44 Musée d'Histoire Naturelle
45 Musée Dobrée
47 Change Graslin
50 SNCF Boutique
51 Librairie Beaufreton
52 Palais de la Bourse; FNAC Store
53 Tourist Office
54 Tourist Office's Bike Rental Kiosk
55 TAN Bus Information Office
56 Laundrette
57 Southbound Bus Station; Eurolines
58 Le Petit Marais; Le Duguesclin
59 CHR de Nantes (Hospital) Emergency Room
= Fountain

The old-fashioned but excellent **Musée d'Histoire Naturelle** (Natural History Museum; ☎ 02 40 99 26 20), 12 Rue Voltaire, founded in 1799, features a **vivarium** with live pythons, crocodiles and a green iguana. It is open from 10 am to noon and 2 to 6 pm (closed Sunday morning, Monday and holidays). Entry costs 20FF (10FF for students and seniors). The most interesting way to get to the museum from Cours des 50 Otages is to walk via **Place Royale**, laid out in 1790, and **Place Graslin**, on the northern side of which stands the **Théâtre Graslin**, built in 1788.

The Musée Dobrée (☎ 02 40 71 03 50), 18 Rue Voltaire, part of which is housed in Manoir de la Touche, a 15th century bishop's palace, has exhibits of classical antiquities, medieval artefacts, Renaissance furniture and items related to the French Revolution. It's open from 10 am to noon and 1.30 to 5.30 pm (closed Monday and holidays). Entry costs 20FF (10FF for children, students and people over 65).

The 133m-long French navy destroyer *Maillé Brézé* (☎ 02 40 69 56 82), in service from 1957 to 1988, is moored at Quai de la Fosse, about 1km west of the main tourist office. From June to September it can be visited daily from 2 to 6 pm; the rest of the year it's open on Wednesday, weekends and holidays from 2 to 5 pm. The excellent (and obligatory) guided tour – usually available in English in summer – costs 30/45FF for the one-hour/1½-hour version (15/25FF for children under 12); the latter includes a visit to the engine room. Written information in English is available.

The **Musée Jules Verne** (☎ 02 40 69 72 52), about 2km south-west of the tourist office at 3 Rue de l'Hermitage, has documents, models, posters and first-edition books connected in some way with Jules Verne, the visionary sci-fi writer who was born in Nantes in 1828. It is open from 10 am to noon and 2 to 5 pm (closed Sunday morning, Tuesday and holidays). Entry costs 8FF (4FF for children).

Promenade de l'Erdre

This network of riverside paths follows both banks of the Erdre River from the Monument des 50 Otages north for about 7km. The **Île de Versailles**, an island 500m north of the monument, is home to a Japanese garden and, at its northern end, a children's playground.

Organised Tours

Bateaux Nantais (☎ 02 40 14 51 14; tram stop Motte Rouge), Quai de la Motte Rouge, 1km north-east of the Monument des 50 Otages near the Hôtel de Police, runs 1¾-hour boat excursions on the Erdre River (75FF) daily during school holiday periods and from June to September. In April, May, October and November there are excursions on weekends and possibly on Wednesdays.

Places to Stay

Nantes is a gold mine of excellent cheap hotels. Most hotels have plenty of rooms in July and August; during the rest of the year, they are least full at the weekend.

Places to Stay – Budget

Camping *Camping du Petit Port* (☎ 02 40 74 47 94), open year-round, is a bit over 3km due north of the Gare Centrale at 21 Blvd du Petit Port. A tent site/car costs 25/10FF; each adult pays 18FF. To get there, take tram No 2 northbound to the Morrhonnière stop.

Hostels Travellers are welcome year-round at ***Résidence Porte Neuve*** (☎ 02 40 20 63 63; fax 02 40 20 63 79), 7 Place Sainte Elisabeth, a dormitory for young people run by a nonprofit organisation. Beds cost 72FF (87 or 105FF in a single), including breakfast. Reception is staffed 24 hours a day.

The 66 bed ***Auberge de Jeunesse*** (in summer, ☎ 02 40 29 29 20 and fax 02 40 20 08 94; during the academic year, ☎ /fax 02 40 74 61 86) is at 2 Place de la Manu, 600m east of the train station's northern entrance. It functions as a hostel from July to mid-September and as the Cité Universitaire Internationale, a university dorm (travellers welcome), the rest of the year. A bed in a plain, well lit room costs 74FF; an HI card is mandatory year-round. Kitchen facilities are available. During the school year, reception is open Monday to Friday from 9 am to noon and 1 to 10 pm and on Sunday from 5 to 10 pm (closed Saturday).

Hotels In the old city, the 22 room ***Hôtel Renova*** (☎ 02 40 47 57 03; fax 02 51 82 06 39), 11 Rue Beauregard, has been run by the same family since 1966. Doubles start at 130FF (160FF with shower and toilet). There are no hall showers. Reception is often closed on Sunday from noon to 6 or 7 pm. The ***Hôtel Saint Daniel*** (☎ 02 40 47 41 25; fax 02 51 72 03 99), 4 Rue du Bouffay, has fairly spacious but ordinary doubles for 150FF (with shower) and 170FF (with shower and toilet). Reception is closed on Sunday from noon to 9 pm.

Next to the Médiathèque tram stop, the ***Hôtel de la Bourse*** (☎ 02 40 69 51 55; fax 02 40 71 73 89), a family-run place at 19 Quai de la Fosse is one of the best deals in town. It has tidy doubles starting at 105FF (120FF with shower, 146FF with shower and toilet). Hall showers are 18FF. Reception is closed on Sunday from 1 to 7 pm. Parking is free in the vast lot across the street, except in the first few rows marked *payant*. Up the block, the 19 room ***Hôtel Fourcroy*** (☎ 02 40 44 68 00), 11 Rue Fourcroy, run by the same family since 1978, has pleasant and exceptionally well kept doubles with upholstered doors for 137FF (with shower) and 157FF (with shower and toilet). Reception closes at 9 pm. There is free parking in the courtyard.

Founded by an Irish couple many years ago, the 24 room ***Hôtel Saint Patrick*** (☎ 02 40 48 48 80), 7 Rue Saint Nicolas, has simple, modern doubles from 120FF (140FF with shower, 20FF more with toilet). Reception is on the 3rd floor (no lift). Hall showers are free.

The friendly, 15 room ***Hôtel d'Orléans*** (☎ 02 40 47 69 32), 12 Rue du Marais, has plain but comfortable doubles from 130FF (155FF with shower). Rooms with shower and toilet are 180/220FF for two/four people. Hall showers are free. Reception is closed on Sunday from noon to 7 pm.

Places to Stay – Mid-Range

There are a number of two and three-star hotels in the charmless area right across from the train station's northern entrance. One of the cheapest is the 31 room ***Hôtel de la Gare*** (☎ 02 40 74 37 25; fax 02 40 93 33 71), 5 Allée Commandant Charcot, which has small doubles/quads with shower and toilet from 190/280FF. The three doubles with washbasin go for 155FF; the hall shower is free.

The ***Hôtel de France*** (☎ 02 40 73 57 91; fax 02 40 69 75 75), 24 Rue Crébillon, is a venerable, three star place that occupies a converted 18th century mansion in Nantes' commercial heart. Bath-equipped singles/doubles, which boast high ceilings, start at 345/369FF. The rooms priced at 450/480FF are huge.

Places to Eat

Nantes has an exceptionally varied selection of ethnic restaurants. The least expensive way to dine out is to take advantage of the many weekday lunch *menus* that go for around 50FF.

In the old city, two blocks west of the chateau in the lively area around Rue de la Juiverie, Rue des Petites Écuries and Rue de la Bâclerie, there are dozens of cafés, bars and small restaurants, many of them French regional or ethnic. Offerings include pizza, tapas, couscous, crêpes and Asian cuisines.

Restaurants – French There are a number of ***cafés*** and ***brasseries*** with inexpensive steak and chips in and around Place du Commerce.

Le Pain Perdu (☎ 02 40 47 74 21), 12 Rue Beauregard, has tasty, family-style French cuisine and specialities from the Landes region, including foie gras, *confit de canard* and *magret de canard*. The *menus* cost 60FF (lunch, except weekends and holidays), 89 and 119FF. It is open from noon to 1.45 pm and 7 to 10.30 pm (11 pm on Saturday; closed on Saturday for lunch and on Monday).

Some of Nantes' best savoury and sweet crêpes (10 to 44FF) are on offer at ***Au Vieux Quimper*** (☎ 02 40 35 63 99), 10 Rue de la Bâclerie, open daily from 11.45 am to 2.30 pm and 6.30 to 11 pm (11.30 pm on Friday and Saturday).

The aptly named ***Brasserie Le Carnivore*** (☎ 02 40 47 87 00), a huge, Louisiana/Old West-style place at 7 Allée des Tanneurs, serves all sorts of meats, including bison, ostrich and kangaroo, as well as smoked salmon and paella. The *menus* cost 55FF (lunch, Monday to Saturday), 88, 138 and 182FF. It is open daily from noon to midnight, with a slightly reduced selection from 3 to 6 pm.

L'Alsace (☎ 02 40 12 19 12), 6 Allée d'Erdre, has *choucroute* for 70FF; the French and Alsatian *menus* cost 130 and 160FF. It is closed on Saturday for lunch, Sunday and Monday night.

The exquisite ***Brasserie La Cigale*** (☎ 02 51 84 94 94), 4 Place Graslin, is grandly decorated with 1890s tilework and painted ceilings that mix the baroque with Art Nouveau. Breakfast is served daily from 7.30 to 11 or 11.30 am, lunch from 11.45 am to 2.30 pm, and dinner from 6.45 pm to 12.30 am; many dishes are available all afternoon. The *menus* cost 75 and 135FF at lunch, and 100 and 150FF at dinner.

Restaurants – Vegetarian ***L'Arbre de Vie*** (☎ 02 40 08 06 10), 8 Allée des Tanneurs, offers a vegetarian, organic alternative to Le Carnivore next door. The lunch *menus* cost 64, 74 and 84FF. Lunch (noon to 1.45 pm) is served Tuesday to Saturday; dinner (7.30 to 10 pm) is only available on Thursday, Friday and Saturday.

Restaurants – Other The ***Nantes Marrakech*** (☎ 02 40 48 08 08), 14 Rue Capitaine Corhumel, serves Moroccan *tajines* and couscous (52 to 89FF) daily, except Sunday, from 11 am to 3.30 pm and 6.30 pm to 1 am.

Le Viet Nam (☎ 02 40 20 06 26), 14 Rue Beauregard, has Vietnamese *menus* for 38FF (lunch, weekdays), 60FF (not available on Friday night) and 85FF. It is closed on Sunday and for lunch on holidays.

At ***La Tasca*** (☎ 02 40 74 23 40), 91 Rue Maréchal Joffre, Latin American cuisine is served from 11 am to 3 pm (except Sunday and Monday) and from 7.30 pm to 2 or 3 am (except Monday night).

Self-Catering The small ***covered market*** at Place du Bouffay and the huge ***Marché de Talensac*** on Rue Talensac are open until about 1 pm (closed Monday).

The ***Monoprix*** supermarket at 2 Rue du Calvaire is open Monday to Saturday from 9 am to 9 pm. In the old city area, the huge ***Decré*** department store, across the street from 5 Rue du Moulin, has a basement food section which is open Monday to Saturday from 9 am to 7 pm.

Entertainment

Listings *Nantes Poche* (6.50FF), issued each Wednesday and available at *tabacs* (tobacconists) and newsagents, has details on films, live music etc. The tourist office has a free monthly, *Le Mois Nantais*, with day-by-day details of cultural events and exhibitions. Tickets for many cultural events are available either at the tourist office or across the hall at the ***FNAC billeterie*** (ticket counter; ☎ 02 51 724 723; open Monday to Saturday from 10 am to 8 pm).

Cinema *Cinéma Katorza* (☎ 08 36 68 06 66 for an answering machine), 3 Rue Corneille (facing Théâtre Graslin), screens nondubbed films. Schedules appear in *Nantes Poche*.

Clubs & Bars ***Pannonica Jazz Café*** (☎ 02 40 48 74 74), down the stairway at 9 Rue Basse Porte, is open when there are live performances, generally on Thursday and Friday at 9 pm; entry costs 40 to 80FF, depending on the event. It is closed in July and August.

La Route du Rhum (☎ 02 40 74 48 57), on a two storey houseboat a bit under 1km north-east of the Monument des 50 Otages (on the east shore of the Erdre River across from the northern tip of the Île de Versailles), is a bar with live music (blues, rock, reggae etc) on Thursday, Friday and Saturday nights at 11.30 pm. It is open daily from 8 pm to 4 am. There's no cover charge except during concerts (30FF).

Up the hill from Théâtre Graslin, there are lots of little pubs and cafés along Rue Scribe. ***Paddy Dooley's*** (☎ 02 40 48 29 00), a spacious Irish-owned pub nearby at 9 Rue Franklin, has live music two to four times a month. Guinness goes for 30FF a pint. A favourite with Anglophone students, it is open daily until 2 am; happy hour is from 7.30 to 9 pm.

In the old city, ***Le Fly*** (☎ 02 40 20 58 89), 8 Rue de l'Emery, is a sleek bar which tries to be both trendy and mellow. It is open from 8 pm to 4 am (closed Sunday night). There's a wooden deck out back.

La Tasca (see Places to Eat), popular with students, is a tapas bar with a small area for dancing the salsa and the merengue. Live Latin American music is on offer twice a month (every other Thursday) starting at 9 or 10 pm. Sangria costs 15FF. This place is open daily, except Monday, from 7.30 pm to 4 am.

Gay & Lesbian Venues *Le Guide Ouest*, issued twice a year, lists gay establishments in Brittany and the Nantes area.

Le Petit Marais (☎ 02 40 20 15 25), a friendly, mainly gay bar at 15 Rue Kervégan, has beer from 14FF. It is open daily from 5 pm to 2 am. ***Le Deguesclin*** (☎ 02 40 89 14 89), next door at No 13, is also mainly gay.

Getting There & Away

Air Nantes-Atlantique airport (☎ 02 40 84 80 00) is about 12km south-east of the centre of town.

Bus The southbound bus station (☎ 02 40 47 62 70), across from 13 Allée de la Maison Rouge, is used by CTA buses serving areas of the Loire-Atlantique department that are south of the Loire River, including the seaside towns of Pornic (60FF; 1¼ hours) and Saint Brévin-les-Pins (60FF; 1½ hours). The information office is open from 6.30 am to 7.30 pm (1.30 pm on Saturday; closed Sunday). The northbound bus office (☎ 02 40 20 46 99), 1 Allée Duquesne (on Cours des 50 Otages), run by Cariane Atlantique, handles buses to destinations north of the Loire.

SNCF buses to Pornic, Saint Gilles-Croix-de-Vie and Poitiers (141FF; 3¼ hours; one a day at 5.30 pm) stop across the street from the train station's southern entrance. For details, ask in the station.

The Eurolines (☎ 02 51 72 02 03) office in the southbound bus station is open until 6.30 pm (5.30 pm on Saturday; closed from noon to 1.30 or 2 pm and on Sunday).

Train The train station (☎ 08 36 35 35 35) has two entrances: the Accès Nord at 27 Blvd de Stalingrad, across the street from the wonderful Jardin des Plantes; and the Accès Sud, across the tracks on Rue de Lourmel. The information offices are open from 9 am to 7 pm (closed Sunday and holidays).

Tickets and information are also available at the SNCF Boutique, near the tourist office at 12 Place de la Bourse. It is open from 9 am to 7 pm (closed on Sunday, holidays and Monday morning).

Nantes is well connected to most of the country. The trip to/from Paris' Gare Montparnasse (284 to 345FF; 10 to 17 a day) takes two to 2½ hours by TGV. Other destinations served by direct trains include Bordeaux (219FF; four hours; four or five a day), La Rochelle (126FF; two hours; five a day), Lyon (384 to 457FF and 4½ hours by TGV; 330FF and at least 6½ hours by non-TGV), Quimper (148FF; 2¾ to four hours; two or three a day) and Tours (137FF; 1½ to two hours; four to eight a day).

Car Budget, Europcar and Hertz have offices right outside the train station's southern entrance. Apache (☎ 02 51 25 26 27), nearby at 45 Quai Malakoff, has cars from 170FF a day, including 100km and a deductible/excess of 3500FF (closed Saturday afternoon and Sunday).

Getting Around

To/From the Airport A public bus known as TAN-Air links the airport with the Gare Centrale bus/tram hub and the train station's southern entrance (38FF; 20 minutes; 15 on weekdays, 10 on Saturday, four on Sunday evening).

Bus & Tram Nantes' urban mass transit system is run by TAN (☎ 08 01 44 44 44). The city's modern tram system (an earlier tram network was phased out in 1958) has two lines that intersect at the Gare Centrale (Commerce), the city centre's main bus/tram transfer point.

Most bus lines run until 8 or 9 pm. From 9.15 pm to 12.15 am, TAN runs an hourly Service de Nuit, which includes the two tram lines and seven bus lines; all pass by the Gare Centrale.

Bus/tram tickets, sold individually (8FF) by bus (but not tram) drivers and in carnets of five/ten (33/58FF), are valid for one hour after being time-stamped for travel in any direction. A *ticket journalier*, good all day long, costs 21FF; time-stamp it only the first time you use it. Tickets and carnets are sold at tram stop ticket machines and tabacs.

TAN's information and ticket office at 2 Allée Brancas (across the street from the Gare Centrale hub) is open Monday to Saturday from 7.15 am to 7 pm.

Taxi At the train station, taxis are easiest to catch outside the southern entrance. To order a taxi, call ☎ 02 40 69 22 22.

Bicycle From mid-June to mid-September, the tourist office rents out bikes from a kiosk across the street from its office (next to the tram tracks). It can also supply you with a free map of bicycle paths.

POITIERS

• pop 107,600 ✉ 86000 alt 116m

Poitiers, the former capital of Poitou, is not a particularly captivating city (it's very constricted and fits very tightly into its hilltop site), but it is home to some of France's most remarkable Romanesque churches.

Orientation

The train station is about 600m west – and down the slope – from the partly pedestrianised old city and commercial centre, which begins just north of Poitiers' main square, Place du Maréchal Leclerc, and stretches north-east to Église Notre Dame la Grande. Rue Carnot leads south from Place du Maréchal Leclerc.

Information

The tourist office (☎ 05 49 41 21 24; fax 05 49 88 65 84; www.pcl.fr/poitiers), 150m north of Place du Maréchal Leclerc at 8 Rue des Grandes Écoles, is open from 9 am to noon and 1.30 (2 pm on Saturday) to 6 pm (closed on Sunday and certain holidays). From mid-June to late September it's open from 9 am to 7 pm (9.45 am to 6.45 pm on Saturday, 9.45 am to 1 pm and 2.45 to 6 pm on Sunday). City maps cost 3FF.

The Banque de France, a block from the tourist office at 1 Rue Henri Oudin, is open weekdays from 9 am to 12.15 pm and 1.45 to 3.30 pm. Commercial banks can be found around Place du Maréchal Leclerc.

Churches

The superb **Église Notre Dame la Grande** is at Place Charles de Gaulle in the pedestrianised old city, 300m north-east of the tourist office. The 57m-long Romanesque church, which has no transept arms, dates from the 11th and 12th centuries – except for three of the five choir chapels (added in the 15th century) and all six chapels along the north wall of the nave (added in the 16th century). The atrociously painted decoration in the nave is from the mid-19th century; the only original frescoes are the faint 12th or 13th century works that adorn the U-shaped dome above the choir. The modern organ, erected in 1996, is occasionally used for concerts. The celebrated **west façade** is decorated with three layers of stone carvings based on the Old and New Testaments (eg Adam and Eve, the Serpent and the Tree of Knowledge, on the left; and the Infant Jesus getting a bath in what looks like a baptismal font, on the right). The Romanesque belfry above the choir has a steep, pinecone-like roof. The church can be visited daily from 8 am to 7 pm.

At the bottom of Rue de la Cathédrale (500m east of Église Notre Dame la Grande), the vast, Angevin (or Plantagenet) Gothic-style **Cathédrale Saint Pierre** – so unlike its Gothic cousins to the north – was built from 1162 to 1271 and consecrated in 1379. The west façade and the towers date from the 14th and 15th centuries. The stained-glass window at the far end of the choir, which illustrates the Crucifixion and the Ascension, is among the oldest in France. The choir stalls are from the mid-13th century; the magnificent, angel-topped organ dates from 1791. The church can be visited from 8 am to 7.30 pm (6 pm in winter).

The 11th and 12th century **Église Saint Hilaire**, across the street from 20 Rue Saint Hilaire (600m south-west of Place du Maréchal Leclerc), was named after the city's first known bishop, who lived in the 4th century and over whose tomb it was built. The transept, the choir (decorated with late 11th century frescoes) and the five apsidal chapels are 3m higher than the nave (mostly rebuilt in the 19th century), which is covered by three cupolas and has three rows of columns on each side. Earlier churches on this site were burned by the Arab general 'Abd ar-Rahmãn shortly before his defeat by the cavalry of Charles Martel (not far from here in the famed Battle of Poitiers, 732 AD) and again during the Norman invasions of the 9th century. The church is open daily until 7.15 pm (7 pm on Sunday).

Museums

Constructed in the 4th and 6th centuries on the foundations of Roman buildings destroyed during the 'barbarian invasions' (276 AD), **Baptistère Saint Jean**, Rue Jean Jaurès, one block south of the cathedral and 600m east of the tourist office, is one of the oldest Christian structures in France. Rebuilt in the 10th century and used as a parish church, it is now a museum of Merovingian (5th to 7th century) sarcophagi. The octagonal hole under the 11th and 12th century frescoes was used for total-immersion baptisms, practised by the Church until the 7th century. It's open from 10.30 am to 12.30 pm and 3 (2.30 pm in July and August) to 6 pm. From November to March it's open daily, except Tuesday, from 2.30 to 4.30 pm. Entry costs 4FF.

Across the lawn, the worthwhile **Musée Sainte Croix** (☎ 05 49 41 07 53), 3 Rue Jean Jaurès, built atop Gallo-Roman walls that were excavated and left *in situ*, has exhibits on the history of Poitou from prehistoric times through the Roman period and the Middle Ages to the 19th century. The collection of 19th and 20th century painting and sculpture includes three works by Camille Claudel. It is open daily from 1 pm (10 am on Tuesday) to 5 pm (from 2 to 6 pm on weekends). From June to September it open daily from 10 am to noon and 1 to 6 pm (closed on Monday morning). Tickets cost 15FF (free for under 18s) and also afford access to the **Musée Rupert de Chièvre**, 9 Rue Victor Hugo, which houses a collection of bric-a-brac assembled in the late 19th century, and the **Hypogée des Dunes**, a Merovingian funerary chapel at 101 Rue du Père de la Croix (farther out along Rue Jean Jaurès from the city centre).

Places to Stay

In the unattractive area around the train station, the best budget choice is the family-run, 10 room ***Hôtel de Paris*** (☎ 05 49 58 39 37) at 123 Blvd du Grand Cerf, whose doubles start at 145FF (190FF with shower). Reception is closed on Monday. The two star, 39 room ***Hôtel Continental*** (☎ 05 49 37 93 93; fax 05 49 53 01 16), across the street from the train station at 2 Blvd Solférino, has good singles/doubles/triples for 255/295/330FF.

Half a block north of Place du Maréchal Leclerc (through the arch next to the Théatre), the two star, 24 room ***Hôtel du Plat d'Étain*** (☎ 05 49 41 04 80; fax 05 49 52 25 84), 7-9 Rue du Plat d'Étain, has pleasant doubles from 145FF (255FF with shower and toilet). Hall showers are free. Private parking is 15FF a day.

At the southern tip of the city centre, the family-run ***Hôtel Jules Ferry*** (☎ 05 49 37 80 14; fax 05 49 53 15 02), 27 Rue Jules Ferry, is about 1km south of the train station (go up Blvd du Pont Achard and then, if on foot, up the ramp known as Rue Jean Brunet) and the same distance south-west of Place du Maréchal Leclerc (by car take Rue Carnot to the very end and turn right twice). It has clean, simply furnished doubles from 140FF (180FF with shower, 210FF with shower and toilet). Reception is closed on Sunday from about 1 to 7.30 pm.

Places to Eat

Restaurants The most promising area for dining or sipping a beer is south of Place du Maréchal Leclerc, especially along Rue Carnot. ***Restaurant Le Saint Nicolas*** (☎ 05 49 41 44 48), down the alleyway at 7 Rue Carnot, serves traditional French cuisine. It is closed on Wednesday and for lunch on Sunday and holidays. *Menus* cost 89 and 119FF. A bit farther south, ***Le Poitevin*** (☎ 05 49 88 35 04), 76 Rue Carnot, serves regional cuisine daily, except Sunday. *Menus* cost 95 to 230FF.

Self-Catering The ***Marché Notre Dame*** next to Église Notre Dame la Grande at Place Charles de Gaulle is open Tuesday to Saturday from 7 am to 1 pm (2 pm on Saturday). About 200m to the south, the ***Monoprix*** across from 29 Rue du Marché Notre Dame (behind the Palais de Justice) is open from 9 am to 8.30 pm (7.30 pm on Saturday; closed Sunday).

Getting There & Away

The train station, Blvd du Grand Cerf, has direct links to Bordeaux (172FF), La Rochelle (109FF), Tours (83FF) and many other cities. TGV tickets from Paris' Gare Montparnasse cost 254 to 316FF; non-TGVs from the capital's Gare d'Austerlitz (two a day) cost 201FF. The SNCF bus to Nantes (141FF; 3¼ hours) leaves daily at 7.45 am.

AROUND POITIERS

Futuroscope

Futuroscope (☎ 05 49 49 30 80), a bit over 10km north of Poitiers in Jaunay-Clan, is a unique cinema theme park in which 20 innovative and visually striking pavilions (more are being added every year) display the latest technologies for making on-screen action seem more immediate. Attractions include the **Tapis Magique** (Magic Carpet), which shows action underfoot – from a bird's-eye perspective – as well as in front of you. At **Le Solido**, the 180° images appear in 3-D thanks to special liquid-crystal glasses. **Le 360°** is a round projection hall in which nine screens give you a 360° view from the centre of the action, eg from among the Tour de France cyclists as they speed through the Pyrenees. At the **Cinéma Dynamique**, the seats shake and tilt to create a virtual-reality roller coaster ride that lasts just three minutes but seems like an eternity.

The specially made films – mostly documentaries, many of them with nature themes – are in French, but an infrared headset (available free at the Office du Tourisme) lets you pick up a parallel soundtrack in English, German or Spanish.

Futuroscope is open daily from 9 am to 6 pm. On Saturday, Sunday and holidays from March to mid-November and daily in July and August, closing time is after the laser and fireworks show, ie sometime between 10.30 pm and midnight. Entry costs 140 to 185FF, depending on the season (130 to 175FF for students, 110 to 150FF for children aged five to 16). You can exit and re-enter so long as you get your hand stamped. When the park is open at night, the fee is 100FF (70FF for children) if you arrive after 6 pm.

Tickets are also sold at the Futuroscope office (☎ 05 49 37 04 18) inside the Poitiers train station. It is open daily from 8.45 am to 6.30 pm (7.30 pm in summer).

Place to Eat There's an ***Auchan*** hypermarket a few hundred metres from the park's main entrance.

Getting There & Away If you're driving from Poitiers, take the A10 northbound.

Local bus Nos 16 and 17 (8FF one way) link Poitiers' train station and Place du Maréchal Leclerc with Futuroscope; one or the other runs once or twice an hour, except Sunday and holidays, until 7.30 or 8 pm.

Futuroscope's *taxis-navettes* (shuttle taxi; 45FF return per person) link the Poitiers train station with the park every 30 to 60 minutes from 8.30 am to 6 pm (and at 6.45 pm when the park is open at night).

LA ROCHELLE

• pop 100,000 ✉ 17000

The lively and very attractive port city of La Rochelle, midway down France's Atlantic seaboard, gets lots of tourists, especially in July and August, but most of them are of the domestic, middle-class variety: unpretentious families or young people out to have fun. The ever expanding Université de La Rochelle, opened in 1993, has added to the city's attraction for young people. The quays of the old ports, grandly illuminated at night, are lined with cafés and bars.

Although the city centre does not have a beach, the nearby Île de Ré is encircled by kilometres of fine-sand beaches.

History

La Rochelle was one of France's foremost seaports from the 14th to 17th century, and local shipowners were among the first to establish trade links with the New World. Many of the early French settlers in Canada – including the founders of Montreal – set sail from here in the 17th century.

During the 16th century, La Rochelle, whose spirit of mercantile independence made it fertile ground for Protestant ideas, incurred the wrath of Catholic loyalists, especially during the Wars of Religion. After the notorious Saint Bartholomew's Day Massacre of 1572, many of the Huguenots who survived took refuge here.

In 1627, La Rochelle – by that time an established Huguenot stronghold – was besieged by Louis XIII's forces under the personal command of his principal minister, Cardinal Richelieu. When they surrendered after 15 months of resistance, all but 1500 of the city's 20,000 residents had died of starvation. The city recovered, albeit slowly, but was dealt further blows by the revocation of the Edict of Nantes in 1685 and the loss of French Canada – and the right to trade with North America – to the English in 1763.

During WWII, the German submarine base here was repeatedly attacked by Allied aircraft, devastated the town. The so-called La Rochelle pocket did not surrender to the Allies until V-E Day, 8 May 1945, making it the last city in France to be liberated.

Orientation

La Rochelle is centred around the Vieux Port (Old Port), to the north of which lies the old city. The tourist office is on the south side of the Vieux Port in an area known as Le Gabut. The train station is linked to the Vieux Port by the 500m-long Ave du Général de Gaulle.

Place du Marché is 1km north of the train station and 250m north of the old city. Place de Verdun, 250m west of Place du Marché, is linked to Tour de la Grosse Horloge by Rue du Palais and Rue Chaudrier.

The university campus is midway between the Vieux Port and the seaside neighbourhood of Les Minimes, 3km south-west of the city centre. The city's commercial port is 5.5km west of town at La Pallice, not far from the bridge to the Île de Ré.

Information

Tourist Office The tourist office (☎ 05 46 41 14 68; fax 05 46 41 99 85), on Place de la Petite Sirène in Le Gabut, is open Monday to Saturday from 9 am to 12.30 pm and 2 to 6 pm, and also on Sunday from 10.30 am to 12.30 pm. From June to September it's open Monday to Saturday from 9 am to 7 pm (8 pm during July and August), and Sunday from 11 am to 5 pm. Local hotel reservations cost 10FF.

Money The Banque de France at 22 Rue Réaumur is open Monday to Friday from 8.30 am to noon and 1.30 to 3.30 pm.

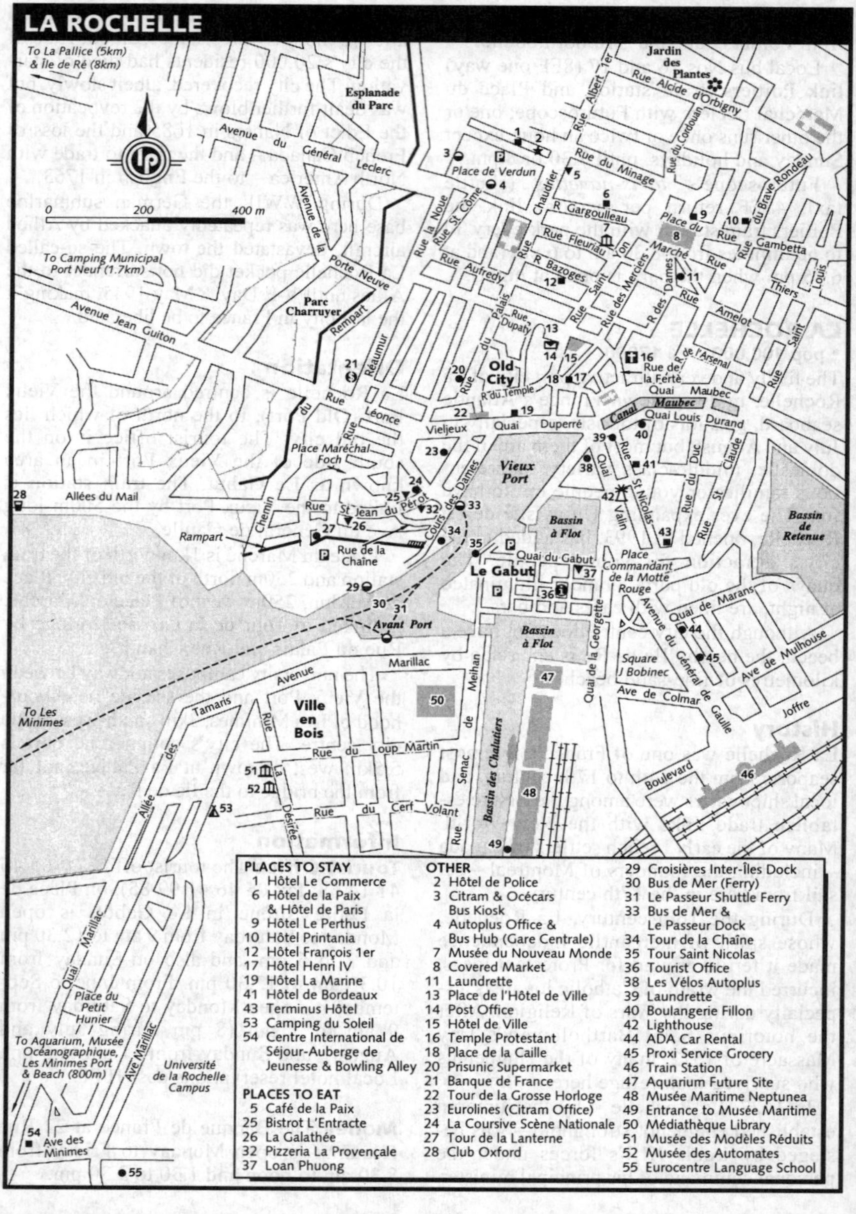

PLACES TO STAY
1 Hôtel Le Commerce
6 Hôtel de la Paix & Hôtel de Paris
9 Hôtel Le Perthus
10 Hôtel Printania
12 Hôtel François 1er
17 Hôtel Henri IV
19 Hôtel La Marine
41 Hôtel de Bordeaux
43 Terminus Hôtel
53 Camping du Soleil
54 Centre International de Séjour-Auberge de Jeunesse & Bowling Alley

PLACES TO EAT
5 Café de la Paix
25 Bistrot L'Entracte
26 La Galathée
32 Pizzeria La Provençale
37 Loan Phuong

OTHER
2 Hôtel de Police
3 Citram & Océcars Bus Kiosk
4 Autoplus Office & Bus Hub (Gare Centrale)
7 Musée du Nouveau Monde
8 Covered Market
11 Laundrette
13 Place de l'Hôtel de Ville
14 Post Office
15 Hôtel de Ville
16 Temple Protestant
18 Place de la Caille
20 Prisunic Supermarket
21 Banque de France
22 Tour de la Grosse Horloge
23 Eurolines (Citram Office)
24 La Coursive Scène Nationale
27 Tour de la Lanterne
28 Club Oxford
29 Croisières Inter-Îles Dock
30 Bus de Mer (Ferry)
31 Le Passeur Shuttle Ferry
33 Bus de Mer & Le Passeur Dock
34 Tour de la Chaîne
35 Tour Saint Nicolas
36 Tourist Office
38 Les Vélos Autoplus
39 Laundrette
40 Boulangerie Fillon
42 Lighthouse
44 ADA Car Rental
45 Proxi Service Grocery
46 Train Station
47 Aquarium Future Site
48 Musée Maritime Neptunea
49 Entrance to Musée Maritime
50 Médiathèque Library
51 Musée des Modèles Réduits
52 Musée des Automates
55 Eurocentre Language School

In the old city there are a number of banks on Rue du Palais, just north of the Tour de la Grosse Horloge.

Post The branch post office across from the Hôtel de Ville is open Monday to Friday until 6.30 pm and on Saturday until noon. Exchange services are available.

Laundry The Salon Lavoir at 4 Rue des Dames is open daily until 7.30 pm (10 pm from about June till September). The Laverie 7/7 on the corner of Quai Louis Durand and Rue Saint Nicolas is open daily from 8.30 am to 8.30 pm.

Emergency The Hôtel de Police (☎ 05 46 51 36 36) at 2 Place de Verdun is staffed 24 hours a day.

Medieval Towers

To protect the harbour at night and defend it in times of war, an enormous chain used to be stretched between the two 14th century stone towers at the harbour entrance. **Tour de la Chaîne** (☎ 05 46 34 11 81) affords fine views from the top and has displays on the history of Protestantism in La Rochelle in the basement. Across the harbour you can also climb to the top of the 36m-high, pentagonal **Tour Saint Nicolas** (☎ 05 46 41 74 13).

From Tour de la Chaîne, you can walk west along the medieval walls to the cylindrical mid-15th century **Tour de la Lanterne** (☎ 05 46 41 56 04), topped with a steeple. It is also known as Tour des Quatre Sergents in memory of four sergeants from the local garrison who were executed in 1822 for plotting to overthrow the newly reinstated monarchy. Long used as a prison and later as a lighthouse, it now houses a **museum**. The English-language graffiti on the walls was carved by English privateers held here during the 18th century. There's a great view from below the octagonal spire.

All three towers are open daily from 10 am to 12.30 pm and 2 to 5.30 pm; from April to September they're open from 10 am to 7 pm. Entry to each costs 25FF (15FF for people aged from 12 to 25); a ticket good for all three is 45FF.

Tour de la Grosse Horloge, the imposing Gothic-style clock tower on Quai Duperré, has a 14th century base and an 18th century top. The street that passes under the tower leads to arcaded **Rue du Palais**, La Rochelle's main shopping street, which is lined with 17th and 18th century shipowners' homes. Two blocks to the east, Rue des Merciers is also lined with arcades.

Hôtel de Ville

The Flamboyant Gothic outer wall of the City Hall (☎ 05 46 41 14 68), Place de l'Hôtel de Ville, was built in the late 15th century; the Renaissance-style courtyard dates from the last half of the 16th century. Guided tours (11/17FF for students/adults) of the mostly 19th century interior, run by the tourist office, are held on Saturday and Sunday at 3 pm. In July and August and during school holiday periods, tours depart daily at 3 and 4 pm.

Musée du Nouveau Monde

The Museum of the New World (☎ 05 46 41 46 50), 10 Rue Fleuriau, housed in the mid-18th century Hôtel de Fleuriau, has a large collection of material on early French exploration and settlement of the Americas, including Quebec and Louisiana. It is open from 10.30 am to 12.30 pm and 1.30 (3 pm on Sunday) to 6 pm; closed Sunday morning and on Tuesday. Entry costs 20FF (free for under 18s).

Temple Protestant

The austere Protestant church at 2 Rue Saint Michel is remarkable for its contrast to most of France's Catholic churches. An earlier building on this site served La Rochelle's Protestant community from 1563 until the siege of 1627-28. The current building, which dates from the late 17th century, became a Protestant church after the Revolution. The interior took on its present form during the last 75 years of the 19th century. The building houses the small **Musée Protestant** (☎ 05 46 50 88 03), whose documents and artefacts connected with La

Rochelle's Huguenot history can be viewed from July to mid-September. It's open from 2.30 to 6 pm (closed Sunday).

Musée Maritime Neptunea

This maritime museum (☎ 05 46 28 03 00) at Bassin des Chalutiers, soon to be the permanent home of Jacques Cousteau's research ship the *Calypso*, occupies what was once the city's wholesale fish market. In the 'wind pool', radio-controlled miniature sailing ships demonstrate the principles of sailing (eg tacking into the wind). The entry fee (45FF, 30FF for under 16s and students) includes tours of a *chalutier* (fishing boat) and the frigate *France I*, outfitted for meteorological research. It is open daily from 10 am to 7 pm (ticket sales end at 6 pm). From November to January or February it may only be open from 2 to 6 pm.

Les Minimes

The modern resort neighbourhood of Les Minimes, 3km south-west of the city centre, has a small **beach** and the largest pleasure craft port on Europe's Atlantic seaboard.

The innovative **Aquarium** (☎ 05 46 34 00 00) on Ave du Lazeret has lots of tanks of colourful fish, including large ones for sharks, and a series of informative exhibits. It is open daily from 10 am to noon and 2 to 7 pm (9 am to 7 pm from April to June and in September, and until 11 pm in July and August). The admission fee is 42FF (37FF for students, 25FF for children aged from four to 11). The aquarium is supposed to relocate to Bassin des Chalutiers (next to the Musée Maritime Neptunea) in 2000.

About midway between the Vieux Port and Les Minimes is the **Musée des Automates** (☎ 05 46 41 68 08), 14 Rue La Désirée, which displays – in action – some 300 automated dolls from the last two centuries. Next door at the **Musée des Modèles Réduits** (☎ 05 46 41 64 51), children of all ages can marvel at the miniature cars, ships (including a naval version of Vietnamese water puppetry) and railroad villages. Both are open daily from 10 am to noon and 2 to 6 pm (in the afternoon only from November to January, and until 7 pm from June to August, when there's no midday closure). Entry to each museum costs a steep 40FF (25FF for children aged three to 10); a ticket good for both is available for 65FF (35FF for children).

Special Events

The Francofolies, a six day festival held each year in mid-July, brings together vocalists and performing artists from all over La Francophonie (the French-speaking world). The official festival is accompanied by a *festival off* (fringe festival). Both events, and the simultaneous Festival de l'Inattendu of gospel, blues, jazz and classical music, attract lots of young people.

La Rochelle's 10-day Festival International du Film runs from the end of June to early July.

Places to Stay

La Rochelle has a shortage of cheap hotels that offer good value. Most places charge high-season rates from sometime in the spring until September or October, making warm-season bargains pretty hard to find. During July and August, virtually all the hotels are full by noon.

Places to Stay – Budget

Camping During the warmer months, dozens of camping grounds open up around La Rochelle and on the Île de Ré. Many of them are so full in July and August that even hikers with small tents are turned away.

The camping ground nearest the city centre is ***Camping du Soleil*** (☎ 05 46 44 42 53), also known as Camping Municipal Les Minimes, which is on Ave Marillac about 1km south-west of the centre of town. It is open from mid-May to mid-September and is often completely full. Two people with a tent and car are charged 60FF. To get there, take bus No 10.

Camping Municipal Port Neuf (☎ 05 46 43 81 20), on Blvd Aristide Rondeau in the Port Neuf area, open year-round, is 3km west of the city centre along Ave Jean Guiton. The charge for a site and one adult is 37FF. To get there, take bus No 6 from the train station or Quai Valin.

Hostel The ***Centre International de Séjour-Auberge de Jeunesse*** (☎ 05 46 44 43 11; fax 05 46 45 41 48) is 2km south-west of the train station on Ave des Minimes in Les Minimes. A dorm bed/double room costs 72/179FF, including breakfast. Except in summer, there's a curfew of midnight (10 pm in the winter). Check-in is possible from 8 am to midnight. In summer it may be possible to rent bicycles. From late June to late August, the hostel usually runs one week mountain bike and windsurfing courses. To get there, take bus No 10, which runs until about 7.30 pm (and later still from June to September).

Hotels The friendly, 24 room ***Hôtel Henri IV*** (☎ 05 46 41 25 79; fax 05 46 41 78 64) occupies a late 16th century building in the middle of the pedestrianised old city at Place de la Caille; the postal address is 31 Rue des Gentilshommes. Doubles start at 160FF (205FF with shower and toilet). Hall showers are free. You can only drive into (or out of) the pedestrian zone until 10.30 am.

Near the port, the welcoming, 22 room ***Hôtel de Bordeaux*** (☎ 05 46 41 31 22; fax 05 46 41 24 43), 43 Rue Saint Nicolas, has modern, quiet doubles from 165FF (210FF from May to September); doubles with shower and toilet go for 220FF (275FF in the high season).

The two star ***Hôtel Le Commerce*** (☎ 05 46 41 08 22; fax 05 46 41 74 85), 6-10 Place Verdun, is near lots of parking. Depending on the season, rather plain doubles with washbasin cost 135 or 150FF (229FF, including breakfast, from May to September). Hall showers are free. Doubles/quads with shower and toilet are 235/245 or 255/285FF (354/463FF, including breakfast, in season).

The slightly dilapidated, 19 room ***Hôtel de la Paix*** (☎ 05 46 41 33 44; fax 05 46 50 51 28), in a late 18th century building at 14 Rue Gargoulleau, has serviceable doubles with shower and toilet from 180FF (260FF from about April to September). A huge, old-fashioned room for five people with a fireplace is 390FF (450FF in high season).

The eight room ***Hôtel Le Perthus*** (☎ 05 46 41 10 16), next to the covered market at 17 Rue Gambetta, has passable doubles/quads from 130/200FF; doubles with shower and toilet are 200FF. Hall showers are free. During July and August, half-board is obligatory. Reception (at the bar) closes on Sunday at 2.30 pm – call ahead if you'll be arriving after that.

You might also try the inefficient ***Hôtel Printania*** (☎ 05 46 41 22 86; fax 05 46 35 19 58), 9 Rue du Brave Rondeau, which has doubles from 150FF (195FF with shower and toilet); quads with shower start at 250FF. Hall showers cost 10FF.

Places to Stay – Mid-Range

The two star, 13 room ***Hôtel La Marine*** (☎ 05 46 50 51 63), a friendly, family-run place at 30 Quai Duperré (2nd floor), has doubles/triples/quads with shower and toilet from 215/290/340FF (280/360/390FF from late June to early September); nondescript but clean doubles with shower start at 185FF (240FF in summer). Reception is closed from noon on Sunday.

The ***Terminus Hôtel*** (☎ 05 46 50 69 69; fax 05 46 41 73 12), 7 Rue de la Fabrique (on Place du Commandant de la Motte Rouge), has unsurprising doubles with shower and toilet starting at somewhere between 250FF (November to March) and 300FF (July to late September).

The 38 room ***Hôtel François 1er*** (☎ 05 46 41 28 46; fax 05 46 41 35 01), 15 Rue Bazoges, has decent but smallish doubles for 390 to 475FF (less in winter) plus a couple of rooms with washbasin for 215FF. A number of French kings stayed in this building in the 15th and 16th centuries.

The extremely pleasant ***Hôtel de Paris*** (☎ 05 46 41 03 59; fax 05 46 41 03 24), 18 Rue Gargoulleau, provides clean and tidy doubles/triples/quads with shower and toilet for between 190/240/280FF (November to March) and 310/370/430FF (July to September).

Places to Eat

According to local people, La Rochelle has so many restaurants that you could stay in town for a whole year, dining out every day, and never have dinner at the same place twice. Dozens of eateries can be found along the north side of the Vieux Port, especially on Quai Duperré, Cours des Dames, Rue de la Chaîne and Rue Saint Jean du Pérot. Le Gabut is home to a number of cafés, crêperies, brasseries and ethnic places. The Place du Marché area has several inexpensive restaurants and pizzerias.

A local speciality you might want to try is *mouclade Rochelaise* (mussels in a cream and curry sauce).

Restaurants – French Classic French cuisine is available at the elegantly rustic ***La Galathée*** (☎ 05 46 41 17 06), 45 Rue Saint Jean du Pérot, where *menus* cost 80, 120 and 180FF. It is open daily, except Tuesday evening and Wednesday (daily, except Wednesday in July and August). The elegant ***Bistrot l'Entracte*** (☎ 05 46 50 62 60), 22 Rue Saint Jean du Pérot, specialises in fish. The four-course *menu* costs 155FF. It's open from 12.15 to 1.45 pm and 9.15 to 9.45 pm (closed Sunday).

At ***Café de la Paix*** (☎ 05 46 41 39 79), 54 Rue Chaudrier (Place de Verdun), you can sip beer (15FF) and dine on brasserie food (49 to 76FF for mains) amid gilded columns and turn-of-the-century marble, mouldings and mirrors.

Restaurants – Other The ***Pizzeria La Provençale*** (☎ 05 46 41 43 68), 15 Rue Saint Jean du Pérot, has pizzas (40 to 65FF), meat mains (50 to 70FF) and three *menus* (for 69, 89 and 120FF). Except from July to September and on holidays, it is closed on Sunday.

The ethnic places in Le Gabut include ***Loan Phuong*** (☎ 05 46 41 90 20), Quai du Gabut, which has an all-you-can-eat Chinese and Vietnamese lunch/dinner buffet for 69/75FF (39/45FF for children under 12). The weekday lunch *menu* costs just 40FF.

Self-Catering The best place to pick up edibles is the lively ***covered market*** at Place du Marché, open daily from 7 am to 1 pm. It expands to fill nearby streets (including Rue Amelot) on Wednesday and Saturday. There are lots of ***food shops*** in the vicinity; at least one of the ***boulangeries*** on nearby Rue Gambetta (at Nos 8 and 29) is open every day of the week.

In the old city, the ***Prisunic*** across from 55 Rue du Palais is open Monday to Saturday from 8.30 am to 8 pm. In July and August it's open on Sunday morning until 12.30 pm. Near the train station, the ***Proxi Service*** grocery at 33 Ave du Général de Gaulle is open Monday to Saturday from 8 am to 12.45 pm and 3 to 7.45 pm (open on Sunday morning in July and August).

Boulangerie Fillon, 18 Quai Louis Durand, is open all day until at least 2 am (8 pm on Tuesday; closed Wednesday and Sunday).

Entertainment

Le Gabut is home to a number of pubs. ***Club Oxford*** (☎ 05 46 41 51 81), a waterfront disco about 500m west of Tour de la Lanterne, is open nightly from 11 pm. In Les Minimes, the ***bowling alley*** (☎ 05 46 45 40 40) next to the hostel is open daily from 11 am to 2 am.

The two auditoriums of ***La Coursive Scène Nationale*** (☎ 05 46 51 54 00) at 4 Rue Saint Jean du Pérot host concerts (classical, world music, jazz), operas and nondubbed art films. The centre is closed from late July to early September.

In July and August there are free organ concerts at the ***Temple Protestant*** (☎ 05 46 50 88 03) every Friday at 6 pm.

Getting There & Away

Bus For information on buses to the Île de Ré see Getting There & Around under Île de Ré. Eurolines (☎ 05 46 50 53 57) reservations can be made at the Citram office at 30 Cours des Dames.

Train The train station (☎ 08 36 35 35 35) information office is open from 9 am to 7 pm (closed Sunday and holidays).

If you're coming from Paris, you can take either a TGV from Gare Montparnasse (305 to 365FF; three hours) or a non-TGV train from Gare d'Austerlitz (256FF; five hours; one a day, several a day in summer). Only three to five TGVs a day are direct – the rest of the time you have to change at Poitiers.

Other destinations served by direct trains include Bordeaux (131FF; 2¼ hours; four to seven a day), Nantes (126FF; two hours; five a day), Toulouse (246FF; one direct a day) and Nice (481FF; one overnight train a day). Getting to most other places, including Bayonne (223FF) and Tours (about 170FF), involves a change of trains.

Car ADA (☎ 05 46 41 02 17), 19 Ave du Général de Gaulle, is open Monday to Saturday from 8 am to noon and 2 to 7 pm. Other companies have offices along the same block or facing the train station.

Boat From April to September, Croisières Inter-Îles (☎ 05 46 50 51 88) has ferries from 14 Cours des Dames to the Île de Ré (30FF return to Sablanceaux – the pier is just south of the bridge) and the Île d'Aix (with a close-up view of Fort Boyard; 89 to 130FF return). Irregular boats also go to the Île d'Oléron (89 to 130FF return to Boyardville, tides permitting).

Getting Around

The city centre, an impossible maze of one-way streets, turns into a giant traffic jam in summer. The situation is at its worst on market mornings (Wednesday and Saturday). The area also has a parking shortage, though the new underground garage at Place de Verdun should improve things.

Bus The innovative local transport system, Autoplus (☎ 05 46 34 02 22), has its main bus hub and an information kiosk (open Monday to Saturday from 6.45 am to 7.30 pm) at Place de Verdun. Most lines run until sometime between 7.15 and 8 pm.

A ticket for a single ride, valid for 45 minutes after it's time-stamped, costs 8FF; a seven ride ticket is 39.20FF. A bus pass valid for 24 hours after it's time-stamped costs 24FF; a three day pass is 58FF.

Bus No 10 links Place de Verdun, the Vieux Port (Quai Valin) and the train station with the hostel and Les Minimes.

Electric Car & Scooter Autoplus, Place de Verdun, rents electrically powered motorcars (Renault 106s and Citroën AXs) for 60/100FF per half-day/day. Electric Barigo scooters cost 40/70FF. Both require a 2500FF cash or credit card deposit.

Taxi Taxis can be ordered 24 hours a day by calling ☎ 05 46 41 55 55 or ☎ 05 46 41 22 22.

Bicycle In 1976, in an effort to encourage people to leave their cars at home, the La Rochelle municipality bought 250 yellow one-speed bikes for the free use by both locals and visitors. The scheme, inspired by a similar program in Amsterdam, has since been modified to prevent theft, but its late 1990s incarnation, Les Vélos Autoplus (☎ 05 46 34 02 22) is alive and well. Bikes are available daily at Place de Verdun from 7.30 am (1 pm on Sunday) to 7 pm; from May to September they can also be picked up at the Vieux Port (across the street from 11 Quai Valin) daily from 9 am to 12.30 pm and 1.30 to 7 pm (no midday closure in July and August). An adult's or child's bike (lock included) is free for the first two hours; after that the charge is 6FF per hour. Keeping the bike overnight will earn you a 60FF fine. You must leave some sort of ID as a deposit. Child seats are available for no charge.

Boat Autoplus' *Le Passeur*, a small ferry that links Tour de la Chaîne with the Avant Port and the Ville en Bois, runs daily whenever there are passengers – just press the red button on the board at the top of the gangplank. It runs from 10 am to 7 pm (8 pm from April to September). A ticket costs 4FF.

The *Bus de Mer*, also run by Autoplus, links Tour de la Chaîne with Les Minimes (20 minutes). From April to September, boats from the Vieux Port depart every hour on the hour from 9 or 10 am to 7 pm (except at 1 pm). In July and August, frequency is increased to twice an hour and service continues until 11.30 pm. The rest of the year the Bus de Mer runs only on weekends and holidays and during school vacation periods from 10 am to 6 pm (except at 1 pm). A single journey costs 10 or 11FF.

AROUND LA ROCHELLE

The crescent-shaped **Île d'Aix** (pronounced something like 'Eel Day'), a 1.33 sq km, car-less island 16km due south of La Rochelle, was fortified by Vauban and later used as a prison. It has some nice beaches. **Fort Boyard**, built during the first half of the 19th century, is a curious, oval-shaped island/fortress between the Île d'Aix and the nearby **Île d'Oléron**. For information on boat trips to Aix and Oléron, see Boat under Getting There & Away for La Rochelle.

ÎLE DE RÉ

• pop 14,000

Île de Ré, the eastern tip of which is 9km west of the centre of La Rochelle, has been connected to the mainland by a graceful, 3km toll bridge since 1988. The island gets more hours of sunshine than any part of France away from the Mediterranean coast.

In summer, the island's many beaches and seasonal camping grounds are a favourite destination for families with young children, in part because the water is shallow and safe and the sun is bright and warming but less harsh than along the Mediterranean. People in their teens and 20s also flock here, helping to increase the island's population 20-fold in August. The island can easily be visited as a day trip from La Rochelle.

Île de Ré's main town is the fishing port of Saint Martin de Ré, on the north coast about 12km from the bridge. The island's interior is covered with low pine forests, fields of wild grasses and areas where grapes, asparagus, potatoes, hay and other crops are cultivated when the tourists aren't around. In most villages, the houses are traditional in design: one or two-storey whitewashed buildings with green shutters and red Spanish tile roofs.

The island boasts 70km of coastline, including 20 or 30km of fine-sand beaches. Most of the north coast is taken up by mudflats and oyster beds. The island's western half curves around a bay known as the Fier d'Ars, which is lined with *marais salants* (salt evaporation pools), saltwater marshes and a nature reserve for birds, **Lilleau des Niges**. Sea walls have been built along some exposed parts of the coast to protect villages from violent storms.

Orientation

The Île de Ré is about 30km long and from 100m to 5km wide. The D735 runs from Sablanceaux (at the bridge end of the island) along the northern coast to Saint Martin de Ré; on to La Couarde-sur-Mer on the south coast; and finally past the salt pools to Phare des Baleines, the lighthouse at the island's westernmost tip.

Information

In summer, almost every village has its own *syndicat d'initiative* that can provide details on outdoor activities (horse riding, water sports etc). The tourist office (☎ 05 46 09 20 06; fax 05 46 09 06 18) in Saint Martin is on Ave Victor Bouthillier a block east of the port (across the street from the Rébus stop). This is a good place to pick up maps of the island. It is open from 10 am to noon and 3.30 to 5.30 pm (closed Wednesday afternoon, Sunday and holidays). In July and August it's open from 10 am to 1 pm and 2 to 7 pm (10 am to noon on Sunday and holidays).

Saint Martin de Ré

• pop 2500 ✉ 17410

This picturesque fishing village, entirely surrounded by Vauban's 17th century fortifications, is especially attractive when the white houses and sailboats are bathed in the bright coastal sun. You can stroll along most of the ramparts but the **Citadelle** (built in 1681), which has been a prison for over two centuries (Alfred Dreyfus was held here before being shipped to Devil's Island), is closed to the law-abiding public.

The fortified, mostly Gothic **church**, three blocks south of the port along Rue de

Sully, was damaged in 1692 in artillery attacks launched by an Anglo-Dutch fleet, but it still functions with an incongruous wood-and-tile roof. There's a great view from the neoclassical **bell and clock tower** over the east front.

Phare des Baleines

At the western tip of the island is the 57m Phare des Baleines (Lighthouse of the Whales), built of stone in 1854 and still operating. You can climb the 257 steps to the top daily from 10 am to noon and 2 to 6 pm (a bit later in summer, 5 pm in winter). Behind it is an old lighthouse (built in 1679), a shady garden and tidal pools. The pines and cypresses of the **Forêt du Lizay** stretch along the coast north-west of here.

Beaches

The best beaches on the Île de Ré are along the southern edge of the main part of the island (ie east and west of La Couarde) and around the island's western tip (ie north-east and south-east of Phare des Baleines). Near Sablanceaux, there are sandy beaches along the south coast towards Sainte Marie. Many of the beaches are bound by dunes that have been fenced off to protect the vegetation.

Plage de la Conche des Baleines is on the north-west coast between Phare des Baleines and the town of Les Portes. Scenes from *The Longest Day* (1962), a Hollywood film about the D-day landings, were shot here. There's an unofficial **naturist beach** near the outskirts of Les Portes; access is via the Forêt du Lizay.

Places to Stay

There are virtually no budget hotels on the Île de Ré, so if you're on a shoestring budget and don't have a tent you'll have to commute from La Rochelle. Every hotel and camping ground on the island is *totally* full from 14 July to 25 August, though carless pedestrians with a small tent may be able to find something. Reservations for July and August should be made in March, certainly no later than May.

Camping All but a handful of the island's many dozens of camping grounds are seasonal. Places open year-round include ***Les Chardons Bleus*** (☎ 05 46 30 23 75), a 260 site, inland camping ground on the road towards La Flotte from La Noue. Three people with a tent are charged 90FF (20% less in the low season). In Saint Martin, the grassy, shaded ***Camping Municipal*** (☎ 05 46 09 21 96), a few hundred metres south of the church, is open from March to mid-October. Three people with a tent or caravan are charged 67FF.

Pitching your tent anywhere but in a camping ground is forbidden.

Hotels – Saint Martin de Ré The one star, 15 room ***Hôtel de Sully*** (☎ 05 46 09 26 94), 150m south of the port on Rue Jean Jaurès, has doubles with shower for 180FF (230FF in summer); doubles with shower and toilet start at 230FF (280FF in summer). If it looks closed, inquire at the two star ***Hôtel du Port*** (☎ 05 46 09 21 21; fax 05 46 09 06 85) on Quai de la Poithevinière (the south side of the port), run by the same company. Comfortable doubles/family quins with shower and toilet start at 310/420FF (380/500FF from July to September).

The two star, 30 room ***Hôtel des Colonnes*** (☎ 05 46 09 21 58; fax 05 46 09 21 49), on the south side of the port at 19 Quai Job Foran, is open year-round except from mid-December to January. Doubles start at 300FF (430FF from early July to late September).

Places to Eat

It's a lot cheaper to buy food in La Rochelle than on the island. In Saint Martin de Ré, the ***covered market*** on the south side of the port at Rue Jean Jaurès is open daily from 8.30 am to 1 pm. There is a cluster of ***food shops*** nearby. There are a lot of touristy restaurants in the port area.

Getting There & Around

Bus The island is served by two excruciatingly slow bus systems: Rébus and, in summer, La Rochelle's Autoplus.

Rébus (☎ 05 46 09 20 15 in Saint Martin) has infrequent buses to the island from three places in La Rochelle: the train station parking lot, the Vieux Port (next to Tour de la Grosse Horloge) and Place de Verdun. The line to Saint Martin de Ré (28FF; 55 minutes; eight a day, three or four on Sundays and holidays, a dozen a day in July and August) also stops at Sablanceaux (15.50FF) and La Flotte (23.50FF; 45 minutes). Rébus also covers intra-island routes.

On Wednesday, weekends and holidays from May to late June and daily from late June to August, Autoplus bus Nos 1 and 50 (known as No 21 for part of the route) link La Rochelle's train station, Quai Valin and Place de Verdun with Sablanceaux (10FF; 25 minutes).

Car For automobiles, the bridge toll (paid on your way *to* the island) is 60FF (a whopping 110FF from mid-June to mid-September); a car with a camping trailer costs 100FF (180FF in summer).

Bicycle Cycling is an extremely popular way to get around the island, which is flat and has an extensive network of paved bicycle paths. A biking map is available at tourist offices. In summer, practically every hamlet has somewhere to rent bikes.

At Sablanceaux, bicycles can be rented from Cycland, which occupies a kiosk in one of the little buildings to the left as you come off the bridge. Three-speeds/mountain bikes/tandems cost 56/75/100FF a day; helmets *may* be available (no extra charge). The kiosk is staffed daily in July and August; the rest of the time, call Cycland's office in La Flotte (☎ 05 46 09 65 27), open daily, and they'll deliver a bike to the bridge. If you rent for more than one day, the bike can be returned to any Cycland office. From mid-March to October, Cycland has a bureau in Saint Martin at 8 Rue de Sully (open daily).

Hitching To hitch to the island, the best place to stand is just past the bridge's toll plaza.

Boat See Getting There & Away under La Rochelle for details on Croisières Inter-Îles ferries from Sablanceaux to the Île d'Aix and the Île d'Oléron.

COGNAC

• pop 19,500 ✉ 16100

The only real reason to come to Cognac is to learn first-hand about the production of the world-famous, double-distilled spirit that bears the town's name – and on which the local economy is based. The town is surrounded by rolling vineyards and quiet villages.

Orientation

The train station is on the southern edge of the city centre, while all three of the cognac distilleries mentioned are on the other side of town, 1.5km to the north, near the Charente River. To get from the train station to the tourist office, turn right (north-east) on Blvd de Paris for 500m and then left (north-west) on Rue Lomehyer for 700m (all the way to the end). Place François 1er, 200m north-east of the tourist office (follow Rue du 14 Juillet), is linked to the river by Blvd Denfert Rochereau.

Information

The tourist office (☎ 05 45 82 10 71; fax 05 45 82 34 47; office.tourisme.cognac@wanadoo.fr) at 16 Rue du 14 Juillet is open from 9 am to 12.30 pm and 2 to 6.15 pm (closed Sunday and holidays). In July and August it's open from 9 am to 8 pm (10.30 am to 4 pm on Sunday and holidays).

The Banque de France branch at 39 Blvd Denfert Rochereau is open from Tuesday to Saturday from 8.45 am to noon and 1.30 to 4 pm.

Cognac Houses

Several of Cognac's most famous distilleries offer tours of their production facilities. Reservations are not necessary, except for groups.

Martell The free, informative guided tours of the sprawling Martell complex (☎ 05 45

TERESA FISHER

In the Pyrenees, Arreau is known for its craft shops and a sticky cake called *gâteau à la broche*.

TERESA FISHER

In the Vallée d'Aspe in the Pyrenees, the town of Borce offers good access to the national park.

MARK HONAN

Across France, if the landscape isn't red with poppies or purple with lavender then it's …

TERESA FISHER

In the Pyrenees, sometimes you'll have to share your view with hikers, other times with the locals.

36 33 33) at Place Édouard Martell (250m north-west of the tourist office) last 45 minutes to an hour and are sometimes conducted in English. At the end, there's a tasting session, and participants are given a tiny bottle of VSOP. From October to May, tours begin on weekdays (except Friday afternoon) at 9.30 and 11 am and 2.30, 3.45 and 5 pm. The rest of the year the tours begin on weekdays from 9.30 to 11 am and 2 to 5 pm (no midday closure in July and August, when there are tours on weekends from 10 am to 4.15 pm).

The Production of Cognac

Cognac is made of grape *eaux de vie* (brandies) of various vintages, aged in oak barrels and then blended by an experienced *maître de chai* (cellar master). Each year, some 3% of the volume of the casks – *la part des anges* (the angels' share) – evaporates through the pores in the wood, nourishing the tiny black mushrooms that thrive on the walls of cognac warehouses.

Since the mid-18th century – when the process for turning 9L of mediocre, low-alcohol wine into 1L of fine cognac was invented – many of the key figures in the cognac trade have been Anglophones: Jean Martell was born on Jersey, Richard Hennessey hailed from County Cork in Ireland and Baron Otard was of Scottish descent. To this day, several of the most common cognac classifications are in English: VS (very special), aged for five to seven years; VSOP (very special old pale), aged for eight to 12 years; Napoleon, aged for 15 to 25 years; and XO (extra old), aged for about 40 years.

All but a tiny fraction of Cognac's cognac is sold outside of France, especially in the UK and Japan, where the major producers have spent a couple of centuries building brand loyalty, and other markets (such as the exclusive world of duty-free shops).

Otard The Château de Cognac at 127 Blvd Denfert Rochereau (650m north of Place François 1er) was the birthplace in 1494 of François I and has been home to Otard (☎ 05 45 36 88 88) since 1795. Since it's less famous than its competitors, the company tries harder with its one-hour tours (in French with a printed translation in English), which begin at 10 and 11 am and at 2, 3, 4 and 5 pm on weekdays (weekends also from April to September). Tours cost 15FF (10FF for children) and end with a sampling session.

Hennessey The 1½-hour tours of the Hennessey facilities (☎ 05 45 35 72 68) at 8 Rue Richonne (100m up the hill from Quai des Flamands, which runs along the river) include a film (in English) and a boat trip across the Charente to visit the *chais* (cellars). They begin daily, one to four times an hour, from 10 to 11.30 am and 1.30 to 5 pm. From June to early October, tours begin every day from 10 am to 6 pm. The cost is 30FF (15FF each if you're in a group of more than six; free for under 18s). There's a tasting session at the end.

Places to Stay

The 14 room ***Hôtel Le Cheval Blanc*** (☎ 05 45 82 09 55; fax 05 45 36 19 37), 6 Place Bayard (100m west of the tourist office), has simple, slightly dreary singles/doubles/triples with washbasin and bidet for 130/150/180FF; hall showers are free. On Sunday, ring the bell.

The three star ***Hôtel François 1er*** (☎ 05 45 32 07 18; fax 05 45 35 33 89), 3 Place François 1er, built in the mid-19th century, has spacious but plain rooms for two/four people for 270/360FF.

Places to Eat

There is a ***Cocodis*** supermarket at Place François 1er. About 300m to the north, the ***marché couvert*** (covered market) at 57 Blvd Denfert Rochereau is open every morning until 1 pm (2 pm on Saturday); only a handful of stalls are staffed on Monday.

Getting There & Away

Cognac's train station (☎ 08 36 35 35 35), at the southern end of Ave du Maréchal Leclerc, is on the line that links Angoulême with Royan. There's one direct train a day from La Rochelle (77FF).

BORDEAUX

• pop 700,000 ✉ 33000

Bordeaux is known for its neoclassical architecture, wide avenues and well tended public squares and parks, all of which give the city a certain 18th century grandeur. The generally grimy state of the buildings may give the impression that Bordeaux has seen better (or at least more prosperous) days, but its excellent museums, ethnic diversity, lively university community (the city has some 60,000 students) and untouristed atmosphere make it much more than just a convenient stop on the way from Paris to Spain.

Bordeaux, which is about 100km from the Atlantic at the lowest bridging point on the Garonne River, was founded by the Romans in the 3rd century BC. From 1154 to 1453, it prospered under the rule of the English, whose fondness for the region's red wine – known across the Channel as claret (with the final T pronounced) – provided the impetus for the eventual creation of Bordeaux's international reputation for quality wine. Today, not surprisingly, the city's single most important economic activity is the marketing and export of wines.

Orientation

The city centre lies between Place Gambetta and the 350m to 500m-wide Garonne River, which is usually a muddy brown as it flows either towards the sea or inland, depending on the tides. From Place Gambetta, Place de Tourny is 500m to the north-east, and the tourist office is 500m to the east.

The train station, known as Gare Saint Jean, is in a seedy area about 3km south-east of the city centre. Cours de la Marne stretches from the train station to Place de la Victoire, which is linked to Place de la Comédie by the 1.1km-long Rue Sainte Catherine pedestrian mall.

Bordeaux, Capital of France

Bordeaux served briefly as the capital of France on three occasions when the country was on the verge of defeat: during the Franco-Prussian War of 1870-71; at the beginning of WWI (1914); and for two weeks in 1940, just before the Vichy government was proclaimed.

Information

Tourist Offices The helpful, well-informed tourist office (☎ 05 56 00 66 00; fax 05 56 00 66 01; otb@bordeaux-tourisme.com; www.bordeaux-tourisme.com) at 12 Cours du 30 Juillet is open Monday to Saturday from 9 am to 7 pm and on Sunday from 9.45 am to 4.30 pm. From May to September, it's open until 8 pm (7 pm on Sunday). The free city map suggests a walking tour itinerary. Hotel reservations in the Bordeaux area are free.

The tourist office annexe at the train station is open Monday to Saturday from 9 am to 6 pm. From May to September, it's open daily until 7 pm.

For brochures on the Gironde department, you might stop by the Maison du Tourisme de la Gironde (☎ 05 56 52 61 40; fax 05 56 81 09 99) at 21 Cours de l'Intendance, open Monday to Saturday until 6.30 or 7 pm.

Money The Banque de France around the corner from the tourist office at 15 Rue Esprit des Lois is open weekdays from 9 am to noon and 1 to 3.30 pm.

Most commercial banks are open weekdays, though a few are also open on Saturday morning. Lots of them can be found near the tourist office on Cours de l'Intendance, Rue Esprit des Lois and Cours du Chapeau Rouge.

American Express (☎ 05 56 00 63 33) at 14 Cours de l'Intendance is open Monday to Friday (and perhaps on Saturday) from 8.45 am to noon and 1.30 to 6 pm.

The Thomas Cook bureau at the train station is open until 5.30 pm (6.30 pm in the warmer months; closed on Sunday from November to April).

Post & Communication The branch post office at Place Saint Projet (on Rue Sainte Catherine) is open until 6.30 pm (noon on Saturday). The post office at 29 Allées de Tourny is open until 6 pm (noon on Saturday), with a break from 12.30 pm to 2 pm.

Cyberstation (☎ 05 56 01 15 15; info@cyberstation.fr), 23 Cour Pasteur (across the street from the Musée d'Aquitaine), is open from 11 am to 2 am (from 2 pm to midnight on Sunday).

Bookshop Bradley's Bookshop (☎ 05 56 52 10 57), 8 Cours d'Albret, has a very wide selection of English-language books, including lots of fiction and a few Lonely Planet titles. It's open from 9.30 am to 12.30 pm and 2 to 7 pm (closed Monday morning and Sunday).

Laundry Near Place de Tourny, the Espace Laverie at 5 Rue de Fondaudège lets you start your wash from 7 am to 8 pm. Two blocks south-west, the laundrette at 3 Rue Lafaurie de Monbadon is open from 7 am to 9 pm. Laverie Lincoln at 31 Rue du Palais Gallien is open until 8 pm.

Medical Services Hôpital Saint André (☎ 05 56 79 56 79, ext 43230), 1 Rue Jean Burguet, open 24 hours a day, is 400m south of Cathédrale Saint André.

Emergency The Hôtel de Police (☎ 05 56 99 77 77) at 29 Rue Castéja is staffed 24 hours a day.

Museums

The outstanding **Musée d'Aquitaine** (Museum of Aquitaine; ☎ 05 56 01 51 00), 20 Cours Pasteur, illustrates the history and ethnography of the Bordeaux area from 25,000 years ago to the 19th century. The prehistoric period is represented by a number of exceptional artefacts, including several stone carvings of women. Signs are in French.

Museum Hours & Prices

Bordeaux's museums are open daily, except Monday and holidays (daily except Tuesday and holidays for the Beaux-Arts and Arts Décoratifs), from 11 am to 6 pm (from 2 pm on weekends for the Centre Jean Moulin and on Sunday for the Arts Décoratifs). On Wednesday, the Art Contemporain stays open until 8 pm. The Centre Jean Moulin is free, but the others cost 20FF (10FF for seniors; free for students and, on the first Sunday of each month, for everyone), and about 10FF more if there's a special exhibit.

The **Musée des Beaux-Arts** (Fine Arts Museum; ☎ 05 56 10 16 93), 20 Cours d'Albret, occupies two wings of the Hôtel de Ville complex (built in the 1770s); between them there's a verdant public park, the **Jardin de la Mairie**. The museum, founded in 1801, has a large collection of paintings, including Flemish, Dutch and Italian works from the 17th century and a particularly important work by Delacroix. Down the block at Place du Colonel Raynal, the **Galerie des Beaux-Arts** (☎ 05 56 96 51 60), an annexe of the Musée des Beaux-Arts, hosts short-term exhibitions. The nearby **Musée des Arts Décoratifs** (Museum of Decorative Arts; ☎ 05 56 00 72 50), 39 Rue Bouffard, specialises in faïence, porcelain, silverwork, glasswork, furniture and the like.

Entrepôts Lainé, built in 1824 as a warehouse for the rare and exotic products of France's colonies (coffee, cocoa, peanuts, vanilla etc), now houses the **Musée d'Art Contemporain** (Museum of Contemporary Art; ☎ 05 56 00 81 50), whose entrance is opposite 16 Rue Ferrère. The exhibits and installations are all temporary.

The **Centre National Jean Moulin** (Jean Moulin Documentation Centre; ☎ 05 56 79 66 00), facing the north side of the cathedral, has exhibits on France during WWII: the occupation, Resistance and liberation. It's

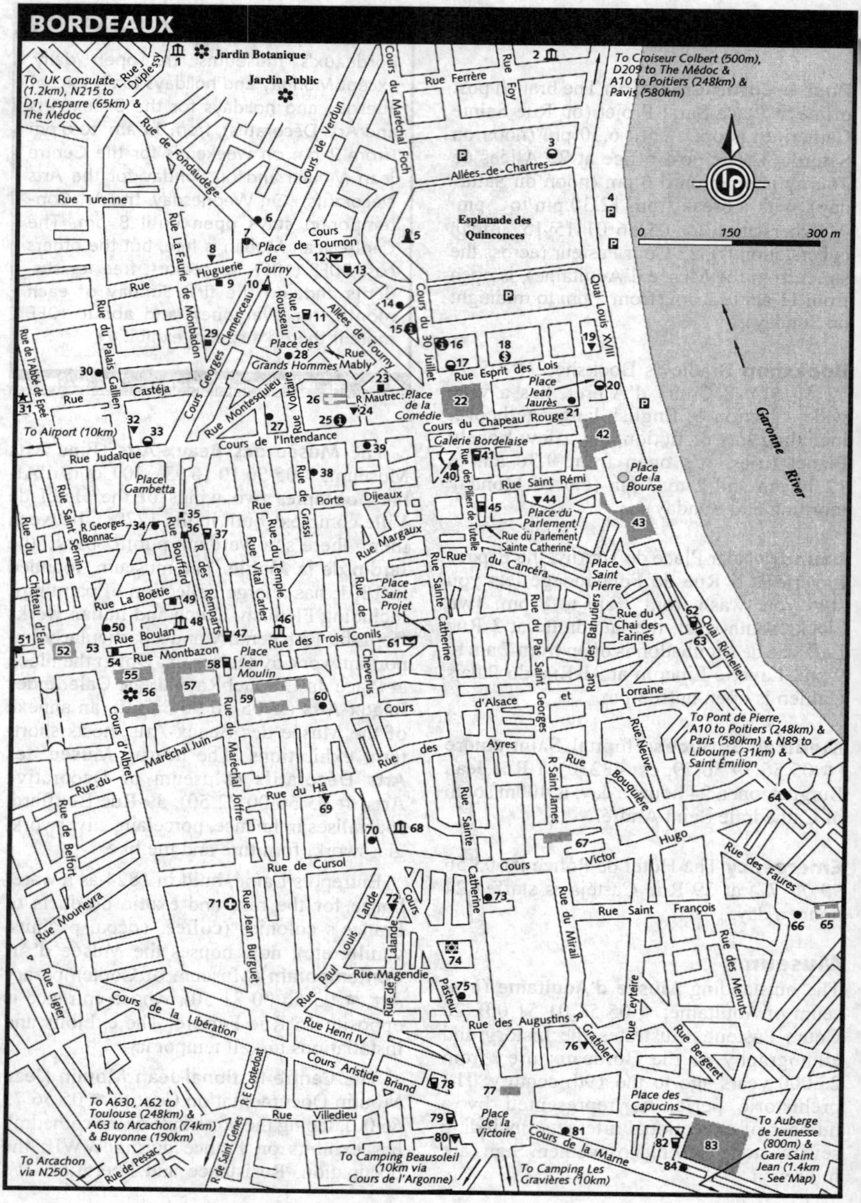

ATLANTIC COAST

open from 11 am (2 pm on weekends) to 6 pm; closed Monday.

Le Croiseur Colbert (☎ 05 56 44 96 11), a 180m-long French navy missile cruiser, was in service with a crew of some 600 from 1957 to 1991. Now permanently docked at Quai des Chartrons, 700m north-east of the centre, it can be visited daily from 10 am to 6 pm (7 pm on weekends in the warmer months and holidays and in July and August; closed on Monday and Friday from October to March). Entry costs 42FF; reduced tariffs apply to children, students and over 65s.

Walking Tour

The sights mentioned below appear pretty much from north to south.

The beautifully landscaped **Jardin Public** along Cours de Verdun, established in 1755 and laid out in the English style a century later, includes the meticulously catalogued **Jardin Botanique** (☎ 05 56 52 18 77), founded in 1629 and at its present site since 1855 (open from 8 am to 6 pm). The **Musée d'Histoire Naturelle** (Natural History Museum; ☎ 05 56 48 29 86) is closed on Saturday and Sunday mornings and on Tuesday. Entry costs 30FF (15FF for students and seniors). There's a **children's playground** on the island.

The most prominent feature of **Esplanade des Quinconces**, a vast square laid out in 1820, is the fountain monument to the Girondins, a group of moderate, bourgeois National Assembly deputies during the French

BORDEAUX

PLACES TO STAY

- 9 Hôtel Touring & Hôtel Studio
- 10 Hôtel de Famille
- 13 Hôtel Royal Médoc & Hôtel de Sèze
- 23 Hôtel Blayais & Hôtel de Dax
- 29 Hôtel Balzac & Laundrette
- 36 Hôtel Bristol
- 49 Hôtel La Boëtie
- 54 Hôtel Boulan

PLACES TO EAT

- 8 Restaurant Baud et Millet
- 19 Restaurant Jean Ramet
- 24 La Chanterelle
- 32 Restaurant Agadir
- 44 Chez Édouard
- 69 Ethnic Restaurants
- 72 Le Fournaise
- 76 La Dakaroise
- 80 Cassolette Café

OTHER

- 1 Musée d'Histoire Naturelle
- 2 Musée d'Art Contemporain
- 3 Halte Routière (Bus Depot)
- 4 Inexpensive Parking Lot
- 5 Monument des Girondins
- 6 Laundrette
- 7 Fromagerie Antonin
- 11 La Factory
- 12 Post Office Branch
- 14 Bordeaux Magnum
- 15 Maison du Vin de Bordeaux
- 16 Tourist Office & Vinothèque
- 17 La Navette (Airport Bus) Stop
- 18 Banque de France
- 20 Bus Hub
- 21 CGFTE Bus Information Office
- 22 Grand Théâtre
- 25 Maison du Tourisme de la Gironde
- 26 Église Notre Dame
- 27 Cinéma Trianon
- 28 Marché des Grands Hommes (Food Market)
- 30 Laundrette
- 31 Hôtel de Police
- 33 La Navette (Airport Bus) Stop
- 34 Virgin Megastore
- 35 Porte Dijeaux
- 37 Le Moyen Age
- 38 Théâtre Femina
- 39 American Express
- 40 Jouets Maurice Verdeun
- 41 Bodega Bodega
- 42 Bourse du Commerce
- 43 Hôtel de la Douane
- 45 Calle Ocho
- 46 Centre National Jean Moulin
- 47 Seven Café
- 48 Musée des Arts Décoratifs
- 50 Bradley's Bookshop
- 51 Auchan Supermarket & Centre Commercial Mériadeck
- 52 Galerie des Beaux-Arts
- 53 Place du Colonel Raynal
- 55 Musée des Beaux-Arts
- 56 Jardin de la Mairie
- 57 Hôtel de Ville
- 58 BHV
- 59 Cathédrale Saint André
- 60 Tour Pey-Berland
- 61 Post Office Branch
- 62 La Reine Carotte
- 63 Porte Cailhau
- 64 Porte des Salinières
- 65 Église Saint Michel
- 66 Tour Saint Michel
- 67 Porte de la Grosse Cloche
- 68 Musée d'Aquitaine
- 70 Cyberstation
- 71 Hôpital Saint André (Hospital)
- 73 Champion Supermarket
- 74 Synagogue
- 75 Cycles Peugeot Pasteur
- 77 Porte d'Aquitaine
- 78 The Down Under
- 79 Le Plana
- 81 Espérance Grocery
- 82 La Lune dans le Caniveau
- 83 Halles des Capucins (Wholesale Food Market)
- 84 Le Fournil des Capucins

Revolution, 22 of whom were executed in 1793 for alleged counter-Revolutionary activities. The entire 50m-high ensemble, completed in 1902, was dismantled in 1943 by the Germans so the statues could be melted down for their 52 tonnes of bronze; restoration work was not completed until 1983.

Bordeaux's neoclassical **Grand Théâtre**, built in the 1770s, is surrounded by a Corinthian colonnade decorated with 12 figures of the Muses and Graces. The nearby riverside area is a lifeless string of parking lots that cries out for redevelopment.

Nowadays, **Place Gambetta** is an island of calm and flowers in the midst of the city centre's hustle and bustle, but during the Reign of Terror that followed the Revolution, a guillotine placed here severed the heads of 300 alleged counter-Revolutionaries.

The city's main shopping area is east of Place Gambetta along the pedestrianised **Rue Porte Dijeaux**, named after **Porte Dijeaux**, a former city gate built in 1748; the upscale, boutique-lined **Cours de l'Intendance**; and **Rue Sainte Catherine**, where you'll find several major department stores. **Galerie Bordelaise**, a 19th century shopping arcade, is at the intersection of Rue Porte Dijeaux and Rue Sainte Catherine.

In 1137, the future King Louis VII married Eleanor of Aquitaine in the **Cathédrale Saint André**. The exterior wall of the nave dates from 1096; most of the rest of the structure was built in the 13th and 14th centuries. The 15th century belfry, **Tour Pey-Berland**, stands behind the choir. The chapels are nestled among the flying buttresses. The interior, which is much more attractive than the stained, crumbling exterior would suggest, can be visited from 7.30 to 11.30 am (12.30 pm on Sunday) and 2 to 6 or 6.30 pm (closed on Sunday afternoon except perhaps in summer).

Porte de la Grosse Cloche, a 15th century clock tower which was once the city hall's belfry, spans Rue Saint James. It was restored in the 19th century.

The architecture of the **Synagogue** (☎ 05 56 91 79 39) on Rue du Grand Rabbin Joseph Cohen, inaugurated in 1882, is a mixture of Sephardic and Byzantine styles. Ripped apart and turned into a prison by the Nazis, it was painstakingly rebuilt after the war according to the original plans. Visits are possible Monday to Thursday from 5 to 6 or 6.30 pm – just ring the bell marked *gardien* at 213 Rue Sainte Catherine.

Organised Tours

The tourist office runs guided walking tours of the city, in French and English, every day at 10 am (40FF, 35FF for students and over 65s).

Places to Stay – Budget

Bordeaux has lots of reasonably priced hotels. You're much better off *not* staying in the seedy area around the train station.

Camping *Camping Beausoleil* (☎ 05 56 89 17 66), open all year, is about 10km south-west of the city centre at 371 Cours du Général de Gaulle (the N10) in Gradignan. Two people with a tent are charged 60FF (85FF with a car). To get there, take bus G from Place de la Victoire towards Gradignan Beausoleil and get off at the last stop.

Camping Les Gravières (☎ 05 56 87 00 36), also open all year, is 10km south-east of the centre of Bordeaux at Place de Courréjean in Villenave d'Ornon. Tariffs are 22FF for a tent site (30FF with a car) and 19FF per adult. To get there, take bus B from Place de la Victoire towards Corréjean and get off at the terminus.

Hostels The charmless *Auberge de Jeunesse* (☎ 05 56 91 59 51; fax 05 56 94 02 98) at 22 Cours Barbey charges 62FF (72FF if you don't have an HI card) for a bed in a utilitarian, eight-bed room. The women's section (on the 1st floor) and the men's section (on the 2nd floor) are reached by separate staircases! The curfew is 11 pm – talk to the manager in advance if you'll be staying out later. Reception is staffed from 8 to 10 am and 4 to 11 pm; bags can be dropped off any time except between noon and 2 pm. The hostel will be closed for renovations during part of 1999.

Hotels – City Centre One of the best cheapies in town is the ***Hôtel Touring*** (☎ 05 56 81 56 73; fax 05 56 81 24 55) at 16 Rue Huguerie. This 12 room, two star hotel has gigantic and spotless singles/doubles for 120/140FF (200/220FF with shower and toilet). Some of the rooms have fireplaces.

Hôtel Studio (☎ 05 56 48 00 14; fax 05 56 81 25 71; www.hotel-bordeaux.com; studio@hotel-bordeaux.com), 26 Rue Huguerie, is the headquarters of Bordeaux's cheap hotel empire – the family owns three other inexpensive places on the same street, all of them offering charmless and small but eminently serviceable singles/doubles with flimsy showers, toilets, mini-fridges and cable TV for 98/120FF; slightly larger doubles are 135FF. Rooms for three to five people go for 180 to 250FF.

The quiet, 16 room ***Hôtel Boulan*** (☎/fax 05 56 52 23 62), 28 Rue Boulan, has rather modest singles/doubles with high ceilings for 100/110FF (120/140FF with shower). Toilets are on the half-floor. Hall showers cost 10FF. ***Hôtel La Boëtie*** (pronounced 'bo-eh-SEE'; ☎ 05 56 81 76 68, fax 05 56 51 24 06), 4 Rue La Boëtie, features modern singles/doubles/quads with toilet and shower from 120/135/200FF.

The very central, 11 room ***Hôtel de Dax*** (☎ 05 56 48 28 42) at 7 Rue Mautrec has large and simple (though hardly spotless) rooms with vintage furnishings for one/two/three people from around 120/125/135FF. Showers are free. The two star ***Hôtel Blayais*** (☎ 05 56 48 17 87; fax 05 56 52 47 57), 17 Rue Mautrec, has fairly large but simple singles/doubles with shower and toilet for 190/200FF.

You might also try the 29 room ***Hôtel de Famille*** (☎ 05 56 52 11 28; fax 05 56 51 94 43) at 76 Cours Georges Clemenceau, which has rather ordinary but homey singles/doubles/triples from 110/120/160FF (190/200/220FF with shower and toilet). Hall showers are free.

Hotels – Train Station Area The choice around here is limited in both quality and quantity. The 14 room ***Hôtel Les Deux Mondes*** (☎ 05 56 91 63 09; fax 05 56 92 12 11), 10 Rue Saint Vincent de Paul, has unexciting singles/doubles/triples with shower and toilet for 120/165/210FF. There are a couple of slightly more expensive places on the same block.

Places to Stay – Mid-Range

The two star, 27 room ***Hôtel Bristol*** (☎ 05 56 81 85 01; fax 05 56 51 24 06; bristol@hotel-bordeaux.com) at 2 Rue Bouffard has cheerful and very comfortable doubles/triples with 4m-high ceilings, bathroom, toilet and minibar from 210/290FF.

The three star, 45 room ***Hôtel Royal Médoc*** (☎ 05 56 81 72 42; fax 05 56 51 74 98), 3 Rue de Sèze, offers comfortable, sound-proofed singles/doubles/triples for 220/250/310FF. Next door at No 7, the ***Hôtel de Sèze*** (☎ 05 56 52 65 54; fax 05 56 44 31 83) has similar prices.

The 13 room ***Hôtel Balzac*** (☎ 05 56 81 85 12), 14 Rue Lafaurie de Monbadon, between Place Gambetta and Place de Tourny, has rather large, modern shower and toilet-equipped singles/doubles/triples for 160/180/200FF.

Facing the train station, ***Hôtel Le Faisan*** (☎ 05 56 91 54 52; fax 05 56 92 93 83), a 62 room, two star establishment at 28 Rue Charles Domercq, has pleasant singles/doubles/triples with shower, toilet and TV for 230/270/330FF.

Places to Eat

Quite a few restaurants offer reasonably priced lunch *menus*.

Restaurants – French The inexpensive cafés and restaurants around Place de la Victoire, popular with students, include the ***Cassolette Café*** (☎ 05 56 92 94 96) at No 20, which offers great value by serving family-style French food in a unique way: each small/large *cassolette* (terracotta plate) that you order from a check-off *carte* costs 11/33FF. It is open from noon to 2.30 pm and 6 to 11.30 pm (closed Sunday).

The very popular ***Chez Édouard*** (☎ 05 56 81 48 87) at 16 Place du Parlement offers

French bistro-style meat and fish dishes. *Menus* cost 57.50FF (weekday lunches), 79.50, 125 and 139.50FF. It is open daily from noon to 2.15 pm and 7.15 to 11.15 pm. There are a number of other ***cafés*** and ***restaurants***, some with terraces, at Place du Parlement and along nearby Rue de Parlement Sainte Catherine and Rue des Piliers de Tutelle.

La Chanterelle (☎ 05 56 81 75 43) at 3 Rue de Martignac serves moderately priced traditional French and regional cuisine. The lunch *menus* cost 65 and 70FF; the other *menus* go for 90 to 150FF. They're closed on Wednesday night and Sunday.

Restaurant Baud et Millet (☎ 05 56 79 05 77), 19 Rue Huguerie, serves cheese-based cuisine (most dishes are vegetarian), including all-you-can-eat meals of *raclette* (110FF) and fondue Savoyarde (95FF); the *menus* cost 140 to 170FF. The basement buffet has 100 to 150 kinds of cheese. This place is open Monday to Saturday from 11 am to 11 pm. The same street is home to several other eateries.

Restaurant Jean Ramet (☎ 05 56 44 12 51), 7 Place Jean Jaurès, serves classic French and Bordelais cuisine amid mirrors, white tablecloths and sparkling tableware. *Menus* cost 160FF (lunch only), 260 and 320FF. It is closed on Saturday for lunch and on Sunday.

Restaurants – Other ***La Fournaise*** (☎ 05 56 91 04 71) at 23 Rue de Lalande serves the cuisine of Réunion, which has strong Indian, Chinese, Basque and Breton elements. The *menus* cost 55FF (weekday lunches only), 75, 95 and 130FF (closed Sunday and Monday).

La Dakaroise (☎ 05 56 92 77 32), 9 Rue Gratiolet, serves simple but tasty dishes from Senegal and the Antilles. The selection consists of only one item: a fixed *menu* (55FF) whose three courses change each night. This place is open Tuesday to Saturday from 7.30 pm to 2 am.

The richly ornamented ***Restaurant Agadir*** (☎ 05 56 52 28 04), 14 Rue du Palais Gallien, has Moroccan couscous and tajines for 60 to 80FF; *menus* are 60FF (lunch), 100 and 150FF. It is open daily from 11.30 am to 2.30 pm and 6.30 to 11.30 pm (12.30 am on Friday and Saturday nights). There are a number of other restaurants on the same street.

Near the Musée d'Aquitaine, there are several ***ethnic restaurants*** (Vietnamese, Indian, Lebanese) on Rue du Hâ. Half a dozen ***Chinese restaurants*** can be found along Rue Saint Rémi, a block north of Place du Parlement.

Self-Catering The upmarket food stalls in the basement of the modern, mirror-plated ***Marché des Grands Hommes*** at Place des Grands Hommes are open Monday to Saturday from 7 am to 7.30 pm.

The vast, cheap ***Auchan*** supermarket in the Centre Commercial Mériadeck, whose eastern entrance is opposite 58 Rue du Château d'Eau, is open Monday to Saturday from 8.30 am to 10 pm. The ***Champion*** supermarket at 190 Rue Sainte Catherine is open daily, except Sunday, from 8.30 am to 8 pm.

Close to Place de Tourny, ***Fromagerie Antonin*** at 6 Rue de Fondaudège is open until 7.30 pm (closed on Monday morning and Sunday and, in July and August, Saturday afternoon); the midday closure lasts from 12.45 to 4 pm. There are several other ***food shops*** in the immediate vicinity.

Near Place de la Victoire, ***Le Fournil des Capucins***, a boulangerie at 62-64 Cours de la Marne, is open 24 hours a day. ***Espérance***, a grocery shop at 10 Cours de la Marne, is open daily until midnight (2 am on Thursday, Friday and Saturday nights).

Entertainment

Bordeaux has a really hopping nightlife scene; details on events appear in a free brochure called *Clubs & Concerts*. Student nightlife centres around Place de la Victoire.

Tickets for sporting events, bullfights etc are available from the ***Virgin Megastore billeterie*** (☎ 05 56 56 05 55) at 17 Place Gambetta, open from 10 am to 7.30 pm (11.30 pm on Friday and Saturday; closed Sunday).

Cinema Nondubbed films are frequently screened at ***Cinéma Trianon*** (also known as Centre Jean Vigo; ☎ 05 56 44 35 17), an art cinema and cultural centre at 6 Rue Franklin.

Classical Music The 18th century ***Grand Théâtre*** (☎ 05 56 48 58 54), Place de la Comédie, stages operas, ballets and concerts of orchestral and chamber music. The ticket office, which also handles ticketing for the plays, dance performances and variety shows held at the ***Théâtre Femina*** (on nearby Rue de Grassi), is open Monday to Saturday from 11 am to 6 pm.

Clubs For zoning reasons, many of the city's late night dance venues are a few blocks north-east of Gare Saint Jean along Quai de Paludate. ***Le Zoo*** (☎ 05 56 85 71 85) at No 48, whose techno, dance and house music is definitely on the mass-market side of things, is open on Thursday, Friday and Saturday nights from 11 pm to 5 am. Entry costs 20FF. This place attracts a young crowd, mainly 25 and under. ***Les Bains Bleus*** (☎ 05 56 85 71 85) at 14-18 Rue de Commerce, under the same management as Le Zoo, attracts somewhat older crowd revellers. It is open Thursday, Friday and Saturday nights from midnight to 6 am. Entry costs 50FF, including a drink.

Pierced eyebrows are recommended but not mandatory at ***La Lune dans le Caniveau*** (☎ 05 56 31 95 92), 39 Place des Capucins, a hardcore disco whose down-and-out surroundings, nonpop sound track (punk rock, 'hard', reggae, ska) and live concerts (about twice a month at 9 pm) attract the grungiest members of the local counter-culture scene. It is open Wednesday to Saturday from 11 pm to 5 am, but things don't get going until about 2 am. There's no cover charge, except for some concerts.

The Cricketers (☎ 05 56 49 69 56), a blues bar at 72 Quai de Paludate, has live concerts (including some by well known overseas groups) two or three times a week (40 to 80FF). It is open daily from 6 pm to 5 am. ***Le Plana*** (☎ 05 56 91 73 23), a bar at 22 Place de la Victoire, has live jazz every Sunday at 10 pm and concerts of pop, funk etc – some of them jam sessions by students – on most Mondays and Tuesdays at 10.30 pm. A beer costs 13FF (15FF after 9 pm). This place, vastly popular with students, is open daily from 7 pm to 2 am.

Gay & Lesbian Venues The streets north of the cathedral form Bordeaux's own little Marais. ***BHV*** (☎ 05 56 44 05 08) at 4 Rue de l'Hôtel de Ville, which is 95% gay, has an evening for *transformistes* (transvestites) every two or three Sundays at 11 pm. It is open daily from 11.30 am (6 pm on weekends) to 2 am. Around the corner at 73 Rue des Trois Conils, ***Seven Café*** (☎ 05 56 48 13 79) is a friendly, mainly gay bar which is open daily from 6 pm to 2 am. The mixed disco in the basement is open on Saturdays, Sundays and holidays from 5 am (when La Factory closes) to noon or 1 pm. The friendly, mellow ***Le Moyen Age*** (☎ 05 56 44 12 87) at 8 Rue des Remparts, one of the oldest gay bars in France, is open from 10 pm to 2 am (closed Tuesday).

La Factory (☎ 05 56 01 10 11) at 28 Rue Mably is a mixed but mainly gay disco with techno upstairs and disco downstairs. It is open daily from midnight to 5 am. On Friday and Saturday and when there are special events entry costs 50FF, including a drink; the rest of the time there's no cover charge.

La Reine Carotte (☎ 05 56 01 26 68), a lesbian bar at 32 Rue du Chai des Farines, is open on Friday and Saturday nights.

Bars ***The Down Under*** (☎ 05 56 94 52 48), 104 Cours Aristide Briand, run by an ex-Aucklander, is a favourite of Aussie and Kiwi rugby players and other Anglophones. Fosters is 15/27FF per half-pint/pint. There are theme parties about twice a month. Daily hours are 7 or 8 pm to 2 am.

One of the hottest places in town is a Cuban-style bar called ***Calle Ocho*** (☎ 05 56 48 08 68) at 24 Rue des Piliers de Tutelle. The house specialty, the *mojito* (a mint drink made with lemon and rum), costs

20FF. Cuban cigars go for 25 to 100FF each. They're open from 5 pm to 2 am (closed Sunday). Down the road at No 4, ***Bodega Bodega*** (☎ 05 56 01 24 24) is a popular tapas bar which is open from noon to 3.15 pm and 7 pm to 2 am (closed for lunch on Sunday and holidays).

Shopping

Bordeaux wine in all price ranges is on sale at several speciality shops near the tourist office, including Bordeaux Magnum (☎ 05 56 48 00 06) at 3 Rue Gobineau and Vinothèque (☎ 05 56 52 32 05) at 8 Cours du 30 Juillet. Both are open Monday to Saturday until 7.30 pm.

Jouets Maurice Verdeun (☎ 05 56 81 63 18), a toy store housed in three shops around 34 Galerie Bordelaise, carries a fabulous selection of miniature cars, model trains, remote control boats and other neat stuff.

Several antique shops can be found along Rue Bouffard, near the Musée des Arts Décoratifs.

Getting There & Away

Air Bordeaux airport (☎ 05 56 34 50 50) is 10km west of the city centre.

Bus Buses to places all over the Gironde (and parts of nearby departments) leave from the Halte Routière on Allées de Chartres (in the north-east corner of Esplanade des Quinconces; schedules are posted) and, in certain cases, from the train station. The information kiosk at the Halte Routière (☎ 05 56 43 68 43) is open weekdays from 6 to 8.30 am and 1 to 8.30 pm, Saturday from 9 am to 12.30 pm and 5 to 8.30 pm, and Sunday from 8.30 to 10.30 am and 5 to 8.30 pm. For details on buses to Pointe de Grave, Soulac-sur-Mer and Euronat in the Médoc, and Saint Émilion, see those listings.

Eurolines (☎ 05 56 92 50 42), facing the train station at 32 Rue Charles Domercq, is open Monday to Saturday from 9 am to noon and 2 to 7 pm.

Train Bordeaux is one of France's most important rail transit points. The train station, Gare Saint Jean (☎ 08 36 35 35 35), is about 3km from the city centre at the southern terminus of Cours de la Marne. The SNCF information office, next to platform No 1 at Gate 14, is open from 9 am to 7 pm (closed Sunday and holidays). The left-luggage office, on Quai 1 at Gate 54, is open daily from 8 am to 12.15 pm and 1.30 to 8 pm. The showers (20FF, including a towel), on Quai 1 at Gate 42, are open daily from 5 am to 10 pm. Be extra careful with your bags here.

Destinations served include Bayonne (132FF; 1¾ hours; seven or eight a day), Clermont-Ferrand (225FF), Nantes (219FF; four hours; four or five a day), La Rochelle (131FF; 2¼ hours; four to seven a day), Nice (416FF), Quimper (324FF), Sarlat (2½ to three hours; five a day, two on Sunday) and Toulouse (161FF; 2¼ hours; 10 a day). For information on getting to the Médoc, Saint Émilion and Arcachon, see those sections.

From Paris, you can take either the TGV Atlantique from Gare Montparnasse (337 to 387FF; three or 3½ hours; at least 16 a day) or a non-TGV departing from Gare d'Austerlitz (295FF; 5½ hours; one to three a day, at least four on Fridays).

Car AA Location (☎ 05 56 92 84 78) at 185 Cours de la Marne rents small cars for 199/510FF a day/weekend with 100/500km free and a 3000FF excess (deductible). Rent-a-Car Système (☎ 05 56 33 60 75) at 204 Cours de la Marne is open Monday to Saturday until 7 pm.

Getting Around

Parking is hard to find in the city centre, and some meters won't allow you to pay the night before for parking after 9 am the next morning. There are inexpensive parking areas along the Garonne – the lot between Esplanade des Quinconces and the river charges 7/25FF for one/12 hours during the day.

To/From the Airport La Navette (☎ 05 56 34 50 50) links the train station, the Grand Théâtre (29 rue Esprit des Lois) and Place Gambetta (the stop for bus line Nos 13 and M) with the airport every 30/45 minutes on weekdays/weekends until at least 9.30 pm (until 10.45 pm from the airport). The trip takes 35 minutes and one-way trips cost 34FF for adults, and 25FF for under 26s and seniors.

Bus Bordeaux's urban bus network, known as CGFTE (☎ 05 57 57 88 88), has *espaces accueil* (information bureaus) at the train station, Place Gambetta (4 Rue Georges Bonnac) and Place Jean Jaurès. They can supply you with an easy-to-use *Plan Poche* (pocket route map). The train station is linked with the city centre by bus Nos 7 and 8.

Single tickets, sold on board, cost 7.50FF and are *not* valid for transfers. Carnets of 10 tickets (54FF), available at tabacs, come with two *talons* (coupons) bearing the same serial number as the tickets – you may be asked to show one of the coupons when transferring. You can transfer up to three times after your initial ride but don't forget to time-stamp your ticket each time you board. The last time-stamping must be done less than 60 minutes after the first.

The Carte Bordeaux Découverte, sold at the tourist office, allows unlimited bus travel for one day (23.50FF) to six days (77FF). Time-stamp it only the first time you use it.

Taxi To order a taxi 24 hours a day, call ☎ 05 56 91 47 05 (Place de la Victoire). For a taxi to the airport, call ☎ 05 56 97 11 27.

Bicycle Cycles Peugeot Pasteur (☎ 05 56 92 68 20), 42 Cours Pasteur (near Place de la Victoire), rents mountain bikes for 70/250FF a day/week. It's open from 10 am to noon and 2 to 7 pm (closed on Sunday and, for July and August, on Monday morning and Saturday afternoon).

BORDEAUX WINE-GROWING REGION

The 1000 sq km wine-growing area around the city of Bordeaux is – along with Burgundy – France's most important producer of top-quality wines. The region is divided into 57 *appellations* (production areas whose soil and microclimate impart distinctive characteristics upon the wine produced there) that are grouped into six *familles* and subdivided into a hierarchy of designations (eg *premier grand cru classé*, the most prestigious) that often vary from appellation to appellation.

The majority of the region's many wines – reds, rosés, sweet and dry whites, sparkling wines – have earned the right to include the abbreviation AOC (Appellation d'Origine Contrôlée) on their labels, indicating that the contents have been grown, fermented and aged according to strict regulations governing such matters as the number of vines permitted per hectare and acceptable pruning methods. In 1997, the region produced 855 million bottles of wine.

Bordeaux has over 5000 *châteaux* (also known as *domaines*, *crus* or *clos*), a term that in this context refers not to palatial residences but rather to the properties where grapes are raised, picked, fermented and then matured as wine. The smaller chateaus sometimes accept walk-in visitors, but at many of the better-known ones you have to make an appointment. Many are closed in August and during the *vendange* (grape harvest) in October.

Traditionally, Bordelais wine-makers have dealt with city-based *négociants* (merchants) to market their wine rather than selling direct from source, which may explain why many chateaus here – even ones 'open to the public' – seem less-than-welcoming to casual visitors. You'll probably have better luck tasting and purchasing wines at retail wine merchants, such as those in Saint Émilion, than at the wineries.

Information

In Bordeaux, the Maison du Vin de Bordeaux (☎/fax 05 56 00 22 88; civb@vins-bordeaux.fr; www.vins-bordeaux.fr) at 3 Cours du 30 Juillet (across the street from the tourist office) has a great deal of information on chateau visits, including a free colour-coded map of production areas, entitled *Vignoble de Bordeaux*. Details on visiting chateaus appear in a series of brochures, one for each sub-region (the Médoc, Entre Deux Mers, Graves etc). Such information is also available from local *maisons du vin* (tourist offices that deal mainly with winery visits), whose addresses appear on the colour-coded map.

The Maison du Vin de Bordeaux is open weekdays from 8.30 am to 6 pm (5.30 pm on Friday). From early June to mid-October, it is also open on Saturday from 9 am to 4 pm; during this period (and by appointment the rest of the year), there are free wine tastings, usually at 11 am and sometimes at 3 pm.

Organised Tours

The Bordeaux tourist office runs half-day bus tours in French and English to chateaus in the area on Wednesday and Saturday (daily from May to October) at 1.15 pm. The cost is 160FF (140FF for students and seniors over 65). More information on winery tours appears under Organised Tours in the Saint Émilion listing.

THE MÉDOC

North-west of Bordeaux, along the western shore of the Gironde Estuary – formed by the confluence of the Garonne and the Dordogne rivers – lie some of Bordeaux's most celebrated vineyards, those of Haut Médoc, Margaux and neighbouring appellations. To the west, beaches of fine sand, bordered by dunes and *étangs* (lagoons), stretch for some 200km from Pointe de Grave (where the Gironde estuary meets the Atlantic) south to the Bassin d'Arcachon and beyond. The coastal dunes abut a vast pine forest planted in the 19th century to stabilise the drifting sands and prevent them from encroaching on areas farther inland.

Getting There & Away

The northern tip of the Médoc, Pointe de Grave, is linked with Royan – on the other side of the estuary – by car ferry (☎ 05 46 38 35 15; 25 minutes; six to 17 a day). Fees are 16FF for bicycles, 53FF for motorcycles and 120FF for cars, plus 16FF per person. It runs until 6.30 pm (7.15 pm from Royan) in winter, and until 8.30 pm (9.30 pm from Royan) in July and August.

A total of four SNCF and Citram Aquitaine buses a day (two on Saturday) link Pointe de Grave with points south, including Soulac-sur-Mer and Bordeaux (87FF; 2¼ hours).

Vineyards & Chateaus

The gravelly soil of the Médoc's gently rolling hills supports orderly rows of meticulously tended grape vines (mainly Cabernet Sauvignon) that produce some of the world's most sought-after red wines. The rose bushes at the end of each row serve a purpose similar to that of canaries in coal mines: they're more susceptible to disease (especially mildew) than the vines, and tell the grower when prophylactic treatment is necessary. The most beautiful part of this renowned wine-growing area is north of **Pauillac**, along the D2 and the D204 (towards Lesparre). To the north, the vines give way to evergreen forests.

Chateaus in the Pauillac appellation that welcome visitors include the beautifully landscaped **Château Lafitte Rothschild** (☎ 05 56 89 78 00), famed for its premier *grand cru classé* (open Tuesday to Thursday from 1.30 to 6 pm, by appointment only); and the equally illustrious **Château Mouton Rothschild** (☎ 05 56 73 21 29), which can be visited on weekdays and, from April to October, on weekends and holidays (20FF; by appointment only). Nearby in the Saint Julien appellation, the impressive **Château Beychevelle** (☎ 05 56 73 20 70) allows weekday visits year-round (on Saturday as well in July and August, by appointment only from November to March).

About 20km to the south in Margaux, you can visit the celebrated **Château Margaux** (☎ 05 57 88 83 83) on weekdays (by appointment only). No reservations are necessary for **Château Palmer** (☎ 05 57 88 72 72), on the D2 3km south of Margaux in Issan, which is open on weekdays (daily from April to October). The last 30-minute tour of the ultra-modern production facilities, which ends with a short *dégustation*, begins at 4.30 pm (5.30 pm from April to October).

Information on the Médoc, and help with reservations for chateau visits, is available at the Maison du Tourisme et du Vin (☎ 05 56 59 03 08) in Pauillac, open daily year-round until 6 or 7 pm. The annual, map-equipped brochure *Médoc Guide Découverte* has details on chateaus that welcome visitors. Finding some of the chateaus can be a bit tricky, though a few of the best known are marked on Michelin's yellow road maps.

By SNCF train or bus, Pauillac is about an hour from Bordeaux (53FF; six on weekdays, four on Saturday, two on Sunday). Bikes can be brought along on most weekday runs.

Soulac-sur-Mer

Soulac (population 2800), which has a wide, safe beach fronted by a promenade, is a lively seaside resort in summer and a very quiet seaside town the rest of the year. The commercial centre is along pedestrianised Rue de la Plage, which runs perpendicular to the beach.

Information The tourist office (☎ 05 56 09 86 61; fax 05 56 73 63 76), across from 68 Rue de la Plage, is next to the Marché Municipal (a covered food market, which is open daily until 1 pm). It's open Monday to Saturday from 9 am to 12.30 pm and 2 to 6 pm; in July and August it's open daily from 9 am to 7 pm. Bus and ferry schedules are posted in the window.

The post office, which does currency exchange, is down the street at 81 Rue de la Plage. It's open weekdays from 9 am to noon and 2 to 5 pm and on Saturday until noon.

Places to Stay Rooms and camping grounds are impossible to come by in July and August.

The two star, 13 room ***Hôtel La Dame de Cœur*** (☎ 05 56 09 80 80; fax 05 56 09 97 47), 103 Rue de la Plage, open throughout the year, has fairly ordinary singles/doubles/triples/quads for 160/200/250/280FF. The two star ***Hôtel L'Hacienda*** (☎ 05 56 09 81 34; fax 05 56 73 65 57), on Rue des Lacs 150m south of the church, is open year-round. Fairly basic doubles cost between 230FF (in winter) and 300FF (June to September).

Getting There & Away Soulac is 9km south of Pointe de Grave and 90km north of Bordeaux.

From Bordeaux, the trip to Soulac takes 1¾ hours by SNCF train and/or bus (81FF; four or five a day, two on Sunday and holidays) and two hours by Citram Aquitaine bus (75FF; five a day, three on Sunday and holidays). Soulac's railway station, on the Bordeaux-Pointe de Grave line, is 700m south of the town's Romanesque church, buried by the dunes in 1757 and dug out a century later. Citram buses stop near the church, at the roundabout with a crucifix in the middle.

Euronat

The relaxed naturist village of Euronat (☎ 05 56 09 33 33; fax 05 56 09 30 27) is about 80km north of Bordeaux. The facilities, which can accommodate up to 7500 people, cover 3.3 sq km of pine forest and broom that abut 1.5km of dune-lined beachfront, dotted with German pillboxes from WWII. The restaurants and commercial centre are open from about April to October, but the centre itself is open year-round. Sporting activities on offer during the warmer months – mainly in July and August – include cycling (rental available), swimming in the heated pool, archery, tennis, yoga, judo, and gymnastics.

For Saturday to Saturday rental, the least expensive bungalows for two/five people cost between 930/1260FF (in winter) and 2400/3300FF (in July and August). Rentals for less than a week are possible except in July and August. Caravan sites, including two adults, cost 60 to 170FF a night; tent sites for two people cost 40 to 110FF.

Euronat's office is open daily from 8 am to 5.30 pm (9 am to 5 pm on weekends and holidays); June to September hours are 8 am to 9 pm. Reservations are necessary only in July and August – bungalows and caravan sites need to be reserved by May, though tent sites are usually available on short notice. Euronat's mailing address is: 33590 Grayan-et-L'Hôpital.

For general information on naturism in France, see Naturism under Activities in the Facts for the Visitor chapter.

Getting There & Away Soulac-sur-Mer, 10km north of Euronat, is linked with Bordeaux by the SNCF and Citram Aquitaine. From there you have to take a taxi (☎ 05 56 09 79 57), though rumour has it that a few Citram Aquitaine buses stop at the entrance to Euronat.

SAINT ÉMILION

• pop 2800 **✉ 33330**

The medieval village of Saint Émilion, 39km east of Bordeaux, is renowned for its full-bodied, deeply coloured red wines. Situated on two limestone hills that look out over the Dordogne River valley, its ramparts (begun in the 13th century) and the rest of the town take on a luscious golden hue as the sun sets. Over the last few years, Saint Émilion's vintages have been attracting ever greater numbers of eager tourists.

In the 8th century, a Benedictine monk from Brittany named Émilion moved into a cave fed by a spring; a monastery was later established around the site. During the Middle Ages, Saint Émilion was a resting place on one of the routes to Santiago de Compostella.

Orientation

Rue Guadet (as the D122 is known as it passes through town) is Saint Émilion's main commercial street and runs north-south. Place du Marché is in the centre of town next to the Église Monolithe.

Information

Tourist Office The tourist office (☎ 05 57 55 28 28; fax 05 57 55 28 29) at Place des Créneaux has quite a few brochures in English and a list of chateaus in the area that can be visited, noting those where English is spoken. Before visiting a chateau, it's a good idea to phone ahead – except in summer when someone at the tourist office may be able to help with this if the office isn't busy. The tourist office is open daily from 9.30 am to 12.30 pm and 1.45 to 6 or 6.30 pm. In July and August, hours are from 9.30 am to 7 pm.

Money The Caisse d'Épargne on Rue Guadet is open from 8.30 am to noon and 1.30 to 4.30 pm (closed Saturday afternoon, Sunday and Monday). The Crédit Agricole on Rue des Girondins has an ATM.

Post The post office on Rue Guadet, open weekdays from 8.30 am to noon and 2.30 to 5.30 pm and on Saturday until noon, will change foreign currency.

Books Wine connoisseurs may want to pick up a copy of the outdated but useful *Wine Buyers' Guide – Saint Émilion* by Philippe Barbour & David Ewens (50FF). It is available at the Maison du Vin (☎ 05 57 55 50 55), around the corner from the tourist office at Place Pierre Meyrat, which is open daily from 9.30 am to 12.30 pm and 2 or 2.30 to 6.30 pm (6 pm from December to February, 7 pm in August).

Église Monolithe Tour

Saint Émilion's most interesting historical sites can be visited only if you take one of the tourist office's 45-minute guided tours (in French with printed English text), which depart every 45 minutes from 10 to 11.30 am and 2 to 5 pm (5.45 pm from April to October). The cost is 33FF (20FF for students, 16FF for children aged 13 to 18).

The 13th century **Chapelle de la Trinité**, a small Benedictine chapel that still has its original frescoes, is just above **Grotte de l'Ermitage**, which is the cave where Émilion – renowned in popular tradition for his ability to perform miracles (though he was never canonised) – lived from 750 to 767 AD.

The **Catacombes** were first used for burials in the 9th century. There are lots of other caves under Saint Émilion (some 200 in total), but archaeologists can't excavate them because of fears the buildings above may collapse.

The **Église Monolithe**, carved out of solid limestone from the 9th to the 12th centuries, measures 20 by 38m and has an 11m-high ceiling. The **bell tower** directly above the church – the entrance is at Place des Créneaux – has a Romanesque base and a Gothic spire; it was built from the 12th to the 15th centuries. You can climb to the top whenever the tourist office is open – to get the key, you have to leave ID and pay 6FF.

Other Sights

The impressive former **Collégiale** (collegiate church), now a parish church, has a long, narrow Romanesque nave (12th century) and a spacious, almost square choir (14th to 16th century). Except during services, it can be visited from 9 am to noon and 2 to 6.30 pm (later on sunny days). **Cloître de l'Église Collégiale**, the church's 14th century cloister, is accessible via the tourist office.

Several of the city's medieval gates survive, including **Porte de la Cadène** (Gate of the Chain), just off Rue Guadet. Next door is **Maison de la Cadène**, a half-timbered house from the early 16th century. **Cloître des Cordeliers**, a ruined monastery on Rue des Cordeliers, is open all year for no

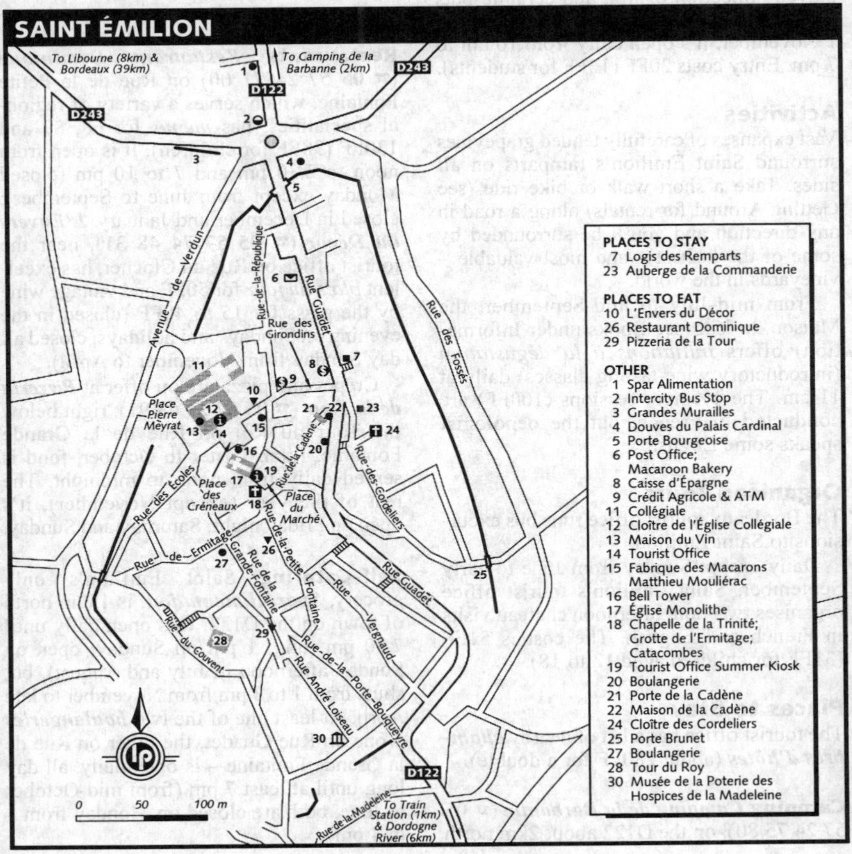

charge. The eponymous winery that has occupied part of the site for over a century makes sparkling wine; tours of their cellars take place daily at 3, 4, 5 and 6 pm.

The rectangular, 13th century **Tour du Roi** (King's Tower) affords fine views of the town and the Dordogne Valley. From about May to October, it is supposed to be open daily from 10.30 am to 12.45 pm and 2.15 to 6.45 pm (later in summer). The rest of the year, it's open mainly in the afternoon. Entry costs 6FF.

The **Musée de la Poterie des Hospices de la Madeleine** (☎ 05 57 55 51 65) at 21 Rue André Loiseau has an attractively displayed collection of iron and ceramic pots and jugs from centuries past. From Easter to 1 November, it's open daily from 10 am to 7 pm. Entry costs 20FF (10FF for students).

Activities

Vast expanses of carefully tended grapevines surround Saint Émilion's ramparts on all sides. Take a short walk or bike ride (see Getting Around for rentals) along a road in any direction and you'll be surrounded by some of the lushest – and most valuable – vineyards in the world.

From mid-July to mid-September, the Maison du Vin (see Books under Information) offers *initiations à la dégustation* (introductory wine-tasting classes) daily at 11 am. The 1½-hour sessions (100FF) are conducted in French, but the oenologist speaks some English.

Organised Tours

The Bordeaux tourist office runs bus excursions to Saint Émilion.

Daily except Sunday from June to early September, Saint Émilion's tourist office organises two-hour afternoon chateau visits in French and English. The cost is 51FF (31FF for children aged 12 to 18).

Places to Stay

The tourist office has a list of nearby ***chambres d'hôtes*** (about 280FF for a double).

Camping ***Camping de la Barbanne*** (☎ 05 57 24 75 80), on the D122 about 2km north of Saint Émilion, is open from April to September. Two adults with a tent are charged 75.20FF (10FF more in July and August).

Hotels The two star, 18 room ***Auberge de la Commanderie*** (☎ 05 57 24 70 19; fax 05 57 74 44 53) on Rue des Cordeliers has spacious, flowery doubles/quads from 280/480FF (380/550FF in June and most of September). It is closed from mid-January to mid-February. The three star ***Logis des Remparts*** (☎ 05 57 24 70 43; fax 05 57 74 47 44) on Rue Guadet has a 12m pool and pleasant doubles starting at 350FF. It is closed in December.

Places to Eat

Restaurants ***Restaurant Dominique*** (☎ 05 57 24 71 00) on Rue de la Petite Fontaine, which serves a variety of regional specialities, has *menus* for 68, 89 and 130FF (38FF for children). It is open from noon to 2.30 pm and 7 to 10 pm (closed Monday except from June to September); closed in December and January. ***L'Envers du Décor*** (☎ 05 57 74 48 31), near the tourist office on Rue du Clocher, has excellent *plats du jour* for 50FF and vintage wine by the glass for 15 to 40FF (closed in the evening on Sundays and holidays; closed all day Sunday from November to April).

Crêpes and pizza are on offer at ***Pizzeria de la Tour*** (☎ 05 57 24 68 91), right below the Tour du Roi on Rue de la Grande Fontaine. From Easter to October, food is served daily from noon to midnight. The rest of the year (except November), it's open on Friday night, Saturday and Sunday.

Self-Catering Saint Émilion's only grocery, ***Spar Alimentation***, is 150m north of town on the D122. It is open daily until 7.30 pm (until 1 pm on Sunday; open on Sunday afternoon in July and August), but shuts from 1 to 3 pm from November to late April. At least one of the two ***boulangeries*** – one on Rue Guadet, the other on Rue de la Grande Fontaine – is open daily, all day long until at least 7 pm (from mid-October to June, both are closed on Monday from 1 to 4 pm).

Shopping

Wine Saint Émilion's quaint streets and squares (eg Place du Marché) are lined with wine shops. Most offer free tasting to serious buyers.

The cooperative Maison du Vin (see Information) is owned by the 225 chateaus whose wines it sells.

Macaroons The recipe for *macarons* – soft cookies made from almond powder, egg whites and sugar that are baked on sheets of paper for about 12 minutes at 180 to 200°C – was brought to Saint Émilion in the 17th century by Ursuline nuns. Fabrique des Macarons Matthieu Mouliérac on Tertre de la Tente charges 30FF per two dozen. There's another macaroon bakery next to the post office.

Getting There & Away

Bus When school is in session, there are Citram Aquitaine buses (☎ 05 56 43 68 43) from Bordeaux (32FF), with a change in Libourne to a Marchesseau bus (☎ 05 57 40 60 79; 11FF), at 6.40 am (Monday to Friday) and, except on Monday and Thursday, at 11.30 am (10.30 am on Sunday and holidays). Year-round, the last bus back leaves Saint Émilion at 5.10 pm (4.45 pm on Sunday and holidays). Buses stop at the northern edge of town (see map).

Train The SNCF's tertiary line from Bordeaux to Bergerac links Bordeaux's Gare Saint Jean with Saint Émilion (43FF; 35 to 45 minutes) two or three times a day. Trains leave Bordeaux at 7.10 am (9.10 am on Sunday) and, most of the time, at 1.30 pm. The last autorail (rail carriage) back to Bordeaux leaves Saint Émilion's train station, a bit over 1km south of town, daily (during most of the year) at 6.30 pm. Buy your ticket on the train.

Getting Around

The tourist office rents bicycles for 60/90FF per half-day/day.

ARCACHON

• pop 11,800 ✉ 33120

The beach resort of Arcachon became popular with bourgeois residents of Bordeaux at the end of the 19th century. Its major attractions are the town's sandy seashore and the extraordinary Dune du Pilat (see Around Arcachon), Europe's highest sand dune. Arcachon, which is somnolent in winter and extremely crowded in summer, is well served by trains and makes an easy day trip from Bordeaux.

Orientation

Arcachon is on the south side of the triangular Bassin d'Arcachon (Arcachon Bay), which is linked to the Atlantic by a 3km-wide channel just west of town. The narrow peninsula of Cap Ferret is on the other side of the outlet. The Dune du Pilat begins 8km south of Arcachon along the D218.

Arcachon's main commercial streets run parallel to the beach: Blvd de la Plage, Cours Lamarque de Plaisance and Cours Héricart de Thury. Perpendicular to the beach, busy streets include Ave Gambetta and Rue du Maréchal de Lattre de Tassigny. The train station, 500m south of the beach, is linked to Jetée Thiers (Thiers Pier) and Blvd de la Plage by Blvd Général Leclerc and Ave Gambetta.

Information

Tourist Office The tourist office (☎ 05 57 52 97 97; fax 05 57 52 97 77; tourisme@arcachon.com; www.arcachon.com) is at Place Président Roosevelt, 200m to the left as you exit the train station. It is open Monday to Saturday from 9 am to 12.30 pm and 2 to 6 pm (7 pm in July and August, when there's no midday closure). Between April and September, it is also open on Sunday and holidays from 9 am to 1 pm.

Money The Banque de France, across the street from the tourist office at 55 Blvd Général Leclerc, is open Monday to Friday from 9 am to noon and 1.15 to 3.30 pm.

There are a number of banks right around the *mairie* (town hall) and along Blvd de la

Plage. The Crédit Agricole next to 252 Blvd de la Plage changes money Tuesday to Saturday from 8.30 to 11.30 am and 1.50 to 4.30 pm.

Post The main post office, at Place Président Roosevelt, is open Monday to Friday from 8 am to 6.15 pm (7 pm in July and August) and on Saturday until noon. Exchange services are available.

Laundry The Laverie at the corner of Blvd Général Leclerc and Rue Molière is open daily from 7 am to 10 pm.

Central Arcachon

The flat area that abuts the **Plage d'Arcachon**, the town's beach, is known as the **Ville d'Été** (Summer Quarter). The liveliest section is around the pier known as **Jetée Thiers**.

The delightful **Musée de la Maquette Marine** (☎ 05 57 52 00 03) at 19 Blvd Général Leclerc displays a multitude of truly exquisite 1:100 scale ship models commissioned by shipyards as prototypes. From Easter to early July and in September, it is open on weekends from 2 to 6 pm. From early July through

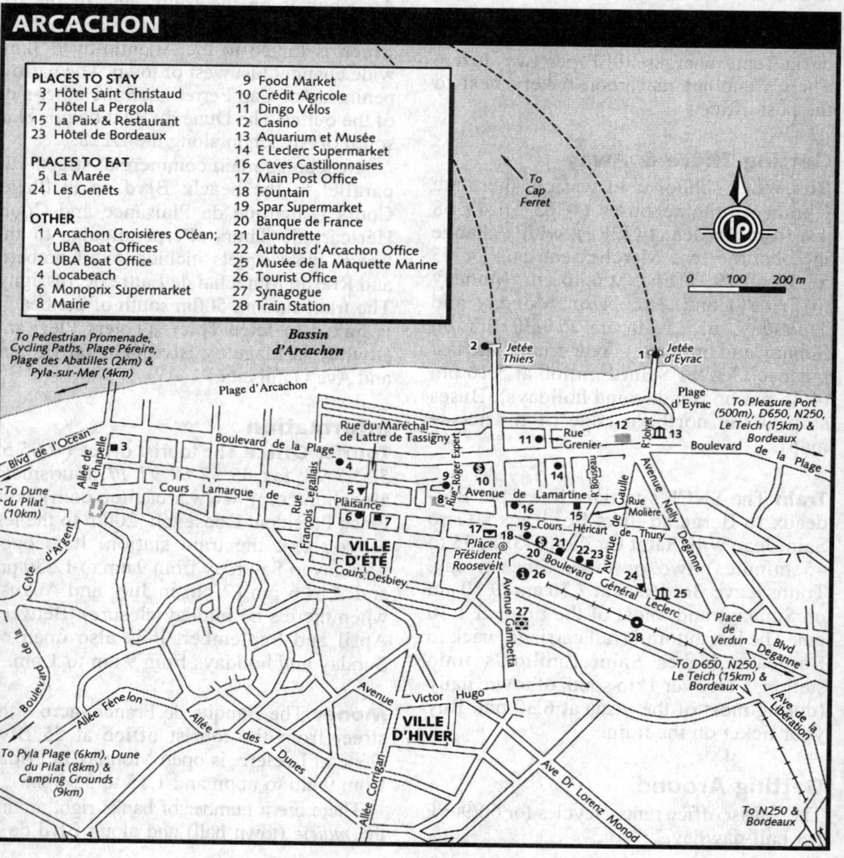

August, it's open daily from 10 am to 12.30 pm and 3 to 7 pm. Entry costs 30FF (15FF for children aged four to 12).

The uninspiring **Aquarium et Musée** (☎ 05 56 54 89 28) at 2 Rue du Professeur Jolyet is open daily from mid-March to early November; hours are 10 am to 12.30 pm and 2 to 7 pm (11 pm in July and August). Tickets cost 24FF (15FF for children aged three to 10 and students).

The **Ville d'Hiver** (Winter Quarter), on the tree-covered hillside south of the Ville d'Été, dates from the turn of the century. In decades past, rich people came here either to amuse themselves with other rich people or to recover from tuberculosis.

A lovely pedestrian promenade lined with trees, grass and playgrounds runs west and then south from the Plage d'Arcachon to **Plage Péreire**, **Plage des Abatilles** and **Pyla-sur-Mer**. **Pistes cyclables** (cycling paths) link Arcachon with Biscarosse, 30km to the south, and towns all around the Bassin d'Arcachon.

Boat Excursions

UBA (see Boat under Getting There & Away) runs cruises around the Île aux Oiseaux (Bird Island, in the Bassin d'Arcachon) daily, year-round at 3 pm (five times a day in July and August; 70FF). Arcachon Croisières Océan (☎ 05 57 52 24 77) has similar excursions from April to October; departures are from Jetée Eyrac.

Daily in July and August, and in June on weekends and when there's demand, UBA has boat excursions to the Banc d'Arguin (a sand bank off the Dune du Pilat; 70FF; daily at 11 am). During especially high tides the company also has trips up the Leyre River.

Places to Stay

During July and August, it is extremely difficult to find accommodation and many hotels require that you take half-pension.

Places to Stay – Budget

Camping See Around Arcachon for details on camping grounds.

Hotels The ***La Paix*** (☎ 05 56 83 05 65), a friendly, down-to-earth hotel at 8 Ave de Lamartine, is open from May to early October. Doubles/triples/quads with washbasin and bidet are 167/220/279FF; toilets for some rooms are in the courtyard. Doubles with toilet cost 189FF (211FF with shower and toilet). Prices, which include breakfast, are 25% higher from June to early September. Hall showers are free. Studio apartments are available year-round for 1000 to 2800FF a week, depending on the season.

The 17 room ***Hôtel Saint Christaud*** (☎ 05 56 83 38 53) at 8 Allée de la Chapelle open year-round, has simply furnished doubles for 99 to 145FF (129 to 185FF with shower and toilet), depending on the season. Hall showers are free. Half-pension (100FF extra per person) is obligatory in July and August.

Places to Stay – Mid-Range

The two star, 20 room ***Hôtel La Pergola*** (☎ 05 56 83 07 89; fax 05 56 83 14 21) at 40 Cours Lamarque de Plaisance is open year-round. Modern doubles with shower and toilet cost between 230FF (from November to Easter) and 417FF (in July and August, including breakfast). The two rooms with washbasin go for 150 to 250FF. There's a charge of 90FF to add a 3rd or 4th person. Studios cost 1000 to 2600FF a week.

Across from the train station, the 12 room ***Hôtel de Bordeaux*** (☎ 05 56 83 80 30; fax 05 56 83 69 02) at 39 Blvd Général Leclerc has ordinary singles/doubles/triples with shower and toilet for between 140/ 200/360FF (in winter) and 200/300/420FF (mid-June to September). It is open year-round.

Places to Eat

Arcachon is known for its seafood, especially *huîtres* (oysters).

Restaurants In the warm months, the beachfront promenade between Jetée Thiers and Jetée Eyrac is lined with ***tourist restaurants*** and places offering pizza and crêpes.

Les Genêts (☎ 05 56 83 40 28) at 25 Blvd Général Leclerc specialises in seafood and fresh dishes made with local produce. The *menus* start at 98FF. It is closed on Sunday night and Monday (open daily except Monday night in July and August). ***La Marée*** (☎ 05 56 83 24 05), a popular seafood place at 21 Rue du Maréchal de Lattre de Tassigny, offers six/12 small oysters for 35/62FF; the *menu* is 99FF. It is open from early February to October and, except during school holiday periods, is closed on Monday night and Tuesday.

From June to mid-September, ***La Paix*** (see Places to Stay) has French *menus* from 59FF. It is open daily from noon to 2 pm and 7.30 to 10 pm.

Self-Catering The lively ***food market*** on Rue Roger Expert, just north of the Mairie on the ground floor of a parking garage, is open daily from 8 am to 1 pm. ***Caves Castillonnaises*** at 32 Ave de Lamartine, open from 9 am to 1 pm and 3 to 8 pm (closed on Sunday afternoon and, except in July and August, on Monday), sells wine both in bottles and from vats; the latter costs as little as 7.50FF per litre.

Across from the tourist office, the ***Spar*** supermarket at 57 Blvd Général Leclerc is open until 8 pm (closed from 12.45 to 3 or 3.30 pm and on Sunday afternoon). The ***E Leclerc*** supermarket at 224 Blvd de la Plage is open Monday to Saturday from 9 am to 12.30 pm and 2.30 to 7.30 pm (no midday closure on Friday and Saturday). In July and August it's open from 9 am to 8 pm and on Sunday until 1 pm. The ***Monoprix*** at 46 Cours Lamarque de Plaisance has almost identical year-round and summer hours but closes at 7 pm (8 pm in July and August).

Getting There & Away

Train Some of the trains from Bordeaux to Arcachon (54FF; 45 minutes; nine to 17 a day) are coordinated with Paris-Bordeaux TGVs. The last train back to Bordeaux leaves Arcachon at 8 pm (9.50 pm on Sundays and holidays, 9 pm on weeknights in July and August).

Boat From June to September, UBA (☎ 05 56 54 60 32) has hourly ferries from Jetée Thiers (and Jetée Eyrac in summer) to Cap Ferret (30/50FF one way/return, 20/35FF for children four to 12). The rest of the year, there is at least one run a day on Monday, Wednesday, Friday and Sunday (four a day in April, May and October).

Getting Around

Car & Motorcycle There is unmetered parking north of the casino along Ave de Gaulle.

Locabeach (☎ 05 56 83 39 64) at 326 Blvd de la Plage, open from April to September, rents out scooters starting at 170FF a day and also has larger motorbikes; the excess ranges from 4000 to 8000FF. It is open daily from 9 am to 7.30 pm (midnight in July and August).

Taxi To order a cab, call ☎ 05 56 83 11 11.

Bicycle A bike path links Arcachon with Biscarosse, 30km to the south.

From Easter to September, Dingo Vélos (☎ 05 56 83 44 09) on Rue Grenier rents tandems, *triplos*, *quatros* and *quintuplos* (bikes with places for two to five riders) and pushme-pullyous (tandems whose riders face in opposite directions) for 30/50FF per person per half-hour/hour. Regular five-speeds/mountain bikes start at 50/80FF a day. It is open daily from 9.30 am to 7 pm (until midnight in July and August).

Locabeach (see Car & Motorcycle), rents five-speeds for 35/50FF per half-day/day; mountain bikes are 60/80FF.

AROUND ARCACHON

Dune du Pilat

The remarkable Dune du Pilat (also called Dune de Pyla) is a sand dune approximately 114m high that stretches from the mouth of the Bassin d'Arcachon southward for almost 3km. Its inland side is steep enough to ski down. At the bottom, the tops of dead trees smothered by the dune as it moves relentlessly eastward – studies have shown it to be moving at about 4.5m a year – poke out of the sand. The slope facing the Atlantic, dotted with tufts of grass, is much gentler.

The view from the top is magnificent. To the west you can see the sandy shoals at the mouth of the Bassin d'Arcachon, including the **Banc d'Arguin bird reserve** and **Cap Ferret**. In the other direction, the dense pine forests of the Landes stretch from the base of the dune eastward almost as far as the eye can see. The GR8 passes not far from the dune.

Caution is advised while swimming in this area: powerful currents swirl around the coast's sandy *baïnes* (baylets), especially when the sea is rough. Also, don't count on being able to buy anything to eat around the dune.

Places to Stay The steep, inland side of the dune is lined with five large and rather pricey camping grounds, most of them half hidden in a forest of pine trees. The ***La Forêt*** (☎ 05 56 22 73 28; fax 05 56 22 70 50; camping .foret@hol.fr), open from Easter to October, charges 75FF for two adults with a tent or caravan.

Getting There & Away The parking lot at the north end of the dune charges 20FF for the whole day.

From June to September, Autobus d'Arcachon (☎ 05 56 83 07 60), based at 47 Blvd du Général Leclerc, has four daily buses (two in June and September) from the train station to the five camping grounds along the dune's eastern side (19FF). During the same period, buses to the Dune du Pilat parking lot (16FF; 30 minutes) run about every 45 minutes (and, in May and October, by request). The rest of the year, buses go only as far south as Pyla Plage (Haïtza), 1km north of the dune (11FF; seven a day, five on Sunday and holidays). Schedules are available at the tourist office.

Parc Ornithologique

The **Bassin d'Arcachon** is a shallow, 250 sq km tidal bay. Since only 20% of this area is underwater at low tide, it is an ideal habitat for birds. Indeed, some 260 bird species, both migratory and non-migratory, visit the area each year.

The Parc Ornithologique (bird reserve; ☎ 05 56 22 80 93) at Le Teich, in the south-east corner of the bay at the mouth of the multi-channelled Leyre (l'Eyre) River, is an important centre for the preservation of endangered bird species and an outstanding place to see some of Europe's rarest and most beautiful birds, such as the spoonbill, little egret, blue throat and black kite. The Parc has about two dozen nesting pairs of *cigognes* (storks) who take to the air every day at around noon. Two circuits – the 2.5km Petit Parcours and the 6km Grand Parcours – take you along dike-topped paths to a series of observation hides (blinds). A longer circuit, the Grand Boucle, is set to open in 2000.

Birds can be seen year-round. From August to October, migratory birds from Scandinavia and Greenland, including lots of waders, pass through. May is a good time to observe species that are rarely seen farther north (eg in the UK). From late summer through the winter, it's easiest to observe the birds at high tide (at low tide the waders are out eating). Tidal schedules are available by Minitel on 3615 SHOM and on the back page of the regional daily, *Sud Ouest*, available at all newsagents. *Pleine* means high tide; *basse* means low tide.

The Parc is open daily, year-round, from 10 am to 6 pm (7 pm from mid-April to mid-September, 10 pm in July and August). Entry costs 35FF (24FF for children aged five to 14). *Jumelles* (binoculars) can be rented for 20FF; *graines* (bird food) costs 4FF a bag.

Activities The **Sentier du Littoral** footpath passes by the Parc. It goes 5km south-east to Lamothe, following the forested banks of the Leyre River, and 5km west to the oyster port of Gujan Mestras.

The Maison de la Nature du Bassin d'Arcachon (☎ 05 56 22 80 93) at the Parc runs nature discovery trips: guided sea kayak tours of the Leyre Delta (100FF per person; three hours) and the Bassin d'Arcachon (200FF per person; all day), held year-round; and, from June to September, unguided canoe cruises on the Leyre River (200FF for up to two adults and two children). For reservations, ring them a couple of days ahead (a week ahead in August).

Places to Stay The grassy, 70 site *Camping du Parc* (☎ 05 56 22 62 36; fax 05 56 22 82 22), a few hundred metres south-east of the Parc at 16 Rue du Port in Le Teich, is open from April to October. Two people with a tent are charged 60FF.

The 11 room ***Hôtel Le Central*** (☎/fax 05 56 22 65 64) at 61 Ave de la Côte d'Argent (the D650) in Le Teich, across the street from the church, has bright doubles/triples with washbasin and shower for 170/200FF.

Getting There & Away The Parc is 15km east of Arcachon on the D650. Le Teich's train station, 1200m south of the Parc, is on the line that links Bordeaux (43FF) with Arcachon (17FF).

Limousin, Périgord & Quercy

The adjacent regions of Limousin, Périgord and Quercy are tucked away in south central and south-western France between the Massif Central and the coastal Aquitaine basin. Although they share similar histories and are firmly steeped in rural life, each has its own distinctive landscape, ambience and cuisine.

HIGHLIGHTS

- **Limoges** – view one of the outstanding porcelain collections
- **Aubusson** – marvel at the famous tapestries
- **Lascaux** – take in the prehistoric cave paintings
- **Rocamadour** – visit this pilgrimage town, France's second most visited site
- **Pretty Villages** – explore some of the prettiest villages in France: Collonges-la-Rouge, Turenne, Domme, La Roque Gageac or Saint Cirq Lapopie

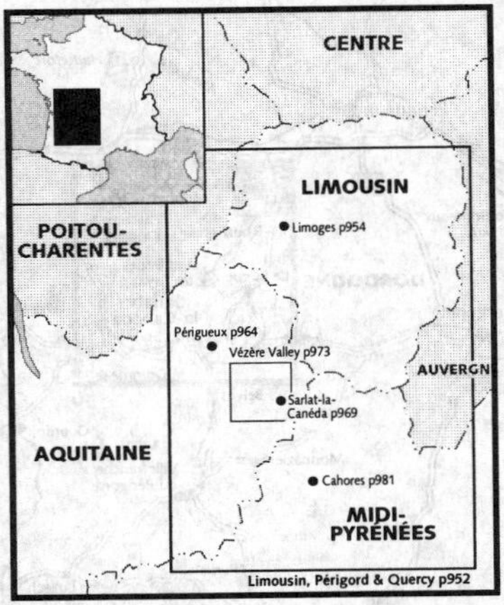

any dish in the *à la périgourdine* style – usually garnished with truffles and sometimes foie gras

pâtés de foie gras

***confit* of duck, goose or pork**

truffles

Limousin

The tranquil, green hills of Limousin, dotted with old churches and castles, present the quintessential image of rural France. Long overlooked by tourists, the region's many rivers, springs and lakes now attract visitors interested in such outdoor pursuits as sailing, canoeing, kayaking and fishing. The local economy is based on agriculture, in particular cattle and sheep farming.

Limousin, the least densely populated area of France, is made up of three departments. Haute-Vienne, in the west, has as its prefecture the city of Limoges; the rural Creuse is in the north-east; and the Corrèze department, blessed with many of the region's most beautiful sights is in the south-east.

LIMOGES

• pop 133,000 ✉ 87000 alt 200m

The pleasant though hardly compelling city of Limoges, once the capital of the Gallic tribe of the Lémovices, served as a main stop on one of the medieval pilgrimage routes to Santiago de Compostela in Spain. The city has long been acclaimed for its production of enamel and fine porcelain, and museums dedicated to these arts are one of Limoges' main attractions.

Orientation

The train station, Gare des Bénédictins, is at the end of Ave du Général de Gaulle, 500m north-east of Place Jourdan. The hillside

LIMOUSIN, PÉRIGORD & QUERCY

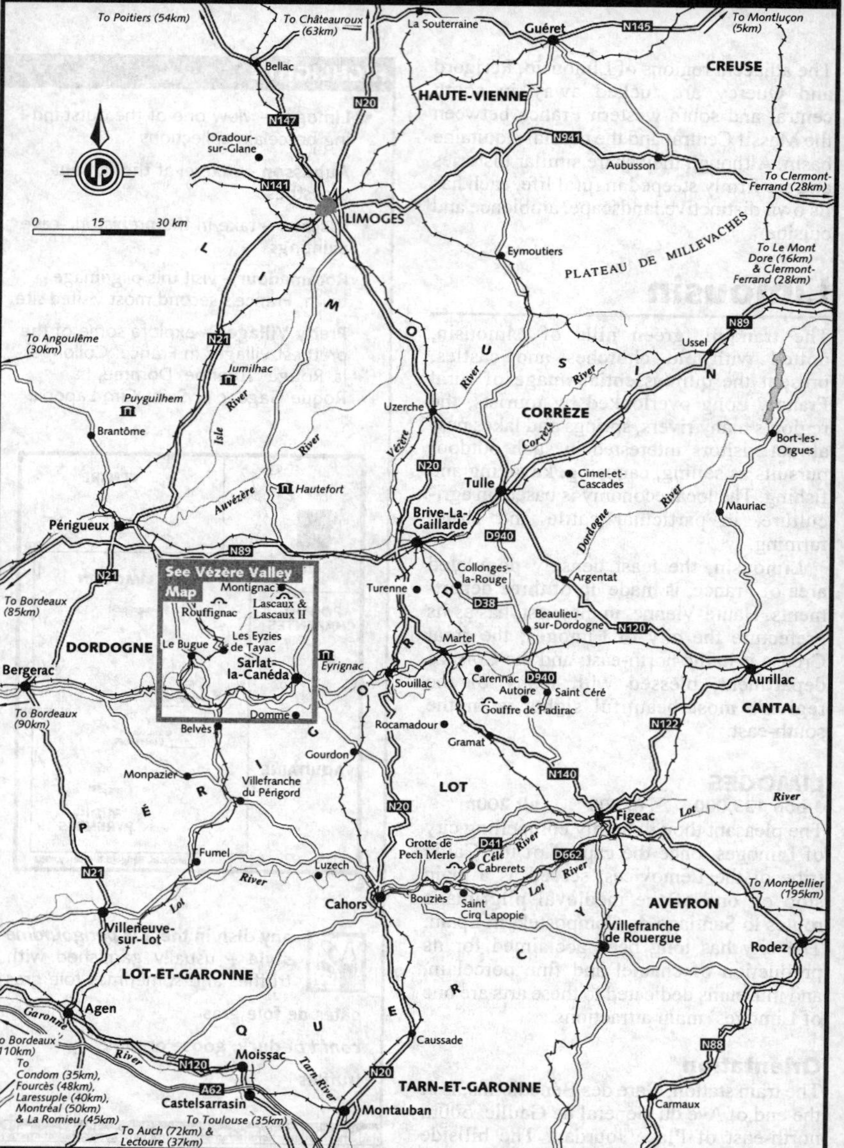

Cité Quarter and its cathedral are south of Place Jourdan and east of the partly pedestrianised commercial centre, the chateauless Château Quarter.

Information

Tourist Office The tourist office (☎ 05 55 34 46 87; fax 05 55 34 19 12) on Blvd de Fleurus is open Monday to Saturday from 9 am to noon and 2 to 6.30 pm. In July and August hours are 9 am to 7 pm (and from 10 am to 2 pm on Sunday).

The welcoming Maison du Tourisme (☎ 05 55 79 04 04), located at 4 Place Denis Dussoubs, has excellent English-language information on the Haute-Vienne department and it also sells topoguides. The office is open weekdays from 8.30 am to noon and 1.30 to 5.30 pm. From June to mid-September it is also open on Saturday from 10 am to noon and from 1.30 to 5 pm.

Money The Banque de France at 8 Blvd Carnot (down the steps from Place de la République) is open weekdays from 8.45 am to noon and 1.30 to 3.30 pm. There are several banks on Place Jourdan and Place Wilson. When the commercial banks are closed (ie in the evening and on Sunday and holidays), money can be exchanged at the tourist office.

Post The main post office on Place Stalingrad is open weekdays from 8 am to 7 pm and Saturday from 8 am to noon. Currency exchange is available.

Laundry The Lavomatique at 28 Rue Delescluze is open daily from 7 am to 9 pm. The GTI laundrette at 9 Rue Monte a Regret (20m down the hill from Place d'Aine) is open daily from 6 am to 10 pm.

Musée National Adrien Dubouché

Limoges' Adrien Dubouché Museum (☎ 05 55 33 08 50) at 8bis Place Winston Churchill is home to one of France's two most outstanding ceramics collections (the other is in Sèvres, south-west of Paris). Housed in an ornate building constructed between 1894 and 1900, its 12,000 pieces include local products as well as works from elsewhere in Europe, the Islamic world and China. It is open from 10 am to 12.30 pm and 2 to 5.45 pm (closed Tuesday and no midday break in July and August). Entry costs 22FF (15FF for people aged 18 to 25 or over 60 and, on Sunday, for everyone; free for under 18s). A brochure with English text is available at the entrance.

Just about the only remnants of Gallo-Roman Limoges – a few stones from the city's amphitheatre, now surrounded by boules courts and a children's playground – can be seen in the **Jardin d'Orsay** on Rue R Couraud, 200m south of the museum.

Château Quarter

All that remains of the great pilgrimage abbey of Saint Martial, founded in 848 AD, is an outline on Place de la République. The 9th century **Crypt of Saint Martial**, containing the tomb of Limoges' first bishop who converted the population to Christianity, can be visited from July to September; daily hours are from 9.30 am to noon and 2.30 to 7 pm.

Église Saint Pierre du Queyroix, half a block south-east of Place de la République, was built shortly after an earlier structure was destroyed by fire in 1213. It has an impressive 13th century tower. Across Place Saint Pierre is the **Pavillon du Verdurier**, an octagonal, porcelain-faced structure that dates from 1900.

Église Saint Michel des Lions on Rue Adrien Dubouché (just north of Place de la Motte), named for the two granite lions standing on either side of the tower door, has a huge copper ball perched atop its 65m-high spire. Built between the 14th and 16th centuries, it contains Saint Martial's relics – including his head, a number of beautiful 15th century stained-glass windows and some 17th and 18th century statuary.

Just off Place Saint Aurélien, the pedestrianised **Rue de la Boucherie** – so named because of the butchers' shops that lined the street in the Middle Ages – and nearby streets are graced with half-timbered houses.

LIMOGES

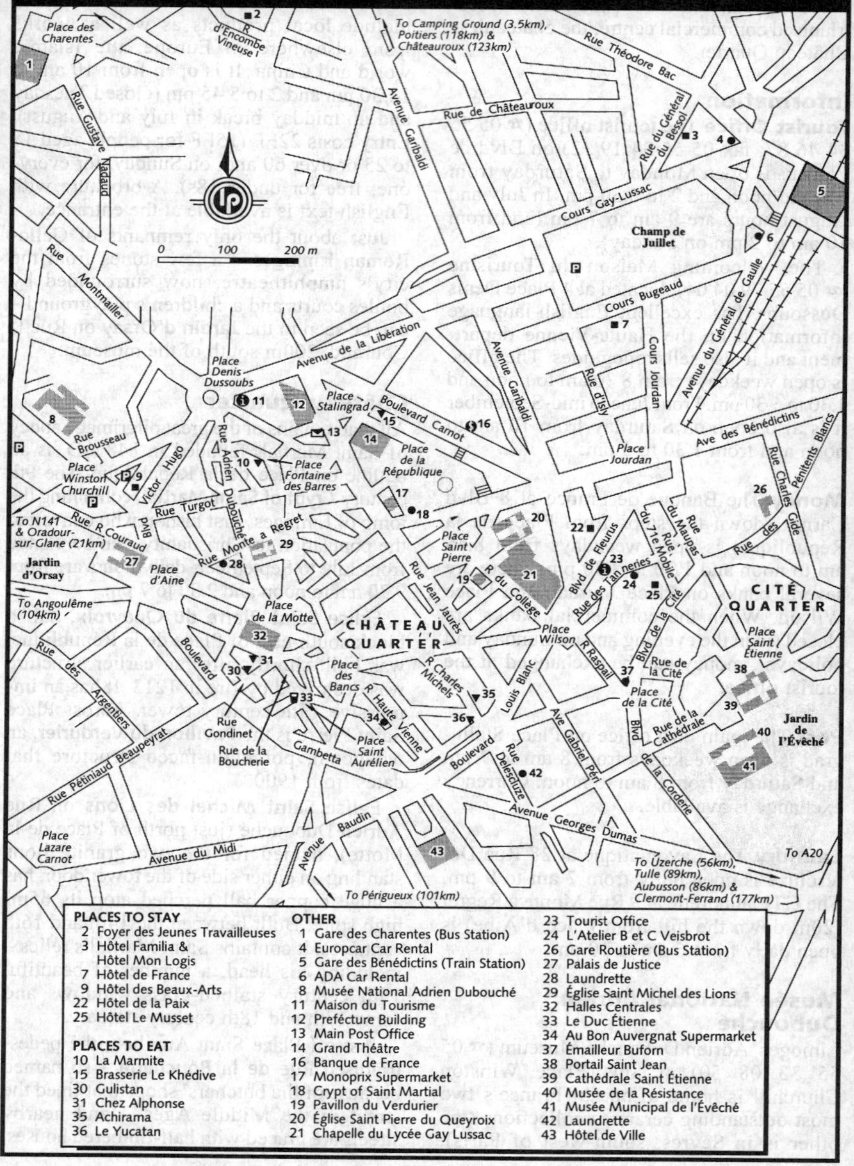

PLACES TO STAY
2 Foyer des Jeunes Travailleuses
3 Hôtel Familia & Hôtel Mon Logis
7 Hôtel de France
9 Hôtel des Beaux-Arts
22 Hôtel de la Paix
25 Hôtel Le Musset

PLACES TO EAT
10 La Marmite
15 Brasserie Le Khédive
30 Gulistan
31 Chez Alphonse
35 Achirama
36 Le Yucatan

OTHER
1 Gare des Charentes (Bus Station)
4 Europcar Car Rental
5 Gare des Bénédictins (Train Station)
6 ADA Car Rental
8 Musée National Adrien Dubouché
11 Maison du Tourisme
12 Prefécture Building
13 Main Post Office
14 Grand Théâtre
16 Banque de France
17 Monoprix Supermarket
18 Crypt of Saint Martial
19 Pavillon du Verdurier
20 Église Saint Pierre du Queyroix
21 Chapelle du Lycée Gay Lussac
23 Tourist Office
24 L'Atelier B et C Veisbrot
26 Gare Routière (Bus Station)
27 Palais de Justice
28 Laundrette
29 Église Saint Michel des Lions
32 Halles Centrales
33 Le Duc Étienne
34 Au Bon Auvergnat Supermarket
37 Émailleur Buforn
38 Portail Saint Jean
39 Cathédrale Saint Étienne
40 Musée de la Résistance
41 Musée Municipal de l'Évêché
42 Laundrette
43 Hôtel de Ville

Cité Quarter

The crumbly granite **Cathédrale Saint Étienne** – the only major Gothic cathedral in this part of France – was begun in 1273 on a site occupied since the 3rd century by a succession of churches, including a Romanesque structure of which the crypt (closed to the public) and the lower stories of the 62m belfry are the only remnants. Facing Place Saint Étienne, the Flamboyant Gothic **Portail Saint Jean** (the carved portal of the north transept arm) dates from between 1515 and 1530.

Inside, the richly decorated Renaissance rood screen, once situated at the entrance to the late 13th and early 14th century choir, is now in a less conspicuous location at the far end of the nave under the modern organ. Note the cathedral's remarkably slender pillars. It is open from 10 am (2.30 pm on Sunday) to 6 pm (6.30 pm on Sunday).

Behind the cathedral, the 18th century former bishop's palace houses the **Musée Municipal de l'Évêché** (☎ 05 55 34 44 09), which specialises in enamel (12th to 20th century) but also contains well presented collections of Egyptian and Gallo-Roman antiquities and a handful of lesser known works by Auguste Renoir, born in Limoges in 1841. It is open from 10 to 11.45 am and 2 to 5 pm (6 pm from June to September), and closed Tuesday except from July to September. Entry is free.

Across the courtyard from the museum is the **Musée de la Résistance et de la Déportation** (☎ 05 55 34 44 09), with photos, handbills, maps and military equipment illustrating the exploits of the Resistance and the suffering of the deportees. It is open from 2 to 5 pm; from June to mid-September, the hours are from 10 to 11.45 am and 2 to 6 pm. It is closed on Tuesday except from July to mid-September. Entry is free.

The cathedral is surrounded by the **Jardin de l'Évêché**, Limoges' botanical garden, whose formal beds include medicinal and toxic herbs and lots of flowers.

Places to Stay

Limoges has a good range of cheap and mid-range accommodation.

Places to Stay – Budget

Camping The three star ***Vallée de l'Aurence*** (☎ 05 55 38 49 43) on Ave d'Uzurat, on the edge of the Bastide forest about 3.5km north of the train station, is open all year. Fees are 16FF per adult, 7FF per child, 8FF per tent and 5FF per car. To get there, take bus No 20 from Place Jourdan to the Louis Armand stop and then walk along the lake for about 500m.

Hostel The 93 room ***Foyer des Jeunes Travailleuses*** (☎ 05 55 77 63 97), 20 Rue d'Encombe Vineuse, a charmless co-ed hostel for young working people, accepts travellers year-round. Reception is open all day long until 1 am. Singles (which is all they have) are 85FF, including breakfast.

Hotels Near the train station at 18 Rue du Général du Bessol, the quiet, friendly 14 room ***Hôtel Familia*** (☎ 05 55 77 51 40) has singles/doubles with shower from 175/195FF. Next door at No 16, the ***Hôtel Mon Logis*** (☎ 05 55 77 41 43) has rooms with shower for 125/150FF, while doubles/quads with shower and toilet are 183/220FF.

Across from the Champ de Juillet gardens, the welcoming ***Hôtel de France*** (☎ 05 55 77 78 92; fax 05 55 77 71 75) at 23 Cours Bugeaud has pastel-toned singles/doubles from 140/160FF (175/200FF with shower, 195/220FF with shower and toilet). The hall shower is free.

In the Château Quarter, an excellent bet is the one star ***Hôtel des Beaux-Arts*** (☎ 05 55 79 42 20; fax 05 55 79 29 13) at 28 Blvd Victor Hugo, whose tastefully decorated but small doubles start at 130FF (175FF with shower). Doubles/triples with shower and toilet are 205/235FF.

Places to Stay – Mid-Range to Top End

The ***Hôtel de la Paix*** (☎ 05 55 34 36 00; fax 05 55 32 37 06), 25 Place Jourdan, has a fantastic collection of 250 museum-quality gramophones and comfortable shower-equipped doubles for 200FF (260FF with toilet). There's free parking out front. The ***Hôtel Le Musset*** (☎ 05 55 34 34 03; fax 05 55 32 45 28) at 3 Rue du 71e Mobile, decorated with stained glass, has lovely rooms with shower for 180/225FF (250/295FF with toilet).

Places to Eat

Restaurants *Chez Alphonse* (☎ 05 55 34 34 14), an unpretentious bistro at 5 Place de la Motte, has a *menu* for 100FF. They're closed Sunday. Around the corner, the intimate ***Gulistan*** (☎ 05 55 34 73 71) at 20 Rue Gondinet serves an excellent Kurdish *menu* for 55FF (lunchtime only); à la carte main dishes cost 45 to 70FF. It is open from noon to 1.30 pm and 7 to 10.30 pm (closed Sunday).

Périgord specialities are served at the timber-framed ***La Marmite*** (☎ 05 55 33 38 34) at 1 Place Fontaine des Barres; *menus* start at 90FF (closed Monday lunch and Sunday). For salads (38 to 45FF) and *feuilletés* (light, triangular pastries filled with salmon, mussels etc), try ***Brasserie Le Khédive*** (☎ 05 55 79 96 69) at 39 Blvd Carnot, decorated with stained-glass windows. Meals are served from noon to 2 pm and 7 pm to 1 am; in the afternoon you can sip a beer or enjoy a dessert (closed Sunday and holidays).

In the Château Quarter, there's a cluster of ***ethnic restaurants*** at the bottom end of Rue Charles Michels. ***Le Yucatan*** (☎ 05 55 33 67 77), a popular, reasonably priced Tex-Mex place at No 3, has smallish tacos, burritos and enchiladas for 40FF. It is open daily from noon to 2 pm, except Sunday for lunch. ***Achirama*** (☎ 05 55 34 33 00), an Indian place at No 6, has *vindaloos* from 45FF and *menus* from 85FF (open Monday to Saturday).

Self-Catering All of Limoges' green spaces – including the Champ de Juillet, Place Jourdan, the Jardin d'Orsay and the Jardin de l'Évêché – are amply supplied with picnic benches.

The ***Halles Centrales*** (covered market) on Place de la Motte is open every morning until 1 pm. The ***food market*** at nearby Place des Bancs is open Tuesday to Saturday, all day long.

The ***Monoprix*** supermarket, located at 42 Rue Jean Jaurès, is open Monday to Saturday from 8.30 am to 7.30 pm and has a second entrance at 12 Place de la République. On the pedestrianised Rue Haute Vienne, the ***Au Bon Auvergnat*** supermarket (opposite No 28) is closed from 12.15 to 3 or 3.30 pm and on Sunday.

Entertainment

The city's meagre nightlife focuses on the brasseries around Place Denis Dussoubs and, near the train station, along Ave du Général de Gaulle. ***Le Duc Étienne*** on Place Saint Aurélien, a small rock and roll pub popular with locals and English-speaking students, has beers from 8FF. It is open daily from 10 am (4 pm on Sunday) to 2 am.

Shopping

Shops selling colourful enamel (*émail* or *émaux*), produced here since the 12th century, and porcelain can be found all over town including Place Wilson.

Original enamel works are available at many small storefront workshop/galleries

The Art of Enamel

The basic enamel-making process involves fixing powdered-lead glass coloured with metallic oxides to a base made of gold, silver, bronze, copper or some other metal. It acquires its translucent quality by being fired several times at about 800°C. Deposits of rare metallic oxides near Limoges enable the town's enamel-makers to create the rich, deep colours for which the town's enamelware is renowned.

The best time to see enamel in Limoges is during the Biénnale d'Émail Contemporain, an innovative international exhibition held on even-numbered years in July and August.

around the bottom of Rue Raspail, including Émailleur Buforn (☎ 05 55 32 43 82) at 4 Place de la Cité, where you can watch a master artisan at work. It is open from about 9 am to 12.30 pm and 2 to 7 pm (closed Sunday). On Rue des Tanneries (right below the tourist office), you can visit L'Atelier B et C Veisbrot (☎ 05 55 34 34 95) at No 19, another place with an *atelier* (workshop) open to the public (daily from 8 am to 7 pm).

On the second Sunday of each month, a flea market takes on Place Saint Étienne. The antiques market on Rue Brousseau (near the Musée National Adrien Dubouché) is open weekdays.

Getting There & Away

Bus Limoges has two bus terminals. Gare des Charentes (☎ 05 55 10 31 00) on Place des Charentes is used by the Régie DTHV, Haute-Vienne's departmental bus company (no service on Sunday and holidays). It is staffed from 7.45 am to 11.30 am and 1.45 to 5.30 pm (closed Saturday afternoon and Sunday). Destinations served include Oradour-sur-Glane.

Porcelain

The name Limoges has been synonymous with fine porcelain since the 1770s, when European artists set out to copy techniques that the Chinese had perfected five centuries earlier.

Three factors distinguish porcelain from other baked-clay ceramics: it is white, very hard and translucent. Made from kaolin (a fine white clay), quartz and feldspar, hard-paste porcelain became popular in Limoges after an exceptionally pure form of kaolin was found in the nearby village of Saint Yrieix. Porcelain is fired three times: first at about 950°C; again, after being covered with liquid enamel, at about 1450°C; and one last time, at 900°C or so, to ensure the hand-painted or machine-applied decoration adheres to the surface.

Five private carriers use the Gare Routière (☎ 05 55 34 47 77) on Rue Charles Gide, staffed on weekdays from 8.45 am to 12.15 pm and 2 to 6.15 pm.

Train Limoges' green-domed main train station, Gare des Bénédictins (☎ 08 36 35 35 35), is one of the most striking stations in all of France. Built in 1929, it has a distinctive tower and colourful stained-glass windows. The information office is open from 9 am to 7 pm (closed Sunday and holidays). The ticket windows are open 24 hours.

There are direct trains to Paris' Gare d'Austerlitz (245FF; three hours; six a day), Bordeaux (147FF; 2¾ hours; at least six a day), Brive-la-Gaillarde (97FF), Cahors (153FF; 2¼ hours; six a day), Clermont-Ferrand (141FF via Ussel; 3¾ hours; two a day), Figeac (146FF), Périgueux (79FF; one hour; five to eight a day), Poitiers (120FF; two hours; three a day), Toulouse (206FF; 3½ hours; six a day) and Uzerche (74FF; five to nine a day; 40 minutes).

Car ADA (☎ 05 55 79 61 12) is opposite the train station at 27 Ave du Général de Gaulle. Europcar (☎ 05 55 77 64 52) is also near the train station at 8 Cours Gay-Lussac.

Getting Around

Local buses, run by TCL (☎ 05 55 32 46 46), stop at various points around town, including Place Jourdan, the Hôtel de Ville and Gare des Bénédictins. The tourist office has free route maps. Single tickets cost 6.50FF; a magnetic card good for 10 journeys costs 51FF at the tourist office or *tabacs* (tobacconists).

AROUND LIMOGES

Oradour-sur-Glane

Oradour-sur-Glane, 21km north-west of Limoges on the D9, was an unexceptional Limousin town until the afternoon of 10 June 1944, when German lorries bearing an SS detachment rumbled into town.

The town's entire population was ordered to assemble at the market square. The men were divided into groups and forced into *granges* (barns), where they were gunned down before the structures were set alight. Several hundred women and children were herded into the church, inside a bomb was detonated; those who tried to escape through the windows were shot before the building was set on fire. The Nazi troops then burned down the entire town; inside the 328 buildings left smouldering that evening were the corpses of dozens of civilians who had hidden to avoid capture. Of the people rounded up that day – among them refugees from Paris and a couple of Jewish families living under assumed names – only one woman and five men survived; 642 people, including 205 children, were killed.

Since these events, the entire village has been left untouched to serve as a memorial. The café still has its tables and chairs, two rusting vehicles are still parked inside the ruins of the garage, and the houses are furnished with moss-covered bedposts, bicycles, pots and treadle sewing machines. The tram tracks and overhead wires, the prewar style electricity lines and the rusting hulks of 1930s automobiles give a pretty good idea of what the town must have looked like on the morning of the massacre. The crypt-like **Mémorial**, under the altar-shaped platform next to the cemetery, displays personal effects found in the debris. The site is open 24 hours a day, all year. There's no entry charge. To get there, follow the road signs to the *village martyr* (martyred village).

After the war, a larger Oradour was built a few hundred metres west of the ruins.

Place to Stay & Eat The ***Hôtel Le Milord*** (☎ 05 55 03 10 35), in the new town on Ave du 10 Juin 1944 (across from the church), has doubles with shower for 140FF. Their ground floor restaurant has *menus* from 63FF.

Getting There & Away Buses from Limoges' Gare des Charentes to Oradour (16.50FF; 30 to 40 minutes; three or four times a day) run from Monday to Saturday.

AUBUSSON

• pop 5100 ✉ 23200 alt 300m

Aubusson is located 86km east of Limoges on the main road to the Massif Central and has been acclaimed for its tapestries and carpets since the 16th century. The **Musée Départemental de la Tapisserie** (☎ 05 55 66 33 06), in the Centre Culturel Jean Lurçat on Ave des Lissiers, has exhibits of antique and contemporary tapestries and displays illustrating the art of tapestry weaving, still practised here. It is open from 9.30 am to noon and 2 to 6 pm (closed Tuesday). From July to mid-September, the hours are 10 am to 6 pm (closed Tuesday morning). Entry costs 14FF (10FF reduced price) except in summer, when the fees are 18FF (14FF reduced). The **École Nationale d'Art Décoratif** (National School of Decorative Art; ☎ 05 55 66 14 28), Place Villeneuve, features temporary exhibitions throughout the year and is open Monday to Saturday from 2 to 7 pm.

The tourist office (☎ 05 55 66 32 12) on Rue Vieille is open Monday to Saturday from 9.30 am to noon and 1.30 to 6 pm; from July to September, hours are from 10 am to 7 pm (10 am to 12.30 pm and 2.30 to 5.30 pm on Sunday).

Getting There & Away

Aubusson is linked to Limoges' train station (1½ hours) by two SNCF buses a day.

PLATEAU DE MILLEVACHES

South of Aubusson, the rocky, sparsely populated Millevaches Plateau (978m at its highest point) is the source of the Vézère River, which flows past the most famous prehistoric sites of Périgord. The area is at its best in autumn, when everything is covered in purple heather; in spring, the dominant colour is yellow, provided by the dandelion-carpeted pastures. Striking reddish brown Limousin cattle speckle the countryside, their highly valued beef dominates the local gastronomy. By the way, the name Millevaches, of Celtic origin, refers to the many springs in the area, not to a thousand cows!

The area is covered by Chamina's *La Corrèze* topoguide, which details 40 short hikes.

UZERCHE

• pop 3270 ✉ 19140 alt 450m

Set on a promontory rising high above the Vézère River, the picturesque town of Uzerche is known for its 15th and 16th century **Maisons à Tourelles**, which look like small castles thanks to their turrets. Some fine examples can be seen around Porte Bécharie, a 14th century town gate near Place Marie Colein.

At the top of the hill, high above the steep, dark grey slate roofs, is **Église Saint Pierre**, a barrel-vaulted Romanesque abbey church with a typically Limousin-style belfry and an 11th century crypt, reached through a squat door in the outside wall of the choir. It is open daily, all day long. From June to September, there's an exhibition of Limousin archaeology in the 17th century **Hôtel du Sénéchal** (☎ 05 55 73 26 07) at 14 Rue de la Justice, a few hundred metres north-east of the church (take Rue Pierre Chalaud down the hill from Place de la Libération).

A panoramic view of the town can be had from the right bank of the river, reached by taking the D3 under the railway viaduct.

Orientation

The old city is perched on a hill almost entirely surrounded by a hairpin curve in the Vézère River. The N20, known as Ave de Paris as it runs along the east side of the old city, intersects the D3 (the road to Eymoutiers) near the disused rail viaduct. About 500m up the hill, just past the post office, is the shop-lined Place Marie Colein, where you'll find the only street into the old city.

Information

The tourist office (☎ 05 55 73 15 71), behind the church, is open daily all year (except weekends in winter); daily hours are from 10 am to 12.30 pm and 2.30 or 3 to 6 or 6.30 pm.

Places to Stay & Eat

The attractive, two star ***Hôtel Jean Teyssier*** (☎ 05 55 73 10 05; fax 05 55 98 43 31), at the intersection of the N20 and the D3, has doubles from 260FF (320FF with shower and toilet) and quads from 330FF. Reception is closed on Wednesday (except from mid-July to mid-September when it opens after 5 pm). The hotel's restaurant (closed Wednesday) has *menus* from 120 to 250FF.

The less-than-welcoming ***Hôtel Bellevue*** (☎ 05 55 73 14 43) on Place Marie Colein (next to the post office) has doubles/triples with washbasin and bidet from 120/160FF.

Getting There & Away

Uzerche is on the N20, 56km south of Limoges and 35km north of Brive-la-Gaillarde.

Buses to/from Brive (29FF; 1¼ hours; two a day except Sunday and holidays) stop at the train station and, depending on which way you're going, just up or down the hill from Place Marie Colein. In Brive, there are stops on Place du 14 Juillet (next to the tourist office) and at the Gare Routière.

The train station, 2km north of the old city along the N20, is on the rail line linking Paris' Gare d'Austerlitz (four hours) and Limoges (40 minutes) with Brive (30 minutes). It is served by five to nine trains a day.

BRIVE-LA-GAILLARDE

• pop 50,000 ✉ 19100 alt 320m

Brive-la-Gaillarde, 93km south of Limoges on the left bank of the Corrèze River, is of no special interest but can be used as a transport, provisioning and accommodation base. A major rail junction, Brive earned the moniker *la gaillarde* (the bold one) in 1356 as a reward for its martial gallantry. Nearby agricultural lands are known for their mild climate and *primeurs* (early-ripening vegetables and fruits).

Brive is centred around the heavily restored **Église Saint Martin** on Place Charles de Gaulle, which has a Romanesque apse and choir and tall, cylindrical pillars of exceptional slenderness. Some 10 streets – many of them pedestrianised – radiate in all directions from the church and one of them, Rue de l'Hôtel de Ville, becomes Ave Jean Jaurès as it heads to the train station, 900m to the south-west. The town is very poorly signposted.

The **Musée Labenche** (☎ 05 55 24 19 05) at 26bis Blvd Jules Ferry (one of the avenues that encircles the old city), housed in the most outstanding of Brive's Renaissance mansions, covers archaeology, regional history and tapestries. It is open from 10 am to 6.30 pm (closed Tuesday). Entry costs 27FF (13.50FF reduced price). The **Centre Édmond Michelet** (☎ 05 55 74 06 08) at 4 Rue Champanatier (600m south-west of the church) has exhibits on the French Resistance during WWII and the deportations to Nazi concentration camps. Admission is free and it is open from 10 am to noon and 2 to 6 pm (closed on Sunday and holidays).

Information

The tourist office (☎ 05 55 24 08 80; fax 05 55 24 58 24), housed in a 19th century water tower on Place du 14 Juillet (400m north of Église Saint Martin), is open Monday to Saturday (except holidays) from 9 am to noon and 2 to 6 pm (9am to 7 pm in July and August, when it's also open on Sunday from 10 am to 1 pm).

The Banque de France at 3 Blvd Général Koenig is open weekdays from 8.45 am to noon and 1.45 to 3.45 pm.

Places to Stay

Near the train station, the cluster of cheap, basic and rather dreary hotels along Ave Jean Jaurès includes the 24 room ***Hôtel Le France*** (☎ 05 55 74 08 13) at No 60, the ***Hôtel Majestic et Voyageurs*** (☎ 05 55 24 10 20) at No 67 and the ***Hôtel Le Progrès*** (☎ 05 55 24 04 52) at No 32 (reception closed on Sunday).

Getting There & Away

Bus The bus station (☎ 05 55 74 20 13), on Place du 14 Juillet, is staffed from Monday to Saturday from 8.15 am to noon and 2 to 6 pm. Buses do not run on Sunday and holidays. Destinations served include Beaulieu-sur-Dordogne (34.50FF; two a day when school is in session), Uzerche (29.50FF; two a day, except Sunday and holidays), Collonges-la-Rouge (15.50FF; 30 minutes; four a day) and Sarlat-la-Canéda (41FF; 1¾ hours; one a day in the late afternoon).

Train The train station (☎ 08 36 35 35 35), at the top of Ave Jean Jaurès, is on the north-south line from Paris' Gare d'Austerlitz (265FF) to Toulouse (140FF), whose stops include Limoges and Cahors, and on the east-west line linking Bordeaux (134FF) with Ussel, which passes through Périgueux and continues east to Clermont-Ferrand. Three SNCF buses a day go to Sarlat (55 minutes). The information office is open from 9 am to 6.30 pm (closed on Sunday and holidays).

Car Near the train station on Ave Jean Jaurès, Europcar (☎ 05 55 74 14 41), Hertz (☎ 05 55 24 26 75) and Avis (☎ 05 55 24 51 00) are at Nos 52, 54, 56 respectively.

AROUND BRIVE-LA-GAILLARDE

Gimel-les-Cascades

This tiny village 37km north-east of Brive-la-Gaillarde, is perched high above the highest waterfalls in Limousin. The three falls have a total drop of 143m into a gorge aptly named the Inferno. It is popular with walkers but requires sturdy footwear.

Other sights include a ruined chateau, the remains of the Romanesque church of Saint Étienne de Braguse (just outside the village) and a 15th century church built in typical Limousin style. Nearby Lac Ruffaud offers a refreshing dip and a shady retreat for a picnic.

Information

The tourist office (☎ 05 55 21 44 32) is near the village church in the main square. It is open Easter to November from 10.30 am to 12.30 pm and 2.30 to 7 pm.

Places to Stay & Eat

Two star ***Hostellerie de la Vallée*** (☎ 05 55 21 40 60; fax 05 55 21 38 74) has small, simple doubles with shower/bath from 240/260FF, and a traditional style restaurant overlooking the gorge, with *menus* from 105FF. It is closed from November to March.

Hôtel-Restaurant Maurianges-Monteil (☎ 05 55 32 28 88) on the RN89 by the train station serves a filling *menu* for 75FF (120FF on Sundays). Clean but basic doubles with washbasin cost 110FF. There is a private lake where hotel guests can swim. The restaurant is closed weekends in winter.

BEAULIEU-SUR-DORDOGNE

• pop 1300 ✉ 19120 alt 140m

The verdant, aptly named town of Beaulieu explain (literally, 'beautiful place'), one of the most attractive medieval villages along the upper Dordogne, is famed for its majestic **Abbatiale**, a 12th century Romanesque abbey church that was once a stop on the way to Santiago de Compostela. The south portal's brilliant **tympanum** (circa 1130) illustrates the Last Judgement with vivid medieval scenes. Based on prophesies from the books of Daniel and the Apocalypse, the graphic figures include monsters devouring the heads and arms of the condemned and a seven-headed dragon from hell. The treasury, open in summer (ask at the tourist office), has a 12th century gilded Virgin and a 13th century enamel reliquary. Nearby streets have picturesque houses that date from the 14th and 15th century.

The tourist office has an English-language brochure of suggested walking trails. Lovely spots for a stroll include the banks of the Dordogne, which can be crossed on foot at the dam. The GR480, a spur of the GR46, passes by here. Beaulieu is covered by IGN map No 2236O, entitled *Saint Céré*.

Orientation & Information

Beaulieu's two main squares, Place Marbot and Place du Champ de Mars, are on the south-west side of Rue du Général de Gaulle (as the D940 is known in the town centre). The old city is across the street, between Rue du Général de Gaulle and the river. Rue Rodolphe de Turenne begins across the street from Place du Champ de Mars.

From April to mid-September, the tourist office (☎ 05 55 91 09 94) on Place Marbot is open daily from 9.30 am to 12.30 pm and 3 to 6 or 7 pm. Hours are shorter in the off season.

The post office, also on Place Marbot, is open from 9 am to noon and 2 to 5 pm and on Saturday until noon. Currency exchange is available.

Places to Stay

Camping The lovely, shaded ***Camping des Îles*** (☎ 05 55 91 02 65), on the other side of the old city from the tourist office on an island sandwiched between two branches of the Dordogne, is open from May to September. Adults pay 21FF; a site costs 24FF.

Hostel The delightful, homely ***Auberge de Jeunesse de la Riviera Limousine*** (☎ 05 55 91 13 82; fax 05 55 91 26 06), along the river on Place du Monturu, occupies a 14th century building with a wooden balcony. A bunk costs 42FF. Kitchen facilities are available. The owner is a great hiker.

Hotels The welcoming one star ***Hôtel L'Étape Fleurie*** (☎ 05 55 91 11 04) on Place du Champ de Mars has bright, modern doubles from 170FF (220FF with shower and toilet). The rustic ***restaurant*** serves local specialities and has *menus* for 60FF (lunch only) and 88 to 109FF. The recently renovated ***Auberge Les Charmilles*** (☎ 05 55 91 29 29), right on the river at 20 Blvd Rodolphe de Turenne, has smart doubles with shower and toilet from 280FF. Both these places are open year-round. Reception is closed on Sunday except from mid-May to mid-September.

The cosy two star ***Central Hôtel Fournié*** (☎ 05 55 91 01 34; fax 05 55 91 23 57), 4 Place du Champ de Mars, open from mid-March to mid-November, has large, pleasant doubles/quads with shower and toilet for 240/320FF. The charming, two star, 15 room ***Hôtel Le Turenne*** (☎ 05 55 91 10 16; fax 05 55 91 22 42) at 1 Blvd Rodolphe de Turenne has singles/doubles/triples for 235/270/335FF. It is closed from December to February.

Places to Eat

On Wednesday and Saturday mornings, there's an ***open-air market*** next to the Abbatiale.

At least one of the two grocers on Place Marbot – the ***Suprette*** and the ***Casino*** – will be open each day except Sunday afternoon. Both are closed from 12.30 to 2.30 or 3 pm.

Getting There & Away
Beaulieu is 44km south-east of Brive, 70km east of Sarlat-la-Canéda and 47km north-east of the Gouffre de Padirac (see the Quercy section).

When school is in session (except on Sunday and holidays), there are two buses a day to/from Brive (34.50FF). Schedules are posted at the bus shelter on Place du Champ de Mars (opposite the Hôtel L'Étape Fleurie) and outside the tourist office.

Getting Around
Beaulieu Sports (☎ 05 55 91 13 87) at 21 Rue du Général de Gaulle, open year-round, rents mountain bikes for 60FF/80FF a half-day/day. It is closed from noon to 2 pm and on Sunday afternoon.

COLLONGES-LA-ROUGE
• pop 50   ✉ 19500   alt 400m

On a gently angled slope situated above a tributary of the Dordogne River, the narrow and quaint alleyways of 'Collonges-the-Red' (built entirely of bright red sandstone) squeeze between old, wisteria-covered houses topped with round turrets. Surrounded by lush greenery – and, in the spring, flowers of every colour – the tiny hamlet is a truly delightful place for a stroll, in part because after about three minutes you'll be out in the countryside.

The partly Romanesque **church**, built from the 11th to the 15th century on the foundations of an 8th century Benedictine priory, was once an important resting place on the pilgrimage to Santiago de Compostela. In the late 16th century, local Protestants held prayers in the south nave and their Catholic neighbours prayed in the north nave, where a gilded wood retable erected in the 17th century still stands. Nearby, the ancient wood and slate roof of the **old covered market**, held up by stone columns, shelters an ancient baker's oven.

Information
The tourist office (☎ 05 55 25 47 57), known as Collonges Accueil, is housed in a little wooden building on the D38. It is open from mid-April to September from 2.30 to 5.30 pm (closed Sunday). In July and August it is also open daily from 10.30 am to 12.30 pm and 2.30 pm to 7 pm.

Places to Stay & Eat
The only place to stay is the 16 room ***Relais de Saint Jacques de Compostelle*** (☎ 05 55 25 41 02; fax 05 55 84 08 51), in a partly medieval building in the centre of the village. Doubles with shower and toilet start at 310FF. It is closed from mid-November to mid-March. The attached ***restaurant***, open daily during the same period, has *menus* of Périgord and Quercy-style dishes for 85 to 240FF. Hours are noon to 2 pm and 7 to 8.30 pm (to 9 pm in summer). Cheaper fare is on offer at ***Le Tourtou*** (☎ 05 55 25 34 15), a crêperie and restaurant open daily from April to September.

Getting There & Away
Except on Sunday and holidays, Collonges is linked with Brive – 18km to the north-west along the D38 – by four buses a day (15.50FF; 30 minutes). The bus stop is near Collonges Accueil.

TURENNE
• pop 740   ✉ 19500   alt 480m

Dubbed 'the small town with a great past', Turenne is named after the family of that name. The Turenne family ruled their own territory for centuries – ie didn't come under the control of the French Crown – but the 'Great Turenne' put a stop to this in 1611, giving way to French rule and thereby becoming the first 'French ruled' Turenne. The **Tour de César** (Caesar's Tower), with stunning views and a 13th century red-stone clock tower are all that remain of his once mighty castle, destroyed during the Revolution. The rest of the village has steep, narrow streets, attractive cream-coloured stone houses and grey-slate turrets.

Information
The helpful tourist office (☎ 05 55 85 94 38) is open mid-June to mid-September, from 10 am to noon and 2 to 5 pm (6 pm in July and August). During the rest of the year, contact the Mairie (☎ 05 55 85 91 15).

Places to Stay & Eat

La Maison des Chanoines (☎ 05 55 85 93 43) on Route de l'Église, near the church and the castle, has just three stylish double rooms costing from 300 to 370FF, and a popular ***restaurant*** with *menus* from 100FF. The restaurant, with its tree-shaded terrace, is open daily except Tuesday and Wednesday evenings. Both hotel and restaurant are closed from mid-November to February.

Getting there and Away

The train station (☎ 08 36 35 35 35) is just over 1km south of town, with infrequent services to Brive-la-Gaillarde, Rocamadour, Figeac and Limoges.

Périgord

Périgord, better known to English speakers as the Dordogne (the name of the most important of the region's seven rivers and of the department that administers most of the area), was one of the prehistoric cradles of human civilisation. The remains of Neanderthal and Cro-Magnon people have been discovered throughout the region, and quite a number of local caves – including the world-famous Lascaux – are colourfully adorned with extraordinary works of prehistoric art. Périgord's numerous hilltop chateaus and defensive *bastides* (fortified villages), many from the 14th and 15th century, testify to the bloody battles waged here during the Middle Ages and the Hundred Years' War.

To make the region's other attractions more accessible to visitors, Périgord has been divided into four areas and assigned colours according to their most prominent features. The fields and forests to the north are known as Périgord Vert (green). In the centre, the limestone area surrounding the capital, Périgueux, is known as Périgord Blanc (white). The wine-growing area of Périgord Pourpre (purple) lies to the south around Bergerac. Périgord Noir (black) encompasses the Vézère valley and, to the south, the Dordogne River Valley, known for its dark oak and pine forests and its many chateaus; between the two valleys lies the attractive medieval town of Sarlat-la-Canéda.

Warm season sports popular in the area include canoeing, kayaking, fishing, rock climbing, horse riding and cycling. Tourist offices have details and can supply you with informative English-language brochures.

During the warmer months, Périgord is a land of mass domestic tourism, and one often comes across 60-seat coaches navigating back roads barely wide enough for two Twingos. In winter, the region goes into deep hibernation, and many hotels, restaurants and tourist sites close.

Chateaus

Périgord isn't in the same league as the Loire Valley, but it does have a number of impressive medieval chateaus. They include the turreted 15th to 17th century **Jumilhac**, about 50km north-east of Périgueux along the N21 and D78; the Renaissance-influenced **Puyguilhem** (☎ 05 53 54 82 18), some 30km north of Périgueux; the imposing neoclassical **Hautefort** (☎ 05 53 50 51 23), 40km east of Périgueux, with its English-style garden and French flower terraces; **Eyrignac** (☎ 05 53 28 99 71), 13km north-east of Sarlat, famed for its exceptional 18th century French-style gardens; the castle-like **Puymartin** (☎ 05 53 59 29 97), 8km north-west of Sarlat; **Losse** (☎ 05 53 50 80 08), in the Vézère Valley 5km south-west of Montignac, decorated with 16th and 17th century tapestries and furniture; and the feudal, hilltop **Beynac-et-Cazenac** (☎ 05 53 29 50 40), 10km south-west of Sarlat on the Dordogne River. For details on several of the chateaus around Domme, see the Dordogne Périgourdine listing. Many chateaus are open for only part of the year, so call before dropping by.

PÉRIGUEUX

• pop 30,000   ✉ 24000   alt 106m

Périgueux, capital of Périgord and prefecture of the Dordogne department, has a restored medieval and Renaissance quarter and one of France's best museums of prehistory. Founded over 2000 years ago on a hill bounded by a

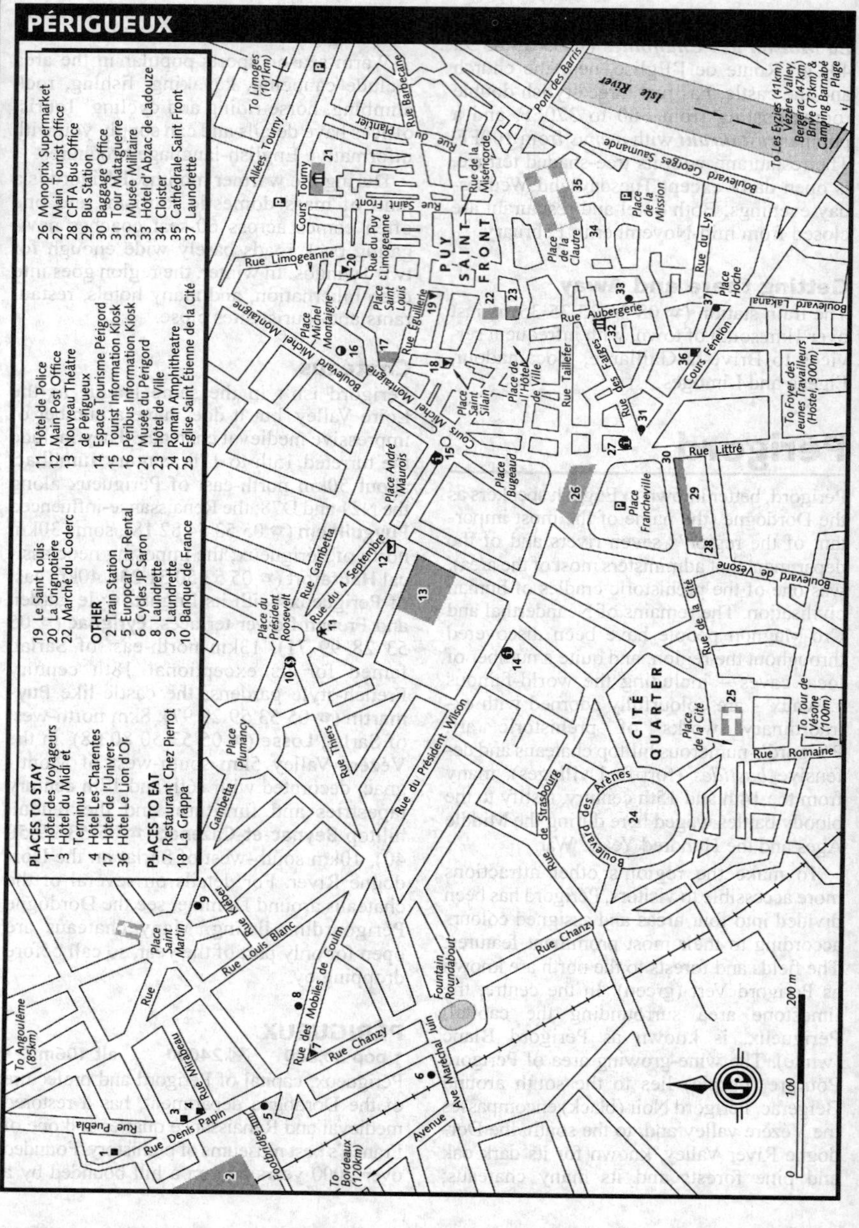
PÉRIGUEUX
PLACES TO STAY
1 Hôtel des Voyageurs
3 Hôtel du Midi et Terminus
4 Hôtel Les Charentes
17 Hôtel de l'Univers
36 Hôtel Le Lion d'Or
PLACES TO EAT
7 Restaurant Chez Pierrot
18 La Grappa
19 Le Saint Louis
20 La Grignotière
22 Marché du Coderc
OTHER
2 Train Station
5 Europcar Car Rental
6 Cycles JP Saron
8 Laundrette
9 Laundrette
10 Banque de France
11 Hôtel de Police
12 Main Post Office
13 Nouveau Théâtre de Périgueux
14 Espace Tourisme Périgord
15 Tourist Information Kiosk
16 Péribus Information Kiosk
21 Musée du Périgord
23 Hôtel de Ville
24 Roman Amphitheatre
25 Église Saint Étienne de la Cité
26 Monoprix Supermarket
27 Main Tourist Office
28 CFTA Bus Office
29 Bus Station
30 Baggage Office
31 Tour Mataguerre
32 Musée Militaire
33 Hôtel d'Abzac de Ladouze
34 Cloister
35 Cathédrale Saint Front
37 Laundrette
To Limoges (101km)
To Angoulême (85km)
To Bordeaux (120km)
To Les Eyzies (41km), Vézère Valley, Bergerac (47km) & Brive (73km)
Camping Barnabé Plage
To Foyer des Jeunes Travailleurs (Hostel; 300m)
To Tour de Vésone (100m)
Isle River
Pont des Barris
Boulevard Georges Saumande
PUY SAINT FRONT
CITÉ QUARTER
Place de la Clautre
Place de la Mission
Place Hoche
Place Francheville
Place Bugeaud
Place de l'Hôtel de Ville
Place Saint Silain
Place Saint Louis
Place Michel Montaigne
Place André Maurois
Place du Président Roosevelt
Place Plumancy
Place Saint Martin
Place de la Cité
Cours Tourny
Allées Tourny
Rue Limogeanne
Rue Saint Front
Rue Éguillerie
Rue Aubergerie
Rue Taillefer
Rue des Farges
Cours Fénelon
Rue du Lys
Boulevard Lakanal
Rue Littré
Boulevard de Vésone
Rue de la Cité
Rue Romaine
Boulevard des Arènes
Rue de Strasbourg
Rue Chanzy
Rue du Président Wilson
Rue Gambetta
Rue du 4 Septembre
Rue Thiers
Rue Louis Blanc
Rue Kléber
Rue des Mobiles de Coulm
Avenue Maréchal Juin
Fountain Roundabout
Rue Denis Papin
Rue Mirabeau
Rue Puebla
Footbridge
Boulevard Michel Montaigne
Cours Michel Montaigne
Rue Barbecane
Rue du Plantier
Rue de la Miséricorde
0
100
200 m

curve in the gentle Isle River, Périgueux is at its liveliest for the Wednesday and Saturday truffle and foie gras markets. The city is 45km north-west of the Vézère Valley.

Orientation

The medieval and Renaissance old city, known as Puy Saint Front, is on the hillside between the Isle River (to the east) and Blvd Michel Montaigne and Place Bugeaud (to the west). On the other side of Place Bugeaud is the old city's historic rival, the largely residential Cité Quarter, centred around the ruins of the amphitheatre. The train station is about 1km north-west of the old city.

Information

Tourist Office The main tourist office (☎ 05 53 53 10 63; fax 05 53 09 02 50) at 26 Place Francheville, next to Tour Mataguerre, is open from 9 am to 12.15 pm and 1.30 to 6 pm (closed Sunday and holidays). From mid-June to mid-September, daily hours are from 9 am to 7 pm (10 am to 6 pm Sunday and holidays).

In summer, the municipality sets up an information kiosk on Place André Maurois.

Espace Tourisme Périgord (☎ 05 53 35 50 24) at 25 Rue du Président Wilson, which has information on the Périgord region, is open weekdays from 8.30 am to 12.30 and 2 to 5 pm.

Money The Banque de France at 1 Place du Président Roosevelt is open weekdays from 8.45 am to 12.15 pm and 1.35 to 3.35 pm. Several banks can be found on Place Bugeaud.

Post The main post office at 1 Rue du 4 Septembre is open weekdays from 8 am to 7 pm and Saturday from 8 am to noon. Exchange operations are available.

Laundry In Puy Saint Front, La Lavandière on Place Hoche (around the corner from 25 Cours Fénelon) opens daily from 8 am to 8 pm.

Near the train station, La Lavandière at 18 Rue des Mobiles de Coulm is open daily from 8 am to 9.30 pm. Its counterpart at 61 Rue Gambetta is open from 8 am to 9 pm (8 pm on Saturday).

Emergency The Hôtel de Police (☎ 05 53 01 17 67) at 17 Rue du 4 Septembre is open 24 hours.

Puy Saint Front

When seen against the evening sky, the **Cathédrale Saint Front**, topped with five bump-studded domes and many more equally bumpy domelets, looks like something you might come across in Istanbul. But by day, the sprawling structure, 'restored' by Abadie (the creator of Paris' Sacré Cœur) in the late 19th century, looks contrived and overwrought in the finest pseudo-Byzantine tradition. The carillon sounds the same hour chime as Big Ben. The best views of the cathedral (and the town) are from Pont des Barris.

The unadorned interior of the cathedral, whose entrance faces the south end of Rue Saint Front, is shaped like a Greek cross. It is noteworthy only for the spectacularly carved 17th century baroque **retable** in the choir. It is open from 8 am to 12.30 pm and 2.30 to 7.30 pm. The eclectic cloister, next to Place de la Clautre, is equally unexceptional.

The **Musée du Périgord** (☎ 05 53 06 40 70) at 22 Cours Tourny is renowned for its rich collection of prehistoric tools and implements. It also has Gallo-Roman and medieval artefacts. Hours are from 10 am to 6 pm; closed Tuesday. Admission is 20FF (10FF for students, free for under 18s).

Established around the abbey of Saint Front in the 5th century, Puy Saint Front is Périgueux's most appealing neighbourhood for a relaxing stroll.

The ancient cobblestone streets north of the cathedral include **Rue du Plantier**. A few blocks west, the area's main thoroughfare, **Rue du Puy Limogeanne**, has graceful Renaissance buildings at Nos 3 and 12. Nearby streets, including Rue Éguillerie (eg across from No 28) and Rue de la Miséricorde, have more such structures. The 15th and 16th century houses along Rue Aubergerie include the **Hôtel d'Abzac de Ladouze**, across from No 19, with its two octagonal towers.

The **Musée Militaire** (☎ 05 53 53 47 36), 32 Rue des Farges, founded right after WWI, has a particularly varied collection of swords, weapons, uniforms and insignia from the Napoleonic wars and the two world wars. Hours are from 10 am to noon and 2 to 6 pm (closed Sunday); closed in the morning from October to December. From January to March, it's only open on Wednesday and Saturday afternoons. Entry costs 20FF.

Of the 28 towers that once made up Puy Saint Front's medieval fortifications, only **Tour Mataguerre**, a stout, round bastion on Place Francheville (next to the tourist office), remains. It was given its present form in the late 15th century.

Cité Quarter

Only a few arches of Périgueux's 1st century **Roman amphitheatre** are still standing – the rest of the massive structure, designed to hold 30,000 spectators, was disassembled and carried off in the 3rd century to construct the city walls. It can be visited from 7.30 am to 6 pm (8 pm from April to September).

Église Saint Étienne de la Cité, an 11th and 12th century church on Place de la Cité, served as Périgueux's cathedral until 1669. Only two cupolas and two bays survived the devastation wrought during the Wars of Religion (1562-98) by the Huguenots.

Tour de Vésone, shaped like a gargantuan anklet, is the only remaining section of a Gallo-Roman temple thought to have been dedicated to the goddess Vesuna, protectress of the town. To get there from Église Saint Étienne de la Cité, follow Rue Romaine southward for 250m.

Places to Stay

Camping ***Barnabé Plage*** (☎ 05 53 53 41 45), about 2km south of the train station along the Isle River, is open year-round. Prices are 16FF per adult, 15.50FF for a site and 10FF for parking. To get there, take the hourly bus No D from Place Michel Montaigne to the Rue des Bains stop (last bus at 6.20 pm; no service on Sunday).

Hostel The 16 place ***Foyer des Jeunes Travailleurs*** (☎ 05 53 53 52 05), also called Résidence Lakanal, is just off Blvd Lakanal, 600m south of the cathedral. A bed costs 73FF a night, including breakfast. Reception is staffed from 5 pm, and it is open year-round. To get there, take bus No G from Place Michel Montaigne to the Lakanal stop.

Hotels The pleasant and welcoming two star ***Hôtel de l'Univers*** (☎ 05 53 53 34 79) at 18 Cours Michel Montaigne has three small attic doubles for 180FF as well as plenty of other rooms, all with shower, starting at 220FF (280FF with bath and toilet, too). The somewhat unfriendly ***Hôtel Le Lion d'Or*** (☎ 05 53 53 49 03; fax 05 53 35 19 62) at 17 Cours Fénelon offers ordinary singles/doubles/quads with washbasin and bidet from 100/160/200FF; doubles with shower and toilet are 280FF. From November to Easter, reception is closed on Monday after 3 pm. Free parking is available nearby.

Near the train station, there are half a dozen inexpensive hotels along Rue Denis Papin and Rue des Mobiles de Coulm. One of the cheapest is the ***Hôtel des Voyageurs*** (☎ 05 53 53 17 44) at 26 Rue Denis Papin, where doubles with cracked linoleum cost only 80FF (100FF with shower). Reception may be closed on weekend afternoons. The amiable ***Hôtel du Midi et Terminus*** (☎ 05 53 53 41 06; fax 05 53 08 19 32) at 18 Rue Denis Papin has singles/doubles from 140/145FF; doubles/quads with shower are 170/215FF (195/255FF with toilet). Hall showers are free. You might also try the one star ***Hôtel Les Charentes*** (☎ 05 53 53 37 13) at 16 Rue Denis Papin, where doubles with shower are 165FF (225FF with toilet). Reception (at the bar) is closed on Sunday from 2 to 7 pm.

Places to Eat

Restaurants In Puy Saint Front, there are a number of eateries on Rue Éguillerie and the streets that branch off it. ***La Grignotière*** (☎ 05 53 53 86 91) at 6 Rue du Puy Limogeanne specialises in salads (48 to 65FF) and has *menus* from 58FF to 95FF. ***Le Saint Louis*** (☎ 05 53 53 53 90), a bar-brasserie at 26bis Rue Éguillerie, serves tasty sandwiches at lunchtime and three-course *menus* in the evening from 55FF. It is open daily from 7 am to 2 am (8 pm from October to Easter, when it's closed on Sunday).

La Grappa (☎ 05 53 09 74 88) at 13 Place Saint Silain has outdoor tables in a pleasant shady area. Pizzas are 35 to 54FF, meat dishes are 58 to 75FF, and the lunch *menu* costs 85FF. The ***Hôtel de l'Univers*** (see Places to Stay) has a vine-covered terrace and a popular lunch *menu* for 85FF.

A few hotels around the train station have *menus* starting at about 78FF – the ***Hôtel du Midi et Terminus*** (see Places to Stay) is a favourite with locals. ***Restaurant Chez Pierrot*** (☎ 05 53 53 43 22), open daily at 78 Rue Chanzy, has a hearty 50FF *menu* including 500mL of wine.

Self-Catering From mid-November to March, black truffles, wild mushrooms, walnuts, foie gras, *confits* (conserve, typically of duck or goose), pork dishes, cheeses and other delicacies are sold on Place Saint Louis in Puy Saint Front on Wednesday and Saturday mornings. Near the cathedral, a ***food market*** is held on Place de la Clautre on Wednesday and Saturday mornings.

There are quite a few ***food shops*** and ***traiteurs*** (places with ready-made dishes) along Rue du Puy Limogeanne; the ***Marché du Coderc***, near the southern end, is open daily until about 1.30 pm.

The ***Monoprix*** supermarket between Place Bugeaud and Place Francheville is open Monday to Saturday from 8.30 am to 8 pm.

Getting There & Away

Bus The bus station is on the south side of Place Francheville. Hours are posted at the platforms. Information is available at the baggage office (☎ 05 53 08 91 06), usually staffed on weekdays from 8 to 9.45 am, 11 am to noon, 2 to 3 pm and 5 to 6 pm. One of the carriers, CFTA (☎ 05 53 08 43 13), has an office (open weekdays) on the storey overlooking the waiting room at the terminal's west end. The tourist office has copies of the schedules.

Except on Sunday and holidays, destinations served include Bergerac (40FF; 1½ hours; three a day), Le Bugue (one hour; one a day during the school year), Hautefort (1½ hours; one or two a day) and Sarlat (49.50FF; 1½ hours; one a day at 6 pm) via the Vézère Valley town of Montignac (34FF; one hour).

Train The information office (☎ 08 36 35 35 35) in the train station, on Rue Denis Papin, is open daily from 9 am to 7.30 pm (closed Sunday). It is connected to Place Michel Montaigne by buses A and C.

Destinations with direct services include Bordeaux (97FF; 1½ hours; six to nine a day), Brive-la-Gaillarde (63FF; one hour; four a day), Clermont-Ferrand (191FF; two to four a day), Les Eyzies de Tayac (40FF; 30 minutes; two to four a day) and Limoges (79FF; one hour; five to eight a day).

Service to Paris' Gare d'Austerlitz (291FF; 4½ hours) is via Limoges. The cheapest way to get to Toulouse, via Agen, costs 192FF and takes four hours. To get to Sarlat (74FF), you have to change at Le Buisson or Libourne.

Car Europcar (☎ 05 53 08 15 72) is near the train station at 7 Rue Denis Papin.

Getting Around

Bus Péribus, the local bus company, has an information kiosk (☎ 05 53 53 30 37; open weekdays) on Place Michel Montaigne, the main bus hub. Single tickets cost 7FF; a 10 ticket carnet costs 45FF. The tourist office has timetables.

Bicycle Cycles JP Saron (☎ 05 53 53 41 91) at 96 Ave Maréchal Juin is next to a bizarre fountain-cum-roundabout representing the rivers of Périgord; the best view of the work is from on top. Ten-speeds/mountain bikes cost 55/80FF a day (cheaper for the second and subsequent days). A deposit of 500FF is required. It is open year-round from 8.30 am to noon and 2 to 5 pm (closed Sunday).

SARLAT-LA-CANÉDA

• pop 10,000 ✉ 24200 alt 173m

The beautiful, well restored town of Sarlat, administratively twinned with nearby La Canéda, is the capital of Périgord Noir. Established around a Benedictine abbey founded in the late 8th century, it became prosperous in the Middle Ages but was ravaged during the Hundred Years' War (when it was on the border between French and English territory) and the Wars of Religion. These days, Sarlat's medieval and Renaissance townscape – much of it built of tan sandstone in the 16th and 17th century – attracts large numbers of tourists, especially for the year-round Saturday market.

Sarlat is an excellent base for car trips to the prehistoric sites of the Vézère Valley and the Dordogne Périgourdine (the section of the Dordogne River in Périgord).

Orientation

Sarlat stretches north for 2km from the train station to the Auberge de Jeunesse. The heart-shaped Cité Médiévale (Medieval Town) is bisected by the ruler-straight Rue de la République (La Traverse), laid out during the last century. The medieval town is centred around Place de la Liberté, Rue de la Liberté and Place du Peyrou.

Information

Tourist Office The main tourist office (☎ 05 53 31 45 45; fax 05 53 59 19 44) on Place de la Liberté occupies the beautiful Hôtel de Maleville, made up of three 15th and 16th century Gothic houses. It is open Monday to Saturday from 9 am to noon and 2 to 6 pm (7 pm from June to September, when it's also open on Sunday from 10 am to noon and 2 to 6 pm). There's no midday break in July and August.

During July and August, the tourist office annexe (☎ 05 53 59 18 87) on Ave du Général de Gaulle is open Monday to Saturday from 9 am to noon and 2 to 6 pm. Both offices charge 10FF for hotel bookings.

Money There are several banks along Rue de la République; open Tuesday to Saturday.

Post The main post office on Place du 14 Juillet is open from 9 am to 6 pm and on Saturday until noon. Currency exchange is available.

Laundry Le Lavandou at 10 Place de la Bouquerie is open daily from 6 am to 10 pm. The Laverie at 74 Ave de Selves is open daily from 6 am to 9 pm.

Medieval Town

The tourist office's free brochure *Visitors' Map of the Medieval Town* takes you on a walking tour of Sarlat's historic centre.

Cathédrale Saint Sacerdos, once part of Sarlat's Cluniac abbey, is a hotchpotch of styles. The wide, airy nave and its chapels date from the 17th century; the cruciform chevet (at the far end from the entrance) is from the 14th century; and the west entrance and much of the belfry above it are 12th century Romanesque. The organ dates from 1752.

Behind the cathedral is the **Jardin des Enfeus**, Sarlat's first cemetery, and the 12th century **Lanterne des Morts** (Lantern of the Dead), which looks like the top of a missile. It may have been built to commemorate Saint Bernard, who visited Sarlat in 1147 and whose relics were given to the abbey.

Across the square from the front of the cathedral is the ornate façade of the Renaissance **Maison de la Boétie**, which is the birthplace of the writer Étienne de la Boétie (1530-63).

The quiet, largely residential area west of Rue de la République is also worth exploring. Rue Jean-Jacques Rousseau makes a good starting point.

Museums

From April to October, the vintage motor vehicles on display at the **Musée de l'Automobile** (☎ 05 53 31 62 81) at 17 Ave Thiers can be viewed from 2 to 6.30 pm; July and August hours are 10.30 am to 7 pm. Admission costs 35FF (15FF for kids aged eight to 12).

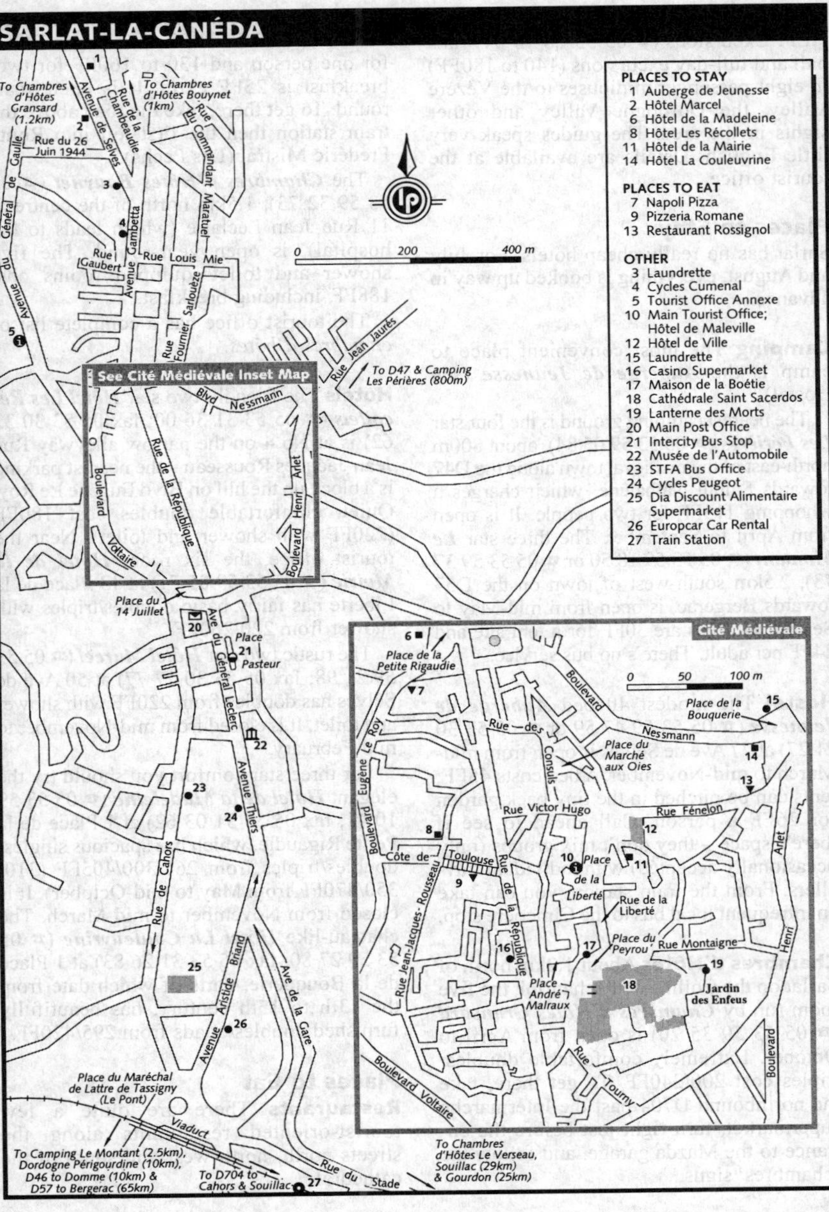
SARLAT-LA-CANÉDA
PLACES TO STAY
1 Auberge de Jeunesse
2 Hôtel Marcel
6 Hôtel de la Madeleine
8 Hôtel Les Récollets
11 Hôtel de la Mairie
14 Hôtel La Couleuvrine
PLACES TO EAT
7 Napoli Pizza
9 Pizzeria Romane
13 Restaurant Rossignol
OTHER
3 Laundrette
4 Cycles Cumenal
5 Tourist Office Annexe
10 Main Tourist Office; Hôtel de Maleville
12 Hôtel de Ville
15 Laundrette
16 Casino Supermarket
17 Maison de la Boétie
18 Cathédrale Saint Sacerdos
19 Lanterne des Morts
20 Main Post Office
21 Intercity Bus Stop
22 Musée de l'Automobile
23 STFA Bus Office
24 Cycles Peugeot
25 Dia Discount Alimentaire Supermarket
26 Europcar Car Rental
27 Train Station
0 200 400 m
To Chambres d'Hôtes Gransard (1.2km)
To Chambres d'Hôtes Bouynet (1km)
Rue du 26 Juin 1944
Avenue de Selves
Rue de la Chambeaudie
Rue du Commandant Maratuel
Avenue du Général de Gaulle
Avenue Gambetta
Rue Gaubert
Rue Louis Mie
Rue Fournier Sarlouèze
Rue Jean Jaurès
To D47 & Camping Les Périères (800m)
See Cité Médiévale Inset Map
Blvd Nessmann
Rue de la République
Boulevard Voltaire
Boulevard Henri Arlet
Place du 14 Juillet
Ave du Général Leclerc
Place Pasteur
Avenue Thiers
Rue de Cahors
Avenue Aristide Briand
Ave de la Gare
Place du Maréchal de Lattre de Tassigny (Le Pont)
Viaduct
To Camping Le Montant (2.5km), Dordogne Périgourdine (10km), D46 to Domme (10km) & D57 to Bergerac (65km)
To D704 to Cahors & Souillac
Rue du Stade
To Chambres d'Hôtes Le Verseau, Souillac (29km) & Gourdon (25km)
Cité Médiévale
0 50 100 m
Place de la Petite Rigaudie
Boulevard Eugène Le Roy
Boulevard Nessmann
Place de la Bouquerie
Rue des Consuls
Place du Marché aux Oies
Rue Victor Hugo
Rue Fénelon
Côte de Toulouse
Rue Jean-Jacques-Rousseau
Rue de la République
Place de la Liberté
Rue de la Liberté
Place du Peyrou
Rue Montaigne
Place André Malraux
Jardin des Enfeus
Rue Tourny
Boulevard Henri Arlet
Boulevard Voltaire

Organised Tours

HEP! Excursions (☎ 05 53 28 10 04) runs half and full-day excursions (140 to 180FF) in eight-passenger minibuses to the Vézère Valley, the Dordogne Valley and other sights in the area. The guides speak very little English. Details are available at the tourist office.

Places to Stay

Sarlat has no really cheap hotels. For July and August, everything is booked up way in advance.

Camping The most convenient place to camp is the ***Auberge de Jeunesse*** (see Hostel).

The nearest camping ground is the four star ***Les Périères*** (☎ 05 53 59 05 84), about 800m north-east of the medieval town along the D47 towards Sainte Nathalène, which charges a whopping 115FF for two people. It is open from April to September. The three star ***Le Montant*** (☎ 05 53 59 18 50 or ☎ 05 53 59 37 73), 2.5km south-west of town on the D57 towards Bergerac, is open from mid-May to September. Fees are 30FF for a tent site and 24FF per adult. There's no bus service.

Hostel The modest 40 bed ***Auberge de Jeunesse*** (☎ 05 53 59 47 59 or ☎ 05 53 30 21 27) at 77 Ave de Selves is open from mid-March to mid-November. A bed costs 45FF; tents can be pitched in the tiny back garden for 26FF a person. Call ahead to see if there's space – they don't mix groups (only occasionally accepted) with individual travellers. From the train station, you can take an infrequent local bus to the Cimetière stop.

Chambres d'Hôtes About 1.2km north of Sarlat on the Colline de Péchauriol, the five room run by ***Chambres d'Hôtes Gransard*** (☎ 05 53 59 35 20) is open from April to October. Extremely comfortable doubles/triples cost 200/240FF. To get there, take the northbound D704 past the Intermarché supermarket, turn right just before the entrance to the Mazda garage, and follow the 'chambres' signs.

The seven room ***Chambres d'Hôtes Le Verseau*** (☎ 05 53 31 02 63) charges 100FF for one person and 130 to 160FF for two; breakfast is 25FF extra. It is open year-round. To get there, take the road above the train station then the first left into Route Frédéric Mistral (Les Pechs).

The ***Chambres d'Hôtes Bouynet*** (☎ 05 53 59 32 73), 1.5km north of the centre at 11 Rue Jean Leclaire (which leads to the hospital), is open year-round. The five shower and toilet-equipped rooms cost 188FF, including breakfast.

The tourist office has a complete list of *chambres d'hôtes*.

Hotels The friendly two star ***Hôtel Les Récollets*** (☎ 05 53 31 36 00; fax 05 53 30 32 62) is at No 4 on the narrow alleyway Rue Jean-Jacques Rousseau – the nearest parking is a block up the hill on Blvd Eugène Le Roy. Quiet, comfortable doubles cost 180FF (220FF with shower and toilet). Near the tourist office, the six room ***Hôtel de la Mairie*** (☎ 05 53 59 05 71) at 13 Place de la Liberté has fairly basic doubles/triples with shower from 220/260FF.

The rustic two star ***Hôtel Marcel*** (☎ 05 53 59 21 98; fax 05 53 30 27 77) at 50 Ave de Selves has doubles from 220FF with shower and toilet. It is closed from mid-November to mid-February.

For three star comfort you should try the elegant ***Hôtel de la Madeleine*** (☎ 05 53 59 10 41; fax 05 53 31 03 62) at 1 Place de la Petite Rigaudie, which has spacious singles/doubles/triples from 265/300/405FF (310/350/470FF from May to mid-October). It is closed from November to mid-March. The chateau-like ***Hôtel La Couleuvrine*** (☎ 05 53 59 27 80; fax 05 53 31 26 83) at 1 Place de la Bouquerie, parts of which date from the 13th to 15th century, has beautifully furnished doubles/quads from 295/420FF.

Places to Eat

Restaurants There are quite a few tourist-oriented restaurants along the streets north, north-west and south of the cathedral.

Périgord-style cuisine is available at a number of upmarket establishments. ***Restaurant Rossignol*** (☎ 05 53 31 02 30) at 15 Rue Fénelon has *menus* from 87 to 290FF; dishes on offer include fish. It is open from noon to 1.30 pm and 7 to 8.30 pm (closed Wednesday). The elegant restaurant attached to the ***Hôtel de la Madeleine*** (see Places to Stay), open daily from mid-March to November, has *menus* for 105 to 295FF. Closed Monday for lunch (except in July and August).

Napoli Pizza (☎ 05 53 31 26 93), a rustic, informal place at 2 Blvd Eugène Le Roy, has pizzas for 35 to 60FF, pasta for 30 to 51FF and red meat dishes for 50 to 90FF. It is open from noon to 2.30 pm and 7 to 11.30 pm (closed Sunday at midday). ***Pizzeria Romane*** (☎ 05 53 59 23 88) at 3 Côte de Toulouse (just off Rue de la République) has pizzas, spaghetti and a Périgord-style *menu* (80FF) that includes *confit de canard*. It is closed on Sunday at midday and on Monday.

Self-Catering Long a driving force in the town's economy, Sarlat's ***Saturday market*** on Place de la Liberté offers edibles in the morning and durables (eg clothing) all day long. Depending on the season, Périgord delicacies on offer include truffles, foie gras, mushrooms and geese and their various products. A smaller ***fruit and vegetable market*** is held here on Wednesday morning. Quite a few shops around town sell foie gras and other pricey regional specialities.

The ***Casino*** supermarket at 32 Rue de la République is open Tuesday to Saturday from 8 am to 1.15 pm and 2.30 to 7.15 pm and on Sunday from 8 am to noon. Hours are longer in July and August. ***Dia Discount Alimentaire***, an inexpensive supermarket between Rue de Cahors and Ave Aristide Briand, is open on weekdays from 9 am to 12.30 pm and 2.30 to 7.30 pm and on Saturday from 9 am to 7 pm.

Getting There & Away

Bus Bus services are very limited; schedules are available at the tourist office. There's no bus station – departures are from the train station, Place Pasteur or Place de la Petite Rigaudie, depending on your final destination.

With the exception of Sunday, the STFA bus to Périgueux via Montignac (25.50FF; 25 minutes), the town nearest Lascaux II, leaves from Place de la Petite Rigaudie at 6 am (8.25 am in July and August); the bus back leaves Montignac at 7.15 pm (1 pm on Saturday; 4.35 pm in July and August). The STFA office (☎ 05 53 59 01 48) at 31 Rue de Cahors is usually open weekdays from 9 am to noon and 2 to 6 pm.

The SNCF bus (50 minutes; three a day), whose stops in Sarlat are at the train station and Place Pasteur, passes through Rouffillac, Peyrillac and Cazoulès. Brive is served by one non-SNCF bus a day (1¾ hours; no service on Sunday and holidays), which leaves from Place Pasteur.

Train The train station (☎ 05 53 59 00 21), 1.3km south of the old city at the southern end of Ave de la Gare, is poorly linked with the rest of the region. The ticket windows are staffed from 6.30 am to 7 pm.

Destinations served include Bordeaux (116FF; 2½ hours; four or five a day) via Bergerac, Périgueux (with a change at Le Buisson or Libourne; 74FF) and Les Eyzies de Tayac (with a change at Le Buisson; 46FF; 50 minutes; three a day). To get to/from Paris' Gare d'Austerlitz, you have to change at Souillac, linked to Sarlat by three SNCF buses a day (see Bus).

Car Europcar (☎ 05 53 30 30 40) has an office near the train station at 15 Ave Aristide Briand.

Getting Around

Bicycle The Sarlat area has nine bike-rental outlets. Cycles Cumenal (☎ 05 53 31 28 40) at 8 Ave Gambetta has city/mountain bikes for 50/80FF a day. It is open Tuesday to Sunday from 9 am to 7 pm. You might also try Cycles Peugeot (☎ 05 53 28 51 87) at 36 Ave Thiers, who charge 70FF a day.

PREHISTORIC SITES & THE VÉZÈRE VALLEY

Of the Vézère Valley's 175 known prehistoric sites, the most famous ones (including the world-renowned cave paintings in Lascaux) are situated between Le Bugue (near where the Vézère joins the Dordogne) and, 25km to the north-east, Montignac. The sites mentioned below – and they're just the highlights – are listed roughly from south-west to north-east.

Many of the villages in the area, including Les Eyzies de Tayac and Montignac, have one or more hotels. Other bases from which the area can be explored include Sarlat, 20km south-east of Les Eyzies, and Périgueux, 45km to the north-west. Most of the valley's sites are closed in winter – the best time to come is in spring or autumn, when things are open but the crowds are not overwhelming.

Getting Around

The Vézère Valley is very well signposted, and road signs direct you to sights major and minor at every crossroad. Public transport in the area is limited – see Getting There & Away under Les Eyzies de Tayac, Montignac, Périgueux and Sarlat-la-Canéda.

For details on day tours by minibus, see Organised Tours in the Sarlat section.

Les Eyzies de Tayac

• pop 850 ✉ 24620

The two museums in the touristy village of Les Eyzies, spread out along the north-south oriented D47, are a good place to start a visit of the valley's prehistoric sites.

Information The tourist office (☎ 05 53 06 97 05; fax 05 53 06 90 79) is on Les Eyzies' main street right below the most prominent part of the cliff. It is open from 9 or 10 am to noon and 2 to 6 pm; closing time is 5 pm from November to mid-March and 8 pm (6 pm on Sunday) in July and August, when there's no midday break. From November to mid-March, it's also closed on Saturday and Sunday.

IGN maps and topoguides are on sale directly across from the tourist office at the Maison de la Press (open daily except from 12.30 to 2.30 pm; closed in the afternoon from December to February).

The post office, 200m south of the tourist office, is open from 9 am to noon and 2 to 5 pm and on Saturday until noon. Currency exchange is available both here and at the tourist office.

Things to See The very interesting **Musée National de la Préhistoire** (National Museum of Prehistory; ☎ 05 53 06 45 45), built into the cliff above the tourist office, provides a great introduction to the area's prehistoric human habitation. Its well presented collection of artefacts can be visited daily, except Tuesday, from 9.30 am to noon and 2 to 5 pm (6 pm from April to November); in July and August there's no midday closure and it's open daily until 7 pm. Admission is 22FF (15FF for people aged 18 to 25 or over 60 and, on Sunday, for everyone; free for under 18s). An English book about the museum is available at the ticket window for 28FF.

About 250m north of the Musée National de la Préhistoire along the cliff face is the **Abri Pataud** (☎ 05 53 06 92 46), a Cro-Magnon shelter inhabited over a period of 15,000 years starting some 37,000 years ago; bones and other artefacts discovered during the excavations are on display. The ibex carved into the ceiling is about 19,000 BC. It is open daily except Monday; one-hour guided tours – the guides generally know some English – begin from 10 to noon and 2 to 6 pm (closed in the morning in November and December; closed in January). July and August hours are 10 am to 7 pm. Entry costs 28FF (14FF for kids aged 6 to 12).

Places to Stay & Eat The tiny ***Camping a la Ferme Le Queylou*** (☎ 05 53 06 94 71) is situated 2.5km west of Les Eyzies on the D706 heading towards Le Bugue, and costs 21FF per person including use of a fridge. The owners speak English and also rents out two cottages (for four to six people) starting from 750FF a week (1600FF in July and August).

Hôtel des Falaises (☎ 05 53 06 97 35), across the street from the Abri Pataud, has doubles with shower and toilet starting at 165FF. The two star, 19 room ***Hôtel du Centre*** (☎ 05 53 06 97 13; fax 05 53 06 91 63), on the square next to the tourist office, has doubles from 280FF. It is open from February to 4 November.

The ***grocery*** across from the tourist office is open daily, except Sunday afternoon.

Le Trois As (☎ 05 53 08 41 57), on Place de la Mairie at Le Bugue (about 10km from Les Eyzies) has *menus* costing 92,142,178 and 245FF. It's closed on Tuesday and Wednesday for lunch.

Getting There & Away The train station (☎ 05 53 06 97 22) is 600m north of the tourist office (and 200m off the D47). The ticket windows are staffed from about 6 am to 9 pm (or later).

Destinations served include Bordeaux (change at Le Buisson; 105FF; two to three hours; four a day), Périgueux (40FF; 30 minutes; two to four a day), Sarlat (change at

VÉZÈRE VALLEY & DORDOGNE PÉRIGOURDINE

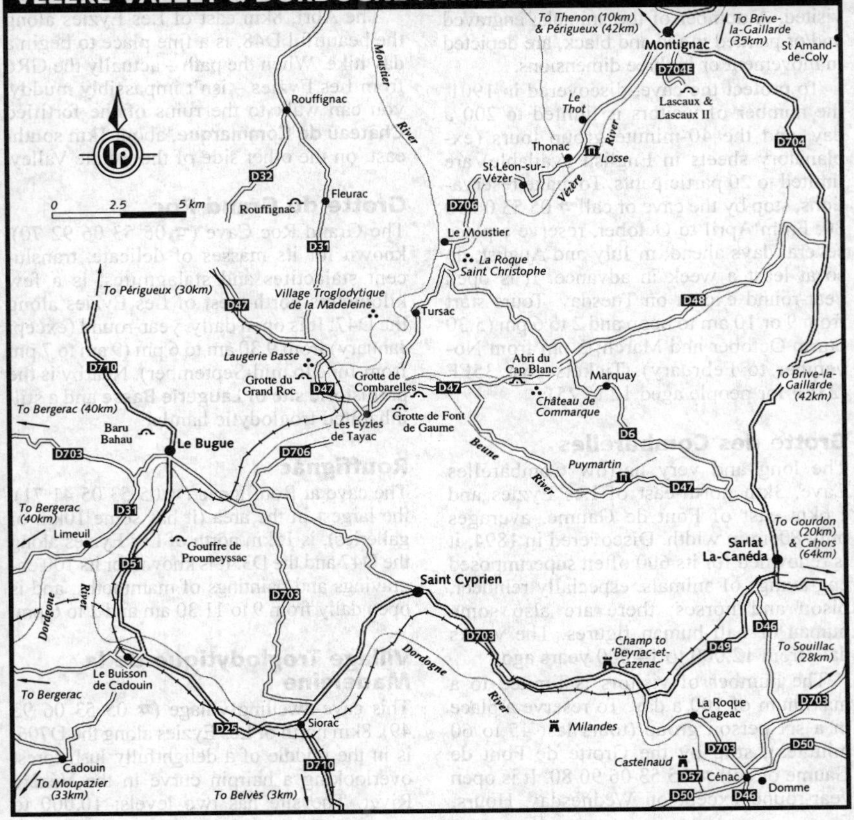

Le Buisson; 46FF; 50 minutes; three a day) and Paris' Gare d'Austerlitz (280FF; 5½ hours; three to five a day, including one direct).

Getting Around Bicycles can be rented at the tourist office.

Grotte de Font de Gaume

This cave, just over 1km north-east of Les Eyzies on the D47, has one of the most astounding collections of prehistoric paintings still open to the public. About two dozen of its 230 remarkably sophisticated polychrome figures of bison, reindeer, horses, bears, mammoths and other creatures, created by Cro-Magnon people 14,000 years ago, can be visited. A number of the animals, engraved and/or painted in red and black, are depicted in movement or in three dimensions.

To protect the cave, discovered in 1901, the number of visitors is limited to 200 a day, and the 40-minute group tours (explanatory sheets in English available) are limited to 20 participants. To make reservations, stop by the cave or call ☎ 05 53 06 90 80. From April to October, reserve a place several days ahead; in July and August, do so at least a week in advance. It is open year-round except on Tuesday. Tours start from 9 or 10 am to noon and 2 to 6 pm (5.30 pm in October and March; 5 pm from November to February). Tickets cost 35FF (23FF for people aged 12 to 25).

Grotte des Combarelles

The long and very narrow Combarelles Cave, 3km north-east of Les Eyzies and 1.6km east of Font de Gaume, averages only 80cm in width. Discovered in 1894, it is renowned for its 600 often superimposed engravings of animals, especially reindeer, bison and horses; there are also some human or half-human figures. The works date from 12,000 to 14,000 years ago.

The number of visitors is limited to a maximum of 100 a day. To reserve a place in a six person group (tours last 45 to 60 minutes), stop by the Grotte de Font de Gaume or call ☎ 05 53 06 90 80. It is open year-round except on Wednesday. Hours, tariffs and reservations guidelines are the same as for the Grotte de Font de Gaume.

Abri du Cap Blanc

High and low-relief figures of horses, reindeer and bison, created 14,000 years ago, decorate this natural shelter, formed by an overhanging rocky outcrop. Situated on a pristine, forested hillside, the privately owned Abri (☎ 05 53 59 21 74) is open from April to October. Guided tours lasting 45 minutes (English explanatory sheets available) begin daily from 10 to 12.30 am and 2 to 6 pm (9.30 am to 7 pm in July and August, with no midday closure). Entry costs 30FF (15FF for kids aged seven to 15).

The Abri, 8km east of Les Eyzies along the beautiful D48, is a fine place to begin a day hike. When the path – actually the GR6 from Les Eyzies – isn't impassibly muddy, you can walk to the ruins of the fortified **Château de Commarque**, about 1km south-east, on the other side of the Beune Valley.

Grotte du Grand Roc

The Grand Roc Cave (☎ 05 53 06 92 70), known for its masses of delicate, translucent stalactites and stalagmites, is a few kilometres north-west of Les Eyzies along the D47. It is open daily, year-round (except January) from 9.30 am to 6 pm (9 am to 7 pm from June to mid-September). Nearby is the prehistoric site of **Laugerie Basse** and a still inhabited troglodytic hamlet.

Rouffignac

The cave at Rouffignac (☎ 05 53 05 41 71), the largest in the area (it has some 10km of galleries), is 15km north of Les Eyzies along the D47 and the D3. It is known for its 100 engravings and paintings of mammoths, and is open daily from 9 to 11.30 am and 2 to 6 pm.

Village Troglodytique de la Madeleine

This cave-dwelling village (☎ 05 53 06 92 49), 8km north of Les Eyzies along the D706, is in the middle of a delightfully lush forest overlooking a hairpin curve in the Vézère River. The site has two levels: 10,000 to

14,000 years ago, prehistoric people lived on the bank of the river in an area now closed to the public; and five to seven centuries ago, medieval French people built a fortified village – now in ruins – halfway up the cliff face. Their chapel, dedicated to Sainte Madeleine, gave its name to the site – and to the entire Magdalenian era. On the plateau above the cliff are the ruins of a 14th century castle (closed to the public). Many of the artefacts discovered here are at the prehistory museum in Les Eyzies. Several walking trails pass by here.

The site is closed on Tuesday (except in July and August) and from mid-November to early February. Guided tours in French (40 minutes) begin from 10.30 to 11.15 am and 2 to 5.15 pm (8 pm from July to early September, when there's no midday break). In February and March and from mid-October to mid-November, the site is closed in the morning and tours leave from 2 to 4.15 pm. Entry costs 30FF (17FF for kids aged 7 to 12). A free English-language brochure is available.

La Roque Saint Christophe

This 900m-long series of terraces and caves (☎ 05 53 50 70 45 for information), on a sheer cliff face 30m above the Vézère River, has had an extraordinary history as a natural bastion, serving Mousterian (Neanderthal) people some 50,000 years ago, enemies of the Normans in the 10th century, the English from 1401 to 1416 and Protestants in the late 16th century.

La Roque Saint Christophe is on the D706, 9km north-east of Les Eyzies. It's open daily year-round from 10 am to 6 pm (5 pm from December to February, when it's also closed from noon to 2 pm, and 7 pm in July and August). Tickets cost 33FF (25FF for children over 13 and students, 17FF for children aged five to 13). The informative brochure in English, which can be borrowed at the ticket kiosk, makes a valiant effort to make the now empty rooms and caverns come alive.

Place to Stay & Eat Across the Vézère River, 1km north of La Roque Saint Christophe in Le Moustier (finds here gave the Mousterian era its name), is the two star, seven room ***Hôtel La Roque Saint Christophe*** (☎ 05 53 50 70 61; fax 05 53 50 81 29), which is open year-round. Doubles start at 180FF. There a hostel in nearby Saint Léon sur Vézère.

Saint Léon-de-Vézère

This atmospheric village is situated 7km south-west of Montignac in a picturesque loop of the Vézère River. It contains two castles – the squat 14th century Château La Salle and the more refined Renaissance turreted Château de Clérens – and one of Périgord's finest Romanesque churches. Once part of a Benedictine priory, it was built on the ruins of a Roman villa, part of which can still be seen today between the church and the river.

There is accommodation at ***L'Auberge du Pont*** (☎ 05 53 50 73 07), who have basic singles with washbasin and bidet for 130FF and a ***restaurant*** with a *menu* at 68FF, which is excellent value.

Le Thot

The museum and animal park known as Le Thot – Espace Cro-Magnon (☎ 05 53 50 70 44), intended as an introduction to the world of prehistoric people, has models of animals that appear in prehistoric art, live specimens of similar animals, and exhibits on the creation of Lascaux II. Admission costs 28FF (14FF for children) but is free with a Lascaux II ticket. It is open from 10 am to 12.30 pm and 1.30 to 7 pm (closed on Monday and in January). In July and August, when tickets must be purchased in Montignac near the tourist office, it's open daily from 10 am to 7 pm. Le Thot is 1.5km off the D706 from a point 5km south-west of Montignac.

Montignac

• pop 2900 ✉ 24290 alt 300m

The relaxing and very picturesque town of Montignac, on the Vézère River, achieved sudden fame after the discovery of the nearby Grotte de Lascaux.

Montignac's attractive old city and commercial centre is on the river's right bank, but of more use for touristic logistics is the left bank area around Place Tourny and along Rue du Quatre Septembre, which links the D65 with the D704 and the D704E to Lascaux.

Information The tourist office (☎ 05 53 51 82 60), 150m west of Place Tourny at 22 Rue du Quatre Septembre, is next to the 14th century Église Saint Georges le Prieuré. It is open Monday to Saturday from 9 am to 12.30 pm and 2 to 5.30 pm (open daily with no midday closure in July and August). IGN maps are sold at the Maison de la Presse just across the street.

There are a couple of banks on the right bank of the river. The post office on Place Tourny is open from 8.30 am to noon and 2 to 5 pm and on Saturday until noon. Currency exchange is available.

Places to Stay & Eat The nine room ***Hôtel de la Grotte*** (☎ 05 53 51 80 48; fax 05 53 51 05 96), 200m east of the tourist office at 63 Rue du Quatre Septembre, has doubles/triples for 165/195FF (215/275FF with shower and toilet). It is open year-round. Their ***restaurant*** has Périgord-style *menus* for 70FF (lunch only) and 78 to 195FF.

On the right bank, the riverside ***Restaurant Pizzeria Les Pilotis*** (☎ 05 53 50 88 15) at 6 Rue Laffitte has salads, pizzas (35 to 44FF) and meat dishes. It is open daily from mid-February to November.

The ***Casino*** supermarket, on Place Tourny next to the post office, is closed from 12.30 to 3 pm on Sunday afternoon and on Monday.

Bar Le Tourny, 38 Rue du 4 Septembre, is open daily until 2 am and sometimes features light music. Breakfast costs 25FF.

Getting There & Away For information on buses to/from Montignac, see Getting There & Away in the Sarlat-la-Canéda and Périgueux sections. The bus stop is at on Rue du Quatre Septembre (Place Tourny).

Grotte de Lascaux & Lascaux II

Lascaux Cave, 2.5km south of Montignac at the end of a sealed road off the D704, is adorned with some of the most extraordinary prehistoric paintings ever discovered.

Discovered in 1940 by four teenage boys who, it is said, were out searching for their dog, Robot, the cave's main room and a number of steep galleries are decorated with figures of wild oxen, deer, horses, reindeer and other creatures depicted in vivid reds, blacks, yellows and browns.

The drawings and paintings, shown by carbon dating to be between 15,000 and 17,000 years old, are thought to have been done by members of a hunting cult.

The cave – in pristine condition when found – was opened to the public in 1948 but was closed 15 years later when it became clear that human breath and the resulting carbon dioxide and condensation were causing a green fungus and even tiny stalactites to grow over the paintings and their colours to fade.

To respond to massive public curiosity about prehistoric art, a precise replica of the most famous section of the original was meticulously re-created a few hundred metres away. The idea of Lascaux II (☎ 05 53 51 95 03) sounds kitschy, but the reproductions are surprisingly evocative and well worth a look.

The 40m-long Lascaux II, which can handle 2000 visitors a day (in groups of 40), is open daily from 9 am to 7 pm from April to October (closed Monday in October); 10 am to 12.30 pm and 1.30 to 5.30 pm from November to March (closed on Monday and for three weeks starting mid-January). Tickets cost 48FF (20FF for kids aged 6 to 12), which also get you into Le Thot; they are sold at the entrance except in July and August, when they must be purchased in Montignac, next to the tourist office (get there early as queues are long). Individual visitors do not need reservations.

Saint Amand-de-Coly

Near the Vézère Valley, 10km east of Montignac, the old slate-tiled houses of Saint Amand-de-Coly are dominated by the village's tall yellow limestone abbey-church – a splendid example of the region's fortified churches, with its high defensive walls. At one time there were 400 monks here, but following the Hundred Years' War only two remained.

DORDOGNE PÉRIGOURDINE

The term Dordogne Périgourdine is used to describe a small part of the Périgord region, running alongside the Dordogne River.

Domme

• pop 1030 ✉ 24250 alt 150m

Set on a steep promontory high above the Dordogne River, the trapezoid-shaped walled village of Domme is one of the few bastides to have retained most of its 13th century ramparts, including three fortified gates: Porte del Bos, Porte des Tours and Porte de la Combe. The village, which is a bit too perfectly restored, attracts more than its share of coach tours, but they in no way spoil the stunning panorama of the Dordogne River from the cliff-side **Esplanade du Belvédère** and the adjacent Promenade de la Barre, which stretches west along the forested slope to the Jardin Public (a public park).

The tourist office (☎ 05 53 31 71 00) on Place de la Halle, has information on day hikes in the area. It is open daily from 10 am to 7 pm from April to September; the rest of the year, weekday hours (except on holidays) are from 2 to 5 pm.

Across from the tourist office, the 19th century reconstruction of a 16th century *halle* (covered market) houses the entrance to the **grottes**, 450m of stalactite-filled galleries underneath the village; a lift whisks you back up at the end of the 30-minute tour. It is open from March to mid-November and during the Christmas and February-March school holidays. Tours begin whenever the tourist office – which sells tickets (22FF) – is open. In July and August it's open from 10.15 am to 6.40 pm.

On the far side of the square from the tourist office, the **Musée d'Arts et Traditions Populaires** (14FF) has nine rooms of clothing, toys, tools etc from the past (especially the 19th century). From April to November, open from 10 am to noon and 2 pm to 6 pm daily.

Place to Stay The 15 room, one star *Nouvel' Hôtel* (☎ 05 53 28 38 67; fax 05 53 28 27 13), two buildings down the hill from the tourist office, has doubles with shower and toilet for 210FF. It is open from Easter to October.

The Dordogne River

The mighty Dordogne rises on the Puy de Sancy high in the Massif Central, flowing south-westward and then due west for 472km – through five dams – to a point about 20km north of Bordeaux, where it joins the Garonne River to form the Gironde Estuary. Towns along the Dordogne with entries in this book include Le Mont Dore (see the Massif Central chapter); Beaulieu-sur-Dordogne (see Limousin in this chapter); Domme, La Roque Gageac, Cénac, Beynac-et-Cazenac and Bergerac (see the Périgord section); Autoire (see the Quercy section); and Saint Émilion (see the Atlantic Coast chapter).

Cénac

The village of Cénac, just west of Domme on the D46 (near where the road to Domme meets the D50 to Castelnaud), offers a number of outdoor activities. Bicycles can be rented at the Élan petrol station (☎ 05 53 28 30 08), 100m north of the intersection, for 80/400FF a day/week. It is open daily from 8 am to noon and 2 to 7 pm.

Year-round, **canoe and kayak trips** can be arranged at Canoë Cénac (also known as Randonnée Dordogne; ☎ 05 53 28 22 01; fax 05 53 28 53 00), a highly professional, English-speaking outfit whose base is 300m to the right as you approach the D46 bridge over the Dordogne River from the south (ie from Domme). Day trips cost 130FF for a one person kayak and 200FF for a two-person canoe, including transport. Longer trips – from two days (230FF a person) to seven days (730FF a person) – are also possible.

Château de Castelnaud

The 12th to 16th century Castelnaud chateau (☎ 05 53 31 30 00), 11km west of Domme along the D50 and D57, has everything you'd expect from a cliff-top castle: walls up to 2m thick (as you can see from peering out the loopholes, some designed for crossbows, others for small cannon); a superb panorama of the meandering Dordogne; and fine views of the fortified chateaus that dot the nearby hilltops. The interior rooms are occupied by a **museum of medieval warfare**, whose displays range from daggers and spiked halberds to huge catapults. The houses of the medieval village of Castelnaud cling to the steep slopes below the fortress.

From March to mid-November, the chateau is open daily (including holidays) from 10 am to 6 pm (7 pm in May, June and September; 9 am to 8 pm in July and August). For the remainder of the year, hours are 2 to 5 pm (closed Saturday). Admission costs 30FF (16FF for children aged from 10 to 17). An comprehensive English-language guidebook can be borrowed at the ticket counter.

La Roque Gageac

This attractive hamlet of tan stone houses, nestled under a cliff on the right bank of one of the *cingles* (hairpin curves) in the Dordogne River, has a number of cave dwellings known as the **Fort Troglodyte**. There's a tiny tourist office shed (☎ 05 53 29 17 01 or ☎ 05 53 29 52 37) in the carpark, but for much of the year the place to go for brochures is the post office. Canoes can be rented from Canoë La Roque Gageac (☎ 05 53 29 58 50; fax 05 53 29 38 92) in the park next to the carpark. The cost depends on how far you wish to go (120/150/190FF for two people travelling 7/14/21km).

Places to Stay The place with the sign reading ***Bar-Hôtel*** (☎ 05 53 29 51 63), open from Easter to October, has doubles with shower for 180FF. The two star ***Hôtel La Belle Étoile*** (☎ 05 53 29 51 44; fax 05 53 29 45 63) has bath/shower-equipped doubles with toilet from 200/260FF. It is open from early April to mid-October.

Beynac-et-Cazenac

For centuries Beynac and Cazenac were arch enemies and today their names remain inextricably linked. Beynac's dramatic **fortress** (☎ 05 53 29 50 40), rising from the cliff face, was once one of the greatest Périgord strongholds, dominating a strategic bend in the Dordogne and rivalling the fortress at Castelnaud on the other bank of the river. It is open daily from 10 am to noon and 2 to 6 pm (4.30 pm in November; 4 pm from December to February and 6.30 pm from July to September) and costs 35/16FF per adult/child.

In the village, there is a small **folklore museum** (☎ 05 53 29 51 28) and, behind the castle, an open-air **Parc Archaeologique** (☎ 05 53 29 51 28 or ☎ 05 53 04 85 02), containing a series of reconstructed Neolithic dwellings and tools. It is open daily, except Saturday, from July to mid-September from 10 am to 7 pm. Admission is 30/20FF for adults/children.

The tourist office (☎ 05 53 29 43 08), beside the river, is open Tuesday to Saturday from 9 am to 12.30 pm and 2 to 5.30 pm (daily in July and August from 9 am to 1 pm and 2 to 7 pm) and has information on boat trips, fishing, canoe hire and hikes in the area.

The neighbouring hilltop hamlet of Cazenac is worth a visit for its **Gothic church** and exceptional views.

Place to Stay & Eat The two star 18 room ***Hôtel-Restaurant du Château*** (☎ 05 53 29 50 13; fax 05 53 28 53 05), overlooking the river on the main road through Beynac, has comfortable doubles with shower from 230FF. The restaurant specialises in regional cuisine, with *menus* from 80FF.

Château des Milandes

The claim to fame of the smallish, late 15th century Milandes chateau (☎ 05 53 07 16 38) is its post-war role as the home of the African-American dancer and music-hall star Josephine Baker (1906-75), who helped bring black American culture to Paris in the 1920s with her *Revue Nègre* and created a sensation by appearing on stage wearing nothing but a skirt of bananas.

Awarded the Croix de Guerre and the Legion of Honour for her very active work with the French Resistance during WWII, and later participating in the US civil rights movement, Baker established her Rainbow Tribe here in 1949, adopting 12 children from around the world as 'an experiment in brotherhood'.

The chateau is open from March to October (but you can phone when it's closed). Visits, guided by a laser-disk commentary (English text available), can be started from 10 am to noon and 2 to 6 pm; from June to August, hours are 9 am to 7 pm. Entry costs 43FF (35FF for students, 33FF for kids aged 4 to 15). When the weather is good, the chateau's courtyard is home to a number of fierce-looking falcons, buzzards and goshawks (the present owner is a falconry fan).

BERGERAC

• pop 27,000 ✉ 24100

The less-than-thrilling town of Bergerac, on the right bank of the Dordogne, makes a convenient stopover on the way from Périgueux (47km to the north-east) to Bordeaux (93km to the west). The main city in the wine-growing area known as Périgord Pourpre, it is surrounded by vineyards. Bergerac is also an important tobacco-growing centre, and has an interesting **Musée du Tabac** (Tobacco Museum), housed in the elegant, early 17th century Maison Peyrarède at 10 Rue de l'Ancien Port (closed on Sunday morning and Monday morning).

A Protestant stronghold in the 16th century, Bergerac sustained heavy damage during the Wars of Religion. However, the old city and the old harbour quarter have retained some of their pre-modern ambience and are worth a stroll.

The dramatist and satirist Savinien Cyrano de Bergerac (1619-55) may have put the town on the map, but his connection with his namesake is extremely tenuous; it is believed that he stayed here a few nights at most.

Information

The well stocked tourist office (☎ 05 53 57 03 11; fax 05 53 61 11 04) at 97 Rue Neuve d'Argenson has useful brochures in English. It is open from 9.30 am to 12.30 pm and 2 to 6.30 pm (closed Sunday and holidays). July and August hours are from 9 am to 7.30 pm (on Sunday from 4 to 7 pm).

Places to Stay

Near the train station, Ave du 108e RI has two small hotels: ***Le Moderne*** (☎ 05 53 57 19 62) at No 19, whose rooms cost 160 to 220FF, and ***L'Ovale*** (☎ 05 53 57 78 75) at Nos 27-29, with rooms for 140 to 230FF.

Getting There & Away

Bergerac is on the tertiary rail line that links Bordeaux and Saint Émilion with Sarlat.

MONPAZIER

• pop 530 ✉ 24540 alt 180m

Of all the bastides in south west France, Monpazier, 45km south-east of Bergerac, is considered the best model. Perfectly laid out in rectangular grid-style, most of its buildings date from the 13th century. Over 30 are classified as historic monuments. Of particular note is the main square **Place des Cornières** with its covered arcades, the covered market with its set of 15th century measures and the town's three fortified gateways.

Today, Monpazier is an essential market town that thrives on the region's produce of tobacco, chestnuts, mushrooms and strawberries.

The tourist office (☎ 05 53 22 68 59 or ☎ 05 53 22 60 38) in the main square is open daily, except Sunday, from 10 am to noon and from 2 to 6 pm (9 am to 12.30 pm and 2.30 to 7 pm in July and August).

Quercy

South of Limousin and east of Périgord lies the warm, unmistakably southern region of Quercy, many of whose residents still speak Occitan. The dry limestone plateau in the north, known as Haut Quercy, is covered with oak trees and cut by dramatic canyons created by the serpentine Lot River and its tributaries. The main city, Cahors, is surrounded by some of the region's finest vineyards.

Activities

Boating One of the most relaxing ways to see the cliffs and villages along the 65km-long navigable stretch of the Lot between Saint Cirq Lapopie and Luzech – Cahors is about midway between the two – is to rent a houseboat.

For detailed information, contact the Centrale de Réservation Loisirs Accueil (see Organised Tours under Cahors) or Les Bateaux Safaraid (☎ 05 65 30 22 84; fax 05 65 30 23 87) in Bouziès; Baboumarine (☎ 05 65 30 08 99; fax 05 65 23 92 59) in Cahors; Blue Line (☎ 05 65 20 08 79, fax 05 65 30 97 96) in Douelle; or Locaboat Plaisance (☎ 03 86 91 72 72, fax 03 86 62 42 41) in Luzech.

For general information on boating in France, see Canal Boating under Activities in the Facts for the Visitor chapter.

Hiking In addition to the GR36 and the GR65, both of which pass through Cahors, the area has numerous marked trails for day hikes. Other Grande Randonnée trails that cross the Lot department include the GR6, GR46, GR64 and GR652.

Details on day hikes in the area between Bouziès (see East of Cahors) and Figeac appear in *Entre Lot et Célé* (39FF), a topoguide in the Promenades et Randonnées series published by the Comité Départemental du Tourisme du Lot. Nine short hikes are covered by another topoguide, *Les Chemins Qui Parlent: Sentiers Pédestres – Pays de Saint Cirq Lapopie* (40FF), which is also available at tourist offices.

Cahors is right in the corner of four IGN Série Bleue maps: 2038E, 2038O, 2039E and 2039O.

Cycling Backroads and off-road options for cyclists are detailed in the French-language topoguides *Cyclotourisme en Quercy* (about 40FF), *Guide du Cyclotourisme dans le Lot* (about 40FF) and *VTT 36 Circuits – Le Lot en Quercy* (50FF), and in the Promenades et Randonnées topoguide series (see Hiking).

Horse Riding For details on *fermes équestres* (farms where you can hire horses), contact the Association Départementale de Tourisme Rural (see Rural Accommodation under Places to Stay in the Cahors section).

CAHORS

• pop 19,700 ✉ 46000 alt 128m

Cahors, the former capital of the Quercy region, is a quiet town with a relaxed atmosphere. Surrounded on three sides by a bend in the Lot River and circled by a ring of hills, it is endowed with a couple of minor Roman sites, a famous medieval bridge and a large (if unspectacular) medieval quarter. The weather is mild in winter, hot and dry in summer and generally delightful in the spring and autumn.

In the Middle Ages, Cahors was a prosperous commercial and financial centre. Pope John XXII, a native of Cahors and the second of the Avignon popes, established a university here in 1331.

Orientation

The main commercial thoroughfare, the north-south oriented Blvd Léon Gambetta, is named after Cahors-born Léon Gambetta (1838-82), one of the founders of the Third Republic and briefly premier of France (1881-82). This avenue shaded by plane trees divides Vieux Cahors (Old Cahors), to the east, from the new quarters, to the west. At its northern end is Place Charles de Gaulle, essentially a giant parking lot; about 500m south is Place François Mitterrand (until recently called Place Aristide Briand), central Cahors' lively main square and the home of the tourist office. An even-numbered street address is often blocks away from a similar odd-numbered one.

Blvd Léon Gambetta is linked to the train station, 600m to the west, by Rue Joachim Murat. Two blocks south, Rue Président Wilson links Blvd Léon Gambetta with Pont Valentré.

Information

Tourist Offices The efficient tourist office (☎ 05 65 35 09 56; fax 05 65 23 98 66) on Place François Mitterrand is open Monday to Saturday from 10 am to noon and 2 to 6 pm

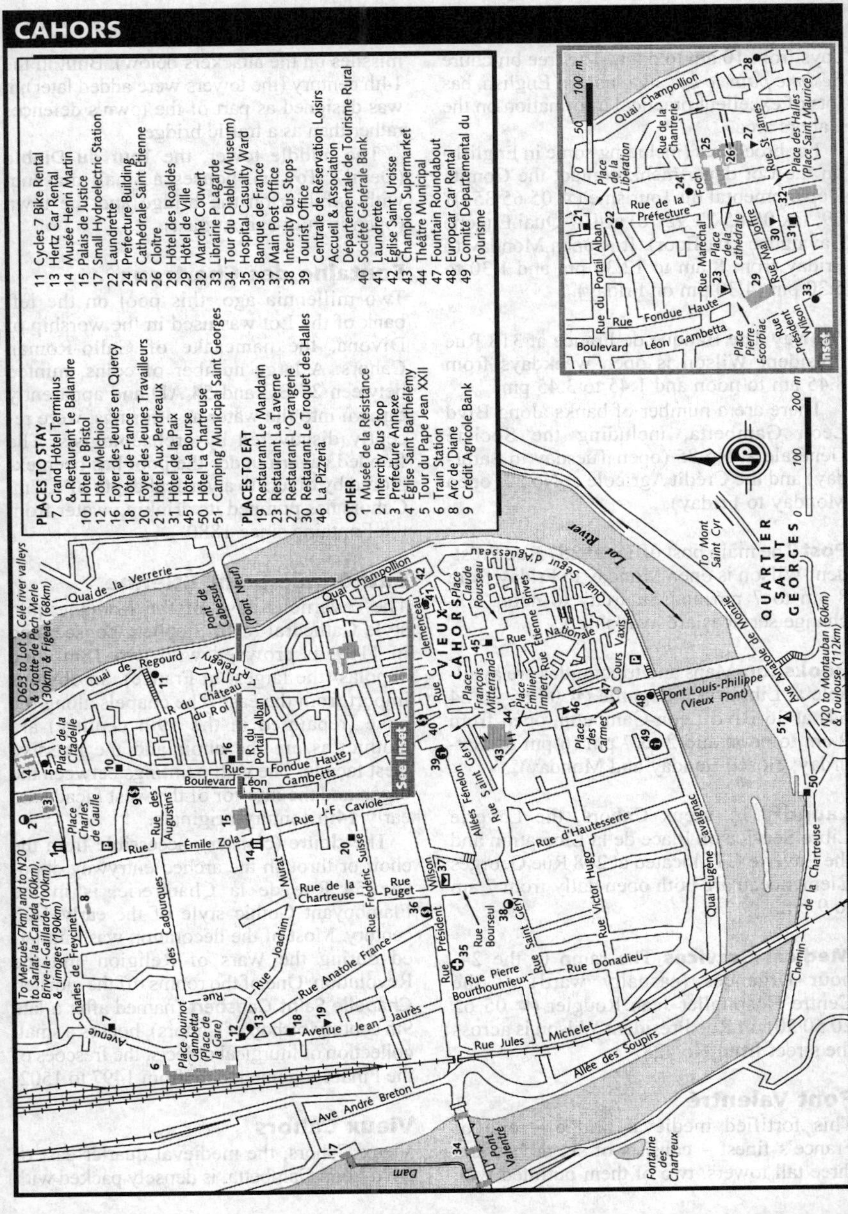
CAHORS
PLACES TO STAY
7 Grand Hôtel Terminus & Restaurant Le Balandre
10 Hôtel Le Bristol
12 Hôtel Melchior
16 Foyer des Jeunes en Quercy
18 Hôtel de France
20 Foyer des Jeunes Travailleurs
21 Hôtel Aux Perdreaux
31 Hôtel de la Paix
45 Hôtel La Bourse
50 Hôtel La Chartreuse
51 Camping Municipal Saint Georges
PLACES TO EAT
19 Restaurant Le Mandarin
23 Restaurant La Taverne
27 Restaurant L'Orangerie
30 Restaurant Le Troquet des Halles
46 La Pizzeria
OTHER
1 Musée de la Résistance
2 Intercity Bus Stop
3 Prefecture Annexe
4 Église Saint Barthélémy
5 Tour du Pape Jean XXII
6 Train Station
8 Arc de Diane
9 Crédit Agricole Bank
11 Cycles 7 Bike Rental
13 Hertz Car Rental
14 Musée Henri Martin
15 Palais de Justice
17 Small Hydroelectric Station
22 Laundrette
24 Prefecture Building
25 Cathédrale Saint Étienne
26 Cloître
28 Hôtel des Roaldès
29 Hôtel de Ville
32 Marché Couvert
33 Librairie P Lagarde
34 Tour du Diable (Museum)
35 Hospital Casualty Ward
36 Banque de France
37 Main Post Office
38 Intercity Bus Stops
39 Tourist Office
Centrale de Réservation Loisirs Accueil & Association Départementale de Tourisme Rural
40 Société Générale Bank
41 Laundrette
42 Église Saint Urcisse
43 Champion Supermarket
44 Théâtre Municipal
47 Fountain Roundabout
48 Europcar Car Rental
49 Comité Départemental du Tourisme
See Inset
Inset
Lot River
VIEUX CAHORS
QUARTIER SAINT GEORGES
Pont Valentré
Pont Louis-Philippe (Vieux Pont)
Pont de Cabessut
To Mercuès (7km) and to N20 to Sarlat-la-Canéda (60km), Brive-la-Gaillarde (100km) & Limoges (190km)
D653 to Lot & Célé river valleys & Grotte de Pech Merle (30km) & Figeac (68km)
N20 to Montauban (60km) & Toulouse (112km)
To Mont Saint Cyr

(6.30 pm from May to August). From May to August, it's also open on Sunday and holidays from 10 am to noon. The free brochure *Sésame pour le Lot*, available in English, has lots of excellent practical information on the Cahors area.

For brochures (including some in English) on the Lot department, contact the Comité Départemental du Tourisme (☎ 05 65 35 07 09; fax 05 65 23 92 76) at 107 Quai Eugène Cavaignac (1st floor). It is open Monday to Friday from 8 am to 12.30 pm and 1.30 to 5.30 pm (4.30 pm on Friday).

Money The Banque de France at 318 Rue Président Wilson is open weekdays from 8.45 am to noon and 1.45 to 3.45 pm.

There are a number of banks along Blvd Léon Gambetta, including the Société Générale at No 85 (open Tuesday to Saturday) and the Crédit Agricole at No 22 (open Monday to Friday).

Post The main post office at 257 Rue Président Wilson is open Monday to Friday from 8 am to 7 pm and Saturday to noon. Exchange services are available.

Bookshop Maps and topoguides are available at Librairie P Lagarde (☎ 05 65 35 24 64) at 36 Blvd Léon Gambetta, open from 9 am to noon and 2 to 7 pm (6 pm on Saturday; closed Sunday and Monday).

Laundry In Vieux Cahors, the Laverie Libre Service on Place de la Libération and the Laverie GTI located at 208 Rue Georges Clemenceau are both open daily from 7 am to 9 pm.

Medical Services The ramp to the 24-hour Urgences (casualty ward) of the Centre Hospitalier Jean Rougier (☎ 05 65 20 50 50) on Rue Président Wilson is across the street from No 428.

Pont Valentré

This fortified medieval bridge – one of France's finest – consists of six arches and three tall towers, two of them outfitted with machicolations (projecting parapets equipped with openings that allow defenders to drop missiles on the attackers below). Built in the 14th century (the towers were added later), it was designed as part of the town's defences rather than as a traffic bridge.

The middle tower, the **Tour du Diable** (Devil's Tower), houses a small museum with exhibits on the bridge and the town (open in July and August).

Fontaine des Chartreux

Two millennia ago, this pool on the left bank of the Lot was used in the worship of Divona, the namesake of Gallo-Roman Cahors. A large number of coins, minted between 27 BC and 54 AD and apparently thrown into the water as offerings, were recently discovered by archaeologists. The flooded cavern under the pool has been explored by divers to a vertical depth of 137m. Cahors has pumped its drinking water from the Fontaine since 1880.

Cathédrale Saint Étienne

The cavernous nave of the Romanesque-style Cathedral of St Stephen, consecrated in 1119, is crowned with two 18m-wide cupolas (the largest in France), an obvious import from the east. The chapels along the nave (repainted in the 19th century) are Gothic, as are the choir and the massive west façade. The wall paintings between the organ and the interior of the west façade are early 14th century originals.

The **cloître** (cloister), accessible from the choir or through the arched entryway opposite 59 Rue de la Chantrerie, is in the Flamboyant Gothic style of the early 16th century. Most of the decoration was mutilated during the Wars of Religion and the Revolution. One of the rooms off the cloister, **Chapelle Saint Gausbert** (named after a late 9th century bishop of Cahors), houses a small collection of liturgical objects; the frescoes of the Final Judgement date from 1497 to 1502.

Vieux Cahors

Vieux Cahors, the medieval quarter east of Blvd Léon Gambetta, is densely packed with old (though not necessarily picturesque) four-storey houses linked by streets and alleyways so narrow you can almost touch both walls.

In 1580, during the Wars of Religion, the Protestant Henri of Navarre (later to become the Catholic King Henri IV) captured the Catholic stronghold of Cahors and stayed in the **Hôtel des Roaldès** (☎ 05 65 35 04 35) at 271 Quai Champollion for one night. It is open to the public on major holidays and from mid-June to October.

The **Tour du Pape Jean XXII**, a square, crenellated tower at 1-3 Blvd Léon Gambetta – at 34m the tallest structure in town – was built in the 14th century as part of the home of Jacques Duèse, later Pope John XXII (reigned 1316-34). The interior is closed to the public. Next door is the 14th century **Église Saint Barthélémy**, with its massive brick and stone belfry.

It is possible to walk around three sides of Cahors by following the quays along the town's riverside perimeter.

West of Blvd Léon Gambetta

The **Musée Henri Martin** (☎ 05 65 30 15 13) at 792 Rue Émile Zola, also known as the Musée Municipal, has some archaeological artefacts and a collection of works by the Cahors-born pointillist painter Henri Martin (1893-1972). It is open only when there are temporary exhibitions, usually from June to September (closed on Tuesday).

The small **Musée de la Résistance** (☎ 05 65 22 14 25), on the north side of Place Charles de Gaulle, has illustrated exhibits on the Resistance, the concentration camps and the liberation of France. It is open daily from 2 to 6 pm. Entry is free.

Die-hard fans of Roman architecture might want to visit the **Arc de Diane**, a stone archway with red-brick stripes that once formed part of a Gallo-Roman bathhouse. It is opposite 24 Ave Charles de Freycinet.

Hiking

Mont Saint Cyr The 264m-high, antenna-topped hill across the river from Vieux Cahors affords excellent views of the town and the surrounding countryside. It can easily be climbed on foot – the trail begins near the south end of Pont Louis-Philippe (1838).

Organised Tours

The Centrale de Réservation Loisirs Accueil (☎ 05 65 53 20 90; fax 05 65 30 06 11), open weekdays from 8 am to 12.30 pm and 1.30 to 6 pm, in the Chambre d'Agriculture du Lot in Place François Mitterrand, can arrange canoe, bicycle and horse-riding excursions, cookery courses and boat rental on the Lot River. If you want a hassle-free hike, they can provide an itinerary and arrange for accommodation, meals and even the transport of your bags. Such activities, some of which are not available in July and August, can often be booked at short notice. It is open Monday to Friday from 8 am to 12.30 pm and 1.30 to 6 pm.

Special Events

Le Printemps de Cahors, a two week exhibition of photography and the visual arts, is held in May or early June. Immediately following Bastille Day (14 July) celebrations, the four-day Festival de Blues brings big-name jazz stars to town.

Places to Stay

Rooms are hardest to come by in July and August. Many cheapies do not register new guests on Sunday unless you make advance arrangement by phone.

Places to Stay – Budget

Camping The riverside two star *Camping Municipal Saint Georges* (☎ 05 65 35 04 64), on Ave Anatole de Monzie is hemmed in by heavily trafficked roads. It is open from Easter to mid-November. Fees are 14FF for a site and 15FF per adult. The office is generally closed from 11.30 am to 4.30 pm.

Hostels The *Foyer des Jeunes Travailleurs* (☎ 05 65 35 64 71; fax 05 65 35 95 92) at 20 Rue Frédéric Suisse, also known as Résidence Frédéric Suisse, serves as a 42 bed hostel throughout the year. Beds cost 49FF (57FF if you lack an HI card). The office is staffed from 9 am to 7 pm (closed Saturday afternoon and Sunday). Telephone reservations are advisable.

The antiquated ***Foyer des Jeunes en Quercy*** (☎ 05 65 35 29 32) at 129 Rue Fondue Haute, run by nuns, provides accommodation for students during the academic year but welcomes travellers of all religions, sexes and ages (from late June to early September). A simple bed in a very basic single or triple with washbasin costs 68FF including breakfast; dinner (available on weekdays) is 32FF. There's no curfew. Reservations can be made by telephone.

Rural Accommodation For information on staying out in the countryside (in *gîtes ruraux*, chambres d'hôtes etc) contact the Association Départementale de Tourisme Rural (☎ 05 65 53 20 75) at Place François Mitterrand, open Monday to Friday from 8 am to 12.30 pm and 1.30 to 6 pm.

On the ground floor, the Centrale de Réservation Loisirs Accueil (see Organised Tours), can help make reservations. Most places require advance booking and have a one week minimum stay.

Hotels In Vieux Cahors, the friendly ***Hôtel La Bourse*** (☎ 05 65 35 17 78), a decent sort of place at 7 Place Claude Rousseau, has large doubles/quads with washbasin and bidet for 110/185FF. Hall showers are free. Reception (at the bar) is closed on Sunday.

Next to the Marché Couvert, the 22 room ***Hôtel de la Paix*** (☎ 05 65 35 03 40) on Place des Halles (Place Saint Maurice) has basic but clean doubles from 150FF (190FF with shower). Hall showers are free. Reception is closed on Sunday and holidays.

The eight room ***Hôtel Aux Perdreaux*** (☎ 05 65 35 03 50) at 137 Rue du Portail Alban (on Place de la Libération) has smallish, nondescript doubles with shower for 160FF. Except in July and August, reception (at the bar) is closed on Sunday.

Places to Stay – Mid-Range

Near the train station, the three star, 79 room ***Hôtel de France*** (☎ 05 65 35 16 76; fax 05 65 22 01 08), 252 Ave Jean Jaurès, has basic but comfortable singles/doubles for 234/238FF, breakfast is 40FF extra. Facing the train station, the two star ***Hôtel Melchior*** (☎ 05 65 35 03 38; fax 05 65 23 92 75) has adequate but hardly attractive one/two-bed doubles from 235/250FF. Except from July to mid-October, reception (at the bar) is closed on Sunday.

Across the Lot from the south end of town in Quartier Saint Georges, the riverside three star ***Hôtel La Chartreuse*** (☎ 05 65 35 17 37; fax 05 65 22 30 03) on Chemin de la Chartreuse can provide singles/doubles for 230/260FF.

On Place Charles de Gaulle, you might try the four room ***Hôtel Le Bristol*** (☎ 05 65 23 93 01) at 17 Blvd Léon Gambetta, whose doubles start at 200FF.

Places to Stay – Top End

The elegant three star ***Grand Hôtel Terminus*** (☎ 05 65 35 24 50; fax 05 65 22 06 40) at 5 Ave Charles de Freycinet (one block up the hill from the train station), a 22 room, stained-glass adorned place built around 1920, has very comfortable singles/doubles with shower starting at 300/350FF.

About 7km north-west of Cahors in the village of Mercuès, ***Le Mas Azemar*** (☎ 05 65 30 96 85) on Rue du Mas de Vinssou is a delightful chambre d'hôte establishment in an 18th century house. It is open year-round by reservation only, with doubles from 360FF.

Places to Eat

Most restaurants are closed on Sunday.

Restaurants – French The friendly and unpretentious ***Restaurant Le Troquet des Halles*** (☎ 05 65 22 15 81), on Rue Saint Maurice near Place des Halles, is popular with the people who make their living in Vieux Cahors. The *menu* costs only 55FF, including wine; the *plat du jour* is 35FF. In the morning (from 7 to 10 am), the soup (16FF) comes with a glass of wine so you can *faire chabrot* (add the wine to the soup and drink it together); you can also buy a steak at the nearby Marché Couvert and have the chef cook it for you for an extra 9FF. The bar is open from 7 am to 8.30 or 9 pm (10 pm in summer). Lunch is on from noon to 2 pm, while dinner – available only from June to September – is served from 7 to 9.30 pm.

The rustic yet sophisticated ***Restaurant La Taverne*** (☎ 05 65 35 28 66) on Place Pierre Escorbiac specialises in French and regional cuisine. *Menus* cost 95 to 250FF; main dishes are 78 to 120FF. It is open from noon to 2 pm and 7.30 to 10 pm (closed weekends except in July and August). Reservations are recommended on Friday and Saturday nights.

The elegant ***Restaurant Le Balandre*** (☎ 05 65 30 01 97), 5 Ave Charles de Freycinet, attached to the ***Grand Hôtel Terminus*** (see Places to Stay), serves creative cuisine based on traditional regional dishes and ingredients, including fish. There is a good lunchtime *menu* for 170FF (coffee or wine included) and dinner *menus* for 150, 250 and 350FF. It is open from noon to 2 pm and 7.30 to 10 pm (closed on Sunday night and all day Monday, although this may alter during peak season).

Restaurants – Vegetarian The attractive, 100% vegetarian ***Restaurant L'Orangerie*** (☎ 05 65 22 59 06) at 41 Rue Saint James has salads for 20 to 35FF, main dishes from 42FF and *menus* for 68 and 98FF. It is open Tuesday to Saturday from noon to 2 pm and 7 to 9 pm (9.30 pm in summer).

Restaurants – Other The popular ***La Pizzeria*** (☎ 05 65 35 12 18) at 58 Blvd Léon Gambetta has pizzas (30 to 50FF), pasta (35 to 45FF) and large salads (30 to 42FF). It is open from noon to 2.15 pm and 7 to 11.30 pm (closed on Sunday at midday and, from November to April, on Sunday evening).

Near the train station, ***Restaurant Le Mandarin*** (☎ 05 65 22 22 93), a Chinese-Vietnamese place at 216 Ave Jean Jaurès (1st floor), has main courses for around 40 to 70FF; the lunch *menu* is 70FF. It is open daily.

Self-Catering Regional specialities, available at tourist-oriented shops as well as food markets, include deep-red Cahors wine, foie gras, truffles and *cabécou* (a small, round goat's cheese).

The ***Marché Couvert*** (also known as Les Halles) on Place des Halles is open Tuesday to Saturday from 7.30 am to 12.30 pm and 3 to 7 pm and on Sunday and holidays from 9 am to noon. There's an ***open-air market*** around the Marché Couvert and on Place de la Cathédrale on Wednesday and Saturday (or the previous day if it clashes with holidays). Nearby, ***food shops*** can be found around Place des Halles and along Rue de la Préfecture.

Near the tourist office, the ***Champion*** supermarket across from 109 Blvd Léon Gambetta is open from 9 am to 12.30 pm and 2.30 to 7.15 pm (closed Sunday; no midday closure on Friday and Saturday).

Getting There & Away

Bus The bus services linking Cahors with destinations around the Lot department (designed primarily to transport school children) are a mess. To sort things out, find a copy of the annual *Guide Horaire des Transports* (timetable) published by the Conseil Général du Lot; it is usually available at tourist offices.

In Cahors, intercity buses stop at one or more of the following three locations: in front of the train station at three anonymous shelters (hours for some lines – mainly SNCF – are posted); along Rue Saint Géry, just west of Allées Fénelon; and in the unmarked parking lot on the north side of Place Charles de Gaulle, next to the Palais des Sports (hours are not posted).

Train The train station (☎ 08 36 35 35 35) is on Place Jouinot Gambetta (Place de la Gare). The information office is open daily from 6.20 am to 9.30 pm.

Cahors is on the main SNCF line that links Paris' Gare d'Austerlitz (324FF; 5½ hours during the day; five a day) with Limoges (153FF; 2¼ hours; six a day), Souillac, Brive-la-Gaillarde, Montauban (54FF; 45 minutes; five to seven a day) and Toulouse

(106FF; 70 minutes; five to seven a day). To get to Bordeaux (186FF) you have to change trains at Montauban; change at Toulouse to get to Marseille (300FF) and Nice (385FF). To get to Sarlat-la-Canéda, take a train to Souillac and an SNCF bus from there.

For details on the daily SNCF bus services from Cahors' train station (and, for certain runs, Place Charles de Gaulle) to Bouziès, Tour de Faure (Saint Cirq Lapopie) and Figeac, see those sections.

Car Europcar (☎ 05 65 22 35 55) is at 68 Blvd Léon Gambetta (closed on Saturday afternoon and Sunday). Hertz (☎ 05 65 35 34 69) is opposite the train station at 385 Rue Anatole France.

Getting Around

Cycles 7 (☎ 05 65 22 66 60) at 417 Quai de Regourd rents mountain bikes for 80FF a day. It's open Tuesday to Saturday from 9 am to noon and 2 to 7 pm.

EAST OF CAHORS

The limestone hills between Cahors and Figeac are cut by the dramatic, cliff-flanked Lot and Célé rivers. The narrow, winding and supremely scenic D662 (signposted 'Vallée du Lot') follows the Lot River, while the even narrower and more spectacular D41 (signposted 'Vallée du Célé') follows the tortuous route of the Célé.

Bouziès

The quiet hamlet of Bouziès, on the left bank of the Lot River between the cliffs and the riverbank, is home to the welcoming 39 room ***Hôtel Les Falaises*** (☎ 05 65 31 26 83; fax 05 65 30 23 87). The hotel rents out a variety of sports equipment to guests and nonresidents alike, including mountain bikes, canoes, kayaks, rowboats, motorboats, *gabarres* (flat-bottomed river boats) and five-person houseboats. The magnificent 65km stretch of the Lot between Luzech and Saint Cirq Lapopie is navigable from April to October.

Double rooms at the hotel cost 255 to 355FF, depending on the season. It is closed in December and January. The hotel's ***restaurant***, which has a lovely terrace, serves regional cuisine (including home-made pâté de foie gras and *confit d'oie*) daily whenever the hotel is open. The *menus* cost 85, 99, 129 and 230FF.

Getting There & Away The SNCF bus that links Cahors (27FF; 25 minutes; five to seven a day) with Figeac (one hour) stops on the D662 across the narrow suspension bridge from Bouziès.

The hotel will send its minivan to pick up guests at Cahors' train station or drop you off at the starting point of a hike.

Cabrerets

The village of Cabrerets, on the Célé River 3km upriver from where it joins the Lot, is about midway between Bouziès and the Grotte de Pech Merle.

Places to Stay & Eat The ***Camping Familial Cantal*** (☎ 05 65 31 27 12 at the tourist office), 700m north-east of the turn-off to the D13 (which goes to the grotte), is on a shaded, grassy site on the right bank of the Célé. A site costs 12FF; adults pay 12FF. It is open all year.

The two star ***Hôtel des Grottes*** (☎ 05 65 31 27 02; fax 05 65 31 20 15), on the D41 overlooking the river, has doubles from 175FF; doubles/triples/quads with shower and toilet cost 250/370/450FF (20FF more in summer). It's open from April to October. The hotel's restaurant serves a hearty three course regional-style *menu* for 75FF.

Getting There & Away SNCF buses on the Cahors-Figeac route stop just under 4km south of Cabrerets at the intersection of the D662 and the D41.

Grotte de Pech Merle

The spectacular, 1200m-long Pech Merle Cave (☎ 05 65 31 27 05), 30km east of Cahors, is first and foremost a natural wonder, with thousands of stalactites and stalagmites of all varieties and shapes. It also has dozens of paintings of mammoths, horses and 'negative' human handprints, drawn by Cro-Magnon people 16,000 to 20,000 years ago in red, black, blue and dark grey. Prehistoric artefacts found in the area are on display in the museum.

From April to October, one-hour guided tours (English text available) begin every 45 minutes (every 15 minutes in summer) daily from 9.30 am to noon and 1.30 to 5 pm. Tickets cost 44FF (30FF for children aged five to 18) and are well worth the price. During the months when there are lots of tourists around, get there early as only 700 people a day are allowed to visit. Reservations are accepted.

The Grotte de Pech Merle is 8km from the Bouziès bridge and 3km from Cabreret along the D41, D13 and D198. On foot, the cave is about 3km from Bouziès via the GR651.

SAINT CIRQ LAPOPIE

• pop 50 ✉ 46330 alt 147m

Saint Cirq Lapopie, 25km east of Cahors and 44km south-west of Figeac, is perched on a cliff top 100m above the Lot River. The spectacular views and the area's natural beauty make up for the village's overstated charm.

The fortified early 16th century **Gothic church** is of no special interest except for its stunning location. The ruins of the 13th century **chateau** at the top of the hill also afford a fine panorama. Below, along the narrow alleyways, the restored stone and half-timbered houses – topped with steep, red-tile roofs – shelter **artisans' studios** offering leather goods, pottery, jewellery and items made of wood. The **Musée Rignault** (15/10FF per adult/child), open daily, except Tuesday, from 10 am to 1 pm and 3 pm to 6 pm (in July and August open every day until 7 pm), has a delightful garden and an eclectic collection of French furniture and art from Africa and China.

Saint Cirq Lapopie is named after Saint Cirq, a child martyred in Asia Minor under Diocletian; his relics, it is believed, later found their way here. Lapopie, a word of Celtic origin that refers to an elevated place, was the family name of the local lords during the Middle Ages.

Information

The tourist office (☎/fax 05 65 31 29 06), in the Mairie has an English brochure on the village. From April to November it is open weekdays from 10 am to 7 pm (6 pm on Monday). The rest of the year it's open daily (except Saturday) to 6 pm.

Activities

The tourist office rents laser disks (in French only), from a collection *Les Chemins qui Parlent*, for a walk around the countryside. It costs 40FF for 24 hours with a 500FF deposit.

Camping de la Plage (see Places to Stay) arranges half-day/day (11/22km) canoe trips for 70/115FF a person, including transport.

Places to Stay & Eat

The riverside ***Camping de la Plage*** (☎ 05 65 30 29 51), on the left bank of the Lot at the bridge linking the D662 (Tour de Faure) with the road up to Saint Cirq Lapopie, charges 30FF per person. It is open all year.

The ***Auberge du Sombral*** (☎ 05 65 31 26 08; fax 05 65 30 26 37), directly across the square from the tourist office, has rooms for 260 to 375FF. It is open from April to mid-November. The ***restaurant***, whose *menus* cost 100 to 200FF, and the hotel's reception are closed on Wednesday, except from July to September.

Getting There & Away

Saint Cirq Lapopie is 2km across the river and up the hill from the D662 and Tour de Faure, whose SNCF bus shelter is a few hundred metres upriver from the bridge. Buses run to Cahors (28FF; 40 minutes; five or six a day) and Figeac (one hour).

Getting Around

Kalapcar (☎ 05 65 30 29 51), below the village at the camp site, rents mountain bikes for 80/100FF per half-day/day.

FIGEAC

• pop 9500 ✉ 46100 alt 250m

The riverside town of Figeac, on the Célé, 68km north-east of Cahors, has a picturesque **old city**, with many houses dating from the 12th to 18th century. Founded in the 9th century by Benedictine monks, it became a prosperous medieval market town, an important stopping place for pilgrims travelling to Santiago de Compostela and, later, a Protestant stronghold (1576-1623).

Orientation

The main commercial roadway is the north-south Blvd Docteur G Juskiewenski, which runs perpendicular to the river Célé and its right-bank quays. Pedestrianised Rue Gambetta, four short blocks east, is also perpendicular to the river. The train station is across the river from the centre of town at the end of Ave Georges Clemenceau; the two banks of the Célé are linked by Pont Gambetta, the bridge at the southern end of Rue Gambetta.

Information

The tourist office (☎ 05 65 34 06 25) is on Place Vival, one block north of the river and two blocks east of Blvd Docteur G Juskiewenski. It sells a locally produced topoguide, *Figeac et Son Pays* (30FF), which has details on a dozen short hikes. It is open Monday to Saturday from 10 am to noon and 2.30 to 6 pm (10 am to 1 pm and 2 to 7 in July and August); open from 10 am to 1 pm on Sunday (10 am to 12.30 pm and 2.30 to 7 pm in July and August).

The post office, a block west of Blvd Docteur G Juskiewenski at 6 Ave Fernand Pezet, is open weekdays from 9 am to 5.30 pm and on Saturday until noon. Currency exchange is available. There are a couple of banks along the same street.

Maps and topoguides are available at the Maison de la Presse at 2 Rue Gambetta (closed Sunday afternoon).

Things to See

The tourist office is housed in a handsome 13th century building known as the **Oustal de la Mounédo** (meaning 'mint' in Occitan; in French: Hôtel de la Monnaie), though coins were never actually minted here. Upstairs is the **Musée du Vieux Figeac** (10/5FF for adults/children), which has a varied collection of antique clocks, coins, minerals and a propeller blade made by a local aerospace firm. It is open the same hours as the tourist office.

Figeac's most illustrious son is the brilliant linguist and founder of the science of Egyptology, Jean-François Champollion (1790-1832), who managed to decipher the written language of the pharaohs by studying the Rosetta Stone, an edict issued in 196 BC in Greek and two Egyptian scripts, demotic and hieroglyphic. Discovered by Napoleon's forces in 1799 during their abortive invasion of Egypt, the stone was captured by the English in 1801 and taken to the British Museum, where it remains to this day; an enlarged copy fills the ancient courtyard next to Champollion's childhood home, now the **Musée Champollion** (☎ 05 65 50 31 08) on tiny Rue des Frères Champollion (four blocks north of the tourist office along pedestrianised Rue de la République). The small collection of Egyptian antiquities can be visited from 10 am to noon and 2.30 to 6.30 pm (closed Monday, except in July and August); from November to February, hours are 2 to 6 pm. Entry costs 20FF (17FF for seniors, 12FF for children and students). Some of the explanatory signs are in English.

North of the Musée Champollion and Place Champollion, **Rue de Colomb**, which was favoured by the local aristocracy in the 18th century, is lined with centuries-old mansions in sandstone, half-timbers and brick. Near the river, the musty **Église Saint Sauveur** on Rue du Chapitre, a Benedictine abbey church, built from the 12th to 14th century, features stained glass installed during the last half of the 19th century.

Places to Stay

In the old city, the two star, 10 room ***Hôtel Champollion*** (☎ 05 65 34 04 37) at 3 Place Champollion has double/triple rooms with bathroom for 250/280FF.

Directly across the square from the train station, the ***Hôtel Le Terminus*** (☎ 05 65 34 00 43; fax 05 65 50 00 94) at 27 Ave Georges Clemenceau has doubles with shower and toilet for 245FF. A few blocks west of the train station on the other side of the tracks, the 10 room ***Hôtel Le Toulouse*** (☎ 05 65 34 22 95) at 4 Ave de Toulouse (the D922) has serviceable doubles with shower and toilet from 180FF.

Places to Eat

À l'Escargot (☎ 05 65 34 23 84) at 2 Ave Jean Jaurès, just across Pont Gambetta from the centre of town, has been run by the same family since 1950. *Menus* of family-style Quercy cuisine cost 85, 95 and 168FF; the plat du jour is 55FF. It is closed on Monday night. ***Restaurant Vimean Ekreach*** (☎ 05 65 34 79 65) at 10 Rue Baudel (a bit south of Place Champollion) serves Chinese food from Tuesday to Sunday; *menus* cost 58FF (lunch only), 85 and 125FF.

The ***Leclerc*** supermarket at 32 Rue Gambetta is closed on Sunday and, except on Saturday, from 12.30 to 2 pm. Place Carnot (two long blocks north of the tourist office along Rue de la République) has a ***food market*** on Saturday morning; the nearby ***food shops*** are closed on Sunday afternoon and Monday. Several stores around town sell regional specialities.

Getting There & Away

The SNCF bus from Cahors (61FF; 1¾ hours; four or five times a day, including Sunday and holidays) via Bouziès and Tour de Faure (Saint Cirq Lapopie) stops at Figeac's train station and, nearer the town centre, on Ave Maréchal Joffre (which runs along the river) at its oblique intersection with Rue de Cordeliers.

The train station (☎ 05 65 80 29 06), staffed from 4 am to midnight, is on two major rail lines: the one that links Toulouse (112FF; 2¼ hours; five a day) with Aurillac (58FF) and Clermont-Ferrand (149FF; four hours; three to five a day); and the one from Paris' Gare d'Austerlitz (300FF; about six hours; five a day, two of them direct) to Limoges, Brive (71FF; 1½ hours; five a day), Rocamadour-Padirac (41FF; 40 minutes) and Rodez (61FF; 1¼ hours; five a day).

Getting Around

The Larroque et Fils (☎ 05 65 34 10 28), a garage at 10 Quai Bessières (along the river), rents mountain bikes for 90FF a day. It is open daily from 9 am to noon and 2 to 6 pm.

NORTHERN QUERCY

The northern edge of Quercy is midway between Cahors and Brive-la-Gaillarde and is not far from Collonges-la-Rouge and Beaulieu-sur-Dordogne (see the Limousin section).

Rocamadour

• pop 630 ✉ 46500 alt 250m

Except in winter, when it's nearly dead, the spectacularly situated pilgrimage centre of Rocamadour, 59km north of Cahors and 51km east of Sarlat, is a tourist's nightmare, overrun with coaches and filled to overflowing with souvenir shops.

Perched on a 150m-high cliff face above the Alzou River, the old city – known as the **Cité** – was, from the 12th to 14th century, an important stop on one of the pilgrimage routes to Santiago de Compostela.

These days, coach tourists with glazed eyes obediently plod through a number of over-restored Gothic chapels, including **Chapelle Notre Dame**, home to a 12th century Black Madonna said to have miraculous powers. Other sights in the Cité include the **Musée du Jouet Ancien Automobile** (☎ 05 65 33 60 75), which has a fine display of over one hundred kiddie cars with pedals made between 1905 and 1960. It is open daily year-round and costs 20FF (free for children).

The Cité's only street is connected to the chapels and the plateau above, known as **L'Hospitalet**, by the **Grand Escalier** (Great Staircase) – once climbed by the pious on their knees – and a path whose switchbacks are marked with graphic Stations of the Cross. At the top, a short walk or drive from L'Hospitalet's tourist office, is the 14th century **chateau** (12FF for a view from the ramparts).

Sights in L'Hospitalet include the freshwater **Aquarium** (☎ 05 65 33 73 61) on

Place de l'Europe, just across the street from the tourist office; it is open daily from Easter to October and weekends and holidays only in winter months. The **Grotte des Merveilles** (☎ 05 65 33 67 92), which is a one room cave 100m towards Peyrat from the tourist office, has some mediocre stalactites and prehistoric cave paintings (open April to October).

Information The tourist office (☎ 05 65 33 62 59) on the Cité's only street is open daily from April to June and September from 10 am to 12.30 pm and 1.30 to 7 pm; July and August from 9.30 am to 7.30 pm; October from 10 am to noon and 2 to 6 pm; November to March daily, except Tuesday, from 2.30 pm to 5.30 pm. The tourist office (☎ 05 65 33 62 80) in L'Hospitalet, housed in a copy of a stone *berger* (shepherd's hut), is open daily in July and August from 10 am to 8 pm; 10 am to noon and 2 to 7 pm daily for the rest of the year.

Places to Stay In the middle of the Cité, the one star, seven room ***Hôtel du Globe*** (☎ 05 65 33 67 73), open from February to November (weekends only in December and January), has rooms with shower and toilet for two/four people from 190/270FF.

If you don't mind the bad pun (Santiago de Compostela translates as Saint Jacques de Compostelle in French), the two star, 15 room ***Comp' Hostel*** (☎ 05 65 33 73 50; fax 05 65 33 69 60), near the tourist office on Place de l'Europe, has characterless, modern doubles/quads for 200/280FF (220/340FF from July to September). It's open from April to September.

Behind the Comp' Hostel, the grassy ***Relais du Campeur*** (☎ 05 65 33 73 50) costs 65FF for two people. It is open from April to September.

Getting There & Away Rocamadour is 4km south-west of the Rocamadour-Padirac train station, which is on the line that links Brive-la-Gaillarde with Figeac and Rodez. Taxis are available for transport to/from the station.

Autoire

No other village in Quercy boasts as many towers and turrets as Autoire, one of the most beautiful villages in France, 31km north-east of Rocamadour. It is situated in a deep gorge leading to the Dordogne River in what was once an important wine-growing area. The village is largely made up of Renaissance manor houses built by wealthy *vignerons* in the style of miniature chateaus. At the top of the cliffs behind the village, it is just possible to make out the ruins of a folly-like fortress dating from the Hundred Years' War. It is called the **Château des Anglais**, a name given to many ancient ruins of uncertain history in the region.

There is no hotel, restaurant or tourist office in the village, but you can get limited information from the Mairie (☎ 05 65 38 05 26).

Gouffre de Padirac

The truly spectacular Padirac Cave (☎ 05 65 33 64 56), 15km north-east of Rocamadour along the D673, offers the closest thing – at least in *this* world – to a cruise to Hades across the Styx River. Discovered in 1889, the cave's navigable river – 103m below ground level – is reached through a 75m-deep, 33m-wide chasm. Boat pilots who speak only Occitan and Midi-accented French ferry visitors along a 500m stretch of the subterranean waterway, guiding them up and down a series of stairways to otherworldly pools and vast, floodlit caverns. The whole operation is unashamedly mass-market, but it retains an innocence and style reminiscent of the 1930s, when the first lifts were installed. The temperature inside the cave is a constant 13°C.

From April to the 2nd Sunday in October, hour-long visits begin from 9 am to noon and 2 to 6 pm; hours are extended in July (8.30 am to 6.30 pm) and August (8 am to 7 pm). Entry costs 46FF (27FF for kids aged 6 to 9).

Martel

Twelfth century Martel, the 'Town of the Seven Towers', 24km north of Rocamadour, has for centuries been the centre of the regional nut trade and the ancient weighing measures can still be seen at the wooden marketplace in the square.

The town was named after Charles Martel, who built an abbey here in 632. It later became the capital of the Viscounts of Turenne, its strong fortifications bearing witness to its violent past – even the church is comprised of battlements and buttresses.

The accommodating tourist office (☎ 05 65 37 43 44) at Place de la Halle is open daily from 10 am to noon and 3 to 6 pm (9 am to 12.30 pm and 3 to 7 pm in July and August).

Saint Céré

The old market town of Saint Céré, 30km from Rocamadour in the valley of the Bave River, is known for its strawberries and plums, and you can still see the *taouilé* (stone bench) in the **Place du Mercadial** where fishermen once displayed their catch.

Saint Céré's museums pay tribute to their most famous resident, Jean Lurçat, celebrated around the world for his textile designs and techniques. Some of his brilliantly coloured tapestries are on display at the **Casino Gallery** (☎ 05 65 38 19 60) in Rue Moussinac, open daily from 9 am to noon and 2 to 7 pm (closed Tuesday from October to June). Entrance is free.

Just behind the gallery, a footpath leads to the medieval **castle of Saint Laurent** (☎ 05 65 38 28 21) on a hill overlooking the town, which also contains a **museum** dedicated to Lurçat, which costs 15/8FF for adults/children up to 13 years. It is open for two weeks at Easter, then from mid-July to September, daily from 9.30 am to noon and 2.30 to 6.30 pm.

Ask at the helpful tourist office (☎ 05 65 38 11 85) in Place de la République for information on 1½-hour guided tours of the town or the free leaflet and walking route *Saint Céré – Visite de la Ville*. It is open Monday to Saturday from 10 am to noon and 2 to 6 pm (9 am to 12.30 pm and 2.30 to 7 pm in July and August, when it is also open Sunday mornings).

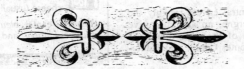

Massif Central

The striking mountain landscape of the Massif Central, dimpled with the cones of extinct volcanoes, is unique in France. Blessed with an abundance of mineral hot springs, the area is also known for its spa towns, among them Vichy and Le Mont Dore.

Except in the few small cities and the regional capital, Clermont-Ferrand, life is primarily rural. The rich volcanic soil supports maize, tobacco and vineyards, while at higher elevations, cows and sheep produce some of the country's most popular (and cheapest) cheeses – you'll come across the powerful *bleu d'Auvergne* and the slightly sour-tasting *cantal* everywhere in France.

Two large regional parks, the dramatic Parc Naturel Régional des Volcans d'Auvergne and its tamer eastern neighbour, the Parc Naturel Régional du Livradois-Forez, together make up France's largest environmentally protected area.

Geography

Formed millions of years before the Alps or Pyrenees, the volcanic landscape of the Massif Central is best known for its *puys* (pronounced 'pwee'), or volcanic cones. The Puy de Dôme west of Clermont-Ferrand is one of the most spectacular, but there are many more, most notably in the Parc des Volcans d'Auvergne. Some of the puys are merely the lava 'plugs' that remained when the surrounding cones eroded away – Saint Michel d'Aiguilhe chapel in Le Puy-en-Velay is perched atop a particularly steep plug.

The region gives rise to some of France's great rivers, including the Dordogne, Allier and Loire. Many of the area's lakes are volcanic craters that have filled with rainwater; others were created when lava flows acted as dams.

The Massif Central covers roughly the area of the Auvergne, an administrative region comprised of the departments of Allier, Puy de Dôme, Cantal and Haute-Loire.

HIGHLIGHTS

- **Vichy** – absorb the old-time atmosphere of this remarkably inexpensive spa town
- **Orcival** – admire the Romanesque basilica in this delightful mountain hamlet
- **Col de Guéry** – marvel at the spectacular view of the surrounding mountains
- **Scenic Drive** – drive up the Cheylade Valley to the Col de Serre along the D62
- **Puy Mary** – hike up to the summit

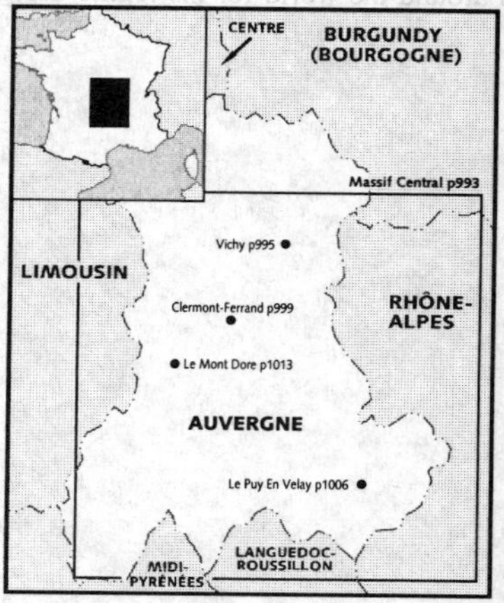

truffade (or *truffado*) – a potato (mashed or shredded) and cheese (usually Tomme) dish

cheeses – cantal, *bleu d'Auvergne*, *fourme d'ambert* and *Saint-Nectaire*

Activities

Local tourist offices are generally the best source of information on outdoor activities. Ask for a copy of *The Wide Open Spaces in the Auvergne*, an excellent two-part brochure (make sure you get both the 'Discovery Guide' and the 'Practical Guide') that is filled with useful information on outdoor activities. It is published by the Comité Régional du Tourisme d'Auvergne.

Hiking & Cycling Hiking is the region's most popular activity. There are 13 GR tracks (including the GR4) and hundreds of smaller footpaths and walking circuits wind through the region, which is dotted with *gîtes d'étape* for overnight stops. Mountain bike enthusiasts can also make use of many of these tracks. Chamina publishes a series of topoguides for the region.

One of the most useful hiking maps is IGN's Top 25 Série Bleue No 2432ET (57FF), entitled *Massif du Sancy*, which covers the area south-east of Le Mont Dore. The area from Orcival to Volvic, including the Puy de Dôme, is covered by IGN map No 2531ET.

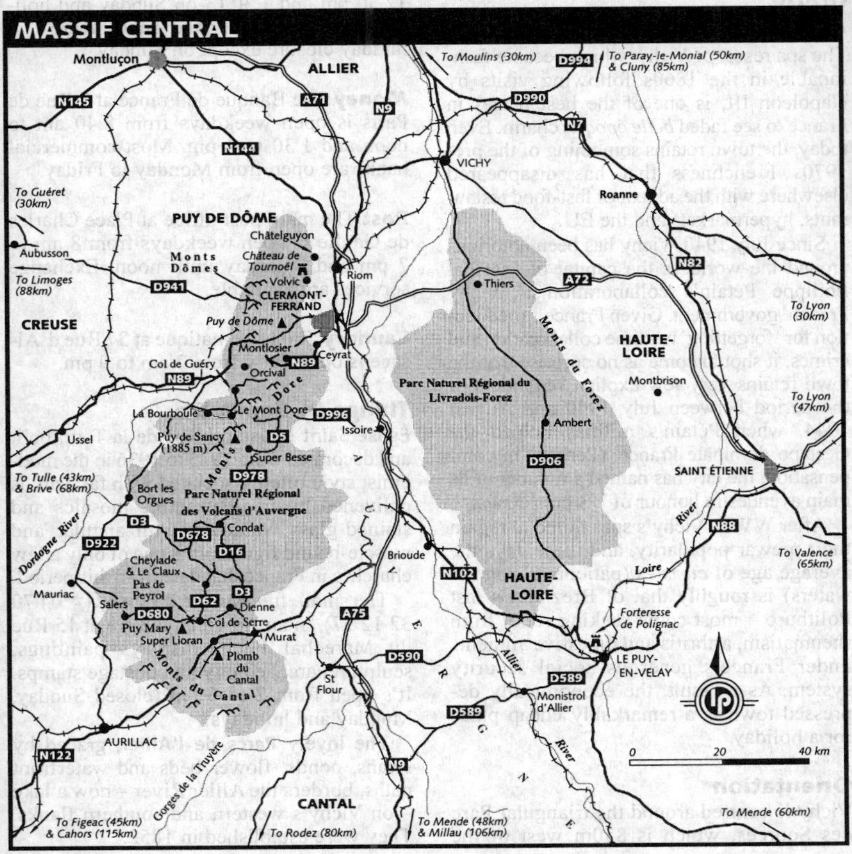

Skiing Several ski resorts, particularly Le Mont Dore and neighbouring Super Besse and Super Lioran (near Murat), have downhill runs and provide full Alpine skiing facilities (lifts etc). The Massif Central's undulating terrain is great for cross-country skiing.

Hang-Gliding The region's topography and thermal currents make it ideal for hang-gliding and parapente (paragliding) flights, for which the puys are used as take-off platforms. For details, see the Puy de Dôme listing and Parapente under Le Mont Dore.

VICHY

• pop 27,700 ✉ 03200 alt 340m

The spa resort of Vichy, which became fashionable in the 1860s following visits by Napoleon III, is one of the best places in France to see faded *belle époque* charm. Even today, the town retains something of the pre-1970s Frenchness that has disappeared elsewhere with the advent of fast-food restaurants, hypermarkets and the EU.

Since July 1940, Vichy has been notorious around the world as the capital of Marshal Philippe Pétain's collaborationist 'Vichy French' government. Given France's predilection for 'forgetting' wartime collaboration and crimes, it should come as no surprise that the town retains very few explicit reminders of the period between July 1940 and August 1944, when Pétain's militias helped the Gestapo dominate France. (Perhaps in compensation, the city has named a number of its main avenues in honour of US presidents.)

After WWII, Vichy's spas failed to regain their prewar popularity, and these days the average age of *curistes* (patients taking the waters) is roughly that of Brezhnev's last Politburo – most come seeking relief from rheumatism, arthritis and digestive ailments under France's generous social security system. As a result, the economically depressed town is a remarkably cheap place for a holiday.

Orientation

Vichy is centred around the triangular Parc des Sources, which is 850m west of the train station along Rue de Paris. Rue Georges Clemenceau, the main shopping thoroughfare, cuts through the partly pedestrianised city centre.

Information

Tourist Office The building at 19 Rue du Parc from which the Vichy government ruled now houses the overly spacious tourist office (☎ 04 70 98 71 94; fax 04 70 31 06 00), open Monday to Saturday from 9 am to noon and 2 to 6.30 pm (6 pm on Saturday), and from 2.30 to 5.30 pm on Sunday. From April to September, it's open from 9 am to 12.30 pm and 1.30 (3 on Sunday and holidays) to 7 pm. In July and August there's no midday closure except on Sunday.

Money The Banque de France at 7 Rue de Paris is open weekdays from 8.40 am to noon and 1.30 to 4 pm. Most commercial banks are open from Monday to Friday.

Post The main post office at Place Charles de Gaulle is open weekdays from 8 am to 7 pm and Saturday until noon. Exchange services are available.

Laundry The Lavomatique at 37 Rue d'Alsace is open daily from 7 am to 9 pm.

Things to See & Do

Église Saint Blaise on Rue de la Tour, built and decorated from 1925 to 1936 in the modernist style often associated with fascism, is enlivened by neo-Byzantine mosaics and stained-glass windows, with angular and muscle-bound figures. It is one of only a few churches in France that date from this period.

The small, free **Musée de Vichy** (☎ 04 70 32 12 97), in an Art Deco theatre at 15 Rue du Maréchal Foch, displays paintings, sculpture, archaeology and postage stamps. It's open from 2 to 6 pm (closed Sunday, Monday and holidays).

The lovely **Parcs de l'Allier**, graced by swans, ponds, flower beds and waterfront paths, borders the Allier River – now a lake – on Vichy's western and southern flanks. They were established in 1852.

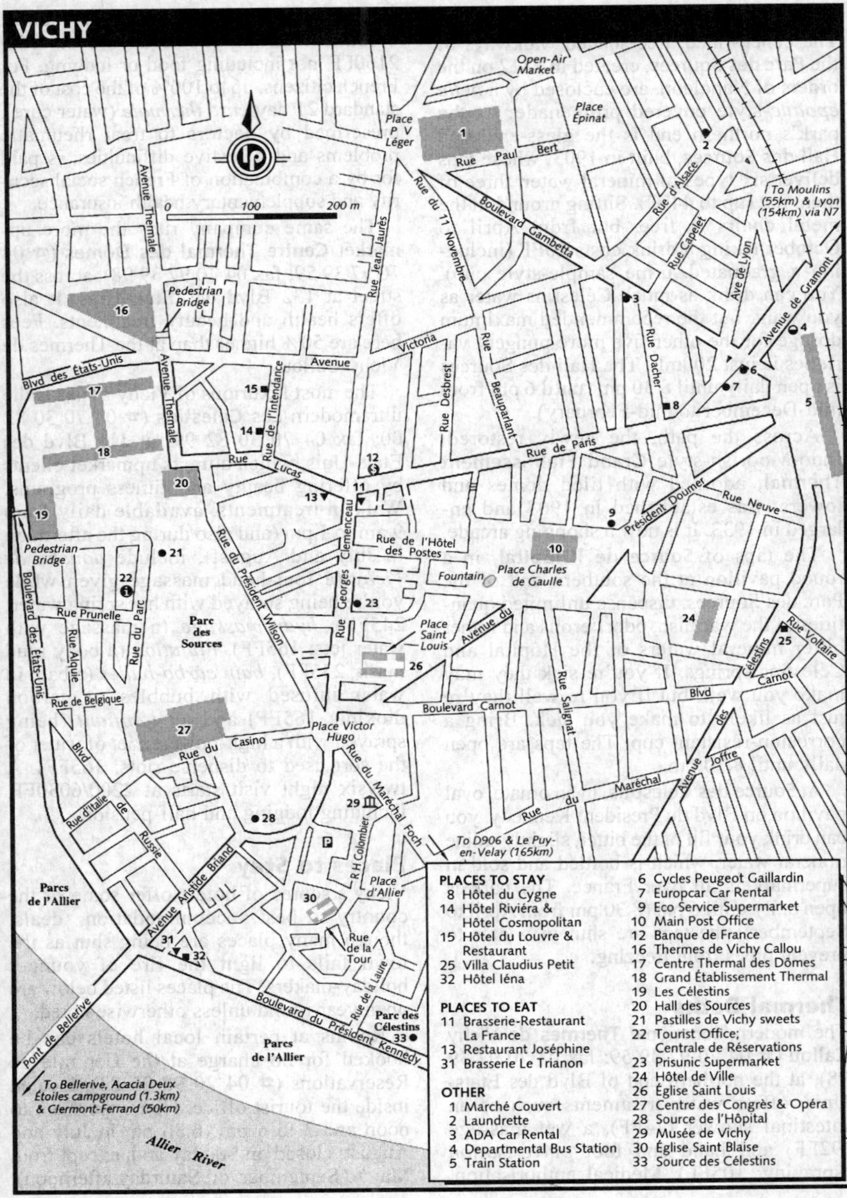
VICHY
Open-Air Market
Place Épinat
Place P V Léger
Rue Paul Bert
Rue d'Alsace
Boulevard Gambetta
Rue du 11 Novembre
Rue Jean Jaurès
To Moulins (55km) & Lyon (154km) via N7
Rue Capelet
Ave de Lyon
Avenue de Gramont
0
100
200 m
Avenue Thermale
Pedestrian Bridge
Blvd des États-Unis
Avenue Victoria
Rue de l'Intendance
Rue Desbrest
Rue Beauparlant
Rue Dacher
Rue de Paris
Rue Lucas
Rue Président Doumer
Rue Neuve
Pedestrian Bridge
Rue Georges Clemenceau
Rue de l'Hôtel des Postes
Fountain
Place Charles de Gaulle
Rue du Président Wilson
Boulevard des États-Unis
Rue du Parc
Rue Prunelle
Rue Alquie
Parc des Sources
Place Saint Louis
Avenue du Célestins
Rue Voltaire
Rue de Belgique
Boulevard Carnot
Rue Salignat
Blvd des Célestins
Carnot
Place Victor Hugo
Rue du Casino
Blvd de Russie
Rue du Maréchal Foch
Avenue Joffre
Rue du Maréchal
Rue d'Italie
To D906 & Le Puy-en-Velay (165km)
Avenue Aristide Briand
R H Colombier
Place d'Allier
Parcs de l'Allier
Rue de la Tour
Rue de la Laure
Parc des Célestins
Boulevard du Président Kennedy
Pont de Bellerive
Parcs de l'Allier
To Bellerive, Acacia Deux Étoiles campground (1.3km) & Clermont-Ferrand (50km)
Allier River
PLACES TO STAY
8 Hôtel du Cygne
14 Hôtel Riviéra & Hôtel Cosmopolitan
15 Hôtel du Louvre & Restaurant
25 Villa Claudius Petit
32 Hôtel Iéna
PLACES TO EAT
11 Brasserie-Restaurant La France
13 Restaurant Joséphine
31 Brasserie Le Trianon
OTHER
1 Marché Couvert
2 Laundrette
3 ADA Car Rental
4 Departmental Bus Station
5 Train Station
6 Cycles Peugeot Gaillardin
7 Europcar Car Rental
9 Eco Service Supermarket
10 Main Post Office
12 Banque de France
16 Thermes de Vichy Callou
17 Centre Thermal des Dômes
18 Grand Établissement Thermal
19 Les Célestins
20 Hall des Sources
21 Pastilles de Vichy sweets
22 Tourist Office; Centrale de Réservations
23 Prisunic Supermarket
24 Hôtel de Ville
26 Église Saint Louis
27 Centre des Congrès & Opéra
28 Source de l'Hôpital
29 Musée de Vichy
30 Église Saint Blaise
33 Source des Célestins

Mineral Springs

The bench-lined, tree-shaded walkways of the **Parc des Sources**, created in 1812 on the orders of Napoleon, are enclosed by a *belle époque*-style covered promenade. At the park's northern end is the glass-enclosed **Hall des Sources**, built in 1903, whose taps deliver six types of mineral water, three of them hot (up to 44°C). Sitting around in the metal chairs is free, but from April to October taking a drink costs 10FF (including a graduated, urine sample-style cup). You can drink as much Célestins water as you want, but the recommended maximum dosage for the other five more pungent varieties is just 200mL. The Hall des Sources is open daily until 8.30 pm (until 6 pm from mid-December to mid-February).

Across the path, the newly restored, Indo-Moorish-style **Grand Établissement Thermal**, adorned with tiled domes and towers, was established in 1903 and enlarged in 1933. It is now a shopping arcade.

The taps of **Source de l'Hôpital**, in a round pavilion at the southern end of the Parc des Sources, dispense unlimited quantities of the warmish, odoriferous and rather bitter mineral waters of the Hôpital and Célestins springs. If you're sick they may make you well, but if you're well they're just as likely to make you sick. Bring a corrosion-resistant cup. The taps are open daily until 8.30 pm.

At **Source des Célestins**, in an ornate, oval pavilion on Blvd du Président Kennedy, you can drink your fill of the bitter, slightly saline mineral water, which is bottled and sold in supermarkets all over France. The park is open daily until 6 pm (8.30 pm from April to September); the taps are shut in winter to prevent pipes from freezing.

Thermal Baths

The modern, functional **Thermes de Vichy Callou** (☎ 04 70 97 39 59; fax 04 70 97 39 98), at the northern end of Blvd des États-Unis, offers water treatments such as an intestinal shower (74FF), a wet massage (92FF) and hand and foot *pulvérisation* (spraying; 105FF). Medical authorisation, available from the house doctor, is required. Treatment lasting six/12 days costs 850/2160FF, not including food or lodging. For French citizens, up to 100% of the cost of the standard 21 day *cure thermale* (water cure), prescribed by doctors to treat rheumatic problems and digestive difficulties, is paid for by a combination of French social security and supplementary health insurance.

The same company runs the more upmarket **Centre Thermal des Dômes** (☎ 04 70 97 39 59; fax 04 70 97 39 98), across the street at 132 Blvd des États-Unis. It also offers health and beauty treatments. Fees here are 50% higher than at the Thermes de Vichy Callou.

The most luxurious of Vichy's spas is the ultramodern **Les Célestins** (☎ 04 70 30 82 00; fax 04 70 30 82 99) at 111 Blvd des États-Unis, which attracts upmarket clients by offering beauty and fitness programs. Walk-in treatments, available daily from 9 am to 1 pm (and also during the afternoon in July and August), include *douche de Vichy* (a four-hand massage given while you're being sprayed with hot spring water; 245FF), *hydromassage* (a massage with water jets; 165FF), *illutation* (a body mud mask; 245FF), *bain carbo-bulles* (a bath in water infused with bubbles of carbon dioxide; 165FF) and *jet tonifiant* (being sprayed with a high-powered jet of water of the sort used to disperse riots; 165FF). A two/six night visit starts at 2200/6030FF, including lodging and half-pension.

Places to Stay

Vichy's scores of hotels offer some of the country's best accommodation deals, though many places are being shut as the town fails to light the fire of younger holiday-makers. The places listed below are open year-round unless otherwise noted.

Rooms at certain local hotels can be booked for no charge at the Centrale de Réservations (☎ 04 70 98 23 83), located inside the tourist office. Hours are 9 am to noon and 2 to 6 pm (6.30 pm in July and August; closed on Sunday and, except from May to September, on Saturday afternoon).

Camping South of Vichy in Bellerive (cross Pont de Bellerive and turn left along the river), ***Acacias Deux Étoiles*** (☎ 04 70 32 36 22), at the end of Rue Claude Décloître, is open from May to mid-September. Two adults with a tent are charged 46FF (65FF in July and August).

Hostel The ***Villa Claudius Petit*** (☎ 04 70 98 43 39; fax 04 70 98 43 74), 76 Ave des Célestins, a hostel for students and young working people, accepts travellers when they have space, which is most likely from May to August. It is obligatory to phone ahead, in part because reception (closed weekends) has variable hours. A single with shower and toilet costs 75FF.

Hotels – City Centre Rue de l'Intendance is home to a cluster of hotels offering good value. The one star ***Hôtel Riviéra*** (☎ 04 70 98 22 32; fax 04 70 96 14 09), at No 5, has large, simple rooms from 140FF (180FF with shower and toilet). Hall showers are free. The two star, 27 room ***Hôtel Cosmopolitan*** (☎ 04 70 98 29 14; fax 04 70 98 46 00), at No 7, has spacious, pleasant singles/doubles from 125/155FF (155/185FF with shower and toilet). The hall shower is free. The two star, 45 room ***Hôtel du Louvre*** (☎ 04 70 98 27 71; fax 04 70 98 86 85), 15 Rue de l'Intendance, has spacious, attractive rooms with toilet from 180/220FF (200/240FF with shower, too). It is open from April to mid-October.

Hotels – Riverfront Near the Parcs de l'Allier, there are a number of inexpensive hotels around the south-west end of Ave Aristide Briand. The ***Hôtel Iéna*** (☎ 04 70 32 01 20), 56 Blvd du Président Kennedy, has singles/doubles with washbasin and bidet from 105/130FF; rooms for two/three/four people with shower and toilet cost 160/180/210FF. Reception is closed on Sunday from October to April.

Hotels – Train Station Area In the unattractive area around the station, the 26 room ***Hôtel du Cygne*** (☎ 04 70 98 21 03), 4 Rue Dacher, has some of the cheapest rooms in town: very simple, clean doubles start at 90FF (105FF with shower, 140FF with shower and toilet). Hall showers are free.

Places to Eat

Many of the hotels that offer full pension also function as restaurants with reasonably priced *menus*.

Restaurants Daily from April to mid-October, the ***Hôtel du Louvre*** (see Places to Stay) serves delicious, copious four-course *menus* for 60 and 80FF (90 and 120FF on Sunday) that include an hors d'oeuvre buffet, a main course, a dessert buffet and wine. Meal hours are noon to 2 pm and 7 to 8.30 or 9 pm.

Restaurant Joséphine (☎ 04 70 98 08 14), a popular crêperie-restaurant at 30 Rue Lucas, has 20 kinds of salads (30 to 50FF), crêpes (20 to 56FF) and a 90FF *menu*. It's open daily except Sunday at midday and on Monday. ***Brasserie-Restaurant La France*** (☎ 04 70 98 20 16), 34 Rue Georges Clemenceau, has a 62FF *formule* and a 69FF *menu*. Meals are served from 11.30 am to 2.30 pm and 7 to 11 pm (closed on Sunday night from November to March). Snacks are available all day.

The popular, sunny ***Brasserie Le Trianon*** (☎ 04 70 32 14 40), 60 Blvd du Président Kennedy, has a formule for 55FF and *menus* for 69.50 and 98FF. Except from mid-June to mid-September, it's closed on Tuesday night and Wednesday.

Self-Catering The cavernous ***marché couvert*** on Place Léger, built in the mid-1930s, sells good produce until 1 pm (closed Monday). There's an ***open-air market*** at Place Épinat on Wednesday morning.

The ***Prisunic*** supermarket at 16 Rue Georges Clemenceau is open from 9.30 am to 1.30 pm and 3.30 to 7 pm (closed on Sunday and holidays). The small ***Eco Service*** supermarket at 18 Place Charles de Gaulle is open Monday to Saturday from 8 am to 12.30 pm and 3 to 7.30 pm and on Sunday from 9 am to 12.30 pm.

Entertainment

Information on cultural and sports activities is printed in the fortnightly, partly English *La Quinzaine à Vichy*, issued from May to October, and in *Vichy Mensuel*, a monthly publication available the rest of the year. Both are available free in hotels and at the tourist office.

Believe it or not, Vichy was once known as the 'French Bayreuth'. From May to mid-October, operas, operettas, ballet and concerts (classical and jazz) are staged several times a week in the ornate **Salle d'Opéra** (1902) in the Centre des Congrès (formerly the Grand Casino; ☎ 04 70 30 50 50) on Rue du Casino.

Shopping

The octagonal mint, aniseed and lemon lozenges known as *pastilles de Vichy*, pride of the city since 1825 (and now American-owned), can be sampled and purchased in the sweets pavilion in the Parc des Sources, across the street from the tourist office. From April to October, it's open daily (except perhaps Monday) until 7 pm. Free samples are on offer, but beware – they're irresistible.

Getting There & Away

Train In the train station (☎ 08 36 35 35 35), the information office is open daily until 6 pm (closed from noon to 2 pm on Sunday). Destinations include Paris' Gare de Lyon (209FF; three hours; five to seven a day), Clermont-Ferrand (49FF; 40 minutes; 14 to 22 a day), Dijon (157FF; at least 2¼ hours; one direct a day), Lyon (119FF; 2¼ hours; six to eight a day) and Riom (41FF; 25 minutes; 13 to 21 a day).

Car Near the train station, Europcar (☎ 04 70 98 47 30) is at 6 Ave de Gramont, and ADA (☎ 04 70 98 49 49) is a bit to the north-west at 32 Blvd Gambetta.

Getting Around

Bicycle Cycles Peugeot Gaillardin (☎ 04 70 31 52 86) at 48 Blvd Gambetta rents 10-speeds/mountain bikes for 50/80FF a day. It is open from 9 am to noon and 2 to 7 pm (closed on Monday morning and Sunday).

CLEMONT-FERRAND

• pop 254,000 ✉ 63000 alt 401m

The lively city of Clermont-Ferrand, by far the largest city in the Massif Central, is situated to the east of a series of puys known as the Monts Dômes, the highest of which is the Puy de Dôme (1465m). The city makes a good base for exploring the northern part of the Massif Central. The town centre, considerably enlivened by the student population of some 34,000, is situated on a long-extinct volcano.

Clermont-Ferrand was Christianised in the 3rd century. In 1095, it was the meeting place for the synod at which Pope Urban II preached the First Crusade. It was also the birthplace of Blaise Pascal (1623-62), the physicist, mathematician and philosopher who helped formulate the theory of probability and made important contributions to fluid dynamics and geometry. These days, Clermont is the hub of France's rubber industry, better known to the rest of the world as the Michelin tyre empire. The company, which produced the world's first steel-belted radial in 1948, got into the sideline of guidebook publishing in 1898 in an effort to promote motorcar tourism – and thus the use of its pneumatic tyres.

Orientation

Clermont's cathedral is situated on the highest point in the old city, which is bounded by Ave des États-Unis, Rue André Moinier and Blvd Trudaine. The partly pedestrianised commercial centre stretches west from the cathedral to Blvd des États-Unis and Place de Jaude, and then along Rue Blatin. The old city's main thoroughfare is sloping, shop-lined Rue des Gras, which is reserved for pedestrians.

The train station is east of the city centre, 1km from the cathedral.

Information

Tourist Offices The main tourist office (☎ 04 73 98 65 00; fax 04 73 90 04 11), in the new Maison du Tourisme at Place de la Victoire (facing the cathedral), is open weekdays from 8.45 am to 6.30 pm, on Saturday from 9 am to noon and 2 to 6 pm, and on

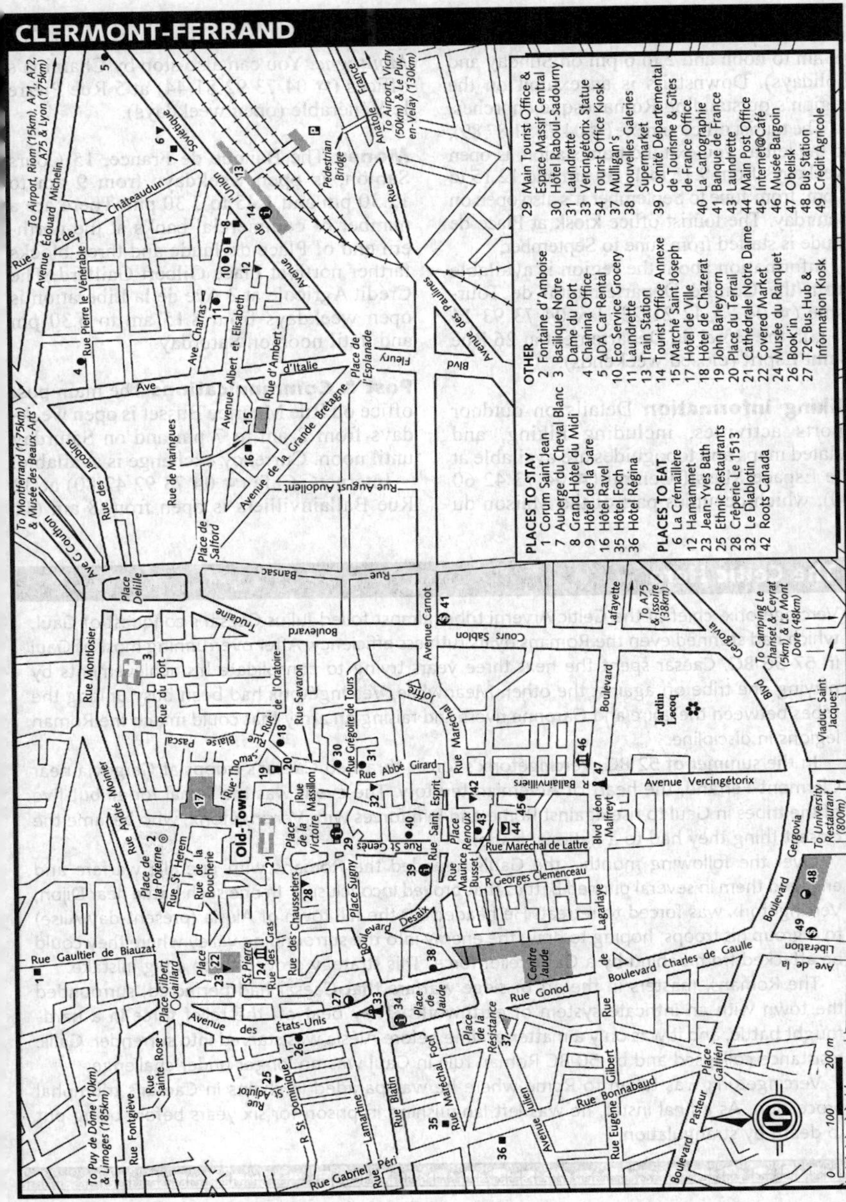
CLERMONT-FERRAND
PLACES TO STAY
1 Corum Saint Jean
7 Auberge du Cheval Blanc
8 Grand Hôtel du Midi
9 Hôtel de la Gare
16 Hôtel Ravel
35 Hôtel Foch
36 Hôtel Régina
PLACES TO EAT
6 La Crémaillère
12 Hamammet
23 Jean-Yves Bath
25 Ethnic Restaurants
28 Crêperie Le 1513
32 Le Diablotin
42 Roots Canada
OTHER
2 Fontaine d'Amboise
3 Basilique Notre Dame du Port
4 Chamina Office
5 ADA Car Rental
10 Eco Service Grocery
11 Laundrette
13 Train Station
14 Tourist Office Annexe
15 Marché Saint Joseph
17 Hôtel de Ville
18 Hôtel de Chazerat
19 John Barleycorn
20 Place du Terrail
21 Cathédrale Notre Dame
22 Covered Market
24 Musée du Ranquet
26 Book'in
27 T2C Bus Hub & Information Kiosk
29 Main Tourist Office & Espace Massif Central
30 Hôtel Raboul-Sadourny
31 Laundrette
33 Vercingétorix Statue
34 Tourist Office Kiosk
37 Mulligan's
38 Nouvelles Galeries Supermarket
39 Comité Départemental de Tourisme & Gîtes de France Office
40 La Cartographie
41 Banque de France
43 Laundrette
44 Main Post Office
45 Internet@Café
46 Musée Bargoin
47 Obelisk
48 Bus Station
49 Crédit Agricole

Sunday and holidays from 9 am to 1 pm. June to September hours are 8.30 am to 7 pm (9 am to noon and 2 to 6 pm on Sunday and holidays). Downstairs is an exhibit on the region's outstanding Romanesque churches.

The tourist office annexe (☎ 04 73 91 87 89), to the left as you exit the train station, is open weekdays from 9.15 to 11.30 am and 12.15 to 5 pm; from June to September it's also open on Saturday. The tourist office kiosk at Place de Jaude is staffed from June to September.

Information about the region is available from the Comité Départemental de Tourisme (☎ 04 73 42 21 23; fax 04 73 93 14 41), in the Hôtel du Département at 26 Rue Saint Esprit (closed weekends).

Hiking Information Details on outdoor sports activities, including hiking, and related maps and topoguides are available at the Espace Massif Central (☎ 04 73 42 60 00), which occupies part of the Maison du Tourisme. It is run by Chamina (the topoguide publishers) and the regional daily, *La Montagne*. You can also stop by Chamina's offices (☎ 04 73 92 81 44) at 5 Rue Pierre le Vénérable (open weekdays).

Money The Banque de France, 15 Cours Sablon, is open weekdays from 9 am to 12.30 pm and 1.45 to 3.30 pm. There are a number of commercial banks at the northern end of Place de Jaude and three blocks farther north at Place Gilbert Gaillard. The Crédit Agricole at 3 Ave de la Libération is open weekdays from 8.15 am to 6.30 pm and until noon on Saturday.

Post & Communications The main post office on Rue Maurice Busset is open weekdays from 8 am to 7 pm and on Saturday until noon. Currency exchange is available.

Internet@Café (☎ 04 73 92 42 80) at 32 Rue Ballainvilliers is open from 8 am (11

The Celtic Hero

Vercingétorix, chief of the Celtic Arverni tribe, almost foiled Julius Caesar's conquest of Gaul, which had stunned even the Romans by its ruthless efficiency. After overrunning most of Gaul in 57-56 BC, Caesar spent the next three years trying to consolidate his achievements by playing one tribe off against the other. Meanwhile, Vercingétorix had been busy uniting the tribes between the Loire and Garonne rivers and raising an army that could match the Roman legions in discipline.

In the summer of 52 BC, Vercingétorix's forces thrashed Caesar's troops at Gergovia near Clermont-Ferrand, the heart of Arvernian territory. The event was the signal for all but five of the tribes in Gaul to rise against Rome and join forces with Vercingétorix, who became the closest thing they had to a national leader.

Over the following months, the Gauls hounded the Romans with guerrilla warfare and engaged them in several pitched battles that proved inconclusive. In one such battle near Dijon, Vercingétorix was forced to retreat. He headed for the hill town of Alésia (present-day Alise) to regroup his troops, hoping to draw the enemy into the surrounding valley where they could be attacked from behind by a Gallic relief force. This strategy proved to be a big mistake.

The Romans, masters in the art of siege warfare that Caesar had perfected, surrounded the town with an intricate system of earthworks. They beat off the relief force in a hard-fought battle, and it was only a matter of time before Alésia was starved into surrender. Gallic resistance collapsed and by 50 BC Roman rule in Gaul was no longer under challenge.

Vercingétorix was taken to Rome where he was paraded in chains in Caesar's triumphal procession. As a final insult, he was left languishing in prison for six years before being put to death by strangulation.

am on Monday and Saturday) to 11 pm (closed Sunday). A half-hour costs 25FF.

Bookshops Book'in (☎ 04 73 36 40 06) at 38 Ave des États-Unis has a small selection of used English-language books. It is closed on Monday morning and Sunday.

La Cartographie (☎ 04 73 91 67 75) at 23 Rue Saint Genès has a huge selection of maps (IGN, Didier-Richard etc) and topoguides. Hours are 9.45 am to noon and 2 to 7 pm (closed Monday morning and Sunday).

Laundry The Lavomatique at 2 Rue Grégoire de Tours and the laundrette at 6 Place Hippolyte Renoux are open daily from 7 am to 8 pm. Near the train station, the laundrette at 62 Ave Charras is open from 7 am to 8.30 pm.

Walking Tour

The tourist office's free historical walking guide, *Welcome to Clermont-Ferrand*, takes you through the more attractive parts of town, mainly in the old city. The narrow, shop-lined streets east of the cathedral are home to some of the city's most interesting buildings, including the **Hôtel de Chazerat** at 4 Rue Blaise Pascal and, nearby at 9 Rue Savaron, the **Hôtel Raboul-Sadourny**, a group of 18th century houses built around a lovely courtyard. **Place de Jaude** is dominated by Bartholdi's equestrian statue of Vercingétorix (see the boxed text 'The Celtic Hero'), the chief of the Arverni who in 52 BC almost turned back the Roman conquest of Gaul.

The quiet suburb of **Montferrand**, 2.5km north-east of the cathedral, is well worth exploring for its many **Gothic and Renaissance houses** and the **Musée des Beaux-Arts** (☎ 04 73 23 08 49) at Place Louis Deteix, open from 10 am to 6 pm (closed Monday). Entry costs 23FF (13FF for children and students). To get there, take bus No 1, 9, 16 or 17.

Another tourist office brochure, *Tour of Fountains*, guides you past the city's many **fountains**. The largest is the early 16th century **Fontaine d'Amboise**, two blocks north of the cathedral at Place de la Poterne, which affords a fine view of the Puy de Dôme and its neighbouring summits.

Cathédrale Notre Dame

Clermont's soaring Gothic cathedral looks like a smog-blackened preservationist's nightmare, but in fact the structure's volcanic stones, dug from the quarries of nearby Volvic, were the same blackish-grey hue the day the finishing touches were put on the choir seven centuries ago. The twin towers are from the 19th century; the west façade, utterly lacking in nuance, was restored by the Gothic Revivalist Viollet-le-Duc.

The architects took full advantage of the great strength and lightness of Volvic stone to create a vast, double-aisled nave held aloft by particularly slender pillars and vaults. The third chapel on the right-hand side of the choir is decorated with **15th century frescoes** that can be viewed with the help of timer-activated lights. A number of the windows in the choir and chapels date from the 13th and 14th centuries. The cathedral is open daily until 6 pm (7 pm on Sunday); closed from noon to 2 pm (3 pm on Sunday).

Basilique Notre Dame du Port

Hidden away in the north-east corner of the old city just off Rue du Port (and most interestingly reached via Rue Blaise Pascal, with its ancient lava edifices), this 12th century basilica is a beautiful example of Auvergne-style Romanesque architecture. The sunken entrance gives way to sculptured stone columns and capitals and, at the far end, an apse that is warmly lit (in the morning) by the fiery stained glass windows. Daily hours are 9 am to noon and 2 to 6 pm.

Museums

The **Musée Bargoin** (☎ 04 73 91 37 31), 45 Rue Ballainvilliers, has an excellent prehistory section on the ground floor and colourful 18th to 20th century carpets (from Turkey, Iran etc) on the 1st floor. It's open from 10 am to 6 pm (closed Monday). Entry costs 23FF (13FF for children, students and seniors).

The exterior ornamentation of the 16th century mansion that houses the **Musée du Ranquet** (☎ 04 73 37 38 63) at 34 Rue des Gras is more interesting than the displays, which include a small exhibition dedicated to Pascal. It's open from 10 am to 6 pm (closed Monday). Tickets cost 13FF (free for under 12s).

Places to Stay

Camping The three star, municipal ***Le Chanset*** (☎ 04 73 61 30 73), Ave Jean Baptiste, about 5km south-west in Ceyrat (on the N89 to Tulle), is open all year. A tent site for two people and a car costs 58FF from June to September (less the rest of the year). Take bus No 4C from Place de Jaude or the train station to the Préguille stop.

Hostels A bit north of the city centre, the modern ***Corum Saint Jean*** (☎ 04 73 31 57 00; fax 04 73 31 59 99), 17 Rue Gaultier de Biauzat, also known as the Foyer des Jeunes Travailleurs, accepts travellers year-round. A bed costs 80FF (10FF more if you don't have an HI card or equivalent), including breakfast. Check-in is possible 24 hours a day. Bus No 2 or 4 will get you there from the train station; get off at the Gaillard stop.

In a pinch, you might try the ***Auberge du Cheval Blanc*** (☎ 04 73 92 26 39), near the train station at 55 Ave de l'Union Soviétique, whose reception is open from 7 to 9.30 am and 5 to 11 pm; the building is deserted all day long and is closed from November to February. A bed costs 60FF, including breakfast.

Gîtes The Gîtes de France office (☎ 04 73 42 21 23; fax 04 73 93 14 41) in the Hôtel du Département at 26 Rue Saint Esprit has brochures on gîtes and *chambres d'hôtes* and handles reservations for *gîtes ruraux*. The reservation service is open weekdays from 8.30 am to 12.15 pm and 1.45 to 6 pm (5.30 pm on Friday).

Hotels – West of Place Jaude The cheery, 19 room ***Hôtel Foch*** (☎ 04 73 93 48 40; fax 04 73 35 47 41), 22 Rue Maréchal Foch, has singles/doubles from 145/155FF (190/195FF with shower and toilet). An extra bed costs 45FF. On Sunday, reception is closed from 1 to 5.30 pm. The two star, 27 room ***Hôtel Régina*** (☎ 04 73 93 44 76; fax 04 73 35 04 63) at 14 Rue Bonnabaud has tidy rooms from 150/170FF (250/270FF with shower and toilet).

Hotels – Train Station Area An excellent bet is the old-fashioned, 21 room ***Hôtel Ravel*** (☎ 04 73 91 51 33; fax 04 73 92 28 48), four blocks west of the station at 8 Rue de Maringues, whose singles/doubles with shower start at 150/170FF (200/220FF with toilet). Free parking is available nearby.

The 39 room ***Grand Hôtel du Midi*** (☎ 04 73 92 44 98; fax 04 73 92 29 41), an unsurprising two star establishment at 39 Ave de l'Union Soviétique, has rooms from 150/160FF (210/220FF with shower and toilet).

Some of the sorriest, most decrepit budget hotels in all of France line Ave Charras. The best of the bunch is the two star, 20th century ***Hôtel de la Gare*** (☎ 04 73 92 07 82; fax 04 73 90 74 36), at No 76, whose doubles start at 160FF (185/240FF for doubles/quads with shower and toilet). On Sunday and holidays, reception is closed from 10 am to 6 pm.

Places to Eat

Restaurants – French A number of small restaurants can be found along medieval, pedestrians-only Rue des Chaussetiers. The cosy ***Crêperie Le 1513*** (☎ 04 73 92 37 46) at No 3 (through the arch), housed in a sumptuous mansion built in 1513, has savoury and sweet crêpes (11 to 60FF), salads and other dishes. It's open daily from 11.30 am straight through to 1 am (1.30 or 2 am on Friday and Saturday nights).

In the old city, ***Le Diablotin*** (☎ 04 73 92 85 20), a rustically elegant fish restaurant at 8 Rue Abbé Girard, has *menus* from 89FF. It is open for dinner only (closed on Sunday and Monday).

Near the train station, ***La Crémaillère*** (☎ 04 73 90 89 25), 61 Ave de l'Union, Soviétique has *menus* of family-style

Auvergnat cuisine for 50 and 79FF (closed Saturday evening and Sunday).

For a splurge, you might try the elegantly modern ***Jean-Yves Bath*** (☎ 04 73 31 23 23), at Place Saint Pierre in the west side of the covered market building, which has one Michelin star. *Menus* of Auvergnat and 'evolutionary' French cuisine cost 260 and 350FF. It's open from noon to 2 pm and 7.30 to 10 pm (closed all day Sunday and Monday).

Restaurants – Other ***Roots Canada*** (☎ 04 73 90 73 74) at 16 Rue Ballainvilliers – the front window is graced by a plywood moose – has steaks (66 to 115FF), *carbonade de caribou* (61FF) and other *specialités Canadiennes*. Hours are 11.30 am to 2.30 pm and 7.30 pm to midnight (closed Monday at midday and Sunday).

Two blocks north of Place de Jaude, Rue Saint Dominique and nearby alleys (eg Rue Saint Adjutor) are home to quite a few inexpensive brasseries and ***ethnic restaurants*** (Tunisian, Indian, Vietnamese, Italian, Tex-Mex etc).

Near the train station, ***Hamammet*** (☎ 04 73 92 08 93) at 48 Ave Albert et Elisabeth has tasty Tunisian couscous from 42FF (closed Sunday).

University Restaurant The ***restaurant universitaire*** (☎ 04 73 34 44 02) at 25 Rue Étienne Dolet is open daily for lunch and dinner (closed in holidays and, in summer, on Sunday). Tickets are sold Monday to Thursday from 11.30 am to 1 pm (12.30 pm in summer); the rest of the time, buy one from a student. To get there, walk about 800m south from the bus station; by bus, take line No 12 to the Dolet stop.

Self-Catering Despite the fearless pigeons, the park around the Fontaine d'Amboise is a fine place for a picnic. The immaculately tended lawns and flower beds of Jardin Lecoq make this park another ideal spot for lunch.

The jumble of blue, yellow and grey cubes that fills Place Saint Pierre is the city's ***covered market***, open from 6 am to 7 pm (closed Sunday). Nearby Rue de la Boucherie, one of the city's oldest streets, is lined with ***food shops***.

The basement supermarket in the ***Nouvelles Galeries*** department store on Place de Jaude is open Monday to Saturday from 8.30 am to 7 pm. Near the train station, the ***Eco Service*** grocery at 66 Ave Charras is open daily until 7.30 pm (until noon on Sunday and holidays; closed from 12.30 to 3 pm).

Entertainment

The cafés and pubs around Place du Jaune include ***Mulligan's*** (☎ 04 73 93 36 70), an Irish-style pub at 2 Place de la Résistance. Hours are 8 am to 1 am (closed Sunday). In the old city, ***John Barleycorn*** (☎ 04 73 92 31 67), an Irish pub at 9 Rue de Terrail, is open Monday to Saturday from 6 pm until 2 am.

Getting There & Away

Air The Clermont-Ferrand-Aulnat airport (☎ 04 73 62 71 00), 7km east of the city, only handles domestic flights.

Bus The bus station is at 69 Blvd Gergovia. The efficient information office (☎ 04 73 93 13 61) is open Monday to Saturday from 8.30 am to 6.30 pm. Destinations include Super Besse (56FF; 1½ hours; one a day on most days, except Sunday). Eurolines has an office (☎ 04 73 35 02 68) in the bus station.

Train Clermont-Ferrand's train station (☎ 08 36 35 35 35) is on Ave de l'Union Soviétique and is the most important rail junction in the Massif Central. The main tourist office houses an SNCF information counter, open weekdays from 10 am to 5.30 pm.

Destinations include Paris' Gare de Lyon (233 to 283FF; 3½ hours; six to eight a day), Limoges (141FF via Brive; four hours; one or two direct a day), Lyon (135FF via Saint Étienne; three hours; five or six direct a day) and Toulouse (221FF; 6¼ hours; one direct a day via Aurillac). The trip through the mountains southward to Nîmes (182FF; five hours; two or three a day) is one of the most scenic in France; the route, which begins in Paris, is known as Le Cévenol.

There are short-haul SNCF services to La Bourboule (61FF), Le Mont Dore (64FF; 1½ hours; four or five a day), Le Puy-en-Velay (106FF; 2¼ hours; four a day), Murat (90FF; 1¾ hours; four to six a day), Riom (18FF; 10 minutes; 20 to 28 a day) and Vichy (49FF; 40 minutes; 14 to 22 a day).

Car ADA car rental (☎ 04 73 91 66 07) at 79 Ave de l'Union Soviétique is open Monday to Saturday.

Getting Around

To/From the Airport A shuttle bus links the train station and the Place de Jaude bus hub with the airport (25FF; four to six a day). You can also take T2C bus Nos 10A and 10M (No 10/13 on Sunday and holidays) to the Aviation stop, from where it's a 10 minute walk.

Bus The local bus company, T2C (☎ 04 73 28 56 56), has an information kiosk at the northern end of Place de Jaude, next to the city's main bus hub. Route maps are also available at the main tourist office. Most lines operate until 8 or 9 pm; service is greatly reduced at night, when the *bus de nuit* line operates, and on Sunday and holidays. Bus Nos 2, 4 and 14 (Nos 2/17 and 14/16 on Sunday and holidays) link the train station with Place de Jaude.

Drivers sell single-ride tickets for 7FF; a 10-ticket carnet costs 53FF. The *Carte Un Jour*, valid for a day and sold only at the T2C kiosk, costs 25FF.

Taxi To order a taxi 24 hours a day, call Taxi Radio (☎ 04 73 19 53 53).

AROUND CLERMONT-FERRAND

Puy de Dôme

Covered in snow in winter and outdoor adventurers in summer, the balding Puy de Dôme (1465m) affords a fantastic, panoramic view of Clermont-Ferrand and some 70 extinct volcanoes. The Celts and later the Romans worshipped gods from the summit (there are remains of a Roman temple dedicated to Mercury), but nowadays the summit is dominated by a TV transmission tower that looks like a giant rectal thermometer.

Parapente and hang-gliding enthusiasts use the summit as a launching platform. Introductory flights with an instructor cost about 350FF; five-day courses are about 1600FF. Several companies organise flights – the main tourist office in Clermont-Ferrand has details.

Getting There & Away The summit can be reached either by the 'mule track' – an hour's climb starting at the Col de Ceyssat, 4km off the D941A – or by the 7km toll road (22FF) which spirals steeply up to the summit (open until sometime between 5 and 10 pm, depending on the season). The latter is closed to private cars between 11 am and 6 pm in July and August and on Sunday in September, when you're required to take a shuttle bus (21/5FF for adults/children).

Riom

• **pop 18,800** ✉ **63200** **alt 363m**

Riom, 15km north of Clermont-Ferrand, was the capital of Auvergne in the Middle Ages. The streets of the austere old city are lined with magistrates' mansions built of dark Volvic stone. Riom makes an easy day trip from Clermont-Ferrand.

Orientation The main streets of the old city, surrounded by tree-lined boulevards, are north-south Rue du Commerce (and its northern extension, Rue de l'Horloge) and east-west Rue de l'Hôtel de Ville. The train station is 400m south-east of the old city at the end of Ave Virlogeux.

Information The tourist office (☎ 04 73 38 59 45; fax 04 73 38 25 15), at No 16 on pedestrianised Rue du Commerce (100m south of Rue de l'Hôtel de Ville), can supply you with an English version of its walking tour brochure. It's open Monday to Saturday from 9 am to noon and 2 to 6.30 pm (6 pm on Saturday). In July and August it's open on Sunday from 10 am to 12.30 pm and 2.30 to 4 pm.

Things to See About 200m down Rue du Commerce from the tourist office, the 15th century **Église Notre Dame du Marthuret** is famous for the *Vierge à l'Oiseau* (Virgin with Bird), a painted stone sculpture from the 14th century that depicts Mary with the Infant Jesus holding a small bird. The figure over the entrance is a copy – the original is inside, in the first chapel to the right, illuminated by a timer-activated light.

The **Musée F Mandet** (☎ 04 73 38 18 53), housed in handsome 17th and 18th century mansions at 14 Rue de l'Hôtel de Ville, has a collection of classical antiquities, medieval sculptures and 17th to 19th century paintings. About 200m down Rue Delille is the excellent **Musée d'Auvergne** (☎ 04 73 38 17 31), whose displays document rural life in Auvergne in past centuries. Both are open from 10 am to noon and 2 or 2.30 to 5.30 or 6 pm (closed on Tuesday and holidays). Entry costs 25FF (10FF for students) for each museum or 35FF for both; free on Wednesday.

About 1.5km west of Riom's town centre is the former Benedictine abbey of **Mozac**, whose church is famed for the superb medieval **capitals** atop the columns in the Auvergnat-Romanesque nave. The choir and transept are Gothic. To get there, follow the signs to Volvic and then the arrows to the 'Abbaye'.

About 7km south-west of Riom is the town of **Volvic**, famous for its spring water and its quarries, which provided the lightweight but strong volcanic stone used in so many buildings in the area, including Clermont-Ferrand's cathedral. The ruins of the nearby **Château de Tournoël** dominate the countryside and are worth visiting.

Places to Stay The ***Hôtel Le Terminus*** (☎ 04 73 38 01 26), across the street from the train station at 8 Rue Gregoire de Tours, has 10 rooms with washbasin and bidet for 120FF each. Hall showers are free. Reception (at the bar) is closed on Monday after 2 pm.

Getting There & Away Riom's train station (☎ 08 36 35 35 35) is linked with Paris' Gare de Lyon, Lyon, Clermont-Ferrand (18FF; 10 minutes; 20 to 28 a day) and Vichy (41FF; 25 minutes; 13 to 21 a day). The last train to Clermont is at 10.20 pm or later; the last train to Vichy leaves at 8.30 pm (there's usually one a bit after 11 pm, too).

LE PUY-EN-VELAY

• pop 21,700 ✉ 43000 alt 629m

The beautiful little town of Le Puy, capital of the department of Haute-Loire, sits amid striking volcanic plugs in a fertile valley near the source of the Loire River. During the Middle Ages, it was an important stop on the pilgrimage trail to Santiago de Compostela, and local people are still known for their devout Catholic faith. These days, Le Puy continues to attract pilgrims.

Each of Le Puy's three lava pinnacles is topped by a religious edifice: the largest, on which the old city is built, by the cathedral; the highest, a bit north of the cathedral, by a giant statue of the Virgin; and the steepest, a few hundred metres farther north, by a 10th century chapel.

Orientation

North of the main square, Place du Breuil, lies the pedestrianised old city, whose narrow streets head up the hill to the cathedral. Le Puy's commercial centre is around the Hôtel de Ville and between Blvd Maréchal Fayolle and Rue Chaussade. The train and bus stations are 600m east of Place du Breuil.

Information

Tourist Offices The main tourist office (☎ 04 71 09 38 41; fax 04 71 05 22 62) on Place du Breuil has an English-language brochure with details on three walking tours. It's open every day of the year from 8.30 am to noon and 1.45 to 6.30 pm (10 am to noon on Sunday). In July and August, it's open from 8.30 am to 7.30 pm (9 am to noon and 2 to 6 pm on Sunday).

The tourist office annexe (☎ 04 71 05 99 02), down the hill from the cathedral at 23 Rue des Tables, is open from late June to August (closed Sunday and Monday).

You can get into Le Puy's four major sights – the cloister of the cathedral, Rocher

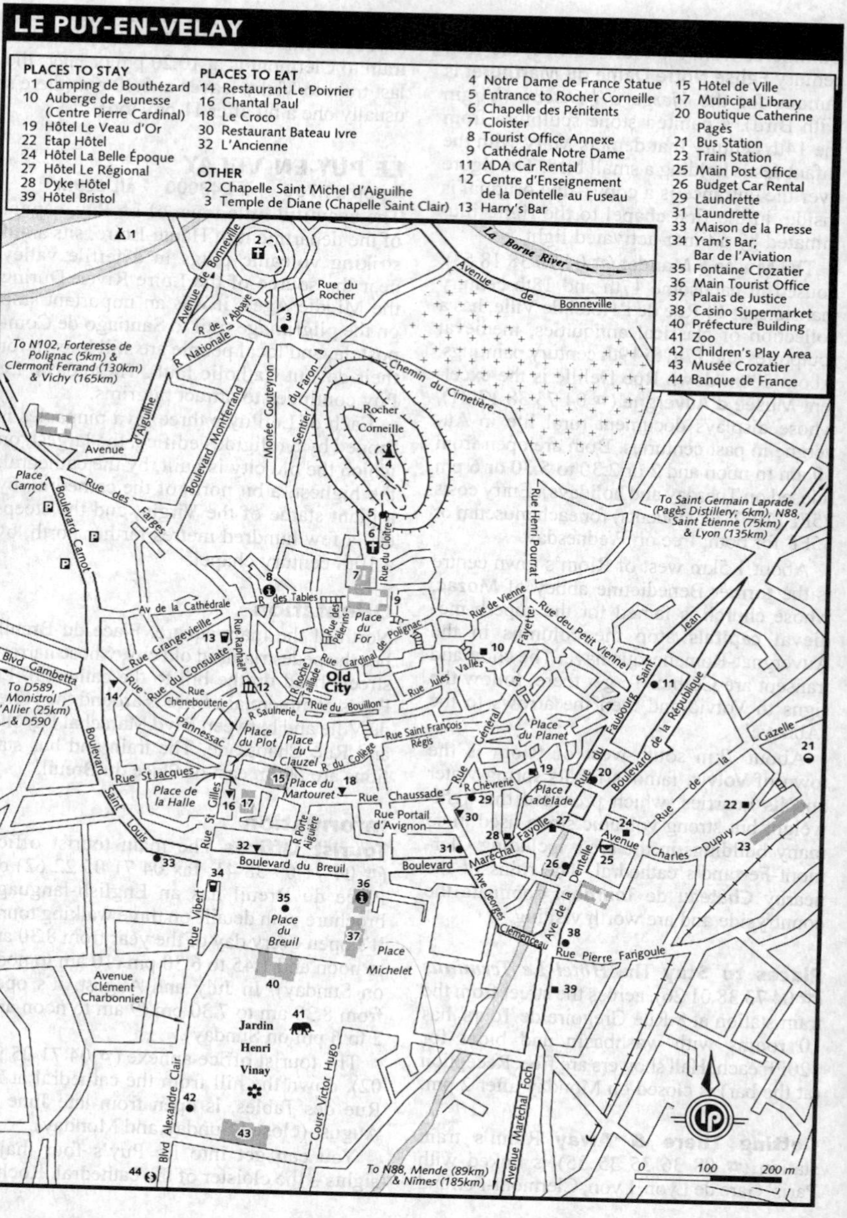
LE PUY-EN-VELAY
PLACES TO STAY
1 Camping de Bouthézard
10 Auberge de Jeunesse (Centre Pierre Cardinal)
19 Hôtel Le Veau d'Or
22 Etap Hôtel
24 Hôtel La Belle Époque
27 Hôtel Le Régional
28 Dyke Hôtel
39 Hôtel Bristol
PLACES TO EAT
14 Restaurant Le Poivrier
16 Chantal Paul
18 Le Croco
30 Restaurant Bateau Ivre
32 L'Ancienne
OTHER
2 Chapelle Saint Michel d'Aiguilhe
3 Temple de Diane (Chapelle Saint Clair)
4 Notre Dame de France Statue
5 Entrance to Rocher Corneille
6 Chapelle des Pénitents
7 Cloister
8 Tourist Office Annexe
9 Cathédrale Notre Dame
11 ADA Car Rental
12 Centre d'Enseignement de la Dentelle au Fuseau
13 Harry's Bar
15 Hôtel de Ville
17 Municipal Library
20 Boutique Catherine Pagès
21 Bus Station
23 Train Station
25 Main Post Office
26 Budget Car Rental
29 Laundrette
31 Laundrette
33 Maison de la Presse
34 Yam's Bar; Bar de l'Aviation
35 Fontaine Crozatier
36 Main Tourist Office
37 Palais de Justice
38 Casino Supermarket
40 Préfecture Building
41 Zoo
42 Children's Play Area
43 Musée Crozatier
44 Banque de France
La Borne River
Avenue de Bonneville
Rue du Rocher
R de l'Abbaye
R Nationale
To N102, Forteresse de Polignac (5km) & Clermont Ferrand (130km) & Vichy (165km)
Chemin du Cimetière
Rocher Corneille
Sentier du Faron
Monée Gouteyron
Boulevard Montferrand
Avenue d'Aiguilhe
Place Carnot
Rue des Farges
Boulevard Carnot
Rue Henri Pourrat
To Saint Germain Laprade (Pagès Distillery; 6km), N88, Saint Étienne (75km) & Lyon (135km)
Rue du Cloître
R des Tables
Av de la Cathédrale
Rue des Pèlerins
Place du For
Rue Cardinal de Polignac
Rue de Vienne
Rue du Petit Vienne
Rue Grangevieille
Rue Raphaël
Rue du Consulat
Blvd Gambetta
To D589, Monistrol d'Allier (25km) & D590
Rue Chenebouterie
Pannessac
Old City
R Roche Taillade
Rue du Bouillon
R Saulnerie
Rue Jules Vallès
Rue Général la Fayette
Rue du Faubourg Saint Jean
Boulevard de la République
Place du Plot
Place du Clauzel
R du Collège
Rue Saint François Régis
Place du Planet
Rue Gazelle
Rue St Jacques
Place de la Halle
Rue St Gilles
Place du Martouret
Rue Chaussade
R Chèvrerie
Place Cadelade
Rue Portail d'Avignon
R Porte Aiguière
Boulevard Saint Louis
Boulevard du Breuil
Boulevard Maréchal Fayolle
Avenue Charles Dupuy
Ave de la Dentelle
Ave Georges Clemenceau
Rue Vibert
Place du Breuil
Place Michelet
Rue Pierre Farigoule
Avenue Clément Charbonnier
Jardin Henri Vinay
Blvd Alexandre Clair
Cours Victor Hugo
Avenue Maréchal Foch
To N88, Mende (89km) & Nîmes (185km)
100
200 m

Corneille, Chapelle Saint Michel and the Musée Crozatier – with a discount combination ticket (39FF), available at the tourist office and the sites.

Money The Banque de France, just southwest of the Musée Crozatier at 30 Blvd Alexandre Clair, is open weekdays from 8.15 am to noon and 1.30 or 1.45 to 4 pm. You'll find a number of commercial banks – most open Tuesday to Saturday – around the perimeter of Place du Breuil.

Post The main post office at 8 Ave de la Dentelle is open weekdays from 8 am to 7 pm and on Saturday to noon. Exchange services are available.

Bookshop The Maison de la Presse at 5 Blvd Saint Louis has lots of maps and topoguides. It is open daily until 7.15 pm (until 12.15 pm on Sunday and holidays).

Laundry The Lav' Flash at 24 Rue Portail d'Avignon is open daily until 8.30 pm (6.30 pm on Sunday and holidays). Around the corner the Lavo-Self at 12 Rue Chèvrerie is open from 7.30 am to noon and 1 to 7.45 pm (closed Sunday and holidays).

Old City

If you picture today's tourists as pilgrims (which they are, in a way), the narrow, cobbled streets of the old city look much as they did 800 years ago. Medieval, Gothic and Renaissance houses made of dark volcanic stone can be found along (from east to west) Rue Chaussade, Rue du Collège, Rue Porte Aiguière and Rue Pannessac.

Cathédrale Notre Dame

The most impressive way to enter this heavily restored Romanesque cathedral, begun in the 11th century on the site of a Roman temple, is by passing through the massive arches at the top of Rue des Tables. The structure's Byzantine and Moorish elements include the six domes over the nave and the ornately patterned stonework. A 17th century **Black Madonna**, which replaced the one burned during the Revolution, takes pride of place on the baroque high altar. Like much of the interior, the **11th century frescoes** in the north transept arm and the **stairway** linking Rues des Tables with the nave have recently undergone extensive restoration. The **Chapelle d'Hiver** (Winter Chapel), off the nave, is adorned with a 15th century allegorical fresco known as *Les Arts Libéraux*.

The beautiful **cloister**, built in the 11th and 12th centuries, would look right at home in southern Spain. Many of the capitals are elegantly ornamented. The attached **Chapelle des Morts**, once used as a burial place, has, on the south wall, an early 13th century fresco of the Crucifixion.

The Renaissance ceiling panels of the richly decorated **Chapelle des Pénitents**, across the alley from the entrance to the cloister, date from 1630.

The cathedral is open daily from 8 am to 7 pm (6 pm in winter). The cloister (25FF; 15FF if you're under 25) is open from 9.30 am to 12.30 pm and 2 to 6 pm (4.30 pm from October to March; 6.30 pm from July to September, when there's no midday closure).

Rocher Corneille

The massive Corneille Rock, just north of the cathedral and accessible via Rue du Cloître, was crowned in 1860 by a jarringly red, 16m-high statue of **Notre Dame de France** made from melted-down cannons captured in the Crimean War. The view – from 130m above Place du Breuil – is superb. It's open from 9 am to 6 pm (7 or 7.30 pm from May and August, 5 pm from October to mid-March); closed in December and January except during school holiday periods and on Sunday afternoons from 2 to 5 pm. Entry costs 20FF (10FF for children and students).

Chapelle Saint Michel d'Aiguilhe

This dark, silent and very medieval chapel, built of black, brown and white volcanic stones, is perched at the summit of an 85m-high volcanic plug. The entrance and irregularly shaped nave, Romanesque in style, date from the 12th century; the 10th

MASSIF CENTRAL

century choir is pre-Romanesque. Traces of the 12th century murals can still be seen. The stained glass was installed in 1955.

The chapel is open from 10 am to noon and from 2 until sometime between 4 (in winter) and 7 pm (from mid-June to mid-September, when there's no midday closure); it's closed if there's snow or frost and in the morning from mid-November to mid-March. Entry costs 12FF (6FF for under 14s). The 268-step climb begins at the bottom of Rue du Rocher. To get there, you can take bus No 6 from Place Michelet, which is east of Place du Breuil.

Centre d'Enseignement de la Dentelle au Fuseau

You can admire antique and modern lace, watch master lacemakers at work and take lacemaking classes at this museum cum educational centre (☎ 04 71 02 01 68) at 38-40 Rue Raphaël. It's open weekdays from 10 am to noon and 2 to 5.30 pm; from mid-June to mid-September, the hours are 9 am to noon and 1.30 to 6.30 pm (closed Sunday). Entry costs 12FF.

Musée Crozatier

This worthwhile museum (☎ 04 71 09 38 90) is at the southern end of **Jardin Henri Vinay**, a lovely informal garden with a swan lake, neat flower patches, a small zoo, a creative **children's play area** and lots of benches.

The museum's exhibits cover Gallo-Roman archaeology, religious items and folk art made since the Middle Ages, 16th to 19th century lace (once an important local industry), painting, sculpture and some clever mechanical devices from the late 19th century. It's open daily, except Tuesday, from 10 am to noon and 2 to 6 pm (4 pm from October to April, when it's also closed on Sunday morning). Entry costs 20FF (10FF for children and students); from October to April, it's free on Sunday afternoon.

Pagès Distillery

Pagès Distillery (☎ 04 71 03 04 11), 6km east of town in Saint Germain Laprade (take the N88 and then the C150), is famous for its pricey, bright green firewater known as Verveine du Velay, first distilled in 1859. Visits of the production facilities lasting 45 minutes take place on weekdays from 10 am to noon and 1.30 to 6.30 pm (on Saturday, too, from June to September). Entry costs 20FF (10FF for children).

Special Events

The arrival of spring is celebrated with the kids-oriented Festival Carnavalesque held on the Friday night and Saturday nearest 21 March. On the evening of Maundy Thursday (the Thursday before Easter), the Pènitent Blanc, a hooded penitent dressed in white, leads a procession up to the cathedral. For a week in mid-July, the Festival Folklorique International brings to town about a dozen folklore troupes from around the world. On the afternoon of Assumption Day (15 August), the cathedral's Black Madonna is paraded around town, followed by some 15,000 people. The Fêtes Renaissance du Roi de l'Oiseau, a frolicking revival of 16th century life, usually take place in the second week of September.

Places to Stay

Camping The impressively situated, riverside *Camping de Bouthézard* (☎ 04 71 09 55 09), a few hundred metres west of Chapelle Saint Michel d'Aiguilhe, charges 49FF for two people with a tent and car. It's open from one week before Easter until mid-October. Bus No 6 stops out front.

Hostel The *Auberge de Jeunesse* (☎ 04 71 05 52 40; fax 04 71 05 61 24) at 9 Rue Jules Vallès, in the old city's Centre Pierre Cardinal (a municipal cultural centre), has beds for 40FF a night; breakfast is 10.50FF. Reception is generally open from 8 am to noon and 2 to 11.30 pm; Sunday hours are 8 to 10 am and 8 to 10 pm; from October to March, it is closed on weekends and holidays. Kitchen facilities are available.

Hotels The *Hôtel Le Régional* (☎ 04 71 09 37 74) at 36 Blvd Maréchal Fayolle has adequate doubles from 120FF (160FF with shower and toilet), 200FF for three people with bath and toilet. Hall showers cost 15FF. Reception is closed on Sunday after noon. Around the corner, the 12 room ***Hôtel La Belle Époque*** (☎ 04 71 02 29 20), 5 Ave Charles Dupuy, set to reopen in mid-1999 after renovations, has doubles with shower and toilet for about 160FF.

The unpretentious ***Hôtel Le Veau d'Or*** (☎ 04 71 09 07 74), above the little café at 7 Place Cadelade, has seven simple, washbasin equipped rooms for one to three people for 110 to 190FF. The hall shower is free.

In the two star category, the garden-equipped, 40 room ***Hôtel Bristol*** (☎ 04 71 09 13 38; fax 04 71 09 51 70), 7 Ave Maréchal Foch, a member of the Logis de France group, is an excellent choice. Singles/doubles start at 200/240FF. The modern ***Dyke Hôtel*** (☎ 04 71 09 05 30; fax 04 71 02 58 66) at 37 Blvd Maréchal Fayolle – a *dyke* (pronounced 'deek') is a volcanic spire – has 15 singles/doubles with shower and toilet from 190/230FF. Reception may be closed on Sunday from 1 to 5 pm.

The ***Etap Hôtel*** (☎ 04 71 02 46 22; fax 04 71 02 14 28), across from the train station at 25 Ave Charles Dupuy, is one of those postmodern, automatic-check-in jobs. Singles/triples start at 185/210FF (a bit less from November to March).

Places to Eat

Restaurants ***Chantal Paul*** (☎ 04 71 09 09 16), a small eatery on Place de la Halle, offers a four course lunch *menu* for 55FF (served daily from 12.15 to 3 pm). ***Restaurant Le Poivrier*** (☎ 04 71 02 41 30) at 69 Rue Pannessac has French and regional *menus* for 69, 79, 110 and 150FF. It's open from noon to 2 pm and 7 to 9.30 pm (closed Monday). In the old city, there are a number of restaurants on or around Rue Raphaël, near the Centre d'Enseignement de la Dentelle au Fuseau.

Le Croco (☎ 04 71 02 40 13) at 5 Rue Chaussade, a cheery and very popular eatery with meat dishes as well as lighter fare (various large salads and baked potatoes), is open from noon to 2 pm and 7 to 10 pm (closed Sunday). For pizzas, pastas, fondues, meat dishes and sweet crêpes, you might try ***L'Ancienne*** (☎ 04 71 09 21 59) at 13 Blvd du Breuil, open daily from noon to 3.30 pm and 7 to 10.30 or 11 pm.

The elegant ***Restaurant Bateau Ivre*** (☎ 04 71 09 67 20) at 5 Rue Portail d'Avignon specialises in classic French and Auvergnat cuisine; *menus* cost 105, 145 and 185FF. It's open from noon to 2.30 pm and 7.30 to 10 pm (closed Sunday and Monday).

Self-Catering Behind the Hôtel de Ville, there's a Saturday morning ***food market*** at Place du Plot and Place de la Halle. Quite a few ***food shops*** – most, except the boulangeries, are closed on Sunday – can be found nearby, especially all along Rue Pannessac.

The ***Casino*** supermarket at 2 Ave de la Dentelle is open Monday to Saturday from 8.30 am to 8 pm.

Entertainment

A couple of popular cafés that become bars at night – ***Yam's Bar*** and ***Bar de l'Aviation*** (open daily until 1 am) – are situated opposite 1 Blvd du Breuil. ***Harry's Bar*** (☎ 04 71 02 23 02), a cosy place at 37 Rue Raphaël, is open from 5 pm to 1 am (closed Sunday).

Shopping

Boutique Catherine Pagès (☎ 04 71 05 25 84) at 2 Rue du Faubourg Saint Jean – topped by a fanciful, early 20th century advertising tower – is an elegant boutique that sells various products of the Auvergne region (honeys, jams, sweets etc) and a variety of liquors distilled by Pagès. It is open until 7 pm (closed from noon to 2 pm, except in summer, and on Sunday from October to April).

Getting There & Away

Bus The bus station (☎ 04 71 09 25 60) is to the right as you exit the train station. The information office is staffed from 7.30 am until 12.30 pm and from 2 to 7 pm (closed Saturday afternoon and Sunday). Autocars Hugon Tourisme (☎ 04 66 49 03 81) has three buses a day (except Sunday) to Mende (83.50FF; two hours).

Train Le Puy's sleepy train station (☎ 08 36 35 35 35), at the eastern end of Ave Charles Dupuy, has limited rail links with the rest of the country. Destinations served include Lyon (106FF; 2¼ hours; six to eight a day), Nîmes (164FF; a beautiful trip via Brioude), Clermont-Ferrand (106FF; 2¼ hours; four a day) and Toulouse (231FF).

Car ADA (☎ 04 71 05 23 17) is at 34 Rue du Faubourg Saint Jean (closed 12.30 to 2 pm and on Sunday). Budget (☎ 04 71 09 06 24) is at 3 Ave de la Dentelle.

Getting Around

TUDIP, the local bus company, has an information desk (☎ 04 71 09 38 41) inside the tourist office (closed Sunday and holidays). All the lines pass by Place du Breuil.

AROUND LE PUY-EN-VELAY

On the outskirts of Le Puy, about 5km northwest of the town centre, the remains of the 9th to 15th century **Forteresse de Polignac** (also known as the Château and the Donjon de Polignac; ☎ 04 71 02 46 57) sit on a volcanic plateau formed as the surrounding countryside eroded away. The place was once home to the powerful Polignac family, who virtually ruled Velay from the 11th to the 14th century. It can be visited in the afternoons from Easter to 1 November (daily from 10 am to 7 pm from June to September).

The roads around Le Puy offer plenty of scenic drives if you have your own transport. West of Le Puy, the wild **Allier River**, once famed for its salmon fishing (a fish reintroduction program is being implemented, complete with fish ladders on the dams), has cut some pretty impressive gorges that are home to small villages lost in time. Head north from **Monistrol d'Allier** (southwest of Le Puy along the D589) to admire the local churches.

Hiking

The many local hiking trails include the **Chemin de Saint Jean-François Régis**, a circuit that passes through the villages east of Le Puy. Long-distance trails include the **GR3**, **GR40** and the **GR65**; the latter goes all the way to Santiago de Compostela in Spain. The tourist office in Le Puy can supply details.

Parc Naturel Régional des Volcans d'Auvergne

The 3250 sq km Parc des Volcans d'Auvergne stretches for 120km from the smooth, cone-shaped volcanoes known as the **Monts Dômes** (the Puys) in the north near Clermont-Ferrand; south to the spectacular **Monts Dore**, around Le Mont Dore, to the older, more rugged **Monts du Cantal** farther south around the Puy Mary and Murat. The volcanic activity in this region started about 20 million years ago, with the last eruptions (in the Monts Dômes) petering out about 6000 years ago.

Many buildings in the 150 towns and villages in the park are built of volcanic stone. The countryside is wild and beautiful and ideal for hiking.

Information

The park's head office is in Montlosier (☎ 04 73 65 64 00), about 20km south-west of Clermont-Ferrand on the D5, a small road off the main N89 from Clermont-Ferrand to Tulle. The exhibition on volcanism and area wildlife (18FF) is open daily from May to 2 November; hours are 10.30 am to 12.30 pm and 1.30 to 6 pm; in July and August, afternoon hours are 2.30 to 7 pm. The park's **Musée des Volcans** (Volcano Museum; ☎ 04 71 48 07 00) in Aurillac, housed in the Château Saint Étienne, is open from February to October. Hours are 10 am to noon and 2 to 6 pm (closed Sunday). From mid-June to mid-September, it is open Monday to Saturday from 10.30 am to 6.30 pm and, on Sunday, from 2 to 6 pm.

From May to 1 November, the department runs a *centre d'accueil* (information bureau; ☎ 04 73 62 21 45) on the summit of the Puy de Dôme (open daily).

Monts Dômes
This northern range, west of Clermont-Ferrand, consists of a chain of 80 'recent' volcanoes, the best known of which is the **Puy de Dôme** (see the Around Clermont-Ferrand section).

Monts Dore
Three million years older than their northern neighbours, the Monts Dore culminate in the **Puy de Sancy** (1885m), the Massif Central's highest point. In winter it's a popular downhill ski station. At its base lies the spa town of **Le Mont Dore**, an ideal summer and winter base for exploring the area. For more information, see the sections on Orcival and Le Mont Dore.

Monts du Cantal
The south of the park is dominated by the bald slopes of the Monts du Cantal, the remains of a super-volcano worn down over the millennia and form one of the Massif Central's wildest areas. The highest point is the **Plomb du Cantal** (1855m), a lonely, desolate peak which is often shrouded in heavy, swirling clouds, even in summer. The town of **Murat** is the best place to base yourself if you want to explore this area, including the **Puy Mary**. For details, see the sections on Puy Mary and Murat.

ORCIVAL
• pop 283 ✉ 63210 alt 860m

The delightful, slate-roofed village of Orcival, about midway between the Puy de Dôme and Le Mont Dore, is surrounded by some of the most spectacular forests and pastures in the Massif Central. Built on the banks of the gurgling Sioulet River, it's a perfect base for day hikes – and, despite the coachloads of tourists, a lovely spot to spend a soothing few days. Hiking trails that pass through Orcival include the GR30; hiking maps are on sale at the *tabac* (tobacconist) next to the *boulangerie*.

The exceptionally fine 12th century, Auvergnat-Romanesque **basilica** dating from the 12th century, a massive structure built of dark grey volcanic blocks, houses a statue of the Virgin made of gilded silver on wood (12th century), which is protected by an infrared alarm system. There are prisoners' balls and chains hanging on the outside, above the entrance.

The *syndicat d'initiative* (tourist office; ☎ 04 73 65 92 25), across the main road from the downhill side of the church, is open during the February and Easter school holidays and from early July to August.

Places to Stay
Nearby camping grounds include ***Camping de l'Étang de Fléchat*** (☎ 04 73 65 82 96), open from June to mid-September. It is 2km from Orcival.

The cluster of reasonably priced one and two-star hotels around the church includes the seven room ***Les Bourelles*** (☎ 04 73 65 82 28), which has a lovely, flowery terrace. Simple doubles/triples with washbasins, bidets and beautiful views cost 135/175FF (closed from October to Easter). The nine room ***Hôtel Notre Dame*** (☎ 04 73 65 82 02) has shower-equipped doubles from 150FF (190FF with toilet). It's closed from December to February and, except in July and August, on Wednesday. The two star ***Hôtel des Touristes*** (☎ 04 73 65 82 55; fax 04 73 65 91 11) has doubles/quads with shower and toilet from 200/280FF (closed from mid-November to December and, except for weekends, in January).

Places to Eat
Regional specialities (cured meats, cheeses, honey etc) are on sale at ***Aux Saveurs des Volcans***, 50m down the hill from the basilica (towards the post office). The ***boulangerie*** facing the basilica is open all day long (closed on Monday except in summer; closed in the afternoon in November).

Getting There & Away
Orcival is on the D27, 27km south-west of Clermont-Ferrand and 18km north of Le Mont Dore. Three buses a day (one on Sunday) link Clermont-Ferrand with Rochefort-Montagne (43FF; 40 minutes), a town 4km west of Orcival.

AROUND ORCIVAL

The D27 from Orcival to the **Col de Guéry** (1268m), 8.5km to the south, passes through some really spectacular mountain scenery.

From late May to mid-September, the **Maison des Fleurs d'Auvergne** (☎ 04 73 65 20 09), at the Col de Guéry overlooking the lake, functions as a visitors centre for people interested in the area's flora (open daily). When there's snow (usually from about January to March), it becomes the **Foyer Ski de Fond Orcival Guéry**, a cross-country skiing centre with at least 25km of pistes. The area has several hiking trails.

LE MONT DORE

• pop 2000 ✉ 63240 alt 1050m

The lovely (though no longer fashionable) little spa town of Le Mont Dore is brilliantly situated for exploring the Puy de Sancy area on foot, by bicycle or with a car. It lies in a narrow, wooded valley along the Dordogne River, not far from its source. Built from the dark local stone, it bustles with skiers in winter and hikers, hang-gliders and curistes attracted by the hot springs in summer.

Orientation

The centre of town is around Place du Panthéon and Place de la République. The train station is about 500m to the north.

Information

Tourist Office The tourist office (☎ 04 73 65 20 21; fax 04 73 65 05 71) on Ave de la Libération, at the southern end of the complex that houses the public ice-skating rink and the bowling alley, is open Monday to Saturday from 9 am to 12.30 pm and 2 to 6.30 pm; Sunday hours are variable. Topoguides are on sale. Hotel reservations (☎ 04 73 65 09 00) are free.

Money The small Banque Chalus on Rue Ramond changes money on weekdays until 5.25 pm (closed from noon to 1.35 pm).

Post The main post office at Place Charles de Gaulle is open weekdays from 8 am to 12.30 pm and 2 to 5 pm (6 pm from mid-June to late September) and on Saturday until noon. Currency exchange is available.

Bookshop The Maison de la Presse at 21 Place du Panthéon, open daily from 7 am to 12.30 pm and 2 to 7 pm (until 8 pm in July and August, when there's no midday closure), has a good selection of maps and topoguides.

Laundry The laundrette in the park below 10 Ave des Belges is open Monday to Saturday from 10 am to noon and 5 to 7 pm.

Établissement Thermal

The huge hot springs complex (☎ 04 73 65 05 10) on Place du Panthéon, whose waters are said to cure respiratory ailments (particularly asthma), sits on the site of a Roman spa. It offers a wide range of hydrotherapies from mid-May to late October.

There are half-hour guided tours (12FF) of the cavernous, neo-Byzantine interior, whose sumptuous décor dates from the early and mid-19th century (with vestiges from the Roman period), which begin at 2.30, 3.30, 4.30 and 5.30 pm when the spa is open and during school holiday periods. The rest of the year (except November and December), tours are usually held on weekday mornings (hours posted).

Funiculaire du Capucin

The best way to get to the **Pic du Capucin**, the 1270m-high wooded plateau above the town, is to take the *belle époque*-style funicular railway (☎ 04 73 65 01 25) on Ave René Cassin, built in 1898. From mid-May to September, it runs daily from 10 am to 12.10 pm and 2 to 6.40 pm (19.50/25.50FF one way/return; every 20 minutes). From the upper station, you can link up with the GR30, which wends its way southward to the Puy de Sancy, or walk back to town.

Téléphérique du Sancy

This cable car (☎ 04 73 65 02 23), about 3.5km south of town, swings dramatically to the summit of the Puy de Sancy (also known as the Pic de Sancy), where you can take in the stunning panorama of the northern puys and the Monts du Cantal before starting a hike or, in winter, slip-sliding down the slopes. Except in October and November, it operates every day until 5 pm (5.50 pm in July and August). One-way/return tickets cost 30/36FF (22/29FF for children). In winter, a free skiers' shuttle bus links Le Mont Dore's tourist office with the téléphérique.

Skiing

Le Mont Dore is a pleasant and relatively cheap ski resort, with 42km of runs on the northern side of the Puy de Sancy, a few kilometres south of town, and another 40km of runs over the hill at **Super Besse** (☎ 04 73 79 52 84), on the mountain's south-eastern slopes; generally sunnier, the latter area tends to have less snow. The cross-country network around Le Mont Dore is excellent, with 30km of runs (280km in the whole Sancy-Ouest area) in relatively unspoilt wilderness.

A lift ticket good for both Le Mont Dore and Super Besse costs 107/275FF (75/190FF for kids under 11) for one/three days; if you

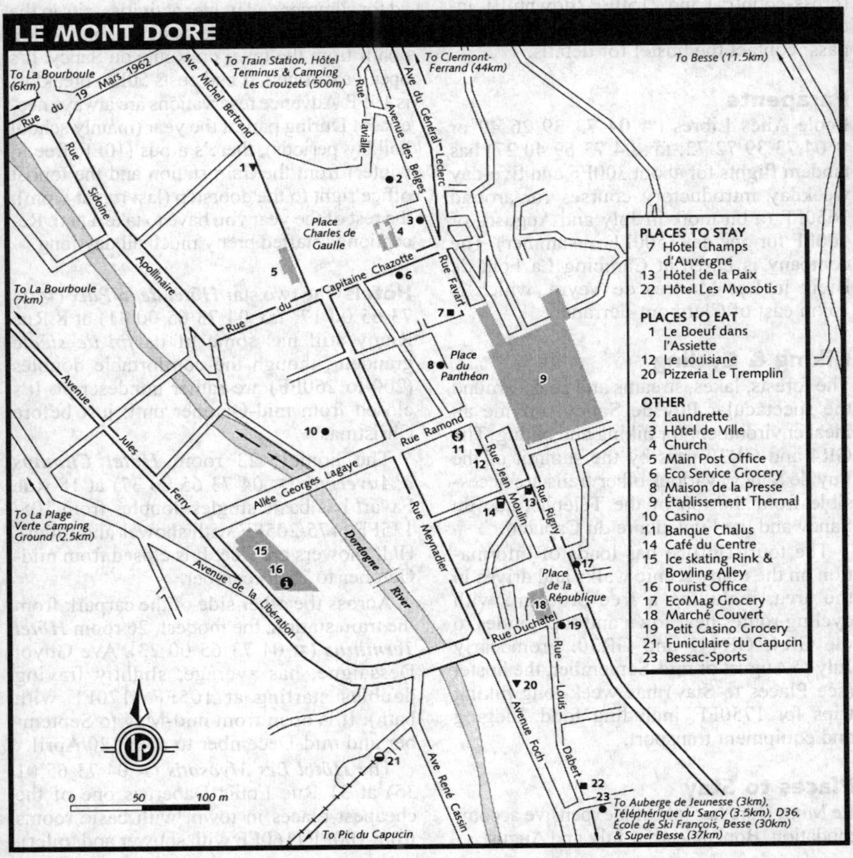

stay four or more days, there are discounts early and late in the season. Renting downhill skis, including boots, costs 55 to 120FF a day; cross-country skis range from 35 to 80FF. Monoskis are about 90FF. Equipment can be hired from quite a few sport shops around town, including Intersport (☎ 04 73 65 01 72) at 2 Rue Duchatel.

Near the Téléphérique du Sancy, the École de Ski Français (ESF; ☎ 04 73 65 07 43) charges 90FF for a two-hour beginners skiing lesson (450FF for six lessons).

FUAJ, the hostel association, offers week-long skiing packages from 1560FF (cross-country) and 2150FF (downhill), including bed, board, equipment and a lift pass; contact the hostel for details.

Parapente

École Ailes Libres (☎ 04 73 39 26 49 or ☎ 04 73 39 72 72; fax 04 73 69 40 27) has tandem flights for about 300FF and five-day weekday introductory courses for around 1650FF (a bit more in July and August), or 400FF for one day (500FF in summer). The company is based at Camping La Font de Bleix in Les Martres de Veyre, which is 15km east of Clermont-Ferrand.

Hiking & Cycling

The forests, lakes, streams and peaks around the spectacular Puy de Sancy provide an ideal environment for hiking and biking. The GR4 and GR30 pass by the summit of the Puy de Sancy; various other trails are accessible from the top of the Téléphérique du Sancy and the Funiculaire du Capucin.

The tourist office has loads of information on the many scenic walks and drives in the area, including a free brochure with cycling routes near town and topoguides to the GR4, GR441 and GR30. From early July to August or mid-September, the hostel (see Places to Stay) has week-long hiking trips for 1750FF, including food, lodging and equipment transport.

Places to Stay

Le Mont Dore has lots of inexpensive accommodation. Book ahead in July and August.

Camping The municipal, two star ***Les Crouzets*** (☎ 04 73 65 21 60), on Ave des Crouzets just across the river as you exit the train station, is open from mid-May to September. It charges about 12FF per adult and 11FF for a tent site. ***La Plage Verte*** (☎ 04 73 65 04 30) on Route de la Tour d'Auvergne (the D213), open from mid-May to September, is 2.5km north-west of town on the Rigolet plateau. Fees are similar. There's no public transport.

Hostel The ***Auberge de Jeunesse*** (☎ 04 73 65 03 53; fax 04 73 65 26 39), ideally situated for summer and winter activities, sits in the shadow of the Puy de Sancy about 3.5km uphill from the town on Route du Sancy. It's open year-round. A bed costs 50FF; breakfast is 19FF. Advance reservations are always necessary. During part of the year (mainly school holiday periods), there's a bus (10FF, free in winter) from the train station and the tourist office right to the doorstep (last run at 6 pm); the rest of the year you have to take a taxi. Reception is staffed pretty much all day long.

Hotels The two star ***Hôtel de la Paix*** (☎ 04 73 65 00 17; fax 04 73 65 00 31) at 8 Rue Rigny still has some of its *fin de siècle* grandeur, though the comfortable doubles (200 to 260FF) are rather nondescript. It's closed from mid-October until just before Christmas.

The homey, 23 room ***Hôtel Champs d'Auvergne*** (☎ 04 73 65 00 37) at 18 Rue Favart has basic singles/doubles from 105/135FF (175/205FF with shower and toilet). Hall showers are free. It is closed from mid-October to 25 December.

Across the other side of the carpark from the train station, the modest, 26 room ***Hôtel Terminus*** (☎ 04 73 65 00 23), Ave Guyot Dessaigne, has average, slightly fraying doubles starting at 105FF (170FF with bath). It is open from mid-May to September and mid-December to about 20 April.

The ***Hôtel Les Myosotis*** (☎ 04 73 65 01 35) at 31 Rue Louis Dabert is one of the cheapest places in town, with basic rooms from 100FF (160FF with shower and toilet).

It is open from late December to mid-April and from mid-May to mid-September.

Places to Eat

Many of Le Mont Dore's hotels have restaurants with moderately priced *menus*.

Restaurants The restaurant in the ***Hôtel Champs d'Auvergne*** (see Places to Stay) specialises in Auvergnat cuisine such as *truffade* (potatoes prepared with very young cantal cheese), *tripoux* (mutton and veal tripe cooked in a white wine sauce) and *fondue Auvergnate* (cantal cheese fondue); the *menus* cost 58, 68, 80 and 95FF. Except from mid-October to 25 December, meals are served daily from noon to 1 pm and 7 to 8.30 pm.

Fresh regional fare, including fish (eg trout), is the speciality of ***Le Louisiane*** (☎ 04 73 65 03 14) at 2 Rue Jean Moulin, whose *menus* cost 85 to 145FF (35FF for children). Hours are noon to 2 pm and 7 to 9.30 pm (closed on Wednesday except from May to mid-October).

Le Boeuf dans l'Assiette (☎ 04 73 65 01 23) at 9 Place Charles de Gaulle, whose wood-panelled interior is reminiscent of a giant sauna, has hearty beef and mutton dishes for 58 to 92FF; the *menus* cost 68 and 89FF (39FF for kids). It is closed on Monday except from early July to September.

Pizzeria Le Tremplin (☎ 04 73 65 25 90) on Ave Foch has pizzas for 38 to 54FF. It's open year-round in the evening (6 to 11 pm or later) and, during the Christmas and February school holidays, for lunch; it's closed on Monday in the spring and autumn.

Self-Catering The best place to purchase edibles is Place de la République, where either the ***Petit Casino*** grocery, the ***EcoMag*** grocery or the small ***marché couvert*** is open daily except, perhaps, on Sunday afternoon. Most places are closed between 12.30 and 3 pm.

The ***Eco Service*** grocery at 7 Rue du Capitaine Chazotte is open daily until 8 pm; it is closed from 12.30 to 3 pm (4 pm on Sunday) except from May to mid-October and mid-December to late February.

Getting There & Around

Le Mont Dore is 44km to the south-west of Clermont-Ferrand.

Train The sleepy train station (☎ 04 73 65 00 02 or ☎ 08 36 35 35 35), at the north-western end of Ave Michel Bertrand, is staffed from 6 am to 7 pm (8 pm on Sunday). To get to Paris' Gare de Lyon (264FF; 5½ hours; one direct a day in the warm months) you usually have to change trains in Clermont-Ferrand (64FF; 1½ hours; four or five a day). To get to Limoges and Bordeaux (202FF), you have to change at Laqueuille, Ussel and/or Brive. The resort town of La Bourboule (8FF; five or six a day) is only eight minutes away.

Bike Mountain bikes can be hired from a number of places, including Bessac-Sports (☎ 04 73 65 02 29) at the southern end of Rue Louis Dabert.

PUY MARY

The immense and majestic Puy Mary (1787m), near the southern edge of the Parc des Volcans, remains snowcapped until late July or early August. In summer, it's an easy, 30 minute climb from the **Pas de Peyrol**, a 1582m pass on the D680, to the summit; the panorama is astounding. The pass and the upper reaches of the D680 are blocked by snowdrifts except from late May (or even early June) to late October. Nearby slopes, forests, valleys and streams can be explored on foot thanks to a number of hiking trails, including the GR4 and GR400.

For a spectacularly beautiful drive, take the D16 south from Condat and turn onto the D62 a few kilometres south of town, near Lugarde. The D62 follows the verdant Cheylade River valley, taking you through rich pastures, deciduous forests and the villages of **Cheylade** and **Le Claux** (population 300) before making a tortuous climb to the 1364m **Col de Serre** (open year-round). The GR4 passes by the col, as do a number of cross-country ski trails. In the spring, when the Pas de Peyrol (3km to the south-west) is closed, you can walk or drive along the D680 to the snow line for a late-season snow frolic.

From the Col de Serre, the D680 follows the gentle Santoire Valley eastward to the tidy village of **Dienne** and the town of Murat (see the following section).

Places to Stay

In Dienne, the 10 room ***Hôtel de la Poste*** (☎ 04 71 20 80 40), on the D680 opposite the post office, has doubles/triples/quads with shower and toilet for 200/260/290FF. It's closed in January.

Places to Eat

The friendly ***Chalet du Col de Serre*** (☎ 04 71 78 93 97), right at the Col de Serre, serves Auvergnat cuisine daily, except from mid-November to mid-December. The *menus* cost 69 to 192FF (49FF for children).

MURAT

• pop 2400 ✉ 15300 alt 930m

The town of Murat, situated in a natural amphitheatre at the foot of a basaltic, crag (with a statue of the Virgin Mary on top) known as the Rocher de Bonnevie, is a good base for exploring the southern reaches of the Parc des Volcans, including Puy Mary, the Plomb du Cantal and the ski station of Super Lioran, 10km to the south-west.

Orientation & Information

The main square, Place du Balat, is 200m up Ave de la République from the train station. The church and the iron-and-brick covered market are 200m farther up the hill along Ave des 12 et 24 Juin 1944.

The tourist office (☎ 04 71 20 09 47), in the Hôtel de Ville at the top end of Place du Balat, is open daily from 10 am to noon and 2 to 5 pm (closed Sunday and most holidays; during school holiday periods it's open on Sunday from 10 am to noon). From June to sometime in September, its open daily from 9.30 am to noon and 2 (3 on Sunday) to 7 pm.

There are a couple of banks, open Tuesday to Saturday, near the tourist office. The post office, across the street from the tourist office, is open weekdays from 8.30 am to noon and 2 to 5 pm and on Saturday until noon. It also exchanges currency.

Hiking maps and topoguides are sold at the Maison de la Presse, across the street from the uphill side of the covered market. It is open until 7 pm (closed from noon to 2 pm and on Sunday afternoon).

Things to See & Do

The **Maison de la Faune** (☎ 04 71 20 00 52), in the turreted stone building up the stairs to the left as you face the Hôtel de Ville, is a better-than-average museum of stuffed and mounted wildlife. It's open daily except Sunday morning from 10 am to noon and 2 to 5 pm (6 pm during school holiday periods, when it's open seven days a week); in July and August, afternoon hours are 3 to 7 pm. Entry costs 25FF (18FF for students, 15FF for children aged from six to 12).

The **GR4** and **GR400** pass through Murat. Hiking destinations include Chastel-sur-Murat (three hours); La Molède and Albepierre (three hours); Bredons-La Molède via Le Bois du Roy (five hours); and the 1855m Plomb du Cantal (six hours) via Prat de Bouc.

The Murat area is covered by IGN's Top 25 Série Bleue map No 2435OT, entitled *Monts du Cantal*. Chamina's *Volcan Cantalien* topoguide (72FF) covers 56 short hikes in the area.

Places to Stay

The ***Camping Municipal*** (☎ 04 71 20 01 83), south of town on Rue de la Stade, charges 9FF for a tent site and 9FF per adult. It's open June to September and, perhaps, during the February-March school holidays.

The friendly, seven room ***Hôtel du Stade*** (☎ 04 71 20 04 73) at 35 Rue du Faubourg Notre Dame, 300m to the right as you exit the train station, has doubles from 120FF; hall showers are free. The two star ***Hôtel Les Messageries*** (☎ 04 71 20 04 04; fax 04 71 20 02 81), across from the train station at 18 Ave du Docteur Mallet, has singles/doubles/quads for 220/260/370FF. It's closed in December.

Getting There & Away

The train station (☎ 04 71 20 07 20) is linked to Clermont-Ferrand (90FF; 1¾ hours; four to six a day) and Aurillac (47FF; 45 minutes) daily. One or two direct trains a day serve Toulouse (168FF).

Getting Around

Mountain bikes (80FF a day) can be rented from the Peugeot shop (☎ 04 71 20 07 83) on the downhill side of the covered market building. It's open from Tuesday to Saturday and the staff can also help with maps.

Toulouse Area

The Toulouse area (le Pays Toulousain), which touches on parts of three different departments, is in something of a geographical limbo. When France's new regional boundaries were mapped out in the 1960s, Languedoc's traditional centre, Toulouse, was excluded from Languedoc-Roussillon. Thus it is no longer Languedoc and not quite the Pyrenees. Nevertheless, it is a fascinating region to visit with heaps of historical sights and activities on offer.

Central to the area is Toulouse itself, a vibrant centre with a large student population and one of the fastest-growing cities in France. Close by are two cities with strong historical connections: Albi, 75km to the north-east, and Montauban, 52km to the north.

Montauban suffered tremendously during the Albigensian Crusade, which was launched against the Cathars (see the boxed text 'The Cathars' in the Languedoc-Roussillon chapter) in Albi in 1208.

HIGHLIGHTS

- **Space Age** – visit Aérospatiale and the Cité de l'Espace museum
- **Toulouse-Lautrec** – visit the painters birthplace, and the most extensive exhibition of his work at the Musée Toulouse-Lautrec
- **After Dark** – enjoy the city's vibrant nightlife

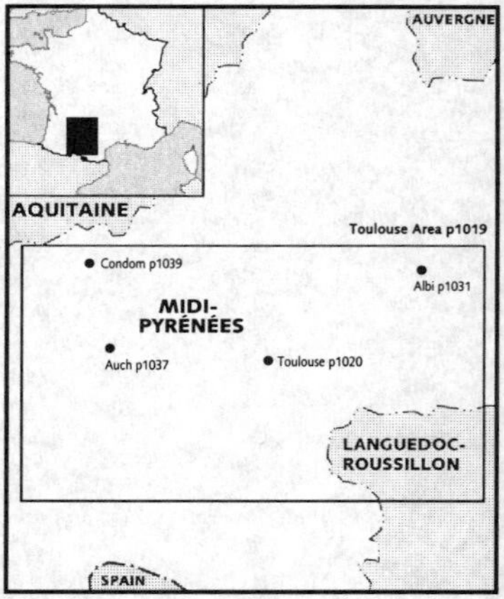

cassoulet – a casserole with white beans, garlic, bacon, herbs and a variety of meats

saucisse de Toulouse – sausages prepared in the Toulouse style

Armagnac brandy

TOULOUSE

• pop 650,000 ✉ 31000 alt 147m

Toulouse is France's fourth largest city (after Paris, Lyon and Marseille). It is renowned for its high tech industries, including some of the most advanced aerospace facilities in Europe. It is also a major centre of higher education: the city's universities, founded in the 13th century to combat Catharism, and its *grandes écoles* (of which there are 14) and other institutes have 110,000 students, more than any other French provincial city.

But while Toulouse is a sunny, dynamic city with some of the friendliest people you'll meet in France, it is not a very attractive place. There are no stone quarries anywhere near Toulouse so all the older buildings in the city centre are made of rose-red brick, earning the city the nickname *la ville rose* (the pink city). Unfortunately, some bricks weather faster than others, so many of the façades are chipped and cracked, imparting a look of dereliction. Still, Toulouse, prefecture of the Haute-Garonne department, does have a number of very good museums and several exceptional churches, including the Romanesque Basilica of Saint Sernin.

History

Toulouse, known as Tolosa during the Roman period, served as the Visigoth capital from 419 to 507. It was unsuccessfully besieged by the Saracens in 721. In the 12th and 13th centuries the counts of Toulouse supported the Cathars; however, three centuries later, during the Wars of Religion, the city sided with the Catholic League. Many Toulouse merchants grew rich in the 16th and 17th centuries from the woad (blue dye) trade, however, this trade collapsed when the Portuguese began importing indigo from India. The Toulouse Parliament ruled Languedoc from 1420 until the Revolution.

Around WWI, the French government chose Toulouse as a centre for the manufacture of arms and aircraft, in large part because it was thought prudent to keep such industries as far from Germany as possible. In the 1920s, Antoine de Saint-Exupéry, who was the author of *Le Petit Prince* (The Little Prince) and whose portrait appears on the blue 50FF note, and other daring pilots pioneered mail flights from Toulouse to north-west Africa, the south Atlantic and South America. After WWII, the French government decided to build on the city's aeronautical base by making it the centre of the country's aerospace industry. Passenger planes built here have included the Caravelle, the Concorde and the Airbus; local factories also produce the Ariane rocket.

Orientation

The centre of Toulouse lies between Blvd de Strasbourg and its continuation, Blvd Lazare Carnot, to the east, and the Garonne River to the west. The train station is about 1km north-east of the centre of town on the dirty Canal du Midi, which is linked to Place Wilson by the wide Allées Jean Jaurès.

The city centre's main square is the lovely Place du Capitole, which is one block west of the tourist office. Rue du Taur links Place du Capitole with Basilique Saint Sernin to the north. A pedestrian mall (deserted at night) running along Rue Saint Rome, Rue des Changes and Rue des Filatiers goes from Place du Capitole southward to Place Esquirol and Place des Carmes. Place Saint Georges, a lively nightlife area, is a few blocks north-east of Place Esquirol.

TOULOUSE AREA

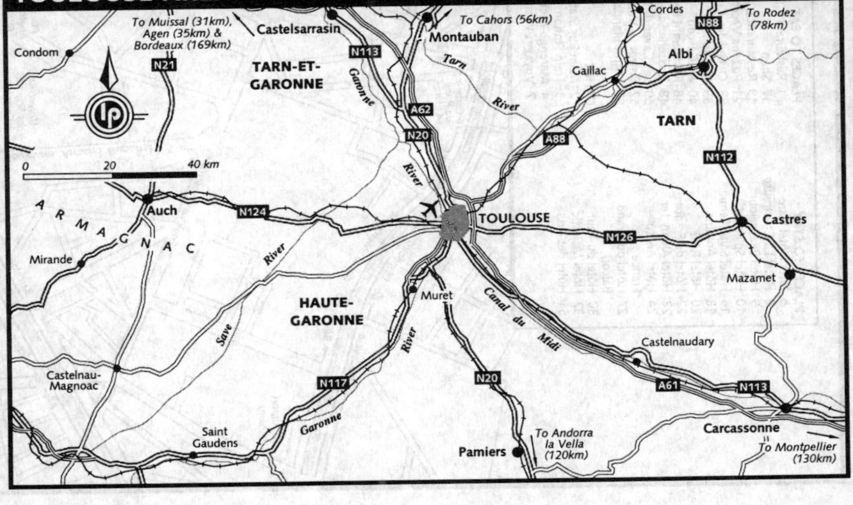

TOULOUSE

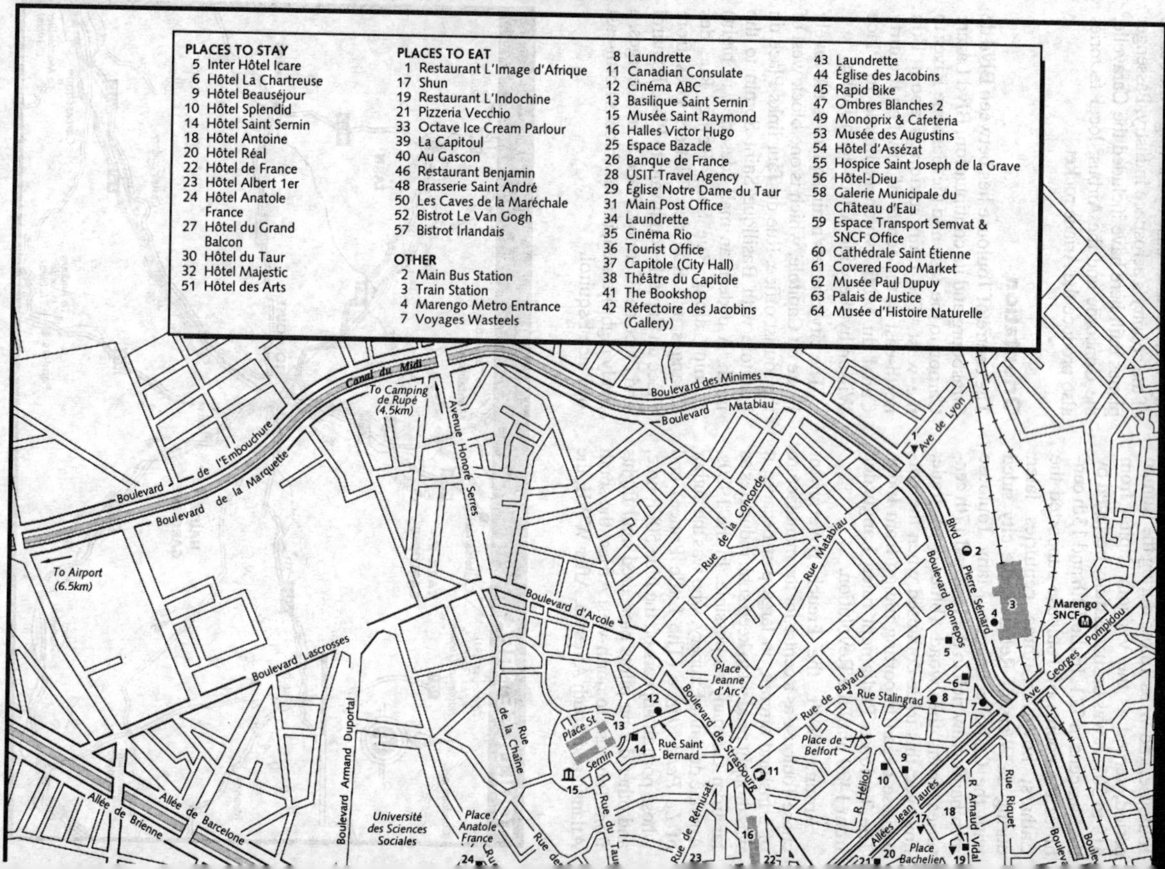

PLACES TO STAY
- 5 Inter Hôtel Icare
- 6 Hôtel La Chartreuse
- 9 Hôtel Beauséjour
- 10 Hôtel Splendid
- 14 Hôtel Saint Sernin
- 18 Hôtel Antoine
- 20 Hôtel Réal
- 22 Hôtel de France
- 23 Hôtel Albert 1er
- 24 Hôtel Anatole France
- 27 Hôtel du Grand Balcon
- 30 Hôtel du Taur
- 32 Hôtel Majestic
- 51 Hôtel des Arts

PLACES TO EAT
- 1 Restaurant L'Image d'Afrique
- 17 Shun
- 19 Restaurant L'Indochine
- 21 Pizzeria Vecchio
- 33 Octave Ice Cream Parlour
- 39 La Capitoul
- 40 Au Gascon
- 46 Restaurant Benjamin
- 48 Brasserie Saint André
- 50 Les Caves de la Maréchale
- 52 Bistrot Le Van Gogh
- 57 Bistrot Irlandais

OTHER
- 2 Main Bus Station
- 3 Train Station
- 4 Marengo Metro Entrance
- 7 Voyages Wasteels
- 8 Laundrette
- 11 Canadian Consulate
- 12 Cinéma ABC
- 13 Basilique Saint Sernin
- 15 Musée Saint Raymond
- 16 Halles Victor Hugo
- 25 Espace Bazacle
- 26 Banque de France
- 28 USIT Travel Agency
- 29 Église Notre Dame du Taur
- 31 Main Post Office
- 34 Laundrette
- 35 Cinéma Rio
- 36 Tourist Office
- 37 Capitole (City Hall)
- 38 Théâtre du Capitole
- 41 The Bookshop
- 42 Réfectoire des Jacobins (Gallery)
- 43 Laundrette
- 44 Église des Jacobins
- 45 Rapid Bike
- 47 Ombres Blanches 2
- 49 Monoprix & Cafeteria
- 53 Musée des Augustins
- 54 Hôtel d'Assézat
- 55 Hospice Saint Joseph de la Grave
- 56 Hôtel-Dieu
- 58 Galerie Municipale du Château d'Eau
- 59 Espace Transport Semvat & SNCF Office
- 60 Cathédrale Saint Étienne
- 61 Covered Food Market
- 62 Musée Paul Dupuy
- 63 Palais de Justice
- 64 Musée d'Histoire Naturelle

TOULOUSE

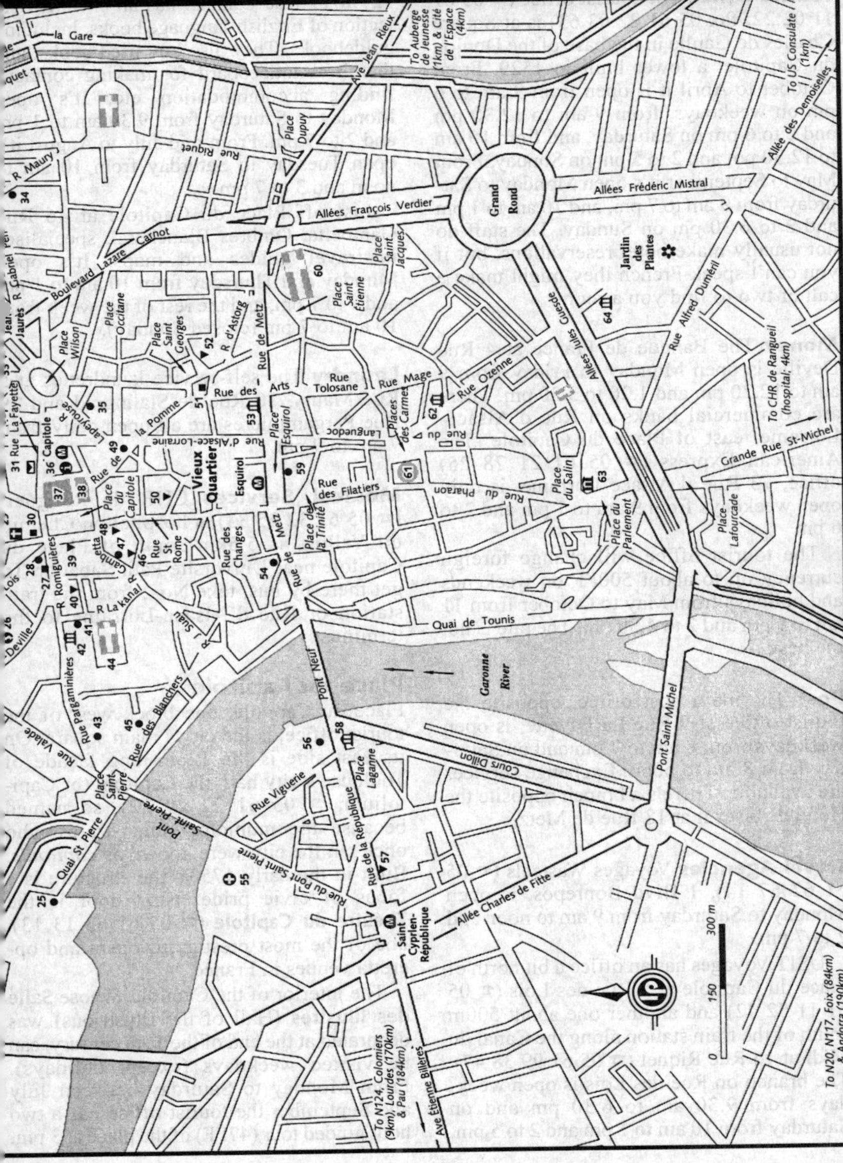

la Gare
To Auberge de Jeunesse (1km) & Cité de l'Espace (4km)
Ave Jean Rieux
To US Consulate (1km)
Allée des Demoiselles
Place Dupuy
Rue Riquet
R Maury
Allées Frédéric Mistral
Grand Rond
Allées François Verdier
Boulevard Lazare Carnot
Jardin des Plantes
Place Saint Jacques
Place Saint Étienne
Rue Alfred Duméril
Allées Jules Guesde
Place Occitane
Place Wilson
Place Saint Georges
R d'Astorg
Rue de Metz
Jean Jaurès
R Gabriel Péri
Rue des Arts
Rue Tolosane
Rue Mage
Rue Ozenne
To CHR de Rangueil (hospital; 4km)
Rue La Fayette
Capitole
Lapeyrouse
la Pomme
Rue d'Alsace-Lorraine
Place Esquirol
Places des Carmes
Langueduc
Rue du Languedoc
Grande Rue St-Michel
Rue de
Vieux Quartier
Esquirol
Rue des Filatiers
Rue du Pharaon
Place du Salin
Place du Capitole
Place de la Trinité
Place du Parlement
Place Lafourcade
R Romiguières
Gambetta
Rue St Rome
Rue des Changes
Rue de Metz
R Lakanal
Deville
Quai de Tounis
R Pargaminières
Pont Neuf
Garonne River
Rue Valade
Rue des Blanchers
Place Saint Pierre
Pont Saint Pierre
Rue Viguerie
Place Laganne
Cours Dillon
Pont Saint Michel
Quai St Pierre
Rue du Pont Saint Pierre
Rue de la République
Allée Charles de Fitte
Saint Cyprien-République
300 m
150
0
To N124, Colomiers (9km), Lourdes (170km) & Pau (184km)
Ave Étienne Billières
To N20, N117, Foix (84km) & Andorra (190km)

Information

Tourist Office The tourist office (☎ 05 61 11 02 22; fax 05 61 22 03 63) is at Square Charles de Gaulle in the base of the Donjon du Capitole, a tower built in 1529. From October to April it is open from 9 am to 6 pm on weekdays, from 9 am to 12.30 pm and 2 to 6 pm on Saturday, and from 10 am to 12.30 pm and 2 to 5 pm on Sunday. From May to September it's open Monday to Saturday from 9 am to 7 pm, and 10 am to 1 pm and 2 to 6.30 pm on Sunday. The staff do not usually make hotel reservations, but if you can't speak French they might make a call or two to find you a room.

Money The Banque de France at 4 Rue Deville is open Monday to Friday from 9 am to 12.20 pm and 1.20 to 3.30 pm. There are commercial banks on Rue d'Alsace-Lorraine, east of Place du Capitole. The American Express (☎ 05 61 21 78 25) office, 73 Rue d'Alsace Lorraine, is only open weekdays from 9 am to 1 pm and 2 to 6 pm.

The tourist office will change foreign currency up to about 500FF on weekends and holidays from May to October from 11 am to 1 pm and 2 to 4.30 pm. The rate is not the best.

Post The main post office, opposite the tourist office at 9 Rue La Fayette, is open weekdays from 8 am to 7 pm and on Saturday from 8 am to noon. Exchange services are available. There's a branch opposite the Hôtel d'Assézat at 18 Rue de Metz.

Travel Agencies Voyages Wasteels (☎ 05 61 62 67 14), 1 Blvd Bonrepos, is open Monday to Saturday from 9 am to noon and 2 to 7 pm.

USIT Voyages has an office a bit north of Place du Capitole at 5 Rue des Lois (☎ 05 61 11 52 42) and another one about 500m south of the train station along the Canal du Midi at 16 Rue Riquet (☎ 05 61 99 38 47). The branch on Rue des Lois is open weekdays from 9.30 am to 6.30 pm and on Saturday from 10 am to 1 pm and 2 to 5 pm.

Bookshops The Bookshop (☎ 05 61 22 9 92) at 17 Rue Lakanal has an excellent se lection of English-language books, includin guidebooks. They also buy used books, an there's a noticeboard for making contacts finding accommodation etc. It's ope Monday to Saturday from 9.30 am to 1 pn and 2 to 7 pm. From mid-July to August it' open Tuesday to Saturday from 10 am t noon and 3 to 7 pm.

Just off Place du Capitole at 46 Ru Gambetta, Ombres Blanches 2 specialise in travel guides and maps. It's ope Monday and Thursday from 10 am to 1 pn and 2 to 7 pm, and the rest of the week fron 10 am to 7 pm (closed Sunday).

Laundry The self-service laundrettes at 5 Rue Maury, 10 Rue de Stalingrad and 2 Rue Pargaminières are all open daily fron 7 am to 9 pm.

Medical Services CHR de Ranguei (☎ 05 61 32 25 33), a hospital on Chemin du Vallon, is 5.5km south of Place du Capitole near Université Paul Sabatier. To get there by bus, take No 2 from the train station or Rue d'Alsace-Lorraine to the terminus.

Place du Capitole

Place du Capitole, one block west of the tourist office, is the city's main square. On its east side is the 128m-long façade of Toulouse's city hall, the **Capitole** (or Capitolium; ☎ 05 61 22 29 22), so named because the municipal magistrates who once ran the city were known as *capitouls*. Built in the early 1750s, the structure is a focus of civic pride. Next door is the **Théâtre du Capitole** (☎ 05 61 63 13 13), one of the most prestigious opera and operetta venues in France.

The interior of the Capitole, whose **Salle des Illustres** (Hall of the Illustrious) was decorated at the end of the 19th century, can be visited weekdays (except holidays). From Monday to Saturday between July and September the tourist office has a two hour guided tour (47FF) of the place at 3 pm.

Henri II, the duke of Montmorency who had the audacity to rebel against Cardinal Richelieu, was executed in the interior double courtyard in 1632.

The **Vieux Quartier** (Old Quarter), which has hardly changed since the 18th century, is south of Place du Capitole around Rue Saint Rome and Rue des Changes, both of which are reserved for pedestrians.

Basilique Saint Sernin

The chancel of this 115m-long basilica (☎ 05 61 21 80 45 from 5 to 8 pm only), the largest and most complete Romanesque structure in France, was built of brick between 1080 and 1096; the nave was added in the 12th century. No significant architectural changes have been made since 1271. Once a Benedictine abbey church, Saint Sernin was an important stop on the way to Santiago de Compostela in Spain, where the cathedral, begun about the same time, is almost identical in design.

The basilica is topped by a magnificent eight-sided **tower** whose lower three storeys (the ones with rounded arches) date from the early 13th century; the upper two storeys were added in the mid-13th century. The spire is from the 15th century.

Inside, the **déambulatoire** (ambulatory) is lined with chapels containing gilded 17th century reliquaries. The two-level **crypt**, rebuilt in the 13th and 14th centuries, has a number of medieval tombs. Directly above the crypt is the sculpted mid-18th century **tomb of Saint Sernin**, topped by a sumptuous canopy. The north transept arm is decorated with a **12th century fresco** of Christ's Resurrection.

The basilica is open daily from 8 am to noon and 2 to 6 pm. During July and August it's open from 8 am to 6.30 pm (9 am to 7.30 pm on Sunday). The ambulatory and crypt, which cost 10FF to visit, are open daily (except Sunday morning) from 10 to 11.30 am and 2.30 to 5 pm; in July and August opening hours are 10 am (12.30 pm on Sunday) to 6 pm.

Église Notre Dame du Taur

Église Notre Dame du Taur, whose entrance is opposite 21-23 Rue du Taur, was built in the southern (or Meridional) Gothic style in the 14th century. It was built to honour Saint Saturninus (Sernin), a local evangelist who was martyred in 257 by being tied to the tail of a *taureau* (wild bull). At the end of the nave are three chapels; the middle one contains a 16th century Black Madonna known as Notre Dame du Rempart. The church can be visited daily from 8.30 am to noon and 2.30 to 7 pm.

Église des Jacobins

The Church of the Jacobins was begun in 1230, shortly after the Dominicans (also known as Jacobins), founded by Saint Dominic in 1215 to preach Church doctrine to the Cathars, established their first chapter in Toulouse. Construction was completed in 1385.

Inside the Gothic structure a single row of seven 22m-high columns runs down the middle of the nave, supporting the roof by means of fan vaulting that makes them look like palm trees. The remains of **Saint Thomas Aquinas** (1225-74), one of the early leaders of the Dominican order and a so-called Doctor of the Church, are now interred below the modern, grey marble altar on the north side, having been moved from the Basilique Saint Sernin. The 45m-high octagonal belfry was built between 1265 and 1298. The church was used as an artillery barracks during the 19th century. It is open daily, except Sunday morning, from 10 am to noon and 2 to 6 pm; all day long in summer.

The Jacobins under Robespierre, who ruled France during the Reign of Terror following the Revolution, were so named because they used to meet in Paris in a Dominican convent.

Réfectoire des Jacobins

The 14th century Dominican refectory (☎ 05 61 22 21 92), just north-west of the Église des Jacobins at 69 Rue Pargaminières, has rotating exhibits, many from the collection of the Musée d'Art Modern et Contemporain, as well as from the Musée Saint Raymond. Admission ranges from 10 to 20FF, depending on the exhibition.

Hôtel d'Assézat

The Hôtel d'Assézat, whose entrance is on Place d'Assézat opposite the post office at 18 Rue de Metz, was built by a rich woad merchant in the late 1550s. The design superimposes three of the five classical orders: Doric, Ionic and Corinthian. The upper storey was added in the 17th century. In 1896 the building was donated to a number of local learned societies, including the Académie des Jeux Floraux, named after an annual poetry competition begun by seven troubadours in 1323 and dedicated to promoting poetry in both French and Occitan (Provençal).

The Hôtel d'Assézat houses the art collection of the **Fondation Bemberg** (☎ 05 61 12 06 89), with paintings, bronzes and *objets d'art* donated by local philanthropist Georges Bemberg. Admission is 25FF (15FF for students).

Musée de l'Histoire de la Médecine

The Museum of the History of Medicine is located in the Hôtel-Dieu on Rue de la République.

Musée des Augustins

The Musée des Augustins (☎ 05 61 22 21 82), 21 Rue de Metz, has a superb collection of paintings and stone artefacts, many of them seized by the Revolutionary government or gathered from the vandalised monuments. The stone carvings, most of which are Romanesque and Gothic, include religious statuary, capitals, *clefs de voûte* (keystones), sarcophagi, gargoyles, tombstones and inscriptions, a few of them in Hebrew. The museum is housed in an Augustinian monastery whose two **cloisters** date from the 14th century. The **gardens** in the cloister are among the prettiest in southern France.

The museum keeps regular hours (10 am to 6 pm daily, except Tuesday) but on Wednesday stays open until 9 pm (10 pm from June to September). Entry costs 12FF (free for students) unless there's a special exhibition, in which case the price jumps to 20FF.

Cathédrale Saint Étienne

The Cathedral of Saint Étienne (Saint Stephen), whose main entrance is south of Rue de Metz, has a rather peculiar layout. The vast nave, begun around 1100 and modified in 1211, is out of line with the choir, built in the northern French Gothic style as part of an ambitious (and unfinished) late 13th century plan to rebuild the cathedral along a different axis. Especially interesting is the improvised Gothic vaulting that links the two sections. The rose window to the west dates from 1230, and the organ case above the entrance to the nave is from four centuries later. The choir is filled with carved wooden stalls and 16th century tapestries. Both the west and north (main) portals are worth a look; the former was added in the 15th century, the latter in 1929. The cathedral is open daily from 7.30 am to 7 pm.

Musée Paul Dupuy

The Paul Dupuy Museum (☎ 05 61 22 21 83), 13 Rue de la Pléau, which occupies the 17th and 18th century Hôtel de Besson, has a fine collection of *objets d'art*, glasswork, medieval religious art, faïence (tin-glazed earthenware), armaments and rare clocks and watches. The **pharmacy**, dating from the mid-17th century, is from Toulouse's Jesuit college. Entry costs 10FF (free for students to the museum only) or 20FF if there's a special exhibition on. It is open daily from 10 am to 5 pm (6 pm in summer).

Gardens

The **Grand Rond**, a huge roundabout-cum-park, and the **Jardin des Plantes** (Botanic Gardens), two of the greenest parts of central Toulouse, are a few blocks southwest of Musée Paul Dupuy.

Cité de l'Espace

You can't miss the amazing new Space Park museum and planetarium complex (☎ 05 62 71 48 71) at Ave Jean Gonord on the eastern outskirts of the city, marked by a 55m-high space rocket. The museum includes interactive attractions, and fascinating displays on life in space, satellite systems and future life on board space stations. There is even talk of a space rocket simulator in the near future. It is open daily from June to September from 9.30 am to 7 pm (from 9.30 am to 6 pm for the rest of the year) and costs 50/30FF for adults/children. Take bus No 19 from the train station then walk for 15 minutes in the direction of the rocket.

Galerie Municipaledu Château d'Eau

Housed in a *château d'eau* (water-pumping station) built in 1822, this municipal photography museum (☎ 05 61 77 09 40) at Place Laganne at the western end of Pont Neuf puts on superb and thought-provoking temporary exhibitions of works by some of the world's finest photographers. There is at least one new exhibition in one of the three galleries each month. Founded in 1974, it is Toulouse's most visited museum, despite tough competition from the Cité de l'Espace. The museum's documentation centre, open to the public, is the only one of its kind in France.

The gallery is open daily, except Tuesday and holidays, from 1 to 7 pm. Entry costs 15FF (10FF for students, free if you're under 12). Everyone gets in for 10FF on Sunday.

EDF Bazacle

Espace Bazacle (☎ 05 62 30 16 00) at 11 Quai Saint Pierre, owned by Electricité de France, hosts all sorts of temporary exhibitions. It is housed in a 12th century mill and is part of a working 19th century hydroelectric plant, which can also be visited. It is open weekdays from 10 am to noon and 2 to 6 pm and weekends from 2 to 7 pm. It is closed from July to mid-September. Entry is free.

Organised Tours

Aérospatiale From Monday to Saturday, the aerospace company Aérospatiale has 1½-hour tours (55FF; 45FF for students) of its huge Clément Ader aircraft factory (where Airbus A330s and A340s are assembled) at Ave Jean Monnet in Colomiers, about 10km west of the city centre. For information and reservations, call ☎ 05 61 15 44 00 a few days in advance and be sure to bring along a passport or national ID card. In August you can make reservations at the tourist office.

Places to Stay

Most of Toulouse's hotels cater to business people, so rooms are easiest to find on Friday, Saturday and Sunday nights, as well as during most of July and August (the annual holiday period).

Places to Stay – Budget

Camping The three star *Camping de Rupé* (☎ 05 61 70 07 35) is 6km north-west of the train station at 21 Chemin du Pont de Rupé. From Ave des États-Unis, go west for 300m along Chemin du Pont de Rupé. This is not the most appealing camping ground you'll ever come across and the 300 sites are often full, but it is easily accessible by bus; from Place Jeanne d'Arc, which is 600m south-west of the train station and something of a hub, take bus No 59 to the Rupé stop. The last bus leaves at 7.25 pm. A tent/caravan site for two people costs 62FF (16FF for each additional person) and a parking space is 5FF. The camp site is open all year.

Hostels At the time this guide went to press the ***Auberge de Jeunesse Villa des Rosiers***, just under 3km south-east of the train station at 125 Ave Jean Rieux, was closed, although the tourist office was hoping that it would reopen soon. Contact the tourist office (☎ 05 61 11 02 22) for an update on the situation.

Hotels Almost all the cheap hotels around the train station and the nearby red-light district, centred around Place de Belfort, are dirty, noisy and run by unpleasant people. If you arrive by rail, your best bet is to walk to Allées Jean Jaurès or take the metro into town.

TOULOUSE

Hotels – Allées Jean Jaurès The ***Hôtel Antoine*** (☎ 05 61 62 70 27), 21 Rue Arnaud Vidal, is a pleasant, friendly place on a quiet street and has singles/doubles from 90/140FF; doubles/quads with shower and toilet are 160/215FF. Hall showers are 10FF. You might also try the ***Hôtel Réal*** (☎ 05 61 62 47 55), 30 Allées Jean Jaurès, whose plain doubles cost 110FF with washbasin, 130FF with shower, and 155FF with shower and toilet. Simple rooms for three or four people are 205FF. Reception is open 24 hours a day – after 1 am, ring the bell.

Your best option north of Allées Jean Jaurès is probably the ***Hôtel Beauséjour*** (☎ 05 61 62 77 59), which is at 4 Rue Caffarelli. Singles/doubles start at 75/95FF; doubles with shower and toilet are 150FF. An extra bed is 40FF. The shower costs 10FF. At the risk of being treated uncivilly, you might try the ***Hôtel Splendid*** (☎ 05 61 62 43 02; fax 05 61 40 52 76) at 13 Rue Caffarelli, whose 14 basic, run-down singles/doubles start at 80/105FF (120/145FF with shower). Hall showers are 10FF.

Hotels – City Centre You can't beat the location of the ***Hôtel du Grand Balcon*** (☎ 05 61 21 48 08; fax 05 61 21 59 98), which is just off Place du Capitole at 8 Rue Romiguières. A faded but still elegant place, the Grand Balcon was where Antoine de Saint-Exupéry holed up (in room No 32, if you must know) between flights in the early 1920s, and the lobby is a veritable shrine to the aviator-author. Spacious singles/ doubles/ triples cost around 110/130/150FF (150/190/200FF with shower); hall showers are 11FF. It is closed for most of August.

Hôtel des Arts (☎ 05 61 23 36 21), 1bis Rue Cantegril, just off Place Saint Georges, is another place with a good location. Adequate singles/doubles (some are noisy), cost 80/125FF with washbasin, and 135/170FF with shower and toilet. Showers cost 10FF per person or 15FF per room.

Just south of Halles Victor Hugo at 9bis Rue du Rempart Villeneuve, the ***Hôtel Majestic*** (☎ 05 61 23 04 29) has large but slightly run-down singles/doubles with shower and toilet for 120/140FF; rooms with washbasin are 110/120. Hall showers are free.

The ***Hôtel Anatole France*** (☎ 05 61 23 19 96), 46 Place Anatole France, has doubles with washbasin for 110FF, with shower for 135FF, and with shower and toilet for 160FF.

Places to Stay – Mid-Range

Many of Toulouse's mid-range hotels offer much better value for money than the budget ones.

Train Station Area The two star, 34 room ***Inter Hôtel Icare*** (☎ 05 61 63 66 55; fax 05 61 63 00 53), 11 Blvd Bonrepos, has spacious, soundproofed singles/doubles with shower from 180/250FF. The family-run ***Hôtel La Chartreuse*** (☎ 05 61 62 93 39; fax 05 61 62 58 17), 4bis Blvd Bonrepos, has small, clean rooms with shower, toilet and TV from 165FF.

City Centre Just east of Halles Victor Hugo, Rue d'Austerlitz is lined with two-star hotels. The well run 64 room ***Hôtel de France*** (☎ 05 61 21 88 24; fax 05 61 21 99 77), whose entrances are at 5 Rue d'Austerlitz and 4 Rue Victor Hugo, has spotless, comfortable doubles/quads with shower (baths in the quads) and toilet from 195/360FF; the rates are cheaper on Friday, Saturday and Sunday nights.

Two blocks west of Halles Victor Hugo at 8 Rue Rivals, the pleasant ***Hôtel Albert 1er*** (☎ 05 61 21 17 91; fax 05 61 21 09 64) has comfortable singles/doubles/quads with shower, toilet, TV and minibar for 200/240/370FF. Prices are about 30FF less on weekends, during school holidays and in July and August.

Just north of Place du Capitole at 2 Rue du Taur, the 40 room ***Hôtel du Taur*** (☎ 05 61 21 17 54) has quiet and fairly spacious singles/doubles with shower and toilet for 200/225FF. Reception is on the mezzanine floor. Saint-Exupéry used to stay here in the late 1920s, evidently having grown tired of the noise from Place du Capitole at the Hôtel du Grand Balcon.

The lovely and very quiet ***Hôtel Saint Sernin*** (☎ 05 61 21 73 08; fax 05 61 22 49 61), in the eastern shadow of the basilica at 2 Rue Saint Bernard, has singles/doubles/triples with all the mod-cons for 220/270/300FF. Parking in the hotel garage is 40FF.

Places to Eat

For the most part restaurants in Toulouse offer what the French call *bon rapport qualité-prix* – good value for money. Without a doubt, the best places in town for lunch (only) are the little restaurants on the 1st floor of Halles Victor Hugo. Catering to market vendors and shoppers alike, they serve up generous amounts of hearty fare for about 55FF per *menu*.

When the weather is good, Place Saint Georges is almost entirely taken over by café tables; at night it's one of the liveliest outdoor spots in town. Both Blvd de Strasbourg and the perimeter of Place du Capitole are lined with restaurants and cafés. Lots of places around town have lunch *menus* for 50 to 60FF.

Restaurants – French ***Les Caves de la Maréchale*** (☎ 05 61 23 89 88), through the arch at 3 Rue Jules Chalande (east of Rue Saint Rome), specialises in both regional cuisine and dishes created by its convivial chef. Housed in the magnificently vaulted brick cellar of a pre-Revolution convent, it is open daily (except on Sunday and for lunch on Monday) from noon to 2 pm and 8 to 11 pm. *Menus* cost 75FF (lunch), 110 and 145FF (dinner). There's also a *formule rapide* for 56FF available at lunch. It's a good idea to make reservations for dinner.

The excellent ***Restaurant Benjamin*** (☎ 05 61 22 92 66), 7 Rue des Gestes (west of Rue Saint Rome), in a setting that is a mixture of classical columns and modern décor, serves nouvelle cuisine. *Menus* start at 59FF (lunch) and 89FF (dinner). It's open daily from noon to 2 pm and 8 to 11 pm.

An excellent place for *canard*, *canard* and more duck is the intimate ***Au Gascon*** (☎ 05 61 21 67 16) at 9 Rue des Jacobins. Its generous *menus* cost 45, 85 and 128FF, and it is open seven days a week.

Bistrot Le Van Gogh (☎ 05 61 21 03 15), 21 Place Saint Georges, has regional specialities such as *cassoulet* (85FF) and *parillade* (eight different kinds of fish; 120FF). The *menus* cost 65FF (lunch) and 120FF (dinner). Le Van Gogh is open daily from noon to 2.30 pm and from 7 to 11 pm (last orders by 10.30 pm). The huge terrace is open whenever the weather allows.

The mellow ***Brasserie Saint André*** (☎ 05 61 22 56 37), 39 Rue Saint Rome, is two floors below street level in a cellar with a rounded ceiling that makes you feel as though you're in the upper half of a brick submarine. The *menus* (75 and 95FF), soups, omelettes and main courses (35 to 78FF) attract a varied clientele that includes lots of young people. Meals are served all night long, from 7.45 pm to 7 am (7.30 am on Saturday and Sunday mornings). It is closed Sunday evening.

Restaurants – Other The ***Shun*** (☎ 05 61 99 39 20), an elegantly designed Japanese eatery at 35 Rue Bachelier, is open for lunch and dinner daily (except on Monday and for lunch on Sunday) till 10.30 pm. Lunch/dinner *menus* start at 80/145FF. Close by at 46 Place Bachelier, ***Restaurant L'Indochine*** (☎ 05 61 62 17 46) serves Chinese and Vietnamese cuisine daily from noon to 2 pm and 7 to 11 pm. The *menus* cost 48 and 67FF. Unusually for a Chinese-Vietnamese restaurant, the portions are large. There are other Asian eateries in the area.

Restaurant L'Image d'Afrique (☎ 05 61 58 48 10), run by an immigrant from Senegal, is one long block north of the train station at 7 Ave de Lyon. Main dishes are 55 to 75FF. L'Image d'Afrique is open daily (except Sunday) from 8 to 10 pm.

Ever think you'd have Irish food in France? The ***Bistrot Irlandais*** (☎ 05 61 42 12 12), across the Pont Neuf at 50 Rue de la République, serves lunch (*menus* at 43, 53 and 63FF) and dinner (88FF) on weekdays only. Try some fresh Irish salmon – there's none better.

Pizzeria Vecchio (☎ 05 61 62 96 26), 22 Allées Jean Jaurès, a thriving place with a large warm-weather terrace, is open daily from 12 to 2.30 pm and 7 to 11.30 pm. Pizzas start at 32FF; pasta dishes are 37 to 55FF.

Le Capitoul (☎ 05 61 21 49 52), 11 Place du Capitole, serves unusual salads from 65FF, *moules frites* (mussels with chips/French fries; 55FF) and quiche (25FF) on a sunny terrace. It is open daily (except Saturday) from 11 am to 10 pm.

Self-Catering ***Halles Victor Hugo***, the large covered food market at Place Victor Hugo, is on the ground floor of a multi-level parking garage. It is open Tuesday to Sunday from 6 am to 1 pm. At Place des Carmes, which is at the southern end of the Rue Saint Rome-Rue des Filatiers pedestrian mall, you'll find another large ***covered food market***. There's a small ***market*** selling organically grown food at Place du Capitole on Tuesday and Saturday until about 1 pm.

Monoprix at 39 Rue d'Alsace-Lorraine, whose supermarket section is on the 1st floor, is open Monday to Saturday from 8.30 am to 9 pm. The ***cafeteria*** (☎ 05 61 21 71 80) on the 2nd floor has *plats du jour* from 23.90FF and *menus* from 38FF. It is open from 11 am to 6.30 pm.

Octave (☎ 05 62 27 05 21) has outlets at 9 Place du Capitole and 11 Allées du Président Roosevelt, it serves incredibly rich ice cream daily from 10 am (2 pm on Monday) to about 2 am. Cones with one to five scoops cost 11 to 39FF. Avoid breathalyser tests after eating the Armagnac pruneaux or Grand Marnier flavours.

Entertainment

The tourist office has all sorts of up-to-date information on Toulouse's vibrant cultural life. In July and August the office sells tickets (80FF) for a series of concerts known as Musique d'Été (Summer Music).

Daytime and night-time café activity is centred around Place Saint Georges and, less so, Blvd de Strasbourg and Blvd Lazare Carnot. Rue des Blanchers, south-west of the Église des Jacobins, has a number of 'alternative' pubs and bars that go on till late. Get a copy of the map-guide *Toulouse La Nuit*, available in many bookshops for 18FF. There are around 20 discos to choose from in Toulouse, but the hottest ones in town are ***La Stada*** (☎ 05 61 62 56 31), 4 Rue Gabriel Perin; ***L'Ubu*** (☎ 05 61 23 26 75), 16 Rue Saint Rome; and ***Le Clap*** (☎ 05 61 52 87 47), 146 Chemin des Etroits.

Cinemas Two cinemas have nondubbed foreign films. ***Cinéma Utopia*** (☎ 05 61 21 22 11), 24 Rue Montardy, has screenings in its three *salles* every day in the afternoon and in the evening. Tickets cost 33FF. The ***Cinéma ABC*** (☎ 05 61 29 81 00), 13 Rue Saint Bernard, changes films every Wednesday. It is closed for most of August. Tickets cost 42FF (32FF for students), depending on the program.

Gay Venues Toulouse is a very gay city – it ain't called *la ville rose* just for those pink bricks – and some of the best discos and bars this side of the Marais in Paris are here. Try the popular ***Pub Les 2-G*** on Rue des Tourneurs, ***Pub-Disco B-Machine*** in Place des Carmes, or the ***Shanghai Express*** (☎ 05 61 23 37 80) south-east of Place du Capitole at 12 Rue de la Pomme.

Shopping

Toulouse's main shopping district, filled with department stores and expensive boutiques, is around Rue du Taur, Rue d'Alsace-Lorraine, Rue de la Pomme, Rue des Arts and nearby streets. Place Saint Georges is also surrounded by fashionable shops. On Wednesday Place du Capitole hosts a flea market, and there's an antiquarian book market on Place Saint Étienne west of the cathedral on Saturday.

Getting There & Away

Air Toulouse-Blagnac international airport (☎ 05 61 42 44 00) is about 8km north-west of the city centre in the suburb of Blagnac.

Bus Toulouse's modern bus station (☎ 05 61 61 67 67), just north of the train station on Blvd Pierre Sémard and about 1km north-east of the city centre, is among the most efficient and helpful in France. Buses from here (all run by different lines) go to destinations including Agen, Albi (52FF), Auch, Carcassonne (55FF), Castelnaudary, Montauban (34FF) and two gateways to Andorra: Ax-les-Thermes and Pas de la Casa (70FF return). Semvat's intercity Arc-en-Ciel buses, which serve local destinations in the Haute-Garonne and nearby departments, also use the main bus station. The information counters are open Monday to Saturday from 7 am to 8 pm.

The Intercars office (☎ 05 61 58 14 53) at the bus station handles buses to Andorra (135FF; Sunday at 8 am), Poland, Portugal and parts of Spain. It's open Monday to Saturday from 9 am to noon and 2 to 7 pm (3 to 7 pm on Thursday and 5 to 7 pm on Saturday). Brussels, Amsterdam, Morocco and other parts of Spain (including Burgos, San Sebastián, Bilbao, Barcelona, Valencia, Murcia and Seville) are handled by Eurolines (☎ 05 61 26 40 04), whose office in the bus station is staffed on weekdays from 9 am till noon and 2 to 6.30 pm. Saturday hours are 9 till noon and 2 to 5 pm.

Train Toulouse's train station, Gare Matabiau (☎ 08 36 35 35 35), is just south of the bus station on Blvd Pierre Sémard. The information office is open daily from 5.30 am to 10.30 pm (Friday and Sunday from 6 am to midnight). The station itself is closed from 1.30 to 4.30 am. Ticket window Nos 17 to 19 will change enough foreign currency to cover the cost of your ticket.

Destinations served by direct trains include Albi (62FF; 70 minutes; up to a dozen a day), Bayonne (200FF; four hours; six a day), Bordeaux (163FF; 2¼ hours; 10 a day), Cahors (86FF; eight a day; 1¼ hours), Marseille (252FF; four hours; nine a day), Montpellier (174FF; 2½ hours) and Nice (317FF; at least six hours; five a day). The route to Paris is covered by TGVs via Bordeaux to Gare Montparnasse (423FF; five hours) and non-TGVs via Cahors to Gare d'Austerlitz (363FF; 6½ to seven hours).

In the city centre at 7 Place Esquirol, SNCF has an information and ticketing office in Espace Transport Semvat (see Bus & Metro under Getting Around). It is open on weekdays from 2 to 6 pm.

Getting Around

To/From the Airport The Navette Airport (airport shuttle; 25FF, or 30FF after 9 pm) service, run by TRG (☎ 05 61 30 04 89), links Toulouse with Toulouse-Blagnac airport. Buses to the airport run about every 20 minutes (every 30 minutes on weekends) from 5.20 am to 9 pm (from 6 am on weekends); they can be picked up at the bus station (bay No 2) as well as from stops on Allées Jean Jaurès (near the entrance to the metro) and Place Jeanne d'Arc (where bus No 1 stops).

Bus & Metro The local public transport network is run by Semvat (☎ 05 61 41 70 70). A single-ride ticket, available from the three Semvat outlets, machines at each metro stop and bus drivers, costs 7.50FF (9FF to the suburbs). A carnet of 10 tickets costs 62FF (70FF to the suburbs) and there's a weekly pass for 73FF. Tickets are valid for 45 minutes (one hour on suburban routes) after they've been time-stamped and can be used for up to three transfers. Most bus lines run daily until 8 or 9 pm. The seven Bus de Nuit (night bus) lines, all of which start at the train station, run from 10.05 pm to just after midnight.

Toulouse's pride and joy, the single-line, fully automatic metro with 15 stations, runs north-east to south-west from Jolimont to Basso Cambo (with a connection to the western suburban Gare de Colomiers at the Arènes stop). The major city stops are Marengo SNCF (the train station), Jean Jaurès, Capitole and Esquirol. The metro's logo is a white 'M' against a grey background with the name of the stop in red.

The Semvat ticket kiosk at the Marengo SNCF metro entrance in front of the train station can supply you with a route map. It is open weekdays from 6.30 am to 7.30 pm, on Saturday from 12.30 to 7 pm and on Sunday from 4.30 to 10 pm. To get from the train station to the city centre, take the metro for two stops (direction Basso Cambo) to Capitole.

In the city centre Semvat has another information and ticket office (Espace Transport Semvat) at 7 Place Esquirol. It is open Monday to Friday from 8.30 am to 6.30 pm and on Saturday until 12.30 pm. There's a Semvat ticket window at 9 Place du Capitole.

Car In the city centre there's a huge parking garage under Place du Capitole. Except on Sunday you can park for free at Place Saint Sernin. Near Blvd de Strasbourg there's a multistorey parking garage above the Halles Victor Hugo.

Taxi There are 24-hour taxi stands at the train station (☎ 05 61 21 00 72), Place Wilson (☎ 05 61 21 55 46), Place Esquirol (☎ 05 61 80 36 36), Place des Carmes (☎ 05 61 52 29 33) and Allées Jean Jaurès (☎ 05 61 52 22 22).

Bicycle Rapid Bike (☎ 05 61 21 29 56), 30 Rue des Blanchers, rents bikes for 70/100FF half-day/day.

ALBI

• pop 47,000 ✉ 81000 alt 169m

Almost all of central Albi, including the huge, fortress-like Gothic cathedral begun in the late 13th century, is built from bricks of reddish clay dug from the nearby Tarn River. Albi is best known for the so-called Albigensian heresy of the 12th and 13th centuries and the violent crusade that crushed it (see the boxed text 'The Cathars' in the Languedoc-Roussillon chapter).

Heavily influenced by both Toulouse and Languedoc, the prefecture of the Tarn department has a very southern feel. It is laid-back and not overrun with tourists, though English holiday-makers are beginning to migrate here from overcrowded Périgord to the north. One of Albi's most famous natives was Henri de Toulouse-Lautrec (1864-1901), who is best known for his posters and lithographs of people in the bars, brothels and music halls of Montmartre in *belle époque* Paris. A large amount of his work is on display in the Musée Toulouse-Lautrec.

Orientation

The cathedral dominates the western side of the centre; from it several pedestrianised streets lead eastward towards Place du Vigan, Albi's centre of commerce and nightlife. The lonely train station area lies about 1km to the south-west.

Information

Tourist Office The tourist office (☎ 05 63 49 48 80; fax 05 63 49 48 98), which is in the shadow of the cathedral at the entrance of the Palais de la Berbie on Place Sainte Cécile, is open Monday to Saturday from 9 am to 12.30 pm and 2 to 6 pm and Sunday from 10.30 am to 12.30 pm and 3.30 to 5.30 pm. In July and August it's open Monday to Saturday from 9 am to 7.30 pm, and on Sunday from 10.30 am to 1 pm and 3.30 to 6.30 pm. It is closed from January to April, and again in November until Christmas. Hotel bookings in Albi cost 10FF, and 20FF for out of town. On Sunday, when the banks are closed, the tourist office has an exchange service.

Money The Banque Populaire at 1 Rue Sainte Cécile is open Tuesday to Saturday from 8.35 to 11.55 am and 1.35 to 5.45 pm (to 4.45 pm on Saturday) and has an ATM, as does the Caisse d'Épargne nearby on Place Sainte Cécile.

Post The main post office, Place du Vigan, is open weekdays from 8 am to 7 pm and Saturday until noon.

Laundry The Lavomatique at 10 Rue Émile Grand is open daily from 7 am to 9 pm.

Walking Tour

For an excellent overall picture of the town just head north to **Pont 22 Août 1944**, one of the bridges over the Tarn. The view is very good on cool mornings as the sun starts to warm up the town's red brick and highlights the arched bridges. In the old town a plaque on the wall of the privately owned **Maison Natale de Toulouse-Lautrec**, situated at 14 Rue Henri de Toulouse-Lautrec, marks the house where the artist was born.

Cathédrale Sainte Cécile

As much a fortress as a church, this mighty cathedral on Place Sainte Cécile was begun in 1282, less than four decades after the Cathar movement was crushed. Built entirely of red brick in the southern (or Meridional) Gothic style, it was finished (mostly) in 1392 and consecrated in 1480. It is certainly not what you would call attractive – indeed, its most impressive feature is its sheer bulk. But when it is illuminated at night in summer the cathedral is breathtaking. The **tower** is 78m high.

In contrast with the plain, sunburned exterior, the interior is elaborately decorated; not a single surface was left untouched by the Italian artists who painted it in around 1512. An intricately carved **rood screen**

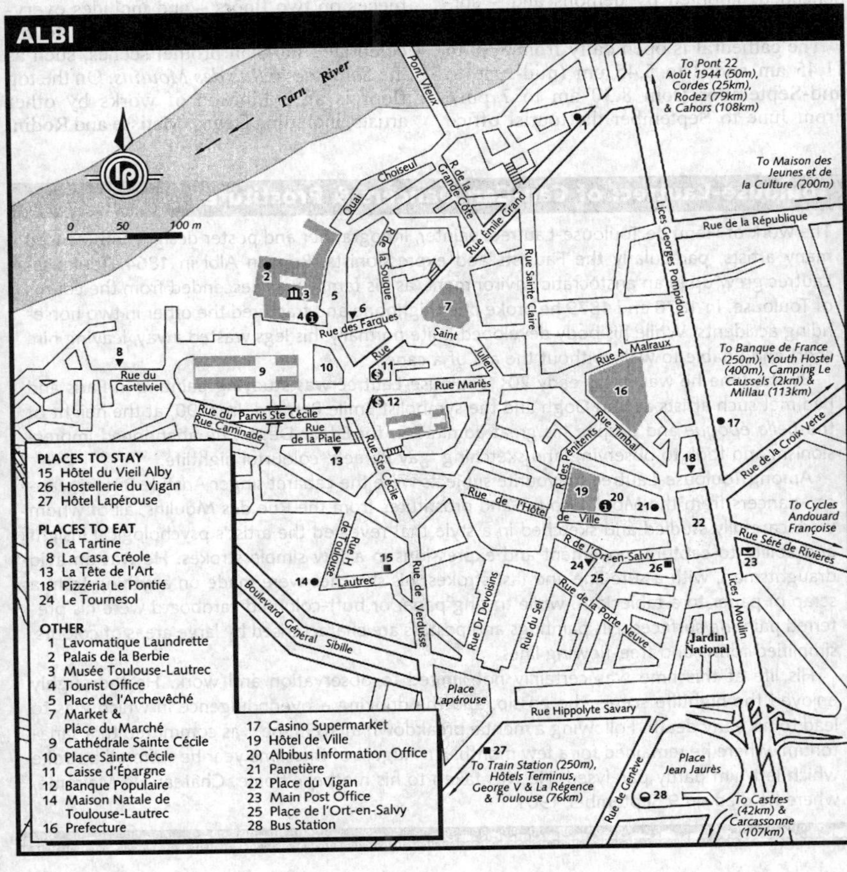

from around 1500, which lost many of its statues in 1792 to Revolutionary guards who deemed them 'superstition', spans the 18m-wide sanctuary. The **stained-glass windows** in the apse and choir date from the 14th to the 16th centuries. On no account should you miss the **grand chœur** (great choir; 3FF) with some 30 Old Testament polychrome figures carved in stone, frescoes and chapels. Below the massive 18th century organ behind today's main altar to the west is *Le Jugement Dernier* (1490), the usual Doomsday horror show of the damned being boiled in oil, tortured, beheaded, gobbled by demons and – surprise, surprise – not enjoying it one bit.

The cathedral is open daily from 8.30 to 11.45 am and 2 to 5.45 pm (mid-June to mid-September from 8.30 am to 7 pm). From June to September the tourist office has daily (except Saturday) tours of the cathedral (27FF; 13.50FF for students) in French at 10 am and 2.30 pm.

Musée Toulouse-Lautrec

Next to the cathedral, this museum (☎ 05 63 49 48 70) is housed in the **Palais de la Berbie**, a fortress-like archbishop's palace built between the 13th and 15th centuries. The entrance of the palace contains the tourist office.

The Toulouse-Lautrec Museum houses the most extensive collection of the artist's works to be found anywhere – over 500 pieces on two floors – and includes everything from simple pencil sketches to his celebrated Parisian brothel scenes, such as the *Salon de la Rue des Moulins*. On the top floor is an exhibition of works by other artists, including Degas, Matisse and Rodin.

Toulouse-Lautrec: of Can-Can Dancers & Prostitutes

The work of Henri de Toulouse-Lautrec, painter, lithographer and poster designer, influenced many artists, particularly the Fauvists and expressionists. Born in Albi in 1864, Toulouse-Lautrec grew up in an aristocratic environment, as his family was descended from the counts of Toulouse. In 1878 and 1879 he broke one thighbone and fractured the other in two horse-riding accidents. While his body developed quite normally, his legs wasted away, leaving him short and unable to walk without the aid of a cane.

By the time he was in his early 20s, Toulouse-Lautrec was studying painting in Paris and had met such artists as Van Gogh and the symbolist Émile Bernard. In 1890, at the height of the *belle époque* and despite his great admiration for Edgar Degas, he abandoned impressionism and took to observing and sketching 'gay Paree's' colourful nightlife.

Among Toulouse-Lautrec's favourite subjects were the cabaret singer Aristide Bruant, can-can dancers from the Moulin Rouge and prostitutes from the Rue des Moulins, all of whom were carefully studied and sketched in a style that revealed the artist's psychological insight and ability to capture movement and expressions in a few simple strokes. He was an avid draughtsman, with a sure line and fast strokes; his sketches were made on anything from a scrap of paper to a tablecloth, while tracing paper or buff-coloured cardboard were his preferred painting surfaces. His paintings and posters are characterised by large areas of colours, simplified forms and free-flowing lines.

His life at this time was certainly not limited to observation and work. He thoroughly enjoyed the nightlife scene, the gossip, and the drinking – overindulgence in which was to lead to his early death. Following a mental breakdown in 1899, he was committed to a sanatorium, where he remained for a few months. In August of the same year he suffered a stroke which left him partly paralysed. He was taken to his mother's home, Château de Malromé, where he died on 9 September 1901.

From October to March the museum is open daily (except Tuesday) from 10 am to noon and 2 to 5 pm. The rest of the year it's open daily from 9 or 10 am to noon and from 2 to 6 pm. Entry costs 24FF (12FF for students). The ornamental palace gardens and courtyard keep to the same schedule but charge no admission. The tourist office has tours of the museum (38FF; 19FF for students) on weekdays from June to September at 10 am and 2.30 pm, and on Saturday and Sunday at 11 am and 4 pm.

Special Events

The biggest events on Albi's cultural calendar are the Festival Théâtral, a theatre festival held at the end of June and beginning of July (100FF per ticket), and a three-day series of ancient music concerts at the end of July.

Places to Stay

Albi is not overendowed with budget hotels. There are a few near the train station along Ave Maréchal Foch and a couple more in the town centre.

Camping The closest camping ground is the two star ***Le Caussels*** (☎ 05 63 60 37 06) just off Route de Millau, about 2km north-east of Place du Vigan. It charges 52FF for two people with a tent/caravan and car and 18FF for one person with a bicycle. It's open from April to mid-October and there's a small grocery and a pool nearby. Bus No 5 from Place du Vigan stops nearby. From the train station you can either walk or take bus No 1 to Place du Vigan.

Hostel The ***Maison des Jeunes et de la Culture*** (MJC; ☎ 05 63 54 53 65; fax 05 63 54 61 55), 13 Rue de la République, is about 400m north-east of Place du Vigan. It has dormitory beds for as little as 26FF, breakfast for 12FF and other meals for 38FF, but no food is served on the weekend. To get there from the train station, take bus No 1 to the République stop on Lices Georges Pompidou and head east down Rue de la République.

Hotels – Train Station Area The cheapest rooms in town are those at the ***Hôtel Terminus*** (☎ 05 63 54 00 99), opposite the station at 33 Ave Maréchal Joffre. This place looks a bit rough and the bar below may get pretty noisy, but the rooms are decent enough. Basic attic singles/doubles start at 120/130FF and doubles with shower at 145FF.

A couple of doors down at No 29 on this tree-lined avenue is the ***Hôtel George V*** (☎ 05 63 54 24 16; fax 05 63 49 90 78) with shower-equipped doubles from 160FF (200FF with toilet). The neighbouring ***Hôtel La Régence*** (☎ 05 63 54 01 42), at No 27, has basic rooms from 110FF or from 160FF with shower. A hall shower costs 15FF. It's easy to park in this area.

Hotels – City Centre On the edge of the town centre, the mustard-toned ***Hôtel Lapérouse*** (☎ 05 63 54 69 22; fax 05 63 38 03 69), 21 Place Lapérouse, has cosy rooms, all with showers, from 150FF (200FF with shower and toilet). There's also a pool at the back. Much more central is the ***Hôtel du Vieil Alby*** (☎ 05 63 54 14 69; fax 05 63 54 96 75) at 25 Rue Henri de Toulouse-Lautrec, just at the beginning of the pedestrianised area. It has rooms with shower for 240FF and triples for 320FF. Parking, which is difficult in these parts, costs 40FF. This place closes during the second half of January and from mid-June to early July.

If you're looking for something even more upmarket, the three star ***Hostellerie du Vigan*** (☎ 05 63 54 01 23; fax 05 63 47 05 42), 16 Place du Vigan, is centrally located and has spacious modern rooms starting from 240FF with shower, and a popular restaurant with *menus* at 90, 120 and 135FF.

Places to Eat

Restaurants The restaurant scene in Albi is somewhat limited – the streets around the cathedral are your best hunting ground. Place du Vigan is the nightlife area, and many brasseries here stay open until late.

Down atmospheric little Rue de la Piale, ***La Tête de l'Art*** (☎ 05 63 38 44 75) at No 7 has a 75FF four course *menu*. On Rue du

Castelviel is ***La Casa Créole*** (☎ 05 63 54 63 39), serving up slightly more exotic dishes from Martinique starting at 48FF. The lunch *menu* is 59FF. Both restaurants are closed on Wednesday.

Opposite the tourist office, both Albigeois and foreigners are attracted to the large terrace of ***La Tartine*** (☎ 05 63 54 50 60) on Place de l'Archevêché. It offers a 65FF *menu* and main courses from 40FF. The traffic noise – not to mention the fumes – may drive you inside.

The ***Buffet de la Gare*** (☎ 05 63 54 28 30), on Place Stalingrad at the train station, has an unpretentious 67FF three-course *menu*. ***Le Tournesol*** (☎ 05 63 38 38 14) is a small vegetarian restaurant at 11 Rue de l'Ort-en-Salvy that serves a *plat du jour* for 47FF; salad platters start at the same price. It is open Tuesday to Saturday from noon to 2 pm and Friday and Saturday from 7.15 to 9.30 pm.

On Place du Vigan, ***Pizzéria Le Pontié*** (☎ 05 63 54 16 34) has pizzas from 39FF. It is open until 1 am.

Self-Catering Fresh fare can be picked up daily (except Monday) from the ***marché couvert***, a lovely covered market on Place du Marché, north-east of the cathedral. The ***Casino*** supermarket opposite the prefecture on Lices Georges Pompidou is open Monday to Saturday from 8.30 am to 7.30 pm. Its cafeteria serves main courses from 22FF and is open daily from 11.30 am to 9.30 pm. ***Panetière*** on Place du Vigan sells bread and other baked goods daily from 7 am to 8 pm.

TOULOUSE

Entertainment

There are free ***organ concerts*** in the cathedral in July and August on Wednesday at 5 pm. A ***flea market*** is held at Foirail du Castelviel, behind the cathedral, on Saturday morning in summer.

Getting There & Away

Bus The bus station, known as the Halle des Autobus, is on Place Jean Jaurès, but there's no real office there. If you're after information or timetables, ask at the tourist office. There are services to Cordes (23FF; 45 minutes; line No 12), Castres (29FF; 50 minutes; line No 5), Toulouse (50FF; 1 hour; line No 4) and Montauban (59FF; 2½ hours; line No 12).

Train The train station (☎ 05 63 54 50 50) is at Place Stalingrad, about 1km south-west of the tourist office in an isolated part of town. The ticket windows are open from between 5 and 6 am to about 9.50 pm. To get into town you can take bus No 1 (last one at 7 pm), which goes to Place du Vigan and the bus station at Place Jean Jaurès. If you're walking, head up Ave Maréchal Joffre (to the left as you leave the station), then turn left into Ave du Général de Gaulle, which leads onto Place Lapérouse. From here Rue de Verdusse leads straight to the cathedral.

There is a service from Albi to Rodez (68FF; 1¼ hours), Millau (109FF; 2½ hours), Toulouse (62FF; one hour; hourly) and Cordes (35FF; one hour). To reach Montauban (91FF) from Albi, you must change at Toulouse. Lockers cost 5FF for 24 hours.

Getting Around

Bus Local buses are run by Albibus (☎ 05 63 38 43 43), which has an information office next to the *mairie* (town hall) at 14 Rue de l'Hôtel de Ville. It's open Monday from 2 to 6 pm and Tuesday to Friday from 8.45 am to noon and 2 to 6 pm. Single tickets cost 5FF or 43FF for a carnet of 10. Buses don't run on Sunday.

Taxi You can order a taxi on ☎ 05 63 47 99 99 or ☎ 05 63 54 85 03.

Bicycle Cycles Andouard Françoise (☎ 05 63 38 44 47), 7 Rue Séré de Rivières, east of the post office, rents mountain bikes for 80/100/500FF for a half-day/day/week.

MONTAUBAN

• pop 55,000   ✉ 82000   alt 80m

Situated on the right bank of the Tarn River, Montauban is the capital of the department of Tarn-et-Garonne. The town was founded in 1144 by Count Alphonse Jourdain of

Toulouse, who, local legend tells us, was so attracted by the high eastern bank of the Tarn covered with flowering trees in spring that he named the place Mont Alba (White Mountain). It is southern France's second oldest *bastide* – a fortified settlement on a rectangular grid plan around a central arcaded square – after Mont de Marsan in the Aquitaine region. Although the town sustained significant damage during the Albigensian Crusade and the subsequent Inquisition in the 13th century, it was named the head of a diocese in 1317.

Montauban became a Huguenot stronghold around 1570, and was chosen as one of the four cities where Protestants were able to worship freely. The Edict of Nantes (1598), decreed by Henry IV, brought further royal concessions to the Huguenots. After the repeal of the Edict of Nantes by Louis XIV in 1685, the town's Protestants again suffered persecution.

Orientation

Place Nationale, a lovely square surrounded by arcaded 17th century brick buildings, is the heart of the old city but today's real centre is the less-attractive Place Franklin Roosevelt to the south. The train station is west of the centre, across the Tarn River at the end of Ave de Mayenne. There is a good view of the town from the mid-14th century Pont Vieux, which you must cross to reach the station.

Information

Tourist Office The tourist office (☎ 05 63 63 60 60) is in the Ancien Collège at 2 Rue du Collège. It is open Monday to Saturday from 9 am to noon and 2 to 7 pm. During July and August it is also open on Sunday from 10 am to noon and 3 to 6 pm.

Money The Banque de France is at 39 Rue de la Banque, two blocks south-east of Place Franklin Roosevelt.

Post The main post office is at 4 Blvd Midi-Pyrénées, three blocks east of Place Nationale.

Musée Ingres

A large portion of the works of the neoclassical painter Jean Auguste Dominique Ingres, a native Montalbanais who also played the violin with great skill (see the boxed text 'Ingres' Hobby'), are exhibited in the **Musée Ingres** (☎ 05 63 22 12 92), 19 Rue de l'Hôtel de Ville, a former bishop's palace and the site of an earlier castle of the counts of Toulouse.

The museum is open from Tuesday to Sunday from 10 am to noon and 2 to 6 pm; in July and August it is open daily from 9.30 am to noon and 1.30 to 6 pm. Admission is 20FF (free for children, students and seniors).

Churches

In Place Franklin Roosevelt, the classical **Cathédrale Notre Dame de l'Assomption**, dating from the 17th and 18th centuries, contains one of Ingres' masterpieces, *Le Vœu de Louis XIII* (The Vow of Louis XIII; 1824).

Ingres' Hobby

The artist Jean Auguste Dominique Ingres (1780-1867) was born in Montauban but at the age of 27 left for Rome, where he studied and painted for 17 years. Ingres became a leading exponent of the neoclassical style, in direct opposition to the often soppy romanticism prevailing in France at the time. His most celebrated works include the *Odalisque* series of sensuous female nudes and highly detailed portraits, including several of Napoleon.

But while Ingres is celebrated for the purity and grace of his drawing and has taken his rightful place in the pantheon of great painters, most French people know of him in a different context altogether. Away from his easel, Monsieur Ingres would relax by playing the violin. Today the French phrase for 'hobby' is *violon d'Ingres*.

Special Event
Montauban's main event is the annual Jazz-Montauban (Jazz in Montauban) held during the third week of July. Tickets, available from the tourist office, cost between 100 and 190FF.

Places to Stay & Eat
Montauban can be visited on a day trip from Toulouse, but there are several decent hotels here if you decide to stay the night. The ***Hôtel Le Lion d'Or*** (☎ 05 63 20 04 04; fax 05 63 66 77 39), near the train station at 22 Ave de Mayenne, has singles with washbasin for 110FF and singles/doubles with shower for 210/240FF. Much more central is the ***Hôtel du Commerce*** (☎ 05 63 66 31 32; fax 05 63 03 18 46), 9 Place Franklin Roosevelt. Singles/doubles with washbasin are only 110/140FF. Rooms with bath and toilet start at 190FF.

For something more upmarket, try the three star ***Hôtel Ingres*** (☎ 05 63 63 36 01; fax 05 63 66 02 90), near the train station at 10 Ave de Mayenne, which has pleasant rooms with private bath from 380FF, and a swimming pool. Parking is available.

The ***Hôtel Le Lion d'Or*** has a decent and inexpensive restaurant, but for more atmosphere try the ***Brasserie des Arts*** (☎ 05 63 20 20 90) at 4 Place Nationale.

TOULOUSE

Getting There & Away
Bus Buses to Albi (59FF), Moissac and Toulouse (34FF) leave from Place Lalaque, just off Ave de Mayenne, a short distance north-east of the train station.

Train The train station (☎ 08 36 35 35 35) is on Ave Roger Salengro at the end of Ave de Mayenne. The information office is open Monday to Saturday from 8 am to 8 pm. There are regular trains to Paris' Gare d'Austerlitz (345FF; six hours) and TGVs to the capital's Gare Montparnasse (425FF; 4½ hours), Toulouse (45FF; 30 minutes), Cordes (91FF; two hours) and Albi (92FF; 1½ hours) via Toulouse, Bordeaux (156FF; two hours), Agen (57FF; 40 minutes) and Moissac (28FF; 20 minutes).

Getting Around
Bus Local buses are run by Transports Montalbanais (☎ 05 63 63 52 52), 15 Blvd Midi-Pyrénées. Its eight lines run from Monday to Saturday; tickets, available from the driver, are 5FF each or 40FF for a carnet of 10. Bus No 3 connects the train and bus stations with the town centre.

Taxi You can order a taxi by ringing Radio Taxis on ☎ 05 63 66 99 99.

Gascony
Stretching west of Toulouse to the Atlantic, the departments of Gers and Landes are popularly known as the region of Gascony (Gasgogne). Famous for its lush rolling countryside, sleepy *bastides* (fortified villages), fine wines, foie gras and Armagnac, Gascony is an ideal region for those looking to experience the slower pace of life and some of the finest examples of medieval and Renaissance architecture in France. Locals sometimes also describe the region as the Pays d'Artagnan, after the famous Gascon hero immortalised by the novelist Alexandre Dumas in *Les Trois Mousquetaires* (The Three Musketeers).

AUCH
• pop 23,000 ✉ 32003 alt 166m

Auch, capital of Gascony, has been an important trade crossroads since Roman times, but had its heyday in the Middle Ages when it was run by the Counts of Armagnac and their archbishops, who built the city's cathedral.

Orientation
Auch is divided into two levels, split by the Gers River: the upper level (to the west of the river) centres around the cathedral, Place de la Libération and Rue Dessoles, the main pedestrianised shopping street. This part contains most of the sights, restaurants, shops and hotels; the lower part of town (east of the river) is more modern and the main residential area. The two parts are bisected by a broad riverside boulevard called Ave Sadi-Carnot.

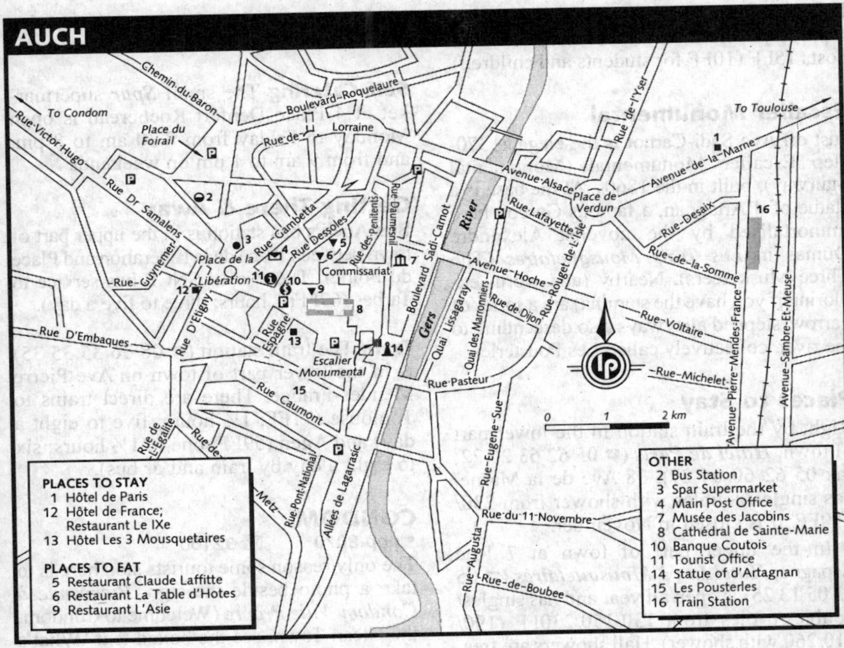

Information

Tourist Office The tourist office (☎ 05 62 05 22 89; fax 05 62 05 92 04) is at 1 Rue Dessoles. From September to May it's open daily (except Sunday) from 10 am to noon and 2 to 6 pm. These hours are extended during peak season, when it is also open Sunday from 10.30 am to noon and 3.30 to 6.30 pm.

Money Banque Courtois on the corner of Rue Arnaud de Moles and Rue Dessoles (near the entrance to the cathedral) is open Tuesday to Friday from 8.40 am to 12.20 pm and from 1.35 to 6 pm, and on Saturday from 8.45 am to noon.

Post The main post office is on Rue Gambetta, and is open weekdays from 8 am to 7 pm and Saturday until noon.

Cathédrale de Sainte-Marie

This magnificent cathedral so impressed Napoleon II when he visited Auch in 1808 he said 'A cathedral like this should be put in a museum!' Built by the Counts of Armagnac over a period of four centuries, the cathedral demonstrates an astonishing variety of architectural styles. Other remarkable features include the Renaissance choir stalls with over 1500 oak carvings and the 16th century stained-glass windows surrounding the choir, which depict Biblical scenes.

Musée des Jacobins

Auch's main museum (☎ 05 62 05 74 79) is housed in a 17th century monastery at 4 Place Louis Blanc, and is considered one of the best (if not a little unconventional) provincial museums in France. From April to October it is open daily, except Monday and holidays, from 10 am to noon and from 2 to 6 pm (5 pm from November to March), and costs 15FF (10FF for students and children).

Escalier Monumental

Just off Ave Sadi-Carnot is the elegant, 370-step Escalier Monumental (Monumental Stairway), built in the 1860s. At the base is a statue of d'Artagnan, a famous Gascon hero immortalised by the novelist Alexandre Dumas in *Les Trois Mousquetaires* (The Three Musketeers). Nearby (and worth exploring if you have the stamina) are a series of narrow, stepped alleyways also descending to the river, collectively called Les Pousterles.

Places to Stay

Right by the train station in the lower part of town, ***Hôtel de Paris*** (☎ 05 62 63 26 22; fax 05 62 60 04 27), 38 Ave de la Marne, has singles/doubles with shower from 230/250FF. It is closed in November.

In the upper part of town at 7 Rue Espagne, ***Hôtel Les 3 Mousquetaires*** (☎ 05 62 05 13 25) is open all year and has singles/doubles/triples from 130/150/230FF (190/210/260 with shower). Hall showers are free. ***Hôtel de France*** (☎ 05 62 61 71 71; fax 05 62 61 71 81), 2 Place de la Libération, is open all year, with singles/doubles from 295/265FF, and a popular restaurant (see Places to Eat).

Places to Eat

Restaurants The popular brasserie-style ***Restaurant Claude Laffitte*** (☎ 05 62 05 04 18), 38 Rue Dessoles, specialises in regional dishes, with a good lunch *menu* for 100FF and a plat du jour for 75FF. Away from the main shopping precinct and less well known, ***Restaurant La Table d'Hotes*** also serves Gascon specialities with *menus* at 60, 90 and 145FF.

Restaurant Le IXe (☎ 05 62 61 71 99), attached to the Hôtel de France (see Places to Stay), has a small terrace and *menus* at 79 and 100FF. Near the cathedral at 3 Rue Arnaud de Moles, ***L'Asie*** (☎ 05 62 05 93 17) is open daily (except Monday) and offers a huge choice of unpretentious Asian dishes from 26 to 50FF.

Self-Catering The small ***Spar*** supermarket at 4 Place Denfert Rochereau is open Monday to Friday from 8.30 am to 8 pm, and from 9 am to 1 pm on weekends .

Getting There & Away

Bus Auch's bus station is in the upper part of town between Place de la Libération and Place du Foirail. There is an SNCF bus service to Tarbes (67FF; 2 hours; three to five a day).

Train The train station (☎ 08 36 35 35 35) is in the lower part of town on Ave Pierre Mendes-France. There are direct trains to Toulouse (71FF; 1½ hours; five to eight a day) and Agen (59FF; one to 1½ hours; six to eight a day by train and/or bus).

CONDOM

• pop 8070 ✉ 32100

The only reason some tourists stop here is to take a photo beside the sign, *Bienvenue à Condom, Ville Propre* (Welcome to Condom, the Clean Town; see the boxed text 'What's in a Name?'). But this small, sleepy town in the heart of Armagnac country is well worth a visit for its Renaissance mansion, and its cathedral.

Condom also makes an ideal base for touring the sights and vineyards of Gascony.

Information

Tourist Office The town's small but accommodating tourist office (☎ 05 62 28 00 80) is on Place Bossuet, behind the cathedral. From November to April it's open Monday to Saturday from 9 am to noon and from 2 to 6 pm. In May, June, September and October, it is open Monday to Saturday from 9 am to 12.30 pm and from 2 to 6.30 pm; and in July and August it is open daily from 10 am to 1 pm and from 2.30 to 7.30 pm.

Money There are several banks by the cathedral in Place Saint-Pierre. There's also a Caisse d'Épargne at No 1, which has a 24 hour ATM. Banks are open weekdays only.

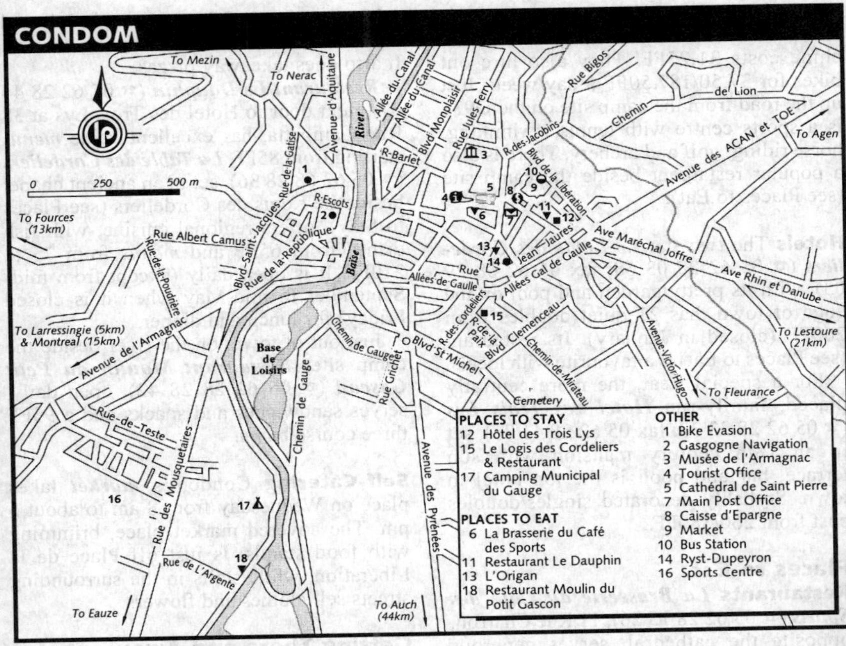

Things to See & Do

The 14th to 16th century **Cathédral de Saint Pierre**, an excellent example of southern Flamboyant Gothic architecture, still contains some of its original stained glass and is worth a look.

Nearby at Rue Jules Ferry, the **Musée de l'Armagnac** (☎ 05 62 28 31 41), housed in the former episcopal stables, provides an insight into the old-fashioned way of producing Armagnac, the finest of French brandies. **Ryst-Dupeyron** (☎ 05 62 28 08 08), on the corner of Rue Daunou and Rue Jean Jaurès, is just one of several Armagnac producers offering free guided tours of their cellars and contemporary production processes. From June to September it's open Monday to Friday from 9 am to noon and 2 to 5 pm, Saturday from 10 am to noon and 2 to 7 pm; it's possible to visit all year-round if you phone ahead.

River Cruise Gasgogne Navigation (☎ 05 62 28 46 46) organises daily, except Sunday, boat trips (1½ hours) from Condom up the Baïse River. Cruises leave at 3 and 4 pm in July and August and cost 45/35FF for adults/children. You can also hire small motor boats (for up to 8 people) for 150/350/500FF per hour/half-day/day.

Special Events

The International Folklore Festival of Gascony and a series of classical concerts called *Nuits Musicales* take place during the first two weeks of July.

Places to Stay

Camping The peaceful, three star ***Camping Municipal de Gauge*** (☎ 05 62 28 17 32; fax 05 62 28 48 32), beside a lock on the Baïse River, is just 1km out of town and clearly signed off the D931 to Eauze. It costs 18.75/17.50/7.50FF per night for a tent/adult/child. Use of the washing machine costs 31.25FF. They also hire out bikes for 37.50/187.50FF a day/week. Just up the road from the camp site on the D931 is a sports centre with tennis, swimming, horse riding, golf and archery. There is also a popular restaurant beside the camp site (see Places to Eat).

Hotels The two star ***Le Logis des Cordeliers*** (☎ 05 62 28 03 68; fax 05 62 68 29 03), with its pretty garden and pool on the edge of town, has 21 quiet doubles from 260FF (closed in January). Its restaurant (see Places to Eat) is a favourite with locals.

For a special treat, the more centrally placed, family-run ***Hotel des Trois Lys*** (☎ 05 62 28 33 33; fax 05 62 28 41 85), set in an 18th century mansion with sun terrace, bar and pool, is the top hotel in town. Stylishly decorated singles/doubles cost from 260/380FF.

Places to Eat

Restaurants ***La Brasserie du Café des Sports*** (☎ 05 62 28 15 26), 11 Rue Charron, opposite the cathedral, serves generous salads and cheap snacks daily from noon until 7.30 pm. Nearby at 4 Rue Cadéot, ***L'Origan*** (☎ 05 62 68 24 84), opposite the school, is a rustic restaurant serving generous pizzas and pasta dishes from 39FF. It is open Tuesday to Saturday from noon to 1.30 pm and from 7.30 to 11 pm; in July and August it's open Monday evening as well. It also does takeaway pizzas.

Restaurant Le Dauphin (☎ 05 62 28 44 67), next door to Hotel des Trois Lys at 38 Rue Gambetta, has excellent value *menus* starting from 85FF. ***La Table des Cordeliers*** (☎ 05 62 68 28 36), set in an ancient chapel beside Le Logis des Cordeliers (see Places to Stay), offers regional cuisine, with fish dishes from 65FF and *menus* from 75 to 210FF. It is open daily (except from mid-September to mid-May when it is closed Friday) for lunch and dinner.

Just out of town, on the river beside the camp site, ***Restaurant Moulin du Petit Gascon*** (☎ 05 62 28 28 42), open daily, serves sandwiches and snacks and a 95FF three course *menu*.

Self-Catering Condom's ***market*** takes place on Wednesday from 8 am to about 5 pm. The covered market place, brimming with food stands, is just off Place de la Libération, while stalls in the surrounding streets sell clothes and flowers.

Getting There and Away

ATR buses (☎ 05 62 05 46 24) operate a daily (except Sunday and holidays) bus service from Toulouse via Auch to Condom at 4.15 pm. The journey takes 2¼ hours. Return buses leave the bus station on Blvd de la Libération at 6.45 am, arriving in

What's in a Name?

Nobody seems to know where the name 'Condom' originated, and local people have been slow to realise the tourist potential of their small town, quite simply because the word 'condom' does not mean the same in French as in English. (In France a contraceptive sheath is a *preservatif*). Now, tired of endless jokes by English-speaking visitors, the people of Condom have decided to cash in on its notoriety.

Soon visitors to Condom will be able to buy some most unusual souvenirs – special chocolates with a hard chocolate exterior and a creamy fig-flavoured filling called *Le Bonheur de Condom* (Condom Happiness; the fig is a Mediterranean symbol of female sexuality) and Armagnac-flavoured condoms, among other things. And there are also plans to open a *Musée des Préservatifs* by the year 2000.

Toulouse at 9.15 am. There are also two or three buses a day to Agen and Bordeaux.

Citram Pyrénées (☎ 05 59 27 22 22) also has a weekday bus to Pau (2½ hours) at 11.15 am and on weekends at 9.10. A return bus leaves at 5.15 pm Monday to Saturday, and at 3 pm on Sunday.

Getting Around

Bicycle Bike Evasion (☎ 05 62 28 00 47), 14 Blvd St Jacques, rents bikes for 50/70/120FF per half-day/day/weekend (30/50/90FF for children). It is open Tuesday to Saturday from 9 am to noon and 2 to 6 pm. The camp site also rents out bikes (see Places to Stay).

AROUND CONDOM

Condom is ideally placed for exploring the surrounding Armagnac countryside and its countless attractive villages. However, there are no buses so you will need to have a bike (see Getting Around in Condom) or a car.

Fourcès

Fourcès is a picturesque bastide on the Auzoue River, 13km north-west of Condom. It follows a highly unusual circular plan, with well restored, medieval houses ringing its tree-shaded main square. It lies at the heart of Armagnac country, and the village prayer tellingly reads: 'O Lord, give me good health, for a long time; love from time to time; work, not much of the time; and Armagnac all the time'.

Special Events The Marché aux Fleurs (Flower Market), on the last weekend of April, always attracts thousands of visitors.

Places to Eat The recently renovated ***L'Auberge*** (☎ 05 62 29 49 53), in the main square, is a great place to enjoy a drink and a light snack. Lunch/dinner *menus* start from 85FF/105FF. It is open daily, except Wednesday evening, from noon to 2 pm and from 7 to 10 pm.

Larressingle

Often nicknamed 'the Carcassonne of the Gers', this 13th century fortified village 5km west of Condom bears testimony to the troubled times of medieval Gascony, a country ravaged by political unrest and Anglo-French discord. Its sturdy church dates from the 6th century, while the traditional Gascon-style castle, once the principal residence of the bishops of Condom, was constructed in the 16th century. There is also a rather poor medieval museum (☎ 05 62 28 11 58), which costs 18/10FF per adult/child, a small crêperie and a couple of craft shops within the walls of this tiny settlement.

Montréal

Montréal was one of the very first bastides in Gascony, founded in 1289, although the site was occupied as early as Celtic times. It contains a massive church and an attractive arcaded main square, scene of a bustling Friday market. However, its real treasure is the Roman villa of Séviac, just south of the town. Discovered only in 1961, it has now been completely excavated. Entry costs 15FF. The most impressive ruins include the baths, pool and some spectacular mosaics. Look out also for two 6th century skeletons, nicknamed *Les Amants* (The Lovers). Other finds from the villa can be seen in a small museum attached to the Montréal tourist office (☎ 05 62 29 42 85) in Place de la Mairie. Entry costs 2.50FF or, combined with a ticket to Séviac, for 12FF.

Places to Stay & Eat The ***Hôtel de la Gare*** (☎ 05 62 29 43 37; fax 05 62 29 49 82), just south of town on the Route d'Eauze (D29), was once the local train station. It now has basic rooms from 190FF, and good value set *menus* at 68, 98 and 160FF. There is rail memorabilia everywhere and even the occasional recorded train noise.

La Romieu

The ancient walled town of La Romieu, takes its name from the pilgrims or *roumieu* (an old local dialect) as they used to be called in the Middle Ages, when it was a stopover on the way to Santiago de Compostella in Spain. The 13th century collegiate church dominates the village. For guided tours call the tourist office (☎ 05 62 28 86 33). On the edge of town at La Bordette the Arboretum Coursiana (☎ 05 62 68 22 80) has over 600 species of trees and rare plants. Entry costs 25FF or 35FF for a guided tour (from April to November).

Lectoure

• pop 4000 ✉ 32700 alt 110m

Lectoure's main claim to fame is its **Musée Lapidaire** (☎ 05 62 68 70 22) in the cellars of the former episcopal palace, which today houses the mairie. The collection began a century ago, following the discovery of several Gallo-Roman altar-shaped *tauroboles* (funeral monuments), decorated with bulls' heads, beneath the cathedral. There is also some fine Roman jewellery, mosaics and an early Christian marble sarcophagus carved with vine leaves. Entrance costs 15FF.

The massive **Cathédrale Saint Gervais et Saint Protais** dates from the 15th century. From the top of the tower on a clear day, you can see most of Gascony and as far as the Pyrenees.

Information The tourist office (☎ 05 62 68 76 98) is on Rue Nationale beside the cathedral. It's open Monday to Friday from 8.30 am to noon and 2 to 6 pm, and mornings only on Saturday. In July and August it opens Monday to Saturday from 9 am to 12.30 pm and 2.30 to 7 pm, and Sunday from 9 am to 12.30 pm and 3 to 7 pm. It provides a useful free walking route of the town, which takes in all the main sights.

Places to Stay & Eat *Camping Lac des Trois Vallées* (☎ 05 62 68 82 33; fax 05 62 68 88 82), just south of the centre, is pricey at 114FF per night (for one, two or three people). However, it does have exceptional facilities, including a huge lake, pool, open-air cinema, tennis, mini-golf and archery. You can also go windsurfing, kayaking or hire *pédalo* (aquatic bike).

Hotels The two star ***Hôtel-Restaurant de Bastard*** (☎ 05 62 68 82 44; fax 05 62 68 76 81), Rue Lagrange, has 28 comfortable doubles from 250FF and set *menus* in its vaulted dining room from 88FF. There is also a pool for guests.

The tourist office also has a list of ***chambres d'hôtes***.

Getting There & Away SNCF buses (☎ 08 36 35 35 35) run a regular service between Agen and Auch, stopping at Lectoure, with eight buses Monday to Friday, five on Saturday and seven on Sunday. Ask at the tourist office for a timetable.

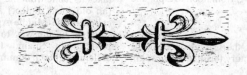

Andorra

The Catalan-speaking principality of Andorra, whose mountainous territory comprises only 468 sq km, is nestled between France and Spain in the middle of the Pyrenees. Though it is tiny, this political anomaly contains some of the most dramatic scenery in south-western Europe. You will never forget the drive from France over Port d'Envalira (2408m), the highest pass in the Pyrenees.

More remote parts of the principality are equally spectacular and remain relatively unspoiled by the overdevelopment and motor traffic that plagues Andorra's towns. There's relatively little of cultural or historical importance, with the exception of a number of Romanesque-style parish churches and some simple but quite elegant stone bridges.

HIGHLIGHTS

- **Skiing** – ski some of the most spectacular slopes in the Pyrenees
- **Shopping** – there's loads of shops and no VAT in Andorra
- **Other Activities** – go hiking, hang-gliding or horse riding in the mountains

escalivada – a roasted salad of peppers, onions, aubergine, garlic etc

escudella – a thick stew-like soup

cromer catalanon – a dessert

Facts about Andorra

HISTORY

By tradition, Andorra's independence is credited to Charlemagne, who captured the region from the Muslims in 803. It was Charlemagne's son Louis I (Louis the Pious) who presented the area's inhabitants with a charter of liberties.

The earliest known document concerning Andorra (Andorre in French) is an order from Charlemagne's grandson Charles II (Charles the Bald) that granted the Valls d'Andorra (Valleys of Andorra) to Sunifred, Count of Urgell, in 843. The Act of Consecration for the cathedral in the nearby Spanish town of La Seu d'Urgell, which dates from around 860, mentions Andorra's parishes as part of the territory of the Count of Urgell.

The country's first constitutional documents, the Pareatges (Acts of Joint Overlordship) of 1278 and 1288, were drawn up to settle conflicting claims of seigniorial rights made by the Spanish Bishop of Urgell and the Count of Foix in France. These feudal agreements, under which the bishop and the count agreed to share sovereignty, form the basis of Andorra's government to this day and are thus among the oldest such documents still in force. The Pareatges ended up creating a peculiar political equilibrium that has saved

Andorra from being swallowed up by its powerful neighbours and thus sharing the fate of all but a handful of Europe's medieval principalities, earldoms and duchies.

Over the centuries, there have been numerous periods of tension between the co-princes as well as conflicts of interest between the powers they represent. After the Revolution, France, inheritor of the lands and prerogatives of the Count of Foix, abolished all feudal rights, including the role of the French head of state in Andorran affairs. However, in 1806, at the request of the Andorrans (who feared Spanish hegemony), it was reinstated by Napoleon. Andorra remained neutral during WWI, the Spanish Civil War and WWII.

GEOGRAPHY

Situated on the southern slopes of the Pyrenees, Andorra measures 25km from north to south and 29km from east to west. Most of its 40 or so towns and hamlets (some with just a few dozen people) are situated in a group of mountain valleys whose streams join to form the country's main river, the Gran Valira, created near the capital, Andorra la Vella, by the confluence of the Valira del Orient and the Valira del Nord.

Pic de Coma Pedrosa (2942m), in western Andorra, is the principality's highest mountain. The lowest point, which is on the Spanish frontier at La Farga de Moles, is 838m above sea level. Andorra's mountain peaks remain snowcapped until early July or even later.

GOVERNMENT & POLITICS

For the seven centuries preceding 1993, Andorra had a unique form of government known as a 'co-principality' with its sovereignty vested in two 'princes': the president of the French Republic, who inherited the job from France's pre-Revolutionary kings, and the Catholic bishop of La Seu d'Urgell (Seo de Urgel) in Spain. The Bishop of Urgell is the last Catholic bishop – other than the Pope – who retains temporal powers.

In March 1993, about 75% of the 9123 native Andorrans who were eligible to vote (less than one-sixth of the population) cast ballots in a constitutional referendum that established Andorra as an independent, democratic 'parliamentary co-principality'. Under the new constitution, which placed full sovereignty in the hands of the Andorran people, the French and Spanish co-princes continue to function as joint heads with much reduced powers (though you'll still see portraits of Jacques Chirac and the Bishop of Urgell in public buildings everywhere). The constitution also provided for separate legislative, executive and judicial branches; gave the government the power to raise revenue through income tax; and allowed Andorran citizens to form trade unions and political parties. In 1994 Andorra became the 33rd member state of the Council of Europe.

For administrative purposes, Andorra is divided into seven parishes (*parròquies* in Catalan).

ECONOMY

The Andorran economy is based on duty-free shopping, tourism (eight million people pass through the principality every year) and banking. The most important components of the agricultural sector, which makes up only 1.2% of total economic activity, are the growing of tobacco and cattle-raising. The government has a very considerable operating deficit.

POPULATION & PEOPLE

Only about one-quarter of Andorra's 65,000 inhabitants (most of whom live in Andorra la Vella) are Andorran nationals. The rest are Spaniards (27,000), French (4000), Portuguese (4000) and others.

LANGUAGE

The official language is Catalan (Català), a Romance language most closely related to Provençal but with roots in Castilian Spanish and, to a lesser degree, French. Local lore has it that everyone in Andorra speaks Catalan, Spanish and French, but there are plenty of people who can't understand more than 10 words of French. Very few people speak English.

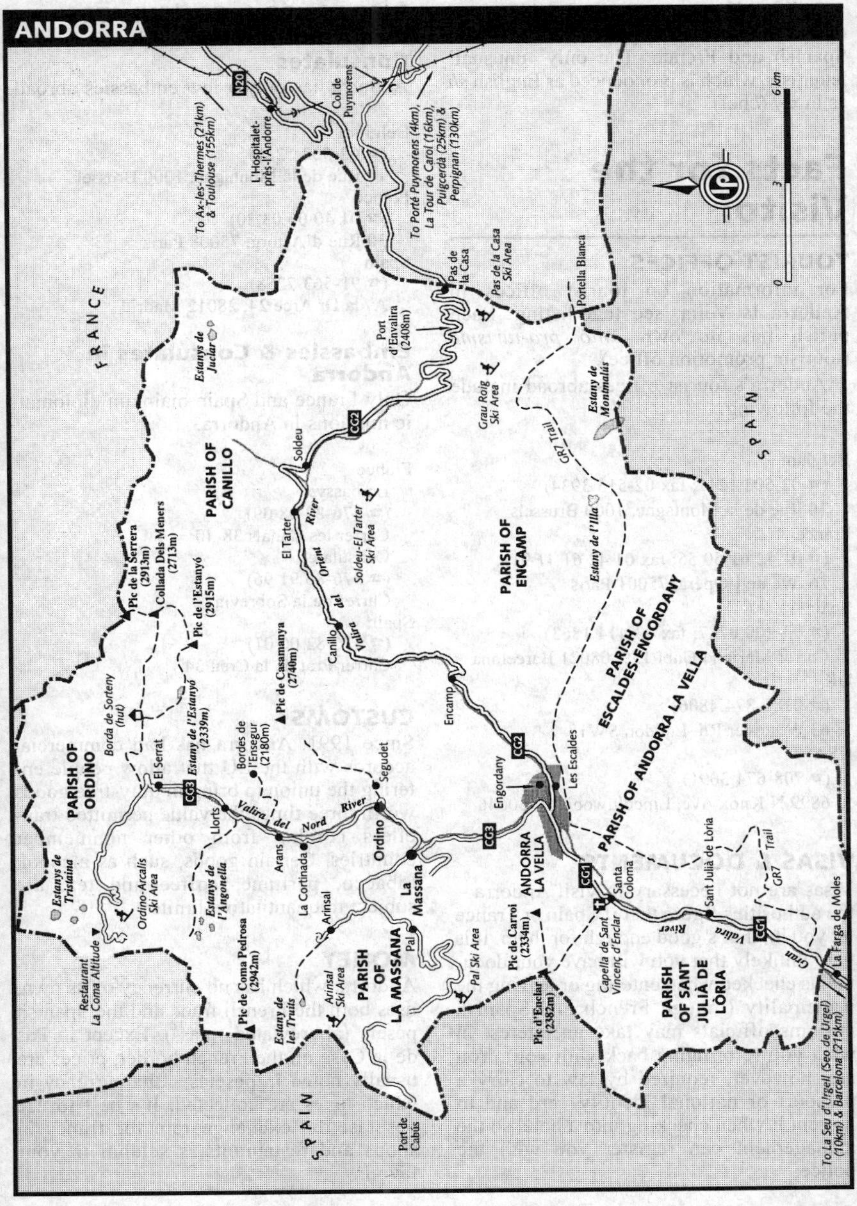
ANDORRA
FRANCE
SPAIN
SPAIN
SPAIN
PARISH OF ORDINO
PARISH OF CANILLO
PARISH OF ENCAMP
PARISH OF ESCALDES-ENGORDANY
PARISH OF ANDORRA LA VELLA
PARISH OF LA MASSANA
PARISH OF SANT JULIÀ DE LÒRIA
ANDORRA LA VELLA
To Ax-les-Thermes (21km) & Toulouse (155km)
N20
L'Hospitalet-près-l'Andorre
Col de Puymorens
To Porté Puymorens (4km), La Tour de Carol (16km), Puigcerdà (25km) & Perpignan (130km)
Pas de la Casa
Pas de la Casa Ski Area
Portella Blanca
Port d'Envalira (2408m)
Estanys de Juclar
Grau Roig Ski Area
Estany de Montmalús
GR7 Trail
CG2
Soldeu
El Tarter
Soldeu-El Tarter Ski Area
Orient River
Valira del
Canillo
Estany de l'Illa
Pic de la Serrera (2913m)
Collada Dels Meners (2713m)
Pic de l'Estanyó (2915m)
Pic de Casamanya (2740m)
Borda de Sorteny (hut)
Estany de l'Estanyó (2339m)
Bordes de l'Ensegur (2180m)
El Serrat
CG3
Llorts
Valira del Nord River
Arans
La Cortinada
Segudet
Ordino
Encamp
Engordany
Les Escaldes
La Massana
Arinsal
Pal
Estanys de Tristaina
Ordino-Arcalís Ski Area
Estanys de l'Angonella
Restaurant La Coma Altitude
Pic de Coma Pedrosa (2942m)
Estany de les Truits
Arinsal Ski Area
Pal Ski Area
Pic de Carroi (2334m)
Pic d'Enclar (2382m)
Capella de Sant Vicenç d'Enclar
Santa Coloma
CG1
Sant Julià de Lòria
GR7 Trail
Gran Valira River
La Farga de Moles
Port de Cabús
To La Seu d'Urgell (Seo de Urgel) (10km) & Barcelona (215km)
0
3
6 km

ANDORRA

Trilingual restaurant *cartes* provide a good opportunity to compare Catalan with Spanish and French. The only 'unusual' letter is *x*, which is pronounced as English *sh* as in *xef* (chef).

Facts for the Visitor

TOURIST OFFICES

For information on tourist offices in Andorra la Vella, see that listing. Each parish has its own *unió pro-turisme* (tourism promotion office).

Andorra's tourist offices abroad include the following:

Belgium
  (☎ 02-502 1211; fax 02-513 3934)
  10 Rue de la Montagne, 1000 Brussels
France
  (☎ 01 42 61 50 55; fax 01 42 61 41 91)
  26 Ave de l'Opéra, 75001 Paris
Spain
  (☎ 93-200 0787; fax 93-414 1863)
  Carrer Mariano Cubí 159, 08021 Barcelona
UK
  (☎ 0181-874 4806)
  63 Westover Rd, London SW18
USA
  (☎ 708-674 3091)
  6899 N Knox Ave, Lincolnwood, IL 60646

VISAS & DOCUMENTS

Visas are not necessary to visit Andorra – the authorities figure that if Spain or France let you in, that's good enough for them. It is very unlikely that you will have your documents checked when entering or leaving the principality (though French and Spanish customs officials may take an interest in what you're bringing back with you). You are, however, required by law to carry a passport or national identity card and to present it when checking into a hotel so the management can register you with the police.

EMBASSIES & CONSULATES

Andorran Embassies & Consulates

Andorra has only a few embassies abroad.

Belgium
  (☎ 02-502 1211)
  10 Rue de la Montagne, 1000 Brussels
France
  (☎ 01 40 06 03 30)
  30 Rue d'Astorg, 75008 Paris
Spain
  (☎ 91-563 7258)
  Avda Dr Arce 24, 28012 Madrid

Embassies & Consulates in Andorra

Only France and Spain maintain diplomatic missions in Andorra.

France
  Embassy:
  (☎ 376-82 08 09)
  Carrer les Canals 38-40
  Consulate:
  (☎ 376-86 91 96)
  Carrer de la Sobrevia
Spain
  (☎ 376-82 00 01)
  Carrer Prat de la Creu 34

CUSTOMS

Since 1991, Andorra has had commercial accords with the EU that allow people entering the union to bring in duty-free goods worth three times the value permitted travellers coming from other nonmember countries. Certain goods, such as alcohol, tobacco, perfume, coffee and tea, are subject to quantitative limits.

MONEY

Andorra, which has no currency of its own, uses both the French franc and the Spanish peseta (abbreviated 'ptas'). Except in Pas de la Casa on the French border, prices are usually noted in pesetas – the currency in which taxes are collected. It's best to use pesetas: the exchange rate for francs in shops and restaurants is seldom in your favour.

Exchange Rates

country	unit		franc		peseta
Australia	A$1	=	3.70FF	=	93.2 pta
Canada	C$1	=	4.10FF	=	103.3 pta
euro	€1	=	6.60FF	=	166.3 pta
Germany	DM1	=	3.35FF	=	84.4 pta
Japan	¥100	=	4.30FF	=	108.4 pta
New Zealand	NZ$1	=	3.15FF	=	79.3 pta
UK	UK£1	=	9.80FF	=	246.9 pta
USA	US$1	=	6FF	=	151.2 pta

POST & COMMUNICATIONS

Post

Andorra has no post office of its own: France and Spain operate separate postal systems with their own Andorran stamps. Those printed, issued and sold by La Poste (France) are in francs, while the Spanish ones are in pesetas. Andorran stamps of both types are valid only for items posted within Andorra and are necessary only for international mail – letters mailed to destinations within the country are free and do not need stamps.

International postal rates are the same as those of the issuing country, with the French tariffs slightly cheaper. Andorrans say that you are better off routing all international mail (except letters to Spain) through the French postal system. There are two kinds of postboxes, but should you use the wrong one your letter will be transferred.

Letters to Andorra la Vella marked 'poste restante' are sent to the town's French post office (see Post under Information in the Andorra la Vella section). There's a charge of about 3FF for each letter that you pick up.

Telephone

International Andorra's telephone country code is ☎ 376. To call Andorra from France, dial 00 (the French international access code) followed by 376 and the six-digit local number, all of which begin with 8. From Spain, dial 07-376 before the six-digit number. To call Andorra from other countries, dial the international access code, then 376 and the local number.

To call France from Andorra, dial 00-33 and then the 10-digit local number. To call Spain, dial 00-34 followed by the regional prefix and the local number. To call other countries, dial 00 and then the country code, area code and local number. Directory assistance is available on ☎ 111; operators speak Catalan, Spanish and French. The international operator can be reached by dialling ☎ 821 111. To France and Spain, telephone rates are 50% cheaper between 10 pm and 8 am and all day on Sunday and holidays. Reverse-charge (collect) calling is not available from Andorra.

Public Telephones Public telephones take pesetas (francs in Pas de la Casa) or an Andorran *teletarja* (telephone card). Cards with 50 and 100 units can be purchased at post offices, tobacconists and tourist offices for 500 and 900 ptas and there's also a 150 unit teletarja (1350 ptas). One unit is good for a local call of about three minutes and far less for an international one.

TIME

Andorra, just like France and Spain, is one hour ahead of GMT/UTC. During summer time (daylight saving time) it is two hours ahead of GMT/UTC.

ELECTRICITY

The electric current is either 220V or 125V, both at 50Hz.

USEFUL ORGANISATIONS

For weather information, call ☎ 84 88 53 (French), ☎ 84 88 52 (Spanish) or ☎ 84 88 51 (Catalan). Ring ☎ 85 56 74 for information about road conditions.

DANGERS & ANNOYANCES

The attitude of the Andorran government towards pretty much everything can be described as laissez-faire, which makes for cheap shopping but some minor hassles. Unlike France, the country's minimal legislation to protect the consumer often remains unenforced, so that hotels (unclassified by any star-rating system) and petrol stations sometimes neglect to post their prices, and restaurants are free to refuse to serve tap water with meals.

The road system is underdeveloped and inadequate, leading to traffic chaos amidst the unsightly buildings erected with very little regard for aesthetics in the towns.

Emergency telephone numbers include:

Police	☎ 110
Medical emergency	☎ 116
Fire or ambulance	☎ 118
Mountain rescue service	☎ 444
Car assistance & towing	☎ 86 99 86

BUSINESS HOURS

Most small stores and banks take a siesta between 1 and 3 or 4 pm.

ACTIVITIES

Skiing

Andorra has the best inexpensive skiing and snowboarding in the Pyrenees. For more detailed information on the principality's five *estaciós d'esquí* (downhill ski areas), all of which are covered in this chapter, inquire at one of the capital's two tourist offices or contact Ski Andorra (☎ 86 43 89; fax 86 59 10) at Avinguda Carlemany 65 in Les Escaldes.

Pas de la Casa-Grau Roig, which has about 30 lifts, is on the Franco-Andorran border a bit south of Port d'Envalira. Pas de la Casa lies on the eastern slopes of the col, while Grau Roig is on the western side. Soldeu-El Tarter is midway between Port d'Envalira and Canillo. The two resorts of Arinsal and Pal are in the west of the country in the parish of La Massana. Ordino-Arcalís is in the Parish of Ordino, north-west of Andorra la Vella.

Pas de la Casa-Grau Roig and Soldeu-El Tarter are the best resorts because of their sizes, higher elevations and many lifts, but they are more expensive than the smaller ones. The skiing is mainly good for beginners and intermediates, with little of interest for experts. The ski season normally lasts from December to April, depending on snow conditions, which in the last decade have not been reliable. All the Andorran resorts have snow-making machines for their major trails.

Hiking

The tranquillity of Andorra's beautiful and relatively unspoiled back country begins only a few hundred metres from the bazaar-like bustle of the towns. The country's north-west region (see the Parish of Ordino section) has some especially nice areas for hiking. All told, Andorra has over 50 lakes hidden among its soaring mountains.

The GR11 trail, which traverses the Pyrenees from the Mediterranean to the Atlantic, passes through the southern part of Andorra and has a number of variations. The GR7 also passes through the principality. Hikers can sleep for free in the *refugis* or shelters (see Accommodation). A 1:50,000 scale *mapa topogràfic* of the country called *Les Valls d'Andorra* costs 565 ptas in bookshops. Maps of individual parishes in 1:10,000 scale (275 ptas) are also available.

Tourist offices have a number of useful publications in English including one called *Sport Activities*, which contains 52 recommended walking tours and seven mountain bike itineraries, each with a small map, as well as useful information on horse riding, rock climbing, white-water rafting, canoeing and fishing.

ACCOMMODATION

Almost all of Andorra's hotels stay open year-round. They are fullest in July and August and from December to March, but since the turnover is high (except in winter), as most people stay just long enough to do a bit of shopping, rooms are almost always available in the morning. The use of hall showers is included in the price of the room. Many smaller hotels have no-one on the staff who speaks English or even French, so it may prove difficult to make reservations by telephone if you don't know Catalan or Spanish.

There are no hostels in Andorra. The 26 unstaffed *refugis* – mountain huts for the use of both shepherds and hikers (one room for each) – are free and do not require reservations.

Most have bunks, fireplaces and sources of potable water but no cooking facilities. Tourist offices have brochures and maps indicating the location of the shelters.

Tourist offices can also provide information on apartments and *xalets* (chalets) available for short-term rental.

SHOPPING

Because customs duties and excise taxes are very low and there's no value-added tax (VAT), Andorra has become famous as a duty-free bazaar for electronics, photographic equipment, alcohol, cigarettes, perfume, leather goods, designer clothing, luxury foods, running shoes, toys etc. If you know exactly what you're looking for, you can probably find it (or something similar from among last year's models). But if you don't know what you want, Andorra is not such a great place to shop around since most places sell a little bit of everything (a few car radios, some watches etc), and salespeople know very little about the merchandise on offer and usually can't produce more than a few roughly similar models for comparison.

Getting There & Away

AIR

The major airports nearest Andorra are those in Toulouse (180km to the north), Perpignan (166km to the east) and Barcelona (225km to the south). Viatges Relax, the American Express agent in Andorra la Vella (see Money in that section), runs minibuses between the Andorran capital and the airport in Barcelona daily at 5 and 8 am (4500 ptas one way). It returns to Andorra la Vella at 1 and 5 pm.

LAND

Short-Haul Bus

Societat Franco-Andorrana de Transports and its sister company, La Hispano Andorrana (☎ 82 13 72 for both), link Andorra la Vella and other Andorran towns to destinations just over the border in France and Spain. The company's main office is in Andorra la Vella at Avinguda Santa Coloma 85-87, west of the centre, but it is easier to seek information from the municipal tourist office (see Information under Andorra la Vella), which posts schedules and fares.

Both companies' buses stop at Plaça Guillemó in Andorra la Vella. Tickets are sold on board. When Col d'Envalira is closed because of snow, buses are rerouted via La Tour de Carol.

To/From France Buses run from Andorra la Vella to L'Hospitalet-près-l'Andorre (925 ptas; 2½ hours), the train station closest to Andorra, via the 2408m-high Port d'Envalira. They leave Andorra la Vella daily year-round at 5.45 am and 5 pm, with an extra run from July to September at 1.30 pm. Buses from L'Hospitalet to Andorra depart at 7.35 am and 7.45 pm (and 6.30 pm between July and September).

From mid-May to mid-October there is a daily service to/from Ax-les-Thermes (1125 ptas; 2½ to 3¼ hours), another SNCF railhead. Buses to Ax-les-Thermes leave from Andorra la Vella at 8.15 am (and 11 am from mid-July to mid-September); departures from Ax-les-Thermes are at 4.20 pm (and noon in summer).

Autos Pujol Huguet (☎ 82 13 72), based in Sant Julià de Lòria, runs a bus daily at 7.15 am (and 2 pm from July to September) from Sant Julià de Lòria via Plaça Guillemó in Andorra la Vella to Pas de la Casa on the French border, Porté Puymorens and La Tour de Carol (1125 ptas; 2½ hours). La Tour de Carol, just across the border from the Spanish town of Puigcerdà, is served by trains from Toulouse, Perpignan and Barcelona. Buses from La Tour de Carol head for Andorra daily at 8 am (and 2 pm from July to September).

To/From Spain There are seven or eight daily runs (five or six on Sunday) between Andorra la Vella and La Seu d'Urgell (400 ptas; 30 minutes), which is about 10km south of the Andorran frontier. Buses leave

Andorra la Vella from Monday to Saturday at 8, 9.05 and 11.30 am and at 1.30, 4.05, 6 and 8.05 pm; all but the 8 am and 6 pm buses run on Sunday as well. From La Seu d'Urgell, buses depart from Monday to Saturday at 8 and 9.30 am and 12.15, 2, 3.20, 4.15 and 7.15 pm. On Sunday, the 3.20 pm bus does not operate.

For details on buses from La Seu d'Urgell to the Spanish railhead of Puigcerdà, see the following section.

Long-Haul Bus

Alsina Graells (☎ 82 73 79), at the bus station (*estació d' autobuses*) on Carrer Bonaventura Riberaygua in Andorra la Vella, links Andorra la Vella with Barcelona. The company also has buses from Puigcerdà (see To/From Spain under Train) to La Seu d'Urgell, from where it's a short bus ride to Andorra (see the earlier Short-Haul Bus section). The office is open each day from 9.30 am to 2.30 pm and 4.30 to 5 pm. Its Barcelona office (☎ 93-265 6866) is at Carrer Alí Bei 80 at Estació del Nord. It also has a bureau in La Seu d'Urgell (☎ 73-350 020) at Carrer Bisbe Benlloch 1.

Alsina Graells buses to Barcelona (2600 ptas) leave Andorra la Vella daily at 6 and 7 am and 2.30 and 5 pm. The trip takes 3¾ hours if you go via the Cadí Tunnel and four hours if you don't. Buses from Puigcerdà to La Seu d'Urgell (600 ptas; one hour) leave daily at 7.30 am and 2.30 and 5.30 pm; buses from La Seu d'Urgell to Puigcerdà depart at 9.30 am and 12.30 and 7 pm.

A number of other companies organised under Andor-Inter (☎ 82 62 89), which is based at the window next to Alsina Graells at the bus station, handle long-distance transport to Spain and south-eastern France. The office has extremely convoluted opening hours but is always closed on Friday.

Samar (☎ 82 62 89) runs a bus on Tuesday, Thursday and Sunday at 1 pm from Andorra southward to Saragossa (2200 ptas; five hours) and Madrid (4500 ptas; 8½ hours). The company's Madrid office (☎ 91-468 4190) is at Estación Sur Autobus, Calle Canarias 17. A Samar (☎ 6861 2654 or ☎ 6861 3111) bus heads from Andorra down the east coast of Spain to Murcia and Cartagena (3900 ptas; 11½ hours) on Saturday at 5 pm. The same company has a service to the French city of Toulouse (2500 ptas; 2½ hours) on Saturday at 8.30 am; a bus also goes from Toulouse to Andorra on Sunday at 8 am.

Autocars Fernàndez (☎ 82 78 10) goes to the Spanish Mediterranean port of Almería (8000 ptas; 17 hours) via Murcia on Monday and Thursday. Autocars Nadal (☎ 82 11 38) has weekly buses to a number of Spanish and French towns, including Perpignan (Sunday at 4 pm) in France. There is a special service for students only during school periods. The trip takes three hours and costs 2500 ptas. A bus leaves for Barcelona each day at 7 am and 2.30 pm. The trip takes 3½ hours and costs 2600 ptas.

For information on other bus services, consult the schedules posted at the municipal tourist office. For information on buses from Toulouse, see Getting There & Away for that city in the Toulouse Area chapter.

Train

There is no railway service within Andorra, but a number of train stations not far away in France and Spain are linked to the principality by bus.

To/From France Buses to Andorra operate from three train stations along SNCF's line from Toulouse to La Tour de Carol: L'Hospitalet (☎ 05 61 05 20 78; 102FF; two hours), which has daily bus links all year; Ax-les-Thermes (☎ 05 61 64 20 72; 90FF; 1½ hours), from where there are one or two buses a day from May to October; and La Tour de Carol (☎ 05 68 04 80 69; 112FF; 2½ hours), served by one or two buses a day. La Tour de Carol is linked to Perpignan (114FF; 3½ hours; six a day) via Villefranche by SNCF, and to Barcelona (55FF; three hours) via Puigcerdà by rather slow Spanish trains.

For information on getting from these railheads to Andorra, see the Short-Haul Bus listing.

To/From Spain The Spanish train station nearest Andorra is at Puigcerdà, which is 5km by rail south-east of La Tour de Carol in France. Puigcerdà – from where there are trains to Barcelona and, via La Tour de Carol, to Toulouse and Perpignan – is one hour by Alsina Graells bus from La Seu d'Urgell; for details, see the Long-Haul Bus listing. For information on getting to Andorra from La Tour de Carol and La Seu d'Urgell, see the Short-Haul Bus listing.

Car

By road, Andorra is 885km from Paris, 853km from Madrid, 464km from Nice, 225km from Barcelona, 180km from Toulouse and 166km from Perpignan. The drive into the principality from France over the 2408m Port d'Envalira is long and exhausting but full of mountain panoramas.

The Puymorens tunnel links the French towns of L'Hospitalet and Porta, bypassing Andorra altogether.

Petrol can be as much as 25% cheaper in Andorra than in France. There are a number of petrol stations between Port d'Envalira and Pas de la Casa so you can enter France with a full tank.

Getting Around

BUS

The Cooperativa Interurbana (☎ 82 04 12) is responsible for Andorra's eight bus lines. The front window of each of the company's red and white buses displays a sign listing the names of both the town where the bus started its run and the town where it will end up.

Buses from Les Escaldes to Sant Julià de Lòria (105 ptas) stop in Andorra la Vella near the Pyrénées department store, Avinguda Meritxell 21, and at Plaça Guillemó. Buses to La Massana (105 ptas) and Ordino (120 ptas) leave from the Plaça Príncep Benlloch stop, opposite 6 Avinguda Príncep Benlloch. Buses to Encamp (105 ptas) also leave from the Plaça Príncep Benlloch stop. All three lines operate daily every 30 minutes from 7 am (7.30 am on Sunday) to 9.30 pm (9 pm to Ordino).

Buses link Andorra la Vella with the neighbouring parish of Escaldes-Engordany (85 ptas) every 20 minutes from 8.30 am to 9.30 pm. There are buses to Canillo (215 ptas) and Soldeu (325 ptas), both in the Parish of Canillo, once an hour from 8 or 9 am to 8 pm. From Andorra la Vella there is one bus a day at 9 am to Pas de la Casa (560 ptas), up to three a day to El Serrat (215 ptas) in the Parish of Ordino, and three a day to Arinsal (Parish of La Massana; 175 ptas).

CAR

Andorra's road system consists of three main highways. The CG1 (CG stands for Carretera General) links Andorra la Vella with Sant Julià de Lòria and the Spanish border, from where it's another 10km to La Seu d'Urgell. The CG2 goes from Andorra la Vella via Les Escaldes, Encamp, Canillo, Soldeu, Port d'Envalira and Pas de la Casa to France. The CG3 begins in the capital and passes through La Massana, Ordino and Llorts on its way to the Ordino-Arcalís ski area.

The speed limit in populated areas is 40km/h. Because of road conditions (lots of twists and turns) it's almost impossible to reach the inter-hamlet speed limit of 90km/h. Andorra la Vella suffers from near gridlock traffic for much of the year. Using a seat belt is not mandatory but motorcycle helmets are.

Andorra la Vella

• **pop 21,731 alt 1010m**

Andorra la Vella (Vella, meaning 'old', is pronounced 'VEY-yah'), the capital of the principality and its largest town, is located in the Valira River valley. It is surrounded by mountains up to 2400m high. There is good transport by public bus from here to most parts of the principality.

The town is given over almost entirely to the retailing of duty-free electronics, jewellery and other luxury goods. With its mountains, constant din of jackhammers and 'mall' architecture, travellers familiar

ANDORRA LA VELLA

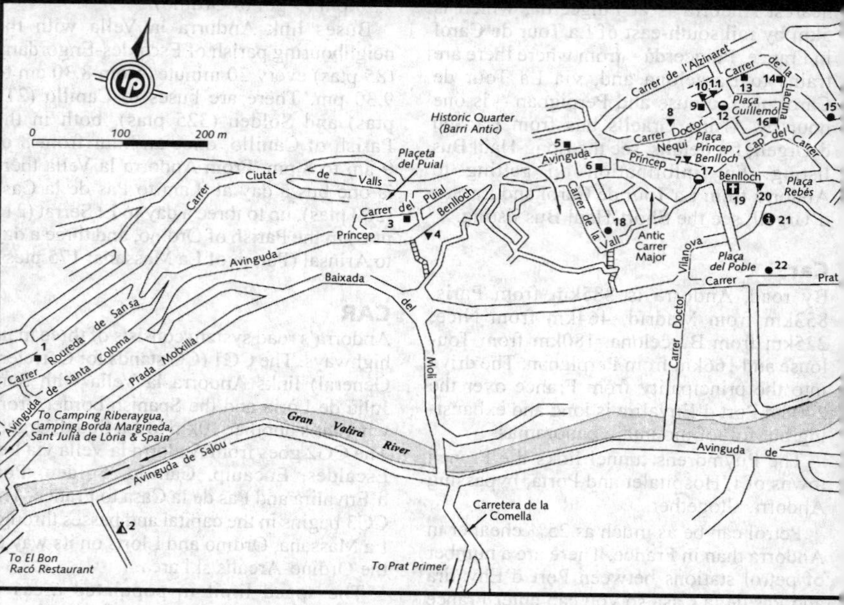

ANDORRA LA VELLA

PLACES TO STAY
1 Hotel Enclar
2 Camping Valira
3 Residència Baró
5 Hôtel Pyrénées
6 Pensió La Rosa
9 Hotel des Arcades
13 Residència Benazet
14 Hotel Florida
16 Hotel Festa Brava
28 Hotel Costa & Restaurant Martí
34 Hotel Residència Albert

PLACES TO EAT
4 Tex-Mex Café
7 Papanico
8 Pizzeria Primavera
10 La Cantina
11 Vilarrasa
20 Pans & Company
32 Pizzeria La Mossega

OTHER
12 Bus Stops
15 American Express/Viatges Relax
17 Bus Stop
18 Casa de la Vall
19 Església Parroquial de Sant Esteve
21 National Tourist Office
22 Public Lift
23 Spanish Embassy
24 Banc Internacional
25 Pyrénées Department Store & Supermarket
26 French Embassy
27 French Consulate
29 Police
30 Crèdit Andorrà
31 Tourist Office
33 Banca Reig
35 STA Telephone Office
36 Spanish Post Office
37 French Post Office
38 Bus Station

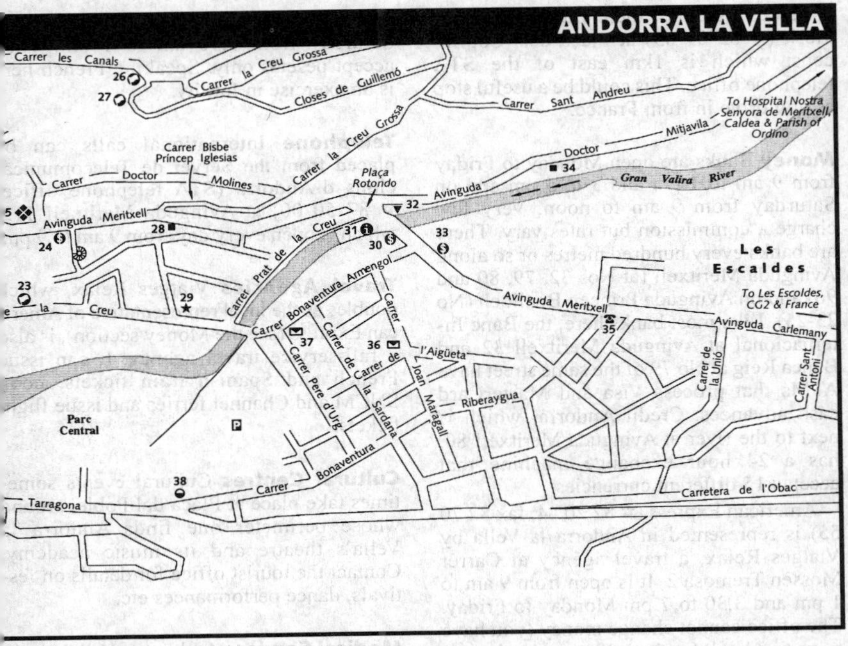

with Asia will be reminded of Hong Kong. The only differences seem to be the snow-capped peaks and the lack of noodle shops!

Orientation

Andorra la Vella is strung out along one main street, the name of which changes from Avinguda Meritxell to Avinguda Príncep Benlloch at Plaça Rebés. The Barri Antic (Historic Quarter) stretches from the Església Parroquial de Sant Esteve to Plaçeta del Puial. Many intercity buses stop at Plaça Guillemó.

The suburb of Santa Coloma is south-west of Andorra la Vella along Avinguda Príncep Benlloch, which becomes Avinguda de Santa Coloma and then the CG1 (the highway to Spain). The spa town of Les Escaldes is along the eastern extension of Avinguda Meritxell, Avinguda Carlemany, which turns into the CG2 (the highway to France).

Information

Tourist Offices The helpful municipal tourist office (*oficina de turisme*; ☎ 82 71 17) on Plaça Rotonda is open every day from 9 am to 1 pm and 2 to 8 pm (7 pm on Sunday). In July and August, it's open daily from 9 am to 9 pm (7 pm on Sunday). The office has maps, all sorts of brochures (including a useful one entitled *The Parish of Andorra la Vella*) and postage stamps and telephone cards for sale.

The national tourist office (*sindicat d'iniciativa*; ☎ 82 02 14; fax 82 58 23) is at the top of Carrer Doctor Vilanova between Plaça del Poble and Plaça Rebés. The office is open Monday to Saturday from 10 am (9 am from July to September) to 1 pm and 3 to 7 pm, and on Sunday morning.

ANDORRA

In Les Escaldes, there's a tourist office kiosk (☎ 82 09 63) at Plaça dels Coprínceps, which is 1km east of the STA telephone office. This could be a useful stop as you drive in from France.

Money Banks are open Monday to Friday from 9 am to 1 pm and 3 to 5 pm and on Saturday from 9 am to noon. Very few charge a commission but rates vary. There are banks every hundred metres or so along Avinguda Meritxell (at Nos 32, 79, 80 and 96) and on Avinguda Príncep Benlloch (No 23-25). Like most banks here, the Banc Internacional at Avinguda Meritxell 32 and Banca Reig at No 79 of the same street have ATMs that process Visa and MasterCard cash advances. Crèdit Andorrà, which is next to the river at Avinguda Meritxell 80, has a 24 hour exchange machine that accepts 15 different currencies.

American Express (☎ 82 20 44; fax 82 70 55) is represented in Andorra la Vella by Viatges Relax, a travel agency at Carrer Mossèn Tremosa 2. It is open from 9 am to 1 pm and 3.30 to 7 pm Monday to Friday. The office cannot change money (you have to go to a bank for that), but it can reissue a lost or stolen American Express card, provide a reimbursement for lost or stolen travellers cheques, cash personal cheques for American Express card holders (payment is made in travellers cheques, not cash) and receive poste restante mail. Reimbursements usually take less than an hour.

Post La Poste (☎ 82 04 08), the main French post office, is at Carrer Pere d'Urg 1. It is open weekdays from 8.30 am to 2.30 pm and on Saturday from 9 am to noon. In July and August, weekday hours are 9 am to 7 pm. All purchases must be made with French francs. No exchange operations are available. Poste restante mail is directed to this post office. Almost no-one here speaks Spanish.

Correus Espanyols (☎ 82 02 57), the main Spanish post office, is three blocks away at Carrer Joan Maragall 10. It is open weekdays from 8.30 am to 2.30 pm and o[n] Saturday from 9.30 am to 1 pm. The[y] accept pesetas only. Speaking French her[e] is an exercise in futility.

Telephone International calls can b[e] placed from the Servei de Telecomunica[cions] d'Andorra (STA telephone office ☎ 87 50 00) at Avinguda Meritxell 112 which is open every day from 9 am to 9 pm.

Travel Agencies Viatges Relax, which doubles as the local representative of American Express (see the Money section), is also a full-service travel agency. It can issue French and Spanish train tickets, book SNCM and Channel ferries and issue flight tickets.

Cultural Centres Cultural events sometimes take place at Plaça del Poble, around whose perimeter one finds Andorra la Vella's theatre and its music academy. Contact the tourist office for details on festivals, dance performances etc.

Medical Services Andorra la Vella's main medical centre is the modern Hospital Nostra Senyora de Meritxell (☎ 87 10 00), Avinguda Fiter i Rossell 1-13, which is about 1.5km east of Plaça Guillemó, just beyond Avinguda Doctor Mitjavila.

Emergency The main police station (*servei de policia/despatx central*; ☎ 82 12 22) is currently at Carrer Prat de la Creu 16, although it may have moved by the time you read this. The tourist office or your hotel reception should be able to inform you of any change of address.

Barri Antic

The Barri Antic was the heart of Andorra la Vella when the principality's capital was little more than a small Pyrenean village. The narrow cobblestone streets between Església Parroquial de Sant Esteve and Casa de la Vall and from there to Plaçeta del Puial are lined with stone houses.

ANDORRA

Casa de la Vall

The pride of the Barri Antic is Casa de la Vall (House of the Valley; ☎ 82 12 34), which has served as Andorra's parliament building since 1702. This three storey stone structure was built in 1580 as the private home of a wealthy family. The Andorran coat of arms featured over the door dates from 1761, and the monument in the plaça in front commemorates the constitution of 1993.

Downstairs is the **Sala de la Justicia**, the only courtroom in the whole country. Upstairs is the **Sala del Consell** (Council General Chamber). The 28 members of the Andorran parliament sit in the red chairs along the walls, the *consellers de govern* (appointed government councillors) sit in the blue ones, while the three red chairs at the far end of the room are for the two presiding officers and the parliamentary secretary. The **Set Panys** (Chest of the Seven Locks) once held Andorra's most important official documents and could only be opened if a key-bearing representative from each of the parishes was present.

Free, 30-minute guided tours of Casa de la Vall in Catalan, French, Spanish and sometimes English take place Monday to Saturday about every 30 minutes from 9.30 am to 1 pm and 3 to 7 pm. It is best to book ahead (☎ 82 91 29).

Plaça del Poble

This large public square occupies the roof of the Edifici Administratiu Govern d'Andorra, a modern government office building at Carrer Prat de la Creu 62-64 that also houses a number of Andorra la Vella's cultural institutions. It is a popular gathering place for local people, especially in the evenings. Various cultural events are held here. The lift in the south-east corner of Plaça del Poble takes you down to the carpark at 54-58 Carrer Prat de la Creu.

Caldea

Caldea (☎ 80 09 99), in the eastern suburb of Les Escaldes, is an enormous spa complex of pools, hot tubs and saunas fed by thermal springs and enclosed in what looks like a futuristic cathedral. Tickets (2500 ptas) are available from the tourist offices. Caldea is at Parc de la Mola 10, just east of Avinguda Fiter i Rossell, the continuation of Avinguda Doctor Mitjavila, and about a 2km walk from Plaça Guillemó. It is open daily from 10 am to 9 pm (last entry at 8 pm).

Organised Tours

Excursions Nadal (☎ 82 11 38; fax 82 06 42), in the bus station at Avinguda Tarragona 42 (and at Avinguda del Pessebre 94 in Les Escaldes), offers half-day/day bus excursions around the principality.

Places to Stay – Budget

Camping The *Camping Valira* (☎ 82 23 84), at the southern edge of town just off Avinguda de Salou, charges 510 to 525 ptas per person and the same for a tent or caravan and car. There's a small indoor swimming pool, and the campsite is open all year. Telephone reservations are accepted; during July and August, they are accepted a maximum of 24 hours in advance.

Two more camping grounds in Santa Coloma are *Camping Riberaygua* (☎ 82 66 99) by the river, which charges 490 to 525 ptas (depending on the season) for a tent, car and per person, and *Camping Borda Margineda* (☎ 82 39 83), which costs 400 ptas. Both are open all year.

Hotels – Plaça Guillemó Area The 15 room *Residència Benazet* (☎ 82 06 98), Carrer de la Llacuna 21, has large, serviceable singles/doubles/triples and cold showers in the hallway for 1300/2600/3600 ptas.

Nearby at Plaça Guillemó 5, the *Hotel des Arcades* (☎ 82 13 55) has singles/doubles with shower and toilet from 2500/3500 ptas. An extra bed costs an additional 1100 ptas.

Hotels – East of Plaça Guillemó The *Hotel Costa* (☎ 82 14 39), Avinguda Meritxell 44, has basic but clean singles/doubles for 1600/3000 ptas. Reception is on the 3rd floor; take the stairs on the left of the shopping arcade on the ground level.

The 21 room ***Hotel Residència Albert*** (☎ 82 01 56), Avinguda Doctor Mitjavila 16, offers friendly service and several newly renovated doubles with shower for 4000 ptas.

Hotels – West of Plaça Guillemó In the Barri Antic, the ***Pensió La Rosa*** (☎ 82 18 10), with 19 rooms on the 1st floor of Antic Carrer Major 18, has reasonably nondescript singles/doubles for 1700/3000 ptas and triples/quads for 3900/5200 ptas.

The ***Residència Baró*** (☎ 82 14 84) is at Carrer del Puial 21, which is at the top of the stairs opposite Avinguda Príncep Benlloch 53. This place, one of the cheapest in town, has rooms for 1500 to 3000 ptas, but telephone first as there is not always someone in attendance.

At the western end of town at Carrer Roureda de Sansa 18, the ***Hotel Enclar*** (☎ 82 03 10) has doubles without/with shower and toilet for 3200/3950 ptas including breakfast, but be prepared for a lengthy trek into the centre of town.

Places to Stay – Mid-Range

In the heart of the Barri Antic at Carrer La Llacuna 7, the quiet ***Hotel Festa Brava*** (☎ 86 02 66) has plain but comfortable singles/doubles with shower from 3000/4000 ptas or with bath from 3000/5500 ptas. Large rooms for three/four people cost from 6500 ptas.

Places to Stay – Top End

The Francophile 74 room ***Hôtel Pyrénées*** (☎ 86 00 06; fax 82 02 65) is only one block from Casa de la Vall at Avinguda Príncep Benlloch 20. It has a tennis court and a swimming pool behind it. Singles/doubles/triples cost 5000/8000/11,200 ptas, including breakfast. At certain times of year (in August and around Christmas) half-board is mandatory. Parking in the hotel garage costs 1000 ptas a day. Ask for a room away from the street if you want a good night's sleep.

The delightful ***Hotel Florida*** (☎ 82 01 05; fax 86 19 25), Carrer de la Llacuna 15 (just one block from Plaça Guillemó), is the equivalent of a three star hotel. Modern doubles, reached by a lift, cost 6850 ptas (including breakfast) in the low season. The price jumps to 8500 ptas on weekends, around Easter and at Christmas. In August and at the height of the ski season, expect to pay around 9600.

Places to Eat

Restaurants The restaurant at the ***Hotel des Arcades*** has a decent *menu* for 900 ptas with some Catalan specialities, such as *cunillo* (rabbit) cooked in tomato sauce, and excellent sangria. ***La Cantina*** (☎ 82 30 65), next door at Plaça Guillemó 4, has a 975 ptas *menu* including wine. Or try the friendly ***Vilarrasa***, with good value two/three course *menus* at 950/1450 ptas.

Restaurant Martí (☎ 82 43 84), which is hidden at the back of the 1st floor of the building at Avinguda Meritxell 44, is a popular place with travellers and has multilingual *menus* for 1100 and 1425 ptas. It is open daily from noon to 3.30 pm (4 pm on weekends) and 8 to 10 pm (11 pm on weekends).

Pizzeria La Mossegada (☎ 82 31 31) overlooks the Valira River at Avinguda Doctor Mitjavila 2. It is open from noon to 4 pm and 8 to 11 pm (closed Wednesday, except during summer). Pizzas cost between 750 and 875 ptas and grilled meat dishes from 975 to 1150 ptas. Near Plaça Guillemó at Carrer Doctor Nequi 4, ***Pizzeria Primavera*** (☎ 82 19 03) has pizzas for 500 to 750 ptas and a *menu* for 800 ptas. Meat dishes are also available. It is open daily from noon to 4 pm and 8 pm to midnight. ***Pans & Company***, which has entrances at Plaça Rebés 2 and Avinguda Meritxell 91, is a popular place for sandwiches and salads (from 345 ptas).

Fancy Mexican in Andorra? The ***Tex-Mex Café*** (☎ 82 01 25), Avinguda Príncep Benlloch 49, has tacos and chilli (850 ptas) and Mexican spareribs (1200 ptas). Or for a truly Spanish experience, ***Papanico*** (☎ 86 73 33), a jolly bar at Avinguda Princep Benlloch 4, serves typical *tapas* dishes such as *tortilla* (Spanish omelette), anchovies, squid and snails from 260 ptas each.

Clearly the best restaurant in town for Catalan/Andorran cooking is the atmospheric ***El Bon Racó*** (☎ 82 20 85) in Santa Coloma, about 1km west of Camping Valira at 86 Avinguda de Salou. Meat – especially *xai* (lamb) – roasted in an open hearth is the speciality (3900 ptas for two), but you might also try *escudella*, a stew of chicken, sausage and meatballs, or *trinxat*, prepared with cabbage, potatoes and bacon.

Self-Catering The huge ***supermarket*** on the 2nd floor of the Pyrénées department store, 21 Avinguda Meritxell, has vast quantities of imported luxury goods but also carries bread, pastries, vegetables, fruits, cheese and the like. It is open Monday to Friday from 9.30 am to 8 pm (9 pm on Saturday) and on Sunday from 9.30 am to 7 pm.

Getting There & Away

Buses to France and Spain and domestic buses to Sant Julià de Lòria leave from Plaça Guillemó. Buses to Ordino, Encamp and elsewhere depart from the Plaça Príncep Benlloch stop, which is in front of the parish church, Església Parroquial de Sant Esteve. For details, see Getting There & Away and Getting Around in this chapter's introductory section.

Getting Around

You can order a taxi in Andorra la Vella by ringing ☎ 86 30 00.

AROUND ANDORRA LA VELLA

Església de Santa Coloma

The Church of Santa Coloma, mentioned in documents from the 9th century, is Andorra's oldest, but its pre-Romanesque form has been modified over the centuries. The four storey, almost round bell tower was built in the 12th century, apparently in two stages. All the church's 12th century Romanesque murals except one, entitled *Agnus Dei* (Lamb of God), were taken to a museum in Berlin for conservation in the 1930s and are still there. The church is 5km south-west of Plaça Guillemó; to get there, follow Avinguda Príncep Benlloch and then Avinguda de Santa Coloma.

Hiking

From Santa Coloma, a path leads northward up the hill to **Capella de Sant Vincenç d'Enclar** (20 minutes), which, before the Pareatges of 1288, was the site of an important castle. Nowadays, in addition to the view, you'll see a renovated church, a cemetery, several silos and some ruins. The trail continues up to **Pic d'Enclar** (2382m), which is on the Spanish border. A path can then be followed eastward along the ridge to **Pic de Carroi** (2334m), which overlooks Santa Coloma from the north.

The 1100m-high **Rec del Solà** is an almost flat, 2.5km path that follows a small irrigation canal running along the hillside a bit north of Andorra la Vella. Another option is to hike south-eastward from Andorra la Vella's Carretera de la Comella up to the shelter of **Prat Primer** (2250m), where it's possible to stay overnight. The walk up takes about two hours.

Parish of Ordino

This mountainous parish to the north and north-west of Andorra la Vella is arguably the country's most beautiful, with slate and fieldstone farmhouses, gushing streams and picturesque stone bridges. Virtually everything of interest is along the 35km-long CG3 highway.

ORDINO

• pop 1008 alt 1304m

Ordino is much larger than other villages in the area, but despite recent development (holiday homes and English-speaking residents abound), it manages to retain its Andorran character.

Information

The tourist office kiosk (☎ 83 69 63), on the CG3 highway, is open Monday to Saturday from 9 am to 1 pm and 3 to 7 pm and on Sunday from 9 am to noon. The Banc Agricol i Comercial d'Andorra opposite the tourist office is open weekdays from 9 am to 1 pm and 3 to 5 pm. Saturday hours are 9 am to noon. It also has a 24 hour ATM. There are more banks at the central Plaça Major, which is 50m up the hill.

Casa d'Areny de Plandolit

The ancestral home (☎ 83 69 08) of the d'Areny de Plandolit family, built in the 17th century and modified in the mid-19th century, is now a museum. The family's most illustrious member was Don Guillem, who was a syndic and leader of the political reform movement of the 1860s. The house has furnished rooms (the library and dining room are particularly fine) and is of typically rugged Andorran design. A half-hour guided visits cost 200 ptas. It is open from 9.30 am to 1.30 pm and 3 to 6.30 pm from Tuesday to Saturday and on Sunday morning.

Hiking

There is a trail from Ordino via the village of Segudet northward up the mountainside towards **Pic de Casamanya** (2740m). It does not go all the way to the summit. The round trip takes about four hours.

Places to Stay & Eat

Just off the Plaça Major, in the alley behind the Crèdit Andorrà bank, is the ***Hotel Quim*** (☎ 83 50 13), which is run by a friendly older woman. Doubles/triples with shower cost 3500/4500 ptas. Much more expensive is the ***Hotel Santa Bàrbara de la Vall d'Ordino*** (☎ 83 71 00; fax 83 70 92), on Plaça Major, with doubles from 6500 ptas (8500 ptas in summer).

Also on Plaça Major, the ***Restaurant Armengol*** (☎ 83 59 77) has an excellent *menu* of Catalan dishes for 1500 ptas, while next door the ***Snack-Bar Quim*** (☎ 83 56 45) serves sandwiches (including toasties) from 500 to 1500 ptas along with generous helpings of the most unusual salads for 300 to 850 ptas.

Getting There & Away

The bus from Andorra la Vella (130 ptas) runs daily from 7 am (7.30 am on Sunday) to 9.30 pm every 20 or 30 minutes.

LLORTS

• pop 105 alt 1413m

The tiny mountain hamlet of Llorts has traditional architecture set amidst tobacco fields and a pristine mountain setting. This is one of the most unadulterated spots in the whole country. Llorts (pronounced 'Yorts') is 6km north of Ordino.

Hiking

A trail leads up the valley west of town (along Riu de l'Angonella) to a group of lakes, **Estanys de l'Angonella**. Count on about 3½ hours to get there.

From slightly north of the village of El Serrat (population 60; 1600m), which is about 3km up the valley from Llorts, a secondary road leads to the Borda de Sorteny mountain shelter (1969m). From there, a trail continues on to a lake called **Estany de l'Estanyó** (2339m) and a mountain known as **Pic de l'Estanyó** (2915m).

From Arans (population 80; 1360m), a village 2km south of Llorts, a trail goes north-eastward to **Bordes de l'Ensegur** (2180m), where there is an old shepherd's hut.

The **Església de Sant Martí**, a tiny Romanesque church in La Cortinada, 1km south of Arans, has 12th century frescoes in remarkably good condition. They were only discovered in 1968.

Places to Stay

Some 200m north of Llorts, the attractive ***Camping Els Pardassos*** (☎ 85 00 22) is open from mid-June to mid-September and costs 300 ptas per person, per tent and per car. Bring your own provisions.

The ***Hotel Vilaró*** (☎ 85 02 25), 200m south of the village limits, has doubles with washbasin and bidet for 3800/3925 ptas. It is open all year. The ***Hotel Subirá*** (☎ 85 00 37; fax 85 00 00) in El Serrat has fabulous views of the valley and surrounding mountains. It is open all year and singles/doubles cost from 4500/6000 ptas.

Getting There & Away

Three buses a day run from Andorra la Vella to El Serrat. Buses leave El Serrat at 7.45 am and 2.45 pm; departures from Andorra la Vella are at 7.15 am (not every day) and 1 and 8.30 pm. Ordino, which is 6km down the valley, is served by more frequent buses.

ORDINO-ARCALÍS SKI AREA

The Ordino-Arcalís ski area (☎ 83 63 20; fax 83 92 25) is in the parish's far north-western corner. During winter there are 12 lifts (mostly drag lifts) covering 24km of trails for beginners and intermediates over 378 hectares. The skiing and snowboarding is between 1940 and 2600m, with a vertical drop of 660m. Experts can have some fun on a mogul run, and there are some excellent prospects for ski touring in the area. Heliskiing is possible, but the vertical drop is only 1000m. There are also 5km of official cross-country trails. In summer, this beautiful mountainous area – a number of the rugged peaks reach 2800m – has some of Andorra's most rewarding hiking trails.

Orientation & Information

There are three carparks along the road from where the lifts commence. Restaurant La Coma Altitude is at the end of the paved road near the uppermost carpark at an altitude of 2200m. The closest accommodation is at El Serrat, which is several kilometres down the valley. There are more hotels as well as banks and post offices in Ordino.

Skiing

In winter, Ordino-Arcalís has enough snow and a decent selection of runs, but it can be rather cold and is often windy. The Telecadira La Coma chair lift (see the following section) operates for skiers from December to mid-May. A lift ticket costs 2575/3625/19,075 ptas per half-day/day/seven days. You can rent ski equipment for about 1800 ptas and snowboards with boots for around 3000 ptas.

Hiking

The trail behind the Restaurant La Coma Altitude leads eastward across the hill then north and over the ridge to a group of beautiful mountain lakes called the **Estanys de Tristaina**. The very pleasant walk to the first lake takes about 30 minutes. It's also a great spot for a picnic.

In the warmer months, walks can also be started from the 2700m-high upper terminus of Telecadira La Coma, the chair lift opposite the Restaurant La Coma Altitude's parking lot. Outside the skiing season it operates daily from late June to August from 10 am to 4.45 pm. Summer fees are 450/750 ptas one way/return for adults and 350/550 ptas for children.

Other Activities

The souvenir kiosk, which is opposite the chair lift's lower station, rents mountain bikes from the end of June to early September. During this period it's open from 10 am to 5.30 pm every day. Charges are 625 ptas for one hour, 1775 ptas for a half-day and 3500 ptas for a full day.

Mountain guides are also available. The charge is 4000 ptas per person for half a day.

Places to Eat

Restaurant La Coma Altitude, with both snacks and a full *carte*, is closed in May and November. From the end of June to early September it's open from 10 am to 6 pm daily, except Monday (daily in August and September).

Getting There & Away

The only way up here is to drive or hitch in summer, but in winter there are five free ski shuttle buses a day between Arinsal, La Massana and the first carpark.

Public buses serve Ordino and El Serrat (see Bus under Getting Around at the start of this chapter).

Parish of La Massana

The Parish of La Massana is situated north-west of Andorra la Vella along the Spanish frontier.

ARINSAL & PAL SKI AREAS

Arinsal (☎ 83 58 22; fax 83 62 42), covering some 330 hectares, has 13 lifts, 28km of trails and a vertical drop of 1010m. It is the only ski village that has a lift system within walking distance of its centre. Both the skiing and snowboarding are good for beginners and intermediates, and Arinsal's après-ski scene is lively. Pal (☎ 83 62 36; fax 83 62 42) has 12 lifts over 363 hectares with 32km of trails and a vertical drop of 578m. Pal's gentler slopes make it an ideal ski resort for families. Transport to the lifts is by free shuttle bus.

Skiing

Lift tickets cost 2375/3375/17,675 ptas at Arinsal and 2575/3625/19,075 ptas at Pal for a half-day/day/seven days. Both areas have joined up with Ordino-Arcalís to issue a common lift pass. They have also introduced a complimentary bus system that transports skiers and snowboarders between the three ski resorts, giving them access to a total 84km of trails.

Other Activities

In summer, mountain bikes are available at Pal for 800/1950/2700 per hour/half-day/day. Horse riding costs from 1700 ptas an hour.

Places to Stay & Eat

The large ***Camping Xixerella*** (☎ 83 66 13) between Pal and Arinsal is open all year and features an outdoor swimming pool. The charges are 450 ptas per adult, tent or caravan and car.

In Arinsal, the basic ***Hotel Baró*** (☎ 83 51 75) has rooms for 2500/5000 ptas. Better value is the smaller ***Hotel Micolau*** (☎ 83 50 52), with clean rooms for 5000/6000 ptas. One of the more popular top-end places is the ***Hotel Solana*** (☎ 83 51 27; fax 83 73 95), with large rooms with bath and toilet for 6000/8000 ptas (half-board). One of the few restaurants around is ***El Bosc*** (☎ 83 55 19), which specialises in Andorran cuisine and has a hearty *menu* for 2200 ptas.

Getting There & Away

Buses between Andorra la Vella and La Massana (110 ptas; 20 minutes) operate every 30 minutes or so from 7 am (7.30 am on Sunday) to 9 pm. In winter there are 17 free ski shuttles a day between La Massana and Arinsal, four to Pal and up to five to Ordino-Arcalís.

Parish of Canillo

SOLDEU-EL TARTER SKI AREA

The Soldeu-El Tarter ski area (☎ 85 11 51; fax 85 13 37) is 19km north-east of Andorra la Vella, midway between the town of Canillo, which has a splendid Romanesque church (Sant Joan de Caselles) dating from the 11th century, and Port d'Envalira. Actually two separate villages, Soldeu and El Tarter are 2km apart and are connected by ski lifts. Together they form the largest ski area in Andorra.

Soldeu and El Tarter are popular with British and French tourists. The 21 lifts, which are mostly tow lines, connect 62km of runs over an area of 850 hectares with a vertical drop of 850m. The skiing is similar to that at Pas de la Casa (see the Parish of Encamp section), except that the black runs into the village are steeper and more picturesque. Soldeu, higher than El Tarter at 1826m, has the bulk of the accommodation and facilities. A bridge over a valley connects the village with the lifts.

Skiing

Plenty of shops rent ski equipment from about 1400 ptas a day (a snowboard and boots go for about 2700 ptas). Lift tickets for a half-day/day/seven days cost 2750/3750/19,250 ptas. Group lessons are 3000/11,000 ptas per person for three/15 hours, while one hour of private tuition costs 3725 ptas.

Other Activities

In summer the chair lift costs 900 ptas return or 2000 ptas for a day pass. Mountain bikes, which can be taken aboard and ridden down, rent for 650/1900/2600 for an hour/half-day/day. There's also horse riding (1600 ptas per hour) and hang-gliding (10,000 ptas with an instructor) available at nearby Tosa d'Espiolets.

Places to Stay & Eat

Most of the accommodation and restaurants are along the main road, the CG2. ***Hotel Soldeu*** (☎ 85 10 35; fax 85 29 29) is not bad for the price: doubles are 2850 ptas. For better value though, try the ***Residència Supervalira*** (☎ 85 10 82; fax 85 10 62) at Carretera Principal 20, where the more expensive doubles cost from 3800 ptas. A more upmarket place to stay is the popular ***Sport Hotel*** (☎ 85 10 51; fax 85 15 93), with rooms for 5400/8200 ptas (half-board).

The restaurant at the ***Hotel Soldeu*** has a *menu* with tasty dishes for 1200 ptas. At the top end, the ***Restaurant Espiolets*** (☎ 85 11 76) near the ski area has been recommended, with à la carte meals for around 10,000 ptas.

Getting There & Away

Buses go to/from Andorra la Vella (340 ptas; 40 minutes) once an hour between 8 or 9 am and 8 pm. You can also reach Pas de la Casa (20 minutes) from Soldeu-El Tarter.

Parish of Encamp

ENCAMP

• pop 9380 alt 1266m

Encamp has one of the few museums in all of Andorra: the **Museu Nacional de l'Automòbil** (National Automobile Museum; ☎ 83 22 66). Located at Avinguda Príncep Episcopal 64, it has about 80 motorcars dating from 1898 to 1950 as well as 100 antique motorcycles and bicycles. It is open Tuesday to Saturday from 9.30 am to 1.30 pm and 3 to 6 pm and on Sunday from 10 am to 2 pm. Entry is 200/100 ptas for adults/students. The museum can be reached from Andorra la Vella by public bus (100 ptas).

PAS DE LA CASA-GRAU ROIG SKI AREA

Pas de la Casa (2091m) is east of Port d'Envalira on the border with France. It lies on the eastern side of the col while Grau Roig is on the western side. Pas de la Casa is a large, unattractive village catering mainly to French visitors with its duty-free shopping and relatively inexpensive skiing.

Information

Tourist Office The tourist office (☎ 85 52 92) is opposite the Andorran customs station beside the church. Hotel reservations can be organised by calling the accommodation service (☎ 86 20 00).

Money & Post The Crèdit Andorrà at Carrer Sant Jordi 7 is open Monday to Friday from 9.30 am to 1 pm and 2 to 4 pm. The bank changes major currencies and travellers cheques and gives cash advances on credit cards. The post office is opposite Carrer de les Abelletes 4. It is open Monday to Friday from 10 am to 1 pm and Saturday to noon.

Skiing

The Pas de la Casa ski area (☎ 85 56 92; fax 82 03 99) boasts the highest skiing in the country at an elevation of between 2050m and 2600m and has the most reliable snow conditions. There is a network of 27 lifts, covering 87km of trails over 600 hectares, with a vertical drop of 590m. Pas de la Casa is linked by several lifts to the Grau Roig ski area in the next valley, which can also be reached by road. The skiing and snowboarding is well suited to beginners and intermediates, and there is also the possibility of night skiing. Grau Roig has 10km of cross-country trails and ski touring is also possible in the surrounding area.

There are several ski rental shops, which hire complete ski equipment from 1300 ptas and snowboards from 2600 ptas a day. Lift tickets cost 2875/4125/20,125 ptas for a half-day/day/seven days. Ski school costs 1800 ptas per person for a two hour group lesson and 3900 ptas for an hour of private instruction, and 11,475 ptas for a 15 hour group lesson.

Places to Stay & Eat

Pas de la Casa offers plenty of accommodation. One of the least expensive places is ***Hotel Llac Negre*** (☎ 85 51 98; fax 85 51 37) at Carrer Sant Jordi 43. Its basic rooms are 5000/6250 ptas. A reasonable mid-range place is ***Hotel Les 4 Estacions*** (☎ 85 53 29), Avinguda d'Encamp 9, with rooms from 5750 ptas for two. At the top end, the ***Hotel Residència Envalira*** (☎ 85 50 95; fax 85 53 71), Carrer Bearn 8, has rooms from 7100/10,200 ptas.

A popular place for breakfast is the bar a ***Hotel Els Cims*** (☎ 85 54 33), Carrer Majo 4. ***Restaurant Les Neus*** (☎ 85 50 85), Carre Comte de Foix, offers inexpensive *menu* from 1300 ptas. At the top end, the ***Restau-rant Marseillais*** (☎ 85 57 34), Carrer Bear 10, has à la carte meals for about 1800 ptas

Getting There & Away

From Andorra la Vella there is one bus a day at 9 am to Pas de la Casa (590 ptas). I returns at 11.30 am. Three daily buse operate to/from L'Hospitalet (30 minutes) the train station nearest Andorra, but only two continue on to Andorra la Vella. In winter there are two extra daily buses (fou on Saturday) to/from Andorra la Vella and Soldeu-El Tarter.

ANDORRA

The Pyrenees

The Pyrenees Mountains stretch for 430km west to east from the Bay of Biscay on the Atlantic coast to the Mediterranean Sea, forming a natural boundary between France and Spain. Some of the most spectacular peaks and mountain valleys are in and around the long, skinny Parc National des Pyrénées, which runs for about 100km along the Franco-Spanish border from the Vallée d'Aspe in the west to the Vallée d'Aure in the east, its width never exceeding 15km. Pau is the transport gateway to the Vallée d'Aspe, while the pilgrimage city of Lourdes has bus links to the mountain town of Cauterets.

For information on the far western section of the Pyrenees, see the French Basque Country chapter. The eastern end of the chain is in Roussillon, which is described in the Languedoc-Roussillon chapter. There's additional information on the Pyrenees in the Andorra chapter.

HIGHLIGHTS

- **Lourdes** – visit one of the world's most important pilgrimage sites
- **Parc National des Pyrénées** – go hiking, skiing, parapenting or rafting
- **Cauterets** – relax in a thermal spa
- **Le Clos aux Ours** – visit the Pyrenean bear information centre

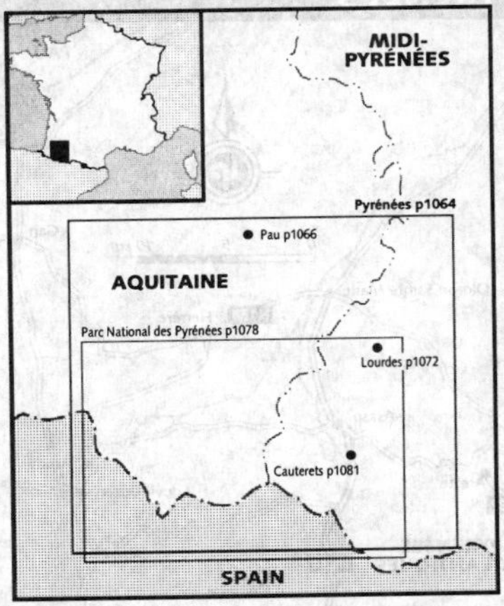

regional delicacies – game dishes (venison, wild boar etc) and mountain goats' cheese

Information

In Paris, information on the Pyrenees region is available at the Maison des Pyrénées (☎ 01 42 86 51 86; métro Quatre Septembre), 15 Rue Saint Augustin (2e).

PAU

• pop 82,000 ✉ 64000 alt 207m

The pleasant, easy-going city of Pau, the former capital of the historical Béarn region and préfecture of the Pyrénées-Atlantiques department, is famed for its mild climate, flower-filled public parks and magnificent views of the Pyrenees. In the mid-19th century, it was a favourite wintering spot for wealthy English people, who introduced steeplechases, golf and fox hunting. These days, the city owes its prosperity to a high tech industrial base, the huge natural gas field at Lacq, 20km to the north-west, and an abundance of Spanish tourists and shoppers. The city's university was founded in 1970.

If you have a car, Pau – well supplied with cheap hotels – makes a good base for forays into the Pyrenees.

Orientation

The train station, near the Pau River (Gave de Pau), is separated from Blvd des Pyrénées, Place Clemenceau and the centre of town by a hill, which is outfitted with a tiny funicular railway. The chateau and the small Vieille Ville (Old Town) are at the western end of Blvd des Pyrénées, while Parc Beaumont is at its eastern end. The semipedestrianised Rue des Cordeliers, in the heart of the shopping district, connects the main drag, Rue Maréchal Joffre, with Place de la Libération. Centre Bosquet is a big, modern commercial and residential complex on Cours Bosquet. The large food market is to the north of the centre.

Information

Tourist Office The tourist office (☎ 05 59 27 27 08; fax 05 59 27 03 21) is on Place Royale, across the square from the upper end of the funicular railway. It opens Monday to Saturday from 9 am to 12.30 pm and 1.30 to 6 pm (5.30 pm Saturday). In July and August it's open daily from 9 am to 6 pm. Hotel reservations in the Pau area are free. The brochure entitled *Pau – Ville Authentique*, available in English, includes a 20 stop walking tour of the Vieille Ville.

PYRÉNÉES

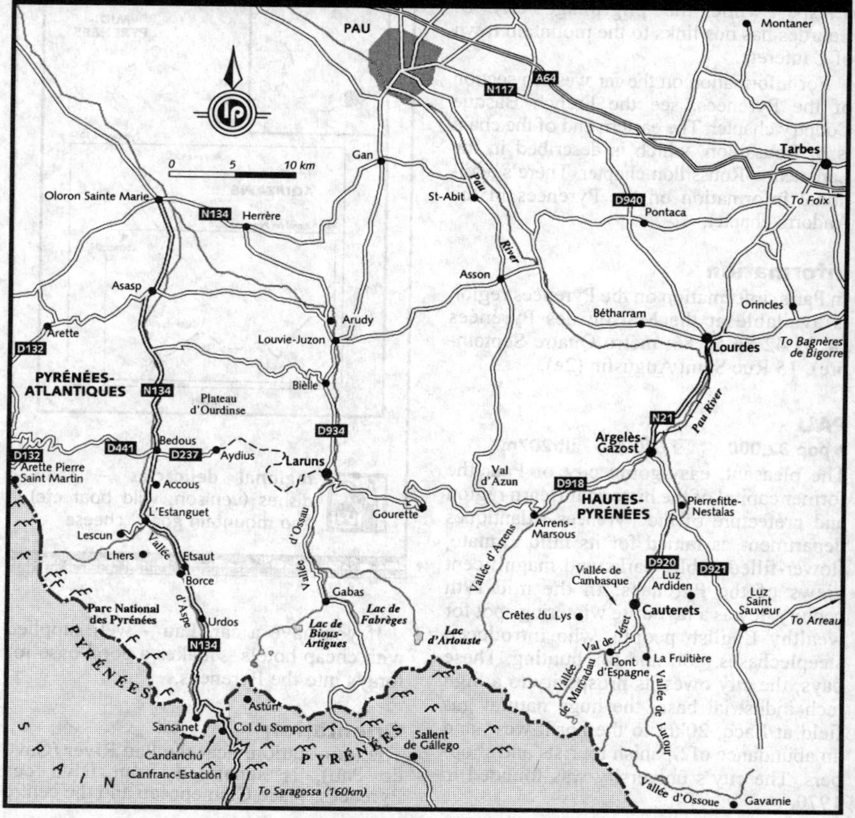

Money The Banque de France at 7 Rue Louis Barthou is open Monday to Friday from 8.30 am to noon and 1.30 to 3.30 pm.

There are commercial banks along Rue Maréchal Foch. If you have a cash crunch on a Sunday or holiday, try the front desk of the Hôtel Continental (see Places to Stay).

Post The main post office, 21 Cours Bosquet, is open weekdays from 8 am to 6.30 pm and on Saturday until noon. Exchange services are available.

Bookshop Hiking maps, topoguides (including *Walking in the Pyrenees*), a wide selection of books on the region and some Lonely Planet titles are all available at the Librairie des Pyrénées (☎ 05 59 27 78 75), 14 Rue Saint Louis, half a block north of the tourist office. It's open Monday to Saturday from 9 am (9.30 am Monday) to 12.30 pm and from 2 to 7.30 pm.

Laundry The Laverie Automatique at 66 Rue Émile Garet is open daily from 7 am to 10 pm.

Medical Services The Centre Hospitalier (☎ 05 59 92 48 48), 3.5km north-east of the centre at 4 Blvd Hauterive (ie the northern end of Ave Pouguet), is the last stop on bus No 6.

Walking Tour

Majestic **Blvd des Pyrénées**, laid out at the beginning of the 19th century, runs along the crest of the hill overlooking the train station. On a clear day you can see a variety of Pyrenean peaks – there is a small *table d'orientation* (viewpoint indicator) opposite 20 Blvd des Pyrénées will tell you what you're looking at. At the eastern end of Blvd des Pyrénées is the 12 hectare **Parc Beaumont**, an English-style park. The lawn, flowers and park are shaded by trees of many species.

The western end of Blvd des Pyrénées leads to the chateau and the narrow streets of the picturesque **Vieille Ville**.

Chateau

The chateau (☎ 05 59 82 38 00) at 2 Rue du Château, former home of the kings of Navarre, was built as a fortress in the 13th and 14th centuries and then transformed into a Renaissance palace by Margaret of Angoulême (also known as Margaret of Navarre) in the 16th century. Neglected in the 18th century and turned into a barracks after the Revolution, it was in a terrible condition by 1838, when Louis-Philippe initiated the renovation of the interior, a process that Napoleon III later completed. Most of the ornamentation and furniture, including the oak dining-room table that seats 100 people, date from the 19th century. The chateau's most outstanding feature is its superb collection of 16th to 18th century **Gobelins tapestries**, which is among the finest in Europe.

The collection of Sèvres porcelain includes a number of *bourdalous*, decorated chamber pots from the 17th and 18th centuries. During the long sermons delivered by Jesuit preachers, known as bourdalous, the aristocratic women in the congregation could relieve themselves without having to leave the hall by placing the pots under their skirts. In the room where Henry IV was born in 1553, you can see what is said to be his **cradle**, an upturned tortoise shell that, it was hoped, would bring the future king longevity and strength.

The interesting **Musée Béarnais** (☎ 05 59 27 07 36), reached by taking the spiral staircase at the far end of the courtyard to the 3rd floor, has displays on the architecture, furniture, costumes etc of the Béarn region. The natural history section has some ghastly stuffed animals. One display case shows how Béarn berets – worn by the Basques to the west as well as armies around the world – are made. The museum is open daily from 9.30 am to noon and 2 to 5.30 pm. Entry costs 10FF (free for children under 18 accompanied by an adult).

On the side of the chateau overlooking the river are two square 14th century towers: the 33m **Tour Gaston Phoébus**, made of brick, and the brick-and-stone **Tour de la Monnaie**,

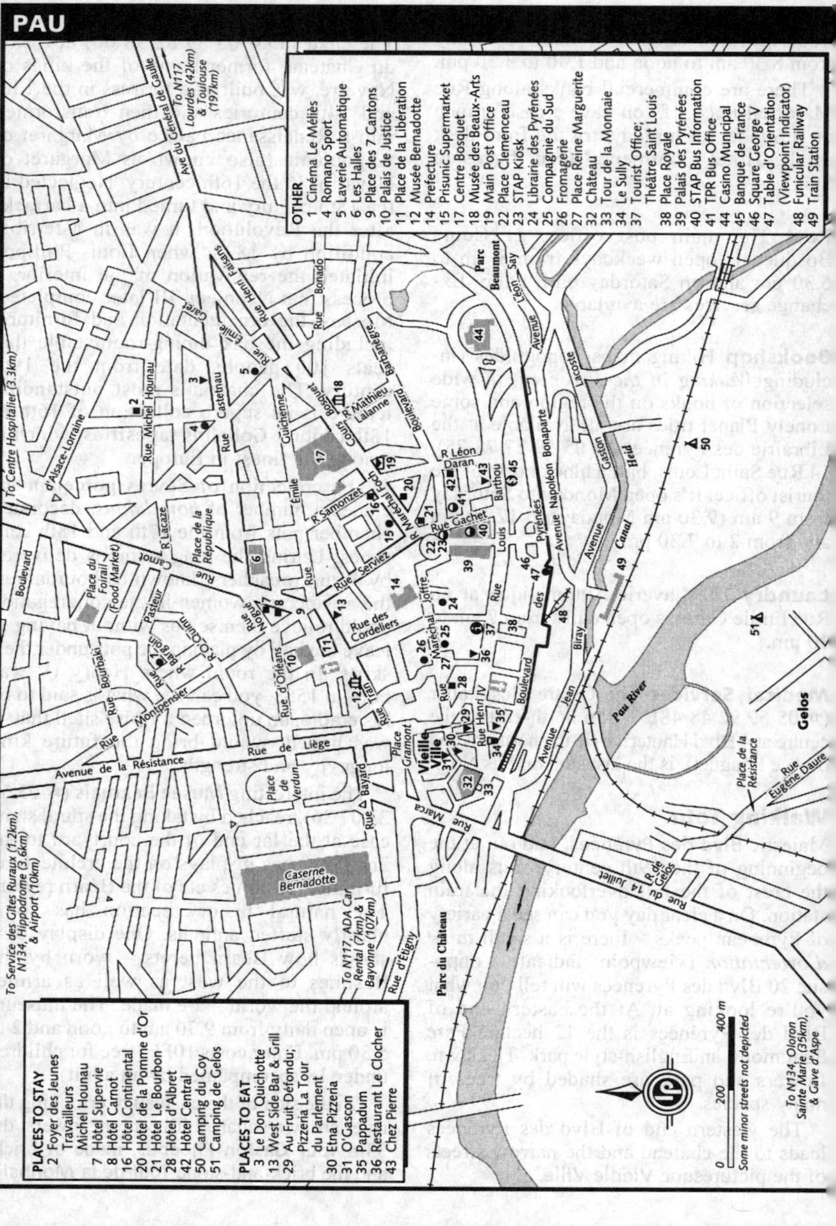
PYRENEES
PAU
PLACES TO STAY
2 Foyer des Jeunes Travailleurs Michel Hounau
7 Hôtel Supervie
8 Hôtel Carnot
16 Hôtel Continental
20 Hôtel de la Pomme d'Or
21 Hôtel Le Bourbon
28 Hôtel d'Albret
42 Hôtel Central
50 Camping du Coy
51 Camping de Gelos
PLACES TO EAT
3 Le Don Quichotte
13 West Side Bar & Grill
29 Au Fruit Défondu; Pizzeria La Tour du Parlement
30 Etna Pizzeria
31 O'Gascon
35 Pappadum
36 Restaurant Le Clocher
43 Chez Pierre
OTHER
1 Cinéma Le Méliès
4 Romano Sport
5 Laverie Automatique
6 Les Halles
9 Place des 7 Cantons
10 Palais de Justice
11 Place de la Libération
12 Musée Bernadotte
14 Prefecture
15 Prisunic Supermarket
17 Centre Bosquet
18 Musée des Beaux-Arts
19 Main Post Office
22 Place Clemenceau
23 STAP Kiosk
24 Librairie des Pyrénées
25 Compagnie du Sud
26 Fromagerie
27 Place Reine Marguerite
32 Château
33 Tour de la Monnaie
34 Le Sully
37 Tourist Office; Théâtre Saint Louis
38 Place Royale
39 Palais des Pyrénées
40 STAP Bus Information
41 TPR Bus Office
44 Casino Municipal
45 Banque de France
46 Square George V
47 Table d'Orientation (Viewpoint Indicator)
48 Funicular Railway
49 Train Station
0 200 400 m
Some minor streets not depicted

which has a lift. Nearby are some of the flower gardens for which Pau is famous. West of the chateau is the shady **Parc du Château**.

The chateau is open daily from 9.30 to 11.45 am and 2 to 5.15 pm. Entrance, including the obligatory one-hour guided tour, costs 27FF (18FF if you're under 26 and free for under-18s). An information sheet in English is available.

Musée Bernadotte

The Bernadotte Museum (☎ 05 59 27 48 42), 8 Rue Tran, has exhibits illustrating the peculiar story of how a Pau-born French general became the king of Sweden and Norway (see the boxed text 'Bernadotte'). Displays include letters, documents, engravings, paintings and memorabilia. The museum, which flies the Swedish flag, is open Tuesday to Sunday from 10 am to noon and 2 to 6 pm. Entry costs 10FF (5FF for children and students).

Bernadotte

Jean-Baptiste Bernadotte, born in 1763 in the building now occupied by Pau's Musée Bernadotte, enlisted in the French army at the age of 17. An enthusiastic supporter of the Revolution, he spent the 1790s as a distinguished general and diplomat, serving both the Revolutionary government and Napoleon and acquiring a reputation as a talented and humane administrator.

Meanwhile, in Stockholm, the Swedish Riksdag concluded that the only way out of the country's dynastic and political crisis was to install a foreigner on the throne. Full of respect for French military prowess, they turned to Bernadotte, electing him crown prince in 1810.

Contrary to Napoleon's expectations, Bernadotte did not follow a pro-French foreign policy. Indeed, in the Battle of Leipzig (1813), Swedish troops under his command helped the allied army deal Napoleon his first major defeat. In 1818, after several years as regent, Bernadotte became King Charles XIV John; he died in office in 1844. The present king of Sweden is the seventh ruler in the Bernadotte dynasty.

Musée des Beaux-Arts

Pau's Fine Arts Museum (☎ 05 59 27 33 02), facing Cours Bosquet but with its entrance opposite 15 Rue Mathieu Lalanne, is a good provincial museum. Among the works on exhibit are a variety of 17th to 20th century European paintings, including some by Rubens, El Greco and Degas. It is open from 10 am to noon and from 2 to 6 pm (closed Tuesday). Admission costs 10FF (5FF for children and students).

Activities

Compagnie du Sud (☎ 05 59 27 04 24; fax 05 59 27 63 25) at 27 Rue Maréchal Joffre offers guided treks for small groups in the French and Spanish Pyrenees. Most routes are open from May to October (June to September at higher elevations), though a few winter hikes are also possible in the Spanish province of Aragón as is snowshoe cross-country touring. The guides speak English. Accommodation is in mountain huts.

The company can also arrange accommodation, food etc for unaccompanied hikes and biking trips. This logistical support, known as Randokits, costs 1500 to 2200FF per person for four to seven days. The office is open from Monday to Saturday from 10 am to 7 pm (5 pm on Saturday).

Romano Sport (☎ 05 59 98 48 56) at 1 rue Jean Reveil rents equipment for hiking (boots 35FF a day), mountain climbing, skiing (71FF a day) and spelunking. It's open Monday to Saturday (daily from December to March) from 9 am to noon and 3 to 7 pm.

Special Event

The Festival de Pau, a three week extravaganza of dance, music and theatre, is held from mid-June to early July at the Théâtre Saint Louis, on Rue Saint Louis behind the tourist office and in the Cour du Château.

Places to Stay

Pau's hotels, which offer some of the best value for money anywhere in France, are busiest during April, May, June, September and October, when tourists and business-people are in town. But even during these months, you can always find a room in the morning.

Places to Stay – Budget

Camping Although it's directly across the Pau River from the train station, ***Camping de Gelos*** (☎ 05 59 06 57 37) is 2.5km from the train station by road at the Base de Plein Air recreational area, which is in the southern suburb of Gelos. To get there by bus, take the No 1 from Place Clemenceau or Rue Marca. It's open from mid-May to September. Tariffs are 23FF for a tent site (including parking), 30FF for a caravan and 15/9FF per adult/child.

Closer to the station and easier to get to on foot (about a 20 minute walk) is ***Camping du Coy*** (☎ 05 59 27 71 38), which is in the south-eastern suburb of Bizanos. It costs 12FF for a tent site, 6FF for a car and 12.50FF per person. Reception is open daily from 10 am to 1 pm and 3 to 7 pm.

Hostel From mid-June to mid-September the friendly ***Foyer des Jeunes Travailleurs Michel Hounau*** (☎ 05 59 72 61 00), 30 Rue Michel Hounau, has a few single rooms for travellers. Even during the school year, when it functions as a *foyer* for young people working or studying in Pau, there are always at least five rooms available for people passing through. Singles (all they have) with washbasin cost 52FF (on presentation of a hostelling card). Sheets are 18FF extra. You can check in 24 hours a day – if the door is locked, just ring the bell. Kitchen facilities are available on the 3rd and 4th floors and there's a cafeteria.

Rural Accommodation The tourist office has a list of *chambres d'hôtes, gîtes d'étape* and *campings à la ferme* in the Pau area. For more information on rural accommodation and help with reservations, contact the Service des Gîtes Ruraux (☎ 05 59 80 19 13; fax 05 59 30 60 65) in the Maison de l'Agriculture at 124 Blvd Tourasse, north of the city centre. It is open Monday to Friday from 9 am to 12.30 pm and 2 to 5 pm.

Hotels The friendly, family-run, 12 room ***Hôtel d'Albret*** (☎ 05 59 27 81 58), 11 Rue Jeanne d'Albret (near Place Reine Marguerite), has large, clean doubles with washbasin and bidet for only 90FF; rooms with shower are 120FF (155FF with shower and toilet). Hall showers are 10FF. Except during summer, reception may be closed on Sunday from noon to 7 pm.

The 20 room ***Hôtel de la Pomme d'Or*** (☎ 05 59 27 78 48), which is on the 1st floor of a former *relais de chevaux* (coaching inn) at 11 Rue Maréchal Foch, can provide singles/doubles/triples with washbasin and bidet for 85/100/140FF. Those with shower are 105/125/170FF and those with shower and toilet are 115/140/180FF. Hall showers are 10FF. To get in or out of the ground floor entrance, push the button on the door-post. If you arrive after midnight, ring the bell to wake up the night clerk.

Somewhat farther from the train station, the 13 room ***Hôtel Supervie*** (☎ 05 59 27 83 32), on the 1st floor at 1 Rue Nogué, has simple singles/doubles for 90/130FF (130/165FF with shower). There are hall showers here, and there's a TV room for guests. Reception is closed on Sunday and for the first two weeks of August.

Around the corner at 13 Rue Carnot (2nd floor), you might try the friendly, no star, eight room ***Hôtel Carnot*** (☎ 05 59 27 88 70), whose large, simple rooms with washbasin, bidet and linoleum floors are great value at 70/108FF. Hall showers are 11FF.

Places to Stay – Mid-Range & Top End

The central ***Hôtel Le Bourbon*** (☎ 05 59 27 53 12; fax 05 59 82 90 99), 12 Place Clemenceau, boasts extremely comfortable singles/doubles/triples with shower, toilet and TV starting at 215/310/360FF. Some of the rooms have air-conditioning.

Another excellent bet is the 28 room ***Hôtel Central*** (☎ 05 59 27 72 75; fax 05 59 27 33 28) at 15 Rue Léon Daran. Large rooms with quite spacious bathrooms and soundproofed windows cost 185/235/300FF for one/two/four people.

Pau's landmark hotel is the 80 room, three star ***Hôtel Continental*** (☎ 05 59 27 69 31; fax 05 59 27 99 84) at 2 Rue Maréchal Foch. Singles/doubles with washbasin and toilet or shower are 230/270FF; those with all the amenities are 400/500FF.

Places to Eat

Restaurants There's a wide variety of restaurants near the chateau on Rue Sully, Rue Henri IV, Rue du Moulin and Rue du Château. You'll find a number of brasseries and cafés along Blvd des Pyrénées around Square George V.

Restaurants – French The ***Restaurant Le Clocher*** (☎ 05 59 27 72 83), 8 Rue de Foix, has *menus* of cuisine from Béarn and the Landes regions for 50, 65FF (both lunch only), 75, 110 and 134FF. It is open Monday to Saturday from noon to 2 pm and 7 to 10 pm.

Au Fruit Défondu (☎ 05 59 27 26 05), 3 Rue Sully, has cheese, fish, meat and chocolate fondues (75 to 90FF), *pierrades* (meats that you must grill yourself; 75 to 90FF) and *raclette* (melted cheese with cold cuts and pickles; 98FF). There are also *menus* for 80 and 100FF. Food is served from 7 pm to 12.30 am daily.

If you really want to treat yourself, head for ***Chez Pierre*** (☎ 05 59 27 76 86), a sophisticated restaurant at 16 Rue Louis Barthou, and feast on things like a salad of fresh baby artichokes and prawns or a *cassoulet* of lobster and saffron. The *menu* costs 185FF, otherwise it's all à la carte. Chez Pierre is closed for Saturday lunch and on Sunday.

Restaurants – International The ***West Side Bar & Grill*** (☎ 05 59 82 90 78), south-east of Place de la Libération at 3 Rue Saint Jacques, has a wood plank floor, 1950s American memorabilia on the walls, groovy music and a miniature train that runs continuously on a track suspended from the ceiling. The inspiration for the all-American and Tex-Mex *menu*, like the décor, came from one of the owners, who spent 15 years in California and Hawaii. Starters such as *nachos* and clam chowder are about 35FF, while steaks, fried chicken, ribs and other main dishes are 65 to 80FF. The 75FF three-course *menu* is excellent value and portions are huge. Food is served from noon to 2 pm and 8 to 10.30 pm on weekdays (8 to 10.30 pm on Saturday). The restaurant is closed on Sunday.

Pappadum (☎ 05 59 27 51 67) is at 9 Impasse Honset. It is one of three Indian restaurants in Pau, has biryanis of various sorts from 58FF, and lunch *menus* for 50, 60 and 80FF.

Pizzeria La Tour du Parlement (☎ 05 59 27 38 29), 36 Rue du Moulin, open daily except Tuesday lunch in winter months, is popular with local Palois as well as visitors. The ***Etna Pizzeria*** (☎ 05 59 27 77 94), 16 Rue du Château, has pizza or pasta from 40FF. It is open daily for lunch and dinner until midnight.

North-east of the centre at 30 Rue Castetnau, ***Le Don Quichotte*** (☎ 05 59 27 63 08) serves tapas (from 15FF) and Spanish main dishes (including the Basque fish soup called *ttoro*) for 45 to 65FF until 1 am (closed for lunch on Saturday, Sunday and Monday).

Self-Catering ***Les Halles***, a large food market at Place de la République, is open Monday to Saturday (closed 1 to 3.30 pm except Saturday). On Wednesday and Saturday mornings there's a ***food market*** at Place du Foirail.

The ***Prisunic*** at 22 Rue Maréchal Foch, whose supermarket section is in the back, is open Monday to Saturday from 8.30 am to 8 pm. On Cours Bosquet the Centre Bosquet contains a ***Champion*** supermarket.

Near the Vieille Ville there's a cluster of ***food shops*** around Place Reine Marguerite. The ***fromagerie*** at 24 Rue Maréchal Joffre is open Monday to Saturday from 9 am to 12.30 pm and 3.15 to 7.30 pm. There are several ***boulangeries*** nearby.

Entertainment

Cinema The only cinema in Pau with non-dubbed English films is ***Cinéma Le Méliès*** (☎ 05 59 27 60 52 or, for a recording, ☎ 08 36 68 68 87) at 6 Rue Bargoin, just off Rue Pasteur. Tickets are 35FF (28FF for students, 20FF for children and 22FF for everyone after 10 pm). The cinema is closed from mid July to mid August.

Bars The Vieille Ville is full of convivial little bars and pubs including ***O'Gascon*** (☎ 05 59 27 64 74), 13 Rue du Château, and ***Le Sully*** (☎ 05 59 82 86 56), a popular watering hole at 13 Rue Henri IV, open daily from 2 pm to 2 am.

The bar of the ***West Side Bar & Grill*** (see Places to Eat) is open on weekdays from 11 am to 2 am and 2 pm to 2 am on Saturday.

Casino The ***Casino Municipal*** (☎ 05 59 27 06 92), in the Parc Beaumont, is open daily from 10 am to 3 am (4 am on Friday and Saturday night). Remember to bring some identification.

Horse Racing The renowned ***Hippodrome du Pont Long*** (☎ 05 59 32 07 93), north of the centre on Blvd du Cami-Salié, has seasonal steeplechases from December and April. You can reach the racecourse on bus No 3 (direction Perlic).

Getting There & Away

Air The Pau-Pyrénées airport (☎ 05 59 33 33 00) is about 10km north-west of central Pau.

Bus TPR (☎ 05 59 27 45 98), 2 Place Clemenceau (actually a bit south of the square on Rue Gachet), has three runs a day (one a day on Sunday and holidays from mid-June to August) to Bayonne (80.50FF; 2¼ hours) and Biarritz (86.50FF; 2½ hours). It also has buses to Lourdes (36.50FF; 1¼ hours; six to seven times a day), Mauléon, Orthez, Monein and other towns in the area.

Train The train station (☎ 08 36 35 35 35) is at the eastern end of Ave Jean Biray below the Vieille Ville. The information office is open from 9 am to 6 pm daily.

Pau is linked to destinations in the Pyrenees including Bedous in the Vallée d'Aspe (52FF; 70 minutes; five a day), Oloron Sainte Marie (36FF; 40 minutes; five a day), the Spanish railhead of Canfranc-Estación (72FF; 2¼ hours; six a day), Laruns in the Vallée d'Ossau (39FF; one hour) and Lourdes (39FF; 30 minutes; 19 a day).

Long-haul destinations served by direct trains include Bayonne (81FF; 1¼ hours; nine a day), Bordeaux (159FF; 2¼ hours; 11 a day), Marseille (341FF; seven to eight hours; two direct trains a day), Nice (403FF; 10 to 11 hours; four a day) and Toulouse (142FF; 2¾ hours; eight a day). There are six daily trains to Paris: four TGVs to Gare Montparnasse (428FF; five hours) and two non-overnight TGVs to Gare d'Austerlitz (383FF; 10 hours).

Car Eurorent (☎ 05 59 27 44 41) is at 15 Rue d'Étigny, the street that runs along the northern edge of Parc du Château. ADA (☎ 05 59 72 94 40) has an office at 3bis Route de Bayonne in the western suburb of Billère. If you call ahead, they'll deliver the car to you in town. The office is open Monday to Saturday from 8 am to noon and 2 to 7 pm.

Getting Around

To/From the Airport The Navette Aéroport (airport shuttle; ☎ 05 59 02 45 45) service meets most incoming flights and costs 30FF each way. There are eight runs a day (six on Sunday) to the airport; pick-up points are at the train station and 5 Place Clemenceau.

Bus The local bus company STAP (☎ 05 59 27 69 78) has an office in the Palais des Pyrénées on Rue Gachet and an information and ticket kiosk at the south-eastern corner of Place Clemenceau, open weekdays from 9 am to 12.15 pm and 1.45 to 5.30 pm. Bus maps are also available at the tourist office. Bus No 7 links the train station with Place Clemenceau, but most people walk or take the funicular.

All nine local bus lines run daily, except Sunday and holidays, from about 6 am to 7 or 7.30 pm and stop somewhere on Place Clemenceau (consult the map at the kiosk). Single tickets, sold on board, cost 6FF. A carnet of four tickets (good for eight rides) costs 31FF and is available at some *tabacs* (tobacconists). The Carte Contact, good for unlimited travel for a week (Monday to Saturday), costs 41FF, but you need a photo. Tickets are valid for one hour after they've been time-stamped.

Funicular Railway The train station is linked to Blvd des Pyrénées by a *funiculaire*, a funny little contraption that saves you over five minutes of easy uphill walking. It was built in 1908 by the hotels along Blvd des Pyrénées to save their guests from cardiovascular fitness, which was unfashionable at the time. From Monday to Saturday cars leave every three to four minutes between 7 am and 9 pm; Sunday hours are 1.30 to 9 pm. Travel is free.

Taxi There's a taxi stand (☎ 05 59 02 22 22) at Place Clemenceau.

LOURDES

• pop 17,000 ✉ 65100 alt 400m

Lourdes, 43km south-east of Pau, was just a sleepy market town on the edge of the snow-capped Pyrenees in 1858 when Bernadette Soubirous (1844-79), a near-illiterate, 14-year-old peasant girl, saw the Virgin Mary in a series of 18 visions that took place in a grotto near the town. The girl's account was eventually investigated by the Vatican, which confirmed them as bona fide apparitions. Bernadette, who lived out her short life as a nun, was canonised as Saint Bernadette in 1933.

These events set Lourdes on the path to becoming one of the world's most important pilgrimage sites. Some five million pilgrims from all over the world converge on Lourdes annually, including many sick people seeking cures.

But accompanying the fervent, almost medieval piety of the pilgrims is a simply astounding display of commercial exuberance that can seem unspeakably tacky. Wall thermometers, shake-up snow domes and plastic holy water bottles shaped like the Virgin are easy to mock; just remember that some people have spent their life savings to come here and for many of the Catholic faithful, Lourdes is as sacred a place as the Wailing Wall in Jerusalem is to Jews, Mecca to Muslims or the Ganges to Hindus.

Orientation

Lourdes' two main east-west streets are Rue de la Grotte and, 300m north, Blvd de la Grotte. Both lead to the Sanctuaires Notre Dame de Lourdes, but Blvd de la Grotte takes you to the main entrance at Pont Saint Michel. The principal north-south thoroughfare, known as Chaussée Maransin when it passes over Blvd de la Grotte, connects Ave de la Gare and the train station with Place Peyramale, where the tourist office is.

Information

Tourist Office The horseshoe-shaped glass-and-steel tourist office (☎ 05 62 42 77 40; fax 05 62 94 60 95), Place Peyramale, is open Monday to Saturday from 9 am to noon and 2 to 6 pm (7 pm from Easter to mid-October, when it is also open on Sunday from 10 am to 6 pm). From June to September, there is no midday closure. The office sells a pass called Visa Passeport Touristique (159/80FF for adults/children under 12) allowing entry to five museums in Lourdes and rides on the Pic du Jer funicular and the *petit train* that circumnavigates the town.

Sanctuaries For information on the Sanctuaires Notre Dame de Lourdes, including brochures in a variety of languages, drop by the Forum Information office (☎ 05 62 42 78 78) on the Esplanade des Processions. It is open daily from 9 am to noon and 2 to 6 pm. Visitors to the Sanctuaires should be dressed modestly – at the very least, don't wear very short skirts or shorts or T-shirts. Smoking is strictly forbidden throughout the complex.

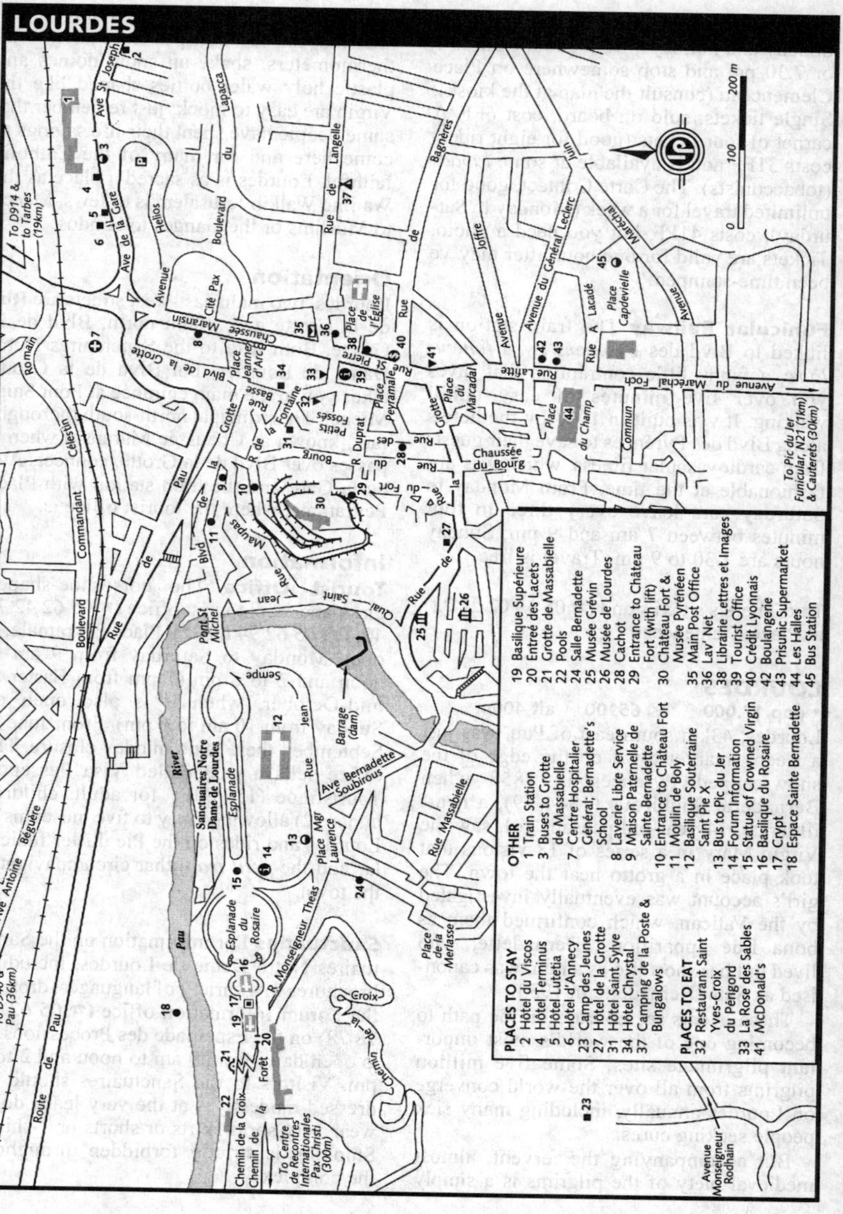
LOURDES
PLACES TO STAY
2 Hôtel du Viscos
4 Hôtel Terminus
5 Hôtel Lutetia
6 Hôtel d'Annecy
23 Camp des Jeunes
27 Hôtel de la Grotte
31 Hôtel Saint Sylve
34 Hôtel Chrystal
37 Camping de la Poste & Bungalows
PLACES TO EAT
32 Restaurant Saint Yves-Croix du Périgord
33 La Rose des Sables
41 McDonald's
OTHER
1 Train Station
3 Buses to Grotte de Massabielle
7 Centre Hospitalier Général; Bernadette's School
8 Laverie Libre Service
9 Maison Paternelle de Sainte Bernadette
10 Entrance to Château Fort (with lift)
11 Moulin de Boly
12 Basilique Souterraine Saint Pie X
13 Bus to Pic du Jer
14 Forum Information
15 Statue of Crowned Virgin
16 Basilique du Rosaire
17 Crypt
18 Espace Sainte Bernadette
19 Basilique Supérieure
20 Entrée des Lacets
21 Grotte de Massabielle
22 Pools
24 Salle Bernadette
25 Musée Grévin
26 Musée de Lourdes
28 Cachot
29 Entrance to Château Fort
30 Château Fort & Musée Pyrénéen
35 Main Post Office
36 Lav' Net
38 Librairie Lettres et Images
39 Tourist Office
40 Crédit Lyonnais
42 Boulangerie
43 Prisunic Supermarket
44 Les Halles
45 Bus Station

Money Crédit Lyonnais at 11 Rue Saint Pierre is open weekdays from 8.20 am to noon and 1.10 to 4.40 pm, and has an automatic teller machine that gives cash advances for most major foreign credit cards. There are several other banks nearby.

Post The main post office, 1 Rue de Langelle, is open Monday to Friday from 8.30 am to 6.30 pm and on Saturday until noon. It has foreign currency services and a 24 hour banknote exchange machine that accepts 15 different currencies.

Bookshop Hiking maps, guidebooks and a few English-language novels are available at Librairie Lettres et Images (☎ 05 62 94 00 29), 7 Rue Saint Pierre. It is open Monday to Saturday from 8.30 am to 12.30 pm and 2 to 7.30 pm.

Laundry The little Lav' Net in the arcade at 4 Rue de Langelle (opposite the main post office) is open daily from 8 am to 9 pm. Each washing machine load costs 29FF. There's a Laverie Libre Service on the ground floor of 10 Chaussée Maransin (opposite the Hôtel Ibis). It is open daily from 8 am to 7 pm and costs 26FF per load.

Medical Services The Centre Hospitalier Général (☎ 05 62 42 42 42) is at 2 Ave Alexandre Marqui, about 300m west of the train station.

Sanctuaires Notre Dame de Lourdes

The Sanctuaries of Our Lady of Lourdes, the huge religious complex that has grown up around the cave where Bernadette's visions took place, are west across the Pau River from the town centre. Development of this area began within a decade of the events of 1858, and the expansion has gone on ever since. You won't be alone if you find it difficult to understand how the gaudy late 19th century architecture, more reminiscent of Disneyland than of the majesty of a Gothic cathedral, inspires awe and devotion, but clearly it does. The grounds can be entered 24 hours a day via the Entrée des Lacets, which is on Rue Monseigneur Theas, off Place Monseigneur Laurence. The Pont Saint Michel entrance is open from 5 am to midnight.

The most revered site in the complex is known variously as the **Grotte de Massabielle** (Massabielle Cave or Grotto), the Grotte Miraculeuse (Miraculous Cave) and the Grotte des Apparitions (Cave of the Apparitions). It is hung with the crutches of generations of cured cripples. Nearby are 17 **pools** – six for men, 11 for women – in which 400,000 people seeking to be healed immerse themselves each year. Miraculous cures are becoming rarer and rarer; the last medically certifiable case took place in 1976.

The cave can be visited daily at any time. The pools are open Monday to Saturday from 9 (10 in winter) to 11 am and 2.30 to 4 pm, and on Sunday from 2 to 4 pm.

The main 19th century section of the Sanctuaries has three parts. On the west side of Esplanade du Rosaire, between the two ramps, is the neo-Byzantine **Basilique du Rosaire** (Basilica of the Rosary), inaugurated in 1889.

One level up is the **crypt**, opened in 1866 and reserved for silent worship. Above that is the spire-topped, neo-Gothic **Basilique Supérieure** (Upper Basilica), completed in 1876. All are open from 6 am to 7 pm between Easter and All Saints' Day (1 November) and from 8 am to 6 pm during the rest of the year.

From Palm Sunday (the Sunday before Easter) to at least mid-October there are solemn **torch-light processions** nightly at 8.45 pm from the Massabielle Grotto. The **Procession Eucharistique** (Blessed Sacrament Procession), in which groups of pilgrims carrying banners march along the Esplanade des Processions, takes place daily during the same period at 4.30 pm. In the event of rain, it is held inside the bunker-like **Basilique Souterraine Saint Pie X** (Underground Basilica of St Pius X), which is a most unattractive church described by some as a cross between a football stadium and an underground carpark. It was built in 1959 in the fallout shelter-style then all the rage. It is 200m long, 80m wide and can hold 20,000 people. Instead of stained-glass windows, it has back-lit works of *gemmail* – superimposed pieces of coloured glass embedded in a colourless enamel. The Underground Basilica keeps the same hours as the other three places of worship.

The modern complex north of the Massabielle Grotto, the **Espace Sainte Bernadette**, is where the sick and ailing receive assistance and those distinctive covered wheelchairs.

Chemin de la Croix Also known as the Chemin du Calvaire (Way of Calvary), the 1.5km Way of the Cross leads up the forested hillside from near the Basilique Supérieure. Inaugurated in 1912, it is lined with life-size versions of the 14 Stations of the Cross. The devout mount the stairs to the first station on their knees. The path is open from 7 am to 7 pm (8 am to 6 pm in the winter months).

Other Bernadette Sites

Four other places that figured largely in the life of Saint Bernadette are open to the public and charge no admission. Her birthplace, the **Moulin de Boly** (Boly Mill), is down the alley next to 55 Blvd de la Grotte at 12 Rue Bernadette Soubirous. On the same road, the **Maison Paternelle de Sainte Bernadette** is the house that the town of Lourdes bought for the Soubirous family after the apparitions. The **Cachot**, a former prison at 15 Rue des Petits Fossés, is where Bernadette lived during the apparitions. **Bernadette's school**, where she studied and lived from 1860 to 1866 with the Sœurs de Notre Dame de Nevers (Sisters of Our Lady of Nevers), is now part of the town's Centre Hospitalier Général west of the train station on Chaussée Maransin, and contains some of her personal effects.

Musée Grévin

The town's wax museum (☎ 05 62 94 33 74), 87 Rue de la Grotte, also known as the Musée de Cire de Lourdes, has life-size dioramas of important events in the lives of both Jesus Christ and Bernadette Soubirous. It is open daily from April to October from 9 to 11.40 am and 1.30 to 6.30 pm. During July and August it's also open in the evening from 8.30 to 10 pm. Entry costs 35FF (18FF for students).

Musée de Lourdes

The Lourdes Museum (☎ 05 62 94 28 00), due west of the Cinéma Pax in the Parking de l'Égalité, deals with the life of Saint Bernadette as well as the general history of Lourdes. It is open daily from 9 am to noon and from 1.30 to 6.30 pm. Admission is 30FF (20FF for students).

Château Fort

The eyrie-like medieval Château Fort des Comtes de Bigorre (Fortified Castle of the Counts of Bigorre), most of whose buildings date from the 17th and 18th centuries, houses a small **Musée Pyrénéen**, open daily from 9 am till noon and 2 to 6 pm.

If you want to take a lift up to the Château Fort, go to the entrance opposite 42 Rue du Fort on Rue Le Bondidier; otherwise, you can walk up the ramp at the north end of Rue du Bourg. Both entrances are open daily from 9 am to noon and 2 to 5 pm; to 7 pm from April to September.

Pic du Jer

The Pic du Jer, whose 948m summit affords a panoramic view of Lourdes and the central Pyrenees, can be reached by a six minute ride in a funicular (☎ 05 62 94 00 41), whose lower station is on Blvd d'Espagne about 1.5km due south of the tourist office. It operates from April to October. The first ascent is at 9.30 am; the last descent of the morning is at 11.50 am. In the afternoon, the first trip up is at 2 pm and the last trip down is usually at 6.20 pm. A return ticket costs 45FF (30FF for children aged six to 12). The funicular is linked with the Sanctuaries by a local bus (20FF return) from Place Monseigneur Laurence.

Alternatively, the walk (three hours return) to the top of Pic du Jer is quite pleasant. The trail starts just near the funicular railway.

Places to Stay

Lourdes has over 350 hotels, more than any other city in France (outside of Paris). The busiest periods are around Easter, Pentecost and Ascension Thursday and during May, August, the first half of September and the first week of October. Rooms are most difficult to find from about 12 to 17 August, when France's Pèlerinage Nationale (national pilgrimage) is held in honour of Assumption Day (15 August). In winter the town is very, very quiet and most of the hotels shut down.

Streets in the town centre that have lots of hotels include Blvd de la Grotte, Rue Basse, Rue de la Fontaine, Rue du Bourg, Rue Baron Duprat and Chaussée du Bourg. Near the train station, there are hotels along Ave de la Gare, Ave Helios, Chaussée Maransin and Cité Pax.

Places to Stay – Budget

Camping The camping ground nearest the centre of town is the tiny but friendly ***Camping de la Poste*** (☎ 05 62 94 40 35) at 26 Rue de Langelle, a few blocks east of the main post office. It is open from April to late October and charges 14FF per person and 19FF for a tent site. They also rent doubles/quads with washbasin and bidet for 130/180FF (150/200FF with shower) in a nearby building.

There are several larger camping grounds on the way to Argelès-Gazost, 12km southwest of Lourdes along the N21.

From June to September pilgrims (but not curious tourists) can pitch a tent at the ***Camp des Jeunes*** (☎ 05 62 42 79 95), 1km south-west of the Sanctuaries off Ave Monseigneur Rodhain, for 17FF per person.

Hostel Young pilgrims can stay at the ***Camp des Jeunes*** (see Camping). Run by the Oblates of Mary Immaculate order, it resembles a summer camp, with all sorts of group religious activities for young people. Space in a dorm room costs 27FF. Bring your own sheets or sleeping bag. Reception is staffed 24 hours a day.

Hotels Lourdes has a wide selection of cheap hotel rooms. Those listed under Town Centre offer the best value.

Hotels – Train Station Area The family-run ***Hôtel du Viscos*** (☎ 05 62 94 08 06; fax 05 62 94 26 74), 6bis Ave Saint Joseph, to the left as you leave the train station, is open from February to mid-December. Unadorned singles/doubles cost 100/150FF with washbasin and bidet and 130/200FF with prefab bathrooms. Hall showers are free.

The two star, 50 room ***Hôtel Lutetia*** (☎ 05 62 94 22 85; fax 05 62 94 11 10), 19 Ave de la Gare, is open from mid March to mid November. Ordinary rooms cost from 106/135FF (with washbasin) to 200/218FF (with shower and toilet). Hall showers are 18FF.

Nearby, the friendly ***Hôtel d'Annecy*** (☎ 05 62 94 13 75), 13 Ave de la Gare, is open from the week before Easter to late October. Plain singles/doubles/triples/quads cost 90/145/170/192FF with washbasin and 135/185/205/215FF with shower and toilet. Hall showers are 10FF.

Hotels – Town Centre ***Hôtel Saint Sylve*** (☎ 05 62 94 63 48), 9 Rue de la Fontaine, has large singles/doubles with washbasin for 70/130FF. With shower they're 100/160FF. The Saint Sylve is open from April to October.

Places to Stay – Mid-Range & Top End

Almost all the mid-range hotels have a selection of rooms with shower and toilet.

Train Station Area The two star ***Hôtel Terminus*** (☎ 05 62 94 68 00; fax 05 62 42 23 89), 31 Ave de la Gare, is open from Easter to mid-November. Singles/doubles cost 140/160FF with washbasin and bidet and 160/180FF with shower and toilet. There are also a few simple singles for 105FF.

Town Centre ***Hôtel Chrystal*** (☎ 05 62 94 00 36; fax 05 62 94 80 32), 16 Rue Basse, has cheap, modern rooms with washbasin and bidet from 110FF and ones with shower and toilet from 140FF. It is open from February to November.

One of the more stylish places in town (which is priced accordingly) is the *fin de siècle* ***Hôtel de la Grotte*** (☎ 05 62 94 58 87; fax 05 62 94 20 50), 66 Rue de la Grotte, with balconies and a really pretty garden. Singles/doubles with all the mod-cons start at 345/370FF (370/390FF from July to October). The Hôtel de la Grotte is open from April to October.

Places to Eat

Restaurants Most hotels offer pilgrims half or full-board plans; some even require guests to stay on those terms. It usually works out cheaper than eating outside, but the food is seldom very inspiring. Restaurants close early in this pious town; even ***McDonald's***, 7 Place du Marcadal, is slammed shut at 10.30 pm.

The ***Restaurant Saint Yves-Croix du Périgord*** (☎ 05 62 94 26 65), 13-15 Rue Basse, just west of the tourist office, serves up steak frites and a salad at lunch for only 45FF; pasta dishes start at 30FF and cassoulet is 50FF. ***La Rose des Sables*** (☎ 05 62 42 06 82), across from the tourist office at 8 Rue des Quatre Frères Soulas, specialises in couscous (from 58FF) and is open for lunch and dinner every day except Monday.

Self-Catering ***Les Halles***, the covered market on Place du Champ Commun, south of the tourist office, is open Monday to Saturday (daily from Easter to October) from 7 am to 1 pm. The ***Prisunic*** supermarket across the square at No 7 is open Monday to Saturday from 8.30 am to 7.30 pm (and on Sunday morning till noon in summer). Nearby, the ***boulangerie*** at 1 Place du Champ Commun is open from 7 am to 1 pm and 2.30 to 7.15 pm (closed Monday). From July to mid-September it's open daily from 7 am to 7.30 pm.

Getting There & Away

Bus The bus station (☎ 05 62 94 31 15), down Rue Anselme Lacadé from Les Halles, has services to Pau (36.50FF; 1¼ hours; four to six times a day), Argelès-Gazost (12.50FF), Bagnères de Bigorre, Bétharram (west of Lourdes), Pierrefitte-Nestalas (south of Argelès-Gazost; 30 minutes) and Tarbes (19FF; 30 minutes; 12 a day). The ticket windows are open weekdays from 8 am to noon and 2 to 6 pm. All the buses also stop at the train station, where tickets are sold on board.

An SNCF bus to the Pyrenean town of Cauterets (36FF; one hour; four to six a day), and another to Luz Saint Sauveur and Luz Ardiden (38FF; one hour; six to seven a day), leave from the train station parking lot; they also stop near the bus station, but only if you flag them down.

Train The train station (☎ 08 36 35 35 35) is 1km east of the Sanctuaries on Ave de la Gare.

Since so many pilgrims arrive by rail, Lourdes is well connected by direct train to cities all over France, including Bayonne (104FF; five a day; 1¾ hours), Bordeaux (178FF; three hours), Dijon (via Lyon; 471FF; 12 hours), Geneva (442FF; 12 hours; two a day), Lyon (382FF; 9½ hours), Marseille (327FF; eight hours), Nice (409FF; 10½ hours; three a day), Pau (39FF; 30 minutes; nine a day) and Toulouse (122FF; 2¼ hours; seven a day). Options to Paris include three non-TGV trains to Gare d'Austerlitz (487FF; nine hours), two of which are overnight sleepers, and TGVs to Gare Montparnasse (439FF; 5½ hours).

Getting Around

Bus From the Sunday before Easter to mid-October, local buses link the train station (the stop is next to the Hôtel Terminus) with the Grotte de Massabielle. A ride costs 11FF (6.50FF from the station to the centre of town). Buses run every 15 minutes from 7.30 to noon and 1.30 to 6.30 pm.

Taxi There's a taxi stand (☎ 05 62 94 31 30) in the carpark of the train station.

Car Lourdes is one big traffic jam in summer. If you have a vehicle, your best bet is to park near the train or bus station, where there are spaces, and walk.

ARREAU

Arreau is situated 60km south-east of Lourdes and accessible only by car (take the D937 to Bagnéres then the D935 over the Col d'Aspin to Arreau). Strategically placed at the crossing of two converging rivers, the Neste du Louron and Neste d'Aure, Arreau prospered for many centuries as the ancient capital of four valleys, equidistant from the Mediterranean and the Atlantic and on one of the main trading routes with Spain. The most attractive buildings here are the Renaissance **Maison des Lys**, covered in fleurs-de-lis timberwork, and the Romanesque **Church of St-Exupére**, Bishop of Toulouse. The tourist office (☎ 05 62 98 63 15) is housed in the **Château de Nestes**, together with an interesting museum of Pyrenean craftwork. Both are open from 9.30 am to noon and from 2 to 5.30 pm. Entrance to the museum is free.

The village is known for its craft shops, and a sticky cake called *gâteau à la broche*, brought to the Pyrenees from the Balkans by Napoleon's armies.

GAVARNIE

During summer months, Gavarnie, 52km south of Lourdes, at the end of the D921, is a popular base for walkers and mountaineers. Footpaths from this small village lead to the Cirque de Gavarnie, a gigantic, amphitheatre-like formation of rock right on the Franco-Spanish border, over 4km wide at its base and 14km around the crest line, with ice-capped peaks of over 3000m. A round trip to the Cirque takes two to three hours on foot (horses and donkeys can be hired in the village for 90FF). ***Camping La Bergerie***, the cheapest place to stay, costs 8/10/8FF per tent/person/car. In mid July, an arts festival at the Cirque attracts thousands of visitors. For further information and tickets, contact the tourist office (☎ 05 62 92 49 10).

PARC NATIONAL DES PYRÉNÉES

The Pyrenees National Park, one of six national parks in France, stretches for about 100km along the Franco-Spanish border from the Vallée d'Aspe in the west to the Vallée d'Aure in the east. Its width varies from 1.5 to 15km. Created in 1967, it covers an area of 457 sq km that includes 230 high-altitude lakes and the highest point in the French Pyrenees, the 3298m Sommet du Vignemale.

About 12% of the park is forested. The many rivers and cascades are fed both by springs and by some 2000mm of annual precipitation, much of which falls as snow (the park is usually covered with snow from November to May). The French side of the range, especially the western section, is much wetter and greener than the Spanish side.

To the north, the park is bordered by 2060 sq km of populated land, which is also managed by the national park but is not fully protected. The area has a population of about 35,000. To the south, on the other side of the border, is a Spanish national park, the 150 sq km Parque Nacional de Ordesa, and 1000 sq km of game reserves.

Information

National Park Offices National park offices with visitors centres are located at Arrens-Marsous, Arudy, Cauterets, Etsaut, Gabas, Gavarnie, Luz Saint Sauveur and Saint Lary-Soulon. Most – though not the one at Cauterets – are closed during the cold half of the year. If you'd like advance information, contact the main office (☎ 05 62 56 48 00; fax 05 62 93 69 90) at 6 Rue Eugene Tenot, 65000 Tarbes.

Weather For weather information in the department of Hautes-Pyrénées (ie for Cauterets), call the *météo* (weather bureau) on ☎ 08 36 68 02 65. The météo number for Pyrénées-Atlantiques (ie the Vallée d'Aspe) is ☎ 08 36 68 02 64.

Maps Each of the six valleys of the national park is covered by a *pochette* (folder) of hiking itineraries in French entitled *Promenades dans le Parc National des*

PARC NATIONAL DES PYRÉNÉES

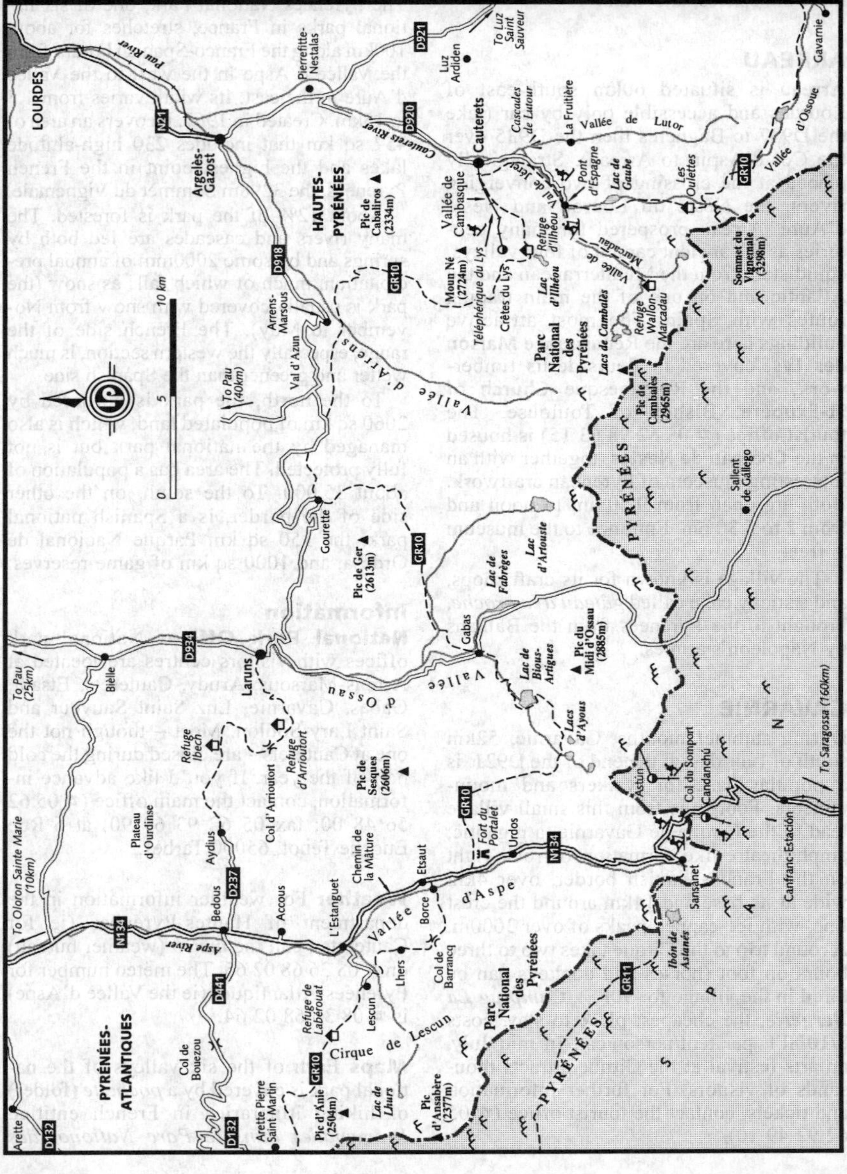

Pyrénées. Intended for use with hiking maps, they are on sale (35FF) at national park offices and local tourist offices.

Hiking

The Parc National des Pyrénées is criss-crossed by 350km of trails (including the GR10), some of which link up with trails in Spain. For hiking suggestions, see Hiking in the sections on Cauterets and Vallée d'Aspe. Map recommendations appear under Maps in the Information section of each listing. Park boundaries are marked by paintings (on rocks, trees etc) of a red *isard* (chamois) head on a white background.

Within the park's boundaries there are about 20 *refuges* (mountain huts or lodges), most of them run by the Club Alpin Français. Most are staffed in the warmer months only but are open all year. *Cabanes* are less comfortable *refuges*.

Rafting

For information on rafting trips in the Pyrenees, contact the Centre de Sports Nautiques (☎ 05 59 39 61 00; fax 05 59 39 65 16) at Soeix, 64400 Oloron Sainte Marie. They have day-long rafting and canoeing trips for 195/160FF for adults/children. There's plenty of rafting done on the Pau River along the N21 four or five kilometres south-west of Lourdes.

Skiing

The Pyrenees receive less snow than the much higher Alps, and what snow falls is generally wetter and heavier. Despite this, there are good alpine skiing and snowboarding for beginners and intermediates. Cross-country skiing and ski touring are also quite good along the various valleys, plateaux and ridges. The ski season normally lasts from December to early April, but this varies from year to year according to snow conditions.

Resorts There are many ski resorts dotting both sides of the Pyrenees, with France counting some 16 downhill and six cross-country areas. One of the oldest resorts is Cauterets, which usually has the longest season and most reliable snow conditions. Another resort is Piau Engaly (tourist office ☎ 05 62 39 61 69), 81km south-east of Tarbes, with 40km of trails between 1420 and 2500m (the vertical drop is 1100m). Its 37 trails, including seven black (expert) runs, are suited to all levels of skiing. Annual downhill speed skiing races are held at Luz Saint Sauveur (tourist office ☎ 05 62 92 81 60), 47km south of Lourdes. Luz Ardiden has 45km of trails between 1730 and 2450m with enough variety for all types of skiers. Both of these resorts have limited cross-country skiing, but for some of the best cross-country skiing head for Val d'Azun (tourist office ☎ 05 62 97 49 49 in Arrens-Marsous), which is about 30km south-west of Lourdes. It has 50km of trails between 1350 and 1500m.

Organised Tours

The Pau-based Compagnie du Sud (☎ 05 59 27 04 24; fax 05 59 27 63 25) has guided treks and other activities in the Pyrenees. See Activities in the Pau section for more details.

CAUTERETS

• pop 1200 ✉ 65110 alt 930m

The lovely thermal spa and ski resort of Cauterets is nestled in a narrow valley surrounded by steep slopes (up to 2800m) of the Pyrenees. In summer it makes a superb base for exploring the forests, meadows, lakes and streams of the Parc National des Pyrénées, though in July and August the trails can get a bit crowded. In winter, Cauterets is blessed with an abundance of snow – it is the first of France's Pyrenean ski stations to open and the last to close. Lourdes, the gateway to Cauterets, is less than 30km to the north.

Orientation

Cauterets is spread out for about 1km along the small Cauterets River (Gave de Cauterets). The main road from Lourdes, the D920, becomes Route de Pierrefitte as it enters town, taking you straight to Place de la Gare, where you'll find the bus station (but no train), the national park office and the Téléphérique du Lys, the cable car that will take you 1850m up to the Cirque du Lys. The tourist office is on Place Maréchal Foch, at the end of Ave Leclerc.

Information

Tourist Office The helpful tourist office (☎ 05 62 92 50 27; fax 05 62 92 59 12) at Place Maréchal Foch is open daily all year from 9 am to 12.30 pm and 2 to 6.30 pm. During school holidays (Christmas, Easter, July and August), the hours are 9 am to 7 pm. The reservation service can help you find both hotel rooms and apartments available by the week.

National Park Office The Maison du Parc National des Pyrénées (☎ 05 62 92 52 56), Place de la Gare, is open daily all year from 9.30 am till noon and 2 to 6.30 pm (3 to 7 pm from June to September). It is one of the few park offices that doesn't close in the off season, and it also houses a free, permanent exhibit on Pyrenean flora and fauna and how they've adapted to different altitudes. See Maps under Information and the Rock Climbing section for maps and brochures you might want to purchase.

Money There are a couple of banks along Rue de Belfort, including a Caisse d'Épargne in the Galerie Aladin shopping mall and a Société Générale at No 5. They are open weekdays only from 9 or 9.30 am till noon and 2 to 4 or 4.15 pm.

Post The post office is on Rue de Belfort. It's open Monday to Friday from 9 am to noon and 2 to 5 pm, and on Saturday until noon. From July to early September, weekday hours are 9 am to 6 pm with no midday break.

Maps The area west of Cauterets is covered by IGN's 1:25,000 scale Série Bleue map No 1647OT, entitled *Vignemale, Ossau, Arrens, Cauterets*; the area east of town is covered by map No 1748OT, *Gavarnie, Luz Saint Sauveur*. Each costs 55FF.

The Maison du Parc National sells the excellent packet of 15 hiking itineraries in French entitled *Promenades dans le Parc National des Pyrénées – Vallée de Cauterets* (40FF) while, for information on short, easy walks around Cauterets, ask the tourist office for a copy of *Cauterets à Deux Pas* (35FF). If you have questions about itineraries, the staff at the Maison du Parc National can help.

Laundry The laundrette at 19 Rue Richelieu is open daily from 7 am to 10 pm. The laundrette on Rue César, a bit up the hill from Place Maréchal Foch and opposite the Hôtel César, is open Monday to Saturday from 8 am to 9 pm.

Hiking

If you take one of the chair lifts that continue to run during the summer and begin your hike from the top, you'll be able to do more walking at higher elevations. For information on the Téléphérique du Lys, see the Getting Around section.

Contact the Bureau des Guides et Accompagnateurs (☎ 05 62 92 62 02) if you'd like to hike with a guide. Its office (shared with the École de Ski Français) next to the Hôtel de Ville on Place Georges Clemenceau is open weekdays from 9 am till noon and 3 to 7 pm.

Around Cauterets The GR10 trail follows the **Vallée de Cambasque**, which is west of Cauterets, and the **Val de Jéret**, south of town.

Possible hiking destinations in the area include the **Pic de Cabaliros** (2334m), north-west of Cauterets; the **Lac d'Ilhéou** (1988m) and the Refuge d'Ilhéou (☎ 05 62 92 75 07; staffed late May to mid October) at the **Col d'Ilhéou** (2242m), south-west of town; and the **Cascades de Lutour**, south of town in the Vallée de Lutour.

You can also take the Téléphérique du Lys and its chair-lift continuation to the 2300m **Crêtes du Lys** and then walk back to town via Lac d'Ilhéou.

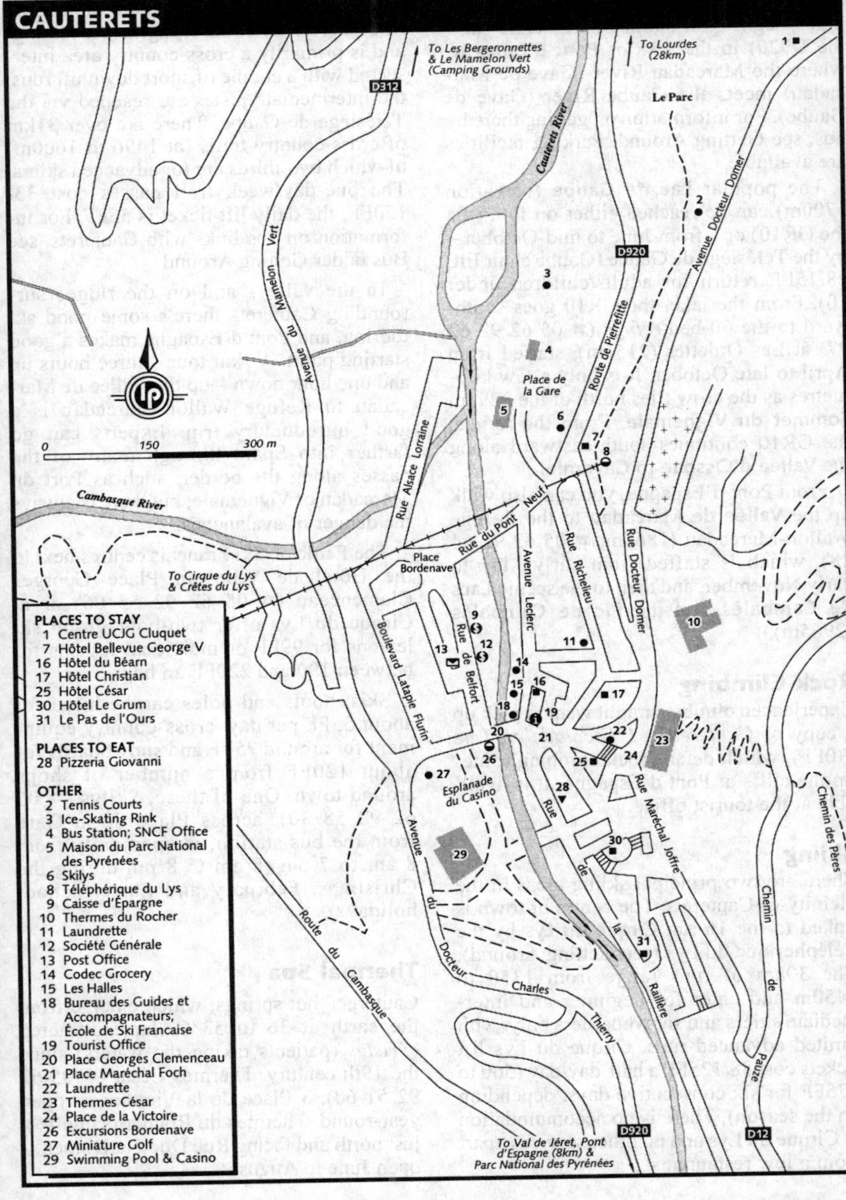
CAUTERETS
To Les Bergeronnettes & Le Mamelon Vert (Camping Grounds)
To Lourdes (28km)
D312
D920
D12
Le Parc
Cauterets River
Cambasque River
Place de la Gare
Place Bordenave
Esplanade du Casino
Avenue du Mamelon Vert
Route de Pierrefitte
Avenue Docteur Domer
Rue Alsace Lorraine
Rue du Pont Neuf
Rue Richelieu
Rue Docteur Domer
Avenue Leclerc
Rue de Belfort
Boulevard Latapie Flurin
Rue Maréchal Joffre
Rue de la Raillère
Avenue du Docteur Charles Thierry
Route du Cambasque
Chemin des Pères
Chemin de Pauze
To Cirque du Lys & Crêtes du Lys
To Val de Jéret, Pont d'Espagne (8km) & Parc National des Pyrénées
0 150 300 m
PLACES TO STAY
1 Centre UCJG Cluquet
7 Hôtel Bellevue George V
16 Hôtel du Béarn
17 Hôtel Christian
25 Hôtel César
30 Hôtel Le Grum
31 Le Pas de l'Ours
PLACES TO EAT
28 Pizzeria Giovanni
OTHER
2 Tennis Courts
3 Ice-Skating Rink
4 Bus Station; SNCF Office
5 Maison du Parc National des Pyrénées
6 Skilys
8 Téléphérique du Lys
9 Caisse d'Épargne
10 Thermes du Rocher
11 Laundrette
12 Société Générale
13 Post Office
14 Codec Grocery
15 Les Halles
18 Bureau des Guides et Accompagnateurs; École de Ski Francaise
19 Tourist Office
20 Place Georges Clemenceau
21 Place Maréchal Foch
22 Laundrette
23 Thermes César
24 Place de la Victoire
26 Excursions Bordenave
27 Miniature Golf
29 Swimming Pool & Casino

From Pont d'Espagne A number of fine hikes begin 8km south of Cauterets (take the D920) in the area of **Pont d'Espagne**, where the Marcadau River (Gave de Marcadau) meets the Gaube River (Gave de Gaube). For information on getting there by bus, see Getting Around. Parking facilities are available.

The popular **Lac de Gaube** (elevation 1700m) can be reached either on foot (via the GR10) or – from June to mid-October – by the Télésiège de Gaube (Gaube chair lift; 28/15FF return for adults/children under 10). From the lake, the GR10 goes southward to the 60-bed *refuge* (☎ 05 62 92 62 97) at Les Oulettes (2151m), staffed from April to late October. It is only a few kilometres as the crow flies north of the 3298m **Sommet du Vignemale**. From the *refuge*, the GR10 continues south-eastward along the **Vallée d'Ossoue** to **Gavarnie**.

From Pont d'Espagne, you can also walk up the **Vallée de Marcadau** to the Refuge Wallon-Marcadau (1866m; ☎ 05 62 92 64 28), which is staffed from early May to early November, and then to the scenic **Lacs de Cambalès** and the **Pic de Cambalès** (2965m).

Rock Climbing

Experienced climbers might want to pick up a copy of *Cauterets – L'Escalade en Tête* (30FF), which details rock climbing routes up the cliffs at Pont d'Espagne. It is available at the tourist office.

Skiing

There are two principal skiing areas in the vicinity of Cauterets. The centre of town is linked to the 16-run **Cirque du Lys** by the Téléphérique du Lys (see Getting Around). The 30km of runs range from 1350 to 2450m and cater for beginner and intermediate skiers and snowboarders only, with limited advanced runs. Cirque du Lys lift tickets cost 88/125FF a half-day/day (560 to 675FF for six consecutive days, depending on the season). There is no accommodation at Cirque du Lys and no other services apart from a few restaurants.

The second ski area is about 8km south of Cauterets at **Pont d'Espagne** (see Hiking) and is primarily a cross-country area intersected with a couple of short downhill runs; the intermediate pistes are reached via the Télésiège de Gaube. There are over 31km of cross-country trails (at 1496 to 1600m) of which two-thirds are for advanced skiers. The one-day/week trail passes cost 33/150FF; the daily lift ticket is 55FF. For information on bus links with Cauterets, see Bus under Getting Around.

In the valleys and on the ridges surrounding Cauterets there's some good ski touring, and Pont d'Espagne makes a good starting point. A 7km tour – three hours up and one hour down – up the Vallée de Marcadau to Refuge Wallon-Marcadau is a good introductory trip. Experts can go farther into Spain through many of the passes along the border, such as Port du Marcadau or Vignemale, but there is always the danger of avalanches.

The École de Ski Français centres next to the Hôtel de Ville on Place Georges Clemenceau (☎ 05 62 92 55 06) or at Cirque du Lys offer two-hour group ski lessons for 99FF or individual lessons for between 190 and 220FF an hour.

Skis, boots and poles can be hired for about 55FF per day, cross-country equipment for around 75FF and snowboards for about 120FF from a number of shops around town. One of these, Skilys (☎ 05 62 92 58 30), across Place de la Gare from the bus station, is open daily from 8 am to 7 pm (8 am to 8 pm during the Christmas, February and Easter school holidays).

Thermal Spa

Cauterets' hot springs, which emerge from the earth at 36 to 53°C, have attracted *curistes* (patients taking the waters) since the 19th century. Thermes César (☎ 05 62 92 51 60), 3 Place de la Victoire, is open year-round. Thermes du Rocher (same ☎), just north and facing Rue Docteur Domer, is open June to August.

Other Activities

About 200m south-west of the tourist office is Esplanade du Casino, also known as Esplanade des Œufs, where you'll find cafés, an indoor swimming pool (☎ 05 62 92 61 30; 20/10FF for adults/children), a miniature golf course and the town's large casino. There's a *patinoire* (ice-skating rink; ☎ 05 62 92 58 48) at Place de la Gare. It is open daily from 3 to 6 pm on Wednesday, Saturday and Sunday (and daily from 3 to 6 pm in July and August). The charge is 30/15FF for adults/children. Skates cost 15FF to rent.

Places to Stay

Cheap beds are thin on the ground in July and August. Many hotels require that you take at least half-pension.

Camping & Bungalows There are a number of camping grounds slightly north of town along Ave du Mamelon Vert, including ***Les Bergeronnettes*** (☎ 05 62 92 50 69) and ***Le Mamelon Vert*** (☎ 05 62 92 51 56).

The friendly ***Centre UCJG Cluquet*** (☎ 05 62 92 52 95) is on Ave Docteur Domer, about 300m north of the tennis courts. From mid-June to mid-September, a bed in one of the three tents, each of which sleeps about a dozen people, costs 40FF, including use of the shower and the fully equipped kitchen. Space is almost always available. You can also pitch a tent here for 20FF per person. This place also has beds in a dormitory for 55FF and nine extremely basic wood-and-cement bungalows, each with two or three beds, that are available year-round despite the lack of heating. Rental costs 55FF per person per night.

Refuges For detailed information on getting to *refuges* ***Wallon-Marcadau***, ***d'Ilhéou*** and ***Les Oulettes***, which charge 78FF per person, see the preceding Hiking section.

Gîte d'Étape ***Le Pas de l'Ours*** (☎ 05 62 92 58 07; fax 05 62 92 06 49), 21 Rue de la Raillère, is open from 1 May to 15 October and 15 December to 20 April. A bed in one of the two dorm rooms costs 65FF, including use of the kitchen. Doubles with shower and toilet start at 240FF. This place has a sauna (45FF).

Hotels Behind the tourist office at 4 Ave Leclerc, the 17 room ***Hôtel du Béarn*** (☎ 05 62 92 53 54) is open all year except October and November. Plain but large and well-lit doubles with washbasin and bidet cost 140 to 180FF. Hall showers are 6FF.

The friendly, 20 room ***Hôtel Le Grum*** (☎ 05 62 92 53 01), 4 Rue Victor Hugo, is open all year except November to mid December. Rooms for one/two/three/four people cost 110/150/180/210FF with washbasin and bidet, and 150/190/210/240FF with shower and toilet. Hall showers are free. The ***Hôtel Christian*** (☎ 05 62 92 50 04), 10 Rue Richelieu, open from February to September, has big doubles with high ceilings for 145FF with washbasin and bidet, 175FF with shower, and 232FF with shower and toilet. Triples/quads with shower and toilet are also available for 294/342FF. Hall showers are free.

The two star, 17 room ***Hôtel César*** (☎ 05 62 92 52 57), 3 Rue César, half a block down the hill from Thermes César, is open all year except May and October. Attractive rooms with shower start at 230FF.

The venerable, 41 room ***Hôtel Bellevue George V*** (☎ 05 62 92 50 21; fax 05 62 92 62 54), opposite the bus station on Place de la Gare, has rooms with shower from 260FF.

In the more secluded Pont d'Espagne, there are also several options, including the ***Auberge de la Frutière*** (☎ 05 62 92 52 04), open from April to late November, where simple rooms with breakfast start at about 260FF, and ***Le Pont d'Espagne*** (☎ 05 62 92 54 10; fax 05 62 92 51 72) with rooms from 120FF. The ***Chalet du Clot*** (☎ 05 62 92 61 27) has dormitory rooms with four beds costing 90FF per person.

Places to Eat

Restaurants The best areas for restaurant-hunting are Rue de la Raillère, Place Maréchal Foch and Rue Richelieu.

Pizzeria Giovanni (☎ 05 62 92 57 80), 5 Rue de la Raillère, is open from mid-June to early November and mid-December to mid-May. Except during school holidays, it may be open only in the evening. Pizzas start at 39FF and there's a *menu* for 75FF.

Self-Catering Around the corner from the tourist office, ***Les Halles***, the covered market at 5 Ave Leclerc, is open from 7 am to 12.30 pm and 4 pm (3.30 pm in summer) to 7.30 pm (closed Sunday afternoon). During February, July and August, a few stalls stay open on Sunday afternoon. There's a ***Codec*** grocery next door at No 5bis, open Monday to Saturday from 8.30 am to 12.30 pm and 4 to 7.30 pm, and on Sunday morning. The ***Casino*** supermarket is at No 18 Ave Leclerc.

Getting There & Away

All public transport to Cauterets passes through Lourdes, 29km to the north, on the way to Tarbes.

Bus The wonderful wooden bus station (☎ 05 62 92 53 70), Place de la Gare, looks like a cross between the set of a western movie and a giant cuckoo clock. It is open weekdays from 9 am to noon and 3 to 6 pm from October to April (9 am to 12.30 pm and 3.30 to 7 pm the rest of the year, also Saturday afternoon and Sunday from June to September).

SNCF buses link the Lourdes train station with Cauterets's bus station (36FF; one hour; four to six a day). The last bus to Lourdes leaves at about 7.30 pm. The bus continues on to Tarbes.

Train Cauterets is not served by train, but the SNCF office in the bus station can handle ticketing and reservations.

Getting Around

Bus Excursions Bordenave (☎ 05 62 92 53 68) has buses to Pont d'Espagne (15FF one way; 25FF return) several times a week during July and August and three times a week in June and September – unless it rains or no one shows up. Buses leave Cauterets at 9.30 am and 2 pm; the last bus back to Cauterets leaves Pont d'Espagne at about 5 pm. From 20 December to approximately the end of March, the company has daily buses to the Télésiège de Gaube at Pont d'Espagne. Hours are about the same as they are in the summer.

Bordenave's buses leave from the bus station. Tickets are sold at the company's office at 8 Place Georges Clemenceau (facing the Hôtel de Ville), which is open from 10.30 am to 12.30 pm and 4 to 7 pm.

Taxi To order a taxi call Excursions Bordenave on ☎ 05 62 92 53 68 or, after hours, on ☎ 05 62 92 52 74.

Bicycle Skilys (☎ 05 62 92 58 30), which is across Place de la Gare from the bus station, rents mountain bikes for 60/100FF a half-day/day. An ID is required as a deposit.

Téléphérique The Téléphérique du Lys (☎ 05 62 92 50 27), 1 Ave Docteur Domer, operates from mid-June to mid or late September and from December to the end of the ski season (sometime in April). It goes to the 1850m Cirque du Lys, where you can catch the Télésiège du Grum up to Crêtes du Lys (2300m); the total travel time is 25 minutes. The one-way/return trip costs 30/40FF for adults and 15/20FF for children to Cirque du Lys and another 22/12FF for adults/children return to Crêtes du Lys, but there's an all-in return package for adults/children for 50/25FF. Transporting a mountain bike or parapente costs 45FF one way. The téléphérique runs every half-hour from 9 am to 12.15 pm and 1.45 to 5.45 pm. The télésiège's schedule is 9.30 am to 12.10 pm and 1.45 to 5.10 pm The last ascent, which will allow you to get back to Cauterets by nightfall, is the one at 4.30 pm.

VALLÉE D'ASPE

The Aspe Valley, which is on the western edge of the Parc National des Pyrénées, is drained by the Aspe River (Gave d'Aspe), which flows north from the 2000m peaks around the Col du Somport to the town of Oloron Sainte Marie, 40km away. The valley gets a lot of vehicular traffic, but the nearby hills, mountains and valleys, accessible only on foot, remain relatively untouched by the 20th century. The whole area is remarkably green, even in summer. Pau is the gateway.

Bedous (population 1100), the largest village in the area, is set in a wide, fairly flat part of the valley. The starting point for several lower-elevation hikes, it is also a good place to stock up on food. Accous (population 200), about 3km south by road, has a couple of places offering parapente and hang-gliding courses.

In the narrow upper valley, Etsaut and nearby Borce, surrounded by the valley's steep slopes, are good bases for higher-elevation hikes. About 3km south of Etsaut is the privately owned **Fort du Portalet**, an early 19th century fortress that overlooks a particularly narrow and defensible bit of the valley. From 1941 to 1945 the Germans used it as a prison.

Orientation

The N134 runs along the length of the Vallée d'Aspe from Oloron Sainte Marie to the Col du Somport, which is on the Franco-Spanish border (see Getting There & Away).

Bedous is about 22km south of Oloron Sainte Marie; the N134 is known as Rue Gambetta as it passes through town. About 2.5km to the south is the turn-off to Accous, whose tiny centre is about 800m east of the N134.

Etsaut is another 9km south. Tiny Borce is a short way up the western side of the valley from Etsaut. Lescun is 3km south-west of the N134 at a point midway between Bedous and Etsaut.

Information

Informal sources of information on the area (eg hiking itineraries, outdoor activities, equipment rental) include Le Choucas Blanc in Bedous and the Maison de l'Ours in Etsaut (see Places to Stay), and the Maison des Jeunes et de la Culture in Etsaut (see Places to Stay).

Tourist Offices Bedous' tourist office (☎ 05 59 34 71 48) is at Place François Sarrail in the arcaded *mairie* (town hall) building, opposite the church. To get there, turn east on Rue Gambetta (the N134) at No 17 and walk down Rue Pierre Portes. It's open Monday to Saturday from 9.30 am to 12.30 pm and 2 to 5.30 pm (2 to 6 pm in summer). Among the useful brochures they distribute is the English-language *Trail Guide*, which identifies the flora you're likely to encounter on a hike.

National Park Office You may be able to extract some hiking information and tips from the less-than-helpful staff at the Maison du Parc National des Pyrénées (☎ 05 59 34 88 30) in Etsaut, housed in the former train station at the northern end of town. It is open from mid-May to mid-November from 9.30 am to 12.30 pm and 1.30 to 6.30 pm.

Entry to the small visitor centre, which has exhibits on the rare brown bear, is free. A 15 minute walk to the north-west will take you to another bear centre, the **Clos aux Ours** (☎ 05 59 34 88 88; see the boxed text 'Pyrenean Bears'). The centre is open June to September from 10 am till noon and 2 to 8 pm, and on Wednesday, Saturday and Sunday from 2 to 7 pm the rest of the year. Admission is 19/12FF for those over/under 16 years.

Money In Bedous, money can be changed at the Caisse d'Épargne, located on the western side of the mairie building facing Rue Pierre Portes. It is open Tuesday to Saturday from 8.30 am to 12.30 pm and 1.50 to 5 pm (3.35 pm on Saturday). The Crédit Agricole on Rue Pierre Portes has an ATM.

Post The Bedous post office, on Rue Gambetta between Nos 28 and 30, is open Monday to Friday from 9 am to noon and 1.45 to 4.45 pm, and on Saturday until noon.

In Etsaut, the post office is in the centre of the village next to the church. Foreign currency services are available. It is open Monday to Friday from 9 am to noon and 1.30 to 4.30 pm, and on Saturday from 8.30 am until 11.30 am. The postcode for Bedous, Accous and Etsaut is 64490.

Maps The best general hiking map of the area is the 1:50,000 scale *Pyrénées Carte No 3*, published by Édition Randonnées Pyrénées. A more detailed option is IGN's 1:25,000 scale Série Bleue map No 1547OT (*Ossau, Vallée d'Aspe*), which costs 55FF.

Promenades dans le Parc National des Pyrénées – Vallée d'Aspe (40FF) is a useful packet of information sheets in French on 12 hikes in and around the Vallée d'Aspe.

If you'd like to trek with a guide, call the Bureau des Guides et Accompagnateurs on ☎ 05 59 39 58 50 (in Etsaut) or the Maison Despourrins on ☎ 05 59 34 53 50 (in Accous; see the Gîtes d'Étape section in Places to Stay).

Laundry The Maison des Jeunes et de la Culture in Etsaut (see Places to Stay) has a washing machine and dryer. The cost is 40FF for a 5kg load.

Hiking

Hikers starting in Bedous have a number of options. To the east,you can walk via the viewpoint indicator to the Plateau d'Ourdinse and then to **Aydius**. Aydius can also be reached by taking the D237; regardless of how you get there, you can return to Bedous via Accous, the **Col d'Arrioutort** or even Etsaut. East of Aydius there are two *refuges*: the Refuge Ibech and the Refuge d'Arrioutort.

Another option from Bedous is to head westward to the **Col de Bouezou**. The trail later links up with the GR10, which you can take back to the Vallée d'Aspe via Lescun or even Etsaut. The Refuge de Labérouat is a few kilometres north-west of Lescun.

From Lescun (population 200; 950m), whose slate roofs once sheltered a leper colony, you get a good view of the **Cirque de Lescun**, the jagged mountains that overlook the town to the west. Another trail leads south-westward to the **Lac de Lhurs** (1691m). Another possible destination in this area is the **Cabane d'Ansabère** at Pic d'Ansabère (2377m).

From Etsaut, you can walk south and then east along a part of the GR10 known as the **Chemin de la Mâture**, used in the 18th century to harvest timber for the Bayonne shipyards.

A difficult segment of the trail continues south-eastward to the **Lacs d'Ayous**. West of Etsaut, the GR10 goes via the village of Borce to the **Col de Barrancq**, from where

Pyrenean Bears

The rugged Aspe Valley near the Franco-Spanish border is the last Pyrenean home of the brown bear (*Ursos arctos*). Hidden deep in the valley near the Franco-Spanish border, the tiny village of Borce would have remained virtually undiscovered by tourists had two young boys not returned from a picnic in 1971 carrying a tiny baby bear, its mother presumedly shot by poachers. Named Jojo, the cub soon became a popular tourist attraction and remained the village mascot until his death 20 years later.

Since then, volunteers in the village, anxious to maintain interest in Pyrenean bears, set up an information centre – Le Clos aux Ours – to show the life of the bears in the mountains and their bleak future (only an estimated half-dozen remain), along with two resident bears, Antoine and Ségolène.

The centre is currently trying to raise support to import two bears from Slovenia to save the local bear population from extinction.

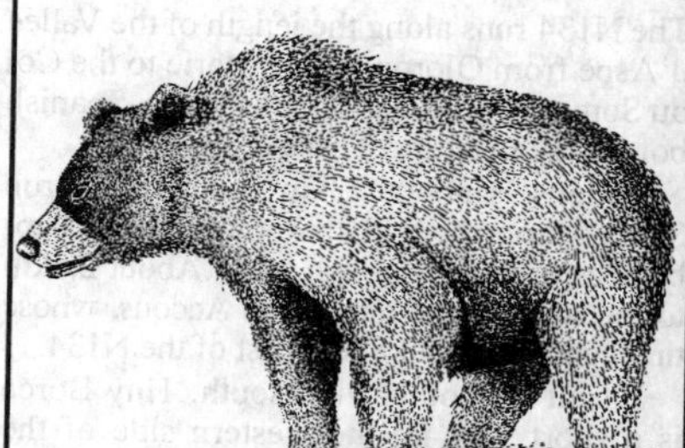

here are trails back to the valley via Lhers and Lescun.

From Sansanet, a carpark at a hairpin curve in the N134 a few kilometres towards Etsaut from the Spanish border, a trail leads to the **Ibón de Astanés** (also spelled Ibon de Estanès and Lac d'Estaens), the largest lake in the area. The walk up and back, an international event given that the lake is in Spain, takes about five hours. The GR11 passes by the Ibón de Astanés.

About 15km west of Bedous, a number of fine hikes begin at Arette Pierre Saint Martin (see Skiing).

Parapente

In Accous near the Maison Despourrins (see Places to Stay), the École de Parapente Ascendance (☎ 05 59 34 52 07) offers accompanied *baptêmes de l'air* (introductory flights) for 350FF. A five day intro course, held regularly from June to September, cost about 2100FF plus board and lodging; more advanced courses are also available. Flights begin from mountainsides 800m above the valley floor. From October to June, Parapente Ascendance is open only on weekends.

Cycling

For information on renting mountain bikes, see Getting Around.

Hang-Gliding

Virvolta (☎ 05 59 34 50 30), also near the Maison Despourrins, has half-day, accompanied baptêmes de l'air for 380FF.

Skiing

The **Le Somport** cross-country skiing area is below **Col du Somport**, but the area's major ski stations are just across the border in the Spanish province of Aragón: **Candanchú** (☎ 00-34 97 437 3025), a favourite of King Juan Carlos, which has 23 lifts and 22 runs between 1560 and 2400m, and **Astún** (☎ 00-34 97 437 2011), whose 13 lifts and 35 runs are at 1700 to 2200m. Both are rather expensive. For transport information see Getting There & Away.

Le Somport (1592m) has 30km of cross-country trails for skiers of all levels. The area is connected by the green (easy) trail to Candanchú.

Le Somport has very limited facilities including a *refuge*, snack bar-restaurant, ski shack for equipment rental and a ski school. Cross-country equipment costs 45/250FF per day/week, while trail passes cost 29/125FF. Group lessons are available at 50FF an hour. The only place to stay is the *refuge*, where a bed costs 75FF per person. It can be booked through the tourist office (☎ 05 59 36 00 21; fax 05 59 34 52 51) and is only open during winter.

About 15km (and a half-hour drive) almost due west of Bedous is the ski station of **Arette Pierre Saint Martin** (☎ 05 59 66 20 09 from December to April; or ☎ 05 59 88 95 38 from April to December; ☎ 05 59 34 12 46 from July and August), known for its abundance of snow at a low elevation the station has a peak height of 2140m.

This small resort is best suited for beginner and intermediate skiers, with no black (expert) runs on its 24 pistes. To get there, take the D442 and the D441 (if these are snowbound you have to take the D918 and the D132, which takes twice as long).

The Maison des Jeunes et de la Culture (see Places to Stay) has skis for hire from 41 to 49FF a day, including boots and poles. Snowboards cost from 85FF a day; snowshoes and poles are 30FF.

Horse Riding

From May to December you can hire horses at the Auberge Cavalière (see Places to Stay), 3km south of Accous. The charge is 250/395FF for half-day/day rides. Pony rides are 35/60FF per half-hour/hour. Advance reservations are necessary.

Places to Stay

The Vallée d'Aspe is filled with cheap but very basic accommodation.

Camping In Bedous, the pleasant ***Camping Municipal*** (☎ 05 59 34 70 45 at the village hall), which has 46 places, is 300m down the hill along the street that intersects Rue Gambetta between Nos 26 and 28. It is open from early March to November. Tent sites cost 8FF and adults/children under seven pay 12.50/6.25FF.

At the intersection of the N134 and the turn-off to Accous, just short of the tourist office, is the grassy, 30-site ***Camping Despourrins*** (☎ 05 59 34 71 16). It is open almost all year-round, but only has hot water from May to October. In summer, charges are 16.50FF for a tent site and 14.50/10FF for adults/children.

About 1.5km uphill from Borce along the D739, ***Camping du Parc National*** (☎ 05 59 34 87 29 in July and August; ☎ 05 59 34 86 15 in other months) is open from about mid-June to mid-September, but you can stay there at other times of the year if you call ahead. Fees are 14FF for a tent site and 15FF per adult. Camping du Parc National is on the GR10.

Hostel In Etsaut, the 60 bed ***Maison des Jeunes et de la Culture*** (MJC; ☎ 05 59 34 88 98; fax 05 59 34 86 91) has beds in barracks-like dorms for 48FF (42FF with a hostelling card). Meals cost from 18 to 48FF and kitchen facilities are available. Sheets are 16FF extra.

To get there from the centre of the village, take the alleyway next to the church. There's no curfew and rooms are accessible all day. Reception is open weekdays from 9 am till noon and 2 to 6 pm; on Saturday from 9 to 11 am and 4 to 6 pm; and on Sunday from 8 to 10.30 am and 4 to 6 pm.

Refuges For information on some of the *refuges* in the mountains around the Vallée d'Aspe, see Hiking.

Gîtes d'Étape In Bedous, the friendly, 40 bed ***Le Choucas Blanc*** (☎ 05 59 34 53 71; fax 05 59 87 19 88), 4 Rue Gambetta, is open all year. Basic dorm beds cost 43FF, but you must buy a membership card valid for three/12 months for 5/15FF. Half pensions costs 110FF and a packed picnic is 30FF. You can use the kitchen facilities for 5FF. The owner can supply tips on hiking itineraries and can even drop you off at the trailhead.

In Accous, the 20 place ***Maison Despourrins*** (☎ 05 59 34 53 50), which is open throughout the year, has beds for 58FF. Lunch or dinner, including wine and coffee, starts at 53FF.

In Etsaut, the 20-bed ***Maison de l'Ours*** (☎ 05 59 34 86 38), also known as the Centre d'Hébergement Léo Lagrange, is next to the carpark in the centre of the village. A place in a two to four-bed room with breakfast costs 75FF (65FF for kids under 12). It's open all year. People staying here can participate in all sorts of outdoor activities, including mountain biking and *tir à l'arc* (archery).

Hotels In Etsaut, the two star ***Hôtel des Pyrénées*** (☎ 05 59 34 88 62; fax 05 59 34 86 96), the only hotel in the village, has doubles for 150FF with washbasin and bidet, and 260FF with shower and toilet. It is open all year.

About 3km south of Accous just off the N134, the 12 room ***Auberge Cavalière*** (☎ 05 59 34 72 30; fax 05 59 34 51 97) is open all year. Doubles with shower cost 240FF.

Places to Eat

Self-Catering In Bedous, there is a ***food market*** next to the mairie on Thursday morning. The ***Casino*** grocery at 5 Rue Gambetta is open daily, except on Sunday afternoon and Monday (also open Monday from June to early September). Its hours are 7.30 am to 12.30 pm and 3 to 7.30 pm. There's an *épicerie* (grocery), ***Guyenne et Gascognén***, two doors down at No 9.

In Etsaut, the ***alimentation*** (general store) on the corner of the main square is open seven days a week, and is ideal for picnic supplies.

Restaurants The popular ***Auberge Cavalière*** (see Places to Stay), south of Accous, has all sorts of tasty Pyrenean specialities cooked on a wood fire, including *garbure* (a thick soup made with fresh vegetables, beans, cabbage and ham) and *poule au pot* (chicken stuffed with vegetables and prepared with tomato sauce). The *menus* cost 98 to 155FF. This place is open daily from noon to 2 pm and 8 to 9.30 pm.

In Etsaut, the restaurant of the ***Hôtel des Pyrénées*** (see Places to Stay) has *menus* for 68, 85 and 110FF.

Shopping

Lots of places sell the valley's excellent cheeses; look for hand-lettered signs advertising *fromage* (or, for Spanish clients, *queso*).

Getting There & Away

The Vallée d'Aspe has been a trans-Pyrenean transport route since before the time of Julius Caesar, whose legionaries marched through the area. It has also served as a crossing point to Spain for medieval pilgrims on their way to Santiago de Compostela as well as for Napoleon's armies.

As part of an EU initiative to improve road links between France and Spain, the N134 is currently being widened and a road tunnel built under the Col du Somport.

The project still faces a great deal of local opposition – not only will the increased traffic devastate the area's pastoral calm, but also the narrow southern reaches of the valley will end up being almost completely buried under asphalt.

The 1632m Col du Somport is the only pass in the central Pyrenees open through the winter.

Bus & Train All public transport to the Vallée d'Aspe goes through Pau. SNCF has services from Pau to the Spanish railhead of Canfranc-Estación, an enormous train station from where there are trains to Saragossa and other parts of Spain.

Traffic is handled by trains only as far south as Oloron Sainte Marie; the rest of the route is covered by four daily SNCF buses, which follow the N134 all the way up the Vallée d'Aspe to the Col du Somport (47FF; 1½ hours), Candanchú and finally Canfranc.

The bus route up the valley parallels the derelict railway tracks, built between 1908 and 1928 and abandoned in 1970 when the bridge at L'Estanguet collapsed under the weight of an overloaded train.

Oloron Sainte Marie's train station (☎ 05 59 39 00 61) is linked by rail with Pau (36FF; 40 minutes; six trains daily). Destinations served by bus daily from Oloron Sainte Marie include Bedous (24FF; 35 minutes), the Accous turn-off, Lescun, Etsaut, and the terminus, Canfranc (4FF; 1¾ hours). In Bedous, there are stops at the carpark near Le Choucas Blanc and in front of the *gendarmerie* (police station). To get to the Accous town centre, you'll have to walk or hitch about 800m from the N134. The bus stop in Etsaut is at the main square, which doubles as a carpark.

Getting Around

Given the relative infrequency of buses on the Oloron Sainte Marie-Canfranc run getting around the valley is very difficult, so it helps if you have a car or are prepared to hitch.

Bicycle In Bedous, VTT Nature (☎ 05 59 34 75 25), on Route d'Espagne (the N134 south of town), has mountain bikes for about 60/100FF a half-day/day. A 2000FF deposit is required.

The staff can provide free maps of suggested cycling routes in the area. Guided rides, with the option of driving to a high spot so you end up going mostly downhill, cost around 150/280FF per adult for a half-day/day (110/200FF for children).

In Etsaut, mountain bikes can be hired at the MJC (see Places to Stay) for 50/90FF a half-day/day. The Auberge Cavalière (see Places to Stay) also has them.

Taxi In Bedous, you can order a taxi on ☎ 05 59 34 70 06.

FOIX

• pop 10,000 ✉ 09000 alt 380m

The attractive town of Foix, distinguished by its castle, 11th century church and ancient streets lined with medieval, half-timbered houses, has been the county-seat of the department of Ariege since the French Revolution.

Orientation

Foix is located on the RN20 at the gateway to Andorra and at the junction of the Ariege and Arget rivers. The oldest, most attractive part of town is on the western bank of the river. The main thoroughfare is Cours Gabriel Fauré, which runs past the main square and the tourist office.

Information

The tourist office (☎ 05 61 65 12 12; fax 05 61 65 64 63) is at 45 Cours Gabriel Fauré. It's open Monday to Saturday from 9 am to noon and 2 to 6 pm (to 7 pm without a break in July and August).

Château des Comtes de Foix

This imposing castle (☎ 05 61 65 56 05), with its three towers standing guard over the town, was constructed in the 10th century as a stronghold for the Counts of Foix. From the 16th century onwards it was used as a prison, and some prisoners' graffiti can still be seen engraved on the stones. Today it houses the Ariege Departmental museum's collection of Prehistoric, Gallo-Roman and Medieval archaeology. It's open daily, except Monday and Tuesday, from October to April from 10.30 am to noon and from 2 to 5.30 pm; daily in May and June from 9.45 am to noon and from 2 to 6 pm; and daily from 9.45 am to 6.30 pm in July and August. Entry costs 25/12FF for adults/children.

Places to Stay – Budget

Camping The two star *Camping du Lac* (☎ 05 61 65 11 58; fax 05 61 06 32 62), on the RN20 just north of Foix, costs 45/12/8FF per tent or caravan/adult/child. Reception is open from 8.30 am to 12.30 pm and from 2 to 7.30 pm.

Hotels There are only four hotels in central Foix. The best value are the three star ***Hotel Audoye-Lons*** (☎ 05 61 65 52 44; fax 05 61 02 68 18), with rooms with shower from 160FF (ask for one overlooking the river), and the more modest two star ***Hotel La Barbacane*** (☎ 05 61 65 50 44; fax 05 61 02 74 33), with 20 rooms from 160FF.

Places to Eat

Vanille Chocolat (☎ 05 61 65 36 90), 19 Rue des Marchands, serves delicious salads and grills from 40FF. It is open daily (except Sunday) for lunch and dinner. ***La Bodega*** (☎ 05 61 02 91 26), 7 Rue Lafaurie, specialises in tapas and generous portions of paella from 68FF, and is open for lunch and dinner seven days a week. At ***Self-Service Gros*** (☎ 05 61 65 00 07), 27 Cours Gabriel Faur, you can help yourself to steak, salad and chips from 45FF (open daily from 11.30 am until 11 pm).

Getting there & Away

Train The information office at the train station (☎ 05 61 02 03 60), on Rue Pierre Semard, is open daily from 9 am to noon and from 2.30 to 6 pm (5 pm on Sunday). Foix can be reached by SNCF train from Toulouse approximately six times a day (70FF; 1 hour).

Around Foix

About 6km from Foix, on Route D1, the **Underground River of Labouiche** (☎ 05 61 65 04 11) is the longest navigable underground river in Europe. For 42FF, you can take a boat for a 1500m trip that lasts 75 minutes. Boats operate on weekdays between Easter and Whitsunday from 2 to 6 pm, and Sunday from 10 am to noon and from 2 to 6 pm, and daily in July and August from 9.30 am to 6 pm.

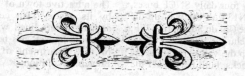

French Basque Country

The department of Pyrénées-Atlantiques in France's far south-western corner is the only part of the Basque Country (Euskadi in Basque) located north of the Pyrenees. Known in French as the Pays Basque, the region is a good base for day trips to the verdant western Pyrenees and the Spanish Basque Country (País Vasco), both of which begin less than 25km south of the two main cities, the cultural capital of Bayonne and the glitzy beach resort of Biarritz.

HIGHLIGHTS

- **Sports** – attend a game of *pelota* (traditional Basque racquet sport) or a *corrida* (bullfight)
- **Biarritz** – go surfing
- **La Rhune** – climb the mountain half in France, half in Spain
- **Pyrenees** – walk in the lush Pyrenean foothills

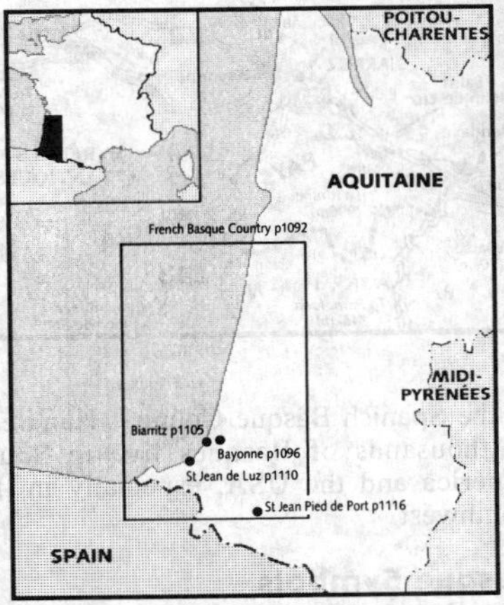

ttoro – a fish soup or casserole with white wine, tomatoes and sweet peppers

Bayonne smoked ham

History

The early history of the Basques, who live in a region on the Bay of Biscay that straddles the French-Spanish border, is largely unknown. Roman sources mention a tribe called the Vascones living in the area. The Basques took over what is now south-western France in the 6th century. They were converted to Christianity in the 10th century and are still known for their strong devotion to Catholicism.

After resisting invasions by the Visigoths, Franks, Normans and Moors, the Basques on both sides of the Pyrenees emerged from the turbulent Middle Ages with a fair degree of local autonomy, which they lost in France during the Revolution. The French Basque Country, part of the duchy of Aquitaine, was under English rule from the mid-12th century – when Eleanor of Aquitaine, divorced by French king Louis VII, remarried Henry of Anjou, later King Henry II of England – until the mid-15th century.

Basque nationalism flourished before and during the Spanish Civil War (1936-39), when German aircraft flying for Francisco Franco's fascists destroyed the Spanish city of Guernica (1937), symbol of the Basque nation and a centre of Basque nationalist activities. Until Franco's death in 1975, many Spanish Basque nationalists and anti-Franco guerrillas sheltered in France. Some Basques still dream of carving an Euskadi state out of the Basque areas of Spain and France, and a few support the terrorist organisation ETA (Euskadi ta Azkatasuna, which means Basque Nation and Liberty). Bombings and other violent activities are not uncommon

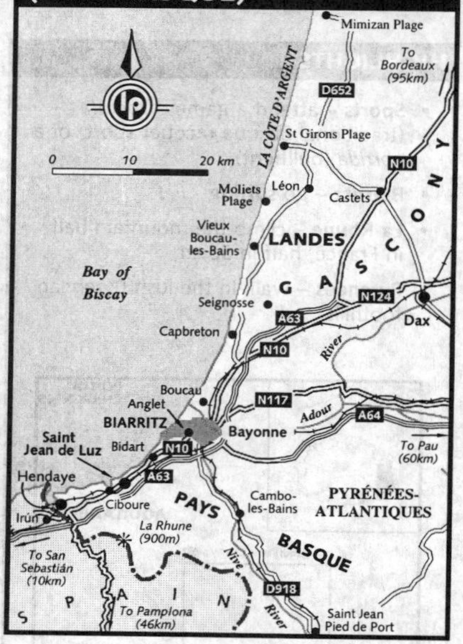

FRENCH BASQUE COUNTRY (PAYS BASQUE)

in the Spanish Basque Country. Hundreds of thousands of Basques live in South America and the USA, especially in the Southwest.

Basque Symbols

The Basque flag is similar in general layout to the UK flag but the field is red, the arms of the vertical cross are white and the arms of the diagonal cross are green. Another common Basque symbol resembles a swastika but is perhaps best described as looking like a skinny Greek cross with the head of a golf driver attached to each end.

Language

Basque (Euskara) is the only language in south-western Europe to have withstood the onslaught of Latin and its derivatives, and it is probably unrelated to any other tongue spoken on earth. Its origins are shrouded in mystery. Theories tying it to languages spoken in the Caucasus region of the former USSR have been discredited, and it is thought that similarities with the long-dead language Iberian may have resulted from contact between the Iberians and Basques rather than from a common origin.

The first book in Basque was printed in 1545 and marked the beginning of Basque literature. Basque is now spoken by about a million people in Spain and France, most of whom are bilingual. In the French Basque Country, the language is widely spoken in Bayonne but is even more common in the hilly hinterland. Two television stations in Spain and one in France now broadcast in Basque. You'll occasionally see '*Hemen Euskara emaiten dugu*' on shop doors, which means 'Basque spoken here'.

Spectator Sports

Corrida, Spanish-style bullfighting in which the bull is killed, has devotees all over the Basque Country. Tournaments are held about half a dozen times each summer. Tickets cost 80 to 450FF. Advance reservations are usually necessary – information is available at tourist offices. The matadors are either French or Spanish.

For information on *pelota* see the boxed text 'Pelote Basque'.

Shopping

For information on Basque linen and sweets, see Shopping under Saint Jean de Luz.

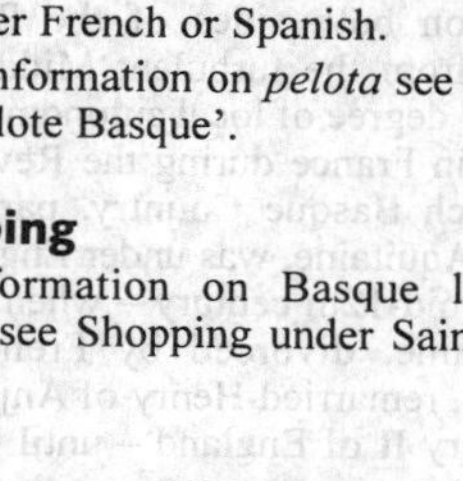

Basque symbol

Pelote Basque

TERESA FISHER

Pelote basque, known in both Basque and English as *pelota*, is the name given to a group of games native to the Basque Country, which are played with a hard ball with a rubber core (a *pelote*) and either *mains nues* (bare hands) or a scoop-like racquet made of wicker, leather or wood.

In the Basque Country, *cesta punta*, also known as *jaï alaï*, the world's fastest ball game, is the most popular variety of pelota. Developed from a type of handball, it became faster and faster after the introduction of rubber made it possible to produce balls with more bounce. In the 1920s and 30s, cesta punta was a big hit in Chicago and New Orleans but lost popularity when betting on it was outlawed. Introduced to Cuba in 1900, the game was banned after the 1959 Revolution.

Cesta punta is played with a *chistera*, a curved wicker scoop that is worn strapped to the wrist, with which players catch the ball and hurl it back with great force. Matches take place in a jaï alaï, which is also known as a *cancha*, a court with three walls that is usually 53m long.

The walls and floor are made of special materials that can withstand the repeated impact of the ball, which can reach speeds of 300km/h. A cancha and its tiers of balconies for spectators constitute a *fronton*. Other types of pelota (eg *joko-garbi*, main nue, *pala*, *paleta*, *pasaka*, *rebot* and *xare*) are played in outdoor, one-wall courts, also known as frontons, and in enclosed structures called *trinquets*.

For information on pelota tournaments, see Entertainment in the Bayonne and Biarritz sections and Spectator Sport in the Saint Jean de Luz and Saint Jean Pied de Port sections. Expect to pay anything from 40 to 150FF for a ticket. For information on pelota lessons, see Pelote Basque in the Biarritz section.

Getting There & Away

Train to Spain For rail travel to Spain, you have to switch trains at Irún because the track gauge is narrower in Spain. The best way to get to the Spanish Basque city of San Sebastián is to catch an SNCF train to Hendaye, from where you can take El Topo, a privately operated shuttle train that runs every half-hour. ATCRB (see Bus under Getting There & Away in the Bayonne, Biarritz and Saint Jean de Luz sections) runs regional buses along the coast and to San Sebastián.

BAYONNE

• pop 40,000 ✉ 64100

Bayonne (Baiona in Basque) is the cultural and economic capital of the French Basque Country. Unlike the upmarket beach resort of Biarritz, a short bus ride away, Bayonne retains much of its Basqueness: the riverside buildings with their faded green, red and white shutters are typical of the region, you'll hear almost as much Euskara as French in certain quarters and every male over the age of 40, it seems, wears a beret.

Most of the graffiti you'll see around town – like *Amnistia!* in huge letters on the massive Château Neuf – is the work of nationalist groups seeking an independent Basque state.

The city, founded as Lapurdum by the Romans, is known for its smoked ham, chocolate and marzipan. The latter two products were introduced in the late 15th century by Jews fleeing the Spanish Inquisition. According to tradition, the *baïonnette* (bayonet) was developed here in the early 17th century.

Bayonne reached the height of its commercial prosperity in the 18th century, when Basque pirate ships landed cargoes much more valuable than the cod caught by the Basque fishing fleet off the coast of Newfoundland.

Orientation

The Adour and Nive rivers split Bayonne into three parts: Saint Esprit, the area north of the Adour, where the train station is located; Grand Bayonne, the oldest part of the city, on the west bank of the Nive; and the very Basque Petit Bayonne quarter to the east.

Pont Saint Esprit over the Adour River links Place de la République with Place du Réduit and the adjacent Place de la Liberté, which abuts the Hôtel de Ville. Rue Port Neuf, Rue Lormand and Rue Victor Hugo nearby are lively, shop-lined pedestrian malls. The bridge spanning the Adour 500m north of the tourist office opened in July 1995.

The nondescript suburban area of Anglet (the final 't' is pronounced) fills the area between Bayonne and Biarritz, 8km to the west. The urban area made up of Bayonne, Anglet and Biarritz (population 120,000) is sometimes abbreviated as BAB. The best map of the conurbation is STAB's local bus map.

Information

Tourist Offices The tourist office (☎ 05 59 46 01 46; fax 05 59 59 37 55) at Place des Basques is open weekdays from 9 am to 6.30 pm and on Saturday from 10 am to 6 pm. During July and August, it is open Monday to Saturday from 9 am to 7 pm and on Sunday from 10 am to 1 pm. It offers a free hotel reservation service here.

The brochure entitled *Fêtes* is useful for cultural and sporting events throughout the Basque Country, while the freebie *Guide Loisirs* is indispensable for organising hiking, biking, climbing, diving etc. The tourist office has guided tours of the city at 3 pm on Tuesday and 10 am on Wednesday, Friday and Saturday in summer. Adults pay 30FF, children go free.

During July and August, the tourist office has an annexe (☎ 05 59 55 20 45) at the train station. It is open Monday to Saturday from 9 am to 12.30 pm and 2 to 6.30 pm.

Money Most banks in Bayonne are open Monday to Friday, while those in Anglet are open Tuesday to Saturday (or Saturday morning).

The Banque de France at 18 Rue Albert 1er is open weekdays from 9 am to noon and 1.30 to 3.35 pm.

Near the train station, there are a number of banks at Place de la République and Blvd Alsace-Lorraine. Most are open Monday to Friday, but the Crédit Mutuel at 7 Blvd Alsace-Lorraine is open Tuesday to Saturday from 8.30 am to 12.30 pm and 1.30 to 5 pm (from 1 pm on Saturday).

In Grand Bayonne, there are lots of banks near the Hôtel de Ville, along Rue Thiers and on Rue du 49ème Régiment d'Infanterie (east of the post office). Some ATMs in Bayonne distribute Spanish pesetas as well as francs.

Post The post office at 11 Rue Jules Labat is open weekdays from 8 am to 6 pm and on Saturday till noon. Exchange services are available. Poste restante items addressed to '64100 Bayonne-Labat' come here, but all other poste restante mail goes to the main post office, which is 1.5km north-west of town on Ave des Allées Marines (just past the Elf petrol station). It is open weekdays from 8 am to 6.30 pm and on Saturday till noon. To get there, take bus No 4 (direction: La Barre) from the train station or the Hôtel de Ville to the Pont de l'Aveugle stop.

The post office near the train station at 21 Blvd Alsace-Lorraine is open weekdays from 8 am to 6 pm and Saturday till noon.

Travel Agencies Pascal Voyages (☎ 05 59 25 48 48) at 8 Allées Boufflers is open Monday to Friday from 8.30 am to 6.30 pm and, except in August, on Saturday from 9 am to noon.

Laundry In Saint Esprit, the laundrette at 16 Blvd Alsace-Lorraine is open seven days a week from 8 am to 8 pm.

Medical Services & Emergency The Centre Hospitalier (☎ 05 59 44 35 35) is south of the centre on Ave de l'Interne Jacques Loeb, the continuation of Ave Raymond de Martres. To get there, take bus No 3 (direction: Panorama) to the Hôpital stop. The police station (☎ 05 59 46 22 22) at 6 Ave Marhum is open 24 hours a day.

Walking Tour

You can get a pretty good sense of central Bayonne with the following itinerary, which begins at the train station.

Cross Pont Saint Esprit from Place de la République to Place du Réduit. Walk to the Hôtel de Ville and then along the arcaded Rue Port Neuf to Cathédrale Sainte Marie. The **old city**, with its narrow streets, retains an essentially medieval layout.

Via Pont Pannecau, cross the Nive River, which is lined with traditional houses. **Rue Bourgneuf**, the heart of strongly nationalistic Petit Bayonne, retains much of its old-time charm, with Basque-language signs and a number of small bars and cafés. ETA guerillas from Spain often hid out here during the Franco era.

Circle back to Pont Saint Esprit via Place Paul Bert (next to the fortified **Château Neuf**, which dates from 1489 and is now a closed military area), **Église Saint André** and the Musée Bonnat.

Ramparts

Thanks to Vauban's 17th century fortifications (see the boxed text 'Vauban's Citadels' in the Facts about France chapter), now covered with grass and dotted with trees, the city centre is surrounded by a green belt. You can walk along the old ramparts by following **Rue du Rempart Lachepaillet**, south of the tourist office and lined with stately, Basque-style stately apartment buildings, and its continuation **Rue Tour de Sault**.

Cathédrale Sainte Marie

Bayonne's Gothic cathedral is on Rue de la Monnaie, at the southern end of the Rue du Port Neuf pedestrian mall in the heart of the oldest part of town. Construction of the cathedral was begun in the 13th century, when Bayonne was ruled by the English, and completed after the area came under French control in 1451. These political changes are reflected in the ornamentation on the vaulted ceiling of the nave, which includes both the English coat of arms (three leopards) and that most French of emblems, the fleur-de-lis. Some of the stained glass dates from the Renaissance (restored in the 19th century), but many of the statues that once graced the church's very crumbly exterior were smashed during the Revolution. The cathedral is open from Monday to Saturday from 10 am to noon and 3.30 to 6 pm, and from 3 to 6 pm on Sunday. The **cloître**, the cathedral's lovely 13th century cloister to the south on Place Louis Pasteur, is open daily, except Saturday, from 9.30 am to 12.30 pm and 2 to 5 pm (6 pm from Easter to October). Entry is free.

Musée Bonnat

This museum (☎ 05 59 59 08 52), 5 Rue Jacques Laffitte in Petit Bayonne, has a diverse collection of works, including paintings by El Greco, Goya and Degas and a whole room of works by Peter Paul Rubens. It is open daily, except Tuesday, from 10 am to noon and 2.30 to 6.30 pm (to 8.30 pm on Friday). The entry fee is 20FF (10FF for children and students).

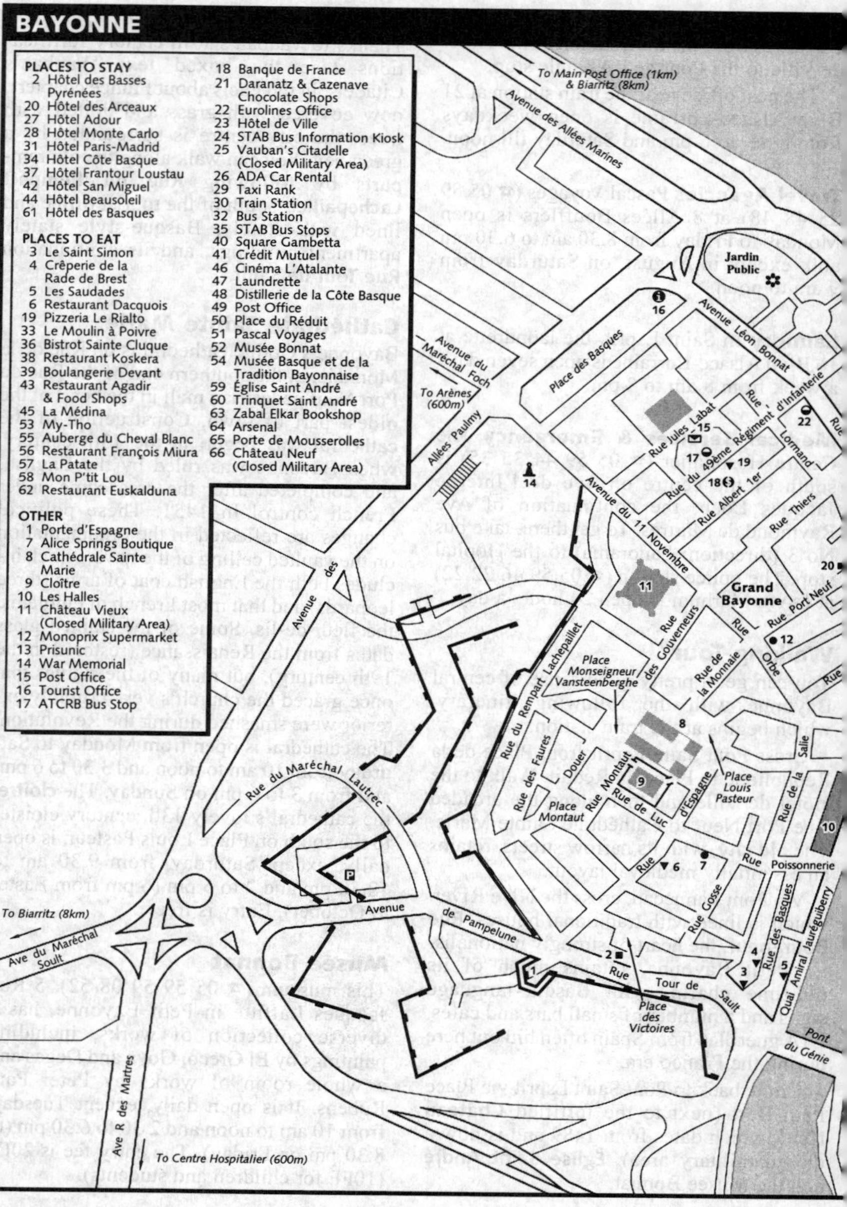
BAYONNE
PLACES TO STAY
2 Hôtel des Basses Pyrénées
20 Hôtel des Arceaux
27 Hôtel Adour
28 Hôtel Monte Carlo
31 Hôtel Paris-Madrid
34 Hôtel Côte Basque
37 Hôtel Frantour Loustau
42 Hôtel San Miguel
44 Hôtel Beausoleil
61 Hôtel des Basques
PLACES TO EAT
3 Le Saint Simon
4 Crêperie de la Rade de Brest
5 Les Saudades
6 Restaurant Dacquois
19 Pizzeria Le Rialto
33 Le Moulin à Poivre
36 Bistrot Sainte Cluque
38 Restaurant Koskera
39 Boulangerie Devant
43 Restaurant Agadir & Food Shops
45 La Médina
53 My-Tho
55 Auberge du Cheval Blanc
56 Restaurant François Miura
57 La Patate
58 Mon P'tit Lou
62 Restaurant Euskalduna
OTHER
1 Porte d'Espagne
7 Alice Springs Boutique
8 Cathédrale Sainte Marie
9 Cloître
10 Les Halles
11 Château Vieux (Closed Military Area)
12 Monoprix Supermarket
13 Prisunic
14 War Memorial
15 Post Office
16 Tourist Office
17 ATCRB Bus Stop
18 Banque de France
21 Daranatz & Cazenave Chocolate Shops
22 Eurolines Office
23 Hôtel de Ville
24 STAB Bus Information Kiosk
25 Vauban's Citadelle (Closed Military Area)
26 ADA Car Rental
29 Taxi Rank
30 Train Station
32 Bus Station
35 STAB Bus Stops
40 Square Gambetta
41 Crédit Mutuel
46 Cinéma L'Atalante
48 Laundrette
48 Distillerie de la Côte Basque
49 Post Office
50 Place du Réduit
51 Pascal Voyages
52 Musée Bonnat
54 Musée Basque et de la Tradition Bayonnaise
59 Église Saint André
60 Trinquet Saint André
63 Zabal Elkar Bookshop
64 Arsenal
65 Porte de Mousserolles
66 Château Neuf (Closed Military Area)
To Main Post Office (1km) & Biarritz (8km)
Avenue des Allées Marines
Jardin Public
Avenue Léon Bonnat
Place des Basques
Avenue du Maréchal Foch
To Arènes (600m)
Allées Paulmy
Rue Jules Labat
Rue du 49ème Régiment d'Infanterie
Rue Lormand
Rue Albert 1er
Rue Thiers
Avenue du 11 Novembre
Grand Bayonne
Rue Port Neuf
Avenue des ...
Rue des Gouverneurs
Rue Orbe
Rue de la Monnaie
Place Monseigneur Vansteenberghe
Rue du Rempart Lachepaillet
Rue des Faures
Rue Douer
Rue Montaut
Rue de Luc
Rue d'Espagne
Place Louis Pasteur
Rue de la Salie
Place Montaut
Rue du Maréchal Lautrec
Rue Poissonnerie
Rue Gosse
Rue des Basques
Quai Amiral Jauréguiberry
Avenue de Pampelune
Rue Tour de Sault
Place des Victoires
Pont du Génie
To Biarritz (8km)
Ave du Maréchal Soult
Ave R des Martres
To Centre Hospitalier (600m)

BAYONNE

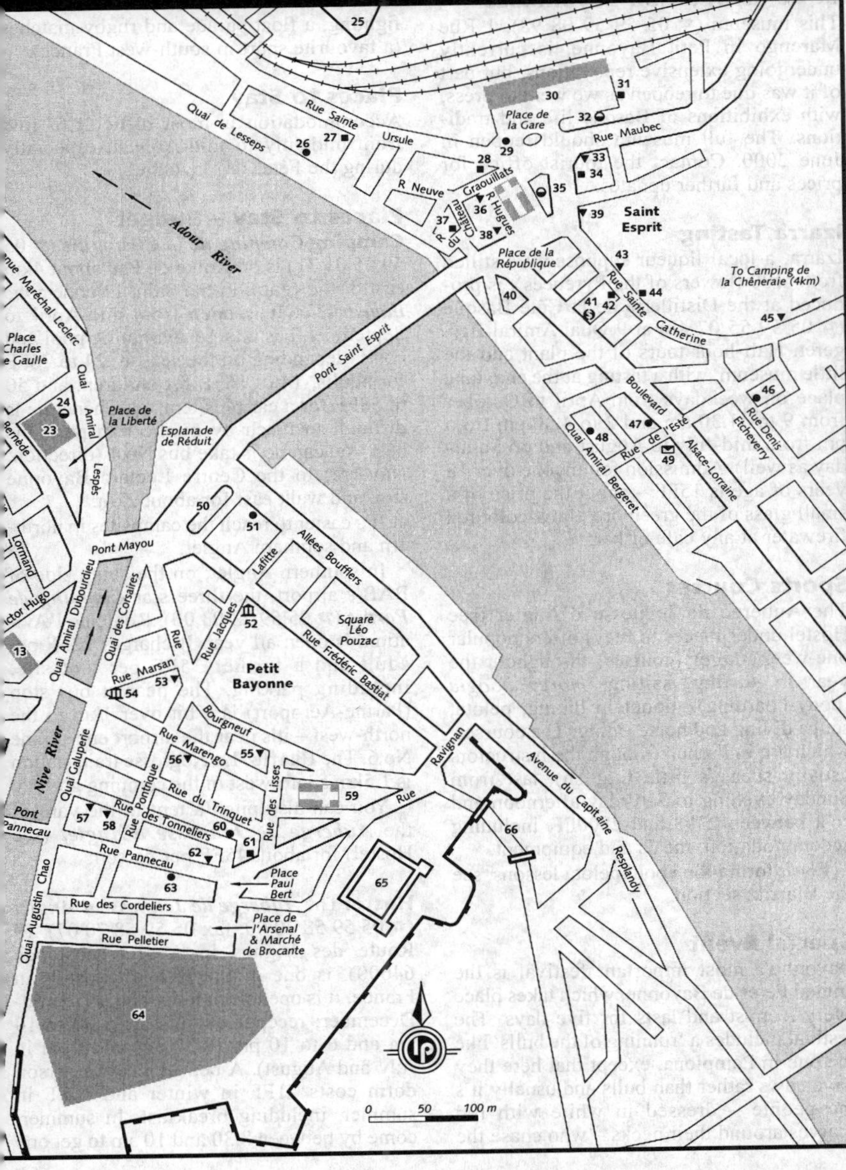

Adour River
Nive River
Quai de Lesseps
Rue Sainte Ursule
R Neuve
Graouillats
R du Château
R Hugues
Place de la Gare
Rue Maubec
Saint Esprit
Place de la République
Rue Sainte Catherine
To Camping de la Chêneraie (4km)
Boulevard Alsace-Lorraine
Rue Denis Etcheverry
Rue de l'Este
Quai Amiral Bergeret
Pont Saint Esprit
Place Charles de Gaulle
Place de la Liberté
Esplanade de Réduit
Quai Amiral Lespès
Pont Mayou
Quai Amiral Dubourdieu
Quai des Corsaires
Rue Jacques Lafitte
Allées Boufflers
Square Léo Pouzac
Rue Frédéric Bastiat
Petit Bayonne
Rue Marsan
Bourgneuf
Rue Marengo
Quai Galuperie
Rue Pontrique
Rue du Trinquet
Rue des Lisses
Rue des Tonneliers
Rue Pannecau
Pont Pannecau
Rue Ravignan
Avenue du Capitaine Resplandy
Place Paul Bert
Place de l'Arsenal & Marché de Brocante
Rue des Cordeliers
Rue Pelletier
Quai Augustin Chao
0 50 100 m

Musée Basque et de la Tradition Bayonnaise

This museum (☎ 05 59 59 08 98), 1 Rue Marengo in Petit Bayonne, is currently undergoing extensive renovations, but part of it was due to reopen as we went to press, with exhibitions of Basque life and traditions. The full museum should reopen in June 2000. Contact the tourist office for prices and further updates.

Izarra Tasting

Izarra, a local liqueur supposedly distilled from '100 flowers of the Pyrenees', is produced at the Distillerie de la Côte Basque (☎ 05 59 55 07 48) at 9 Quai Amiral Bergeret. Half-hour tours of the plant and the little museum, with a tasting at the end, take place on weekdays from April to October from 9 to 11.30 am and 2 to 4.30 pm (to 6 pm from mid-July to August and on Saturday as well). Admission for anyone over 18 years of age is 15FF – about the price of a small glass of the green or yellow-coloured firewater at any café or bar.

Sports Courses

The Auberge de Jeunesse d'Anglet (see Hostel under Places to Stay) offers popular one-week *stages* (courses) throughout the year in surfing, sailing, *morey boogie* (body-boarding), mountain biking, pelota, scuba diving and horse riding. The courses, which are in French (though the instructors usually speak a little English), last from Sunday evening to Saturday afternoon and cost between 2395 and 2800FF, including accommodation, meals and equipment.

For information about pelota lessons, see the Biarritz section.

Special Event

Bayonne's most important festival is the annual Fêtes de Bayonne, which takes place every August and lasts for five days. The festival includes a 'running of the bulls' like the one in Pamplona, except that here they have cows rather than bulls and usually it's the people – dressed in white with red scarves around their necks – who chase the cows rather than the other way around. The festival also includes Basque music, bullfighting, a float parade and rugby matches (a favourite sport in south-west France).

Places to Stay

Accommodation is most difficult to find from mid-July to mid-August, especially during the Fêtes de Bayonne.

Places to Stay – Budget

Camping *Camping de la Chêneraie* (☎ 05 59 55 01 31) is on Route de Pau about 4km east of the centre in the Saint Étienne *zone industrielle*. It is open from mid-April to September, has a large swimming pool and costs, depending on the season, 24 to 26FF for adults, 14 to 16FF for children, and 50 to 58FF for a car plus tent. La Chêneraie is difficult to reach by public transport; the best you can do is take bus No 1 (direction: Navarre) to the Centre Leclerc Bayonne stop and walk east for about 2km.

It's easier to reach the campsites in northern and southern Anglet.

In southern Anglet, on the south side of BAB's airport, the three star ***Camping de Parme*** (☎ 05 59 23 03 00), Route de l'Aviation, is open all year. It charges 22FF per adult and a further 35FF per tent site, including parking. The nearest bus stop (Parme-Aéroport) is a bit over 1km to the north-west – it's near the airport end of line No 6. The Biarritz-La Négresse train station is 1.5km south-west of the camping ground.

You can also pitch a tent in the yard of the ***Auberge de Jeunesse d'Anglet*** (see Hostel) for about 45FF per person.

Hostel The ***Auberge de Jeunesse d'Anglet*** (☎ 05 59 58 70 00; fax 05 59 58 70 07), 19 Route des Vignes in Anglet (postcode 64600), is one of the liveliest hostels in France. It is open from mid-January to mid-December; reception hours are 8.30 to 10 am and 6 to 10 pm (8.30 am to 10 pm in July and August). A bed in a seven person dorm costs 71FF in winter and 80FF in summer, including breakfast. In summer, come by between 8.30 and 10 am to get one of the few spots that open up each morning. For information on sports activities, see the earlier Sports Courses section. Guests can rent surfboards for 60 to 100FF a day.

To get to the hostel from the Bayonne train station, take bus No 4 heading for Biarritz and get off at the Auberge de Jeunesse stop. This bus runs regularly in summer but has a much more limited schedule in winter. From the Biarritz-La Négresse train station, take bus No 2 to the Hôtel de Ville and change to the No 4 going north to La Barre.

Hotels – Saint Esprit The ***Hôtel Paris-Madrid*** (☎ 05 59 55 13 98; fax 05 59 55 07 22) is to the left (east) as you exit the train station in Bayonne. Run by a friendly English-speaking couple who have lived in Canada and England, the hotel is popular with young travellers. The cheapest singles cost 90FF, and big, pleasant doubles without/with shower start at 120/145FF. Doubles/riples/quads with shower and toilet cost from 165/200/240FF, and hall showers are 5FF. Reception is open 24 hours a day in July and August.

The ***Hôtel Monte Carlo*** (☎ 05 59 55 02 68), opposite the train station at 1 Rue Sainte Ursule, has rooms from 90FF (150FF with shower); hall showers are free. The ***Hôtel Beausoleil*** (☎ 05 59 55 00 10), south of the train station at 23 Rue Sainte Catherine, has singles/doubles starting at 110/130FF; showers are free.

The pleasant ***Hôtel San Miguel*** (☎ 05 59 55 17 82), opposite at No 8, is slightly more expensive. Spacious doubles with big beds cost 140/170FF without/with shower; doubles with shower and toilet are 190FF with one bed and 220FF with two. Hall showers are 15FF.

Hotels – Grand Bayonne The one star ***Hôtel des Arceaux*** (☎ 05 59 59 15 53) is right in the middle of Grand Bayonne at 26 Rue Port Neuf. Large but rather bare doubles/triples with washbasin and bidet start at 130/170FF, while doubles with bath, toilet and TV are 230FF.

Hotels – Petit Bayonne The least expensive hotel in the colourful Petit Bayonne quarter is the ***Hôtel des Basques*** (☎ 05 59 59 08 02), on Place Paul Bert and next to 3 Rue des Lisses. Large, pleasant singles and doubles with washbasin and bidet start at 130FF (160FF with two beds). Rooms with shower, toilet, TV, and overlooking the square are 150FF (210FF with two beds). Showers cost 10FF. This place is closed from mid-October to early November. Parking is available in Place Paul Bert below the Château Neuf.

Places to Stay – Mid-Range

The two star ***Hôtel Adour*** (☎ 05 59 55 11 31; fax 05 59 55 86 40), 13 rue Sainte Ursule, has comfortable singles/doubles/triples with shower for 195/240/ 290FF, with parking and bike storage for 20FF. An extra bed in a room costs 50FF (or 20FF for an extra person).

The two star, 42 room ***Hôtel Côte Basque*** (☎ 05 59 55 10 21; fax 05 59 55 39 85), 2 Rue Maubec, has unsurprising doubles with fairly spacious bathrooms for 180FF (with washbasin) or 295FF (with shower, toilet and TV). Two-bed doubles/quads with shower, toilet and TV are 310/360FF.

The two star, 41 room ***Hôtel des Basses Pyrénées*** (☎ 05 59 59 00 29; fax 05 59 59 42 02) has entrances at Place des Victoires and 12 Rue Tour de Sault. Doubles/triples/quads with shower and toilet start at 280/350/400FF. There are also a few rooms with washbasin for 150 to 190FF. You can park in nearby Place des Victoires.

Places to Stay – Top End

Saint Esprit's nicest hotel is the three star ***Hôtel Frantour Loustau*** (☎ 05 59 55 08 08; fax 05 59 55 69 36), which faces the Adour River on Quai de Lesseps (the actual address is 1 Place de la République) in an 18th century building. Standard doubles/triples with shower and toilet are 360/430FF or 410/455FF in summer. Off-street parking costs 50FF.

FRENCH BASQUE COUNTRY

Places to Eat

Restaurants – French The unpretentious ***Restaurant Dacquois*** (☎ 05 59 59 29 61), 48 Rue d'Espagne, is open Monday to Saturday from 8 am to 8.30 pm for breakfast, lunch and dinner. Sandwiches cost from 12FF and its 65FF *menu* provides a good choice of main dishes and hors d'œuvres.

Over in Saint Esprit, an excellent choice is the ***Bistrot Sainte Cluque*** (☎ 05 59 55 82 43), 9 Rue Hugues. Its speciality is paella (55FF), other main courses are 40 to 75FF and there are *menus* from 55FF. It's open daily from 12 to 2 pm and from 7 to 11 pm.

Crêperie de la Rade de Brest (☎ 05 59 59 13 62), 7 Rue des Basques, uses traditional Breton recipes brought here by the restaurant's Brest-born *patron*. Both crêpes and *galettes* cost 10 to 36FF. It is open Tuesday to Saturday from noon to 2 pm and 7 to 10 pm (11 pm on Friday and Saturday). From May to September it is also open on Monday.

One of Bayonne's best restaurants is the elegant ***Auberge du Cheval Blanc*** (☎ 05 59 59 01 33), 68 Rue Bourgneuf, which boasts a Michelin star. *Menus* cost 118/185/260FF. It is open Tuesday to Sunday for lunch (daily in July and August). Reservations are necessary on holidays. Two other excellent choices (and perhaps a bit more experimental) in this category are the postmodern ***Restaurant François Miura*** (☎ 05 59 59 49 89), in Petit Bayonne at 24 Rue Marengo, with *menus* at 110 and 185FF and, in Grand Bayonne at 1 Rue des Basques, the charming ***Le Saint Simon*** (☎ 05 59 59 27 71). The award-winning young chef at the latter creates some superb dishes. *Menus* cost 99/139/197FF.

Restaurants – Basque It's not as easy as you'd think to sample Basque cuisine in Bayonne.

In Saint Esprit at 3 Rue Hugues, ***Restaurant Koskera*** (☎ 05 59 55 20 79) has inexpensive plats du jour of hearty Basque fare and *menus* for 70 and 95FF. It is open Monday to Saturday from noon to 2 pm only. From mid-June to September it's also open in the evening from 8 to 10.30 pm.

The homey ***Le Moulin à Poivre*** (☎ 05 59 55 56 91), in Saint Esprit, has Basque, French and Moroccan dishes in the 42 to 69FF range. It's open for lunch and dinner daily, except Sunday, and Wednesday for dinner.

In Petit Bayonne, ***Restaurant Euskalduna*** (☎ 05 59 59 28 02), near the Hôtel des Basques (see Places to Stay) at 61 Rue Pannecau, has a Basque *menu* for 60FF and main dishes for 35 to 50FF. Most of the clients are locals. It's open Monday to Friday for lunch.

Restaurants – Other Chinese restaurant ***My-Tho*** (☎ 05 59 59 15 07), 40 Rue Bourgneuf in Petit Bayonne, has excellent value *menus* at 69/79/99/119FF including wine. It is open daily, except for lunch on Tuesday and Wednesday. ***Restaurant Agadir*** (☎ 05 59 55 66 56), near the train station at 3 Rue Sainte Catherine, has southern Moroccan-style couscous for 60 to 80FF and *menus* for 80FF and 100FF. It is open daily (except Monday for lunch) from noon to 2 pm and 7 to 11 pm.

Tunisian restaurant ***La Médina*** (☎ 05 59 55 85 17) at 13 Blvd Jean d'Amou in Saint Esprit serves salads from 26FF, couscous (60 to 75FF) and grills from 65FF. On the river in Grand Bayonne at 15 Quai Amiral Jauréguiberry is ***Les Saudades*** (☎ 05 59 25 60 13), a Portuguese restaurant with *menus* at 72 and 105FF and delicious fish dishes from 22 to 71FF. Nearby, at 14 Rue des Tonneliers in Petit Bayonne, try jacket potatoes with their various fillings at ***La Patate*** (☎ 05 59 59 85 66).

The small ***Mon P'tit Lou*** (☎ 05 59 25 59 03), next door to La Patate at 16 Rue des Tonneliers, serves pizzas from 30 to 45FF and pasta from 32 to 45FF. It's only open in the evenings (except in July and August when they open at lunchtime too). In Grand Bayonne at 7 Rue du 49ème Régiment d'Infanterie, ***Pizzeria Le Rialto*** (☎ 05 59 59 02 30) is open daily, except Sunday and holidays, from noon to 2 pm and 7 to 11 pm. Pizzas and pasta dishes cost 34 to 70FF with salads 18 to 65FF.

Self-Catering Most food stores are closed on Sunday and, often, all or part of Saturday or Monday as well.

Near the train station at 36 Place de la République, ***Boulangerie Devant*** is open Monday to Saturday from 7 am to 1 pm and 3 to 7.30 pm, and on Sunday from 7 am to 1 pm and 4 to 7.30 pm. Along nearby Rue Sainte Catherine, there's a ***fruit & vegetable shop*** at No 29 (closed Sunday and on Monday afternoon), a ***grocery*** at No 39 (closed Saturday afternoon and Sunday) and a ***boulangerie*** at No 43.

Grand Bayonne's central market, ***Les Halles***, is in a wonderful building on the west quay (Quai Amiral Jauréguiberry) of the Nive River and is open every morning (except Sunday) from 6 or 7 am to 1.30 or 2 pm. On Friday and Saturday it reopens again from 3.30 to 7 pm.

Prisunic, with entrances at 27 Rue Victor Hugo and 1-3 Quai Amiral Dubourdieu, is open Monday to Saturday from 8 or 8.30 am to 7.30 pm. The food section is on the 1st floor. The ***Monoprix*** supermarket at 8 Rue Orbe, open the same days and hours, has a small food section at the back. There are a number of ***food stores*** along Rue Port Neuf and Rue d'Espagne.

Entertainment

Cinema The ***Cinéma L'Atalante*** (☎ 05 59 55 76 63), 7 Rue Denis Etcheverry in Saint Esprit, screens nondubbed films but is closed in July and August. A ticket costs 37FF (25FF for students).

Pubs & Bars There are lots of small bars scattered around Petit Bayonne, especially along Rue Pannecau, and along Rue Port Neuf in Grand Bayonne.

Spectator Sports

Pelote Basque From October to May or June, Trinquet Saint André (☎ 05 59 59 18 69), 2 Rue du Jeu de Paume (a tiny side street just off Rue des Tonneliers) in Petit Bayonne, has professional *main nue* matches every Thursday at 4.10 pm sharp. Tickets cost 50FF.

Bullfighting In summer, corridas are held at the *arènes* (arena), which is 800m west of Grand Bayonne along Ave du Maréchal Foch. Two *ferias* with daily corridas take place each year in mid-August (Feria de l'Assomption) and early September (Feria de l'Atlantique). Tickets sell for between 80 and 450FF.

Shopping

Bayonne is famous throughout France for its ham and chocolate. Buy the former at Charcuterie Brouchican (☎ 05 59 59 27 18), 20 Quai Augustin Chaho; the latter at the very traditional *chocolateries* Cazenave (☎ 05 59 59 03 16), 19 Rue Port Neuf, and Daranatz (☎ 05 59 59 03 05), at No 15.

Zabal Elkar (☎ 05 59 25 43 90), 52 Rue Pannecau, has a large selection of cassettes and CDs of Basque music. It also carries lots of books (including some English titles) on Basque history and culture and hiking in the Basque Country as well as a few maps. The shop is open daily, except Monday morning and Sunday, from 9.15 am to 12.30 pm and 2.30 to 7.30 pm.

Homesick Aussies should check out Alice Springs (☎ 05 59 59 13 72), a *boutique australienne* at 25 Rue Poissonnerie that's open Monday to Saturday from 10 am to 7 pm (closed between 1 and 2 pm).

There's a colourful *marché de brocante* (flea market) at Place de l'Arsenal in Petit Bayonne every Friday morning from 8 am to noon and every third Saturday from 8 am to 5 pm.

Getting There & Away

Air The airport serving Bayonne, Biarritz and Anglet, (☎ 05 59 43 83 83), is 5km south-west of central Bayonne and 2.5km south-east of the centre of Biarritz.

Bus ATCRB's rather slow regional buses (☎ 05 59 26 06 99 in Saint Jean de Luz) follow the coast from Bidart (11FF) to Saint Jean de Luz (20FF; 40 minutes) and also serve Hendaye (33.50FF; 1½ hours). There are 10 runs a day Monday to Saturday between 8 am and 7.15 pm. The six runs on Sunday start at 9.15 am and finish at 7.30 pm. From Monday to Saturday between June and mid-October there are buses at 8.15 am and 1.45 pm to the Spanish city of San Sebastián (40.50FF; 1¾ hours). The rest of the year they leave on Tuesday, Thursday and Saturday only. Both lines leave from the ATCRB bus stop at 9 Rue du 49ème Régiment d'Infanterie. Because of the beach traffic in summer, the trips can sometimes take twice as long as scheduled.

Bayonne's tiny bus station (☎ 05 59 55 17 59) is situated in front of the train station at Place de la Gare. It is open weekdays from 9 am to 12.15 pm and 2 to 5.30 pm. Tickets are sold on the buses. The RDTL (☎ 05 59 55 17 59) line serves destinations in Landes, the department north of Bayonne, including Capbreton, Dax (43FF), Léon, Seignosse and Vieux Boucau-les-Bains. To get to the beaches along the coast north of Bayonne (eg Mimizan Plage and Moliets Plage), take the line to Vieux Boucau (37FF; 1¼ hours). TPR (☎ 05 59 27 45 98) has buses to Pau (76FF).

Eurolines (☎ 05 59 59 19 33), 3 Place Charles de Gaulle, has buses to London (20 hours), Tangier (23 hours), Madrid and other places all over Spain and Portugal, Amsterdam, Brussels and, in summer, Prague. It is open on weekdays from 9 am to noon and 2 to 6 pm. In July and August it's open Monday to Saturday from 10 am to noon and 2 to 6 pm.

Train The train station (☎ 08 36 35 35 35) is in Saint Esprit at Place de la Gare. The information office is open Monday to Saturday from 9 am to noon and 2 to 6.30 pm. In July and August, it's open daily from 9 am to 7.30 pm. There are luggage lockers with a 72 hour time limit on platform No 1.

TGVs to/from Paris' Gare Montparnasse (413FF) take five hours. The two daily non-TGV trains overnight to Paris' Gare d'Austerlitz (371FF) take about eight hours. Within the Basque Country, there are fairly frequent trains to Biarritz (13FF; 10 minutes), Saint Jean de Luz (26FF; 20 minutes) and Saint Jean Pied de Port (46FF; one hour) and the Franco-Spanish border towns of Hendaye (46FF; 35 minutes) and Irún. There are also trains to Bordeaux (142FF; 1½ hours by TGV; about a dozen a day), Lourdes (104FF; 1¾ hours; six a day), Nice (438FF; 11 hours; one overnight and one all-day train), Pau (81FF; 1¼ hours; eight a day) and Toulouse (190FF; 3½ hours).

Car ADA (☎ 05 59 50 37 10) has an office two blocks from the train station at 11 Quai de Lesseps. It is open Monday to Saturday from 8 am to noon and 2 to 7 pm. Cars with 400km free start at about 379FF a day.

Getting Around

To/From the Airport Bus No 6 links the airport servicing the region with Bayonne and Biarritz.

Bus The bus network linking Bayonne, Biarritz and Anglet is known as STAB. Individual tickets cost 7.50FF; a carnet of 10 is 62FF. Tickets remain valid for an hour after they have been time-stamped.

STAB's information and ticket office (☎ 05 59 59 04 61) is in Grand Bayonne, in the north-eastern corner of the Hôtel de Ville facing Place Charles de Gaulle. It is open Monday to Friday from 8 am to 12 pm and 1.30 to 6 pm.

Bus line No 1 links Bayonne's train station with the centre of Biarritz (stop: Hôtel de Ville) via Anglet. Line No 2 starts at Bayonne's train station and passes through the centre of Bayonne and Biarritz before continuing on to the Biarritz-La Négresse train station. Bus No 4 links the train station in Bayonne and the centre of Biarritz via the Anglet coast and its beaches. Bus No 6 links Bayonne and Biarritz via the airport. Bus No 9 is a scenic – if slow – way to get from Bayonne to Biarritz.

Taxi To order a taxi, call ☎ 05 59 59 48 48. There's a large rank in front of the train station.

BIARRITZ

• pop 30,000 ✉ 64200

The classy coastal town of Biarritz, 8km west of Bayonne, got its start as a resort in the mid-19th century when Napoleon III and his Spanish-born wife, Eugénie, began coming here. In later decades, Biarritz became popular with wealthy Britons and was visited by Queen Victoria and King Edward VII, both of whom have streets named in their honour. These days, the Biarritz area is known for its fine beaches and some of the best surfing in Europe.

Biarritz can be a real budget-buster. Consider making it a day trip from Bayonne or the hostel in Anglet.

Orientation

The centre of Biarritz is the long Place Clemenceau, which is 200m south of the main beach (Grande Plage). Pointe Saint Martin, topped with a lighthouse, is at the northern end of Plage Miramar, the northern continuation of the Grande Plage.

The hilltop Port Vieux area is 400m west of Place Clemenceau around the old port, the little inlet just south of the rock known as Rocher de la Vierge. The Biarritz-La Négresse train station is 4km south-east of the centre.

Information

Tourist Offices The tourist office (☎ 05 59 22 37 10; fax 05 59 24 97 80), is only one block east of Ave Édouard VII at 1 Square d'Ixelles, is open daily from 9 am to 6.45 pm. From June to September it's open from 8 am to 8 pm when there is also an annexe at the train station open from 8.30 am to 7.30 pm. The city's monthly guide to sporting events, concerts and other cultural activities is called *Biarritzcope*. The tourist office does not handle hotel reservations.

Money There are lots of commercial banks around Place Clemenceau. The Bureau de Change Atollíssimo (☎ 05 59 22 27 27), 27 Place Clemenceau, offers some of the best rates in town and is open from 9 am to 6.30 pm from Monday to Saturday (daily from 9 am to 8 pm from mid-June to mid-September).

Post The main post office is between Place Clemenceau and Ave Jaulerry on Rue de la Poste. It's open weekdays from 8.30 am to 7 pm and on Saturday from 8.30 am to noon.

Bookshop The Bookstore (☎ 05 59 24 48 00) next to the Bureau de Change Atollíssimo on Place Georges Clemenceau has a small selection of English books.

Walking Tour

The most imposing landmark along the **Grande Plage** (see Beaches) is the stately **Hôtel du Palais**, a large villa built for the Empress Eugénie in 1854 and now a luxury hotel. King Edward VII stayed here in 1906 and 1910. Across Ave de l'Impératrice at No 8 is **Église Alexandre Newsky**, a Russian Orthodox church built to serve the spiritual needs of the Russian aristocrats who used to come here before the Russian Revolution of 1917. Russians are once again very much in evidence in Biarritz. Divine Liturgy is said one weekend each month at 6 pm on Saturday and 10.30 am on Sunday. The **Chapelle Impériale** south of the church on Ave de la Marne was built for Eugénie in 1864. It is currently closed to the public, but may open to groups. Call the tourist office for further details.

To the north on Pointe Saint Martin is the **Phare de Biarritz**, the town's 73m-high lighthouse erected in 1834.

From below the Espace Bellevue congress centre at the south end of the Grande Plage, a **promenade** follows the rocky coast above the old **Port des Pêcheurs**, the fishing port that is now filled with expensive pleasure craft. The Byzantine and Moorish-style **Église Sainte Eugénie**, on the seafront at Place Sainte Eugénie, was built in 1864 for – who else? – Empress Eugénie.

The mauve cliffs continue westward to **Rocher de la Vierge** (Rock of the Virgin), a stone island reached by a footbridge, which gets splashed in stormy weather. It is named after the white statue of the Virgin and the Infant Jesus on top, protected by some nasty-looking steel spikes (no doubt to prevent the faithful from getting too carried away). From the rock, you can see the coast of the Landes department stretching northward and, far to the south, the mountains of the Spanish Basque Country.

Just east of Rocher de la Vierge is the interesting Musée de la Mer. The narrow streets of the **Port Vieux area**, which overlooks a tiny beach, are a few hundred metres to the south-east.

Along the south side of the promontory is a hillside road aptly named **Perspective de la Côte Basque**. It affords views of Plage de la Côte des Basques and the coastal cliffs that run southward.

Musée de la Mer

Biarritz's Sea Museum (☎ 05 59 24 02 59) is on Esplanade des Anciens Combattants, next to the footbridge to Rocher de la Vierge. The ground floor **aquarium** has 24 tanks of 150 species of underwater beasties from the Bay of Biscay (Golfe de Gascogne), the area of the Atlantic bounded by the south-west coast of France and the north coast of Spain. The 1st floor has exhibits on commercial fishing and whaling, as Biarritz was once a whaling port. The four *phoques* (seals) are fed in their seawater pool daily at 10.30 am and 5 pm. A nearby pool holds *requins* (sharks).

The Sea Museum is open daily from 9.30 am to 12.30 pm and 2 to 6 pm. From mid-July to August the museum stays open till midnight. Entry is 45FF (30FF for students and children aged 5 to 16).

Musée Historique du Vieux Biarritz

The Museum of Old Biarritz (☎ 05 59 24 86 28), in a desanctified Anglican church (Église Saint Andrew) opposite 10 Rue Broquedis, has exhibits on the history of Biarritz. It is open from 10 am to noon and 2.30 to 6.30 pm daily, except Thursday and Sunday. Admission costs 15/5FF for adults/children.

Beaches

Biarritz's fashionable beaches are wall-to-wall with people on hot summer days. They are especially crowded at high tide, when row after row of sunbathers get chased up the beach to the dwindling strip of dry sand. Lifeguards are on duty from 10 am to 7 or 8 pm.

In season, the **Grande Plage** is lined with brightly striped bathing tents. North of the Hôtel du Palais is **Plage Miramar**, bounded on the north by Pointe Saint Martin. At low tide, there is **nude bathing** at the northern end of Plage Miramar (beyond the boulders).

North of Pointe Saint Martin, the fine beaches of **Anglet** stretch northward for 4km. They are served by bus No 4 in season.

South of Rocher de la Vierge, there is a small, protected beach at the **Port Vieux**. The long, exposed **Plage de la Côte des Basques**, which completely disappears at high tide, begins some 500m farther down the coast. The cliff above the Plage de la Côte des Basques has been stabilised at great expense and is quite an eyesore.

At the southern end of Plage de la Côte des Basques are two more beaches: **Plage de Marbella** and **Plage de la Milady**. By bus, take line No 9 (stop: Marbella).

Surfing

Rip Curl Surf Shop (☎ 05 59 24 38 40), 2 Ave de la Reine Victoria, which is open Tuesday to Saturday (Monday to Saturday from April to October) from 10 am to noon or 12.30 pm and 3 to 7 or 7.30 pm, rents surfboards or body boards for 50/80FF per half-day/day. They also offer instruction at 200FF for a two hour lesson (500FF/1000FF for a course of three/seven two hour lessons).

Pelote Basque

Introductory one/two hour pelota lessons are available in Biarritz for 100/180FF per person (including equipment) for a minimum of four people. For information, contact Fronton Couvert Plaza Berri (☎ 05 59 22 15 72), 42 Ave du Maréchal Foch. You will probably need to book a few days in advance.

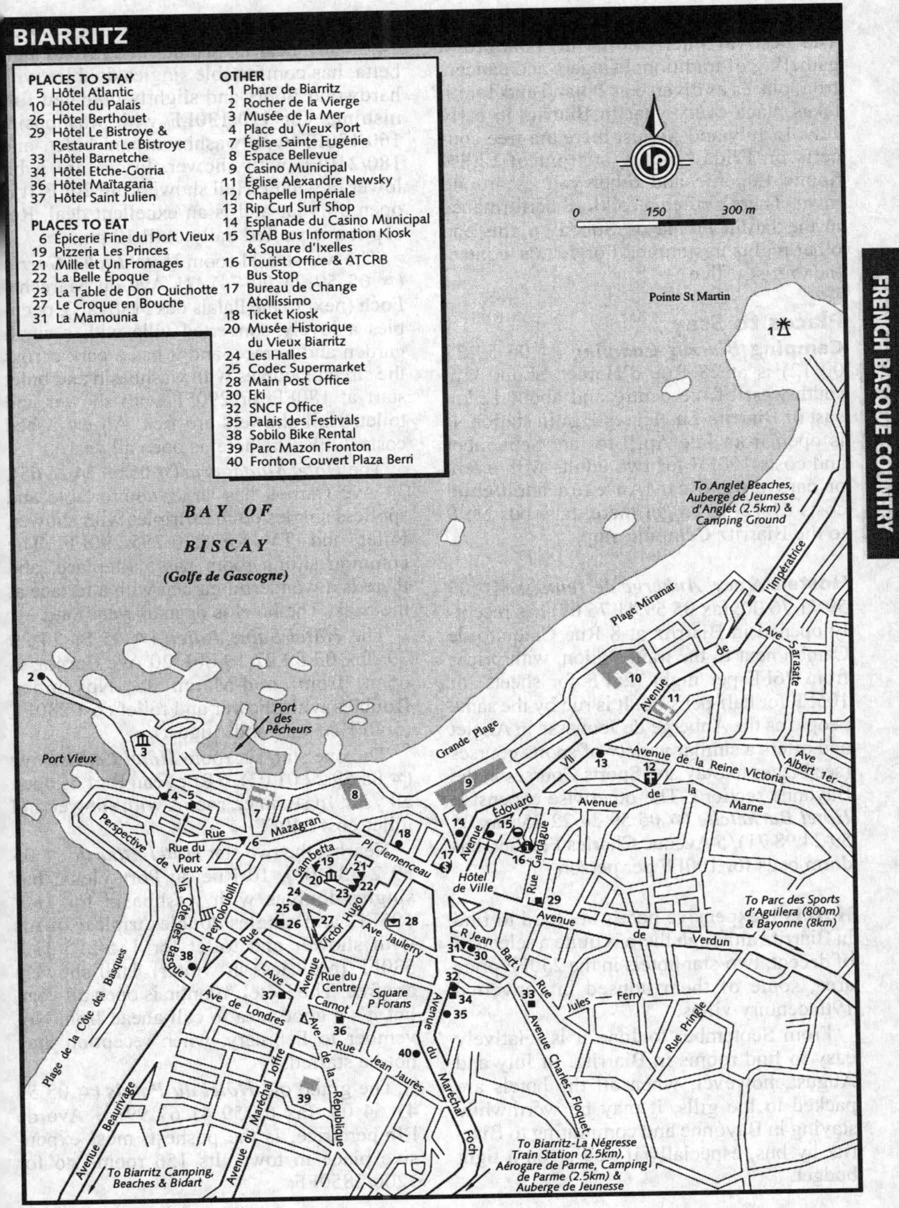
BIARRITZ
PLACES TO STAY
5 Hôtel Atlantic
10 Hôtel du Palais
26 Hôtel Berthouet
29 Hôtel Le Bistroye & Restaurant Le Bistroye
33 Hôtel Barnetche
34 Hôtel Etche-Gorria
36 Hôtel Maïtagaria
37 Hôtel Saint Julien
PLACES TO EAT
6 Épicerie Fine du Port Vieux
19 Pizzeria Les Princes
21 Mille et Un Fromages
22 La Belle Époque
23 La Table de Don Quichotte
27 Le Croque en Bouche
31 La Mamounia
OTHER
1 Phare de Biarritz
2 Rocher de la Vierge
3 Musée de la Mer
4 Place du Vieux Port
7 Église Sainte Eugénie
8 Espace Bellevue
9 Casino Municipal
11 Église Alexandre Newsky
12 Chapelle Impériale
13 Rip Curl Surf Shop
14 Esplanade du Casino Municipal
15 STAB Bus Information Kiosk & Square d'Ixelles
16 Tourist Office & ATCRB Bus Stop
17 Bureau de Change Atollissimo
18 Ticket Kiosk
20 Musée Historique du Vieux Biarritz
24 Les Halles
25 Codec Supermarket
28 Main Post Office
30 Eki
32 SNCF Office
35 Palais des Festivals
38 Sobilo Bike Rental
39 Parc Mazon Fronton
40 Fronton Couvert Plaza Berri
0
150
300 m
Pointe St Martin
BAY OF BISCAY
(Golfe de Gascogne)
To Anglet Beaches, Auberge de Jeunesse d'Anglet (2.5km) & Camping Ground
Plage Miramar
Ave de l'Impératrice
Ave Sarasate
Avenue de la Reine Victoria
Ave Albert 1er
Avenue de la Marne
Grande Plage
Avenue Édouard VII
Port des Pêcheurs
Port Vieux
Rue Mazagran
Rue du Port Vieux
Perspective de la Côte des Basques
Pl Clemenceau
Gambetta
Hôtel de Ville
Rue Gardague
Avenue de Verdun
To Parc des Sports d'Aguilera (800m) & Bayonne (8km)
R Peyroloubilh
Rue Victor Hugo
Ave Jaulerry
R Jean Bart
Rue du Centre
Square P Forans
Ave Carnot
Ave de Londres
Ave de la République
Rue Jean Jaurès
Avenue du Maréchal Foch
Avenue Charles Floquet
Rue Jules Ferry
Rue Pringle
Plage de la Côte des Basques
Avenue Beaurivage
Avenue du Maréchal Joffre
To Biarritz Camping, Beaches & Bidart
To Biarritz-La Négresse Train Station (2.5km), Aérogare de Parme, Camping de Parme (2.5km) & Auberge de Jeunesse

Special Events

The Festival International de Folklore, a gathering of traditional singers and dancers from places as diverse as Poland and Tahiti, takes place every year in Biarritz in early July. In July and August there are free concerts on Friday nights in front of Église Sainte Eugénie and other venues around town. There's often a folklore performance in the Jardin Public on Sunday nights and other nights in summer. For details, contact the tourist office.

Places to Stay

Camping *Biarritz Camping* (☎ 05 59 23 00 12) is at 28 Rue d'Harcet, about 3km south-west of the centre and about 1.5km east of Biarritz-La Négresse train station. It is open from late April to late September and costs 100FF for two adults with a tent or caravan and car. An extra adult/child costs 21/12FF. To get there, take bus No 9 to the Biarritz Camping stop.

Hostels A new *Auberge de Jeunesse* (☎ 05 59 41 76 00; fax 05 59 41 76 07) has recently opened in Biarritz at 8 Rue Chiquito de Cambo next to the train station, with prices from 76FF per night (25FF for sheets) or 105FF for half-pension. It is run by the same people as the Auberge de Jeunesse in Anglet and offers a similar variety of sports courses (see Places to Stay and Sports Courses in the Bayonne section). The otherwise expensive *Hôtel Barnetche* (☎ 05 59 24 22 25; fax 05 59 24 98 71), 5 Avenue Charles Floquet, has dorm beds for 100FF per person.

Hotels Inexpensive hotels are hard to find in Biarritz although there is quite a selection of decent, two-star hotels in the 250FF price area, some of them housed in converted 19th century villas.

From September to June it is relatively easy to find rooms in Biarritz. In July and August, however, when all the hotels are packed to the gills, it may be worthwhile staying in Bayonne and commuting to Biarritz by bus, especially if you're on a tight budget.

The friendly *Hôtel Berthouet* (☎ 05 59 24 63 36), near Les Halles at 29 Rue Gambetta, has comfortable singles/doubles with hardwood floors and slightly outdated furnishings for 110/130FF with washbasin 160/190FF with washbasin and bidet, and 180/210FF with shower. Prices are a bit lower in winter. Hall showers are 20FF. It is open all year and is an excellent deal. Reception is staffed daily until 10 pm.

The two star, 11 room *Hôtel Etche-Gorria* (☎ 05 59 24 00 74), 21 Ave du Maréchal Foch (next to the Palais des Festivals), occupies a lovely converted villa with a small garden and terrace, and it has a park across the street. Doubles with washbasin and bidet start at 180FF, or 290FF with shower and toilet. Hall showers are free. An extra bed costs 70FF. The hotel is open all year.

The *Hôtel Maïtagaria* (☎ 05 59 24 26 65), 34 Ave Carnot, has large, comfortable and spotless singles/doubles/triples with shower, toilet and TV for 220/255/290FF. The common sitting room has a fireplace, and there is a wonderful garden with a terrace at the back. The hotel is open all year long.

The *Hôtel Saint Julien* (☎ 05 59 24 20 39; fax 05 59 22 19 80), 20 Ave Carnot, is open from mid-March to November. Doubles with shower and toilet cost 230FF (360FF in July and August).

The one star, six room *Hôtel Le Bistroye* (☎ 05 59 22 01 02), 6 Rue Jean Bart, is open all year. In summer, rooms with shower and toilet cost 240FF.

Nearby, the two star *Hôtel Atlantic* (☎ 05 59 24 34 08), 10 Rue du Port Vieux, has singles/doubles with washbasin for 160/195FF, and singles/doubles/triples/ quads with shower and toilet for 185/275/310/330FF (a bit less in winter). Hall showers are free. The Hôtel Atlantic is open all year, but it's a good idea to call ahead from November to February, when reception may not be staffed.

The grand old *Hôtel du Palais* (☎ 05 59 41 64 00; fax 05 59 41 67 99), 1 Ave de l'Impératrice, is the poshest, most expensive place in town. Its 156 rooms go for 1200/2850FF.

Places to Eat

Restaurants There are quite a few decent little restaurants scattered around Les Halles.

Le Croque en Bouche (☎ 05 59 22 06 57), 5 Rue du Centre, serves high-quality regional cuisine in an elegant dining room. Starters/main courses/desserts start from 65/75/35FF or you can choose a *menu* at 90 or 145FF. The restaurant is closed Sunday evening, Monday and the second half of January.

Not far away, ***La Belle Époque*** (☎ 05 59 24 66 06), 10 Rue Victor Hugo, has a variety of French regional dishes as well as a few items from Spain and the Antilles. The décor was inspired by the *belle époque*, but the background music is 1930s-style jazz. Fish costs 60 to 80FF, meat dishes are 60 to 99FF, or there is a *menu* for 68FF. It is open daily from 12.15 to 2.30 pm and 7.15 to 10.30 pm (11 pm in summer).

The restaurant at the ***Hôtel Le Bistroye*** (see Places to Stay) has delicious hot dishes starting from 48FF. It is closed Wednesday evening and all day Sunday. An excellent place for lunch is ***La Mamounia*** (☎ 05 59 24 76 08), next door at 4 Rue Jean Bart, with couscous from 75 to 105FF and other Moroccan specialities starting from 89FF.

Pizzeria Les Princes (☎ 05 59 24 21 78), 13 Rue Gambetta, has pizzas for 40 to 50FF and pasta from 38 to 50FF. It's open from Monday afternoon to Saturday for lunch and dinner (to 11.30 pm).

Self-Catering Biarritz's covered market, ***Les Halles***, is two blocks south of Place Clemenceau with entrances on Rue Gambetta and Ave Victor Hugo. It is open daily from 7 am to 1.30 pm. There are lots of ***food shops*** in the immediate vicinity, including a ***Codec*** supermarket at 2 Rue du Centre, which is open Monday to Saturday from 8.45 am to 12.25 pm and from 3 to 7.10 pm.

Just downhill from Les Halles at 12 Ave Victor Hugo, ***La Table de Don Quichotte*** sells all sorts of Spanish hams, sausages and wines, while further down the hill at No 8 you'll find a tempting array of cheeses at ***Mille et Un Fromages***.

In the Port Vieux area at 41bis Rue Mazagran, ***Épicerie Fine du Port Vieux*** has cheese, wine, fruit, vegetables and prepared foods, including foie gras and gâteau Basque (Basque-style cake). A convenient if pricey place to assemble a gourmet picnic, it is open daily from 7 am to 1.30 pm and 3 to 8 pm (7 am to 9 pm from June to October).

Entertainment

Information about the many cultural and sporting events can be obtained at the ticket kiosk (☎ 05 59 24 69 20), 15 Place Clemenceau, during summer months.

Spectator Sports

To experience the lightning-fast game of pelota (see the boxed text 'Pelote Basque'), try to attend a tournament at the Fronton Couvert Plaza Berri (☎ 05 59 22 15 72), 42 Ave du Maréchal Foch in Biarritz, where there is a match every Tuesday and Friday night at 9.15 pm from June to early September. Tickets cost about 40FF.

During the rest of the year, various tournaments – including the Basque and French championships of *paleta cuir* and *pala corta* (kinds of pelota played with wooden racquets) as well as main nue – are held here, often on Sunday afternoons.

Entry is free except for the semifinals and finals. When no matches are being played, you can visit the ball-scarred court – overlooked by three tiers of narrow balconies – by walking through the Bar Plaza Berri, next door.

From July to mid-September, the outdoor *fronton* (☎ 05 59 23 91 09 for information) at Parc Mazon, which is off Ave du Maréchal Joffre, has *chistera* matches on Monday at 9 pm and sometimes on other nights.

Parc des Sports d'Aguilera (☎ 05 59 23 91 09), 2km east of central Biarritz on Ave Henri Haget, has professional *cesta punta* matches from mid-June to mid-September every Wednesday and Saturday evening at 9 pm. Tickets cost 40 or 50FF. The Parc des Sports is linked to Biarritz and Bayonne by bus No 1 (stop: Aguilera).

Shopping

Basque music, crafts and guidebooks are available at Eki (☎ 05 59 24 79 64), 21 Ave de Verdun, which is open from 9 am to 1 pm and 3.30 to 7.30 pm daily, except Sunday and Monday.

Delicious chocolates and Basque sweets (see Shopping under Saint Jean de Luz) can be purchased at Robert Pariès (☎ 05 59 22 07 52), next to the Bureau de Change Atollíssimo at 27 Place Clemenceau.

Getting There & Away

Air See Air under Getting There & Away in the Bayonne section for details on BAB's airport.

Bus The rather slow buses run by ATCRB (☎ 05 59 26 06 99 in Saint Jean de Luz), which stop right outside the tourist office, follow the coast southward to Bidart, Saint Jean de Luz and Hendaye. Between June and mid-October there are buses daily (except Sunday) at 8.30 am and 2 pm to San Sebastián in Spain (33.50FF). The rest of the year they leave at 12.15 and 6.45 pm on Tuesday, Thursday and Saturday only.

Train The Biarritz-La Négresse train station (☎ 08 36 35 35 35) is 4km south-east of the centre of Biarritz at the southern end of Ave du Président John F Kennedy, which is the continuation of Ave du Maréchal Foch. To get there from the centre of Biarritz or the Bayonne train station, take bus No 2 to the terminus.

SNCF has a downtown office (☎ 05 59 24 00 94) at 13 Ave du Maréchal Foch, which is open Monday to Friday from 9 am to noon and 2 to 6 pm.

Hitching Don't even bother trying to hitch between Bayonne and Biarritz – people don't stop.

Getting Around

To/From the Airport BAB's airport is linked to Biarritz by STAB bus No 6. On Sunday, line C links Biarritz (Hôtel de Ville) with the airport 17 times a day between 7.36 am and 7.50 pm.

Bus For a run down on the STAB bus system, which serves Bayonne, Anglet and Biarritz, see Getting Around under Bayonne.

Biarritz has a STAB information kiosk (☎ 05 59 52 59 52) on Ave Louis Barthou, which is across Square d'Ixelles from the tourist office. It is open Monday to Saturday from 8 am to noon and 1.30 to 6 pm.

Taxi To summon a taxi, call ☎ 05 59 23 05 50, ☎ 05 59 03 18 18 or ☎ 05 59 63 17 17.

Motorcycle & Bicycle Two-wheeled conveyances of all sorts can be rented from Sobilo (☎ 05 59 24 94 47), 24 Rue Peyroloubilh, south of Place Clemenceau where Rue Gambetta becomes Ave Beaurivage. Mountain bikes cost 50FF a day (plus 1000FF deposit); scooters are from 100FF (plus a 6000FF deposit), including helmet. The shop is open daily (except Sunday) March to November from 10 am to 1 pm and 3 to 7 pm. In July and August it's open daily from 9 am to 1 pm and 3 to 7 pm.

SAINT JEAN DE LUZ

• pop 13,000 ✉ 64500

The attractive seaside town of Saint Jean de Luz (Donibane Lohizune in Basque), 21km south-west of Bayonne at the mouth of the Nivelle River, is the most Basque of the region's beach resorts. Built along one side of a sheltered bay, it has a colourful history of whaling and piracy. Saint Jean de Luz and the twin town of Ciboure make a perfect day trip from Bayonne or Biarritz.

Saint Jean de Luz is still an active fishing port and is known for its large catches of sardines (from the waters off Portugal and Morocco), tuna (from the Bay of Biscay and West Africa) and anchovies (from the Bay of Biscay).

Orientation

The train station is 500m south of the beach at the southern end of Ave de Verdun; the tourist office is between the two. Main streets in the town centre are the pedestrianised Rue de la République and Rue Gambetta. The beach is on the south-east side of an oval-shaped bay (Baie de Saint Jean de Luz) and protected from the open ocean by three mid-19th century *digues* (breakwaters).

Ciboure (Ziburu in Basque; population 5800), Saint Jean's twin town, is on the left bank of the Nivelle, which is spanned by Pont Charles de Gaulle.

Information

Tourist Office The helpful tourist office (☎ 05 59 26 03 16; fax 05 59 26 21 47), Place Maréchal Foch, is open Monday to Saturday from 9 am to 12.30 pm and 2 to 6.30 pm. During July and August it's open Monday to Saturday from 9 am to 8 pm, and on Sunday and holidays from 10 am to 1 pm and from 3 to 7 pm. The staff do not usually make hotel reservations but will assist foreigners who don't speak French. This is a good place to pick up ATCRB bus schedules.

Money The Société Générale at 9 Blvd Victor Hugo is open Tuesday to Saturday from 8.30 am to 12.20 pm and 1.55 to 5.05 pm. Change Plus (☎ 05 59 51 03 43), an exchange bureau at 32 Rue Gambetta, is open Monday to Saturday from 9 am to 12.30 pm and 2 to 7 pm. Between July and mid-September it's open Monday to Saturday from 8 am to 8 pm, and on Sunday from 10 am to 1 pm and 4 to 7 pm.

Socoa Voyages (☎ 05 59 26 06 27; fax 05 59 51 09 27), 31 Blvd Thiers, the only American Express office between Bordeaux and the Spanish border, is open from 9 am to 12.30 pm and 2.30 to 6.30 pm daily, except Sunday and holidays.

Post The post office at 44 Blvd Victor Hugo is open weekdays from 9 am to noon and 1.30 to 5.30 pm (9 am to 6 pm in July and August) and on Saturday till noon.

In Ciboure, the post office at 3 Quai Maurice Ravel is open Monday to Friday from 9 am to noon and 2 to 5 pm and on Saturday morning.

Walking Tour

At **Place Louis XIV**, north-west of the tourist office, there are two buildings of interest: the **mairie**, erected in 1657, and the **Maison Louis XIV** (☎ 05 59 26 01 56), also known as the Maison Lohobiague, where Louis XIV stayed for over a month before his marriage in 1660. From June to September, the structure, built in 1643 by a rich shipowner and furnished in the style of the 17th century, can be visited daily except Sunday morning from 10.30 am to noon and from 2.30 to 5.30 pm (to 6.30 pm in July and August). Guided tours, with English text available, cost 25FF (20FF for students and children). During the Revolution, a guillotine was set up nearby.

Maison de l'Infante, Quai de l'Infante, where Marie-Thérèse stayed before marrying Louis XIV, is a few blocks to the west. The interior is closed to the public, but the **Musée Grévin** (☎ 05 59 51 24 88), next door at 3 Rue Mazarin, contains wax figures of all the nobles who graced Saint Jean de Luz with their presence (and presents) over the centuries. It is open from April to October from 10 am to noon and 2 to 6.30 pm. In July and August the hours are 10 am to 12.30 pm and 2 to 8 pm. Admission is 34/17FF for adults/children under 13 years.

There is a fine **view** of the commercial fishing port from Quai de l'Infante.

The most popular street for window shopping is **Rue Gambetta**, but **Blvd Thiers,** whose northern reaches run along the beach, is more elegant. Like **Promenade Jacques Thibaud**, which runs parallel for much of the length of the beach, it is lined with modern buildings, most of them white or in light pastel colours.

Pointe Sainte Barbe, a promontory that juts into Baie de Saint Jean de Luz in its north-eastern corner, is about 1km north of the Saint Jean de Luz beach. To get there, walk along Blvd Thiers and **Promenade des Rochers**, which runs along the shore.

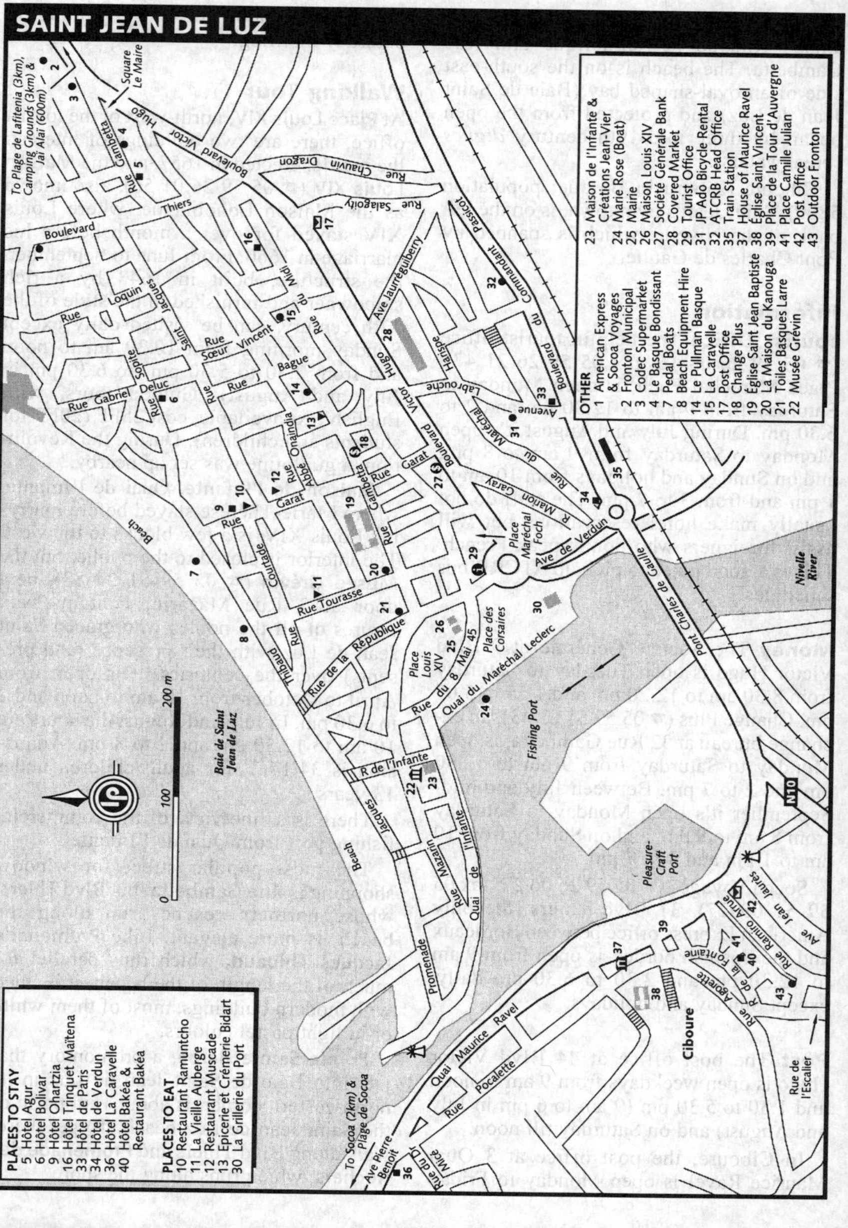
SAINT JEAN DE LUZ
FRENCH BASQUE COUNTRY
PLACES TO STAY
5 Hôtel Agur
6 Hôtel Bolivar
9 Hôtel Ohartzia
16 Hôtel Trinquet Maïtena
33 Hôtel de Paris
34 Hôtel de Verdun
36 Hôtel La Caravelle
40 Hôtel Bakéa & Restaurant Bakéa
PLACES TO EAT
10 Restaurant Ramuntcho
11 La Vieille Auberge
12 Restaurant Muscade
13 Epicerie et Crémerie Bidart
30 La Grillerie du Port
OTHER
1 American Express & Socoa Voyages
2 Fronton Municipal
3 Codec Supermarket
4 Le Basque Bondissant
7 Pedal Boats
8 Beach Equipment Hire
14 Le Pullman Basque
15 La Caravelle
17 Post Office
18 Change Plus
19 Église Saint Jean Baptiste
20 La Maison du Kanouga
21 Toiles Basques Larre
22 Musée Grévin
23 Maison de l'Infante & Créations Jean-Vier
24 Marie Rose (Boat)
25 Mairie
26 Maison Louis XIV
27 Société Générale Bank
28 Covered Market
29 Tourist Office
31 JP Ado Bicycle Rental
32 ATCRB Head Office
35 Train Station
37 House of Maurice Ravel
38 Église Saint Vincent
39 Place de la Tour d'Auvergne
41 Place Camille Julian
42 Post Office
43 Outdoor Fronton
To Plage de Lafitenia (3km), Camping Grounds (3km) & Jaï Alaï (600m)
To Socoa (2km) & Plage de Socoa
Baie de Saint Jean de Luz
Fishing Port
Pleasure-Craft Port
Nivelle River
Ciboure
Place Louis XIV
Place Maréchal Foch
Place des Corsaires
Quai du Maréchal Leclerc
Port Charles de Gaulle
Boulevard Thiers
Boulevard Victor Hugo
Rue Gambetta
Rue de la République
Quai Maurice Ravel
N10
0 100 200 m

Église Saint Jean Baptiste

This church on Rue Gambetta, whose magnificent interior dates from the latter half of the 17th century, is among the largest and most famous Basque churches in France. On 9 June 1660, Louis XIV and the child Marie-Thérèse of Austria, daughter of King Philip IV of Spain, were married here, as provided for in the Treaty of the Pyrenees of 1659, which ended 24 years of war between France and Spain. The **portal** on the south side, through which the newlyweds exited the church, was sealed after the ceremony and the outline can be seen opposite 20 Rue Gambetta. The church is closed from noon to 2 pm.

Until the Second Vatican Council (1962-65), there was separate seating for men and women. The men, who sat in the three tiers of **oak balconies** (four tiers at the back) and reached by a wooden stairway, used to sing as a chorus, while the women sat near the family sepulchres, which were once located under the church floor.

The gilded wooden statues that ornament the exceptional **altar screen**, made between 1665 and 1670, exhibit a mixture of classical severity and Spanish baroque exuberance. A votive model of the ship *L'Aigle*, a gift of the Empress Eugénie after the real thing narrowly escaped sinking off Ciboure, hangs in the middle of the church.

Ciboure Walking Tour

The fishing town of Ciboure, quieter and less touristy than Saint Jean de Luz, is right across the river from Saint Jean de Luz. **Rue Agorette**, **Rue de la Fontaine** and **Rue de l'Escalier** all retain their typically Basque architecture. The buildings are white with either green or reddish-brown shutters and balconies.

Église Saint Vincent, on Rue Pocalette, built during the 16th and 17th centuries, is topped by an unusual octagonal bell tower with a three tiered roof. The beautiful wood interior is typically Basque.

The composer Maurice Ravel (1875-1937), whose mother was Basque (his father was Swiss), was born in the house at 27 Quai Maurice Ravel.

The village of **Socoa** is 2.5km north-west of Ciboure along Quai Maurice Ravel and its beachside continuation, Blvd Pierre Benoit. The **fort** was built in 1627 and was later improved by Vauban. You can walk out to the **Digue de Socoa**, the breakwater at the western tip of Baie de Saint Jean de Luz. Socoa is served by ATCRB buses.

Beaches

Saint Jean de Luz's sandy beach, popular with families, is fairly wide at low tide but gets progressively narrower as the tide comes in. In 1749 a tsunami (sometimes incorrectly called a tidal wave) devastated much of the town.

Bathing tents, set up from June to September, cost 40FF a day and can be rented below the northern end of Rue Tourasse. Parasols are 28FF a day. The daily rate for a *transat* (deck chair) is 15FF. You can also rent by the week, fortnight and month.

The **Plage de Socoa** is several kilometres west of Ciboure along Blvd Pierre Benoit. It is served by ATCRB buses (see Bus under Getting There & Away).

Activities

Pedal Boats From July to the first week in September, you can rent *pédalos* on the beach between Rue Garat and Rue Tourasse for 30/50FF per 30 minutes/hour.

Surfing The sheltered Baie de Saint Jean de Luz is much too calm for surfing, but locals do manage to catch a few waves at **Plage de Lafitenia**, which is almost 4km north-east of the centre of town near the camping grounds. It is served by ATCRB buses going to Bayonne and Biarritz.

Bullfighting Saint Jean de Luz does not have its own bullfighting arena, but tickets for corridas in other parts of the Basque Country are on sale during July and August at Le Pullman Basque (☎ 05 59 26 03 37), 33 Rue Gambetta.

Organised Tours

From June to September Le Pullman Basque has half-day/day excursions for

90/160FF to San Sebastián, Pamplona, Guernica and other destinations in Spain. Buses leave from in front of the tourist office. The company's office is open daily (except Sunday) from 9.30 am to noon and 2.30 to 7 pm. From July to mid-September it's open daily, except Sunday afternoon, from 8.30 am (9 am on Sunday) to 12.30 pm and 2.30 to 7.30 pm.

Special Events

The *fête patronale* (saint's day) of Saint Jean Baptiste (St John the Baptist) is celebrated on the weekend before 24 June. The festivities begin on Friday night with a concert by local choral groups at Église Saint Jean Baptiste. On Saturday, bonfires are lit in front of the church and the *mairie*. On Sunday, there are outdoor music and dance performances around town.

La Nuit de la Sardine (Night of the Sardine) is not a horror movie but rather an evening of music, folklore and dancing held twice each summer: on a Saturday in early July and the Saturday that falls on or before 14 August. Staged outdoors next to the *jaï alaï* (a court used for chistera) on Ave André Ithurralde, each of the 2000 places costs 40 to 80FF. Sardines, tuna, cakes, cheese, sandwiches etc are on sale. Doors open at 7 pm and the festivities start an hour or so later.

La Fête du Thon (Tuna Festival), which falls on the first Saturday after 1 July, brings wandering musicians to Place Maréchal Foch, Place des Corsaires, Quai Maréchal Leclerc and Ciboure. Local sports organisations set up stands and sell tuna dishes. There are also two balls: at Place Maréchal Foch a local orchestra plays traditional Basque music and rock, while a larger orchestra plays in a more formal venue. There is a fireworks display at the port around midnight.

Places to Stay – Budget

Many hotels get the same summer clients year after year, so it is extremely difficult to find a room in July and August, when prices rise by 50% or more and some hotels require that you take half-board.

Camping About 3.5km north of the centre of Saint Jean de Luz, eight camping grounds are located in an area not too far from the coast. ***Camping Luz Europ*** (☎ 05 59 26 51 90) in Quartier Acotz, open from Easter to October, charges about 25FF per adult, 11FF per child, and 38FF for a tent site, including parking.

Camping Elgar (☎ 05 59 26 85 85), Quartier Erromardie, is open from mid-April to September. Two people with a tent are charged 57.50FF (69.50FF with a car). To get there, you can take any of the ATCRB buses linking Saint Jean de Luz with Biarritz and Bayonne (see Bus under Getting There & Away).

Hotels Near the train station at 13 Ave de Verdun, a good option off-season is the 14 room ***Hôtel de Verdun*** (☎ 05 59 26 02 55). Ordinary but large doubles cost 150FF with washbasin and bidet, 170FF with shower, and 185FF with bath and toilet (190/215/275FF from July to September). Hall showers are 10FF. Some of the doubles have two large beds and can sleep up to four people. In July and August *demi-pension* (170FF per person extra) is obligatory. This place is closed in December.

Hôtel Trinquet Maïtena (☎ 05 59 26 05 13; fax 05 59 26 09 90), 42 Rue du Midi, has basic singles from 115FF, doubles with shower/bath from 220/240FF, and triples/quads from 320FF.

Two blocks from the beach at 18 Rue Sopite, the two star ***Hôtel Bolivar*** (☎ 05 59 26 02 00) is open from May to September. Singles/doubles cost 170/195FF with washbasin, and 230/295FF with bath and toilet (doubles only). Prices are slightly lower in June and September.

Places to Stay – Mid-Range

Saint Jean de Luz Opposite the train station at 1 Blvd du Commandant Passicot, ***Hôtel de Paris*** (☎ 05 59 26 00 62; fax 05 59 26 90 02), has fairly nondescript, medium-sized singles/doubles/triples/quads that include shower, toilet and TV for 180/200/260/280FF (about 50% more in July and August). This two star, 30 room establishment is closed in January and February. Reception is staffed until 11 pm.

The ***Hôtel Agur*** (☎ 05 59 51 91 11), 96 Rue Gambetta, with a Scottish proprietor, is open from mid-March to mid-November. Modern and extremely functional singles/doubles/triples with shower, toilet and TV start at 275/295/395FF (375/ 395/495FF from July to mid-September). Some rooms have recently been converted into self-catering flats for two, which cost 1490FF per week in the off season and 3490FF in summer.

Ciboure In the centre of Ciboure at 9 Place Camille Julian, the friendly, one star ***Hôtel Bakéa*** (☎ 05 59 47 34 40) has doubles and triples with shower and toilet for 200 to 250FF. It is open from March to December.

The 20 room ***Hôtel La Caravelle*** (☎ 05 59 47 18 05), open all year, is at the western end of Blvd Pierre Benoit, next to the mouth of the harbour. Doubles/quads with shower and toilet are 260/360FF. ATCRB buses to Socoa pass by here.

Places to Stay – Top End

The two star, 17 room ***Hôtel Ohartzia*** (☎ 05 59 26 00 06; fax 05 59 26 74 75), half a block from the beach at 28 Rue Garat, is open all year. The pleasant rooms cost 330FF with shower, 360FF with bath (390 and 440FF in summer), including breakfast.

Places to Eat

Considering its size, Saint Jean has quite a few excellent dining options. A number of rather pricey establishments are to be found along Rue de la République, and there are lots of cafés at Place Louis XIV.

Restaurants – Saint Jean de Luz ***La Vieille Auberge*** (☎ 05 59 26 19 61), 22 Rue Tourasse, serves generous portions of traditional French and Basque cuisine, including *ttoro* (Basque fish casserole; 99FF). *Moules marinières* (mussels cooked in their own juice with onions) are 49FF. The different *menus* cost 75, 99, 115 and 129FF. From April to October, it is open daily, except Tuesday evening and Wednesday (daily, except Tuesday lunch, in July and August).

The rustic ***Restaurant Ramuntcho*** (☎ 05 59 26 03 89), 24 Rue Garat, has a mix of French regional and south-western French dishes you're unlikely to find elsewhere. The cook's husband is from Normandy, so the sauces are made with lots of fresh cream. Specialities include duck and fish. The *menus* cost 90, 125 and 160FF. They close off-season on Monday.

Restaurant Muscade (☎ 05 59 26 96 73), 20 Rue Garat, specialises in two things: *tartes* (tarts or pies; 28 to 60FF), both savoury ones made with cheese, mushrooms, fish, vegetables etc and sweet ones for dessert; and *salades composées* (mixed salads; 42 to 98FF). The restaurant is open daily from noon to 2.30 pm and 7 to 9 or 10 pm (slightly longer hours in July and August). It is closed in January.

For a truly unique dining experience, it's hard to beat the informal and enormously popular ***La Grillerie du Port*** (☎ 05 59 51 18 29), in an old shack between Place Maréchal Foch and the fishing port. Open from mid-June to mid-September, it serves only freshly cooked sardines (35FF for a plate of about five), *thon* (tuna; 45 to 50FF) and one kind of omelette (25FF). The whole set up is designed to maximise the number of sardines eaten, and the one giant dining room is continually abuzz with young waiters rushing about with plates of fish and bread. It is open daily from 11.30 am to 2.30 pm and 6 to 10 pm. There is often a queue in the evening.

Restaurants – Ciboure The restaurant on the ground floor of the ***Hôtel Bakéa*** is a superb choice for a splurge. Its spectacularly good seafood dishes include *chipirones à l'encre* (cuttlefish; 80FF), ttoro (220FF for two), *merlu koskera* (hake; 220FF for two) and a *plateau de fruits de mer* (seafood platter; 150FF) with over a dozen kinds of edible sea creatures. There are also *menus* priced at 90/120/155FF. Bakéa is open daily, except Tuesday night and Wednesday (daily in July and August).

Self-Catering A ***food market*** is held in Saint Jean de Luz every Tuesday and Friday morning (and Saturday morning in July and August) around the *marché couvert* (covered market) along Blvd Victor Hugo.

Epicerie et Crémerie Bidart, 29 Rue Gambetta, sells a fine selection of cold meats and cheeses from 7 am to 12.30 pm and 3 to 7.30 pm Monday to Saturday, and there is a good ***fruit and vegetable shop*** opposite (which is also open Sunday morning in summer). There are a number of other ***food shops*** along Rue Gambetta.

The ***Codec*** supermarket at 87 Rue Gambetta is open Monday to Saturday from 8.30 am to 12.30 or 1 pm and 3 to 7 pm (7.30 pm in July and August).

Spectator Sports

Pelote Basque Cesta punta matches take place at the jaï alaï (☎ 05 59 51 65 30) across the street from 43 Ave André Ithurralde (also known as the Route de Bayonne and the N10), which is 1km north-east of the train station. From late June to early September, tournaments are held every Tuesday and Friday from 9.15 pm to about midnight. Music or dance performances liven up the half-time interval. Tickets cost 50 to 120FF, depending on the match.

In Ciboure, there is an outdoor fronton on Rue Ramiro Arrue.

Rugby Saint Jean de Luz's Fête du Rugby is held each year around 15 August.

Shopping

Sweets Saint Jean de Luz is an excellent place to try Basque pastries and sweets such as *mouchous* (almond biscuits), *gochuak* (biscuits made with hazelnuts), *kanouga* (cubes of rich, chewy chocolate or coffee candy, wrapped in metallic paper), *macarons* (macaroons) and gâteau Basque.

La Maison du Kanouga (☎ 05 59 26 01 46), a somewhat pricey *pâtisserie* and chocolate shop located at 9 Rue Gambetta, has scrumptious biscuits for about 4FF each and tiny cream or cherry gâteaux Basques for 6FF (from 32FF for a large one). It is open daily from 8.30 am to 1 pm and 2 to 7.30 pm (8 am to midnight in July and August, and until 8 pm around Christmas and Easter).

Linen Saint Jean de Luz is one of the best places in the Basque Country to buy tea towels (45FF), tablecloths, serviettes (napkins; 195FF for six), oven gloves and potholders (44FF), and aprons made of colourful *linge Basque* (Basque linen).

A good selection of such items is available at La Caravelle (☎ 05 59 26 28 61), 64 Rue Gambetta. It is open Tuesday to Saturday from 10 am to 12.15 pm and 3 to 7 pm. From April to September it's open Monday to Saturday from 9.30 am to 12.30 pm and 3 to 7.30 pm (Sunday from 10.30 am to 12.30 pm and 3.30 to 7 pm). Alternatively, Toiles Basques Larre (☎ 05 59 26 02 13), 4 Rue de la République, just off Place Louis XIV, is open daily (except Sunday and Monday morning) from 9.30 am to 12.30 pm and 2.30 to 7 pm. From July to September it's open daily from 9 am to 1 pm and 2.30 to 8 pm.

Basque linen with more designer flair is available at Créations Jean-Vier (☎ 05 59 26 66 26), on the ground floor of Maison de l'Infante on Quai de l'Infante. It is open daily from mid-April to mid-November from 9.30 am to 12.30 pm and from 2.30 to 7 pm (to around midnight from July to mid-September).

Getting There & Away

Bus The head office of ATCRB (☎ 05 59 26 06 99) at La Halte Routiere, opposite the train station on Blvd du Commandant Passicot, is open from 8 am to 7 pm on weekdays and Saturday morning. About 15 buses a day (eight on Sunday and holidays) follow the coast to Bidart, Biarritz (15.50FF) and Bayonne (20FF; 40 minutes). Some of the company's 20 runs to Hendaye (15.50FF) go along the coast, while others pass through inland villages. The short run to Socoa (6FF), which goes through Ciboure, departs five times a day (except on Sunday and holidays). Tickets are sold on the bus. Because of traffic, ATCRB buses are slow and often late, especially in summer.

ATCRB also has buses to the Spanish city of San Sebastián (23FF; one hour) at 9 am and 2.30 pm on Tuesday, Thursday and Saturday (Monday to Saturday from June to mid-October). Pesa, a Spanish bus company that shares its bus stops with ATCRB, has year-round services from Monday to Saturday to San Sebastián at 12.45 and 7.15 pm. In summer there are also buses to Hendaye, and the Spanish border town of Irún (10km south), from where you can catch a bus every half an hour to Fontarabie (5FF) with its wonderful castle.

Train The Saint Jean de Luz-Ciboure train station (☎ 08 36 35 35 35 for information) sells tickets from 9 am to 7.30 pm; the information office is open daily from 10.15 am to 7 pm. The luggage lockers are open from 6 am to 11 pm.

There are at least 20 trains a day to Bayonne (26FF; 20 minutes), Biarritz (17FF; 13 minutes) and the French border town of Hendaye (17FF; 12 minutes), from where there are shuttle trains to San Sebastián in Spain. For details on trains serving Saint Jean de Luz, pick up the timetable entitled *Dax-Hendaye*.

Getting Around

Taxi There is a taxi rank to the left as you exit the train station. To order a cab by phone, call ☎ 05 59 26 10 11.

Motorcycle & Bicycle JP Ado (☎ 05 59 26 14 95), 7 Ave Labrouche, rents bicycles for 60/294FF a day/week, mountain bikes for 80/365FF, and 50cc motorbikes for 430 to 535FF a week. The shop is open Tuesday to Saturday from 8 am to noon and 2 to 7 pm (and Sunday morning in July and August).

LA RHUNE

La Rhune, a 900m-high, antenna-topped mountain 10km south-east of Saint Jean de Luz, which is half in France and half in Spain, is something of a symbol of the French Basque Country. There are spectacular views of the whole region from the summit, which can be reached from **Col de Saint Ignace** on foot or by a 4km *train à crémaillère* (cog-wheel railway; ☎ 05 59 54 20 26). The train, built in 1924, runs from Easter to mid-November. There are departures roughly every 35 minutes from 9 am (8.30 am in July and August) depending on the crowds. The return fare is 50/35FF for adults/children. The trip takes 30 minutes.

From June to September, Le Basque Bondissant (☎ 05 59 26 25 87), 100 Rue Gambetta in Saint Jean de Luz, has buses from Blvd du Commandant Passicot, near the train station, to Col de Saint Ignace (7.50FF each way; 30 minutes). There are three return trips daily, except on weekends and holidays. The first two leave Saint Jean de Luz at 11 am and 2.30 pm; the last (7 pm) would not get you to Col de Saint Ignace in time to make the ascent. Buses return from Col de Saint Ignace at 1.55, 3.10 and 6.05 pm. Le Basque Bondissant is open from 9 am to noon and 2 to 6 pm on weekdays and Saturday morning.

SAINT JEAN PIED DE PORT

• pop 1400 ✉ 64220 alt 160m

The walled Pyrenean town of Saint Jean Pied de Port (Donibane Garazi in Basque), 53km south-east of Bayonne and 8km from the Spanish border, was once the last stop in France for pilgrims heading south to Santiago de Compostela. Today, the town, set in a river valley surrounded by hills, retains much of its rural Basque character despite its popularity with visitors.

Saint Jean Pied de Port makes an easy day trip from Bayonne. Half the reason for coming here is the scenic trip from Bayonne – both the rail line and the main road, the D918, pass through rocky hills, forests and lush meadows dotted with white farmhouses with dark red shutters, shepherds and their flocks and signs announcing *ardi* ('cheese' in Basque) for sale. If you really want to get away from it all, you can rent a bike and head off into the hills.

Orientation

The centre of town, Place Charles de Gaulle and nearby Place du Trinquet, is 600m south of the train station along Ave Renaud. Place Floquet is on the southern side of the Nive River. Rue de la Citadelle, up the hill from Place du Trinquet, is linked to Rue d'Espagne by the Vieux Pont. The Citadelle is at the top of the hill that borders the east side of town.

Information

Tourist Office The tourist office (☎ 05 59 37 03 57; fax 05 59 37 34 91), 14 Place Charles de Gaulle, is open from 9 am to noon and 2 to 7 pm weekdays (to 6 pm on Saturday). From mid-June to mid-September it's also open on Sunday and holidays from 10.30 am to 12.30 pm and 3 to 6 pm.

Money Crédit Agricole just up the hill from the post office on Ave Renaud will exchange foreign currency. It is open weekdays from 9 am to 12.15 pm and 2 to 5 pm.

The Caisse d'Épargne, near the campsite at 9 Ave du Jaï Alaï, is open weekdays from 9 am to 12.30 and from 1 to 5 pm.

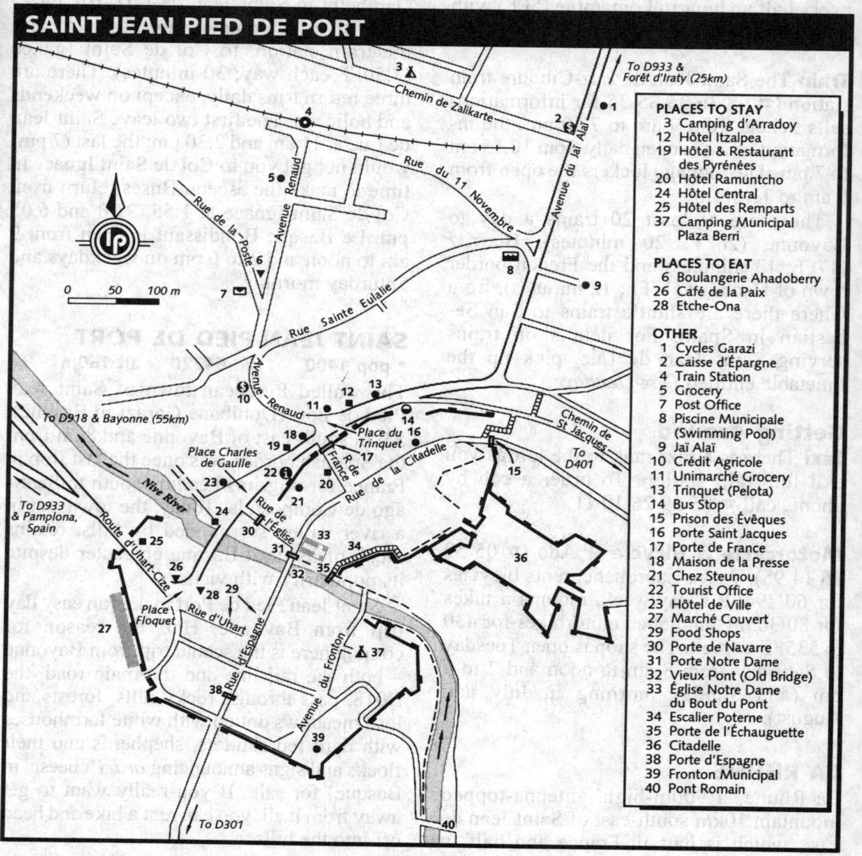

Post The post office, 1 Rue de la Poste, is open from 9 am to noon and 2 to 5 pm weekdays and on Saturday morning.

Bookshop The Maison de la Presse (☎ 05 59 37 07 13), 23 Place Charles de Gaulle, carries hiking maps of the area. It is open Monday to Saturday from 6.30 am to 12.30 pm and 2 to 7.30 pm, and on Sunday from 8 am to 12.30 pm.

Walking Tour

From Place du Trinquet, walk through **Porte de France**, one of the gates in the town's 15th century **ramparts**, which were built by the Navarres. Rue de France leads up the slope to **Rue de la Citadelle** in the heart of the old town, many of its 16th and 17th century houses have the date of construction carved into the lintel. The walled city is for pedestrians only from 2 to 7 pm. **Église Notre Dame du Bout du Pont**, the church at the bottom of Rue de la Citadelle at **Porte Notre Dame**, was built in the 17th century. **Rue de l'Église**, the town's main thoroughfare in the 17th century, leads to **Porte de Navarre**.

From the **Vieux Pont**, you can often see 40cm-long trout swimming away happily in the crystal-clear water. As the Nive River passes through town, fishing is forbidden – and the fish seem to know it. **Rue d'Espagne** heads southward from the bridge.

The **Pont Romain**, a stone bridge 500m upriver from the Vieux Pont on the pastoral outskirts of town, is a perfect place for a picnic.

From the right bank of the Nive, just behind the church, a narrow *escalier poterne* (back staircase) leads through the **Porte de l'Échauguette** (Watchtower Gate) and along the lichen and moss-covered stone ramparts to the **Citadelle**, built in 1628 and rebuilt by military engineers of the Vauban school around 1680. It has been under renovation for years and now serves as a school. The Citadelle, which affords really picturesque views of the town, the Nive River Valley and the surrounding hills, can also be reached by walking up a rough cobblestone street that heads up the hill from Rue de la Citadelle.

The tiny **Prison des Évêques** (☎ 05 59 37 03 57), 41 Rue de la Citadelle, served as a prison from the 16th century until WWII, when the Germans used it to intern people caught while trying to flee to Spain. The vaulted, Gothic-style 13th century **dungeon** looks and feels like one, with moist stone walls, a single tiny barred window and general gloominess. The ground floor, built in the 16th century, houses a few less-than-thrilling displays. The prison is open daily from Easter to October from 9.30 or 10 am to noon and 2 to 6.30 or 8 pm. Entry costs 10FF (5FF for children under 12).

Hiking & Cycling

The GR10 and the GR65 pass right through Saint Jean Pied de Port. See Bookshop under Information for details on where to buy hiking maps.

Saint Jean Pied de Port is a great place to begin a bike ride into the Pyrenean foothills, where the only sounds you'll hear are cowbells and sheep munching grass. Just take any of the secondary or tertiary roads leading out of town. You can bring along bicycles free of charge on certain SNCF trains (eg the 9 am train from Bayonne) and then cycle back down to the coast.

The tourist office sells a folder of rudimentary maps (10FF) for five circular backroad walks of between 2km and 16km from Saint Jean Pied de Port. The routes are perfect for mountain biking. The tourist office also has a brochure on six beautiful hikes in the **Forêt d'Iraty**, 25km south-east of here on the Spanish border and famed for its beech trees. The only way to get there is by car.

If you plan to do some hiking in the region and the weather looks dodgy, call the Météo service (☎ 08 36 68 02 64) for updates and forecasts.

Swimming

The Piscine Municipale (Municipal Swimming Pool; ☎ 05 59 37 05 56), Rue du 11 Novembre, is open from mid-June to mid-October. Entry is 11FF (8.50FF for children aged six to 14).

Places to Stay

Camping The ***Camping Municipal Plaza Berri*** (☎ 05 59 37 11 19), Ave du Fronton, occupies a lovely, riverside site with lush grass and thick tree cover. It is open from May to September. Tariffs are 15/10FF per adult/child, 8FF for a tent or caravan site and 8FF to park.

Near the train station at 4 Chemin de Zalikarte, ***Camping d'Arradoy*** (☎ 05 59 37 11 75) is open between April and September and adults/children pay 8.50/4.30FF, while a tent or caravan site plus parking is 6FF.

Chambres d'Hôtes & Gîtes Ruraux Ask the tourist office for information on accommodation with families in the vicinity and rural B&Bs.

Hotels Saint Jean Pied de Port is not over-endowed with inexpensive places to stay. One of the cheapest is ***Hôtel des Remparts*** (☎ 05 59 37 13 79), which is on Route d'Uhart-Cize but gives its address as 16 Place Floquet. It is open all year, except on Saturday and Sunday nights from October to March. Its smallish singles/doubles, all of which now have showers, cost 195/200FF.

The classy ***Hôtel Central*** (☎ 05 59 37 00 22; fax 05 59 37 27 79), 1 Place Charles de Gaulle, built in the 19th century, is open from mid-February to just before Christmas. Large, comfortable doubles with shower and toilet cost 290/320/450FF for one/two/three people. The back rooms look out on to a small waterfall on the Nive River, and there's a lovely terrace in front.

The ***Hôtel Ramuntcho*** (☎ 05 59 37 03 91; fax 05 59 37 35 17), up the hill from the Porte de France at 1 Rue de France, is the only hotel within the old walls, and is open from January to mid-November. Doubles with shower and toilet cost from 260 to 295FF, depending on the season.

The ***Hôtel Itzalpea*** (☎ 05 59 37 03 66; fax 05 59 37 33 18), 5 Place du Trinquet, has doubles with shower, toilet and TV from 200FF. It is open all year.

The three star ***Hôtel des Pyrénées*** (☎ 05 59 37 01 01; fax 05 59 37 18 97), 19 Place Charles de Gaulle, is the classiest place i town with a much acclaimed restaurant (se Places to Eat). Doubles start at 550FF.

Places to Eat

There are a number of restaurants aroun Place du Trinquet, Place Charles de Gaull and Place Floquet. Some places offer trou dishes – the area is known for its trou fishing – and *poulet Basquaise* (Basque-style chicken).

Restaurants The impeccable***Restauran des Pyrénées*** at the Hôtel des Pyrénées ha two Michelin stars and *menus* of classica French and Basque cuisine cost 230, 300, 400 and 500FF. It's closed on Tuesday (except from July to mid-September), Monday at dinner from November to March, from 20 November to 22 December and during most of January.

Etche-Ona (☎ 05 59 37 01 14), a couple of notches below at 15 Place Floquet, has *menus* for 100/155/255FF. The restaurant in the ***Hôtel Itzalpea*** (see Places to Stay), which serves family-style regional cuisine all year long, is open daily except Saturday (daily in July and August). *Menus* cost 58, 88 and 170FF. The restaurant in the ***Hôtel Ramuntcho*** is open daily except Wednesday (daily in July and August). *Menus* cost 78, 95 and 98FF.

Café de la Paix (☎ 05 59 37 00 99), 4 Place Floquet, has pizzas from 33FF, paella (58FF) and salads from 35FF. The *menus* cost 62, 95 and 135FF.

Self-Catering There's a ***food market*** every Monday at Place Charles de Gaulle.

Near the train station at 35 Ave Renaud, the small ***grocery*** is open Monday to Saturday from 7.30 am to 12.30 pm and 2.30 to 7.30 or 8 pm, and on Sunday from 7.30 am to 12.30 pm. The little ***Ahadoberry bakery***, 2 Rue de la Poste, across from the post office, has gâteau Basque. It is open Monday to Saturday from 8 am to 8 pm and on Sunday from 8 am to 1 pm.

Close to the tourist office, there's an ***Unimarché*** grocery at 3 Place du Trinquet open and Sunday afternoons) from 8 am to 12.30 pm and 3 to 7.30 pm.

On Rue d'Espagne, the ***grocery store*** at No 12 is open Monday to Saturday and, in July and August, on Sunday morning also. There are other food shops nearby, including a ***dépôt de pain*** (bread shop; closed Wednesday except in July and August) at No 9, a ***boulangerie*** at No 38, and a ***boucherie*** nearby at 8 Rue d'Uhert.

Spectator Sport

Pelote Basque All year long, the *trinquet* at 7 Place du Trinquet has professional main nue and pala matches every Monday at 4.30 pm. Tickets cost about 50FF. For detailed information, call the Bar du Trinquet (☎ 05 59 37 09 34).

The huge jaï alaï plays host to cesta punta championships in July and August on Saturday nights at 9 pm.

In July and August the open-air Fronton Municipal has pelota matches on Friday at 5 pm.

Bullfight A two-hour running of the bulls Landes-style (*course de vaches landaises*) and a 'fight' in which the bovines are simply teased, jumped over, chased and, gratefully, live to tell the tale, takes place mid-July to early September every Monday at 9 pm at the jaï alaï.

Getting There & Away

Bus Buses to/from Tardets, Mauléon and Bayonne (three or four a day, Monday to Saturday) run by Transports Basques (☎ 05 59 65 73 11 in St Palais) stop opposite the trinquet on Place du Trinquet.

Train Saint Jean Pied de Port is the terminus of a rail line that begins in Bayonne (45FF; one hour). There are three or four trains a day (five a day in July and August). Bags can be stored with the station staff for 30FF each. The tiny station (☎ 05 59 37 02 00) is open from Monday to Thursday from 6.20 am to 7.40 pm, and on Friday, Saturday and Sunday from 6.20 am to 9.40 pm.

For a day trip from Bayonne, your best bet is the train that leaves Bayonne at 9.50 am. The last train back to Bayonne leaves Saint Jean Pied de Port at 4.52 pm.

Getting Around

Taxi To order a taxi, call ☎ 05 59 37 05 00, ☎ 05 59 37 02 92 or ☎ 05 59 37 05 70.

Bicycle From late June to early September, bikes can be rented daily at Chez Steunou (☎ 05 59 37 25 45), a souvenir shop at 12 Place Charles de Gaulle right next to the tourist office. Three and five-speeds are 35/50FF per half-day/day. A 200FF deposit is required.

Near the train station at 1 Place Saint Laurent, Cycles Garazi (☎ 05 59 37 21 79) rents bikes from mid-May to September. Mountain bikes cost 50/80FF per half-day/day. The shop is open from 9 am to noon and 2 to 7 pm.

Language

Modern French developed from the *langue d'oïl*, a group of dialects spoken north of the Loire River that grew out of the vernacular Latin used during the late Gallo-Roman period. The langue d'oïl – particularly the Francien dialect spoken in the Île de France – eventually displaced the *langue d'oc*, the dialects spoken in the south of the country and from which the Mediterranean region of Languedoc got its name.

Standard French is taught and spoken in France, but its various accents and sub-dialects are an important source of identity in certain regions. In addition, some of the peoples subjected to French rule many centuries ago have preserved their traditional languages. These include Flemish in the far north; Alsatian in Alsace; Breton (a Celtic tongue similar to Cornish and Welsh) in Brittany; Basque (a language unrelated to any other) in the Basque Country; Catalan in Roussillon (Catalan is the official language of nearby Andorra and the first language of many in the Spanish province of Catalonia); Provençal in Provence; and Corsican on the island of Corsica.

Around 122 million people worldwide speak French as their first language; it is an official language in Belgium, Switzerland, Luxembourg, the Canadian province of Quebec and over two dozen other countries, most of them former French colonies in Africa. It is also spoken in the Val d'Aosta region of north-western Italy. Various forms of Creole are used in Haiti, French Guiana and parts of Louisiana. France has a special government ministry (Ministère de la Francophonie) to deal with the country's relations with the French-speaking world.

While the French rightly or wrongly have a reputation for assuming that all human beings should speak French – until WWI it was *the* international language of culture and diplomacy – you'll find that any attempt to communicate in French will be much appreciateded. Probably your best bet is always to approach people politely in French, even if the only sentence you know is *Pardon, madame/monsieur/mademoiselle, parlez-vous anglais?* (Excuse me, madam/sir/miss, do you speak English?).

For a more comprehensive guide to the French language get hold of Lonely Planet's French phrasebook.

Grammar

An important distinction is made in French between *tu* and *vous*, which both mean 'you'. *Tu* is only used when addressing people you know well, children or animals. When addressing an adult who is not a personal friend, *vous* should be used unless the person invites you to use *tu*. In general, younger people insist less on this distinction, and they may use *tu* from the beginning of an acquaintance.

All nouns in French are either masculine or feminine and adjectives reflect the gender of the noun they modify. The feminine form of many nouns and adjectives is indicated by a silent *e* added to the masculine form, as in *étudiant* and *étudiante*, the masculine and feminine for 'student'. In the following phrases we have indicated both masculine and feminine forms where necessary. The masculine form comes first, separated from the feminine by a slash. The gender of a noun is often indicated by a preceding article: 'the/a/some', *le/un/du* (m), *la/une/de la* (f); or a possessive adjective, 'my/your/his/her', *mon/ton/son* (m), *ma/ta/sa* (f). With French, unlike English, the possessive adjective agrees in number and gender with the thing possessed: 'his/her mother', *sa mère*.

Pronunciation

Most letters in French are pronounced more or less the same as their English equivalents. A few which may cause confusion are:

j   as the 's' in 'leisure', eg *jour* (day)

c before **e** and **i**, as the 's' in 'sit'; before **a**, **o** and **u** it's pronounced as English 'k'. When undescored with a 'cedilla' (ç) it's always pronounced as the 's' in 'sit'.

French has a number of sounds that are difficult for Anglophones to produce. These include:

- The distinction between the 'u' sound (as in *tu)* and 'oo' sound (as in *tout)*. For both sounds, the lips are rounded and projected forward, but for the 'u' the tongue is towards the front of the mouth, its tip against the lower front teeth, whereas for the 'oo' the tongue is towards the back of the mouth, its tip behind the gums of the lower front teeth.
- The nasal vowels. With nasal vowels the breath escapes partly through the nose and partly through the mouth. There are no nasal vowels in English; in French there are three, as in *bon vin blanc*, (good white wine). These sounds occur where a syllable ends in a single **n** or **m**; the **n** or **m** is silent but indicates the nasalisation of the preceding vowel.
- The **r**. The standard **r** of Parisian French is produced by moving the bulk of the tongue backwards to constrict the air flow in the pharynx while the tip of the tongue rests behind the lower front teeth. It's similar to the noise made by some people before spitting, but with much less friction.

Basics

Yes.	*Oui.*
No.	*Non.*
Maybe.	*Peut-être.*
Please.	*S'il vous plaît.*
Thank you.	*Merci.*
You're welcome.	*Je vous en prie.*
Excuse me.	*Excusez-moi.*
Sorry/Forgive me.	*Pardon.*

Greetings

Hello/Good morning.	*Bonjour.*
Good evening.	*Bonsoir.*
Good night.	*Bonne nuit.*
Goodbye.	*Au revoir.*

Small Talk

How are you?	*Comment allez-vous?* (polite)
	Comment vas-tu?/ Comment ça va? (informal)
Fine, thanks.	*Bien, merci.*
What's your name?	*Comment vous appelez-vous?*
My name is ...	*Je m'appelle ...*
I'm pleased to meet you.	*Enchanté* (m)/ *Enchantée* (f).
How old are you?	*Quel âge avez-vous?*
I'm ... years old.	*J'ai ... ans.*
Do you like ...?	*Aimez-vous ...?*
Where are you from?	*De quel pays êtes-vous?*
I'm from ...	*Je viens ...*
Australia	*d'Australie*
Canada	*du Canada*
England	*d'Angleterre*
Germany	*d'Allemagne*
Ireland	*d'Irlande*
New Zealand	*de Nouvelle Zélande*
Scotland	*d'Écosse*
Wales	*du Pays de Galle*
the USA	*des États-Unis*

Language Difficulties

I understand.	*Je comprends.*
I don't understand.	*Je ne comprends pas.*
Do you speak English?	*Parlez-vous anglais?*
Could you please write it down?	*Est-ce que vous pouvez l'écrire?*

Getting Around

I want to go to ...	*Je voudrais aller à ...*
I'd like to book a seat to ...	*Je voudrais réserver une place pour ...*
What time does the ... leave/arrive?	*À quelle heure part/arrive ...?*
aeroplane	*l'avion*
bus (city)	*l'autobus*
bus (intercity)	*l'autocar*
ferry	*le ferry(-boat)*
train	*le train*
tram	*le tramway*

Where is (the) ...?	*Où est ...?*
bus stop?	*l'arrêt d'autobus*
metro station	*la station de métro*
train station	*la gare*
tram stop	*l'arrêt de tramway*
ticket office	*le guichet*

I'd like a ... ticket.	*Je voudrais un billet ...*
one-way	*aller-simple*
return	*aller-retour*
1st class	*première classe*
2nd class	*deuxième classe*

How long does the trip take?	*Combien de temps dure le trajet?*

The train is ...	*Le train est ...*
delayed	*en retard*
on time	*à l'heure*
early	*en avance*

Do I need to ...?	*Est-ce que je dois ...?*
change trains	*changer de train*
change platform	*changer de quai*

left-luggage locker	*consigne automatique*
platform	*quai*
timetable	*horaire*

I'd like to hire ...	*Je voudrais louer ...*
a bicycle	*un vélo*
a car	*une voiture*
a guide	*un guide*

Signs

ENTRÉE	ENTRANCE
SORTIE	EXIT
COMPLET	NO VACANCIES
RENSEIGNEMENTS	INFORMATION
OUVERT/FERMÉ	OPEN/CLOSED
INTERDIT	PROHIBITED
(COMMISSARIAT DE) POLICE	POLICE STATION
CHAMBRES LIBRES	ROOMS AVAILABLE
TOILETTES, WC	TOILETS
HOMMES	MEN
FEMMES	WOMEN

Around Town

I'm looking for ...	*Je cherche ...*
a bank/ exchange office	*une banque/ un bureau de change*
the city centre	*le centre-ville*
the ... embassy	*l'ambassade de ...*
the hospital	*l'hôpital*
my hotel	*mon hôtel*
the market	*le marché*
the police	*la police*
the post office	*le bureau de poste/ la poste*
a public phone	*une cabine*
a public toilet	*les toilettes téléphonique*
the tourist office	*l'office de tourisme*

Where is (the) ...?	*Où est ...?*
beach	*la plage*
bridge	*le pont*
castle/mansion	*le château*
cathedral	*la cathédrale*
church	*l'église*
island	*l'île*
lake	*le lac*
main square	*la place centrale*
mosque	*la mosquée*
old city (town)	*la vieille ville*
the palace	*le palais*
quay/bank	*le quai/la rive*
ruins	*les ruines*
sea	*la mer*
square	*la place*
tower	*la tour*

What time does it open/close?	*Quelle est l'heure d'ouverture/ de fermeture?*
I'd like to make a telephone call.	*Je voudrais téléphoner.*

I'd like to change ...	*Je voudrais changer ...*
some money	*de l'argent*
travellers cheques	*chèques de voyage*

Directions

How do I get to ...?	*Comment dois-je faire pour arriver à ...?*
Is it near/far?	*Est-ce près/loin?*

Can you show me on the map/ city map?	*Est-ce que vous pouvez me le montrer sur la carte/le plan?*
Go straight ahead.	*Continuez tout droit.*
Turn left.	*Tournez à gauche.*
Turn right.	*Tournez à droite.*
at the traffic lights	*aux feux*
at the next corner	*au prochain coin*
behind	*derrière*
in front of	*devant*
opposite	*en face de*
north	*nord*
south	*sud*
east	*est*
west	*ouest*

Accommodation

I'm looking for ...	*Je cherche ...*
the youth hostel	*l'auberge de jeunesse*
the campground	*le camping*
a hotel	*un hôtel*
Where can I find a cheap hotel?	*Où est-ce que je peux trouver un hôtel bon marché?*
What's the address?	*Quelle est l'adresse?*
Could you write it down, please?	*Est-ce vous pourriez l'écrire, s'il vous plaît?*
Do you have any rooms available?	*Est-ce que vous avez des chambres libres?*
I'd like to book ...	*Je voudrais réserver ...*
a bed	*un lit*
a single room	*une chambre pour une personne*
a double room	*une chambre double*
a room with a shower and toilet	*une chambre avec douche et WC*
I'd like to stay in a dormitory.	*Je voudrais coucher dans un dortoir.*
How much is it ...?	*Quel est le prix ...?*
per night	*par nuit*
per person	*par personne*
Is breakfast included?	*Est-ce que le petit déjeuner est compris?*
Can I see the room?	*Est-ce que je peux voir la chambre?*
Where is ...?	*Où est ...?*
the bathroom	*la salle de bains*
the shower	*la douche*
Where is the toilet?	*Où sont les toilettes?*
I'm going to stay ...	*Je resterai ...*
one day	*un jour*
a week	*une semaine*

Shopping

How much is it?	*C'est combien?*
It's too expensive for me.	*C'est trop cher pour moi.*
Can I look at it?	*Est-ce que je peux le/la voir?* (m/f)
I'm just looking.	*Je ne fais que regarder.*
Do you accept credit cards?	*Est-ce que je peux payer avec ma carte de crédit?*
Do you accept travellers cheques?	*Est-ce que je peux payer avec des chèques de voyage?*
It's too big/small.	*C'est trop grand/petit.*
more/less	*plus/moins*
cheap	*bon marché*
cheaper	*moins cher*
bookshop	*la librairie*
chemist/pharmacy	*la pharmacie*
laundry/laundrette	*la laverie*
market	*le marché*
newsagency	*l'agence de presse*
stationers	*la papeterie*
supermarket	*le supermarché*

Time & Dates

What time is it?	*Quelle heure est-il?*
It's (two) o'clock.	*Il est (deux) heures.*
When?	*Quand?*
today	*aujourd'hui*
tonight	*ce soir*
tomorrow	*demain*

day after tomorrow	*après-demain*
yesterday	*hier*
all day	*toute la journée*
in the morning	*du matin*
in the afternoon	*de l'après-midi*
in the evening	*du soir*
Monday	*lundi*
Tuesday	*mardi*
Wednesday	*mercredi*
Thursday	*jeudi*
Friday	*vendredi*
Saturday	*samedi*
Sunday	*dimanche*
January	*janvier*
February	*février*
March	*mars*
April	*avril*
May	*mai*
June	*juin*
July	*juillet*
August	*août*
September	*septembre*
October	*octobre*
November	*novembre*
December	*décembre*

Numbers

1	*un*
2	*deux*
3	*trois*
4	*quatre*
5	*cinq*
6	*six*
7	*sept*
8	*huit*
9	*neuf*
10	*dix*
11	*onze*
12	*douze*
13	*treize*
14	*quatorze*
15	*quinze*
16	*dix-sept*
20	*vingt*
100	*cent*
1000	*mille*
one million	*un million*

Emergencies

Help!	*Au secours!*
Call a doctor!	*Appelez un médecin!*
Call the police!	*Appelez la police!*
Leave me alone!	*Fichez-moi la paix!*
I've been robbed.	*On m'a volé.*
I've been raped.	*On m'a violée.*
I'm lost.	*Je me suis égaré/égarée.* (m/f)

Health

I'm sick.	*Je suis malade.*
I need a doctor.	*Il me faut un médecin.*
Where is the hospital?	*Où est l'hôpital?*
I have diarrhoea.	*J'ai la diarrhée.*
I'm pregnant.	*Je suis enceinte.*
I'm ...	*Je suis ...*
diabetic	*diabétique*
epileptic	*épileptique*
asthmatic	*asthmatique*
anaemic	*anémique*
I'm allergic ...	*Je suis allergique ...*
to antibiotics	*aux antibiotiques*
to penicillin	*à la pénicilline*
to bees	*aux abeilles*
antiseptic	*antiseptique*
aspirin	*aspirine*
condoms	*préservatifs*
contraceptive	*contraceptif*
medicine	*médicament*
nausea	*nausée*
sunblock cream	*crème solaire haute protection*
tampons	*tampons hygiéniques*

FOOD

breakfast	*le petit déjeuner*
lunch	*le déjeuner*
dinner	*le dîner*
grocery store	*l'épicerie*
I'd like the set menu.	*Je prends le menu.*

I'm a vegetarian. *Je suis végétarien/ végétarienne.*
I don't eat meat. *Je ne mange pas de viande.*

Starters (Appetisers)

assiette anglaise
plate of cold mixed meats and sausages
assiette de crudités
plate of raw vegetables with dressings
entrée
starter
fromage de tête
pâté made with pig's head set in jelly
soufflé
a light, fluffy dish made with egg yolks, stiffly beaten egg whites, flour and cheese or other ingredients

Soup

bouillabaisse
Mediterranean-style fish soup, originally from Marseille, made with several kinds of fish, including *rascasse* (spiny scorpion fish); often eaten as a main course
bouillon
broth or stock
bourride
fish stew; often eaten as a main course
croûtons
fried or roasted bread cubes, often added to soups
potage
thick soup made with puréed vegetables
soupe au pistou
vegetable soup made with a basil and garlic paste
soupe de poisson
fish soup
soupe du jour
soup of the day

Meat, Chicken & Poultry

agneau – lamb
aiguillette – thin slice of duck fillet
andouille or *andouillette* – sausage made from pork or veal tripe
bifteck – steak
bœuf – beef
bœuf haché – minced beef
boudin noir – blood sausage (black pudding)
brochette – kebab
canard – duck
caneton – duckling
cervelle – brains
charcuterie – cooked or prepared meats (usually pork)
cheval – horse meat
chèvre – goat
chevreau – kid (goat)
chevreuil – venison
côte – chop of pork, lamb or mutton
côtelette – cutlet
cuisses de grenouilles – frogs' legs
entrecôte – rib steak
dinde – turkey
épaule d'agneau – shoulder of lamb
escargot – snail
faisan – pheasant
faux-filet – sirloin steak
filet – tenderloin
foie – liver
foie gras de canard – duck liver pâté
gibier – game
gigot d'agneau – leg of lamb
jambon – ham
langue – tongue
lapin – rabbit
lard – bacon
lardon – pieces of chopped bacon
lièvre – hare
mouton – mutton
oie – goose
pieds de porc – pigs' trotters
pigeonneau – squab (young pigeon)
pintade – guinea fowl
porc – pork
poulet – chicken
rognons – kidneys
sanglier – wild boar
saucisson – large sausage
saucisson fumé – smoked sausage
steak – steak
tournedos – thick slices of fillet
tripes – tripe
veau – veal
venaison – venison
viande – meat
volaille – poultry

Common Meat & Poultry Dishes

blanquette de veau or *d'agneau*
veal or lamb stew with white sauce
bœuf bourguignon
beef and vegetable stew cooked in red wine (usually burgundy)
cassoulet
Languedoc stew made with goose, duck, pork or lamb fillets and haricot beans
chapon
capon
chou farci
stuffed cabbage
choucroute
sauerkraut with sausage and other prepared meats
confit de canard or d'oie
duck or goose preserved and cooked in its own fat
coq au vin
chicken cooked in wine
civet
game stew
fricassée
stew with meat that has first been fried
grillade
grilled meats
marcassin
young wild boar
quenelles
dumplings made of a finely sieved mixture of cooked fish or (rarely) meat
steak tartare
raw ground meat mixed with onion, raw egg yolk and herbs

Ordering a Steak

bleu
nearly raw
saignant
very rare (literally, 'bleeding')
à point
medium rare but still pink
bien cuit
literally, 'well cooked', but usually like medium rare

Fish & Seafood

anchois anchovy
anguille eel
brème bream
brochet pike
cabillaud cod
calmar squid
carrelet plaice
chaudrée fish stew
colin hake
coquille Saint-Sacques scallop
crabe crab
crevette grise shrimp
crevette rose prawn
écrevisse small, freshwater crayfish
fruits de mer seafood
gambas king prawns
goujon gudgeon (small fresh water fish)
hareng herring
homard lobster
huître oyster
langouste crayfish
langoustine very small saltwater 'lobster' (Dublin Bay prawn)
maquereau mackerel
merlan whiting
morue cod
moules mussels
oursin sea urchin
palourde clam
poisson fish
raie ray
rouget mullet
sardine sardine
saumon salmon
sole sole
thon tuna
truite trout

Vegetables, Herbs & Spices

ail garlic
aïoli or *ailloli* garlic mayonnaise
aneth dill
anis aniseed
artichaut artichoke
asperge asparagus
aubergine aubergine (eggplant)
avocat avocado
basilic basil
betterave beetroot
cannelle cinnamon
carotte carrot

céleri celery
cèpe cepe (boletus mushroom)
champignon mushroom
champignon de Paris button mushroom
chou cabbage
citrouille pumpkin
concombre cucumber
cornichon gherkin (pickle)
courgette courgette (zucchini)
crudités small pieces of raw vegetables
échalotte shallot
épice spice
épinards spinach
estragon tarragon
fenouil fennel
fève broad bean
genièvre juniper
gingembre ginger
haricots beans
haricots blancs white beans
haricots rouge kidney beans
haricots verts French (string) beans
herbe herb
laitue lettuce
légume vegetable
lentilles lentils
maïs sweet corn
menthe mint
navet turnip
oignon onion
olive olive
origan oregano
panais parsnip
persil parsley
petit pois pea
poireau leek
poivron green pepper
pomme de terre potato
ratatouille casserole of aubergines, tomatoes, peppers and garlic
riz rice
salade salad or lettuce
sarrasin buckwheat
seigle rye
tomate tomato
truffe truffle

Cooking Methods

à la broche spit-roasted
à la vapeur steamed
au feu de bois cooked over a wood-burning stove
au four baked
en croûte in pastry
farci stuffed
fumé smoked
gratiné browned on top with cheese
grillé grilled
pané coated in breadcrumbs
rôti roasted
sauté sautéed (shallow fried)

Sauces & Accompaniments

béchamel
basic white sauce
huile d'olive
olive oil
mornay
cheese sauce
moutarde
mustard
pistou
pesto (pounded mix of basil, hard cheese, olive oil and garlic)
provençale
tomato, garlic, herb and olive oil dressing or sauce
tartare
mayonnaise with herbs
vinaigrette
salad dressing made with oil, vinegar, mustard and garlic

Fruit & Nuts

abricot apricot
amande almond
ananas pineapple
arachide peanut
banane banana
cacahuète peanut
cassis blackcurrant
cerise cherry
citron lemon
datte date
figue fig
fraise strawberry
framboise raspberry

grenade	pomegranate
groseille	red currant/gooseberry
mangue	mango
marron	chestnut
melon	melon
mirabelle	type of plum
myrtille	bilberry (blueberry)
noisette	hazelnut
noix de cajou	cashew
orange	orange
pamplemousse	grapefruit
pastèque	watermelon
pêche	peach
pistache	pistachio
poire	pear
pomme	apple
prune	plum
pruneau	prune
raisin	grape

Desserts & Sweets

crêpe
thin pancake

crêpes suzettes
orange-flavoured crêpes flambéed in liqueur

bergamotes
orange-flavoured confectionary

dragée
sugared almond

éclair
pastry filled with cream

far
flan with prunes (a Breton speciality)

flan
egg-custard dessert

frangipane
pastry filled with cream and flavoured with almonds or a cake mixture containing ground almonds

galette
wholemeal or buckwheat pancake; also a type of biscuit

gâteau
cake

gaufre
waffle

gelée
jelly

glace
ice cream

glace au chocolat
chocolate ice cream

île flottante
literally 'floating island'; beaten egg white lightly cooked, floating on a creamy sauce

macarons
macaroons (sweet biscuit made of ground almonds, sugar and egg whites)

sablé
shortbread biscuit

farine de semoule
semolina flour

tarte
tart (pie)

tarte aux pommes
apple tart

yaourt
yoghurt

Snacks

croque-monsieur
a grilled ham and cheese sandwich

croque-madame
a croque-monsieur with a fried egg

frites
chips (French fries)

quiche
quiche; savoury egg, bacon and cream tart

Basics

beurre	butter
chocolat	chocolate
confiture	jam
crème fraîche	cream
farine	flour
huile	oil
lait	milk
miel	honey
œufs	eggs
poivre	pepper
sel	salt
sucre	sugar
vinaigre	vinegar

Utensils

bouteille	bottle
carafe	carafe
pichet	jug
verre	glass
couteau	knife
cuillère	spoon
fourchette	fork
serviette	serviette (napkin)

Glossary

(m) indicates masculine gender, (f) feminine gender and (pl) plural

accueil (m) – reception
alimentation (f) – grocery store
arrondissement (m) – administrative division of large city; abbreviated on signs as 1er (1st arrondissement), 2e or 2ème (2nd) etc
auberge de jeunesse (f) – (youth) hostel

baie (f) – bay
bastide (f) – medieval settlement in southwestern France, usually built on a grid plan and surrounding an arcaded square
billet (m) – ticket
billeterie (f) – ticket office or counter
billet jumelé (m) – combination ticket, good for more than one site, museum etc
boulangerie (f) – bakery, bread shop
boules (f pl) – a game not unlike lawn bowls played with heavy metal balls on a sandy pitch; also called *pétanque*
brasserie (f) – restaurant usually serving food all day (original meaning: brewery)
bureau de poste (m) or **poste** (f) – post office
bureau de change (m) – exchange bureau

capitainerie (f) – harbour master's office
carnet (m) – a book of five or 10 bus, tram or metro tickets sold at a reduced rate
carrefour (m) – crossroad
carte (f) – card; menu; map
caserne (f) – military barracks
cave (f) – wine cellar
chambre (f) – room
chambre de bonne (f pl) – maids' quarters
chambre d'hôte (f) – B&B
charcuterie (f) – pork butcher's shop and delicatessen
chars à voile (m pl) – sand yachts
cimetière (m) – cemetery
coffre (m) – hotel safe
col (m) – mountain pass
consigne (f) – left-luggage office
consigne automatique (f) – left-luggage locker
consigne manuelle (f) – left-luggage office
correspondance (f) – linking tunnel or walkway, eg in the metro; rail or bus connection
couchette (f) – sleeping berth on a train or ferry
cour (f) – courtyard
crémerie (f) – dairy, cheese shop
cyclisme (m) – cycling

dégustation (f) – tasting
demi (m) – 330mL glass of beer
demi-pension (f) – half-board (B&B with either lunch or dinner)
département (m) – administrative division of France
douane (f) – customs

église (f) – church
embarcadère (m) – pier, jetty
épicerie (f) – small grocery store

fauteuil (m) – seat on trains, ferries or at the theatre
fête (f) – festival
forêt (f) – forest
formule or **formule rapide** (f) – similar to a *menu* but allows choice of whichever two of three courses you want (eg starter and main course or main course and dessert)
fouilles (f pl) – excavations at an archaeological site
foyer (m) – workers or students hostel
fromagerie (f) – cheese shop
funiculaire (m) – funicular railway

galerie (f) – covered shopping centre or arcade
gare or **gare SNCF** (f) – railway station
gare maritime (f) – ferry terminal

gare routière (f) – bus station
gaufre (f) – waffle with various toppings, usually eaten as a snack
gendarmerie (f) – police station; police force
gîte d'étape (m) – hikers accommodation, usually in a village
gîte rural (m) – country cottage
golfe (m) – gulf
grande école (f) – prestigious educational institution offering training in such fields as business management, engineering and the applied sciences

halles (f pl) – covered market, central food market
halte routière (f) – bus stop
horaire (m) – timetable or schedule
hôte payant (m) – paying guest
hôtel de ville (m) – city or town hall
hôtes payants (m pl) or **hébergement chez l'habitant** (m) – homestays
hydroglisseur (m) – hydrofoil or hydroplane

intra-muros – old city (literally, 'within the walls')

jardin (m) – garden
jardin botanique (m) – botanic garden
jours fériés (m pl) – public holidays

laverie (f) or **lavomatique** (m) – laundrette

mairie (f) – city or town hall
maison de la presse (f) – newsagent
maison du parc (f) – a national park's headquarters and/or visitors' centre
mandat postal (m) – postal money order
marché (m) – market
marché aux puces (m) – flea market
marché couvert (m) – covered market
mas (m) – farmhouse; tiny hamlet
menu (m) – fixed-price meal with two or more courses
mistral (m) – incessant north wind in southern France said to drive people crazy
Mobylette (f) – moped
musée (m) – museum

navette (f) – shuttle bus, train or boat

palais de justice (m) – law courts
parlement (m) – parliament
pâtisserie (f) – cake and pastry shop
pensions de famille (f pl) – similar to B&Bs
pétanque (f) – a game not unlike lawn bowls played with heavy metal balls on a sandy pitch; also called *boules*
piste cyclable (f) – bicycle path
pied noir (m) – literally, 'black feet'; the name given to Algerian-born French people
place (f) – square, plaza
plage (f) – beach
plan (m) – city map
plan du quartier (m) – map of nearby streets (hung on the wall near metro exits)
plat du jour (m) – daily special in a restaurant
pont (m) – bridge
port (m) – harbour, port
port de plaisance (m) – marina or pleasure-boat harbour
porte (f) – gate in a city wall
poste (f) or **bureau de poste** (m) – post office
poste (m) – telephone extension
préfecture (f) – prefecture (capital of a *département)*
presqu'île (f) – peninsula
pression (f) – draught beer

quai (m) – quay, railway platform
quartier (m) – quarter, district

refuge (m) – mountain hut, basic shelter for hikers
rez-de-chaussée (m) – ground floor
rive (f) – bank of a river
riverain (m) – local resident
rond point (m) – roundabout
routier (m) – trucker or truckers restaurant

sentier (m) – trail
service des urgences (f) – casualty ward
sortie (f) – exit

spectacle (m) – performance, play, theatrical show
square (m) – public garden
supplément (m) – supplement, additional cost
syndicat d'initiative (m) – tourist office

tabac (m) – tobacconist (also selling bus tickets, phonecards etc)
table d'orientation (f) – viewpoint indicator
taxe de séjour (f) – municipal tourist tax
télécarte (f) – phonecard
téléphérique (m) – cableway or cable car
télésiège (m) – chair lift
téléski (m) – ski lift, tow
tour (f) – tower
tour d'horloge (f) – clock tower

vallée (f) – valley
v.f. (f) – *version française*; a film dubbed in French
vieille ville (f) – old town or old city
ville neuve (f) – new city, new town
v.o. (f) – *version originale*; a nondubbed film with French subtitles
voie (f) – train platform

ACRONYMS

The French love acronyms as much as the British and Americans do. Many transport companies are known by acronyms whose derivations are entirely unknown by the average passenger.

BP – *boîte postale* (post office box)
FN – Front National (National Front)
GR – *grande randonnée* (long-distance hiking trail)
ONU – Organisation des Nations Unies (the UN)
PC – Parti Communiste
PS – Parti Socialiste
RPR – Rassemblement pour la République (right-wing political party)
SNCF – Société Nationale des Chemins de Fer (state-owned railway company)
SNCM – Société Nationale Maritime Corse-Méditerranée (state-owned ferry company linking Corsica and mainland France)
TGV – *train à grande vitesse* (high-speed train, bullet train)
UDF – Union pour la Démocratie Française (right-wing political party)
VTT – *vélo tout terrain* (mountain bike)

Food Glossary

Abbreviations

A&L – Alsace and Lorraine
AC – Atlantic Coast
B – Brittany
BU – Burgundy
C – Champagne
CA&M – Côte d'Azure and Monaco
CO – Corsica
FA&J – French Alps and the Jura
FBC – French Basque Country
FNF – Far Northern France
L – Lyon
L-R – Languedoc-Roussillon
LPQ – Limousin, Périgord and Quercy
LV – Loire Valley
MC – Massif Central
N – Normandy
P – Paris
PR – Provence
T&P – Toulouse and the Pyrenees

à la Languedocienne (L-R) – dishes with a garlicky garnish of tomatoes, aubergines and *cèpes*
à la Provençale (PR) – dish with garlic-seasoned tomatoes
agneau chilindron (FBC) – sautéed lamb with potatoes and garlic
ail – garlic
aïoli (CA&M) – garlic mayonnaise
aïoli garni (CA&M) – boiled fish with garlic mayonnaise
alouêttes sans têtes (CO) – beef olives
anchoïade (PR) – anchovy-paste dipping sauce
anchois (L-R) – anchovies
andouilles (B) – tripe sausages
andouillettes (L) – tripe sausages
assiette Provençale (PR) – a mixture of regional savouries

baeckeoffe (A&L) – stew made of several meats (often pork, mutton and beef) and vegetables that have been marinated for two days; traditionally prepared at home before being cooked in the oven of a nearby bakery
bergamote (A&L) – tiny golden squares made with essence of bergamot, a pear-shaped citrus fruit grown in southern Europe
bleu des causses (L-R) – cheese
bœuf bourguignon (BU) – beef marinated and cooked in red wine with mushrooms, onions and bacon
boles de picolat (L-R) – spicy pork meatballs in a casserole
bonhomme Normand (N) – duck in a cider and cream sauce
boudin (L) – blood sausage (black pudding)
bouillabaisse (PR) – at least three kinds of fresh fish cooked in broth with onions, tomatoes, saffron and various herbs, including bay leaves, sage and thyme
bouilliture (AC) – eel stew with wine, mushrooms and prunes
bourride (CA&M) – a rich fish soup
bouzigues – mussels
brebis (FBC) – ewe's milk cheese
brocciu (CO) – soft white cheese

calisson (PR) – a small confection made with almond paste
Calvados (N) – apple-flavoured brandy
Camembert (N) – a soft creamy cheese
canard à la Montmorency (P) – duck with cherries
canard flambé au Calvados (N) – duck with Calvados
cargolade (L-R) – grilled snails
cassis (BU) – liqueur made with blackcurrants
cassoulet (T&P) – a rich casserole containing beans, knuckle of pork, preserved goose, bacon and sausage
cèpes (L-R) – boletus mushrooms
charcuterie (A&L) – bacon, little Strasbourg sausages, knackwurst, smoked ham and smoked pork chops
chaudrée (AC) – fish stew

chèvre (PR) – goat's cheese that has been marinated for 15 days in herbs and olive oil and then sprinkled with *marc*
choucroute (L) – sauerkraut served with meat
choucroute Alsacienne (or **choucroute garnie**) (A&L) – sauerkraut served hot with charcuterie
choux au lard (A&L) – cabbage with bacon
civet (L-R) – spiny lobster cooked in wine
confit de canard (LPQ) – preserved duck
confit d'oie (LPQ) – preserved goose **coq à la bière** (FNF) – carbonade-like chicken stew
coq au vin (BU) – chicken cooked in wine
coquilles St-Jacques – scallops
corniottes (BU) – cheese cake
cotriade (B) – fish and potato stew
cou d'oie farci (LPQ) – goose's neck stuffed with pork and veal mince
couscous – a spicy North African dish consisting of steamed semolina and a meat stew
crêpe or **krampouez** – thin pancake
crêpe au buerre (B) – buttered crêpe
crêpes Languedociennes (L-R) – rum-flambéed pancakes filled with vanilla cream

daube de bœuf (PR) – beef stew with red wine, cooked in a pot-bellied casserole called daubière
diots au vin blanc (FA&J) – little spicy sausages cooked with white wine
douillon (N) – pear cooked in pastry

escargots – snails
esqueixade de bacallà (L-R) – salt cod salad
estocaficado (PR) – salt cod and tomato stew

faire chabrot (LPQ) – the addition of wine to soup just before consumption
faisan au verjus (LPQ) – pheasant cooked in verjuice (unripe grape juice)
far breton (B) – prune and custard flan
feuilleté (LPQ) – light, triangular pastries filled with salmon, mussels, etc
figatelli (CO) – a rich liver sausage
flammeküche or **tarte flambée** (A&L) – a thin layer of pastry topped with cream, onion, bacon and sometimes cheese or mushrooms and cooked in a wood-fired oven
fleichkechele (A&L) – mixed grilled meats
foie gras d'oie – goose liver pâté
fondue au chocolat (T&P) – melted chocolate with fruits
fondue Auvergnate (MC) – cheese fondue made with Cantal
fondue bourguignonne (BU) – meat fondue with sauces
fondue Savoyarde (FA&J) – cheese fondue
fricandeau (L-R) – fresh tuna braised in a fish stock with olives or anchovies
fromage de chèvre (LV) – goat's milk cheese
fruits glacés (CA&M) – glazed or candied fruits

galettes (B) – buckwheat crêpes
garbure (FBC) – a filling cabbage and bean soup
garbure (T&P) – a thick soup made with fresh vegetables, beans, cabbage and ham
gochuak (FBC) – hazelnut biscuits
gougère (BU) – salted soft cheese balls

huile d'olive – olive oil
huîtres – oysters

jambon de Bayonne (FBC) – Bayonne ham
jambon en croûte (A&L) – ham wrapped in a crust of bread
jambon persillé (BU) – ham and parsley in aspic
jambonneau braisé (A&L) – ham

kanouga (FBC) – cubes of rich, chewy chocolate or coffee candy, wrapped in metallic paper
kir (BU) – sweet blackcurrant liqueur combined with white wine as an apéritif
kougelhopf (A&L) – sultana and almond cake easily identified by its ribbed, dome-like shape; traditionally eaten at breakfast

and became popular in France thanks to Marie-Antoinette, who tasted it for the first time when on a visit to Alsace
kouing-aman (B) – heavy buttery cake

Lyon mustard (L) – sharp mustard

macarons (AC) – soft biscuits made from almond flour, egg whites and sugar; brought to Saint Émilion in the 17th century by Ursuline nuns
madeleines (A&L) – small lemon teacakes adored by Proust
marc (PR) – spirit distilled from the debris left after the final pressing of grapes for wine
marrons (L) – chestnuts
mesclun (CA&M) – a rather bitter salad of dandelion greens and other leaves
michettes (CA&M) – savoury bread stuffed with cheese, olives, anchovies and onions
miroton lyonnais (L) – beef with onion
mojhettes (AC) – white beans
moules – mussels
morue pochée (PR) – poached cod
mouchous (FBC) – almond biscuits
mouclade rochelaise (AC) – mussels in a cream and curry sauce
moules marinières (FBC) – mussels cooked in their own juice with onions
moutarde (BU) – mustard, flavoured with anything from tarragon to honey and ranging in taste from delicate to fiery
Munster (A&L) – strong-smelling soft cheese

pain brié (N) – thick white bread
pain d'épice (BU) – gingerbread made with honey and spices that traditionally takes six to eight weeks to prepare
Paris-Brest (P) – stuffed choux pastry ring
pescajoun aux fruits (LPQ) – egg pancake with fruit
pibales (AC) – baby eels
piccata (FA&J) – veal escalope in batter
pierrade (T&P) – meats that you grill yourself
pierre à feu (C) – meat that you cook for yourself on a hot volcanic rock
piperade (FBC) – a rich stew of tomatoes and peppers mixed with eggs and then scrambled
pochouse (BU) – freshwater fish stew
potage Saint-Germain (P) – garden pea soup
poule au pot (T&P) – chicken stuffed with vegetables and prepared with tomato sauce, a favorite of King Henri IV
poulet au vinaigre (L) – chicken in sour cream and vinegar
poulet Basquaise (FBC) – Basque-style chicken
poulet vallée d'Auge (N) – chicken in cream and cider

quenelles (L) – light fish dumplings, often made with pike

raclette (T&P) – melted cheese with cold cuts and pickles
ragoût de mouton (B) – lamb baked for five hours under a layer of roots and herbs
ratafia (C) – an apéritif liqueur flavoured with almonds
ratatouille (PR) – tomatoes, eggplant and squash, stewed together along with green peppers, garlic and various aromatic herbs
rillettes – pork pâté
rouille – spicy condiment made from red chillis, garlic, olive oil and fish stock

salade fécampoise (N) – salad of potatoes, smoked herring and eggs
salade Lyonnaise (L) – green salad with croutons, bacon and egg
salmis de palombe (FBC) – wood pigeon partially roasted then simmered in a rich sauce of wine and vegetable purée
sarrasin – buckwheat
saumon – salmon
socca (CA&M) – a thin layer of chickpea flour and olive oil batter friend on a griddle
sole Normande (N) – sole with mussels, shrimps and mushrooms
soupe au pistou (PR) – a soup of vegetables, noodles, beans, basil and garlic
spaetzle (A&L) – Alsatian noodles

tajines – slow cooked stews of meat and

vegetables flavoured with herbs and spices from North Africa

tarte Alsacienne (A&L) – a custard tart made with local fruits, especially the wonderful Alsatian plums called *quetsches*

tarte Lyonnaise (L) – custard tart with kirsch and almonds

tartiflette (FA&J) – a filling concoction of oven-cooked potatoes and reblochon cheese

teurgoule (N) – a sweet, cinnamon-flavoured rice pudding typical of the Bayeux region

toro à la gardianne (L-R) – a rich stew of beef, herbs and red wine

tourte (A&L) – raised pie with ham, bacon or ground pork, eggs and leeks

tripes à la mode de Caen (N) – a heavily spiced tripe stew

tripoux (LPQ) – lamb's tripe with herbs

tripoux (MC) – mutton and veal tripe cooked in a white wine sauce

trois viandes sur pierre chaude (FA&J) – thinly sliced pieces of beef, veal and duck that you fry yourself on a hot ceramic plate

truffade (MC) – potatoes prepared with very young Cantal cheese

truffes (PR) – truffles

ttorro (FBC) – Basque fish soup

vacherin (L) – strawberry meringue tart

Welsh rarebit (FNF) – fondue prepared with dark beer

ziebelküche or **tarte à l'oignon** (A&L) – an onion tart

Acknowledgments

FROM THE AUTHORS

Steve Fallon A number of people helped in the updating of France and I would like to thank all the staff at the Lonely Planet office in Paris for help beyond the call of duty, especially ma copine de table, Zahia Hafs, and the very active Laurence Billiet, whose enthusiasm for le sport is fetching but not quite catching (yet). Thanks too to Brenda Turnnidge, Frank Viviano, Chew Terrière and Danielle 'Pixie' Garno (née Garnaut) for assistance, encouragement and companionship and to my fellow authors, Teresa Fisher, Daniel Robinson and Nicola Williams for their timely cooperation. The staff at Lonely Planet in London threw me a lifeline (in this case, a desk) when I was adrift at sea. Caroline Birch and Pat Read, who loves paprika, did that too, and it is much appreciated. Last (but hardly least) to all those wonderful, infuriating French people I met along the way – elegant and stylish, cultured and entertaining, bitchy and full of attitude – merci à tous. You're just what the world needs more of.

Daniel Robinson I found a number of readers' letters particularly helpful as I prepared to start work on the update. For their insights on how to improve this book, special thanks go to Philippe D Gray, who hails from I know not where; Roland Hellmann of Grenoble, France; Tobien Peters of Utrecht, the Netherlands; Michael Stolt of Germany; and Nick Williams of Cotham, Bristol in England. Keep the letters coming, folks! By the way, I'm especially fond of letters that help us ferret out errors, omissions and misleading impressions.

As in the past, the SNCF's Paris-based overseas and pan-European sales team, Philippe Kirsanovv and Barbara Grau – both long-time LP fans – went out of their way to make sure our rail information is both comprehensive and up-to-the-minute. Also in the French capital, I'd like to thank Eric Kam and Michel Lavandier of Pantin-based SDTE for their help with my *informatique* problems; Agnés Satory and Carole Molero of Renault Eurodrive, who helped arrange the Megane on which I clocked up some 8000km over the course of my 100 days of in-country research; and Sylvia Chezeau of Eurolines' Rue Saint Jacques office. Once again, I was showered with hospitality by lots of people: Sylvia Turjansky and Michel Loustic and their delightful daughter Ilona Sue; the Haouzi family, including Sabrina, former French teacher to Tony and Maureen Wheeler; and the Bebe family: Eliane, Antoine, Pauline, Tom, Tali and Shana. Sadly, Dr Maurice Bebe passed away in the course of my research – *y'hi zichro baruch* (may his memory be a blessing).

My work way up north was enlivened by Marie-Héléne Girard, Line Boursier, Michel Dhorne, Jean-Marie Regnier, a slightly expanded version of LP's usual team of 'Lillexperts'. Other Lillois who helped out include Mathias Dellacherie and Christophe Boulanger of Micropuce, who did their best to get my stubborn modem working, and M Delanoy of the Renault garage in La Madeleine.

In Lorraine, Rabbi Bruno Fiszon and his family, and Cantor Aaron and Michal Hayoun showed exceptional hospitality during my visit to Metz. Covering Verdun was something of a nightmare, but Bruno Launai was kind enough to show me around the not-yet-open exhibits of the Centre Mondial de la Paix.

In Alsace, I'd like to thank Nancy Mayne-Waechter of the Bookworm in Strasbourg for providing so many excellent tips on her adopted city; Mme Dany Fournil of the Strasbourg tourist office; Bernard Holz of Schiltigheim; Nicole Bézu of the Colmar tourist office; and the Kempf family, fourth-generation owners of the Hôtel Kempf in Colmar, including little Cassandra (accent on the last syllable), Aurelien and Adrien. Emily Silverman of Freiburg, Germany, a loyal cyberspace companion, managed to pop across the Rhine to help me explore the Vosges mountains.

As in 1995, I again spent a warm, family-style Passover Seder with the Ben Simon family of Lyon – my thanks to Julien, Elsa, Beatrice, Melanie, Samuel and Rebecca, as well as to Marcel Ben Simon and his family and Suzette and Guy Slama. The choice of Lyon as a venue to sit hunched over my beloved, guidebook-sized Libretto computer, keying in my notes, gave me the chance to get to know my enthusiastic co-author Nicola Williams and her husband Matthias Lüfkens. As usual, it was a pleasure working with coordinating author Steve Fallon, though regrettably this time our paths crossed but once.

In the south-west, I am indebted to Lisa Madarasz of The Down Under in Bordeaux, who provided loads of information on her city's hopping nightlife; Pierre and Claudy Marcoueille of Hôtel La Paix in Arcachon; Vivian Newman and Alanna Jackson of Victoria, BC; and Sarinah Kalb, presently of Philadelphia, PA.

In Burgundy, my thanks go to Belinda Debrito of the Beaune tourist office; Fabrice Sautot of Club Le Privé in Dijon; Ann Mullin of Montreal, who provided some insider's tips on cycling from Dijon to Beaune; and finally Matthew Sigel of New Rochelle, NY, who, though he works for the wrong publisher, seems like a nice guy.

It is a rare treat for an LP author to work in a country with its very own LP office. Alas, since I didn't cover Paris this time around I got to hang out only briefly with Zahia Hafs and her super staff: the editors Jean-Bernard Carillet, Sophie Le Mao, Michel MacLeod and Isabelle Muller; the artists and cartographers Jean-Noël Doan, Philippe Maître, Soph' Rivoire and Caroline Sahanouk; the promotions staff, Laurence Billiet, Didier Buroc and Arnaud Lebonnois; office coordinator Caroline Guilleminot; and accountant Rachida Habbad.

Teresa Fisher I would like to thank the long list of individuals and organisations who have given information and other forms of assistance to me while researching and producing this book. I am sorry that I am unable to single out everyone who has helped. However, I would specifically like to thank Brittany Ferries, Air France and the countless tourist offices I visited throughout France and Andorra. Special thanks also to Steve Fallon, my coordinating author, fellow authors Nicola Williams and Daniel Robinson, Richard I'Anson of Lonely Planet Images for his inspirational photographic training, and all the staff at the Lonely Planet offices in London and Melbourne for their invaluable support.

Nicola Williams Big thanks and smiles to rising politician and Belfort historian Christophe Grudler of the Journal Alsace; Christophe Mey of Radio France Besançon; Bruno Cadene of Radio France Isère; Véronique Poty of Lyon's Musée Urbain; Tony Garnier; Renaud from the Cyberdrome cybercafé in Avignon; and Isabelle and Eric for dinner Le Corbusier-style. On the slopes, thanks to Christa, Karl Otto, Peter and Marianne for being such great skiing companions. By the sea, many thanks to Anne Van der Linden of Saint Tropez and Yves d'Hanens for welcoming me to Célèrine, and to Reine and George for a wonderful wedding. Thanks too, to Pascal and Fréderique Imbs in Annecy, my fellow authors; and to fab coordinating author Steve Fallon (bisous ...) and the editors in LP Oz who painstakingly ploughed through my texts. Eternal gratitude as always to my family for their moral support, and to Matthias Lüfkens for his love, wit and insatiable appetite for life (and French food).

THANKS

Many thanks to the travellers who used the last edition and wrote to us with helpful hints, useful advice and interesting anecdotes:

Stephanie Abba, Dr R Alexander, Jeff Adams, Jan Andrucci-Haig, Betty & Michael Allan, Geffroy Annik, Rhiannon Batten, Pamela Baumbarger,

David Beauchamp, Stephen Beck, Anne Bernie, Gerald Berstell, Eric Bertrand, Paul Bethell, Jon, Jean & Mandy Blue, Glynn Bowen, Ian Bradley, Michael Brady, Luc Braeuer, A Brind, Anne Buchler, RW Buckland, Fiona Buley, Matt Burgess, Paul Burley, Teresa Buttler, George Buxton, Nicolas Canzian, Ron & Peg Caouette, Eric Carlson, James Carty, Les Cashin, Dean Chan, Michael Clarke, Richard Colebourn, John Cock, Mr & Ms Connellan, Max Cooper, Yitschak Copperman, Warwick Cox, Rosemary Craig, Chris Cunningham, Jay Davidson, Carmel Davidson, Ian Deacon, Julia DeBaecke, Eric Desmet, Janneke Dijkstra, Felicie Doizelet, Doug Drysdale, Lauraine Dube, Todd Dusenbery, Robert Egg, Jerry Eicher, Dorothy Eisengart, Elaine Ellsworth, Corine Englander, Tracey Farrell, Christopher Feierabend, Barrett Felman, Peter Finnegan, Marie Fischer, Thierry Floretin, Louise Fogarty, Michel Fougeres, Liz Freebairn, Bernez Gestin, Billy R Gilleland, Norma & Ron Godzinski, Phillipe D Gray, Vivian Green, Kelly Gunton, Marco Haakmeester, Bob Hammon, Julie Harper, Ray Hartwell, Annie Hawkins, Joan Healy, David Heffernan, Dr Philip Henschke, Linda Hirsch, Alan Hobbs, Chris Honeysett, Allan Hough, G S Houghton, Nery Howard, Josephine Hsieh, Tim Hughes, Sophie Jacques, Elmi Jamial, Dave Johnson, Cathryn Jones, Masako Kakui, Dr Clovis Karam, Cheryl Kaufman, Mrs F Kell, Karen Kepke, Taylor Kirby, Bob Klepner, Rebecca Kopke-Bennett, O Kvisla, MA Laird, Ron Lamothe, Rich Lamureu, Rob Lance, John Lavabre, Robert L Lenard, Maryanne Lewell, Helene Leydier, Simon Li, Marie Lippens, Samantha Livingstone, Pat Lloyd, Albert Lo, Curtis Long, Adrian Lush, Gill Maddox, Ofra Magidor, MJ Makepeace, Linda Manoll, Ramona Mapp, Alex Marcovitch, Lisa Marsden, David McCormick, Lynn McDonald, William McIntyre, Mike Meakin, Betty Mekeel, Nolan Menachemson, Richard Mikael, George & Delores Merchant, Ronei Miotto, David Morgan, Jessica Morris, Dave Mountain, Richard Moyer, Hillary Munro, Alessandro Naldi, FC Napies, Matt Neil, Lyda Ness, R Nicholson, K Nicholson, Anthony Oakley, Jennifer Oats-Sargent, Mike O'Carroll, Andrea van Oort, Richard Parr, Gordon S Patton, D Paulsrud, Karen Pearce, Mark Pennington, Stephen K Percival Fabien Peters, Michael G Petkos, Papadimitriou Philippe, James AM Phillips, Heather Phillips, Loo Pi Li, Miriam Pizzoferrato, Barry Pollard, Tim Pollock, James Preston, Robert Preston, A Price, Reg Quelch, Emma Reynish, Gina Roberts, Thomas & Norma K Roling, Antonella Rosati, Leslie Rossi, Ethan G Salwen, Scott T Sanders, Axel Schauf, Aysha Schurman, Dick Scotton, Paul Sechi, Phyl Shimfield, Leif Sjoblom, Jenny Slaughter, Peter Sluijter, David Smith, George Speight, DA Spencer, L Stafford, Michael Stolt, Joan Sulser, Len Tabicman, Kuo-Ken Tai, Drake Taylor, Meredith Thompson, Robin Thompson, Peter Torley, Ailsa Townley, Claudia Turner, Michael Tyler, Othmar Ulrich, Balazs & Eva Vajda, Frank Vergona, Dr B Voigt, Daniel Walfish, Ryan Wallach, Lisa Warren, SB Watkins, Paul Watts, Lawrence Webb, Nathan & Leslie Wilkes, Nick Williams, Tina Wolf, Martha Bays Wolfser, H Wood, James Wood and Yan Zhang.

LONELY PLANET

FREE Lonely Planet Newsletters

We love hearing from you and think you'd like to hear from us.

Planet Talk

Our FREE quarterly printed newsletter is full of tips from travellers and anecdotes from Lonely Planet guidebook authors. Every issue is packed with up-to-date travel news and advice, and includes:

- a postcard from Lonely Planet co-founder Tony Wheeler
- a swag of mail from travellers
- a look at life on the road through the eyes of a Lonely Planet author
- topical health advice
- prizes for the best travel yarn
- news about forthcoming Lonely Planet events
- a complete list of Lonely Planet books and other titles

To join our mailing list, residents of the UK, Europe and Africa can email us at go@lonelyplanet.co.uk; residents of North and South America can email us at info@lonelyplanet.com; the rest of the world can email us at talk2us@lonelyplanet.com.au, or contact any Lonely Planet office.

Comet

Our FREE monthly email newsletter brings you all the latest travel news, features, interviews, competitions, destination ideas, travellers' tips & tales, Q&As, raging debates and related links. Find out what's new on the Lonely Planet Web site and which books are about to hit the shelves.

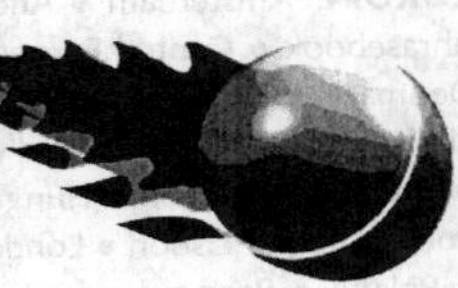

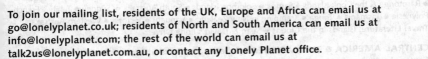

Subscribe from your desktop: www.lonelyplanet.com/comet

LONELY PLANET

Guides by Region

Lonely Planet is known worldwide for publishing practical, reliable and no-nonsense travel information in our guides and on our Web site. The Lonely Planet list covers just about every accessible part of the world. Currently there are nine series: travel guides, shoestring guides, walking guides, city guides, phrasebooks, audio packs, travel atlases, diving and snorkeling guides and travel literature.

AFRICA Africa – the South • Africa on a shoestring • Arabic (Egyptian) phrasebook • Arabic (Moroccan) phrasebook • Cairo • Cape Town • Central Africa • East Africa • Egypt • Egypt travel atlas • Ethiopian (Amharic) phrasebook • The Gambia & Senegal • Kenya • Kenya travel atlas • Malawi, Mozambique & Zambia • Morocco • North Africa • South Africa, Lesotho & Swaziland • South Africa, Lesotho & Swaziland travel atlas • Swahili phrasebook • Trekking in East Africa • Tunisia • West Africa • Zimbabwe, Botswana & Namibia • Zimbabwe, Botswana & Namibia travel atlas
Travel Literature: The Rainbird: A Central African Journey • Songs to an African Sunset: A Zimbabwean Story • Mali Blues: Traveling to an African Beat

AUSTRALIA & THE PACIFIC Australia • Australian phrasebook • Bushwalking in Australia • Bushwalking in Papua New Guinea • Fiji • Fijian phrasebook • Islands of Australia's Great Barrier Reef • Melbourne • Micronesia • New Caledonia • New South Wales & the ACT • New Zealand • Northern Territory • Outback Australia • Papua New Guinea • Papua New Guinea (Pidgin) phrasebook • Queensland • Rarotonga & the Cook Islands • Samoa • Solomon Islands • South Australia • Sydney • Tahiti & French Polynesia • Tasmania • Tonga • Tramping in New Zealand • Vanuatu • Victoria • Western Australia
Travel Literature: Islands in the Clouds • Sean & David's Long Drive

CENTRAL AMERICA & THE CARIBBEAN Bahamas and Turks & Caicos • Barcelona • Bermuda • Central America on a shoestring • Costa Rica • Cuba • Dominican Republic & Haiti • Eastern Caribbean • Guatemala, Belize & Yucatán: La Ruta Maya • Jamaica • Mexico • Mexico City • Panama
Travel Literature: Green Dreams: Travels in Central America

EUROPE Amsterdam • Andalucía • Austria • Baltic States phrasebook • Berlin • Britain • British phrasebook • Central Europe • Central Europe phrasebook • Croatia • Czech & Slovak Republics • Denmark • Dublin • Eastern Europe • Eastern Europe phrasebook • Edinburgh • Estonia, Latvia & Lithuania • Europe • Finland • France • French phrasebook • Germany • German phrasebook • Greece • Greek phrasebook • Hungary • Iceland, Greenland & the Faroe Islands • Ireland • Italian phrasebook • Italy • Lisbon • London • Mediterranean Europe • Mediterranean Europe phrasebook • Paris • Poland • Portugal • Portugal travel atlas • Prague • Provence & the Côte D'Azur • Romania & Moldova • Russia, Ukraine & Belarus • Russian phrasebook • Scandinavian & Baltic Europe • Scandinavian Europe phrasebook • Scotland • Slovenia • Spain • Spanish phrasebook • St Petersburg • Switzerland • Trekking in Spain • Ukrainian phrasebook • Vienna • Walking in Britain • Walking in Italy • Walking in Ireland • Walking in Switzerland • Western Europe • Western Europe phrasebook
Travel Literature: The Olive Grove: Travels in Greece

INDIAN SUBCONTINENT Bangladesh • Bengali phrasebook • Bhutan • Delhi • Goa • Hindi/Urdu phrasebook • India • India & Bangladesh travel atlas • Indian Himalaya • Karakoram Highway • Nepal • Nepali phrasebook • Pakistan • Rajasthan • South India • Sri Lanka • Sri Lanka phrasebook • Trekking in the Indian Himalaya • Trekking in the Karakoram & Hindukush • Trekking in the Nepal Himalaya
Travel Literature: In Rajasthan • Shopping for Buddhas

LONELY PLANET

Mail Order

Lonely Planet products are distributed worldwide. They are also available by mail order from Lonely Planet, so if you have difficulty finding a title please write to us. North and South American residents should write to 150 Linden St, Oakland, CA 94607, USA; European and African residents should write to 10a Spring Place, London NW5 3BH, UK; and residents of other countries to PO Box 617, Hawthorn, Victoria 3122, Australia.

ISLANDS OF THE INDIAN OCEAN Madagascar & Comoros • Maldives • Mauritius, Réunion & Seychelles

MIDDLE EAST & CENTRAL ASIA Arab Gulf States • Central Asia • Central Asia phrasebook • Iran • Israel & the Palestinian Territories • Israel & the Palestinian Territories travel atlas • Istanbul • Jerusalem • Jordan & Syria • Jordan, Syria & Lebanon travel atlas • Lebanon • Middle East on a shoestring • Turkey • Turkish phrasebook • Turkey travel atlas • Yemen
Travel Literature: The Gates of Damascus • Kingdom of the Film Stars: Journey into Jordan

NORTH AMERICA Alaska • Backpacking in Alaska • Baja California • California & Nevada • Canada • Florida • Hawaii • Honolulu • Los Angeles • Miami • New England USA • New Orleans • New York City • New York, New Jersey & Pennsylvania • Pacific Northwest USA • Rocky Mountain States • San Francisco • Seattle • Southwest USA • USA • USA phrasebook • Vancouver • Washington, DC & the Capital Region
Travel Literature: Drive Thru America

NORTH-EAST ASIA Beijing • Cantonese phrasebook • China • Hong Kong • Hong Kong, Macau & Guangzhou • Japan • Japanese phrasebook • Japanese audio pack • Korea • Korean phrasebook • Kyoto • Mandarin phrasebook • Mongolia • Mongolian phrasebook • North-East Asia on a shoestring • Seoul • South-West China • Taiwan • Tibet • Tibetan phrasebook • Tokyo
Travel Literature: Lost Japan

SOUTH AMERICA Argentina, Uruguay & Paraguay • Bolivia • Brazil • Brazilian phrasebook • Buenos Aires • Chile & Easter Island • Chile & Easter Island travel atlas • Colombia • Ecuador & the Galapagos Islands • Latin American Spanish phrasebook • Peru • Quechua phrasebook • Rio de Janeiro • South America on a shoestring • Trekking in the Patagonian Andes • Venezuela
Travel Literature: Full Circle: A South American Journey

SOUTH-EAST ASIA Bali & Lombok • Bangkok • Burmese phrasebook • Cambodia • Hill Tribes phrasebook • Ho Chi Minh City • Indonesia • Indonesian phrasebook • Indonesian audio pack • Jakarta • Java • Laos • Lao phrasebook • Laos travel atlas • Malay phrasebook • Malaysia, Singapore & Brunei • Myanmar (Burma) • Philippines • Pilipino (Tagalog) phrasebook • Singapore • South-East Asia on a shoestring • South-East Asia phrasebook • Thailand • Thailand's Islands & Beaches • Thailand travel atlas • Thai phrasebook • Thai audio pack • Vietnam • Vietnamese phrasebook • Vietnam travel atlas

ALSO AVAILABLE: Antarctica • Brief Encounters: Stories of Love, Sex & Travel • Chasing Rickshaws • Not the Only Planet: Travel Stories from Science Fiction • Travel with Children • Traveller's Tales

Index

Text

Bold indicates maps.
Italics indicates boxed text.

Bold indicates maps.
Italics indicates boxed text.

Bold indicates maps.
Italics indicates boxed text.

Bold indicates maps.
Italics indicates boxed text.

N

O

P

Bold indicates maps.
Italics indicates boxed text.

Boxed Text

MAP LEGEND

BOUNDARIES

International
State
Disputed
Arrondissement

HYDROGRAPHY

Coastline
River, Creek
Lake
Intermittent Lake
Canal
Rapids
Waterfalls
Swamp

ROUTES & TRANSPORT

Freeway
Highway
Major Road
Minor Road
Unsealed Road
City Freeway
City Highway
City Road
City Street, Lane

Pedestrian Mall
Tunnel
Train Route & Station
Metro & Station
Tramway
Cable Car or Chairlift
Walking Track
Walking Tour
Ferry Route

AREA FEATURES

Building
Park, Gardens
Cemetery

Market
Beach, Desert
Urban Area

MAP SYMBOLS

CAPITAL National Capital
CAPITAL State Capital
CITY City
Town Town
Village Village
Point of Interest

Place to Stay
Camping Ground
Caravan Park
Hut or Chalet

Place to Eat
Pub or Bar

Airport
Ancient or City Wall
Archaeological Site
Bank
Beach
Border Crossing
Castle or Fort
Church
Cliff or Escarpment
Embassy
Hospital
Monument
Mountain or Hill
Museum

One-Way Street
Parking
Pass
Police Station
Post Office
Shopping Centre
Ski Field
Stately Home
Telephone
Temple
Toilet
Tourist Information
Transport
Zoo

Note: not all symbols displayed above appear in this book

LONELY PLANET OFFICES

Australia
PO Box 617, Hawthorn, Victoria 3122
☎ (03) 9819 1877 fax (03) 9819 6459
email: talk2us@lonelyplanet.com.au

UK
10a Spring Place, London NW5 3BH
☎ (0171) 428 4800 fax (0171) 428 4828
email: go@lonelyplanet.co.uk

USA
150 Linden St, Oakland, CA 94607
☎ (510) 893 8555 TOLL FREE: 800 275 8555
fax (510) 893 8572
email: info@lonelyplanet.com

France
1 rue du Dahomey, 75011 Paris
☎ 01 55 25 33 00 fax 01 55 25 33 01
email: bip@lonelyplanet.fr
minitel: 3615 lonelyplanet *(1,29 F TTC/min)*

World Wide Web: www.lonelyplanet.com *or* AOL keyword: lp
Lonely Planet Images: lpi@lonelyplanet.com.au